To

For

Happy Christmas
All My Love
Hely xxx

THE
PUB
GUIDE
2016

AA Lifestyle Guides

Published by AA Publishing, a trading name of AA Media Limited, whose registered office is Fanum House, Basing View, Basingstoke RG21 4EA. Registered number 06112600.

19th edition September 2015.
© AA Media Limited 2015.

Assessments of AA inspected establishments are based on the experience of the Hotel and Restaurant Inspectors on the occasion(s) of their visit(s) and therefore descriptions given in this guide necessarily contain an element of subjective opinion which may not reflect or dictate a reader's own opinion on another occasion. See pages 8–9 for a clear explanation of how, based on our Inspectors' inspection experiences, establishments are graded. If the meal or meals experienced by an Inspector or Inspectors during an inspection fall between award levels the restaurant concerned may be awarded the lower of any award levels considered applicable.

AA Media Limited strives to ensure accuracy of the information in this guide at the time of printing. Nevertheless, the Publisher cannot be held responsible for any errors or omissions, or for changes in the details given in this guide, or for the consequences of any reliance on the information provided by the same. This does not affect your statutory rights. Due to the constantly evolving nature of the subject matter the information is subject to change. AA Media Limited is grateful for any advice from readers about necessary updates.

Please contact:
Advertising Sales Department: advertisingsales@theAA.com
Editorial Department: lifestyleguides@theAA.com
AA Hotel and B&B Scheme Enquiries: 01256 844455

Website addresses are included in some entries and specified by the respective establishment. Such websites are not under the control of AA Media Limited and as such AA Media Limited will not accept any responsibility or liability in respect of any and all matters whatsoever relating to such websites including access, content, material and functionality. By including the addresses of third party websites the AA does not intend to solicit business or offer any security to any person in any country, directly or indirectly.

Photographs in the gazetteer are provided by the establishments.

Typeset/Repro: Servis Filmsetting Ltd, Stockport.
Printed and bound in Italy by Printer Trento SRL
Directory compiled by the AA Lifestyle Guides Department and managed in the Librios Information Management System.

Pub descriptions have been contributed by the following team of writers: Jackie Bates, Phil Bryant, Neil Coates, David Halford and Mark Taylor.

Maps prepared by the Mapping Services Department of AA Publishing.

Maps © AA Media Limited 2015.

Contains Ordnance Survey data © Crown copyright and database right 2015.

Information on National Parks in England provided by the Countryside Agency (Natural England).

Information on National Parks in Scotland provided by Scottish Natural Heritage.

Information on National Parks in Wales provided by The Countryside Council for Wales.

A CIP catalogue for this book is available from the British Library.

ISBN: 978-0-7495-7723-0

A05288

Contents

Welcome to the AA Pub Guide 2016

We aim to bring you the country's best pubs, selected for their atmosphere, good beer and great food. Updated every year, this popular and well-established guide includes lots of old favourites, plus many new and interesting destinations for drinking and eating across England, Scotland and Wales.

Who's in the guide?

We make our selection by seeking out pubs that are worth making a detour for – 'destination' pubs – where publicans show real enthusiasm for their trade and offer a good selection of well-kept drinks and great food. We also choose neighbourhood pubs which are supported by locals and prove attractive to passing motorists or walkers. Our selected pubs make no payment for their inclusion in the guide*; they appear entirely at our discretion.

That special place

We find pubs that offer something special: pubs where the time-honoured values of a convivial environment for conversation while supping or eating have not been forgotten. They may be attractive, interesting, unusual or in a good location. Some may be very much a local pub or they may draw customers from further afield, while others appear because they are in an exceptional place. Interesting towns and villages, eccentric or historic buildings and rare settings can all be found within this guide.

Tempting food

We look for menus that show a commitment to home cooking, that make good use of local produce wherever possible, and offer an appetising range of freshly prepared dishes. Pubs presenting well-executed traditional dishes like ploughman's or pies, or those offering innovative bar or restaurant food, are all in the running. In keeping with recent trends in pub food, we are keen to include those where particular emphasis is placed on imaginative modern dishes. Occasionally we include pubs that serve no food, or just snacks, but are distinctive in other ways.

Pick of the Pubs

Some of the pubs included in the guide are particularly special, and we have highlighted these as Pick of the Pubs. For 2016, over 640 pubs have been selected using the personal knowledge of our editorial team, our AA Inspectors, and suggestions from our readers. These pubs have a more detailed description, and this year over 150 have chosen to enhance their entry by purchasing two photographs to create a full-page entry.

Beer and cider festivals

As well as keeping their ales and ciders in tip-top condition throughout the year, many of the pubs in this guide hold beer and cider festivals, either just once a year or on several occasions. If they have told us that they do, we have indicated these events in the pub entries, and where possible have also mentioned the month/s of the year or bank holidays when they are held. You'll find lists of these festivals at the back of the guide.

Tell us what you think

We welcome your feedback about the pubs included, and about the guide itself. We would also be pleased to receive suggestions about good pubs you have visited that do not feature in this guide. A Readers' Report form appears at the back of the guide, so please write in or email us at **lifestyleguides@theAA.com**.

* Once chosen for the guide, pubs may decide to enhance their text entry or include advertising for which there is a charge.

How to use the guide

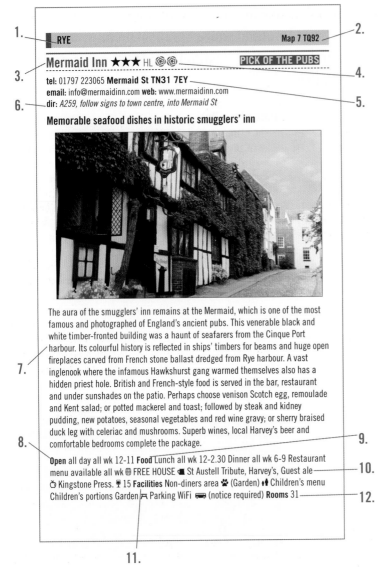

RYE — 1.

Map 7 TQ92 — 2.

Mermaid Inn ★★★ HL ◉◉ — 3. / 4.

PICK OF THE PUBS

tel: 01797 223065 **Mermaid St TN31 7EY**
email: info@mermaidinn.com **web:** www.mermaidinn.com
dir: A259, follow signs to town centre, into Mermaid St — 5. / 6.

Memorable seafood dishes in historic smugglers' inn

The aura of the smugglers' inn remains at the Mermaid, which is one of the most famous and photographed of England's ancient pubs. This venerable black and white timber-fronted building was a haunt of seafarers from the Cinque Port harbour. Its colourful history is reflected in ships' timbers for beams and huge open fireplaces carved from French stone ballast dredged from Rye harbour. A vast inglenook where the infamous Hawkshurst gang warmed themselves also has a hidden priest hole. British and French-style food is served in the bar, restaurant and under sunshades on the patio. Perhaps choose venison Scotch egg, remoulade and Kent salad; or potted mackerel and toast; followed by steak and kidney pudding, new potatoes, seasonal vegetables and red wine gravy; or sherry braised duck leg with celeriac and mushrooms. Superb wines, local Harvey's beer and comfortable bedrooms complete the package. — 7.

Open all day all wk 12-11 **Food** Lunch all wk 12-2.30 Dinner all wk 6-9 Restaurant menu available all wk ⊕ FREE HOUSE ◀ St Austell Tribute, Harvey's, Guest ale ◌ Kingstone Press. ♟ 15 **Facilities** Non-diners area ♣ (Garden) ♦♦ Children's menu Children's portions Garden ⌫ Parking WiFi ▭ (notice required) **Rooms** 31 — 8. / 9. / 10. / 11. / 12.

1. Location

Guide order Country; county; town or village. Pubs are listed under their town or village name alphabetically within their county, within their country. There is a county map at the back of the guide. Some village pubs prefer to be listed under the nearest town, in which case the village name appears in their address.

2. Map reference

Each town or village is given a map reference – the map page number and a two-figure reference based on the National Grid. For example: **Map 7 TQ92**
7 refers to the page number of the map section at the back of the guide
TQ is the National Grid lettered square (representing 100,000sq metres) in which the location will be found
9 is the figure reading across the top and bottom of the map page
2 is the figure reading down at each side of the map page
London Maps: A Central London map and a Greater London map follow the map section at the back of the guide. The pub location will either appear on Plan 1 or Plan 2.

3. Pub name

Where the name appears in italic type the information that follows has not been confirmed by the pub for 2016.

4. AA ratings/designators/awards

★★★★ Star rating under AA Hotel or B&B Schemes (see pages 8–9) followed by a designator (i.e. HL) which shows the type of hotel or B&B.

@ AA Rosette award for food excellence (see page 9).

PICK OF THE PUBS (see page 5)

5. Address and contact details

6. Directions
Brief details are given on how to find the pub.

7. Description

8. Opening times
Times are given for when the pub is open, and closed.

9. Food
Indicates the days and times that food can be ordered, followed by the average price of a main course (as supplied to us by the pub). Please be aware that last orders could vary by up to 30 minutes. We also show if a separate restaurant menu is offered and on what days it is available.

Food Allergies From December 2014 a new EU regulation came into force making it easier for those with food allergies to make safer food choices when eating out. There are 14 allergens listed in the regulation, and pubs and restaurants are required to list any of these that are used in the dishes they offer. These may be highlighted on the menus or customers can ask staff for full information. Remember, if you are allergic to a food and are in any doubt, speak to a member of the pub or restaurant's staff.

For further information see www.food.gov.uk/science/allergy-intolerance/label/labelling-changes

10. Brewery and Company
@ indicates the name of the brewery to which the pub is tied, or the company that owns it. FREE HOUSE is shown if the pub is independently owned and run.

◀ indicates the principal beers sold by the pub. The pub's top cask or hand-pulled beers are listed. Many pubs have a much greater selection, with several guest beers each week.

ŏ indicates the real ciders sold by the pub.

♀ indicates the number of wines available by the glass.

11. Facilities
⊼ indicates that the pub serves food outside.

❀ indicates that the pub has told us they are happy to be described as dog-friendly. If possible we also show whereabouts the dogs are accepted (i.e. bar, restaurant, garden and/or outside area).

♦ indicates that the pub welcomes children and they offer a children's menu and/or children's portions.

Further information in this section shows if the pub has a non-diners' area; holds a beer and/or cider festival; has a children's play area, a garden or outside area; if parking is available; if they accept coach parties and if so, if prior notice is required; if WiFi is available.

Key to Symbols

★★★★	Accommodation rating. See explanation on pages 8 & 9
U	Accommodation rating not yet confirmed
@	Rosettes – The AA's food award. See explanation on page 9
⊕	Name of Brewery; Company; Free House
◀	Principal beers sold
ŏ	Real ciders sold
♀	At least eight wines available by the glass. The number of wines may be shown beside the symbol
❀	Dog-friendly pubs: dogs can be accepted in bar, restaurant, garden and/or outside area
♦	Children welcome
⊼	Outside eating area
🚌	Coach parties accepted; pre-booking may be required
⊠	Credit and debit cards not accepted
NEW	Pubs appearing in the guide for the first time

12. Rooms
The number of bedrooms is only shown if the pub's accommodation is rated by the AA.

Notes
⊠ As so many establishments take one or more of the major credit or debit cards, we only indicate if a pub does not accept any cards.

AA classifications and awards

Many of the pubs in this guide offer accommodation. Where a star rating appears next to an entry's name in the guide, the establishment has been inspected by the AA under common Quality Standards agreed between the AA, VisitBritain, VisitScotland and VisitWales. These ratings are for the accommodation, and ensure that the establishment meets the highest standards of cleanliness, with an emphasis on professionalism, proper booking procedures and prompt and efficient service. Some of the pubs in this guide offer accommodation but do not belong to an AA rating scheme; in this case reference to the accommodation is not included in their entry.

AA recognised establishments pay an annual fee that varies according to the classification and the number of bedrooms. The establishments receive an unannounced inspection from a qualified AA Inspector who recommends the appropriate classification. Return visits confirm that standards are maintained; the classification is not transferable if an establishment changes hands.

The annual *AA Hotel Guide* and *AA Bed & Breakfast Guide* give further details of the classification schemes. Details of AA recognised hotels, guest accommodation, restaurants and pubs are also available at theAA.com, and on AA apps.

AA hotel classification

Hotels are classified on a 5-point scale, with one star (★) being the simplest, and five stars offering a luxurious service at the top of the range. The AA's top hotels in Britain and Ireland are identified by red stars (★). Hotels with silver stars (★) are highly recommended for their standards of hotel keeping and quality of food within their star rating. In addition to the main **Hotel** (HL) classification which applies to some pubs in this guide, there are other hotel categories which may be applicable to pubs, as follows:

Town House Hotel (TH) – A small, individual city or town centre property.
Country House Hotel – (CHH) Quietly located in a rural area.
Small Hotel (SHL) – Owner-managed with fewer than 20 bedrooms.

AA guest accommodation

Guest accommodation is also classified on a scale of one to five black stars, with one star (★) being the most simple, and five being more luxurious. Gold stars (★) indicate the very best B&Bs, Guest Houses, Farmhouses, Inns, Restaurant with Rooms and Guest Accommodation in the 3, 4 and 5 star ratings. Establishments with silver stars (★) are highly recommended for their levels of hospitality, service and cleanliness within their star rating.
Guest accommodation is designated as follows:

Inn (INN) – Accommodation provided in a fully licensed establishment. The bar will be open to non-residents and food is provided in the evenings.

Bed & Breakfast (B&B) – Accommodation provided in a private house, run by the owner and with no more than six paying guests.

Guest House (GH) – Accommodation provided for more than six paying guests and run on a more commercial basis than a B&B. Usually more services, for example dinner, provided by staff as well as the owner.

Farmhouse (FH) – B&B or guest house rooms on a working farm or smallholding.

Restaurant with Rooms (RR) – Destination restaurant offering overnight accommodation. The restaurant is the main business and is open to non-residents. A high standard of food should be offered, at least five nights a week. A maximum of 12 bedrooms. Most Restaurants with Rooms have been awarded AA Rosettes for their food.

Guest Accommodation (GA) – Any establishment which meets the entry requirements for the Scheme can choose this designator.

[U] A small number of pubs have this symbol because their star classification was not confirmed at the time of going to press.

Rosette awards

Out of the thousands of restaurants in the British Isles, the AA identifies, with its Rosette awards, around 2,000 as the best. What to expect from restaurants with AA Rosette awards is outlined here; for a more detailed explanation of Rosette criteria please see theAA.com

◉ Excellent local restaurants serving food prepared with care, understanding and skill and using good quality ingredients.

◉◉ The best local restaurants, which consistently aim for and achieve higher standards and where a greater precision is apparent in the cooking. Obvious attention is paid to the selection of quality ingredients.

◉◉◉ Outstanding restaurants that demand recognition well beyond their local area.

◉◉◉◉ Among the very best restaurants in Britain, where the cooking demands national recognition.

◉◉◉◉◉ The finest restaurants in Britain, where the cooking stands comparison with the best in the world.

AA Pub of the Year

The prestigious annual awards for the AA Pub of the Year for England, Scotland and Wales have been selected with the help of our AA inspectors and we have chosen three very worthy winners. These pubs stand out for being great all-rounders, combining a convivial atmosphere, well-kept beers and ciders, excellent food, and of course, a warm welcome from the friendly and efficient hosts and their staff.

ENGLAND

THE PORCH HOUSE ★★★★★ ◉◉
STOW-ON-THE-WOLD, GLOUCESTERSHIRE   page 214

In the heart of picturesque market town Stow-on-the-Wold, this charming Cotswold inn, allegedly the oldest in England (it dates from 947AD) welcomes everyone – except witches. The fireplace in the dining room is incised with symbols meant to ward them off, and a square-toed shoe of the type not fashionable since 1600 was found up the chimney – another device for kicking the backside of evil spirits. A recent makeover has ensured that public areas ooze with character. Warm, soft lighting, limestone floors, wood-burning stoves and cosy alcoves create a relaxing atmosphere in which to enjoy real ales and a host of other beers, wines and spirits from around the world. Comfortably seated at one of the candlelit tables, you may also be tempted to try one of the home-brewed drinks including still or slushy lemonade from a 100-year old recipe, ginger ale or a spicy Bloody Mary made with home-roasted tomatoes. There's a huge choice of where to eat the award-winning food, too – the dining room, bar, lounge or conservatory are all options, as is the contemporary-style garden, with its Raffles-style armchairs and planters. Local produce is a feature of the menus, and if you wish you can stay the night in one of the 13 luxuriously appointed rooms where a coffee machine, Roberts radio, sumptuous bed linen and free newspaper comes as standard. All in all The Porch House is a very worthy winner.

SCOTLAND

THE SCRAN & SCALLIE
CITY OF EDINBURGH page 604

Tucked away slightly off the tourist track in the trendy Stockbridge area of Edinburgh's New Town, rustic-chic Scran & Scallie is the vibrant new enterprise of two renowned Scottish chefs – Tom Kitchin and Dominic Jack. With such stellar names at the helm and James Chapman as head chef, this stylish gastro-pub is, as expected, a great meeting place, big on atmosphere and even bigger on food; the delicious modern Scottish menu featuring a host of old favourites is presented with delightfully innovative twists and follows their 'nature to the plate' ethos. Attracting a very mixed clientele – many travel miles just to visit this place while some are yummy mummies from around the corner – this family-friendly venue operates as much as a traditional pub as an award-winning restaurant. An extensive drinks menu, served all day, includes a range of traditionally brewed ales, wines and whiskies. Enthusiastic diners pass through the buzzing bar to the dining room with its mismatched wooden chairs, some draped with fur throws, amid walls of open brickwork and wood panelling, bristling antlers and soft-hued tartan – a kind of Scots meets Scandi mash-up. Both food and decor are a fabulous mixture of old and modern, taking the best from both and creating something new and wonderful. Friendly, knowledgeable staff provide the finishing touch. This 'public house with dining' as they style themselves certainly deserves this prestigious accolade.

WALES

THE KINMEL ARMS ★★★★★
RESTAURANT WITH ROOMS
ABERGELE, CONWY page 630

Situated in the foothills of the Elwy Valley, this handsome rural inn delights visitors to this relatively unknown corner of Conwy with its top-notch food and stylish accommodation. Husband-and-wife team Tim and Lynn Cunnah-Watson had both visited the pub since childhood; in 2002 they bought it and immediately embarked on a refurbishment that reflected elements of their travels and their personalities. Behind the old inn's mellow sandstone exterior, light and airy rooms filled with contemporary furnishings create a cheerful, relaxed mood. The cared-for, highly polished vibe extends to the bar and sunny conservatory-dining room with its glorious sea views, where an extensive, seasonally inspired menu makes excellent use of the best local produce – fresh fish, local meats and artisan-made breads and cheeses. Bar meals are simpler but still of fine quality. For those who want to stay a while there are just four individually designed luxury suites furnished with enormous and blissfully comfortable hand-made oak and maple beds. Egyptian cotton sheets, plasma screens and fluffy bathrobes provide further cosseting touches, and the walls are decorated with Tim's imaginative artworks. Expect to be welcomed and looked after by a friendly and engaging team who all deserved to be crowned winners. Whether you want a quick pint, a top-notch meal or an overnight stay, The Kinmel Arms has it all.

Licensed to chill

There's more to some pubs than meets the eye. Phil Bryant investigates tales of otherworldly happenings in Britain's licensed premises, from a ghostly smuggler who causes glasses to jump off shelves to sightings of a grey lady and her spectral horse in Scotland.

You are, presumably, no stranger to visiting pubs. After all, you're reading this guide.

Imagine then, that you are enjoying a meal in a pub restaurant when something near the fireplace catches your eye. Your forkful of salmon en croûte hovers halfway to your mouth. Your companion clearly wonders why you appear to be so transfixed by the dancing flames.

What only you have seen is a sad-looking woman with black hair. She seems to be floating. Suddenly, she speaks: "My name is Sarah and I am 35 years old." Then she vanishes. So spooked are you that you leave the table, your salmon unfinished, your companion totally mystified. A day or two later, you seek advice from your vicar, who tells you, much to your relief, that he too once saw a ghost. He's certain that's what you saw.

One evening in 2005 this sighting happened to a woman in The Swettenham Arms, a 16th-century Cheshire village pub that is haunted, according to local legend, by the ghost of a nun. It was once a nunnery, where coffins were often 'rested' overnight before being taken through an underground tunnel to the nearby church.

The Crown Inn at Pishill, Oxfordshire

Whether or not you believe in ghosts, it's a good story, so good that the pub has even published a brochure about it. Some pubs, of course, prefer to remain silent on the subject, but a surprising number in this guide are happy to mention their ethereal residents, promoting them as enthusiastically as they do their chef's pedigree, range of real ales and wonderful views.

For instance, there's The Crown Inn at Shorwell on the Isle of Wight, where a female ghost shows her disapproval of customers playing cards by throwing them on the floor (the cards, that is). In the southern Cotswold village of Sherston, legendary Saxon warrior John Rattlebones makes his spectral presence felt at the pub named after him, The Rattlebone Inn. And in Walberswick, Suffolk, one of Britain's most haunted villages, the ghostly goings-on at The Bell Inn include the apparition of a fisherman who sits there smoking away without a care in the world, and the infamous Black Shuck, a huge, red-eyed, phantom dog, sometimes seen on the road between the Bell and the vicarage. The name of the Adnams beer 'Ghost Ship' was inspired by tales from this pub and the wrecks of many smuggling ships said to lie off this part of the Suffolk coast.

Liz Jackson, landlady of The Hare Inn in the North York Moors National Park, says that although she doesn't believe in ghosts, she still wonders about Alice, the resident spirit of a witch who lived there in the 13th century, before it became a pub. One night, apparently, Alice, having assumed the form of a hare, was chased by hunters back to her cottage, where she changed back into human form and promptly died of exhaustion. Had the customer who told Liz she had just "felt a presence" encountered Alice?

Shropshire is particularly rich in pub ghosts. Greg Williams of The Bear at Hodnet, for example, tells of Jasper Neilsen, a 16th-century regular, who was thrown out into the bitterly cold night after an argument over yet another unpaid drinks bill, later dying of

"Sometimes when I'm working, the hairs go up on the back of my neck, so I assume Hammond's around and I just talk to him."

hypothermia. "Today," says Greg, "when anyone asks if they can run a tab, some claim you can hear Jasper's anguished cry."

Below the limestone escarpment of Wenlock Edge is The Crown Country Inn (Munslow), once used as a type of court known as a Hundred House, where the infamous 'Hanging' Judge Jeffreys occasionally presided over proceedings. Was Charlotte, the black-swathed figure that sometimes appears, sentenced to death by him? In 14 years as landlady, Jane Arnold has never seen her. "Some ghosthunters asked if they could mount a vigil, but I refused," she says. "Whoever's here is happy here."

Also in Shropshire is The Old Three Pigeons at Nesscliffe, once frequented by Sir Humphrey Kynaston, a highwayman who, Robin Hood-like, robbed the rich to help the poor. Owner Mike Brooks grew up in the pub and knows all about his spooky antics, and those of Kynaston's horse Beelzebub. "I once saw Sir Humphrey walking about a foot above the floor, which was its level before it was lowered. More recently, a couple were eating here when the man saw a ghostly horse go right through the hedge outside. He got up and left, white and shaking."

Lee Keirman runs the part 13th-century Boot Inn at Flyford Flavell, Worcestershire. One day a customer told him about the day he was dining with his wife in The Dairy, the oldest part of the pub: "I know it sounds daft, but she said that every time she looked up she could see cows, and when she looked down she could

see a dog at her feet. Mind you, she's a very spiritual person." Another couple, also eating in The Dairy, were amazed, Lee says, when chrysanthemums apparently started dropping down from the ceiling.

The late-Victorian Coach & Horses in London's Clerkenwell has had only six landlords since it opened. Boss today is Giles Webster, who says his staff have seen the figure of a young woman with a bunch of flowers, dressed like Eliza Doolittle in *My Fair Lady*. According to Giles, "There's a lot of spooky activity down in the cellar, where I understand a former landlord was murdered in the 1930s."

From Selling in Kent comes the story of the night in 1889 that Hammond John Smith left the Rose and Crown for home, following a heated argument with two men about who could cut an acre of corn the fastest. The next day Hammond was found dead in a barn and landlord Tim Robinson believes he haunts the pub to this day: "Sometimes when I'm working, the hairs go up on the back of my neck, so I assume Hammond's around and I just talk to him. He sometimes gets up to mischief with the ladies, like the member of staff he regularly followed, until one day she turned round and told him to stop. After that, he never followed her again."

Kim Pruett at The Laughing Dog, an old drovers' stop-over in Llandrindod Wells, tells of heavy filing cabinets being moved around when nobody is in the room used as an office. "Shortly after we bought the pub," he adds, "my wife saw an old lady dressed like a maid sitting in a chair, sewing. Then there was the customer who asked about the smartly dressed man in a top hat he'd just seen in the gents', but when another chap went to investigate, the place was empty."

A tragic incident occurred in the 1880s at The Blue Cow Inn & Brewery in South Witham, Lincolnshire, when a woman left the pub a little the worse for wear and was killed by a passing horse and cart. Perhaps it's her ghost that customers today sometimes see walking through a bay window? Recently, two couples were sitting

Above: a former courthouse presided over by 'Hanging' Judge Jeffries - The Crown Country Inn, Sherston

in the bay, chatting to landlord Simon Crathorn, who takes up the story: "Although the fire was blazing away nearby, both ladies suddenly complained that their arms had gone icy cold. About 20 minutes later they said the cold feeling had gone. They were really intrigued when I told them that a ghost might have been passing between them." The pub also used to have a ghost dog. In the 1940s, the landlord died in his bedroom. "Apparently, his dog never got over it," says Simon. "When I came here, some guests in that room would wake up feeling a dog lying across their legs. When I refurbished the room, it stopped happening."

One night in 1687, pirate-turned-smuggler John Trenchman was attacked by the King's Men; mortally wounded, he managed to reach The Fox & Hounds in South Godstone, Surrey, where he died. Landlady Ellie Conway has seen him twice: "The first time it was broad daylight, and he was staggering towards the door leading to the oldest part of the building. Rather pointlessly, I shot over to the door and bolted it. On the second occasion he walked past the bar grinning at me. I was dumbfounded." Staff have seen him too, sitting on a barrel in the cellar, his head in his hands. And, adds Ellie: "Glasses jump off shelves, too. It costs me a fortune."

In the days when Catholic priests were persecuted, their salvation was often a priest's hole, like the one at The Crown Inn, a pretty brick and flint building at Pishill, not far from Henley-on-Thames. Unfortunately, it led to a sticky end for a Father Dominique who, while hiding out, was either seduced by a serving girl and, overcome with guilt, killed himself, or was murdered because he tried to protect the girl from a drunken

assailant. Whichever version is true, his ghost is said to still haunt The Crown.

Tucked away in the warren of streets near Winchester Cathedral is The Wykeham Arms. Four years ago, a couple staying overnight found the eyes in a painting of a Mr Redman, husband of a landlady in the 1950s, rather disturbing, so they placed a towel over the frame. Twice during night, the husband woke up and could make out that the towel had dropped to the floor. Twice he replaced it. In the morning, the towel was on the floor again, but this time a gravity-defying 10ft away from the wall. At breakfast, the duty manager confirmed that, yes, the room was allegedly haunted. Perhaps Mrs Redman's ghost disapproved of his painting being covered up.

Finally, we head for The Inn at Lathones, near St Andrews in Scotland, where set above the large fireplace is the wedding stone of Iona and Ewan, who married in the local kirk in 1718. The Inn's Greg Jenkins explains that when Iona died in 1736, the stone mysteriously cracked, and Ewan died shortly afterwards. Staff believe Iona is The Grey Lady, a friendly spirit that some overnight guests claim to have seen walking through their bedroom; often she's seen with her spectral horse. One lady woke up thinking it must be her husband creeping around until she realised he was sound asleep beside her.

So, if you like a pub filled with both kinds of spirits, consider visiting one haunted by Sarah, Father Dominique, the Grey Lady or by one of many other phantom presences described here. You'll also find quite a few references to other ghosts and apparitions in the following pages. But if you want to meet them in the flesh, well that might be a bit tricky.

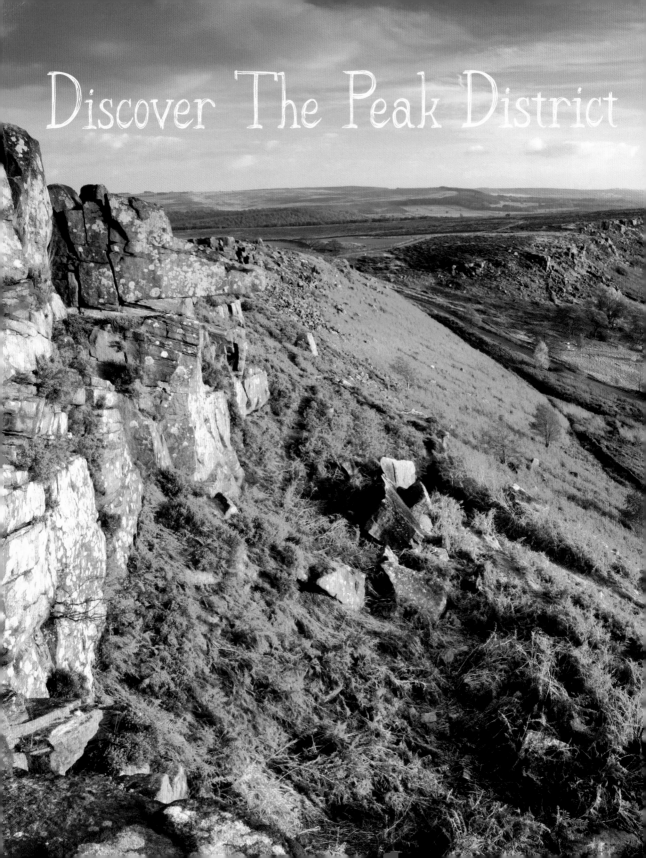

Discover The Peak District

What makes The Peak District National Park such a popular place to visit? We asked Roly Smith, author of the *AA Guide to The Peak District*, to highlight its attractions.

The Peak District – the first, most popular and inevitably, most pressurised national park in Britain – has two contrasting faces, one White the other Dark. These 'Twin Peaks' offer sharply contrasting, yet complementary, landscapes, each of which have their own loyal aficionados.

In fact, nowhere in Britain offers such a variety of landscapes in such a small area as the Peak District, from the wild, bleak moors of the Dark Peak in the north, to the gentler, pastoral limestone dales of the White Peak in the south. There's no chance of getting bored by the scenery; if you don't like what you're seeing, travel a couple of miles further on and you can find yourself in a totally different landscape.

The White Peak

The predominant rock in the south and central area of the 555 square mile national park is Carboniferous limestone. It was the pearly-grey colour of this 350-million-year-old, fossil-filled rock that gave it the generic name of the White Peak.

The landscape of the White Peak consists of a 1,000ft high plateau of gently rolling pastureland, split by dramatic, steep-sided dales and threaded by sparkling, clear rivers like the Dove, Manifold, Wye and Lathkill, which mysteriously disappear underground during dry spells. Most of these delightful dales can be entered only on foot, unlike the broader, more spacious Yorkshire Dales further north. This gives them an intimacy and peacefulness not found elsewhere, and it makes them a haven for some rare and beautiful wildlife.

Many of the Peakland dales are protected as nature reserves, such as the Derbyshire Dales National Nature Reserve, which covers parts of Lathkill, Cressbrook, Monk's, Long and Hay Dales. The reserve includes superb examples of all the major wildlife habitats of the White Peak, particularly flower-rich grasslands and ash woodlands. Lime-loving flowers, such as common rock-rose and salad burnet, are abundant here, with up to 45 different species of flowers found within a square yard.

Baslow Edge from Curbar Edge

The Dark Peak moors are the home of the mountain hare, the ubiquitous red grouse, the curlew and the golden plover

In spring, visitors enjoy the breathtaking sight of thousands of early purple orchids and cowslips. Breeding birds include the redstart, wood warbler and pied flycatcher, and the rivers and streams (especially the Lathkill, which flows for its entirety over limestone) are among the purest in the country.

The Dark Peak

The more rugged Dark Peak occupies the northern part of the Peak District, extending in two enclosing arms down either side of the White Peak, like the hair on the head of a balding man. Before the last Ice Age, the limestone was completely covered by layer upon layer of gritstone, laid down by huge rivers flowing from the north. Then the devastating power of glaciers and aeons of wind and rain scoured it all away, exposing, once again, the bare, bleached skeleton of the limestone beneath.

Abrasive millstone grit (it gets its name from its former use for making millstones) is the predominant rock in the Dark Peak. It outcrops in the Peak's famous gritstone edges, which frown down for many miles on the valley of the Derwent in the east, and in the more complex system of cloughs (rocky streams) in the west, where the Roaches in the Staffordshire moorlands offer an equally dramatic, serrated skyline.

The heather-clad moors above and beyond the edges rise to the high points of Kinder Scout at 2,088ft and Bleaklow at 2,077ft in the north – surprisingly, the largest area of land above 2,000ft in England.

The Dark Peak moors are the home of the mountain hare, the ubiquitous red grouse, the curlew and the golden plover, plus dashing raptors such as the merlin and peregrine falcon.

Human history

The human history of the Peak goes back to the first evidence of mankind in Britain. Monuments like the 5,000-year-old Neolithic henge and stone circle of Arbor Low, near Youlgreave, and the scores of 'lows' (burial mounds) which punctuate almost every hilltop on the limestone plateau, bear silent witness to those earliest settlers.

In Saxon times, the local tribe was known as the *Pecsaetan*, which simply meant 'the dwellers of the Peak'. The Anglo-Saxon

The Roaches

word *peac* could mean any knoll or hill, and the Peak District was first known as *Pecsaetna lond*, 'the land of the settlers of the Peak'.

The timeless stone villages of the White Peak, such as Bakewell, Tideswell, Hartington and the famous 'plague village' of Eyam, remain virtually unchanged, to the delight of modern visitors. They come to admire the unique and beautiful folk art of well dressing, which can be seen in various villages throughout the summer months. This is thought originally to have been a pagan ceremony, giving thanks for the gift of water on the fast-draining limestone plateau. It later became adopted by the Christian church, and now takes place annually in about 40 Peakland villages.

'The Great Escape'

It's not unusual to see a well-equipped walker kitted out in rucksack, anorak, breeches and boots striding out along Piccadilly in Manchester or Fargate in Sheffield, heading towards the railway station and a day's walking in the Peak. It was the late broadcaster, Council for National Parks president and Peak-lover Brian Redhead who accurately dubbed the Peak 'The Great Escape'.

But for many years before the creation of the national park, most of the highest points of the Peak District, including the moorlands of Kinder Scout and Bleaklow, were forbidden mountains, strictly out of bounds to walkers from the surrounding cities. Grouse-shooting landlords erected

'Trespassers Will Be Prosecuted' signs at every access point, and gamekeepers, who were not averse to using strong-arm tactics to forcibly evict transgressors, patrolled the moors. So it was here that 'the gentle art of trespass' – as described by one early access campaigner – was born.

It was the pressure from its surrounding towns and cities that was largely responsible for the Peak District becoming Britain's first national park in 1951. Huge open-air 'access to mountains' rallies had culminated in the celebrated mass trespass on Kinder Scout and arrest and imprisonment of five ramblers in 1932. These events undoubtedly proved to be important catalysts for the creation of national parks.

The Pennine Way is the first, and some would say the

toughest, of Britain's National Trails. It starts in the shadow of Kinder Scout at Edale, and runs for 258 miles along the crest of the Pennines and the Cheviot Hills of Northumberland across the Scottish Border to the village of Kirk Yetholm.

Fancy a pint of the local brew?

Like many other places in Britain, the Peak District is today home to an astonishing variety of acclaimed breweries and microbreweries.

They include the award-winning **Thornbridge Brewery** that first started brewing in 2005 after establishing a 10-barrel brewery in the grounds of Victorian Thornbridge Hall, near Hassop. Thornbridge now operates from two breweries, the original one at the hall, which uses the traditional infusion mash ale system, and the Riverside Brewery in Bakewell, which concentrates on innovations through technology. Their beers, such as Jaipur IPA and Twin Peaks, are sold at pubs like The Plough at Hathersage; The Maynard at Grindleford, and The Red Lion at Birchover.

Peak Ales, which also launched in 2005, produces traditionally brewed ales from a barn on the Chatsworth Estate. It is now a 20-barrel microbrewery supplying both cask and bottled ales to local pubs, hotels and retail outlets such as The Yorkshire Bridge at Bamford; the Devonshire Arms at Beeley, and The Chequers Inn at Froggatt.

Whim Ales Brewery at Whim Farm, Hartington, is a 10-barrel microbrewery specialising in cask ale using the finest Maris Otter malt, whole cone hops, their own freshly cropped yeast and Derbyshire spring water. Making use of redundant farm buildings, the brewery started in 1993, and its ales are sold at The Jug and Glass, Hartington; The Barley Mow, Bonsall and The Royal Oak at Hurdlow.

Ashover Brewery is a small brewery next door to The Old Poet's Corner pub in Ashover where, not unsurprisingly, a favourite ale is called Poet's Tipple. It is also sold at two other associated local pubs, The Poet and Castle at Codnor and The Princess Victoria at Matlock Bath.

The park today

The exodus from the industrial towns and cities surrounding the Peak (comprising half the population of England) which continues today is largely thanks to mass car ownership, aided by a superb public transport network. With an estimated 22 million annual day visits, the Peak is one of the most heavily visited national parks in the world.

The Park Authority has pioneered many ground-breaking schemes in order to extract visitors from their cars. Starting with an experiment in 1971 in the Goyt Valley, on the western side of the national park near Buxton, it closed cul-de-sac valley roads to traffic at busy times such as Bank Holidays and summer weekends. This successful idea was later repeated in the Upper Derwent Valley in the northeast of the park.

The conversion of former railway lines such as the Tissington, High Peak Monsal and Manifold Trails into pleasant walking and riding routes with cycle-hire facilities is another scheme that has proved very popular with visitors, and taken traffic off the roads.

Chrome and Parkhouse Hills

Great houses and estates

The Peak has much more to offer though than beautiful landscapes and physical challenges. Stately homes such as Chatsworth House, Haddon Hall, and the National Trust's Lyme Park on the outskirts of Stockport, show the benign influence of great landowners through their extensive parklands and neat estate villages, providing further major attractions for modern visitors to enjoy. Minor stately homes include 17th-century Eyam Hall (NT), home of the Wright family for more than 300 years, and Tudor Tissington Hall, seat of the Fitzherberts since the early 1600s.

Many of these manorial estates, including Chatsworth House and Haddon Hall, homes of the Dukes of Devonshire and Rutland respectively, occupy superbly landscaped parklands in the shale valleys carved by the great Peakland rivers of the Derwent and Wye.

So, if you want to visit a land of contrasts, where moors and dales, springs and caves, market towns and historic houses abound, The Peak District has it all, with a plethora of atmospheric pubs and microbreweries along the way.

If you've enjoyed this feature on one of England's most special places, The Peak District, find out more by seeking out *The AA Guide to the Peak District*, packed with information on this popular region.

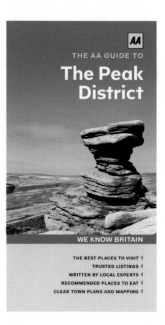

THE AA GUIDE TO

The Peak District

WE KNOW BRITAIN

THE BEST PLACES TO VISIT
TRUSTED LISTINGS
WRITTEN BY LOCAL EXPERTS
RECOMMENDED PLACES TO EAT
CLEAR TOWN PLANS AND MAPPING

Island of darkness

If you look at a satellite photograph of Britain at night, the Peak District stands out as an island of darkness, surrounded by the street lights of the enclosing towns and cities. The Peak District National Park Authority, Nottingham Trent University and the Science and Technology Facilities Council have worked together to identify 'Dark Sky discovery sites' away from the worst of local light pollution and offering optimum conditions for stargazing. **The three Dark Sky sites, all based at National Park car parks, are:**

- **Surprise View, off the A6187 near Hathersage**
- **Parsley Hay, off the A515 near Hartington (nearest postcode SK17 0DG)**
- **Minninglow, also off the A515 at Pikehall (nearest postcode DE4 2PN)**

Astronomy interpretation panels, which are changed each season, help beginners to identify constellations and explore the night skies. The Parsley Hay and Minninglow panels are both located beside the High Peak Trail.

England

BEDFORDSHIRE

BEDFORD   Map 12 TL04

The Embankment

tel: 01234 261332 **6 The Embankment MK40 3PD**
email: embankment@peachpubs.com
dir: *From M1 junct 13, A421 to Bedford. Left onto A6 to town centre. Into left lane on river bridge. Into right lane signed Embankment. Follow around St Paul's Square into High St, into left lane. Left onto The Embankment*

Mock-Tudor riverside pub with a hospitable atmosphere

This imposing pub sits behind an outdoor terrace overlooking the River Great Ouse on the edge of Bedford's beautifully landscaped Embankment gardens. Dating from 1891, the building has been renovated and its Victorian features brought back to life. Among its delights are the open fire, antique mirrors, vintage tables, sofas in racing green and silk lampshades. Food choices range from deli boards to full meals, such as Brixham crab Benedict, spinach, poached egg and hollandaise, followed by slow-cooked pork belly, spring vegetable salsa, roast apple and green sauce.

Open all day all wk Closed 25 Dec **Food** Lunch all wk 12-6 Dinner all wk 6-10 Av main course £15 Set menu available ⊕ PEACH PUBS ◀ Wells Eagle IPA & Bombardier, Young's ☼ Aspall. ☗ 16 **Facilities** Non-diners area ✿ (Bar Outside area) ♦♦ Children's portions Outside area ⊓ Parking WiFi ▭ (notice required)

The Knife and Cleaver ★★★★ INN

tel: 01234 930789 **The Grove, Houghton Conquest MK45 3LA**
email: info@theknifeandcleaver.com **web:** www.theknifeandcleaver.com
dir: *A6 from Bedford towards Luton. In 5m right to Houghton Conquest. Or B530 from Bedford towards Ampthill left to Houghton Conquest*

Highly regarded rustic pub

The Shuttleworth aeroplane collection and Bletchley Park are easily reached from this pub in a village named after the Conquest family, who lived here between the 13th and 18th centuries. The bar and All Saints Restaurant welcome customers throughout the day, every day, even for just for a pint of Wells Eagle IPA. The choice is good: starters include wild rabbit and ham hock terrine; and hot smoked mackerel with buttermilk pancake, horseradish crème fraîche and grapefruit jam: among the mains are Woburn venison haunch with celeriac and potato rösti; and grilled lobster tail, thermidor croquettes, red pepper mayonnaise and samphire.

Open all day all wk **Food** Lunch all day Dinner all day Av main course £12 Set menu available Restaurant menu available all wk ⊕ CHARLES WELLS ◀ Eagle IPA, Courage Directors, Guest ale ☼ Symonds. ☗ 35 **Facilities** Non-diners area ♦♦ Children's menu Children's portions Family room Garden Outside area ⊓ Parking WiFi ▭ (notice required) **Rooms** 9

The Park Pub & Kitchen   PICK OF THE PUBS

tel: 01234 273929 **98 Kimbolton Rd MK40 2PA**
email: info@theparkbedford.co.uk
dir: *M1 junct 14, A509 follow Newport Pagnell signs, then A422, A428 onto A6. Right into Tavistock St (A600). Left into Broadway, 1st left into Kimbolton Rd. Pub 0.5m*

Smart, bright and spacious, a stylish mix of old and new

Built in the 1900s, this fine-looking pub is a stone's throw from Bedford Park, just a little way out of town. The smartly decorated exterior promises a similarly well cared for interior, and you won't be disappointed – fireplaces, flagstone floors and beamed ceilings combine to create a traditional welcoming atmosphere. Beyond the wrap-around bar are a spacious restaurant, relaxing conservatory and airy garden room; this leads to an outdoor area where heaters permit comfortable drinking and dining if there's a chill in the air. Eagle IPA and Bombardier from the town's Wells and Young's brewery are served in the bar, along with over 30 wines sold by the glass. Most of the pub's suppliers are proudly detailed on the menu, while the

kitchen team produces the pub's own bread, pasta, ice creams and chutneys. In addition, snacks and sandwiches with home-cut chips are served on Saturday from 3pm to 6pm.

Open all day all wk **Food** Lunch Mon-Sat 12-3, Sun 12-8 Dinner Mon-Sat 6-10, Sun 12-8 Set menu available Restaurant menu available all wk ⊕ CHARLES WELLS ◀ Bombardier, Eagle IPA, Guest ales ☼ Aspall. ☗ 33 **Facilities** Non-diners area ✿ (Bar Garden) ♦♦ Children's portions Garden ⊓ Parking WiFi ▭ (notice required)

The Three Tuns

tel: 01234 354847 **57 Main Rd, Biddenham MK40 4BD**
email: info@thethreetunsbiddenham.co.uk
dir: *On A428 from Bedford towards Northampton 1st left signed Biddenham. Into village, pub on left*

Thatched pub with food of a high standard

In a pretty village, this stone-built pub has a large garden with a patio and decking, and a separate children's play area. Owner Chris Smith worked for celebrity chef Jean-Christophe Novelli for a number of years and now produces dishes such as white onion and cumin soup; creamy chicken, bacon and ale pot pie; and pineapple carpaccio with coconut and tarragon sorbet and lime jelly. Each dish on the à la carte is matched with a recommended wine. The two-course set menu is excellent value. In the garden is a long-disused, possibly haunted, morgue, the oldest building hereabouts.

Open all wk 12-3 5.30-late (Fri-Sat all day Sun 12-6) **Food** Lunch Tue-Sat 12-2.30, Sun 12-4 Dinner Tue-Sat 6-9.30 Set menu available Restaurant menu available Tue-Sun ⊕ GREENE KING ◀ IPA, Guinness, Guest ale ☼ Thatchers Gold. ☗ 16 **Facilities** Non-diners area ♦♦ Children's portions Play area Garden ⊓ Parking WiFi ▭ (notice required)

BOLNHURST   Map 12 TL05

The Plough at Bolnhurst ⊛   PICK OF THE PUBS

tel: 01234 376274 **Kimbolton Rd MK44 2EX**
email: reservations@bolnhurst.com
dir: *On B660, N of Bedford*

Tudor inn with notable food and wine

This whitewashed 15th-century country inn six miles north of Bedford has fresh, country-style decor coupled with original features such as thick walls, low beams and great open fires. The impressive choice of real ales and inspired wine list are matched by a delicious menu prepared by Raymond Blanc-trained Martin Lee and his team of skilled chefs. The menu is driven by the freshest local and regional produce and specialist foods gathered from all corners. The result is an ever-changing choice of unique dishes, which have gained The Plough an AA Rosette. Start with seared Cornish mackerel, smoked fennel, anchovy dressing and garlic crisps; or fresh potato gnocchi, rabbit ragout, aged parmesan, Sicilian olive oil and marjoram; follow up with slow-cooked Aberdeenshire beef cheek, sautéed cavalo nero, roasted garlic mash and red wine sauce. Rhubarb soufflé with vanilla anglaise makes a tempting dessert but do leave room for the cheeseboard, with its fantastic choice of British, Italian and French varieties.

Open Tue-Sat 12-3 6.30-11 (Sun 12-3) Closed 1 Jan, 2wks Jan, Mon & Sun eve **Food** Lunch Tue-Sun 12-2 Dinner Tue-Fri 6.30-9, Sat 6.30-9.30 Set menu available ⊕ FREE HOUSE ◀ Adnams Southwold Bitter, Potton, Fuller's London Pride, Church End Goat's Milk ☼ Aspall Harry Sparrow. ☗ 13 **Facilities** Non-diners area ✿ (Bar) ♦♦ Children's portions Garden Parking WiFi ▭

HARROLD
Map 11 SP95

The Muntjac

tel: 01234 721500 **71 High St MK43 7BJ**
email: muntjacharrold@hotmail.co.uk
dir: *Phone for detailed directions*

Free house with an Indian restaurant

This 17th-century former coaching inn in a pretty village has a lot on offer. Six real ales on handpump, 30 gins and 13 vodkas for a start; a real fire in the winter, pool table and Sky Sport TV for the big matches. Attached to the pub is Harrolds Indian Cuisine that offers an extensive range of traditional dishes cooked to order, to eat in or take away; you can even 'challenge the chef' to create your own dish if you ask.

Open Mon-Thu 5.30-11 (Fri 12.30-12 Sat 12-12 Sun 1-10.30) Closed L only Mon-Thu **Food** Contact pub for food times ⊕ FREE HOUSE ◼ Regularly changing ales. **Facilities** Non-diners area ♦♦ Children's portions Garden Parking ▭ (notice required) **Notes** ☺

IRELAND
Map 12 TL14

The Black Horse

tel: 01462 811398 **SG17 5QL**
email: ctaverns@aol.com **web:** www.blackhorseireland.com
dir: *From S: M1 junct 12, A5120 to Flitwick. Onto A507 by Redbourne School. Follow signs for A1, Shefford (cross A6). Left onto A600 towards Bedford*

Traditional and modern comfortably combined

Original beams, slate floors, inglenook fireplaces, original artwork and low ceilings combine to create a chic and modern interior in this family-run, 17th-century inn. The flower-rich garden and courtyard offer alfresco dining in the warmer months. Grab a pint of Adnams, or choose from the excellent wine list, and settle down in comfort to appreciate the tempting seasonally inspired dishes made from locally sourced produce – maybe smoked trout and horseradish pâté with apricot and ginger chutney; spiced roasted duck leg, Puy lentils, with light chicken and orange jus; or griddled Dingley Dell pork chop with sage and apple sauce.

Open all wk 12-3 6-12 (Sun 12-6) Closed 25-26 Dec, 1 Jan **Food** Lunch Mon-Sat 12-2.30, Sun 12-5 Dinner Mon-Sat 6.30-10 Set menu available ⊕ FREE HOUSE ◼ Adnams, Sharp's Doom Bar, Fuller's London Pride Ⓣ Westons Mortimers Orchard. ☕ 16 **Facilities** Non-diners area ♦♦ Children's portions Garden ▭ Parking WiFi ▭ (notice required)

KEYSOE
Map 12 TL06

The Chequers

tel: 01234 708678 **Pertenhall Rd, Brook End MK44 2HR**
email: chequers.keysoe@tesco.net
dir: *On B660, 7m N of Bedford. 3m S of Kimbolton*

Classic pub grub in a tranquil country pub

This peaceful 15th-century country pub has been in the same safe hands for over a quarter of a century. No games machines, pool tables or jukeboxes disturb the simple pleasures of well-kept ales and great home-made food. The menu offers pub stalwarts like ploughman's; home-made steak and ale pie; chicken curry and rice; chilli con carne and a variety of grilled steaks; and a blackboard displays further choice plus the vegetarian options. For a lighter meal try the home-made chicken liver pâté or soup, garlic mushrooms on toast, or plain or toasted sandwiches.

Open 11.30-2.30 6.30-11 Closed Sun eve, Mon & Tue, Wed L **Food** Lunch Thu-Sun 12-2 Dinner Wed-Sat 6.30-11 ⊕ FREE HOUSE ◼ Hook Norton Hooky Bitter, Fuller's London Pride Ⓣ Westons Stowford Press. **Facilities** Non-diners area ♦♦ Children's menu Children's portions Play area Family room Garden Parking ▭ (notice required) **Notes** ☺

LEIGHTON BUZZARD
Map 11 SP92

The Heath Inn ★★★ INN

tel: 01525 237816 **76 Woburn Rd, Heath and Reach LU7 0AR**
email: enquiries@theheathinn.com **web:** www.theheathinn.com
dir: *Phone for detailed directions*

Great cask ales in a traditional setting

This privately-owned free house on the outskirts of the charming market town of Leighton Buzzard hosts live music throughout the year. The wood-beamed bar is cosy with an open fire; or take your refreshments out to the pretty courtyard garden in summer, where children are well catered for with swings and a slide in the play area. Cask ales are well represented by the likes of Tring, Hopping Mad and Marston's, ably supported by cider from Westons, draft lagers and quality wines. Food served in the bar or in Balens Restaurant follows traditional lines, from ploughman's and jackets to grills and Sunday roasts.

Open all day all wk **Food** Lunch all wk 12-2.30 Dinner Mon-Sat 6-9 ⊕ FREE HOUSE ◼ Tring, Marston's, Hopping Mad Ⓣ Westons Stowford Press. **Facilities** Non-diners area ♦♦ Children's menu Children's portions Play area Outside area ▭ Parking WiFi ▭ (notice required) **Rooms** 16

NORTHILL
Map 12 TL14

The Crown

tel: 01767 627337 **2 Ickwell Rd SG18 9AA**
email: info@crownnorthill.co.uk
dir: *In village centre, adjacent to church*

Greene King pub with a wide-ranging menu

A delightful 16th-century pub with smart, modern interior decor. A number of guests ales are very well kept, and make a delightful companion to almost anything on the menu. Dig into sharing deli boards or sub rolls and panini with fillings such as brie and bacon, or fish fingers and ketchup. Or how about mains such as roasted cod loin with bacon mustard leeks and poached egg, or soy and honey marinated duck with spiced vegetable and noodle stir-fry? The garden has plenty of tables for alfresco eating, and a children's play area.

Open all day all wk **Food** Lunch Mon-Fri 12-3, Sat 12-10, Sun 12-6 Dinner Mon-Fri 6.30-10, Sat 12-10 Av main course £11 ⊕ GREENE KING ◼ IPA & Abbot Ale, Morland Old Speckled Hen, Hardys & Hansons Olde Trip, Guest ales Ⓣ Aspall. ☕ 9 **Facilities** Non-diners area ✿ (Bar Garden) ♦♦ Children's menu Children's portions Play area Garden ▭ Parking WiFi ▭

OAKLEY
Map 11 TL05

Bedford Arms

tel: 01234 822280 **57 High St MK43 7RH**
email: bedfordarmsoakley@btconnect.com
dir: *From A6 N of Bedford follow Oakley signs*

Pretty village inn specialising in fresh fish dishes

Bounded on three sides by the River Ouse in the heart of the pretty village of Oakley, this 16th-century inn is surrounded by beautiful countryside but only a short drive from Bedford. Enjoy a pint of Charles Wells Eagle in the cosy, traditional beamed bar or head to the large garden and decked alfresco dining area for a meal. Fresh fish is a speciality here, and the fish board changes daily to reflect the very best at the market that day; typical dishes include white crabmeat and smoked salmon tagliatelle, and roast rump of lamb with buttered spinach and mint hollandaise. Just let them know if gluten-free dishes are required and they will make sure a wide range is available.

Open all day all wk **Food** Lunch Mon-Sat 12-2.30, Sun 12-4 Dinner Mon-Sat 6-9.30 Restaurant menu available Mon-Sat ⊕ CHARLES WELLS ◀ Eagle IPA, Bombardier Burning Gold, Courage Directors, Guest ale Ŏ Aspall. ☷ 35 **Facilities** Non-diners area ❄ (Bar Garden) ♦️ Children's menu Children's portions Garden ⌂ Parking WiFi ▰ (notice required)

RAVENSDEN
Map 12 TL05

The Horse & Jockey

tel: 01234 772319 **Church End MK44 2RR**
email: horseandjockey@live.com
dir: *N of Bedford. Phone for detailed directions*

Quiet country pub with a caring approach

Sarah Smith's friendly staff ensure a happy welcome at this quiet country pub, which sits atop a hill next to the village church. Locals and visitors feel equally at home, enjoying an Adnams ale or Aspall cider in the bar, or relaxing in the peaceful garden where birdsong is all that can be heard; the pub supplies fleece blankets for cooler evenings. Sarah's husband Darron runs the kitchen, and is passionate in his distinctly British approach to food. Expect the likes of lobster macaroni to start, chargrilled sirloin or rib-eye steaks to follow, and caramel cheesecake with walnut praline to finish.

Open all wk 12-3 6-11 **Food** Lunch all wk 12-2 Dinner all wk 6-9.30 Set menu available Restaurant menu available Mon-Sat ⊕ FREE HOUSE ◀ Adnams Southwold Bitter, Sharp's Doom Bar Ŏ Aspall. ☷ 26 **Facilities** Non-diners area ❄ (Bar Garden) ♦️ Children's portions Garden ⌂ Parking WiFi ▰ (notice required)

SALFORD
Map 11 SP93

The Swan
PICK OF THE PUBS

tel: 01908 281008 **2 Warendon Rd MK17 8BD**
email: swan@peachpubs.com
dir: *M1 junct 13, follow signs to Salford*

Smart gastro-pub that appeals to everyone

Located in a pretty village, the tile-hung, Edwardian-era Swan, run by an enthusiastic team, has a lively bar with comfy leather armchairs that make you feel instantly at home, as does the eating area, where the big French doors can be thrown open to the garden. Peer through the feature window into the kitchen to watch the chefs preparing dishes from the best, locally supplied or own-grown ingredients. Sandwiches, snacks and deli boards are available throughout the day. The pub has its own smokehouse so the likes of home-smoked pork loin and home-smoked mackerel appear on the deli boards. Main courses include pumpkin and Swiss chard pancake with gruyère sauce; bangers and mash with sage and onion gravy; or slow-cooked venison bourguignon with parsnip and thyme purée. Puddings

are very tempting – who could resist iced apple parfait and warm cinnamon fritter? The restored barn with a large central dining table can be used for a private dinner. There's a busy social calendar of events.

Open all day all wk 11am-mdnt (Sun 12-10.30) Closed 25 Dec **Food** Lunch all wk 12-6 Dinner Mon-Sat 6-9.45, Sun 6-9.30 Restaurant menu available all wk ⊕ PEACH PUBS ◀ Sharp's Doom Bar & Cornish Coaster Ŏ Aspall. ☷ 12 **Facilities** Non-diners area ❄ (Bar Garden) ♦️ Children's portions Garden ⌂ Parking WiFi ▰

SOULDROP
Map 11 SP96

The Bedford Arms

tel: 01234 781384 **High St MK44 1EY**
email: thebedfordarms@tiscali.co.uk
dir: *From Rushden take A6 towards Bedford. In 6m right into Stocking Lane to Souldrop. Pub 50mtrs on right*

Children welcome at this village free house

Set in a secluded no-through-road village deep in the Bedfordshire countryside, the very traditional attractions of this 300-year-old establishment – pub games, cottage-style interior and decor – contrast with the modern-day speedfest that is the nearby Santa Pod Raceway. Petrolheads will find it pleasant to wind down here with a good range of real ales and ciders, sipped in a beer garden overlooking fields and distant woodland. Appetites may be sated from a fulfilling menu including yellow fin sole stuffed with smoked haddock and spinach; or rack of baby ribs. Children have their own menu, and there's a wide choice of light bites.

Open 12-3 6-11 (Fri-Sat 12-11 Sun 12-10) Closed Mon (ex BHs) **Food** Lunch Tue-Sat 12-2, Sun 12-4 Dinner Tue-Sat 6.30-9 Av main course £9.95 ⊕ FREE HOUSE ◀ Phipps NBC Red Star, Greene King IPA, Black Sheep, 2 guest ales Ŏ Evershed's Cider, Thatchers Gold, Saxby's Cider. ☷ 13 **Facilities** Non-diners area ❄ (Bar Garden) ♦️ Children's menu Children's portions Garden ⌂ Parking WiFi

STANBRIDGE
Map 11 SP92

The Five Bells

tel: 01525 210224 **Station Rd LU7 9JF**
email: fivebells@fullers.co.uk
dir: *A505 from Leighton Buzzard towards Dunstable, turn left to Stanbridge*

Relaxed village pub with large garden

This whitewashed 400-year-old village inn, now in new hands, has been delightfully renovated and revived. The bar features lots of bare wood as well as comfortable armchairs and rustic wood and tiled floors. The modern decor extends to the bright, airy 75-cover dining room with its oak beams and paintings. The inn uses local suppliers whenever possible to offer farm-assured chicken and beef, and sustainable seafood. The menu typically includes dishes such as beer battered cod and chips, and steak and ale suet pudding, which are complemented by light lunches, blackboard daily specials and Sunday roasts. There's also a spacious lawned garden and patio.

Open all day all wk 11-11 (Sun 12-10.30) **Food** Lunch Mon-Sat 12-10, Sun 12-9 Dinner Mon-Sat 12-10, Sun 12-9 ⊕ FULLER'S ◀ London Pride, Guest ale Ŏ Aspall, Westons Stowford Press. ☷ 8 **Facilities** Non-diners area ❄ (Bar Garden) ♦️ Children's menu Children's portions Garden ⌂ Parking WiFi ▰ (notice required)

The Bell in Studham

Studham is the southern-most village in Bedfordshire & there you'll find the highest lying pub – *The Bell*. The Grade II listed, 500 year old freehold, is amidst Bedfordshire's finest countryside. With panoramic views and character, this haven is just 10 minutes from Dunstable & Hemel Hempstead and 5 minutes from Dunstable Downs and Whipsnade Zoo.

We pride ourselves on providing 'Food and Gifts we Love' and our team aim to provide a warm welcome… Enjoy Home-made Pies, Sunday Roasts with all the trimmings, freshly beer battered Cod & triple cooked chips, to eat in or take-away and '99 soft Ice creams! Also authentic pasta dishes, fresh fish & fine meats. Be enticed with the aroma of fresh dough pizzas, cooked in our stone clay oven. Wines are recommended and there's gifts and goodies to buy. Home accessories, clocks, signs, candles, fudge, jams, chutney and more – perfect as a gift or to keep!

Enjoy a 'Brew & Bakery Treat', a snack at lunchtime with our 'Cask 2 Glass Ale'. Free Wi-Fi 'n' revive with fresh 'Bean to Cup' Coffees or an evening of champagne. Holding a function or dining with family & friends… *The Bell* is there to welcome you.

The Bell, Dunstable Road, Studham, Bedfordshire LU6 2QG • **Tel:** 01582 872460
Website: www.thebellinstudham.co.uk • **Email:** info@thebellinstudham.co.uk

STUDHAM | Map 11 TL01

The Bell in Studham

tel: 01582 872460 **Dunstable Rd LU6 2QG**
email: info@thebellinstudham.co.uk **web:** www.thebellinstudham.co.uk
dir: *M1 junct 9, A5 towards Dunstable. Left onto B4540 to Kensworth, B4541 to Studham*

Nostalgic home cooking and ideal for walkers

Surrounded by some of Bedfordshire's prettiest countryside, but also handy for visitors to Whipsnade zoo and Dunstable Downs, this Grade II listed, 15th-century pub is a gem for walkers and those with dogs (who are welcome to join their owners in the bar). Although bar snacks, sandwiches and sharing boards are available, the main menu puts the emphasis on good proper home cooking with home-made pies, filled jacket potatoes, steaks and chicken Kiev alongside the stone-baked pizzas and fish specials. In summer, grab a table in the large garden with great views.

Open all day all wk **Food** Lunch Mon-Fri 12-2.30, Sat-Sun all day Dinner Mon-Fri 5-9.30, Sat-Sun all day Set menu available ⊕ FREE HOUSE ◀ Greene King IPA, Sharp's Doom Bar, Guest ales ♂ Thatchers Gold & Heritage. ♀ 10
Facilities Non-diners area ♣ (Bar Garden) ♦ Children's portions Garden ♁ Parking WiFi ▄▄ (notice required)

See advert on page 27

SUTTON | Map 12 TL24

The John O'Gaunt

PICK OF THE PUBS

tel: 01767 260377 **30 High St SG19 2TP**
email: thejohnogauntsutton@hotmail.co.uk
dir: *From A1 at Biggleswade at rdbt take A6001, straight on at 2 rdbts, right onto B1040. Pub in village centre*

Village pub owned by couple with accolades galore

First licensed in 1835, Jago and Jane Hurt's 18th-century free house takes its name from the 1st Duke of Lancaster, son of King Edward III and 14th-century lord of the

manor. Set back from the road it stands near an ancient, double-arched packhorse bridge beside a ford running across Potton Brook. Featured on the pub sign is Paige, the owners' pet Staffie. Ale pump badges in the bar declare loyalty to Adnams, with Aspall's Harry Sparrow for real cider drinkers. Jago uses local ingredients for pulled pork pancake with coleslaw and barbecue sauce; lemon sole goujons with fine chips and tartare sauce; short-rib of beef braised in beer with bubble-and-squeak; and hand-rolled gnocchi with roasted butternut squash, spinach, parmesan and pine nuts. Open toasted sandwiches are served at lunchtime. A new flagstone floor has given the green light to muddy boots and dogs.

Open 12-2 6-11 Closed Mon (ex BH) **Food** Lunch Tue-Sat 12-2, Sun 12-3 Dinner Tue-Sat 6.30-9 ⊕ FREE HOUSE ◀ Woodforde's Wherry, Adnams Broadside & Lighthouse ♂ Aspall Harry Sparrow. ♀ 12 **Facilities** Non-diners area ♣ (Bar Garden) ♦ Children's portions Garden ♁ Parking WiFi

TILSWORTH | Map 11 SP92

The Anchor Inn

tel: 01525 211404 **1 Dunstable Rd LU7 9PU**
dir: *Exit A5 at Tilsworth. In 1m pub on right at 3rd bend*

Classic Victorian country dining pub with a garden that's great for kids

The only pub in this Saxon village, The Anchor dates from 1878. The new team pride themselves on their fresh food and well-kept beers and guest ales. An acre of garden includes patio seating for alfresco dining, an adventure playground and a barbecue.

Open all day all wk 12-11.30 **Food** Lunch Mon-Fri 12-2.30, Sat 12-9, Sun 12-7 Dinner Mon-Fri 6-9, Sat 12-9, Sun 12-7 Set menu available ⊕ GREENE KING ◀ Rotating Guest ales ♂ Thatchers. **Facilities** Non-diners area ♦ Children's menu Children's portions Play area Garden ♁ Parking WiFi ▄▄ (notice required)

WOBURN | Map 11 SP93

The Birch at Woburn

tel: 01525 290295 **20 Newport Rd MK17 9HX**
email: ctaverns@aol.com **web:** www.birchwoburn.com
dir: *Phone for detailed directions*

Serious about good, locally sourced food

Close to Woburn Abbey and the Safari Park, this smart family-run establishment has built its reputation on friendly service and freshly cooked food; the kitchen team is passionate about sourcing ingredients from local farms and estates. The contemporary restaurant is welcoming and the menu might offer grilled mackerel fillet to start; and then pork Wellington; or confit duck leg; while the griddle can provide steaks and fish, cooked to your liking by the chefs.

Open 12-3 6-12 Closed 25-26 Dec, 1 Jan, Sun eve **Food** Lunch all wk 12-2.30 Dinner Mon-Sat 6-10 Set menu available ⊕ FREE HOUSE ◀ Sharp's Doom Bar, Adnams ♂ Westons Mortimers Orchard. ♀ 14 **Facilities** Non-diners area ♦ Children's portions Outside area ♁ Parking ▄▄ (notice required)

The Black Horse

tel: 01525 290210 **1 Bedford St MK17 9QB**
email: blackhorse@peachpubs.com
dir: *In town centre on A4012*

Georgian coaching inn serving seasonal fare

'Courtyard Garden' it says above the arch through which stagecoaches once entered and left this 18th-century inn, conveniently in the middle of pretty Woburn. Behind the Georgian frontage the cosy bar is lined with old leather-upholstered settles and the chic, relaxing dining area is where locally sourced, modern British menus offer venison from the Duke of Bedford's Woburn Estate; roast free-range chicken breast; Devon mussels and king prawn linguine; caramelised red onion and spinach tart; and daily specials. Bands play live music on the last Friday evening of the month.

Open all day all wk 11-11 (Sat 11am-11.30pm) Closed 25 Dec **Food** Lunch Mon-Fri 12-3, Sat 12-10, Sun 12-9 Dinner Mon-Fri 6-10, Sat 12-10, Sun 12-9 Av main course £14 ⊕ GREENE KING ◄ IPA & Abbot Ale, Guest ales Ö Aspall. ♀ **Facilities** Non-diners area ❖ (Bar Garden) ♦ Children's portions Garden ⋒ Cider festival WiFi ▭ (notice required)

BERKSHIRE

ALDWORTH Map 5 SU57

The Bell Inn

tel: 01635 578272 **RG8 9SE**
dir: *Just off B4009 (Newbury to Streatley road)*

Well-kept local ales in timewarp setting

Beginning life as a manor hall in 1340, The Bell has reputedly been in the same family for 200 years: ask landlady Mrs Macaulay, she's been here for over 75 years. A 300-year-old, one-handed clock still stands in the taproom 'keeping imperfect time', and the rack for the spit-irons and clockwork roasting jack are still over the fireplace. One might be surprised to discover that an establishment without a restaurant can hold its own in a world of smart gastro-pubs. But The Bell survives thanks to hot, filled rolls and cracking pints of Arkell's or a West Berkshire brew or a monthly guest ale plus local farmhouse ciders.

Open Tue-Sat 11-3 6-11 (Sun 12-3 7-10.30) Closed 25 Dec, Mon (open BH Mon L only) **Food** Lunch Tue-Sat 11-2.30, Sun 12-2.30 Dinner Tue-Sat 6-9.30, Sun 7-9 ⊕ FREE HOUSE ◄ Arkell's Kingsdown Special Ale & 3B, West Berkshire Old Tyler & Maggs' Magnificent Mild, Guest ales Ö Upton's Farmhouse, Tutts Clump, Lilley's Pear & Apple. **Facilities** Non-diners area ❖ (Bar Garden) ♦ Garden ⋒ Parking Notes ◙

ASCOT Map 6 SU96

The Thatched Tavern

tel: 01344 620874 **Cheapside Rd SL5 7QG**
email: enquiries@thethatchedtavern.co.uk
dir: *Follow Ascot Racecourse signs. Through Ascot 1st left (Cheapside). 1.5m, pub on left*

Modern grub in a historic pub

En route to Windsor Castle, Queen Victoria's carriage was allegedly sometimes spotted outside this 400-year-old, flagstone-floored, low-ceilinged pub, while what the history books call 'her faithful servant' John Brown knocked a few back inside. The sheltered garden makes a fine spot to enjoy a Fuller's real ale, a glass of wine

and, for lunch, perhaps sausage and red onion marmalade ciabatta or a ploughman's. For something more substantial try warm mackerel fillet, pickled winter vegetables and home-made guacamole, then lemon and thyme marinated corn-fed chicken breast, rustic ratatouille and dauphinoise potatoes.

Open all wk Mon-Thu 12-3 5.30-11 (Fri-Sun all day) **Food** Lunch Mon-Sat 12-2.30, Sun 12-8 Dinner Mon-Sat 6.30-9.30, Sun 12-8 ⊕ FREE HOUSE ◄ Fuller's London Pride, Thatched Best (pub's own from a local brewery), Guinness Ö Westons Stowford Press. ♀ 11 **Facilities** Non-diners area ♦ Children's portions Garden Parking WiFi

ASHMORE GREEN Map 5 SU56

The Sun in the Wood

tel: 01635 42377 **Stoney Ln RG18 9HF**
email: info@thesuninthewood.co.uk
dir: *From A34 at Robin Hood Rdbt left to Shaw, at mini rdbt right then 7th left into Stoney Ln. 1.5m, pub on left*

Country pub surrounded by woodland

The Sun is a country pub and restaurant surrounded by beautiful mature woodland; the interior is smart and modern. The menu proffers stone baked pizzas and sharing boards and reliable starters such as twice baked goats' cheese soufflé, rocket and parmesan cream; a typical main course might be pork belly, pulled pork croquette, smoked carrot purée, creamed mash, purple sprouting broccoli and red wine jus. Chocolate brownie, hazelnuts and Ray's salted caramel ice cream might make the perfect finish. A change of hands.

Open all wk 12-11 (Sun 12-10.30) **Food** Lunch Mon-Sat 12-3, Sun 12-6 Dinner Mon-Sat 5.30-9.30 ⊕ WADWORTH ◄ 6X, Henry's Original IPA, Horizon & Swordfish Ö Westons Stowford Press, Aspall. ♀ 15 **Facilities** Non-diners area ❖ (Bar Garden) ♦ Children's menu Children's portions Play area Garden ⋒ Parking WiFi ▭

BOXFORD Map 5 SU47

The Bell at Boxford

tel: 01488 608721 **Lambourn Rd RG20 8DD**
email: paul@bellatboxford.com
dir: *M4 junct 14, A338 towards Wantage. Right onto B4000 to x-rds, signed Boxford. Or from A34 junct 13 towards Hungerford, right at rdbt onto B4000. At x-rds right to Boxford. Pub signed*

Seafood specials in a pretty setting

At the heart of the lovely Lambourn Valley, close to Newbury Racecourse, this mock-Tudor country pub boasts a period main bar in the part of the building dating back to the 17th century, and the very occasional visit from Mr Merritt, the resident ghost. Alfresco dining in flower-laden heated terraces offers hog roasts and barbecues and there's a good range of local ales, and also Stowford Press cider on draught; all 60 wines on the list are available by the glass. Feast on seafood specials (whole lobster available if the season's right); tiger prawn linguine; duck egg, black pudding and hollandaise; or mushroom risotto.

Open all day all wk **Food** Lunch Mon-Fri 12-2.30, Sat & Sun 12-6.30 (pizza all wk 2.30-10.30) Dinner Mon-Fri 7-9.30, Sat & Sun 12-6.30 (pizza all wk 2.30-10.30) Set menu available Restaurant menu available all wk ⊕ FREE HOUSE ◄ Wadworth The Bishop's Tipple, 6X & Henry's Original IPA, West Berkshire Good Old Boy, Guinness Ö Westons Stowford Press, Lilley's Apples & Pears. ♀ 60 **Facilities** Non-diners area ❖ (Bar Garden) ♦ Children's portions Garden ⋒ Parking WiFi ▭ (notice required)

BRAY | Map 6 SU97

The Crown Inn ◉◉ | PICK OF THE PUBS

tel: 01628 621936 **High St SL6 2AH**
email: reservations@thecrownatbray.co.uk
dir: M4 junct 8, A308(M) signed Maidenhead (Central). At next rdbt, right onto A308 signed Bray & Windsor. 0.5m, left onto B3028 signed Bray. In village, pub on left

Cosy, Thames-side village inn

Half-timbered outside, this Tudor building explodes with the character of days long gone, with heavy beaming, open fires and all the trimmings. It's been an inn for several centuries; its name possibly derives from regular visits made by King Charles II when visiting Nell Gwynn nearby. Assignations today are firmly rooted in the desire to enjoy the dishes that have gained this Heston Blumenthal-owned pub two AA Rosettes for the distinctly traditional English menu. Diners (restaurant bookings essential, but not for bar meals) may commence with a starter such as Morecambe Bay shrimp, shrimp butter and cucumber salad, setting the standard for mains the like of roasted fillet of Loch Duart salmon; or chargrilled Hereford sirloin steak, marrowbone sauce and fries, finishing with 'Duffy Sheardown' chocolate parfait, blackberry and vanilla. The enclosed courtyard is sheltered by a spreading vine, and there's a large garden in which to quaff Caledonian Golden XPA.

Open all day all wk **Food** Lunch Mon-Fri 12-2.30, Sat 12-3, Sun 12-8 Dinner Mon-Thu 6-9.30, Fri-Sat 6-10, Sun 12-8 ⊕ FAT DUCK GROUP ◀ Courage Best Bitter & Directors, Caledonian Flying Scotsman & Golden XPA, Guest Ales. ♚ 19
Facilities Non-diners area ♣ (Bar Garden Outside area) ♦♦ Children's menu Children's portions Garden Outside area 🎋 Parking WiFi 🚍 (notice required)

The Hinds Head ◉◉◉ | PICK OF THE PUBS

tel: 01628 626151 **High St SL6 2AB**
email: info@hindsheadbray.com
dir: M4 junct 8/9 take Maidenhead Central exit. Next rdbt take Bray/Windsor exit. 0.5m, B3028 to Bray

Old-English fare with a modern twist

This Heston Blumenthal's establishment in Bray has become, not surprisingly, a gastronomic destination, yet the striking 15th-century building remains very much a village local. Its origins as a pub are a little obscure, but the bar's atmosphere created by beams and sturdy oak panelling, log fires, leather chairs, and Windsor and Eton seasonal ales is reassuringly traditional. The main restaurant is on the ground floor, while upstairs are two further dining areas: the Vicar's Room and the larger Royal Room. Having worked alongside the team in the Tudor kitchens at Hampton Court Palace, Heston elaborates on original British cuisine, reintroducing classic recipes from the pub's Tudor roots. Hash of snails; and spiced goose ham with foie gras are indicative starters. Gutsy main courses vary from oxtail and kidney pudding to bone-in sirloin of veal. 'Wassailing' caramelised butter loaf with apple and Pomona is a typical – or rather an atypical – pudding.

Open all wk 11.30-11 (Sun 12-7 Mon 12-11) Closed 25 Dec **Food** Lunch Mon-Sat 12-2.30, Sun 12-4 Dinner Mon-Sat 6.30-9.30 Set menu available ⊕ FREE HOUSE ◀ Rebellion IPA & Seasonal ales, Windsor & Eton Seasonal ale Ⓩ Harry's Cider. ♚ 15
Facilities Non-diners area ♣ (Bar) ♦♦ Children's menu Parking WiFi 🚍 (notice required)

BURCHETT'S GREEN | Map 5 SU88

The Crown

tel: 01628 824079 **Burchett's Green Rd SL6 6QZ**
email: info@thecrownburchettsgreen.com
dir: From Maidenhead take A4 towards Reading. At mini rdbt right signed Burchett's Green. Pub in village centre

Village pub in spirited and capable hands

Now owned by chef-landlord Simon Bonwick, this early-Victorian village local reflects his delightfully quirky persona. Take, for example, his declaration that, although there's no table service in the bar or eating areas, he promises, despite being virtually a one-man band, "to continuously look after you in a friendly manner, like the pubs of yesterday!" Or that, in the bar, dogs are welcome, "apart from Pit Bulls, Rottweilers and other belligerent animals like lions and tigers". His starters include artichokes 'like when in Provence', and among his mains are roast rump of salt marsh lamb, garlic and thyme. For a traditional pudding, there can be nothing better than the aptly described 'treacle sponge hot'. Children are not allowed in the bar, but Simon happily serves them smaller portions of his 'really nice grub'. Abbot is the real ale bar staple, with regularly-changing guests and craft beers.

Open Tue-Sun 12-2 6-11 (Mon 6-11) Closed Mon L **Food** Lunch Summer Thur-Sun 12-2, Winter Sun 12-2 Dinner Summer Mon-Sat 6-9, Winter Wed-Sat 6-9 Restaurant menu available Mon-Sat ⊕ FREE HOUSE ◀ Greene King Abbot Ale, Guest ales.
Facilities Non-diners area ♦♦ Children's portions Garden 🎋 Parking

---

COLNBROOK | Map 6 TQ07

The Ostrich

tel: 01753 682628 **High St SL3 0JZ**
email: enquiries@theostrichcolnbrook.co.uk
dir: M25 junct 14 towards Poyle. Right at 1st rdbt, over next 2 rdbts. Left at sharp right bend into High St. Left at mini rdbt, pub on left

900 years of hospitality and still going strong

One of England's oldest pubs can be found, perhaps surprisingly, close to Heathrow and minutes from the M25. Dating from 1106, the vast and rambling Ostrich oozes history. Some of its legends are particularly gruesome, as would befit the heavily timbered façade, cobbled courtyard, wonky oak beams, massive fireplaces and crooked stairs. Yet the interior has acquired a contemporary style, so expect glass doors, a steel bar, chunky furnishings and vibrant colours. The menu of pub food embraces potato skins with sour cream and salsa; braised lamb shank; and warm walnut fudge with chocolate brownie.

Open all wk 12-3 5-11 (Sun all day) **Food** Lunch Mon-Sat 12-2.30, Sun 12-9 Dinner Mon-Sat 6-9.30, Sun 12-9 ⊕ SHEPHERD NEAME ◀ Master Brew, Spitfire, Whitstable Bay Pale Ale Ⓩ Symonds. ♚ 10 **Facilities** Non-diners area ♦♦ Children's menu Children's portions Garden 🎋 Parking WiFi 🚍 (notice required)

COOKHAM | Map 6 SU88

The White Oak ◉

tel: 01628 523043 **The Pound SL6 9QE**
email: info@thewhiteoak.co.uk
dir: From A4 E of Maidenhead take A4094 signed Cookham. Left into High St (B4447) signed Cookham Rise/Cookham Dean. Pass through common. Left at mini rdbt, pub on right

Modern British menus at friendly pub and restaurant

After a spell in London, Henry and Katherine Cripps returned to their roots to transform and run what is now a successful, contemporary village pub and restaurant. Diners can tuck into award-winning, daily changing, modern British dishes, so perhaps start with split pea and ham hock soup with mint oil; or roast chicken ravioli; then skate wing with nut-brown butter, capers, spinach and chips; or oxtail and cheek cottage pie, finishing with lardy cake, salted whisky caramel and vanilla ice cream; or steamed treacle sponge and custard. A separate 'Auberge' menu is inspired by French country cooking.

Open all wk **Food** Lunch Mon-Sat 12-2.30, Sun 12-3.30 Dinner Mon-Sat 6.30-10, Sun 5.30-9 Set menu available Restaurant menu available all wk ⊕ GREENE KING ◀ IPA & Abbot Ale ♻ Aspall. ᵠ 24 **Facilities** Non-diners area ◖◗ Children's menu Children's portions Garden 🎜 Parking WiFi

---

COOKHAM DEAN
Map 5 SU88

The Chequers Brasserie
PICK OF THE PUBS

tel: 01628 481232 **Dean Ln SL6 9BQ**
email: info@chequersbrasserie.co.uk
dir: From A4094 in Cookham High St towards Marlow, over rail line. 1m on right

Historic pub with an established brasserie

Tucked away between Marlow and Maidenhead, The Chequers is in one of the prettiest villages in the Thames Valley. Striking Victorian and Edwardian villas around the green set the tone, while the surrounding wooded hills and dales have earned Cookham Dean a reputation as a centre for wonderful walks. Wooden beams, an open fire and comfortable seating welcome drinkers to the small bar, perhaps to sample Rebellion's fine ales. Dining takes place in the older part of the building, or in the conservatory; a private dining room can be reserved for parties. The menus of expertly prepared dishes are based on fresh, quality ingredients enhanced by careful use of cosmopolitan flavours. A starter of Scotch duck egg, black pudding, red onion jam and a balsamic reduction could be followed by seafood risotto; butternut squash and wild mushroom linguine; or chicken breast wrapped in Parma ham with cream Savoy and fondant potato. Dogs are welcome in the garden only.

Open all wk Mon-Fri 10-3 5.30-11 (Sat-Sun all day) **Food** Lunch all wk 12-2.30 Dinner Sun-Thu 6.30-9.30, Fri-Sat 6.30-10 Set menu available Restaurant menu available all wk ⊕ FREE HOUSE ◀ Rebellion IPA ♻ Westons Stowford Press. ᵠ 14 **Facilities** Non-diners area ◖◗ Children's portions Garden 🎜 Parking WiFi 🚍 (notice required)

CURRIDGE
Map 5 SU47

The Bunk Inn

tel: 01635 200400 **RG18 9DS**
email: info@thebunkinn.co.uk
dir: M4 junct 13, A34 N towards Oxford. Take 1st slip road. At T-junct right signed Hermitage. In approx 1m right at mini rdbt into Long Ln, 1st right signed Curridge

Village tavern handy for Newbury Racecourse

One of the oldest village buildings, the inn was lovingly refurbished in 2013 by Upham Brewery, whose tasty beers populate the handpulls on the bar. The log fire-warmed village snug remains a comfy focus for chatter or contemplation, whilst an airy restaurant with eye-catching decor or a heated patio offer alternative locations to sit, sup and study the compact, well-balanced menu. The chefs home-in on local suppliers and create dishes such as glazed pork faggot with black pudding, baked potato purée, Savoy cabbage and honeyed parsnip; and curried Brixham crab and leek omelette. Specials may feature game from the local estates and woods that characterise this green heart of Berkshire.

Open all day all wk **Food** Lunch Mon-Fri 12-2.30, Sat 12-3, Sun 12-3.30 Dinner Mon-Sat 6.30-9.30, Sun 6.30-9 Av main course £11-£12 Set menu available Restaurant menu available Mon-Sat ⊕ UPHAM BREWERY ◀ Punter, Tipster, 1st Drop & Stakes ♻ The Orchard Pig. ᵠ 9 **Facilities** Non-diners area ✿ (Bar Garden) ◖◗ Children's menu Children's portions Family room Garden 🎜 Beer festival Parking WiFi 🚍 (notice required)

EAST GARSTON
Map 5 SU37

The Queen's Arms Country Inn ★★★★ INN ⊛
PICK OF THE PUBS

tel: 01488 648757 **RG17 7ET**
email: info@queensarmshotel.co.uk **web:** www.queensarmshotel.co.uk
dir: M4 junct 14, 4m onto A338 to Great Shefford, then East Garston

Stylish pub in the heart of racehorse country

Pleasantly located in the Lambourn Valley, home to over 2,000 racehorses and more than 50 racing yards, this charming pub acts as a quasi-headquarters for British racing with owners, trainers and jockeys among its clientele. The inn's oldest part was a farmer's cottage in the 18th century; its name derives from being licensed around 1856, the year of Queen Victoria's Silver Jubilee. The welcome is warm and the setting stylishly traditional. So with a glass of Doom Bar in hand, and a listening ear tuned for an indiscreet racing tip, choose from the menu: a sandwich of Kelmscott Farm cured bacon, roasted tomato and wholegrain mustard mayo perhaps. Or a pub favourite – smoked chicken, ham and leek pie served with skinny chips and pea purée. After a gallop two courses could be called for: try spiced and sweetened crispy pork cheeks with baby watercress and chipotle peppers, followed by whole lemon sole with roasted courgettes and lemon butter.

Open all day all wk 11am-mdnt Closed 25 Dec **Food** Lunch Mon-Sat 12-2.30, Sun 12-3.30 Dinner Mon-Sat 6.30-9.30 ⊕ FREE HOUSE ◀ Sharp's Doom Bar, Loose Cannon Abingdon Bridge, Guinness, Guest ales ♻ Thatchers Gold. **Facilities** Non-diners area ✿ (Bar Garden) ◖◗ Children's portions Garden 🎜 Parking WiFi 🚍 (notice required) **Rooms** 8

FRILSHAM
Map 5 SU57

The Pot Kiln ⊛
PICK OF THE PUBS

tel: 01635 201366 **RG18 0XX**
email: info@potkiln.org
dir: From Yattendon follow Pot Kiln signs, cross over motorway. 0.25m, pub on right

Locally sourced game dishes drive the menu here

Hidden down narrow lanes, this 18th-century pub can be a bit elusive, but when you find it – and you will – you'll also find it was worth the effort. A former kiln-workers' beer house, the bar has a choice of West Berkshire Brewery ales and Somerset cider. Game and wild food has long fascinated owner Mike Robinson, a passion that lies behind the success of this idyllic red-brick pub. A big draw is the venison from the deer herd that Mike manages nearby. Once out of the pot, it is served in various ways, such as a main course of pavé of fallow deer with roast bone marrow. Other signature dishes include warm salad of wild wood pigeon, artichoke purée, bacon and black pudding; or linguine of winter chanterelles and trumpet mushrooms. On summer Sunday evenings, pizzas are cooked in a wood-fired oven in the garden.

Open Mon & Wed-Fri 12-3 6-11 (Sat-Sun 12-11) Closed 25 Dec, Tue **Food** Lunch Wed-Mon 12-2.30 Dinner Wed-Mon 6.30-8.30 Restaurant menu available Wed-Mon ⊕ FREE HOUSE ◀ Brick Kiln, West Berkshire Mr Chubb's Lunchtime Bitter & Maggs' Magnificent Mild ♻ Thatchers, Cotswold. ᵠ 10 **Facilities** Non-diners area ✿ (Bar Garden) ◖◗ Children's menu Children's portions Play area Garden 🎜 Parking WiFi 🚍 (notice required)

HAMPSTEAD NORREYS
Map 5 SU57

NEW The White Hart

tel: 01635 202248 **Church St RG18 0TB**
email: the.white.hart@hotmail.co.uk
dir: *M4 junct 13, A34 signed Oxford. Left signed Hermitage. Through Hermitage. At T-junct left signed Hampstead Norreys. At mini rdbt in village turn right. Pub on left*

Steeped in history and surrounded by beautiful countryside

An extensively refurbished, but still charming, traditional building of 16th-century origin. Absolutely everything on the menu, from stocks and sauces to the desserts, is made from scratch. Meats come from an award-winning butcher and game-dealer down the road. On the main menu, cod and chips; duck breast; and stuffed mushroom. Look to the specials board for constantly changing dishes such as piri piri pork with sweet potato mash and mango and coriander salsa; roasted monkfish wrapped in Parma ham with chorizo risotto; and minted lamb steak with red wine jus and dauphinoise potatoes. Arrive on the last weekend in June for the annual beer festival.

Open 12-3 6-close (Sat-Sun 12-close) Closed 1 Jan, Mon **Food** Lunch Tue-Sat 12-2.30, Sun 12-3 Dinner Tue-Thu 6-9, Fri-Sat 6-9.30, Sun 6-8.30 ⊕ GREENE KING ◀ Morland Original Ò Aspall. **Facilities** Non-diners area ❖ (Bar Garden) ◆ Children's menu Children's portions Play area Garden ⌂ Beer festival Parking WiFi ▥ (notice required)

HERMITAGE
Map 5 SU57

The White Horse of Hermitage

tel: 01635 200325 **Newbury Rd RG18 9TB**
email: whitehorsehermitage@gmail.com
dir: *5m from Newbury on B4009. From M4 junct 13 follow signs for Newbury Showground, right into Priors Court Rd, left at mini rdbt, pub approx 50yds on right*

Enjoyable home-cooked food and large garden

Under new ownership, this family-friendly pub dates back at least 160 years and is now run by experienced operator Sarah Sweeney. The White Horse has achieved a solid reputation for its pub food, using the freshest and finest local produce to create a daily menu that typically includes burgers, pies, steaks and other daily specials, all washed down with pints of Abbot Ale or Aspall cider. The interior bar and restaurant is contemporary in decor, and outside you can choose between the Mediterranean-style patio or the large garden, which is equipped with swings and climbing frames for younger visitors.

Open all day all wk **Food** Lunch Mon-Sat 12-3, Sun 12-6 Dinner Mon-Thu 5-9, Fri-Sat 5-9.30, Sun 12-6 Av main course £12 Set menu available ⊕ GREENE KING ◀ Abbot Ale & IPA, Guinness, Guest ales Ò Thatchers, Aspall. ▾ 9 **Facilities** Non-diners area ❖ (Bar Restaurant Garden) ◆ Children's menu Children's portions Play area Garden ⌂ Beer festival Cider festival Parking WiFi ▥ (notice required)

HOLYPORT
Map 6 SU87

The Belgian Arms

tel: 01628 634468 **SL6 2JR**
email: reservations@thebelgianarms.com
dir: *M4 junct 8, A308(M). At rdbt take A330 signed Ascot. At Holyport village green left signed Bray & Windsor. 1st left into Holyport St. Belgian Arms on right*

Earthy decor, friendly staff and classy food

The name of this wisteria-draped village pub, just off the green and overlooking the pond, begs the question – what's the connection with Belgium? Apparently, during the First World War many local men fought in Flanders and so its name was changed from The Eagle as a tribute to them. Today's reputation is founded on serving good British food, featuring fresh, daily-delivered produce, often from artisan suppliers. Menus typically feature steak béarnaise; cottage pie; chestnut and mushroom pithivier; 'fish n chips'; and Sunday roasts.

Open all day all wk Mon 5-9 Tue-Thu 12-3 5-11 Fri-Sat 12-11 Sun 12-9.30 **Food** Lunch Tue-Sat 12-2.30, Sun 12-4 Dinner Tue-Thu 6.30-9.30, Fri-Sat 6-10, Sun 6-9 Set menu available Restaurant menu available all wk ⊕ BRAKSPEAR ◀ Brakspear Best & Special, Marston's Pedigree Ò Symonds. ▾ 12 **Facilities** Non-diners area ❖ (Bar Garden) ◆ Children's menu Children's portions Garden ⌂ Parking WiFi

HUNGERFORD
Map 5 SU36

The Pheasant Inn

tel: 01488 648284 **Ermin St, Shefford Woodlands RG17 7AA**
email: info@pheasantinnlambourn.co.uk
dir: *M4 junct 14, A338 towards Wantage. Left onto B4000 towards Lambourn*

Welcoming atmosphere, chic interior and good food

Originally called The Paraffin House because it was licensed to sell fuel alongside ale, this old drovers' retreat in the Lambourn Valley is a notable food pub. Its interior retains original features such as beams, wood-panelling and a stone floor. Food choices include sharing boards crammed with the likes of houmous, tzatziki, olives and pitta bread, or full meals such as chicken liver parfait with spiced pear chutney and toasted brioche, followed by fresh tagliatelle with hare and vegetable ragout; with sticky toffee pudding for dessert. Wash it down with Ramsbury Gold or Symonds Founders Reserve cider.

Open all day all wk Closed 25 Dec **Food** Lunch all wk 12-2.30 Dinner Mon-Sat 6.30-9.30, Sun 6.30-8.30 Restaurant menu available all wk ⊕ FREE HOUSE ◀ Ramsbury Gold, Upham Punter Ò Symonds Founders Reserve. ▾ 12 **Facilities** Non-diners area ❖ (Bar Restaurant Garden) ◆ Children's menu Children's portions Garden Parking WiFi ▥

The Swan Inn ★★★★ INN
PICK OF THE PUBS

tel: 01488 668326 **Craven Rd, Lower Green, Inkpen RG17 9DX**
email: enquiries@theswaninn-organics.co.uk web: www.theswaninn-organics.co.uk
dir: *S on Hungerford High St, past rail bridge, left to Hungerford Common, right signed Inkpen*

Beamed village inn with excellent walks on the doorstep

Idyllically positioned on the North Wessex Downs, this 17th-century pub has its own farm shop, which is the first clue that owners Mary and Bernard Harris are also beef farmers. All the meat on the menu here is organic, with beef from the owners' own farm and chicken from Otter Valley. The beers are organic too, with Jester Bitter from nearby Great Shefford among the regular pumps. Almost everything on the menu is prepared using fresh farm produce, including some vegetables and soft fruit. Most pasta is handmade on the premises, maybe making an appearance on the menu as tagliatelle with chicken and mushrooms in creamy tomato sauce; or ricotta and spinach cannelloni. Other main course choices might include award-winning home-made sausages and mash; or chilli con carne with basmati rice. There is an attractive terraced garden and ten en suite bedrooms.

Open all wk 12-2.30 7-11 (Sat 12-11 Sun 12-4) Closed 25-26 Dec **Food** Lunch all wk 12-2.30 Dinner Mon-Sat 7-9.30 Restaurant menu available all wk ⊕ FREE HOUSE ◪ Butts Traditional, Jester & Blackguard Porter, Guest ales. **Facilities** Non-diners area ◈ Children's menu Children's portions Play area Garden Outside area ⊟ Parking WiFi ☛ (notice required) **Rooms** 10

HURLEY
Map 5 SU88

The Olde Bell Inn ★★★★★ INN ◉◉ PICK OF THE PUBS

tel: 01628 825881 **High St SL6 5LX**
email: oldebellreception@coachinginn.co.uk **web:** www.theoldebell.co.uk
dir: M4 junct 8/9 follow Henley signs. At rdbt take A4130 towards Hurley. Right to Hurley, inn 800yds on right

Ancient inn widely known for its good food

As long ago as 1135, pilgrims to Hurley Priory would stay here in what used to be its guest house; the priory's nave survived to become today's parish church. In truth, the inn is not all quite that ancient, but it reckons to be the country's oldest still-operating inn and its nooks, crannies and crooked doors strongly suggest it's a fair claim. Age apart, attractions include the accomplished food, awarded two AA Rosettes, with daily-changing menus based firmly on produce from local farms and suppliers. A bar menu displays pub favourites such as beer-battered haddock with chunky chips and mushy peas, while the fixed price two- or three-course lunch menu represents excellent value. Look to the carte for a starter of pan-fried herring with Devon crab and horseradish mayonnaise; mains such as pan-fried sea bass with pea, chorizo and mussel risotto; and treacle tart with apple purée for pudding. The terrace and wildflower-meadow beer garden are delightful.

Open all day all wk 11am-mdnt (Sun 11-11) **Food** Lunch Mon-Sat 12-2.30, Sun 12.30-3.30 Dinner Mon-Sat 6-9.30, Sun 6.30-9 Set menu available Restaurant menu available all wk ⊕ FREE HOUSE ◪ Rebellion, Theakston ☍ Burrow Hill. ♈ 10 **Facilities** Non-diners area ❀ (Bar Garden) ◈ Children's menu Children's portions Play area Garden ⊟ Parking WiFi ☛ **Rooms** 48

HURST
Map 5 SU77

The Green Man

tel: 0118 934 2599 **Hinton Rd RG10 0BP**
web: www.greenmanhurst.co.uk
dir: From Wokingham on A321 towards Twyford. Right after Hurst Cricket Club cricket ground on right into Hinton Rd

Ever-reliable village retreat

A homely half-timbered cottage pub situated close to the village cricket pitch and now with capable new hands at the helm. Older parts of the building predate its

---

first licence granted in 1602; thick beams were recycled from Tudor warships and offer a memorable interior in this appealing rustic retreat. Brakspear Brewery bitter and seasonal ales continue to keep drinkers happy. Diners can anticipate a seasonally adjusted, solidly British menu with mains like chicken, rabbit and bacon stew, with bread and butter pudding to follow. There's a tree-shaded beer garden with serene country views and the pub is very dog friendly.

Open all day all wk **Food** Lunch all wk 12-3 Dinner Mon-Fri 6-9.30, Sat-Sun all day ⊕ BRAKSPEAR ◪ Bitter & Seasonal ales, Wychwood Hobgoblin ☍ Addlestones. ♈ 20 **Facilities** Non-diners area ❀ (Bar Garden) ◈ Children's menu Children's portions Play area Garden ⊟ Parking WiFi

---

KNOWL HILL
Map 5 SU87

Bird In Hand Country Inn PICK OF THE PUBS

tel: 01628 826622 & 822781 **Bath Rd RG10 9UP**
email: info@birdinhand.co.uk
dir: On A4, 5m W of Maidenhead, 7m E of Reading

Friendly country pub

Three generations of landlady Caroline Shone's family have run this part 14th-century inn; it's said that George III sometimes stopped here when he resided at Windsor Castle. The choice of real ales in the wood-panelled bar, the oldest part of the pub, runs to five guests and that's in addition to Binghams locally brewed Twyford Tipple. The 50-bin wine list includes a white and a rosé from nearby Stanlake Park vineyard. In the attractive restaurant, which overlooks a courtyard and fountain, the menu (this also applies in the bar) offers light meals such as Yorkshire rarebit (that's Welsh rarebit with a fried egg), or whitebait. Classic mains include various steaks; pan-roasted duck breast; and scampi and chips. A selection of home-made desserts is available, and they also have cake. Beer festivals take place in June and November.

Open all day all wk **Food** Lunch all wk 12-10 Dinner all wk 12-10 Av main course £12.95 ⊕ FREE HOUSE ◪ Binghams Twyford Tipple, 5 guest ales ☍ Thatchers. ♈ 20 **Facilities** Non-diners area ❀ (Bar Garden) ◈ Children's menu Children's portions Garden ⊟ Beer festival Parking WiFi ☛ (notice required)

LECKHAMPSTEAD
Map 5 SU47

The Stag

tel: 01488 638436 **Shop Ln RG20 8QG**
dir: 6m from Newbury on B4494

A great spot after a country walk

The white-painted Stag lies just off the village green in a sleepy downland village, close to the Ridgeway long-distance path and Snelsmore Common, home to nightjar, woodlark and grazing Exmoor ponies. Inside old black-and-white photographs tell of village life many years ago. Traditional home-cooked food is the order of the day, and the special board changes weekly. Sunday lunches are available.

Open 12-3 6-11 Closed Sun eve & Mon **Food** Lunch Tue-Sat 12-2, Sun 12-2.30 Dinner Tue-Sat 6-9 Av main course £9.95 ⊕ FREE HOUSE ◪ Morland Original, West Berkshire Good Old Boy, Guest ales ☍ Aspall. **Facilities** Non-diners area ❀ (Bar Garden Outside area) ◈ Children's menu Children's portions Garden Outside area ⊟ Parking WiFi ☛ (notice required)

MARSH BENHAM
Map 5 SU46

The Red House

tel: 01635 582017 **RG20 8LY**
email: info@theredhousepub.com
dir: *From Newbury A4 towards Hungerford. Pub signed. in approx 3m. Left onto unclassified road to Marsh Benham*

Thatched country pub with gluten-free menu specialities

Tucked away in the verdant Kennet Valley, trim thatched roofs cap this tranquil retreat just a modest stroll (dog walkers welcome) from the Kennet & Avon Canal. Indulge in a beer from the respected West Berkshire brewery whilst contemplating views from the sheltered beer garden, or slumber beside the log fire, anticipating your choice from the kitchen overseen by experienced French chef-patron Laurent Lebeau. His essentially British menu might include braised ox cheeks in red wine with celeriac mash or, from the thoughtful gluten-free menu, South Coast bream fillets and roasted root vegetables. As for the wines, Laurent chooses well.

Open all day all wk **Food** Lunch Mon-Sat 12-9, Sun 12-8 Dinner Mon-Sat 12-9, Sun 12-8 Set menu available ⊕ FREE HOUSE ◀ West Berkshire Good Old Boy & Mr Chubb's Lunchtime Bitter, Guinness, Guest ales Ò Aspall Harry Sparrow. **Facilities** Non-diners area ☂ (Bar Garden) ◀ Children's menu Children's portions Garden ⋒ Parking WiFi ▭ (notice required)

MONEYROW GREEN
Map 6 SU87

The White Hart

tel: 01628 621460 **SL6 2ND**
email: admin@thewhitehartholyport.co.uk
dir: *2m S from Maidenhead. M4 junct 8/9, follow Holyport signs then Moneyrow Green. Pub by petrol station*

Perfect stop for Windsor visitors

The close proximity to the M4 makes this traditional 19th-century coaching inn a popular spot for those heading to nearby Maidenhead and Windsor. The wood-panelled lounge bar is furnished with leather chesterfields, and quality home-made food and award-winning real ales can be enjoyed in a cosy atmosphere with an open fire. Typical mains are grilled chicken and chorizo salad; Argentine rib-eye steak; chilli con carne; and sausage and mash. Sandwiches, jacket potatoes and filled omelettes are offered at lunchtime. There are large gardens to enjoy in summer with a children's playground and petanque pitch. Time a visit for the annual summer cider and beer festival.

Open all day all wk **Food** Lunch all wk 12-2.30 Dinner all wk 6-9 Av main course £9.50 ⊕ GREENE KING ◀ IPA, Morland Old Speckled Hen, Guest ales Ò Westons Stowford Press. **Facilities** Non-diners area ☂ (Bar Garden) ◀ Children's menu Children's portions Play area Garden ⋒ Beer festival Cider festival Parking WiFi ▭ (notice required)

NEWBURY
Map 5 SU46

The Lord Lyon ★★★ INN

tel: 01488 657578 **Ermin St, Stockcross RG20 8LL**
web: www.lordlyon.co.uk
dir: *A4 from Newbury towards Hungerford. At rdbt take B4000 signed Stockcross. Pub on left*

Just the place after a day at the races

Lord Lyon was a famous racehorse, but older villagers still call the pub The Nag's Head, its original name. Equine connections, especially its location close to Newbury Racecourse, make it popular with trainers and jockeys. As an Arkell's house, it serves the brewery's Moonlight and Wiltshire Gold, as well as 13 wines by the glass. Pub food includes the Lord Lyon beefburger with onion rings and spicy tomato and onion chutney; beer-battered cod and chips; American-style chicken

breast marinated in barbecue sauce with bacon and cheese; and spinach and mushroom lasagne. There are weekly specials too.

Open all day 11.30-11.30 (Sun 12-6) Closed Sun eve **Food** Lunch Tue-Sun 12-3 Dinner Tue-Sat 6-9 Restaurant menu available Tue-Sun ⊕ ARKELL'S ◀ Moonlight & Wiltshire Gold Ò Westons Stowford Press. ♙ 13 **Facilities** Non-diners area ☂ (Bar Garden Outside area) ◀ Children's menu Children's portions Family room Garden Outside area ⋒ Parking WiFi ▭ (notice required) **Rooms** 5

NEW The Newbury

tel: 01635 49000 **137 Bartholomew St RG14 5HB**
email: bar@thenewburypub.co.uk **web:** www.thenewburypub.co.uk
dir: *Phone pub for detailed directions*

Sophisticated town-centre gastro-pub

Until 2012, when director Peter Gumber and head chef Clark Oldfield revamped it, this was the Bricklayers Arms. And exceedingly well it's done since. Through the elegant portico from the street there's a spacious bar, lounge and dining areas, and a roof terrace. House ales from the West Berkshire brewery are joined by other local beers and the occasional rough cider. Spirits are a big thing, and good wines are a given. Using mostly locally sourced artisan produce, the open kitchen delivers Newbury mixed grill; half Selsey lobster; braised ox-cheek, mash and wild mushrooms; and roast rabbit saddle with Stornoway black pudding.

Open all day all wk **Food** Lunch 12-3 Dinner 5.30-11 Restaurant menu available ⊕ SPIRIT PUB COMPANY ◀ Two Cocks Cavalier & Roundhead, West Berkshire Good Old Boy & Mr Swift's Pale Ale Ò Westons Stowford Press. ♙ 26 **Facilities** Non-diners area ☂ (Bar Garden) ◀ Children's portions Garden ⋒ WiFi ▭ (notice required)

See advert on opposite page

OAKLEY GREEN
Map 6 SU97

The Greene Oak

tel: 01753 864294 **SL4 5UW**
email: info@thegreeneoak.co.uk
dir: *M4 junct 8, A308(M) signed Maidenhead Central. At rdbt take A308 signed Bray & Windsor. Right into Oakley Green Rd (B3024) signed Twyford. Pub on left*

Thriving dining-pub near Windsor

The refinement that the Metropolitan Pub Company brings here draws those who enjoy classy yet relaxed drinking and dining. On parade in the bar is Guardsman, which was Windsor's first new brew for 80 years when launched in 2010; the same year saw the rebirth of Truman's, whose Swift is also on tap. Considerable thought lies behind the daily-changing modern menus, as shown by pavé of lamb with lamb shoulder croquette and smoked aubergine purée; roasted hake fillet with charred cucumber and fennel crumb fish velouté; and confit onion tart. Take the children - they have a menu all to themselves.

Open all day all wk **Food** Lunch Mon-Sat 12-2.30, Sun 12-5 Dinner Mon-Sat 6.30-9.30 ⊕ FREE HOUSE ◀ Greene King IPA & Abbot Ale, Truman's Swift, Windsor & Eton Guardsman Ö Aspall. ☕ 26 **Facilities** Non-diners area ♦♦ Children's menu Children's portions Garden ⌂ Parking WiFi ➡ (notice required)

PALEY STREET
Map 5 SU87

The Royal Oak Paley Street ⓢⓢⓢ   PICK OF THE PUBS

tel: 01628 620541 **Littlefield Green SL6 3JN**
email: reservations@theroyaloakpaleystreet.com
dir: *M4 junct 8/9a A308(M) signed Maidenhead (Central)*

Award-winning food in celebrity-owned village pub

With a cottagey aspect outside, the interior continues the theme with a distinctly welcoming, nostalgic feel; time-honoured decor and furnishings enhanced by contemporary artwork. Bang up to date is the white pebble and waterfall garden, a pleasant, alfresco retreat of shrub and herb planters. The team behind this success story includes former TV chat-show host Sir Michael Parkinson, and his son Nick who brings a wealth of experience to the helm, and having won numerous awards. The head chef, Michael Chapman, sources the best seasonal British produce to create the ever-changing range of dishes such as a starter of smoked River Test eel with pickled baby onions, Granny Smith apple and bacon. Then graduate perhaps to the main event of Wiltshire pheasant with braised lentils and roast cauliflower purée; or Berkshire guinea fowl, wood pigeon and chestnut pie. There's ample opportunity to match food and wine, with 25 available by the glass, whilst beers from Fuller's and Gales complete the picture.

Open all wk 12-3 6-11 (Sun 12-4) **Food** Lunch Mon-Sat 12-2.30, Sun 12-3.30 Dinner Mon-Thu 6.30-9.30, Fri-Sat 6.30-10 Set menu available Restaurant menu available all wk ⊕ FULLER'S ◀ London Pride, George Gale & Co Seafarers. ☕ 25 **Facilities** Non-diners area ♦♦ Children's portions Garden Parking WiFi

PEASEMORE
Map 5 SU47

The Fox at Peasemore

tel: 01635 248480 **Hill Green Ln RG20 7JN**
email: info@foxatpeasemore.co.uk
dir: *M4 junct 13, A34 signed Oxford. Immediately left onto slip road signed Chieveley, Hermitage & Beedon. At T-junct left, through Chieveley to Peasemore. Left at phone box, pub signed*

Ever-successful village pub

The awards Philip and Lauren Davison have won between them over the years would fill several mantelpieces. Admittedly, some were earned before they came to The Fox, but the way things are going more display space will soon be needed. Charmingly rustic, with elegant modern touches, they didn't just refurbish the pub, they transformed it. The bar, warmed by a log-burner, serves Good Old Boy and Butts Traditional, plus Tutts Clump cider. On the main menu are crispy fried brie with Cumberland sauce; Mediterranean vegetable timbale and gazpacho dressing; pan-fried duck breast (cooked pink) with savoury potatoes and rich red wine and berry jus; sticky toffee pudding with black treacle sauce and toffee ice cream. Pub classics are on a blackboard, and sandwiches, baguettes and ploughman's are available too. Outside seating overlooks beautiful countryside – great for a traditional Sunday roast, subject inevitably to Britain's roller-coaster weather.

Open 12-3 6-11 (Sat-Sun 12-late) Closed Mon **Food** Lunch Tue-Sun 12-2 Dinner Tue-Sun 6-9 Av main course £11 Set menu available Restaurant menu available Wed-Sun ⊕ FREE HOUSE ◀ Butts Traditional, West Berkshire Good Old Boy Ö Tutts Clump. ☕ 16 **Facilities** Non-diners area ✿ (Bar Garden Outside area) ♦♦ Children's menu Children's portions Garden Outside area ⌂ Parking WiFi ➡ (notice required)

READING
Map 5 SU77

The Flowing Spring

tel: 0118 969 9878 **Henley Rd, Playhatch RG4 9RB**
email: info@theflowingspringpub.co.uk
dir: *3m N of Reading on A4155 towards Henley*

Cosy country pub at the edge of the Chilterns

Unusually this pub is on the first floor, which slopes steeply from one end of the bar to the other; the verandah overlooks Thames Valley countryside. The pub has been recognised for its well-kept ales and cellar, and the menu of no-nonsense pub favourites is backed by a comprehensive range of vegetarian, vegan and gluten-free and dairy-free options. The pub hosts beer festivals, astronomy nights, outdoor live music, stand-up comedy nights and many other exciting events throughout the year. The huge garden is bounded by streams.

Open all day Closed Mon **Food** Lunch Tue-Sun 12-2.30 Dinner Tue-Sat 6-9 ⊕ FULLER'S ◀ London Pride & ESB, George Gale & Co Seafarers, Guest ale Ö Aspall. ☕ 10 **Facilities** Non-diners area ✿ (Bar Restaurant Garden) ♦♦ Children's portions Play area Garden ⌂ Beer festival Cider festival Parking WiFi ➡ (notice required)

Silver Stars The AA Silver Star rating denotes a Hotel or B&B that we highly recommend. They have a superior level of quality within their star rating, high standards of hospitality, service and cleanliness.

The Shoulder of Mutton

tel: 0118 947 3908 **Playhatch RG4 9QU**
email: shoulderofmutton@hotmail.co.uk
dir: *From Reading follow signs to Caversham, take A4155 to Henley-on-Thames. At rdbt left to Binfield Heath, signed, 1st pub on left*

Village pub that is true to its name

Close to Caversham Lakes and the River Thames; a pleasant walled cottage garden, beams and open fire grace this long-established local favourite in tiny Playhatch. Beer lovers pop in for ales brewed just up the road by Loddon Brewery, whilst others travel from afar to indulge in chef-patron Alan Oxlade's astonishing mutton dishes. The 7-hour roasted shoulder of mutton is famous; the 5-hour shepherd's pie deserves equal consideration; reserve a seat in the airy conservatory and indulge. The wider menu is equally impressive – braised venison and beef pie cooked with beetroot-infused gravy, or the 'Alternative Shoulder', that's pork shoulder cooked for 30 hours, with creamed potato and smoked barbecue sauce.

Open 12-3 6-11 (Mon & Sun 12-3 Sat 12-3 6.30-11) Closed 26 Dec, 2 Jan, Sun eve, Mon eve **Food** Lunch all wk 12-2 Dinner Tue-Sat 6.30-9 Av main course £8.50 Restaurant menu available Tue-Sat ⊕ GREENE KING ◼ Ruddles Best, Loddon Ferrymans's Gold ⓑ Aspall. **Facilities** Non-diners area ◆◆ Children's portions Garden ⊟ Parking ☎ (notice required)

Buratta's at the Royal Oak

tel: 0118 934 5190 **Ruscombe Ln RG10 9JN**
email: enquiries@burattas.co.uk
dir: *From A4 (Wargrave rdbt) take A321 to Twyford (signed Twyford/Wokingham). Straight on at 1st lights, right at 2nd lights onto A3032. Right onto A3024 (Ruscombe Rd which becomes Ruscombe Ln). Pub on left on brow of hill*

Relaxed pub with its own antiques shop

Originally a one-bar pub, the Royal Oak has been extended over the years and the cottage next door is now the kitchen. With Binghams Brewery and Fuller's London Pride as resident ales, the relaxed restaurant offers a range of meals, from hearty bar snacks and sandwiches to à la carte choices such as deep-fried tempura prawns with chilli dip followed by monkfish wrapped in Parma ham, green peppercorn sauce and new potatoes. The large garden, complete with resident ducks, is dog friendly, and the pub has its own antiques shop, which is open during restaurant hours. Nearly everything in the pub is for sale.

Open Tue-Sat 12-3 6-11 (Sun-Mon 12-3) Closed Sun eve & Mon eve **Food** Lunch all wk 12-2.30 Dinner Tue-Sat 7-9.30 ⊕ ENTERPRISE INNS ◼ Fuller's London Pride, Binghams, Guest ales. ☗ 12 **Facilities** Non-diners area ❁ (Bar Restaurant Garden) ◆◆ Children's menu Children's portions Garden ⊟ Parking WiFi ☎ (notice required)

NEW The Shurlock Inn

tel: 0118 934 9094 **The Street RG10 0PS**
email: info@shurlockinn.com

Family-friendly village pub serving local food

This lovely 17th-century pub was bought by a group of villagers in 2009 and refurbished to a high standard, while retaining its exposed timbers and open fireplace. The large family garden and sheltered courtyard are a draw during the warmer months, or you could head to the cosy bar to enjoy pints of Rebellion IPA or one of several well-considered wines. The seasonally-driven menu champions local produce: duck and green peppercorn terrine might be followed by pan-fried fillet of hake with seafood chowder. Desserts are their speciality – try the peppermint pannacotta topped with mint chocolate.

Open all wk 12-3 6-11 (Fri-Sat 12-11 Sun 12-9) **Food** Lunch Mon-Sat 12-2.30, Sun 12-8 Dinner Mon-Sat 6-9.30, Sun 12-8 ⊕ FREE HOUSE ◼ West Berkshire Mr Chubb's, Rebellion IPA ⓑ Westons Stowford Press. ☗ 9 **Facilities** Non-diners area ❁ (Bar Garden) ◆◆ Children's menu Children's portions Play area Garden ⊟ Parking WiFi ☎ (notice required)

The Walter Arms

tel: 0118 977 4903 **Bearwood Rd RG41 5BP**
email: mail@thewalterarms.com
dir: *A329 from Wokingham towards Reading. 1.5m, left onto B3030. 5m, left into Bearwood Rd. Pub 200yds on left*

Welcoming pub with interesting menu of global dishes

A typically solid Victorian building built about 1850 by John Walter III, grandson of the man who founded *The Times* newspaper. The idea was that it should be a working men's club for the workers on the Bearwood Estate, where Walter lived. Now a popular dining pub, the seasonal menus offer traditional English dishes, such as pan-roasted rump of lamb, and beer-battered sustainable haddock; as well as pasta, stone-baked pizzas and oriental- and Arabian-style 'smörgåsbord'. The beer garden is a good spot for a pint of Courage Best.

Open all day all wk 12-11 (Sat 12-12 Sun 12-10) **Food** Lunch Mon-Fri 12-2.30, Sat 12-10, Sun 12-9 Dinner Mon-Fri 6-10, Sat 12-10, Sun 12-9 ⊕ ENTERPRISE INNS ◼ Courage Best Bitter, Guest ale ⓑ Westons Stowford Press. **Facilities** Non-diners area ◆◆ Children's menu Children's portions Garden ⊟ Parking

The Bull Inn

tel: 0118 969 3901 **High St RG4 6UP**
email: bullinn@fullers.co.uk
dir: *From Reading take A4 towards Maidenhead. Left onto B4446 to Sonning*

Welcoming olde-worlde inn

Two minutes' walk from the River Thames in the pretty village of Sonning, this black-and-white timbered inn can trace its roots back 600 years or so; it can also boast visits by former owner Queen Elizabeth I and a mention in Jerome K Jerome's classic novel *Three Men in a Boat*. With Fuller's ales on tap, comfy leather chairs and log fires in the grate, The Bull charms locals and visitors alike. It's a great place to eat too, with an interesting menu of British and world cuisine. Dishes could include a slow braised blade of beef; roasted pheasant stew; Greek meze platter; jerk spiced ham; butternut squash gnocchi and chicken fajita wraps.

Open all day all wk 11-11 **Food** Lunch all wk 10-9.30 Dinner all wk 10-9.30 Set menu available Restaurant menu available all wk ⊕ FULLER'S ◼ London Pride, Chiswick Bitter, Discovery & Organic Honey Dew, George Gale & Co HSB, Guest ale. ☗ 24 **Facilities** Non-diners area ❁ (Bar Garden) ◆◆ Children's portions Garden ⊟ Parking WiFi ☎ (notice required)

STANFORD DINGLEY   Map 5 SU57

NEW The Bull Inn

tel: 0118 974 4582 **RG7 6LS**
email: enquiries@thebullinnstanforddingley.co.uk
web: www.thebullinnstanforddingley.co.uk
dir: *M4 junct 12, A4 towards Newbury, A340 towards Pangbourne. 1st left to Bradfield. Through Bradfield, 0.3m left into Back Lane. At end left, pub 0.25m on left*

Historic country inn in the Pang Valley

Run by the Maton family, with Laura front of house and Andy as chef; baby Noah is currently unassigned. The pub dates from the 15th century, so prepare to duck and grouse. Pump badges promise West Berkshire and Two Cocks ales, and Wyatt's Berkshire Gold cider. For simple rustic surroundings, eat in the Tap Room or the Saloon; the Dining Room is more formal. Choose from dishes featuring rare-breed meats, local game and Brixham-landed fish and shellfish, as well as sandwiches and bar snacks. From May to September, on the second Saturday of the month, classic cars gather in the adjoining meadow.

Open all day all wk **Food** Lunch all wk 12-2.30 Dinner Mon-Sat 6-9.30 Restaurant menu available all wk ⊕ FREE HOUSE ◀ West Berkshire Good Old Boy, Two Cocks Cavalier, Black Sheep ♂ Wyatt's Berkshire Gold. ☎ 13 **Facilities** Non-diners area ♣ (Bar Garden) ♦ Children's portions Garden ⚲ Parking WiFi ▨ (notice required)

The Old Boot Inn

tel: 0118 974 4292 **RG7 6LT**
email: johnintheboot@hotmail.co.uk
dir: *M4 junct 12, A4, A340 to Pangbourne. 1st left to Bradfield. Through Bradfield, follow Stanford Dingley signs*

Peaceful situation and well known for good food

Oak beams and half-timbering feature inside this cottagey inn remote along lanes in the peaceful Pang Valley. The rustic theme continues with log fires and an

enormous beer garden rolling back to merge with pastureland backed by wooded hills. The modern conservatory restaurant is light and airy; just the place to settle down with a pint of local Dr Hexters beer and seek inspiration on the menus. Old school bar meals are the tip of the iceberg, complemented by an à la carte selection and robust specials, perhaps beef Wellington; or lamb shank, mash and vegetables.

Open all wk 11-3 6-11 (Sat-Sun all day) **Food** Lunch all wk 12-2 Dinner all wk 6-9 ⊕ FREE HOUSE ◀ Bass, West Berkshire Dr Hexters, Fuller's London Pride ♂ Westons Stowford Press. ☎ 10 **Facilities** Non-diners area ♣ (Bar Garden) ♦ Children's menu Children's portions Play area Garden ⚲ Parking WiFi ▨ (notice required)

SUNNINGHILL   Map 6 SU96

NEW Dog & Partridge

tel: 01344 623204 **92 Upper Village Rd SL5 7AQ**
email: info@oxandfire.co.uk
dir: *From either A329 or A330 into High St. Into Truss Hill Rd, 1st right into Upper Village Rd, pub on left*

Tucked behind the High Street, but worth finding

If the weather's favourable, make for the courtyard garden, where a small, marble fountain will gently burble away as you ease into your Pinot Grigio, or a Windsor & Eton brewery real ale. Start with marinated chicken skewers and peanut sauce; or maybe thyme- and chilli-marinated squid. Then, monkfish and tiger prawn Thai curry; fillet of beef with wilted spinach, and Calvados and peppercorn sauce; or stuffed courgettes with feta, pine nuts and toasted red pepper sauce. Cheesecake of the day for dessert. No-one need go hungry at lunchtime, when sandwiches, pies, jacket potatoes and pasta are on offer.

Open 12-3 5-11 (Fri-Sat 12-11 Sun 12-10.30) Closed Mon **Food** Contact pub for food times Restaurant menu available Tue-Sun ◀ Fuller's London Pride, Sharp's Doom Bar, Windsor & Eton ♂ Symonds. ☎ 10 **Facilities** Non-diners area ♣ (Bar Garden) ♦ Children's menu Children's portions Garden ⚲ Parking

SWALLOWFIELD   Map 5 SU76

The George & Dragon

tel: 0118 988 4432 **Church Rd RG7 1TJ**
email: dining@georgeanddragonswallowfield.co.uk
dir: *M4, junct 11, A33 towards Basingstoke. Left at Barge Ln to B3349 into The Street, right into Church Rd*

Country pub dating back to the 17th century

This country pub and restaurant looks very much the part with its low, stripped beams, log fires, rug-strewn floors and warm earthy tones. Expect internationally inspired seasonal menus. Starters could be herbed spinach and button mushroom pancake with mornay sauce; and soy- and chilli-braised octopus with pineapple, orange and tomato salsa. Typical main courses include local venison loin steak with haggis mash and redcurrant jus; baked meatballs in a rich Barolo wine tomato sauce, with zesty gremolata and pasta; and monkfish on sweet potato bubble-and-squeak. The garden overlooks beautiful countryside and makes a great place to head for after walking the long-distance Blackwater Valley Path.

Open all day all wk **Food** Lunch Mon-Sat 12-2.30, Sun 12-3 Dinner Mon-Sat 7-9.30, Sun 7-9 ⊕ FREE HOUSE ◀ Ringwood Best Bitter, Sharp's Doom Bar, Upham Punter, Guest ale ♂ Aspall. **Facilities** Non-diners area ♣ (Bar Garden) ♦ Children's menu Children's portions Garden ⚲ Parking

WALTHAM ST LAWRENCE · Map 5 SU87

The Bell

tel: 0118 934 1788 **The Street RG10 0JJ**
email: info@thebellwalthamstlawrence.co.uk
dir: On B3024 E of Twyford. From A4 turn at Hare Hatch

Good ciders and beers at very old inn

This 14th-century free house is renowned for its ciders and an ever-changing range of real ales selected from small independent breweries. The building was given to the community in 1608 and profits from the rent continue to help village charities. Iain and Scott Ganson have built a local reputation for good food and everything possible is made on the premises, including all charcuterie and preparation of game. Start with game terrine, gherkins and toasted beer bread; or caramelised swede and cardamom soup, then continue with seven-hour shoulder of lamb, carrots, mash and caper and anchovy dressing; spatchcock partridge, sage, rainbow chard and braised cannellini beans. Leave room for nectarine crumble and vanilla ice cream.

Open all wk 12-3 5-11 (Sat 12-11 Sun 12-10.30) **Food** Lunch Mon-Fri 12-2, Sat-Sun 12-3 Dinner all wk 6-9.30 ⊕ FREE HOUSE ◀ Loddon Hoppit, 5 guest ales ♻ Pheasant Plucker, Westons Old Rosie. ♀ 19 **Facilities** Non-diners area ✿ (Bar Restaurant Garden) ♦♦ Children's menu Children's portions Garden ⋈ Beer festival Parking

WHITE WALTHAM · Map 5 SU87

The Beehive ◉◉ · PICK OF THE PUBS

tel: 01628 822877 **Waltham Rd SL6 3SH**
dir: M4 junct 8/9, A404, follow White Waltham signs

A cracking country local in an idyllic village setting

In parts this four-square, brick-built village pub dates back to the 18th century. Overlooking the cricket pitch, the distant prospect from the beer-garden is one of pocket woods and rich pastureland. Inside, the pub is distinctly contemporary, with some discrete nods to the local of old. Dominic Chapman arrived in 2014 and determined to retain the pub's function as a focus of village life, hence there are bar stools and hooks where drinkers may enjoy beers from nearby microbreweries. It's for the exemplary menu that visitors beat a path to the door. Dominic's an award-winning chef with an astonishing pedigree and his mission here is 'to provide a solid menu of seasonal food, cooked with a flourish from the heart'. Taking your eye on the menu may be a starter of pickled Cornish mackerel with beetroot and horseradish cream; then choose rabbit and bacon pie with mash and curly kale; or roast haunch of venison with a cocoa sauce, finishing with quince and plumb crumble.

Open all wk 11-3 5-11 (Sat 11am-mdnt Sun 12-10.30) Closed 25-26 Dec
Food Lunch Mon-Fri 12-2.30, Sat 12-9.30, Sun 12-8.30 Dinner Mon-Fri 5-9.30, Sat 12-9.30, Sun 12-8.30 Restaurant menu available all wk ⊕ ENTERPRISE INNS ◀ Fuller's London Pride, Greene King Abbot Ale, Rebellion, Brakspear, Sharp's Doom Bar, Loddon guest ale ♻ Cornish Orchards. ♀ **Facilities** Non-diners area ✿ (Bar Garden) ♦♦ Children's menu Children's portions Garden ⋈ Parking WiFi ▥ (notice required)

WINKFIELD · Map 6 SU97

The Winning Post

tel: 01344 882242 **Winkfield St SL4 4SW**
email: info@winningpostwinkfield.co.uk
dir: M4 junct 6, A355. 3rd exit at rdbt into Imperial Rd (B3175). Right at lights into Saint Leonards Rd (B3022). At 2nd rdbt 2nd exit into North St signed Winkfield. Through Winkfield, at sharp left bend turn right into Winkfield St. Pub 200yds on right

Tranquil village pub popular with the racing fraternity

A short canter from Ascot and Windsor racecourses, this charming 18th-century pub has long been a favourite with the equine-inclined. The Winning Post is off the beaten track and surrounded by stunning Berkshire countryside but it's also a convenient pit stop for Heathrow Airport. The open fire and stone floors retain the building's original character and the beer garden offers alfresco opportunities. Enjoy a pint of Tipster & Punter ale as you order from an enticing menu that might offer roast quail breast with confit leg terrine, crispy egg and fig purée; and pan-fried fillet of Loch Duart salmon with new potatoes and grain mustard beurre blanc.

Open all day all wk **Food** Lunch Mon-Thu 12-9.30, Fri-Sat 12-5.30 Dinner Mon-Thu 12-9.30, Sun 7-9 Restaurant menu available Mon-Sat ⊕ UPHAM PUB CO ◀ Tipster & Punter ♻ Thatchers. ♀ **Facilities** Non-diners area ✿ (Bar Garden) ♦♦ Children's menu Garden ⋈ Parking WiFi

WINTERBOURNE · Map 5 SU47

The Winterbourne Arms

tel: 01635 248200 **RG20 8BB**
email: mail@winterbournearms.com
dir: M4 junct 13 into Chieveley Services, follow Donnington signs to Winterbourne. Right into Arlington Ln, right at T-junct, left into Winterbourne

Idyllic pub with large gardens, now in new hands

Steeped in 300 years of history, warmth and charm, yet only five minutes from the M4, this pretty village pub once housed the village bakery and shop. The real ales may include Ramsbury Deer Stalker or Gold, while 12 wines served by the glass. The traditional and modern British menus and daily-changing specials offer starters like deep-fried butterfly prawns or pan-fried wild mushrooms, followed by chicken fillet filled with garlic herb butter or slow braised flaked ham hock with butter beans, which can be enjoyed by candlelight or alfresco in summer. Local game is served in season. There was a change of hands in early 2015.

Open all wk 12-3 6-11 (Sun 12-10.30) **Food** Lunch all wk 12-2.30 Dinner all wk 6-10 Restaurant menu available all wk ⊕ FREE HOUSE ◀ Ramsbury Gold & Deer Stalker. ♀ 12 **Facilities** Non-diners area ✿ (Bar Garden) ♦♦ Children's portions Garden ⋈ Parking ▥ (notice required)

PICK OF THE PUBS

The Royal Oak Hotel

YATTENDON Map 5 SU57

tel: 01635 201325
The Square RG18 0UG
email: info@royaloakyattendon.com
web: www.royaloakyattendon.co.uk
dir: *M4 junct 12, A4 to Newbury, right at 2nd rdbt to Pangbourne then 1st left. From junct 13, A34 N 1st left, right at T-junct. Left then 2nd right to Yattendon*

Village pub with pretty garden

Yattendon doesn't make much of a footprint on the Berkshire countryside, but although small, it's a delightful village. It once had a castle, but this was wrecked during the Civil War, and locals tell a story of a wealthy family who fled the village after having first hidden a vast fortune in gold down a deep well. The search goes on. Forming part of a row of 16th-century cottages, the pub offers log fires in the bar, oak beams, and quarry-tiled and wooden floors in the adjoining lounge and dining rooms. Not surprisingly, owner Rob McGill serves real ales from the village's West Berkshire Brewery, including Good Old Boy and Mr Chubb's Lunchtime Bitter. Abundant local produce from top suppliers helps head chef Toby Barrett create unfussy seasonal dishes that have gained recognition in many a foodie guide. Consider, for example, cream of cauliflower and cumin soup; venison carpaccio, orange and rosemary

sea salt and horseradish crème fraîche to start. Then mains shown on the regularly changing carte could be wild boar sausage 'toad in the hole', curly kale and onion gravy; grilled sea bass fillet, saffron potato purée and creamed fennel; and on-the-bone chargrilled 10oz Sussex Cross rib steak with chips. Gather a party of eight, give four days' notice, and a feasting menu enables you to dine on roast suckling pig, roast rib of beef, venison Wellington or whole roasted sea bass. French windows lead to a walled rear garden with a vine-laden trellis. Quizzes are held fortnightly, and there are rib and crab nights, seafood weekends, local bands playing and weekend barbecues in the summer months.

Open all day all wk **Food** Lunch Mon-Fri 12-2.30, Sat-Sun 12-3 Dinner Mon-Thu 6.30-9.30, Fri-Sat 6.30-10, Sun 6.30-9 ⊕ FREE HOUSE ◼ West Berkshire Good Old Boy & Mr Chubb's Lunchtime Bitter, Guest ale ♂ Westons Stowford Press. ♟ 10 **Facilities** Non-diners area ✿ (Bar Restaurant Garden) ✦ Children's menu Children's portions Garden ⊼ Parking WiFi

WOKINGHAM
Map 5 SU86

The Broad Street Tavern

tel: 0118 977 3706 **29 Broad St RG40 1AU**
email: broadstreettavern@wadworth.co.uk
dir: In town centre, adjacent to Pizza Express

Family-friendly pub with appealing menu

A handsome detached period building fronted by elegant railings, this town-centre pub offers a friendly atmosphere and spacious indoor and outdoor seating areas. A management change has introduced a more relaxed approach to families; children and dogs are welcome until 6pm. Indeed regular child-centric events are an intrinsic element of the pub's busy social diary, which includes two ale festivals and one for cider in summer. The menu has introduced modern and tasty twists on classic pub food: nibble on salt and pepper squid; share a platter of nachos with guacamole, salsa, sour cream and cheese; or dig into a whole rack of BBQ ribs with corn on the cob and sweet potato fries.

Open all day all wk Closed 25 Dec **Food** Lunch Mon-Fri 12-2.30, Sat 12-4, Sun 12-5 Dinner Mon-Sat 6-9.30 Av main course £9.95 ⊕ WADWORTH ◀ Swordfish, Horizon, 6X, Henry's Original IPA, The Bishop's Tipple ○ Westons Old Rosie. ☗ 15 **Facilities** Non-diners area ❧ (Bar Restaurant Garden) Garden 丹 Beer festival Cider festival WiFi ➠ (notice required)

NEW The Crooked Billet

tel: 0118 978 0438 **Honey Hill RG40 3BJ**
web: www.crookedbilletwokingham.co.uk
dir: Phone pub for detailed directions

Early 19th-century rural gem

A little tucked away, but once on the right road you really shouldn't miss this cute, white-painted, weatherboarded pub. Brakspear's real ales are accompanied by two monthly guests. Typical dishes include beer-battered pollock with chunky chips and peas; roast chicken breast with braised greens and mushrooms; pan-fried calves' liver with spinach, bacon and onions; and leek, potato and cheddar pie. Winter menus will feature local game. Sandwiches and light meals, such as mussels steamed in cider with shallots and smoked bacon, are available at lunchtime. The cheeseboard is good enough to win a prize.

Open all day all wk **Food** Lunch 12-9.30 Dinner 12-9.30 Av main course £12-£14 ⊕ BRAKSPEAR ◀ Brakspear, Wychwood Hobgoblin, Guest ales. ☗ 9 **Facilities** Non-diners area ❧ (Bar Garden) ♦ Children's menu Children's portions Garden 丹 Parking WiFi ➠ (notice required)

WOOLHAMPTON
Map 5 SU56

The Rowbarge

tel: 0118 971 2213 **Station Rd RG7 5SH**
email: rowbarge@brunningandprice.co.uk
dir: From A4 (Bath Rd) at Midgham into Station Rd, signed to station & pub. Over rail crossing, over canal, pub on right

Traditional pub by the Kennet Canal

This early 18th-century pub that sits alongside a busy lock on the Kennet & Avon Canal retains its traditional character; the large garden runs down to the canal towpath so cyclists and walkers can easily pop in for a pint. The bar serves half a dozen cask ales – King John and Saxon Archer among them – Aspall cider and 16 wines by the glass. For something light, try smoked haddock kedgeree, or a rump steak sandwich; main meals include calves' liver and bacon; baked salmon Wellington; and pan-fried parmesan gnocchi.

Open all day all wk 11-11 (Sun 11-10.30) **Food** Lunch Mon-Sat 12-10, Sun 12-9.30 Dinner Mon-Sat 12-10, Sun 12-9.30 ⊕ FREE HOUSE ◀ Original, Andwell, Three Castles, Guest ales ○ Aspall. ☗ 16 **Facilities** Non-diners area ❧ (Bar Garden) ♦ Children's menu Children's portions Garden 丹 Beer festival Parking WiFi ➠ (notice required)

YATTENDON
Map 5 SU57

The Royal Oak Hotel
`PICK OF THE PUBS`

See Pick of the Pubs on opposite page

BRISTOL

BRISTOL
Map 4 ST57

The Albion

tel: 0117 973 3522 **Boyces Av, Clifton BS8 4AA**
email: info@thealbionclifton.co.uk
dir: From A4 take B3129 towards city centre. Right into Clifton Down Rd. 3rd left into Boyces Ave

Popular from brunch time through to the evening

This handsome Grade II listed coaching inn dates from the 17th century. Owned by the St Austell Brewery, it's a popular place to enjoy West Country ales and ciders, as well as being a gastro-pub. In the enclosed courtyard you can order jugs of Pimm's in summer or sip mulled cider under heaters in the winter. The modern British cooking uses local produce in dishes such as smoked venison, beef and ale pie with mash and wilted greens; or John Dory with spaghetti de mer, prawn salsa, sauté potato and rocket pesto. Brunch and Sunday lunch menus are also available. There is an annual cider festival in May.

Open all day 10am-mdnt Closed 25-26 Dec, Mon L **Food** Lunch Tue-Fri 12-3, Sat 11-3, Sun 11-3.30 Dinner Tue-Sat 7-10 ⊕ ST AUSTELL BREWERY ◀ Proper Job, Tribute & Cornish Best, Otter Bitter ○ Thatchers Cheddar Valley, Thatchers Gold. ☗ 12 **Facilities** Non-diners area ❧ (Bar Outside area) ♦ Children's portions Outside area 丹 Cider festival WiFi ➠ (notice required)

BRISTOL *continued*

The Alma Tavern & Theatre

tel: 0117 973 5171 **18-20 Alma Vale Rd, Clifton BS8 2HY**
email: info@almatavernandtheatre.co.uk
dir: *Phone for detailed directions*

Traditional pub with its own theatre and good food

Down a leafy side street in the heart of Clifton, this bustling Victorian pub has the unique and added attraction of a small theatre upstairs. The team here continues to draw in the theatre crowd and maintain a pubby atmosphere for the locals, while also enticing others with their good food offering. As well as an appealing lunchtime menu of sandwiches and light bites, the bar menu offers pub classics and a carte that might include pan-fried haunch of venison with white truffle and thyme dauphinoise potatoes, kale, butternut purée and a port jus; or haloumi and roast squash salad served with pumpkin seeds and honey and balsamic dressing.

Open all day all wk **Food** Lunch Mon-Fri 12-3, Sat-Sun 12-5 Dinner Mon-Sat 6-9.30 Av main course £10 Set menu available Restaurant menu available Mon-Fri ⊕ SPIRIT ◀ Bath Ales Gem, Sharp's Doom Bar, St Austell Tribute ♂ Addlestones, Thatchers Gold. ♀ 12 **Facilities** Non-diners area ❀ (Bar Garden) ♦♦ Children's menu Children's portions Garden ╦ Beer festival Cider festival WiFi ▭ (notice required)

Highbury Vaults

tel: 0117 973 3203 **164 St Michaels Hill, Cotham BS2 8DE**
email: highburyvaults@youngs.co.uk
dir: *A38 to Cotham from inner ring dual carriageway*

Ever-popular unpretentious city escape

A classic little city pub which oozes the character of a Victorian drinking house; lots of dark panelled nooks and crannies, dim lighting, impressive original bar and a cosmopolitan crowd of locals, many of whom retreat from their labours in academia and medicine at this corner of the university area of Bristol. Condemned Victorian prisoners took their last meals here; today's crowd are more fortunate, revelling in beers such as Bath Ales and chowing down on no-nonsense pub fare like fish pie, sausage and mash or burgers. Other benefits include no music or fruit machines and a heated garden terrace. An added attraction of a rather eccentric nature, is the model train that runs the length of the bar.

Open all day all wk 12-12 (Sun 12-11) Closed 25 Dec eve, 26 Dec L, 1 Jan L **Food** Lunch Mon-Fri 12-2, Sat 12-2.30, Sun 12-3 Dinner Mon-Fri 5.30-8.30 Av main course £8 ⊕ YOUNG'S ◀ London Gold & Bitter, Bath Gem, St Austell Tribute, Guest ales ♂ Addlestones, Thatchers Gold. **Facilities** Non-diners area ♦♦ Garden ╦ WiFi ▭ (notice required) **Notes** ⊚

Read all about pubs and **their friendly ghosts in our feature on page 12**

The Kensington Arms

PICK OF THE PUBS

tel: 0117 944 6444 **35-37 Stanley Rd BS6 6NP**
email: info@thekensingtonarms.co.uk
dir: *From Redland Rail Station into South Rd, then Kensington Rd. 4th right into Stanley Rd*

Good food in this buzzy backstreet local

In the quiet backstreets of Bristol's leafy Redland district, this Victorian corner pub still attracts discerning local drinkers but the food has a much wider reach. The elegant dining room is packed with mismatched antique furniture, Victorian prints and views into the open kitchen. The modern British food utilises the very best local produce and the menu changes daily, with meat from the region's farms, and fish delivered daily from Cornwall. In the bar, try the burger or venison pie with your pint of Olde Trip ale or Thatchers Gold. Typical restaurant dishes in the evening are starters of crab and butternut squash tartlet with pickled vegetables; and partridge faggot and parsley root. These might be followed by ricotta dumplings, cauliflower and parmesan; or mallard, blood orange, port, swede and bacon. Finish with pear and almond crumble with honey ice cream; spiced fig doughnuts or a selection of artisan cheeses.

Open all day all wk Closed 25 & 26 Dec **Food** Lunch Mon-Fri 12-3, Sat 10-3, Sun 12-4 Dinner all wk 6-10 Av main course £12 Restaurant menu available all wk ⊕ GREENE KING ◀ Morland Old Golden Hen, Hardys & Hansons Olde Trip ♂ Westons Stowford Press, Thatchers Gold. ♀ 14 **Facilities** Non-diners area ❀ (Bar Restaurant Outside area) ♦♦ Children's portions Outside area ╦ WiFi ▭ (notice required)

BUCKINGHAMSHIRE

AMERSHAM | Map 6 SU99

Hit or Miss Inn

tel: 01494 713109 **Penn Street Village HP7 0PX**
email: hit@ourpubs.co.uk
dir: *M25 junct 18, A404 (Amersham to High Wycombe road) to Amersham. Past crematorium on right, 2nd left into Whielden Ln (signed Winchmore Hill). 1.25m, pub on right*

A dining pub that is certainly a hit

Overlooking the cricket ground from which its name is taken, this is an 18th-century cottage-style dining pub. It has a beautiful country garden with lawn, patio and picnic tables for warmer days, while inside you'll find fires, old-world beams, Badger ales and a warm welcome from landlords Michael and Mary Macken, who have been running the pub for over 12 years. Options on the menu range from tempting sandwiches and baked potatoes to dishes like guinea fowl with spinach, sunblush tomatoes, dauphinoise potatoes and brandy reduction; or slow-cooked lamb shank with crispy pancetta, broad beans and new potatoes. There are daily specials, Sunday roasts and a children's menu, too. There is a village beer and cider festival in mid July.

Open all day all wk 11-11 (Sun 12-10.30) **Food** Lunch Mon-Fri 12-2.30, Sat 12-3, Sun 12-8 Dinner Mon-Sat 6.30-9.30, Sun 12-8 ⊕ HALL & WOODHOUSE ◀ Badger Dorset Best, Tanglefoot, K&B Sussex, Badger Firkin Fox ♂ Westons Stowford Press. ♀ 14 **Facilities** Non-diners area ❀ (Bar Restaurant Garden) ♦♦ Children's menu Children's portions Garden ╦ Beer festival Cider festival Parking WiFi ▭ (notice required)

ASHENDON
Map 11 SP71

NEW The Hundred of Ashendon

tel: 01296 651296 **Lower End HP18 OHE**
email: info@thehundred.co.uk **web:** www.thehundred.co.uk
dir: *Phone pub for detailed directions*

An inn where everyone is very welcome

The interiors of The Hundred ooze charisma, thanks to dark polished wood floors, half plastered walls, mismatched furniture and eclectic decorative artefacts. Walkers, cyclists, families with children and dogs – all receive the same warm welcome from chef and landlord Matthew and his partner Pia who are fulfilling their dream here. A splendid array of real ales greets the thirsty, notably Side Pocket for a Toad from Tring Brewery. Daily-changing menus are a good indication of Matthew's kitchen skills: red mullet soup to start, followed by braised duck leg with turnips and green sauce; finish with quince jelly and shortbread if you want to make a proper meal of it.

Open 12-3.30 6-11 Closed Mon **Food** Lunch 12-3 Dinner 6.30-9 Restaurant menu available Tue-Sun ⊕ FREE HOUSE ◼ Tring Side Pocket for a Toad, XT4, Chiltern Beechwood Bitter Ò Hitchcox. ⬤ 10 **Facilities** Non-diners area ❀ (Bar Garden) ◆◆ Children's portions Garden ⋈ Parking WiFi ⬛ (notice required)

AYLESBURY
Map 11 SP81

The King's Head

tel: 01296 718812 **Market Square HP20 2RW**
email: info@farmersbar.co.uk
dir: *Access on foot only. From Market Square access cobbled passageway. Pub entrance under archway on right*

Brewery tap for the Chiltern microbrewery

Henry VIII reputedly wooed Anne Boleyn when staying at this coaching inn that dates from 1455. Today, The King's Head is the award-winning brewery tap for the Chiltern Brewery, one of the oldest microbreweries in the country. There is a special weekly gravity beer, served from a wooden cask atop the bar. Enjoy a pint in the ancient cobbled courtyard, or dine on house specialities and home-cooked dishes – Buckinghamshire rarebit, and Shearers' lamb stew with minted dumplings to name but two. Rothschild's supplies the wines from its former family seat at nearby National Trust-owned Waddesdon Manor. Contact the pub for details of the beer festivals.

Open all day all wk 11-11 (Sun 12-10.30) Closed 25 Dec **Food** Lunch Mon-Fri 12-2, Sat-Sun 12-3 ⊕ FREE HOUSE/CHILTERN BREWERY ◼ Beechwood Bitter, Chiltern Ale, 300s Old Ale Ò Westons Stowford Press. ⬤ 12 **Facilities** Non-diners area ◆◆ Children's menu Children's portions Garden ⋈ Beer festival WiFi ⬛ (notice required)

BEACONSFIELD
Map 6 SU99

The Red Lion Knotty Green

tel: 01494 680888 **Penn Rd, Knotty Green HP9 2TN**
email: info@myredlion.com
dir: *M40 junct 2, A355 signed Beaconsfield. At 2nd mini rdbt right onto A355 signed Amersham. Over railway, left into Ledborough Ln signed Penn. At T-junct right on B474 Haslemere & Penn. Pub on left*

Delightful country pub with a literary past

The gallery of original Noddy prints and library of Enid Blyton books in the Snuggery is explained by the fact that the famous children's author lived most of her life in the hamlet, and this old pub was her local. From a menu declaring, somewhat tongue in cheek, "The finest food in all of Knotty Green!", dining possibilities include salmon and watercress Wellington; spicy Mexican chicken; mushroom or seafood risotto; a selection of pizzas; lemon sponge pudding and Belgian waffles. At the front, there's decking with tables and chairs.

Open all wk 12-3 5-11 (Mon 5-11, Fri 12-3 5-1am, Sat 12-12, Sun 12-8) **Food** Lunch Tue-Fri 12-3, Sat 12-9, Sun 12-5 Dinner Tue-Thu 5-8.30, Fri 6-9.30, Sat 12-9 Restaurant menu available Tue-Sun ⊕ PUNCH TAVERNS ◼ Young's, Wells Bombardier, Fuller's London Pride, Marston's Tina's Bitty Ò Westons Stowford Press. ⬤ 10 **Facilities** Non-diners area ❀ (Bar Garden) ◆◆ Children's menu Children's portions Garden ⋈ Beer festival Parking WiFi ⬛ (notice required)

The Royal Standard of England
PICK OF THE PUBS

tel: 01494 673382 **Brindle Ln, Forty Green HP9 1XT**
email: theoldestpub@btinternet.com
dir: *A40 to Beaconsfield, right at church rdbt onto B474 towards Penn, left into Forty Green Rd, 1m*

Historic inn renowned for its beers and game dishes

Tucked away in The Chilterns on a site where ale has been provided since Saxon times, this is said to be the oldest free house in England. Many people visit this gabled, idyllic pub to quaff the ales flowing from the pub's own microbrewery, complementing other beers brewed in the surrounding chalk hills and a range of Somerset farm ciders and Herefordshire perry. Hearty food is the order of the day on the quality menus, served amid the leaded windows, quirky artefacts, ancient pillars and beams and flagstone floors, warmed in winter by log-burners and an inglenook. Comforting pub classics include devilled lamb's kidneys or poached salmon salad, followed perhaps by steak and kidney suet pudding or chicken, leek and mushroom pie. Leave a corner for Eton mess or treacle tart. Keep an eye on the specials boards for seasonal game, rabbit, pigeon or venison dishes. There's a bank holiday beer and cider festival in August.

Open all day all wk 11-11 **Food** Contact pub for food times ⊕ FREE HOUSE ◼ Chiltern Ale, Windsor & Eton Conqueror 1075 Ò The Orchard Pig, Westons Perry, Bridge Farm Artisan Cider. ⬤ 11 **Facilities** Non-diners area ❀ (Bar Restaurant Garden) ◆◆ Children's portions Family room Garden Beer festival Cider festival Parking WiFi ⬛

BLEDLOW
Map 5 SP70

The Lions of Bledlow

tel: 01844 343345 **Church End HP27 9PE**
web: www.lionsofbledlow.co.uk
dir: *M40 junct 6, B4009 to Princes Risborough, through Chinnor into Bledlow*

Lovely old pub often in the spotlight

This lovely old free house dates back to the 1500s and is often used as a filming location for dramas such as *Midsomer Murders, Miss Marple* and *Restless.* Low beams and careworn flooring give the pub a timeless feeling, underlined by the steam trains chugging past on the heritage railway beyond the village green. Ramblers who drop down from the wooded Chiltern scarp can fill up on generously filled baguettes and rustic home-made meals like beef lasagne with garlic bread; and hot smoked mackerel fillets with salad and boiled potatoes, boosted by daily-changing specials.

Open all wk 11.30-3 6-11 (wknds all day) **Food** Lunch all wk 12-2.30 Dinner Mon-Sat 6.30-9.30, Sun 7-9 ⊕ FREE HOUSE ◀ Wadworth 6X, Guest ales ⚲ Westons Stowford Press. ☗ 12 **Facilities** Non-diners area ◀ Children's menu Children's portions Family room Garden ☶ Parking ▭

BOVINGDON GREEN
Map 5 SU88

The Royal Oak
PICK OF THE PUBS

See Pick of the Pubs on opposite page

BRILL
Map 11 SP61

The Pheasant Inn

tel: 01844 239370 **Windmill St HP18 9TG**
email: info@thepheasant.co.uk
dir: *In village centre, by windmill*

Stunning views from a popular inn

This 17th-century hilltop inn, now in new hands, stands next to Brill Windmill and occupies a fine position on the edge of Brill Common, with impressive views over the Vale of Aylesbury and the Chilterns. A simple menu offers hearty modern dishes, including starters of crispy duck with Asian salad, citrus fruit and sesame marinade, and main courses like braised shoulder steak and ale pie with creamed potatoes and greens; and honey-roasted Wiltshire ham with Burford eggs and hand-cut chips. Salads, filled baps and ploughman's lunches are served at lunchtime – best enjoyed in the garden in summer.

Open all day all wk 12-11 (Fri-Sat 12-12 Sun 12-10.30) **Food** Lunch Mon-Sat 12-9, Sun 12-6 Dinner Mon-Sat 12-9, Sun 12-6 ⊕ FREE HOUSE ◀ A Very Pleasant Pheasant Ale (pub's own), Guest ales ⚲ Symonds, Guest ciders.
Facilities Non-diners area ❁ (Bar Restaurant Garden) ◀ Children's portions Garden ☶ Cider festival Parking WiFi ▭ (notice required)

NEW The Pointer ◉◉

tel: 01844 238339 **27 Church St HP18 9RT**
email: ester@thepointerbrill.co.uk **web:** www.thepointerbrill.co.uk
dir: *Phone pub for detailed directions*

Impressively restored hilltop village pub and restaurant

David Howden and Ester Gill admit that buying the old Red Lion in 2011 cost them "a little more than" the five shillings it was once valued at. Now comprehensively spruced up, and having regained its original, 16th-century name, it serves the village as pub, restaurant, butcher's and delicatessen. In the bar, real ale pump badges declare Brill's own Vale Brewery and Pointer from XT near Thame, whose spent grains and yeast feed the pub's Longhorn cattle; 3Cs Vintage cider comes from Brackley. For lunch consider pot-roast pheasant, and for dinner rare-breed Middle White pork, or Cornish day-boat pollock.

The Pointer

Open all day Closed Mon L **Food** Lunch Tue-Sat 12-2.30, Sun 1-5 Dinner Tue-Thu 6.30-9, Fri-Sat 6.30-10 Av main course £20 Restaurant menu available Tue-Sun ⊕ FREE HOUSE ◀ XT The Pointer, Vale Pale Ale ⚲ Thatchers, 3Cs Vintage Cider.
☗ 12 **Facilities** Non-diners area ❁ (Bar Garden Outside area) ◀ Children's menu Children's portions Garden Outside area ☶ WiFi ▭ (notice required)

PICK OF THE PUBS

The Royal Oak

BOVINGDON GREEN   Map 5 SU88

tel: 01628 488611
Frieth Rd SL7 2JF
email: info@royaloakmarlow.co.uk
web: www.royaloakmarlow.co.uk
dir: *A4155 from Marlow. 300yds right signed Bovingdon Green. 0.75m, pub on left*

Successful pub strong on seasonality

'Dogs, children and muddy boots welcome' is the friendly motto at this little old whitewashed pub, just up the hill from town on the edge of Marlow Common, and standing in sprawling, flower-filled gardens. Now refurbished, the inside is spacious yet cosy, with dark floorboards, heritage colours, rich fabrics, and a wood-burning stove. All this sets the tone for early evening regulars gathered round a challenging crossword with a pint of Rebellion from Marlow, or Mortimer's Orchard draught cider from Westons in West Berkshire. The imaginative modern British and international menu, put together with good food ethics in mind, is designed to appeal to all, beginning with 'small plates', such as Wobbly Bottom goats' cheese, basil quinoa, walnuts and local damson vinaigrette; and sautéed mushrooms, parmesan polenta and hazelnut aïoli. Main courses cover ground from roast salmon, Bombay

spiced potato cake, Bucksum winter greens and coconut curry cream; slow-cooked beef cheek bourguignon with slow-roast garlic mash; to Jerusalem artichoke risotto with roast chervil root, beetroot jelly and toasted almond dressing. Perhaps treat yourself to warm pecan pie with burnt orange ice cream and caramel sauce; or Thai infused rice pudding with caramelised pineapple, mango and chilli syrup to finish. An exclusively European wine list has 24 by the glass and a wide choice of pudding wines, including one from Worcestershire. Outside there's a sunny summer terrace, pétanque piste and more than likely, red kites wheeling around in the sky.

Open all day all wk 11-11 (Sun 12-10.30) Closed 25-26 Dec
Food Lunch Mon-Fri 12-2.30, Sat 12-3, Sun 12-9.30 Dinner Mon-Thu 6.30-9.30, Fri-Sat 6.30-10, Sun 12-9.30
⊕ SALISBURY PUBS LTD ◀ Rebellion IPA, Smuggler Ŏ Westons Mortimers Orchard. ¶ 24 **Facilities** Non-diners area ❖ (Bar Garden) ♦ Children's portions Garden ⅋ Parking WiFi

BUCKINGHAM
Map 11 SP63

The Old Thatched Inn

tel: 01296 712584 **Main St, Adstock MK18 2JN**
email: manager@theoldthatchedinn.co.uk **web:** www.theoldthatchedinn.co.uk
dir: *A413 from Buckingham towards Aylesbury. Approx 4m left to Adstock*

Spacious pub with plenty of original character

Once called the Chandos Arms, this lovely 17th-century thatched inn still boasts traditional beams and inglenook fireplace. The spacious interior consists of a formal conservatory and a bar with comfy furniture and a welcoming, relaxed atmosphere. Using the freshest, seasonal ingredients from local and regional suppliers, the evening menu takes in smoked mackerel rillette with cucumber and dill salad; and braised lamb neck fillet with roasted root vegetables and minted red wine gravy. Typical lunchtime dishes include pan-fried fillet of pollock with chorizo and potato hash; and Cumberland sausages with mash and onion gravy.

Open all day all wk Closed 26 Dec **Food** Lunch Mon-Fri 12-2.30, Sat 12-3, Sun 12-9 Dinner Mon-Sat 6-9.30, Sun 12-9 Set menu available Restaurant menu available all wk ⊕ FREE HOUSE ◀ Hook Norton Hooky Bitter, Morland Old Speckled Hen, Fuller's London Pride, Timothy Taylor Landlord, Sharp's Doom Bar ☼ Aspall. ₹ 14 **Facilities** Non-diners area ❤ (Bar) ◀◀ Children's menu Children's portions Outside area ⊓ Parking WiFi

See advert on opposite page

CADMORE END
Map 5 SU79

NEW The Tree at Cadmore ★★★ INN ◉

tel: 01494 881183 **HP14 3PF**
email: cadmore@freehotel.co.uk **web:** http://cadmore.treehotel.co.uk
dir: *M40 junct 5 signed Stokenchurch. In Stokenchurch right onto B482 signed Cadmore End. Pub 2m on left*

International cuisine in a country pub

Lovers of Indian and European food will enjoy the choice at this Chiltern Hills pub which holds an AA Rosette for a mouthwatering menu featuring murgh (chicken) kalami kebab; Amritsari fried fish; and maas ke sholey (marinated lamb) as starters, then continuing with tangy and spicy Goan fish and prawn curry; Kashmiri rogan josh (lamb); and chicken jalfrezi. Non-Indian possibilities include confit of pork belly; smoked salmon Caesar salad; and baked tomato and basil pesto gnocchi. Brakspear's Oxford Gold is the house real ale.

Open all day all wk **Food** Contact pub for food times Av main course £12 Restaurant menu available all wk ⊕ MARSTON'S ◀ Brakspear Oxford Gold ☼ Westons Stowford Press. ₹ 9 **Facilities** Non-diners area ◀◀ Children's menu Children's portions Outside area ⊓ Parking WiFi ▭ **Rooms** 16

CHALFONT ST PETER
Map 6 TQ09

The Greyhound Inn
PICK OF THE PUBS

tel: 01753 883404 **SL9 9RA**
email: reception@thegreyhoundinn.net
dir: *M40 junct 1/M25 junct 16, follow signs for Gerrards Cross, then Chalfont St Peter*

Good food from Savoy-trained chef

Over the centuries, this old coaching inn has welcomed many a traveller, Oliver Cromwell and Winston Churchill among them. Judge Jeffreys presided over some of his famous assize courts here, often sending miscreants to the gallows overlooking the adjacent River Misbourne. Much of the pub's 14th-century character survives, particularly the massive beams, huge brick chimneys, and imposing panelled and flagstoned bar. Here you can join the villagers supping pints of Fuller's, watch the big game, and order a bar snack at half time. The refurbished restaurant specialises in English and continental dishes devised by The Savoy-trained head chef Nana Akuffo. Start with the hot and cold Var salmon with asparagus and cream cheese dressing. Next may come a pub favourite such as a home-made burger with back bacon, cheese, fries and relish; or a simple grilled rump steak cooked to your liking. A warm chocolate brownie with orange ice cream makes a satisfying finish.

Open all day all wk Mon-Wed 6.30am-10.30pm (Thu 6.30am-11.30pm Fri-Sat 6.30am-1am Sun 8.30am-10.30pm) **Food** Lunch Mon-Sat 12-2.30, Sun 12-6 Dinner Mon-Sat 6-9.30 Restaurant menu available all wk ⊕ ENTERPRISE INNS ◀ Fuller's London Pride, Sharp's Doom Bar, Adnams. ₹ 10 **Facilities** Non-diners area ❤ (Bar Garden) ◀◀ Children's menu Children's portions Garden ⊓ Parking WiFi

CHENIES
Map 6 TQ09

The Red Lion
PICK OF THE PUBS

tel: 01923 282722 **WD3 6ED**
email: theredlionchenies@hotmail.co.uk
dir: *Between Rickmansworth & Amersham on A404, follow signs for Chenies & Latimer*

A true local with good food

Mike and Heather Norris like to describe their white-painted, 17th-century, Chess Valley village pub as 'autarkic'. It's a real word, meaning self-sufficient, which, as a privately-run free house, it is. Expect a simply furnished main bar, and a charming dining area in the original cottage to the rear, with a tiled floor, inglenook and rustic furniture. Mike is an expert custodian of his beers, from Vale in Brill, Wadworth in Devizes, and guest ales. A typical menu includes lamb's kidneys in creamy mustard and cayenne pepper sauce on toast; fresh daily pies – try the chicken and haggis; chilli con carne; the day's grilled flat fish; and chef's risotto. Daily specials are chalked up, along with home-made puddings. There are also light meals, sandwiches and filled jacket potatoes. Outside, on the pub's sunny side, is a small seating area.

Open all wk Mon-Fri 11-2.30 5.30-11 (Sat 11-11 Sun 12-10.30) **Closed** 25 Dec **Food** Lunch Mon- Fri 12-2, Sat 11-10, Sun 12-9 Dinner Mon-Fri 7-10, Sat 11-10, Sun 12-9 ⊕ FREE HOUSE ◀ Wadworth 6X, Vale Best Bitter, Guest ales ⚬ Westons Stowford Press. ℧ 10 **Facilities** ❋ (Bar Garden) Garden Outside area ⌁ Parking

CHESHAM
Map 6 SP90

The Black Horse Inn

tel: 01494 784656 **Chesham Vale HP5 3NS**
email: blackhorsechesham@aol.co.uk
dir: *A41 from Berkhamsted, A416 through Ashley Green, 0.75m before Chesham right to Vale Rd, at bottom of Nashleigh Hill, 1m, inn on left*

Traditional Chilterns' pub

This 500-year-old pub, now in new hands, is set in some beautiful valley countryside and is ideal for enjoying a cosy, traditional environment without electronic games or music. During the winter there are roaring log fires to take the chill off those who may spot one of the resident ghosts. An ever-changing menu includes an extensive range of snacks, while the main menu features home-made pies. In summer, why not eat in the large garden?

Open all day 12-11 (Sun 12-10.30 Mon 6-11) **Closed** Mon L **Food** Lunch Tue-Sun 12-3 Dinner all wk 6-8.45 Set menu available ⊕ PUNCH TAVERNS ◀ Adnams Broadside & Ghost Ship, Fuller's London Pride, 2 guest ales.
Facilities Non-diners area ❋ (Bar Garden) ⚐ Children's menu Children's portions Garden ⌁ Beer festival Parking WiFi ⛟ (notice required)

The Swan

tel: 01494 783075 **Ley Hill HP5 1UT**
email: swanleyhill@btconnect.com
dir: *1.5m E of Chesham by golf course*

A warm welcome and a cosy fire

Set in the delightful village of Ley Hill, this beautiful 16th-century pub was once the place where condemned prisoners would drink a 'last and final ale' on the way to the nearby gallows. During World War II, Glen Miller and Clark Gable cycled here for a pint from the Air Force base at Bovingdon. These days, it is a free house offering a warm welcome, real ales and good food, plus a large inglenook fireplace and original beams. Pan-fried fillet of sea bream with Lyonnaise potato, poached baby

fennel and roasted cherry tomatoes; steak and kidney pie; or chicken and chorizo tagliatelle are typical choices. Look out for the Bank Holiday beer festival in August.

Open 12-2.30 5.30-11 (Sun 12-4) **Closed** Mon **Food** Lunch Tue-Sat 12-2.30 Dinner Tue-Sat 6.30-9.30 ⊕ FREE HOUSE ◀ St Austell Tribute, Timothy Taylor Landlord, Tring Side Pocket for a Toad, Guest ales. **Facilities** Non-diners area ❋ (Garden) ⚐ Children's menu Garden ⌁ Beer festival Parking ⛟ (notice required)

CUBLINGTON
Map 11 SP82

The Unicorn ⊛⊛

tel: 01296 681261 **High St LU7 0LQ**
email: theunicornpub@btconnect.com
dir: *2m N of A418 (between Aylesbury & Leighton Buzzard). In village centre*

Top Aylesbury Vale village free house

That the 17th-century Unicorn overflows with character is not surprising, given its low-beamed bar, wooden floors and real fires. Even the mismatched furniture plays its part. Relax, maybe in the secluded garden, with a pint of Sharp's Doom Bar or Long Crendon XT. Two AA Rosettes recognise the inventive dishes on the seasonal menus, such as monkfish in Parma ham with lobster beignets and lobster bisque; venison burger with smoked cheese and bacon; or pan-fried sea trout with vegetable ratatouille. Finish with plum frangipane tart and clotted cream perhaps. Events include quiz nights and May and Summer Bank Holiday beer festivals featuring 12 real ales and ciders.

Open 12-3-5-11 (Fri 10.30am-mdnt, Sat 9.30am-mdnt, Sun 12-7) **Closed** Sun eve **Food** Lunch Mon-Sat 12-3, Sun 12-4 Dinner Mon-Sat 6.30-9 Av main course £11 Set menu available Restaurant menu available all wk (ex Sun eve) ⊕ FREE HOUSE ◀ Sharp's Doom Bar, Timothy Taylor Landlord, Long Crendon XT ⚬ Westons Stowford Press, Thatchers. **Facilities** Non-diners area ❋ (Bar Garden) ⚐ Children's menu Children's portions Play area Garden ⌁ Beer festival Parking WiFi ⛟ (notice required)

CUDDINGTON
Map 5 SP71

The Crown
PICK OF THE PUBS

tel: 01844 292222 **Spurt St HP18 0BB**
email: david@djbbars.com
dir: *From A418 between Thame & Aylesbury follow Cuddington signs. Pub in village centre*

Atmospheric pub offering a modern menu with international influences

This thatched and whitewashed listed pub sits in the picturesque village of Cuddington. The Crown's atmospheric interior includes a locals' bar and several low-beamed dining areas lit by candles in the evening. Fuller's London Pride, Adnams and guest ales are on tap, and there's also an extensive wine list, with 12 by the glass. The well thought out and modern menu might include starters of baked camembert with red onion; or a fish board of calamari, mackerel pâté, whitebait and crayfish, followed by mains such as winter game casserole, baby potatoes and seasonal vegetables; slow roasted shoulder of lamb, braised shallots, mash and red wine jus; sea bass fillet, sauté potatoes, grilled asparagus, tomato and spinach coulis; or wild mushroom and sage risotto. Look to the blackboard for daily specials or the set menu for good value options. A compact patio area provides outside seating.

Open all wk 12-3 6-11 (Sun all day) **Food** Lunch all wk 12-2.15 Dinner Mon-Sat 6.30-9.15 Av main course £7.50 ⊕ FULLER'S ◀ London Pride, Adnams, Guest ales. ℧ 12 **Facilities** Non-diners area ⚐ Children's portions Outside area ⌁ Parking WiFi ⛟ (notice required)

DENHAM
Map 6 TQ08

The Falcon Inn ★★★★ INN

tel: 01895 832125 **Village Rd UB9 5BE**
email: mail@falcondenham.com **web:** www.falcondenham.com
dir: *M40 junct 1, follow A40/Gerrards Cross signs. Approx 200yds, right into Old Mill Rd. Pass church on right. Pub opposite village green on left*

The heart and soul of a conservation village

Barely 17 miles as the crow flies, yet central London seems light years away from this lovely 16th-century coaching inn opposite the village green. Expect well-kept Brakspear, Timothy Taylor and Wells real ales. Brasserie food includes pan-fried sea bass; stuffed chicken with chorizo; and steak and Merlot pie with chips and seasonal vegetables. The menu also lists pub classics such as beer-battered cod; and ham, egg and chips; check the daily specials too. Other attractions are a south-facing terraced garden and four bedrooms, two of which have original oak beams.

Open all day all wk **Food** Lunch Mon-Sat 11-3, Sun 12-6 Dinner Mon-Sat 5-9.30, Sun 12-6 Av main course £13 Restaurant menu available Mon-Sat ⊕ ENTERPRISE INNS ◀ Timothy Taylor Landlord, Wells Bombardier, Brakspear ☼ Westons Stowford Press. ☕ 10 **Facilities** Non-diners area ❧ (Bar Garden) ♦️ Children's portions Family room Garden ⊨ Beer festival Cider festival WiFi ▭ (notice required) **Rooms** 4

DORNEY
Map 6 SU97

The Palmer Arms

tel: 01628 666612 **Village Rd SL4 6QW**
email: chrys@thepalmerarms.com
dir: *From A4 take B3026, over M4 to Dorney*

Community pub with a suntrap garden

Built in the 15th century with wooden beams and open fires, this family-friendly pub in the pretty conservation village of Dorney is just a short stroll from the Thames Path and Boveney Lock. The interior is contemporary and the menu combines both modern and classic British dishes, which can be accompanied by wines from the comprehensive list. Scottish salmon gravad lax may precede a main of pan-fried venison medallions. There is a lighter lunch menu, roasts on Sundays and tasting menu evenings. An early autumn beer festival features local beers and ciders.

Open all day all wk 11a m-11.30pm (Sun 12-10.30) **Food** Lunch Mon-Fri 12-9, Sat-Sun 12-10 Dinner Mon-Fri 12-9, Sat-Sun 12-10 ⊕ GREENE KING ◀ Abbot Ale, IPA & Palmer Arms Ale, Guinness ☼ Aspall. ☕ 18 **Facilities** Non-diners area ❧ (Bar Garden) ♦️ Children's menu Children's portions Play area Garden ⊨ Beer festival Parking ▭ (notice required)

EASINGTON
Map 5 SP61

Mole and Chicken

PICK OF THE PUBS

tel: 01844 208387 **HP18 9EY**
email: chef@themoleandchicken.co.uk
dir: *M40 juncts 8 or 8a, A418 to Thame. At rdbt left onto B4011 signed Long Crendon & Bicester. In Long Crendon right into Carters Lane signed Dorton & Chilton. At T-junct left into Chilton Rd signed Chilton. Approx 0.75m to pub*

Secluded former cider house with panoramic views

On the Oxfordshire-Buckinghamshire border, Steve and Suzanne Bush's pub was built in 1831 as housing for estate workers, later becoming the village store and beer and cider house. The far-reaching views from its high terraced garden are magnificent, while inside it's a combination of exposed beams, flagged floors and

smart, contemporary furniture. Village-brewed XT4 and Vale brewery's Easington Best are on tap, alongside Long Crendon cider. From a British and eastern Mediterranean-influenced menu, a typical meal would be coriander and white pepper squid, aïoli, chorizo and endive, then braised ox cheek, carrots, horseradish mash, herb crumbs and bone marrow sauce; ending with apple and blackberry crumble and custard. Bar dishes include spaghetti, creamed wild mushrooms, truffle oil and parmesan; and pork belly Thai curry. And if you were wondering about the whimsical name, it recalls two long-gone landlords, 'Moley' and 'Johnny Chick'.

Open all day all wk Closed 25 Dec **Food** Lunch Mon-Sat 12-2.30, Sun 12-4 Dinner Mon-Sat 6.30-9.30, Sun 6-9 Restaurant menu available all wk ⊕ FREE HOUSE ◀ XT4, Easington Best (pub's own) ☼ Long Crendon Ciders. **Facilities** Non-diners area ♦️ Children's menu Children's portions Play area Garden ⊨ Parking WiFi ▭

FARNHAM COMMON
Map 6 SU98

The Foresters

tel: 01753 643340 **The Broadway SL2 3QQ**
email: info@theforesterspub.com
dir: *Phone for detailed directions*

Well-chosen dishes in an eclectic setting

This handsome 1930s building has an interior where old meets new – crystal chandeliers and log fires, real ales and cocktails, glass-topped tables and wooden floors, chesterfields and velvet thrones. Opt for a starter of English asparagus with poached egg and hollandaise sauce, or one of the 'mini dishes' – perhaps prawn popcorn with sweet and sour sauce, or tempura green beans with sake dip. Typical main dishes include sea bream stuffed with aromatic herbs, under a sea salt crust with fennel salad; and pulled pork and cider risotto with crispy sage leaves and 'petty pommes'. Choose something sweet from the list of dessert tapas. There are front and rear gardens.

Open all day all wk **Food** Lunch all wk 12-3 Dinner all wk 6.30-10 Set menu available Restaurant menu available all wk ⊕ PUNCH TAVERNS ◀ Fuller's London Pride, Young's, Sharp's Doom Bar, Guest ales ☼ Thatchers Gold. ☕ 16 **Facilities** Non-diners area ❧ (Bar Garden) ♦️ Children's menu Children's portions Garden ⊨ Parking WiFi ▭ (notice required)

FARNHAM ROYAL
Map 6 SU98

The Emperor

tel: 01753 643006 **Blackpond Ln SL2 3EG**
email: bookings@theemperorpub.co.uk
dir: *Phone for detailed directions*

A pub for all seasons

Off the beaten track, this village inn with an attractive whitewashed façade is over 100 years old. Polished wood floors and original beams run through the bar, conservatory and barn, and there is a log fire in winter and alfresco tables in the summer. Owned by actor Dennis Waterman and his friend Martin Flood, The Emperor has continued to be a friendly local pub with traditional values. British favourites based on fresh seasonal fare, drive the daily specials and menus, which might include duck liver parfait with toasted brioche and kumquat marmalade, followed by poached fillet of smoked haddock, spinach and poached egg; or slow-roasted belly pork with pease pudding. Contact the pub for details of their beer festival.

Open all day all wk 12-11 (Thu-Sun 12-12) **Food** Lunch Mon-Sat 12-2, Sun 12-3 Dinner Mon-Sat 6-9 Av main course £12 ⊕ ORIGINAL PUB CO LTD ◀ Fuller's London Pride, Rebellion, 3 guest ales. ☕ 8 **Facilities** Non-diners area ❧ (Bar Garden) ♦️ Children's menu Children's portions Garden ⊨ Beer festival Parking WiFi ▭ (notice required)

FRIETH
Map 5 SU79

The Prince Albert

tel: 01494 881683 **RG9 6PY**
dir: *4m N of Marlow. Follow Frieth road from Marlow. Straight across at x-rds on Fingest road. Pub 200yds on left*

A peaceful retreat and traditional pub grub

There's no TV, jukebox or electronic games in this cottagey Chiltern Hills pub. What you get instead, surprise, surprise, is just good conversation, probably much as when it was built in the 1700s. In the bar, low beams, a big black inglenook stove, high-backed settles and lots of copper pots and pans; an alternative place to enjoy a pint of Brakspear is a seat in the garden, while admiring the woods and fields. A short menu sources locally for dishes such as sandwiches; filled jacket potatoes; Thai cod and prawn fishcake and salad; chicken goujons and chilli mayo dip; and deep-fried fish and chips.

Open all day all wk 11-11 (Sun 12-10.30) **Food** Lunch Mon-Sat 12.15-2.30, Sun 12.30-3 Dinner Fri-Sat 7.30-9.30 ⊕ BRAKSPEAR ◀ Bitter, Seasonal ales ♂ Thatchers Gold. ♥ 9 **Facilities** Non-diners area ♣ (Bar Garden) ♦ Children's portions Garden ⋒ Parking WiFi

GERRARDS CROSS
Map 6 TQ08

The Three Oaks

tel: 01753 899016 **Austenwood Ln SL9 8NL**
email: info@thethreeoaksgx.co.uk
dir: *From A40 at lights take B416 (Packhorse Rd) signed Village Centre. Over railway. Left signed Gold Hill into Austenwood Ln. Pub on right*

Contemporary gastro-pub with relaxed feel

The Three Oaks, in the heart of affluent Gerrards Cross, is a stylish dining venue with a smart, contemporary feel, yet the vibe is relaxed and informal. Drop by for a pint of local Rebellion Ale or a glass of unoaked Chardonnay and tuck into the cracking value set lunch menu, or perhaps crispy baby squid, Merguez sausage, red pepper and basil mayonnaise, followed by lemon and thyme marinated chicken, black trumpet mushrooms, roast pumpkin, sweetcorn and truffle mayonnaise, and then sticky toffee pudding, Guinness sauce, walnut and Devonshire ice cream. There's a super terrace for alfresco dining, and don't miss the summer beer festival.

Open all wk **Food** Lunch Mon-Sat 12-2.30, Sun 12-6 Dinner Mon-Sat 6.30-9.30 Set menu available Restaurant menu available all wk ⊕ ENTERPRISE INNS ◀ Fuller's London Pride, Rebellion & IPA ♂ Aspall. ♥ 24 **Facilities** Non-diners area ♦ Children's menu Children's portions Garden ⋒ Beer festival Parking WiFi ⊷ (notice required)

GREAT HAMPDEN
Map 5 SP80

The Hampden Arms

tel: 01494 488255 **HP16 9RQ**
email: louise.lucas@outlook.com
dir: *M40 junct 4, A4010, right before Princes Risborough. Great Hampden signed*

Home-cooked food at lovely countryside inn

The large garden of this mock-Tudor free house on the wooded Hampden Estate sits beside the common, where you might watch a game of cricket during the season. Chef-proprietor Constantine Lucas includes Greek signature dishes such as kleftiko and Greek salad alongside more traditional choices such as fish crumble; aubergine and tomato lasagne; and duck breast with a wild mushroom and brandy sauce; blackboard specials add to the choices. The pub has a secure beer garden, ideal for private functions.

Open all wk 12-3 6-12 **Food** Lunch Mon-Sat 12-2, Sun 12-3 Dinner Mon-Sat 6-9.30, Sun 7-9.30 Set menu available Restaurant menu available all wk ⊕ FREE HOUSE ◀ Fuller's London Pride, Chiltern, Rebellion, Guest ales ♂ Addlestones. **Facilities** Non-diners area ♦ Children's menu Children's portions Family room Garden ⋒ Beer festival Parking WiFi

GREAT MISSENDEN
Map 6 SP80

The Nags Head ★★★★ INN ⊛
PICK OF THE PUBS

See Pick of the Pubs on opposite page

The Polecat Inn
PICK OF THE PUBS

tel: 01494 862253 **170 Wycombe Rd, Prestwood HP16 OHJ**
email: info@thepolecatinn.co.uk
dir: *On A4128 between Great Missenden & High Wycombe*

Wine and beer taken seriously here

In the spring of 2014, Philip Whitehouse took over this 17th-century Chiltern Hills free house following its two decades in the same hands. Essentially though, the pub hasn't changed: flower baskets carry on adorning the exterior, while inside, the small, low-beamed rooms radiating from the bar still offer a choice of dining and drinking options. From the village's own Malt The Brewery, which you can visit, comes Prestwood Best; 30 wines are sold by the glass. Dishes are prepared from local ingredients, including herbs from the huge garden. If you enjoy beef Wellington or magret of duck, you could be in luck; ditto Cumberland sausage; Alan's 'amazing' pork spare ribs; or baked salmon with celeriac dauphinoise, sun-blushed tomatoes and gruyère cheese. Home-made venison and wild rabbit pie, blackboard specials, baguettes and filled jacket potatoes add further choices. Children are well catered for, too. Check on summer beer festival dates.

Open all day all wk 11-11 (closed 2.30-6 in Jan) **Food** Lunch all wk 12-3 Dinner Mon-Sat 6.30-9 Av main course £11 Set menu available ⊕ FREE HOUSE ◀ Brakspear Oxford Gold, Malt The Brewery Prestwood's Best, Rebellion IPA ♂ Thatchers Gold. ♥ 30 **Facilities** Non-diners area ♣ (Bar Restaurant Garden) ♦ Children's menu Children's portions Play area Family room Garden ⋒ Beer festival Parking WiFi ⊷

GROVE
Map 11 SP92

Grove Lock

tel: 01525 380940 **LU7 OQU**
email: grovelock@fullers.co.uk
dir: *From A4146 (S of Leighton Buzzard) take B4146 signed Ivinghoe & Tring. Pub 0.5m on left*

Perfect atmosphere in summer and winter

This pub is situated next to Lock 28 on the Grand Union Canal, and is less than a mile from the scene of the 1963 Great Train Robbery. Its lofty open-plan bar has leather sofas, assorted tables and chairs and canal-themed artworks. The restaurant, once the lock-keeper's cottage, serves breaded chicken Caesar salad; butternut squash risotto; sausages and mash; and smoked belly of pork. Plenty of outdoor seating means you can watch the canal traffic, while enjoying a pint of Fuller's.

Open all day all wk Mon-Sat 11-11 (Sun 11-10.30) **Food** Lunch Mon-Sat 12-9, Sun 12-7 Dinner Mon-Sat 12-9, Sun 12-7 ⊕ FULLER'S ◀ London Pride, Organic Honey Dew & ESB ♂ Aspall. ♥ 14 **Facilities** Non-diners area ♦ Children's menu Children's portions Garden ⋒ Parking WiFi

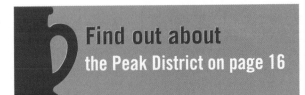

Find out about the Peak District on page 16

PICK OF THE PUBS

The Nags Head ★★★★ INN ✿

GREAT MISSENDEN   Map 6 SP80

tel: 01494 862200
London Rd HP16 0DG
email: goodfood@nagsheadbucks.com
web: www.nagsheadbucks.com
dir: *N of Amersham on A413, left at Chiltern hospital into London Rd signed Great Missenden*

Charming rural pub with excellent Anglo-French cooking

The late Roald Dahl used to be a regular here and the dining room is decorated with limited edition prints by the children's author, who drew inspiration from the pub for his famous book *Fantastic Mr Fox.* Originally three small workers' cottages whose inhabitants made spindles for chairs, The Nags Head became a coaching inn in the 16th-century and was a popular stop for travellers and their horses commuting from the midlands to London. Tucked away in the sleepy valley of the River Misbourne in the picturesque Chiltern Hills, the pub has been restored by the Michaels family, who sprinkled similar magic dust on sister pub the Bricklayers Arms in Flaunden, Hertfordshire. The family has helped the Nags Head to gain a formidable reputation for food and hospitality. Low oak beams and an inglenook fireplace have been carefully retained as a backdrop for the stylish bar, where drinkers can enjoy one of the real ales, perhaps from the Tring

brewery. Food is taken seriously here, and executive head chef Claude Paillet sources the finest ingredients from local suppliers wherever possible, for a menu fusing English with French. Lunch and dinner menus may offer starters like duck liver parfait and roasted pistachios in a jar with pear chutney and toasted brioche. Main courses range from slow-cooked, honey glazed short rib of beef, ale jus and champ; to duck breast and confit leg, black fig jus and the potato dish of the day. Leave room for lemon tart and cassis sorbet; or coffee and Baileys cheesecake. In summer, relax over a drink or a meal whilst gazing out across the Chiltern Hills from the pub's lovely garden. Alternatively, stay overnight in one of the five beautiful bedrooms.

Open all day all wk Closed 25 Dec **Food** Lunch Mon-Sat 12-2.30, Sun 12-3.30 Dinner Mon-Sat 6.30-9.30, Sun 6-8.30 Set menu available Restaurant menu available all wk ⊕ FREE HOUSE ◀ Rebellion, Tring, Vale, Sharp's Doom Bar, Malt ♻ Aspall. ♀ 19 **Facilities** Non-diners area ❤ (Bar Garden) ♦♦ Children's portions Garden ㅈ Parking WiFi **Rooms** 5

HAMBLEDEN — Map 5 SU78

The Stag & Huntsman Inn ★★★★ INN

tel: 01491 571227 **RG9 6RP**
email: enquiries@thestagandhuntsman.co.uk **web:** www.thestagandhuntsman.co.uk
dir: *5m from Henley-on-Thames on A4155 towards Marlow, left at Mill End towards Hambleden*

Lovingly restored inn retaining old world charm

Close to the glorious beech-clad Chilterns, this 400-year-old brick and flint village pub has featured in countless films and TV series. Ever-changing guest ales are served in the public bar, larger lounge bar and cosy snug. Food is available in the bars as well as the dining room, from an extensive menu of home-made pub favourites prepared with local seasonal produce. Opt for the likes of pan-fried fillet of salmon; rib-eye steak; or oven-roasted peppers filled with spiced couscous. Hambleden Estate game features strongly when in season, and there is a pizza and barbecue menu to enjoy in the garden during the summer months.

Open all day all wk **Food** Lunch Mon-Sat 12-2.30, Sun 12-3 Dinner all wk 6-9.30 FREE HOUSE Rebellion, Sharp's, Loddon, Guest ales Westons Stowford Press. **Facilities** (Bar Garden) Garden Parking **Rooms** 9

HEDGERLEY — Map 6 SU98

The White Horse

tel: 01753 643225 **SL2 3UY**
dir: *Phone for detailed directions*

One for the beer festival follower

An ale drinker's paradise if ever there was one, parts of which date back 500 years. With three beer festivals a year (Easter, Spring Bank Holiday and Summer Bank Holiday) and barely a pause between them, this pub can almost claim to run a single year-long celebration, with over 1,000 real ales consumed annually. Real cider and Belgian bottled beers augment the already mammoth range. A large well-kept garden at the rear hosts summer barbecues; otherwise the menu of home-cooked pub favourites ranges from a salad bar with quiches, sandwiches and ploughman's through to curries, chilli, pasta dishes, pies and steaks (lunchtime only).

Open all wk 11-2.30 5-11 (Sat 11-11 Sun 11-10.30) **Food** Lunch Mon-Fri 12-2, Sat-Sun 12-2.30 FREE HOUSE 8 rotating ales 3 guest ciders. 10 **Facilities** Non-diners area (Bar Garden) Children's portions Family room Garden Beer festival Parking

LACEY GREEN — Map 5 SP80

The Whip Inn

tel: 01844 344060 **Pink Rd HP27 0PG**
dir: *1m from A4010 (Princes Risborough to High Wycombe road). Adjacent to windmill*

Traditional pub popular with walkers and cyclists

Standing high above the Vale of Aylesbury in the heart of the Chiltern Hills, the beer garden of this 200-year-old pub overlooks the Lacey Green windmill. Ramblers on the Chiltern Way join locals in appreciating some of 800 different real ales offered each year, as well as real Millwhites cider. A robust menu of home-made classic favourites such as ham, egg and chips and chargrilled steaks seals the deal at this rustic, music- and fruit-machine-free country inn. The Whip holds a beer festival twice a year in May and September.

Open all day all wk **Food** Lunch Mon-Sat 12-2.30, Sun 12-3 Dinner Mon-Sat 6.30-9 FREE HOUSE Over 800 guest ales a year Thatchers, Millwhites. 22 **Facilities** Non-diners area (Bar Garden) Children's menu Children's portions Garden Beer festival Parking

LANE END — Map 5 SU89

Grouse & Ale — PICK OF THE PUBS

See Pick of the Pubs on opposite page

LITTLE KINGSHILL — Map 6 SU89

The Full Moon

tel: 01494 862397 **Hare Ln HP16 0EE**
email: email@thefullmoon.info
dir: *SW of Great Missenden, accessed from either A413 or A4128*

Perfect for post-walk ales and meals

A popular post-ramble refuelling stop, especially as both dogs and children are warmly welcomed inside, this pub has a wealth of wonderful walks through the Chiltern Hills radiating from its doorstep. It is noted for its tip-top Fuller's London Pride and the weekly-changing guest ales, and the pub throngs during the mid-July beer festival. Walking appetites will be satisfied with one of the starters to share; a chargrilled Philly steak sandwich; gnocchi, pear, walnuts and blue cheese sauce; or a hearty and adventurous main like crocodile fillet with a lemongrass, white wine and butter sauce. The apple toffee fudge cake could round things off nicely.

Open all day all wk **Food** Lunch all wk 12-3 Dinner all wk 6-10 Av main course £13 PUNCH TAVERNS Fuller's London Pride, Young's, Adnams, Guest ale Aspall. 21 **Facilities** Non-diners area (Bar Garden) Children's menu Children's portions Play area Garden Beer festival Parking (notice required)

PICK OF THE PUBS

Grouse & Ale

LANE END Map 5 SU89

tel: 01494 882299 **High St HP14 3JG**
email: info@grouseandale.co.uk
web: www.grouseandale.com
dir: *On B482 in village*

Smart pub, modern menus, friendly service

This was the Clayton Arms for nearly a century before a major refurbishment a few years ago; it was named after Sir Robert Clayton who built it in 1679 on becoming Lord Mayor of London. Today the house's spacious spick-and-span interior mixes cosy corners with comfortably furnished drinking and dining areas, to create a smart country town pub in the true British tradition. The staff's smiling faces, well cared for real ales, and impressive modern menus all combine to make the Grouse & Ale an inviting venue for family and friends. With a drink and a menu, relax in the sun-trap courtyard. Choice is extensive and high on comfort appeal, but attention to detail, top quality ingredients and beautiful presentation have won awards for the kitchen. Deal with hungry children first: proper chicken goujons with skinny chips is a firm favourite, while sausage and mash with onion gravy appeals to those with more grown-up tastes. The picante pizza, however, with pepperoni, chorizo, tomatoes and jalapeños, is not recommended for junior tastebuds. Pub

favourites list a gourmet burger, Courage beer-battered haddock, and treacle-glazed gammon ham with Lacey's free-range eggs; all are served with proper hand-cut chips. With the variety and high gastro appeal on offer, choosing a three-course special occasion dinner is not difficult. Crayfish and prawn salad, bisque dressing, parsley crème and cheese straw makes a mouthwatering starter. Follow with chicken saltimbocca — breast of chicken stuffed with cheddar and sage and wrapped in streaky bacon; it's served with sweet chilli and brie sauce, wilted spinach and fondant potato. A tarte au citron with raspberry sorbet rounds things off nicely — unless the artisan British cheese plate is too much of a temptation. As you would expect from an

establishment that aims to please, the list of coffees and teas is exemplary.

Open all day all wk **Food** Lunch Mon-Sat 12-2.30, Sun 12-4 Dinner Mon-Sat 6-9.30 ⊞ STAR PUBS & BARS ◀ Adnams Broadside, Caledonian Deuchars IPA, Courage. ▆ 27 **Facilities** Non-diners area ☙ (Bar Outside area) ▮▮ Children's menu Children's portions Outside area ☴ Parking WiFi

LITTLE MARLOW
Map 5 SU88

The Queens Head

tel: 01628 482927 **Pound Ln SL7 3SR**
email: tqhlittlemarlow@yahoo.co.uk
dir: *From A404 take Marlow exit towards Bourne End. Approx 1m, right by church into Church Rd. Approx 100mtrs right into Pound Ln*

A rose-clad gem of a pub

Dating from the 16th century and called 'Marlow's little secret', this is a pretty collection of buildings from three different periods. Standing opposite the manor house, its beamed, open fire-warmed interior feels immediately welcoming. Since it's just a tankard's throw from the Marlow Rebellion Brewery, expect IPA and from November to January, Roasted Nuts (surely the only real ale named after a bar snack). Dishes include carrot and ginger soup; and chicken, Parma ham and tomato terrine; pan-seared cod fillet with potato and chorizo, tomato sauce with thyme vinaigrette. More substantial are braised shin of beef, spiced potatoes, Savoy cabbage and port jus; and steamed venison suet pudding and truffle mash.

Open all day all wk Closed 25-26 Dec **Food** Lunch Mon-Fri 12-2.30, Sat-Sun 12-4 Dinner all wk 6.30-9.30 Av main course £15 ⊕ PUNCH TAVERNS ◀ Rebellion IPA ℧ Westons Stowford Press. **Facilities** Non-diners area ✚ Children's portions Garden ⌐ Parking WiFi ☎ (notice required)

LONG CRENDON
Map 5 SP60

The Angel Inn ◉
PICK OF THE PUBS

tel: 01844 208268 **47 Bicester Rd HP18 9EE**
email: info@angelrestaurant.co.uk
dir: *M40 junct 7, A418 to Thame, B4011 to Long Crendon. Inn on B4011*

Great food in an exceptional village inn

Situated in the Vale of Aylesbury and close to the rippling Chiltern Hills, the village of Long Crendon was a centre for lace-making in medieval times. Certain buildings retain a real sense of history, including the old courthouse, picturesque rows of cottages and the gabled Angel Inn. This old coaching stop still has much of its original character, with ancient fireplaces and wattle-and-daub walls alongside modern features including an airy conservatory. Refreshments centre on Vale Brewery's Wychert and the village's own XT Brewing Company's ales. A good wine list offers many sold by the glass, and an extensive range of spirits includes Scottish, Irish and Japanese whiskies. Turning to the AA Rosette-worthy food, check out the fixed price lunch menu for the likes of Italian ceci soup followed by beef and ale cottage pie. Fish options, such as steamed Cornish rope-grown mussels, and lightly curried hake with spinach and potato sag aloo, are on the specials list.

Open all day Closed 1-2 Jan, Sun eve **Food** Lunch all wk 12-2.30 Dinner Mon-Sat 7-9.30 Av main course £10.95 Set menu available Restaurant menu available all wk ⊕ FREE HOUSE ◀ Vale Wychert, XT-4 & XT-6. ☘ 12 **Facilities** Non-diners area ✚ Children's portions Garden ⌐ Parking WiFi ☎ (notice required)

MARLOW
Map 5 SU88

NEW The Coach ◉◉◉
PICK OF THE PUBS

3 West St SL7 2LS
dir: *From A404 to Marlow. Pub in town centre*

Stylish new enterprise from celebrity chef

In the heart of Marlow, a stone's throw from his award-winning flagship business, The Hand & Flowers, TV chef Tom Kerridge has created something quite special at The Coach. With its glazed wall tiles, soft leather furnishings and open kitchen, the look is timeless yet contemporary, as is head chef Nick Beardshaw's modern British cooking. So sit yourself down on a bar stool or at a table and decide from the concise menu with headings of 'Meat, No meat and Sweet'. Start perhaps with salmon tartare with rye bread cracker, or cauliflower cheese soup with fried ox; before moving on to steak and ale pie with suet pastry, or whole stuffed rotisserie quail. Banana custard with dates and honeycomb, and whisky and rye pudding are just two ways to finish. You can't pre-book to eat here – it's first-come-first-served – so it's all fingers crossed you'll time your visit just right.

Open all day all wk Closed 25 Dec **Food** Lunch all wk 12-2.30 Dinner all wk 6.30-10.30 ⊕ ENTERPRISE INNS ◀ Rebellion IPA, Wells Bombardier Burning Gold, Young's Bitter ℧ Westons Rosie's Pig. ☘ 20 **Facilities** ✚ Children's portions WiFi

The Hand & Flowers ◉◉◉◉
PICK OF THE PUBS

tel: 01628 482277 **126 West St SL7 2BP**
email: contact@thehandandflowers.co.uk
dir: *M4 junct 9, A404 to Marlow, A4155 towards Henley-on-Thames. Pub on right*

Unpretentious but highly acclaimed gastro-pub

In 2005 chef Tom Kerridge and his sculptor wife Beth turned their simple concept into reality: to create in this 18th-century pub the sort of place where they would like to eat. My, how well it has worked as Tom's TV stardom, four AA Rosettes and chock-a-block reservations diary testify. Housing all the desired historic features – flagstone floors, old timbers and log fires – the bar offers the unusual opportunity to drink a pint of Roasted Nuts (actually a real ale from Marlow's Rebellion brewery). Sourcing some ingredients from his own allotment, Tom's menus combine modern British and rustic French cooking, such as the potato risotto with baked potato stock, Pied de Mouton and fresh chestnut starter. Mouth-wateringly descriptive mains include Scottish halibut with Portobello mushroom purée, crispy beef suet and sesame-braised parsnip; and tenderloin of Wiltshire pork with pickled mustard leaf, malt-glazed cheek, garlic sausage and potato dauphine. Booking to eat here is essential and must be arranged months in advance.

Open 12-2.45 6.30-9.45 (Sun 12-3.15) Closed 24-26 Dec, 1 Jan Dinner, Sun eve **Food** Lunch Mon-Sat 12-2.30, Sun 12-3.15 Dinner Mon-Sat 6.30-9.30 Set menu available ⊕ GREENE KING ◀ Abbot Ale, Morland Old Speckled Hen, Rebellion Roasted Nuts ℧ Aspall & Perronelle's Blush. ☘ 17 **Facilities** Non-diners area ✚ Children's portions Outside area ⌐ Parking WiFi

The Kings Head

tel: 01628 484407 **Church Rd, Little Marlow SL7 3RZ**
email: clive.harvison@sky.com
dir: *M40 junct 4, A4040 S, then A4155 towards Bourne End. Pub 0.5m on right. Or M4 junct 8/9, A404(M) signed High Wycombe. Then A4155 towards Bourne End. Pub 0.5m*

Good range of real ales close to the Thames Path

This charming 16th-century pub with a large garden is only a few minutes' walk from the Thames Path. The open-plan interior features original beams and log fires. A great selection of ales awaits visitors to The Kings Head, including a couple from the Rebellion Brewery in Marlow. As well as sandwiches, baguettes, paninis and jacket potatoes, the food includes substantial salads, steaks, grilled salmon, chilli con carne, wholetail scampi and aubergine cannelloni. Tell staff you've parked the car, go for a walk and return for a meal.

Open all day all wk Closed 26 Dec **Food** Lunch Mon-Sat 12-2.30, Sun 12-7 Dinner Mon-Sat 6.30-9.30, Sun 12-7 ⊕ ENTERPRISE INNS ◀ Fuller's London Pride, Timothy Taylor Landlord, Adnams Broadside, Rebellion IPA & Smuggler ℧ Thatchers Gold, Aspall. ☘ 13 **Facilities** Non-diners area ✚ Children's menu Children's portions Garden ⌐ Parking WiFi ☎ (notice required)

MILTON KEYNES
Map 11 SP83

The Swan Inn

tel: 01908 665240 **Broughton Rd, Milton Keynes Village MK10 9AH**
email: info@theswan-mkvillage.co.uk
dir: *M1 junct 14 towards Milton Keynes. Pub off V11 or H7*

Rustic rural charm with orchard garden

In the heart of the original Milton Keynes village, the beautiful 13th-century Swan Inn, now in new hands, offers everything you could wish for from an ancient thatched pub. The interior is an eclectic mix of traditional charm and contemporary chic; it has flagstone floors, an open fire in the inglenook in winter keeps things cosy, and an orchard garden for those warmer days. The open-plan kitchen creates tempting dishes such as sharing plates and starters of warm guinea fowl ballotine, star anise jus and hazelnuts; or pan-fried artichoke gnocchi stuffed with goats' cheese, and pesto cream. Follow on with the chef's pie of the day; free-range pork sausages, creamy mash and onion gravy; or braised heel of beef, parsnip purée and roasted bone marrow.

Open all day all wk Mon-Thu 11-11 (Fri-Sat 11-mdnt Sun 12-10.30) **Food** Lunch Mon-Thu 12-3, Fri-Sat 12-10, Sun 12-8 Dinner Mon-Thu 6-9.30, Fri-Sat 12-10, Sun 12-8 ⊕ FRONT LINE INNS ◀ Wells Bombardier, Young's, Guest ales ♂ Symonds. ♟ 34 **Facilities** Non-diners area ✿ (Bar Garden) ♠ Children's portions Garden ⼌ Parking WiFi ▄ (notice required)

MOULSOE
Map 11 SP94

The Carrington Arms

tel: 01908 218050 **Cranfield Rd MK16 0HB**
email: enquiries@thecarringtonarms.co.uk
dir: *M1 junct 14, A509 to Newport Pagnell 100yds, turn right signed Moulsoe & Cranfield. Pub on right*

Traditional countryside inn which is all about customer choice

Only a short hop from the rush and noise of the M1, the family-run Carrington in the pretty village of Moulsoe combines tradition with modern hospitality. Real ales and a good wine list are a given, but the pub is most famous for its fresh meat counter where customers can talk through their selection with the chef; locally-raised Bedfordshire beef is a highlight. The choice starts with sandwiches and pub favourites, but other options are a modern take on a prawn cocktail, then pink Woburn venison loin with smoked venison boudin, fondant potato with a red wine and port jus. The large garden hosted a beer and cider festival in mid June.

Open all day all wk 12-11 **Food** Lunch all wk 12-10 Dinner all wk 12-10 Restaurant menu available all wk ⊕ FREE HOUSE ◀ Fuller's London Pride, Marston's Pedigree, Guest ales ♂ The Orchard Pig. ♟ 15 **Facilities** Non-diners area ♠ Children's portions Garden ⼌ Beer festival Cider festival Parking WiFi ▄ (notice required)

NEWTON BLOSSOMVILLE
Map 11 SP95

The Old Mill ★★★ INN

tel: 01234 881273 **MK43 8AN**
email: enquiries@oldmill.uk.com **web:** www.oldmill.uk.com
dir: *A509 N of Milton Keynes. Right to village. Or A428 from Bedford. In Turvey left to village*

Much loved village local with reliable cuisine

A handsome stone inn in a village of thatched cottages tucked away in the tranquil Ouse Valley; The Old Mill is an ideal base to stay-over in its attractive bedrooms. The beer range changes with the seasons, whilst the choice on the menu relies heavily on what's available from local suppliers. There's a solid base of pub favourites, complemented by daily specials; perhaps home-made lamb and mint

pie or the Friday fish dish. There's a peaceful, dog-friendly grassy garden, whilst a wood-burner flickers in the cosy bar. Regulars keep warm playing skittles in the local league.

Open all wk 12-3 5-11 (Fri-Sun 12-11) **Food** Lunch Mon-Sat 12-2.30, Sun 12-4 Dinner Mon-Sat 6-9 Restaurant menu available all wk ⊕ FREE HOUSE ◀ Greene King Ruddles Best, Guest ales ♂ Aspall. **Facilities** Non-diners area ✿ (Bar Garden) ♠ Children's menu Children's portions Garden WiFi ▄ (notice required) **Rooms** 5

NORTH MARSTON
Map 11 SP72

NEW The Pilgrim

tel: 01296 670969 **25 High St MK18 3PD**
email: info@thepilgrimpub.co.uk **web:** www.thepilgrimpub.co.uk
dir: *From Aylesbury take A413 towards Buckingham. In Whitchurch turn left & follow North Marston sign. Right to North Marston, approx 1m to pub*

Tranquil haven overlooking Aylesbury Vale

A holy well in the village, reputedly the site of many miracles in the Middle Ages, was reason enough for pilgrims to make the journey to North Marston. Brett and Nadia Newman took over this 300-year-old pub (formerly The Bell) in 2014, the husband-and-wife team managing the kitchen and front of house respectively. They are working hard to build local loyalty and wider appeal, with burgers, quizzes, curries and wines each having a dedicated evening in the month's social calendar. Home-grown produce is planned too, to accompany dishes such as grilled free-range pork steak with sautéed sprout tops; and pan-roasted sea bass fillet with roasted root vegetables.

Open 12-3 5-11 (Fri 12-3 5-12 Sat 12-12 Sun 12-6) Closed Sun eve & Mon **Food** Lunch Tue-Sat 12-2, Sun 12-3 Dinner Tue-Sat 6-9 Av main course £13.50 Restaurant menu available Tue-Sun ⊕ FREE HOUSE ◀ XT 4, Sharp's Doom Bar ♂ Millwhites Hedge Layer, Westons Family Reserve. ♟ 10 **Facilities** Non-diners area ✿ (Bar Garden) ♠ Children's portions Garden ⼌ Parking WiFi ▄ (notice required)

PENN
Map 6 SU99

The Red Lion

tel: 01494 813107 **Elm Rd HP10 8LF**
email: redlionpub@btconnect.com
dir: *Phone for detailed directions*

Traditional village pub popular with Chiltern walkers

Set in the pretty village of Penn, this 16th-century pub is an ideal base for exploring the beautiful Chiltern Hills and nearby Penn Wood. For those in need of more leisurely pursuits, sit on the sunny front terrace overlooking the village green with a pint of Chiltern Beechwood Bitter and watch the world go by. Inside, log fires warm the cosy, antique-strewn bar in winter as good conversation abounds. The food here is home cooked and hearty with traditional dishes including liver and bacon with creamy mash and onion gravy; moules et frites; or vegetarian cassoulet.

Open all day all wk **Food** Lunch all day Dinner all day Restaurant menu available all wk ⊕ ENTERPRISE INNS ◢ Chiltern Beechwood Bitter, Guest ales Ö Westons Mortimers Orchard. ♟ 11 **Facilities** Non-diners area ❄ (Bar Restaurant Garden) ♦∮ Children's menu Children's portions Garden ⌁ Parking WiFi ▭ (notice required)

RADNAGE
Map 5 SU79

The Three Horseshoes Inn

tel: 01494 483273 **Horseshoe Rd, Bennett End HP14 4EB**
email: threehorseshoe@btconnect.com
dir: *M40 junct 5, A40 towards High Wycombe, after unrestricted mileage sign turn left signed Radnage (Mudds Bank). 1.8m, 1st left into Bennett End Rd, inn on right*

European flavours in a pretty Chiltern pub

When chef-patron Simon Crawshaw bought this beautiful old building, he knew it would be something special. Down a leafy lane, it is truly traditional – worn flagstones, blackened beams and original inglenook fireplace. On his modern English and European menus he typically offers rillette of poached and smoked Scottish salmon with home-made Hovis-style loaf, then roast rump of lamb with ratatouille, Suffolk kale, gratin potatoes and red wine jus. Enjoy Marlow's Rebellion ale in the bar or in the lovely garden.

Open 12-3 6-11 (Mon 6-11 Sat all day Sun 12-6) Closed Sun eve, Mon L **Food** Lunch Tue-Sat 12-2.30, Sun 12-3 Dinner Mon-Thu 6-9, Fri-Sat 6-9.30 ⊕ FREE HOUSE ◢ Rebellion, Brakspear Oxford Gold. ♟ 12 **Facilities** Non-diners area ❄ (Bar Garden) ♦∮ Children's portions Garden ⌁ Parking WiFi ▭ (notice required)

Find out more about the AA's awards for food excellence on page 9

SEER GREEN
Map 6 SU99

The Jolly Cricketers ◉

tel: 01494 676308 **24 Chalfont Rd HP9 2YG**
email: amanda@thejollycricketers.co.uk
dir: *M40 junct 2, A355 signed Beaconsfield A40, Amersham. At Pyebush rdbt 1st exit, A40 signed Beaconsfield, Amersham, A355. At rdbt, A355 signed Amersham. Right into Longbottom Ln signed Seer Green. Left into Bottom Ln, right into Orchard Rd, left into Church Rd, right into Chalfont Rd*

Top notch food in a homely setting

Chris Lillitou and Amanda Baker's 19th-century, wisteria-clad free house in the heart of the picture-perfect Seer Green appeals to all-comers: locals chatting over pints of Marlow's Rebellion IPA, quiz addicts on Sunday nights, live music fans, beer festival-goers and dog-walkers. The modern, AA-Rosette menu could include crispy Cornish squid with chilli and lemon sauce; spicy chorizo and razor clams with shallots, tomatoes and black-eye beans as typical starters. Follow with pan-fried stone bass, wild mushrooms, braised fennel in orange and saffron. For dessert, maybe vanilla cheesecake with rhubarb and rhubarb sorbet. Beer festivals on Easter weekend and Summer Bank Holiday.

Open all day all wk Mon-Thu 12-11.30 (Fri-Sat 12-12 Sun 12-10.30) **Food** Lunch Mon-Fri 12-2.30, Sat 12-3, Sun 12-7 Dinner Mon-Sat 6.30-9, Sun 12-7 Av main course £7.50 Restaurant menu available all wk ⊕ FREE HOUSE ◢ Rebellion IPA, Fuller's London Pride, Chiltern Beechwood Bitter, Vale VPA Ö Millwhites, Artisan bottle selection. ♟ 16 **Facilities** Non-diners area ❄ (Bar Garden) ♦∮ Children's menu Children's portions Garden ⌁ Beer festival Parking WiFi

SKIRMETT
Map 5 SU79

The Frog
`PICK OF THE PUBS`

tel: 01491 638996 **RG9 6TG**
email: info@thefrogatskirmett.co.uk
dir: *Exit A4155 at Mill End, pub in 3m*

Quality choices in both refreshment and food

An 18th-century coaching inn within the Chilterns Area of Outstanding Natural Beauty, with the Hamble Brook flowing gently behind. In summer the garden is a relaxing place to be, perhaps after a ramble to the famous windmill on nearby Turville Hill. Winter warmth is guaranteed in the charming public bar where oak beams, bare floorboards and leather seating combine with colourful textiles to create a welcoming atmosphere. Where better to settle with a pint of Leaping Frog or Henry's Original IPA? Alternatively 15 wines are sold by the glass, or push the boat out and share a sparkler from the Hambleden vineyard just down the road. Head chef and co-owner Jim Crowe uses superb ingredients in flavoursome dishes to satisfy the most discerning of palates. The menu offers deli boards and perhaps a starter of crisp fried south coast squid; or haggis, neeps and tatties, followed by fillet of pork Wellington; pie of the day; or slow-braised ox tail.

Open 11.30-3 6-11 Closed 25 Dec, Sun eve (Oct-Apr) **Food** Lunch all wk 12-2.30 Dinner all wk 6.30-9.30 Av main course £12.85 ⊕ FREE HOUSE ◢ Leaping Frog, Rebellion IPA, Sharp's Doom Bar, Wadworth Henry's Original IPA Ö Thatchers. ♟ 15 **Facilities** Non-diners area ❄ (Bar Garden) ♦∮ Children's menu Children's portions Family room Garden ⌁ Parking ▭

STOKE MANDEVILLE
Map 5 SP81

The Bell

tel: 01296 612434 **29 Lower Rd HP22 5XA**
email: info@bellstokemandeville.co.uk **web:** www. bellstokemandeville.co.uk
dir: *From S & E follow signs from Stoke Mandeville towards Stoke Mandeville Hospital, pub on left in 200yds after primary school. From N & W pass Stoke Mandeville Hospital on left, pub approx 1m on right*

An honest-to-goodness great British dining pub

The Bell has a sign that reads 'Dogs, children and muddy boots welcome', thereby setting the friendly tone of a visit to this traditional country village pub. Physiotherapists caring for those with spinal injuries at nearby Stoke Mandeville hospital have been known to set The Bell as an objective for their newly mobile patients. The reward could be a pint of Wells Bombardier or Aspall cider, with a plate of fresh seasonal food. James Penlington has some star kitchens on his CV, so expect proper bar snacks and hearty full-flavoured meals – typical are pan-roast cod fillet with wholegrain mustard mash and parsley sauce; or seared pigeon breast with winter vegetable rémoulade and vegetable crisps. Be sure to leave a corner for delicious desserts like coconut pannacotta with pineapple and chilli salsa, or sticky toffee pudding with butterscotch sauce.

Open all day all wk Closed 25-26 Dec **Food** Lunch Mon-Sat 12-6.30 Restaurant menu available all wk ⊕ CHARLES WELLS ◀ Bombardier, Young's Bitter, Guest ale ♂ Aspall. ☻ 16 **Facilities** Non-diners area ♣ (Bar Restaurant Garden) ♦ Children's menu Children's portions Garden ⋒ Parking WiFi ▬ (notice required)

TURVILLE
Map 5 SU79

The Bull & Butcher
PICK OF THE PUBS

See Pick of the Pubs on page 58

TURWESTON
Map 11 SP63

NEW The Stratton Arms

tel: 01280 704956 **Main St NN13 5JX**
email: thestrattonarms@aol.com
dir: *From A43 (NE of Brackley) take A422 towards Buckingham. Left to Turweston. Through village, pub on left*

Warmly regarded village local

Just like many of the other buildings in this rather straggly village, the pub is built of mellow local stone. Landlord Philip Caley offers a good range of ales – Bass, London Pride, Otter and more. His menu is full of tried and tested, home-made pub food, such as chilli con carne with rice; wholetail scampi, chips and peas; Barnsley chop and mash; and spinach ricotta cannelloni with jacket potato. Freshly baked pizzas can be taken home to eat. At the far end of its large garden flows the River Great Ouse.

Open all day all wk **Food** Lunch Fri-Sun 12-2 Dinner Fri-Sun 6-9 Av main course £5.50 Set menu available ⊕ ENTERPRISE INNS ◀ Otter, Timothy Taylor Landlord, Fuller's London Pride, Bass, Sharp's Doom Bar ♂ Westons Stowford Press. ☻ **Facilities** Non-diners area ♣ (Bar Garden Outside area) ♦ Children's menu Children's portions Play area Family room Garden Outside area ⋒ Beer festival Parking WiFi ▬ (notice required)

WEST WYCOMBE
Map 5 SU89

The George and Dragon Hotel

tel: 01494 535340 **High St HP14 3AB**
email: georgeanddragon@live.co.uk
dir: *On A40*

Delightful timber-framed hotel reached through a cobbled archway

After a hard day touring the West Wycombe Caves, and stately houses at Cliveden and Hughenden, relax at this traditional coaching inn located in a National Trust village. The 14th-century inn was once a hideout for highwaymen stalking travellers between London and Oxford; indeed, one unfortunate guest, robbed and murdered here, is rumoured still to haunt its corridors. Reliable real ales include St Austell Tribute and Skinner's Smugglers. The varied menu offers freshly-prepared dishes cooked to order such as beef and ale pie; beer-battered haddock; button mushroom, brie and cranberry filo parcel; and succulent rib-eye steaks.

Open all day all wk 12-12 (Fri-Sat noon-1am Sun 12-11.30) **Food** Lunch Mon-Sat 12-2.30, Sun 12-3 Dinner Mon-Thu 6-9, Fri-Sat 6-9.30 Restaurant menu available all wk ⊕ ENTERPRISE INNS ◀ St Austell Tribute, Skinner's Smugglers Ale ♂ Symonds. ☻ 9 **Facilities** Non-diners area ♣ (Bar Restaurant Garden) ♦ Children's menu Children's portions Play area Family room Garden ⋒ Parking WiFi ▬ (notice required)

WHEELER END
Map 5 SU89

The Chequers Inn

tel: 01494 883070 **Bullocks Farm Ln HP14 3NH**
email: landlord@chequerswheelerend.co.uk
dir: *4m N of Marlow*

Families welcome at this Fuller's pub

This picturesque 16th-century inn, with its low-beamed ceilings, roaring winter fires and two attractive beer gardens, is ideally located for walkers on the edge of Wheeler End Common (families and dogs are welcome). Lunchtime dishes include pub favourites such as spaghetti bolognaise or bangers and mash with gravy; and there's a sandwich menu too. Typical evening choices are spicy chicken wings with blue cheese dressing; bacon and Stilton beefburger with chips; or pie of the day.

Open 12-3 6-11 (Sat 12-11 Sun 12-6) Closed Sun eve, Mon L ⊕ FULLER'S ◀ London Pride & ESB, George Gale & Co Seafarers, Guest ale ♂ Aspall. **Facilities** ♣ (Bar Garden) ♦ Children's menu Children's portions Garden Parking WiFi

PICK OF THE PUBS

The Bull & Butcher

TURVILLE   Map 5 SU79

tel: 01491 638283 **RG9 6QU**
email: info@thebullandbutcher.com
web: www.thebullandbutcher.com
dir: *M40 junct 5, follow Ibstone signs.
Right at T-junct. Pub 0.25m on left*

Quintessential English pub in the Chilterns

Built in 1550, Turville's village pub nestles in the Hambledon Valley, an Area of Outstanding Natural Beauty not far from Henley-on-Thames. Stunning countryside vistas include the windmill from *Chitty Chitty Bang Bang* perched on a steep ridge overlooking the village, and the 10th-century church that starred in *The Vicar of Dibley* and many episodes of *Midsomer Murders*. The pub was originally known as the 'Bullen Butcher', a reference to Henry VIII's treatment of his second wife Anne Boleyn. The Grade II listed building is divided into two main areas: the Well Bar and the Windmill Lounge, both of which have large open fires, original beams and a relaxed atmosphere. Outside, a large sunny garden and patio areas are ideal for summertime refreshment; children and dogs are welcome. The Bull Room, with glass barn doors leading out to the lawn, offers a private dining and special occasion venue for larger groups. Handles for Brakspear and guest ales populate the bar, and a good selection of wines has something for every palate. High quality

and locally sourced produce are the keynotes of the menus, mixing pub favourites with cosmopolitan flavours. A new and dedicated lunch menu offers a short selection of straightforward and well-priced choices: trio of sausages with wholegrain mustard mash, for example. At dinner time starters may include coquilles St Jacques; or duck and chestnut ravioli with Jerusalem artichoke sauce. Move on to pot-roasted chicken leg with wild mushroom mousse, hunter sauce, roasted kohlrabi and Parmentier potatoes; or ox cheeks in stout with horseradish mash, roasted vegetables and crispy shallot sprinkles. Finally dessert: apple and toffee crumble with custard, perhaps, or brioche bread and butter pudding with double cream. Live music, last Friday of the month.

Open all wk summer 12-11 (Sat noon-1am) winter 12-3 5.30-11 **Food** Lunch Mon-Fri 12-2.30, Sat 12-3, Sun 12-4, summer all day Dinner Mon-Sat 6-9, summer all day ⊞ BRAKSPEAR ◀ Bitter & Oxford Gold, Guest ales ♂ Symonds. ♀ 36 **Facilities** Non-diners area ❀ (Bar Garden) ♦ Children's menu Garden ☶ Parking WiFi 🚌 (notice required)

WOOBURN COMMON
Map 6 SU98

Chequers Inn ★★★ HL ◉◉
PICK OF THE PUBS

tel: 01628 529575 **Kiln Ln HP10 OJQ**
email: info@chequers-inn.com **web:** www.chequers-inn.com
dir: *M40 junct 2, A40 through Beaconsfield towards High Wycombe. Left into Broad Ln, signed Taplow/Burnham/Wooburn Common. 2m to pub*

Pub grub meets fine dining in the Chilterns

The atmosphere of much of this 17th-century coaching inn is still firmly of the past, especially in the open-fired bar, where the hand-tooled oak beams and posts, and timeworn flagstone and wooden floors shrug off the passage of time. Contrast then the 21st-century chic lounge, with leather sofas and chairs, low tables and greenery while outside, sheltering the patio and flowery garden, stands a magnificent old oak tree. Beers are from Marlow's Rebellion and the St Austell breweries, and 14 wines are by the glass. The two-AA Rosette restaurant menu features ever-changing dishes such as calves' liver with olive oil mash, bacon and green beans; coconut crusted cod with wilted spinach and chorizo butter sauce; and Stilton and red onion tart. Accommodation comprises 17 designer rooms.

Open all day all wk 12-12 **Food** Lunch Mon-Fri 12-2.30, Sat 12-10, Sun 12-9.30 Dinner Mon-Thu 6-9.30, Fri 6-10, Sat 12-10, Sun 12-9.30 Set menu available Restaurant menu available all wk ⊕ FREE HOUSE ◄ Rebellion IPA & Smuggler, St Austell Tribute ♂ Westons Stowford Press. ▼ 14 **Facilities** Non-diners area ♦ Children's menu Children's portions Garden ⋒ Parking WiFi **Rooms** 17

CAMBRIDGESHIRE

ABBOTS RIPTON
Map 12 TL27

The Abbot's Elm ★★★★ INN ◉◉

tel: 01487 773773 **PE28 2PA**
email: info@theabbotselm.co.uk **web:** www.theabbotselm.co.uk
dir: *From A141 or Huntingdon follow Abbots Ripton signs*

Thatched village inn with a very warm welcome

Situated in the delightful village of Abbots Ripton, the exterior of this pub looks pretty much as it has done over the centuries but step inside and you'll find that the open-plan bar and restaurant are bathed in natural light. Owners John and Julia Abbey are genial hosts and visitors are welcome whether it's for coffee or a seven-course tasting dinner. A chalkboard menu of pub classics runs alongside a carte featuring dishes such as Herefordshire snails, wild mushrooms and coriander broth; poach-roast guinea fowl breast, confit leg, sage fondant potatoes, and Madeira sauce; and milk chocolate mousse torte with caffè latte ice cream.

Open all day Closed Sun eve **Food** Lunch all wk 12-2.15 Dinner Mon-Sat 6-9 Set menu available Restaurant menu available all wk ⊕ FREE HOUSE ◄ Oakham Ales JHB, Guest ales ♂ Symonds. ▼ 29 **Facilities** Non-diners area ♦ (Bar Garden) ♦ Children's menu Children's portions Garden ⋒ Parking WiFi **Rooms** 3

BALSHAM
Map 12 TL55

The Black Bull Inn ★★★★ INN ◉

tel: 01223 893844 **27 High St CB21 4DJ**
email: info@blackbull-balsham.co.uk **web:** www.blackbull-balsham.co.uk
dir: *From S: M11 junct 9, A11 towards Newmarket, follow Balsham signs. From N: M11 junct 10, A505 signed Newmarket (A11), onto A11, follow Balsham signs*

Transformed inn for excellent food and a good night's sleep

An AA Rosette for food and four AA stars for accommodation are just two of the awards acquired by this 16th-century pub, run by the same team as The Red Lion in

nearby Hinxton. The bar serves East Anglian real ales and ciders, sandwiches, baguettes, hot meals and shortcrust pastry pie. The restaurant is in an adjoining converted barn, where main dishes, depending on the season, may include prawn bisque, red pepper arancini, tiger prawn, parmesan crisp and charred leek; and rack of lamb, fondant potato, vegetable purée and red wine jus. Out front is a tree-lined sandstone patio, and at the back a south-facing beer garden.

Open all day all wk **Food** Lunch Mon-Thu 12-2, Fri-Sun 12-2.30 Dinner Mon-Thu 6.30-9, Fri-Sat 6.30-9.30, Sun 7-9 ⊕ FREE HOUSE ◄ Woodforde's Wherry, Adnams Southwold Bitter, Red & Black, Nethergate ♂ Aspall & Harry Sparrow. ▼ 12 **Facilities** Non-diners area ♦ (Bar Garden) ♦ Children's menu Children's portions Garden ⋒ Beer festival Parking WiFi ➡ (notice required) **Rooms** 5

BARRINGTON
Map 12 TL34

The Royal Oak

tel: 01223 870791 **31 West Green CB22 7RZ**
email: info@royaloakbarrington.co.uk
dir: *From Barton off M11, S of Cambridge*

Quintessential English pub by village green

One of the oldest thatched and timbered pubs in England, this rambling 16th-century building overlooks a 30-acre village green. With a pretty 'chocolate-box' image on the outside, the smart interior is now contemporary in design; the menu lists the classic dishes for which the pub has long been known, such as pie of the day, toad-in-the-hole, beer battered haddock, and aubergine parmigiana. In addition there's a regularly changing specials menu, a collection of salads and sandwiches, and a choice of ales that includes Buntingford Twitchell and Adnams.

Open all wk 12-3 6-11 (Sun 12-11) **Food** Lunch all wk 12-2 Dinner all wk 6-9 Av main course £10 ⊕ FREE HOUSE ◄ Woodforde's, Buntingford Twitchell, Adnams, Hanlons Royal Oak ♂ Aspall, Thatchers Gold. ▼ 8 **Facilities** Non-diners area ♦ (Bar Garden) ♦ Children's menu Children's portions Garden ⋒ Parking WiFi ➡ (notice required)

BOURN
Map 12 TL35

The Willow Tree

tel: 01954 719775 **29 High St CB23 2SQ**
email: contact@thewillowtreebourn.com
dir: *From Royston on A1198, right on B1046 signed Bourn. Pub in village on right (8m from Cambridge)*

Village pub with candlelit restaurant

Just off Ermine Street, the old Roman road from London to York, is Craig and Shaina Galvin-Scott's mansard-roofed village pub. A white picket fence surrounds the street frontage, while in the rear garden are the majestic eponymous willow tree, a heated terrace, a children's play area and, when warm, striking purple deckchairs. The shabby-chic interior incorporates an open fireplace and a medley of non-matching dining chairs. From a winter menu come blow-torched scallop with peas and pancetta; roasted venison haunch rolled in chervil and walnut crush; Mediterranean sea bass and squid stew; and aubergine, red pepper and lentil moussaka.

Open all day all wk **Food** Lunch all wk 12-3 Dinner all wk 5.30-9.30 Set menu available ⊕ FREE HOUSE ◄ Milton Pegasus, Woodforde's Wherry ♂ Addlestones, Aspall. ▼ 20 **Facilities** Non-diners area ♦ (Garden) ♦ Children's menu Children's portions Garden ⋒ Beer festival Cider festival Parking WiFi ➡ (notice required)

The Crown Inn

tel: 01487 824428 **Bridge Rd PE28 3AY**
email: info@thecrowninnrestaurant.co.uk
dir: *A141 from Huntingdon towards Warboys. Left to Broughton*

Picturesque inn at the heart of the community

In the mid-19th century, this village inn incorporated a saddler's shop, thatched stables and piggeries. Today it focuses on being a popular pub and restaurant in a thriving local community. The bar offers real ales from Suffolk and national breweries, and you'll also find Aspall cider. The restaurant combines a traditional pub look with contemporary design, and it's here you'll be able to eat modern European dishes cooked using the best sustainable fish caught by day boats, the highest quality meats and excellent seasonal vegetables. Menus change regularly, so you may find one offering seared pigeon breast; roast cod with sautéed celeriac; and cappuccino and hazelnut praline gâteau.

Open all wk Mon-Sat 11.30-3.30 6.30-11 (Sun 11.30-6) **Food** Lunch Mon-Sat 11.30-2.30, Sun 12-3.30 Dinner Mon-Sat 6.30-9.15 ⊕ FREE HOUSE ◀ Rotating Local ales Ỏ Aspall, Glebe Farm. ♀ 10 **Facilities** Non-diners area ❀ (Bar Garden) ◀❙ Children's menu Children's portions Play area Garden ⊨ Parking

The Anchor Pub, Dining & River Terrace

tel: 01223 353554 **Silver St CB3 9EL**
email: info@anchorcambridge.com
dir: *Phone for detailed directions*

Popular riverside pub

Bordering Queens' College is a medieval lane, at the end of which stands this attractive pub, right by the bridge over the River Cam. Head for the riverside patio with a local real ale, or a Hazy Hog cider, and watch rookie punters struggling with their tricky craft – another definition of pole position, perhaps. A good choice of food includes sea bass fillet with pumpkin and sage risotto; honey-glazed Barbary duck leg with parsnip mash; and beer-battered fish and chips. Sandwiches, sausage rolls and Scotch eggs are available too. A change of hands.

Open all day all wk Mon-Thu & Sun 11-11 (Fri-Sat 11am-mdnt) **Food** Lunch Mon-Sat 11.30-4, Sun 11.30-9 Dinner Mon-Sat 5-10, Sun 11.30-9 Restaurant menu available all wk ⊕ METRO COUNTRY PUBS ◀ Meantime, Rotating Guest ales Ỏ Aspall, Hogs Back Hazy Hog. ♀ 12 **Facilities** Non-diners area ◀❙ Children's menu Outside area ⊨ WiFi ▥ (notice required)

The Old Spring

tel: 01223 357228 **1 Ferry Path CB4 1HB**
email: theoldspring@hotmail.co.uk
dir: *Just off Chesterton Rd, (A1303) in city centre, near Midsummer Common*

Neighbourhood pub with a lengthy and varied menu

You'll find this bustling pub in the leafy suburb of De Freville, just a short stroll from the River Cam and its many boatyards. The bright and airy interior offers rug-covered wooden floors, comfy sofas and large family tables. Sip a pint of Abbot Ale, one of the five real ales on tap, or one of 20 wines by the glass while choosing from over a dozen main courses plus specials, perhaps Old Spring fish pie with potato and parmesan crust; lamb burger with tzatziki, salad and fries; corned beef hash, crushed potatoes, white onion, fried egg and crusty bread; or chicken and bacon on toasted ciabatta. Leave some room for pudding though, hot Belgian waffle with butterscotch sauce and ice cream, for example.

Open all day all wk 11.30-11 (Sun 12-10.30) **Food** Lunch Mon-Fri 12-2.30, Sat 12-4, Sun 12-9.30 Dinner Mon-Sat 6-9.30, Sun 12-9.30 ⊕ GREENE KING ◀ IPA & Abbot Ale, Guest ales Ỏ Aspall. ♀ 20 **Facilities** Non-diners area ◀❙ Children's menu Children's portions Outside area ⊨ Parking WiFi ▥

The Punter

tel: 01223 363322 **3 Pound Hill CB3 OAE**
email: info@thepuntercambridge.co.uk
dir: *Phone for detailed directions*

Seasonal food and a great atmosphere

Two minutes' walk from the city centre, this former coaching house is popular with post-grads, locals and dog lovers alike who create a happy mood with their chatter and laughter. The interior is an eclectic mix of previously loved hand-me-downs, comfy sofas, sturdy school chairs, and an assortment of pictures and painting jostling for space on the walls. Drinkers can enjoy local ales but it seems it's the food that draws people in. The modern menu might offer mushroom and red wine risotto with crispy leeks; and beef bourguignon, mash and curly kale.

Open all day all wk Closed 25-26 Dec **Food** Lunch all wk 12-3 Dinner Mon-Sat 6-10, Sun 6-9 Av main course £13 ⊕ PUNCH TAVERNS ◀ Punter ale, Punter Blonde, Guest ales Ỏ Addlestones. ♀ 13 **Facilities** Non-diners area ❀ (Bar Restaurant Outside area) ◀❙ Children's portions Outside area ⊨ WiFi

The Plough

tel: 01954 210489 **2 High St CB23 7PL**
email: info@theploughcoton.co.uk
dir: *M11 juncts 12 or 13. Follow Coton signs*

Fine food in Cambridge-edge countryside

Nudging the cricket pitches and grassy recreation ground, this much upgraded village pub caters for savvy diners escaping the hubbub of nearby Cambridge. The cool, chic interior is a model of contemporary decor, with colourful rugs, leather sofa and colourwashed walls producing a relaxing atmosphere in which to enjoy the modern, gastro-style menu. Sharing 'planks' of cured meats and cheeses; inspired upmarket pizzas or mains like pan-fried loin of pollock with oyster fritter; or Jerusalem artichoke, truffle and almond risotto typify an evening's repast. The wine list features around 30 bins and beers are from East Anglian breweries.

Open all day all wk **Food** Lunch Mon-Sat 12-3, Sun 12-6 Dinner Mon-Thu 6-9, Fri-Sat 6-9.30, Sun 12-6 ⊕ ENTERPRISE INNS ◀ Sharp's Doom Bar, Adnams Lighthouse, Greene King Ruddles Best, Woodforde's Wherry, Rotating guest ale Ỏ Aspall. ♀ **Facilities** Non-diners area ❀ (Bar Garden) ◀❙ Children's menu Children's portions Play area Garden ⊨ Beer festival Parking WiFi ▥

The Black Horse

tel: 01954 782600 **35 Park St CB23 8DA**
email: deniseglover@hotmail.co.uk
dir: *A14 junct 30, follow signs for Dry Drayton. In village turn right to pub (signed)*

Renowned for its ales and good food

Just five miles from Cambridge, The Black Horse has been at the heart of this quiet village for more than 300 years. Gary and Denise Glover and chef Daniel Walker have built a reputation for notable food. Many local ales are showcased in the bar, and local suppliers dominate the menu in the restaurant. A starter of pan-seared pigeon breast, black pudding and game jus might be followed by Aldeburgh stone bass with green lentils, spinach and mussel sauce. The pub holds an annual beer festival over the St George's Day weekend in April.

Open 12-3 6-11 (Sat 12-11 Sun 12-4) Closed Mon **Food** Lunch Wed-Sat 12-3, Sun 12-4 Dinner Wed-Sat 6-9.30 ⊕ FREE HOUSE ◀ Black Horse, Adnams & Broadside, Guest ale Ỏ Aspall. **Facilities** Non-diners area ❀ (Bar Garden) ◀❙ Children's portions Garden ⊨ Beer festival Parking WiFi

PICK OF THE PUBS

The Anchor Inn ★★★★ INN ⊛

ELY Map 12 TL58

tel: 01353 778537
Sutton Gault CB6 2BD
email: anchorinn@popmail.bta.com
web: www.anchorsuttongault.co.uk
dir: *From A14, B1050 to Earith, take B1381 to Sutton. Sutton Gault on left*

Riverside inn beneath big Fenland skies

The Fens were lawless and disease-ridden until, in 1630, the Earl of Bedford commissioned Dutch engineer Cornelius Vermuyden to drain them. By digging the Old and New Bedford Rivers, the Dutchman ended the constant danger of flooding and began the process that created today's rich agricultural landscape. Using thick gault clay, he built raised river banks and beside the New Bedford (or 'The Hundred Foot Drain') constructed the Anchor for his workforce; it has been a pub ever since. Today, low beams, dark wood panelling, scrubbed pine tables, gently undulating tiled floors, antique prints and log fires create the intimate character of this family-run free house. Ten wines by the glass and East Anglian real ales Buntingford Twitchell and Milton Sparta will be found in the bar. The modern British cuisine is strong on local produce, including hand-dressed crabs from Cromer, Brancaster oysters and mussels, samphire, fresh asparagus, and venison from the Denham Estate. In the winter there'll be pheasant, partridge, pigeon and wild duck. Making an interesting starter is 'fish finger' with poached egg, bacon and pickled samphire; this could be followed by braised beef cheek, pearl barley and parsley risotto, star anise carrots and sticky glaze; or olive crust rump of lamb, celeriac purée, re-hydrated tomatoes and confit sweet potato. Desserts may include blackberry fool mille feuille and vanilla ice cream; and coffee and hazelnut Battenburg with Ameretto ice cream. Sunday roasts – indeed, any meal – may be enjoyed on the terrace overlooking the river. The cathedral cities of Ely and Cambridge are both within easy reach.

Open all wk Mon-Fri 12-2.30 7-10.30 (Sat 12-3 6.30-11 Sun 12-4 6.30-10) Closed 25-26 Dec eve **Food** Lunch Mon-Fri 12-2, Sat-Sun 12-2.30 Dinner Mon-Fri 7-9, Sat-Sun 6.30-9 Set menu available ⊕ FREE HOUSE ◄ Buntingford Twitchell, Milton Sparta. ☗ 10 **Facilities** Non-diners area ♦ Children's portions Garden ㅈ Parking WiFi ▭ (notice required) **Rooms** 4

DUXFORD — Map 12 TL44

The John Barleycorn — PICK OF THE PUBS

tel: 01223 832699 **3 Moorfield Rd CB22 4PP**
email: info@johnbarleycorn.co.uk
dir: *Exit A505 into Duxford*

Seventeenth-century traditional village pub

Built in 1660, this thatched and whitewashed former coach house became the John Barleycorn in the mid-19th century. The name first appeared in an old folksong as the personification of malting barley and the beer and whisky that results. During World War II the brave young airmen of Group Captain Douglas Bader's Duxford Wing drank here in what today is a softly-lit bar with country furniture, a large brick fireplace, old tiled floor, cushioned pews and hop-adorned beams. Food is a big draw, from the sandwiches and jacket potatoes, to the tzatziki and charcuterie grazing boards; from the smoked Gressingham duck cassoulet with Puy lentils and pancetta, to the chargrilled supreme of tuna marinated in lime and coriander, stir-fried pak choi and ginger and carrot broth; and from the Hereford and Limousin steaks, to the vanilla and strawberry crème brûlée. Eating and drinking on the flower-decorated patio is extremely pleasant.

Open all day all wk **Food** Lunch Mon-Thu 12-3, Fri-Sat 12-10, Sun 12-8.30 Dinner Mon-Thu 5-9.30, Fri-Sat 12-10, Sun 12-8.30 ⊕ GREENE KING ◀ Greene King IPA & Abbot Ale, Guest ales Ö Thatchers. ♟ 12 **Facilities** Non-diners area ✿ (Bar Restaurant Garden) ♦️ Children's menu Children's portions Play area Garden ⌷ Parking WiFi ▦ (notice required)

ELY — Map 12 TL58

The Anchor Inn ★★★★ INN ◉ — PICK OF THE PUBS

See Pick of the Pubs on page 61

FEN DITTON — Map 12 TL46

Ancient Shepherds

tel: 01223 293280 **High St CB5 8ST**
email: marycullen@ancientshepherds.com
dir: *From A14 take B1047 signed Cambridge/Airport*

Popular pub in a peaceful riverside village

Three miles from Cambridge, this heavily beamed pub is a popular dining destination away from the bustle of the city. Built as three cottages in 1540, it was named after the Loyal and Ancient Order of Shepherds that once met here. The pub is free of music, darts and pool, and is a cosy place to sup a pint beside one of the inglenook fires. The bar lunch menu offers an extensive range of filled baguettes as well as jackets and snacks. In the restaurant, perhaps choose marinated crayfish tails; braised lamb shank with minted red wine and rosemary gravy, then apple strudel for dessert. Specials could include fishcakes, lasagne or cannelloni.

Open 12-2.30 6-11 Closed 25-26 Dec, 1 Jan, Sun eve **Food** Lunch Tue-Sat 12-2, Sun 12-2.30 Dinner Tue-Sat 7-9 ⊕ PUNCH TAVERNS ◀ Greene King IPA, Rotating Guest ales Ö Aspall. ♟ 8 **Facilities** Non-diners area ✿ (Bar Garden) ♦️ Children's portions Garden ⌷ Parking WiFi

FENSTANTON — Map 12 TL36

King William IV

tel: 01480 462467 **High St PE28 9JF**
email: kingwilliamfenstanton@btconnect.com
dir: *On A14 between Hunstanton & Cambridge follow Fenstanton signs*

Rustic village inn with good food

This rambling 17th-century village pub features oak beams, old brickwork and a wonderful central fireplace. Lunchtime offerings include a range of hot and cold sandwiches but also light bites such as sliced ham, fried egg and hand-cut chips; or minute steak and French fries. Diners looking for something more substantial can choose from the restaurant or classics menus – seared duck breast, potato rösti, braised red cabbage and balsamic glaze; liver, bacon, greens, mash and gravy; or butternut squash and garlic risotto. Occasionally, there's live music on a Sunday afternoon.

Open all wk Mon-Thu 12-3 5-11 (Fri-Sun all day) **Food** Lunch all wk 12-2.30 Dinner Mon-Thu 6-9, Fri-Sat 6-9.30 Set menu available Restaurant menu available all wk ⊕ GREENE KING ◀ IPA, Guest ales Ö Aspall. ♟ 13 **Facilities** Non-diners area ✿ (Bar Garden) ♦️ Children's portions Garden ⌷ Parking WiFi ▦ (notice required)

FORDHAM — Map 12 TL67

White Pheasant ◉◉ — PICK OF THE PUBS

tel: 01638 720414 **CB7 5LQ**
email: whitepheasant@live.com
dir: *From Newmarket A142 to Ely, approx 5m to Fordham. Pub on left in village*

Carefully constructed menu of select options

This 18th-century building stands in a fenland village between Ely and Newmarket. While enjoying a pint of Adnams or glass of wine, choose between the dishes of good English fare on the two AA-Rosette menu. Cooking is taken seriously here, with quality, presentation and flavour taking top priority; specials change daily. Starters may include beetroot mousse, pine nut, feta and pear; or smoked quail, pickled quail egg, watercress, carrot and hazelnut. Followed by Suffolk chicken, creamy potato, sweetcorn and chorizo; or seared lamb's liver, rustic purée, Suffolk bacon and red wine jus. Desserts could be a temptation of vanilla pannacotta, raspberry and white chocolate; blackcurrant mousse with cinnamon ice cream; or dark chocolate marquise, parsnip and hazelnut.

Open Tue-Sat 12-2.30 6.30-9.30 (Sun 12-2.30) Closed Sun eve & Mon **Food** Lunch Tue-Sun 12-2.30 Dinner Tue-Sat 6.30-9.30 Set menu available Restaurant menu available Tue-Sat ⊕ FREE HOUSE ◀ Adnams Ö Aspall Harry Sparrow. ♟ 12 **Facilities** Non-diners area ✿ (Garden) ♦️ Children's portions Garden ⌷ Parking WiFi ▦ (notice required)

GLINTON — Map 12 TF10

NEW The Blue Bell

tel: 01733 252285 **10 High St PE6 7LS**
email: info@thebluebellglinton.co.uk web: www.thebluebellglinton.co.uk
dir: *Phone pub for detailed directions*

Contemporary dining and old-world charm

The oak beams and log fires provide a relaxed, old-world feel to this charming 18th-century village pub run by chef Will Frankgate and his wife Kelly. The excellent food at The Blue Bell is more contemporary with innovative new dishes rubbing shoulders with old favourites. Typical choices include marinated Cornish mackerel fillet, pickled turnips, preserved lemon, coriander yogurt; or Gressingham duck breast with carrot purée, braised red cabbage, fondant potato and glazed fig sauce; with steaks, burgers and fish and chips for more traditional palates. Lunchtime sandwiches are also served.

Open all day all wk **Food** Contact pub for food times Av main course £11.95 Set menu available Restaurant menu available all wk ⊕ GREENE KING ◀ IPA, Morland Old Speckled Hen, Guest ales. **Facilities** Non-diners area ✿ (Bar Garden) ♦ Children's menu Children's portions Garden ⋈ Beer festival Parking WiFi 🚐 (notice required)

GRANTCHESTER   Map 12 TL45

NEW The Rupert Brooke

tel: 01223 841875 **2 Broadway CB3 9NQ**
email: info@therupertbrooke.com
dir: M11 junct 12, follow Grantchester signs

Idyllic riverside pub with literary links

Named after the English poet who once lived at the Old Vicarage in the pretty village of Grantchester, this stylish pub reopened in October 2014. Located alongside the River Cam, it is just a couple of miles from the centre of Cambridge, which can be accessed via the river path, although some customers are known to arrive by punt. A range of ales including Woodforde's Wherry are dispensed from the bar, which also offers a dozen wines by the glass to accompany enjoyable dishes like wild mushroom and truffle macaroni; and braised collar of ham with duck egg and chips.

Open all day all wk **Food** Lunch all wk 12-2.30 Dinner Mon-Sat 6.30-9.30 Av main course £15 Set menu available ⊕ FREE HOUSE ◀ Woodforde's Wherry, Local guest ale Ö Aspall. ☗ 12 **Facilities** Non-diners area ✿ (Bar Restaurant Garden) ♦ Children's menu Children's portions Garden ⋈ Parking WiFi 🚐 (notice required)

GREAT ABINGTON   Map 12 TL54

NEW Three Tuns ★★★★ INN

tel: 01223 891467 **75 High St CB21 6AB**
email: email@thethreetuns-greatabington.co.uk
web: www.thethreetuns-greatabington.co.uk
dir: A11 onto A1307 (Haverhill). Right signed Abington. Pub on left

A 16th-century free house with excellent Thai food

A rashly shouted 'Oi!' here might well bring the chef running out from his kitchen, for that's his name. The highly experienced Oi is from Thailand and his huge range of traditional Thai food embraces starters and soups; beef, chicken, duck, pork and prawn stir-fries; classic green, red, yellow, Massaman, Penang and jungle curries; fish dishes, such as sea bass in chilli sauce; pad Thai and other noodle dishes; and vegetables and rice cooked different ways. Among the 200 beers, many from local breweries, available in the bar is Austrian Stiegl lager on tap.

Open all wk 12-2 6-11 (Fri-Sun 12-11) Closed 1 Jan **Food** Lunch 12-2 Dinner 6-9.30 Av main course £8 ⊕ FREE HOUSE ◀ Greene King IPA, Woodforde's Wherry, Adnams Ö Aspall. **Facilities** ✿ (Bar Garden) ♦ Garden ⋈ Parking WiFi 🚐 (notice required)
Rooms 9

GREAT WILBRAHAM   Map 12 TL55

The Carpenters Arms

tel: 01223 882093 **10 High St CB21 5JD**
email: contact@carpentersarmsgastropub.co.uk
web: www.carpentersarmsgastropub.co.uk
dir: From A11 follow "The Wilbraham" signs. Into Great Wilbraham, right at junct, pub 150yds on left

Traditional free house, microbrewery and French-inspired food

A beer house since 1729, this smart pub restaurant is still brewing – today they're called Crafty Beers, such as Carpenter's Cask and Sauvignon Blonde. Landlords Rick and Heather Hurley previously ran an award-winning restaurant in France, so expect French – eg tartiflette – Catalan, Italian and even Thai dishes on the menus. Other possibilities include warm confit of duck salad; chicken breast with coriander butter, walnut sauce, sautéed potatoes and carrots; cider slow-roasted belly pork, creamy mash and braised red cabbage; and sea bass fillet, ginger and lemongrass sauce, rice and cucumber, tomato salsa, while Sunday roasts remain decidedly English. A Suffolk white features among the world-sourced wine list.

Open 11.30-3 6.30-11 Closed 26 Dec, 1 Jan, 1wk Nov & 1wk Feb, Sun eve & Tue **Food** Lunch Wed-Mon 12-2.30 Dinner Wed-Sat & Mon 7-9 Av main course £10.95 Restaurant menu available Wed-Sat ⊕ FREE HOUSE ◀ Crafty Carpenter's Cask & Sauvignon Blonde Ö Aspall. **Facilities** Non-diners area ♦ Children's menu Children's portions Garden Outside area ⋈ Parking WiFi 🚐 (notice required)

See advert on page 64

The Carpenters Arms
Great Wilbraham
Brew Pub & Restaurant

FREE HOUSE

CAMRA
AWARD
WINNER
CAMBS

A traditional country pub with
award winning food & beer.
All food freshly made from
fresh local produce, some home grown!

our own real ales brewed on site

Hospitality - Sit long Talk much !
in front of the fire in winter, in the garden in summer...let us spoil you!

The Carpenters Arms, Great Wilbraham
Cambridgeshire CB21 5JD
Tel 01223 882093
www.carpentersarmsgastropub.co.uk

tripadvisor
The world's largest travel site

2014 Winner
Certificate of Excellence

LOO
OF THE YEAR
Awards
2015
PLATINUM

HEMINGFORD GREY   Map 12 TL27

The Cock Pub and Restaurant   PICK OF THE PUBS

See Pick of the Pubs on page 66

HINXTON   Map 12 TL44

The Red Lion Inn ★★★★ INN ◉   PICK OF THE PUBS

tel: 01799 530601 **32 High St CB10 1QY**
email: info@redlionhinxton.co.uk **web:** www.redlionhinxton.co.uk
dir: *N'bound only: M11 junct 9, towards A11, left onto A1301. Left to Hinxton. Or M11 junct 10, A505 towards A11/Newmarket. At rdbt take 3rd exit onto A1301, right to Hinxton*

Country pub, restaurant and B&B with super garden

With many awards for what goes on inside, this 16th-century pink-washed free house and restaurant has much going for it outside too, with a pretty walled garden and dovecote, and a patio overlooking the church. Four local real ales await your order in the low-ceilinged and wood-floored bar; three of them – Woodforde's Wherry, Crafty Sauvignon Blonde and own label Red & Black – are fixtures, the fourth a local guest brew. Over 20 wines are served by the glass. It's good to eat in the bar, but you might prefer the high-raftered, L-shaped restaurant, which is furnished with high-backed settles similar to those in the bar. The menu gives a taste of the modern British approach to food, in dishes such as a seafood flan with French beans dressed with truffle oil; and spring vegetable tagliatelle. Puddings also show twists on the traditional: try sticky toffee, date and coconut pudding with butterscotch sauce and vanilla ice cream.

Open all day all wk **Food** Lunch Mon-Thu 12-2, Fri-Sun 12-2.30 Dinner Mon-Thu 6.30-9, Fri-Sat 6.30-9.30, Sun 7-9 Restaurant menu available all wk ⊕ FREE HOUSE ◀ Crafty Sauvignon Blonde, Woodforde's Wherry, Adnams, Red & Black (own ale), Guest ales ♉ Aspall Harry Sparrow. ♟ 22 **Facilities** Non-diners area ❤ (Bar Garden) ✦ Children's menu Children's portions Garden ⋔ Parking WiFi ⛟ (notice required) **Rooms** 8

HISTON   Map 12 TL46

Red Lion

tel: 01223 564437 **27 High St CB24 9JD**
dir: *M11 junct 14, A14 towards. Exit at junct 32 onto B1049 for Histon*

Village pub with good choice of real ales

A pub since 1836, this popular village local on Cambridge's northern fringe has been run by Mark Donachy for more than two decades. A dyed-in-the-wool pub man, Mark's real ales include Oakham Bishops Farewell, as well as Pickled Pig Porker's Snout cider. There are also over 30 different bottled beers from around the world. Expect quality pub food in a traditional environment, along side cheerful service, winter log fires and a good-sized neat garden. Typical of the specials board: steak and kidney suet pudding; and quinoa, sweet potato and black bean chilli. Fresh fish is a draw on Tuesday evenings and Wednesdays. Time a visit for the Easter or early September beer and cider festivals.

Open all day all wk 10.30am-11pm (Fri 10.30am-mdnt Sun 12-11) **Food** Lunch Mon-Fri 12-2.30, Sat 10.30-9.30, Sun 12-5 Dinner Tue-Thu 6-9.30, Sat 10.30-9.30 Av main course £9 ⊕ FREE HOUSE ◀ Oakham Bishops Farewell, Batemans Yella Belly, Adnams Ghost Ship, Tring Side Pocket for a Toad ♉ Pickled Pig Porker's Snout, Westons Perry. **Facilities** Non-diners area ✦ Children's portions Family room Garden ⋔ Beer festival Cider festival Parking WiFi ⛟ (notice required)

HORNINGSEA   Map 12 TL46

The Crown & Punchbowl

tel: 01223 860643 **CB25 9JG**
email: crown@cambscuisine.com
dir: *Phone for detailed directions*

Friendly coaching inn with a commitment to local produce

Dating back to 1764, the tiled and whitewashed Crown & Punchbowl (now in new hands) stands in a little one-street village. Soft colours and wooden floors create a warm atmosphere, while in the low-beamed restaurant, the new owners demonstrate their commitment to providing fresh, seasonal and locally sourced produce on the menus. While deciding on your choices nibble on pork crackling and apple sauce, then take a seat and enjoy devilled lamb's kidneys; or clam, leek and saffron risotto, followed by home-made pork and herb sausages; or coley and crayfish fishcakes. The puddings are just as appealing – sticky toffee pudding, toffee sauce and vanilla ice cream.

Open Mon-Sat 12-3 6.30-9.30 (Sun 12-3) Closed Sun eve & BHs eve **Food** Contact pub for food times ⊕ FREE HOUSE ◀ Milton Justinian. ♟ 14 **Facilities** Non-diners area ✦ Children's portions Garden ⋔ Parking WiFi

KEYSTON   Map 11 TL07

Pheasant Inn ◉◉   PICK OF THE PUBS

tel: 01832 710241 **Village Loop Rd PE28 0RE**
email: info@thepheasant-keyston.co.uk
dir: *0.5m from A14, clearly signed, 10m W of Huntingdon, 14m E of Kettering*

Thatched 16th-century village inn with excellent food

In a sleepy farming village, this pretty thatched pub was bought by the Hoskins family in 1964 and it has been serving good food ever since. Continuing that tradition are today's owners, Simon Cadge and Gerda Koedijk, while John Hoskins, a Master of Wine, compiles the wine list. In the large, oak-beamed bar, locals sup pints of Brewster's Hophead and Digfield Ales Barnwell Bitter. At the rear, the Garden Room surveys a sunny patio. Simon relies greatly on local produce for his menus, but not so much that he can't offer Portland crab linguine with chilli, lemon, fennel, garlic and flat-leaf parsley; or pan-fried sea trout with shellfish risotto, cavolo nero and tarragon. His comprehensive menu also lists beetroot risotto with goats' cheese, and chargrilled Scotch beef with Wagyu oxtail croquette, horseradish mash and confit swede. A dessert to catch the eye is spotted dick with vanilla custard.

Open 12-3 6-11 (Sun 12-5) Closed 2-16 Jan, Mon & Sun eve **Food** Lunch Tue-Sat 12-2, Sun 12-3.30 Dinner Tue-Sat 6.30-9.30 Set menu available ⊕ FREE HOUSE ◀ Adnams Broadside, Brewster's Hophead, Nene Valley NVB, Digfield Ales Barnwell Bitter ♉ Aspall. ♟ 16 **Facilities** Non-diners area ❤ (Bar Garden) ✦ Children's menu Children's portions Garden ⋔ Parking WiFi ⛟ (notice required)

PICK OF THE PUBS

The Cock Pub and Restaurant

HEMINGFORD GREY   Map 12 TL27

tel: 01480 463609
47 High St PE28 9BJ
email: cock@cambscuisine.com
web: www.cambscuisine.com
dir: *Between A14 juncts 25 & 26, follow village signs*

Confident cooking in a pretty village close to the River Ouse

A handsome 17th-century pub on the main street of the charming village of Hemingford Grey, The Cock stands among thatched, timbered and brick cottages. Although it's only a mile from the busy A14, it feels like a world away and it's the ideal place to relax with peaceful views across the willow-bordered Great Ouse. Other than the peaceful location, the detour is well worth taking as the food on offer is excellent – the set lunch menu is a steal. The stylish interior comprises a contemporary bar for drinks only, and a restaurant with bare boards, dark or white-painted beams, wood-burning stoves, and church candles on an eclectic mix of old dining tables. Cooking is modern British, with the occasional foray further afield, and fresh local produce is used in preparing the short, imaginative carte, while daily deliveries of fresh fish dictate the chalkboard menu choice. A typical meal might kick off with walnut-crusted goats' cheese mousse and beetroot

three-ways; beef carpaccio with tomato and chilli jam; or pork and game terrine with pear chutney. Follow with venison haunch steak, fondant potato, roast carrots, fried sprouts with chestnuts and pancetta and port sauce; hake fillet, chorizo, butterbean and tomato stew; or pork, pig cheek and apple faggot, creamed potatoes, black pudding, salt-baked carrots and onion sauce, then round off with tiramisù, chocolate jelly and almond praline; or cherry and bramble jelly, stewed cherries and cherry sorbet; or a plate of unusual cheeses. The wine list specialises in the Languedoc-Roussillion area and the choice of real ales favours local microbreweries, perhaps Elgood's Cambridge Bitter or Brewster's Hophead. A beer festival is held in mid August.

Open all wk 11.30-3 6-11 **Food** Contact pub for details Set menu available Restaurant menu available all wk ⊕ FREE HOUSE ◼ Brewster's Hophead, Great Oakley Wagtail, Elgood's Cambridge Bitter Ö Cromwell. ♀ 18 **Facilities** Non-diners area ♦♦ Children's portions Garden ⋒ Beer festival Parking WiFi 🚐 (notice required)

| **LITTLE WILBRAHAM** | Map 12 TL55 |

Hole in the Wall ◉◉ | PICK OF THE PUBS

tel: 01223 812282 **2 High St CB21 5JY**
email: info@holeinthewallcambridge.com
dir: *Phone for detailed directions*

Enjoyable food from an award-winning chef

The name of this 16th-century village pub and restaurant between Cambridge and Newmarket comes from the days when farm workers used to collect their jugs of beer through a hole in the wall so as not to upset the gentry in the bar. Customers nowadays can enjoy ales from the Milton Brewery and the Indian Summer Brewing Company. The heavily-timbered pub is owned by former BBC *MasterChef* finalist Alex Rushmer, and first-class modern British cooking is prepared from fresh local produce. You could explore the five or seven course tasting menus, or stick to the set menu, with choices like game terrine with carrot and pear chutney and sourdough; Suffolk pork belly, roasted cauliflower, curried granola and raisin agrodolce; or fillet of hake, chorizo hash, red pepper sauce and wild rocket. Finish with Cambridge burnt cream, mango compôte and black pepper shortbread.

Open 11.30-3 6.30-11 Closed 2wks Jan, 25 Dec, Mon, Tue L, Sun eve **Food** Lunch Wed-Sun 12-2 Dinner Tue-Sat 7-9 Set menu available Restaurant menu available Tue-Sat evenings only ⊕ FREE HOUSE ⬛ Milton Brewery, Indian Summer Brewing Co ♻ Aspall. ☕ 10 **Facilities** Non-diners area ♦ Children's portions Garden ⊼ Parking WiFi

| **MADINGLEY** | Map 12 TL36 |

The Three Horseshoes | PICK OF THE PUBS

tel: 01954 210221 **High St CB23 8AB**
email: 3hs@btconnect.com
dir: *M11 junct 13, 1.5m from A14*

Cutting edge meals in traditional pub

Chimneys of mellow brick pierce the thick thatch of this cute village inn outside Cambridge. Between the reed-roofed main building and the extensive beer garden, a substantial conservatory restaurant bathes in the dappled light cast by mature trees edging this plot in one of the county's most charming villages. With tasty beers from the likes of City of Cambridge brewery and 22 wines by the glass, the wet side of the business attracts a good following. The meals emerging from the kitchen overseen by chef-patron Richard Stokes take the treat to another level again. A meal could start with house-cured and tea-smoked halibut with edamame beans, mushrooms and crispy rice, shoots and miso, then mains may continue with slow-cooked pork cheeks with seared scallops, celeriac purée, kohlrabi, lardo, cider vinegar and tarragon; or roast mallard with blueberries, smoked potato purée, cime di rapa and toasted hazelnuts. Still room, perhaps, for fig ice cream and milk crumbs? Menus change weekly and seasonally; children's portions are available.

Open all wk 11.30-3 6-11 (Sun 11.30-3 6-9.30) **Food** Lunch Mon-Fri 12-2, Sat-Sun 12-2.30 Dinner all wk 6.30-9.30 Av main course £17 Restaurant menu available all wk ⊕ FREE HOUSE ⬛ Adnams Southwold Bitter, Hook Norton Old Hooky, Smiles Best Bitter, City of Cambridge Hobson's Choice, Guest ales ♻ Westons Stowford Press. ☕ 22 **Facilities** Non-diners area ♦ Children's portions Garden Outside area ⊼ Parking WiFi 🚌 (notice required)

| **NEWTON** | Map 12 TL44 |

The Queen's Head

tel: 01223 870436 **Fowlmere Rd CB22 7PG**
dir: *6m S of Cambridge on B1368, 1.5m off A10 at Harston, 4m from A505*

No nonsense food and good beer in old fashioned pub

The same family has owned and operated this tiny and very traditional village pub for some 50 years. Unchanging and unmarred by gimmickry, the stone-tiled bars,

replete with log fires, pine settles and old school benches, draw an eclectic clientele, from Cambridge dons to local farm workers. They all come for tip-top Adnams ale direct from the barrel, the friendly, honest atmosphere and straightforward pub dishes. Food is simple – at lunch, soup, sandwiches and Aga-baked potatoes. In the evening, just soup, toast and beef dripping, and cold platters. Village tradition is kept alive with time-honoured pub games – dominoes, table skittles, shove ha'penny and nine men's Morris.

Open all wk 11.30-2.30 6-11 (Sun 12-2.30 7-10.30) Closed 25-26 Dec **Food** Lunch all wk 12-2.15 Dinner all wk 7-9.30 ⊕ FREE HOUSE ⬛ Adnams Southwold Bitter, Broadside, Ghost Ship & Old Ale ♻ Crones, Hogan's. ☕ 10 **Facilities** Non-diners area ❄ (Bar Outside area) ♦ Children's portions Family room Outside area ⊼ Parking 🚌 (notice required) **Notes** ◉

| **OFFORD D'ARCY** | Map 12 TL26 |

The Horseshoe Inn

tel: 01480 810293 **90 High St PE19 5RH**
email: info@theoffordshoe.co.uk
dir: *Between Huntingdon & St Neots. 1.5m from Buckden on A1*

Inventive cooking at inn close to the river

Behind this substantial, gabled old farmhouse, a long, grassy beer garden stretches to meadows fringing the Great Ouse Valley with its countless ponds and lakes. Tranquil territory in which to sup on a brace of renowned East Anglian real ales, supplemented each mid-summer by a beer festival. At the pub, known locally as The Offord Shoe, the modern, pan-European menu is changed every two months to allow chef-patron Richard Kennedy to utilise seasonal ingredients to the full. Graduate, perhaps, from pan-fried scallops with chorizo and chilli to mains like game, wild mushroom and pancetta casserole; or brown sugar and mustard glazed salmon with charred broccoli, complementing popular pub classics.

Open all wk **Food** Lunch Mon-Fri 12-2.30, Sat-Sun all day Dinner Mon-Fri 6-9.30, Sat-Sun all day Set menu available Restaurant menu available all wk ⊕ FREE HOUSE ⬛ Adnams Southwold Bitter, Nethergate Old Growler, Sharp's Doom Bar. ☕ 17 **Facilities** Non-diners area ❄ (Bar Garden) ♦ Children's portions Play area Garden ⊼ Beer festival Parking WiFi 🚌 (notice required)

| **PETERBOROUGH** | Map 12 TL19 |

The Brewery Tap

tel: 01733 358500 **80 Westgate PE1 2AA**
email: brewerytap.manager@oakagroup.com
dir: *Opposite bus station*

Award-winning brewpub with American style and local ales

Located in the old labour exchange on Westgate, this striking American-style pub is home to the multi-award winning Oakham Brewery and it is one of the largest brewpubs in Europe. Visitors can see the day-to-day running of the brewery through a glass wall spanning the length of the bar. As if the appeal of the 12 real ales and the vast range of bottled beers was not enough, Thai chefs beaver away producing delicious snacks, soups, salads, stir-fries and curries. Look out for live music nights, and DJs on Saturday nights.

Open all day all wk Closed 25-26 Dec, 1 Jan **Food** Lunch Mon-Thu 12-2.30, Fri-Sat 12-10.30, Sun 12-3.30 Dinner Mon-Thu 5.30-10.30, Fri-Sat 12-10.30, Sun 5.30-9.30 ⊕ FREE HOUSE ⬛ Oakham Inferno, Citra, JHB & Bishops Farewell, Guest ales ♻ Westons Old Rosie, Rosie's Pig, Raspberry Twist & Wyld Wood Vintage, Oakham Opale. ☕ 10 **Facilities** Non-diners area ❄ (Bar) ♦ WiFi 🚌

PETERBOROUGH *continued*

Charters Bar & East Restaurant

tel: 01733 315700 & 315702 (bookings) **Upper Deck, Town Bridge PE1 1FP**
email: manager@charters-bar.com
dir: *A1/A47 towards Wisbech, 2m to city centre & town bridge (River Nene). Barge moored at Town Bridge (west side)*

Moored barge on the River Nene

The largest floating real ale emporium in Britain can be found moored in the heart of Peterborough. The 176-foot converted barge motored from Holland across the North Sea in 1991, and is now a haven for real-ale and cider-lovers. Twelve handpumps dispense a continually changing repertoire of cask ales, while entertainment, dancing, live music and an Easter beer festival are regular features. The 'East' part of the name applies to the oriental restaurant on the upper deck which offers a comprehensive selection of pan-Asian dishes.

Open all day all wk 12–11 (Fri-Sat noon-2am) Closed 25-26 Dec, 1 Jan **Food** Lunch all wk 12-2.30 Set menu available Restaurant menu available all wk ⊕ FREE HOUSE ◀ Oakham Ales JHB, Bishops Farewell, Citra, Inferno, Rotating local guest ales Ö Glebe Farm. ♚ 11 **Facilities** Non-diners area ✿ (Bar Garden) ♦♦ Garden ⨅ Beer festival Cider festival Parking WiFi ▰ (notice required)

REACH	Map 12 TL56

Dyke's End

tel: 01638 743816 **CB25 0JD**
dir: *Phone for detailed directions*

At the heart of village life

Located in the centre of the village, overlooking the green, this pub was saved from closure by villagers in the 1990s. They ran it as a co-operative until 2003, when it was bought by Frank Feehan, who further refurbished and extended it. Frank's additions included the Devil's Dyke microbrewery, which continues to be run by owners Catherine and George Gibson. The pub has a strong local following for its food and beers. The menu is seasonal with daily-changing specials, although pub favourites like beer-battered haddock and steak frites are always popular.

Open 12-2.30 6-11 (Sat-Sun 12-11) Closed Mon L **Food** Lunch Tue-Sun 12-2 Dinner Tue-Sun 7-9 Av main course £12 ⊕ FREE HOUSE ◀ Thwaites Wainwright, Adnams Southwold Bitter, Sharp's Special Ö Aspall. **Facilities** Non-diners area ✿ (Bar Restaurant Garden) ♦♦ Children's portions Garden ⨅ Parking WiFi

SPALDWICK	Map 12 TL17

The George

tel: 01480 890293 **5-7 High St PE28 0TD**
email: info@thegeorgespaldwick.co.uk
dir: *In village centre. Just off A14 junct 18. 5m W of Huntingdon*

Highly-praised village centre inn

Dating from 1679, this former coaching inn is a successful pub and restaurant; it has moved with the times, yet retained its rustic charm and character. The bar, with its low ceilings and wooden floor, serves local real ales and bar snacks, while the restaurant menu majors on all the pub favourites: baked camembert served with home-made marmalade and warm crusty bread; chicken breast wrapped in bacon and stuffed with cream cheese and asparagus; and chocolate brownie served with warm chocolate sauce and vanilla ice cream. Tables on the lawns and a terraced

patio are much sought after, especially during the pub's popular annual ale and cider festival.

Open all wk 11.30-3 5.30-11 (Sat 11.30am-mdnt Sun 12-10.30) **Food** Lunch Mon-Sat 12-2.30, Sun 12-7 Dinner Mon-Sat 6-9, Sun 12-7 Restaurant menu available all wk ⊕ PUNCH TAVERNS ◀ Woodforde's Wherry, Timothy Taylor Landlord, Black Sheep. ♚ 9 **Facilities** Non-diners area ✿ (Bar Garden Outside area) ♦♦ Children's menu Children's portions Garden Outside area ⨅ Beer festival Cider festival Parking WiFi ▰ (notice required)

STAPLEFORD	Map 12 TL45

The Rose at Stapleford

tel: 01223 843349 **81 London Rd CB22 5DG**
email: info@rose-stapleford.co.uk
dir: *Phone for detailed directions*

Great home-cooked food and accredited ales

Paul and Karen Beer have woven some magic at The Rose, a traditional village pub close to Cambridge and Duxford Imperial War Museum. Expect a stylish interior, replete with low beams and inglenook fireplaces, and traditional unfussy menus majoring on local produce, fresh Lowestoft fish, and quality Scottish steaks. As well as a good selection of appetisers, typical main dishes include slow-roasted Suffolk pork belly, marinated in cider and sage and served with mashed potatoes, apple purée and seasonal vegetables; and home-made beef lasagne with garlic bread and mixed salad. For the sweet of tooth, bread and butter pudding with custard is a favourite.

Open all wk 12-3 5.30-11 (Sun 12-10.30) **Food** Lunch Mon-Sat 12-2, Sun 12-8.30 Dinner Mon-Sat 5.30-9.30, Sun 12-8.30 Av main course £11-£14 Set menu available Restaurant menu available Mon-Sat ⊕ CHARLES WELLS ◀ Wells Bombardier, Courage Directors, Young's Ö Symonds. ♚ 12 **Facilities** Non-diners area ♦♦ Children's menu Children's portions Garden ⨅ Parking WiFi ▰ (notice required)

STILTON	Map 12 TL18

The Bell Inn Hotel ★★★ HL ⊚   PICK OF THE PUBS

tel: 01733 241066 **Great North Rd PE7 3RA**
email: reception@thebellstilton.co.uk **web:** www.thebellstilton.co.uk
dir: *From A1(M) junct 16 follow signs for Stilton. Hotel on main road in village centre*

Handsome stone inn with historic Stilton pedigree

A Bell Inn has stood here since 1500, although this one is mid-17th century and it is reputedly the oldest coaching inn on the old Great North Road, with an impressive stone façade, a splendid inn sign and a fine original interior with an upbeat feel. It once welcomed (or maybe not!) highwayman Dick Turpin, as well as Lord Byron and Clark Gable, who was stationed nearby in 1943. Famous as the birthplace of Stilton cheese, the pub is again making their own, called Bell Blue, and the Stilton cheese sampler is a must to try. Modern British dishes in the Bar/Bistro include oak-smoked salmon and citrus potato salad; cod loin, butternut risotto, wilted spinach, tomato and basil sauce; slow-braised brisket of beef with bourguignon sauce; sausages of the day with mash; and spiced rice pudding with brandy-steeped apricots. All the en suite bedrooms are round the old courtyard — two have four-posters.

Open all wk 12-2.30 6-11 (Sat 12-12 Sun 12-11) Closed 25 Dec **Food** Lunch Mon-Sat 12-2.30, Sun 12-3 Dinner all wk 6-9.30 Av main course £13.95 Restaurant menu available Mon-Sat evening, Sun L ⊕ FREE HOUSE ◀ Greene King IPA, Morland Old Speckled Hen, Oakham Bishops Farewell, Digfield Fool's Nook, Guest ales Ö Aspall. ♚ 11 **Facilities** Non-diners area ✿ (Garden) ♦♦ Children's menu Children's portions Garden ⨅ Parking WiFi ▰ (notice required) **Rooms** 22

STRETHAM
Map 12 TL57

The Lazy Otter ★★★★ INN

tel: 01353 649780 **Cambridge Rd CB6 3LU**
email: thelazyotter@btconnect.com **web:** www.lazy-otter.com
dir: *Phone for detailed directions*

Welcoming waterside focal point amidst the Fens

A pub here has served fenland watermen for several centuries; today's bustling incarnation is popular with leisure boaters on the River Ouse, which glides past the extensive beer garden, from which are cracking views over the rich farmland. Barley from these acres goes into the good range of East Anglian beers, including the house ale from Milton Brewery; an annual beer and cider festival is also held. The restaurant offers dishes like seafood grill; chicken Stroganoff; wild mushroom puff pastry pillow with thyme couscous; and pheasant breast with bacon and chestnut stuffing, bubble-and-squeak and Madeira reduction.

Open all day all wk 7am-11pm (Sun 8.30am-10.30pm) **Food** Contact pub for food times Restaurant menu available all wk ⊕ FREE HOUSE ◀ Adnams Broadside, Milton Lazy Otter, Milton Tiki, Oakham JHB, Woodforde's Wherry, Guest ales Ŏ Westons Stowford Press & Old Rosie. ₹ 10 **Facilities** Non-diners area 🐾 (All areas) ♦ Children's menu Children's portions Play area Garden Outside area ⊞ Beer festival Cider festival Parking WiFi ➡ **Rooms** 3

The Red Lion

tel: 01353 648132 **47 High St CB6 3LD**
email: redlion@charnwoodpubco.co.uk
dir: *Exit A10 between Cambridge & Ely into Stretham. Left into High St, pub on right*

Busy local with traditional food

Just ten miles north of Cambridge, in the village of Stretham, this former coaching inn has a busy locals' bar where you can enjoy a pint of Adnams beer or Pickled Pig cider with bar meals such as a chicken fajita wrap with chips and salad, or a whole baked camembert with crusty bread. Alternatively, head to the conservatory-style restaurant for traditional home-made favourites such as battered fish and chips; lasagne; steak and ale pie; home-cooked ham, eggs and chips; or one of the steaks from the grill, served with chips and salad.

Open all day all wk **Food** Lunch all wk 12-2.30 Dinner all wk 6-9 ⊕ CHARNWOOD PUB CO ◀ Greene King IPA, Wychwood Hobgoblin, Adnams, Marston's Ŏ Pickled Pig. ₹ 8 **Facilities** Non-diners area 🐾 (Bar Garden) ♦ Children's menu Children's portions Garden ⊞ Parking WiFi ➡ (notice required)

THORNEY
Map 12 TF20

NEW Dog In A Doublet

tel: 01733 202256 **Northside PE6 0RW**
email: info@doginad.co.uk
dir: *On B1040 between Thorney & Whittlesey*

Excellent food in the Fens

John McGinn gave up his day job as a civil engineer to compete for BBC's *MasterChef* before restoring this riverside pub, which had been closed for four years. In the heart of the Fens, this 16th-century inn sits on the banks of the River Nene, next to one of the biggest lock gates in Europe. Local ales and home-made cider draw drinkers to the bar with its open fire, whilst the shabby-chic farmhouse-style restaurant serves classics with a twist, perhaps smoked poacher rarebit on corn bread with chocolate-spiked chilli beef; and ox shin and oyster pie.

Open 12-2.30 5-10 (Sat-Sun 12-10) Closed Mon L & Tue L **Food** Lunch Wed-Fri 12-2.30, Sat-Sun 12-10 Dinner Mon-Fri 5-10, Sat-Sun 12-10 Av main course £10 Set menu available Restaurant menu available all wk ⊕ FREE HOUSE ◀ Marston's Pedigree, KCB 66 Ŏ Westons Old Rosie. ₹ 20 **Facilities** Non-diners area 🐾 (Bar Garden) ♦ Children's menu Children's portions Play area Garden ⊞ Cider festival Parking WiFi ➡ (notice required)

UFFORD
Map 12 TF00

The White Hart ★★★★ INN

tel: 01780 740250 **Main St PE9 3BH**
email: info@whitehartufford.co.uk **web:** www.whitehartufford.co.uk
dir: *From Stamford take B1443 signed Barnack. Through Barnack, follow signs to Ufford*

Pretty pub supplied by the family farm

Salvaged old agricultural tools and other farming memorabilia embellish the bar of this 17th-century country inn. Among its four real ales is Oakham's JHB; Aspall supplies the cider and 10 wines are by the glass, selected from an extensive cellar. The Orangery, The Pantry and the garden are three of the five dining areas, where options include Hereford sirloin steak with roasted tomato, grilled mushroom and double-fried chips; fillet of Scottish salmon with sautéed potatoes and wilted spinach; and spring vegetable risotto with aged parmesan. You don't have to have a Sunday roast - steak and kidney pie is an alternative.

Open all day all wk Mon-Thu 9am-11pm (Fri-Sat 9am-mdnt Sun 9-9) **Food** Lunch Mon-Sat 12-2.30, Sun 12-6 Dinner Mon-Sat 6-9.30 ⊕ FREE HOUSE ◀ Adnams, Fuller's London Pride, Oakham Ales JHB Ŏ Aspall. ₹ 10 **Facilities** Non-diners area 🐾 (Bar Garden) ♦ Children's menu Children's portions Play area Garden ⊞ Parking WiFi ➡ (notice required) **Rooms** 10

WHITTLESFORD
Map 12 TL44

The Tickell Arms

tel: 01223 833025 **North Rd CB22 4NZ**
email: tickell@cambscuisine.com
dir: *M11 junct 10, A505 towards Saffron Walden. Left signed Whittlesford*

Food prepared and served by a knowledgeable team

Part of the Cambscuisine (that's cuisine from Cambridgeshire) group, this blue-washed village pub stands behind a neat, white picket fence. The car park is entered through wrought-iron gates. Inside the pub are elegant fireplaces, gilt mirrors and whimsical bowler hat-shaped lampshades. Among the four local real ales is Pegasus from Milton Brewery in Cambridge, and from Hemingford Grey comes Cromwell cider. The restaurant serves seasonal modern British and European food from a regularly-changing menu. Examples are Israeli couscous and chive yogurt, roast apple and beetroot; guinea fowl terrine; braised ox cheek, creamed potato, sprout tops and caramelised onions. The tempting fish menu might include hake fillet, bouillabaisse sauce, mussels and fennel.

Open all wk 12-3 6-11 (Sat-Sun all day) **Food** Lunch Mon-Fri 12-2.30, Sat-Sun 12-5 Dinner Mon-Fri 6-11, Sat-Sun 5-11 Set menu available Restaurant menu available all wk ⊕ FREE HOUSE ◀ Milton Pegasus, Brewster's Hophead, Elgood's Cambridge Bitter Ŏ Cromwell. ₹ 16 **Facilities** Non-diners area 🐾 (Bar Garden) ♦ Children's menu Children's portions Garden ⊞ Beer festival Parking WiFi ➡ (notice required)

CHESHIRE

ALDFORD
Map 15 SJ45

The Grosvenor Arms
PICK OF THE PUBS

tel: 01244 620228 **Chester Rd CH3 6HJ**
email: grosvenor.arms@brunningandprice.co.uk
dir: On B5130, S of Chester

Freshly cooked food with broad appeal

With its red brick and black and white timbering, this higgledy-piggledy Brunning & Price pub was designed by Victorian architect John Douglas, who designed around 500 buildings, many of them in Cheshire. The spacious, open-plan interior includes an airy conservatory and a panelled, book-filled library. The range of real ales from small breweries around the country changes all the time so it's no wonder the locals are fond of it. On the bistro-style menu, starters may feature potted mackerel and shrimp with horseradish butter, potato cakes and pickled cucumber, which might precede main courses of Red Leicester, potato and onion pie; or pan-fried duck breast with confit carrot, roasted beetroot, dauphinoise potato, redcurrant and balsamic jus. Leave room for glazed lime tart with passionfruit sauce, mascarpone and citrus fruit salad. A terrace leads into a small but pleasing garden, and on out to the village green.

Open all day all wk **Food** Lunch Mon-Thu 12-9.30, Fri-Sat 12-10, Sun 12-9 Dinner Mon-Thu 12-9.30, Fri-Sat 12-10, Sun 12-9 ⊕ FREE HOUSE/BRUNNING & PRICE ◀ Original Bitter, Weetwood Eastgate Ale, Phoenix, Guest ales ♂ Westons Stowford Press, Aspall. ♀ 20 **Facilities** Non-diners area ♣ (Bar Garden) ♦ Children's menu Children's portions Garden ⊟ Parking WiFi

ALLOSTOCK
Map 15 SJ77

The Three Greyhounds Inn

tel: 01565 723455 **Holmes Chapel Rd WA16 9JY**
email: info@thethreegreyhoundsinn.co.uk **web:** www.thethreegreyhoundsinn.co.uk
dir: S from Allostock on A50. Right on B5082 signed Northwich. Over M6, pub on right

A real find at a rural crossroads

This 300-year-old former farmhouse is now a stylishly eclectic dining pub. Inside is a warren of atmospheric rooms, replete with exposed beams, rugs on wooden floors, crackling log fires in brick fireplaces, fat candles on old dining tables, and a host of quirky touches to make you smile. Go there for a choice of five local ales and over

50 brandies behind the bar, and some cracking pub food – seafood sharing plate; potted beef with stout piccalilli; cod loin with shrimp butter; duck leg and haricot bean stew; apple and Calvados crumble, and an imaginative choice of sandwiches. Book ahead for the memorable Sunday lunches. Dogs are welcome in the snug and the garden.

The Three Greyhounds Inn

Open all day all wk **Food** Lunch all wk 12-9.30 Dinner all wk 12-9.30 ⊕ FREE HOUSE ◀ Almighty Allostock Ale, Byley Bomber, Merlins Gold, Three Greyhound Bitter, Weetwood Ales Cheshire Cat. ♀ 15 **Facilities** Non-diners area ♣ (Bar Garden) ♦ Children's portions Garden ⊟ Parking WiFi ⇔ (notice required)

ASTON
Map 15 SJ64

The Bhurtpore Inn
PICK OF THE PUBS

See Pick of the Pubs on opposite page

BROXTON
Map 15 SJ45

Egerton Arms

tel: 01829 782241 **Whitchurch Rd CH3 9JW**
email: egertonarms@woodwardandfalconer.com
dir: On A41 between Whitchurch & Chester

Spacious pub with sun-trap garden

This elegant, eye-catching Victorian roadhouse is part of a small group of quality dining pubs bringing together excellent local beers with top-notch food from the generous larders of the area. It's handy for active visitors making the most of Cheshire's hilly sandstone spine, with its castles, hill fort and countless byways. Wind down in the extensive garden, enjoying a glass of Weetwood beer and discerning your choices from the well-balanced, regularly updated menu which is strong on seafood (lobster thermidor is a signature dish) and generous with both meat and vegetarian options. There's an airy country-house feel to the inside, where myriad local photos add interest.

Open all day all wk 12-11 (Sun 12-10.30) Closed 25 Dec & 31 Dec eve **Food** Lunch Mon-Sat 12-9.30, Sun 12-9 Dinner Mon-Sat 12-9.30, Sun 12-9 Set menu available Restaurant menu available all wk ⊕ WOODWARD & FALCONER PUBS LTD ◀ Piffle & Balderdash, Weetwood Ales. ♀ 16 **Facilities** Non-diners area ♦ Children's menu Children's portions Play area Family room Garden ⊟ Parking WiFi ⇔

PICK OF THE PUBS

The Bhurtpore Inn

ASTON Map 15 SJ64

tel: 01270 780917
Wrenbury Rd CW5 8DQ
email: simonbhurtpore@yahoo.co.uk
web: www.bhurtpore.co.uk
dir: *Just off A530 between Nantwich & Whitchurch. Follow Wrenbury signs at x-rds in village*

Friendly traditional inn with real community spirit

A pub since at least 1778, when it was called the Queen's Head. It subsequently became the Red Lion, but it was Lord Combermere's success at the Siege of Bhurtpore in India in 1826 that inspired the name that has stuck. Simon and Nicky George came across it in 1991, boarded-up and stripped out. Simon is a direct descendant of Joyce George, who leased the pub from the Combermere Estate in 1849, so was motivated by his family history to take on the hard work of restoring the interior. Since then, 'award-winning' hardly does justice to the accolades heaped upon this hostelry. In the bar, 11 ever-changing real ales are always available, mostly from local microbreweries, as are real ciders, continental draught lagers and around 150 of the world's bottled beers. An annual beer festival, reputedly Cheshire's largest, is in its 19th year, with around 130 real ales. The pub has also been shortlisted many times for the 'National Whisky Pub of the Year' award, and there is a long soft drinks menu. Recognition extends to the kitchen too, where unfussy dishes of classic pub fare are prepared. Among the hearty British ingredients you'll find seasonal game, such as pigeon breast on roasted field mushrooms, red wine and bacon sauce; or three bird game roast. Curries and balti dishes are always on the blackboard. Vintage vehicles bring their owners here on the first Thursday of the month, and folk musicians play on the third Tuesday.

Open all wk 12-2.30 6.30-11.30 (Fri-Sat 12-12 Sun 12-11) Closed 25-26 Dec, 1 Jan **Food** Lunch Mon-Fri 12-2, Sat 12-9.30, Sun 12-9 Dinner Mon-Fri 6.30-9.30, Sat 12-9.30, Sun 12-9 Av main course £10.95 ⊕ FREE HOUSE

🍺 Salopian Golden Thread, Abbeydale Absolution, Weetwood Oast-House Gold, Hobsons Twisted Spire, Hobsons Mild, Acorn Yorkshire Pride, Merlins Gold Ŏ Thatchers Cheddar Valley, Wrenbury Cider. 🍷 15 **Facilities** Non-diners area 🐾 (Bar Garden Outside area) 👫 Children's portions Garden Outside area 🎪 Beer festival Parking WiFi 🚌 (notice required)

PICK OF THE PUBS

The Pheasant Inn ★★★★★ INN ❀

BURWARDSLEY Map 15 SJ55

tel: 01829 770434
CH3 9PF
email: info@thepheasantinn.co.uk
web: www.thepheasantinn.co.uk
dir: *A41 (Chester to Whitchurch) left signed Tattenhall. Through Tattenhall to Burwardsley. In Burwardsley follow Cheshire Workshops signs*

Popular pub with magnificent rural views

High on the sandstone ridge known as the Peckforton Hills stands Beeston Castle. Enjoying a similarly lofty position on its west-facing slopes overlooking the Cheshire Plain, is this 300-year-old former farmhouse and barn, where only five families have been licensees since it became an alehouse. Such is its elevation that you can see the Welsh hills and two cathedrals, Liverpool's 23 miles away and, much nearer, Chester's. Particularly familiar with the Pheasant are walkers and hikers on the Sandstone Trail long-distance footpath that links Frodsham on the Mersey with Whitchurch in Shropshire. On a fine day the obvious place to be is in the flower-filled courtyard or on the terrace, but when the weather dictates otherwise grab a space by the big open fire in the wooden-floored, heftily-beamed bar. Here you'll find four real ales, three from the Weetwood Brewery near Tarporley.

The kitchen makes extensive use of local produce, while much of the seafood comes from Fleetwood in Lancashire. With the daily-changing restaurant menu offering a wide choice of modern British and European dishes, think about starting with ham hock and leek terrine, cornichons, piccalilli and rocket; or crispy ox cheek, celeriac and horseradish remoulade. Follow with venison haunch, fig jam, parsnips, crispy kale and chocolate oil; spiced pork cheeks, seared scallops, crispy black pudding, trompette mushrooms and pickled cauliflower; or Ridlings Reserve steak and kidney suet pudding. And don't miss the choices on the specials board. Comfortable en suite accommodation is available.

Open all day all wk **Food** Mon-Thu 12-9.30, Fri-Sat 12-10, Sun 12-9 ⊕ FREE HOUSE ◖ Weetwood Old Dog Premium Bitter, Eastgate Ale & Best Bitter, Guest ale ♺ Kingstone Press. ♟ 12 **Facilities** Non-diners area ❀ (Bar Restaurant Garden) ♦ Children's menu & portions Garden ☂ Parking WiFi ⛟ (notice required) **Rooms** 12

BUNBURY
Map 15 SJ55

The Dysart Arms
PICK OF THE PUBS

tel: 01829 260183 **Bowes Gate Rd CW6 9PH**
email: dysart.arms@brunningandprice.co.uk
dir: Between A49 & A51, by Shropshire Union Canal

Well defined English hostelry

A classic English village pub with open fires, lots of old oak, full-height bookcases and a pretty garden with views to two castles and the neighbouring parish church. Built as a farmhouse in the mid-18th century and licensed since the late 1800s, it once functioned simultaneously as a farm, an abattoir and a pub; the abattoir building was demolished by a German bomber crew on their way home from 'rearranging' the Liverpool docks. The hostelry is named after local landowners, the Earls of Dysart, whose coat of arms is above the door. An ever-changing line-up of ales is served in the central bar, around which are several airy rooms perfect for drinking and eating. Light bites include seared haloumi and red pepper salad; starters may list smoked salmon with beetroot and fennel salad; and main courses range from roast loin of pork with stuffing and apple sauce, to spicy Vietnamese king prawn and rice noodle salad. Have some hot waffles or bread and butter pudding for your afters.

Open all day all wk 11.30-11 (Sun 12-10.30) **Food** Lunch Mon-Sat 12-9.30, Sun 12-9 Dinner Mon-Sat 12-9.30, Sun 12-9 ⊕ BRUNNING & PRICE ◀ Original Bitter, Weetwood Best Cask, Guest ales Ō Aspall. ☗ 18 **Facilities** Non-diners area ✿ (Bar Garden Outside area) ♦️ Children's menu Children's portions Garden Outside area ⊼ Parking WiFi

BURLEYDAM
Map 15 SJ64

The Combermere Arms

tel: 01948 871223 **SY13 4AT**
email: combermere.arms@brunningandprice.co.uk
dir: From Whitchurch take A525 towards Nantwich, at Newcastle/Audlem/Woore sign, turn right at junct. Pub 100yds on right

Classic coaching inn with impressive menu

Local shoots, walkers and town folk frequent this classic 17th-century country inn. Full of character and warmth, it has three roaring fires and a wealth of oak, nooks and crannies, pictures and old furniture. Food options range from light bites such as Shropshire Blue and butternut squash quiche to full meals — maybe smoked pigeon breast with blackberry, hazelnut salad and black pudding croutons, followed by smoked haddock and salmon fishcakes; or rabbit and prune faggots with celeriac mash, buttered kale and wild mushroom gravy. You could finish with a hot waffle, warm blackberries and salted caramel ice cream. There is a great choice of real ales and ciders, an informative wine list and impressive cheese board.

Open all day all wk 11.30-11 **Food** Lunch Sun-Thu 12-9, Fri-Sat 12-10 Dinner Sun-Thu 12-9, Fri-Sat 12-10 ⊕ FREE HOUSE/BRUNNING & PRICE ◀ Original Bitter, Weetwood Cheshire Cat, Wadworth 6X, Guest ales Ō Westons Stowford Press, Thatchers Green Goblin, Aspall. ☗ 20 **Facilities** Non-diners area ♦️ Children's menu Children's portions Garden ⊼ Parking WiFi

BURWARDSLEY
Map 15 SJ55

The Pheasant Inn ★★★★★ INN ❀
PICK OF THE PUBS

See Pick of the Pubs on opposite page

CHELFORD
Map 15 SJ87

Egerton Arms

tel: 01625 861366 **Knutsford Rd SK11 9BB**
email: jeremy@chelfordegertonarms.co.uk
dir: On A537 (Knutsford to Macclesfield road)

Family-run and family welcoming pub/restaurant

Sited in Cheshire's best countryside in the affluent area known as the 'golden triangle', the Egerton Arms is efficiently and enthusiastically run by Jeremy Hague. Low beams, large fireplaces, eccentric antiques and a long bar with brass pumps characterise the interior of this 16th-century building, whose history is closely tied to Lord Egerton and his Tatton Park estate which is nearby. Local real ales are briskly served in the bar, while the 100-seat restaurant caters to hungry families with a comprehensive menu full of pub classics, including deli boards, grills, and pizzas from the stone-baked oven. There is now a deli adjoining the pub which sells a wide choice of artisan produce from all over the country.

Open all day all wk **Food** Lunch all day Dinner all day Restaurant menu available all wk ⊕ FREE HOUSE ◀ Wells Bombardier, Copper Dragon, Local ales Ō Westons Stowford Press. ☗ 9 **Facilities** Non-diners area ✿ (All areas) ♦️ Children's menu Children's portions Play area Garden Outside area ⊼ Parking WiFi ⛟ (notice required)

CHESTER
Map 15 SJ46

The Brewery Tap

tel: 01244 340999 **52-54 Lower Bridge St CH1 1RU**
email: drink@the-tap.co.uk
dir: From B5268 in Chester into Lower Bridge St towards river

Great ale in historic city surroundings

This historic pub is situated in part of Gamul House, named after Sir Francis Gamul, a wealthy merchant and mayor of Chester who built it in 1620. It is reputedly where Charles I stayed when his troops were defeated at Rowton Moor, shortly before the king's final flight to Wales. Relax with a Thirstquencher ale and enjoy the pub's numerous period details, then choose from a menu of hearty pub favourites such as smoked mackerel, beetroot and horseradish; braised beef and Old Wavertonian pie, pickled red cabbage and fat chips.

Open all day all wk Closed 25-26 Dec **Food** Lunch Mon-Sat 12-9.30, Sun 12-9 Dinner Mon-Sat 12-9.30, Sun 12-9 ⊕ FREE HOUSE/SPITTING FEATHERS ◀ Thirstquencher, Old Wavertonian Stout Ō Westons Stowford Press, Guest ciders. ☗ 14 **Facilities** Non-diners area ♦️ WiFi

CHESTER *continued*

Old Harkers Arms

tel: 01244 344525 **1 Russell St CH3 5AL**
email: harkers.arms@brunningandprice.co.uk
dir: *Close to railway station, on canal side*

A buzzy city watering hole

Housed in a former Victorian chandler's warehouse beside the Shropshire Union Canal, the tall windows, lofty ceilings, wooden floors and bar constructed from salvaged doors make this one of Chester's more unusual pubs. The bar offers over 100 malt whiskies and ales from a range of breweries. The daily-changing menu from light dishes such as ham hock and parsley pie through to main courses like grilled whole plaice with caper, lemon and parsley butter; shredded duck salad with orange and pistachio nut and pomegranate dressing; or smoked haddock and salmon fishcakes. The pub holds events such as 'Pudding, Pie and Great British Beers Week' in February or March time, where over 20 award-winning ales can be tried, plus a 'Pie and Champion Ale' week in October.

Open all day all wk 10.30am-11pm (Sun 12-10.30) Closed 25 Dec **Food** Lunch all wk 12-9.30 Dinner all wk 12-9.30 Av main course £12.95 ⊕ FREE HOUSE/BRUNNING & PRICE ◾ Brunning & Price Original Bitter, Weetwood Cheshire Cat, Flowers Original, Salopian, Derby, Facer's North Star Porter ♂ Westons Country Perry, Gwynt y Ddraig Black Dragon. ♟ 15 **Facilities** Non-diners area Outside area ⼏ Beer festival Cider festival WiFi

The Stamford Bridge

tel: 01829 740229 **CH3 7HN**
email: stamfordbridge@woodwardandfalconer.com
dir: *A51 from Chester towards Tarporley, left at lights, pub on left*

Attractive city-limits inn with fine food and beers

New landlord Chris Askew's attractive, city-outskirts inn has extensive views from its beer garden across the Cheshire Plain. Inside, country-house formality meets cottage homeliness – heavy beams, open fires with precision-cut logs, and well-stocked bookshelves. Real ales include Piffle and Balderdash, brewed specially for pub owners Woodward & Falconer. Lunchtime offers sandwiches, baps and focaccias, while evening diners can expect a good choice of fish (plaice, cod, smoked haddock, sea bass...) and meats (Gressingham duck, steaks, lamb, pork belly...). Steak and kidney, and venison bourguignon are pie possibilities, while an option for vegetarians is roasted red pepper, tomato and spinach gnocchi.

Open all day all wk 12-11 (Sun 12-10.30) Closed 25 Dec & 31 Dec eve **Food** Contact pub for food times ⊕ WOODWARD & FALCONER PUBS LTD ◾ Piffle, Balderdash, Weetwood, Conwy. ♟ 14 **Facilities** Non-diners area ♦ Children's menu Children's portions Play area Family room Garden ⼏ Parking WiFi ⍾

The Cholmondeley Arms   PICK OF THE PUBS

See Pick of the Pubs opposite page

Ring O'Bells

tel: 01244 335422 **Village Rd CH3 7AS**
email: info@ringobellschester.co.uk
dir: *3m from Chester between A51 towards Nantwich & A41 towards Whitchurch*

Chester-fringe pub with local ales and enjoyable food

Much of the appeal of this spruced-up village pub is the scope of events that draw drinkers and diners. Wine tastings, live music and lunchtime networking meetings are just a few of the reasons why people keep on returning, not to mention the choice of outdoor dining areas, particularly the decked suntrap terrace. The bar stocks real ale from Chester's Spitting Feathers brewery, as well as representatives from Mobberley Ales and Weetwood. Good use of local produce is evident on seasonal menus that might start with BBQ pork ribs and continue with seafood risotto or Thai fishcakes.

Open all day all wk **Food** Lunch Mon-Fri 12-3, Sat-Sun 12-5 Dinner Mon-Thu 5-9, Fri-Sat 5-9.30, Sun 5-8 ⊕ TRUST INNS ◾ Spitting Feathers, Weetwood, Big Hand, Mobberley. ♟ **Facilities** Non-diners area ♥ (Bar Restaurant Garden) ♦ Children's menu Children's portions Play area Garden ⼏ Parking WiFi ⍾ (notice required)

Egerton Arms Country Inn

tel: 01260 273946 **Astbury Village CW12 4RQ**
email: egertonastbury@totalise.co.uk
dir: *1.5m SW of Congleton off A34, by St Mary's Church*

Good pub food in an attractive village

Opposite the parish church, the pub dates from the early 1700s, taking its name from former lords of the manor. After 20 years, Allen and Grace Smith are past-masters at looking after their customers, whether in the bar for a sandwich and a pint of Robinsons Dizzy Blonde (to the brewery she's 'Peggy'), or in the restaurant, where the wish-list might encompass grilled halibut; sirloin steak; roast turkey; or spinach and ricotta cannelloni. Food allergies are catered for. Grounds incorporate a beer garden, terrace and play area. Children are allowed inside until 9pm, and dogs are welcomed with gravy bones and water.

Open all day all wk **Food** Lunch Mon-Sat 11.30-2, Sun 12-8 Dinner Mon-Sat 6-9, Sun 12-8 Set menu available Restaurant menu available all wk ⊕ ROBINSONS ◾ Unicorn, Dizzy Blonde, Double Hop, Seasonal ales. ♟ 12 **Facilities** Non-diners area ♥ (Outside area) ♦ Children's menu Children's portions Play area Garden ⼏ Parking WiFi

---

Silver Stars The AA Silver Star rating denotes a Hotel or B&B that we highly recommend. They have a superior level of quality within their star rating, high standards of hospitality, service and cleanliness.

PICK OF THE PUBS

The Cholmondeley Arms

CHOLMONDELEY Map 15 SJ55

tel: 01829 720300 **SY14 8HN**
email: info@cholmondeleyarms.co.uk
web: www.cholmondeleyarms.co.uk
dir: *On A49, between Whitchurch & Tarporley*

Friendly inn with imaginative menus and 140 gins

Set in rolling Cheshire countryside virtually opposite Cholmondeley Castle on the A49, and still part of the Viscount's estate, is this red-brick former schoolhouse. Quirky and eclectic, it's surely one of England's more unusual pubs, the decor and artefacts, including family heirlooms, educational memorabilia, bell tower without and blackboards within add tremendously to the atmosphere of the cavernous interior. No longer a draughty institute, owners Tim and Mary Bird have created a warm and inviting interior, with church candles on old school desks, fresh flowers, glowing log fires and a relaxing atmosphere. After exploring the local countryside, visiting the castle, or the fabulous ruins at Beeston, stapled to Cheshire's hilly sandstone spine, it's the perfect place to unwind, sup a pint of Cholmondeley Best or another local guest (only microbrewery beers from a 30-mile radius can be found on the five hand pumps), or delve into the mindboggling list of over 140 different gins behind the bar. Allow time to taste

some of the best produce from Cheshire's burgeoning larder, including seasonal game from the estate. Nibble and natter over little potted shrimps on toast, or black pudding Scotch egg, then start with a trawler's seafood board; pan-fried devilled lamb's kidneys; or treacle cured sea trout with pickled fennel and caper berry salad. The 'Old School Favourites' mains take in Wagyu beef gourmet burger; their 'legendary' steak and kidney pie, chips and 'not so mushy' peas; and fish pie with crispy mash and spiced cauliflower; leaving room for steamed Yorkshire rhubarb and ginger pudding – school meals were never like this! There's a gin festival each year. Please note that children under ten are not allowed after 7pm in the bar, or 9pm in the garden.

Open all day all wk **Food** Lunch Mon-Fri 12-3, Sat 12-9.30, Sun 12-8.45 Dinner Mon-Fri 5.30-8.45, Sat 12-9.30, Sun 12-8.45 ⊕ FREE HOUSE
🍺 Cholmondeley Best Bitter, 4 Rotating Guest ales ⚫ Westons Old Rosie, South West Orchards. ♀ 16
Facilities Non-diners area 🐾 (Bar Restaurant Garden) 👫 Children's portions Garden ⋒ Parking WiFi 🚌 (notice required)

CHESTER *continued*

The Plough At Eaton ★★★★ INN

tel: 01260 280207 **Macclesfield Rd, Eaton CW12 2NH**
email: enquiries@theploughinncheshire.com **web:** www.theploughinncheshire.com
dir: *On A536 (Congleton to Macclesfield road)*

Popular inn with barn restaurant

Set well back from the main road in the hamlet of Eaton, this 400-year-old Cheshire-brick inn is a far cry from its genesis as a farmhouse. It's now a popular destination dining pub with a traditional interior; the restaurant is housed in a remarkable cruck barn moved here from Wales. Choose your refreshment, a pint of Tatton or a guest ale perhaps, before perusing the wide-ranging menu of pub food. Here you'll find bang-bang chicken wings; fisherman's pie; and 'three little pigs': belly pork, sticky ribs and sausage barrel wrapped in pancetta with apple and potato croquettes.

Open all day all wk 11am–mdnt Closed 1 Jan **Food** Lunch Mon-Fri 12-2.30, Sat 12-9.30, Sun 12-8 Dinner Mon-Fri 6-9.30, Sat 12-9.30, Sun 12-8 Av main course £10 ⊕ FREE HOUSE ◀ Storm, Wells Bombardier, Tatton, Local guest ales ♻ Thatchers. ♟ 10 **Facilities** Non-diners area ♣ (Bar Garden) ♠ Children's menu Children's portions Garden ⊟ Parking WiFi 🚌 **Rooms** 17

COTEBROOK   Map 15 SJ56

Fox & Barrel

tel: 01829 760529 **Foxbank CW6 9DZ**
email: info@foxandbarrel.co.uk
dir: *On A49, 2.8m N of Tarporley*

Countryside pub offering a warm welcome and excellent food

The rather cute explanation for the pub's name is that a fox being chased by the local hunt ran into the cellar, where the landlord gave it sanctuary. And who's to say

otherwise? Interior features include a huge open log fire, old beams and half-panelled walls; the snug bar is the perfect spot for a pint of Weetwood. Classic pub food with an adventurous angle includes twice baked Cheshire cheese soufflé; and white onion soup with cheddar and sage as starters; then game suet pudding, garlic mash and juniper sauce; smoked salmon omelette; lamb hotpot with red cabbage; or hand-made goats' cheese gnocchi as main courses. Outside is a secluded landscaped garden surrounded by unspoilt Cheshire countryside.

Open all day all wk Closed 25-26 Dec pm, 31 Dec am, 1 Jan pm **Food** Lunch Mon-Sat 12-9.30, Sun 12-9 Dinner Mon-Sat 12-9.30, Sun 12-9 ⊕ FREE HOUSE ◀ Weetwood Eastgate Ale, Caledonian Deuchars IPA. ♟ 20 **Facilities** Non-diners area ♣ (Bar Garden) ♠ Children's menu Children's portions Garden ⊟ Parking WiFi

DELAMERE   Map 15 SJ56

The Fishpool Inn

tel: 01606 883277 **Fishpool Rd CW8 2HP**
email: info@thefishpoolinn.co.uk
dir: *Phone for detailed directions*

Striking village pub with quirky interior

Idyllically positioned on the edge of the Delamere Forest in the stunning Cheshire countryside, this 18th-century pub seamlessly blends the traditional with the contemporary. The quirky interior is really impressive, especially the Victorian tiles and antlered stags' heads. The cellar keeps Cheshire real ales and Herefordshire cider in tip-top condition alongside a globetrotting wine list. From an open kitchen comes seasonal, regionally sourced, modern British and European cooking, including a pie of the day; local beef steaks; Welsh Valley lamb; sea bass a la plancha; coq au vin; and thin-crust pizzas cooked in the woodstone oven.

Open all day all wk **Food** Lunch Mon-Thu 12-9.30, Fri-Sat 12-10, Sun 12-9 Dinner Mon-Thu 12-9.30, Fri-Sat 12-10, Sun 12-9 ⊕ FREE HOUSE ◀ Weetwood Ales Best Bitter, Eastgate & Cheshire Cat, Guest ales ♻ Herefordshire Cider. ♟ 14 **Facilities** Non-diners area ♣ (Bar Garden Outside area) ♠ Children's menu Children's portions Garden Outside area ⊟ Parking WiFi 🚌 (notice required)

FARNDON   Map 15 SJ45

The Farndon ★★★★ INN

tel: 01829 270570 **High St CH3 6PU**
email: enquiries@thefarndon.co.uk **web:** www.thefarndon.co.uk
dir: *From Wrexham take A534 towards Nantwich. Follow signs for Farndon on left*

Fine food in the tranquil Dee Valley

This most imposing magpie inn commands Farndon's High Street as it winds down to the ancient, haunted stone bridge across the River Dee, which forms the England/Wales border. Coaches stopped here en route between the Midlands and Holyhead; centuries of hospitality are continued in the contemporary, comfy interior, a relaxing mix of colour-washed walls and modern furnishings all warmed by a seasonal roaring fire. Cheshire beers such as Weetwood accompany an impressive menu – the chef's deli platter; smoked haddock fishcakes with tomato salsa; braised ox cheek with bourguignon sauce; and Belgian waffle with rum and raisin ice cream are typical choices from the regularly changing fare. Five boutique guest bedrooms complete the picture.

Open all wk 5-11 (Sat 12-11 Sun 12-10.30) **Food** Lunch Sat-Sun 12-9.30 Dinner Mon-Fri 6-9, Sat-Sun 12-9.30 Av main course £10 Restaurant menu available Wed-Sun ⊕ FREE HOUSE ◀ Timothy Taylor Landlord, Weetwood Cheshire Cat & Eastgate Ale, Spitting Feathers Thirstquencher, Sandstone, Big Hand. ♟ 10 **Facilities** Non-diners area ♣ (Bar Garden) ♠ Children's menu Children's portions Garden ⊟ Parking WiFi 🚌 (notice required) **Rooms** 5

GAWSWORTH
Map 16 SJ86

Harrington Arms

tel: 01260 223325 **Church Ln SK11 9RJ**
dir: *From Macclesfield take A536 towards Congleton. Turn left for Gawsworth*

Lovely pub on a working farm

Part farmhouse, part pub, the little-changed interior comprises a main bar serving Robinsons real ales and quirky rooms with open fires and rustic furnishings. Memorable for its impression of timelessness, it dates from 1664 and has been licensed since 1710. On offer is good pub food made extensively from the wealth of local produce, including home-made pies; rib-eye, sirloin and gammon steaks; fish and chips; vegetarian dishes; hot sandwiches; roast turkey crown and daily specials. Early October sees the annual conker championship here.

Open all wk 12-2.30 5-11.30 (Fri 12-2.30 4.30-12 Sat 12-11.30 Sun 12-11) Closed 25 Dec **Food** Lunch Mon-Fri 12-2.30, Sat 12-9, Sun 12-8 Dinner Mon-Thu 5-8.30, Fri 5-9, Sat 12-9, Sun 12-8 ⊕ ROBINSONS ◀ Unicorn, 1892, Dizzy Blonde & Seasonal ale, Guinness ♂ Westons Stowford Press. ☻ 8 **Facilities** Non-diners area ♨ (Bar Garden) ♦ Children's portions Garden ⊨ Parking ▄▄ (notice required)

GOOSTREY
Map 15 SJ77

The Crown

tel: 01477 532128 **111 Main Rd CW4 8DE**
email: info@thecrowngoostrey.co.uk
dir: *In village centre. Follow Goostrey signs either from A50, or from A535 in Tremlow Green*

Charming village local with good food and local ales

A traditional pub set in the heart of the Cheshire farming village of Goostrey, The Crown has been an integral part of community life since the 18th century. Beyond its red-bricked façade, the pub has been sympathetically refurbished but retains much charm with oak beams and real fireplaces. Local breweries including Weetwood and Dunham Massey are well represented, perhaps accompanied by home-made crackling. The extensive modern menu takes in slow-roasted lamb shank with roasted root vegetables, parsley mash and minted gravy; and salmon and cod fishcakes. Check with the pub for details of its summer beer festival and its annual gooseberry-growing competition.

Open all wk 11.30-11 **Food** Lunch Mon-Sat 12-9, Sun 12-8 Dinner Mon-Sat 12-9, Sun 12-8 ⊕ FREE HOUSE ◀ Weetwood Ales, Dunham Massey Ales, Tatton Ales White Queen. **Facilities** Non-diners area ♨ (Bar Garden Outside area) ♦ Children's menu Children's portions Garden Outside area ⊨ Beer festival Parking WiFi ▄▄ (notice required)

GREAT BUDWORTH
Map 15 SJ67

George and Dragon

tel: 01606 892650 **High St CW9 6HF**
email: thegeorge-dragon@btinternet.com
dir: *From M6 junct 19 or M56 junct 10 follow signs for Great Budworth*

Village local steeped in history

Painstakingly restored, this charming inn has many original features, including a stone tablet in the bar dated 1722 and inscribed 'Nil nimium cupito' ('I desire

nothing to excess'). Also visible is a verse above a door written by local Astley Hall estate-owner, Rowland Egerton-Warburton, who had the inn remodelled in 1875. Regular real ales are Lees Bitter from Manchester and the pub's own Great Budworth Best Bitter. Start your meal with home-made pâté, or smoked haddock and mozzarella fishcake, followed by honey roast ham, egg and chip; bangers and mash; or slow roast lamb shank.

Open all day all wk **Food** Lunch Mon-Sat 11.30-3, Sun 12-8.30, snacks 3-5 Dinner Mon-Sat 5-9.30, Sun 12-8.30 Av main course £11.95 Restaurant menu available all wk ⊕ J W LEES ◀ Lees Bitter, Great Budworth Best Bitter, MPA, The Governor. ☻ 12 **Facilities** Non-diners area ♨ (Bar Outside area) ♦ Children's menu Children's portions Outside area ⊨ Parking WiFi ▄▄ (notice required)

HANDLEY
Map 15 SJ45

The Calveley Arms

tel: 01829 770619 **Whitchurch Rd CH3 9DT**
email: calveleyarms@btconnect.com
dir: *5m S of Chester, signed from A41. Follow signs for Handley & Aldersey Green Golf Course*

Old inn, old beams, great beer

This spruced-up old coaching inn, first licensed in 1636, stands opposite the church with views of the distant Welsh hills. Chock full of old timbers, jugs, pots, pictures, prints and ornaments, the rambling bars provide an atmospheric setting in which to sample some cracking beers and decent pub food. Typically, tuck into lunchtime filled baguettes (tuna mayo, cheese or prawn for example), lamb cutlets, salmon teriyaki, speciality salads, and a good selection of pasta dishes. There are spacious gardens to enjoy in summer.

Open all wk 12-3 6-11 (Sun 12-3 7-11) **Food** Lunch all wk 12-3 Dinner Mon-Sat 6-9, Sun 7-9 ⊕ ENTERPRISE INNS ◀ Castle Eden Ale, Marston's Pedigree, Theakston Black Bull Bitter, Wells Bombardier, Greene King IPA, Black Sheep ♂ Aspall. **Facilities** Non-diners area ♦ Children's portions Play area Garden Parking ▄▄

HAUGHTON MOSS
Map 15 SJ55

The Nags Head

tel: 01829 260265 **Long Ln CW6 9RN**
email: manager@nagsheadhaughton.co.uk
dir: *Exit A49 S of Tarporley at Beeston/Haughton sign into Long Ln. 2.75m to pub*

Secluded country inn with finest Cheshire produce

Deep in the Cheshire countryside near to a dramatic wooded sandstone ridge, is this half-timbered country inn. There's no hiding the near-400-year heritage of the place, though; the huge cruck frame and crackling fire create rustic character and charm, which set-off nicely the light, conservatory-inspired dining extension which overlooks the tranquil garden and increasingly rare bowling green. The riches of the northern Welsh Marches are liberally sourced, with great beers from Cheshire's Weetwood brewery matched by the wide-ranging menu of steaks, classic pub pies and seafood options.

Open all day all wk **Food** Lunch Sun-Thu 12-9, Fri-Sat 12-9.30 Dinner Sun-Thu 12-9, Fri-Sat 12-9.30 Set menu available Restaurant menu available all wk ⊕ FREE HOUSE ◀ Weetwood Ales, Thwaites, Guest ales ♂ Westons Stowford Press. ☻ **Facilities** ♨ (Bar Garden) ♦ Children's menu Children's portions Garden ⊨ Parking WiFi

KERRIDGE
Map 16 SJ97

The Lord Clyde ◉◉◉
PICK OF THE PUBS

tel: 01625 562123 **SK10 5AH**
email: hello@thelordclyde.co.uk
dir: *From Macclesfield A523 towards Poynton. At rdbt follow Bollington sign onto B5090. 1st right into Clark Ln*

Extremely good country dining

Tables outside this converted terrace of weavers' cottages look out to the wood-dappled Kerridge Edge, the fringe of the Peak District. There are good local beers in the bar if that's your thing, but it's the restrained and interesting menu that draws in the diners. Chef-proprietor Ernst van Zyl has worked in some of the world's top restaurants; his seasonally changing menu reflects the very best of Cheshire's produce. Ox cheek and oyster, salsify and kale might kick things off, with monkfish and Brussel sprouts, parsley root and pork skin to follow, showcasing the thoroughly modern approach that's championed here. The wine list is both extensive and impressive.

Open all wk 12-3 5-11 (Fri-Sun all day) **Food** Lunch all wk 12-3 Dinner all wk 6.30-9 Restaurant menu available Mon-Sat ⊕ PUNCH TAVERNS ◀ Morland Old Speckled Hen, Weetwood Ales Cheshire Cat, Thwaites Original ♂ Westons Stowford Press. ▼ 12 **Facilities** Non-diners area ♣ (Bar Outside area) ♦ Children's portions Outside area ⋒ Parking WiFi ▭ (notice required)

KETTLESHULME
Map 16 SJ97

Swan Inn

tel: 01663 732943 **SK23 7QU**
email: the.swan.kettleshulme@gmail.co.uk
dir: *On B5470 between Whaley Bridge (2m) & Macclesfield (5m)*

Charming village pub renowned for its beer and seafood dishes

Huddled in the shadow of the craggy Windgather Rocks in the Cheshire Peak District, the Swan is a glorious 15th-century village inn. With a new dining room now added, the eclectic and international menu has interesting dishes such as Greek-style rabbit stew slow-cooked with red wine, cinnamon, shallots and currants; and an extensive seafood menu including bouillabaisse and scallops Thermidor. Local craft ales such as Thornbridge keep ramblers and locals very contented, especially at the pub's beer festival on the first weekend in September.

Open all wk Mon 5-11 Tue-Sun all day Closed 25-26 Dec, 1 Jan, Mon L **Food** Lunch Tue 12-8.30, Wed & Sat 12-9, Thu-Fri 12-7, Sun 12-4 Dinner Tue 12-8.30, Wed & Sat 12-9, Thu-Fri 12-7 ⊕ FREE HOUSE ◀ Marston's, Marble, Thornbridge, Phoenix ♂ Thatchers Gold. **Facilities** Non-diners area ♣ (Bar Garden Outside area) ♦ Children's portions Garden Outside area ⋒ Beer festival Parking WiFi

KNUTSFORD
Map 15 SJ77

The Dog Inn
PICK OF THE PUBS

tel: 01625 861421 **Well Bank Ln, Over Peover WA16 8UP**
email: info@thedogpeover.co.uk
dir: *S from Knutsford take A50. Turn into Stocks Ln at The Whipping Stocks pub. 2m to inn*

Friendly inn with good food and local ales

This row of cottages housed village industries before being joined together to form a public house in 1860. In summer colourful flowerbeds, tubs and hanging baskets create quite a display, while the interior – rich with dark wood furniture and gleaming brass – generates year-round appeal. A range of cask-conditioned Cheshire ales from Weetwood in Tarporley is supported by a good selection of wines sold by the glass. The menu is strong on comfort food, such as classic prawn cocktail, or corned beef hash with egg and brown sauce. Interspersed are more complex choices such as main courses of sticky sesame chilli beef with cashew nuts and noodle salad; moules frites served with skinny fries and ciabatta; and smoked duck breast and orange salad, with toasted walnuts, sultanas, star anise and orange dressing. Comfort is again the keynote in desserts such as lemon tart with Chantilly cream, or chocolate torte with boozy cherries.

Open all day all wk **Food** Contact pub for food times Av main course £12 ⊕ FREE HOUSE ◀ Weetwood Best Bitter & Cheshire Cat, Hydes. ▼ 10 **Facilities** Non-diners area ♣ (Bar Garden) ♦ Children's menu Children's portions Garden ⋒ Beer festival Parking WiFi ▭

LACH DENNIS
Map 15 SJ77

The Duke of Portland

tel: 01606 46264 **Penny's Ln CW9 7SY**
email: info@dukeofportland.com
dir: *M6 junct 19, A556 towards Northwich. Left onto B5082 to Lach Dennis*

Good all-day food at country pub

This family-run pub continues to make a name for itself through a committed use of local and regional produce from across the Cheshire and Lancashire area. In the bar, enjoy a pint of Jennings Cocker Hoop or Cumberland Ale or one of the 10 wines by the glass. Sandwiches and menu choices are available all hours – typical dishes are beetroot-cured salmon with potato and dill blini; duo of pork belly and hickory-smoked ribs; and lemon tart and raspberry coulis. A sunny, landscaped garden is the ideal place to relax and unwind.

Open all day all wk **Food** Lunch all wk 12-5.30 Dinner all wk 5.30-9.30 Set menu available Restaurant menu available all wk ⊕ MARSTON'S ◀ Banks's Original, Brakspear Oxford Gold, Jennings Cocker Hoop & Cumberland Ale, Marston's Pedigree ♂ Thatchers Gold. ▼ 10 **Facilities** Non-diners area ♣ (Bar Garden) ♦ Children's menu Children's portions Garden ⋒ Parking WiFi ▭

LOWER WITHINGTON
Map 15 SJ87

NEW The Black Swan

tel: 01477 571770 **Trap St SK11 9EQ**
email: enquiries@blackswancheshire.com
dir: *From A34 N of Congleton into Giantswood Rd signed Black Swan (brown sign). Pub on right before Lower Withington*

Good pub grub in the heart of the Cheshire countryside

Just 15 minutes from Alderley Edge, The Black Swan is a quaint old pub, full of character. The atmosphere is friendly and welcoming, and the eclectic mix of decor and furnishings make for a relaxed setting for something to eat (food is served all day) or just a drink and a chat. Dogs are welcome in the bar and there are plenty of good walks round about. A wood-fired oven in the garden is lit on sunny weekends in the summer, and you can play boules in the pretty beer garden. Menus feature classic pub grub and some modern lighter dishes – lamb shank pie or home-made burgers.

Open all day all wk **Food** Lunch all wk 12-9 Dinner all wk 12-9 Av main course £11.95 ⊕ FREE HOUSE ◀ Jennings Cumberland, Red Willow Mucky Duck ♂ Westons Stowford Press. ▼ 12 **Facilities** Non-diners area ♣ (Bar Garden) ♦ Children's menu Children's portions Garden ⋒ Parking WiFi

PICK OF THE PUBS

The Bulls Head

MOBBERLEY Map 15 SJ77

tel: 01565 873395 **Mill Ln WA16 7HX**
email: info@thebullsheadpub.com
web: www.thebullsheadpub.com
dir: *From Knutsford take A537, A5085 to Mobberley*

A 200-year-old pub with lots going on

This little gem thrives as both a village local and as a destination pub. One attraction is the real ales from Cheshire microbreweries all within a radius of 30-35 miles — Dunham Massey, Merlin, Mobberley, Redwillow, Storm, Tatton and Wincle — but you'll need to spread your visits to make acquaintance with them all. Yet another, Weetwood, brews Mobberley Wobbly (aka Mobb Wobb) exclusively for the pub; it's a pint of this that comes with the 'legendary' handcrafted steak and ale pie with chips and 'not so mushy' peas. Smart, traditionally-styled rooms provide a comfortable and convivial setting for wholesome home-cooked food, including delicious Sunday roasts; slow-cooked ox casserole in rich caramelised port gravy with celery, carrot, onion and celeriac; local organic pork sausages with creamy mash, red cabbage and shallot gravy; pan-fried Old Winchester cheese-breadcrumbed chicken with fresh tomato, basil sauce and salad; and smoked fish pie with haddock, salmon, trout, and carrot and celeriac mash. One of the home-made puddings is Irish whiskey sticky toffee pudding with vanilla ice cream. Wheat-free and gluten-free dishes are also available. The pub hosts two car clubs: The 3p, which stands for 'Pub, Porsche and Pint', and for which you have to own, borrow or regularly hire said German vehicle; and The Goodfellows, for which you must own anything but a Porsche. (Membership isn't quite that simple — see the pub website for details.) There's a garden and a June beer festival. Finally, you may be interested to know that, just after the First World War, The Bulls Head was run by the parents of a young man who later established the Umbro sportswear chain — his stock room was a cupboard in the pub.

Open all day all wk **Food** Contact pub for details Av main course £13 ⊕ FREE HOUSE ◼ Bulls Head Bitter, Mobberley Wobbly Ale, 1812 Overture Ale, White Bull Ď South West Orchards. ♈ 16 **Facilities** Non-diners area ❤ (Bar Garden) ♦❢ Children's portions Garden ⊼ Beer festival Parking WiFi 🚐 (notice required)

MARTON — Map 16 SJ86

The Davenport Arms — PICK OF THE PUBS

tel: 01260 224269 **Congleton Rd SK11 9HF**
email: info@thedavenportarms.co.uk
dir: *2m from Congleton on A34*

Charming pub with pleasing home-made dishes

Dating from the 18th century, this former farmhouse with a large garden is steeped in history. It enjoys a picturesque site opposite the oldest half-timbered church still in use in Europe. Inside, many period details make for a comfortable atmosphere. Pull up a leather armchair or flop among cushions on the sofa by the roaring fire in the traditional bar, and choose from the good selection of Cheshire ales. There's something for everyone on the crowd-pleasing menu, all freshly made on the premises. Lunchtime favourites include curry of the day; wraps such as Cajun chicken with lettuce, citrus mayonnaise and sweet chilli; and baguettes. Evening choices could kick off with Portobello mushroom stuffed with goats' cheese accompanied by toasted pine nuts, spinach and red onion marmalade. Follow perhaps with Capesthorne pheasant and game hotpot with braised red cabbage. Alternatively look to the chef's specials list for dishes full of freshly delivered seasonal and local produce.

Open 12-3 6-12 (Fri-Sun 12-11) Closed Mon L (ex BHs) **Food** Lunch Tue-Fri 12-2.30, Sat 12-9, Sun 12-8. No food available 25-26 Dec Dinner Tue-Fri 6-9, Sat 12-9, Sun 12-8 ⊕ FREE HOUSE ◀ Copper Dragon, Storm, Theakston, Beartown, Courage Directors, Wincle, Moorhouses. ☎ 9 **Facilities** Non-diners area ☙ (Bar Garden) ⢾ Children's menu Play area Garden ⌁ Parking WiFi ⛟ (notice required)

MOBBERLEY — Map 15 SJ77

The Bulls Head — PICK OF THE PUBS

See Pick of the Pubs on page 79

The Church Inn — PICK OF THE PUBS

See Pick of the Pubs on opposite page

MOULDSWORTH — Map 15 SJ57

The Goshawk

tel: 01928 740900 **Station Rd CH3 8AJ**
email: goshawk@woodwardandfalconer.com
dir: *A51 from Chester onto A54. Left onto B5393 towards Frodsham. Into Mouldsworth, pub on left*

Old railway inn popular with cyclists and walkers

This sturdy inn has a hint of Edwardian grandeur whilst benefiting from contemporary comforts; print-clad walls and dado rails, comfy sofas and open fires. Its village setting makes the most of the area's delights, including the many miles of footpaths, cycle trails and meres of nearby Delamere Forest; Chester is just one stop away on the train. Local ales draw an appreciative crowd, whilst the wide-ranging menu is matched by an extensive wine list. The menus, that include good fish and vegetarian choices, change every six weeks. The terrace and large grassy beer garden overlooks the well-kept bowling green which is frequently used in the summer months.

Open all day all wk 12-11 (Sun 12-10.30) Closed 25 Dec, 1 Jan **Food** Contact pub for food times ⊕ WOODWARD & FALCONER PUBS LTD ◀ Piffle, Balderdash, Weetwood, Conwy, Guest ales. ☎ 14 **Facilities** Non-diners area ⢾ Children's menu Children's portions Play area Family room Garden ⌁ Parking WiFi ⛟ (notice required)

NANTWICH — Map 15 SJ65

The Thatch Inn

tel: 01270 524223 **Wrexham Rd, Faddiley CW5 8JE**
email: johntribe@gmail.com
dir: *From Nantwich follow Wrexham signs, inn on A534 in 4m*

Enjoyable food in traditional pub with large beer garden

There may have been a change of hands in 2014, but the Thatch is still believed to be one of the oldest pubs in south Cheshire, if not the prettiest. This black-and-white inn has a three-quarter acre garden, while inside there are plentiful oak beams and open fires in winter. Enjoy a pint of Salopian Shropshire Gold with main courses such as pan-fried fillet of salmon with oven-roasted sun-blushed tomatoes, saffron risotto and pea shoots. Finish with lemon and lime parfait with gin and tonic sorbet. Children can choose from their own menu.

Open Mon-Tue 5.30-11, Wed-Thu 12-3 5.30-11, Fri-Sat 12-11, Sun 12-10.30 Closed Mon L & Tue L **Food** Lunch Wed-Fri 12-3, Sat 12-9, Sun 12-8.30 Dinner Mon-Fri 5.30-9, Sat 12-9, Sun 12-8.30 Set menu available Restaurant menu available all wk ⊕ ENTERPRISE INNS ◀ Salopian Shropshire Gold, Timothy Taylor Landlord. **Facilities** Non-diners area ⢾ Children's menu Children's portions Play area Garden ⌁ Parking WiFi ⛟

NORTHWICH — Map 15 SJ67

The Red Lion ★★★ INN

tel: 01606 74597 **277 Chester Rd, Hartford CW8 1QL**
email: cathy.iglesias@tesco.net web: www.redlionhartford.com
dir: *From A556 take Hartford exit. Red Lion at 1st junct on left next to church*

Popular village inn with stylish accommodation

This engaging inn was the village fire station until a century or so ago, and many artefacts remain from that time. Hunker down with a pint of Black Sheep, tuck in to hearty pub grub like home-made lamb hotpot, or take on the locals at darts or dominoes. This is a thriving community local where visitors to the nearby Delamere Forest or Oulton Park motor-racing circuit can also bed down in the en suite accommodation here. Log fires in winter, and at the back there is an enclosed beer garden.

Open all day all wk **Food** Lunch Mon-Sat 12-2 Dinner Mon-Sat 6-8 Av main course £6.95 ⊕ FREE HOUSE ◀ Marston's Pedigree, Black Sheep, John Smith's Cask, Timothy Taylor Landlord. ☎ 9 **Facilities** Non-diners area ☙ (Bar Garden) ⢾ Family room Garden ⌁ Parking WiFi **Rooms** 3

PARKGATE — Map 15 SJ27

The Boat House

tel: 0151 336 4187 **1 The Parade CH64 6RN**
email: boathouse@woodwardandfalconer.com
dir: *On B5135, 3m from Heswall*

Welcoming pub with unbeatable estuary location

The salt marshes begin right in front of The Boat House, so there's nothing to spoil the views of North Wales across the estuary. Once a thriving Deeside port, Parkgate's silted-up waters are now a nature reserve, although exceptionally high tides do still reach the walls of this striking black-and-white-timbered pub. Real ales include Weetwood Eastgate Ale, while for food stay in the bar or head for the Dee-facing dining room. Menus, always with a good fish and seafood selection, might offer seared scallops and pork belly, followed by classic fish pie.

Open all day all wk 12-11 (Sun 12-10.30) Closed 25 Dec, 1 Jan **Food** Contact pub for food times ⊕ WOODWARD & FALCONER PUBS LTD ◀ Piffle & Balderdash, Weetwood Eastgate Ale, Monty's, Conwy. ☎ 16 **Facilities** Non-diners area ⢾ Children's menu Children's portions Outside area ⌁ Parking WiFi ⛟ (notice required)

PICK OF THE PUBS

The Church Inn

MOBBERLEY   Map 15 SJ77

tel: 01565 873178 **WA16 7RD**
email: info@churchinnmobberley.co.uk
web: www.churchinnmobberley.co.uk
dir: *From Knutsford take B5085 towards*
Wilmslow. In Mobberley left into Church
Ln. Pub opposite church

Local produce drives the menu of this stylish village pub

Tim Bird and Mary McLaughlin have certainly put this old inn back on the map, alongside their other pub in the village, The Bulls Head. The Church Inn is a stylish country pub that appeals to locals and destination diners alike. On the edge of the village and opposite the 12th-century St Wilfrid's church, it is ideally situated between the bustling towns of Wilmslow and Knutsford and only eight miles from Manchester Airport. Surrounded by rolling Cheshire countryside, the rear garden and attractive summer dining terrace leads down to an old bowling green that boasts panoramic views across neighbouring fields. In the bar and boot room, a range of locally sourced ales includes Mallory's Mobberley Best, named after Mobberley-born mountaineer George Mallory. A choice of intimate dining areas offers a relaxed and comfortable setting for the extensive food offering, which takes in pub classics (shepherd's pie; lamb burgers; fish and chips) alongside the

main menu. Start a meal by sharing either the English butchers' board or the seafood trawler board perhaps, then follow on with a seasonal dish of slow-cooked treacle and ale beef, caramelised onion mash and sesame baby carrots; pot roast pork belly, slow-roasted apple, creamy mash potato and cider gravy. Sticky ginger pudding, whisky ice cream with vanilla sauce is a typical dessert, although the board of Cheshire artisan cheeses changes daily. Canines are more than welcome in the bar and the boot room and there is a bowl of dog biscuits on the bar, as well as dog 'beer' (meat-based stock) for them to drink. There are two private dining rooms and the pub holds wine-tasting classes.

Open all day all wk **Food** Lunch all wk, all day Dinner all wk, all day Av main course £13 Restaurant menu available all wk ◂ Dunham Massey Mallory's Mobberley Best, Tatton Brewery Ale-Alujah, Guest ales Ö Ty Gwyn. 🍷 16 **Facilities** Non-diners area 🐾 (Bar Garden) 🚼 Children's portions Garden 🎋 Parking WiFi 🚌 (notice required)

PARKGATE *continued*

The Ship Hotel

tel: 0151 336 3931 **The Parade CH64 6SA**
email: info@the-shiphotel.co.uk
dir: *A540 from Chester towards Neston. Left onto B5134 to Neston town centre. At T-junct right onto B5136. Next left onto B5135 to Parkgate. Hotel 50yds on right on The Parade*

Free house with fine views of the Welsh mountains

Parkgate's port is now silted up, but the views from The Parade across what is now the RSPB's Dee Estuary bird reserve to the Welsh coast don't change. With 18th-century origins, The Ship was regularly visited by Lord Nelson and his mistress Lady Hamilton, who had been born in nearby Neston. Real ale names to conjure with in the contemporary bar include Trapper's Hat from Wirral brewery Brimstage and Weetwood Oast-House Gold, also from Cheshire. Enjoy home-made food by the fire, with options such as pheasant wrapped in pancetta; Cumberland sausage and mash; surf and turf; Thai green curry, and specials.

Open all day all wk **Food** Lunch all wk 12-9 Dinner all wk 12-9 Av main course £10 ⊕ FREE HOUSE ◀ Brimstage Trapper's Hat, Weetwood Oast-House Gold, Jennings Cumberland Ale, Tatton Gold. ♀ 15 **Facilities** Non-diners area ◀ Children's menu Children's portions Outside area ⊼ Parking WiFi ▭ (notice required)

PRESTBURY   **Map 16 SJ87**

The Legh Arms

tel: 01625 829130 **The Village SK10 4DG**
email: legharms@hotmail.co.uk
dir: *On A538 (New Road)*

Serving good food all day every day

Trendy Prestbury is popular with Premiership footballers and they're lucky to have the gabled and part-timbered Legh Arms on their doorstep. Fine ales from nearby Robinsons Brewery are served in the bar with its oak beams and roaring fires. You'll find simpler fare on offer there, such as salads, sharing platters, sandwiches and pub favourites. For a celeb-spotting dinner, eat in the restaurant, where dishes use herbs from the pub's own walled garden. You might choose Cheshire game terrine followed by pan-fried calves' liver. The beer garden has a wood-burning stove for cooler nights.

Open all day all wk **Food** Lunch all wk 12-10 Dinner all wk 12-10 Set menu available Restaurant menu available all wk ⊕ ROBINSONS ◀ 1892, Hatters & Unicorn. ♀ **Facilities** Non-diners area ❀ (Garden) ◀ Children's portions Garden ⊼ Parking WiFi

---

SPURSTOW   **Map 15 SJ55**

The Yew Tree Inn

tel: 01829 260274 **Long Ln CW6 9RD**
email: info@theyewtreebunbury.com
dir: *400mtrs from A49*

Seriously good ales and food

Built by the Earl of Crewe, this is a sympathetically refurbished 19th-century pub. Inside, the original beams and open fires are a reminder of the pub's history, while the terrace is a more modern addition and perfect for summer dining. Up to eight real ales and two draught ciders testify to the pub's serious attention to quality refreshments, and the Easter weekend beer festival should not be missed. But diners are well rewarded too, with the kitchen producing seasonal menus driven

by local produce. Sticky baby back ribs with braised cabbage, fennel and apple make an irresistible starter, and any main course served with beef dripping chips will not disappoint.

Open all day all wk **Food** Lunch Mon-Thu 12-9.30, Fri-Sat 12-10, Sun 12-9 Dinner Mon-Thu 12-9.30, Fri-Sat 12-10, Sun 12-9 ⊕ FREE HOUSE ◀ Stonehouse Station Bitter, 7 guest ales ○ Westons Stowford Press, Guest cider. ♀ 14 **Facilities** Non-diners area ❀ (Bar Garden Outside area) ◀ Children's menu Children's portions Garden Outside area ⊼ Beer festival Parking WiFi ▭ (notice required)

STYAL   **Map 15 SJ88**

The Ship Inn

tel: 01625 444888 **Altrincham Rd SK9 4JE**
email: info@theshipstyal.co.uk
dir: *From B5166 N of Wilmslow, left signed Styal into Altrincham Rd*

All that's good in a pub still casting its spell

Styal's history is closely bound to that of the local cotton industry; many of the Ship's customers call in after visiting nearby Quarry Bank Mill. The 350-year-old building was once a shippon, an ancient term for a farm's cattle shed; it became a pub when the farmer owner started brewing for the locals. Happily craft ales are still high in the pub's attractions, with Weetwood Cheshire Cat and Big Tree Bitter by Dunham Massey usually among the five on offer. There's something for everyone on the menu, with traditional favourites often given a creative spin. Children have their own selection, and are welcome until 8pm. Beer festival in summer.

Open all wk 11.30-11 (Sun 12-10.30) **Food** Lunch all wk 12-9 Dinner all wk 12-9 ⊕ FREE HOUSE ◀ Weetwood Best & Cheshire Cat, Dunham Massey Big Tree Bitter, Timothy Taylor Boltmaker, Guest Ales ○ Hereford Cider. ♀ 11 **Facilities** Non-diners area ◀ Children's menu Children's portions Garden ⊼ Beer festival Parking WiFi ▭ (notice required)

SUTTON LANE ENDS   **Map 16 SJ97**

Sutton Hall   **PICK OF THE PUBS**

tel: 01260 253211 **Bullocks Ln SK11 0HE**
email: sutton.hall@brunningandprice.co.uk
dir: *A523 from Macclesfield. At lights left into Byron's Ln (signed Sutton, Langley & Wincle). Left into Bullocks Ln. Pub on left*

Former manor house turned spacious pub

The family seat of the Earls of Lucan, this striking half-timbered and gritstone manor house is surrounded by its own estate. Dating from the 16th century, but considerably added to since, it conceals a wealth of nooks and crannies, a snug, a library and seven different dining areas, with terraces and gardens outside. The Macclesfield Canal runs nearby, while in the other direction are the steeply wooded hills and crags of Macclesfield Forest. As part of the Brunning & Price chain of dining pubs, it offers the company's own Original Bitter alongside Lord Lucan, a local brew whose whereabouts are no mystery; the wine list is well compiled and there are over 100 whiskies. A typical starter is potted smoked mackerel, crayfish, apple and fennel salad. Sample mains include honey-roast duck breast; pan-fried sea bass with chorizo, caper and tomato dressing; and Moroccan spiced pepper with couscous, aubergine and okra salad.

Open all day all wk 11.30-11 (Sun 11-10.30) ⊕ FREE HOUSE/BRUNNING & PRICE ◀ Brunning & Price Original Bitter, Flowers Original, Wincle Lord Lucan ○ Aspall, Westons Wyld Wood Organic. **Facilities** ❀ (Bar Garden) ◀ Children's portions Play area Garden Parking WiFi

PICK OF THE PUBS

The Bear's Paw ★★★★★ INN ✿

WARMINGHAM Map 15 SJ76

tel: 01270 526317
School Ln CW11 3QN
email: info@thebearspaw.co.uk
web: www.thebearspaw.co.uk
dir: *M6 junct 18, A54, A533 towards Sandbach. Follow signs for village*

Refined gastro-pub cooking

With its prominent central gable and some nods towards typical Cheshire black-and-white half-timbering, this stylish 19th-century gastro-inn has clearly had a lot of money spent on it. Acres — well it seems like acres — of reclaimed antique oak flooring, leather sofas surrounding a huge open fireplace, bookshelves offering plenty of choice for a good read, and more than 200 pictures and archive photos lining the oak-panelled walls. The bar, in which stands a carved wooden bear with a salmon in its mouth, offers a half dozen cask ales from local microbreweries, including the somewhat appropriate Beartown in Congleton, Weetwood in Tarporley, and Tatton in Knutsford, as well as Hereford dry cider. Whether you're sitting out front looking across to the churchyard or in the clubby interior, there's plenty of comfortable dining space in which to sample wholesome, locally sourced food from wide-ranging daily menus that expertly blend the classic with the modern. Take, for example, starters like

home-made black pudding with poached duck egg, pea purée and mustard jus; or goats' cheese and pickled beetroot ballotine with balsamic walnuts; and main dishes such as eight-hour braised shin of beef, carrot purée, creamy mash, confit garlic and red wine jus; beer-battered North Sea haddock, mushy peas, tartare sauce and chunky chips; or tomato, chorizo and basil spaghetti. Great for sharing are the imaginative deli boards, which come laden with local cheeses, charcuterie or pickled and smoked fish, and don't miss the Sunday roast lunches. For something lighter, think in terms of a filled baguette or ciabatta, or sandwich. The Bear's Paw also offers distinctive, boutique-style en suite bedrooms.

Open all day all wk **Food** Mon-Thu 12-9.30, Fri-Sat 12-10, Sun 12-8 ⊕ FREE HOUSE ◼ Weetwood Best Bitter, Cheshire Cat & Eastgate Ale, Spitting Feathers, Beartown, Tatton ♻ Hereford Dry Cider. ☐ 10 **Facilities** Non-diners area ✿ (Bar Restaurant Garden) ♠ Children's menu Children's portions Garden ☍ Parking WiFi ➡ (notice required) **Rooms** 17

SWETTENHAM

Map 15 SJ86

The Swettenham Arms

PICK OF THE PUBS

tel: 01477 571284 **Swettenham Ln CW12 2LF**
email: info@swettenhamarms.co.uk
dir: M6 junct 18 to Holmes Chapel, then A535 towards Jodrell Bank. 3m right (Forty Acre Lane) to Swettenham (NB do not use postcode for Sat Nav; enter Swettenham Lane)

Popular with ramblers and diners

In the depths of the Cheshire countryside, this remote ancient inn close to the renowned Lovell Quinta Arboretum is ideally situated for taking gentle rambles into the tranquil valley of the nearby River Dane. A comfy pub full of quiet corners, the best of Cheshire food and drink draws an appreciative crowd year-round. In summer the neighbouring lavender meadow is a fragrant location to sit and sup Moorhouse's Pride of Pendle or Tatton Best, musing on the enjoyable menu created by talented chef Thomas Lüdecke. Roast Goosnargh chicken breast with chestnut and red pepper mousse, gnocchi, green beans, carrots and green pepper sauce; or wild mushroom and butternut squash risotto hit the mark; many dishes benefit from the inn's own-grown vegetables. The building itself is tucked into a former Tudor nunnery; one of its three working fireplaces is said to be haunted by a black-clad nun named Sarah.

Open all wk 11.30am-close (Closed Mon-Fri 3.30-6 Winter) **Food** Lunch Mon-Fri 12-2.30, Sat-Sun 12-6 Dinner Mon-Sat 6-9.30, Sun 6-8.30 Av main course £13 ⊕ FREE HOUSE ◀ Timothy Taylor Landlord, Sharp's Doom Bar, Bollington Best, Courage Directors, Moorhouse's Pride of Pendle, Slater's Top Totty, Black Sheep, Beartown, Wells Bombardier, Fuller's London Pride, Tatton, Thwaites Wainwright Ŏ Addlestones, Westons Old Rosie. ♀ 12 **Facilities** Non-diners area ❀ (Bar Garden) ♦ Children's menu Children's portions Play area Garden 🎄 Parking WiFi ☕ (notice required)

TARPORLEY

Map 15 SJ56

Alvanley Arms Inn ★★★★ INN

tel: 01829 760200 **Forest Rd, Cotebrook CW6 9DS**
email: info@alvanleyarms.co.uk **web:** www.alvanleyarms.co.uk
dir: On A49, 1.5m N of Tarporley

Local produce features on the menus

This lovely 16th-century former coaching inn has links to the Cotebrook Shire Horse Centre next door, so expect a horse-themed decor – harnesses and horseshoes – in the traditional oak-beamed bar. Hand-pulled ales complement a range of freshly prepared dishes, based on ingredients from local family businesses; the chef patron makes his own bread from local Walk Mill flour. Dishes range from starters such as home-made pad Thai 'pot noodle'; and potted chicken liver pâté; and to main courses of spicy lamb bhuna; grilled Cumberland sausage with mash; mussels and chips; game pie; and lasagne al forno. Lighter options such as sandwiches with fries and a tasting cup of soup are available at lunchtime.

Open all day all wk 12-11 **Food** Lunch Mon-Fri 12-2, Sat-Sun 12-9 Dinner Mon-Fri 6-9, Sat-Sun 12-9 Av main course £8.95 Set menu available Restaurant menu available all wk ⊕ ROBINSONS ◀ Dizzy Blonde, Trooper, Unicorn, Guest ales Ŏ Westons Stowford Press. ♀ 12 **Facilities** Non-diners area ♦ Children's menu Children's portions Garden 🎄 Parking WiFi ☕ (notice required) **Rooms** 7

The Swan, Tarporley

tel: 01829 733838 **50 High St CW6 0AG**
email: info@theswantarporley.co.uk
dir: From junct of A49 & A51 into Tarporley. Pub on right in village centre

Restored coaching inn where hospitality rules

The 16th-century Swan has been the hub of Cheshire's picturesque Tarporley village for over 500 years; in days gone by it was a convenient resting place for travellers journeying between London and Chester. Tastefully restored by the current owners, The Swan opens early – 7am on weekdays, and 8am at weekends. While locals stop by for a pint of Weetwood's Eastgate, the chef prepares local produce for the seasonal menus which change weekly. Bar nibbles include home-pickled cockles and clams, while main courses may proffer a fish pie of salmon, cod and smoked haddock. Look out for the summer beer festival.

Open all wk 7am-11pm (Sat 8am-11pm Sun & BH Mon 8am-10.30pm) **Food** Lunch Mon-Sat 12-10, Sun & BH Mon 12-8 Dinner Mon-Sat 12-10, Sun & BH Mon 12-8 ⊕ FREE HOUSE ◀ Weetwood Best Bitter, Cheshire Cat & Eastgate Ale, Timothy Taylor Boltmaker. ♀ 13 **Facilities** Non-diners area ❀ (Bar Garden) ♦ Children's menu Children's portions Family room Garden 🎄 Beer festival Parking WiFi ☕ (notice required)

WARMINGHAM

Map 15 SJ76

The Bear's Paw ★★★★★ INN ◉

PICK OF THE PUBS

See Pick of the Pubs on page 83

WRENBURY

Map 15 SJ54

The Dusty Miller

tel: 01270 780537 **CW5 8HG**
email: info@thedusty.co.uk
dir: Phone for detailed directions

Transformed former corn mill on Llangollen Canal

This beautifully converted 18th-century corn mill is beside the Llangollen Canal in the rural village of Wrenbury. The pub's large arched windows offer views of passing boats, while a black-and-white lift bridge, designed by Thomas Telford, completes the picture-postcard setting. Alongside a good choice of real ales, the modern British menu, which mainly relies on ingredients from the region, offers frequently changing options to suit everyone.

Open 12-12 Closed Mon in winter **Food** Lunch Mon-Fri 12-3, Sat 12-9.30, Sun 12-8 Dinner Mon-Fri 6-9, Sat 12-9.30, Sun 12-8 ⊕ ROBINSONS ◀ Unicorn, Old Tom & Dizzy Blonde, Guest ales Ŏ Westons Stowford Press & Traditional. ♀ 12 **Facilities** Non-diners area ❀ (All areas) ♦ Children's menu Children's portions Garden Outside area 🎄 Parking WiFi ☕ (notice required)

Find out more about the AA's accommodation rating schemes on page 8

CORNWALL & ISLES OF SCILLY

ALTARNUN — Map 2 SX28

Rising Sun Inn

tel: 01566 86636 **PL15 7SN**
email: risingsuninn@hotmail.co.uk
dir: *From A30 follow Altarnun signs onto unclassified road. Through Altarnun & Treween to T-junct. Inn 100yds on left*

Moorland free house worth leaving the A30 for

It's still fine to arrive by horse at this inviting, 18th-century moorland inn – there's a hitching post in the car park. On horseback could be the best way home, too, given the real ales from the village's Penpont brewery (which celebrates its birthday at a beer festival here in mid November), Skinner's Betty Stogs, and also Cornish Orchards and Press Gang ciders. Lunch and dinner dishes include all kinds, from bangers and mash to lobster. The specials board changes daily, but always focuses on seasonal and locally sourced produce. Home of the original 'Boxeater' steak.

Open all wk 12-2.30 5.30-11 (Sat 12-11 Sun & BHs 12-10.30) **Food** Lunch all wk 12-2 Dinner all wk 6-9 ⊕ FREE HOUSE ◀ Penpont St. Nonna's, Skinner's Betty Stogs, Guest ales ♂ Cornish Orchards, Skinner's Press Gang. ♀ 10 **Facilities** Non-diners area ♣ (Bar Garden) ♦♦ Children's menu Children's portions Garden ☴ Beer festival Parking WiFi ◼ (notice required)

BODINNICK — Map 2 SX15

The Old Ferry Inn ★★★ INN

tel: 01726 870237 **PL23 1LX**
email: info@oldferryinn.co.uk **web:** www.oldferryinn.co.uk
dir: *From Liskeard on A38 to Dobwalls, left at lights onto A390. After 3m left onto B3359 signed Looe. Right signed Lerryn/Bodinnick/Polruan for 5m*

Traditional Cornish pub with splendid estuary views

Daphne du Maurier wrote many of her novels at 'Ferryside', the house next door to this 400-year-old inn by the River Fowey. You can watch people messing about in boats from one of the sun terraces, stay in the bar among the nautical memorabilia, or cosy up in the stone-walled snug. A long list of snacks includes Cornish Pasties, while among the mains are cod in Sharp's ale batter; wholetail scampi and chips; roast chicken breast with local cider, cream and apple sauce; and wild mushroom and thyme penne pasta. The adjacent ferry carries cars over to Fowey town.

Open all day all wk **Food** Lunch all wk 12-3 Dinner all wk 6-9 ⊕ FREE HOUSE ◀ Sharp's Cornish Coaster & Own, Guest ale ♂ Haye Farm, Sharp's Orchard Cornish Cider. **Facilities** Non-diners area ♣ (Bar Outside area) ♦♦ Children's menu Family room Outside area ☴ Parking WiFi **Rooms** 12

BOLINGEY — Map 2 SW75

Bolingey Inn

tel: 01872 571626 **Penwartha Rd TR6 0DH**
email: michaelsanders@bolingeyinn.co.uk
dir: *From B3285 in Perranporth at rdbt into Station Rd. Approx 0.5m right signed Bolingey. Pub 0.5m on right*

Delightful pub associated with Cornwall's former mining industry

In a previous life, the Bolingey Inn was reputedly a count house for the vicinity's mines; doubtless the money men would have appreciated ale on tap without needing to leave the building. 'More landlords than can be researched', the menu tells us, have served here since its change of use, some making structural changes during their tenure. Today the Bolingey charms its clients with its atmosphere, serves four bitters from the likes of Sharp's and Fuller's, and prepares good home-cooked dishes in the kitchen. Most ingredients are sourced locally, with the specials board listing fresh fish options. Beer festivals in April and October.

Open all day all wk **Food** Lunch all wk 12-2.30 Dinner all wk 6-9.30 ⊕ PUNCH TAVERNS ◀ Sharp's Doom Bar, Greene King Abbot Ale, Butcombe, St Austell Proper Job, Fuller's London Pride ♂ Thatchers. **Facilities** Non-diners area ♣ (Bar Outside area) ♦♦ Children's menu Children's portions Outside area ☴ Beer festival Parking WiFi ◼ (notice required)

BOSCASTLE — Map 2 SX09

The Wellington Hotel ★★★ HL ◉◉   PICK OF THE PUBS

See Pick of the Pubs on page 86

CADGWITH — Map 2 SW71

Cadgwith Cove Inn

tel: 01326 290513 **TR12 7JX**
email: garryandhelen@cadgwithcoveinn.co.uk
dir: *A3083 from Helston towards Lizard. Left to Cadgwith*

Local seafood and beer in a former smugglers' haunt

A visit to this 300-year-old pub in the largely unspoilt fishing hamlet on the Lizard coastline will illustrate why it once appealed to smugglers. Relics in the atmospheric bars attest to a rich seafaring history; the cove itself is just across the old pilchard cellar from its sunny front patio. Traditional favourites include fish and chips; crab salad and vegetarian trio of the day. Quiz nights are on Mondays, folk music on Tuesdays, the Cadgwith Singers perform every Friday and there are seafood buffets on Saturdays throughout the summer; or you could time a visit for the October beer and cider festival.

Open all day all wk **Food** Lunch all wk 12-3 Dinner all wk 6-9 Restaurant menu available all wk ⊕ PUNCH TAVERNS ◀ Sharp's, Skinner's, Guest ales ♂ Westons Stowford Press, Thatchers. ♀ 9 **Facilities** Non-diners area ♣ (Bar Restaurant Outside area) ♦♦ Children's menu Children's portions Outside area ☴ Beer festival Cider festival WiFi

CHAPEL AMBLE — Map 2 SW97

The Maltsters Arms

tel: 01208 812473 **PL27 6EU**
dir: *A39 from Wadebridge towards Camelford. In 1m left signed Chapel Amble. Pub on right in village*

Traditional home-cooking in charming Cornish village inn

In the pretty Cornish village of Chapel Amble and a short drive from Rock and Port Isaac, The Maltsters Arms oozes old-world charm and character, from slate floors and copper pots to 'mind-your-head' beams and open fires. A pub at the heart of the community with a quiz night and must-book Sunday carvery, the food is home-cooked and traditional. Pub favourites of burgers and beer-battered fish and chips appear alongside main menu dishes such as roasted cod loin, mussels, prawns and saffron linguine; and local lamb shank with garlic and spring onion mash and redcurrant jus. There's a beer and cider festival on the Spring Bank Holiday weekend in late May.

Open all wk 11-3 6-11 **Food** Lunch all wk 11-3 Dinner all wk 6-9 Set menu available ⊕ FREE HOUSE ◀ Sharp's Doom Bar & Atlantic IPA ♂ Westons Old Rosie. ♀ 11 **Facilities** Non-diners area ♣ (Bar Outside area) ♦♦ Children's menu Children's portions Outside area ☴ Beer festival Cider festival Parking WiFi ◼ (notice required)

PICK OF THE PUBS

The Wellington Hotel ★★★ HL 🌹🌹

BOSCASTLE	Map 2 SX09

tel: 01840 250202
The Harbour PL35 0AQ
email: info@wellingtonhotelboscastle.com
web: www.wellingtonhotelboscastle.com
dir: *A30/A395 at Davidstow follow Boscastle signs. B3266 to village. Right into New Rd*

Popular pub and fine dining restaurant on the Cornish coast

This listed 16th-century coaching inn with its castellated tower sits on one of England's most stunning coastlines, at the end of a glorious wooded valley where the rivers Jordan and Valency meet; in 1852 it was renamed in honour of the Duke of Wellington. Known affectionately as 'The Welly' by both locals and loyal guests, it retains much of its original charm as in the traditional Long Bar, complete with minstrels' gallery, where a good selection of Cornish ales, ciders such as Cornish Orchards, and malt whiskies are to be found. Bar snacks here embrace sandwiches with or without soup of the day, along with small plates. For a proper lunch, look to the blackboard for daily specials or the carte for the likes of crab linguine; sausages and mash; or grilled leg of lamb steak with crispy polenta. Follow perhaps with Eton Mess; or chocolate brownie with poached cherries and cherry ripple ice cream. Children are

well catered for with their own menu, and some adult main courses can be served in half-size portions. For fine dining, head to the first floor of the hotel to find the Waterloo Restaurant. The kitchen team prepares fresh local produce — none fresher or more local than the seafood landed by the boats in the harbour a few yards away. Starters may include smoked chicken terrine with honeycomb and pickles, then continue with pork tenderloin, black pudding, celeriac, truffle and peas; roasted cod risotto and bisque; and finally orange cheesecake, lemon posset, orange salad and shortbread.

Open all day all wk 11-11 **Food** Lunch Mon-Fri 12-3, Sat-Sun 12-9 Dinner Mon-Fri 6-9, Sat-Sun 12-9 Av main

course £13.50 Restaurant menu available Tue-Sat ⊕ FREE HOUSE 🍺 St Austell Tribute, Sharp's Doom Bar, Skinner's Betty Stogs ♂ Cornish Orchards, Healey's Cornish Rattler. **Facilities** Non-diners area 🐾 (Bar Garden Outside area) 👶 Children's menu Children's portions Family room Garden Outside area 🍴 Parking WiFi 🚌 (notice required) **Rooms** 14

CONSTANTINE
Map 2 SW72

Trengilly Wartha Inn
PICK OF THE PUBS

tel: 01326 340332 **Nancenoy TR11 5RP**
email: reception@trengilly.co.uk
dir: *Follow signs to Constantine, left towards Gweek until 1st sign for inn, left & left again at next sign, continue to inn*

Friendly, family retreat in a sheltered valley

In this charming 600-year-old inn near the Helford River, Will and Lisa Lea have created a popular bistro and local. The Cornish name means 'a settlement above the trees', although it actually lies at the foot of a densely wooded valley. In the black-beamed bar, oft-changing local real ales might include Penzance Potion No 9, served from the stillage shared with Healey's Cornish Rattler and Ty Gwyn ciders; 15 wines are sold by the glass, and over 40 malts clamour for attention. A typical dish, most likely sourced from a local farm or fishing boat, could be one of the specials, such as spring onion with roasted crab meat; chicken satay with fragrant rice; or wild mushroom and cheddar cheese risotto. Pub classics include 8oz Cornish sirloin steaks with home-made chips and mushrooms; and Thai pork burger with chilli mayonnaise. Meadows surround the pretty beer garden and its vine-shaded pergola.

Open all wk 11-3 6-12 **Food** Lunch all wk 12-2.15 Dinner all wk 6.30-9.30 Av main course £11 ⊕ FREE HOUSE ◖ Sharp's, Penzance Potion No 9, Guest ales ♨ Healey's Cornish Rattler, Thatchers Gold, Ty Gwyn. ♟ 15 **Facilities** Non-diners area ☺ (Bar Garden) ♦ Children's menu Children's portions Play area Family room Garden ⋒ Beer festival Cider festival Parking WiFi ☷ (notice required)

CRAFTHOLE
Map 3 SX35

The Finnygook Inn

tel: 01503 230338 **PL11 3BQ**
email: eat@finnygook.co.uk
dir: *10m W of Tamar Bridge take A374 S. In 3m right signed Crafthole & follow pub signs. From Torpoint take A374, 5m to Antony. Left in Antony, 1m to T-junct. 3m to Crafthole*

Old coaching inn serving peninsula-brewed beers

There's been a change of hands at this 16th-century pub, located in a hamlet above Portwrinkle's cove-nibbled coast. They say the ghost of smuggler Silas Finny walks the cliffs and byways hereabouts; so, too, do ramblers and visitors seeking to share the local beers from St Austell, Penpont, Harbour and Bays breweries, and tempting fodder available here. The Finnygook serves a host of reliable pub favourites – garlic mushrooms or pan-seared Cornish scallops to start, followed by calves' liver with champ mash, crispy bacon, red onion marmalade and red wine jus – taken by the log fire, in the library room or on the terrace with distant views up the Tamar estuary.

Open all day all wk **Food** Lunch all wk 12-9 (Nov-Mar 12-2.30) Dinner all wk 12-9 (Nov-Mar 6-9) ⊕ FREE HOUSE ◖ St Austell Tribute & Proper Job, Penpont Cornish Arvor, Dartmoor, Harbour, Bays ♨ Thatchers, Healey's Cornish Rattler. ♟ 10 **Facilities** Non-diners area ☺ (Bar Garden) ♦ Children's menu Children's portions Garden ⋒ Parking WiFi ☷ (notice required)

CUBERT
Map 2 SW75

The Smugglers' Den Inn

tel: 01637 830209 **Trebellan TR8 5PY**
email: hello@thesmugglersden.co.uk
dir: *From Newquay take A3075 to Cubert x-rds, then right, then left signed Trebellan, 0.5m to inn*

Classic coastal pub with plenty of local seafood

Jason and Helen Allen took over here in March 2015 and they have quickly stamped their personality on this thatched 16th-century pub, just 15 minutes from Newquay.

Popular with locals and visitors alike, the pub comprises a long bar, family room, children's play area, courtyards and huge beer garden. Local ingredients are the cornerstone of the family-friendly menu, which might kick off with Cornish mussels cooked in cider, shallots, garlic and cream. Home-made fish pie; chicken curry; and wild mushroom Stroganoff are typical main courses. Leave a space for the lemon and lime posset.

Open all wk 11.30-3 6-11 (Sun 11-11) **Food** Lunch Mon-Sat 12-3, Sun 12-4 Dinner Mon-Thu & Sun 6-9, Fri-Sat 6-9.30 ⊕ FREE HOUSE ◖ Sharp's Doom Bar, St Austell Tribute, Guest ales ♨ Healey's Cornish Rattler, Thatchers Gold. **Facilities** Non-diners area ☺ (Bar Garden) ♦ Children's menu Play area Family room Garden ⋒ Beer festival Parking WiFi ☷

DULOE
Map 2 SX25

NEW The Plough

tel: 01503 262556 **PL14 4PN**
email: enquiries@ploughduloe.co.uk
dir: *From A38 to Dobwalls. In Dobwalls follow Duloe signs*

Low-mileage food and cider

Richard Shepherd and Louisa Duggie took over Duloe's only pub late in 2014. Set in deep Cornish countryside, the village is a quiet getaway midway between the bustling towns of Liskeard to the north and Looe to the south. Duloe is also home to the Cornish Orchards Company, so no surprise to find its ciders on tap alongside St Austell ales in The Plough's bar. Richard and Louisa's use of local produce extends when possible to the menus. A starter of Cornish crab and wild garlic croquettes with Cumberland sauce, for example, could be followed by a home-made burger topped with Cornish cheddar.

Open all wk 12-3 6-11 **Food** Lunch Mon-Sat 12-2, Sun 12-3 Dinner Mon-Sat 6-9, Sun 6-8 Av main course £11 Restaurant menu available all wk ⊕ FREE HOUSE ◖ Sharp's Doom Bar, St Austell Tribute, Guest ale ♨ Cornish Orchards Gold Cider. **Facilities** Non-diners area ☺ (Bar Restaurant Garden) ♦ Children's menu Children's portions Family room Garden ⋒ Parking WiFi ☷ (notice required)

DUNMERE
Map 2 SX06

The Borough Arms

tel: 01208 73118 **PL31 2RD**
email: borougharms@staustellbrewery.co.uk
dir: *From A30 take A389 to Wadebridge, pub approx 1m from Bodmin*

Welcome refreshment in a Cornish valley

One of England's best loved recreational trails, the Camel Trail, skims past this considerably updated Victorian railway pub in the Cornish countryside outside Bodmin. Trains carrying china clay along the old line have been replaced by cyclists and ramblers, accessing the pub car park directly from the trail to indulge in a range of West Country real ales and ever-reliable pub grub. Ploughman's, steaks, curry of the day and freshly battered fish and chips revive flagging lovers of the outdoors, or they can try the carvery. Families are well catered for, with a children's play area to burn off extra energy.

Open all day all wk **Food** Lunch all wk 12-9 Dinner all wk 12-9 ⊕ ST AUSTELL BREWERY ◖ Tribute, Cornish Best, George Gale & Co HSB, Guest ales ♨ Healey's Cornish Rattler. **Facilities** Non-diners area ☺ (Bar Garden) ♦ Children's menu Children's portions Play area Family room Garden ⋒ Parking WiFi ☷

FEOCK
Map 2 SW83

The Punchbowl & Ladle

tel: 01872 862237 **Penelewey TR3 6QY**
email: punchbowlandladle@googlemail.com
dir: *From Truro take A39 towards Falmouth, after Shell garage at Playing Place rdbt follow King Harry Ferry signs. 0.5m, pub on right*

Local produce served in this gorgeous thatched inn

Local rumour has it that the fireplace in the bar of this lovely old pub close to the King Harry Ferry was used to burn contraband when customs officers dropped by. Settle down in the cosy low-beamed bar and make your choices from a menu that uses seasonal ingredients sourced from local Cornish suppliers. Typical dishes are Cornish mussels; and pulled pork bap with fries, onion rings and cabbage coleslaw, although salads and sandwiches are also on offer. In summer, head for the suntrap walled garden or patio with a glass of Trelawny ale or Cornish Rattler cider.

Open all day all wk **Food** Lunch Mon-Sat 12-2.30, Sun 12-3 Dinner all wk 6-9 Av main course £10-£13 ⊕ ST AUSTELL BREWERY ◀ Tribute, Proper Job, Trelawny & HSD Ò Healey's Cornish Rattler. ☐ 16 **Facilities** Non-diners area ☙ (Bar Garden) ♦ Children's menu Children's portions Garden ⊓ Parking WiFi ⊟

FOWEY
Map 2 SX15

The Ship Inn

tel: 01726 832230 **Trafalgar Square PL23 1AZ**
dir: *From A30 take B3269 & A390*

Very old inn situated in Fowey's narrow streets

One of Fowey's oldest buildings, the Ship was built in 1570 by John Rashleigh, who sailed to the Americas with Walter Raleigh. Given Fowey's riverside position, assume a good choice of fish, including River Fowey mussels as a starter or main; and grilled sardines in garlic. Other options include Mr Kittow's pork sausages and mash; spinach, asparagus and wild mushroom risotto. St Austell ales, real fires and a long tradition of genial hospitality add the final touches. There's been a change of hands at The Ship Inn.

Open all day all wk 11am-mdnt (Fri-Sat 11am-1am) **Food** Lunch all wk 12-2.30 Dinner all wk 6-9 ⊕ ST AUSTELL BREWERY ◀ Tribute & Proper Job, Dartmoor IPA Ò Healey's Cornish Rattler & Pear Rattler. ☐ 10 **Facilities** Non-diners area ☙ (Bar) ♦ Children's menu Children's portions Family room WiFi ⊟ (notice required)

GUNNISLAKE
Map 3 SX47

The Rising Sun Inn

tel: 01822 832201 **Calstock Rd PL18 9BX**
email: therisingsungunnislake@yahoo.co.uk
dir: *From Tavistock take A390 to Gunnislake. Left after lights into Calstock Rd. Inn approx 500mtrs on right*

Traditional picture-postcard pub in a lovely valley

Although ownership of this two-roomed pub changed in autumn 2014, nothing has changed the fabulous views from the pretty terraced gardens of the Tamar Valley and the river flowing towards Plymouth. Gunnislake is just in Cornwall, so it's understandable that Dartmoor Brewery's Jail Ale and Legend draught beers are served, while in a nod to neighbouring Devon, so is Otter. Good old British menu favourites include home-made beef chilli and curries; grilled gammon; sustainable cod in Symonds cider batter; and chicken goujons in a basket. Brie, hazelnut and cranberry Wellington is a vegetarian option. Great walks start and finish from the pub.

Open all day all wk **Food** Contact pub for food times Restaurant menu available all wk ⊕ FREE HOUSE ◀ Exmoor Ales, Driftwood Spars, Otter, Dartmoor Legend, Dartmoor Jail Ale, Local guest ales Ò Symonds, Thatchers Gold, Guest ciders. ☐ 25 **Facilities** Non-diners area ☙ (Bar Garden) ♦ Children's menu Children's portions Play area Garden ⊓ Beer festival Cider festival Parking WiFi ⊟ (notice required)

GUNWALLOE
Map 2 SW62

The Halzephron Inn
PICK OF THE PUBS

tel: 01326 240406 **TR12 7QB**
email: enquiries@halzephron-inn.co.uk
dir: *3m S of Helston on A3083, right to Gunwalloe, through village. Inn on left*

Stunning views and lots of local seafood on the menu

The name of the inn derives from Als Yfferin, old Cornish for 'Cliffs of Hell', an appropriate description for this hazardous stretch of Atlantic coastline. Located high above Gunwalloe Fishing Cove, this 500-year-old, rugged stone inn commands an enviable position, with breathtaking views across Mount's Bay. On sunny days grab a front bench and enjoy a pint of St Austell Tribute while looking out to St Michael's Mount. The two interconnecting bars feature cosy log fires, fishing memorabilia, and watercolours of local scenes. The à la carte and daily changing specials utilise the best Cornish produce available, including fresh seafood. Everything is home made, with the likes of crab cake with sweet chilli dipping sauce; and pan-fried strips of fillet steak with walnuts and balsamic dressing among the starters. Main courses include roast breast of guinea fowl with spiced thigh terrine on rösti and braised curly kale; creamy macaroni cheese bake; or medallions of pork fillet and black pudding in creamy garlic and rosemary sauce.

Open all day all wk 11-11 (Sun 12-10.30) **Food** Lunch Mon-Sat 12-2, Sun 12-3 Dinner all wk 6-9 ⊕ FREE HOUSE ◀ Sharp's Own, Doom Bar & Special, St Austell Tribute, Skinner's Betty Stogs Ò Symonds Founders Reserve. ☐ 10 **Facilities** Non-diners area ☙ (Bar Garden) ♦ Children's menu Children's portions Play area Family room Garden ⊓ Parking WiFi ⊟ (notice required)

GWEEK
Map 2 SW72

Black Swan ★★★★ INN

tel: 01326 221502 **TR12 6TU**
email: alec@alecrobertson.co.uk **web:** www.blackswangweek.co.uk
dir: *In village centre*

Home-cooked food and Cornish beers

This delightful inn is located in the picturesque village of Gweek on the River Helford, a stone's throw from the popular National Seal Sanctuary. The Black Swan has become famous for their sirloin steaks, but also offers signature dishes of steak and Guinness pie with creamy mash, and Cajun chicken breast, chips and peas. There's a choice of regularly changing specials too to widen the options. Not to be missed is a selection of Cornish ales and guest ales. If you'd like to stay over the pub has stylish bedrooms delightfully named Raspberry, Blackberry, Gooseberry and Mulberry.

Open all day all wk **Food** Lunch all wk, all day Dinner all wk, all day ⊕ PUNCH TAVERNS ◀ Sharp's Doom Bar, Bass, St Austell Tribute, Skinner's Betty Stogs, Guest ales Ò Thatchers, Addlestones. ☐ 9 **Facilities** Non-diners area ☙ (Bar Garden) ♦ Children's menu Children's portions Garden ⊓ Parking WiFi ⊟ (notice required) **Rooms** 4

GWITHIAN
Map 2 SW54

The Red River Inn

tel: 01736 753223 **1 Prosper Hill TR27 5BW**
email: louisa.saville@googlemail.com
dir: *Exit A30 at Loggans Moor rdbt, follow Hayle signs. Immediately take 3rd exit at mini rdt onto B3301 signed Gwithian. 2m to pub in village centre*

A village pub that offers something for everyone

The name of this 200-year-old pub recalls the colour of the village river when tin was mined locally. Close by runs the South West Coastal Path, and the beach is popular with surfers who, even in their wetsuits, are warmly welcomed here. Among its attractions are up to five, ever-changing Cornish real ales, an Easter weekend beer and cider festival, and food that ranges from fresh crab sandwiches and haloumi salad to fresh sea bass, steaks and Middle Eastern, Mexican and Indonesian dishes. Burgers are named Firebolt and Stinky Pig. An in-house shop sells artisan bread, pastries and farm produce from April to October.

Open 12-11 summer (Tue-Fri 12-2 5.30-11 Sat-Sun 12-11 winter) Closed Mon (winter only) **Food** Lunch all wk 12-2 Dinner all wk 6-9 ⊕ FREE HOUSE ◀ Sharp's Own, Spingo, Cornish Chough, Tintagel Harbour Special ♂ Thatchers Gold, Healey's Cornish Rattler & Cornish Gold. **Facilities** Non-diners area ✿ (Bar Restaurant Garden) ♦ Children's menu Children's portions Garden ⊟ Beer festival Cider festival Parking WiFi ▄ (notice required)

HALSETOWN   Map 2 SW43

The Halsetown Inn   PICK OF THE PUBS

tel: 01736 795583 **TR26 3NA**
email: info@halsetowninn.co.uk
dir: On B3311, 1m for St Ives

Smart country gastro-pub showcasing local produce

Built in 1831, The Halsetown Inn is named after the village's architect and benefactor, James Halse. From the outside, little changes at this stone-built pub, but the interior reveals a more contemporary style although the open fires remain and dogs are welcome. Run by the same team as the award-winning Blas Burgerworks restaurant in St Ives, local produce drives the menus here; typical starters on the concise menu are crab and sweetcorn soup; and Jerusalem artichoke, kale and feta empanadas. Then for mains, perhaps go for crispy fried whole mackerel, black olive and black bean dressing, spring onion and mint salad; or red duck curry, tea-smoked duck, green mango and pear salad, rice and greens. Puds could be the Halsetown 'Jaffa Cake' – orange cake, blood orange, and chocolate mousse; or crema catalana with caramel oatmeal biscuit. The team here are environmental aware, and dedicated to sustainability, be that composting, recycling or using low carbon electricity. Look out for the beer festival and village fête in August.

Open 11-3 5.30-close Closed 1st 2wks Jan, Sun eve **Food** Lunch Mon-Sat 12-2, Sun 12-3 Dinner Mon-Sat 6-9 (5.30-9.30 summer) Av main course £14 Set available ⊕ PUNCH TAVERNS ◀ Sharp's Doom Bar, Skinner's Betty Stogs ♂ Cornish Orchards. **Facilities** Non-diners area ✿ (Bar Outside area) ♦ Children's menu Children's portions Outside area ⊟ Beer festival Parking WiFi ▄ (notice required)

HELFORD PASSAGE   Map 2 SW72

The Ferryboat Inn

tel: 01326 250625 **TR11 5LB**
email: manager@ferryboatinnhelford.com
dir: In village centre, 1st turn after Trebah Gardens

Wonderful views and great seafood

There are fabulous views over the Helford estuary from this waterside pub, which dates back 300 years. Whether it's a plate of oysters and a glass of fizz on the sunny, south-facing terrace or Cornish rump steak, smoked tomato butter, kale and mash by the warmth of the granite fireplace inside, this is a venue for all weathers. Everything is made on the premises and the Ferryboat burger is especially popular. The pub is owned by Wright Brothers, custodians of the Duchy of Cornwall's oyster farm, so the quality of the shellfish and seafood speaks for itself. If available, perhaps try Cornish brown crab rarebit, white crab and pickled vegetables.

Open all day all wk **Food** Lunch all wk 12-3 Dinner all wk 6-9 (summer 6-10) Av main course £10-£12 ⊕ ST AUSTELL ◀ Tribute, Dartmoor, Proper Job ♂ Healey's Cornish Rattler. ☗ 12 **Facilities** Non-diners area ✿ (Bar Restaurant Outside area) ♦ Children's menu Children's portions Outside area ⊟ Parking WiFi ▄ (notice required)

LANLIVERY   Map 2 SX05

The Crown Inn ★★★ INN   PICK OF THE PUBS

tel: 01208 872707 **PL30 5BT**
email: thecrown@wagtailinns.com **web:** www.wagtailinns.com
dir: Signed from A390. Follow brown sign approx 1.5m W of Lostwithiel

One of Cornwall's oldest pubs

In a moorland village above a tributary of the Fowey River is this former longhouse, with characteristic thick stone walls, low beams, granite and slate floors, open fires and an unusual bread oven. Much of the present building dates from the 12th century, when it housed the stonemasons constructing the nearby church. The pub has been extensively but sympathetically restored over the years; at one point the work uncovered a deep well, now covered by glass, under the porch. With the sea only a few miles away, expect a menu offering plenty of fresh fish and seafood, as well as other local produce. A popular main course is Cornish ale-battered fish with chips, crushed peas and home-made tartare sauce. At lunchtime in warm weather, enjoy a fresh Fowey crab sandwich or a proper Cornish Pasty and a pint of Skinner's Betty Stogs in the lovely garden.

Open all day all wk **Food** Lunch all wk 12-2.30 Dinner all wk 6-9 ⊕ FREE HOUSE ◀ Harbour Amber Ale, Skinner's Betty Stogs, Guest ales ♂ Healey's Cornish Rattler. **Facilities** Non-diners area ✿ (Bar Garden) ♦ Children's menu Children's portions Garden ⊟ Parking WiFi ▄ (notice required) **Rooms** 8

LOOE   Map 2 SX25

The Ship Inn ★★★ INN

tel: 01503 263124 **Fore St PL13 1AD**
dir: In town centre

Busy pub on a narrow street

This lively St Austell Brewery-owned pub stands on a corner in the heart of this charming old fishing town, a minute's walk from the working harbour. Locals and tourists join together in the appreciation of a pint of Tribute, and select their favourites from the menu – a burger or hot baguette for some, while others go for steak and ale pie or hunter's chicken. A quiz is held on Mondays throughout the year, live bands play regularly, and well-equipped bedrooms are available for those wanting to tarry awhile.

Open all day all wk **Food** Contact pub for food times ⊕ ST AUSTELL BREWERY ◀ Tribute, Trelawny, HSD ♂ Healey's Cornish Rattler. ☗ **Facilities** Non-diners area ✿ (Bar) ♦ Children's menu Children's portions Family room **Rooms** 8

LUXULYAN   Map 2 SX05

The Kings Arms

tel: 01726 850202 **Bridges PL30 5EF**
dir: From A30 at Innis Downs junct take A39 signed St Austell. Left signed Luxulyan. Over railway & river. Inn on right at bottom of hill

Well-kept beers, good pub grub and a friendly welcome

Walkers, cyclists, families, dog owners – all are most welcome at this traditional stone-built village pub. Owned by St Austell Brewery, it offers their HSD, Trelawny, Proper Job and Tribute real ales, an occasional guest, and Healey's Cornish Rattler cider; wine drinkers have a choice of 12 by the glass. The menu of locally sourced produce offers a selection of no-nonsense home-made snacks and main meals that should leave everybody happy – Trelawny pie; rabbit casserole; fish and chips; and 'build a burger'. A takeaway service serves home-made pizzas.

Open all day all wk Sun-Thu 11-11 (Fri-Sat 11am-mdnt) **Food** Lunch all wk 12-2.30 Dinner all wk 6-9 ⊕ ST AUSTELL BREWERY ◀ HSD, Tribute, Trelawny & Proper Job, Guest ale ♂ Healey's Cornish Rattler. ☗ 12 **Facilities** Non-diners area ✿ (Bar Restaurant Garden) ♦ Children's menu Children's portions Garden ⊟ Parking WiFi ▄ (notice required)

MEVAGISSEY — Map 2 SX04

The Ship Inn

tel: 01726 843324 **Fore St PL26 6UQ**
email: shipinnmeva2013@hotmail.co.uk
dir: *7m S of St Austell*

A popular tavern a few steps from the harbour

This 400-year-old inn stands just a few yards from Mevagissey's picturesque fishing harbour, so the choice of fish and seafood dishes comes as no surprise on a menu of home-cooked dishes: moules marinière, beer-battered cod, and oven-baked fillet of haddock topped with prawns and Cornish Tiskey cheese. The popular bar has low-beamed ceilings, flagstone floors and a strong nautical feel.

Open all day all wk 11am-mdnt **Food** Lunch all wk 12-3 Dinner all wk 6-9 ⊕ ST AUSTELL BREWERY ◀ St Austell Tribute & Proper Job, Guest ale ☼ Healey's Cornish Rattler. ☗ 8 **Facilities** Non-diners area ❄ (Bar) ♦ Children's menu WiFi ▭

MITCHELL — Map 2 SW85

The Plume of Feathers ★★★★ INN   PICK OF THE PUBS

tel: 01872 510387 **TR8 5AX**
email: theplume@hospitalitycornwall.com **web:** www.theplumemitchell.co.uk
dir: *From A30 follow Mitchell signs*

Friendly atmosphere in a historic inn

From the impressive pillared porch at this sturdy old Cornish inn, John Wesley preached the benefits of Methodism to farmers and miners in the 1750s. Elements of the old place still survive, with low beams, wood-burning stove and a natural well in the bar blending with the contemporary artworks on display. As the village inn, it's popular with locals who can rely on regional real ales and farm cider from Healey's, made on the north coast a few miles distant. The airy conservatory is an appealing place in which to dine, while seven stylish bedrooms provide the perfect overnight retreat. Local Cornish produce takes centre stage on the modern British menu and there's always a good showing of fish and locally reared meats. To start, consider smoked mackerel and horseradish pâté; advancing then to mains like crispy slow-cooked Cornish pork belly with mustard mash, smoked bacon, peas and baby onion gravy. The raised, tree-shaded beer garden is a tranquil retreat.

Open all day all wk 9am-11pm/mdnt (25 Dec 11-4) **Food** Lunch all wk 12-6 Dinner all wk 6-10 ⊕ FREE HOUSE ◀ Sharp's Doom Bar, John Smith's Extra Smooth, Skinner's, St Austell Tribute ☼ Healey's Cornish Rattler. ☗ **Facilities** Non-diners area ❄ (Bar Garden) ♦ Children's menu Play area Garden ⌂ Beer festival Parking WiFi ▭ (notice required) **Rooms** 7

MITHIAN — Map 2 SW75

The Miners Arms

tel: 01872 552375 **TR5 0QF**
email: minersarms@live.co.uk
dir: *From A30 at Chiverton Cross rdbt take A3075 signed Newquay. At Pendown Cross left onto B3284 signed Perranporth. Left, left again to Mithian*

Fascinating history at centuries' old pub

The curiously light interior of this historic 16th-century pub adds yet another layer of mystery to the legends of its past. Over the centuries it has served as a courthouse, a venue for inquests, a smugglers' lair and even a house of ill repute. Relax beneath the low-beamed ceilings while admiring the wall paintings of Elizabeth I, and choose from the menu of dishes freshly cooked to order from local produce: hake topped with pesto; steak of the day; vegetable tagine; and the Miners' fish pie is a must.

Open all day all wk 12-11.30 **Food** Lunch all wk 12-2.30 Dinner all wk 6-9 ⊕ PUNCH TAVERNS ◀ Sharp's Doom Bar, St Austell Tribute, Skinner's Betty Stogs ☼ Westons Stowford Press, Thatchers Gold. **Facilities** Non-diners area ❄ (Bar) ♦ Children's menu Children's portions Garden ⌂ Parking ▭

MYLOR BRIDGE — Map 2 SW83

The Pandora Inn   PICK OF THE PUBS

See Pick of the Pubs on opposite page

NEWQUAY — Map 2 SW86

The Lewinnick Lodge Bar & Restaurant ★★★★ RR

tel: 01637 878117 **Pentire Headland TR7 1NX**
email: thelodge@hospitalitycornwall.com **web:** www.lewinnicklodge.co.uk
dir: *From Newquay take Pentire Rd 0.5m, pub on right*

Recommended for its fresh seafood and stunning views

Lewinnick Lodge perches on the cliff top of the Pentire Headland, enjoying a timeless panorama of sea views. This is a destination eatery, but real ales, local cider, crisp wines and premium lagers are all on offer in the bar. Wraps and baps and gourmet burgers can be ordered, but fresh seafood, much of it from Cornish waters, is the menu's key attraction; expect the likes of pan-fried stone bass fillets with patatas bravas, chorizo, spinach, spring onion and salsa verde; or whole roasted plaice with sautéed potatoes, griddled asparagus and cockle butter. Meats from the county include slow-roasted lamb and beef. Leave room for the lemon posset with black forest berries, shortbread and meringue.

Open all day all wk **Food** Lunch all wk 12-5 Dinner all wk 5-10 ⊕ FREE HOUSE ◀ Sharp's Doom Bar, Skinner's Betty Stogs, St Austell Tribute ☼ Cornish Orchards. ☗ 8 **Facilities** Non-diners area ❄ (Bar Garden) ♦ Children's menu Children's portions Garden ⌂ Parking WiFi ▭ **Rooms** 11

PAR — Map 2 SX05

The Britannia Inn & Restaurant ★★★★ INN

tel: 01726 812889 **St Austell Rd PL24 2SL**
email: info@britanniainn.com **web:** www.britanniainn.com
dir: *On A390 between Par & St Austell, adjacent to Cornish Market World*

Family-owned and family friendly, with large garden

Sixteenth-century, solidly built free house, where Sharp's Doom Bar, St Austell Tribute and Healey's Cornish Rattler wave the black and white county flag. The three dining areas do likewise by offering prime-cut Cornish steaks and other locally sourced dishes, typically battered cod and chips; steak and ale pie; scampi, chips and peas; and pulled pork with home-made barbecue sauce on toasted ciabatta. A short pub classics selection is offered at £15 for two, Monday to Saturday, with daily chef's specials adding further choice. The Sunday carvery is popular.

Open all day all wk **Food** Lunch all wk 12-9 Dinner all wk 12-9 ⊕ FREE HOUSE ◀ Sharp's Doom Bar, St Austell Tribute, Bass ☼ Thatchers Gold, Healey's Cornish Rattler. ☗ **Facilities** Non-diners area ❄ (Bar Garden) ♦ Children's menu Children's portions Play area Family room Garden ⌂ Parking WiFi ▭ (notice required) **Rooms** 7

PICK OF THE PUBS

The Pandora Inn

MYLOR BRIDGE   Map 2 SW83

tel: 01326 372678
Restronguet Creek TR11 5ST
email: info@pandorainn.com
web: www.pandorainn.com
dir: *From Truro/Falmouth follow A39, left at Carclew, follow signs to pub*

Historic waterside inn

When you visit the Pandora, it's easy to forget you're in the 21st century – its spectacular setting on the edge of Restronguet Creek is timeless. Parts of the inn date back to the 13th century and, with its flagstone floors, low-beamed ceilings and thatched roof it's not difficult to believe that little has changed since that time. While the Pandora's wonderful setting remains unchanged, everything else in this cosy traditional inn is 21st-century comfort and quality. Publicans John Milan and Steve Bellman pay attention to detail in everything – from the food and service, to the decor and furniture, and have established the Pandora as an award-winning pub that aims to give customers an enjoyable and memorable experience whenever they visit. Alongside an excellent wine list and the local ales from St Austell Brewery, chef Tom Milby uses the freshest local and seasonal produce, including fish and shellfish bought from boats landing at

the Pandora's own pontoon. Dine on that very pontoon, at a table by the water's edge, or in one of the series of little rooms inside, perhaps on Cornish shellfish in white wine, garlic, butter, herbs and cream, followed by seared pork cutlet with boulangère potatoes, pan-fried black pudding and a quince and red wine jus. Alternatively, start with seared scallops, winter squash purée, Serrano ham crisps and dill pickled cucumber, then rare-breed 8oz rib-eye steak. Orange marmalade and chocolate chip bread and butter pudding, or steamed honey and pecan nut pudding are two ways to round off a very enjoyable meal.

Open all day all wk 10.30am-11pm
Food all wk 10.30-9.30 Av main course £12.50 ⦾ ST AUSTELL BREWERY
◗ HSD, Tribute, Proper Job & Trelawny
♻ Healey's Cornish Rattler & Pear Rattler. ⚲ 17 **Facilities** Non-diners area
♣ (Bar Outside area) ♦ Children's menu Children's portions Outside area
⨅ Parking WiFi

PAR *continued*

The Royal Inn ★★★★ INN

tel: 01726 815601 **66 Eastcliffe Rd PL24 2AJ**
email: info@royal-inn.co.uk **web:** www.royal-inn.co.uk
dir: *A3082 Par, follow brown tourist signs for 'Newquay Branch line' or railway station. Pub opposite rail station*

Welcoming pub on the Rail Ale Trail

This 19th-century inn was named after a visit by King Edward VII to a local copper mine and was originally frequented by travellers and employees of the Great Western Railway. The pub is now on the Atlantic Coast Line of the 'Rail Ale Trail', and the building is much extended, with an open-plan bar serving a variety of beers including Tintagel Arthur's Ale. The bar menu offers everything from pizzas and burgers to salads and omelettes, while the restaurant menu includes smoked fish platter; steak, mushroom and ale pie; and battered cod and chips. Fifteen bedrooms are available.

Open all day all wk 11-11 (Sun 12-10.30) **Food** Lunch all wk 12-2 Dinner all wk 6.30-9 ⊕ FREE HOUSE ◀ Sharp's Doom Bar & Special, Cotleigh Barn Owl, Tintagel Arthur's Ale, Bays Devon Dumpling Ö Healey's Cornish Rattler, Thatchers Gold. ☂ 13 **Facilities** Non-diners area ♣ (Bar Garden) ♦ Children's menu Children's portions Garden ⋒ Parking WiFi ⛟ (notice required) **Rooms** 15

| PENZANCE | Map 2 SW43 |

The Coldstreamer Inn ★★★ INN ⊛

tel: 01736 362072 **Gulval TR18 3BB**
email: info@coldstreamer-penzance.co.uk **web:** www.coldstreamer-penzance.co.uk
dir: *From Penzance take B3311 towards St Ives. In Gulval right into School Ln. Pub in village centre*

Expect the best local produce at this traditional village inn

This unassuming inn tucked away in a sleepy village close to Penzance and St Ives makes an ideal setting for the chef's simple yet accomplished regional cooking. Produce from local fishermen, farmers and growers is used to good effect in dishes such as Newlyn crab rarebit with bloody Mary dressing; or Cornish Yarg fritters with romanesco and almonds to start; a main course of Terras Farm duck breast with celeriac gratin, black kale and star anise; and yogurt pannacotta, poached rhubarb and apple curd; or sticky toffee pudding, honey and clotted cream ice cream to finish. Well kept local and guest ales, good value home-made bar snacks, a roaring fire and contemporary bedrooms complete the picture.

Open all day all wk **Food** Lunch all wk 12-2 Dinner all wk 6-9.30 (summer), 6-9 (winter) ⊕ PUNCH TAVERNS ◀ Skinner's Ginger Tosser, Bays Topsail, Guest ale. ☂ 12 **Facilities** Non-diners area ♣ (Bar Outside area) ♦ Children's menu Children's portions Outside area ⋒ Beer festival WiFi ⛟ (notice required) **Rooms** 3

Dolphin Tavern ★★★ INN

tel: 01736 364106 **Quay St TR18 4BD**
email: dolphin@tiscali.co.uk **web:** www.dolphintavern.com
dir: *From rail station follow road along harbour. Tavern on corner opposite Scilonian Ferry Terminal*

Interesting history and fish always on the menu

Sir Walter Raleigh is said to have smoked the first pipe of tobacco in England at this lovely 16th-century pub, the central part of which was once used as a courtroom by Judge Jeffreys. These days, the Dolphin serves great home-made food accompanied by a full range of St Austell beers, plus accommodation. Fresh, locally caught fish features on the daily specials board, and the menu offers a tempting selection of meat, vegetarian and children's dishes. A typical menu might feature steak and ale pie or Newlyn crab salad.

Open all day all wk Closed 25 Dec **Food** Contact pub for food times ⊕ ST AUSTELL BREWERY ◀ HSD, Cornish Best, Tribute Ö Healey's Cornish Rattler. ☂ 10 **Facilities** Non-diners area ♣ (Bar Restaurant Garden) ♦ Children's menu Children's portions Family room Garden WiFi ⛟ (notice required) **Rooms** 3

The Turks Head Inn

tel: 01736 363093 **Chapel St TR18 4AF**
email: turks@fsmail.net
dir: *Phone for detailed directions*

Historic tucked-away town pub

This popular terraced side-street local is the oldest pub in Penzance, dating from around 1233, and was the first in the country to be given the Turks Head name. Sadly, a Spanish raiding party destroyed much of the original building in the 16th century, but an old smugglers' tunnel leading directly to the harbour still exists. Wash down hearty pub food – steaks, burgers, fish pie – or perhaps seafood broth, green Thai monkfish curry or braised lamb shank, with a cracking pint of Sharp's Doom Bar, best enjoyed in the sunny flower-filled garden. Don't miss the annual beer festival.

Open all day all wk **Food** Lunch all wk 12-2.30 Dinner all wk 6-10 ⊕ PUNCH TAVERNS ◀ Sharp's Doom Bar, Turk's Head Ale Ö Westons Old Rosie. ☂ 12 **Facilities** Non-diners area ♣ (Bar Restaurant Garden) ♦ Children's menu Children's portions Family room Garden ⋒ Beer festival WiFi ⛟ (notice required)

| PERRANUTHNOE | Map 2 SW52 |

The Victoria Inn   PICK OF THE PUBS

tel: 01736 710309 **TR20 9NP**
email: enquiries@victoriainn-penzance.co.uk
dir: *Exit A394 (Penzance to Helston road), signed Perranuthnoe*

Coastal pub with new chef patron

Its history spans nine centuries, so this striking pink-washed village inn could be Cornwall's oldest public house. Decorated with seafaring memorabilia, its typically Cornish stone-walled interior attracts families strolling up from Perran Sands and walkers from the South West Coastal Path. Real ales, lager and cider – all from Cornwall – enjoy pride of place in the wood-fire-warmed, softly lit bar; there is even a Cornish wine. After making your choice, take a menu outside to the Mediterranean-style patio garden if the weather is clement. Dishes are modern British in style, again making good use of locally sourced produce. Cornish crab with aïoli, herbs, gazpacho sauce and garlic croûtons makes a tasty starter. Continue the seafood theme with roasted Cornish megrim sole, new potatoes, cherry tomatoes, courgettes, anchovies and pesto sauce. A sample dessert would be white chocolate and mascarpone mousse, with chocolate crumble, Cornish raspberries and chocolate sorbet.

Open all day all wk Closed 25 Dec **Food** Lunch Mon-Sat 12-2, Sun 12-2.30 Dinner all wk 6.30-9 Av main course £10-£15 Set menu available ⊕ FREE HOUSE ◀ Sharp's Doom Bar, St Austell Tribute, Skinner's Betty Stogs, Cornish Chough Serpentine Ö Healey's Cornish Orchards. ☂ **Facilities** Non-diners area ♣ (Bar Garden) ♦ Children's menu Children's portions Garden ⋒ Parking WiFi

---

| PHILLEIGH | Map 2 SW83 |

Roseland Inn

tel: 01872 580254 **TR2 5NB**
email: contact@roselandinn.co.uk
dir: *From Truro take A39 towards Falmouth. Left onto B3289 towards St Mawes. Left at sharp right bend for Philleigh*

Traditional Cornish pub with welcoming, cosy interior

Owner Phil Heslip and chef Brian Green take pride in the quality of the home-prepared modern British cooking at this highly appealing, rural 16th-century inn.

The character of the interior owes much to the low-beamed ceilings, brassware, paintings and prints. Phil brews his ornithologically themed Cornish Shag, Chough to Bits and High-as-a-Kite beers on site. So, in winter cosy up to the fire for a drink or a meal of perhaps slow-roasted shoulder of Cornish lamb, or oven-baked hake with pan-fried new potatoes; in warmer weather head outside to the picnic tables. Just to the west is the famous King Harry Ferry over the River Fal.

Open all wk 11-3 6-11.30 (summer all day) **Food** Lunch all wk 12-2.30 Dinner all wk 6-9 Av main course £11.95 ⊕ PUNCH TAVERNS ◧ Skinner's Betty Stogs, Roseland Cornish Shag, High-as-a-Kite & Chough to Bits, Sharp's Doom Bar Ö Westons Stowford Press. **Facilities** Non-diners area ❧ (Bar Garden) ⅰ Children's menu Children's portions Garden ⋈ Beer festival Parking WiFi ◉ (notice required)

POLKERRIS   Map 2 SX05

The Rashleigh Inn

tel: 01726 813991 **PL24 2TL**
email: jonspode@aol.com
dir: From A3082 between Fowey & Par follow Polkerris signs

Right on the beach

Once a coastguard station, this 300-year-old pub at the end of a no-through road to Polkerris Beach faces west, so watching the sun set over St Austell Bay is a delight. In the bar there's a good selection of real ales from the South West, real cider, local organic soft drinks and a water bowl and Bonio biscuits for visiting dogs. Good, locally sourced food majors on the county's fresh seafood, with river mussels from Fowey, Looe scallops, and local crab. For meat lovers, a prime Cornish sirloin or the home-made steak and ale pie will hit the spot.

Open all day all wk **Food** Lunch all wk 12-3, snacks 3-5 Dinner all wk 6-9 Av main course £9.95 ⊕ FREE HOUSE ◧ Timothy Taylor Landlord, Skinner's Betty Stogs, St Austell HSD, Otter Bitter, Black Sheep Best Bitter, Bath Ales Gem, Guest ales Ö Westons Stowford Press, Addlestones. ▾ 11 **Facilities** Non-diners area ❧ (Bar Garden) ⅰ Children's menu Children's portions Garden ⋈ Parking WiFi

PORT GAVERNE   Map 2 SX08

Port Gaverne Hotel   **PICK OF THE PUBS**

tel: 01208 880244 **PL29 3SQ**
email: eat@portgavernehotel.co.uk
dir: Signed from B3314, S of Delabole via B3267, E of Port Isaac

The freshest local fish and seafood

Pretty Port Gaverne has two main attractions: the secluded cove where women once loaded sea-bound ketches with slate from Delabole's great quarry, and this delightful 17th-century inn, now in new hands. With the slate industry long dead, the inn today reaps the reward of being right on the South West Coastal Path, most of whose walkers are ready for a thirst-quenching Cornish real ale or cider, or refreshing glass of wine, in the slate-floored (what else?), low-beamed bar or small beer garden. Locally supplied produce includes plenty of fresh fish, such as mackerel from Jim's boat, 50 yards from the front door; Porthilly mussels; and Port Isaac lobster thermidor. Not everything is from the Atlantic, of course, so look out for Josper-oven-grilled Aberdeen Angus rump steak; rare-breed belly pork with salt-baked celeriac; and autumn mushroom, roast root and shiitake crumb risotto. Finish with a Cornish ice cream or home-made pudding.

Open all day all wk **Food** Lunch all wk 12-2.30 Dinner all wk 6-9 Restaurant menu available ⊕ FREE HOUSE ◧ St Austell Tribute & Proper Job, Timothy Taylor Landlord, Skinner's Betty Stogs. ▾ 16 **Facilities** Non-diners area ❧ (Bar Garden) ⅰ Children's menu Children's portions Garden ⋈ Parking WiFi ◉

PORTHLEVEN   Map 2 SW62

The Ship Inn

tel: 01326 564204 **TR13 9JS**
dir: From Helston follow signs to Porthleven (B3304), 2.5m. On entering village continue to harbour. Follow road to other side of harbour. 1st left to inn

Unspoilt pub in an unspoilt fishing port

Dating from the 17th century, this smugglers' inn is actually built into the cliffs, and is approached by a flight of stone steps. During the winter, a log fire warms the interior, while the flames of a second flicker in the separate Smithy party room. Expect a good selection of locally caught fish and seafood, such as pan-fried hake with salsa verde; or the smoked fish platter, all smoked in Cornwall. Meat eaters might choose steak and ale pie, or a hearty rump steak. August cider festival.

Open all day all wk 11am-11.30pm **Food** Lunch all wk 12-2.30 Dinner all wk 6.30-9 ⊕ FREE HOUSE ◧ Sharp's Doom Bar & Own, Skinner's Porthleven, Rebel Penryn Pale Ale Ö Cornish Orchards. ▾ 8 **Facilities** Non-diners area ❧ (Bar Restaurant Garden) ⅰ Children's portions Family room Garden ⋈ Cider festival WiFi

PORT ISAAC   Map 2 SW98

The Slipway

tel: 01208 880264 **Harbour Front PL29 3RH**
email: slipway@portisaachotel.com
dir: From A39 take B3314 signed Port Isaac. Through Delabole & Pendoggett, right onto B3267. 2m to Port Isaac, pass Co-op on right, 100mtrs into Back Hill (one way) to harbour (NB no parking by pub; car park at top of village)

Harbourside pub noted for fish and seafood

This 16th-century, one-time ship's chandlery could hardly be closer to Port Isaac's tiny harbour, so no wonder it has a reputation for seriously good fresh fish and seafood. Cornish Orchards cider, and real ales from Tintagel and Sharp's breweries are on handpump in the bar, while in the heavy-beamed, galleried restaurant locally sourced dishes include Porthilly mussels; Doom Bar battered fish and chips; roast belly pork; and slow-braised ox cheek. On summer evenings the covered terrace overlooking the harbour is the perfect place to dine and enjoy music from the local bands.

Open all day all wk Closed 25 Dec **Food** Lunch all wk 12-2.30 Dinner all wk 6.30-8.30 (9 summer) Restaurant menu available all wk ⊕ FREE HOUSE ◧ Tintagel Harbour Special, Sharp's Doom Bar Ö Cornish Orchards. **Facilities** Non-diners area ❧ (Bar Outside area) ⅰ Children's menu Children's portions Outside area ⋈ WiFi

PORTREATH   Map 2 SW64

Basset Arms

tel: 01209 842077 **Tregea Ter TR16 4NG**
email: bassettarms@btconnect.com
dir: From Redruth take B3300 to Portreath. Pub on left near seafront

Local seafood a speciality

Built as a pub to serve harbour workers, at one time this early 19th-century Cornish stone cottage served as a mortuary for ill-fated seafarers, so there are plenty of ghost stories. Tin-mining and shipwreck photographs adorn the low-beamed interior of the bar where you can wash down a meal with a pint of Skinner's real ale. The menu makes the most of local seafood, such as seafood stew; and home-made fish pie, but also provides a wide selection of alternatives, including beef lasagne; cottage pie; and vegetable pasta bake.

Open all day all wk 11-11 (Fri-Sat 11am-mdnt Sun 11-10.30) **Food** Lunch all wk 12-2, summer 12-3 Dinner all wk 6-9, summer 5-9 ⊕ FREE HOUSE ◧ Sharp's Doom Bar, Skinner's, Dartmoor Legend, St Austell Tribute Ö Thatchers Gold. **Facilities** Non-diners area ❧ (Bar Outside area) ⅰ Children's menu Children's portions Play area Outside area ⋈ Parking WiFi ◉ (notice required)

RUAN LANIHORNE   Map 2 SW84

The Kings Head

tel: 01872 501263 **TR2 5NX**
email: contact@kings-head-roseland.co.uk
dir: *3m from Tregony Bridge on A3078*

Country pub with delightful summer garden

This traditional country pub set deep in the Roseland countryside has a warm and welcoming atmosphere. Roaring winter fires, beamed ceilings and mulled wine contrast with summer days relaxing on the terrace with a jug of Pimm's, a pint of Betty Stogs or Cornish Orchards cider. Whatever the time of year, the chef responds with seasonal dishes using the best local produce, including duo of local sausages with red onion and marmalade mash to chicken breast stuffed with prunes and leeks and wrapped in bacon. Look out for the signature dish, too – Ruan duck three ways: confit leg, pan-fried breast and drakes pudding.

Open 12-2.30 6-11 Closed Sun eve, Mon (Oct-Etr) **Food** Contact pub for food times ⊕ FREE HOUSE ◀ Skinner's Betty Stogs, Keltek Even Keel, Sharp's Doom Bar ⊙ Cornish Orchards. ♀ 9 **Facilities** Non-diners area ♦ Children's portions Garden Outside area ⊫ Parking

ST AGNES   Map 3 SW75

Driftwood Spars ★★★★ GA   PICK OF THE PUBS

tel: 01872 552428 **Trevaunance Cove TR5 0RT**
email: info@driftwoodspars.co.uk **web:** www.driftwoodspars.co.uk
dir: *A30 onto B3285, through St Agnes, down steep hill, left at Peterville Inn, follow Trevaunance Cove sign*

Great 16th-century find near coastal path

"I can see the sea" will doubtless be heard from any children in the car as you approach this pub, just before St Agnes' relatively secret 'best' beach and redundant harbour. During its time, the whitewashed, three-storey building fulfilled many functions, not least as a smugglers' rendezvous – secret tunnel and all. The roof timbers are spars from a wreck, while nautical artefacts recall its time as a chandlery. Assorted furnishings, open fires and dressed stone walls provide additional character in the warren of rooms, including the summer-only, ocean-facing Fitty Pysk seafood bistro. Up to six hand-pulled real ales, including those from the on-site microbrewery, are served in the three fire-warmed bars, as are Rattler Cornish cider and a few English wines. A seasonal bar menu features leek and Cornish Yarg vegetarian sausages; pan-roast hake fillet; and lamb three ways. Beer festivals are in mid March and early May.

Open all day all wk 11-11 (Fri-Sat 11am-1am 25 Dec 11am-2pm) **Food** Lunch all wk 12-2.30 Dinner all wk 6-9.30 (winter 6.30-8.30) Av main course £12 Restaurant menu available Tue-Sat (peak season) ⊕ FREE HOUSE ◀ Driftwood Spars, Sharp's Doom Bar, Guest ales ⊙ Healey's Cornish Rattler, Thatchers. ♀ 11 **Facilities** Non-diners area ♣ (Bar Garden Outside area) ♦ Children's menu

Children's portions Garden Outside area ⊫ Beer festival Parking WiFi ⛟ (notice required) **Rooms** 15

ST EWE   Map 2 SW94

The Crown Inn

tel: 01726 843322 **PL26 6EY**
email: thecrownstewe@hotmail.co.uk
dir: *From St Austell take B3273. At Tregiskey x-rds turn right. St Ewe signed on right*

Local ales and home-cooking in this pretty village inn

Only a mile away from the famous 'Lost Gardens of Heligan', this attractive 16th-century village inn is the ideal place to refuel, whether it's by the fire in the traditional bar or in the peaceful flower-festooned garden in summer. Quaff a pint of Proper Job ale and tuck into the home-cooked food, perhaps traditional prawn cocktail followed by slow-roasted belly pork with apple sauce and cider gravy; or home-made curry of the day. Lunchtime sandwiches, jacket potatoes and smaller portions of main dishes are also available.

Open all wk 12-3 5.30-close **Food** Lunch all wk 12-2 Dinner Mon-Sat 5.30-9 ⊕ ST AUSTELL BREWERY ◀ Tribute, Cornish Best & Proper Job ⊙ Healey's Cornish Rattler. **Facilities** Non-diners area ♣ (Bar Garden) ♦ Children's menu Children's portions Play area Family room Garden ⊫ Parking WiFi ⛟

ST IVES   Map 2 SW54

The Queens ★★ HL ◉

tel: 01736 796468 **2 High St TR26 1RR**
email: info@queenshotelstives.com **web:** www.queenshotelstives.com
dir: *Phone for detailed directions*

Winning combination of fine food and stylish accommodation

There's an easy-going mix of chic and contemporary design with a nod to times past in this thriving hostelry at the heart of the old town. It's worth the stroll from the harbour or the resort's beaches to discover this solid granite-built, late-Georgian building, where local art works vie for attention with local cider, Cornish beers and a great menu inspired by the wealth of the county's larder. A sample lunch menu includes tiger prawn, saffron, sping onion and parmesan risotto; venison, poached egg and herb salad; and a selection of sandwiches. A chalkboard holds much additional promise. Some of the stylish bedrooms have views to Carbis Bay.

Open all day all wk **Food** Lunch Mon-Sat 12-2.30, Sun 12-4 Dinner Mon-Sat 6.30-9.30 Av main course £10 ⊕ ST AUSTELL BREWERY ◀ Tribute, HSD ⊙ Healey's Cornish Rattler. ♀ 16 **Facilities** Non-diners area ♣ (Bar Restaurant) ♦ Children's menu Children's portions WiFi ⛟ (notice required) **Rooms** 10

The Sloop Inn ★★★ INN

tel: 01736 796584 **The Wharf TR26 1LP**
email: sloopinn@btinternet.com **web:** www.sloop-inn.co.uk
dir: *On St Ives harbour by middle slipway*

Famous St Ives inn by picturesque harbour

A trip to St Ives wouldn't be complete without visiting this 700-year-old pub perched right on the harbourside. Slate floors, beamed ceilings and nautical artefacts dress some of the several bars and dining areas, whilst the cobbled forecourt is an unbeatable spot for people- and harbour-watching, preferably with a pint of local Doom Bar. The menu majors on local seafood, from line-caught St Ives Bay mackerel and fries to home-made Newlyn cod, smoked haddock and smoked bacon fishcakes. Most of the comfortably appointed bedrooms overlook the pretty bay.

Open all day all wk **Food** Lunch all wk 12-3 Dinner all wk 5-10 Av main course £9 Restaurant menu available all wk ⊕ ENTERPRISE INNS ◀ Sharp's Doom Bar ⊙ Thatchers Gold. ♀ 10 **Facilities** Non-diners area ♣ (Bar Outside area) ♦ Outside area ⊫ WiFi ⛟ (notice required) **Rooms** 22

The Watermill

tel: 01736 757912 **Lelant Downs, Hayle TR27 6LQ**
email: watermill@btconnect.com
dir: *Exit A30 at junct for St Ives/A3074, turn left at 2nd mini rdbt*

Converted mill with food to suit everyone

Set in extensive gardens on the old St Ives coach road, with glorious valley views towards Trencrom Hill, The Watermill is a cosy, family-friendly pub and restaurant created in the 18th-century Lelant Mill. The old mill machinery is still in place and the iron waterwheel continues to turn, gravity fed by the mill stream. Downstairs is the old beamed bar and wood-burning stove, while upstairs in the open-beamed mill loft is the atmospheric restaurant where steaks and fish (sea bass, sardines and mackerel perhaps) are specialities. There are beer festivals in June and November with live music all weekend.

Open all day all wk 12-11 **Food** Lunch all wk 12-2.30 Dinner all wk 6-9 ⊕ FREE HOUSE ◀ Sharp's Doom Bar, Skinner's Betty Stogs, Guest ales Ò Healey's Cornish Rattler. **Facilities** Non-diners area ❤ (Bar Garden) ♦♦ Children's menu Play area Garden ⊫ Beer festival Parking WiFi ▭

◗ **ST KEW** Map 2 SX07

St Kew Inn

tel: 01208 841259 **Churchtown PL30 3HB**
email: stkewinn@btconnect.com
dir: *From Wadebridge N on A39. Left to St Kew*

A chocolate-box village pub with plenty of local seafood

Visit this 15th-century, stone-built pub in summer and you will be rewarded with flower tubs and creepers enhancing its pretty façade, whilst traditional features inside include a huge open fire. Cornish St Austell beers and Rattler cider are the prime refreshments, while menus proffer carefully sourced British dishes, often featuring local fish and seafood. Choose between four eating areas – five if you include the garden – when ordering your lunchtime snack. Alternatively, in the evening try piri piri marinated goats' cheese and tomato salsa, follow with pheasant, bacon and mushroom pie, and finish with cranberry brownie and clotted cream.

Open all wk 11-3 5.30-11 (summer all day) **Food** Lunch all wk 12-2, summer all day Dinner all wk 6-9, summer all day Av main course £14 Set menu available ⊕ ST AUSTELL BREWERY ◀ Tribute, HSD, Proper Job Ò Healey's Cornish Rattler. **Facilities** Non-diners area ❤ (Bar Garden) ♦♦ Children's menu Children's portions Family room Garden ⊫ Parking

---

◗ **ST MAWES** Map 2 SW83

The Victory Inn **PICK OF THE PUBS**

tel: 01326 270324 **Victory Hill TR2 5DQ**
email: contact@victory-inn.co.uk
dir: *A3078 to St Mawes. Pub adjacent to harbour*

Seafood takes top billing on the menus

Named after Nelson's flagship, this friendly fishermen's local near the harbour adopts a modern approach to its daily lunch and dinner menus. You may eat downstairs in the traditional bar, or in the modern and stylish first-floor Seaview Restaurant (white walls, white linen and wicker chairs), with a terrace that looks across the town's rooftops to the harbour and the River Fal. High on the list of ingredients is fresh seafood – all from Cornish waters – the choice changing daily to include crab risotto, fisherman's pie, and beer-battered cod and hand-cut chips, with chicken breast cordon bleu, lamb shank Provençale, and curry or casserole of the day among the other favourites. Wines are all carefully chosen and excellent in quality, as are the real ales from Cornwall's own Roseland, Sharp's and Skinner's breweries. There is outside seating with views over the harbour. Booking for meals is definitely advisable in the summer.

Open all day all wk 11-3 6-11 (summer all day) **Food** Lunch all wk 12-2.30 Dinner all wk 6-9 ⊕ PUNCH TAVERNS ◀ Skinner's Betty Stogs, Sharp's Doom Bar, Roseland Cornish Shag Ò Westons Stowford Press. **Facilities** Non-diners area ❤ (Bar Garden) ♦♦ Children's menu Children's portions Garden ⊫ WiFi ▭

◗ **ST MAWGAN** Map 2 SW86

The Falcon Inn ★★★★ INN **PICK OF THE PUBS**

See Pick of the Pubs on page 96

◗ **ST MERRYN** Map 2 SW87

The Cornish Arms **PICK OF THE PUBS**

tel: 01841 532700 **Churchtown PL28 8ND**
email: reservations@rickstein.com
dir: *From Padstow follow signs for St Merryn, up hill, pub on right*

Simple British pub food the Rick Stein way

St Merryn, just outside Padstow, is home to this ancient village pub, part of the Stein portfolio. Situated across the road from the parish church and overlooking a peaceful valley, the pub has remained very much the village boozer certainly to the happiness of the locals. The pub oozes character, with slate floors, beams and roaring log fires, and they've kept the food offering equally traditional. The chalkboard lists simple pub classics prepared from fresh produce: ham, egg and chips, rump steak, or sausage and mash, followed perhaps by apple and blackberry pie or sticky toffee pudding. Wash it down with a glass of Chalky's Bark, named after the scene-stealing Jack Russell that once appeared in his owner's TV programmes. Check with the pub for details of themed nights and the beer and mussels festival in March.

Open all day all wk 11.30-11 **Food** Lunch all wk 12-2.30 Dinner all wk 6-8.30 Av main course £7.80 Set menu available ⊕ ST AUSTELL BREWERY ◀ Tribute, Proper Job, Trelawny, Chalky's Bite, Chalky's Bark Ò Healey's Cornish Rattler. ▾ 17 **Facilities** Non-diners area ❤ (Bar Restaurant Garden) ♦♦ Children's menu Children's portions Garden ⊫ Beer festival Parking WiFi ▭

PICK OF THE PUBS

The Falcon Inn ★★★★ INN

ST MAWGAN   Map 2 SW86

tel: 01637 860225
TR8 4EP
email: thefalconinnstmawgan
@gmail.com
web: www.thefalconinnstmawgan.co.uk
dir: *From A30 (8m W of Bodmin) follow signs to Newquay Airport. Turn right 200mtrs before airport terminal into St Mawgan, pub at bottom of hill*

Traditional Cornish village inn

This wisteria-clad, stone-built inn situated in the Vale of Lanherne is just four miles from Newquay. It can trace its ancestry back as far as 1758, but is thought to be even older. By 1813 the pub had been renamed more than once, and in about 1880 it changed again to The Falcon Inn, an allusion to the nearby estate's coat of arms. Throughout much of the 20th century the inn was run by members of the Fry family; the present innkeepers are David Carbis and Sarah Lawrence. The Falcon's interior is cosy and relaxed, with flagstone floors and log fires in winter; there's a large attractive garden, magnificent magnolia tree and cobbled courtyard for alfresco summer dining. An ever-changing selection of predominantly West Country real ales is augmented by rotating real ciders, and a dozen wines are served by the glass. Lunchtime brings snacks like Cornish pasty and breaded scampi, plus an appetising range of sandwiches.

There's also a good choice of hot dishes, all home made, such as soup of the day, pâté, pie, fish and curry every day. The evening menu is served in the more formal restaurant; starters could be trio of pâtés and terrines with piccalilli; then main courses include 'Bubble and Smoke' — roasted smoked haddock, with wok-fried bubble-and-squeak, poached egg and pea shoots; chandra malai kofta — chickpea, courgette and almond kofta with lentil and coconut sauce; osso bucco with saffron risotto and gremolata. Three comfortable, individually furnished en suite bedrooms are also available, and events like charity quiz nights run throughout the year. Contact the pub for details of the beer and cider festival.

Open all wk 11-3 6-11 (Jul-Aug all day) Closed 25 Dec (open 12-2) **Food** Lunch all wk 12-2 Dinner all wk 6-9 ⌾ FREE HOUSE ◀ Rotating Real ales ♻ Rotating Real ciders. ♟ 12 **Facilities** Non-diners area ☺ (Bar Garden) ⅙ Children's menu Children's portions Garden ⋈ Beer festival Cider festival Parking WiFi ⊟ **Rooms** 3

ST TUDY
Map 2 SX07

St Tudy Inn

tel: 01208 850656 **PL30 3NN**
email: hello@harbourkitchen.com
dir: *Follow St Tudy signs from A39 between Camelford & Wadebridge. Pub in village centre*

Fresh pub, fresh management, fresh cooking

Emily Scott, one of Cornwall's most admired female chefs, took over this much-loved village pub in time for Christmas 2014. Previously called the Cornish Arms and completely refurbished five years ago, the building's exterior stonework and interior warm terracotta decor create a welcoming ambience. Emily's short and sweet menus with no-nonsense pricing indicate treats in store: snacks such as Welsh rarebit; starters like celeriac, fennel and orange soup; a main course of sea bream with herb dressing, new potatoes and watercress; and puddings such as flourless chocolate cake with crème Anglaise are typical. Doom Bar and Sharp's Orchard cider are the bar's staples.

Open 12-3 6-12 Closed Sun eve & Mon **Food** Lunch Tue-Sun 12-2.30 Dinner Tue-Sat 6.30-9 Av main course £15 ⊕ FREE HOUSE ◀ Sharp's Doom Bar ♂ Sharp's Orchard. ♚ 10 **Facilities** Non-diners area ♣ (Bar Outside area) ♦♦ Children's portions Outside area ⌐ Parking WiFi

SALTASH
Map 3 SX45

The Crooked Inn ★★★★ INN

tel: 01752 848177 **Stoketon Cottage, Trematon PL12 4RZ**
email: info@crooked-inn.co.uk **web:** www.crooked-inn.co.uk
dir: *Phone for detailed directions*

Family-run inn with good food and great children's facilities

Overlooking the lush Lyher Valley and run by the same family for more than 25 years, this delightful inn once housed staff from Stoketon Manor, whose ruins lie on the other side of the courtyard. It is set in 10 acres of lawns and woodland, yet is only 15 minutes from Plymouth. There is an extensive menu including evening specials with plenty of fresh fish and vegetarian dishes. The children's playground has friendly animals, swings, slides and a treehouse. The spacious bedrooms are individually designed.

Open all day all wk 11-11 (Sun 12-10.30) Closed 25 Dec **Food** Lunch all wk 11-2.30 Dinner all wk 6-9.30 Av main course £9.95 ⊕ FREE HOUSE ◀ St Austell HSD, Dartmoor Jail Ale, Guest ales ♂ Thatchers Gold, Cornish Orchards. ♚ 9 **Facilities** Non-diners area ♣ (All areas) ♦♦ Children's menu Children's portions Play area Garden Outside area ⌐ Parking WiFi ⇔ **Rooms** 15

ISLES OF SCILLY

See Tresco

TORPOINT
Map 3 SX45

Edgcumbe Arms
PICK OF THE PUBS

tel: 01752 822294 **Cremyll PL10 1HX**
dir: *Phone for detailed directions*

A 15th-century pub with glorious views over the Tamar estuary

Close to the foot ferry from Plymouth, this inn next to Mount Edgcumbe Country Park offers fabulous views from its bow window seats and waterside terrace, which take in Drakes Island, the Royal William Yard and the marina. Real ales from St Austell like Tribute, plus Healey's Cornish Rattler cider, and quality home-cooked food are served in a series of rooms, which are full of character with American oak panelling and flagstone floors. The same extensive menu is offered throughout and dishes are a mixture of international and traditional British pub favourites: garlicky Cornish sardines on toasted ciabatta or shredded duck pancakes with hoi-sin sauce to start, followed by toad-in-the-hole; fish pie; or chilli braised beef. Vegetarian

options might include Mediterranean vegetable and nut strudel. Sandwiches, loaded potato skins and platters are also available. The inn has a courtyard garden.

Open all day 11-11 Closed Jan-Feb Mon & Tue eve **Food** Lunch all wk 12-5 Dinner all wk 12-9 ⊕ ST AUSTELL BREWERY ◀ Tribute, Proper Job, Trelawny ♂ Healey's Cornish Rattler. ♚ 10 **Facilities** Non-diners area ♣ (Bar Garden) ♦♦ Children's menu Children's portions Garden ⌐ Parking WiFi ⇔ (notice required)

TREBARWITH
Map 2 SX08

The Mill House Inn
PICK OF THE PUBS

tel: 01840 770200 **PL34 0HD**
email: management@themillhouseinn.co.uk **web:** www.themillhouseinn.co.uk
dir: *From Tintagel take B3263 S, right after Trewarmett to Trebarwith Strand. Pub 0.5m on right*

Family-friendly inn with good food and live entertainment

Set in seven acres of woodland on the north Cornish coast, close to Tintagel Castle, the Mill House is half a mile from the surfing beach at Trebarwith Strand, one of the finest in Cornwall. The log fires in this atmospheric stone building – a charming former corn mill dating from 1760 – warm the residents' lounge and slate-floored bar, where wooden tables and chapel chairs help create a relaxed, family-friendly feel. Locally brewed real ales are supplied by Sharp's and Tintagel breweries, and the ciders are Cornish Orchards and Healey's Cornish Rattler. Lunches, evening drinks and barbecues are particularly enjoyable out on the attractive terraces, while a more intimate dinner in the Millstream Restaurant might involve Porthilly mussels in tarragon, white wine and coconut cream reduction, followed by Battenburg of pork tenderloin, hog's pudding and chorizo wrapped in bacon; or baked fillet of sea bass in lemon butter, grilled courgette, beetroot with crab and butterbean lobster bisque. Regular live entertainment events feature local musicians and comedians.

Open all day all wk 11-11 (Fri-Sat 11am-mdnt Sun 12-10.30) **Food** Lunch Mon-Sat 12-2.30, Sun 12-3 Dinner all wk 6.30-8.30 Restaurant menu available all wk evening ⊕ FREE HOUSE ◀ Sharp's Doom Bar, Tintagel Cornwall's Pride, Castle Gold & Arthur's Ale ♂ Cornish Orchards, Healey's Cornish Rattler. **Facilities** Non-diners area ♣ (Bar Garden) ♦♦ Children's menu Children's portions Play area Family room Garden ⌐ Parking WiFi ⇔ (notice required)

The Port William

tel: 01840 770230 **Trebarwith Strand PL34 0HB**
email: portwilliam@staustellbrewery.co.uk
dir: *From A39 onto B3314 signed Tintagel. Right onto B3263, follow Trebarwith Strand signs, then brown Port William signs*

Stunning location by the sea

Occupying one of the best locations in Cornwall, this former harbourmaster's house lies directly on the coastal path, 50 yards from the sea, which means the views of the Trebarwith Strand are amazing. There is an entrance to a smugglers' tunnel at

continued

TREBARWITH *continued*

the rear of the ladies' toilet! Obviously there's quite an emphasis on fresh fish, but there's no shortage of other options. A typical menu starts with pulled pork with smoky barbecue sauce and toasted crouton, or sautéed Cornish mushrooms with peppercorn sauce and crumbled blue cheese; then moves on to mains such as gourmet burger with chunky chips; ocean pie; local mussels or vegetable red Thai curry. If you've room, check the specials board for the desserts of the day.

Open all day all wk 10am-11pm (Sun 10am-10.30pm) **Food** Lunch all wk 12-9 Dinner all wk 12-9 ⊕ ST AUSTELL BREWERY ◀ Tribute, Proper Job & Trelawny, Guest ales ♂ Healey's Cornish Rattler. ♟ 8 **Facilities** Non-diners area ♣ (Bar Restaurant Garden) ♦♦ Children's menu Children's portions Family room Garden ⊼ Parking WiFi

TREBURLEY — Map 3 SX37

The Springer Spaniel — PICK OF THE PUBS

tel: 01579 370424 **PL15 9NS**
email: enquiries@thespringerspaniel.org.uk
dir: *On A388 halfway between Launceston & Callington*

Popular gastro-pub in Cornish village setting

Set above the valley of the River Inny in the pretty hamlet of Treburley, a few miles south of Launceston. This 18th-century pub is owned and run by Anton Piotrowski, a former winner of BBC's *MasterChef The Professionals*. Anton heads a close-knit team dedicated to serving guests with top-notch ales, ciders and food. A tree-shaded garden to the rear is a pleasant place to relax with a pint of Jail Ale from the increasingly popular Dartmoor Brewery, or a bottle of Healey's Cornish Rattler cider. Choosing from the menu of pub classics and specials may be a struggle. A robust start could be game terrine with pickles and toast; or a pheasant and bacon Scotch egg with home-made brown sauce. Follow perhaps with roast guinea fowl, pearl barley and green beans. Dessert selections may include chocolate and orange bread and butter pudding; and lemon curd cheesecake.

Open all day Closed 25-26 Dec, Mon **Food** Lunch all day Dinner all day Restaurant menu available Tue-Sun ⊕ FREE HOUSE ◀ St Austell Tribute & Proper Job, Dartmoor Jail Ale ♂ Thatchers, Cornish Orchards, Healey's Cornish Rattler.
Facilities Non-diners area ♣ (Bar Garden) ♦♦ Children's portions Garden ⊼ Parking WiFi ⛌ (notice required)

TREGADILLETT — Map 3 SX28

Eliot Arms

tel: 01566 772051 **PL15 7EU**
email: humechris@hotmail.co.uk
dir: *From Launceston take A30 towards Bodmin. Then follow brown signs to Tregadillett*

Creeper-covered inn with lots of nostalgia

The extraordinary decor in this charming creeper-clad coaching inn, dating back to 1625, includes Masonic regalia, horse brasses and grandfather clocks. It was believed to have been a Masonic lodge for Napoleonic prisoners, and even has its own friendly ghost. Customers can enjoy real fires in winter and lovely hanging baskets in summer. Food, based on locally sourced meat and fresh fish and shellfish caught off the Cornish coast, is served in the bar or bright and airy restaurant. Expect home-made soups, pie and curry of the day; steak and chips; chargrills; and home-made vegetarian dishes.

Open all day all wk 11.30-11 (Fri-Sat 11.30am-mdnt Sun 12-10.30) **Food** Lunch Mon-Fri 12-2, Sat-Sun 12-9 Dinner Mon-Fri 6-9, Sat-Sun12-9 ⊕ FREE HOUSE ◀ St Austell Tribute, Wadworth 6X, Wychwood Hobgoblin ♂ Symonds. ♟ 9 **Facilities** Non-diners area ♣ (Bar Outside area) ♦♦ Children's menu Children's portions Family room Outside area Parking WiFi ⛌ (notice required)

TRESCO (ISLES OF SCILLY) — Map 2 SV81

The New Inn ★★★★ INN ⊛ — PICK OF THE PUBS

tel: 01720 422849 **New Grimsby TR24 0QQ**
email: newinn@tresco.co.uk **web:** www.tresco.co.uk
dir: *By New Grimsby Quay*

Sub-tropical splendour and local bounty at the edge of Britain

Just a few steps away from this old inn is the quay at New Grimsby and the first of a string of white-sand beaches that garland this sub-tropical island out in the Atlantic. The new hands at the tiller here are steering the inn into a secure future, with subtle changes made to improve the overall ambience whilst retaining the terrific character that is the pub's signature – the bar is partly created from salvage from local wrecks giving a rustic maritime feel. Scilly-brewed beers populate some of the handpulls on the bar, whilst Scillonian provender forms the backbone of the well-balanced menu. Clock a fishing boat from your breakfast table and by lunchtime you could be ensconced on the sunny terrace, eating grilled megrim sole caught by that fisherman. Island beef is a mainstay, whilst shellfish dishes are legion. Three beer and cider festivals are held over the summer.

Open all day all wk (Apr-Oct) phone for winter opening **Food** Lunch all wk 12-2 Dinner all wk 6.30-9 Av main course £20 ⊕ FREE HOUSE ◀ Skinner's Betty Stogs, Ales of Scilly Scuppered & Firebrand, St Austell Tribute, Harbour Pale Ale No.5 ♂ Healey's Cornish Rattler, Cornish Gold & Pear Rattler. ♟ 14 **Facilities** Non-diners area ♦♦ Children's menu Children's portions Garden ⊼ Beer festival Cider festival WiFi **Rooms** 16

TRURO — Map 2 SW84

Old Ale House

tel: 01872 271122 **7 Quay St TR1 2HD**
email: jamie@oahtruro.com
dir: *In town centre*

Architecturally distinctive city-centre pub

Close to the old riverside quays, this bare-boarded, heavily-beamed pub is Skinner's Brewery tap, so a reliable pint is a cert; guest ales and Truro-made Apple Slayer and Lyonesse real ciders are first-rate too. A collaboration between Skinner's and Devon's River Cottage trained chefs lies behind the new upstairs restaurant, that showcases Cornwall's best produce. Menus offer Cornish Blue cheese croquettes with honey and mustard dipping sauce; Betty Stogs real-ale-battered fish platter; pulled pork with melted Cornish Yarg and potato wedges; and hot, crispy mackerel bap with pickled cucumber and horseradish crème fraîche. The pub holds a beer and cider festival every spring.

Open all day all wk 11-11 (Fri-Sat 11am-1am Sun 12-10.30) Closed 25-26 Dec, 1 Jan **Food** Lunch all wk 12-2.30 Dinner 5-9 Av main course £8.95 Restaurant menu available all wk ⊕ ENTERPRISE INNS ◀ Skinner's, Guest ales ♂ Cornwall Cider Co Apple Slayer & Lyonesse. ♟ 9 **Facilities** Non-diners area ♣ (Bar) ♦♦ Children's menu Beer festival Cider festival WiFi ⛌ (notice required)

The Wig & Pen

tel: 01872 273028 **Frances St TR1 3DP**
email: wigandpentruro@hotmail.com
dir: *In city centre near Law Courts*

Friendly city centre pub where everything is made in-house

This pub has both an L-shaped ground-floor bar and Quills restaurant in the basement which opens in the evenings. Food is freshly made in-house, and that even includes the crisps and the pork scratchings that go with HSD and Tribute beers. Choose a casual meal in the bar which serves modern pub classics such as beer battered fish and chips and gourmet burgers, or venture downstairs to Quills for a more fine dining experience.

Open all day all wk Closed 26 Dec, 1 Jan **Food** Lunch Mon-Sat 12-2.30, Sun 12-3 Dinner Mon Sat 6-9 ⊕ ST AUSTELL BREWERY ◀ Tribute, HSD, Cornish Best Ŏ Healey's Cornish Rattler & Pear Rattler. ♀ 16 **Facilities** Non-diners area ✿ (Bar Garden) ♦♦ Children's portions Garden ⋒ 🚍 (notice required)

| **VERYAN** | Map 2 SW93 |

The New Inn

tel: 01872 501362 **TR2 5QA**
email: info@newinn-veryan.co.uk
dir: From St Austell take A390 towards Truro, in 2m left to Tregony. Through Tregony, follow signs to Veryan

Traditional home cooking and good ales

This unspoiled pub started life as a pair of cottages in the 16th century. In the centre of a pretty village on the Roseland Peninsula, The New Inn has open fires, a beamed ceiling, a single bar serving St Austell ales and a warm, welcoming atmosphere. Sunday lunch is a speciality; other choices during the week might include traditional lasagne; creamy tarragon chicken; mushroom Stroganoff; steak and ale pie; and vegetable chilli. Traditional puddings take in warm chocolate fudge cake; zingy lemon cheesecake; and sticky toffee pudding – some served with Cornish clotted cream.

Open all day all wk 12-3 5.30-11 (Sun 7-11) Closed 25 Dec **Food** Lunch all wk 12-2 Dinner Mon-Sat 6.30-9, Sun 7-9 Set menu available ⊕ ST AUSTELL BREWERY ◀ Tribute, Proper Job, Dartmoor Ŏ Healey's Cornish Rattler. ♀ **Facilities** Non-diners area ✿ (Bar Garden) ♦♦ Children's menu Children's portions Garden ⋒ WiFi 🚍 (notice required)

| **WADEBRIDGE** | Map 2 SW97 |

The Quarryman Inn

tel: 01208 816444 **Edmonton PL27 7JA**
email: thequarryman@live.co.uk
dir: From A39 (W of Wadebridge) follow Edmonton sign (opposite Royal Cornwall Showground)

Tucked away in the Cornish countryside

Close to the famous Camel Trail, this family-owned free house was originally a group of 18th-century slate workers' cottages, built around a courtyard. A bow window featuring a stained-glass quarryman adds character to this unusual inn. The pub's menus change frequently, but look out for regular house speciality hake, monkfish, king prawns and River Exe mussels in Portuguese-style sauce. Other sample dishes include hot and spicy Thai red chicken curry; grilled trio of moorland lamb chops; and roasted Mediterranean vegetable lasagne arrabbiata. Enjoy one of the good range of beers and ciders in the slate courtyard.

Open all day all wk 12-11 **Food** Lunch all wk 12-2.30 Dinner all wk 6-9 ⊕ FREE HOUSE ◀ Timothy Taylor Landlord, Sharp's, Skinner's, Otter, Guest ales Ŏ Cornish Orchards Gold Cider. **Facilities** Non-diners area ♦♦ Children's menu Children's portions Garden ⋒ Parking WiFi 🚍 (notice required)

NEW The Ship Inn

tel: 01208 813845 **Gonvena Hill PL27 6DF**
email: info@shipinnwadebridge.co.uk
dir: From A39 (E of River Camel) at rdbt follow Rock sign. Straight on at mini rdbt, pass Wadebridge School, inn on right

A local with a busy social diary

Naval paraphernalia is only to be expected within a pub called The Ship, and this one in Wadebridge is no exception. But it's not overdone, instead lending an air of

quiet sophistication to this popular local. Dating to the 16th century and refurbished not long ago, the interior's three levels are warmed by two open fires in winter; a decking area outside is much sought-after in summer. Local ales populate the bar, as do local suppliers on the menus. Davidstow Cheddar rarebit makes a tasty snack, or choose from the mains such as hake fillet with olive oil mash, grilled vegetables and gremolata.

Open all wk 12-2.30 5-11 **Food** Lunch 12-2 Dinner Sun-Thu 5-9, Fri-Sat 5-9.30 (no food Sun eve in winter) ⊕ PUNCH TAVERNS ◀ Sharp's Atlantic IPA & Doom Bar, Padstow Windjammer. ♀ 12 **Facilities** Non-diners area ✿ (Bar) ♦♦ Children's menu Children's portions Outside area ⋒ Parking WiFi 🚍 (notice required)

| **WIDEMOUTH BAY** | Map 2 SS20 |

Bay View Inn

tel: 01288 361273 **Marine Dr EX23 0AW**
email: thebayviewinn@aol.com
dir: Adjacent to beach

Ocean views and good food

Dating back around 100 years, this welcoming, family-run pub was a guest house for many years before becoming an inn in the 1960s. True to its name, the pub has fabulous views of the rolling Atlantic. It also has three dining areas: Driftwood Restaurant, which has patio doors that lead out onto a decking area; Surf Restaurant, with its atmospheric lighting and quirky paintings; and Beach Hut Restaurant, running along the front of the original building. Menus make excellent use of local produce, as in the signature dish of fish pie; Cornish gammon steak; or Big Bad Boy Bay View Burger – Cornish mince steak topped with red onion marmalade. Other choices include home-made pies and casseroles.

Open all day all wk **Food** Lunch Mon-Fri 12-2.30, Sat-Sun 12-9 Dinner Mon-Fri 5.30-9, Sat-Sun 12-9 ⊕ FREE HOUSE ◀ Skinner's Betty Stogs & Spriggan Ale, Sharp's Doom Bar Ŏ Somersby Cider. ♀ 14 **Facilities** Non-diners area ✿ (Bar Garden) ♦♦ Children's menu Children's portions Play area Garden ⋒ Parking WiFi 🚍 (notice required)

| **ZENNOR** | Map 2 SW43 |

The Tinners Arms   `PICK OF THE PUBS`

tel: 01736 796927 **TR26 3BY**
email: tinners@tinnersarms.co.uk
dir: Take B3306 from St Ives towards St Just. Zennor approx 5m

Timeless village inn with local ales and good food

Its closeness to the South West Coastal Path almost guarantees that muddy-booted walkers will be found among the Tinners Arms' clientele, enjoying the timelessness of its stone floors, low ceilings, cushioned settles, winter open fires and the revivifying Cornish real ales or Burrow Hill cider from Somerset. Built of granite in 1271 for masons working on ancient St Senara's church next door (famous for its richly carved Mermaid Chair), many may welcome the fact that the only pub in the village has no TV, jukebox or fruit machine, nor can a mobile phone signal reach it. Based on ingredients from local suppliers, the dinner menu offers leek and Stilton crumble with kale and chips; Thai green chicken curry; or smoked haddock, creamy mash with spinach and a poached egg. Sandwiches and light meals are available at lunchtime. Outside is a peaceful garden and large terrace with sea views.

Open all day all wk **Food** Lunch all wk 12-3 Dinner all wk 6.30-9 (ex Sun & Mon eve winter) ⊕ FREE HOUSE ◀ Zennor Mermaid, St Austell Tinners Ale & Tribute Ŏ Burrow Hill. ♀ 10 **Facilities** Non-diners area ✿ (Bar Restaurant Garden) ♦♦ Children's menu Children's portions Garden ⋒ Parking WiFi

CUMBRIA

AMBLESIDE
Map 18 NY30

Drunken Duck Inn
PICK OF THE PUBS

tel: 015394 36347 **Barngates LA22 0NG**
email: info@drunkenduckinn.co.uk
dir: *From Kendal on A591 to Ambleside, then follow Hawkshead sign. In 2.5m inn sign on right, 1m up hill*

Traditional inn with wonderful Lakeland views

The quirky name dates from Victorian times, when a landlady's ducks overindulged in beer-soaked feed. High above Ambleside, at a lonely crossroads, this 17th-century pub enjoys breathtaking views of the fells towards Lake Windermere. Beer is still brewed here in the adjoining Barngates Brewery and served on a counter of local black slate in the oak-floored bar, where hops adorn the old beams, and Herdwick wool coverings soften the wooden settles. Add candlelight and a log fire, and what more could you ask, except perhaps for corn-fed chicken, gnocchi and wild garlic; cod, mashed potato, capers and leeks; or charred and braised broccoli, Jerusalem artichoke and spiced almonds. Then, for dessert, treacle tart, prunes and clotted cream ice cream or poached rhubarb, hazelnut crumb and rhubarb sorbet. Complete with its own tarn, the peaceful garden is home to a rich variety of wildlife.

Open all day all wk Closed 25 Dec **Food** Lunch all wk 12-4 Restaurant menu available ⊕ FREE HOUSE ◀ Barngates Cracker Ale, Chesters Strong & Ugly, Tag Lag, Cat Nap, Brathay Gold. ♚ 17 **Facilities** Non-diners area ♦ Children's portions Garden ⊼ Parking WiFi

Wateredge Inn

tel: 015394 32332 **Waterhead Bay LA22 0EP**
email: stay@wateredgeinn.co.uk
dir: *M6 junct 36, A591 to Ambleside, 5m from Windermere station*

Family-run inn on the shores of Lake Windermere

The Wateredge Inn was converted from two 17th-century fishermen's cottages, and now offers a stylish bar and restaurant. With large gardens and plenty of seating running down to the lakeshore, the inn has been run by the same family for nearly 30 years. The lunch menu offers sandwiches, salads, pub classics and slates – platters of smoked fish, charcuterie or cheese and antipasti. Meanwhile the dinner menu has choices ranging from baby pork back ribs to Cumbrian lamb hotpot, and chicken curry. Specials and a children's menu are also available.

Open all day all wk 10.30am-11pm Closed 23-26 Dec **Food** Lunch Mon-Fri 12-2.30, Sat-Sun 12-4 Dinner all wk 6-9 ⊕ FREE HOUSE ◀ Theakston, Barngates Tag Lag & Cat Nap, Watermill Collie Wobbles Ŏ Symonds. ♚ 15 **Facilities** Non-diners area ♣ (Bar Garden) ♦ Children's menu Children's portions Garden ⊼ Parking WiFi

Find out more about this county with *The AA Guide to Lake District & Cumbria* – see shop.theAA.com

APPLEBY-IN-WESTMORLAND
Map 18 NY62

Tufton Arms Hotel
PICK OF THE PUBS

tel: 017683 51593 **Market Square CA16 6XA**
email: info@tuftonarmshotel.co.uk
dir: *In town centre*

Elegant coaching inn with renowned fish dishes

This imposing, gabled building sits at the foot of Appleby's main street, close to the River Eden below the curvaceous fells of the wild North Pennines. There's an elegant, country house feel to the public rooms, where co-owner Teresa Milsom's design skills shine through, with astonishing attention to detail producing classic atmosphere and contemporary comforts. At the heart of the hotel, overlooking a cobbled mews courtyard, is the Conservatory Fish Restaurant, where David Milsom and his kitchen team's cuisine is complemented by a serious wine list. The menu covers all bases, with lamb shank, belly pork or home-made steak and ale pie as comforting standards, and local game presented as available. It's for the fresh fish dishes, however, that the Tufton has a particular reputation. Daily deliveries from Fleetwood are crafted into starters like smoked haddock and mushroom hotpot baked in cheese sauce; progressing to mains of seafood tagliatelle, or pan-fried hand-picked crab and salmon cake. Beer connoisseurs may enjoy the hotel's own house ale.

Open all day all wk 7.30am-11pm Closed 25-26 Dec **Food** Lunch all wk 12-2 Dinner all wk 6-9 ⊕ FREE HOUSE ◀ Tufton Arms Ale, Cumberland Corby Ale. ♚ 15 **Facilities** Non-diners area ♣ (Bar Outside area) ♦ Children's portions Outside area ⊼ Parking WiFi ▭

BASSENTHWAITE
Map 18 NY23

The Pheasant ★★★ HL ⊛
PICK OF THE PUBS

See Pick of the Pubs on opposite page

BEETHAM
Map 18 SD47

The Wheatsheaf at Beetham
PICK OF THE PUBS

tel: 015395 62123 **LA7 7AL**
email: info@wheatsheafbeetham.com
dir: *On A6, 5m N of M6 junct 35*

Family-owned traditional village free house

In the 17th century, this was a farmhouse and the farmer's wife would feed the labourers; it later became a coaching inn. Today its long history of providing refreshment continues with an intriguing offer from owners Jean and Richard Skelton: order a main course and pay just 1p for your starter or dessert. So, having raided the piggy bank, what do your pennies buy? Among the starters are chicken and pork pâté with home-made chutney; and goats' cheese and tomato tart. Main courses include pan-fried minute steak with mushroom, onion, potato and red wine ragout; and home-made fish pie with haddock and prawns, mash and melted cheese. A dessert could be rich warm chocolate fudge cake and cream; or apple crumble and custard. The Old Tap Bar offers Thwaites Wainwright, Tirril Queen Jean and Cross Bay Nightfall real ales, as well as Kingstone Press cider.

Open all day all wk 10am-11pm Closed 25 Dec **Food** Lunch Mon-Sat 12-9, Sun 12-8.30 Dinner Mon-Sat 12-9, Sun 12-8.30 Av main course £12.95 Set menu available Restaurant menu available all wk ⊕ FREE HOUSE ◀ Thwaites Wainwright, Tirril Queen Jean, Cross Bay Nightfall Ŏ Kingstone Press. **Facilities** Non-diners area ♦ Children's menu Children's portions Outside area ⊼ Parking WiFi ▭ (notice required)

PICK OF THE PUBS

The Pheasant ★★★ HL ❀

BASSENTHWAITE
Map 18 NY23

tel: 017687 76234 **CA13 9YE**
email: info@the-pheasant.co.uk
web: www.the-pheasant.co.uk
dir: *A66 to Cockermouth, 8m N of Keswick on left*

Accomplished food in peaceful Lake District setting

At the foot of the Sale Fell and close to Bassenthwaite Lake, this 17th-century former coaching inn occupies a peaceful spot in the Lake District and is surrounded by lovely gardens. Once a farmhouse, the pub today combines the role of traditional Cumbrian hostelry with that of an internationally renowned modern hotel. Even so, you still sense the history the moment you walk through the door – the legendary foxhunter John Peel, whose "view halloo would awaken the dead", according to the song, was a regular here. In the warmly inviting bar, with polished parquet flooring, panelled walls and oak settles, hang two of Cumbrian artist and former customer Edward H Thompson's paintings. Here, you can order a pint of Coniston Bluebird or Hawkshead Bitter, or cast your eyes over the extensive selection of malt whiskies. The high standard of food, recognised by an AA Rosette, is well known for miles around; meals are served in the attractive beamed restaurant, bistro,

bar and lounges overlooking the gardens. Light lunches served in the lounge and bar include open sandwiches, baguettes and Scotch eggs, as well as main courses such as beef and ale pie; goujons of plaice with pea purée; and blue cheese and spinach soufflé. A three course dinner in the restaurant could feature carrot and sweet potato soup; stone bass fillet, sprouting broccoli; crayfish bisque and pickled cucumber, perhaps with a side dish of triple cooked chips; and crème brûlée with a Pheasant butter shortbread. Treat the family to afternoon tea with home-made scones and rum butter. The Pheasant can get pretty busy, so booking ahead for meals may be required.

Open all day all wk Closed 25 Dec
Food Lunch all wk 12-4.30 Dinner all wk 6-9 Restaurant menu available Tue-Sun
⊕ FREE HOUSE ◼ Coniston Bluebird Bitter, Cumberland Corby Ale, Hawkshead Bitter ♉ Thatchers Gold.
♟ 12 **Facilities** Non-diners area ❀ (Bar Garden) ♦ Children's menu Children's portions Garden ⊼ Parking WiFi
Rooms 15

BOOT
Map 18 NY10

Brook House Inn ★★★★ INN
PICK OF THE PUBS

tel: 019467 23288 **CA19 1TG**
email: stay@brookhouseinn.co.uk **web:** www.brookhouseinn.co.uk
dir: M6 junct 36, A590 follow Barrow signs. A5092, then A595. Pass Broughton-in-Furness, right at lights to Ulpha. Cross river, next left signed Eskdale to Boot. (NB not all routes to Boot are suitable in bad weather conditions)

Tranquil location for tempting, home-made food

Few locations can rival this: Lakeland fells rise behind the inn to England's highest peak, while golden sunsets illuminate tranquil Eskdale. Footpaths wind to nearby Stanley Ghyll's wooded gorge with its falls and red squirrels, and the charming La'al Ratty narrow-gauge railway steams to and from the coast. It's a magnet for ramblers and cyclists, so a small drying room is greatly appreciated. Up to seven real ales are kept, including Yates Best Bitter and Langdale from Cumbrian Legendary Ales, and an amazing selection of 175 malt whiskies. Home-made food prepared from Cumbria's finest showcases the menus, so temper the drizzle with a warming bowl of home-made soup, or grilled scallops with cheese, garlic and lemon, followed by wild mushroom and fettuccine; beef and beer pie; or smoked haddock on mashed potato with leeks. Raspberry meringues or chocolate fudge cake with hot berry sauce, make a fine finish. This great community pub also takes a full role in the famous Boot Beer Festival each June.

Open all day all wk Closed 25 Dec **Food** Contact pub for food times ⊕ FREE HOUSE ◀ Hawkshead Windermere Pale, Cumbrian Legendary Langdale, Yates Best Bitter, Guest ales Ö Westons. ♛ 10 **Facilities** Non-diners area ♦ Children's menu Children's portions Family room Garden ⊓ Beer festival Parking WiFi ▄ **Rooms** 8

BORROWDALE
Map 18 NY21

The Langstrath Country Inn

tel: 017687 77239 **CA12 5XG**
email: info@thelangstrath.com
dir: From Keswick take B5289, through Grange & Rosthwaite, left to Stonethwaite. Inn on left after 0.5m

Picturesque village inn, a favourite with ramblers

Sitting in the stunning Langstrath Valley in the heart of the Lakes and on the coast-to-coast and Cumbrian Way walks, this lovely family-run, 16th-century inn was originally a miner's cottage. It is an ideal base for those attempting England's highest peak, Scafell Pike, and the restaurant is ideally positioned to maximise the spectacular views. Here hungry ramblers enjoy high-quality Lakeland dishes based on local ingredients. A typical choice could include the meat sharing dish of venison Parma ham, chicken pâté, home-made terrine and Cumbrian; slow-roasted Hardwick lamb, mash, seasonal vegetables and red wine gravy. Local cask-conditioned ales include some from the Keswick Brewery.

Open all day 12-10.30 Closed Dec & Jan, Mon **Food** Lunch Tue-Sun 12-2.30 Dinner Tue-Sun 6-9 ⊕ FREE HOUSE ◀ Jennings Bitter & Cocker Hoop, Keswick Thirst Rescue, Theakston Old Peculier Ö Thatchers Gold. ♛ 9 **Facilities** Non-diners area ♣ (Bar Garden) ♦ Children's menu Children's portions Garden ⊓ Parking WiFi ▄ (notice required)

BOWLAND BRIDGE
Map 18 SD48

Hare & Hounds Country Inn
PICK OF THE PUBS

tel: 015395 68333 **LA11 6NN**
email: info@hareandhoundsbowlandbridge.co.uk
dir: M6 junct 36, A590 signed Barrow. Right onto A5074 signed Bowness & Windermere. Approx 4m at sharp bend left & follow Bowland Bridge sign

Fabulous views and local produce

Very much at the heart of the community, this 17th-century coaching inn even hosts the Post Office on Tuesday and Thursday afternoons. In the pretty little hamlet of Bowland Bridge, not far from Bowness, the pub has gorgeous views of Cartmel Fell. Its traditional country-pub atmosphere is fostered by the flagstone floors, stacked logs, wooden tables and mis-matched chairs. Strong links with local food producers result in exclusively reared pork and lamb featuring on the menu alongside Cumbrian brewed beers. Visit at lunchtime and take your pick from sandwiches and salads or hearty meals such as lamb hot pot with local black pudding; braised lamb shank with redcurrant and mint gravy; or savoury cheesy bread and butter pudding. Finish with honey and lemon pannacotta or sticky ginger pudding.

Open all day all wk 12-11 Closed 25 Dec **Food** Lunch Mon-Fri 12-2, Sat 12-9, Sun 12-8.30 Dinner Mon-Fri 6-9, Sat 12-9, Sun 12-8.30 Restaurant menu available all wk ⊕ FREE HOUSE ◀ Tirril, Coniston, Ulverston, Hawkshead, Kirkby Lonsdale Ö Cowmire Hall. ♛ 10 **Facilities** Non-diners area ♣ (Bar Garden) ♦ Children's menu Children's portions Garden ⊓ Parking WiFi ▄ (notice required)

BRAITHWAITE
Map 18 NY22

Coledale Inn

tel: 017687 78272 **CA12 5TN**
email: info@coledale-inn.co.uk
dir: M6 junct 40, A66 signed Keswick. Approx 18m. Exit A66, follow Whinlatter Pass & Braithwaite sign, left on B5292. In Braithwaite left at pub sign, over stream bridge to inn

An atmospheric place to finish a walk

Originally a woollen mill, the Coledale Inn dates from around 1824 and had stints as a pencil mill and a private house before becoming the inn it is today. The interior is attractively designed, whilst footpaths leading off from the large gardens make it ideal for exploring the nearby fells. Two homely bars serve a selection of local ales while traditional lunch and dinner menus are served in the dining room. Typical choices include duo of black pudding and haggis; chilli con carne; rosemary and garlic chicken; and hot chocolate and fudge cake; there's further options on the specials board.

Open all day all wk **Food** Lunch all wk 12-2 Dinner all wk 6-9 Set menu available ⊕ FREE HOUSE ◀ Cumberland Corby Ale, Hesket Newmarket, Yates, Keswick, Tirril, Geltsdale, Marston's. ♛ 8 **Facilities** Non-diners area ♣ (Bar Garden) ♦ Children's menu Children's portions Play area Garden ⊓ Parking WiFi ▄ (notice required)

The Royal Oak ★★★★ INN

tel: 017687 78533 **CA12 5SY**
email: tpfranks@hotmail.com **web:** www.royaloak-braithwaite.co.uk
dir: *M6 junct 40, A66 towards Keswick, approx 18m (bypass Keswick), exit A66 left onto B5292 to Braithwaite. Pub in village centre*

Delightful country pub surrounded by beautiful landscapes

Surrounded by high fells and beautiful scenery, The Royal Oak is set in the centre of the village and is the perfect base for walkers. The interior is all oak beams and log fires, and the menu offers hearty pub food, such as slow-roasted pork belly and apple flavoured mash; Thai red chicken curry; smoky bacon and chorizo sausage pasta; and giant Yorkshire pudding filled with Cumberland sausage casserole, all served alongside local ales, such as Sneck Lifter or Cumberland Ale. Visitors can extend the experience by staying over in the comfortable en suite bedrooms.

Open all day all wk **Food** Lunch all wk 12-2 Dinner all wk 6-9 ⊕ MARSTON'S ◪ Jennings Lakeland Stunner, Cumberland Ale, Cocker Hoop & Sneck Lifter. ⬤ 8 **Facilities** Non-diners area ◉ Children's menu Children's portions Garden ⌂ Parking WiFi ◻ **Rooms** 10

BRAMPTON Map 21 NY56

Blacksmiths Arms ★★★★ INN

tel: 016977 3452 **Talkin CA8 1LE**
email: blacksmithsarmstalkin@yahoo.co.uk **web:** www.blacksmithstalkin.co.uk
dir: *M6 junct 43, A69 E. 7m, straight on at rdbt, follow signs to Talkin Tarn then Talkin Village*

Attractive free house serving good home-cooked food

With cartwheels lined up outside, this former smithy faces a small green by the crossroads in the centre of the village. On its doorstep is northern Cumbria's wildly beautiful countryside. The menu of good, traditional home cooking makes extensive use of fresh local produce for sweet and sour chicken; medallions of beef; rainbow trout; and spinach and ricotta cannelloni. Likely contenders as blackboard specials are lamb chump with redcurrant and port gravy; liver, bacon and onion casserole; and smoked haddock florentine. Two of the real ales come from the Geltsdale Brewery in neighbouring Brampton. There's a beer garden, and out front a couple of tables with seating.

Open all day all wk 12-12 **Food** Lunch all wk 12-2 Dinner all wk 6-9 ⊕ FREE HOUSE ◪ Yates, Black Sheep, Guest ales. ⬤ 16 **Facilities** Non-diners area ◉ Children's menu Children's portions Garden ⌂ Parking WiFi **Rooms** 8

BROUGHTON-IN-FURNESS Map 18 SD28

Blacksmiths Arms PICK OF THE PUBS

tel: 01229 716824 **Broughton Mills LA20 6AX**
email: blacksmithsarms@aol.com
dir: *A593 from Broughton-in-Furness towards Coniston, in 1.5m left signed Broughton Mills, pub 1m on left*

Ancient pub surrounded by quiet fells and farms

Originally a farmhouse and then an inn and blacksmith's (hence the name), this whitewashed Lakeland pub dates from 1577 and stands in the secluded Lickle Valley, with miles of glorious walks radiating from the front door. The interior remains largely unchanged, with oak-panelled corridors, slate floors, oak-beamed ceilings and log fires. The Lanes own and run the Blacksmiths, Michael dividing his time between the kitchen and the bar, and Sophie running front of house. The bar is reserved for drinking only, with ales from Barngates and Tirril and Westons Old Rosie cider. The Lanes use only suppliers who guarantee quality produce for their

menus. Apart from lunchtime sandwiches, there are options such as Cajun-spiced chicken salad and roasted pork tenderloin. The evening menu typically features honey-roast breast of duck and roasted rump of lamb. The sheltered, flower-filled front patio garden is great for alfresco dining.

Open all wk Mon 5-11 Tue-Fri 12-2.30 5-11 Sat 12-11 Sun 12-10.30 (Summer school hols 12-11 ex Mon) Closed 25 Dec, Mon L **Food** Lunch Tue-Sun 12-2 Dinner Tue-Sun 6-9 ⊕ FREE HOUSE ◪ Barngates Cracker Ale, Dent Golden Fleece, Tirril, Rotating ales ○ Westons Old Rosie. **Facilities** Non-diners area ◉ Children's menu Garden ⌂ Beer festival Parking

CALDBECK Map 18 NY34

Oddfellows Arms

tel: 016974 78227 **CA7 8EA**
email: info@oddfellows-caldbeck.co.uk
dir: *Phone for detailed directions*

Hearty Lake District pub food

Caldbeck's famous resident, the huntsman John ("D'ye ken...") Peel lies in the churchyard opposite this 17th-century coaching inn. The pub serves Jennings real ales, lunchtime snacks — typically jacket potatoes and sandwiches — and offers a menu on which representative dishes include salmon and haddock fishcakes; traditional Cumberland sausage ring; Herdwick lamb cobbler; and cheese ploughman's. From the garden you can admire the dramatic northern fells of the Lake District National Park, before hitting the Cumbrian Way, which passes the front door, or pedalling off to the Reivers cycling route from Whitehaven to Tynemouth two miles away.

Open all day all wk **Food** Lunch Mon-Sat 12-2, Sun 12-8 Dinner Mon-Sat 5.30-9, Sun 12-8 ⊕ MARSTON'S ◪ Jennings Bitter, Cumberland Ale. ⬤ 13 **Facilities** Non-diners area ❀ (Bar Garden) ◉ Children's menu Children's portions Garden ⌂ Parking WiFi ◻ (notice required)

CARTMEL Map 18 SD37

The Cavendish Arms PICK OF THE PUBS

tel: 015395 36240 **LA11 6QA**
email: info@thecavendisharms.co.uk
dir: *M6 junct 36, A590 signed Barrow-in-Furness. Cartmel signed. In village take 1st right*

Cosy retreat in a medieval village

A babbling stream flows past the tree-lined garden of this 450-year-old coaching inn situated within Cartmel's village walls, its longest-surviving hostelry. Many traces of its history remain, from the mounting block outside the main door to the bar itself, which was once the stables. Low, oak-beamed ceilings, uneven floors, antique furniture and an open fire create a traditional, cosy atmosphere. As well as Cumbrian ales, the food owes much to its local origins. The menu changes every six weeks, listing lunchtime sandwiches and starters such as mixed game pâté. Then moves on to oven-baked fillet of hake or tagliatelle primavera. Desserts include banoffee crunch sundae and blackcurrant fool. The owners have teamed up with a local company that offers carriage tours of the village. This popular area is ideal for walking, horse riding, and visiting Lake Windermere.

Open all day all wk 9am-11pm Closed 25 Dec **Food** Lunch all wk 12-9.30 Dinner all wk 12-9.30 ⊕ STAR PUBS & BARS ◪ Caledonian Golden XPA, Cumberland Corby Ale, Theakston, Cavendish Fox, Guest ales ○ Symonds. ⬤ 8 **Facilities** Non-diners area ❀ (Bar Garden) ◉ Children's menu Children's portions Garden ⌂ Beer festival Parking WiFi ◻

CARTMEL *continued*

The Masons Arms

tel: 015395 68486 **Strawberry Bank LA11 6NW**
email: info@masonsarmsstrawberrybank.co.uk
dir: *M6 junct 36, A590 towards Barrow. Right onto A5074 signed Bowness/Windermere. 5m, left at Bowland Bridge. Through village, pub on right*

Attractive inn in a beautiful spot

An atmospheric, charmingly decorated pub with a stunning location overlooking the Winster Valley and beyond, The Masons Arms has an atmospheric interior with low, beamed ceilings, old fireplaces and quirky furniture. Waiting staff manoeuvre through the busy bar, dining rooms and heated, covered terraces carrying popular dishes such as warm pitta bread and home-made houmous to nibble; Masons Arms ribs with sticky sauce and fries or Cullen skink to start; followed by smoked haddock, scampi and lemon fishcakes; or braised belly pork with a sage jus. If there's room, try some apple and blackberry crumble, jam roly poly or honeycomb cheesecake. Wash it down with a pint of Thwaites Wainwright.

Open all day all wk 9.30am–11pm **Food** Lunch Mon-Fri 12-2.30, Sat-Sun 12-9 Dinner Mon-Fri 6-9, Sat-Sun 12-9 ⊕ FREE HOUSE/INDIVIDUAL INNS LTD ◀ Thwaites Wainwright, Hawkshead Bitter, Guest ales ♂ Kingstone Press. ₹ 12
Facilities Non-diners area ◀ Children's menu Children's portions Outside area ⟊ Parking WiFi

Pig & Whistle

tel: 015395 36482 **Aynsome Rd LA11 6PL**
email: info@pigandwhistlecartmel.co.uk
dir: *M6 junct 36, A590 towards Barrow. Left at Cartmel sign, pub in village centre*

A genuine local with first-class food

The co-landlord here with Penny Tapsell is Simon Rogan, one of the UK's most accomplished chefs. The pub has long been his local, and he likes it that way. His short but perfectly formed menu offers remarkably good value-for-money dishes, starting with twice-baked sweet potato soufflé; moving on to the Pig & Whistle burger, Cumbrian veal rib eye, sirloin of beef, or honey glazed pork belly with Savoy cabbage and black pudding. Leave room for ginger pudding with milk ice cream or caramelised banana bread with rum and raisin ice cream. Real ale drinkers may find a Dizzy Blonde in the bar – it's one of Robinsons of Stockport's seasonal brews.

Open all wk Summer 12-11 (Winter Mon & Tue 4-11 Fri-Sun 12-11) **Food** Lunch Wed-Sat 12-2, Sun 12-8.30 Dinner Wed-Sat 5.30-8.30, Sun 12-8.30 Av main course £14.70 ⊕ ROBINSONS ◀ Dizzy Blonde, Hartleys Cumbria Way ♂ Westons Stowford Press. **Facilities** Non-diners area ♣ (Bar Garden) ◀ Children's menu Garden ⟊ WiFi ▭

CLIFTON Map 18 NY52

George and Dragon **PICK OF THE PUBS**

tel: 01768 865381 **CA10 2ER**
email: enquiries@georgeanddragonclifton.co.uk
dir: *M6 junct 40, A66 towards Appleby-in-Westmorland, A6 S to Clifton*

Historic pub majoring on local produce

This lovely pub is more peaceful today than it was in 1745, when the retreating army of Bonnie Prince Charlie was defeated in the nearby village of Clifton. Set on the historic Lowther Estate near Ullswater; the ruined castle-mansion is set at the heart of pasture, woodland and fells alongside the rushing River Lowther and pretty village of Askham. Meticulously renovated by owner Charles Lowther, it is a traditional inn with contemporary comforts. The appealing menu majors on the bountiful produce of the estate. Beef is from pedigree Shorthorns; pork from home-reared rare breed stock; game and most fish from local waters. Settle in with a pint of Cumberland Corby Blonde and secure a starter of braised pig's cheek with

parsnip purée, followed by roast monkfish tail, herb risotto, crispy ham; or pan-fried lambs' liver, sweet potato and thyme jus. Sharing plates, salads, sandwiches and burgers all vie for space on the menu. There is a secluded courtyard and garden.

Open all day all wk Closed 26 Dec **Food** Lunch all wk 12-2.30 Dinner all wk 6-9 Av main course £15.95 Set menu available ⊕ FREE HOUSE ◀ Hawkshead Bitter, Eden Gold, Cumberland Corby Blonde ♂ Westons Stowford Press. ₹ 17
Facilities Non-diners area ♣ (Bar Garden) ◀ Children's menu Children's portions Garden ⟊ Parking WiFi

---

COCKERMOUTH Map 18 NY13

The Trout Hotel ★★★★ HL

tel: 01900 823591 **Crown St CA13 0EJ**
email: enquiries@trouthotel.co.uk **web:** www.trouthotel.co.uk
dir: *In town centre*

Town-centre hotel overlooking the River Derwent

Until he was eight, the poet William Wordsworth lived next door, although then this 17th-century building was a private house. Much remains to remind us of its heritage: stone walls, exposed beams, marble fireplaces, restored plasterwork, period stained-glass, and a carefully-preserved oak staircase. At the bar ales from town brewery Jennings are joined by Carlisle-brewed guest, Corby Blonde. Fresh, locally sourced ingredients drive the menu, from smoked haddock fishcake, made with Thornby Moor Stumpies goats' cheese, to Cumbrian beef sirloin fajitas. A drink or a meal in the gardens overlooking the River Derwent is an enjoyable way of passing time.

Open all day all wk **Food** Lunch all wk 12-9.30 Dinner all wk 12-9.30 Restaurant menu available all wk ⊕ FREE HOUSE ◀ Jennings Cumberland Ale, Cooper Hoop, Cumberland Corby Blonde ♂ Thatchers. ₹ 24 **Facilities** Non-diners area ◀ Children's menu Children's portions Garden ⟊ Parking WiFi ▭ (notice required) **Rooms** 49

CONISTON Map 18 SD39

The Black Bull Inn & Hotel **PICK OF THE PUBS**

tel: 015394 41335 & 41668 **1 Yewdale Rd LA21 8DU**
email: ian@conistonbrewery.com
dir: *M6 junct 36, A590. 23m from Kendal via Windermere & Ambleside*

Four-hundred-year-old Lake District heartland pub

Beside a stream, or beck as they say round here, stands this traditional Lakeland pub. Its bare stone walls, oak beams, log-burning stove and part-slate floor all contribute to its appeal, while of further interest, at least to beer drinkers, is its own microbrewery's Bluebird Bitter, commemorating Donald Campbell's attempts on the world water speed record; it also brews Old Man Ale, named for the local 2,634-ft mountain. Those out walking all morning or all day can look forward to sandwiches or filled jacket potatoes. Chances are they'll want something heartier, such as roast rib of beef with Yorkshire pudding and gravy; poached sole fillets with dill and cucumber cream; or roast loin and belly of pork with sage and onion stuffing, crackling and gravy. Ask about beer festival dates.

Open all day all wk Closed 25 Dec **Food** Lunch all wk 12-9 Dinner all wk 12-9 Av main course £10 ⊕ FREE HOUSE ◀ Coniston Bluebird Premium XB, Old Man Ale, Winter Warmer Blacksmiths Ale, Special Oatmeal Stout ♂ Broadoak Premium Perry & Moonshine, Gwynt y Ddraig Haymaker, Guest ciders. ₹ 10 **Facilities** Non-diners area ♣ (Bar Garden) ◀ Children's menu Children's portions Family room Garden ⟊ Beer festival Parking WiFi ▭ (notice required)

CROSTHWAITE Map 18 SD49

The Punch Bowl Inn ★★★★★ INN ◉◉ **PICK OF THE PUBS**

See Pick of the Pubs on opposite page

PICK OF THE PUBS

The Punch Bowl Inn ★★★★★ INN ✿✿

CROSTHWAITE Map 18 SD49

tel: 015395 68237 **LA8 8HR**
email: info@the-punchbowl.co.uk
web: www.the-punchbowl.co.uk
dir: *M6 junct 36, A590 towards Barrow,
A5074, follow Crosthwaite signs. Pub by
church*

Luxury Lake District inn and restaurant

Very much a destination dining inn, The Punch Bowl stands alongside the village church in the delightfully unspoilt Lyth Valley. The slates on the bar floor were found beneath the old dining room and complement the Brathay slate bar top and antique furniture, while in the restaurant are polished oak floorboards, comfortable leather chairs and an eyecatching stone fireplace. Two rooms off the bar add extra space to eat or relax with a pint and a daily paper in front of an open fire. Head chef Scott Fairweather focuses on the best local and seasonal produce and has two AA Rosettes to show for his expertise. Sourcing extensively from the area's estates, farms and coastal villages, the lunch and dinner menus in both the bar and the restaurant might begin with rabbit terrine with celeriac remoulade and mushrooms à la Greque; venison tartare with blue cheese, capers and smoked egg yoke purée; or black pudding with bubble-and-squeak. For a

main course, possibly spinach and olive linguine with local duck egg, chestnut mushrooms and parmesan cream; pan-fried stone bass with cauliflower purée, shrimp and hazelnut butter and sautéed potatoes; or maple-glazed duck breast with braised red cabbage, golden raisin, and dauphinoise potatoes. And for dessert, round things off with caramel cheesecake, blood orange soufflé, or coconut pannacotta. The owners are great supporters of Cumbrian microbreweries, witness Westmorland Gold from Barngates, and Bluebird from the Coniston brewery. In addition to a good list of dessert wines, champagne is available by the glass. Individually furnished guest rooms with freestanding roll-top baths are available.

Open all day all wk **Food** Lunch Mon-Fri 12-5.30, Sat-Sun 12-4 Dinner all wk 5.30-9 ⊕ FREE HOUSE ◖ Barngates Westmorland Gold, Coniston Bluebird Bitter, Winster Valley Old School ♂ Thatchers Gold. ▾ 14
Facilities Non-diners area ❀ (Bar Garden) ♦ Children's menu Children's portions Garden ⊼ Parking WiFi
Rooms 9

ELTERWATER

Map 18 NY30

The Britannia Inn

`PICK OF THE PUBS`

tel: 015394 37210 **LA22 9HP**
email: info@britinn.co.uk
dir: *In village centre*

Village inn well placed for Lake District walkers

Walks and mountain-bike trails head off in all directions from the front door of this free house in the Langdale Valley, just a short drive from Ambleside, Grasmere, Windermere, Hawkshead and Coniston. Built as a farmhouse and cobbler's more than 500 years ago, the whitewashed building only became an inn some 200 years back and the bar area is essentially a series of small, cosy rooms with low-beamed oak ceilings and winter coal fires. Bar staff pull pints of guest beers nineteen to the dozen, as well as the house special brewed by Coniston. An even wider selection of real ales is available during the two-week beer festival in mid-November. The inn offers a wide choice of fresh, home-cooked food, with an evening meal typically featuring grilled sea bass fillet; or home-made chicken, ham and leek pie. Dine alfresco in the garden and take in the views of the village and tarns.

Open all day all wk 10.30am-11pm **Food** Lunch all wk 12-9.30 Dinner all wk 12-9.30 ⊕ FREE HOUSE ◀ Jennings Bitter, Coniston Bluebird Bitter & Britannia Inn Special Edition, Dent Aviator, Hawkshead Bitter, Guest ales.
Facilities Non-diners area ❁ (Bar Garden) ♦ Children's menu Children's portions Garden ⚲ Beer festival WiFi

ENNERDALE BRIDGE

Map 18 NY01

NEW Shepherds Arms

tel: 01946 861249 **Kirkland Rd CA23 3AR**
email: shepherdsarmshotel@btconnect.com **web:** www.shepherdsarms.com
dir: *From A66 at Cockermouth take A5086 to Egremont. 7.3m, left towards Ennerdale. Through Kirkland Down to Ennerdale Bridge*

Cumbrian hospitality in a remote valley

Popular with coast-to-coast walkers and cyclists of various nationalities, the bar is usually populated by a cosmopolitan crowd mixing merrily with local farmers. In fact, this was once a village-centre farmhouse which also dispensed beer to the local countrymen. Today, an excellent array of Cumbrian ales is served, alongside plates of good home-made food based on local produce. All appetites are catered for, starting with lunchtime snacks and finishing with robust dinner dishes such as pork belly and black pudding; or duck breast with a port and marmalade reduction.

Open all day all wk (winter times may vary) Closed 25-26 Dec **Food** Lunch all wk 12-5 Dinner all wk 5-9 ⊕ FREE HOUSE ◀ Cumbrian Legendary Ales Loweswater Gold, Yates Best Bitter, Ennerdale Blonde, Hesket Newmarket High Pike, Stringers Wolf Warrior. **Facilities** Non-diners area ♦ Children's portions Outside area ⚲ Parking WiFi 🚌 (notice required)

FAUGH

Map 18 NY55

The String of Horses Inn

tel: 01228 670297 **CA8 9EG**
email: info@stringofhorses.com
dir: *M6 junct 43, A69 towards Hexham. In approx 5m right at 1st lights at Corby Hill/Warwick Bridge. 1m, through Heads Nook, in 1m sharp right. Left into Faugh. Pub on left down hill*

Traditional coaching inn in historic area

Close to Hadrian's Wall in the peaceful village of Faugh, this traditional 17th-century Lakeland inn may be tucked away but it's just 10 minutes from Carlisle. There are oak beams, wood panelling, old settles and log fires in the restaurant, where imaginative pub food is on offer, and in the bar, where you'll find real ales from Brampton Brewery. Creamy tomato and basil soup; spicy prawn casserole; Moroccan lamb tagine; chilli lasagne; and half shoulder of lamb with mint gravy admirably represent what's on a typical menu.

Open Tue-Sun 6-11 Closed Mon **Food** Dinner Tue-Sun 6-8.45 ⊕ FREE HOUSE ◀ Allendale Pennine Pale, Brampton Best, Geltsdale Cold Fell ♨ Westons Family Reserve. ☗ 8 **Facilities** Non-diners area ♦ Children's menu Outside area Parking WiFi 🚌 (notice required)

GRASMERE

Map 18 NY30

The Travellers Rest Inn

tel: 015394 35604 **Keswick Rd LA22 9RR**
email: stay@lakedistrictinns.co.uk **web:** www.lakedistrictinns.co.uk
dir: *A591 to Grasmere, pub 0.5m N of Grasmere*

Old-world charm and a mountain backdrop

Located on the edge of picturesque Grasmere and handy for touring and exploring the ever-beautiful Lake District, the Travellers Rest has been a pub for more than 500 years. Inside, a roaring log fire complements the welcoming atmosphere of the beamed and inglenook bar area. Along with ales like Sneck Lifter, an extensive menu of traditional home-cooked fare is offered, ranging from steak and kidney pudding with potatoes and vegetables, to roasted aubergine with haricot bean ratatouille. Leave room for sticky toffee pudding or red berry sundae.

Open all day all wk 12-11 **Food** Lunch all wk 12-9.30 Dinner all wk 12-9.30 ⊕ FREE HOUSE ◀ Jennings Bitter, Cocker Hoop, Cumberland Ale & Sneck Lifter, Guest ales. ☗ 10 **Facilities** Non-diners area ❁ (Bar Garden) ♦ Children's menu Children's portions Family room Garden ⚲ Parking WiFi 🚌

GREAT SALKELD
Map 18 NY53

The Highland Drove Inn and Kyloes Restaurant
PICK OF THE PUBS

tel: 01768 898349 **CA11 9NA**
email: highlanddrove@kyloes.co.uk
dir: M6 junct 40, A66 E'bound, A686 to Alston. 4m, left onto B6412 for Great Salkeld & Lazonby

Convivial village pub deep in the pretty Eden Valley

On an old drove road, this 300-year-old country inn recalls the long-vanished days when hardy Highland cattle were driven across open water from Scotland's Western Isles to markets in England. A reputation for high-quality food might suggest it's a destination pub, as indeed it is, but it's more than that, because locals love it too, one attraction being a cask-conditioned ale called Kyloes Kushie. The attractive brick and timber bar, where snacks are available, is furnished with old tables and settles; the more formal dining takes place upstairs in the hunting lodge-style restaurant, where a verandah offers fine country views. The kitchen depends on locally-sourced game, fish and meat, examples including venison rendang, an Indonesian curry with coconut milk and spices; Cumbrian lamb shank slow-braised in Guinness; duck breast marinated in pineapple, chilli and soy sauce; and baked fillet of halibut.

Open Tue-Fri 12-2 (all wk 6pm-12am Sat 12pm-2am) Closed 25 Dec, Mon L **Food** Lunch Tue-Sun 12-2 Dinner all wk 6-9 ⊕ FREE HOUSE ◀ Theakston Black Bull Bitter, Best & Traditional Mild, John Smith's Cask & Smooth, Eden Brewery Kyloes Kushie, Guest ale ♂ Symonds. ♀ 10 **Facilities** Non-diners area ✿ (Bar Garden) ⋔ Children's menu Children's portions Garden ⋒ Parking WiFi ▭ (notice required)

GREAT URSWICK
Map 18 SD27

General Burgoyne

tel: 01229 586394 **Church Rd LA12 0SZ**
email: contact@generalburgoyne.com
dir: M6 junct 36, A590 towards Barrow-in-Furness. Through Ulverston, left after Swarthmoor signed Great Urswick, 1.5m to pub

Traditional country pub continuing to make a big impression

General Burgoyne, or Gentleman Johnny as he was known, was a British army officer, politician and dramatist, infamous for surrendering his men to the enemy during the American War of Independence. A skull – not Burgoyne's – found during renovations in 1995 is displayed in the fire-warmed bar, where Robinsons beers are served, and the comprehensive menu includes pub classics and sandwiches. In the modern Orangery Restaurant, look for roast rump of Duddon Valley lamb; 'partridge in a pear tree' – roasted breast, confit leg, pomme Elizabeth, smooth pear, smoked garlic, and thyme jus; and toffee vodka and praline profiteroles. Walkers, cyclists, bikers and dogs are always welcome.

Open all day Closed 26 Dec & 1st wk Jan, Mon **Food** Lunch Tue-Sat 12-2, Sun 12-8 Dinner Tue-Sun 5-9, Sun 12-8 Av main course £15 ⊕ ROBINSONS ◀ Dizzy Blonde, Hartleys Cumbria Way. **Facilities** Non-diners area ✿ (Bar Outside area) ⋔ Children's menu Children's portions Outside area ⋒ Parking WiFi ▭ (notice required)

HAWKSHEAD
Map 18 SD39

Kings Arms ★★★ INN

tel: 015394 36372 **The Square LA22 0NZ**
email: info@kingsarmshawkshead.co.uk **web:** www.kingsarmshawkshead.co.uk
dir: M6 junct 36, A590 to Newby Bridge, right at 1st junct past rdbt, over bridge, 8m to Hawkshead

Homely inn in Beatrix Potter village

In the charming square at the heart of this Lakeland village, made famous by Beatrix Potter who lived nearby, this 16th-century inn throngs in summer. In colder weather, bag a table by the fire in the traditional carpeted bar, quaff a pint of Hawkshead Bitter and tuck into lunchtime food such as hot Cumberland sausage with a jacket potato and gravy or evening meals along the lines of Morecambe Bay potted shrimps; or Lakeland tapas followed by baked chicken supreme; or lamb, black pudding and chunky vegetable casserole. Look out for the carved figure of a king in the bar. Cosy, thoughtfully equipped bedrooms are available.

Open all day all wk 11am-mdnt **Food** Lunch all wk 12-2.30 Dinner all wk 6-9.30 ⊕ FREE HOUSE ◀ Hawkshead Gold & Bitter, Coniston Bluebird Bitter, Cumbrian Legendary, Guest ales. ♀ 10 **Facilities** Non-diners area ✿ (Bar Outside area) ⋔ Children's menu Children's portions Outside area ⋒ Beer festival WiFi ▭ (notice required) **Rooms** 8

The Queen's Head Inn & Restaurant ★★★★ INN
PICK OF THE PUBS

tel: 015394 36271 **Main St LA22 0NS**
email: info@queensheadhawkshead.co.uk **web:** www.queensheadhawkshead.co.uk
dir: M6 junct 36, A590 to Newby Bridge, 1st right, 8m to Hawkshead

Excellent food and hospitality in the southern Lakes

Hawkshead has impressive literary links – William Wordsworth attended the local grammar school, and Beatrix Potter lived just up the road. The 17th-century Queen's Head on the village's main street is a stone's throw from Esthwaite Water and surrounded by fells and forests. Behind the pub's flower-bedecked exterior, low oak-beamed ceilings, wood-panelled walls, slate floors and welcoming fires create a relaxed, traditional setting. Ales include Hartleys Cumbria Way and Robinsons Double Hop, and nearly a dozen wines are served by the glass. Local suppliers are proudly listed on the menu, which brims with their fresh, quality ingredients. At lunchtime, sandwiches such as Appleby cheddar with home-made piccalilli refuel the ramblers. In the evening you might start with game terrine, mushroom salad, dill pickles and toasted sour dough; and continue with 'three little pigs' – crispy pork belly, loin and croquette, served with apple purée, Savoy cabbage and wholegrain mustard jus.

Open all day all wk 11am-11.45pm (Sun 12-11.45) **Food** Lunch Mon-Sat 12-3, Sun 12-4 Dinner all wk 6-9 Av main course £12-£15 ⊕ ROBINSONS ◀ Double Hop, Hartleys Cumbria Way, Guest ale. ♀ 11 **Facilities** Non-diners area ✿ (Bar Garden) ⋔ Children's menu Garden ⋒ WiFi ▭ (notice required) **Rooms** 13

The Sun Inn

tel: 015394 36236 **Main St LA22 0NT**
email: rooms@suninn.co.uk
dir: N'bound on M6 junct 36, A591 to Ambleside, B5286 to Hawkshead. S'bound on M6 junct 40, A66 to Keswick, A591 to Ambleside, B5286 to Hawkshead

A popular hostelry in a busy village

This listed 17th-century coaching inn is at the heart of the charming Hawkshead village and makes a great base for exploring the Lakes. The wood-panelled bar has low, oak-beamed ceilings, and hill walkers and others will enjoy the log fires, real ales and locally sourced food. Choices range from potted rabbit with carrot and pea shoot salad, to crab meat and brown shrimp cannelloni for starters; and for mains from beef and chorizo burger; slow-roasted lamb shoulder, celeriac fondant and minted crushes peas; to potato and cauliflower curry.

Open all day all wk 10am-mdnt **Food** Lunch all wk 12-2.30 Dinner all wk 6-9 ⊕ FREE HOUSE ◀ Jennings, Bowness Bay Swan Blond, Watermill Collie Wobbles, Guest ale. **Facilities** Non-diners area ✿ (Bar Garden) ⋔ Children's menu Children's portions Garden ⋒ Beer festival WiFi ▭

KENDAL
Map 18 SD59

NEW The Punch Bowl ★★★★ INN

tel: 015395 60267 **Barrows Green LA8 0AA**
email: punch-bowl@hotmail.co.uk **web:** www.thepunchbowla65.com
dir: M6 junct 36, A65. Pub in 5m on left

A 'proper' Lakeland pub

If, when heading for The Lakes, your route involves leaving the M6 at junction 36, this is the first pub you'll encounter. In the inviting bar the real ales change frequently, and you can play pool, darts and dominoes. Committed to local sourcing, the kitchen has a mantra: "Proud to serve proper pub food in decent portions". Expect cheesy leek-stuffed chicken; steak and Theakston's ale pie; gently baked salmon fillet; roasted and stuffed bell pepper; chargrills and gourmet burgers. Expect good wines: the three top men at the pub's wine merchant have knocked up 100 years' experience between them.

Open all day all wk **Food** Lunch Mon-Fri 12-3, Sat-Sun 12-9 Dinner Mon-Fri 6-9, Sat-Sun 12-9 Av main course £10 ⊕ HEINEKEN ◀ Theakston, Caledonian Deuchars IPA, Guest ales. ♀ 10 **Facilities** Non-diners area ❀ (Bar Garden) ⊕ Children's menu Children's portions Garden ♫ Parking WiFi ▄▄ (notice required) **Rooms** 2

KESWICK
Map 18 NY22

The George ★★★★ INN

tel: 017687 72076 **3 Saint John's St CA12 5AZ**
email: rooms@thegeorgekeswick.co.uk **web:** www.thegeorgekeswick.co.uk
dir: M6 junct 40, A66, filter left signed Keswick, pass pub on left. At x-rds left into Station St, inn 150yds on left

Imposing coaching inn with plenty of character

Keswick's oldest coaching inn is a handsome 17th-century building in the heart of this popular Lakeland town. Restored to its former glory, retaining its traditional black panelling, Elizabethan beams, ancient settles and log fires, it makes a comfortable base from which to explore the fells and lakes. Expect to find local Jennings ales on tap and classic pub food prepared from local ingredients. Typical dishes include brie and almond wedges or haggis fritters with creamy whisky sauce to start; then there could be main dishes such as pumpkin and red onion tagine; local pheasant breast stuffed with Cumberland sausage and wrapped in bacon; or caramelised duck breast on potato rösti, or Mediterranean vegetable and goats' cheese lasagne. There are 12 comfortable bedrooms available.

Open all day all wk **Food** Lunch Mon-Thu 12-2.30, Fri-Sun 12-5 Dinner all wk 5.30-9 Av main course £12 Restaurant menu available all wk ⊕ JENNINGS ◀ Bitter, Cumberland Ale, Sneck Lifter & Cocker Hoop, Guest ales. ♀ 10 **Facilities** Non-diners area ❀ (Bar) ⊕ Children's menu Children's portions Parking WiFi ▄▄ (notice required) **Rooms** 12

The Horse & Farrier Inn
PICK OF THE PUBS

tel: 017687 79688 **Threlkeld Village CA12 4SQ**
email: info@horseandfarrier.com
dir: M6 junct 40, A66 signed Keswick, 12m, right signed Threlkeld. Pub in village centre

Classic Lakeland inn with hard-to-beat views

From this lovely, late 17th-century Lakeland inn at the foot of Blencathra there are wonderful views across to the Helvellyn range. Within its thick, whitewashed stone walls you'll find slate-flagged floors, beamed ceilings and open log fires, with hunting prints decorating the traditional bars and panelled snug. Cockermouth's Jennings and a guest brewery supply the real ales. Now in new hands, the pub maintains a reputation for good food, dependent on a long-standing commitment to local, seasonal produce and continuing with its preparation in the 'gleaming kitchen'. Restaurant starters include buffalo mozzarella, vine tomato and air-dried prosciutto; and seared fresh scallops with black pudding roulade. Likely contenders among the mains could be Cumberland sausage with spring onion and chive mash; steamed fillet of salmon with wilted spinach and linguine; home-made curry of the day; and bean and celery chilli. Six walks start or end here, including ones to Blencathra and Skiddaw.

Open all day all wk 7.30am-mdnt **Food** Lunch all wk 12-9 Dinner all wk 12-9 ⊕ JENNINGS ◀ Bitter, Sneck Lifter & Cumberland Ale, Guest ale. ♀ 10 **Facilities** Non-diners area ❀ (Bar Garden) ⊕ Children's menu Children's portions Family room Garden ♫ Parking WiFi ▄▄ (notice required)

The Kings Head
PICK OF THE PUBS

tel: 017687 72393 **Thirlspot CA12 4TN**
email: stay@lakedistrictinns.co.uk **web:** www.lakedistrictinns.co.uk
dir: M6 junct 40, A66 to Keswick then A591, pub 4m S of Keswick

Lovely valley views south of Keswick

Helvellyn, the third highest peak in England, towers above this 17th-century coaching inn; the long, whitewashed building and its delightful beer garden enjoy great views of the surrounding fells, while indoors the traditional bar features old beams and an inglenook fireplace. In addition to several regulars from the Cumberland brewery, there are guest real ales and a fine selection of wines and malt whiskies. In the bar, paninis, sandwiches and jacket potatoes head the lunchtime options, which also feature a deli board and ploughman's. It's in the restaurant, which looks out to the glacial valley of St Johns in the Vale that dinner might begin with warm pigeon breast salad; or oven-baked whole camembert to start; home-made steak and kidney pie; slow-braised lamb shank; or garlic-infused wild mushroom risotto. Finish with warm poached pear, mulled wine syrup and vanilla ice cream. There's a separate set price steak menu Mondays to Saturdays.

Open all day all wk 11-11 **Food** Lunch all wk 12-9.30 Dinner all wk 12-9.30 Av main course £10.95 Set menu available Restaurant menu available all wk ⊕ FREE HOUSE ◀ Jennings Bitter, Cumberland Ale, Sneck Lifter & Cocker Hoop, Guest ales. ♀ 9 **Facilities** Non-diners area ❀ (Bar Garden) ⊕ Children's menu Children's portions Family room Garden ♫ Parking WiFi ▄▄ (notice required)

PICK OF THE PUBS

The Royal Oak at Keswick ★★★★ INN

KESWICK   Map 18 NY22

tel: 017687 74584 **Main St CA12 5HZ**
email: relax@theinnkeswick.co.uk
web: www.royaloakkeswick.com
dir: *M6 junct 40, A66 to Keswick town centre to war memorial x-rds. Left into Station St. Inn 100yds*

Popular inn at the heart of walking country

One of Thwaites' Inns of Character, on the corner of a pedestrian-only street leading to Keswick's busy market square, this friendly 18th-century coaching inn combines modern amenities with charming reminders of its past. In the 19th century, when it was known as Keswick Lodge, Coleridge, Wordsworth, Tennyson, Ruskin, Shelley and other literary titans either met or passed through here, as the plaque on an outside wall testifies. By its very nature the Lake District attracts outdoor types, so today's inn is understandably popular with walkers, climbers, sailors and cyclists. That dogs are permitted in the bar, and in some of the bedrooms, will please their owners (and probably Buster too). In the bar the real ales to remind you of your location are Thwaites' Wainwright, and Lancaster Bomber; also on tap are representatives from the brewery's Signature Range, Kingstone Press cider and 12 wines by the glass. The kitchen's careful sourcing of ingredients ensures sustainability as well as quality, all the way from sandwiches on fresh crusty bread to specialities such as Fellside lamb hotpot. Among the starters are stuffed Spanish olives; smoked haddock fishcakes with rocket salad; and ham hock and chorizo terrine. Sharing platters come in butcher's, fishmonger's and ploughman's varieties; from the grill come sirloin, rib-eye and rump steaks, Barnsley chops and burgers; and from the rotisserie, whole and half chickens. Last, but not least, are pie of the day; blackened chicken breast with sweet chilli sauce; ale-battered haddock, hand-cut chips and mushy peas; and field and wild mushroom Stroganoff. For those with a sweet tooth, Baileys cheesecake, and English Lakes ice creams are tempting options.

Open all day all wk 9am-mdnt
Food Mon-Sat 11-10, Sun 12-9
Av main course £9 Set menu available
⏣ THWAITES INNS OF CHARACTER
◀ Wainwright, Original, Lancaster
Bomber ⏣ Kingstone Press. ♟ 12
Facilities Non-diners area 🐾 (Bar
Restaurant) ⅰ Children's menu
Children's portions WiFi 🚌 (notice
required) **Rooms** 19

KESWICK *continued*

Pheasant Inn

tel: 017687 72219 **Crosthwaite Rd CA12 5PP**
dir: *On A66 Keswick rdbt towards town centre, 60yds on right*

Local food and ales, an ideal stop after a Lakeland walk

An open-fired, traditional Lakeland inn, owned by Jennings Brewery, so expect their regular range on tap, and a monthly guest. For the seasonal menus, the kitchen produces home-cooked, locally sourced food, including starters of whitebait with smoked paprika sauce; and 'gooey' baked camembert with ciabatta dipping sticks and chilli, red onion and tomato relish. Follow with a favourite like red Thai chicken and mango curry, or a chef's special (of which there are many), such as prime Cumbrian rump steak; lamb Henry with red wine gravy; and whole roasted rainbow trout with Mediterranean vegetables.

Open all day all wk Closed 25 Dec **Food** Lunch all wk 12-4 (12-2 low season) Dinner all wk 6-9 ⊕ JENNINGS ◼ Bitter, Cumberland Ale, Cocker Hoop & Sneck Lifter, Pheasant Ale, Guest ale ⌥ Thatchers Gold. ☗ 8 **Facilities** Non-diners area ❀ (Bar Garden) ◀◆ Children's menu Garden ☶ Parking WiFi

The Royal Oak at Keswick ★★★★ INN [PICK OF THE PUBS]

See Pick of the Pubs on page 109 and advert below

See Pick of the Pubs on page 109 and advert below

KIRKBY LONSDALE	Map 18 SD67

The Pheasant Inn ★★★★ INN ◉ [PICK OF THE PUBS]

tel: 01524 271230 **Casterton LA6 2RX**
email: info@pheasantinn.co.uk **web:** www.pheasantinn.co.uk
dir: *M6 junct 36, A65 for 7m, left onto A683 at Devils Bridge, 1m to Casterton centre*

Peaceful inn with lovely views of the fells

Below the fell on the edge of the beautiful Lune Valley is this sleepy hamlet with its whitewashed 18th-century coaching inn. It's perfectly situated for exploring the Dales, the Trough of Bowland and the Cumbrian Lakes. The Wilson family and staff ensure a warm welcome in the bar and stylish oak-panelled dining room. Guest ales and beers from Theakston can be sampled while perusing the interesting menu. It

mixes home-grown seasonal produce from valley farms with favourite recipes from foreign fields: starters, for example, include warm wood pigeon and quail salad, new potatoes, shallot and pistachio dressing; and home-made country pâté. The Pheasant's 'proper' braised steak, mushroom and onion pie is served with dauphinoise potatoes, white cabbage and beef jus. The excellent dessert choice ranges from old fashioned sticky syrup sponge pudding with stem ginger custard, to a classic tiramisù. Food can be served on the lawn in fine weather.

Open all day all wk **Food** Lunch all wk 12-2 Dinner all wk 6-9 ⊕ FREE HOUSE ◼ Theakston, Tirril, Guest ales. ☗ 8 **Facilities** Non-diners area ❀ (Bar Garden Outside area) ◀◆ Children's menu Children's portions Garden Outside area ☶ Parking WiFi **Rooms** 10

The Sun Inn ★★★★★ RR ◉◉ [PICK OF THE PUBS]

tel: 01524 271965 **Market St LA6 2AU**
email: email@sun-inn.info **web:** www.sun-inn.info
dir: *M6 junct 36, A65 for Kirkby Lonsdale. 5m to mini rdbt, 1st exit, left at next junct. At bottom of hill right, inn on left*

Terrific period inn with top-notch menu

JMW Turner captured the town's beauty on canvas; John Ruskin did the same in prose. Kirkby Lonsdale retains immense character and charm, beautifully evidenced in the classic period building that is The Sun Inn. It burrows back from a pretty pillared frontage into a comfy mix of low-slung beams, oak and flagstone flooring and cosy alcoves focussed on a feature fireplace at the heart of the pub. The enthusiastic owners are keen supporters of locally produced goods; expect beer from the town's microbrewery to accompany the uplifting bill of fare sourced from the surrounding countryside. Sam Carter's accomplished, modish bar and dinner menus feature starters such as ham hock and guinea fowl terrine which complements a main dish of treacle-cured wild duck breast, braised leg, potato rösti, pumpkin and gingerbread. Eleven bedrooms make The Sun an ideal base from which to explore the Lake District and Yorkshire Dales.

Open Mon 3-11, Tue-Sun 10am-11pm Closed Mon L **Food** Lunch Tue-Sun 12-3 Dinner all wk 6.30-9 Set menu available ⊕ FREE HOUSE ◼ Kirkby Lonsdale, Thwaites Wainwright, Hawkshead Bitter. ☗ 9 **Facilities** Non-diners area ❀ (Bar) ◀◆ Children's portions WiFi **Rooms** 11

PICK OF THE PUBS

Kirkstile Inn ★★★★ INN

LOWESWATER　　Map 18 NY12

tel: 01900 85219 **CA13 0RU**
email: info@kirkstile.com
web: www.kirkstile.com
dir: *From A66 Keswick take Whinlatter Pass at Braithwaite. Take B5292, at T-junct left onto B5289. 3m to Loweswater. From Cockermouth B5289 to Lorton, past Low Lorton, 3m to Loweswater. Left at red phone box*

Traditional pub set among woods, fells and lakes

Stretching as far as the eye can see, the woods, fells and lakes are as much a draw today as they must have been in the inn's infancy some 400 years ago. The beck below meanders under a stone bridge, oak trees fringing its banks with the mighty Melbreak towering impressively above. Tucked away next to an old church, this classic Cumbrian inn stands just half a mile from the Loweswater and Crummock lakes and makes an ideal base for walking, climbing, boating and fishing. The whole place has an authentic, traditional and well-looked-after feel – whitewashed walls, low beams, solid polished tables, cushioned settles, a well-stoked fire and the odd horse harness remind you of times gone by. You can call in for afternoon tea, but better still would be to taste one of the Cumbrian Legendary Ales – Loweswater Gold, Grasmoor Dark Ale, Esthwaite Bitter – brewed by landlord Roger Humphreys in Esthwaite Water near Hawkshead. Traditional pub food is freshly prepared using local produce and the lunchtime menu brims with wholesome dishes that will satisfy the most hearty appetites. For a light meal, tuck into sandwiches or ciabatta panini rolls. Evening additions and daily specials may take in deep-fried brie, coated in Loweswater ale batter with Melbreak chutney; a Cumberland sausage and black pudding 'Scotch egg'; chicken, Cumbrian ham and leek pudding; slow roasted Lakeland lamb shoulder, buttered mash and red wine and orange jus. Leave room for rum nicky, a pudding of dates, orange, ginger and rum with lattice pastry, based on a 17th-century recipe.

Open all day all wk Closed 25 Dec **Food** Lunch all wk 12-2, light menu 2-4.30 Dinner all wk 6-9 ⊕ FREE HOUSE ◀ Cumbrian Legendary Loweswater Gold, Esthwaite Bitter, Grasmoor Dark Ale, Langdale ♻ Westons Stowford Press. ⏰ 9 **Facilities** Non-diners area ⅋ Children's menu Children's portions Family room Garden ⊼ Beer festival Parking **Rooms** 10

KIRKBY LONSDALE *continued*

The Whoop Hall

tel: 015242 71284 **Skipton Rd LA6 2GY**
email: info@whoophall.co.uk
dir: *M6 junct 36, A65. Pub 1m SE of Kirkby Lonsdale*

Comfy inn in stunning countryside

Set in the gorgeous Lune Valley with fells rising to over 2,000ft just up the lane, this considerably modernised 400-year-old coaching inn is a grand base for exploring the nearby Yorkshire Dales National Park. Yorkshire also provides beers such as Black Sheep and excellent local produce used on the enticing menus in the restaurant and bistro bar. Slow-cooked pork belly with braised leeks and cider jus or roasted chump of lamb with bubble-and-squeak satisfy major appetites; or snack on stone-baked pizzas or hot deli sandwiches while sitting on the terrace.

Open all day all wk **Food** Lunch all wk 12-9 Dinner all wk 12-9 ⊕ FREE HOUSE ◀ Jennings Cumberland Cream & Cumberland Ale, Black Sheep ♂ Thatchers Gold. ⬤ 14 **Facilities** Non-diners area ❤ (Bar Garden) ◀ Play area Family room Garden ⋈ Parking ▭

LITTLE LANGDALE — Map 18 NY30

Three Shires Inn ★★★★ INN   PICK OF THE PUBS

tel: 015394 37215 **LA22 9NZ**
email: enquiry@threeshiresinn.co.uk **web:** www.threeshiresinn.co.uk
dir: *Exit A593, 2.3m from Ambleside at 2nd junct signed 'The Langdales'. 1st left 0.5m. Inn in 1m*

Popular stop-over in a wonderful setting

Comfortably fitting into a break in the drystone walls and thick hedges bordering the winding lane leading to the Wrynose and Hard Knott Passes, is this slate-built Lake District pub. Ian Stephenson and his family have run it since 1983. It's Lakeland through and through, from its Cumbrian-sourced food, and real ales from Hesket Newmarket, Hawkshead and Ennerdale, to its comfortable accommodation. Everyone – including families with children and dogs – is welcome in the beamed bar for a ploughman's, a warm ciabatta, a sandwich, or even a lamb stew. When it's cold there's a fire; when it's warm the place to be is the landscaped garden, views over the fells a bonus. For an evening meal, battered black pudding with herb mash and balsamic onion gravy, followed by grilled fresh Lakeland trout, or marinated pork loin steak, finishing with spiced sultana sponge and vanilla custard.

Open all wk 11-3 6-10.30 Dec-Jan, 11-10.30 Feb-Nov (Fri-Sat 11-11) Closed 25 Dec **Food** Lunch all wk 12-2 (ex 24-25 Dec) Dinner all wk 6-8.45 (ex mid-wk Dec-Jan) ⊕ FREE HOUSE ◀ Cumbrian Legendary Melbreak Bitter, Jennings Bitter & Cumberland Ale, Coniston Old Man Ale, Hawkshead Bitter, Ennerdale Blonde. **Facilities** Non-diners area ❤ (Bar Garden) ◀ Children's menu Garden ⋈ Parking WiFi **Rooms** 10

LOWESWATER — Map 18 NY12

Kirkstile Inn ★★★★ INN   PICK OF THE PUBS

See Pick of the Pubs on page 111

LOW LORTON — Map 18 NY12

The Wheatsheaf Inn

tel: 01900 85199 & 85268 **CA13 9UW**
email: j.williams53@sky.com
dir: *From Cockermouth take B5292 to Lorton. Right onto B5289 to Low Lorton*

Good beers, good food and good views

Occasionally, landlord Mark Cockbain crosses the lane from his white-painted, 17th-century pub to fish for salmon and trout in the River Cocker. For visitors it's the panoramic views of the lush Vale of Lorton from the child-friendly beer garden that matter. The quaint, open-fired bar looks like a gamekeeper's lodge: "We like our locals to feel at home," says Mark's wife, Jackie. Real ales from Jennings in Cockermouth also help in that respect. On the menu are sticky sesame ribs; lemon pepper chicken goujons; local trout with lime, almond and parsley butter; and chilli con carne in a tortilla basket. The end of March is beer festival time.

Open Tue-Sun Closed Mon & Tue eve in Jan & Feb **Food** Lunch Fri 12-2, Sat 12-3, Sun 12-8.30 Dinner Tue-Sat 6-8.30, Sun 12-8.30 ⊕ MARSTON'S ◀ Pedigree, Jennings Bitter & Cumberland Ale, Brakspear Oxford Gold ♂ Scrumpy Jack. **Facilities** Non-diners area ❤ (Bar Garden) ◀ Children's menu Children's portions Family room Garden ⋈ Beer festival Parking ▭

LUPTON — Map 18 SD58

The Plough Inn ★★★★★ INN ⊛   PICK OF THE PUBS

tel: 015395 67700 **Cow Brow LA6 1PJ**
email: info@theploughatlupton.co.uk **web:** www.theploughatlupton.co.uk
dir: *M6 junct 36, A65 towards Kirkby Lonsdale. Pub on right in Lupton*

Affectionately held in the locals' hearts

Below Farleton Knott, a hill from which locals once warned of Scottish unrest, stands this apparently simple roadside pub. Any notion of simplicity, however, is quickly dispelled on entering what turns out to be an extensively refurbished 1760s inn; the latest improvements were made in early 2015. Oak beams, leather sofas, colourful rugs and antique furniture impart a farmhouse feel. Brathay slate tops the bar, where Lakeland brewers such as Tirril and Bowness Bay augment Kirkby Lonsdale's own Monumental ale; more than a dozen wines are served by the glass. Polished oak floors lead into the restaurant, where open fires and wood-burning stoves do a sterling job when needed. Food is served from noon through to 9pm, with quality and local provenance the keynotes. Mussels poached in cider with smoked bacon, garlic and parsley make an excellent starter. Continue perhaps with pan-fried Cumbrian free-range chicken served with buttered parsley mash, curly kale and honey-glazed parsnips.

Open all day all wk **Food** Lunch all wk 12-9 Dinner all wk 12-9 ⊕ FREE HOUSE ◀ Kirkby Lonsdale Monumental, Thwaites Wainwright, Tirril, Bowness Bay ♂ Kingstone Press. ⬤ 14 **Facilities** Non-diners area ❤ (Bar Garden) ◀ Children's menu Children's portions Garden ⋈ Parking WiFi **Rooms** 6

NEAR SAWREY — Map 18 SD39

Tower Bank Arms   PICK OF THE PUBS

See Pick of the Pubs on opposite page

PICK OF THE PUBS

Tower Bank Arms

NEAR SAWREY Map 18 SD39

tel: 015394 36334 **LA22 0LF**
email: enquiries@towerbankarms.co.uk
web: www.towerbankarms.co.uk
dir: *On B5285 SW of Windermere.1.5m
from Hawkshead. 2m from Windermere
via ferry*

Popular rustic pub

This 17th-century village pub on the
west side of Lake Windermere is owned
by the National Trust (although run
independently), as is Beatrix Potter's old
home, Hill Top, which can be found just
behind the inn. It has been known as
the Tower Bank Arms for over a century
and Potter illustrated it perfectly in her
Tale of Jemima Puddleduck, although
history fails to record whether she ever
slipped in for a drink during a break
from sketching. This cosy, bustling inn
is popular not only with visitors to Hill
Top, but also walkers, cyclists,
holidaymakers and locals. In the low-
beamed slate-floored main bar are an
open log fire, fresh flowers and ticking
grandfather clock, with local brews on
hand-pump from the Cumbrian
Legendary and Hawkshead breweries.
Lunch and dinner menus are both
served throughout all areas. Hearty
country food makes good use of local
produce, whether in a midday snack
such as a Cumbrian baked ham
sandwich with wholegrain honey
mustard; or dishes of traditional

Cumberland sausages supplied by
Woodall's of Waberthwaite, who hold a
royal warrant; or deep-fried beer-
battered haddock with mushy peas,
chips and tartare sauce. In the evening,
try perhaps warm goats' cheese and fig
salad with honey and wholegrain
mustard dressing; and Cumbrian beef
and ale stew with herb suet dumplings.
Puds, however, are confirmed favourites:
chocolate orange brownie sundae; and
raspberry Eton mess are two examples.
Alternatively an assorted slate of
Cumbrian cheeses is accompanied with
red onion marmalade. Food and drink
can be served in the garden, where the
panorama of farms, fells and fields
makes a relaxing vista.

Open all wk (all day Etr-Oct) Closed 1wk

Dec & Jan **Food** Lunch all wk 12-2
Dinner Mon-Sat 6-9, Sun & BHs 6-8
(Mon-Thu Oct-Apr) Av main course £13
⊕ FREE HOUSE ◼ Hawkshead Bitter &
Brodie's Prime, Cumbrian Legendary
Ales Loweswater Gold & Langdale
♂ Westons Wyld Wood, Rosie's Pig & Old
Rosie ♇ 9 **Facilities** Non-diners area
🐾 (Bar Garden) ♣ Children's (evening)
menu & portions Garden 🎪 Parking WiFi
🚌 (notice required)

OUTGATE
Map 18 SD39

Outgate Inn

tel: 015394 36413 **LA22 0NQ**
email: info@outgateinn.co.uk
dir: *M6 junct 36, by-passing Kendal, A591 towards Ambleside. At Clappersgate take B5285 to Hawkshead, Outgate 3m*

Traditional welcoming Cumbrian inn with a secluded beer garden

For 80 years until 1921, aerated waters were produced in this 18th-century building, sourced from deep underground. It's owned by Robinsons Brewery, so Hartleys Cumbrian XB and Dizzy Blonde are the real ale mainstays. Newish tenants Nigel and Julie Brayne offer a wide selection of home-cooked food, including hearty sandwiches, freshly made soups, wholetail scampi, local Cumberland sausage and chilli con carne; sticky toffee pudding, and raspberry and white chocolate cheesecake are typical desserts. Vegetarian and gluten-free options are available. Several Lakeland walks start here; since they also finish here, the real fire is often a welcome sight.

Open all day all wk **Food** Lunch all wk 12-5 Dinner all wk 5-8 ⊕ ROBINSONS ◀ Dizzy Blonde, Hartleys Cumbrian XB Ŏ Westons Stowford Press. **Facilities** Non-diners area ❤ (Bar Garden) ◗◗ Children's menu Children's portions Garden ﹉ Parking WiFi

PENRITH
Map 18 NY53

Cross Keys Inn

tel: 01768 865588 **Carleton Village CA11 8TP**
email: crosskeys@kyloes.co.uk
dir: *From A66 in Penrith take A686 to Carleton Village, inn on right*

Lovely views and traditional food

This much-refurbished old drovers' and coaching inn at the edge of Penrith offers sweeping views to the nearby North Pennines from the upstairs restaurant where timeless, traditional pub meals are the order of the day; Scottish wholetail battered scampi or Cumberland lamb hotpot for example. Kyloes Grill here is particularly well thought of, with only Cumbrian meats used. Beers crafted in nearby Broughton Hall by Tirril Brewery draw an appreciative local clientele, warming their toes by the ferocious log-burner or laying a few tiles on the domino tables.

Open all wk Mon-Fri 12-2.30 5-12 (Sat-Sun all day) **Food** Lunch all wk 12-2.30 Dinner Mon-Thu 6-9, Fri-Sat 5.30-9, Sun 6-8.30 ⊕ FREE HOUSE ◀ Tirril 1823, Guest ale. ♟ 10 **Facilities** Non-diners area ❤ (Bar Garden) ◗◗ Children's menu Children's portions Garden ﹉ Parking WiFi (notice required)

RAVENSTONEDALE
Map 18 NY70

The Black Swan ★★★★ INN   PICK OF THE PUBS

See Pick of the Pubs on opposite page

The Fat Lamb Country Inn ★★★★ INN   PICK OF THE PUBS

tel: 015396 23242 **Crossbank CA17 4LL**
email: enquiries@fatlamb.co.uk web: www.fatlamb.co.uk
dir: *On A683 between Sedbergh & Kirkby Stephen*

Old-fashioned hospitality and idyllic countryside

Tables outside this 350-year-old former coaching inn come with some of the most outstanding views in England. Vast fells create an undulating patchwork that completely surrounds the stone inn. A source of the River Lune here has been

tapped to create the heart of the inn's own nature reserve, where sightings have included otters, roe deer and countless upland birds. Rambling parties can pop in for breakfast before tackling the local trails; less-active travellers can explore the very traditional interior of the inn, where quirks like a huge aircraft propeller and a stuffed ram's head provoke comment. Lounge at the bar near the old Yorkshire range, quaff Yorkshire beer and peruse a menu of pub stalwarts and daily-changing specials that cater for most diets. Look for slow-roast pulled beef cooked in a barbecue sauce served with horseradish rösti potato and parsnip crisps; or pan-seared salmon fillet with Morecambe Bay shrimps. Twelve refurbished en suite rooms complete the picture here.

Open all day all wk **Food** Lunch Mon-Fri 12-2, Sat-Sun 12-6 Dinner all wk 6-9 Av main course £11 Set menu available Restaurant menu available all wk ⊕ FREE HOUSE ◀ Black Sheep Best Bitter Ŏ Westons Stowford Press. **Facilities** Non-diners area ❤ (Bar Garden) ◗◗ Children's menu Children's portions Play area Garden ﹉ Parking WiFi (notice required) **Rooms** 12

The King's Head

tel: 015396 23050 **CA17 4NH**
email: enquiries@kings-head.com
dir: *M6 junct 38, A685 towards Kirkby Stephen. Approx 7m, right to Ravenstonedale. Pub 200yds on right*

Set in beautiful rolling Cumbrian countryside

It's hard to believe that this old whitewashed pub was, at one time, closed for three years. There are real fires in the restaurant, where a three-course lunch or evening meal might be wood pigeon breast with celeriac remoulade; braised belly of pork with black pudding potato cake; and sticky toffee pudding. Vegetarians will find dishes such as Cumberland farmhouse cheese and onion soufflé; and wild mushroom and courgette bouché. Three regularly-changing real ales and eight wines by the glass are served in the open-plan bar. Cyclists will appreciate the lock-up facility for their bikes.

Open all day all wk Closed 25 Dec **Food** Lunch all wk 12-6 Dinner all wk 6-9 Av main course £13.50 ⊕ FREE HOUSE ◀ 3 regularly changing guest ales. ♟ 8 **Facilities** Non-diners area ❤ (Bar Garden) ◗◗ Children's menu Children's portions Garden ﹉ Parking WiFi (notice required)

SANTON BRIDGE
Map 18 NY10

Bridge Inn

tel: 019467 26221 **CA19 1UX**
email: info@santonbridgeinn.co.uk
dir: *From A595 at Gosforth follow Eskdale & Wasdale sign. Through Santon to inn on left. Or inn signed from A595 S of Holmkirk*

New ownership at this country inn

The Lake District was formed, not by ice or volcanic action, but by large moles and eels. Actually, that's a lie, one of the many told in this comfortable old inn at the annual World's Biggest Liar competition, held every November. No doubt pints of Jennings Sneck Lifter, Cocker Hoop and Thatchers Gold help to inspire such outrageous fibbing. With the new owners come new set menus and the chef's specials chalked up on the board. The inn, in the beautiful valley of Wasdale, is licensed for civil marriages, when, hopefully, "I do" is not a lie!

Open all day all wk **Food** Lunch all wk 12-9 Dinner all wk 12-9 ⊕ JENNINGS ◀ Cumberland Ale, Sneck Lifter, Cocker Hoop, Guest ales Ŏ Thatchers Gold. ♟ 10 **Facilities** Non-diners area ❤ (Bar Outside area) ◗◗ Children's menu Children's portions Family room Outside area ﹉ Parking WiFi (notice required)

PICK OF THE PUBS

The Black Swan ★★★★ INN

RAVENSTONEDALE Map 18 NY70

tel: 015396 23204 **CA17 4NG**
email: enquiries@blackswanhotel.com
web: www.blackswanhotel.com
dir: *M6 junct 38, A685 E towards*
Brough; or A66 onto A685 at Kirkby
Stephen towards M6

One of Lakeland's best family-run residential inns

In a pretty conservation village, stands this handsome, multi-gabled Victorian proudly run by enterprising owners Alan and Louise Dinnes. The building has been refurbished to its former glory, and has friendly bars and a lounge warmed by an open fire. In its tranquil riverside gardens below Wild Boar Fell and the headwaters of the River Eden you might spot a red squirrel or two. An acclaimed real ale line-up features regulars from the Black Sheep brewery and guests from Dent, Hawkshead, Hesket Newmarket and Tirril microbreweries. Meals may be eaten in both bar areas, the lounge or in either of the two beautifully restored and decorated restaurants. As with the beers, reliance on local produce is key, which is evident in the names of some of the dishes. New chef Bryan Parsons brings a wealth of experience and new ideas, so maybe try spicy lamb and rosemary meatballs, chorizo and aubergine tomato sauce with egg tagliatelle; fresh crab, pepperdew and spring onion croquette

with dill and curry mayonnaise; sticky lime marmalade-glazed roast chicken breast; slow cooked shin of Galloway beef with ginger and soy, mixed greens, coriander and sweet pepper noodles; butternut squash, coconut and peanut curry. A children's option is Cumberland sausage with French fries and beans. On a memorable day in 2008 HRH Prince Charles opened the Black Swan's on-site village store where essential groceries, stationery and locally-made gifts, crafts and organic soaps and toiletries – as used in the guest rooms – are on sale. A beer festival is held in the garden in the summer. In such a lovely area of the country it is certainly worth considering stopping over in one of the inn's individually designed bedrooms.

Open all day all wk 8am-1am **Food** All day from 8am Dinner all wk 6-9 Set menu available ⊕ FREE HOUSE ◀ Black Sheep Ale & Best Bitter, John Smith's Cask, Guinness, Rotating local guest ales ♂ Westons Stowford Press. ♟
Facilities Non-diners area ☙ (Bar Garden) ♯ Children's menu & portions Play area Garden ⊼ Beer festival Parking WiFi 🚌 (notice required)
Rooms 15

SATTERTHWAITE
Map 18 SD39

The Eagles Head

tel: 01229 860237 **LA12 8LN**
email: theeagleshead@gmail.com
dir: *Phone for detailed directions*

Traditional food and local beers in family-run Lake District pub

More than 400 years old, The Eagles Head occupies a lovely spot in the tiny village of Satterthwaite in the Grizedale Forest. A traditional, family-run Cumbrian inn with a crackling log fire in winter and pretty beer garden for sunnier days, the pub has a good reputation for serving tip-top quality beers from local microbreweries such as Hawkshead and Barngates. Local meat and vegetables, as well as fish from the east coast appear in straightforward, enjoyable dishes. Whole Lakeland trout with new potatoes and salad; and Cumberland sausage, mash and onion gravy are typical main courses.

Open all day all wk **Food** Lunch all wk 12-3 Dinner all wk 5-9 ⊕ FREE HOUSE ◀ Hawkshead Pale, Cumbrian Legendary Ales Loweswater Gold, Barngates Cracker Ale, Ulverston ♂ Westons Stowford Press. **Facilities** Non-diners area ♣ (Bar Restaurant Garden) ♦ Children's menu Children's portions Garden ⋒ Beer festival Parking WiFi ➡ (notice required)

SEATHWAITE
Map 18 SD29

Newfield Inn

tel: 01229 716208 **LA20 6ED**
dir: *From Broughton-in-Furness take A595 signed Whitehaven & Workington. Right signed Ulpha. Through Ulpha to Seathwaite, 6m (NB it is advisable not to use Sat Nav)*

Classic walkers' pub with view-filled garden

Tucked away in the peaceful Duddon Valley, Wordsworth's favourite, is Paul Batten's 16th-century cottage-style pub. Hugely popular with walkers and climbers, the slate-floored bar regularly throngs with parched outdoor types quaffing pints of local ales. Served all day, food is hearty and traditional and uses local farm meats; the choice ranges from fresh rolls, salads and lunchtime snacks like double egg and chips, to home-made spicy bean casserole; Cumberland sausages; and pineapple upside down pudding. Retreat to the garden in summer and savour cracking southern fells views, or come for the beer festival in October.

Open all day all wk **Food** Lunch all wk 12-9 Dinner all wk 12-9 Av main course £10 ⊕ FREE HOUSE ◀ Cumberland Corby Ale, Jennings Cumberland Ale & Sneck Lifter, Barngates Cat Nap. ♛ 8 **Facilities** Non-diners area ♣ (Bar Garden) ♦ Children's portions Play area Garden ⋒ Beer festival Parking ➡

SEDBERGH
Map 18 SD69

NEW The Dalesman Country Inn

tel: 015396 21183 **Main St LA10 5BN**
email: info@thedalesman.co.uk
dir: *M6 junct 37, A684 to Sedbergh. Inn in town centre*

Good food and local ales in the Lakes

A 30-minute drive from Windermere, this family-run 16th-century coaching inn in the pretty market town of Sedbergh is an ideal base for Lake District walkers. A range of ales from local breweries such as Coniston and Hawkshead are served in the character bar with its warming log-burner. Once the village smithy, the restaurant serves seasonal food showcasing local producers. Try the award-winning Cumberland sausages or the lamb and root vegetable casserole with mash and pickled red cabbage. Alternatively, the home-made gourmet pizzas are a popular choice, as are the 'native breed' steaks.

Open all day all wk **Food** Lunch all wk 12-9 Dinner all wk 12-9 Av main course £14 ⊕ FREE HOUSE ◀ Cumbrian Legendary Ales Loweswater Gold, Bowness Bay, Hawkshead, Coniston ♂ Thatchers Gold. ♛ 14 **Facilities** Non-diners area ♦ Children's menu Children's portions Outside area ⋒ WiFi ➡

TEMPLE SOWERBY
Map 18 NY62

The Kings Arms ★★★★ INN

tel: 017683 62944 **CA10 1SB**
email: enquiries@kingsarmstemplesowerby.co.uk
web: www.kingsarmstemplesowerby.co.uk
dir: *M6 junct 40, E on A66 to Temple Sowerby. Inn in town centre*

Hostelry in charming village

In 1799, when Temple Sowerby was known as 'The Queen of Westmorland Villages', romantic poets William Wordsworth and Samuel Coleridge began their tour of the Lake District at this 17th-century coaching inn on the Penrith to Appleby turnpike. The kitchen serves plenty of old favourites, including Cumberland sausage, grain mustard vegetable mash with cider and red onion gravy; Thai stir-fried chicken with egg noodles; Sowerby hot-pot; and specials of honey-roast shank of lamb; pan-fried breast of Gressingham duck; and butter-grilled salmon steak. There's also a good vegetarian choice, home-made desserts and a children's menu.

Open all wk 10-3 6-11 **Food** Lunch all wk 12-2 Dinner all wk 6-9 Av main course £10.50 ⊕ FREE HOUSE ◀ Black Sheep, Guest ales ♂ Westons Stowford Press. **Facilities** Non-diners area ♣ (Bar Garden) ♦ Children's menu Children's portions Garden ⋒ Parking WiFi ➡ (notice required) **Rooms** 8

ULVERSTON
Map 18 SD27

Farmers Arms Hotel

tel: 01229 584469 **Market Place LA12 7BA**
email: roger@thefarmers-ulverston.co.uk
dir: *In town centre*

A warm welcome and crowd-pleasing pub grub

Perhaps the oldest inn in the Lake District, there's a hospitable welcome here at the Farmers Arms, whether in the traditionally decorated restaurant with its oak beams and impressive views of the Crake Valley or in the 14th-century stable bar complete with a log fire and original slate floors. The wide-ranging menus include meat or seafood deli boards for sharing; slow-cooked belly pork with black pudding, local sausage, buttered and gravy; piri piri chicken with feta, coriander and sweet potato mash; and Cumbrian mature cheese, broccoli and leek pie. Local ales include Hawkshead Bitter and there's both beer and cider festivals annually.

Open all day all wk **Food** Lunch all wk 9-3 Dinner all wk 6-9 ⊕ FREE HOUSE ◀ Hawkshead Bitter, John Smith's, Courage Directors, Yates ♂ Symonds. ♛ 12 **Facilities** Non-diners area ♦ Children's menu Children's portions Garden ⋒ Beer festival Cider festival WiFi ➡ (notice required)

Old Farmhouse

tel: 01229 480324 **Priory Rd LA12 9HR**
email: oldfarmhouse@hotmail.co.uk
dir: *From A590 in Ulverston take A5087 signed Bardsea. Pub on right*

Community-focused pub in a converted barn

Located just south of the town and a short distance from Morecambe Bay, the Old Farmhouse is a busy pub housed within a beautifully converted barn. Its very popular restaurant area in the main barn area offers an extensive traditional menu – choose a classic such as their celebrated Cumberland pie, or an Aberdeen Angus, chicken or fish burger; Cumberland meatballs and linguine; or grilled mackerel fillets, and leave room for the apple and cinnamon crumble. Local Cumbrian ales, a sun-trap courtyard garden, a big screen for live sports and a function room for private hire complete the picture.

Open all day all wk **Food** Lunch all wk 12-9 Dinner all wk 12-9 Set menu available Restaurant menu available all wk ⊕ FREE HOUSE ◀ Ulverston Harvest Moon, Lancaster Blonde, Cumberland, Sharp's Doom Bar, Copper Dragon. ♛ 9 **Facilities** Non-diners area ♣ (Bar Garden Outside area) ♦ Children's menu Children's portions Garden Outside area ⋒ Parking WiFi ➡

The Stan Laurel Inn

tel: 01229 582814 **31 The Ellers LA12 0AB**
email: thestanlaurel@aol.com
dir: M6 junct 36, A590 to Ulverston. Straight on at Booths rdbt, left at 2nd rdbt in The Ellers, pub on left after Ford garage

Local ales and hearty food

When the old market town of Ulverston's most famous son – the comic actor Stan Laurel – was born in 1890, this town-centre pub was still a farmhouse with two cottages surrounded by fields and orchards. Owners Trudi and Paul Dewar serve a selection of locally brewed real ales and a full menu of traditional pub food plus a specials board. Take your pick from starters such as Thai fishcakes; seafood pancake; Greek salad; or spicy chicken strips. Among tasty mains are green vegetable korma; liver, onions and bacon and mash; and the ever popular 'Stan's renowned lasagne'.

Open Mon 7pm-11pm Tue-Thu 12-2.30 6-11 Fri-Sat 12-2.30 6-12 Sun 12-11.30 Closed Mon L **Food** Lunch Tue-Sat 12-2, Sun 12-8 Dinner Tue-Sat 6-9, Sun 12-8 ⊕ FREE HOUSE ◖ Thwaites Original, Ulverston, Barngates, Salamander. **Facilities** Non-diners area ❤ (Bar Outside area) ◈ Children's menu Children's portions Outside area ⛱ Parking WiFi

▌ WASDALE HEAD ▐ Map 18 NY10

Wasdale Head Inn ★★★★ INN

tel: 019467 26229 **CA20 1EX**
email: reception@wasdale.com **web:** www.wasdale.com
dir: From A595 follow Wasdale signs. Inn at head of valley

Welcoming inn surrounded by record breakers

Dramatically situated at the foot of England's highest mountain, adjacent to England's smallest church and not far from the deepest lake, this Victorian inn is reputedly the birthplace of British climbing – photographs decorating the oak-panelled walls reflect the passion for this activity. Ritson's Bar is named after Will Ritson who was awarded the very first title of 'The World's Biggest Liar'. Expect local ales and hearty food such as Wasdale Particular (pea and Cumberland ham soup); followed by Wasdale lamb cobbler; or Cumberland sausage. The Wasdale Show on the 2nd Saturday in October is a great reason to hang up the climbing boots for a day and maybe stay over in one of the comfortable bedrooms.

Open all day all wk **Food** Lunch all wk 12-8.30 Dinner all wk 12-8.30 Av main course £10.50 Restaurant menu available Wed-Sun ⊕ FREE HOUSE ◖ Cumbrian Legendary Ales Loweswater Gold & Esthwaite Bitter, Jennings, Hesket Newmarket High Pike ♻ Westons. **Facilities** Non-diners area ❤ (Bar Restaurant Garden) ◈ Children's menu Children's portions Garden ⛱ Beer festival Parking **Rooms** 20

▌ WINDERMERE ▐ Map 18 SD49

Eagle & Child Inn

tel: 01539 821320 **Kendal Rd, Staveley LA8 9LP**
email: info@eaglechildinn.co.uk
dir: M6 junct 36, A590 towards Kendal then A591 towards Windermere. Staveley approx 2m

Free house with a riverside beer garden

Surrounded by miles of excellent walking, cycling and fishing country in a quiet village, this friendly inn shares the same name with several pubs in Britain, which refers to a legend of a baby found in an eagle's nest during the time of King Alfred.

The rivers Kent and Gowan meet at the pub's gardens with its picnic tables for outdoor eating and local-ale drinking. Dishes include ingredients from village suppliers, such as slow-roasted lamb shank, Cumberland sausage and hunter's chicken. Non-meat choices might be Malaysian vegetable curry or roast vegetable pasta.

Open all day all wk **Food** Lunch Mon-Fri 12-2.30, Sat-Sun 12-9 Dinner Mon-Fri 6-9, Sat-Sun 12-9 ⊕ FREE HOUSE ◖ Hawkshead Bitter, Yates Best Bitter, Tirril, Coniston, Dent, Jennings Cumberland ♻ Westons, Thatchers Gold, Guest cider. ☕ 10 **Facilities** Non-diners area ❤ (Bar Restaurant Garden) ◈ Children's menu Children's portions Garden ⛱ Parking WiFi ⛟

▌ WINSTER ▐ Map 18 SD49

The Brown Horse Inn

tel: 015394 43443 **LA23 3NR**
email: steve@thebrownhorseinn.co.uk
dir: On A5074 between Bowness-on-Windermere & A590 (Kendal to Barrow-in-Furness road)

An inn of many talents

Despite all the time-worn charm of this 1850s inn in the beautiful and tranquil Winster Valley, the decor has a subtly modern edge. The inn is virtually self-sufficient: vegetables and free-range meat come from the owners' surrounding land, and ales are brewed on site. The innovative cooking is a contemporary take on traditional fare and dinner could see a starter of tempura soft shell crab, wasabi dressing, lime and coriander. Mains range from home-made pie of the week to pork, chilli and chocolate sausages, smoked cheese and ham black pudding with creamed potatoes.

Open all day all wk **Food** Lunch Mon-Fri 12-2, Sat-Sun, BHs & School Hols 12-4 Dinner all wk 6-9 ⊕ FREE HOUSE ◖ Winster Valley Best Bitter, Old School, Hurdler, Chaser ♻ Somersby Cider. ☕ 12 **Facilities** Non-diners area ❤ (Bar Outside area) ◈ Children's menu Children's portions Outside area ⛱ Parking WiFi ⛟ (notice required)

▌ WORKINGTON ▐ Map 18 NY02

The Old Ginn House

tel: 01900 64616 **Great Clifton CA14 1TS**
email: enquiries@oldginnhouse.co.uk
dir: Just off A66, 3m from Workington & 4m from Cockermouth

Converted farm building offering good food

When this was a farm, ginning was the process by which horses were used to turn a grindstone that crushed grain. It took place in the rounded area known today as the Ginn Room and which is now the main bar, serving local ales. The dining areas, all butter yellow, bright check curtains and terracotta tiles, rather bring the Mediterranean to mind, although the extensive menu and specials are both cosmopolitan and traditional. The pub has a good reputation for steaks but others options are cod loin with streaky bacon and smoked cheese sauce; whole shoulder of lamb marinated in mint, honey and garlic; pan-fried sea bass fillet with cracked black pepper and lemon butter. A good vegetarian choice is available.

Open all day all wk Closed 24-26 Dec, 1 Jan **Food** Lunch all wk 12-2 Dinner all wk 6-9.30 ⊕ FREE HOUSE ◖ John Smith's, Coniston Bluebird Bitter, Local guest ales. **Facilities** Non-diners area ◈ Children's menu Children's portions Garden ⛱ Parking WiFi ⛟ (notice required)

YANWATH
Map 18 NY52

The Yanwath Gate Inn
PICK OF THE PUBS

tel: 01768 862386 **CA10 2LF**
email: info@yanwathgate.co.uk
dir: *Phone for detailed directions*

Known for its Cumbrian craft beers and good food

Well placed for excursions to the shores of Ullswater or the great, scalloped fells of the high Pennines, this one-time tollgate house dates from 1683, evolving into a pub several centuries later. Its favoured location between the fells and lakes, in an area of country estates and the rich pasturelands of the Eden Valley, holds the promise of great food and drink. Some of the best Cumbrian microbrewery beers from the likes of Yates and Barngates draw guests into the country-style interior with lots of beams, and old pine. Lunch and evening menus vary, and content depends on seasonal or specialist availability. A Gate Inn platter of fish, game and cheese gives a great flavour of the area, whilst more heavyweight mains can cover hogget steak with three-bean ragout and onion mash, or lemon and aubergine risotto with thyme crème fraîche. For lighter eaters there's an impressive tapas menu. Change of hands.

Open all day all wk **Food** Lunch all wk 12-2.30 Dinner all wk 6-9 ⊕ FREE HOUSE ◀ Barngates, Yates, Guest ales ♻ Westons Old Rosie. ♟ 12 **Facilities** Non-diners area ♣ (Bar Garden) ♦♦ Children's menu Garden ⌂ Parking WiFi

DERBYSHIRE

ASHOVER
Map 16 SK36

NEW The Crispin Inn

tel: 01246 590911 **Church St S45 0AB**
dir: *From Matlock take A632 towards Chesterfield. Right onto B6036 to Ashover*

Popular village pub with a past

Ashover was the scene of a confrontation between Cavaliers and Roundheads during the English Civil War; a sign on the front wall of this 14th-century pub tells of its bit-part role in the skirmish. Jennings delivers its real ales from Cumbria, Brakspear from Oxfordshire, and Marston's from Burton upon Trent. There's plenty of good pub food to be had, including hot torpedo cobs and ciabattas; jacket potatoes; seafood platter; home-made lasagne and chips; pan-fried liver and bacon; and beef and ale with dumplings. Adding to the options are such specials as kangaroo, ostrich, wild boar and other speciality sausages, and dishes suitable for vegetarians and vegans.

Open all wk 12-3 6-11.30 (Sun 12-11.30) Closed 25 Dec **Food** Lunch 12-2 Dinner 6-9 Av main course £10 ◀ Jennings Cumberland Ale & Cocker Hoop, Brakspear Oxford Gold, Marston's Pedigree. ♟ **Facilities** Non-diners area ♣ (Bar Garden) ♦♦ Children's portions Garden ⌂ Parking WiFi ⛟ (notice required)

The Old Poets Corner

tel: 01246 590888 **Butts Rd S45 0EW**
email: enquiries@oldpoets.co.uk
dir: *From Matlock take A632 signed Chesterfield. Right onto B6036 to Ashover*

Ever-popular pub with great walks all around

It's no wonder that ale and cider aficionados flock to this traditional village local; it dispenses eight ciders, and ten cask ales including choices from the Ashover Brewery behind the pub. The March and October beer festivals see these numbers multiply. There's live music here twice a week, quizzes, special events and Sunday night curries. Hearty home-cooked pub dishes range from creamy garlic mushrooms

on sourdough bread to braised liver and onions in a rich gravy made with the pub's own Coffin Lane Stout. Walk it off in the scenic Derbyshire countryside.

Open all day all wk **Food** Lunch Mon-Fri 12-2, Sat all day, Sun 12-3 Dinner Mon-Thu 6.30-9, Fri 6-9.30, Sat all day, Sun 6-9 Av main course £8.25 ⊕ FREE HOUSE ◀ Ashover, Oakham, Guest ales ♻ Broadoak Perry & Moonshine, Westons Old Rosie, Ashover & Poets' Pippin. **Facilities** Non-diners area ♣ (Bar Outside area) ♦♦ Family room Outside area ⌂ Beer festival Cider festival Parking WiFi ⛟

BAKEWELL
Map 16 SK26

The Monsal Head Hotel
PICK OF THE PUBS

tel: 01629 640250 **Monsal Head DE45 1NL**
email: enquiries@monsalhead.com
dir: *A6 from Bakewell towards Buxton. 1.5m to Ashford. Follow Monsal Head signs, B6465 for 1m*

Extensive range of local ales on draught

Only a few minutes from Chatsworth House and the famous railway viaduct at Monsal Head, the hotel's Stables bar reflects its earlier role as the home of railway horses collecting passengers from Monsal Dale station. It has a rustic ambience with an original flagstone floor, seating in horse stalls and a log fire – the perfect place to enjoy a range of cask ales from microbreweries such as Tollgate. The Longstone restaurant is spacious and airy with large windows to appreciate the views, again with an open fire in the colder weather. Although the menu has influences from around the world, it demonstrates an extensive use of local produce. Breakfasts and morning coffee are available everyday, and the same menu is offered in the bar, restaurant and the large outdoor seating area.

Open all day all wk 8am-mdnt **Food** Lunch Mon-Sat 12-9, Sun 12-8.30 Dinner Mon-Sat 12-9, Sun 12-8.30 ⊕ FREE HOUSE ◀ Wincle, Pennine Brewery Co, Tollgate Brewery, Welbeck Abbey Brewery ♻ Symonds. ♟ 17 **Facilities** Non-diners area ♣ (Bar Garden Outside area) ♦♦ Children's menu Children's portions Garden Outside area ⌂ Beer festival Parking ⛟ (notice required)

BAMFORD
Map 16 SK28

The Yorkshire Bridge Inn
PICK OF THE PUBS

See Pick of the Pubs on page 120 and advert on opposite page

BARROW UPON TRENT
Map 11 SK32

Ragley Boat Stop

tel: 01332 703919 **Deepdale Ln, Off Sinfin Ln DE73 7FY**
email: pippa@king-henrys-taverns.co.uk
dir: *Phone for detailed directions*

Canalside pub ideal for watching the world go by

This timbered and whitewashed free house features a lovely garden sloping down to the Trent and Mersey Canal. A huge balcony overlooking the canal and the grassy garden complete with picnic benches are both great spots for a quiet drink. The smart, spacious interior is cool and contemporary with muted colours, stripped wood and plenty of comfy sofas. The menu of freshly prepared dishes has choices to suit every appetite. Beef in all its forms is a major attraction; alternatively international flavours abound in dishes such as vegetable fajitas, chicken korma, swordfish steak, and a Cajun chicken and ribs combo.

Open all day all wk 11.30-11 **Food** Lunch all wk 12-10 Dinner all wk 12-10 ⊕ FREE HOUSE/KING HENRY'S TAVERNS ◀ Greene King IPA, Marston's Pedigree, Guinness. ♟ 16 **Facilities** Non-diners area ♦♦ Children's menu Children's portions Garden Parking ⛟

BEELEY
Map 16 SK26

The Devonshire Arms at Beeley ★★★★ INN ⚜⚜
PICK OF THE PUBS

tel: 01629 733259 **Devonshire Square DE4 2NR**
email: res@devonshirehotels.co.uk **web:** www.devonshirebeeley.co.uk
dir: *B6012 towards Matlock, pass Chatsworth House. After 1.5m turn left, 2nd entrance to Beeley*

Chatsworth Estate scene of Royal trysts

Surrounded by classic Peak District scenery, this handsome, 18th-century former coaching inn often welcomed Charles Dickens and, so rumour has it, King Edward VII often entertained his mistress, Alice Keppel, here. The original part of the inn is much the same as they would remember it, with low-beamed ceilings, wooden settles, flagstone floors and open fires in winter. Far more 21st century are the floor-to-ceiling windows in the bright, stripey-chaired Brasserie, which overlooks a brook and the village square, while up a few steps in the Malt Vault is the 'big table', ideal for family get-togethers. Among the modern British dishes that have earned chef-patron Alan Hill two AA Rosettes are harissa-glazed Scottish salmon; Chatsworth Estate venison haunch bourguignon; and parsnip and winter squash tarte Tatin. Alan makes good use of local produce, including game, while his Barter Board offers estate-brewed and other local beers in exchange for villagers' home-grown produce.

Open all day all wk **Food** Lunch all wk 12-3 Dinner all wk 6-9.30 ⊕ FREE HOUSE/ DEVONSHIRE HOTELS & RESTAURANTS ◀ Peak Chatsworth Gold, Thornbridge Jaipur, Theakston Old Peculier Ŏ Aspall. ♀ 10 **Facilities** Non-diners area ♦♦ Children's menu Children's portions Garden ⋈ Parking WiFi **Rooms** 14

BIRCHOVER
Map 16 SK26

The Druid Inn
PICK OF THE PUBS

tel: 01629 653836 **Main St DE4 2BL**
email: r.innes228@btinternet.com
dir: *From A6 between Matlock & Bakewell take B5056 signed Ashbourne. In approx 2m, left to Birchover*

Well-appointed village inn with dynamic menu choices

Set on a wooded ridge at the fringe of a pretty Peak District village, this classic stone-built inn has been here for over four centuries. The all-day menus make the place an ideal retreat for ramblers exploring the evocative stone circles and rock formations of the local vales and moors. It's also increasingly popular as a dining destination. Home-in first on the great selection of top-notch real ales – Blue Monkey and Abbeydale amongst many – and grab a seat on the terrace before studying a revelatory menu that offers both stalwart pub grub choices and cutting-edge dishes from a talented chef and creative team. Beetroot and potato pie with whipped goats' cheese, apple and walnut is a great starter; chased up by mains like Toulouse cassoulet; or perhaps baked wild halibut and oxtail with caramelised salsify. The blackboard menus change weekly and are complemented with occasional specialist taster menus. There's a beer festival here each May.

Open all day noon-late Closed Mon L **Food** Lunch Tue-Sat 12-9, Sun 12-8 Dinner Tue-Sat 12-9, Sun 12-8 Set menu available ⊕ FREE HOUSE ◀ Abbeydale, Cumbrian Legendary Ales, Hawkshead, Oakham Ales, Blue Monkey, Sarah Hughes, Guest ales Ŏ Hogan's. **Facilities** Non-diners area ❧ (Bar Restaurant Garden) ♦♦ Children's menu Children's portions Family room Garden ⋈ Beer festival Parking WiFi ▬ (notice required)

Red Lion Inn

tel: 01629 650363 **Main St DE4 2BN**
email: red.lion@live.co.uk
dir: *5.5m from Matlock, off A6 onto B5056*

Good beer plus Sardinian dishes on the menu

Built in 1680, the Red Lion's old well, now glass-covered, still remains in the taproom. Follow a walk to nearby Rowter Rocks and cosy up in the oak-beamed bar with its exposed stone walls, scrubbed oak tables and worn quarry-tiled floor. Quaff a pint of locally brewed Nine Ladies or one of the other weekly-changing real ales on tap, and refuel with a plate of home-cooked food. Start with a Sardinian speciality from owner Matteo Frau's homeland, perhaps a selection of cured meats, cheese and olives, then follow with pork loin medallions with lemon, caper and sage butter, or field mushroom tart Tatin with Birchover Blue cheese. Their Sardinian evenings prove popular and there's a beer and cider festival mid July.

Open 12-2.30 6-11.30 (Sat & BH Mon 12-12 Sun 12-11) Closed Mon in winter ex BHs **Food** Lunch Mon-Fri 12-2.30, Sat 12-9, Sun-12-8 Dinner Mon-Fri 6-9, Sat 12-9, Sun-12-8 Av main course £10.95 Set menu available ⊕ FREE HOUSE ◀ Peak Swift Nick, Nine Ladies, Peakstones Rock, Buxton, Thornbridge, Ichinusa (Sardinian) Ŏ Traditional Local ciders. **Facilities** Non-diners area ♦♦ Children's portions Garden Beer festival Cider festival Parking WiFi ▬

The Yorkshire Bridge Inn

Ashopton Road, Bamford, Hope Valley, Derbyshire S33 0AZ
Tel: 01433 651361 · Email: info@yorkshire-bridge.co.uk
Website: www.yorkshire-bridge.co.uk

Set in a glorious location, *The Yorkshire Bridge Inn* is an ideal base from which to explore the exceptional beauty of the Peak District. With a magnificent backdrop of some of the most stunning scenery in the Peak District National Park, the Upper Derwent reservoir area is a simply spectacular location and is considered by many to be the jewel in the Peak District's crown.

The quality and integrity of our food is something special. We have fine food prepared to order using fresh local produce. There is a great choice of beers as well as an imaginative well priced wine list.

We have 14 bedrooms offering comfortable accommodation, as well as 5-star self catering apartments located in the recently restored former pump house to the reservoir.

Our award winning success and desire to please our guests go hand in hand. Together with our friendly, loyal and helpful staff, we will endeavour to make your stay a real home from home.

PICK OF THE PUBS

The Yorkshire Bridge Inn

BAMFORD   Map 16 SK28

tel: 01433 651361
Ashopton Rd S33 0AZ
email: info@yorkshire-bridge.co.uk
web: www.yorkshire-bridge.co.uk
dir: *From Sheffield A57 towards Glossop,*
left onto A6013, pub 1m on right

In the heart of wonderful Peak District walking country

Named after the old packhorse bridge over the River Derwent, this early 19th-century free house is only a short distance away from the Ladybower Reservoir. Between 1935 and 1943, when it was created, two local villages were drowned and during periods of drought it's possible to see the remains of one of them. It was in 1943 that the RAF's 617 Squadron, known as 'The Dambusters', used Ladybower and two other nearby reservoirs for testing Barnes Wallis's famous bouncing bombs, later to destroy two important German dams. Back inside, views from the beamed and chintz-curtained bars take in the peak of Whin Hill, making it a jolly good spot for enjoying a pint of the unique Bombs Gone specially brewed for the inn at the Bradfield Brewery, and good-quality pub food made with fresh local produce. Sandwiches are all freshly prepared, with fillings from home-baked ham to hot tuna melt. Main meal starters include home-made asparagus soup;

and oak-smoked salmon and prawn cocktail, and a sharing platter in which nachos with melted cheese, jalapeño peppers and baked spare ribs marinated in barbecue sauce are just a pointer to what will arrive on the plate. Next could come warm Spanish quiche; chargrilled rosemary and garlic lamb steaks; grilled salmon fillet with béarnaise sauce; or one of the various salad platters. If you've walked to one of the reservoirs and back, look to the grill for a calorie replacing T-bone, sirloin or gammon steak, cooked to your liking without demur from a chef who doesn't insist on doing it his way. Bakewell pudding, or New York vanilla cheesecake finish a meal off well. A beer and cider festival is held in mid-May.

Open all day all wk **Food** Lunch Mon-Sat 12-2.30, Sun 12-8.30 Dinner Mon-Thu 5.30-8.30, Fri-Sat 5-9, Sun 12-8.30 Av main course £11 🛢 FREE HOUSE 🍺 Peak Ales Bakewell Best Bitter, Bradfield Farmers Blonde, Farmers Bitter & Bombs Gone 🍏 Thatchers. 🍷 11 **Facilities** Non-diners area 🍴 Children's menu & portions Garden 🪑 Beer festival Cider festival Parking WiFi 🚌 (notice required)

BONSALL
Map 16 SK25

The Barley Mow

tel: 01629 825685 **The Dale DE4 2AY**
email: david.j.wragg@gmail.com
dir: *S from Matlock on A6 to Cromford. Right onto A5012 (Cromwell Hill). Right into Water Ln (A5012). Right in Clatterway towards Bonsall. Left at memorial into The Dale. Pub 400mtrs on right*

Good food, real ales and fast fowl

There are several reasons to visit this intimate, former lead miner's cottage: Bonsall is apparently Europe's UFO capital; the pub hosts the World Championship Hen Races; and landlords Colette and David display an unshakeable commitment to Peak District and other regional real ales, as their bank holiday beer festivals help to confirm. The simple menu is all about home-cooked pub grub, such as ham, egg and chips; scampi and chips; extra-mature rump steak; chicken curry; sausages and mash; beef chilli; and gammon steak.

Open 6-11 (Sat-Sun 12-12) Closed Mon (ex BHs) **Food** Lunch Sat-Sun 12-3 Dinner Tue-Fri 6-9, Sat-Sun 5-8 ⊕ FREE HOUSE ◀ Thornbridge, Whim, Abbeydale, Blue Monkey ♂ Hecks, Westons Perry. ♟ 10 **Facilities** Non-diners area ❀ (Bar Restaurant Outside area) ⬩ Children's menu Children's portions Outside area ⊼ Beer festival Cider festival Parking WiFi ▄▄

BRADWELL
Map 16 SK18

The Samuel Fox Country Inn ★★★★★ INN ◉◉

tel: 01433 621562 **Stretfield Rd S33 9JT**
email: enquiries@samuelfox.co.uk **web:** www.samuelfox.co.uk
dir: *M1 junct 29, A617 towards Chesterfield onto A623 (Chapel-en-le-Frith). B6049 to Bradwell. Pub on left*

Fine food and real ales in the Hope Valley

In the heart of the Peak District National Park and handy for the Pennine Way, this village inn is named after the local man credited with inventing the steel-ribbed umbrella – hence the pub sign showing a fox sheltering beneath one. Owner and chef, James Duckett, has worked in and run restaurants in several countries and ensures that there's a warm welcome and pleasant atmosphere for villagers and visitors alike. Contemporary and cosmopolitan notes creep into the food, which is firmly based on fresh local produce. Expect the likes of hake fritters; beef cheek braised in red wine; and poached lemon sole with Jerusalem artichokes, cavolo nero and market mushrooms.

Open 12-3 6-11 Closed 2-18 Jan, Mon & Tue **Food** Lunch Wed-Sat 12-2.30, Sun 1-8 Dinner Wed-Sat 6-9, Sun 6-8 Set menu available Restaurant menu available Wed-Sun ⊕ FREE HOUSE ◀ Bradfield, Kelham Island ♂ Thatchers Heritage, Westons. ♟ 19 **Facilities** Non-diners area ⬩ Children's menu Children's portions Outside area ⊼ Parking WiFi **Rooms** 4

CASTLETON
Map 16 SK18

The Peak Hotel

tel: 01433 620247 **How Ln S33 8WJ**
email: info@thepeakhotel.co.uk
dir: *On A6187 in centre of village*

Plenty on offer at this Peak District magnet

The Peak Hotel is where to aim for after climbing Lose Hill, or walking along the Hope Valley. Standing below Peveril Castle, this 17th-century stone building is a real magnet, seducing visitors with its leather armchairs, open log fires and locally brewed cask beers, real ciders and wines by the glass; alternative places to recover are the restaurant/coffee shop and raised sun terrace. Regional ingredients are used to good effect in dishes such as winter vegetable and lentil broth; steak and ale casserole with dumplings; and Derbyshire venison burger.

Open all day all wk **Food** Lunch all wk 12-5 Dinner all wk 5-9 ⊕ PUNCH TAVERNS ◀ Adnams Southwold Bitter, Kelham Island Easy Rider, Castle Rock Harvest Pale, Guest ales ♂ Westons Old Rosie & Stowford Press. ♟ 9 **Facilities** Non-diners area ❀ (All areas) ⬩ Children's menu Children's portions Garden Outside area ⊼ Beer festival Cider festival Parking WiFi ▄▄ (notice required)

Ye Olde Nags Head

tel: 01433 620248 **Cross St S33 8WH**
email: info@yeoldenagshead.co.uk
dir: *A625 from Sheffield, W through Hope Valley, through Hathersage & Hope. Pub on main road*

A warm welcome and crowd-pleasing food

Close to Chatsworth House and Haddon Hall, this traditional 17th-century coaching inn is situated in the heart of the Peak District National Park. The owner continues to welcome thirsty travellers, and the miles of wonderful walks and country lanes favoured by walkers and cyclists means that there are plenty of them willing to occupy the cosy bars warmed by open fires. The interior is a successful mix of contemporary and traditional, a theme also reflected on the menu: expect a variety of stone-baked pizzas, sandwiches, salads, grills and sharing platters. Main dishes include beef, ale and potato pie, and classic nut roast topped with roast tomato sauce and goats' cheese. There's also a beer festival in the summer.

Open all day all wk **Food** Lunch all wk 12-9 Dinner all wk 12-9 ⊕ FREE HOUSE ◀ Timothy Taylor Landlord, Buxton Kinder Sunset, Kelham Island Riders on the Storm, Black Sheep, Sharp's Doom Bar, Bradfield Farmers Blonde, Guinness ♂ Westons Old Rosie, Rosie's Pig, Family Reserve. **Facilities** Non-diners area ❀ (Bar) ⬩ Children's menu Children's portions Beer festival Parking WiFi ▄▄ (notice required)

CHESTERFIELD
Map 16 SK37

Red Lion Pub & Bistro ★★★★ HL ◉◉ **PICK OF THE PUBS**

tel: 01246 566142 **Darley Rd, Stone Edge S45 0LW**
email: dine@peakedgehotel.co.uk **web:** www.peakedgehotel.co.uk
dir: *Phone for detailed directions*

Innovative food close to good walking country

Dating back to 1788, the Red Lion has seen many changes but it has retained much of its character. Located on the edge of the beautiful Peak District National Park, the original wooden beams and stone walls are complemented by discreet lighting and comfy leather armchairs which add a contemporary edge. Striking black-and-white photographs decorate the walls, whilst local bands liven up the bar on Thursday evenings. Meals are served in the bar and bistro, or beneath umbrellas in the large garden. Seasonal produce drives the menu and the chefs make everything, from sauces to the chips. Typical choices might start with crab lasagne, or carpaccio of beef with pickled vegetables, followed by stone bass, confit radishes, pak choi and chicken oysters; or poached and roasted rabbit, carrot variations and rabbit bolognese. Leave space for 'The Bakewell' with custard, or one of the home-made ice creams.

Open all day all wk **Food** Lunch Sun-Thu 12-9, Fri-Sat 12-9.30 Dinner Sun-Thu 12-9, Fri-Sat 12-9.30 ⊕ FREE HOUSE ◀ Guest ales. ♟ 12 **Facilities** Non-diners area ⬩ Children's menu Children's portions Garden ⊼ Parking WiFi ▄▄ (notice required) **Rooms** 27

CHINLEY
Map 16 SK08

Old Hall Inn
PICK OF THE PUBS

See Pick of the Pubs on opposite page

The Paper Mill Inn

tel: 01663 750529 **Whitehough SK23 6EJ**
email: info@papermillinn.co.uk
dir: *In village centre*

A cosy beer haven with frequently changing menus

Run by the same team as the adjacent Old Hall Inn, the pub is a veritable haven for beer and sport lovers. Flagstone floors, open fires and sporting events on TV combine to create a highly satisfactory ambience for customers enjoying real ales such as Thornbridge, or a world beer from the list of many; the choice peaks at festivals in February and September, with the latter also hosting draught ciders. The food on offer is just tapas-style small plates as the main restaurant is over at the Old Hall Inn.

Open all wk 5-11 (Sat-Sun 12-11) **Food** Contact pub for food times ⊕ FREE HOUSE ◀ Thornbridge, Marston's. **Facilities** Non-diners area ❖ (Bar Restaurant Outside area) ♦ Outside area ⌷ Beer festival Cider festival Parking WiFi ▭

DALBURY
Map 10 SK23

The Black Cow ★★★★ INN ◉

tel: 01332 824297 **The Green DE6 5BE**
email: info@blackcow.co.uk **web:** www.theblackcow.co.uk
dir: *From A52 (W of Derby) take B5020 signed Mickleover. On left bend right signed Long Ln & Longford. Left signed Lees Dalbury. Pub on left in village. (NB if using Sat Nav follow directions not postcode)*

Recommended for its hospitality, accommodation and cuisine

Facing the village green and its iconic red telephone box, this free house champions real ales from county-based Dancing Duck, Mansfield and Mr Grundy's breweries. In the one AA-Rosette restaurant, award-winning head chef Jaswant Singh's seasonal menus might feature red Thai vegetable stir-fry; spicy meatballs in tomato parsley sauce with melted cheddar and pasta; and breaded scampi with home-made chips. Since this is Derbyshire, expect Bakewell tart with crème Anglaise to make an appearance. Tastefully decorated guest rooms offer free WiFi. A small store/farm shop even sells ramblers' and cyclists' requirements.

Open all wk 12-3 5-close (Sat & Sun 12-close) **Food** Lunch Mon-Fri 12-2, Sat 12-9.30, Sun 12-4 Dinner Mon-Thu 6-9, Fri 6-9.30, Sat 12-9.30 ⊕ FREE HOUSE ◀ Guest real ales. ⏲ 10 **Facilities** Non-diners area ♦ Children's menu Children's portions Play area Family room Garden Outside area ⌷ Beer festival Parking WiFi ▭ (notice required) **Rooms** 6

Find out more about this county with *The AA Guide to The Peak District* **– see shop.theAA.com**

DERBY
Map 11 SK33

The Alexandra Hotel

tel: 01332 293993 **203 Siddals Rd DE1 2QE**
email: alexandrahotel@castlerockbrewery.co.uk
dir: *150yds from rail station*

Victorian railway hotel with an excellent choice of real ales

This small hotel was built in 1871 and is named after the Danish princess who married the Prince of Wales, later Edward VII. It was also known as the Midland coffee house after the Midland Railway company, one of Derby's major employers. It is noted for its real ales with between six and eight pumps on the go at any one time; real ciders, and bottled and draught continental beers complete the line-up at the bar. Simple food offerings include pies and filled rolls.

Open all day all wk 12-11 (Fri 12-12 Sat 11am-mdnt) **Food** Contact pub for food times ⊕ CASTLE ROCK ◀ Harvest Pale ♂ Westons Old Rosie. **Facilities** Non-diners area ❖ (Bar Outside area) ♦ Outside area Parking WiFi

DOE LEA
Map 16 SK46

Hardwick Inn

tel: 01246 850245 **Hardwick Park S44 5QJ**
email: hardwickinn@hotmail.co.uk
dir: *M1 junct 29, A6175. 0.5m left signed Stainsby/Hardwick Hall. After Stainsby, 2m, left at staggered junct. Follow brown tourist signs*

Step back in time at this village inn

Dating from the 15th century and built of locally quarried sandstone, this striking building was once the lodge for Hardwick Hall (NT) and stands at the south gate of Hardwick Park, not far from Chesterfield. Owned by the Batty family for three generations, the pub has a rambling interior and features period details such as mullioned windows, oak beams and stone fireplaces. Traditional food takes in a popular carvery roast, a salad bar, hearty home-made pies and casseroles, as well as selections of fish and vegetarian dishes. A handy pitstop for M1 travellers.

Open all day all wk **Food** Lunch Mon-Sat 11.30-9.30, Sun 12-9 Dinner Mon-Sat 11.30-9.30, Sun 12-9 Set menu available ⊕ FREE HOUSE ◀ Theakston Old Peculier & XB, Bess of Hardwick, Black Sheep, Peak Ales Chatsworth Gold ♂ Symonds Scrumpy Jack. ⏲ 10 **Facilities** Non-diners area ❖ (Bar Garden) ♦ Children's menu Children's portions Play area Family room Garden ⌷ Parking ▭

ELMTON
Map 16 SK57

The Elm Tree

tel: 01909 721261 **S80 4LS**
email: enquiries@elmtreeelmton.co.uk
dir: *M1 junct 30, A616 signed Newart through 5 rdbts. Through Clowne, right at staggered x-rds into Hazelmere Rd to Elmton*

Contemporary dining pub with a passion for local produce

Food is very much the focus at this 17th-century pub tucked away in pretty Elmton. Chef-patron Chris Norfolk is passionate about sourcing seasonal and fully traceable produce from local suppliers, including fruit and vegetables from neighbour's gardens, and everything, from bread, pasta and pastry, is made on the premises. Changing menus (served all day) may deliver roast partridge with creamed cabbage and bacon; lentil, potato and spinach curry, their award-winning burger (topped with Stilton and jalapeño peppers), and baked vanilla cheesecake with raspberry sorbet. There's a contemporary feel in the stone-floored bar and 'The Library' private dining room with four real ales on tap.

Open all day Closed Tue **Food** Lunch Mon, Wed-Sat 12-9, Sun 12-6 Dinner Mon, Wed-Sat 12-9, Sun 12-6 Set menu available ⊕ PUNCH TAVERNS ◀ Black Sheep, Kelham Island Easy Rider, Elm Tree Bitter ♂ Westons Old Rosie & Perry. ⏲ **Facilities** Non-diners area ❖ (Bar Garden) ♦ Children's portions Play area Garden ⌷ Parking ▭ (notice required)

PICK OF THE PUBS

Old Hall Inn

CHINLEY　　　　**Map 16 SK08**

tel: 01663 750529
Whitehough SK23 6EJ
email: info@old-hall-inn.co.uk
web: www.old-hall-inn.co.uk
dir: *B5470 W from Chapel-en-le-Frith.
Right into Whitehough Head Ln. 0.8m
to inn*

An ideal stop for serious walkers

Prime Peak District walking country surrounds this family-run 16th-century pub attached to Whitehough Hall. It's within easy reach are the iconic landscape features of Kinder Scout, Mam Tor and Stanage Edge, popular with climbers and fell-walkers who head here for refreshment following their exertions. And no wonder. The drinks list is as long as your arm, with local breweries to the fore; beers from Kelham Island, Red Willow, Thornbridge and many more all have their enthusiasts, which makes for a lively atmosphere in the bar. Sheppy's from Somerset is among the real ciders and perries – a cider festival is held on the third weekend in September. All manner of bottled beers, particularly Belgian wheat, fruit and Trappist varieties, a remarkable choice of malts and gins and around 80 wines round off the excellent drinks range. Food service is busy too; the pub opens into the Minstrels' Gallery restaurant in the old manor house, where a short seasonal

menu and daily specials offer freshly made 'small plates' of haddock, leek and smoked bacon gratin; confit pork belly and fresh apple salad; and whitebait and home-made tartare sauce. Main courses range from Derbyshire steaks hung for one month, served with grilled tomato, mushroom, peas and home-made chips; and other pub classics such as Cumberland pork sausages; and honey home-roasted ham, free range eggs and chips, to pan-seared monkfish with vegetarian Thai green curry and rice. Half a dozen desserts, award-winning British cheeses, artisan teas and freshly roasted coffee complete the all-embracing menu.

Open all day all wk **Food** Lunch Mon-Sat 12-2, Sun 12-7.30 Dinner Mon-Thu 5-9, Fri-Sat 5-9.30, Sun 12-7.30 Av main course £10 Set menu available ⊕ FREE HOUSE ◀ Marston's, Thornbridge, Phoenix, Abbeydale, Storm, Kelham Island, Red Willow Ö Thatchers, Sheppy's, Westons. ☻ 12 **Facilities** Non-diners area ♦♦ Children's menu & portions Garden ☂ Beer festival Cider festival Parking WiFi ⛟

EYAM — Map 16 SK27

Miners Arms

tel: 01433 630853 **Water Ln S32 5RG**
dir: Off B6521, 5m N of Bakewell

Children, dogs and walkers all welcome

This welcoming 17th-century inn and restaurant was built just before the plague hit Eyam; the village tailor brought damp cloth from London and hung it to dry in front of the fire so releasing the infected fleas. The pub gets its name from the local lead mines of Roman times. Owned by Greene King, there's always the option to pop in for a pint of their IPA or Ruddles Best bitter, or enjoy a meal. A beer festival is held three times a year.

Open all wk Mon 12-3 5.30-12 Tue-Sun 12-12 **Food** Lunch Mon-Sat 12-2, Sun 12-3 Dinner Mon 6-8, Tue-Fri 6-9, Sat 7-9 ⊕ GREENE KING ◄ IPA, Ruddles Best, Guest ales ♂ Westons Old Rosie. **Facilities** Non-diners area ♣ (Bar Garden) ♦ Children's menu Children's portions Garden ⌂ Beer festival Parking WiFi ⚌ (notice required)

FENNY BENTLEY — Map 16 SK14

Bentley Brook Inn ★★★ INN — PICK OF THE PUBS

tel: 01335 350278 **DE6 1LF**
email: all@bentleybrookinn.co.uk **web:** www.bentleybrookinn.co.uk
dir: 2m N of Ashbourne at junct of A515 & B5056

Local specialities at the edge of the Peak District

Just a short distance from the glories of Dovedale, this eye-catching black-and-white country property was created over 200 years ago on the footprint of a medieval farmhouse. It became a pub only in the 1970s. Many period features remain, including a splendid central log fireplace. Outside are several acres of landscaped gardens which host the World Toe-Wrestling Championship every summer. From this you may deduce that real ales play an important part in the daily life of the inn; Leatherbritches (which originated here), Marston's and Falstaff brews are all on offer. Service starts with breakfast at 8am (8.30am in winter), but check the inn's diary if you're planning an evening out – the week is dotted with special attractions such as the Chinese buffet on Thursdays. With a menu proffering popular pub meals, there's something for everyone: from tandoori chicken skewers to scampi in a basket. Children and dogs are made very welcome, and the Sunday carvery lunch is popular.

Open all day all wk 12-12 **Food** Lunch all wk 12-9 (Winter Mon-Fri 12-3) Dinner all wk 12-9 (Winter Mon-Fri 6-9) Set menu available Restaurant menu available Mon-Sat ⊕ FREE HOUSE ◄ Leatherbritches Dr Johnson, Falstaff, Marston's Pedigree. ♥ 10 **Facilities** Non-diners area ♣ (Bar Garden) ♦ Children's menu Children's portions Play area Garden ⌂ Beer festival Parking WiFi ⚌ **Rooms** 11

Looking for a beer or cider festival?
Check our listings at the end of this guide

The Coach and Horses Inn

tel: 01335 350246 **DE6 1LB**
email: coachandhorses2@btconnect.com **web:** www.coachandhorsesfennybentley.co.uk
dir: On A515 (Ashbourne to Buxton road), 2.5m from Ashbourne

17th-century coaching inn offering good, honest cooking

A cosy refuge in any weather, this family-run, 17th-century coaching inn stands on the edge of the Peak District National Park. Besides the beautiful location, its charms include stripped wood furniture and low beams, real log-burning fires plus a welcoming and friendly atmosphere. Expect a great selection of real ales and good home cooking that is hearty and uses the best of local produce. Specials could include baked salmon en croûte with white wine and watercress cream sauce; chicken breast wrapped in bacon and stuffed with haggis; or pan-fried Gressingham duck breast with black cherry and vodka sauce. Hot and cold sandwiches and baguettes provide lighter options.

Open all day all wk 11-11 (Sun 12-10.30) **Food** Lunch all wk 12-9 Dinner all wk 12-9 ⊕ FREE HOUSE ◄ Marston's Pedigree, Oakham JHB, Peak Swift Nick, Whim Hartington Bitter, Derby. **Facilities** Non-diners area ♦ Children's menu Family room Garden ⌂ Parking ⚌ (notice required)

FOOLOW — Map 16 SK17

The Bulls Head Inn ★★★★ INN

tel: 01433 630873 **S32 5QR**
email: wilbnd@aol.com **web:** www.thebullatfoolow.co.uk
dir: Just off A623, N of Stoney Middleton

Traditional English country pub serving good food

In an upland village surrounded by a lattice-work of dry-stone walls, this 19th-century former coaching inn is the epitome of the English country pub. Well, with open fires, oak beams, flagstone floors, great views and good food and beer, it has to be. The bar serves Black Sheep and Peak Ales, lunchtime snacks and sandwiches, while main meals include Cumberland sausages and Yorkshire pudding; beef Wellington with red wine gravy; sea bream fillets with lemon butter; Mediterranean vegetable hotpot. The bedrooms are well equipped.

Open 12-3 6.30-11 (Sun all day) Closed Mon (ex BHs) **Food** Lunch Tue-Sun 12-2 Dinner Tue-Sun 6.30-9 ⊕ FREE HOUSE ◄ Black Sheep, Peak, Adnams, Tetley. **Facilities** Non-diners area ♣ (Bar) ♦ Children's menu Children's portions ⌂ Parking ⚌ **Rooms** 3

PICK OF THE PUBS

The Maynard ★★★ HL ❀❀

GRINDLEFORD   Map 16 SK27

tel: 01433 630321
Main Rd S32 2HE
email: info@themaynard.co.uk
web: www.themaynard.co.uk
dir: *M1 junct 30, A619 into Chesterfield,
then onto Baslow. A623 to Calver, right
into Grindleford*

Imposing Peak District hotel with a fine-dining restaurant

Renowned attractions lie within easy reach of this former coaching inn. Chatsworth House is the family seat of the Dukes of Devonshire, and near Castleton is the Blue John Cavern, where the semi-precious mineral is still mined. Above the pub are the steep, wooded crags of Froggatt Edge, while below is the village of Grindleford and, beyond, the Derwent Valley. Although decorated in a contemporary style, the interior of this stone-built inn retains plenty of original features to make visitors aware of its Edwardian origins. Local artists are invited to display their work around the walls, alongside photographs of Peak District scenes. In the Longshaw Bar, with its leather sofas and log fires, real ales include Abbeydale Moonshine, and Peak Ales Bakewell Best, brewed on the Chatsworth Estate. Here, lime and ginger cod fishcake is offered as a starter, perhaps followed by lamb, shallot and garden pea pie, or teriyaki-style salmon fillet. The alternative place in which to find out why The Maynard has earned two AA Rosettes is the contemporary restaurant overlooking the gardens and countryside, where seasonal menus might offer starters of a pork tasting plate, or crisp sea bass fillet; main courses of 28-day aged Derbyshire rib-eye steak; pan-fried gilt-head bream fillet; or Moroccan-style vegetable and chickpea stew; and desserts of home-made Yorkshire parkin with spiced rum custard, or mulled fruit crumble. The large beer garden offers stunning panoramas across moorland and river valley. Beautifully appointed en suite bedrooms offer a king-size bed, flat-screen TV, tea and coffee facilities and complimentary WiFi. Dogs are most welcome.

Open all day all wk **Food** Lunch all wk 12-2 Dinner all wk 7-9 Restaurant menu available all wk ⊕ FREE HOUSE ◖ Abbeydale Moonshine, Peak Bakewell Best Bitter. **Facilities** Non-diners area ❤ (Bar) ⭧ Children's menu Garden ⋈ Parking WiFi ᓚ (notice required) **Rooms** 10

FROGGATT

Map 16 SK27

The Chequers Inn ★★★★ INN ◉

PICK OF THE PUBS

tel: 01433 630231 **Froggatt Edge S32 3ZJ**
email: info@chequers-froggatt.com web: www.chequers-froggatt.com
dir: *On A625, 0.5m N of Calver*

A Peak District favourite

Walk, cycle or drive to this 16th-century pub, standing on a wooded hillside below the gritstone escarpment of Froggatt Edge. You won't be disappointed. Wooden floors, antiques and blazing log fires create a welcoming interior that's perfect for a pint of Peak Ales Chatsworth Gold, brewed on the nearby estate of the Duke of Devonshire. The kitchen's loyalty to local produce and suppliers is reflected in the pub menu with dishes such as Derbyshire wood pigeon with spiced popcorn, radish, autumn berries and charcoal mayonnaise; lamb rump with mini-turnips, Chantenay carrots, sweetbreads and elderflower jus; and East Coast beer-battered haddock with twice-cooked chips and mushy peas. In addition, there's a range of lunchtime sandwiches and an ever-changing selection of blackboard specials, including vegetarian options. Popular with walkers, Froggatt Edge itself can be reached by a steep, wild woodland footpath from the pub's elevated secret garden.

Open all day all wk Closed 25 Dec **Food** Lunch Mon-Fri 12-2.30, Sat 12-9.30, Sun 12-9 Dinner Mon-Fri 6-9.30, Sat 12-9.30, Sun 12-9 ⊕ FREE HOUSE ◄ Kelham Island Easy Rider, Peak Ales Bakewell Best Bitter & Chatsworth Gold, Bradfield Farmers Blonde, Guest ales. ♀ 10 **Facilities** ♦♦ Children's portions Garden ⋈ Parking WiFi **Rooms** 6

GREAT HUCKLOW

Map 16 SK17

The Queen Anne Inn ★★★ INN

tel: 01298 871246 **SK17 8RF**
email: angelaryan100@aol.com web: www.queenanneinn.co.uk
dir: *A623 onto B6049, exit at Anchor pub towards Bradwell, 2nd right to Great Hucklow*

Great hospitality in a country setting

The inn dates from 1621, a licence has been held for over 300 years and the names of all the landlords are known. The sheltered south-facing garden enjoys wonderful open views, and it's an ideal space for children during the warmer months. Inside you'll find an open fire in the stone fireplace, an ever-changing range of cask ales, and a short menu of popular pub dishes. These embrace starters of traditional prawn cocktail or smoked trout with seafood sauce; and main courses of Whitby scampi with chips and peas; or kung po chilli chicken with egg-fried rice.

Open 12-2.30 5-11 (Fri-Sun 12-11) Closed Mon **Food** Lunch Tue-Sun 12-2 Dinner Tue-Thu 6-8.30, Fri-Sat 6-9, Sun 6-8 Set menu available Restaurant menu available Tue-Sun ⊕ FREE HOUSE ◄ Tetley's Cask, Bass, Local guest ales ♂ Westons Stowford Press. ♀ 9 **Facilities** Non-diners area ♥ (Bar Garden) ♦♦ Children's menu Children's portions Family room Garden ⋈ Parking WiFi ⚐ (notice required) **Rooms** 2

GREAT LONGSTONE

Map 16 SK27

The White Lion

tel: 01629 640252 **Main St DE45 1TA**
email: info@whiteliongreatlongstone.co.uk
dir: *Take A6020 from Ashford-in-the-Water towards Chesterfield. Left to Great Longstone*

Stylish pub in an unspoilt Peak District village

Whether arriving on foot, on two wheels, or on four legs, visitors to Great Longstone's White Lion are sure to recuperate from their exertions. Sitting under the mass of Longstone Edge not far from Bakewell, Greg and Libby Robinson's gastro-pub has a peaceful outside patio and dog-welcoming snug bar. Very much food

focussed, the monthly-changing menus use locally-sourced produce whenever possible. A fixed-price two- or three-course lunch represents excellent value: a starter of smoked haddock and chive tart; or warm crab and salmon mousse could be followed by a plate of seafood ravioli; basil pesto risotto, or oven-baked salmon with lime and ginger linguine.

Open all wk 12-3 6-9 (Sat 12-9 Sun 12-8) **Food** Contact pub for food times Set menu available ⊕ ROBINSONS ◄ Dizzy Blonde. **Facilities** Non-diners area ♥ (Bar Outside area) ♦♦ Children's menu Children's portions Outside area ⋈ Parking WiFi ⚐ (notice required)

GRINDLEFORD

Map 16 SK27

The Maynard ★★★ HL ◉◉

PICK OF THE PUBS

See Pick of the Pubs on page 125

HARDSTOFT

Map 16 SK46

COCO Bar Bistro at the Shoulder ★★★★ INN

tel: 01246 850276 **Deep Ln S45 8AF**
email: book@cocoattheshoulder.co.uk web: www.cocoattheshoulder.co.uk
dir: *From B6039 follow signs for Hardwick Hall. 1st right into car park*

Inviting menu in Derbyshire countryside inn

Just ten minutes from the M1, this 300-year-old pub, now in new hands, is an ideal base for exploring the Peak District and Sherwood Forest. Peak Ales' Bakewell Best Bitter is one of the local beers available in the bar, with its open log fires. The kitchen sources all ingredients within 15 miles of the pub where possible, with the exception of fish, which is from sustainable sources. In the restaurant look forward to a pan-seared scallop or basil and spinach gnocchi starter, a taster for mains such as poached salmon fishcakes with poached egg and tartare sauce; or wild mushroom and goats' cheese risotto. 'Perfect puds' include chocolate tart and apple tarte Tatin.

Open all day all wk 12-11 **Food** Lunch Mon-Sat 12-5, Sun 12-6 Dinner Mon-Thu 5-9, Fri-Sat 5-9.30 ⊕ FREE HOUSE ◄ Peak Bakewell Best Bitter, Greene King Abbot Ale, Guest ales ♂ Symonds. ♀ 10 **Facilities** Non-diners area ♥ (Bar Restaurant) ♦♦ Children's portions ⋈ Parking WiFi ⚐ (notice required) **Rooms** 4

HARTINGTON

Map 16 SK16

NEW The Jug & Glass Inn ★★★ INN

tel: 01298 84848 **Ashbourne Rd SK17 0BA**
email: enquiries@jugandglass.biz web: www.jugandglass.biz
dir: *From Buxton take A515 towards Ashbourne. Approx 10m to pub*

Family-run hostelry in High Peak walking country

An ideal base for hiking the trails of Derbyshire's Peak District, strolling through the streets of Ashbourne and Bakewell, or visiting famous sights such as Chatsworth. Ales include Church End, and Whim from nearby Hartington, while the menu lists all the comfort food you could wish for: starters of lemon sole goujons or prawn cocktail; cottage pie, chilli con carne, steak and kidney pudding, and pan-fried lamb's liver are among the traditional and home-made main courses; dessert lovers are spoilt for choice with favourites such as profiteroles, apple crumble and treacle sponge. Nine newly-appointed rooms and superb views complete the picture.

Open 12-3 6-10 (Fri-Sat 12-10.30 Sun 12-9.30) Closed Mon-Tue **Food** Lunch Wed-Thu 12-3, Fri-Sat 12-8.30, Sun 12-7.30 Dinner Wed-Thu 6-8.30, Fri-Sat 12-8.30, Sun 12-7.30 Av main course £9 ⊕ FREE HOUSE ◄ Church End, Whim Hartington. **Facilities** Non-diners area ♥ (Bar Garden Outside area) ♦♦ Children's menu Children's portions Garden Outside area ⋈ Parking WiFi ⚐ (notice required) **Rooms** 9

PICK OF THE PUBS

The Plough Inn ★★★★ INN ❀

HATHERSAGE   Map 16 SK28

tel: 01433 650319 & 650180
Leadmill Bridge S32 1BA
email: sales@theploughinn-hathersage.co.uk
web: www.theploughinn-hathersage.co.uk
dir: *M1 junct 29, take A617W, A619, A623, then B6001 N to Hathersage*

Stylish, riverside award-winner with extensive menu choices

The 16th-century Plough stands in nine acres by the River Derwent where the 18th-century, three-arched Leadmill Bridge carries the Derwent Valley Heritage Way over the rapids that disturb the otherwise gently flowing waters. Inside, smart red tartan carpets work well with the open fires and wooden beams of the bar, which serves hand-pulled Adnams, Black Sheep and Timothy Taylor ales. An extensive British menu features locally sourced starters such as black pudding Scotch egg with a foie gras yolk, apple purée, pickled walnut and watercress; and citrus fruit cured salmon, cucumber confit, caper berries and gazpacho dressing. Next choose from the best part of 20 main courses, including rump of lamb with rissole potatoes, baby vegetables and port jus; Oriental-marinade fillet of

place, coconut rice and pak choi; and beef and Guinness pie, mash, thyme roast shallots and Guinness gravy. If you prefer, there's traditional pub grub too, typically a home-made burger with all the extras; and breaded scampi, fries garden peas and salad. Roast meats are only part of the Sunday line-up, with dishes featuring lemon sole, pork medallions, chicken and pissaladière also on offer. The Plough's well-stocked cellar combines Old and New World wines, from France to Chile one way, and New Zealand the other. Guests may stroll through the landscaped grounds before retiring to one of the bedrooms in the inn itself, or in the converted barn across the cobbled courtyard.

Open all day all wk 11-11 (Sun 12-10.30) Closed 25 Dec **Food** all wk 12-9.30 Av main course £14 Set menu available ⊕ FREE HOUSE ◼ Adnams, Black Sheep, Timothy Taylor, Bass Extra Smooth, Local ales. ⬤ 15
Facilities Non-diners area 🐾 (Bar Restaurant Garden) 👶 Children's menu Children's portions Garden 🪑 Parking WiFi **Rooms** 5

HARTSHORNE   Map 10 SK32

The Mill Wheel ★★★★ INN ⦿

tel: 01283 550335 **Ticknall Rd DE11 7AS**
email: info@themillwheel.co.uk **web:** www.themillwheel.co.uk
dir: *From A511 between Burton upon Trent & Ashby-de-la-Zouch take A514 at Woodville signed Derby. 1.8m to Hartshorne*

Award-winning food in a lovely setting

Close to the National Trust's remarkable Calke Abbey, many trades have used this old building over the centuries; today it's a feel-good, rustic pub in an attractive setting. The mill wheel, which has powered bellows, grindstones and hoists only momentarily diverts attention from Colin Brown's enticing menus, which have gained an AA Rosette. A typical dinner might include potted, thyme-infused chicken liver parfait; followed by vegetable Wellington; roast rump of lamb; pan-fried duck breast with plum sauce; or local steaks from the grill. There are modern bedrooms for those wishing to stay overnight.

Open all wk (Sat-Sun all day) **Food** Lunch Mon-Fri 12-2.30, Sat 12-9.15, Sun 12-6 Dinner Mon-Thu 6-9.15, Fri 6-9.30, Sat 12-9.15, Sun 12-6 Av main course £8.95 Set menu available Restaurant menu available all wk ⊕ FREE HOUSE ◀ Greene King Abbot Ale, Hop Back Summer Lightning, Marston's Pedigree. ♥ 8
Facilities Non-diners area ♦♦ Children's menu Children's portions Garden ⋤ Parking WiFi ➡ **Rooms** 4

HASSOP   Map 16 SK27

The Old Eyre Arms

tel: 01629 640390 **DE45 1NS**
email: nick@eyrearms.com
dir: *On B6001 N of Bakewell*

A perfect Peak District escape

In a village-edge location between the formality of Chatsworth's vast estate, bold gritstone edges and the memorable wooded limestone dales of Derbyshire's River Wye, this comfortably unchanging, creeper-clad old inn ticks all the right boxes for beers and food too. Real ales from Peak Ales and Bradfield breweries couldn't be more local, whilst all meals are prepared in-house: kick off with smoked mackerel or Thai-style fishcakes, and follow with duckling in a Grand Marnier sauce; baked rainbow trout with butter and almonds; or bulgar wheat and walnut casserole to take the chill off a long ramble. Oak beams and furnishing and log fires complete the picture.

Open all wk 11-3 6-11 Closed 25-26 Dec, 2wks in Jan **Food** Lunch Mon-Fri 12-2, Sat-Sun 12-2.30 Dinner all wk 6-9 Av main course £11.95 Set menu available ⊕ FREE HOUSE ◀ Peak Ales Swift Nick & Chatsworth Gold, Black Sheep Ale, Bradfield Farmers Blonde ♂ Westons Stowford Press. ♥ 9 **Facilities** Non-diners area ♦♦ Children's menu Children's portions Garden ⋤ Parking

HATHERSAGE   Map 16 SK28

The Plough Inn ★★★★ INN ⦿   **PICK OF THE PUBS**

See Pick of the Pubs on page 127

The Scotsmans Pack Country Inn

tel: 01433 650253 **School Ln S32 1BZ**
email: scotsmans.pack@btinternet.com
dir: *From A6187 in Hathersage turn at church into School Lane*

A warm welcome for locals and visitors alike

Set in the beautiful Hope Valley on one of the old packhorse trails used by Scottish 'packmen', this traditional inn is a short walk from Hathersage church and Little John's Grave. Weather permitting, head outside onto the sunny patio, next to the

trout stream. The pub offers a good choice of hearty daily specials – six starters, ten main and eight desserts – perhaps best washed down with a pint of Jennings Cumberland. This is a perfect base for walking and touring the Peak District.

Open all day all wk Closed 25 Dec **Food** Lunch all wk 12-9.30 Dinner all wk 12-9.30 ⊕ MARSTON'S ◀ Burton Bitter, EPA & Pedigree, Jennings Cumberland Ale ♂ Thatchers Gold. ♥ 10 **Facilities** Non-diners area ♦♦ Children's menu Children's portions Family room Garden ⋤ Parking WiFi ➡

HAYFIELD   Map 16 SK08

The Royal Hotel

tel: 01663 742721 **Market St SK22 2EP**
email: enquiries@theroyalathayfield.com
dir: *From A624 follow Hayfield signs*

Village-centre pub on the Peak District border

Up in the High Peak, below the windswept plateau of Kinder Scout, the hotel dates from 1755. Its period charm still very evident, one place to relax with a pint of Thwaites Original or Happy Valley Kinder Falldown is the oak-panelled, log-fired bar. Others are the Cricket Room, popular with the local cricket team, whose ground is next door, and the Ramblers Bar which has hiking boots strung along the beams. The bar menu keeps things simple: sausage and mash; roast beef and Yorkshire pudding; and breaded wholetail scampi. There's also a separate sandwich menu, and on Fridays and Saturdays, a bistro menu. Meals can be served on the patio overlooking the moorland.

Open all day all wk Mon-Thu 11-11 (Fri-Sat 11am-11.30pm Sun 11-10.30) **Food** Lunch Mon-Fri 12-2.30, Sat 12-9, Sun 12-7 Dinner Mon-Fri 6-8, Sat 12-9, Sun 12-7 Av main course £9.95 Set menu available Restaurant menu available Fri-Sun ⊕ FREE HOUSE ◀ Thwaites Original, Happy Valley Kinder Falldown ♂ Westons Stowford Press, Thatchers Green Goblin, Hogan's. ♥ **Facilities** Non-diners area ❀ (Bar Outside area) ♦♦ Children's menu Children's portions Family room Outside area ⋤ Parking WiFi ➡ (notice required)

HOGNASTON   Map 16 SK25

The Red Lion Inn

tel: 01335 370396 **Main St DE6 1PR**
email: enquiries@redlionhognaston.org.uk **web:** www.redlionhognaston.org.uk
dir: *From Ashbourne take B5035 towards Wirksworth. Approx 5m follow Carsington Water signs. Turn right to Hognaston*

Traditional country pub awash with character

Here in 1997 for a wedding, John F Kennedy's son and his wife stayed at this whitewashed, 17th-century village pub overlooking Carsington Water. With beams, bare brick, old photos, bric-a-brac and antique furniture spread liberally around an open-fire warmed interior, traditional character isn't hard to find. Settle with a pint, perhaps from the Wincle Brewery in Cheshire, and start considering the menu, on which appear fresh Conwy mussels cooked in dark ale; oven-roasted sea bass with tarragon and Pernod sauce; chicken supreme topped with Wensleydale and cranberry cheese; and vegetable Wellington. In the garden is a boules court.

Open all wk 12-2.30 6-11 **Food** Lunch all wk 12-2.30 Dinner all wk 6.30-9 summer, 6-8.30 winter ⊕ FREE HOUSE ◄ Marston's Pedigree, Greene King Ruddles County, Black Sheep, Wincle, Timothy Taylor Landlord. ♈ 10 **Facilities** Non-diners area ♣ (Bar Garden) ♦♦ Children's portions Garden ⋒ Parking WiFi

HOPE
Map 16 SK18

The Old Hall Hotel

tel: 01433 620160 **Market Place S33 6RH**
email: info@oldhallhotelhope.com
dir: On A6187 in town centre

Fine old inn with a tea room and café

For generations Hope Hall, as this early 16th-century building was once called, was the Balguy family seat. In 1730 it became an inn, The Cross Daggers, then in 1876 it was renamed The Hall Hotel. In the 18th century a cattle market was held here; today, on bank holidays, the Hope Valley Beer and Cider Festival draws the crowds. Main menus promise dishes such as pan-seared salmon with prawn linguine; calves' liver and bacon; Gressingham duck, wilted spinach, roast beetroot and thyme mash. For lunch there's also soup and sandwiches, hot ciabatas and light bites.

Open all day all wk **Food** Lunch all wk 12-5 Dinner all wk 5-9 ⊕ HEINEKEN/THEAKSTON ◄ Theakston Best, Old Peculier, Castle Rock Harvest Pale, Adnams, Caledonian Deuchars IPA, 2 guest ales Ö Guest ciders. ♈ 10 **Facilities** Non-diners area ♣ (Bar Garden Outside area) ♦♦ Children's menu Children's portions Garden Outside area ⋒ Beer festival Cider festival Parking WiFi ⚌ (notice required)

HURDLOW
Map 16 SK16

The Royal Oak

tel: 01298 83288 & 07866 778847 **SK17 9QJ**
email: hello@peakpub.co.uk
dir: From A515 between Buxton & Ashbourne follow Hurdlow signs

Popular pitstop for walkers and cyclists on the Tissington Trail

Situated in the southern Peak District, this warm-hearted hostelry welcomes one and all, at any time of day. Tired ramblers and cyclists head straight for the pumps, where five real ales include locals such as Whim Hartington, Thornbridge and Peak Ales. Families with children and dogs add to the fun, arriving whenever suits them in the knowledge that generous plates of home-cooked pub food are served throughout the day. Most ingredients are seasonal and sourced within 20 miles of the pub from suppliers with trusted reputations. Look out for the likes of trio of lamb chops with leek mash, roast vegetable and Stilton tart; Cajun chicken salad with jalapeño peppers; or poached salmon with prawns and white wine sauce.

Open all day all wk **Food** Lunch Mon-Fri 10-9, Sat-Sun 8.30am-9pm Dinner Mon-Fri 10-9, Sat-Sun 8.30am-9pm ⊕ FREE HOUSE ◄ Whim Hartington Bitter, Thornbridge, Buxton, Wincle, Peak Ales Ö Aspall. **Facilities** Non-diners area ♣ (Bar Restaurant Garden) ♦♦ Children's menu Children's portions Garden ⋒ Parking WiFi ⚌ (notice required)

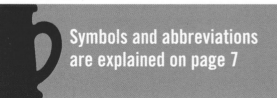
Symbols and abbreviations are explained on page 7

INGLEBY
Map 11 SK32

The John Thompson Inn & Brewery

tel: 01332 862469 **DE73 7HW**
email: nick@johnthompsoninn.com
dir: From A38 between Derby & Burton upon Trent take A5132 towards Barrow upon Trent. At mini rdbt right onto B5008 (signed Repton). At rdbt 1st exit into Brook End. Right into Milton Rd. Left, left again to Ingleby

Friendly brewpub serving hearty lunches

A pub since 1968, this 15th-century former farmhouse took its name from licensee and owner John Thompson. Now run by son Nick, it is a traditional brewpub set in idyllic countryside beside the banks of the River Trent with views of the neighbouring National Forest. Inside, a wealth of original features make it an atmospheric place to enjoy a pint of home-brewed JTS XXX and tuck into lunches ranging from sandwiches to a roast beef carvery or a trio of cheese and pasta broccoli bake. Finish with home-made bread and butter pudding.

Open Tue-Fri 11-2.30 6-11 (Sat-Sun 11-11 Mon 6-11) Closed Mon L **Food** Lunch Tue-Sun 12-2 ⊕ FREE HOUSE ◄ John Thompson JTS XXX, St Nick's, Gold, Rich Porter. ♈ 9 **Facilities** Non-diners area ♦♦ Children's portions Family room Garden Parking WiFi ⚌

KIRK IRETON
Map 16 SK25

Barley Mow Inn

tel: 01335 370306 **DE6 3JP**
dir: Phone for detailed directions

Step back in time at this traditional pub

Built on the edge of the Peak District National Park by the Storer family of yeomen farmers in the 16th century, the building became an inn during the early 1700s. The imposing free house has remained largely unchanged over the years. Six nine-gallon barrels of beer stand behind the bar, with cheese and pickle or salami rolls and bar snacks on offer at lunchtime. Tea and coffee are always available. Close to Carsington Water, there are good walking opportunities on nearby marked paths.

Open all wk 12-2 7-11 (Sun 12-2 7-10.30) Closed 25 Dec, 1 Jan **Food** Lunch 12-2 ⊕ FREE HOUSE ◄ Whim Hartington Bitter, Rotating ales Ö Thatchers. **Facilities** Non-diners area ♦♦ Garden Parking **Notes** ⊛

LITTLE HAYFIELD
Map 16 SK08

Lantern Pike

tel: 01663 747590 **45 Glossop Rd SK22 2NG**
email: tomandstella@lanternpikeinn.co.uk
dir: On A624 between Glossop & Chapel-en-le-Frith

Welcoming pub in hilly terrain

Set in a tiny mill village at the edge of the Kinder Scout moors and below the shapely Lantern Pike hill, site of an Armada beacon, the sublime views from the beer garden of the wooded Peak District hills are reason enough to seek out this fine pub. Add a well-considered selection of real ales and an ever-changing menu – perhaps grilled lemon sole; pork chasseur; or sirloin steak with onions, mushrooms, tomatoes and chips – and it's little wonder that this ultra-traditional 170-year-old inn is a highly popular destination for diners and outdoor pursuits enthusiasts alike. Unique *Coronation Street* ephemera add fascination for the faithful.

Open Mon 5-12, Tue-Fri 12-3 5-12 (Sat-Sun all day) Closed 25 Dec, Mon L **Food** Lunch Tue-Fri 12-2.30, Sat-Sun 12-8.30 Dinner Mon 5-8, Tue-Fri 5-8.30, Sat-Sun 12-8.30 Av main course £10 Restaurant menu available all wk ⊕ ENTERPRISE INNS ◄ Timothy Taylor Landlord, Castle Rock Harvest Pale, Ossett Silver King, Theakston Black Bull. **Facilities** Non-diners area ♦♦ Children's menu Children's portions Garden ⋒ Parking WiFi ⚌ (notice required)

LITTON
Map 16 SK17

Red Lion Inn

tel: 01298 871458 **SK17 8QU**
email: theredlionlitton@aol.com
dir: *Just off A623 (Chesterfield to Stockport road), 1m E of Tideswell*

Pub paradise beside the village green

New owners are at the helm of this tiny pub in a terrace of green-side, stone-built cottages which has served locals and visitors to this pretty White Peak village for two centuries. The warren of hobbit-sized rooms ooze character, shadows cast by log-fires flit across the low beams, murmuring village chit-chat and happy ramblers returning from nearby limestone gorges add to the timeless atmosphere. Beers from local microbreweries such as Peak Ale and Abbeydale major on the bar, whilst diners can happily chomp away on homity pie, or braised blade of beef with cheddar cheese and bacon mash. Space constraints mean that children under six cannot be accommodated inside the pub.

Open all day all wk **Food** Lunch Sun-Mon 12-8, Tue-Sat 12-9 Dinner Sun-Mon 12-8, Tue-Sat 12-9 ⊕ ENTERPRISE INNS ◀ Abbeydale Absolution, Peak Ales Bakewell Best Bitter, 2 guest ales Ò Westons Stowford Press. ₹ 10 **Facilities** Non-diners area ✿ (Bar Restaurant Outside area) Outside area ⋈ Beer festival WiFi

MATLOCK
Map 16 SK35

The Red Lion ★★★ INN

tel: 01629 584888 **65 Matlock Green DE4 3BT**
dir: *From Chesterfield, A632 into Matlock, on right just before junct with A615*

An all-rounder in the heart of Derbyshire's county town

This friendly, family-run free house makes a good base for exploring local attractions like Chatsworth House, Carsington Water and Dovedale. Spectacular walks in the local countryside help to work up an appetite for bar lunches, or great tasting home-cooked dishes in the homely restaurant. On Sunday there's a popular carvery with freshly cooked gammon, beef and turkey. In the winter months, open fires burn in the lounge and games room, and there's a boules area in the attractive beer garden for warmer days. Some of the ales from the bar were brewed on the Chatsworth Estate. There are six comfortable bedrooms.

Open all day all wk **Food** Lunch Tue-Fri 12-2 Dinner Tue-Sat 6-9 Restaurant menu available Tue-Sat ⊕ FREE HOUSE ◀ Morland Old Speckled Hen, Peak, Guest ales. **Facilities** Non-diners area Children's menu Children's portions Garden ⋈ Beer festival Cider festival Parking WiFi ⭦ **Rooms** 6

MIDDLE HANDLEY
Map 16 SK47

Devonshire Arms

tel: 01246 434800 **Lightwood Ln S21 5RN**
email: enquiries@devonshirearmsmiddlehandley.com
dir: *B6052 from Eckington towards Chesterfield. 1.5m*

Great local beers and thoughtful menu

A contemporary dining pub which has not forgotten its roots as a time-honoured local. The stylish interior has original features including a grandfather clock and wood-burning stove, perfect to sit beside in winter with a glass of Sheffield's Kelham Island beer or Aspall cider. Modern, locally-sourced British ingredients form the backbone of the busy kitchen's output; a good mix of pub classics and inspirations such as Moss Valley belly pork slowly cooked overnight in cloudy cider, with apple and potato terrine. The Devonshire Arms certainly welcomes dogs, just as long as they keep to the tiled floor areas.

Open 12-3 5-9 (Sat 12-10 Sun 12-5) Closed Mon **Food** Lunch Tue-Fri 12-3, Sat 12-10, Sun 12-5 Dinner Tue-Fri 5-9, Sat 12-10 ⊕ FREE HOUSE ◀ Bradfield Farmers Blonde, Kelham Island Pride of Sheffield, Peak Chatsworth Gold, Guest ales Ò Aspall. ₹ 10 **Facilities** Non-diners area ✿ (All areas) ◀ Children's menu Children's portions Garden Outside area ⋈ Parking WiFi

PILSLEY
Map 16 SK27

The Devonshire Arms at Pilsley ★★★ INN

tel: 01246 583258 **High St DE45 1UL**
email: enquiries@devonshirepilsley.co.uk **web:** www.devonshirepilsley.co.uk
dir: *From A619, in Baslow, at rdbt take 1st exit onto B6012. Follow signs to Chatsworth, 2nd right to Pilsley*

Traditional inn on the Chatsworth Estate

Set in an estate village amidst the rolling parkland that surrounds Chatsworth House, the 'Palace of The Peaks', this fabulous old stone pub is an ideal base for visiting Matlock Bath and Castleton. There are open fires, Peak Ales from the estate's brewery and meats, game and greens from the adjacent estate farm shop, all sourced from these productive acres at the heart of the Peak District. After a day's exploration, classics like fish pie; ham, egg and chips; or steak and ale pie will hit the spot. Finish with Eton mess, and stop over at the luxurious accommodation designed by the Duchess of Devonshire.

Open all day all wk **Food** Lunch all wk 12-2.30 Dinner all wk 5-9 Av main course £12.95 ⊕ FREE HOUSE ◀ Thornbridge Jaipur, Peak Chatsworth Gold, Guest ales. **Facilities** Non-diners area ◀ Children's portions Outside area ⋈ Parking WiFi **Rooms** 13

ROWSLEY
Map 16 SK26

The Grouse & Claret ⸆

tel: 01629 733233 **Station Rd DE4 2EB**
web: www.grouseclaretpub.co.uk
dir: *On A6 between Matlock & Bakewell*

Angling connections and a menu for everyone at this popular pub

A venue popular with local anglers, this 18th-century pub takes its name from a fishing fly. Situated at the gateway to the Peak District National Park, it is handy for visits to the stately homes of Haddon Hall and Chatsworth House. After quenching the thirst with a pint of Wychwood Hobgoblin, the comprehensive menu promises a selection of well-priced and tasty pub meals: courgette and halloumi stack; salmon Florentine tart; beef lasagne; rotisserie chicken or ham; gourmet burgers (perhaps wild boar and chorizo) and roast root vegetable crown pie. From the dessert choices there's gingerbread cheesecake; and Sicilian lemon tart. Dogs are very welcome in the outside areas.

Open all day all wk **Food** Lunch Mon-Sat 11.30-10, Sun 11.30-9 Dinner Mon-Sat 11.30-10, Sun 11.30-9 Av main course £7 Set menu available ⊕ MARSTON'S ◀ Pedigree, Wychwood Hobgoblin, Guest ale. ₹ 16 **Facilities** Non-diners area ◀ Children's menu Children's portions Play area Garden ⋈ Beer festival Parking WiFi ⭦ **Rooms** 8

SHARDLOW
Map 11 SK43

The Old Crown Inn

tel: 01332 792392 **Cavendish Bridge DE72 2HL**
email: jamesvize@hotmail.co.uk
dir: *M1 junct 24, A50 signed Stoke & Shardlow. Take slip road signed B6540. At rdbt right, follow Shardlow sign. Left at Cavendish bridge sign to inn*

Traditional inn with regular evening events

Up to nine real ales are served at this family-friendly pub on the south side of the River Trent, where there's a beer festival twice a year. Built as a coaching inn during the 17th century, it retains its warm and atmospheric interior. Several hundred water jugs hang from the ceilings, while the walls display an abundance of brewery and railway memorabilia. Food is lovingly prepared by the landlady; main meals focus on pub classics such as home-made steak and kidney pie; ham, eggs and chips; lasagne; curry; steaks; and daily specials. There's also a good choice of baguettes, sandwiches and jackets. Monday night is quiz night; folk music on the first and third Tuesday of every month; curry night on Wednesdays.

Open all wk 11am-11.30pm (Mon 3-11 Fri-Sat 11am-12.30am Sun 11-11) **Food** Lunch Tue-Fri 12-2, Sat 12-8, Sun 12-3 Dinner Tue-Fri 5-8, Sat 12-8 Av main course £6.95 Set menu available ⊕ MARSTON'S ◀ Pedigree & Old Empire, Jennings Cocker Hoop, Guest ales ○ Thatchers Gold. **Facilities** Non-diners area ❤ (Bar Restaurant) ❉ Children's menu Children's portions Play area Garden ⊼ Beer festival Cider festival Parking ☞ (notice required)

The Saracen's Head

tel: 01335 360330 **Church Ln DE6 3AS**
email: info@saracens-head-shirley.co.uk
dir: A52 from Ashbourne towards Derby. Right in 4m to Shirley

A gastro-pub where traditional meets contemporary

Overlooking the front garden and village street, the 1791-built Saracen's Head takes its name from the family crest of Sewallis de Scyrle (pronounced Shirley), a Holy Land crusader. All dishes are made on the premises from local, ethical sources. Starting with creamy garlic button mushrooms, it's an easy move to, say, slowly braised beef bourguignon with creamy mash and vegetables; or warm cheddar and caramelised onion quiche. For a quintessential country pub experience, visit on a Sunday at lunchtime.

Open all wk 11-3 6-11 (Sun 11-10.30) **Food** Lunch Mon-Sat 12-2, Sun 12-2.30 Dinner all wk 6-9 ⊕ GREENE KING ◀ IPA, St Edmunds, Morland Old Speckled Hen, Guest ales. **Facilities** Non-diners area ❤ (Bar Garden) ❉ Children's portions Garden ⊼ Parking WiFi ☞ (notice required)

The Flying Childers Inn

tel: 01629 636333 **Main Rd DE4 2LW**
dir: From A6 (between Matlock & Bakewell) follow Youlgrave signs. Onto B5056 to Ashbourne. Follow Stanton in Peak signs

Enchanting old-style village pub

Above this instantly likeable, charmingly old-fashioned village pub looms Stanton Moor, riddled with Neolithic stone monuments. At the heart of a pretty old Peak District estate village, The Flying Childers was named after a champion racehorse owned by the 4th Duke of Devonshire. Little log fires warm the cosy, beamed interior, where settles and magpie-furniture fit an absolute treat. The lunchtime-only menu is small but perfectly formed; home-made soups, casseroles, filled cobs, toasties, and hearty ploughman's, all with locally sourced ingredients. Local real ales, a beer garden and a great welcome for canine companions, too.

Open all wk 12-2 7-11 (Mon-Tue 7pm-11pm Sat-Sun 12-3 7-11) **Food** Lunch Wed-Sun 12-2 ⊕ FREE HOUSE ◀ Wells Bombardier, Guest ales. **Facilities** ❤ (Bar Garden) ❉ Garden Parking **Notes** ⊗

The George

tel: 01298 871382 **Commercial Rd SK17 8NU**
email: info@georgeinn.co.uk
dir: A619 to Baslow, A623 towards Chapel-en-le-Frith, 0.25m

Charming coaching inn with traditional food

Set in the shadow of St John the Baptist's church (known locally as the Cathedral of the Peak), this delightful stone-built coaching inn dates from 1730 and is

conveniently placed for exploring the National Park and visiting Buxton, Chatsworth and Eyam. The simple, unfussy menu focuses on traditional pub fare — lunchtime sandwiches and full meals such as mushroom and Stilton crumble followed by traditional rag pudding with gravy, and sticky toffee pudding for dessert. There's a good selection from the grill, ranging from steaks to a fish medley or Cajun chicken.

Open all day all wk **Food** Lunch all wk 12-3 Dinner all wk 5-9 Set menu available Restaurant menu available ⊕ GREENE KING ◀ Morland, Ruddles, Guest ale ○ Aspall. **Facilities** Non-diners area ❤ (All areas) ❉ Children's menu Children's portions Garden Outside area ⊼ Parking WiFi ☞ (notice required)

The White Horse Inn

tel: 01246 590319 **Badger Ln DE55 6FG**
dir: From A61 at Stretton take B6014, then B6036 Woolley Moor

Spick and span bar and restaurant near Matlock

This 200-year-old pub sits in two acres of gardens amidst beautiful countryside; the nearby Ogston Reservoir is where Dame Ellen MacArthur learned her sailing skills. The building's interior has been meticulously updated, with exposed solid stone walls and precisely laid flagstone floors providing the backdrop for an abundance of polished tables and chairs in both the bar area and bright garden conservatory. Peak Ales are well kept and wines sold by the glass are numerous, but this is primarily a food destination. Salt and pepper squid with aïoli dip makes a flavoursome starter, to be followed perhaps with Barbary duck breast, dauphinoise potatoes and blackberry jus.

Open all wk 12-3 5.30-11 (Sun 12-5) **Food** Lunch Mon-Sat 12-1.45, Sun 12-4 Dinner Mon-Sat 6-8.45 Set menu available Restaurant menu available all wk ⊕ FREE HOUSE ◀ Peak Ales Bakewell Best Bitter & Chatsworth Gold. ☙ 13 **Facilities** Non-diners area ❉ Children's portions Garden ⊼ Parking WiFi ☞ (notice required)

NEW The Farmyard Inn

tel: 01629 636221 **DE45 1UW**
email: suzidayfarmyard@hotmail.co.uk
dir: Phone for detailed directions

A little gem in the Peak District National Park

This old farmhouse, which became an inn in 1829, looks south across Bradford Dale and its picturesque stretches of tree-hung, crystal-clear water. Warm and friendly, the bar offers two guest real ales and a good selection of wines by the glass. Home-made, locally-sourced dishes include Derbyshire mushrooms with grilled blue cheese; warm black pudding and bacon salad; fish pie with North Atlantic prawns; Derbyshire homity pie filled with leek and apple; and red bean, tomato and brazil nut flan. The area abounds with walks and places to visit, such as Chatsworth and Haddon Hall.

Open all wk 5pm till late **Food** Dinner all wk 5-9 Av main course £10 ⊕ GREENE KING ◀ Abbot, IPA Gold, Morland, Guest ales ○ Aspall, Thatchers Gold. ☙ 9 **Facilities** ❤ (Bar Restaurant Garden) ❉ Children's menu Children's portions Garden ⊼ Parking WiFi ☞ (notice required)

DEVON

ASHBURTON
Map 3 SX77

The Rising Sun ★★★ INN

tel: 01364 652544 **Woodland TQ13 7JT**
email: admin@therisingsunwoodland.co.uk **web:** www.therisingsunwoodland.co.uk
dir: *From A38 E of Ashburton follow Woodland & Denbury signs. Pub on left, approx 1.5m*

Family-friendly pub with large garden near Dartmoor

This former drovers' pub is in the hands of the capable Reynolds family who are putting this family- and dog-friendly pub firmly on the map. Surrounded by gorgeous countryside, and with a large garden in which to sup a pint of Dartmoor Jail Ale, you're on the edge of Dartmoor National Park. Renowned for their pies, chips and specials board, they also offer light snacks at lunchtime, and a great children's menu. Sample specials include pork belly with vanilla mashed potatoes, spinach and caramelised apple jus; and braised lamb shoulder with colcannon and black trumpet mushrooms.

Open 12-3 6-11 (Sun 12-3 6.30-11) Closed Mon (ex BH) **Food** Lunch Tue-Sat 12-2.15, Sun 12-2.30 Dinner Mon-Thu 6-9, Fri-Sat 6-9.30, Sun 6.30-9 ⊕ FREE HOUSE ◂ Dartmoor Jail Ale, Guest ales ♂ Annings Fruit Cider, Thatchers Gold. **Facilities** Non-diners area ☺ (Bar Restaurant Garden) ♦ Children's menu Children's portions Play area Garden ⋈ Parking WiFi ▦ (notice required) **Rooms** 4

AVONWICK
Map 3 SX75

The Turtley Corn Mill
PICK OF THE PUBS

tel: 01364 646100 **TQ10 9ES**
email: eat@turtleycornmill.com
dir: *From A38 at South Brent/Avonwick junction, take B3372, then follow signs for Avonwick, 0.5m*

Seasonal menus in an idyllic riverside setting

This sprawling old free house is set among six acres of gardens and fields in the South Hams on the edge of Dartmoor, and includes a lake complete with ducks, and its own small island. Originally a corn mill, it spent many years as a chicken hatchery before being converted to a pub. The interior is light and fresh with old furniture and oak and slate floors. You'll find plenty of newspapers and books to browse through while enjoying a whisky or supping a pint of Summerskills Start Point. The daily-changing modern British menus for breakfast/brunch, lunch and dinner are extensively based on local produce from around the pub's idyllic location. Choices from a sample menu start with chickpea fritters with a minted yogurt dressing or chicken liver pâté on toast; continue with warm Cornish scallop salad, diced game pie with creamy mash and buttered curly kale, or seafood casserole; and wind up with steamed apple and honey sponge or sticky toffee pudding.

Open all day all wk Closed 25 Dec **Food** Lunch all wk 12-10 Dinner all wk 12-10 Set menu available ⊕ FREE HOUSE ◂ St Austell Tribute, Sharp's Doom Bar, Summerskills Start Point, Guest ales ♂ Thatchers. ♥ 10 **Facilities** Non-diners area ☺ (Bar Restaurant Garden) ♦ Children's portions Garden ⋈ Parking WiFi

BAMPTON
Map 3 SS92

Exeter Inn

tel: 01398 331345 **EX16 9DY**
email: enquiries@the-exeter-inn.co.uk
dir: *From Bampton take B3227 (Brook St) signed Tiverton A396. Approx 1.2m to pub on rdbt (junct with A396)*

Historic 15th-century inn and restaurant

Set below wooded hills in the Exe Valley just a short distance from Exmoor National Park, is this long, low, white-painted inn. Beer lovers will be heartened by the sight of up to six barrels stillaged behind the snug little old bar here, with West Country ales favoured brews. This timeless scene complements the rest of the interior of the inn which has stood here for around six centuries; you'll find flagstone floors, beams, log fires and cosy corners; there's a well-appointed restaurant, too. The menu changes weekly and offers traditional English favourites, fish specials and a range of dishes with worldwide inspirations. There's a hog roast on bank holidays and a new tea room is planned (noon until 5pm).

Open all day all wk **Food** Lunch all wk 12-2.30 (Bkfst Mon-Sat 7.30am-11am) Dinner all wk 5.30-9 ⊕ PUNCH TAVERNS ◂ Exmoor, Cotleigh, Whitbread ♂ Thatchers, Addlestones. **Facilities** Non-diners area ☺ (Bar Outside area) ♦ Children's menu Children's portions Outside area ⋈ Parking WiFi ▦ (notice required)

The Swan ★★★★ INN ❀

tel: 01398 332248 **Station Rd EX16 9NG**
email: info@theswan.co **web:** www.theswan.co
dir: *M5 junct 17, A361 towards Barnstaple. At rdbt NW of Tiverton take A396 to Bampton*

Seriously good food at this village gem

Originally used as accommodation by masons and other craftsmen enlarging the church in 1450, renovation has endowed the bar with a contemporary style; at the solid oak counter you'll find Devon Storm, Otter and Proper Job real ales, Sandford Orchards Devon Red cider and many wines by the glass. Smoked haddock and leek fishcake with pea sauce gets a meal off to a good start, followed by fillet of Brixham hake, rarebit, buttered leeks, tomato dressing and bacon jam; or slow-roasted spiced lamb shoulder and butterbean cassoulet with buttered Savoy cabbage. Private dining for 20 people is available.

Open Tue-Thu 12-11 (Fri-Sat 12-12 Sun 12-10.30 Mon 5-11) Closed 25 Dec, Mon L **Food** Lunch Tue-Sat 12-2, Sun 12-2.30 Dinner Tue-Sat 6-9.30 ⊕ FREE HOUSE ◂ Red Rock Devon Storm, Otter, St Austell Proper Job ♂ Sandford Orchards Devon Red. ♥ **Facilities** Non-diners area ☺ (Bar Outside area) ♦ Children's menu Children's portions Family room Outside area ⋈ Parking WiFi ▦ (notice required) **Rooms** 3

BEER
Map 4 SY28

Anchor Inn ★★★★ INN

tel: 01297 20386 **Fore St EX12 3ET**
email: 6403@greeneking.co.uk **web:** www.oldenglish.co.uk
dir: *A3052 towards Lyme Regis. At Hangmans Stone take B3174 into Beer. Pub on seafront*

Enjoy sea views and sample fresh fish

A traditional inn overlooking the bay in the picture-perfect Devon village of Beer, this pretty colour-washed pub is perfectly situated for walking the Jurassic coastline. Fish caught by local boats features strongly on the menu, and the tempting starters might include ham hock and black pudding terrine or nachos, followed by roasted pork belly with black treacle and bourbon glaze; salmon and spring onion fishcakes; or roasted butternut squash and feta couscous. Leave space for Bramley apple pie or gingerbread, pear and caramel crumble pudding. Six comfortable guest rooms are also available.

Open all day all wk 8am-11pm **Food** Lunch Sun-Thu 11-9, Fri-Sat 11-9.30 Dinner Sun-Thu 11-9, Fri-Sat 11-9.30 Set menu available Restaurant menu available all wk ⊕ GREENE KING ◂ IPA & Abbot Ale, Otter Ale ♂ Aspall, Symonds Scrumpy Jack. ♥ 14 **Facilities** Non-diners area ☺ (Bar Garden) ♦ Children's menu Garden ⋈ WiFi ▦ (notice required) **Rooms** 6

BEESANDS
Map 3 SX84

The Cricket Inn ★★★★ INN ⚜
PICK OF THE PUBS

tel: 01548 580215 **TQ7 2EN**
email: enquiries@thecricketinn.com **web:** www.thecricketinn.com
dir: *From Kingsbridge take A379 towards Dartmouth. At Stokenham mini rdbt turn right to Beesands*

This seaside inn is a must for seafood lovers

The Cricket Inn first opened its doors in 1867 and has since survived storms, a World War II bomb and a mudslide. Located in a small South Hams fishing village, the inn encompasses a dog-friendly bar serving West Country ales, an AA-Rosette restaurant with sea views, and bright and airy accommodation. Cooking just metres from the sloping beach and clear waters of Start Bay, the head chef works closely with local fishermen who bring their catch straight to the kitchen door. From the lunch menu, sample Beesands crab soup with brandy cream; hand-dived scallops with bacon, garlic butter and chive mash; or the 'almost world famous' seafood pancake. Choices at dinner could be king prawn linguine; local 10oz rib-eye steak with baked blue cheese and walnut cream; or whole lemon sole, all made with produce from the Devonshire countryside and its waters.

Open all wk 11-3 6-11 (May-Sep all day) **Food** Lunch all wk 12-2.30 Dinner all wk 6-8.30 Restaurant menu available all wk ⊕ HEAVITREE ◀ Otter Ale & Bitter, St Austell Tribute ♂ Aspall, Heron Valley, Thatchers. ♈ 12 **Facilities** Non-diners area ❤ (Bar Restaurant) ♦ Children's menu Children's portions Outside area ⊞ Parking WiFi **Rooms** 7

BICKLEIGH
Map 3 SS90

Fisherman's Cot

tel: 01884 855237 **EX16 8RW**
email: fishermanscot.bickleigh@marstons.co.uk
dir: *Phone for detailed directions*

Riverside hostelry popular with locals and visitors alike

Just a short drive from Tiverton and Exmoor, this well-appointed thatched inn stands by Bickleigh Bridge over the River Exe. With food all day and beautiful gardens, The Waterside Bar is the place for doorstep sandwiches, pies, snacks and afternoon tea, while the restaurant incorporates a carvery (on Sunday) and carte menus. Expect dishes such as Thai green chicken curry; chilli and lime sea bass fillets with pilau rice and roasted vegetables; slow-cooked lamb shank in rosemary, redcurrant and red wine jus; chuck steak chilli con carne; and for dessert, lemon meringue.

Open all day all wk 11-11 (Sun 12-10.30) **Food** Lunch all wk 12-9 Dinner all wk 12-9 ⊕ MARSTON'S ◀ Wychwood Hobgoblin, Ringwood ♂ Thatchers. ♈ 8 **Facilities** Non-diners area ❤ (Bar Garden) ♦ Children's portions Garden ⊞ Parking WiFi ▤ (notice required)

BLACKAWTON
Map 3 SX85

The George Inn ★★★ INN

tel: 01803 712342 **Main St TQ9 7BG**
email: tgiblackawton@yahoo.co.uk **web:** www.blackawton.com
dir: *From Totnes on A381 through Halwell. Left onto A3122 towards Dartmouth, turn right to Blackawton*

Family-friendly village pub close to Dartmouth

In the South Hams village of Blackawton, The George is an ideal base for visitors to nearby Totnes and Dartmouth, as well as Woodlands Leisure Park. The pub gained its name during George III's reign but it was rebuilt after a fire in 1939, after which it became the rallying point for the forced evacuation of the parish in WW2. Now a family-friendly pub with comfortable accommodation, it's a place to relax over a pint of Teignworthy Spring Tide and a traditional menu including pizzas, curries and pub classics.

Open all wk 12-3 5-11 (Sun 12-3 7-10.30) **Food** Lunch all wk 12-2 Dinner Mon-Sat 6-9, Sun 7-9 ⊕ FREE HOUSE ◀ Teignworthy Spring Tide, Guest ales ♂ Thatchers Gold, Somersby Cider, Healey's Cornish Rattler. ♈ 12 **Facilities** Non-diners area ❤ (Bar Restaurant Outside area) ♦ Children's menu Children's portions Play area Garden Outside area ⊞ Beer festival Parking WiFi **Rooms** 4

The Normandy Arms

tel: 01803 712884 **Chapel St TQ9 7BN**
email: info@thenormandyarms.co.uk
dir: *From Dartmouth take A3122 towards Halwell. Right at Forces Tavern to Blackawton*

16th-century free house with south-facing garden

Why Normandy? In 1944, soldiers trained for D-Day and the Normandy landings on nearby Slapton Sands, which explains why there's a salvaged Sherman tank in nearby Torcross (but why Blackawton hosts the annual International Festival of Wormcharming, you'll have to ask). The pub's character comes from the clean lines of the slate-floored bar and relaxing dining room, both with log-burners. In the bar, local and regional guest ales support Otter Ale and Thatchers Cheddar Valley cider. The pub serves traditional bar meals and modern European restaurant dishes.

Open 5.30pm-11pm Closed 2 Jan-1 Feb, Sun & Mon **Food** Dinner Tue-Sat 6.30-9.30 Set menu available ⊕ FREE HOUSE ◀ Otter Ale, Hunter's ♂ Thatchers Cheddar Valley. ♈ 12 **Facilities** Non-diners area ❤ (Bar Restaurant Garden) ♦ Garden ⊞ Parking WiFi

BRAMPFORD SPEKE
Map 3 SX99

The Lazy Toad
PICK OF THE PUBS

tel: 01392 841591 **EX5 5DP**
email: thelazytoad@outlook.com
dir: *From Exeter take A377 towards Crediton 1.5m, right signed Brampford Speke*

Thatched village country inn

Harriet and Mike Daly took over in early 2015 what, until 2007, had been The Agricultural Inn. Oak-beamed, it dates from the late 18th century, when the village farrier and wheelwright worked in the cobbled courtyard, although its core may be even older. Polished slate tiles surround a bar serving ales from Devon's Hanlons and Otter breweries, Sandford Orchards ciders from Crediton, and wines from Sharpham near Totnes, and Camel Valley near Bodmin. A smallholding behind the pub supplies vegetables, fruits and herbs for dishes on the short, daily changing menus. These offer starters of cream of parsnip soup; and smoked haddock risotto; and mains of pan-fried hake, buttered spinach and mussel chowder; steak and kidney pudding, creamed Savoy cabbage and roasted young carrots; and Devon Blue cheese, spinach and hazelnut tortellini with onion purée and crispy kale. Dogs on leads are welcome in the bar and walled beer den.

Open all day 12-11 (Sun 12-4) Closed 3wks Jan, Sun eve **Food** Lunch all wk 12-2 Dinner Mon-Sat 6.30-9 Av main course £14 ⊕ FREE HOUSE ◀ Otter Bitter, St Austell Tribute, Hanlons ♂ Sandford Orchards Devon Red & Devon Mist. **Facilities** Non-diners area ❤ (Bar Garden Outside area) ♦ Children's menu Children's portions Family room Garden Outside area ⊞ Parking WiFi

BRANSCOMBE — Map 4 SY18

The Fountain Head

tel: 01297 680359 **EX12 3BG**
email: thefountainhead@btconnect.com
dir: *From Seaton on A3052 towards Sidmouth left at Branscombe Cross to pub*

Often packed with walkers and locals

This 500-year-old forge and cider house is a true rural survivor, in a peaceful village just a short walk from the coastal path. The traditional worn flagstones, crackling log fires, rustic furnishings, village-brewed beers from Branscombe Vale, and the chatty atmosphere (no intrusive music or electronic games here) charm both locals and visitors. Hearty pub food includes tempura battered squid; braised lamb shank, sweet parsnip mash, honey-roast shallots and red wine jus; and home-made vegetable lasagne. There's a spit-roast and barbecue every Sunday evening between July and September. Don't miss the midsummer beer festival.

Open all wk 11-3 6-11 (Sun 12-10.30) **Food** Lunch all wk 12-2 Dinner all wk 6.30-9 ⊕ FREE HOUSE ◀ Branscombe Vale Branoc, Jolly Geff & Summa That ♖ Westons, Pip. **Facilities** Non-diners area ✿ (Bar Restaurant Garden) ♦♦ Children's menu Children's portions Family room Garden ⊼ Beer festival Parking ➠ (notice required)

The Masons Arms

`PICK OF THE PUBS`

tel: 01297 680300 **EX12 3DJ**
email: masonsarms@staustellbrewery.co.uk
dir: *Exit A3052 towards Branscombe, down hill, Masons Arms at bottom of hill*

Ancient pub close to the sea

Just a 10-minute stroll from the beach and located in a picturesque village, the peaceful gardens of this inn have sea views across a picturesque valley. Creeper-clad, it dates from 1360 when it was a cider house. Back then it was a smugglers' haunt and its interior has barely changed since those days: slate floors, stone walls, ships' beams, an old jail railing and a huge open fireplace used for spit roasts on Sundays all add to the time-warp charm. Food is a serious business here; where possible all ingredients are grown, reared or caught locally. Kick off with a starter of steamed River Exe mussels, white wine, garlic, cream, parsley and rustic bread and follow it with the baked pie of the day or a chargrilled Devonshire steak. Time your visit for the July beer and cider festival.

Open all day all wk 11-11 (Sun 12-10.30) **Food** Lunch all wk 12-2.15 Dinner all wk 6.30-9 ⊕ ST AUSTELL BREWERY ◀ Tribute & Proper Job, Otter ♖ Thatchers Gold, Healey's Pear Rattler. ♔ 14 **Facilities** Non-diners area ✿ (Bar Outside area) ♦♦ Children's menu Children's portions Outside area ⊼ Beer festival Cider festival Parking WiFi

BRAUNTON — Map 3 SS43

The Williams Arms

tel: 01271 812360 **Wrafton EX33 2DE**
email: info@williamsarms.co.uk
dir: *On A361 between Barnstaple & Braunton*

Family-owned free house with popular carvery

This postcard-pretty thatched free house beside the popular Tarka Trail dates back to the 16th century and has been owned by the Squire family since the mid-70s. Its prime location sees weary walkers, cyclists and local diners pile in for the pub's famous daily carvery, which always features locally reared meat and seasonal vegetables. Alternatively, you can try Devon scallops in white wine and cream sauce; steak and real ale pie or lighter options like prawn salad or roast turkey ciabatta — perfect when washed down with a pint of Sharp's Doom Bar. The carvery proves very popular.

Open all day all wk 8.45am-11pm **Food** Lunch all wk 12-9 Dinner all wk 12-9 ⊕ FREE HOUSE ◀ Worthington's Creamflow, Sharp's Doom Bar, Exmoor Ales Gold, Guinness ♖ Thatchers Gold & Red, Somersby. ♔ 10 **Facilities** Non-diners area ♦♦ Children's menu Children's portions Play area Garden ⊼ Parking WiFi ➠ (notice required)

BRENDON — Map 3 SS74

Rockford Inn

tel: 01598 741214 **EX35 6PT**
email: enquiries@therockfordinn.com
dir: *A39 through Minehead follow signs to Lynmouth. Left to Brendon*

Popular Exmoor hideaway

Standing alongside the East Lyn River in the tucked-away Brendon Valley, this traditional 17th-century free house stands at the heart of Exmoor and is handy for several walking routes. Thatchers ciders complement local cask ales such as Barn Owl and Devon Darter, and there's a choice of good home-made pub meals. Venison casserole cooked with shallots, Chantenay carrots and port; wild mushroom and leek crumble; and steak and Devon Blue shortcrust pie are typical menu choices; the specials board changes daily. Eat in the garden in warm weather, or head inside to the open fire when the weather changes.

Open all day all wk **Food** Lunch all wk 12-2.30 Dinner all wk 6-8.30 ⊕ FREE HOUSE ◀ Cotleigh Barn Owl & 25, St Austell Tribute, Clearwater Proper Ansome, Devon Darter & Real Smiler, Exmoor ♖ Thatchers, Addlestones. **Facilities** Non-diners area ✿ (Bar Restaurant Garden) ♦♦ Children's menu Children's portions Garden ⊼ Parking WiFi

BRIDFORD — Map 3 SX88

The Bridford Inn

tel: 01647 252250 **EX6 7HT**
email: info@bridfordinn.co.uk
dir: *Phone for detailed directions*

Traditional inn with Dartmoor views

Converted from three 17th-century cottages, this elevated Dartmoor village inn and shop is set in the pretty village of Bridford overlooking the stunning Teign Valley. Oak beams, exposed stonework and a huge inglenook fireplace with log-burner retains the pub's original character and the bar serves Dartmoor Jail Ale alongside three weekly guest beers. The menu changes quarterly but might offer a pie of the day; fish and chips; and a veggie-friendly potato gnocchi with Devon blue cheese cream sauce. Look out for the pub's bank holiday beer and cider festivals.

Open all day all wk **Food** Lunch Mon-Fri 12-2, Sat-Sun 12-3 Dinner Mon-Thu 6.30-8.30, Fri-Sat 6.30-9 ⊕ FREE HOUSE ◀ Dartmoor Jail Ale, Guest ales ♖ Sandford Orchards, Westons. **Facilities** Non-diners area ✿ (All areas) ♦♦ Children's menu Children's portions Garden Outside area ⊼ Beer festival Cider festival Parking WiFi ➠ (notice required)

BROADHEMBURY
Map 3 ST10

NEW The Drewe Arms

tel: 01404 841267 **EX14 3NF**
email: info@drewearmsinn.co.uk
dir: M5 junct 28, A373 towards Honiton. Left to Broadhembury

Renowned time-warp in pretty village

What differentiates this classic old free house even from other classic pubs is that, instead of over a bar counter, drinks are served through hatches. One serves a room with benches, tables and an open log fire, another the snug, with a wood-burner and the traditional pub games of bar billiards and shove ha'penny. Barrels of Devonshire-brewed real ales line up alongside Tricky cider from the Blackdown Hills. On the uncomplicated menu, steak and ale pie, fries and peas; pan-fried lamb's liver, bacon, mash and red onion gravy; and butternut squash with sage pearl barley risotto. Easter is beer festival time.

Open all day all wk **Food** Lunch all wk 12-3 Dinner Mon-Sat 6-9 Av main course £10 ⊕ FREE HOUSE ◀ Otter Amber & Ale, Exeter Avocet, Bays Devon Dumpling, Branscombe Vale Branoc Ŏ Tricky. **Facilities** Non-diners area ♥ (Bar Garden) ♦️ Children's menu Children's portions Garden ⊼ Beer festival WiFi

BUCKLAND MONACHORUM
Map 3 SX46

Drake Manor Inn

tel: 01822 853892 **The Village PL20 7NA**
email: drakemanor@drakemanorinn.co.uk
dir: From A386 (Plymouth) turn left before Yelverton, follow signs to Buckland Monachorum. Left into village, on left next to church

12th-century inn known for its warm welcome and good food

In the 12th century, when nearby St Andrew's church was being built, the masons needed a house to live in. Today's licensee of that now very old house is Mandy Robinson, who prides herself on running a 'proper pub', with a menu of locally-sourced delights. Start with grilled goats' cheese salad or whitebait with chilli mayo; follow on with a butterfly chicken breast with chilli and lime rub; beef lasagne; Mediterranean vegetable tarts with feta; or a minted lamb burger. Leave space for some delicious home-made dessert. There's a lovely cottage garden to the side of the pub, and a wood-burner in the winter.

Open all wk Mon-Thu 11.30-2.30 6.30-11 (Fri-Sat 11.30-11.30 Sun 12-11) **Food** Lunch Mon-Fri 11.30-2, Sat-Sun 11.30-2.30 Dinner Sun-Thu 6.30-9.30, Fri-Sat 6.30-10 ⊕ PUNCH TAVERNS ◀ Dartmoor Jail Ale, Sharp's Doom Bar, Otter Amber Ŏ Thatchers Gold & Heritage. ♥ 9 **Facilities** Non-diners area ♥ (Bar Garden) ♦️ Children's menu Children's portions Family room Garden ⊼ Parking WiFi

BUTTERLEIGH
Map 3 SS90

The Butterleigh Inn

tel: 01884 855433 **EX15 1PN**
email: thebutterleighinn1@btconnect.com
dir: M5 junct 28, B3181 signed Cullompton. In Cullompton High St right signed Butterleigh. 3m to pub

Regularly changing real ales and home-made food

Set in a delightful village opposite the 13th-century St Matthew's church and in the heart of the rolling Devon countryside, the 400-year-old Butterleigh is a traditional free house. There is a mass of local memorabilia throughout this friendly local,

where customers can choose from a selection of changing real ales including Dartmoor Jail Ale, ciders including Devon Scrumpy from Sandford Orchards, and around 15 malt whiskies. Expect home-made dishes such as steak and kidney pie; curry; beer battered cod and hand-cut chips; home-cooked ham; local sausages and mash. On fine days, the garden is very popular.

Open 12-2.30 6-11 (Fri-Sat 12-2.30 6-12 Sun 12-3) Closed Sun eve, Mon L **Food** Lunch Tue-Sat 12-2 Dinner Tue-Sat 7-9 ⊕ FREE HOUSE ◀ Cotleigh Tawny Owl, Otter Ale & Amber, Dartmoor IPA & Jail Ale, Guest ale Ŏ Sandford Orchards Devon Scrumpy, Sheppy's, Winkleigh Sam's. ♥ 9 **Facilities** Non-diners area ♥ (Bar Garden) ♦️ Children's portions Garden ⊼ Parking WiFi

CHAGFORD
Map 3 SX78

Sandy Park Inn

tel: 01647 433267 **TQ13 8JW**
email: info@sandyparkinn.co.uk
dir: From A30 exit at Whiddon Down, left towards Moretonhampstead. Inn 3m

Lovely thatched pub with a timeless quality

In a beautiful setting near the River Teign on the edge of Dartmoor, this inn attracts locals and tourists alike, with their dogs comfortably slumped in front of the fire. Homely horse brasses and sporting prints adorn the walls of the beamed bar, where a good range of traditional ales like Otter and Dartmoor Jail Ale are pulled. A change of management has introduced a daily-changing menu of home-cooked pub food with a twist. Sample dishes are cherry tomato and goats' cheese tart with crispy baby leaf salad and quail eggs; haunch of venison in red wine; and Devon clotted cream gâteau.

Open all day all wk **Food** Lunch all wk 12-2.30 Dinner all wk 6-9 ⊕ FREE HOUSE ◀ Otter Bitter, Dartmoor Jail Ale, Sharp's Doom Bar Ŏ Thatchers, Autumn Devon Scrumpy. **Facilities** Non-diners area ♥ (Bar Garden) ♦️ Children's menu Children's portions Family room Garden ⊼ Parking WiFi 🚌 (notice required)

CLAYHIDON
Map 4 ST11

The Merry Harriers

tel: 01823 421270 **Forches Corner EX15 3TR**
email: merryharriers.bookings@gmail.com
dir: M5 junct 26, A38 signed Wellington. At next rdbt left signed Exeter/A38. Left into Ford St (follow brown pub sign). At next x-rds left signed Merry Harriers 1.5m

Family- and dog-friendly free house high on the Blackdown Hills

Although not immediately apparent from its black-and-white-timbered, two-storey façade, this delightful pub was built in 1492 as a traditional Devon longhouse. Interior features include beamed ceilings, an inglenook fireplace with wood-burner, and attractive dining areas, where Peter and Angela Gatling's seasonal menus offer filled baguettes; steak and kidney pie; cod and chips, and other fish fresh from Lyme Bay; and daily specials. The large garden is popular, not least because there's a children's play area. Bar favourites include Exmoor, Cotleigh and Otter real ales, Bollhayes cider, and 14 wines by the glass. Check for summer beer festival dates.

Open 12-3 6.30-11 Closed Sun eve & Mon **Food** Lunch Tue-Sat 12-2, Sun 12-2.15 Dinner Tue-Sat 6.30-9 Set menu available Restaurant menu available Tue-Sun ⊕ FREE HOUSE ◀ Exmoor, Cotleigh & Otter Ales Ŏ Thatchers Gold, Bollhayes. ♥ 14 **Facilities** Non-diners area ♥ (Bar Garden) ♦️ Children's menu Children's portions Play area Garden ⊼ Beer festival Cider festival Parking WiFi 🚌 (notice required)

CLEARBROOK
Map 3 SX56

The Skylark Inn

tel: 01822 853258 **PL20 6JD**
email: skylvic@btinternet.com
dir: *5m N of Plymouth on A386 towards Tavistock. Take 2nd right signed Clearbrook*

Child-friendly pub set in the Dartmoor National Park

Originally used by miners in the 18th century, the Skylark is just 10 minutes from Plymouth. The village and surrounding area are ideal for cyclists and walkers. Children are welcome at this attractive pub and there is a special play area for them. Local ales and good wholesome food are served in the beamed bar with its large fireplace and wood-burning stove. Dishes include sizzling steaks, Mediterranean-style tuna, prawn salad, spinach and mascarpone lasagne, and classics like breaded scampi and barbecued ribs. Jackets and baguettes are also on offer. There is a beer festival on the Summer Bank Holiday and monthly charity quiz nights.

Open all wk 11.30-3 6-11.30 (Sat-Sun all day) **Food** Lunch Mon-Fri 12-2, Sat-Sun all day Dinner Mon-Fri 6.30-9, Sat-Sun all day ⊕ ENTERPRISE INNS ◀ Otter Ale, St Austell Tribute, Dartmoor Jail Ale, Sharp's Doom Bar ♂ Somersby, Symonds. **Facilities** Non-diners area ✿ (Bar Garden) ♦ Children's menu Children's portions Play area Family room Garden ☲ Beer festival Parking WiFi ▬ (notice required)

CLOVELLY
Map 3 SS32

Red Lion Hotel ★★ HL
PICK OF THE PUBS

tel: 01237 431237 **The Quay EX39 5TF**
email: redlion@clovelly.co.uk
dir: *From Bideford rdbt, A39 to Bude, 10m. At Clovelly Cross rdbt right, pass Clovelly Visitor Centre entrance, bear left. Hotel at bottom of hill*

Excellent home-cooked food in unspoilt fishing village

This charming whitewashed hostelry sits right on the quay in Clovelly, the famously unspoilt 'village like a waterfall', which descends down broad steps to a 14th-century harbour. Guests staying in the whimsically decorated bedrooms can fall asleep to the sound of waves lapping the shingle. Originally a beer house for fishermen and other locals, the Red Lion has plenty of character and offers Cornish ales such as Sharp's Doom Bar in its snug bar, where you can rub shoulders with the locals. Alternatively, you could settle in the Harbour Bar, and sample the home-cooked food, the modern seasonal menu specialising in fresh seafood, which is landed daily right outside the door. Choose pan-fried fillet of sea bass with cream bean cassoulet, or opt for medallions of wild venison; or beetroot risotto served with parsnip chips. There is an annual beer festival at Spring Bank Holiday in late May.

Open all day all wk **Food** Lunch all wk 12-2.30 Dinner all wk 6-8.30 Set menu available Restaurant menu available all wk ⊕ FREE HOUSE ◀ Sharp's Doom Bar, Clovelly Cobbler, Guinness ♂ Thatchers, Winkleigh, Somersby Cider. **Facilities** ✿ (Bar) ♦ Children's menu Children's portions Family room Outside area ☲ Beer festival Parking WiFi ▬ (notice required) **Rooms** 17

CLYST HYDON
Map 3 ST00

The Five Bells Inn

tel: 01884 277288 **EX15 2NT**
email: info@fivebells.uk.com
dir: *B3181 towards Cullompton, right at Hele Cross towards Clyst Hydon. 2m turn right, then sharp right at left bend at village sign*

16th-century pub saved by the villagers

The pub and the church were neighbours until early last century, when the rector's objections forced the inn to move into this old thatched farmhouse, its new name intended as a raspberry to the rector. Otter and Butcombe real ales hold sway in the bar – note the original counter. Exposed brick and cream-papered walls are adorned with signed Exeter Chiefs rugby shirts, and there's a German-style 'stammtisch', or regulars' table. Simple pub food includes bangers and mash; Jerusalem artichoke risotto; South Devon Herd rump steak; and fresh fish pie, plus daily specials. The inn is very child friendly. The beer festival is held during the second week of August.

Open all wk 12-3 6-12 (Sun 12-10) **Food** Lunch Mon-Sat 12-2, Sun 12-5 Dinner Sun-Thu 6-9, Fri-Sat 6-9.30 Set menu available ⊕ FREE HOUSE ◀ Otter Ale, Otter Amber, Butcombe Bitter ♂ Berry Farm. ☘ 9 **Facilities** Non-diners area ✿ (Bar Garden Outside area) ♦ Children's menu Children's portions Garden Outside area ☲ Beer festival Cider festival Parking WiFi ▬ (notice required)

COCKWOOD
Map 3 SX98

The Anchor Inn

tel: 01626 890203 **EX6 8RA**
email: scott.anchor@hotmail.co.uk **web:** www.anchorinncockwood.com
dir: *From A379 between Dawlish & Starcross follow Cockwood sign*

Waterside pub specialising in seafood

Originally a Seamen's Mission, this 450-year-old inn overlooks a small landlocked harbour on the River Exe and was once the haunt of smugglers. There is even a friendly ghost with his dog. In summer, customers spill out onto the verandah and harbour wall, while real fires, nautical bric-a-brac and low beams make the interior cosy in winter. For fish dish lovers, the comprehensive menu will make decisions difficult – there are over 20 different ways to eat mussels, and plenty of scallop dishes and fish platters. Meat-eaters and vegetarians are not forgotten. Beer festivals twice a year around Easter and Halloween.

Open all day all wk 11-11 (Sun 12-10.30 25 Dec 12-2) **Food** Lunch Mon-Sat 12-10, Sun 12-9.30 Dinner Mon-Sat 12-10, Sun 12-9.30 Restaurant menu available all wk ⊕ HEAVITREE ◀ Otter Ale, St Austell Tribute & Proper Job, Dartmoor Jail Ale, 3 guest ales. **Facilities** Non-diners area ✿ (Bar Outside area) ♦ Children's menu Children's portions Outside area ☲ Beer festival Parking ▬ (notice required)

PICK OF THE PUBS

Royal Castle Hotel ★★★ HL

DARTMOUTH Map 3 SX85

tel: 01803 833033
11 The Quay TQ6 9PS
email: enquiry@royalcastle.co.uk
web: www.royalcastle.co.uk
dir: *In town centre, overlooking inner harbour*

Historic pub and hotel with great estuary views

An iconic 17th-century building in the centre of this bustling town, the Royal Castle Hotel commands a prime site overlooking the Dart estuary. Originally four Tudor houses built on either side of a narrow lane, which now forms the lofty hallway, this handsome old coaching inn offers plenty of original features in the shape of period fireplaces, spiral staircases, oil paintings and priest holes. The choice of real ales from local breweries includes Dartmoor Jail Ale and Otter Amber, and there is an impressive number of carefully selected wines served by the glass; a wider range of high quality wines appears on the Castle Collection list. A supporter of Taste of the West's 'buy local' campaign, the kitchen showcases plenty of Devon produce on both the all-day bar menu and the Grill Room restaurant. Typical choices in the pubby Harbour Bar and Galleon Lounge might take in local crab sandwiches; seafood chowder; chargrilled South Devon sirloin steak and chips; or the vegetarian quesadilla

baked with cheddar cheese, peppers, onion and roasted jalapeño peppers. With its lovely river views, the Grill Room upstairs is a great setting to enjoy starters such as South Devon mussels marinière or ham hock terrine with duck liver mousse, home-made piccalilli and root vegetable vinaigrette. These might be followed by braised turbot on the bone with wilted spinach, Parisienne potatoes and lemongrass and coriander emulsion; or oven-roasted venison loin with sweet potato gratin, aubergine and courgette cannelloni, slow-roasted celeriac purée and juniper jus. Finish, perhaps, with mascarpone and raspberry trifle terrine, raspberry sorbet and strawberry gremolata; or a board of West Country cheeses with local ale chutney.

Open all day all wk 8am-11.30pm
Food all wk 11.30-10 Set menu available Restaurant menu available all wk ⊕ FREE HOUSE ◀ Dartmoor Jail Ale, Otter Amber, Sharp's Doom Bar ♻ Thatchers Gold, Orchard's. ♟ 29
Facilities Non-diners area ❖ (Bar) ⋔ Children's menu Children's portions Family room WiFi **Rooms** 25

COLEFORD
Map 3 SS70

The New Inn ★★★★ INN
PICK OF THE PUBS

tel: 01363 84242 **EX17 5BZ**
email: enquiries@thenewinncoleford.co.uk **web:** www.thenewinncoleford.co.uk
dir: *From Exeter take A377, 1.5m after Crediton left for Coleford, 1.5m to inn*

Local ales and food in secluded Devon valley

The attractive 13th-century building with thatched roof makes a perfect home for this friendly inn. The ancient slate-floored bar with its old chests and polished brass blends effortlessly with fresh white walls, original oak beams and simple wooden furniture in the dining room. Set beside the River Cole, the garden is perfect for alfresco summer dining, when you can ponder on the pub's history: it was used by travelling Cistercian monks long before Charles I reviewed his troops from a nearby house during the English Civil War. Menus change regularly, and special events such as 'posh pies week' or 'sea shanty evening' are interspersed throughout the year. Home-made bar food includes a range of soups, omelettes and platters, while a larger meal might include poached Brixham skate wing with parmesan crust; or sautéed pork tenderloin fillet, black pudding and Madeira sauce. The pub's talking Amazon Blue parrot, called Captain, has been a famous fixture here for nearly 30 years, greeting bar regulars and guests booking into the six well-appointed bedrooms.

Open all wk 12-3 6-11 (Sun 12-3 6-10.30) **Food** Lunch all wk 12-2 Dinner all wk 6-9.30 ⊕ FREE HOUSE ◗ Sharp's Doom Bar, Otter Ale Ö Winkleigh Sam's, Thatchers Gold. ♟ 15 **Facilities** Non-diners area ♣ (Bar Garden Outside area) ♦️ Children's menu Children's portions Garden Outside area ⛺ Parking WiFi ⛟ (notice required) **Rooms** 6

DARTMOUTH
Map 3 SX85

Royal Castle Hotel ★★★ HL
PICK OF THE PUBS

See Pick of the Pubs on page 137

DODDISCOMBSLEIGH
Map 3 SX88

The NoBody Inn ★★★★ INN ⊛
PICK OF THE PUBS

See Pick of the Pubs on opposite page

DOLTON
Map 3 SS51

Rams Head Inn

tel: 01805 804255 **South St EX19 8QS**
email: ramsheadinn@btopenworld.com
dir: *8m from Torrington on A3124*

Traditional pub in Devon's lovely countryside

This 15th-century free house has retained much of its original character with huge old fireplaces, bread ovens and pot stands. The inn's central location places it on many inland tourist routes, whilst the Tarka Trail and Rosemoor Gardens are both nearby. Expect a selection of cask ales on tap, accompanied by popular and traditional meals on the restaurant menu, served at lunchtime and in the evening.

Open 10-3 6-11 (Fri-Sat 12-12 Sun 12-4 6-11) Closed Mon winter **Food** Lunch all wk 12-2.30 Dinner Mon-Sat 6.30-9 Restaurant menu available Tue-Sat ⊕ FREE HOUSE ◗ Sharp's Own, Guest ales Ö Winkleigh. ♟ 14 **Facilities** Non-diners area ♣ (Bar Outside area) ♦️ Garden Outside area ⛺ Parking WiFi ⛟

EAST ALLINGTON
Map 3 SX74

The Fortescue Arms

tel: 01548 521215 **TQ9 7RA**
email: reception@thefortescuearms.com
dir: *Phone for detailed directions*

Pretty free house in a South Hams village

Named after a local landowner, this 19th-century pub retains the charms of yesteryear with wooden tables, flagstone floors and beamed ceilings. Open fires burn in winter, warming the informal and candlelit interior where a range of proper ales is served. New owners mean new menus, and the results are nicely priced dishes of popular home-made fare: Welsh rarebit, followed by beef stew with root vegetables and horseradish dumplings makes a warming and fulfilling combination. The quiet and comfortable cottage garden is a great place to eat if you're visiting this Area of Outstanding Natural Beauty on a fine day. A beer and cider festival is promised.

Open 12-3 6-11 (Sat-Sun all day Tue 6-11) Closed Mon & Tue L (ex BH) **Food** Lunch Wed-Sun 12-2 Dinner Tue-Sun 6-9 Av main course £10.95 ⊕ FREE HOUSE ◗ Dartmoor Legend & Jail Ale, Wadworth Henry's Original IPA, St Austell Tribute, Guinness Ö Westons Stowford Press. ♟ **Facilities** Non-diners area ♣ (Bar Restaurant Garden) ♦️ Children's menu Children's portions Garden ⛺ Beer festival Cider festival Parking WiFi ⛟ (notice required)

EAST PRAWLE
Map 3 SX73

The Pigs Nose Inn

tel: 01548 511209 **TQ7 2BY**
email: info@pigsnoseinn.co.uk
dir: *From Kingsbridge take A379 towards Dartmouth. After Frogmore turn right signed East Prawle. Approx 5m to pub in village centre*

A 500-year-old inn overlooking the village green

Smugglers used to store their shipwreck booty here but, rather than hiding contraband, today's owners Lesley and Peter Webber prefer to demonstrate their adherence to old-fashioned values by banning juke boxes and games machines, and by their provision of a 'knitting corner', games and toys. Devon-sourced real ales are served straight from the barrel in the wonderfully cluttered bar. Food here is never a 'minuscule blob on an oversized square plate', but good helpings of traditional pub grub, such as chicken curry; scampi and chips; cod and chips; and vegetarian Mediterranean pasta. There's also a dog menu!

Open 12-3 6-11.30 Closed Sun (Nov-Mar) **Food** Lunch all wk 12-2 Dinner all wk 6.30-9 ⊕ FREE HOUSE ◗ The South Hams Eddystone & Devon Pride, Otter Ö Thatchers Heritage. **Facilities** Non-diners area ♣ (Bar Restaurant Outside area) ♦️ Children's menu Children's portions Play area Family room Outside area ⛺ WiFi ⛟ (notice required) **Notes** ⊛

PICK OF THE PUBS

The NoBody Inn ★★★★ INN ❁

DODDISCOMBSLEIGH   Map 3 SX88

tel: 01647 252394 **EX6 7PS**
email: info@nobodyinn.co.uk
web: www.nobodyinn.co.uk
dir: *3m SW of Exeter Racecourse (A38)*

All the old-world charm you could want

For over 400 years, this old building has stood in the rolling countryside between the Haldon Hills and the Teign Valley. Remodelling over the centuries has reflected its several roles, including a long spell as a centre for parish affairs and meeting place until in 1838 Pophill House, as it was then known, formally became The New Inn. Among the five landlords since was the poor chap in 1952 whose body undertakers mistakenly left in the mortuary, so that his funeral went ahead with an empty coffin — which is how the inn acquired its name. Inside, providing all the expected old-world charm, are low ceilings, blackened beams, an inglenook fireplace and antique furniture. The bar serves 30-odd wines by the glass, selected from a range of more than 250 bins, some quite rare, and the shelves groan under the weight of a mind-boggling 280 whiskies, mostly malts. Branscombe Vale brewery supplies NoBody's Bitter, with other Devon and Cornwall guest ales adding to the choice. Crisp white napkins define the restaurant, where the seasonally

changing menus, awarded an AA Rosette, rely extensively on fine Devon produce. A typical lunch or dinner would be beetroot carpaccio, Vulscombe goats' cheese mousse, candied walnuts and celery and apple salad; followed by herb-crusted confit sea bream fillet and mussel chowder; or the ever-popular steak and NoBody ale pie; and, to finish, pistachio olive oil cake with raspberry sorbet. Daily specials might be panko crumb squid and sweet chilli mayo; and rack of Devon lamb, oregano crust, pesto mash, roast butternut squash and Madeira jus. If you want a bar snack, there's homity pie; and ploughman's, featuring Sharpham Brie, Devon Blue or Devon Oke cheese.

Open all day all wk 11-11 (Sun

12-10.30) Closed 1 Jan **Food** Lunch Mon-Sat 12-2, Sun 12-3 Dinner Mon-Thu 6.30-9, Fri-Sat 6.30-9.30, Sun 7-9 Restaurant menu Tue-Sat ⊕ FREE HOUSE ◑ Branscombe Vale NoBody's Bitter, Guest ales ⏚ Westons Old Rosie, Ashridge Devon Gold, Winkleigh Sam's Poundhouse Crisp. ♟ 28 **Facilities** Non-diners area ❅ (Bar Garden) ♟ Children's portions Garden ⊼ Cider festival Parking **Rooms** 5

EXETER
Map 3 SX99

The Hour Glass

tel: 01392 258722 **21 Melbourne St EX2 4AU**
email: ajpthehourglass@yahoo.co.uk
dir: *M5 junct 30, A370 signed Exeter. At Countess Weir rdbt 3rd exit onto Topsham Rd (B3182) signed City Centre. In approx 2m left into Melbourne St*

Quirky end-of-terrace pub with friendly staff

This distinctively shaped backstreet pub has built up a reputation for its friendly service and inventive food, not to mention its impressive range of local real ales. Expect beams, wood floors, an open fire and resident cats in the bar, where handpulled pints of Otter Bitter or Exeter Avocet can be enjoyed with curried eggs and watercress; or lamb, quince and Rioja stew with anchovy dumplings.

Open 12-2.30 5-close (Sat-Sun all day Mon 5-close) Closed 25-26 Dec, 2 Jan, Mon L **Food** Lunch Tue-Fri 12-2.15, Sat-Sun 12-3 Dinner Mon-Sat 7-9.30, Sun 6-9 ⊕ ENTERPRISE INNS ◀ Otter Bitter, Exeter Avocet, Bath Ales Special Pale Ale, Rotating local ales Ở Burrow Hill. ☂ 24 **Facilities** Non-diners area WiFi

Red Lion Inn

tel: 01392 461271 **Broadclyst EX5 3EL**
dir: *On B3181 (Exeter to Cullompton road)*

Tucked away in a quiet corner of the Killerton Estate

You'll find the Red Lion in a 16th-century listed building set at the heart of a delightful village in the National Trust's Killerton Estate. The interior has a wealth of beams and warming open fires, where pints of Tribute are cheerfully served and supped. The typical menu may offer lamb's liver, onion and bacon casserole; pot roasted lamb shank; grilled sea bass; or Exmoor ale rabbit stew. Treat yourself to a home-made pud afterwards. Vegetarians and coeliacs are catered for, as are the canine contingent, who have their own bar menu.

Open all wk 12-2.30 5.30-11 (Sat-Sun 12-11) **Food** Lunch all wk 12-1.45 Dinner all wk 6-8.45 ⊕ FREE HOUSE ◀ St Austell Tribute, Local guest ale Ở Thatchers Gold, Sandford Orchards Devon Scrumpy. ☂ 8 **Facilities** Non-diners area ✿ (Bar Garden) ♦ Children's menu Children's portions Garden ⋈ Parking ▤ (notice required)

The Rusty Bike

tel: 01392 214440 **67 Howell Rd EX4 4LZ**
email: tiny@rustybike-exeter.co.uk
dir: *Phone for detailed directions*

Truly unique gastro-pub a stone's throw from Exeter University

Now into their sixth year, The Rusty Bike is a place for the kitchen team to show what they can do with the wealth of local produce available. The pub offers tempting choices ranging from Exmoor deer, black pudding and duck Scotch egg to classic Ruby Red beef bourguignon and mash – all locally sourced, or as they say, 'from welly to belly'. Beer and cider aficionados will also enjoy the Fat Pig Brewery's own creations, Pigmalion Ale, John Street Ale and Rusty Pig Cider.

Open all wk 5-11 (Fri-Sat 5-12 Sun 12-11) **Food** Lunch Sun 12-7 Dinner Mon-Sat 6-10, Sun 12-7 Av main course £16 ⊕ FREE HOUSE ◀ Fat Pig Ham 69, John Street Ale & Pigmalion Ở Rusty Pig. ☂ 18 **Facilities** Non-diners area ✿ (Bar Restaurant Outside area) ♦ Children's portions Outside area WiFi ▤ (notice required)

EXTON
Map 3 SX98

The Puffing Billy
PICK OF THE PUBS

tel: 01392 877888 **Station Rd EX3 OPR**
email: enquiries@thepuffingbilly.co.uk
dir: *A376 signed Exmouth, through Ebford. Follow signs for pub, right into Exton*

Smart modern setting for seasonal British food

The neighbouring Exe estuary and the distant upwellings of Dartmoor's hills and woods may be glimpsed from the tables set in front of this old whitewashed pub. The building might be 16th century; the name 19th century and referring to the nearby railway line; the food is absolutely 21st century, served in a chic, modern dining pub-restaurant. The traditional exterior disguises the crisp, clean lines and finish within, where reliable West Country beers such as Branscombe Vale Branoc and Hanlons Yellow Hammer and a zesty menu combine to make The Puffing Billy a favourite destination dining bar. The menu is energetically English, seasonally changing and based on the best that Devon can provide – and all home cooked. Crab cakes with beetroot and apple relish and watercress salad is a possible starter; continuing then with sage and garlic stuffed West Country belly pork with baked pear and cider sauce. To finish – steamed treacle pudding with, what else, Devon clotted cream.

Open all day all wk **Food** Lunch 12-2.15 Dinner 6-9.15 Set menu available Restaurant menu available Mon-Sat ⊕ FREE HOUSE ◀ Branscombe Vale Branoc, Hanlons Yellow Hammer Ở Sandford Orchards Devon Red, Thatchers Gold. ☂ 15 **Facilities** Non-diners area ✿ (Bar Garden) ♦ Children's menu Children's portions Garden ⋈ Parking WiFi ▤ (notice required)

GEORGEHAM
Map 3 SS43

The Rock Inn

tel: 01271 890322 **Rock Hill EX33 1JW**
email: therockgeorgeham@gmail.com
dir: *From A361 at Braunton follow Croyde Bay signs. Through Croyde, 1m to Georgeham. Pass shop & church. Turn right (Rock Hill), inn on left*

A mixture of dining options at this popular inn

Handy for the famous surfing beaches at Woolacombe, this old inn is also a lovely watering hole for walkers and cyclists. Its friendly atmosphere, comprising a mix of happy banter from the locals and gentle jazz played at lunchtime, adds to the enjoyment of a pint selected from the five ales on offer, including Exmoor Gold. Choose between the bar, the slightly more contemporary lower bar, or a bright conservatory. The tasty menu is hard to resist, extending from a lunch of shredded duck wraps, to dinner dishes such as linguine with tiger prawns, mussels, chilli, garlic and white wine.

Open all day all wk 11am-mdnt **Food** Lunch Mon-Sat 12-2.30, Sun 12-9 Dinner Mon-Sat 6-9.30, Sun 12-9 ◀ Timothy Taylor Landlord, Exmoor Ale & Gold, St Austell Tribute, Sharp's Doom Bar, Otter, Braunton Bitter Ở Thatchers Gold, Addlestones. ☂ 12 **Facilities** Non-diners area ✿ (Bar Garden) ♦ Children's menu Children's portions Garden ⋈ Parking WiFi ▤

Visit shop.theAA.com
for a wide variety of AA publications, including Walking books, Lifestyle Guides, Atlases, and International Travel Guides

HAYTOR VALE

Map 3 SX77

The Rock Inn ★★★★ INN ⚹

PICK OF THE PUBS

tel: 01364 661305 **TQ13 9XP**
email: info@rock-inn.co.uk **web:** www.rock-inn.co.uk
dir: *A38 from Exeter, at Drum Bridges rdbt take A382 for Bovey Tracey, 1st exit at 2nd rdbt (B3387), 3m left to Haytor Vale*

An oasis of calm and comfort on wild Dartmoor

Just inside Dartmoor National Park, below the Haytor Rocks, this beamed and flagstoned 18th-century coaching inn occupies a stunning location with wonderful surrounding walks. The traditional interior is full of character, with antique tables, settles, prints and paintings, a grandfather clock, and pieces of china over the two crackling fireplaces. After a day walking, healthy appetites can be satisfied with some robust and contemporary British cooking, using top-notch local produce in attractively presented dishes of duck Scotch egg with chilli jam and salad leaves or pan-roasted lamb rump with tenderstem broccoli, wilted spinach, colcannon mash and red wine sauce. Leave room for a dark chocolate delice or pear bavarois. Meals can be enjoyed alfresco in the courtyard or in the peaceful garden across the lane. West Country cheese is a particular feature, alongside wine from the Sharpham Vineyard in Totnes and locally brewed Dartmoor Jail Ale.

Open all day all wk 11-11 (Sun 12-10.30) Closed 25-26 Dec **Food** Lunch all wk 12-2 Dinner all wk 7-9 Set menu available Restaurant menu available all wk ⊕ FREE HOUSE ◖ Dartmoor Jail Ale & IPA ♂ Sandford Orchards. ♟ 12 **Facilities** Non-diners area ❤ (Garden) ⚬ Children's menu Children's portions Family room Garden �🄿 Parking WiFi **Rooms** 9

HONITON

Map 4 ST10

The Holt ⚹⚹

PICK OF THE PUBS

tel: 01404 47707 **178 High St EX14 1LA**
email: enquiries@theholt-honiton.com
dir: *Phone for detailed directions*

A chic pub, restaurant and smokehouse

Successfully run by brothers Joe and Angus McCaig, this popular split-level establishment is just where the High Street crosses a stream called The Gissage. The downstairs bar is stocked with the full range of Otter beers from nearby Luppitt, ciders from Sheppy's and Honiton's own Norcotts, and Joe's wine selection; it's also where the open-plan kitchen is; for the candlelit, two-AA Rosette restaurant, head upstairs. The cooking style is modern British, with regularly changing menus showcasing local suppliers in a big way and making good use of meats and fish from Angus's smokehouse. Tapas is served at lunchtime and in the evening, and daily specials supplement main dishes such as seared wild venison haunch steak with celeriac, dauphinoise potatoes and red wine jus; and apple wood smoked haddock rarebit with champ potato, celeriac, leek and wholegrain mustard. The Holt hosts quarterly musical events, from jazz to rock to reggae to folk.

Open 11-3 5.30-12 Closed 25-26 Dec, Sun & Mon **Food** Lunch Tue-Sat 12-2 Dinner Tue-Sat 6.30-9 ⊕ FREE HOUSE ◖ Otter Bitter, Ale, Bright, Amber, Head ♂ Sheppy's, Thatchers Gold, Norcotts Cider. ♟ 9 **Facilities** Non-diners area ❤ (Bar) ⚬ Children's portions Beer festival WiFi 🚌

The Railway

tel: 01404 47976 **Queen St EX14 1HE**
email: sue@gochef.co.uk
dir: *From High St into New St (Lloyds bank on corner). 1st left into Queen St, follow road around to right. Pub on left before the railway bridge*

Local ale and good food in this friendly town pub

The Railway dates back to 1869, when it was built as a cider house for thirsty GWR workers. Melanie and Jean Sancey have breathed new life into the place, which offers a warm, family-friendly atmosphere. Whether it's in the bar with its cosy log-burner and range of real ales, or in the restaurant, the appealing menu offers plenty of choice including meze and gourmet pizzas; there is an emphasis on quality local ingredients. A typical starter of creamed Arbroath haddock and gambas prawn chowder might be followed by guinea fowl breast 'schnitzel' with melted Taleggio cheese.

Open 12-3 6-close Closed Sun & Mon **Food** Lunch Tue-Sat 12-2 Dinner Tue-Sat 6-9 Restaurant menu available all wk ⊕ FREE HOUSE ◖ St Austell Proper Job, Bath Ales Gem, Branscombe Vale Branoc, Hanlons Yellow Hammer ♂ Bath Ciders Bounders, Thatchers. ♟ 12 **Facilities** Non-diners area ❤ (Bar Outside area) ⚬ Children's portions Outside area �🄿 Parking

IDDESLEIGH

Map 3 SS50

The Duke of York

PICK OF THE PUBS

tel: 01837 810253 **EX19 8BG**
email: john@dukeofyorkdevon.co.uk
dir: *Phone for detailed directions*

High on a hill with views of the tors

In a tiny village of pretty cottages, this thatched, cob and stone inn is where local author Michael Morpurgo embarked on his novel *War Horse*, following conversations in front of the fire with a First World War veteran. Another literary link is Henry Williamson's *Tarka the Otter*, the Tarka Trail now passing the pub door. An enticing range of real ales includes Bays Topsail from Paignton, and Winkleigh cider from that Devon village. Around 640 years old, the interior bursts at the seams with signs of antiquity: ancient beams and pillars, huge inglenooks and timeworn furniture. The short menu typically offers a three-course meal of smoked duck breast with avocado and mixed leaf salad; whole brill stuffed with prawns, and rich white wine and parsley sauce; and Dunstaple Farm ice cream. Daily specials appear on a blackboard. There's a beer festival in August.

Open all day all wk 11-11 **Food** Lunch all wk 11-10 Dinner all wk 11-10 Av main course £12 Restaurant menu available all wk ⊕ FREE HOUSE ◖ Adnams Broadside, Bays Topsail, Guest ales ♂ Winkleigh. ♟ 10 **Facilities** Non-diners area ❤ (Bar Garden) ⚬ Children's menu Children's portions Garden �🄿 Beer festival WiFi 🚌 (notice required)

KILMINGTON
Map 4 SY29

The Old Inn

tel: 01297 32096 **EX13 7RB**
email: pub@oldinnkilmington.co.uk web: www.oldinnkilmington.co.uk
dir: *From Axminster on A35 towards Honiton. Pub on left in 1m*

Delightful Devon longhouse offering classic pub meals

Duncan and Leigh Colvin's thatched Devon longhouse dates from 1650, when it was a staging house for changing post horses, and stands beside the A35 just west of Axminster. Weary travellers will find a cosy, beamed interior with a relaxed atmosphere, crackling log fires, and a fine range of local ales on tap. Order a pint of Otter to accompany a traditional pub meal, perhaps a baked aubergine with Mediterranean vegetables and sweet potato, topped with a three-cheese crust; Cumberland ring, mash and gravy; a jacket potato with a choice of toppings; or chargrilled belly pork with bubble-and-squeak and a fried egg. The south-facing garden is the venue for the Spring Bank Holiday beer festival in late May.

Open all wk 11-3 6-11 Closed 25-26 Dec **Food** Lunch all wk 12-2 Dinner all wk 6-9 Av main course £11 ⊕ FREE HOUSE ◀ Otter Bitter, Branscombe Vale Branoc ♂ Branscombe Vale PIP. ▼ 10 **Facilities** Non-diners area ✿ (Bar Garden) ♦ Children's menu Children's portions Garden ◚ Beer festival Parking WiFi ▭ (notice required)

KINGSBRIDGE
Map 3 SX74

The Crabshell Inn

tel: 01548 852345 **Embankment Rd TQ7 1JZ**
email: info@thecrabshellinn.com
dir: *A38 towards Plymouth, follow signs for Kingsbridge*

Gourmet pizzas and great views

The Crabshell Inn is a traditional sailors' watering hole on the Kingsbridge estuary – you can moor up to three hours either side of high tide. As you would expect, the

views from the outside tables – with a glass of Proper Job or Thatchers Gold in hand – and from the first-floor restaurant are unbeatable. As well as a good selection of salads, meat, poultry and fish dishes using locally sourced ingredients, the pub has introduced a gourmet pizza menu. Made with thin sourdough bases, there are more than a dozen mouthwatering toppings to choose from: quattro formaggi (four cheeses), fiorentina (spinach and egg), and 'go figa' (gorgonzola, fig, pancetta and cherry tomatoes).

Open all day all wk **Food** Lunch all wk 12-3, all day Jul-Aug Dinner all wk 6-9, all day Jul-Aug ⊕ FREE HOUSE ◀ Sharp's Doom Bar, St Austell Proper Job, Tribute, Dartmoor Jail Ale ♂ Thatchers Gold, Heron Valley. ▼ **Facilities** Non-diners area ✿ (Bar Restaurant Garden) ♦ Children's menu Children's portions Play area Family room Garden ◚ Parking WiFi ▭

KINGSKERSWELL
Map 3 SX86

Bickley Mill Inn
`PICK OF THE PUBS`

tel: 01803 873201 **TQ12 5LN**
email: info@bickleymill.co.uk
dir: *From Newton Abbot take A380 towards Torquay. Right at Barn Owl Inn, follow brown tourist signs*

A charming mix of old and new in a rural mill

With the resorts and beaches of the English Riviera just to the east and the wilderness of Dartmoor an easy drive to the west, this country pub in the Stoneycombe Valley started life as a flour mill some 700 years ago. Lovingly converted into a homely inn, the owners have effortlessly blended the old with on-trend contemporary design and furnishings. Thirsty ramblers can rest easy beside a roaring log fire in the bar, supping beers from local microbreweries like Teignworthy and Otter. The stimulating menu melds modern British and international dishes, with the ingredients favouring Devon suppliers. A typical starter may be pan-fried scallops with chorizo, apple, watercress and a sherry dressing. Those with larger appetites should look for a trio of lamb cutlets with rosemary potatoes, crushed peas and fresh mint sauce; a vegetarian option may be roasted red pepper and tomato cannelloni. Alfresco dining takes advantage of a tree-shaded garden above the inn.

Open all day all wk **Food** Lunch Mon-Sat 12-2.30, Sun 12-3 Dinner Mon-Sat 6-9, Sun 6-8 ⊕ FREE HOUSE ◀ Otter Ale, Teignworthy, Bays. ▼ 12 **Facilities** Non-diners area ✿ (Bar Garden) ♦ Children's menu Children's portions Garden ◚ Parking WiFi ▭

KINGS NYMPTON
Map 3 SS61

The Grove Inn
`PICK OF THE PUBS`

tel: 01769 580406 **EX37 9ST**
email: eatdrink@thegroveinn.co.uk
dir: *2.5m from A377 (Exeter to Barnstaple road). 1.5m from B3226 (South Molton road). Follow brown pub signs*

Classic English village pub

The Grove Inn has everything one expects of an English pub: thatched, whitewashed, beamed ceilings, stone walls, rustic furnishings, flagstone floors and winter log fires. It is, of course, a listed building, just like many others in this secluded village. Moreover, the owners work closely with nearby farmers to provide the fresh, seasonal produce we all demand these days – count the local farm names on the various menus. From the well thought out dishes there may be roast leg of rare-breed pork with apple sauce; chicken breast stuffed with thyme, Devon Blue and Parma ham; pastry-topped fish pie; or brie and apricot compôte Wellington with cranberry sauce. An accompanying drink could be one of the 26 wines by the glass, a pint of Hunter's Devon Dreamer or Otter Ale for example, or a Sam's Dry cider from Winkleigh. Afterwards, investigate the collection of 65 single malts. A beer and cider festival takes place in July.

Open 12-3 6-11 (Sun 12-4 7-10 BH 12-4) Closed Mon L (ex BHs) **Food** Lunch Tue-Sat 12-2, Sun 12-3 Dinner Tue-Sat 6.45-9 ⊕ FREE HOUSE ◪ Exmoor Ale, Skinner's Betty Stogs, Otter Ale, Chuffin' Ale, Hunter's Devon Dreamer, Exe Valley DOBS Best Bitter ♂ Winkleigh Sam's Dry. ♟ 26 **Facilities** Non-diners area ♣ (Bar Restaurant Outside area) ♦ Children's menu Children's portions Outside area ♬ Beer festival Cider festival WiFi ▭ (notice required)

KINGSTON
Map 3 SX64

The Dolphin Inn

tel: 01548 810314 **TQ7 4QE**
email: info@dolphininn.eclipse.co.uk
dir: From A379 (Plymouth to Kingsbridge road) take B3233 signed Bigbury-on-Sea, at x-rds straight on to Kingston. Follow brown inn signs

Off the beaten track for precious tranquillity

Church stonemasons lived here in the 15th century, and later it was taken over by fishermen and their families. The inn is close to the beautiful Erme estuary and the popular surfing beaches of the South Hams. Teignworthy Spring Tide is one of several real ales, alongside Thatchers cider. Home-made food includes pan-set pigeon breast, chocolate, foie gras and cherries; wild mushroom and pesto linguine; pork belly, hogs pudding, scallops and creamed potato; and tiramisù with honeycomb ice cream. A circular walk from the pub takes in woodland, the estuary and the South West Coastal Path.

Open 12-3 6-11 (Sun 12-3 7-10.30) Closed Sun eve & Tue winter **Food** Lunch Mon-Sat 12-3, Sun 12-2.30 Dinner all wk 6-9 Av main course £9.95 Set menu available Restaurant menu available Mon-Sun evenings (ex Sun eve in winter) ⊕ PUNCH TAVERNS ◪ Exmoor Ale, Teignworthy Spring Tide, Sharp's Doom Bar, Otter, Dartmoor Jail Ale ♂ Thatchers. **Facilities** Non-diners area ♣ (Bar Restaurant Garden) ♦ Children's menu Children's portions Play area Family room Garden ♬ Parking WiFi

KNOWSTONE
Map 3 SS82

The Masons Arms ◉◉
PICK OF THE PUBS

tel: 01398 341231 **EX36 4RY**
email: enqs@masonsarmsdevon.co.uk
dir: Follow Knowstone signs from A361

Village local crossed with high-end restaurant

A thatched 13th-century inn on the edge of Exmoor, where excellent food and drink are preceded by a genuinely warm welcome. Villagers and visiting walkers mix happily in the low-beamed bar, where pints of Cotleigh Tawny Owl and Sam's Poundhouse cider are supped around the warmth of the huge fireplace. The bright rear dining room offers long views, an extraordinary ceiling mural, and food worthy of two AA Rosettes. Chef and owner Mark Dodson can boast cooking under the guidance of Michel Roux, and now runs his own monthly masterclass which culminates in a two-course lunch. As befits the menu's sophisticated adult tastes, the dining room is out of bounds for under 5s in the evening. Typical of choices are wood pigeon breasts with curried Brussels sprouts purée and stuffing; fillets of John Dory with crab risotto and bouillon tempura of mangetout; and Amaretto mousse with poached plums.

Open 12-2 6-11 Closed 1st wk Jan, Feb half term & last wk Aug, Sun eve & Mon **Food** Lunch Tue-Sun 12-2 Dinner Tue-Sat 6-11 Av main course £24 Set menu available Restaurant menu available Tue-Sun ⊕ FREE HOUSE ◪ Cotleigh Tawny Owl ♂ Winkleigh Sam's Poundhouse. ♟ 10 **Facilities** Non-diners area ♣ (Bar Garden Outside area) Children's portions Garden Outside area ♬ Parking WiFi

LIFTON
Map 3 SX38

The Arundell Arms ★★★ HL ◉◉
PICK OF THE PUBS

tel: 01566 784666 **PL16 0AA**
email: reservations@arundellarms.com **web:** www.arundellarms.com
dir: 1m from A30 dual carriageway, 3m E of Launceston

Internationally acclaimed fishing and country sports hotel

A spit from Cornwall, this former coaching inn has a 250-year-old cock-fighting pit in the garden, and from the car park you can see the window bars of the cells of the neighbouring old police station. The Courthouse Bar dispenses the aptly named Dartmoor Jail Ale, and Ashridge cider; sensibly priced wines come from around the world. Holding two AA Rosettes for many years, Devon-born Master Chef of Great Britain Steve Pidgeon's restaurant makes good use of produce from local shoots and estates, the hotel's kitchen garden and villagers; he'll cook fish caught by guests, too. Menus feature pan-fried grey mullet; roast best-end of English lamb; fillet of Aylesbury duck; and vegetable croustade provençale. There's also a five-course 'Taste of the West' menu. With Dartmoor close by, the big decisions are: lunch? dinner? breakfast? or all three? Professional advice is available for guests using the inn's fishing beats on the Tamar and six tributaries.

Open all wk 12-3 6-11 **Food** Lunch all wk 12-2 Dinner all wk 6-10 Av main course £14 Restaurant menu available all wk ⊕ FREE HOUSE ◪ St Austell Tribute, Dartmoor Jail Ale, Guest ales ♂ Ashridge. ♟ 9 **Facilities** Non-diners area ♣ (Bar Garden) ♦ Children's menu Children's portions Garden ♬ Parking WiFi **Rooms** 24

LUSTLEIGH
Map 3 SX78

The Cleave Public House

tel: 01647 277223 **TQ13 9TJ**
email: ben@thecleavelustleigh.uk.com
dir: From Newton Abbot take A382, follow Bovey Tracey signs, then Moretonhampstead signs. Left to Lustleigh

Delightful thatched pub beside the village cricket pitch

Set on the edge of Dartmoor National Park, and dating from the 16th century, this thatched, family-run pub is the only one in the village and is adjacent to the cricket pitch. It has a traditional snug bar, with beams, granite flooring and log fire; to the rear, formerly the old railway station waiting room, is now a light and airy dining area leading to a lovely cottage garden. The pub/bistro has gained a reputation for an interesting and varied, daily-changing menu. Dishes include Ligurian fish stew; River Teign mussels; sausages in ale gravy with bubble-and-squeak; or hand-made pumpkin ravioli with sage butter and balsamic onions.

Open all day all wk 11-11 (Sun 12-9) **Food** Lunch Mon-Sat 12-9, Sun 12-7 Dinner Mon-Sat 12-9, Sun 12-7 ⊕ HEAVITREE ◪ Otter Ale, Bitter, Guest ales ♂ Aspall. **Facilities** Non-diners area ♣ (Bar Garden) ♦ Children's menu Children's portions Garden ♬ Parking WiFi

Who are the AA's award-winning pubs? For details see pages 10 & 11

LUTON (NEAR CHUDLEIGH)   Map 3 SX97

The Elizabethan

tel: 01626 775425 **Fore St TQ13 OBL**
email: contact@elizabethaninn.co.uk **web**: www.elizabethaninn.co.uk
dir: *Between Chudleigh & Teignmouth*

Good honest Devon food and drink

Known locally as the Lizzie, this smart, welcoming 16th-century free house attracts diners and drinkers alike. There's a great selection of West Country ales like Teignworthy Reel Ale to choose from, as well as Thatchers Gold and local Reddaway's Farm cider. Sit beside a log fire in winter or in the pretty beer garden on warmer days. The pub prides itself on using the best local ingredients. The regularly-changing menus includes salad bowls, risottos and traditional dishes, while the daily specials boards might offer River Teign mussels; fish and chips; and roasted red peppers filled with Mediterranean risotto. A monthly-changing set menu on weekdays and a take-away menu are both offered.

Open all wk 12-3 6-11.30 (Sun all day) Closed 25-26 Dec, 1 Jan **Food** Lunch Mon-Sat 12-2, Sun 12-8.30 Dinner Mon-Sat 6-9.30, Sun 12-8.30 Set menu available ⊕ FREE HOUSE ◀ Teignworthy Reel Ale, St Austell Tribute, Sharp's Doom Bar, Exeter Avocet Ŏ Thatchers Gold, Reddaway's Farm. ▼ **Facilities** Non-diners area ❤ (Bar Garden) ♦♦ Children's menu Children's portions Garden ⋒ Parking WiFi

See advert on opposite page

LYNMOUTH   Map 3 SS74

Rising Sun Hotel ★★ HL ⦾   PICK OF THE PUBS

tel: 01598 753223 **Harbourside EX35 6EG**
email: reception@risingsunlynmouth.co.uk **web**: www.risingsunlynmouth.co.uk
dir: *M5 junct 25 follow Minehead signs. A39 to Lynmouth*

Historic inn with literary connections

Overlooking Lynmouth's tiny harbour and bay is this 14th-century thatched smugglers' inn. In turn, overlooking them all, are Countisbury Cliffs, the highest in England. The building's long history is evident from the uneven oak floors, crooked ceilings and thick walls. Literary associations are plentiful: R D Blackmore wrote some of his wild Exmoor romance, *Lorna Doone*, here; the poet Shelley is believed to have honeymooned in the garden cottage, and Coleridge stayed here too. Immediately behind rises Exmoor Forest and National Park, home to red deer, wild ponies and birds of prey. With moor and sea so close, game and seafood are in plentiful supply; appearing in dishes such as braised pheasant with pancetta and quince and Braunton greens; and roast shellfish – crab, mussels, clams and scallops in garlic, ginger and coriander. At night the oak-panelled, candlelit dining room is an example of romantic British inn-keeping at its best.

Open all day all wk 11am-mdnt Closed 25 Dec **Food** Lunch all wk 12-2.30 Dinner all wk 6-9 ⊕ FREE HOUSE ◀ Exmoor Gold, Exmoor Ales Stag, Sharp's Atlantic IPA Ŏ Thatchers Gold, Addlestones. ▼ **Facilities** Non-diners area ❤ (Bar Outside area) Outside area ⋒ WiFi ⊨ **Rooms** 14

MARLDON   Map 3 SX86

The Church House Inn

tel: 01803 558279 **Village Rd TQ3 1SL**
dir: *From Torquay ring road follow signs to Marldon & Totnes, follow brown signs to pub*

Grade II listed 18th-century inn with contemporary touches

Built as a hostel for the stonemasons of the adjoining village church, this ancient country inn dates from 1362. It was rebuilt in 1740 and many features from that period still remain, including beautiful Georgian windows; happily some of the original glass is intact despite overlooking the cricket pitch. These days it has an uncluttered, contemporary feel with additional seating in the garden. The menu might include roasted butternut squash soup with cinnamon cream; Dartmoor smoked fish platter; pork, tomato and basil with leek mash and red wine gravy; and hot chicken and bacon salad bowl. Sandwiches and baguettes too – perhaps hot sirloin of beef with rocket and horseradish; or English cheddar with home-made pear and ginger chutney.

Open all wk 11.30-2.30 5-11 (Fri-Sat 11.30-2.30 5-11.30 Sun 12-3 5.30-10.30) **Food** Lunch all wk 12-2 Dinner all wk 6.30-9.30 ⊕ FREE HOUSE ◀ St Austell Dartmoor & Tribute, Teignworthy Gundog. ▼ 12 **Facilities** Non-diners area ❤ (Bar Garden) ♦♦ Children's portions Garden ⋒ Parking

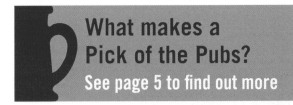

The Elizabethan

Whether you're popping in for a drink and a chat with friends, dining or collecting a takeaway you will always receive a warm welcome at "The Lizzie".

Since 2002 Nick and Anne have been the Proprietors of this Free House and together with their Manager Matt Goldsworthy and loyal staff work hard at maintaining its reputation for good food and service. Originally a farmhouse the pub can trace its title back to Elizabethan times and since 1840 has been a Licensed Premises first known as The Albert Inn then renamed The Elizabethan in 1953 to celebrate the Queen's Coronation. Situated in the farming community of Luton it is only a 5 minute drive away from either the A380 or B3192.

When choosing from the Special Boards, Bar Menu or the Weekday Set Menu you will become aware of just how many of the tempting dishes are made with very local ingredients. Meat and vegetables, herbs and, when in season, game comes from suppliers based in the surrounding countryside, and fresh fish is delivered daily direct from Brixham Fish Market. All these are then used in the dishes prepared by Nick and team of Chefs using classic, traditional and their own recipes and they rightly pride themselves for producing "good, honest Devon Food". Having been awarded the Cask Marque for well-kept beers and cellar a good pint of beer is guaranteed. There is always a choice of two real ales available as well as an array of other drinks to tempt you including award winning Reddaway's Cider which is made in the village by a neighbouring farmer.

The Elizabethan is open every day for food which is served 12 noon to 2 pm and from 6 pm to 9.30pm and ALL DAY on Sundays when the Special Roast Menu is added to the extensive choice.

Extra Information:
- Large carpark
- Pub Garden
- Childrens Menu available and Highchairs
- Takeaway Menu
- Dogs allowed in bar area only and garden
- Free WiFi

Fore Street, Luton, Nr Newton Abbot, Devon TQ13 0BL • **Tel:** 01626 775425
Email: contact@elizabethaninn.co.uk • **Website:** www.elizabethaninn.co.uk

MEAVY — Map 3 SX56

The Royal Oak Inn

tel: 01822 852944 **PL20 6PJ**
email: info@royaloakinn.org.uk
dir: B3212 from Yelverton to Princetown. Right at Dousland to Meavy, past school. Pub opposite village green

At the heart of the community in Dartmoor village

This traditional 15th-century inn is situated by a village green within Dartmoor National Park. Flagstone floors, oak beams and a welcoming open fire set the scene at this free house popular with cyclists and walkers. Local cask ales, ciders and fine wines accompany the carefully sourced ingredients in a menu ranging from lunchtime light bites to steak and ale pie; home-cooked ham, egg and chips; or local bangers and mash.

Open all wk Mon-Fri 11-3 6-11 (Sat-Sun & Apr-Oct all wk 11-11) **Food** Lunch Mon-Fri 12-2.30, Sat-Sun 12-3 Dinner all wk 6-9 ⊕ FREE HOUSE ◀ Dartmoor Jail Ale & IPA, Meavy Oak Ale, Guest ale ♂ Westons Old Rosie, Sandford Orchards Scrumpy & Old Kirton. ♟12 **Facilities** Non-diners area ✿ (Bar Garden) ✦ Children's menu Children's portions Garden ♫ ⟺ (notice required)

MODBURY — Map 3 SX65

California Country Inn — PICK OF THE PUBS

See Pick of the Pubs on opposite page

MORETONHAMPSTEAD — Map 3 SX78

The Horse

tel: 01647 440242 **George St TQ13 8PG**
email: info@thehorsedartmoor.co.uk
dir: In village centre

One for those who enjoy Italian food

Once virtually derelict, The Horse is an object lesson in pub revival, as its beautiful dining room, Mediterranean-style courtyard and stunning barn conversion testify. The chesterfield-furnished bar offers Devon-brewed real ales and ciders, and the same menu as the restaurant, which, with its clear Italian ring, could mean antipasto; hand-rolled gourmet pizzas; or hand-made meatballs in rich tomato sauce, while the courtyard smokery is responsible for smoked pastrami, salmon and salt beef. For dinner, bouillabaisse; crispy Dartmoor lamb breast; or slow-braised Dartmoor beef pie may be on offer. Local folk musicians have a sing-song on the last Monday of every month.

Open 12-3.30 5-12 (Sun-Mon 5-12) Closed 25 Dec, Sun L & Mon L **Food** Lunch Tue-Sat 12.30-2.30 Dinner all wk 6.30-9 (pizza only Sun-Mon) Av main course £12 ⊕ FREE HOUSE ◀ Dartmoor Legend & IPA, Otter Ale, Pedigree New World Pale Ale ♂ Addlestones, Symonds, Winkleigh Sam's Poundhouse. ♟12 **Facilities** Non-diners area ✿ (Bar) ✦ Children's menu Children's portions Outside area ♫ WiFi ⟺ (notice required)

NEWTON ABBOT — Map 3 SX87

The Wild Goose Inn

tel: 01626 872241 **Combeinteignhead TQ12 4RA**
dir: From A380 at Newton Abbot rdbt take B3195 (Shaldon road) signed Milber, 2.5m to village, right at pub sign

Flying the flag for West Country ales and ciders

Set in the heart of Combeinteignhead at the head of a long valley, this charming free house boasts a sunny walled garden, overlooked by the ancient village church.

The former farmstead was originally licensed as the Country House Inn in 1840 and renamed in the 1960s when nearby geese began intimidating the pub's customers. A good range of West Country real ales and ciders accompanies home-made pub food prepared from local ingredients. The lunch menu lists roast hake with a chorizo and white bean cassoulet, while an example from the à la carte is pork belly, braised lentils, choucroute and sage jus. There is a beer festival in early May.

Open all wk 11-3 5.30-11 (Sun 12-3 7-11) **Food** Lunch all wk 12-2.30 Dinner Mon-Sat 6-9, Sun 7-9 ⊕ FREE HOUSE ◀ Otter Ale, Skinner's Best Bitter, Teignworthy, Branscombe Vale, Exe Valley, Cotleigh, Sharp's ♂ Skinner's Press Gang, Wiscombe Suicider, Milltop Gold. ♟10 **Facilities** Non-diners area ✿ (Bar Garden) ✦ Children's menu Children's portions Family room Garden ♫ Beer festival Parking

NEWTON ST CYRES — Map 3 SX89

The Beer Engine

tel: 01392 851282 **EX5 5AX**
email: info@thebeerengine.co.uk
dir: From Exeter take A377 towards Crediton. Signed from A377 towards Sweetham. Pub opposite rail station, over bridge

Ever popular railway brewpub

This pretty whitewashed free house originally opened as a railway hotel in 1852. It sits opposite the Tarka Line on the banks of the River Creedy, much favoured by dogs and their walkers. Home to one of Devon's oldest microbreweries, it produces ales with names such as Rail Ale and Sleeper Heavy. Freshly baked bread uses the wort (beer yeast) from the brewery; dishes may include a home-made fishcake with sweet chilli sauce and fresh bread; fresh fish in Beer Engine batter; and chicken curry with rice. Vegetarians will rejoice in the range of soups and bakes, and the pub also caters for vegans and coeliacs.

Open all day all wk Tue-Sat 11-11 (Sun 12-10.30 Mon 11-10.30) **Food** Lunch all wk 12-2.15 Dinner Tue-Sat 6.30-9.15, Sun-Mon 6.30-8.15 ⊕ FREE HOUSE ◀ The Beer Engine Piston Bitter, Rail Ale, Sleeper Heavy, Silver Bullet ♂ Green Valley Cyder, Dragon Tears, Sandford Orchards Devon Red. ♟9 **Facilities** Non-diners area ✿ (Bar Garden) ✦ Children's portions Garden ♫ Parking WiFi ⟺ (notice required)

NORTH BOVEY — Map 3 SX78

The Ring of Bells Inn — PICK OF THE PUBS

tel: 01647 440375 **TQ13 8RB**
email: mail@ringofbells.net
dir: 1.5m from Moretonhampstead off B3212. 7m S of Whiddon Down junct on A30

Dog-friendly Dartmoor village pub

Dating back to the 13th-century, this thatched Dartmoor pub was originally built to house the stonemasons building the parish church. Overlooking the village green, the Ring of Bells draws Dartmoor visitors and walkers in for good food and regularly changing guest ales. The kitchen uses fresh, locally sourced produce and menus reflect the changing seasons with both traditional and contemporary dishes; suppliers are proudly listed. Served in cosy low-beamed bars, with heavy oak doors, rustic furnishings, crackling winter log fires and evening candlelight, the daily menu may list grilled game Scotch egg or chicken liver parfait as starters, followed by main dishes such as venison, pheasant and pork lasagne; Exmouth mussels in garlic and white wine cream sauce; and slow-cooked beef cheek and mushroom shortcrust pastry pie. Round off with lemon and lime posset with shortbread.

Open all day all wk **Food** Lunch all wk 12-2.30 Dinner all wk 6-9 Av main course £10.95 ⊕ FREE HOUSE ◀ Teignworthy Reel Ale, Dartmoor IPA, Guest ales ♂ Thatchers, Winkleigh Sam's Poundhouse. ♟12 **Facilities** Non-diners area ✿ (Bar Garden) ✦ Children's menu Children's portions Family room Garden ♫ Parking WiFi ⟺ (notice required)

PICK OF THE PUBS

California Country Inn

MODBURY   Map 3 SX65

tel: 01548 821449
California Cross PL21 0SG
email: enquiries@californiacountryinn.
co.uk
web: www.californiacountryinn.co.uk
dir: *On B3196 (NE of Modbury)*

A real find in the South Hams area

This centuries-old inn stands in some of the most tranquil countryside in southern England, just a few miles from Dartmoor to the north and the cliffs and estuaries of the coast to the south. In fact, this Area of Outstanding Natural Beauty encompasses the hills and vales which can be seen from the pub's landscaped gardens. Dating from the 14th century, its unusual name is thought to derive from local adventurers in the mid-19th century who heeded the call to 'go west' and waited at the nearby crossroads for the stage to take them on the first part of their journey to America's west coast. They must have suffered wistful thoughts of home when recalling their local pub, with its wizened old beams, exposed dressed stone walls and a fabulous, huge stone fireplace. Old rural prints and photographs, copper kettles, jugs, brasses and many other artefacts add to the rustic charm of the whitewashed pub's atmospheric interior. A family-run free house, the beers on tap are likely to include Sharp's and St Austells', the

wine list has award-winning Devon wines from nearby Sharpham Vineyard, and the good-value house wines come from Chile. Having won accolades as a dining pub, head chef Tim Whiston's food is thoughtfully created and impressively flavoursome. Most ingredients are sourced from the bounty of the local countryside and waters, with meats from a supplier in nearby Loddiswell. Meals can be taken from the bar menu, but why not indulge in the à la carte menu from the inn's dining room? Appetising starters include twice baked goats' cheese soufflé, and the main course selection may include roasted monkfish, smoked bacon, potato and sweetcorn chowder. The special board adds to the choices.

Open all day all wk **Food** Lunch Mon-Sat 12-2, Sun 12-2.30 Dinner Mon-Sat 6-9, Sun 6-8.30 Restaurant menu available Wed-Sun eve ⊕ FREE HOUSE
◀ Dartmoor Jail Ale, Sharp's Doom Bar, St Austell Tribute Ŏ Addlestones, Thatchers Gold, Westons Old Rosie, Hunt's. ♀ 12 **Facilities** Non-diners area ♣ (Bar Garden) ♦♦ Children's menu Children's portions Family room Garden ⊨ Parking WiFi ▭

NOSS MAYO
Map 3 SX54

The Ship Inn
PICK OF THE PUBS

tel: 01752 872387 **PL8 1EW**
email: ship@nossmayo.com
dir: *5m S of Yealmpton. From Yealmpton take B3186, then follow Noss Mayo signs*

Waterside free house popular with sailing enthusiasts

Surrounded by wooded hills, Noss Mayo lies on the south bank of the tidal Yealm; opposite is Newton Ferrers. The waterside location means you can, if you wish, sail to this deceptively spacious pub, which has been superbly renovated using reclaimed local stone and English oak. Log fires, wooden floors, old bookcases and dozens of local pictures characterise the interior spaces. The cellar keeps a good range of beers, mostly from brewers that know the Ship well. Whether eating in the bar, panelled library or by the river, daily-changing home-made dishes include starters like grilled flat mushroom topped with Welsh rarebit, or chicken liver pâté with red onion marmalade and toast; and mains such as seared scallops with bacon and sautéed potatoes; or oven-baked cod with smoked haddock and saffron chowder. For chicken curry and rice; steak and kidney pie; or ploughman's and baguettes, see the bar menu. Dogs are allowed downstairs.

Open all day all wk **Food** Lunch Mon-Sat 12-9.30, Sun 12-9 Dinner Mon-Sat 12-9.30, Sun 12-9 Av main course £10.95 ⊕ FREE HOUSE ◀ Dartmoor Jail Ale & IPA, St Austell Tribute & Proper Job, Otter, Palmers. ♟ 13 **Facilities** Non-diners area ✿ (Bar Garden) ♦ Children's portions Garden ⊅ Parking

OTTERY ST MARY
Map 3 SY19

The Talaton Inn

tel: 01404 822214 **Talaton EX5 2RQ**
dir: *A30 to Fairmile, then follow signs to Talaton*

Black-and-white timbered, traditional inn

This well-maintained timber-framed 16th-century inn is run by a brother and sister partnership. There is a good selection of real ales (Otter Ale, Otter Amber) and malts, and a fine collection of bar games. The regularly-changing evening blackboard menu might include brie wedges with cranberry dip; surf and turf; tuna steak au poivre; or gammon and egg. At Sunday lunchtimes (booking advisable), as well as the popular roast, there is also a pie and vegetarian choice. Lunchtime special deals available. There is a patio for summer dining and themed food nights.

Open 12-3 7-11 Closed Mon **Food** Lunch Tue-Sun 12-2 Dinner Wed-Sat 7-9 Set menu available Restaurant menu available all wk ⊕ FREE HOUSE ◀ Otter Ale & Amber, Sharp's Doom Bar, Guest ale ♂ Westons Stowford Press. **Facilities** Non-diners area ✿ (Bar Outside area) ♦ Children's menu Children's portions Outside area ⊅ Parking ➡ (notice required)

PLYMTREE
Map 3 ST00

The Blacksmiths Arms

tel: 01884 277474 **EX15 2JU**
email: blacksmithsplymtree@yahoo.co.uk
dir: *From A373 (Cullompton to Honiton road) follow Plymtree signs. Pub in village centre*

Well-kept ales and locally-sourced food

Alan and Susie Carter have been at the helm for a numbers of years and the pub has become the hub of this idyllic Devon village. A traditional free house with exposed beams and log fire, it has a reputation for serving quality food using local ingredients, and is known for generous portions of classics like game pie and local steaks, as well as curries, sharing platters and fish dishes. Up to 14 well-kept local ales include Otter Amber, and there is a fine selection of wines. A beer festival is held in July every even-numbered year. A large beer garden and alfresco dining area complete the picture.

Open Tue-Fri 6-11 (Sat 12-11 Sun 12-4) Closed Mon, Tue-Fri L, Sun eve **Food** Lunch Sat-Sun 12-2 Dinner Tue-Sat 6-9 ⊕ FREE HOUSE ◀ Hanlons Yellow Hammer, Otter Amber, St Austell Proper Job & Tribute, Sharp's Doom Bar ♂ Thatchers Gold. ♟ 8 **Facilities** Non-diners area ✿ (Bar Restaurant Garden) ♦ Children's menu Children's portions Play area Family room Garden ⊅ Beer festival Parking WiFi ➡ (notice required)

RATTERY
Map 3 SX76

Church House Inn

tel: 01364 642220 **TQ10 9LD**
email: ray.hardy@btconnect.com
dir: *1m from A38 (Exeter to Plymouth road) & 0.75m from A385 (Totnes to South Brent road)*

Centuries of conversation and hospitality

Tracing its history as far back as 1028, this venerable inn burgeons with brasses, bare beams, large fireplaces and other historic features. Some customers encounter the wandering spirit of a monk; fortunately he seems to be friendly. In the character dining room, dishes on the specials board include duck and orange pâté followed by trio of lamb steaks with redcurrant and rosemary sauce; moussaka; and chilli con carne. Fresh fish (grilled plaice; fisherman's pie, and pan-fried hake perhaps) features strongly. For dessert, maybe choose Bakewell tart or bread and butter pudding, served with double cream, vanilla ice cream or custard. There is a large lawned beer garden and patio where you can enjoy a pint of Dartmoor Jail Ale in warmer months.

Open all wk 11-2.30 6-11 (Sun 12-3 6-10.30) **Food** Lunch Mon-Sat 11.30-2, Sun 12-2 Dinner all wk 6.30-9 ⊕ FREE HOUSE ◀ Dartmoor Jail Ale & Legend, St Austell Proper Job, Guest ale ♂ Thatchers Gold. ♟ 10 **Facilities** Non-diners area ✿ (Bar Garden) ♦ Children's menu Children's portions Garden ⊅ Parking WiFi ➡ (notice required)

ROCKBEARE
Map 3 SY09

Jack in the Green Inn ◉◉
PICK OF THE PUBS

tel: 01404 822240 **London Rd EX5 2EE**
email: info@jackinthegreen.uk.com
dir: *M5 junct 29, A30 (dual carriageway) towards Honiton. Left onto B3184 (old A30) to Rockbeare*

Top notch pub food for everyone

Empty plates, diners' contented smiles and two AA Rosettes testify to the Jack's well-deserved reputation for upmarket modern British food, but this family-friendly roadside pub also offers good West Country brews on tap. The smart interior with its low beamed rooms, soft brown leather chairs and a wood-burning stove create a contemporary pub atmosphere. In the restaurant, the simple philosophy is to serve the best seasonal Devon produce in stylish surroundings. Local artisan producers underpin chef Matthew Mason's innovative menus with punchy flavours, be it game from local shoots, or salad leaves and seasonal vegetables from growers just six miles away. A three-course 'Totally Devon' selection could start with cured pork shoulder and smoked ham hock with apple and a green mustard vinaigrette. Next may come loin eye of Whimple lamb with mutton and caper pudding and swede purée. Finish with Sharpham brie; or hazelnut cake with caramelised pears and Devon cider brandy syrup.

Open all wk 11-3 5.30-11 (Sun 12-11) Closed 25 Dec-5 Jan **Food** Lunch Mon-Sat 12-2, Sun 12-9 Dinner Mon-Sat 6-9, Sun 12-9 Av main course £12.50 Set menu available Restaurant menu available all wk ⊕ FREE HOUSE ◀ Otter Ale & Amber, Sharp's Doom Bar, Butcombe Bitter, Hanlons Firefly & Yellow Hammer ♂ Dragon Tears, Luscombe, St Georges. ♟ 12 **Facilities** Non-diners area ♦ Children's menu Children's portions Family room Outside area ⊅ Parking WiFi ➡ (notice required)

SALCOMBE

Map 3 SX73

The Victoria Inn

tel: 01548 842604 **Fore St TQ8 8BU**
email: info@victoriainn-salcombe.co.uk
dir: *In town centre, overlooking estuary*

Friendly town pub with excellent local seafood

Tim and Liz Hore's pub has something unique among Salcombe's licensed premises – a really big garden with sun terraces. Where better for that glass of Cornish Rattler cider? From the first-floor restaurant you can watch the fishing boats bringing in the catch, destined perhaps to reappear as sauté of mild Thai-spiced monkfish and king prawns with coconut and coriander rice. Other internationally-influenced dishes include chicken souvlaki with tzatziki and salad; and, from a generous vegetarian selection, red lentil, potato and aubergine moussaka. Cottage pie with bacon and cheddar crust helps restore British balance. Treats await well-behaved children and dogs.

Open all day all wk 11.30-11 Closed 25 Dec **Food** Lunch all wk 12-9 Dinner all wk 12-9 ⊕ ST AUSTELL BREWERY ◼ Tribute, Proper Job, Guest ales ♂ Healey's Cornish Rattler. ☐ 20 **Facilities** Non-diners area ❤ (Bar Garden) ◗ Children's menu Children's portions Play area Garden ⋒ WiFi

SANDFORD

Map 3 SS80

The Lamb Inn

tel: 01363 773676 **The Square EX17 4LW**
email: thelambinn@gmail.com web: www.lambinnsandford.co.uk
dir: *A377 from Exeter to Crediton. 1st right signed Sandford & Tiverton. Left, left again, up hill. 1.5m left into village square*

A thriving community local

Mark Hildyard has worked hard at making this 16th-century former coaching inn a cracking all-round pub. Set in a sleepy Devon village, the pub's upstairs room is used as an art gallery, skittle alley, cinema, theatre, venue for open-mic nights, conferences and a meeting room for village groups. Downstairs, expect to find three log fires, candles on scrubbed tables and an imaginative chalkboard menu. Using the best Devon produce, top-notch dishes may include Holsworthy pork fillet and cheek with Sandford apples, baby gem and Jersey Royals; or new season Kenford lamb rump with spring vegetables. Everyone is welcome, including dogs and walkers in muddy boots.

The Lamb Inn

Open all day all wk 11am-11.30pm **Food** Lunch all wk 12.30-2.30 Dinner all wk 6.30-9.30 ⊕ FREE HOUSE ◼ Otter Bitter, Hanlons Yellow Hammer, Dartmoor Jail Ale & Legend, Skinner's, St Austell Proper Job ♂ Sandford Orchards. ☐ 9 **Facilities** Non-diners area ❤ (Bar Restaurant Garden) ◗ Children's portions Garden ⋒ Beer festival WiFi ⊞ (notice required)

SHEBBEAR

Map 3 SS40

The Devil's Stone Inn

tel: 01409 281210 **EX21 5RU**
email: churst1234@btinternet.com
dir: *From Okehampton turn right opposite White Hart, follow A386 towards Hatherleigh. At rdbt outside Hatherleigh take Holsworthy road to Highampton. Just after Highampton right, follow signs to Shebbear*

A village pub with an interesting history

Reputedly one of England's most haunted pubs, The Devil's Stone Inn was a farmhouse before it became a coaching inn some 400 years ago. Country sports lovers use this pub as a base for their activities; it is especially a haven for fly-fishermen, with beats, some of which the pub owns, on the middle and upper Torridge. The pub's name comes from the village tradition of the turning the Devil's Stone (situated opposite the pub), which happens every year on 5th November. The beamed and flagstone-floored interior has several open fires. Locally sourced and home-cooked food, a selection of real ales and ciders, a games room, separate dining room and large garden complete the picture.

Open all wk 12-3 6-11 (Fri-Sun all day fr 12) **Food** Lunch all wk 12-2.30 Dinner all wk 6-9.30 Restaurant menu available all wk ⊕ FREE HOUSE ◼ St Austell Tribute, Otter Ale, Fuller's London Pride ♂ Healey's Cornish Rattler, Thatchers Gold. **Facilities** Non-diners area ❤ (Bar Garden) ◗ Children's menu Children's portions Play area Garden ⋒ Parking WiFi ⊞ (notice required)

PICK OF THE PUBS

The Tower Inn

SLAPTON   Map 3 SX84

tel: 01548 580216 **Church Rd TQ7 2PN**
email: towerinn@slapton.org
web: www.thetowerinn.com
dir: *Exit A379 S of Dartmouth, left at Slapton Sands*

West Country ales and seasonal menus

Tucked up a narrow driveway behind cottages and the church in this unspoilt Devon village, the ancient ivy-clad tower (which gives this charming 14th-century inn its name) looms hauntingly above the pub. It is all that remains of the old College of Chantry Priests – the pub was built to accommodate the artisans who constructed the monastic college. Six hundred years on and this truly atmospheric village pub continues to welcome guests and the appeal, other than its peaceful location, is the excellent range of real ales on tap and the eclectic choice of modern pub grub prepared from locally sourced ingredients, which include smoked fish from Dartmouth, quality Devon-reared beef, and fresh fish and crab landed at Brixham. Expect hearty lunchtime sandwiches alongside the ploughman's platter laden with pork pie, cheddar cheese, home-made relish and crusty bread; and Thai fishcakes. A typical evening meal may take in seared scallops with haggis and fried leeks;

followed by West Country loin of lamb with slow-cooked bean cassoulet; or pan-fried hake with French dumplings, crab bisque and braised fennel. Round off with apple and blueberry crumble with vanilla ice cream and wash down with a pint of Devon Pride or St Austell Proper Job. Stone walls, open fires, low beams, scrubbed oak tables and flagstone floors characterise the welcoming interior, the atmosphere enhanced at night with candlelit tables. There's a splendid landscaped rear garden, perfect for summer alfresco meals. Visitors exploring Slapton Ley Nature Reserve and Slapton Sands should venture inland to seek out this ancient inn.

Open 12-3 6-11 (Sun 6-10.30) Closed 1st 2wks Jan, Sun eve in winter
Food Lunch all wk 12-2.30 Dinner all wk 6.30-9.30 ⊕ FREE HOUSE ◼ Butcombe Bitter, Otter Bitter, St Austell Proper Job, The South Hams Devon Pride ♻ Addlestones, Sharp's Orchard.
Facilities Non-diners area ☙ (Bar Restaurant Garden) ♦ Children's menu Children's portions Garden ⏚ Beer festival Parking WiFi 🚌

SIDBURY
Map 3 SY19

The Hare & Hounds

tel: 01404 41760 **Putts Corner EX10 0QQ**
email: contact@hareandhounds-devon.co.uk web: www.hareandhounds-devon.co.uk
dir: *From Honiton take A375 signed Sidmouth. In approx 0.75m pub at Seaton Rd x-rds*

Whitewashed free house serving classic pub dishes

Behind the whitewashed walls of this traditional Devon free house you'll find a comfortable interior with wooden beams and winter log fires. There's also a large garden and an extension which both enjoy fantastic views down the valley to the sea at Sidmouth. Besides the daily carvery, the extensive menu features classic pub dishes and snacks. Main course options include beef lasagne and steak and kidney pudding, as well as fish dishes and vegetarian options. The permanent cask ales are brewed less than 10 miles away by the Otter Brewery.

Open all day all wk 10am-11pm (Sun 11-10.30) Closed 25 Dec eve **Food** Lunch all wk 12-9 Dinner all wk 12-9 ⊕ FREE HOUSE ◀ Otter Bitter & Ale, Guest ales ☼ Wiscombe Suicider. **Facilities** Non-diners area ♣ (Bar Garden) ♦️ Children's menu Children's portions Play area Garden ⊢ Parking WiFi

SIDMOUTH
Map 3 SY18

Blue Ball Inn
PICK OF THE PUBS

tel: 01395 514062 **Stevens Cross, Sidford EX10 9QL**
email: enquiries@blueballinnsidford.co.uk
dir: *M5 junct 30, A3052, through Sidford towards Lyme Regis, inn on left*

Family-friendly pub with a warm welcome

Postcard-pretty under its thatched roof, the 14th-century cob-and-flint Blue Ball in Sidford is popular with locals and visitors alike. Lovingly maintained, colourful and attractive gardens surround the inn. A wide selection of freshly prepared food from traditional beer battered fish and chips, and steak and kidney pudding to a wide range of fresh fish including crab, lobster, sole and mussels; in addition there are many other dishes from the regularly changing specials board. The wine list ranges from new world and more traditional choices that will suit all pockets. The real ales include local Otter Bitter, St Austell Tribute, Sharp's Doom Bar and Bass. The inn is within easy reach of the M5, A303 and Exeter, and just minutes from stunning walks inland and along the coast. Families are very welcome here.

Open all day all wk Closed 25 Dec eve **Food** Lunch all wk 12-2.30 Dinner all wk 6-9 Set menu available ⊕ PUNCH TAVERNS ◀ Otter Bitter, St Austell Tribute, Sharp's Doom Bar, Bass, Guest ale ☼ Thatchers Gold. ♚ 13 **Facilities** Non-diners area ♣ (Bar Garden) ♦️ Children's portions Garden Outside area ⊢ Parking WiFi ▭

SLAPTON
Map 3 SX84

The Tower Inn
PICK OF THE PUBS

See Pick of the Pubs on opposite page

SOUTH POOL
Map 3 SX74

The Millbrook Inn
PICK OF THE PUBS

See Pick of the Pubs on page 152

SPARKWELL
Map 3 SX55

The Treby Arms ◎◎
PICK OF THE PUBS

See Pick of the Pubs on page 153

SPREYTON
Map 3 SX69

The Tom Cobley Tavern
PICK OF THE PUBS

tel: 01647 231314 **EX17 5AL**
dir: *From A30 at Whiddon Down take A3124 towards North Tawton. 1st right after services, 1st right over bridge*

Fabulous views and a huge range of ales

Close to the village green in this village of cob and thatch cottages, guests in the tree-shaded beer garden here can enjoy views across to the distant moors of northern Dartmoor. It was from this pub one day in 1802 that Thomas Cobley and his companions set forth for Widecombe Fair, an event immortalised in song; his cottage still stands in the village. The inn's unspoilt main bar has a roaring log fire, cushioned settles, and benefits from a stillage where an impressive selection of casks of Devon microbrewery beers are always on tap. Being a firmly traditional Devon pub, there are draught ciders here too, all served from the unusual thatched bar. Time-honoured hearty English fare is the mainstay of the menus, and there's a particularly strong suite of vegetarian and vegan dishes. Mushroom, brie and cranberry Wellington; duck and cherry pie; or steak and kidney suet pudding give a flavour of the home-cooked dishes here.

Open 12-3 6-11 (Sun 12-4 7-11 Mon 6.30-10.30 Fri-Sat 12-3 6-12) Closed Mon L **Food** Lunch Tue-Sun 12-2 Dinner all wk 7-9 ⊕ FREE HOUSE ◀ Teignworthy Gundog, St Austell Tribute & Proper Job, Dartmoor Jail Ale & Legend, Holsworthy Tamar Black ☼ Winkleigh, Westons Stowford Press, Healey's Berry Rattler & Pear Rattler, Sandford Orchards, Gwynt y Ddraig, Lilley's. **Facilities** Non-diners area ♣ (Bar Garden) ♦️ Children's menu Children's portions Garden ⊢ Parking ▭ (notice required)

STAVERTON
Map 3 SX76

Sea Trout Inn

tel: 01803 762274 **TQ9 6PA**
email: info@theseatroutinn.co.uk
dir: *From A38 take A384 towards Totnes. Follow Staverton & Sea Trout Inn sign*

Long, white-painted pub offering a modern British menu

Apart from the occasional puff of a steam train drifting across the pretty Dart Valley from the South Devon Railway, this character village inn is the epitome of tranquillity. Dating back 600 years, the Sea Trout ticks all the boxes for the authentic country pub, from the delightful locals' bar to the stylish restaurant, where trying to choose from the modern British menu can be agonising; fresh figs wrapped in Parma ham with melted blue cheese and pine nut salad to start, followed by seafood risotto; Thai green curry; or perhaps lamb's liver, smoked bacon, mash, spinach and onion rings, with well-kept Palmers ales the icing on the cake.

Open all day all wk **Food** Lunch Mon-Fri 12-2, Sat 12-2.30, Sun 12-3 Dinner Mon-Thu 6-9, Fri-Sat 6-9.30, Sun 6.30-9 Av main course £12 ⊕ PALMERS ◀ 200, Copper Ale, Best Bitter & Dorset Gold ☼ Thatchers Gold. ♚ 11 **Facilities** Non-diners area ♣ (Bar Garden) ♦️ Children's menu Children's portions Garden ⊢ Parking WiFi ▭ (notice required)

PICK OF THE PUBS

The Millbrook Inn

tel: 01548 531581 **TQ7 2RW**
email: info@millbrookinnsouthpool.co.uk
web: www.millbrookinnsouthpool.co.uk
dir: *A379 from Kingsbridge to Frogmore. In Frogmore right signed South Pool. 2m to village*

French country cooking meets good pub grub

This quaint, white-painted 16th-century village pub is little more than a good mooring rope's throw from South Pool creek on the Salcombe estuary. No surprise then that it attracts boat-owners from all along the coast. Its compact courtyard with bench tables is at one side, while at the rear a small terrace overlooks a pretty stream and fields. Open fires warm the two traditionally decorated beamed bars, and there's a small dining room, whose charm you may not be able to enjoy if you don't book. A pint of something from the South Hams brewery, or a guest ale, will no doubt be uppermost in the minds of arrivals by boat after all that belaying and tacking. The wine list is designed to complement the food, the big draw being chef Jean-Philippe Bidart's auberge-type food, based on French family recipes and the best South Hams meats and fish. A close look at his menus reveals poached eggs in red wine sauce with smoked bacon stock and shallots; snails with garlic, parsley and brioche; Devon crab and mackerel; guinea fowl cassoulet; and the famous warm duck gizzard, smoked duck, black pudding and duck egg salad. The lighter bar menu offers pan-fried chorizo with new potatoes, spinach and duck egg; smoked haddock and butterbean cassoulet; and pig's cheeks with mash and apple sauce, known as Bath Chaps. Monsieur Bidart turns out seductive desserts too, such as cardamom pannacotta with mango and berry sorbet; and sticky toffee pudding with toffee sauce and Devon clotted cream. Rural West Country and French cheeses – among them Wookey Hole cave aged cheddar; Ragstone and Dorset Blue Vinny – are served with celery, quince, apple, grapes and oat cakes. A 24-hour Veg Shed with an honesty box helps to replace a long-lost village shop.

Open all day all wk 12-11 (Sun 12-10.30)
Food Lunch all wk 12-2 (summer 12-5)
Dinner all wk 7-9 Set menu available
Restaurant menu available all wk
⊕ FREE HOUSE ◖ South Hams
Pandemonium & Wild Blonde, Guest ales
Ö Thatchers Heritage & Gold. ♀ 10
Facilities Non-diners area ♣ (Bar
Restaurant Garden) ♦♦ Children's portions
Garden Outside area ⋒ WiFi ⌦

PICK OF THE PUBS

The Treby Arms ❀❀

SPARKWELL   Map 3 SX55

tel: 01752 837363
1 Newton Row PL7 5DD
email: trebyarms@hotmail.co.uk
web: www.thetrebyarms.co.uk

Village pub that punches above its weight

This once humble, 17th-century, end-of-terrace local has successfully become a destination dining pub due to the initiative and hard work of chef-patron Anton Piotrowski and his wife Clare. Anton's achievement as a BBC MasterChef in 2012 has undoubtedly helped to ramp up interest, so booking is essential if you want to experience his inspired cooking. But first the bar, where Dartmoor Jail and IPA share counter space with St Austell Tribute, Otter Amber, and Symonds and Rekorderlig ciders. The restaurant's achievement of two AA Rosettes acknowledges the passion Anton and his staff have for their food, all, it goes without saying, prepared, cooked and presented to a very high standard. They use fresh seasonal produce, including locally-caught fish, estate game and village allotment vegetables, for the daily carte and set menus. A typical three-course option might be truffle brie, pickled onion, charcoal and nut soil with micro vegetables; Devon rose veal rump steak, triple cooked chips and onion rings; and a tasting of apples. Turn to the carte for

crispy ox tongue, roasted foie gras and pan-fried quail egg; smoked halibut, avocado ice cream, Devon crab and pomegranate; Cajun lamb rump, lamb samosa, curried leeks, squash purée and houmous; and hay-baked poussin with sage and onion croquettes. As it says on the menu 'a meal isn't complete without a dessert', so you could try the Yorkshire forced rhubarb, vanilla parfait, meringue with sage and ginger gel. Alternatively, there's a cheeseboard, on which Miss Muffet from Bude and Sharpham Rustic from Totnes are possible choices. Anton also puts together a six-course taster menu with wines. His monthly Master Class is for 'students' wanting to learn how to prepare pasta, venison, fish and the dishes that form their post-course meal.

Open 12-3 6-11 (Fri-Sun 12-11) Closed 25-26 Dec & 1-2 Jan, Mon **Food** Lunch Tue-Thu 12-3, Fri-Sun 12-9 Dinner Tue-Thu 6-9, Fri-Sun 12-9 Set menu available Restaurant menu available Tue-Sun ⊕ FREE HOUSE ◧ St Austell Tribute, Otter Amber, Dartmoor Jail Ale & IPA ♉ Thatchers, Symonds, Rekorderlig. **Facilities** Non-diners area ❤ (Bar Outside area) ♦ Children's portions Outside area ⌁ Parking WiFi

STOKE FLEMING
Map 3 SX84

The Green Dragon Inn

tel: 01803 770238 **Church Rd TQ6 OPX**
email: pcrowther@btconnect.com
dir: *From A379 (Dartmouth to Kingsbridge coast road) follow brown pub sign, into Church Rd. Pub opposite church*

A haven of boating memorabilia

Opposite the village church, this South Hams pub has many seafaring connections, being only two miles from Dartmouth. Although there has been a building on this site since the 12th century, the first recorded landlord took charge in 1607. The current landlord has decorated the interior in a seafaring theme with charts and sailing pictures. Local beers such as Otter and Exmoor slake the thirst of walkers, whilst the great-value menu can satisfy the largest of appetites with hearty baguettes, hand-picked crab, cottage pie, bangers and mash, surf 'n' turf burger or a West Country sirloin steak.

Open all wk 11.30-3 5.30-11 (Sun 12-3.30 6.30-10.30) Closed 25-26 Dec
Food Lunch all wk 12-2 Dinner all wk 6.30-8.30 ⊕ HEAVITREE ◼ Otter Ale, Exmoor Ale, St Austell Tribute, Guest ales ♂ Aspall, Addlestones. ♟ 10
Facilities Non-diners area ♣ (Bar Garden) ♦ Children's menu Children's portions Play area Garden ♠ Parking WiFi

TAVISTOCK
Map 3 SX47

The Cornish Arms

tel: 01822 612145 **15-16 West St PL19 8AN**
email: info@thecornisharmstavistock.co.uk
dir: *Phone for detailed directions*

Cosy and welcoming pub on the edge of Dartmoor

Historically the last coaching inn before reaching Cornwall, The Cornish Arms is run by husband and wife team John and Emma Hooker. Whether inside the modern but cosy interior or out in the garden, guests will find an unpretentious menu of pub favourites, from ploughman's; steak and kidney pudding with mash and buttered swede to lamb's liver and smoked bacon. The bar is well stocked with ales including St Austell's Trelawny and ciders such as Cornish Rattler, and the real ale and cider festival in August is a must-attend occasion for visitors.

Open all day all wk **Food** Lunch Mon-Sat 12-6, Sun 12-3 Dinner Mon-Sat 6-9.30, Sun 6-9 ⊕ ST AUSTELL ◼ Tribute, Proper Job & Trelawny ♂ Healey's Cornish Rattler, Sandford Orchards Devon Red. **Facilities** Non-diners area ♣ (Bar Garden Outside area) ♦ Children's menu Children's portions Garden Outside area ♠ Beer festival Cider festival Parking WiFi ▭ (notice required)

Peter Tavy Inn

tel: 01822 810348 **Peter Tavy PL19 9NN**
email: chris@wording.freeserve.co.uk
dir: *From Tavistock take A386 towards Okehampton. In 2m right to Peter Tavy*

Dartmoor inn recommended for its pies

It is thought this inn was originally built in the 15th century as a Devon longhouse for the stonemasons rebuilding the village church. On the western flanks of Dartmoor, it is likely that it became a pub by the early 17th century and a further floor was added. It is now as much a draw for its range of local real ales and ciders as it is for its food, much of it sourced locally. The pies are popular main dishes, but other choices could be lamb, chorizo and butterbean casserole; Thai chicken curry; Barnsley chop with colcannon; and whole sea bass with spring onion and ginger.

Open all wk 12-3 6-11 (Sun 12-3 6-10.30); all day Etr-Autumn Closed 25 Dec
Food Lunch all wk 12-2 Dinner all wk 6.30-9 Av main course £9.95-£12.95 ⊕ FREE HOUSE ◼ Dartmoor Jail Ale, Branscombe Vale Drayman's Best Bitter, Tavy Ideal Pale Ale ♂ Winkleigh Sam's Poundhouse & Crisp. ♟ 9 **Facilities** Non-diners area ♣ (Bar Restaurant Garden) ♦ Children's menu Children's portions Garden ♠ Parking WiFi

THURLESTONE
Map 3 SX64

The Village Inn

tel: 01548 563525 **TQ7 3NN**
email: enquiries@thurlestone.co.uk
dir: *Take A379 from Plymouth towards Kingsbridge, at Bantham rdbt take B3197, right signed Thurlestone, 2.5m*

Minutes from the beach and South West Coastal Path

Recycling came naturally to the 16th-century builders of The Village Inn, for they used timbers salvaged from wrecked Spanish Armada warships. In 2014 the Grose family, who also own the nearby Thurlestone Hotel, refurbished it to create a modern, yet still pleasingly traditional, look. The menu offers freshly prepared sandwiches and salads; signature dishes such as West Country kedgeree; pub classics including scampi, chips and peas; and daily blackboard specials. Palmers Best, Doom Bar and guest ales are on tap. Children and dogs are welcome. Live entertainment is arranged throughout the year.

Open all wk 11.30-3 6-11.30 (Sat-Sun, summer & school holidays all day)
Food Lunch Mon-Fri 12-2.30, Sat-Sun 12-9 Dinner Mon-Fri 6-9, Sat-Sun 12-9 Av main course £12.95 ⊕ FREE HOUSE ◼ Palmers Best Bitter, Sharp's Doom Bar, Guest ale ♂ Heron Valley, Thatchers, Rekorderlig. **Facilities** Non-diners area ♣ (Bar Restaurant Outside area) ♦ Children's menu Children's portions Outside area ♠ Parking WiFi ▭ (notice required)

TIPTON ST JOHN
Map 3 SY09

The Golden Lion Inn
PICK OF THE PUBS

See Pick of the Pubs on opposite page

TOPSHAM
Map 3 SX98

Bridge Inn
PICK OF THE PUBS

tel: 01392 873862 **Bridge Hill EX3 0QQ**
email: tom@cheffers.co.uk
dir: *M5 junct 30 follow Sidmouth signs, in approx 400yds right at rdbt onto A376 towards Exmouth. In 1.8m cross mini rdbt. Right at next mini rdbt to Topsham. 1.2m, cross River Clyst. Inn on right*

True brewing heritage with royal approval

This 'museum with beer' is substantially 16th century, although its constituent parts vary considerably in age. Most of the fabric is local stone, while the old brewhouse at the rear is traditional Devon cob. Four generations of the same family have run it since great-grandfather William Gibbings arrived in 1897, and it remains eccentrically and gloriously old fashioned. Usually around 10 real ales from local and further-flung breweries are served straight from their casks, the actual line-up varying by the week. There are no lagers and only a few wines, two from a local organic vineyard. Traditional, freshly prepared lunchtime bar food includes granary ploughman's, pork pies, veggie or meat pasties, and sandwiches, all made with local ingredients. Queen Elizabeth II visited in 1998; it is believed this is the only time she has officially stepped inside an English pub.

Open all wk 12-2 6-10.30 (Fri-Sat 12-2 6-11 Sun 12-2 7-10.30) **Food** Lunch all wk 12-2 ⊕ FREE HOUSE ◼ Branscombe Vale Branoc, Adnams Broadside, Exe Valley, Hanlons, Teignworthy, Jollyboat Plunder. **Facilities** Non-diners area ♣ (Bar Garden) ♦ Garden ♠ Parking WiFi **Notes** ☺

PICK OF THE PUBS

The Golden Lion

TIPTON ST JOHN   Map 3 SY09

tel: 01404 812881 **EX10 0AA**
email: info@goldenliontipton.co.uk
web: www.goldenliontipton.co.uk
dir: *Phone for detailed directions*

Mediterranean slant to excellent menus

Michelle and Francois Teissier have been at the helm of this welcoming Devon village pub for over a decade. So many things contribute to its traditional feel – the low wooden beams and stone walls, the winter log fire, the art-deco prints and Tiffany lamps, not to mention the paintings by Devonian and Cornish artists. And there's the bar, of course, where locally brewed Otter ales are the order of the day. Chef-patron Franky (as everyone calls him) trained in classical French cooking at a prestigious establishment in the Loire Valley, a grounding that accounts today for his rustic French, Mediterranean and British menus. Their delights may include home-smoked duck salad with onion marmalade; chunky fish soup with rouille and croutons; crevettes with garlic butter; moules frites; steak frites; escargots de Bourgogne; magret de canard; and crayfish salad with lime and garlic dressing. Given that the genteel seaside town of Sidmouth is just down the road, the seafood specials depend totally on that day's catch – cod, hake and sea bass are all

candidates. Tempting white and granary bread sandwiches are filled with fresh Lyme Bay crab, mature cheddar or home-cooked ham. The Sunday lunch menu offers roast West Country beef with Yorkshire pudding; roast lamb with mint sauce; and winter vegetable crêpe. As Franky sums up: 'When Michelle and I took over in 2003, our aim was to create a friendly, inviting village pub offering great value, high-quality food made from the freshest ingredients; with our combination of rustic French dishes and traditional British food with a Mediterranean twist, there's something for everyone!' Outside there is a grassy beer garden and walled terrace area with tumbling grapevines.

Open 12-2.30 6-11 (Sun 12-2.30)
Closed Sun eve **Food** Lunch all wk 12-2
Dinner Mon-Sat 6.30-8.30 Av main
course £15 ⊕ HEAVITREE
🍺 Bass, Otter Ale & Bitter. 🍷 12
Facilities Non-diners area
🚻 Children's menu Children's portions
Garden 🎋 Parking 🚌 (notice required)

TOPSHAM *continued*

The Globe

tel: 01392 873471 **34 Fore St EX3 0HR**
email: theglobe@staustellbrewery.co.uk
dir: *M5 junct 30, A379 to Topsham. At rdbt take B3182. In Topsham at mini rdbt straight ahead into Fore St. Pub approx 500yds on left*

16th-century coaching inn in appealing estuary town

Rich textures and colours meet the eye on entering this sympathetically updated old inn, close to the River Exe. You can enjoy a pint of Tribute in the comfortable fire-warmed bar, while the wood-panelled Elizabethan restaurant makes excellent use of locally grown, reared or caught ingredients. There are chargrilled West Country rump and fillet steaks on offer; or wild mushroom and Somerset brie risotto or River Exe mussels with tomato, chilli and coriander. Daily-changing specials make the most of West Country produce too.

Open all day all wk **Food** Lunch all day Dinner all day ⊕ ST AUSTELL ◀ Tribute, Proper Job & Trelawny ♂ Thatchers Gold. ♟ 10 **Facilities** Non-diners area ❖ (Bar Outside area) ♦♦ Children's menu Children's portions Outside area ⋒ Parking WiFi ◄ (notice required)

TORCROSS   Map 3 SX84

Start Bay Inn

tel: 01548 580553 **TQ7 2TQ**
email: clair@startbayinn.co.uk
dir: *Between Dartmouth & Kingsbridge on A379*

Ancient pub serving the very freshest seafood

Located on the beach and with a freshwater reserve on its other side, the patio of this 14th-century inn overlooks the sea. The fishermen working from Start Bay deliver their catch direct to the kitchen; so does a local crabber, who leaves his catch at the back door to be cooked by the pub. The former landlord (father of landladies Clair and Gail) continues to dive for scallops. Be in no doubt therefore about the freshness of the seafood on the specials board. Look also for locally sourced steaks, burgers from the local butcher, and Salcombe Dairy ice creams. Ploughman's, sandwiches and jackets are also available.

Open all day all wk 11.30-11 **Food** Lunch all wk 11.30-2.15 Dinner all wk 6-9.30 winter, 6-10 summer Av main course £10 ⊕ HEAVITREE ◀ Otter Ale & Bitter, St Austell Tribute & Trelawny, Guest ale ♂ Heron Valley, Addlestones. ♟ 8 **Facilities** Non-diners area ♦♦ Children's menu Children's portions Family room Garden ⋒ Parking WiFi

---

TORQUAY   Map 3 SX96

Cary Arms ★★★★★ INN   PICK OF THE PUBS

See Pick of the Pubs on opposite page

Read all about pubs and their friendly ghosts in our feature on page 12

TOTNES   Map 3 SX86

The Durant Arms   PICK OF THE PUBS

tel: 01803 732240 **Ashprington TQ9 7UP**
email: contact@durantarms.co.uk
dir: *From Totnes take A381 towards Kingsbridge, 1m, left for Ashprington*

Village free house high above the River Dart

A 1725-built village pub that goes from strength to strength after its relaunch a couple of years ago. The stylish bar 'in all its solid-oak glory' has a wood-burning stove and the original stone-flag floor – here you'll find West Country ales and ciders, and award-winning Luscombe organic soft drinks and wines from Sharpham Vineyard just down the hill (tours are available). Ingredients sourced from in and around Totnes appear on a seasonal menu listing home-cooked dishes such as courgette and parmesan soup; River Exe mussels steamed in cider, thyme and shallots; Mr Gribble's pork and honey sausages, mash and onion gravy; and pheasant, bacon and leek pie. Waving the flag for the desserts section might be Bramley apple crumble and vanilla custard; or the chocolate nemesis and mousse duo. Simple snacks, sandwiches and salads are available at lunchtime. Doors from the dining room lead to a sheltered courtyard.

Open 11-3 6-11 Closed Mon (out of season) **Food** Lunch Mon-Sat 12.30-2.30, Sun 12-3 Dinner all wk 6-9 Set menu available ⊕ FREE HOUSE ◀ Dartmoor, Otter, Guest ales ♂ Sandford Orchards Devon Red. ♟ 12 **Facilities** Non-diners area ❖ (Bar Restaurant Outside area) ♦♦ Children's menu Children's portions Outside area ⋒ Beer festival WiFi ◄ (notice required)

Royal Seven Stars Hotel

tel: 01803 862125 **The Plains TQ9 5DD**
email: enquiry@royalsevenstars.co.uk
dir: *From A382 signed Totnes, left at 'Dartington' rdbt. Through lights towards town centre, through next rdbt, pass Morrisons car park on left. 200yds on right*

Town centre favourite

This Grade II listed property in the heart of Totnes has three character bars and a grand ballroom. The champagne bar, an addition to the TQ9 brasserie, is where bubbly is served by the glass or bottle from 5pm onwards, along with cocktails and wines. Excellent local brews and ciders are always on tap. Quality food at affordable prices is another strength – expect the likes of smoked trout mousse with home-made horseradish cream; braised Devon lamb rump with root vegetables, creamed potato and red wine jus; and a choice of steaks from the grill.

Open all day all wk **Food** Lunch all wk 11-9.30 Dinner all wk 11-9.30 Av main course £12.95 Set menu available Restaurant menu available Mon-Sat ⊕ FREE HOUSE ◀ Sharp's Doom Bar, Bays Gold, Jail Ale, Guest ales ♂ Thatchers, Orchard's, Ashridge. ♟ 26 **Facilities** Non-diners area ❖ (Bar Outside area) ♦♦ Children's menu Children's portions Family room Outside area ⋒ Beer festival Cider festival Parking WiFi

---

Rumour

tel: 01803 864682 **30 High St TQ9 5RY**
dir: *Follow signs for Totnes castle/town centre. On main street up hill above arch on left. 5 mins' walk from rail station*

Stylish bar serving exciting European food

Named after Fleetwood Mac's landmark 1977 album, this 17th-century building at the top of the high street has had a chequered history including stints as a milk bar, restaurant and wine bar. They offer an ever-changing blackboard menu, hand-made pizzas, and a popular steak night on Sundays.

Open all wk Mon-Sat 10am-11pm (Sun 6-10.30) **Food** Lunch Mon-Sat 12-3 Dinner Mon-Sat 6-10, Sun 6-9 ⊕ FREE HOUSE ◀ St Austell Tribute, New Lion Pandit IPA ♂ Westons Rosie's Pig. ♟ 17 **Facilities** Non-diners area ♦♦ WiFi

PICK OF THE PUBS

Cary Arms ★★★★★ INN

TORQUAY Map 3 SX96

tel: 01803 327110
Babbacombe Beach TQ1 3LX
email: enquiries@caryarms.co.uk
web: www.caryarms.co.uk
dir: *Into Teignmouth, at bottom of hill at lights, right signed Torquay/A379. Cross river. At mini rdbt follow Babbacombe signs. Pass Babbacombe Model Village, through lights, left into Babbacombe Downs Rd, left into Beach Rd*

Beachside inn that has it all

Right on the beach, the rambling and whitewashed Cary Arms is a real find in Babbacombe Bay. This 'boutique inn' is so much more than just a pub; unwind in the beamed bar with its original stone walls, perhaps with a pint of Bays Topsail or Otter Ale in hand, contemplating the stunning views across the bay; stay in one of the luxury sea-facing bedrooms; and sample the delicious gastro-inn food from the daily-changing menu. The informal bar is perfect for playing a board game and relaxing after a bracing walk or a day on the beach. If it's a glorious summer's day, you will unquestionably wish to eat in the terraced gardens that lead down to the water's edge; this is when the barbecue and wood-fired oven come into their own. The watchwords in the kitchen are freshness and seasonality, underpinned by a respect for the local pastures and waters. Catch of the day

will be a must for fish-lovers — perhaps pan-fried Brixham scallops, pea purée and crispy Parma ham; or a crab salad — but the menu reflects coast and country in equal measure. Hard to resist are fish bouillabaisse; Dunterton Farm steak, Otter Ale and mushroom pie, dauphinoise potatoes and red wine jus; and trio of Gribbles sausages (venison, pork and apple, lamb and mint) with mash and red onion jus. Gastro evenings are regular events; the barbecue is often booked by groups, and a menu is available for the 'nippers'. If staying over, the bedrooms are classic and cool with echoes of New England beachside-chic, and most have a private terrace or balcony overlooking the sea.

Open all wk 12-4 6-11 **Food** Lunch all wk 12-3 Dinner all wk 6.30-9 Restaurant menu available all wk ⊕ FREE HOUSE ◀ Otter Ale, Bays Topsail, Hunter's Devon Dreamer ⌀ Sandford Orchards Devon Mist & Devon Red. ♟ 11 **Facilities** Non-diners area ♣ (Bar Restaurant Garden) ♦ Children's menu Children's portions Family room Garden ♫ WiFi **Rooms** 8

TOTNES *continued*

Steam Packet Inn

tel: 01803 863880 **St Peter's Quay TQ9 5EW**
email: steampacket@buccaneer.co.uk
dir: *Exit A38 towards Plymouth, 18m. A384 to Totnes, 6m. Left at mini rdbt, pass Morrisons on left, over mini rdbt, 400yds on left*

Popular inn on the River Dart

Named after the passenger, cargo and mail steamers that once plied the Dart, this riverside pub (alongside which you can moor your boat) offers great views, particularly from the conservatory restaurant and heated waterside patio, where there is plenty of seating. A real log fire warms the bar in the colder months. The mainly traditional choices at lunch and dinner might include plaice goujons, gammon steak, lamb rump and Mexican fajitas. There are daily fish specials on the blackboard. Look out for the three-day beer festival in mid-May, occasional live music and summer barbecues.

Open all day all wk **Food** Lunch Mon-Fri 12-2.30, Sat 12-3, Sun 12-8 Dinner Mon-Sat 6-9.30, Sun 12-8 ⊕ FREE HOUSE/BUCCANEER ◀ Sharp's Doom Bar, Dartmoor Jail Ale, Guest ale Ö Westons Stowford Press & GL, Ashridge. ⛾ 11 **Facilities** Non-diners area ❀ (Bar Garden) ♦ Children's menu Garden ⊨ Beer festival Parking WiFi ➡ (notice required)

The White Hart Bar & Restaurant   PICK OF THE PUBS

tel: 01803 847111 **Dartington Hall TQ9 6EL**
email: bookings@dartingtonhall.com
dir: *A38 onto A384 towards Totnes. Turn at Dartington church into Dartington Hall Estate*

Focal point on an 880-acre estate

Surrounded by landscaped gardens and leafy woodland paths, the White Hart is part of the splendid 14th-century Dartington Hall, home of a famous arts trust. Ancient tapestries, open fires, flagstones, Gothic chandeliers and limed oak settles characterise the interior. Devonshire and Cornish real ales and Dartington's own cider are available in the bar; outside there's a patio. Starters on Anuj Thakur's menu include line-caught mackerel escabeche; Exmouth mussels; and Vulscombe goats' cheese. Further local sourcing is evident from mains such as Devon lamb rump with polenta and charred courgette and gazpacho fondue; Salcombe- and Dartmouth-reared pork with salsify, ham hock bonbon and toasted-nut muesli; and roasted butternut with wild mushrooms and Sharpham cheese. Desserts are few, but delicious nonetheless – chocolate mousse with Cointreau sorbet; glazed lemon tart with clotted cream; roast pineapple with Breton sablé biscuit; and sticky toffee pudding with honeycomb ice cream. Curries are served every Thursday night.

Open all day all wk 12-11 **Food** Lunch all wk 12-3 Dinner all wk 5.30-9 Av main course £15 Set menu available ⊕ FREE HOUSE ◀ St Austell Tribute & Proper Job, Bays Topsail, Local guest ales. **Facilities** Non-diners area ♦ Children's menu Children's portions Garden Outside area ⊨ Parking WiFi ➡ (notice required)

TRUSHAM   Map 3 SX88

Cridford Inn   PICK OF THE PUBS

tel: 01626 853694 **TQ13 0NR**
email: reservations@vanillapod-cridfordinn.com
dir: *From A38 exit at junct for Teign Valley, right, follow Trusham signs for 4m*

Historic pub near Dartmoor with great food

Over a thousand years of history are packed into the rough stone walls and thatched roof of this heritage gem of a pub, right down to the medieval masons' marks still visible above the bar. Find a seat on the terrace beneath mature trees

for views over the Teign Valley. You can eat in either the bar, where Teignworthy is one of the local brewery's showcased, or the popular Vanilla Pod restaurant, where food with an excellent local pedigree and seasonal flavours delights locals and visitors alike. Start with Tregida smoked salmon and pickled beetroot, or River Teign mussels poached in dry white wine, garlic, onion, tarragon and cream; follow with rabbit pie; honey-baked ham with free-range eggs and chunky chips; or classic chilli con carne with basmati and coriander rice. Home-made desserts include raspberry marshmallow cheesecake or steamed lemon and golden syrup sponge pudding with crème Anglaise.

Open all wk 11-3 6.15-11 (Sat 11-11 Sun 12-10.30) **Food** Lunch Mon-Fri 12-2.30, Sat & Sun (Mar-Sep) all day, Sun (Oct-Feb) 12-3 Dinner all wk 7-9.30 ⊕ FREE HOUSE ◀ Sharp's Doom Bar, Teignworthy, Guest ales Ö South West Orchards. ⛾ 10 **Facilities** Non-diners area ❀ (Bar Garden Outside area) ♦ Children's menu Children's portions Family room Garden Outside area ⊨ Parking WiFi ➡ (notice required)

▌ TUCKENHAY   Map 3 SX85

The Maltsters Arms

tel: 01803 732350 **TQ9 7EQ**
email: maltsters@tuckenhay.com
dir: *A381 from Totnes towards Kingsbridge. 1m, at hill top turn left, follow signs to Tuckenhay, 3m*

Arrive by road or river at this waterside pub and restaurant

A white-painted, 18th-century inn standing just where tidal Bow Creek tapers to an end. Predictably, it was once a malthouse, malt being one of many commodities handled on the wide quay, now a lovely place to sit with a pint of Otter or Bays Topsail and admire the steep wooded river banks. Dine in the restaurant overlooking the creek, in the bar, or the fire-warmed Dart Cabin on seasonal, locally sourced home-smoked fish and shellfish; Exmoor venison; or Creedy Carver duck breast. To finish a meal, try the West Country cheeses. Events include an annual beer festival, live music, winter quizzes, and pie, curry and Thai nights.

Open all day all wk Mon-Thu & Sun 9am-11pm (Fri-Sat 9am-mdnt) **Food** Lunch Mon-Thu 12-2.30, Fri-Sun all day Dinner Mon-Thu 6-9, Fri-Sun all day ⊕ FREE HOUSE ◀ Dartmoor Jail Ale, Otter Ale, Bays Topsail Ö Thatchers Gold, Sheppy's. ⛾ 10 **Facilities** Non-diners area ❀ (Bar Restaurant Garden) ♦ Children's menu Children's portions Garden ⊨ Beer festival Parking WiFi

▌ TYTHERLEIGH   Map 4 ST30

The Tytherleigh Arms

tel: 01460 220214 **EX13 7BE**
email: tytherleigharms@gmail.com
dir: *Between Chard & Axminster on A358*

Local produce at a smart 16th-century inn

This 16th-century coaching inn on the borders of Devon, Dorset and Somerset still retains plenty of original features, including beamed ceilings and huge fires, which make for a lovely setting if you are popping in for a pint of Branoc ale, or making a beeline for the daily-changing menu. Local produce drives the menu, whether it's Jerusalem artichoke and gruyère tartlet, sorrel and pine nut pesto; or roast guinea fowl supreme, wild mushroom and tarragon risotto.

Open 11-4 6-12 Closed 25 Dec, Sun eve winter **Food** Lunch Mon-Fri 12-2.30, Sat 12-3, Sun 12-4 Dinner Mon-Fri 6-9.30, Sat 6-10, Sun 6-9 ⊕ FREE HOUSE ◀ Otter Ale & Amber, Branscombe Vale Branoc Ö Thatchers Gold, Westons Wyld Wood Organic, Perry's Barn Owl. ⛾ 10 **Facilities** Non-diners area ❀ (Bar Garden) ♦ Children's portions Garden ⊨ Parking WiFi

PICK OF THE PUBS

The Digger's Rest

WOODBURY SALTERTON   Map 3 SY08

tel: 01395 232375 **EX5 1PQ**
email: bar@diggersrest.co.uk
web: www.diggersrest.co.uk
dir: *2.5m from A3052. Signed from Westpoint Showground*

Picturesque thatched pub offering the best of seasonal produce

It may have new owners in Marc and Donna Slater but The Digger's Rest has been welcoming drinkers for more than 500 years. This picturesque free house is just a few minutes' drive from the Exeter junction of the M5, and stands in the delightful east Devon village of Woodbury Salterton. Originally a cider house, its vintage can be identified from its thatched roof, thick stone and cob walls, heavy beams and log fire. These days, the choice on the bar is much wider but cider is still well represented with Westons Scrumpy and Stowford Press. Real ales feature Otter Bitter from Devon with guest appearances from other West Country brewers such as Yellow Hammer. Wine fans will appreciate the wine list which has been created by the independent wine merchant, Tanners of Shrewsbury. The food menus are created to make the best of seasonal produce. Sourcing locally plays a big role in freshness and quality control, and English and West

Country organic produce is used wherever possible. The kitchen is also committed to supporting farmers who practise good husbandry. Menus feature fish landed at Brixham and Looe, West Country beef hung for 21 days and pork from a farm just up the road. As well as the main menu there is a blackboard which features dishes the chef has created from prime cuts or rarer seasonal ingredients he has sought out. Start perhaps with potted seafood and prawns; or pork and pistachio terrine before moving on to slow-braised local venison pie, or roast salmon fillet with new potatoes, braised fennel, watercress and orange salad. It's worth timing a visit for the May beer festival.

Open all wk 11-3 5.30-11 (Fri-Sun all day) **Food** Lunch all wk 12-2 Dinner all wk 6-9 Set menu available ⊕ FREE HOUSE ◀ Otter Bitter, Hanlons Yellow Hammer, Exeter Avocet, Hunter's Crack Shot Ö Westons & Stowford Press, Symonds. ♀ 10 **Facilities** Non-diners area ❖ (Bar Garden) ⁑ Children's menu Children's portions Garden ⋈ Beer festival Parking WiFi 🚌 (notice required)

WIDECOMBE IN THE MOOR   Map 3 SX77

The Rugglestone Inn   PICK OF THE PUBS

tel: 01364 621327 **TQ13 7TF**
email: enquiries@rugglestoneinn.co.uk
dir: *From village centre take road by church towards Venton. Inn down hill on left*

Pretty, wisteria-clad Dartmoor pub

Originally a cottage, this unaltered Grade II listed building was converted to an inn around 1832. Set in the picturesque village of Widecombe in the Moor, the pub is surrounded by tranquil moorland and streams; the Rugglestone stream rises behind the pub, and Widecombe's famous church acts as a beacon for ramblers and riders seeking out the inn's rural location. Cosy little rooms and comforting wood-burners encourage appreciative visitors and locals alike to tarry awhile and sup ales such as Dartmoor Legend; farmhouse ciders such as Ashridge are stillaged behind the snug bar and tapped straight from the barrel. The filling fare is a decent mix of classic pub staples and savoury dishes, keeping the cold away in winter or fulfilling a summer evening's promise in the streamside garden. The Rugglestone platter of ham, cheddar and Stilton served with salad, pickles, home-made coleslaw and crusty bread is a great Dartmoor experience.

Open all wk Mon-Thu 11.30-3 6-11.30 Fri 11.30-3 5-12 Sat 11.30am-mdnt Sun & BH 12-11 **Food** Lunch all wk 12-2 Dinner all wk 6.30-9 Av main course £10.50 ⊕ FREE HOUSE ◀ Bays Gold, Otter Bitter, Teignworthy Rugglestone Moor, Dartmoor Legend Ō Ashton Press, Lower Widdon Farm, Ashridge, North Hall Manor. ♜ 10 **Facilities** Non-diners area ❤ (Bar Restaurant Garden) ◀♦ Children's menu Children's portions Garden ♰ Parking ➡ (notice required)

WOODBURY SALTERTON   Map 3 SY08

The Digger's Rest   PICK OF THE PUBS

See Pick of the Pubs on page 159

YEALMPTON   Map 3 SX55

Rose & Crown   PICK OF THE PUBS

tel: 01752 880223 **Market St PL8 2EB**
email: info@theroseandcrown.co.uk
dir: *Phone for detailed directions*

Classy dining among enticing countryside

Close to the pretty Yealm Estuary and the seductive wilderness of southern Dartmoor, foodies make a bee-line here to experience Simon Warner's modern British cooking. There's a cool, airy, bistro-like atmosphere in this classy dining pub at the heart of the South Hams. Village locals and beer-lovers can sample beers from the St Austell Brewery stable, perhaps in the walled courtyard garden with its fishpond and fountain, but it is as a destination dining pub that the Rose & Crown shines out. The menu proffers traditional classics with an extra touch of class, allowing the kitchen's focus on quality and local supply to be maintained. A choice of pub favourites such as curry of the day or home-made burger runs alongside a carte that might kick off with Jerusalem artichoke soup or Thai crab cake; and continue with a main course of duck breast with bubble-and-squeak, or roast red onion and wild mushroom suet pudding.

Open all day all wk **Food** Lunch all wk 12-2.30 Dinner all wk 6.30-9.30 Av main course £14 Set menu available Restaurant menu available all wk ⊕ ST AUSTELL BREWERY ◀ Tribute & Proper Job, Bath Ales Gem, Dartmoor Jail Ale Ō Thatchers Gold, Healey's Cornish Rattler. **Facilities** Non-diners area ❤ (Bar Garden) ◀♦ Children's menu Children's portions Garden ♰ Parking WiFi ➡ (notice required)

DORSET

ASKERSWELL   Map 4 SY59

The Spyway Inn ★★★★ INN

tel: 01308 485250 **DT2 9EP**
email: spywaytime@hotmail.com web: www.spyway-inn.co.uk
dir: *From A35 follow Askerswell sign, then follow Spyway Inn sign*

Oak beams, cask ales and stunning views

Handy for Dorchester and Bridport, this old beamed country inn offers magnificent views of the glorious Dorset countryside. Close to West Bay, who's memorable cliffs have been made even more memorable by two series of *Broadchurch*, the pub boasts a landscaped beer garden with a pond, stream and children's play area. It all makes for a lovely setting to enjoy a glass of Otter Ale and sample locally sourced, home-made fare like slow-roast belly pork with cider sauce; pan-fried fillets of sea bass with Savoy cabbage and bacon; or steak and ale pie. Accommodation is also available.

Open all wk 12-3 6-close **Food** Lunch all wk 12-3 Dinner all wk 6-9 Av main course £12 ⊕ FREE HOUSE ◀ Otter Ale, Bitter Ō West Milton, Kingcombe Cider. ♜ 10 **Facilities** Non-diners area ◀♦ Children's menu Children's portions Play area Garden ♰ Parking WiFi ➡ (notice required) **Rooms** 3

BOURTON   Map 4 ST73

The White Lion Inn

tel: 01747 840866 **High St SP8 5AT**
email: office@whitelionbourton.co.uk
dir: *Off A303, opposite B3092 to Gillingham*

Beautiful inn with popular ales and dishes

Dating from 1723, the White Lion is a beautiful stone-built, creeper-clad Dorset inn. The bar is cosy with beams, flagstones and an open fire. Here you will find a range of real beers and ciders, and menus drawing on the wealth of quality local produce. Starters range from devilled kidneys on toast, to Jackson's of Newton Abbot smoked haddock with spinach and creamy gruyère sauce. Select a main course from the classics list, such as Barclay's Butchers stack: Cumberland sausage, faggot and bacon with mash and gravy; or the half-pound cheese burger with chips and salad. There's a cider festival in July.

Open all day all wk **Food** Lunch Mon-Sat 12-2, Sun 12-4 Dinner all wk 6-9 ⊕ FREE HOUSE ◀ Otter Amber, St Austell Tribute Ō Thatchers, Rich's Farmhouse. **Facilities** Non-diners area ❤ (Bar Restaurant Garden) ◀♦ Children's menu Children's portions Garden ♰ Cider festival Parking WiFi ➡ (notice required)

BRIDPORT   Map 4 SY49

The Shave Cross Inn ★★★★★ INN   PICK OF THE PUBS

tel: 01308 868358 **Shave Cross, Marshwood Vale DT6 6HW**
email: roy.warburton@virgin.net web: www.theshavecrossinn.co.uk
dir: *From Bridport take B3162. In 2m left signed 'Broadoak/Shave Cross', then Marshwood*

Caribbean food in the heart of Hardy country

Off the beaten track down narrow lanes in the beautiful Marshwood Vale, deep in Thomas Hardy country, this thatched 14th-century cob-and-flint inn was once a resting place for pilgrims and other monastic visitors on their way to Whitchurch Canonicorum to visit the shrine to St Candida and St Cross. While they were at the inn they had their tonsures trimmed, hence the pub's name. Step inside the cosy bar to find low beams, stone floors, a huge inglenook fireplace, rustic furnishings, and local Dorset ale on tap, as well as real farm ciders. The food here is both unusual and inspirational, with a strong Caribbean influence together with dishes originating as far afield as Fiji. A starter of jerk chicken salad with plantain, crispy bacon and aïoli might be followed by a main course of hot and spicy Cuban seafood bouillabaisse or Jamaican jerk pork tenderloin with pineapple compôte.

Open 11-3 6-11.30 Closed Mon (ex BHs) **Food** Lunch Tue-Sun 12-2.30 Dinner Tue-Sat 6-8.30, Sun 6-8 Set menu available Restaurant menu available Tue-Sun ⊕ FREE HOUSE ▣ Branscombe Vale Branoc, Dorset, Local guest ales ♂ Westons Old Rosie, Thatchers, Pitfield Thunderbolt. ₹ 12 **Facilities** Non-diners area ❖ (Bar Garden) ♦ Children's menu Children's portions Play area Garden ⚘ Parking WiFi ▥ (notice required) **Rooms** 7

■ BUCKHORN WESTON   Map 4 ST72

Stapleton Arms   PICK OF THE PUBS

See Pick of the Pubs on page 162

■ CATTISTOCK   Map 4 SY59

Fox & Hounds Inn

tel: 01300 320444 **Duck St DT2 0JH**
email: lizflight@yahoo.co.uk
dir: *On A37, between Dorchester & Yeovil, follow signs to Cattistock*

Popular inn in pretty Dorset village

Expect a bar full of locals, children, dogs and even chickens under foot at this attractive pub. Situated in a picturesque village, the 17th-century inn has a welcoming and traditional atmosphere engendered by ancient beams, open fires in winter and huge inglenooks, one with an original bread oven. Palmers ales are on tap, along with Taunton cider, while home-made meals embrace whitebait and tartare sauce; goats' cheese soufflé; roast pork belly, mash, braised cabbage with ground mustard and cider gravy. Regular events include folk music and poetry.

Open 12-2.30 6-11 (Sun 12-10) Closed Mon L **Food** Lunch Tue-Sun 12-2 Dinner Mon-Sat 7-9, Sun 6-8 ⊕ PALMERS ▣ Best Bitter, Copper Ale, 200, Dorset Gold ♂ Taunton Traditional, Thatchers Gold, Sheppy's. **Facilities** Non-diners area ❖ (Bar Restaurant Garden) ♦ Children's portions Play area Garden ⚘ Parking WiFi ▥ (notice required)

■ CERNE ABBAS   Map 4 ST60

The New Inn   PICK OF THE PUBS

tel: 01300 341274 **14 Long St DT2 7JF**
email: info@thenewinncerneabbas.co.uk
dir: *Take A352 from Dorchester to Cerne Abbas. Pub in village centre*

Old coaching inn serving accomplished cooking

The village of Cerne Abbas has a reasonable claim to be one of the prettiest in England, with its delightful stone buildings and thatched cottages. In the past, it was famous for brewing – at one time there were 16 pubs here. One that remains is The New Inn, a beautifully restored 16th-century coaching inn that re-opened to much acclaim. The Palmers ales are much in demand, but it's the mix of contemporary British and pub classic dishes that brings in the punters. You could try the whole grilled mackerel with samphire and chargrilled peppers from the bar menu, maybe, or start a three-course dinner with pressed ham, globe artichoke and truffle terrine with piccalilli, and follow that with slow-roast pork belly and crackling, braised red cabbage, apple sauce and champ; or a mushroom 'Scotch

egg' with curly kale, Jerusalem artichoke and mustard dressing. Finish with crêpes Suzette soufflé and orange blossom ice cream, or the plate of mini puds ('to share or not…'as it says on the menu). You can walk it off afterwards around the nearby Cerne Abbas giant.

Open all wk 12-3 6-close Closed 25-26 Dec **Food** Lunch all wk 12-2.15 Dinner all wk 7-9 Av main course £13 Restaurant menu available all wk ⊕ PALMERS ▣ IPA, Copper, Dorset Gold. ₹ 12 **Facilities** Non-diners area ❖ (Bar Garden) ♦ Children's menu Children's portions Garden ⚘ Parking WiFi

---

■ CHEDINGTON   Map 4 ST40

Winyard's Gap Inn

tel: 01935 891244 **Chedington Ln DT8 3HY**
email: enquiries@winyardsgap.com
dir: *5m S of Crewkerne on A356*

Extravagant views, craft ciders and seasonal produce

Situated beside National Trust woodlands in a corner of the Dorset Area of Outstanding Natural Beauty, the old inn's garden commands an extraordinary view across Somerset from the eponymous gap in the sinuous chalk hills. The two counties provide the wherewithal for the August cider festival here, whilst beers from Exmoor and Otter breweries anoint the bar, with its solid rustic seating and tables and a log-burner for the winter nip. The impressive 'Ultimate Ploughman's' takes in the cheeses of the area, or enjoy chicken liver parfait with real ale chutney and Evershot Bakery toast, then chargrilled matured West Country beef with hand-cut chips, field mushrooms, tomatoes and herb butter. Leave space for chocolate fondant with clotted cream, or pineapple tarte Tatin and lime cream.

Open all wk 11.30-3 6-11 (Sat-Sun 11.30-11) Closed 25-26 Dec **Food** Lunch Mon-Sat 12-2 Dinner all wk 6-9 Set menu available Restaurant menu available all wk ⊕ FREE HOUSE ▣ Sharp's Doom Bar, Dorset Piddle, Exmoor Ale, Otter Ale ♂ Thatchers Gold, Westons Old Rosie & 1st Quality, Dorset Nectar. ₹ 12 **Facilities** Non-diners area ❖ (Bar Garden) ♦ Children's menu Children's portions Garden ⚘ Cider festival Parking WiFi ▥ (notice required)

■ CHETNOLE   Map 4 ST60

The Chetnole Inn

tel: 01935 872337 **DT9 6NU**
email: enquiries@thechetnoleinn.co.uk
dir: *A37 from Dorchester towards Yeovil. Left at Chetnole sign*

Tranquil village pub with garden overlooking fields

A change of hands ushers in a new era at this bright and airy village inn opposite a pretty church deep in Thomas Hardy country. Plenty of walks thread their way through the rich countryside; it's handy, too, for the historic town of Sherborne. The flagstone-floored snug, bar and restaurant make an ideal setting for the West Country meats and Bridport-landed seafood that fill the British menu. Choose perhaps pan-roasted chicken breast with cherry vine tomatoes and asparagus, or the home-made beefburger, and enjoy at a table in the tree-shaded garden, home to the pub's hens. Local beers include Yeovil Ales Star Gazer and Wriggle Valley Copper Hoppa.

Open 12-3 6-close Closed Sun eve **Food** Lunch all wk 12-2 Dinner Mon-Sat 6.30-9 ⊕ FREE HOUSE ▣ Sharp's Doom Bar, Yeovil Ales Star Gazer, Wriggle Valley Copper Hoppa ♂ Burrow Hill, Thatchers Gold. ₹ 9 **Facilities** Non-diners area ❖ (Bar Garden) ♦ Children's menu Children's portions Garden ⚘ Parking WiFi ▥ (notice required)

PICK OF THE PUBS

Stapleton Arms

BUCKHORN WESTON   Map 4 ST72

tel: 01963 370396 **Church Hill SP8 5HS**
email: relax@thestapletonarms.com
web: www.thestapletonarms.com
dir: *3.5m from Wincanton in village centre*

Serious about cider, ale and local produce

Clean, modern lines within belie the Georgian exterior of this progressive village inn. It sits on the edge of Blackmoor Vale in Thomas Hardy's rolling Dorset countryside; classic walking country enjoyed by many of the inn's patrons. With a multitude of artisanal producers on the doorstep, it's no surprise that the bar majors on farmhouse ciders: Thatchers Cheddar Valley and Gold are among a handful on offer, along with a tantalising range of earthy apple juices. The pub hosts an annual beer festival, always a good indication of a serious attitude to ales. Handles pulling pints from Plain Ales Brewery in Warminster and regional guests are complemented by a comprehensive range of world bottled beers. The pub's stylish and unstuffy attitude creates a welcoming and relaxing ambience in which to enjoy these drinks. For more of Dorset's larder, look no further than the menu, overflowing with fresh and local produce, ethically raised and delivered with minimum food miles. Light bites in

the bar range from Scotch eggs and pork pies, to Dorset bouillabaisse served with rouille and soda bread; or potted hare with pickled cucumber and beef dripping toast. Sandwiches are prepared with home-made bread and quality fillings such as smoked salmon or rare roast beef with horseradish. Lunchtime classics include butternut squash risotto with goats' curd, parmesan and poached egg; and home-made game pie with buttered greens. For a dinner treat, start with watercress velouté with crispy hen's egg and pancetta; continue with whole roast partridge, red cabbage, salt-baked turnip, blackberries and bacon potato cake; and round off with white peach and apple crumble with raspberry sorbet.

Open all wk 11-3 6-11 (Sun 12-10.30) **Food** Lunch all wk 12-3 Dinner all wk 6-10 ⊕ FREE HOUSE ◀ Butcombe, Plain Ales Ö Thatchers Cheddar Valley & Gold, The Orchard Pig, Ashton Press, Guest ciders. ♀ 30 **Facilities** Non-diners area ❤ (Bar Garden) ♦️ Children's menu Children's portions Play area Garden ☂ Beer festival Parking WiFi 🚐 (notice required)

CHIDEOCK
Map 4 SY49

The Anchor Inn

tel: 01297 489215 **Seatown DT6 6JU**
email: contact@theanchorinnseatown.co.uk
dir: *From A35 in Chideock turn opposite church & follow single track road for 0.75m to beach*

Set in a little cove beneath Golden Cap

A former smugglers' haunt, the Anchor enjoys an incredible setting in a cove surrounded by National Trust land. The large sun terrace and cliffside beer garden overlooking the beach make it a premier destination for throngs of holidaymakers in the summer, while on winter weekdays it can be blissfully quiet. The menu starts with snacks and light lunches – two types of ploughman's, salads, sharing platters and a range of ciabattas might take your fancy. For something more substantial choose Balson's award-winning sausages, butternut squash, mustard mash and red onion gravy; griddled chicken breast with wild mushroom and goats' cheese sauce; or smoked haddock and salmon gratin accompanied by one of the Palmers real ales.

Open all wk 10am-11pm (10-3 6-11 Dec-Feb) **Food** Lunch all wk 12-9 (12-2.30 Dec-Feb) Dinner all wk 12-9 (6-9 Dec-Feb) Av main course £12 ⊕ PALMERS ◀ 200, Best Bitter, Copper Ale & Dorset Gold ♂ Thatchers Gold. **Facilities** Non-diners area ❧ (Bar Restaurant Garden) ♦ Children's menu Children's portions Family room Garden ⊼ Parking WiFi

CHRISTCHURCH
Map 5 SZ19

The Ship In Distress

tel: 01202 485123 **66 Stanpit BH23 3NA**
email: shipindistress@rocketmail.com
dir: *Phone for detailed directions*

Community pub with lots of seafood

The seafood menu at this 300-year-old smugglers' pub reflects the closeness of Mudeford Quay and the English Channel. Nautical memorabilia is everywhere, so bag a seat by the wood-burner with a pint of Ringwood Best Bitter and traditional fish and chips or cottage pie; alternatively, head into the restaurant for salmon and scallion fishcake; fruits de mer; locally caught lobster; or whole Dorset crab. The full carte, including steaks, is on the blackboard. In summer enjoy the Shellfish Bar on the suntrap terrace.

Open all day all wk 11am-mdnt (Sun 11-11) **Food** Lunch Mon-Fri 12-2, Sat-Sun 12-2.30 Dinner Sun-Thu 6.30-9, Fri-Sat 6.30-9.30 Set menu available Restaurant menu available all wk ⊕ PUNCH TAVERNS ◀ Ringwood Best Bitter, Guest ales ♂ Aspall. **Facilities** Non-diners area ❧ (Bar Garden) ♦ Children's portions Garden ⊼ Parking WiFi (notice required)

CHURCH KNOWLE
Map 4 SY98

The New Inn

tel: 01929 480357 **BH20 5NQ**
email: maurice@newinn-churchknowle.co.uk
dir: *From Wareham take A351 towards Swanage. At Corfe Castle right for Church Knowle. Pub in village centre*

16th-century, part-thatched village inn

The Estop family have been here for over three decades, landlord Maurice being only the fourth licensee in 150 years. The inn's old-world charm includes inglenook fireplaces and a brick alcove once the farmhouse oven. Real ales include Dorset Jurassic and guests, with draught ciders too. Son and head chef Matthew Estop makes much of locally caught fish and seafood – hake, Dover sole, black bream, gurnard, mussels and crab – as well as local meats, in the restaurant and the

carvery. Blue Vinny cheese soup is a long-standing fixture. Don't expect a wine list, because customers can browse for the right bottle in the 'Wine Shack'.

Open 10-3 6-11 (10-3 5-11 summer) Closed Mon Jan-Mar **Food** Lunch all wk 12-2.15 Dinner all wk 6-9.15 (5-9.15 summer) Set menu available ⊕ PUNCH TAVERNS ◀ Dorset Jurassic, Sharp's Doom Bar, St Austell Tribute, Guest ales ♂ Westons Old Rosie, Stowford Press & Traditional. ⬤ 10 **Facilities** Non-diners area ❧ (Garden Outside area) ♦ Children's menu Children's portions Family room Garden Outside area ⊼ Parking WiFi (notice required)

CRANBORNE
Map 5 SU01

The Inn at Cranborne ★★★★ INN

tel: 01725 551249 **5 Wimborne St BH21 5PP**
email: info@theinnatcranborne.co.uk **web:** www.theinnatcranborne.co.uk
dir: *On B3078 between Fordingbridge & Wimborne Minster*

Hearty food and Dorset ales in a delightful village

Jane Gould searched long and hard for somewhere to turn into her vision of a traditional English country pub. Since finding this 17th-century, former coaching inn she has skilfully transformed it into a must-visit destination in Cranborne Chase, nearly 400-square miles of rolling chalk downland. The inn's own Fleur Ale, brewed specially by Hall & Woodhouse, shares bar space with Dorset and Somerset ciders. Choose a table near one of the wood-burning stoves for something hearty from the daily-changing menu, such as seared sea trout with cavolo nero, herb gnocchi and quince jam; slow-cooked shin of beef with mash and roasted roots; or wild mushroom and parmesan risotto.

Open all day all wk **Food** Lunch Tue-Fri 12-2, Sat-Sun 12-2.30 Dinner Tue-Thu 6-9, Fri-Sat 6-9.30 ⊕ HALL & WOODHOUSE ◀ Badger First Gold, The Fleur ♂ Westons Stowford Press, Badger Pearwood & Applewood. ⬤ 10 **Facilities** Non-diners area ❧ (Bar Restaurant Outside area) ♦ Children's menu Children's portions Outside area ⊼ Beer festival Parking WiFi (notice required) **Rooms** 9

See advert on page 164

EAST MORDEN
Map 4 SY99

The Cock & Bottle
PICK OF THE PUBS

tel: 01929 459238 **BH20 7DL**
email: cockandbottle@btconnect.com
dir: *From A35 (W of Poole) turn right onto B3075, pub 0.5m on left*

Crowd-pleasing range of ales and food options

The low-beamed ceilings and wealth of nooks and crannies are a reminder that parts of this Dorset longhouse were built around 400 years ago. The simply furnished locals' bar is comfortably rustic, with a large wooden settle on which to while away a winter's evening beside the cosy log fire. The fine range of real ales from the nearby Hall & Woodhouse brewery is also available in the lounge bar, while a modern restaurant at the back completes the picture. The ever-changing menu ranges from light lunches and bar meals to pub favourites. The carte menu choices might include a starter of crispy duck and green onion spring roll with cucumber and sweet and sour sauce. Moving on, venison Wellington, and steak and kidney pudding are typical main course options, and home-made desserts like apple and rhubarb make a fitting finale. There are lovely pastoral views over the surrounding farmland.

Open 11.30-2.30 6-11 (Sun 12-3) Closed Sun eve **Food** Lunch all wk 12-1.45 Dinner Mon-Sat 6-8.45 Restaurant menu available all wk ⊕ HALL & WOODHOUSE ◀ Badger Dorset Best & Tanglefoot, Guest ale. **Facilities** Non-diners area 🐾 (Bar Restaurant Garden) ⬤ Children's menu Children's portions Play area Garden ☰ Parking 🚃

EVERSHOT
Map 4 ST50

The Acorn Inn ★★★★ INN ◉
PICK OF THE PUBS

See Pick of the Pubs on opposite page and advert on page 166

FARNHAM
Map 4 ST91

The Museum Inn ★★★★ INN ◉◉
PICK OF THE PUBS

tel: 01725 516261 **DT11 8DE**
email: enquiries@museuminn.co.uk **web:** www.museuminn.co.uk
dir: *From Salisbury take A354 to Blandford Forum, 12m. Farnham signed on right. Pub in village centre*

A great combination of tip-top ales and quality food

This part-thatched country pub lies on Cranborne Chase, where kings used to hunt and where, in the 19th century, General Augustus Pitt Rivers pioneered modern archaeological fieldwork. He built the inn for visitors to a small museum, now gone, where he displayed his finds. The interior features the original inglenook fireplace, flagstone floors, a fashionable mismatch of furniture and a book-filled sitting room. If you're passionate about your ales, a pint of Sixpenny 6D Best, or Orchard Pig cider if you prefer, never tasted better. Dishes are prepared with quality seasonal ingredients, many sourced from local estates and farms and with two AA Rosettes, expect dishes of accomplished cuisine; an entrée such as Dorset snails on cheese rarebit toast with prosciutto crisp could be followed by a sea bream fillet with cockle and saffron sauce. Desserts are no less focussed, and a fine selection of teas and coffees confirms the attention to detail.

Open all day all wk **Food** Lunch Mon-Sat 12-2.30, Sun 12-3 Dinner all wk 6-9.30 ⊕ FREE HOUSE ◀ Sixpenny 6D Best, Fuller's London Pride, Ringwood Best Bitter, Guest ale ♻ The Orchard Pig. ♀ 12 **Facilities** Non-diners area 🐾 (Bar Restaurant Garden) ⬤ Children's menu Children's portions Garden ☰ Parking WiFi 🚃 (notice required) **Rooms** 8

PICK OF THE PUBS

The Acorn Inn ★★★★ INN ❀

EVERSHOT   Map 4 ST50

tel: 01935 83228 **DT2 0JW**
email: stay@acorn-inn.co.uk
web: www.acorn-inn.co.uk
dir: *From A37 between Yeovil & Dorchester, follow Evershot & Holywell signs, 0.5m to inn*

Surrounded by unspoilt rolling countryside

Jack and Alex Mackenzie continue to run this highly successful, pretty, 16th-century village inn. Wessex novelist and poet Thomas Hardy called the pub the 'Sow and Acorn' in *Tess of the d'Urbervilles*. Much would still be familiar to him, from the unusual porch to the old beams, low ceilings, oak panelling, flagstone floors and carved Hamstone fireplaces. He'd also recognise the bedroom names, taken from places in his books, such as Kingsbere, his pseudonym for Bere Regis. The lively bar is a big draw for villagers, who enjoy the real ales, quiz nights and the occasional yard-of-ale-drinking challenges. In the softly lit, AA Rosette restaurant you'll find smartly laid tables and terracotta tiles. An elegant stone fireplace is carved with oak leaves and, as it happens, acorns. Sustainability is the watchword for a modern British menu that uses local, seasonal produce for dishes such as

home-made soup; light and crispy beer-battered fish from the nearby coast; beetroot risotto; truffle gnocchi; slow-roasted pork belly; and chargrilled sirloin steak. Lunch and bar menus offer sandwiches, anti pasti sharing platters, deep-fried whitebait, burgers and ploughman's. Beer drinkers can choose from an excellent range of real ales which change every week; plus there's 34 wines by the glass and an impressive stock of malt whiskies. The pub also features a lovely old skittle alley and a beer garden, while some of the rooms feature four-poster beds. Good walks radiate from the village, so stick your wellies in the car.

Open all day all wk 11am-11.30pm
Food Lunch all wk 12-2 Dinner all wk 7-9 Restaurant menu available all wk
⛃ FREE HOUSE ◧ Otter, Rotating guest ales ♂ Thatchers Gold. ♗ 34
Facilities Non-diners area ☙ (Bar Garden) ♦ Children's portions Family room Garden ⋈ Parking WiFi
🚌 (notice required) **Rooms** 10

FERNDOWN
Map 5 SU00

The Kings Arms

tel: 01202 577490 **77 Ringwood Rd, Longham BH22 9AA**
email: thekingsarmslongham@yahoo.co.uk
dir: On A348

An upward trajectory for this free house serving tempting food

The Kings Arms continues to improve, gaining a good local reputation for its British classics, especially beef, and other locally-sourced dishes prepared by chefs Mark Miller and Tim Butler. From their main menu come a variety of steaks, including a 100-day, grain-fed rib-eye, and a 16-18oz Chateaubriand for sharing. Also, pan-roasted cod loin; Dorset home-cooked ham, egg and chips; lamb two ways; and risottos, both chicken and chorizo, and vegetarian. Fresh seared tuna loin with wilted spinach; and wild mushroom, courgette and asparagus ragoût are specials. The bar usually keeps three real ales, among them Ringwood Best, from a few miles east, and various traditional ciders. Some 15 wines are by the glass, the reds chosen very much with the beef dishes in mind.

Open all day all wk **Food** Lunch Sun-Thu 12-9, Fri-Sat 12-9.30 Dinner Sun-Thu 12-9, Fri-Sat 12-9.30 Set menu available ⊕ FREE HOUSE ◀ Ringwood Best, Otter Ale, Fuller's London Pride, Timothy Taylor ♂ Westons. ♒ 15 **Facilities** Non-diners area ♣ (Bar Outside area) ♦ Children's portions Outside area ⌨ Parking WiFi ▄ (notice required)

FONTMELL MAGNA
Map 4 ST81

The Fontmell ★★★★ INN

tel: 01747 811441 **SP7 0PA**
email: info@thefontmell.com **web:** www.thefontmell.com
dir: Halfway between Shaftesbury & Blandford Forum, on A350

Smart inn with seasonally inspired menus

On the A350, between Shaftesbury and Blandford Forum is The Fontmell, a stylish and comfortable country pub, complete with a stream flowing between the bar and the dining room. Linger over a pint of one of the weekly changing guest ales at the bar, or curl up on the sofa and peruse the newspapers. Most visitors and guests cannot resist chef/patron Tom Shaw's frequently changing menus which feature flavour packed dishes such as Cornish mackerel bhaji; rustic rabbit terrine; moules marinière and frites; and rump of Dorset lamb, chorizo, goats' cheese and wilted greens. From Monday to Thursday a set menu is available at lunchtime.

Open all day all wk **Food** Lunch Mon-Thu 12-2, Fri-Sun 12-2.30 Dinner Mon-Thu 6-9, Fri-Sat 6-9.30, Sun 6-8.30 Av main course £12 ⊕ FREE HOUSE ◀ Keystone Mallyshag, Seasonal ale, Rotating Guest ales ♂ Rotating Guest ciders. ♒ 13 **Facilities** Non-diners area ♣ (Bar Garden) ♦ Children's menu Children's portions Garden ⌨ Parking WiFi **Rooms** 6

GILLINGHAM
Map 4 ST82

The Kings Arms Inn

tel: 01747 838325 **East Stour Common SP8 5NB**
email: nrosscampbell@aol.com
dir: 4m W of Shaftesbury on A30

Family-run pub with a Scottish flavour

Scottish touches – paintings by artist Mavis Makie, quotes by Robert Burns, the presence of haggis, skirlie and cranachan on the menus, and a wide choice of single malts – reflect the origin of this inn's landlord and landlady. A 200-year-old, family-run village free house where Victorian fireplaces sit comfortably alongside modern wooden furniture and subtly coloured fabrics, it offers an extensive choice of dishes ranging from salmon and hoki fillets with garden pea purée, tempura king prawns and sweet chilli drizzle to slow roast belly pork on bubble-and-squeak with black pudding, cider sauce, apple fritter and crackling. Look out for the £7 pub lunch specials.

Open all wk 12-3 5.30-11.30 (Sat-Sun 12-12) **Food** Lunch Mon-Sat 12-2.30, Sun 12-9.15 Dinner Mon-Sat 5.30-9.15, Sun 12-9.15 Restaurant menu available all wk ⊕ FREE HOUSE ◀ Sharp's Doom Bar, St Austell Tribute, Butcombe. ♒ **Facilities** Non-diners area ♣ (Bar Garden) ♦ Children's menu Children's portions Family room Garden ⌨ Parking WiFi ▄ (notice required)

The Acorn Inn

28 Fore Street, Evershot, Dorset DT2 0JW
Tel: 01935 83228 • Website: www.acorn-inn.co.uk • Email: stay@acorn-inn.co.uk

An unspoilt 16th century coaching inn, set deep in the heart of Hardy's Wessex, and featured in his novel *Tess of the d'Urbervilles* – perfect for exploring the delights of the legendary Jurassic Coast. Ten individually designed and recently refurbished rooms, three with four poster beds. The feel is comfortable and traditional with strikingly modern bathrooms. With two bars, skittle alley and a restaurant, it's equally popular with drinkers and diners alike – not just a local, or a gastro-pub, but both! The highly rated menu features dishes that make inspired use of the finest seasonal produce, from local and sustainable sources.

LYME REGIS
Map 4 SY39

The Mariners ★★★★ INN ⊛

tel: 01297 442753 **Silver St DT7 3HS**
email: enquiries@hotellymeregis.co.uk **web:** www.hotellymeregis.co.uk
dir: *A35 onto B3165 (Lyme Rd). The Mariners is pink building opposite road to The Cobb (Pound Rd)*

Try the local seafood specials

Once a coaching inn in the 17th century, this restored property in the heart of the town is steeped in Lyme's fossil history, having once been home to the Philpot sisters, famed as collectors in the early 19th century. Beatrix Potter is said to have stayed here too, reputedly writing *The Tale of Little Pig Robinson* – The Mariners is illustrated in the book. The building combines traditional character with modern style. Simple menus feature the best of local seafood and other quality ingredients in dishes such as scallops with crispy pancetta, asparagus and watercress pesto; wild mushroom and ricotta tortellini; and mango pannacotta to finish. Only bottled beers are available.

Open all day all wk **Food** Lunch all wk 12-2 Dinner all wk 6.30-9 Set menu available Restaurant menu available all wk ⊕ FREE HOUSE ◀ Otter Bright, Mighty Hop Mighty Red IPA & Mariners Ale ♂ Thatchers Gold. ♀ 9 **Facilities** Non-diners area ♣ (Bar Garden) ♦ Children's menu Children's portions Garden ♩ Parking WiFi ➡ (notice required) **Rooms** 14

MILTON ABBAS
Map 4 ST80

The Hambro Arms ★★★★ INN

tel: 01258 880233 **DT11 0BP**
email: info@hambroarms.com **web:** www.hambroarms.com
dir: *From A354 (Dorchester to Blandford road), exit at Milborne St Andrew to Milton Abbas*

A community-owned pub in a unique village

Picture-perfect Milton Abbas, including the charming Hambro Arms, was built in 1780. It replaced a nearby medieval hamlet which was demolished by the privacy-seeking landowner, the Earl of Dorchester; thus Milton Abbas may claim to be the first planned village in England. Today the long thatched and whitewashed pub thrives in the ownership of the community. Its two spacious bars stock local guest ales, spirits and quality wines. Menus cater for all appetites, from lighter lunchtime bites to full à la carte dining in the elegant Library Restaurant; you couldn't do better than choose a starter of Rosary goats' cheese mousse; a main of herb-crusted rack of lamb, and a lemon posset dessert.

Open all wk 11.30-3 6-11 (Sat-Sun 11.30-11.30) **Food** Lunch Mon-Fri 12-2.30, Sat-Sun 12-3 Dinner Mon-Thu 6-9, Fri-Sat 6-9.30 ⊕ FREE HOUSE ◀ Sharp's Doom Bar, Ringwood, Guest ales ♂ Westons Stowford Press. ♀ 8 **Facilities** Non-diners area ♦ Children's menu Children's portions Garden ♩ Beer festival Parking WiFi ➡ **Rooms** 4

MOTCOMBE
Map 4 ST82

The Coppleridge Inn ★★★ INN

tel: 01747 851980 **SP7 9HW**
email: thecoppleridgeinn@btinternet.com **web:** www.coppleridge.com
dir: *Take A350 towards Warminster for 1.5m, left at brown tourist sign. Follow signs to inn*

Former farmhouse in beautiful surroundings

Chris and Di Goodinge took over this 18th-century farmhouse and farm about 25 years ago and converted it into the pub you see today. As well as retaining the flagstone floors and log fires, they have kept the farm's 15 acres of meadow and woodland, where they raise their own cattle. The bar offers a wide range of real ales, as well as constantly changing old favourites such as beer battered haddock and chips, or seasonal dishes, perhaps pork beef Wellington, carrot and red pepper purée and dauphinoise potatoes. Ten spacious bedrooms are situated around a converted courtyard and there is a secure children's playground. New additions are the woodland wedding venue and a marquee.

Open all day all wk **Food** Lunch all wk 12-2.30 Dinner all wk 6-9 Av main course £11.50 ⊕ FREE HOUSE ◀ Butcombe Bitter, Wadworth 6X, Fuller's London Pride, Sharp's Doom Bar, Ringwood Best Bitter ♂ Ashton Press, Thatchers. ♀ 10 **Facilities** Non-diners area ♣ (Bar Garden) ♦ Children's menu Children's portions Play area Family room Garden ♩ Parking WiFi ➡ (notice required) **Rooms** 10

NETTLECOMBE
Map 4 SY59

Marquis of Lorne

tel: 01308 485236 **DT6 3SY**
email: info@themarquisoflorne.co.uk
dir: *From A3066 (Bridport-Beaminster road) approx 1.5m N of Bridport follow Loders & Mangerton Mill signs. At junct left past Mangerton Mill, through West Milton. 1m to T-junct, straight over. Pub up hill, approx 300yds on left*

Recommended for its interesting menus and lovely views

In a picturesque hamlet and close to the market town of Bridport, The Marquis of Lorne is surrounded by beautiful views. Built as a farmhouse in the 16th century and converted into a pub in 1871, it is now run by Steve and Tracey Brady. They have renewed the focus on local produce throughout the menus, and locally brewed Palmers ales are on tap. Home-made duck liver pâté spiked with pistachio makes an interesting starter, while international influences are at play in a main course of tenderloin of Dorset pork wrapped in Serrano ham with flageolet bean and spinach ragout. Look out for special dinner evenings. The attractive gardens are family friendly, too.

Open all wk 12-2.30 6-11 **Food** Lunch all wk 12-2 Dinner all wk 6-9 ⊕ PALMERS ◀ Copper Ale, Best Bitter, Dorset Gold. ♀ 9 **Facilities** Non-diners area ♣ (Bar Garden) ♦ Children's menu Children's portions Play area Garden ♩ Parking WiFi ➡ (notice required)

NORTH WOOTTON
Map 4 ST61

The Three Elms

tel: 01935 812881 **DT9 5JW**
dir: *From Sherborne take A352 towards Dorchester then A3030. Pub 1m on right*

Village store, post office...and pub

Incorporating a shop and post office, this family-friendly pub near the beautiful Blackmore Vale has become the heart of the community. The bar is well stocked with weekly changing guest real ales and ciders, and freshly cooked pub classics include West Country mixed grill; chilli con carne; and spinach and ricotta cannelloni. Among the 'two for £10' deals are chicken, beef and veggie burgers, fishcakes and faggots; takeaways are available, too. The large beer garden hosts summer barbecues and beer festivals.

Open all day 11-11 (Sun 12-10.30) Closed 26 Dec, Mon **Food** Lunch Tue-Sat 12-2.30, Sun 12-3 Dinner Tue-Sat 6-9.30, Sun 6-9 Av main course £7.95 ⊕ FREE HOUSE ◀ St Austell Tribute, Guest ale ♂ Thatchers & Gold, St Austell Copper Press. **Facilities** Non-diners area ♣ (Bar Restaurant Garden) ♦ Children's menu Children's portions Play area Garden ♩ Beer festival Parking WiFi ➡

PIDDLEHINTON
Map 4 SY79

The Thimble Inn

tel: 01300 348270 **DT2 7TD**
email: info@thimbleinn.co.uk
dir: *Take A35 W'bound, right onto B3143, Piddlehinton in 4m*

Thatched village local in huge grounds

Following refurbishment by Bridport brewery Palmers, this 18th-century pub and restaurant is run by French-trained chef Mark Ramsden and his wife Lisa. The now-stunning interior features antique furniture, sandstone and oak floors and a glass-covered well. Its patio overlooks the River Piddle, or Puddle, as prim Victorians preferred. Mark uses the best local produce for dishes such as honey- and wholegrain mustard-glazed ham with macaroni cheese; slow-cooked pork belly with crackling and apple sauce; and grilled salmon fillet with potato and spinach hash. Sundays see roast Dorset Red beef and free-range local pork. Desserts include Black Forest gâteau; and apple crumble with cream.

Open 11.30-3 6-11 (Sat-Sun 11.30-11) Closed Mon **Food** Lunch Tue-Fri 12-3, Sat-Sun 12-9 Dinner Tue-Fri 6-9, Sat-Sun 12-9 Restaurant menu available Tue-Sun ⊕ PALMERS ◀ Copper Ale, Best Bitter, 200 Ď Thatchers Gold. ♥ 10 **Facilities** Non-diners area ❤ (Bar Garden) ♦ Children's menu Children's portions Garden ⊨ Parking WiFi ⛊ (notice required)

PIDDLETRENTHIDE
Map 4 SY79

The Poachers Inn

tel: 01300 348358 **DT2 7QX**
email: info@thepoachersinn.co.uk
dir: *6m N from Dorchester on B3143. At church end of village*

Good range of food and garden with swimming pool

Located in the pretty little village of Piddletrenthide in the heart of Thomas Hardy country, this 17th-century riverside pub is perfectly situated for exploring west Dorset and the Jurassic Coast. The kitchen makes good use of Dorset suppliers to create both classic pub meals (scampi, pie of the day, gourmet burger, lamb cutlets) and contemporary alternatives (butternut squash and Mediterranean vegetable risotto) for the extensive menu. Relax with a glass of ale in the beer garden, which even has a heated swimming pool to enjoy throughout the summer. Details of three circular walks are available at the bar.

Open all day all wk 8am-mdnt **Food** Lunch all wk 12-2.30 Dinner all wk 6-9.30 Set menu available ⊕ FREE HOUSE ◀ Sharp's Doom Bar, Morland Old Speckled Hen Ď Thatchers Gold. ♥ 9 **Facilities** Non-diners area ❤ (Bar Garden) ♦ Children's menu Children's portions Garden ⊨ Parking WiFi ⛊ (notice required)

PLUSH
Map 4 ST70

The Brace of Pheasants ★★★★ INN

tel: 01300 348357 **DT2 7RQ**
email: info@braceofpheasants.co.uk web: www.braceofpheasants.co.uk
dir: *A35 onto B3143, 5m to Piddletrenthide, then right to Mappowder & Plush*

Village inn popular with walkers

Tucked away in a fold of the hills in the heart of Hardy's beloved county, this pretty 16th-century thatched village inn is an ideal place to start or end a walk. With its welcoming open fire, oak beams and fresh flowers, it is the perfect setting to enjoy a selection of real ales and ciders and 18 wines by the glass. Food options might

include pan-fried lamb's kidneys with mustard cream sauce or local venison steak with red wine reduction. The inn offers eight en suite bedrooms, four above the pub and four in the old skittle alley.

Open all wk 12-3 7-11 **Food** Lunch all wk 12-2.30 Dinner all wk 7-9 ⊕ FREE HOUSE ◀ Flack Manor Flack's Double Drop, Palmers, Ringwood Best Bitter, Sunny Republic, Guest ales Ď Westons Traditional, Purbeck Dorset Draft, Cider by Rosie. ♥ 18 **Facilities** Non-diners area ❤ (Bar Restaurant Garden) ♦ Children's portions Garden ⊨ Parking WiFi ⛊ (notice required) **Rooms** 8

POOLE
Map 4 SZ09

NEW The Plantation

tel: 01202 701531 **53 Cliff Dr, Canford Cliffs BH13 7JF**
email: info@the-plantation.co.uk
dir: *From A35 between Poole & Bournemouth into Archway Rd (leads to Canford Cliffs Rd). At mini rdbt left into Haven Rd, right into Cliff Drive*

Fresh and refreshing pub and restaurant

Light and airy interiors in classic colonial style characterise this beautifully upgraded pub and restaurant. Within the Poole conservation area and close to some of Bournemouth's best beaches, The Plantation is ideally sited for visitors sampling the delights of this picturesque coast. At the bar Upham ales are ably supported by Orchard Pig's range of bottled ciders, while short menus showcase high quality, fresh, local and seasonal ingredients. A typical three-course choice could begin with winter salad, pickled pear, pecans and poppy seed yogurt; continue with pressed lamb shoulder, chilli, polenta and smoked aubergine; and finish with baked Alaska, rhubarb compôte and jelly.

Open all day all wk **Food** Lunch 12-5.30 Dinner 6-9.30 Restaurant menu available all wk ⊕ FREE HOUSE ◀ Upham Punter, Tipster & Stakes Ď Orchard Pig Reveller, Charmer & Truffler. ♥ 15 **Facilities** Non-diners area ❤ (Bar Garden Outside area) ♦ Children's menu Children's portions Garden Outside area ⊨ Parking WiFi ⛊

POWERSTOCK
Map 4 SY59

Three Horseshoes Inn
PICK OF THE PUBS

tel: 01308 485328 **DT6 3TF**
email: threehorseshoespowerstock@live.co.uk
dir: *3m from Bridport off A3066 (Beaminster road)*

Good reputation for locally-sourced food

Under new management since the start of 2015, this pretty late-Victorian inn is owned by Palmers, a part-thatched brewery in nearby Bridport. The food owes much to the kitchen's devotion to seasonal, locally sourced ingredients, some from the garden and some foraged from surrounding hedgerows. Daily-changing menus lean towards game dishes in winter and fresh fish in summer, but inventiveness is present all year round. Your visit may coincide with starters of rabbit and veal terrine with apricot chutney, or celeriac and Bramley apple soup with blue cheese. For mains, try the venison pie; fillet of sea bass with roast cherry tomatoes and tapenade; or shin of beef braised in best bitter. Those with a sweet tooth look to the blackboards for the dessert choices. The pub patio and terraced garden look out over the village, above which rises the National Trust's Eggardon Hill Fort.

Open 12-3 6.30-11.30 (Sun 12-3 6.30-10.30) Closed Mon L **Food** Lunch Tue-Sat 12-2.30, Sun 12-3 Dinner all wk 6.30-9.30 ⊕ PALMERS ◀ Best Bitter, Copper Ale, Tally Ho! & 200 Ď Thatchers Gold & Traditional. **Facilities** Non-diners area ❤ (Bar Garden) ♦ Children's portions Garden ⊨ Parking WiFi

PICK OF THE PUBS

The Kings Arms ★★★★★ INN ❁

SHERBORNE   Map 4 ST61

tel: 01963 220281
North Rd, Charlton Horethorne DT9 4NL
email: admin@thekingsarms.co.uk
web: www.thekingsarms.co.uk
dir: *On A3145, N of Sherborne. Pub in village centre*

Enjoyable food in elegantly converted country pub

On the Somerset and Dorset border, three miles from the historic market towns of Sherborne and Wincanton, this Edwardian building has been transformed into a chic country pub and modern restaurant with boutique-style accommodation. Locals and visitors head to the bar to order local ales which include Wadworth, and Lawrence's cider from nearby Corton Denham. The wine list details 50 bottles, with 13 sold by the glass. Stay in the bar if you're looking for a light snack in relaxed surroundings, otherwise follow a wide walkway past a theatre-style kitchen to the more formal Georgian-mirrored dining room; from here, doors open on to an extensive dining terrace overlooking a croquet lawn. The cooking style is both traditional and modern British; add in influences from around the world and the result is an AA Rosette-winning menu. Everything is made in-house, including bread, pasta and ice creams. Starters range from cream of sweetcorn soup; to twice baked Smokeacre soufflé with sweet fig chutney. The kitchen's specialist charcoal grill oven is kept busy with main courses such as a local rib-eye steak with watercress salad and peppercorn sauce. Alternatively you may find pan-seared hake, pea purée, fennel, saffron potatoes, mouli and rocket salad, with caper and parsley butter; or Jerusalem artichoke and goats' cheese risotto on the menu. Pudding favourites are sticky toffee pudding with honeycomb ice cream, while chocolate mocha mousse with blood orange jelly; or lemon and lime posset, raspberry sorbet and stem ginger thins brim with interesting flavours. A short selection of dishes just for children is prepared to the same high standards. The ten individually designed bedrooms complete the picture.

Open all day all wk **Food** Lunch all wk 12-2.30 Dinner Mon-Thu 7-9.30, Fri-Sat 7-10, Sun 7-9 ⊕ FREE HOUSE
◀ Butcombe, Otter, Wadworth 6X
Ŏ Lawrence's. ♟ 13
Facilities Non-diners area ❤ (Bar Garden) ♦ Children's menu Children's portions Garden ☶ Parking WiFi
🚌 (notice required) **Rooms** 10

PUNCKNOWLE — Map 4 SY58

The Crown Inn

tel: 01308 897711 **Church St DT2 9BN**
email: email@thecrowninndorset.co.uk
dir: *From A35 through Litton Cheney to Puncknowle. Or from Swyre on B3157 follow Puncknowle signs*

Chocolate-box thatched inn

This picturesque 16th-century pub was once the haunt of smugglers on their way from nearby Chesil Beach to visit prosperous customers in Bath. There's a traditional, welcoming atmosphere within the rambling, child- and dog-friendly bars with their log fires, comfy sofas and low beams. Home-cooked food ranges from pizzas, tapas slates, jackets and multi-grain sandwiches to seasonally changing dishes prepared using local fish and meat. Enjoy a glass of real ale or one of the wines by the glass with a meal, or while playing one of the many traditional board games that are dotted around the pub. The lovely garden overlooks the Bride Valley.

Open all day (Nov-Etr 11-3 5.30-10.30) Closed Sun eve in winter **Food** Lunch Mon-Sat 12-2.30, Sun 12-9 (winter) Dinner Mon-Sat 6-9 Av main course £11 ⊕ PALMERS ◀ Best Bitter, 200, Copper Ale, Seasonal ales ♂ Thatchers Gold. **Facilities** Non-diners area ♣ (Bar Restaurant Garden) ♦♦ Children's menu Children's portions Garden ℞ Parking WiFi ▄ (notice required)

SHAPWICK — Map 4 ST90

The Anchor Inn

tel: 01258 857269 **West St DT11 9LB**
email: anchor@shapwick.com
dir: *From Wimborne or Blandford Forum take B3082. Pub signed*

Village-owned pub with great local food

Rescued by a village collective, the Anchor is now home to the Magrath family. 'Our landlords are our neighbours,' they point out 'it doesn't get much more independent than that!' And this independence pays off, with all their produce sourced from within a 20-mile radius of the village. For lunch you could go for the venison burger, or the house ham, egg and chips; they also do filled baguettes and chips. At dinner, start with smoked duck breast, pomegranate seed and hazelnut salad before moving on to braised and roasted beef brisket with confit cabbage mash, truffle butter and caramelised onions; or salt and vinegar batter cod fillet.

Open all day Closed Sun eve **Food** Lunch all wk 12-3 Dinner Mon-Sat 6-9.30 Set menu available Restaurant menu available ⊕ FREE HOUSE ◀ Sharp's Doom Bar, Local guest ales ♂ Westons Stowford Press, Aspall. ♥ 20 **Facilities** Non-diners area ♣ (Bar Restaurant Garden) ♦♦ Children's menu Children's portions Garden ℞ Parking WiFi ▄ (notice required)

SHERBORNE — Map 4 ST61

The Kings Arms ★★★★★ INN ◉   PICK OF THE PUBS

See Pick of the Pubs on page 169

SHROTON OR IWERNE COURTNEY — Map 4 ST81

The Cricketers   PICK OF THE PUBS

See Pick of the Pubs on opposite page

STRATTON — Map 4 SY69

Saxon Arms

tel: 01305 260020 **DT2 9WG**
email: rodsaxonlamont1@yahoo.co.uk
dir: *3m NW of Dorchester on A37. Pub between church & village hall*

Thatched flint-stone pub serving good food

Popular with villagers as much as visiting fishermen, cycling clubs and ramblers, this handsome, thatched flint-stone free house is ideally situated for riverside walks. Flagstone floors, a wood-burning stove and solid oak beams create a comfortable setting for a traditional English inn that offers a friendly welcome, a range of well-kept real ales and simple, carefully cooked food. Menu choices include smoked haddock and spring onion soufflé; chargrilled Hampshire pork tenderloin with bubble-and-squeak; pan-fried buffalo liver and crispy Parma ham; whole lemon sole with prawn, capers, lemon and parsley butter; and white chocolate and Baileys pannacotta. There's also a deli counter and a selection of baguettes and jackets.

Open all wk 11-3 5.30-late (Fri-Sun 11am-late) **Food** Lunch Mon-Thu 11-2.15, Fri-Sat 11.30-9.30, Sun 12-9 Dinner Mon-Thu 6-9.15, Fri-Sat 11.30-9.30, Sun 12-9 Set menu available ⊕ FREE HOUSE ◀ Fuller's London Pride, Palmers Best Bitter, Greene King Abbot Ale & Ruddles, Otter, Ringwood, Timothy Taylor, Butcombe, Guest ales ♂ Westons Stowford Press, Guest ciders. ♥ 15 **Facilities** Non-diners area ♣ (Bar Garden) ♦♦ Children's menu Children's portions Garden ℞ Parking WiFi ▄ (notice required)

STUDLAND — Map 5 SZ08

The Bankes Arms Hotel

tel: 01929 450225 **Watery Ln BH19 3AU**
dir: *B3369 from Poole, take Sandbanks chain ferry, or A35 from Poole, A351 then B3351*

Creeper-clad 16th-century pub close to Studland Bay

Standing above the wide sweep of Studland Bay, this 16th-century creeper-clad inn was once a smugglers' dive. Nowadays the pub hosts an annual four-day festival in mid-August, featuring live music and some 200 beers and ciders that include award-winning ales from its own Isle of Purbeck brewery. Fresh fish and seafood salads are a speciality, but slow-braised lamb shank with rosemary mash; chilli con carne; and a daily curry are other examples from the menu.

Open all day all wk 11-11 (Sun 11-10.30) Closed 25 Dec **Food** Lunch all wk 12-3 (summer & BH 12-9.30) Dinner Mon-Sat 6-9.30, Sun 6-9 (summer & BH 12-9.30) ⊕ FREE HOUSE ◀ Isle of Purbeck IPA & Fossil Fuel, Studland Bay Wrecked, Solar Power ♂ Broadoak. **Facilities** Non-diners area ♣ (Bar Restaurant Garden) ♦♦ Children's menu Garden ℞ Beer festival Cider festival WiFi ▄

PICK OF THE PUBS

The Cricketers

SHROTON OR IWERNE COURTNEY Map 4 ST81

tel: 01258 860421
DT11 8QD
email: info@thecricketersshroton.co.uk
web: www.heartstoneinns.co.uk
dir: *7m S of Shaftesbury on A350, turn right after Iwerne Minster. 5m N of Blandford Forum on A360, past Stourpaine, in 2m left into Shroton. Pub in village centre*

Award-winning free house in secluded gardens

Under Hambledon Hill, where General Wolfe trained his troops before his assault on Quebec in 1759, lies what maps show as both Iwerne Courtney and Shroton; ask locals for the latter when looking for this early 20th-century pub and you'll be pointed in the right direction. Built to replace a much earlier establishment, over the years it has become not only a real community local, but also a popular pit-stop for walkers on the Wessex Way, who, since the path passes conveniently right by, are rarely so unwise as to wander through without stopping for Joe and Sally Grieves' genuine hospitality. In the light, open-plan interior, where in winter there's a cosy log-burner, the real beers are Butcombe and Otter Bitter, while wine drinkers will find up to nine by the glass; there's no separate restaurant. The menu changes seasonally and makes use of locally sourced, home-

cooked ingredients to offer starters or light options such as grilled onglet steak; and spiced tomato crumble. Main dishes include braised ox cheek, horseradish and orange dumpling, roasted shallots and carrots with red wine sauce; and pan-fried buffalo's liver and bacon. For vegetarians there's twice-baked cheddar soufflé; and macaroni, porcini and parmesan. Sandwiches are available at lunchtime, and on Sunday a choice of roast meats is always on offer; specials are forever changing. Events include occasional summer barbecues and a beer festival weekend with live music. The pub is proud of its long association with the Shroton Cricket Club, from which it takes its name.

Open all wk 12-3 6-11 (Sun 12-10.30)
Food Lunch all wk 12-2.30 Dinner Mon-Thu 6.30-9, Fri-Sat 6.30-9.30
⊕ FREE HOUSE ◪ Butcombe, Otter Bitter ♻ Westons Stowford Press. ♟ 9
Facilities Non-diners area ♦♦ Children's menu Children's portions Garden ⌂ Beer festival Parking WiFi 🚌 (notice required)

SYDLING ST NICHOLAS
Map 4 SY69

NEW The Greyhound Inn
PICK OF THE PUBS

tel: 01300 341303 **26 High St DT2 9PD**
email: info@dorsetgreyhound.co.uk
dir: *From A37 (Yeovil to Dorchester road), exit at staggered x-rds signed Sydling St Nicholas & Cerne Abbas*

Good food in the heart of Hardy country

Deep in Thomas Hardy country, this 18th-century pub is tucked away among pastel-hued flint and stone houses in a valley formed by Sydling Water. With many lovely walks starting from the pub, the staff are accustomed to welcoming muddy-booted families and wet dogs. Relax in the open-plan bar with a pint of Trelawny, a glass of Sandford Orchards Devon Red craft cider, or one of over 20 wines sold by the glass. Next, choose where to eat: the bar, with its open fire; the conservatory with oak, fruitwood and scrubbed wood tables and a deep chesterfield; the refurbished restaurant with an exposed well; or the suntrap front terrace. The food is modern British in approach, and menus change daily. Look to the specials list for fresh fish, the pub's strength; it's ordered the night before from the quaysides in Weymouth and Bridport. There's a good vegetarian selection too.

Open all wk 11-3 5.30-late (Sun 12-late Summer & BH hours may vary) **Food** Lunch Mon-Sat 12-2.30, Sun 12-5 Dinner Mon-Sat 6-9.30 ⊕ FREE HOUSE ◀ Fuller's London Pride, St Austell Proper Job & Trelawny, Otter Ale ♂ Sandford Orchards Devon Red, Westons Old Rosie. ♀ 22 **Facilities** Non-diners area ♣ (Bar Garden) ♦ Children's portions Garden ♫ Parking WiFi

TARRANT MONKTON
Map 4 ST90

The Langton Arms ★★★★ INN
PICK OF THE PUBS

tel: 01258 830225 **DT11 8RX**
email: info@thelangtonarms.co.uk **web:** www.thelangtonarms.co.uk
dir: *A31 from Ringwood, or A357 from Shaftesbury, or A35 from Bournemouth*

Family-friendly thatched inn located in beautiful countryside

A short walk from the village church and surrounded by countryside immortalised by Thomas Hardy, this lovely 17th-century thatched inn has two bars, both of which are relaxing places to savour a pint from the ever-changing choice of outstanding local ales and ciders. Traditional pub dishes are served in the bars, as well as in the Stables restaurant and conservatory. Expect choice West Country fare made from local produce – sourced in Dorset whenever possible, including beef from the owners' own herd at Rawston Farm. Apart from the beef, main courses might include local pheasant game pie, or fillet of wild sea bream. Desserts are English favourites such as bread and butter pudding. Children, if you can persuade them to leave the fully-equipped play area, are spoilt for choice with their own menu or smaller portions from the adult carte. Comfortable bedrooms are situated around an attractive courtyard.

Open all day all wk **Food** Lunch Mon-Fri 12-2.30, Sat-Sun all day Dinner Mon-Thu 6-9.30, Fri 6-10, Sat-Sun all day ⊕ FREE HOUSE ◀ Local guest ales ♂ Purbeck Dorset Draft, Westons Stowford Press. ♀ 10 **Facilities** Non-diners area ♣ (Bar Garden) ♦ Children's menu Children's portions Play area Family room Garden ♫ Parking WiFi (notice required) **Rooms** 6

TRENT
Map 4 ST51

The Rose and Crown Inn, Trent ★★★★★ INN
PICK OF THE PUBS

See Pick of the Pubs on opposite page

WEST BEXINGTON
Map 4 SY58

The Manor Hotel

tel: 01308 897660 **DT2 9DF**
email: relax@manorhoteldorset.com
dir: *On B3157, 5m E of Bridport. In Swyre turn opposite The Bull Inn into 'No Through Road'*

Cosy old pub overlooking Chesil Beach

Overlooking the Jurassic Coast's most famous feature, Chesil Beach, parts of this 16th-century manor house are thought to date from the 11th century. It offers an inviting mix of flagstones, Jacobean oak panelling, roaring fires and a cosy cellar bar serving Otter ales and locally sourced dishes. Eat in the Manor Restaurant or in the Cellar Bar. With a pint of Otter Ale in hand study the chalkboards displaying modern British dishes; perhaps mackerel pâté followed by pan-fried venison steak and triple cooked celeriac chips. The large free car park is a bonus.

Open all wk 11.30-3 6-10 Closed 1st 2wks Jan **Food** Lunch all wk 12-2 Dinner Mon-Sat 6.30-9, Sun 6-8 ⊕ FREE HOUSE ◀ Otter Ale & Bitter ♂ Thatchers Gold, Lilley's. ♀ 10 **Facilities** Non-diners area ♣ (Bar Garden) ♦ Children's menu Garden ♫ Parking WiFi (notice required)

WEST LULWORTH
Map 4 SY88

Lulworth Cove Inn

tel: 01929 400333 **Main Rd BH20 5RQ**
email: lulworthcoveinn@hall-woodhouse.co.uk
dir: *From A352 (Dorchester to Wareham road) follow Lulworth Cove signs. Inn at end of B3070, opposite car park*

A short stroll from Lulworth Cove and the Jurassic Coast

Lulworth Cove's famous horseshoe bay is just steps away from the front door of this inn. It was once a distribution point for the mail service arriving by stagecoach, plus many smugglers' stories can be heard. Ramblers can sate their appetites from the extensive menu, which features light bites, filled baguettes and jacket potatoes, as well as main course dishes like the ever-popular steak and Tanglefoot ale pie; haddock smokie pie; and crisp parmesan chicken.

Open all day all wk **Food** Lunch all wk 12-9 Dinner all wk 12-9 ⊕ HALL & WOODHOUSE ◀ Badger ♂ Westons Stowford Press. ♀ 10 **Facilities** Non-diners area ♣ (Bar Restaurant Garden) ♦ Children's menu Children's portions Garden ♫ WiFi

WEST STOUR
Map 4 ST72

The Ship Inn

tel: 01747 838640 **SP8 5RP**
email: mail@shipinn-dorset.com
dir: *On A30, 4m W of Shaftesbury (4m from Henstridge)*

Combining old and new in a rural setting

Walkers can explore the footpaths, which pass through the picturesque Dorset countryside surrounding this coaching inn built in 1750. The main bar has a traditional flagstone floor, low ceiling and log fire, while the lounge bar has stripped oak floorboards and chunky farmhouse furniture. Both offer a selection of beers and ciders, with weekly-changing guest ales. An evening menu includes open bison burger with fries and onion rings; wild mushroom, blue cheese, spinach and hazelnut Wellington; and game pie. Home-made desserts may include dark chocolate and brandy torte. Outside there's a suntrap patio and large child-friendly garden. Perhaps time your visit for the beer and cider festival in August.

Open all wk 12-3 6-11.30 (Sat-Sun 12-11.30) **Food** Lunch all wk 12-2.30 Dinner Mon-Sat 6-9 Av main course £12.95 Set menu available ⊕ FREE HOUSE ◀ Palmers IPA, Sharp's Doom Bar, Ringwood Fortyniner, Butcombe, Guest ale ♂ Thatchers Cheddar Valley & Heritage, Westons Stowford Press, The Orchard Pig, Landshire Cider. ♀ 13 **Facilities** Non-diners area ♣ (Bar Garden) ♦ Children's menu Children's portions Garden ♫ Beer festival Cider festival Parking WiFi

PICK OF THE PUBS

The Rose and Crown Inn, Trent ★★★★★ INN

TRENT   Map 4 ST51

tel: 01935 850776 **DT9 4SL**
email: info@theroseandcrowntrent.co.uk
web: www.theroseandcrowntrent.co.uk
dir: *Just off A30 between Sherborne & Yeovil*

Much loved by generations of locals and visitors

When 14th-century workmen were building the slender church spire, one of only three of such vintage in Dorset, this is where they lived. Now ivy-clad, it owes more to its days as a farmhouse in the 18th century than to its medieval origins, but the beams and flagstone floors of this Dorset gem don't date. Located on the Ernest Cook Trust estate that surrounds Trent, the inn has a lounge with a large, log-surrounded open fire and comfortable leather sofa; the main bar looks out over the fields, and from the restaurant you can survey the valley of the Trent Brook. At the bar, there is always a selection of Wadworth's ales such as 6X and Henry's IPA as well as guest ales like Butcombe Bitter and St Austell's Proper Job. Essential to the country cooking on the regularly changing menus are Lyme Bay fish, Dorset lamb, Blackmore Vale cream, Dorset Blue Vinny cheese, Somerset beef and locally shot game. Lunchtime classics include mustard-glazed ham with free-range eggs and triple-cooked chips; ploughman's and fish finger sandwiches

with tartare sauce. On the main menu you'll find River Exe mussels in Addlestone's Somerset cider cream with warm apple bread to get you started, followed by red mullet with grilled polenta, roasted baby carrots, glazed shallots, black cabbage and tomato salsa; calves' liver with black pudding and sage doughnuts, Lyonnaise potatoes and bacon gravy; and warm confit fennel tarte Tatin with creamy blue cheese, pickled walnuts and watercress. Couples could share a Chateaubriand steak with home-made chips, tomato, field mushroom, onion rings and peppercorn sauce. The steak may not leave much room for winter fruit crumble and vanilla custard, but a scoop of mulled wine sorbet should hardly prove daunting.

Open all day all wk **Food** Lunch Mon-Sat 12-2.30, Sun 12-3 Dinner all wk 6-9 ⊕ WADWORTH ◧ 6X, Henry's IPA, Guest Ales (Butcombe Bitter, St. Austells Proper Job, Hardys & Hansons Olde Trip) ♂ Addlestones Cloudy Cider, Thatchers Gold. ♀ 23 **Facilities** Non-diners area ♣ (Bar Restaurant Garden) ♦♦ Children's menu Children's portions Family room Garden 🎋 Parking WiFi 🚌 (notice required) **Rooms** 3

WEYMOUTH
Map 4 SY67

The Old Ship Inn

tel: 01305 812522 **7 The Ridgeway DT3 5QQ**
email: info@theoldshipupwey.co.uk
dir: *3m from Weymouth town centre, at bottom of The Ridgeway*

Weymouth views and real ales

Thomas Hardy refers to this 400-year-old pub in his novel *Under the Greenwood Tree*, and copper pans, old clocks and a beamed open fire create a true period atmosphere. Expect a good selection of real ales of tap, perhaps Dorset Jurassic, Otter and Sharp's Doom Bar, with Addlestones cloudy cider as an alternative. A frequently changing menu of good home-cooked pub food offers crispy whitebait; grilled goats' cheese bruschetta; the very popular pork belly braised in Addlestones cider with black pudding and dauphinoise potatoes; home-made pie of the day; and parmesan crusted cod. On sunny days bag a bench in the garden and enjoy the views across Weymouth.

Open all wk Mon 5-11 Tue-Fri 12-3 5-11 Sat 12-11 Sun 12-10 **Food** Lunch Tue-Sat 12-2.30, Sun 12-6 Dinner Mon-Sat 6-9 Av main course £10 ⊕ PUNCH TAVERNS ◖ Sharp's Doom Bar, Ringwood Best Bitter, Dorset Jurassic, Otter, Guest ales Ö Addlestones, Westons Stowford Press. ♟ 13 **Facilities** Non-diners area ❤ (Bar Garden) ♦❙ Children's menu Children's portions Garden ⌱ Parking WiFi ▭

The Red Lion

tel: 01305 786940 **Hope Square DT4 8TR**
email: info@theredlionweymouth.co.uk **web:** www.theredlionweymouth.co.uk
dir: *Opposite Brewers Quay*

Rums, real ale and extensive food choices

Directly opposite the old Devenish Brewery in the heart of Weymouth, the former brewery tap has long been a famous ale house, popular with locals and visitors, and with strong links with the local RNLI – it is after all the lifeboat crew's nearest pub. Expect a comfortably rustic feel to the rambling rooms, with wood floors, candles on scrubbed tables, eclectic furnishings, period fireplaces, walls adorned with lifeboat pictures and artefacts, newspapers to peruse, and a cracking bar serving 80 rums, five ales and traditional ciders. To eat, there are platters to share; a pint or half pint of prawns; proper surf 'n' turf; and the 'legendary' home-made steak and Life Boat Ale pie, chips and 'not so mushy' peas.

The Red Lion

Open all day all wk 11-11 (Fri-Sat 11am-mdnt Sun 12-10.30) **Food** Lunch all wk 12-3, Apr-Sep all day Dinner all wk 6-9, Apr-Sep all day ⊕ FREE HOUSE ◖ Otter Brewery Life Boat Ale, Dorset Jurassic, Sharp's Doom Bar, St Austell Tribute Ö Westons Traditional Scrumpy & Country Perry. ♟ 12 **Facilities** Non-diners area ❤ (Outside area) ♦❙ Children's menu Children's portions Outside area ⌱ WiFi ▭ (notice required)

WORTH MATRAVERS
Map 4 SY97

The Square and Compass

tel: 01929 439229 **BH19 3LF**
dir: *Between Corfe Castle & Swanage. From B3069 follow signs for Worth Matravers*

Lovely pub with beer but no bar and limited food

Little has changed at this stone-built pub for the past century, during which time it has been run by the same family. This tucked-away inn boasts a simple interior with no bar, just a serving hatch and an abundance of flagstone floors, oak panels and a museum of local artefacts and fossils from the nearby Jurassic Coast. Award-winning West Country beers and ciders come straight from the barrel and food is limited to just pasties and pies. On the first Saturday in October there's a beer and pumpkin festival, and in early November there's a cider festival.

Open all wk 12-3 6-11 (summer & Fri-Sun 12-11) **Food** Contact pub for food times ⊕ FREE HOUSE ◖ Palmers Copper Ale, Wessex Longleat Pride, Hatty Browns Mustang Sally Ö Hecks Farmhouse, home made cider. **Facilities** Non-diners area ❤ (All areas) ♦❙ Garden Outside area Beer festival Cider festival ▭ **Notes** ⊛

COUNTY DURHAM

AYCLIFFE
Map 19 NZ22

The County ★★★★ RR

tel: 01325 312273 **13 The Green, Aycliffe Village DL5 6LX**
email: info@thecountyaycliffevillage.com **web:** www.thecountyaycliffevillage.com
dir: A1 (M) junct 59, off A167 into Aycliffe Village

Picturesque village green setting and TV location

Prettily perched on the village green, the Hairy Bikers filmed here on location in 2012. The smart restaurant and terrace is a lovely place to eat, as is the homely bar where you can sup a pint of Black Sheep or Cocker Hoop. With superb local produce on the doorstep, the seasonally changing menus offer the likes of ham hock terrine with pineapple pickle and fried quail's egg, then fillet of wild halibut with cavolo nero and Shetland mussels with fig and mascarpone tart with honey to finish.

Open all day all wk Closed 25-26 Dec, 1 Jan **Food** Lunch Mon-Sat 12-2, Sun 12-9 Dinner Mon-Sat 5.30-9, Sun 12-9 Restaurant menu available all wk ⊕ FREE HOUSE ◗ Cocker Hoop, Black Sheep, Yorkshire Dales, Hawkshead ੭ Thatchers Gold. ♟ 10 **Facilities** Non-diners area ♦ Children's portions Outside area ⊓ Parking **Rooms** 7

BARNARD CASTLE
Map 19 NZ01

The Morritt Hotel ★★★★ HL ◉◉
PICK OF THE PUBS

tel: 01833 627232 **Greta Bridge DL12 9SE**
email: relax@themorritt.co.uk **web:** www.themorritt.co.uk
dir: From A1(M) at Scotch Corner take A66 towards Penrith, in 9m exit at Greta Bridge. Hotel over bridge on left

Country house atmosphere

This fine building dates from the late 17th century, when it served Carlisle- and London-bound coach travellers. Traditionally a fine-dining venue, the restaurant has been brought bang up to date with vibrant colours, a touch of black leather, comfortable armchairs, silk blinds over window seats and works by local artists. This association with art began in 1946, when local portraitist Jack Gilroy painted the mural of Dickensian characters you'll find in the bar. Restaurant dishes might include local rabbit ballotine; scorched North Sea mackerel; and Orkney scallops 'Waldorf' as starters. With 57 degree lamb rump, swede mash, parsnip purée, leek dumpling and warm pea mousse; or pan-fried halibut, saffron potatoes, mussel meat, salify purée, kale and curried broth to follow.

Open all day all wk 7am-11pm (Sun 7am-10.30pm) **Food** Lunch all wk 12-6 Dinner all wk 6-9 Restaurant menu available Tue-Sun ⊕ FREE HOUSE ◗ Timothy Taylor Landlord, Rotating local guest ales. ♟ 12 **Facilities** Non-diners area ✿ (Bar Garden) ♦ Children's menu Children's portions Play area Family room Garden ⊓ Beer festival Parking WiFi ◛ **Rooms** 26

Three Horseshoes ★★★★ INN

tel: 01833 631777 **5-7 Galgate DL12 8EQ**
email: info@three-horse-shoes.co.uk **web:** www.three-horse-shoes.co.uk
dir: In town centre on A67

Local produce in family-run pub

In the centre of the historic market town of Barnard Castle, the Three Horseshoes is an ideal base for walkers exploring the nearby Teesdale Valley and the North Pennines. The Green family are now firmly established at this popular 17th-century coaching inn. Enjoy a pint of Black Sheep as you scan the menus, which take in sandwiches at lunchtime. The evening menu focuses on local produce – start perhaps with chicken liver parfait before moving on to the chef's curry of the day with pilaf rice. Accommodation available.

Open all day all wk **Food** Lunch Mon-Sat 11.30-3, Sun 12-4 (early bird menu Mon-Fri 3-6.30) Dinner Mon-Sat 5.30-9 Set menu available ⊕ FREE HOUSE ◗ Black Sheep Best Bitter, Wychwood Hobgoblin, Ringwood Boondoggle. ♟ 12

Facilities Non-diners area ♦ Children's menu Children's portions Garden Outside area ⊓ Parking WiFi ◛ **Rooms** 11

CASTLE EDEN
Map 19 NZ43

NEW Castle Eden Inn

tel: 01429 835137 **Stockton Rd TS27 4SD**
email: info@castleedeninn.com
dir: Phone pub for detailed directions

Great reputation for locally sourced good food

The village of Castle Eden was mentioned in the Domesday Book (although it seems there is no evidence that there was a castle there at the time) and the inn dates from the 18th century. You'll find Castle Eden Ale and Timothy Taylor Landlord in the bar, and the kitchen is certainly building a good reputation for dishes such as ox tongue, pickles and croutons; North Sea smoked salmon and prawn fishcakes with sweetcorn chowder; bacon and black pudding salad with free-range poached egg; and marmalade roast bacon loin, mustard mash and leeks. The pub's events calendar is pretty full and includes a beer festival in early summer.

Open all day all wk 11am-mdnt (Sun 12-10.30) **Food** Lunch Mon-Sat 12-2.30, Sun 12-5.30 Dinner Mon-Thu 5-9, Fri-Sat 5-9.30 Av main course £9 Set menu available Restaurant menu available all wk ⊕ ENTERPRISE INNS ◗ Castle Eden Ale, Timothy Taylor Landlord ੭ Rekorderlig. ♟ 10 **Facilities** Non-diners area ✿ (Bar Garden) ♦ Children's menu Children's portions Family room Garden ⊓ Beer festival Cider festival Parking WiFi ◛ (notice required)

CHESTER-LE-STREET
Map 19 NZ25

The Moorings Hotel

tel: 0191 370 1597 **Hett Hill DH2 3JU**
email: info@themooringsdurham.co.uk
dir: A1(M) junct 63 to Chester-le-Street. Take B6313. Hotel on left

Tranquil Tees Valley setting

Handy both for the fascinating open air museum at Beamish and the historic heart of Chester-le-Street, this thriving hotel bar attracts much custom from ramblers and riders enjoying the glorious countryside along the valley of the River Tees. Thirsts are quenched by beers from the respected microbrewery at the Beamish complex, whilst keen appetites can be sated by dishes created from the freshest local produce. The menu of modern classics ranges across the spectrum, from breaded cod, haddock and crayfish tail fishcakes with ratatouille to sirloin steak and garlic butter tiger prawns, finishing with warm Scotch pancakes with chocolate sauce.

Open all day all wk **Food** Lunch Mon-Thu 11.45-9, Fri-Sat 11.45-9.30, Sun 11.45-8.30 Dinner Mon-Thu 11.45-9, Fri-Sat 11.45-9.30, Sun 11.45-8.30 Set menu available ⊕ FREE HOUSE ◗ The Stables Beamish Hall Bitter, Guest ales. **Facilities** ♦ Children's menu Family room Garden Outside area ⊓ Parking WiFi ◛ (notice required)

COTHERSTONE
Map 19 NZ01

The Fox and Hounds

tel: 01833 650241 **DL12 9PF**
email: ianswinburn999@btinternet.com
dir: 4m W of Barnard Castle. From A66 onto B6277, signed

Picturesque village setting

At the heart of beautiful Teesdale and just a stone's throw from the river's wooded gorge, The Fox and Hounds is huddled above one of the village greens in pretty Cotherstone. Beams, open fires and thickly cushioned wall seats tempt you to linger at this 360-year-old coaching inn, admiring the local photographs and country pictures while you sip a pint of Black Sheep Best Bitter or Symonds cider. From the

continued

COTHERSTONE *continued*

menu, tuck into dishes made from the best of fresh, local ingredients: mini salmon, smoked mackerel and prawn fishcakes; or gammon steak, tomato and cheese melt and chunky chips.

Open 12-2.30 6-11 (Sun 12-2.30 6-10.30) Closed 25-26 Dec, Mon L, Tue L, Wed L winter **Food** Lunch all wk 12-2 Dinner all wk 6-8.30 Av main course £9.90 Set menu available ⊕ FREE HOUSE ◖ Black Sheep Best Bitter & Ale, York Yorkshire Terrier, Daleside, Hawkshead Lakeland Gold, Rudgate ♂ Aspall, Symonds, Westons Rosie's Pig. **Facilities** Non-diners area ♦♦ Children's menu Children's portions Outside area 🅿 Parking WiFi 🚐 (notice required)

| **COXHOE** | Map 19 NZ33 |

NEW The Clarence Villa

tel: 0191 377 3773 **DH6 4HX**
email: info@theclarencevilla.co.uk **web:** www.theclarencevilla.co.uk
dir: *Phone pub for detailed directions*

Brewery tap serving excellent local food

Home to the Sonnet 43 Brewhouse based in Coxhoe, the birthplace of 19th-century poet Elizabeth Barrett Browning, The Clarence Villa dates back to 1857. The name can be traced back to the days when coal was transported from the neighbouring Clarence Railway, and the pub still retains its Victorian charm. A full range of the brewery's ales are served in the bar, including Steam Beer and Bourbon Milk Stout. The pub also rears its own pigs and uses local suppliers for dishes such as Dropswell Farm and Sonnet 43 bangers and mash; and chicken, mustard and leek pie.

Open all day all wk **Food** Lunch Mon-Sat 12-9, Sun 12-8 Dinner Mon-Sat 12-9, Sun 12-8 Av main course £7.95 Set menu available Restaurant menu available Mon-Sat ⊕ TAVISTOCK HOSPITALITY ◖ Sonnet 43 American Pale Ale, Steam Beer, Bourbon Milk Stout, India Pale Ale & Blonde Beer. **Facilities** Non-diners area ♦♦ Children's menu Children's portions Garden Outside area 🅿 Parking WiFi 🚐 (notice required)

| **DARLINGTON** | Map 19 NZ21 |

Number Twenty 2

tel: 01325 354590 **22 Coniscliffe Rd DL3 7RG**
email: no22@btconnect.com
dir: *In town centre, off A67*

An ale drinkers' heaven with new microbrewery

Looking just like other shop fronts in the street, the door of Number Twenty 2 opens to reveal a classic Victorian pub. Multiple awards recognise that real ales are the name of the game here – up to 13 being pulled at busy times; expect to find Bull Premium and White Boar. Even more interesting perhaps will be the ouput from the new onsite microbrewery and nano-distillery. Add to all this, nine continental beers, wines chosen for easy quaffing, and a select list of fine spirits and you have a drinker's paradise. Whether by popular demand or applied common sense, a seating area known as 'the canteen' is where bar bites, soups and sandwiches are served from midday until 7pm.

Open all day Closed 25-26 Dec, 1 Jan & BH Mon, Sun **Food** Lunch Mon-Sat 12-7 Dinner Mon-Sat 12-7 Av main course £6 ⊕ FREE HOUSE ◖ The Village Brewer White Boar Bitter, Bull Premium Bitter & Old Raby ♂ Kingstone Press, Guest ciders. ♟ 22 **Facilities** Non-diners area ♦♦ WiFi

---

| **DURHAM** | Map 19 NZ24 |

Victoria Inn

tel: 0191 386 5269 **86 Hallgarth St DH1 3AS**
dir: *In city centre*

Traditional red brick street pub at the heart of the city

This unique listed inn has scarcely changed since it was built in 1899 – not a jukebox, pool table or TV to be found. Just five minutes' walk from the cathedral, it has been carefully nurtured by the Webster family for over three decades. Small rooms warmed by coal fires and a congenial atmosphere include the tiny snug, where a portrait of Queen Victoria still hangs above the upright piano. You'll find a few simple snacks to tickle the taste buds, but it's the cracking well-kept local ales, single malts, and over 40 Irish whiskies that are the main attraction.

Open all wk 11-11 **Food** Contact pub for food times ⊕ FREE HOUSE ◖ Wylam Gold Tankard, Durham Magus, Big Lamp Bitter, Fyne Ales Jarl, Hill Island, Saltaire Blonde. **Facilities** Non-diners area ♥ (Bar Restaurant) ♦♦ Family room Parking WiFi 🚐

| **FIR TREE** | Map 19 NZ13 |

Duke of York Inn

tel: 01388 767429 **DL15 8DG**
email: info@dukeofyorkfirtree.co.uk
dir: *On A68, 12m W of Durham. From Durham take A690 W. Left onto A68 to Fir Tree*

A warm welcome, modern interior and good food

On the tourist route (A68) to Scotland, the Duke of York is a former drovers' and coaching inn dating from 1749. It is appointed inside and out to a high standard, keeping the traditional country feel with contemporary touches. Look for Black Sheep and Camerons beers to accompany the food served all day. There's light bites, sandwiches and omelettes plus main menu choices such as the signature dish of chicken in creamy leek and pancetta sauce with crushed potatoes; or full rack of smokey BBQ baby ribs and hand-cut chips.

Open all day all wk **Food** Lunch all wk 12-9 Dinner all wk 12-9 Set menu available ⊕ CAMERONS BREWERY ◖ Black Sheep Best Bitter, Camerons Guest ales. **Facilities** Non-diners area ♥ (Bar Garden) ♦♦ Children's menu Children's portions Garden 🅿 Parking WiFi 🚐

FROSTERLEY

Map 19 NZ03

The Black Bull Inn

tel: 01388 527784 **DL13 2SL**
dir: *From A68 onto A689 towards Stanhope. Left into Frosterley. Inn adjacent to railway station*

Great ales with bells on

Uniquely, this family-run, independent country pub has its own church bells – not to mention a great range of real ales to enjoy after a spot of bell-ringing. Located next to Weardale steam railway station, it has cosy, music-free rooms, a stone-flagged bar and open fires in Victorian ranges. The ad hoc beer festivals demonstrate unwavering backing for local microbreweries, while the kitchen is equally supportive of the regional suppliers behind the food. A meal might take in potted North Shields crab; herb crusted lamb shoulder with apricot and walnut stuffing, dauphinoise potatoes and rosemary jus; and raspberry and white chocolate cheesecake.

Open all day Closed 1 Jan for 1wk, Sun eve, Mon, Tue & Wed **Food** Lunch Thu-Sun 12.30-2.30 Dinner Thu-Sat 7-9 ⊕ FREE HOUSE ◀ Allendale, Wylam, Consett, York, Jarrow ♂ Wilkins Farmhouse, Westons. **Facilities** ✿ (Bar Garden) ♦♦ Children's portions Garden ♩ Beer festival Cider festival Parking WiFi ☰ (notice required)

HURWORTH-ON-TEES

Map 19 NZ30

The Bay Horse

tel: 01325 720663 **45 The Green DL2 2AA**
email: mail@thebayhorsehurworth.com
dir: *From A66 at Darlington Football Club rdbt follow Hurworth sign*

Fine dining in pretty Tees Valley village

Savvy diners may get 'Bitter and Twisted' at the bar in this sublime gastro-pub; its one of the real ales there to satisfy devotees seeking out the culinary magic conjured up by talented chef-proprietors Jonathan Hall and Marcus Bennett. The ancient pub retains considerable character enhanced by carefully chosen period furnishings. Thoroughly modern cuisine sets this ambience off to a tee. At dinner expect starters like French black pudding with beetroot remoulade and Worcestershire sauce mayonnaise; or pan-fried scallops with pork kofta, butternut squash purée and curried apple dressing; and mains such as slow-cooked daube of beef with broad beans and bacon fricassée; or roasted stone bass with fish burger, pickled cucumber, mussel and saffron chowder. There's a good vegetarian choice and a delightful dessert selection.

Open all day all wk Closed 25-26 Dec **Food** Lunch Mon-Sat 12-2.30, Sun 12-4 Dinner all wk 6-close Set menu available Restaurant menu available Mon-Sat & Sun eve ⊕ FREE HOUSE ◀ Harviestoun Bitter & Twisted, Jennings Cumberland Ale. ♀ 12 **Facilities** Non-diners area ♦♦ Children's menu Garden ♩ Parking WiFi

Find out more about this county with *The AA Guide to Durham & Northumberland* – see shop.theAA.com

NEW The Otter & Fish

tel: 01325 720019 **1 Strait Ln DL2 2AH**
email: r.weeks@btconnect.com **web:** www.otterandfish.co.uk
dir: *Phone pub for detailed directions*

Contemporary style and traditional food

Overlooking the River Tees in the picturesque village of Hurworth, close to the North Yorkshire border, this pub has been family owned and run since 2006. A refurbishment has given the place a relaxed and welcoming contemporary style, with an emphasis on good food and great service. Traditional bar meals are available, as well as a full carte, offering plenty of choice, from beer battered haddock and chips; or chef's burger on toasted ciabatta; to beef and Black Sheep ale pie, pan-roast duck breast and confit leg, or trio of pork.

Open all wk **Food** Lunch Mon-Sat 12-2, Sun 12-5 Dinner Mon-Sat 6-9 Set menu available ⊕ PUNCH TAVERNS ◀ Black Sheep ♂ Westons Stowford Press. **Facilities** Non-diners area ♦♦ Children's menu Children's portions Outside area ♩ Parking WiFi ☰ (notice required)

HUTTON MAGNA

Map 19 NZ11

The Oak Tree Inn ◉◉

PICK OF THE PUBS

tel: 01833 627371 **DL11 7HH**
dir: *From A1 at Scotch Corner take A66 W. 6.5m, right for Hutton Magna*

Excellent cooking with a pedigree

Books by Raymond Blanc, Gordon Ramsay, Stéphane Reynaud and other top chefs casually repose around this whitewashed, part 18th-century free house. They suggest that food is taken seriously here – seriously enough to warrant two AA Rosettes, that's for sure. Responsible are Alastair and Claire Ross, he with a CV listing The Savoy, Leith's and a London private members' club. In the simply furnished dining room, Alastair's refined dishes change daily, combining classic techniques and modern flavours to offer such starters as celeriac and parmesan soup with white truffle oil; and ballotine of guinea fowl with wild mushrooms, chicken liver pâté and apple. Then, maybe turbot with king prawns, Shetland mussels, turmeric, coconut- and cashew-tempered rice; or best end of lamb with fondant potato, tenderstem broccoli, onion and rosemary. As well as fine real ales from Timothy Taylor and Jennings, there are world-sourced bottled beers and over 20 malt whiskies.

Open 6-11 (Sun 5.30-10.30) Closed Xmas & New Year, Mon **Food** Contact pub for food times Restaurant menu available Tue-Sun ⊕ FREE HOUSE ◀ Jennings Cumberland Ale, Timothy Taylor Landlord, Copper Dragon. ♀ 10 **Facilities** Non-diners area ✿ (Bar) Parking

LONGNEWTON
Map 19 NZ31

Vane Arms ★★★★ INN

tel: 01642 580401 **Darlington Rd TS21 1DB**
email: thevanearms@hotmail.com **web:** www.vanearms.com
dir: W end of village, just off A66 midway between Stockton-on-Tees & Darlington

Village pub with two beer festivals

This 18th-century pub is now successfully run by villagers Jill and Paul Jackson. There's no jukebox, pool or gaming machine, and the TV is on only for special events; background music plays quietly in the lounge. Sensibly priced home-made restaurant food includes haloumi stuffed pepper; crispy salmon and haddock fishcakes; butternut squash risotto; short-crust steak, mushroom and Black Sheep ale pie; and steamed spotted dick with bayleaf custard and seasonal berries. Grill night is Tuesday, French cuisine and tapas are available on alternate Wednesday evenings, roasts on Sunday, and there is a Black Sheep beer festival in October and a mini beer festival in July. A large garden looks towards the Cleveland Hills and the North Yorkshire Moors.

Open all wk Tue-Thu 12-2 5-11 (Mon 5-11 Fri-Sat 12-2 5-12 Sun 12-11)
Food Contact pub for food times Set menu available Restaurant menu available all wk ⊕ FREE HOUSE ◀ Black Sheep Best Bitter, Guest ales Ŏ Hereford Dry, Somersby Cider. **Facilities** Non-diners area ❤ (Garden) ♦️ Children's portions Garden ⊼ Beer festival Parking WiFi ▄ (notice required) **Rooms** 4

MICKLETON
Map 18 NY92

The Crown

tel: 01833 640381 **DL12 0JZ**
email: info@thecrownatmickleton.co.uk
dir: B6277 from Barnard Castle. Approx 6m to Eggleston. Follow Mickleton signs

In the upper Tees Valley

This old stone inn stands on Mickleton's main street, surrounded by the heather-covered moors of the North Pennines Area of Outstanding Natural Beauty. Candlelight and a log-burning stove illuminate the interior, lovingly updated by the Rowbotham family whom, it's good to report, are enthusiastic supporters of local craft breweries, such as Cumberland, Jarrow and Sonnet. The specials blackboard might catch your eye with chicken and 'Barney Banger' ballotine, or Portuguese fish stew. On the regular menu are Aberdeen Angus steaks; roasted haunch of venison; and Mediterranean vegetable lasagne, with cornflake tart and custard to follow. The dog-friendly garden is a real treat.

Open all day all wk **Food** Contact pub for food times ⊕ FREE HOUSE ◀ Cumberland Corby Ale, Jarrow Rivet Catcher, Sonnet 43 Steam Beer. ♟ 9
Facilities Non-diners area ❤ (All areas) ♦️ Children's portions Garden Outside area ⊼ Parking WiFi ▄ (notice required)

NEWTON AYCLIFFE
Map 19 NZ22

Blacksmiths Arms

tel: 01325 314873 **Preston le Skerne, (off Ricknall Lane) DL5 6JH**
dir: Exit A167 (dual carriageway) at Gretna Green pub signed Great Stanton, Stillington & Bishopton, into Ricknall Ln. Blacksmiths Arms 0.5m

Large dining pub in a rural setting serving good food

Dating from the 1700s, this former smithy may still be relatively isolated but certainly enjoys an excellent local reputation as a good dining pub. The menu offers starters of sautéed black pudding and smoked bacon; farmhouse pâté with home-made chutney; or the classic prawn cocktail. Fish dishes get their own page on the menu – you might find baked salmon with a ginger and honey glaze, and chilli and lime salsa, oven-baked sea bass fillets, and the luxury fish pie. There's also a page of chef's specialities, a good selection of vegetarian dishes and a gluten-free menu. An ever-changing selection of real ales is served in the bar.

Open 11.30-2.30 6-11 Closed 1 Jan, Mon **Food** Lunch Tue-Sun 11.30-2 Dinner Tue-Sun 6-9 ⊕ FREE HOUSE ◀ Guest ales. ♟ 10 **Facilities** Non-diners area ♦️ Children's menu Play area Garden ⊼ Parking ▄ (notice required)

ROMALDKIRK
Map 19 NY92

The Rose & Crown ★★★ HL ◉◉ [PICK OF THE PUBS]

See Pick of the Pubs on opposite page

SEAHAM
Map 19 NZ44

The Seaton Lane Inn ★★★★ INN

tel: 0191 581 2036 **Seaton Ln SR7 0LP**
email: info@seatonlaneinn.com **web:** www.seatonlaneinn.com
dir: S of Sunderland on A19 take B1404 towards Houghton-le-Spring. In Seaton turn left for pub

Traditional pub with stylish, contemporary interior and good food

With a traditional bar area as well as a stylish restaurant and lounge, this boutique-type inn offers four real ales to keep the regulars happy, served from the central bar. The menu proffers dishes such as smooth chicken liver parfait; and classic Caesar salad with hot kiln smoked salmon flakes as starters, followed by beef cheeks braised in stout, mash and honey-roasted carrots; fillet of monkfish cassoulet; Thai vegetable risotto; or Wallington Estate prime rib-eye steak. Bedrooms are modern, spacious and smartly furnished.

Open all day all wk 11am-mdnt **Food** all wk 7am-9.30pm Set menu available Restaurant menu available all wk ⊕ FREE HOUSE ◀ Timothy Taylor Landlord, Wells Bombardier, Caledonian Deuchars IPA, Sharp's Doom Bar. ♟ 10
Facilities Non-diners area ❤ (Bar Garden Outside area)
♦️ Children's menu Children's portions Garden Outside area ⊼ Parking WiFi ▄
Rooms 18

Follow us on twitter
@TheAA_Lifestyle

PICK OF THE PUBS

The Rose & Crown ★★★ HL 🌹🌹

ROMALDKIRK   Map 19 NY92

tel: 01833 650213
DL12 9EB
email: hotel@rose-and-crown.co.uk
web: www.rose-and-crown.co.uk
dir: *6m NW from Barnard Castle on B6277*

A real rural dining pub with a long pedigree

Overlooking the village's old stocks and water pump, this creeper-clad stone built coaching inn stands on the village green, while next door is the Saxon church known as 'The Cathedral of the Dale'. Step inside the 18th-century pub to be greeted by fresh flowers, varnished oak panelling, old beams, and gleaming copper and brass artefacts, then enter the quirky little bar and you'll encounter oak settles, a vast dog grate, old prints, carriage lamps and rural curios. In the secluded lounge you can retire to a wing-backed chair and be lulled by the ticking of a grandfather clock, with maybe a glass of Thwaites Wainwright or Black Sheep. The chefs use the best local produce sourced from Teesdale farms and sporting estates, as well as fish from the north-east coast, to create their imaginative, seasonal menus. Drop in at lunchtime for a just light bite or from the à la carte choose perhaps a home-made steak pie or a seasonally inspired fish dish. In the evening food can be enjoyed either in the bar area or in the oak-panelled restaurant. The cuisine style combines modern British cooking with a nod to the traditional Dales setting of The Rose & Crown. Typical dinner menu dishes are black treacle marinated beef short rib with pickled artichoke and horseradish; roast breast and confit leg of woodpigeon, creamed cabbage, dauphinoise potato, pickled kale and blueberry gastrique; baked fillet of Dover sole, nut brown butter, shrimps, sea vegetables and fondant potato; and ginger pannacotta with textures of rhubarb and champagne sorbet. The service is professional yet friendly and the overall ambience is relaxed and comfortable.

Open all day all wk Closed 24-26 Dec & 1wk Jan **Food** Lunch all wk 12-2.30 Dinner all wk 6.30-9 Av main course £12 Restaurant menu available all wk ⊕ FREE HOUSE 🍺 Black Sheep Best Bitter, Thwaites Wainwright Ŏ Kingston. ⬤ 9 **Facilities** Non-diners area 🐾 (Bar Outside area) 🚻 Children's menu Children's portions Outside area 🪑 Parking WiFi **Rooms** 14

SHINCLIFFE — Map 19 NZ24

NEW Seven Stars Inn

tel: 0191 384 8454 **DH1 2NU**
email: info@sevenstarsinn.co.uk
dir: *A1(M) junct 61, A177 towards Durham. Approx 2m to Shincliffe. Pub in village centre*

Country inn with walks to Durham city

In a peaceful village a short hop from Durham's historic city centre, the family-run Seven Stars has been refreshing travellers since it was built as a coaching inn in 1724. The cosy traditional bar with open fire offers ales from the Durham Brewery, while the separate restaurant serves modern British dishes with occasional international influences. Expect the likes of salt and pepper squid with tomato and saffron salsa; pan-fried venison haunch; and Mississippi mud pie with vanilla ice cream. Lighter lunchtime bites include a small Thai red curry with chicken or vegetables, and stone-baked hand-rolled pizzas are home made.

Open all day all wk **Food** Lunch all wk 12-2.30 Dinner Mon-Sat 5.30-9, Sun 6-8 Set menu available ⊕ ENTERPRISE INNS ◀ Timothy Taylor Landlord, Black Sheep Best Bitter, Durham Magus. ⬤ 10 **Facilities** Non-diners area ❖ (Bar Outside area) ◀❖ Children's menu Children's portions Outside area ⋒ WiFi

STANLEY — Map 19 NZ15

The Stables Pub and Restaurant

tel: 01207 288750 & 233733 **Beamish Hall Hotel, Beamish DH9 OYB**
email: info@beamish-hall.co.uk
dir: *A693 to Stanley. Follow signs for Beamish Hall Country House Hotel & Beamish Museum. Left at museum entrance. Hotel on left 0.2m after golf club. Pub within hotel grounds*

Own-brewed beer and ever-popular food

The stone-floored, beamed bar is the perfect spot to sample the pub's own real ales, brewed on site at their microbrewery. The beer festival in the third week of September will get you even more closely acquainted, while a cider festival is held during the second weekend of December. The pub, in the former mansion house stables, was a courtyard for alfresco eating and drinking, but if the weather's on the chilly side there's always the option to cheer up your day by enjoying a pint by a roaring fire. Regional producers supply the best local ingredients from which are crafted exemplary meals. Try perhaps Thai crab cakes with lime and chilli jam; followed by the trio of Knitsley Farm sausages, buttered mash, Beamish Ale gravy and crispy onion rings; or a classic fish pie and winter greens.

Open all day all wk Mon-Thu 11-11 (Fri-Sat 11am-mdnt Sun 11-10.30) **Food** Lunch Mon-Thu 12-9, Fri-Sat 12-9.30, Sun 12-8 Dinner Mon-Thu 12-9, Fri-Sat 12-9.30, Sun 12-8 Set menu available Restaurant menu available all wk ⊕ FREE HOUSE ◀ The Stables Beamish Hall Bitter, Beamish Burn Brown Ale, Old Miner Tommy, Silver Buckles ⚬ Gwynt y Ddraig Haymaker & Farmhouse Pyder. ⬤ **Facilities** Non-diners area ❖ (Garden) ◀❖ Children's menu Children's portions Play area Garden ⋒ Beer festival Cider festival Parking WiFi 🚌

THORPE THEWLES — Map 19 NZ32

The Vane Arms

tel: 01740 630458 **TS21 3JU**
email: tom@thevanearms.com
dir: *Take A177 from Stockton-on-Tees towards Sedgefield. Left to Thorpe Thewles*

Long-established village pub

Named after the Vane-Tempest family of Raby, higher up the valley, this handsome pub has served its peaceful Tees Valley village for over 200 years. Tables out-front overlook the green, and Village Brewer's White Boar is served in the bar as well as a guest ale. The menu is now the same at lunch and dinner – Guinness and leek Welsh rarebit or hot haggis Scotch egg and piccalilli to start, perhaps, followed by a

classic like beer-battered Hartlepool cod with chips, tartare sauce and Yorkshire caviar, or a 21 day dry-aged steak (rib-eye, fillet, or 32oz T-bone). There's a beer festival in June.

Open 12-2 5-11 (Sat 12-11 Sun 12-5) Closed Sun eve & Mon **Food** Lunch Tue-Sat 12-2, Sun 12-4 Dinner Tue-Sat 5.30-9 ⊕ FREE HOUSE ◀ The Village Brewer White Boar Bitter, Rotating Guest ale ⚬ Aspall. ⬤ 12 **Facilities** Non-diners area ◀❖ Children's portions Garden Outside area ⋒ Beer festival Parking

WINSTON — Map 19 NZ11

The Bridgewater Arms

tel: 01325 730302 **DL2 3RN**
email: paul.p.grundy@btinternet.com
dir: *Exit A67 between Barnard Castle & Darlington, onto B6274 into Winston*

Former schoolhouse serving fresh seafood

Set in a former schoolhouse, this Grade II listed pub is decorated with original photographs of the building and its pupils. It prides itself on offering high quality, simple meals made with local produce, particularly seafood. Cheddar and spinach soufflé, followed by confit leg of duck with garlic mash and red wine sauce is a typical meal, while fishy offerings could include tiger prawn and monkfish curry with pilau rice; and grilled cod chunk, spring onion mash, mussels and curry cream. Afterwards, the historic Winston Bridge and beautiful views to the church are a short stroll away.

Open 12-2.30 6-11 Closed 25-26 Dec, 1 Jan, Sun & Mon **Food** Lunch Tue-Sat 12-2 Dinner Tue-Sat 6-9 Av main course £12 ⊕ FREE HOUSE ◀ Timothy Taylor Landlord, Marston's, Cumberland, Mithril Ales, Rudgate ⚬ Thatchers. ⬤ 15 **Facilities** Non-diners area ◀❖ Children's portions Outside area ⋒ Parking WiFi

ESSEX

ARKESDEN — Map 12 TL43

Axe & Compasses — PICK OF THE PUBS

See Pick of the Pubs on opposite page

AYTHORPE RODING — Map 6 TL51

Axe & Compasses

tel: 01279 876648 **Dunmow Rd CM6 1PP**
email: axeandcompasses@msn.com
dir: *From A120 follow signs for Dunmow*

Nostalgic pub with great home cooking

The owners of this weather-boarded, 17th-century pub like to create a 'nostalgic pub experience'. In the bar, ales from brewers such as Adnams, are backed by Westons ciders. David Hunt, a skilled self-taught chef, uses the best of seasonal produce and loves to offer dishes such as chicken liver and brandy parfait; pigeon breast with bacon lardons, Savoy cabbage, Puy lentils and game gravy; and a choice of five home-made pies. The pub also serves breakfast daily and offers a great range of bar snacks such as pork crackling with warm apple sauce or a home-made Scotch egg.

Open all day all wk 9am-11.30pm (Sun 9am-11pm) **Food** Lunch Mon-Sat 12-2.30, Sun 12-8 Dinner Mon-Sat 6-9.30, Sun 12-8 (Bkfst all wk 9am-11.30am) ⊕ FREE HOUSE ◀ Sharp's Doom Bar, Adnams Broadside & Lighthouse, Guest ale ⚬ Westons Old Rosie, Rosie's Pig & Cider Twist Raspberry. ⬤ 15 **Facilities** Non-diners area ❖ (Bar Garden) ◀❖ Children's menu Children's portions Garden ⋒ Parking WiFi 🚌

PICK OF THE PUBS

Axe & Compasses

ARKESDEN Map 12 TL43

tel: 01799 550272 **High St CB11 4EX**
email: axeandcompasses@mail.com
web: www.axeandcompasses.co.uk
dir: *From Buntingford take B1038 towards Newport, left for Arkesden*

Lovely inn with Greek dishes on the menus

The Axe & Compasses is the centrepiece of this sleepy, picture-postcard village, whose narrow main street runs alongside gentle Wicken Water, spanned by a succession of footbridges that give access to white, cream and pink washed cottages. The thatched central part of the pub dates from 1650; the right-hand extension was added during the early 19th century and is now the public bar. It's run by Themis and Diane Christou from Cyprus, who between them have knocked up a good few awards for the marvellous things they do here. Easy chairs and settees, antique furniture, clocks and horse brasses fill their comfortable lounge and, in winter, there's an open fire. The pumps of Greene King hold sway in the bar, and it's with a pint of Olde Trip that you can have a sandwich or light meal, such as monkfish served on a roasted red pepper sauce. In the softly lit restaurant area, which seats 50 on various levels, and where agricultural implements adorn the old beams, the slightly Greek-influenced menus offer a

good selection of starters, including flat field mushrooms baked with garlic, thyme, lemon juice and olive oil; and avocado, bacon and blue cheese crostini. There's a good choice of main courses too, examples being moussaka; supreme of chicken Kiev with mushroom duxelles in puff pastry and wholegrain mustard cream; tender rump of lamb with mint and red wine gravy; grilled halibut steak with creamed leeks; and fried spinach and potato cakes with tomato and basil sauce. Rounding off the menu are desserts from the trolley, such as trifle of the day, and summer pudding. The wine list is easy to navigate, with house reds and whites coming in at modest prices. On fine days many drinkers and diners head for the patio.

Open all wk 12-2.30 6-11 (Sun 12-3 6-10.30) **Food** Lunch all wk 12-2 Dinner all wk 6.30-9.15 Av main course £15.95 Restaurant menu available all wk
🍺 GREENE KING ◀ IPA, Hardys & Hansons Olde Trip, Guest ale
⚗ Thatchers Gold. 🍷 14
Facilities Non-diners area ♟ Children's portions Outside area 🎪 Parking WiFi
🚌 (notice required)

BELCHAMP ST PAUL   Map 13 TL74

NEW The Half Moon

tel: 01787 277402 **Cole Green CO10 7DP**
email: enquiries@halfmoonbelchamp.co.uk
dir: *From Braintree take A131 towards Halstead. Left onto A1017 to Great Yeldham. In Great Yeldham follow 'The Belchamps' signs. Approx 4m to pub*

Delightful thatched free house overlooking village green

Many pubs claim to be quintessentially English; this one deserves the claim. Dating from the 1520s, many of its original features, including low beams, leaded windows and an open fire have survived – no wonder scenes in TV's *Lovejoy* were filmed here. Locally sourced, freshly made food maintains an ever-changing seasonal menu offering such treats as venison and sloe gin pie; chicken stuffed with Serrano ham-wrapped brie and bubble-and-squeak; and herb-crusted cod loin with tarragon cream sauce. Essex-brewed beers are in the bar and again in August for the bank holiday beer and cider festival.

Open all wk 12-3 6-11 (Sat-Sun 12-11) **Food** Lunch Mon-Fri 12-2.30, Sat 12-3, Sun 12-5 Dinner Mon-Sat 6-9 ⊕ FREE HOUSE ◀ Greene King IPA, Sharp's Doom Bar, Mighty Oak, Colchester, Nethergate ♂ Westons, Gwynt y Ddraig, Orchard Pig. ♥ 8 **Facilities** Non-diners area ♦ Children's portions Family room Garden ⊨ Beer festival Cider festival Parking WiFi ᓮ (notice required)

BLACKMORE   Map 6 TL60

The Leather Bottle   PICK OF THE PUBS

tel: 01277 823538 & 821891 **The Green CM4 0RL**
email: leatherbottle@btconnect.com
dir: *M25 junct 8 onto A1023, left onto A128, 5m. Left onto Blackmore Rd, 2m. Left towards Blackmore, 2m. Right then 1st left*

Enjoyable food in village pub with large beer garden

With its creeper-clad exterior and spacious garden, The Leather Bottle still continues to draw the crowds after 400 years. The stone-floored bar is a cosy, welcoming place to savour East Anglian real ales and cider, while the restaurant is smart, with modern furnishings, and an airy conservatory opens on to the large garden and covered patio. The cuisine is a blend of European and traditional English, prepared with top-quality ingredients mainly from local suppliers. The lunchtime meal deal (Tuesdays to Saturdays) options include a starter of ham hock terrine, piccalilli, cornichons and mixed leaves; and lamb's liver and bacon with creamy mash, gravy and seasonal vegetables. Typical evening dishes are rib-eye steak, wild mushrooms, spinach, chunky chips and mushroom sauce; and pan-seared duck breast, creamy mash, smoked bacon lardons, peas, Savoy cabbage and cherry jus.

Open all day all wk **Food** Lunch Mon-Sat 12-2, Sun 12-4 Dinner Tue-Sat 7-9 Set menu available Restaurant menu available all wk ⊕ FREE HOUSE ◀ Adnams Southwold Bitter & Broadside, Courage Directors, Sharp's Doom Bar, Woodforde's Wherry, Cottage Cactus Jack, Young's Special ♂ Aspall, Westons Old Rosie. ♥ 9 **Facilities** Non-diners area ♥ (Bar Garden) ♦ Children's portions Garden Parking

BURNHAM-ON-CROUCH   Map 7 TQ99

Ye Olde White Harte Hotel

tel: 01621 782106 **The Quay CM0 8AS**
email: whiteharthotel@gmail.com
dir: *Along high street, right before clocktower, right into car park*

Quayside hotel with an old-world atmosphere

Situated on the waterfront overlooking the River Crouch, the hotel dates from the 17th century and retains many original features, including beams and fireplaces. It also has its own private jetty. Enjoy fresh local produce and fish in The Waterside Restaurant, or eat in the bar or on the terrace. The dining room offers a wide range of starters, as well as main course options that include vegetarian dishes and a daily roast. The bar menu might feature lasagne and salad; or locally caught skate with new potatoes and vegetables.

Open all day all wk **Food** Lunch all wk 12-2.15 Dinner all wk 6.30-9 Restaurant menu available all wk ⊕ FREE HOUSE ◀ Adnams Southwold Bitter, Crouch Vale Brewers Gold. **Facilities** ♥ (Bar Outside area) ♦ Children's portions Outside area ⊨ Parking WiFi ᓮ (notice required)

CASTLE HEDINGHAM   Map 13 TL73

The Bell Inn   PICK OF THE PUBS

See Pick of the Pubs on opposite page

CHELMSFORD   Map 6 TL70

Admiral J McHardy

tel: 01245 256783 **37 Arbour Ln CM1 7RG**
email: admiraljmchardy@gmail.com
dir: *Phone for detailed directions*

Customer-focused white clapboard alehouse

This late 19th-century pub was previously called The Alma; it was renamed to commemorate the first Chief Constable of Essex, appointed in 1840. A year after acquiring the pub, a new management team subtly refreshed and lightened the mood of the dining area, and set about metaphorically embracing their customers with a warm welcome and a listening ear. The result is a menu of popular pub grub ranging from sandwiches to liver and bacon, from roast shoulder of lamb to pork and leek sausages. Guest ales, Somersby fruit ciders and a dozen wines by the glass meet most refreshment demands.

Open all wk 12-3 5-11 (Fri-Sun all day) **Food** Lunch Mon-Sat 12-2, Sun 12-5 Dinner Mon-Sat 6-9 Av main course £10 Set menu available ⊕ FREE HOUSE ◀ Sharp's Doom Bar, Guest ales ♂ Somersby Cider. ♥ 12 **Facilities** Non-diners area ♥ (Bar Garden) ♦ Children's menu Children's portions Garden ⊨ Beer festival Parking WiFi ᓮ (notice required)

CHRISHALL   Map 12 TL43

The Red Cow

tel: 01763 838792 **11 High St SG8 8RN**
email: thepub@theredcow.com
dir: *M11 junct 10, A505 towards Royston. 2m, pass pet crematorium, 1st left signed Chrishall. 3.5m, pub in village centre*

Recommended for local game dishes

Conveniently positioned between Saffron Walden and Royston, this 500-year-old thatched pub is very much the hub of the local community. Ales such as Nelson's Revenge, and ciders from Aspall, are locally brewed or from East Anglia. The seasonally changing restaurant carte typically offers prawn mornay with crusty bread, followed by Barbary duck breast with dauphinoise potatoes and butternut squash purée. The pub's social calendar is full to bursting, with music (or 'moosic' to use one of the pub's favoured beef-based puns) particularly high on the agenda. If a quieter life is preferred, a proper English afternoon tea is served at weekends.

Open 12-3 6-12 (Sat 12-12 Sun 12-11) Closed Mon **Food** Lunch Tue-Sun 12-3 Dinner Tue-Thu 6-9, Fri-Sat 6-9.30 ⊕ FREE HOUSE ◀ Adnams Southwold Bitter, Woodforde's Wherry & Nelson's Revenge, Morland Old Speckled Hen, Purity Mad Goose, Sharp's Doom Bar, Timothy Taylor Landlord ♂ Aspall Harry Sparrow. **Facilities** Non-diners area ♥ (Bar Garden) ♦ Children's menu Children's portions Play area Garden ⊨ Beer festival Parking WiFi ᓮ (notice required)

PICK OF THE PUBS

The Bell Inn

CASTLE HEDINGHAM   Map 13 TL73

tel: 01787 460350
Saint James St CO9 3EJ
web: www.hedinghambell.co.uk
dir: *On A1124 N of Halstead, right to Castle Hedingham*

British and Turkish cooking in a traditional village local

A 15th-century former coaching inn situated in the charming medieval village of Castle Hedingham, The Bell has been run by the Ferguson family for over 45 years. From the late 1700s the pub was a popular stop for coaches en route between Bury St Edmunds and London and it remains a traditional pub serving good quality real ales and honest food using local ingredients including herbs and vegetables from the pub's own allotment at the back. Exposed stone walls, heavy beams and real log fires create a welcoming atmosphere in which to enjoy a Mighty Oak Maldon Gold, Adnams Southwold Bitter or one of the guest ales. The Turkish chef puts his stamp on the menu, with Mediterranean fish nights on Mondays, and Turkish stone-baked pizzas on Wednesdays, Thursdays and Fridays. In the summer, the wood-fired oven and barbecue are fired up for guests to enjoy Middle Eastern dishes and fish specials alfresco in the walled patio and hop garden, once home to cock-fighting, croquet and quoits.

At lunchtime, Italian paninis are one option, alongside favourites such as ploughman's. Otherwise, enjoy unpretentious dishes like grilled lamb shish and sweet red pepper in a tortilla wrap with bulgur wheat; salmon and broccoli fishcakes with salad and potato salad; lemon roast chicken with root vegetables; or lentil pottage pie (a vegan alternative to cottage pie); with chocolate brownie for afters. Half-size portions of many dishes are available for younger visitors. The annual July beer festival that showcases up to 40 ales proves popular, as is live music every Friday night and jazz on the last Sunday of the month.

Open all wk 12-3 5.30-11 (Fri-Sat 12-12 Sun 12-11) Closed 25 Dec eve

Food Lunch Mon-Fri 12-2, Sat 12-2.30, Sun 12-3 Dinner Sun-Mon 7-9, Tue-Sat 7-9.30 Av main course £10 ⊕ GRAY & SONS ◼ Mighty Oak Maldon Gold, Adnams Southwold Bitter, Guest ales ♂ Aspall, Delvin End.
Facilities Non-diners area ❤ (Bar Restaurant Garden) ♦ Children's menu Children's portions Play area Family room Garden ⋒ Beer festival Parking WiFi ▭ (notice required)

CLAVERING
Map 12 TL43

The Cricketers
PICK OF THE PUBS

tel: 01799 550442 **CB11 4QT**
email: info@thecricketers.co.uk
dir: M11 junct 10, A505 E, A1301, B1383. At Newport take B1038

Famous dining pub in rural Essex

The Cricketers has served the community for almost 500 years and all the signs are here – from the beams and forest of wooden pillars to the old fireplaces and wisteria surrounding the door. Located in the lovely village of Clavering with winding lanes, extensive woodland and thatched cottages, the pub serves seasonally changing dishes prepared by head chef Justin Greig and his team. Meats are properly hung, the fish is always fresh, and local produce is used wherever possible. Jamie Oliver, son of landlords Trevor and Sally (over 30 years behind the bar), supplies the vegetables and herbs from his certified organic garden that is nearby. Begin perhaps with twice-baked cauliflower and gorgonzola soufflé and follow with Trev's chicken Kiev or pork belly, roasted celeriac, shallots and pancetta with apple and cider jus. The extensive wine list changes regularly, while beers are mostly East Anglian. Children are particularly welcome.

Open all day all wk Closed 25-26 Dec **Food** Lunch Mon-Sat 12-2, Sun 12-8 Dinner Mon-Sat 6.30-9.30, Sun 12-8 ⊕ FREE HOUSE ◼ Adnams Broadside & Southwold Bitter, Tetley's Bitter, Greene King IPA, Woodforde's Wherry & Norfolk Nog Ö Aspall. ₹ 17 **Facilities** Non-diners area ◖ Children's menu Children's portions Garden ⊨ Parking WiFi ▭ (notice required)

COLCHESTER
Map 13 TL92

The Rose & Crown Hotel ★★★ HL

tel: 01206 866677 **East St CO1 2TZ**
email: info@rose-and-crown.com **web:** www.rose-and-crown.com
dir: M25 junct 28, A12 N. Follow Colchester signs

Ancient, black-and-white oak-framed hotel

Just a few minutes' stroll from Colchester Castle, this beautiful timber-framed building dates from the 14th century and is believed to be the oldest hotel in the oldest town in England. The Tudor bar with its central roaring fire is a great place to relax with a drink. Food is served in the Oak Room or the Tudor Room brasserie, an informal alternative serving classic bar food. Typically, start with ham hock terrine or a sharing platter of shellfish, then follow with pork belly with butterbean, pancetta and chorizo cassoulet. Leave room for warm pear and almond tart.

Open all wk ⊕ FREE HOUSE ◼ Rose & Crown Bitter, Tetley's Bitter, Adnams Broadside. **Facilities** ◖ Children's portions Family room Outside area Parking WiFi **Rooms** 39

COPFORD GREEN
Map 7 TL92

NEW The Alma

tel: 01206 210607 **CO6 1BZ**
email: mail@thealma.org.uk
dir: From rdbt junct of A12 & A120 follow Colchester signs. At next rdbt follow Copford sign (B1408). In Copford right into School Rd. Pub 0.75m on left

Traditional country village pub for all-comers

On the edge of Copford Green, the staff at The Alma warmly welcome their guests, with or without their children and dogs. A Greene King house, there are always four ales and various lagers to choose from; its beer credentials are confirmed by the festival held here every Spring Bank Holiday weekend. The menus are crowd-pleasers too, featuring main dishes such as home-made deep-filled pie of the day; butcher's hand-carved ham with a brace of fried eggs and thick-cut chips; and Thai chicken burger with sweet chilli sauce. Children are well catered for with smaller portions from the main menu, or their own choices such as creamy pasta carbonara.

Open all wk 12-3 5-close **Food** Lunch all wk 12-3 Dinner all wk 6-9 Av main course £7.50 Set menu available Restaurant menu available Wed-Sun ⊕ GREENE KING ◼ IPA & Abbot, Red Fox Hunter's Gold, Guest ale Ö Aspall. **Facilities** Non-diners area ◖ (Bar Garden Outside area) ◖ Children's menu Children's portions Play area Garden Outside area ⊨ Beer festival Parking WiFi ▭

DEDHAM
Map 13 TM03

Marlborough Head Inn ★★★ INN

tel: 01206 323250 **Mill Ln CO7 6DH**
email: jen.pearmain@tiscali.co.uk **web:** www.marlborough-head.co.uk
dir: E of A12, N of Colchester

Comfortable and cosy inn serving hearty food

Tucked away in glorious Constable Country, this 16th-century building was once a clearing-house for local wool merchants. In 1660, after a slump in trade, it became an inn. Today it is as perfect for a pint, sofa and newspaper as it is for a good home-cooked family meal. Traditional favourites such as deep-fried whitebait; steak and kidney pie; and breaded whole tail scampi appear on the menu, plus fish is given centre stage on Fridays. There is a terrace and walled garden to enjoy in the warmer weather and an open log fire to sit beside in winter. Three en suite bedrooms are available.

Open all day all wk 11.30-11 **Food** Contact pub for food times Av main course £6.95 ⊕ PUNCH TAVERNS ◼ Greene King IPA, Adnams Southwold Ö Aspall. ₹ 12 **Facilities** Non-diners area ◖ (Bar Garden) ◖ Children's menu Children's portions Family room Garden ⊨ Parking WiFi ▭ (notice required) **Rooms** 3

The Sun Inn ★★★★★ INN ◉◉
PICK OF THE PUBS

tel: 01206 323351 **High St CO7 6DF**
email: office@thesuninndedham.com **web:** www.thesuninndedham.com
dir: From A12 follow signs to Dedham for 1.5m, pub on High Street

A centuries-old inn with Mediterranean-influenced cuisine

Independently owned and run, this lovely old inn has a smart yellow-painted exterior. Inside are two informal bars, an open dining room, a snug oak-panelled lounge, three open fires, and exposed timbers; outside is a suntrap terrace and walled garden overlooked by the church tower. So take your pick of where to enjoy your chosen refreshment, be it a pint of Crouch Vale Brewers Gold or Aspall Harry Sparrow cider; for wine drinkers, the choice extends beyond two dozen served by the glass. Locally sourced seasonal ingredients drive the daily-changing menu of traditional Mediterranean-style dishes, many with a strong Italian influence. Two AA Rosettes have been awarded for tastebud-tingling dishes such as grilled salt marsh leg of lamb with roasted red and yellow beetroot; and Gloucester Old Spots pork loin with braised black cabbage and Spello lentils. AA Wine Award Winner for England & Overall Winner 2015-16.

Open all day all wk 11-11 Closed 25-27 Dec **Food** Lunch Mon-Thu 12-2.30, Fri-Sun 12-3 Dinner Sun-Thu 6.30-9.30, Fri-Sat 6.30-10 Av main course £8.50 Set menu available ⊕ FREE HOUSE ◼ Crouch Vale Brewers Gold, Adnams Broadside, 2 guest ales Ö Aspall Harry Sparrow. ₹ 25 **Facilities** Non-diners area ◖ (Bar Garden) ◖ Children's menu Children's portions Garden ⊨ Parking WiFi **Rooms** 7

FEERING
Map 7 TL82

The Sun Inn

tel: 01376 570442 **Feering Hill CO5 9NH**
email: hello@sunninnfeering@.co.uk
dir: *On A12 between Colchester & Witham. Village 1m*

Ancient pub with two annual beer festivals

A pretty pub dating from 1525 with heavily carved beams to prove it, this Grade II listed building has two inglenook fireplaces and a large garden and courtyard. The traditional bar, which sells Shepherd Neame's real ales, has no TV or games machines. Home-cooked pub classics are backed by mains like beef, mushroom and Stilton pie, and haddock in ale batter with chips, peas and tartare sauce. From May to September wood-fired pizzas are available. Three roasts, together with other options, are offered on Sundays. Over 30 real ales and ciders are showcased at the June and September festivals.

Open all wk Sat-Sun all day **Food** Lunch Mon-Sat 12-2.30, Sun 12-8 Dinner Mon-Sat 6-9.30, Sun 12-8 ⊕ SHEPHERD NEAME ◀ Master Brew, Spitfire & Bishops Finger, Whitstable Bay Pale Ale, Guest ales ♂ Thatchers Heritage. ♈ 12
Facilities Non-diners area ✿ (Bar Garden) ♦♦ Children's menu Children's portions Garden ⋒ Beer festival Cider festival Parking WiFi ☞ (notice required)

FINGRINGHOE
Map 7 TM02

The Whalebone

tel: 01206 729307 **Chapel Rd CO5 7BG**
email: info@thewhaleboneinn.co.uk
dir: *Phone for detailed directions*

British cuisine and breathtaking views

This Grade II listed 18th-century free house enjoys beautiful views from its position at the top of the Roman River Valley. Its name comes from the bones of a locally beached whale, which were once fastened above the door of the pub. Wooden floors, exposed beams, bespoke furniture, a roaring fire and unique artwork all combine to create a feeling of warmth and character. Hearty British fare is prepared from local ingredients, along with Adnams and Woodforde's ales. A lunchtime snack can be enjoyed in one of the garden pavilions. The carte menu options include pan-fried red snapper to chargrilled rib-eye steak and roast topside of local beef.

Open all wk 12-3 5.30-11 (Sat 12-11 Sun 12-10.30 Winter Sun 12-6) ⊕ FREE HOUSE ◀ Adnams Southwold Bitter, Woodforde's Wherry, 2 guest ales ♂ Aspall.
Facilities ✿ (Bar Restaurant Garden) ♦♦ Children's menu Children's portions Play area Family room Garden Parking

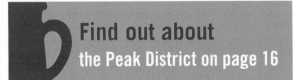

Find out about
the Peak District on page 16

FULLER STREET
Map 6 TL71

The Square and Compasses

tel: 01245 361477 **CM3 2BB**
email: info@thesquareandcompasses.co.uk **web:** www.thesquareandcompasses.co.uk
dir: *From A131 (Chelmsford to Braintree) take Great Leighs exit, enter village, right into Boreham Rd. Left signed Fuller St & Terling. Pub on left*

A prominent feature of village life

Known locally as The Stokehole, this beautifully restored 17th-century village pub is set in lovely countryside but is just 10 minutes from Chelmsford. Originally two farm cottages, the privately owned and run free house still retains its original beams and inglenook fireplaces, with antique furnishings. The locally sourced food is straightforward, served alongside a good selection of ciders and ales. As well as pub classics, the daily-changing seasonal specials might include pan-fried scallops with pea purée and truffle infused oil, followed by mains such as whole grilled Dover sole; or pan-roasted duck breast with pea and smoked ham risotto. For your dessert what better than lemon tart with lemon crisps and syrup?

Open all day all wk 11.30-11.30 **Food** Lunch Mon-Fri 12-2, Sat 12-2.30, Sun 12-6 Dinner Mon-Sat 6.30-9.30 ⊕ FREE HOUSE ◀ Farmers Ales A Drop of Nelsons Blood, Wibblers Dengie Gold ♂ Westons, Aspall. ♈ 14 **Facilities** Non-diners area ✿ (Bar Garden) ♦♦ Children's portions Garden ⋒ Parking

FYFIELD
Map 6 TL50

NEW The Queen's Head

tel: 01277 899231 **Queen St CM5 0RY**
email: sglamprecht@gmail.com
dir: M11 junct 7, A414 towards Chelmsford. In Chipping Ongar at rdbt left to Fyfield on B184

Family-run free house with river garden

With a history dating back to the 15th century, The Queen's Head is a traditional free house with log fires and private dining room. Adnams and Crouch Vale are the ales on offer, backed by Aspall cider and a wide-ranging choice of wines. An annual beer festival over the bank holiday in August is when the pub's river garden comes into its own. The kitchen's modern British approach produces starters such as blow-torched confit salmon; and crispy aromatic quail with sweet and sour tamarind. Scan the daily specials board for the likes of potted crab followed by pan-fried skate wing with caper beurre noisette.

Open 11-3.30 6-11 (Sat 11am-11.30pm Sun 12-10.30) Closed 26 Dec, Mon **Food** Lunch Tue-Fri 12-2.30, Sat 12-4, Sun 12-6 Dinner Tue-Sat 6.30-9.30 Set menu available Restaurant menu available Tue-Sun ⊕ FREE HOUSE ◀ Adnams Southwold Bitter & Broadside, Crouch Vale Brewers Gold ○ Aspall. ♀ 17
Facilities Non-diners area ♦ Children's portions Garden ⋒ Beer festival Parking WiFi (notice required)

GESTINGTHORPE
Map 13 TL83

The Pheasant ★★★★★ INN ◎
PICK OF THE PUBS

See Pick of the Pubs on opposite page

GOLDHANGER
Map 7 TL90

The Chequers Inn

tel: 01621 788203 **Church St CM9 8AS**
email: chequersgoldhang@aol.com
dir: From B1026, 500mtrs to village centre

'Low' pub in a riverside village

Built in 1410, The Chequers can be found next to the church in picturesque Goldhanger, on the River Blackwater. The pub name comes from a chequerboard used by the tax collector in the pub many, many years ago. At around 30 feet above sea level, it reputedly has the 'lowest' bar in Britain, where you can enjoy a pint of Adnams Ghost Ship. Several rooms decorated with farming and fishing implements surround the bar area. Pride is taken in the preparation and presentation of food, which includes whole sea bass baked with fennel and thyme; lamb and mint suet pudding; and aubergine, butternut and walnut bake. There are beer festivals in March and September.

Open all day all wk **Food** Lunch all wk 12-3 Dinner Mon-Sat 6.30-9 ⊕ PUNCH TAVERNS ◀ Young's Bitter, Crouch Vale Brewers Gold, Sharp's Doom Bar, Adnams Ghost Ship, Fuller's Bengal Lancer ○ Westons Traditional & Perry. ♀ 13
Facilities Non-diners area ♣ (Bar Garden) ♦ Children's menu Children's portions Garden ⋒ Beer festival Parking WiFi (notice required)

GREAT TOTHAM
Map 7 TL81

The Bull at Great Totham ★★★★ RR ◎◎
PICK OF THE PUBS

tel: 01621 893385 **2 Maldon Rd CM9 8NH**
email: reservations@thebullatgreattotham.co.uk **web:** www.thebullatgreattotham.co.uk
dir: Exit A12 at Witham junct to Great Totham

A highly regarded destination gastro-pub and restaurant

The Bull, overlooking the cricket green, is a 16th-century coaching inn and proud holder of two AA Rosettes. It offers not far short of 20 fine wines by the glass, real ales from Adnams and Greene King, and a bar menu of baguettes, sausage and mash, and beer-battered cod tail. Named after the ancient tree in the lavender-filled garden is the fine-dining Willow Room, where you might start with charred mackerel with Devon crab, apple, fennel and carrot salad, then follow with pan-fried loin of Atlantic cod, bean and chorizo bouillabaisse; or braised ox cheek, smoked mash potato, pancetta, oyster mushrooms and crispy onions. If you're a vegetarian, the basil gnocchi, arrabiata sauce, spinach and pecorino might take your fancy. Finish in style with salted caramel tart and crème fraîche ice cream. Musical and themed dining evenings and other events are held frequently.

Open all day all wk **Food** Lunch Mon-Fri 12-2.30 (light bites till 5.30), Sat 12-10, Sun 12-6.45 Dinner Mon-Thu 5.30-9, Fri 5.30-10, Sat 12-10, Sun 12-6.45 Set menu available Restaurant menu available Mon-Sat ⊕ FREE HOUSE ◀ Adnams, Greene King. ♀ 17 **Facilities** Non-diners area ♣ (Bar Garden Outside area) ♦ Children's menu Children's portions Play area Garden Outside area ⋒ Parking (notice required) **Rooms** 4

GREAT YELDHAM
Map 13 TL73

The White Hart ★★★★★ INN ◎◎
PICK OF THE PUBS

tel: 01787 237250 **Poole St CO9 4HJ**
email: mjwmason@yahoo.co.uk **web:** www.whitehartweddingvenue.co.uk
dir: On A1017 between Haverhill & Halstead

Character old inn with contemporary cooking

A huge, grassy, stream-side beer garden folds round part of this eye-catching old coaching inn deep in the Essex countryside. Its timber framed bulk and vast brick chimneys are reflected inside by wall panelling, solid fireplaces and polished wood flooring. One hidey-hole was apparently used as a lock-up to contain highwaymen. Maturing over five centuries, the inn's heritage makes it a popular venue for weddings. The hard work put in by the establishment's owner, Matthew Mason, has resulted in many awards, including two AA Rosettes for the food and a high rating for the luxury accommodation in adjoining converted barns. The bar menu offers comforting reading; a starter of Yeldham wood pigeon with 'kale bubble' and shallot jus complements main dishes of grilled black bream fillet with potato rösti, samphire and saffron cream; or home-made venison pudding with cream potato and red wine jus. Beer lovers will find a welcome selection of local ales at the bar. Please note, dogs are only allowed in the inn's grounds.

Open all day all wk **Food** Lunch all wk 12-3 Dinner all wk 6-9 Av main course £12.95 Restaurant menu available Tue-Sat ⊕ FREE HOUSE ◀ Brandon Rusty Bucket, Nethergate Old Growler. ♀ 10 **Facilities** Non-diners area ♣ (Garden) ♦ Children's menu Children's portions Garden ⋒ Parking WiFi (notice required) **Rooms** 11

PICK OF THE PUBS

The Pheasant ★★★★★ INN ✸

GESTINGTHORPE   Map 13 TL83

tel: 01787 465010
Audley End, Church St CO9 3AU
email: thepheasantpb@aol.com
web: www.thepheasant.net
dir: *A131 from Sudbury towards Castle Hedingham. Right, follow Castle Hedingham sign, through Gestingthorpe to Audley End*

Gastro-pub with top-notch plot-to-plate cooking

A previous winner of the AA Pub of the Year for England, The Pheasant continues to go from strength-to-strength thanks to hands-on owners James and Diana Donoghue. On the Essex and Suffolk border and surrounded by lovely countryside, this stylish gastro-pub is blessed in that James was an award-winning garden designer and he has created a kitchen garden which now provides a steady and abundant supply of seasonal organic fruit and vegetables for the restaurant. The one-acre garden is located across the road from the pub and produces soft fruits, onions, leeks, artichokes, beetroots, courgettes and various herbs and lettuces. Potatoes destined for the chips, mash and Sunday lunch roasties are grown ten miles away in Wormingford and the kitchen staff peel ten sacks of them a week. Enterprising James even keeps bees and he also smokes his own fish, much of it sourced from south coast day boats and delivered up to four times a week. Starters typically include grilled goats' cheese with a green salad and sweet chilli dressing; and tempura tiger prawns with garlic mayonnaise dip, followed by mains of garlic chicken, new potatoes and kale; Gressingham duck breast with orange and fennel salad; or home-made pie of the day with hand-cut chips. Home-made apple and cider crumble; and sticky toffee pudding with caramel sauce and honeycomb crunch ice cream are two typical desserts. Accompany your meal with a pint of Adnams ale or the pub's own Pheasant Bitter, brewed by Woodforde's in Norfolk. Alternatively, enjoy a glass of Suffolk-made Aspall cider.

Open all day all wk Closed 1st 2wks Jan **Food** Lunch all wk 12-2.30 Dinner all wk 6.30-9.30 ⊕ FREE HOUSE 🛢 Adnams Southwold Bitter, Woodforde's Pheasant Bitter, Guest ales ⚖ Aspall.
Facilities Non-diners area 🐾 (Bar Garden Outside area) 🚸 Children's portions Garden Outside area 🪑 Parking WiFi 🚌 (notice required) **Rooms** 5

HASTINGWOOD

Map 6 TL40

Rainbow & Dove

tel: 01279 415419 **Hastingwood Rd CM17 9JX**
email: rainbowanddove@hotmail.co.uk
dir: Just off M11 junct 7

Little pub with a varied history

Dating back to at least the 16th century, the Rainbow & Dove was a farmhouse, staging post, village shop and post office before it became a pub. English Heritage has given it Grade II historical building status. There are cask-conditioned real ales, a selection of whiskies and a good wine list. Menus revolve around fresh seasonal produce. On the snack menu you'll find ciabattas, baguettes sandwiches and jacket potatoes, but if it's something more substantial that you require then the carte lists dishes such as sharing platters; carpaccio of wild venison; stuffed rabbit loin; fresh, whole, grilled lemon sole; Tuscan-style roast pork belly; and asparagus, broad bean and roasted garlic risotto.

Open 11.30-3 6-11 (Sun 12-5 Mon 11.30-3.30) Closed Sun eve, Mon eve **Food** Lunch Mon-Sat 12-2.30, Sun 12-4 Dinner Tue-Sat 6-9 Restaurant menu available all wk ⊕ FREE HOUSE ◀ Rainbow & Dove, Adnams Broadside, Sharp's Doom Bar, Guest ales Ò Aspall, Thatchers, Westons Wyld Wood Organic. ♟ 10
Facilities Non-diners area ❀ (Bar Garden) ♦♦ Children's menu Children's portions Garden ⊟ Beer festival Parking ☞ (notice required)

HATFIELD BROAD OAK

Map 6 TL51

The Duke's Head

tel: 01279 718598 **High St CM22 7HH**
email: info@thedukeshead.co.uk **web:** www.thedukeshead.co.uk
dir: M11 junct 8, A120 towards Great Dunmow. Right into B183 to Hatfield Broad Oak. Pub on left at 1st bend in village

Friendly village gastro-pub

Standing behind a white-painted picket fence, this 185-year-old pub's proprietors are Justin and Liz Flodman. Spacious, with two wood-burners, the pub's customers can enjoy good wines by the glass, real ales from Essex and surrounding counties, and Justin's seasonal, modern British food. Maybe choose steamed Shetland mussels with Thai green curry sauce and noodles; veal escalope Holstein with fried egg, polenta chips and sherry jus; or a Turkish dish of baked 'imam bayildi' (which translates as 'the imam swooned', allegedly at his wife's cooking) and haloumi fritters, with spiced aubergine and tomato ragout, and pomegranate tabbouleh.

Open all day all wk Closed 25-26 Dec **Food** Lunch Mon-Fri 12-2.30, Sat 10.30-10, Sun 10.30-9 Dinner Mon-Thu 6.30-9.30, Fri 6.30-10, Sat 10.30-10, Sun 10.30-9 Av main course £12.50 ⊕ ENTERPRISE INNS ◀ Greene King IPA, Sharp's Doom Bar, Timothy Taylor Landlord, Purity Mad Goose Ò Aspall. ♟ 25 **Facilities** Non-diners area ❀ (Bar Garden) ♦♦ Children's menu Children's portions Garden ⊟ Parking WiFi ☞ (notice required)

HATFIELD HEATH

Map 6 TL51

The Thatcher's

tel: 01279 730270 **Stortford Rd CM22 7DU**
email: thethatcherspub@yahoo.co.uk
dir: In village on A1060 (Bishop's Stortford road)

Quaint old pub serving home-made food

A pretty, thatched 16th-century pub overlooking the village green with oak beams and a welcoming inglenook wood-burning stove. The dishes are all prepared on the premises and might start with grilled tiger prawns with parsley and garlic butter; black pudding and duck Scotch egg with tomato relish; or natural smoked haddock rarebit with cherry vine tomatoes, followed by a pressed pork belly with mustard mash, braised red cabbage and apple sauce; or roast butternut squash risotto with goats' cheese fritter. Finish with treacle tart or milk chocolate brownie. Also enjoy a pint from the Mighty Oak brewery among others.

Open all wk 11.30-3.30 5.30-11 (Sat-Sun all day) **Food** Lunch all wk 12-2 Dinner all wk 6-9 ⊕ FREE HOUSE ◀ St Austell Tribute, Nethergate, Mighty Oak, Adnams. ♟ 11 **Facilities** Non-diners area ♦♦ Children's portions Family room Garden ⊟ Parking ☞ (notice required)

HORNDON ON THE HILL

Map 6 TQ68

Bell Inn & Hill House

`PICK OF THE PUBS`

tel: 01375 642463 **High Rd SS17 8LD**
email: info@bell-inn.co.uk
dir: M25 junct 30 or 31, follow Thurrock signs

Historic family-run inn with plenty of talking points

In the same family since 1938, this 15th-century coaching inn is steeped in history – you might notice hot cross buns hanging from the original king post supporting the ancient roof timbers. Every year the oldest willing villager hangs another one, an unusual tradition that dates back 100 years to when the pub changed hands on a Good Friday. In the wood-panelled bar, regular brews like Crouch Vale Brewers Gold are backed by a selection of changing guest ales. The lunchtime bar menu offers sandwiches and light meals but booking is essential in the popular restaurant, where the daily-changing menu is driven by seasonal produce. Venison and pigeon terrine with sauce gribiche, fried duck egg and blackberry, might be followed by mustard roast loin of pork with sage and onion sausage roll and sweet potato purée. Leave room for desserts like dark chocolate marquis with caramelised banana and cream.

Open all day all wk 11-11 (Sun 12-10.30) Closed 25-26 Dec **Food** Lunch all wk 12-1.45 Dinner Mon-Fri 6.30-9.45, Sat 6-9.45, Sun 7-9.45 Restaurant menu available all wk ⊕ FREE HOUSE ◀ Greene King IPA, Crouch Vale Brewers Gold, Sharp's Doom Bar, Bass, Guest ales. ♟ 16 **Facilities** Non-diners area ❀ (Bar Garden) ♦♦ Children's portions Garden ⊟ Parking WiFi

INGATESTONE

Map 6 TQ69

The Red Lion

tel: 01277 352184 **Main Rd, Margaretting CM4 0EQ**
dir: From Chelmsford take A12 towards Brentwood. Margaretting in 4m

A proper English pub

Emphatically a traditional inn and not a restaurant (although it does sell quality food), the 17th-century Red Lion is best described as a 'quintessential English pub'. The bar is decorated in burgundy and aubergine, the restaurant in coffee and cream. From an extensive menu choose prawn tostada; home-made balti curry; or classic moules marinière. Every Thursday you can get two steaks and a bottle of wine for £25. Wash it down with a pint of Greene King IPA or guest ales, and look out for Mr Darcy and Mr Gray, the house donkeys.

Open all wk 12-11 (Sun 12-6) **Food** Lunch all wk 12-3 Dinner Mon-Sat 6-9 Restaurant menu available all wk ⊕ GREENE KING ◀ IPA, 4 weekly changing guest ales Ø Westons Stowford Press. ☕ 14 **Facilities** Non-diners area ◀ Children's menu Children's portions Play area Garden ⋒ Parking WiFi ⚌ (notice required)

◼ LANGHAM Map 13 TM03

The Shepherd

tel: 01206 272711 **Moor Rd CO4 5NR**
email: info@shepherdlangham.co.uk
dir: A12 from Colchester towards Ipswich, take 1st left signed Langham

Stylish village food pub in Constable Country

In the pretty village of Langham, deep in Constable Country on the Suffolk/Essex border, is this Edwardian pub. Richard and Esther Brunning have given this family-friendly free house a stylish and contemporary makeover and the pub is open all day. Adnams and Woodforde's are among the ales served at the bar, alongside an extensive list of wines and cocktails. A typical meal could take in salt and pepper calamari with sweet chilli mayonnaise, followed by Suffolk ham, bubble-and-squeak cake, poached eggs and hollandaise.

Open all day all wk **Food** Lunch all wk 12-3 Dinner Tue-Sat 6-9 Restaurant menu available ⊕ FREE HOUSE ◀ Adnams Southwold & Ghost Ship, Woodforde's Wherry Ø Aspall. **Facilities** Non-diners area ♣ (Bar Garden) ◀ Children's menu Children's portions Garden ⋒ Parking WiFi ⚌ (notice required)

◼ LITTLE BURSTEAD Map 6 TQ69

The Dukes Head

tel: 01277 651333 **Laindon Common Rd CM12 9TA**
email: enquiry@dukesheadlittleburstead.co.uk
dir: From Basildon take A176 (Noah Hill Rd) N toward Billericay. Left into Laindon Common Rd to Little Burstead. Pub on left

Welcoming pub known for its themed food events

Smart interiors and a friendly team characterise the atmosphere in this large hostelry between Brentwood and Basildon. Chunky wood tables, leather-upholstered stools and relaxing armchairs surround the open fire in the bar area, where the ales vie for selection with an excellent range of wines served by the glass. Modern British food ranges from pizzas and pastas to the chef's daily specials.

Open all day all wk **Food** Lunch Mon-Sat 12-10, Sun 12-9 Dinner Mon-Sat 12-10, Sun 12-9 Set menu available ⊕ MITCHELLS & BUTLERS ◀ Sharp's Doom Bar, Adnams Southwold Bitter, Guest ales Ø Aspall. ☕ 21 **Facilities** Non-diners area ♣ (Bar Garden) ◀ Children's menu Children's portions Garden ⋒ Parking WiFi ⚌ (notice required)

◼ LITTLEBURY Map 12 TL53

The Queens Head Inn Littlebury ★★ INN

tel: 01799 520365 **High St CB11 4TD**
email: queensheadlittlebury@aol.co.uk **web:** www.thequeensheadinn.net
dir: M11 junct 9A, B184 towards Saffron Walden. Right onto B1383, S towards Wendens Ambo

Popular community pub with good home-made food

A beautiful family-run former coaching inn with open fires, exposed beams and one of only two remaining full-length settles in England. Very much at the centre of the local community, the pub runs darts and football teams and pétanque

competitions; a large beer garden with a children's play area confirms its family-friendly credentials. The kitchen aims to produce good home-made pub grub at realistic prices, with a menu of popular favourites from fresh baguettes, fish and chips, a choice of home-made gourmet burgers and curries to the chef's specials. If you need to stay over after an evening in the bar, there are six en suite bedrooms.

Open all day all wk Mon-Thu 12-11.30 Fri-Sat 12-12 Sun 12-10.30 **Food** Lunch Mon-Sat 12-2.30, Sun 12-4 Dinner Mon-Sat 6-9.30 Restaurant menu available all wk ⊕ GREENE KING ◀ IPA, Morland Old Speckled Hen, Guest ales Ø Westons Stowford Press, Aspall. ☕ 9 **Facilities** Non-diners area ♣ (Bar Garden) ◀ Children's menu Children's portions Play area Garden ⋒ Beer festival Parking WiFi ⚌ **Rooms** 6

◼ LITTLE CANFIELD Map 6 TL52

The Lion & Lamb

tel: 01279 870257 **CM6 1SR**
email: info@lionandlamb.co.uk
dir: M11 junct 8, B1256 towards Takeley & Little Canfield

Perfect for a pre-flight meal

Ideal for business or leisure, this former coaching inn was built on what used to be the main East Coast road. Now a traditional country pub and restaurant, it's a popular stop for travellers on the way to Stansted Airport. Inside are oak beams, winter log fires and plenty of real ales, although the large and well-furnished garden is the place to relax in summer. A typical meal might be Scottish smoked salmon with granary bread, followed by a rack of salt marsh lamb, creamed potatoes, vegetables with red wine and rosemary jus. Finish with apple and berry crumble.

Open all day all wk 11-close (Sun 12-close) Closed 1 Jan **Food** Lunch Mon-Sat 11-10, Sun 12-10 Dinner Mon-Sat 11-10, Sun 12-10 Restaurant menu available all wk ⊕ GREENE KING ◀ IPA, Morland Old Golden Hen, Guest ales Ø Aspall Harry Sparrow. ☕ 11 **Facilities** Non-diners area ◀ Children's menu Children's portions Play area Garden ⋒ Parking WiFi ⚌

◼ LITTLEY GREEN Map 6 TL71

The Compasses

tel: 01245 362308 **CM3 1BU**
email: compasseslittleygreen@googlemail.com
dir: Phone for detailed directions

Unspoilt country local deep in rural Essex

Joss Ridley left London and a top job and snapped up this pub in 2008 to revive the family link with the former Ridley Brewery, and hasn't looked back. The traditional inn stands in a sleepy hamlet and thrives selling tip-top ales straight from the barrel, including Bishop Nick, brewed by Joss's brother Nelion, and fresh, hearty pub food. Using local ingredients, the menu and chalkboard specials include filled 'huffer' baps, ploughman's, and beer battered cod and chips. The interior is timeless and unspoilt, the garden large and peaceful.

Open all wk 12-3 5.30-11.30 (Thu-Sun all day) **Food** Lunch Mon-Fri 12-2.30, Sat-Sun 12-5 Dinner Sun-Fri 7-9.30, Sat 5-9.30 Av main course £10 ⊕ FREE HOUSE ◀ Bishop Nick, Crouch Vale, Mighty Oak Ø Westons, The Orchard Pig, Abrahalls. **Facilities** Non-diners area ♣ (Bar Restaurant Garden) ◀ Children's portions Garden ⋒ Beer festival Parking WiFi ⚌ (notice required)

MANNINGTREE · Map 13 TM13

The Mistley Thorn ◉◉ · **PICK OF THE PUBS**

tel: 01206 392821 **High St, Mistley CO11 1HE**
email: info@mistleythorn.co.uk
dir: *From Ipswich A12 junct 31 onto B1070, follow signs to East Bergholt, Manningtree & Mistley. From Colchester A120 towards Harwich. Left at Horsley Cross. Mistley in 3m*

Seafood a speciality

With views of the Stour estuary from its street-corner position, this light and airy pub will keep Adnams real ale fans very happy, and with 17 options available by the glass, wine drinkers won't be disappointed either. For those who want to eat there's a bonus, for Californian co-owner and executive chef Sherri Singleton (who also runs a cookery school next door) specialises in seafood. Not to do so would surely be unthinkable, for nearby are both Mersea Island and Colchester, whence come fine oysters. Changing daily, one of Sherri's two AA-Rosette menus might offer a starter of oak-smoked, peel-and-eat prawns with mayo, followed by an Italian-style seafood stew; chargrilled Suffolk Red Poll beef with hand-cut fries; or home-made potato gnocchi with butternut squash cream. On 'Moules Madness' Thursday evenings, the mussels, fries and a drink combo is on offer for a very good price.

Open all wk 12-2.30 6.30-9.30 (Fri 6-9.30 Sat-Sun all day) **Food** Lunch Mon-Fri 12-2.30, Sat-Sun & BHs 12-5 Dinner Mon-Thu 6.30-9.30, Fri-Sun 6-9.30 Set menu available Restaurant menu available all wk ⊕ FREE HOUSE ◀ Adnams Southwold Bitter & Ghost Ship. ♟ 17 **Facilities** Non-diners area ☻ (Bar Restaurant) ♦♦ Children's menu Children's portions Parking WiFi

MARGARETTING TYE · Map 6 TL60

The White Hart Inn

tel: 01277 840478 **Swan Ln CM4 9JX**
email: liz@thewhitehart.uk.com **web:** www.thewhitehart.uk.com
dir: *From A12 junct 15, B1002 to Margaretting. At x-rds in Margaretting left into Maldon Rd. Under rail bridge, left. Right into Swan Ln, follow Margaretting Tye signs. Follow to pub on right*

Two popular beer festivals held here

Parts of this pub, sitting proudly on a green known locally as Tigers Island, are 250 years old. Landlady Liz and her team revel in offering a great choice of the best regional and local beers and ciders. The pub's interior, all match boarding, old pictures, brewery memorabilia, dark posts, pillars, beams and fireplaces, oozes character, while the solidly traditional menu and specials board shout quality. Start with an Italian meat platter, and move on to lamb's liver and bacon casserole; grilled extra mature rib-eye steak; or grilled haddock served on creamy spring onion mash with a wild mushroom fricasée.

Open all wk 11.30-3 6-12 (Sat-Sun 12-12) Closed 25 Dec **Food** Lunch Mon-Sat 12-2.30, Sun 12-7.30 Dinner Tue-Thu 6.30-9, Fri-Sat 6-9.30, Sun 12-7.30 ⊕ FREE HOUSE ◀ Adnams Southwold Bitter & Broadside, Mighty Oak IPA & Oscar Wilde Mild ♂ Aspall, Rekorderlig. ♟ 10 **Facilities** Non-diners area ☻ (Bar Garden) ♦♦ Children's menu Family room Garden ⋈ Beer festival Parking WiFi ➤ (notice required)

MESSING · Map T TL81

NEW The Old Crown

tel: 01621 815575 **Lodge Rd CO5 9TU**
email: theoldcrownmessing@hotmail.co.uk
dir: *From Chelmsford: A12 junct 23, B1024 (Kelvedon). In Kelvedon right onto B1023 (Maldon). Left to Messing. From Colchester: A12 junct 24, B1024 (Kelvedon) left onto B1023*

Bistro pub in a lovely village

After many years as regulars, Malcolm and Penny Campbell took over this lovely old pub about two years ago. The Old Crown calls itself a 'bistro pub' and is right in the heart of the lovely village of Messing, proving very popular with walkers and cyclists. Dogs are welcome in the bar and the atmosphere throughout is warm and cosy, with open fires in the winter and outside tables in summer. The food is all home cooked and sourced locally whenever possible, and there's a delicatessen on site. There's plenty of choice on the handwritten menu — from warm pigeon breast and sautéed wild mushroom bruschetta, to lamb curry; steamed game pudding; or cassoulet of belly pork, pancetta and Toulouse sausages.

Open all day all wk **Food** Lunch 12-2.30 Dinner 6-9.30 Av main course £8.50 Restaurant menu available Mon-Sat ⊕ FREE HOUSE ◀ Adnams Southwold Bitter & Broadside, Crouch Vale ♂ Aspall Harry Sparrow. **Facilities** Non-diners area ☻ (Bar Garden) ♦♦ Children's menu Children's portions Garden ⋈ Parking WiFi ➤ (notice required)

MOUNT BURES · Map 13 TL93

The Thatchers Arms

tel: 01787 227460 **Hall Rd CO8 5AT**
email: hello@thatchersarms.co.uk
dir: *From A12 onto A1124 towards Halstead. Right immediately after Chappel Viaduct. 2m, pub on right*

Bustling rural pub with well thought-out menus

There's something for all comers at this cheery country pub in the lovely Stour Valley, a perfect rural setting for weddings, birthdays and celebrations of all types in a function room and private patio area. Challenge the quoits beds in the beer garden, or ramble on paths that Constable may once have walked; the pub even hosts cinema nights, quiz nights and theatre productions. Popular with locals and visitors drawn to the real ales and interesting wines, delicious home-cooked dishes include rack of lamb, guinea fowl, scallops and the legendary Mars Bar cheesecake. Food allergy sufferers are well catered for.

Open all day all wk **Food** Lunch Mon-Fri 12-2.30, Sat 12-9, Sun 12-8 Dinner Mon-Fri 6-9, Sat 12-9, Sun 12-8 Set menu available Restaurant menu available all wk ⊕ FREE HOUSE ◀ Adnams Southwold Bitter, Crouch Vale Brewers Gold, Guest ales. ♈ 11 **Facilities** Non-diners area ❦ (Bar Restaurant Garden) ♦♦ Children's menu Children's portions Garden ⊞ Beer festival Parking WiFi ☞ (notice required)

MOUNTNESSING — Map 6 TQ69

The George & Dragon

tel: 01277 352461 **294 Roman Rd CM15 0TZ**
email: enquiry@thegeorgeanddragonbrentwood.co.uk
dir: In village centre

Flavoursome food in a laid-back gastro-pub

Spruced-up in true contemporary gastro-pub style, the interior of this 18th-century former coaching inn successfully blends bold artwork, colourful leather chairs and chunky modern tables with preserved original wooden floors, exposed beams and brick fireplaces. In this relaxed and convivial setting tuck into Mediterranean-inspired British dishes from an extensive menu that should please all tastes and palates. There are sharing platters, salads and pasta dishes, a selection of stone-baked pizzas and main courses like slow-cooked pork belly and seared scallops with sticky ginger beer glaze, crackling, black pudding and mash; or king prawn, crab and chorizo linguine.

Open all day all wk **Food** Lunch all wk 12-10 Dinner all wk 12-10 Av main course £15 Set menu available ⊕ MITCHELLS & BUTLERS ◀ Fuller's London Pride, St Austell Tribute Ȫ Aspall. ♈ 21 **Facilities** Non-diners area ❦ (Bar Garden Outside area) ♦♦ Children's menu Children's portions Garden Outside area ⊞ Parking WiFi ☞ (notice required)

NEWNEY GREEN — Map 6 TL60

The Duck Pub & Dining

tel: 01245 421894 **CM1 3SF**
email: theduckinn1@btconnect.com
dir: From Chelmsford take A1060 (Sawbridgeworth). Straight on at mini rdbt, 4th left into Vicarage Rd (signed Roxwell & Willingate), left into Hoe St, becomes Gravelly Ln, left to pub

Peace and quiet at a quintessential country inn

Formed from two agricultural cottages, this 17th-century inn is situated in the tiny hamlet of Newney Green. Fully restored by the current owners, the friendly Duck offers up to six real ales, including weekly guests, and menus that reflect the region's produce. Choose from the extensive menu in the beamed dining room, from classics like steak and ale pie and scampi and chips, to game casserole with dumplings, and lamb shank braised in honey and mint. Soak up the sun in the garden with its children's play area. There is an Summer Bank Holiday beer festival.

Open all day Closed Mon **Food** Lunch Tue-Sun 12-9.30 Dinner Tue-Sun 12-9.30 ⊕ FREE HOUSE ◀ Woodforde's Wherry, Adnams Broadside, Sharp's Doom Bar, Guest ales. ♈ 14 **Facilities** Non-diners area ♦♦ Children's menu Children's portions Play area Family room Garden ⊞ Beer festival Parking WiFi ☞

NORTH FAMBRIDGE — Map 7 TQ89

The Ferry Boat Inn

tel: 01621 740208 **Ferry Ln CM3 6LR**
email: ferryboatinn1@hotmail.com
dir: From Chelmsford take A130 S, then A132 to South Woodham Ferrers, then B1012. Turn right to village

Traditional riverside village inn

Believed to have been an inn for at least 200 years, the 500-year-old weatherboarded building was originally three fishermen's cottages. Known locally as the FBI, the pub sits beside a yacht haven on the River Crouch. Low beams and winter fires characterise the bars where pints of Greene King and Mighty Oak Maldon Gold are pulled. Food follows pub grub lines but is home-cooked and good value; look out for specials served all day, deals for OAPs, steaks on Tuesdays and curries on Thursdays. Next door is the 600-acre Essex Wildlife Trust nature reserve, a winter feeding ground for flocks of Brent geese.

Open all day all wk **Food** Lunch Mon-Thu 12-2.30, Fri-Sun all day Dinner Mon-Thu 6-8.30, Fri-Sun all day Av main course £8.95 ⊕ FREE HOUSE ◀ Greene King IPA & Abbot Ale, Mighty Oak Maldon Gold. **Facilities** Non-diners area ❦ (Bar Garden) ♦♦ Children's menu Children's portions Family room Garden Outside area ⊞ Parking WiFi ☞ (notice required)

PATTISWICK — Map 13 TL82

The Compasses at Pattiswick **PICK OF THE PUBS**

tel: 01376 561322 **Compasses Rd CM77 8BG**
email: info@thecompassesatpattiswick.co.uk
dir: A120 from Braintree towards Colchester. After Bradwell 1st left to Pattiswick

Destination pub, an ideal rural retreat

Years ago, two farm workers' cottages were amalgamated to form this friendly pub, still surrounded by the meadows and pocket woodlands of the Holifield Estate. The pub's owners source some of the raw materials for their menu direct from the estate. Support for local producers is at the centre of the pub's ethos, with minimising food miles being a guiding principle. Hearty rural recipes and uncomplicated cooking allow the dishes to do the talking. The main menu is supplemented by a daily specials board, allowing the chefs to take full advantage of seasonal produce. The dinner menu might feature toad-in-the-hole; Mediterranean vegetable linguine; and roast mutton shepherd's pie. The wine list is very comprehensive and features some exclusive Bordeaux and Burgundies. A roaring log fire makes a welcoming sight in winter after a local walk, while in summer the large garden is inviting. Families are very well catered for here, with a play area and toy box to keep little diners entertained.

Open all wk 11-3 5.30-11 (Sat 11-3 5.30-12 Sun 12-4) **Food** Lunch Mon-Sat 12-2.30, Sun 12-3 Dinner Mon-Thu 6-9.30, Fri-Sat 6-9.45 ⊕ FREE HOUSE ◀ Woodforde's Wherry, Adnams Southwold Bitter Ȫ Aspall. ♈ 13 **Facilities** Non-diners area ♦♦ Children's menu Children's portions Play area Garden Parking WiFi

Follow us on Facebook
www.facebook.com/TheAAUK
Find us on Facebook

PELDON
Map 7 TL91

The Peldon Rose

tel: 01206 735248 **Colchester Rd CO5 7QJ**
email: enquiries@thepeldonrose.co.uk
dir: On B1025 Mersea Rd, just before causeway

Historic inn, modern food

Contraband was once big business at this early 15th-century inn, understandably given its proximity to The Strood, which bridges the network of channels and creeks separating mainland Essex from Mersea Island. You can easily imagine the smugglers in the original-beamed bar with its leaded windows, but less so in the contemporary conservatory leading to the garden. A well-deserved reputation for good food begins with regularly changing menus offering dishes such as chicken and chorizo terrine; and beetroot-cured salmon as starters, and main courses of Thai-style vegetable linguine; Moroccan-style lamb tagine; and beer-battered fish and chips.

Open all day all wk Closed 25 Dec **Food** Lunch all wk 12-2.30 Dinner all wk 6-9 ⊕ FREE HOUSE ◀ Adnams Southwold Bitter, Woodforde's Wherry, IPA, Guest ales ♂ Aspall. ⬗ 15 **Facilities** Non-diners area ◀◀ Children's menu Children's portions Garden ⊨ Parking ➡ (notice required)

PURLEIGH
Map 7 TL80

NEW The Bell

tel: 01621 828348 **The Street CM3 6QJ**
email: kirsten@purleighbell.co.uk
dir: Between Chelmsford & Burnham-on-Crouch on B1010. (5m S of Maldon). In Purleigh, pub on top of hill adjacent to church

Some of the best views in Essex

A direct ancestor of George Washington is believed to have lived here in 1634 when he was the local rector. The building was old even then, going back to the 14th century. Purleigh Hill on which it stands is only 45 metres above sea level, but still high enough for sweeping views south. Drink Essex- and Suffolk brewed real ales or try neighbouring New Hall Vineyard's Sauvignon Blanc in the inglenook fireplace-warmed bar. Daily menus and weekly specials boards inspire with deep-fried camembert with cranberry sauce; guinea fowl with chasseur sauce; and monkfish with whisky provençale sauce. Check dates for the early Autumn beer festival.

Open 11.30-3 6-11 (Sat 12-4 6-11 Sun 12-5) Closed Sun eve, Mon **Food** Lunch Tue-Fri 12-2, Sat 12-2.30, Sun 12-4 Dinner Tue-Fri 7-9, Sat 6.30-9 Restaurant menu available ⊕ FREE HOUSE ◀ Crouch Vale Brewers Gold, Adnams IPA, Mighty Oak Captain Bob. ⬗ 13 **Facilities** Non-diners area ◀ (Bar Restaurant Garden) ◀◀ Children's menu Children's portions Garden ⊨ Beer festival Parking WiFi ➡ (notice required)

RICKLING GREEN
Map 12 TL52

The Cricketers Arms

tel: 01799 543210 **CB11 3YG**
email: info@thecricketersarmsricklinggreen.co.uk
dir: M11 junct 10, A505 E. 1.5m, right onto B1301, 2.2m, right onto B1383 at rdbt. Through Newport to Rickling Green. Right into Rickling Green Rd, 0.2m to pub, on left

Classic village green pub – perfect for cricket fans

Well-placed for Saffron Walden and Stansted Airport, this inn enjoys a peaceful position overlooking the village green and cricket pitch in sleepy Rickling Green. The rambling bar and dining rooms have a comfortable, contemporary feel, with squashy sofas by the log fire providing the perfect winter evening refuge for tucking into vegetarian tapas; locally caught rabbit with mustard sauce; Thai fishcake with clam broth; or oven baked whole sea bass with ginger and lemongrass cream. Arrive early on summer weekends to bag a table on the terrace – a popular spot in which to relax with a pint of Doom Bar and watch an innings or two.

Open all day all wk ⊕ PUNCH TAVERNS ◀ Sharp's Doom Bar, Woodforde's Wherry, Guest ale ♂ Westons Stowford Press. **Facilities** ◀ (Bar Outside area) ◀◀ Children's menu Children's portions Outside area Parking WiFi

SAFFRON WALDEN
Map 12 TL53

The Crown Inn ★★★ INN

tel: 01799 522475 **Little Walden CB10 1XA**
email: pippathecrown@aol.com **web:** www.thecrownlittlewalden.co.uk
dir: 2m from Saffron Walden on B1052

A family-friendly beamed country pub

The Crown's rural situation just outside the pretty market town of Saffron Walden makes it a good choice for local businessmen in need of a change of scene, and for families wanting to tire out children and dogs on one of the many walks in the surrounding countryside. Mums and dads can return for a well-earned glass of Adnams Broadside or a glass of wine, and hungry children can choose from the half dozen options on their dedicated menu. The short but reasonably priced menus embrace all the classic pub grub dishes. There's live jazz on Wednesday evenings.

Open all wk 11.30-2.30 6-11 (Sun 12-10.30) **Food** Lunch Mon-Sat 11.30-2, Sun 12-3 Dinner Tue-Sat 6.30-9 ⊕ FREE HOUSE ◀ Woodforde's Wherry, Adnams Broadside, Greene King Abbot Ale, Guest ales. **Facilities** Non-diners area ◀ (Bar Restaurant Outside area) ◀◀ Children's menu Children's portions Outside area ⊨ Parking WiFi ➡ (notice required) **Rooms** 3

Old English Gentleman

tel: 01799 523595 **11 Gold St CB10 1EJ**
email: goodtimes@oldenglishgentleman.com **web:** www.oldenglishgentleman.co.uk
dir: *M11 junct 9a, B184 signed Saffron Walden. Left at High St lights into George St, 1st right into Gold St (one-way system)*

A warm, friendly town-centre local

Regulars call Jeff and Cindy Leach's 19th-century, town centre pub the OEG, an informality which the top-hatted dandy on the sign over the front door might frown upon. Ancient beer taps line a wall of the central bar area, which extends into a dining space with a log-burner and air conditioning, while outside is a heated patio garden. Resident ales Adnams Southwold and Woodforde's Wherry are backed up by changing guests and Aspall cider; a portfolio that earns customers' respect. Hearty main meals include beer-battered catch of the day; OEG pie of the week; and sausages and mash. For a lighter bite try a panini or hand-cut sandwiches.

Open all day all wk **Food** Lunch all wk 12-2.30 ◀ Woodforde's Wherry, Adnams Southwold Bitter, 2 guest ales ◌ Aspall. ♀ 10 **Facilities** Non-diners area ♨ (Bar Outside area) ♦♦ Outside area ⊼ WiFi

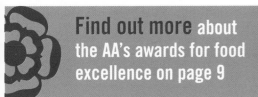

Find out more about the AA's awards for food excellence on page 9

See Little Canfield

NEW The Cock Public House

tel: 01279 812964 **30 Silver St CM24 8HD**
email: info@thecockatstansted.co.uk
dir: *Phone pub for detailed directions*

Family-run and proudly traditional

The Cock sits on a busy road running through Stansted Mountfitchet, but today's locals are given just the same warm welcome as their ancestors received when it opened for business back in the quieter 1800s. The pub hosts quizzes, live music and charity events, as well as private parties; Greene King ales and home-cooked pub food are its keys to success. Snacks include sandwiches, paninis and jackets, while a typical three-course choice could embrace chipotle chilli battered prawns; a build-your-own burger with a toppings selection of bacon, fried egg, onion rings, sautéed mushrooms, Stilton or brie; and home-made salted caramel brownie.

Open all day all wk **Food** Lunch Mon-Sat 12-2.30, Sun 12-6 Dinner Mon-Sat 6-9 Av main course £11 Set menu available Restaurant menu available all wk ⊕ GREENE KING ◀ IPA & Abbot, Morland Old Speckled Hen. ♀ 10 **Facilities** Non-diners area ♦♦ Children's menu Children's portions Play area Garden Outside area ⊼ Parking WiFi ⌨ (notice required)

The Hoop ®

tel: 01277 841137 **21 High St CM4 9BD**
email: thehoopstock@yahoo.co.uk **web:** www.thehoop.co.uk
dir: *On B1007 between Chelmsford & Billericay*

Traditional pub with a focus on food

This 15th-century free house on Stock's village green is every inch the traditional country pub, offering a warm welcome, authentic pub interiors and a pleasing absence of music and fruit machines. There's an emphasis on food here, with dishes ranging from traditional pie, mash and liquor to roast halibut with sticky oxtail, pan-fried cepes and Jerusalem artichoke. You could finish with lemon cake or crumble tart of the day. The annual beer festival (late May) has been going from strength to strength for over 30 years; you'll have over 100 real ales to choose from, not to mention fruit beers, perries and more.

Open all day all wk **Food** Lunch Mon-Fri 12-2.30, Sat 12-9.30, Sun 12-5 Dinner Mon-Thu 6-9, Fri 6-9.30, Sat 12-9.30 Av main course £10 Restaurant menu available Tue-Sat ⊕ FREE HOUSE ◀ Adnams Southwold Bitter, Crouch Vale Brewers Gold, Young's, Wibblers, Guest ales ◌ Thatchers Gold. ♀ 12
Facilities Non-diners area ♨ (Bar Garden) ♦♦ Children's portions Garden ⊼ Beer festival WiFi

WENDENS AMBO
Map 12 TL53

The Bell

tel: 01799 540382 **Royston Rd CB11 4JY**
email: thebellwenden@hotmail.com
dir: *Phone for detailed directions*

Traditional old English pub with beams galore

First mentioned in 1576 as a farm, evidence of its great age is everywhere, particularly the fine Elizabethan chimney stack. Other attributes include acres of gardens, a willow-edged pond, a woodland walk, play equipment, open fires and a resident ghost. Then there's the traditional country pub food, such as the hugely popular Bell beef and real ale pie; lamb Marrakesh; battered 'catch of the day'; and roasted vegetable and goats' cheese strudel. Cask ales and real ciders are always on tap. Ambo, incidentally, means 'both' in Latin and reflects a 17th-century merging of parishes. There's a beer festival over Summer Bank Holiday weekend.

Open all day Closed Mon L (winter) **Food** Lunch Tue-Thu 12-2, Fri-Sat 12-3, Sun 12-4 Dinner Tue-Sat 6-9 Set menu available ⊕ FREE HOUSE ◼ Woodforde's Wherry, Oakham Ales JHB, Adnams, Guest ales ♂ Thatchers Cheddar Valley.
Facilities Non-diners area ❖ (Bar Garden) ♦ Children's menu Children's portions Play area Garden ⋈ Beer festival Parking WiFi ⚏ (notice required)

WOODHAM MORTIMER
Map 7 TL80

Hurdlemakers Arms

tel: 01245 225169 **Post Office Rd CM9 6ST**
email: info@hurdlemakersarms.co.uk
dir: *From Chelmsford A414 to Maldon (Danbury). 4.5m, through Danbury into Woodham Mortimer. Over 1st rdbt, 1st left, pub on left. Behind golf driving range*

Family-run pub with a great beer festival

This pretty old village institution slumbers contentedly beside a lane in tranquil countryside just inland from Maldon's creeks and sea-marshes. Muscular posts and rippling beams inside hint at the age of the building, which is much older than its first licence in 1837. There's a simply enormous garden here, dappled with ancient fruit trees; an ideal location for their June beer festival. Year-round treats on the bar include beers from Dark Star and Wibblers, who also provide the local cider. The consummate menu covers all bases: pigeon pie; walnut and almond roast; and smoked haddock Florentine are typical choices on the locally sourced bill of fare.

Open all day all wk 12-11 (Sun 12-9) **Food** Lunch Mon-Fri 12-3, Sat 12-9.30, Sun 12-8 Dinner Mon-Fri 6-9.30, Sat 12-9.30, Sun 12-8 ⊕ GRAY & SONS ◼ Mighty Oak, Farmers, Wibblers, Dark Star, Guest ales ♂ Westons Old Rosie, Wibblers Dengie Cider. ⏍ 8 **Facilities** Non-diners area ♦ Children's menu Children's portions Play area Garden ⋈ Beer festival Parking WiFi ⚏

GLOUCESTERSHIRE

ALDERTON
Map 10 SP03

The Gardeners Arms

tel: 01242 620257 **Beckford Rd GL20 8NL**
email: gardeners1@btconnect.com
dir: *M5 junct 6, A46 towards Evesham. At rdbt take B4077 signed Stow. Left to Alderton*

Tapas, fresh fish and seasonal specials

Operating as a pub since the 16th century, this pretty, family-run, thatched free house is popular with walkers, cyclists and car clubs. You can play boules in the large beer garden, and traditional games in the stone-walled bar, where Cotswold Way numbers among the real ales. Menus change with the seasons, as you might expect from a pub with the word 'gardener' in its name. There's an early bird lunch menu, offering plenty of choice, as well as fresh fish and seasonal specials. The food is hearty and traditional, including the likes of lasagne, chilli con carne, lamb's liver and bacon, fish and chips, and beef topside with roasted turnips. Spring Bank Holiday and Boxing Day both kick off five-day beer festivals, while cider drinkers' turn is on the Summer Bank Holiday in August.

Open all wk 9.30-2.30 5.30-10 (Fri 9.30-2.30 5.30-12 Sat 9.30-2.30 5.30-10.30 Sun 10-9) Closed 3 days in Jan **Food** Lunch all wk 12-2 Dinner all wk 5.30-9 Av main course £9.95 Set menu available ⊕ FREE HOUSE ◼ Sharp's Doom Bar, Prescott Track Record, Wickwar Cotswold Way, Gloucester, Local guest ales ♂ Westons Stowford Press. **Facilities** Non-diners area ❖ (Bar Garden) ♦ Children's menu Children's portions Garden ⋈ Beer festival Cider festival Parking ⚏ (notice required)

ALMONDSBURY
Map 4 ST68

The Swan Hotel

tel: 01454 625671 **14 Gloucester Rd BS32 4AA**
email: garth@swanhotelbristol.com
dir: *M5 junct 16, A38 to Almondsbury*

Comfortable village pub with family-friendly food

On the outskirts of Bristol, parts of this former coaching inn date back to the 16th century and its hilltop position offers views across the Bristol Channel towards Wales. A family-friendly pub where children get their own menu (and half-size Sunday roasts), head chef Nigel Bissett champions local produce and keeps things interesting with Tuesday steak nights and Thursday seafood evenings. The daily menu might offer steak and mushroom suet pudding; honey-glazed ham hock with braised red cabbage and mustard mash; or grilled paneer and peppers with yogurt and spiced couscous. The pub holds a beer and cider festival in July.

Open all day all wk **Food** Lunch all wk 12-4 Dinner Mon-Sat 4-9.30, Sun 4-8.30 ⊕ MARSTON'S ◼ Pedigree, Wychwood Hobgoblin, Brakspear Oxford Gold ♂ Thatchers Gold & Cheddar Valley, Westons Stowford Press. ⏍ 12
Facilities Non-diners area ♦ Children's menu Children's portions Play area Garden ⋈ Beer festival Cider festival Parking WiFi ⚏ (notice required)

ARLINGHAM
Map 4 SO71

The Old Passage Inn ★★★★ RR ◉◉ PICK OF THE PUBS

See Pick of the Pubs on opposite page

PICK OF THE PUBS

The Old Passage Inn ★★★★★ RR ⚜️⚜️

ARLINGHAM   Map 4 SO71

tel: 01452 740547
Passage Rd GL2 7JR
email: oldpassage@btconnect.com
web: www.theoldpassage.com
dir: *A38 onto B4071 through Arlingham. Through village to river*

Famous for its seafood and river views

Overlooking the River Severn and set against the backdrop of the Forest of Dean, this was once the site of the ford across the River. This seafood restaurant-with-rooms on the riverbank once provided refreshment to ferry passengers across the tidal river but now attracts people from afar for its quality food and air of tranquillity. Eating in the open and airy dining room, or on the popular riverside terrace in summer is a delight. A selection of oysters and pre-starters such as deep-fried squid, passionfruit and chilli sauce, or soft shell crab with spicy kumquat jam act as a delicious curtain raiser to the main menu. Head chef Mark Redwood uses only the freshest fish and seafood and keeps things simple to let the ingredients shine, whether it's scallops from Looe or oysters from the Camel estuary. Dishes may include treacle-cured salmon,

pickled beetroot and stem ginger syrup; the lightly spiced zarzuela – a traditional Spanish fish stew; roast wild halibut, braised bok choi, celeriac purée, girolles and oxtail; or lobsters from the pub's own seawater tank – try one grilled with parsley and garlic butter. Carnivores will not be disappointed with seared breast of pigeon, celeriac gratin, pickled girolles and apple purée; and roast fillet of beef, braised oxtail, fondant potatoes and braised red cabbage. Leave room for the local Cerney Ash goats' cheese or chocolate brownie with yogurt ice cream. There's a six-course tasting menu too.

Open 10-3 7-close Closed 25 Dec, Jan-Feb Tue & Wed eve, Sun eve & Mon
Food Lunch Tue-Sat 12-2, Sun 12-3 Dinner Tue-Sat 7-9 Set menu available Restaurant menu available Tue-Sun
⊕ FREE HOUSE ♟ 12
FacilitiesNon-diners area ♟ Children's portions Garden ㅈ Parking WiFi
Rooms 3

ASHLEWORTH
Map 10 SO82

The Queens Arms
PICK OF THE PUBS

tel: 01452 700395 **The Village GL19 4HT**
dir: *From Gloucester N on A417 for 5m. At Hartpury, right at Broad St to Ashleworth. Pub 100yds past village green*

Rural free house offering an interesting menu

Set between rolling hills and the River Severn in a delightful rural village, this 16th-century inn is owned by Tony and Gill Burreddu. Although alterations have been made over the years, the original beams and iron fireplaces have been kept, simply complemented with comfortable armchairs, antiques and a gallery of local artists' work. As a free house, the Queens offers ales from a range of breweries including Brecon Brewing and Shepherd Neame. Tony and Gill have built a loyal customer base and an excellent reputation for imaginative dishes made from the best local produce. Specials board entries may include a starter of filo prawns in a sweet and sour sauce; a main course of Greek lamb studded with garlic and herbs, braised in rich red wine gravy and topped with mint yogurt; and Cape brandy pudding – a South African speciality made with light sponge and brandy-soaked dates.

Open 12-3 7-11 Closed 25-26 Dec, 1 Jan, Sun eve & Mon (ex BHs wknds)
Food Lunch Tue-Sun 12-2 Dinner Tue-Sat 7-9 ⊕ FREE HOUSE ◀ Timothy Taylor Landlord, Donnington BB, Brains The Rev. James, Shepherd Neame Spitfire, Sharp's Doom Bar, Brecon Brewing Gold Beacons Ŏ Westons Stowford Press. ♟ 14
Facilities Non-diners area ◗◗ Garden ⋒ Parking

BARNSLEY
Map 5 SP00

The Village Pub ★★★★★ INN ⊛
PICK OF THE PUBS

tel: 01285 740421 **GL7 5EF**
email: reservations@thevillagepub.co.uk **web:** www.thevillagepub.co.uk
dir: *On B4425 4m NE of Cirencester*

Non-touristy traditional local in an Area of Outstanding Natural Beauty

Surprising perhaps to find a Barnsley in the Cotswolds, although this one is far older than its Yorkshire namesake. The interior is warmly furnished and decorated, as befits the flagstones, oak floorboards, exposed timbers and open fireplaces. Also contributing to its appeal is a contemporary approach to English pub food, holder of an AA Rosette, with regularly-changing, largely locally-sourced menus. Vegetables, for example, come from 17th-century Barnsley House. Starters include Butts Farm Old Spots pork pie with home-made piccalilli; and Cornish scallops with quinoa, chorizo, capers and herb salad. Main course choices might include braised brisket with red cabbage and dauphinoise potato; whole Cotswold chicken, roast new potatoes, rosemary and bacon; and smoked haddock fishcakes, spinach and lemon butter sauce. A Welsh rarebit fritter bar snack goes well with a pint of Hooky bitter, an Ashton Press cider or one of the 10 wines by the glass.

Open all day all wk all wk 7am-11pm **Food** Lunch Mon-Fri 12-2.30, Sat-Sun 12-3 Dinner Mon-Thu 6-9.30, Fri-Sat 6-10, Sun 6-9 ⊕ FREE HOUSE ◀ Hook Norton Hooky Bitter, Butcombe Gold, Guest ales Ŏ Ashton Press. ♟ 10 **Facilities** Non-diners area ❧ (Bar Restaurant Outside area) ◗◗ Children's portions Outside area ⋒ Parking WiFi ▰ (notice required) **Rooms** 6

BERKELEY
Map 4 ST69

The Malt House ★★★ INN

tel: 01453 511177 **Marybrook St GL13 9BA**
email: the-malthouse@btconnect.com **web:** www.themalthouse.uk.com
dir: *M5 junct 13/14, A38 towards Bristol. Pub on main road towards Sharpness*

Village charm in the pretty Vale of Berkeley

At the heart of historic Berkeley, close to the remarkable castle and the Edward Jenner (the pioneer immunologist) Museum, this village free house is a popular place with walkers on the spectacular Severn Way along the nearby estuary shoreline; comfy accommodation and good food tempt overnight stops here. Ease into the copiously beamed old bar and consider a menu rich with modern British dishes – steak and ale pie; lamb shank; or halibut steak with sweet chilli dip will satisfy; there's a good vegetarian selection including nut roast, a specials board and a great sausage choice.

Open all wk Mon-Thu 6-11 (Fri 6-12 Sat 12-12 Sun 12-3) **Food** Lunch Sat-Sun 12-2 Dinner Mon-Sat 6.30-8.30 Av main course £10 ⊕ FREE HOUSE ◀ Theakston Best Bitter, Wickwar Cotswold Way Ŏ Westons Stowford Press, Thatchers Gold.
Facilities Non-diners area ◗◗ Children's menu Children's portions Garden ⋒ Parking WiFi ▰ (notice required) **Rooms** 9

BIBURY
Map 5 SP10

Catherine Wheel ★★★★ INN

tel: 01285 740250 **Arlington GL7 5ND**
email: info@catherinewheel-bibury.co.uk **web:** www.catherinewheel-bibury.co.uk
dir: On B4425, W of Bibury

Welcoming Cotswold inn offering a crowd-pleasing menu

The beautiful Cotswold-stone building, stable courtyard and orchard date back to the 15th century but plenty of historical features remain. This former blacksmith's has changed hands many times since J Hathaway opened it as an inn in 1856 but a warm welcome, a good selection of accredited ales such as Hook Norton and quality food remain its hallmarks. The appetising menu might include ham hock and chicken terrine; and Asian-marinated beef short ribs. Classics such as steak and red wine pie; and Gloucester Old Spots sausages and mash satisfy traditional tastes.

Open all day all wk 9am-11pm **Food** Lunch Mon-Fri 12-3, Sat 12-9.30, Sun 12-9 Dinner Mon-Fri 6-9.30, Sat 12-9.30, Sun 12-9 ⊕ FREE HOUSE/WHITE JAYS LTD ◀ Sharp's Doom Bar, Hook Norton Ö Westons Stowford Press, Aspall. ♈ 9 **Facilities** Non-diners area ♣ (Bar Garden) ♦ Children's menu Children's portions Garden ♒ Parking WiFi ☞ (notice required) **Rooms** 4

BIRDLIP
Map 10 SO91

The Golden Heart

tel: 01242 870261 **Nettleton Bottom GL4 8LA**
email: info@thegoldenheart.co.uk
dir: On A417 (Gloucester to Cirencester road). 8m from Cheltenham. Pub at base of dip in Nettleton Bottom

Traditional pub with some exotic dishes

A traditional 17th-century Cotswold-stone inn that was once a drovers' resting place, this lovely pub boasts stunning views of the valley from the terraced gardens. The main bar is divided into four cosy areas with log fires and traditional built-in settles. Excellent local ales and ciders are backed by a good selection of wines, while the extensive menus demonstrate commitment to local produce, particularly prize-winning meat from the region. Perhaps try salmon, sweet potato and coriander fishcake; or bubble-and-squeak with Gloucester Old Spots sausages. The more adventurous should aim for an exotic taster of croc, ostrich, kangaroo and camel meatball, or glazed kangaroo steak with sweet cranberry and honey. Vegetarian, vegan and gluten-free options are available.

Open all day all wk **Food** Lunch all wk 11-11 Dinner all wk 11-11 Av main course £11.95 ⊕ FREE HOUSE ◀ Otter Bitter, Cotswold Lion, Brakspear, Jennings, Flying Monk Ö Westons, Henney's, Thatchers. ♈ 10 **Facilities** Non-diners area ♣ (Bar Restaurant Garden) ♦ Children's portions Family room Garden ♒ Parking WiFi ☞

BISLEY
Map 4 SO90

NEW The Bear Inn

tel: 01452 770265 **George St GL6 7BD**
email: info@bisleybear.co.uk
dir: Phone pub for detailed directions

Striking 17th-century inn serving traditional food

David and Amanda Terry took over the Bear in December 2014, but there has been a pub here for almost 400 years. Stories and legends abound here and there is even a priest hole halfway up the inglenook fireplace. The pub's original character and charm is still evident, from the friendly bar serving pints of Butcombe beer to the dining room where food is traditional and comforting. If one of the weekly pie specials doesn't take your fancy, the likes of home-made beef madras; home-baked ham with fried eggs; and poached salmon fillet with chive and lemon sauce will.

Open all day all wk **Food** Lunch all wk 12-3 Dinner all wk 6-9 Av main course £10 ⊕ PUNCH TAVERNS ◀ Wells Bombardier & Golden, Butcombe, St Austell Tribute Ö Westons Stowford Press. **Facilities** Non-diners area ♣ (Bar Garden) ♦ Children's menu Children's portions Family room Garden ♒ Parking WiFi ☞ (notice required)

BLAISDON
Map 10 SO71

The Red Hart Inn

tel: 01452 830477 **GL17 0AH**
dir: Take A40 (NW of Gloucester) towards Ross-on-Wye. At lights left onto A4136 signed Monmouth. Left into Blaisdon Lane to Blaisdon

Village inn with tranquil country views

On the fringe of the Forest of Dean, this old whitewashed pub exudes the charm of a village local, all flagstoned floor, log fire, low beams and friendly pub dog to-boot. Four guest ales whet the whistle of passing ramblers, whilst those dining out will appreciate the quality pork raised by the pub's owners. Specials introduce dishes featuring venison or pheasant to the well-balanced menu, taken in the bar or restaurant. The sunny garden is a good place to sit with a glass of local cider.

Open all wk 12-3 6-11.30 (Sun 12.30-4 7-11) **Food** Lunch all wk 12-2.15 Dinner all wk 6.30-9 ⊕ FREE HOUSE ◀ Young's, Bespoke, 4 guest ales Ö Westons Stowford Press, Traditional & 1st Quality. **Facilities** Non-diners area ♣ (Bar Garden) ♦ Children's menu Children's portions Play area Garden ♒ Parking WiFi ☞ (notice required)

BLEDINGTON
Map 10 SP22

The Kings Head Inn ★★★★ INN ◉
PICK OF THE PUBS

tel: 01608 658365 **The Green OX7 6XQ**
email: info@kingsheadinn.net **web:** www.kingsheadinn.net
dir: On B4450, 4m from Stow-on-the-Wold

Sublime Cotswold free house

It's axiomatic that people make pubs – on both sides of the bar. They certainly do here. On one side, long-term owners Archie and Nicola Orr-Ewing; on the other, their customers, drawn by a reputation for well-kept real ales and top-quality, locally sourced food. Facing the village green, this stone-built pub dates back to the 15th century; it's been called the quintessential Cotswolds inn. Original structure survives in the low-beamed ceilings, flagstone floors, exposed stone walls and an inglenook fireplace. On the beer pumps, the labels of Hooky Bitter, Purity Gold and Wye Valley appear alongside local lagers; 10 wines are served by the glass. Among choices in the AA Rosette restaurant are deep-fried Windrush goats' cheese salad; vodka-and-tonic soft-shell crab; wood pigeon tart; seafood and saffron risotto; and Tamworth pork and black pudding burger. For dessert, how about affogato?

Open all day all wk Closed 25-26 Dec **Food** Lunch Mon-Fri 12-2, Sat-Sun 12-3 Dinner Sun-Thu 6.30-9, Fri-Sat 6.30-9.30 ⊕ FREE HOUSE ◀ Hook Norton Hooky Bitter, Purity Gold, Wye Valley, Butcombe, Butts, Bath Ales Ö Westons Stowford Press. ♈ 10 **Facilities** Non-diners area ♦ Children's menu Children's portions Garden ♒ Parking WiFi **Rooms** 12

BOURTON-ON-THE-HILL
Map 10 SP13

Horse and Groom
PICK OF THE PUBS

tel: 01386 700413 **GL56 9AQ**
email: greenstocks@horseandgroom.info
dir: *2m W of Moreton-in-Marsh on A44*

Elegant Georgian inn with views offering excellent locally-sourced food

The Greenstock brothers run this handsome Grade II listed Cotswold stone pub and it is both a serious dining destination and a friendly place for a drink. The building combines a contemporary feel with plenty of original period features and the mature garden is a must-visit in summer with its panoramic hilltop views. The beer selection mixes local brews such as Goffs Jouster and over 20 carefully selected wines are served by the glass. The blackboard menu changes daily, providing plenty of appeal for even the most ardent regulars. With committed local suppliers backed up by the pub's own abundant vegetable patch, the kitchen has plenty of good produce to work with. A typical menu might feature deep-fried salt and pepper squid with Vietnamese salad; griddled Dexter sirloin steak, garlic, parsley and shallot butter; or pan-fried John Dory fillet, sautéed spinach, brown shrimps and café de Paris butter; followed by vanilla gingernut cheesecake with spiced clementines.

Open 11-3 6-11 Closed 25 Dec, Sun eve **Food** Lunch all wk 12-2 Dinner Mon-Sat 7-9 ⊕ FREE HOUSE ◖ Wye Valley Bitter, Purity Pure UBU, Goffs Jouster, Cotswold Wheat Beer, Stroud Organic Ŏ Hogan's. ♟ 21 **Facilities** Non-diners area ⚬⦀ Children's portions Garden 舟 Parking WiFi

BROCKHAMPTON
Map 10 SP02

Craven Arms Inn

tel: 01242 820410 **GL54 5XQ**
email: cravenarms@live.co.uk
dir: *From Cheltenham take A40 towards Gloucester. In Andoversford, at lights, left onto A436 signed Bourton & Stow. Left, follow signs for Brockhampton*

Secluded village setting in fine walking country

Inside and out, this set-back, gabled old village inn glows with mellow honeyed stone; log fires, beams and mullioned windows add to the charm of its setting beneath the gently undulating horizon of the Cotswolds. Drinkers appreciate the selection of real ales; ciders and perry from regional orchards; and the mid-September beer festival. Diners can self-cook their fish and steaks on grill-stones at the table, or choose from the list of starters and bar meals. Here you may find smoked mackerel rillettes with crostini and pea shoot salad; and home-made monkfish tail scampi with chips, crushed peas and tartare sauce. There's a gluten-free menu too.

Open 12-3 6-11 Closed Sun eve & Mon **Food** Lunch Tue-Fri 12-2, Sat 12-2.30, Sun 12-3 Dinner Tue-Thu 6.30-9, Fri-Sat 6.30-9.30 ⊕ FREE HOUSE ◖ Otter, Butcombe Legless Bob Ŏ Westons Stowford Press, Dunkertons. ♟ 9 **Facilities** Non-diners area ⚬ (Bar Garden) ⦀ Children's menu Children's portions Garden 舟 Beer festival Parking WiFi ⟺ (notice required)

CHELTENHAM
Map 10 SO92

The Gloucester Old Spot

tel: 01242 680321 **Tewkesbury Rd, Piff's Elm GL51 9SY**
email: eat@thegloucesteroldspot.co.uk
dir: *On A4019 on outskirts of Cheltenham towards Tewkesbury*

Traditional pub with enthusiastic owners

Simon and Kate Daws own this free house and it ticks all the boxes with its quarry tile floors, roaring log fires, farmhouse furnishings and real ales such as Wye Valley; they also own another Cheltenham pub, The Royal Oak Inn. Local ciders and perries are on offer at the bar and there is an Early May Bank Holiday beer festival, too. The baronial dining room takes its inspiration from the local manor, and game and rare-breed pork make an appearance on a menu that includes pork mixed grill and slow roasted belly pork with braised pig cheek bourguignon; and Old Spots pork loin steak with hand-cut chips. The newly renovated gardens are just the place for enjoying a drink or lunch, or a perhaps a barbecue that is available for private groups.

Open all day all wk Closed 25-26 Dec **Food** Lunch Mon-Sat 12-2, Sun 12-8 Dinner Mon-Sat 6-9, Sun 12-8 Set menu available ⊕ FREE HOUSE ◖ Timothy Taylor Landlord, Purity Mad Goose, Wye Valley HPA & Butty Bach, Butcombe Bitter Ŏ Thatchers, Westons Stowford Press, Black Rat. **Facilities** Non-diners area ⚬ (Bar Garden) ⦀ Children's menu Children's portions Garden 舟 Beer festival Cider festival Parking WiFi ⟺ (notice required)

The Royal Oak Inn

tel: 01242 522344 **The Burgage, Prestbury GL52 3DL**
email: eat@royal-oak-prestbury.co.uk
dir: *From town centre follow signs for Winchcombe/Prestbury & Racecourse. In Prestbury follow brown signs for inn from Tatchley Ln*

Welcoming pub recommended for its beer and cider festivals

Close to Cheltenham's famous racecourse, this 16th-century pub was once owned by England cricket legend Tom Graveney. Current owners Simon and Kate, who have been here for over a decade, also own The Gloucester Old Spot, Cheltenham. Enjoy well-kept local cask ales, real ciders and delicious food in the snug, the comfortable dining room or the heated patio overlooking a pretty beer garden. Menus include king prawns, wood pigeon, slow-cooked pork belly and Cotswold game sausages. There is a beer and sausage festival on the Spring Bank Holiday and a cider festival on the Summer Bank Holiday.

Open all day all wk Closed 25 Dec **Food** Lunch Mon-Sat 12-2, Sun 12-8 Dinner Mon-Sat 6-9, Sun 12-8 Av main course £14 ⊕ FREE HOUSE ◖ Timothy Taylor Landlord, Purity Mad Goose, Butcombe Bitter Ŏ Thatchers, Westons Stowford Press, Sandford Orchards Devon Red. **Facilities** Non-diners area ⦀ Children's menu Children's portions Garden 舟 Beer festival Cider festival Parking WiFi

CHIPPING CAMPDEN
Map 10 SP13

The Bakers Arms

tel: 01386 840515 **Broad Campden GL55 6UR**
email: lutti.asf@live.co.uk
dir: *1m from Chipping Campden*

Sublime Cotswold pub with friendly welcome

Ease into the compact little bar here, squeeze into a space near the eye-catching inglenook and live the Cotswold dream, with local Stanney Bitter mirroring the colour of the mellow thatched stone cottages in this picture-postcard hamlet. The patio, terrace and garden are all ideal on summer evenings in this most tranquil spot, lost amidst lanes and tracks below tree-fringed hilltops. The traditional, well-considered menu may offer a creamy beetroot risotto starter with chicken, ham and leek pie or lamb shank to follow; the intimate dressed-stone walled restaurant area is a peaceful retreat from the popular bar.

Open 11.30-2.30 5.30-close (Fri-Sat 11.30-11 Sun 12-10.30) Closed 25 Dec, Mon L (ex BH) **Food** Lunch Tue-Sat 12-2, Sun 12-3 Dinner Mon-Thu 6-8.30, Fri-Sat 6-9 ⊕ FREE HOUSE ◖ Stanway Stanney Bitter, Wickwar, Wye Valley, North Cotswold Windrush Ŏ Thatchers Heritage. **Facilities** Non-diners area ⚬ (Bar Garden) ⦀ Children's menu Children's portions Play area Garden 舟 Parking WiFi ⟺ (notice required)

PICK OF THE PUBS

Seagrave Arms ★★★★ RR ❀❀

CHIPPING CAMPDEN   Map 10 SP13

tel: 01386 840192 **Friday St, Weston Subedge GL55 6QH**
email: enquiries@theseagravearms.com
web: www.seagravearms.co.uk
dir: *From Moreton-in-Marsh A44 towards Evesham. 7m, right onto B4081 to Chipping Campden. Left at junct with High St. 0.5m, straight on at x-rds to Weston Subedge. Left at T-junct*

Prime Cotswold country inn where quality counts

In mid-2014, Cirrus Inns acquired this handsome Georgian inn. Built as a farmhouse around 1740 and Grade II listed, the four-square building in Cotswold stone is approached between a display of neatly trimmed, globe-shaped bushes in stone planters. Briefly closed for a sympathetic restoration, it re-opened under the new management of Hannah Brown and Newstead Sayer. The previously large restaurant/bar combination has been reconfigured so that the bar has its own space; here you'll find real ales from Hook Norton and guest breweries, and the recently introduced 3Cs cider from Northampton. The same menu is served in the bar and the restaurant, and a garden and sheltered courtyard offer alfresco dining options. Local sourcing and sustainability are the basic tenets behind compact seasonal menus. Expect asparagus from Evesham, pork

from Gloucester Old Spots pigs, local venison, Dexter beef and Cotswold lamb; pheasant, wild duck and partridge are delivered after winter shoots. A typical choice could begin with a Salcombe Bay crab with avocado, quail egg and crab mayonnaise. Next, Cotswold white chicken with mash, mushrooms, peas, winter truffle and smoked almond. Finish with a classic apple tart made with slow-cooked Cox's apples, puff pastry and served with vanilla ice cream. A board of regional cheeses may display Lincolnshire Poacher, St Eadburgha from Gorsehill Abbey, and the award-winning Oxford Blue. Chalk boards offer pub classics and specials. Pie lovers should arrange their visit for a Monday evening when this great British favourite is celebrated — a range

of different home-made pies served with chips or mash for a bargain price.

Open all day all wk **Food** Lunch Mon-Fri 12-2.30, Sat 12-9.30, Sun 12-8 Dinner Mon-Sat 6-9.30, Sat 12-9.30, Sun 12-8 ⊕ CIRRUS INNS ◼ Hook Norton, Guest ale ♂ The Orchard Pig, 3Cs Vintage Cider. ♟ 11 **Facilities** Non-diners area ❧ (Bar Garden) ♦♦ Children's menu Children's portions Garden ⩎ Parking WiFi **Rooms** 8

CHIPPING CAMPDEN *continued*

Eight Bells
PICK OF THE PUBS

tel: 01386 840371 **Church St GL55 6JG**
email: neilhargreaves@bellinn.fsnet.co.uk
dir: *In town centre*

Tranquil town inn with finest Cotswold hospitality

There's a golden glow both inside and outside of this glorious, hanging basket bedecked Cotswold inn. The mellow Ham stone was recycled about 400 years ago from an earlier inn, which originated in medieval times when the set of church bells was stored here prior to hanging. The cobbled entranceway leads into two beamed bars with open fireplaces and, in the floor of one, a surviving priest's hole; rough-hewn stone walls add further period character. Outside is an enclosed courtyard and terraced garden overlooking the almshouses and church. Beers such as Goffs Jouster and Hook Norton Hooky are sourced from the Cotswolds; in a similar vein the produce of these limestone hills and vales is used in many of the seasonally-adjusted dishes from the kitchen. Anticipate roasted loin of Gloucester Old Spots pork with all the trimmings; or seared lamb's liver on bubble-and-squeak with rich onion gravy. A specials board includes fish and seafood dishes.

Open all day all wk 12-11 (Sun 12-10.30) Closed 25 Dec **Food** Lunch Mon-Thu 12-2, Fri-Sat 12-2.30, Sun 12-9 Dinner Mon-Thu 6.30-9, Fri-Sat 6.30-9.30, Sun 12-9 ⊕ FREE HOUSE ◀ Hook Norton Hooky Bitter, Purity Pure UBU & Gold, Goffs Jouster, Wye Valley HPA Ö Westons Old Rosie & Family Reserve. ☂ 8
Facilities Non-diners area ♣ (Bar Garden) ♦ Children's menu Children's portions Garden ♒ WiFi ➡ (notice required)

The Kings ★★★★ RR ◉◉
PICK OF THE PUBS

tel: 01386 840256 **The Square GL55 6AW**
email: info@kingscampden.co.uk **web:** www.kingscampden.co.uk
dir: *Phone for detailed directions*

Wide choice of dining options in charming town centre pub

Facing the square of one of England's prettiest towns, this sympathetically restored old townhouse is packed with character, the oldest parts including the 16th-century stone mullioned windows on the first floor. The bar offers at least two real ales, including local North Cotswold Windrush, as well as daily papers and traditional pub games, but no noisy gaming machines. Bar snacks include a good range of sandwiches and baguettes, while main meals are served in the informal bar

brasserie or more formal AA Rosette restaurant overlooking the square. The packed menu offers some imaginative delights: pressed ham hock roulade, pickled vegetables and Scotch quail's egg; fillet of pollock, violet potato gnocchi, samphire, saffron and crab velouté; and chargrilled vegetable tian with mozzarella arancini. The large grassed garden and dining terrace is surprising to find in a town centre pub. Individually decorated bedrooms offer period features with plenty of modern comforts too.

Open all day all wk 7am-11pm (Sat-Sun 8am-11pm) **Food** Lunch all wk 12-2.30 Dinner all wk 6.30-9.30 Av main course £12.50 Set menu available Restaurant menu available all wk ⊕ FREE HOUSE ◀ Hook Norton Hooky Bitter, North Cotswold Windrush Ö Thatchers Gold. ☂ 10 **Facilities** Non-diners area ♦ Children's menu Children's portions Garden Outside area ♒ Parking WiFi ➡ (notice required) **Rooms** 19

Noel Arms Hotel
PICK OF THE PUBS

tel: 01386 840317 **High St GL55 6AT**
email: reception@noelarmshotel.com
dir: *On High St, opposite Town Hall*

Delightful inn with its own curry club

The Noel Arms is one of the oldest hotels in the Cotswolds, a place where traditional appeal has been successfully preserved and interwoven seamlessly with contemporary comforts. Charles II reputedly stayed in this golden Cotswold-stone 16th-century coaching inn. It was through the carriage arch that packhorse trains used to carry bales of wool, the source of Chipping Campden's prosperity, to Bristol and Southampton. Absorb these details of the hotel's history while sipping a pint of Butty Bach in front of the log fire in Dover's Bar; read the papers over a coffee and pastry in the coffee shop; and enjoy brasserie-style food in the restaurant. An alternative to the modern English dishes is brought by Indunil Upatissa who creates his trademark curries daily, and enthusiasts arrive for his Curry Club on the last Thursday evening of every month.

Open all day all wk **Food** Lunch all wk 12-2 Dinner all wk 6-9.30 ⊕ FREE HOUSE ◀ Wye Valley Butty Bach, Noel Arms Ale (pub's own), Guest ale Ö Westons Stowford Press. ☂ **Facilities** Non-diners area ♣ (Bar) ♦ Children's menu Children's portions Outside area ♒ Parking WiFi ➡

Seagrave Arms ★★★★ RR ◉◉
PICK OF THE PUBS

See Pick of the Pubs on page 199

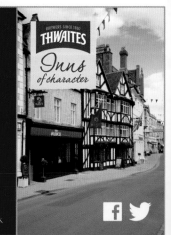

The Volunteer Inn

tel: 01386 840688 **Lower High St GL55 6DY**
email: info@thevolunteerinn.net
dir: *From Shipston on Stour take B4035 to Chipping Campden*

Cotswold character and cuisine with a twist

The beautiful, honey-coloured Cotswold stone glowing beside Chipping Campden's main street continues within; the convivial, log-fire warmed stone floored bar a welcoming retreat for guests hunting through the town's antique shops or pausing on a stroll along the Cotswold Way footpath. Once a recruiting centre for volunteer militia, today's clients sign on for some very interesting dishes from the Maharaja Restaurant located here. As well as traditional dishes like dhansak, bhuna, jalfrezi and so on, there are less well known options like nowabi lamb, jalil hash, begun bhari and moglai chicken. The grassy beer garden is a quiet town centre retreat.

Open all wk Mon-Thu 3-12 (Fri-Sun 11am-late) **Food** Contact pub for food times ⊕ FREE HOUSE ◀ Sharp's Doom Bar Ö Westons Stowford Press.
Facilities Non-diners area ◀ Children's portions Play area Family room Garden WiFi ➡ (notice required)

CIRENCESTER Map 5 SP00

The Crown of Crucis ★★★ HL **PICK OF THE PUBS**

tel: 01285 851806 **Ampney Crucis GL7 5RS**
email: reception@thecrownofcrucis.co.uk **web:** www.thecrownofcrucis.co.uk
dir: *On A417 to Lechlade, 2m E of Cirencester*

Quintessential Cotswold coaching inn

Five minutes' drive out of Cirencester will bring you to this 16th-century former coaching inn; it overlooks a cricket green, and Ampney Brook meanders past its lawns. Its name is derived from the 'crucis' or ancient cross in the churchyard. Although modernised, the interior still feels old, and the traditional beams and log fires create a warm, friendly atmosphere. Atlantic and Wickwar are among the real ales, along with some 17 wines served by the glass. Sandwiches, salads, pastas and grills are served from midday, while in the evening the restaurant's dinner menu proffers popular pub dishes such as starters of breaded whitebait with salad and tartare sauce; or smoked mackerel pâté with toasted home-made brioche. Move on to a special of herb-crusted cod loin with spring onion and pea risotto and tomato salsa; or a dish from the chargrill stove: pan-fried calves' liver with crispy bacon, bubble-and-squeak cake and Madeira sauce.

Open all day all wk Closed 25 Dec **Food** Lunch all wk 12-5 Dinner all wk 5-10 Av main course £12.95 ⊕ FREE HOUSE ◀ Crown Bitter, Sharp's Doom Bar & seasonal ales, Wickwar, Atlantic Ö Westons Stowford Press. ♟ 17
Facilities Non-diners area ✿ (Bar Garden) ◀ Children's menu Children's portions Garden ⋔ Parking WiFi ➡ (notice required) **Rooms** 25

The Fleece at Cirencester ★★★★★ INN

tel: 01285 658507 **41 Dyer St, Market Place GL7 2NZ**
email: relax@thefleececirencester.co.uk **web:** www.thefleececirencester.co.uk
dir: *In centre of Cirencester*

Cotswold dining pub with royal links

This is a 17th-century coaching inn, once visited by Charles II. The bar, restaurant and lounge retain their original charms with wooden beams, a log fire and an outdoor courtyard for long summer days. A range of Thwaites beers are on offer at the bar, including Lancaster Bomber, and the extensive menu features deli boards; chargrilled steaks; and mains of roasted butternut squash risotto; or blade of beef cooked in ale with parsnip and potato mash. There are 28 bedrooms if you want to extend your visit and explore the Cotswolds.

Open all day all wk **Food** Lunch all wk 12-6 Dinner Mon-Sat 6-9.30, Sun 6-8.30 ⊕ THWAITES INNS OF CHARACTER ◀ Wainwright, Lancaster Bomber & Signature Ales, Guest ales Ö Westons Stowford Press. ♟ 10 **Facilities** Non-diners area ✿ (Bar Outside area) ◀ Children's menu Children's portions Outside area ⋔ Parking WiFi **Rooms** 28

See advert on opposite page

CLEARWELL
Map 4 SO50

The Wyndham Arms ★★★ HL ◉

tel: 01594 833666 **The Cross GL16 8JT**
email: dine@thewyndhamhotel.co.uk **web:** www.thewyndhamhotel.co.uk
dir: *M4 junct 21 onto M48 for Chepstow. Exit at junct 2 signed A48/Chepstow. At rdbt take A48 towards Gloucester. Take B4228 to Coleford & The Forest of Dean. 10m, through St Briavels, in 2m Clearwell signed on left*

Cosy hotel between the Forest of Dean and the Wye Valley

Open log-burners and oak flooring create the sort of rustic charm that's ideal for enjoying a pint of Kingstone's real ales, brewed at nearby Tintern, or Severn Sider Cider from Newnham. In the domed stone vaults of the Old Spot Country Restaurant, the AA has awarded a Rosette for the classic British food, as in smoked fish pâté and potato salad; Wyndham raised Gloucester Old Spots ham and turkey pie; liver and bacon, onion gravy and crushed potatoes; bread and butter pudding; and apple crumble and custard. Staying in Wyndham's accommodation is perfect for those visiting Clearwell Castle, a popular wedding venue.

Open all day all wk Closed 1st wk Jan **Food** Lunch Mon-Sat 12-2, Sun 12-2.30 Dinner all wk 6.30-9 Restaurant menu available all wk ⊕ FREE HOUSE ◀ Kingstone Humpty's Fuddle IPA, Kingstone Gold Fine Ale ☼ Severn Sider Cider. ☂ 10 **Facilities** Non-diners area ☙ (Bar Outside area) ♦ Children's menu Children's portions Outside area ⅁ Parking WiFi **Rooms** 18

CLEEVE HILL
Map 10 SO92

The Rising Sun ★★★ INN

tel: 01242 676281 **GL52 3PX**
email: 9210@greeneking.co.uk **web:** www.oldenglish.co.uk
dir: *On B4632, 4m N of Cheltenham*

Hilltop inn offering stunning vistas

On a clear day you can see south Wales from this Victorian property on Cleeve Hill, which also boasts views across Cheltenham and the Malverns. Whether you are staying overnight or just popping in to relax, settle in the nicely modernised bar or, in summer, out in the garden, which is well furnished with trestle tables and benches. The wide ranging menu includes sandwiches, wraps, ciabattas, steaks and grills, burgers, jacket potatoes and roasts on Sundays.

Open all day all wk ⊕ GREENE KING ◀ IPA, Abbot Ale ☼ Aspall. **Facilities** ♦ Children's menu Children's portions Family room Garden Parking WiFi **Rooms** 24

CLIFFORD'S MESNE
Map 10 SO72

The Yew Tree
PICK OF THE PUBS

tel: 01531 820719 **GL18 1JS**
email: unwind@yewtreeinn.com **web:** www.yewtreeinn.com
dir: *From Newent High Street follow signs to Clifford's Mesne. Pub at far end of village on road to Glasshouse*

Hidden pub with great views and glorious home cooking

You may need to rely on the Sat Nav to find this former cider press tucked away down a little lane. It's on the slopes of May Hill (National Trust), Gloucestershire's highest point, from which the Welsh mountains, the Malvern Hills and the River Severn can all be seen on a clear day. The pub has a quarry-tiled floor warmed by log fires in winter. A good choice of real ales from breweries like Gloucester and Sharp's is backed by an excellent range of ciders. As for the food, the emphasis is on tasty home cooking using seasonal local produce, with daily-changing menus and specials. Starters could include hot crab pot with warm toast; and goujons of pheasant with redcurrant dip. House specialities are beef Wellington; and a seafood skillet comprising salmon, tuna, sea bass, tiger prawns and mussels served with

savoury rice and hand-cut chips. Puddings such as treacle and pecan tart are home made. Beer and cider festival in October.

The Yew Tree

Open 12-2.30 6-11 (Sun 12-5) Closed Mon, Tue L, Sun eve **Food** Lunch Wed-Sat 12-2, Sun 12-4 Dinner Tue-Sat 6-9 Av main course £16 ⊕ FREE HOUSE ◀ Wye Valley HPA, Cotswold Spring Stunner, Sharp's Own, Gloucester Mariner, Local ales ☼ Westons Stowford Press, Lyne Down, Severn Cider & Perry, Swallowfield Cider & Perry, Three Choirs. ☂ 12 **Facilities** Non-diners area ☙ (Bar Restaurant Garden) ♦ Children's menu Children's portions Play area Garden ⅁ Beer festival Cider festival Parking WiFi

COATES
Map 4 SO90

The Tunnel House Inn
PICK OF THE PUBS

tel: 01285 770280 **Tarlton Rd GL7 6PW**
email: info@tunnelhouse.com
dir: *A433 from Cirencester towards Tetbury, 2m, right towards Coates, follow brown inn signs*

Delightfully timeless Cotswold village inn

Built for the navvies who spent five years constructing the two-mile long Sapperton Tunnel, this rural inn overlooks the entrance to the tunnel which hasn't been navigated by a barge since 1911. Three winter log fires warm the curio-filled bar, where oddities include an upside-down table suspended from the ceiling. Food, all home cooked, is served every day from noon onwards and you may eat in the bar or restaurant, starting perhaps with prawns and smoked salmon platter, followed by wild mushroom risotto. The garden is tailor-made for relaxing with a pint of one of the mostly local real ales – typically from Uley, Wye Valley and Hook Norton breweries – or a Somerset or Herefordshire real cider, while enjoying the views over the fields. A children's play area and delightful walks add to the pub's popularity.

Open all day all wk noon-late ⊕ FREE HOUSE ◀ Uley Old Spot & Bitter, Wye Valley Bitter, Stroud Budding Pale Ale, Hook Norton, Butcombe ☼ Healey's Cornish Rattler, Black Rat, Westons Wyld Wood Organic. **Facilities** ☙ (All areas) ♦ Children's menu Children's portions Play area Family room Garden Outside area Parking WiFi

COLD ASTON
Map 10 SP11

NEW The Plough Inn

tel: 01451 822602 **GL54 3BN**
email: hello@coldastonplough.com
dir: *In village centre*

Country pub enjoying a new lease of life

Locals Nick and Laura Avery bought the 17th-century Plough in 2012 and embarked on a much-needed restoration that, while fully respecting the period charm of its Cotswold flagstones, oak beams and big open fire, has left it looking very smart ndeed. Rotating real ales, such as local Stroud Budding, are served from casks, and there are real ciders, too. Try devilled lamb's kidneys on toast; followed by Gloucester Old Spots sausages, mash and onion gravy; or beer-battered haddock, chips and crushed peas; then custard tart, nutmeg and fresh summer berries. A charcoal oven cooks perfect steaks and fish.

Open 12-3 6-11 (Sat-Sun all day) Closed 1-16 Jan, Mon Food Lunch Tue-Sun 12-3 Dinner Tue-Sun 6.30-9 ⊕ FREE HOUSE ◀ Cotswold Spring Stunner, Stroud Budding, Wye Valley Butty Bach ♂ Aspall Spadger, Orchard Pig Reveller. Facilities Non-diners area ❤ (Bar Restaurant Outside area) ♦ Children's portions Outside area ㅈ Parking WiFi ▄ (notice required)

COLEFORD
Map 4 SO51

NEW The Dog & Muffler

tel: 01594 832444 Joyford, Berry Hill GL16 7AS
dir: Phone pub for detailed directions

Traditional food in the heart of the forest

Set in the ancient and beautiful Forest of Dean, where wild boar and deer roam free, The Dog & Muffler was once a cider house with its own orchard and cider press; the press can still be found in the large garden. Once a favourite watering hole of playwright Dennis Potter, visitors can now mingle with locals supping pints of Wye Valley ale or one of several ciders on offer. Traditional, home-cooked food includes beef lasagne, barbecue ribs, curry of the day and prize-winning pies served with double-cooked chips and peas.

Open 12-3.30 6-11.30 Closed Mon Food Lunch Tue-Sun 12-3 Dinner Tue-Sun 6-9.30 Av main course £7.95 Restaurant menu available Tue-Sun ⊕ FREE HOUSE ◀ Wye Valley Butty Bach, Sharp's Doom Bar ♂ Westons Stowford Press, Lilley's Apples & Pears. ♚ 10 Facilities Non-diners area ❤ (Bar Restaurant Garden) ♦ Children's menu Children's portions Garden ㅈ Parking ▄ (notice required)

COLESBOURNE
Map 10 SP01

The Colesbourne Inn

tel: 01242 870376 GL53 9NP
email: colesbourneinn@wadworth.co.uk
dir: Midway between Cirencester & Cheltenham on A435

Georgian country inn full of character

This handsome, stone-built inn is just a short meadow walk from the source of the Thames; you can sit in the two-acre grounds with a pint of Wadworth 6X and Swordfish and savour the glorious country views. Dating back to 1827, the inn oozes historic charm and character with its original beams and roaring log fires aplenty. The seasonal menus combine traditional pub classics, including ham, egg and chips, with modern ideas, perhaps Puy lentil, chickpea and sweet potato curry; lamb and mint burger on a toasted brioche bun with goats' cheese and red onion relish; or duck leg with a port, blackberry and thyme sauce.

Open all day all wk Food Lunch Mon-Sat 12-9.30, Sun 12-8 Dinner Mon-Sat 12-9.30, Sun 12-8 Av main course £13.95 Set menu available Restaurant menu available all wk ⊕ WADWORTH ◀ 6X, Horizon & Swordfish ♂ Westons Stowford Press. ♚ 20 Facilities Non-diners area ❤ (Bar Garden) ♦ Children's portions Garden ㅈ Parking WiFi ▄ (notice required)

COWLEY
Map 10 SO91

The Green Dragon Inn ★★★★ INN   PICK OF THE PUBS

See Pick of the Pubs on page 204

CRANHAM
Map 10 SO81

The Black Horse Inn

tel: 01452 812217 GL4 8HP
dir: A46 towards Stroud, follow signs for Cranham

A great rest-stop for walkers

Near the Cotswold Way and the Benedictine Prinknash Abbey, in a small village surrounded by woodland and commons, this inn is popular with walkers, the cricket team and visiting Morris dancers. Mostly home-cooked traditional pub food includes grilled lamb chops; roast pork, beef or turkey; kleftiko (half-shoulder of slow-cooked lamb in red wine, lemon and herbs); haggis and bacon; fresh trout with garlic and herb butter; and roast vegetable, cranberry and goats' cheese nut roast. Among the real ales are Stroud Tom Long, Sharp's and Otter, and there are good ciders too in the cosy, open-fire-warmed bar.

Open 12-2 6.30-11 (Sun 12-2 8.30-11) Closed 25 Dec, Mon (ex BHs L) Food Lunch Tue-Sun 12-2 Dinner Tue-Sun 6.30-9 ⊕ FREE HOUSE ◀ Sharp's Doom Bar, Otter, Stroud Tom Long, Guest ales ♂ Thatchers Gold & Cheddar Valley, Westons Stowford Press & Country Perry. ♚ 8 Facilities Non-diners area ❤ (Bar Outside area) ♦ Children's portions Outside area ㅈ Parking ▄ (notice required)

PICK OF THE PUBS

The Green Dragon Inn ★★★★ INN

COWLEY Map 10 SO91

tel: 01242 870271
Cockleford GL53 9NW
email: green-dragon@buccaneer.co.uk
web: www.green-dragon-inn.co.uk
dir: *Phone for detailed directions*

Cotswolds inn featuring Mouseman furniture

With a pretty rose- and creeper-covered Cotswold-stone façade, this building was recorded as an inn in 1675. However, it was 1710 before Robert Jones, a churchwarden, became the first landlord, splitting his time between pew and pump for the next 31 years. In summer the secluded patio garden overlooking a lake is an obvious spot to head for. Step inside the stone-flagged Mouse Bar and you will notice that each piece of English oak furniture features a carved mouse, the trademark of Robert Thompson, the Mouseman of Kilburn. He died in 1955, but North Yorkshire craftsmen continue the tradition. There's even one of the little beggars running along the edge of the bar in front of the Butcombe, Hook Norton and Sharp's beer pumps. Lunchtime light meals and sandwiches can be served on the patio, weather permitting. An evening dinner starter could be spicy lamb kofta meatballs with banana curry

sauce; or chilled tian of crabmeat, risotto rice and avocado with lemon and chive yogurt. Steak and kidney pudding, home-made minted mushy peas with fries or new potatoes; or Dimity pie (farmhouse cheddar, parsnip, apple, onion and potato) with a green salad could follow. Children are catered for with a range of favourites. The comfortable and individually furnished en suite bedrooms, and the St George's Suite (which has its own sitting room overlooking Cowley lakes), make the Green Dragon an ideal base for exploring the Cotswolds; the local Miserden Gardens and Chedworth Roman Villa should not be missed.

Open all day all wk Closed 24 Dec eve, 25 Dec eve & 1 Jan eve **Food** Lunch Mon-Fri 12-2.30, Sat 12-3, Sun 12-3.30 Dinner all wk 6-9.30 Av main course £15 ⊕ FREE HOUSE/BUCCANEER
◄ Hook Norton, Butcombe, Sharp's Doom Bar, Guest ale ♨ Westons Stowford Press. ⬤ 12
Facilities Non-diners area ⊪ Children's menu Outside area ⊼ Parking WiFi ⊞
Rooms 9

DUNTISBOURNE ABBOTS
Map 4 SO90

NEW Five Mile House

tel: 01285 821432 **Old Gloucester Rd GL7 7JR**
email: thefivemilehouse@gmail.com
dir: On A417 between Air Balloon rdbt (E of Gloucester) & Cirencester. Take slip road signed Services & Duntisbourne Abbots, pub on left

Appealing mix of historic buildings and modern dining

This Grade II listed 17th-century coaching inn has an original bar and tap room furnished with rare high-backed settles. Here hang photographs of the Ruck family, who ran the pub for 100 years until landlady Ivy Ruck died in 1995; the Snug was Ivy's sitting room and now gives additional dining space. Open fires in both bar and restaurant warm the cockles in winter months. Chef/proprietor Stephen Rawicki presents carefully prepared modern cosmopolitan dishes such as artichoke and wild mushroom risotto with shaved Manchego. The garden room, originally the cellar, opens out to the back, where a seating area enjoys splendid views over rolling Cotswold countryside.

Open 11-2.30 5.30-11 (Sat 11-11 Sun 11-9.30) Closed Mon **Food** Lunch Tue-Fri 12-2.30, Sat 12-9, Sun 12-5 Dinner Tue-Fri 6-9, Sat 12-9 Restaurant menu available Tue-Sun ⊕ FREE HOUSE ◀ Hook Norton Hooky Bitter, Timothy Taylor Landlord. **Facilities** Non-diners area ❖ (Bar Garden) ◀◀ Children's portions Garden ⌂ Parking WiFi ▬ (notice required)

DURSLEY
Map 4 ST79

The Old Spot Inn
PICK OF THE PUBS

tel: 01453 542870 **Hill Rd GL11 4JQ**
email: enquiries@oldspotinn.co.uk
dir: From Tetbury on A4135 (or Uley on B4066) into Dursley, round Town Hall. Straight on at lights towards bus station, pub behind bus station. Or from Cam to lights in Dursley immediately prior to pedestrianised street. Right towards bus station

Excellent beer at popular village local

This classic 18th-century free house is a real ale champion, so it's worth a visit to sample the tip-top brews on handpump, and to savour the cheerful buzzing atmosphere. It sits smack on the Cotswold Way, and is formed from three terraced farm cottages known as 'pig row'. It's apt, then, that it should derive its name from the Gloucester Old Spots pig. Ale festivals are held in May and October. The one in May also showcases ciders, and fans of fermented apple juice will always find an excellent selection at the bar. Devoid of modern-day intrusions, the rustic and traditional low-beamed bars are havens of peace, with just the comforting sound of crackling log fires and the hubbub of chatting locals filling the rambling little rooms. Wholesome and home-made fodder ranges from jacket potatoes to Moroccan lamb tagine with couscous; puddings include traditional deep-filled apple pie.

Open all day all wk 11-11 (Sun 12-11) **Food** Lunch Mon-Sat 12-6, Sun 12-4 Av main course £10 ⊕ FREE HOUSE ◀ Old Ric, Butcombe, Otter, Guest ales ♂ Westons 1st Quality & Old Rosie, Pheasant Plucker. ♟ 8 **Facilities** Non-diners area ❖ (Bar Garden) ◀◀ Children's portions Family room Garden ⌂ Beer festival Cider festival Parking WiFi ▬ (notice required)

EBRINGTON
Map 10 SP14

The Ebrington Arms ★★★★ INN ◉◉
PICK OF THE PUBS

tel: 01386 593223 **GL55 6NH**
email: reservations@theebringtonarms.co.uk **web:** www.theebringtonarms.co.uk
dir: From Chipping Campden on B4035 towards Shipston on Stour. Left to Ebrington signed after 0.5m

Home-brewed ales at this quintessential village pub

Built in 1640, this award-winning Cotswold gem has an abundance of character thanks to the heavy beams and original flagstones in both the bar and Old

Bakehouse dining room; the large inglenook fireplaces recall the building's days as the village bakery. Very much the hub of community life, lucky locals (and visitors too, of course) are spoilt for choice. Now brewing three of its own beers: Yubberton Yubby, Yawnie and YPA, which sit alongside guests such as Stroud and Cotswold Brewing's cider and lagers. Recognised with two AA Rosettes, the pub's carte offers the likes of Cornish crab cake with aïoli, followed by roasted cod with basil mash.

Open all day all wk noon-close ⊕ FREE HOUSE ◀ Stroud Budding Pale Ale, North Cotswold Windrush Ale, Prescott Hill Climb, Yubberton Yubby Bitter, Yawnie & YPA ♂ Cotswold. **Facilities** ❖ (Bar Garden) ◀◀ Children's menu Children's portions Garden Parking WiFi **Rooms** 5

EWEN
Map 4 SU09

The Wild Duck ★★★★ INN

tel: 01285 770310 **GL7 6BY**
email: duckreservations@aol.com **web:** www.thewildduckinn.co.uk
dir: From Cirencester take A429 towards Malmesbury. At Kemble left to Ewen. Inn in village centre

Cotswold pub with an excellent choice of ales

Built from honeyed Cotswold stone in 1563, this pub has been owned by the same family for more than 20 years and is close to the Cotswold Water Park. Deep red walls give the Post Horn Bar a warm feel, as does the extensive choice of real ales. The rambling restaurant has a lunch menu of pub favourites, while dinner may extend to king prawns pan-fried with chorizo sausage, lemon and parsley dressing, followed by roast rack of lamb, mint mash, rosemary and redcurrant gravy. There's an enclosed courtyard garden.

Open all day all wk Closed 25 Dec (eve) **Food** Lunch Mon-Fri 12-2, Sat-Sun all day Dinner all wk 6.30-10 ⊕ FREE HOUSE ◀ The Wild Duck Duckpond Bitter, Butcombe Bitter, Wye Valley Dorothy Goodbody's Country Ale, Greene King Abbot Ale, Morland Old Speckled Hen, Bath Ales Gem ♂ Ashton Press, Westons Stowford Press, Aspall. ♟ 32 **Facilities** Non-diners area ❖ (Bar Garden) ◀◀ Children's menu Children's portions Garden ⌂ Beer festival Parking WiFi ▬ (notice required) **Rooms** 12

FRAMPTON MANSELL
Map 4 SO90

The Crown Inn ★★★★ INN
PICK OF THE PUBS

tel: 01285 760601 **GL6 8JG**
email: enquiries@thecrowninn-cotswolds.co.uk **web:** www.thecrowninn-cotswolds.co.uk
dir: A419 halfway between Cirencester & Stroud

A handsome Cotswold inn perfect for whiling away an hour or two

Right in the heart of the village, the Crown is surrounded by the peace and quiet of the Golden Valley. Once a simple cider house, it's a classic 17th-century Cotswold-stone inn that's full of old-world charm, with honey-coloured stone walls, beams and open fireplaces where logs blaze in winter. Plenty of seating in the large garden allows for contemplative supping during the warmer months. Gloucestershire beers, such as Stroud Organic and Laurie Lee's Bitter, are usually showcased alongside others from the region, and a good choice of wines by the glass is served in the restaurant and three inviting bars. Fresh local food with lots of seasonal specials is the carte's promise. Rabbit wrapped in streaky bacon with pickled mushrooms is a tasty starter, to be followed perhaps by Hailey Farm lamb hotpot and braised red cabbage. For non-meat eaters, the vegetable and lentil Mulligatawny is ideal.

Open all day all wk 12-11 Closed 25 Dec **Food** Lunch Mon-Sat 12-2.30, Sun 12-8.30 Dinner Mon-Sat 6-9.30, Sun 12-8.30 Av main course £10 ⊕ FREE HOUSE ◀ Butcombe Bitter, Uley Laurie Lee's Bitter, Stroud Organic, Guest ales ♂ Addlestones, Guest ciders. ♟ 16 **Facilities** Non-diners area ❖ (Bar Restaurant Garden) ◀◀ Children's portions Garden ⌂ Parking WiFi ▬ **Rooms** 12

| **GLOUCESTER** | Map 10 SO81 |

Queens Head

tel: 01452 301882 **Tewkesbury Rd, Longford GL2 9EJ**
email: queenshead@aol.com
dir: *On A38 (Tewkesbury to Gloucester road) in Longford*

A cracking line-up at the locals' bar

This pretty 250-year-old half-timbered pub/restaurant is just out of town, but cannot be missed in summer when it is festooned with hanging baskets. Inside, a lovely old flagstone-floored locals' bar proffers a great range of real ales and ciders. The owners believe in giving their diners high-quality, freshly prepared food that is great value for money. Menus tempt with modern British food: duck and orange pâté; braised shoulder of Herefordshire beef; and the ever-popular Longford lamb – slow-roasted in chef's own secret recipe gravy. Smart casual dress and no children under 12 years.

Open all wk 11-3 5.30-11 **Food** Lunch all wk 12-2 Dinner all wk 6.30-9.30 ⊕ FREE HOUSE ◖ Wye Valley Butty Bach, Sharp's Doom Bar, Skinner's Betty Stogs, Otter, Butcombe Gold ♂ Ashton Press, Westons Stowford Press. ♚
Facilities Non-diners area Parking WiFi

| **GREAT BARRINGTON** | Map 10 SP21 |

The Fox Inn   PICK OF THE PUBS

tel: 01451 844385 **OX18 4TB**
email: info@foxinnbarrington.com
dir: *From Burford take A40 towards Northleach. In 3m right signed The Barringtons, pub approx 0.5m on right*

Seasonal food in riverside Cotswold pub

With a garden overlooking the River Windrush, this busy centuries-old former coaching house is a perfect base for lovely walks and cycle rides in summer. Set in the picturesque Windrush Valley, the pub is popular with race-goers visiting Cheltenham. A quintessential Cotswold inn built of mellow local stone, the bar proffers a range of well-kept Donnington beers and a concise wine list. The conservatory dining bar, barbecue and alfresco eating area all contribute to the friendly and relaxed atmosphere. Landlord Paul Porter's enthusiasm for tasty food shines through with the menu's descriptions: examples are 'our famous' twice-cooked belly of pork with stuffing, apple compôte, sauté potatoes and vegetables; and a 'classic' pan-fried Barbary duck breast with orange and marmalade gravy. Vegetarians are well catered for, with typical dishes including spinach, leek and chestnut pie. Regular events include curry buffets and the Sunday carvery.

Open all day all wk 11am-close **Food** Lunch Mon-Fri 12-2.30, Sat-Sun all day Dinner Mon-Fri 6.30-9.30, Sat-Sun all day ⊕ DONNINGTON ◖ BB, SBA ♂ Westons Stowford Press & Perry, Addlestones. **Facilities** Non-diners area ♥ (Bar Garden) ♦♦ Children's portions Garden ⼧ Parking WiFi

---

| **HAM** | Map 4 ST69 |

The Salutation Inn

tel: 01453 810284 **GL13 9QH**
dir: *S of Berkeley towards Stone*

Genuine rural free house close to the Severn Estuary

Landlord Peter Tiley says "What makes the Sally so special isn't the range of quality ales and ciders, the heritage pub games, the humble bar snacks, the cosy bars with log fires, or the genuine community spirit. It's something intangible". Maybe Peter's right, although those tangible features sound pretty good. Food is available only at lunchtime when, in addition to the permanent ploughman's, and Gloucestershire ham, eggs and chips, he offers a not-so-humble 'third dish', perhaps 'ham from Ham', hay-baked, cider-soaked belly of pork from his own Gloucester Old Spots pigs. Tiley's own microbrewery launches in 2015.

Open 12-2.30 5-11 (Sat 12-11 Sun 12-10.30) Closed Mon L **Food** Lunch Tue-Sun 12-2.30 ⊕ FREE HOUSE ◖ Butcombe Bitter, Bristol Beer Factory, Cotswold Spring, Severn Vale, Wye Valley ♂ Tom Olivers, Barnes & Adams, Wilkins Farmhouse.
Facilities Non-diners area Garden ⼧ Parking WiFi (notice required)

| **HINTON** | Map 4 ST77 |

The Bull at Hinton

tel: 0117 937 2332 **SN14 8HG**
email: reservations@thebullathinton.co.uk
dir: *From M4 junct 18, A46 to Bath, 1m turn right, 1m, down hill. Pub on right*

Village inn on the southern edge of the Cotswolds

Just 20 minutes from both Bath and Bristol, this 17th-century, stone-built former farmhouse and dairy is packed with original character, with beams in the bar and dining room, flagstone floors, inglenook fireplaces, old pews and big oak tables. Meals are freshly prepared using ingredients mostly from local producers and suppliers (and from home-grown produce), meaning that a typical menu might feature spicy salmon fish cakes; followed by sticky BBQ ribs or spring green risotto; and finally passion fruit pannacotta. The south-facing terrace and garden is where to be when the sun's out.

Open 12-3 6-12 (Sat-Sun & BH open all day) Closed Mon L (ex BHs) **Food** Lunch Tue-Fri 12-2, Sat 12-9.30, Sun 12-8.30 (BHs 12-8) Dinner Mon-Fri 6-9, Sat 12-9.30 Sun 12-8.30 (BHs 12-8) ⊕ WADWORTH ◖ 6X, Henry's Original IPA, The Bishop's Tipple & Summersault, Guest ale ♂ Thatchers Gold, Westons Stowford Press. ♚ 11
Facilities Non-diners area ♥ (Bar Garden) ♦♦ Children's menu Play area Garden ⼧ Parking WiFi (notice required)

| **LECHLADE ON THAMES** | Map 5 SU29 |

The Trout Inn

tel: 01367 252313 **St Johns Bridge GL7 3HA**
email: chefpjw@aol.com
dir: *A40 onto A361 then A417. From M4 junct 15, A419, then A361 & A417 to Lechlade*

Extensive menu served in an ancient inn

When workmen constructed a new bridge over the Thames in 1220, they built an almshouse to live in. It became an inn in 1472, and its flagstone floors and beams now overflow into the old boathouse. The extensive menu features meat, fish and vegetarian options, as well as pizzas, filled jacket potatoes and burgers. This family-friendly pub offers smaller portions for children, who also have their own separate menu. The large garden often hosts live jazz, an annual steam week and a beer festival, both in June, plus a riverfolk festival in July.

Open all wk 10-3 6-11 (summer all wk 10am-11pm) Closed 25 Dec **Food** Lunch all wk 12-2 Dinner all wk 7-10 Av main course £12 ⊕ ENTERPRISE INNS ◖ Courage Best Bitter, Sharp's Doom Bar & Cornish Coaster, Guest ales. ♚ 15
Facilities Non-diners area ♥ (Bar Garden) ♦♦ Children's menu Children's portions Play area Family room Garden Beer festival Parking WiFi (notice required)

PICK OF THE PUBS

The Weighbridge Inn

MINCHINHAMPTON   Map 4 SO80

tel: 01453 832520 **GL6 9AL**
email: enquiries@weighbridgeinn.co.uk
web: www.weighbridgeinn.co.uk
dir: *On B4014 between Nailsworth & Avening*

Recommended for its freshly made pies

Parts of this whitewashed free house date back to the 17th century, when it stood adjacent to the original packhorse trail between Bristol and London. While the trail is now a footpath and bridleway, the road in front (now the B4014) became a turnpike in the 1820s. The innkeeper at the time ran both the pub and the weighbridge for the local woollen mills — serving jugs of ale in between making sure tolls were paid. Associated memorabilia and other rural artefacts from the time are displayed around the inn, which has been carefully renovated to retain original features, like exposed brick walls and open fires. Up in the restaurant, which used to be the hayloft, the old roof timbers reach almost to the floor. The inn prides itself on its decent ales and ciders, and the quality of its food, with everything cooked from scratch. Starters to get the taste buds going could be baked Cotswold brie and red onion marmalade; and mascarpone gnocchi. The hearty main courses include cottage pie; goats' cheese and pesto Wellington;

and the Weighbridge burger. Lighter meals are available, such as salads, omelettes, fritattas and filled baguettes. The Weighbridge is also the home of 'the famous 2 in 1 pies', one half containing a filling of your choice from a selection of seven (such as pork, bacon and celery) and topped with pastry, the other half home-made cauliflower cheese — all cooked to order and available to take away or even bake at home. Typical desserts are apple and blackberry crumble, and crème brûlée. From the patios and sheltered, landscaped garden the Cotswolds are in full view.

Open all day all wk 12-11 (Sun 12-10.30) Closed 25 Dec **Food** all wk 12-9.30 ⊞ FREE HOUSE ◀ Wadworth 6X, Uley Old Spot, Palmers Best Bitter,

Box Steam Chuffin Ale, Stroud Budding ♂ Bath Ciders Bounders, Westons Rosie's Pig. ♟ 15
Facilities Non-diners area
♣ (Bar Restaurant Garden)
♦♦ Children's menu Children's portions Family room Garden ⊼ Parking WiFi
🚌 (notice required)

LEIGHTERTON
Map 4 ST89

The Royal Oak

tel: 01666 890250 **1 The Street GL8 8UN**
email: info@royaloakleighterton.co.uk
dir: M4 junct 18, A46 towards Stroud. After Dunkirk continue on A46. Right signed Leighterton

Pub majoring on local, seasonal produce

Set in a picture-postcard Cotswold village, close to Westonbirt Arboretum, Paul and Antonia Whitbread's pub thrives as a popular dining venue. The bright, contemporary bar and dining room successfully blends exposed beams, open fires and antiques with modern furnishings. Enjoy a pint of Bath Ales with a lunchtime sandwich or platter or dive into the main menu. Food is classic British and everything is made on the premises from local ingredients. In addition to pub classics (fish and chips, burgers and pies) typically, tuck into lobster ravioli and vermouth butter sauce; game casserole with juniper berry dumplings; and ginger and cinnamon sponge, warm poached apples and whipped cream.

Open 12-3 5.30-11 (Sat 12-11 Sun 12-10.30) Closed Mon **Food** Lunch Tue-Fri 12-2, Sat 12-2.30, Sun 12-3 Dinner Tue-Thu 6-9, Fri-Sat 6-9.30 Av main course £15 Set menu available ⊕ FREE HOUSE ◀ Bath Ales Gem, Butcombe Adam Henson's Rare Breed, Guest ales ⚫ Westons Stowford Press, Sherston, Wilce's Herefordshire. ▾ 10 **Facilities** Non-diners area ✿ (Bar Garden) ◀◀ Children's menu Children's portions Garden ⋈ Beer festival Parking WiFi (notice required)

LONGHOPE
Map 10 SO61

The Glasshouse Inn

tel: 01452 830529 **May Hill GL17 0NN**
email: glasshouseinn@gmail.com
dir: From A40 approx 8m SE of Ross-on-Wye, follow signs for May Hill. Through May Hill to pub on left

Gimmick-free traditional pub

The Glasshouse gets its name from Dutch glassmakers who settled locally in the 16th century but its origins can be traced back further, to 1450. A gimmick-free traditional pub, it is located in a fabulous rural setting with a country garden and an elegant interior. The inn serves a range of real ales including Butcombe and Sharp's Doom Bar, plus home-cooked dishes such as fish pie; cod and chips; beef curry; steak and kidney served in Yorkshire puddings; and chilli. At lunch you can also choose from a range of sandwiches, ploughman's lunches or basket meals of chips with the likes of scampi or sausage. There's a choice of roasts at Sunday lunch – booking is advisable.

Open 11.30-3 7-11 (Sun 12-3) Closed Sun eve **Food** Lunch all wk 12-2 (booking required for parties of 6 or more) Dinner Mon-Sat 7-9 (booking required for parties of 6 or more) ⊕ FREE HOUSE ◀ Sharp's Doom Bar, Butcombe ⚫ Westons Stowford Press. ▾ 12 **Facilities** Garden ⋈ Parking WiFi

LOWER SLAUGHTER
Map 10 SP12

NEW The Slaughters Country Inn ★★★★★ INN ◉◉

tel: 01451 822143 **GL54 2HS**
email: info@theslaughtersinn.co.uk **web:** www.theslaughtersinn.co.uk
dir: Between Stow-on-the-Wold & Bourton-on-the-Water on A429 follow 'The Slaughters' signs

Much-loved Cotswold-stone village inn with beautiful rooms

Formerly the Washbourne Court, it stands close to the River Lye, soon to join the Windrush and eventually the Thames. The spacious beamed bar is a good example of how to successfully balance the appealing qualities of a 17th-century building with the demands of the 21st century. Two AA Rosettes signify that good food is paramount, from sandwiches and light bites to the chargrilled Hereford Shorthorn

rib-eye steak with fries. In between might come Cornish day-boat fish pie thermidor and buttered vegetables; traditional faggots with garden peas and onion gravy; and baked potato gnocchi, goats' cheese and spinach.

Open all day all wk **Food** Lunch all wk 12-3 Dinner all wk 6.30-9 ⊕ FREE HOUSE ◀ Brakspear, Wychwood Hobgoblin. ▾ 11 **Facilities** Non-diners area ✿ (Bar Garden) ◀◀ Children's menu Children's portions Garden ⋈ Parking WiFi (notice required) **Rooms** 31

MARSHFIELD
Map 4 ST77

The Catherine Wheel

tel: 01225 892220 **39 High St SN14 8LR**
email: roo@thecatherinewheel.co.uk
dir: M4 junct 18, A46 signed Bath. Left onto A420 signed Chippenham. Right signed Marshfield

Traditional Cotswold inn with sunny patio

On the edge of the Cotswolds, this mainly 17th-century inn has the expected exposed brickwork and large open fireplaces offset by a simple, stylish decor. Menus are also simple and well presented, with favourites at lunchtime including steak and kidney pie; and jacket potatoes. In the evening look forward to potted smoked mackerel, lemon and herb pâté or tomato and goats' cheese tartlets, followed perhaps by venison stew and thyme dumplings or fish pie. A small but sunny patio is a lovely spot for a summertime pint of Butcombe Bitter or Thatchers cider.

Open all day all wk **Food** Lunch Mon-Fri 12-2, Sat-Sun 12-3 Dinner Mon-Thu 6.30-9, Fri-Sat 6.30-9.30, Sun 6-8.30 Set menu available ⊕ FREE HOUSE ◀ Butcombe Bitter, Sharp's Doom Bar, Cotswold Spring Stunner ⚫ Ashton Press, Thatchers. ▾ 10 **Facilities** Non-diners area ✿ (Bar Garden) ◀◀ Children's portions Garden ⋈ Parking WiFi (notice required)

MEYSEY HAMPTON
Map 5 SP10

The Masons Arms

tel: 01285 850164 **28 High St GL7 5JT**
dir: 6m E of Cirencester off A417, beside village green

Family- and dog-friendly village pub

This 17th-century, stone-built Cotswold inn used to be Paul Fallows' local, so when the opportunity arose he decided to buy it. Standing conveniently alongside the village green, on to which tables and benches have surreptitiously migrated, it's the hub of the community, offering a warming log fire in the large inglenook, and well-kept Arkell's ales, and Westons and Rekorderlig ciders in the convivial beamed bar. Good value home-made food includes twice-baked Applewood cheese soufflé; and carrot and butternut squash soup as starters, and mains such as chicken curry and rice; salmon and haddock fishcakes; and sausage and mash.

Open all day all wk 8.30-3 5-11 (Sat-Sun all day) **Food** Lunch Mon-Fri 12-2, Sat 12-9, Sun 12-8 Dinner Mon-Fri 6.30-9, Sat 12-9, Sun 12-8 ⊕ ARKELL'S ◀ Wiltshire Gold, Three B's ⚫ Westons Stowford Press, Rekorderlig. ▾ 12 **Facilities** Non-diners area ✿ (Bar Garden) ◀◀ Children's menu Children's portions Garden ⋈ Beer festival WiFi (notice required)

MINCHINHAMPTON
Map 4 SO80

The Weighbridge Inn
PICK OF THE PUBS

See Pick of the Pubs on page 207

NETHER WESTCOTE
Map 10 SP22

The Feathered Nest Country Inn ★★★★★ INN ◉◉◉
PICK OF THE PUBS

See Pick of the Pubs on opposite page

PICK OF THE PUBS

The Feathered Nest Country Inn ★★★★★ INN ✿✿✿

NETHER WESTCOTE   Map 10 SP22

tel: 01993 833030 **OX7 6SD**
email: info@thefeatherednestinn.co.uk
web: www.thefeatherednestinn.co.uk
dir: *A424 between Burford &*
Stow-on-the-Wold, follow signs

Award-winning food in a beautiful rural location

In the picturesque village of Nether Westcote on the border of Gloucestershire and Oxfordshire, The Feathered Nest has marvellous views over the Evenlode Valley. Originally an old malthouse, the pub has been thoughtfully designed to retain the original character, especially in the cosy log-fired bar, where local and award-winning real ales are on offer. Herbs and vegetables are grown in the kitchen garden, with local produce forming the backbone of the menus. As well as bar snacks, the modern British cuisine brings a daily set lunch menu for relaxed eating in the bar, and on the garden terrace (shaded by a sycamore tree) when the weather allows. Blackboard specials could include darne of hake, sautéed potatoes, kale and caper butter. The seasonal à la carte offers a modern take on classic combinations, such as wood pigeon pastrami, red cabbage, celeriac, apple and flat bread; and stone bass, squid ink pearl millet, sea purslane and langoustine bisque. For simpler tastes

there's a selection from the charcoal grill; maybe 28-day aged rib-eye steak with skinny chips, béarnaise or peppercorn sauce and mixed leaf salad. Be sure to leave room for desserts such as passionfruit parfait with caramel sauce and pine nuts. Afternoon tea and Sunday lunch are also served. Individually decorated bedrooms furnished with antiques and comfortable beds are available; the pub makes an excellent base from which to explore the countryside and the quaint and charming villages nearby. Look out for enjoyable events that run throughout the year, including a pie and pint tasting evening, live jazz, and a quiz night.

Open all day Closed 25 Dec, Mon **Food** Lunch Tue-Sat 12-2.30, Sun 12-3.30 Dinner Tue-Sat 6.30-9.30 ⊕ FREE HOUSE ◪ Rotating Local ales ♂ Aspall Harry Sparrow. ♟ 19 **Facilities** Non-diners area ☺ (Bar Garden) ♦♦ Children's menu Children's portions Family room Garden ☊ Parking WiFi **Rooms** 4

NEWENT
Map 10 SO72

Kilcot Inn ★★★★ INN

tel: 01989 720707 **Ross Rd, Kilcot GL18 1NA**
email: info@kilcotinn.com **web:** www.kilcotinn.com
dir: *M50 junct 3, B4221 signed Newent. Approx 2m to pub on left*

Welcoming country inn offering great hospitality

A restored country inn on the borders of Gloucestershire and Herefordshire, the Kilcot offers the best traditions of hospitality, food and drink. From the selection of local real ales and ciders on tap to the high quality produce used in the dishes in the bar and restaurant, there is something for everyone. The menu might include warm bruschetta of grilled mackerel with tomato and olive salsa, followed perhaps by slow-cooked shoulder of lamb in red wine and redcurrant jelly with feta and spring onion potato cake. Outdoor seating is available, including a pleasant garden area to the rear.

Open all day all wk **Food** Lunch all wk 12-2.30 Dinner Mon-Wed 6-9, Thu-Sat 6-9.30 ⊕ FREE HOUSE ◀ Wye Valley Butty Bach, Marston's EPA Ò Westons Stowford Press, Old Rosie & Country Perry. **Facilities** Non-diners area ♣ (Bar Garden Outside area) ♦ Children's menu Children's portions Play area Garden Outside area ⟨ Parking WiFi ▭ (notice required) **Rooms** 4

NEWLAND
Map 4 SO50

The Ostrich Inn
PICK OF THE PUBS

tel: 01594 833260 **GL16 8NP**
email: kathryn@theostrichinn.com
dir: *Follow Monmouth signs from Chepstow (A466), Newland signed from Redbrook*

Huge range of real ales here

On the western edge of the Forest of Dean and adjoining the Wye Valley in a pretty village, the 13th-century Ostrich is thought to have taken its name from the family emblem of the Probyns, local landowners in previous centuries; it retains many of its ancient features, including a priest hole. With its warm welcome, The Ostrich is a thriving social centre for the village. An open log fire burns in the large lounge bar throughout the winter, and customers can relax immediately in the friendly atmosphere with a pint of their chosen brew. And what a choice. Eight cask-conditioned real ales such as Butty Bach are served at any one time; real ciders, too, are strongly represented. Diners settle down in the small and intimate restaurant, in the bar or out in gardens.

Open all wk 12-3 (Mon-Fri 6.30-11.30 Sat 6-11.30 Sun 6.30-10.30) **Food** Lunch all wk 12-2.30 Dinner Sun-Fri 6.30-9.30, Sat 6-9.30 ⊕ FREE HOUSE ◀ Wye Valley Butty Bach, Guest ales Ò Westons Stowford Press, Mortimers Orchard & Old Rosie. **Facilities** Non-diners area ♣ (Bar Restaurant Garden) ♦ Garden ⟨

NORTH CERNEY
Map 5 SP00

Bathurst Arms

tel: 01285 832150 **GL7 7BZ**
email: pub@bathurstarms.com
dir: *5m N of Cirencester on A435*

17th-century Cotswolds free house

The River Churn, the infant Thames's first tributary, runs through the garden of this creeper-camouflaged, 17th-century pub on the Earl of Bathurst's estate. Even when the log fires aren't lit, the beamed and flagstoned bar is inviting, but then so too is the pretty riverside garden. Under the pub's new ownership, the equally fresh kitchen team prepares form locally sourced ingredients dishes such as trio of Cotswolds sausages; beer-battered fish and chips; and roasted beetroot, horseradish and rosemary risotto. In addition to Hooky, Ramsbury Gold awaits real ale drinkers, with many more local brews at the January, April, July and October beer festivals.

Open all day all wk **Food** Lunch Mon-Fri 12-3, Sat-Sun 12-9 Dinner Mon-Fri 6-9, Sat-Sun 12-9 Av main course £12 Restaurant menu available Wed-Sun ⊕ FREE HOUSE ◀ Hook Norton Hooky Bitter, Ramsbury Gold Ò Hogan's. ♀ 23 **Facilities** Non-diners area ♣ (Bar Garden) ♦ Children's menu Children's portions Play area Garden ⟨ Beer festival Parking WiFi ▭

NORTHLEACH
Map 10 SP11

The Wheatsheaf Inn

tel: 01451 860244 **West End GL54 3EZ**
email: reservations@cotswoldswheatsheaf.com
dir: *Just off A40 between Oxford & Cheltenham*

Stylish pub worth seeking out

A beautiful Cotswold-stone 17th-century inn on the square of the pretty former wool town of Northleach, The Wheatsheaf is everything anyone could wish for, with flagstone floors, beams, log fires and a vibrant, smartened-up feel throughout. It's the perfect place for enjoying bracing walks then chilling out in the bar with the papers or sampling some seriously good food. Monthly menus evolve with the season and may take in duck leg cassoulet with white beans, pancetta and Morteau sausage; calves' liver with sage and balsamic onions; sticky toffee pudding and cheeses from Neal's Yard Dairy.

Open all day all wk **Food** Lunch all wk 12-3 Dinner all wk 6-10 Set menu available ⊕ FREE HOUSE ◀ Bath Ales Barnsey, Wye Valley HPA, Sharp's Atlantic Ò Dunkertons Premium Organic. ♀ 15 **Facilities** Non-diners area ♣ (Bar Restaurant Garden) ♦ Children's menu Children's portions Play area Garden ⟨ Parking WiFi ▭ (notice required)

OLDBURY-ON-SEVERN
Map 4 ST69

The Anchor Inn

tel: 01454 413331 **Church Rd BS35 1QA**
email: info@anchorinnoldbury.co.uk
dir: *From N A38 towards Bristol, 1.5m then right, village signed. From S A38 through Thornbury*

Homely inn in tranquil Severnside village

Set beside a tree-lined pill (stream) that meanders down to the nearby Severn Estuary, this family-friendly pub is on the Severn Way footpath and a popular stopping place for ramblers. Parts of the stone-built inn are nearly 500 years old, and an olde-worlde welcome is assured for travellers to this charming, out-of-the-way village. Appetite-busters on the good-value bar and dining room menu include smoked haddock and salmon fish pie; kashmiri lamb curry; roast guinea fowl breast with shallot and red wine sauce; and steal and kidney pudding. Reliable real ales include guests like Severn Sins, plus there's a good range of bottled cider and perry.

Open all wk Mon-Thu 11.30-2.30 6-11 (Fri-Sat 11.30am-mdnt Sun 12-10.30) **Food** Lunch Mon-Fri 12-2, Sat 12-2.30, Sun 12-3 Dinner all wk 6-9 Set menu available ⊕ FREE HOUSE ◀ Bass, Butcombe Bitter, St Austell Trelawny, Guest ales Ò Ashton Press & Still, Thatchers. ♀ 16 **Facilities** Non-diners area ♦ Children's menu Family room Garden ⟨ Parking ▭ (notice required)

PAINSWICK
Map 4 SO80

The Falcon Inn ★★★★ INN

tel: 01452 814222 **New St GL6 6UN**
email: info@falconpainswick.co.uk **web:** www.falconpainswick.co.uk
dir: *On A46 in centre of Painswick, opposite St Mary's church*

Historic inn with wide-ranging menus

Dating from 1554, this pub spent over 200 years as a courthouse and occupies a lovely spot in the heart of the town and opposite the church with its iconic 99 yew trees. Expect a good choice of local real ales, including Hook Norton, Wye Valley HPA and various guest ales. Lunch and dinner menus are varied, offering something for everyone. A typical dinner might start with a Greek-inspired sharing platter or chicken liver parfait with apple and plum chutney and move on to blade of beef and bean cassoulet with dauphinoise potatoes.

Open all day all wk 10am-11pm **Food** Lunch all wk 12-2.30 Dinner all wk 7-9.30 Restaurant menu available ⊕ PARSNIP INNS LTD ◀ Hook Norton, Wye Valley HPA, Guest ales ○ Westons Stowford Press. ☎ 10 **Facilities** Non-diners area ♣ (All areas) ♦ Children's menu Children's portions Garden Outside area ⊨ Parking WiFi ⟺ (notice required) **Rooms** 11

POULTON   Map 5 SP00

The Falcon Inn

tel: 01285 851597 & 850878 **London Rd GL7 5HN**
email: bookings@falconinnpoulton.co.uk **web:** www.falconinnpoulton.co.uk
dir: *From Cirencester 4m E on A417 towards Fairford*

Informal atmosphere and locally brewed cask ales

Taking centre stage at the heart of a village of pretty Cotswold stone cottages and villas, this centuries-old pub is run with passion by Gianni Gray and Natalie Birch. Their dedication to all things local ensures a reliable pint of real ale from some of the area's independent breweries, enjoyed in a pub that marries contemporary comforts with age-old tradition. The fresh, zingy menu changes every month to make the most of locally available produce. Diners may find included hand-dived scallops with cauliflower purée, florets and chorizo; or perhaps breast of pigeon with butternut squash, roast beetroot, baby onions and chocolate soil with truffle.

The Falcon Inn

Open Tue-Sat 12-3 5-11 (Sun 12-4) Closed 25 Dec, Mon **Food** Lunch Tue-Sat 12-2.15, Sun 12-3 Dinner Tue-Sat 6-9 Set menu available ⊕ FREE HOUSE ◀ Hook Norton Hooky Bitter, Guest ale ○ Westons Stowford Press. ☎ 11 **Facilities** Non-diners area ♦ Children's menu Children's portions Garden ⊨ Parking WiFi

See advert below

SAPPERTON   Map 4 SO90

The Bell at Sapperton   PICK OF THE PUBS

See Pick of the Pubs on page 212

SHEEPSCOMBE   Map 4 SO81

The Butchers Arms   PICK OF THE PUBS

See Pick of the Pubs on page 213

PICK OF THE PUBS

The Bell at Sapperton

SAPPERTON   Map 4 SO90

tel: 01285 760298 **GL7 6LE**
email: info@bellsapperton.co.uk
web: www.bellsapperton.co.uk
dir: *From A419 between Cirencester &*
Stroud follow Sapperton signs

Village free house, very much part of the community

The Cotswold stone exterior of this village inn has been quietly mellowing for over 300 years; still gently maturing too are the beamed ceilings, unrendered walls, polished flags, bare boards and open fireplaces of the interior. Although most people arrive by car or on foot, horse riders and their mounts are also welcome, and will be able to tie up and water them. Liquid refreshment for humans includes real ales from Butcombe, Hook Norton, Otter and Stroud, and a dozen wines by the glass. Food, from home-made bread to the chocolate truffles that complement an after-dinner coffee, is always freshly prepared. In the garden the chef oversees cultivation of vegetables and salads, while top local suppliers furnish other ingredients. Meals are served throughout four cosy dining areas, each with its own individual character; outside, a secluded rear courtyard and a landscaped front garden make fine-weather dining a pleasure. For lunch or dinner, you might start with ham hock terrine with brioche and chutney;

beetroot-cured gravad lax with vanilla mayo; or devilled crab on toast. Main course possibilities include beef cheek bourguignon, parsley mash and heritage chantenay carrots; stew of cod, mussels, tiger prawns, squid, butterbeans and saffron; beer-battered haddock, chips and crushed peas; and parmesan gnocchi, butternut squash purée, kale and pine nuts. There are specials too, as well as ideas for children. And should you want a dessert, try white chocolate cheesecake with raspberry compôte; or sticky toffee pudding with vanilla ice cream. Cirencester Park close by, stretches all the way to the town, although it is screened from it by the world's tallest yew hedge.

Open all day all wk 11-11 (Sun 12-9) Closed 25 Dec **Food** Lunch Mon-Sat 12-2.30, Sun 12-4 Dinner Mon-Sat 6-9.30 🛢 FREE HOUSE 🍺 Flying Monk, Otter Bitter, Hook Norton Hooky Bitter, Butcombe, Stroud Budding Ö Westons Stowford Press. 🍷 12 **Facilities** Non-diners area 🐾 (Bar Restaurant Garden) 👶 Children's menu Children's portions Garden 🎪 Beer festival Parking WiFi

PICK OF THE PUBS

The Butchers Arms

SHEEPSCOMBE   Map 4 SO81

tel: 01452 812113 **GL6 7RH**
email: mark@butchers-arms.co.uk
web: www.butchers-arms.co.uk
dir: *1.5m S of A46 (Cheltenham to Stroud road), N of Painswick*

Rural Cotswold gem with stunning views

Tucked into the western scarp of the Cotswolds and reached via narrow winding lanes, pretty Sheepscombe radiates all of the mellow, sedate, bucolic charm you'd expect from such a haven. The village pub, dating from 1670 and a favourite haunt of *Cider with Rosie* author Laurie Lee, lives up to such expectations and then some. Views from the gardens are idyllic whilst within is all you'd hope for: log fires, clean-cut rustic furnishings, village chatter backed up by local beers from Prescotts of Cheltenham Brewery. Walkers, riders and locals all beat a path to the door beneath the pub's famous carved sign showing a butcher supping a pint of ale with a pig tied to his leg. The pub takes its name from its association with Henry VIII's Royal Deer Park, which was located nearby, when deer carcasses were hung in what is now the bar. The fulfilling fodder here includes locally sourced meats, including beef from Beech Farm; the beef, ale and Stilton pie is a perennial favourite, as is the home-made burger

– try one with a blue cheese and chorizo topping. Alternative main courses take in pork, apple and cider sausages and specials like seared tuna steak salad Niçoise, or Dell Farm rack of lamb with minted mash, purple sprouting broccoli and a redcurrant jus. Nibblers can graze on a delicious bacon, West Country brie and cranberry sandwich or a chicken, pesto and mozzarella panini; others can share a baked camembert or a huge farmhouse platter, while those thinking of tucking into the memorable Sunday roasts should book well ahead. To drink, there's a cracking range of ales, and a traditional farmhouse scrumpy cider. Following a sympathetic extension late in 2014 there is now a better bar and more room to enjoy the delights of this lovely pub.

Open all wk 11.30-2.30 6.30-11 (Sat 11.30-11.30 Sun 12-10.30) **Food** Lunch Mon-Fri 12-2.30, Sat-Sun all day Dinner Mon-Sat 6.30-9.30, Sun 6.30-8 (ex Sun Jan-Mar) ⊕ FREE HOUSE ◖ Prescotts Hill Climb, Otter Bright, St Austell Proper Job, Wye Valley H.P.A. ♂ Westons Stowford Press & Rosie's Pig Traditional Cider. **Facilities** Non-diners area ☙ (Bar Garden) ♦♦ Children's menu Children's portions Garden ⊓ Parking WiFi

SOMERFORD KEYNES
Map 4 SU09

The Bakers Arms

tel: 01285 861298 **GL7 6DN**
email: enquiries@thebakersarmssomerford.co.uk
dir: *Exit A419 signed Cotswold Water Park. Cross B4696, 1m, follow signs for Keynes Park & Somerford Keynes*

Chocolate-box Cotswold pub

The beautiful Bakers Arms dates from the 17th century and was formerly the village bakery; it still has its low-beamed ceilings and inglenook fireplace. Only a stone's throw from the Thames Path and Cotswold Way, the pub is a convenient watering hole for walkers. The mature gardens are ideal for alfresco dining, with discreet children's play areas. The home-cooked food on offer runs along the lines of baguettes, specials and pub favourites – trio of sausages with mash, onion gravy and parsnip chips; breaded scampi and chips; rib-eye steak; or vegetable curry.

Open all day all wk 12-11 **Food** Lunch Mon-Sat 12-9, Sun 12-4 Dinner Mon-Sat 12-9, Sun 6-8 Av main course £12 Set menu available ⊕ ENTERPRISE INNS ◄ Butcombe Bitter, Stroud Budding, Sharp's Doom Bar ♂ Somersby Cider, Westons Stowford Press. **Facilities** Non-diners area ♣ (Bar Restaurant Garden) ♦ Children's menu Children's portions Play area Garden ⌐ Parking WiFi ➡ (notice required)

SOUTHROP
Map 5 SP10

NEW The Swan
PICK OF THE PUBS

tel: 01367 850205 **GL7 3NU**
email: admin@theswanatsouthrop.co.uk
dir: *Follow Southrop signs from A361 between Lechlade & Burford*

Beautifully appointed, early 17th-century Cotswolds inn

Overlooking the green, The Swan is clearly the village focal point. Summer ivy covers the external walls, while those in the stone-floored bar and restaurant are painted white, soft grey-blue or left unrendered. A good real ale line-up includes Hook Norton Hooky, Bath Ales Gem and Sharp's Atlantic, with six red and six white wines by the glass. Owner Terry Hibbert's close links with local food producers lead to crayfish from nearby gravel pits, Macaroni Farm lamb, Hatherop Estate partridge, Kelmscott pork, quail and geese from Thyme, eggs from his own chickens and Southrop Manor gardeners Joff and Peter supplying vegetables and salads. Translating such affinities to the plate results typically in roasted pumpkin and sage risotto; roast Ropsley pheasant forestière with Jerusalem artichoke; calves' liver with rosemary polenta, chard and prosciutto crisp; and wild sea bass fillet with salsify, spinach, persillade and lie de vin sauce.

Open 12-2.30 6-11 (Sat 12-3 6-11 Sun 12-4) Closed Sun eve **Food** Lunch Mon-Fri 12-2.30, Sat 12-3, Sun 12-3.30 Dinner Mon-Thu 6-9, Fri-Sat 6-9.30 Restaurant menu available all wk ⊕ FREE HOUSE ◄ Hook Norton Hooky Bitter, Bath Ales Gem, Sharp's Doom Bar & Atlantic, Otter ♂ Sharp's Orchard Keg. ♀ 15
Facilities Non-diners area ♣ (Bar Restaurant Garden) ♦ Children's menu Children's portions Garden ⌐ WiFi ➡ (notice required)

STANTON
Map 10 SP03

NEW The Mount Inn

tel: 01386 584316 **Old Snowshill Rd WR12 7NE**
email: info@themountinn.co.uk
dir: *Follow Stanton signs from B4632 between Broadway & Winchcombe*

Amazing sunsets and local ales

Stanton, a pretty and unspoilt village with houses built from honey-coloured local stone, is located just off the Cotswold Way long-distance path, in an Area of Outstanding Natural Beauty. The Mount Inn is a traditional country pub and, as its name suggests, it's at the top of a hill, with great views across the Vale of Evesham to the Malverns. Pub classics on the menu might include breaded scampi; gammon steak, egg and chips; or cod fillet encased in the pub's own Donnington ale batter. There's a specials board, too.

Open 12-3 6-11 Closed 1wk Jan, Mon (Oct-Apr) **Food** Lunch 12-2 Dinner 6-9 Av main course £14 ⊕ DONNINGTON ◄ BB, SBA & Gold ♂ Westons Mortimers Orchard & Stowford Press. **Facilities** Non-diners area ♣ (All areas) ♦ Children's portions Garden Outside area ⌐ Parking WiFi

STOW-ON-THE-WOLD
Map 10 SP12

The Bell at Stow

tel: 01451 870916 **Park St GL54 1AJ**
email: bellatstow@youngs.co.uk
dir: *In town centre on A436*

Handsome Cotswold pub with modern British dishes

This ivy-clad stone pub in lovely Stow offers a warm welcome to all, including dogs. Open-plan with flagstone floors, beamed ceilings and log fires, it's a relaxed setting to enjoy a pint of Young's Special or one of the 10 wines sold by the glass. Seafood dominates the daily-changing specials boards – typical dishes including smoked haddock and coriander fishcakes; and chargrilled Cajun-spiced swordfish steaks. Non-fish options might be game pie and a vegetarian roast butternut squash, spinach and gorgonzola tagliatelle.

Open all day all wk 11-11 **Food** Lunch Mon-Sat 12-9.30, Sun 12-9 Dinner Mon-Sat 12-9.30, Sun 12-9 Restaurant menu available all wk ⊕ YOUNG'S ◄ Bitter & Special, Guest ales. ♀ 10 **Facilities** Non-diners area ♣ (Bar Garden) ♦ Children's portions Garden ⌐ Parking WiFi

AA PUB OF THE YEAR FOR ENGLAND 2015–2016

NEW The Porch House ★★★★★ INN ◉◉
PICK OF THE PUBS

tel: 01451 870048 **Digbeth St GL54 1BN**
email: james@porch-house.co.uk web: www.porch-house.co.uk
dir: *A429 into Stow, off main square at end of Digbeth St*

Award-winning, historic Cotswold inn

In the centre of pretty Stow-on-the-Wold, this stone-built inn claims to be the oldest pub in England. Parts of the historic building date back to 947AD, when it is believed to have been a hospice built by the order of Aethelmar, Duke of Cornwall, on land belonging to Evesham Abbey. More recent additions include vast 16th-century fireplaces and low 'mind your head' beams. The Porch received an extensive and stylish makeover in 2013 and there's a relaxed feel about the place, especially in the bar which dispenses a range of real ales, including several from the pub's brewery owners Brakspear. Served in the bar, conservatory and dining room, the food is a worthy recipient of two AA Rosettes. A typical meal might begin with Severn & Wye smoked trout, potato salad, pea shoots and horseradish; and move on to sirloin steak, skin-on chips, Stilton hollandaise and watercress.

Open all day all wk **Food** Lunch all wk 12-3 Dinner all wk 6-9.30 Av main course £12 ⊕ BRAKSPEAR ◄ Bitter, Oxford Gold, Special, Ringwood Boondoggle. ♀ **Facilities** Non-diners area ♣ (Bar Garden Outside area) ♦ Children's menu Children's portions Garden Outside area ⌐ Parking WiFi ➡ (notice required)
Rooms 13

STROUD
Map 4 SO80

Bear of Rodborough Hotel ★★★ HL ◉ **PICK OF THE PUBS**

tel: 01453 878522 **Rodborough Common GL5 5DE**
email: info@bearofrodborough.info **web:** www.cotswold-inns-hotels.co.uk/bear
dir: *From M5 junct 13 follow signs for Stonehouse then Rodborough*

Surrounded by 300 acres of National Trust land

Located amidst the rolling, windswept grassland of Rodborough Common with its
far-reaching views of the Stroud Valley and Severn Vale, and cattle roaming free in
the summer months, this 17th-century former alehouse takes its name from the
bear-baiting that used to take place nearby. Head to the bar for a pint of Wickwar
before seeking a seat on the York stone terrace or in the gardens with their walled
croquet lawn. The bar menu has many delights, such as afternoon tea, sharing
platters and ploughman's, and fond favourites: fisherman's pie, cornfed chicken
supreme and chargrilled steaks. Look to the Library Restaurant for a more formal
affair, where you can try smoked Scottish scallops with butternut squash and
chorizo; followed by rump of lamb and braised shoulder, dauphinoise potatoes,
wilted spinach and rosemary jus; and lastly raspberry crème brûlée with a cassis
smoothie and vanilla, all the while enjoying panoramas of the Cotswold countryside.
Guest rooms are distinctively furnished and decorated with rich fabrics.

Open all day all wk 10.30am-11pm **Food** Lunch all wk 12-3 Dinner all wk 6.30-9.30
Restaurant menu available all wk ⊕ FREE HOUSE ◀ Butcombe, Stroud, Wickwar
⊙ Ashton Press. ♥ 10 **Facilities** Non-diners area ❀ (Bar Garden) ⑪ Children's menu
Children's portions Play area Garden ⋒ Parking WiFi ☞ (notice required) **Rooms** 46

NEW Bisley House

tel: 01453 751328 **Middle St GL5 1DZ**
email: info@bisleyhousecafe.co.uk
dir: *From A419 rdbt follow hospital signs. 1st right into Field Road. 3rd left into Whitehall
(leads to Middle St). Pub on right*

Town centre pub designed for family dining

Built in Victorian times, this bar and restaurant was given a fresh look two years
ago. It takes its regular real ales from Stroud Brewery, including their ever-popular
Budding, while draught lager and cider come from Bourton-on-the-Water's
Cotswold Brewery. Smoked Scottish salmon with lemon mayonnaise might begin
lunch or dinner, followed by pan-fried hake with white wine and saffron sauce; an
8oz rib-eye steak with mushrooms and cherry tomatoes; or Moroccan spiced
vegetable tagine with roasted baby courgettes and heritage carrots. On the
extensive wine list are bins from France, Italy and Spain, chosen to complement the
cooking's Mediterranean flavours.

Open all day Closed Mon **Food** Lunch 11-3 Dinner 6-9 Av main course £12 ⊕ FREE
HOUSE ◀ Stroud Budding, Beerd Monterey ⊙ Cotswold. ♥ **Facilities** Non-diners area
❀ (Bar Restaurant Garden) ⑪ Children's menu Children's portions Garden ⋒ WiFi

The Ram Inn

tel: 01453 873329 **South Woodchester GL5 5EL**
dir: *A46 from Stroud to Nailsworth, right after 2m into South Woodchester, follow brown
tourist signs*

17th-century inn with splendid Cotswold views

In winter the warmth from its huge fireplace might prove more appealing than
standing on the terrace of this 17th-century Cotswold-stone inn, admiring the
splendid views. Originally a farm, it became an alehouse in 1811 and is still full of
historic little gems. Typical dishes are starters of black pudding tapas, Scotch egg,
chorizo chips or chicken goujons, followed by main courses such as fillet steak,
beer-battered cod or haddock, or the Woodchester Whopper burger. Paninis are also
served at lunchtime.

Open all day all wk **Food** Lunch Mon-Fri 12-2, Sat-Sun 12-3 Dinner all wk 6-9
Av main course £12.95 ⊕ FREE HOUSE ◀ Butcombe Bitter, Wickwar Cotswold Way,

Otter Amber, Gloucester Gold ⊙ Westons Stowford Press, Lilley's Apples & Pears &
Bee Sting Pear, Pheasant Plucker. **Facilities** Non-diners area ❀ (Bar Restaurant
Garden) ⑪ Children's portions Garden ⋒ Parking WiFi ☞ (notice required)

TETBURY
Map 4 ST89

Gumstool Inn
PICK OF THE PUBS

tel: 01666 890391 **Calcot Manor GL8 8YJ**
email: reception@calcotmanor.co.uk
dir: *3m W of Tetbury at A4135 & A46 junct*

Stylish gastro-pub with good wine choices

A popular and stylish free house, this stone farmhouse was originally built by
Cistercian monks in the 14th century, and is now part of Calcot Manor Hotel. The
buzzy and comfortable Gumstool Inn has a real country-pub atmosphere and stocks
a good selection of ales such as Butcombe Bitter, and local ciders including Ashton
Press. An excellent choice of wines is offered by the glass or bottle. The food here is
top-notch and there is a pronounced use of local suppliers. Kick off with starters of
smoked salmon with egg mayonnaise and buttered brown bread; or seared scallops
with warm spicy lentil salsa. Among the main courses may be found roasted
haunch of venison with apple and braised red cabbage; and corn-fed chicken
breast with forestière and rösti potatoes. In the summer, grab a table on the pretty,
flower-filled sun terrace, while indoor winter evenings are warmed with log fires.

Open all day all wk **Food** Lunch all wk 12-2.30 Dinner Mon-Sat 5.30-9.30, Sun
5.30-9 Av main course £15 ⊕ FREE HOUSE ◀ Butcombe Bitter, Sharp's Doom Bar
⊙ Ashton Press. ♥ 23 **Facilities** Non-diners area ⑪ Children's menu Children's
portions Play area Family room Garden ⋒ Parking WiFi ☞ (notice required)

The Priory Inn ★★★ SHL
PICK OF THE PUBS

tel: 01666 502251 **London Rd GL8 8JJ**
email: info@theprioryinn.co.uk **web:** www.theprioryinn.co.uk
dir: *M4 junct 17, A429 towards Cirencester. Left into B4014 to Tetbury. Over mini rdbt into
Long St, pub 100yds after corner on right*

Family-friendly Cotswold pub and hotel

An enormous 'walk-around' open log fire greets visitors to this thriving gastro-pub
and small hotel. Its high exposed beams date from the 16th century, when it was
the stable-block and grooms' cottages for the neighbouring priory. Local
microbreweries, typically Uley and Cotswold Lion, supply the real ales; a white wine
and a sparkling rosé come from a vineyard in Malmesbury; and damson brandy,
sloe gin and quince liqueur come from the banks of the River Severn. Meals in the
bare-boarded, beamed bar and more contemporary restaurant use fresh ingredients
sourced from within a 30-mile radius – for roasted chicken breast, rösti, creamed
leeks, smoked bacon and thyme sauce; grilled 8oz steak topped with tarragon
butter, grilled tomato and a Portobello mushroom; or root vegetable pie, topped with
mash and Double Gloucester cheese. Children can create personalised wood-fired
pizzas. The Early May Bank Holiday beer and cider festival is a big draw.

Open all day all wk 7am-11pm (Fri 7am-mdnt Sat 8am-mdnt Sun 8am-11pm)
Food Lunch Mon-Thu 12-3, Fri-Sun & BH all day (bkfst served all wk 7-10.30)
Dinner Mon-Thu 5-10, Fri-Sun & BH all day ⊕ FREE HOUSE ◀ Uley Bitter, Cotswold
Lion, Guest ale ⊙ Thatchers Gold, Cotswold, Guest cider. ♥ 13 **Facilities** Non-diners
area ⑪ Children's menu Children's portions Play area Family room Garden ⋒ Beer
festival Cider festival Parking WiFi ☞ (notice required) **Rooms** 14

TETBURY *continued*

NEW The Royal Oak Tetbury

tel: 01666 500021 **1 Cirencester Rd GL8 8EY**
email: stay@theroyaloaktetbury.co.uk **web:** www.theroyaloaktetbury.co.uk
dir: *From town centre at mini rdbt by Market House (yellow building) into Chipping St. Pass car park on right. Royal Oak on right at bottom of hill*

An impressive Arts and Crafts-style free house and dining room

For owners Chris York and Kate Lewis, restoration of this Cotswolds inn was a labour of love, a feeling shared by the team of craftsmen and other experts. Stroud Brewery's Tom Long, Bath Ales Gem, the rotating Moor Beer's Nor'Hop and So'Hop, and Severn cider occupy the bar pumps; they appear too at the beer and cider festival on the Bank Holiday in late May. Organic bar food includes Workers' Pot, a hearty stew and, if you dine 'up in the rafters', shellfish linguine with tomato chowder sauce; pan-fried duck breast with Thai potato rösti; and porcini mushroom and herb burger.

Open all day all wk Closed 1st wk Jan Mon-Thu **Food** Lunch Mon-Sat 12-2.30, Sun 12-5 Dinner Mon-Sat 5-9.30 Av main course £11 ⊕ FREE HOUSE ◀ Bath Ales Gem, Stroud Brewery Tom Long, Moor Beer So' Hop & Nor' Hop ♂ Severn. ♀ 10
Facilities Non-diners area ♣ (Bar Garden) ♦♦ Children's portions Garden ⋒ Beer festival Cider festival Parking WiFi ➡ (notice required)

Snooty Fox Hotel ★★★ SHL

tel: 01666 502436 **Market Place GL8 8DD**
email: res@snooty-fox.co.uk **web:** www.snooty-fox.co.uk
dir: *In town centre opposite covered market hall*

Draw up a chair by the log fire

Occupying a prime spot in the heart of Tetbury, this 16th-century coaching inn and hotel retains many of its original features. Sit in a leather armchair in front of the log fire with a pint of Wadworth 6X and order from the extensive bar menu – eggs Benedict or a bowl of mussels maybe. Alternatively, head for the restaurant and enjoy the likes of pan-fried scallops with cauliflower purée and crisp black pudding followed by slow-roast lamb shank with leeks, bacon, creamed mash and onion sauce. Traditional puddings include Cambridge burnt cream, and rhubarb and apple crumble.

Open all day all wk **Food** Lunch all wk 12-3, snacks 3-6 Dinner all wk 6-9.30 ⊕ FREE HOUSE ◀ Wadworth 6X, Butcombe Bitter ♂ Ashton Press. ♀
Facilities Non-diners area ♦♦ Children's menu Children's portions Outside area ⋒ WiFi ➡ (notice required) **Rooms** 12

UPPER ODDINGTON — Map 10 SP22

The Horse & Groom Inn — PICK OF THE PUBS

tel: 01451 830584 **GL56 0XH**
email: info@horseandgroom.uk.com
dir: *1.5m S of Stow-on-the-Wold, just off A436*

Cotswold-stone inn specialising in local beer and food

In a conservation village in the Evenlode Valley, this pretty 16th-century inn has been owner-operated for more than a decade. The bar boasts pale polished flagstones, stripped stone walls, oak beams in the ochre ceiling, and a double-sided inglenook fireplace. Well-kept ales, cider and lager from the Cotswold Brewing Company, plenty of wines by the glass and 20 malt whiskies add up to a faultless choice of drinks. After ordering refreshment, take a menu out to the terrace or walled garden for a seat beneath a green parasol. Three courses of classic but imaginative pub food could start with salmon, cod and smoked haddock fishcake with dill mayonnaise. Follow perhaps with one of the pub's most popular dishes, such as Gloucester Old Spots sausages with mustard mash; or lamb chump with honey-roast parsnips, curly kale and fondant potato. Puddings may include a chocolate marquise with meringue, toasted almonds and brandy crème Anglaise.

Open all wk 12-3 5.30-11 (Sun 12-3 6.30-10.30) **Food** Lunch all wk 12-2 Dinner Mon-Sat 6.30-9, Sun 7-9 ⊕ FREE HOUSE ◀ Wye Valley Bitter & HPA, Goffs Tournament, Prescott Hill Climb, Otter Bitter, North Cotswold Shagweaver ♂ Cotswold. ♀ 25 **Facilities** Non-diners area ♣ (Bar Restaurant Garden) ♦♦ Children's menu Children's portions Garden ⋒ Parking WiFi ➡ (notice required)

WINCHCOMBE — Map 10 SP02

The Lion Inn

tel: 01242 603300 **37 North St GL54 5PS**
email: reception@thelionwinchcombe.co.uk
dir: *In town centre (parking in Chandos St)*

Shabby-chic, friendly and caring town centre hostelry

This attractive watering hole in the ancient town of Winchcombe is buzzy and welcoming. With 15th-century origins, care has been taken over the years to make sure the building's quirky charms remain. Lovers of wine and real ale are spoilt for choice in the spacious and relaxed bar – a pint of Brakspear Oxford Gold or a Prescott ale might be just the thing. The menu features pigeon breast, pearl barley and chorizo ragu; or slow-braised brisket of Wagyu beef, mash, French beans and rich beef jus.

Open all day all wk **Food** Lunch all wk 12-3 Dinner all wk 6-9.30 ⊕ FREE HOUSE ◀ Brakspear Oxford Gold, Ringwood, Prescott ♂ Thatchers Gold. ♀ 19
Facilities Non-diners area ♣ (Bar Garden) ♦♦ Children's portions Garden ⋒ WiFi

GREATER MANCHESTER

CHORLTON-CUM-HARDY
Map 15 SJ89

The Horse & Jockey

tel: 0161 860 7794 **Chorlton Green M21 9HS**
email: info@horseandjockeychorlton.com
dir: *M60 junct 7, A56 towards Stretford. Right onto A5145 towards Chorlton. After lights, 2nd right into St Clements Rd. Pub left on green*

Facing Chorlton's wooded town green

Assuming this Tudor pub's interior designers had a free hand when it was last refurbished, they certainly made the most of it. Wherever you look – the bar, the restaurant, the rooms, the beer garden – the results are impressive. The pub doubles as the home of the Bootleg Brewery, run by an all-too-rare female head brewer. The brewery is open to the public on occasions such as their Oktoberfest. Home-made gourmet pies; Lancashire lamb hotpot; seafood platter; hanging kebabs; and burger boards all feature on a comprehensive menu.

Open all day all wk **Food** Lunch Mon-Sat 12-10, Sun 12-8 Dinner Mon-Sat 12-10, Sun 12-8 Av main course £9 ⊕ JOSEPH HOLT ◄ Bootleg Chorlton Pale Ale, Twisted Groove & Urban Fox ♂ Westons Stowford Press. ♟ **Facilities** Non-diners area ♣ (Bar Outside area) ♦♦ Children's menu Children's portions Outside area ⋒ WiFi ⛴

DELPH
Map 16 SD90

The Old Bell Inn ★★★★ INN ⊕

tel: 01457 870130 **5 Huddersfield Rd OL3 5EG**
email: info@theoldbellinn.co.uk web: www.theoldbellinn.co.uk
dir: *M62 junct 22, A672 to Denshaw junct (signed Saddleworth). Left onto A6052 signed Delph. Through Delph to T-junct. Left onto A62, pub 150yds on left*

Historic coaching inn with excellent food

Legend has it that highwayman Dick Turpin rested here on his way to the gallows; more certain is that young Queen Victoria stayed when visiting York. Standards are high throughout, whether for a well-kept pint of Black Sheep in the bar, a relaxing snack in the brasserie, a special-occasion dinner in the restaurant, or a night in one of the bedrooms. If you're sitting down to eat, the menu may offer starters like smoked salmon and chive fishcakes, creamy garlic and parsley steamed mussels; or squab pigeon Wellington with parsnip and apple purée. Moving onto mains you may find steak and ale pie; haddock and chips; baked sea bass fillet with braised celery, shellfish risotto and bisque; or cheddar, leek and roast red onion pie. Leave enough room for apple and granola crumble tart or sticky toffee pudding with butterscotch sauce.

Open all day all wk **Food** Lunch all wk 12-5 Dinner Mon-Sat 5-9.30, Sun 5-9 Set menu available Restaurant menu available all wk ⊕ FREE HOUSE ◄ Timothy Taylor Landlord & Golden Best, Black Sheep Best Bitter ♂ Thatchers. **Facilities** Non-diners area ♦♦ Children's menu Children's portions Garden Outside area ⋒ Parking WiFi ⛴ (notice required) **Rooms** 18

DENSHAW
Map 16 SD91

The Rams Head Inn

tel: 01457 874802 **OL3 5UN**
email: info@ramsheaddenshaw.co.uk
dir: *M62 junct 22, A672 towards Oldham, 2m to inn*

A gastro-pub, farm shop and tea room

At 1,212 feet above sea level, this 450-year-old family-owned country inn has fabulous moorland views and is just two miles from the M62. Log fires and collections of memorabilia are features of the interior, which includes The Pantry, an in-house farm shop, deli, bakery and tea room selling everything from cheeses to chocolates. Game and seafood figure strongly on the menu, with dishes ranging from gratinated haddock fillet, spring onion mash and cheddar sauce to whole grilled Whitby plaice. There are also plenty of vegetarian options. Finish with the inn's 'famed' sticky toffee pudding. There's a garden area to the rear of the inn with bench seating and panoramic views.

Open Tue-Fri 12-2.30 5.30-10 (Sat 12-10.30 Sun 12-8.30) Closed 25-26 Dec, 1 Jan, Mon (ex BHs) **Food** Lunch Tue-Fri 12-2.30, Sat 12-10, Sun 12-8.30 Dinner Tue-Thu 5.30-8.30, Fri 5.30-9.30, Sat 12-10, Sun 12-8.30 Set menu available Restaurant menu available Tue-Sun ⊕ FREE HOUSE ◄ Timothy Taylor Landlord. ♟ 16 **Facilities** Non-diners area ♦♦ Children's portions Garden ⋒ Parking WiFi ⛴ (notice required)

DIDSBURY
Map 16 SJ89

The Metropolitan

tel: 0161 438 2332 **2 Lapwing Ln M20 2WS**
email: info@the-metropolitan.co.uk
dir: *M60 junct 5, A5103, right into Barlow Moor Rd, left into Burton Rd. Pub at x-rds. Right into Lapwing Ln for car park*

Airy Victorian railway hotel and gastro-pub

'The Met' is well situated in the leafy suburb of West Didsbury on the old Midland Railway line into Manchester. Its Victorian heritage – decorative floor tiling, ornate windows and huge airy interior filled with antique tables, chairs and deep sofas – attracts a mainly young and cosmopolitan crowd. The drinks choice matches customer demand with nearly 30 wines sold by the glass, popular beers and bottled craft ciders. The bar and terrace menu offers pizzas and salads, while the restaurant carte is high on brasserie appeal: confit duck and kale hash, with fried duck egg and brown sauce, for example; and the famous Met burger made from 28-day aged beef.

Open all day all wk 11.30-11 (Wed-Thu 11.30-11.30 Fri-Sat 11.30am-mdnt Sun 12-11) Closed 25 Dec **Food** Lunch Mon-Thu 12-9.30, Fri-Sat 12-10, Sun 12-9 (bkfst Mon-Fri 10am-11.45am, Sun 10am-11.30am) Dinner Mon-Thu 12-9.30, Fri-Sat 12-10, Sun 12-9 Restaurant menu available Mon-Sat evenings ⊕ ENTERPRISE INNS ◄ Timothy Taylor Landlord, Caledonian Deuchars IPA, Guinness ♂ Hogan's, The Orchard Pig, Cornish Heritage. ♟ 28 **Facilities** Non-diners area ♦♦ Children's menu Children's portions Outside area ⋒ Parking WiFi ⛴ (notice required)

LITTLEBOROUGH
Map 16 SD91

The White House

tel: 01706 378456 **Blackstone Edge, Halifax Rd OL15 0LG**
dir: *On A58, 8m from Rochdale, 9m from Halifax*

A favourite with walkers and cyclists

Known as The White House for over 100 years, this 17th-century coaching house has been in the same hands for almost 30 of them. On the Pennine Way, 1,300 feet above sea level, it has panoramic views of the moors and Hollingworth Lake far below. Not surprising then, that it attracts walkers and cyclists who rest up and sup on Black Sheep and Theakston Best Bitter. A simple menu of pub grub ranges from sandwiches and salads, to grills, international and vegetarian dishes, and traditional mains such as home-made steak and kidney pie, and haddock and prawn Mornay.

Open all wk Mon-Sat 12-3 6-10 (Sun 12-10.30) Closed 25 Dec **Food** Lunch Mon-Sat 12-2, Sun 12-9 Dinner Mon-Sat 6.30-9.30, Sun 12-9 Av main course £8.50 ⊕ FREE HOUSE ◄ Theakston Best Bitter, Black Sheep, Guest ales. **Facilities** Non-diners area ♦♦ Children's menu Children's portions Outside area Parking WiFi ⛴

MANCHESTER
Map 16 SJ89

Marble Arch

tel: 0161 832 5914 **73 Rochdale Rd M4 4HY**
dir: *In city centre (Northern Quarter)*

Victorian pub popular with ale aficionados

A listed building famous for its sloping floor, glazed brick walls and barrel-vaulted ceiling, the Marble Arch is a fine example of Manchester's Victorian heritage. Part of the award-winning organic Marble Brewery, the pub was built in 1888 by celebrated architect Alfred Darbyshire for Manchester brewery B&J McKenna. An established favourite with beer aficionados and offering six regular ales and eight seasonal house beers, the pub offers a well-considered menu offering traditional bar meals of burgers and hot salt beef bagels to innovative mains including pan-fried halibut with Madras curry sauce and polenta cakes. It hosts its own beer festivals.

Open all day all wk Closed 25 Dec **Food** Lunch Mon-Sat 12-8.45, Sun 12-7.45 Dinner Mon-Sat 12-8.45, Sun 12-7.45 ⊕ FREE HOUSE ◀ Marble Manchester Bitter, Lagonda IPA, Ginger Marble, Pint & Earl Grey IPA Ŏ Moonshine.
Facilities Non-diners area ❤ (Bar Garden) ♦ Garden ⊼ Beer festival WiFi

MARPLE BRIDGE
Map 16 SJ98

Hare & Hounds

tel: 0161 427 4042 **19 Mill Brow SK6 5LW**
email: haremillbrow@gmail.com
dir: *From A626 in Marple Bridge (at lights at river bridge) follow Mellor signs into Town St. 1st left into Hollins Ln. Right at T-junct into Ley Ln. Pub 0.25m on left*

Idyllic rural retreat in lovely countryside

Tucked away in a secluded hamlet in the hills fringing the Peak District, this comfortable community local first opened its doors in 1805. It retains much of the character of days gone by and is a popular stop with ramblers exploring the countless paths threading the ridges, moors and wooded cloughs hereabouts. Roaring winter fires take away the chill; or you could settle down outside with a glass of Stockport-brewed Robinsons beer and anticipate freshly cooked mains such as wild mushroom, smoked garlic and spinach risotto; or venison pie with roasted root vegetables, braised red cabbage and gravy, with bread and butter pudding with double cream to finish.

Open Mon-Tue 5-10 (Wed-Thu 5-12 Fri 12-3 5-12 Sat 12-12 Sun 12-10) Closed Mon-Thu L **Food** Lunch Fri-Sat 12-2, Sun 1-7 Dinner Wed-Sat 6-9.30, Sun 1-7 ⊕ ROBINSONS ◀ Unicorn, Hatters, Dizzy Blonde, Seasonal Ales Ŏ Westons Stowford Press. **Facilities** Non-diners area ❤ (Bar Restaurant Outside area) ♦ Children's portions Outside area ⊼ Parking WiFi

Find out more about the AA's accommodation rating schemes on page 8

MELLOR
Map 16 SJ98

NEW Oddfellows Arms

tel: 0161 449 7826 **73 Moor End Rd SK6 5PT**
email: info@oddfellowsmellor.com **web:** www.oddfellowsmellor.com
dir: *In village centre*

Stylishly refurbished pub with good food and local ales

A pub since 1803, the 'Oddies' was taken over by a group of regulars who set about refurbishing it and restoring it to its 17th-century splendour. Situated in the High Peak National Park, the pub boasts three log burners, oak floors and a stylish upstairs dining room. In the bar, cask ales such as Abbeydale Deception and Marble Manchester Bitter keep drinkers happy but the excellent food attracts diners from far and wide. Local produce drives the menu, with typical dishes including Bury black pudding, poached egg and pepper sauce, and Saddleback pork sausages with parsley mash.

Open 4-late (Fri-Sun 12-late) Closed Mon **Food** Lunch Fri 12-3, Sat 12-9.30, Sun 12-8 Dinner Tue 5-8, Wed 5-9, Thu-Fri 5-9.30, Sat 12-9.30, Sun 12-8 Av main course £12 ⊕ FREE HOUSE ◀ Marble Manchester Bitter, Marston's Pedigree, Abbeydale Deception, Thornbridge Jaipur Ŏ Thatchers Gold. ♚ 13
Facilities Non-diners area ❤ (Bar Outside area) ♦ Children's menu Children's portions Family room Outside area ⊼ Parking ⛟ (notice required)

OLDHAM
Map 16 SD90

The Roebuck Inn

tel: 0161 624 7819 **Strinesdale OL4 3RB**
email: sehowarth1@hotmail.com
dir: *From Oldham Mumps Bridge take Huddersfield Rd (A62), right at 2nd lights into Ripponden Rd (A672), 1m right at lights into Turfpit Ln, 1m*

Country pub not far from Oldham

A thousand feet up in Strinedale on the edge of Saddleworth Moor, this traditionally styled inn provides a menu with plenty of choice. Starters include lamb samosas served with a mint yogurt dip, or fresh mushrooms in a creamy garlic butter sauce, then comes a long list of main courses, including strips of beef fillet cooked in red wine sauce and topped with grilled Stilton; salmon fillet, dill mash and prawn sauce; chicken fajitas with all the trimmings, or a vegetarian option such as mushroom, cranberry, nut and brie Wellington served with a cranberry sauce. Beers come from a variety of local breweries.

Open all wk 12-3 5-11 (Fri-Sun 12-11) **Food** Lunch all wk 12-2.15 Dinner all wk 5-9.15 Set menu available Restaurant menu available all wk ⊕ FREE HOUSE ◀ Greenfield Silver Owl. ♚ 9 **Facilities** Non-diners area ❤ (Bar Garden) ♦ Children's menu Children's portions Play area Garden Parking WiFi ⛟

The White Hart Inn ★★★★ INN ◉◉   PICK OF THE PUBS

tel: 01457 872566 **51 Stockport Rd, Lydgate OL4 4JJ**
email: bookings@thewhitehart.co.uk **web:** www.thewhitehart.co.uk
dir: *From Manchester A62 to Oldham. Right onto bypass, A669 through Lees. In 500yds past Grotton, at brow of hill right onto A6050*

Charming dining pub with award-winning gardens

High on the hillside overlooking Oldham and Manchester, The White Hart is owned by Charles Brierley, who converted the ground floor into a smart bar and brasserie, and who also put together the wine list after months of research. There's been a pub on this site since 1788, when its vast cellars were used for brewing beer. The inn has retained its period charm of beams, exposed stonework and open fireplaces, blending these with contemporary decor. The kitchen team believe in creating 'meals, not sculptures on a plate' and in making good use of local ingredients to offer cosmopolitan dishes. In the rustic brasserie try quail ballotine, roast chestnut and fried quail's egg, followed by rump of lamb, curds, courgette, onion ash and chilli oil, then hot prune soufflé with tarragon ice cream. Book the contemporary restaurant for the seven-course chef's tasting menu, and there's also an intimate library dining area.

Open all day all wk Closed 26 Dec, 1 Jan **Food** Lunch Mon-Sat 12-2.30, Sun 12-8 Dinner Mon-Sat 6-9.30, Sun 12-8 Set menu available Restaurant menu available Wed-Sat eve ⊕ FREE HOUSE ◖ Timothy Taylor Landlord & Golden Best, JW Lees Bitter, Thwaites Wainwright Ö Westons Mortimers Orchard. ₹ 9
Facilities Non-diners area ◖ Children's menu Garden ⊨ Beer festival Parking WiFi
Rooms 12

■ SALFORD	Map 15 SJ89

The King's Arms

tel: 0161 839 8726 **11 Bloom St M3 6AN**
email: kingsarmssalford@gmail.com
dir: *Phone for detailed directions*

Impressive Victorian pub with Bohemian atmosphere

Redevelopment has swept away much of old Salford. Fortunately this striking street-corner edifice survives intact amidst the concrete, steel and glass, across the River Irwell from Manchester's gleaming centre. It's a grass-roots venue renowned for arts, festivals and creative exhibitions. Music and theatre feature in the busy function room; co-owner Paul Heaton is a celebrated musician whilst the pub itself features in the cult TV series *Fresh Meat*. At this drinks-led pub (no food except Sunday roasts) you'll find an ever-changing range of up to six beers, mostly from Greater Manchester's renowned microbrewery culture; guest ciders and continental bottled beers add to the lively jigsaw.

Open all wk Mon-Wed 4-close (Thu-Sun 12-close) ⊕ FREE HOUSE ◖ 6 changing guest ales Ö 2 changing guest ciders. **Facilities** ✿ (Bar Restaurant Garden) ◖ Garden WiFi

---

■ STOCKPORT	Map 16 SJ89

The Arden Arms

tel: 0161 480 2185 **23 Millgate SK1 2LX**
email: steve@ardenarms.com
dir: *M60 junct 27 to town centre. Across mini rdbt, at lights turn left. Pub on right of next rdbt behind Asda*

Timeless gem with interesting real ales

In the centre of Stockport, this Grade II listed late-Georgian coaching inn retains its unspoilt multi-roomed layout and original tiled floors. The building was last

modernised in 1908, giving drinkers the opportunity to order from the traditional curved bar before settling down by the coal fire or in the tiny snug behind the bar. Outside, the large cobbled courtyard is used for alfresco dining and summer concerts. The lunch menu has an extensive list of hot and cold sandwiches and daily-changing specials, while pan-fried fillet of plaice, fish stew or roasted vegetable and buffalo mozzarella lasagne may be dinner options. There's always a traditional Sunday roast, as well as jazz nights and charity quizzes.

Open all wk 12-12 Closed 25-26 Dec, 1 Jan **Food** Lunch Mon-Fri 12-2.30, Sat 12-4, Sun 12-6.30 Dinner Thu-Sat 6-9 ⊕ ROBINSONS ◖ Unicorn, Trooper, 1892, Dizzy Blonde, Double Hop, Seasonal ales Ö Westons Stowford Press. ₹ 9
Facilities Non-diners area ✿ (Bar Restaurant Garden) ◖ Garden ⊨ WiFi

---

The Nursery Inn

tel: 0161 432 2044 **Green Ln, Heaton Norris SK4 2NA**
email: nurseryinn@hydesbrewery.com
dir: *M60 junct 1, A5145 towards Didsbury. At lights right into Bankhall Rd (B5169), 5th right into Green Ln. Pass rugby club. Right onto narrow cobbled road, pub 100yds on right*

A heritage pub unspoilt by progress

Built in 1939 to replace its predecessor, this well-preserved hostelry is down a narrow street of late 19th-century terraced houses. The spacious interior evokes pre-World War II days, with its oak-panelled lounge, former smoke room and other mid 20th-century pub features. Good-value, home-cooked lunchtime snacks (the kitchen is closed in the evening) comprise sandwiches, toasties, jacket potatoes and mains of gammon, egg and chips; beer-battered fish and chips; and rib-eye steak baguette with salad. The pub's bowling green is reached by a passage lined with team trophies. The Hydes real ales in the bar are joined by guests at the three annual beer festivals.

Open all day all wk **Food** Lunch Tue-Fri 12-2.30, Sat-Sun 12-4 Av main course £6.95 ⊕ HYDES BREWERY ◖ Original, The Beer Studio, Seasonal ales, Guest ales. ₹ 9
Facilities Non-diners area ✿ (Bar Garden) ◖ Children's menu Children's portions Family room Garden ⊨ Beer festival Parking WiFi ▭

■ WALMERSLEY	Map 15 SD81

The Lord Raglan

tel: 0161 764 6680 **Nangreaves BL9 6SP**
dir: *M66 junct 1, A56 to Walmersley. Left into Palatine Drive, left into Ribble Drive, left into Walmersley Old Rd to Nangreaves*

Recommended for its own microbrewery beers

The rambling, stone-built Lord Raglan is set beside a cobbled lane high on the moors above Bury, at the head of a former weaving hamlet, where lanes and tracks dissipate into deep, secluded gorges rich in industrial heritage. Beers brewed at the on-site Leyden microbrewery may be taken in the garden, where the throaty cough of steam engines on the East Lancashire Railway echoes off the River Irwell's steep valley sides below the towering Peel Monument. Reliable, traditional pub grub and changing specials take the edge off walkers' appetites. Try the chicken and mushroom pie, hot steak sandwich, or grilled halibut steak served with a lime and tomato salsa. There are beer festivals in the summer and autumn.

Open all wk 12-2.30 6-11 (Fri-Sun all day) **Food** Lunch Mon-Thu 12-2, Fri-Sat 12-9, Sun 12-8 Dinner Mon-Thu 6-9, Fri-Sat 12-9, Sun 12-8 ⊕ FREE HOUSE ◖ Leyden Nanny Flyer, Crowning Glory, Light Brigade, Black Pudding Ö Wilce's Herefordshire. ₹ 10 **Facilities** ✿ (Bar Garden) ◖ Children's menu Children's portions Garden Beer festival Parking WiFi ▭

HAMPSHIRE

ALTON
Map 5 SU73

The Anchor Inn ★★★★★ RR ◉◉
PICK OF THE PUBS

tel: 01420 23261 **Lower Froyle GU34 4NA**
email: info@anchorinnatlowerfroyle.co.uk **web:** www.anchorinnatlowerfroyle.co.uk
dir: From A31 follow Bentley signs

Celebrating the traditional English country inn

A 16th-century, tile-hung farmhouse forms the nucleus of the Anchor. It's one of the Miller's Collection of traditional English inns in Hampshire and Berkshire, all four of which focus on fine food and beer and country sports. Low ceilings, wooden floors, exposed beams and open fires suggest that little has changed for decades in the intimate snug and saloon bar, source of local beers Triple fff Alton's Pride, Andwell King John, and Bowman Wallops Wood. The restaurant's two AA Rosette award recognises the quality of the regularly changing, locally sourced food that at lunchtime or dinner could be pan-fried cod fillet with potato gnocchi, Jerusalem artichoke, spinach, and mushroom and chestnut sauce; pulled pork with pan haggerty, cabbage and bacon; or butternut squash ravioli with rocket, aged balsamic and toasted pumpkin seeds.

Open all day all wk Closed 25 Dec ⊕ FREE HOUSE/MILLER'S COLLECTION ◼ Triple fff Alton's Pride, Andwell King John, Bowman Wallops Wood ♂ Westons Stowford Press. **Facilities** ♣ (Bar Garden) ♦ Children's menu Children's portions Garden Parking WiFi **Rooms** 5

NEW The George

tel: 01420 82331 **Butts Rd GU34 1LH**
email: georgeatalton@gmail.com
dir: From A31 onto A339 towards Basingstoke. At mini rdbt take 2nd exit signed Town Centre (Butts Rd). Pub on right

Small, friendly town pub

Fronting the street, The George is a long, white-painted building with a rather fine portico. The bar, set out with pale-wood tables and chairs, stocks real ales from across the country, although local brews get a good look-in too. Seasonal menus – we quote from a winter one – might offer moules marinière; or vegetable croquette with parsnip crisps, sesame and honey dressing as a starter. Possible main courses might be the day's curry; crispy chicken wings marinated in spicy hot sauce; or Whitby scampi. Sandwiches are available at lunchtime and there's a short menu for children.

Open all day all wk Closed 1 Jan **Food** Contact pub for food times Av main course £8 ⊕ PUNCH TAVERNS ◼ St Austell Tribute, Sharp's Atlantic & Doom Bar, Surrey Hills Shere Drop, Bowman Ales Swift One. ♚ 24 **Facilities** Non-diners area ♣ (All areas) ♦ Children's menu Children's portions Garden Outside area ⌐ Beer festival Parking WiFi ▭ (notice required)

AMPFIELD
Map 5 SU42

White Horse at Ampfield

tel: 01794 368356 **Winchester Rd SO51 9BQ**
email: whitehorseinn@hotmail.co.uk
dir: From Winchester take A3040, then A3090 towards Romsey. Ampfield in 7m. Or M3 junct 13, A335 (signed Chandler's Ford). At lights right onto B3043, follow Chandler's Ford Industrial Estate then Hursley signs. Left onto A3090 to Ampfield

Traditional village inn once frequented by pilgrims

With roots as a pilgrims' inn in the 16th century, the timber-framed White Horse is the only pub in the village in which The Rev W. Awdry, *Thomas the Tank Engine's*

creator, lived as a boy. The building is home to three large inglenooks, the one in the public bar having an iron fireback decorated with the crest of Charles I and hooks on which to hang bacon sides for smoking. Typical dishes are mushroom mille feuille with mixed bean and chickpea cassoulet and pea purée; roast chicken breast with sweet chilli and honey sauce; and smoked trout with new potatoes and salad.

Open all day all wk 11-11 (Sun 12-9) **Food** Lunch Mon-Sat 12-2.30, Sun 12-4 Dinner Mon-Sat 6-9 ⊕ GREENE KING ◼ IPA, Morland Old Speckled Hen & Original ♂ Somersby Cider, Aspall. ♚ 14 **Facilities** Non-diners area ♣ (Bar Garden Outside area) ♦ Children's menu Children's portions Play area Garden Outside area ⌐ Parking WiFi ▭ (notice required)

AMPORT
Map 5 SU34

The Hawk Inn

tel: 01264 710371 **SP11 8AE**
email: info@hawkinnamport.co.uk
dir: From Andover towards Thruxton on A303 exit signed Hawk Conservancy & Amport. 1m to Amport. Or A303 onto A343 (S of Andover) follow Abbots Ann & Amport signs

Both modern and traditional British food

In the light and spacious interior of adjoining rooms, the bar offers Ramsbury Gold real ale, while a meal at one of the widely-spaced tables could feature crispy squid with smoked paprika aïoli, or Jerusalem artichoke soup with truffle oil to start, followed by thyme and garlic roasted whole poussin with caramelised onions and hand-cut chips; or The Hawk Burger with smoked Applewood cheddar, bacon and fries. The terrace area affords great views towards Pill Hill Brook.

Open all day all wk Closed 25 Dec **Food** Lunch all wk 12-2.30 Dinner Mon-Sat 6.30-9.30, Sun 6-9 Av main course £13 ⊕ FREE HOUSE ◼ Ramsbury Gold. ♚ 14 **Facilities** Non-diners area ♣ (Bar Outside area) ♦ Children's menu Children's portions Outside area ⌐ Parking WiFi

ANDOVER
Map 5 SU34

Wyke Down Country Pub & Restaurant

tel: 01264 352048 **Wyke Down, Picket Piece SP11 6LX**
email: info@wykedown.co.uk
dir: 3m from Andover town centre on A303 follow signs for Wyke Down Caravan Park

Converted barn and conservatory dining

A diversified farm on the outskirts of Andover, this establishment combines a pub/restaurant with a golf driving range, but still raises its own beef cattle. The pub started in a barn over 25 years ago and the restaurant was built some years later. A typical meal might be baked avocado topped with smoked chicken and cheese followed by beef, mushroom and Stilton steam pudding. Other choices include plenty from the grill and international favourites such as chilli, lasagne and Cajun chicken. You might want to time your visit for a summer Sunday car boot sale, held in an adjacent field.

Open all wk 12-3 6-11 Closed 25 Dec-2 Jan **Food** Lunch all wk 12-2 Dinner Sun-Tue 6-8, Wed-Sat 6-9 ⊕ FREE HOUSE ◼ Fuller's London Pride ♂ Aspall. **Facilities** Non-diners area ♦ Children's menu Children's portions Play area Garden ⌐ Parking WiFi ▭ (notice required)

PICK OF THE PUBS

The Wellington Arms ❀❀

BAUGHURST Map 5 SU56

tel: 0118 982 0110
Baughurst Rd RG26 5LP
email: hello@thewellingtonarms.com
web: www.thewellingtonarms.com
dir: *From A4, E of Newbury, through Aldermaston. At 2nd rdbt 2nd exit signed Baughurst, left at T-junct, pub 1m*

Drawing discerning diners from miles around

Hidden down a maze of lanes in peaceful countryside between Basingstoke and Newbury is the stylish 'Welly', a former hunting lodge for the Duke of Wellington. Inside are wooden tables, tiled floors and attractively patterned curtains and blinds. Jason King and Simon Page have never looked back since arriving here around ten years ago. Their ethos is simple: local, well-priced and delicious food. Jason's award-winning, daily chalkboard menus offer plenty of interest and imagination and much of the produce is organic, local or home grown; they are very conscious of keeping the food miles down. Salad leaves, herbs and vegetables are grown in the pub's polytunnel and raised vegetable beds, free-range eggs come from their rare-breed and rescue hens, and there are also rare-breed sheep, Tamworth pigs and five beehives. This might translate to a starter of twice-baked Westcombe

cheddar soufflé, braised young leeks with double cream and parmesan; Sarah's pheasant, rabbit and pork terrine with home-produced apple chutney. Follow with flaky pastry potpie of home-reared Jacob lamb; or Brixham market's pan-fried skate wing with brown butter, capers and Anya potatoes. One of the Wellington's home-made desserts will make the perfect finish – perhaps the dark chocolate squidgy and vanilla ice cream; or lemon posset with berries and shortbread. The dining room is rather small so booking is certainly advisable, or maybe just arrive early to secure a table. The well-tended garden is an extension for diners when the sun shines but if the weather is on the chilly side, just ask to borrow a cosy mohair rug to keep you warm.

Open 12-3 6-11 (Sun 12-3) Closed Sun eve **Food** Lunch all wk 12-3 Dinner Mon-Sat 6-9 Set menu available Restaurant menu available all wk ⊕ FREE HOUSE ◆ Longdog, West Berkshire, Two Cocks, Wild Weather Ales ◌ Tutts Clump. ♀ 9
Facilities ❀ (Bar Restaurant Garden) ♦ Children's portions Garden ☍ Parking WiFi ▭ (notice required)

BALL HILL
Map 5 SU46

The Furze Bush Inn

tel: 01635 253228 **Hatt Common, East Woodhay RG20 ONQ**
email: info@furzebushinn.co.uk
dir: *From Newbury take A343 (Andover Road), pub signed*

Hearty food in a handy location

A popular rural free house, this is a perfect place for refreshment following a day at the Newbury Races, walking the Berkshire Downs, or visiting Highclere Castle (the location for the TV series *Downton Abbey*). The bar menu features a good range of favourites, such as tempura prawns with salad and chilli sauce; herb-crusted salmon fillet with parsley and caper butter; gamekeeper's casserole with herb dumplings and creamed potatoes; and warm chocolate fudge cake for afters. There's a large front garden, a children's play area and a rear patio with parasols – perfect for summer drinking.

Open all day all wk **Food** Lunch Mon-Fri 12-3, Sat 12-9, Sun 12-8.30 Dinner Mon-Fri 5-9, Sat 12-9, Sun 12-8.30 Restaurant menu available all wk ⊕ FREE HOUSE ◀ Greene King Abbot Ale & IPA. ♀ 9 **Facilities** Non-diners area ⬩ Children's menu Play area Garden ⊨ Beer festival Parking WiFi ⬛

BAUGHURST
Map 5 SU56

The Wellington Arms ◉◉
PICK OF THE PUBS

See Pick of the Pubs on page 221

BEAULIEU
Map 5 SU30

The Drift Inn

tel: 023 8029 2342 **Beaulieu Rd SO42 7YQ**
email: bookatable@driftinn.co.uk
dir: *From Lyndhurst take B3056 (Beaulieu Rd) signed Beaulieu. Cross railway line, inn on right*

Family-friendly New Forest inn

This inn is surrounded by the glorious New Forest National Park. The word 'drift' refers to the centuries-old, twice a year, round-up of the 3,000-plus free-wandering ponies. Beers from Ringwood on the western side of the forest and a guest ale are served in the bar, while in the restaurant the menu lists beef chilli; chargrilled local 28-day matured sirloin steak; goats' cheese and vegetable lasagne; and a selection of sandwiches, baguettes and jacket potatoes. Outside are two children's play areas and large gardens, although no one minds if you come inside wearing walking boots or wellies and with your dog in tow.

Open all day all wk 10am-11pm (Sat 9am-11pm Sun 9am-10.30pm) **Food** Lunch all wk 12-3 (Etr-Oct 12-9) Dinner all wk 6-9 (Etr-Oct 12-9) Set menu available ⊕ FREE HOUSE ◀ Ringwood Best Bitter, Old Thumper & Fortyniner, Guest ales Ŏ Thatchers. **Facilities** Non-diners area ⬩ (Bar Restaurant Garden) ⬩ Children's menu Children's portions Play area Garden ⊨ Beer festival Cider festival Parking WiFi ⬛ (notice required)

BEAUWORTH
Map 5 SU52

The Milburys

tel: 01962 771248 **SO24 OPB**
email: martin1949@gma.co.uk
dir: *A272 towards Petersfield, 6m, turn right for Beauworth*

Popular community pub with great views and traditional pub grub

Dating from the 17th century and taking its name from the Bronze Age barrow nearby, this rustic hill-top pub is noted for its massive, 250-year-old treadmill that used to draw water from the 300-ft well in the bar. In summer, sweeping views across Hampshire can be savoured from the lofty garden. Inside you will find a great selection of real ales which you can enjoy by the warming winter fires. Traditional pub food, such as steak and ale pie and battered cod, is served all week in the bar and restaurant. There's a skittle alley, and car, motorcycle and caravan rallies are held here.

Open all wk **Food** Lunch all wk 12-2 Dinner all wk 6-9 Av main course £9.95 Restaurant menu available ⊕ FREE HOUSE ◀ Milburys Best, Goddards Ale of Wight, Hop Back Summer Lightning & Crop Circle, Palmers, Wadworth Ŏ Westons Stowford Press, Thatchers. **Facilities** Non-diners area ⬩ (Bar Garden) ⬩ Children's menu Children's portions Play area Family room Garden ⊨ Parking ⬛

BENTLEY
Map 5 SU74

The Bull Inn

tel: 01420 22156 **GU10 5JH**
email: enquiries@thebullinnbentley.co.uk
dir: *2m from Farnham on A31 towards Winchester*

Period details and an extensive menu

Exposed beams, real fires and plenty of alfresco seating make this 15th-century coaching inn well worth a visit. There's also a great selection of food. Lunch choices brings The Bull platter, sandwiches, salads and a two-course lunch special; the à la carte menu includes chargrill dishes. There's a good selection of wines, and real ales such as Fuller's London Pride, Ringwood Best Bitter and St Austell Tribute.

Open all day all wk 11-11 (Sun 12-10.30) Closed 1 Jan **Food** Lunch Mon-Sat 12-2.30, Sun 12-7 Dinner Mon-Sat 6-9.30, Sun 12-7 Set menu available ⊕ ENTERPRISE INNS ◀ Fuller's London Pride, St Austell Tribute, Ringwood Best Bitter Ŏ Aspall. ♀ 9 **Facilities** Non-diners area ⬩ (Bar Outside area) ⬩ Children's menu Children's portions Outside area ⊨ Parking WiFi ⬛ (notice required)

BENTWORTH
Map 5 SU64

The Sun Inn
PICK OF THE PUBS

See Pick of the Pubs on page 224 and advert on opposite page

BISHOP'S WALTHAM
Map 5 SU51

The Hampshire Bowman

tel: 01489 892940 **Dundridge Ln SO32 1GD**
email: info@hampshirebowman.com
dir: *From Bishop's Waltham on B3035 towards Corhampton. Right signed Dundridge. 1.2m to Pub*

Rustic rural gem lost down lanes

A true rural local, set in 10 acres beside a country lane in rolling downland, this unassuming Victorian pub remains delightfully old fashioned. In the beamed, simply furnished and brick-floored bar you'll find time-honoured pub games and barrels of beer on racks behind the bar. Ale-lovers come for foaming pints of Bowman Ales Swift One or Oakleaf Quercus Folium, or a glass of heady Black Dragon cider, best enjoyed in the rambling orchard garden. Soak it up with a traditional bar meal, perhaps ham, egg and chips; liver and bacon with mash and shallot jus; or fish and chips. Don't miss the beer and cider festival in late July.

Open all day all wk **Food** Lunch Mon-Thu 12-2, Fri-Sun 12-9 Dinner Mon-Thu 6-9, Fri-Sun 12-9 ⊕ FREE HOUSE ◀ Bowman Ales Swift One, Oakleaf Quercus Folium, Guest ales Ŏ Gwynt y Ddraig Black Dragon, Lilley's Crazy Goat, Guest ciders. ♀ 10 **Facilities** Non-diners area ⬩ (Bar Restaurant Garden) ⬩ Children's menu Children's portions Play area Garden ⊨ Beer festival Cider festival Parking WiFi ⬛ (notice required)

The Sun Inn

Bentworth, Hampshire GU34 5JT • **Tel:** 01420 562338

Website: www.thesuninnbentworth.co.uk • **Email:** info@thesuninnbentworth.co.uk

Hidden down a lane on the edge of Bentworth Village in Hampshire, *The Sun Inn* is a pretty flower-adorned and unspoilt rural free-house dating back to the 17th century when it was a pair of traditional cottages.

The landlady Mary Holmes has been at *The Sun* for the past 17 years and has ensured the pub has kept its original character. The brick and board floors are laid with a rustic mix of scrubbed pine tables, benches and settles, the original beams are hung with sparkling horse brasses, while the walls are adorned with plates and prints depicting the history of the village of Bentworth.

Nestle in front of one of the three crackling log fires warming each of the interlinked rooms. Peruse a magazine, enjoy the fresh flowers and relax in a cosy candlelit atmosphere with friendly helpful service. A thriving free house, the Sun offers a selection of real ales from around the local Hampshire area all on hand pump. These include *Andwells Resolute*, *Hogsback T.E.A*, *Bowman's Swift One* and *Ringwood Best*. As well as local real ales there is a wide range of guest beers including *Fuller's London Pride*, *Timothy Taylor's Landlord*, and *Sharps Doombar*, plus many more regular favourites.

As well as *The Sun's* charm and extensive range of real ales and lagers, this freehouse really comes into its own by serving hearty home-cooked dishes that make a trip to this pub well worth the visit. Dishes range from ploughman's lunches, home-made soups and sandwiches to more filling options such as beer-battered cod, calves liver and bacon, tiger prawns and scallops in garlic butter, steak and Guinness pie, and half-shoulder of lamb with redcurrant and mint jelly. Game is also served in season including venison, partridge and pheasant.

If that is not enough to fill you up indulge in some of the home-made puddings like apple and rhubarb crumble, warm chocolate brownie, sticky toffee pudding, banoffee pie or strawberry and white chocolate cheesecake. When visiting *The Sun Inn* you will be sure to receive a warm and friendly welcome from Mary and her team.

PICK OF THE PUBS

The Sun Inn

BENTWORTH   Map 5 SU64

tel: 01420 562338 **Sun Hill GU34 5JT**
email: info@thesuninnbentworth.co.uk
web: www.thesuninnbentworth.co.uk
dir: *From A339 between Alton & Basingstoke follow Bentworth signs*

A step back in time to a pretty pub with hearty food

Just as you think you're about to leave the village behind, this pretty, foliage covered, rural free house comes into view. Dating from the 17th century, when it was built as a pair of traditional cottages, little can have changed inside in recent years, which is how landlady Mary Holmes intends things to stay. The floors in the three interlinked rooms are laid with brick and board; the furniture is a mix of scrubbed pine tables, benches and settles; the old ceiling beams are hung with horse brasses; and assorted prints and plates decorate the walls. Log fires may be burning, while tasteful cosmetic touches – magazines, fresh flowers, flickering candlelight – enhance the period feel still further. Apart from The Sun's overall charm, people come here for its good selection of real ales, including from Andwell, Sharp's, Fuller's, Ringwood and Stonehenge breweries, as well as Aspall cider. They come too for the extensive range of hearty home-cooked dishes, which run from ploughman's, home-made soup and sandwiches, to tiger

prawns and scallops in garlic butter; chicken breast in Stilton and walnut sauce; steak, mushroom and ale pie; and Yorkshire pudding with vegetable sausages. Game in season includes pheasant, and venison cooked in Guinness with pickled walnuts. The uncomplicated desserts are typically warm chocolate brownie, banoffee pie, and treacle tart. There's a lot to see and do in the area: in Selborne, there's the house where naturalist Gilbert White lived and where the Oates (of Scott's ill-fated 1911-12 Antarctic expedition fame) Collection is now found, and Jane Austen's House at Chawton is an easy drive too. A ride on the Watercress Line from Alton about 15 minutes away takes you on a 10-mile steam train journey through the Hampshire countryside.

Open all wk 12-3 6-11 (Sun 12-10.30) **Food** Lunch all wk 12-2 Dinner all wk 7-9.30 ⊕ FREE HOUSE ◼ Andwell Resolute, Ringwood Fortyniner, Sharp's Doom Bar, Stonehenge Pigswill, Fuller's London Pride, Black Sheep ♂ Aspall. ♟ 12 **Facilities** Non-diners area ❖ (Bar Garden) ♦♦ Children's menu Children's portions Family room Garden ♫ Parking WiFi

BOLDRE
Map 5 SZ39

The Hobler Inn

tel: 01590 623944 **Southampton Rd, Battramsley SO41 8PT**
email: hedi@alcatraz.co.uk
dir: *From Brockenhurst take A337 towards Lymington. Pub on main road*

New Forest pub popular with families

On the main road between Brockenhurst and Lymington, The Hobler has a large grassed area and trestle tables ideal for families visiting the New Forest. The Hobler Inn is more London wine bar with its stylish leather furniture than a village local, but still serves a well-kept pint of Ringwood. The food, served all day, is locally sourced and freshly cooked.

Open all day all wk 10am-11pm **Food** Lunch Mon-Sat 12-9.30, Sun 12-9 Dinner Mon-Sat 12-9.30, Sun 12-9 Set menu available ⊕ ENTERPRISE INNS ◖ Ringwood Best Bitter, Timothy Taylor. ♥ 10 **Facilities** Non-diners area ♦♦ Children's menu Garden Parking WiFi ▦ (notice required)

The Red Lion
`PICK OF THE PUBS`

tel: 01590 673177 **Rope Hill SO41 8NE**
dir: *M27 junct 1, A337 through Lyndhurst & Brockenhurst towards Lymington, follow Boldre signs*

15th-century pub for all seasons

Mentioned in the Domesday Book, The Red Lion sits at the crossroads in the ancient village of Boldre. The rambling interior contains cosy, beamed rooms, log fires and rural memorabilia; the rooms glow with candlelight on antique copper and brass. Expect a genuinely warm welcome and traditional values, with Ringwood ales on offer at the bar. The kitchen places an emphasis on traditional meals made using the very best of the forest's produce. Typical starters include tea-smoked Hampshire trout with home-made potato salad; and twice baked goats' cheese soufflé. Typical of the pub's traditional favourites are lamb shank slow braised with redcurrant, rosemary and honey, mash and root vegetables; and free-range chicken supreme, crispy bacon, smoked cheese sauce and chunky chips. In the summer, you can enjoy full table service outside on the herb patio.

Open all wk 11-3 5.30-11 (Sun 12-8) (summer Sat 11-11) Closed 25 Dec **Food** Lunch Mon-Sat 12-2.30, Sun 12-8 (summer Sat 12-9.30) Dinner Mon-Sat 6-9.30 Sun 12-8 (summer Sat 12-9.30) Restaurant menu available all wk ⊕ FREE HOUSE ◖ Ringwood Best Bitter & Fortyniner, Guinness, Guest ales Ö Thatchers Gold. ♥ 15 **Facilities** Non-diners area ♣ (Bar Restaurant Garden) ♦♦ Children's portions Garden ㅠ Parking WiFi ▦ (notice required)

Looking for a beer or cider festival?
Check our listings at the end of this guide

BRAISHFIELD
Map 5 SU32

NEW The Wheatsheaf

tel: 01794 368652 **SO51 0QE**
email: thewheatsheafbraishfield@aol.co.uk
dir: *On A3090 from Romsey towards Winchester, left for Braishfield*

Dog-friendly pub with great beer

Close to the Test Valley Way, The Wheatsheaf welcomes walkers, cyclists and especially dogs. Your four-legged friends will appreciate the barrel of treats on the bar while you sample a pint of Sharp's Doom Bar or Flack's Double Drop. The pub has lovely gardens and great views, and there's always something going on — live music and 'jam' nights, quiz nights, theme nights, and 'pie nite' where there's a choice of nine or more home-made pies. In the summer there are barbecues and an annual bottled cider festival. Sandwiches, jackets and ploughman's are available, or try local sausages and mash.

Open all day all wk **Food** Lunch Mon-Sat 12-2, Sun all day Dinner Mon-Sat 6-9, Sun all day Av main course £11.95 ⊕ ENTERPRISE INNS ◖ Sharp's Doom Bar, Flack Manor Flack's Double Drop, St Austell Tribute. ♥ 10 **Facilities** Non-diners area ♣ (Bar Garden) ♦♦ Children's menu Children's portions Play area Garden ㅠ Beer festival Cider festival Parking WiFi ▦ (notice required)

BRANSGORE
Map 5 SZ19

The Three Tuns Country Inn ⊛
`PICK OF THE PUBS`

tel: 01425 672232 **Ringwood Rd BH23 8JH**
email: threetunsinn@btconnect.com
dir: *1.5m from A35 Walkford junct. 3m from Christchurch & 1m from Hinton Admiral railway station*

Thatched, yet spacious, New Forest pub with a large garden

This chocolate box 17th-century inn is adorned with a riot of flowers in the spring and summer. It's set in a south-facing garden with over 2,500 square metres of lawn surrounded by fields, trees and grazing ponies. The excellent food and drink is served in all of the five public areas. The comfortable lounge bar warmed by log fire stocks an admirable range of cask-conditioned real ales and ciders, with mulled wine and cider in winter; an oak-beamed snug, similarly warmed, has biscuits and water for the dog; a large terrace with a water feature suits summer alfresco dining; and the 60-seat restaurant serves AA Rosette-quality dishes. Favourites such as fish and chips and burger with cheese and bacon sit alongside menu specials like sea bass with fricasée of squid, olives and tomato; or lentil and bean fajitas. A cider festival is held during the summer holidays, followed by a beer festival at the end of September. The pub also has a civil ceremony licence so you could even get married at one of the festivals.

Open all day all wk 11-11 (Sun 12-10.30) **Food** Lunch Mon-Fri 12-2.15, Sat-Sun 12-9.15 Dinner Mon-Fri 6.30-9.15, Sat-Sun 12-9.15 Set menu available Restaurant menu available all wk ⊕ ENTERPRISE INNS ◖ St Austell Tribute, Ringwood Best Bitter & Fortyniner, Exmoor Gold, Otter Bitter, Timothy Taylor, Skinner's Betty Stogs & Cornish Knocker Ö Rekorderlig, Thatchers Gold & Katy, New Forest Traditional, Westons Stowford Press. ♥ 9 **Facilities** Non-diners area ♣ (Bar Garden) ♦♦ Children's menu Children's portions Garden ㅠ Beer festival Cider festival Parking WiFi ▦ (notice required)

BROOK
Map 5 SU21

NEW The Bell Inn ★★★★ INN ⊛

tel: 023 8081 2214 **SO43 7HE**
email: bell@bramshaw.co.uk web: www.bellinnbramshaw.co.uk
dir: *M27 junct 1, B3079 signed Brook. Inn 1m on right*

Sumptuous hostelry serving New Forest delights

Owned by the same family for generations, this lavishly furnished inn is more akin to a country house than a pub. Stately in its dimensions, it has a garden with forest views, comfortable dining areas, a huge bar and accommodation for those just can't tear themselves away. In the bar you'll find local ales from Ringwood and Romsey's Flack Manor Brewery, and the AA Rosette menu has its focus firmly on modern British dishes of fresh, local and seasonal provender. Start perhaps with Lymington Bay crab cakes; continue with a trio of lamb rump, rack and faggot; and finish with warm carrot cake, or apple crumble parfait.

Open all day all wk **Food** Lunch 12-3 Dinner 6-9.30 Set menu available Restaurant menu available all wk ⊕ FREE HOUSE ◀ Ringwood Best Bitter, Flack Manor Flack Catcher, Guest Ales Ö Thatchers, Aspall. **Facilities** Non-diners area ♣ (Bar Restaurant Garden) ♦♦ Children's menu Children's portions Family room Garden ⌐ Parking WiFi ➡ (notice required) **Rooms** 27

BURLEY
Map 5 SU20

The Burley Inn

tel: 01425 403448 **BH24 4AB**
email: info@theburleyinn.co.uk
dir: *4m SE of of Ringwood*

Favoured forest village setting

A great base from which to explore the tracks, paths and rides of the surrounding New Forest National Park, this imposing Edwardian edifice, in neat grounds behind picket fencing, is one of a small local chain of dining pubs combining the best of local real ales – Flack Manor and Fuller's breweries often feature – with homely, traditional pub grub from an extensive menu. Toast wintery toes before log fires or relax on the decking patio, looking forward to olde English fish pie or venison casserole, with key lime pie to finish, whilst idly watching free-roaming livestock amble by on the village lanes.

Open all day all wk **Food** Lunch all wk 12-10 Dinner all wk 12-10 ⊕ FREE HOUSE ◀ Flack Manor Flack's Double Drop, Fuller's London Pride, Guest ales Ö Thatchers. ♥ 10 **Facilities** Non-diners area ♣ (Bar Outside area) Children's menu Children's portions Outside area ⌐ Parking WiFi ➡

CADNAM
Map 5 SU31

Sir John Barleycorn

tel: 023 8081 2236 **Old Romsey Rd SO40 2NP**
email: sjb@alcatraz.co.uk
dir: *From Southampton M27 junct 1 into Cadnam*

The oldest inn in the New Forest

The name of this friendly thatched establishment comes from a folksong celebrating the transformation of barley to beer. It is formed from three 12th-century cottages, one of which was reputedly home to the charcoal burner who discovered the body of King William Rufus. Beers on offer are Fuller's London Pride and HSB, while ciders are represented by Westons Stowford Press. The menu has something for everyone with quick snacks and sandwiches, a children's menu and traditional dishes like home-made steak and ale pudding and toad-in-the-hole. More inventive options are crab and lobster ravioli and slow-cooked lamb shank.

Open all day all wk 11-11 **Food** Lunch Mon-Sat 12-6, Sun 12-8 Dinner Mon-Sat 6-9, Sun 12-8 Av main course £12 Set menu available Restaurant menu available Mon-Fri ⊕ FULLER'S ◀ London Pride, George Gale & Co HSB, Guest ales Ö Westons Stowford Press, Guest cider. ♥ 10 **Facilities** Non-diners area ♦♦ Children's menu Children's portions Family room Garden ⌐ Parking WiFi ➡ (notice required)

CHALTON
Map 5 SU71

The Red Lion

tel: 023 9259 2246 **PO8 0BG**
email: redlion.chalton@fullers.co.uk
dir: *Just off A3 between Horndean & Petersfield. Follow signs for Chalton*

Traditional English pub with South Downs views

Said to be the oldest pub in Hampshire, dating back to 1147, when it was built to house craftsmen constructing St Michael's church opposite. It retains an olde worlde English charm, with a thatched roof, whitewashed exterior, brass knick-knacks, beams and roaring fires. A large purpose-built dining room is kept busy serving plates of pub grub. The expansive garden gives lovely views of the South Downs, and there's a beer festival on the first weekend in August.

Open all day all wk 11.30-11 (Sun 12-10.30) **Food** Lunch Mon-Sat 12-9, Sun 12-8 Dinner Mon-Sat 12-9, Sun 12-8 Av main course £11.95 ⊕ FULLER'S ◀ London Pride, George Gale & Co Seafarers & HSB, Guest ales Ö Aspall, Rekorderlig. ♥ 20 **Facilities** Non-diners area ♣ (Bar Garden) ♦♦ Children's menu Children's portions Garden ⌐ Beer festival Parking WiFi ➡ (notice required)

CHARTER ALLEY
Map 5 SU55

The White Hart Inn

tel: 01256 850048 **White Hart Ln RG26 5QA**
email: enquiries@whitehartcharteralley.com
dir: *M3 junct 6, A339 towards Newbury. Right signed Ramsdell. Right at church, then 1st left into White Hart Ln*

A must for lovers of good beer

When this free house opened in 1818, on the northern edge of the village overlooking open farmland and woods – just as today – it must have delighted the woodsmen and coach drivers visiting the farrier next door. Real ale pumps lined up on the herringbone-patterned, brick-fronted bar include Triple fff Moondance, Red Cat Prowler, West Berkshire Good Old Boy and Bowman Swift One. The menu changes daily to offer typical locally sourced dishes as Greenfield's traditional pork sausages, two free-range fried eggs and chips; chicken Madras and basmati rice; and vegetable hotpot and new potatoes. A patio leads into an attractive little garden. Contact the inn for its occasional beer festival dates.

Open Mon 7-11 (Tue-Wed 12-2.30 7-11 Thu-Fri 12-2.30 5.30-11 Sat 12-3 6.30-11 Sun 12-4) Closed 25-26 Dec, 1 Jan, Mon L, Sun eve **Food** Lunch Tue-Sun 12-2

Dinner Tue-Sat 7-9 ⊕ FREE HOUSE ◼ Triple fff Moondance, Bowman Swift One, Red Cat Prowler Pale, West Berkshire Good Old Boy. ⛉ 9 **Facilities** Non-diners area ✿ (Bar Outside area) ◗◖ Children's menu Children's portions Family room Outside area ⋒ Beer festival Parking WiFi ⇌ (notice required)

CHAWTON	Map 5 SU73

The Greyfriar

tel: 01420 83841 **Winchester Rd GU34 1SB**
email: hello@thegreyfriar.co.uk **web:** www.thegreyfriar.co.uk
dir: *Just off A31 near Alton. Access to Chawton via A31/A32 junct. Follow Jane Austen's House signs. Pub opposite*

Old-fashioned values and family-friendly

Opposite Jane Austen's House Museum stands this 16th-century pub. As well as its friendly atmosphere and delightful village setting, the south-facing suntrap garden is another draw. The pub is Fuller's-owned and offers London Pride and Seafarers along with great food. A sample menu includes crayfish and prawn cocktail, and oven-roasted figs with Stilton and pesto dressing to start, followed by seafood linguine; roast rack of lamb; chilli con carne; ham and eggs; or steak and Guinness pie. Sandwiches and jackets are also available for lunch.

Open all day all wk 12-11 (Sun 12-10.30) **Food** Lunch Mon-Sat 12-2.30, Sun 12-7 Dinner Mon-Sat 6-9.30 Restaurant menu available all wk ⊕ FULLER'S ◼ London Pride, George Gale & Co Seafarers, Seasonal ales ♂ Aspall. ⛉ **Facilities** Non-diners area ✿ (Bar Garden) ◗◖ Children's portions Garden ⋒ Parking WiFi ⇌ (notice required)

CHERITON	Map 5 SU52

The Flower Pots Inn

tel: 01962 771318 **SO24 0QQ**
dir: *A272 towards Petersfield, left onto B3046, pub 0.75m on right*

Popular village pub with its own microbrewery

Known almost universally as The Pots, this pub used to be a farmhouse and home to the head gardener of nearby Avington Park. These days, local beer drinkers know the pub well for its award-winning Flower Pots Bitter and Goodens Gold, brewed across the car park in the microbrewery. Simple home-made food includes hearty filled baps, toasted sandwiches, jacket potatoes, cheese and meat ploughman's and different hotpots – chilli con carne, lamb and apricot, steak and ale, spicy mixed bean. A large, safe garden, with a covered patio, allows children to let off steam (no under 14s in the bar). The pub holds a beer festival in August.

Open all wk 12-2.30 6-11 (Sun 12-3 7-10.30) **Food** Lunch all wk 12-1.45 Dinner Mon-Sat 7-8.45 ⊕ FREE HOUSE ◼ Flower Pots Bitter, Goodens Gold ♂ Westons Old Rosie. **Facilities** Non-diners area ✿ (Bar Garden) Garden Beer festival Parking **Notes** ⊜

NEW The Hinton Arms

tel: 01962 771252 **Petersfield Rd SO24 0NH**
email: info@hintonarms.co.uk
dir: *A272 between Petersfield & Winchester*

Great food and colourful floral displays

Weary walkers and cyclists, and well-behaved children and dogs are all very welcome at this privately owned bar and restaurant. So too are those interested in the English Civil War, keen to follow the trail to the nearby site of the Battle of Cheriton, fought in 1644. Food is a high point, especially the game and fresh fish; portions are reputedly generous. Seasonal menus cover all bases, with dishes such as Malaysian chicken korma; Atlantic wholetail scampi; gammon steak and eggs; sausages and mash; and mushroom Stroganoff. Real ale policy favours those brewed in Hampshire.

Open all wk 10-3 6-11 (Sat-Sun 10am-11pm) **Food** Lunch Mon-Sat 12-2.30, Sun 12-9.30 Dinner Mon-Sat 6-9.30, Sun 12-9.30 ⊕ FREE HOUSE ◼ Itchen Valley Hampshire Rose, Triple fff Moondance, Bowman Ales Swift One & Wallops Wood ♂ Westons Stowford Press. ⛉ 12 **Facilities** ✿ (Bar Garden) ◗◖ Children's menu Children's portions Play area Garden ⋒ Parking WiFi ⇌ (notice required)

CLANFIELD	Map 5 SU71

The Rising Sun Inn ★★★ INN

tel: 023 9259 6975 **North Ln PO8 0RN**
email: enquiries@therisingsunclanfield.co.uk **web:** www.therisingsunclanfield.co.uk
dir: *A3(M) then A3 towards Petersfield. Left signed Clanfield. Follow brown inn signs*

Traditional village inn just inside the South Downs National Park

Although it looks two centuries old, the flint-faced Rising Sun was built in 2003. Apparently, in 1960, its predecessor was constructed in one day, even serving its first pint at 6pm. Today the bar sells a variety of real ales and ciders, as well as a selection of single malt whiskies. The menu focuses on pub classics such as liver and bacon, beer battered cod and lasagne, with support from leek and potato bake, tapas, salmon steak in prawn, mushroom and dill sauce, and a choice of baguettes and sandwiches. Tuesday night is steak night, curries are Thursday and it's Friday for music. The B&B accommodation is popular with walkers and cyclists on the South Downs Way.

Open all day all wk **Food** Lunch all wk 12-9 Dinner all wk 12-9 ⊕ ENTERPRISE INNS ◼ George Gale & Co HSB, Ringwood Best Bitter, Sharp's Doom Bar, Guest ales ♂ Westons Old Rosie, Thatchers Gold. ⛉ 15 **Facilities** Non-diners area ✿ (All areas) ◗◖ Children's menu Children's portions Garden Outside area ⋒ Beer festival Parking WiFi ⇌ (notice required) **Rooms** 3

CROOKHAM VILLAGE
Map 5 SU75

The Exchequer

tel: 01252 615336 **Crondall Rd GU51 5SU**
email: bookings@exchequercrookham.co.uk
dir: *M3 junct 5, A287 towards Farnham for 5m. Left to Crookham Village*

Welcoming dining pub with top-notch ales

Amongst the quiet villages of north Hampshire in the beautiful setting of Crookham Village, this whitewashed free house is just a stone's throw from the A287. The Exchequer serves carefully chosen wines and local ales straight from the cask, and offers a great seasonal menu with dishes featuring the best local produce. Start with a sharing board of meze or perhaps a sweet pepper and goats' cheese tart. Main course dishes include crushed new potato, salmon and smoked haddock fishcake; and roast chicken breast wrapped in Parma ham and stuffed with pâté. Leave room for blackberry and apple crumble with custard. Sandwiches and pub classics are available at lunchtime.

Open all wk 12-3 6-11 (Fri-Sun 11-11) Closed 25 Dec **Food** Lunch Mon-Thu 12-2.30, Fri-Sun 12-9.30 Dinner Mon-Thu 6-9.30, Fri-Sun 12-9.30 Restaurant menu available all wk ⊕ FREE HOUSE ◀ Andwell, Hogs Back TEA, Guest ales ♂ Hogs Back Hazy Hog. ♀ 10 **Facilities** Non-diners area ◀◀ Children's menu Children's portions Garden ♁ Parking WiFi

DROXFORD
Map 5 SU61

The Bakers Arms ◉
PICK OF THE PUBS

tel: 01489 877533 **High St SO32 3PA**
email: enquiries@thebakersarmsdroxford.com
dir: *10m E of Winchester on A32 between Fareham & Alton. 7m SW of Petersfield*

Small village pub with first-rate food

In 2011 the pretty village of Droxford found itself in the newly created South Downs National Park – so that's one good reason to head for this unpretentious, white-painted pub. In addition, it has abundant country charm, the staff are friendly and locals clearly love the place. The Bowman Brewery a mile away supplies the bar with Swift One and Wallops Wood, so why look any further afield, asks owner Adam Cordery. Also in the bar you'll find home-made Cornish pasties, pickled eggs and onions, and hot filled baguettes, while over the big log fire a blackboard lists the day's AA Rosette-standard main dishes. Among these will be the day's pie, burgers, sausages or steaks; and maybe slow-cooked Hampshire pork belly with pork and black pudding croquette; butter-poached roast crown of partridge with parsnip purée; and garlic and black rice risotto. Adam shoots or grows much of the produce himself.

Open 11.45-3 6-11 (Sun 12-3) Closed Sun eve **Food** Lunch all wk 12-2 Dinner Mon-Sat 7-9 Set menu available ⊕ FREE HOUSE ◀ Bowman Ales Swift One & Wallops Wood ♂ Thatchers. ♀ 11 **Facilities** Non-diners area ❤ (Bar Restaurant Garden) ◀◀ Children's portions Garden ♁ Parking WiFi

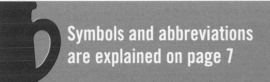

Symbols and abbreviations are explained on page 7

DUMMER
Map 5 SU54

The Queen Inn

tel: 01256 397367 **Down St RG25 2AD**
email: richardmoore49@btinternet.com
dir: *From M3 junct 7 follow Dummer signs*

Country inn just off the M3

You can dine by candlelight in the restaurant at this low-beamed, 16th-century inn with a huge open log fire. The main menu offers a wide choice: steaks and burgers; supreme of chicken with leek, bacon and Stilton; trio of minted lamb cutlets; steak and ale pie; and grilled goats' cheese, walnut and beetroot salad. Children are encouraged to have small adult portions, but have their own menu if all entreaties fail. There's a good real ale line-up, including Sharp's Doom Bar, Otter Bitter and guest ales.

Open all wk 11-3 6-11 (Sun 12-3 7-10.30) **Food** Lunch all wk 12-2.30 Dinner Mon-Sat 6.30-9.30, Sun 7-9 ⊕ ENTERPRISE INNS ◀ Otter Bitter, Sharp's Doom Bar, Guest ale ♂ Thatchers Gold, Westons Stowford Press. ♀ 9 **Facilities** Non-diners area ◀◀ Children's menu Children's portions Garden Parking WiFi

The Sun Inn

tel: 01256 397234 **Winchester Road A30 RG25 2DJ**
email: thesuninndummer@hotmail.co.uk
dir: *M3 junct 7, A30 (Winchester Rd) towards Basingstoke. Left onto A30 towards Winchester. Inn on right*

Certainly worth a detour from a motorway journey

The Sun has stood for many years alongside the main coaching route from London to Exeter, today's A30. Passing traffic is not a problem since most West Country travellers now use the M3, accessible from nearby junction 7. Moondance from Triple fff takes pole position in the bar, alongside Symonds cider, while in the restaurant the well-conceived menu might list cider and fennel steamed Cornish mussels; trio of pork (belly, loin and hock) with potato purée, vegetables, cider gel and red wine jus; and vegetarian hot pot, alongside pub classics such as ale-battered fish and triple cooked chips. A lovely garden lies at the back.

Open all wk 12-11 **Food** Lunch all wk 12-3 Dinner Mon-Sat 6-9 ⊕ FREE HOUSE ◀ Triple fff Moondance, Sharp's Doom Bar ♂ Symonds. ♀ 8 **Facilities** Non-diners area ❤ (Bar Garden) ◀◀ Children's menu Children's portions Play area Garden ♁ Parking WiFi 🚍

DUNBRIDGE
Map 5 SU32

The Mill Arms ★★★★ INN

tel: 01794 340401 **Barley Hill SO51 0LF**
email: mill.arms@btconnect.com **web:** www.millarms.co.uk
dir: *From Romsey take A3057 signed Stockbridge & Winchester. Left onto B3084 through Awbridge to Dunbridge. Pub on left before rail crossing*

Smart country pub offering good food not far from the River Test

There's been a change of hands at this attractive Victorian country inn. With its flagstone floors, oak beams and open fires, it's traditional and welcoming, and in a great location in the heart of the Test Valley close to the River Test, one of the finest chalk streams in the world. Not surprisingly, the pub is popular with fly fishermen from far and wide. On the menu you'll find everything from patatas bravas and chorizo, to a good choice of sandwiches, as well as more substantial dishes like game cobbler or beer battered fish and chips. There's also a function room, a skittle alley and large landscaped gardens.

Open all day Closed 25 Dec, Sun eve **Food** Lunch Mon-Sat 12-3, Sun 12-4 Dinner Mon-Sat 6-9 ⊕ ENTERPRISE INNS ◀ Flack Manor Flack's Double Drop, Guest ales ♂ Symonds. ♀ 10 **Facilities** Non-diners area ❤ (Bar Garden) ◀◀ Children's menu Children's portions Garden ♁ Parking WiFi 🚍 (notice required) **Rooms** 6

DURLEY
Map 5 SU51

NEW The Robin Hood

tel: 01489 860229 **Durley St S032 2AA**
email: robinhooddurley@gmail.com

A village pub with lots of personality

The Robin Hood is a friendly, welcoming place. There's a cosy seating area with comfy sofas, not one but two open fires and loos which are hidden behind a false bookcase door. The garden is huge, with a play area for children that includes a pirate ship. If you're (sadly) too old to make use of that, there's a decked area with lovely country views for drinks and alfresco dining. In the bar you'll find Black Sheep and Timothy Taylor Landlord, and on the menu are pub classics such as baked brie with chilli jam and salad, followed by steak and ale pie; beer-battered cod or haddock; or lamb's liver and mash.

Open all wk 11-3 5.30-11 (Sun 11-10.30) Closed 25 Dec **Food** Lunch Mon-Sat 12-2, Sun 12-8.30 Dinner Mon-Thu 6-9, Fri-Sat 6-9.30, Sun 12-8.30 ⊕ GREENE KING ◼ Timothy Taylor Landlord, Black Sheep ♂ Westons Stowford Press. ♥ 14
Facilities Non-diners area ✿ (Bar Garden Outside area) ♦♦ Children's menu Children's portions Play area Garden Outside area ⊼ Parking WiFi ☞ (notice required)

EAST BOLDRE
Map 5 SU30

Turfcutters Arms

tel: 01590 612331 **Main Rd S042 7WL**
email: enquiries.turfcutters@gmail.com
dir: *From Beaulieu take B3055 towards Brockenhurst. Left at Hatchet Pond onto B3054 towards Lymington, turn left, follow signs for East Boldre. Pub approx 0.5m*

Off the beaten track and offering good value food

Five miles south of Beaulieu, this New Forest pub, easily recognised by its white picket fence, attracts cyclists, ramblers, dog-walkers and locals all year round. In winter the open fires warm the cockles, while the lovely garden comes into its own in summer. Good beer including Ringwood and draught ciders such as Thatchers complement a menu of unpretentious pub grub including baguettes, jacket potatoes and main meals such as fish and chips, BBQ belly pork, chicken curry, chicken burger and hommity pie. Children have their own menu, and canine treats are handed out at the bar. Time a visit for the annual beer festival.

Open all day all wk **Food** Lunch Mon-Fri 12-2.30, Sat 12-3, Sun 12-8 Dinner Mon-Tue 6-8, Wed-Sat 6-9, Sun 12-8 Set menu available ⊕ ENTERPRISE INNS ◼ Ringwood Best Bitter, Fortyniner, Guest ales ♂ Thatchers Gold.
Facilities Non-diners area ✿ (Bar Restaurant Garden) ♦♦ Children's menu Children's portions Play area Garden ⊼ Beer festival Parking WiFi ☞ (notice required)

EAST END
Map 5 SZ39

The East End Arms
PICK OF THE PUBS

tel: 01590 626223 **Main Rd S041 5SY**
email: manager@eastendarms.co.uk
dir: *From Lymington towards Beaulieu (past Isle of Wight ferry), 3m to East End*

Striking all the right notes

Find the East End Arms by threading your way through lanes along the southern edge of the New Forest National Park; the Solent is just a short stroll south, and the delightful village of Buckler's Hard is nearby. It's a happy mix of community village inn and restaurant, with menus drawing on local produce and changing daily. The inviting Foresters Bar is pleasingly old-fashioned, with flagstoned floors and roaring fire adding to the pleasure of a gravity-drawn pint of Andwell's ale or a bottle of Brothers cider. Lunchtime sandwiches are served on granary or white bloomer with French fries or crisps. The bright and airy restaurant is decorated with photographs of musicians, reflecting the pub's owner, Dire Straits' bass player John Illsley. Starters such as crispy poached duck egg with prosciutto ham and parmesan shavings could be followed by turbot with king prawns, pea and broad bean risotto with vanilla oil.

Open all wk 11.30-3 6-11 (Fri-Sun 11.30-11) **Food** Lunch all wk 12-2.30 Dinner Mon-Sat 7-9 Restaurant menu available lunch all wk ⊕ FREE HOUSE ◼ Ringwood Best Bitter & Fortyniner, Andwell's, Jennings, Cottage ♂ Thatchers Gold.
Facilities Non-diners area ✿ (Bar Garden Outside area) ♦♦ Children's portions Garden Outside area ⊼ Parking WiFi

EAST MEON
Map 5 SU62

Ye Olde George Inn

tel: 01730 823481 **Church St GU32 1NH**
email: yeoldegeorge@live.co.uk
dir: *S of A272 (Winchester/Petersfield). 1.5m from Petersfield turn left opposite church*

Medieval inn set in a lovely village

In the beautiful countryside of the Meon Valley, the setting for this delightful 15th-century coaching inn is hard to beat. The village boasts a magnificent Norman church where tapestry designs similar to Bayeux can be found. If you want heavy beams, inglenook fireplaces and wooden floors, look no further – they're all here, creating an ideal atmosphere for a choice of Hall & Woodhouse ales and Westons cider. The monthly changing menus reflect the seasons, with lighter dishes in the summer and hearty, warming food in the winter – such as confit Gressingham duck with chorizo rösti, baby spinach, fried hen's egg and harissa jus. There are tables outside on the pretty patio.

Open all wk 11-3 6-11 (Sun 11-10) Closed 25 Dec, 26 Dec eve & 1 Jan eve **Food** Lunch Mon-Sat 12-2.30, Sun 12-3 Dinner Mon-Sat 6.30-9.30, Sun 6.30-9 ⊕ HALL & WOODHOUSE ◼ Badger First Gold, K&B Sussex, Tanglefoot ♂ Westons Stowford Press. ♥ 9 **Facilities** Non-diners area ✿ (Bar Outside area) ♦♦ Children's menu Children's portions Outside area ⊼ Parking WiFi ☞ (notice required)

EASTON
Map 5 SU53

The Chestnut Horse

tel: 01962 779257 **S021 1EG**
email: info@thechestnuthorse.com
dir: *M3 junct 9, A33 towards Basingstoke, then B3047. 2nd right, 1st left*

Hidden away in the idyllic Itchen Valley

This gem of a 16th-century pub has an abundance of traditional English character and atmosphere. Old tankards hang from the low-beamed ceilings in the two bar areas, and a large open fire is the central focus through the winter months. Hall & Woodhouse beers, such as Pickled Partridge and Chestnut Horse Special, along with Westons ciders, can be enjoyed in the bar or the garden. Carte food choices are several cuts above the average. An indicative starter and main course could be venison carpaccio with Asian salad and gremolata dressing; and rigatoni with local Hampshire 'quattro formaggi' cream sauce, spinach, sun-dried tomatoes and truffle oil. The two-course fixed-price lunch menu represents excellent value.

Open all wk 12-3.30 5.30-11 (Fri-Sat 12-11.30 Sun 12-10.30) **Food** Lunch Mon-Sat 12-2.30, Sun 12-8 Dinner Mon-Sat 6-9.30, Sun 12-8 Av main course £12 Set menu available ⊕ HALL & WOODHOUSE ◼ Badger First Gold & Pickled Partridge, Chestnut Horse Special ♂ Westons Stowford Press & Old Rosie. ♥ 12
Facilities Non-diners area ✿ (Bar Garden) ♦♦ Children's menu Children's portions Garden ⊼ Parking WiFi ☞

EAST STRATTON
Map 5 SU54

Northbrook Arms

tel: 01962 774150 **SO21 3DU**
email: northbrookarms@hotmail.com
dir: *Follow brown pub sign from A33, 4m S of junct with A303*

Social centre of a small but perfectly formed village

Memo to Hollywood: if you need an English pub location, look no further. Bang opposite the village green and architecturally perfect, it endears itself to local bar-proppers with six or seven real ales and three ciders, a May beer festival and a September cider celebration. The compact menu gets the thumbs up too, with dishes such as spicy duck parcels with chilli and apple purée; wild mushroom and thyme mille feuille; baked lemon and pepper salmon; and buttermilk pudding with cardamom strawberries. There are light bites and deli options such as Indian potato cake, and smoked cod Scotch egg.

Open all day all wk **Food** Lunch all wk 12-3 Dinner all wk 6-9 ⊕ FREE HOUSE ◀ Otter, Bowman Swift One, Flack Manor Flack's Double Drop, Amber Sharp's Cornish Coaster, Alfred's Saxon Bronze Ŏ Aspall, Mr Whiteheads, Westons Stowford Press. ♥ 12 **Facilities** Non-diners area ♣ (All areas) ♦♦ Children's menu Children's portions Play area Garden Outside area ⋒ Beer festival Cider festival Parking WiFi ▨ (notice required)

EMSWORTH
Map 5 SU70

The Sussex Brewery

tel: 01243 371533 **36 Main Rd PO10 8AU**
email: info@sussexbrewery.com
dir: *On A259, E of Emsworth towards Chichester*

Friendly roadside pub with a winning ale-and-sausage combination

No prizes for guessing this pub was once a brewery, and this ethos continues with its pride in offering good honestly-priced food and drink served by friendly staff in a happy atmosphere. Young's ales sit beside guests, with Addlestones and Thatchers ciders served too. Locally made sausages form the backbone of the menu, and have done for over 10 years; differing flavours, including a special made with Young's bitter, are served with creamy mash, caramelised onions and gravy. Equally in demand are light bites such as a bucket of whitebait with home-made tartare sauce, and main courses like ale-battered hake with chips.

Open all day all wk **Food** Lunch Mon-Sat 12-2.30, Sun 12-3 Dinner Mon-Sat 6-9, Sun 6.30-9 Restaurant menu available all wk ⊕ YOUNG'S ◀ London Gold & Special, Wells Bombardier, St Austell Tribute Ŏ Addlestones, Thatchers. ♥ 12 **Facilities** Non-diners area ♣ (Bar Outside area) ♦♦ Children's portions Outside area ⋒ Parking WiFi ▨ (notice required)

EVERSLEY
Map 5 SU76

The Golden Pot
PICK OF THE PUBS

tel: 0118 973 2104 **Reading Rd RG27 0NB**
email: info@golden-pot.co.uk
dir: *Between Reading & Camberley on B3272 approx 0.25m from Eversley cricket ground*

Innovative home-cooked food and a good range of beers

This well-established free house dates back to the 1700s and offers a fine selection of real ales and nine wines by the glass. A double-sided warming fire connects the bar and restaurant, while outside the Snug and Vineyard, surrounded by colourful tubs and hanging baskets, are just the ticket for summer relaxation. Tuck into home-cooked food such as steak and ale pie; fish pie; organic salmon Wellington; and calves' liver and bacon with creamed potatoes and red wine sauce. Desserts are all home made too, perhaps chocolate and orange trifle; apple and plum tart with custard; or strawberry and vanilla cheesecake. Dogs are welcome in the bar area and the garden.

Open all day all wk 11.30-11 Closed 25-26 & 31 Dec, 1 Jan **Food** Lunch all wk 12-2.30 Dinner all wk 5.30-10 ⊕ FREE HOUSE ◀ Andwell, Bowman, Ascot, Rebellion, Windsor & Eton, Upham Ale, Church End, Longdog Ales, Hammerpot Ales, Guest ale Ŏ Rekorderlig, Aspall, Henney's. ♥ 9 **Facilities** Non-diners area ♣ (Bar Garden) ♦♦ Children's menu Children's portions Garden ⋒ Beer festival Cider festival Parking WiFi

EVERSLEY CROSS
Map 5 SU76

NEW The Chequers

tel: 0118 402 7065 **RG27 0NS**
email: thechequers@peachpubs.com
dir: *On B3272 (W of Yateley) in village centre*

Welcoming and warm-hearted gastro-pub

Belonging to the Peach Pubs group, which pursues the tenet of 'small is beautiful', The Chequers welcomes all-comers from breakfast onwards. Quality is the focus for all aspects of the operation, from ales such as Hogs Back to a carte packed with seasonal goodies. Deli boards are generous: order the cold cuts and a mini shepherd's pie, free-range chicken, bacon and leek terrine, honey mustard sausages, air-dried British beef, crunch slaw and toasted sourdough are all yours, along with Mark's brown sauce. Brasserie-type dishes range from chargrilled Cornish lamb cutlets with roasted Parmentier potatoes; to dry-aged beef steaks served with chips, watercress and béarnaise sauce.

Open all day all wk Closed 25 Dec **Food** Lunch Mon-Sat 12-10, Sun 12-9 Dinner Mon-Sat 12-10, Sun 12-9 Av main course £15 ⊕ FREE HOUSE ◀ Hogs Back TEA, Sharp's Doom Bar Ŏ Aspall. ♥ **Facilities** Non-diners area ♣ (Bar Garden) ♦♦ Children's portions Garden ⋒ Beer festival Parking WiFi ▨ (notice required)

EXTON
Map 5 SU62

The Shoe Inn

tel: 01489 877526 **Shoe Ln SO32 3NT**
email: theshoeexton@googlemail.com
dir: *On A32 between Fareham & Alton*

Good food with many ingredients from the pub's own garden

On warmer days, you can enjoy views of Old Winchester Hill from the garden of this popular pub in the heart of the Meon Valley. Food is key – local ingredients include those from its ever-expanding herb and vegetable garden. A typical selection of dishes could include local home-made pea and ham soup; Southdown lamb's liver, bacon, onion gravy and mashed potato; beer battered haddock, hand-cut chips and mushy peas. The bar offers well-kept Wadworth ales, weekly changing guest ales, and 11 wines served by the glass.

Open all wk 11-3 6-11 (Sat-Sun all day) Closed 25 Dec **Food** Lunch all wk 12-2.15 Dinner all wk 6-9 ⊕ WADWORTH ◀ 6X, Henry's Original IPA, The Bishop's Tipple, Guest ales Ŏ Westons Stowford Press. ♥ 11 **Facilities** ♣ (Bar Garden) ♦♦ Children's menu Children's portions Garden ⋒ Parking

FORDINGBRIDGE
Map 5 SU11

The Augustus John

tel: 01425 652098 **116 Station Rd SP6 1DG**
email: enquiries@augustusjohnfordingbridge.co.uk
dir: *12m S of Salisbury on A338 towards Ringwood*

Village pub with artistic associations

The Welsh painter Augustus John lived in Fordingbridge for some years until his death in 1961; he was a regular when the pub served the now long-vanished, adjacent railway station. Today, under new landlord Bryan Greenwood, Ringwood and guest real ales continue to attract locals and visitors. So too do such characteristic dishes as local rib-eye steak with port and Stilton sauce; chef's home-made shortcrust pastry pies; grilled salmon fillet with lemon and chive cream sauce; and spinach and mushroom pancakes. Why not time a visit for the Early May Bank Holiday beer festival?

Open all wk 11.30-3 5-11 (Sat-Sun all day) **Food** Lunch all wk 12-2.30 Dinner Mon-Sat 6.30-9, Sun 7-9 (booking advised Fri-Sun) Av main course £11.95 Set menu available ⊕ MARSTON'S ◀ Ringwood Best Bitter & Fortyniner, Guest ale ♂ Thatchers Gold. **Facilities** Non-diners area ❄ (Bar Garden) ♦♦ Children's menu Children's portions Garden ⌂ Beer festival Parking WiFi ➤ (notice required)

FREEFOLK
Map 5 SU44

NEW The Watership Down Inn

tel: 01256 892254 **RG28 7NJ**
dir: *From Whitchurch take B3400 towards Basingstoke. Pub in 1.5m*

19th-century Test Valley country pub with large garden

The downland that Richard Adams made famous in his classic 1972 novel lies four miles north of here. The inn's country-style interior features oak and quarry-tile flooring, a wood-burner and hardwood bar, from where some 100 different locally brewed real ales are offered – over time, of course. The wine list is similarly comprehensive. At lunchtime snails in garlic butter may be available; more conventional possibilities are beer-battered haddock, and home-made pie of the day. Evening choices could well include brie-filled chicken supreme in Parma ham; an 8oz rib-eye steak; and wild mushroom, thyme and pumpkin risotto. There's a beer festival on the first May weekend.

Open all wk 12-3 6-11 (Fri-Sun all day) **Food** Lunch 12-2.30 Dinner 6.30-9 Av main course £12 ⊕ FREE HOUSE ◀ Rotating guest ales. **Facilities** Non-diners area ❄ (Bar Garden) ♦♦ Children's menu Children's portions Play area Garden ⌂ Beer festival Parking WiFi ➤ (notice required)

HAMBLE-LE-RICE
Map 5 SU40

The Bugle ◉
PICK OF THE PUBS

tel: 023 8045 3000 **High St SO31 4HA**
email: manager@buglehamble.co.uk
dir: *M27 junct 8, follow signs to Hamble. In village centre turn right at mini rdbt into one-way cobbled street, pub at end*

Enjoyable food in restored waterside pub with views

Rescued from proposed demolition, this famous waterside pub was taken over by Matthew Boyle who has lovingly refurbished it using traditional methods and materials. Old features include exposed beams and brickwork, natural flagstone floors and the wonderful oak bar, plus there's a large heated terrace with lovely views over the River Hamble – perfect for outdoor dining. A pint of locally brewed

Itchen Valley ale makes an ideal partner for one of the 'small plates' (great for sharing), a fish finger, tartare sauce and cucumber sandwich, or pub classics like moules frites or seasonal meat pie. From the dining room menu, go for pressed rabbit and prune terrine to start, then order the bream fillet with creamed leeks, warm kale and potato salad. Round off with apple crumble tart and vanilla ice cream. The Bugle is the sister pub to The White Star Tavern in Southampton.

Open all day all wk Mon-Thu 11-11 (Fri-Sat 11-mdnt Sun 12-10.30) **Food** Lunch Mon-Thu 12-2.30, Fri 12-3, Sat 12-4, Sun 12-9 Dinner Mon-Thu 6-9.30, Fri-Sat 6-10, Sun 12-9 ⊕ FREE HOUSE ◀ Itchen Valley, Rotating local ales. ☗ 10 **Facilities** Non-diners area ♦♦ Children's portions Outside area ⌂ WiFi ➤

HANNINGTON
Map 5 SU55

The Vine at Hannington

tel: 01635 298525 **RG26 5TX**
email: info@thevineathannington.co.uk
dir: *Follow Hannington signs from A339 between Basingstoke & Kingsclere*

A favourite with walkers and cyclists

Given the nature of North Hampshire's rolling chalk downland, you can expect rambling and cycling devotees to patronise this gabled Victorian inn. A wood-burning stove heats the spacious, traditionally furnished bar areas and conservatory. Seasonal menus and daily specials feature home-made pies and burgers, vegetarian and gluten-free options. Sharp's Doom Bar and guest ales, 11 wines by the glass as well as teas, coffee and hot chocolate are always available. There is a large, secure garden with a children's play area, and a summer beer festival.

Open 12-3 6-11 (Sat all day Sun 12-5) Closed Mon **Food** Lunch Tue-Sat 12-2, Sun 12-4 Dinner Tue-Sat 6-9 Av main course £12 ⊕ PUNCH TAVERNS ◀ Sharp's Doom Bar, Guest ales ♂ Thatchers Gold. ☗ 11 **Facilities** Non-diners area ❄ (Bar Restaurant Garden) ♦♦ Children's menu Children's portions Play area Family room Garden ⌂ Beer festival Parking WiFi ➤ (notice required)

HAVANT
Map 5 SU70

NEW The Wheelwright's Arms

tel: 023 9247 6502 **27 Emsworth Rd PO9 2SN**
email: info@wheelwrightshavant.co.uk
dir: *A27 into Emsworth Rd towards Havant. Pub on right*

Sensitively restored character pub

A major revamp in 2014 followed acquisition by the Upham Group of this handsome, twin-gabled pub. This fast-expanding enterprise, until not so long ago a simple village microbrewery, supplies the real ales; the cider is Orchard Pig Reveller. Lunch on honey- and mustard-glazed ham; ale-battered hake; or fried Havant rabbit. For dinner, pressed smoked mackerel, River Test trout and saffron potato terrine with Alresford watercress; then steak and kidney suet pudding; and finally Wheelwright's waffle, strawberries and cream. Picking up on the pub's name, over-65s can choose from the Pounds & Penny Farthings menu, children from one called Trikes.

Open all day all wk **Food** Lunch 12-3 Dinner 6-9.30 ⊕ UPHAM PUB COMPANY ◀ Punter, Tipster & Stakes ♂ Orchard Pig Reveller. ☗ 10 **Facilities** Non-diners area ❄ (Bar Restaurant Outside area) ♦♦ Children's menu Children's portions Outside area ⌂ Parking WiFi ➤ (notice required)

HAWKLEY
Map 5 SU72

The Hawkley Inn ★★★★ INN

tel: 01730 827205 **Pococks Ln GU33 6NE**
email: info@hawkleyinn.co.uk **web:** www.hawkleyinn.co.uk
dir: *From A3 (Liss rdbt) towards Liss on B3006. Right at Spread Eagle, in 2.5m left into Pococks Ln*

Friendly pub with seriously good food

An inn sign saying 'Free Hoose' owes something to the moose head hanging above one of the fires. It sums up this pub's quirky decor. With seven beer engines, the pub is well known to local real ale enthusiasts and cider lovers; a festival takes place over June's first weekend. Menus change daily and proffer the likes of grilled smoked salmon with asparagus; and calves' liver with lentils. These and the vegetarian specials are all locally sourced and freshly prepared on the premises, and any dietary need can be catered for.

Open all wk Mon-Fri 12-3 5.30-11 (Sat-Sun all day) **Food** Lunch Mon-Sat 12-2, Sun 12-4 Dinner Mon-Sat 6-9 Av main course £13 Set menu available ⊕ FREE HOUSE ◀ 7 constantly changing ales, Guest ales Ö Mr Whitehead's. ⏱ 8 **Facilities** Non-diners area ✿ (Bar Restaurant Garden) ◀◗ Children's portions Garden ⊟ Beer festival WiFi ▄ (notice required) **Rooms** 6

HERRIARD
Map 5 SU64

The Fur & Feathers

tel: 01256 384170 **Herriard Rd RG25 2PN**
email: bookings@thefurandfeathers.co.uk
dir: *From Basingstoke take A339 towards Alton. After Herriard follow pub signs. Turn left to pub*

Bag a table in the garden when the weather allows

Its high-ceilinged Victorian proportions translate into light and airy spaces for drinkers and diners, and comfort too, with log-burning fireplaces at each end of the bar. Purpose-built 120 years ago for local farm workers, The Fur & Feathers has to this day obligations in the upkeep of the church roof. In the bar, a trio of ales are rotated, and menus of modern British cooking are perused. Typical dishes are crispy duck breast with orange and redcurrant sauce; pan-fried mackerel fillet with pepper, orange and caper butter; or poached egg with vegetarian bubble-and-squeak cakes and creamy spinach. A large garden hosts entertainment, and is home to chickens laying eggs for the pub's kitchen.

Open Tue-Thu 12-3 5-11 (Fri-Sat 12-11 Sun 12-6) Closed 1wk end of Dec, Sun eve & Mon **Food** Lunch Tue-Sat 12-2, Sun 12-3 Dinner Tue-Sat 6.30-9 Restaurant menu available Tue-Sun ⊕ FREE HOUSE ◀ Local ales, rotating Flack Manor Flack's Double Drop, Hogs Back, Sharp's, Wild Weather Ales, Long Dog, Red Cat Ö Hogs Back Hazy Hog, Sharp's Orchard. ⏱ 28 **Facilities** Non-diners area ◀◗ Children's menu Children's portions Garden ⊟ Parking WiFi ▄ (notice required)

HIGHCLERE
Map 5 SU45

The Yew Tree ★★★★ INN ◉◉

tel: 01635 253360 **Hollington Cross, Andover Rd RG20 9SE**
email: info@theyewtree.co.uk **web:** www.theyewtree.co.uk
dir: *M4 junct 13, A34 S, 4th junct on left signed Highclere/Wash Common, turn right towards Andover A343, inn on right*

Delightful 17th-century pub

After visiting nearby Highclere Castle, where *Downton Abbey* was filmed, have lunch here. Or vice versa. Either way, enjoy its high standards of food and service, starting in the bar with tartan high back seats and comfy leather chairs, which offers 13 wines by the glass, real ales from the Two Cocks Brewery and Orchard Pig Reveller cider. Admired for his locally sourced fresh fish and game, chef Simon Davis presents frequently-changing menus featuring bar snacks, sharing plates and, typically, salt and pepper Brixham squid with mango, chilli and lime dressing; Laverstoke Park mozzarella crostini with chargrilled aubergine; and wild line-caught black bream with squid and potato chowder.

Open all day all wk **Food** Lunch all wk 12-2.30 Dinner Mon-Sat 6.30-9.30, Sun 7-8.30 ⊕ CIRRUS INNS ◀ Two Cocks Cavalier, Ringwood Best Bitter, Ramsbury Gold Ö Orchard Pig Reveller. ⏱ 13 **Facilities** Non-diners area ✿ (Bar Restaurant Garden) ◀◗ Children's menu Children's portions Garden ⊟ Parking WiFi ▄ (notice required) **Rooms** 8

HOLYBOURNE
Map 5 SU74

The White Hart Hotel

tel: 01420 87654 **139 London Rd GU34 4EY**
dir: *M3 junct 5, follow Alton signs (A339). In Alton take A31 towards Farnham. Follow Holybourne signs*

Friendly village pub

The village of Holybourne is steeped in history: an old Roman fort lies under the cricket field, and the village also stands on the Pilgrims' Way. Rebuilt in the 1920s on the site of the original inn, The White Hart provides a comfortable, welcoming setting for enjoying a well-kept pint and a hearty meal. Children are welcome and there's a bouncy castle in the summer.

Open all day all wk **Food** Lunch Mon-Fri 12-3, Sat 12-9, Sun 12-8 Dinner Mon-Fri 5-9, Sat 12-9, Sun 12-8 Av main course £12 Set menu available Restaurant menu available Mon-Sat ⊕ GREENE KING ◀ Hardys & Hansons, Morland Old Speckled Hen, 3 guest ales Ö Mr Whitehead's Holybourne Cider, Aspall, Rekorderlig. ⏱ 10 **Facilities** Non-diners area ✿ (Bar Garden) ◀◗ Children's menu Children's portions Play area Garden ⊟ Parking WiFi ▄ (notice required)

Silver Stars The AA Silver Star rating denotes a Hotel or B&B that we highly recommend. They have a superior level of quality within their star rating, high standards of hospitality, service and cleanliness.

HOOK — Map 5 SU75

The Hogget

tel: 01256 763009 **London Rd, Hook Common RG27 9JJ**
email: home@hogget.co.uk
dir: *M3 junct 5, A30, 0.5m, between Hook & Basingstoke*

Value for money just off the M3

Just off the London Road, The Hogget goes from strength to strength, and its reputation for good food and service continues to grow. Ringwood Best is the session beer, while the stronger candidates are either Ringwood 49er, Marston's Pedigree or Wychwood Hobgoblin. Carefully prepared English favourites include a number of slow-cooked dishes; gourmet burgers; and local sausages, but you'll also find butternut squash risotto; pork and sage meatballs with linguine; Shipyard's pale ale battered cod; and Hereford-Angus beef from a friend's farm in Wiltshire.

Open all wk 12-3 5.30-11 (Sat 12-11 Sun 12-10.30) Closed 25-26 Dec **Food** Lunch all wk 12-2.30 Dinner all wk 6.30-9 Av main course £12 ⊕ MARSTON'S ◄ Ringwood Best Bitter, Wychwood Hobgoblin, Guest ales ♂ Thatchers Gold. ♈ 12 **Facilities** Non-diners area ✿ (Bar Outside area) ♦ Children's menu Children's portions Outside area ♒ Parking WiFi

HOUGHTON — Map 5 SU33

The Boot Inn

tel: 01794 388310 **SO20 6LH**
email: bootinnhoughton@btconnect.com
dir: *Phone for detailed directions*

Quality pub dining with fishing by arrangement

The River Test is renowned as one of the world's best fly fishing waters, and The Boot enjoys a tranquil location on its banks. The 18th-century timber-framed bar serves a choice of beers and ciders, while its restaurant strives to serve good food without earning the gastro-pub sobriquet. Pub grub, then, of a higher order – in lunchtime plates of home-made steak and kidney pie; and evening dishes like haddock mornay with broad beans and mash; or pork fillet Wellington.

Open all wk 10-3 6-11 **Food** Lunch all wk 12-2 Dinner all wk 6.30-9 Restaurant menu available Lunch all wk, Dinner Tue-Sat ⊕ FREE HOUSE ◄ Ringwood Best Bitter, Upham Punter ♂ Westons Stowford Press. **Facilities** Non-diners area ✿ (Bar Garden Outside area) ♦ Children's menu Children's portions Garden Outside area ♒ Parking WiFi (notice required)

HURSLEY — Map 5 SU42

The Dolphin Inn

tel: 01962 775209 **SO21 2JY**
dir: *Phone for detailed directions*

16th-century coaching inn close to South Downs National Park

Like most of the village, this old coaching inn with magnificent chimneys once belonged to the Hursley Estate, which is now owned by IBM. It was built between 1540 and 1560, reputedly using timbers from a Tudor warship called HMS *Dolphin* (today's less glamorous 'ship' is a shore establishment in Gosport). On tap in the beamed bars are Ringwood Best, George Gale & Co HSB and Green Goblin oak-aged cider. In addition to sandwiches, baguettes and jacket potatoes, favourites include Hursley-made faggots; lamb's liver and bacon; scampi and chips; and macaroni cheese.

Open all day all wk Mon-Sat 11-11 (Sun 12-10.30) **Food** Lunch Mon-Sat 12-2.30, Sun 12-8.30 Dinner Mon-Thu 6-9, Fri-Sat 6.30-9.30, Sun 12-8.30 ⊕ ENTERPRISE INNS ◄ George Gale & Co HSB, Ringwood Best Bitter ♂ Thatchers & Green Goblin. ♈ 12 **Facilities** Non-diners area ✿ (Bar Garden) ♦ Children's menu Children's portions Play area Family room Garden ♒ Parking (notice required)

The Kings Head ★★★★ INN

tel: 01962 775208 **Main Rd SO21 2JW**
email: enquiries@kingsheadhursley.co.uk web: www.kingsheadhursley.co.uk
dir: *On A3090 between Winchester & Romsey*

A winning mix of modernity and tradition

Close to historic Winchester and with pleasant walks nearby, The Kings Head is owned five local farming families. The 'Taste of Hampshire Menu', available Monday to Friday lunchtime in addition to sandwiches and pub classics, offers pan-fried fillet of red mullet with tabouleh salad and saffron aïoli to start; followed by braised daube of Hampshire beef, choucroute cabbage and creamed piper potatoes; and bread-and-butter pudding with vanilla custard. The dinner menu includes Shetland mussels, confit belly of pork, and curried monkfish. Two guest ales change on a weekly basis. A beer festival is held on the Summer Bank Holiday weekend.

Open all day all wk 7.30am-11pm **Food** Lunch all wk 12-9 Dinner all wk 12-9 Set menu available ⊕ FREE HOUSE ◄ Sharp's Doom Bar, Ringwood, Flack Manor, Guest ale ♂ The Orchard Pig. ♈ 10 **Facilities** Non-diners area ✿ (Bar Garden) ♦ Children's menu Children's portions Garden ♒ Beer festival Parking WiFi (notice required) **Rooms** 8

LEE-ON-THE-SOLENT — Map 5 SU50

The Bun Penny

tel: 023 9255 0214 **36 Manor Way PO13 9JH**
email: bar@bunpenny.co.uk web: www.bunpenny.co.uk
dir: *From Fareham take B3385 to Lee-on-the-Solent. Pub 300yds before High St*

Classic country free house a short walk from the water

A short walk from the waterfront, this former farmhouse occupies a prominent position on the road into Lee-on-the-Solent. Every inch a classic country free house, it has a large patio at the front and an extensive back garden that's ideal for summer relaxation, while real fires and cosy corners are welcome in winter. Otter beer is sold direct from the cask, backed by hand-pulls including ales from the local Oakleaf Brewery. A typical meal might be paprika-crusted calamari with garlic mayonnaise and sweet chilli dip followed by fillet of pork Wellington, roasted root vegetables with a light scrumpy sauce.

Open all day all wk 11-11 (Fri-Sat 11am-mdnt Sun 12-10.30) **Food** Lunch Mon-Sat 12-2.30, Sun 12-9 Dinner Mon-Sat 6-9, Sun 12-9 ⊕ FREE HOUSE ◄ Otter Bitter, Oakleaf Hole Hearted, Guest ales ♂ Westons. ♈ 13 **Facilities** Non-diners area ✿ (Bar Garden) ♦ Children's menu Children's portions Garden ♒ Parking WiFi (notice required)

LISS
Map 5 SU72

The Jolly Drover ★★★★ INN

tel: 01730 893137 **London Rd, Hillbrow GU33 7QL**
email: thejollydrover@googlemail.com **web:** www.thejollydrover.co.uk
dir: *From station in Liss at mini rdbt right into Hill Brow Rd (B3006) signed Rogate, Rake, Hill Brow. At junct with B2071, pub opposite*

Just out of town at the top of the hill

This pub was built in 1844 by a drover, Mr Knowles, to offer cheer and sustenance to other drovers on the old London road. For nearly 20 years it has been run by Anne and Barry Coe, who welcome all-comers with a large log fire, secluded garden, a choice of real ales including guests, and home-cooked food. The same menu is served in the bar and restaurant. Dishes include roast beef and Yorkshire pudding, 'Hodgepodge Pie' (pork, veal and lamb), chicken breast with bacon and Stilton sauce, and grilled whole plaice with white wine and parsley sauce. Gluten-free and vegetarian choices are also available.

Open all wk 10.30-3 5.30-11 (Sat 10.30-3 5.30-11 Sun 12-4) Closed 25-26 Dec, 1 Jan, Sun eve **Food** Lunch Mon-Sat 12-2.15, Sun 12-2.30 Dinner Mon-Sat 7-9.30 Av main course £10-£12 Restaurant menu available all wk ⊕ ENTERPRISE INNS ◀ Sharp's Doom Bar, Timothy Taylor Landlord, Guest ale. ☗ 10 **Facilities** Non-diners area ◀ Children's portions Garden ⴴ Parking WiFi ▄▄▄ (notice required) **Rooms** 6

LITTLETON
Map 5 SU43

The Running Horse ★★★★ INN ◉◉   PICK OF THE PUBS

See Pick of the Pubs on opposite page

LONGPARISH
Map 5 SU44

The Plough Inn ◉◉   PICK OF THE PUBS

tel: 01264 720358 **SP11 6PB**
email: eat@theploughinn.info
dir: *M3 junct 8, A303 towards Andover. In approx 6m take B3048 towards Longparish*

Traditional country pub with a contemporary feel

Perfectly placed for Test Way walkers (the long-distance path runs through the pub car park) and just off the A303, this charming, early 18th-century inn is found in the village of Longparish. Since taking over here, chef James Durrant and his wife Louise have focused on food – worthy of two AA Rosettes – but not at the expense of its role as a local, with a snug bar offering Timothy Taylor Landlord and Ringwood Best, and continental lagers, draught and bottled ciders and over a dozen wines by the glass. There are some tasty snacks on the bar menu, like whitebait, or a fab Scotch egg, and there's a grill if you just fancy a steak. Otherwise, check out the

short carte for the likes of roe deer tartare with picked and baked beetroot and juniper mayonnaise, followed by slow-cooked pork shoulder with burnt onion ketchup, choucroute and jacket potato. To really get a feel for the food, try the six-course 'Taste of the Plough'. The garden is just the ticket for outdoor dining.

Open Tue-Thu 12-3.30 6-11 (Fri-Sat all day Sun 12-6) Closed Sun eve, Mon **Food** Lunch Tue-Sat 12-2.30, Sun 12-4.30 Dinner Tue-Sat 6-9.30 Restaurant menu available Tue-Sat ⊕ ENTERPRISE INNS ◀ Timothy Taylor Landlord, Ringwood Best Bitter, Local guest ale ♂ The Orchard Pig, Wessex Cider. ☗ 14 **Facilities** Non-diners area ♣ (Bar Garden) ◀ Children's menu Children's portions Garden ⴴ Parking WiFi ▄▄▄ (notice required)

LOVEDEAN
Map 5 SU61

The Bird in Hand

tel: 023 9259 1055 **269 Lovedean Ln PO8 9RX**
email: enquiries@lovedeanbirdinhand.co.uk
dir: *A3(M) junct 2, A3 signed Portsmouth. At next rdbt left (A3/Portsmouth). Right into Lovedean Ln (signed Lovedean). Pub on left*

Country pub with inspiring menus

This Tudor-look, 200-year-old pub marks the village edge, from where cornfields and copses ripple across the gently rolling Hampshire countryside. At the start of World War II, locals are rumoured to have drunk beer out of the FA Cup, which was despatched here for safe-keeping by the then-holders, Portsmouth. Today's drinkers lack such silverware, but still have great local beers to sample. The inspiring, multiple menus include generous dairy and gluten-free selections for bar or restaurant consumption. Main menu options include sea bass fillet with crab, tomato and chilli linguine; or venison saddle, with plum and poppy seed crumble to finish.

Open all day all wk **Food** Lunch Mon-Sat 12-3, Sun 12-7.30 Dinner Mon-Sat 6-9.30, Sun 12-7.30 Set menu available ⊕ ENTERPRISE INNS ◀ Ringwood Best Bitter, Bowman Ales Wallops Wood, Havant Finished, Guest ales ♂ Westons Stowford Press. ☗ 11 **Facilities** Non-diners area ♣ (Bar Garden) ◀ Children's menu Children's portions Garden ⴴ Parking WiFi ▄▄▄ (notice required)

LOWER SWANWICK
Map 5 SU40

The Navigator

tel: 01489 572123 **286 Bridge Rd SO31 7EB**
email: info@thenavigatorswanwick.co.uk
dir: *M27 junct 8, A3024 signed Bursledon. 1st exit at next rdbt onto A27 (Bridge Rd). Cross river, pub 300yds on left*

Food-driven hostelry on the River Hamble

With its prime location on the magnificent marina front at Lower Swanwick, The Navigator's ambience reflects the strong sea-faring traditions of this area. It's one owned by the Upham Group, so no surprise to find ales from its own brewery behind the bar. Head chef Gareth Longhurst moved here from The Navigator's well-regarded sister pub in West Meon, The Thomas Lord. So food of a higher order can be expected, and the carte does not disappoint. The sample dinner menu, for example, details a smoked ham hock with garlic and parsley terrine, piccalilli and toast; pan-fried pollock fillet with crispy chorizo, herb risotto and samphire; and guinea fowl breast and leg ballotine, wilted black cabbage and cider, mustard and herb cream.

Open all day all wk **Food** Lunch Mon-Sat 12-2.30, Sun 12-3.30 Dinner Mon-Sat 6.30-9.30, Sun 6.30-9 ⊕ UPHAM PUB CO ◀ Tipster, Punter & Stakes. **Facilities** Non-diners area ♣ (Bar Outside area) ◀ Children's menu Children's portions Outside area ⴴ Parking WiFi ▄▄▄ (notice required)

PICK OF THE PUBS

The Running Horse ★★★★ INN ❀❀

LITTLETON   Map 5 SU43

tel: 01962 880218
88 Main Rd SO22 6QS
email: info@runninghorseinn.co.uk
web: www.runninghorseinn.co.uk
dir: *3m from Winchester, 1m from Three Maids Hill, signed from Stockbridge Rd*

Upmarket pub and restaurant on Winchester's fringe

Belonging to the Upham Group, this judiciously restored and rejuvenated country pub lies in one of Winchester's satellite villages. Dating from the mid-1850s, by the latter years of the 20th century it was being run by a succession of landlords, many of whom, says Upham "had taken [it] as a route to peaceful semi-retirement." Things are different today, the pub's new lease of life coming with a thoroughly professional team. The light, spacious interior shows just what a good designer can achieve: heritage-red walls, wooden flooring, bookcases crammed with old tomes, and a large hatch revealing the kitchen. Needless to say, given its ownership, the real ales are from Upham's as well as from a guest brewery. Cider fans will find Orchard Pig, and wine drinkers a good selection by the glass. Two AA Rosettes prove the continuing high quality of the food, all from trusted local suppliers, and its careful preparation under the watchful eye of a new chef. Look out for starters of pork pâté with macerated raisins and

chive shallot dressing; and carpaccio of beetroot with roasted golden beetroot, goats' cheese croquette and beetroot dressing. To follow might be whole gurnard with triple-cooked chips and brown caper butter; lamb rump with fondant potato, wild mushrooms and rosemary jus; and butternut squash risotto with crispy sage, burnt butter and amaretti crumb. For dessert, mango pannacotta with coconut macaroon, burnt pineapple, green tea sorbet and crystallised mint; and toffee apple crumble with nutty granola topping and salted caramel ice cream. An open area at the front features a cosy thatched cabana, and at the rear are tables and benches, beyond which overnight accommodation is arranged around the garden.

Open all day all wk Closed 25, 26 & 31 Dec Evenings **Food** Lunch Mon-Sat 12-2.30, Sun 12-3.30 Dinner Mon-Sat 6.30-9.30, Sun 6.30-9 Restaurant menu available all wk ⊞ FREE HOUSE/UPHAM PUB CO ◖ Tipster, Punter & Stakes, Guest ale ♻ The Orchard Pig. ♟ 12 **Facilities** Non-diners area ❦ (Bar Garden) ♦♦ Children's menu Children's portions Garden ⊼ Beer festival Parking WiFi ▭ (notice required) **Rooms** 9

LOWER WIELD

Map 5 SU64

The Yew Tree

PICK OF THE PUBS

tel: 01256 389224 **SO24 9RX**
dir: *A339 from Basingstoke towards Alton. Turn right for Lower Wield*

Good selection of fine wines and local ales

The eponymous, 650-year-old yew tree was just getting into its stride when this free house started serving real ale in 1845. Set in wonderful countryside, opposite a picturesque cricket pitch, the popular landlord's simple mission statement promises 'Good honest food; great local beers; fine wines (lots of choice); and, most importantly, good fun for one and all'. Triple fff Moondance is the house beer, with 20 guest ale brewers on rotation, including Bowman Ales and Hogs Back. Most of the food is sourced from Hampshire or neighbouring counties, and the menu reflects the seasons while keeping the favourites 'to avoid uproar'. Sample dishes include warm Chinese duck and noodle salad with sesame and oriental dressing; or garlic and blue cheese mushrooms with toasted ciabatta, followed by red snapper fillet, basmati rice and lightly curried cream sauce; or belly of pork, mash and toffee apple cream sauce. Finish off with chocolate and raisin biscuit cake for afters. There is an annual cricket match and sports day in summer, and quizzes in the winter months.

Open Tue-Sat 12-3 6-11 (Sun all day) Closed 1st 2wks Jan, Mon **Food** Lunch Tue-Sun 12-2 Dinner Tue-Sat 6.30-9, Sun 6.30-8.30 ⊕ FREE HOUSE ◀ Flower Pots Cheriton Pots, Bowman Swift One, Triple fff Moondance, Hogs Back TEA, Hop Back GFB, Andwell Gold Muddler. ♟ 14 **Facilities** Non-diners area ♣ (Bar Garden) ◀♦ Children's menu Children's portions Garden Parking WiFi

LYMINGTON

Map 5 SZ39

Mayflower Inn

tel: 01590 672160 **Kings Saltern Rd SO41 3QD**
email: manager@themayflowerlymington.co.uk
dir: *A337 towards New Milton, left at rdbt by White Hart, left to Rookes Ln, right at mini rdbt, pub 0.75m*

Mock-Tudor inn serving good food, right next to the yacht haven

A favourite with yachtsmen and dog walkers, this solidly built mock-Tudor inn overlooks the Lymington River, with glorious views to the Isle of Wight. There's a magnificent garden with splendid sun terraces where visitors can enjoy a pint of Goddards Fuggle-Dee-Dum, and an on-going summer barbecue in fine weather. Menu prices are reasonable, with dishes that range from sizzling platters of steak or Cajun chicken, to main courses of lasagne bolognese, battered hake fillet and chips or Quorn and cashew stir-fry.

Open all day all wk **Food** Lunch Mon-Sat 12-9.30, Sun 12-9 Dinner Mon-Sat 12-9.30, Sun 12-9 Set menu available ⊕ ENTERPRISE INNS/COASTAL INNS & TAVERNS LTD ◀ Ringwood Best Bitter, Sharp's Doom Bar, Goddards Fuggle-Dee-Dum ♻ Thatchers. ♟ 9 **Facilities** Non-diners area ♣ (Bar Garden) ◀♦ Children's menu Children's portions Play area Garden ⊟ Parking WiFi ▭ (notice required)

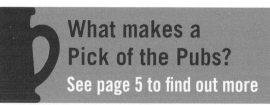

What makes a Pick of the Pubs?

See page 5 to find out more

The Walhampton Arms

tel: 01590 673113 **Walhampton Hill SO41 5RE**
email: enquiries@walhamptonarms.co.uk **web:** www.walhamptonarmslymington.co.uk
dir: *From Lymington take B3054 towards Beaulieu. Pub in 2m*

Order a meal from the popular carvery

Originally a farm building in the early 19th-century that included a model dairy supplying Walhampton Estate, this friendly pub serves real ales from Ringwood, with guest ales from local microbreweries throughout the year. This pub is also known for its excellent value carvery, but the steaks and surf 'n' turf are two other reasons why people flock here. Looking for different options? Then other dishes might include lamb's liver and bacon; steak and ale pie or the chef's curry with rice. Children too will find all their favourites on their own menu.

Open all day all wk 11-11 (Sun 12-10.30) **Food** Lunch Tue-Sat 12-9, Sun-Mon 12-8 Dinner Tue-Sat 12-9, Sun-Mon 12-8 ⊕ FREE HOUSE ◀ Ringwood Best Bitter, Local guest ales. ♟ 10 **Facilities** Non-diners area ♣ (Bar Outside area) ◀♦ Children's menu Children's portions Outside area ⊟ Parking WiFi ▭ (notice required)

LYNDHURST

Map 5 SU30

New Forest Inn

tel: 023 8028 4690 **Emery Down SO43 7DY**
email: info@thenewforestinn.co.uk
dir: *M27 junct 1 follow signs for A35/Lyndhurst. In Lyndhurst follow signs for Christchurch, turn right at Swan Inn towards Emery Down*

Friendly 18th-century inn with large garden

New Forest ponies occasionally wander into this traditional local, a distraction that only serves to enhance its friendly atmosphere. There's incumbents Fortyniner, Flack's Double Drop and Aspall cider on tap. The menu showcases a multitude of items – doorstep sandwiches, snacks, chargrills, toasted paninis, vegetarian and chef's choices. In there somewhere are smoked haddock kedgeree with poached egg; pork cutlet with ratatouille and mash; herb crusted salmon fillet on chorizo and pea risotto; and leek and gruyère tart. The beer festival is in July.

Open all day all wk **Food** Lunch Mon-Sat 11.30-9.30, Sun 12-9 Dinner Mon-Sat 11.30-9.30, Sun 12-9 ⊕ ENTERPRISE INNS ◀ Ringwood Fortyniner, Flack Manor Flack's Double Drop, Guest ales ♻ Aspall. ♟ 12 **Facilities** Non-diners area ♣ (Bar Restaurant Garden) ◀♦ Children's menu Children's portions Garden ⊟ Beer festival Cider festival Parking WiFi ▭ (notice required)

PICK OF THE PUBS

The Gamekeepers

MAPLEDURWELL Map 5 SU65

tel: 01256 322038 & 07786 998994
Tunworth Rd RG25 2LU
email: info@thegamekeepers.co.uk
web: www.thegamekeepers.co.uk
dir: *M3 junct 6, A30 towards Hook. Right across dual carriageway after The Hatch pub. Pub signed*

Weatherboarded pub with a large garden overlooking fields

The 1841 census records that Joseph Phillips, a shoemaker, lived here with his wife Elizabeth, four children and his brother, a farm labourer. By 1861 Joseph was multi-tasking, having added innkeeping to his repertoire, with his cottage now doubling as The Queen's Head. He probably made his big decision a few years earlier, in 1854, because that's the date that appears on two fireplace bricks in the dining room, one with his initials and the other with Elizabeth's. It has been The Gamekeepers since 1973, owners Phil and Sandra Costello arriving here some 30 years later. Standing on its own down a leafy lane in a village comfortably beyond Basingstoke's eastern limits, the pub is part-clapboard and the low-beamed, flagstone-floored interior features an indoor well. Armed with a drink, perhaps a Hampshire-brewed real ale, or a Norcotts real cider from Devon, settle into a leather sofa and study the menu, on which starters might include 'Welsh-style' mussels cooked in cider with leeks and smoked bacon; and Arbroath smokies with smoked fish pâté, cream cheese, horseradish and chives. Among the mains look for chargrilled fillet of beef with blue cheese and peppercorn butter, dauphinoise potatoes, wilted baby spinach, cherry tomatoes, organic shimeji mushrooms and red wine jus; or pan-fried fillet of sea bream with king prawns, new potatoes, market vegetables, tomato and caper butter. Vegetarian options include Sicilian ravioli with chillies, garlic, cumin and coriander, wild mushrooms, spinach and shaved parmesan. To round off, perhaps peach and Champagne sorbet; or the Hampshire cheeseboard of Barkham Blue, Stoney Cross and Tunworth.

Open all wk Mon-Fri 11-2.30 5.30-11 (Sat 11-11 Sun 11-10.30) Closed 31 Dec, 1 Jan **Food** Lunch Mon-Fri 11-2.30, Sat-Sun 11-9.30 Dinner Mon-Fri 5.30-9.30, Sat-Sun 11-9.30 ⊕ FREE HOUSE ◄ Andwell Gold Muddler, Hogs Back, Longdog, Upham, Resolute & King John, Triple fff, Fuller's London Pride ♻ Sharp's Orchard, Norcotts Cider, Westons Stowford Press. ♟ 10 **Facilities** Non-diners area ♣ (Bar Garden) ♦♦ Children's portions Garden ⌁ Parking WiFi ⚌ (notice required)

LYNDHURST *continued*

The Oak Inn

tel: 023 8028 2350 **Pinkney Ln, Bank SO43 7FD**
email: oakinn@fullers.co.uk
dir: *From Lyndhurst signed A35 to Christchurch, follow A35 for 1m, left at Bank sign*

Reliable oasis on New Forest trails

At the heart of the National Park, patrons enjoying Gales ales in the garden of this bare-boarded, bric-a-brac full country pub may idly watch local residents' pigs snuffling for acorns, New Forest ponies grazing or even fallow deer fleetingly flitting amidst the trees. It's a popular stop with cyclists and walkers exploring the Forest's tracks, breaking for a while to partake of the enticing menu which is strong on meals prepared using produce of the parish; perhaps a doorstop sandwich with New Forest ham and Loosehanger cheese, or cider braised pork belly, celeriac and sage purée, gratin potatoes and spiced apple compôte as a main. Booking for meals is advised. Children are welcome, but only eight years and over after 8pm.

Open all wk Mon-Fri 11.30-3 5.30-11 (Sat 11.30-11 Sun 12-10.30) **Food** Lunch Mon-Fri 12-2.30, Sat 12-9.30, Sun 12-9 Dinner Mon-Fri 6-9.30, Sat 12-9.30, Sun 12-9 ⊕ FULLER'S ◧ London Pride, George Gale & Co HSB & Seafarers ♂ Aspall. ⚑ 12 **Facilities** Non-diners area ☻ (Bar Garden) ♦♦ Children's menu Children's portions Garden ⊸ Parking WiFi

---

MAPLEDURWELL	**Map 5 SU65**

The Gamekeepers   PICK OF THE PUBS

See Pick of the Pubs on page 237

MARCHWOOD	**Map 5 SU31**

The Pilgrim Inn

tel: 023 8086 7752 **Hythe Rd SO40 4WU**
email: pilgrim.inn@fullers.co.uk
dir: *M27 junct 2, A326 towards Fawley. Follow brown sign for inn, turn left into Twiggs Lane. At T-junct right into Hythe Rd. Pub on right*

Family-friendly dining on the edge of the New Forest

Only nine miles from Southampton and on the edge of New Forest National Park, The Pilgrim comprises two handsome thatched buildings complete with exposed beams, stone walls and log fire. It all makes for a genial setting to enjoy a pint of London Pride in the bar, or to settle down in the dining area and choose from a family-friendly menu showcasing local produce. Typical mains include faggots, red cabbage and mash; and pan-fried cod fillet with celeriac, bacon and mushroom fricassée. Leave room for plum crumble with cinnamon ice cream.

Open all day all wk **Food** Lunch Mon-Fri 12-3, Sat-Sun 12-6 Dinner Mon-Fri 6-9.30, Sat 6-10, Sun 6-8 ⊕ FULLER'S ◧ London Pride, Gales HSB. ⚑ 17 **Facilities** Non-diners area ☻ (Bar Garden) ♦♦ Children's menu Children's portions Garden ⊸ Parking WiFi (notice required)

MICHELDEVER	**Map 5 SU53**

Half Moon & Spread Eagle

tel: 01962 774339 **Winchester Rd SO21 3DG**
email: hmoonseagle@gmail.com
dir: *From Winchester take A33 towards Basingstoke. In 5m left after Class tractors. Pub 1m on right*

Traditional pub with large garden in thatched village

New, but highly experienced, landlords are successfully maintaining the real village pub feel here, while also attracting customers from well beyond the parish

boundary. The only pub in the country with this name, incidentally, it comprises a beamed central bar, a pool room and a restaurant, although the convivial bar has tables too. Interesting guest beers change frequently. Among the home-cooked dishes are chilli with rice or chips; rump and rib-eye steaks; Southern fried chicken; salads and ploughman's. Sunday naturally means roasts, with alternatives such as haddock and spinach bake; rack of ribs; and goats' cheese and beetroot salad.

Open 12-3 6-10.30 (Fri 12-3 6-12 Sat 12-12 Sun 12-8) Closed Mon (winter) **Food** Lunch Tue-Sat 12-3, Sun 12-4 Dinner Tue-Sat 6-9 Av main course £10 ⊕ GREENE KING ◧ London Glory, Moon Best, 3 guest ales ♂ Westons Stowford Press. ⚑ 12 **Facilities** Non-diners area ☻ (Bar Garden) ♦♦ Children's menu Children's portions Play area Garden ⊸ Parking WiFi (notice required)

NEW ALRESFORD	**Map 5 SU53**

The Bell Inn

tel: 01962 732429 **12 West St SO24 9AT**
email: info@bellalresford.com
dir: *In village centre*

Small, family-run free house in charming town centre

A well-restored former coaching inn in Georgian Alresford's main street, where Hampshire real ales hold their own against contenders from Cornwall and Devon, and over 18 wines are available by the glass. The bar dining area and candlelit restaurant offer game terrine, apple, pear and fig chutney; and smoked haddock and mussel chowder to start; then steak and Guinness pie, mash, greens and gravy; and confit of French duck leg, dauphinoise potatoes, spinach and cassis sauce. There's a good value two-course menu available at various times during the week. Station Road, opposite the inn, leads to the famous Watercress Line.

Open all day Closed Sun eve **Food** Lunch Mon-Sat 12-3, Sun 12-4 Dinner Mon-Sat 6-9 Av main course £15 Set menu available Restaurant menu available Lunch all wk ⊕ FREE HOUSE ◧ Sharp's Doom Bar, Itchen Valley, Upham Ale, Otter Bitter, Bowman Ales Swift One ♂ Aspall. ⚑ 18 **Facilities** Non-diners area ☻ (Bar Outside area) ♦♦ Children's menu Children's portions Outside area ⊸ WiFi (notice required)

NORTHINGTON	**Map 5 SU53**

The Woolpack Inn ★★★★ INN ⊛   PICK OF THE PUBS

tel: 01962 734184 **Totford SO24 9TJ**
email: info@thewoolpackinn.co.uk **web:** www.thewoolpackinn.co.uk
dir: *From Basingstoke take A339 towards Alton. Under motorway, turn right (across dual carriageway) onto B3036 signed Candovers & Alresford. Pub between Brown Candover & Northington*

Welcoming country inn with cracking food and local ales

Set in stunning Hampshire countryside, this Grade II listed drovers' inn has a sense of calm modernity while still retaining the classic feel of a country pub. Standing in a tiny hamlet in the peaceful Candover Valley, The Woolpack welcomes walkers and their dogs, families, cyclists and foodies. Ales change weekly, while an up-market wine list will please the cognoscenti. Eat in the traditional bar, where rugs on tiled or wood floors and a roaring log fire create a relaxing atmosphere; alternatives are the smart dining room or a heated terrace. The bar menu proffers classics such as pie of the day or bangers and mash with onion gravy. Typical dining room main courses are confit pork belly, smoked bacon and potato gratin; or spiced winter vegetable hotpot, carrot and onion fritters and garlic flatbread.

Open all day all wk **Food** Lunch Mon-Thu 12-2.30, Fri-Sun 12-3 Dinner Mon-Sat 6.30-9, Sun 5.30-8.30 ⊕ FREE HOUSE ◧ Palmers Copper Ale, The Ramshead (pub's own), Weekly changing Guest ale ♂ Thatchers Gold. ⚑ 11 **Facilities** Non-diners area ☻ (Bar Restaurant Garden) ♦♦ Children's menu Children's portions Play area Garden ⊸ Parking WiFi (notice required) **Rooms** 7

PICK OF THE PUBS

The Fox

NORTH WALTHAM　　　Map 5 SU54

tel: 01256 397288 **RG25 2BE**
email: info@thefox.org
web: www.thefox.org
dir: *M3 junct 7, A30 towards Winchester. North Waltham signed on right. Take 2nd signed road, then 1st left at Y junct*

Family-friendly pub with a large garden

Built as three farm cottages in 1624, a feature of the bar in this peaceful village pub is its collection of miniatures — over 1,100 so far, and counting. It's an easy place to get to whether travelling on the A303 or the M3. The Fox welcomes families, as you might guess from the children's adventure play area in the extensive beer garden which blazes with colour in summer when the pretty flower borders and hanging baskets are in bloom. In the bar, landlord Rob MacKenzie serves well-looked after real ales from Sharp's, Brakspear, West Berkshire and a guest brewery, and an impressive malt whisky selection among which you'll find the relatively scarce Auchentoshan, Dalmore and Singleton. Bar choices include a ciabatta bacon butty; and steak and beef sausage pie and mash. Rob's wife Izzy is responsible for the monthly menus and daily specials board in the tartan-carpeted restaurant, which list the house specialities of cheese soufflé,

and Hampshire venison served with glazed shallots, field mushrooms, spinach, creamed swede, sauté potatoes and port glaze. Among typical main courses there might be sea bass with coriander butter; lobster and crab risotto; or, in season, pan-fried pheasant breast and confit leg in apricot and wine sauce with dauphinoise potatoes and steamed green beans. Home-made desserts are tempting too — there's pineapple Alaska; passionfruit crème brûlée; and bread and butter pudding with caramelised apples, toffee sauce and ice cream. The Fox's events calendar features monthly wine tasting dinners, and a beer festival in late April.

Open all day all wk 11-11 Closed 25 Dec **Food** Lunch all wk 12-2.30 Dinner all wk 6-9.30 Restaurant menu available all wk ⊕ FREE HOUSE ◾ West Berkshire Good Old Boy, Brakspear, Sharp's Doom Bar, Guest ale ♻ Aspall. ♟ 14 **Facilities** Non-diners area 🐾 (Bar Garden) 🚻 Children's menu Children's portions Play area Garden ⊼ Beer festival Parking 🚐 (notice required)

NORTH WALTHAM   Map 5 SU54

The Fox   PICK OF THE PUBS

See Pick of the Pubs on page 239

OLD BASING   Map 5 SU65

The Crown

tel: 01256 321424 **The Street RG24 7BW**
email: sales@thecrownoldbasing.com
dir: *M3 junct 6 towards Basingstoke. At rdbt right onto A30. 1st left into Redbridge Ln, to T-junct. Right into The Street, pub on right*

Village local with well-kept ales

Just outside Basingstoke is the picturesque village of Old Basing, in the heart of which is The Crown. Reliable and popular national ales are backed by local brews like Andwell King John and a good wine list. Here, they take great pride in the fact that every dish is prepared from scratch in the pub's kitchen. Food takes the form of bar snacks like filled rolls, salads and deli boards, and on the main menu, a typical choice could be a starter of crispy breaded Tunworth cheese with Doom Bar chutney, followed by crisp belly of lamb with cauliflower purée and spiced lentils. Lemon posset or warm coffee and walnut sponge both make for a delicious finale.

Open all wk 11.30-2.30 5-11 (Fri-Sat 11.30-11.30 Sun 11.30-10) Closed 1 Jan **Food** Lunch Mon-Thu 12-2, Fri-Sun 12-2.30 Dinner Mon-Thu 6-9, Fri-Sat 6-9.30 Restaurant menu available ⊕ ENTERPRISE INNS ◀ Sharp's Doom Bar, Fuller's London Pride, Andwell King John Ŏ Thatchers Gold. ▾ 9 **Facilities** Non-diners area ✿ (Bar Garden) ♦♦ Children's menu Children's portions Garden ⋒ Parking WiFi ▬ (notice required)

OVINGTON   Map 5 SU53

The Bush   PICK OF THE PUBS

tel: 01962 732764 **SO24 0RE**
email: thebushinn@wadworth.co.uk
dir: *A31 from Winchester towards Alton & Farnham, approx 6m, left to Ovington. 0.5m to pub*

On the banks of the River Itchen

Pubs are often described as traditional, full of character, cosy and even rose-covered. All of these, The Bush is tucked down a short track that's part of the historic Pilgrim's Way running from nearby Winchester to Canterbury. Small rooms off the bar are characterised by subdued lighting, dark-painted walls, sturdy tables and chairs, high-backed settles, and other rustic artefacts. Add the comforting log fire and one of Wadworth's real ales and the result is, well, pub heaven. Regularly changing menus include sandwiches; butcher's and ploughman's boards; starters and small plates, such as sautéed lamb's kidneys in brandy and mushroom cream sauce; and Cumberland sausage ring on scallion mash with braised red cabbage; and mains including sea bass fillet on lemon and fennel risotto; rump and sirloin steaks; fish of the day in beer batter; and roasted pepper, onion and spinach polenta cake topped with goats' cheese.

Open all wk Mon-Thu 11-3 6-11 Fri-Sat 11-11 Sun 12-10.30 (summer hols Mon-Sat 11-11 Sun 12-10.30) **Food** Lunch Mon-Fri 12-2.30, Sat-Sun 12-9.30, summer hols all wk 12-9.30 Dinner Mon-Fri 6-9.30, Sat-Sun 12-9.30, summer hols all wk 12-9.30 ⊕ WADWORTH ◀ 6X, Henry's Original IPA, Horizon, Seasonal ales Ŏ Westons Rosie's Pig. ▾ 19 **Facilities** Non-diners area ✿ (Bar Restaurant Garden) ♦♦ Children's menu Children's portions Garden ⋒ Parking WiFi

PETERSFIELD   Map 5 SU72

The Old Drum ★★★★ INN ⊛

tel: 01730 300544 **16 Chapel St GU32 3DP**
email: info@theolddrum.co.uk **web:** www.theolddrum.co.uk
dir: *From A3 follow town centre signs (Winchester Rd). At mini rdbt, 2nd exit. Over rail crossing, 3rd right into Chapel St. Pub on right*

A contemporary pub in the centre of town

Two old school friends and their wives decided to buy and transform Petersfield's oldest pub, discovering on the way original 16th-century features, including a superb beamed ceiling and, of perhaps less pulse-racing potential, a tongue-and-groove 1960s ceiling. The bar where author H G Wells once sat with a pint of mild now serves five frequently-changing, locally micro-brewed real ales. The food too has moved considerably on from H G's pickled-egg-if-he-was-lucky days to include AA Rosette-standard mussels in Conqueror stout; roast monkfish, saffron and shellfish ragout, braised fennel and mash; and breast and confit of Hampshire mallard, celeriac purée and savoury blackberry crumble.

Open 10-3 5-11 Closed 25 Dec, 1st wk Jan, Sun eve **Food** Lunch Mon-Sat 12-2, Sun 12-3 Dinner Mon-Sat 6.30-9.30 ⊕ FREE HOUSE ◀ Dark Star Hophead, American Pale Ale & The Art of Darkness, Bowman Ales Wallops Wood, Suthwyk Ales Liberation, Triple fff Moondance Ŏ Westons Bounds. ▾ 12 **Facilities** Non-diners area ✿ (Bar Restaurant Garden) ♦♦ Children's portions Garden ⋒ Beer festival WiFi **Rooms** 5

The Trooper Inn   PICK OF THE PUBS

tel: 01730 827293 **Alton Rd, Froxfield GU32 1BD**
email: info@trooperinn.com
dir: *From A3 follow A272 Winchester signs towards Petersfield (NB do not take A272). 1st exit at mini rdbt for Steep. 3m, pub on right*

Within the South Downs National Park

It calls itself the Pub on the Hill and, at an elevation of 220 metres, it's entitled to, although it sits in a dip. Allegedly a recruiting centre during the run-up to WWI, it backs on to Ashford Hangers National Nature Reserve. Inside are winter log fires, a spacious bar and a charming restaurant with a vaulted ceiling and wooden settles. Hampshire real ales Ballards and Ringwood Best are served in the bar, as are spicy potato wedges; home-cooked ham with free-range eggs and bubble-and-squeak; Aberdeen Angus burger and other snacks. Trooper speciality of slow-roasted lamb shoulder is on the main menu, alongside wild mushroom and Madeira baked risotto; and fillet of cod with mussels in creamy shallot sauce. Selected dishes from this menu are Sunday roast alternatives. Among the desserts are pomegranate and almond cake; and pistachio meringue with Turkish Delight ice cream.

Open 12-3 6-11 Closed 25-26 Dec, 1 Jan, Sun eve & Mon L **Food** Lunch Tue-Sat 12-2, Sun 12-2.30 Dinner Mon-Fri 6.30-9, Sat 7-9.30 ⊕ FREE HOUSE ◀ Ringwood Best Bitter, Ballards, Local guest ales. **Facilities** Non-diners area ✿ (Bar Restaurant Garden) ♦♦ Children's menu Children's portions Garden ⋒ Parking WiFi ▬ (notice required)

Read all about pubs and their friendly ghosts in our feature on page 12

PICK OF THE PUBS

Purefoy Arms

PRESTON CANDOVER Map 5 SU64

tel: 01256 389777
Alresford Rd RG25 2EJ
email: info@thepurefoyarms.co.uk
web: www.thepurefoyarms.co.uk
dir: *On B3046, S of Basingstoke*

Fabulous food in the Candover Valley

Heavy on the bare brick and chunky wooden furnishings, there's nevertheless an air of quiet sophistication to this rural roadside dining pub in one of Hampshire's most appealing valleys. With the possible exception of the real ales, which are down-to-earth and delicious from breweries such as Itchen Valley, the word 'sophisticated' is an appropriate description for the entire operation. Take the wine list and throw caution to the winds with a Kung Fu Girl Riesling from Washington State, USA; if the wallet will not stretch that far, at least one of 17 wines sold by the glass is bound to appeal. The menus are equally astonishing. Settle into a fireside chesterfield to study the hand-written cartes, perhaps with an appetiser of gordal olives; or Manchego with membrillo, a popular Spanish paste made with quince. Then enjoy trying to decide which of head chef, Andy Yates' creative dishes to sample. Some dishes are more familiar than others: a starter of confit Middlewhite, rhubarb and beetroot compôte, and

morcilla may be considered more adventurous than wild mushroom parfait, porcorina parmentiers and tomato jam. The Spanish accent continues with main courses such as rack of Ropley lamb, faggot, Catalan spinach and white bean purée. For dessert, you can stay in Spain for the likes of churros con chocolate, or calasperra rice pudding with honey roast figs. If your visit is timed for lunch rather than dinner, the 'simple lunch' is a fixed-price menu offering exceptional value: black pudding hash with duck egg and HP sauce could be followed by slow-cooked rump of Galician beef with dripping chips and salad. On a lovely summer's evening the garden is a peaceful place to relax with a drink and tapas-style nibbles.

Open 12-3 6-11 (Sun 12-4) Closed 26 Dec, 1 Jan, Sun eve & Mon **Food** Lunch Tue-Sat 12-3, Sun 12-4 Dinner Tue-Sat 6-10 Set menu available ⊕ FREE HOUSE ◀ Flack Manor Flack's Double Drop, Itchen Valley, Irving Frigate Golden Bitter, Purefoy ale ♉ Westons Old Rosie. ♟ 17 **Facilities** Non-diners area ♣ (Bar Restaurant Garden) ♦♦ Children's menu Childre's portions Garden ☍ Parking WiFi ⛟ (notice required)

PETERSFIELD continued

The White Horse Inn

tel: 01420 588387 **Priors Dean GU32 1DA**
email: info@pubwithnoname.co.uk
dir: *From Petersfield through Steep, 5m, right at small x-rds to East Tisted (follow brown pub sign), 2nd right*

Former forge with excellent beers

Originally used as a forge for passing coaches, this splendid 17th-century farmhouse is also known as the 'Pub With No Name' as it has only an empty frame where a sign should hang. The blacksmith sold beer to the travellers while their horses were attended to. Today there is an excellent range of beers including No Name Strong. Menus offer the likes of red onion, feta and olive tart; duck breast with red cabbage and pork reduction; and a selection of burgers and sharing platters. The pub holds a beer festival every June and a cider festival in September.

Open all day all wk 12-11 **Food** Lunch Mon-Fri 12-2.30, Sat-Sun 12-9 Dinner Mon-Fri 6-9.30, Sat-Sun 12-9 ⊕ FULLER'S ◄ London Pride, No Name Best & No Name Strong, Ringwood Fortyniner, Guest ales Ö Aspall. ♀ 10 **Facilities** Non-diners area ✿ (Bar Garden) ♦♦ Children's menu Children's portions Family room Garden ⊨ Beer festival Cider festival Parking ▄▄

PRESTON CANDOVER — Map 5 SU64

Purefoy Arms — PICK OF THE PUBS

See Pick of the Pubs on page 241

RINGWOOD — Map 5 SU10

The Star Inn

tel: 01425 473105 **12 Market Place BH24 1AW**
email: thestarringwood@yahoo.co.uk
dir: *From A31 follow market place signs*

Specialising in Thai and Asian cuisine

Ian Pepperell, the landlord of this 470-year-old pub on the square has played a character in BBC Radio 4's *The Archers* for over 15 years. Away from his radio career he pulls pints of Ringwood Best for locals and helps serve the authentic Thai and oriental food that dominates the menu. Typical dishes include salt and pepper squid, deep-fried sea bass with chilli sauce, chicken in black bean sauce, and aromatic crispy duck. At lunch, you can also tuck into rib-eye steak and chips and tuna mayonnaise sandwiches.

Open all day all wk **Food** Lunch Mon-Sat 12-2.30 Dinner Mon-Sat 6-9.30 Set menu available Restaurant menu available Mon-Sat ⊕ ENTERPRISE INNS ◄ Ringwood Best Bitter, Hop Back Summer Lightning, Brains, Timothy Taylor Landlord Ö Black Rat, Thatchers Green Goblin, Aspall. ♀ 11 **Facilities** Non-diners area ✿ (Bar) ♦♦ Outside area ⊨ WiFi ▄▄ (notice required)

ROCKBOURNE — Map 5 SU11

The Rose & Thistle

tel: 01725 518236 **SP6 3NL**
email: enquiries@roseandthistle.co.uk
dir: *Follow Rockbourne signs from either A354 (Salisbury to Blandford Forum road) or A338 at Fordingbridge*

Pretty, quintessentially English pub

A spectral presence is occasionally abroad here; hardly surprising that the spirit of a former landlord is loathe to leave such an idyllic thatched pub at the fringe of the New Forest. For mortal visitors it's the lure of the local beers, the discovery of top-notch home cooking and the bright, shrubby cottage garden that will detain them. In chillier weather they can settle inside to be warmed by huge log fires. A tasty lunchtime snack of locally smoked salmon, or a full-blown pan-fried venison steak with red wine sauce and hint of chocolate could easily fit the bill. There has been a change of hands at The Rose & Thistle.

Open all wk 11-3 6-11 (Sat 11-11 Sun 12-8) **Food** Lunch all wk 12-2.30 Dinner Mon-Sat 7-9.30 ⊕ FREE HOUSE ◄ Ringwood Best, Sharp's Doom Bar, Butcombe Bitter Ö Westons, Black Rat. ♀ 10 **Facilities** Non-diners area ✿ (Bar Garden) ♦♦ Children's portions Garden ⊨ Parking WiFi ▄▄ (notice required)

ROMSEY — Map 5 SU32

The Cromwell Arms

tel: 01794 519515 **23 Mainstone SO51 8HG**
email: cromwellarms@fullers.co.uk
dir: *From Romsey take A27 signed Ringwood, Bournemouth, Salisbury. Cross River Test, pub on right*

Offering locally sourced food and ales

With Broadlands, former home of Lord Mountbatten and current home of Lord and Lady Brabourne, as its neighbour, The Cromwell Arms derives its name from Romsey's links with the English Civil War. It offers fresh, home-cooked food and attentive service with some unique twists on traditional gastro-pub favourites. Typical locally sourced dishes are rosemary- and garlic-studded baked local Tunworth cheese; and slow-cooked Romsey pork belly, cannellini bean and bacon casserole, Savoy cabbage and cider sauce. Its Hampshire-skewed offering of real ales includes Double Drop from the town's Flack Manor brewery, Cornish Orchards cider and a diverse selection of wines (17 by the glass).

Open all day all wk Closed 25 Dec **Food** Lunch Mon-Fri 12-3, Sat 12-9.30, Sun 12-5 Dinner Mon-Fri 6-9, Sat 12-9.30, Sun 6-7.30 ⊕ FULLER'S ◄ London Pride, Flack Manor Flack's Double Drop, Guest ale Ö Cornish Orchards. ♀ 17 **Facilities** Non-diners area ♦♦ Children's menu Children's portions Garden ⊨ Parking WiFi ▄▄ (notice required)

The Three Tuns ◉◉ — PICK OF THE PUBS

tel: 01794 512639 **58 Middlebridge St SO51 8HL**
email: manager@the3tunsromsey.co.uk
dir: *From Romsey bypass (A27) follow town centre sign. Left into Middlebridge St*

Award-winning market-town pub, near Broadlands

Owned by the same team as Winchester's much-praised Chesil Rectory restaurant, it stands to reason that this 300-year-old pub holds AA Rosettes. Its smart wood panelling, vintage chandeliers and botanical prints blend happily with low oak beams and open fireplaces to create a predominantly traditional feel. A simple British menu depends on local ingredients for seasonal classics, sharing platters and Sunday roasts. For a starter, maybe South Coast crab cakes with mint yogurt, cucumber and coriander; then a main of beef, mushroom and horseradish pie with mash and seasonal vegetables; or herb gnocchi with roasted beetroot, broccoli, almond butter and soft-poached egg; and, to finish, black cherry bread and butter pudding with raisin purée and rum and raisin ice cream. For a quiet fireside pint, there's Romsey's own Flack Manor's Double Drop, Ringwood or a guest ale.

Open all wk 12-3 5-11 (Fri-Sun 12-11) summer all day (Sun 11-10.30) **Food** Lunch Mon-Thu 12-2.30, Fri-Sun 12-3 Dinner Mon-Thu 6-9, Fri-Sat 6-9.30 Av main course £12.95 ⊕ ENTERPRISE INNS ◄ Ringwood Best Bitter, Flack Manor Flack's Double Drop, 2 guest ales Ö Westons Stowford Press. ♀ 11 **Facilities** Non-diners area ✿ (Bar Garden) ♦♦ Children's portions Garden ⊨ Cider festival Parking WiFi

PICK OF THE PUBS

The Plough Inn

SPARSHOLT   Map 5 SU43

tel: 01962 776353
Woodman Ln SO21 2NW
dir: *B3049 from Winchester towards Salisbury, left to Sparsholt, 1m*

Ever-popular inn down a country lane

Built as a coach house to serve Sparsholt Manor opposite, this village pub just a few miles from Winchester has been a popular local alehouse for more than 150 years. Inside, the main bar and dining areas blend harmoniously together, with farmhouse-style pine tables, wooden and upholstered seats, stone jars, miscellaneous agricultural implements, wooden wine box end-panels and dried hops. Wadworth of Devizes supplies all the real ales, and there's a good wine selection. Lunchtime regulars know that 'doorstep' is a most apt description for the great crab and mayonnaise, beef and horseradish and other sandwiches, plus good soups and chicken liver parfait. The dining tables to the left of the entrance look over open fields to wooded downland, and it's at this end of the pub you'll find a daily changing blackboard offering dishes such as salmon and crab fishcakes with saffron sauce; lamb's liver and bacon with mash and onion gravy; beef, ale and mushroom pie; and whole baked

camembert with garlic and rosemary. The menu board at the right-hand end of the bar offers the more substantial venison steak with celeriac mash and roasted beetroot; roast pork belly with bubble-and-squeak, five spice and sultana gravy; chicken breast filled with goats' cheese mousse; and fillet of sea bass with olive mash. Puddings include sticky toffee pudding and crème brûlée. The Plough is very popular, so it's best to book for any meal. The delightful flower- and shrub-filled garden has plenty of room for children to run around and play in. There's a jazz night on the first Sunday in August and carol singing with Father Christmas on 23rd December.

Open all wk 11-3 6-11 (Sun 12-3 6-10.30) Closed 25 Dec **Food** Lunch all wk 12-2 Dinner Sun-Mon 6-8.30, Tue-Thu 6-9, Fri-Sat 6-9.30 ⊕ WADWORTH ◀ Henry's Original IPA, 6X, The Bishop's Tipple, Horizon. ♟ 15
Facilities Non-diners area ❖ (Bar Garden) ♦ Children's menu Children's portions Play area Family room Garden ⊨ Parking WiFi

ROTHERWICK
Map 5 SU75

The Coach and Horses

tel: 01256 768976 **The Street RG27 9BG**
email: ian027@btinternet.com
dir: *Follow brown signs from A32 (Hook to Reading road)*

A cosy, welcoming and unpretentious atmosphere

Close to the church in Rotherwick – a picturesque village that has appeared in TV's *Midsomer Murders* – parts of this smart, cream-washed inn can be traced back to the 17th century. With log fires in winter, board games, exposed brickwork and red-and-black tiled or wooden floors, the interior is pleasingly traditional. The south-facing garden with views of fields is a draw in the summer as a place for a relaxed pint of Badger First Call, an afternoon tea or a sensibly priced meal; in summer wood-fired pizzas are available. Look out for visiting Morris dancers throughout the summer, and visits by vintage tractors and classic cars.

Open 12-3 5-11 (Sat 12-11 Sun 12-6) Closed Sun eve & Mon **Food** Lunch Tue-Sat 12-3, Sun 12-3.30 (booking advisable Sun) Dinner Tue-Sat 6-9 ⊕ HALL & WOODHOUSE ◼ Badger First Call, Tanglefoot ♂ Westons Stowford Press & Old Rosie. ♟ 9 **Facilities** Non-diners area ♣ (Bar Restaurant Garden) ◈ Children's menu Children's portions Garden ☄ Parking WiFi ☞ (notice required)

SELBORNE
Map 5 SU73

The Selborne Arms

tel: 01420 511247 **High St GU34 3JR**
email: info@selbornearms.co.uk
dir: *From A3 take B3006, pub in village centre*

Microbrewery delights in a friendly village pub

A huge chimney, known as a baffle entry, blocks your way on entering this 17th-century pub. You have to turn left or right, but it doesn't matter which, for either way you'll find homely bars with hop-strewn beams, a huge fireplace, Courage Best, Ringwood Fortyniner, local guest ales and Mr Whitehead's cider. The menu will please those who enjoy, for example, Welsh rarebit with Suthwyk Ale; local hand-made pork sausages and mash; smoked Scottish salmon salad; or Hampshire beefburger. A beer festival takes place on the first weekend in October. Eighteenth-century naturalist Gilbert White lived at The Wakes just up the road.

Open all wk 11-3 6-11 (Sat-11-11 Sun 12-11) **Food** Lunch Mon-Sat 12-2, Sun 12-3 Dinner Mon-Sat 7-9, Sun 7-8.30 ⊕ FREE HOUSE ◼ Courage Best Bitter, Ringwood Fortyniner, Bowman Ales Swift One, Local guest ales ♂ Mr Whitehead's. ♟ 10 **Facilities** Non-diners area ◈ Children's menu Children's portions Play area Garden ☄ Beer festival Parking ☞ (notice required)

SILCHESTER
Map 5 SU66

Calleva Arms

tel: 0118 970 0305 **Little London Rd, The Common RG7 2PH**
email: thecalleva@gmail.com
dir: *A340 from Basingstoke, signed Silchester*

A country pub in the finest tradition

The ancient walls of Calleva Atrebatum, known today as Silchester Roman Town, are some of the best preserved in Britain. The ruins are not far away from this 19th-century Fuller's pub overlooking the common and cricket pitch. Two bar areas, with a log-burner in the middle, lead to a pleasant conservatory and pretty garden. A full lunch and evening menu includes baguettes, ciabattas, baked jacket potatoes and fresh salads; vegetable moussaka; home-made pie of the day; hand-carved Wiltshire ham, eggs and chips; beer-battered hake fillet; and aromatic duck with stir-fried hoisin noodles. Also outside is a pétanque piste.

Open all day all wk **Food** Lunch Mon-Fri 12-2.30, Sat 12-9, Sun 12-6 Dinner Mon-Fri 5.30-9, Sat 12-9 ⊕ FULLER'S ◼ London Pride, George Gale & Co HSB, Guinness ♂ Westons Stowford Press. ♟ 11 **Facilities** Non-diners area ♣ (Bar Garden) ◈ Children's portions Garden ☄ Parking WiFi ☞ (notice required)

SOUTHAMPTON
Map 5 SU41

The White Star Tavern, Dining & Rooms
★★★★★ INN ⊕⊕

tel: 023 8082 1990 **28 Oxford St SO14 3DJ**
email: reservations@whitestartavern.co.uk web: www.whitestartavern.co.uk
dir: *M3 junct 13, A33 to Southampton. Follow Ocean Village & Marina signs*

Seasonal cooking amid ocean-liner decor

Named after the famous White Star Line shipping company that used to set sail from Southampton, this stylish gastro-pub with rooms is set in cosmopolitan Oxford Street. The restaurant provides modern British cooking typified by bream fillet with chorizo, chickpea, red pepper and tomato; chestnut crusted cod loin with artichoke purée and dauphinoise potato; and sticky toffee pudding with butterscotch sauce and vanilla ice cream. Watch the world go by from the pavement tables, or stay a little longer in one of the smart and comfortable bedrooms.

Open all day all wk 7am-11pm (Fri-Sat 7am-mdnt Sun 8.30am-10.30pm) Closed 25 Dec **Food** Lunch Mon-Thu 7am-11am (bkfst) 12-2.30, Fri-Sat 7am-11am (bkfst) 12-3, Sun 8.30am-11am (bkfst) 12-8 Dinner Mon-Thu & Sat 6-9.30, Fri 6-10, Sun 12-8 ⊕ ENTERPRISE INNS ◼ Fuller's London Pride, Bowman Swift One, Ringwood. ♟ 11 **Facilities** Non-diners area ◈ Children's menu Children's portions ☄ WiFi **Rooms** 13

SPARSHOLT
Map 5 SU43

The Plough Inn
PICK OF THE PUBS

See Pick of the Pubs on page 243

STEEP
Map 5 SU72

Harrow Inn
PICK OF THE PUBS

tel: 01730 262685 **GU32 2DA**
dir: *From A272 in Petersfield to Sheet, left opposite church (School Ln), over A3 by-pass bridge. Inn signed on right*

Real ales, hearty food and serious charity fundraiser

This 16th-century tile-hung gem is situated in a lovely rural location and has changed little over the years. The McCutcheon family has run it since 1929; sisters Claire and Nisa, both born and brought up here, are now the third generation with their names over the door. Tucked away off the road, it comprises two tiny bars – the 'public' is Tudor, with beams, tiled floor, inglenook fireplace, scrubbed tables, wooden benches, tree-trunk stools and a 'library'; the saloon (or Smoking Room, as it is still called) is Victorian. Beers are dispensed from barrels, there is no till and the toilets are across the road. Food is in keeping: ham and pea soup; hot Scotch eggs (some days); cheddar ploughman's; and various quiches. The large garden has plenty of tables surrounded by country-cottage flowers and fruit trees. Quiz nights raise huge sums for charity, for which Claire's partner Tony grows and sells flowers outside. Ask about the Harrow Cook Book, a collection of customers' recipes on sale for charity.

Open 12-2.30 6-11 (Sat 11-3 6-11 Sun 12-3 7-10.30) Closed Sun eve in winter **Food** Lunch all wk 12-2 Dinner all wk 7-9 Av main course £11 ⊕ FREE HOUSE ◼ Ringwood Best Bitter, Hop Back GFB, Bowman, Dark Star Hophead, Flack Manor Flack's Double Drop, Langham Hip Hop ♂ Thatchers Heritage. **Facilities** Non-diners area ♣ (Bar Garden Outside area) Garden Outside area ☄ Parking **Notes** ⊕

STOCKBRIDGE
Map 5 SU33

NEW The Greyhound on the Test ★★★★ RR ◉◉

tel: 01264 810833 **31 High St SO20 6EY**
email: info@thegreyhoundonthetest.co.uk **web:** www.thegreyhoundonthetest.co.uk
dir: In village centre

High quality food and accommodation

Hampshire's famous fly-fishing river runs right behind this early 19th-century free house on Stockbridge's wide, picturesque high street. The wood-floored interior is laid out with interestingly styled tables and chairs under a beamed ceiling, while en route to the restaurant local artist Soraya French's artwork is on show. Very much a dining pub, The Greyhound has two AA Rosettes, so expect high quality in dishes such as Broughton buffalo carpaccio; best end of lamb, haggis and faggots; monkfish and scallop céviche; and roasted celeriac soup with honey and chestnut. Saturday's regular special is Barbary duck breast.

Open all day all wk Closed 25-26 Dec **Food** Lunch 12-3 Dinner 6.30-9 Set menu available ⊕ FREE HOUSE ◄ Rotating Guest ales. **Facilities** Non-diners area ✿ (Bar Garden) ◖ Children's portions Garden ◿ Parking WiFi ⛽ (notice required) **Rooms** 10

Mayfly

tel: 01264 860283 **Testcombe SO20 6AZ**
dir: Between A303 & A30, on A3057. Between Stockbridge & Andover

Famous pub on the River Test

Standing right on the banks of the swiftly flowing River Test, the Mayfly is an iconic drinking spot. Inside the beamed old farmhouse with its traditional bar and bright conservatory you'll find a choice of draught ciders and up to six real ales. All-day bar food might include grilled black pudding and poached egg; chicken and five bean chilli; baked sea bream stuffed with fennel and red peppers; or steak and Stilton pie. Be sure to arrive early to guarantee a space in the small car park, and on warm spring and summer days to grab a bench on the large riverside terrace.

Open all day all wk 10am-11pm **Food** Lunch all wk 11.30-9 Dinner all wk 11.30-9 ⊕ FREE HOUSE ◄ George Gale & Co Seafarers & HSB ⚬ Aspall, Thatchers Green Goblin & Gold. ₹ 20 **Facilities** Non-diners area ✿ (Bar Restaurant Garden) ◖ Children's portions Garden ◿ Parking WiFi ⛽

The Peat Spade Inn ★★★★ INN ◉

PICK OF THE PUBS

tel: 01264 810612 **Longstock SO20 6DR**
email: info@peatspadeinn.co.uk **web:** www.peatspadeinn.co.uk
dir: Phone for detailed directions

Test Valley pub famous for its fishing connections

Now in new hands following acquisition by the fast-growing Upham Pub Company, The Peat Spade stands very close to the River Test. Nearby is Stockbridge, sometimes referred to as the country's fly-fishing capital. A gabled, red-brick Victorian building, its unusual windows overlook a peaceful village lane and thatched cottages. In the cosy fishing- and shooting-themed bar and dining room the short, daily changing menu lists dishes reliant on local and regional family-firm suppliers. Among them at lunchtime may be Huntsham Longhorn burger with bourguignon relish and fries; Tipster ale-battered hake and chips; and ploughman's, featuring Old Winchester cheese. The shorter dinner menu might offer guinea fowl with fondants, pumpkin, kale, onion and quince; and wild sea bass with barley, almonds, wild mushroom, ham hock and fennel. Outside is a sheltered and enclosed terrace.

Open all day all wk 11-11 (Sun 11-10.30) Closed 25 Dec **Food** Lunch all wk 12-2.30 Dinner all wk 6.30-9.30 Av main course £18 Set menu available ⊕ FREE HOUSE/ UPHAM PUB COMPANY ◄ Punter & Tipster. ₹ 11 **Facilities** Non-diners area ✿ (Bar Restaurant Garden) ◖ Children's menu Children's portions Garden ◿ Parking WiFi ⛽ (notice required) **Rooms** 8

The Three Cups Inn ★★★★ INN ◉

PICK OF THE PUBS

tel: 01264 810527 **High St SO20 6HB**
email: manager@the3cups.co.uk **web:** www.the3cups.co.uk
dir: M3 junct 8, A303 towards Andover. Left onto A3057 to Stockbridge

Charming pub with low beams and a river in the garden

The pub's name apparently comes from an Old English phrase for a meeting of three rivers, although there's only one river here. That river happens to be The Test, generally regarded as the birthplace of modern fly fishing. One of these channels flows through the delightful rear garden of this 15th-century, timber-framed building, where brown trout may be spotted from the patio. The low-beamed bar to the right of the front door can be warmed by the centrally placed log fire; Itchen Valley and Flower Pots — Hampshire real ales — and a guest, are served here. You can eat in the bar, but the main, candlelit dining area is at the other end of the building. Modern European and traditional selections blend fresh regional ingredients to create starters such as beetroot-cured trout, horseradish pannacotta, beetroot purée and lemon oil; and main courses of smoked haddock and leek risotto; and pan-fried chicken supreme, sauté potatoes, creamed wild mushrooms, fine green beans and redcurrant jus. Suites provide excellent overnight accommodation.

Open all day all wk 10am-11pm (Fri-Sun 8am-11pm) **Food** Lunch all wk 12-2.30 Dinner all wk 6-9.30 Restaurant menu available all wk ⊕ FREE HOUSE ◄ Itchen Valley Fagins, Young's Bitter, Flower Pots, Guest ales ⚬ Westons Stowford Press. ₹ **Facilities** Non-diners area ✿ (Bar Garden) ◖ Children's menu Children's portions Garden ◿ Beer festival Cider festival Parking WiFi ⛽ **Rooms** 8

SWANMORE
Map 5 SU51

The Rising Sun

tel: 01489 896663 **Hill Pound SO32 2PS**
dir: M27 junct 10, A32 through Wickham towards Alton. Left into Bishop's Wood Rd, right at x-rds into Mislingford Rd to Swanmore

Homely pub with its own brewery

Tucked in the heart of the beautiful Meon Valley, this 17th-century coaching inn has winter fires, low beams, uneven floors and lots of nooks and crannies. In summer, enjoy a home-brew or pint of Palmers, Dorset Gold or Sharp's Doom Bar in the secluded rear garden. Home-cooked food makes good use of locally sourced ingredients in simple snacks such as a sandwiches and salads through to full meals along the lines of devilled whitebait; or creamy garlic mushrooms followed by Sue's home-made faggots with creamed potatoes, mushy peas and gravy; or spicy curry of the day. There's a beer, cider and wine festival on the Summer Bank Holiday Saturday in August.

Open all wk Mon-Sat 11.30-3 5.30-11 (Sun 12-4 5.30-10.30) **Food** Lunch Mon-Sat 12-2, Sun 12-2.30 Dinner Mon-Sat 6-9, Sun 6-8.30 Av main course £9.95 Set menu available ⊕ FREE HOUSE ◄ Sharp's Doom Bar, Palmers, Dorset Gold, Irving Type 42, Itchen Valley Hampshire Rose ⚬ Thatchers Gold. ₹ 13 **Facilities** Non-diners area ✿ (Bar Garden) ◖ Children's menu Children's portions Garden ◿ Beer festival Cider festival Parking ⛽ (notice required)

TANGLEY
Map 5 SU35

The Fox Inn

tel: 01264 730276 **SP11 0RU**
email: info@foxinntangley.co.uk
dir: From rdbt (junct of A343 & A3057) in Andover follow station signs (Charlton Rd). Through Charlton & Hatherden to Tangley

Local ales and spicy treats in rural seclusion

Curiously, among the team at The Fox Inn, is a former chef to the Thai Royal Family who now dedicates his skills to providing a startling menu to pub-goers who adventure along the country lanes that cross outside this secluded inn in the North

continued

TANGLEY *continued*

Wessex Downs Area of Outstanding Natural Beauty. Their reward is a superb setting beside coppice woodland with relaxing views across sloping arable fields that stretch to the horizons. This 300-year-old brick and flint cottage has been a pub since 1830; inside it is largely furnished in a casual-contemporary style featuring an unusual log-end bar design, where guests may enjoy a wide choice of genuine Thai dishes and some fine local beers.

Open all day all wk 12-11 (Sun 12-10.30) Closed 25 Dec, 1 Jan **Food** Lunch all wk 12-2.30 Dinner Mon-Sat 6-9.30, Sun 6-8 Set menu available Restaurant menu available all wk ⊕ FREE HOUSE ◀ Ramsbury Gold, Flack Manor Flack's Double Drop, Upham Punter, Red Rock Devon Coast, Two Cocks Leveller Ö Symonds. ♟ 12 **Facilities** Non-diners area ❤ (Bar Restaurant Garden) ♦ Children's menu Children's portions Garden ⌒ Parking WiFi 🚐 (notice required)

The White Horse Inn & Restaurant ★★★ INN

tel: 01264 772401 **Mullens Pond SP11 8EE**
email: enquiries@whitehorsethruxton.co.uk **web:** www.whitehorsethruxton.co.uk
dir: *S of Thruxton. Phone for detailed directions*

Thatched, 15th-century pub with lovingly-tended garden

There's plenty of old-time, Grade II listed atmosphere in this Test Valley pub, thought to date from around 1450. The spacious bar does its bit for local breweries by offering Romsey's Flack's Manor Double Drop, and King John from Andwell, near Basingstoke. Australian chef-patron Norelle Oberin shows her hand with twice-baked mature cheese soufflé; chorizo and lamb croquettes with saffron mayo; herb-crusted lamb rump, new potatoes, seasonal greens and mint jus; and roast cherry tomato, feta and thyme risotto. For dessert try one of the ice creams or sorbets, or coffee crème brûlée perhaps. Baguettes and sandwiches are available at lunchtime.

Open all day all wk **Food** Lunch all wk 12-3 Dinner Mon-Sat 6-9 Set menu available Restaurant menu available all wk ⊕ FREE HOUSE ◀ Sharp's Doom Bar, Andwell

King John, Flack Manor Flack's Double Drop Ö Thatchers. ♟ 24
Facilities Non-diners area ❤ (Bar Garden) ♦ Children's menu Children's portions Garden ⌒ Parking WiFi **Rooms** 4

The Tichborne Arms   **PICK OF THE PUBS**

tel: 01962 733760 **SO24 0NA**
email: tichbornearms@xln.co.uk
dir: *Follow pub signs from B3046, S of A31 between Winchester & Alresford*

In a village with a tale to tell

Not as old as its thatched roof might suggest, for this village pub was built in the mid-20th century to replace its burnt-down predecessor. If the pub's name rings a bell, it's probably because of the famous 1870s trial of The Tichborne Claimant, a crooked East End butcher pretending to be heir to a local baronetcy, and the subject of a 1998 film, starring John Gielgud. Antiques, prints and other artefacts attractively clutter the rustically furnished, dried-hop-strung bar, so there's plenty to look at as you relax with a pint of Hop Back or Red Cat real ale, or JJ's SuEcider (sic). Owner-chef Patrick Roper's short daily menus may well feature fillet of sea bream with creamy prawn sauce; medallions of pork tenderloin with apple and cider sauce; and mushroom tagliatelle, as well as at least one vegetarian option. A beer festival takes place in the tree-shaded garden in June.

Open all wk 11.45-3 6-10.30 (Sat all day Sun 12-7.30) **Food** Lunch Mon-Fri 12-2, Sat 12-2.30, Sun 12-4 Dinner Tue-Sat 6-9 Set menu available Restaurant menu available all wk ⊕ FREE HOUSE ◀ Downton, Hop Back, Palmers, Bowman, Red Cat, Stonehenge Ales Ö JJ's SuEcider. ♟ 10 **Facilities** Non-diners area ❤ (Bar Restaurant Garden) ♦ Children's portions Garden ⌒ Beer festival Parking WiFi 🚐 (notice required)

NEW The Brushmakers Arms

tel: 01489 860231 **2 Shoe Ln SO32 1JJ**
email: thebrushmakers@gmail.com
dir: *Phone pub for detailed directions*

Genuine traditional country local

Over 600 years old, this tucked-away village pub has also been many other things, including a brushmaker's, so both pub name and the display of all manner of brushes around the dark-beamed interior make perfect sense. The village is home to the fast-expanding Upham Brewery, whose real ales, along with Ringwood Best, you'll find at the bar. As well as bar snacks, food on offer includes omelettes and ploughman's (lunchtime only); home-made chicken curry and rice; beef fajitas; honey-glazed gammon steak; and various pies with chips and beans, or peas. A beer festival takes place in mid-August.

Open all wk 11-3 5.30-11 (Sun all day) **Food** Lunch Mon-Sat 12-2, Sun 12-8 Dinner Mon-Thu 6-9, Fri-Sat 6-9.30, Sun 12-8 Av main course £10 ⊕ FREE HOUSE ◀ Ringwood Best Bitter & Fortyniner, Upham Punter & Sprinter Ö Addlestones, Westons Stowford Press. ♟ **Facilities** Non-diners area ❤ (Bar Garden) ♦ Children's portions Garden ⌒ Beer festival WiFi 🚐 (notice required)

Follow us on twitter
@TheAA_Lifestyle

UPPER CLATFORD | Map 5 SU34

NEW Crook & Shears

tel: 01264 361543 **SP11 7QL**
dir: *Phone pub for detailed directions*

Quiet village inn with picture postcard credentials

Old photographs show the thatched and whitewashed exterior looking much as it did 100 years ago, when the Crook & Shears first became a pub; parts of the building date to the 17th century, when it was probably built as a farmhouse. The interiors ooze character, ideal surroundings in which to enjoy a quiet pint of Ringwood or glass of wine. Menus are wholesome and traditional, ranging from freshly baked baguettes and jacket potatoes at lunchtime, to pub favourites in the evening such as breaded garlic mushrooms; home-made steak and ale pie; and jam roly poly. Food and drink can be served in the large rear garden.

Open 12-3 6-11 (Fri-Sat 12-3 6-12 Sun 12-3 7-10.30) Closed Mon L **Food** Lunch Tue-Sun 12-2.30 Dinner Tue-Sat 6.30-9 Av main course £10 ⊕ ENTERPRISE INNS ◀ Ringwood Best Bitter, Otter Ale ♂ Thatchers Gold. ♥ 10 **Facilities** Non-diners area ❀ (Bar Garden) ◀◗ Children's portions Play area Garden ㅈ WiFi ☕ (notice required)

UPPER FROYLE | Map 5 SU74

The Hen & Chicken Inn

tel: 01420 22115 **GU34 4JH**
email: info@henandchicken.co.uk
dir: *2m from Alton towards Farnham on A31. Adjacent to petrol station. Signed from A31*

Character coaching inn off the A31

Highwaymen, hop-pickers and high clergy have all supped and succoured here in this noble, three-storey Georgian road house. They'd still recognise some of the comfortably traditional interior – timeless panelling, beams, old tables and inglenook; maybe, too, the little wooden barn in a corner of the grassy garden, stood on its painted staddle stones. The reliable country menu is strong on local produce and vegetables from the garden; start with coarse game terrine and spiced fruit chutney; then move onto barbecue whole rack of pork ribs; sea bream, ratatouille and basil oil; or apple and walnut risotto. It may be hard to resist the treacle tart and clotted cream.

Open all day all wk 9am-11pm **Food** Lunch all wk 12-9 Dinner all wk 12-9 Av main course £8 ⊕ HALL & WOODHOUSE ◀ Badger Tanglefoot & First Call, K&B Sussex ♂ Westons Stowford Press & Rosie's Pig. **Facilities** Non-diners area ❀ (Bar Garden) ◀◗ Children's menu Children's portions Play area Garden ㅈ Parking WiFi ☕ (notice required)

WARNFORD | Map 5 SU62

The George & Falcon ★★★★ INN

tel: 01730 829623 **Warnford Rd SO32 3LB**
email: reservations@georgeandfalcon.com **web:** www.georgeandfalcon.com
dir: *M27 junct 10, A32 signed Alton. Approx 10.5m to Warnford*

Country inn with modern cuisine

The lively little River Meon slides past the garden of this imposing inn, first recorded over 400 years ago. The cosy, fire-warmed snug is the place to settle with a pint of Ringwood Fortyniner and reflect on a grand winter walk on nearby Old Winchester Hill; or discover the terrace and consider the enticing modern British menu. Kick off with roasted award-winning haggis with whisky, wholegrain mustard

sauce, then perhaps choose venison sausage cassoulet; pie of the day; or Mediterranean vegetable tart. Six en suite residential rooms complete the scene.

Open all day all wk 11-11 (Oct-Mar 11-3 6-11) **Food** Lunch all wk 11-3 Dinner all wk 6-9 Restaurant menu available all wk ⊕ MARSTON'S ◀ Ringwood Best Bitter & Fortyniner ♂ Thatchers Gold. ♥ 9 **Facilities** Non-diners area ❀ (Bar Restaurant Garden) ◀◗ Children's menu Children's portions Family room Garden ㅈ Parking WiFi ☕ (notice required) **Rooms** 6

WELL | Map 5 SU74

The Chequers Inn

tel: 01256 862605 **RG29 1TL**
email: thechequers5@hotmail.co.uk
dir: *From Odiham High St into King St, becomes Long Ln. 3m, left at T-junct, pub 0.25m on top of hill*

Locally renowned little cracker

A lovely country pub with a multitude of low beams testifying to its 15th-century origins. Paul and Nichola Sanders have a proven track record of running successful pubs; their forte is preparing classic English dishes and daily specials based on fresh fish, steaks and duck, and serving well-kept pints of Hall & Woodhouse ales. A brasserie menu proffers the likes of salmon and crab fishcakes, while the carte overflows with favourites such as avocado and prawn cocktail, and pan-fried calves' liver with bacon. Eat and drink by a log fire, out front under sheltered grapevines, or in the rear garden overlooking the countryside on the new decking.

Open all wk 12-3 6-11 (Fri-Sun & Jun-Sep all day) **Food** Lunch Mon-Fri 12-3, Sat 12-9.30, Sun 12-8 Dinner Mon-Thu 6.30-9, Fri 6.30-9.30, Sat 12-9.30, Sun 12-8 Restaurant menu available all wk ⊕ HALL & WOODHOUSE ◀ Badger First Gold & Tanglefoot, Seasonal ales ♂ Westons Stowford Press, Badger Applewood & Pearwood. ♥ 12 **Facilities** Non-diners area ❀ (Bar Garden Outside area) ◀◗ Children's portions Garden Outside area ㅈ Parking WiFi ☕ (notice required)

WEST MEON | Map 5 SU62

The Thomas Lord ◉ | PICK OF THE PUBS

tel: 01730 829244 **High St GU32 1LN**
email: info@thethomaslord.co.uk
dir: *M3 junct 9, A272 towards Petersfield, right at x-roads onto A32, 1st left*

Country inn with impressive cricket connections

Named after the founder of Lord's Cricket Ground, who retired to the pretty village of West Meon in 1830 and is buried in the churchyard, this beautifully restored pub has a bar decorated with cricketing memorabilia and well furnished with drinkers' tables and chairs; it's an agreeable setting for a well-kept Ringwood ale, or a chilled glass of white chosen from the sophisticated range of wines. Herbs, salads and vegetables are grown in the pub's own garden; otherwise the kitchen is supplied by local farms and small-scale producers; the result is a menu of seasonal delights. A typical meal might start with guinea fowl leg, curried dumplings and lentil stew, with a poached smoked duck egg, followed by shepherd's pie, or fillet of cod with burnt apple purée, hazelnuts, citrus caramelised onions, potato pressing, pork cheek, honey roast swede, sprouts and pancetta.

Open all day all wk **Food** Lunch Mon-Fri 12-2.30, Sat 12-3, Sun 12-4 Dinner Mon-Thu 6-9.30, Fri-Sat 6-10, Sun 6-9 Set menu available ⊕ FREE HOUSE ◀ Upham Ales, Ringwood Best Bitter ♂ Thatchers Cheddar Valley. ♥ 15
Facilities Non-diners area ❀ (Bar Garden) ◀◗ Children's portions Garden ㅈ Parking WiFi ☕

WEST TYTHERLEY   Map 5 SU22

The Black Horse

tel: 01794 340308 **The Village SP5 1NF**
email: info@theblackhorsepublichouse.co.uk
dir: *In village centre*

Ideal spot for walkers and cyclists

This traditional 17th-century former coaching inn is the perfect spot to rest and refuel. Located on the Clarendon Way, the popular walking/cycling trail between Winchester and Salisbury, it's a proper village community pub, replete with skittle alley, regular quiz nights and locals supping pints of Hop Back and Flower Pots ales by the blazing fire in the oak-beamed main bar. Food ranges from lunchtime filled ciabatta sandwiches to curries, pie of the day, burgers and main courses like tarragon chicken or creamy vegetable risotto. Fish is a speciality on Fridays, Thursday is steak night, and there is also a good-value and extensive Sunday lunch menu.

Open 12-3 6-11 (Sun 12-8) Closed 2 days after New Year BH, Mon L & Tue L **Food** Lunch Wed-Sun Dinner Tue-Sun ⊕ FREE HOUSE ◀ Hop Back, Stonehenge, Bowman, Flower Pots Ö Westons 1st Quality. ♀ 8 **Facilities** Non-diners area ❤ (Bar Restaurant Garden) •♦ Children's menu Children's portions Play area Garden ⊟ Parking WiFi ➡ (notice required)

WEST WELLOW   Map 5 SU21

NEW The Rockingham Arms

tel: 01794 324798 **Canada Rd SO51 6DE**
email: info@rockinghamarms.co.uk
dir: *M27 junct 2, A36 towards Salisbury. In Wellow left into Canada Rd*

Old village pub full of character

Having undergone a major facelift in 2014, Upham Pub Company's outpost on the edge of the New Forest National Park is firing on all cylinders. Its 1840 origin is still evident from the outside, although the pleasingly modernised interior today retains few clues. House policy is to source food from local, family owned suppliers. If a lunchtime sandwich might not be enough, consider a four-egg omelette, or a cured-meat platter. Dinner might begin with crispy whitebait, or sautéed field mushrooms on toast; with Upham beer-battered pollock and chips; confit duck leg; or vegetarian tart of the day to follow.

Open all day all wk **Food** Lunch all wk 12-3 Dinner Mon-Sat 6-9, Sun 6-8 ⊕ UPHAM PUB COMPANY ◀ Punter, Tipster & Stakes Ö The Orchard Pig. **Facilities** Non-diners area ❤ (Bar Restaurant) •♦ Children's menu Children's portions Garden ⊟ Parking WiFi ➡ (notice required)

WHITCHURCH   Map 5 SU44

The White Hart ★★★ INN

tel: 01256 892900 **Newbury St RG28 7DN**
email: thewhitehart.whitchurch@arkells.com **web:** www.whiteharthotelwhitchurch.co.uk
dir: *On B3400 in town centre*

Tasty pub grub near the source of the River Test

Strategically located where the old London to Exeter and Oxford to Southampton roads cross, this was Swindon brewery Arkell's first Hampshire pub. Dating from 1461, its rich history includes patronage by the late Lord Denning, Master of the Rolls, who was born opposite. What he dined on is unknown, but today's menu lists jacket potatoes; steak and ale pie; Somerset pork casserole; beer-battered fish and chips; and sizzling home-made fajitas. For vegetarians, there's three-cheese macaroni, and vegetable Madras. Just over the road is Whitchurch Silk Mill, the oldest of its type in the UK in its original building, and still using 19th-century machinery.

Open all day all wk **Food** Lunch all wk 12-2 Dinner Mon-Sat 6-9 ⊕ ARKELL'S ◀ 3B & Wiltshire Gold Ö Westons Stowford Press. **Facilities** Non-diners area ❤ (Bar Restaurant Outside area) •♦ Children's menu Family room Outside area ⊟ Parking WiFi **Rooms** 10 **Notes** ⊜

WICKHAM   Map 5 SU51

Greens Restaurant & Bar

tel: 01329 833197 **The Square PO17 5JQ**
dir: *M27 junct 10, A32 to Wickham*

Hardy perennial of the pub world

It's hard to miss Greens' black-and-white timbered building, standing prominently on a corner of Wickham's medieval market square, the second largest in England. Its proprietors for nearly 30 years, Frank and Carol Duckworth still use their original slogan – 'Nothing is too much trouble', a promise evident in the modern British seasonal menus and, more importantly, on the plate. Starters include steamed mussels; and Gressingham duck, apricot and orange terrine; while main dish options are local free-range pork with black pudding mash; Hampshire rib-eye steak; and pan-fried fillet of hake. Bowmans, in nearby Droxford, supplies two of its prize-winning ales.

Open 10-3 6-11 (Sat 11-11 Sun & BH 12-5 May-Sep all day) Closed 19-20 May, Sun eve & Mon **Food** Lunch Tue-Sat 12-2.30, Sun 12-5 Dinner Tue-Sat 6-9.30 ⊕ FREE HOUSE ◀ Bowman Ales Wallops Wood & Swift One. ♀ 12 **Facilities** Non-diners area •♦ Children's portions Garden ⊟

WINCHESTER   Map 5 SU42

The Bell Inn

tel: 01962 865284 **83 St Cross Rd SO23 9RE**
dir: *M3 junct 11, B3355 towards city centre. Approx 1m pub on right*

Community local close to pretty watermeadows

Close to the 12th-century Hospital of St Cross & Almshouse of Noble Poverty, this is a real community local. Expect a warm welcome, good ales, and good value food which is either served in the main bar, lounge or walled garden. Daily specials include pan-fried sirloin steak; oven-roasted chicken supreme stuffed with mozzarella and chorizo; pan-seared salmon fillet; and wild mushroom risotto. There's a children's selection too. A walk through the River Itchen water meadows leads to Winchester College and the city centre.

Open all day all wk 11-11 (Fri-Sat 12-12 Sun 12-10.30) **Food** Lunch Mon-Sat 12-9, Sun 12-4 Dinner Mon-Sat 12-9 Av main course £11 ⊕ GREENE KING ◀ Ruddles Best, Belhaven Grand Slam, Morland Old Speckled Hen, Red Cat Ö Westons Stowford Press. ♀ 15 **Facilities** Non-diners area ❤ (Bar Garden) •♦ Children's menu Children's portions Play area Garden ⊟ Beer festival Parking WiFi ➡ (notice required)

The Black Boy

tel: 01962 861754 **1 Wharf Hill SO23 9NQ**
email: enquiries@theblackboypub.com
dir: *Off Chesil St (B3300)*

Traditional pub with the emphasis firmly on local ales

This old fashioned whitewashed pub in the ancient capital of Wessex is a decidedly beer-led hostelry. As well as three regular regional ales from the Cheriton, Ringwood and Hop Back breweries, The Black Boy offers two Hampshire guests, perhaps from Triple fff or Itchen Valley. A small selection of good French wines is also available. The interior features old wooden tables and a quirky decor with all manner of objects hanging from the ceiling, while the short daily menu on the blackboard could include sandwiches, home-made burgers and fish and chips. There is a sheltered garden with patio heaters.

Open all day all wk **Food** Lunch all wk 12-2 Dinner Mon-Sat 7-9 Av main course £9.50 ⊕ FREE HOUSE ◀ Flower Pots Cheriton Pots, Ringwood Best Bitter, Bowman Ales Swift One, Hop Back Summer Lightning, Guest ales Ö Westons Stowford Press. **Facilities** Non-diners area ❤ (All areas) •♦ Garden Outside area ⊟ WiFi

The Golden Lion

99 Alresford Road, Winchester, Hants SO23 0JZ • **Tel:** 01962 865512
Website: www.thegoldenlionwinchester.co.uk • **Email:** bridphelan@me.com

We warmly invite you to *The Golden Lion Pub*, Winchester, for our cosy vintage style interiors, excellent home cooked food and great Irish welcome! We are located just on the Eastern edge of the city, within very easy reach of the M3, the A272 and the A34, and just a 10 minute walk into the beautiful heart of the city with all of its historic attractions and wealth of independent shops. We have a large car park as well as patio areas and beer gardens to the front and back, including a special enclosed area for doggies to have a run. We also have disabled access and facilities inside. We are a TV and gaming machine free zone so that you can relax in our friendly atmosphere and enjoy our great background music. We also welcome children who are eating with their parents/guardians.

We are very proud to have received many awards for the services that we offer, including 'The Casque Mark' and 'Master Cellerman' for our real ales, the certificate of 'Excellent' for our food hygiene, and we have won many awards for our floral displays and hanging baskets. We were very honoured to have been awarded as the Wadworth Brewery 'Retailer of the Year'. We were also delighted to receive the Quality Assured Award in Hampshire Hospitality Awards 2014 and the 'Certificate of Excellence' from TripAdvisor.

We have regular live music sessions such as Bluegrass music on the last Tuesday evening of the month, and Irish music on the second Thursday evening of the month.

Our new 'Regal Room' is now open and would be perfect for any occasion, a birthday, small wedding, a christening and many more! We offer a large range of buffet menus and set-menus, and brand new for 2015, afternoon cream teas and corporate breakfasts, details for all of these can be found on our website.

Follow us on Facebook at facebook.com/goldenlionwinchester
Or on Twitter @GoldenLionWinch
We very much look forward to welcoming you very soon!

WINCHESTER *continued*

The Golden Lion

tel: 01962 865512 **99 Alresford Rd SO23 OJZ**
email: bridphelan@me.com **web:** www.thegoldenlionwinchester.co.uk
dir: *From Union St in town centre follow 'All other routes' sign. At rdbt 1st exit into High St. At rdbt 1st exit into Bridge St (B3404) signed Alton/Alresford, (becomes Alresford Rd)*

Charming, dog-friendly pub

As a brewer, Wadworth must be delighted not just with the trade-related awards this 1932-built, city-edge pub has picked up; those for its wonderful floral displays too. Brid and Derek Phelan are strong on Irish charm and straightforward, hearty pub meals, such as grilled rib-eye steak; breaded plaice fillet; roast pork belly; and vegetable cottage pie. Ginger, rum and raisin sponge pudding with custard is a tempting dessert. Soft cushions are provided for those sitting in the large beer garden, or smoking shelter. Evening music sessions include bluegrass on the last Tuesday of the month, and Irish on the second Thursday.

Open all wk Mon-Sat 11.30-3 5.30-11 (Sun 12-10.30) **Food** Lunch all wk 12-2.30 Dinner all wk 6-9 ∰ WADWORTH ◀ 6X, Henry's Original IPA, Seasonal ales ♂ Westons Stowford Press. ♈ 8 **Facilities** Non-diners area ♣ (Bar Restaurant Garden) ♦♦ Children's menu Children's portions Garden ⊨ Parking WiFi ☷ (notice required)

See advert on page 249

The Green Man

tel: 01962 866809 **53 Southgate St SO23 9EH**
email: greenmanwinchester@gmail.com
dir: *Phone for detailed directions*

Cool, quirky and central

With its retro-furnished bar, Jayne Gillin's Green Man is one of her five city bars and restaurants, all showing her enviable talent for trendy makeovers. Upstairs is an

Edwardian-style dining room with rich fabrics, candelabras and chandeliers, while The Outhouse, formerly the skittle alley, is now a cool, 1930s industrial-style function room, where platter suppers, pitchers of wine and buckets of beer are served at a huge refectory table. The evening menu offers pork and leek sausages and mash with onion gravy; seared haloumi burger with roasted vegetables and seasoned fries; coq au vin; and fish catch of the day.

Open all day all wk 12-12 (Sun-Mon 12-10.30) Closed 25-26 Dec **Food** Lunch all wk 12-3 Dinner all wk 6-10 Av main course £10-£14 ∰ GREENE KING ◀ St Edmunds, Morland ♂ Aspall. ♈ 16 **Facilities** Non-diners area WiFi

The Old Vine ★★★★ INN

tel: 01962 854616 **8 Great Minster St SO23 9HA**
email: reservations@oldvinewinchester.com **web:** www.oldvinewinchester.com
dir: *M3 junct 11, follow Saint Cross & City Centre signs. 1m, right at Green Man pub right into Saint Swithun St, bear left into Symonds St (one-way). Right into Great Minster St (NB for Sat Nav use SO23 9HB)*

Cathedral views and top hospitality

An elderly vine rambles all over the street frontage of this elegant pub, built on Saxon foundations in the 18th century. Directly opposite is Winchester's fine cathedral and the City Museum. There are four guest beers, including local ales, in the oak-beamed bar, where you can eat sandwiches, salads and light meals. Freshly prepared, in the restaurant are, typically, starters like fresh pear and Dorset Blue Vinny cheese salad; creamy smoked trout, potato, leek and dill tartlet; followed by wild mushroom, pea and mascarpone risotto; baked cod loin fillet with garlic and herb butter; or slow-braised lamb shank with a rich red wine, redcurrant and mint sauce. Puddings include mini French almond macaroons; butterscotch and treacle sponge pudding; banoffee cheesecake with cream; or melting chocolate pudding. At the back of the pub is a flower-filled patio.

Open all day all wk Closed 25 Dec **Food** Lunch Mon-Thu 12-2.30, Fri-Sun 12-6 Dinner Mon-Sat 6.30-9.30, Sun 6.30-9 Av main course £12.95 ∰ ENTERPRISE INNS ◀ Guest ales. ♈ 11 **Facilities** Non-diners area ♣ (Bar Outside area) ♦♦ Family room Outside area ⊨ WiFi **Rooms** 6

The Westgate Inn ★★★ INN

tel: 01962 820222 **2 Romsey Rd SO23 8TP**
email: wghguy@yahoo.co.uk **web:** www.westgateinn.co.uk
dir: *On corner of Romsey Rd & Upper High St, opposite Great Hall & Medieval West Gate*

Top of the hill landmark hostelry

Standing boldly on a street corner, the curving, Palladian-style façade of this 1860s inn overlooks the city's medieval Westgate. A well-known interest in real ales and ciders is backed up by an annual beer festival. Full English breakfasts and mid-morning brunches are followed by made-to-order lunchtime sandwiches, soups and uncomplicated three-egg omelettes with various fillings; bangers and mash, along with many other pub classics. Attractive and good-sized accommodation is available.

Open all day all wk 12-11.30 **Food** Lunch all wk 12-2.30 Dinner all wk 6-9.30 Av main course £8.50 ∰ MARSTON'S ◀ Jennings Cumberland Ale, Ringwood Best Bitter & Fortyniner, Guest ales ♂ Westons Stowford Press & Old Rosie. **Facilities** Non-diners area ♣ (Bar) ♦♦ Children's menu Children's portions Beer festival WiFi **Rooms** 8

The Wykeham Arms ★★★★ INN ⊛⊛ `PICK OF THE PUBS`

See Pick of the Pubs on opposite page

PICK OF THE PUBS

The Wykeham Arms ★★★★ INN

WINCHESTER Map 5 SU42

tel: 01962 853834
75 Kingsgate St SO23 9PE
email: wykehamarms@fullers.co.uk
web: www.wykehamarmswinchester.co.uk
dir: *Near Winchester College & Winchester Cathedral*

Sophisticated gastro-pub in Winchester's historic heart

It's quite hard to convey just how much character The Wyk has. For it's more than a pub and a restaurant with accommodation; it's a Winchester institution. Beyond the cathedral from the High Street, with Winchester College as a neighbour, this 270-year-old building is entered from the pavement through curved, etched-glass doors straight into two bars, one dead ahead, the other to your left. Both have open fires and are furnished with old pine tables and redundant college desks. Everywhere, and that's no understatement – are portraits and prints, pewter tankards and miscellaneous ephemera. It all creates a warm feeling – gemütlichkeit as they say in Germany. Perhaps this is why it attracts such a varied clientele - business people, barristers, clergy, college dons, ladies who lunch, tourists and, yes, locals, for this is a desirable residential quarter. You may eat in the bars, but serious dining is done in tucked-away rooms, where modern

British menus ring the seasonal changes to include crispy Kings Somborne egg, pickled mushrooms, shallots and cep purée; and pan-seared scallops, hazelnut crumb, sesame purée and compressed apple as typical starters. Equally representative are main dishes of roast halibut, parmentiers, black cabbage, capers and beef cromesquis; and braised blade of beef, snails, carrots and burnt aubergine purée. 'Home Comforts' include confit pork belly, chorizo hash and roast swede. Finish with warm treacle tart, bay leaf ice cream and citrus curd. It's one of the Fuller's flagship pubs, although there's guest real ales too, perhaps one from the nearby Flower Pots microbrewery. The wine list is impressive.

Open all day all wk **Food** Lunch all wk 12-3 Dinner all wk 6-9.30 Av main course £15 Set menu available Restaurant menu available all wk ⊞ FULLER'S ◼ London Pride, George Gale & Co HSB & Seafarers, Flower Pots Goodens Gold, Guest ales. ♉ 20 **Facilities** Non-diners area ♣ (Bar Outside area) Outside area ⊼ Parking WiFi **Rooms** 14

HEREFORDSHIRE

AYMESTREY

Map 9 SO46

The Riverside Inn

PICK OF THE PUBS

tel: 01568 708440 **HR6 9ST**
email: theriverside@btconnect.com
dir: On A4110, 18m N of Hereford

Friendly hostelry in countryside setting

Built in 1580, this character inn started catering to the passing sheep drovers in 1700; it's midway along the Mortimer Trail, just by the ford across the River Lugg. All the country pursuits are here: choose between 10 circular walks and look out for otters, kingfishers, herons and deer on the way. The wood-panelled interior with low beams and log fires makes a cosy setting for the enjoyment of ales such as Wye Valley Butty Bach and Hobsons Best; ciders include Westons and Robinsons. The pub's vegetable, herb and fruit garden is the source of many ingredients for the seasonal menus – Shropshire ham hock terrine, pickled apple relish and caramelised walnuts might precede seared freshwater trout fillet, parsley and almond gremolata and cauliflower purée; Heritage carrot, Monkland cheese and leek risotto; or slow-cooked Herefordshire beef, oxtail sauce, smoked mash and salt-baked shallots.

Open Tue-Sat 11-3 6-11 (Sun 12-3) Closed 26 Dec, 1 Jan, Sun eve, Mon L, Mon eve in winter **Food** Lunch Tue-Sun 12-2.15 Dinner Tue-Sat 7-9 Av main course £12 Restaurant menu available Tue-Sun evening ⊕ FREE HOUSE ◀ Wye Valley Bitter & Butty Bach, Hobsons Best Bitter ♂ Westons Stowford Press, Robinsons Flagon. **Facilities** Non-diners area ❤ (Bar Restaurant Garden) ♦ Children's portions Garden ☶ Parking WiFi ▨ (notice required)

BREDWARDINE

Map 9 SO34

NEW The Red Lion ★★★ INN

tel: 01981 500303 **HR3 6BU**
email: info@redlion-hotel.com **web:** www.redlion-hotel.com
dir: Take A438 from Hereford towards Eardisley. Follow signs for Bredwardine

Tranquil rural pub serving enjoyable local food

Handy for both Hereford and Hay-on-Wye, the 17th-century Red Lion is tucked away in the sleepy hamlet of Bredwardine, set against a backdrop of fields and cider orchards. Once a coaching inn, the lounge was used as the courtroom for the circuit judge, although these days the only judgement being passed is on the well-kept Butty Bach beer and Gwatkin cider, and the highly-regarded food. A starter of lime and garlic marinated pigeon breast with spinach, tomato and coriander salsa might precede lamb, beetroot and black pudding casserole. Wye River fishing is also available here.

Open all wk 12-2.30 6.30-11 **Food** Lunch 12-2 Dinner 7-9 Av main course £10.75 ⊕ FREE HOUSE ◀ Wye Valley Butty Bach, Mulberry Duck ♂ Westons Stowford Press, Gwatkin. **Facilities** ❤ (Bar Garden) ♦ Children's portions Garden ☶ Parking WiFi **Rooms** 10

BRINGSTY COMMON

Map 10 SO75

Live and Let Live

tel: 01886 821462 **WR6 5UW**
email: theliveandletlive@tiscali.co.uk
dir: From A44 (Bromyard to Worcester road) turn at pub sign (black cat) onto track leading to common. At 1st fork bear right. Pub 200yds on right

Ancient cider house offering local ales and ciders

One of the oldest buildings in the area is this 16th-century thatched cider house set amidst bracken and old orchards on Bringsty Common. Local Oliver's cider is joined

by beers from Herefordshire breweries. Bar meals and the intimate Thatch Restaurant major on seasonal food from the home area. A typical main course option is chicken breast stuffed with sun-dried tomatoes, topped with melted mozzarella and served with duchess potatoes, fresh vegetables and home-made cheese sauce.

Open Tue-Thu 12-2.30 6-11 (Fri-Sun & summer all day) Closed Mon (ex BHs) **Food** Lunch Tue-Sun 12-2 (12-3 summer) Dinner Tue-Sun 6-9 ⊕ FREE HOUSE ◀ Wye Valley, Ludlow, Otter, Ledbury Ales ♂ Oliver's, Hogan's. **Facilities** Non-diners area ❤ (Bar Garden) ♦ Children's menu Children's portions Garden ☶ Beer festival Parking ▨ (notice required)

BROMYARD DOWNS

Map 10 SO65

NEW The Royal Oak

tel: 01885 482585 **HR7 4QP**
email: info@royaloakbromyard.com
dir: From A44 at Bromyard take B4203 towards Stourport-on-Severn. Approx 1.5m, pub signed

Definitely one for the walking fraternity

A 300-year-old, black-and-white free house, 200 metres above sea level and the only pub left on the lovely Bromyard Downs. Breweries not too far away supply Shropshire Lad, Black Pear and Pure Gold real ales. A look at the menu reveals a comforting list of home-made dishes, including steak and kidney pie; beef chilli; and Stilton, leek and apple crumble. Curries make a good showing too, with Thai green, chicken tikka masala and vegetable balti. Batting for the fish team are breaded wholetail scampi; plaice goujons; and battered haddock. Burgers, jacket potatoes, sandwiches, baguettes and salads are other possibilities.

Open 12-3 6-10/11 Closed 25 Dec, 2wks Jan, Sun eve & Mon **Food** Lunch Tue-Sun 12-3 Dinner Tue-Sat 6-9 ⊕ FREE HOUSE ◀ Wood's Shropshire Lad, Malvern Hills Black Pear, Purity Pure Gold. ⬥ 9 **Facilities** Non-diners area ❤ (Bar Garden) ♦ Children's menu Children's portions Play area Garden ☶ Parking ▨ (notice required)

CAREY

Map 10 SO53

Cottage of Content

tel: 01432 840242 **HR2 6NG**
dir: From x-rds on A49 between Hereford & Ross-on-Wye, follow Hoarwithy signs. In Hoarwithy branch right, follow Carey signs

Cracking inn secluded in the Wye Valley

Lost along narrow lanes in bucolic countryside close to the meandering River Wye, this pretty streamside inn has been licensed for 530 years. Now, as then, local ciders and beers flow from the bar which boasts log fire and flagged floors, with heavy timbering and pubby furnishings. From the sloping, family-friendly grassy garden are relaxing views across the tranquil countryside. Making the most of the county's produce, dishes on the concise menu might be baked mushroom and Stilton gratin; or potted pulled pork, jerk butter and crisp olive toasts to start, followed by slow-cooked Hereford beef brisket, grain mustard mash and balsamic roasted roots; or seared marinated duck breast, caramelised red cabbage with fig and Madeira sauce; and chocolate and peanut butter pie and praline ice cream.

Open 12-2 6.30-11 (times vary summer & winter) Closed 1wk Feb, 1wk Oct, Sun eve, Mon (Tue winter only) **Food** Lunch Tue-Sat 12-2 Dinner Tue-Sat 6.30-9.30 Restaurant menu available Tue-Sun Lunch, Tue-Sat Dinner ⊕ FREE HOUSE ◀ Wye Valley Butty Bach, Hobsons Best Bitter ♂ Ross-on-Wye, Carey Organic, Westons Stowford Press. **Facilities** Non-diners area ♦ Children's menu Children's portions Garden ☶ Parking ▨ (notice required)

CLIFFORD
Map 9 SO24

The Castlefields

tel: 01497 831554 **HR3 5HB**
email: info@thecastlefields.co.uk
dir: On B4352 between Hay-on-Wye & Bredwardine

Traditional country pub and restaurant in Golden Valley

After hours spent browsing in nearby Hay-on-Wye, the 'Town of Books', a 10-minute drive will get you to this family-run, 16th-century former coach house. The interior is furnished with elegantly modern tables and chairs, although a reminder of the pub's long life is the glass-covered, 39ft-deep well. Home-cooked, locally-sourced food served all day includes roast half-duck with orange sauce; pan-fried liver and crispy bacon; tagliatelle carbonara; wholetail scampi; and lots of grills. Wednesday is curry night and traditional roasts are served on Sundays. The Rev. James and his companions, Doom Bar and Butty Bach, will be in the bar.

Open all day 11.45am-close Closed Mon (Nov-Feb) **Food** Lunch Tue-Sat 12-9, Sun 12-8 Dinner Tue-Sat 12-9, Sun 12-8 Restaurant menu available Tue-Sun ⊕ FREE HOUSE ◀ Sharp's Doom Bar, Brains The Rev. James, Wye Valley Butty Bach Ō Westons Stowford Press. ▾ **Facilities** Non-diners area ♦ Children's menu Children's portions Play area Garden ⊨ Parking WiFi ▬ (notice required)

CRASWALL
Map 9 SO23

The Bulls Head

tel: 01981 510616 **HR2 0PN**
dir: From A465 at Pandy follow Walterstone, Oldcastle & Longtown signs. In Longtown follow Craswall sign. Village in 11m

Weekend-only refuelling stop

You'll find this old drovers' inn south of Hay-on-Wye in a remote spot at the foot of the Black Mountains. Only open at weekends, it is popular with walkers and riders, who tie their horses at the rail outside. Real ales and farmhouse ciders are served through the hole in the wall servery in the bar with its flagstone floors and log fires. There is a Mediterranean feel to the menu, which might take in soup au pistou; Italian style meatballs; ragu of boar with chestnuts and creamed polenta; and clementine cake for dessert.

Open Fri-Sun 12-3 7-11 Closed Mon-Thu **Food** Lunch Fri-Sun 12-2.30 Dinner Fri-Sat 7-8.30 ⊕ FREE HOUSE ◀ Wye Valley Butty Bach & Bitter Ō Oliver's, Dunkertons Premium Organic & Black Fox. **Facilities** Non-diners area ♣ (Bar Garden) ♦ Garden WiFi

EARDISLEY
Map 9 SO34

The Tram Inn

tel: 01544 327251 **Church Rd HR3 6PG**
email: info@thetraminn.co.uk
dir: On A4111 at junct with Woodeaves Rd

Family- and dog-friendly free house with a beautiful garden

With its name recalling a 19th-century, narrow-gauge, horse-drawn railway, this 16th-century inn is one of Eardisley's many traditional, black-and-white-timbered

buildings. Wood-burning stoves warm the bar for the Wye Valley Butty Bach drinkers who, in summer, might be found playing boules in the garden. Landlords Mary and Kerry Vernon like to champion their 28-day-aged steaks. And quite right, too, as a visit will confirm, although they'd understand if instead you chose honey-roast ham with free-range eggs and chunky chips; pan-roast chicken breast with spinach and sweet potato stuffing, steamed rice, sag aloo and curry sauce; or battered hake with mushy peas.

Open 12-3 6-12 (Fri-Sat 12-3 6-12.30 Sun 12-3 7-11) Closed Mon (ex BHs) **Food** Lunch Tue-Sun 12-3 Dinner Tue-Sat 6-9 ⊕ FREE HOUSE ◀ Wye Valley Butty Bach, Hobsons Best Bitter Ō Westons Stowford Press, Dunkertons Organic. **Facilities** Non-diners area ♣ (Bar Garden) ♦ Children's portions Play area Garden ⊨ Parking WiFi ▬ (notice required)

EWYAS HAROLD
Map 9 SO32

NEW The Temple Bar Inn ★★★★ INN ❀❀

tel: 01981 240423 **HR2 0EU**
email: phillytemplebar@btinternet.com **web:** www.thetemplebarinn.co.uk
dir: From Pontrilas on A465 take B4347 to Ewyas Harold. 1m turn left into village centre. Inn on right

Smart village pub popular with walkers and cyclists

Just a few miles from the Welsh border, The Temple Bar Inn is a popular pit-stop for walkers and cyclists exploring the Black Mountains and Herefordshire Trail. Painstakingly restored by the Jinman family in 2012, this handsome building was first licensed in the 1850s but before that it had been a court house, corn exchange, school room and stable. It is now very much the hub of the community, with locals popping in for pints of Wye Valley ales or foodies enjoying well-executed classics such as beef and root vegetable curry; ham, egg and triple-cooked chips; or steak sandwiches.

Open all wk 11-3 5-close (Sat-Sun & BH 11am-close) Closed 25 Dec **Food** Lunch Mon-Sat 12-2.30 (Sat brunch 11am-1pm) Dinner Wed-Sat 5-7 Av main course £8 Restaurant menu available Wed-Sat 7-9, Sun Lunch ⊕ FREE HOUSE ◀ Wye Valley Butty Bach, Ludlow Gold, Butcombe Bitter Ō Westons Stowford Press & Gold Label. **Facilities** Non-diners area ♣ (Bar Outside area) ♦ Children's portions Outside area ⊨ Parking WiFi ▬ (notice required) **Rooms** 3

GARWAY
Map 9 SO42

Garway Moon Inn ★★★★ INN

tel: 01600 750270 **HR2 8RQ**
email: info@garwaymooninn.co.uk **web:** www.garwaymooninn.co.uk
dir: *From Hereford S on A49. Right onto A466, right onto B4521. At Broad Oak turn right to Garway*

Eat, drink and relax in this privately owned country inn

A family-run free house dating back to 1750, overlooking the peaceful and picturesque common. Ask at the bar for three circular walks which will take you to a Knights Templar church of 1180, Skenfrith Castle, and panoramic views of Garway Hill. A good selection of real ales includes Butcombe and Otter Brewery, with Westons cider also on tap. Traditional pub food is based on high quality local ingredients – many of the producers are regulars in the bar. Share a platter of charcuterie or go for a starter of pulled pork, black pudding and chorizo cake with red onion marmalade, followed by a steak, a burger, a pub favourite such as steak and ale pie; or curry of the day.

Open Mon-Tue 6-11 (Wed-Fri 12-2.30 5-11 Sat-Sun 11-11) Closed Mon & Tue L **Food** Lunch Wed-Sun 12-2.30 Dinner Tue-Sun 6-9.30 Restaurant menu available Tue-Sun ⊕ FREE HOUSE ◀ Wye Valley Butty Bach & HPA, Butcombe, Kingstone Brewery, Otter ☼ Westons Stowford Press. **Facilities** Non-diners area ❀ (Bar Garden) ♣ Children's menu Children's portions Play area Family room Garden ⋒ Parking WiFi ➡ (notice required) **Rooms** 3

HOARWITHY
Map 10 SO52

The New Harp Inn

tel: 01432 840900 **HR2 6QH**
email: booking@thenewharpinn.co.uk **web:** www.thenewharpinn.co.uk
dir: *From Ross-on-Wye take A49 towards Hereford. Turn right for Hoarwithy*

A real country pub

The New Harp's slogan reads: 'Kids, dogs and muddy boots all welcome' – and it's certainly popular with locals, fishermen, campers and visitors to the countryside. Situated on the River Wye in an Area of Outstanding Natural Beauty, the pub has

---

extensive gardens and a real babbling brook. Begin your visit with a local real ale or the home-produced cider. The menu includes starters such as chef's fishcake with tartare sauce; or chicken liver and pork pâté, then moves on to mains like game pie; or duck, wild mushroom and port pudding with gratin dauphinoise and roast vegetables. There's also a board for specials. Look out for bank holiday beer festivals and a cider festival on the Summer Bank Holiday.

The New Harp Inn

Open all wk 12-3 6-11 (Fri-Sun all day) **Food** Lunch Mon-Fri 12-3, Sat-Sun all day Dinner Mon-Fri 6-9, Sat-Sun all day Set menu available Restaurant menu available all wk ⊕ FREE HOUSE ◀ Wye Valley Butty Bach & Dorothy Goodbody's Country Ale, Otter, Purity, Sharp's, Wood's Shropshire Lad Ö Westons Stowford Press & Gold Label, Mortimers Orchard, New Harp Reserve. ℗ 10 **Facilities** Non-diners area ✿ (Bar Garden Outside area) ♦♦ Children's menu Children's portions Garden Outside area ⌦ Beer festival Cider festival Parking WiFi ▄▄

See advert on opposite page

KENTCHURCH
Map 9 SO42

NEW The Bridge Inn

tel: 01981 240408 **HR2 0BY**
email: bridgeinnkentchurch@hotmail.com
dir: *From A465 between Hereford & Abergavenny onto B4347 at Pontrilas signed Kentchurch. Pub on right*

Delightful 400-year-old pub on the River Monnow

Before going in, take a look at the inn sign. It shows Jack O' Kent, a legendary hero of the Welsh Marches who regularly took on the devil and usually got the better of him. From the beer garden stretching 100 metres along the banks of the river, which here forms the England-Wales border, enjoy fine views of the Black Mountains. The simple menu offers traditional and not-so-traditional pub food, typified by beef bourguignon; slow-cooked hoisin belly pork; chicken curry with pilau rice; and Mediterranean risotto. In addition, there are specials and regular Oriental, Italian and tapas themed nights.

Open 12-2 6-11 Closed 2nd wk Feb & 1st 2wks Oct, Tue **Food** Lunch Wed-Mon 12-2 Dinner Wed-Sat & Mon 6-9 Av main course £12 Restaurant menu available Wed-Sat & Mon ⊕ FREE HOUSE ◀ Otter Bitter & Wye Valley HPA. **Facilities** Non-diners area ♦♦ Children's menu Children's portions Garden ⌦ Parking WiFi ▄▄ (notice required)

KILPECK
Map 9 SO43

The Kilpeck Inn

tel: 01981 570464 **HR2 9DN**
email: booking@kilpeckinn.com **web:** www.kilpeckinn.com
dir: *From Hereford take A465 S. In 6m at Belmont rdbt left towards Kilpeck. Follow church & inn signs*

A warm welcome awaits at this green inn

Kilpeck is famous for its Romanesque church, a few minutes' walk from this 250-year-old whitewashed pub that's run by chef patron Ross Williams. Commendably green, the pub uses a wood-pellet burner for underfloor heating; rainwater to flush the loos; and solar panels for hot water. Typical dishes might include pan-fried duck livers with brandy and pink peppercorn sauce and sourdough toast; local venison braised with red wine and chestnuts, parsnip mash and flower sprouts; roast breast and confit pheasant leg, straw potatoes and bread sauce; and rhubarb crème brûlée. The bar stocks local real ales, and draught cider from Westons in Much Marcle.

Open 12-2.30 5.30-11 (Sun 12-5.30) Closed 25 Dec, Sun eve **Food** Lunch Mon-Sat 12-2, Sun 12-3 Dinner Mon-Sat 6-9 Set menu available Restaurant menu available Mon-Sat ⊕ FREE HOUSE ◀ Wye Valley Butty Bach & Bitter, Boddingtons Ö Westons Stowford Press. ℗ 9 **Facilities** Non-diners area ♦♦ Children's portions Garden ⌦ Parking WiFi ▄▄ (notice required)

KIMBOLTON
Map 10 SO56

Stockton Cross Inn

tel: 01568 612509 **HR6 0HD**
email: mb@ecolots.co.uk
dir: *From A49 take A4112 between Leominster & Ludlow*

Chocolate-box pretty, inside and out

Standing at a lonely crossroads where witches were allegedly hanged, this 16th-century, black-and-white former drovers' inn is picture-book pretty, and is regularly photographed by tourists as well as appearing on calendars. There's a good range of ales, including local Wye Valley Butty Bach, and regular guest beers. A typical evening meal could include Thai-style salmon fishcakes; chicken and leek pie; chargrilled swordfish steaks; home-made Shropshire fidget pie; and vegetarian Wellington. Lunchtime choices include sandwiches and salads; in summer, enjoy them in the pretty garden. It is fish night every second Friday of the month.

Open all day all wk 11-11 **Food** Lunch all wk 12-3 (Fri-Sun 12-9 in winter, 12-9 all wk in summer) Dinner all wk 6-9 (Fri-Sun 12-9 in winter, 12-9 all wk in summer) Av main course £10 ⊕ FREE HOUSE ◀ Wye Valley Butty Bach & HPA, Three Tuns, Guest ales Ö Robinsons Flagon, Westons Stowford Press. **Facilities** Non-diners area ✿ (Bar Restaurant Garden) ♦♦ Children's menu Children's portions Garden ⌦ Beer festival Parking WiFi ▄▄ (notice required)

KINGTON
Map 9 SO25

The Stagg Inn and Restaurant ◉◉   PICK OF THE PUBS

tel: 01544 230221 **Titley HR5 3RL**
email: reservations@thestagg.co.uk
dir: *Between Kington & Presteigne on B4355*

A fusion of village local and child-friendly fine-dining restaurant

This celebrated rural gastro-pub stands in a little corner of heaven, where the wooded ridges of west Herefordshire meet with the higher commons and hills of the Welsh border. Lucky locals in this dispersed community mingle at the small bar tucked away amidst rambling dining areas; beers from Ludlow and full-bodied local ciders are a given here. Awash with awards, including two AA Rosettes, long-established chef-proprietor Steve Reynolds creates memorable dishes that draw heavily on the bounty of the Marches, adjusted regularly to take full advantage of seasonality. Contemplate a starter of campfire trout with horseradish and potato, following with venison loin and haunch with mushroom, artichoke and sprout leaves. From local shoots may come partridge, matched with sweet and sour parsnips, kale and smoked mash. A specials board widens the scope, whilst a set Sunday lunch could be the introduction to Steve's cutting-edge contemporary menu; a palate-cleanser may be a Herefordshire wine from Broadfield Court Vineyard. There's an inspired vegetarian menu available, too.

Open 12-3 6.30-11 Closed 25-27 Dec, 2wks Nov, 2wks Jan & Feb, Mon & Tue **Food** Lunch Wed-Sun 12-3 Dinner Wed-Sun 6.30-9 Av main course £12 Restaurant menu available Wed-Sat, Sun Dinner ⊕ FREE HOUSE ◀ Ludlow Gold, Wye Valley Butty Bach ♂ Dunkertons, Westons. ☎ 12 **Facilities** Non-diners area ❄ (Bar Garden Outside area) ◑ Children's menu Children's portions Garden Outside area ⊓ Parking WiFi

LEDBURY
Map 10 SO73

Prince of Wales

tel: 01531 632250 **Church Ln HR8 1DL**
email: pebblewalk@gmail.com
dir: *M50 junct 2, A417 to Ledbury. Pub in town centre behind Market House (black & white building) on cobbled street (parking nearby)*

Character inn with home-made pies and excellent local beers

In an enchanting spot hidden between Ledbury's memorable half-timbered market house and the ancient church, a cobbled alley lined by eye-catching medieval houses hosts this cracking little pub. All low beams with bags of character, folk nights add to the craic at this half-timbered gem, where home-made pies or pork and beef sausages from an award-winning local butcher are firm favourites on the traditional pub menu. The local theme continues, with Westons Rosie's Pig scrumpy from neighbouring Much Marcle and beers from Wye Valley Brewery just down the road complementing a huge range of guest ales.

Open all day all wk **Food** Lunch all wk 12-2.30 Dinner Mon-Sat 6-8.30 ⊕ FREE HOUSE ◀ Hobsons Best Bitter, Wye Valley Butty Bach & HPA, Otter Bitter, Ledbury Dark, Courage Best, Guest ales ♂ Westons Rosie's Pig, Robinsons Flagon. **Facilities** Non-diners area ◑ Children's menu Outside area ⊓ WiFi ▭ (notice required)

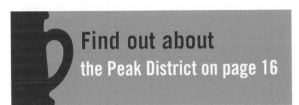

Find out about
the Peak District on page 16

The Talbot

tel: 01531 632963 **14 New St HR8 2DX**
email: talbot.ledbury@wadworth.co.uk
dir: *From A449 in Ledbury into Bye St, 2nd left into Woodley Rd, over bridge to junct, left into New St. Pub on right*

Beautiful inn in historic town

This higgledy-piggledy marvel is one of the stars of Ledbury's extensive suite of amazing half-timbered buildings. Parts of it date back to 1550; the interior of the coaching inn oozes the character of great age, with fine beams and panelling in the refined dining room. Holes caused by musket shot fired during a Civil War skirmish are just another quirky talking point of the gabled building, where Wadworth's beers slake the thirst of ramblers fresh from the challenging local countryside. Indulge in tasty platters (boards), small plates, salads, sandwiches or temping starters and main courses, and perhaps sit in the sun-trap courtyard garden.

Open all day all wk **Food** Lunch all wk 12-3 Dinner Mon-Sat 5.30-9, Sun 5-8 ⊕ WADWORTH ◀ 6X, Henry's Original IPA & Wadworth guest ales, Wye Valley Butty Bach ♂ Westons Stowford Press, Wyld Wood Organic & Perry, Thatchers Gold. ☎ 15 **Facilities** Non-diners area Children's portions Garden ⊓ WiFi

The Trumpet Inn

tel: 01531 670277 **Trumpet HR8 2RA**
email: thetrumpetinn@mail.com
dir: *4m from Ledbury, at junct of A438 & A417*

Beamed inn dating from the Middle Ages

This very striking half-timbered inn has stood at a rural crossroads for upwards of 600 years. The name recalls Georgian times when stagecoach guards blew a horn to warn of their approach. New management here continues to ensure a warm welcome remains at the heart of today's pub; whether it's the cheery open fires in the well-beamed and posted interior or a filling meal from the accomplished menu of both traditional and modern dishes. Contrast an oyster mushroom, champagne and rocket risotto starter with mains such as grilled chicken breast with BBQ sauce topped with smoky bacon and mature cheddar, or a vegetarian choice from the specials board.

Open all day all wk 11-11 (Sun 11-10.30) **Food** Lunch Mon-Sat 12-3, Sun 12-8 Dinner Mon-Sat 6-9, Sun 12-8 Av main course £10.95 Set menu available Restaurant menu available Mon-Sat ⊕ WADWORTH ◀ 6X, Henry's Original IPA, Guest ales ♂ Westons Stowford Press. **Facilities** Non-diners area ❄ (Bar Garden) ◑ Children's portions Garden ⊓ Parking WiFi ▭ (notice required)

LEOMINSTER
Map 10 SO45

The Grape Vaults

tel: 01568 611404 **Broad St HR6 8BS**
email: jusaxon@tiscali.co.uk
dir: *Phone for detailed directions*

In the heart of the town centre

This unspoilt, 15th-century pub is so authentic that even its fixed seating is Grade II listed. Its many charms include a small, homely bar complete with a coal fire. A good selection of real ale is a popular feature, and includes microbrewery offerings. The unfussy food encompasses favourites like cottage pie, lasagne, chicken curry and various fresh fish and vegetarian choices. There are also plenty of jackets, baguettes, omelettes and other lighter meals available. No jukebox, gaming machines or alcopops but there is live music every Sunday from 3pm to 6pm.

Open all day all wk 11-11 **Food** Lunch all wk 12-2 Dinner Mon-Sat 5.30-9 ⊕ FREE HOUSE ◀ Ludlow Best, Mayfields, Wood's, Malvern Hills, Guest ales ♂ Westons Stowford Press. ☎ 10 **Facilities** Non-diners area ❄ (Bar Restaurant) ◑ Children's portions WiFi **Notes** ◉

MADLEY
Map 9 SO43

The Comet Inn

tel: 01981 250600 **Stoney St HR2 9NJ**
email: thecometinn-madley@hotmail.co.uk
dir: *6m from Hereford on B4352*

Hearty food served in converted cottages with plenty of character

Set at a crossroads deep in rural Herefordshire, the space-age parabolic dishes of the Madley Earth Station and the distant smudge of the Black Mountains provide contrasting skylines visible from the large grounds of this convivial local. Within, it retains much of the character of the old cottages from which it was converted over 100 years ago, including a roaring fire in the winter months. Vicky Willison, the enthusiastic and welcoming owner, serves a select range of Herefordshire- and Worcestershire-brewed beers to accompany simple and hearty home-cooked pub food in the conservatory off the main bar, with smaller portions for smaller appetites if required. In summer visitors can enjoy the large garden that has a children's play area.

Open all wk 12-3 6-11 (Fri-Sun & BHs all day) **Food** Lunch all wk 12-3 Dinner Mon-Sat 6-9 (Sun bookings only) Restaurant menu available all wk (Sun eve bookings only) ⊕ FREE HOUSE ◖ Wye Valley, St George's, Hereford, Otter ⊘ Westons Stowford Press, Gold Label & Vintage. **Facilities** Non-diners area ⁑ Children's menu Children's portions Play area Garden ⊓ Parking WiFi ⛟ (notice required)

MICHAELCHURCH ESCLEY
Map 9 SO33

The Bridge Inn

tel: 01981 510646 **HR2 OJW**
email: thebridgeinn@hotmail.com
dir: *From Peterchurch take B4348 towards Hereford, turn right in Vowchurch to Michaelchurch Escley. At T-junct in village turn left*

A truly welcoming inn by a river

With its 16th-century origins, traditional wood-burning stoves and friendly atmosphere, this delightful riverside inn exudes a warm welcome. It makes an ideal base for exploring the Golden Valley, the Brecon Beacons National Park and Offa's Dyke. Cask-conditioned ales and a selection of local ciders are bar highlights; over the Bank Holiday weekend in August, a festival celebrates both forms of refreshment. Heartwarming dishes on their interesting menus are venison bourguignon, mash and steamed vegetables; Persian lamb served with za'atar potatoes, coconut salad and curried houmous; and vegetables curry. If you have room you could be tempted by plum crumble or sticky toffee pudding.

Open all wk 12-3 5.30-10 (Sat-Sun all day) **Food** Lunch Tue-Fri 12-2.30, Sat-Sun 12-3 Dinner Mon-Thu 5.30-8.30, Fri-Sat 5.30-9.30, Sun 5.30-8 Restaurant menu available all wk ⊕ FREE HOUSE ◖ Wye Valley Butty Bach ⊘ Gwatkin Pyder & Yarlington Mill, Westons Wyld Wood. ⚑ 20 **Facilities** Non-diners area ⁑ (Bar Garden) ⁑ Children's menu Children's portions Garden ⊓ Beer festival Cider festival Parking WiFi ⛟ (notice required)

Follow us on Facebook
www.facebook.com/TheAAUK
f Find us on Facebook

ORLETON
Map 9 SO46

The Boot Inn

tel: 01568 780228 **SY8 4HN**
email: hello@thebootinnorleton.co.uk **web:** www.thebootinnorleton.co.uk
dir: *Follow A49 S from Ludlow (approx 7m) to B4362 (Woofferton), 1.5m off B4362 turn left. Inn in village centre*

Atmospheric hostelry with many tall tales

A black and white, half-timbered, 16th-century village inn characterised by a large inglenook fireplace, oak beams, mullioned windows, and exposed wattle-and-daub. Herefordshire real ales and Robinsons cider accompany dishes such as slow-cooked belly pork; line-caught sea bass; and wild mushroom and spinach linguine. In the back room is a painting from which the figure of one-time regular Joe Vale was obliterated after arguing with the landlord. Occasionally, old Joe's ghost returns.

Open all wk 12-3 5.30-11 (Sat-Sun all day) **Food** Lunch Mon-Sat 12-2, Sun 12-3 Dinner all wk 6.30-9 ⊕ FREE HOUSE ◖ Hobsons Best Bitter, Wye Valley, Local guest ales ⊘ Robinsons, Thatchers Gold. **Facilities** Non-diners area ⁑ (Bar Garden) ⁑ Children's menu Play area Garden ⊓ Beer festival Cider festival Parking ⛟

PEMBRIDGE
Map 9 SO35

New Inn

tel: 01544 388427 **Market Square HR6 9DZ**
dir: *From M5 junct 7 take A44 W through Leominster towards Llandrindod Wells*

Traditional inn for good beer and home-cooked food

Formerly a courthouse and jail, and close to the site of the last battle of the War of the Roses, this 14th-century black and white timbered free house has been under the same ownership for over 30 years. Worn flagstone floors and winter fires characterise the cosy bar, and in summer customers spill out into the pub's outdoor seating area on the Old Market Square. Don't expect to find any background music or a TV screen. Home-cooked English fare, using local produce, might include beef steak and ale casserole with horseradish dumplings; hot game pie with Cumberland sauce; or garlic cheese stuffed chicken stuffed, wrapped in bacon in cream wine sauce.

Open all wk 11-2.30 6-11 (summer 11-3 6-11) Closed last wk Feb, Tue L Jan-Etr **Food** Lunch all wk 12-2 Dinner all wk 6.30-9 ⊕ FREE HOUSE ◖ Hobsons Town Crier, Sharp's Doom Bar, Hook Norton, Three Tuns, Ludlow ⊘ Westons Stowford Press & Wyld Wood Organic, Dunkertons. ⚑ 10 **Facilities** Non-diners area ⁑ Children's portions Family room Garden Outside area ⊓ Parking

STAPLOW

Map 10 SO64

The Oak Inn

PICK OF THE PUBS

tel: 01531 640954 **HR8 1NP**
email: oakinn@wyenet.co.uk
dir: *M50 junct 2, A417 to Ledbury. At rdbt take 2nd exit onto A449, then A438 (High St). Take B4214 to Staplow*

17th-century pub in the heart of rural Herefordshire

Set in bucolic Herefordshire countryside richly endowed with orchards and hopyards. The Oak enjoys an enviable location close to the lovely old market town of Ledbury, with the striking ridge of the Malvern Hills a sublime horizon. Ramblers can enjoy a walk along the nearby course of the former Herefordshire and Gloucestershire Canal before retiring to the lovingly extended cottage-style pub, complete with log-burning stoves, flagstone floors and old wooden beams adorned with hops. Both the drinks and food menus draw lavishly on the county's larder; beers from Ledbury and Wye Valley breweries adorn the bar, whilst local cider adds interest. Dishes from the starter menu include Madgett's Farm (Wye Valley) chicken liver and brandy parfait, whilst a sharing platter includes Severn and Wye smoked Var salmon. Juniper braised blade of Herefordshire beef with roasted beetroot and carrots and wild berry sauce examples the comfortable mains menu here. Dogs are very welcome both inside and in the orchard-side garden.

Open all day all wk **Food** Lunch Mon-Sat 12-2.30, Sun 12-3 Dinner Mon-Sat 6.30-9.30, Sun 7-8.30 ⊕ FREE HOUSE ◀ Bathams Best Bitter, Ledbury Gold, Wye Valley Bitter, Guest ales ○ Westons Stowford Press, Robinsons.
Facilities Non-diners area ❀ (Bar Restaurant Garden) ◖ Children's portions Garden ⊼ Parking WiFi

SYMONDS YAT (EAST)

Map 10 SO51

The Saracens Head Inn ★★★★ INN

PICK OF THE PUBS

See Pick of the Pubs on opposite page and advert below

TILLINGTON

Map 9 SO44

The Bell

tel: 01432 760395 **HR4 8LE**
email: glenn@thebellinntillington.co.uk
dir: *From A4103 (N Hereford) follow Tillington sign*

Village pub with something for everybody

Amidst blossoming fruit trees (in the spring, that is) this traditional, village pub has been run since 1988 by the Williams family. With two bars, one with an open fire and a screen for sporting events, dining room, extensive gardens, patio and grassed play area, it offers something for everybody. Home-made ciders are served alongside Herefordshire ales such as brews from Wye Valley. Prepared from locally-sourced ingredients are sandwiches, baguettes, light lunches, and dishes such as Dexter minced beef cottage pie with roast root vegetables; slow-roast pork belly; and smoked paprika chicken cassoulet. If you have a sweet tooth, go for the Mars Bar cheesecake.

Open all day all wk **Food** Lunch Mon-Fri 12-2.30, Sat all day, Sun 12-3 Dinner Mon-Fri 6-9.30, Sat all day Av main course £12.50 ⊕ FREE HOUSE ◀ Fuller's London Pride, Wye Valley Bitter, Local ales ○ Tillington Belle (pub's own).
Facilities Non-diners area ◖ Children's menu Play area Garden ⊼ Parking WiFi 🚌 (notice required)

The Saracens Head Inn

Symonds Yat East, Ross-on-Wye, Herefordshire HR9 6JL   Tel: 01600 890435
Website: www.saracensheadinn.co.uk • Email: contact@saracensheadinn.co.uk

For centuries the *Saracens Head Inn* has occupied its spectacular position on the east bank of the River Wye, where the river flows into a steep wooded gorge. The Inn's own ferry across the river still operates by hand, just as it has for the past 200 years.

There's a relaxed atmosphere throughout the Inn, from the flagstoned bar to the cosy lounge and dining room. The riverside terraces are a great place to watch the world go by.

The Inn has a reputation for high quality food, using fresh local ingredients where possible, with a regularly changing menu and daily specials – not to mention a tempting choice of 6 real ales (featuring local breweries), and freshly-ground coffee.

Symonds Yat East is situated in an Area of Outstanding Natural Beauty on the edge of the Forest of Dean, so a stay in one of the ten guest bedrooms is a must for exploring the unspoilt local countryside.

The Wye Valley Walk passes the Inn, as does the Peregrine cycle trail. Walking, cycling, mountain biking, river cruises, canoeing, kayaking, climbing and fishing are all available nearby.

PICK OF THE PUBS

The Saracens Head Inn ★★★★ INN

SYMONDS YAT (EAST)   Map 10 SO51

tel: 01600 890435
HR9 6JL
email: contact@saracensheadinn.co.uk
web: www.saracensheadinn.co.uk
dir: *A40 onto B4229, follow Symonds Yat East signs, 2m*

Former cider mill in an unrivalled location

Occupying a stunning position on the east bank of the River Wye where it flows into a steep wooded gorge on the edge of the Royal Forest of Dean, The Saracens Head can be reached by the inn's own ferry, which still operates by hand, just as it has for the past 200 years. Symonds Yat East ('yat' being the local name for a gate or pass) was named after Robert Symonds, a Sheriff of Herefordshire in the 17th century, and has been designated an Area of Outstanding Natural Beauty. There's a relaxed atmosphere throughout the 16th-century inn, from the bar (serving Wye Valley ales), the cosy lounge and stylish dining room, and two sunny terraces overlooking the Wye. If you come at lunchtime, try roasted topside, horseradish and watercress sandwich, or bacon, brie and cranberry baguette. Seasonal menus and daily specials boards offer both the traditional and modern: ham hock, prune and fennel terrine, ginger breaded quail's egg, and

cognac poached cherry jelly could be followed by hand-made Monmouthshire faggots, mash, mushy peas and red wine gravy. Main courses at dinner might include Toulouse sausage and duck cassoulet; or trio of Welsh lamb — garlic and rosemary lamb cutlet, sweet potato shepherd's pie and lamb frickadella. Complete your meal with one of the home-made desserts on the blackboard or you might opt for a slate of three local cheeses — Hereford Hop, Per Las and Tintern — served with grapes, crackers, and quince and rose petal jelly. A stay in one of the ten en suite bedrooms is a must if you're exploring this area.

Open all day all wk Closed 25 Dec
Food Lunch all wk 12-2.30 Dinner all wk 6.30-9 ⊕ FREE HOUSE ◀ Wye Valley HPA & Butty Bach, Bespoke Saved by the Bell, Sharp's Doom Bar, Kingstone Llandogo Trow, Wickwar BOB ♨ Westons Stowford Press & Country Perry. ♟ 10
Facilities Non-diners area ❖ (Bar Garden) ♦ Children's menu Children's portions Garden ⊫ Parking WiFi
Rooms 10

WALFORD
Map 10 SO52

The Mill Race
PICK OF THE PUBS

See Pick of the Pubs on opposite page

WALTERSTONE
Map 9 SO32

Carpenters Arms

tel: 01873 890353 **HR2 0DX**
email: carpentersarms1@btinternet.com
dir: *Exit A465 between Hereford & Abergavenny at Pandy*

Step back in time inside the cosy Carpenters

Located on the edge of the Black Mountains and overlooked by Offa's Dyke, there's plenty of character in this pub. You'll find beams, antique settles and a leaded range with open fires that burn all winter; a perfect cosy setting for enjoying a pint of Ramblers Ruin. Popular food options include crispy battered cod; gammon steak with pineapple or an egg; and vegetarian lasagne. Ask about the large choice of home-made desserts. There are a few tables outside which can be a suntrap in summer. Half a mile from the Welsh border, the 300-year-old Carpenters Arms has been owned by the Watkins for three generations.

Open all day all wk 12-11 Closed 25 Dec **Food** Contact pub for food times ⊕ FREE HOUSE ◀ Wadworth 6X, Breconshire Golden Valley & Ramblers Ruin Ö Westons. **Facilities** Non-diners area ◀▮ Children's portions Play area Family room Garden Parking ▭ **Notes** ⊚

WELLINGTON
Map 10 SO44

The Wellington

tel: 01432 830367 **HR4 8AT**
email: info@wellingtonpub.co.uk
dir: *Exit A49 into village centre. Pub 0.25m on left*

Country pub ideal for families

The garden of this pub is sunny and secure, an ideal venue for enjoying a pint of the local brew or a glass of wine. If the weather is inclement, the pub's restaurant and conservatory are also at the disposal of family groups. Here, a typical lunch could comprise potted crab, cottage pie topped with cheddar mash, and sticky toffee pudding. Dinner choices include seared scallops, pancetta and apple and mustard sauce; steak au poivre and chunky chips; and chocolate pudding cake with clotted cream. Ales are local, coming from Wye Valley Brewery in Herefordshire.

Open 12-2.30 5.30-11 Closed Mon ⊕ FREE HOUSE ◀ Wye Valley Butty Bach & HPA, Butcombe, Guest ales Ö Westons. **Facilities** ✿ (Bar Garden) ◀▮ Children's portions Garden Parking WiFi

WEOBLEY
Map 9 SO45

Ye Olde Salutation Inn
PICK OF THE PUBS

tel: 01544 318443 **Market Pitch HR4 8SJ**
email: info@salutation-inn.com
dir: *A44, then A4112, 8m from Leominster*

Timber-framed free house run by a chef-proprietor

Known to locals as 'the Sal', this 17th-century black-and-white pub is in the heart of the medieval village of Weobley. The inn, sympathetically converted from an old alehouse and adjoining cottage, is the perfect base for exploring the Welsh Marches and the Black-and-White Villages Trail. The book capital of Hay-on-Wye and the cathedral city of Hereford are close by, as are the Wye Valley and Black Mountains. Chef-proprietor Stuart Elder's menu specials and old favourites are served in the traditional lounge bar with its welcoming atmosphere and cosy inglenook fireplace. The inn's restaurant offers a range of tempting dishes created with the use of locally sourced ingredients. Start, perhaps, with deep-fried artichoke hearts in a light batter, and continue with half a roast duck with orange and ginger sauce, and finish with lemon tart and raspberry sorbet.

Open all day all wk 12-11 (Sun 12-10.30) **Food** Lunch all wk 12-2.30 Dinner all wk 6-9 Set menu available ⊕ FREE HOUSE ◀ Wye Valley Butty Bach, Local guest ales Ö Westons Stowford Press, Robinsons. **Facilities** Non-diners area ✿ (Bar Restaurant Outside area) ◀▮ Children's portions Outside area ▭ Parking WiFi ▭ (notice required)

WINFORTON
Map 9 SO24

The Sun Inn

tel: 01544 327677 **HR3 6EA**
email: richard23457@btinternet.com
dir: *In village centre on A438 (Hereford to Brecon road)*

Small, intimate pub with a friendly atmosphere

Owners Gail and Richard Greenwood and their chefs have established a network of local Herefordshire food producers in order to create their monthly changing menus. 'Local' really doesn't get much closer than the pork and lamb from the chef's own farm, and beef from less than a mile away; fish travels a little further but is fresh from Cornwall. With that in mind perhaps choose new season Hay-on-Wye lamb loin chop, vodka mint jelly, lamb and mint jus from a spring menu; or on another occasion pan-fried scallops in brandy; slow-roasted pork belly and soured apple compôte with crispy crackling.

Open 12-3 6.30-last orders (Sun 12-2 winter) Closed Sun eve & Mon (Tue Oct-Apr) **Food** Lunch Tue-Sat 12-2, Sun 12-3, Wed-Sun 12-2 winter Dinner Tue-Sat 6.30-9, Wed-Sat 6.30-9 winter ⊕ FREE HOUSE ◀ Wye Valley Butty Bach, Brecon Gold Beacons Ö Gwatkin, Westons Old Rosie, Local cider. **Facilities** Non-diners area ◀▮ Children's menu Children's portions Garden ▭ Parking WiFi

WOOLHOPE
Map 10 SO63

The Crown Inn

tel: 01432 860468 **HR1 4QP**
email: menu@crowninnwoolhope.co.uk
dir: *B4224 to Mordiford, left after Moon Inn. Pub in village centre*

Locally sourced food and great choice of ciders and perries

A traditional village free house with large gardens, The Crown Inn is popular with walkers and well supported by locals and visitors alike. Excellent food and drink are a priority here, with good ales as well as 24 local ciders and perries. Typical starter dishes on the concise menu could be crispy chilli beef with coriander salad; or seared black pudding, sautéed baby potatoes, soft boiled egg and wholegrain mustard. Follow on with pheasant, leek and bacon pie, creamed mash and flower sprouts; or beer battered Cornish whiting, chunky chips, mushy peas and tartare sauce. There is an outside summertime bar in the garden on Saturday nights and an Early May Bank Holiday beer and cider festival.

Open all wk 12-2.30 6-11 (Sat-Sun all day) **Food** Lunch all wk 12-2 Dinner all wk 6-9 ⊕ FREE HOUSE ◀ Wye Valley HPA, Ledbury Bitter, Guest ales Ö Westons Stowford Press, Country Perry & Bounds, Local ciders. ☗ 8 **Facilities** Non-diners area ◀▮ Children's menu Children's portions Garden ▭ Beer festival Cider festival Parking WiFi ▭ (notice required)

PICK OF THE PUBS

The Mill Race

WALFORD   Map 10 SO52

tel: 01989 562891
HR9 5QS
email: enquiries@millrace.info
web: www.millrace.info
dir: *B4234 from Ross-on-Wye to Walford. Pub 3m on right*

The best local produce, direct from its own nearby farm

There's another Walford in the north of the county, so make sure you've put the right postcode into your Sat Nav. It lies on the banks of the River Wye, just upstream from the picturesque gorge at Symonds Yat, and the Forest of Dean. Standing majestically on the other bank is Goodrich Castle, home to 'Roaring Meg', the only surviving Civil War mortar, which the Parliamentarians used to breach its walls. The pub's interior is suitably cosy and welcoming, with a beamed and flagstone-floored bar and rustically furnished dining areas. Warm up in winter by one of the log fires, or in summer relax on the terrace and watch the buzzards drifting overhead. At nearby Bishopwood is the pub's own 1,000-acre farm estate, which together with a dedicated supply chain of local producers, allows landlord Luke Freeman and his team to dedicate their days to producing the food that is highly regarded within the Herefordshire

Slow Food movement. Lunch and evening menus vary; a typical meal might begin with walnut and cracked wheat salad with honey and cumin; or wood pigeon, blackcurrant and juniper purée and bacon lardons; followed by red legged partridge Wellington, wild mushrooms, truffle-infused mash, carrots and turnips; or beetroot tart Tatin, pickled candy beetroot and fig salad. The Mill Race offers a great choice sharing plates for two – seafood; shoulder of spring lamb; and rack of Gloucester Old Spots pork being just three. Wednesday night is fish night. Wines from Herefordshire are on the globe-spanning list.

Open all wk 12-3 5-11 (Sat 12-11.30 Sun 12-11) **Food** Lunch Mon-Sat 12-2, Sun 12-4 Dinner Mon-Fri 6-9.30, Sat-Sun 6-9 Set menu available ⊕ FREE HOUSE ◖ Wye Valley Bitter & Butty Bach, Butcombe Rare Breed Ŏ Westons Stowford Press, Gwynt y Ddraig ciders. ♟ 25 **Facilities** Non-diners area ♦♦ Children's menu & portions Garden ⊼ Parking WiFi ⛐ (notice required)

HERTFORDSHIRE

ALDBURY
Map 6 SP91

The Greyhound Inn

tel: 01442 851228 **19 Stocks Rd HP23 5RT**
email: greyhound@aldbury.wanadoo.co.uk
dir: *Phone for detailed directions*

A traditional village inn offering good food in a relaxed atmosphere

The village's ancient stocks and duck pond are popular with film-makers who frequently use Aldbury as a location, allowing the pub's customers the chance to witness every clap of the clapperboard. In the oak-beamed restaurant, the comprehensive menu includes salads and platters, as well as smoked haddock, mash, broccoli and poached egg; salmon supreme, creamed leeks and noisette potatoes; butternut squash, sage and pine nut risotto, shaved parmesan and butter sauce. Among the desserts are baked figs with mascarpone cheese, and warm almond and treacle tart with custard. The bar snacks are a local legend, especially when accompanied by Badger Dorset Best or Tanglefoot ale.

Open all day all wk 11.30-11 (Sun 12-10.30) Closed 25 Dec **Food** Lunch all wk 12-2.30 Dinner all wk 6.30-9.30 Av main course £12.75 Set menu available ⊕ HALL & WOODHOUSE ◀ Badger Dorset Best, Tanglefoot, K&B Sussex. ♀ 13
Facilities Non-diners area ♣ (Bar Garden) ♦ Children's menu Children's portions Family room Garden Parking WiFi ▦ (notice required)

The Valiant Trooper

tel: 01442 851203 **Trooper Rd HP23 5RW**
email: valianttrooper@gmail.com
dir: *A41 at Tring junct, follow rail station signs 0.5m, at village green turn right, pub 200yds on left*

Pretty pub with good food

Named in honour of the Duke of Wellington who allegedly discussed strategy with his troops here, this old pub has been enjoyed by lucky locals for centuries. Located in the quintessential Chilterns' village of Aldbury, beneath the beech woods of Ashridge Park, the Trooper's bar proffers six real ales and beer festivals usually take place on Bank Holidays. Bar food encompasses jackets, sandwiches, ploughman's and pub favourites. The restaurant menu features more creative dishes like braised spring vegetable medley with shredded ham hock, parmesan, cheddar scones and wholegrain mustard.

Open all day all wk 12-11 (Sun 12-10.30) **Food** Lunch Mon-Fri 12-3, Sat 12-9, Sun 12-4 Dinner Wed-Fri 6-9, Sat 12-9 Set menu available Restaurant menu available Wed-Sun ⊕ FREE HOUSE ◀ Fuller's London Pride, Tring Side Pocket for a Toad, Chiltern Beechwood, Guest ales ♂ Lilley's Apples & Pears, Millwhites Hedge Layer, Westons. **Facilities** Non-diners area ♣ (Bar Restaurant Garden) ♦ Children's menu Children's portions Play area Family room Garden Beer festival Parking WiFi ▦ (notice required)

ARDELEY
Map 12 TL32

Jolly Waggoner

tel: 01438 861350 **SG2 7AH**
email: adrian@churchfarmardeley.co.uk
dir: *From Stevenage take B1037, through Walkern, in 2m right to Ardeley*

Ancient village pub with a 'one-mile menu'

All meat on the Jolly Waggoner's menu, including heritage varieties and rare breeds, is traditionally reared at Church Farm across the road, together with over 100 different vegetables, fruits and herbs. As Church Farm runs this 500-year-old pub, the food on offer is truly local, being sourced from within a one-mile radius. Start with sweet potato curry or macaroni cheese, and continue with slow-cooked

shoulder of lamb or pan-fried salmon fillet from the market menu. Regular beers are Buntingford and Fuller's London Pride. The annual beer festival takes place in August.

Open all day all wk 12-11.30 **Food** Lunch Mon-Fri 12-2, Sat 12-9, Sun 12-7 Dinner Mon-Fri 6.30-9, Sat 12-9, Sun 12-7 Av main course £13.50 ⊕ FREE HOUSE ◀ Buntingford Highwayman, Fuller's London Pride, Adnams Broadside, Dark Star, Mauldons Mole Trap, Tring ♂ Aspall. ♀ 13 **Facilities** Non-diners area ♣ (Bar Garden) ♦ Children's menu Children's portions Garden ⋈ Beer festival Parking WiFi ▦ (notice required)

ASHWELL
Map 12 TL23

NEW The Three Tuns

tel: 01462 743343 **6 High St SG7 5NL**
email: info@thethreetunsashwell.co.uk **web:** www.thethreetunsashwell.co.uk
dir: *A1(M) junct 10, A507 (Baldock) then follow Ashwell signs*

Popular destination pub

Behind this early 19th-century inn are Ashwell Springs, source of The Cam, the river that from here heads for nearby Cambridge. A handsome brick building, the pub has a pergola-shaded patio and lovely gardens to the rear. For lunch try a Reuben salt beef sandwich, or bubble-and-squeak potato cake. South Coast lemon sole; poached Dingley Dell pork tenderloin; and beetroot and pearl barley risotto are dinner possibilities. Highlighted on the menu as favourites are Thai salmon fishcakes; beer-battered fish and chips; and steak frites. Potential dessert candidates include Jaffa mousse, and damson and almond tart. Wines are from Argentina to New Zealand, by way of Austria.

Open all day all wk **Food** Lunch Mon-Sat 12-3, Sun 12-5 Dinner Mon-Thu 6-9, Fri-Sat 6-10 Restaurant menu available all wk ⊕ GREENE KING ◀ St Austell Tribute, Hogs Back TEA, Hook Norton Old Hooky ♂ Thatchers. ♀ **Facilities** Non-diners area ♣ (Bar Garden) ♦ Children's menu Children's portions Garden Outside area ⋈ Parking WiFi ▦ (notice required)

AYOT GREEN | Map 6 TL21

The Waggoners

tel: 01707 324241 **Brickwall Close AL6 9AA**
email: laurent@thewaggoners.co.uk
dir: *Ayot Green on unclassified road off B197, S of Welwyn*

Modern French cuisine in the Hertfordshire countryside

Close to the large, traditional village green and with good English real ales flowing in the beamed bar, it comes as a surprise that the menu has a strong French bent to it. Cue the Gallic owners, whose culinary skills have gained an AA Rosette for their inspired cuisine at this former waggoners' and coaching stop in the low Hertfordshire hills. Menus may include moules marinière; sweetcorn risotto with smoked chicken; salmon confit with apple and hazelnut salad; Chateaubriand (for two), grilled plum tomato, flat mushroom and red wine sauce; and roast turbot fillet with celeriac, steak, kidney and oyster sauce. The wine list stretches to 100 bins.

Open all day all wk **Food** Lunch all wk 12-2.45 Dinner all wk 6.30-9.30 Set menu available Restaurant menu available all wk ⊕ PUNCH TAVERNS ◖ Fuller's London Pride, St Austell Tribute, Adnams Broadside, Greene King Abbot Ale & IPA, Sharp's Doom Bar ♂ Westons Stowford Press. ♟ 50 **Facilities** Non-diners area ♣ (Bar Garden Outside area) ♦ Children's portions Garden Outside area ⋒ Parking WiFi ▭ (notice required)

BERKHAMSTED | Map 6 SP90

The Old Mill

tel: 01442 879590 **London Rd HP4 2NB**
email: oldmill@peachpubs.com
dir: *At east end of London Rd in town centre*

Historic waterside pub buzzing throughout the week

There are safe new hands at the helm at this imposing, multi-gabled old mill building right beside the Grand Union Canal. Ghosts of its former life add character to the pub, the mill race off the River Bulbourne still flows by the secluded courtyard, whilst absorbing photos and ephemera are spread throughout the part-beamed rooms. Artisan beers from the local Red Squirrel Brewery feature at the bar in the thoughtfully updated interior, where modern British dishes lead on the well balanced menu. Expect dishes like mulled Cornish lamb casserole; or roasted cod supreme with River Exe mussel and bacon chowder. Vegetarian choices are equally inspired.

Open all day all wk Closed 25 Dec **Food** Lunch all wk 12-6 Dinner all wk 6-10 Set menu available ⊕ PEACH PUBS ◖ Red Squirrel Conservation Bitter, Tring Side Pocket for a Toad & Bring Me Sunshine, Sharp's Doom Bar ♂ Aspall. ♟ 16 **Facilities** Non-diners area ♣ (Bar Garden) ♦ Children's portions Garden ⋒ Parking WiFi ▭ (notice required)

BISHOP'S STORTFORD | Map 6 TL42

NEW Water Lane Bar and Restaurant

tel: 01279 211888 **31 Water Ln CM23 2JZ**
email: reservations@waterlane.co
dir: *From A1250 in town centre at mini rdbt into North St. 2nd left into Barrett Ln (one way). At T-junct left into Water Lane*

Slickly converted brewery proud of their food sourcing

The old Hawkes Brewery, dating from 1780, has undergone a total restoration, but contemporary fixtures and fittings only enhance the retained original features. It's a dog-free zone that welcomes families, who are entertained on occasion by a strolling magician as they dine in the vaulted cellar bar or high-ceilinged restaurant. Drinks range from Sharp's Doom Bar to speciality cocktails, while the kitchen prepares freshly-baked bread; smoked haddock bubble-and-squeak Scotch egg with curried leeks; and chargrilled bourbon-glazed belly ribs served with chipotle slaw.

Open 12-11 (Fri-Sat 12-1am Sun 12-6) Closed Mon **Food** Lunch Tue-Sat 12-10, Sun 12-4 Dinner Tue-Sat 12-10 Av main course £13 ⊕ FREE HOUSE ◖ Woodforde's Wherry, Brancaster Best, Sharp's Doom Bar. ♟ 12 **Facilities** Non-diners area ♦ Outside area WiFi

BRAUGHING | Map 12 TL32

The Golden Fleece

tel: 01920 823555 **20 Green End SG11 2PG**
email: pub@goldenfleecebraughing.co.uk **web:** www.goldenfleecebraughing.co.uk
dir: *A10 N from Ware. At rdbt right onto B1368 signed Braughing. Approx 1m to village*

Lovingly restored village inn on the way to Cambridge

This Grade II-listed Georgian coaching inn was closed for a decade until Peter and Jessica Tatlow bought it at auction and reopened it after a major renovation. Their hard work has clearly paid off as the pub has gained a good reputation for its local real ales and ciders, but also its food, which specialises in gluten- and dairy-free dishes. The menu changes every month, but popular dishes are brought back time and time again. Chicken breast with chestnut and fig stuffing and mustard, red onion sauce; and Quorn and mushroom puff parcel served with vegetables and dauphinoise potatoes are typical choices, and the monthly tapas night is a popular fixture on the last Wednesday of each month.

Open all wk 11.30-3 5.30-11 (Fri 11.30-3 5.30-12 Sat 11.30am-mdnt Sun 12-10) Closed 25 Dec **Food** Lunch Mon-Sat 12-2.30, Sun 12-6 Dinner Mon-Thu 6-9, Fri-Sat 7-10, Sun 12-6 Set menu available ⊕ FREE HOUSE ◖ Adnams, Nethergate, Buntingford, Mauldons, Church End, Cottage ♂ Aspall Harry Sparrow. ♟ 15 **Facilities** Non-diners area ♦ Children's menu Children's portions Play area Garden ⋒ Parking WiFi ▭ (notice required)

BROOKMANS PARK　　　　　　　　　　　Map 6 TL20

Brookmans

tel: 01707 664144 **Bradmore Green AL9 7QW**
email: brookmans@peachpubs.com
dir: *A1000 from Hatfield towards Potters Bar. Right signed Brookmans Park. Through Bradmore Green. Pub on right*

Enjoyable local food in a buzzy village hub

Built as a hotel in the 1930s, Brookmans may no longer offer a bed for the night but it remains the social hub of the village. Racing Green leather upholstery and silk lampshades add a touch of class to the bar, where a rotating choice of guest ales is complemented by 15 wines by the glass. Local produce and named suppliers drive the modern British menu and daily specials, which might include chilli and lime crab cake with wasabi mayo; Cornish lamb casserole and creamy mash, finishing off with Valrhona white chocolate cheesecake and Baileys cream.

Open all day all wk Closed 25 Dec **Food** Lunch all wk 12-6 Dinner Mon-Sat 6-10, Sun 6-9 ⊕ FREE HOUSE ◀ Sharp's Doom Bar & Cornish Coaster, Guest ales ♂ Aspall. ♚ 15 **Facilities** Non-diners area ♣ (Bar Garden) ♦ Children's portions Play area Garden ⊨ Parking WiFi ➠ (notice required)

BUNTINGFORD　　　　　　　　　　　Map 12 TL32

The Sword Inn Hand ★★★★ INN

tel: 01763 271356 **Westmill SG9 9LQ**
email: welcome@theswordinnhandrestaurant.co.uk **web:** www.theswordinnhand.co.uk
dir: *Off A10, 1.5m S of Buntingford*

Welcoming travellers since the 14th century

Midway between London and Cambridge, this old inn provides an excellent stopping off point. Inside are the original oak beams, flagstone floors and open fireplace; outside is a large garden and pretty patio. As a free house, there is a varied selection of real ales from the likes of Greene King and Young's. Fresh produce is delivered daily for a good selection of bar snacks including salads, omelettes, sandwiches and light dishes. Taken from a typical evening menu are mozzarella-stuffed peppers with couscous; basil-crusted salmon fillet with Mediterranean vegetables; and calves' liver and bacon. Smart accommodation is available.

Open all wk 12-3 5-11 (Fri-Sat all day, Sun 12-7) **Food** Lunch Mon-Sat 12-2.30, Sun 12-4 Dinner Mon-Sat 6.30-9 ⊕ FREE HOUSE ◀ Greene King IPA, Young's Bitter, Guest ales ♂ Westons Stowford Press. ♚ 9 **Facilities** Non-diners area ♦ Children's menu Children's portions Play area Garden ⊨ Parking WiFi ➠ **Rooms** 4

BUSHEY　　　　　　　　　　　Map 6 TQ19

NEW The Horse & Chains

tel: 020 8421 9907 **79 High St WD23 1BL**
email: info@thehorseandchains.co.uk
dir: *Phone pub for detailed directions*

Family-run and a clear hit with locals

First referred to in 1698, its location halfway up a hill was ideal for wagoners and their horses needing refreshment. Although sympathetically redesigned, its great age remains evident, particularly the big open fireplace that dwarfs its modern wood-burner. If more than a sandwich, bar snack or sharing platter is called for,

then maybe grilled whole lemon sole; Japanese-style chicken katsu, shredded Asian greens and sticky jasmine rice; or a salad will do the trick. Theme nights include fish (Mondays), mussels (Tuesdays), and tapas and Greek. Between 5 and 6.30pm on Saturdays buy a starter, main or dessert and get another free.

Open all day all wk **Food** Lunch all wk 12-6 Dinner all wk 6-10 Av main course £13.50 Set menu available Restaurant menu available all wk ⊕ ENTERPRISE INNS ◀ Sharp's Doom Bar. ♚ 19 **Facilities** Non-diners area ♣ (Bar Garden) ♦ Children's menu Children's portions Garden ⊨ Parking WiFi ➠ (notice required)

COTTERED　　　　　　　　　　　Map 12 TL32

The Bull at Cottered

tel: 01763 281243 **SG9 9QP**
email: darren.perkins@tiscali.co.uk
dir: *On A507 in Cottered between Buntingford & Baldock*

Charming, traditional village local

The four key things that sum up this member of the Greene King portfolio – low beams, antique furniture, cosy fires and teamwork. Then, of course, there's the food. You can eat in one of two traditional bars with open fires, in the pretty beamed dining room, or in the large, well-kept gardens. Everything that can be is home-made, the brasserie-style cooking typified by starters of pan-seared scallops, black pudding and chive cream; smoked duck breast with wasabi mayonnaise; the wild mushroom and parmesan risotto; roast cod, red wine lentils, bacon and kurly kale; and pork fillet stuffed with mature cheddar and smoked bacon.

Open all wk 11.30-3 6.30-11 (Sun 12-10.30) **Food** Lunch Mon-Sat 12-2, Sun 12-4 Dinner Mon-Sat 6.30-9.30, Sun 6-9 Restaurant menu available all wk ⊕ GREENE KING ◀ IPA & Abbot Ale. **Facilities** Non-diners area ♦ Children's portions Garden Outside area ⊨ Parking WiFi ➠ (notice required)

DATCHWORTH　　　　　　　　　　　Map 6 TL21

The Tilbury ◉◉

tel: 01438 815550 **Watton Rd SG3 6TB**
email: info@thetilbury.co.uk
dir: *A1(M) junct 7, A602 signed Ware & Hertford. At Bragbury End right into Bragbury Ln to Datchworth*

Elegant country pub serving exciting menus

At The Tilbury you'll find varied menus that include popular pub classics such as game cottage pie, and an à la carte of refined modern British dishes. The three owners and their head chef have created award-winning, tempting choices such as oxtail Eccles cakes, English mustard ice cream; braised rabbit, carrot cake, rabbit and jus; pigeon breast, black pudding pie, mash and braised red cabbage; and beetroot rösti, candied beetroot, poached egg and sage custard. The large terrace and garden is perfect for enjoying a drink or meal on sunny days, and with several dining areas, The Tilbury can offer private dining options. A set menu is available at both lunch and dinner, and there is an extensive wine list.

Open all day Closed Sun eve & Mon **Food** Lunch Tue-Sun 12-2 Dinner Tue-Sat 6-9.30 Set menu available Restaurant menu available Tue-Sun ⊕ BRAKSPEAR ◀ Bitter ♂ Westons Wyld Wood Organic, Symonds. ♚ 20 **Facilities** Non-diners area ♦ Children's menu Children's portions Garden ⊨ Parking WiFi ➠ (notice required)

PICK OF THE PUBS

The Bricklayers Arms ❀

FLAUNDEN   Map 6 TL00

tel: 01442 833322
Hogpits Bottom HP3 0PH
email: goodfood@bricklayersarms.com
web: www.bricklayersarms.com
dir: *M25 junct 18, A404 (Amersham road). Right at Chenies for Flaunden*

Country inn with Anglo-French cuisine

The creeper-clad Bricklayers Arms is a low, cottagey tiled pub formed from a pair of 18th-century cottages. It was in 1832 that Benskin's brewery converted the first of the cottages into an alehouse; the other joined it in the 1960s. Lost down leafy Hertfordshire lanes in a peaceful and inviting location, the pub has featured in many fictional films and TV programmes, and is a favourite with locals, walkers, horse-riders and, well, just about everyone. In summer, the flower festooned garden is the perfect place to savour an alfresco pint or meal. An ivy covered façade gives way to an immaculate interior, complete with low beams, exposed brickwork, candlelight and open fires. The award-winning restaurant is housed in a converted outbuilding and barn. Here you'll find a happy marriage of traditional English and French cooking. The Gallic influence comes from experienced head chef, Claude Pallait, and his team who use

fresh organic produce from local suppliers to create seasonal lunch and dinner menus, plus daily specials. For starters try venison coarse terrine with Kentish pear chutney; or charcuterie for two to share. To follow pan-fried duck breast with duck leg confit marinated in salt and duck fat, with sweet and sour cranberry jus; or roast breast of guinea fowl with pheasant sausage and a liver mousse feuillete. But don't stop there, from the puddings perhaps choose sticky toffee pudding with a date mascarpone and vanilla ice cream, or lemon tart with pannacotta and raspberry ice cream. Opt for one of the 120 wines from all corners of the world and, in the summer, enjoy it with your lunch in the terraced garden.

Open all day all wk 12-11.30 (Sun 9.15am-10.30pm 25 Dec 12-3)
Food Lunch Mon-Sat 12-2.30, Sun 12-3.30 Dinner Mon-Sat 6.30-9.30, Sun 6.30-8.30 Av main course £13 Set menu available ⊕ FREE HOUSE ◼ Tring Jack O'Legs, Sharp's Doom Bar, Rebellion ♻ Aspall, Thatchers Gold. ♟ 20
Facilities Non-diners area ❖ (Bar Garden) ♦❶ Children's portions Garden ⊟ Parking WiFi

EPPING GREEN
Map 6 TL20

The Beehive

tel: 01707 875959 **SG13 8NB**
email: squirrell15@googlemail.com
dir: *B158 from Hertford towards Hatfield. Left signed Little Berkhamsted. Left at war memorial signed Epping Green*

Popular family-run country free house

Weatherboarded under a tiled roof, this family-run pub has held a liquor licence for over 200 years. Hanging baskets and window boxes adorn the frontage, while the interior feels traditional to the core, with black beams, a log burner and ornamental brasses; outside is decked and grassed. Fresh fish is a speciality – maybe poached fish pie; sea bass fillets; or conventional fish and chips. Among the meats are chicken, ham hock and leek pie; lamb shoulder in minted gravy; bacon and brie beefburger; steaks and specials. Vegetarians and coeliacs have a good choice too. On the beer pumps are Greene King and a changing guest ale.

Open all wk Mon-Sat 11.30-3 5.30-11 (Sun 12-10.30) **Food** Lunch Mon-Sat 12-2.30, Sun 12-4 Dinner Mon-Sat 6-9.30, Sun 6-8.30 Restaurant menu available all wk ⊕ FREE HOUSE ◀ Greene King IPA & Abbot Ale, Guest ale. ♟ 12
Facilities Non-diners area ♦♦ Children's portions Garden ⼞ Parking WiFi ☞ (notice required)

FLAUNDEN
Map 6 TL00

The Bricklayers Arms ⊛
PICK OF THE PUBS

See Pick of the Pubs on page 265

HEMEL HEMPSTEAD
Map 6 TL00

Alford Arms
PICK OF THE PUBS

See Pick of the Pubs on opposite page

HERONSGATE
Map 6 TQ09

The Land of Liberty, Peace and Plenty

tel: 01923 282226 **Long Ln WD3 5BS**
email: beer@landoflibertypub.com
dir: *M25 junct 17, follow Heronsgate signs. 0.5m, pub on right*

Top-quality beers and ciders in single-bar pub

Named after a Chartist settlement established in Heronsgate in 1847, this inn is believed to have the second longest pub name in the British Isles. A traditional pub with a large garden and covered decked area, the cosy single bar has a buzz of conversation from locals. The focus here are the real ales and real ciders, all of which can be enjoyed with bar snacks of pork pies, pasties and pots of nuts. Please note that no children or the use of mobile phones are allowed in the bar. Regular events and beer festivals are held during the year.

Open all wk 12-11 (Fri-Sat 12-12) **Food** Contact pub for food times ⊕ FREE HOUSE ◀ 8 guest ales ♨ 4 Guest ciders or perry. **Facilities** Non-diners area ❣ (Bar Garden) Garden ⼞ Beer festival Parking WiFi ☞ (notice required)

HERTFORD HEATH
Map 6 TL31

NEW The College Arms

tel: 01992 558856 **40 London Rd SG13 7PW**
email: info@thecollegearmshertfordheath.com
dir: *From A10 onto A1170 towards Hoddesdon. At rdbt left towards Ware. At next rdbt left signed Hertford Heath*

Dog-friendly village gastro-pub

With links to the old East India Company College, now Haileybury College, the pub backs on to woodland, making it an ideal halfway house for walkers. Thoughtful renovation is particularly evident inside, where exposed brickwork, large rugs and gentlemen's-club-style wingback chairs are harmoniously juxtaposed. An easy-to-digest menu suggests pork dumplings with rocket salad as a starter; oven-baked crusted cod fillet with chickpea and tiger prawn masala; and sausages and mash as mains; and chocolate marquis for dessert. Some of the cheeses come from the smirk-inducing Wobbly Bottom Farm in Hitchin. Sunday roasts are all served with large Yorkshire puddings.

Open all day all wk **Food** Lunch Mon-Sat 12-3, Sun 12-9 Dinner Mon-Fri 6-9, Sat 6-9.30, Sun 12-9 ⊕ ENTERPRISE INNS ◀ Sharp's Doom Bar, Guest ale ♨ Aspall. ♟ 19 **Facilities** Non-diners area ❣ (Bar Garden) ♦♦ Children's menu Children's portions Play area Garden ⼞ Beer festival Parking WiFi ☞ (notice required)

HEXTON
Map 12 TL13

The Raven

tel: 01582 881209 **SG5 3JB**
email: theraven@emeryinns.com
dir: *5m W of Hitchin. 5m N of Luton, just outside Barton-le-Clay*

Family-friendly pub

This neat 1920s pub is named after Ravensburgh Castle in the neighbouring hills. Comfortable bars witness the serving of four weekly-changing guest ales, perhaps Fuller's London Pride or Greene King IPA, while outside a large garden with heated terrace and a play area ensure family friendliness. Extensive menus and blackboard specials embrace pub classics, salads, jackets, baguettes and wraps, vegetarian options, fish dishes and 'combination' meat plates like ribs and/or steak with Cajun chicken, and surf 'n' turf. So a three-course meal could see ginger and chilli chicken goujons; chargrilled lamb chops; or crab linguine; and sticky figgy pudding.

Open all day all wk **Food** Lunch all wk 12-9 Dinner all wk 12-9 ⊕ FREE HOUSE ◀ Greene King IPA, Morland Old Speckled Hen, Fuller's London Pride, Timothy Taylor Landlord, Sharp's Doom Bar. ♟ 24 **Facilities** Non-diners area ♦♦ Children's menu Children's portions Play area Garden ⼞ Parking WiFi ☞ (notice required)

PICK OF THE PUBS

Alford Arms

HEMEL HEMPSTEAD　　　Map 6 TL00

tel: 01442 864480
Frithsden HP1 3DD
email: info@alfordarmsfrithsden.co.uk
web: www.alfordarmsfrithsden.co.uk
dir: *From Hemel Hempstead on A4146, 2nd left at Water End. 1m, left at T-junct, right in 0.75m. Pub 100yds on right*

Professional but relaxed pub with understated style

With a flower-filled garden overlooking the green in the untouched hamlet of Frithsden, this pretty Victorian pub is surrounded by National Trust woodland and has historic Ashridge Park on its doorstep. Cross the threshold and you'll immediately pick up on the warm and lively atmosphere, derived from the buzz of conversation, some soft jazz in the background, and from the rich colours and eclectic mix of old furniture and antique pictures in the dining room and bar from Tring's well known salerooms. Also from Tring is real ale called Side Pocket for a Toad, which shares bar space with Sharp's Doom Bar and Chiltern Brewery's Beechwood Bitter. The seasonal menus and daily specials are a balance of modern British with more traditional dishes, all prepared from fresh local produce whenever possible. There's a great choice of light dishes or 'small plates', from crispy chilli squid with coriander and chorizo aïoli, to

pigeon, duck and pancetta terrine with piccalilli and toasted soda brioche. Equally imaginative 'big plates' include ale-braised shin of beef with dauphinoise potatoes, cavolo nero and liquor reduction; pan-fried gilt-head bream fillet, polenta chips, watercress and chilli, with roasted red pepper dressing. Dark chocolate truffle terrine and beetroot ice cream; and rice pudding brûlée with caramelised banana are just two ways to finish, or there's also home-made sorbets and ice creams, and the plate of British cheeses with oatcakes and green tomato and apple chutney.

Open all day all wk 11-11 (Sun 12-10.30) Closed 25-26 Dec
Food Lunch Mon-Fri 12-2.30, Sat 12-3,

Sun 12-9.30 Dinner Mon-Thu 6.30-9.30, Fri-Sat 6.30-10, Sun 12-9.30
🌐 SALISBURY PUBS LTD 🛢 Sharp's Doom Bar, Tring Side Pocket for a Toad, Chiltern Beechwood Bitter Ŏ Westons Mortimers Orchard. ⚑ 24 **Facilities** Non-diners area 🐾 (Bar Garden) ⛾ Children's portions Garden 🇫 Parking WiFi

HITCHIN
Map 12 TL12

Hermitage Rd.

tel: 01462 433603 **20-21 Hermitage Rd SG5 1BT**
email: reservations@hermitagerd.co.uk
dir: *From lights on B656 in town centre into Hermitage Rd*

A bar, restaurant and coffee house

Once a ballroom and nightclub, this is not your typical town-centre pub. Although original features survive, like the high vaulted ceiling and arched windows, the stage once graced by Sixties pop stars is now a dining area. Also part of the transformation is the open-plan kitchen, from which come cauliflower, leek and white onion soup; Norfolk mussels in white wine and parsley cream; wild mushroom, leek and tarragon pie with truffle mash; and pan-fried bream with lobster bisque chowder and caramelised scallop. Local brews like Brancaster Oyster Catcher are complemented by a globe-trotting wine list.

Open all day all wk **Food** Lunch Mon-Sat 12-9.30, Sun 12-8 Dinner Mon-Sat 12-9.30, Sun 12-8 Av main course £10 Restaurant menu available all wk ⊕ FREE HOUSE ◀ Adnams Southwold Bitter, Sharp's Doom Bar, Brancaster Oyster Catcher ♂ Symonds Founders Reserve. ♚ 13 **Facilities** Non-diners area ♦♦ Children's menu Children's portions WiFi ➡ (notice required)

NEW The Highlander

tel: 01462 454612 **45 Upper Tilehouse St SG5 2EF**
dir: *From Hitchen centre take A505 towards Luton. Pub on right*

English pub and French bistro in *entente cordiale*

Close to Hitchin's historic town centre, with rustic charm intact, open fire, and secluded garden with terrace. The Highlander continues to thrive in the capable hands of the Prutton family, who have run this Grade II listed pub for nearly 40 years. Today's partnership between Charlotte Prutton and Eric Ransinangue has introduced a French flavour to proceedings. Excellent real ales such as Tring's Side Pocket for a Toad are on tap (a beer festival is hosted in late May), the wine list is eco-friendly, and there is an extensive choice of malt whiskies. Concise menus worthy of a French bistro complete the picture, proposing the likes of grilled pork chop in bois boudrin sauce with boulangère potatoes.

Open all wk 12-3 6-11 (Fri-Sat all day Sun 12-5 7-10.30) **Food** Lunch Mon-Thu 12-2, Fri-Sun 12-2.30 Dinner Mon-Sat 6.30-9 Av main course £12.75 ⊕ FREE HOUSE ◀ Greene King IPA, Tring Side Pocket for a Toad, XT 1,2,3,4, 3 Brewers Special. ♚ **Facilities** ♣ (Bar Restaurant Garden) ♦♦ Children's portions Garden ♬ Beer festival Parking WiFi ➡ (notice required)

HUNSDON
Map 6 TL41

The Fox and Hounds
PICK OF THE PUBS

tel: 01279 843999 **2 High St SG12 8NH**
email: info@foxandhounds-hunsdon.co.uk **web:** www.foxandhounds-hunsdon.co.uk
dir: *From A414 between Ware & Harlow take B180 in Stanstead Abbotts N to Hunsdon*

Mediterranean-inspired menu in a renowned gastro-pub

A major internal revamp awaits those who haven't been here for a year or so, while the new look will also make a good impression on first-timers. Eye-catching features include the smart grey and white decor, the unusual white-tiled bar-back, and a striking poster reading "Nous sommes les soiffards", which, tactfully translated, suggests a fondness for drink. Chef James and wife Bianca run things and together they've created an easy-going place, where Adnams and local ales hold court at the bar, and lunch and dinner can be taken in the elegant, chandeliered dining room. James uses his new Josper charcoal oven to cook squid, merguez and chermoula marinade; spatchcocked French quail with aubergine caponata and aïoli; and wild sea bass fillet. Or try the home-made venison sausages. Finish with pannacotta and poached Yorkshire rhubarb; or chocolate and hazelnut torte. Outside is a tree-shaded garden with a covered terrace.

The Fox and Hounds

Open 12-4 6-11 Closed 26 Dec, Sun eve, Mon & BHs eve (Tue after BHs) **Food** Lunch Tue-Sat 12-2.30, Sun 12-3.30 Dinner Tue-Sat 6-9 Av main course £17.50 Set menu available ⊕ FREE HOUSE ◀ Adnams Southwold Bitter & Broadside, Local ales ♂ Aspall. ♚ 9 **Facilities** Non-diners area ♣ (Bar Garden) ♦♦ Children's menu Children's portions Play area Garden ♬ Parking WiFi

LITTLE HADHAM
Map 6 TL42

The Nags Head

tel: 01279 771555 **The Ford SG11 2AX**
email: paul.arkell@virgin.net
dir: *M11 junct 8, A120 towards Puckeridge & A10. Left at lights in Little Hadham. Pub 1m on right*

Along the country byways just south of Little Hadham

This warm and relaxed country pub was built in 1595 and still retains its traditional atmosphere, with an old bakery oven and a good range of real ales at the bar. Fish dishes such as poached skate wing with black butter and capers feature strongly on the full à la carte menu, which also includes a choice of steaks and vegetarian meals. At lunchtime, sandwiches and jacket potatoes offer a lighter alternative to hot main courses. Sit out the front on a good day and enjoy the countryside.

Open all wk 11.30-2.30 6-11 (Sun 12-10.30) **Food** Lunch Mon-Sat 12-2, Sun all day Dinner Mon-Sat 6-9, Sun all day Set menu available Restaurant menu available all wk ⊕ GREENE KING ◀ Abbot Ale, Ruddles County & IPA, Morland Old Speckled Hen, Marston's Pedigree. ♚ 12 **Facilities** Non-diners area ♦♦ Children's menu Children's portions Garden ♬ WiFi ➡

NORTHAW
Map 6 TL20

The Sun at Northaw

tel: 01707 655507 **1 Judges Hill EN6 4NL**
email: reservations@thesunatnorthaw.co.uk
dir: *M25 junct 24, A111 to Potters Bar. Right onto A1000, becomes High Street (B156). Follow to Northaw, pub on left*

Pretty inn with a skilled chef patron

A Grade II listed inn on a picturesque village green, The Sun has gained a reputation for its real ale, with up to seven available at any time. There is also an excellent wine list to complement cooking from chef and owner Oliver Smith, whose menus are driven by local, seasonal produce. An appetiser of smoked sprats and horseradish might precede a starter of potted beef, pickled prunes and Yorkshire pudding, followed by a main course of venison saddle, swede, haggis mash, wild cabbage and sloe gin. Finish with salted caramel rice pudding, rum and raisins.

Open 12-4 5-11 Closed Sun eve & Mon **Food** Lunch Tue-Sun 12-4 Dinner Tue-Sat 5-11 Set menu available ⊕ FREE HOUSE ◀ Adnams, Buntingford, Saffron, Nethergate, Red Squirrel RSX ♂ Millwhites, Aspall. ♚ 13 **Facilities** Non-diners area ♣ (Bar Garden) ♦♦ Children's menu Children's portions Garden ♬ Parking WiFi

PERRY GREEN
Map 6 TL41

The Hoops Inn

tel: 01279 843568 **SG10 6EF**
email: reservations@hoops-inn.co.uk
dir: *From Ware on B1004 towards Bishop's Stortford right onto unclassified road to Perry Green*

Stylish inn with links to famous sculptor

Once home to Henry Moore, Perry Green is dotted with his famous sculptures. This comfortable dining inn is part of the estate and it boasts a chic country decor, contemporary furnishings and Moore-inspired artefacts. The food here draws a crowd thanks to dishes such as five-spice battered soft shell crab with oriental salad; and seared haunch of venison with carrot and horseradish purée. Excellent Sunday roasts can be walked off by visiting The Henry Moore Foundation's estate just across the village green. There is a large front terrace and back garden to enjoy in the warmer weather.

Open all day 11.30-11 Closed Mon **Food** Lunch Wed-Sat 12-3, Sun 12-6 Dinner Wed-Sat 5-9.30 Set menu available Restaurant menu available Wed-Sun ⊕ FREE HOUSE ◼ Adnams Southwold Bitter, Guinness Ö Aspall. **Facilities** ◆◆ Children's menu Children's portions Garden 🎗 Beer festival Cider festival Parking 🚌 (notice required)

POTTEN END
Map 6 TL00

Martins Pond

tel: 01442 864318 **The Green HP4 2QQ**
dir: *A41 onto A416 signed Chesham, follow signs to Berkhamsted town centre. At lights straight over into Lower Kings Rd. Pass station, into Station Rd. Left at pub on opposite side of village green*

Innovative food and good walks directly from the pub

The unusual name refers to the village green where this welcoming pub is located. A section of Grim's Dyke, an ancient bank-and-ditch earthwork, is clearly visible nearby. By comparison the pub – dating from 1924 – is relatively new, but there's been a public house here since the 17th century. These days it's a good destination for home-cooked food such as smoked haddock kedgeree fishcake with curried coleslaw, followed by venison and smoked bacon meatballs, buttered Savoy cabbage, red wine and cranberry gravy.

Open all day all wk Closed 26 Dec **Food** Lunch Mon-Sat 12-2.30, Sun 12-4 Dinner Mon-Sat 6-9 ⊕ FREE HOUSE ◼ Fuller's London Pride, Red Squirrel. ☻ 13 **Facilities** Non-diners area ☻ (Bar Garden) ◆◆ Children's portions Garden 🎗 Parking WiFi

POTTERS CROUCH
Map 6 TL10

The Holly Bush

tel: 01727 851792 **AL2 3NN**
email: info@thehollybushpub.co.uk
dir: *Village accessed from A4147 & A405*

Country pub with old-world charm

Tucked away in a hamlet, The Holly Bush is a picturesque 17th-century pub with a large enclosed garden complete with wooden benches and tables. There is a delightfully welcoming atmosphere, with antique dressers, log fires and exposed beams setting the interior style. Traditional and modern pub fare is offered. At lunch there's ploughman's, baked potatoes, garden salads, deli platters, burgers and toasted sandwiches; while on the evening menu there might be farmed salmon fillet with buttered spinach, baked potato and tomato chutney; or wild mushroom, asparagus, white wine and cream pie. The pub is close to St Albans with its Roman ruins and good local walks.

Open all wk 12-2.30 6-11 (Sun 12-3) **Food** Lunch Mon-Sat 12-2, Sun 12-2.30 Dinner Wed-Sat 6-9 ⊕ FULLER'S ◼ London Pride, ESB, George Gale & Co Seafarers, Seasonal ales. **Facilities** Non-diners area ◆◆ Garden 🎗 Parking WiFi 🚌 (notice required)

SARRATT
Map 6 TQ09

The Cock Inn

tel: 01923 282908 **Church Ln WD3 6HH**
email: enquiries@cockinn.net
dir: *M25 junct 18, A404 signed Chorleywood, Amersham. Right follow signs to Sarratt. Pass church on left, pub on right*

Welcoming rustic pub oozing character and charm

A warm and friendly welcome is guaranteed at this traditional village inn standing opposite Sarratt's Norman church. Originally called the Cock Horse, the 17th-century pub is in the heart of the Chess Valley, an area favoured by walkers. It has head-cracking low beams, an inglenook fireplace and Hall & Woodhouse ales at the bar, while the ancient timbered barn houses the restaurant. Expect classic pub dishes such as cottage pie; pork and leek sausages; or liver and bacon casserole. Light bites and sandwiches are served in the bar or garden.

Open all day all wk **Food** Lunch Mon-Fri 12-2.30, Sat 12-9, Sun 12-5 Dinner Mon-Fri 6-9, Sat 12-9, Sun 12-5 Restaurant menu available Tue-Sun ⊕ HALL & WOODHOUSE ◼ Badger Tanglefoot & First Call, K&B Sussex Ö Westons Stowford Press. **Facilities** Non-diners area ☻ (Bar Restaurant Garden) ◆◆ Children's menu Children's portions Play area Garden 🎗 Parking WiFi 🚌 (notice required)

SHENLEY
Map 6 TL10

The White Horse, Shenley

tel: 01923 853054 **37 London Rd WD7 9ER**
email: enquiry@whitehorseradlett.co.uk
dir: *M25 junct 22, B556 then B5378 to Shenley*

Village pub with an interesting menu

The White Horse belies its 170-year-old foundation as a village pub, offering contemporary comforts and dining at the fringe of this green-belt village, with country walks to the Hertfordshire Way from the door. Bright, light and cheerful inside, with some quirky decor, it's an ideal place to sup a Sharp's Doom Bar bitter over a Sunday roast or crack a bottle from the extensive wine list and indulge in soft shell crab with crispy calamari, soy, ginger and chilli dip followed by pork fillet wrapped in sage and prosciutto with pistachio and blue cheese sauce, with white chocolate brûlée for dessert. There's also a children's menu.

Open all day all wk 11-11 **Food** Lunch Mon-Sat 12-10, Sun 12-9 Dinner Mon-Sat 12-10, Sun 12-9 ⊕ FREE HOUSE/MITCHELLS & BUTLERS ◼ Sharp's Doom Bar, Marston's Pedigree Ö Aspall. ☻ 12 **Facilities** Non-diners area ☻ (Bar Restaurant Garden) ◆◆ Children's menu Children's portions Garden 🎗 Parking 🚌 (notice required)

THERFIELD
Map 12 TL33

NEW The Fox and Duck

tel: 01763 287246 **The Green SG8 9PN**
email: info@thefoxandduck.co.uk
dir: *From Royston take A505 towards Baldock. At rdbt left (Therfield). 1st right signed (Therfield)*

Lovely old pub in great walking country

A quintessential country pub with plenty of original features – flagstone floors and exposed beams – The Fox and Duck is right on the village green in picturesque Therfield and ideally situated for walking the Icknield Way, which passes directly outside. Ramblers and walking groups use the pub as a start and finish point, stopping in for a pint of IPA or one of the rotating guest ales. Food wise, there's a bar menu and a carte and you can mix and match from either, maybe starting with chicken liver parfait and moving on to a trio of pork – loin, braised cheek and white pudding.

Open 12-3 5.30-11.30 (Sat-Sun all day) Closed Mon (ex BH) **Food** Lunch Tue-Fri 12-2, Sat 12-2.30, Sun 12-4 Dinner Tue-Thu 6.30-9, Fri-Sat 6.30-9.30 ⊕ GREENE KING ◖ IPA, Rotating Guest ales Ö Aspall, Rekorderlig. ♀ 18
Facilities Non-diners area ❈ (Bar Garden) ♦◗ Children's menu Children's portions Play area Garden ⋒ Parking WiFi ▭

WATTON-AT-STONE
Map 6 TL31

The Bull

tel: 01920 831032 **High St SG14 3SB**
email: info@thebullwatton.co.uk
dir: *A602 from Stevenage towards Ware. At rdbt follow Watton-at-Stone sign. Right at mini rdbt (Datchworth & Walkern) into High St. Pub on right*

Village pub infused with love and vitality by local family

The Bramley family were living in this pretty village when The Bull became available. Using their experience in managing gastro-pubs, they've made sure that this inn is once again extending warm hospitality to all-comers. Families gather for Christmas carols around the huge inglenook fireplace, Morris dancers entertain in summer, and beer and cider festivals are hosted in May and October. Seasonality is also key to the kitchen's work, together with the provenance of high-grade ingredients; rare breed meats, for example, are reared just outside the village. So expect menus of hearty British fare such as pork belly with black pudding and apple bon bons; duck leg cassoulet with toulouse sausage, root vegetables, haricot beans and fondant potato; or butternut squash and pea pappardelle.

Open all day all wk **Food** Lunch Mon-Sat 12-3, Sun 12-6 Dinner Mon-Sat 6-10 Set menu available ⊕ PUNCH TAVERNS ◖ Sharp's Doom Bar, Adnams Ghost Ship, Guest ale Ö Westons Mortimers Orchard. ♀ 10 **Facilities** Non-diners area ❈ (Garden Outside area) ♦◗ Children's menu Children's portions Play area Garden Outside area ⋒ Beer festival Cider festival Parking WiFi ▭ (notice required)

WELWYN
Map 6 TL21

The Wellington ★★★★★ INN ◉

tel: 01438 714036 **High St AL6 9LZ**
email: info@wellingtonatwelwyn.co.uk **web:** www.wellingtonatwelwyn.co.uk
dir: *A1(M) junct 6 to Welwyn*

Stylish village pub with notable food

Opposite the Saxon church in the attractive village of Welwyn, this 13th-century coaching inn offers six comfortable bedrooms alongside its one AA-Rosette food.

Inside, it's cosy and stylish but when the weather allows, grab a table on the terrace or enjoy a drink by the river at the bottom of the garden. There is plenty of choice when it comes to food, from lunchtime sandwiches and wraps to sharing plates and modern British dishes listed on the 'clipboard' menus and blackboard specials.

Open all day all wk **Food** Lunch Mon-Fri 12-3, Sat-Sun 12-10 Dinner Mon-Fri 5.30-10, Sat-Sun 12-10 Set menu available Restaurant menu available all wk ⊕ GREENE KING ◖ Morland Old Speckled Hen, Wellington Ale Ö Aspall. ♀ 37 **Facilities** Non-diners area ♦◗ Children's menu Children's portions Garden ⋒ Parking WiFi ▭ (notice required) **Rooms** 6

WELWYN GARDEN CITY
Map 6 TL21

The Brocket Arms

tel: 01438 820250 & 07867 537718 **Ayot St Lawrence AL6 9BT**
email: bookings@brocketarms.com
dir: *A1(M) junct 4 follow signs to Wheathampstead, then Shaw's Corner. Pub past Shaw's Corner on right*

Great ales in a traditional setting

Encircled by a picturesque village that was once home to George Bernard Shaw, The Brocket Arms dates in parts to 1378 when it was built as a monks' hostel; it became a tavern in the 1630s. Huge oak beams and hefty hearths greet you along with a great range of real ales and wines. Food options range from snacks such as a Scotch egg with home-made chutney through to full meals such as pan-seared scallops with caramelised cauliflower purée and parsnip crisp followed by pan-fried pork loin with black pudding mash, thyme jus and creamed leeks.

Open all day all wk 12-11 (Sun 12-10.30) **Food** Lunch all wk 12-2.30 Dinner Mon-Sat 6-9 ⊕ FREE HOUSE ◖ Nethergate Brocket Bitter, Greene King IPA & Abbot Ale, Sharp's Doom Bar, 3 Brewers, Tring Side Pocket for a Toad, Guest ales Ö Aspall, Westons Mortimers Orchard. ♀ 18 **Facilities** Non-diners area ❈ (Bar Garden) ♦◗ Children's menu Children's portions Play area Garden ⋒ Parking WiFi ▭

WEST HYDE
Map 6 TQ09

NEW The Oaks

tel: 01895 822118 **Old Uxbridge Rd WD3 9XP**
email: info@theoakspub.co.uk
dir: *From rdbt on A412 between Rickmansworth & Denham into Chalfont Ln. At T-junct right, pub on left*

Brewers' Tudor-style country pub

Surrounded by a white picket-fence, The Oaks stands on a corner, with lakes and woodland behind; handy for an outing from Harefield, Chalfont St Peter, Rickmansworth or Denham. Expect to find St Austell and Brakspear on handpump along with guest ales. A typical meal could be brochette of fried wild mushrooms, house-smoked cheddar and shallots, followed by haddock in Symonds cider batter, chips, peas and home-made tartare sauce; a 28-day-aged rump, sirloin or rib-eye steak; or honey-roast ham hock with beetroot and potato gratin, mustard and cider sauce. Snacks include spiced barbecue chicken and pulled pork sandwiches. Among the desserts, quince crème caramel is quite unusual.

Open all day all wk **Food** Contact pub for food times Set menu available ⊕ ENTERPRISE INNS ◖ St Austell Tribute, Brakspear, Guest ales. ♀ 16 **Facilities** Non-diners area ❈ (Bar Garden) ♦◗ Children's menu Children's portions Garden ⋒ Parking WiFi ▭ (notice required)

WESTON
Map 12 TL23

NEW The Cricketers

tel: 01462 790273 **Damask Green Rd SG4 7DA**
email: info@thecricketersweston.co.uk
dir: *Phone pub for detailed directions*

A warm welcome at this on-the-up pub

In situ for barely a year, landlord Howard Nye has lively plans for this village watering hole. Indeed renovations and an extension may have been completed by the time you visit. But whatever condition you find The Cricketers in, the warmest of welcomes is assured, for adults with or without children, muddy boots and dogs. The open fire, range of ales and Symonds cider, and menu of home-cooked pub food meld into the pub's relaxed ambience; the large garden and kids' play area are especially popular in the warmer months. Excellent green credentials and menus meeting gluten-free and other dietary requirements complete the picture.

Open all wk 12-2 5.30-11 (Sat 12-11 Sun 12-10) **Food** Lunch all wk 12-2.30 Dinner all wk 6-9 Av main course £9.50 ⊕ FREE HOUSE ◗ Woodforde's Wherry, Sharp's Doom Bar, Adnams Bitter Ö Symonds. **Facilities** Non-diners area ❀ (Bar Restaurant Garden) ⦿ Play area Garden ⊨ Parking WiFi ▱ (notice required)

WILLIAN
Map 12 TL23

The Fox ◉◉
PICK OF THE PUBS

tel: 01462 480233 **SG6 2AE**
email: info@foxatwillian.co.uk
dir: *A1(M) junct 9 towards Letchworth, 1st left to Willian, pub 0.5m on left*

Fine dining pub with a smart, contemporary interior

Sitting opposite the village pond and right next to the church, this imposing 18th-century pub is an award-winning destination, attracting locals, walkers and cyclists alike. A clean, crisp look defines the interior, while the laid-back bar, restaurant atrium, enclosed courtyard and two beer gardens are all pleasant places to settle down with the modern British menus. In the bar and restaurant, expect East Anglian ales such as Adnams Southwold Bitter accompanying fresh fish brought in from Norfolk and plenty of other produce sourced locally. There's lots of choice on the menus – from bar snacks such as crispy pepper squid and Brancaster Staithe oysters, to main courses of tomato and smoked mozzarella risotto or baked whole plaice with parsley new potatoes, lemon and cockle butter. Look out for 'bin end' wine deals and the themed food nights that take place throughout the year.

Open all day all wk **Food** Lunch Mon-Fri 12-2, Sat 12-6, Sun 12-3 Dinner Mon-Fri 7-9 Av main course £11.95 Restaurant menu available Mon-Sat & Sun Lunch ⊕ FREE HOUSE ◗ Adnams Southwold Bitter, Woodforde's Wherry, Sharp's Doom Bar, Brancaster Best. ☗ 15 **Facilities** Non-diners area ❀ (Bar Garden Outside area) ⦿ Children's portions Garden Outside area ⊨ Beer festival Parking WiFi ▱ (notice required)

ISLE OF WIGHT

ARRETON
Map 5 SZ58

The White Lion

tel: 01983 528479 **Main Rd PO30 3AA**
email: whitelioniow@gmail.com
dir: *On A3056 (Blackwater to Shanklin/Sandown road)*

Traditional pub food and reliable real ales

A 200-year-old coaching inn in the heart of Arreton village. Reliable ales like Doom Bar and Timothy Taylor Landlord are the top refreshments, while prices on the short wine list are commendably affordable. Food ranges from paninis and sandwiches to light bites and children's choices, and then on to classic starters, favourites main courses, and traditional desserts. A typical choice could kick off with blue cheese and Ventnor Bay crab beignets served with a port and Stilton sauce. Next may come the short-crust pie of the day from the blackboard, with a home-made berry Pavlova with crème Chantilly to finish.

Open all day all wk 11.30-11 (Sun 12-10.30) **Food** Lunch all wk 12-9.30 Dinner all wk 12-9.30 ⊕ ENTERPRISE INNS ◗ Sharp's Doom Bar, Timothy Taylor Landlord. **Facilities** Non-diners area ❀ (Bar Garden) ⦿ Children's menu Children's portions Family room Garden ⊨ Parking

BEMBRIDGE
Map 5 SZ68

The Crab & Lobster Inn ★★★★ INN

tel: 01983 872244 **32 Forelands Field Rd PO35 5TR**
email: info@crabandlobsterinn.co.uk web: www.crabandlobsterinn.co.uk
dir: *From High St in Bembridge, 1st left after Boots into Forelands Rd. At right bend, left into Lane End Rd, 2nd right into Egerton Rd. At T-junct left into Howgate Rd. Road bears right & becomes Forelands Field Rd, follow brown inn signs*

Great sea views and seafood at beamed inn

This inn is bedecked with flower baskets in summer and the stunning coastal location beside Bembridge Ledge means the raised deck and patio is a perfect place to sup locally brewed Goddards Fuggle-Dee-Dum bitter whilst watching yachts and fishing boats out in the eastern approach to the Solent. Locally caught seafood is one of the pub's great attractions, with dishes such as crab and lobster soup; hot seafood platter for two; and linguine con gamberetti e rucola. There are of course meat and vegetarian dishes too, and sandwiches at lunchtime. Some of the light and airy bedrooms have outstanding sea views.

Open all day all wk 11-11 (Sun 11-10.30) **Food** Lunch all wk 12-2.30 (wknds & BHs all day) Dinner Sun-Thu 6-9, Fri-Sat 6-9.30 (wknds & BHs all day) ⊕ ENTERPRISE INNS ◗ Sharp's Doom Bar, Goddards Fuggle-Dee-Dum, Greene King IPA Ö Westons Stowford Press. ☗ 12 **Facilities** Non-diners area ❀ (Bar Garden) ⦿ Children's menu Children's portions Garden ⊨ Parking WiFi **Rooms** 5

BEMBRIDGE *continued*

The Pilot Boat Inn

tel: 01983 872077 **Station Rd PO35 5NN**
email: george@thepilotboatinn.com
dir: *Follow B3395 (Embankment Rd) around harbour. Pub on junct with Station Rd*

Welcoming harbourside local beside coastal footpath

With a startling, quirky look of a beached ark, this lively pub makes the most of its setting beside Bembridge Harbour, with an ever-varying choice of daily seafood specials progressing straight from creel to galley. Slow-cooked lamb shank with all the trimmings is another staple at this accommodating local in what is said to be England's largest village, where beers from the Isle of Wight's own Goddards Brewery keep seafarers old and new in chatty mode. A winter fire warms the brightly appointed interior, dressed with nautical and other flags, whilst morris dancers may enliven a summer's afternoon.

Open all day all wk **Food** Lunch all wk 12-2.30 Dinner all wk 6-8.30 Restaurant menu available all wk ⊕ FREE HOUSE ◄ Goddards Ale of Wight Ö Westons Old Rosie, Stowford Press. **Facilities** Non-diners area ♥ (Bar Restaurant Garden) ♦♦ Children's menu Children's portions Garden ⋒ Parking WiFi ➡ (notice required)

| BONCHURCH | Map 5 SZ57 |

The Bonchurch Inn

tel: 01983 852611 **Bonchurch Shute PO38 1NU**
email: gillian@bonchurch-inn.co.uk
dir: *Signed from A3055 in Bonchurch*

Family-run free house with an Italian emphasis

Tucked away in a secluded Dickensian-style courtyard, this small inn is in a quiet, off-the-road location. In fact, little has changed here since this former coaching inn and stables was granted a licence in the 1840s. Food is available lunchtime and evenings in the bar; choices range from sandwiches and salads to plenty of daily-fresh fish (sea bass, pollock and crab among the choices) and traditional meat dishes. Italian specialities are a prominent feature on account of the owners' heritage; try one of the pizzas, the spinach cannelloni, or the king prawn portofino (mushrooms, Pernod, cream and rice). Desserts also have an Italian bias – perhaps zabaglione, tiramisù or cassata. If you want something not-so-Italian, there's still plenty of choice.

Open all wk 12-3 6.30-11 Closed 25 Dec **Food** Lunch all wk 12-2 Dinner all wk 6.30-9 ⊕ FREE HOUSE ◄ Courage Best Bitter, Wells Bombardier. **Facilities** Non-diners area ♥ (Bar Outside area) ♦♦ Children's menu Children's portions Family room Outside area ⋒ Parking WiFi

---

| COWES | Map 5 SZ49 |

Duke of York Inn ★★★ INN

tel: 01983 295171 **Mill Hill Rd PO31 7BT**
email: bookings@dukeofyorkcowes.co.uk **web:** www.dukeofyorkcowes.co.uk
dir: *In town centre*

Pub with a nautical theme

A former coaching inn close to Cowes town centre, ferry terminals and the marina, it has been run by the Cass family for over 40 years. Even sopping wet yachtsmen are made welcome here. Fuggle-Dee-Dum from the island's Goddards Brewery is one of several real ales, with the rest coming from the mainland. Quality home-cooked food with an emphasis on fresh seafood available in the bar and restaurant includes grilled sardines; baked sea bass; and traditional battered cod. Possible alternatives are chicken curry; several varieties of pie; and steak burgers, all home made, as well as daily blackboard specials and Sunday roasts.

Open all day all wk **Food** Lunch all wk 12-10 Dinner all wk 12-10 Restaurant menu available Mon-Sat & Sun evening ⊕ ENTERPRISE INNS ◄ Goddards Fuggle-Dee-Dum, Sharp's Doom Bar, Ringwood Best Bitter Ö Westons 1st Quality & Old Rosie. **Facilities** Non-diners area ♥ (Bar Restaurant Outside area) ♦♦ Children's menu Children's portions Outside area ⋒ Parking WiFi ➡ **Rooms** 13

The Fountain Inn ★★★ INN

tel: 01983 292397 **High St PO31 7AW**
email: 6447@greeneking.co.uk **web:** www.oldenglish.co.uk
dir: *Adjacent to Red Jet passenger ferry in town centre*

Quayside contentment at the heart of Cowes

An imposing foursquare Georgian building built to cater for travellers awaiting the mainland ferry that still plies from the dock behind the inn. Character oozes from the nooks and crannies peppering the public areas, where French King Charles X and family also took sustenance in 1830. The decking patio overlooking the bustling West Cowes Quay is a fine base at which to appreciate the Greene King beers or chow down on a robust menu of pub favourites like roasted cod loin, pan-seared black pearl scallops or Suffolk pork sausages with cheddar mash. Some of the en suite bedrooms have sea views.

Open all day all wk **Food** Lunch all wk 11-5 Dinner all wk 5-10 ⊕ GREENE KING ◄ IPA, Morland Old Golden Hen, Ferryman's Tipple Ö Aspall. ♥ **Facilities** Non-diners area ♥ (Bar Outside area) ♦♦ Children's menu Children's portions Outside area ⋒ WiFi **Rooms** 20

| FISHBOURNE | Map 5 SZ59 |

The Fishbourne ★★★★ INN

tel: 01983 882823 **Fishbourne Ln PO33 4EU**
email: info@thefishbourne.co.uk **web:** www.thefishbourne.co.uk
dir: *From East Cowes ferry terminal to rdbt. 3rd exit signed Ryde & Newport. At T-junct left onto A3021 signed Ryde & Newport. At next rdbt 1st exit signed Newport. At next rdbt 1st exit onto A3054 signed Ryde. Left at lights into Fishbourne Ln signed Portsmouth. Pass ferry terminal to pub*

Top-quality eating in a pub environment

Time your ferry crossing to Portsmouth carefully and, since it's down the same cul-de-sac as the Wightlink terminal, you'll be able to visit this mock-Tudor dining pub. A design-savvy approach to furnishing is apparent in the spacious bar, where there are smart leather sofas, and in the elegant dining area, where lunchtime sees sandwiches, baguettes, seafood specialities, deli boards and sharing platters, as well as old favourites like fish and chips, and sausage and mash. Daily-changing blackboard specials may include pork and leek sausages with mash and gravy; pie of the day; and warm chicken and bacon salad with boiled egg and ranch dressing. The en suite bedrooms are stylishly decorated with modern amenities.

Open all day all wk **Food** Lunch all wk 12-2.30 Dinner all wk 6-9.30 (varies with season) ⊕ ENTERPRISE INNS ◄ Goddards Fuggle-Dee-Dum, Sharp's Doom Bar, Ringwood Best Bitter Ö Westons Stowford Press. ♥ 12 **Facilities** Non-diners area ♦♦ Children's menu Children's portions Garden ⋒ Parking WiFi **Rooms** 5

| FRESHWATER | Map 5 SZ38 |

The Red Lion

tel: 01983 754925 **Church Place PO40 9BP**
dir: *In Old Freshwater follow signs for All Saints Church*

Friendly village pub a short walk from Yarmouth Harbour

Its two big gables and red-brick walls give no indication of its great age but, like the neighbouring church, the pub's origins go back to the 11th century. Like his predecessor, new landlord Mark McDonald serves Goddards Special Bitter and Fuggle-Dee-Dum in the shiny-flagstoned bar, where settles and sofas partner well-scrubbed pine tables. Meals feature herbs and vegetables from the pub's large garden, and many other ingredients are from elsewhere on the island or its coastal waters. Menu fixtures include crab mornay with toasted ciabatta; beer-battered fresh fish; daily changing pies; and home-made tagliatelle. Further choice is afforded by specials.

Open all wk 11-11 (Sun 11-10.30) **Food** Lunch 12-2.30 Dinner 6-9 Av main course £12 ⊕ ENTERPRISE INNS ◀ Goddards Special Bitter & Fuggle-Dee-Dum, Sharp's Doom Bar, West Berkshire Good Old Boy Ö Symonds. ♀ 12 **Facilities** Non-diners area ❀ (Bar Garden) ♦ Garden ⊨ Parking WiFi

---

| GODSHILL | Map 5 SZ58 |

The Taverners   PICK OF THE PUBS

tel: 01983 840707 **High St PO38 3HZ**
dir: Phone for detailed directions

Village pub incorporating its own food shop

At the heart of the island's prettiest village, The Taverners fits the heritage jigsaw perfectly. With heavy ribbed beams and posts, slab flooring, log fires and scrubbed rustic furnishings it's the archetypical village inn. Real ales and village-made cider are stalwarts on the bar here, where there's an impressive commitment to keeping food and drink miles low. Meats and dairy products all come from Isle of Wight farmers, fish are from local waters, island fruit and vegetables are used when in season, and much else is locally caught, shot or foraged. Time-honoured pub grub is a given, including home-made beef and ale pie; whilst the daily-changing specials open up wider horizons. Cue a starter of Egyptian-style dukka eggs with chickpea salad; progressing then to organic venison meatballs wrapped in bacon, with swede purée and curly kale. In the garden, adjoining the vegetable plots, is a toddlers' play area. The pub has its own shop selling wines and artisanal goods.

Open all day all wk Closed 1st 3wks Jan **Food** Lunch all wk 12-3 Dinner Mon-Thu 6-9, Fri-Sat 6-9.30 Av main course £11 ⊕ PUNCH TAVERNS ◀ Taverners Own, Sharp's Doom Bar, Brains The Rev. James, Black Sheep, Butcombe Ö Westons Stowford Press, Godshill. ♀ 10 **Facilities** Non-diners area ❀ (Bar Garden) ♦ Children's menu Children's portions Play area Garden ⊨ Parking WiFi ▭ (notice required)

| HULVERSTONE | Map 5 SZ38 |

The Sun Inn at Hulverstone

tel: 01983 741124 **Main Rd PO30 4EH**
email: info@sun-hulverstone.com
dir: Between Mottistone & Brook on B3399

Village-edge inn in stunning location

All flagstones, floorboards, beams, settles and fires, this lovely ancient thatched pub occupies an enviable position in the gently rolling countryside towards the western tip of the island. With English Channel views from the pleasant garden here, customers can indulge in Wight-brewed beers from Goddards and choose from a menu almost entirely sourced from the island's own producers. The village bakery, farm shop, local fishmongers and cheesemaker ensure the produce is the freshest possible. Expect to find moules marinière, deep-fried whitebait; Mottistone Farm sausages, mash and onion gravy; and 10oz local rump steak with all the trimmings, whilst the specials board details the home-made pie of the day. Different diets can be catered for, please ask. Restaurant booking is advised.

Open all day all wk **Food** Lunch all wk 12-9 Dinner all wk 12-9 ⊕ ENTERPRISE INNS ◀ Ringwood Fortyniner, Goddards Fuggle-Dee-Dum, Adnams Southwold Bitter, Otter Ale, Island Ales, Rotating ales Ö Westons Stowford Press. **Facilities** Non-diners area ❀ (Bar Garden) ♦ Children's portions Garden ⊨ Parking WiFi ▭ (notice required)

| NEWPORT | Map 5 SZ48 |

The Stag

tel: 01983 522709 **Stag Ln PO30 5TW**
email: info@thestagiow.co.uk
dir: On A3020 between Cowes & Newport

Family dining pub

New landlords Martin and Lisa Bullock arrived in December 2014 to run this pub in the middle of the island. Pale-coloured wood predominates in the attractive long bar, where Sharp's Doom Bar takes the lead and sandwiches and baguettes come with dressed salad or chips. Variously filled burgers include Eastern-spiced falafel with chilli sauce. Other attractions are salads and grills; rotisserie half-chicken; beer-battered fresh fish; beef and ale pie; local sausages with mash and rich onion gravy; and roasted beef tomato filled with Stilton and squash risotto.

Open all day all wk **Food** Lunch all wk 12-2.30 Dinner all wk 6-9 Set menu available ⊕ PUNCH TAVERNS ◀ Sharp's Doom Bar. ♀ 12 **Facilities** Non-diners area ♦ Children's portions Play area Garden ⊨ Parking WiFi

---

| NINGWOOD | Map 5 SZ38 |

Horse & Groom

tel: 01983 760672 **Main Rd PO30 4NW**
email: info@horse-and-groom.com
dir: On A3054 (Yarmouth to Newport road)

Great for families with young children

Just a couple of miles west of Yarmouth on the Newport road, this large landmark pub, now with a new landlord, is certainly family-friendly. There's a pleasant garden with a large children's play area, and an extensive and well-priced kids' menu. Food is served daily from noon until 9pm, and the offering ranges from jacket potatoes and light bites to pub favourites like home-made lasagne; steak and ale pie; and sticky toffee pudding plus a specials board offering seasonal specialities. Four-footed family members are also welcome on the stone and wood-floor indoor areas.

Open all day all wk **Food** Lunch all wk 12-9 Dinner all wk 12-9 Av main course £10 ⊕ ENTERPRISE INNS ◀ Ringwood, Sharp's Doom Bar Ö Westons Stowford Press, Somersby Cider. ♀ 11 **Facilities** Non-diners area ❀ (Bar Restaurant Garden) ♦ Children's menu Children's portions Play area Garden ⊨ Parking WiFi ▭ (notice required)

| NITON | Map 5 SZ57 |

Buddle Inn

tel: 01983 730243 **St Catherines Rd PO38 2NE**
email: sayhi@buddleinn.co.uk
dir: From Ventnor take Whitwell Rd (signed Niton). In Whitwell left after church into Kemming Rd (signed Niton). In Niton, left opposite Norris (shop), right into St Catherines Rd

Popular with hikers and ramblers

With the English Channel on one side and the coastal path on the other, this 16th-century, former cliff-top farmhouse and smugglers' inn is one of the island's oldest hostelries. The interior has the full traditional complement – stone flags, oak beams and a large open fire, great real ales on tap, and muddy boots are welcome. Expect hearty home-made food, deep-filled Buddle pies, a large specials board full of seasonal dishes, and a great variety of freshly caught local fish. Two beer festivals a year take place – in June and September.

Open all day all wk 12-10.30 (Wed 12-11 Fri-Sat 12-11.30) **Food** Lunch all wk 12-9 Dinner all wk 12-9 ⊕ ENTERPRISE INNS ◀ Sharp's Doom Bar, Yates' Dark Side of the Wight & Buddle Inn, Timothy Taylor Landlord Ö Westons Old Rosie. ♀ 12 **Facilities** Non-diners area ❀ (All areas) ♦ Children's menu Children's portions Garden Outside area ⊨ Beer festival Parking ▭ (notice required)

PICK OF THE PUBS

The New Inn

SHALFLEET   Map 5 SZ48

tel: 01983 531314
Main Rd PO30 4NS
email: info@thenew-inn.co.uk
web: www.thenew-inn.co.uk
dir: *6m from Newport towards Yarmouth on A3054*

Recommended for their seafood

Set on the National Trust-owned Newtown River estuary, this charming whitewashed pub is an absolute mecca for sailing folk. One of the island's best-known dining pubs, The New Inn's name refers to how it rose phoenix-like from the charred remains of an older hostelry, which burnt down in 1743. Original inglenook fireplaces, flagstone floors and low-beamed ceilings give the place bags of character. The waterside location sets the tone for the menu; the inn has a reputation for excellent seafood dishes, with lobster and cracked local crab usually available. Daily specials are chalked on blackboards around the place. Further fish options may include smoked salmon with home-made horseradish mayonnaise; fish pie in lemon and tarragon sauce; or the seafood Royale platter. Meat lovers could try the home-made pie of the day or Isle of Wight sirloin steak with cherry tomatoes, chestnut mushrooms, onion rings and chips. Vegetarians can enjoy the likes

of wild mushroom and roasted chestnut risotto with crispy leeks and truffle oil or tagliatelle with slow-roast tomato and saffron sauce with chilli and rocket. There's also a list of dishes for 'smaller appetites', including chicken goujons with chips and peas; and locally made sausages with chips and peas – but if it's a light lunch you're seeking, be sure to consider the best-selling hand-picked crabmeat sandwiches and baguettes or the ploughman's featuring local cheeses and home-made chutneys. At the bar you'll find Goddards Fuggle-Dee-Dum and Cornish Sharp's Doom Bar among others, Westons Stowford Press cider and over 60 worldwide wines comprise one of the island's most extensive selections.

Open all day all wk **Food** Lunch Mon-Sat 12-2.30, Sun 12-3 Dinner all wk 6-9.30 (varies with season) ⊕ ENTERPRISE INNS ◼ Goddards Fuggle-Dee-Dum, Sharp's Doom Bar ♉ Westons Stowford Press. ♟ 11 **Facilities** ✿ (Bar Garden) ⁛ Children's menu Children's portions Garden ⨝ Parking WiFi

NORTHWOOD
Map 5 SZ49

Travellers Joy

tel: 01983 298024 **85 Pallance Rd PO31 8LS**
email: thetravellersjoy@hotmail.co.uk
dir: *Phone for detailed directions*

Family-friendly haven for ale lovers

A little way inland from Cowes, this 300-year-old alehouse is known for its eight real ales on handpump all year round; there's a great selection of real ciders too, and beer festivals in July and September. Classic home-made pub dishes are the mainstays of the menu, with local sourcing and seasonal availability playing their part. Expect the likes of fishcakes with sweet chilli sauce and cucumber salad, followed by creamy chicken and bacon tagliatelle with garlic bread. The appeal is to all-comers – from walkers and cyclists to locals and tourists, especially families. So children, smaller appetites, vegetarians and coeliacs are all well catered for.

Open all day all wk 12-12 **Food** Lunch all wk 12-9 Dinner all wk 12-9 Av main course £8.95 ⊕ FREE HOUSE ◀ Island Wight Gold, Courage Directors, Caledonian Deuchars IPA, St Austell Tribute, Timothy Taylor Landlord, Goddards Wight Squirrel, Brains The Rev. James, Theakston Old Peculier ○ Biddenden Bushels, Westons Old Rosie & Family Reserve, Scrumpy. ♟ 9 **Facilities** Non-diners area ❄ (Bar Garden) ♦ Children's menu Children's portions Play area Garden ⚲ Beer festival Parking WiFi ▭ (notice required)

SEAVIEW
Map 5 SZ69

The Boathouse ★★★★ INN

tel: 01983 810616 **Springvale Rd PO34 5AW**
email: info@theboathouseiow.co.uk **web:** www.theboathouseiow.co.uk
dir: *From Ryde take A3055. Left onto A3330, left into Puckpool Hill. Pub 0.25m on right*

Watch the ocean liners from this seaside location

At the rather chic and certainly aptly-named Seaview, the powder-blue-painted Boathouse overlooks the eastern Solent. The setting really is spectacular. Well-kept ales and an extensive global wine listing complement specials boards that make the most of freshly landed local fish. Other choices include lunchtime baguettes and sandwiches; Isle of Wight reared rump and rib-eye steaks; whole cracked crab salad; cold seafood platter for two; and the Boathouse fisherman's pie. Children might like dishes such as sausages with chips and peas; or breaded whole-tail scampi, chips, peas and home-made tartare sauce. Sea views are available in some of the stylish en suite bedrooms.

Open all day all wk 9am-11pm (varies with season) **Food** Lunch all week 12-2.30 Dinner all week 6-9.30 (varies with season) Set menu available ⊕ PUNCH TAVERNS ◀ Sharp's Doom Bar, Goddards ○ Westons Stowford Press. ♟ 12 **Facilities** Non-diners area ♦ Children's menu Children's portions Garden ⚲ Parking WiFi **Rooms** 4

Find out more about the AA's accommodation rating schemes on page 8

The Seaview Hotel & Restaurant
PICK OF THE PUBS

tel: 01983 612711 **High St PO34 5EX**
email: reception@seaviewhotel.co.uk
dir: *B3330 from Ryde, left signed Puckpool, along seafront, hotel on left*

Great combination of coastal views and island produce

One of life's great pleasures has to be sitting on the terrace outside here, sipping beer from Wight brewers like Yates and drinking in the views over racing dinghies to one of the Solent's remarkable sea forts. Warm and welcoming, The Pump Bar is a hidden gem and perfect for ladies who lunch, old friends spinning yarns or families chilling out; its decor reflects the seaside location with a quirky selection of lobster pots, oars, masts and other nautical memorabilia. Fittingly, seafood features strongly on the menu, with a smoked haddock Scotch egg with curry mayonnaise starter or Ale of Wight fish and chips ticking all the right boxes. The owners raise deer, highland cattle and pigs on their farm, ensuring traceability and top quality for the carte and specials. Salt-beef hash, spinach, fried egg and HP sauce; poached pigs' cheeks, Savoy cabbage and mash; and cheddar and stout rarebit, fried hen's egg and pickled red onion are typical of the choices.

Open all wk 10-3 6-11 **Food** Lunch all wk 12-2.30 Dinner all wk 6.30-9.30 Av main course £9.95 Set menu available Restaurant menu available all wk ⊕ FREE HOUSE ◀ Goddards, Island Ales, Yates ○ Westons Stowford Press. **Facilities** Non-diners area ❄ (Bar Restaurant Outside area) ♦ Children's menu Children's portions Outside area ⚲ Parking WiFi

SHALFLEET
Map 5 SZ48

The New Inn
PICK OF THE PUBS

See Pick of the Pubs on opposite page

SHORWELL
Map 5 SZ48

The Crown Inn
PICK OF THE PUBS

See Pick of the Pubs on page 276

WHIPPINGHAM
Map 5 SZ59

The Folly

tel: 01983 297171 **Folly Ln PO32 6NB**
dir: *Phone for detailed directions*

Extensive menus and a large beer garden

The Folly stands beside the River Medina and you can, if you wish, travel here from Cowes on the pub's own waterbus. In the bar are timbers from the hull of an old barge, and even the restaurant tables are named after boats. The menus offer a wide choice of lighter bites – sandwiches, wraps, jacket potatoes and salads – as well as 'ultimate' burgers, steaks and grills, and classic pub grub. In addition, there are sharing plates, daily specials and international mains such as chicken tikka masala; beef lasagne; and sizzling chicken fajitas. Wednesday evening is 'Get Spicy' curry night.

Open all day all wk **Food** Lunch all wk 12-5 Dinner all wk 5-10 Set menu available ⊕ GREENE KING ◀ Abbot Ale, IPA, Morland Old Speckled Hen ○ Aspall. ♟ 11 **Facilities** Non-diners area ❄ (All areas) ♦ Children's menu Children's portions Garden Outside area ⚲ Parking WiFi ▭ (notice required)

PICK OF THE PUBS

The Crown Inn

SHORWELL Map 5 SZ48

tel: 01983 740293 **Walkers Ln PO30 3JZ**
email: enquiries@crowninnshorwell.co.uk
web: www.crowninnshorwell.co.uk
dir: *Left at top of Carisbrooke High
Street. Shorwell approx 6m*

Family-friendly village pub beside a delightful stream

A traditional country pub in the pretty
village of Shorwell, a short hop south-
west from Newport. After World War II,
the Crown was one of the first pubs to
boast an island-wide trade thanks to
the entertainment value of its then
landlord, Vivian 'Nutty' Edwards, who
entertained customers nightly with his
music hall approach to tales from his
army days; Nutty retired in the 1960s to
become the island's last Chelsea
Pensioner. Today's owners, Nigel and
Pamela Wynne, are continuing this
heritage of welcoming hospitality, with
a family-friendly approach throughout
the all-day operation. The rear garden
boasts a children's play area, bounded
by a spring-fed stream where trout,
ducks and moorhens can be spotted.
Parts of the Crown date from the 17th
century, although its varying floor levels
suggest many subsequent alterations.
The most recent building work has
increased the floor area significantly,
but the pub's character has been
preserved with log fires burning and
antique furniture in abundance. Real

ales include Goddards that's brewed on
the island, while cider comes from
Healey's Farm in Cornwall. If you
overindulge, you might glimpse the
female ghost who is friendly but shows
her disapproval of customers playing
cards by throwing them on the floor (the
cards, that is, not the customers). The
kitchen makes good use of locally
sourced lamb, beef, game and fish in
daily specials. Otherwise pub staples
include lasagne, curries, scampi or
beer-battered fish with chips, a range of
pizzas, and sausages with mash.
Steaks, gammon and burgers from the
chargrill are understandably popular,
but vegetarian choice is good too with
dishes such as wild mushroom and
spinach gratin.

Open all day all wk **Food** all wk 12-9.30
Av main course £10 ⊕ ENTERPRISE INNS
◀ Sharp's Doom Bar, Adnams
Broadside, Goddards, St Austell Tribute
Ŏ Westons Stowford Press, Healey's.
♟ 12 **Facilities** Non-diners area ❤ (Bar
Restaurant Garden) ♦ Children's menu
Children's portions Play area Garden ☶
Parking WiFi ▭ (notice required)

KENT

BADLESMERE
Map 7 TR05

NEW The Red Lion

tel: 01233 740320 **Ashford Rd, Badlesmere Lees ME13 0NX**
email: theredlionbadlesmere@gmail.com
dir: *M2 junct 6, A251 towards Ashford. Approx 5m to Badlesmere Lees*

Family- and dog-friendly free house with large garden

Built as a farmhouse in 1546, and an inn since 1728, today's pub is known for affordable home-cooked food and locally brewed beers, and as a live-music venue. Diners after something regional should try a Kentish huffkin, a traditional stone-ground flour bread roll with Kentish Blue cheese and spiced plum chutney. Or there's lamb hotpot and moglai lamb curry – the animals reared on the Kentish salt-marshes. Alternatives are locally shot pheasant in rich red wine and port sauce; fresh cod, smoked haddock and salmon fish pie; and breadcrumb-topped cauliflower, broccoli and leeks with mature cheddar sauce. Beer festivals are held throughout the year.

Open all day 12-11 (Sun-Mon 12-7) Closed Sun eve & Mon eve **Food** Lunch all wk 12-3 Dinner Tue-Sat 6.30-9 Av main course £9.50 ⊕ FREE HOUSE ◀ Gadds' The Ramsgate No 7, Shepherd Neame Master Brew ♂ Kentish Pip. ☂ 10 **Facilities** Non-diners area ❤ (Bar Restaurant Garden) ♦♦ Children's menu Children's portions Garden ⊓ Beer festival Parking WiFi ▥ (notice required)

BEARSTED
Map 7 TQ85

The Oak on the Green

tel: 01622 737976 **Bearsted Green ME14 4EJ**
email: headoffice@villagegreenrestaurants.com
dir: *In village centre*

Beefy treats beside the village green

Kentish hops drape the beams in this lively old pub, which dates from 1665 and is known for its good quality menu and the sometimes unusual real ales. The oak-shaded terrace overlooks a corner of the immense village green and cricket pitch, great for those long summer evenings. The kitchens were once the village gaol; escaping from them today are freshly-prepared dishes with a distinct nod towards Scottish beef – the steaks are impressive, from the 28- to 35-day dry-aged rib eye to the 28-day dry-aged fillet. For dessert, try the gypsy tart or warm chocolate fudge cake.

Open all day all wk Closed 25 Dec **Food** Lunch Mon-Sat 12-10.30, Sun 12-10 Dinner Mon-Sat 12-10.30, Sun 12-10 ⊕ FREE HOUSE ◀ Harvey's Sussex Best Bitter, Old Dairy Red Top & Guest ale ♂ Biddenden. ☂ **Facilities** Non-diners area ❤ (Bar Restaurant Outside area) ♦♦ Children's menu Children's portions Outside area ⊓ Parking WiFi ▥

BENENDEN
Map 7 TQ83

The Bull at Benenden
PICK OF THE PUBS

tel: 01580 240054 **The Street TN17 4DE**
email: enquiries@thebullatbenenden.co.uk
dir: *From A229 onto B2086 to Benenden. Or from Tenterden take A28 S towards Hastings. Right onto B2086*

One for all the family

Set in a lovely village in the Kentish Weald, The Bull dates back to 1601 and overlooks the village green. Hard-to-miss features include the unusual chinoiserie windows, the huge brick inglenook fireplace, the rounded wooden bar, and the antique furniture collection. Dark Star, Harvey's and Larkins breweries man the pumps, with Biddenden's own Bushels cider also ready for duty. The traditional pub

menu offers scampi and chips in a basket; a hearty ploughman's; steak of the day; and Mrs Bull's home-made pies and suet puddings with a top, bottom and side. Mr Bull lends his name to a range of burgers, including Moroccan spiced lamb; chickpea and bean; and American beef with Monterey Jack cheese. For children there's wholetail scampi, home-cooked ham with free-range eggs, and pasta pomodoro. Colouring pens and paper, and high chairs are also provided. Outside is a 'secret' garden.

Open all day all wk 12-12 **Food** Lunch Mon-Sat 12-2.30, Sun 12-4 Dinner Mon-Sat 6-9.20 Set menu available ⊕ FREE HOUSE ◀ Dark Star Hophead, Larkins, Harvey's, Guest ales ♂ Biddenden Bushels. ☂ 9 **Facilities** Non-diners area ❤ (Bar Garden) ♦♦ Children's menu Children's portions Garden ⊓ Parking ▥ (notice required)

BIDBOROUGH
Map 6 TQ54

NEW The Kentish Hare ◉◉

tel: 01892 525709 **95 Ridborough Ridge TN3 0XB**
email: enquiries@thekentishhare.com
dir: *Phone pub for detailed directions*

Family-friendly pub where under-fives eat free

The impressive CVs of chefs and brothers James and Chris Tanner log their numerous prestigious assignments to include Britain, France and the USA. They care passionately about where their food comes from (Kent, of course). Curried gurnard is served with spiced lentils, cucumber and honey yogurt; duck breast comes with orange and caramel glaze, turnips, kale and pommes Anna; and caramelised cauliflower floret risotto with pine nuts and truffle oil. From Kamado Joe's grill you can order a 16oz Chateaubriand. House-brewed real ale The Kentish Hare joins Harvey's Sussex and cider from the Kent village of Biddenden.

Open 11-3 5-11 (Sat 11-11 Sun 11-4) Closed 2-9 Jan, Sun eve & Mon **Food** Lunch Tue-Sun 12-2.30 Dinner Tue-Sat 6-9.30 Set menu available Restaurant menu available Tue-Sun ⊕ FREE HOUSE ◀ Harvey's, The Kentish Hare ♂ Biddenden. ☂ 29 **Facilities** Non-diners area ♦♦ Children's menu Children's portions Garden ⊓ Parking WiFi

BIDDENDEN
Map 7 TQ83

The Three Chimneys
PICK OF THE PUBS

tel: 01580 291472 **Biddenden Rd TN27 8LW**
email: info@thethreechimneys.co.uk
dir: *From A262 midway between Biddenden & Sissinghurst, follow Frittenden signs. (Pub visible from main road). Pub immediately on left*

Pretty village pub with excellent cooking

Its original small-roomed layout and old-fashioned furnishings make this 15th-century timbered pub a classic. Further atmosphere is provided by low beams, wood-panelled walls, worn brick floors, log fires, evening candlelight and nothing electronic except the till. From the Garden Room and conservatory customers can access the secluded heated patio and huge shrub-filled garden. Bar snacks are served all day, but the kitchen is at the top of its game so a meal here should not disappoint. You could start with three cheese risotto balls on a tomato and basil sauce, or Kentish blue cheese rarebit on toast with a salad of poached pear and walnuts. Continue with pan-roasted fillet of haddock on creamed leeks and crushed new potatoes. Harvey's and Adnams ales and the heady (8.4 per cent ABV) Biddenden cider are tapped direct from the cask. The village sign depicts The Biddenden Maids, who were conjoined twins born here in 1100.

Open all day all wk 11.30-11 Closed 25 Dec **Food** Lunch all wk 12-3 Dinner all wk 6.30-9.30 Av main course £10 Restaurant menu available all wk ⊕ FREE HOUSE ◀ Harvey's Sussex Old Ale, Adnams ♂ Biddenden. ☂ 10 **Facilities** Non-diners area ❤ (Bar Garden) ♦♦ Children's portions Garden ⊓ Parking WiFi

BRABOURNE
Map 7 TR14

The Five Bells Inn

tel: 01303 813334 **The Street TN25 5LP**
email: visitus@fivebellsinnbrabourne.com
dir: *5m E of Ashford*

Blowing the trumpet for fine Kent produce

Environmental responsibility is important to the owners of this old village inn which trims the North Downs. Locally sourced wood supplies 25% of the energy here, whilst most of the food and drink is traceable locally. Thus the beers travel the few miles from Goacher's Maidstone brewery, wines are from Biddenden, meats arrive from Kent's Romney Marsh or the Alkham Valley, and seafood from boats at Hythe. Tempting in ramblers from the popular walking country hereabouts may be Kentish blue cheese soufflé; chestnut-roasted pork ribs (to share); or apple, thyme and almond crumble and Calvados cream. The on-site deli/shop is a trove of all things comestible and Kentish.

Open all day all wk **Food** Contact pub for food times ⊕ FREE HOUSE ◀ Goacher's, Hopdaemon, Brabourne Stout, Guest ales Ö Biddenden. **Facilities** Non-diners area ❤ (All areas) ◀ Children's portions Garden Outside area ⋈ Parking WiFi ➡ (notice required)

CANTERBURY
Map 7 TR15

The Chapter Arms

tel: 01227 738340 **New Town St, Chartham Hatch CT4 7LT**
email: info@chapterarms.com
dir: *A28 from Canterbury towards Ashford. Right signed Chartham Hatch. 1m to pub*

An acre of gardens and a talented kitchen team

This charming and picturesque free house was once three cottages owned by Canterbury Cathedral's Dean and Chapter – hence the name. It sits on the North Downs Way overlooking apple orchards and oast houses. The à la carte includes beef fillet carpaccio with blue cheese purée; and red wine marinated fig with goats' cheese and walnut salad to start, followed by game venison haunch steak, dauphinoise potatoes and thyme and crushed pepper sauce; and pea and mint risotto. A barbecue is available for special events. Look out for the Spoofers' Bar, where you can enjoy a game of spoof; The Chapter Arms hosted the World Spoofing Championships a few years ago and was featured in Rory McGrath and Will Mellor's TV programme *Champions of the World.*

Open all wk 11-3 6-11 (Sun 12-5) **Food** Lunch all wk 12-2.30 Dinner Mon-Sat 6.30-9 Set menu available Restaurant menu available Tue-Sun ⊕ FREE HOUSE ◀ Greene King IPA & London Glory, Seasonal Ales Ö Thatchers. ♚ 10 **Facilities** Non-diners area ❤ (Bar Garden) ◀ Children's menu Children's portions Play area Garden ⋈ Parking WiFi ➡

The Dove Inn ◉
PICK OF THE PUBS

See Pick of the Pubs on opposite page

NEW Duke of Cumberland ★★★ INN

tel: 01227 831396 **The Street, Barham CT4 6NY**
email: info@dukeofcumberland.co.uk **web:** www.dukeofcumberland.co.uk
dir: *A2 from Canterbury towards Dover. Follow Barham signs. In village centre into The Street. Pub 200yds on left*

Pub grub in a village near Canterbury

A traditional country inn, the Duke of Cumberland was built in 1749 and has been licensed to sell ale since 1766. It's named after the commander of the English army

victorious at Culloden, although no one knows exactly why. You'll find a good choice of ales in the bar, including Greene King IPA, St Austell Tribute and Harvey's Sussex Best. If you're peckish there's a selection of sandwiches available, or go all out with crispy whitebait followed by a 10oz rib-eye steak and chips, or the Duke burger. There's a great children's play area, and bedrooms if you want to stay over. There's a beer festival in July or August.

Open all day all wk 12-11 (Fri-Sat 12-12 Jan-Feb Mon-Fri 12-3 5-11) **Food** Lunch Mon-Fri 12-3, Sat-Sun 12-9 Dinner Mon-Fri 6-9, Sat-Sun 12-9 Av main course £11 Set menu available ⊕ PUNCH TAVERNS ◀ Greene King IPA, St Austell Tribute, Harvey's Sussex Best Bitter, Timothy Taylor Landlord Ö Thatchers Gold, Kingswood, Kentish Pip. **Facilities** Non-diners area ❤ (Bar Garden) ◀ Children's menu Children's portions Play area Garden Beer festival Parking WiFi ➡ (notice required) **Rooms** 3

The Granville

tel: 01227 700402 **Street End, Lower Hardres CT4 7AL**
email: thegranville.canterbury@gmail.com
dir: *On B2068, 2m from Canterbury towards Hythe*

Ever-changing art at pub with contemporary character

As well as a striking feature central fireplace/flue, this light and airy pub not far from Canterbury displays an interesting series of roll-over art exhibitions and installations (lino cuts, photographs, sculptures). Ample parking, a patio and large beer garden where summer barbecues take place make this Shepherd Neame pub good for families and dogs, whilst locals head for the public bar. The kitchen team has a confident approach to utilising the best that Kent and the enfolding seas can provide. You could start with warm salad of teal, beetroot and orange, followed perhaps by roast venison haunch with celeriac and wild mushrooms; or roast cod fillet with tartare sauce. Finish with roast plums on French toast with cinnamon ice cream.

Open all wk 12-3.30 5.30-11 Closed 25-26 Dec **Food** Lunch Tue-Sat 12-2.30 Dinner Tue-Sat 6.30-9 Set menu available Restaurant menu available Tue-Sun ⊕ SHEPHERD NEAME ◀ Master Brew, Seasonal ale Ö Thatchers. **Facilities** Non-diners area ❤ (Bar Garden) ◀ Children's portions Garden ⋈ Parking WiFi

The Red Lion
PICK OF THE PUBS

tel: 01227 721339 **Stodmarsh CT3 4BA**
email: info@theredlionstodmarsh.com
dir: *From Canterbury take A257 towards Sandwich, left into Stodmarsh Rd to Stodmarsh*

Modern British food in a pretty Kent village

An inn full of character on the edge of the renowned Stodmarsh National Nature Reserve, where rare raptors and waterbirds co-exist amidst tidal creeks and reedy marshland. The Red Lion is also ideally placed for explorers keen to escape the busy medieval streets of nearby Canterbury. Kent-boarding and hang-tiling catch the eye outside; the inside is busy with ephemera, boarded flooring and beams dressed with hop-bines, with gravity-dispensed beers stillaged behind the bar. Add cracking log fires in winter and a secluded, flowery beer garden for long summer days; the scene is completed by a menu of solidly British dishes with a modern twist. Typically a starter of sloe gin cured salmon with rye bread and dill cream, followed by a mains choice of braised shin of veal with celeriac, saffron and tomato risotto; or oxtail slow cooked in ale for eight hours.

Open all day 11.30-11 (Sat 11.30-11.30 Sun 12-5) Closed Sun eve **Food** Lunch Mon-Sat 11.30-2.30, Sun 12-3.30 Dinner Mon-Sat 6.30-9 ⊕ FREE HOUSE ◀ Greene King IPA, Sharp's, Wantsum Ö Thatchers. **Facilities** Non-diners area ❤ (Bar Restaurant Garden) ◀ Children's menu Children's portions Play area Family room Garden ⋈ Parking WiFi ➡

PICK OF THE PUBS

The Dove Inn ❀

tel: 01227 751360
Plum Pudding Ln, Dargate ME13 9HB
email: bookings@thedovedargate.co.uk
web: www.thedovedargate.co.uk
dir: *6m from Canterbury; 4m from Whitstable. Phone for detailed directions*

Friendly village pub that welcomes walkers, families and dogs

About halfway between Faversham and Whitstable, this single-gabled, 18th-century village inn stands amid wooded hills and fruit orchards – this is the Garden of England, after all. It's run by Chris, Dee and Ben who, within its matchboarded, wooden-floored and log-stove-warmed interior, have created comfortable surroundings in which to enjoy a simple tea or coffee, light lunch or full-blown dinner. Sitting at country-style, candlelit tables, diners may study menus offering a balanced choice of AA Rosette-awarded, contemporary country dishes that make maximum use of quality local produce. Bearing in mind that dishes change, the menu might list starters of chicken liver parfait with red onion jam and sourdough toast; and hand-dived scallops with black pudding, pea velouté and bacon crisps. To follow, choices might include venison sausages with black pudding mash, green beans and red wine jus; or pan-roasted salmon with pommes purée,

sautéed new potatoes, smoked bacon and samphire. For vegetarians, gnocchi with pesto, wilted spinach, smoked goats' cheese and semi-dried tomatoes. In addition to a cheeseboard, desserts include chocolate brownie with vanilla ice cream; and orange and cardamom crème brûlée. Outside is a gorgeous cottage garden where – don't be too surprised – a dovecote complete with doves makes an agreeable backdrop for enjoying a real ale from Shepherd Neame. Here too is the pitch where during the summer a Dove team plays 'bat and trap', an old pub game that survives in Kent. There's live music on the last Friday of the month, outside or inside depending on the season, while on the last Sunday of the month, classic car owners turn up for a barbecue.

Open 12-3 6-12 (Fri 12-12 Sun 12-5) Closed Mon **Food** Lunch Wed-Sat 12-2.30 Dinner Wed-Sat 6.30-9 ⊕ SHEPHERD NEAME ◖ Master Brew, Spitfire, Whitstable Pale Ale, Seasonal ales. ♟ 10 **Facilities** Non-diners area ❖ (Bar Garden) ♦♦ Children's portions Garden ⚹ Parking WiFi ▭ (notice required)

CHIDDINGSTONE
Map 6 TQ54

Castle Inn
PICK OF THE PUBS

See Pick of the Pubs on opposite page

CHILHAM
Map 7 TR05

The White Horse

tel: 01227 730355 **The Square CT4 8BY**
email: thewhitehorsechilham@outlook.com
dir: *Take A28 from Canterbury then A252, in 1m turn left*

One of the most photographed pubs in Britain

The White Horse is situated opposite Chilham Castle in the 15th-century village square that is a delightfully haphazard mix of gabled, half-timbered houses, shops, and inns dating from the late Middle Ages – it's often used as a film location. This 'chocolate box' inn, newly redecorated, offers a traditional atmosphere and a wide selection of real ales from breweries like Sharp's, White Horse and Shepherd Neame. The modern cooking is based on fresh local produce. The bar menu offers a variety of sandwiches, ploughman's and dishes like pie of the week and vegetable curry. An evening menu might tempt with duo of Ardennes and Brussels pâté; chicken cake and home-made lemon mayo; and dark and white chocolate mousse.

Open all day all wk 12–12 Closed 25 Dec eve **Food** Lunch Mon-Fri 12–3, Sat 12–8, Sun 12–4 Dinner Mon-Fri 6–9, Sat 12–8 Av main course £8.95 Set menu available Restaurant menu available all wk ⊕ ENTERPRISE INNS ◀ Shepherd Neame Master Brew, Sharp's Doom Bar, White Horse Ale, Guest ale ♂ Thatchers Gold. ♟ 10 **Facilities** Non-diners area ✿ (All areas) ♦♦ Children's menu Children's portions Garden Outside area ♫ Beer festival Parking WiFi ☕ (notice required)

CHIPSTEAD
Map 6 TQ55

George & Dragon

tel: 01732 779019 **39 High St TN13 2RW**
email: info@georgeanddragonchipstead.com
dir: *Phone for detailed directions*

Sincerity in everything is the watchword here

The delights of this 16th-century village gastro-pub are easily summarised: the welcoming open fires, the heavy oak beams and solid furnishings; the splendidly beamed upstairs restaurant; and the tree-house-inspired private dining room. Then there's Westerham Brewery's specially-produced George's Marvellous Medicine ale; and finally, the food, using top free-range or organic meats from farms in Kent and neighbouring counties, and sustainable fish from south-east coastal waters. Daily-changing menus might list grilled skate wing with lemon and caper butter; seared haunch of Chart Farm venison with Jerusalem artichoke and truffle; and beetroot and goats' cheese risotto.

Open all day all wk 11–11 Closed 1 Jan **Food** Lunch Mon-Fri 12–3, Sat-Sun 12–4 Dinner Mon-Sat 6–9.30, Sun 6–8.30 ⊕ FREE HOUSE ◀ Westerham George's Marvellous Medicine & Grasshopper ♂ Westons Stowford Press. ♟ 18 **Facilities** Non-diners area ✿ (Bar Garden) ♦♦ Children's menu Children's portions Play area Garden ♫ Parking WiFi ☕ (notice required)

Looking for a beer or cider festival?
Check our listings at the end of this guide

CRANBROOK
Map 7 TQ73

The George Hotel

tel: 01580 713348 **Stone St TN17 3HE**
email: georgehotel@shepherd-neame.co.uk
dir: *From A21 follow signs to Goudhurst. At large rdbt take 3rd exit to Cranbrook (A229). Hotel on left*

Former courthouse offers brasserie and restaurant dining

One of Cranbrook's landmark buildings, the 14th-century George Hotel traditionally served visiting buyers of locally-made Cranbrook cloth. Magistrates held court here for over 300 years, and today the sophisticated interior mixes period features with contemporary decor. Two separate menus have been created; the brasserie offers a take on classic English cuisine – grilled veal escalope with crushed sweet potatoes, grilled vegetables and a port jus, perhaps, while in the restaurant diners can sample modern English dishes like pan-roasted lamb noisettes with dauphinoise potatoes, chicory, red onion and apricot Tatin and rosemary jus.

Open all day all wk **Food** Lunch all wk 12–3 Dinner Mon-Sat 6–9.30, Sun 6–9 Restaurant menu available ⊕ SHEPHERD NEAME ◀ Master Brew, Spitfire, Whitstable Bay, Seasonal ales ♂ Symonds. ♟ 10 **Facilities** Non-diners area ✿ (Bar Outside area) ♦♦ Children's menu Children's portions Outside area ♫ Parking WiFi ☕ (notice required)

DARTFORD
Map 6 TQ57

The Rising Sun Inn ★★★ INN

tel: 01474 872291 **Fawkham Green, Fawkham, Longfield DA3 8NL**
web: www.risingsun-fawkham.co.uk
dir: *0.5m from Brands Hatch Racing Circuit & 5m from Dartford*

Traditional 16th-century pub opposite the village green

Standing on the green in a picturesque village not far from Brands Hatch, The Rising Sun is a 16th-century building, which has been a pub since 1702. Inside you will find a bar full of character, complete with inglenook log fire, and Inglenooks restaurant where home-made traditional house specials and a large fresh fish menu, using the best local produce, are served. Among the mains you may find a selection of steaks; pork fillet with Stilton, bacon and chives wrapped in Parma ham; veal with paprika sauce; and lamb shank with a redcurrant jus. There is also a front patio and garden for alfresco dining in warmer weather, plus comfortable en suite bedrooms if you would like to stay over.

Open all day all wk **Food** Contact pub for food times Av main course £9.90 Set menu available Restaurant menu available all wk ⊕ FREE HOUSE ◀ Courage Best Bitter & Directors, Fuller's London Pride, Sharp's Doom Bar. ♟ 9 **Facilities** Non-diners area ♦♦ Children's portions Garden ♫ Parking WiFi ☕ (notice required) **Rooms** 5

PICK OF THE PUBS

Castle Inn

CHIDDINGSTONE Map 6 TQ54

tel: 01892 870247 **TN8 7AH**
email: info@castleinn-kent.co.uk
web: www.castleinn-kent.co.uk
dir: *1.5m S of B2027 between Tonbridge & Edenbridge*

Historic inn in film-set village

Arguably one of England's prettiest villages, Chiddingstone is a fine example of a Tudor one-street village. To ensure its preservation, the National Trust bought it in 1939, part of the deal included the Castle Inn, built in 1420 when it was known as Waterslip House. It was over three centuries later that two brothers opened it as the Five Bells. Timber-framed and tile-hung, the inn — indeed, the whole village — may seem familiar, because it has been the backdrop to numerous films requiring scenes of a rural England now largely vanished. The heavily beamed saloon bar serves beers from Larkins, brewed a few hundred yards away, and Harvey's from Lewes in neighbouring East Sussex; about 150 wines are on the wine list. Although chef John McManus is also the proprietor, it's really because of what he and his team do in the kitchen and restaurant that attracts the most attention. For a start, they ensure a good lunchtime range of bar snacks and main and light meals, from a ploughman's to smoked haddock fishcake, and specials too. There's also

plenty of choice at dinner: start maybe with grilled goats' cheese, crispy shallot, Puy lentil and sage salad with piccalilli; follow with whole baked plaice with crayfish, capers, lemon and samphire; or Kentish rib-eye steak, triple cooked chips, garlic butter and rocket; and finish with treacle tart, almonds and Chantilly cream. On Sundays a set three-course lunch might feature crayfish cocktail; sirloin of Kentish beef with crispy roast potatoes, Yorkshire pudding and pan gravy; and lemon posset with home-made shortbread. Behind the inn is a vine-hung courtyard with its own bar, then over a bridge are a beautifully tended lawn and flowerbeds.

Open all day all wk 11-11 (Sun 12-10.30) **Food** Lunch Mon-Fri 12-2, Sat-Sun 12-4 Dinner Mon-Sat 7-9.30 ⊕ FREE HOUSE ◀ Larkins Traditional, Porter & Platinum Blonde, Harvey's Sussex Ö Westons Stowford Press. ♛ 9 **Facilities** Non-diners area ❤ (Bar Garden) ❂ Children's menu Children's portions Garden ⋒ WiFi 🚐 (notice required)

FAVERSHAM

Map 7 TR06

Albion Taverna

tel: 01795 591411 **29 Front Brents ME13 7DH**
email: contact@albiontaverna.com
dir: *Phone for detailed directions*

Mexican and English cook house on the waterfront

Located next to the Shepherd Neame Brewery near the Faversham swing bridge, the Albion Taverna looks directly onto the attractive waterfront area. The colourful menu is a combination of Mexican and English dishes. On the Mexican side are fajitas and quesadillas with a choice of fillings, enchiladas, nachos, buffalo wings, marinated ribs, chipotle meatballs and beef or bean chilli pots. English options include a gourmet beefburger; scampi and chips; and egg, ham and chips. Other treats are mussels cooked country style, Thai style or Mexican style. For dessert, try churros with dark chocolate fondue. There is an annual hop festival in early September.

Open all wk 12-3 6-11.30 (Sat-Sun 12-11.30) **Food** Contact pub for food times ⊕ SHEPHERD NEAME ◀ Master Brew, Whitstable Bay, Early Bird, IPA Ö Thatchers Gold. ♟ **Facilities** Non-diners area ♥ (Garden) ♦♦ Children's menu Children's portions Play area Garden ♬ Beer festival Parking WiFi ➡ (notice required)

Shipwright's Arms

PICK OF THE PUBS

tel: 01795 590088 **Hollowshore ME13 7TU**
dir: *A2 through Ospringe then right at rdbt. Right at T-junct then left opposite Davington School, follow signs*

Walk in the footsteps of pirates, smugglers and sailors

The creekside Shipwright's Arms was first licensed in 1738, when the brick and weatherboarded pub's remote location on the Swale Marshes made it a popular haunt for briny ne'er-do-wells; it's been a favoured watering hole for sailors and fishermen ever since. Best reached on foot or by boat, the effort in getting here is well rewarded, as this charming and unspoilt tavern oozes historic character. Step back in time in the relaxed and comfortable bars, which boast nooks and crannies, original timbers, built-in settles, well-worn sofas, wood-burning stoves, and a wealth of maritime artefacts. Locally-brewed Hopdaemon and Goacher's ales are tapped straight from the cask, and make for a perfect match with simple, traditional bar food such as baguettes and jacket potatoes. Alternatively look to the specials board for fresh fish, or the carte for the likes of steak and Merlot pie, or roast chicken. In summer come and support the pub's Bat and Trap team.

Open all wk 11-3 6-10 (Sat 11-11; Sun 12-6 in winter 12-10.30 in summer) **Food** Lunch Mon-Sat 11-2.30, Sun 12-2.30 Dinner Tue-Sat 7-9 (no food Tue-Thu eve in winter) Av main course £8.95 ⊕ FREE HOUSE ◀ Goacher's, Hopdaemon, Whitstable, Local ales. ♟ 12 **Facilities** Non-diners area ♥ (Bar Garden) ♦♦ Children's menu Children's portions Family room Garden ♬ Parking ➡

GOUDHURST

Map 6 TQ73

Green Cross Inn

tel: 01580 211200 **TN17 1HA**
dir: *A21 from Tonbridge towards Hastings left onto A262 towards Ashford. 2m, Goudhurst on right*

Dining pub specialising in seafood

In an unspoiled corner of Kent, close to Finchcocks Manor, and originally built to serve the Paddock Wood to Goudhurst railway line, this thriving dining pub

specialises in fresh seafood. Arrive early to bag a table in the dining room, prettily decorated with fresh flowers, and tuck into grilled skate wing, halibut with cream and spinach sauce; seafood paella; or go for the slow-roasted pork belly with crackling, gravy and apple sauce, followed by pineapple sorbet or lemon chiffon; all freshly prepared by the chef-owner who is Italian and classically trained.

Open all wk 12-3 6-11 Closed Sun eve **Food** Lunch all wk 12-2.30 Dinner Mon-Sat 7-9.45 Restaurant menu available all wk ⊕ FREE HOUSE ◀ Harvey's Sussex Best Bitter, Guinness Ö Biddenden. **Facilities** ♦♦ Children's portions Garden ♬ Parking WiFi ➡ (notice required)

The Star & Eagle ★★★★ INN

PICK OF THE PUBS

See Pick of the Pubs on opposite page

GRAVESEND

Map 6 TQ67

The Cock Inn

tel: 01474 814208 **Henley St, Luddesdowne DA13 0XB**
email: andrew.r.turner@btinternet.com
dir: *Phone for detailed directions*

Adults-only pub with cask-conditioned English ales

Dating from 1713, this whitewashed free house in the beautiful Luddesdowne Valley has two traditional beamed bars with wood-burning stoves and open fires. Always available are eight well-kept real ales, Köstritzer and other German beers, and not a fruit machine, jukebox or TV in sight. All food is ordered at the bar: expect filled submarine rolls, basket meals and home-made lamb shank; chicken, leek and ham pie; or roasted vegetable and Wensleydale bake. As an adults-only pub, no-one under 18 is allowed in.

Open all day all wk 12-11 (Sun 12-10.30) **Food** Lunch all wk 12-3 Dinner all wk 5-8 ⊕ FREE HOUSE ◀ Adnams Southwold Bitter, Broadside & Lighthouse, Goacher's Real Mild Ale, St Austell Trelawny, Truman's Swift. **Facilities** Non-diners area ♥ (Bar Restaurant Garden) Garden ♬ Parking

HALSTEAD

Map 6 TQ46

Rose & Crown

tel: 01959 533120 **Otford Ln TN14 7EA**
email: info@roseandcrownhalstead.co.uk
dir: *M25 junct 4, A21, London (SE)/Bromley/Orpington signs. At Hewitts Rdbt 1st exit onto A224 signed Dunton Green. At rdbt 3rd exit into Shoreham Ln. In Halstead left into Station Rd, left into Otford Ln*

Bustling community local

This handsome Grade II listed pub, situated in the lee of the North Downs, is all a good village pub should be; traditional pub games including bat and trap, family friendly, supporting local microbreweries (with no less than three beer festivals held each year) and a welcoming base for walks into the peaceful countryside on the doorstep. With a lively bar, peaceful lounge, Stables Restaurant and tranquil garden to suit all tastes, home-made pub grub is the icing on the cake, from home-made venison and ale pie to breaded plaice, chips and peas.

Open all day all wk **Food** Lunch all wk 12-11 Dinner all wk 12-11 Av main course £7 Set menu available ⊕ FREE HOUSE ◀ Larkins Traditional, Elgood's Rose & Crown Best, Guest ales Ö Symonds. ♟ **Facilities** Non-diners area ♥ (Bar Garden Outside area) ♦♦ Children's menu Children's portions Play area Garden Outside area ♬ Beer festival Parking WiFi ➡

PICK OF THE PUBS

The Star & Eagle ★★★★ INN

GOUDHURST   Map 6 TQ73

tel: 01580 211512 **High St TN17 1AL**
email: starandeagle@btconnect.com
web: www.starandeagle.co.uk
dir: *Just off A21 towards Hastings. Take A262 into Goudhurst. Pub at top of hill adjacent to church*

Outstanding views, historic interiors, and cooking with a European twist

If a visit to the old spa town of Royal Tunbridge Wells is in your plans, or perhaps a stroll around the gardens at Sissinghurst Castle, The Star & Eagle in Goudhurst's High Street would make an ideal port of call. Its 14th-century origins can be seen in vaulted stonework that suggests that this rambling, big-beamed building may once have been a monastery; the tunnel from the cellars probably surfaces beneath the neighbouring parish church. In the 18th century it was a base for the infamous Hawkhurst gang, who hatched smuggling plans over their ales and terrorised the surrounding area with their thieving. Standing 400 feet above sea level, The Star & Eagle's breathtaking views survey the orchards and hop fields that have earned Kent the accolade 'The Garden of England'. Harvey's, Wychwood Hobgoblin and a guest ale are always on offer, and a good selection of wine is served by the glass. While quaffing, unwind and enjoy choosing between fine traditional and continental dishes prepared by head

chef Scott Smith and his team under the watchful eyes of proprietors Karin and Enrique Martinez. Tapas-style starters such as deep-fried whitebait sprinkled with Spanish paprika, or large pan-fried Portuguese sardines, can be served in large portions for sharing. The blackboard displays daily specials, or look to the house specialities for the likes of roast guinea fowl with Chantenay carrots, bubble and squeak cake, orange and ginger sauce. For fish lovers, a lemon-spiced fillet of salmon, or a whole lemon sole with prawn and lemon butter sauce, are typical choices. Desserts follow English favourite lines: apple and blackberry crumble and sticky toffee sponge pudding are both served with vanilla custard; or choose a selection of Kentish cheeses served with grapes and chutney.

Open all day all wk 11-11 (Sun 12-3 6.30-10.30) **Food** Lunch all wk 12-2.30 Dinner all wk 7-9.30 ⊕ FREE HOUSE ◀ Harvey's, Brakspear Oxford Gold, Wychwood Hobgoblin ♂ Biddenden. ♟ 14 **Facilities** Non-diners area ♂♀ Children's menu Children's portions Family room Outside area ⊼ Parking WiFi 🚐 **Rooms** 10

HAWKHURST
Map 7 TQ73

The Black Pig at Hawkhurst

tel: 01580 752306 **Moor Hill TN18 4PF**
email: enquiries@theblackpigathawkhurst.co.uk
dir: *On A229, S of Hawkhurst*

Local produce to the fore

From the pub's village-edge hillside location, footpaths burrow deep into the commons and woodland of the High Weald Area of Outstanding Natural Beauty. This rural aspect is mirrored in the eclectic mix of country-rustic furnishings which comfortably dapple the open-plan, pale-beamed interior. To the rear a hidden garden is the ideal retreat in which to savour local beers such as Old Dairy Copper Top. The daily-changing menu is home cooked and locally sourced. Contemporary British dishes predominate; grilled pork chops with Biddenden cider cream sauce, or beer and hop bangers with red wine gravy are typical fare. The fish, meat or vegetarian sharing platters prove popular.

Open all day all wk 11am-mdnt **Food** Lunch Mon-Sat 12-2.30, Sun 12-4 Dinner all wk 6.30-9.30 ⊕ FREE HOUSE ◀ Dark Star Hophead, Larkins Traditional, Old Dairy Copper Top, Harvey's ○ Biddenden. **Facilities** Non-diners area ♣ (Bar Garden) ◀ Children's menu Children's portions Garden ☏ ▥ (notice required)

The Great House
PICK OF THE PUBS

tel: 01580 753119 **Gills Green TN18 5EJ**
email: enquiries@thegreathouse.net
dir: *Just off A229 between Cranbrook & Hawkhurst*

Family-friendly free house in the heart of the Kentish Weald

Tucked away along a lane in a tranquil hamlet is this eye-catching Kentish weatherboard inn. Over 400 years old, it displays equally appealing character in the range of rooms that cater well both for drinkers – beers from the ever-reliable Harvey's Brewery are stocked – and diners. With beams and trusses; open fires and stone floors; country furniture and very eclectic decor, there's a relaxed atmosphere here. This spreads informally through the three dining areas; whilst an orangery and secluded terrace suggest undertones of the Mediterranean linking to the peaceful beer garden. The menus combine classic English dishes with a dash of French brasserie-style cooking. Offering starters like potted wild duck with kohlrabi and carrot salad; mains run to braised local pig's cheeks with potato and apple gratin; or halibut fillet with tarragon mash, girolle mushrooms and brown shrimp butter sauce. Accompanying a meal can be Kentish cider and wines and the pub hosts a beer festival every year.

Open all day all wk 11.30-11 **Food** Lunch Mon-Fri 12-3, Sat-Sun 12-9.45 Dinner Mon-Fri 6-9.45, Sat-Sun 12-9.45 ⊕ FREE HOUSE ◀ Harvey's, Sharp's Doom Bar, Guinness ○ Biddenden, Aspall. ☗ 20 **Facilities** Non-diners area ♣ (All areas) ◀ Children's menu Children's portions Garden Outside area ☏ Beer festival Parking WiFi

HODSOLL STREET
Map 6 TQ66

The Green Man

tel: 01732 823575 **TN15 7LE**
email: the.greenman@btinternet.com
dir: *Between Brands Hatch & Gravesend off A227*

Recommended for its fish dishes

The picturesque village of Hodsoll Street on the North Downs, surrounded by beautiful Kent countryside, is home to this 300-year-old, family-run pub, much loved for its decent food and real ales. There's a large garden for warmer weather, and Sharp's Doom Bar and Timothy Taylor Landlord are a couple of the four real ales on tap. Food is prepared to order using fresh local produce, and the evening menu includes a wide variety of fish, such as whole plaice, skate wing and smoked

haddock, as well as dishes like roast lamb shank, steak and kidney filo parcel, and various steaks.

Open all wk 11-2.30 6-11 (Fri-Sun all day) **Food** Lunch Mon-Thu 12-2, Fri-Sun all day Dinner Mon-Thu 6.30-9.30, Fri-Sun all day Set menu available ⊕ HAYWOOD PUB COMPANY LTD ◀ Timothy Taylor Landlord, Harvey's, Sharp's Doom Bar, Guest ale ○ Thatchers Gold. **Facilities** Non-diners area ♣ (Bar Restaurant Garden) ◀ Children's menu Children's portions Play area Garden ☏ Parking WiFi ▥

HOLLINGBOURNE
Map 7 TQ85

The Dirty Habit
PICK OF THE PUBS

tel: 01622 880880 **Upper St ME17 1UW**
email: enquiries@thedirtyhabit.net
dir: *M20 junct 8, follow A20 signs, then Hollingbourne signs on B2163. Through Hollingbourne, pub on hill top on right*

Historic watering hole on the Pilgrims Way

There's been a pub on this site since the 11th century, when monks brewed ale for pilgrims plodding from Winchester to the shrine of Thomas à Becket at Canterbury. The building retains much period charm – look, for instance, at the long Georgian oak bar and panelling, and the Victorian furniture, all beautifully restored by skilled local craftsmen. Harvey's of Lewes is one of the real ales on tap, and there's cider from Biddenden too. The Monks Corner, with oak beams to the apex and a bread oven in the corner, is ideal for private dining, while outside is a quiet terrace. The kitchen prepares dishes such as fish, tapas and meat sharing boards; salt and pepper squid with lemon mayo; Aga-cooked Bedgebury game stew (rabbit, partridge and venison), new potatoes and seasonal vegetables; king prawn and chorizo linguine; and fig pudding with honeycomb ice cream.

Open all day all wk **Food** Lunch Mon-Sat 12-3, Sun all day Dinner Mon-Sat 6-9.45, Sun all day ⊕ ENTERPRISE INNS ◀ Harvey's, Old Dairy Red Top, Timothy Taylor Landlord ○ Biddenden, Aspall. ☗ 28 **Facilities** ♣ (Bar Restaurant Outside area) ◀ Children's menu Children's portions Outside area ☏ Parking WiFi

NEW The Windmill

tel: 01622 889000 **32 Eyhorne St ME17 1TR**
email: reservations@thewindmillbyrichardphillips.co.uk
dir: *M20 junct 8, A20 towards Lenham. Straight on at 1st rdbt, left at 2nd rdbt into Eyhorne St*

TV chef's latest venture

The latest in chef Richard Phillips' (you might have seen him on the BBC's *Saturday Kitchen*) collection of pubs and restaurants, The Windmill is found in the beautiful village of Hollingbourne. Full of distinctive character and very much part of the local community, it's the ideal place for a relaxing lunch, a quiet drink (Doom Bar, Hoppin' Robin or Flintlock Pale Ale are the real ales on offer) or a more formal dinner. A lunchtime menu might feature poached plaice with duck egg linguine and cockles; while at dinner you could start with locally foraged mushroom tart and move on to braised belly of Charing pork.

Open all day all wk **Food** Lunch all wk 11am-mdnt Dinner all wk 11am-mdnt Av main course £14.50 Set menu available Restaurant menu available all wk ⊕ ENTERPRISE INNS ◀ Sharp's Doom Bar, Rockin' Robin Hoppin Robin, Coach House Flintlock Pale Ale ○ Aspall, Westons Stowford Press. ☗ **Facilities** Non-diners area ♣ (Bar Garden) ◀ Children's menu Children's portions Play area Garden ☏ Beer festival Parking WiFi ▥ (notice required)

PICK OF THE PUBS

The Plough at Ivy Hatch

IVY HATCH   Map 6 TQ55

tel: 01732 810100
High Cross Rd TN15 0NL
email: miles@theploughivyhatch.co.uk
web: www.theploughivyhatch.co.uk
dir: *Exit A25 between Borough Green & Sevenoaks, follow Ightham Mote signs*

Village pub near the National Trust's Ightham Mote

This 17th-century, tile-hung pub in the picturesque village of Ivy Hatch is but a short walk from the National Trust's Ightham Mote, Britain's best-preserved medieval manor house. From spring to autumn, The Plough keeps its own pigs and chickens in a cobnut coppice in the back garden. During the week it's open for breakfast and a wide range of teas and coffees. In the bar, the real ales come from a select roster of Kentish breweries, and food includes sandwiches with chips or soup; and a choice of fish, ploughman's and deli farm charcuterie boards. On the daily-changing restaurant menus are British- and European-style dishes featuring rare-breed steaks (Longhorn T-bones, Dexter sirloin and Shorthorn burgers) seafood, game and, courtesy of those pigs, country pork terrines; home-made bacon, pork and apple burgers; and mouth-watering, slow-cooked legs and shoulders. Looking to other options, a starter of gin cured salmon, pickled cherries and dill cream cheese might be

followed by a main course of Chart Farm venison bourguignon with thyme and rosemary dumplings; polenta-coated deep-fried squid with chilli, parsley, aïoli and mixed leaves; or smoked chicken Caesar salad. Desserts include Seville orange curd and cinnamon mille feuille with passionfruit and orange sorbet; and chocolate fondant with vanilla ice cream and chocolate sauce. There are many excellent walks through the countryside surrounding The Plough, and the road- and mountain-biking opportunities are excellent too. Muddy boots and cycling gear, if not necessarily de rigueur, are definitely not frowned upon and wearers caught in the rain will be able to dry off either in front of the winter open fire, or, if the sun's out, on the terrace.

Open all wk 9-3 6-11 (Sat 10am-11pm Sun 10-6) Closed 26 Dec **Food** Lunch Mon-Sat 12-2.45, Sun 12-6 Dinner Mon-Sat 6-9.30 ⊕ FREE HOUSE ◖ Tonbridge Coppernob & Rustic, Old Dairy Red Top, Ringwood Best Bitter Ŏ Thatchers Gold. ⬤ 10 **Facilities** Non-diners area ♦ Children's menu Children's portions Garden ⋒ Parking WiFi 🚐 (notice required)

ICKHAM
Map 7 TR25

The Duke William

tel: 01227 721308 & 721244 **The Street CT3 1QP**
email: goodfood@dukewilliam.biz
dir: *A257 Canterbury to Sandwich. In Littlebourne left opposite The Anchor, into Nargate St. 0.5m right into Drill Ln, right into The Street*

Child-friendly village inn with daily changing dishes

This whitewashed free house is in the heart of the village, and traditional, locally sourced (from surrounding farms) and home-cooked food is the keynote here; in fact the kitchen team relish produce 'in all its knobbly and unperfected glory'. The menu is 'on the board' as the dishes change from day to day to reflect the freshest seasonal ingredients. A typical main dish is blackened beef fillet with pommes Anna and textures of onion. This family-friendly pub believes that little people should be able to choose healthy, home-made food too – and even if they are a little fussy it's not a problem they say. The lovely garden features a covered patio, as well as a children's play area with a swing and slide.

Open all day all wk all day **Food** Lunch Mon-Sat 12-3, Sun 12-8 Dinner Mon-Sat 6-10, Sun 12-8 Restaurant menu available Mon-Sat ⊕ FREE HOUSE ◀ Shepherd Neame Whitstable Bay, Sharp's Doom Bar, Harvey's, Guest ale Ö Aspall. ♀ 9 **Facilities** Non-diners area ❖ (Bar Garden) ♦♦ Children's menu Children's portions Play area Garden ♫ WiFi ➡ (notice required)

IDEN GREEN
Map 6 TQ73

The Peacock

tel: 01580 211233 **Goudhurst Rd TN17 2PB**
dir: *A21 from Tunbridge Wells to Hastings, onto A262, pub 1.5m past Goudhurst*

Family-friendly inn

Dating from the 14th century, this Grade II listed former smugglers' haunt has exposed brickwork, low beams, an inglenook fireplace, and ancient oak doors. Kent Best and Bishops Finger can be found among several ales in the convivial bar. Popular with families, The Peacock offers a wide range of traditional pub food made using produce from local farmers; maybe garlic tiger prawns on toast followed by ham, egg and chips; steak and ale pie; chicken and bacon salad; or liver and bacon. In summer enjoy the large enclosed garden with fruit trees and picnic tables on one side of the building.

Open all day all wk 12-11 (Sun 12-9) **Food** Lunch Tue-Thu 12-3, Fri-Sat 12-9, Sun 12-4 Dinner Tue-Thu 6-9 ⊕ SHEPHERD NEAME ◀ Master Brew, Kent, Bishops Finger, Seasonal ales. **Facilities** Non-diners area ❖ (Bar Garden) ♦♦ Children's menu Children's portions Family room Garden ♫ Beer festival Parking WiFi ➡ (notice required)

IGHTHAM
Map 6 TQ55

The Harrow Inn
PICK OF THE PUBS

tel: 01732 885912 **Common Rd TN15 9EB**
dir: *1.5m from Borough Green on A25 to Sevenoaks, signed Ightham Common, left into Common Rd. Inn 0.25m on left*

Worth seeking out for imaginative food

Tucked away down country lanes, yet easily accessible from both the M20 and M26, this creeper-hung, stone-built free house dates back to at least the 17th century. The two-room bar area has a great brick fireplace, open to both sides and piled high with logs, while the restaurant's vine-clad conservatory opens on to a terrace that's ideal for a pint of Loddon Hoppit or Gravesend Shrimpers and warm weather dining. Menus vary with the seasons, and seafood is a particular speciality: fish lovers can enjoy dishes such as crab and ginger spring roll; swordfish with Cajun spice and salsa; or pan-fried fillets of sea bass with lobster cream and spinach. Other main courses may include baked sausage with gammon, fennel, red onions

and garlic; and tagliatelle with wild mushroom, fresh herb, lemongrass and chilli ragout. The car park is fairly small, although there's adequate street parking.

Open 12-3 6-11 Closed 1wk between Xmas & New Year, Sun eve & Mon-Wed ⊕ FREE HOUSE ◀ Loddon Hoppit, Gravesend Shrimpers. **Facilities** ♦♦ Children's portions Family room Outside area Parking

IVY HATCH
Map 6 TQ55

The Plough at Ivy Hatch
PICK OF THE PUBS

See Pick of the Pubs on page 285

LAMBERHURST
Map 6 TQ63

The Vineyard
PICK OF THE PUBS

tel: 01892 890222 **Lamberhurst Down TN3 8EU**
email: enquiries@thevineyard.com
dir: *From A21 follow brown Vineyard signs onto B2169 towards Lamberhurst. Left, continue to follow Vineyard signs. Straight on at x-rds, pub on right*

Robust Anglo-French cooking with good ale and wines to match

Built more than 300 years ago, original elements of this country roadside pub are reflected in the quirky stuffed boar's head mounted above the huge brick-built fireplace. Leather sofas, wingback and parlour chairs mix easily with the rustic look and chunky wooden furniture, whilst the eye is taken by a mural illustrating the well-established wine-making craft in the area. The pub is next door to one of England's oldest vineyards and there's a carefully chosen wine list and 20 served by the glass. Fans of the hop are rewarded with firkins from microbreweries such as Old Dairy. From the kitchen comes a pleasing mix of top-notch traditional English and regional French brasserie dishes: Roquefort and apple salad with celery and toasted walnuts to start, then halibut fillet with tarragon mash, girolles and brown shrimps in butter sauce, finishing with apple and pear crumble.

Open all day all wk 11.30-11 **Food** Lunch Mon-Fri 12-6, Sat-Sun 12-9.30 Dinner Mon-Fri 6-9.45, Sat-Sun 12-9.30 ⊕ FREE HOUSE ◀ Sharp's Doom Bar, Harvey's, Old Dairy Ö Aspall. ♀ 20 **Facilities** Non-diners area ❖ (Bar Garden Outside area) ♦♦ Children's portions Garden Outside area ♫ Parking

LEIGH
Map 6 TQ54

The Greyhound Charcott

tel: 01892 870275 **Charcott TN11 8LG**
email: ghatcharcott@aol.com
dir: *From Tonbridge take B245 towards Hildenborough. Left onto Leigh Rd, right onto B2027 (Stocks Green Rd). Through Leigh, right then left at T-junct, right into Charcott (Camp Hill)*

Village pub where tradition matters

Music, pool table, games machine? Not in this cosy pub, where, on cold days customers can look forward to log fires, and on warm ones to the prospect of a pint of Lewes-brewed Harvey's, or perhaps one of the 12 wines by the glass, in the garden. The regularly-changing menu might suggest a light lunch/main meal starter of leek and mussel crumble; or home-made pork and brandy pâté. Mains typically include monkfish and crayfish risotto with chilli and coriander dressing; braised shank of local lamb; and baked avocado, goats' cheese and sun-blushed tomatoes. Snacks include ploughman's and sandwiches.

Open 12-3 5.30-11 (Sat all day Sun 12-6) Closed Sun eve & Mon L **Food** Lunch Tue-Sat 12-2, Sun 12-3 Dinner Mon-Sat 6.30-9.30 ⊕ ENTERPRISE INNS ◀ Harvey's, Otter, Adnams Lighthouse Ö Westons Stowford Press. ♀ 12
Facilities Non-diners area ❖ (Bar Garden) ♦♦ Children's menu Children's portions Garden Parking WiFi ➡ (notice required)

LEYSDOWN-ON-SEA
Map 7 TR07

The Ferry House Inn ★★★★ INN

tel: 01795 510214 **Harty Rd ME12 4BQ**
email: info@theferryhouseinn.co.uk **web:** www.theferryhouseinn.co.uk
dir: From A429 towards Sheppey. At rdbt take B2231 to Eastchurch. From Eastchurch High St into Church Rd. At rdbt into Rowetts Way signed Leysdown. Right into Harty Ferry Rd to village

A family-owned, delightfully remote island pub

Named for the ferry that crossed the Swale to the mainland until the onset of World War II, this 16th-century pub stands in three acres of terraced lawns. The views over the water to Faversham, Whitstable and the North Downs alone are worth the journey, while its open log fires, wooden beams and solid oak floors add to the tally. And then there's the food, with the inn's membership of 'Produced in Kent' meaning locally caught fish of the day; pan-fried Harty Estate partridge crowns with Parmentier potatoes, carrots, Biddenden cider and thyme jus; and roasted tomato and winter-green risotto with grilled haloumi.

Open Tue-Fri & Mon (Apr-Sep) 11-3 6.30-11 (Sat all day Sun 11-5) Closed 24-31 Dec, Mon (Oct-Mar) **Food** Lunch Mon-Fri 12-2.30, Sat & Sun 12.30-4 Dinner Mon-Sat 6.30-9 ⊕ FREE HOUSE ◀ Shepherd Neame Spitfire, Young's Special Ò Sheppy's, Hush Heath Jake's Orchard. **Facilities** Non-diners area ♦♦ Children's menu Children's portions Play area Family room Garden ⋒ Parking WiFi ▭ (notice required) **Rooms** 5

LINTON
Map 7 TQ75

The Bull Inn

tel: 01622 743612 **Linton Hill ME17 4AW**
email: food@thebullatlinton.co.uk
dir: S of Maidstone on A229 (Hastings road)

Rural pub ideal for alfresco eating and drinking

Built in 1674, this part-timbered former coaching inn stands high on the Greensand Ridge, with wonderful views and sunsets over the Weald. The award-winning garden includes two oak gazebos and a large decked area for alfresco bistro dining and afternoon tea. Inside there is an imposing inglenook fireplace, lots of beams and a bar serving Shepherd Neame ales. The wide-ranging menu offers hearty sandwiches and pub classics – perfect sustenance for walkers tackling the Greensand Way. The inn offers seasonal menus, daily delivered seafood, and home-made desserts.

Open all day all wk 11am-11.30pm (Sun 12-10.30) **Food** Lunch all wk 12-9 Dinner all wk 12-9 Av main course £12 Set menu available ⊕ SHEPHERD NEAME ◀ Shepherd Neame Master Brew, Kent's Best, Late Red Ò Thatchers Gold. **Facilities** Non-diners area ♣ (Bar Garden) ♦♦ Children's menu Children's portions Garden ⋒ Parking WiFi ▭

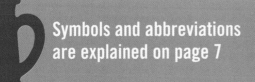

Symbols and abbreviations are explained on page 7

LOWER HALSTOW
Map 7 TQ86

The Three Tuns

tel: 01795 842840 **The Street ME9 7DY**
email: info@thethreetunsrestaurant.co.uk
dir: From A2 between Rainham & Newington turn left, follow Lower Halstow sign. At T-junct right signed Funton & Iwade. Pub on right

Quality dining, pub grub and Kentish real ales

Built in 1468 and licensed to sell ale since 1764, Chris and Carol Haines's traditional fire-warmed bar is paradise for lovers of local real ales and cider. They stock Millis Kentish Best, Goacher's Real Mild and Dudda's Tun Kentish cider, while Summer Bank Holiday sees the Kentish Ale and Cider Festival, with a hog-roast, seafood and live music. Farms supply much of the food on the ever-changing restaurant menu, where items might include pan-fried plaice with spinach, rice noodles and tomato, cockle and king bream broth; or gratinated brie Portobello mushroom with sage and chestnut crumble topping. A large beer garden with decking flanks a stream that soon flows into nearby Halstow Creek.

Open all day all wk **Food** Lunch all wk 12-9 Dinner all wk 12-9 Restaurant menu available Mon-Sat ⊕ FREE HOUSE ◀ Millis Brewing Co Kentish Best, Goacher's Real Mild Ale, Guest ales Ò Dudda's Tun Kentish Cider, Core Fruit Products Hard Core. ☻ 10 **Facilities** Non-diners area ♣ (Bar Garden) ♦♦ Children's menu Children's portions Garden ⋒ Beer festival Cider festival Parking WiFi ▭ (notice required)

MAIDSTONE
Map 7 TQ75

The Black Horse Inn ★★★★ INN

tel: 01622 737185 **Pilgrim's Way, Thurnham ME14 3LD**
email: info@wellieboot.net **web:** www.wellieboot.net
dir: M20 junct 7, A249, right into Detling. Turn opposite Cock Horse Pub into Pilgrim's Way

Charming free house on the Pilgrim's Way

Tucked beneath the North Downs on the Pilgrim's Way, this 18th-century former forge welcomes guests with an open log fire in the colder months. Dine in the conservatory restaurant that has stunning countryside views or in the cosy candlelit restaurant. Real ales change weekly and the kitchen uses local ingredients in fish or meat sharing plates, or in mains like pan-roasted rump of Romney Marsh lamb; crispy lamb belly and fondant potato; or hot smoked breast of Gressingham duck with pommes Anna, warm figs, wilted spinach and plum sauce; a daily-changing specials board adds to the choices.

Open all day all wk **Food** Lunch all wk 12-6 Dinner all wk 6-10 Set menu available Restaurant menu available all wk ⊕ FREE HOUSE ◀ Greene King IPA, Wychwood Hobgoblin, Westerham Grasshopper, Harvey's Sussex Best Bitter, Black Sheep Ò Biddenden. ☻ 21 **Facilities** Non-diners area ♣ (Bar Garden) ♦♦ Children's menu Children's portions Garden ⋒ Parking ▭ (notice required) **Rooms** 27

MARKBEECH

Map 6 TQ44

The Kentish Horse

tel: 01342 850493 **Cow Ln TN8 5NT**
dir: *3m from Edenbridge & 7m from Tunbridge Wells*

Popular free house in the Garden of England

Britain's only Kentish Horse honours Invicta, the county's prancing white stallion. Popular with ramblers and cyclists, the locals rate it too, partly because Chiddingstone-brewed Larkins and Lewes-brewed Harvey's are available, with guest ales on high days and holidays. Owners Trevor and Tina Jobson serve home-cooked, traditional food, such as pan-fried lamb's liver and onions; beer-battered fresh fillet of haddock; and tagliatelle with Stilton and mushroom cream sauce. The four-acre grounds include an extensive garden and a children's play area, and you also get a terrific view over Winnie the Pooh's home, Ashdown Forest.

Open all day all wk **Food** Lunch Mon-Sat 12-2.30, Sun 12-3 Dinner Mon-Sat 7-9.30 ⊕ FREE HOUSE ◀ Harvey's, Larkins Ŏ Westons Stowford Press, Symonds. **Facilities** Non-diners area ✿ (Bar Garden) ✚ Children's menu Children's portions Play area Garden Parking ➡ (notice required)

MATFIELD

Map 6 TQ64

The Poet at Matfield

tel: 01892 722416 **Maidstone Rd TN12 7JH**
email: info@thepoetatmatfield.co.uk **web:** www.thepoetatmatfield.co.uk
dir: *From Tonbridge on A21 towards Hastings left onto B2160 signed Paddock Wood. Approx 1.5m to pub on left in Matfield*

Smart village inn with impressive literary links

Named after poet Siegfried Sassoon, who was born in this quintessentially English village just outside Tunbridge Wells, this Grade II listed pub is more than 350 years old. The pub retains its original character with the beams and antiques, but comfortable leather chesterfield sofas and armchairs add an elegant edge.

Provenance is the cornerstone of the menu, which lists local suppliers including the Tonbridge Brewery responsible for the Coppernob ale served at the bar. The concise carte could kick off with smoked haddock risotto and move on to Kentish pork belly with boudin noir, carrots, sprouts and apple.

Open all day all wk **Food** Lunch Mon-Sat 12-2.30, Sun 12-4 Dinner all wk 6-9 Restaurant menu available all wk ⊕ ENTERPRISE INNS ◀ Tonbridge Coppernob, Harvey's Sussex Best Bitter, Guest ale. ₹ 12 **Facilities** Non-diners area ✿ (Bar Garden) ✚ Children's portions Garden ➤ Parking WiFi ➡ (notice required) *See advert on opposite page*

OARE

Map 7 TR06

NEW The Three Mariners

tel: 01795 533633 **2 Church Rd ME13 0QA**
email: info@thethreemarinersoare.co.uk
dir: *M2 junct 7, A2 towards Sittingbourne. Through Ospringe. At rdbt right onto B2045 (Western Link). At T-junct left signed Oare. Pub on right*

Coastal pub popular with walkers and bird-watchers

Dating back to the late 18th century, the Grade II listed Three Mariners occupies an enviable position in the village of Oare just outside Faversham. With the Saxon Shore Way, the Swale Heritage Trail and the marshes close by, this coastal pub is popular with walkers and wildlife enthusiasts. Log fires warm the bar in winter, whilst the sunny terrace is a real draw in summer. Enjoy a pint of local Shepherd Neame ale and order from a menu that might include potted crab on toast; fillet of local turbot with white wine and dill sauce; or beef fillet Stroganoff.

Open all day all wk 12-11 (Sun 12-10) Closed 24 Dec eve & 25 Dec eve **Food** Contact pub for food times Set menu available Restaurant menu available all wk ⊕ SHEPHERD NEAME ◀ Master Brew, Late Red, Early Bird. ₹ 13 **Facilities** ✿ (Bar Garden Outside area) ✚ Children's portions Garden Outside area ➤ Parking

PENSHURST

Map 6 TQ54

The Bottle House Inn   PICK OF THE PUBS

See Pick of the Pubs on page 290

The Spotted Dog   PICK OF THE PUBS

tel: 01892 870253 **Smarts Hill TN11 8EE**
email: thespotteddogpub@gmail.com
dir: *Off B2188 between Penshurst & Fordcombe*

Sitting in the folds of the Weald

This independently run, weatherboarded inn started life as a row of cottages in the 15th century, and is now a rambling building with open fires, a forest of low beams and oak-board floors. There are tiered beer gardens to the front and rear, the latter offering fantastic views in the summer. Kentish ales from Larkins and cider from Chiddingstone are just another excellent reason to stop here, along with the bang up-to-date menu, making the most of the produce grown in this richly endowed countryside. Sample a starter of deep-fried crispy duck rolls drizzled with hoi sin sauce, precursor to Thai green chicken curry; steak and kidney pie; or loin of lamb with a red wine, rosemary and redcurrant jus. These are enhanced by a daily-changing specials board and lunchtime baguettes, sandwiches and ploughman's. The Spotted Dog is close to two magnificent stately homes, Penshurst Place and Hever Castle.

Open all day all wk 11.30-11 (Sun 12-9 Mon 11.30-9) **Food** Lunch Mon-Fri 12-2.30, Sat-Sun 12-4 Dinner Mon-Sat 6-9 ⊕ FREE HOUSE ◀ Larkins Traditional, Harvey's, Guest ale Ŏ Chiddingstone, Thatchers Gold. **Facilities** Non-diners area ✿ (Bar Garden Outside area) ✚ Children's menu Children's portions Garden Outside area ➤ Parking WiFi ➡ (notice required)

PLUCKLEY
Map 7 TQ94

The Dering Arms
PICK OF THE PUBS

tel: 01233 840371 **Station Rd TN27 0RR**
email: jim@deringarms.com
dir: M20 junct 8, A20 to Ashford. Right onto B2077 at Charing to Pluckley

Great selection of seafood dishes

Creeper-clad stone gables and arched windows mark out this imposing building as something special. There's a touch of Victorian Gothic and 'Hammer' films about this eye-catching pub, built originally as a hunting lodge. The grandeur remains inside, with open fires, bare boards, scrubbed old tables and a hop-bine dressed bar groaning with venerable handpumps. The separate clubroom has comfy settees, log-burner and a baby grand just itching to be played. It's a popular destination for seafood lovers, with ever-changing dishes filling the specials board. A starter of oysters from County Cork; or provençale fish soup with rouille could be followed by confit of duck with bubble-and-squeak; or monkfish with bacon, orange and cream sauce. If you really want to push the boat out, and the time of year is right, ask for the fruit de mer – just give the chef 24 hours notice. Drinkers are rewarded with a fine cellar, plus a selection of Kentish ales and ciders.

Open Mon-Fri 11.30-3.30 6-11 (Sat 9am-11pm Sun 12-4) Closed 26-27 Dec, Sun eve **Food** Lunch Mon-Fri 12-2.30, Sat 12-3, Sun 12-4 Dinner Mon-Sat 6.30-9 Restaurant menu available all wk ⊕ FREE HOUSE ◀ Goacher's Best Dark Ale, Gold Star Ale, Old Ale, Dering Ale ♂ Biddenden, Hush Heath Jake's Orchard, Wise Owl. ⬺ 11 **Facilities** Non-diners area ✿ (Bar Garden) ◀ Children's portions Family room Garden ⋒ Parking WiFi

ROLVENDEN
Map 7 TQ83

The Bull

tel: 01580 241212 **1 Regent St TN17 4PB**
email: info@thebullinnrolvenden.co.uk
dir: Just off A28, approx 3m from Tenterden

The beer garden overlooks the village cricket pitch

This handsome, tile-hung village inn dates, in part, back to the 13th century and is located close to the walled garden that inspired Frances Hodgson Burnett's classic tale *The Secret Garden*. Handy, too, for steam trains of the Kent and East Sussex Railway, there's a welcome focus on local beers and produce, with a heart-warming, pubby menu. Look out for warm chicken and chorizo salad with sun-blushed tomatoes to start, followed by calves' liver and bacon or wild boar sausages with wholegrain mustard mash and tomato confit. There's a lovely beer garden overlooking the village cricket ground.

Open all day all wk **Food** Lunch all wk 12-3 Dinner all wk 6-10 Av main course £11 Restaurant menu available Mon-Sat ⊕ FREE HOUSE ◀ Red Top, Harvey's, Old Dairy Gold Top ♂ Westons Stowford Press. ⬺ 12 **Facilities** Non-diners area ✿ (Bar Garden) ◀ Children's menu Children's portions Garden ⋒ Beer festival Parking WiFi ⛟ (notice required)

SANDWICH
Map 7 TR35

George & Dragon Inn

tel: 01304 613106 **Fisher St CT13 9EJ**
email: enquiries@georgeanddragon-sandwich.co.uk
dir: Between Dover & Canterbury (park at Quay Car Park, walk through Fisher Gate to Fisher St)

Charming family-run pub serving modern British food

Built in 1446, ale was first sold here in 1549, but was only licensed under the name of George & Dragon in 1615. This town centre pub oozes charm and character, with its wood floors and open fires, and makes a welcome pit stop when exploring historic Sandwich on foot. Run by two brothers, you can refuel with a pint of well-kept Wantsum, Otter or a guest ale. On the monthly-changing evening menu, you might find chicken croquettes with garlic and herb mayonnaise, followed by grilled lamb rump and liver, parsley mash, sautéed onions and red wine sauce. Head outside to the picturesque suntrap courtyard in summer.

Open all day 11-11 (Sun 12-4) Closed Sun eve **Food** Lunch all wk 12-2 Dinner Mon-Sat 6-9 Set menu available ⊕ ENTERPRISE INNS ◀ Wantsum, Otter Amber, Butcombe, Guest ales ♂ Aspall. ⬺ 9 **Facilities** Non-diners area ✿ (Bar Garden) Garden ⋒ WiFi

---

The Poet at Matfield

Situated in the quintessential English village of Matfield, in the heart of rural Kent, our unique Grade II listed building is steeped in history and offers a relaxing ambience with a few quirky twists.

We have chosen to call ourselves The Poet, after the famous war poet Siegfried Sassoon who was born just a stone's throw from the pub. We felt having a local link with our name also reflected our passion to support and promote all things local. We strive to offer dishes which encompass as many local elements as possible. We can trace the provenance of everything we use.

If you're thinking of having a private party, school reunion, or want to impress business clients, give us a call and our in-house team will take away the stress of organisation and ensure you have the perfect event. Our restaurant has a wide range of flexible dining and event areas to suit groups of all sizes.

Maidstone Road, Matfield, Kent TN12 7JH • Tel: 01892 722416
Email: info@thepoetatmatfield.co.uk • Website: www.thepoetatmatfield.co.uk

PICK OF THE PUBS

The Bottle House Inn

PENSHURST Map 6 TQ54

tel: 01892 870306
Coldharbour Rd TN11 8ET
email:
info@thebottlehouseinnpenshurst.co.uk
web:
www.thebottlehouseinnpenshurst.co.uk
dir: *A264 W from Tunbridge Wells onto B2188 N. After Fordcombe left towards Edenbridge & Hever. Pub 500yds after staggered x-rds*

Historic pub off the beaten track

Built as a farmhouse in 1492, this historic building formed part of a local estate during Henry VII's reign. A handsome, weatherboarded inn set down a country lane, it wasn't until 1806 that it was granted a licence to sell ales and ciders, later diversifying to function as a shop, farrier's and cobbler's too. Refurbishment in 1938 unearthed hundreds of old bottles, which inspired its unusual name. Later improvements included ancient oak beams sandblasted back to their natural colour, brickwork exposed and walls painted in neutral shades. At the copper-topped bar counter choose between Harvey's of Lewes and Chiddingstone-brewed Larkins handpumped beers, or a wine from one of the 19 served by the glass, then settle at a table on the patio or on the terrace. The menus in the stylish dining room change regularly to capitalise on

the availability of seasonal produce, and the chef's recommendations change frequently. Light bites might include BBQ pulled pork roll; or chargrilled chicken open sandwich. Starters are equally enticing – smoked paprika dusted whitebait with chive mayo, for instance. Among the main courses are steak and chestnut mushroom shortcrust pie, wholegrain mash, broccoli and gravy; pan-fried sea bass fillets, pecan mash, buttered spinach, roast cherry tomatoes with caper and lemon dressing; and winter vegetable and butterbean cheesy crumble. From the home-made desserts, you're likely to find sticky toffee pudding, toffee sauce and vanilla ice cream.

Open all day all wk 11-11 (Sun 11-10.30) Closed 25 Dec **Food** Mon-Sat 12-10, Sun & BH 12-9 ⊕ FREE HOUSE ◀ Harvey's Sussex Best Bitter, Larkins Traditional, Guest ales from Westerham Brewery. ♟ 19 **Facilities** Non-diners area ❀ (Bar Outside area) ♦ Children's menu & portions Outside area ⊼ Parking ▭ (notice required)

SELLING
Map 7 TR05

The Rose and Crown

tel: 01227 752214 **Perry Wood ME13 9RY**
email: info@roseandcrownperrywood.co.uk
dir: *From A28 right at Badgers Hill, left at end. 1st left signed Perry Wood*

Pretty country pub with a long history

The ghost of Hammond Smith, murdered after a boozy day in 1889, may join you for a pint but don't let his friendly presence detract from the pleasure of this rambling, low-beamed 16th-century inn. Packed with character via the inglenooks, horse brasses and corn dollies, Goldings hops are draped around a bar offering Harvey's and Adnams real ales plus Biddenden cider. Descend to the restaurant for home-cooked Kent fish pie; confit duck; game pie; or brie, bacon and walnut jacket potato. The flower-festooned garden is made for summer eating and drinking.

Open 12-3 6.30-11 (Sat-Sun all day) Closed 25-26 Dec eve, 1 Jan eve, Mon **Food** Lunch Tue-Sun 12-2 Dinner Tue-Sat 6.30-9 ⊕ FREE HOUSE ◀ Adnams Southwold Bitter, Harvey's Sussex Best Bitter, Guest ale Ö Westons Stowford Press, Biddenden. **Facilities** Non-diners area ❤ (Bar Restaurant Garden) ♦ Children's menu Children's portions Play area Garden ⊼ Parking ☷ (notice required)

SHIPBOURNE
Map 6 TQ55

The Chaser Inn

tel: 01732 810360 **Stumble Hill TN11 9PE**
email: enquiries@thechaser.co.uk
dir: *N of Tonbridge take A227 towards Shipbourne. Pub on left*

Popular pub with famous connections

Once a haunt for stars such as Richard Burton and Elizabeth Taylor, The Chaser Inn is an informal, relaxed village inn, next to the church and overlooking the common. Well-kept real ales and plenty of wines by the glass are complemented by an extensive menu of sandwiches, light bites and main courses such as whole grilled plaice, caper and citrus butter; or steak and vegetable suet pudding. There is a lovely beer garden and the covered courtyard comes into its own in the winter months. The pub takes its name from its long association with the nearby Fairlawne racing stables.

Open all day all wk 10am-mdnt **Food** Lunch Mon-Sat 12-9.30, Sun 12-9 Dinner Mon-Sat 12-9.30, Sun 12-9 ⊕ WHITING & HAMMOND ◀ Greene King IPA, Larkins Traditional, Guest ales. ♟ 16 **Facilities** Non-diners area ❤ (Bar Garden) ♦ Children's portions Garden ⊼ Parking WiFi ☷ (notice required)

SISSINGHURST
Map 7 TQ73

NEW The Milk House

tel: 01580 720200 **The Street TN17 2JG**
email: fresh@themilkhouse.co.uk
dir: *In village centre*

Excellent locally-sourced food in convivial village inn

In picturesque Sissinghurst, this former 16th-century hall house is very much the hub of the village. With its timber beams and Tudor fireplace, the pub has considerable charm and locals supping pints of Kentish-brewed Musket Brewery ale mingle with destination diners tempted by the acclaimed food. Most of the produce comes from a 20-mile radius of the pub and dishes such as navarin of Romney Marsh lamb with root vegetables and minted pearl barley, or grilled gurnard with borage and chervil root mash sit happily alongside innovative home-made pizzas and a top-notch children's menu.

Open all day all wk **Food** Lunch 12-9 Dinner 12-9 Av main course £9 Restaurant menu available all wk ⊕ ENTERPRISE INNS ◀ Old Dairy, Harvey's, Musket, Westerham Ö Symonds, The Orchard Pig, Rubens Curious Apple, Hush Heath Jake's Kentish Cider. ♟ 11 **Facilities** Non-diners area ❤ (Bar Garden) ♦ Children's menu Children's portions Play area Garden ⊼ Beer festival Cider festival Parking WiFi

---

SMARDEN
Map 7 TQ84

The Chequers Inn
PICK OF THE PUBS

tel: 01233 770217 **The Street TN27 8QA**
email: spaldings@thechequerssmarden.com
dir: *From Maidstone take A229. Left, through Sutton Valence & Headcorn. Left signed Smarden. Pub in village centre*

Ancient pub with courtyard and lovely gardens

The former weavers' village of Smarden has around 200 buildings of architectural and historical interest, one of which is the clapboarded 14th-century Chequers Inn. Its beautiful landscaped garden features a large carp pond and an attractive south-facing courtyard. Ales brewed by Harvey's, Sharp's, Fuller's, Wadworth and the Old Dairy Brewery are served in the low-beamed bars. Seasonal ingredients are sourced locally for the menus of traditional and modern food. Typical of the restaurant choices are starters of potted ham with piccalilli; home-made Scotch egg; whole lemon sole, lemon and caper butter, green vegetables and new potatoes; and rabbit pie, braised cabbage and bacon. The bar menu, carte and children's menu are all served on Sundays too, when traditional beef, lamb and pork roasts are joined by gammon and turkey.

Open all day all wk **Food** Lunch all wk 12-3 Dinner all wk 6-9 Restaurant menu available all wk ⊕ FREE HOUSE ◀ Sharp's Doom Bar, Fuller's London Pride, Wadworth 6X, Old Dairy, Harvey's Ö Westons Stowford Press. **Facilities** Non-diners area ♦ Children's menu Children's portions Garden ⊼ Parking WiFi ☷

SPELDHURST
Map 6 TQ54

George & Dragon
PICK OF THE PUBS

tel: 01892 863125 **Speldhurst Hill TN3 ONN**
email: julian@speldhurst.com
dir: *Phone for detailed directions*

Kentish ales, wine and fare in ancient timber-framed inn

Set in a part of Kent dappled with architectural gems like Penshurst Place and Hever Castle, this wonderful village inn more than holds its own. Much of the heavy tiled roof, vast chimneys and ancient timbers have been here since the pub was built over 800 years ago; the interior is equally mature with log fires and rippling oak beams creating a timeless setting for guests keen to savour the wet and dry sides of the inn. The wine list is extensive (including a Kent sparkling white), whilst lovers of the hop will appreciate beers from some of the area's burgeoning microbrewery sector. The seasonal menu promises organic, free-range and GM-free produce whenever possible. Provenance is king, with rare-breed pork and venison coming from named farms nearby, fish from a Kentish fishmonger and vegetables from local suppliers. A starter of seared local pigeon breast with smoked bacon and watercress walnut salad sets a high standard; mains cover Ashdown Forest venison rump and chop with hand-cut chips and aïoli, or seared fillet of sea bass with samphire and mussels.

Open all day all wk **Food** Lunch all wk 12-2.30 Dinner Mon-Sat 7-9.45 Set menu available ⊕ FREE HOUSE ◀ Harvey's Sussex Best Bitter, Westerham George's Marvellous Medicine, Larkins Ö Westons Stowford Press. ♟ 11 **Facilities** Non-diners area ❤ (Bar Garden) ♦ Children's portions Family room Garden ⊼ Parking WiFi ☷

STALISFIELD GREEN   Map 7 TQ95

The Plough Inn

tel: 01795 890256 **ME13 0HY**
email: info@theploughinnstalisfield.co.uk
dir: *From A20 (dual carriageway) W of Charing follow Stalisfield Green signs. Approx 2m to village*

Downland pub with a passion for Kentish produce

The Plough Inn is a splendid, 15th-century Wealden hall house situated by the green in an unspoilt hamlet high up on the North Downs. A real country pub, it enjoys far-reaching views across the Swale estuary and is worth seeking out for the array of Kentish drinks – microbrewery beers, ciders and juices – and modern pub food prepared from ingredients sourced from local farms and artisan producers. The menus evolve with the seasons; there's a bar snack menu plus a set menu at lunchtime that may start with grilled sardines with walnut croûte, caramelised onions and tomato coulis; continue with pavé of cod with Norfolk brown shrimp and buttered leek risotto; and end with a sticky toffee pudding, date purée and cinnamon ice cream.

Open 12-3 6-11 (Sat 12-11 Sun 12-6) Closed Mon **Food** Lunch Tue-Fri 12-2, Sat 12-3, Sun 12-3.30 Dinner Tue-Sat 6-9 Set menu available Restaurant menu available Tue-Sun ⊕ FREE HOUSE ◀ Local guest ales ♂ Biddenden Bushels, Kent. ⚑ 13 **Facilities** Non-diners area ♣ (Bar Restaurant Garden) ♦♦ Children's menu Children's portions Play area Family room Garden ⊨ Beer festival Parking ▥ (notice required)

STOWTING   Map 7 TR14

The Tiger Inn

tel: 01303 862130 **TN25 6BA**
email: info@tigerinn.co.uk
dir: *Phone for detailed directions*

Classic village pub with rustic charm and hearty food

Lost down winding lanes in a scattered North Downs hamlet, the 250-year-old Tiger Inn oozes traditional character and rural charm. The front bar is delightfully rustic and unpretentious, with stripped oak floors, two warming wood-burning stoves, old cushioned pews and scrubbed old pine tables. Mingle with the locals at the bar with a pint of Master Brew or the pub's own Tiger Top, then order a hearty meal from the inviting chalkboard menu – perhaps Romney Marsh rack of lamb with redcurrant jus; whole Dover sole; and chicken, ham and leek pie with shortcrust pastry. In summer dine alfresco on the suntrap front terrace. There are super walks all around.

Open all day Closed Mon & Tue **Food** Lunch Wed-Sun 12-9 Dinner Wed-Sun 12-9 Av main course £14 ⊕ FREE HOUSE ◀ Shepherd Neame Master Brew, Harvey's, Old Dairy, Gadds', Hop Fuzz, Tiger Inn Tiger Top ♂ Biddenden. ⚑ 10 **Facilities** Non-diners area ♣ (Bar Garden) ♦♦ Children's menu Children's portions Garden ⊨ Parking WiFi ▥

TENTERDEN   Map 7 TQ83

White Lion Inn

tel: 01580 765077 **57 High St TN30 6BD**
email: info@whiteliontenterden.com
dir: *On A28 (Ashford to Hastings road)*

Thoroughly 21st-century town centre inn

Beside the broad tree-lined street in Tenterden, 'the Jewel of the Weald', stands this stylish inn, which combines many original features with a contemporary look and feel. Reasonably priced fresh food ranges from starters of baked camembert with onion jam to share, or salmon and crab cakes with tartare sauce, to mains such as steak, mushroom and ale pie; battered haddock and fat chips; or grilled salmon Niçoise. Look out for special offers on pub classics served all day. Reliable Marston's and Wychwood Hobgoblin ales are the mainstay in the bar. Takeaway pizzas are available too.

Open all wk 10am-11pm (wknds 10am-mdnt) **Food** Lunch Mon-Sat 12-10, Sun 12-9 Dinner Mon-Sat 12-10, Sun 12-9 ⊕ MARSTON'S ◀ EPA, Old Dairy, Ringwood Best Bitter, Wychwood Hobgoblin, Guest ales ♂ Symonds. **Facilities** Non-diners area ♦♦ Children's menu Children's portions Outside area ⊨ Parking WiFi ▥ (notice required)

TONBRIDGE   Map 6 TQ54

See also Penshurst

The Little Brown Jug

tel: 01892 870318 **Chiddingstone Causeway TN11 8JJ**
email: enquiries@thelittlebrownjug.co.uk
dir: *On B2027 between Tonbridge & Bough Beech*

Warm and welcoming village favourite

Under new management since October 2014, this village treasure always feels as warm as toast thanks to two open fires in the bar and heated Polynesian-style huts in the garden, each seating up to 10 for lunch or dinner. Amenities of a more conventional kind include the bar, dispensing Chiddingstone-brewed Larkins beers, and the restaurant, which does a great home-made burger; Highfield Farm shoulder of lamb; ham, egg and chips and sausage and mash, and gluten-free dishes too. Events are a big thing here, with sausage and pie weeks, and the May and September beer festivals.

Open all day all wk **Food** Contact pub for food times ⊕ WHITING & HAMMOND ◀ Greene King Abbot Ale, Larkins, Guest ales ♂ Aspall. ⚑ 16 **Facilities** Non-diners area ♣ (Bar Garden) ♦♦ Children's portions Play area Garden ⊨ Beer festival Cider festival Parking WiFi ▥

TUDELEY   Map 6 TQ64

The Poacher & Partridge

tel: 01732 358934 **Hartlake Rd TN11 0PH**
email: enquiries@thepoacherandpartridge.com
dir: *A21 S onto A26 E, at rdbt turn right. After 2m turn sharp left into Hartlake Rd, 0.5m on right*

Stylish rural pub with good food

Set amongst Kentish orchards, this pretty country pub has a rustic, down-to-earth feel with sturdy old wood furniture and unique features such as a beautiful old wine cellar and deli kitchen. Outside, you'll discover a large garden with a children's play area, ideal for a refreshing summer pint of Harvey's from the wide selection of local ales and ciders. Traditional English cuisine and regional French brasserie-style fare feature on the pub's well-considered menu, perhaps venison carpaccio and Venetian salad, followed by honey and mustard crusted lamb rump, potato rösti, baby vegetable and Jerez jus.

Open all day all wk 11.30-11 **Food** Lunch all wk 12-3 Dinner all wk 6-9.45 ⊕ FREE HOUSE ◀ Sharp's Doom Bar, Shepherd Neame Spitfire, Tonbridge, Harvey's, Old Dairy ♂ Thatchers Gold, Aspall, Biddenden. ⚑ 30 **Facilities** Non-diners area ♣ (Bar Garden) ♦♦ Children's menu Children's portions Play area Garden ⊨ Parking WiFi ▥ (notice required)

TUNBRIDGE WELLS (ROYAL) Map 6 TQ53

The Crown Inn

tel: 01892 864742 **The Green, Groombridge TN3 9QH**
email: crown.inn.groombridge@gmail.com
dir: *Take A264 W of Tunbridge Wells, then B2110 S*

Good food and bags of character

In the 18th century this charming free house was the infamous headquarters for a gang of smugglers who hid their casks of tea in the passages between the cellar and Groombridge Place, later home to Sir Arthur Conan Doyle. Doyle made this 16th-century pub his local and today, its low beams and an inglenook fireplace are the setting for some great food and drink. Favourites include trio of local pork sausages, mash, kale and red onion gravy; beer battered fish and chips, peas and home-made tartare sauce, and daily specials based on fresh local produce. Eat alfresco during the summer months.

Open all day all wk **Food** Lunch Mon-Fri 12-2.30, Sat 12-9, Sun 12-5 Dinner Mon-Fri 6-9, Sat 12-9 ⊕ FREE HOUSE ◀ Harvey's Sussex Best Bitter, Black Cat, Larkins ♻ Westons Stowford Press. **Facilities** Non-diners area ❄ (Bar Garden) ♦ Children's menu Children's portions Play area Garden ⚤ Parking WiFi 🚌 (notice required)

The Hare on Langton Green **PICK OF THE PUBS**

tel: 01892 862419 **Langton Rd, Langton Green TN3 0JA**
email: hare@brunningandprice.co.uk
dir: *From Tunbridge Wells take A264 towards East Grinstead. Pub on x-rds at Langton Green*

Imposing village pub

Overlooking a village green just outside Tunbridge Wells, The Hare dates from 1901, its architect drawing nostalgically on Tudor-style half-timbering to replace its fire-razed, 18th-century predecessor. Pub group Brunning & Price lease it from Greene King, whose Bury St Edmunds brewery supplies the real ales, while real ciders include Biddenden Bushel and Wyld Wood Organic. Extensive daily menus offer a good variety of ways to enjoy a three-course meal, beginning perhaps with goats' cheese terrine with fig chutney, mulled pear, watercress and walnut salad; or pan-fried scallops with creamed leeks and pancetta. Among the light bites might be crisp thyme polenta with sautéed wild mushrooms, while mains range from Sicilian fish stew, by way of Kentish sausages with buttered mash; and honey- and mustard-glazed ham with free-range eggs and chips, to chargrilled tandoori haloumi with toasted coconut. For dessert, mixed berry crumble; or hot waffle with toffee apple sauce.

Open all day all wk **Food** Lunch Sun-Thu 12-9.30, Fri-Sat 12-10 Dinner Sun-Thu 12-9.30, Fri-Sat 12-10 Av main course £12 ⊕ BRUNNING & PRICE ◀ Greene King IPA, Ruddles Best & Abbot Ale, Morland Original, Hardys & Hansons Olde Trip ♻ Westons Old Rosie & Wyld Wood Organic, Aspall, Biddenden Bushel. ₹ 20 **Facilities** Non-diners area ❄ (Bar Garden) ♦ Children's menu Children's portions Garden ⚤ Parking WiFi

NEW Sankey's

tel: 01892 511422 **39 Mount Ephraim TN4 8AA**
email: sankeys@sankeys.co.uk
dir: *Phone pub for detailed directions*

Cask ales and beers from around the world

A respected family business in the Tonbridge area for over 50 years, Sankey's houses a unique collection of enamel signs, family memorabilia and antique church pews. But the focal points are the large open fire encircled with comfy armchairs, and the bar. Here you will need time to peruse the 23 draught options, which include ales from the town's brewery such as Coppernob, and from overseas such as Denmark's Mikkeller; also among the taps are two cider specials. A mouth-watering selection of pub favourites will soak up your refreshment, or head down to the old cellars for a feast of fish in the Seafood Brasserie.

Open all day all wk **Food** Lunch Mon-Fri 12-3, Sat-Sun 12-5, Dinner all wk 6-10 Av main course £10.50 Set menu available Restaurant menu available Tue-Sun ⊕ FREE HOUSE ◀ Tonbridge Coppernob, Brewdog, Mikkeller, Rotating guest ales ♻ Westons Stowford Press, Guest ciders. ₹ 12 **Facilities** Non-diners area ❄ (Bar Garden Outside area) ♦ Children's menu Children's portions Garden Outside area ⚤ Beer festival WiFi 🚌

WESTERHAM Map 6 TQ45

The Fox & Hounds

tel: 01732 750328 **Toys Hill TN16 1QG**
email: pub@foxandhoundstoyshill.co.uk
dir: *From A25 in Brasted follow brown signs for pub into Chart Lane. 2m to pub*

Great ale house, especially for dog owners

Chartwell, where Sir Winston Churchill lived for most of his adult life, is not far from this late 18th-century alehouse surrounded by National Trust land high on Kent's Greensand Ridge. All food served in the bar and traditionally styled restaurant is made on the premises from locally sourced produce. Start with some tiger prawns in garlic butter or crusty bread with smoked mackerel and horseradish pâté, before moving on to a more substantial main. Look out for pan-fried hake with lemon and caper butter; chicken, chorizo and chilli linguine; or sausage and mash with peas and onion gravy. The landlord describes the pub as very dog friendly.

Open all wk 11.30-3 6-11 (Fri-Sun all day) **Food** Lunch Mon-Sat 12-2.30, Sun 12-4 Dinner Mon-Sat 6-9 Av main course £13 ⊕ GREENE KING ◀ IPA, Abbot Ale, Morland Original. ₹ 10 **Facilities** Non-diners area ❄ (Bar Garden Outside area) ♦ Children's menu Children's portions Garden Outside area ⚤ Parking WiFi 🚌 (notice required)

Grasshopper on the Green

tel: 01959 562926 **The Green TN16 1AS**
email: info@grasshopperonthegreen.com
dir: *M25 junct 5, A21 towards Sevenoaks, then A25 to Westerham. Or M25 junct 6, A22 towards East Grinstead, A25 to Westerham*

Local brews and modern home-cooked cuisine

Overlooking Westerham's pretty green, the 700-year-old Grasshopper takes its name from the arms of local merchant Thomas Gresham, founder of London's Royal Exchange in 1565. The bar's low-beamed ceilings, hung with antique jugs, and its winter log fire are particularly appealing, as are Westerham brewery's Grasshopper and British Bulldog real ales. House specials include spicy chicken wrap; and home-made roasted vegetable lasagne, while regular cast members include grilled fresh tuna, lemon butter and capers; and slow-roasted lamb shank with red wine and rosemary jus. Ask long-term hosts Neale and Anne Sadlier for directions to Chartwell, Sir Winston Churchill's former home.

Open all day all wk **Food** Lunch all wk 12-9 Dinner all wk 12-9 ⊕ FREE HOUSE ◀ Adnams Broadside, Harvey's Sussex Best Bitter, Courage Best Bitter, Westerham British Bulldog BB & Grasshopper ♻ Symonds. ₹ 12 **Facilities** Non-diners area ❄ (Bar Garden) ♦ Children's menu Children's portions Play area Garden ⚤ Parking WiFi 🚌 (notice required)

WEST MALLING
Map 6 TQ65

The Farm House
PICK OF THE PUBS

tel: 01732 843257 **97 The High St ME19 6NA**
email: enquiries@thefarmhouse.biz
dir: *M20 junct 4, S on A228. Right to West Malling. Pub in village centre*

Elegant gastro-pub adding a French accent to local ingredients

Well positioned in the heart of the Kentish market town of West Malling, with a pretty walled garden overlooking 15th-century stone barns. The handsome Elizabethan building offers a friendly welcome, whether stopping for refreshment in the stylish bar or eating in one its two dining areas. Local seasonal ingredients are expertly used in menus with a strong French influence. So a glass of wine may be called for – choose from 20 sold by the glass. In addition to the tapas, fish or meat sharing boards typical starters are pea and mint soup; and crab rarebit. Main courses vary from pub favourites such as free range chicken Caesar salad; to slow-cooked squid and chorizo stew, chickpeas, tomatoes, confit peppers and new potatoes. There is a good choice for children, perhaps Lamberhurst pork sausage with French fries, peas and gravy. There's a beer festival in early May.

Open all day all wk 10am-11pm **Food** Lunch Mon-Thu 10-3, Fri-Sat 10-9.45, Sun 10-9.30 Dinner Mon-Thu 6-9.45, Fri-Sat 10-9.45, Sun 10-9.30 ⊕ ENTERPRISE INNS ◀ Harvey's, Sharp's Doom Bar, Guinness ⬚ Biddenden, Aspall. ☗ 20 **Facilities** Non-diners area ⬤ Children's menu Garden ⌂ Beer festival Parking WiFi

WEST PECKHAM
Map 6 TQ65

NEW The Swan on the Green

tel: 01622 812271 **The Green ME18 5JW**
email: bookings@swan-on-the-green.co.uk
dir: *From A228 from West Malling towards Tonbridge, at rdbt take B2016 (Wrotham). At x-rds left to West Peckham. Pub opposite church*

Well-crafted home brews and modern food

First licensed over 330 years ago, The Swan on the Green's microbrewery has revived the 18th-century principles of 'pure ale', using only natural and, when possible, local ingredients for its eight craft ales; these are colourfully celebrated during the pub's October beer festival when Morris dancing may hinder through traffic. A full menu includes light bites such as boar burger with fried egg and mushroom, or a whole baked camembert with crusty bread. Typical of the main dishes is Serrano-rolled loin of pork on a chorizo and mixed bean cassoulet. Home-made puddings may proffer American-style pancakes with either maple syrup or berry compôte with ice cream.

Open all wk 12-3 6-late **Food** Lunch 12-2 Dinner 6.30-9 Av main course £13 ⊕ FREE HOUSE ◀ Swan Fuggles & Trumpeter ⬚ Biddenden Bushels. **Facilities** ⬤ (Bar Restaurant) ⬤ Children's portions Outside area ⌂ Beer festival Parking ⬛ (notice required)

WHITSTABLE
Map 7 TR16

Pearson's Arms

tel: 01227 773133 **Sea Wall CT5 1BT**
email: info@pearsonsarmsbyrichardphillips.co.uk
dir: *In town centre. On one-way system, left at end of High St*

Relaxed seafront hostelry serving the county's best

Once owned by the Kray twins, this beach-facing pub was built to accommodate workers building the railway line between the town and Canterbury – now a popular rambling route called the Crab and Winkle Way. Today this friendly pub proffers all good Kentish things, including ales such as Timothy Taylor Landlord, and Symonds cider; drinks can be served in plastic cups for taking to the beach. Chef Richard Phillips' flavoursome food is fresh and also sourced as locally as possible: fresh Whitstable rock oysters with sherry vinegar shallots and tabasco could precede a plate of roast saddle of Kentish rabbit; or organic salmon and crab fishcake.

Open all day all wk **Food** Lunch Mon-Sat 12-9.30 Dinner Mon-Sat 12-9.30 Av main course £15.95 Set menu available Restaurant menu available all wk ⊕ ENTERPRISE INNS ◀ Timothy Taylor Landlord, Whitstable IPA, Harvey's Sussex Best Bitter ⬚ Aspall, Symonds. ☗ 16 **Facilities** Non-diners area ⬤ (Bar) ⬤ Children's menu Children's portions WiFi ⬛ (notice required)

WROTHAM
Map 6 TQ65

The Bull ★★★★ INN ⑳⑳
PICK OF THE PUBS

tel: 01732 789800 **Bull Ln TN15 7RF**
email: info@thebullhotel.com web: www.thebullhotel.com
dir: *M20 junct 2, A20 (signed Paddock Wood, Gravesend & Tonbridge). At rdbt 3rd exit onto A20 (signed Wrotham, Tonbridge, Borough Green, M20 & M25). At rdbt take 4th exit into Bull Ln (signed Wrotham)*

Ancient pub featuring micro-beers

First licensed under Henry VII in 1495, this three-storey building can be traced to 1385. More recently, World War II pilots relaxed here – stamps on the restaurant ceiling mark downed German planes. Ales from the award-winning Dark Star microbrewery are supported by a vast wine list. A Big Green Egg BBQ is the workhorse of the two AA Rosette kitchen and it's used daily for smoking, slow roasting and grilling. Be tempted by a starter of barbecued aubergine, cucumber shot, crème fraîche, lemon oil; or chicken liver parfait, caramelised onion with saffron fruit bread, and follow on with slow-braised lamb shoulder, creamy mash, shallot purée, oxtail horseradish beignet and minted lamb jus; or pan-fried sea bass fillet, rice noodles, mushroom ginger lemongrass broth. The bar offers the likes of slow-cooked ribs and 10-hour smoked pulled pork, perhaps washed down with one of several craft beers. Pub classic dishes are also available.

Open all day all wk **Food** Lunch Mon-Fri 12-2.30, Sat 12-9, Sun 12-8 Dinner Mon-Fri 6-9, Sat 12-9, Sun 12-8 Restaurant menu available all wk ⊕ FREE HOUSE ◀ Dark Star Hophead, Old Dairy Red Top, Guest Ales ⬚ Burrow Hill. ☗ 12 **Facilities** Non-diners area ⬤ (Bar Garden) ⬤ Children's portions Garden ⌂ Parking WiFi ⬛ (notice required) **Rooms** 11

LANCASHIRE

ALTHAM
Map 18 SD73

The Walton Arms

tel: 01282 774444 **Burnley Rd BB5 5UL**
email: walton-arms@btconnect.com
dir: *M65 junct 8, A678, pub between Accrington & Padiham*

Popular pub serving good pub food

A long-established way-station on an ancient highway linking Yorkshire and Lancashire, this sturdy, stone-built dining pub oozes history. Pilgrims to Whalley Abbey called at an inn here when Henry VII was king. Beams and brasses, rustic furniture and slabbed stone floors welcome today's pilgrims intent on sampling the comprehensive menu, either as a bar meal or in the atmospheric dining room. Typical choices include sea bass fillets, crayfish, chorizo and lemon risotto; spinach, cherry tomato and mozzarella suet pudding; or the inn's signature dish – shoulder of local lamb with roasted vegetables.

Open 12-2.30 5.30-11 (Sun 12-10.30) Closed Mon **Food** Lunch Tue-Fri 12-2, Sun 12-7 Dinner Tue-Sat 6-9, Sun 12-7 Set menu available Restaurant menu available Tue-Sun ⊕ J W LEES ◀ Bitter. ☻ 16 **Facilities** Non-diners area ◀ Children's menu Children's portions Outside area ⌂ Parking ☞ (notice required)

BARLEY
Map 18 SD84

NEW Barley Mow ★★★★ INN

tel: 01282 690868 **BB12 9JX**
email: info@barleymowpendle.co.uk **web:** www.seafoodpubcompany.com
dir: *M65 junct 13, at rdbt exit onto A682. Left into Pasture Ln, right into Ridge Ln, continue on Barley New Rd. Turn right*

Upmarket gastro-pub with good walks

Owned by the Seafood Pub Company, the Barley Mow is located at the start and end of a lovely walk on Pendle Hill, after which you should be in need of a glass of Wainwright ale and a hearty meal. The menu focuses on the grill, which might be employed to produce a full rack of baby back ribs served with slaw, skin-on fries, corn on the cob and BBQ sauce, or pork satay skewers with sweet potato fries and peanut sauce. Jam roly poly with vanilla custard is one traditional end to a meal.

Open all day all wk Mon-Thu 7.30am-11pm Fri-Sat 8.30am-mdnt Sun 8.30am-10pm **Food** Lunch Mon-Thu 12-8.30, Fri-Sat 11.30-9.30, Sun 11.30-8.30 Dinner Mon-Thu 12-8.30, Fri-Sat 11.30-9.30, Sun 11.30-8.30 Av main course £13.95 ⊕ FREE HOUSE ◀ Thwaites Wainwright, Timothy Taylor Landlord, Moorhouses Pride of Pendle ♂ Kingstone Press. ☻ 8 **Facilities** Non-diners area ◀ (All areas) ◀ Children's portions Garden Outside area ⌂ Parking WiFi ☞ (notice required) **Rooms** 6

BARROW
Map 18 SD73

The Eagle at Barrow

tel: 01254 825285 **Clitheroe Rd BB7 9AQ**
email: info@theeagleatbarrow.co.uk
dir: *Off A59, N of Whalley. Phone for detailed directions*

Successful pub with great interior

At the heart of The Eagle is the oak-panelled public bar with a log fire, antique pews and chairs, and a baby grand piano providing lively entertainment on Friday and Saturday evenings. Taylor's champagne bar is for those seeking a little more privacy. The wide choice of food in the Brasserie, sourced from the very best local produce, includes beef bourguignon; steamed suet steak pudding; fish pie; and spiced aubergine. Buy take-away award-winning sausages and other regional treats from the in-house Berkins Deli.

Open all day all wk 12-11 (Fri-Sat noon-1am) **Food** Lunch Mon-Sat 12-2.30, Sun 12-8 Dinner Mon-Sat 6-9 Set menu available ⊕ FREE HOUSE ◀ Courage Directors, Caledonian Deuchars IPA, Local guest ales ♂ Old Mout. ☻ **Facilities** Non-diners area ◀ (Bar Outside area) ◀ Children's menu Children's portions Outside area ⌂ Parking WiFi

BILSBORROW
Map 18 SD53

Owd Nell's Tavern

tel: 01995 640010 **Guy's Thatched Hamlet, Canal Side PR3 0RS**
email: info@guysthatchedhamlet.com
dir: *M6 junct 32 N on A6. In approx 5m follow brown tourist signs to Guy's Thatched Hamlet*

Canalside eating, drinking and shopping complex

The Wilkinson family's pub forms part of Guy's Thatched Hamlet, a group of refreshment outlets and craft shops beside the Lancaster Canal. Aimed at all ages, it bills itself "For eatin', drinkin', stayin', playin' and dancin'". The stone-flagged, low-beamed bar serves Owd Nell's Canalside Bitter, Moorhouse's Pendle Witches Brew and other local ales. An all-day menu offers hot potato skins; black pudding and poached egg stack; Cottam's Cumberland sausage, egg and chips; lamb cutlets; local seafood platter; and grilled goats' cheese salad. Children's menus are also available. Events include a July cider festival and a celebration for oysters in September.

Open all day all wk 7am-2am Closed 25 Dec **Food** Lunch all wk 12-9 Dinner all wk 12-9 Restaurant menu available all wk ⊕ FREE HOUSE ◀ Moorhouse's Pendle Witches Brew, Owd Nell's Canalside Bitter, Bowland, Copper Dragon, Black Sheep, Thwaites, Hart ♂ Thatchers Heritage & Cheddar Valley. ☻ 20 **Facilities** Non-diners area ◀ (Bar Garden Outside area) ◀ Children's menu Children's portions Family room Garden Outside area ⌂ Beer festival Cider festival Parking WiFi ☞ (notice required)

BLACKBURN
Map 18 SD62

The Clog and Billycock ◉
PICK OF THE PUBS

tel: 01254 201163 **Billinge End Rd, Pleasington BB2 6QB**
email: enquiries@theclogandbillycock.com
dir: *M6 junct 29 to M65 junct 3, follow Pleasington signs*

Landmark village pub that ticks all the boxes

The unusual pub name celebrates the favourite attire of an early 20th-century landlord, a billycock being a felt hat. The Ribble Valley Inns group, which owns it, styled the decor to include wall lights fashioned from old weaving shuttles, lamps from cobblers' shoe stretchers, and artwork by north-west artist, Nicholas Saunders. Background music is played in some parts of the building. The real ales are from Thwaites of Blackburn, while the award-winning wine list is compiled by leading authority, Craig Bancroft. All contributing towards its AA Rosette are Nigel Haworth's Lancashire hotpot; cheese and onion pie; chicken kebab and curried lentil sauce; pan-roasted sea bass with yellow beets; Garstang Blue, pear and walnut salad; and smoked fish pie. If the weather's good, eat and drink outdoors on the dining terrace. Out on Blackburn's western fringes, the pub is well placed for walks through pleasantly wooded countryside.

Open all wk 12-11 (Sun 12-10) **Food** Lunch Mon-Fri 12-2, Sat & BHs 12-9, Sun 12-8.30, (afternoon bites Mon-Fri 2-5.30) Dinner Mon-Thu 5.30-8.30, Fri 5.30-9, Sat & BHs 12-9, Sun 12-8.30 Av main course £13 Set menu available ⊕ RIBBLE VALLEY INNS ◀ Thwaites Lancaster Bomber, Original, Wainwrights & Nutty Black ♂ Kingstone Press. ☻ 11 **Facilities** Non-diners area ◀ (Bar Outside area) ◀ Children's menu Outside area ⌂ Parking WiFi

BLACKBURN *continued*

The Millstone at Mellor ★★★★★ INN ◉◉

PICK OF THE PUBS

See Pick of the Pubs on opposite page and advert below

BLACKO
Map 18 SD84

Moorcock Inn

tel: 01282 614186 **Gisburn Rd BB9 6NG**
email: moorcockinn@gmail.com
dir: *M65 junct 13, A682, inn halfway between Blacko & Gisburn*

Country pub with many walks around

Beyond the folly of Blacko Tower, high on the road towards Gisburn on the Upper Admergill area, lies this family-run, 18th-century inn with traditional log fires, splendid views towards the Pendle Way and locally brewed cask ales in the bar. There's a wide choice on the menu and specials board including salads and sandwiches, and vegetarian and children's meals. Main dishes are hearty and include home-made pies, steaks, salads, sandwiches and specials that might include corned beef hash, bratwursts and schnitzels. Vegetarian options are available too.

Open 12-2 6-9 (Sat 12-9 Sun 12-6) Closed Mon **Food** Lunch Tue-Fri 12-2, Sat 12-9, Sun 12-6 Dinner Tue-Fri 6-9, Sat 12-9, Sun 12-6 Av main course £7.95 ⊕ FREE HOUSE ◀ Reedley Hallows ♺ Kingstone Press. **Facilities** Non-diners area ❖ (Bar Restaurant Outside area) ♦ Children's menu Children's portions Outside area ☐ Parking ⛟ (notice required)

BURROW
Map 18 SD67

The Highwayman ◉

PICK OF THE PUBS

tel: 01524 273338 **LA6 2RJ**
email: enquiries@highwaymaninn.co.uk
dir: *M6 junct 36, A65 to Kirkby Lonsdale. A683 S. Burrow approx 2m*

Flying the flag for Lancashire produce

Part of The Ribble Valley Inns group, The Highwayman is a stylishly appointed 18th-century coaching inn with craggy stone floors, warm wooden furniture and log fires. Thwaites and Wainwright supply the real ales, Kingstone Press its draught cider, and wine expert Craig Bancroft chooses the extensive wine list, with 10 by the glass. Experienced chef Jason 'Bruno' Birkbeck, who trained with owner Nigel Haworth, has created a menu that picks up local and regional favourites, such as potato and back bacon soup with smoked Lancashire puffs; and rabbit pie. Other possibilities are braised shoulder of Kitridding lamb with root vegetables; breast of duck with shallot tart, duck leg bon bon, green peppercorn sauce and chips in dripping; or mushroom suet pudding, mash, honey roast carrots and onion gravy. There are seasonal alternatives, a good children's menu and a gluten-free one too. Butterflies and birds love the terraced gardens, where there is comfortable seating and outdoor heating.

Open all day all wk 12-11 (Sun 12-10.30) **Food** Lunch Mon-Fri 12-2, Sat 12-9, Sun 12-8.30 Dinner Mon-Thu 5.30-8.30, Fri-Sat 5.30-9, Sat 12-9, Sun 12-8.30 Set menu available ⊕ FREE HOUSE ◀ Thwaites Wainwright & 1816 ♺ Kingstone Press. ♟ 10 **Facilities** Non-diners area ❖ (Bar Garden Outside area) ♦ Children's menu Garden Outside area ☐ Parking WiFi

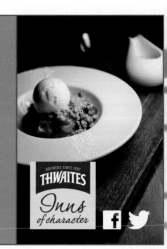

PICK OF THE PUBS

The Millstone at Mellor ★★★★★ INN ❀❀

BLACKBURN   Map 18 SD62

tel: 01254 813333
Church Ln, Mellor BB2 7JR
email: relax@millstonehotel.co.uk
web: www.millstonehotel.co.uk
dir: *M6 junct 31, A59 towards Clitheroe,
past British Aerospace. Right at rdbt
signed Blackburn/Mellor. Next rdbt 2nd
left. At top of hill on right*

Country-edge inn with superb cuisine

This handsome coaching inn stands in
an old village at the edge of Mellor Moor
above Blackburn. With the beautiful
Ribble Valley and Forest of Bowland
Area of Natural Beauty to the north,
Pendle Hill nearby and the half-
timbered wonder that is Samlesbury
Hall just along the lanes, it's little
wonder that this inn is a popular place.
It's very much a village inn at the heart
of the community, presided over by chef-
patron Anson Bolton, whose culinary
skills have repeatedly gained two AA
Rosettes in recognition of his innovative
take on classic dishes. Warm up by the
log fire in the well-appointed bar or
relax in the oak-panelled Miller's
restaurant, perhaps picking at the
nibbles board — black pudding fritters,
bhajis and chipolatas with dips and
pondering the attractive menu options.
The selection of starters ranges from
duck spring rolls to chicken Caesar

salad; or settle for the charcuterie deli
board featuring home-cured meats with
pickles, rocket, oils and bread. Mains
reflect the strong tradition of good pub
food, with a fish curry a popular option,
whilst the Bowland steak, kidney and
Thwaites Wainwright Ale suet pudding
is a great winter warmer. Let your eyes
drift to the 'Inn Season' specials board,
drawing on the extravagant produce for
which the Ribble Valley is widely
renowned; 28-day aged Bowland steaks
are also a favourite. Walkers passing
from the local footpath network can
expect beers from the local Thwaites
brewery, founded over 200 years ago by
Daniel Thwaite, who is buried in the
churchyard near this, one of his first
pubs.

Open all day all wk **Food** Mon-Sat
12-9.30, Sun 12-9 Av main course £14
🌐 THWAITES INNS OF CHARACTER
🛢 Lancaster Bomber, Original,
Wainwright Ŏ Kingstone Press. ♟ 10
Facilities Non-diners area ⫯ Children's
menu Children's portions Outside area
⌶ Parking WiFi **Rooms** 23

CARNFORTH
Map 18 SD47

The Longlands Inn and Restaurant

tel: 01524 781256 **Tewitfield LA6 1JH**
email: info@longlandshotel.co.uk
dir: *Phone for detailed directions*

Confident cooking of local produce

Although very much Lancastrian, this traditional country inn is only minutes away from the Cumbria border. With its nooks and crannies, old beams and uneven floors, this family-run dog-friendly inn stands next to Tewitfield Locks on the Lancaster Canal and is an ideal base for the Lake District. The bar, with Tirril ales on tap, rocks to live bands on Mondays while hungry music lovers consume plates of stone-baked pizzas and pasta. Otherwise look to the restaurant for good country cooking and local produce, with Lakeland steaks and Morecambe Bay shrimps on the appetising menu. Children are well catered for.

Open all day all wk 11-11 **Food** Lunch Mon-Fri 12-2.30, Sat 12-4, Sun 12-9 Dinner Mon-Sat 6-9.30, Sun 12-9 ⊕ FREE HOUSE ◀ Tirril Old Faithful, Black Sheep, Bowland Hen Harrier, Old School Brewery. ♀ 9 **Facilities** Non-diners area ✿ (Bar Garden) ♦♦ Children's menu Garden ⌂ Parking WiFi ➡ (notice required)

CHIPPING
Map 18 SD64

Dog & Partridge

tel: 01995 61201 **Hesketh Ln PR3 2TH**
dir: *M6 junct 31A, follow Longridge signs. At Longridge left at 1st rbdt, straight on at next 3 rdbts. At Alston Arms turn right. 3m, pub on right*

Tudor pub with a restored barn restaurant

Dating back to 1515, this pleasantly modernised rural pub in the Ribble Valley enjoys delightful views of the surrounding fells. The barn has been transformed into a welcoming dining area, where home-made food on the comprehensive bar snack menu is backed by a specials board featuring fresh fish and game dishes. A typical menu shows a starter of deep-fried garlic mushrooms; and chilled melon with cream curry sauce; then mains of braised pork chops with home-made apple sauce and stuffing; poached salmon with prawn sauce; or home-made steak and kidney pie.

Open 11.45-3 6.45-11 (Sat 11.45-3 6-11 Sun 11.45-10.30) Closed Mon **Food** Lunch Tue-Sat 12-1.45 Set menu available Restaurant menu available Tue-Sun ⊕ FREE HOUSE ◀ Black Sheep, Marston's EPA, Moorhouse's Premier Bitter, Tetley's Dark Mild, Guest ales. ♀ 8 **Facilities** Non-diners area ♦♦ Children's menu Children's portions Parking WiFi ➡

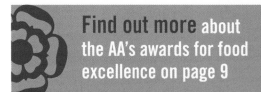

Find out more **about the AA's awards for food excellence on page 9**

CHORLEY
Map 15 SD51

NEW The Yew Tree Inn

tel: 01257 480344 **Dill Hall Brow, Heath Charnock PR6 9HA**
web: www.yewtreeinnanglezarke.co.uk
dir: *From A6 x-rds in Anderton (S of Heath Charnock) into Babylon Ln. At T-junct right signed Rivington. Over M6. Left signed Anglezarke. Pub on right*

Secluded pub-restaurant in stunning setting

This stone-built country inn stands at the fringe of Bolton's remarkable lakeland; a string of reservoirs wrapped around the foot of the West Pennine Moors. No surprises, then, that the peaceful beer garden is a target for ramblers slaking their thirst with beers from the local Blackedge Brewery. At heart The Yew Tree is a popular destination dining pub, with hearty British dishes to the fore – typically Rivington pork ribs with home-made BBQ sauce; or herb crusted lamb rump with butternut squash and wilted spinach. Log fires warm the light interior of this refurbished rural retreat; whilst Easter sees a beer and cider festival here.

Open 12-3 6-9.30 (Fri 12-3 6-10.30 Sat 12-10.30 Sun 12-8) Closed Mon **Food** Lunch Tue-Fri 12-3, Sat 12-9.30, Sun 12-6.30 Dinner Tue-Thu 6-9, Fri 6-9.30, Sat 12-9.30, Sun 12-6.30 Av main course £13 Set menu available ⊕ FREE HOUSE ◀ Blackedge Anglezarke, Gold & Treacle Stout Ò Herefordshire Cider, South West Orchards Raspberry Craft Cider. ♀ 13 **Facilities** Non-diners area ✿ (Bar Garden Outside area) ♦♦ Children's menu Children's portions Garden Outside area ⌂ Beer festival Cider festival Parking WiFi ➡ (notice required)

CLAUGHTON
Map 18 SD54

The Fenwick Seafood Pub

tel: 01524 221157 **Hornby Rd LA2 9LA**
email: info@fenwickarms.co.uk
dir: M6 junct 34, A683. Follow Kirkby Lonsdale signs. Approx 5m to pub on left

Specialist seafood pub

Joycelyn Neve founded her Seafood Pub Company on the back of her family's long-standing maritime associations. One of her several pubs, this 250-year-old inn, with open fires, low-beamed ceilings and oak-planked floors, combines its traditional role with that of specialist fish and seafood restaurant. Top quality produce arrives daily from the family business in Fleetwood, to emerge from the kitchen perhaps as wild mushroom and brown shrimp on brioche; or Malaysian seafood curry. Other attractions include chicken, ham and leek pot pie; and twice baked Lancashire cheese soufflé. In the bar there's Timothy Taylor and Thwaites Wainwright beers.

Open all day all wk **Food** Lunch Mon-Thu 12-9, Fri-Sat 12-10, Sun 12-8.30 Dinner Mon-Thu 12-9, Fri-Sat 12-10, Sun 12-8.30 ⊕ FREE HOUSE ◀ Black Sheep, Thwaites Wainwright, Timothy Taylor Boltmaker. ¶ 14 **Facilities** Non-diners area ♣ (Bar Outside area) ♦ Children's menu Children's portions Outside area ⊓ Parking WiFi ➡ (notice required)

CLITHEROE
Map 18 SD74

The Assheton Arms ★★★★★ RR ◉   PICK OF THE PUBS

tel: 01200 441227 **Downham BB7 4BJ**
email: info@asshetonarms.com **web:** www.asshetonarms.com
dir: A59 to Chatburn, then follow Downham signs

Historic village inn with seafood specialities

Originally a farmhouse brewing beer to refresh its workers, this pub became the George and Dragon in 1872. In 1950 it was renamed in honour of the contribution made by Ralph Assheton, Lord Clitheroe, during World War II. A few years ago it was taken over by the family-owned and operated Seafood Pub Company, which just refreshed the stylish restaurant while preserving its village inn credentials; a great choice of real ales includes Moorhouse's Pride of Pendle. Local sourcing is a priority here, with fresh fish and seafood supplied daily. Snack on haddock goujons with Marie Rose sauce, or push the boat out by starting with devilled crab, salmon and brown shrimp with radish and cress salad and sea salt croûtes; and continuing with a main course such as roast hake with smoked salmon potato pancake and steamed baby spinach. There's plenty of choice for those who aren't so keen on fish, and the kids' own menu is mouthwatering.

Open all day all wk 12-10.30 (Fri-Sat 12-12) **Food** Lunch Mon-Sat 12-3, Sun 12-8 Dinner Mon-Thu 6-8.30, Fri-Sat 6-9, Sun 12-8 Av main course £15.50 ⊕ FREE HOUSE ◀ Thwaites Wainwright, Black Sheep, Timothy Taylor, Moorhouse's Pride of Pendle Ŏ Thatchers Gold. ¶ 10 **Facilities** Non-diners area ♣ (Bar Garden Outside area) ♦ Children's menu Children's portions Garden Outside area ⊓ Parking WiFi ➡ (notice required) **Rooms** 11

ELSWICK
Map 18 SD43

The Ship at Elswick

tel: 01995 672777 **High St PR4 3ZB**
email: mail@theshipelswick.co.uk
dir: M55 junct 3, A585 signed Fleetwood. Right onto Thistleton Rd (B5269). 1m to pub

Former farmhouse in a quiet village, offering hearty food

In a quiet village on the Fylde and handy both for Blackpool and the quieter resorts of Cleveleys and Fleetwood, this former farmhouse is now a reliable village local and dining inn. From Fleetwood come some of the fish inhabiting the very traditional menu here; corned beef hash, and cheese and onion pie are other favourites, or start with smoked salmon and crayfish fishcakes. There are also pasta choices, salads and a Sunday roast. The owners are proud to use Lancashire produce in most of their dishes, although the standard beer is Yorkshire's Black Sheep.

Open all day all wk **Food** Lunch Mon-Sat 12-9, Sun 12-8 Dinner Mon-Sat 12-9, Sun 12-8 Av main course £10 ⊕ PUNCH TAVERNS ◀ Jennings Cumberland Ale, Black Sheep, Guest ales. ¶ 8 **Facilities** Non-diners area ♦ Children's menu Children's portions Play area Garden ⊓ Parking WiFi ➡

FENCE
Map 18 SD83

Fence Gate Inn

tel: 01282 618101 **Wheatley Lane Rd BB12 9EE**
email: info@fencegate.co.uk
dir: From M65 junct 13 towards Fence, 1.5m, pub set back on right opposite T-junct for Burnley

Village inn with a bustling brasserie

Once a private house, this imposing 300-year-old building next to the village church only became an inn as recently as 1982. At the edge of beautiful open countryside, the pub's brasserie and dining suites reveal its function as a foodie destination, but drinkers aren't forgotten, with a wood-panelled bar featuring a grand log fire and high-quality furnishings, where Lancashire-brewed beers are the order of the day. The Lancashire theme continues with the locally sourced food going into dishes such as Bowland beef steak burger, pulled pork sandwich, chicken schnitzel, lamb kofta salad and vegetable Thai green curry.

Open all day all wk noon-close **Food** Lunch Mon-Sat 12-2.30, Sun 12-8 Dinner Mon-Sat 6-9, Sun 12-8 ⊕ FREE HOUSE ◀ Courage Directors, Caledonian Deuchars IPA, Theakston Best Bitter, Moorhouse's, Bowland, Guest ales. ¶ 10 **Facilities** Non-diners area ♣ (Bar Garden) ♦ Children's menu Children's portions Garden Parking WiFi ➡

FENISCOWLES
Map 18 SD62

Oyster & Otter   PICK OF THE PUBS

tel: 01254 203200 **631 Livesey Branch Rd BB2 5DQ**
email: info@oysterandotter.co.uk
dir: M65 junct 3, right at lights, right at mini rdbt into Livesey Branch Rd

Seafood-led gastro-pub with global influences

This clapboard and stone-fronted pub is run by former Fleetwood fish wholesaler Chris Neve, who comes from a long line of North Sea and Irish Sea trawlermen. His daughter Joycelyn studied the coastal food industry in South America before becoming head of operations here, and the third lynch-pin is executive chef Antony Shirley, formerly head chef at Raffles in the West Indies. This Blackburn-fringe pub may look more New England than Lancashire mill-town but the menu gets its inspiration from all over the world. You might try fish starters such as citrus-crumbed squid with smoked chilli mayo, while main courses include fish pie and seafood ramen packed with king prawns, squid, mussels and salmon. Alternatively, there's duck red curry; or slow-cooked shin of beef in ale with parsley mash and roast carrots. A typical dessert is lemon curd and ginger nut cheesecake with poached blackberries.

Open all day all wk **Food** Lunch all wk 12-5 Dinner Sun-Thu 5-9, Fri-Sat 5-10 Av main course £15 ⊕ THWAITES ◀ Wainwright, Lancaster Bomber, Original Ŏ Kingstone Press. ¶ 9 **Facilities** Non-diners area ♦ Children's menu Children's portions Garden Outside area ⊓ Parking WiFi ➡ (notice required)

FORTON

Map 18 SD45

The Bay Horse Inn

PICK OF THE PUBS

tel: 01524 791204 **LA2 0HR**
email: craig@bayhorseinn.com
dir: *M6 junct 33 take A6 towards Garstang, turn left for pub. Pub approx 1m from M6*

Stylish family-run inn with imaginative menu

In one direction lanes percolate through to the sea-marshes of Morecambe Bay; in the other the destination is the Forest of Bowland, a magical landscape of moors, crags and gorge-like valleys. Rural Lancashire at its most sublime. There's good Lancashire beer here too, from Moorhouses' Burnley brewery, perhaps supped in the extended gardens which lead to open fields where pheasants and deer can often be spotted. Mismatched furniture and a handsome stone fireplace with roaring winter log fire characterise the inn, offering a tantalising flavour of the small coaching inn it once was. The kitchen, managed by chef-patron Craig Wilkinson, makes full use of the wealth of produce the county has to offer. So from the concise menu be tempted by a starter of grilled black pudding, celeriac coleslaw, cured ham, apple purée and brown sauce; progress then to slow-cooked shank of lamb with pearl barley, mash and rosemary, and round off with damson fool with cinder toffee and hazelnuts.

Open 12-3 6-12 Closed Mon-Tue (ex BHs L) **Food** Lunch Wed-Sat 12-2, Sun 12-3 Dinner Wed-Sat 6.30-9, Sun 6-8 Av main course £15 Set menu available ⊕ FREE HOUSE ◪ Moorhouse's Pendle Witches Brew, Black Sheep, Guest ale. ♟ 11 **Facilities** Non-diners area ♣ (Bar Garden) ♦♦ Children's portions Garden ➤ Parking WiFi

GREAT ECCLESTON

Map 18 SD44

Farmers Arms

tel: 01995 672018 **Halsalls Square PR3 0YE**
email: info@greatecclestonpub.co.uk
dir: *M55 junct 3, A585, A586 to Great Eccleston. From High St into Chapel St, pub on left*

Family-friendly gastro-pub specialising in seafood

Just off the main Garstang to Blackpool road, this two-storey pub-restaurant belongs to the Seafood Pub Company. It was set up by Joycelyn Neve who decided to capitalise on her family's long-standing involvement with deep-sea fishing. Naturally, there's plenty of fish and seafood on the menu, from seaside fritto misto with proper chips and Marie Rose sauce to smoked haddock with bubble-and-squeak, poached egg and mustard butter sauce. An excellent children's menu offers dishes in two sizes for 'hungry young 'uns'.

Open all day all wk **Food** Lunch all wk 12-5 Dinner Sun-Thu 5-9, Fri-Sat 5-10 Av main course £15.50 ⊕ FREE HOUSE ◪ Timothy Taylor Landlord, Thwaites Wainwright, Lancaster Blonde Ŏ Thatchers Gold. ♟ 12 **Facilities** Non-diners area ♣ (Bar Garden Outside area) ♦♦ Children's menu Children's portions Garden Outside area ➤ Parking WiFi ▭

GRINDLETON

Map 18 SD74

Duke of York

tel: 01200 441266 **Brow Top BB7 4QR**
email: info@dukeofyorkgrindleton.com
dir: *From A59 N of Clitheroe left to Chatburn. In Chatburn right into Ribble Ln. Over river, right at T-junct. Pub at brow of hill on left*

A leading Ribble Valley dining pub

Built of local stone, with an interior characterised by low ceilings, stone-flagged floors and little nooks and crannies, this creeper-clad village pub is at least 150

years old. Food takes the lead, although the bar still gets its fair share of Lancaster Blonde real ale drinkers. Driving things from the kitchen is chef/proprietor Michael Heathcote, on whose daily menu appears a short, but carefully chosen, choice of dishes, such as smoked Goosnargh duck with apple and pickled carrot; chargrilled rump of lamb with pea and broad bean broth; pan-fried fillet of cod with pork belly and mussel chowder; and lobster thermidor. There's a lovely garden too.

Open 12-3 6-11 (Sun 12-3 5-10.30) Closed 25 Dec, Mon (ex BHs, closed Tue following BHs) **Food** Lunch Tue-Sun 12-2 Dinner Tue-Sat 6-9, Sun 5-7.30 Set menu available ⊕ PUNCH TAVERNS ◪ Timothy Taylor Landlord, Lancaster Blonde. ♟ 20 **Facilities** Non-diners area ♣ (Bar Garden) ♦♦ Children's menu Children's portions Garden ➤ Parking WiFi ▭ (notice required)

HESKIN GREEN

Map 15 SD51

Farmers Arms

tel: 01257 451276 **85 Wood Ln PR7 5NP**
email: andy@farmersarms.co.uk
dir: *On B5250 between M6 & Eccleston*

Handsome family-run pub

This fine 17th-century pub used to be called the Pleasant Retreat, but in 1902 the name was changed. Never mind, because this long, creeper-covered building is still pleasant, very pleasant actually, and its flagstone Vault Bar is still a retreat. Malcolm and Ann Rothwell have been here for a quarter of a century, and run it together with their son Andrew who is the chef, and daughter-in-law Sue who oversees the restaurant. The menu may include minted lamb cutlets or baked haddock gratin, while the main menu features Cumberland sausage, lasagne verdi, grills and steaks, and a selection of salads, jacket potatoes and sandwiches. Hand-pulled real ales include Silver Tally, named after the token that miners would exchange for a lamp.

Open all day all wk **Food** Contact pub for food times ⊕ ENTERPRISE INNS ◪ Timothy Taylor Landlord, Marston's Pedigree, Prospect Silver Tally, Black Sheep, Tetley's. **Facilities** Non-diners area ♣ (Bar Garden) ♦♦ Children's menu Children's portions Play area Garden Parking WiFi

HEST BANK

Map 18 SD46

Hest Bank Inn

tel: 01524 824339 **2 Hest Bank Ln LA2 6DN**
email: chef.glenn@btinternet.com
dir: *From Lancaster take A6 N, after 2m left to Hest Bank*

Historic inn with lots to offer

First licensed in 1554, this former coaching inn is awash with history: it was occupied by Cromwell's officers in the Civil War and was also the haunt of highwaymen. Comedian Eric Morecambe used to drink at the canalside Hest Bank, which offers cask ales and a wide selection of meals all day, with local suppliers playing an important role in maintaining food quality. The good value menu ranges from piri piri chicken to steamed venison and beef pudding. Enjoy a pint of Thwaites Wainwright in the terraced garden. Wednesday evening is quiz night, while steak night is every Thursday. Call the pub for details of their beer festival.

Open all day all wk 11.30-11.30 (Sun 11.30-10.30) **Food** Lunch Mon-Fri 12-3, Sat 12-9, Sun 12-8 Dinner Mon-Fri 5-9, Sat 12-9, Sun 12-8 ⊕ PUNCH TAVERNS ◪ Thwaites Wainwright, Black Sheep Best Bitter, Guest ales. **Facilities** Non-diners area ♣ (Bar Garden) ♦♦ Children's menu Children's portions Play area Garden ➤ Beer festival Parking WiFi ▭ (notice required)

LANCASTER
Map 18 SD46

The Borough

tel: 01524 64170 **3 Dalton Square LA1 1PP**
email: jodie@theboroughlancaster.co.uk **web:** www.theboroughlancaster.co.uk
dir: *Phone for detailed directions*

Superb Lancashire produce in town house pub

This Grade II Georgian pub, in the city centre, with a Victorian frontage has wooden floors, chunky tables, chesterfield sofas, warm green hues and masses of light from a huge bay window. All this creates a friendly, relaxed vibe for enjoying their own microbrewery's Borough pale, dark and bitter and a quality food offering. Using top-notch ingredients from local suppliers, including meat and eggs from surrounding farms, the seasonal menu may take in BBQ pulled pork croquettes; Morecambe Bay mariners' pie; and the chance of 'building' your own burger from the grill section. Platters are available, and home-made desserts include sticky toffee pudding.

Open all wk 8am-11pm (Fri noon-12.30am Sat 8am-12.20am) **Food** Lunch Sun-Thu 12-9, Fri-Sat 12-9.30 Dinner Sun-Thu 12-9, Fri-Sat 12-9.30 Set menu available ⊕ FREE HOUSE ◀ Lancaster Amber, Young's Bitter, Wells Eagle IPA, Bowland Hen Harrier, Borough Brewery Bitter, Pale & Dark. ♥ 11 **Facilities** Non-diners area ✿ (Bar Garden) ♦ Children's menu Garden ⋒ WiFi ⛟ (notice required)

Penny Street Bridge ★★★★ INN   PICK OF THE PUBS
See Pick of the Pubs on page 302 and advert below

The Stork Inn

tel: 01524 751234 **Conder Green LA2 0AN**
email: tracy@thestorkinn.co.uk
dir: *M6 junct 33 take A6 N. Left at Galgate & next left to Conder Green*

Traditional coaching inn with South African influences

The Stork is a white-painted coaching inn spread along the banks of the tidal Lune estuary, with a colourful 300-year-history that includes several name changes. The quaint sea port of Glasson Dock is a short walk along the Lancashire Coastal Way. In the bar you will find local ales such as Lancaster Black, Amber and Blonde. Seasonal specialities join home-cooked English and South African food like pan-fried chicken breast topped with Lancashire cheese and bacon; Boerewors – lightly spiced pure beef sausage, served with sweet potato mash and balsamic, red onion and tomato relish; and Cape Malay Kerrie – slow braised mutton and apricots in Cape Malay spices.

Open all day all wk 7.30am-11pm **Food** Lunch Sun-Mon 7.30am-8pm, Tue-Sat 7.30am-9pm Dinner Sun-Mon 7.30am-8pm, Tue-Sat 7.30am-9pm ⊕ ENTERPRISE INNS ◀ Timothy Taylor Landlord & Golden Best, Black Sheep, Lancaster Blonde, Amber & Black. ♥ 10 **Facilities** Non-diners area ✿ (Bar Restaurant Garden) ♦ Children's menu Children's portions Play area Garden ⋒ Parking WiFi ⛟

PICK OF THE PUBS

Penny Street Bridge ★★★★ INN

LANCASTER Map 18 SD46

tel: 01524 599900 **Penny St LA1 1XT**
email: relax@pennystreetbridge.co.uk
web: www.pennystreetbridge.co.uk
dir: *In city centre*

Quirkily elegant, canal-side, city centre townhouse offering the best of Lancashire produce

Right in the centre of the city, the listed Penny Street Bridge was once a Corporation Toll House. Demolished in 1901, it was then rebuilt as two separate pubs, which Thwaites Brewery joined together again in 2007 to create a smart town-house, bar and brasserie. Its wonderfully high ceilings make it feel light and modern, although retained period features can be seen everywhere, from the listed staircase to the servant bell hooks, and from the stained-glass windows to the rather special wardrobe in one of the bedrooms that the owners can't, and wouldn't ever want to, move. The atmosphere is quirkily elegant, with wooden floors in the brasserie, mismatched tables and tub chairs in the traditional bar and grill, and a stylish, contemporary feel in the refurbished bedrooms. The kitchen team prepare all food on the premises. Served all day, their seasonal menus make the most of the excellent Lancashire produce available locally, from smoked

haddock fishcakes or tempura tiger prawns for a starter, to main courses such as steamed steak and ale pudding; Lancashire cheese, onion and potato pie; or lamb hotpot. Steaks aged for 28 days are seared on the charcoal grill and served with thick cut chips and a Caesar side salad. Stone-baked pizzas made with fresh dough come with all the popular toppings, like pepperoni, or goats' cheese and red onion. For pudding, try the banoffee sundae, apple and blackberry crumble, or sticky toffee pudding. Opposite the pub is Penny Street Bridge itself, under which runs the Lancaster Canal on its 42-mile journey from Tewitfield to Kendal.

Open all day all wk 9am-mdnt
Food all wk 11.30-9 ⊕ THWAITES INNS OF CHARACTER ◀ Wainwright, Lancaster Bomber, Original Ŏ Kingstone Press. ♟ 11 **Facilities** Non-diners area ♦♦ Children's menu Children's portions Garden ⋈ Parking WiFi 🚌 (notice required) **Rooms** 28

LANCASTER *continued*

The Sun Hotel and Bar — PICK OF THE PUBS

tel: 01524 66006 **LA1 1ET**
email: info@thesunhotelandbar.co.uk
dir: *6m from M6 junct 33*

Famous for its hospitality over the centuries

The oldest building in Lancaster, The Sun was first licensed as 'Stoop Hall' in 1680 as the town's premier coaching inn. Generals from the occupying Jacobean Army lodged here in 1745, and the artist JMW Turner stayed whilst making sketches of Heysham in 1812. Original features include a bottomless well and beautiful old door. Owned by the Lancaster Brewery, the pub has a wide selection of cask ales, world beers and wines. The bar is frequented throughout the day; from hotel guests and business breakfasters, to shoppers enjoying mid-morning coffee or brunch, and customers tucking into the locally sourced food at lunch and dinner, as well as wine and ale connoisseurs. The experienced kitchen brigade prepares sea bass Niçoise; baby carrot and fennel risotto; and sausages and mash. The extensive cheese board menu is especially popular, and also includes cold meats, pâtés and fish. There is a patio for alfresco dining in warmer weather, regular quiz nights and an annual beer festival in the summer.

Open all day all wk from 7.30am-late **Food** Lunch Mon-Sat 12-3, Sun 12-8 Dinner Mon-Thu 4-9, Fri 4-8, Sat 4-7, Sun 12-8 ⊕ FREE HOUSE ◖ Lancaster Amber & Blonde ♂ Kingstone Press. ♟ 23 **Facilities** Non-diners area ♦♦ Children's menu Children's portions Garden ⊨ Beer festival WiFi ☵ (notice required)

The White Cross

tel: 01524 33999 **Quarry Rd LA1 4XT**
email: twcpub@yahoo.co.uk
dir: *S on one-way system, left after Town Hall. Over canal bridge, on right*

Enjoy good food as canal boats go by

Set in a 130-year-old former cotton mill warehouse on the edge of the Lancaster Canal, The White Cross is a short stroll from the city centre. A regularly changing selection of up to 14 cask ales includes beers from Copper Dragon, Timothy Taylor and Theakston breweries, but food is an equal draw at this popular waterfront venue. Look out for starters like potted prawn and crayfish, or black pudding fritter; follow with Lancashire hotpot or creamy sweet potato, chickpea and spinach curry. If there's still room after all that, try white chocolate and honeycomb cheesecake, or dark chocolate and rum torte. Sandwiches, burgers, salads and deli boards also available. A beer and pie festival takes place in late April.

Open all day all wk **Food** Contact pub for food times ⊕ ENTERPRISE INNS ◖ Copper Dragon Golden Pippin, Timothy Taylor Landlord, Theakston Old Peculier ♂ Westons Stowford Press & Old Rosie, Ribble Valley Gold. ♟ 13 **Facilities** Non-diners area ♦♦ Children's menu Children's portions Garden ⊨ Beer festival Parking WiFi ☵ (notice required)

LANESHAW BRIDGE — Map 18 SD94

The Alma Inn ★★★★ INN

tel: 01282 857830 **Emmott Ln BB8 7EG**
email: reception@thealmainn.com web: www.thealmainn.com
dir: *M65, A6068 towards Keighley. At Laneshaw Bridge left into Emmott Ln. 0.5m, inn on left*

Country inn serving local produce

With magnificent views to Pendle Hill from tables on the paved patio, this old, hill-top stone inn deep in the Lancashire countryside is a real find. The rambling interior has some fine panelling, real fires and stone floors, whilst chic accommodation and extensive dining facilities mean it's popular for weddings. Reliable beers from Moorhouse's slake the thirst after a decent stroll. The wide-ranging contemporary menu covers most bases, from starters like pan-fried woodland pigeon; and mussels marinara via mains of pies, puddings, pasta and risotto dishes to the butcher's selection choices of game stew and herb dumplings; confit leg of duck; and slow-braised lamb shank. Sticky toffee sundae medley is a filling final fling.

Open all day all wk **Food** Lunch all wk 12-9 Dinner all wk 12-9 ⊕ FREE HOUSE ◖ Moorhouse's Pride of Pendle, Guest ales ♂ South West Orchards. ♟ 10 **Facilities** Non-diners area ♣ (Bar Restaurant Garden) ♦♦ Children's menu Children's portions Garden ⊨ Parking WiFi ☵ **Rooms** 9

LITTLE ECCLESTON — Map 18 SD44

The Cartford Inn — PICK OF THE PUBS

See Pick of the Pubs on page 304

LONGRIDGE — Map 18 SD63

NEW Derby Arms ★★★★ INN

tel: 01772 782370 **Chipping Rd PR3 2NB**
email: info@derbyarmslongridge.co.uk web: www.seafoodpubcompany.com

One for fish and seafood aficionados

A delightful village inn owned by Joycelyn Neve's Seafood Pub Company, with a central bar leading into three dining rooms, two with feature fireplaces. A tap room is set aside for bar games. Its very ownership dictates fish by the boatload – for instance, baked queenie scallops with white wine and cheese; devilled crab; salmon and brown shrimps with country toast; grilled lime and oregano swordfish steaks; and sea bass tagine with prawn koftas. In addition, expect salt-beef and potato pie with caper and mustard relish; and twice-baked Lancashire cheese soufflé. Wainwright, Timothy Taylor and Copper Dragon ales await in the bar.

Open all day all wk **Food** Lunch Bkfst Mon-Fri 7.30am-9.30am, Sat-Sun 8.30am-10.30am, Sun-Thu 12-9, Fri-Sat 12-10 Dinner Sun-Thu 12-9, Fri-Sat 12-10 Av main course £15.50 ⊕ FREE HOUSE ◖ Thwaites Wainwright, Timothy Taylor Landlord, Copper Dragon ♂ Kingstone Press. ♟ 10 **Facilities** Non-diners area ♦♦ Children's menu Children's portions Outside area ⊨ Parking WiFi ☵ (notice required) **Rooms** 6

NEWTON-IN-BOWLAND — Map 18 SD65

Parkers Arms — PICK OF THE PUBS

tel: 01200 446236 **BB7 3DY**
email: enquiries@parkersarms.co.uk
dir: *From Clitheroe take B6478 through Waddington to Newton-in-Bowland*

Imaginative cooking and delightful countryside views

In a beautiful hamlet amidst the rolling hills of the Trough of Bowland, this Georgian dining inn is just yards from the River Hodder and enjoys panoramic views over Waddington Fell. It celebrates its rural location by serving the best of Lancashire produce. This includes ales from the local breweries, meats raised on nearby moorland, vegetables from Ribble Valley farms and fresh fish from nearby Fleetwood. French chef-patron Stosie Madi even forages for ingredients herself. The simple, but elegant, modern dishes on the daily-changing, seasonal menu include Goosnargh corn-fed chicken and leek pie; slow-braised shin of Bowland beef in ale with creamed mash; and fillet of sea bass with pea gnocchi and a lemon reduction. Pudding could be 'Wet Nelly', a classic north-west dessert originally created for Lord Nelson in Liverpool and reworked by co-owner Kathy Smith.

Open 12-3 6-close (Sat-Sun & BH 12-close) Closed Mon (Tue in winter) **Food** Lunch Tue-Sun 12-3 Dinner Tue-Sun 6-8.30 Set menu available Restaurant menu available Tue-Sun ⊕ FREE HOUSE/ENTERPRISE LEASE ◖ Lancaster, Bowland ♂ Westons Stowford Press. **Facilities** Non-diners area ♣ (Bar Restaurant Garden) ♦♦ Children's menu Children's portions Garden ⊨ Parking WiFi ☵ (notice required)

PICK OF THE PUBS

The Cartford Inn

LITTLE ECCLESTON   Map 18 SD44

tel: 01995 670166 **PR3 0YP**
email: info@thecartfordinn.co.uk
web: www.thecartfordinn.co.uk
dir: *N of A586 (W of Great Eccleston)*

17th-century inn with eclectic interiors and excellent food

Set in an idyllic location adjoining a toll bridge across the tidal Rive Wyre, this award-winning 17th-century coaching inn enjoys extensive views over the countryside towards the Trough of Bowland and the Lake District. Owners Julie and Patrick Beaume have created a relaxed family-run inn: the stylish and contemporary interior is an appealing blend of striking colours, natural wood and polished floors, whilst the smart open fireplace and an eclectic selection of furniture adds a comfortable and relaxed feel to the bar lounge. There's a choice of eating areas – the Riverside Lounge, Fire Lounge and alcove, and outside on the terrace – where you can enjoy an imaginative range of dishes based on quality ingredients from local suppliers. Lunchtime sandwiches like cold poached salmon or Cumbrian cured ham and chutney come on Pebby's fresh bread and are served with organic crisps, whilst wooden platters are the showcase for local antipasti, Fleetwood seafood, and organic crudités. Cartford favourites include beef and oxtail in real

ale suet pudding; and the ever popular Cartford cassoulet. Other main course options range from pan-roasted saddle of Pilling Marsh lamb served with rosemary and goats' cheese croquette, salsa verde, and minted crumbs, to a spiced seafood combo with a Thai green curry and jasmine rice and classic moules frites. Rhubarb rice pudding with toasted marshmallow, and fresh mango tarte Tatin with rum ice cream are just two of the choices for dessert. The Cartford Inn makes an ideal spot from which to explore the surrounding area; Lancaster, the Royal Lytham Golf Club, and Blackpool with its Winter Gardens and Grand Theatre are all within easy reach.

Open all day Closed 25 Dec, Mon L
Food Lunch Tue-Sat 12-2, Sun 12-8.30
Dinner Mon-Thu 5.30-9, Fri-Sat 5.30-10
🍺 FREE HOUSE 🛢 Moorhouse's Pride of Pendle, Hawkshead Lakeland Gold, Giddy Kipper Ö Westons Stowford Press.
Facilities Non-diners area 🚼 Children's menu Children's portions Garden 🪑 Parking WiFi

PARBOLD
Map 15 SD41

The Eagle & Child
PICK OF THE PUBS

tel: 01257 462297 **Maltkiln Ln, Bispham Green L40 3SG**
dir: *M6 junct 27, A5209 to Parbold. Right onto B5246. 2.5m, Bispham Green on right*

A country dining pub in a pretty and peaceful location

Set in the tranquil valley of the River Douglas and close to some lovely rambles on Parbold Hill, this thriving village inn caters admirably for all-comers. Part of a small group of select rural dining pubs, the emphasis is on high-quality modern cooking using locally sourced seasonal produce. On the restaurant menu confit corn-fed Goosnargh duck leg, rhubarb and chilli compôte with celeriac crisps is a typical opening gambit. Progress to grilled wild turbot with artichoke purée, Parmentier potatoes, wild mushrooms and red wine sauce; or roast pigeon, confit leg stuffing and blackberry compôte. The bar menu is equally appealing; perhaps creamy Lancashire cheese and onion pie with tomato and red onion, sour cream, chives and triple cooked chips. The traditionally styled pub is a popular village local, with an ever-changing array of beers from local microbreweries such as Southport and farmhouse ciders, while the annual Early May Bank Holiday beer festival attracts up to 2,000 people to a huge marquee in the pub grounds. A pub deli completes the scene.

Open all day all wk 12-11 (Sun 12-10.30) **Food** Lunch all wk 12-2 Dinner Sun-Thu 5.30-8.30, Fri-Sat 5.30-9 Av main course £14 Set menu available Restaurant menu available ⊕ FREE HOUSE ◀ Moorhouse's Black Cat, Thwaites Original, Southport Golden Sands, Guest ales Ö Kingstone Press, Farmhouse Cider Scrumpy. **Facilities** Non-diners area ✿ (Bar Restaurant Garden) ♦ Children's menu Children's portions Family room Garden ⋈ Beer festival Parking ☷ (notice required)

PENDLETON
Map 18 SD73

The Swan with Two Necks

tel: 01200 423112 **BB7 1PT**
email: swanwith2necks@yahoo.co.uk
dir: *Exit A59 between Whalley & Chatburn follow Pendleton signs, 0.5m to pub*

Charming inn set in a beautiful stone-built Lancashire village

Hidden away in the pretty village of Pendleton, the award-winning Swan with Two Necks is a traditional village inn dating back to 1722. Pendleton sits under Pendle Hill, which is famous for its witches, and that's not the only curious piece of history attached to this place; the inn's name refers to the tradition of marking the necks of swans belonging to the Worshipful Company of Vintners with two 'nicks' to distinguish them from swans belonging to the king or queen. Of course you won't find swan on the menu here, but this pub is renowned for its ales and ciders, so be sure to try the likes of Phoenix Wobbly Bob or Ribble Valley Gold.

Open 12-3 6-11 (Sun 12-10.30) Closed 25 Dec, Mon L **Food** Lunch Tue-Sat 12-1.45, Sun 12-6 Dinner Mon 6-8, Tue-Sat 6-8.30 ⊕ FREE HOUSE ◀ Phoenix Wobbly Bob, Copper Dragon Golden Pippin, Prospect Nutty Slack, Marble, Salamander Ö Westons Traditional & Country Perry, Ribble Valley Gold. ☙ 14 **Facilities** Non-diners area ♦ Children's menu Children's portions Garden ⋈ Parking WiFi ☷ (notice required)

RAMSBOTTOM
Map 15 SD71

NEW Eagle + Child

tel: 01706 557181 **3 Whalley Rd BL0 0DL**
email: glen@eagle-and-child.com
dir: *M66 junct 1, A56 towards Edenfield. Pub on left in outskirts of Ramsbottom*

A unique social enterprise

Youngsters are introduced to the hospitality and horticultural industries at this pub with a social purpose. The result of landlord Glen Duckett's vision, with

wholehearted support from the Thwaites Brewery, the pub has won many local and national food awards. An acre of 'incredible edible' beer garden is a work in progress, but is already inspiring children and the pub's clientele to grow, cook and eat delicious high quality produce with minimum food miles. Look out for Lancashire sausage with Eve's black pudding; Butler's Lancashire cheese and ham hock with devilled black peas; and Goosnargh turkey pie with clapshot.

Open all day all wk **Food** Lunch Mon-Fri 12-2.30, Sat 12-9.30, Sun 12-7 Dinner Mon-Fri 5-9, Sat 12-9.30, Sun 12-7 Av main course £14.95 Set menu available ⊕ THWAITES ◀ Lancaster Bomber & Wainwright Ö Westons Rosie's Pig. **Facilities** Non-diners area ✿ (Garden) ♦ Children's menu Children's portions Play area Garden ⋈ Beer festival Parking WiFi ☷ (notice required)

SAWLEY
Map 18 SD74

The Spread Eagle
PICK OF THE PUBS

tel: 01200 441202 **BB7 4NH**
email: spread.eagle@zen.co.uk
dir: *Just off A159 between Clitheroe & Skipton, 4m N of Clitheroe*

Well-appointed trendy pub focusing on modern dishes

This handsome old stone inn stands on a quiet lane in the glorious Ribble Valley, flanked on one side by the ruins of Sawley Abbey, and on other by the River Ribble. Inside, choose between the elegant, light-filled dining room with its lush river views through picture windows, or the charming 17th-century bar, where you'll find traditional stone-flagged floors, old oak furniture and roaring fires alongside trendy wallpaper, painted settles strewn with bright cushions, colourful upholstered chairs, eclectic objets d'art and cool Farrow & Ball hues. All this adds up to a cosy and relaxing setting for savouring a pint of something from the Black Horse Brewery and some good modern pub food. Served throughout the inn and changing daily, the menu may include black pudding Scotch egg with piccalilli mayonnaise; fish pie with cheesy mash; spiced cauliflower and chickpea terrine; and warm chocolate brownie with maple ice cream. Then don your boots and walk it all off in the Bowland Hills.

Open all day all wk 11-11 (Sun 12-10.30) **Food** Lunch Mon-Sat 12-2, Sun 12-7 Dinner Mon-Fri 5.30-9, Sat 6-9.30, Sun 12-7 Set menu available ⊕ INDIVIDUAL INNS ◀ Thwaites Wainwright, Moorhouse's, Black Horse Brewery Ö Kingstone Press. ☙ 16 **Facilities** Non-diners area ✿ (Bar Garden) ♦ Children's menu Children's portions Garden ⋈ Parking ☷

SLAIDBURN
Map 18 SD75

NEW Hark to Bounty Inn

tel: 01200 446246 **Townend BB7 3EP**
email: manager@harktobounty.co.uk

Good beer in a lovely location

The pretty village of Slaidburn is in the Forest of Bowland, an Area of Outstanding Natural Beauty and perfect for walking, fishing, bird-watching and cycling. Have a pint of Theakston's Old Peculier and check out the pub classics on the menu; gammon steak; fish and chips; or steak and ale pie. If you're wondering about the unusual name, the story goes that in the 19th century the local squire, out hunting one day with his hounds, stopped at the pub for a drink. Disturbed by prolonged baying from the pack, he could hear above the noise his favourite dog, prompting him to call out 'Hark to Bounty!'

Open all day all wk **Food** Lunch Mon-Sat 12-2, Sun 12-8 Dinner Mon-Thu 6-8, Fri-Sat 6-9 (winter), Mon-Sat 6-9 (summer), Sun 12-8 ⊕ FREE HOUSE ◀ Theakston Best Bitter & Old Peculier, Lancaster Blonde. **Facilities** Non-diners area ✿ (Bar Restaurant Garden) ♦ Children's menu Children's portions Garden ⋈ Parking WiFi ☷ (notice required)

TOCKHOLES
Map 15 SD62

The Royal Arms

tel: 01254 705373 **Tockholes Rd BB3 OPA**
dir: *M65 junct 4 follow Blackburn signs. Right at lights, 1st left. Up hill left at Three B's Brewery into Tockholes Rd. Pub in 1m on left*

Rich with pickings from Lancashire microbreweries

High in the West Pennine Moors is this appealing old stone pub situated in a tiny fold of mill-workers' cottages. There's an engaging hotchpotch of furnishings in the fire-warmed, flagstoned and beamed rooms together with fascinating old photos of the local villages in their mill-town heyday. Take a glass of ale out to tables on the lawn and study the regularly changing menu of home-cooked goodies, such as lamb kleftico, and braised steak in red wine. There are walks from the door – drop into Roddlesworth Woods or you can climb to the imposing Jubilee Tower on nearby Darwen Hill.

Open all wk 12-11 (Mon 4-8 Sun 12-10.30) **Food** Lunch Tue-Fri 12-2, Sat 12-3, Sun 12-5.30 Dinner Wed-Sat 6-8.45 Restaurant menu available Wed-Sun ⊕ FREE HOUSE ◀ Banks's Bitter, Copper Dragon Golden Pippin, Moorhouse's Pendle Witches Brew, Three B's, York Dark Knight, Guest ales. **Facilities** Non-diners area ♣ (Bar Garden) ♦ Children's menu Children's portions Garden ⊟ Beer festival Parking WiFi ▬ (notice required)

TUNSTALL
Map 18 SD67

The Lunesdale Arms

tel: 015242 74203 **LA6 2QN**
email: info@thelunesdale.co.uk
dir: *M6 junct 36. A65 Kirkby Lonsdale. A638 Lancaster. Pub 3m on right. Or: M6 junct 34, A638 (Kirkby Lonsdale) pub 10m on left*

Destination pub showcasing locally sourced produce

In a small village in the beautiful Lune Valley, this bright and cheery pub has quite a reputation for its regional ales, wines and food. Owner and chef Nigel Brigstock and his team draw diners from far and wide with a seasonal menu whose highlights include bread baked on the premises; and locally sourced meats, vegetables and salad leaves, with typical dishes of creamy king prawn and haddock pie; Lune Valley lamb hot-pot; smoked chicken stew; and whole baked onion stuffed with roasted vegetable quinoa. Pizzas may be eaten within or taken home; Thai evenings (Thursdays) are proving popular.

Open 11-3 6-12 (Sat Sun & BH 11-4 6-1am) Closed 25-26 Dec, Mon (ex BHs) **Food** Lunch Tue-Fri 12-2, Sat-Sun 12-2.30 Dinner Tue-Sun 6-9 ⊕ FREE HOUSE ◀ Dent Aviator, Black Sheep, Brysons, Lancaster Blonde, Guinness Ŏ Westons Stowford Press. **Facilities** Non-diners area ♣ (Bar Outside area) ♦ Children's menu Children's portions Family room Outside area ⊟ Parking WiFi ▬ (notice required)

WADDINGTON
Map 18 SD74

The Lower Buck

tel: 01200 423342 **Edisford Rd BB7 3HU**
email: thelowerbuck@aol.com
dir: *From A671 at rdbt onto B6478 (Well Terrace) signed Waddington. In Waddington at x-rds left into Waddow View. At T-junct right signed Bashall Eaves. At next T-junct right, pub on left*

Easily missed gem in a 'Best Kept Village'

In the chocolate box village of Waddington, winner of 'Best Kept Village' on several occasions, look for St Helen's church and you'll find The Lower Buck just behind it. The 250-year-old pub has been affectionately run by Andrew Warburton for 10 years now, without music or fruit machines disturbing the peace. The emphasis is on warmth of welcome, four excellent ales – with Bowland Hen Harrier among them – and a classic pub menu of quality dishes. Snacks include superior sandwiches such as hot topside of beef with fried onions, while the fisherman's salad overflows with smoked salmon, prawns, poached salmon and cockles.

Open all day all wk **Food** Lunch Mon-Fri 12-2.30, Sat-Sun 12-9 Dinner Mon-Fri 5-9, Sat-Sun 12-9 ⊕ FREE HOUSE ◀ Bowland Hen Harrier, Timothy Taylor Landlord, Guest ales Ŏ Ribble Valley Gold. ♀ 10 **Facilities** Non-diners area ♣ (Bar Outside area) ♦ Children's menu Children's portions Outside area ⊟ WiFi ▬

Waddington Arms

tel: 01200 423262 **West View, Waddington Rd BB7 3HP**
email: info@waddingtonarms.co.uk
dir: *In village centre*

Local produce drives the menu here

Close to the A59, this former coaching inn occupies an enviable position in the heart of the Ribble Valley. In the bar and on the pavement outside cushioned wickerwork chairs are ideal for watching village life and perfect for relaxing with a pint of Bowland Sawley Tempted. Dining is available throughout, including two cosy side rooms off the main bar. Strong on local specialities, the menu offers Goosnargh duck Wellington with potato gratin, chestnut mushrooms and Madeira sauce; and curry-spiced cod loin with saag aloo and basmati rice. Look out for the October beer festival.

Open all day all wk **Food** Lunch Mon-Fri 12-2.30, Sat 12-9.30, Sun 12-9 Dinner Mon-Fri 6-9.30, Sat 12-9.30, Sun 12-9 ⊕ FREE HOUSE ◀ Bowland Hen Harrier & Sawley Tempted, Lancaster Blonde Ŏ Ribble Valley Gold. ♀ 14 **Facilities** Non-diners area ♣ (Bar Garden) ♦ Children's menu Children's portions Play area Family room Garden ⊟ Beer festival Parking WiFi ▬ (notice required)

PICK OF THE PUBS

The Inn at Whitewell ★★★★★ INN ❀

WHITEWELL Map 18 SD64

tel: 01200 448222
Forest of Bowland BB7 3AT
email: reception@innatwhitewell.com
web: www.innatwhitewell.com
dir: *From B6243 follow Whitewell signs*

Historic inn with spectacular valley views

This must be one of the most enchantingly-sited inns in England. The River Hodder swirls by verdant meadows abutting wooded clefts in the glorious Forest of Bowland. Here the partly 13th-century inn slumbers by a tiny Georgian chapel, with slippery paths down to stepping stones across the torrent. All around the high moors, pastures and estates burst with provisions destined for the inn's renowned kitchen. The engaging multi-roomed interior is liberally decorated with antiques, ephemera and pictures; there's also an art gallery and independent wine shop. All in all, there is plenty to entertain the residential guests who book into one of the individually designed, luxury period bedrooms. Jamie Cadman has been masterminding the kitchen's output for 18 years. His enduring passion for quality local produce shines through in consistently good dishes, which have been awarded an AA Rosette. A light lunch could comprise a rustic terrine of pork fillet and smoked bacon with home-made piccalilli and crusty bread;

or home-made black pudding grilled with sweet onions, Lancashire cheese mash and a Bramley apple purée. At dinner, the full carte features starters such as venison carpaccio with rocket and parmesan shavings lead to main dishes of Burholme Lonk lamb rack with rosemary and garlic, roasted tomatoes and crushed new potatoes; or chargrilled fillet of local beef with roast shallots, flat mushrooms and tarragon butter. For fish lovers, king scallops wrapped in pancetta followed by the kitchen's signature Whitewell fish pie will do the trick. Puddings are traditional and home made. Ramblers dropping in from the heights will delight in beers from Bowland and Copper Dragon, enjoyed on a terrace overlooking the fabulous fell landscape.

Open all day all wk 10am-1am **Food** Lunch all wk 12-2 Dinner all wk 7.30-9.30 Restaurant menu available all wk evenings only ⊕ FREE HOUSE ◀ Timothy Taylor Landlord, Bowland, Copper Dragon, Moorhouse's, Hawkshead ⚬ Dunkertons Premium Organic. ♟ 16 **Facilities** Non-diners area ❤ (Bar Garden) ♦ Children's portions Garden ⊼ Parking WiFi ▭ (notice required) **Rooms** 23

WHALLEY   Map 18 SD73

The Three Fishes ⊛   PICK OF THE PUBS

tel: 01254 826888 **Mitton Rd, Mitton BB7 9PQ**
email: enquiries@thethreefishes.com
dir: M6 junct 31, A59 to Clitheroe. Follow Whalley signs, B6246, 2m

Contemporary hostelry championing local food and drink

People have stopped for refreshment at this inn for more than two centuries and although the focus is now on the AA Rosette-standard food, well-kept pints of Bowland and Thwaites ales can still be supped in the bar. As you settle with your refreshment of choice, you'll notice black-and-white photographs of local food producers on the walls. Some new cooking techniques have been introduced in the quest to keep pace with trends, but owner Nigel Haworth has retained many classics, and even reinstated old favourites such as Lancashire hotpot. Well-trained staff are adept at friendly and professional service, ushering starters of sticky pulled Bowland venison and twice-baked Lancashire cheese soufflés from kitchen to table. Next may come wild rabbit pie or breast of Goosnargh chicken with mash and red wine sauce. Dessert choices may include Bramley apple tart or rhubarb and lemon verbena trifle.

Open all day all wk 12-11 (Sun 12-10.30) **Food** Lunch Mon-Fri 12-2, Sat 12-9, Sun 12-8.30 Dinner Mon-Thu 5.30-8.30, Fri 5.30-9, Sat 12-9, Sun 12-8.30 Set menu available ⊕ FREE HOUSE ◢ Bowland Hen Harrier, Thwaites Wainwright ⚲ Westons Stowford Press. ₹ 11 **Facilities** Non-diners area ✿ (Bar Garden) ⁂ Children's menu Garden ⊟ Parking WiFi

WHEELTON   Map 15 SD62

The Dressers Arms

tel: 01254 830041 **Briers Brow PR6 8HD**
email: info@dressersarms.co.uk
dir: M61 junct 8, A674 to Blackburn. Follow sign for pub on right

Dog-friendly, welcoming fires and good pub grub

Until the 1960s, this was the smallest pub in Lancashire. The long, low, creeper-festooned old gritstone building is crammed with local photos, collectables and artefacts spread through a clutch of separate drinking areas; partly flagged floors are warmed by roaring fires in winter. Its appeal is enhanced by the choice of ales and a reliable raft of home-made pub grub: perhaps a hot tuna melt sandwich, a salad or a jacket potato will hit the spot; otherwise look to the main for lamb Henry, gammon steak, chilli con carne, Cumberland sausage or poached salmon.

Open all day all wk **Food** Lunch all wk 12-9 Dinner all wk 12-9 ⊕ FREE HOUSE ◢ The Dressers Arms Dressers Bitter, Black Sheep ⚲ Westons. ₹ 20 **Facilities** Non-diners area ✿ (Bar Restaurant Garden) ⁂ Children's menu Children's portions Family room Garden ⊟ Parking WiFi ⛟

WHITEWELL   Map 18 SD64

The Inn at Whitewell ★★★★★ INN ⊛   PICK OF THE PUBS

See Pick of the Pubs on page 307

LEICESTERSHIRE

BIRSTALL   Map 11 SK50

The White Horse

tel: 0116 267 1038 **White Horse Ln LE4 4EF**
email: info@thewhitehorsebirstall.co.uk
dir: M1 junct 21A, A46 towards Newark 5.5m. Exit A46 at Loughborough towards Leicester, follow brown signs for White Horse

Delivering the very best expected of a village inn

A former canal-worker's beerhouse whose tranquil garden was once a coal wharf serving the village of Birstall, The White Horse overlooks Watermead Country Park. Rebuilt in the 1920s, the pub has matured over the years into today's restful retreat offering reliable beers, good company and a sought-after range of dishes. Boaters and ramblers alike look forward to classic main courses such as a hand-made burger with chips and onion rings; gammon with egg and chips; or beef lasagne with dressed salad and garlic bread. Or follow the locals' lead and tuck in to the pie of the week with all the trimmings.

Open all wk winter 12-3 5.30-11 (Sun 12-10.30); summer all day all wk **Food** Lunch Mon-Sat 12-2.30, Sun 12-4 Dinner Mon-Sat 6-9 ⊕ TRUST INNS ◢ Timothy Taylor Landlord, Thwaites Wainwright, Guest ale. ₹ 8 **Facilities** Non-diners area ✿ (Bar Garden) ⁂ Children's menu Children's portions Play area Garden ⊟ Parking WiFi ⛟ (notice required)

BREEDON ON THE HILL   Map 11 SK42

The Three Horseshoes

tel: 01332 695129 **Main St DE73 8AN**
email: ian@thehorseshoes.com
dir: 5m from M1 junct 23a. Pub in village centre

Welcoming old pub with a chocolate workshop next door

Originally a farrier's, the buildings here are around 250 years old; the pub has been here for at least a century, while the main kitchen, a farm shop and a chocolate workshop now occupy the smithy and stables in the courtyard. Inside, numerous original features and old beams are supplemented by antique furniture, and sea-grass matting completes the warm and welcoming atmosphere. Typical dishes start with smoked salmon with dill mayonnaise or fish and spinach pancake with cheese, followed by beef hotpot with Yorkshire pudding, or blackened salmon with crème fraîche. Try bread and butter pudding or treacle oat tart for dessert.

Open 11.30-2.30 5.30-11 (Sun 12-3) Closed 25-26 & 31 Dec-1 Jan, Sun eve & Mon **Food** Lunch Tue-Sat 12-2, Sun 12-3 Dinner Tue-Sat 6-9 Restaurant menu available Tue-Sun ⊕ FREE HOUSE ◢ Marston's Pedigree, Guest ales. **Facilities** Non-diners area ✿ (Bar Garden) ⁂ Children's portions Garden ⊟ Parking

BRUNTINGTHORPE   Map 11 SP68

The Joiners

tel: 0116 247 8258 **Church Walk LE17 5QH**
email: stephen@thejoinersarms.co.uk
dir: 4m from Lutterworth

Food-led village gastro-pub

Yesteryear's modest village pub is today's popular eating place, thanks to Stephen and Tracy Fitzpatrick and their dedicated team. You'll find stripped oak beams, flagstone floors, an open fire and candles. Menus change constantly, with ingredients sourced from wherever Stephen thinks best – beef from Scotland, seafood from Cornwall, black pudding from Clonakilty. A typical example lists medallions of beef fillet with dauphinoise potatoes and Diane sauce; calves' liver with smoked bacon and garlic mash; monkfish in Parma ham with butternut squash and sage risotto; and goats' cheese and beetroot orzo. Every Tuesday there's a three-course fixed-price 'Auberge Supper' (booking is advisable).

Open 12-2 6.30-11 Closed Mon **Food** Lunch Tue-Sun 12-2 Dinner Tue-Sat 6.30-9.30 Set menu available ⊕ FREE HOUSE ◀ Sharp's Doom Bar. ♀ 16 **Facilities** Non-diners area Outside area ⋈ Parking WiFi 🚐 (notice required)

BUCKMINSTER   Map 11 SK82

Tollemache Arms

tel: 01476 860477 **48 Main St NG33 5SA**
email: info@tollemache-arms.co.uk **web:** www.tollemache-arms.co.uk
dir: *4m from A1, between Colsterworth & Melton Mowbray on B676*

Family-friendly village dining pub

An impressive 19th-century stone-built country pub and restaurant, a short hop from the A1. The aroma of freshly baked bread, large bunches of flowers, table lamps, wood floors and old pews characterise the rustic but homely ambience. Oakham and Grainstore Brewery's ales, a range of bottled beers and a good wine selection meet most people's refreshment demands. The restaurant carte shows a short selection of British classics, such as smoked salmon roulade followed by rack of lamb with dauphinoise potatoes. Look to the bar menu for a range of hot drinks, a sandwich, or chicken in a basket with hand-cut chips and the chef's coleslaw.

Open Tue-Fri 10.30-3 6-11 (Sat 11-11 Sun 12-5) Closed Sun eve, Mon **Food** Lunch Tue-Fri 12-3, Sat 12-9, Sun 12-4 Dinner Tue-Fri 6-9, Sat 12-9 Av main course £21 Restaurant menu available Tue-Sun ⊕ FREE HOUSE ◀ Oakham Ales JHB, The Grainstore Red Kite, Guest ale. ♀ 11 **Facilities** Non-diners area ❀ (Bar Garden Outside area) ♦ Children's menu Children's portions Garden Outside area ⋈ Parking WiFi 🚐 (notice required)

See advert on page 310

COLEORTON   Map 11 SK41

George Inn

tel: 01530 834639 **Loughborough Rd LE67 8HF**
email: janice@jwilkinson781.orangehome.co.uk
dir: *A42 junct 13 onto A512*

Relaxing country pub in National Forest

A comfortable old local bristling with homely touches, with crackling log-burners in the main rooms and a tree-shaded beer garden looking over the rich pasturelands of this corner of Leicestershire. It's at the heart of extensive National Forest, whilst Calke Abbey is a leisurely drive away. Bright and airy inside, with colourwash and panelled walls and nooks and crannies to explore, Marston's Pedigree complements the sturdy menu. Kick in with goats' cheese and poached pear, following up with wild boar sausages or steak and ale pie with Stilton; some gluten-free options, too.

Open 12-3 5.30-11 (Fri-Sat 12-11 Sun 12-4) Closed Sun eve, Mon **Food** Lunch Tue-Sat 12-2, Sun 12-3 Dinner Tue-Sat 6-9 ⊕ FREE HOUSE ◀ Marston's Pedigree, Guest ales ♂ Thatchers Gold. ♀ 12 **Facilities** Non-diners area ♦ Children's menu Children's portions Play area Garden ⋈ Parking WiFi

EVINGTON   Map 11 SK60

The Cedars

tel: 0116 273 0482 **Main St LE5 6DN**
email: pippa@king-henrys-taverns.co.uk
dir: *From Leicester take A6 towards Market Harborough. Left at lights, onto B667 to Evington. Pub in village centre*

'Something for everyone' menus

At The Cedars you can choose to eat in the restaurant with its panoramic windows overlooking the fountain and pond, dine alfresco in the gardens, or just enjoy a drink in the lounge bar with its leather sofas and relaxed atmosphere. The menu of freshly prepared dishes offers something for everyone – small and large appetites alike. Choose from steaks, grills and burgers, as well as traditional favourites such as fish pie, vegetarian options and international dishes like lamb rogan josh. Smaller plates include paninis, salads and jackets. For dessert, the chocolate fudge cake or pecan pie is a treat for those with a sweet tooth.

Open all day all wk 11.30-11 **Food** Lunch all wk 12-10 Dinner all wk 12-10 ⊕ FREE HOUSE/KING HENRY'S TAVERNS ◀ Greene King IPA, Marston's Pedigree, Guinness. **Facilities** Non-diners area ♦ Children's menu Children's portions Garden ⋈ Parking WiFi 🚐

GRIMSTON   Map 11 SK62

The Black Horse

tel: 01664 812358 **3 Main St LE14 3BZ**
email: amanda.wayne@sky.com
dir: *Phone for detailed directions*

Family pub in the countryside

At the foot of the hill dropping from the medieval church, The Black Horse commands the sloping green in this peaceful village outside Melton Mowbray. The trim, flowery garden, alfresco dining area and rich, warm interior reflect this village setting, where Leicestershire produce leads on the highly traditional menu. Steak and ale pie, lamb shank, or chicken breast with Stilton and bacon are classic dishes, whilst daily specials, fresh fish dishes and a vegetarian board enliven the choice. On the beer front, two weekly-changing guest ales complement regional favourites.

Open all wk 12-3 6-11 (Sun 12-6) **Food** Lunch Mon-Sat 12-2, Sun 12-3 Dinner Mon-Sat 6-9 ⊕ FREE HOUSE ◀ Marston's Pedigree, Adnams, Guest ales ♂ Thatchers Gold. **Facilities** Non-diners area ❀ (Bar Garden Outside area) ♦ Children's menu Children's portions Garden Outside area ⋈ 🚐

Tollemache Arms
at Buckminster

Re-Furbished
e-Energised
e-Opened
and Under New Management

The Tollemache Arms is an impressive 19th century stone built country inn located in the beautiful village of Buckminster just five minutes from the A1 serving delicious food and a wide range of drinks and with ample car parking and free Wi-Fi throughout. The "Tolle" can host private functions such as birthdays, christenings, weddings and other special events with bespoke menus to suit the specific occasion.

The Accommodation at the Tollemache Arms provides a really comfortable place to stay in one of the recently renovated en-suite bedrooms with sumptuous beds, flat screen tv and tea/coffee making faculties.

The Bar is open to everyone including little ones, dogs and their muddy feet and offers a relaxed family friendly atmosphere to enjoy a drink or sample the food in front of our roaring open log fire in winter or al fresco in the summer in our extensive garden.

You will find a comprehensive selection of draught beers, locally brewed guest ales, bottled beers, spirits, malt whiskeys and fine wines including prosecco, all to suit most tastes. Traditional classic pub food, sandwiches and salads are available during the day and evening together with freshly ground speciality coffee, such as espresso, cappuccino, latte, Americano, mocha, etc.

The Restaurant is a perfect place to sample our range of à la carte dishes prepared daily by our Chef using the best quality fresh local produce. Experience dishes such as roast venison or just simply try one of our beautiful char-grilled steaks. Try our delicious desserts made daily in our kitchen to complete the experience.

The Library adjoins the main restaurant and offers a separate dining area and being a quieter room, is also ideal for those wishing a more intimate dining experience or for small venues such as business meetings, social gatherings, clubs and similar functions or just pre-dinner/after dinner drinks.

www.tollemache-arms.co.uk
For Reservations Call 01476 860 477 or
E-Mail: dine@tollemache-arms.co.uk
Tollemache Arms 48 Main Street Buckminster Grantham Lincolnshire NG33 5SA

KNOSSINGTON — Map 11 SK80

The Fox & Hounds

tel: 01664 452129 **6 Somerby Rd LE15 8LY**
dir: *4m from Oakham in Knossington*

Cosy, inviting interior and good food

High-quality food and helpful, friendly service are the hallmarks of this 500-year-old pub. Set in the leafy village of Knossington close to Rutland Water, the building retains lots of traditional features, and the large rear garden and sitting area are ideal for alfresco summer dining. All food is freshly cooked to order and comes with fresh vegetables and potatoes of the day.

Open Tue-Fri 6-11 (Sat 6.30-11 Sun 12-4) Closed 10 days in summer, Sun eve & Mon **Food** Dinner Tue-Sat 6.30-9 ⊕ ENTERPRISE INNS ◀ Fuller's London Pride. **Facilities** Non-diners area ❀ (Bar Garden Outside area) Garden Outside area ☶ Parking WiFi ⇌ (notice required)

LEICESTER — Map 11 SK50

The Rutland & Derby

tel: 0116 262 3299 **Millstone Ln LE1 5JN**
email: rutlandandderby@ssoosh.co.uk
dir: *Phone for detailed directions*

City centre pub that pleases on many levels

Everything here seems carefully considered, and nothing is without some special quality. Handy for city-centre attractions, and not far from the city's rugby ground, the pub is worth seeking out for a craft ale such as Everards, a glass of wine from the 20 on offer, or a carefully prepared cocktail. Attention to detail is evident too in the food. Ethically sourced ingredients feature in quirky but flavoursome dishes such as Wymeswold Scotch egg with Stokes brown sauce. Hand-stretched and stone-cooked flatbreads are a speciality: salami Milano and fresh chilli, mozzarella, sundried tomato and fresh pesto makes a winning combination.

Open all day Closed Sun **Food** Contact pub for food times ⊕ FREE HOUSE ◀ Adnams Broadside, Everards Tiger ♂ Westons. ₹ 20 **Facilities** Non-diners area ♦ Children's portions Garden ☶ WiFi ⇌ (notice required)

LONG WHATTON — Map 11 SK42

The Falcon Inn

tel: 01509 842416 **64 Main St LE12 5DG**
email: enquiries@thefalconinnlongwhatton.com
dir: *Phone for detailed directions*

Western Mediterranean spice in classic British pub

There's a taste of the Middle East to this traditional country inn in the shape of Lebanese-born proprietor Jad Otaki; the Mezzeh is akin to a tasting menu of some half dozen starters and four main courses. If spice is not your thing, you can plump for familiar bar meals such as home-made steak and ale pie; or salmon fillet in a cream, mushroom and seafood sauce. However, The Falcon is at heart an English pub, decked out with flower displays and hosting real ale drinkers on the striking heated rear terrace.

Open all day all wk **Food** Lunch Mon-Sat 12-2, Sun 12-4 Dinner Mon-Sat 6.30-9 ⊕ EVERARDS ◀ Tiger & Original, Guest ale. **Facilities** Non-diners area ♦ Children's portions Family room Garden Outside area ☶ Parking WiFi ⇌ (notice required)

The Royal Oak ★★★★ INN ◉ **PICK OF THE PUBS**

tel: 01509 843694 **26 The Green LE12 5DB**
email: enquiries@theroyaloaklongwhatton.co.uk **web:** www.theroyaloaklongwhatton.co.uk
dir: *M1 junct 24, A6 to Kegworth. Right into Whatton Road (becomes Kegworth Ln) to Long Whatton. From Loughborough, A6 towards Kegworth. Left onto B5324, right into Hathern Rd leading to The Green*

Stylish village inn with rooms

Ideally situated in a picturesque village close to Loughborough and East Midlands Airport, The Royal Oak is an award-winning gastro-pub, offering high quality, locally sourced food. Popular brews are on offer in the smart bar, and the carefully selected wine list has 13 by the glass. In the stylish AA-Rosetted restaurant diners can expect some tough decisions: pan-fried ox cheek boudin with horseradish jam; sharing platter of mixed tapas; Applewood smoked cheddar and aubergine schnitzel with a macaroni pasta and ratatouille crumble; or a pub classic such as fish pie. Leave room for desserts like the 'Retro Trio' — gypsy tart with crème Anglaise, rice pudding with strawberry jam, and Amaretto jelly with pistachio and almond ice cream. An annual summer beer festival offers 30 real ales and 10 ciders. The impeccably furnished guest bedrooms are in a separate building.

Open all day all wk **Food** Lunch Mon-Sat 12-2.30, Sun 12-4 Dinner Mon-Sat 5.30-9.30 ⊕ FREE HOUSE ◀ St Austell Tribute, Bass, Blue Monkey, Sharp's Doom Bar, Guest ales ♂ Westons Old Rosie, Thatchers. ₹ 13 **Facilities** Non-diners area ♦ Children's menu Children's portions Garden ☶ Beer festival Cider festival Parking WiFi **Rooms** 7

LUTTERWORTH — Map 11 SP58

The Man at Arms

tel: 01455 552540 **The Green, Bitteswell LE17 4SB**
email: pippa@king-henrys-taverns.co.uk
dir: *From Lutterworth take Lutterworth Rd towards Ullesthorpe. Turn left at small white cottage. Pub on left after college on village green*

Contemporary decor and hearty pub grub

Close to the market town of Lutterworth, this large village pub is named after a bequest by the Dowse Charity to the nearby village of Bitteswell in return for providing a 'man at arms' for times of war. It was the first pub bought by the King Henry's Taverns group; now, 29 years later, it has a smart, contemporary interior, all clean lines, wooden floorboards and high-backed leather seats, and shares a common menu with its sister pubs. Along with traditional favourites, there are international, fish and vegetarian dishes. Sizeable options include the Titanic Challenge — a rump steak weighing some three pounds.

Open all day all wk 11.30-11 **Food** Lunch all wk 12-10 Dinner all wk 12-10 ⊕ FREE HOUSE/KING HENRY'S TAVERNS ◀ Greene King IPA, Wells Bombardier, Bass, Guinness. ₹ 16 **Facilities** Non-diners area ♦ Children's menu Children's portions Garden Parking ⇌

MOUNTSORREL · Map 11 SK51

The Swan Inn

tel: 0116 230 2340 **10 Loughborough Rd LE12 7AT**
email: danny.harwood@hotmail.com
dir: *On A6 between Leicester & Loughborough*

17th-century cottage beside the river

Originally built as two terraced cottages in 1688, this Grade II listed free house stands on the banks of the River Soar and has a secluded riverside garden, ideal for summer sipping and dining. Exposed beams, flagstone floors and roaring winter log fires characterise the cosy bar and dining areas. Fine wines and cask-conditioned beers from Black Sheep accompany a varied, weekly-changing menu of British and European classics, as well as light lunches and snacks: smoked haddock and mustard fishcakes, followed by pan-fried trout fillet with balsamic beetroot and horseradish yogurt, or maybe a steak chimmichurri. Children are welcome only until 8pm unless they're eating along with adults.

Open all wk 12-2.30 5.30-11 (Fri 12-2.30 4.30-12 Sat 12-12 Sun 12-11) **Food** Lunch Mon-Sat 12-2, Sun 12-4 Dinner Mon-Sat 6.30-9.30 Set menu available Restaurant menu available ⊕ FREE HOUSE ◀ Black Sheep Best Bitter, Greene King Abbot Ale, Morland Old Speckled Hen, Castle Rock Harvest Pale, Guest ales Ò Symonds , Guest ciders. **Facilities** Non-diners area ❖ (Bar Garden) ♦♦ Children's portions Garden ⌱ Beer festival Parking

MOWSLEY · Map 11 SP68

The Staff of Life · PICK OF THE PUBS

tel: 0116 240 2359 **Main St LE17 6NT**
dir: *M1 junct 20, A4304 to Market Harborough. Left in Husbands Bosworth onto A5199. In 3m turn right to pub*

Fresh look for a charming village inn

Tucked away in the countryside, this pub has been in the same hands for over a decade during which time it has been very well looked after. Were they to return, the former residents of this well-proportioned Edwardian house would surely be amazed by the transformation of their home into such an appealing community local. The bar has high-backed settles, a flagstone floor and large wood-burning stove. Look up to see not only a fine wood-panelled ceiling but also, not quite where you'd expect it, the wine cellar. The dining area overlooking the garden sees the serving of dishes using the best of British seasonal produce, with a strong emphasis on local game: duck liver pâté and plum chutney or seared wood pigeon breast wrapped in bacon with black pudding are typical starters. Follow with roast leg of lamb with apricot and rosemary stuffing, or smoked salmon and dill fish cakes with aïoli mayonnaise.

Open Mon-Fri 6-close (Sat 12-3 6-close Sun 12-10.30) Closed Mon-Fri L **Food** Lunch Sat 12-2.15, Sun 12-3 Dinner Tue-Sat 6-9.15 Set menu available ⊕ FREE HOUSE ◀ Thwaites Wainwright, Okells, Sharp's Doom Bar. ♊ 19 **Facilities** Non-diners area ♦♦ Children's portions Garden Outside area ⌱ Parking WiFi ➡ (notice required)

OADBY · Map 11 SK60

The Cow & Plough · PICK OF THE PUBS

tel: 0116 272 0852 **Gartree Rd, Stoughton Farm LE2 2FB**
email: cowandplough@googlemail.com
dir: *From Leicester on A6 towards Oadby. Left at hospital sign at lights. At next rdbt follow Spire Hospital sign into Gartree Rd*

Former farm building famous for its pies

Housed in old Victorian farm buildings, The Cow & Plough continues to thrive, hosting functions and events including quarterly beer festivals. The pub also brews its own award-winning Steamin' Billy beers and ciders, named in honour of the owners' Jack Russell terrier. The interior is decorated with historic inn signs and brewing memorabilia, providing a fascinating setting in which to enjoy food from the regularly changing menus. Typical choices include terrine of prawn and smoked salmon, or quail Scotch egg with pig's head croquettes followed by confit duck leg with celeriac pommes Anna, green beans and red cabbage, or a vegetarian-friendly chargrilled vegetable tarte Tatin. A separate list of 'traditional dishes' offers the likes of lamb's liver and crispy bacon or a pie of the day (Thursday is pie night). Puddings continue in a traditional vein with the likes of lemon posset or baked blueberry and white chocolate cheesecake.

Open all day all wk **Food** Lunch Mon-Fri 12-2.30, Sat 12-9, Sun 12-5 Dinner Mon-Fri 6-9, Sat 12-9 ⊕ FREE HOUSE ◀ Steamin' Billy Bitter & Skydiver, Fuller's London Pride, Guest ales Ò Steamin' Billy Country Cider, Westons, Old Mout Cider. ♊ 10 **Facilities** Non-diners area ❖ (Bar Outside area) ♦♦ Children's menu Children's portions Family room Outside area ⌱ Beer festival Parking WiFi ➡

REDMILE · Map 11 SK73

NEW The Windmill

tel: 01949 842281 **4 Main St NG13 0GA**
email: kirsten.rutt@btopenworld.com
dir: *From A52 between Bingham & Grantham follow signs for Redmile. Pub in village centre*

Lovely village pub with TV connections

Located in the centre of Redmile, three miles from the A52 and within walking distance of Belvoir Castle, The Windmill featured in the TV series *Auf Wiedersehen Pet* and still draws fans of the show. A comfortable lounge bar with a fireplace is a cosy place to enjoy a pint of Oldershaw Heavenly Blonde, or head to the magnificent sunny terrace at the front. Lunchtime sandwiches and snacks are augmented by a full lunch and dinner menu, which might start with smoked haddock, salmon and prawn fishcakes and move on to braised Derbyshire beef with creamed potato and roast root vegetables.

Open all day all wk **Food** Contact pub for food times Set menu available Restaurant menu available all wk ⊕ FREE HOUSE ◀ Oldershaw Heavenly Blonde, Newby Wyke HMS Warrior, Adnams Southwold Bitter Ò Cornish Orchards. ♊ **Facilities** Non-diners area ♦♦ Children's menu Children's portions Outside area ⌱ Parking WiFi ➡ (notice required)

Silver Stars The AA Silver Star rating denotes a Hotel or B&B that we highly recommend. They have a superior level of quality within their star rating, high standards of hospitality, service and cleanliness.

| SADDINGTON | Map 11 SP69 |

NEW The Queens Head

tel: 0116 240 2536 **Main St LE8 0QH**
email: info@queensheadsaddington.co.uk **web:** www.queensheadsaddington.co.uk
dir: M1 junct 20, A4304 signed Market Harborough. At Husbands Bosworth left onto A5199 signed Leicester. In 4m right signed Saddington. Pub in village centre

Country pub and kitchen with views

Set in the rolling hills of south Leicestershire with views over Saddington Reservoir, this spacious family-friendly pub promises a welcoming and relaxing experience. Everards and a brace of guest ales, plus 11 wines by the glass and the occasional guest cider, are the prime refreshments, while the work of Chris Lewis-Sharman in the kitchen pleases all-comers. A lighter menu offers the likes of Cajun spiced whitebait with lemon and lime salsa. Mains from the carte are favourites such as beef stew and dumplings; or slow-braised shank of lamb. Children have their own menu, and there's plenty of room to play outside.

Open all wk 12-11 (Sun 12-10 Mon 12-2.30 5.30-10 Tue 12-2.30 5.30-11) **Food** Lunch Mon-Fri 12-2.30, Sat 12-9.30, Sun 12-6 Dinner Mon-Fri 5.30-9, Sat 12-9.30 Set menu available Restaurant menu available all wk ⊕ EVERARDS ◙ Tiger, Guest ales Ö Guest ciders. ♥ 11 **Facilities** Non-diners area ✿ (Bar Garden) ♦♦ Children's menu Children's portions Play area Garden ⊟ Parking WiFi ▄▄ (notice required)

| SHAWELL | Map 11 SP58 |

NEW The White Swan

tel: 01788 860357 **Main St LE17 6AG**
email: info@whiteswanshawell.co.uk
dir: M6 junct 1, A426, at rdbt into Gibbet Ln (by garage) to Shawell. Or M1 junct 19, A5 towards Nuneaton. Under M6, at rdbt into Gibbet Ln (by garage)

High-quality food close to the M1

Between Rugby and Lutterworth, in the pretty village of Shawell, The White Swan is just a few minutes from the M1, making it a perfect place to stop for a pint of local Dow Bridge Gladiator ale. Rory McLean and Samantha Laye took over in 2012 and they have retained the pub's character with log-burning fires and a cosy snug. Chef Rory used to cook in some of London's most notable restaurants and his modern British food is worth a detour. A starter of duck leg papardelle, parmesan and parsley might precede pork belly, smoked mash and tenderstem broccoli.

Open all day Closed Mon **Food** Lunch 12-2.30 Dinner 6-9.30 Av main course £13 Set menu available Restaurant menu available Tue-Sun ⊕ FREE HOUSE ◙ Dow Bridge Acris & Gladiator, Church End Goat's Milk Ö Westons Old Rosie. ♥ 37 **Facilities** Non-diners area ✿ (Bar Outside area) ♦♦ Children's menu Children's portions Outside area ⊟ Beer festival Parking WiFi ▄▄ (notice required)

| SILEBY | Map 11 SK61 |

The White Swan

tel: 01509 814832 **Swan St LE12 7NW**
email: tamiller56@googlemail.com
dir: From Leicester A6 towards Loughborough, right for Sileby; or take A46 towards Newark-on-Trent, left for Sileby

A reputation for home-cooked food

Behind the unassuming exterior of this 1930s building, you'll find a free house of some character, with a book-lined restaurant and a homely bar with an open fire and pictures and knick-knacks adorning the walls. Menus change weekly, and there are blackboard specials, too. Menu favourites include beef cobbler (diced beef cooked in Guinness with onions, mushrooms and Stilton scone topping), salmon and prawn pasta, and sliced potato cakes with garlic mushrooms and butternut squash. There's a good range of gourmet 8oz beefburgers with various toppings, and if you've still got room, you could try and fit in a chocolate brownie or chocolate tiffin for afters. Sunday lunch is also a popular event.

Open Wed-Fri & Sun 12-2 Tue-Sat 6-11 Closed 27 Dec & 1 Jan, Sat & Tue L, Sun eve & Mon **Food** Lunch Wed-Fri & Sun 12-1.30 Dinner Tue-Sat 7-8.30 ⊕ FREE HOUSE ◙ Bass, Guest ales. ♥ 8 **Facilities** Non-diners area ♦♦ Children's menu Children's portions Outside area ⊟ Parking WiFi

| SOMERBY | Map 11 SK71 |

Stilton Cheese Inn

tel: 01664 454394 **High St LE14 2QB**
web: www.stiltoncheeseinn.co.uk
dir: From A606 between Melton Mowbray & Oakham follow signs to Pickwell & Somerby. Enter village, 1st right to centre, pub on left

Village pub surrounded by beautiful countryside

An attractive, mellow sandstone building dating from the 17th century, whose interior frequently prompts customers to liken it to stepping back in time. Its reputation for good food stems from deep-fried fillet of cod; home-made cottage pie; grilled steaks; chilli con carne; macaroni cheese, and regularly changing specials. Stilton comes as a cheese option for a ploughman's, and for a steak sauce topping. In addition to the food, also attracting custom is the wide selection of wines by the glass or mini-bottle, and locally brewed real ales from Belvoir, The Grainstore, Newby Wyke and others. Furthermore, there's a choice of 25-plus malt whiskies.

Open all wk 12-3 6-11 (Sun 12-3 7-11) **Food** Lunch all wk 12-2 Dinner Mon-Sat 6-9, Sun 7-9 ⊕ FREE HOUSE ◙ The Grainstore Ten Fifty, Brewster's Hophead, Belvoir Star, Oakham Ales JHB, Newby Wyke Kingston Topaz Ö Westons Old Rosie & Bounds. ♥ 15 **Facilities** Non-diners area ♦♦ Children's menu Children's portions Family room Garden ⊟ Parking ▄▄ (notice required)

STATHERN
Map 11 SK73

Red Lion Inn
PICK OF THE PUBS

tel: 01949 860868 **Red Lion St LE14 4HS**
email: info@theredlioninn.co.uk
dir: *From A1 (Grantham), A607 towards Melton, turn right in Waltham, right at next x-rds then left to Stathern*

An inn for all seasons

Located in the beautiful Vale of Belvoir, details like the flagstone bar, the elegant dining room and the comfortable lounge (complete with plenty of reading material) make this establishment stand out. The Red Lion has plenty to offer all year round: logs crackling in the stove in winter, 'country cocktails' in summer, Sunday lunches, cookery demonstrations and wine evenings. There's a great line-up of regional ales, farmhouse ciders and local fruit beers at the bar. Menus change seasonally in accordance with locally supplied produce, and offer a mix of classic pub food and innovative country cooking. Typical of chef Sean Hope's dishes are haricot bean, white onion and thyme soup; oven-baked cod with parsnip hash browns, cavolo nero, lemon and thyme velouté; and roast breast of guinea fowl with butternut squash risotto and caramelised onion. Desserts reflect an attention to detail and are listed with suggested wines, ports and beers: try vanilla and blood orange pannacotta; or pistachio and honey cheesecake. There are good value set meals too.

Open 12-3 6-11 (Fri-Sat 12-11 Sun 12-7) Closed Sun eve & Mon **Food** Lunch Tue-Sat 12-2, Sun 12-3 Dinner Tue-Thu 6-9, Fri 5.30-9.30, Sat 7-9.30 Set menu available ⊕ FREE HOUSE/RUTLAND INN COMPANY LTD ◖ The Grainstore Red Lion Ale, Brewster's Marquis, Fuller's London Pride, Castle Rock Harvest Pale ♂ Aspall, Sheppy's, Westons. ♟ 8 **Facilities** Non-diners area ♣ (Bar Garden) ♦ Children's menu Children's portions Garden Outside area ⩎ Parking WiFi ▄▄ (notice required)

SUTTON CHENEY
Map 11 SK40

NEW Hercules Revived

tel: 01455 699336 **Main St CV13 0AG**
email: herculesrevived@yahoo.co.uk **web:** www.herculesrevived.co.uk
dir: *Phone pub for detailed directions*

Great British produce at revitalised village inn

Hercules was an 18th-century racehorse and – the story goes – his 'revival' has led to him becoming an innkeeper – described as a 'strong silent type and rarely seen'. Whether or not it's run by a horse, this 17th-century inn has undergone its own revival; complete renovation resulted in a relaxed bar and simple dining on the ground floor, with a cosy and elegant restaurant upstairs. Local producers supply pretty much everything. A winter evening menu might include a seafood platter for grazing, as well as classics like slow-braised beef with cheddar mash, hot pickled

red cabbage and bacon; or maybe teriyaki salmon, carrot, ginger and potato rösti, with toasted sesame and broccoli.

Hercules Revived

Open all day all wk **Food** Lunch all wk 12-2.30 Dinner all wk 6-9 Av main course £12.95 ⊕ FREE HOUSE ◖ Church End What The Fox's Hat, Tunnel Brewery Henry Tudor ♂ Thatchers Gold. ♟ 12 **Facilities** Non-diners area ♣ (Bar Outside area) ♦ Children's portions Outside area ⩎ Beer festival Parking ▄▄ (notice required)

SWITHLAND
Map 11 SK51

The Griffin Inn

tel: 01509 890535 **174 Main St LE12 8TJ**
email: thegriffininn@swithland.info
dir: *From A46 into Anstey. Right at rdbt to Cropston. Right at x-rds, 1st left, 0.5m into Swithland. Follow brown signs for inn*

Unpretentious food in a traditional walkers' inn

Parts of this welcoming, traditional, family-run country inn date back to the 15th century. There are three cosy bar areas serving a range of real ales, two dining rooms, a skittle alley, large patio and 'secret' garden with a stream. Menus and a wide range of specials offer unfussy, good-value internationally inspired food including moules marinière; chicken and chorizo linguine; traditional Spanish paella; and rhubarb and ginger sponge, lemon curd and vanilla ice cream. Dogs are only allowed in one room near the bar. The area is popular with walkers heading for Swithland Woods, Beacon Hill and the Old John folly, and there's also a steam railway nearby.

Open all day all wk **Food** Lunch Mon-Thu 12-2, Fri-Sun 12-9 Dinner Mon-Thu 6-9, Fri-Sun 12-9 Set menu available ⊕ EVERARDS ◖ Tiger & Original, Adnams Southwold Bitter, 2 guest ales ♂ Symonds, Guest cider. ♟ 15
Facilities Non-diners area ♦ Children's menu Children's portions Garden ⩎ Parking WiFi ▄▄

THORPE LANGTON
Map 11 SP79

The Bakers Arms

tel: 01858 545201 **Main St LE16 7TS**
dir: *Take A6 S from Leicester then left signed 'The Langtons', at rail bridge continue to x-rds. Straight on to Thorpe Langton. Pub on left*

Intimate thatched pub with great fish nights

A pretty thatched pub set in an equally pretty village, The Bakers Arms has the requisite low beams, rug-strewn quarry-tiled floors, large pine tables and open fires. Its weekly-changing menu of modern pub food has gained it a keen local following. Expect dishes like crevettes with asparagus, soft boiled eggs and garlic mayonnaise; confit of duck with red pepper and ginger marmalade; and apple and cinnamon crêpes with vanilla ice cream. Fish lovers should be sure to visit on a Thursday, when fish specials might include pan-fried sea bass fillets with spinach and chive butter sauce. The area is popular with walkers and mountain bikers.

Open 6.30-11 (Sat 12-2.30 6.30-11 Sun 12-2.30) Closed 1-7 Jan, Sun eve, Mon **Food** Contact pub for food times Restaurant menu available all wk ⊕ FREE HOUSE ◀ Langton Bakers Dozen Bitter. ☕ 9 **Facilities** Non-diners area Garden ⋈ Parking WiFi

---

WELHAM — Map 11 SP79

The Old Red Lion

tel: 01858 565253 **Main St LE16 7UJ**
email: pippa@king-henrys-taverns.co.uk
dir: NE of Market Harborough take B664 to Weston by Welland. Left to Welham

Tranquil setting in rolling countryside

The airy, split-level, contemporary interior of today's pub blends well with vestiges of its origins as a coaching inn. Polished floorboards, leather seating and open fire are a welcome retreat for ramblers drifting in from the area's popular walking routes. Views from the windows stretch across this rural corner of Leicestershire where the River Welland meanders through rich pastureland. One of a small chain of local dining pubs; the menu covers all bases, from British classics such as steak and ale pie to a select choice of international dishes, with vegetarian options including mushroom, cranberry and brie Wellington. Beers include Marston's Pedigree.

Open all day all wk 11.30-11 **Food** Lunch all wk 12-10 Dinner all wk 12-10 ⊕ FREE HOUSE/KING HENRY'S TAVERNS ◀ Greene King IPA, Marston's Pedigree, Fuller's London Pride, Guinness. ☕ 15 **Facilities** Non-diners area ♦ Children's menu Children's portions Outside area ⋈ Parking WiFi ▦

WOODHOUSE EAVES — Map 11 SK51

NEW The Curzon Arms

tel: 01509 890377 **44 Maplewell Rd LE12 8QZ**
email: info@thecurzonarms.com
dir: M1 junct 23, A512 towards Loughborough. Right signed Nanpantan. Through Nanpantan to Woodhouse Eaves

Contemporary but still pleasingly old-fashioned village pub

Traditional and lounge bars, a restaurant, wood-burning stoves, wooden floors, a large terrace and a beer garden just about sum up this Charnwood Forest pub. Other essentials are the four rotating real ales, hand-picked wines and seasonal British food, with monthly changing, well-compiled menus offering light bar meals, three-course dinners and 'funky' bar snacks. Possible choices include rabbit, carrot and leek stew; crispy risotto balls with chilli and tomato dressing; whole baked sea bream; confit leg of Gressingham duck; Woodhouse honey and mustard roast ham; and pan-fried polenta cake with winter vegetable ragout. For dessert, maybe Baileys crème brûlée with mulled berry compôte.

Open all wk 12-3 5.30-12 (Fri-Sat 12-12 Sun 12-11.30) **Food** Lunch Mon-Fri 12-2.30, Sat 12-9, Sun 12-6 Dinner Mon-Fri 5.30-9.30, Sat 12-9 Set menu available ⊕ ENTERPRISE INNS ◀ Sharp's Doom Bar, Timothy Taylor Landlord. ☕ 16 **Facilities** ✿ (Bar Garden) ♦ Children's menu Children's portions Garden ⋈ Parking WiFi ▦ (notice required)

The Wheatsheaf Inn ★★★★ INN

tel: 01509 890320 **Brand Hill LE12 8SS**
email: richard@wheatsheafinn.net **web:** www.wheatsheafinn.net
dir: M1 junct 22, follow Quorn signs

Old village inn at heart of Charnwood Forest

A rambling, creeper dressed stone inn (it was a quarrymen's watering hole 200 years ago) with contemporary bed and breakfast accommodation, a comfortably traditional bar and 'The Mess' dining area based on RAF connections. Charnwood Forest's stirring countryside is all around and the Great Central Railway (steam) is close-by. Explorers may choose to sit in the flowery courtyard garden, indulging in Timothy Taylor Landlord bitter and select from an ever-changing menu, perhaps haddock in beer batter with mushy peas, fries and home-made tartare sauce; the always popular Woodhouse smokies; and the Wheatsheaf burger. There's a decent list of wines to accompany.

Open all wk 12-3 6-11 (Sat 12-11 Sun 12-4) Closed Sun eve **Food** Lunch Mon-Fri 12-2.30, Sat 12-3, Sun 12-4 Dinner Mon-Fri 6-9.15, Sat 6-9.30 Av main course £14 ⊕ FREE HOUSE ◀ Greene King Abbot Ale, Timothy Taylor Landlord, Adnams Broadside, Tetley's Smoothflow, Marston's Pedigree, Guest ale Ö Thatchers. ☕ 16 **Facilities** Non-diners area ✿ (Bar Garden) ♦ Children's menu Children's portions Garden ⋈ Parking WiFi ▦ (notice required) **Rooms** 2

WYMESWOLD — Map 11 SK62

The Windmill Inn

tel: 01509 881313 **83 Brook St LE12 6TT**
email: info@thewindmillwymeswold.com
dir: From A46 N of Six Hills left onto A606 signed Wymeswold. In village left into Church Ln, left into Brook St. Or from M1 junct 24, A6 signed Loughborough & Kegworth, A6006 to Wymeswold

Family-friendly local with large beer garden

It may be a traditional village inn but the Windmill has a contemporary feel in both the bar and restaurant, with a mix of wood and stone tiled floors, wood-burners, warm heritage colours and comfortable seating creating the informal scene. Monthly menus combine pub classics with modern British dishes, perhaps pan-fried scallops, thermidor sauce and watercress followed by honey-roast duck, fondant potato, pumpkin purée, kale and cherry jus, and banana and caramel parfait. Dogs and children are most welcome and there's a lovely garden for alfresco dining.

Open all wk 12-3 5.15-11.30 (Mon 12-3 5.15-11 Fri-Sat 12-12 Sun 12-9) **Food** Lunch Mon-Thu 12-2.30, Fri-Sat 12-9.30, Sun 12-5 Dinner Mon 5.30-9, Tue-Thu 5.30-9.30, Fri-Sat 12-9.30 Set menu available ⊕ FREE HOUSE ◀ Sharp's Doom Bar, Castle Rock Harvest Pale, Guest ale Ö Symonds. ☕ **Facilities** Non-diners area ✿ (Bar Garden Outside area) ♦ Children's menu Children's portions Family room Garden Outside area ⋈ Parking WiFi

WYMONDHAM
Map 11 SK81

The Berkeley Arms

tel: 01572 787587 **59 Main St LE14 2AG**
email: info@theberkeleyarms.co.uk
dir: *In town centre*

Locally sourced, freshly prepared meals and fine wines

Having fulfilled their long-held ambition to own a pub, Neil and Louise Hitchen have seen their appealing, stone-built Berkeley Arms go from strength to strength. They are dedicated to sourcing fresh, local produce for the daily-changing menus. So a winter menu may offer chargrilled rare local wood pigeon breast with a Waldorf salad; haunch of local sika deer with swede purée, poached pear and caramelised walnuts; and David Cox of Stathern Lincolnshire sausages, mash and red onion gravy. Leave a little room for poached pear with chocolate sauce and vanilla ice cream. Well thought out two- and three- course lunches are served on Sundays.

Open 12-3 6-11 (Sun 12-5) Closed 1st 2wks Jan & 1wk summer, Sun eve & Mon **Food** Lunch Tue-Sat 12-2 Dinner Tue-Sat 6.30-9.30 Set menu available ⊕ FREE HOUSE ◀ Castle Rock Harvest Pale, Batemans XB, Marston's Pedigree Ò Westons Stowford Press. ♚ 10 **Facilities** Non-diners area ♣ (Bar Garden) ♦♦ Children's portions Garden ♠ Parking

LINCOLNSHIRE

BARNOLDBY LE BECK
Map 17 TA20

The Ship Inn

tel: 01472 822308 **Main Rd DN37 0BG**
email: the_ship_inn@btinternet.com
dir: *M180 junct 5, A18 past Humberside Airport. At Laceby Junction rdbt (A18 & A46) straight over follow Skegness/Boston signs. Approx 2m turn left signed Waltham & Barnoldby le Beck*

Traditional village pub with coal fires and great seafood

Set in a picturesque village on the edge of the Lincolnshire Wolds, this 300-year-old inn has always attracted an interesting mix of customers, from Grimsby's seafarers to aviators from the county's World War II airstrips. The bar is filled with maritime bric-à-brac and serves a grand choice of ales such as Black Sheep or Tom Wood's, and there's also a beautiful garden. Seafood is a speciality, so tuck into pan-fried cod cheeks with pea purée and chorizo, and then whole salt-crusted sea bass, coriander, chilli rice and stir-fried vegetables.

Open 12-3 6-11 (Fri-Sat 12-3 6-12 Sun 12-5) Closed 25 Dec, Sun eve **Food** Lunch Mon-Sat 12-2, Sun 12-5 Dinner Mon-Sat 6-9 Av main course £12 ⊕ FREE HOUSE/ INNOVATIVE SIGHT LTD ◀ Black Sheep Best Bitter, Tom Wood's, Guinness Ò Thatchers Gold. ♚ 9 **Facilities** Non-diners area ♣ (Garden) ♦♦ Children's portions Garden ♠ Parking WiFi ⌨ (notice required)

BELCHFORD
Map 17 TF27

The Blue Bell Inn

tel: 01507 533602 **1 Main Rd LN9 6LQ**
email: bluebellbelchford@gmail.com
dir: *From Horncastle take A153 towards Louth. Right signed Belchford*

In the heart of the Lincolnshire Wolds

Pantiles on the roof, white walls reflecting the sun, this family-run free house stands on the Viking Way long-distance path from the Humber to Rutland Water. Diners from all over the county are attracted by its many culinary temptations, among them local wild fallow venison and red wine pie; Lincolnshire sausages and mash; lamb chump marinated in garlic and rosemary; guinea fowl au vin; and smoked haddock, salmon and prawn fish pie. Anyone just after a glass of wine or

pint of Wainfleet-brewed Batemans XXXB, Greene King IPA or a guest beer, will find plenty of armchairs to sink into.

Open all wk 11.30-2.30 6.30-11 (Sun 12-10.30) Closed 2nd & 3rd wk Jan **Food** Lunch all wk 12-2 Dinner all wk 6.30-9 Av main course £12 ⊕ FREE HOUSE ◀ Batemans XXXB, Greene King IPA, Guest ale. **Facilities** Non-diners area ♣ (Bar Garden) ♦♦ Children's menu Children's portions Garden ♠ Parking WiFi

BURTON COGGLES
Map 11 SK92

NEW The Cholmeley Arms

tel: 01476 550225 **Village St NG33 4JS**
email: berrylesley@aol.com
dir: *From A1 at Colsterworth onto A151 towards Corby Glen. Left onto B1176 signed Burton Coggles*

Village free house with a royal tale to tell

Descendants of Sir Henry Cholmeley, who in 1592 bought the manor of Easton, which embraces the inn, still live in the village. In addition to quality food and drink, the inn has a farm shop, where in 2011, on a visit accompanied by HRH The Prince of Wales, The Duchess of Cornwall bought a home-made cake and the Royal couple chatted to regulars and staff. Sadly, what they did not have the opportunity to try dishes such as Mediterranean mixed seafood salad; Gressingham duck breast with redcurrant and port sauce; steak, mushroom and ale pie; and fresh Grimsby haddock with mushy peas.

Open 11.30-3 5-11 Closed Mon L & Tue L **Food** Lunch Wed-Sat 12-2, Sun 12-3.30 Dinner Mon-Sat 6-9 Restaurant menu available all wk ⊕ FREE HOUSE ◀ John Smith's Extra Smooth, Guest ales Ò Thatchers. **Facilities** Non-diners area ♣ (Bar Garden) ♦♦ Children's menu Children's portions Garden ♠ Parking WiFi

CLEETHORPES
Map 17 TA30

NEW The Nottingham House ★★★★ INN

tel: 01472 505150 **5-7 Seaview St DN35 8EU**
email: nottinghamhousehotel@gmail.com **web:** www.nottinghamhousehotel.com
dir: *Phone for detailed directions*

Real ale haven in seaside town centre

To locals this is The Notts, an intimate, family-run pub in narrow Seaview Street, from which you can indeed see the briny. Landlords Anne and Roger Gott speak of the "amazing views across the Humber Estuary" from upstairs. A strong commitment to real ales and ciders is evident in the bar, where in addition 25 wines are sold by the glass. Menus offer pub grub – for example, eggs, chips and beans – and dishes such as pan-fried Gressingham duck with red wine and redcurrant gravy; paupiettes of plaice stuffed with smoked salmon and spinach; and three-cheese vegetable bake.

Open all day all wk **Food** Lunch 12-3 Dinner 6-9 Restaurant menu available Wed-Sun ⊕ PUNCH TAVERNS ◀ Tetley's Bitter & Dark Mild, Wychwood Hobgoblin, Timothy Taylor Landlord, Guinness Ò Westons Old Rosie, Rosie's Pig, Perry & Raspberry Twist. ♚ 25 **Facilities** Non-diners area ♣ (Bar) ♦♦ Children's menu Children's portions Family room Beer festival Cider festival WiFi ⌨ (notice required) **Rooms** 3

CONINGSBY
Map 17 TF25

The Lea Gate Inn

tel: 01526 342370 **Leagate Rd LN4 4RS**
email: theleagateinn@hotmail.com
dir: *From Coningsby take A153 towards Horncastle. Right onto B1192 signed Boston. Pub on left*

The oldest licensed premises in the county

Dating from 1542, this was the last of the Fen Guide Houses that provided shelter before the treacherous marshes were drained. Among the oak-beamed pub's features are a priest's hole, low ceilings, a very old inglenook fireplace, extensive gardens and a yew tree dating from the 1600s. The same family has been running the pub for 30 years and they source their produce locally (including game in season). All food is home made, and dishes on the seasonal menu could include wild game pie, slow roasted blade of beef, fisherman's pie and double-dipped full rack of BBQ ribs. Wednesday night is steak night.

Open all wk 11.30-3 6-11 (Sun 12-10.30) **Food** Lunch Mon-Sat 11.45-2, Sun 12-9 Dinner Mon-Sat 6-9, Sun 12-9 ⊕ FREE HOUSE ◀ Timothy Taylor Landlord, Woodforde's Wherry, Guest ales ♂ Aspall. ♈ 10 **Facilities** Non-diners area ♣ (Bar Garden) ♦♦ Children's menu Children's portions Play area Garden ⋒ Parking WiFi ☞

DRY DODDINGTON
Map 11 SK84

Wheatsheaf Inn

tel: 01400 281458 **NG23 5HU**
email: wheatsheafdrydoddington@hotmail.co.uk
dir: *From A1 between Newark-on-Trent & Grantham. Turn into Doddington Ln for Dry Doddington*

Village inn with a good selection of ales on tap

The church, with its leaning tower, faces this pantile-roofed inn across the village green. No one's sure of the inn's age, but at least they can put a date on the pre-Jurassic era stones used to build it as being around 200-million-years old. Abbot Ale and Timothy Taylor Landlord are the regular real ales, with Lincolnshire easily the biggest contributor of produce on the menus. Enjoy a starter of pea, mint and crème fraîche risotto, followed by slow-braised shoulder of lamb; fish of the day; or honey-roasted pepper and goats' cheese tart, either in the bar, restaurant or sheltered garden.

Open 12-3 5-11 (Sat-Sun 12-11) Closed Mon **Food** Lunch Tue-Fri 12-2, Sat 12-2.30, Sun 12-3 Dinner Tue-Fri 6-9, Sat 6-9.30 ⊕ FREE HOUSE ◀ Timothy Taylor Landlord, Greene King Abbot Ale, Guest ales ♂ Thatchers Gold, Hogan's. ♈ 12 **Facilities** Non-diners area ♣ (Bar Garden) ♦♦ Children's menu Children's portions Garden ⋒ Parking WiFi ☞ (notice required)

FULBECK
Map 17 SK95

The Hare & Hounds

tel: 01400 273322 **The Green NG32 3JJ**
email: harefulbeck@yahoo.co.uk
dir: *On A607, N of Grantham*

Village pub with imaginative food

Overlooking an attractive village green, this is a 17th-century, Grade II listed pub where a log fire does the business in winter; on warmer days, an outside eating area awaits. The beer pumps in the bar announce Adnams Broadside and Woodforde's Wherry among others. The chef and his team work with only the best locally sourced ingredients, producing a typical three-course dinner of curried smoked haddock risotto with poached egg and crispy pancetta; breast of chicken with pan haggerty, green beans and wild mushroom sauce; and Baileys crème brûlée. Pub classics include Lincolnshire sausages with mash and onion gravy; and barbecued sticky ribs.

Open 12-2 5.30-11 (Sun 12-4) Closed Sun eve **Food** Lunch Mon-Sat 12-2, Sun 12-3 Dinner Mon-Sat 6-9 ⊕ FREE HOUSE ◀ Adnams Broadside, Harvey's Pale, Wadworth 6X, Woodforde's Wherry. ♈ 11 **Facilities** Non-diners area ♦♦ Children's menu Children's portions Family room Outside area ⋒ Parking WiFi

GEDNEY DYKE
Map 12 TF42

The Chequers

tel: 01406 366700 **PE12 0AJ**
email: info@the-chequers.co.uk **web:** www.the-chequers.co.uk
dir: *From A17 between Holbeach & Sutton Bridge left at rdbt onto B1359 (signed Gedney Dyke)*

Destination eatery with beguiling warmth

You can just sit at the spotless bar and enjoy a pint of Woodforde's Wherry, but chances are most people arriving here will have booked a table. The contemporary decor, crisp white napery and smartly dressed front of house staff all indicate a quality food destination. That said, dogs are welcome in the bar, children have their own menu, and the welcome from the staff matches the warmth of the atmosphere. So choose your refreshment and settle down to enjoy the labours of a highly-qualified kitchen brigade – roast saddle of venison; roast sea bass in a Thai-style broth; and butternut squash and feta cheese bake are indicative dishes. If you aren't too full, why not try the vanilla poached apple with blackberries and hazelnut crumble.

Open 11.30-3 5-11 Closed Mon & Tue **Food** Lunch Wed-Sat 12-2.30, Sun 12-3 Dinner Wed-Sat 6-9 Set menu available Restaurant menu available Wed-Sun ⊕ FREE HOUSE ◀ Woodforde's Wherry, Guest ales ♂ Aspall. ♈ 12 **Facilities** Non-diners area ♣ (Bar Garden) ♦♦ Children's menu Children's portions Garden ⋒ Parking WiFi ☞

GOSBERTON
Map 12 TF23

The Black Horse

tel: 01775 840995 **66 Siltside, Gosberton Risegate PE11 4ET**
dir: *From Spalding take A16 towards Boston. Left onto A152. At Gosberton take B1397 to Gosberton Risegate. Pub set back from road*

No poker faces at this friendly Fenland local

This lovely creeper-clad hostelry is tucked away in a village outside Spalding. Poker and nap nights feature in the pub's social calendar along with quiz nights, and indoor barbecues if the weather is unaccommodating. Huddle up to the wood-burning stove with a pint of Black Sheep or Fuller's London Pride while perusing the extensive choices of pub grub on the menu. All the favourites are here, from starters of whitebait or prawn cocktail, to main plates of scampi with chips and peas, or pie of the day. Chef's home-made cheesecake with fruit coulis and honeycomb ice cream rounds things off nicely.

Open Wed-Thu 5.30-10.30 (Fri-Sat 12-2 5.30-10.30 Sun 12-10.30) Closed Mon-Tue **Food** Lunch Fri-Sat 12-2, Sun 12-4 Dinner Wed-Sat 6-9 ⊕ FREE HOUSE ◀ Black Sheep, Fuller's London Pride. **Facilities** Non-diners area ♦♦ Children's portions Garden ⊼ Parking WiFi ☜

GRIMSTHORPE
Map 11 TF02

NEW The Black Horse Inn

tel: 01778 591093 **Main St PE10 0LY**
email: enquiries@theblackhorsegrimsthorpe.co.uk
dir: *On A151, NW of Bourne*

In the shadow of Grimsthorpe Castle

The Black Horse, along with the rest of the village, is part of an estate belonging to the castle owners. The former coaching inn has been integral to village life for centuries, with passing travellers always warmly welcomed. Its impressive frontage sits back in a large courtyard where a walnut tree provides welcome shade in summer. Its interior walls create several separate rooms, pleasing those looking for intimate dining as well as for family groups. Fresh local produce, with game high on the list, is the kitchen's priority. A well-priced two-course meal could start with smoked haddock croquettes, and continue with a home-ground venison burger.

Open Wed-Sat 12-2 6-9 (Sun 12-3) Closed Mon-Tue **Food** Lunch Wed-Sat 12-2, Sun 12-3 Dinner Wed-Sat 6-9 Av main course £12 ⊕ FREE HOUSE ◀ The Grainstore Triple B & Rutland Osprey ♨ Thatchers Gold. ☉ **Facilities** Non-diners area ♣ (Bar Garden Outside area) ♦♦ Children's portions Garden Outside area ⊼ Parking WiFi ☜ (notice required)

Who are the AA's award-winning pubs? For details see pages 10 & 11

HOUGH-ON-THE-HILL
Map 11 SK94

The Brownlow Arms ★★★★★ INN ☺

tel: 01400 250234 **High Rd NG32 2AZ**
email: armsinn@yahoo.co.uk **web:** www.thebrownlowarms.com
dir: *From A607 (Grantham to Sleaford road), Hough-on-the-Hill signed from Barkston*

Country-house-style village inn

This 17th-century stone inn ticks all the boxes. Named after former owner Lord Brownlow, it still looks, inside and out, every inch the country house it once was. Enjoy a pint of Timothy Taylor Landlord or Black Sheep in the convivial bar, while browsing the menu for AA-Rosette standard dishes such as whole baked sea bass; butter-poached supreme of chicken; and Moroccan sweet potato and aubergine tagine. The landscaped terrace invites outdoor drinking and dining, although please note that children must be eight or over to be allowed in the pub.

Open Tue-Sat 6pm-11pm Sun 12-3 Closed Mon, Sun eve **Food** Dinner Tue-Sat 6-9 Restaurant menu available ⊕ FREE HOUSE ◀ Timothy Taylor Landlord, Black Sheep. ☉ 10 **Facilities** Non-diners area Garden ⊼ Parking WiFi **Rooms** 6

INGHAM
Map 17 SK98

Inn on the Green

tel: 01522 730354 **34 The Green LN1 2XT**
email: enquiries@innatthegreeningham.co.uk **web:** www.innonthegreeningham.co.uk
dir: *From Lincoln take A15 signed Scunthorpe. Left into Ingham Ln signed Ingham, Cammeringham. Right onto B1398 (Middle St), left to Ingham*

Village favourite offering some excellent pub food

This lovely old limestone and pantile pub stands at a corner of the huge green in a secluded village at the foot of Lincoln Edge. Drinkers relaxing at garden tables and enjoying a real ale from Horncastle or Welbeck Abbey may be startled by the Red Arrows, practicing from nearby RAF Scampton. The pub's three bars and restaurant area exude the character that has gained it Grade II listing; an appealing destination in which to enjoy highly individual seasonal dishes crafted by a talented kitchen team. Pigeon pie starter gives the measure of the locally sourced produce; continue then with chilli con carne made with seared venison haunch; or charred salmon fish stew. A summer beer festival is held.

Open 11.30-3 6-11 (Sat 11.30-11 Sun 12-10.30) (Sat 11.30-3 6-11 in winter) Closed Mon **Food** Lunch Tue-Sat 12-2, Sun 12-4 Dinner Tue-Sat 6-9 ⊕ FREE HOUSE ◀ Horncastle, Sharp's Doom Bar & Special, Springhead, Welbeck Abbey Red Feather ♨ Thatchers Gold. ☉ 10 **Facilities** Non-diners area ♦♦ Children's portions Garden ⊼ Beer festival Parking ☜ (notice required)

KIRKBY LA THORPE Map 12 TF04

Queens Head

tel: 01529 305743 & 307194 **Church Ln NG34 9NU**
email: info@thequeensheadinn.com **web:** www.thequeensheadinn.com
dir: Pub signed from A17 (dual carriageway)

Offering ales brewed in a windmill

Heavy beams, open log fires, antique furnishings and original watercolours – this destination dining pub fulfills the brief when it comes to original features and traditional character. The French-trained chef-proprietor prepares everything on site, from breads to desserts, and local ingredients get star billing on the extensive seasonal menus. Wild boar terrine; or salmon and coriander fishcakes might make way for slow-roast rump of lamb, creamed greens with smoked bacon, and lightly minted lamb jus; or an individual wild venison and red wine pie. Wash it down with Lincolnshire ales from the 8 Sail Brewery, brewed in Heckington Windmill, or wines from a well-considered list.

Queens Head

Open all wk 12-3 6-11 (Sun 12-11) **Food** Lunch Mon-Sat 12-2.30, Sun 12-8.30 Dinner Mon-Fri 6-9.30, Sat 6-10, Sun 12-8.30 Set menu available Restaurant menu available all wk ⊕ FREE HOUSE ◀ Batemans XB, 8 Sail Brewery, Guest ales. ♟ 9 **Facilities** Non-diners area ☺ (Bar Outside area) ♦ Children's menu Children's portions Outside area ☂ Parking WiFi ☎ (notice required)

See advert below

The Queens Head

Kirkby La Thorpe, Sleaford, Lincolnshire NG34 9NU
Tel: 01529 305743 or 01529 307194 • **Website:** www.thequeensheadinn.com

KIRTON IN LINDSEY
Map 17 SK99

The George

tel: 01652 640600 **20 High St DN21 4LX**
email: enquiry@thegeorgekirton.co.uk
dir: *From A15 take B1205, turn right onto B1400*

Country inn near Ermine Street

Lincoln and the Wolds are within easy reach of this extensively restored yet traditional pub. The 18th-century former coaching inn serves locally brewed ales and seasonally changing menus. Customers can dine in the comfortable bar area or in the informal restaurant. Favourite starters such as prawn cocktail, and bar meals such as lasagne with salad and hand-cut chips, are topped by regularly changing specials such as chicken schnitzel with a brandy and mushroom sauce; and game and blackcurrant pie.

Open all wk 5-11 (Sun 12-2.30) **Food** Lunch Sun 12-2 Dinner Mon-Sat 5-9 ⊕ FREE HOUSE ◀ Rotating Guest ales. **Facilities** Non-diners area ♦♦ Children's menu Children's portions Play area Garden Outside area ☷

LINCOLN
Map 17 SK97

The Pyewipe

tel: 01522 528708 **Fossebank, Saxilby Rd LN1 2BG**
email: enquiries@pyewipe.co.uk
dir: *From Lincoln on A57 towards Worksop, pub signed in 0.5m on left*

Waterside inn with home-made food

There's a great view of nearby Lincoln Cathedral from the grounds of this waterside inn, which takes its name from the local dialect for lapwing. Set in four wooded acres beside the Roman-built Fossedyke Navigation, it serves real ales and home-made, locally sourced food. Expect dishes such as partridge and black pudding stack with a red wine sauce; pork belly with a cider and grain mustard sauce and mash; or loin of cod poached in Thai broth with noodles and stir-fried vegetables. There is a beer garden and riverside patio where you can enjoy your meal, a refreshing ale or a glass of wine.

Open all day all wk 11-11 **Food** Lunch all wk 12-9 Dinner all wk 12-9 ⊕ FREE HOUSE ◀ Guest ales. **Facilities** Non-diners area ♦♦ Children's portions Garden ⊓ Parking WiFi ☷

The Victoria

tel: 01522 541000 **6 Union Rd LN1 3BJ**
email: jonathanjpc@aol.com
dir: *From city outskirts follow signs for Cathedral Quarter. Pub 2 mins' walk from all major up-hill car parks. Adjacent to West Gate of Lincoln Castle*

Good real ales in the city

Situated right next to the West Gate entrance of the castle and a short stroll from Lincoln Cathedral, a long-standing drinkers' pub with a range of real ales, including three changing guest beers, ciders and perries. As well as the fantastic views of the castle, the pub also offers great meals made from home-prepared food including hot baguettes and filled rolls. House specials include sausage and mash, various pies, chilli con carne and home-made lasagne. Facilities include a large beer garden with children's play area. There are annual Halloween and winter beer festivals.

Open all day all wk 11am-mdnt (Fri-Sat 11am-1am Sun 12-12) **Food** Lunch all wk 12-2.30 ⊕ BATEMANS ◀ XB & Yella Belly Gold, Timothy Taylor Landlord, Castle Rock Harvest Pale, Guest ales ♂ Westons. **Facilities** Non-diners area ♣ (Bar Garden) ♦♦ Children's portions Play area Garden ⊓ Beer festival WiFi ☷ (notice required)

Wig & Mitre
PICK OF THE PUBS

tel: 01522 535190 **32 Steep Hill LN2 1LU**
dir: *At top of Steep Hill, adjacent to cathedral & Lincoln Castle car parks*

Old-fashioned values and contemporary cuisine

Just yards from the magnificent edifice of Lincoln Cathedral, this two-storey pub has a pedigree nearly as long; parts of it date back over 700 years. It's the ideal place for a quick pick-me-up snack, drink or leisurely meal from breakfast to evening. Notably music-free; instead you'll find a reading room, eclectic decor and furnishings – note the caricatures and prints of clergy and lawyers – and beers from both local and national breweries to slake the thirst. The set menu, regularly refreshed during the year, adds modern twists to traditional dishes. Thus roast rump of lamb comes with pine nut and herb couscous and minted yogurt; or slow-cooked pork collar with Lincolnshire sausage bread pudding, creamed white beans and sage may be listed. Daily blackboard specials considerably extend the choice and include vegetarian and gluten-free options. Gourmet evenings (pre-booking essential) are regularly held, while wine-lovers have a choice of 24 by the glass.

Open all day all wk 8.30am-mdnt Closed 25 Dec **Food** Lunch all wk 8.30am-10pm Dinner all wk 8.30am-10pm Set menu available Restaurant menu available all wk ⊕ FREE HOUSE ◀ Oakham Ales JHB, Young's London Gold, Black Sheep ♂ Aspall. ♇ 24 **Facilities** Non-diners area ♣ (Bar) ♦♦ Children's menu Children's portions WiFi

LITTLE BYTHAM
Map 11 TF01

The Willoughby Arms

tel: 01780 410216 **Station Rd NG33 4RA**
email: info@willoughbyarms.co.uk
dir: *B6121 (Stamford to Bourne road), at junct follow signs to Careby & Little Bytham, inn 5m on right*

Former railway property now a traditional inn

This beamed, traditional stone country inn started life as the booking office and waiting room for Lord Willoughby's private railway line. These days it has a fresher look whilst retaining its traditional charms. Expect a good selection of real ales – including several from local microbreweries – with great, home-cooked food available every lunchtime and evening. Dishes may include steak and kidney pie, Lincolnshire sausage and mash, or meat or vegetable lasagne. Omelettes, jacket potatoes, and hot and cold baguettes are also on offer. As well as a cosy bar with open fire, and a light and airy sun lounge, there is also a large beer garden with stunning views to enjoy on warmer days. A summer holiday beer festival is held.

Open all day all wk 12-11 **Food** Lunch Mon-Sat 12-2, Sun 12-3 Dinner all wk 6-9 Av main course £9.50 ⊕ FREE HOUSE ◀ Hopshackle Simmarillo, Abbeydale Absolution ♂ Aspall, Westons Stowford Press, Guest cider. ♇ 10 **Facilities** Non-diners area ♣ (Bar Garden) ♦♦ Children's menu Children's portions Garden ⊓ Beer festival Parking WiFi ☷ (notice required)

MARKET RASEN
Map 17 TF18

The Advocate Arms ★★★★★ RR ◉

tel: 01673 842364 **2 Queen St LN8 3EH**
email: info@advocatearms.co.uk web: www.advocatearms.co.uk
dir: *In town centre*

Convenient town-centre location

This 18th-century, three-storey corner property in the town centre has a contemporary veneer. Until 11am there's a wide choice of breakfasts, including kippers, then for lunch there are sandwiches, omelettes, salads and light meals, or more substantial main meals. Taken from a sample evening carte are seared red snapper with tomato, green bean and courgette salsa; roast duck breast with celeriac chips, pickled Jerusalem artichoke, shallot purée, smoked bacon and kale; roast turbot with oyster chowder; or pumpkin and butternut squash cannelloni.

Open all day all wk **Food** Lunch all wk 12-6 Dinner all wk 6-9.30 Restaurant menu available Mon-Sat ⊕ FREE HOUSE ◀ Wells Bombardier, Greene King IPA ♂ Aspall, Westons Rosie's Pig. ♥ 8 **Facilities** Non-diners area ♦ Children's menu Children's portions Outside area ⊨ Parking WiFi ⇒ (notice required) **Rooms** 10

MINTING
Map 17 TF17

NEW The Sebastopol Inn

tel: 01507 578577 **Church Ln LN9 5RS**
email: thesebastopol@hotmail.co.uk **web:** www.thesebastopol.com
dir: From A158 from Lincoln towards Horncastle. After Wragby follow signs for Minting on right

Cosy old inn with great local food

First licensed in 1836, and named after the famous 11-month siege during the Crimean War, the Sebastopol was taken over by the Reed family around five years ago. Successfully brought back to life from an empty shell, it's a cosy place with a log fire, comfy seating, and plenty of old photos and other memorabilia. The highest quality ingredients from the best local producers and suppliers take pride of place on the menu. Try the treacle ham hock to start with, perhaps, and then the Minting Park Farm mutton leg; or Lop pork loin and belly. Wild plum clafouti finishes things off nicely.

Open Tue-Sat 12-2.30 6-11 (Sun 12-4) Closed 2-3wks from 1 Jan, Mon **Food** Lunch Tue-Sun 12-1.45 Dinner Tue-Sat 6-10 Av main course £14 ⊕ FREE HOUSE ◀ Batemans, Tom Wood's, Springhead, Horncastle, Oldershaw, Milestone ♂ Skidbrooke. **Facilities** Non-diners area ❀ (Bar Garden) ♦ Children's menu Garden ⊨ Parking

PARTNEY
Map 17 TF46

Red Lion Inn

tel: 01790 752271 **PE23 4PG**
email: enquiries@redlioninnpartney.co.uk
dir: On A16 from Boston, or A158 from Horncastle

Sound reputation for good, home-cooked food

Here is a welcoming village inn especially to walkers and cyclists due to its location, just below the Lincolnshire Wolds; many inevitably more than ready for pint of Black Sheep, or a glass of chilled wine. The pub's solid reputation for home-cooked food can be attributed to dishes such as sweet and sour chicken with rice; moussaka; pheasant, venison and rabbit pie; and cod and prawns in cheese sauce. A formidable selection of desserts includes puddings, sponges, sundaes and tarts.

Open 12-2 6-11 (Sun 12-2 6-10.30) Closed Mon **Food** Lunch Tue-Sun 12-2 Dinner Tue-Sun 6-9 ⊕ FREE HOUSE ◀ Black Sheep, Tetley's, Guinness, Guest ales. **Facilities** Non-diners area ♦ Children's menu Children's portions Parking WiFi ⇒ (notice required)

RAITHBY
Map 17 TF36

Red Lion Inn

tel: 01790 753727 **PE23 4DS**
dir: A158 from Horncastle, through Hagworthingham, right at top of hill signed Raithby

Quiet village setting, cosy in winter, garden in summer

This traditional beamed village pub, parts of which date back 300 years, is situated on the edge of the Lincolnshire Wolds, a great place for walking and cycling. Inside is a wealth of character with log fires providing a warm welcome in winter. Dine in one of the four bars or on the comfort of the restaurant. A varied menu of home-made dishes is prepared using fresh local produce — sea bass with stir-fried vegetables; roast guinea fowl with tomato, garlic and bacon; and medallions of beef with peppercorn sauce. Meals can be enjoyed in the garden in the warmer months.

Open 12-2 6-11 (Mon 7-11) Closed Mon L **Food** Lunch Tue-Sun 12-2 Dinner Tue-Sat 7-8.30 ⊕ FREE HOUSE ◀ Thwaites, Batemans ♂ Thatchers Gold. **Facilities** Non-diners area ♦ Children's menu Children's portions Outside area ⊨ Parking ⇒ (notice required)

SOUTH RAUCEBY
Map 11 TF04

The Bustard Inn & Restaurant ◉   PICK OF THE PUBS

tel: 01529 488250 **44 Main St NG34 8QG**
email: info@thebustardinn.co.uk
dir: A15 from Lincoln. Right onto B1429 for Cranwell, 1st left after village, straight across A17 to South Rauceby

Grade II listed pub with award-winning cooking

Situated above Lincoln Edge, at the heart of a pretty stone-built estate village, this imposing building dates from 1860. The pub's name is based on the legend that the last indigenous great bustard was shot nearby in 1845 by the local lord of the manor. In the beer garden and courtyard, try a pint of Batemans XB or Timothy Taylor Landlord. The light and airy interior is divided between the bar and an elegant restaurant, with dressed stone walls, beamed ceiling and tapestry chairs; an ornate oriel window looks out on to the lovely garden. Head chef Phil Lowe's cooking draws on local produce where possible. The menu for bar and restaurant is one and the same: whole baked camembert for two to share makes an appetising starter, followed perhaps by beef two ways (fillet and rillette), or chargrilled gammon steak.

Open 12-3 5.30-11 (Sun 12-3.30) Closed 1 Jan, Sun eve, Mon **Food** Lunch Tue-Sat 12-2.30, Sun 12-3 Dinner Tue-Sat 6-9.30 Av main course £12.40 Set menu available ⊕ FREE HOUSE ◀ Batemans XB, Timothy Taylor Landlord, Guinness, Guest ale ♂ Aspall. ♥ 15 **Facilities** Non-diners area ♦ Children's menu Children's portions Garden ⊨ Parking WiFi ⇒ (notice required)

SOUTH WITHAM
Map 11 SK91

Blue Cow Inn & Brewery

tel: 01572 768432 **High St NG33 5QB**
email: enquiries@bluecowinn.co.uk
dir: *Between Stamford & Grantham on A1*

Own-brewed real ale and pub classics

Licensee Simon Crathorn has been brewing the award-winning Blue Cow Best Bitter at the small brewery here for more than 10 years – ask for a free viewing, subject to availability. The pub was renamed 'blue' by erstwhile owner the Duke of Buckminster nearly 400 years ago, on account of his political allegiance to his king. Low beams, flagstone floors and dressed-stone walls characterise the ancient interior, with crackling log fires to take the edge off the fenland breezes; any remaining chill may be generated by the pub's ghosts – a lady and a dog. Snacks, salads and sandwiches are offered, as well as mains like gammon steak, sausages and scampi.

Open all day all wk 11-11 **Food** Lunch all wk 12-2.30 Dinner all wk 6-9.30 Av main course £8 ⊕ FREE HOUSE ◀ Blue Cow Best Bitter, Sharp's Doom Bar, Castle Rock Vulcan Bomber. ⏱ 10 **Facilities** Non-diners area ✿ (All areas) ♦♦ Children's menu Children's portions Family room Garden Outside area ⌁ Parking WiFi ⊞ (notice required)

STAMFORD
Map 11 TF00

The Bull & Swan at Burghley ★★★★ INN ◉

tel: 01780 766412 **High St, St Martin's PE9 2LJ**
email: enquiries@thebullandswan.co.uk **web:** www.thebullandswan.co.uk
dir: *A1 onto B1081 (Carpenters Lodge junct). Signed Stamford & Burghley. 1m, pub on right*

Memorable meals in a magnificent market town setting

Commanding a prime position on one of historic Stamford's most stunning streets, this gabled coaching inn is recognised by the AA for both its top-notch accommodation and its very good food. Tucked behind the mellow stone façade is a comfily-appointed, traditional destination which appeals to all-comers, where dining is to the fore but beer lovers aren't short-changed. Local brewers The Grainstore is one reliable supplier to the bar, whilst produce from this corner of the East Midlands plump out the enticing menu. Smoked eel risotto with scorched baby leeks comes as starter or main; or try a taste of Old England with Lincoln Red beef, ale and parsnip steamed pudding.

Open all day all wk **Food** Lunch Mon-Sat 12-2.30, Sun 12-8.30 Dinner Mon-Sat 6-9, Sun 12-8.30 Set menu available ⊕ FREE HOUSE ◀ Nene Valley Blond Session BSA, Adnams Southwold Bitter, The Grainstore Triple B, Sharp's Doom Bar ♂ Westons Stowford Press. ⏱ 10 **Facilities** Non-diners area ✿ (Bar Outside area) ♦♦ Children's menu Children's portions Outside area ⌁ Parking WiFi **Rooms** 7

THE KINGS HEAD

11 Kingsway, Tealby, Market Rasen, Lincolnshire LN8 3YA
Tel: 01673 838347
Website: www.thekingsheadtealby.co.uk

What makes *The Kings Head* one of the top pubs in the county? Dating back to 1367, it is possibly the oldest thatched pub in Lincolnshire; a charming rustic façade concealing a modern and stylish interior. Add to this seamless blend of tradition and innovation, the excellent food, the vast choice of real ales and the friendly welcome that wait for you inside and you have a truly unique gastropub. It is a destination pub like no other in the village of Tealby.

With four real ales permanently available as well as regular guest ales, *The Kings Head* is a fantastic place to enjoy a drink with friends. The food on offer is constantly updated and often features locally caught game and a range of healthy specials, such as steaks, fish and casseroles, on top of the already extensive menu. All dishes are freshly prepared in the pub's kitchens and made using locally sourced ingredients wherever possible. If you've ever thought that delicious, high-end fare like this was out of your price range, a visit to *The Kings Head* will be sure to change your mind.

In the summer time, the pretty outdoor beer garden comes alive as a venue for al-fresco dining.

The Kings Head is open for food from noon daily and the three course set menu begins at just £17.95 for anybody wishing to sample the delightful fayre of this beloved village pub.

The George of Stamford ★★★★ HL ⊛ PICK OF THE PUBS

tel: 01780 750750 **71 St Martins PE9 2LB**
email: reservations@georgehotelofstamford.com **web:** www.georgehotelofstamford.com
dir: *From Peterborough take A1 N. Onto B1081 for Stamford, down hill to lights. Hotel on left*

Magnificent period inn located in heritage town

One of England's most renowned old coaching inns, it shares a stunning streetscape of imposing silver-limestone houses and villas tumbling down to the River Welland. Many period films and TV programmes have been filmed here. The George, with its extraordinary gallows sign (erected as a welcome to some and a warning to others), was built in 1597 to extend an earlier inn, elements of which survive in the crypt and walled garden. In the York Bar northbound coach passengers waited while horses were changed; the London Room fulfilled the same purpose for those heading south. Of the several elegant places to dine here; The York Bar or Garden Room are most informal. The food has gained one AA Rosette for the confident modern menus which change quarterly. Confit duck leg comes with braised red cabbage, Bramley apple and peppercorn sauce; whilst the pappardelle di guancia di manzo incorporates braised beef cheek, mushrooms and smoked bacon lardons. Local beers from The Grainstore and a considerable choice of 24 wines by the glass may accompany.

Open all day all wk 11-11 (Sun 12-11) **Food** Lunch all wk 12-2.30 Set menu available Restaurant menu available all wk ⊕ FREE HOUSE ◀ Adnams Broadside, The Grainstore, Bass, Guest ales Ö Aspall. ₹ 24 **Facilities** Non-diners area ⁑ Children's portions Garden Outside area ⋈ Parking WiFi **Rooms** 47

The Tobie Norris   PICK OF THE PUBS

tel: 01780 753800 **12 Saint Pauls St PE9 2BE**
email: info@tobienorris.com
dir: *From A1 to Stamford on A6121, becomes West St, then East St. After right bend right into Saint Pauls St*

Lively pub in award-winning restored medieval building

A medieval hall house built in 1280, this splendidly restored and renovated building is named after Tobias Norris, who bought it in 1617 for use as a bell foundry. Adnams Southwold Bitter and Castle Rock Harvest Pale are permanent fixtures in the wood-floored bar, while national and regional guest ales are rotated regularly. Having started maybe with a plate of beetroot pickled eggs, your main course, from the rather imaginative menu, could be wild game, ale and brown sugar pie; chorizo sausage and BBQ chicken lasagne; one-pot cod and pancetta cassoulet; and pressed pork belly with black pudding and baked apples. Stone-baked pizzas are cooked in ovens imported from Italy, their toppings ranging from halloumi to Tallington (the pub's own farm) meatballs. Puddings include millionaire chocolate

shortbread tart, and hot apple and cinnamon pie. A large enclosed patio appeals on warmer days. Note that, lunchtimes apart, there's a strict over 21s-only policy.

Open all day all wk **Food** Lunch all wk 12-2.30 Dinner all wk 6-9 Av main course £13.95 ⊕ FREE HOUSE ◀ Adnams Southwold Bitter, Castle Rock Harvest Pale, Guest ales Ö Guest cider. ₹ 18 **Facilities** Non-diners area ⁑ (Bar Garden) Garden ⋈ WiFi

---

SUSWORTH   Map 17 SE80

The Jenny Wren Inn

tel: 01724 784000 **East Ferry Rd DN17 3AS**
email: info@jennywreninn.co.uk
dir: *Phone for detailed directions*

Italian dishes a speciality here

With an upstairs function room overlooking the River Trent, this beamed and wood-panelled former farmhouse has buckets of character. No better place then for the sampling of special cocktails and nibbles now served every evening; ale lovers can stick to the likes of Morland Old Speckled Hen. The pub gains much praise for its food, especially for dishes involving line-caught fresh fish. Otherwise the Italian head chef and his team create both traditional pub favourites and authentic pasta, to be enjoyed in the ground-floor lounge with open fire. Chicken Bologna and smoked haddock with mash and leek sauce are typical main courses.

Open all wk 12-2 5.45-10.30 (Sat-Sun 12-10.30) **Food** Lunch Mon-Fri 12-2, Sat 12-9, Sun 12-8 Dinner Mon-Fri 5.45-9, Sat 12-9, Sun 12-8 ⊕ FREE HOUSE ◀ Morland Old Speckled Hen, Sharp's Doom Bar. **Facilities** Non-diners area ⁑ (Bar Garden) ⁕ Children's menu Children's portions Family room Garden Parking WiFi ⛺

TEALBY   Map 17 TF19

The Kings Head

tel: 01673 838347 **11 Kingsway LN8 3YA**
email: sol.newunion@googlemail.com **web:** www.thekingsheadtealby.co.uk
dir: *At lights in Market Rasen take B1203 (Jameson Bridge St) to Tealby*

The oldest thatched pub in Lincolnshire

Dating from around 1367, The Kings Head stands in an ample garden in a pretty village where former resident and songwriter Bernie Taupin was apparently inspired by the colour of the Lincolnshire stone to pen *Goodbye Yellow Brick Road* for his mate, Elton John. Dogs are welcome in the bar, where the line-up includes real ales from Marston's, Ringwood, Jennings and Wychwood plus ciders. Sausage and mash; and brie, cherry tomato, cranberry and broccoli bake appear on the bar menu, while

continued

TEALBY *continued*

in the converted barn restaurant the mains listing includes slow-cooked lamb shank; pancetta wrapped chicken breast; and vegetable bake.

The Kings Head

Open all day all wk **Food** Lunch Tue-Sat 12-9, Sun-Mon 12-7 Dinner Tue-Sat 12-9, Sun-Mon 12-7 Av main course £12 Set menu available Restaurant menu available all wk ⊕ MARSTON'S ◼ Pedigree, Ringwood Boondoggle, Jennings Cumberland, Wychwood Hobgoblin ○ Thatchers Gold, Rekorderlig. ♟ 9 **Facilities** Non-diners area ✿ (Bar Garden) ◗◆ Children's portions Garden ⊨ Parking WiFi ▭

See advert on page 322

THEDDLETHORPE ALL SAINTS   Map 17 TF48

Kings Head Inn

tel: 01507 339798 **Mill Rd LN12 1PB**
email: lordandladyhutton@hotmail.co.uk
dir: *From A1031 between Mablethorpe & Theddlethorpe, turn left into Mill Rd. Pub on right*

Ultra-low ceilings and old world charm

Two miles from the beach and close to a nature reserve, this thatched 16th-century inn is a sight for sore eyes. Inside are charming bars with traditional furnishings and very low ceilings. All food is locally sourced and vegetables are home grown. Fish is a speciality in the summer; game in the winter. Dishes range from chicken satay, or Welsh rarebit as starters to a rich game pie; steaks, burgers and grills; or oven crisp pork belly with apple and brandy gravy for mains.

Open 12-3 6-11 (Sat 12-11 Sun 12-10.20 summer; Sun 12-5 winter) Closed Mon (winter) **Food** Lunch Sun-Fri 12-2.30, Sat all day Dinner Sun-Fri 6-9, Sat all day Restaurant menu available ⊕ FREE HOUSE ◼ Batemans XB ○ Thatchers Gold, Skidbrooke. **Facilities** Non-diners area ✿ (Bar Garden) ◗◆ Children's portions Family room Garden ⊨ Beer festival Parking WiFi ▭ (notice required)

WOODHALL SPA   Map 17 TF16

Village Limits Country Pub, Restaurant & Motel

tel: 01526 353312 **Stixwould Rd LN10 6UJ**
email: info@villagelimits.co.uk
dir: *At rdbt on main street in Woodhall Spa follow Petwood Hotel signs. Pub 500yds past Petwood Hotel*

Tranquil location beside country park

Handily placed for the southern hills of the Lincolnshire Wolds, and 80 years of aircraft heritage at nearby RAF Coningsby, this friendly pub is on the outskirts of the Edwardian spa town. It's a little country inn that excels at offering beers from Tom Wood's and Dixon's and meals which champion the best of locally sourced ingredients. Home-made port and chicken liver pâté sets the scene for Lincolnshire sausages, mash and onion gravy; or baked salmon with mild paprika and shellfish sauce. Keep an eye on the specials board for the latest dishes.

Open 11.30-3 6.30-11 Closed 26 Dec-2 Jan, Mon L **Food** Lunch Tue-Sun 11.30-2 Dinner all wk 6.30-9 ⊕ FREE HOUSE ◼ Batemans XB, Tom Wood's Best Bitter, Dixon's Major Bitter ○ Thatchers. ♟ 8 **Facilities** Non-diners area ◗◆ Children's menu Children's portions Garden ⊨ Parking WiFi

WOOLSTHORPE   Map 11 SK83

The Chequers Inn ★★★★ INN ⊛   `PICK OF THE PUBS`

tel: 01476 870701 **Main St NG32 1LU**
email: justinnabar@yahoo.co.uk **web:** www.chequersinn.net
dir: *Approx 7m from Grantham. 3m from A607, follow heritage signs for Belvoir Castle*

Country dining pub with charming interior

Leicestershire, Lincolnshire and Nottinghamshire all meet not far from this 17th-century coaching inn overlooking the village cricket pitch. From here you can see Belvoir Castle, a mile or so away. Five real fires warm the interior, and a well-stocked bar does a good line in real ales and cider. Dine in the Snug & Bar, the contemporary Dining Room or the Bakehouse Restaurant, which still features the oven from village bakery days. On the menu may be chargrilled rib-eye steak with hand-cut chips; pavé of venison with celeriac purée; rosette of plaice with rösti potato and brown shrimp and crayfish velouté; and butternut squash and aubergine tagine. Representing the pub classics category are home-made pie; beer-battered cod; and Thai green curry. Typical puddings are apple and berry crumble with custard, and lemon meringue pie with raspberry sorbet.

Open all day all wk **Food** Lunch Mon-Sat 12-2.30, Sun 12-4 Dinner Mon-Sat 6-9.30, Sun 6-8.30 Set menu available ⊕ FREE HOUSE ◼ Rotating Guest ales ○ Guest cider. ♟ 30 **Facilities** Non-diners area ✿ (Bar Garden) ◗◆ Children's menu Children's portions Garden ⊨ Parking WiFi ▭ (notice required) **Rooms** 4

LONDON

E1

Town of Ramsgate PLAN 2 G3

tel: 020 7481 8000 **62 Wapping High St E1W 2PN**
email: peter@townoframsgate.co.uk
dir: *Nearest tube: Wapping*

River Thames gem full of history

Wood panelling, snob screens, leaded windows and a secluded terrace with views across the river; the oldest Thames-side pub makes the most of its heritage and setting. Tucked away amidst converted warehouses, the name recalls the days when fishermen from Ramsgate landed their fresh catches on nearby steps before heading off to market. Its robust past includes use by press-gangs and a visit by the ill-fated Captain Bligh on his way to view HMS *Bounty*. Today's guests are ensured a far more positive outcome, with traditional pub meals including some great hand-made pies and savoury puddings, washed down with reliable real ales and real cider.

Open all day all wk 12-12 (Sun 12-11) **Food** Lunch all wk 12-4 Dinner Sun-Thu 5-9, Fri-Sat 5-10 ⊕ FREE HOUSE ◀ Fuller's London Pride, Sharp's Doom Bar, Young's ♂ Cornish Orchards Gold Cider. ♇ 13 **Facilities** Non-diners area ♣ (Bar Garden) ♦♦ Garden ♩ WiFi ▄▄ (notice required)

E8

The Cat & Mutton PLAN 2 G4

tel: 020 7249 6555 **76 Broadway Market, Hackney E8 4QJ**
dir: *Phone for detailed directions*

Popular food pub

Used by workers on their way to London's livestock markets in the 17th century, this revamped pub was once known as the 'Cattle & Shoulder of Mutton'. Today, the building has been reinvented as one of East London's busiest food pubs. At scrubbed tables in trendy, gentrified surroundings, order a 'small plate' of burnt broccoli, yogurt, pickled mustard seeds and almonds; onglet steak with chimichurri; or octopus, potatoes and black garlic crème fraîche. For bigger appetites there's 'large plates' of jerk chicken and mango coleslaw; lamb belly with smoked aubergine; and a bucket of mutton chops, bean salad and mint sauce. Blood orange sorbet with a glass of Prosecco finishes a meal nicely.

Open all day all wk Mon 12-11 Tue-Thu 12-12 Fri noon-1am Sat 11am-1am Sun 12-11.30 **Food** Lunch Mon-Fri 12-4.30, Sat 12-11, Sun 12-9 Dinner Mon-Thu 6-10, Fri 6-10.30, Sat 12-10.30, Sun 12-9 Restaurant menu available all wk ⊕ THE COLUMBO GROUP ◀ Meantime London Pale Ale, Guest ales ♂ Symonds, Westons, Addlestones, Aspall. ♇ 12 **Facilities** Non-diners area ♣ (Bar Restaurant Outside area) ♦♦ Children's portions Outside area ♩ WiFi

E9

The Empress ◉◉ PLAN 2 G4 **PICK OF THE PUBS**

tel: 020 8533 5123 **130 Lauriston Rd, Victoria Park E9 7LH**
email: info@empresse9.co.uk
dir: *From Mile End Station turn right into Grove Rd, leads into Lauriston Rd*

Café, bar and restaurant pleasing a Bohemian clientele

A classic mid-Victorian East End corner pub, with Gothic revival windows at first-floor level and lofty ceilings. A long bar serves ale and cider from that venerable East End brewer, Truman's. Neighbourhood suppliers are important to The Empress, with meats and fish from Victoria Park suppliers Ginger Pig and Jonathan Norris respectively, and coffee from Climpson & Sons. Head chef Elliott Lidstone's great value bar snacks include whitebait and smoked paprika aïoli; pork rillettes and

caper berries; and cecina. Equally well priced are mains such as braised goat, black lentils, radicchio and anchovy; snails and bone marrow; and baked duck egg, black pudding and leeks. The short list of sweet things may include treacle pannacotta with caramelised banana. There's roasts on Sundays, a popular weekend brunch menu and a meal deal on Monday evenings.

Open all day all wk Closed 25-26 Dec **Food** Lunch all wk 12-3.30 Dinner all wk 6-10.15 Av main course £16 ⊕ FREE HOUSE ◀ East London Foundation Bitter, Truman's Runner ♂ Aspall, Truman's Côte Breton Brut. ♇ 16 **Facilities** Non-diners area ♣ (Bar Outside area) ♦♦ Children's menu Children's portions Outside area ♩ WiFi ▄▄

E14

The Grapes PLAN 2 G3

tel: 020 7987 4396 **76 Narrow St, Limehouse E14 8BP**
email: info@thegrapes.co.uk
dir: *Phone for detailed directions*

Dickensian pub on the Thames

In *Our Mutual Friend*, Charles Dickens immortalised this old Thames-side pub as the Six Jolly Fellowship Porters. While he might recognise the wood-panelled, Victorian long bar and The Dickens Snug, where as a child he reputedly danced on a table, much of surrounding Limehouse has changed beyond recognition. Cask-conditioned ales in the bar include Adnams and Timothy Taylor Landlord and guests, while in the tiny upstairs dining room dishes include devilled whitebait; smoked salmon and haddock fishcakes; fresh pan-fried swordfish, marinated in lemon and olive oil; grilled chicken burger; and Sir Ian's meaty shepherd's pie. Salads, and sandwiches are always available, and there are Sunday roasts. Sorry, no one under 18 years is permitted.

Open all day all wk Closed 25-26 Dec, 1 Jan **Food** Lunch Mon-Fri 12-2.30, Sat 12-9.30, Sun 12-3.30 Dinner Mon-Fri 6.30-9.30, Sat 12-9.30 Restaurant menu available all wk ⊕ SPIRIT LEASED ◀ Marston's Pedigree, Timothy Taylor Landlord, Adnams, Guest ales ♂ Aspall. **Facilities** Non-diners area ♣ (Bar Outside area) Outside area ♩

The Gun ◉ PLAN 2 G3 **PICK OF THE PUBS**

tel: 020 7515 5222 **27 Coldharbour, Docklands E14 9NS**
email: info@thegundocklands.com
dir: *From West Ferry Rd into Marsh Wall to mini rdbt. Turn left, over bridge, 1st right into Coldharbour. Nearest tube stations: Canary Wharf, South Quay & Blackwall*

A surviving riverside gem

Contrasting skylines are revealed from this historic Thames-side pub; adjoining is a terrace of dockers' cottages that overlook the nearby lock, backed by frozen-in-time crane jibs. Dwarfing these are the skyscrapers of Canary Wharf, whilst across the river is the distinctive domed shape of the O2 Arena. Lord Nelson and Lady Hamilton secretly met at The Gun, and the pub still retains a restrained naval and shipping heritage that adds character to the range of panelled dining rooms and snugs. Diners drawn to the AA Rosette menu can anticipate tempting dishes prepared by a highly capable kitchen team. From a choice of menus come first courses like venison, rabbit and pistachio terrine; and confit wild boar collar. Mains choices may include slow-braised Dexter beef cheek; Herdwick lamb rump with smoked bacon, kidney and lentil stew, or 45-day aged rare breed steaks. The chefs look to nearby Billingsgate Market for the best fish and seafood. Guest beers, several beer festivals and a great wine list complement the award-winning menus.

Open all wk 11am-mdnt (Sun 11-11) Closed 25-26 Dec **Food** Lunch Mon-Sat 12-3, Sun 12-4 Dinner Mon-Sat 6-10.30, Sun 6.30-9.30 ⊕ ETM GROUP ◀ Adnams Southwold Bitter, Jugged Hare Pale Ale, Guest ales ♂ Symonds. ♇ 22 **Facilities** Non-diners area ♦♦ Children's portions Outside area ♩ Beer festival WiFi ▄▄ (notice required)

EC1

The Bleeding Heart Tavern ◉◉ PLAN 1 E4

PICK OF THE PUBS

tel: 020 7242 8238 **19 Greville St EC1N 8SQ**
email: bookings@bleedingheart.co.uk
dir: *Close to Farringdon tube station, at corner of Greville St & Bleeding Heart Yard*

City pub with award-winning bistro food

The tavern dates from 1746, when its distinctly non-pc slogan invited customers to get 'drunk for a penny and dead drunk for twopence'. In the hardly surprising absence of a 21st-century equivalent, the tavern wisely promotes its full English breakfasts, with croissants and baguettes from its own bakery, and its bistro fare. Drinks-wise, holding court are traditional ales from Adnams, Aspall cider and an impressive wine list with 450 choices from around the globe. Downstairs in the wood-panelled restaurant you'll find dishes such as spicy chorizo with saffron aïoli; foie gras and chicken liver parfait, quince chutney; suckling pig, roast potatoes, green beans, apple and mustard dressing; smoked haddock and salmon fishcake, spinach and butter sauce; Suffolk Blackface lamburger with red cabbage coleslaw and chips; and squash and beetroot salad with toasted pine nuts. Desserts include baked vanilla rice pudding with ruby plum compôte.

Open all day 7am-11pm Closed BHs, 10 days at Xmas, Sat-Sun **Food** Lunch Mon-Fri 11.30-10.30 Dinner Mon-Fri 11.30-10.30 Av main course £10.50 Set menu available Restaurant menu available Mon-Fri ⊕ FREE HOUSE ◀ Adnams Southwold Bitter, Broadside, Fisherman, May Day ♻ Aspall. ♛ 17 **Facilities** Non-diners area WiFi

The Coach & Horses PLAN 1 E5 **PICK OF THE PUBS**

tel: 020 7278 8990 **26-28 Ray St, Clerkenwell EC1R 3DJ**
email: info@thecoachandhorses.com
dir: *From Farringdon tube station right into Cowcross St. At Farringdon Rd turn right, after 500yds left into Ray St. Pub at bottom of hill*

Archetypal Victorian gastro-pub in Clerkenwell

This wood-panelled, late 19th-century pub was built to serve the myriad artisans, many of them Italian, who once lived in this area. At one time a secret passage led to the long-buried River Fleet, which still runs beneath the pub and is audible from a drain outside the entrance. Unsurprisingly, there are a few ghosts, including an old man and a black cat. Typical 'small plates' include gin cured salmon with pickled cucumber; and rabbit, foie gras and prune terrine, while in the Eduardo Paolozzi-artwork-decorated dining room the modern British menu lists reasonably priced dishes such as venison shoulder casserole, porcini, pancetta and thyme dumplings; ale battered haddock with triple cooked chips; and whole Cornish mackerel, warm potato salad with beetroot relish. Enticing desserts could include lavender brûlée with a chocolate cookie. Enjoy with a pint of Portobello Star, Doom Bar or Bounders cider, or a glass of wine from the well-balanced list.

Open Mon-Fri 12-11 Closed 24 Dec-1st Mon in Jan, BHs, Sat & Sun **Food** Lunch Mon-Fri 12-3 Dinner Mon-Fri 5-8.30 ⊕ PUNCH TAVERNS ◀ Woodforde's Wherry, Brentwood BBC 2, Sharp's Doom Bar, Portobello Star ♻ Bath Ciders Bounders. ♛ 17 **Facilities** Non-diners area ♨ (Bar Restaurant Outside area) ♦♦ Children's portions Outside area ⊞ WiFi ▭ (notice required)

The Eagle PLAN 1 E5

tel: 020 7837 1353 **159 Farringdon Rd EC1R 3AL**
dir: *Nearest tube: Angel or Farringdon. Pub at north end of Farringdon Rd*

One of trendy Clerkenwell's top establishments

Blazing a trail in the early 1990s and paving the way for what we now except as stylish gastro-pubs, The Eagle is still going strong. The lofty interior includes a wooden-floored bar and dining area, a mishmash of vintage furniture, and an open-to-view kitchen that produces a creatively modern, twice-daily changing blackboard menu and tapas selection which revel in bold, rustic flavours. Typical of the range are parsnip soup; grilled whole mackerel with tomato chilli jam and couscous salad; and Dexter rump steak, beetroot, rocket and horseradish.

Open all day 12-11 (Sun 12-5) Closed BHs L (1wk Xmas), Sun eve **Food** Lunch Mon-Fri 12-3, Sat 12-3.30, Sun 12.30-4 Dinner Mon-Sat 6.30-10.30 ⊕ FREE HOUSE ◀ Wells Eagle IPA & Bombardier, Hackney Ales ♻ Westons, Addlestones. ♛ 15 **Facilities** Non-diners area ♨ (Bar) ♦♦ Children's portions

The Jerusalem Tavern PLAN 1 E4 **PICK OF THE PUBS**

tel: 020 7490 4281 **55 Britton St, Clerkenwell EC1M 5UQ**
email: thejerusalemtavern@gmail.com
dir: *100mtrs NE of Farringdon tube station; 300mtrs N of Smithfield*

Historic inn with St Peter's Brewery cask and bottled beers

Owned by Suffolk's St Peter's Brewery, this historic tavern has close links to Samuel Johnson, Oliver Goldsmith, David Garrick and the young Handel, who used to drink here on his visits to London. Named after the Priory of St John of Jerusalem, founded in 1140, the pub can be traced back to the 14th century, having occupied several sites in the area including part of St John's Gate. The current premises date from 1720 although the shop frontage dates from about 1810, when it was a workshop for Clerkenwell's various watch and clock craftsmen. Its dimly lit Dickensian bar, with bare boards, rustic wooden tables, old tiles, candles, open fires and cosy corners, is the perfect film set – which is what it has been on many occasions. A classic pub in every sense, it offers the full range of cask and bottled beers from St Peter's Brewery, as well as a range of simple pub fare.

Open all day 11-11 Closed 25 Dec-1 Jan, Sat-Sun **Food** Lunch Mon-Fri 12-3 Av main course £10 ⊕ ST PETER'S BREWERY ◀ St Peter's (full range) ♻ New Forest Traditional, Oliver's, Once Upon a Tree Tumpy Ground. **Facilities** Non-diners area ♨ (Bar) Outside area WiFi

The Peasant PLAN 1 E5 **PICK OF THE PUBS**

tel: 020 7336 7726 **240 Saint John St EC1V 4PH**
email: eat@thepeasant.co.uk
dir: *Nearest tube: Farringdon. Pub on corner of Saint John St & Percival St*

Restored Victorian pub with reputation for good food

One of the first gastro-pubs, this dining institution stands opposite tree-shaded gardens in the heart of Clerkenwell. With imposing brickwork and a balustrade outside, the eye-catching interior emphasises the Victorian grandeur of the pub with its decorative tiling, plasterwork ceiling, mosaic floor and great horseshoe mahogany bar. The first-floor restaurant continues the theme, with bold chandeliers and a quirky collection of arty circus memorabilia. Beer hounds will not be disappointed by the selection of real ales, including beers from Crouch Vale brewery, whilst Bounders cider quenches a sharper thirst. The good value bar menu indulges most tastes, kicking in with starters typified by confit duck leg with white bean and Morteau sausage cassoulet. Mains impress with braised shoulder of venison and caramelised onion pie with mash and vegetables; or pan-fried fillet of sea bream with chilli, tomato, capers and garlic linguine. The restaurant has a set menu of modern European-inspired dishes; roast herb-crusted cod with mussel stew catches the eye.

Open all day all wk Closed 24 Dec-2 Jan, BHs **Food** Lunch all wk 12-11 Dinner all wk 12-11 Restaurant menu available ⊕ FREE HOUSE ◀ Crouch Vale Brewers Gold, Bath Ales Gem, Guest ales ♻ Bath Ciders Bounders, Westons Wyld Wood Organic, Original Sin. ♛ 15 **Facilities** Non-diners area ♦♦ Children's portions Garden ▭ (notice required)

Ye Olde Mitre PLAN 1 E4

tel: 020 7405 4751 **1 Ely Court, Ely Place EC1N 6SJ**
email: yeoldemitre@fullers.co.uk
dir: From Chancery Lane tube station exit 3 to Holborn Circus, left into Hatton Garden. Pub in alley between 8 & 9 Hatton Garden

Historic, hidden away pub

Built in 1546, extended in 1781, in the shadow of the palace of the Bishops of Ely, this quirky historic corner pub is in Ely Court, off Hatton Garden. It is often used as a film location. Choose from at least six real ales in the magnificent wood-panelled rooms, with a range of bar snacks or 'English tapas' that includes toasted sandwiches, pork pies, Scotch eggs, sausage rolls, olives and picked eggs. Please note that this pub, without music and bar TVs, is closed at weekends and Bank Holidays. Beer festivals are held in May, August and December.

Open all day Closed 25 Dec, 1 Jan, BHs, Sat-Sun (ex 1st wknd Aug) **Food** Lunch Mon-Fri 11.30-9.30 Dinner Mon-Fri 11.30-9.30 ⊕ FULLER'S ◀ London Pride, George Gale & Co Seafarers, Caledonian Deuchars IPA, Adnams Broadside, Guest ales ♂ Biddenden Bushels, Orchard Pig Philosopher, Gwynt y Ddraig Black Dragon. ♟ 8 **Facilities** Non-diners area Garden ♠ Beer festival WiFi

---

EC2

The Fox PLAN 1 F4

tel: 020 7729 5708 **28-30 Paul St EC2A 4LB**
email: info@thefoxpublichouse.co.uk
dir: Nearest tube: Old Street. Take exit 4 for City Road South, into City Rd. 2nd left into Epworth St, 500yds, pub on corner at junct with Paul St

Chill out with good food in this Shoreditch retreat

Not long ago, few visited Shoreditch for pleasure. Now, together with neighbouring Hoxton and Spitalfields, it is one of the capital's buzziest districts, with Victorian pubs like this thriving once more. Carefully selected wines and real ales — Harvey's Sussex and Otter, for example — and simple, straightforward food help to make it the place to head for after the shops and flower market of Columbia Road, the Asian bustle of Brick Lane, or a hard day at the office. Typically on the regularly changing menu are devilled whitebait with tahini; Toulouse sausage, mash and onion gravy; and roasted red onion, fennel and chicory tart with feta.

Open all day all wk Closed 25-28 Dec & BHs ⊕ ENTERPRISE INNS ◀ Harvey's Sussex Best Bitter, Sharp's Doom Bar, Otter Bitter ♂ Addlestones. **Facilities** ✿ (Bar Outside area) ♦♦ Outside area WiFi

---

The Princess of Shoreditch PLAN 1 F4

tel: 020 7729 9270 **76-78 Paul St EC2A 4NE**
email: info@theprincessofshoreditch.com
dir: Nearest tube: Old Street

Well-known City gastro-pub

Dating back to 1742, this popular gastro-pub is a lively pub with three rotating ales on handpump, around 40 bottled beers and canned craft beers and 20 Old World wines under £30. On the pub menu there's Kilravock Farm spiced pork terrine, apple, and sourdough; and beer-battered fish and chips from Cornish day boats. There is a 42-seater candlelit dining room accessed via a spiral staircase where the regularly changing menu might feature whole lemon sole to share; sticky toffee pudding, bourbon toffee sauce and cinnamon ice cream.

Open all day all wk Closed 24-26 Dec **Food** Lunch Mon-Fri 12-3, Sat 12-4, Sun 12-9 Dinner Mon-Sat 6.30-10, Sun 12-9 Restaurant menu available Mon-Sat ⊕ ENTERPRISE INNS ◀ Hackney, Redemption, East London, Truman's ♂ Lilley's. ♟ 17 **Facilities** Non-diners area ♦♦ Children's portions Outside area WiFi

---

EC4

The White Swan ◉ PLAN 1 E4 **PICK OF THE PUBS**

tel: 020 7242 9696 **108 Fetter Ln, Holborn EC4A 1ES**
email: info@thewhiteswanlondon.com
dir: Nearest tube: Chancery Lane. From station towards St Paul's Cathedral. At HSBC bank left into Fetter Ln. Pub on right

Handsome pub on legal London's eastern fringe

This exquisitely fitted-out City pub comprises a traditional ground-floor bar, a galleried mezzanine, and a first-floor dining room. For its cosmopolitan selection of bottled beers and lagers, Adnams on tap, Addlestones cider and a dozen wines by the glass, it has to be the bar, of course, whose cream-coloured walls provide the backdrop for leather-covered stools and assorted tables, chairs and banquettes. Modern British dishes served here include roast Peterhead cod; and artichoke and sprout-top ravioli with duck egg and wild mushrooms. Upstairs is the beautifully restored dining room with mirrored ceiling and linen-clad tables, where the day's choices might include wild Brixham sea bass (fish comes in daily from Billingsgate), fennel and Pernod velouté; pan-fried loin and slow-cooked neck of Herdwick mutton with braised shallot, truffle gnocchi and anchovy jus; or Cumbrian veal cheek with spätzle, roast pumpkin and January King cabbage. Finish with pineapple soufflé and coconut sorbet.

Open all day Closed 25-26 Dec, wknds & BHs, Sat-Sun **Food** Lunch Mon-Fri 12-3 Dinner Mon-Fri 6-10 Set menu available Restaurant menu available Mon-Fri ⊕ PUNCH TAVERNS ◀ Adnams ♂ Addlestones. ♟ 12 **Facilities** Non-diners area ♦♦ WiFi

---

N1

The Albion PLAN 2 F4

tel: 020 7607 7450 **10 Thornhill Rd, Islington N1 1HW**
email: info@the-albion.co.uk
dir: From Angel tube station, cross road into Liverpool Rd past Sainsbury's, continue to Richmond Ave. Left. At junct with Thornhill Rd turn right. Pub on right

Spacious walled garden for alfresco drinking

This is a Georgian gem of a pub in the Barnsbury conservation area of Islington that continues to serve good food using top-notch British produce. In winter, log fires warm the pub's tastefully furnished interior, with the large walled garden and wisteria-covered pergola drawing the crowds in summer. The daily-changing menu includes roast pork tenderloin, wild garlic mash, rhubarb compôte and crab apple jus; whole roast sea bass, Atlantic prawns and chorizo; and pearl barley and celeriac risotto, squash, gorgonzola and roast garlic.

Open all day all wk **Food** Lunch Mon-Fri 12-3, Sat 12-4, Sun 12-9 Dinner Mon-Sat 6-10, Sun 12-9 Av main course £16 ⊕ PUNCH TAVERNS ◀ Ringwood Best Bitter, Caledonian Deuchars IPA ♂ Addlestones. ♟ 12 **Facilities** Non-diners area ✿ (Bar Garden) ♦♦ Children's menu Children's portions Garden ♠ WiFi ▭ (notice required)

The Charles Lamb PLAN 2 F4

tel: 020 7837 5040 **16 Elia St, Islington N1 8DE**
email: food@thecharleslambpub.com
dir: From Angel station turn left, at junct of City Rd turn left. Pass Duncan Terrace Gdns, left into Colebrooke Row. 1st right

A really friendly London local

Named after a local writer who lived in Islington in the 1830s, this cracking neighbourhood pub changed hands late in 2014. Locals beat a path to the door for microbrewery ales and the hearty, home-cooked comfort food listed on the daily chalkboard menu.

Open all wk Mon & Tue fr 4 Wed-Sun fr noon Closed 23 Dec-1 Jan **Food** Lunch Wed-Fri 12-3, Sat 12-4, Sun 12-6 Dinner Mon-Sat 6-9.30, Sun 7-9 ⊕ FREE HOUSE ◀ Dark Star Hophead, Windsor & Eton Windsor Knot, Guest ales ♂ Newton Court. ♟ 9 **Facilities** Non-diners area ✿ (Bar Restaurant Outside area) ♦♦ Outside area ♠ WiFi

LONDON N1 *continued*

The Drapers Arms ⦿   PLAN 2 F4   PICK OF THE PUBS

tel: 020 7619 0348 **44 Barnsbury St N1 1ER**
email: nick@thedrapersarms.com
dir: *Turn right from Highbury & Islington station, into Upper St. Barnsbury St on right opposite Shell service station*

Neighbourhood pub in trendy Islington

Standing beside a quiet tree-lined street of attractive Georgian terraced housing, backed by a tranquil paved patio garden and distinguished by tasteful, cool colourwash above the wood-floored bar, this popular neighbourhood local appeals to all-comers. Founded in the 1830s by one of London's trade guilds, the pub's current owners marry up the best of fine dining with an appealing range of real ales and cider. Plump for a beer from Dark Star or Windsor & Eton breweries – or maybe one of 18 wines by the glass – and prepare to tackle the ever-changing, one AA Rosette menu. Both lunchtime and evening choices are equally rewarding. Exceptional starters may include duck hearts, snails and black cabbage on toast, trumped by a main of cod, grilled leeks and crab broth. A choice for two could include whole mallard with red cabbage and duck fat potatoes. The modern, edgy menu also retains classics like steaks or slow-cooked lamb shoulder, with comfort-food gingerbread pudding with whipped cream and oats to finish.

Open all day all wk Closed 25-26 Dec **Food** Lunch Mon-Sat 12-3, Sun 12-8.30 Dinner Mon-Sat 6-11, Sun 12-8.30 ⊕ FREE HOUSE ◀ Harvey's Sussex, Sambrook's Wandle, Truman's Runner, Dark Star Hophead, Windsor & Eton Windsor Knot, Cornish Crown Bitter, Portobello Star Ò Westons Stowford Press & Wyld Wood Organic, The Orchard Pig. ₹ 18 **Facilities** Non-diners area ❖ (Bar Garden) ♦ Children's portions Garden ⋒ WiFi

The Pig and Butcher   PLAN 2 F4

tel: 020 7226 8304 **80 Liverpool Rd, Islington N1 0QD**
email: crackling@thepigandbutcher.co.uk
dir: *Nearest tube: Angel*

Lovely ales and food 'like Granny used to make'

Before The Pig and Butcher was built in the mid-1800s, the fields here grazed by livestock on its way to Smithfield. Owner Jack Ross embraces this concept by receiving carcasses direct from the farm and then butchering on site. Rare breeds such as White Park cattle, Iron Age pigs and Hebridean lamb are specialities, along with game and vegetables from Kent and south coast fish. In winter, meats are brined, cured, smoked and braised, while summer sees the specially built charcoal grill glowing. Ales from the likes of Sambrook's and Bath complete the ethos behind this pub's carefully considered operation.

Open all wk 5-11 (Thu 5-12 Fri-Sat noon-1am Sun 12-11) Closed 24-26 Dec **Food** Lunch Fri 12-3.30, Sat 12-4, Sun 12-9 Dinner Mon-Sat 6.30-10, Sun 12-9 ⊕ ENTERPRISE INNS ◀ Bath Ales Gem, Sharp's Doom Bar, Sambrook's Wandle. ₹ **Facilities** Non-diners area ❖ (Bar Outside area) ♦ Children's portions Outside area ⋒ WiFi

Smokehouse ⦿⦿   PLAN 2 F4

tel: 020 7354 1144 **63-69 Canonbury Rd N1 2DG**
email: info@smokehouseislington.co.uk
dir: *Phone for directions*

Meat-eaters can't go wrong here

Situated in Islington's prestigious Canonbury district but moments away from the hustle and bustle of Upper Street, this successful gastro-pub serve food steered by award-winning chef Neil Rankin who smokes, barbecues and roasts on Big Green Eggs, offset smokers and a robata grill. Using the finest ingredients sourced from

small, family-owned farms, the Smokehouse offers a refined take on BBQ dishes. You'll find dishes like chopped brisket roll and gochujang; and smoked pork belly, brown shrimp, udon and pear miso. Expect to find a range of 20 craft beers on tap and a further 60 by the bottle; the wine list showcases only wines from small, family-owned vineyards.

Open Mon-Wed 5-11 (Thu & Fri 5-mdnt Sat 11am-mdnt Sun & BHs 12-10.30) Closed 24-26 Dec, Mon-Thu L (ex BHs) **Food** Lunch Sat 11-4, Sun 12-9 Dinner Mon-Fri 6-10, Sat 6-10, Sun 12-9 Av main course £18 ⊕ NOBLE INNS ◀ Rotating craft ales Ò Bath Ciders Bounders, Lilley's Apples & Pears. ₹ 15 **Facilities** Non-diners area ❖ (Bar Garden) ♦ Children's menu Children's portions Garden ⋒ WiFi ▥ (notice required)

▪ N6

The Flask   PLAN 2 E5   PICK OF THE PUBS

tel: 020 8348 7346 **77 Highgate West Hill N6 6BU**
email: theflaskhighgate@london-gastros.co.uk
dir: *Nearest tube: Archway or Highgate*

Landmark gastro-pub with links to Dick Turpin

High on Highgate Hill, The Flask may now be a gastro-pub with a big reputation but its name was made long ago when Dick Turpin frequented it. This Grade II listed pub, dating back to 1663 and made famous by Byron, Keats, Hogarth and Betjeman, has become a London landmark. It retains much of its character and cosy atmosphere and a maze of small rooms is served by two bars, one of which houses the original sash windows. Fuller's and guest real ales from newer London breweries are on offer alongside two dozen bottled ales and ciders, and some sensibly priced wines. Starters include salt and pepper squid with chilli mayonnaise; and crispy pig's cheeks, chorizo salad and pickled vegetables, while typical mains are pheasant, cannellini bean and mushroom ragu and wilted spinach; and pan-fried sea bass, mussel and pea velouté, runner beans and spinach. For dessert, try the lime tart. The large front garden is especially popular in the summer.

Open all day all wk 12-11 (Sun 12-10.30) Closed 25 Dec **Food** Lunch all wk 12-4 Dinner Mon-Sat 6-10, Sun 6-9 ⊕ FULLER'S ◀ London Pride, ESB, George Gale & Co Seafarers, Guest ales Ò Cornish Orchards Gold. ₹ 13 **Facilities** Non-diners area ❖ (Bar Restaurant Garden) ♦ Garden ⋒ WiFi ▥ (notice required)

▪ NW1

The Chapel   PLAN 1 B4

tel: 020 7402 9220 **48 Chapel St NW1 5DP**
email: thechapel@btconnect.com
dir: *By A40 Marylebone Rd & Old Marylebone Rd junct. Off Edgware Rd by tube station*

A popular child-friendly gastro-pub

The Chapel has a bright, open-plan interior of stripped floors and pine furniture, and boasts one of central London's largest enclosed pub gardens – great for the children to let off steam. Owners Alison McGrath and Lakis Hondrogiannis take delivery of the freshest produce for daily-changing menus featuring internationally influenced dishes, as well as Mediterranean antipasti and canapés. A sample menu lists creamy cauliflower soup with bacon and walnuts; rabbit pie; slow-cooked pork belly with braised lentils, buttered spinach and thyme sauce; and risotto with wild mushrooms, aubergines and peppers. There's a good choice of wines by the glass.

Open all day all wk Closed 25-26 Dec, 1 Jan, Etr **Food** Lunch Mon-Sat 12-2.30, Sun 12-3 Dinner all wk 7-10 Set menu available ⊕ FREE HOUSE ◀ Adnams Southwold Bitter, Black Sheep Ò Somersby Cider. ₹ 15 **Facilities** Non-diners area ❖ (Bar Restaurant Garden) ♦ Children's menu Children's portions Garden ⋒ ▥ (notice required)

The Engineer PLAN 2 E4 **PICK OF THE PUBS**

tel: 020 7483 1890 **65 Gloucester Av, Primrose Hill NW1 8JH**
email: enquiries@theengineerprimrosehill.co.uk
dir: *Phone for detailed directions*

World beers and eclectic dishes in a relaxed atmosphere

Built by Isambard Kingdom Brunel in 1841, this unassuming street corner pub stands tucked away in a residential part of Primrose Hill close to Camden Market. It attracts a discerning dining crowd who relish its imaginative and well-prepared food and friendly, laid-back atmosphere. There is a spacious bar area, wood floors, sturdy wooden tables with candles, simple decor and cosy upstairs private dining rooms. A walled, paved and heated garden to the rear is popular in fine weather. In addition to cosmopolitan beers, the drinks list includes hand-crafted teas, freshly ground coffees, interesting wines, and a variety of whiskies. Regularly changing menus feature an eclectic mix of inspired home-made dishes using organic and free-range products. A typical Sunday lunch menu may feature rabbit terrine with piccalilli to start, followed by roast duck with plums and braised red cabbage, or lamb shoulder with confit garlic and mint sauce. Leave room for bitter chocolate pudding with malt ice cream.

Open all day all wk 12-11 (Sat 10am-11pm Sun 12-10.30) **Food** Lunch all wk 12-10 Dinner all wk 12-10 ⊕ MITCHELLS & BUTLERS ◖ Sharp's Doom Bar ♂ Aspall. � 19 **Facilities** Non-diners area ♣ (Bar Garden) ♦ Children's menu Children's portions Family room Garden 戸 Beer festival Cider festival WiFi ⛟

The Prince Albert PLAN 2 F4

tel: 020 7485 0270 **163 Royal College St NW1 0SG**
email: info@princealbertcamden.com
dir: *From Camden tube station follow Camden Rd. Right into Royal College St, 200mtrs on right*

Organic food at character pub

Picnic tables furnish the small paved courtyard, while The Prince Albert's wooden floors and bentwood furniture make a welcoming interior for customers and their four-legged friends. Real ales there are, but you may fancy a refreshing glass of wine and there's plenty of choice. Bar dishes range from home-made sticky pork ribs; salmon Scotch eggs and octopus, chorizo and onion stew; these can be followed by home-made steak and kidney pie, burgers and relish, or fish and chips. Two or three times a year the pub holds a three-day real ale festival.

Open all day all wk **Food** Lunch all wk 12-3 Dinner all wk 6-10 Set menu available ⊕ FREE HOUSE ◖ Dark Star, Sambrook's, Adnams, Redemption. ♉ 14 **Facilities** Non-diners area ♣ (Bar Garden) ♦ Children's portions Garden 戸 Beer festival Cider festival WiFi ⛟ (notice required)

NW5

The Bull and Last PLAN 2 E5

tel: 020 7267 3641 **168 Highgate Rd NW5 1QS**
email: info@thebullandlast.co.uk
dir: *From Kentish Town tube station N into Highgate Rd. (4 mins' walk from Gospel Oak Station)*

Tempting menus and many wines by the glass

A popular free house in a Grade II listed building, a stone's throw from Hampstead Heath. Children and dogs are welcome too, so this really is a relaxing place to sample a pint of Redemption Big Chief or one of the many wines sold by the glass. Wondering whether to eat? A glance at the home-made dishes on the menu will

make up your mind – who can resist mouth watering starters like confit rabbit, smoked eel and ham hock terrine with sour apple purée? Move on to roast cod, hazelnut pesto, Roscoff onions, monk's beard and white kale; or Denham Vale aged côte de boeuf for two if you're determined to push the boat out. Summer picnic hampers and take-away ice creams are available too.

Open all day all wk 12-11 (Fri-Sat 12-12 Sun 12-10.30 Sat-Sun 9am-11am bkfst) Closed 24-25 Dec **Food** Lunch Mon-Fri 12-3, Sat-Sun 9am-11am (bkfst) 12.30-4 Dinner Mon-Sat 6.30-10, Sun 6.30-9 ⊕ FREE HOUSE/ETIVE PUBS LTD ◖ Dark Star Partridge Best Bitter, ELB So Solid Brew, Redemption Big Chief, Red Squirrel London Porter ♂ Addlestones, Snails Bank Tumbledown. ♉ 17 **Facilities** Non-diners area ♣ (Bar Outside area) ♦ Children's menu Children's portions Outside area 戸 WiFi

NW6

The Salusbury Pub and Dining Room PLAN 2 D4

tel: 020 7328 3286 **50-52 Salusbury Rd NW6 6NN**
email: thesalusburypub@btconnect.com
dir: *100mtrs left from Queen's Park tube & train station. (5 mins' walk from Brondesbury Station)*

A community local serving good value fare

A stone's throw from Queen's Park tube, this pub serves the local community well, admitting dogs and children and serving kiddy-sized portions from the uncomplicated menu. Small plates come cold (Dorset crab, quail's egg and watercress) or hot (devilled lamb's kidneys on toast), while main dishes are robust and classically British: grilled Barnsley chop with grain mustard mash and broccoli; or Guinness-braised ox cheek with pearl barley. Desserts may feature Bramley apple and quince crumble with clotted cream. Along with the food, Greene King ales, Aspall cider and a good range of wines can all be served on the outside patio.

Open all day all wk 12-11 (Thu-Sat 12-12 Sun 12-10.30) Closed 25-26 Dec **Food** Lunch all wk 12-4 Dinner Mon-Sat 6-10, Sun 6-9 Av main course £12 Set menu available ⊕ FREE HOUSE ◖ Greene King Abbot Ale & IPA, Moncada Notting Hill ♂ Aspall, Rekorderlig. ♉ 15 **Facilities** Non-diners area ♣ (Bar Outside area) ♦ Children's portions Family room Outside area 戸 WiFi ⛟ (notice required)

NW8

The New Inn PLAN 2 E4

tel: 020 7722 0726 **2 Allitsen Rd, St John's Wood NW8 6LA**
email: thenewinn@gmail.com
dir: *Exit A41 by St John's Wood tube station into Acacia Rd, last right, to end on corner*

British favourites meet international tapas

Colourful flower baskets and troughs break the lines of this street-corner pub, where pavement tables are a popular retreat for locals supping Abbot Ale, Aspall cider or a choice from the extensive wine list. This convivial Regency inn is well-placed for nearby Regent's Park and Lord's Cricket Ground. In the elegant restaurant, diners indulge in the sharing boards, the global tapas selection, fresh salads or a traditional main like bangers and mash or rack of ribs. Desserts include tiramisù and home-made ice creams. There is also a 'Little People's' menu.

Open all day all wk 7.30am-11pm (Fri 7.30am-mdnt Sat 8am-mdnt Sun 8.30am-10.30pm) **Food** Lunch all day Dinner all day Restaurant menu available all wk ⊕ GREENE KING ◖ Abbot Ale, IPA, London Glory, Morland Old Speckled Hen, Guest ales ♂ Aspall, Kopparberg, Rekorderlig. ♉ 14 **Facilities** Non-diners area ♣ (Bar Restaurant) ♦ Children's menu Children's portions WiFi ⛟

SE1

The Garrison   PLAN 1 G2   PICK OF THE PUBS

tel: 020 7089 9355 **99-101 Bermondsey St SE1 3XB**
email: info@thegarrison.co.uk
dir: *From London Bridge tube station, E towards Tower Bridge 200mtrs, right into Bermondsey St. Pub in 100mtrs*

Friendly neighbourhood gastro-pub

No doubt this green-tiled, street-corner pub was once a popular local for generations of Surrey Docks stevedores. The docks are no more, Bermondsey has gone up-market, and The Garrison has moved with the times too. The pub's 21st-century restyling comprises an idiosyncratic mix of decorative themes and antique knick-knacks. The place pulsates from breakfast through to the evening. Start the day with a bowl of porridge or an Orkney streaky bacon butty, or both. At lunch there are entrées, and grills such as roasted duck breast with duck fat potatoes, Savoy cabbage, orange and red wine jus. Desserts may include sticky black treacle pudding with ginger ice cream and coffee sauce. In the evening check out the grilled ox tongue with green beans, radish and tartare vinaigrette; followed by confit pork belly with leek and black pudding mash and baby root vegetables. Menus change every couple of months; ales rotate more frequently.

Open all day all wk 8am-11pm (Fri 8am-mdnt Sat 9am-mdnt Sun 9am-10.30pm) Closed 25-26 Dec **Food** Lunch Mon-Fri 12-3, Sat 12.30-4, Sun 12-9.30 Dinner Mon-Sat 6-10.30, Sun 12-9.30 Restaurant menu available all wk ⊕ FREE HOUSE ◀ Rotating Guest ales. ♀ 17 **Facilities** Non-diners area ♣ (Bar) ♦ Children's portions WiFi

The George Inn   PLAN 1 F3

tel: 020 7407 2056 **77 Borough High St SE1 1NH**
email: 7781@greeneking.co.uk
dir: *From London Bridge tube station, take Borough High St exit, left. Pub 200yds on left*

Unique former haunt of Charles Dickens

The coming of the nearby railway meant demolition of part of what is now London's sole surviving example of a 17th-century, galleried coaching inn, but what's left is impressive. National Trust-owned, it still features some very old woodwork, like the simple wall seats. Serving thirsty Londoners for centuries, the pub is mentioned in Dickens's *Little Dorrit*. As well as Greene King ales and rotating guests, George Inn Ale is the house beer. The pub grub includes a sharing fish slate, potted mackerel, chicken casserole, shepherd's pie, roasted vegetable and cheese filo parcel, and Toulouse sausages.

Open all day all wk 11-11 (Sun 12-10.30) Closed 25-26 Dec ⊕ GREENE KING ◀ IPA, George Inn Ale, Guest ales ♂ Aspall. **Facilities** ♦ Children's portions Garden WiFi

The Market Porter   PLAN 1 F3

tel: 020 7407 2495 **9 Stoney St, Borough Market, London Bridge SE1 9AA**
dir: *Close to London Bridge Station*

A real ale pub with a Harry Potter connection

With as apt a name as you could wish for, this Borough Market pub is blessed with a really good atmosphere, especially on Thursdays, Fridays and Saturdays, when the retail market operates. Harry Potter fans will surely know that the inn became the 'Third Hand Book Emporium' in one of the films. The exceptional choice of real ales includes the resident Harvey's, others changing up to nine times a day along with some international sidekicks. Apart from sandwiches and bar snacks there are dishes such as warm Cajun chicken and bacon salad; Cumberland sausage and mash with red onion marmalade; and for vegetarians, penne pasta with cannellini

bean cassoulet. On weekdays the pub opens its doors at 6am. Children are welcome before 6pm.

Open all day all wk 6am-9am, 11-11 (Sat 12-11 Sun 12-10.30) Closed 25-26 Dec, 1 Jan **Food** Lunch Mon-Thu 12-3, Fri-Sun 12-5 Set menu available Restaurant menu available all wk ⊕ FREE HOUSE ◀ Harvey's Sussex Best Bitter, wide selection of international ales ♂ Traditional Scrumpy. ♀ 10 **Facilities** Non-diners area ♦ Children's portions Outside area ㅠ ▰ (notice required)

SE5

The Crooked Well   PLAN 2 F3

tel: 020 7252 7798 **16 Grove Ln, Camberwell SE5 8SY**
email: info@thecrookedwell.com
dir: *Nearest tube: Denmark Hill*

Neighbourhood restaurant and bar is a Camberwell beauty

Set up and run by three friends, each with stacks of restaurant experience in the kitchen or front of house, this Victorian, street corner pub has rapidly earned some worthy plaudits for its food. A penchant for home-cooked British classics, such as rabbit and bacon pie (for two), still allows continental influences to not so much creep in as enter with brio – for example, roast lamb with spiced aubergine and tzatziki; rose-harissa-toasted couscous; and coley with tagliatelle and salsa verde. Regularly involved with community events, it holds mums' (and dads') mornings and jazz nights.

Open all day all wk Closed 25-27 Dec, Mon L **Food** Lunch Tue-Sat 12.30-3, Sun 12.30-4 Dinner Mon-Thu 6.30-10, Fri-Sat 6.30-10.30, Sun 7-9 Set menu available Restaurant menu available all wk ⊕ PUNCH TAVERNS ◀ Sharp's Doom Bar ♂ Westons Wyld Wood Organic. ♀ 10 **Facilities** Non-diners area ♣ (Bar Restaurant Outside area) ♦ Children's menu Children's portions Outside area ㅠ WiFi ▰ (notice required)

SE10

Greenwich Union Pub   PLAN 2 G3

tel: 020 8692 6258 **56 Royal Hill SE10 8RT**
email: theunion@meantimebrewing.com
dir: *From Greenwich DLR & main station exit by main ticket hall, turn left, 2nd right into Royal Hill. Pub 100yds on right*

A beer-drinker's idea of heaven

In the heart of Greenwich's bustling Royal Hill, this pub's comfortable leather sofas and flagstone floors help to keep its original character intact. Interesting craft beers from the award-winning Meantime Brewing Company, along with lagers from around the world and a beer garden, make this a popular spot. The food is an eclectic range of traditional and modern dishes drawn from around the world. Everything is freshly prepared and sourced locally where possible: fish comes straight from Billingsgate Market, while bread comes from the Greenwich itself. The lunch menu includes sandwiches, and favourites like home-made 28-day-aged Aberdeen Angus beefburger, while at dinner you could opt for Welsh rarebit followed by kedgeree or three bean chilli. All courses, including dessert, can be accompanied by a recommended beer, so you could round off with sticky toffee pudding and a glass of Meantime Chocolate Porter.

Open all day all wk 12-11 (Fri-Sat 12-11 Sun 12-10.30) **Food** Lunch all wk 12-10 Dinner all wk 12-10 ⊕ FREE HOUSE ◀ Meantime Pale Ale & Chocolate Porter, Pilsner, Yakima Red ♂ Sheppy's. **Facilities** ♣ (Bar Restaurant Garden) ♦ Garden ㅠ WiFi

North Pole Bar & Restaurant PLAN 2 G3 PICK OF THE PUBS

tel: 020 8853 3020 **131 Greenwich High Rd, Greenwich SE10 8JA**
email: info@northpolegreenwich.com
dir: *Right from Greenwich rail station, pass Novotel. Pub on right*

The complete package in Greenwich

Dating from 1849, the name originated with the Victorian obsession for polar exploration, and North Pole Road adjoins the pub. It's a stylish, contemporary venue, offering a complete night out under one roof, with a bar, restaurant and basement club. Outside in the beer garden (which is also home to a shisha pipe lounge) is seating for well over 100 people. Refreshments range from international beers such as Staropramen to cocktails, while the all-day bar menu features tapas, platters, sandwiches, grills and salads. The Piano restaurant attracts both visitors and loyal locals with its seasonally changing, modern European à la carte and brasserie menus: Thai-style haddock and crayfish cake, lime curry mayo; roast duck breast, braised red cabbage, roast parsnip and port reduction; pumpkin, mascarpone, mushroom risotto; and seared tuna, sweet chilli pea lentils, horseradish purée and herb oil. Desserts range from date pudding and butterscotch sauce to Bramley apple pie.

Open all day all wk noon-2am **Food** Lunch all wk 12-10 Dinner all wk 12-10 Set menu available Restaurant menu available all wk ⊕ FREE HOUSE ◀ Fuller's London Pride, Meantime ♺ Aspall. ♊ 9 **Facilities** Non-diners area ❤ (All areas) ♦ Children's menu Children's portions Garden Outside area ⊓ WiFi ▭ (notice required)

The Old Brewery PLAN 2 G3

tel: 020 3327 1280 **The Pepys Building, Old Royal Naval College, Greenwich SE10 9LW**
email: info@oldbrewerygreenwich.com
dir: *Nearest tube: Cutty Sark*

Buzzy pub housing the only brewery in a World Heritage Site

By day, the stuccoed façade of The Pepys Building in the grounds of The Old Royal Naval College house a convivial pub/café; in the evening it becomes a vibrant pub/restaurant. It's home also to the Meantime Brewery Company, whose real ales accompany Dark Star and fifty-plus bottled world classics. Pub food is served in the bar and courtyard during the day, while an evening meal amidst the copper tuns and suspended bottles in the main hall might be barbecued ribs marinated in Meantime wheat beer; fisherman's pie; or mushroom and Jerusalem artichoke risotto.

Open all day all wk Closed 26 Dec **Food** Lunch all wk 12-5 Dinner all wk 6-10 Restaurant menu available all wk ⊕ MEANTIME BREWING CO ◀ Meantime Brewing Co beer, Dark Star Hophead & American Pale Ale ♺ Sheppy's.
Facilities Non-diners area ❤ (Bar Garden) ♦ Children's menu Children's portions Garden ⊓ Beer festival WiFi ▭ (notice required)

SE16

NEW The Mayflower PLAN 2 G3

tel: 020 7237 4088 **117 Rotherhithe St SE16 4NF**
email: mayflowerrotherhithe@gmail.com
dir: *Phone pub for detailed directions*

Historic pub with fine Thames views

Named after the famous ship that set sail from Rotherhithe in 1620, this historic Thameside pub is packed with reminders of The Mayflower in the 16th century. Original fireplaces and timber floors add to the timeless character of this pub, which boasts wonderful river views from the upstairs restaurant and the jetty outside. Over a pint of Scurvy Ale, one of several beers on tap, order from the extensive menu. Typical dishes include Gloucester Old Spots sausages and mash

with black pudding and onion gravy or asparagus and pea risotto. Look to the specials board for the pie of the day.

Open all day all wk **Food** Lunch 12-3 Dinner 6-9.30 Av main course £10 ⊕ FREE HOUSE ◀ Mayflower Scurvy Ale, Dark Star Hophead, Thwaites 13 Guns, Purity Pure UBU, Okells, St Austell Tribute ♺ Aspall. ♊ 12 **Facilities** ❤ (Bar Outside area) ♦ Children's portions Outside area ⊓ WiFi ▭ (notice required)

SE21

The Rosendale PLAN 2 F2

tel: 020 8761 9008 **65 Rosendale Rd, West Dulwich SE21 8EZ**
email: info@therosendale.co.uk
dir: *Nearest station: West Dulwich*

Transformed mid-Victorian coach house

Owned by three former schoolmates who also run other South London pubs, The Rosendale, just like the other pubs in the group, has been totally transformed. The owners like keeping things simple but interesting, so the formidably-stocked bar might include Moor Nor' Hop, a Bristol brew, but also Harvey's Sussex classic bitter, several real ciders, and a mind-boggling range of rums, tequilas and vodkas. Traditional British food, using top-quality ingredients such as meats from the boys' own farm in Hampshire, includes bar snacks like Scotch eggs, and the more substantial honey-spiced Goosnargh duck; roast butternut and ricotta ravioli; and artisan pizzas with toppings that include Norfolk chorizo, Oxspring's ham and Laverstoke Park Farm's buffalo mozzarella.

Open all day all wk Closed 26 Dec **Food** Lunch Mon-Fri 12-3.30, Sat 12-4, Sun 12-9 Dinner Mon-Thu 6-10, Fri-Sat 6-10.30, Sun 12-9 ⊕ RENAISSANCE PUBS ◀ Moor Nor' Hop, Adnams Ghost Ship, Harvey's Sussex Best Bitter, Timothy Taylor Landlord, Brixton Atlantic APA, London Beer Factory ♺ Wilkins Farmhouse, Hecks, Sandford Orchards, Thatchers. ♊ 27 **Facilities** Non-diners area ❤ (Bar Garden) ♦ Children's menu Children's portions Play area Garden ⊓ WiFi ▭

SE22

The Palmerston ⊕ PLAN 2 F2

tel: 020 8693 1629 **91 Lordship Ln, East Dulwich SE22 8EP**
email: info@thepalmerston.co.uk
dir: *2m from Clapham, 0.5m from Dulwich Village (10 mins' walk from East Dulwich station)*

Smart London corner pub serving excellent modern food

A striking corner-plot destination dining pub in leafy Dulwich, heavy on the wood panelling, with stripped floorboards and some great floor tiling. Occasional installations of photographic exhibitions add to the interior's flair. Chefs Jamie Younger and Rob Wilcox create modern British menus with a Mediterranean twist. Start with potted shrimp on brown toast; baked escargot with café de Paris butter; or twice baked blue cheese soufflé with wild mushrooms. Then move on to roast fillet of venison, braised red cabbage, faggot and cranberry gravy; or sea bass fillet with black olive and parsley salad and aïoli. Finish with chocolate tart with prune and Armagnac ice cream. Affable locals pop in for some flavoursome beers, too, from the likes of Sharp's and Harvey's, and perhaps one of the 32 wines offered by the glass.

Open all day all wk Closed 25-26 Dec, 1 Jan **Food** Lunch Mon-Fri 12-2.30, Sat-Sun 12-3.30 Dinner Mon-Sat 7-10, Sun 7-9.30 Set menu available Restaurant menu available all wk ⊕ ENTERPRISE INNS ◀ Sharp's Doom Bar, Harvey's, Timothy Taylor Landlord, Sambrook's Wandle ♺ Cornish Orchards Gold. ♊ 32
Facilities Non-diners area ♦ Children's portions Outside area ⊓ Beer festival WiFi ▭ (notice required)

SE23

The Dartmouth Arms   PLAN 2 G2

tel: 020 8488 3117 **7 Dartmouth Rd, Forest Hill SE23 3HN**
email: dartmouth@innpublic.com
dir: *100mtrs from Forest Hill Station*

Smart Georgian pub with modern British cuisine

The original patrons of today's stylish pub would have been boatmen from the Croydon Canal, which ran behind the pub until 1836. Georgian features remain in this popular meeting place, where good beers like Golden from Brockley Brewery quench the thirst. A cosmopolitan choice of menu dishes caters for most tastes; a starter may be rabbit and pork terrine with apple chutney and soda bread. Mains range from spätzle with roasted Jerusalem artichoke and watercress sauce to chickpea, merguez, black pudding and chorizo stew. Rhubarb and ginger crumble should take care of a sweet tooth.

Open all wk Closed 25-26 Dec, 1 Jan **Food** Lunch Mon-Fri 12-3.30, Sat 12-9.30, Sun 12-4 Dinner Mon-Fri 6-9.30, Sat 12-9.30, Sun 5-9 ⊕ ENTERPRISE INNS ◀ St Austell Tribute, Brockley Golden, Guest ale ⭕ Westons Stowford Press. ⵏ 9
Facilities Non-diners area ❀ (Bar Garden) ♦♦ Garden ⋒ Parking WiFi ▭

SW1

The Buckingham Arms   PLAN 1 D2

tel: 020 7222 3386 **62 Petty France SW1H 9EU**
email: buckinghamarms@youngs.co.uk
dir: *Nearest tube: St James's Park*

Forever popular for good beer and top pub food

This elegant Young's pub retains much of its old charm including etched mirrors and period light fittings in the bar. Close to Buckingham Palace, it is popular with pretty much everyone: tourists, business people, politicians, media types and real ale fans. Expect a good range of simple pub food, including grazers (perhaps breaded brie with raspberry and rosemary dip); sandwiches and hearty favourites such as sausages and mash, steak and ale pie and West Country beef burgers.

Open all day 11-11 (Sat 12-6 Sun 12-6 summer) Closed 25-26 Dec, Sun (winter) **Food** Lunch Mon-Fri 12-9, Sat-Sun 12-5 Dinner Mon-Fri 12-9 ⊕ YOUNG'S ◀ Bitter & Special, Wells Bombardier, London Gold, Guest ales ⭕ Aspall. ⵏ 15
Facilities Non-diners area ❀ (Bar) ♦♦ WiFi

The Nags Head   PLAN 1 B2   PICK OF THE PUBS

tel: 020 7235 1135 **53 Kinnerton St SW1X 8ED**
dir: *Phone for detailed directions*

Step back in time at this mews pub

This pub was built in the early 19th century to cater for below-stairs staff and stable hands working in this quiet Belgravia mews near Harrods. With its Dickensian frontage and an interior like a well-stocked bric-à-brac shop, The Nags Head stubbornly resists any contemporary touches. It's a mobile-free zone, and you are politely requested to hang coats and bags on the hooks provided. Compact and bijou, its front and back bars are connected by a narrow stairway and boast wooden floors, low ceilings and panelled walls covered with photos, drawings, and mirrors; other adornments include helmets, model aeroplanes, and even penny-slot machines. The atmosphere is best described as 'entertaining' if you're in the right mood. The waist-high bar is another oddity, but the full Adnams range is served, along with a good value menu of traditional pub grub – real ale sausages, roast of the day; and chilli con carne.

Open all day all wk 11-11 **Food** Lunch all wk 11-9.30 Av main course £8 ⊕ FREE HOUSE ◀ Adnams Southwold Bitter, Broadside, Fisherman, Regatta & Old Ale ⭕ Aspall. **Facilities** Non-diners area ❀ (Bar) ♦♦ Outside area ⋒

The Orange Public House & Hotel   PLAN 1 C1

tel: 020 7881 9844 **37 Pimlico Rd SW1W 8NE**
email: reservations@theorange.co.uk
dir: *Nearest tube: Victoria or Sloane Street*

An ornate corner building offering rustic and uncomplicated food

Recognised for its approach to sustainability, The Orange comprises a number of light and airy adjoining rooms, which have a rustic Tuscan feel with their muted colours and potted orange trees on stripped wooden boards. Well-heeled locals quaff local ales and Italian wines while selecting from menus of modern European dishes. Wood-fired pizzas and oven roasts lead the way, but the carte is full of good things: chilli salt squid and spiced lime dressing; sweet potato, artichoke and fennel risotto; steamed spiced mussels, chorizo and sherry, aïoli and focaccia; and braised pork belly, rosemary white beans, kale, apple and saffron chutney, brandy jus to list but a few.

Open all day all wk 8am-11.30pm (Sun 8am-10.30pm) **Food** Lunch all wk 12-6 Dinner all wk 6-10 ⊕ FREE HOUSE ◀ Florence A Head in a Hat, Capper &Topee ⭕ Westons Mortimers Orchard. ⵏ 15 **Facilities** Non-diners area ♦♦ Children's menu Children's portions Outside area ⋒ WiFi

The Thomas Cubitt   PLAN 1 C2

tel: 020 7730 6060 **44 Elizabeth St SW1W 9PA**
email: reservations@thethomascubitt.co.uk
dir: *Nearest tube: Victoria or Sloane Square*

Distinguished pub in fashionable district

Norfolk-born builder Thomas Cubitt developed Belgravia as a stuccoed rival to swanky Mayfair. This exclusive, white-painted corner pub draws a discerning crowd to its country-house-style interior featuring open fireplaces, detailed panelling and a superb hand-made, oak counter. Floor-to-ceiling glass doors open out on to tables and chairs on the street. In the bar, where A Head in a Hat, Capper and Topee real ales are resident, enjoy Frenchman's Creek rock oysters; and corn-fed chicken Caesar salad. Upstairs the dining room offers dishes such as honeyed Goosnargh duck breast; and warm root vegetable terrine. Booking is essential for the memorable Sunday roast.

Open all day all wk 12-11 (Sun 12-10.30) **Food** Lunch all wk all day Dinner all wk all day Restaurant menu available all wk ⊕ FREE HOUSE ◀ Florence A Head in a Hat, Capper & Topee ⭕ Westons Mortimers Orchard. ⵏ **Facilities** Non-diners area ♦♦ Children's menu Children's portions Outside area ⋒ ▭ (notice required)

The Wilton Arms   PLAN 1 B2

tel: 020 7235 4854 **71 Kinnerton St SW1X 8ED**
email: wilton@shepherd-neame.co.uk
dir: *Between Hyde Park Corner & Knightsbridge tube stations*

Cosy pub serving Shepherd Neame ales

Known locally as The Village Pub, this early 19th-century hostelry's other name is a reference to the 1st Earl of Wilton. In summer it is distinguished by fabulous flower-filled baskets and window boxes. High settles and bookcases create cosy, individual seating areas in the air-conditioned interior, and a conservatory covers the old garden. Shepherd Neame ales, including Spitfire, accompany traditional pub fare: ploughman's, toasted sandwiches, burgers, sausages and mash with onion gravy; and home-made specials such as pies, curries, lasagne and chilli con carne add to the choices.

Open all day all wk Closed 25-26 Dec, BHs **Food** Lunch Mon-Sat 12-3 Dinner Mon-Fri 5.30-9 Av main course £8 ⊕ SHEPHERD NEAME ◀ Spitfire & Bishops Finger, Oranjeboom. ⵏ 8 **Facilities** Non-diners area ❀ (Bar Outside area) ♦♦ Children's portions Outside area ⋒ WiFi ▭

SW3

The Builders Arms   PLAN 1 B1   PICK OF THE PUBS

tel: 020 7349 9040 **13 Britten St SW3 3TY**
email: thebuildersarms@geronimo-inns.co.uk
dir: *From Sloane Square tube station into King's Rd. Right into Chelsea Manor St, at end right into Britten St, pub on right*

Modern English food with a twist

The Builders Arms is a stylish three-storey Georgian pub tucked away in the back streets of Chelsea, just off the King's Road. It was built by the same crew that constructed St Luke's church over the way. Leather sofas and colourfully liveried armchairs furnish the interior, with a line of bar stools fronting the spacious, informal bar. Here you can quickly order a pint of Builders & Monks, or more slowly peruse the wine list to choose one from the three dozen sold by the glass. Food comprises Builder's bites, bar boards or carte options. A typical three-course choice could start with seared terrine of bacon, Lord Burgh cheddar, spring onion and grape molasses; continue with coq au vin cooked with Côte du Rhône and served with rice pilaf; and finish with a comforting dark chocolate brownie with dulce de leche granizado.

Open all day all wk Mon-Wed 11-11 Thu-Sat 11am-mdnt (Sun 12-10.30) **Food** Lunch Mon-Fri 12-3, Sat 12-4, Sun all day Dinner Mon-Sat 6.30-10.30, Sun all day Av main course £13 ⊕ GERONIMO INNS ◼ Sharp's Doom Bar, Builders & Monks ♂ Aspall. ♟ 36 **Facilities** Non-diners area ✤ (Bar Restaurant) ♦♦ Children's portions Outside area ♩ WiFi ▬

Coopers Arms   PLAN 1 B1

tel: 020 7376 3120 **87 Flood St, Chelsea SW3 5TB**
email: coopersarms@youngs.co.uk
dir: *From Sloane Square tube station, into King's Rd. Approx 1m W, opposite Waitrose, turn left. Pub half way down Flood St*

Classy Chelsea pub offering a genial welcome

Just off the King's Road and close to the river, this pub sees celebrities rubbing shoulders with the aristocracy and blue collar workers. The stuffed Canadian moose brings a character of its own to the bar, where at least five real ales grace the pumps. Food is served both in the main bar area and in the first-floor Albert Room, which also plays host to private dinners and parties. The menu offers a range of modern British classics, including beef and bone marrow burger and a pie of the day. There is a weekly Tuesday quiz night.

Open all day all wk 12-11 (Sun 12-10.30) **Food** Lunch Mon-Fri 12-3, Sat 12-10, Sun 12-7 Dinner Mon-Fri 5-10, Sat 12-10, Sun 12-7 Set menu available ⊕ YOUNG'S ◼ Special & Bitter, Sambrook's Wandle, Guinness, Guest ales ♂ Aspall. ♟ 15 **Facilities** Non-diners area ✤ (Bar Garden) ♦ Children's menu Children's portions Garden WiFi

SW4

The Abbeville   PLAN 2 F2

tel: 020 8675 2201 **67-69 Abbeville Rd SW4 9JW**
email: info@theabbeville.co.uk
dir: *Nearest tube: Clapham South*

Smart Clapham neighbourhood pub

The one-time Huguenot enclave around Abbeville Road lacked its own pub until local boys Nick Fox, Tom Peake and Mark Reynolds transformed a former restaurant into the pioneering member of today's Renaissance Group of south London pubs; Massimo Tebaldi joined later as group executive chef. In style terms we're talking

eccentric 16th-century paintings and mismatched furniture, although the long-legged bar chairs are clearly members of the same family. Timothy Taylor Landlord bitter hits the spot with the locals, and dishes include tandoori spiced plaice with chilli and mint couscous; roasted lamb rump with tapenade, chickpeas and tomatoes; and wild mushroom risotto with parmesan, rocket and truffle oil.

Open all day all wk ⊕ FREE HOUSE ◼ Timothy Taylor Landlord ♂ Aspall. **Facilities** ✤ (Bar Restaurant Outside area) ♦♦ Children's menu Children's portions Outside area WiFi

The Stonhouse   PLAN 2 E2

tel: 020 7819 9312 **165 Stonhouse St SW4 6BJ**
email: info@thestonhouse.co.uk
dir: *Nearest tube: Clapham Common*

Modern local on a residential side street

Tucked discreetly away between Clapham's Old Town and its busy High Street is this impressively transformed corner local. In the elegant bar, a local guest beer and Timothy Taylor Landlord vie for real ale drinkers' attention, while cider fans can choose Stowford Press. In the log-fire-warmed dining area, the brasserie-style menu is skewed towards modern British food, in particular steaks, dishes featuring free-range chicken and pork from the pub's Hampshire farm, and sustainably sourced fish. The regularly changing menu could feature Cornish potted crab, caper butter and sourdough; Bulleit Bourbon BBQ beef brisket, chips, red cabbage slaw and pickle; and apple and blackberry crumble and home-made custard. A partially-covered paved garden area lies outside.

Open all day all wk Closed 25-26 Dec **Food** Lunch Mon-Fri 12-3.30, Sat 11-4, Sun 12-9 Dinner Mon-Sat 6-10.30, Sun 12-9 ⊕ PUNCH TAVERNS ◼ Timothy Taylor Landlord, Sambrook's Wandle, Guest ale ♂ Westons Stowford Press. ♟ 19 **Facilities** Non-diners area ✤ (Bar Garden) ♦♦ Children's menu Children's portions Garden ♩ WiFi ▬ (notice required)

SW6

The Atlas   PLAN 2 E3   PICK OF THE PUBS

tel: 020 7385 9129 **16 Seagrave Rd, Fulham SW6 1RX**
email: reservations@theatlaspub.com
dir: *2 mins' walk from West Brompton tube station*

Traditional London pub with a walled garden

Located in a trendy part of town where a great many pubs have been reinvented to become diners or restaurants, The Atlas is one of only a handful of London pubs to have a walled garden. Just around the corner from West Brompton tube, this traditional, relaxed local remains true to its cause with a spacious bar area split into eating and drinking sections. Typical menus might feature starters such as braised veal and tuna salad with baby cress, capers and lemon; or Portobello mushrooms and goats' cheese tart with caramelised red onion and balsamic molasses. Tempting mains demonstrate some European influences in dishes such as penne with Italian sausage ragu; or herb-crusted rack of lamb with vegetable Provençale and black olives tapenade. There are good choices on the wine list, with around 15 by the glass for those who want to match different dishes.

Open all day all wk 12-12 Closed 24-31 Dec **Food** Lunch Mon-Fri 12-2.30, Sat 12-4, Sun 12-10 Dinner Mon-Sat 6-10, Sun 12-10 ⊕ FREE HOUSE ◼ Fuller's London Pride, Guest ales ♂ Symonds. ♟ 15 **Facilities** Non-diners area ♦♦ Children's portions Garden ♩ WiFi ▬ (notice required)

LONDON SW6 *continued*

The Harwood Arms ◉◉ PLAN 2 E3 `PICK OF THE PUBS`

tel: 020 7386 1847 **Walham Grove SW6 1QP**
email: admin@harwoodarms.com
dir: *Phone for detailed directions*

Tip-top dining pub in leafy Fulham

The combined talents of chef Brett Graham and TV chef Mike Robinson, who also owns The Pot Kiln in Berkshire, have transformed this neighbourhood pub in leafy Fulham into a top dining venue. The inspired British cooking makes it worthy of two AA Rosettes, but the Harwood remains a proper pub. Microbrewery ales are on tap, the atmosphere is vibrant and friendly, and bar snacks like venison rissoles with Oxford sauce, or crispy garlic potatoes, can be ordered. The kitchen's passion about the provenance and seasonality of ingredients is key to its success; the pub is renowned for its game and wild food, predominantly from Berkshire, where Mike shoots on various estates. The short, ever-changing menu may list Berkshire game faggots with Jerusalem artichokes, pickled walnuts and grapes; Hereford snails with oxtail braised in stout and parsley; slow-cooked belly of Tamworth pork with apple, burnt onion, cabbage and bacon; and Mrs Gooderson's yummy rhubarb and sherry trifle.

Open all day 12-11 (Mon 5.30-11) Closed 24-27 Dec, 1 Jan, Mon until 5.30pm **Food** Lunch Tue-Sat 12-3, Sun 12-4 Dinner Mon-Sat 6.15-9.30, Sun 7-9 ⊕ ENTERPRISE INNS ◀ Sambrook's Wandle, Bath Ales Gem, Guest ales. ☍ 20 **Facilities** Non-diners area ❤ (Bar Restaurant) ◑ Children's portions WiFi ☞ (notice required)

The Jam Tree PLAN 2 E3

tel: 020 3397 3739 **541 King's Rd SW6 2EB**
email: chelsea@thejamtree.com
dir: *Nearest tube: Imperial Wharf or Fulham Broadway*

Quirky gastro-pub with a vibrant night life

Number two in The Jam Tree gastro-pub family, this Chelsea sibling echoes the quirkiness of its Clapham sister. Antique mirrors, personalised artworks, old chesterfields and mismatched furniture give the interior a decidedly individual look. The modern British menu adds colonial undertones offers curries; cauliflower and cumin fritters, saffron and buttermilk dip; Shahi paneer vegetable curry; and Singapore laska. Other possibilities are blackened Creole hanger steak with hand-cut chips; and a calorie conscious super salad. A long cocktail list, barbecue, plasma screen and resident DJs could be additional reasons for visiting.

Open all day all wk **Food** Lunch Mon-Fri 12-3, Sat-Sun 11-5 Dinner Mon-Fri 6-10, Sat 5-10, Sun 5-9 Av main course £15 ⊕ FREE HOUSE ◀ Timothy Taylor Landlord ◔ Symonds. ☍ 9 **Facilities** Non-diners area ❤ (Bar Restaurant Garden) ◑ Children's menu Children's portions Garden ☶ WiFi

The Malt House PLAN 2 E3

tel: 020 7084 6888 **17 Vanston Place, Fulham SW6 1AY**
email: reservations@malthousefulham.co.uk
dir: *Nearest tube: Fulham Broadway*

A quietly situated, upmarket Fulham pub

Owned by Mayfair restaurateur Claude Bosi and his brother Cedric, the former Jolly Maltster - its old name still appears on a gable-end - is a Brakspear pub, with Marston's Pedigree in support. Kitchen policy is to source the ingredients for the classic British dishes served here from independent local suppliers. To convey an idea of the style, starters include Loch Duart salmon and cucumber with tomato

salsa; cauliflower soup with a curried cauliflower fritter; and confit duck hash with poached hen's egg and mustard dressing. For main courses, braised globe artichoke with caponata vegetables and parsley sauce; and grilled plaice with brown shrimp butter, crushed potatoes and Secrett's Farm asparagus.

Open all day all wk Closed 25 Dec **Food** Lunch Mon-Sat 12-3, Sun 12-9 Dinner Mon-Sat 6-10, Sun 12-9 Av main course £14 ⊕ BRAKSPEAR ◀ Bitter, Marston's Pedigree ◔ Symonds. **Facilities** Non-diners area ❤ (Bar Restaurant Garden) ◑ Children's menu Children's portions Garden ☶ WiFi ☞ (notice required)

The Sands End Pub PLAN 2 E3

tel: 020 7731 7823 **135-137 Stephendale Rd, Fulham SW6 2PR**
email: thesandsend@hotmail.co.uk
dir: *From Wandsworth Bridge Rd (A217) into Stephendale Rd. Pub 300yds at junct with Broughton Rd*

Local, seasonal produce drives the menu here

A stylish country pub in the city is how fashionable Fulham foodies regard this much-loved neighbourhood gem. Expect to find scrubbed farmhouse tables, wooden floors, locals quaffing pints of Chelsea Blonde, chalkboard menus listing terrific bar snacks (the Scotch eggs are legendary). British seasonal cooking makes use of foraged produce and even vegetables from the pub's allotment, resulting in dishes like, chicken liver parfait with white wine jelly and brioche to start; roast underblade fillet of beef with shallot and girolle fricassée, duck fat chips and red wine jus to follow; and a nice bit of apple and blackberry crumble with vanilla ice cream for afters.

Open all day all wk Closed 25 Dec **Food** Lunch Mon-Fri 12-3, Sat 10.30-4, Sun 10.30-9, snacks all day Dinner Mon-Sat 6-10, Sun 10.30-9 Av main course £17 Set menu available ⊕ FREE HOUSE ◀ Greene King IPA, Truman's Swift, London Beer Factory Chelsea Blonde ◔ Aspall. ☍ 24 **Facilities** Non-diners area ❤ (Bar Restaurant Outside area) ◑ Children's portions Outside area ☶ WiFi

The White Horse PLAN 2 E3 `PICK OF THE PUBS`

tel: 020 7736 2115 **1-3 Parson's Green, Fulham SW6 4UL**
email: bookings@whitehorsesw6.com
dir: *140mtrs from Parson's Green tube station*

Beer Academy at the 'Sloaney Pony'

With a triangular walled front terrace overlooking Parson's Green, the former late 18th-century coaching inn and Victorian gin palace is a substantial sandstone pub. It's a destination for lovers of British pub food and interesting real ales and wines, with a restaurant in the former coach house, an upstairs bar, and a luxurious private dining area. The interior is a pleasing blend of polished mahogany and wooden and flagstone floors, open fires and contemporary lighting. Bar snacks are very tempting – tempura cauliflower, chilli mayo; and pan-fried chorizo being just two to get you started. Every dish on the menu comes with a recommended beer to drink, such partnering forming part of the pub's Beer Academy Courses. For instance, a starter of salt and pepper squid with spiced mayonnaise is paired with Goose Island 312; and a main of steak focaccia with caramelised onion, should be washed down with Adnams Broadside. It's good for Sunday brunch, summer barbecues and its four annual beer festivals – American, European, British and Old Ale.

Open all day all wk **Food** Lunch all wk 12-10.30 Dinner all wk 12-10.30 Restaurant menu available all wk ⊕ MITCHELLS & BUTLERS ◀ Adnams Broadside, Harvey's Sussex Best Bitter ◔ Aspall. ☍ 20 **Facilities** Non-diners area ❤ (Bar Garden) ◑ Children's menu Children's portions Garden ☶ Beer festival WiFi

SW10

The Hollywood Arms   PLAN 1 A1

tel: 020 7349 7840 **45 Hollywood Rd SW10 9HX**
email: hollywoodarms@youngs.co.uk
dir: *From Chelsea & Westminster Hospital in Fulham Rd into Hollywood Rd opposite, 200mtrs on right*

Stylish mid-terrace gem of a pub

Deep in Chelsea, this mid 17th-century building was once the home of the Middletons, owners of land in England, Barbados and America's Deep South. To one side, a gated archway leads to a small mews where horses were once stabled. The elegant interior was a runner-up in the prestigious Restaurant & Bar Design Awards, in part for the splendid first-floor Blanchard Room, named after a balloonist who in 1784 ascended from the grounds of the house and landed in Romsey. The ground-floor bar serves Meantime's London-brewed real ales and rather special wines released by Young's brewery (to obtain, discreetly ask a member of staff). Spiced parsnip and apple soup with sourdough toast is a possible starter, with 'posh' chicken Kiev, champ, autumn greens and smoked bacon; or market fish of the day to follow. Finish with sticky toffee pudding and Meantime London Stout-flavoured ice cream.

Open all day all wk 12-11.30 (Thu-Sat 12-12 Sun 12-10.30) **Food** Lunch Mon-Fri 12-3, Sat-Sun 12-9 Dinner Mon-Fri 6-9, Sat-Sun 12-9 Av main course £11.50 Set menu available Restaurant menu available all wk ⊕ YOUNG'S ◀ Wells Bombardier, Young's, Meantime ♂ Aspall. ♟ 12 **Facilities** Non-diners area ❤ (Bar Restaurant) ♦♦ Children's portions Outside area ⊟ Beer festival Cider festival WiFi ➡ (notice required)

SW11

The Bolingbroke Pub & Dining Room   PLAN 2 E2

tel: 020 7228 4040 **172-174 Northcote Rd SW11 6RE**
email: info@thebolingbroke.com
dir: *Nearest tube: Clapham South or Clapham Junction*

Family-friendly dining pub

This refined dining pub stands in a road known colloquially as 'Nappy Valley', due to its popularity with well-heeled young families. Named after the first Viscount Bolingbroke, who managed to be both brilliant politician and reckless rake, the pub caters admirably for children and adults alike. Expect modern British fare along the lines of beetroot and goats' cheese tarte Tatin with balsamic glaze followed by braised beef cheeks with haggerty potatoes and red cabbage. Weekend brunch includes boiled egg and soldiers for the very young.

Open all day all wk Closed 25-26 Dec ⊕ FREE HOUSE ◀ Timothy Taylor Landlord, Sambrook's Junction ♂ Aspall. **Facilities** ❤ (Bar Restaurant Outside area) ♦♦ Children's menu Children's portions Outside area WiFi

The Fox & Hounds   PLAN 2 E2

tel: 020 7924 5483 **66 Latchmere Rd, Battersea SW11 2JU**
email: foxandhoundsbattersea@btopenworld.com
dir: *From Clapham Junction exit into High St turn left, through lights into Lavender Hill. After post office, left at lights. Pub 200yds on left*

Known for its international wine list and Mediterranean food

From the moment you step through the door of this archetypal Victorian corner pub, you'll feel like one of the locals. This is one of those timeless pubs that London still has in abundance, its style simple with bare wooden floors, an assortment of furniture, walled garden, extensive patio planting and a covered and heated seating area. Regulars head here for the good selection of real ales and an international wine list. Fresh ingredients arrive daily from the London markets, enabling the Mediterranean-style menu and specials to change accordingly; all prepared in the open-to-view kitchen. So, you might start with baked king prawns with garlic; or rare roast beef and grilled asparagus salad with horseradish gremolata. Follow with penne with Italian sausage ragu; spinach and gorgonzola risotto; or pan-roast hake fillet with purple sprouting broccoli and pearl barley. A traditional British lunch is served on Sundays.

Open 12-3 5-11 (Mon 5-11 Fri-Sat 12-11 Sun 12-10.30) Closed 24-28 Dec, Mon L **Food** Lunch Fri 12.30-3, Sat 12.30-4, Sun 12-10.30 Dinner Mon-Sat 6.30-10, Sun 12-10.30 Av main course £14 ⊕ FREE HOUSE ◀ St Austell Tribute, Sambrook's, Hogs Back, Twickenham Fine Ales ♂ Cornish Orchards. ♟ 14 **Facilities** Non-diners area ❤ (Bar Restaurant Garden) ♦♦ Children's portions Garden ⊟ WiFi ➡ (notice required)

SW12

The Avalon   PLAN 2 E2

tel: 020 8675 8613 **16 Balham Hill SW12 9EB**
email: info@theavalonlondon.com
dir: *Nearest tube: Clapham South*

Elegant, comfortable and relaxing

Named after the mythical isle of Arthurian legend, the attractions of this Balham member of the Renaissance Group of south London pubs are far from fairytale. For example, there's a three-tiered rear garden that comes alive on summer days, the bar stocks Timothy Taylor Landlord, Sharp's Doom Bar and Aspall cider, and the wine list offers many by the glass. On top of that, house policy is to serve beef aged in-house, sustainable fish from English waters, and free-range pork and chicken from the group's own farm. Bar meals include meze platter; Welsh rarebit; fish and chips; and croque monsieur.

Open all day all wk Closed 26 Dec **Food** Lunch Mon-Fri 12-3.30, Sat 12-4, Sun 12-9 Dinner Mon-Sat 6-10.30, Sun 12-9 Set menu available ⊕ ENTERPRISE INNS ◀ Timothy Taylor Landlord, Sharp's Doom Bar ♂ Aspall, Mortimers. ♟ 15 **Facilities** Non-diners area ❤ (Bar Garden) ♦♦ Children's menu Children's portions Family room Garden ⊟ WiFi

SW13

The Brown Dog   PLAN 2 D2

tel: 020 8392 2200 **28 Cross St, Barnes SW13 0AP**
email: info@thebrowndog.co.uk
dir: *Phone for detailed directions*

Pleasant family oasis a short detour from the Thames

Given the pub's name, it would be odd if The Brown Dog did not welcome canines, albeit that the resident dog is black. The pub also welcomes children, which is perhaps surprising given its location in the exclusive back streets of Barnes and the gastro nature of its operation. However cask ales such as Truman's testify to its drinking credentials, along with a wine list designed to match an enticing menu. Here you'll find oysters among the starters, main courses boasting Tamworth pork or aged Scottish beef, and traditional sweets such as apple and rhubarb crumble with vanilla ice cream. A granite-slabbed terrace furnished with bench tables and parasols completes this altogether rather pleasant establishment.

Open all day all wk **Food** Lunch Mon-Fri 12-3, Sat-Sun 12-4 Dinner Mon-Fri 6.30-10, Sat 6-10, Sun 6-9 ⊕ FREE HOUSE ◀ Hackney Pale Ale, Truman's Runner, Twickenham Original ♂ Westons Stowford Press, Cidre Breton. ♟ 18 **Facilities** Non-diners area ❤ (Bar Restaurant Garden) ♦♦ Children's menu Children's portions Family room Garden ⊟ WiFi

237 Lower Richmond Rd, Putney, London SW15 1HJ
Tel: 020 8788 0640   **Fax:** 01455 221 296
Website: www.thespencerpub.com
Email: info@thespencerpub.com

We at *The Spencer* pride ourselves on serving good food, excellent drinks and having friendly staff going above and beyond, to make your experience a truly memorable one. Our menu is full of British pub classics but also has a few contemporary dishes which makes for a mouth watering selection. We handpick the wines to complement the menu and our knowledgeable staff are always on hand to give you advice.

Our focus is on you, our customer, and we try to ensure that your experience is an enjoyable one. The food is great value for money and the beers and wine are possibly some of the best selected in the area.

The Spencer is situated in the leafy backstreets of Putney, off the beaten track with a beautiful view of the common. There is plenty of space for all the family; children and dogs included. You can relax outside with a Pimm's in the all day sun or toast your feet during those cold winter evenings in front of our fire.

SW14

The Victoria ★★★★ RR ◉◉ PLAN 2 C2 PICK OF THE PUBS

tel: 020 8876 4238 **10 West Temple Sheen, East Sheen SW14 7RT**
email: bookings@thevictoria.net **web:** www.thevictoria.net
dir: *Nearest tube: Richmond*

Family-friendly and a real charmer

Close to Richmond Park, The Victoria offers something for everyone, with a large conservatory dining room and a leafy garden with a safe children's play area. TV chef Paul Merrett and restaurateur Greg Bellamy are at the helm, so you can expect award-winning culinary delights. It could be tough to decide from a menu that brims with interesting, thoroughly modern dishes, and also a few classics. Perhaps make a start with spiced tomato and bell pepper broth with freekeh, roasted squash, okra and fava beans; or Loch Duart salmon sashimi, shallot and chilli crunch, ketjap manis and pickled cucumber. Next might be 28-day aged South Devon rib-eye steak, béarnaise sauce and thrice cooked chips; seared wild Cornish sea bass, bok choi, hot and sour broth, chilli, lime leaf and ginger; yogurt spiced chicken breast, bhel puri salad with chilli, mint and pomegranate and paratha bread. Still not full? Then consider steamed syrup pudding, vanilla ice cream and custard, or a selection of cheeses.

Open all day all wk Closed 1 Jan **Food** Lunch Mon-Fri 12-2.30, Sat 8.30am-10.30am (bkfst) 11-3 (brunch), Sun 12-4 Dinner Mon-Fri 6-10, Sat 5-10, Sun 5-8 Set menu available Restaurant menu available Mon-Sat ⊕ ENTERPRISE INNS ◀ Fuller's London Pride, Timothy Taylor Landlord, Guest ale ○ Aspall. ♟ 28
Facilities Non-diners area ✿ (Bar Garden) ◀ Children's menu Children's portions Play area Garden ⊟ Parking WiFi ▭ (notice required) **Rooms** 7

SW15

Prince of Wales PLAN 2 D2

tel: 020 8788 1552 **138 Upper Richmond Rd, Putney SW15 2SP**
email: princeofwales@foodandfuel.co.uk
dir: *From East Putney station turn left, pub on right. From Putney Station, left into High St, left into Upper Richmond Rd; pub on left*

Victorian pub serving good beer and interesting food

Just two minutes from East Putney tube station, this Victorian corner pub attracts a mix of drinkers and foodies. In the cosy front bar, you can enjoy pints of Sambrook's Wandle and Purity Mad Goose with the locals or head to the rear dining room with its skylight and eclectic country-style decor of stuffed animals and wall-mounted antlers. The food here is not lacking ambition – a starter of crispy pig's cheeks with spicy sweet and sour sauce might be followed by pan-seared brill, squid ink risotto, crab-stuffed cucumber and red wine reduction.

Open all day all wk **Food** Lunch all wk 12-3 Dinner all wk 6.30-10 Set menu available ⊕ PUNCH TAVERNS/FOOD & FUEL ◀ Purity Mad Goose, Sambrook's Wandle ○ Aspall, Addlestones. ♟ 30 **Facilities** Non-diners area ✿ (Bar Outside area) ◀ Children's portions Outside area ⊟ WiFi ▭ (notice required)

The Spencer PLAN 2 D2 PICK OF THE PUBS

See Pick of the Pubs on page 338 and advert on opposite page

The Telegraph PLAN 2 D2

tel: 020 8788 2011 **Telegraph Rd, Putney Heath SW15 3TU**
email: info@thetelegraphputney.co.uk
dir: *Nearest tube: East Putney. Nearest rail station: Putney High St*

A 'country pub' just minutes from the busy streets

This pub was close to an Admiralty telegraph station between London and Portsmouth, and has been involved in the sale of beer since before 1856. Although it's only five minutes from the hustle and bustle of Putney High Street, The Telegraph feels more like a country pub. Certainly the focus on well-kept real ales cannot be faulted, with St Austell Tribute and Fuller's London Pride always available. The menu, with its pub fare and contemporary European dishes, includes grazing boards and chicken, chorizo and haloumi skewers to start, and mains of braised lamb shank, roast duck breast, steaks and burgers.

Open all day all wk 11am-mdnt **Food** Lunch Mon-Sat 12-9.30, Sun 12-9 Dinner Mon-Sat 12-9.30, Sun 12-9 ⊕ FREE HOUSE ◀ St Austell Tribute, Fuller's London Pride, Sambrook's Wandle, Guest ales ○ Thatchers Gold. **Facilities** ✿ (Bar Restaurant Garden) ◀ Children's menu Children's portions Garden Parking ▭

SW18

The Earl Spencer PLAN 2 E2 PICK OF THE PUBS

tel: 020 8870 9244 **260-262 Merton Rd, Southfields SW18 5JL**
dir: *Exit Southfields tube station, into Replingham Rd, left at junct with Merton Rd, to junct with Kimber Rd*

Sophisticated Edwardian gastro-pub

A forecourt enclosed by a brick wall distances this grand Edwardian gastro-pub from the street. It's a popular drinking and dining venue, especially during 'Wimbledon Fortnight', but that still leaves 50 other weeks for its attractions to work their magic. The log fires and polished wood furnishings make their contribution, but for many it's the great choice of refreshments – real ales, ciders and world wines, of course, but not forgetting South London's very own Merton Mule, a cocktail of vodka, ginger beer, ginger ale and crushed lime. Another big draw is the short but daily-changing menu on which everything is home made, including the bread. Start with ham hock and parsley terrine with piccalilli and toast. For a main course, a plate of braised ox cheeks, parsnip mash and root vegetables makes a warming winter treat. Finish with Yorkshire rhubarb mess, or sticky ginger pudding with toffee sauce and vanilla ice cream.

Open all wk 4-11 (Fri-Sat 11am-mdnt Sun 12-10.30) Closed 25 & 26 Dec **Food** Lunch Fri-Sat 12.30-3, Sun 12.30-4 Dinner Mon-Sat 7-10, Sun 7-9.30 ⊕ ENTERPRISE INNS ◀ Adnams Broadside, Sambrook's Wandle, Otter Amber, Harvey's Sussex Best Bitter, Sharp's Cornish Coaster, Timothy Taylor Landlord, Guest ales ○ Aspall, Westons Old Rosie & Wyld Wood Organic. ♟ 17
Facilities Non-diners area ✿ (Bar Restaurant Garden) ◀ Garden Outside area ⊟ WiFi

The Roundhouse PLAN 2 E2

tel: 020 7326 8580 **2 Northside, Wandsworth Common SW18 2SS**
email: info@theroundhousewandworth.com
dir: *Phone for detailed directions*

Recommended for its London microbrewery ales

Between Clapham Junction and Wandsworth, The Roundhouse has the ambience of a friendly local, with a round black walnut bar, open kitchen, and eclectic art on the walls. Ales come from two local microbreweries, including Sambrook's Wandle – an ale named after a nearby river. The short, daily-changing menu may take in free-range jerk chicken, spinach, sweet potato, plantain with mango and pineapple salsa; pan-roasted monkfish with sautéed zucchini, salsa verde and chive mash; or crispy pork belly with creamy mash, home-made apple sauce and spring greens. Finish with chocolate brownie with mascarpone ice cream. There was as change of hands in Summer 2014.

Open all day all wk Mon-Thu 12-11 (Fri-Sat 12-12 Sun 12-10.30) Closed 25-26 Dec **Food** Lunch Mon-Fri 12-3, Sat 12-4, Sun 12-4.30 Dinner Mon-Sat 6-9.30, Sun 6-9 Av main course £12 ⊕ FREE HOUSE ◀ Sambrook's Wandle, Guest ales ○ Symonds, Westons Mortimers Orchard. ♟ 16 **Facilities** Non-diners area ✿ (Bar Garden) ◀ Children's portions Garden ⊟ WiFi ▭ (notice required)

PICK OF THE PUBS

The Spencer

SW15   PLAN 2 D2

tel: 020 8788 0640 **237 Lower Richmond Rd, Putney SW15 1HJ**

email: info@thespencerpub.com
web: www.thespencerpub.com
dir: *Corner of Putney Common & Lower Richmond Rd, opposite Old Putney Hospital*

Well kept ales and family-friendly food

Formerly known as The Spencer Arms, this landmark pub occupies a lofty position on green and leafy Putney Common and its close proximity to the Thames Embankment makes it one of the best vantage points for watching the annual Oxford and Cambridge boat race. The beer garden here is part of the common and the pub's 25 picnic benches are hotly contested in the summer by those in search of an alfresco lunch. A light, bright and airy interior belies the rather traditional look of the place; revamped a few years ago, the emphasis is on good dining in a stylish environment where locals are still welcomed to sup at the bar, with Timothy Taylor Landlord and Fuller's London Pride among the pick of the beers. Meals, in the bar or restaurant area, are a modern take on traditional favourites, such as a starter of garlic and herb mushrooms on toast with a rocket salad, or parfait of chicken livers with toasted brioche and apricot

chutney. Mains take on a seasonal look to reflect the desire to use only the freshest ingredients; look for smoked haddock and salmon fish pie; rump of lamb with roasted vegetables, and polenta with red wine jus; or sweet chilli chicken and haloumi salad with avocado and rocket. Typical desserts might include poached whole pear with cinnamon and marsala wine syrup or apple and blackcurrant crumble. Sunday roasts and rotisserie free-range chickens are a favourite with families, and children get to choose from their own well-priced menu. An extensive breakfast menu (available 9am-noon from Monday to Saturday) is a popular option with early morning dog walkers and cyclists.

Open all day all wk Mon-Sat 9am-mdnt (Sun 11-11) **Food** Mon-Sat 12-10, Sun 12-9 ⊕ FREE HOUSE ◼ Fuller's London Pride, Sharp's Doom Bar, Timothy Taylor Landlord, Guinness ♻ Aspall Draught. ♟ 20 **Facilities** Non-diners area ☻ (Bar Restaurant Garden) ⬩♦ Children's menu Children's portions Play area Garden ⊼ WiFi ▥

SW19

Fox & Grapes ⊛   PLAN 2 D1

tel: 020 8619 1300 **9 Camp Rd, Wimbledon Common SW19 4UN**
email: reservations@foxandgrapeswimbledon.co.uk
dir: *Just off Wimbledon Common*

Ever-successful pub on a secluded edge of Wimbledon Common

Opened nearly five years ago, the Fox & Grapes' success from day one was more or less assured by the pedigree of its chefs. Step inside to an large open-plan interior of parquet flooring, wood panelling, scrubbed wooden tables. Certainly you can enjoy a pint of Doom Bar or Wye Valley, as many dog-walkers do; or consult the wine carte for the small selection of sustainable, organic and biodynamic wines. But AA Rosette-standard cooking based on ingredients from small producers remains the prime attraction, so booking is advisable. A typical dinner menu offers confit of pork jowl with beetroot and russet apple; or octopus carpaccio, blood orange, harissa and almonds; followed by ras-el-hanout partridge with chickpeas and preserved lemon; or roast plaice with Heritage carrots, bacon and pinot noir.

Open all day all wk Closed 25 Dec **Food** Lunch Mon-Sat 12-3, Sun 12-9 Dinner Mon -Sat 6-9.30, Sun 12-9 ⊕ ENTERPRISE INNS ◀ Sharp's Doom Bar, Wye Valley ♂ Symonds. **Facilities** Non-diners area ❧ (Bar Restaurant) ♦ Children's menu Children's portions WiFi ⊜ (notice required)

W1

Duke of Wellington   PLAN 1 B4

tel: 020 7723 2790 **94a Crawford St W1H 2HQ**
email: theduke@hotmail.com
dir: *5 mins' walk from Baker Street Station*

Stylish decor and fine food

A refreshing mix of street-corner local and cosmopolitan restaurant is found here at the busy heart of Marylebone, amidst Georgian-style terraces close to leafy Bryanston Square. Inspired interior design raises The Duke's profile, with gilt mirrors and an eye-catching Roman-style mural acting as foils to the dark-wood bar, rustic tables and fittings. The bright, first-floor restaurant is a tranquil escape and shares many dishes with the bar menu; smoked haddock with quails' eggs a starter before artichoke, sweet potato, chestnut and tomato crumble or chargrilled Galloway onglet steak with béarnaise sauce. Outside tables are popular with drinkers supping a pint.

Open all day all wk Closed 25 Dec-2 Jan **Food** Lunch Mon-Fri 12-3, Sat-Sun 12-4.30 Dinner all wk 6.30-10 ◀ Sharp's Doom Bar, Fuller's London Pride, Black Sheep ♂ Addlestones. ♟ **Facilities** Non-diners area ❧ (Bar) ♦ Children's portions ♫ WiFi ⊜ (notice required)

French House   PLAN 1 D4

tel: 020 7437 2477 **49 Dean St, Soho W1D 5BG**
dir: *Nearest tube: Piccadilly Circus; Tottenham Court Road; Covent Garden. Pub at Shaftesbury Avenue end of Dean St*

The rich and famous beat a path to this Soho spot

This legendary Soho watering hole was known as the Maison Francais a hundred years ago; it was patronised by General de Gaulle during the Second World War, and later by Dylan Thomas, Francis Bacon, Dan Farson and many other louche Soho habitués. Run by Lesley Lewis for over 20 years, the small, intimate and very atmospheric bar only serves half pints of Meteor, Kronenbourg and Guinness. The upstairs is a second bar, offering more informal drinking space; this area is also used as an art gallery. Only lunchtime bar food is served.

Open all day all wk 12-11 (Sun 12-10.30) **Food** Lunch Mon-Fri 12-4 ⊕ FREE HOUSE ◀ Budweiser Budvar, Kronenbourg, Leffe, Meteor, Guinness. ♟ 22 **Facilities** Non-diners area WiFi

The Grazing Goat   PLAN 1 B4

tel: 020 7724 7243 **6 New Quebec St W1H 7RQ**
email: reservations@thegrazinggoat.co.uk
dir: *Behind Marble Arch tube station, off Seymour St*

Stylish London dining pub with plenty of character

Just minutes away from Oxford Street and Marble Arch, this classy, six-storey pub is full of period features including open fireplaces, oak floors and solid oak bars. The name is not mere whimsy; goats did once graze around here because the first Lady Portman was allergic to cow's milk. Expect modern British, seasonal cooking – maybe chilli salt squid with blood orange and thyme dressing; or smoked buffalo ricotta with truffle brioche, orange marmalade, chicory and apple salad to start; followed by South Coast black bream with truffle cauliflower, purple potatoes, and tenderstem broccoli; or pan-fried halibut with Jerusalem artichokes, rainbow chard, and blood orange butter sauce; with cider-glazed apple, raisin almond cake and apple sorbet for dessert. Floor-to-ceiling glass doors are opened in warmer weather for alfresco dining.

Open all day all wk 7.30am-11.30pm (Sun 7.30am-10.30pm) **Food** Contact pub for food times ⊕ FREE HOUSE ◀ A Head In A Hat Capper & Topee ♂ Westons Mortimers Orchard. ♟ 20 **Facilities** Non-diners area ♦ Children's portions Outside area ♫ WiFi ⊜ (notice required)

NEW Newman Street Tavern ⊛   PLAN 1 C4

tel: 020 3667 1445 **48 Newman St W1T 1QQ**
email: reservations@newmanstreettavern.co.uk
dir: *Nearest Tube: Goodge St*

Foodie pub in the heart of Fitzrovia

This classic London street-corner pub is exceedingly well placed for an escape from the rigours of West End shopping. Awaiting escapees are Mighty Oak brewery's real ales in the bar and there's an award-winning, 100-bin wine list. Almost everything for which the AA awarded its Rosette is prepared in house, from butchery to breads, and from full English breakfasts to Sunday roasts. With loads to choose from, why not home in on Helford fishcake with aïoli and rocket salad; Galloway beef steak tartare; Middle White suckling pig with Bramley apple; or omelette Arnold Bennett?

Open all day all wk Closed 25-26 Dec **Food** Lunch Mon-Sat 12-3, Sun 12-4.30 Dinner Mon-Sat 6-10.30 Av main course £16.90 ⊕ FREE HOUSE ◀ Mighty Oak Kings, Maldon Gold & Captain Bob. ♟ 15 **Facilities** Non-diners area ❧ (Bar Outside area) ♦ Children's portions Outside area ♫ WiFi ⊜ (notice required)

The Only Running Footman ⊛   PLAN 1 C3

tel: 020 7499 2988 **5 Charles St, Mayfair W1J 5DF**
email: manager@therunningfootmanmayfair.com
dir: *Nearest tube: Green Park*

Smart Mayfair pub – popular all year round

This central Mayfair pub's full name is 'I Am The Only Running Footman', recalling the manservants who would precede their aristocrat master's carriage, clearing riff-raff out of the way and paying tolls. By the early 1800s, only the 4th Duke of Queensbury's footman remained in service, so His Grace renamed this, their once-favourite pub, after him. The ground floor is traditionally pub-like, with removable windows to create an inside/outside feel in summer, but upstairs is an elegant restaurant serving dishes like home-made pumpkin ravioli; roast Cornish cod, crushed parsley potatoes, wild spinach and brown crab sauce; and lemon posset with blueberries and lavender shortbread.

Open all day all wk **Food** Contact pub for food times Set menu available Restaurant menu available all wk ⊕ THE MEREDITH PUB GROUP ◀ Wells Bombardier, Greene King IPA, Young's Special ♂ Aspall. ♟ 20 **Facilities** Non-diners area ❧ (Bar Outside area) ♦ Children's menu Children's portions Outside area ♫ WiFi ⊜ (notice required)

LONDON W1 *continued*

The Portman   PLAN 1 B4

tel: 020 7723 8996 **51 Upper Berkeley St W1H 7QW**
email: manager@theportmanmarylebone.com
dir: *From Marble Arch into Great Cumberland Place, 3rd left into Upper Berkeley St*

Stylish central London pub with a seasonal British menu

Tucked between the hustle of Oxford Street and the elegant shops of Marylebone, prisoners once stopped here for a final drink on their way to the gallows at Tyburn Cross. These days, this friendly central London pub is the perfect place for weary shoppers to refuel on a St Austell or Timothy Taylor beer and seasonal British classics served all day, 365 days a year. Beer battered fish and chips, and the pie of the day are popular choices in the ground-floor pub but for a fine dining experience there's a restaurant upstairs where meals are served by way of an unpretentious silver service.

Open all day all wk **Food** Lunch all day Dinner all day Set menu available Restaurant menu available all wk ⊕ FREE HOUSE ◀ St Austell Proper Job, Timothy Taylor, Guest ale ♂ Aspall. � 15 **Facilities** Non-diners area ♥ (Bar Outside area) ♦ Children's menu Children's portions Outside area ⊞ WiFi 🚍 (notice required)

W4

NEW The City Barge   PLAN 2 C3

tel: 020 8994 2148 **27 Strand on the Green W4 3PH**
email: info@citybargechiswick.com

Fantastic location by the Thames

Slap bang next to the Thames in Chiswick, The City Barge dates in part to the 14th century. With three open fires, old prints on the walls and photographs of the river and the famous Thames barges, it's certainly full of character. There's a private dining room overlooking the water, and loads of outside seating so you can enjoy a pint of Greene King IPA or the house bitter, Argey Bargey, in the sunshine. On the menu, braised pig's cheek; whole soft shell 'crabacado' burger; braised lamb shoulder; or duck ragu pappardelle.

Open all day all wk **Food** Contact pub for food times Av main course £15 Set menu available Restaurant menu available all wk ⊕ FREE HOUSE/METROPOLITAN PUBS ◀ Greene King IPA, Argey Bargey (house bitter) ♂ Truman's Cote Breton. � 20 **Facilities** Non-diners area ♥ (Bar Garden Outside area) ♦ Children's menu Children's portions Garden Outside area ⊞ Beer festival Cider festival Parking WiFi 🚍 (notice required)

The Swan   PLAN 2 D3   **PICK OF THE PUBS**

tel: 020 8994 8262 **1 Evershed Walk, 119 Acton Ln, Chiswick W4 5HH**
email: reservations@theswanpub.com
dir: *At end of Evershed Walk*

Mediterranean cuisine accompanied by recommended ales

A friendly gastro-pub, The Swan is the perfect spot for all seasons with its welcoming wood-panelled interior and a large lawned garden and patio for summertime refreshments. Good food is at the heart of the operation, and you can sit and eat wherever you like. The menu of modern, mostly Mediterranean cooking has a particular Italian influence, and vegetarians are not forgotten. Start perhaps with cauliflower and sweet onion soup, or pork terrine with spiced pineapple chutney. Next comes the main course: salmon and dill fishcakes with wilted spinach and hollandaise; grilled Tuscan sausages with mash and red onion marmalade; or

roast pumpkin risotto. If you still have an appetite, then finish off with chocolate and almond cake, or sticky toffee pudding. Real ale recommendations are shown on the menu.

Open all wk 5-11.30 (Sat 12-11.30 Sun 12-11) Closed 24-28 Dec **Food** Lunch Sat 12.30-10.30, Sun 12.30-10 Dinner Mon-Thu 6-10, Fri 6-10.30, Sat 12.30-10.30, Sun 12.30-10 Av main course £13.50-£14.50 ⊕ FREE HOUSE ◀ Fuller's London Pride, St Austell Tribute, Dark Star Hophead, Sambrook's, Twickenham Fine Ales ♂ Cornish Orchards. ♟ 12 **Facilities** Non-diners area ♥ (Bar Garden) ♦ Children's portions Garden ⊞ WiFi

---

W5

NEW The Grove   PLAN 2 C3

tel: 07896 231503 **The Green, Ealing W5 5QX**
email: info@thegrovew5.co.uk
dir: *Nearest tube: Ealing Broadway*

Atypical refreshment choices and menu ingredients

Opposite Ealing Green and the famous film studios, The Grove describes itself as a typical London pub. But its extensive range of refreshments sets it apart. At least six beers from independent breweries are always on tap. The choice continues with real lagers, from Camden and Bury St Edmonds, European bottled beers, and 20 bourbon, single malt and blended whiskies. Its cooking is a rung or two higher than usual too. Starters such as scallop and chive boudin blanc with pea purée and sea herbs; and main courses like roast fallow deer saddle, haunch and chestnut pithivier, red cabbage and sauce grand veneur are good indications of the kitchen's capabilities.

Open all day all wk Closed 26 Dec **Food** Lunch 12-4 Dinner 6-10 Av main course £12 Restaurant menu available all wk ⊕ METROPOLITAN PUBS ◀ Dark Star Hophead, Twickenham Naked Ladies, Portobello Chestnut Ale. ♟ 17 **Facilities** Non-diners area ♥ (Bar Garden) ♦ Children's menu Children's portions Garden ⊞ Beer festival WiFi 🚍

W6

Anglesea Arms ⊛   PLAN 2 D3

tel: 020 8749 1291 **35 Wingate Rd W6 0UR**
email: theangleseaarmsw6@gmail.com
dir: *Phone for detailed directions*

Good food in west London

Built in 1866, this traditional Victorian corner pub reopened in 2014 with new owners after 18 successful years under the previous team. New custodians Richard and George Manners are experienced operators with a collection of seven London pubs and they have enhanced the Anglesea Arms' reputation for delicious food, good wine and a rotating choice of real ales. Located between Shepherd's Bush and Hammersmith, the bar offers a fireside drinking area with sofas and an intimate dining area at the rear. With four real ales and a global wine list on offer, the bar appeals to drinkers as much as it does foodies. Chef Phil Harrison's British menu is hard to resist and might start with smoked haddock brandade with charred bread and soft egg before moving on to Gloucester Old Spots pork chop, turnip, prunes, kale and mustard. A cosy outdoor terrace is popular with locals in the summer.

Open all wk 5-11 (Fri-Sat 12-11 Sun 12-10.30) **Food** Lunch Fri-Sat 12-3, Sun 12-9 Dinner Mon-Sat 6-10, Sun 12-9 ⊕ ENTERPRISE INNS ◀ Rotating Guest ales. ♟ 20 **Facilities** Non-diners area ♥ (Bar Garden) ♦ Children's portions Garden ⊞

The Dartmouth Castle   PLAN 2 D3   PICK OF THE PUBS

tel: 020 8748 3614 **26 Glenthorne Rd, Hammersmith W6 OLS**
email: dartmouth.castle@btconnect.com
dir: *Nearest tube: Hammersmith. 100yds from Hammersmith Broadway*

Corner pub with a reputation for imaginative cooking

The Dartmouth Castle is very much a place to relax in, serving a good range of refreshments and plates of very appealing food. It's a child-free zone after 7pm too, adding to its appeal for those seeking a quiet evening pint. Sambrook's have not been brewing long, but have made their mark with ales such as Wandle; or you may come across Twickenham's Naked Ladies, from a brewery just a few years older. Alternatives are Cornish Orchards cider and Sierra Nevada Pale Ale amidst a generous choice of cosmopolitan bottled ciders, beers and lagers; more than a dozen wines are sold by the glass. From the menu, expect imaginative flavours in starters such as grilled chorizo and king prawn skewers with chicory, avocado salad and shallot vinaigrette; or smoked duck breast with celeriac remoulade, prosciutto and crème fraîche. Move on to a main course of grilled Italian sausages, and finish with affogato.

Open all day 12-11 (Sat 5-11 Sun 12-10.30) Closed Etr, 23 Dec-2 Jan, Sat L
Food Lunch Mon-Fri 12-2.30, Sun 12-9.30 Dinner Mon-Sat 6-10, Sun 12-9.30
⊕ FREE HOUSE ◖ Sharp's Doom Bar, Sambrook's Wandle, Otter Bitter, St Austell Tribute, Guest ales ☼ Cornish Orchards, Symonds Founders Reserve. ⬗ 15
Facilities Non-diners area ❤ (Bar Restaurant Garden) ◖◗ Garden ⋒ WiFi

The Hampshire Hog   PLAN 2 D3

tel: 020 8748 3391 **225-227 King St W6 9JT**
email: info@the-hog.com
dir: *Nearest tube: Hammersmith & Ravenscourt Park*

Stylish gastro-pub with its own pantry of home-made delights

Located between Chiswick and Hammersmith, this corner gastro-pub may be Victorian on the outside but it's stylishly contemporary within, with wood floors, white walls and a light and airy conservatory. With three additional private dining rooms, there are plenty of options when it comes to eating here and the seasonal menu might include kale, butternut squash, pecorino and pumpkin seed salad; slow-cooked shoulder of lamb, spiced couscous, pistachio, sultanas and baby artichokes, and apple and blueberry crumble. Brunch is served until midday and you can buy home-made products from the pub's pantry to enjoy at home.

Open all day all wk 11.30-11 (Sat 10am-11pm Sun 10-10) Closed 25-26 Dec
Food Lunch Mon-Sat 12-4, Sun & BHs 12.30-4.30 Dinner Mon-Sat 6-10.30, Sun 6-9.30 Set menu available Restaurant menu available all wk ⊕ STAR PUBS & BARS ◖ Caledonian 80/- & Deuchars IPA ☼ Symonds. ⬗ 11 **Facilities** Non-diners area ❤ (Bar Garden) ◖◗ Children's menu Children's portions Garden ⋒ WiFi ⛟ (notice required)

The Stonemasons Arms   PLAN 2 D3

tel: 020 8748 1397 **54 Cambridge Grove W6 OLA**
email: stonemasonsarms@london-gastros.co.uk
dir: *From Hammersmith tube station into King St, 2nd right into Cambridge Grove, pub at end*

Creative cooking and a tempting alfresco area

Fascinating menu options make this imposing corner pub, just a short hop from Hammersmith tube station, well worth finding; London Porter hot-smoked salmon, pickled cucumber and horseradish remoulade might be a good place to start before 35-day hung, grass-fed Hampshire rump steak, house chips with pepper sauce, or choose one of the seasonal specials. The tasty eating options make the Stonemasons popular with local residents and business people alike. During warmer months a decking area can be used for alfresco dining, and there's a secluded, intimate restaurant area. The pub carries an ever-changing display of works by a local artist, and there are weekly quiz nights.

Open all day all wk 11-11 (Sun 12-10.30) Closed 25-26 Dec **Food** Lunch Mon-Fri 12-3, Sat 12-10, Sun 12-9.30 Dinner Mon-Fri 6-10, Sat 12-10, Sun 12-9.30 ⊕ FULLER'S ◖ London Pride & Organic Honey Dew, Peroni, Guinness ☼ Westons Stowford Press, Cornish Orchards. ⬗ 20 **Facilities** Non-diners area ◖◗ Children's portions Outside area ⋒ WiFi ⛟ (notice required)

W8

The Scarsdale   PLAN 2 E3

tel: 020 7937 1811 **23A Edwardes Square, Kensington W8 6HE**
email: scarsdale@fullers.co.uk
dir: *From Kensington High Street tube station turn left. 0.5m (10 mins' walk) left into Edwardes Square after Odeon Cinema*

19th-century character pub in quiet area

The Scarsdale is a 19th-century free-standing building with colourful hanging baskets and window boxes spilling into the small terraced patio, in a leafy road just off Kensington High Street. The Frenchman who developed the site was supposedly one of Bonaparte's secret agents, but more recently – the 1970s and 80s – the Scarsdale played a role as the local watering hole for Bodie and Doyle, in ITV's *The Professionals*. A typical restaurant menu offers duck leg confit with apple compôte; beef Wellington and red wine sauce; and spinach and ricotta tortellini with sun-dried tomato sauce. There is also an equally tempting bar menu, and an impressive wine list.

Open all day all wk 12-11 (Sun 12-10.30) Closed 25-26 Dec **Food** Lunch all day Dinner all day Av main course £10 Restaurant menu available all wk ⊕ FULLER'S ◖ London Pride & Bengal Lancer, George Gale & Co Seafarers, Butcombe. ⬗ 20 **Facilities** Non-diners area ❤ (Bar Garden) Garden ⋒ WiFi

LONDON W8 *continued*

The Windsor Castle PLAN 2 E3

tel: 020 7243 8797 **114 Campden Hill Rd W8 7AR**
email: enquiry@thewindsorcastlekensington.co.uk
web: www.thewindsorcastlekensington.co.uk
dir: *From Notting Hill tube station into Bayswater Rd towards Holland Park. Left into Campden Hill Rd*

Eccentric and therefore not to be missed

One legend has it that Windsor Castle could be seen from the upstairs windows when the pub was built in the 1830s; another, that the skeleton of Thomas Paine (Rights of Man) was buried in the cellar after his son sold it to settle a beer debt. Such stories add to the fascination of this pub, where wood panelling separates three areas inexplicably called Campden, Private and Sherry. Read the menu before choosing your refreshment – it matches a beer with each dish: Devon crab is paired with Curious Brew, for example; or perhaps you fancy chicken hotpot with a pint of Hop Back's Winter Lightning. Beer and cider festival in July.

Open all wk 12-11 (Sun 12-10.30) **Food** Lunch Mon-Sat 12-10, Sun 12-9 Dinner Mon-Sat 12-10, Sun 12-9 Restaurant menu available Mon-Sat ⊕ MITCHELLS & BUTLERS ◀ Timothy Taylor Landlord, Windsor & Eton Knight of the Garter, Rotating guest ales Ó Westons Old Rosie, Addlestones, Aspall Harry Sparrow. ♠ 21
Facilities Non-diners area ❤ (Bar Garden) ♦♦ Children's menu Children's portions Garden ♬ Beer festival Cider festival WiFi ☞ (notice required)

W9

The Waterway PLAN 2 E4

tel: 020 7266 3557 **54 Formosa St W9 2JU**
email: info@thewaterway.co.uk
dir: *From Warwick Avenue tube station into Warwick Av, turn left into Formosa St*

Canalside pub with a great range of drinks

Enjoying a lovely setting in Maida Vale, The Waterway offers great alfresco opportunities with is outdoor terrace, where popular barbecues are held in summer. In colder weather, the bar is a great place to relax with its sumptuous sofas and open fires. There is a good choice of drinks, including many wines and a couple of champagnes by the glass, as well as draught beers and non-alcoholic cocktails. The menus offer British and European food – devilled chicken liver with French bean and shallot salad; Dorset crab cakes with chilli, lime and garlic, or The Waterway burger with mustard mayo, mixed leaves, salsa and rustic chips. Apple and pear crumble or chocolate sundae make a great way to finish.

Open all day all wk 11am-mdnt (Sat 10-mdnt Sun 10am-11pm) **Food** Lunch all day Dinner all day Av main course £13.50 Set menu available Restaurant menu available all wk ⊕ ENTERPRISE INNS ◀ Sharp's Doom Bar, Fuller's London Pride, Skinner's Cornish Knocker, Red Squirrel Redwood American IPA Ó Aspall. ♠ 16
Facilities Non-diners area ♦♦ Children's menu Children's portions Garden ♬ WiFi ☞

W11

Portobello Gold PLAN 2 E3

tel: 020 7460 4900 **95-97 Portobello Rd, Notting Hill W11 2QB**
email: reservations@portobellogold.com
dir: *From Notting Hill Gate tube station follow signs to Portobello Market*

A touch of gold in Notting Hill

In the heart of famous Portobello Road Market, is this quirky Notting Hill pub/wine bar/brasserie where menus always list game and seafood, including sashimi, British mussels and Irish oysters. All dishes (pasta, tortillas, seafood, burgers, bangers and steaks) are prepared from scratch on the premises. With the landlord's wife, Linda Bell, an established wine writer, 18 wines by the glass should be no surprise. The pub also offers an interesting range of British ales and European beers (including a gluten-free choice) and cocktails. US President Bill Clinton dropped into Portobello Gold with an entire motorcade once, stayed an hour and left without paying! Many other famous visitors have called in or become regulars.

Open all day all wk Closed 25-31 Dec **Food** Lunch all day Dinner all day ⊕ ENTERPRISE INNS ◀ Harvey's Sussex, Freedom, Purity Longhorn IPA, Guinness Ó Thatchers Gold, Katy & Spartan. ♠ 18 **Facilities** Non-diners area ❤ (Bar) ♦♦ Children's portions WiFi ☞ (notice required)

NEW The Red Lemon PLAN 2 D4

tel: 020 7229 5963 **45 All Saints Rd, Notting Hill W11 1HE**
email: info@theredlemon.co.uk
dir: *Nearest tube stations: Westbourne Park & Ladbroke Grove*

Music, food and beer in Notting Hill

The Red Lemon (formerly The Pelican) has been a pub for 130 years and has seen plenty of changes in Notting Hill. Embracing its setting, music is important here, and the clientele is a mix of locals, young professionals, and musicians and artists, some of whom are responsible for the art on the walls. The pub and restaurant areas are separate, so the bar feels properly pub-like. Modern takes on pub classics might bring choices like spiced crab on toast followed by ham, fried duck egg and chips. They do Sunday roasts as well.

Open all day all wk **Food** Contact pub for food times Restaurant menu available all wk ⊕ FREE HOUSE ◀ Portobello. ♠ 14 **Facilities** ❤ (Bar Restaurant Outside area) ♦♦ Children's menu Children's portions Outside area ♬ WiFi ☞

W12

NEW Princess Victoria PLAN 2 D3

tel: 020 8749 5886 **217 Uxbridge Rd W12 9DT**
email: info@princessvictoria.co.uk **web:** www.princessvictoria.co.uk
dir: Nearest tube: Shepherd's Bush Market

Former 'gin palace' keeping its heritage alive

The building dates from 1829 when it was the terminus of a tram route from Acton. Not until it was rebuilt in 1872 did it take on its new vocation and grand 'gin palace' appearance thanks to architect William Bruton; he was known as 'the supreme music hall artist of pub architects'. In keeping with this heritage, today's Princess Victoria maintains a close relationship with a local gin distillery; a distillery tour followed by a meal at the pub is a regular feature of the busy social diary. The brasserie-style menu ranges from fine charcuterie to steaks from the charcoal oven served with triple-cooked chips.

Open all day all wk Closed 24-28 Dec **Food** Lunch Mon-Sat 12-3, Sun 12-4.30 Dinner Mon-Sat 6.30-10.30, Sun 6.30-9.30 Av main course £16.50 Set menu available Restaurant menu available all wk ⊕ FREE HOUSE ◀ Timothy Taylor Landlord, Portobello Pale Ὂ Addlestones, Orchard Pig Reveller, Westons Wyld Wood Organic. ♈ 20 **Facilities** Non-diners area ♣ (Bar Garden) ◗◗ Children's menu Children's portions Garden ♫ Parking WiFi ▬ (notice required)

W14

The Albion PLAN 2 D3

tel: 020 7603 2826 **121 Hammersmith Rd, West Kensington W14 0QL**
email: info@thealbionpub.com
dir: Near Kensington Olympia & Barons Court tube stations

Old pub with a great atmosphere

If you've been wandering around Olympia all day head across the road to The Albion for a pint of London Pride, St Austell Tribute or one of the many wines by the glass. A fine old pub that takes its name from HMS *Albion*, it has the look and feel of an old ship, with bare floor boards and long, scrubbed wooden tables. The menu features a selection of burgers and salads, with jackets, sandwiches and omelettes available at lunchtime. Other choices are sausages, mash, rich onion gravy; Cajun chicken; home-made steak and ale pie; and battered fish and chips. There is an August beer festival.

Open all day all wk **Food** Lunch Mon-Fri 12-3 Dinner all wk 5-10 ⊕ HEINEKEN ◀ Fuller's London Pride, St Austell Tribute, Guest ales Ὂ Symonds. ♈ 13 **Facilities** Non-diners area ♣ (Bar Restaurant Outside area) Outside area ♫ Beer festival WiFi ▬ (notice required)

The Cumberland Arms PLAN 2 D3   **PICK OF THE PUBS**

tel: 020 7371 6806 **29 North End Rd, Hammersmith W14 8SZ**
email: thecumberlandarmspub@btconnect.com
dir: From Kensington Olympia tube station turn left. At T-junct right into Hammersmith Rd. 3rd left into North End Rd, 100yds pub on left

Gastro-pub with a locals' atmosphere

At the heart of cosmopolitan Hammersmith and handy for Olympia, this eye-catching gastro-pub, generously dressed with colourful summer hanging baskets and boxes, is a popular place for people-watching. Bag a bench beside the adjacent flowery enclave on sunny days, or head inside where mellow furniture and stripped floorboards characterise the interior. Friendly staff, a comprehensive wine list and well-kept ales (St Austell Tribute, Skinner's Betty Stogs, Exmoor Gold) are the draw for those seeking after-work refreshment. But it's also a great place for sampling enticing cuisine with an Italian accent from a regularly updated menu and specials selection. Starters embrace spiced butternut squash and red pepper soup; or courgette and walnut tart. Among the mains are ravioli with chicken, spinach and ricotta; smoked haddock and creamed leek risotto; or Tunisian lamb tagine with almond and citrus couscous salad. Desserts are few but sweet: sticky date pudding with caramel, perhaps, or apple and rhubarb crumble with ice cream.

Open all day all wk 12-11 (Sun 12-10.30 Thu-Fri 12-12) Closed 24 Dec-1 Jan **Food** Lunch Mon-Sat 12-3, Sun 12-9.30 Dinner Mon-Sat 6-10, Sun 12-9.30 Av main course £14 ⊕ FREE HOUSE ◀ Exmoor Gold, Sharp's Doom Bar, Skinner's Betty Stogs, St Austell Tribute. ♈ 16 **Facilities** Non-diners area ♣ (Bar Restaurant Garden) ◗◗ Children's portions Garden ♫ WiFi ▬ (notice required)

WC1

The Bountiful Cow PLAN 1 E4   **PICK OF THE PUBS**

tel: 020 7404 0200 **51 Eagle St, Holborn WC1R 4AP**
email: manager@roxybeaujolais.com
dir: 230mtrs NE from Holborn tube station, via Procter St. Walk through 2 arches into Eagle St. Pub between High Holborn & Red Lion Square

Homage to the cow

Pub cookbook author Roxy Beaujolais runs this 'public house devoted to beef', her second pub venture following the delightful Seven Stars in WC2. Two floors are crowded with framed pictures of cows, bullfights, cowgirls, diagrams of meat cuts and posters of cow-themed films; jazzy but discreet music adds to an atmosphere halfway between funky bistro and stylish saloon. The well kept ales are from Adnams or guest breweries, and the short but estimable wine list includes several gutsy reds. The value-priced menu features Bountyburgers and perfectly grilled and tender aged steaks; the meat is sourced from a trusted Smithfield Market supplier. Starters of garlic fried prawns or octopus salad, and desserts like Belgian apple tart with vanilla ice cream might open and close the proceedings, with an oak steak board platter for two in between. Booking for all meals is advisable.

Open all day 11-11 (Sat 12-11) Closed 25-26 Dec, 1 Jan, some BHs, Sun **Food** Lunch Mon-Sat 12-10.30 Dinner Mon-Sat 12-10.30 ⊕ FREE HOUSE ◀ Adnams Southwold Bitter, Guest ales Ὂ Aspall. ♈ **Facilities** Non-diners area ◗◗ Outside area ♫ WiFi ▬ (notice required)

LONDON WC1 *continued*

The Easton PLAN 1 E5

tel: 020 7278 7608 **22 Easton St WC1X ODS**
email: info@theeastonpub.co.uk
dir: *Nearest tube stations: Farringdon; Angel; Kings Cross*

Modern dining in deepest Clerkenwell

Near the famous Sadlers Wells Theatre a short distance from Farringdon tube, this gastro-pub with pavement benches is also just a stroll away from EC1's Exmouth Market. Timothy Taylor, Truman's and Hackney Pale Ale are the top real ales and 16 wines served by the glass. A dozen tasty bar snacks tempt with the likes of porcini arancini; mini smoked haddock fishcakes with tartare sauce; and smoked ham croquettes with aïoli. These indicate the modern approach to cosmopolitan ingredients found on the seasonally-changing main menu, in dishes such as rabbit ravioli with parmesan; pan-fried pollock fillet; and asparagus, tarragon and goats' cheese pie.

Open all day all wk **Food** Lunch Mon-Fri 12-3, Sat 12-4, Sun 12-5 Dinner Mon-Sat 6-10, Sun 6-9 ⊕ ENTERPRISE INNS ◖ Timothy Taylor Landlord, Truman's Runner, Hackney Pale Ale ♻ Westons Stowford Press, Cidre Breton. ♟ 16
Facilities Non-diners area ♥ (Bar Restaurant Outside area) ♦ Children's menu Outside area ♬ WiFi ▄ (notice required)

The Lady Ottoline PLAN 1 E4

tel: 020 7831 0008 **11A Northington St WC1N 2JF**
email: info@theladyottoline.com **web:** www.theladyottoline.com
dir: *Nearest tube: Chancery Lane*

Classic London corner pub and dining rooms

A blue plaque marks the house in nearby Gower Street where Bloomsbury aristocrat and society hostess Lady Ottoline Morrell lived. Her memory also lives on in this attractive corner pub with a log fire, where four rotating real ales, bottled craft beers, several real ciders, and nine wines by the glass are always at the ready. Mount the stairs to the cosy dining rooms for good seasonal British food such as salted cod croquettes with saffron aïoli; Dingley Dell pork, mash, baby onions and black pudding; Hereford beefburger with hand-cut chips; and wild mushroom and baby artichoke risotto with parmesan.

Open all wk 12-11 (Sun 12-5) Closed 25 Dec-2 Jan **Food** Lunch Mon-Fri 12-3, Sat 12-4, Sun 12-5 Dinner Mon-Sat 6.30-10 Set menu available ⊕ PUNCH TAVERNS ◖ Portobello Star, Sambrook's Wandle, Adnams ♻ Addlestones, Aspall, Hoxton. ♟ 9
Facilities Non-diners area ♥ (Bar Outside area) ♦ Children's portions Outside area ♬ WiFi

Norfolk Arms PLAN 1 D5

tel: 020 7388 3937 **28 Leigh St WC1H 9EP**
email: info@norfolkarms.co.uk
dir: *Nearest tube: Russell Square; King's Cross St Pancras; Euston*

Classic London corner pub offering international tapas

Set amidst the elegant terraces of Bloomsbury, this eye-catching partly tile-fronted Victorian pub brings a taste of Spain and the Med to this cosmopolitan corner of London. Its gastro-pub credentials – braised beef cheeks with celeriac mash or whole sea bream with sautéed spinach examples of such – are greatly enhanced by the extensive tapas menu that draws an appreciative clientele from a wide area. Chorizo in cider; fried paprika pork belly; roast biodynamic pumpkin or saganaky (baked feta) give a flavour of the ever-changing tastes of the moment. Mainstream beers and 10 wines by the glass accompany the food, whilst private dining facilities are available.

Open all day all wk Closed 25-26, 31 Dec & 1 Jan **Food** Lunch Mon-Fri 12-3, Sat 12-4, Sun 12-10.15 Dinner Mon-Sat 6-12.15, Sun 12-10.15 Av main course £12.50 Set menu available ⊕ STAR PUBS & BARS ◖ Theakston XB, Greene King IPA. ♟ 10
Facilities Non-diners area ♥ (Bar) ♦ Children's portions ♬ WiFi

▌ WC2

The Seven Stars PLAN 1 E4 `PICK OF THE PUBS`

tel: 020 7242 8521 **53 Carey St WC2A 2JB**
email: roxy@roxybeaujolais.com
dir: *From Temple tube station turn right. 1st left into Arundel St. Right into Strand (walking). Left into Bell Yard. 1st left into Carey St*

A real one-off – stylish saloon style and market driven dishes

The Seven Stars may never have seen better days in its 414 years of existence. Since Roxy Beaujolais took over this Grade II listed pub behind the Royal Courts of Justice 16 years ago, delicate and undisruptive primping has produced nothing but accolades. Look out for the mullioned glass dumbwaiter, designed by Roxy's architect husband, that looks tactfully historic, and the cat, named Ray Brown, who wears a ruff just as his predecessor did. Strengthened by its personalities and ambience, The Seven Stars is considered the ideal pub – the food is simple but well executed, the ales are kept perfectly, the wines are few but very good, and the staff are welcoming and efficient. Roxy cooks most of the time here. The day's dishes, listed on the blackboard, change according to what's best in the market and what tickles Roxy's fancy. Examples are dill cured herring with potato salad; pheasant and pork pie with cranberries; and Spanish scramble – eggs, chorizo, potatoes, garlic, saffron and parsley.

Open all day all wk 11-11 (Sat 12-11 Sun 12-10.30) Closed 25-26 Dec, 1 Jan **Food** Lunch Mon-Fri 12-9.30, Sat-Sun 1-9.30 Dinner Mon-Fri 12-9.30, Sat-Sun 1-9.30 ⊕ FREE HOUSE ◖ Adnams Southwold Bitter & Broadside, Sambrook's Wandle, Sharp's Cornish Coaster ♻ Aspall. **Facilities** Non-diners area WiFi

The Sherlock Holmes PLAN 1 D3

tel: 020 7930 2644 **10 Northumberland St WC2N 5DB**
email: 7967@greeneking.co.uk
dir: *From Charing Cross tube station into Villiers St. Through 'The Arches' (runs underneath Charing Cross station) straight across Craven St into Craven Passage to Northumberland St*

Themed pub serving comforting pub grub

Painted black with etched glass windows and colourful hanging baskets, this traditional corner pub is chock-full of Holmes memorabilia, including photographs of Conan Doyle, mounted pages from manuscripts, and artefacts and pieces recording the adventures of the Master Detective. There's even a replica of Holmes' and Watson's sitting room and study. This split-level establishment has a bar on the ground floor and on the first floor an intimate covered roof garden and the restaurant. There's Sherlock Holmes Ale to drink, hot and cold bar food plus a menu offering Holmesian food choices like Rupert Everett's smoked salmon, Mrs Hudson's home-made steak and ale pie, Mary Sunderland's Cumberland sausages, and (non-Holmesian) vanilla and mascarpone cheesecake for afters.

Open all day all wk Closed 25 Dec **Food** Lunch all wk 11-10 Dinner all wk 11-10 Av main course £10.95 Restaurant menu available all wk ⊕ GREENE KING ◀ Sherlock Holmes Ale & Abbot Ale, Morland Old Speckled Hen ○ Aspall. ♀ 14 **Facilities** Non-diners area ⭐ Outside area ⋒ WiFi ⊷ (notice required)

GREATER LONDON

CARSHALTON   Map 6 TQ26

The Sun

tel: 020 8773 4549 **4 North St SM5 2HU**
email: thesuncarshalton@googlemail.com
dir: From A232 (Croydon Rd) between Croydon & Sutton, turn into North St signed Hackbridge (B277). Pub on right at x-rds

Stylish pub with excellent real ales

This imposing corner-plot pub stands close to the heart of Carshalton village. The enclosed walled garden area houses a wood-fired pizza oven, whilst a private dining room is ideal for group gatherings. Both wet and food sides of the business are increasingly popular; six real ales, such as Sharpe's Doom Bar, Brighton Bier and Slater's attract beer lovers – there's a summer beer festival, too. The gastro-style menu encourages diners to tarry a while in the modish interior. Commence with smoked duck pastrami, haloumi, poached pear and nutmeg parsnip; leaving room for mains such as crab, cockle and prawn tagliatelle; or sausages of the day, mash, red onion gravy and root vegetable crisps.

Open all day all wk **Food** Lunch Mon-Fri 12-3, Sat 12-10, Sun 12-8 Dinner Mon Fri 6-9.30, Sat 12-10, Sun 12-8 Av main course £14 Set menu available Restaurant menu available ⊕ FREE HOUSE ◀ Sharp's Doom Bar, Brighton Bier, Slater's ○ Aspall. ♀ 14 **Facilities** Non-diners area ⭐ (Bar Restaurant Garden) ⭐ Children's menu Children's portions Family room Garden ⋒ Beer festival WiFi ⊷ (notice required)

CHELSFIELD   Map 6 TQ46

The Bo-peep

tel: 01959 534457 **Hewitts Rd BR6 7QL**
dir: M25 junct 4 (Bromley exit). At rdbt follow Well Hill sign. Pub approx 500yds on right

Traditional home cooking close to the M25

Turn off the ever hectic M25 and in just five minutes you could be enjoying the tranquillity of this 14th-century inn. The low timber beams and inglenook in the bar offer plenty of original character, and Adnams, Sharp's Doom Bar, and Westerham (when possible) are on tap to quench your thirst. Everything here is home cooked and typical dishes include belly of pork with cider jus; and fillet of sea bass with ratatouille. On sunny days, take a table in the large garden and admire the views.

Open all day all wk **Food** Contact pub for food times Av main course £12.95 Set menu available ⊕ ENTERPRISE INNS ◀ Adnams, Sharp's Doom Bar, Westerham's Beers on rotation ○ Thatchers. ♀ 12 **Facilities** ⭐ (Bar Garden) ⭐ Children's portions Garden ⋒ Parking WiFi

The Five Bells   PICK OF THE PUBS

tel: 01689 821044 **BR6 7RE**
dir: M25 junct 4, A224 towards Orpington. In approx 1m turn right into Church Rd. Pub on left

Country pub with good food and live music

Dating from 1680, The Five Bells takes its name from the magnificent bells at the St Martin of the Tours church just up the road. This whitewashed Grade II listed building is conveniently located just inside the M25, but also situated in a

protected conservation village, with many lovely walks in the area. There are two bars: one is a dog-friendly front bar boasting an original inglenook fireplace; the other houses the restaurant area. This in turn leads to the patio and extensive garden, which comes complete with a children's play area. The seasonal menu complements the real ales and wines on offer: root vegetable beef cobbler and BBQ chicken breast with smoked bacon and melted cheese are examples from a winter menu. Sandwiches, baguettes, ciabattas and pizzas are available too, and beer festivals take place at Easter and in October along with live music and quizzes.

Open all day all wk **Food** Lunch all wk 12-2.45 Dinner Thu-Sat 6.30-8.45 Av main course £10 Restaurant menu available Thu-Sat eve ⊕ ENTERPRISE INNS ◀ Courage Best Bitter, Sharp's Doom Bar, Otter, Jennings Cumberland. ♀ 13 **Facilities** Non-diners area ⭐ (Bar Garden) ⭐ Children's menu Children's portions Play area Garden ⋒ Beer festival Parking WiFi ⊷ (notice required)

HAREFIELD   Map 6 TQ09

NEW The Old Orchard

tel: 01895 822631 **Park Ln UB9 6HJ**
email: old.orchard@brunningandprice.co.uk
dir: M25 junct 17, follow Harefield signs. Before Harefield follow pub signs

No other buildings in sight, just lakes and countryside

An early 20th-century country house that became a B&B in the Sixties, a Seventies' dance venue and then a restaurant, until 2010 when Brunning & Price bought and transformed it. The outside looks good, and the inside can hold its head high too, with open fires, honest-to-goodness furniture and a decent bar, where the six real ales include Tring Brewery's Side Pocket for a Toad, and whiskies top 130. Daily menus have offered bouillabaisse; deep-fried haddock in beer batter; balsamic-braised lamb shoulder; char siu beef salad; and gnocchi with beetroot. An outside bar and barbecue function in the summer.

Open all day all wk **Food** Lunch Mon-Sat 12-10, Sun 12-9.30 Dinner Mon-Sat 12-10, Sun 12-9.30 Av main course £14 ⊕ FREE HOUSE ◀ Tring Side Pocket for a Toad, Brunning & Price Original Bitter, Mighty Oak Oscar Wilde ○ Thistly Cross, Aspall, Westons Old Rosie & Stowford Press. ♀ 18 **Facilities** Non-diners area ⭐ (Bar Restaurant Garden) ⭐ Children's menu Children's portions Play area Garden ⋒ Parking WiFi ⊷ (notice required)

PINNER

The Queens Head   PLAN 2 B5

tel: 020 8868 4607 **31 High St HA5 5PJ**
email: info@queensheadpinner.co.uk
dir: Nearest tube station: Pinner

Pinner's oldest, maybe spookiest, inn

In 1872, Admiral Nelson's only daughter, Eleanor, was killed by a bolting horse outside this ancient inn. They say her ghost still roams its rooms, but she's supposedly benevolent and with five permanent and two weekly-changing guest real ales to choose from she might even join you for a pint. On the lunch menu are a range of Pieminister pies, all served in the correct manner, with mash and mushy peas, while on Sundays there's a traditional roast. Although dinner is not served, bar snacks are available until 9pm. Beer festivals are held in the spring.

Open all day all wk **Food** Lunch all wk 12-3 Dinner all wk 5-9 Av main course £9 ⊕ SPIRIT PUB COMPANY ◀ Young's Special, Rebellion Mutiny, Greene King Abbot Ale, Adnams, Wells Bombardier, Guest ales ○ Aspall. ♀ 13 **Facilities** Non-diners area ⭐ (Bar Restaurant Garden) Garden ⋒ Beer festival Parking WiFi

RICHMOND UPON THAMES

The White Swan   PLAN 2 C2

tel: 020 8940 0959 **26 Old Palace Ln TW9 1PG**
email: info@whiteswanrichmond.co.uk
dir: *Nearest tube: Richmond*

Excellent food in the heart of Richmond

Tucked away from Richmond's bustling high street, The White Swan dates back to 1777. Whether it's for a pint of Otter Bitter in the cosy bar with its open fire or a meal in the upstairs dining room or suntrap garden, this is a pub to suit every occasion. The kitchen has gained a good reputation for its daily-changing menus. A typical meal might feature Thai-spiced salmon and smoked haddock fish cakes, followed by puff pastry chicken and ham pie with mixed vegetables. Look out for pub dog Jake, a friendly Springer Spaniel.

Open all day all wk **Food** Lunch Mon-Fri 12-3, Sat-Sun 12-4 Dinner Mon-Fri 6.30-9, Sat-Sun 6.30-10 ⊕ FREE HOUSE ◄ Sharp's Doom Bar, Timothy Taylor Landlord, Otter Bitter Ŏ Aspall, Symonds. ♀ 18 **Facilities** Non-diners area ♣ (Bar Outside area) ♦♦ Children's portions Outside area ⊟ WiFi

MERSEYSIDE

BARNSTON   Map 15 SJ28

Fox and Hounds

tel: 0151 648 7685 **107 Barnston Rd CH61 1BW**
email: info@the-fox-hounds.co.uk
dir: *M53 junct 4, A5137 to Heswall, onto A551 signed Barnston*

Home-cooked food in friendly village pub

In the quaint village of Barnston can be found the Fox and Hounds. Built in 1911, the pub's Edwardian character is preserved in its leaded windows, pitch-pine woodwork and open fire. In the Snug, the original bar, are collections of bric-à-brac including brewery clocks and flying ducks. A good variety of real ales includes Theakston and Timothy Taylor; a huge range of malts appeals to whisky aficionados; and Rosie's Llandegla cider is made over the border in North Wales. The frequently-changing menu always includes favourites such as steak pie, curries, sausages and mash, and cottage pie, along with salads and sandwiches. Traditional Sunday roasts showcase Welsh lamb and beef.

Open all day all wk 11am-11.30pm (Sun 11-10.30) **Food** Lunch Mon-Fri 12-2, Sat 12-8, Sun 12-7 Dinner Tue-Fri 5-8, Sat 12-8, Sun 12-7 ⊕ FREE HOUSE ◄ Theakston Best Bitter & Old Peculier, Brimstage Trapper's Hat, Timothy Taylor Ŏ Aspall, Rosie's Llandegla. ♀ 15 **Facilities** Non-diners area ♣ (Bar Garden) ♦♦ Children's portions Garden ⊟ Parking ▦ (notice required)

Food Allergies

A new EU regulation makes it easier for those with food allergies to choose safer foods when eating out. 14 allergens are listed in the regulation, and pubs and restaurants must now list any of these used in the dishes they offer.

GREASBY   Map 15 SJ28

Irby Mill

tel: 0151 604 0194 **Mill Ln CH49 3NT**
email: info@irbymill.co.uk
dir: *M53 junct 3, A552 signed Upton & Heswall. At lights onto A551 signed Upton & Greasby. At lights left into Arrowe Brook Rd. At rdbt 3rd exit into Mill Ln*

Former miller's cottage serving local produce

An eye-catching, solid, sandstone-block built old miller's cottage (the windmill was demolished in 1898, the pub opened in 1980) just a short jog from the airy heights of Thurstaston Common at the heart of The Wirral Peninsula. One of the area's best choices of real ales meets an exceptional, very pubby menu strong on Wirral produce – 'Muffs' sausage and mash comes with black pudding, peas, mushrooms, gravy and onion rings and could be followed by Nicholls of Parkgate ice cream or Belgian waffles. Popular with ramblers and Sunday diners, there's a suntrap grassy garden for summer; a log fire for the winter.

Open all day all wk **Food** Lunch Mon-Sat 12-9, Sun 12-8 Dinner Mon-Sat 12-9, Sun 12-8 ⊕ STAR PUBS & BARS ◄ Wells Bombardier, Greene King Abbot Ale, Jennings Cumberland Ale, 5 guest ales. ♀ 12 **Facilities** ♣ (Bar Garden) ♦♦ Children's menu Children's portions Garden ⊟ Parking WiFi ▦

HESWALL   Map 15 SJ28

The Jug and Bottle

tel: 0151 342 5535 **Mount Av CH60 4RH**
email: info@the-jugandbottle.co.uk
dir: *From A540 in Heswall. At lights into The Mount, 1st left into Mount Ave*

Good locally-sourced food on the Wirral Peninsula

In the heart of Heswall, on the spectacular Wirral Peninsula with its views towards Liverpool and North Wales, 'The Jug' (as the locals call it) is tucked away off the main road but convenient for the M56. With two open fires and surrounded by gardens, this traditional country pub offers a warm welcome all year round, serving good food in the dining room and a range of real ales including local Brimstage Trapper's Hat. Locally-sourced food is served lunchtimes and evenings, typical choices being fisherman's pie with spring greens; and braised oxtail suet pudding with horseradish mash and ale gravy.

Open all day all wk **Food** Lunch Mon-Fri 12-2.30, Sat 12-9.30, Sun 12-8 Dinner Mon-Thu 5.30-9, Fri-5.30-9.30, Sat 12-9.30. Sun 12-8 ⊕ FREE HOUSE ◄ Brimstage Trapper's Hat, Guest ales. **Facilities** Non-diners area ♣ (Bar Garden) ♦♦ Children's menu Children's portions Garden ⊟ Parking WiFi ▦

HIGHTOWN   Map 15 SD30

The Pheasant Inn

tel: 0151 929 2106 **20 Moss Ln L38 3RA**
email: enquiry@thepheasanthightown.co.uk
dir: *From A565 take B5193, follow signs to Hightown*

A different event every day of the week

This attractive pub with a whitewashed wooden exterior is a former alehouse with a sunny garden. It's just minutes from Crosby Beach, where sculptor Antony Gormley's famous 100 cast-iron figures gaze out to sea. Surrounded by fields and golf courses, the pub retains an original brick in the restaurant wall dated 1719. In the bar these days you'll find Thwaites Wainwright alongside Aspall ciders. The menu is changed twice a year so expect dishes like pulled beef and bacon pie or a minted lamb burger. There are also the legendary Sunday platter, fish suppers on 'Fin and Fizz' Fridays and retro dining evenings.

Open all day all wk 12-11 (Sun 12-10.30) **Food** Lunch all wk 12-6 Dinner all wk 6-9.30 ⊕ MITCHELLS & BUTLERS ◄ Thwaites Wainwright Ŏ Aspall Draught & Organic. ♀ 30 **Facilities** Non-diners area ♣ (Bar Garden) ♦♦ Children's menu Garden ⊟ Parking WiFi

LIVERPOOL

Map 15 SJ39

The Monro

tel: 0151 707 9933 **92 Duke St L1 5AG**
email: mail.monro@themonrogroup.com **web:** www. themonro.com
dir: *Phone for detailed directions*

Elegant gastro-pub offering fresh, locally sourced food

In 1746, merchant John Bolton built himself a finely-proportioned house, which today is this popular city gastro-pub. Bolton later entered history as a combatant in Liverpool's last recorded duel (he was the victor). The elegance of the interior would make him feel very nostalgic, although he might struggle with the concept of

naming beers Boondoggle (Ringwood), Cocker Hoop (Jennings) and GingerBeard (Wychwood). Examples from a monthly-changing menu include six-hour confit of pork belly, celeriac mash, apple purée and purple sprouting broccoli; and guinea fowl ballotine, fondant potato, winter vegetables and red wine jus.

The Monro

Open all day all wk Closed 25-26 Dec, 1 Jan **Food** Lunch all wk 12-9.30 Dinner all wk 12-9.30 Set menu available Restaurant menu available Mon-Sat ⊕ FREE HOUSE
◀ Ringwood Boondoggle, Jennings Cocker Hoop, Wychwood GingerBeard
Ŏ Thatchers Katy. ♟ 10 **Facilities** Non-diners area ♦ Children's menu Children's portions Garden ♬ WiFi ═ (notice required)

See advert below

NORFOLK

BAWBURGH
Map 13 TG10

Kings Head
PICK OF THE PUBS

tel: 01603 744977 **Harts Ln NR9 3LS**
email: anton@kingshead-bawburgh.co.uk
dir: *From A47 take B1108 W towards Watton. Right signed Bawburgh*

Worth finding after exploring nearby Norwich

Old English roses and lavender fragrance the lanes in front of this low, rambling 17th-century pub, set in a cosy village of flint and brick cottages beside the River Yare. Behind the roadside brick house rambles an eyecatching half-timbered cottage, complete with bulging walls, wooden floors and log fires. Leather sofas and a vaguely rustic mix of furnishings add to the charm which attracts customers keen to engage with Pamela and Anton Wimmer's enticing menu of pub favourites and something that little bit special. The busy kitchen team relies on East Anglian suppliers for virtually all the ingredients; grilled pigeon breast, salted popcorn, sweetcorn purée and toasted seeds is a typically uplifting starter. There's plenty of seafood on the monthly-changing menu – witness the steamed salmon with warm salad of green beans, courgettes and peas. Gluten free options and daily specials add to the choices.

Open all day Closed Sun eve Oct-Mar **Food** Lunch Mon-Sat 12-2, Sun 12-4, summer Sun 12-3 Dinner Mon-Sat 5.30-9, summer Sun 6-9 ⊕ FREE HOUSE ◀ Adnams Southwold Bitter & Broadside, Woodforde's Wherry, Guest ale ♂ Aspall. ♟ 11 **Facilities** Non-diners area ❀ (Bar Garden) ♦ Children's menu Children's portions Garden ⊟ Parking WiFi ◛ (notice required)

BLAKENEY
Map 13 TG04

The Blakeney White Horse
PICK OF THE PUBS

tel: 01263 740574 **4 High St NR25 7AL**
email: hello@blakeneywhitehorse.co.uk
dir: *From A148 (Cromer to King's Lynn road) onto A149 signed to Blakeney*

Popular pub in fishing village

Since the 17th century, this former coaching inn has been tucked away among Blakeney's flint-built fishermen's cottages, a short, steepish amble up from the small tidal harbour. The tastefully appointed, Adnams-stocked bar is stylish yet informal, the conservatory naturally bright – both are eating areas, where the same menu and daily specials apply. Locally sourced food is a given, especially the lobster, crab and mussels from village fishermen, meats and game from Norfolk estates, soft fruit, salads, asparagus and free-range eggs from local smallholders, while rod- and line-caught mackerel and sea bass find their way through the kitchen door in summer. On the lunch menu there'll be filled bagels, baguettes and pie of the day. In the evening maybe smoked haddock fishcakes with beetroot rémoulade and poached egg; braised beef brisket with horseradish mash, wilted spinach, sautéed garlic, wild mushrooms and red wine jus; and gooseberry jam crème brûlée.

Open all day all wk 10.30am-11pm **Food** Lunch Mon-Sat 12-2, Sun 12-2.30 Dinner all wk 6.30-9 ⊕ ADNAMS ◀ Southwold Bitter & Broadside, Guest ales ♂ Aspall. ♟ 14 **Facilities** Non-diners area ❀ (Bar Restaurant) ♦ Children's menu Children's portions Family room Outside area ⊟ Parking WiFi

The Kings Arms

tel: 01263 740341 **Westgate St NR25 7NQ**
email: kingsarmsnorfolk@btconnect.com
dir: *From Holt or Fakenham take A148, then B1156 for 6m to Blakeney*

Very old pub in lovely seaside village

Tucked away in a popular fishing village close to north Norfolk's coastal path (Peddars Way), this thriving free house is the perfect refreshment stop following an invigorating walk, time spent birdwatching, or a boat trip to the nearby seal colony. Open all day and run by the same family for almost 40 years, it serves an excellent selection of real ales, including Norfolk-brewed Woodforde's Wherry that is backed by menus featuring locally caught fish and seasonal seafood. Perhaps cod, prawn and bacon chowder; mussels in garlic cream sauce – with braised pheasant with bacon jus; steak and Adnams ale suet pudding; and home-made lasagne.

Open all day all wk Closed 25 Dec eve **Food** 8.30am-9.30pm ⊕ FREE HOUSE ◀ Morland Old Speckled Hen, Woodforde's Wherry, Marston's Pedigree, Adnams Southwold Bitter, Greene King. ♟ 10 **Facilities** Non-diners area ❀ (Bar Restaurant Garden) ♦ Children's menu Children's portions Play area Family room Garden ⊟ Parking WiFi ◛

BRANCASTER
Map 13 TF74

The Ship Hotel

tel: 01485 210333 **Main Rd PE31 8AP**
email: thebar@shiphotelnorfolk.co.uk
dir: *On A149 in village centre*

Nautical pub serving cracking food

Set in a prime coastal location close to Brancaster Beach, TV chef and hotelier Chris Coubrough's stylish gastro-pub continues to attract walkers, beach bums and families with its appealing menus of modern pub food prepared from fresh produce sourced from local farmers and fisherman. Be tempted by wild mushroom and herb gnocchi with baby spinach, truffle oil and shaved parmesan, or trio of Norfolk pheasant with roast vegetable medley. Wash it down with a pint of Bitter Old Bustard or Aspall Harry Sparrow cider and relax in the gorgeous bar and dining rooms, where you can expect rug-strewn wood floors, wood-burning stoves, shelves full of books, quirky antiques, scrubbed wooden tables and a distinct nautical feel.

Open all day all wk **Food** Lunch 12-2.30 (school holidays, menu available 3-6) Dinner 6-9 ⊕ FREE HOUSE/FLYING KIWI INNS ◀ Jo C's Norfolk Kiwi & Bitter Old Bustard, Adnams Southwold Bitter ♂ Aspall Harry Sparrow. ♟ 19 **Facilities** Non-diners area ❀ (Bar Outside area) ♦ Children's menu Children's portions Garden Outside area ⊟ Parking WiFi ◛ (notice required)

BRANCASTER STAITHE
Map 13 TF74

The Jolly Sailors

tel: 01485 210314 **PE31 8BJ**
email: info@jollysailorsbrancaster.co.uk
dir: *On A149 (coast road) midway between Hunstanton & Wells-next-the-Sea*

Children, muddy boots and dogs welcome

Focal point of the village, the 18th-century 'Jolly' is the brewery tap for the Brancaster microbrewery, both being run by father and son team, Cliff and James Nye. In the Harbour Snug you can look out over the water, read local books, and play darts and board games. The Nyes' Brancaster ales aren't obligatory – you'll also find Woodforde's, 13 wines by the glass, a selection of cocktails and 30 rums. Pub food is typified by open-fired pizzas (make-your-own, eat in or take away), plus from the blackboard, deep-fried whitebait; toasted goats' cheese salad; Stilton, spinach and mushroom tagliatelle; and hickory BBQ burgers. The beach-themed ice cream hut in the garden is an attraction in the summer. A beer and music festival is held in June.

Open all wk Mon-Thu 12-3 6-11 Fri 12-3 5-11 Sat 12-11 Sun 12-10.30 (all day spring & summer) Closed 25 Dec **Food** Lunch (winter) Mon-Fri 12-2 (all day spring & summer), Sat-Sun 12-9 Dinner (winter) Mon-Thu 6-9, Fri 5-9 (all day spring & summer), Sat-Sun 12-9 Av main course £10.75 ⊕ FREE HOUSE ◀ Brancaster Best & Oyster Catcher, Woodforde's Wherry ♂ Symonds. ♟ 13 **Facilities** Non-diners area ❀ (Bar Restaurant Garden) ♦ Children's menu Children's portions Play area Garden ⊟ Beer festival Parking WiFi ◛ (notice required)

PICK OF THE PUBS

The George Hotel

CLEY NEXT THE SEA   Map 13 TG04

tel: 01263 740652
High St NR25 7RN
email: info@thegeorgehotelatcley.co.uk
web: www.thegeorgehotelatcley.co.uk
dir: *On A149 through Cley next the Sea, approx 4m from Holt*

Village hostelry popular with birdwatchers

This old hotel has been an ornithological focal point for many years – in fact, it is well-known for its 'bird bible' which records sightings by visiting twitchers. The George's beer garden backs on to the salt marshes of the north Norfolk coast, a renowned paradise for birdwatchers. Now in the capable hands of Polina and Steve Cleeve, the George is a welcoming place, proffering several real ales at the bar, including Yetman's just inland towards Holt. You can snack in the lounge bar or dine in the light, painting-filled restaurant. The daily-changing dishes offer the best of local fresh ingredients, and fish and seafood is a real strength. Starters include soup of the day; Cley smoked haddock chowder; and the Cley deli board. Typical main courses are Allards guest sausages of the week, creamy mashed potato, fine green beans, onion rings

and caramelised onion jus; and risotto of Binham Blue, wild mushrooms and spinach, plus daily specials choices. Desserts like mixed berry pannacotta; and the cheese board, 'A selection from Mrs Temple at Wighton' keep the birdwatchers coming back. They can even bring in their dogs, which are welcome in the bar and front restaurant. With a great choice for children, who get to choose from their own menu, and a roaring open fire in winter, the George's welcome is warm at any time of year. Close by are the famous Cley Windmill and Blakeney Harbour.

Open all day all wk 10.30am-11.30pm
Food Mon-Thu 11.30-9, Fri-Sat 11.30-9.30, Sun 11.30-8.30 Av main course £12.95 ⊕ FREE HOUSE ◀ Greene King Abbot Ale, Woodforde's Wherry, Winter's, Yetman's, Guest ales ♻ Aspall. ♟ 11
Facilities Non-diners area
☙ (Bar Restaurant Garden)
⫰ Children's menu Garden ⋒ Parking WiFi 🚌 (notice required)

BRANCASTER STAITHE *continued*

The White Horse ★★★ HL ◎◎ | PICK OF THE PUBS

tel: 01485 210262 **PE31 8BY**
email: reception@whitehorsebrancaster.co.uk **web:** www.whitehorsebrancaster.co.uk
dir: *A149 (coast road), midway between Hunstanton & Wells-next-the-Sea*

Stylish inn with stunning coastal views

The White Horse offers stunning vistas over glorious tidal marshes across to Scolt Head Island, a four-mile long sandbar that's home to a nature reserve rich in birdlife. Reflecting the view, interior colours are muted and natural, with beach-found objects complemented by contemporary artworks. Scrubbed pine tables and high-backed settles in the bar create a welcoming atmosphere, while alfresco dining in the sunken front garden is a popular warm-weather option, perhaps accompanied by a pint of Adnams Ghost Ship. While the bar menu lists grills, salads and sandwiches, the extensive, daily-changing menu in the airy conservatory restaurant (with two AA Rosettes) champions the freshest local seafood, delivered directly to the kitchen by the fishermen. Typically, pan-seared scallops, curried chickpeas, carrot and golden raisin; or duo of local rabbit loin, tortellini, mushroom tea and Marmite jus, could be followed by pan-roasted grey mullet, herring roe, lentils, capers and caviar butter; or slow cooked porchetta, artichoke, Israeli couscous, kale and jus.

Open all day all wk 11-11 (Sun 12-10.30) (open from 9am for breakfast)
Food Lunch all wk 9-9 Dinner all wk 9-9 Av main course £14 Restaurant menu available all wk ⊕ FREE HOUSE ◀ Adnams Ghost Ship, Woodforde's Wherry, Brancaster Best, Malthouse Bitter & Oyster Catcher, Guest ales ♂ Aspall. ⬥ 14 **Facilities** Non-diners area ♥ (Bar Garden Outside area) ♦♦ Children's menu Children's portions Garden Outside area ⋒ Parking WiFi ☞ (notice required) **Rooms** 15

BURNHAM THORPE | Map 13 TF84

The Lord Nelson | PICK OF THE PUBS

tel: 01328 738241 **Walsingham Rd PE31 8HN**
email: enquiries@nelsonslocal.co.uk **web:** www.nelsonslocal.co.uk
dir: *B1355 (Burnham Market to Fakenham road), pub 9m from Fakenham & 1.75m from Burnham Market*

Soak up over 370 years of atmosphere

This pub started life in 1637 as The Plough and was renamed The Lord Nelson in 1798, to honour Horatio Nelson who was born in the village. Located opposite the delightful village cricket ground and bowling green, it has an atmospheric interior that has changed little over the past 370 plus years; you can even sit on Nelson's high-backed settle. Drinks are served from the taproom, with real ales drawn straight from the cask. In the cosy bar you can also partake in unique rum-based tipples such as Nelson's Blood. The kitchen aims to cook dishes with balance between flavours, so that the quality of the ingredients shines. A typical meal is

farmhouse pâté with toast and red onion marmalade followed by pan-fried salmon in a green herb crust with beurre blanc and duchess potatoes, with apple pie and vanilla ice cream for dessert. Children will enjoy the huge garden. From May to September, weekend walking tours of Nelson's village are available.

Open all wk 12-3 6-11 (Jul-Aug & BHs 12-11) **Food** Lunch all wk 12-2.30 Dinner all wk 6-9 ⊕ GREENE KING ◀ Abbot Ale, Woodforde's Wherry ♂ Aspall. ⬥ 12 **Facilities** Non-diners area ♥ (Bar Garden) ♦♦ Children's menu Play area Garden ⋒ Parking WiFi ☞

BURSTON | Map 13 TM18

The Crown

tel: 01379 741257 **Mill Rd IP22 5TW**
email: enquiries@burstoncrown.com
dir: *NE of Diss*

Very much a locals' pub serving inventive food

Steve and Bev Kembery have transformed their 16th-century pub by the green into a cracking community pub, drawing locals in for top-notch ale and food, organising the village fête, hosting three beer festivals a year, and offering a weekly busker's night and regular theme nights. As well as a decent pint of Adnams, you can tuck into nachos with spicy tomato salsa and melted cheese or 'a very Norfolk platter' charcuterie board. From the à la carte, chicken liver parfait with white port and juniper berries to start perhaps, followed by wild mushroom, spinach and gruyère cheese crêpes; or blackened salmon fillet with mango salsa and rice. A pub well worth seeking out.

Open all day all wk **Food** Lunch Tue-Sat 12-2, Sun 12-4 Dinner Tue-Sat 6.30-9 Av main course £10.50 Restaurant menu available Tue-Sun ⊕ FREE HOUSE ◀ Adnams Southwold Bitter & Old Ale, Elmtree Burston's Cuckoo, Morland Old Speckled Hen, Green Jack Orange Wheat Beer ♂ Aspall. **Facilities** Non-diners area ♥ (Bar Garden) ♦♦ Children's menu Children's portions Play area Garden ⋒ Beer festival Parking WiFi ☞ (notice required)

CLEY NEXT THE SEA | Map 13 TG04

The George Hotel | PICK OF THE PUBS

See Pick of the Pubs on page 349

CROMER | Map 13 TG24

The Red Lion Food and Rooms ★★★★ INN

tel: 01263 514964 **Brook St NR27 9HD**
email: info@redlion-cromer.co.uk **web:** www.redlion-cromer.co.uk
dir: *From A149 into Cromer, on one-way system, pass church on left. 1st left after church into Brook St. Pub on right*

Interesting beers on Norfolk's conservation coastline

A firm fixture of the charming Victorian resort of Cromer, guests can gaze through the inn's front windows directly over the fine beach to the sturdy pier. Fishing boats drawn up on the shingle bank may provide the wherewithal for the pub's renowned seafood dishes – try the fish pie, Norfolk ale battered cod or Cromer crab – whilst sharing platters overflow with produce from Norfolk's generous inland larder. The playful menu has suggestions for wines to accompany dishes, whilst beer-lovers will delight at a choice that includes cutting edge local breweries like Wolf and Cromer's own Poppyland. Sea-views feature from many of the bedrooms.

Open all day all wk **Food** Lunch Mon-Fri 12-2.30, Sat-Sun 12-9.30 Dinner Mon-Fri 6-9.30, Sat-Sun 12-9.30 ⊕ FREE HOUSE ◀ Bees Wobble, Green Jack Lurcher Stout, Woodforde's Nelson's Revenge, Humpty Dumpty Railway Sleeper, Adnams Broadside, Wolf, Poppyland ♂ Westons. ⬥ 14 **Facilities** Non-diners area ♥ (Bar) ♦♦ Children's menu Children's portions Parking WiFi ☞ (notice required) **Rooms** 15

EAST RUSTON   Map 13 TG32

The Butchers Arms

tel: 01692 650237 **Oak Ln NR12 9JG**
email: info@thebutchersarms.biz
dir: *From A149 (SE of North Walsham) follow signs for Briggate, Honing & East Ruston. Oak Ln off School Rd*

Local ale and traditional food

A timeless village pub, without jukebox or pool table but with 'Mavis', a 1954 Comma fire engine, parked outside, this quintessential beamed pub started life as three terraced cottages in the early 1800s. Landlady Julie Oatham has been here for over 25 years, and ensures a welcoming atmosphere. Changing guest ales are offered alongside traditional favourites such as home-made cottage pie; beef chilli and a roast of the day. The desserts change daily but are of the comforting, traditional type. There is a beer garden and vine-covered patio for summer dining.

Open 12-2.30 6.30-11 Closed Mon (Sep-Jun) Food Lunch all wk 12-2 Dinner all wk 7-8.30 ⊕ FREE HOUSE ◀ Guest ales Ô Somersby Cider. Facilities Non-diners area ❀ (Bar Garden) ♦ Children's menu Children's portions Garden ⏚ Parking WiFi ➡ (notice required) Notes ⊛

EATON   Map 13 TG20

The Red Lion

tel: 01603 454787 **50 Eaton St NR4 7LD**
email: admin@redlion-eaton.co.uk
dir: *Off A11, 2m S of Norwich city centre*

The menus offer a seemingly endless choice

This heavily beamed 17th-century coaching inn has bags of character, thanks to its Dutch gable ends, panelled walls, suit of armour and inglenook fireplaces. The covered terrace enables customers to enjoy one of the real ales or a glass of wine outside during the summer months. Everyone will find something that appeals on the extensive menus, which include plenty of fish options: pan-fried fillet of brill with roasted shellfish bisque sauce; chargilled swordfish loin with avocado and sun-dried tomato salad; and non-piscatorian dishes like teriyaki glazed pork loin ribs with coleslaw and corn on the cob; or slow-baked Swannington lamb shoulder kleftico style. There's a light meals and snack menu too.

Open all day all wk Food Lunch all wk 12-2.15 Dinner all wk 6.30-9 ◀ Adnams Southwold Bitter, Woodforde's Wherry, Fuller's London Pride Ô Aspall. ⏺ 10 Facilities Non-diners area ♦ Children's portions Garden Parking WiFi

FAKENHAM   Map 13 TF92

The Wensum Lodge Hotel

tel: 01328 862100 **Bridge St NR21 9AY**
email: enquiries@wensumlodge.fsnet.co.uk
dir: *In town centre*

Idyllic riverside hostelry with fishing

Dating from around 1700, this building was originally the grain store for the adjoining mill idyllically located by the River Wensum. Just three minutes' walk from Fakenham, this lovely place has a stream flowing through its garden and offers guests free fishing on the river. An ideal base for cycling, birdwatching, fishing and horse racing, the pub serves a range of real ales are complemented by home-cooked food, with baguettes, jacket potatoes and an all-day breakfast on the

light bite menu. From the carte menu, a typical meal might start with garlic mushrooms and follow with home-made cottage pie.

Open all day all wk Food Lunch all wk 12-3 Dinner all wk 6.30-9 Set menu available Restaurant menu available all wk ⊕ FREE HOUSE ◀ Greene King Abbot Ale & IPA, Old Mill Traditional Bitter, Adnams, Elmtree Beers Ô Thatchers Gold. Facilities Non-diners area ❀ (Bar Garden Outside area) ♦ Children's menu Children's portions Garden Outside area ⏚ Parking WiFi ➡

GREAT HOCKHAM   Map 13 TL99

NEW The Eagle

tel: 01953 498893 **Harling Rd IP24 1NR**
email: mail@hockhameagle.com
dir: *From Thetford take A1075 to Great Hockham. Right into Harling Road. Pub on left*

Good choice of beer and classic pub grub

A traditional country pub in the picturesque village of Great Hockham, close to Thetford Forest and just 10 minutes from the motor racing circuit at Snetterton. Children and dogs are welcome and as well as seating out the front there's an enclosed rear courtyard. The bars serve five real ales, including Woodforde's Wherry and Morland Old Speckled Hen as well as rotating guest ales. Classic pub food is what's on the menu – Sheringham steak and ale pie; ham, egg and chips, or lasagne. There's a weekly-changing specials board, and you can 'build your own burger' from a selection including pork and apple.

Open all wk 12-2.30 6-11 (Fri-Sat 12-12 Sun 12-10.30) Food Lunch Mon-Thu 12-2, Fri 12-9, Sat-Sun 12-7 Dinner Fri 12-9, Sat-Sun 12-7 ⊕ FREE HOUSE ◀ Adnams Southwold Bitter, Woodforde's Wherry, Morland Old Speckled Hen, Greene King Abbot Ale, Guest ale. Facilities Non-diners area ❀ (Bar Outside area) ♦ Children's menu Children's portions Outside area ⏚ Parking WiFi

GREAT MASSINGHAM   Map 13 TF72

The Dabbling Duck

tel: 01485 520827 **11 Abbey Rd PE32 2HN**
email: info@thedabblingduck.co.uk
dir: *From King's Lynn take either A148 or B1145 then follow Great Massingham signs. Or from Fakenham take A148 signed King's Lynn. Or from Swaffham take A1065 towards Cromer, then B1145 signed King's Lynn*

Stylish village-owned inn

The Dabbling Duck on Great Massingham's glorious green thrives as a community local and a stylish inn. Head for the high-backed settles by the raised log fire to peruse the papers with pork scratchings and apple ketchup and a pint of Woodforde's Wherry, Adnams Broadside or Aspall cider. Then move to a scrubbed table in one of the comfortably rustic dining areas, or the garden, and choose pearl barley carbonara, ham and cured back fat; or salt hake Scotch egg, sardine ketchup and n'duja mayonnaise to start, followed by cod, 'Norwich' carrot, sea buckthorn, nasturtium and cobnuts; or Dingley Dell pork belly, piccalilli purée, carrots, cauliflower, apple and cucumber. There are shelves groaning with books and board games, rugs on tiled floors and the atmosphere is informal and relaxed. Everything adds up to create a cracking village pub.

Open all day all wk 8am-11pm Food Lunch all wk 12-2.30 Dinner Mon-Thu & Sun 6.30-9, Fri-Sat 6-9.30 Av main course £12 ⊕ FREE HOUSE ◀ Woodforde's Wherry, Beeston Worth the Wait, Adnams Broadside Ô Aspall, Thatchers. Facilities Non-diners area ❀ (Bar Garden Outside area) ♦ Children's menu Children's portions Play area Garden Outside area ⏚ Parking WiFi ➡ (notice required)

GREAT RYBURGH   Map 13 TF92

The Blue Boar Inn

tel: 01328 829212 **NR21 0DX**
email: eat@blueboar-norfolk.co.uk
dir: *From Fakenham take A1067 towards Norwich. Approx 4m right to Great Ryburgh*

Good food in pretty Wensum Valley inn

Lots to see at this character, listed village inn; beyond the beer garden is a notable round-towered medieval church (once linked to the pub by a secret tunnel), whilst inside are quarry-tile floors, beams and a vast inglenook, spread through a jumble of levels marking alterations to this popular local pub over the centuries. It was used as a recruiting station during the Napoleonic Wars; all that's required of today's visitors is to enjoy the local Yetman's beers and indulge the richly varied, Norfolk-based menu, which may include cassoulet of chicken leg and sausage, or pot roast half guinea fowl.

Open 6-11 (Sun 12-6) Closed Tue **Food** Lunch Sun 12-4.30 Dinner Wed-Sat & Mon 6.30-9 ⊕ FREE HOUSE ◀ Adnams Southwold Bitter, Winter's Golden & Revenge, Staropramen, Yetman's, Guinness ♂ Addlestones, Westons Stowford Press, Aspall. ♈ 8 **Facilities** Non-diners area ♦♦ Children's menu Children's portions Play area Family room Garden ⊟ Parking WiFi ▰

HEVINGHAM   Map 13 TG12

Marsham Arms Coaching Inn

tel: 01603 754268 **Holt Rd NR10 5NP**
email: info@marshamarms.co.uk
dir: *On B1149 (N of Norwich Airport), 2m, through Horsford towards Holt*

Charming inn serving ales from the taproom

Victorian philanthropist and landowner Robert Marsham built the Marsham Arms as a roadside hostel for poor farm labourers, and some original features, including the wooden beams and large open fireplace are still evident. Real ales are served straight from the barrel. The seasonal menu uses fresh local produce and there are always vegetarian and gluten-free options; there's fish and grill nights and regular music evenings too. The spacious garden has a paved patio. The inn holds a Green Tourism award.

Open all day all wk **Food** Lunch Mon-Fri 12-2.30, Sat-Sun all day Dinner Mon-Fri 6-9, Sat-Sun all day ⊕ FREE HOUSE ◀ Adnams Southwold Bitter & Broadside, Woodforde's Wherry, Mauldons, Grain Best Bitter, Humpty Dumpty ♂ Aspall. ♈ **Facilities** Non-diners area ♣ (Bar Restaurant Garden) ♦♦ Children's menu Children's portions Garden ⊟ Parking WiFi ▰ (notice required)

HEYDON   Map 13 TG12

Earle Arms

tel: 01263 587376 **The Street NR11 6AD**
email: theearlearms@gmail.com
dir: *Signed between Cawston & Corpusty on B1149 (Holt to Norwich road)*

One for fans of the turf

"H", the landlord and chef, is responsible for the horseracing memorabilia throughout this 16th-century, Dutch-gabled free house on the village green. As part-owner of a racehorse, he will gladly give you a tip, but says it's probably best not to go nap on it. The privately owned conservation village of Heydon is often used for filming, and many a star of the big and small screen has enjoyed the Earle's off-the-pier-fresh seafood; fillet of beef Marchand de Vin with vegetables; mixed bean chilli with rice; and game stew. A beer festival is held on St George's Day (23rd April).

Open 11-3 6-11 (Sun all day) Closed Mon **Food** Lunch Tue-Sun 12-2 Dinner Tue-Sun 6-8.30 Av main course £11 Restaurant menu available Tue-Sun ⊕ FREE HOUSE ◀ Woodforde's Wherry, Adnams, Guest ales ♂ Addlestones. ♈ 16 **Facilities** Non-diners area ♦♦ Children's menu Children's portions Garden ⊟ Beer festival Parking WiFi ▰

HINGHAM   Map 13 TG00

The White Hart Hotel

tel: 01953 850214 **3 Market Place NR9 4AF**
email: whitehart@flyingkiwiinns.co.uk
dir: *In market square on B1108*

Food that focuses on the larder of East Anglia

A tasteful blend of chic contemporary design and a nod to 'the rustic', characterises this upmarket village inn, an imposing Georgian building at the heart of pretty Hingham. Quirky additions – note the antler chandelier – add a colourful twist to this, one of chef Chris Coubrough's stable of inns. Chris's wife Jo adds further to this eclectic mix with tasty beers from her microbrewery near Fakenham. The menu is equally diverse; start with avocado, pickled walnut and sun-blushed tomato salad, and follow with apricot and chorizo stuffed fillet of pork; or fresh seafood linguine.

Open all day all wk **Food** Lunch all wk 12-2.30 Dinner all wk 6.30-9.30 ⊕ FREE HOUSE ◀ Adnams Southwold Bitter, Jo C's Norfolk Kiwi, Guest ale ♂ Aspall. ♈ **Facilities** ♣ (Bar) ♦♦ Children's menu Children's portions Garden Outside area ⊟ WiFi ▰ (notice required)

HOLT   Map 13 TG03

The Pigs   `PICK OF THE PUBS`

See Pick of the Pubs on opposite page

HUNSTANTON   Map 12 TF64

The Ancient Mariner Inn ★★★★ HL

tel: 01485 536390 **Golf Course Rd, Old Hunstanton PE36 6JJ**
email: gm@lestrangearms.co.uk **web:** www.traditionalinns.co.uk
dir: *Exit A149, 1m N of Hunstanton. Turn left at sharp right bend by pitch & putt course*

Coastal setting with great views and local walks

Summer evenings can be spectacular here; when the sun sets across the sands of The Wash, the light matches the golds of the real ales enjoyed by drinkers in the peaceful gardens, up to seven beers may be on tap. Equally enticing is the menu of modern pub classics such as Cumberland sausage ring or braised lamb shank; daily fish specials boost the choice. The appealing flint and brick inn is creatively incorporated into the stable block of a Victorian hotel, the stylish rooms of which are popular with visitors to the beautiful Norfolk Coast Area of Outstanding Natural Beauty.

Open all day all wk **Food** Lunch all wk 12-9 Dinner all wk 12-9 Av main course £10 ⊕ FREE HOUSE ◀ Adnams, Theakston, Wychwood, Shepherd Neame, Sharp's, Woodforde's ♂ Symonds. ♈ 10 **Facilities** Non-diners area ♣ (Bar Garden) ♦♦ Children's menu Children's portions Play area Family room Garden ⊟ Beer festival Parking WiFi ▰ (notice required) **Rooms** 43

PICK OF THE PUBS

The Pigs

HOLT   Map 13 TG03

tel: 01263 587634 **Norwich Rd, Edgefield NR24 2RL**
email: info@thepigs.org.uk
web: www.thepigs.org.uk
dir: *From Norwich A140 (Airport). Pass airport on right, left onto B1149 at rdbt. Approx 16m to Edgefield*

Bustling village local with pig-inspired menus

Bought by three ambitious co-owners nearly ten years ago, this 17th-century country inn on the edge of a lovely village has been transformed into a thriving local and celebration of all things Norfolk, both on the plate and in the glass. The lovely tranquil setting at the fringe of the village allows for a peaceful garden, whilst locals barter their fresh fruit and vegetables over the bar for a pint or two, practise darts or bar billiards and quaff the Old Spot bitter brewed by local Wolf Brewery — what else. An impressively versatile menu emerges from the kitchen, utilising forgotten cuts of locally sourced meat and produce from the pub's adjoining allotment. If it's genuine 'nose to tail' dining you're looking for, the Honey, Colman's mustard and marmalade glazed pork ribs, followed by the slow-cooked belly of pork with smoky bacon beans, apple chutney, black pudding and crackling should fit the bill. Tapas-style starters called 'Iffits'

include deep-fried 'popcorn' cockles, and a Kilner jar of potted pork which are ideal for sharing. If pork-based treats aren't your thing, then venison faggots with roast chestnut and leek mash; or East coast mussels with Old Spot ale, leeks, parsley sauce and bread to dunk may tempt, along with fish options such as deep-fried line-caught haddock, mushy peas, beef dripping chips and tartare sauce. Leek, wild mushroom and pine nut pot barley stew is one of the meat-free choices. Leave room for one of the tempting desserts, perhaps cinnamon rice crumble with vanilla shortbread. A children's cookery school proves popular.

Open all day all wk 8am-11pm
Food Lunch Mon-Sat 12-2.30, Sun & BH

12-9 Dinner Mon-Sat 6-9, Sun & BHs 12-9 Av main course £12-£15 ⊕ FREE HOUSE 🍺 Woodforde's Wherry, Greene King Abbot Ale, Wolf Old Spot, Adnams Broadside & Southwold Bitter ♻ Aspall 🍷 17 **Facilities** Non-diners area 🐾 (Bar Outside area) 👶 Children's menu Children's portions Play area Family room Outside area 🎪 Parking WiFi 🚌 (notice required)

HUNSTANTON *continued*

The King William IV Country Inn & Restaurant

tel: 01485 571765 **Heacham Rd, Sedgeford PE36 5LU**
email: info@thekingwilliamsedgeford.co.uk
dir: *A149 to Hunstanton, right at Norfolk Lavender in Heacham onto B1454, signed Docking. 2m to Sedgeford*

Food and drink to please all tastes

Tucked away in the village of Sedgeford, this free house has been an inn for over 175 years. It's conveniently close to the north Norfolk coastline and the Peddars Way. Made cosy by winter log fires, it has four dining areas, plus a covered alfresco terrace where you may enjoy a local crab salad in the summer months. You'll find five real ales on tap, and extensive menus (including one for vegetarians) to please everyone: shredded confit of duck leg or breaded plaice goujons for starters, and steak and Adnams Ale pie; or pan-fried monkfish with scallops to follow. Events include quiz Mondays, curry Tuesdays and piano Fridays.

Open all day 11-11 (Sun 12-10.30) Closed Mon L (ex BHs) **Food** Lunch Tue-Sat 12-2, Sun 12-2.30 Dinner all wk 6.30-9 Set menu available Restaurant menu available all wk ⊕ FREE HOUSE ◛ Woodforde's Wherry, Adnams Southwold Bitter, Greene King Abbot Ale, Morland Old Speckled Hen, Guest ale Ò Aspall Harry Sparrow. ♟ 9 **Facilities** Non-diners area ✿ (Bar Garden) ♦ Children's menu Children's portions Family room Garden ⊨ Parking WiFi ⛟ (notice required)

| HUNWORTH | Map 13 TG03 |

The Hunny Bell — PICK OF THE PUBS

tel: 01263 712300 **The Green NR24 2AA**
email: hunnybell@hotmail.com
dir: *From Holt take B1110. 1st right to Hunworth*

Old, charming and tranquil

Just a few miles from Norfolk's heritage coastline, this 18th-century village pub acquired new owners in 2014. The change was virtually seamless, for the new leaseholders are Sean and Penny Chapman; Penny having already been the pub and restaurant manager. In addition, other staff, including 'infamous Phil', with over 20 years behind the bar, have happily stayed on. Well-behaved dogs are welcome in the wooden-floored bar, where Hunny Bell and other East Anglian real ales and cider are served; good spots to drink them are the colourful garden, or the patio overlooking the elongated village green. Meals make optimum use of Norfolk's seafood and other produce for seasonal menus, an example listing dressed Cromer crab; pan-roasted pheasant breast with turnips and sautéed girolles; honey-roast ham with free-range eggs; and beetroot tarte Tatin with Binham Blue cheese and candied walnut salad.

Open all wk 12-3 6-11 (Fri-Sat 12-3 6-12) **Food** Lunch all wk 12-2 Dinner all wk 6-9 Av main course £7.50-£15 Set menu available Restaurant menu available all wk ⊕ FREE HOUSE/COPPERBEECH INNS LTD ◛ Woodforde's Wherry, Adnams, Greene King & Abbot Ale, Hunny Bell Cask Ale, Guest ales Ò Aspall. ♟ 10 **Facilities** Non-diners area ✿ (Bar Garden Outside area) ♦ Children's menu Children's portions Garden Outside area ⊨ Beer festival Parking ⛟ (notice required)

| INGHAM | Map 13 TG32 |

The Ingham Swan ★★★★ RR ⊛⊛ — PICK OF THE PUBS

tel: 01692 581099 **Swan Corner, Sea Palling Rd NR12 9AB**
email: info@theinghamswan.co.uk **web:** www.theinghamswan.co.uk
dir: *From A149 through Stalham to Ingham*

Picture-postcard dining inn

From the tiny village of Ingham you can follow meandering lanes to the nearby Norfolk Coast Area of Outstanding Natural Beauty and a string of broadland nature

reserves, renowned for rare birds. Before you head off though, you should check out The Swan. This ancient, flint-built pub and the majestic church that adjoins it are all that survive of the once-flourishing Ingham Priory. Slumbering beneath trim thatch, the inn was carefully transformed into a destination dining pub and restaurant a few years back, but drinkers are always welcome at the bar for real ales from the local Grain Brewery. Chef-patron Daniel Smith trained at Le Gavroche in London and Blakeney's Morston Hall, and he sticks to his Norfolk roots with an award-winningly creative, modern menu, packed with seasonal local produce. A lazy lunch could start with chicken liver parfait with fig chutney and celeriac remoulade, followed by chorizo roast salmon, or sea salt crackling belly pork with curly kale, fennel duxelle, crispy pork fritter and cocotte potatoes. The menu includes useful matching wine suggestions.

Open all wk 11-3 6-11 Closed 25-26 Dec **Food** Lunch Mon-Sat 12-2, Sun 12-3 Dinner all wk 6-9 Set menu available Restaurant menu available all wk ⊕ FREE HOUSE ◛ Woodforde's Wherry, Nelson's Revenge, Grain Oak & Redwood Ò Aspall. ♟ 10 **Facilities** Non-diners area ♦ Children's portions Garden ⊨ Parking ⛟ (notice required) **Rooms** 4

| ITTERINGHAM | Map 13 TG13 |

The Walpole Arms

tel: 01263 587258 **NR11 7AR**
email: info@thewalpolearms.co.uk **web:** www.thewalpolearms.co.uk
dir: *From Aylsham towards Blickling. After Blickling Hall take 1st right to Itteringham*

Dining pub with inventive food

Owned by a local farming family, this renowned rural dining venue is tucked away down narrow lanes on the edge of sleepy Itteringham, close to the National Trust's Blickling Hall. Its oak-beamed bar offers local Woodforde's and Adnams ales on tap, while menus champion top-notch meats and produce from the family farm and local artisan producers. Typical dishes include roast pheasant breast, carrots and lentil casserole; pan-fried stone bass, smoked haddock fishcake and mussel velouté; and open ravioli with creamy wild mushrooms, basil pesto and spinach. Leave room for baked Alaska; sticky toffee pudding; or chocolate mousse with cinnamon doughnuts.

Open all wk 12-3 6-11 (Sat 12-11 Sun 12-5) **Food** Lunch Mon-Sat 12-2.30, Sun 12-3 Dinner Mon-Sat 6-9.15 Set menu available ⊕ FREE HOUSE ◛ Adnams Broadside & Southwold Bitter, Woodforde's Wherry, Guest ales Ò Aspall. ♟ 20 **Facilities** Non-diners area ✿ (Bar Garden) ♦ Children's menu Children's portions Garden ⊨ Parking WiFi ⛟ (notice required)

KING'S LYNN
Map 12 TF62

The Stuart House Hotel, Bar & Restaurant

tel: 01553 772169 **35 Goodwins Rd PE30 5QX**
email: reception@stuarthousehotel.co.uk
dir: *Follow signs to town centre, pass under Southgate Arch, immediate right, in 100yds turn right*

Small, independent free house

In a central, but nevertheless quiet location, this place, in attractive grounds, is one of the town's favoured eating and drinking places. Top-notch East Anglian ales and traditional snacks are served in the bar, and there's a separate restaurant menu typically featuring Norfolk sausages with creamy mash and red onion gravy; pan-fried fillet of sea bass with herbed sauté potatoes; sweet chilli beef with noodles; and vegetable Kiev with garlic butter sauce. Daily specials, like everything else, are home cooked from fresh local produce. Events include regular live music, murder mystery dinners and a July beer festival.

Open all wk 5-11 **Food** Dinner all wk 6-9.30 Av main course £9.95 ⊕ FREE HOUSE ◀ Oakham Ales JHB, Timothy Taylor Landlord, Adnams, Woodforde's Ö Aspall. **Facilities** Non-diners area ❖ (Bar Garden) Children's portions Play area Garden Beer festival Parking WiFi ▄ (notice required)

LARLING
Map 13 TL98

Angel Inn
PICK OF THE PUBS

tel: 01953 717963 **NR16 2QU**
email: info@angel-larling.co.uk
dir: *5m from Attleborough; 8m from Thetford*

Family-run inn with a range of ales and enjoyable food

On the edge of Breckland and Thetford Forest Park, this 17th-century former coaching inn has been run for more than 80 years by three generations of the Stammers family and has a good local feel and warm welcome. In the beamed public bar, a jukebox, dartboard and fruit machine add to the traditional feel, while the oak-panelled lounge bar has dining tables with cushioned wheel-back chairs, a wood-burner and a collection of water jugs. Five ales, including Crouch Vale Brewers Gold, are served, as well as more than a hundred whiskies. Menus make good use of local ingredients, with lighter snacks including sandwiches, jacket potatoes, ploughman's, burgers and salads. Typically among the mains are poached salmon fillet topped with mushrooms, chicken korma, sweet pepper lasagne or chicken and mushroom Stroganoff. Look out for the August festival, with over 100 real ales.

Open all day all wk 10am-mdnt **Food** Lunch Sun-Thu 12-9.30, Fri-Sat 12-10 Dinner Sun-Thu 12-9.30, Fri-Sat 12-10 Av main course £11.95 Set menu available ⊕ FREE HOUSE ◀ Adnams Southwold Bitter, Crouch Vale Brewers Gold, Timothy Taylor Landlord, Mauldons, Hop Back Ö Aspall. ♀ 10 **Facilities** Non-diners area ♦ Children's menu Children's portions Play area Garden Beer festival Parking WiFi ▄

LETHERINGSETT
Map 13 TG03

The Kings Head
PICK OF THE PUBS

tel: 01263 712691 **Holt Rd NR25 7AR**
email: info@kingsheadnorfolk.co.uk
dir: *On A148, 1m from Holt. Pub on corner*

Vintage-chic gastro-pub recommended for its outdoor areas

From the outside this looks to be a grand, manor-like building, but step through the door to find elegant, rustic-chic decor throughout the rambling dining areas that radiate from the central bar, with warm heritage hues, rugs on terracotta tiles, feature bookcases, an eclectic mix of old dining tables, and squashy sofas and leather chairs fronting blazing winter log fires. The atmosphere is informal, the beer on tap is Woodforde's Wherry, and the modern British food is prepared from top-notch ingredients supplied by local farmers, fisherman and artisan producers. This translates to pub favourites such as venison casserole with herb dumplings and champ mash; wild mushroom and baby spinach risotto with truffle oil and parmesan; and a 10oz chargrilled rump steak with garlic butter and fries. This gastro-pub has superb alfresco areas including an excellent children's garden and a gravelled front terrace with benches and brollies.

Open all day all wk 11-11 **Food** Lunch all wk 12-2.30, BHs all day Dinner Mon-Sat 6.30-9.30, Sun 6.30-8, BHs all day ⊕ FREE HOUSE ◀ Adnams, Norfolk Moon Gazer, Woodforde's Wherry, Guest ales Ö Aspall. ♀ 14 **Facilities** Non-diners area ❖ (Bar Restaurant Garden) ♦ Children's menu Children's portions Play area Garden Parking WiFi ▄

MARSHAM
Map 13 TG12

The Plough Inn
PICK OF THE PUBS

tel: 01263 735000 **Norwich Rd NR10 5PS**
email: enquires@ploughinnmarsham.co.uk
dir: *On A140, 10m N of Norwich, 1m S of Aylsham*

Countryside inn specialising in gluten- and wheat-free dishes

Whether you're touring the Norfolk Broads or on your way to Norwich Airport six miles away, the welcome at this 18th-century country hostelry will be warm, and experienced staff will ensure you enjoy your visit. Greene King IPA and Adnams are the ales on offer, together with a good range of wines. The restaurant uses local and seasonal produce if possible; the varied menus of modern British favourites are prepared in house, and wheat- and gluten-free meals are a speciality. The range of lunchtime sandwiches, jacket potatoes and omelettes offer fillings to suit every palate. Tasty starters are home-made focaccia with olives, and chicken liver pâté. Main courses range from sirloin steak Stroganoff to fillet of salmon with a leek and potato cake, vegetables and a white wine sauce. Children are well catered for with their own menu. The carvery is popular on Sundays.

Open all wk 12-11 **Food** Lunch all wk 12-2.30 Dinner all wk 6-9 Set menu available ⊕ FREE HOUSE ◀ Greene King IPA, Adnams, John Smith's Ö Aspall. ♀ 10 **Facilities** Non-diners area ♦ Children's menu Children's portions Garden Parking WiFi ▄ (notice required)

Silver Stars The AA Silver Star rating denotes a Hotel or B&B that we highly recommend. They have a superior level of quality within their star rating, high standards of hospitality, service and cleanliness.

MUNDFORD

Map 13 TL89

Crown Hotel

tel: 01842 878233 **Crown Rd IP26 5HQ**
email: info@the-crown-hotel.co.uk web: www.the-crown-hotel.co.uk
dir: *A11 to Barton Mills onto A1065 through Brandon to Mundford*

By the small but perfectly formed village green

Roofed with traditional Norfolk pantiles, this historic inn on the edge of Thetford Forest dates from 1652. Originally a hunting lodge, it has also served as a magistrate's court. Today it's a popular pub with two restaurants, the Old Court and the Club Room, whose menus might propose pan-fried sea bass fillets with lemon and crayfish cream; slow-braised Cornish lamb shank in redcurrant and herb sauce; and three-cheese tortellini. In addition to Woodforde's Wherry, guest ales and wines by the glass, the bars stock over 50 malt whiskies. The pub being on a slight rise, the garden is at first-floor level.

Open all day all wk 10.30am-mdnt **Food** Lunch all wk 12-3 Dinner all wk 6.30-10 Av main course £12.95 ⊕ FREE HOUSE ◄ Courage Directors, Greene King Ruddles County, Hardys & Hansons Olde Trip, Woodforde's Wherry, Guest ales. ♀ 9 **Facilities** Non-diners area ❀ (Bar Garden) ◀◀ Children's portions Garden ⊓ Parking WiFi ▦

NORWICH

Map 13 TG20

Adam & Eve

tel: 01603 667423 **Bishopsgate NR3 1RZ**
email: theadamandeve@hotmail.com
dir: *Behind Anglican Cathedral, adjacent to Law Courts*

Historic city-centre bolt hole

This enchanting, brick-and-flint built inn sits beneath trees at the fringe of the grounds of Norwich's Anglican Cathedral, the builders of which lodged at the pub, licensed since 1249. It's a refreshing step back in time, free of electronic diversions whilst rich with beers from Woodforde's and Wolf breweries; spirits here include ghosts of lingering, long-gone former locals. Who can blame them when the food is as rewarding as the ales; visitors resting on a tour of Norwich's finest can expect no-nonsense quality pub classics like filled large Yorkshire pudding, trawlerman's pie, home-made curry or chilli. The hanging basket displays are stunning.

Open all day all wk 11-11 (Sun 12-10.30) Closed 25-26 Dec, 1 Jan **Food** Lunch Mon-Sat 12-7, Sun 12-5 Dinner Mon-Sat 12-7 Av main course £9 ⊕ ENTERPRISE INNS ◄ Adnams Southwold Bitter, Theakston Old Peculier, Wolf Golden Jackal, Woodforde's Sundew ♂ Aspall. ♀ 11 **Facilities** Outside area ⊓ Parking WiFi ▦ (notice required)

The Mad Moose Arms

PICK OF THE PUBS

tel: 01603 627687 **2 Warwick St NR2 3LD**
email: madmoose@animalinns.co.uk
dir: *1m from A11*

A bustling neighbourhood gastro-pub

Belonging to the Animal Inns group (The Wildebeest in Stoke Holy Cross is another), the Mad Moose dates back to the late 1800s. It stands at the apex of two streets lined with terraced housing within Norwich's Golden Triangle, a cosmopolitan mix of students, professionals and families. Its two bars, one on the ground floor, another upstairs, where you'll also find a smart dining room, are popular with locals, of which there are many. One reason for this is the reliability of the good selection of well-kept local and not-so-local real and craft ales, premium lagers and Aspall cider. Applying throughout is a seasonal menu offering plenty of choice: smoked mackerel and parsley parfait; spicy barbecued chicken wings and fries; Norfolk sausages topped with brie; cod loin with curly kale; and wild mushroom linguine carbonara, for example. Outside is a stylish patio. The pub football team plays in the Norwich Sunday League.

Open all day all wk 12-12 **Food** Lunch all wk 12-5 Dinner all wk 5-9 ⊕ FREE HOUSE/ ANIMAL INNS ◄ Banks's Bitter, Ringwood Boondoggle, Wychwood Hobgoblin, Banks's Sunbeam, Greene King Abbot Ale, Lacons Legacy ♂ Aspall. ♀ 10 **Facilities** Non-diners area ❀ (Bar Garden) ◀◀ Children's portions Garden ⊓ Beer festival WiFi ▦ (notice required)

The Reindeer Pub & Kitchen

PICK OF THE PUBS

tel: 01603 612995 **10 Dereham Rd NR2 4AY**
email: enquiries@thereindeerpub.co.uk
dir: *Phone for detailed directions*

Gastro-pub where real ales share star billing with food

Dan and Katie Searle say they focus on the food as much as the beer, although there are still more than 20 ales on offer. Chef Gary Steward is passionate about British produce and you can expect to find anything from duck hearts, pickled blueberries, fennel and wild rice to Norfolk pheasant, fig, artichoke and mushroom on the menu. Also available all day is a tapas and bar snack menu including home-made Swannington pork crackling; plates of British cured meats and cheeses; and beer-battered whitebait. Leave room for desserts such as chocolate and ginger truffle with white chocolate and thyme ice cream and chocolate mousse; or ginger, orange, Yorkshire rhubarb tart and rhubarb ice cream. Wash it all down with one of several real ales from breweries such as Dark Star and Elgood's. Look out for the summer beer festival.

Open all day Closed Mon **Food** Lunch Tue-Sat 12-3, Sun 12-8 Dinner Tue-Sat 6-10, Sun 12-8 Av main course £14 ⊕ ELGOOD'S & SONS ◄ Elgood's, Dark Star, Thornbridge, Green Jack, Humpty Dumpty, Magic Rock ♂ Westons & Bounds, The Orchard Pig. ♀ 12 **Facilities** Non-diners area ❀ (Bar Garden) ◀◀ Children's menu Children's portions Garden ⊓ Beer festival Parking WiFi ▦ (notice required)

Ribs of Beef

tel: 01603 619517 **24 Wensum St NR3 1HY**
email: roger@cawdron.co.uk
dir: *From Tombland (in front of cathedral) turn left at Maids Head Hotel. Pub 200yds on right on bridge*

City centre local with cask ales and river views

On record as an alehouse back in the 18th century, this building has been used variously as an antiques shop, electrical store and fashion boutique, before Roger and Anthea Cawdron relicensed in the mid 1980s. The pub is popular for its range of cask ales, excellent wines, traditional English food using locally sourced produce and comfy leather seats. Breakfast is available until midday and there's live music on Thursday and Saturdays. The varied menus offer hearty choices like beef and ale stew; a bowl of chilli; and sausage platter alongside sandwiches, wedges, burgers and jacket potatoes. Sit outside on the jetty during the warmer months and enjoy the fabulous river views.

Open all day all wk 11-11 (Fri-Sat 11am-1am) **Food** Lunch Mon-Fri 12-2.30, Sat-Sun 12-5 Av main course £8 ⊕ FREE HOUSE ◄ Woodforde's Wherry, Adnams Ghost Ship, Oakham JHB, Fuller's London Pride, Wolf Golden Jackal ♂ Kingfisher Norfolk Cider, Lilley's Bee Sting Still Perry. ♥ 9 **Facilities** Non-diners area ♣ (Bar Garden Outside area) ♦♦ Children's menu Children's portions Family room Garden Outside area ⋈ WiFi ▬ (notice required)

SALTHOUSE · Map 13 TG04

The Salthouse Dun Cow

tel: 01263 740467 **Coast Rd NR25 7XA**
email: salthouseduncow@gmail.com
dir: On A149 (coast road). 3m E of Blakeney, 6m W of Sheringham

An ideal retreat overlooking salt marsh scenery

In a quiet coastal village within an Area of Outstanding Natural Beauty, this traditional brick and flint pub probably originated as a cattle barn built around 1650. Today it overlooks some of Britain's finest salt marshes, so expect to share it, particularly the front garden, with birdwatchers and walkers. The interior decor seems to reflect the surrounding farmland and seascapes with brick walls, bare floorboards and a wood-burning stove. Local suppliers provide high quality produce for select menus prepared from scratch, especially fresh shellfish and game from local shoots. Samphire, asparagus and soft fruit are all sourced within five miles.

Open all day all wk **Food** Lunch all wk 12-9 Dinner all wk 12-9 ⊕ PUNCH TAVERNS ◄ Woodforde's Wherry, Adnams, Greene King Abbot Ale, Guest ales ♂ Aspall. ♥ 19 **Facilities** Non-diners area ♣ (Bar Restaurant Garden) ♦♦ Children's menu Children's portions Garden ⋈ Parking WiFi ▬ (notice required)

SHERINGHAM · Map 13 TG14

The Two Lifeboats

tel: 01263 823144 **2 High St NR26 8JR**
email: bridget@thetwolifeboats.co.uk
dir: In town centre

Traditional pub a few yards from the beach

Once the local Fisherman's Mission building and a coffee shop, this seafront pub was named in honour of the two lifeboats that rescued a crew of eight from a Norwegian brig in the late 19th century. This is a traditional pub where you can either quaff pints of Adnams Broadside alongside the locals or grab a table to enjoy home-cooked dishes such as creamy smoked salmon and dill linguine; lamb's liver and bacon with mustard mash; or roasted butternut squash and red pepper risotto.

Open all day all wk ⊕ PUNCH TAVERNS ◄ Adnams Broadside & Ghost Ship, Woodforde's Wherry, Sharp's Doom Bar ♂ Aspall. **Facilities** ♣ (Bar Outside area) ♦♦ Children's menu Children's portions Outside area WiFi

---

SNETTISHAM · Map 12 TF63

The Rose & Crown ★★★★ INN ◉ · PICK OF THE PUBS

tel: 01485 541382 **Old Church Rd PE31 7LX**
email: info@roseandcrownsnettisham.co.uk **web:** www.roseandcrownsnettisham.co.uk
dir: 10m N from King's Lynn on A149 signed Hunstanton. At Snettisham rdbt take B1440 to Snettisham. Left into Old Church Rd, inn on left

Everything you'd expect from a north Norfolk free house

Roses round the door, fresh seafood and an AA Rosette – just some of what Anthony and Jeannette Goodrich's splendid inn offers. Built in the 14th century for craftsmen working on the beautiful village church, its rose-hung façade conceals twisting

passages and hidden corners, heavy oak beams, uneven red-tiled floors and inglenooks. Three charming bars offer Adnams, Bass, Fuller's and Woodforde's real ales on tap and 15 wines by the glass. Locally supplied produce includes shellfish and samphire from Brancaster, beef from salt marsh-raised cattle, game shot by men in wellies who drink in the back bar, asparagus and strawberries from farmers, and herbs from village allotments. Lunch and dinner menus typically offer smoked haddock gratin, spinach and poached egg; pan-roast guinea fowl breast, warm winter vegetable salad with tahini and maple dressing; and pumpkin risotto, grilled goats' cheese and toasted macadamia nuts. Follow with poached pear Pavlova.

Open all day all wk **Food** Lunch all wk 12-6.30 Dinner Sun-Thu 6.30-9, Fri-Sat 6.30-9.30 Av main course £13.50 ⊕ FREE HOUSE ◄ Adnams Southwold Bitter & Broadside, Bass, Fuller's London Pride, Greene King IPA, Woodforde's Wherry, Guest ales ♂ Aspall. ♥ 15 **Facilities** Non-diners area ♣ (Bar Restaurant Garden) ♦♦ Children's menu Children's portions Play area Family room Garden ⋈ Parking WiFi **Rooms** 16

STIFFKEY · Map 13 TF94

The Stiffkey Red Lion

tel: 01328 830552 **44 Wells Rd NR23 1AJ**
email: redlion@stiffkey.com
dir: On A149, 4m E of Wells-next-the-Sea; 4m W of Blakeney

A perfect spot for walkers and birdwatchers

Dating from the 17th century, this comfortable inn has been a house and even a doctor's surgery in its long life. Located on the north Norfolk coast, it is now a popular bolt-hole for walkers and birdwatchers stepping off the nearby salt marshes. Grab an old pew by one of the four log fires and warm up over a glass of Nelson's Revenge and locally sourced seasonal dishes such as salmon and crab fishcakes with home-made tartare sauce; home honey-roasted ham with egg and chips; and classic spotted dick for dessert. Children's meals are available.

Open all day all wk 12-12 **Food** Lunch Mon-Sat 12-2.30, Sun 12-9 Dinner Mon-Sat 6-9, Sun 12-9 ⊕ FREE HOUSE ◄ The Stiffkey Red Lion Stewkey Brew, Woodforde's Wherry & Nelson's Revenge ♂ Aspall. ♥ 12 **Facilities** Non-diners area ♣ (Bar Restaurant Garden) ♦♦ Children's menu Children's portions Garden ⋈ Parking WiFi

---

STOKE HOLY CROSS · Map 13 TG20

The Wildebeest · PICK OF THE PUBS

tel: 01508 492497 **82-86 Norwich Rd NR14 8QJ**
email: wildebeest@animalinns.co.uk
dir: From A47 take A140, left to Dunston. At T-junct turn left, pub on right

Perfect retreat from city hustle and bustle

Set back behind a patio beer garden in a village just far enough out of Norwich to enjoy tranquillity, a double-take is occasionally taken by first-time visitors here. It's not the wholly traditional beams or lovingly aged floorboards; nor is it the rustic individual hand-carved oak tables. It's the restful ochre-washed walls and the discrete collection of African artefacts – masks, wall-hangings and carvings – that really capture the eye. The look has developed over the past 20 years, during which time the owners have also pursued a fine food policy that makes the pub worth a detour. Contemporary British cuisine tempts with starters like crayfish, salmon and chive terrine, celeriac remoulade and rye toast. Local suppliers are trusted to find top ingredients for mains such as tarragon crusted sea bream fillet with crab and brown shrimp gnocchi, roasted leeks and lobster bisque; vegetarians may find that nut roast ballotine with potato and celeriac terrine, roasted beetroot and smoked aubergine caviar is one dish to savour.

Open all wk 11.30-3 6-11 (Sat-Sun all day) **Food** Lunch all wk 12-2.30 Dinner all wk 6-9 Av main course £15.50 Set menu available ⊕ FREE HOUSE ◄ Adnams, Marston's Burton Bitter, Wychwood Hobgoblin ♂ Thatchers Gold. ♥ 10 **Facilities** Non-diners area ♦♦ Children's menu Children's portions Garden ⋈ Parking

STOW BARDOLPH
Map 12 TF60

The Hare Arms
PICK OF THE PUBS

tel: 01366 382229 **PE34 3HT**
email: trishmc@harearms222.wanadoo.co.uk
dir: *From King's Lynn take A10 to Downham Market. After 9m village signed on left*

Handsome country pub with a good vegetarian selection

Peacocks and hens roam the garden of this ivy-clad pub. It was named after the Hare family, who purchased Stow Bardolph estate in 1553 and still play an important part locally. The fascinating memorabilia that Trish and David McManus have collected during four decades here are on display throughout the music-free, L-shaped bar, where two guest ales partner those of Greene King. There's plenty to contemplate on the menu, so take your time in choosing between, perhaps, haddock goujons or baby Thai chicken cake starters, or, as a main, between Cajun salmon fillet with yogurt and cucumber dip and, say, steak and peppercorn shortcrust pastry pie with cream and brandy sauce. Another good read is the daily specials menu, featuring gazpacho; Brancaster mussels; locally-reared duck breast; and meatballs with pasta. Vegetarian eyes will spot haloumi and roasted vegetable burger; puff pastry Wellington with a choice of fillings; and Quorn chicken burritos.

Open all wk 11-2.30 6-11 (Sat & BH Mon 11-11 Sun 12-10.30) Closed 25-26 Dec **Food** Lunch Mon-Fri 12-2, Sat-Sun & BH Mon 12-10 Dinner Mon-Fri 6.30-10, Sat-Sun & BH Mon 12-10 Av main course £12 ⊕ GREENE KING ◀ Abbot Ale & IPA, Morland Old Speckled Hen, Guest ales ♻ Aspall. ₹ 9 **Facilities** Non-diners area ♦♦ Children's menu Children's portions Family room Garden ⛱ Parking WiFi ⛟ (notice required)

THOMPSON
Map 13 TL99

Chequers Inn
PICK OF THE PUBS

See Pick of the Pubs on opposite page

THORNHAM
Map 12 TF74

The Orange Tree
PICK OF THE PUBS

See Pick of the Pubs on page 360

TITCHWELL
Map 13 TF74

Titchwell Manor Hotel ★★★ HL ◉◉◉ PICK OF THE PUBS

tel: 01485 210221 **PE31 8BB**
email: margaret@titchwellmanor.com web: www.titchwellmanor.com
dir: *A149 between Brancaster & Thornham*

Sublime sea views and extraordinary cuisine

Elegant, bold, contemporary; descriptions both of the interior of the substantial Victorian farmhouse here and the brasserie-style cuisine that has gained three AA Rosettes for Eric Snaith and his team. This smart destination dining inn glories in an enviable situation at the heart of North Norfolk's heritage coast. Premier bird-watching and rambling opportunities are strung along the bays and salt marshes fringing the fields opposite; ideal appetite-builders. Select a spot in the Eating Rooms, bar, sea-view terrace or tranquil conservatory and indulge in a Pandora's box of food choices. Your first choice could be whelk and scallop ravioli with pink shallot and macadamia nut as a starter. Typical main dishes are Brancaster skate with muesli, fermented mushrooms, celeriac and sea purslane on the Conservatory menu; Brancaster mussels followed by a Dexter beefburger; or venison pudding from the Eating Rooms selection. Classic sweets complete the treats here; beers include Norfolk's own Woodforde's Wherry.

Open all day all wk **Food** Lunch all wk 12-5.30 Dinner all wk 6-9.30 Set menu available Restaurant menu available all wk ⊕ FREE HOUSE ◀ Abbot Ale, Woodforde's Wherry ♻ Aspall. ₹ 17 **Facilities** Non-diners area ♣ (Bar Garden) ♦♦ Children's menu Children's portions Garden ⛱ Parking WiFi ⛟ (notice required) **Rooms** 27

WARHAM ALL SAINTS
Map 13 TF94

Three Horseshoes
PICK OF THE PUBS

tel: 01328 710547 **NR23 1NL**
email: mail@warhamhorseshoes.co.uk
dir: *From Wells A149 to Cromer, then right onto B1105 to Warham*

Memorable heritage pub with great pies and ales

In a row of brick-and-flint stands this timeless village pub. Its rambling, quarry-tile floored, period-piece rooms recall long-gone taverns; the bar is lit by gas mantles and beers from the likes of Wolf and Woodforde's breweries are often gravity-served from barrels stillaged behind the servery. Vintage posters, clay pipes, photographs and memorabilia adorn the walls, whilst a curious green and red dial in the ceiling turns out to be a rare example of Norfolk Twister, an ancient drinking game. As befits such a rural pub, robust artisan food is the order of the day and generous home-made pies the undoubted stalwarts of the chalkboard menu. Mushroom and nut, or pork and apricot varieties may stand out, or perhaps a bowl of game and vegetable broth will disperse a winter chill. As the coast is only a short hop away, fish dishes are well represented. Alfresco enjoyment can be taken in a rose-bedecked courtyard or grassy garden, whilst dog-lovers can treat their pooch to the doggy-biscuit menu.

Open all wk 12-2.30 6-11 **Food** Lunch all wk 12-2 Dinner all wk 6-8 ⊕ FREE HOUSE ◀ Woodforde's Wherry, Nelson's Revenge, Wolf Ale, Moon Gazer ♻ Whin Hill. **Facilities** Non-diners area ♣ (Bar Garden) ♦♦ Children's portions Family room Garden ⛱ Parking ⛟ (notice required)

WELLS-NEXT-THE-SEA
Map 13 TF94

The Crown Hotel
PICK OF THE PUBS

tel: 01328 710209 **The Buttlands NR23 1EX**
email: reception@crownhotelnorfolk.co.uk
dir: *10m from Fakenham on B1105*

Modern dishes and locally brewed beers

Owned by Norfolk's Flying Kiwi group, this 17th-century former coaching inn overlooks a tree-lined green. Contemporary decor blends effortlessly with the bar's ancient beams and other old-world charms, leaving the modern marketing punnery of Fakenham brewer Jo Coubrough ('the bird who brews') to bring you back to the future with real ales called Bitter Old Bustard and Knot Just Another IPA. Whether you eat in the bar, the restaurant, the Orangery, or outside with its great views, the menus offer modern British and internationally influenced dishes. For lunch, perhaps cod, bacon, mussel and sage chowder; or slow-braised brisket of beef? In the evening, maybe Norfolk quail with herb risotto and cranberry jus; Holkham venison with butternut squash purée and slow-roast shallots; or haddock goujons in batter with hand-cut chips? And to finish, pistachio meringue with kiwi and passionfruit. Some 14 wines by the glass are available from a professionally stocked cellar.

Open all day all wk **Food** Lunch all wk 12-2.30 Dinner all wk 6.30-9.30 Av main course £17.95 ⊕ FREE HOUSE/FLYING KIWI INNS ◀ Adnams Southwold Bitter, Jo C's Norfolk Kiwi, Guest ale ♻ Aspall. ₹ 14 **Facilities** Non-diners area ♣ (Bar Garden) ♦♦ Children's menu Children's portions Garden ⛱ WiFi

Find out more about this county with *The AA Guide to Norfolk & Suffolk* – see shop.theAA.com

PICK OF THE PUBS

Chequers Inn

THOMPSON Map 13 TL99

tel: 01953 483360 **Griston Rd IP24 1PX**
email: richard@thompsonchequers.co.uk
web: www.thompsonchequers.co.uk
dir: *Exit A1075 between Watton & Thetford*

Breckland pub well off the beaten track

If you can't place Breckland, it's that region of gorse-covered sandy heath straddling south Norfolk and north Suffolk. Within its boundaries you'll find this splendid, long and low, thatched 17th-century inn, and worth finding it is for its peaceful location and unspoilt charm. In the 18th century manorial courts were held here, dealing with rents, letting of land, and petty crime. It's more fun here today. Beneath its steeply-raked thatch lies a series of low-ceilinged, interconnecting rooms served by a long bar at which the principal real ales are Adnams Southwold Bitter, Greene King IPA and Wolf Ale. The overall impression of the interior is of skew-whiff wall timbers, squat doorways, open log fires, rustic old furniture and farming implements. Although not long, the main menu more than adequately covers most bases, with starters of pan-fried mushrooms in Stilton and cream sauce; local asparagus with crispy pancetta and hollandaise sauce; and Cranworth smoked salmon with dill and lemon

mayonnaise. Its seven or eight main dishes may well include seafood tagliatelle with tomato and herb sauce; Chinese-spiced roast belly of pork with stir-fried vegetables and noodles; and roast vegetable and Portobello mushroom puff pastry pie. To add to one's choice, there are specials — typically breast of chicken stuffed with smoked salmon, and steak and kidney pudding. Finally, dessert; perhaps home-made apple crumble; treacle and almond tart; or chocolate profiteroles. You'll find picnic tables in the large rear garden, where dogs are welcome. The inn is an ideal base for walking the Peddars Way and the Great Eastern Pingo Trail — a string of lakelets (the pingos) left behind after the Ice Age.

Open all wk 11-3 6-11 (Sun all day)
Food Lunch Mon-Sat 12-2, Sun all day
Dinner Mon-Sat 6.30-9, Sun all day
🌐 FREE HOUSE 🛢 Adnams Southwold Bitter, Wolf Ale, Greene King IPA, Woodforde's Wherry 🍎 Thatchers, Aspall.
🍷 8 **Facilities** Non-diners area 🐾 (Bar Garden) 👫 Children's menu Children's portions Garden 🎪 Beer festival Parking WiFi 🚐 (notice required)

PICK OF THE PUBS

The Orange Tree

THORNHAM   Map 12 TF74

tel: 01485 512213 **High St PE36 6LY**
email: email@theorangetreethornham.co.uk
web: www.theorangetreethornham.co.uk
dir: *Phone for detailed directions*

Contemporary dining pub in a coastal village

Standing in the centre of the village opposite the church, this family-run pub is a useful stop for walkers on the Peddars Way. Formerly a smugglers' haunt, the 400-year-old whitewashed inn has evolved over the years into the stylish country pub it is today. Develop an appetite with a stroll to the local staithe, where working fishing boats still come and go through the creeks of Brancaster Bay, before returning for meal and a pint of East Anglian-brewed ale. Chef Philip Milner makes the most of freshly landed local seafood, with innovative dishes like fillet of Loch Duart salmon with chorizo jam, crispy espelette polenta, buttered curly kale, baba ganoush and tempura soft-shell crab. But it's not just the seafood that justifies his claim that the restaurant is the jewel in The Orange Tree's crown; the pub has a long-established relationship with local suppliers, and most of the meat is sourced from the Sandringham Estate. Typically found on the restaurant menu are Capricorn goats' cheese and red pepper crème caramel; and rump of

salt marsh lamb, aubergine kofta, spiced vegetable tagine, rose water Israeli couscous. Meanwhile, dishes on the bar classics menu could include Moroccan chickpea, preserved lemon and feta burger with a bucket of chips; or the OT balti with a choice of two heat and spice levels. Look to the board for the daily sandwich selection. Leave space to sample the appetising selection of desserts, the delightfully themed 'Fairground': bubblegum pannacotta, baby toffee apples, candyfloss, butterscotch popcorn and chocolate covered honeycomb. Traditionalists might opt for lemon cheesecake or a home-made ice cream or sorbet. Dogs get their own beer and menu, while children will love the climbing frame in the pub's garden.

Open all day all wk **Food** all wk 12-9.30 ⊕ PUNCH TAVERNS ◼ Woodforde's Wherry, Adnams Southwold Bitter, Guest ales ♂ Aspall, Symonds. ♟ 29 **Facilities** Non-diners area ♣ (Bar Garden) ♦ Children's menu Children's portions Play area Garden ⌂ Parking WiFi 🚐

PICK OF THE PUBS

Wiveton Bell ★★★★ INN ◉

WIVETON   Map 13 TG04

tel: 01263 740101
Blakeney Rd NR25 7TL
email: wivetonbell@me.com
web: www.wivetonbell.com
dir: *From Blakeney take A149 towards Cley next the Sea. Right to Wiveton*

Tranquil country pub championing local fish and game

Immaculately spruced-up though it is, and while rightly renowned for its cuisine, the Bell remains faithful to its roots as a traditional village pub. This means that, even in full walking gear (dog in tow) you are welcome to drift in for just a pint of Woodforde's Wherry, or Norfolk Moon Gazer, and nobody will suggest you should be better dressed, or have left Rex in his basket. In a village pub so close to the unspoilt salt marshes of the North Norfolk coast – an Area of Outstanding Natural Beauty – and just 10 minutes' walk from Blakeney nature reserve, that's a wise approach. Built in the 18th century, it features earthy, heritage-coloured walls, stripped beams, chunky tables and oak-planked floors, with further character imbued by local artworks lining the walls of the bar and conservatory dining room. On a winter's evening head for the tables close to the inglenook fireplace, where, by the light of the masses of candles, your meal might begin with pan-fried mackerel, cauliflower purée,

peppered walnut brittle and caper crisps; or smoked ham hock terrine with soft-boiled, free-range egg and parsley emulsion. For a main course try the 'Wivvy Bell' salt marsh-grazed beefburger, topped with Norfolk Dapple smoked cheese, served with onion rings, hand-cut chips and home-made relish; or roasted local pigeon crown with cherry-braised red cabbage, fondant potato and pea fricassée. Petit pois, baby spinach and Binham Blue cheese risotto is a vegetarian option. On a Sunday there's an excellent choice of roasts, but booking is essential. Two sample desserts to give you a good idea of the Wivvy style are treacle-dipped ginger parkin with vanilla ice cream; and orange and star anise blancmange with candied orange and roast almonds.

Open all day all wk Closed 25 Dec
Food Lunch all wk 12-2.15 Dinner all wk 6-9 ⊞ FREE HOUSE ◗ Woodforde's Wherry, Norfolk Moon Gazer, Yetman's ♉ Aspall. ♟ 14 **Facilities**Non-diners area ✿ (Bar Garden) ♙ Children's menu Children's portions Garden ⋔ Parking WiFi **Rooms** 6

WINTERTON-ON-SEA   Map 13 TG41

Fishermans Return

tel: 01493 393305 **The Lane NR29 4BN**
email: enquiries@fishermansreturn.com **web:** www.fishermansreturn.com
dir: 8m N of Great Yarmouth on B1159

Just round the corner from sandy beaches

This dog-friendly, 350-year-old brick and flint built free house stands close to long beaches and National Trust land, making it the ideal spot to finish a walk. Guest ales support Woodforde's Norfolk Nog and Wherry behind the bar, whilst the menus range from popular favourites like fish and chips; and chicken, bacon and cheese burger to sirloin steak and three bean chilli. Look out for fish and seafood specials on the daily-changing blackboard, where freshly caught mackerel or sea bass may be on offer. The pub hosts a beer festival on Summer Bank Holiday.

Open all wk 11-2.30 5.30-11 (Sat-Sun 11-11) **Food** Lunch all wk 12-2.30 Dinner all wk 6-9 ⊕ FREE HOUSE ◖ Woodforde's Wherry & Norfolk Nog, Greene King Skippers Tipple & IPA, Guest ales ♂ Westons Stowford Press & Old Rosie Scrumpy, Local ciders. ♟ 9 **Facilities** Non-diners area ❖ (Bar Restaurant Garden) ♦♦ Children's menu Children's portions Play area Family room Garden Beer festival Cider festival Parking WiFi ➡

WIVETON   Map 13 TG04

Wiveton Bell ★★★★ INN ◉   PICK OF THE PUBS

See Pick of the Pubs on page 361

WOODBASTWICK   Map 13 TG31

The Fur & Feather Inn

tel: 01603 720003 **Slad Ln NR13 6HQ**
dir: From A1151 (Norwich to Wroxham road), follow brown signs for Woodforde's Brewery. Pub adjacent to brewery

An idyllic thatched country pub ideal for beer lovers

A weeping willow and duckpond in the garden; a creeper-clad façade beneath rolling reed-thatched roof; oh, and a brewery right next door. This pub-lovers' nirvana gets better, with an interior wrested from a brace of artisan's cottages still blissfully free of electronic entertainment. Here, Woodforde's beers from across the yard are gravity dispensed from barrels on the bar stillage. Work up an appetite exploring the Bure Valley's broads just across the fields before selecting from the classic pub-grub menu. Pies, puddings, fish and a good vegetarian choice all feature; top-notch locally made burgers in countless variety are a renowned speciality of the house.

Open all day all wk **Food** Lunch all wk 10-9 Dinner all wk 10-9 Av main course £12 ⊕ WOODFORDE'S LTD ◖ Woodforde's Wherry, Bure Gold, Sundew, Norfolk Nog, Nelson's Revenge, Once Bittern, Headcracker, Mardler's Mild. ♟ 12 **Facilities** Non-diners area ♦♦ Children's menu Garden ⚲ Parking WiFi ➡ (notice required)

NORTHAMPTONSHIRE

ASHBY ST LEDGERS   Map 11 SP56

The Olde Coach House Inn ★★★★ INN

tel: 01788 890349 **CV23 8UN**
email: info@oldecoachhouse.co.uk **web:** www.oldecoachhouse.co.uk
dir: M1 junct 18 follow A361/Daventry signs. Village on left

Good food in a memorable village setting

This mellow stone inn (The OCH) sits amidst thatched cottages in the lovely estate village here; until a century ago it was a farmhouse. Today it's an engaging mix of contemporary and rustic, with a strong emphasis on comfort; deep leather furnishings tempt you to linger by log fires, wondering at the function of the archaic rural artefacts on display. The courtyard dining area is a popular place to sample the extensive fare which ranges from home-made, stone-fired pizzas and 'design your own' grazing boards to dishes such as Ashby rare breed pork sausage, mash and seasonal vegetables; and Portugeuse espetada. Fifteen boutique-style bedrooms are available.

Open all day all wk **Food** Lunch Mon-Sat 12-2.30, Sun 12-8 Dinner Mon-Sat 6-9.30, Sun 12-8 Av main course £11 Set menu available Restaurant menu available all wk ⊕ CHARLES WELLS ◖ Bombardier, Young's. ♟ 12 **Facilities** Non-diners area ❖ (Bar Garden Outside area) ♦♦ Children's menu Children's portions Play area Garden Outside area ⚲ Parking WiFi ➡ (notice required) **Rooms** 15

AYNHO

Map 11 SP53

The Great Western Arms

tel: 01869 338288 **Station Rd OX17 3BP**
email: info@great-westernarms.co.uk
dir: *From Aynho take B4031 (Station Road) W towards Deddington. Turn right to pub*

Run by a young and friendly bunch

The Great Western Railway company disappeared in 1948, but its name lives on in this foliage-covered inn between the line it built to Birmingham, and the Oxford Canal. It's a Hook Norton pub, so the brewery's range of ales is well represented; 10 wines are sold by the glass, and there's a packed whisky and spirit shelf. Good things on chef-patron René Klein's menus include his creamy chicken curry; venison, pheasant, cranberry and port pie; Cajun-dusted salmon fillet; and leek and cheese sausages. The pretty courtyard and garden has Hook Norton's top award.

Open all day all wk 11-11 Closed 25 Dec **Food** Lunch Mon-Sat 12-3, Sun 12-9 Dinner Mon-Sat 6-9, Sun 12-9 ⊕ HOOK NORTON ◀ Old Hooky, Guest ales ♂ Westons Perry, Old Rosie & Stowford Press. ♚ 10 **Facilities** Non-diners area ♣ (Bar Garden) ♦ Children's menu Children's portions Garden �🝐 Parking WiFi ➿ (notice required)

BRAUNSTON

Map 11 SP56

NEW The Admiral Nelson

tel: 01788 891900 **Dark Ln NN11 7HJ**
dir: *Phone pub for detailed directions*

Canal-side freehouse saved by one family's determination

Despite its enviable position beside the Grand Union Canal, The Admiral Nelson has suffered a chequered history. Originally a 1730s farm building, the pub's custom waned as canal traffic declined. There followed many years of unreliable performance under a series of tenant landlords. The Davis family only just succeeded in saving the pub from closure in 2013. Four hand pumps today offer three guest ales and Admiral's Ale, specially made by the local MerriMen microbrewery. The family apply the same care to the provenance of their kitchen ingredients; mince for the chargrilled burgers, for example, comes from a nearby water buffalo farm.

Open all day all wk 12-11 **Food** Lunch 12-3 Dinner 6-9 Av main course £11 Restaurant menu available Tue-Sat ⊕ FREE HOUSE ◀ MerriMen Admiral Ale, Rotating Guest ales ♂ Addlestones, Westons Stowford Press. **Facilities** Non-diners area ♣ (Bar Garden) ♦ Children's menu Children's portions Garden �🝐 Parking WiFi ➿ (notice required)

BULWICK

Map 11 SP99

The Queen's Head

PICK OF THE PUBS

tel: 01780 450272 **Main St NN17 3DY**
email: info@thequeensheadbulwick.co.uk
dir: *Just off A43, between Corby & Stamford*

Village free house supporting local breweries

A 17th-century stone-built free house overlooking the village church, parts of The Queen's Head date back to 1400. The pub is a warren of small rooms with exposed wooden beams, four open fireplaces and flagstone floors. Relax by the fire or on the patio with a pint of real ale from the nearby Oakham or Rockingham breweries. Local shoots supply seasonal game such as teal, woodcock and partridge, and other ingredients often include village-grown fruit and vegetables brought in by customers and friends. Lunchtime brings a good selection of sandwiches, snacks and main dishes. The evening menu might feature local pork sausages, mash with white onion and grainy mustard sauce. The menu is backed by a comprehensive wine list; there's an outdoor oven for outside dining.

Open 12-3 6-11 (Sun 12-7) Closed Mon **Food** Lunch Tue-Sat 12-2, Sun 12-3 Dinner Tue-Sat 6-9 ⊕ FREE HOUSE ◀ Rockingham, Oakham, Digfield Ales, Shepherd Neame ♂ Aspall, Hogan's Scrumpy. ♚ 9 **Facilities** Non-diners area ♣ (Bar Outside area) ♦ Children's portions Outside area �🝐 Parking ➿

COLLYWESTON

Map 11 SK90

NEW The Collyweston Slater ★★★★ INN

tel: 01780 444288 **87 Main Rd PE9 3PQ**
email: enquiries@collywestonslaterpub.co.uk **web:** www.collywestonslaterpub.co.uk
dir: *In village centre on A43*

Traditional 17th-century coaching inn

Before entering, look up at the roof and its Collyweston slates, a locally-quarried, tough limestone. Inside, there's wood panelling, stonework and comfortable furnishings, and all very attractive they are too. An Everards pub, it serves their Tiger and Sunchaser real ales; the cider is from Symonds and there are 12 wines by the glass. Classic main courses include scampi, chips and peas; gammon, egg and chips; bangers 'n' mash; and ricotta cheese with spinach cannelloni. Among a good range of burgers you'll find Southern-fried chicken, and smoky pulled pork. Youngsters can eat from the Colly-flowers menu.

Open all day all wk **Food** Lunch 12-9 Dinner 12-9 Av main course £9.95 ⊕ EVERARDS ◀ Tiger & Sunchaser ♂ Symonds. ♚ 12 **Facilities** Non-diners area ♣ (Bar Outside area) ♦ Children's menu Children's portions Play area Outside area �🝐 Parking WiFi ➿ (notice required) **Rooms** 3

CRICK

Map 11 SP57

The Red Lion Inn

tel: 01788 822342 **52 Main Rd NN6 7TX**
dir: *M1 junct 18, A428, 0.75m, follows signs for Crick from rdbt*

Village inn in the same hands for many years

An old gabled, thatched, coaching inn of mellow ironstone standing beside the pretty main street just a stone's throw from Crick's ancient church. Exposed beams, low ceilings and open fires characterise this village free-house, family-run for the past 35 years. Beers from Adnams or Wells example the varied range of real ales available here, with classic pub meals the order of the day.

Open all wk 11-2.30 6-11 (Sun 12-3 7-11) **Food** Lunch all wk 12-2 Dinner Mon-Sat 6.30-9 ⊕ FREE HOUSE ◀ Adnams Southwold Bitter, Wells Bombardier, Morland Old Speckled Hen, Guest ale. **Facilities** Non-diners area ♣ (Bar Restaurant Garden) ♦ Children's menu Children's portions Garden �🝐 Parking WiFi

EAST HADDON
Map 11 SP66

The Red Lion
PICK OF THE PUBS

tel: 01604 770223 **Main St NN6 8BU**
email: nick@redlioneasthaddon.co.uk
dir: *Just off A428*

Refined destination village gastro-pub

There's something about the yellow Northamptonshire stone and thatched roof of Nick Bonner and Ren Aveiro's Red Lion that declares 'classic English village pub'. Classic food too, from a starter of home-made salt-beef hash with fried egg and brown sauce gravy, to mains of poached smoked haddock with crushed new potatoes, green beans and herb cream sauce; slow-braised lamb pie with creamed potato, crushed peas and minted gravy; and pan-fried haloumi with red pepper, olive and artichoke salad. Golden syrup tart with warm vanilla custard makes a nostalgic-for-some appearance among the desserts, alongside lemon drizzle cake with Seville orange marmalade ice cream. As an accompaniment, a reasonably priced glass of Pino Grigio or Malbec, or maybe a pint of Bombardier. In the grounds, overlooking rolling countryside, Nick and fellow director Wendy Carter run Shires Cookery School.

Open all day all wk 11-11 **Food** Lunch Mon-Fri 12-2.30, Sat-Sun all day Dinner Mon-Fri 6-9, Sat-Sun all day ⊕ CHARLES WELLS ◀ Bomardier, Young's. ♥ 14 **Facilities** Non-diners area ♦️ Children's menu Children's portions Garden ⋒ Parking WiFi ☎ (notice required)

FARTHINGHOE
Map 11 SP53

The Fox

tel: 01295 713965 **Baker St NN13 5PH**
email: enquiries@foxatfarthinghoe.co.uk
dir: *M40 junct 11, A422, towards Brackley. Approx 5.5m to Farthinghoe*

Relaxed and friendly village pub that's close to Silverstone

Only 12 miles from Silverstone, this Charles Wells pub brings its customers fresh, locally sourced food with friendly service and a relaxing village atmosphere. In practice this translates as a varied menu offering pub favourites such as glazed Cotswold ham, sticky BBQ ribs, kedgeree smoked haddock, and chef's fish pie, along with more exotic options such as chicken and chorizo linguine. Sandwiches and wraps are also available, and there is even a take-out menu. A roast is offered every Sunday lunch.

Open all wk 12-3 6-11 (Fri-Sun 12-11) ⊕ CHARLES WELLS ◀ Courage Directors, Young's, Erdinger, Guinness, Guest ale Ŏ Aspall. **Facilities** ♣ (Bar Garden) ♦️ Children's portions Garden Parking WiFi

FARTHINGSTONE
Map 11 SP65

The Kings Arms
PICK OF THE PUBS

tel: 01327 361604 **Main St NN12 8EZ**
email: paul@kingsarms.fsbusiness.co.uk
dir: *M1 junct 16, A45 towards Daventry. At Weedon take A5 towards Towcester. Turn right signed Farthingstone*

Attractive village pub with wildlife-loving garden

Tucked away in perfect walking country, this stone-built 300-year-old free house is close to Canons Ashby, an Elizabethan manor house run by the National Trust. The pub's quirky garden is full of interesting recycled items, decorative trees and shrubs, and secluded corners. Paul and Denise Egerton grow their own salads and herbs here, and it's also a haven for wildlife – 50 different species of birds, 200 species of moth and 20 of butterflies have all been spotted. Have an alfresco drink on the terrace when it's warm, watching red kites and buzzards wheeling overhead; in winter, real fires warm the stone-flagged interior. The Kings Arms is mainly a drinkers' pub, with up to five real ales and Westons Old Rosie cider on tap. At the

weekend you can get a bar lunch, including quality platters – meat, fish or cheese. Other offerings might be local game casserole; or Yorkshire pudding filled with steak and kidney; desserts include lemon pudding or raspberry meringue; and hot gingerbread with maple syrup.

Open 7-11.30 (Fri 6.30-12 Sat 12-12 Sun 12-5 9-11) Closed Mon **Food** Lunch Sat-Sun 12-2.30 Dinner last Fri in month or special events ⊕ FREE HOUSE ◀ Vale VPA, St Austell Trelawny, Thwaites Wainwright, Adnams Ghost Ship Ŏ Westons Old Rosie. **Facilities** Non-diners area ♣ (Bar Restaurant Garden) ♦️ Children's portions Family room Garden ⋒ Parking WiFi

FOTHERINGHAY
Map 12 TL09

The Falcon Inn

tel: 01832 226254 **PE8 5HZ**
email: info@thefalcon-inn.co.uk **web:** www.thefalcon-inn.co.uk
dir: *From A605 between Peterborough & Oundle follow Fotheringhay signs*

Popular locals' inn with designer garden

This attractive 18th-century, stone-built pub stands in gardens overlooking the stunning church. It's a real local, the Tap Bar regularly used by the village darts team, their throwing arms lubricated by pints of Fool's Nook ale. The menus in both the bar and charming conservatory restaurant rely extensively on locally sourced ingredients. In the winter, restaurant offerings are local game terrine with apple and onion chutney or twice baked cheese soufflé with celeriac remoulade to start. Mains might be braised shin of beef with horseradish mash, or steamed sea bass fillet with salmon mousse. Hopefully there'll still be room for spiced fruit crumble with plum custard, or frangipane tart with Armagnac ice cream.

Open all day 12-11 (Sun 12-4 Jan-Mar) Closed Sun eve Jan-Mar **Food** Lunch Mon-Sat 12-2, Sun 12-3 (Sun 12-4 Jan-Mar) Dinner Mon-Sat 6-9 (Sun 6-8 Apr-Dec) Av main course £10 Set menu available Restaurant menu available ⊕ FREE HOUSE ◀ Greene King IPA, Digfield Fool's Nook, Fuller's London Pride Ŏ Aspall. ♥ 14 **Facilities** Non-diners area ♣ (Bar Restaurant Garden) ♦️ Children's menu Children's portions Garden ⋒ Beer festival Parking WiFi ☎ (notice required)

GRAFTON REGIS
Map 11 SP74

The White Hart

tel: 01908 542123 **Northampton Rd NN12 7SR**
email: alan@pubgraftonregis.co.uk
dir: *M1 junct 15, A508 towards Milton Keynes*

Thatched pub offering a friendly welcome

This thatched, stone-built property dating from the 16th century is the focal point for a friendly village with around 100 residents. In 1464 Edward IV married Elizabeth Woodville in this historic place. The pub has been run by the same family for since 1996 and Alan the owner, is also the chef. Menus change frequently according to available produce. Typical choices include salmon and monkfish mornay with pesto tagliatelle; lasagne; steak, Stilton and mushroom pie; and a selection of steaks. Well-kept ales and 14 wines by the glass complete the picture. The garden has a gazebo/band stand.

Open 12-2.30 6-11 Closed Mon **Food** Lunch Tue-Sun 12-2 Dinner Tue-Sun 6-9.30 ⊕ FREE HOUSE ◀ Greene King, Abbot Ale & IPA ♂ Aspall. ♚ 14 **Facilities** Non-diners area ✿ (Garden) ♦♦ Children's portions Garden ⋒ Parking WiFi

---

GREAT HOUGHTON   Map 11 SP75

The Old Cherry Tree

tel: 01604 761399 **Cherry Tree Ln NN4 7AT**
email: info@theoldcherrytree.co.uk
dir: From A45 SE of Northampton take A428 towards Bedford. Right to Great Houghton. Left in The Cross, left into Cherry Tree Ln. Pub at end

Traditional food and relaxing beer garden

East of Northampton and close to the A428 towards Bedford, this tucked away 16th-century thatched pub is a popular country rendezvous for families, and it's dog-friendly too. Enjoy a pint of Charles Wells Eagle IPA by the real log fire, or head to the tranquil beer garden if the weather allows. At lunchtime, soups, jacket potatoes, burgers and baguettes offer a light option but the evening menu moves up a gear with the likes of chicken supreme served with mushroom, thyme and bacon, or beef and Stilton pie. Leave room for the ginger pudding with custard.

Open all wk 11-3 5.30-11 (Sun 12-7) **Food** Lunch all wk 12-2.30 Dinner Tue-Sat 6.30-9 Restaurant menu available Tue-Sat (dinner only) ⊕ CHARLES WELLS ◀ Eagle IPA, Young's London Gold, Courage Directors. ♚ 15 **Facilities** Non-diners area ✿ (Bar Garden) ♦♦ Children's menu Children's portions Garden ⋒ Parking WiFi ➡ (notice required)

KILSBY   Map 11 SP57

The George

tel: 01788 822229 **Watling St CV23 8YE**
dir: M1 junct 18, follow A361/Daventry signs. Pub at rdbt junct of A361 & A5

A great local with home-cooked food

A warm welcome and great local atmosphere characterise this village pub, which has a traditional public bar and a high-ceilinged wood-panelled lounge opening into a smarter but relaxed area with solidly comfortable furnishings. The lunch bar menu includes sandwiches, filled baguettes, faggots with spring onion mash and mushy peas; and a selection of home-made dishes. The evening menu majors on home-made, hearty dishes such as beef and real ale shortcrust pie; lasagne; and the generous chicken and bacon Caesar salad. A children's menu is always available. There is an attractive garden for sunny days.

Open all wk 11.30-3 5.30-11.30 (Sun 12-5 6-11) **Food** Lunch Mon-Sat 12-2, Sun 12-3 Dinner Mon-Sat 6-9, Sun 6-8.30 Restaurant menu available all wk ⊕ PUNCH TAVERNS ◀ Fuller's London Pride, Adnams Southwold Bitter, Timothy Taylor Landlord. ♚ 10 **Facilities** Non-diners area ♦♦ Children's menu Children's portions Garden ⋒ Parking WiFi ➡ (notice required)

LITTLE BRINGTON   Map 11 SP66

The Saracens Head

tel: 01604 770640 **Main St NN7 4HS**
email: info@thesaracensatbrington.co.uk
dir: M1 junct 16, A45 to Flore. In Flore 1st right signed the Bringtons. Straight on at x-rds to Little Brington, pub on left

Old village inn with smallholding produce

Barrel tables and beams; quarry tile and bareboard floors; leaded windows and a fierce wood-burner; the Saracens has character in droves. This 17th-century building of mellow ironstone slumbers in a tiny village where lucky locals enjoy a changing range of beers that includes some from local microbreweries. It's a

popular stop too for horse riders using the network of local bridleways, who can hitch-up in the garden for more sedate views of the countryside. The menu here has a modern twist; witness the confit pig's cheeks starter or main of roast loin of cod wrapped in pancetta, whilst coeliacs and the gluten-intolerant have a good choice of dishes, cooked on the premises.

Open all day all wk ⊕ FREE HOUSE ◀ Greene King IPA, Timothy Taylor Landlord, Guest ale. **Facilities** ✿ (Bar Garden) ♦♦ Children's portions Garden Parking WiFi

---

LITTLE HOUGHTON   Map 11 SP85

Four Pears

tel: 01604 890900 **28 Bedford Rd NN7 1AB**
email: info@thefourpears.com
dir: From Northampton take A428 towards Bedford. Left signed Little Houghton

Smartly renovated village inn with appealing menu

In a peaceful, ironstone-built village just outside Northampton, this 400-year-old hostelry was rescued from closure by local residents not long ago. The fresh, contemporary design owes little to the past. Rather; tip-top real ales are supped in the smart, light bar area, where dog-walkers straying from the nearby Nene Valley lakes will find a warm welcome. The refined, soft-furnishing rich lounge captures the essence of the dining pub; a comfy retreat where bistro meets pub-grub. Start with crispy pig with cured ham and apple chutney, or go straight for spiced salmon and crayfish linguine in the bright restaurant area popular with families.

Open all day all wk **Food** Lunch all wk 12-3 Dinner Mon-Sat 6-9 Restaurant menu available Mon-Sat ⊕ FREE HOUSE ◀ St Austell Tribute, Fuller's London Pride, Phipps IPA ♂ Westons Stowford Press. ♚ **Facilities** Non-diners area ✿ (Bar Outside area) ♦♦ Children's portions Outside area ⋒ WiFi ➡ (notice required)

NASSINGTON   Map 12 TL09

The Queens Head Inn ★★★★ INN ◉◉

tel: 01780 784006 **54 Station Rd PE8 6QB**
email: info@queensheadnassington.co.uk **web:** www.queensheadnassington.co.uk
dir: Exit A1 at Wansford, follow Yarwell & Nassington signs. Through Yarwell. Pub on left in Nassington

Traditional inn with great food

A stone-built inn with exposed beams and traditional furnishings, The Queens Head's name nods to the beheading of Mary, Queen of Scots at nearby Fotheringhay Castle in 1587. Proud of its AA Rosettes, it offers favourites old and new, including pressed ham hock and foie gras terrine with quail's egg, piccalilli and baby onions; slow braised shin of venison with carrot and cinnamon purée, and boulangère potatoes; and banana and tonka bean pannacotta with toffee sauce, banana wafer and peanut brittle. Dine outdoors in warmer weather.

Open all day all wk 11-11 (Sat 11am-mdnt Sun 12-11) **Food** Lunch Mon-Sat 12-2.30, Sun 12-8 Dinner Mon-Sat 6-9, Sun 12-8 ⊕ FREE HOUSE ◀ Greene King IPA, Oakham JHB. ♚ 8 **Facilities** Non-diners area ✿ (Bar Garden) ♦♦ Children's menu Children's portions Garden ⋒ Parking WiFi ➡ (notice required) **Rooms** 10

NORTHAMPTON   Map 11 SP76

Althorp Coaching Inn

tel: 01604 770651 **Main St, Great Brington NN7 4JA**
email: althorpcachinginn@btconnect.com
dir: From A428 pass main gates of Althorp House, left before rail bridge. Great Brington 1m

Thatched pub with old-world charm and locally sourced food

Occupying a lovely position in the pretty village of Great Brington on the Althorp Estate, this 16th-century stone coaching inn has original decor throughout. The

continued

NORTHAMPTON *continued*

cellar restaurant specialises in traditional English cooking based on locally sourced ingredients. A brick and cobbled courtyard is surrounded by stable rooms, and the enclosed flower garden is a peaceful spot in which to sample one of the real ales from a wide selection that includes five guest ales.

Open all day all wk 11-11 (wknds 11am-mdnt) ⊕ FREE HOUSE ◀ Greene King IPA & Abbot Ale, Fuller's London Pride, Cottage Puffing Billy, Tunnell Sweet Parish Ale, 5 guest ales ♂ Farmhouse, Thatchers Heritage. **Facilities** ❀ (Bar Garden) ♦❙ Children's menu Children's portions Garden Parking WiFi

NEW The Hopping Hare ★★★★ INN ◉

tel: 01604 580090 **18 Hopping Hill Gardens, Duston NN5 6PF**
email: info@hoppinghare.com **web:** www.hoppinghare.com
dir: *Take A428 from Northampton towards West Haddon. Left into Hopping Hill Gardens, pub signed*

Top family-owned pub

The mildly eccentric pub signage reflects the 'hopping' element; as it's hard to explain, a visit will clarify. Having seen, enter the bar, where several national real ales accompany Saxby's cider, made on a local farm, and around 11 wines by the glass. For her modern British dishes, head chef Jennie Bowmaker hand-picks her suppliers, so knows how her meats were reared, her fish caught, and her vegetables grown. The result: Parma-ham-wrapped pheasant breast with sautéed Brussels sprouts and chestnuts; pan-fried sea bass fillet with clams and mussels; and crispy potato cake with goats' cheese, and garlic and watercress stuffing.

Open all day all wk **Food** Lunch Mon-Fri 12-2.30, Sat 12-10, Sun 12-8.30 Dinner Mon-Thu 5.30-9.30, Fri 5.30-10, Sat 12-10, Sun 12-8.30 Set menu available Restaurant menu available all wk ⊕ FREE HOUSE ◀ Black Sheep, Adnams Broadside, Guest ale ♂ Aspall, Somersby Cider, Saxby's Cider. ☗ 11 **Facilities** Non-diners area ♦❙ Children's portions Outside area ♩ Parking WiFi **Rooms** 20

NEW The White Horse

tel: 01604 781297 **Walgrave Rd NN6 9QX**
email: whitehorseold@hotmail.co.uk
dir: *From A43 (between Kettering & Northampton) follow Walgrave signs. Through Walgrave to Old*

Sympathetically restored village-centre pub

Whimsical sayings ("The road to success is under construction"), cushions with postage stamp designs and a book exchange characterise the interior of this beautifully refurbished steam-driven mill. Micro-brewed real ales rarely need to travel far, as for instance Gundog from Woodford Halse, and Whistling Kite from Kettering. Food is prepared fresh daily for a smallish menu listing pork four ways; shepherd's pie; classic fish and chips; and butternut squash risotto, with specials changing weekly. A doggy bag is willingly offered if you can't finish. Over the Summer Bank Holiday weekend in August there's a beer and cider festival.

Open 12-3 5-11 (Sat 12-11 Sun 12-7) Closed Mon (ex BH) **Food** Contact pub for food times Av main course £9.95 ⊕ FREE HOUSE ◀ Phipps, Langton, Nene Valley, Whistling Kite, Gun Dog Ales ♂ Westons. ☗ 11 **Facilities** Non-diners area ❀ (Bar Garden Outside area) ♦❙ Children's portions Garden Outside area ♩ Beer festival Cider festival Parking WiFi ⛟ (notice required)

The Chequered Skipper

tel: 01832 273494 **Ashton PE8 5LD**
email: enquiries@chequeredskipper.co.uk
dir: *A605 towards Oundle, at rdbt follow signs to Ashton. 1m, turn left into Ashton*

Well known for their pizzas

The Chequered Skipper has a traditional thatched exterior complemented by a contemporary interior. Located opposite the green in the model village of Ashton, built for the estate workers in the 1880s, the pub plays its part well, with timeless oak floor and beams, and a collection of butterfly display cases diverting attention from a bar stocking locally brewed beers (two beer festivals a year). The menu mixes speciality pizzas and traditional English and European dishes – pork and liver pâté might be followed by braised shoulder of lamb with dauphinoise potatoes.

Open all wk 11.30-3 6-11 (Sat 11.30-11 Sun 11.45-11) **Food** Lunch Mon-Fri 12-2, Sat 12-2.30, Sun 12-3 Dinner Mon-Sat 6.30-9.30, Sun 6.30-9 ⊕ FREE HOUSE ◀ Rockingham Ale, Brewster's Hophead, Oakham. ☗ 8 **Facilities** Non-diners area ❀ (Bar Garden) ♦❙ Children's portions Garden Beer festival Parking WiFi ⛟ (notice required)

The Red Lion — PICK OF THE PUBS

tel: 01858 880011 **43 Welland Rise LE16 9UD**
email: andrew@redlionwinepub.co.uk
dir: *From Market Harborough take A4304, through Lubenham, left through Marston Trussell to Sibbertoft*

A real passion for good wine

The interior of this friendly 300-year-old free house is an appealing blend of contemporary and classic decor, with oak beams, leather upholstery and a smartly turned-out dining room. Andrew and Sarah Banks have built a loyal following here thanks to their special passion for wine: over 200 bins appear on the list, 20 labels are served by the glass, and an annual wine festival is a high point in the pub's busy calendar. After tasting, all wines can be bought at take-home prices, avoiding the guesswork of supermarket purchases. The monthly-changing and reasonably priced menu is served in both bar and restaurant, and could feature home-made sausage roll with piccalilli and brown sauce; battered cod tail, minted mushy peas, tartare sauce and a pale of fries; and date and sticky toffee pudding with vanilla ice cream.

Open 5-11 (Sat 12-3 6-11 Sun 12-6) Closed Mon-Fri L & Sun eve **Food** Lunch Sat 12-3, Sun 12-6 Dinner Mon-Sat 5-11 Av main course £10 Set menu available ⊕ FREE HOUSE ◀ St Austell Tribute, Greene King Abbot Ale ♨ Aspall, Westons. ⬤ 20 **Facilities** Non-diners area ✿ (Garden) ◗ Children's menu Children's portions Play area Garden ⋂ Parking WiFi ➟ (notice required)

STAVERTON   Map 11 SP56

The Countryman

tel: 01327 311815 **Daventry Rd NN11 6JH**
email: thecountrymanstaverton@gmail.com **web:** www.thecountrymanstaverton.co.uk
dir: On A425 between Daventry & Southam

Quality modern cooking in traditional village coaching inn

Built in traditional Northamptonshire ironstone this lovely 17th-century coaching inn retains plenty of original character courtesy of log fires and beamed ceilings. A range of ales from local microbreweries such as Great Oakley and Gun Dog keep beer fans happy, whilst the seasonal menu showcases regional produce in dishes such as roasted rack of lamb with sweet onion tartlet, fondant potato, spring greens and port reduction; or roasted spring vegetable and mushroom strudel with seasonal greens and Shropshire Blue sauce, finishing perhaps with tropical fruit meringue with passion fruit cream and mango coulis.

Open all wk 12-3 6-11 (Sun 12-10.30) Closed 4-14 Jan 2016 **Food** Lunch Mon-Sat 12-2.30, Sun 12-9 Dinner Mon-Sat 6-9.30, Sun 12-9 Set menu available ⊕ FREE HOUSE ◀ Gun Dog Ales, Church End, Great Oakley. ⬤ 9 **Facilities** Non-diners area ✿ (Bar Outside area) ◗ Children's menu Children's portions Outside area ⋂ Parking WiFi ➟ (notice required)

STOKE BRUERNE   Map 11 SP74

The Boat Inn

tel: 01604 862428 **NN12 7SB**
email: info@boatinn.co.uk **web:** www.boatinn.co.uk
dir: In village centre, just off A508 & A5

Family-run free house on the Grand Union Canal

Trim thatch topping a long, low building of golden limestone makes this canalside pub stand out at the heart of the canal system. The busy locks here, together with the National Canal Museum directly opposite, are reflected in the decor; lots of old photos, paintings and ephemera – one bar is shaped like a narrowboat. Beers from the Marston's stable satisfy the thirst, whilst food can be enjoyed in bars, bistro or elegant restaurant. Traditional pub grub is the foundation of robust bar meals; the carte menu in Woodwards Restaurant includes herb-basted, slow-roasted rump of lamb, or pan-fried sea bass fillet with leeks.

Open all day all wk 9.30am-11pm (Sun 9.30am-10.30pm) **Food** Lunch all wk 9.30-9.30 Dinner all wk 9.30-9.30 Set menu available Restaurant menu available all wk ⊕ FREE HOUSE ◀ Banks's Bitter, Marston's Pedigree & Old Empire, Wychwood Hobgoblin, Jennings Cumberland Ale, Ringwood Best ♨ Thatchers Traditional. ⬤ 10 **Facilities** Non-diners area ✿ (Bar Garden) ◗ Children's menu Children's portions Garden ⋂ Parking ➟ (notice required)

THORNBY   Map 11 SP67

The Red Lion

tel: 01604 740238 **Welford Rd NN6 8SJ**
email: enquiries@redlionthornby.co.uk
dir: A14 junct 1, A5199 towards Northampton. Pub on left in village

An oasis just off the A14

Weary A14 travellers should take note of this 400-year-old traditional pub, as it's just a mile from junction 1 in tiny Thornby. Rest and refuel in the glorious summer garden, or bag a seat by the log fire in the comfortable bar on cold winter days. Simon and Louise Cottle offer four ales on handpump and a regularly changing menu of freshly prepared dishes. Menus change every month but they always include the ever popular home-made steak and Stilton pie; other choices might be braised pig cheek, apple sauce, crackling and sage jus; and tandoori chicken with Bombay potatoes, peas, spinach and mint yogurt. For dessert perhaps try dark chocolate and orange tart, confit orange and Chantilly cream. Sandwiches are available at lunchtime. Annual beer festivals are held.

Open all wk 12-3 5-11 (Mon 5-10 Sat-Sun 12-11) **Food** Lunch Tue-Fri 12-2, Sat 12-3, Sun 12-5 Dinner Tue-Sat 6-9 ⊕ FREE HOUSE ◀ Adnams, Black Sheep, The Grainstore, Purity, Nobby's ♨ Westons Stowford Press. **Facilities** Non-diners area ✿ (Bar Garden) ◗ Children's portions Garden ⋂ Beer festival Parking WiFi ➟ (notice required)

TITCHMARSH   Map 11 TL07

The Wheatsheaf at Titchmarsh

tel: 01832 732203 **1 North St NN14 3DH**
email: enquiries@thewheatsheafattitchmarsh.co.uk
dir: A14 junct 13, A605 towards Oundle, right to Titchmarsh. Or from A14 junct 14 follow signs for Titchmarsh

Pretty village pub with smart, modern interior

There's a perfect balance of traditional and contemporary styles at this stone-built village pub. A wide selection of real ales is on offer in the bar and can be enjoyed beside one of the two open fires. Freshly prepared dishes might include roast pepper and sun-dried tomato risotto as a starter followed by pan-friend loin of tuna wrapped in Parma ham with avocado purée and sautéed samphire. Among the lighter dishes are ploughman's, or strips of rumps steak on ciabatta. Real ales include Sharp's Doom Bar, Butcombe and Fuller's London Pride.

Open all wk 12-3 6-11 (Sat 12-11 Sun 12-8) **Food** Lunch Mon-Thu 12-2, Fri-Sat 12-2.30, Sun 12-5 Dinner Mon-Sat 6-9.30 Set menu available Restaurant menu available all wk ⊕ FREE HOUSE ◀ Greene King IPA, Sharp's Doom Bar, Fuller's London Pride, Butcombe, Guest ales ⚲ Aspall. ▾ 11 **Facilities** Non-diners area ❄ (Bar Garden) ♦ Children's menu Children's portions Garden ⋈ Parking WiFi ⛟ (notice required)

TOWCESTER   Map 11 SP64

NEW The Folly Inn

tel: 01327 354031 **London Rd NN12 6LB**
email: info@follyinntowcester.co.uk **web:** www.follyinntowcester.co.uk
dir: On A5 opposite Towcester Racecourse

Quintessential thatched country inn for foodies

Sitting beside the A5 opposite Towcester Racecourse, the Folly beckons with its picture-postcard looks, flower-filled hanging baskets and coaching lamps. The interior reveals all the hallmarks of a proper diners' pub, with neatly laid tables in a clean and fresh setting. Lunchtime classics range from a club sandwich to posh fish and twice-cooked chips. Dinner could feature Perkins Lodge Farm steaks or Gloucestershire Old Spots pork chop from the chargrill. Desserts are tried and tested favourites such as sticky toffee pudding, or baked New York cheesecake. If a glass of ale in the extensive rear garden is all that's required, three of the county's most cherished breweries are on tap.

Open 12-2.30 6-9.30 (Sun 12-7.30) Closed Mon **Food** Contact pub for food times Restaurant menu available Tue-Sun ⊕ FREE HOUSE ◀ Gun Dog Ales, Towcester Mill, Whittlebury. **Facilities** ❄ (Bar Garden) ♦ Children's menu Children's portions Garden ⋈ Parking WiFi

The Saracens Head ★★★ INN

tel: 01327 350414 **219 Watling St NN12 6BX**
email: saracenshead.towcester@greeneking.co.uk
web: www.saracenshead-towcester.co.uk
dir: M1 junct 15A, A43 towards Oxford. Take A5 signed Towcester

400 years old and immortalised by Charles Dickens

This imposing building dates back over 400 years, and is featured in Charles Dickens' first novel, *The Pickwick Papers*. The same home comforts that Dickens enjoyed when visiting Towcester have been updated to modern standards, and discerning customers will find excellent service in the restored pub. Starters might be panko-breadcrumbed calamari rings; or chicken liver pâté with cherry compôte, followed by a main course of beef and ale pie, mash and vegetables; or leek, potato and spring onion homity pie. Sandwiches, jackets, wraps and ciabattas are all available too.

Open all day all wk 11-11 (Fri-Sat 11am-mdnt) **Food** Lunch all wk 11-5 Dinner all wk 5-10 ⊕ GREENE KING/OLD ENGLISH INNS ◀ Abbot Ale & IPA, Morland Old Speckled Hen, Guest ale. ▾ 13 **Facilities** Non-diners area ♦ Children's menu Children's portions Garden ⋈ Beer festival Parking WiFi ⛟ **Rooms** 21

UPPER BODDINGTON   Map 11 SP45

NEW Plough Inn

tel: 01327 260364 **32 Warwick Av NN11 6DH**
email: enquiries@ploughinnboddington.co.uk
dir: Phone pub for detailed directions

Traditional thatched village inn close to Silverstone

Set within lovely Northamptonshire countryside, the Plough Inn is a charming 18th-century thatched coaching inn at the heart of village life in Upper Boddington. Just one mile from the tranquility of Boddington reservoir with its fishing and sailing club, the pub is also convenient for Silverstone race circuit. A traditional pub with flagstones and log burner, this free house serves several real ales, which can be enjoyed in the snug or 'Doll's Parlour'. In the dining room, enjoy dishes such as pork belly with cider gravy or fish and chips. Look out for the bank holiday beer festival in August.

Open all wk 5.30-11 (Fri 5-12 Sat 12-12 Sun 12-10.30) **Food** Lunch Sat 12-5, Sun 12-4 Dinner Tue-Sat 6-9 ⊕ FREE HOUSE ◀ Shepherd Neame Spitfire, Local guest ales. **Facilities** Non-diners area ❄ (Bar Outside area) ♦ Children's menu Children's portions Outside area ⋈ Beer festival Parking WiFi ⛟ (notice required)

WADENHOE

Map 11 TL08

The King's Head

PICK OF THE PUBS

tel: 01832 720024 **Church St PE8 5ST**
email: info@wadenhoekingshead.co.uk
dir: *From A605, 3m from Wadenhoe rdbt. 2m from Oundle*

Pretty pub featuring a shaded riverside garden

Set in the unspoilt village of Wadenhoe, alongside the picturesque River Nene, this stone-built, partially thatched inn has been serving travellers since the 17th century. In the summer, grab a seat in extensive riverside gardens in the shade of the ancient willow trees and watch the colourful narrow boats over a pint of King's Head Bitter. In winter, head for the comfortable bar with its quarry-tiled and bare-boarded floors, heavy oak-beamed ceilings, pine furniture and open log fires. The pub offers the most modern facilities but has lost none of its old world charm. The lunchtime menu offers sandwiches, pies and light bites such as home-made burger topped with cheddar cheese, or a ploughman's. In the evening you can feast like a king on warm pork and black pudding terrine with apple sauce, or roast chicken, tarragon and shallot pot pie, minted new potatoes and purple sprouting broccoli.

Open all day all wk 11-11 (Sun 12-10 winter 11-2.30 5.30-11 Sun 12-6) Closed Sun eve in winter **Food** Lunch all wk 12-2.30 Dinner all wk 6-9 ⊕ FREE HOUSE ◼ King's Head Bitter, Digfield Barnwell Bitter, Brewster's Hop Head ♂ Gaymers. ♥ 15 **Facilities** Non-diners area ♦♦ Children's portions Garden ⊼ Beer festival Parking ⇔

WESTON

Map 11 SP54

The Crown

PICK OF THE PUBS

tel: 01295 760310 **Helmdon Rd NN12 8PX**
email: mike.foalks@live.co.uk
dir: *Accessed from A43 or B4525*

Community-focused village pub with an interesting tale

It is here at this delightful 16th-century inn, on the day after the murder of his children's nanny in 1974, Lord Lucan was allegedly spotted knocking back a pint. Today, The Crown fulfils a role as a true community pub, with a reputation for its family- and dog-friendly attitude, its excellent beers and a range of high-quality, locally-sourced, 'nothing-out-of-a-packet' dishes. The interior is modern and styled in calming colours. A seasonal menu might well feature the following temptations – beetroot cured salmon, chilli cream, honey and mustard; roast chicken breast, mushroom risotto and rocket and rosemary pesto; toad-in-the-hole with mash, seasonal vegetables and gravy. There's always something going on at the pub event-wise including celebrity chef's nights, and Ruby Tuesdays, the rhyming-slang explanation making sense only to those who remember a Northern Irish singer called Ruby Murray, thus curry.

Open all wk 12-3 5-11 (Fri-Sat 12-11 Sun 12-5) Closed Mon L **Food** Lunch Tue-Sat 12-3, Sun 12-3 Dinner Mon-Sat 6-9.30 Av main course ££15 ⊕ FREE HOUSE ◼ Hooky, Fuller's London Pride, St Austell Tribute, Sharp's Doom Bar ♂ Thatchers Gold. **Facilities** Non-diners area ♣ (Bar Garden) ♦♦ Children's menu Children's portions Garden ⊼ Parking WiFi ⇔ (notice required)

WOODNEWTON

Map 11 TL09

The White Swan

tel: 01780 470944 **22 Main St PE8 5EB**
dir: *Phone for detailed directions*

Popular village pub with contemporary interior

When Ian Simmons bought this 19th-century, stone-built pub it was in a bad way, with heavy shutters on the windows and doors, having closed down no less than three times in five years. But with his dedication and strong local support, The White Swan really is making a name for itself. Beer drinkers will find Sharp's Doom

Bar and Woodforde's Wherry. On the menu, pub classics include chef's fish pie; and chargrilled beefburger; other mains are pan-fried sea bass fillet; braised sticky beef; and butternut squash and pine nut tagliatelle. Young ones can choose from their own dedicated menu.

Open all wk 12-3 6-11 (Sat 12-11 Sun 12-10.30) **Food** Lunch all wk 12-2.30 Dinner all wk 6-9.30 Set menu available ⊕ FREE HOUSE ◼ Woodforde's Wherry, Sharp's Doom Bar. **Facilities** Non-diners area ♣ (Bar Garden Outside area) ♦♦ Children's menu Children's portions Garden Outside area ⊼ Parking WiFi ⇔ (notice required)

YARDLEY HASTINGS

Map 11 SP85

Rose & Crown

tel: 01604 696276 **4 Northampton Rd NN7 1EX**
email: info@roseandcrownbistro.co.uk **web:** www.roseandcrownbistro.co.uk
dir: *A428 from Northampton. 1st left to Yardley Hastings*

Great bistro-style food and good ale

Andrew Dunkley's stone-built village pub has been a hostelry since at least 1748, but the Bistro is his own creation. It's here that Andrew's daily-changing menu blends traditional British cuisine with more distant influences to produce dishes such as white crab and chilli tagliatelle; devilled lamb's kidneys; saddle of Black Forest wild boar, pink fir fondant, celeriac purée and sprouting broccoli. A favourite among the desserts is the dark chocolate fudge brownie, while the British cheeseboard has Wodehill Blue from Bedfordshire, Bosworth Ash from Staffordshire and vintage Lincolnshire Poacher from Lincolnshire, of course.

Open 12-11 (Mon 5-11 Fri-Sat 12-11.30 Sun 12-10) Closed Mon L **Food** Lunch Tue-Sun 12-3 Dinner Mon-Sat 6-9, Sun 6-8 Set menu available Restaurant menu available all wk ⊕ FREE HOUSE ◼ Hart Brewery The Local, Greene King Abbot Ale ♂ Aspall, Thatchers. ♥ 20 **Facilities** Non-diners area ♣ (Bar Restaurant Garden) ♦♦ Children's portions Garden ⊼ Parking WiFi

NORTHUMBERLAND

ALNWICK   Map 21 NU11

The Hogs Head Inn ★★★ INN

tel: 01665 606576 **Hawfinch Dr NE66 2BF**
email: info@hogsheadinnalnwick.co.uk web: www.hogsheadinnalnwick.co.uk
dir: *From S: A1 onto A1068 signed Alnwick. 3rd exit at rdbt. Under A1, right at BP garage. From N: A1 onto A1068 signed Alnwick. 1st left, right at BP garage (NB older Sat Nav systems may not recognise pub's postcode)*

Notable local food served at this Harry Potter-inspired pub

Named after the pub featured in the Harry Potter books, this inn is just minutes from Alnwick Castle, which was used as Hogwarts in the first two films. Close to Alnwick Garden, the Hogs Head is an ideal base for exploring Northumberland, and food at this family-friendly pub is served all day. North East produce appears throughout the menu — belly pork and black pudding served with peppercorn sauce and crispy crackling; chicken and pancetta tagliatelle in creamy garlic sauce; or chickpea and coriander burger. Save space for treacle sponge and custard, and wash it down with a pint of Hadrian Border Tyneside Blonde.

Open all day all wk **Food** Contact pub for food times ⊕ FREE HOUSE ◀ Black Sheep Best Bitter, Hadrian Border Tyneside Blonde ☼ Somersby Cider. ♥ **Facilities** Non-diners area ♦ Children's menu Children's portions Play area Garden Outside area ⊨ Parking WiFi ⇔ (notice required) **Rooms** 53

AMBLE   Map 21 NU20

NEW The Wellwood

tel: 01665 714646 **High St NE65 0LD**
email: enquiries@wellwoodamble.co.uk
dir: *At junct of A1068 & High St in Amble*

Traditional meals served alongside Indian classics

On the stunning Northumberland coast in an Area of Outstanding Natural Beauty, The Wellwood started life as a farmhouse and it's the oldest building in Amble. Walkers and locals mingle in the bar over pints of Timothy Taylor Landlord, whilst diners have very different options, with a restaurant, dining room and carvery. As well as a bar menu and traditional pub favourites like bangers and mash and steak pie, there is a separate menu of Asian specialties, cooked by two experienced Indian chefs. Try the tandoori lamb chops and the chicken in lemongrass and coconut.

Open all day all wk **Food** Lunch all wk 12-3 Dinner all wk 5-10 Av main course £7-£10 Set menu available Restaurant menu available ⊕ PUNCH TAVERNS ◀ Wells Bombardier, Timothy Taylor Landlord, Sharp's Doom Bar. ♥ **Facilities** Non-diners area ❧ (Bar Garden) ♦ Children's menu Children's portions Family room Garden ⊨ Parking WiFi ⇔ (notice required)

BARRASFORD   Map 21 NY97

The Barrasford Arms ⊛

tel: 01434 681237 **NE48 4AA**
email: contact@barrasfordarms.co.uk
dir: *From A69 at Hexham take A6079 signed Acomb & Chollerford. In Chollerford by church turn left signed Barrasford*

A destination food pub

Chef Tony Binks's village inn stands close to Hadrian's Wall deep in the glorious Northumbrian countryside, with spectacular views of the Tyne Valley. Despite the emphasis on food, it retains a traditional pub atmosphere, with local Wylam and Hadrian Border ales on tap in the time-honoured bar, which fills with locals and passing walkers and cyclists. Most beat a path to the door for Tony's short, imaginative, one-AA Rosette menus. For dinner, tuck into red onion and goats' cheese tart with cherry tomato salsa; roast wild bass with asparagus, Charlotte potatoes and salad; pheasant and vegetable casserole with braised red cabbage;

and baked pear and almond tart with fresh vanilla sauce for afters. His set and Sunday lunches are great value.

Open 12-3 6-11 (Sat-Sun all day) Closed 1st wk Jan, Mon L (Mon all day Nov-Mar) **Food** Lunch Tue-Sun 12-2.30 Dinner Tue-Sat 6.30-9 Set menu available ⊕ FREE HOUSE ◀ Wylam Gold Tankard, Hadrian Border Gladiator. **Facilities** Non-diners area ♦ Children's portions Garden ⊨ Parking WiFi ⇔ (notice required)

BEADNELL   Map 21 NU22

The Craster Arms ★★★★ INN

tel: 01665 720272 **The Wynding NE67 5AX**
email: michael@crasterarms.co.uk web: www.crasterarms.co.uk
dir: *Exit A1 at Brownieside signed Preston. Left at T-junct signed Seahouses. Right signed Beadnell village. Pub on left*

Within walking distance of beautiful beaches

In the 15th century, the English in this neck of the woods built small fortified watch towers to warn of Scottish invasions — this was one of them. Since becoming a pub in 1818 its role has widened to offer not just food, drink and accommodation, but a programme of live entertainment, including the Crastonbury music festival (an RNLI fundraiser), and a beer and cider festival (last weekend in July). Sandwiches, baguettes, paninis, salads and hot meals are available at lunchtime; in the evening there's braised lamb shank; Thai green chicken curry; seasonal blackboard specials; crab fishcake and other local seafood.

Open all day all wk 11-11 **Food** Lunch all wk 11-9 Dinner all wk 11-9 ⊕ PUNCH TAVERNS ◀ Camerons Strongarm, Black Sheep, Mordue Workie Ticket ☼ Westons Traditional Scrumpy & Old Rosie. **Facilities** Non-diners area ❧ (Bar Garden) ♦ Children's menu Children's portions Garden ⊨ Beer festival Cider festival Parking WiFi ⇔ **Rooms** 3

BELFORD   Map 21 NU13

Blue Bell Hotel

tel: 01668 213543 **Market Place NE70 7NE**
email: enquiries@bluebellhotel.com
dir: *From A1 halfway between Berwick-upon-Tweed & Alnwick follow Belford signs*

Worth leaving the busy A1 for

At one time a busy coaching inn in the village centre on the old London to Edinburgh road, the hotel and its fine gardens still attract many a traveller. Unquestionably, the food has much to do with its appeal, with starters that include bacon, brie and black pudding salad; smoked salmon and dill fishcake; and local Adderstone Scotch egg, while the roll-call of main dishes includes chicken Kiev; pan-fried liver, red onions and bacon; Eyemouth fish pie; rib-eye and sirloin steaks; and tagliatelle pesto. A little further north, over a causeway, is Holy Island, but do be sure to check the times of the tides before visiting.

Open all day all wk 11am-2am **Food** Lunch all wk 12-2.30 Dinner all wk 6-9 ⊕ FREE HOUSE ◀ Tetley's Smoothflow, Black Sheep, Guinness. **Facilities** Non-diners area ❧ (Bar Garden Outside area) ♦ Children's menu Children's portions Play area Garden Outside area ⊨ Parking WiFi ⇔ (notice required)

BLANCHLAND   Map 18 NY95

The Lord Crewe Arms ★★★ CHH ⊛   **PICK OF THE PUBS**

tel: 01434 675469 **DH8 9SP**
web: www.lordcrewearmsblanchland.co.uk
dir: *10m S of Hexham via B6306*

Memorable village inn with unfussy, reliable menu

Blanchland, high in the Durham Dales, is an exquisite little estate village, full of charming houses built from the local honey-coloured stone. The Lord Crewe began life as the Abbot's Lodge and guest house to a Norman abbey. It's owned by the same people as Calcot Manor, Barnsley House and the Village Pub in Gloucestershire, and they certainly know what they're doing when it comes to creating a comfortable, contemporary experience in an historic setting. The impressively vaulted Crypt Bar offers local beers, including their own, Lord Crewe Brewe; from the kitchen equally parochial dishes vary by the season and aim at offering old fashioned nostalgic grub in the bar and two restaurants. Anticipate fulfilling fish dishes — pan-fried cod with whipped potato, buttered spinach and brown shrimps, for example; meatier choices might include roast pork fillet with braised shallots and 'Crewe' cured bacon; venison steak with sweet 'n' sour beetroot and braised red cabbage, or a peppered flat iron steak with chips and onion rings. Finish with Yorkshire rhubarb fool and sponge fingers; or sticky toffee pudding with salted caramel sauce and vanilla ice cream. You can eat alfresco in the beautiful gardens.

Open all day all wk 11-11 **Food** Lunch all wk 12-3 Dinner all wk 6-9 Av main course £15.50 ⊕ FREE HOUSE ◀ Allendale Golden Plover, Wylam Gold Tankard, Lord Crewe Brewe (pub's own) ♂ Westons Stowford Press. ⏷ 9 **Facilities** Non-diners area ❤ (Bar Garden) ♦ Children's menu Children's portions Garden ⋤ Parking WiFi **Rooms** 21

CARTERWAY HEADS — Map 19 NZ05

The Manor House Inn — PICK OF THE PUBS

tel: 01207 255268 **DH8 9LX**
email: themanorhouseinn@gmail.com
dir: A69 W from Newcastle, left onto A68 then S for 8m. Inn on right

Head out of town for this popular all-rounder

When shopping in Newcastle or Durham palls and you fancy a drink or meal out of town, a 30-minute drive will get you to this former coaching inn. As the stone walls, low-beamed ceiling and massive timber support in the bar might suggest, it was built in the mid 18th century. From its lofty position, there are great views of both the Derwent Valley and reservoir. Jostling for real ale drinkers' attention are Old Speckled Hen and local brews. The restaurant is divided into two, the larger area welcoming families with children. Most produce is local and includes game and wild fish from hereabouts. Suggested dishes include toasted walnut, red wine poached pear and Stilton salad; and premium Cumberland sausage and mash, garden peas and rich onion gravy; and crispy real ale battered Barents Sea cod with home-made chips. There's an annual beer festival at the end of August.

Open all day all wk 12-11 (Sun 12-10.30) Closed 26 Dec, 1st Mon in Jan **Food** Lunch Mon-Sat 12-9, Sun 12-8 summer 12-7 winter Dinner Mon-Sat 12-9, Sun 12-8 summer 12-7 winter ⊕ ENTERPRISE INNS ◀ Morland Old Speckled Hen, Local guest ales ♂ Westons Old Rosie. ⏷ 12 **Facilities** Non-diners area ❤ (Bar Garden) ♦ Children's menu Children's portions Garden ⋤ Beer festival Cider festival Parking WiFi ⋙ (notice required)

CHATTON — Map 21 NU02

NEW Percy Arms ★★★★ INN

tel: 07733 936155 **Main Rd NE66 5PS**
email: enquiries@percyarmschatton.co.uk **web:** www.percyarmschatton.co.uk
dir: From A1 between Warenford & Belford, onto B6348 signed Chatton

Classy pub in tranquil village

On a low grassy bank with tables and benches, this beautifully refurbished pub, with an underlying theme of game birds and animals, reflects owner Kris Blackburn's refined approach to styling. The dog-friendly, L-shaped bar is filled with chesterfields, tartan-covered chairs, hunting-scene drapes, horns, horseshoes, riding crops and wellies, all within range of an open fire. Allendale Golden Plover and Acton Golden Cocker real ales are brewed in the North Pennines and Blyth respectively. On a seasonal menu perhaps toad-in-the-hole; battered North Sea cod

and chunky chips; or a Percy pie, perhaps with Northumberland steak and Alnwick ale, or a veggie version.

Open all day all wk **Food** Lunch Wed-Sun 12-9 Dinner Wed-Sun 12-9 ⊕ FREE HOUSE ◀ Allendale Golden Plover, Acton Golden Cocker. **Facilities** Non-diners area ❤ (Bar) ♦ Children's menu Children's portions Garden ⋤ Parking WiFi ⋙ (notice required) **Rooms** 5

CORBRIDGE — Map 21 NY96

The Angel of Corbridge

tel: 01434 632119 **Main St NE45 5LA**
email: info@theangelofcorbridge.com
dir: 0.5m off A69, signed Corbridge

Prime location in historic town

In the heart of Northumberland, this old coaching inn dates to 1726 and is the oldest in Corbridge. There's a real fire in the spacious lounge bar and the barn restaurant offers a solid English menu drawing on local producers. The traditional bar offers beers from the local brewery and serves food all day, with a bar menu as well as chef's specials and sandwiches. Typical dishes from the specials menu might be Thai marinated fillet of beef with a rocket, cucumber and mint salad to start, followed by roast saddle of lamb stuffed with sausage, apricot and prune; or brioche-breaded plaice fillets.

Open all day all wk 11-11 (Fri-Sat 11am-mdnt Sun 11-10.30) **Food** Lunch Mon-Sat 12-9, Sun 12-5 Dinner Mon-Sat 12-9 Av main course £12.50 Set menu available Restaurant menu available ⊕ FREE HOUSE ◀ Hadrian Border Tyneside Blonde, Wylam Angel, Local ales. ⏷ 12 **Facilities** Non-diners area ♦ Children's menu Children's portions Outside area ⋤ Parking WiFi ⋙ (notice required)

CRASTER — Map 21 NU21

The Jolly Fisherman

tel: 01665 576461 **Haven Hill NE66 3TR**
email: info@thejollyfishermancraster.co.uk
dir: Exit A1 at Denwick. Follow Seahouses signs, then 1st sign for Craster

Fine harbourside location

The charm of this historic stone-flagged, low-beamed pub remains undimmed. When it's cold, relax by an open fire; at any time admire impressive Dunstanburgh Castle from the delightful beer garden. When the pub opened in 1847, Craster was a thriving fishing village; now only a few East Coast cobles leave harbour, mostly for the herring that, once smoked, become the famous kippers. House specialities are fresh fish stew; whole line-caught sea bass; breast of chicken in Serrano ham; and slow-roasted pepper with butternut squash and celeriac risotto. At the bar are Black Sheep and Mordue Workie Ticket bitter.

Open all day all wk 11-11 **Food** Lunch Mon-Sat 11-3, Sun 12-3 Dinner Mon-Sat 5-8.30 winter, 5-9 summer, Sun 5-9 ⊕ PUNCH TAVERNS ◀ Mordue Workie Ticket, Black Sheep, Timothy Taylor Landlord, Guest ale ♂ Symonds Scrumpy Jack. ⏷ 12 **Facilities** Non-diners area ❤ (Bar Garden) ♦ Children's menu Children's portions Garden ⋤ Parking WiFi ⋙ (notice required)

FALSTONE — Map 21 NY78

The Pheasant Inn ★★★★ INN — PICK OF THE PUBS

See Pick of the Pubs on page 372

PICK OF THE PUBS

The Pheasant Inn ★★★★ INN

FALSTONE   Map 21 NY78

tel: 01434 240382
Stannersburn NE48 1DD
email: stay@thepheasantinn.com
web: www.thepheasantinn.com
dir: *A69, B6079, B6320, follow signs for Kielder Water*

Perfect base for Northumbrian adventures

In the early 17th century, long, long before nearby Kielder Water and Kielder Forest were created, agricultural workers drank at a beer-house in Stannersburn. This ivy-clad country inn is that beer-house, now finding itself where the Northumberland National Park meets the Border Forest Park, and surrounded by verdant valleys, high moors and tranquil woodlands. It's well positioned too for cycle tracks, a sculpture trail, an observatory, endless walks and wildlife watching, including red squirrels. What you see today is what Irene and Robin Kershaw have achieved since they acquired it, then rather run down, in 1985. Most spaces in the two bars have been filled with historic Northumberland memorabilia, and on the exposed stone walls that support the blackened beams are photos of yesteryear's locals working at forgotten trades like blacksmithing and coalmining. In winter, log fires cast flickering shadows across the furniture.

The restaurant, with terracotta-coloured walls and furnished in mellow pine, looks out over the countryside. Self evidently it's where to enjoy Irene and Robin's daily-changing, traditional British food, all making the most of what Northumbria has to offer, such as slow-roasted local lamb with rosemary and redcurrant jus; grilled fresh salmon with hot pepper marmalade and crème fraîche; fresh dressed crab from the Northumberland coast; and Stilton and vegetable crumble with salad. Excellent beers from Wylam Brewery and Timothy Taylor might cloud the mind, but not the dark night skies, which make the area a mecca for astronomers. There is a tranquil stream-side garden.

Open 12-3 6.30-11 Closed 25-27 Dec, Mon-Tue (Nov-Feb) **Food** Lunch Mon-Sat 12-2.30 Dinner all wk 6-9 (Etr-Oct 6-8.30) ⊕ FREE HOUSE ◼ Timothy Taylor Landlord, Wylam Gold Tankard, Rocket, Red Kite, Red Shot & Angel. **Facilities** Non-diners area ♦ Children's menu Children's portions Play area Family room Garden Outside area ⋔ Parking WiFi **Rooms** 8

FELTON
Map 21 NU10

NEW The Northumberland Arms

tel: 01670 787370 **The Peth, West Thirston NE65 9EE**
email: thenorthumberlandarmsfelton@gmail.com
dir: *Take A1 from Morpeth towards Alnwick. Turn right, follow Felton signs*

Upmarket local and refined eatery

A solid stone-built coaching inn beside the River Coquet, about a mile from the A1. It was built in the 1820s by Hugh Percy, 3rd Duke of Northumberland, as a place for horses to rest and guests to freshen up before being received at Alnwick Castle. Acquired in recent years by the successful artisan bakery opposite, the Northumberland has undergone a complete and tasteful makeover. The bar, where locals and tourists alike sup pints of Harviestoun Bitter & Twisted, is now the focus of weekly quizzes and monthly folk music. The county's pantry furnishes the kitchen with most of its ingredients, for dishes such as chargrilled asparagus tips with Northumberland Nettle cheese; and braised pig's cheeks with white truffle mash.

Open all day all wk **Food** Lunch 12-6 Dinner 6-9 ⊕ FREE HOUSE ◖ Harviestoun Bitter & Twisted, Anarchy Blonde Star ♂ Gwynt y Ddraig Fiery Fox. **Facilities** Non-diners area ♨ (Bar) ♦♦ Children's menu Children's portions Parking WiFi ⛽ (notice required)

HAYDON BRIDGE
Map 21 NY86

The General Havelock Inn

tel: 01434 684376 **Ratcliffe Rd NE47 6ER**
email: generalhavelock@aol.com
dir: *On A69, 7m W of Hexham*

Free house overlooking the River Tyne

Built in the 1760s, this riverside inn is named after a 19th-century British Army officer. The restaurant, in a converted stone barn, is a favourite with local showbusiness personalities. The real ales are all sourced from a 30-mile radius: Mordue Workie Ticket and Nel's Best are but two. Owner and chef Gary Thompson makes everything by hand, including the bread and ice cream. Local ingredients are the foundation of his dishes, which include Cullen skink; chicken, ham and leek pie; and bread and butter pudding with apricot compôte. In summer, the patio area is covered by a marquee.

Open 12-2.30 7-12 (Sun 12-10.30) Closed Mon **Food** Lunch Tue-Sun 12-2.30 Dinner Tue-Sat 7-9 Av main course £10 Set menu available Restaurant menu available Tue-Sat ⊕ FREE HOUSE ◖ High House Farm Nel's Best, Mordue Workie Ticket, Cumberland Corby Blonde, Cullercoats Lovely Nelly, Jarrow Rivet Catcher. ⚑ 15 **Facilities** Non-diners area ♨ (Bar Garden) ♦♦ Children's portions Family room Garden ⊟ WiFi ⛽ (notice required)

HEDLEY ON THE HILL
Map 19 NZ05

The Feathers Inn
PICK OF THE PUBS

See Pick of the Pubs on page 374

HEXHAM
Map 21 NY96

Battlesteads Hotel & Restaurant
PICK OF THE PUBS

tel: 01434 230209 **Wark NE48 3LS**
email: info@battlesteads.com
dir: *10m N of Hexham on B6320 (Kielder road)*

Utterly charming pub, hotel and restaurant

Hadrian's Wall lies to the south of this converted 18th-century farmhouse; surrounding it are some of the country's finest livestock herds, game-shooting and fishing; and Britain's darkest night skies are overhead. There are three dining options: the bar serving, among others, Nel's Best real ale from High House Farm brewery, and Sandford Orchards cider; the conservatory, overlooking the walled herb, salad leaf, fruit and vegetable garden; and the softly-lit main restaurant, decorated with old railway travel posters. Among head chef Eddie Shilton's primarily modern British dishes are carpaccio of beetroot with fresh horseradish and Brinkburn goats' cheese; Cumbrian lamb shank tagine with bulgur wheat and harissa; and Thistleyhaugh organic chicken with shallots, bacon, parsley mash and greens. Desserts include their ever popular whisky and marmalade bread and butter pudding. Given half a chance, owner Richard Slade will show visitors his carbon-neutral heating system and other 'green' features. Check with them for the summer beer festival date.

Open all day all wk **Food** Lunch all wk 12-3 Dinner all wk 6.30-9.30 Set menu available Restaurant menu available all wk ⊕ FREE HOUSE ◖ Durham Magus, High House Farm Nel's Best, Guest ales ♂ Sandford Orchards. ⚑ 15 **Facilities** Non-diners area ♨ (Bar Garden) ♦♦ Children's portions Garden ⊟ Beer festival Parking WiFi ⛽ (notice required)

Dipton Mill Inn
PICK OF THE PUBS

tel: 01434 606577 **Dipton Mill Rd NE46 1YA**
email: ghb@hexhamshire.co.uk
dir: *2m S of Hexham on HGV route to Blanchland, B6306, Dipton Mill Rd*

Converted mill that now brews its own beer

Surrounded by farmland and woods with footpaths for pleasant country walks, and Hadrian's Wall and other Roman sites, this former farmhouse was rebuilt some 400 years ago and has a pretty millstream running right through the gardens. The Dipton Mill is home to Hexhamshire Brewery ales, which include Devil's Water and Whapweasel, plus Blackhall English Stout. All dishes are freshly prepared from local produce where possible. Start with tomato and vegetable soup, followed by mince and dumplings; duck breast with orange and cranberries; or haddock baked with tomatoes and basil. A decent selection of vegetarian options includes cheese and onion flan with salad. Dessert brings comforting favourites such as creamy lemon tart; and syrup sponge and custard, plus a good selection of Northumberland and Durham cheeses. Salads and an extensive selection of sandwiches and ploughman's are always available.

Open 12-2.30 6-11 (Sun 12-3) Closed 25 Dec, Sun eve **Food** Lunch all wk 12-2 Dinner Mon-Sat 6.30-8 ⊕ FREE HOUSE ◖ Hexhamshire Shire Bitter, Devil's Water, Devil's Elbow, Whapweasel, Blackhall English Stout, Seasonal ales ♂ Westons Old Rosie. ⚑ 17 **Facilities** Non-diners area ♨ (Garden) ♦♦ Children's portions Garden ⊟ ⛽ (notice required) **Notes** ⊜

Miners Arms Inn

tel: 01434 603909 **Main St, Acomb NE46 4PW**
email: minersarms2012@gmail.com
dir: *2m W of Hexham on A69*

Traditional food in peaceful family-run village pub

The Greenwell family took over this 18th-century village pub near Hadrian's Wall a few years ago, and it's very much a family business with David and Elwyn helped by their son and two daughters. Among the choice of ales, local Wylam Gold Tankard is always available, with guest beers available every week. Mainly locally sourced dishes, including haggis and black pudding with peppercorn sauce; and home-made steak and ale pie typify the traditional food. Visitors can enjoy the open-hearth fire, the sunny beer garden, or simply sit out front soaking up life in this peaceful village. Beer festivals are held occasionally.

Open all wk 4-12 (Sat-Sun 12-12) **Food** Lunch Sat 12-8, Sun 12-2.30 Dinner Tue-Fri 4-8, Sat 12-8 Av main course £8.95 ⊕ FREE HOUSE ◖ Wylam Gold Tankard, Yates Best Bitter, Guest ale. **Facilities** Non-diners area ♨ (Bar Garden) ♦♦ Children's menu Children's portions Garden ⊟ Beer festival

PICK OF THE PUBS

The Feathers Inn

HEDLEY ON THE HILL   Map 19 NZ05

tel: 01661 843607 **NE43 7SW**
email: info@thefeathers.net
web: www.thefeathers.net
dir: *A695 towards Gateshead. In Stocksfield right into New Ridley Rd. Left at Hedley on the Hill sign to village*

Microbrewery ales and cracking food

This small, 200-year-old stone-built free house is set high above the Tyne Valley with splendid views across the Cheviot Hills. Once frequented by lead miners and cattle drovers, all visitors are charmed by the friendly and relaxed atmosphere created by owners Rhian Cradock and Helen Greer. It's also worth the detour for its rotating choice of microbrewery ales; relax and sup Wylam Red Kite or Northumberland Pit Pony beside a welcoming wood-burning stove. Old oak beams, rustic settles and stone walls decorated with local photographs set the informal scene. There's a good selection of traditional pub games like shove ha'penny and bar skittles and you'll find a good collection of cookery books as well. Rhian's impressive daily menu makes sound use of the freshest local ingredients – including game from local shoots, rare breed local cattle and Longhorn beef – to create great British classics as well as regional dishes from the north east. You could start with black pudding,

poached free-range egg and devilled gravy, or potted brown shrimps with toast, watercress and lemon. Typical main courses include venison and beef Scotch pie with cabbage and bacon and creamy mash; and plaice with heritage potatoes, buttered rainbow chard, anchovy and sorrel butter. Leave room for apple crumble and vanilla custard, or sticky ginger parkin with butterscotch sauce and spiced ice cream. Families are welcome, and a small side room can be booked in advance if required. The Easter beer and food festival includes a barrel race, egg jarping, barbecue and a farmers' market, while the cider festival is on Summer Bank Holiday in August.

Open all wk 12-11 (Mon 6-11 Sun 12-10.30) Closed No food served 1st

2wks Jan **Food** Lunch Tue-Sat 12-2, Sun 12-4.30 Dinner Tue-Sat 6-8.30 Set menu available ⊕ FREE HOUSE ◀ Mordue Workie Ticket, Northumberland Pit Pony, Orkney Red MacGregor, Wylam Red Kite, The Consett Ale Works Red Dust Ö Westons 1st Quality & Old Rosie. ♥ **Facilities** Non-diners area ♦ Children's portions Outside area ⌂ Beer festival Cider festival Parking WiFi

HEXHAM *continued*

Rat Inn
PICK OF THE PUBS

tel: 01434 602814 **Anick NE46 4LN**
email: info@theratinn.com
dir: *2m from Hexham. At Bridge End (A69) rdbt, take exit signed Oakwood. Inn 500yds on right*

Passionate about local food and beer

Opposite the handkerchief-sized green in a tiny hamlet of stone-built cottages and farms, this convivial pub commands a shoulder of land above the River Tyne, looking out over the historic town of Hexham spread below; the tree-shaded terraced garden unlocks these great views. Indulge in a pint of beer from Hexhamshire, the county's oldest brewery, while contemplating whether the pub may have been built with stone liberated from nearby Hadrian's Wall. The stone theme continues within, with grand open fires and flagstone floors in the superbly traditional old bar of this one-time drovers' inn. Join in lively conversation with locals by the fine carved-oak bar, consider their opinions on the origin of the pub's name, and peruse a fine menu of proudly Northumbrian delicacies. Typical of these are beetroot-cured salmon with potato salad; and slow-roast belly pork with Savoy cabbage and potatoes Lyonnaise.

Open all day all wk **Food** Lunch Tue-Sat 12-2, Sun 12-3 Dinner Tue-Sat 6-9 ⊕ FREE HOUSE ◖ Cumberland Corby Ale, High House Farm Nel's Best, Hexhamshire Shire Bitter, Timothy Taylor Landlord, Wylam Gold Tankard. ♀ **Facilities** Non-diners area ♦♦ Children's portions Garden ☞ Parking WiFi

LONGFRAMLINGTON Map 21 NU10

The Anglers Arms
PICK OF THE PUBS

tel: 01665 570271 & 570655 **Weldon Bridge NE65 8AX**
email: info@anglersarms.com
dir: *Take A697 N of Morpeth signed Wooler & Coldstream. 7m, left to Weldon Bridge*

Still welcoming visitors after 250 years

Since the 1760s, this part-battlemented, three-storey, former coaching inn on the road to and from Scotland has commanded the picturesque Weldon Bridge over the River Coquet. It belongs to John and Julie Young, whose knick-knacks and curios, pictures and fishing memorabilia are liberally distributed within. On the bar top pump badges declare the availability of Timothy Taylor Landlord, Theakston Best Bitter and a trio of Greene King brews. A comprehensive menu suggests, for example, kipper salad – warm Craster kippers, new potatoes, endive and soft poached egg with Caesar dressing, followed by Tournedos Flodden – prime fillet steak and Stilton wrapped in bacon with garlic sauce; or glazed ham hock with vine tomatoes, chunky chips and cheese sauce. The carefully tended half-acre of garden is perfect for outdoor dining and includes a children's play park. It is possible to fish for brown trout, salmon and sea trout on the pub's own one-mile stretch of the Coquet.

Open all day all wk 11-11 (Sun 12-10.30) **Food** Lunch all wk 12-9.30 Dinner all wk 12-9.30 ⊕ FREE HOUSE ◖ Timothy Taylor Landlord, Morland Old Speckled Hen, Greene King Abbot Ale, Theakston Best Bitter. **Facilities** Non-diners area ♣ (Bar Garden Outside area) ♦♦ Children's portions Play area Family room Garden Outside area ☞ Parking ➡ (notice required)

NEW The Granby Inn ★★★ INN

tel: 01665 570228 **NE65 8DP**
email: info@thegranbyinn.co.uk **web:** www.thegranbyinn.co.uk
dir: *In village centre*

Popular with visitors to the Northumbrian coast

Once a coaching inn, this family-run pub just north of Morpeth is perfectly situated for exploring the stunning Northumbrian coast and the ancient town of Alnwick. Dating back around 250 years, The Granby Inn prides itself on being a traditional pub for a pint in the cosy bar but the food attracts diners from all over. Local sourcing extends to meat from a nearby butcher and fish from North Shields, all of which turns up in specials such as grilled fillets of sea bass on leek carbonara, or grilled lamb chops glazed with mustard and brown sugar.

Open all wk 9-3 6-11 (Sat-Sun all day) Closed 25-26 Dec & 1 Jan **Food** Lunch 12-3 Dinner 6-9 Av main course £12 Set menu available ⊕ FREE HOUSE/ **Facilities** ♦♦ Children's menu Children's portions Outside area ☞ Parking WiFi ➡ (notice required) **Rooms** 5

LONGHORSLEY Map 21 NZ19

Linden Tree ★★★★ HL ◉◉

tel: 01670 500033 **Linden Hall NE65 8XF**
email: lindenhall@macdonald-hotels.co.uk **web:** www.macdonald-hotels.co.uk/lindenhall
dir: *From A1 onto A697, 1m N of Longhorsley*

The 19th-hole after a round of golf

The friendly and informal Linden Tree pub stands within the 450-acres that surround Linden Hall, an impressive Georgian mansion that is now a popular golf and country club. A sunny patio makes a relaxed setting for lunch in summer and the brasserie-style menu makes good use of Scottish beef and lamb. Dishes might include steak and ale pie; shepherd's pie; battered haddock with chips and mushy peas; or rump or rib-eye steak from the grill. Round off a long day with a nightcap in the golfers' lounge.

Open all day all wk Mon-Sat 11-11 (Sun 11-10.30) **Food** Lunch all wk 12-9 Dinner all wk 12-9 Av main course £13 ⊕ FREE HOUSE ◖ Mordue, Guest ale. ♀ 10 **Facilities** Non-diners area ♣ (Bar Garden) ♦♦ Children's menu Children's portions Play area Garden ☞ Parking WiFi ➡ (notice required) **Rooms** 50

LOW NEWTON BY THE SEA Map 21 NU22

The Ship Inn

tel: 01665 576262 **The Square NE66 3EL**
email: forsythchristine@hotmail.com
dir: *NE from A1 at Alnwick towards Seahouses*

Good, simple food and home-brewed beers

There's a very salty tang about this pretty, late-1700s inn – of course there is, since it overlooks Newton Haven's sandy beach. Then there are the names of the real ales: Sea Coal, Sea Wheat, Ship Hop Ale and Sandcastles at Dawn, all in fact, with Dolly Day Dream brewed next door. The barrels then have to be rolled all of 15 feet to the cellar; from here they are pumped to the small bar, where you can expect plenty of locally caught fresh and smoked fish; toasted sandwiches; ploughman's; bacon, mushroom and tomato stottie (a local flat loaf); and hand-picked crab.

Open all wk seasonal variations, please telephone for details Closed 24-26 Dec **Food** Lunch all wk 12-2.30 Dinner Wed-Sat 7-8 ⊕ FREE HOUSE ◖ The Ship Inn Sea Coal, Dolly Day Dream, Sea Wheat, Ship Hop Ale, Sandcastles at Dawn. **Facilities** ♣ (Bar Restaurant Garden) ♦♦ Garden

MILFIELD   Map 21 NT93

The Red Lion Inn

tel: 01668 216224 **Main Rd NE71 6JD**
email: redlioninn@fsmail.net **web:** www.redlionmilfield.co.uk
dir: *On A697, 9m S of Coldstream (6m N of Wooler)*

Historic inn serving comfort food and guest ales

Dating back to the 1700s, sheep drovers from the northern counties stayed at this stone building before it was used as a stopover for the mail stagecoach en route from Edinburgh and London. Well placed for salmon and trout fishing on the River Tweed and for shooting on the Northumberland estates, the Red Lion offers a relaxing atmosphere, good guest beers and wholesome food. Start with breaded chicken goujons with sweet chilli or garlic mayonnaise before enjoying home-made steak and ale suet crust pie with chips and peas; for pudding choose vanilla crème brûlée or Eton Mess. There's also a beer festival in June.

Open all wk 11-2 5-11 (Sat 11-11 Sun 11-10.30) (summer all day) **Food** Lunch all day all wk summer, winter Mon-Fri 11-2, Sat-Sun 11-9 Dinner all day all wk summer, winter Mon-Fri 5-9, Sat-Sun 11-9 ⊕ FREE HOUSE ◁ Black Sheep, Guinness, Guest ales Ö Westons, Guest cider. **Facilities** Non-diners area ♦♦ Children's menu Children's portions Garden ⊼ Beer festival Parking WiFi ⊟

MORPETH   Map 21 NZ28

NEW St Mary's Inn ★★★★★ INN

tel: 01670 293293 **Saint Mary's Ln, St Mary's Park NE61 6BL**
email: hello@stmarysinn.co.uk **web:** www.stmarysinn.co.uk
dir: *From A1 into Stannington into Church Rd. At T-junct right into Green Ln, into St Mary's Park*

Spacious yet embracing cure for all ills

Occupying the site of a former hospital, this eponymously named pub continues the caring tradition – with hospitality. In-patients have been known to make a speedy recovery while relaxing by the real fires, and enjoying the pub's cosy corners and colourful spaces. Four real ales, including a pale ale brewed especially by Wylam Breweries, 17 wines by the glass, and a huge range of whiskies are dispensed at the huge oak bar. All-day sustenance ranges from good old-fashioned bar snacks such as corned beef and potato pie with brown sauce, to steaming plates of mince and dumplings with seasonal vegetables. Afternoon tea is a speciality.

Open all day all wk **Food** Lunch all day Dinner all day ⊕ FREE HOUSE ◁ Wylam St Mary's Ale Ö Samuel Smith's Organic. ⊈ 17 **Facilities** Non-diners area ✿ (Bar Garden Outside area) ♦♦ Children's menu Children's portions Garden Outside area ⊼ Parking WiFi **Rooms** 11

NETHERTON   Map 21 NT90

The Star Inn

tel: 01669 630238 **NE65 7HD**
dir: *7m from Rothbury*

Old fashioned inn, tip-top cask ales but no food

Little has changed at this timeless gem since the Wilson-Morton family took over in 1917. Lost in superb remote countryside north of Rothbury, The Star Inn retains many period features and the bar is like stepping into someone's living room, comfortable and quiet, with no intrusive fruit machines or piped music. Don't expect any food though, just cask ales in the peak of condition, served from a hatch in the entrance hall. This inn is a real find – just check the days of the week when it's open.

Open Tue-Wed & Sun 7.30pm-10.30pm (Fri-Sat 7.30pm-11pm) Closed Mon, Thu ⊕ FREE HOUSE ◁ Guest ales in summer. **Facilities** Non-diners area Outside area Parking ⊟ (notice required) **Notes** ⊛

NEWTON   Map 21 NZ06

Duke of Wellington Inn

tel: 01661 844446 **NE43 7UL**
email: info@thedukeofwellingtoninn.co.uk
dir: *From Corbridge A69 towards Newcastle. 3m to village*

Hillside, traditional country pub

Just off the A69 near Corbridge, this early 19th-century coaching inn overlooks the Tyne Valley and has stunning views, and is a handy base for exploring the National Park and Hadrian's Wall. The building's original oak and stone construction is complemented by modern furniture and fabrics that create a comfortable pub. On offer are local ales, a comprehensive wine list and enjoyable dishes such as beetroot smoked salmon; or pineapple and prawn cocktail, followed by lamb stew with red cabbage, carrots and new potatoes; or open wild mushroom lasagne. The stone floored bar has a roaring log fire during the colder months but when the sun shines there is ample space on the terrace to enjoy refreshments. Dogs are welcome in the bar and garden.

Open all day all wk 8am-11pm **Food** Lunch all wk 12-9 Dinner all wk 12-9 Set menu available ⊕ FREE HOUSE ◁ Hadrian Border Tyneside Blonde, Timothy Taylor Landlord. ⊈ 11 **Facilities** Non-diners area ✿ (Bar Garden) ♦♦ Children's menu Children's portions Garden ⊼ Parking WiFi ⊟ (notice required)

NEWTON-ON-THE-MOOR   Map 21 NU10

The Cook and Barker Inn ★★★★ INN   **PICK OF THE PUBS**

tel: 01665 575234 **NE65 9JY**
email: info@cookandbarkerinn.co.uk **web:** www.cookandbarkerinn.co.uk
dir: *0.5m from A1 S of Alnwick*

Traditional Northumbrian country inn with far-reaching views

For spectacular views of the North Sea coast and the Cheviot Hills, head for the Farmer family's creeper-covered, flower-adorned, stone-built pub and restaurant. Phil Farmer also runs Hope House Farm eight miles away, source of the organic beef, lamb and pork that feature on the various menus – 'forest and field', grills and roasts, and Oriental; there's also a seafood selection. A suggested dinner starter of seared West Coast scallops, black pudding, fresh green pea purée, and red wine reduction might be followed by either rack of Hope House Farm lamb with parsnips, petit pois, and redcurrant and pork wine sauce; or roasted sea bass fillet, prawn and crab risotto, and tempura herbs. Real ale drinkers can expect – indeed, should be pleased – to find Bass on the bar, as well as Timothy Taylor Landlord and Black Sheep. The en suite bedrooms are smartly furnished, some retaining original exposed beams.

Open all day all wk 12-11 **Food** Lunch all wk 12-2 Dinner all wk 6-9 Set menu available Restaurant menu available all wk ⊕ FREE HOUSE ◁ Timothy Taylor Landlord, Black Sheep, Bass Ö Kopparberg. **Facilities** Non-diners area ♦♦ Children's portions Garden ⊼ Parking WiFi ⊟ (notice required) **Rooms** 18

SEAHOUSES
Map 21 NU23

The Bamburgh Castle Inn ★★★ INN

tel: 01665 720283 **NE68 7SQ**
email: enquiries@bamburghcastleinn.co.uk **web:** www.bamburghcastleinn.co.uk
dir: *A1 onto B1341 to Bamburgh, B1340 to Seahouses, follow signs to harbour*

Harbourside inn with superb Farne Islands views

With its prime location on the quayside giving wraparound sea views as far as the Farne Islands, this is surely one of the best positioned pubs anywhere along Northumberland's stunning coast. Dating back to the 18th century, the inn has been transformed in more recent times to offer superb bar and dining areas plus seating outside. Children and dogs are welcomed, and pub dishes of locally sourced food represent excellent value. Typical of these are Cointreau chicken liver pâté; slow-cooked shoulder of lamb, mash and minted jus; and Nothumberland pheasant Stroganoff.

Open all day all wk **Food** Contact pub for food times ⊕ FREE HOUSE ◀ Black Sheep, Hadrian Border Farne Island ⊘ Somersby Cider. ♟ 11 **Facilities** Non-diners area ❄ (Bar Restaurant Garden) ♦ Children's menu Children's portions Family room Garden ♠ Parking WiFi 🚌 (notice required) **Rooms** 29

The Olde Ship Inn ★★★★ INN

PICK OF THE PUBS

tel: 01665 720200 **9 Main St NE68 7RD**
email: theoldeship@seahouses.co.uk **web:** www.seahouses.co.uk
dir: *Lower end of main street above harbour*

Family-owned inn with a nautical theme

Built on farmland around 1745, this stone-built inn with rooms has been in the present owners' family for the past century. Set above the bustling old harbour of Seahouses, the Olde Ship's interior is lit through stained-glass windows and the main saloon bar is full of character, its wooden floor made from ships' decking. A range of whiskies is supplemented by a selection of real ales, such as Hadrian Border Farne Island and Black Sheep. The inn's corridors and boat gallery are an Aladdin's cave of antique nautical artefacts, ranging from a figurehead to all manner of ship's brasses and dials. Bar food includes locally caught seafood and home-made soups. In the evenings, starters like duck and orange with oatcakes; or potted corned beef salad might be followed by seafood platter; gammon and chips; or chilli bean stew. Some of the bedrooms have views of the Farne Islands.

Open all day all wk 11-11 (Sun 12-11) **Food** Lunch all wk 12-2.30 Dinner all wk 7-8.30 (no Dinner late Nov-late Jan) ⊕ FREE HOUSE ◀ Greene King Ruddles, Courage Directors, Hadrian Border Farne Island, Morland Old Speckled Hen, High House Farm Nel's Best, Black Sheep, Theakston ⊘ Westons Old Rosie & Family Reserve. ♟ 10 **Facilities** Non-diners area ♦ Children's menu Children's portions Family room Garden ♠ Parking WiFi **Rooms** 18

SLAGGYFORD
Map 18 NY65

The Kirkstyle Inn

tel: 01434 381559 **CA8 7PB**
email: mail@andrewmarkland.plus.com
dir: *Just off A689, 6m N of Alston*

Wonderful views of the South Tyne Valley

Slaggyford has no shop or school, but when the South Tynedale Railway, currently being restored, reaches the village it will again have a station and its first trains since 1976. Thankfully, it already has the 18th-century Kirkstyle Inn, named after the stile into the adjacent churchyard and blessed with wonderful views of the river. In winter a log fire heats the bar, where among the real ales are Yates Best Bitter and a summer brew named after the inn. On the menu are local sausages with Alston honey mustard; shepherd's suet pudding; and breaded scampi. Friday is steak night.

Open 12-3 6-11 Closed Mon (Tue in winter) **Food** Lunch Tue-Sun 12-2 Dinner Tue-Sat 6-8.30 ⊕ FREE HOUSE ◀ Kirkstyle Ale, Yates Best Bitter, Guinness.
Facilities Non-diners area ❄ (Bar Outside area) ♦ Children's portions Outside area ♠ Parking WiFi 🚌 (notice required)

WARDEN
Map 21 NY96

The Boatside Inn

tel: 01434 602233 **NE46 4SQ**
email: sales@theboatsideinn.com **web:** www.theboatsideinn.com
dir: *From A69 W of Hexham, follow signs to Warden Newborough & Fourstones*

A traditional haven for walkers and cyclists

Standing beneath Warden Hill at the confluence of the North and South Tyne rivers, The Boatside is surrounded by woodland footpaths and bridleways, and has fishing rights on the river. The name of this stone-built country free house harks back to the days when a rowing boat ferried people across the river before the bridge was built. Black Sheep, Wylam and Mordue ales are on offer in the bar with its log fire and dart board. Meals are served in the conservatory, restaurant or snug, and include a sharing plate of cold Continental meats and cheeses; steak and kidney shortcrust pie; 'posh' fish pie; and beef lasagne. The Boatside welcomes children and dogs too.

Open all day all wk 11-11 (Sun 11-10.30) **Food** Lunch Mon-Sat 11-9, Sun 12-8 Dinner Mon-Sat 11-9, Sun 12-8 ⊕ FREE HOUSE ◀ Black Sheep, Caffrey's Irish Ale, John Smith's, Mordue, Wylam. **Facilities** Non-diners area ❄ (Bar Garden) ♦ Children's menu Children's portions Garden ♠ Parking WiFi 🚌 (notice required)

WARENFORD — Map 21 NU12

The White Swan
PICK OF THE PUBS

tel: 01668 213453 **NE70 7HY**
email: dianecuthbert@yahoo.com
dir: *100yds E of A1, 10m N of Alnwick*

Worth a detour from the main road

This 200-year-old coaching inn stands near the original toll bridge over the Waren Burn. Formerly on the Great North Road, the building is now just a stone's throw from the A1. Inside, you'll find thick stone walls and an open fire for colder days; in summer, there's a small sheltered seating area outside, with further seats in the adjacent field. The Dukes of Northumberland once owned the pub, and its windows and plasterwork still bear the family crests. Visitors and locals alike enjoy the welcoming atmosphere, fine wines and Northumbrian ales. The modern British dishes are created in-house from the county's produce; the bread, preserves and desserts are home made too. Try perhaps pheasant and black pudding terrine with black grape, apricot and cumin chutney; and seared duck breast, apple and hazelnut fricassée with anise velouté. Vegetarians are well catered for, with interesting dishes like baked tower of aubergine, courgette, onion, sweet pepper and mushroom with beetroot sorbet and blue cheese.

Open all wk Mon-Sat 12-2.30 5.30-10 (Sun 12-10) **Food** Lunch all wk 12-2.30 Dinner all wk 6-9 ⊕ FREE HOUSE ◀ Caledonian, Hadrian Border Tyneside Blonde, Greene King IPA. ⚑ 10 **Facilities** Non-diners area ❄ (Bar Garden) ♦♦ Children's menu Children's portions Garden ⌂ Parking WiFi ▭

NOTTINGHAMSHIRE

BEESTON — Map 11 SK53

The Victoria

tel: 0115 925 4049 **Dovecote Ln NG9 1JG**
email: vichotel@btconnect.com
dir: *M1 junct 25, A52 E. Turn right at Nurseryman PH, right opposite Rockaway Hotel into Barton St, 1st left, adjacent to railway station*

Excellent range of beers, ciders, whiskies and trains

This free house combines a welcoming atmosphere with great food and a wide choice of traditional ales and ciders, continental beers and lagers, many wines by the glass and single malt whiskies. The Victoria dates from 1899 when it was built next to Beeston Railway Station, and the large, heated patio garden is still handy for a touch of train-spotting. Main courses could include steak bordelaise; sauté of fresh monkfish and king prawns with mild Thai sauce; or smoked haddock with spinach and prawn lasagne. There are just as many options for vegetarians. Check out the dates of the annual beer festivals – Easter, last two weeks in July, and October.

Open all day all wk 10.30am-11pm (Sun 12-11) Closed 26 Dec **Food** Lunch Sun-Tue 12-9, Wed-Sat 12-9.30 ⊕ FREE HOUSE ◀ Timothy Taylor Boltmaker, Castle Rock Harvest Pale, Everards Tiger, Holden's Black Country Bitter, Blue Monkey, Kelham Island Best Bitter, Guest ales ⚙ Thatchers Traditional, Broadoak, Biddenden Bushels. ⚑ 25 **Facilities** Non-diners area ❄ (Bar Garden) ♦♦ Children's portions Garden ⌂ Beer festival Parking WiFi

---

BLIDWORTH — Map 16 SK55

Fox & Hounds

tel: 01623 792383 **Blidworth Bottoms NG21 0NW**
email: info@foxandhounds-pub.com **web:** www.foxandhounds-pub.com
dir: *From Ravenshead towards Blidworth on B6020, right to Blidworth*

Revitalised country pub with theatrical leanings

A fusion of blues, creams, reds and a change of furniture and fabrics have revitalised the pub without damaging the traditional country-style character that stem from its early 19th-century origins. For nearly 100 years the locals have performed a 'Plough Play' in the pub every January, recalling the days when Blidworth Bottoms was a larger community with shops and a post office. The Greene King ales are reliable as ever, and the menu delivers well-priced dishes of popular home-made favourites, such as beef casserole and herb dumplings or cottage pie.

Fox & Hounds

Open all day all wk 11.30-11.30 (Fri-Sat 11.30am-mdnt) **Food** Lunch all wk 11.30-9 Dinner all wk 11.30-9 ⊕ GREENE KING ◀ Morland Old Golden Hen, Hardys & Hansons Best Bitter & Olde Trip, Black Sheep, Seasonal guest ales ⚙ Thatchers Gold. ⚑ 9 **Facilities** Non-diners area ❄ (Bar Garden) ♦♦ Children's menu Children's portions Play area Garden ⌂ Parking ▭

BLYTH
Map 16 SK68

NEW The White Swan Inn

tel: 01909 591222 **High St S81 8EQ**
email: whiteswanblyth@gmail.com
dir: *From A1 or A1(M) to Blyth. Pub in village centre*

Tastefully decorated, popular village pub

This rather cute, whitewashed pub is sandwiched between two rows of cottages overlooking the village green. Inside it is warm and welcoming, a state of affairs that keeps the locals popping in for a pint, and visitors from further afield dining here. The menu is divided into self-explanatory sections: Salad Garden; The Pie Shed; From the Sea; From the Farm, for example. The one headed Black Rock Grill, though, might need explanation since it involves cooking your steak, kangaroo fillet, wild boar haunch, or bison rump on volcanic rocks at your table. You will be warned not to rest your cutlery on the rocks!

Open all day all wk **Food** Lunch 12-3 Dinner 6-9 Av main course £9 ⊕ ENTERPRISE INNS ◀ Theakston, Wentworth, Black Sheep. ☐ 8 **Facilities** Non-diners area ▪♦ Children's menu Children's portions Garden ⊞ WiFi ▭

CAR COLSTON
Map 11 SK74

The Royal Oak

tel: 01949 20247 **The Green NG13 8JE**
email: rich-vicky@btconnect.com
dir: *From Newark-on-Trent on A46 follow Mansfield, then Car Colston signs. From rdbt N of Bingham on A46 follow Car Colston sign. Left at next rdbt signed Car Colston*

Good pub food and an intriguing past

Some experts attribute origins as a hosiery factory to this 200-year-old inn, citing as evidence its unusual vaulted brick ceiling, undoubtedly capable of supporting any weighty textile machinery above. Much older is the centurion, perhaps from the nearby Roman-British town of Margidunum, whose ghost you may run into. Normally on duty in the bar is owner Richard Spencer, dispensing his carefully tended Marston's, Brakspear and Ringwood real ales, while Vicky, his wife (a dab hand chef) is in the kitchen preparing dishes such as fresh beer-battered or oven-baked haddock; shepherd's pie; and her very popular steak pies.

Open all day all wk **Food** Lunch Mon-Sat 12-2.15, Sun 12-4 Dinner Mon-Sat 6-8.45 ⊕ MARSTON'S ◀ EPA & Burton Bitter, Brakspear Bitter, Ringwood Boondoggle. ☐ 13 **Facilities** Non-diners area ▪ (Bar Garden) ♦ Children's portions Garden ⊞ Parking WiFi ▭ (notice required)

CAUNTON
Map 17 SK76

Caunton Beck
PICK OF THE PUBS

tel: 01636 636793 **NG23 6AB**
email: email@cauntonbeck.com
dir: *6m NW of Newark on A616 to Sheffield*

A village pub-restaurant open early until late

Tucked away beside a byroad deep in the rich farmlands of the Trent Valley, this beck-side village inn is one of a small chain of quality dining pubs owned by the Hope family. An imposing rose arbour, created by a former vicar of the village church across the water, is a feature of the much extended 16th-century cottages at the core of the pub. Fans of the hop can expect a glass of Black Sheep alongside further guest ales; wine-lovers have a choice of 24 by the glass. Beams, oak floorboards and rustic farmhouse-style furnishings characterise the traditional-style interior; outside is a sheltered terrace and lawned garden. Meals start with breakfast and continue well into the evening. The modern, mostly pan-European main menu changes regularly, offering a stimulating choice to satisfy most palates. Starters might be teriyaki salmon fillet with shredded bok choy; leading to pan-

seared red mullet, crayfish and chorizo-spiced paella; or panko pork schnitzel. Gourmet evenings add further spice to the mix.

Open all day all wk 9am-10.30pm Closed 25 Dec **Food** Lunch all wk 9am-10pm Dinner all wk 9am-10pm Set menu available Restaurant menu available all wk ⊕ FREE HOUSE ◀ Black Sheep, Oakham Ales JHB, Guinness, Guest ales Ö Westons Stowford Press. ☐ 24 **Facilities** Non-diners area ▪ (Bar Garden Outside area) ♦ Children's menu Children's portions Garden Outside area ⊞ Parking WiFi

COLSTON BASSETT
Map 11 SK73

The Martin's Arms
PICK OF THE PUBS

See Pick of the Pubs on page 380

EDWINSTOWE
Map 16 SK66

Forest Lodge ★★★★ INN

tel: 01623 824443 **4 Church St NG21 9QA**
email: reception@forestlodgehotel.co.uk web: www.forestlodgehotel.co.uk
dir: *A614 towards Edwinstowe, onto B6034. Inn opposite church*

Lovingly restored coaching inn at the edge of Robin Hood territory

This 18th-century coaching inn stands on the edge of Sherwood Forest opposite the church where Robin Hood is supposed to have married Maid Marian. Sympathetically restored by the Thompson family over the past decade or so, it includes stylish accommodation and a comfortable restaurant and bar. Award-winning cask ales are always on tap in two beamed bars warmed by open fires. An impressive baronial-style dining hall is an ideal setting for wholesome fare such as pan-fried pigeon with parsnip purée, dark chocolate and berries, followed by seared hake fillet with confit chorizo, broccoli purée, champ potatoes and cider jus; or butternut squash and sage risotto.

Open all wk 11.30-3 5.30-11 (Fri 11.30-3 5-11 Sun 12-3 6-10.30) Closed 1 Jan **Food** Lunch all wk 12-2.30 Dinner all wk 6-9 ⊕ FREE HOUSE ◀ Wells Bombardier, Kelham Island Pale Rider, Forest Lodge English Pale Ale, Ossett Silver King. **Facilities** Non-diners area ♦ Children's menu Children's portions Garden ⊞ Parking WiFi ▭ (notice required) **Rooms** 13

FARNDON
Map 17 SK75

The Farndon Boathouse ⊛
PICK OF THE PUBS

tel: 01636 676578 **Off Wyke Ln NG24 3SX**
email: info@farndonboathouse.co.uk
dir: *From A46 rdbt (SW of Newark-on-Trent) take Fosse Way signed Farndon. Right into Main St signed Farndon. At T-junct right into Wyke Ln, follow Boathouse signs*

Delightful riverside pub

Should you arrive here on a mystery tour, you might not guess that the tranquil, wooded view from the terrace of this modern bar and restaurant is the River Trent. The setting is perfect for this old-boathouse-styled pub, with wood cladding, chunky exposed roof trusses, stone floors and warehouse-style lighting. The food, long-term beneficiary of an AA Rosette, reflects a philosophy that champions home cooking and local sourcing, with herbs and salad leaves from the pub garden, and meats, fish and cheeses often smoked in-house. Wide-ranging menus offer goats' cheese salad with roast walnuts, mandarin orange, beetroot, rocket and croûtons; braised oxtail pie with wild mushrooms and herbs, beef jus, duck-fat roast potatoes and sprouting broccoli; and coconut-infused Thai fish bowl. An impressive 46 wines are sold by the glass. There are Spanish evenings, pie and monthly ladies' nights, and live music is played every Sunday evening.

Open all day all wk 10am-11pm **Food** Lunch all wk 12-3 Dinner all wk 6-9.30 Av main course £11.95 Set menu available Restaurant menu available all wk ⊕ FREE HOUSE ◀ Greene King IPA, Guest ales Ö Thatchers. ☐ 46 **Facilities** Non-diners area ♦ Children's menu Children's portions Garden ⊞ Parking WiFi ▭ (notice required)

PICK OF THE PUBS

The Martin's Arms

COLSTON BASSETT   Map 11 SK73

tel: 01949 81361 **School Ln NG12 3FD**
email: martins_arms@hotmail.com
web: www.themartinsarms.co.uk
dir: *Exit A46 between Leicester &*
Newark

Traditional 18th-century pub with seasonally inspired menus

In the pretty village of Colston Bassett in the Vale of Belvoir, this striking Grade II listed building occupies a quintessentially English spot on the corner of a leafy cul-de-sac close to an old cross. At the heart of village life since the 18th century, the pub takes its name from Henry Martin, MP for Kinsale in County Cork, who was the local squire in the early 19th century. Close to National Trust land, the pub is surrounded by ancient trees in the estate parkland to which it belonged until 1990, when the current owners, Jack Inguanta and Lynne Strafford Bryan, bought it, undertaking to maintain its character and unique atmosphere. This they have clearly managed to do, since much of the interior will transport you straight back in time, especially the Jacobean fireplaces and the period furnishings. The bar has an impressive range of real ales, with Castle Rock Harvest Pale waving the flag for the county, while another local 'brew' is elderflower pressé from Belvoir Fruit Farms. Bread,

preserves, sauces, terrines, soups, pasta and much, much more are all made on site. Classic pub dishes include a pie of the day; fish and chips and a beef burger teamed with Colston Bassett's famous Stilton, while mains from the à la carte might include tempura Scottish scallops, pickled cockles, crispy bacon, black pudding and Marie Rose sauce; or smoked Barbary duck breast, Waldorf, pickled walnut and celery cress. Among the desserts are banana cake, roast banana purée, Chantilly, rum and raisin; and chocolate brownie, white chocolate mousse with coconut cronuts. Overlooked by the church spire, the one-acre garden incorporates a croquet lawn.

Open all wk 12-3 6-11 (Sun 12-4 7-11) Closed 25 Dec **Food** Lunch Mon-Sat 12-2, Sun 12-2.30 Dinner Mon-Sat 6-9.30 Restaurant menu available all wk ⏚ FREE HOUSE ◀ Timothy Taylor Landlord, Marston's Pedigree, Bass, Greene King IPA, Castle Rock Harvest Pale ♂ Aspall, Cornish Orchards. ♀
Facilities Non-diners area ♦ Children's portions Family room Garden ⋒ Parking WiFi 🚐 (notice required)

HARBY
Map 17 SK87

Bottle & Glass

tel: 01522 703438 **High St NG23 7EB**
dir: S of A57 (Lincoln to Markham Moor road)

Compact and convivial old free house

One of the Exceedingly Small group's three pubs, the Bottle & Glass is in the village where Edward I's wife, Eleanor, died in 1290. With flagged floors and heavy beams, it offers Young's Bitter and London Gold, Black Sheep real ales, and a generous 24 wines by the glass. Starters on the short, seasonal lunch/dinner menu include tomato and red pepper soup; and ham hock terrine with cucumber pickle: mains typically include herb-crusted rack of lamb with redcurrant jus; linguine with Mediterranean vegetables; and pan-fried sea bass on piperade. On sunny days stake an early claim for a terrace table.

Open all day all wk 10am-11pm Closed 25 Dec **Food** Lunch Mon-Fri & Sun 10-9.30, Sat 10-10 Dinner Mon-Fri & Sun 10-9.30, Sat 10-10 Set menu available Restaurant menu available all wk ⊕ FREE HOUSE ◼ Young's Bitter & London Gold, Black Sheep, Guinness ♂ Thatchers Gold. ▼ 24 **Facilities** Non-diners area ❤ (Bar Garden) ♦♦ Children's menu Children's portions Play area Garden ⊓ Parking WiFi

HOVERINGHAM
Map 11 SK74

The Reindeer Inn

tel: 0115 966 3629 **Main St NG14 7JR**
email: reindeerinn@outlook.com
dir: NE of Nottingham. Phone for detailed directions

Reliable village inn close to lakeside walks

Piles of logs by the door beneath a flowery pergola signal the warm and friendly welcome offered at this traditionally furnished and decorated village pub in the Trent Valley lakeland. Set back from a main street lined by attractive cottages, it has a beer garden that overlooks the cricket ground, where trays of beers from Nottingham's Castle Rock Brewery slake a summer thirst. The quality pub-food menus change daily, but always include the signature dishes of Scotch egg with soft poached egg, leeks and cheese sauce; and dry-aged rib of Nottinghamshire beef. Enjoy pie night on the last Friday of every month. A change of hands.

Open 12-close (Mon 4.30-close) Closed Mon L **Food** Lunch Tue-Sat 12-2.30, Sun 12-3 Dinner Mon-Tue & Fri-Sat 5-8 Set menu available ⊕ FREE HOUSE ◼ Blue Monkey, Castle Rock Harvest Pale, Black Sheep Best Bitter ♂ Somersby Cider. ▼ 12 **Facilities** Non-diners area ❤ (Bar Garden) ♦♦ Children's portions Garden ⊓ Parking 🚌 (notice required)

KIMBERLEY
Map 11 SK44

The Nelson & Railway Inn

tel: 0115 938 2177 **12 Station Rd NG16 2NR**
dir: M1 junct 26, A610 to Kimberley

Family-run former railway inn

This popular village pub has been run by the same family for nearly 45 years. Originally dating from the 17th-century with Victorian additions, it sits next door to the Hardys & Hansons Brewery that supplies many of the beers. Sadly the two nearby railway stations that once made it a railway inn are now derelict. Interesting brewery prints and railway signs decorate the beamed bar and lounge. A hearty menu of pub favourites includes ploughman's and hot rolls, as well as grills and pub classics like lasagne, scampi and chips and home-made steak and ale pie.

Open all day all wk 11am-mdnt **Food** Lunch Mon-Fri 12-2.30, Sat 12-9, Sun 12-6 Dinner Mon-Fri 5.30-9, Sat 12-9 Restaurant menu available all wk ⊕ GREENE KING ◼ Hardys & Hansons Best Bitter, Cool & Dark Mild, Nottingham EPA, Guest ales. **Facilities** Non-diners area ❤ (Bar Garden) ♦♦ Children's menu Children's portions Family room Garden ⊓ Beer festival Parking WiFi 🚌

LAXTON
Map 17 SK76

The Dovecote Inn

tel: 01777 871586 **Cross Hill NG22 0SX**
email: hello@thedovecoteinn.com **web:** www.thedovecoteinn.com
dir: Exit A1 at Tuxford through Egmanton to Laxton

Superb local produce features on the menus

Like most of the village of Laxton, the 18th-century Dovecote is Crown Estate property, belonging to the Royal Family. There's a delightful beer garden with views of the church, while the interior has a bar as well as three cosy wining and dining rooms. The seasonally changing menus offer home-cooked dishes and could include Bury black pudding bon bons, parsnip purée, roasted cherry tomatoes and Parma ham; wild game cobbler (local venison, rabbit, pheasant and partridge); or pan-fried red mullet fillets with chorizo, tomato, potato gnocchi and rocket compôte. The Gourmet Fish Nights are extremely popular and booking is essential.

Open all wk 11.30-3 5.30-11 (Sun 12-10.30) **Food** Lunch Mon-Sat 11.30-3, Sun all day Dinner Mon-Sat 5.30-11, Sun all day Av main course £11.95 Set menu available ⊕ FREE HOUSE ◼ Castle Rock Harvest Pale, Black Sheep Best Bitter, Timothy Taylor Landlord, Guest ales. ▼ 11 **Facilities** Non-diners area ♦♦ Children's menu Children's portions Garden ⊓ Parking WiFi 🚌 (notice required)

MORTON
Map 17 SK75

The Full Moon Inn
PICK OF THE PUBS

tel: 01636 830251 **Main St NG25 0UT**
email: bookings@thefullmoonmorton.co.uk
dir: A617 from Newark towards Mansfield. Past Kelham, left to Rolleston & follow signs to Morton

Pretty red-brick pub with year-round appeal

All pantiles, pale bricks and creeper, this long-established inn stands at the village centre just a short hop from the magnificent Minster at nearby Southwell amidst the rich cornfields of the Trent Valley. Within, it's a contemporary and comfortable pub, with exposed old beams and brickwork retained from the original 18th-century cottages, scattered with reclaimed panelling and furniture. It's a relaxing locale in which to chill out with a glass of pale ale from the popular Navigation Brewery in Nottingham. What's more it's both child- and dog-friendly, with a grassy, tree-shaded garden an additional bonus for summer days. Equally local are the ingredients for the regularly changing menu. Good pub tucker features on the lunchtime bar menu: steak and Guinness pie; or haddock and pea risotto are filling examples. The à la carte extends the choice; perhaps a corned beef hash and soft boiled egg starter followed by Portobello mushroom burger with Stilton and leeks, all at keen prices.

Open all wk fr 11am **Food** Lunch Mon-Fri 12-2, Sat 12-3, Sun 12-5 Dinner Mon-Fri 5.30-9, Sat 6-9.30 Set menu available ⊕ FREE HOUSE ◼ Black Sheep, Navigation Pale, Sharp's Doom Bar, Timothy Taylor. ▼ 9 **Facilities** Non-diners area ❤ (Bar Garden) ♦♦ Children's menu Children's portions Play area Family room Garden ⊓ Parking WiFi 🚌 (notice required)

NEWARK-ON-TRENT
Map 17 SK75

The Prince Rupert

tel: 01636 918121 **46 Stodman St NG24 1AW**
email: rupert@kneadpubs.co.uk
dir: *5 mins walk from castle, on entry road to Market Sq*

Brimming with character and charm

The 15th-century Prince Rupert oozes character and charm and is one of Newark's most historic pubs. Expect old beams, wood floors, crackling log fires and cosy corners in the series of small downstairs rooms; make sure you explore upstairs, as the ancient architectural features are stunning. To drink, Oakham Ales JHB and Brains The Rev. James take pride of place alongside constantly changing choices while menus take in pub classics and excellent stone-baked pizzas. There are regular live music events and beer and cider festivals in the summer months.

Open all day all wk Mon-Tue 11-11 Wed-Thu 11am-mdnt Fri-Sat 11am-1am Sun 12-11 Closed 25 Dec **Food** Lunch Mon-Fri 12-2.30, Sat 12-5, Sun 12-8 Dinner Mon-Sat 6-9, Sun 12-8 ⊕ FREE HOUSE ◀ Brains The Rev. James, Oakham Ales JHB, Rotating guest ales. ♀ 16 **Facilities** Non-diners area ♦♦ Outside area ⊓ Beer festival Cider festival WiFi ▦

NOTTINGHAM
Map 11 SK53

NEW The Hand and Heart

tel: 0115 958 2456 **65-67 Derby Rd NG1 5BA**
email: handandheart@ntlworld.com
dir: *On A610 (2 mins' walk from Canning Circus)*

Great beer in a fascinating building

Originally a house, this Georgian building was also a brewery before becoming a pub in Victorian times. Beer was brewed in the converted stables and stored in the sandstone cave below, which is now a cosy snug. Famous for its excellent selection of real ales, the Hand and Heart holds two beer festivals a year, spring and autumn, and in the bar you can sample Round Heart from the Dancing Duck Brewery as well as the Maypole Brewery's Little Weed, and six changing guest ales. The food is also worthy of attention – confit duck leg; slow braised oxtail; or Hand and Heart belly pork, for example.

Open all day all wk 12-11 (Thu 12-12 Fri-Sat 12-late Sun 12-10.30) Closed 25 Dec & 1 Jan **Food** Lunch Mon-Sat 12-9.30, Sun 12-9 Dinner Mon-Sat 12-9.30, Sun 12-9 Set menu available ⊕ FREE HOUSE ◀ Dancing Duck Round Heart, Maypole Little Weed, Guest ales ♂ Guest ciders. ♀ 18 **Facilities** Non-diners area ♣ (Bar Outside area) Outside area ⊓ Beer festival Cider festival WiFi ▦

Ye Olde Trip to Jerusalem
PICK OF THE PUBS

tel: 0115 947 3171 **1 Brewhouse Yard, Castle Rd NG1 6AD**
email: 4925@greeneking.co.uk
dir: *In town centre*

Medieval gem with history aplenty

Castle Rock, upon which stands Nottingham Castle, is riddled by caves and passageways cut into the sandstone. The builders of this unusual pub made the most of this, incorporating some of the caves into the design of the inn, one of Britain's oldest – founded in AD1189. The name recalls that soldiers, clergy and penitents gathered here before embarking on the Crusade to the Holy Land – doubtless they drank to their quest at the castle's beerhouse before their trip to Jerusalem. Centuries of service impart instant appeal, from the magpie collection

of furnishings in the warren of rooms to the unique Rock Lounge, and quirks such as the cursed galleon and the fertility chair. Beers from the Nottingham Brewery feature strongly, accompanying a reliable menu of old favourites like slow-cooked pork belly and Scottish scampi, to tapas style dishes, sharing plates, lighter mains and fish such as oven-baked cod, crayfish and spinach fishcakes. Several annual beer festivals are held.

Open all day all wk 11-11 (Fri-Sat 11am-mdnt) Closed 25 Dec **Food** Lunch all wk 11-10 Dinner all wk 11-10 ⊕ GREENE KING ◀ IPA & Abbot Ale, Hardys & Hansons Olde Trip, Nottingham guest ales ♂ Aspall. ♀ 13 **Facilities** Non-diners area ♦♦ Garden Beer festival WiFi ▦ (notice required)

SOUTHWELL
Map 17 SK75

NEW The Hearty Goodfellow

tel: 01636 919176 **NG25 0HQ**
email: info@heartygoodfellowpub.co.uk
dir: *From Newark-on-Trent take A617 towards Mansfield. At lights left to Southwell. Pub on right on A612*

Traditional cask ale house and award-winning garden

Close to the picturesque centre of Southwell, a stone's throw from the Minster and racecourse. Inside, a warm and caring welcome embraces one and all, including children and dogs. Settle back with a pint of Hearty Blonde, the house beer, or try a Millwhites Blackberry Blush cider for a change. Light bites include a posh fish-finger sandwich; for a 'Hearty' alternative, look to the home-made beef and ale pie in shortcrust pastry; or the burger with garlic sauce. Children eat proper food too, with smaller portions from the main menu. Ales in July and cider in February are celebrated in two annual festivals.

Open all day Closed Mon L **Food** Lunch Tue-Thu 12-2.30, Fri-Sat 12-9, Sun 12-4 Dinner Tue-Thu 5-9, Fri-Sat 12-9 Av main course £10.95 Set menu available ⊕ EVERARDS ◀ Welbeck The Hearty Blonde, Tiger, Rotating Guest ales ♂ Millwhites. ♀ 11 **Facilities** Non-diners area ♣ (Bar Restaurant Garden) ♦♦ Children's portions Play area Garden ⊓ Beer festival Cider festival Parking WiFi ▦ (notice required)

TUXFORD
Map 17 SK77

The Fountain

tel: 01777 872854 **155 Lincoln Rd NG22 0JQ**
email: icthefountain@gmail.com
dir: *Phone for detailed directions*

Family-oriented pub with a good local reputation

Sir Walter Scott called the Great North Road "the dullest road in the world". Today, as the A1(M), it's even duller, so turn off into Tuxford and find this popular pub with its smart interior. On tap are beers from Welbeck Abbey Brewery and cider from the Scrumpy Wasp company in East Markham. If you want food that's more than basic pub grub without being pretentious, this is the place: for example home-made Scotch egg with crispy pancetta salad and red pepper piperade; shank of lamb braised in red wine with mashed potatoes, root vegetables and mint; and smoked salmon with dill and penne pasta in cream and white wine sauce. Pies come with various fillings – game, fish or roasted root vegetables, and there are steaks and a mixed grill.

Open all day all wk **Food** Contact pub for food times Set menu available ⊕ FREE HOUSE ◀ Welbeck Abbey Brewery ♂ Scrumpy Wasp. ♀ **Facilities** Non-diners area ♦♦ Children's menu Children's portions Play area Garden ⊓ Parking WiFi ▦ (notice required)

The Mussel & Crab

tel: 01777 870491 **Sibthorpe Hill NG22 OPJ**
email: musselandcrab1@hotmail.com **web:** www.musselandcrab.com
dir: *From Ollerton/Tuxford junct of A1 & A57. N on B1164 to Sibthorpe Hill. Pub 800yds on right*

A huge choice of seafood dishes

Bruce and Allison Elliott-Bateman turned this quirky pub in landlocked Nottinghamshire into a renowned seafood restaurant. Beautifully fresh fish and seafood dominate the menu, with food served in a multitude of rooms; the piazza room is styled as an Italian courtyard and the beamed restaurant is big on rustic charm. Over a dozen blackboards offer ever-changing fish dishes, as well as 'things that don't swim'. You could select po pei mussels, followed by lobster thermidore, or twice-cooked two cheese soufflé with a main of pork fillet in puff pastry.

Open all wk 11-3 6-11 **Food** Lunch Mon-Sat 11-2.30, Sun 11-3 Dinner Mon-Sat 6-10, Sun 6-9 Set menu available ⊕ FREE HOUSE ◖ Tetley's Smoothflow & Cask, Guinness ⬡ Somersby Cider. ⬤ 16 **Facilities** Non-diners area ⬤ (Bar Garden) ⬤ Children's menu Family room Garden ⩫ Parking

UPTON
Map 17 SK75

NEW Cross Keys

tel: 01636 813269 **Main St NG23 5SY**
email: info@crosskeysatupton.co.uk
dir: *From A617 W of Newark-on-Trent onto A612 towards Southwell. Pub in village centre*

A 16th-century pub for everyone

Heavily beamed ceilings, open fires, little alcoves, an unusual brick wall with recesses for wine bottles, and candles in the evenings. In a nutshell, that's the Cross Keys. Co-owner Steve Hussey, with partner Alison Ryan, is also head brewer at nearby Maythorne's Mallard microbrewery, which supplies the real ales, with Somerset's Broadoak providing cider and perry. Classically trained French chef Franck Morisseau specialises in fish, such as scallops and tiger prawns quick-fried in butter, but is equally proficient at pan-fried, corn-fed chicken breast on tagliatelle with creamy sherry sauce; beef, smoked bacon and Stilton pie; and root vegetable and vegetarian sausage cassoulet.

Open 12-3 5-11 (Fri-Sun 12-12) Closed Mon **L** **Food** Lunch Tue-Sat 12-3, Sun 12-4 Dinner Tue-Sat 5-8.30 ⊕ FREE HOUSE ◖ Mallard Drake & Duck 'n' Dive ⬡ Broadoak Moonshine & Perry. ⬤ 10 **Facilities** Non-diners area ⬤ (Bar Garden) ⬤ Children's portions Garden ⩫ Parking ▭ (notice required)

OXFORDSHIRE

ABINGDON-ON-THAMES
Map 5 SU49

NEW The Brewery Tap

tel: 01235 521655 **40-42 Ock St OX14 5BZ**
email: thebrewerytap@gmail.com
dir: *Phone pub for detailed directions*

Town-centre favourite with a beer garden

This predominantly late 17th-century pub, has been in the aptly-named Heritage family for nearly 25 years. Flagstone floors and open fireplaces characterise the interior, where the bar staff dispense a changing line-up of six guest ales, and Thatchers Heritage (that name again!) and Hazy Hog ciders. Bar snacks range from grilled jalapeño peppers to pork crackling, while classic dishes include bangers and mash; steak and chips; chicken avocado salad; and Philly steak sandwich. Sunday roasts are a big thing, followed between 5pm and 7pm by live music. Beer and cider festivals are held in March and October.

Open all day all wk **Food** Lunch all wk 12-3 Dinner Mon-Sat 6-9 ⊕ FREE HOUSE ◖ Rotating guest ales ⬡ Thatchers Heritage, Westons Old Rosie, Hogs Back Hazy Hog. ⬤ 12 **Facilities** Non-diners area ⬤ (Bar Restaurant Garden) ⬤ Children's menu Children's portions Garden ⩫ Beer festival Cider festival Parking WiFi

ADDERBURY
Map 11 SP43

Red Lion ★★★ INN

tel: 01295 810269 **The Green OX17 3LU**
email: 6496@greeneking.co.uk **web:** www.oldenglishinns.co.uk
dir: *S of Banbury on A4260*

Historic inn overlooking the village green

A fine stone-built coaching inn overlooking the village green. Dating back to English Civil War times, it was once owned by the Royalists who, a tad sycophantically, called it The King's Arms. A list of landlords since 1690 is displayed inside, where age-blackened 'duck or grouse' beams, oak panelling and great big fireplaces set the scene for daily newspapers, real ales and good wines. Classic dishes include British beef and Ruddles ale pie; slow-cooked lamb shank; chicken tikka masala; and grilled sea bass fillets. Accommodation is provided in 12 individually designed bedrooms.

Open all day all wk Mon-Thu 7am-11pm (Fri 7am-11.30pm Sat 8am-11.30pm Sun 8am-10.30pm) **Food** Lunch Mon-Fri 7am-10pm, Sat-Sun 8am-10pm Dinner Mon-Fri 7am-10pm, Sat-Sun 8am-10pm ⊕ GREENE KING ◖ Rotating ales. ⬤ 11 **Facilities** Non-diners area ⬤ (Bar Restaurant Garden) ⬤ Children's menu Children's portions Garden ⩫ Parking WiFi ▭ (notice required) **Rooms** 12

Read all about pubs and their friendly ghosts in our feature on page 12

BAMPTON
Map 5 SP30

The Romany

tel: 01993 850237 **Bridge St OX18 2HA**
email: theromanyinnbampton@yahoo.co.uk
dir: *Phone for detailed directions*

A warm welcome and live entertainment

This 18th-century building of Cotswold stone was a shop until a couple of decades ago. It's now a pretty inn, and as such The Romany counts a beamed bar, log fires and intimate dining room among its many charms. The choice of food ranges from bar snacks and bar meals to a full carte, with home-made specials like lasagne, chicken Romany, or chilli and chips. There is also a good range of vegetarian choices. The garden might be just the spot to enjoy a pint of Hooky Bitter or London Pride. Regional singers provide live entertainment a couple of times a month.

Open all day all wk 12-12 **Food** Lunch Fri-Sat 12-9, Sun 12-3 Dinner Tue-Thu 4-9, Fri-Sat 12-9 Av main course £8.50 ⊕ PUNCH TAVERNS ◀ Hook Norton Hooky Bitter, Fuller's London Pride, Guest ales. **Facilities** Non-diners area ♦◀ Children's menu Children's portions Play area Garden ☎ WiFi ☎ (notice required)

BANBURY
Map 11 SP44

The Wykham Arms

tel: 01295 788808 **Temple Mill Rd, Sibford Gower OX15 5RX**
email: info@wykhamarms.co.uk
dir: *Between Banbury & Shipston-on-Stour off B4035*

Attractive village inn with modern menu

A beautiful thatched, mellow stone pub in a hilly village of venerable, reed-roofed cottages at the edge of The Cotswolds. With roses round the door and a cosy courtyard for long summer evenings, it's the idyllic rural inn. With a brace and more of real ales, including one from local brewers Whale, proprietors and classically trained chefs Damian and Debbie Bradley skilfully produce a regularly changing menu of contemporary dishes. Snack on a chicken satay light-bite or plump for mains like lentil, mushroom and spinach cottage pie, or pavé of fresh cod with smoked salmon and prawn potato cake, roast fennel and pea cream.

Open 12-3 6-11 Closed 25 Dec, Mon (ex BHs) **Food** Lunch Tue-Sun 12-2.30 Dinner Tue-Sat 6-9.30 Restaurant menu available Tue-Sat ⊕ FREE HOUSE ◀ Wye Valley HPA, St Austell Trelawny, Whale Ale Brewery, Guinness Ô Aspall. ☐ 20 **Facilities** Non-diners area ♣ (Bar Garden Outside area) ♦◀ Children's portions Family room Garden Outside area ☎ Parking WiFi

Find out more about this area with *The AA Guide to The Cotswolds* – see shop.theAA.com

Ye Olde Reindeer Inn

tel: 01295 270972 **47 Parsons St OX16 5NA**
email: thereindeerbanbury@gmail.com **web:** www.ye-olde-reindeer-inn-banbury.co.uk
dir: *1m from M40 junct 11, in town centre just off market square. Car park access via Bolton Rd*

Town pub with interesting history

Cotswold-brewed beers from the renowned Hook Norton Brewery draw in a lively local clientele to this historic pub right at the core of old Banbury, just a stone's throw from the Cross of nursery-rhyme fame. Its origins go back to Tudor times, and during the Civil War, Oliver Cromwell himself is believed to have directed his commanders in the richly panelled Globe Room. Weekly events include live music, steak nights and quizzes. Enjoy good, solid pub grub in the traditional, time-worn, classic interior or indulge in a game of Aunt Sally in the flower-decked courtyard. A sampling of dishes includes venison burger, scampi and chips, rustic chicken Kiev and pies from the Pieminister range.

Open all day all wk Mon-Thu 11-11 (Fri-Sat 11am-mdnt Sun 12-10.30) Closed 25 Dec **Food** Lunch all wk 12-3 Dinner Mon-Sat 6-9 ⊕ HOOK NORTON ◀ Hooky Bitter, Old Hooky, Hooky Lion, Hooky Mild Ô Westons Stowford Press. ☐ 16 **Facilities** Non-diners area ♣ (All areas) ♦◀ Children's menu Children's portions Family room Garden Outside area ☎ Beer festival Cider festival Parking ☎ (notice required)

PICK OF THE PUBS

The Vines

BLACK BOURTON Map 5 SP20

tel: 01993 843559
Burford Rd OX18 2PF
email: info@vineshotel.com
web: www.vinesblackbourton.co.uk
dir: *A40 at Witney onto A4095 to Faringdon, 1st right after Bampton to Black Bourton*

Stylish village retreat with modern British food

The Vines, built of Cotswold stone and discreetly set back from the road, looks for all the world as though it has been an inn for centuries. In fact, it hasn't, and thanks go to American airmen based at nearby Brize Norton during the 1940s that it became one — because so many of them were there, the existing village pub couldn't cope. Today it belongs to Ahdy and Karen Gerges, who are responsible for building and maintaining the excellent reputation of this elegant fine-dining pub. One of the leather sofas in the spacious lounge area close to the log fire is the perfect spot to enjoy a pint of something from the nearby Hook Norton brewery, or maybe saunter out to the patio, with a glass of wine, where you can play Aunt Sally, an old pub game involving throwing sticks at an old woman's head (wooden, of course). The menu lists imaginative, internationally influenced, modern British dishes, all freshly

prepared using locally sourced produce. Typical starters include antipasto misto, a selection of freshly sliced cured meats; and melanzane parmigiana — baked sliced aubergines with tomato and basil sauce and parmesan cheese. Lamb shank is served with horseradish mash and garlic, red wine and rosemary sauce; and chicken breast comes stuffed with Parma ham and Stilton cheese, served with rosemary and garlic-crushed potatoes and creamy dill sauce. Other possibilities are catch of the day, and fresh egg pasta. Typical desserts are Eton mess; and profiteroles with chocolate sauce. There's always a good selection of Old and New World wines.

Open all wk **Food** Dinner Mon-Sat 6-9, Sun 7-9 Restaurant menu available all wk ⊕ FREE HOUSE 🍺 Hook Norton Old Hooky, Tetley's Smoothflow Ö Westons Stowford Press.
Facilities Non-diners area 🐾 (Garden) 🚻 Children's menu Children's portions Garden 🪑 Parking WiFi 🚌 (notice required)

BEGBROKE

Map 11 SP41

NEW The Royal Sun

tel: 01865 374718 **2 Woodstock Road West OX5 1RZ**
email: theroyalsun@hotmail.co.uk
dir: *From Oxford take A44 towards Woodstock. Approx 5m to Begbroke*

Pub classics in an Oxfordshire village

A stone-built inn, dating from the 17th century, and handy for Woodstock and Blenheim Palace. Sir Winston Churchill (who was born at the Palace) and the Duke of Marlborough used to ride to the pub for a drink — and if it was good enough for them, then surely it's good enough for anyone. There's a cosy bar and a smart restaurant where the menus feature classics like honey roast ham and eggs; scampi and chips; or local sausage with bubble-and-squeak. On Sundays there's a carvery.

Open all day all wk **Food** Lunch all wk 12-9 Dinner all wk 12-9 ⊕ PUNCH TAVERNS
◀ Hook Norton Hooky Bitter Ŏ Westons Stowford Press. ₹ 9
Facilities Non-diners area ♦ Children's menu Children's portions Garden ⊓ Parking WiFi 🚗 (notice required)

BLACK BOURTON

Map 5 SP20

The Vines

PICK OF THE PUBS

See Pick of the Pubs on page 385

BLOXHAM

Map 11 SP43

The Elephant & Castle

tel: 01295 720383 **OX15 4LZ**
email: bloxhamelephant1@btconnect.com
dir: *Take A361 from Banbury towards Chipping Norton, 1st left after shops in Bloxham*

Traditional Cotswold stone coaching inn

Locals play Aunt Sally or shove-ha'penny in this 15th-century coaching inn's big wood-floored bar, whilst the lounge boasts a bar-billiards table and a large inglenook fireplace. External features include an arch that used to straddle the former Banbury to Chipping Norton turnpike; at night the gates of the pub were closed, and no traffic could get over the toll bridge. Today the menu offers toasties and baguettes, and favourites like scampi, crispy cod and vegetarian shepherd's pie. The bar serves seasonal and guest ales as well as Westons ciders. The beer festival in May is part of the Bloxfest Music Festival.

Open all wk 10-3 6-12 (Fri 10-3 5-2am Sat 10am-2am Sun 10am-mdnt)
Food Lunch Mon-Sat 12-2 Av main course £6.50 ⊕ HOOK NORTON ◀ Hooky Bitter & Seasonal ales, Guest ales Ŏ Westons 1st Quality, Old Rosie, Wyld Wood, Perry & Rosie's Pig, Thatchers, Hogan's Picker's Passion & Panking Pole.
Facilities Non-diners area ♣ (Bar Restaurant Garden) ♦ Children's menu Children's portions Family room Garden ⊓ Beer festival Cider festival Parking WiFi 🚗

BRIGHTWELL BALDWIN

Map 5 SU69

The Nelson

PICK OF THE PUBS

See Pick of the Pubs on opposite page

BRIGHTWELL-CUM-SOTWELL

Map 5 SU59

The Red Lion

tel: 01491 837373 **The Street OX10 0RT**
email: mark@redlion.biz
dir: *From A4130 (Didcot to Wallingford road) follow Brightwell-cum-Sotwell signs. Pub in village centre*

Friendly village pub

This picture-postcard thatched and timbered 16th-century village pub is not only pretty but also a cracking community local. Behind the bar, beers come from the likes of West Berkshire, and Loddon breweries, while a choice of wine comes from the very local Brightwell Vineyard. The pub holds a beer festival (with live music) for two days every summer. Hearty, traditional pub food is freshly prepared from local produce. Look to the chalkboard for the famous short-crust pastry pies of the day, or the main menu for things like lasagne, pork tenderloin with black pudding and caramelised apple, or vegetable chilli. Don't miss the Sunday roast lunches.

Open all wk 12-3 6-11 **Food** Lunch all wk 12-2 Dinner Tue-Sat 6.30-9 ⊕ FREE HOUSE ◀ West Berkshire Good Old Boy, Loddon Hoppit Ŏ Symonds Founders Reserve, Tutts Clump. **Facilities** Non-diners area ♣ (Bar Garden) ♦ Children's menu Children's portions Garden ⊓ Beer festival Parking WiFi

BRITWELL SALOME

Map 5 SU69

The Red Lion

PICK OF THE PUBS

tel: 01491 613140 **OX49 5LG**
email: info@theredlionbritwellsalome.co.uk
dir: *M40 junct 6, B4009 signed Watlington. Through Watlington, follow Benson & B480 signs to Britwell Salome*

Relaxed village inn with confident cooking

With real ales from West Berkshire Brewery, Red Dog cider from the nearby village of Benson, and a variety of wines by the glass, the pub has a loyal local following, and charms visiting walkers who interrupt their peregrinations in the surrounding Chilterns for well-earned refreshment. Nibbles come in the form of a black pudding Scotch egg; or Colston Bassett Stilton and fruit cake. But make the most of your visit by diving into the flavourful menu: melted Brézain (a raclette-style cheese from the Haute Savoie region of France) with celeriac, mustard and cornichons; and smoked Cuxham wild duck salad with pickled rhubarb and feta are typical starters. Continue with local partridge, curried lentils and griddled cauliflower; or pan-fried Brixham turbot fillet with saffron potatoes, bouillabaisse sauce and rouille.

Open 12-3 6-11 (Fri-Sat 12-3 5.30-11 Sun 12-5) Closed Sun eve, Mon & Tue
Food Lunch Wed-Sun 12-2 Dinner Wed-Sat 6-9 Restaurant menu available all wk
⊕ FREE HOUSE ◀ West Berkshire Mr Chubb's Lunchtime Bitter Ŏ Red Dog. ₹ 18
Facilities Non-diners area ♣ (Bar Restaurant Outside area) ♦ Children's portions Outside area ⊓ Parking WiFi

Follow us on twitter
@TheAA_Lifestyle

PICK OF THE PUBS

The Nelson

BRIGHTWELL BALDWIN   Map 5 SU69

tel: 01491 612497 **OX49 5NP**
email: info@thenelsonbrightwell.co.uk
web: www.thenelsonbrightwell.co.uk
dir: *Off B4009 between Watlington & Benson*

Country inn and restaurant with pretty terraced garden

In Nelson's day the pub was known as the Admiral Nelson but when, in 1797, the great man was elevated to the peerage, the pub's name was elevated accordingly. In 1905 the inn closed following complaints about over-indulgent estate workers, but several years later the building was bought by a couple who gave it a complete makeover. The Lord Nelson finally reopened on Trafalgar Day 1971, but today it's known simply as The Nelson. As you approach down the lane, look for the union flags flying patriotically outside. Its quiet position makes it a great getaway for a country walk before opening time. The interior is full of fresh flowers, and tables lit by candles in the evening are warmed by a splendid inglenook fireplace. In summer the pretty terraced garden with its weeping willow is popular for alfresco eating and drinking; seafood lovers should check out the dates of the annual crab and lobster festival. All food is freshly cooked, using local produce where possible. Starters might include local

pigeon breast on a black pudding rösti; or a twice-baked cheese soufflé on wilted spinach. Main courses reflect the pub's proudly British traditions: expect the likes of English lamb rump, fresh rosemary and red wine sauce, green vegetables and mashed potatoes; or the Nelson burger, served with home-made tomato relish, spicy slaw and skinny chips. Vegetarian options have much appeal: cauliflower and broccoli cheese bake served with garlic bread; or creamy mint and green pea risotto, with roasted tomato and rocket salad. If refreshment is all that's required, ales include Loose Cannon from Abingdon, or North Yorkshire's much respected Black Sheep. Weston's ciders and around 20 wines served by the glass complete the drinks line-up.

Open 12-3 6-11 (Sun 12-4) Closed 25 Dec, Sun eve **Food** Lunch Mon-Sat 12-2, Sun 12-3.30 Dinner Mon-Sat 6-10, Sun 7-9.30 Set menu available ⊞ FREE HOUSE ◪ Rebellion IPA, Loose Cannon, Black Sheep ⏾ Westons Stowford Press. ⏺ 20 **Facilities** Non-diners area ⚐ (Bar Garden Outside area) ⏺ Children's portions Garden Outside area ⋒ Parking WiFi ⛟ (notice required)

BROUGHTON
Map 11 SP43

Saye and Sele Arms

tel: 01295 263348 **Main Rd OX15 5ED**
email: mail@sayeandselearms.co.uk
dir: *From Banbury Cross take B4035 to Broughton. Approx 3m*

Peaceful retreat in historic village

Named after the family who own the astonishing, moated Broughton Castle at the edge of this attractive village; this charming, ironstone-built pub is itself over 400 years old. Beams in the cosy restaurant and bar sag with the weight of over 200 collectable water jugs; at the bar, beer lovers will find ales from several micros that are pleasing to quaff in the tree-shaded garden. There's a very strong, wide-ranging menu, featuring home-made shortcrust pies from chef-patron Danny McGeehan, typically alongside mains like sea bass; vegetable lasagne; sausage and mash; or grilled rump steak. Danny's desserts are also popular, especially the soufflé bread and butter pudding.

Open 11.30-2.30 7-11 (Sat 11.30-3 7-11 Sun 12-5) Closed 25 Dec, Sun eve **Food** Lunch Mon-Sat 12-2 Dinner Mon-Sat 7-9.30 ⊕ FREE HOUSE ◀ Brains The Rev. James, Sharp's Doom Bar, 2 guest ales ◔ Westons Stowford Press, Thatchers Dry. ♟ 9 **Facilities** Non-diners area ♦♦ Children's portions Garden ⊼ Parking ▦ (notice required)

BURCOT
Map 5 SU59

The Chequers

tel: 01865 407771 **OX14 3DP**
email: enquiries@thechequers-burcot.co.uk
dir: *On A415 (Dorchester to Abingdon road) between Clifton Hampden & Dorchester*

Classic British food by the river

Once a staging post for boats on the Thames, this 400-year-old thatched and timber-framed pub is run by chef-patron Steven Sanderson. Locals supply game during the winter, and neighbours' gardens and allotments also yield their bounty. In the kitchen, Steven devises straightforward British classics for his seasonal menus, using carefully chosen meats, fish from Devon and Cornwall markets, mussels from the Norfolk coast, and oysters from Scotland and Jersey. Try diver-caught Orkney scallops with black pudding, parsnip purée, crackling and red wine jus followed by the trio of beef with horseradish mash.

Open all day 12-11 (Sun 12-8) Closed Mon **Food** Lunch Tue-Sat 12-2.30, Sun 12-6 Dinner Tue-Sat 6.15-9 Set menu available Restaurant menu available all wk ⊕ FREE HOUSE ◀ Loose Cannon Abingdon Bridge, Two Cocks, West Berkshire ◔ Westons Stowford Press. ♟ 10 **Facilities** Non-diners area ♦♦ Children's menu Children's portions Garden ⊼ Parking WiFi ▦ (notice required)

BURFORD
Map 5 SP21

The Angel at Burford ★★★★ INN ⊛

tel: 01993 822714 **14 Witney St OX18 4SN**
email: enquiries@theangelatburford.co.uk **web:** www.theangelatburford.co.uk

Well presented 16th-century coaching inn

This welcoming Hook Norton house continues to lure real ale drinkers with pints of perfectly kept Hooky, but it also draws the food crowd. The menu offers an all-day bar menu, including a charcuterie board, sandwiches and burgers, alongside the main carte. Try the spiced pork belly with sweet pepper dip followed by smoked haddock, minted peas, crushed new potatoes, poached egg and smoked cheese sauce. If you still have room, chocolate and Amaretto torte is one choice for those with a sweet tooth. Look out for the summer beer festival.

Open all day all wk **Food** Lunch all wk 12-6 Dinner all wk 6-9.30 Av main course £12.50 Set menu available Restaurant menu available all wk ⊕ HOOK NORTON BREWERY ◀ Hooky bitter ◔ Westons Stowford Press. **Facilities** Non-diners area ♣ (Bar Restaurant Garden) ♦♦ Children's menu Children's portions Garden ⊼ Beer festival WiFi ▦ (notice required) **Rooms** 3

The Highway Inn

tel: 01993 823661 **117 High St OX18 4RG**
email: info@thehighwayinn.co.uk
dir: *From A40 onto A361*

Charming pub in a picturesque Cotswold town

An attractive inn of medieval origin at the heart of pretty Burford; the secluded courtyard garden to the rear is a blissful retreat from the hurly-burly of this ancient town. Beers from the likes of Hook Norton, together with local cider are the order of the day. The relaxing interior, with lots of dressed stone, open fire, bric-à-brac and cosy corners is popular with diners drawn to the unfussy, high-quality menu of seasonal dishes. Cotswold largesse is exampled by mains like oven-roasted breast of pheasant with game jus; home-made pies and the renowned rack of ribs. A beer festival takes place at the beginning of June.

Open all day all wk 12-11 Closed 1st 2wks Jan **Food** Lunch all wk 12-2.30 Dinner all wk 6-9 Av main course £12 Set menu available Restaurant menu available all wk ⊕ FREE HOUSE ◀ Hook Norton Hooky Bitter, Guest ale ◔ Westons Stowford Press, Cotswold. ♟ 15 **Facilities** Non-diners area ♣ (Bar Outside area) ♦♦ Children's menu Children's portions Outside area ⊼ Beer festival WiFi

The Inn for All Seasons ★★★ INN   `PICK OF THE PUBS`

tel: 01451 844324 **The Barringtons OX18 4TN**
email: sharp@innforallseasons.com **web:** www.innforallseasons.com
dir: *3m W of Burford on A40*

Excellent fresh fish specials and extensive wine list

The Sharp family took over in the mid-1980s, but this 17th-century inn has a long history and once witnessed the dispatch of Cotswold stone for buildings like St Paul's Cathedral. The pub's unusual name was chosen by former owner Jeremy Taylor, who had worked on the film *A Man for All Seasons* as a horse choreographer. The interior is a veritable treasure trove of ancient oak beams, leather chairs and interesting memorabilia. The bar offers Otter and St Austell ales, as well as an extensive wine list. Matthew Sharp selects seasonal local produce for his British-continental cuisine; he also offers one of the area's best specials boards for fresh fish, with daily deliveries from Brixham. Main course meat options range from Kelmscott pork chop and kidney pie; to roast grass-fed Cotswold lamb pavé with warm salad of lentils and peppers with duck-fat Parmentier potatoes. If pies are your thing, call in on a Wednesday.

Open all wk 11-3 6-11 (Fri-Sat 11-11) **Food** Lunch all wk 12-3 Dinner all wk 6.30-9.30 Restaurant menu available all wk ⊕ FREE HOUSE ◀ St Austell Tribute, Otter Amber ◔ Kingstone Press. ♟ 16 **Facilities** Non-diners area ♣ (Bar Garden) ♦♦ Children's menu Children's portions Play area Family room Garden ⊼ Parking WiFi ▦ **Rooms** 10

The Lamb Inn ★★★ SHL ⊛⊛   `PICK OF THE PUBS`

tel: 01993 823155 **Sheep St OX18 4LR**
email: info@lambinn-burford.co.uk **web:** www.cotswold-inns-hotels.co.uk/lamb
dir: *M40 junct 8, follow A40 & Burford signs, 1st turn, down hill into Sheep St*

Cotswold charm and style

In a grass-verged, tranquil side street in this attractive Cotswolds town, the 15th-century Lamb is a dyed-in-the-wool award winner, including two AA Rosettes. A welcoming atmosphere is generated by the bar's flagstone floor, log fire, cosy armchairs, gleaming copper, brass and silver and, last but not least, Hook Norton and Wickwar real ales. In fact, old-world charm and stylish interiors are a feature throughout. Take, for example, the elegant columns and mullioned windows of the courtyard-facing restaurant, where chef Sean Ducie presents contemporary English cooking, based extensively on local produce. Starters such as eggs Benedict with ham set you up for mains of cheddar and red onion omelette; macaroni cheese; and whole dressed crab with skinny chips. After that, if you have room, desserts including sticky toffee pudding with vanilla ice cream, or apple and cinnamon crumble with custard may tempt you. An extensive cellar holds over 100 wines.

Open all day all wk Food Lunch all wk 12-9.30 Dinner all wk 12-9.30 Set menu available Restaurant menu available all wk ⊕ FREE HOUSE ◄ Hook Norton Hooky Bitter, Wickwar Cotswold Way ♂ Cotswold. ♥ 16 Facilities Non-diners area ♣ (Bar Garden Outside area) ✦ Children's menu Children's portions Garden Outside area ⊼ Parking WiFi Rooms 17

The Maytime Inn ★★★★ INN

tel: 01993 822068 Asthall OX18 4HW
email: info@themaytime.com web: www.themaytime.com
dir: Phone for detailed directions

Pleasing combination of traditional ambience and eclectic food

Dominic Wood heads up the young and passionate team in this 17th-century countryside pub that once had its own smithy. You'll find it in the pretty Cotswold village of Asthall, where the Mitford sisters were raised. The church is worth a visit, and the manor often hosts public events. Real ales are a strength, and ciders include Black Dragon from Wales. The ambitious kitchen prepares and cooks all dishes using only the finest, fresh local ingredients to create modern English food.

Open all day all wk Food Lunch all wk 12-3 Dinner all wk 6-9.30 Av main course £12-£18 Restaurant menu available all wk ⊕ FREE HOUSE ◄ Otter Amber, Loose Cannon Abingdon Bridge, North Cotswold Windrush, Hook Norton Hooky Bitter

♂ Gwynt y Ddraig Black Dragon & Haymaker, Westons Old Rosie, Pheasant Plucker. ♥ 12 Facilities Non-diners area ♣ (All areas) ✦ Children's portions Garden Outside area ⊼ Parking WiFi (notice required) Rooms 6

NEW The Mermaid

tel: 01993 822193 78 High St OX18 4QF
email: themermaidburford@btconnect.com
dir: In Burford from A40 rdbt onto A361 signed Chipping Norton. Pub in centre of High St by pedestrian crossing

Historic town-centre and family-friendly pub

With a long history dating back to the 14th century, an interior with character is only to be expected. The Mermaid certainly does not disappoint. Part of the building once housed a bakery, and today the baker's fireplace still radiates a warmth to match the welcome extended to guests, their children and dogs. Add in the crooked beams, flagstone floors, a candle-lit first-floor restaurant, a choice of four real ales and home-cooked food, and it's no wonder the pub is popular with townspeople and visitors alike. Fresh fish dishes and home-made pies are a speciality, and vegetarian and gluten-free menus are available.

Open all day all wk Food Lunch Mon-Fri 11-2.30, Sat 10-9.30, Sun 10-9 Dinner Mon-Fri 6-9 (9.30 in summer), Sat 10-9.30, Sun 10-9 Av main course £10 ⊕ GREENE KING ◄ IPA, Morland Old Speckled Hen, Hardys & Hansons Olde Trip. ♥ 10 Facilities Non-diners area ♣ (Bar Outside area) ✦ Children's menu Children's portions Family room Outside area ⊼ WiFi (notice required)

CASSINGTON	Map 5 SP41

The Chequers Inn

tel: 01865 882620 6 The Green OX29 4DG
email: info@chequersoxford.co.uk
dir: From Oxford take A40 towards Witney. Right to Cassington

Smart village inn not far from Oxford

Turn off the busy A40, and you'll find this imposing Cotswold-stone inn next to the church at the end of the village road. The interior is cosy yet stylish, with polished flagstone floors, winter log fires and wooden furniture adorned with pretty candles. Freshly prepared meals include starters of goats' cheese and caramelised plum crostini, or parsnip and sweet potato soup; followed by main courses of Thai chicken curry; honey and cider ham; and rib-eye steak with peppercorn sauce. There is a beautiful orangery, perfect for private parties and functions.

Open all wk Mon-Fri 12-2.30 4.30-11 (Sat 12-11 Sun 12-10.30) Food Lunch Mon-Sat 12-2, Sun 12-4 Dinner Mon-Sat 6-9 ⊕ FREE HOUSE ◄ Hook Norton Hooky Bitter ♂ Westons Stowford Press. ♥ 10 Facilities Non-diners area ✦ Children's menu Children's portions Outside area ⊼ Parking WiFi (notice required)

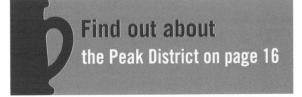

Find out about the Peak District on page 16

CHALGROVE — Map 5 SU69

The Red Lion Inn — PICK OF THE PUBS

tel: 01865 890625 **The High St OX44 7SS**
dir: *B480 from Oxford ring road, through Stadhampton, left then right at mini rdbt. At Chalgrove Airfield right into village*

Historic pub overlooking the village green

Other than the occasional quack of inquisitive ducks, the medieval village of Chalgrove may be tranquil these days but that wasn't the case in 1643 when Prince Rupert clashed with John Hampden's Parliamentarian forces during the first Civil War. The stream-side beer garden of this old inn overlooks the compact green at the heart of the village, where thatched cottages slumber not far from the church which is, unusually, owner of the pub. In the bar, select from the great range of draught beers complementing the appealing menu created from the best local ingredients by chef-patron Raymond Sexton. The choice may include roulade of smoked salmon with cream cheese and chives, an appetiser for lemon sole fillets 'simply grilled in a little butter', or slow-cooked pork belly with braised vegetables and roast gravy. Finish with sticky toffee pudding or warm treacle tart courtesy of Suzanne Sexton, an accomplished pastry chef.

Open all wk 11-3 6-12 (Fri-Sat 11-3 6-1am Sun all day) **Food** Lunch Mon-Sat 12-2, Sun 12-3 Dinner Mon-Sat 6-9.30 ⊕ FREE HOUSE ◀ Fuller's London Pride, Butcombe, Guest ales ♂ Westons Stowford Press, Local cider. ♥ 11 **Facilities** Non-diners area ♣ (Bar Garden) ♦♦ Children's menu Children's portions Play area Garden ⋒ (notice required)

CHARLBURY — Map 11 SP31

The Bull Inn — PICK OF THE PUBS

tel: 01608 810689 **Sheep St OX7 3RR**
email: info@bullinn-charlbury.com
dir: *M40 junct 8, A40, A44 follow Woodstock/Blenheim Palace signs. Through Woodstock take B4437 to Charlbury, pub at x-roads in town*

Imaginative cooking and Cotswold ales

Presiding over Charlbury's main street, this handsome stone-fronted 16th-century free house is a conveniently short hop from Woodstock, Blenheim Palace and other attractions of the Cotswolds. The beamed interior and log fires burning in the inglenook fireplaces add to the charming period character, as does the wooden-floored bar that offers Bull Bitter and weekly guest ales. A tastefully furnished lounge and dining room add to the relaxing space, while outside the vine-covered terrace is a lovely backdrop for a drink or meal in summer. Sandwiches served at lunchtime from Tuesday to Saturday may suffice, but the main menu proves tempting with a starter of smoked salmon with lemon and dill dressing and main courses like trio of sausages with mash, peas and gravy, or the Bull Inn burger with chilli jam and fries. Leave room for the lemon posset or selection of local cheeses.

Open 12-2.30 6-11 Closed 25-26 Dec, 1 Jan, Sun eve & Mon **Food** Lunch Tue-Fri 12-2, Sat-Sun 12-2.30 Dinner Tue-Sat 6.30-9 Av main course £12 ⊕ FREE HOUSE ◀ Bull Bitter (brewed for pub), Guest ales ♂ Thatchers Gold. ♥ 10 **Facilities** Non-diners area ♦♦ Children's portions Garden ⋒ Parking

CHASTLETON — Map 10 SP22

NEW The Greedy Goose

tel: 01608 646551 **Salford Hill GL56 0SP**
email: info@thegreedygoosemoreton.co.uk
dir: *From Chipping Norton towards Moreton-in-Marsh on A44, pub at x-rds junct with A436*

Attractive country pub guarding a crossroads

With no immediate neighbours, The Greedy Goose looks lonely, but it knows how to attract customers. The interior, all intriguingly patterned walls, swathes of polished wood flooring, elegant striped-fabric chairs and much else point to the talents of an interior design pro. A large, part-covered patio also reflects professional design input. In the bar North Cotswold Brewery Windrush Ale, Cotswold Best and Shagweaver monopolise the real ale pumps. The menu favours 'modern, fresh and hearty' dishes such as local sausages with horseradish mash; Moroccan lamb tagine; 'succulent' fish pie; and butternut squash and goats' cheese risotto. Stone-baked pizzas can be ordered to go.

Open all wk **Food** Lunch all wk 12-3 Dinner Mon-Sat 6-9, Sun 6-8 Av main course £12.50 ⊕ FREE HOUSE ◀ North Cotswold Brewery Cotswold Best, Windrush Ale & Shagweaver ♂ Thatchers Gold. **Facilities** Non-diners area ♣ (Bar Garden) ♦♦ Children's menu Children's portions Family room Garden ⋒ Parking WiFi ⋒ (notice required)

CHECKENDON — Map 5 SU68

The Highwayman ⑧ — PICK OF THE PUBS

tel: 01491 682020 **Exlade St RG8 0UA**
email: thehighwaymaninn@btconnect.com
dir: *On A4074 (Reading to Wallingford road)*

Desirable food below Chiltern beech woods

The wooded hills of the Chilterns, criss-crossed by bridleways and footpaths, form a constant horizon drifting above the rural location of this attractive old building. Just a stone's throw away is the remarkable Maharaja's Well at nearby Stoke Row, a bracing circular ramble from the inn. Bare brick and beams predominate in the airy interior, interspersed by alcoves and warmed by log-burning stoves in this much updated 16th-century inn, where contented regulars sup beers supplied from the nearby Loddon brewery. The AA Rosette menu is eclectic and strong on locally sourced raw materials. The speciality here is pies; wild boar pie or venison cottage pie may tempt as a follow-up to a smoked mackerel pâté and whisky jelly starter. Alternatively a crisp snowy walk is well-rewarded with roasted chestnut and winter vegetable hotpot with potato rösti, whilst the steaks are from the Royal Windsor Estate. A peaceful rear garden and suntrap terrace aid laid-back summer drinking.

Open 12-3 6-11 (Sun 12-6) Closed Mon **Food** Lunch Tue-Sat 12-2, Sun 12-3 Dinner Tue-Sat 6-9 Set menu available ⊕ FREE HOUSE ◀ Fuller's London Pride, Loddon Hoppit, Rebellion, Guest ale ♂ Aspall. ♥ 11 **Facilities** Non-diners area ♣ (Bar Garden) ♦♦ Children's portions Garden ⋒ Parking WiFi ⋒ (notice required)

CHINNOR — Map 5 SP70

The Sir Charles Napier ⑧⑧⑧ — PICK OF THE PUBS

tel: 01494 483011 **Spriggs Alley OX39 4BX**
dir: *M40 junct 6, B4009 to Chinnor. Right at rdbt to Spriggs Alley*

A dining experience among the Chiltern beechwoods

Despite being well and truly hidden down rural Oxfordshire lanes, this one is definitely worth seeking out. Named after the British Army general who became commander-in-chief in India in the 19th century, this sublime flint-and-brick destination dining inn is just 10 minutes from the M40. Locally-felled timber fuels the fires in the bars, while further neighbourhood exploitation is evidenced by the hedgerow- and field-sourced herbs, fungi, berries and game that have helped to earn the restaurant three AA Rosettes. You can eat inside, on the vine-covered terrace or under the cherry trees beside Michael Cooper's big, black marble sculptures and watch red kites soaring overhead. Blackboards and printed menus list, for example, wild garlic risotto with morels; bouillabaisse with rouille; loin of local venison with bubble-and-squeak, and braised red cabbage purée; and roast root vegetables with Puy lentils, imam bayildi (Turkish-style stuffed eggplant), pickled beetroot and onion bhaji. The inn is also renowned for its excellent wine list.

Open 12-4 6-12 (Sun 12-6) Closed 25-26 Dec, Mon, Sun eve **Food** Lunch Tue-Fri 12-2.30 Dinner Tue-Sat 6.30-9 Av main course £14.50 Set menu available Restaurant menu available Tue-Sun ⊕ FREE HOUSE ◀ Wadworth 6X, Henry's Original IPA. ♥ 12 **Facilities** Non-diners area ♦♦ Children's menu Children's portions Garden ⋒ Parking WiFi

PICK OF THE PUBS

Bear & Ragged Staff ❀

CUMNOR Map 5 SP40

tel: 01865 862329
28 Appleton Rd OX2 9QH
email:
enquiries@bearandraggedstaff.com
web: www.bearandraggedstaff.com
dir: *A420 from Oxford, right onto B4017 signed Cumnor*

Old World charm and modern menus

In typically tranquil Oxfordshire countryside, this 16th-century, stone-built dining pub has a rich history, not least having served as a billet for troops during the English Civil War. While the soldiers were here, Richard Cromwell, son of Oliver and Lord Protector of England, allegedly chiselled away the Royal Crest that once adorned the lintel above one of the doors in the bar, and Sir Walter Scott mentions this very Bear & Ragged Staff in his novel, *Kenilworth*. The chefs here take full advantage of the fresh, seasonal game available from local estates and shoots, since the surrounding woods and farmland teem with pheasant, partridge, deer, muntjac, rabbit, duck and pigeon. From the kitchen come hearty, country-style casseroles, stews, steaks, bangers and mash and other pub classics. Install yourself in one of the traditional bar rooms, all dressed stone and warmed by log fires, relax on the stone-flagged patio, or settle in the comfortable

restaurant and ask for the eminently manageable menu. Start with meze, charcuterie, crispy duck leg pancakes or home-made soup; then choose vegetable tagine; pork and wild boar faggots; chargrilled venison steak; market fish of the day; or butternut squash, brown cap mushrooms and spinach risotto. Pizzas from an authentic oven are another option. If, to follow, upside-down apple pudding with Calvados crème anglaise, or creamy rice pudding with red plum compôte fail to tick the right box, call for the cheeseboard, full of British classics with crackers, celery, chutney and grapes. The Bear has a climbing frame for children and dogs are welcome in the bar area.

Open all day all wk **Food** Contact pub for details Set menu available Restaurant menu available all wk ⊕ GREENE KING ◧ Guinness, Morland Old Speckled Hen, Guest ales ♉ Aspall, Hogan's. ☖ 16 **Facilities** Non-diners area ☺ (Bar Outside area) ♦ Children's menu Children's portions Play area Garden Outside area ㅠ Parking WiFi ▆ (notice required)

The Crown Inn — PICK OF THE PUBS

tel: 01608 677262 **Mill Ln OX7 4NN**
email: crown_inn@btconnect.com
dir: From A44 at Enstone (15m N of Oxford) onto B4030 signed Church Enstone

Box-ticking Cotswold-stone village pub

If log fires in an inglenook, old village photos on the walls of a traditional rustic bar, and a beamed dining room sound like your type of pub, then look no further. Similarly, if you'd enjoy a pint of Hook Norton Hooky Bitter, or a glass of Pinot Grigio on a cottage garden terrace overlooking thatched, honey-coloured stone cottages, Tony and Caroline Warburton's 17th-century inn will tick even more boxes. The couple have a well-earned reputation for food, based partly on Tony's speciality, fish, although steak pie is also given top billing. In the slate-floored conservatory, the compact menu might offer fettuccine with mushrooms, rocket, pesto and cream; and roast belly of Cotswold pork, with apple sauce, crackling and cider gravy. Among the day's specials might be breaded John Dory fillets with chips and mushy peas; or winter vegetable, sweet potato, bean and spinach curry with rice.

Open all wk 12-3 6-11 (Sun 12-4) Closed 26 Dec, 1 Jan **Food** Lunch all wk 12-2 Dinner Mon-Sat 7-9 Av main course £11.95 Set menu available ⊕ FREE HOUSE ◀ Hook Norton Hooky Bitter, Timothy Taylor Landlord, Wychwood Hobgoblin ♂ Westons Stowford Press. ♟ 8 **Facilities** Non-diners area ♦ Children's portions Garden ⋒ Parking

---

Bear & Ragged Staff ◉ — PICK OF THE PUBS

See Pick of the Pubs on page 391

The Vine Inn

tel: 01865 862567 **11 Abingdon Rd OX2 9QN**
dir: A420 from Oxford, right onto B4017

Well kept ales and a large garden

A vine does indeed clamber over the whitewashed frontage of this 18th-century village pub. In 1560, nearby Cumnor Place was the scene of the suspicious death of the wife of Lord Robert Dudley, favourite of Elizabeth I; the house was pulled down in 1810. There's a selection of rotating real ales in the carpeted bar, and a typical starters include traditional prawn cocktail; whitebait; or calamari and salad; followed by a meat, fish or oven-baked camembert sharing plate; or perhaps chilli con carne or one of the burger choices. Children love the huge garden.

Open all wk 12-3 6-11.30 (Fri-Sun all day) **Food** Lunch Mon-Sat 12-2.30, Sun 12-6 Dinner Mon-Sat 6-9 ⊕ PUNCH TAVERNS ◀ Sharp's Doom Bar, Brakspear, Hobgoblin, Guest ales ♂ Somersby Cider. **Facilities** Non-diners area ♣ (Bar Garden) ♦ Children's menu Children's portions Play area Garden ⋒ Beer festival Parking WiFi ☷ (notice required)

Deddington Arms ★★★ HL — PICK OF THE PUBS

tel: 01869 338364 **Horsefair OX15 0SH**
email: deddarms@oxfordshire-hotels.co.uk **web:** www.deddington-arms-hotel.co.uk
dir: M40 junct 11 to Banbury. Follow signs for hospital, then towards Adderbury & Deddington, on A4260

Good country pub fare in a 16th-century inn

Overlooking Deddington's pretty market square, this striking 16th-century former coaching inn boasts a wealth of timbering, flagstone floors, numerous nooks and crannies, crackling winter log fires and sought-after window seats in the beamed bar. Here you can savour a glass of Hook Norton, Adnams ale or Somersby cider while perusing the menu. Eat in the bar or head for the elegant dining room and kick off a meal with tiger prawns, pea purée and pickled cucumber; or a meat or vegetarian sharing platter, followed by seared calves' liver, creamed potatoes, sweet cabbage, smoked bacon and caramelised onions; or sea bream fillet, aubergine, potato and tartare sauce; finishing with dark chocolate and espresso torte; or traditional treacle tart and clotted cream. Accommodation includes 27 en suite bedrooms with cottage suites and four-poster luxury.

Open all day all wk 11am-mdnt (Sun 11-11) **Food** Lunch all wk 12-2.30 Dinner all wk 6.30-9.30 Set menu available Restaurant menu available all wk ⊕ FREE HOUSE ◀ Adnams, Hook Norton Lion, 2 guest ales ♂ Somersby Cider. ♟ 8 **Facilities** Non-diners area ♦ Children's menu Children's portions Parking WiFi ☷ (notice required) **Rooms** 27

The George — PICK OF THE PUBS

See Pick of the Pubs on opposite page

Eyston Arms

tel: 01235 833320 **High St OX12 8JY**
email: info@eystonarms.co.uk
dir: Just off A417 (Wantage to Reading road)

A family-owned local favourite

Owned, appropriately, by the Eyston family, who have lived in the village since 1443, this old inn stands just north of the prehistoric track known as The Ridgeway. With some of its original look revealed by renovations, the pub greets its customers with a huge log fire, flagstone floor, simple polished tables, leather chairs and cartoons of its regulars. The bar stocks real ales from Wadworth and Hook Norton. Chef Maria Jaremchuk's ever-changing menus may feature cock-a-leekie pie; chargrilled rib-eye steak; and vegetarian pad Thai, while carefully cultivated contacts with south coast fishermen mean excellent fish specials.

Open all wk 11-3 6-11 (Fri-Sat 11-11 Sun 11-9) **Food** Lunch Mon-Sat 12-2, Sun 12-4 Dinner Mon-Sat 6.30-9.30 ⊕ FREE HOUSE ◀ Hook Norton, Wadworth 6X ♂ Westons Stowford Press. **Facilities** Non-diners area ♣ (Bar Outside area) ♦ Children's portions Outside area ⋒ Parking WiFi

---

PICK OF THE PUBS

The George

DORCHESTER (ON THAMES)   Map 5 SU59

tel: 01865 340404 **25 High St OX10 7HH**
email: georgedorchester@relaxinnz.co.uk
web: www.thegeorgedorchester.co.uk
dir: *From M40 junct 7, A329 S to A4074 at Shillingford. Follow Dorchester signs. From M4 junct 13, A34 to Abingdon then A415 E to Dorchester*

Take a step back in time at this friendly inn

The multi-gabled, 15th-century George stands in the old town's picturesque high street, opposite the 12th-century Dorchester Abbey. Believed to be one of the country's oldest coaching inns, it has been a welcome haven for many an aristocrat, including Sarah Churchill, the first Duchess of Marlborough, while much later the non-aristocratic author D H Lawrence favoured it with his presence. Oak beams and inglenook fireplaces characterise the interior, while the elevated restaurant offers a secret garden with a waterfall. The Potboys Bar, apparently named after the Abbey bell-ringers, is a traditional taproom and therefore unquestionably the right place to enjoy a pint from one of the six breweries that make up The George's roll of honour while tucking into pasta carbonara with garlic bread; bangers and mash with gravy; or an 8oz rump steak with fat chips from the bar menu. Food is all locally sourced: the Abbey gardens, for example, supply all

the herbs, customers contribute the occasional home-grown vegetables, and local shoots provide pheasants. In Carriages Restaurant the menu offers confit of crisp belly pork with Puy lentils, local Toulouse sausages and crushed new potatoes; coq au vin with roasted garlic croûtons and celeriac mash; fresh and smoked fish pie with potato and cheddar cheese glaze; and butternut squash risotto with red onion, fresh herbs, white truffle oil and parmesan shavings. Expect white chocolate and marmalade bread-and-butter pudding with Disaronno custard, and Eton Mess for dessert. There are extensive gardens to enjoy.

Open all day all wk 7am-mdnt
Food Lunch all wk 12-3 Dinner all wk 6-9 ⊕ CHAPMANS GROUP ◗ Wadworth 6X, Skinner's Betty Stogs, Fuller's London Pride, Sharp's Doom Bar, Butcombe, Hook Norton ♂ Westons Stowford Press. **Facilities** Non-diners area ♟ Children's menu Children's portions Garden Outside area ⊞ Beer festival Parking WiFi 🚐

FARINGDON
Map 5 SU29

The Lamb at Buckland
PICK OF THE PUBS

tel: 01367 870484 **Lamb Ln, Buckland SN7 8QN**
email: thelambatbuckland@googlemail.com
dir: Just off A420, 3m E of Faringdon

Hearty, well-made food and friendly service

So often the word 'Cotswold' prefixes 'stone', but today it can also appear on the labels of the gin, vodka and lager available at the 17th-century Lamb, because they're all made in nearby Bourton-on-the-Water. The pub lies down a cul-de-sac in a group of similar-vintage cottages. Owners Richard and Shelley Terry are experienced chefs, although Shelley is usually front-of-house. Localness is paramount, as testified, for example, by the real ales, the game shot by a pub regular, and the many vegetables grown in the kitchen garden. Typical dishes include pressed pheasant terrine with home-made chutney; fillet of sea trout with creamy mussels, leek, bacon and cider chowder; pork sausages with creamed potato and onion jus; and wild mushroom risotto with roasted butternut squash. Among the desserts are vanilla cheesecake with caramel sauce and vanilla ice cream; and apple crumble tart. Steak Night is every Wednesday.

Open all wk 11.30-3 6-11 Closed Sun eve, Mon **Food** Lunch Tue-Sat 12-2, Sun 12-3 Dinner Tue-Sat 7-9 ⊕ FREE HOUSE ◄ Flying Monk, Ramsbury Gold, West Berkshire Good Old Boy, Loose Cannon Abingdon Bridge. ♀ 12 **Facilities** Non-diners area ♥ (Bar Restaurant Garden) ♦ Children's portions Garden ♬ Parking WiFi

The Trout at Tadpole Bridge ★★★★ INN ⊛
PICK OF THE PUBS

tel: 01367 870382 **Buckland Marsh SN7 8RF**
email: info@troutinn.co.uk **web:** www.troutinn.co.uk
dir: A415 from Abingdon signed Marcham, through Frilford to Kingston Bagpuize. Left onto A420. 5m, right signed Tadpole Bridge. Or M4 (E'bound) junct 15, A419 towards Cirencester. 4m, onto A420 towards Oxford. 10m, left signed Tadpole Bridge

Award-winning free house by the River Thames

Just 20 minutes from Oxford, this lovely stone pub by an ancient bridge over the River Thames is popular with boaters, and ramblers on the Thames Path that threads along the bank. Up the road is Kelmscott Manor, the remarkable home of 19th-century artist and designer, William Morris. Stretching down to the water is a secluded garden, clearly designed for just lolling about with a pint of Prescott Chequered Flag, Loose Cannon Abingdon Bridge, or Westons Stowford Press cider. To the restaurant or bar (or outside, if you prefer) for Gareth and Helen Pugh's well balanced, AA Rosette-awarded cooking, all based on the best produce – fish and seafood up daily from Cornwall, game from area shoots, and local fruit, herbs and vegetables. Try pig's head and black pudding croquette with piccalilli; hake fillet, roasted fennel and three bean salad; or roast buttenut squash, Oxford Blue and spinach gallette. Tapas features on the menu too.

Open all wk 11.30-3 6-11 (Sat-Sun all day May-Sep all wk all day) Closed 25-26 Dec **Food** Lunch all wk 12-2 Dinner all wk 7-9 ⊕ FREE HOUSE ◄ Ramsbury Bitter, Young's Bitter, White Horse Wayland Smithy, Loose Cannon Abingdon Bridge, Prescott Chequered Flag ♂ Westons Stowford Press, Cotswold. ♀ 12 **Facilities** Non-diners area ♥ (Bar Restaurant Garden) ♦ Children's menu Children's portions Garden ♬ Parking WiFi **Rooms** 6

FERNHAM
Map 5 SU29

The Woodman Inn

tel: 01367 820643 **SN7 7NX**
email: enquiries@thewoodmaninn.net
dir: M4 junct 15, A419 towards Swindon. Right onto A420 signed Oxford/Shrivenham. Straight on at next 2 rdbts. At x-rds left onto B4508 to Fernham

Old inn near famous landmark

An enticing mix of ultra-traditional old village bar wrapped around a tempting stillage, plus an eye-opening Tudor-style banqueting hall welcome guests to this pretty 400-year old pub. In a peaceful village in the Vale of White Horse, the famous Uffington white horse chalk figure is just a handful of miles away. Now in new hands the pub offers Greene King beers and rotating guests ales. The menus are based on the best local produce in dishes such as duck liver pâté with orange and Cognac; home-made steak, mushroom and ale pie; and apple crumble and custard.

Open all day all wk 11-2.30 5.30-11 (Fri-Sat 11-11 Sun 12-10.30) **Food** Lunch Mon-Fri 12-2, Sat 12-2.30, Sun 12-4 Dinner Mon-Sat 6.30-9.30, Sun 7-9 ⊕ FREE HOUSE ◄ Greene King, Guest ales ♂ Aspall, Thatchers. **Facilities** Non-diners area ♥ (Bar Restaurant Garden) ♦ Children's menu Children's portions Family room Garden ♬ Beer festival Parking WiFi ▭

FILKINS
Map 5 SP20

The Five Alls
PICK OF THE PUBS

tel: 01367 860875 **GL7 3JQ**
email: info@thefiveallsfilkins.co.uk
dir: Between Lechlade & Burford, just off A361

A class act in the Cotswolds

The Five Alls, in picture-postcard Filkins, is very successfully run by Sebastian and Lana Snow. The pub's interior oozes warmth and style, with rugs on stone floors, flickering candles on old dining tables, and a leather chesterfield fronting the log fire – the perfect spot to relax with a pint and the papers. The bar bustles with locals, walkers and cyclists supping pints of Wychwood Hobgoblin or Brakspear Oxford Gold and tucking into proper bar snacks (devilled kidneys or a plate of Serrano ham perhaps), while the concise modern British menu bristles with quality, locally sourced ingredients, draws diners from far and wide across the Cotswolds. Typically, you'll find roast rare beef salad; potted shrimps; and eggs Benedict, florentine or royale as a starter, then for the main event, confit duck leg, braised red cabbage, watercress and rösti potato; blackened cod with bok choi, glass noodles, ginger, chilli and scallions; or tagliata of beef with roasties, wild mushrooms and parmesan shavings.

Open all day Closed 25 Dec, Sun eve **Food** Lunch all wk 12-2.30 Dinner Mon-Sat 6-9.30 Av main course £17 Set menu available Restaurant menu available all wk ⊕ BRAKSPEAR ◄ Oxford Gold, Ringwood, Wychwood Hobgoblin ♂ Thatchers. **Facilities** Non-diners area ♥ (Bar Restaurant Garden) ♦ Children's menu Children's portions Play area Garden ♬ Parking WiFi ▭

PICK OF THE PUBS

The White Hart ✿✿

FYFIELD Map 5 SU49

tel: 01865 390585
Main Rd OX13 5LW
email: info@whitehart-fyfield.com
web: www.whitehart-fyfield.com
dir: *7m S of Oxford, just off A420
(Oxford to Swindon road)*

Confident cooking in picturesque village inn

Mark and Kay Chandler's 500-year-old former chantry house is steeped in history and has been a pub since 1580 when St John's College in Oxford leased it to tenants but reserved the right to 'occupy it if driven from Oxford by pestilence' – so far this has not been invoked! The building is breathtaking and boasts a grand hall with a 15th-century arch-braced roof, original oak beams, flagstone floors, and huge stone-flanked windows. For a table with a view there's still a splendid 30ft high minstrels' gallery overlooking the restaurant. Study the wonderful history and architecture over a pint of local Loose Cannon Abingdon Bridge, Loddon Hullabaloo or Sharp's Doom Bar, or one of the 14 wines served by the glass in the character bar – in winter arrive early to bag the table beside the roaring fire. Awarded two AA Rosettes for his food, chef/owner Mark is steadfast in his pursuit of fresh, seasonal food from trusted local suppliers and their own kitchen garden provides a regular supply of fruit and vegetables. Mark's

cooking reveals a high level of technical skill and his menus change daily, perhaps featuring beetroot cured salmon with smoked salmon mousse, pickled beetroot and thyme crisps; or Jerusalem artichoke soup with artichoke crisps and pickled shiitake mushrooms among the starters. To follow, try slow-cooked lamb belly, sweetbreads, carrot and cumin purée, glazed carrots and lentil and thyme jus; or sea bass fillet with crab crushed new potatoes, sea vegetables and crab bisque. Then stem ginger crème brûlée, rhubarb pillows and poached rhubarb. Fish, antipasti or meze sharing boards are great for nibbles. The lunchtime set menu is great value.

Open 12-3 5.30-11 (Sat 12-11 Sun 12-10.30) Closed Mon (ex BHs)

Food Lunch Tue-Sat 12-2.30, Sun 12-3.30 Dinner Tue-Thu 7-9.30, Fri-Sat 6.45-9.30 Av main course £18 Set menu available ⊕ FREE HOUSE ◀ Sharp's Doom Bar, Loddon Hullabaloo, Loose Cannon Abingdon Bridge, Guest ales ⚬ Thatchers Cheddar Valley, Thatchers Gold. ♥ 14 **Facilities** Non-diners area ♦♦ Children's menu Children's portions Play area Garden ⊼ Parking WiFi

---

The Butchers Arms

tel: 01869 277363 **OX27 8EB**
email: tg53@sky.com
dir: *4m from Bicester on A4421 towards Buckingham*

Charming pub next to the village green

Flora Jane Thompson, author of *Lark Rise to Candleford,* was born at Juniper Hill, a couple of miles from this pretty, creeper-covered pub, and her first job was in the Post Office in Fringford. In her writings, Juniper Hill became Lark Rise, Fringford became Candleford Green, and Buckingham and Banbury metamorphosed into Candleford. Handpumps dispense Doom Bar, Adnams and Black Sheep, while the menu offers a good traditional selection, including pie of the day; beef or mushroom Stroganoff; and roast chicken. There's a senior citizens lunch offer six days a week. You can watch the cricket from the patio and in June there's a beer festival.

Open all day all wk **Food** Lunch Mon-Sat 12-2.30 Dinner Tue-Sat 6.30-9 Av main course £10.95 ⊕ PUNCH TAVERNS ◀ Sharp's Doom Bar, Adnams, Black Sheep ♻ Thatchers Katy, Westons Stowford Press. **Facilities** Non-diners area ♣ (Bar Outside area) ♦♦ Children's menu Children's portions Outside area ☞ Beer festival Parking WiFi ➡ (notice required)

The White Hart ◉◉ **PICK OF THE PUBS**

See Pick of the Pubs on page 395

NEW The Reformation

tel: 0118 972 3126 **Horsepond Rd RG4 9BP**
email: info@therefpub.com
dir: *From A4074 between Reading & Wallingford follow signs for Gallowstree Common*

Diners, drinkers, children, muddy boots and dogs very welcome

Set in an Area of Outstanding Natural Beauty, this friendly pub is a busy place, with plenty going on. There are regular charity 'tractor runs' and barbecues in the summer, live music monthly, and themed dining evenings, as well as beer festivals in May and October. You'll find very well-kept Brakspear ales here, and guests too, and the classic pub menu, with ingredients sourced locally where possible, might feature crispy whitebait or an English and continental charcuterie plate; and mains confit duck leg or pan-fried sea bream, with sticky toffee pudding to finish. Their philosophy? 'We're a pub that serves food, not a restaurant that serves beer.'

Open 12-3 5.30-11 (Sat 12-4 6-11 Sun 12-5) Closed Sun eve & Mon **Food** Lunch Tue-Fri 12-2.30, Sat-Sun 12-4 Dinner Tue-Sat 6-9 Av main course £12 ⊕ BRAKSPEAR ◀ Bitter, Wychwood Hobgoblin ♻ Symonds, The Orchard Pig. ♥ 11 **Facilities** Non-diners area ♣ (Bar Restaurant Garden) ♦♦ Children's menu Children's portions Play area Family room Garden ☞ Beer festival Parking WiFi ➡ (notice required)

The Miller of Mansfield ★★★★ RR ◉◉ **PICK OF THE PUBS**

tel: 01491 872829 **High St RG8 9AW**
email: mary.galer@millerofmansfield.com **web:** www.millerofmansfield.com
dir: *From Pangbourne take A329 to Streatley. Right on B4009, 0.5m to Goring*

A beautiful focal point for the village

Creepers cover the front of this 18th-century coaching inn. Run by Nick and Mary Galer, its appealing location in an upmarket village is just a hop, step and a jump from the River Thames, with the rolling Berkshire and Oxfordshire countryside beyond. Shiny wooden floors, fat candles on scrubbed tables, log fires and local ales

Good Old Boy and Old Hooky characterise the bar, while a restaurant overview must mention its Philippe Starck-influenced design. Menus full of flavour have earned two AA Rosettes but remain keenly priced. Who would quibble with a nibble of proper sausage rolls and brown sauce? A typical fixed-price lunch could comprise Jerusalem artichoke soup; smoked pork belly with red cabbage and buttered mash; and apple crumble with spiced ice cream. In the evening, look to the carte for free-range chicken terrine with white onion purée, followed by fillet of local venison with fondant potato, curly kale and roast peppercorn sauce.

Open all day all wk **Food** Lunch Mon-Sat 12-2.30, Sun 12-4 Dinner Mon-Thu 6-9, Fri-Sat 6-9.30, Sun 6-8 Set menu available ⊕ ENTERPRISE INNS ◀ Hook Norton Old Hooky, West Berkshire Good Old Boy ♻ Aspall, Thatchers. ♥ 11 **Facilities** Non-diners area ♣ (Bar Outside area) ♦♦ Children's menu Children's portions Outside area ☞ Parking WiFi ➡ (notice required) **Rooms** 13

The Falkland Arms **PICK OF THE PUBS**

tel: 01608 683653 **OX7 4DB**
email: falklandarms@wadworth.co.uk
dir: *Off A361, 1.25m, signed Great Tew*

Ancient inn replete with English character

Named after Lucius Carey, 2nd Viscount Falkland, who inherited the manor of Great Tew in 1629, this 500-year-old creeper-clad inn can be found at the end of a charming row of Cotswold-stone cottages. The Falkland Arms is a classic: wooden floors, exposed beams, high-backed settles and low stools and an inglenook fireplace characterise the intimate bar, where a huge collection of beer and cider mugs and jugs hangs from the ceiling. Wadworth and guest ales, together with a meal, can be enjoyed in the bar or the lovely pub garden. Sharing plates, pork pie, baked camembert and home-made soup supplement the lunchtime menu of thick-cut bloomer sandwiches. In the evening, booking is essential for dinner in the small dining room. Expect pan-fried potato gnocchi with wild mushrooms and spinach; honey-roast Wiltshire ham; and chef's pie of the day.

Open all day all wk 8am-11pm **Food** Lunch all wk 12-2.30 Dinner all wk 6.30-9.30 ⊕ WADWORTH ◀ 6X, Henry's Original IPA & Horizon, Guest ales ♻ Westons Traditional & Kingstone Press. ♥ 14 **Facilities** Non-diners area ♣ (Bar Restaurant Garden) ♦♦ Children's portions Garden ☞ Beer festival WiFi ➡ (notice required)

NEW The Lamb Inn ◉◉

tel: 01993 708792 **Steep Hill, Crawley OX29 9TW**
email: lambcrawley@yahoo.co.uk
dir: *From Witney (B4047), follow signs for Crawley*

Pretty village inn popular with walkers

In the tiny village of Crawley just outside Witney, this 18th-century pub is popular with walkers because of its routes from Minster Lovell and the Windrush River. Oak beams and Cotswold-stone walls are reminders of the pub's vintage, although a BBQ and brick pizza oven in the garden indicate a more contemporary approach to hospitality. Ales brewed at the nearby Wychwood Brewery can be found on the handpumps, with Somerset cider also on tap. Local produce drives the menu, from grilled wood pigeon with blackcurrant, nut and beetroot granola to braised short rib of Butt's Farm rare breed beef.

Open 11-3 6-12 Closed Sun eve & Mon **Food** Lunch Tue-Thu 12-2, Fri-Sat 12-2.30, Sun 12-3 Dinner Tue-Thu 6.30-9, Fri-Sat 6.30-9.30 Av main course £17 Restaurant menu available Tue-Sat ⊕ BRAKSPEAR ◀ Bitter & Oxford Gold, Guest ale ♻ Thatchers Gold. ♥ 13 **Facilities** Non-diners area ♣ (Bar Garden) ♦♦ Children's menu Children's portions Garden ☞ Parking WiFi ➡ (notice required)

THE LITTLE ANGEL
Henley on Thames

Henley on Thames, South Oxfordshire is just an hour from London & home to the famous Little Angel Pub. Just 80 yards from Henley Bridge & the famous Royal Regatta course on the River Thames, it is renowned the world over. One of the largest & most individual pubs in the area, the focus here is a cracking bar, fantastic food & good times. Open every day, all day & serving only the best local & seasonal food, this award winning pub is one of the busiest in the region & is as happy hosting thousands during regatta week in July, as it is a romantic table for two! A uniquely designed pub, it has several individual areas that can cater for parties of all sizes & with a large car park for its patrons, is highly prized in the town. Daily specials boards deliver delicious foodie treats, as does the daily bar food offer, including enormous home made Scotch eggs that are superb. Cosy in the winter but equally loved for its large patio garden for al fresco dining or drinks. Overlooking the quintessential Henley Cricket Club grounds, you could do worse than while away an afternoon with a good lunch, chilled bottle of rosé & good company. Whether you are enjoying a day trip, passing through or partaking in one of the large annual events in the town, you would not want to pass The Little Angel & not pop in. Their friendly & efficient staff will take great care of you.

THE LITTLE ANGEL REMENHAM LANE   HENLEY ON THAMES   OXON   RG9 2LS
01491 411 008   ENQUIRIES@THELITTLEANGEL.CO.UK   WWW.THELITTLEANGEL.CO.UK

HAMPTON POYLE
Map 11 SP51

The Bell
PICK OF THE PUBS

tel: 01865 376242 **OX5 2QD**
email: contactus@thebelloxford.co.uk
dir: *From N: exit A34 signed Kidlington, over bridge. At mini rdbt turn right, left to Hampton Poyle (before slip road to rejoin A34). From Kidlington: at rdbt (junct of A4260 & A4165) take Bicester Rd (Sainsbury's on left) towards A34. Left to Hampton Poyle*

Good food and welcoming, professional staff

A centuries-old inn that is independent and privately owned, and conveniently sited for Oxford, Bicester Village shopping outlet and Blenheim Palace. The charms of its oak beams and time-worn flagstone floors are complemented by the dining area with an open kitchen featuring an eye-catching wood-burning oven, from which are produced rustic pizzas and other dishes. These, along with burgers and salads, are served in the bar at any time, while in the restaurant a meal might start with pressed game terrine with celeriac remoulade, cornichons and toast; or salt and pepper squid chipotle chilli and lime mayonnaise; continue with golden beetroot and butternut squash risotto with crispy sage and parmesan; or sticky Tamworth pork chaps with Hispi cabbage. Finish with ginger and lemon syrup sponge with rhubarb compôte and custard. Should you have a well-behaved dog, he or she will be welcome to join you in the bar or out on the delightful south-facing terrace.

Open all day all wk 7am-11pm **Food** Lunch Mon-Sat 12-2.30, Sun 12-3 Dinner Sun-Thu 6-9, Fri-Sat 6.30-9.30 Set menu available ⊕ FREE HOUSE ◀ Hook Norton Hooky Bitter, Wye Valley Butty Bach. ♥ 10 **Facilities** Non-diners area ♣ (Bar Garden Outside area) ♠ Children's portions Family room Garden Outside area ⊼ Parking WiFi ☞ (notice required)

HARWELL
Map 5 SU48

The Hart of Harwell

tel: 01235 834511 **High St OX11 OEH**
email: info@hartofharwell.com
dir: *In village centre, accessed from A417 & A4130*

Village pub with unusual wells and great food

Several old wells were found during renovations of this 15th to 16th-century pub, and one now serves as a dining table. You can peer down it while eating – an unusual diversion. The modern barn's stable of Greene King real ales is supplemented by regularly-changing guests. Sandwiches are served at lunchtime only, while the main menu covers both lunch and dinner, so either meal could feature a pulled pork, pickles and toast starter, followed by, say, treacle baked ham with egg, chips and peas; or perhaps beef and Guinness pie with cabbage and mash; and, to end, ginger pear and black cherry crumble with vanilla custard.

Open all wk 12-3 5.30-11 (Fri-Sat 12-12 Sun 12-11) **Food** Lunch Mon-Sat 12-2.30, Sun 12-4 Dinner Mon-Sat 6-9.30 ⊕ GREENE KING ◀ Morland Old Speckled Hen & Original, Hardys & Hansons Olde Trip, Guinness ♂ Thatchers Gold. ♥ 24 **Facilities** Non-diners area ♣ (Bar Garden) ♠ Children's menu Children's portions Garden ⊼ Parking WiFi

HENLEY-ON-THAMES
Map 5 SU78

The Five Horseshoes
PICK OF THE PUBS

tel: 01491 641282 **Maidensgrove RG9 6EX**
email: admin@thefivehorseshoes.co.uk
dir: *From Henley-on-Thames take A4130, 1m, take B480 signed Stonor. In Stonor left, through woods, over common, pub on left*

Popular for its summer hog roasts and barbecues

There's every chance of seeing red kites wheeling around above this 16th-century, brick and flint pub overlooking the Chiltern Hills. Its two snug bar areas are characterised by beams, wrought iron, brasswork, open fires, traditional pub games

and Brakspear's real ales on the handpumps. To dine in the large conservatory restaurant is to enjoy an approach to traditional English dishes that often involves tweaking them to intensify the flavours, thus a menu typically begins with pan-seared pigeon breast, walnuts, grapes and vegetable crisps; and Cornish mussels marinière. Then to follow might be a main course of poached smoked haddock fillet with poached egg, spinach and hollandaise; a 35-day aged steak, hand-cut chips and roast tomatoes; and Lincolnshire sausages, vegetables, mash, and bacon and mushroom sauce. There's sandwiches if you just want a light lunch. Dogs are welcome in the bar and two large beer gardens.

Open 12-3.30 6-11 (Sat 12-11 Sun 12-6) Closed Mon **Food** Lunch Tue-Fri 12-2.30, Sat 12-3, Sun 12-4 Dinner Tue-Sat 6.30-9.30 ⊕ BRAKSPEAR ◀ Bitter, Oxford Gold ♂ Symonds. **Facilities** Non-diners area ♣ (Bar Garden) ♠ Children's portions Garden Parking ☞

The Little Angel

tel: 01491 411008 **Remenham Ln RG9 2LS**
email: enquiries@thelittleangel.co.uk **web:** www.thelittleangel.co.uk
dir: *M4 juncts 8 & 9, A404, A4130 to Henley, then towards Maidenhead. Pub on left*

Spacious and busy pub with an inviting interior

This large whitewashed pub, just over the famous bridge from the town, gets pretty packed, especially at weekends. The chic interior features wooden floorboards, duck-egg blue tones with warming accents, an open fire, and spacious bar and dining areas. Other attractions are the well-compiled wine list, the Brakspear ales, and the exceptional modern menu, which is changed quarterly. Try baked beetroot, balsamic vinegar reduction and parsnip purée; Little Angel sausages, creamed mash and caramelised onion jus; and hedgerow blackberry glazed rice pudding. Sundays are 'unbelievably busy' so booking is essential, but don't worry, lunch is served all day.

Open all day all wk 11-11 (Fri-Sat 11am-mdnt Sun 12-10) **Food** Lunch Mon-Fri 12-3, Sat-Sun all day Dinner Mon-Fri 7-10, Sat-Sun all day Set menu available Restaurant menu available all wk ⊕ BRAKSPEAR ◀ Brakspear, Oxford Gold,

Guinness, Seasonal ales ⟳ Symonds. ☂ 11 **Facilities** Non-diners area 🐾 (Bar Restaurant Garden) ♦️ Children's menu Children's portions Garden ⏟ Parking WiFi 🚌 (notice required)

See advert on page 397

The Three Tuns

tel: 01491 410138 & 01865 891118 **5 The Market Place RG9 2AA**
email: info@threetunshenley.co.uk
dir: *In town centre. Parking nearby*

Known for its warm and friendly service

Mark and Sandra Duggan successfully run this bustling drinking and dining spot. One of the oldest pubs in town, the cosy, matchboarded front bar has scrubbed tables, an open fire and Brakspear Brewery prints from a bygone era. From the adjacent cosy and intimate dining room, a passageway leads to the suntrap terrace garden. Freshly sourced local produce (the butcher is only next door) underpins menus both traditional and modern: goats' cheese soufflé, confit duck leg, and roast loin of cod, for example. There is live music every Sunday evening and live comedy acts on the first Thursday each month.

Open all day 11.30-11 (Sat 11am-mdnt Sun 11-10) Closed 25 Dec, Mon (ex BHs) **Food** Lunch Tue-Sat 12-3, Sun 12-4 Dinner Tue-Sat 6-9.45 Set menu available ⊕ BRAKSPEAR 🍺 Special, Oxford Gold & Bitter ⟳ Symonds. ☂ 20 **Facilities** Non-diners area 🐾 (Bar Garden Outside area) ♦️ Children's portions Garden Outside area ⏟

The White Hart

tel: 01491 641245 **High St, Nettlebed RG9 5DD**
email: whitehart@tmdining.co.uk
dir: *On A4130 between Henley-on-Thames & Wallingford*

History and tradition blend with stylish modernity

Royalist and parliamentary soldiers frequently lodged in taverns during the English Civil War; this 15th-century inn reputedly billeted troops loyal to the King. During the 17th and 18th centuries the area was plagued by highwaymen, including the notorious Isaac Darkin who was eventually caught, tried and hung at Oxford Gaol. Today the beautifully restored property is favoured by a stylish crowd who appreciate the chic bar and restaurant. Heading the beer list is locally-brewed Brakspear, backed by popular internationals and a small selection of cosmopolitan bottles. Food comprises typically English dishes interspersed with South African offerings such as boerewors served as a starter with bread and a spicy dipping sauce. Half a spit-roasted chicken can be cooked either with garlic lemon butter or basted with piri piri sauce. The dessert choice includes stalwarts such as banoffee pie, and sticky toffee pudding with custard.

Open all day all wk 7am-11pm (Sun 8am-10pm) **Food** Lunch Mon-Sat 12-3, Sun 12-8 Dinner Mon-Sat 6-10, Sun 12-8 ⊕ BRAKSPEAR 🍺 Brakspear, Guinness. ☂ 20 **Facilities** Non-diners area 🐾 (Bar Garden) ♦️ Children's menu Children's portions Garden ⏟ Parking 🚌

HETHE	Map 11 SP52

The Muddy Duck

See Pick of the Pubs on page 400 and advert below

PICK OF THE PUBS

The Muddy Duck

HETHE   Map 11 SP52

tel: 01869 278099 **Main St OX27 8ES**
email: dishitup@themuddyduckpub.co.uk
web: www.themuddyduckpub.co.uk
dir: *From Bicester towards Buckingham on A4421 left signed Fringford. Through Fringford, right signed Hethe, left signed Hethe*

Family-run rural pub and restaurant

The Muddy Duck is family-owned and run by a close-knit team who are big on friendly, efficient service and high food standards – without the pompous style. This stone-built village pub is a sympathetic combination of old and new and the real ales are likely to include old favourites Hooky, Landlord and Tribute, from a cellar looked after by the knowledgeable Ian, himself a former innkeeper. The refurbished pub is a lively, welcoming area to enjoy a pint, bar snack or the self-styled 'tummy fillers' by the open fire. Don't miss the infamous giant pork scratchings, the popular Provençale fish stew and authentic French onion soup with rarebit croûte. For more of a dining experience, check out The Malthouse restaurant and explore the full à la carte menu. The Harris family is big on free-range, high welfare and zero tolerance on short-cuts – in their words 'all fresh, no ping-and-ding here' and the only thing that comes frozen is the ice cream, and that's made

by them, too. A rich offering of starters includes smoked salmon Scotch egg with spinach and beurre blanc; carpaccio of beef with horseradish crème fraîche and dressed rocket; or confit duck leg and fig salad with a poached duck egg. Big hearted mains include stuffed and rolled pork belly with sage mash, baby fennel, apple purée and confit apple; pan-fried rump of lamb; or cauliflower macaroni cheese with tenderstem garlic broccoli. If you have room after all that, don't miss the banana parfait with honey figs, caramelised bananas and toffee popcorn. A traditional Valoriani wood-fired oven leads to the heated terrace area, protected by giant parasols for year-round alfresco dining.

Open all wk 11-11 **Food** Lunch Mon-Sat 12-2.30, Sun 12-4 Dinner Mon-Sat 6-9 Restaurant menu available all wk ⊕ FREE HOUSE ◀ Timothy Taylor Landlord & Boltmaker, St Austell Tribute, Hook Norton Hooky Bitter ⓒ Westons Stowford Press. **Facilities** Non-diners area 🐾 (Bar Garden) 👪 Children's portions Garden 🎋 Parking WiFi

---

HIGHMOOR
Map 5 SU78

Rising Sun

tel: 01491 640856 **Witheridge Hill RG9 5PF**
email: info@risingsunwitheridgehill.co.uk
dir: *From Henley-on-Thames take A4130 towards Wallingford. Take B481, turn right to Highmoor*

Intimate, cottagey pub in the Chilterns

Next to the green in a Chilterns' hamlet, you approach this 17th-century pub through the garden. Inside, you'll find richly coloured walls, low-beamed ceilings and open fires. Chalkboards tell you which guest ales are accompanying regulars Brakspear's Bitter and Oxford Gold, and Wyld Wood Organic, the incumbent cider. The three-section restaurant is a cosy place to dine on pan-fried breast of pheasant with roast potatoes, parsnip purée and bacon and mushroom port wine reduction; home-made chicken, mushroom and leek puff pastry pie; or roast loin of pork with roast potatoes, apple sauce and apricot and sage stuffing. Check dates of outdoor music events.

Open all wk Mon-Fri 12-3 5-11 (Sat 12-11 Sun 12-7) **Food** Lunch Mon-Fri 12-2, Sat-Sun 12-3 Dinner Mon-Sat 6.30-9 Av main course £13.50 Restaurant menu available all wk ⊕ BRAKSPEAR ◼ Bitter, Oxford Gold ♻ Westons Wyld Wood Organic, The Orchard Pig. ♟ 10 **Facilities** Non-diners area ♣ (Bar Garden) ♦ Children's menu Children's portions Family room Garden � Parking WiFi ⛙ (notice required)

KINGHAM
Map 10 SP22

The Kingham Plough ★★★★ INN ◉◉◉ **PICK OF THE PUBS**

tel: 01608 658327 **The Green OX7 6YD**
email: book@thekinghamplough.co.uk **web:** www.thekinghamplough.co.uk
dir: *B4450 from Chipping Norton to Churchill. 2nd right to Kingham, left at T-junct. Pub on right*

Relaxed and upmarket village inn with an imaginative menu

In a plum position in the north Cotswolds, this eye-catching, rambling old stone village coaching inn effortlessly satisfies a role as both welcoming local and destination dining inn. The discerning bar-hound can revel in great beers from small breweries such as Purity or Cotswold; relaxing in a character beamed bar that features real fires, a pub dog and regular events like Sunday quizzes, perhaps snacking on Cotswold rarebit on sourdough toast. Media-favourite and multi award-winning chef-proprietor Emily Watkins, together with head chef Ben Dulley, continue to raise the culinary stakes with a crisp, ever-evolving menu of rustic, revealing British dishes based on carefully-sourced, largely local produce. Their three AA Rosette distinction results from consummate starters such as partridge terrine with parsnip and apple croquette and burnt apple purée. The mains' menu may field treats like pheasant Wellington with roasted and puréed parsnip and braised red cabbage; alternatively loin and steam pudding of local hogget may fit the bill. For a final flourish, Guernsey milk and borage honey pudding.

Open all day all wk Closed 25 Dec **Food** Lunch Mon-Sat 12-9, Sun 12-8 Dinner Mon-Sat 12-9, Sun 12-8 Restaurant menu available all wk ⊕ FREE HOUSE ◼ Wye Valley HPA, Purity Mad Goose, Cotswold Wheat Beer, Hook Norton ♻ Ashton Press. **Facilities** Non-diners area ♣ (Bar Garden) ♦ Children's menu Children's portions Garden ⌴ Parking WiFi **Rooms** 6

NEW The Wild Rabbit ★★★★★ RR

tel: 01608 658389 **Church St OX7 6YA**
email: theteam@thewildrabbit.co.uk **web:** www.thewildrabbit.co.uk
dir: *In centre of village*

Organic produce and celebrity clientele

From the family behind nearby Daylesford Organic, The Wild Rabbit has already been heralded 'the poshest pub in Britain' because of its A-list celebrity customers. Renovated in 2013, this 18th-century Cotswold inn has stripped back walls, open fires and simple, handcrafted furniture. Local Hook Norton ale is one of four beers on tap, alongside an impeccably sourced wine list. Food is available from the bar and terrace all day and the seasonal menu features organic produce from Daylesford. Try crisp pig's head, apple and celery, or roast cod, wild garlic, Swiss chard, Jersey royals and thyme vinaigrette.

Open all day all wk Closed 1st wk Jan **Food** Lunch all wk 12-2.30 Dinner all wk 7-9.30 Av main course £11 Restaurant menu available all wk ⊕ FREE HOUSE ◼ Hook Norton, Timothy Taylor Landlord, Sharp's Doom Bar, Otter ♻ Westons Stowford Press. ♟ 14 **Facilities** Non-diners area ♣ (Bar Outside area) ♦ Children's menu Children's portions Outside area ⌴ Beer festival Parking WiFi **Rooms** 12

KIRTLINGTON
Map 11 SP42

The Oxford Arms

tel: 01869 350208 **Troy Ln OX5 3HA**
email: enquiries@oxford-arms.co.uk
dir: *Take either A34 or A44 N from Oxford, follow Kirtlington signs*

Homely village pub serving unpretentious good food

Dating from 1862, this attractive stone-built village inn prides itself on providing a warm welcome mirrored by its real log fire. In summer, head to the patio for alfresco dining near the kitchen garden that produces a supply of herbs, salad leaves and soft fruits. Inside, freshly-cut flowers and wax-encrusted church candles on the tables adds a rustic touch to proceedings. Everything in the kitchen is made from scratch from local produce, although the fish arrives from Devon every day. Start perhaps with crab bisque, or potted shrimps before enjoying a game pie of venison, partridge and pheasant with vegetable purée.

Open all wk 12-3 6-11 **Food** Lunch all wk 12-2.30 Dinner Mon-Sat 6.30-9.30 ⊕ PUNCH TAVERNS ◼ St Austell Tribute, Hook Norton Hooky Bitter ♻ Westons Old Rosie. ♟ 12 **Facilities** Non-diners area ♣ (Bar Restaurant Garden) ♦ Children's portions Garden ⌴ Parking ⛙ (notice required)

LOWER SHIPLAKE — Map 5 SU77

The Baskerville ★★★★ INN ◉ — PICK OF THE PUBS

tel: 0118 940 3332 **Station Rd RG9 3NY**
email: enquiries@thebaskerville.com **web:** www.thebaskerville.com
dir: Just off A4155, 1.5m from Henley-on-Thames towards Reading, follow signs at War Memorial junct

Variety and a relaxed atmosphere are key here

On the popular Thames Path is this modern-rustic pub of real quality. Walkers remove their muddy boots at the door before heading to the bar that's adorned with sporting memorabilia, and where pints of Loddon Hoppit, brewed two miles away, await. There is plenty of choice food-wise; whether it's the bar menu or the à la carte, the objective is to serve great food at reasonable prices in an unpretentious atmosphere. Modern British describes the kitchen's approach, with continental and Eastern influences evident in the sustainably sourced ingredients. For lunch, you could go for an open sandwich or savour seafood linguine. Typical evening choices might be rich chicken liver parfait with truffle butter and spiced fruit chutney; followed by organic salmon, cod and prawn fish pie. The wine list extends to 50 bins, and owner Allan Hannah betrays his origins with 40 malt whiskies. The pub boasts an attractive garden, where summer Sunday barbecues are a common fixture.

Open all day all wk 11-11 (Sun 12-10.30) Closed 1 Jan **Food** Lunch Mon-Sat 12-6, Sun 12-3.30 Dinner Mon-Thu 6-9.30, Fri-Sat 6-10 Av main course £14-£23.50 Set menu available Restaurant menu available all wk ▬ Loddon Hoppit & Ferryman's Gold, Sharp's Doom Bar, Marlow Rebelllion IPA ♨ Thatchers. ☘ 17 **Facilities** Non-diners area ✿ (Bar Garden) ◗◗ Children's menu Children's portions Play area Garden ⌂ Parking WiFi **Rooms** 4

LOWER WOLVERCOTE — Map 5 SP40

The Trout Inn

tel: 01865 510930 **195 Godstow Rd OX2 8PN**
dir: From A40 at Wolvercote rdbt (N of Oxford) follow signs for Wolvercote, through village to pub

Ever-popular waterside inn

The Trout was already ancient when Lewis Carroll, and later CS Lewis took inspiration here; centuries before it had been a hospice for Godstow Nunnery, on the opposite bank of the Thames. It featured in several episodes of *Inspector Morse,*

and has long been a favourite with Oxford undergraduates. Its leaded windows, great oak beams, flagged floors and glowing fireplaces make it arguably the area's most atmospheric inn. On a summer day bag a table on the terrace by the fast flowing water to enjoy a pint and something from the menu that pleases everyone – 18-hour slow cooked British corned salt beef hash; stone-baked pizzas; and beer-battered line-caught cod and twice cooked chunky chips are just three ideas. A change of hands.

Open all day all wk 9am-close **Food** Lunch all wk 12-10 Dinner all wk 12-10 Set menu available ⊕ FREE HOUSE ▬ Brakspear Bitter, Sharp's Doom Bar, Guest ales ♨ Aspall. ☘ 21 **Facilities** Non-diners area ✿ (Bar Garden) ◗◗ Children's menu Children's portions Garden ⌂ Parking WiFi ▭

MARSH BALDON — Map 5 SU59

Seven Stars

tel: 01865 343337 **The Green OX44 9LP**
email: info@sevenstarsonthegreen.co.uk
dir: From Oxford ring road onto A4074 signed Wallingford. Through Nuneham Courtenay. Left, follow Marsh Baldon signs

Thriving community-owned pub

After several closures the exasperated Marsh Baldon residents dug deep into their pockets and bought the historic 350-year-old pub on the pretty village green. Today the Seven Stars has a smart interior, local ales on tap and a modern pub menu offering a good range of dishes prepared from fresh local ingredients. Typical dishes include risottos, sausages and mash, classic Sunday roasts, and specials like fish pie and sticky toffee pudding. For summer, there's a gorgeous garden and an August beer festival. The area has several interesting walks and Oxford Arboretum is a five-minute walk away.

Open all day all wk **Food** Lunch Mon-Fri 12-9, Sat-Sun 10-9 Dinner Mon-Fri 12-9, Sat-Sun 10-9 ⊕ FREE HOUSE ▬ Fuller's London Pride, Loose Cannon Abingdon Bridge, Loddon Hoppit, Shotover Prospect, Village Idiot, White Horse ♨ Aspall. ☘ 9 **Facilities** Non-diners area ✿ (Bar Garden) ◗◗ Children's menu Children's portions Garden ⌂ Beer festival Parking WiFi ▭ (notice required)

MIDDLETON STONEY — Map 11 SP52

Best Western The Jersey Arms ★★ HL

tel: 01869 343234 **OX25 4AD**
email: jerseyarms@bestwestern.co.uk **web:** www.jerseyarms.com
dir: M4 junct 9 or 10, A34 onto B340

British food in a historic property

Until 1951, when a family called Ansell bought it, this 13th-century country inn belonged to the Jersey Estate. In 1985 the Ansells sold it to Donald and Helen Livingston, making them only its third set of owners since 1243. It is just three minutes from Bicester Village shopping outlet if you want to call in for refreshments after grabbing a few bargains. Food can be taken in the Bar & Grill where the British menu is supplemented by daily specials. Start with king-size prawns in hot garlic oil, then move onto confit of duck with caramelised orange, parsnip mash and orange sauce; classic spaghetti bolognaise; or red Thai curry.

Open all day all wk **Food** Lunch all wk 12-2 Dinner all wk 6.30-9 Restaurant menu available all wk ⊕ FREE HOUSE ▬ Flowers. ☘ 9 **Facilities** Non-diners area ◗◗ Children's menu Garden ⌂ Parking WiFi **Rooms** 20

MILCOMBE
Map 11 SP43

The Horse & Groom Inn ★★★★ INN

tel: 01295 722142 **OX15 4RS**

email: horseandgroominn@gmail.com **web:** www.thehorseandgroominn.co.uk
dir: From A361 between Chipping Norton & Bloxham follow Milcombe signs. Pub at end of village

A traditional Cotswold pub with daily-changing menus

The 17th-century Horse & Groom still shows signs of its traditional elements such as stone floors, a wood-burning stove, and delightful snug area but is right in the 21st century otherwise. The contemporary dining room seats 50, and the daily-changing menus are bursting with dishes created from local produce. Start off with potted pheasant and ham with pickles and toasted sourdough; followed by turkey, mushroom and leek pie, or slow-cooked pork shoulder and chorizo lasagne. Vegetarians have interesting choices too – grilled goats' cheese crouton with red onion marmalade; or lentil, cashew and vegetable bake, perhaps.

Open 12-3 6-11 (Sun 12-5) Closed 25 Dec eve & 26 Dec, Sun eve **Food** Lunch Mon-Sat 12-2.30, Sun 12-4 Dinner Mon-Sat 6-9 Av main course £12 ⊕ PUNCH TAVERNS ◀ Sharp's Doom Bar, Hook Norton Hooky Bitter, Young's Bitter, Black Sheep. ♈ 11 **Facilities** Non-diners area ♣ (Bar Outside area) ♦♦ Children's menu Children's portions Outside area ⌨ Parking WiFi ☗ (notice required) **Rooms** 4

MILTON
Map 5 SU49

The Plum Pudding

tel: 01235 834443 **44 High St OX14 4EJ**

email: jez@theplumpuddingmilton.co.uk
dir: From A34 (Milton Interchange) follow Milton signs. 1st left (signed Milton) into High St

Proper village free house serving old-breed pork

The name 'Plum Pudding' derives from the nickname of the Oxford Sandy and Black Pig, one of the oldest of British breeds and bred in this area. The dog-friendly bar of this pub stocks local and regional ales such as Loose Cannon, and the Plum Pudding's pork specialities may include slow-roast belly with wholegrain mustard mash, and different flavours of specially made sausages. Alternatives such as filled baguettes, battered cod with mushy peas, and Oxfordshire sirloin steak complete a menu of confirmed pub favourites. Beer festivals are held in April and October.

Open all wk 11.30-2.30 5-11 (Fri-Sun all day) **Food** Lunch Mon-Sat 12-2, Sun 12-3 Dinner Mon-Sat 6-9 ⊕ FREE HOUSE ◀ Loose Cannon, Brakspear, Ringwood, Guest ales. **Facilities** Non-diners area ♣ (Bar Restaurant Garden) ♦♦ Children's portions Garden ⌨ Beer festival Parking WiFi ☗

MURCOTT
Map 11 SP51

The Nut Tree Inn ◉◉
PICK OF THE PUBS

tel: 01865 331253 **Main St OX5 2RE**

dir: M40 junct 9, A34 towards Oxford. Left onto B4027 signed Islip. At Red Lion turn left. Right signed Murcott, Fencott & Charlton-on-Otmoor. Pub on right in village

Village local and destination dining venue

Local lad Mike North grew up dreaming of owning this thatched, 15th-century free house overlooking the pond. In 2006 his dream came true when he and Imogen, then his fiancée, bought it. Oak beams, wood-burners and unusual carvings are the setting for either a locally brewed, or a more distantly sourced, pint. But, as the Norths point out, real ales and worldwide-sourced wines don't pay the bills, so they (it's actually Mike and his sister Mary who cook) set great store by their food, which is why they've collected two AA Rosettes. Commitment begins outside, where they raise rare-breed pigs for the table and grow fruit and vegetables. A typical menu

promises roast saddle and faggot of lamb; home-smoked and fresh salmon fishcake; and parmesan, potato and rosemary croquette. Thoughtfully, one of the two seven-course tasting menus is for vegetarians. Light meals and sandwiches are served at lunchtime.

Open all day Closed 2wks from 27 Dec, Sun eve & Mon **Food** Lunch Tue-Sat 12-2.30, Sun 12-3 Dinner Tue-Sat 7-9 Av main course £10 Set menu available Restaurant menu available Tue-Sun ⊕ FREE HOUSE ◀ Vale Best Bitter, Fuller's London Pride, Brains The Rev. James, Shepherd Neame Spitfire, Oxfordshire Ales Pride of Oxford. ♈ 11 **Facilities** Non-diners area ♦♦ Children's portions Garden ⌨ Parking ☗ (notice required)

NORTH HINKSEY VILLAGE
Map 5 SP40

The Fishes

tel: 01865 249796 **OX2 ONA**

email: fishes@peachpubs.com
dir: From A34 S'bound (dual carriageway) left at junct after Botley Interchange, signed North Hinksey & Oxford Rugby Club. From A34 N'bound exit at Botley Interchange & return to A34 S'bound, then follow as above

Victorian pub with a huge garden

A short walk from Oxford city centre, this attractive tile-hung pub stands in three acres of tranquil wooded grounds running down to Seacourt Stream, with a decking area and a children's playground. Providing plenty of shade, these grounds are ideal for barbecues and picnics, which can be ordered at the bar. Seasonal menus of modern British dishes include pressed guinea fowl and duck terrine; Enderby's smoked haddock kedgeree; roast cannon of Cornish lamb; and steaks from award-winning butcher Aubrey 'By Royal Appointment' Allen. Soups, sandwiches, deli boards and a handful of mains are served all day. Also seasonal, are the interesting English and French cheese selections.

Open all day all wk Closed 25 Dec **Food** Lunch 12-2.30 Dinner 6.30-9.30 Av main course £13.50 ⊕ PEACH PUBS ◀ Morland Old Speckled Hen, Greene King IPA ♻ Aspall. ♈ **Facilities** Non-diners area ♣ (Bar Garden) ♦♦ Children's portions Garden ⌨ Beer festival Cider festival Parking WiFi ☗

NORTHMOOR
Map 5 SP40

The Red Lion

tel: 01865 300301 **OX29 5SX**

email: info@theredlionnorthmoor.com
dir: A420 from Oxford. At 2nd rdbt take 3rd exit onto A415. Right after lights into Moreton Ln. At end turn right, Pub on right

A reborn pub going from strength to strength

A pretty 17th-century pub with a large garden set on the skew in the middle of the village; experts have deduced from the positioning of its wooden beams and open fireplaces that it was originally two cottages. The local community bought the Red Lion from a brewery chain, and the experienced publicans Ian Neale and Lisa Lyne have certainly made their mark in the last couple of years. The tempting menus offer snacks of chorizo Scotch eggs; and sweet potato chips with blue cheese sauce, and more substantial dishes of smoked Bibury trout, beetroot purée and celeriac remoulade; roast loin of venison, braised spiced red cabbage, Anna potatoes and juniper sauce; and Venetian rice pudding.

Open 11-3 6-11 (Sat all day Sun 12-4) Closed Sun eve & Mon **Food** Lunch Tue-Sat 12-2.30, Sun 12-3.30 Dinner Tue-Sat 6.30-9.30 Av main course £11 Restaurant menu available Tue-Sat ⊕ FREE HOUSE ◀ Wychwood Hobgoblin, Brakspear, Hook Norton Lion, Guest ale ♻ Thatchers Gold. ♈ 11 **Facilities** Non-diners area ♣ (All areas) ♦♦ Children's menu Children's portions Garden Outside area ⌨ Beer festival Parking WiFi ☗ (notice required)

OXFORD
Map 5 SP50

The Magdalen Arms

tel: 01865 243159 **243 Iffley Rd OX4 1SJ**
email: info@magdalenarms.co.uk
dir: *On corner of Iffley Rd & Magdalen Rd*

Busy food pub with a boho vibe

Just a short stroll from Oxford city centre, this bustling food pub is run by the same team as Waterloo's hugely influential Anchor & Hope gastro-pub. There is a similar boho feel to the place with its dark red walls and vintage furniture and the nose-to-tail menu will be familiar to anybody who knows the pub's London sibling. Expect the likes of wild rabbit and pork rillettes; twice-baked cep and parmesan soufflé; braised ox cheek, suet dumplings and horseradish cream; rib of beef, béarnaise, chips and salad; and sticky toffee pudding with double cream. Real ales are complemented by a vibrant modern wine list. There's books and wooden bricks for children in the sofa area.

Open 11-11 (Mon 5-11 Sun 12-10.30) Closed BHs, 24-26 Dec, Mon L **Food** Lunch Tue-Sat 12-2.30, Sun 12-3 Dinner Mon-Sat 6-10, Sun 6-9.30 ⊕ STAR PUBS & BARS ◀ Caledonian XPA & Deuchars IPA, Theakston Black Bull, Guest ale ♂ Symonds. ♟ 16 **Facilities** Non-diners area ♣ (Bar Garden) ♦ Children's portions Garden ♬ Beer festival WiFi ➡ (notice required)

The Oxford Retreat

tel: 01865 250309 **1-2 Hythe Bridge St OX1 2EW**
email: info@theoxfordretreat.com
dir: *In city centre. 200mtrs from rail station towards city centre*

Perched on the river close to the city centre

Right beside the River Isis, this willow-tree-shaded waterside pub is the place to be seen and is best enjoyed after a day exploring the City of Dreaming Spires. Arrive early and relax, start by sipping cocktails or quaffing a pint of Doom Bar, then order from the sharing-inspired global pub menu, tucking into Egyptian dukkah, Spanish guindillas or choosing the slider menu of 15 different mini burgers. In summer, there's nowhere better than the garden for relaxing with friends, and in winter, retreat inside and cosy up around the log fire.

Open all day all wk Closed 25-26 Dec, 1 Jan **Food** Lunch Mon-Thu 12-3, Fri-Sat 12-10, Sun 12-6 Dinner Mon-Thu 6-10, Fri-Sat 12-10 Set menu available Restaurant menu available Tue-Sun ⊕ FREE HOUSE ◀ Fuller's London Pride, Staropramen, Sharp's Doom Bar, Guinness ♂ Westons Wyld Wood Organic, Aspall. ♟ 10 **Facilities** Non-diners area ♣ (Bar Garden) ♦ Children's portions Garden ♬ WiFi ➡ (notice required)

The Punter

tel: 01865 248832 **7 South St, Osney Island OX2 0BE**
email: info@thepunteroxford.co.uk
dir: *Phone for detailed directions*

Quirky Thames-side treasure

If feeling famished on your tour of Oxford, then seek out this rustically-cool pub on Osney Island in the heart of the city – it enjoys a magnificent and very tranquil spot beside the river. The decor is eclectic and interesting, with much to catch the eye, from rugs on flagstone floors and mismatched tables and chairs to bold artwork on whitewashed walls. Come for a relaxing pint of Punter Ale by the river or refuel on something tempting from the daily menu – pheasant and bacon rillettes with plum chutney and toast; artichoke, walnut and goats' cheese tart with green beans; slow-cooked lamb shank with butter bean stew and gremolata; or smoked haddock, pea and lemon salt risotto, poached egg and parmesan.

Open all day all wk **Food** Lunch Mon-Fri 12-3, wknds all day Dinner Mon-Fri 6-10, wknds all day Av main course £11 ⊕ GREENE KING ◀ The Punter Ale

♂ Addlestones. ♟ 12 **Facilities** Non-diners area ♣ (Bar Restaurant Garden) ♦ Children's portions Garden ♬ WiFi

The Rickety Press

tel: 01865 424581 **67 Cranham St OX2 6DE**
email: info@thericketypress.com
dir: *Phone for detailed directions*

In the heart of historic Jericho

The Rickety Press is run by the same three old school friends as The Rusty Bicycle in east Oxford. Deceptively spacious, there's a large conservatory restaurant, a snug and a bar serving Arkell's real ales, handpicked wines, coffees and teas, while the spicy aroma of mulled wine fills the winter air. Big hits on winter-into-spring menus include smoked duck liver parfait; venison 'scotched' egg; pork shoulder with apple ketchup and smoked mash; and 'the well-aged beefburger'. One particularly tempting bar snack is quails' eggs with smokey salt and truffle chips. Be sure to leave space for the spiced roast plums, oat crumble and custard.

Open all day all wk **Food** Lunch Mon-Sat 12-2.30, Sun 12-3 Dinner Sun-Thu 6-9.30, Fri-Sat 6-10 ⊕ ARKELL'S ◀ 3B, Moonlight, Kingsdown. ♟ **Facilities** Non-diners area ♣ (Bar) ♦ Children's menu Children's portions WiFi

The Rusty Bicycle

tel: 01865 435298 **28 Magdalen Rd OX4 1RB**
email: info@therustybicycle.com
dir: *From Oxford ring road (A4142) take A4158 (Iffley Rd) towards city centre. Right into Magdalen Rd*

Great community local with fine pies

You can't miss the hanging sign for this quirky suburban pub – look for a 1950s grocer's bike swinging high above Magdalen Road's pavement. Inside the design is decidedly eccentric and Edwardian. This is a community pub in a very cosmopolitan part of the city, with the ambition of catering for all-comers. The plan appears to work well, with grand beers from owners Arkell's Brewery and carefully chosen guests coupled with a menu that is both traditional and eclectic. Look for burgers (including cod, pulled pork and black bean and mushroom varieties); sour dough pizzas (meat-eaters, vegetarian and vegans catered for), snacks and salads. Bareboard floors, amusing signage, real fires and eclectic furnishing, this is one to discover and savour at length.

Open all day all wk Closed 25-26 Dec **Food** Lunch all wk 12-2.30 Dinner all wk 6-9 Av main course £10 ⊕ ARKELL'S ◀ 3B, Moonlight & Wiltshire Gold ♂ Westons Old Rosie. ♟ 8 **Facilities** Non-diners area ♣ (Bar Restaurant Garden) ♦ Children's menu Children's portions Garden ♬ WiFi ➡

Turf Tavern

tel: 01865 243235 **4 Bath Place, off Holywell St OX1 3SU**
email: 8004@greeneking.co.uk
dir: *Phone for detailed directions*

The hidden haunt of dons and students over many centuries

A jewel of a pub, and consequently one of Oxford's most popular, although it's not easy to find, as it is approached through hidden alleyways, which, if anything, adds to its allure. Previously called the Spotted Cow, it became the Turf in 1842, probably in deference to its gambling clientele; it has also had brushes with literature, film and politics. The Turf Tavern is certainly one of the city's oldest pubs, with some 13th-century foundations and a 17th-century low-beamed front bar. Three beer gardens help ease overcrowding, but the 11 real ales and reasonably priced pub grub keep the students, locals and visitors flowing in.

Open all day all wk 11-11 (Sun 12-10.30) Closed 25 Dec **Food** Lunch Mon-Sat 11-9, Sun 12-9 Dinner Mon-Sat 11-9, Sun 12-9 ⊕ GREENE KING ◀ Guest ales ♂ Westons Old Rosie, Lilley's Apples & Pears, Guest ciders. **Facilities** ♣ (Bar Garden) ♦ Garden ♬ WiFi ➡

PICK OF THE PUBS

The Crown Inn

PISHILL Map 5 SU78

tel: 01491 638364 **RG9 6HH**
email:
enquiries@thecrowninnpishill.co.uk
web: www.thecrowninnpishill.co.uk
dir: A4130 from Henley-on-Thames,
right onto B480 to Pishill

Coaching inn with thatched barn

A pretty 15th-century brick and flint former coaching inn, The Crown has had a colourful history. The building began life in medieval times, serving ale to the thriving monastic community, then providing refuge to Catholic priests escaping Henry VIII's tyrannical rule. It contains possibly the country's largest priest hole, in which one Father Dominique met his end, and whose ghost is occasionally seen around the premises. Before going any further, how should Pishill be pronounced? Old maps show a second 's' in the name, supporting the theory that farm-waggon drivers used to stop at the inn having made the long climb out of Henley-on-Thames, and while the men topped themselves up in the bar, the horses would relieve themselves. Fast-forward to the Swinging 60s, and the neighbouring thatched barn housed a nightclub hosting George Harrison, Dusty Springfield and other big names from the world of pop. Nowadays, the barn is licensed for civil ceremonies, as well as serving as a function room. In

the pub itself, the bar is supplied by mostly local breweries, typically Brakspear, Loddon, Rebellion and West Berkshire. The menu always includes sandwiches and ploughman's at lunchtimes, and features fresh local produce cooked to order. Lunch and dinner are served every day and may be enjoyed inside, where there are three log fires, or in the picturesque garden overlooking the valley. Depending on the season, you might find smoked ham hock stovie, poached hen's egg and beurre blanc; aged Oxfordshire rib-eye steak, Café de Paris butter, string fries and spring leaves; and slow-braised Oxfordshire pork belly, chickpea and chorizo stew with salsa verde. In late September, there's a beer festival.

Open all wk 12-3 6-11 (Sun 12-3 7-10) Closed 25-26 Dec **Food** Lunch all wk 12-2.30 Dinner Mon-Thu 6.30-9, Fri-Sat 6.30-9.30, Sun 7-9 Av main course £13-£14 ⊞ FREE HOUSE ◀ Brakspear, West Berkshire, Loddon, Rebellion, Vale, Otter. **Facilities** Non-diners area 🐾 (Bar Garden) 🚼 Children's portions Garden 🏖 Beer festival Parking WiFi 🚌 (notice required)

PISHILL
Map 5 SU78

The Crown Inn
PICK OF THE PUBS

See Pick of the Pubs on page 405

RAMSDEN
Map 11 SP31

The Royal Oak
PICK OF THE PUBS

See Pick of the Pubs on opposite page

ROTHERFIELD GREYS
Map 5 SU78

NEW The Maltsters Arms

tel: 01491 628400 **RG9 4QD**
email: peter@maltsters.co.uk
dir: *From A4156 in Henley-On-Thames at lights into Greys Rd. Approx 3m to pub on left*

Friendly pub with classic pub grub

Just three miles outside Henley, there's a popular walk up through the Happy Valley to the pub. The atmosphere is friendly and welcoming, and there are two separate seating areas inside, one with original beams and the other decorated with the landlord's collection of cricketing memorabilia. Great British pub classics are what you'll find on the menu, including the famous steamed steak and kidney pudding (only cooked on Tuesdays, October-March, so if you want to try it, make sure you go on the right day). Otherwise you'll find dishes like home-made fish fingers; stuffed pheasant; or roast shoulder of lamb.

Open all wk 12-3 6-11 (Sat-Sun all day) **Food** Lunch 12-2.30 Dinner 6.15-9.15 Restaurant menu available Mon-Sat ⊕ BRAKSPEAR ◀ Bitter & Oxford Gold ⚬ Westons Stowford Press. ☂ 10 **Facilities** Non-diners area ⚬ (Bar Garden) ⦁ Children's menu Children's portions Play area Garden ⊓ Parking WiFi ⚏ (notice required)

SHILTON
Map 5 SP20

Rose & Crown

tel: 01993 842280 **OX18 4AB**
dir: *From A40 at Burford take A361 towards Lechlade on Thames. Right, follow Shilton signs on left. Or from A40 E of Burford take B4020 towards Carterton*

Well-supported village local and destination food pub

A traditional Cotswold-stone inn dating back to the 17th century, whose two rooms retain their original beams and are warmed by a wood-burner and an open log fire. In the bar, Hook Norton Old Hooky might well partner Young's Bitter and Ashton Press cider. As their pedigrees might lead you to expect, chef-landlord Martin Coldicott, who trained at London's Connaught Hotel, and head chef Jamie Webber, from The Ivy, prepare above average, but simply presented food, typically game terrine and red onion marmalade; lamb shoulder with greens, carrots and mash; steak and mushroom pie; and bread and butter pudding. You may eat and drink in the garden if the weather's nice.

Open all wk 11.30-3 6-11 (Sat-Sun & BH 11.30-11) **Food** Lunch Mon-Fri 12-2, Sat-Sun & BH 12-2.45 Dinner all wk 7-9 ⊕ FREE HOUSE ◀ Butcombe, Hook Norton Old Hooky, Loose Cannon, Wye Valley, Young's Bitter ⚬ Ashton Press, Westons Wyld Wood Organic. ☂ 10 **Facilities** Non-diners area ⚬ (Bar Garden) ⦁ Garden ⊓ Parking WiFi

SHIPLAKE
Map 5 SU77

The Plowden Arms

tel: 0118 940 2794 **Reading Rd RG9 4BX**
email: info@doffandbow.co.uk
dir: *On A4155, 4m from Reading (2m from Henley-on-Thames)*

Family-welcoming hostelry offering refreshments from a bygone era

Between Henley-on-Thames and Reading, The Plowden Arms takes its name from the family who occupied Shiplake Court (now Shiplake College) in the 17th century. Period features, original beams and a working fireplace are the setting for Brakspear beers, draught ciders, and a menu that takes its inspiration from forgotten dishes of bygone times. The recipe for Alexis Soyer's Lamb 'Reform', for example, dates from 1839; and the pudding of Barley cream (on the menu with blackcurrant compôte) was first created in 1859 by Robert Kemp Philp. Other dishes that might tempt are devilled kidneys on toast; and whole roast poussin, onion cake, baby vegetables and Madeira gravy.

Open 11-2.30 5-11 (Sun 12-4 7-10.30) Closed Mon **Food** Lunch Tue-Sat 12-2, Sun 12-3.30 Dinner Tue-Sat 6-10, Sun 7-9 ⊕ BRAKSPEAR ◀ Bitter, Ringwood Boondoggle ⚬ Addlestones, Thatchers Heritage. ☂ 13 **Facilities** Non-diners area ⚬ (Bar Garden) ⦁ Children's menu Children's portions Garden ⊓ Parking

SHIPTON-UNDER-WYCHWOOD
Map 10 SP21

The Shaven Crown Hotel

tel: 01993 830500 **High St OX7 6BA**
email: relax@theshavencrown.co.uk
dir: *On A361, halfway between Burford & Chipping Norton*

Historic inn overlooking the picturesque village green and church

This 14th-century coaching inn was built by the monks of Bruern Abbey as a hospice for the poor. Following the Dissolution of the Monasteries, Elizabeth I used it as a hunting lodge before giving it to the village in 1580, when it became the Crown Inn. Thus it stayed until 1930, when a brewery with a sense of humour changed the name as homage to the familiar monastic tonsure. Its interior is full of original architectural features, like the Great Hall. Light meals and real ales are served in the bar, while the restaurant offers modern English dishes.

Open all wk 11-11 (Sun 11-4) **Food** Lunch all wk 12-2.30 Dinner Mon-Sat 6-9.30 Restaurant menu available all wk ⊕ FREE HOUSE ◀ Hook Norton ⚬ Westons Stowford Press. ☂ 10 **Facilities** Non-diners area ⚬ (Bar Garden) ⦁ Children's menu Children's portions Garden ⊓ Parking WiFi ⚏ (notice required)

STANFORD IN THE VALE
Map 5 SU39

NEW The Horse & Jockey

tel: 01367 710302 **25 Faringdon Rd SN7 8NN**
email: info@horseandjockey.org
dir: *On A417 between Faringdon & Wantage*

Stylish village inn with home comforts

A wealth of exposed stone, leather-clad armchairs, and dark wood dining furniture characterise the interior of this stylish 16th-century inn. Children and dogs are made as welcome as their parents, and with a range of pizzas on the menu they are unlikely to leave hungry (the children, that is). Other hearty pub fare options are steaks, Morlands beer battered fish and chips, and sticky BBQ pork ribs served with hand-cut Cajun wedges. A take-away service operates for those in a rush, but if it's just a quiet pint you are looking for, head to the beer garden to sup a Hook Norton Hooky or Belhaven Black.

Open all wk 11-3 5-12 (Fri-Sat 11am-12.30am Sun 12-11) **Food** Lunch 12-2.30 Dinner 6-9 Av main course £9.95 ⊕ GREENE KING ◀ Greene King ales, Hook Norton Hooky Bitter, Belhaven Black. ☂ 8 **Facilities** Non-diners area ⚬ (Bar Garden) ⦁ Children's portions Play area Garden ⊓ Parking WiFi

PICK OF THE PUBS

The Royal Oak

RAMSDEN Map 11 SP31

tel: 01993 868213 **High St OX7 3AU**
email: jonoldham57@gmail.com
web: www.royaloakramsden.com
dir: *B4022 from Witney towards Charlbury, right before Hailey, through Poffley End*

Award-winning pub near many lovely walks

Built of Cotswold stone and facing Ramsden's fine parish church, this former 17th-century coaching inn is a popular refuelling stop for walkers exploring nearby Wychwood Forest and visitors touring the pretty villages and visiting Blenheim Palace. Whether you are walking or not, the cosy inn oozes traditional charm and character, with its old beams, warm fires and stone walls, and long-serving landlords John and Jo Oldham provide a very warm welcome. A free house, it dispenses beers sourced from local breweries, such as Hook Norton Hooky Bitter and Old Hooky, alongside Adnams Broadside and Young's Special. Somerset's Original Cider Company supplies the bar with Pheasant Plucker cider, alongside Westons Old Rosie from Herefordshire. With a strong kitchen team, the main menu, built on the very best of fresh local and seasonal ingredients, regularly features a pie of the week topped with puff pastry, or the popluar steak and kidney suet pudding; there

are popular choices such as starters of oven-baked baby brie; devilled lamb's kidneys with Dijon mustard sauce; or chargrilled aubergine, sun-dried feta cheese and piquant tomato sauce. Typical mains are confit of duck, Puy lentils, garlic potatoes, red berry and quince sauce; seafood pot au feu; Gymkhana Club curry, a traditional Sri Lankan dish, served with rice and pickles; and a choice of Aberdeen Angus steaks and burgers. Carefully selected by the owner, the wine list has over 200 wines, specialising in those from Bordeaux and Languedoc, with 30 of them served by the glass. Every Thursday evening there is a special offer of steak, with a glass of wine and dessert included.

Open all wk 11.30-3 6.30-11 (Sun 11.30-3 7-10.30) Closed 25 Dec
Food Lunch all wk 12-2 Dinner Mon-Sat 7-9.45, Sun 7-9 ⊕ FREE HOUSE ◀ Hook Norton Old Hooky & Hooky Bitter, Adnams Broadside, Young's Special, Wye Valley ♂ Westons Old Rosie, Pheasant Plucker. ⬤ 30
Facilities Non-diners area ❤ (Bar Garden) Children's portions Garden Parking

STEEPLE ASTON

Map 11 SP42

The Red Lion

tel: 01869 340225 **South Side OX25 4RY**
email: redlionsa@aol.com
dir: *0.5m off A4260 (Oxford Rd). Follow brown tourist signs for pub*

Unspoilt 18th-century pub popular with walkers

In an elevated position in the village, this Hook Norton brewery pub offers a number of options: in front of the fire in the bar; in the comfortably furnished, oak-beamed Garden Room; or head for the pretty suntrap terrace, not least for its view of the delightful Cherwell Valley. In addition to generous Sunday roasts, other locally sourced dishes include salads; thin-crust, stone-baked pizzas; Aberdeen Angus burgers; risottos; roast rump of lamb with redcurrant and rosemary; and fresh haddock with or without batter, triple-cooked chips and mushy peas. Children and dogs are welcome.

Open all wk 12-3 5.30-11 (Sat 12-11 Sun 12-5) Closed Sun eve from 5pm **Food** Lunch all wk 12-2.30 Dinner Mon-Sat 6-9 ⊕ HOOK NORTON ◙ Hooky Bitter, Lion & Seasonal ales Ō Westons Stowford Press. ♦ 11 **Facilities** Non-diners area ❤ (Bar Outside area) ♦❙ Children's portions Outside area ⊟ Parking WiFi ▭ (notice required)

STOKE ROW

Map 5 SU68

Crooked Billet

PICK OF THE PUBS

tel: 01491 681048 **RG9 5PU**
dir: *From Henley towards Oxford on A4130. Left at Nettlebed for Stoke Row*

17th-century pub with plenty of character and an excellent menu

Built in 1642, the Crooked Billet was once the hideout of notorious highwayman Dick Turpin. Tucked away down a single track lane in deepest Oxfordshire, this charmingly rustic pub is now a popular hideaway for the well-heeled and the well known. Many of its finest features are unchanged, including the low beams, tiled floors and open fires that are so integral to its character. Local produce and organic fare are the mainstays of the kitchen; the chef-proprietor will even exchange a lunch or dinner for locals' excess vegetables. A set lunch starter and main course could kick off with pumpkin Oxford Blue risotto cakes with chestnuts and trompette mushrooms, and continue with pheasant casserole, mustard dumplings and green herb dressing. Finish with a pud such as plum Bakewell and custard ice cream.

Open all wk 12-3 7-12 (Sat-Sun 12-12) **Food** Lunch Mon-Fri 12-2.30, Sat 12-10.30, Sun 12-10 Dinner Mon-Fri 7-10, Sat 12-10.30, Sun 12-10 Set menu available ⊕ BRAKSPEAR ◙ Organic Best Bitter. ♦ 10 **Facilities** Non-diners area ♦❙ Children's portions Garden ⊟ Parking

STONESFIELD

Map 11 SP31

NEW The White Horse

tel: 01993 891063 **The Ridings OX29 8EA**
email: jalloyd@btinternet.com
dir: *From Oxford take A44 towards Chipping Norton. After Woodstock left signed Charlbury. Through Stonesfield to T-junct, pub opposite*

Contemporary country inn serving great pub classics

Originally built as two mine-workers' cottages, this Cotswold stone free house dates back to the 19th century and is situated in the village of Stonesfield, handy for exploring Woodstock, Blenheim Palace, and Oxford. The atmosphere is welcoming at this family and dog-friendly contemporary country pub, with its wood-burning stove and cosy seating. The menus are strong on pub classics like home-made beefburgers; slow-roast pork belly; or sirloin steak. A double chocolate brownie with ice cream for pudding seals the deal.

Open 5-11 (Sat 12-3 6-11 Sun 12-3) Closed Lunch Tue-Fri, Sun eve & Mon **Food** Lunch Sat-Sun 12-2 Dinner Fri-Sat 6-9 Av main course £11.95 Restaurant menu available Fri-Sun ⊕ FREE HOUSE ◙ Ringwood Best Bitter Ō Westons Stowford Press. **Facilities** Non-diners area ❤ (Bar Garden Outside area) ♦❙ Children's portions Garden Outside area ⊟ Parking WiFi

STONOR

Map 5 SU78

The Quince Tree

tel: 01491 639039 **RG9 6HE**
email: home@thequincetree.com
dir: *From Henley-on-Thames take A4130 towards Wallingford. Right on B480 to Stonor*

Pub, café, shop and more in a pretty Chilterns village

With Henley-on-Thames nearby and Stonor Park's scenic grounds on the doorstep, The Quince Tree is well placed for walkers, cyclists and wildlife lovers. Lots on offer too, within this sensitively restored 17th-century coaching inn – a welcoming mix of pub, café, shop, bakery, pâtisserie and deli. The menus range from bruschettas for starters to main courses like poached sea bream with morels, linguine and broad beans. The bakery works through the night to supply unbeatably fresh breads and pastries. As for liquid refreshments, Marston's and guest ales on tap are accompanied by a terrific range of bottled craft ales and ciders.

Open 12-3 5-11 (Sun 12-4.30 Mon 12-3.30) Closed Sun eve, Mon eve **Food** Lunch Mon-Fri 12-2.30, Sat-Sun 12-3 Dinner Tue-Sat 6.30-9.30 ⊕ FREE HOUSE ◙ Marston's EPA, Guest ales Ō Cotswold. ♦ **Facilities** Non-diners area ❤ (Bar Garden) ♦❙ Children's menu Children's portions Garden ⊟ Parking WiFi ▭ (notice required)

SWERFORD

Map 11 SP33

The Mason's Arms

tel: 01608 683212 **Banbury Rd OX7 4AP**
email: admin@masons-arms.com
dir: *Between Banbury & Chipping Norton on A361*

Large beer garden ideal for families

Here at The Mason's Arms, Jamie Bailey and Louise Robertson continue their successful track record of running pubs. This one is a 300-year-old, stone-built former Masonic lodge, situated in the Cotswolds; it retains its traditional, informal feel and the large garden has stunning views of the surrounding area. Jamie's modern European cooking concentrates on local produce whenever possible and there is an emphasis on fish on the specials board, which might offer pan-fried tiger prawns with chilli and chorizo followed by pan-fried red mullet on crab meat and samphire linguine. Non-fish options include coq au vin and venison Wellington.

Open all wk 10-3 6-11 (Sun 12-dusk) **Food** Lunch Mon-Sat 12-2.30, Sun 12-dusk Dinner Mon-Sat 7-9, Sun 12-dusk Set menu available ⊕ FREE HOUSE ◙ Wychwood Hobgoblin, Brakspear Ō Thatchers Gold. ♦ 15 **Facilities** Non-diners area ❤ (Bar Garden) ♦❙ Children's menu Children's portions Garden ⊟ Parking WiFi ▭ (notice required)

SWINBROOK
Map 5 SP21

The Swan Inn ★★★★ INN ◎◎
PICK OF THE PUBS

tel: 01993 823339 **OX18 4DY**
email: info@theswanswinbrook.co.uk **web:** www.theswanswinbrook.co.uk
dir: *A40 towards Cheltenham, left to Swinbrook*

Tranquillity and class at Cotswold boutique inn

Hidden in the Windrush Valley you will find the idyllic village of Swinbrook where time stands still. Owners Archie and Nicola Orr-Ewing took on the lease of this dreamy, wisteria-clad stone pub from the late Dowager Duchess of Devonshire. The Swan is the perfect English country pub – it stands by the River Windrush near the village cricket pitch, overlooking unspoilt Cotswold countryside. It gets even better inside: the two cottage-style front rooms, replete with worn flagstones, crackling log fires, low beams and country furnishings, lead through to a cracking bar and classy conservatory extension. First-class pub food ranges from simple bar snacks to more substantial main courses of guinea fowl, apricot and chickpea tagine; and Cornish hake with a casserole of butter beans, tomato and chorizo. You won't want to leave, so book one of the stunning en suite rooms in the restored barn.

Open all wk 11.30-11 (Closed afternoons Nov-Feb) Closed 25 Dec **Food** Lunch Mon-Fri 12-2, Sat 12-2.30, Sun 12-3 Dinner Mon-Thu & Sun 7-9, Fri-Sat 7-9.30 ⊕ FREE HOUSE ◀ Hook Norton, Guest ales ♂ Aspall, Westons Wyld Wood Organic & Stowford Press. ₹ 9 **Facilities** Non-diners area ✿ (Bar Restaurant Garden) ♦♦ Children's menu Children's portions Garden ♠ Parking WiFi **Rooms** 6

TETSWORTH
Map 5 SP60

The Old Red Lion

tel: 01844 281274 **40 High St OX9 7AS**
email: info@theoldredliontetsworth.co.uk
dir: *From Oxford ring road at Headington take A40. Follow A418 signs (over M40). Right onto A40 signed Milton Common & Tetsworth*

Village pub ideal for early birds

An airy, contemporary pub with traditional flourishes, ideal for trippers heading for the nearby Chilterns. Birdwatchers pursuing red kites can stop by before or after hitting the hills, whilst cricketers inspecting the wicket on the adjacent village green pitch can call from mid-morning onwards. Not content with two restaurant areas and a bustling bar to run, the owners also host a village shop here. Beers from local microbreweries hit the spot, whilst timeless pub grub meals like sausage and mash fill the gap. Summer barbecues are popular, and there's a mini beer festival every Easter.

Open all day all wk **Food** Lunch Mon-Thu & Sat 10-10, Fri 11am-mdnt, Sun 12-3.30 (open for breakfast 7am-11.30am) Dinner Mon-Thu & Sat 10-10, Fri 11am-mdnt ⊕ FREE HOUSE ◀ Loose Cannon Brewery, White Horse, XT 4 ♂ Somersby Cider. **Facilities** Non-diners area ✿ (Bar Outside area) ♦♦ Children's menu Children's portions Garden Outside area ♠ Beer festival Parking WiFi ▦

THAME
Map 5 SP70

The James Figg

tel: 01844 260166 **21 Cornmarket OX9 2BL**
email: thejamesfigg@peachpubs.com
dir: *In town centre*

Buzzing town centre free house with a beer garden

James Figg, born in Thame in 1684, was the bare-knuckle boxer who Jack Dempsey called the 'father of modern boxing'. The pub's traditional interior of dark wood floors and a double-sided open fire also houses a curving bar stocking ales such as Purity Mad Goose. Snacks include home-made pork scratchings, pork pies, sandwiches and granary baps. Further 'simple and tasty' possibilities are burger and chips; a range of pizzas; pie of the day with mash and peas; breaded wholetail scampi and chips; and honey- and mustard-glazed ham, egg and chips. Beyond The Stables function room you'll find a private garden.

Open all day all wk 11am-mdnt Closed 25 Dec **Food** Lunch Mon-Sat 12-8.30, Sun 12-6 Dinner Mon-Sat 12-8.30 Av main course £10.50 ⊕ FREE HOUSE ◀ Purity Mad Goose, Sharp's Doom Bar ♂ Aspall Draught & Harry Sparrow. ₹ **Facilities** Non-diners area ✿ (Bar Garden) ♦♦ Children's portions Garden ♠ Parking WiFi ▦ (notice required)

The Thatch

tel: 01844 214340 **29-30 Lower High St OX9 2AA**
email: thatch@peachpubs.com
dir: *From rdbt on A418 into Oxford Rd signed town centre. Follow into Thame High St. Pub on right*

Half-timbered pub with a sunny courtyard garden

Originally a row of cottages in the heart of Thame's high street, this thatched pub remains a cosy warren of rooms with inglenook fireplaces and antique furniture. If you make it past the bar without being tempted by coffee, cakes or a pint of Doom Bar, you'll find yourself in the restaurant overlooking the garden. The kitchen focuses on the best seasonal ingredients – a starter of Brixham crab Benedict might be followed by free-range chicken breast with spring cabbage, chorizo and sweet potato croquette. There is a beer festival during National Cask Ale Week.

Open all day all wk Closed 25 Dec **Food** Lunch all wk 12-10 Dinner all wk 12-10 ⊕ PEACH PUBS ◀ Vale Wychert & Best Bitter, Sharp's Doom Bar ♂ Aspall. ₹ 16 **Facilities** Non-diners area ✿ (Bar Garden) ♦♦ Children's portions Garden ♠ Beer festival Parking WiFi ▦ (notice required)

TOOT BALDON
Map 5 SP50

The Mole Inn ◎
PICK OF THE PUBS

tel: 01865 340001 **OX44 9NG**
email: info@themoleinn.com
dir: *5m SE from Oxford city centre off B480*

A foodie destination with great service

The Mole Inn is a lovely 300-year-old, Grade II listed building that has put the village of Toot Baldon on the foodie map with the culinary output of chef and host Gary Witchalls. His dedication in the kitchen is matched by the front-of-house professionalism of his wife, Jenny. Drinks are also a strength: try a pint of Hook Norton, Shepherd Neame Spitfire or The Mole's Pleasure – developed together with Moodley's microbrewery, which is particularly suited to the pub's dry-aged steaks from Aberdeenshire. Pick from rib-eye, rump, sirloin or fillet steaks and then choose your sauce. Other options could include hot roasted mixed beets, whipped goats' cheese and horseradish, hazelnuts, cumin caramelised shallots and orange; cannon of hogget, spiced lamb breast, minted pea purée, pea cress and parmesan crumbed potatoes; and treacle tart with Carnation milk ice cream. Leather sofas, stripped beams, solid white walls and terracotta floors provide the perfect background for a leisurely meal.

Open all day all wk 12-12 (Sun 12-11) Closed 25 Dec **Food** Lunch all wk 12-2.30 Dinner all wk 7-9.30 Set menu available Restaurant menu available all wk ⊕ FREE HOUSE ◀ The Mole's Pleasure, Fuller's London Pride, Shepherd Neame Spitfire, Hook Norton, Guinness ♂ Westons Stowford Press. ₹ 11 **Facilities** Non-diners area ♦♦ Children's menu Children's portions Garden ♠ Parking WiFi

UFFINGTON
Map 5 SU38

The Fox & Hounds ★★★★ INN

tel: 01367 820680 **High St SN7 7RP**
email: enquiries@uffingtonpub.co.uk **web:** www.uffingtonpub.co.uk
dir: *From A420 (S of Faringdon) follow Fernham or Uffington signs*

Traditional food and good beer in timeless village inn

Amidst the thatched cottages and 13th-century church in the charming village of Uffington, The Fox & Hounds boasts unrivalled views of The Ridgeway and the Uffington White Horse. Writer John Betjeman once lived across the road from the pub and Tolkein was a frequent visitor – legend has it that St George slew the dragon at nearby Dragon Hill. A traditional free house with a range of well-kept real ales, the home-cooked food is simple and takes in such pub favourites as pie of the day; wholetail scampi with chips; and home-made burgers. Contact the pub for details of its beer festivals.

Open all day all wk 11-11 (Sun 12-10.30) **Food** Lunch Mon-Fri 12-2, Sat-Sun & BHs 12-3 (ex 25 Dec) Dinner Mon-Sat 6-9 ⊕ FREE HOUSE ◀ Local ales ♂ Thatchers. **Facilities** Non-diners area ✿ (Bar Restaurant Garden) ♦♦ Children's menu Children's portions Garden ⌐ Beer festival Parking WiFi ☎ (notice required) **Rooms** 2

WEST HANNEY
Map 5 SU49

Plough Inn

tel: 01235 868674 **Church St OX12 0LN**
email: ploughpub@hotmail.co.uk
dir: *From Wantage take A338 towards Oxford. Inn in 1m*

Friendly village free house

Thatched with four 'eyebrows', the Plough dates from around 1525, when it was a row of cottages. Steve Potts took over in 2015 and enjoys responsibility for such things as ensuring there are logs for the fires, choosing the six rolling real ales, and organising the Easter, Spring and Summer Bank Holiday beer festivals. From the kitchen come home-cooked, seasonal dishes such as pan-seared devilled lamb's kidneys, coriander, smoked bacon and spring onions; and slow-cooked pork belly with creamy mash, red onions and glazed apples. For a treat, dine in the pretty walled garden.

Open all wk 12-3 5-12 (Sat-Sun all day) **Food** Lunch all wk 12-3 Dinner all wk 6-9 Av main course £12 ⊕ FREE HOUSE ◀ Adnams, Bass, Marston's, Timothy Taylor, Sharp's Doom Bar, Fuller's London Pride, Local guest ales ♂ Westons, Thatchers Gold. ♥ 10 **Facilities** Non-diners area ✿ (Bar Garden) ♦♦ Children's portions Garden ⌐ Beer festival Parking WiFi ☎ (notice required)

WITNEY
Map 5 SP31

The Fleece

tel: 01993 892270 **11 Church Green OX28 4AZ**
email: fleece@peachpubs.com
dir: *In town centre*

Good surroundings and good craic

Overlooking, as the address suggests, the green in front of St Mary's church, this fine Georgian pub was where, in the late 1940s, Dylan Thomas enjoyed a drink when he was living nearby. Then, it was also Clinch's brewery; today it's a Greene King house, with guest ales. The packed menu takes a while to study, so here are some advance suggestions: share a cold cuts or fish deli board, or single-handedly tackle smoked haddock kedgeree; pan-fried sea trout with polenta and sun-dried tomato cake; or free-range pork tomahawk steak with sweet potato wedges. Another thought is a steak from Aubrey Allen, the Queen's butcher.

Open all day all wk Closed 25 Dec **Food** Lunch all wk 12-2.30 Dinner Mon-Sat 6-10, Sun 6-9 Av main course £14.50 Set menu available ⊕ GREENE KING ◀ IPA, Morland Old Speckled Hen, Guest ale ♂ Aspall Draught, Guest cider. ♥ **Facilities** Non-diners area ✿ (Bar Outside area) ♦♦ Children's portions Outside area ⌐ Parking WiFi ☎ (notice required)

NEW Old Swan & Minster Mill ★★★★★ INN @

tel: 01993 774441 **Minster Lovell OX29 0RN**
web: www.oldswanandminstermill.com
dir: *N'bound: M40 junct 8, A40 (S'bound M40 junct 9, A34) towards Oxford. From Oxford ringroad follow Cheltenham signs. 14m, follow Carterton & Minster Lovell signs. Through Minster Lovell, right at T-junct, 2nd left signed Old Swan & Minster Mill*

Romantic bolthole in the heart of the Cotswolds

Idyllically situated alongside the River Windrush in the thatched village of Old Minster, this 600-year-old inn used to be a favourite of Sir Winston Churchill, whose ancestral home is nearby Blenheim Palace. Over the past 30 years, the de Savary family has transformed the place into a luxurious destination, whether it's just for a quiet pint, a meal or overnight stay. In the high-ceilinged, beamed restaurant, pub classics are served alongside more innovative daily specials. A starter of River Windrush crayfish and Devon crab cocktail might be followed by pan-roasted Burford chicken and Madeira jus.

Open all wk 12.30-3 6.30-9 (Fri-Sat 12.30-3 6.30-9.30) **Food** Lunch all wk 12.30-3 Dinner all wk 6.30-9 Restaurant menu available all wk ⊕ FREE HOUSE ◀ Brakspear Bitter & Oxford Gold, Wychwood Hobgoblin ♂ Westons Stowford Press. **Facilities** Non-diners area ✿ (Bar Garden Outside area) ♦♦ Children's menu Children's portions Play area Garden Outside area ⌐ Parking WiFi **Rooms** 60

WOODSTOCK
Map 11 SP41

The Kings Arms
PICK OF THE PUBS

tel: 01993 813636 **19 Market St OX20 1SU**
email: stay@kingshotelwoodstock.co.uk
dir: *In town centre, on corner of Market St & A44*

Smart hotel with bags of style

In the middle of the charming, historic town of Woodstock, this imposing Georgian free house and hotel is less than five minutes' walk from Blenheim Palace. It also makes a good base from which to explore Oxfordshire and the Cotswolds. The comfortable bar areas with stripped wooden floors, a log-burning stove and marble-topped counters, is where regulars Brakspear Bitter, North Cotswold Brewery Cotswold Best and Loose Cannon Gunners Gold are on offer. The all-day bar menu lists sandwiches, sharing boards and cream teas. For rather more stylish surroundings, go to the Atrium Restaurant with its black-and-white tiled flooring and high-backed leather chairs. Here, you might begin with poached Cotswold duck egg with Daylesford Cheddar rarebit, followed perhaps by Cornish lamb rump with apricot glaze, baby leeks and minted cracked wheat.

Open all day all wk ⊕ FREE HOUSE ◀ Brakspear Bitter, Loose Cannon Gunners Gold, North Cotswold Brewery Cotswold Best ♂ Thatchers Green Goblin. **Facilities** ♦♦ Children's portions Outside area WiFi

WOOLSTONE
Map 5 SU28

The White Horse

tel: 01367 820726 **SN7 7QL**
email: info@whitehorsewoolstone.co.uk
dir: Exit A420 at Watchfield onto B4508 towards Longcot signed Woolstone

Old-world thatched Elizabethan pub

Following an invigorating Ridgeway walk across White Horse Hill, this black-and-white timbered village pub is the perfect rest and refuelling stop. Upholstered stools line the traditional bar, where a fireplace conceals two priest holes, visible to those who don't mind getting their knees dirty. Accompany a pint of Arkell's ale with a trio of hand-made sausages and buttered mash; or lamb three ways – roast rump, crispy belly and slow-roast shoulder wrapped in pancetta with sweet potato and roast beetroot. Baileys crème brûlée proves an excellent finish. The pub has a garden, and children and dogs are welcome throughout.

Open all day all wk 11-11 **Food** Lunch all wk 12-2.30 Dinner Mon-Sat 6-9 Set menu available Restaurant menu available all wk ⊕ ARKELL'S ◀ Moonlight & Wiltshire Gold, Arkell's 3B, Guinness Ò Westons Stowford Press. **Facilities** Non-diners area ✿ (Bar Restaurant Garden) ✦ Children's portions Garden ⌖ Parking WiFi ▦ (notice required)

WYTHAM
Map 5 SP40

White Hart

tel: 01865 244372 **OX2 8QA**
email: whitehartwytham@wadworth.co.uk
dir: From A34 (NE of Oxford) follow Wytham signs

Smart, sleepy-village pub

Following restoration, this Cotswold-stone pub reopened under new management in January 2015. Although 17th century, its contemporary interior sits well with the big old fireplace and all those 400-year-old stone flags. The management's marketing stance is that it's as happy to serve a pint of real ale as it is a sit-down meal, from a Small Plate, inspired by the bars and cafés of France, Italy and Spain, to main menu dishes such as spiced cod fishcakes; chargrilled rib-eye and sirloin steaks; Moroccan lamb tagine; or roasted hazelnut, aubergine and mushroom parcels. In summer, dine on the Mediterranean-style terrace.

Open all wk 12-3 6-11 (Sat-Sun 12-11, all day everyday Apr-Oct) **Food** Lunch Mon-Sat 12-3, Sun 12-4.30 Dinner Mon-Sat 6-9 Restaurant menu available Tue-Sun ⊕ WADWORTH ◀ Henry's Original IPA & 6X, Guest ales Ò Westons Stowford Press. ♟ 15 **Facilities** Non-diners area ✿ (Bar Garden) ✦ Children's menu Children's portions Garden ⌖ Beer festival Cider festival Parking WiFi ▦ (notice required)

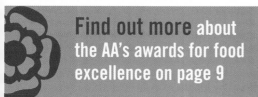

Find out more about the AA's awards for food excellence on page 9

RUTLAND

BARROWDEN
Map 11 SK90

Exeter Arms
PICK OF THE PUBS

tel: 01572 747247 **LE15 8EQ**
email: enquiries@exeterarmsrutland.co.uk
dir: From A47 turn at landmark windmill, village 0.75m S. 6m E of Uppingham & 17m W of Peterborough

Heart of the village and heart of Rutland, too

Overlooking the village green, duck pond and open countryside, this 17th-century, stone-built free house is also a microbrewery, where landlord Martin Allsopp brews at least half a dozen real ales. Expect a traditional, informal feel to the spacious bar and enjoy perhaps one of the 10 wines by the glass and good pub food. More enjoyment at lunchtime, with sandwiches, slow-cooked lamb shank with kale colcannon, or smoked haddock with soft-poached egg and spring onion mash. Dinner could start with breaded whitebait with lemon and tartare sauce, and continue with roast sirloin of beef with Yorkshire pudding and roast potatoes; tandoori chicken with Bombay potatoes, red pepper and spinach; or filo parcel filled with gruyère, leeks, spinach and mushrooms. Out front is a shaded patio, while the large rear garden has sufficient room for a petanque piste.

Open 12-2.30 6-11 (Sat 12-3.30 6-11 Sun 12-8) Closed 1st 2wks Jan, Sun eve, Mon **Food** Lunch Tue-Sat 12-5, Sun 12-5 Restaurant menu available Tue-Sun ⊕ FREE HOUSE ◀ Exeter Arms Beech, Owngear, Hop Gear, Pilot, Blackadder. ♟ 10 **Facilities** Non-diners area ✿ (Bar Garden) ✦ Garden ⌖ Parking WiFi ▦ (notice required)

BRAUNSTON
Map 11 SK80

The Blue Ball

tel: 01572 722135 **6 Cedar St LE15 8QS**
email: blueballbraunston@gmail.com
dir: From Oakham N on B640. Left into Cold Overton Rd, 2nd left into West Rd, into Braunston Rd (becomes Oakham Rd). In village 2nd left into Cedar St. Pub on left opposite church

A warm welcome at a pretty thatched inn

The 17th-century thatched Blue Ball, only a few miles from Rutland Water, makes an excellent stopping-off point for cyclists and walkers. Landlord Dominic Way looks after his ales, as locals in the beamed and cosy bar will testify. Seasonal and local ingredients go into pub classics like steak and kidney pie and risottos plus modern dishes such as goats' cheese, roasted beetroot and caramelised onion tart; oven-baked sea bass with pan-fried chorizo; and a tempting dessert like sticky toffee pudding with vanilla ice cream. There is a Sunday roast menu and young diners are welcome to order small portions of most dishes, confirming the pub's family-friendly credentials. Vegetarian, gluten-free and special diets are catered for.

Open 12-2.30 6-11 (Fri 12-2.30-5.30-11 Sat 12-11 Sun 12-8) Closed 25 Dec, Mon (ex BHs) **Food** Lunch Tue-Fri 12-1.45, Sat 12-2, Sun 12-3 Dinner Tue-Sat 6.30-9 Av main course £10.95 Set menu available ⊕ MARSTON'S ◀ EPA & Burton Bitter, Jennings Cumberland Ale Ò Thatchers Gold. ♟ 10 **Facilities** Non-diners area ✦ Children's portions Outside area ⌖ WiFi ▦ (notice required)

CLIPSHAM
Map 11 SK91

The Olive Branch ★★★★ INN ⊛   PICK OF THE PUBS

tel: 01780 410355 **Main St LE15 7SH**
email: info@theolivebranchpub.com **web:** www.theolivebranchpub.com
dir: *2m from A1 at B664 junct, N of Stamford*

Award-winning hostelry on the fringe of the Wolds

Investigate the bar here for its range of bottled beers, ales from the Grainstore brewery in nearby Oakham, and Sheppy's cider. Note the unusual nurdling chair – used for an archaic pub game when coins are thrown into a hole in the seat. The chair is just one of a range of artefacts enriching the interior of this one-time terrace of farm workers' cottages. The pub's name originated when a local squire made a peace offering by opening the inn in 1890 after closing another in the village. Chef and co-owner Sean Hope has earned an AA Rosette for his well-balanced menus, that are fiercely local in provenance. Set lunch and dinner menus are backed by the carte which proffers the likes of pan-seared bream with griddled leeks, orange and rosemary; pork three ways with cider fondant and farmhouse cabbage; and Danish pastry and butter pudding with marmalade ice cream.

Open all wk 12-3.30 6-11 (Sat 12-11 Sun 12-10.30) Closed 25 Dec eve **Food** Lunch Mon-Sat 12-2, Sun 12-3 Dinner Mon-Sat 6.30-9.30, Sun 7-9 Av main course £16.50 Set menu available Restaurant menu available all wk ⊕ FREE HOUSE/RUTLAND INN COMPANY LTD ◄ The Grainstore Olive Oil, Timothy Taylor Landlord Ò Sheppy's Cider with Honey. ♀ 16 **Facilities** Non-diners area ✿ (Bar Garden) ♦ Children's menu Children's portions Garden ⋒ Parking WiFi **Rooms** 6

EMPINGHAM
Map 11 SK90

The White Horse Inn

tel: 01780 460221 **Main St LE15 8PS**
email: info@whitehorserutland.co.uk
dir: *From A1 take A606 signed Oakham & Rutland Water. From Oakham take A606 to Stamford*

Stone-built pub on the shores of Rutland Water

A 17th-century former courthouse with an interior that's very 21st century. The beamed bar, good selection of real ales and friendly staff makes it an ideal place to relax after a walk or cycle ride. The pub works closely with local suppliers to ensure high-quality seasonal ingredients for the menu of pub classics and more sophisticated choices, such as sausages and mash, and honey-roast duck breast with braised red cabbage.

Open all day all wk Closed 25 Dec **Food** Lunch Mon-Fri 12-2.30, Sat 12-9, Sun 12-5 Dinner Mon-Fri 6-9, Sat 12-9 ⊕ ENTERPRISE INNS ◄ Timothy Taylor Landlord, The Grainstore Rutland Bitter, Oakham Ales JHB, Castle Rock Harvest Pale Ò Symonds. ♀ 10 **Facilities** Non-diners area ✿ (Bar Garden) ♦ Children's menu Children's portions Garden ⋒ Parking WiFi ➟ (notice required)

GREETHAM
Map 11 SK91

The Wheatsheaf

tel: 01572 812325 **1 Stretton Rd LE15 7NP**
email: enquiries@wheatsheaf-greetham.co.uk
dir: *From A1 follow signs for Oakham onto B668 to Greetham, pub on left*

Homely refuge with an emphasis on locally sourced food

Set sideways to the road, this 18th-century, stone-built village pub is lovingly run by Carol and Scott Craddock. Carol notched up more than 20 years working in several renowned kitchens before coming here to put her wide experience to

excellent use. She changes her modern British menu weekly, and cooks using locally sourced meats and high quality sustainable fresh fish; she makes bread daily, too. A typical dinner might feature deep-fried rabbit fritters; or smoked salmon, baby spinach and sweetcorn pancake for starters, then pan-fried tiger prawns and squid; or macaroni cheese with wild mushrooms and leeks for the main course. Rutland-brewed real ales are served in the bar.

Open 12-3 6-close (Fri-Sun all day) Closed 1st 2wks Jan, Mon (ex BHs) **Food** Lunch Tue-Fri 12-2, Sat 12-2.30, Sun 12-3 Dinner Tue-Sat 6.30-9 Av main course £13.50 Set menu available ⊕ PUNCH TAVERNS ◄ Greene King IPA, Oldershaw Newton's Drop, Brewsters Decadence, Oakham Ales Inferno, Grainstore Triple B. ♀ 11 **Facilities** Non-diners area ✿ (Bar Garden) ♦ Children's menu Children's portions Garden ⋒ Parking WiFi

LYDDINGTON
Map 11 SP89

The Marquess of Exeter ★★★★ INN ⊛

tel: 01572 822477 **52 Main St LE15 9LT**
email: info@marquessexeter.co.uk **web:** www.marquessexeter.co.uk
dir: *A1(N) exit towards Leicester/A4. At rdbt onto A47 towards Leicester. At Uppingham rdbt onto A6003/Ayston Rd. Through Uppingham to Stoke Rd. Left into Lyddington, left into Main St. Pub on left*

Smart village inn with great food

Run by renowned local chef Brian Baker, this old village inn fits seamlessly into Lyddington's long, yellow-brown ironstone streetscape. Stylish, contemporary design works well together with traditional pub essentials, to wit, beams, flagstone floors and winter fires. Modern British menus offer starters like Asian prawn broth; or the charcuterie plate with rocket and marinated shallots, and main courses such as pan-fried calves' liver, steamed new potatoes, crispy Parma ham and onion dressing; and Brian's signature sharing dish of grilled rib of Derbyshire beef with frites and béarnaise sauce. Add a shady garden and the mix is complete for an enjoyable visit.

Open all day all wk 11-11 (Sat 11am-mdnt Sun 12-10.30) **Food** Lunch Mon-Sat 12-2.30, Sun 12-3 Dinner Mon-Sat 6.30-9.30, Sun 6-9 Set menu available Restaurant menu available all wk ⊕ MARSTON'S ◄ Help for Heroes, The Marquess Bitter Ò Thatchers. ♀ 14 **Facilities** Non-diners area ✿ (Bar Garden) ♦ Children's menu Children's portions Garden ⋒ Parking WiFi ➟ (notice required) **Rooms** 17

Old White Hart

tel: 01572 821703 **51 Main St LE15 9LR**
email: mail@oldwhitehart.co.uk
dir: *From A6003 between Uppingham & Corby take B672. Pub on main street*

17th-century inn in a rural conservation village

This free house opposite the village green is constructed from honey-coloured sandstone like the surrounding cottages, and has original beamed ceilings and stone walls. Owners Stuart and Holly East have been running the pub for over 15 years and have built a reputation for food. Dishes served in the restaurant include crayfish and smoked salmon thermidor; roast rabbit with spinach tagliatelle and wild mushrooms, and a selection of vegetarian choices. On warm days customers take their pints of Nene Valley bitter or Aspall cider out into the gardens or onto the covered patio. The inn also has a floodlit petanque pitch.

Open all wk 12-11 (Sun 12-4 7-10.30) Closed 25 Dec, 26 Dec eve **Food** Lunch Mon-Sat 12-2, Sun 12-2.30 Dinner Mon-Sat 6.30-9 (Sun 6-8 Summer) Av main course £13 ⊕ FREE HOUSE ◄ Greene King IPA, The Grainstore, Nene Valley, KCB Ò Aspall. ♀ 10 **Facilities** Non-diners area ♦ Children's portions Play area Garden ⋒ Parking WiFi ➟ (notice required)

MANTON
Map 11 SK80

The Horse and Jockey

tel: 01572 737335 **2 St Marys Rd LE15 8SU**
email: enquiries@horseandjockeyrutland.co.uk
dir: *Exit A6003 between Oakham & Uppingham signed Rutland Water South Shore. 1st left in Manton into St Marys Rd*

Handy refuelling stop by Rutland Water

Cyclists and ramblers investigating the recreational tracks around Rutland Water can expect treats in the form of fine Rutland-brewed beers – including one created for the pub – and some robust pub food at this pleasing, stone-built village free house. Privately owned, the innate charm of the traditional, stone-floored, beamed interior complements the wholesome home-cooked menu which is strong on produce with local provenance. Steaks, curries, baked fish or roast loin of pork are amongst the pub favourites helping refuel visitors to the vast reservoir. Vegetarian options may include mushroom and red onion confit pudding, and a specials board is also available.

Open all day all wk **Food** Lunch all wk 12-9 (Apr-Sep) all wk 12-2.30 (Oct-Mar) Dinner all wk 12-9 (Apr-Sep) all wk 6-9 (Oct-Mar) Av main course £10.95 ⊕ FREE HOUSE ◀ The Grainstore Cooking & Ten Fifty (Fall At The First), Guest ales ♂ Jollydale, Kopparberg. ♀ 12 **Facilities** Non-diners area ❤ (Bar Garden) ♦♦ Children's menu Children's portions Garden ⇥ Parking WiFi ➡ (notice required)

MARKET OVERTON
Map 11 SK81

The Black Bull

tel: 01572 767677 **2 Teigh Rd LE15 7PW**
email: enquiry@blackbullrutland.co.uk
dir: *From Oakham take B668 to Cottesmore. Left signed Market Overton*

Convivial village local with good food

Just six miles from Rutland Water nature reserve and a short drive from Stamford and Nottingham, The Black Bull occupies a lovely spot in the picturesque village of Market Overton. Once a coach house, the thatched pub offers a traditional atmosphere with real fires and sumptuous sofas, although walking boots, children and dogs are as welcome as diners. Local produce fills the frequently changing menu here, including steaks from a local farm and lamb from Launde Abbey. Sample dishes include fresh crab cakes, dill, white wine and cream sauce; and trio of pork sausages, mash and rich onion pan gravy.

Open 12-3 6-12 (Sun 12-6) Closed Sun eve & Mon **Food** Lunch Tue-Sat 12-2.30, Sun 12-3 Dinner Tue-Sat 6-9.30 ⊕ FREE HOUSE ◀ Black Sheep, Grainstore Rutland Bitter ♂ Thatchers Gold, Westons Old Rosie, Scrambler. **Facilities** Non-diners area ❤ (Bar Outside area) ♦♦ Children's menu Children's portions Outside area Parking WiFi ➡ (notice required)

OAKHAM
Map 11 SK80

The Grainstore Brewery

tel: 01572 770065 **Station Approach LE15 6RE**
email: enquiries@grainstorebrewery.com
dir: *Adjacent to Oakham rail station*

The largest brewery in the smallest county

One of the best brew pubs in Britain, The Grainstore Brewery is housed in a three-storey Victorian grain store next to Oakham railway station. Founded in 1995, Davis's brewing company uses the finest quality hops and ingredients to make the beers that can be sampled in the pub's taproom. Food is wholesome and straightforward, with the ales playing an important part in recipes for Rutland Panther chilli con carne and pork and Ten Fifty sausages. A full diary of events includes live music, the annual Summer Bank Holiday Rutland beer festival and the Spring Bank Holiday cider and sausage festival in late May. Tours of the brewery can be arranged.

Open all day all wk Mon-Fri 11am-mdnt (Sat-Sun 8.30am-mdnt) **Food** Lunch Mon-Fri 11-3, Sat-Sun 9-5 Dinner Tue-Wed 6-9 Av main course £8 ⊕ FREE HOUSE ◀ The Grainstore Rutland Panther, Triple B, Ten Fifty, Rutland Beast, Nip, Cooking, Seasonal beers ♂ Sheppy's. **Facilities** Non-diners area ❤ (Bar Restaurant Outside area) ♦♦ Children's menu Children's portions Outside area ⇥ Beer festival Cider festival Parking WiFi ➡ (notice required)

SOUTH LUFFENHAM
Map 11 SK90

The Coach House Inn

tel: 01780 720166 **3 Stamford Rd LE15 8NT**
email: thecoachhouse123@aol.com
dir: *On A6121, off A47 between Morcroft & Stamford*

Former stables serving well-kept real ales

Horses were once stabled here while weary travellers enjoyed a drink in what is now a private house next door. This elegantly appointed, attractive stone inn offers a comfortable 40-cover dining room and a cosy bar serving Adnams, Morland and Greene King beers. A short, appealing menu in the Ostler's Restaurant might feature chicken liver pâté with orange and cranberry chutney; and lamb shank with garlic mash, root vegetables and redcurrant jus. In the bar tuck into roast cod with hand-cut chips and pea purée; or beef and ale casserole.

Open 12-2 5-11 (Sat all day) Closed 25 Dec, 1 Jan, Sun eve, Mon L **Food** Lunch Tue-Sat 12-2 Dinner Mon-Sat 6.30-9 ⊕ FREE HOUSE ◀ Morland Old Speckled Hen, Adnams, Greene King IPA, St Austell Tribute, The Grainstore Triple B, Guinness ♂ Aspall. **Facilities** Non-diners area ❤ (Bar Garden Outside area) ♦♦ Children's portions Garden Outside area ⇥ Parking WiFi ➡ (notice required)

STRETTON
Map 11 SK91

The Jackson Stops Country Inn
PICK OF THE PUBS

tel: 01780 410237 **Rookery Rd LE15 7RA**
email: info@thejacksonstops.com
dir: *From A1 follow Stretton signs*

Timeless pub with seasonal dishes

There can be few pubs in the country that have acquired their name by virtue of a 'For Sale' sign. One was planted outside the pub for so long during a previous change of ownership that the locals dispensed with the old name in favour of the name of the estate agent on the board. Robert and Mandy Knowles took over in 2014 and have already stamped their personality on this long, low, stone-built partly thatched building dating from 1721. Inside, the pub has plenty of appeal: stone fireplaces with log fires, quarry-tiled floors, scrubbed wood tables and five intimate dining rooms. In the timeless and beamed snug bar, real ales such as Grainstore Ten Fifty lift the heart, boding well for excellent value dishes like blade of beef with horseradish mash, or pan-fried fillet of sea bass and tiger prawns with pea shoot and dill risotto.

Open 12-3.30 6-11 (Sun 12-5) Closed Sun eve, Mon **Food** Lunch Tue-Sat 12-3, Sun 12-5 Dinner Tue-Sat 6.30-9.30 Set menu available Restaurant menu available Tue-Sun ⊕ FREE HOUSE ◀ The Grainstore Cooking & Ten Fifty. ♀ 10 **Facilities** Non-diners area ❤ (Bar Garden) ♦♦ Children's menu Children's portions Garden ⇥ Parking WiFi ➡ (notice required)

PICK OF THE PUBS

King's Arms Inn ★★★★ INN ❀❀

tel: 01572 737634 **Top St LE15 8SE**
email: info@thekingsarms-wing.co.uk
web: www.thekingsarms-wing.co.uk
dir: *1m off B6003 between Uppingham & Oakham*

Seventeenth century inn with its own smokehouse

The Family Goss — as they like to style themselves — have run this attractive, stone-built free house since 2004, and their expertise is evident. Dating from 1649, its flagstone floors, low-beamed ceilings and two open fires are original. The bar is well stocked with snacks, including home-made salamis, biltong and pork scratchings, any of which would happily accompany a sloe gin, elderflower vodka or Zermatter mulled wine, all made here with locally foraged or donated berries or fruit. Real ales come from Grainstore, Marston's and Shepherd Neame, with real ciders from Sheppy's, Jollydale and Bottle Kicking, named for an ancient Leicestershire village tradition. For his seasonal menus, two-AA-Rosette-earning chef James Goss has a 'buy-local' policy that relies on his network of farmers, millers, brewers, hunters and fishermen; sea fish are all wild or line-caught from British waters. Lunchtime snacks include freshly baked filled cobs; more substantial are pub classics such as fisherman's pie; and smokehouse platter, from the pub's smokery that

James set up based on his knowledge of air-drying and fish-curing from working in Switzerland and Denmark. A starter of soused herrings with curried egg salad might be followed by chump of lamb with crisp sweetbreads, creamed leeks and rosemary-crushed potatoes; or sea bass supreme with potato and crab gratin, Cognac bisque, green beans and pancetta. Leave some space for lemon and lime meringue tartlet. The Bin Ends blackboard lists fine, affordable wines, while a Farmers Market board in The Snug promotes locally grown fruit and vegetables. The eight spacious letting rooms are located in the old village bakery directly opposite the pub.

Open Tue-Sun 12-3 6.30-11 Closed Sun eve, Mon, Tue L (Oct-Mar), Sun eve,

Mon L (Apr-Sep) **Food** Lunch Tue-Sun 12-2.30 Dinner Tue-Sat 6.30-8.30 Restaurant menu Tue-Sun 🍺 FREE HOUSE 🍴 Shepherd Neame Spitfire, The Grainstore Cooking 🍏 Sheppy's, Jollydale, Stamford. 🍷 33 **Facilities** Non-diners area 🐾 (Bar Outside area) 👶 Children's menu & portions Outside area 🪑 Parking WiFi 🚐 (notice required) **Rooms** 8

WHITWELL
Map 11 SK90

The Noel @ Whitwell ★★★ INN

tel: 01780 460347 **Main Rd LE15 8BW**
email: info@thenoel.co.uk **web:** www.thenoel.co.uk
dir: Between Oakham & Stamford on A606, N shore of Rutland Water

North shore village pub for everyone

The part-thatched village inn stands just a 15-minute stroll from the north shore of Rutland Water, so worth noting if you are walking or pedalling the lakeside trail and in need of refreshment. The friendly, smart bar and dining room have a stylish modern feel and feature flagstone floors, heritage colours and a warming winter log fires. Expect to find local Grainstore ales on tap and a wide-ranging menu listing pasta and salad dishes alongside The Noel's chicken, leek and bacon pie; Thai green prawn curry and Moroccan vegetable couscous.

Open 12-3 6-close **Closed** Mon **Food** Lunch Tue-Sat 12-2, Sun 12-3 Dinner Tue-Sat 6.30-9 Restaurant menu available Tue-Sat ⊕ ENTERPRISE INNS ◀ The Grainstore Rutland Bitter ♻ Westons Stowford Press. ₹ 10 **Facilities** Non-diners area ♣ (Bar Garden) ♦ Children's menu Children's portions Garden ⌓ Parking WiFi ⏛ (notice required) **Rooms** 8

WING
Map 11 SK80

King's Arms Inn ★★★★ INN ◉◉　PICK OF THE PUBS

See Pick of the Pubs on opposite page

SHROPSHIRE

ADMASTON
Map 10 SJ61

The Pheasant Inn at Admaston

tel: 01952 251989 **TF5 0AD**
email: info@thepheasantadmaston.co.uk
dir: M54 junct 6, A5223 N. At 4th rdbt left onto B5063 to Admaston. Pub on left

Stylish country inn with good children's menu

Dating from the 19th century, this lovely old country pub offers stylish interior decor and real fire, which add character to the dining areas. The large enclosed garden is ideal for families and there is a good menu for children under ten. Grown-ups certainly aren't overlooked, either – the kitchen uses the best local produce in dishes such as Shropshire Blue and caramelised onion horn, which might be followed by Wickstead aged sirloin steak with balsamic tomatoes, watercress salad and chips. Steamed chocolate pudding, and banana and pecan tart are just two options for dessert. Dogs are allowed in the bar between 2.30pm and 5.30pm.

Open all day all wk 11-11 (Thu 11am-11.30pm Fri-Sat 11am-mdnt) **Food** Lunch Mon-Fri 12-2, Sat 12-9.15, Sun 12-7 Dinner Mon-Fri 6-9 Set menu available ⊕ ENTERPRISE INNS ◀ Salopian Shropshire Gold, Greene King IPA, Guinness. ₹ 10 **Facilities** Non-diners area ♣ (Garden Outside area) ♦ Children's menu Children's portions Play area Garden Outside area ⌓ Parking WiFi ⏛

BASCHURCH
Map 15 SJ42

The New Inn

tel: 01939 260335 **Church Rd SY4 2EF**
email: eat@thenewinnbaschurch.co.uk
dir: 8m from Shrewsbury, 8m from Oswestry

Shropshire beers plus the best local produce on the menus

Near the medieval church, this stylishly modernised old whitewashed village pub is a focal point for all things Welsh Marches, with beers from nearby Oswestry's Stonehouse brewery amongst five ales stocked, meats from the village's Moor Farm or Shrewsbury's renowned market, and cheeses from a Cheshire supplier. In addition

to the interesting sandwich menu, the tempting fare might include a sharing platter (seafood or deli); a starter of Stilton mousse, poached pears, candied walnuts and watercress salad; followed by slow-cooked pork belly with apricot and pistachio stuffing, parsnip mash and cider gravy; or chicken Caesar salad.

Open Tue-Fri 11-3 6-11 (Sat 11-11 Sun 12-6) **Closed** 26 Dec, 1 Jan, Mon **Food** Lunch Tue-Sat 12-2, Sun 12-3 Dinner Tue-Sat 6-9 ⊕ FREE HOUSE ◀ Banks's Bitter, Stonehouse Station Bitter, Hobsons Best Bitter, Guest ales ♻ Thatchers Gold. ₹ 13 **Facilities** Non-diners area ♣ (Bar Outside area) ♦ Children's menu Children's portions Outside area ⌓ Parking WiFi

BISHOP'S CASTLE
Map 15 SO38

The Three Tuns Inn　PICK OF THE PUBS

tel: 01588 638797 **Salop St SY9 5BW**
email: timce@talk21.com
dir: From Ludlow take A49 through Craven Arms, left onto A489 to Lydham, A488 to Bishop's Castle, inn at top of town

Historic inn famed for its microbrewery ales

One of England's most renowned inns fronts the country's oldest brewery. The picture-perfect enclave of compact tower brewery and adjoining inn snuggles beside the top of the steep main street of a pretty hill-town deep in the Welsh Marches. For over 350 years the pub and brewery were a single business, and although ownership has now split, they continue to work together, producing the enticing array of Three Tuns real ales sold here, including 1642, commemorating the date of the inn's first brewing licence. The engaging warren of rooms is generally music and games machine free, although regular live jazz, rock, classical music and morris dancing events prove very popular. An airy dining room overlooks the brewing tower; test out a menu by choosing game terrine and cranberry compôte; or spiced duck, cucumber and pak choi salad for starters. Progressing to the mains, the choice may include pork tenderloin with brandy and apricot sauce; or macaroni with blue cheese and broccoli. A dynamic beer festival over the second weekend of July involves all the town's pubs.

Open all day all wk **Food** Lunch all wk 12-2.30 Dinner Mon-Sat 6.30-9 ⊕ STAR PUBS & BARS ◀ Three Tuns XXX, Solstice, Old Scrooge, Cleric's Cure, 1642. ₹ 12 **Facilities** Non-diners area ♣ (Bar Restaurant Outside area) ♦ Children's menu Children's portions Outside area Beer festival WiFi

BRIDGNORTH
Map 10 SO79

Halfway House Inn ★★★ INN

tel: 01746 762670 **Cleobury Rd, Eardington WV16 5LS**
email: info@halfwayhouseinn.co.uk
dir: M54 junct 4, A442 to Bridgnorth. Or M5 junct 4, A491 towards Stourbridge. A458 to Bridgnorth. Follow tourist signs on B4363

An old-world coaching inn

This 17th-century coaching inn was renamed in 1823 after the very young Princess Victoria stopped here en route between Shrewsbury and Worcester; when she asked where she was, came the diplomatic reply, 'halfway there ma'am'. An original Elizabethan mural has been preserved behind glass for all to enjoy, and the pub is renowned for a good selection of regional real ales, 40 malts, and around 100 wines. The weekend lunch menu ranges from light bites (maybe Cecile's chicken liver pâté or deep-fried breaded brie with hot redcurrant sauce) while the dinner menu offers the likes of Shropshire beef with onions and mushrooms braised in Guinness and ale; and home-made local lamb curry. Finish with one of the home-made puddings.

Open all wk 6-11.30 (Fri-Sat 11am-11.30pm Sun 11-7) **Closed** Sun eve Nov-Mar **Food** Lunch Fri-Sun 12-2 Dinner Mon-Sat 6-9 Set menu available Restaurant menu available all wk ⊕ FREE HOUSE ◀ Holden's Golden Glow, Wood's Shropshire Lad, Guinness ♻ Westons Stowford Press. ₹ 10 **Facilities** Non-diners area ♣ (Bar Garden) ♦ Children's menu Children's portions Play area Garden ⌓ Parking WiFi ⏛ (notice required) **Rooms** 10

BUCKNELL   Map 9 SO37

NEW Baron at Bucknell

tel: 01547 530549 **SY7 0AH**
email: info@baronatbucknell.co.uk **web:** www.baronatbucknell.co.uk
dir: *From Bromfield on A49 onto A4113 towards Knighton. Through Leintwardine. Right to Bucknell. Cross rail line, left & follow brown signs for inn*

Home-made food in great walking country

A stone's throw from Ludlow in the lovely Shropshire Hills Area of Outstanding Natural Beauty, the Baron sits at the foot of Bucknell Mynd. It's beautifully peaceful and there are plenty of great walks if you need to work up an appetite. Good home-made food is what they promise here, and you can eat either in the charming restaurant or the airy conservatory. Start with warm black pudding, bacon and croûton salad, maybe, before moving on to honey-glazed gammon steak or steak, mushroom and Guinness pie. There's a pizza menu, too, and a choice of sandwiches and toasted paninis is available at lunchtime.

Open 6pm-10.30pm (Fri 12-3 6-11 Sat 12-11 Sun 12-6) Closed 2wks Jan, Lunch Mon-Thu & Sun eve **Food** Lunch Fri-Sun 12-2.30 Dinner Mon-Sat 6-8.30 Av main course £12 ⊕ FREE HOUSE ◧ Wye Valley Bitter & Butty Bach, Wood's Shropshire Lad ♂ Robinsons Flagon, Westons Stowford Press. **Facilities** Non-diners area ✿ (Bar Garden) ♦♦ Children's menu Children's portions Garden ⋈ Parking WiFi ⛟ (notice required)

CARDINGTON   Map 10 SO59

The Royal Oak

tel: 01694 771266 **SY6 7JZ**
email: inntoxicated@gmail.com
dir: *N of Church Stretton right to Cardington; or from Much Wenlock take B4371, 2m to Cardington*

Historic pub in a conservation village

Reputedly the oldest continuously licensed pub in Shropshire and set in a conservation village, this free house can trace its roots to the 15th century. The rambling low-beamed bar with vast inglenook (complete with cauldron, black kettle and pewter jugs) and comfortable beamed dining room are refreshingly undisturbed by music, TV or games machines. Choose from the excellent cask ales and ponder your choice of sustenance: good-value home-made fare includes caramelised red onion and cherry tomato tart; sticky belly pork; game pie; and lager battered cod, chips and mushy peas.

Open 12-2.30 6-11 (Sat-Sun 12-11) (Jan-Mar 12-2.30 6.30-11 Sat 12-11 Sun 12-4) Closed Mon (ex BH L) & Sun eve Jan-Mar **Food** Lunch Tue-Sun 12-2.30 Dinner Tue-Sun 6-9 (Tue-Sat 6.30-9 Jan-Mar) Av main course £12.95 ⊕ FREE HOUSE ◧ Ludlow Best, Three Tuns XXX, Wye Valley Butty Bach, Salopian Hop Twister, Sharp's Doom Bar. **Facilities** Non-diners area ✿ (Bar Outside area) ♦♦ Children's menu Outside area ⋈ Parking WiFi ⛟ (notice required)

CHURCH STRETTON   Map 15 SO49

The Bucks Head ★★★★ INN

tel: 01694 722898 **42 High St SY6 6BX**
email: lnutting@btinternet.com **web:** www.the-bucks-head.co.uk
dir: *12m from Shrewsbury & Ludlow*

Traditional pub in the Shropshire Hills

The small market town of Church Stretton is sandwiched between the Long Mynd and Wenlock Edge, and the charming old Bucks Head is without doubt where to stay to explore these impressive landscape features. The pub is known for several essential things: its comfortable, AA four-star accommodation, its well-kept Marston's, Banks's and guest ales, and its restaurant. Where possible, the kitchen uses local fresh meat, poultry and vegetables to create their dishes.

Open all day all wk **Food** Lunch all wk 12-2.30 Dinner Mon-Sat 6-9, Sun 6-8.30 ⊕ MARSTON'S ◧ Pedigree, Banks's Bitter, 3 guest ales. ☕ 9
Facilities Non-diners area ♦♦ Children's menu Children's portions Garden ⋈ WiFi ⛟ (notice required) **Rooms** 4

CLEOBURY MORTIMER   Map 10 SO67

The Crown Inn   PICK OF THE PUBS

tel: 01299 270372 **Hopton Wafers DY14 0NB**
dir: *On A4117, 8m E of Ludlow, 2m W of Cleobury Mortimer*

Delightful old coaching inn with three restaurants

The exterior of this 16th-century coaching inn pushes the description 'creeper-clad' to its limit, and delightful it looks as a result. Birmingham to Ludlow mail coaches used to take on extra horses here for the steep climb up the hill. Much of its period past is evident inside – in the bar, for example, and in Poachers Dining Area, where you'll find exposed beams, stonework and a large inglenook fireplace. The two other eating areas are the Shropshire Restaurant, overlooking the countryside, and the Rent Room, with pine kitchen-style seating, sofas and more rural views. A typical three-course meal might be warm smoked salmon with salad and horseradish, followed by braised shank of local lamb with red wine, rosemary and redcurrant jus; or home-made meat or vegetarian curry with jasmine rice; and finally, Eton mess. The wine list, selected by a local merchant, includes a range of fine ports, Armagnacs and Cognacs.

Open all day all wk **Food** Lunch Mon-Fri 12-2, Sat 12-2.30, Sun 12-8 Dinner Mon-Fri 6-9, Sat 6-9.30, Sun 12-8 Set menu available Restaurant menu available all wk ⊕ FREE HOUSE ◧ Hobsons Best Bitter, Guest ales. ☕ 25 **Facilities** Non-diners area ✿ (Bar Garden) ♦♦ Children's menu Children's portions Play area Garden Parking ⛟

CLUN
Map 9 SO38

The White Horse Inn

tel: 01588 640305 **The Square SY7 8JA**
email: pub@whi-clun.co.uk **web:** www.whi-clun.co.uk
dir: *On A488 in village centre*

Home to the Clun Brewery

In the beautiful Shropshire Hills, this gloriously unspoilt and unpretentious village inn oozes character with beams, wizened wood and slab floors. Three beers brewed in their own microbrewery, the Clun, together with others selected from Shropshire's many craft breweries provide the line-up at the bar. This 'green' pub offers visitors drawn to AE Housman's 'Quietest place under the sun' heart-warming pub grub, derived from very local suppliers. Main courses may include grilled pork belly with ratatouille sauce, topped with Stilton; steak and mushroom pie; or penne pasta with tomato, pepper, mushroom and olive sauce. The traditional suet puddings are a speciality. Regular events take place here, including the Clun Valley beer festival on the first weekend in October.

The White Horse Inn

Open all day all wk **Food** Lunch Mon-Sat 12-2, Sun 12.30-2.30 Dinner all wk 6.30-8.30 Av main course £10.50 ⊕ FREE HOUSE ◀ Clun Pale Ale, Citadel & Loophole, Wye Valley Butty Bach, Hobsons Best Bitter, Guest ales ♂ Robinsons Flagon, Thistly Cross Whisky Cask. **Facilities** Non-diners area ✿ (Bar Garden) ♦♦ Children's menu Children's portions Garden ⌒ Beer festival WiFi ▦ (notice required)

See advert below

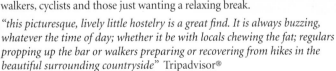

CRAVEN ARMS
Map 9 SO48

The Sun Inn

tel: 01584 861239 **Corfton SY7 9DF**
email: normanspride@btconnect.com
dir: On B4368, 7m N of Ludlow

Family-run pub with an innovative microbrewery

First licensed in 1613, this historic pub is close to the towns of Ludlow and Bridgnorth, and handy for the ramblers' paradise of Clee Hill and Long Mynd. It's been run by the Pearce family since 1984, and from 1997 landlord Norman Pearce has been brewing the Corvedale ales in what was the pub's old chicken and lumber shed, using local borehole water; Herefordshire's Gwatkin cider is another thirst-quenching option. Teresa Pearce uses local produce in a delicious array of traditional dishes — pork and apple in cider gravy; smoked haddock; steaks. There are also vegetarian and some vegan options. The pub holds a beer festival in May.

Open all wk 12-2.30 6-11 (Sun 12-3 7-11) **Food** Lunch Mon-Sat 12-2, Sun 12-2.45 Dinner Mon-Sat 6-9, Sun 7-9 Av main course £10 ⊕ FREE HOUSE ◀ Corvedale Norman's Pride & Golden Dale, Dark & Delicious Ö Gwatkin. ▾ 8
Facilities Non-diners area ❤ (Bar Garden Outside area) ◀❙ Children's menu Children's portions Play area Garden Outside area ⊢ Beer festival Parking WiFi ➡ (notice required)

CRESSAGE
Map 10 SJ50

The Riverside Inn

tel: 01952 510900 **Cound SY5 6AF**
email: info@theriversideinn.net
dir: On A458. 7m from Shrewsbury, 1m from Cressage

Great river views from the conservatory and garden

This inn sits in three acres of gardens alongside the River Severn, offering customers delightful river views both outdoors and from a modern conservatory. Originally a vicarage for St Peter's church in the village, the building also housed a girls' school and a railway halt before becoming a pub in 1878. The pub is popular with anglers. The monthly-changing menu might open with roast parsnip soup or seafood pancake, followed by perhaps oven-baked herb crusted hake; minced steak pie; or vegetarian chilli. Comforting desserts include Bakewell tart and cream. Their own brew, Riverside Inn Bitter, is available in the cosy bar.

Open all day all wk **Food** Lunch all wk 12-9 Dinner all wk 12-9 Av main course £10.50 ⊕ FREE HOUSE ◀ Riverside Inn Bitter, Guest ales. ▾
Facilities Non-diners area ❤ (Bar Garden Outside area) ◀❙ Children's menu Garden Outside area ⊢ Parking WiFi

HODNET
Map 15 SJ62

The Bear at Hodnet

tel: 01630 685214 **TF9 3NH**
email: reception@bearathodnet.co.uk
dir: At junct of A53 & A442 turn right at rdbt. Inn in village centre

Former coaching inn with a ghostly tale

With old beams, open fireplaces and secret passages leading to the church, this black-and-white-timbered, former coaching inn was once known for its bear-baiting pit. In the 1680s, a landlord threw Jasper, a regular down on his luck, out into a bitterly cold night. Within hours both were dead, Jasper from hypothermia, the landlord from fright, as if he'd seen a ghost, which legend suggests was Jasper. Food includes apple and black pudding Scotch egg; pigeon with wild berry salad

and port dressing; beer battered cod, triple cooked chips, mushy peas and tartare sauce; and red onion marmalade sausages, spring onion mash, buttered greens and red wine gravy.

Open all day all wk 12-11 (Sun 12-9) Closed 1 Jan **Food** Lunch Mon-Thu 12-3, Fri-Sat 12-9.30, Sun 12-4 Dinner Mon-Thu 6-9, Fri-Sat 12-9.30 ⊕ FREE HOUSE ◀ Salopian Shropshire Gold, Rotating Guest ales Ö Westons Stowford Press. ▾ 10
Facilities Non-diners area ❤ (Bar Garden) ◀❙ Children's menu Children's portions Play area Garden ⊢ Parking WiFi ➡ (notice required)

IRONBRIDGE
Map 10 SJ60

The Malthouse

tel: 01952 433712 **The Wharfage TF8 7NH**
email: info@themalthouse.co.uk
dir: Phone for detailed directions

Live music and good food

In the Severn Gorge, within a mile of the famous Iron Bridge, the 18th-century Malthouse is known for its Friday and Saturday night live music. But for a different way to spend the evening try the restaurant, where candlelit tables and an extensive menu feature home-made steak and Guinness pie; king prawn linguine; braised shoulder of Shropshire lamb; and mushroom, pepper and spinach Stroganoff. There's pubbier grub too, such as thick pork sausages with black pudding mash. Brakspear, Wood's and Wychwood make up the real ale portfolio.

Open all day all wk 11.30-11 **Food** Lunch all wk 11.30-10 Dinner all wk 11.30-10 ⊕ FREE HOUSE ◀ Wychwood Hobgoblin, Wood's Shropshire Lad, Brakspear Oxford Gold, Sharp's Doom Bar Ö Thatchers Gold, Somersby Cider. ▾ 10
Facilities Non-diners area ◀❙ Children's menu Children's portions Garden ⊢ Parking WiFi ➡

LITTLE STRETTON
Map 15 SO49

NEW The Green Dragon

tel: 01694 722925 **Ludlow Rd SY6 6RE**
email: enquiries@greendragonlittlestretton.co.uk
web: www.greendragonlittlestretton.co.uk
dir: A49 from Shrewsbury towards Ludlow. 1m after Church Stretton right to Little Stretton. Pub in village centre

Traditional village pub in prime walking country

Close to the Long Mynd in the Shropshire Hills and backing on to Small Batch Valley, the 16th-century Green Dragon is in a prime location for walkers and campers but also convenient for the busy market town of Ludlow 14 miles away.

Grab a seat near the log-burner in the bar and enjoy a glass of Wye Valley Butty Bach ale or one of the traditional ciders. Local produce appears on the traditional menu in the form of Paddy Ryan's faggots and peas with mash and onion gravy, or Bert Butler's beef in Butty Bach with herb dumplings.

The Green Dragon

Open all day all wk **Food** Lunch Mon-Sat 11.30-9, Sun 11.30-8 Dinner Mon-Sat 11.30-9, Sun 11.30-8 Av main course £9.95 ⊕ FREE HOUSE ◀ Wye Valley Butty Bach, Bass, Guest ales Ö Westons Stowford Press, Robinsons, Guest ciders. ♚ 10 **Facilities** Non-diners area ❤ (Bar Garden) ♦♦ Children's menu Children's portions Play area Garden ⋈ Parking WiFi 🚐 (notice required)

The Ragleth Inn

tel: 01694 722711 **Ludlow Rd SY6 6RB**
email: wendyjd65@hotmail.com
dir: *From Shrewsbury take A49 towards Leominster. At lights in Church Stretton turn right. 3rd left into High St. Continue to Little Stretton. Inn on right*

Country inn serving home-cooked favourites

This 17th-century country inn sits midway between Shrewsbury and Ludlow in beautiful countryside at the foot of the Long Mynd hills. Its pretty exterior overlooks a large beer garden with plenty of wooden benches and a children's play area. Inside are two traditional bars and a restaurant with oak beams, antiques and inglenook fireplaces. A good range of ales includes Wood's Parish and Wrekin Gold, with Aspall's Harry Sparrow pleasing cider lovers. Food follows classic pub grub lines, though the specials menu may list fresh calamari with sweet chilli; or medallions of pork, black pudding and Dijon sauce.

Open all wk Closed 25 Dec **Food** Lunch Mon-Sat 12-2.15, Sun all day Dinner Mon-Sat 6.30-9, Sun all day Av main course £10 Set menu available ⊕ FREE HOUSE ◀ Wood's Parish Bitter, Wrekin Gold, Wye Valley Butty Bach, Hobsons, Three Tuns, Sharp's Doom Bar Ö Aspall Harry Sparrow, Westons Stowford Press. **Facilities** Non-diners area ❤ (Bar Garden Outside area) ♦♦ Children's menu Children's portions Play area Garden Outside area ⋈ Parking WiFi 🚐 (notice required)

NEW The Charlton Arms ★★★★ INN ◉

tel: 01584 872813 **Ludford Bridge SY8 1PJ**
email: reservations@thecharltonarms.co.uk **web:** www.thecharltonarms.co.uk
dir: *On B4361 from Ludlow towards Leominster (just S of River Teme)*

Enjoyable Anglo-French food and local ale

Frenchman Cedric Bosi and his wife Amy took over this free house in 2013 and it has quickly become one of Ludlow's must-visit food pubs. Whether it's dogs, children or muddy-booted walkers, everybody is made to feel welcome at this pub on the banks of the River Teme. Well-kept local ales such as Ludlow Gold keep beer drinkers happy and there are 11 wines by the glass. The Anglo-French food is excellent – a typical meal might start with Herefordshire snails in garlic butter and continue with saffron seafood bisque, or ox cheeks braised in red wine.

Open all day all wk **Food** Lunch all wk 12-3 Dinner Mon-Sat 6-9.15, Sun 6-8.30 Av main course £12 ⊕ FREE HOUSE ◀ Hobsons Best Bitter, Ludlow Gold, Wye Valley Butty Bach Ö Thatchers Gold, Westons Mortimers Orchard. ♚ 11 **Facilities** Non-diners area ❤ (Bar) ♦♦ Children's portions Outside area ⋈ Parking WiFi 🚐 (notice required) **Rooms** 9

The Church Inn ★★★ INN

tel: 01584 872174 **Buttercross SY8 1AW**
web: www.thechurchinn.com
dir: *In town centre, behind Buttercross*

Real ales and pies in a narrow town centre street

The inn stands on one of the oldest sites in Ludlow town centre, dating back some seven centuries, and through the ages has been occupied by a blacksmith, saddler, apothecary and barber-surgeon. These days it enjoys a reputation for providing a good range of up to 10 real ales in the cosy bar areas alongside the pies for which it has become well known – there's a choice of 30 different pies at any one time. Food is served all day. There are 10 comfortable en suite bedrooms with smart modern bathrooms.

Open all day all wk **Food** Lunch all wk all day Dinner all wk all day ⊕ FREE HOUSE ◀ Hobsons Town Crier & Mild, Weetwood, Wye Valley Bitter, Ludlow Gold & Boiling Well, Guest ales Ö Westons, Aspall, Robinsons. **Facilities** Non-diners area ♦♦ Children's menu WiFi 🚐 **Rooms** 10

LUDLOW *continued*

The Clive Bar & Restaurant with Rooms ★★★★★ RR ◉

PICK OF THE PUBS

tel: 01584 856565 **Bromfield SY8 2JR**
email: info@theclive.co.uk **web:** www.theclive.co.uk
dir: *2m N of Ludlow on A49, between Hereford & Shrewsbury*

Handsome Georgian building with classy bar and restaurant

A former farmhouse, this place has been a pub since the early 1900s, when it catered for thirsty workers on the Earl of Plymouth's estate. Clive of India lived on the estate in the 18th century, hence the name. Untouched until 1997, a refurbishment introduced contemporary style while retaining original features. The bar comprises two areas: an 18th-century lounge with log fire and Clive's original coat of arms; and a more contemporary upper part that leads out to a courtyard with tables and parasols. You'll find Hobsons ales at the bar, plus ciders such as Robinsons Flagon, and 16 wines served by the glass. Lunchtime bar snacks served with home-cut chips proffer the likes of Welsh rarebit with ham and a fried egg; while a three-course choice in the evening could comprise scallops wrapped in pancetta with potato purée; pan-fried duck breast, beetroot dauphinoise, wilted spinach and wild mushrooms; and apple and cinnamon tarte Tatin with toffee apple purée, caramel, and vanilla ice cream. Tastefully converted period outbuildings provide accommodation.

Open all day all wk Closed 25-26 Dec **Food** Lunch Mon-Fri 12-3, Sat-Sun 12-6.30 Dinner Mon-Sat 6.30-10, Sun 6.30-9.30 Restaurant menu available all wk ⊕ FREE HOUSE ◧ Hobsons Best Bitter, Ludlow Gold ♂ Dunkertons, Thatchers Old Rascal, Robinsons Flagon. ♟ 16 **Facilities** Non-diners area ♦♦ Children's portions Garden ⊼ Parking WiFi ▭ (notice required) **Rooms** 15

MAESBURY MARSH   Map 15 SJ32

NEW The Navigation Inn

tel: 01691 672958 **SY10 8JB**
email: info@thenavigation.co.uk **web:** www.thenavigation.co.uk
dir: *From Shrewsbury take A5 to Mile End Services. A483 (Welshpool), 2nd left signed Knockin. Approx 1.5m to Maesbury Marsh*

Country position beside the Montgomery Canal

Otherwise known as 'the Navvy', this canal-side pub maximises the appeal of its red-brick and stone-built industrial heritage; the restaurant was a canal warehouse in the 18th century. Comfortable sofas, a wealth of beams, log fire and piano all add to the bar's appeal, not to mention the range of Oswestry's Stonehouse ales on tap. Outside in summer, benches on the patio by the canal are much sought after. The kitchen applies strong ethical standards to the sourcing of its meats and fish, and deals directly with local producers whenever possible. A typical menu choice

could be goats' cheese and pepper roulade, followed by trio of Home Farm sausages with bubble-and-squeak.

Open 12-2 6-11 (Sun 12-6) Closed 1st 2wks Jan, Sun eve-Tue L **Food** Lunch 12-2 Dinner 6-8.30 Set menu available Restaurant menu available Tue-Sun ⊕ FREE HOUSE ◧ Stonehouse Cambrian Gold & Station Bitter, Wood's Shropshire Lad ♂ Westons Stowford Press. ♟ 11 **Facilities** Non-diners area ❄ (Bar Outside area) ♦♦ Children's menu Children's portions Outside area ⊼ Parking WiFi ▭ (notice required)

MARTON   Map 15 SJ20

The Lowfield Inn

tel: 01743 891313 **SY21 8JX**
email: lowfieldinn@tiscali.co.uk
dir: *From Shrewsbury take B4386 towards Montgomery. Through Westbury & Brockton. Pub on right in 13m just before Marton*

Successful modern interpretation of old village inn

In a stunning location below the west Shropshire Hills, this pub has all the atmosphere of a friendly village local and a fierce dedication to supporting microbreweries dotted along the England/Wales border – Monty's and Three Tuns beers are regularly stocked, as are a range of decent ciders. Modern British pub grub is the order of the day; grilled haggis with bubble-and-squeak to start, maybe, followed by locally made faggots or lamb's liver and bacon. They do a 'pie of the day' as well. The eye-catching brick bar, comfy seating, slab floor, log-burner and duck pond add to the character of this village favourite.

Open all day all wk **Food** Lunch all wk 12-9.30 Dinner all wk 12-9.30 Av main course £11 Set menu available ⊕ FREE HOUSE ◧ Three Tuns XXX & 1642, Monty's Moonrise & Mojo, Wood's Shropshire Lad, Salopian Shropshire Gold ♂ Inch's Stonehouse, Westons Old Rosie, Gwynt y Ddraig Dog Dancer. ♟ 18 **Facilities** Non-diners area ❄ (Bar Restaurant Garden) ♦♦ Children's menu Children's portions Garden ⊼ Parking WiFi ▭

The Sun Inn

tel: 01938 561211 **SY21 8JP**
email: suninnmarton@googlemail.com
dir: *On B4386 (Shrewsbury to Montgomery road), in centre of Marton*

Convivial free house respected for its food

Probably about 300 years old, the attractive, stone-built Sun stands on a corner in a quiet hamlet. Offa's Dyke Path runs nearby on its 177-mile route from Sedbury Cliffs on the Severn estuary to Prestatyn. The Gartell family runs this pub very much as a convivial local, with darts, dominoes, regular quiz nights and Hobsons real ales from Cleobury Mortimer. It's well respected as a dining venue, with the Gartells offering modern British dishes such as smoked salmon, quail egg, buckwheat blinis with soured cream and chives; slow-cooked shin of beef in Merlot; steamed halibut, creamed leeks and mushrooms; and tagine of vegetables with couscous.

Open 12-3 7-12 Closed Sun eve, Mon, Tue L **Food** Lunch Wed-Sat 12-2.30 Dinner Tue-Fri from 7pm Set menu available Restaurant menu available Tue-Sat ⊕ FREE HOUSE ◧ Hobsons Best Bitter, Guest ales ♂ Oldfields Orchard. ♟ 8 **Facilities** Non-diners area ❄ (Bar Garden) ♦♦ Children's portions Garden Outside area ⊼ Parking ▭ (notice required)

PICK OF THE PUBS

The Crown Country Inn ★★★★ INN ❀❀

MUNSLOW Map 10 SO58

tel: 01584 841205 **SY7 9ET**
email: info@crowncountryinn.co.uk
web: www.crowncountryinn.co.uk
dir: *On B4368 between Craven Arms &*
Much Wenlock

Dedication to serving excellent food

The Grade II listed Crown has stood in its lovely setting below the limestone escarpment of Wenlock Edge since Tudor times. An impressive three-storey building, it served for a while as a Hundred House, a type of court, where the infamous 'Hanging' Judge Jeffreys sometimes presided over proceedings. Could it be that the black-swathed Charlotte, whose ghost is sometimes seen in the pub, once appeared before him? The main bar retains its sturdy oak beams, flagstone floors and prominent inglenook fireplace, and on offer are beers from the Three Tuns Brewery. Owners Richard and Jane Arnold are well known for their strong commitment to good food, Richard being not only head chef but Shropshire's only Master Chef of Great Britain, a title he has cherished for many years. Meals based on top-quality local produce from trusted sources are served in the main bar, the Bay dining area, and the Corvedale restaurant, the former court room. These may include dishes such as seared scallops, pea pesto, crispy prosciutto ham and pickled fennel; braised Bridgnorth beef brisket, butterbean fricassée, roasted roots, pickled walnut sauce and crispy polenta fritters; and griddled rib-eye or Hereford sirloin steak. Sundays here are deservedly popular, when a typical lunch might start with cream and coriander soup; followed by roast fore rib of beef and Yorkshire pudding, or pavé of Shetland salmon, with red wine and crayfish butter sauce; and to finish, warm apple and Black Forest fruit crumble pie, or orange crème brûlée. Three large bedrooms are in a converted Georgian stable block.

Open Tue-Sat 12-3.30 6.45-11 (Sun 12-3.30) Closed Xmas, Sun eve, Mon **Food** Lunch Tue-Sun 12-2 Dinner Tue-

Sat 6.45-8.45 Restaurant menu available Tue-Sat ⊕ FREE HOUSE ◼ Three Tuns 1642, Corvedale Golden Dale, Ludlow Best, Rotating local guest ales ○ Westons.
Facilities Non-diners area ♦♦ Children's portions Play area Garden ⊼ Parking WiFi ⛟ (notice required) **Rooms** 3

MUCH WENLOCK   Map 10 SO69

The George & Dragon

tel: 01952 727312 **2 High St TF13 6AA**
email: thegeorge.dragon@btinternet.com
dir: *On A458 halfway between Shrewsbury & Bridgnorth, on right of the High Street*

Good pub food and choice of ales

If you are looking for somewhere dog-friendly, with five cask ales and several draught ciders, and where newspapers are provided, this early 18th-century inn should do nicely. Over the fireplace in the bar, an oak beam features the initials of the Yates family, innkeepers from 1834 to 1958. On the menu are baguettes and light lunches, while in the evening choose from deep-fried breaded scampi; chicken breast wrapped in bacon, stuffed with garlic mushrooms; a selection of pies – beef in ale, traditional fish and Shropshire fidget (pork and apple), and vegetarian options.

Open all day all wk 12-11 (Fri-Sat 12-12) ⊕ PUNCH TAVERNS ◢ Greene King Abbot Ale, Hobsons Best Bitter, St Austell Tribute, Guest ales ♂ Westons Wyld Wood Organic, Thatchers Gold. **Facilities** ♣ (Bar Outside area) ♦ Children's menu Children's portions Outside area WiFi

MUNSLOW   Map 10 SO58

The Crown Country Inn ★★★★ INN ◉◉ **PICK OF THE PUBS**

See Pick of the Pubs on page 421

NESSCLIFFE   Map 15 SJ31

NEW The Old Three Pigeons

tel: 01743 741279 **SY4 1DB**
email: info@3pigeons.co.uk
dir: *Phone pub for detailed directions*

Rural roadside pub with resident ghost

The spirits of Sir Humphrey Kynaston and his horse Beelzebub are said to return occasionally to this ancient watering hole in deepest Shropshire; a local Robin Hood, he was outlawed by Henry VII and in 1493 ultimately pardoned by Henry VIII. Red leather-clad armchairs, a forest of black beams and local real ales set the charming ambience, while the menu's broad range of pub dishes pleases all tastes and appetites. Starters range from roasted pepper and sweet potato soup, to fresh Manx kipper Florentine. Typical main courses are veal schnitzel with rösti potatoes and forestière sauce; and grilled fillet of Irish plaice with spinach and cream. Vegetarians are also well catered for.

Open all wk 12-3 5-11 **Food** Lunch 12-2 Dinner 6-9 ⊕ FREE HOUSE ◢ Stonehouse Station Bitter. ♥ 10 **Facilities** Non-diners area ♣ (Bar Garden) ♦ Children's menu Children's portions Garden ⋒ Parking WiFi ⛟ (notice required)

NORTON   Map 10 SJ70

The Hundred House ★★★★ INN ◉◉ **PICK OF THE PUBS**

tel: 01952 580240 **Bridgnorth Rd TF11 9EE**
email: reservations@hundredhouse.co.uk **web:** www.hundredhouse.co.uk
dir: *On A442, 6m N of Bridgnorth, 5m S of Telford centre*

Award-winning pub with quirky features

Lapped by astonishing gardens, this creeper-clad old Shropshire brick inn dates in part to the 14th century. From its village location, lanes and paths filter down through verdant countryside into the depths of the Severn Gorge. It's from the same countryside that the land-based ingredients for the two AA-Rosette menu overseen by Stuart Philips are garnered. Order a glass of local microbrewery beer and relax in the warren of lavishly decorated bars and dining rooms, replete with quarry-tiled floors, exposed brickwork, beamed ceilings and Jacobean oak panelling. Both à la carte and specials menus are rich in fish and game choices to accompany a starter like griddled scallops with risotto cake and stir-fry vegetables. Then lightly smoked, walnut- and sage-stuffed pheasant breast with orange and red wine sauce is typical fare; or parsley-crusted hake fillet, butterbeans and sautéed chorizo. Memorable, antique-rich accommodation is the icing on the cake here.

Open all day all wk 10am-11pm Closed 25 Dec eve **Food** Lunch all wk 12-2.30 Dinner all wk 6-9.30 Av main course £18.95 Restaurant menu available all wk ⊕ FREE HOUSE ◢ Ironbridge, Three Tuns, Ludlow, Big Shed Engineers Best ♂ Westons Old Rosie. ♥ 10 **Facilities** Non-diners area ♣ (Bar Garden) ♦ Children's menu Children's portions Family room Garden ⋒ Parking WiFi ⛟ (notice required) **Rooms** 9

OSWESTRY   Map 15 SJ22

The Bradford Arms

tel: 01691 830582 **Llanymynech SY22 6EJ**
email: robinbarsteward@tesco.net
dir: *5.5m S of Oswestry on A483 in Llanymynech*

Tip-top ales at a Welsh Borders pub

Once part of the Earl of Bradford's estate, between Oswestry and Welshpool, this 17th-century coaching inn is ideally situated for golfing, fishing and walking. It is well known as a community pub serving first-class real ales. Eating in the spotless, quietly elegant bar, dining rooms and conservatory is a rewarding experience, with every taste catered for. For lunch try beef Stroganoff; or chilli con carne; while a typical dinner menu features hunter's chicken; lamb casserole; or pork medallions.

Open all wk 11.30-3 5-12 **Food** Lunch all wk 11.30-2 Dinner all wk 5.30-9 Set menu available Restaurant menu available all wk ⊕ FREE HOUSE ◢ Black Sheep Best Bitter, 2 guest ales ♂ Westons Stowford Press. **Facilities** Non-diners area ♣ (Bar Outside area) ♦ Children's menu Children's portions Outside area ⋒ Parking WiFi ⛟ (notice required)

PAVE LANE   Map 10 SJ71

The Fox

tel: 01952 815940 **TF10 9LQ**
email: fox@brunningandprice.co.uk
dir: *1m S of Newport, just off A41*

Grand Edwardian pub offering Shropshire ales

Behind The Fox's smart exterior are spacious rooms and little nooks wrapped around a busy central bar, where there is an original wooden fireplace, and plenty of Shropshire real ales demanding attention. The menu offers sandwiches and light meals (crab linguine, wild mushrooms on toast), as well as smoked haddock and salmon fishcakes, steak and ale pie, Malaysian fish stew, or braised lamb shoulder with dauphinoise potatoes. Enjoy the gently rolling countryside and wooded hills from the lovely south-facing terrace with its patio tables and large grassy area.

Open all day all wk 11-11 (Sun 11-10.30) **Food** Lunch all day Dinner all day ⊕ FREE HOUSE/BRUNNING & PRICE ◢ Wood's Shropshire Lad, Titanic Mild, Holden's Golden Glow, Three Tuns XXX, Purple Moose Snowdonia. ♥ 12 **Facilities** Non-diners area ♣ (Bar Garden) ♦ Children's menu Children's portions Play area Garden ⋒ Beer festival Cider festival Parking WiFi

PORTH-Y-WAEN
Map 15 SJ22

NEW The Lime Kiln

tel: 01691 839599 **SY10 8LX**
email: info@limekilnoswestry.co.uk
dir: *From Oswestry take A483 towards Welshpool. Right at Llynclys x-roads. Pub on right opposite Chads garage*

Last pub in England, first in Wales

Below a wooded hillside stands this unassuming white-painted pub, with padded stools lining the counter in the homely bar, and cushioned wooden settles and leather sofas offering more relaxing seating. With Wales so close, expect Welsh real ales, such as Monty's Moonrise and Purple Moose Snowdonia, with Six Bells Back to Basics waving the Union Flag. Menu suggestions in the simply furnished dining area include Welsh Black fillet steak with braised shin of beef and béarnaise tartlet; wild Cornish sea bass with clam risotto; or pear and Perl Las cheese tart. Hidden in the undergrowth nearby are the old lime kilns.

Open 12-3 6-11 Closed Mon **Food** Lunch 12-2 Dinner 6-9 ⊞ FREE HOUSE ◀ Monty's Moonrise, Purple Moose Snowdonia, Six Bells Back to Basics Ŏ Dunkertons Premium Organic. **Facilities** Non-diners area ✿ (Bar Restaurant Garden) ⦿ Children's portions Garden ⋒ Parking WiFi ⛺ (notice required)

SHREWSBURY
Map 15 SJ41

The Boat House

tel: 01743 231658 **New St SY3 8JQ**
email: info@boathouseshrewsbury.co.uk **web:** www.boathouseshrewsbury.co.uk
dir: *From A458 & A488 rdbt (N of River Severn) follow A488 (Porthill & Bishops Castle). 1st left into New St. Pub on left by suspension footbridge*

Riverside ambience and serious Shropshire fare

Paths from the medieval heart of the town drift through Quarry Park and across a footbridge to this half-timbered retreat beside a great loop of the River Severn at Shrewsbury. Lounge on the huge riverside terrace or make a base in the beamed, rambling, airy interior where real ales from Shropshire's best microbreweries, including Three Tuns and Ludlow Gold should delight the most discerning beer-lover. Dishes from the grill are specialities of the house, using meats with a largely Welsh Marches provenance. Otherwise perhaps start with ham hock and pea terrine with piccalilli purée; or wild mushroom and thyme soup, then tuck into steak and ale pie, sauté curly kale, peas and carrots; and finish with lemon posset and raspberry sorbet.

Open all day all wk **Food** Lunch Mon-Fri 12-2.30, Sat 12-10, Sun 12-9 Dinner Mon-Fri 6-10, Sat 12-10, Sun 12-9 ⊞ ENTERPRISE INNS ◀ Salopian Shropshire Gold, Three Tuns, Wood's Shropshire Lad, Purity Mad Goose, Ludlow Gold. ⛾
Facilities ⦿ Children's portions Garden Outside area ⋒ Parking WiFi

Lion & Pheasant Hotel ★★★ TH ⓪⓪

tel: 01743 770345 **50 Wyle Cop SY1 1XJ**
email: info@lionandpheasant.co.uk **web:** www.lionandpheasant.co.uk
dir: *From S & E: pass abbey, cross river on English Bridge to Wyle Cop, hotel on left. From N & W: follow Town Centre signs onto one-way system to Wyle Cop. Hotel at bottom of hill on right*

Boutique hotel luxury in historic market town

The handsome façade of this family-owned hotel and free house graces medieval Wyle Cop, shortly before the street becomes English Bridge over the River Severn. A coolly elegant look is evident throughout, from the ground floor public areas to the spacious, well-equipped bedrooms upstairs. Just off the reception is the wood-floored café-style bar, which leads to the flagstoned Inglenook Bar, serving snacks and a full range of main meals. On the first floor is the split-level restaurant, where Cumbrian rose veal with onion soubise; seafood stew with spicy mussel and saffron sauce; and parmesan gnocchi help to maintain their two AA Rosette status.

Open all day all wk Closed 25-26 Dec **Food** Lunch 12-2.30 Dinner 6-9.30 Restaurant menu available Mon-Sat ⊞ FREE HOUSE ◀ Salopian Shropshire Gold, Guest ales Ŏ Robinsons, Westons Stowford Press. ⛾ 13 **Facilities** Non-diners area ⦿ Children's menu Children's portions Garden ⋒ Parking WiFi ⛺ (notice required) **Rooms** 22

The Mytton & Mermaid Hotel ★★★ HL PICK OF THE PUBS

tel: 01743 761220 **Atcham SY5 6QG**
email: reception@myttonandmermaid.co.uk **web:** www.myttonandmermaid.co.uk
dir: *M54 junct 7, follow Shrewsbury signs, at 2nd rdbt take 1st left signed Ironbridge & Atcham. In 1.5m hotel on right after bridge*

Attractive riverside coaching inn

The River Severn slides past the grounds of this substantial Georgian coaching inn. On one hand is the ancient stone church; on the other a stunning old bridge arching gracefully over the waters. From waterside benches and the grassy garden are restful views of this favoured corner of rural Shropshire. Equally Salopian are the beers stocked here, including Hobsons and Wood's ales. Dating from 1735, the inn is tastefully appointed throughout; the lovingly updated interior reflects the essence of long-past mail-coach days. There's a relaxed feel about the place, especially the bar which features a wood floor, scrubbed tables, comfy sofas and an open log fire. Dining opportunities make the most of the generous larder of the Marches. Local beef, ale and parsnip suet pudding is a comforting winter dish; or perhaps slow-cooked farm belly pork with Wenlock Edge black pudding and a bacon sauce will hit the spot. Smaller meals might include home-smoked breast of pigeon, and deli boards add further spice.

Open all day all wk 7am-11pm Closed 25 Dec **Food** Lunch all wk Brunch 9am-noon, Lunch 12-2.30, Afternoon 2.30-6 Dinner Mon-Sat 6-10, Sun 6-9 Av main course £14 ⊞ FREE HOUSE ◀ Wood's Shropshire Lad, Salopian Shropshire Gold, Hobsons Best Bitter, Wye Valley. ⛾ 12 **Facilities** Non-diners area ⦿ Children's menu Garden ⋒ Parking WiFi ⛺ (notice required) **Rooms** 16

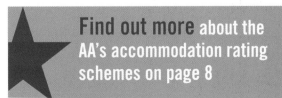

Find out more about the AA's accommodation rating schemes on page 8

SHREWSBURY *continued*

NEW The Prince of Wales

tel: 01743 343301 **30 Brynner St SY3 7NZ**
email: queenprince117@yahoo.co.uk
dir: *Phone pub for detailed directions*

Traditional food and award-winning local ales

Tucked down the back streets of Belle Vue in the heart of Shrewsbury, The Prince of Wales was taken over in 2013 by Victoria Price, who has restored this friendly pub to its former glory. A rotating choice of guest ales has already won the pub several awards and the commitment to real ale continues with February and May beer festivals. Enjoy your pint in the bar or the large sun-trap beer garden overlooking the local bowling green. The traditional food menu includes baguettes, ploughman's, pie of the day, home-made lasagne and local sausages, egg and chips.

Open 5pm-mdnt (Fri-Sun 12-12) Closed Lunch Mon-Thu **Food** Lunch Fri 12-2, Sun 12-2.30 Av main course £4.95 Set menu available ⊕ GRS INNS ◀ Salopian Golden Thread Ŏ Westons Rosie's Pig. ♛ 10 **Facilities** Non-diners area ❤ (Bar Garden) ♦♦ Children's menu Children's portions Garden ⚏ Beer festival Parking WiFi ☕ (notice required)

NEW The Stiperstones Inn

tel: 01743 791327 **SY5 0LZ**
email: inn@stiperstones.net
dir: *Phone pub for detailed directions*

Beautiful location for pub grub

Built in the mid-16th century, the Stiperstones has been a pub since the 1840s and is full of charm and character. Set in the heart of the south Shropshire hills, in an Area of Outstanding Natural Beauty, it's ideally placed for walking the Stiperstones Ridge or the Long Mynd. Afternoon tea is available as well as more traditional pub offerings. Local ales can be found in the two bars, and a comprehensive menu includes favourites such as salads and jacket potatoes, as well as steaks, curries and ribs; or try the steak and kidney pudding. For dessert don't miss the famous whinberry crumble.

Open all day all wk **Food** Lunch all wk 12-9 Dinner all wk 12-9 Av main course £6.95 ⊕ FREE HOUSE ◀ Wood's, Stonehouse, Hobson's, Three Tuns, Six Bells Ŏ Westons Stowford Press. **Facilities** Non-diners area ❤ (Bar Garden) ♦♦ Children's portions Garden ⚏ Parking WiFi ☕ (notice required)

Fighting Cocks

tel: 01746 718270 **1 High St DY14 8TZ**
email: sandrafc_5@hotmail.com
dir: *11m from Bridgnorth off B4376*

Deep-in-the-countryside pub and shop

According to a framed newspaper cutting on the pub wall, 'Nipper Cook' drank 30 pints of cider each night at this unassuming 18th-century rural free house. Today, this lively local hosts regular music nights, as well as an apple day each October and an annual beer festival in November. The menus change daily but expect home-made pâtés, curries, pies and puddings on the menu. The owners' neighbouring shop supplies local meats, home-made pies, sausages, and produce from the gardens.

Open 6pm-mdnt (Fri 5pm-1am Sat 12-12 Sun 12-10.30) Closed Mon (Oct-Mar) **Food** Lunch Sat-Sun 12-2.30 Dinner Tue-Sat 7-9 ⊕ FREE HOUSE ◀ Hobsons Best Bitter, Mild, Twisted Spire & Town Crier, Wye Valley HPA & Bitter, Ludlow Gold, Three Tuns XXX Ŏ Westons Stowford Press, Robinsons Flagon. **Facilities** Non-diners area ♦♦ Children's menu Children's portions Garden Outside area ⚏ Beer festival Parking WiFi

---

The Old Orleton Inn

tel: 01952 255011 **Holyhead Rd TF1 2HA**
email: aapub@theoldorleton.com
dir: *From M54 junct 7 take B5061 (Holyhead Rd), 400yds on left on corner of Haygate Rd & Holyhead Rd*

Grand views and wide-ranging menus

The old and new blend effortlessly throughout this 17th-century former coaching inn. Overlooking the famous Wrekin Hill, it is popular with walkers exploring the Shropshire countryside. Expect a relaxed and informal atmosphere, local Hobsons ales on tap and modern British food prepared from scratch. At lunch in the brasserie taking in soup, sandwiches, salad platters, chef's dish of the day and more. Evening choices include Bar Bites for a just a snack or three-course meals that might include pan-seared, 8oz Border county rib-eye steak; chef's pie of the day; or confit Gressingham duck leg.

Open 12-3 5-11 Closed 1st 2wks Jan, Sun eve **Food** Lunch Mon-Sat 12-2.30, Sun 12-4 Dinner Mon-Sat 6-9.30 Av main course £13 ⊕ FREE HOUSE ◀ Hobsons Best Bitter, Town Crier Ŏ Westons Stowford Press. ♛ 10 **Facilities** Non-diners area Garden ⚏ Parking WiFi ☕ (notice required)

The Crown Inn

tel: 01588 650613 **SY9 5EE**
dir: *From Shrewsbury A49 to Church Stretton, follow signs over Long Mynd to Asterton, right to Wentnor*

A lovely village pub set in a beautiful landscape

Deep amid the Shropshire Hills, this inviting 16th-century timbered inn is popular with walkers who warm themselves at wood-burning stoves in winter and on the outside decking in the summer; here you can sup Three Tuns bitter and gaze at the Long Mynd's lofty ridge. The pub's homely atmosphere, enhanced by beams and horse brasses, makes eating and drinking here a pleasure. Meals are served in the bar or separate restaurant; expect pub classics like garlic mushrooms and chicken balti with rice, chips and naan bread.

Open all day all wk **Food** Lunch all wk 12-9.30 Dinner all wk 12-9.30 ⊕ FREE HOUSE ◀ Brains The Rev. James, Hobsons Old Henry, Three Tuns, Wye Valley Butty Bach Ŏ Westons Scrumpy. ♛ 8 **Facilities** Non-diners area ❤ (Bar Garden) ♦♦ Children's menu Children's portions Play area Garden ⚏ Beer festival Parking WiFi ☕ (notice required)

Willeymoor Lock Tavern

tel: 01948 663274 **Tarporley Rd SY13 4HF**
dir: *2m N of Whitchurch on A49 (Warrington to Tarporley road)*

Canalside pub ideal for families and walkers

Watch narrow boats negotiating the lock from this much-extended former lock-keeper's cottage on the attractive and busy Llangollen Canal. In the bar, Shropshire Gold represents the county, teapots hang from low beams and there are open log fires. Competitively priced food includes plenty of fish and veggie dishes, as well as pub classics and meats from the grill: rump, sirloin or T-bone steaks; gammon steaks; and surf 'n' turf. The children's play area and large beer garden make this an ideal warm weather location, and it's a popular refreshment spot for walkers exploring the nearby Sandstone Trail and the Bishop Bennett Way.

Open all wk 12-2.30 6-11 (Sun 12-2.30 6-10.30) Closed 25 Dec **Food** Lunch all wk 12-2 Dinner all wk 6-9 ⊕ FREE HOUSE ◀ Weetwood Eastgate Ale, Timothy Taylor Landlord, Greene King IPA, Morland Old Speckled Hen, Salopian Shropshire Gold, Stonehouse Ŏ Aspall, Westons. ♛ 9 **Facilities** Non-diners area ❤ (Bar Restaurant Garden) ♦♦ Children's menu Play area Garden Outside area ⚏ Parking ☕ (notice required)

SOMERSET

ASHCOTT
Map 4 ST43

Ring O'Bells

tel: 01458 210232 **High St TA7 9PZ**

email: info@ringobells.com

dir: M5 junct 23 follow A39 & Glastonbury signs. In Ashcott turn left, at post office follow church & village hall signs

Traditional family-run village free house

Successfully run by the same family for more than 25 years, this independent free house dates in parts from 1750, and the interior reflects this with beams, split-level bars, an old fireplace and a collection of bells and horse brasses. The pub is close to the Somerset Levels, the RSPB reserve at Ham Wall and the National Nature Reserve at Shapwick Heath. Local ales and ciders are a speciality, while all food is made on the premises. Expect good-value dishes and daily specials such as cream of broccoli soup; liver braised in cider with sage and apples; and steak, ale and black pudding pie. Treat yourself to an ice cream sundae or raspberry, white chocolate and Amaretto roulade.

Open all wk 12-2.30 7-11 (Sun 12-2.30 7-10.30) **Food** Lunch all wk 12-2 Dinner all wk 7-10 Av main course £10 Set menu available ⊕ FREE HOUSE ◀ Rotating local guest ales Ö Wilkins Farmhouse, The Orchard Pig. ♥ 8 **Facilities** Non-diners area ♣ (Bar Garden) ⬥ Children's menu Children's portions Play area Garden ⋒ Parking WiFi ⬛ (notice required)

ASHILL
Map 4 ST31

Square & Compass ★★★★ INN

tel: 01823 480467 **Windmill Hill TA19 9NX**

email: squareandcompass@tiscali.co.uk **web:** www.squareandcompasspub.com

dir: Exit A358 at Stewley Cross service station onto Wood Rd. 1m to pub in Windmill Hill

Friendly rural pub with high-quality accommodation

Beautifully located overlooking the Blackdown Hills, this traditional family-owned country pub has been a labour of love for owners Chris and Janet Slow for over 17 years. A warm and friendly atmosphere pervades the bar with its hand-made settles and tables. Exmoor and St Austell ales head the refreshments list, while reasonably priced and freshly made meals are prepared in the state-of-the-art kitchen. In addition to classic pub dishes, grills and omelettes, the chef's specials may tempt with sea bass fillets, crushed new potatoes with tomato and basil vinaigrette; and breast of duck with wild berry sauce. The inn offers AA rated accommodation, and the barn next door hosts weddings and regular live music.

Open 12-3 6.30-late (Sun 7-late) Closed 25-26 Dec, Tue-Thu L **Food** Lunch Fri-Mon 12-2 Dinner all wk 7-9.30 Av main course £8.95 ⊕ FREE HOUSE ◀ St Austell Tribute & Trelawny, Exmoor Ö Burrow Hill. **Facilities** Non-diners area ♣ (Bar Garden) ⬥ Children's menu Children's portions Garden ⋒ Parking WiFi **Rooms** 8

AXBRIDGE
Map 4 ST45

Lamb Inn

tel: 01934 732253 **The Square BS26 2AP**

dir: 10m from Wells & Weston-Super-Mare on A370

Plenty of pub favourites at this old inn

Under new ownership since June 2014, parts of this rambling 15th-century building were once the guildhall, but it became an inn in 1830. The bars are heated by log fires and offer Butcombe ales; there's also a skittle alley and large terraced garden. All the food is home made, ranging from pan-seared monkfish to hand-made burgers, with jacket potatoes and fish finger sandwiches offering a lighter option. Opposite is the medieval King John's Hunting Lodge, so christened in 1905 by an owner who chose to ignore the fact that John had died over two centuries before it was built.

Open all day all wk 11-3 6-11 (Thu-Sat 11am-11.30pm Sun 12-10.30) **Food** Lunch Mon-Sat 12-2.30, Sun 12-6 Dinner Mon-Thu 6-9, Fri-Sat 6-9.30 Av main course £9 ⊕ BUTCOMBE ◀ Bitter, Guest ales Ö Thatchers Cheddar Valley, Ashton Press. ♥ 10 **Facilities** Non-diners area ♣ (Bar Garden) ⬥ Children's menu Children's portions Garden ⋒ WiFi ⬛ (notice required)

BABCARY
Map 4 ST52

Red Lion ★★★★ INN

tel: 01458 223230 **TA11 7ED**

email: redlionbabcary@btinternet.com **web:** www.redlionbabcary.co.uk

dir: NE of Yeovil. Follow Babcary signs from A303 or A37

Pretty pub with a great range of food

Rich colour-washed walls, heavy beams and simple wooden furniture characterise this beautifully appointed, thatched free house. The bar offers a great selection of real ales, and you can dine there, in the restaurant or in the garden. The daily menus run from pub favourites such as steak and kidney suet pudding or chargrilled steak with all the trimmings through to pan-roast cod loin, cauliflower purée, beef cheek croquettes and watercress pesto; and whole roast red-legged partridge, crispy bacon, champ mash, curly kale and red wine jus. All bread is baked on the premises and local suppliers are used as much as possible – they have a 24-hour 'port to plate' policy for the fish that's supplied from Brixham.

Open all wk 12-3 6-12 **Food** Lunch all wk 12-2.30 Dinner Mon-Sat 7-9.30 ⊕ FREE HOUSE ◀ Teignworthy, Otter, Bays, Yeovil Ales Ö Thatchers, Lilley's. ♥ 12 **Facilities** Non-diners area ♣ (Bar Garden) ⬥ Children's portions Play area Garden ⋒ Parking WiFi ⬛ **Rooms** 6

BATH
Map 4 ST76

The Blathwayt Arms

tel: 01225 421995 **Lansdown BA1 9BT**

email: info@blathwaytarms.co.uk **web:** www.blathwaytarms.co.uk

dir: 2m N of Bath, next to Bath Racecourse

Classic country pub, traditional fare, interesting ales

Named after William Blathwayt, the 17th-century politician who established the War Office as an official government department. Blathwayt effectively became the country's first Minister for War; his National Trust country house a few miles from the pub is known for its deer park. With its welcoming approach to dogs, children and muddy boots, this is a proper pub serving anything from a pint of Otter to a plate of Blathwayt Czech beef goulash. Mulled wine is supped around log fires in winter, while barbecues in summer are prepared in the large garden, which has a children's play area and overlooks Bath Racecourse.

Open all day all wk **Food** Lunch Mon-Thu 12-9, Fri-Sat 12-9.30, Sun 12-6 Dinner Mon-Thu 12-9, Fri-Sat 12-9.30 Restaurant menu available all wk ⊕ FREE HOUSE/ HEARTSTONE INNS LTD ◀ Otter Bitter, Butcombe Bitter Ö Westons Wyld Wood. ♥ 9 **Facilities** Non-diners area ♣ (Bar Garden) ⬥ Children's menu Children's portions Play area Garden ⋒ Parking WiFi

BATH *continued*

The Chequers ⊛⊛

tel: 01225 360017 **50 Rivers St BA1 2QA**
email: info@thechequersbath.com **web:** www.thechequersbath.com
dir: *In city centre, near Royal Crescent & The Circus*

Smart city gastro-pub

A beautifully appointed gastro-pub that's been serving customers since sedan-chair carriers first quenched their thirst here in 1776. A short walk from The Circus and the Royal Crescent, The Chequers' reputation for excellent ales and great food has made it a firm favourite with city locals and visitors alike; booking is advisable. The upstairs restaurant has the look and feel of the ground floor rooms; a large window into the kitchen introduces an air of modern theatricality to the enjoyment of such dishes as lamb Scotch egg with Jerusalem artichoke and mint vinaigrette, or pigeon pie with chips.

Open all day all wk 12-11 Closed 25 Dec **Food** Lunch Mon-Sat 12-2.30, Sun 12-6 Dinner Mon-Sat 6-9.30 Restaurant menu available all wk ⊕ ENTERPRISE INNS ◀ Butcombe Bitter, Bath Ales Gem ♂ Westons Wyld Wood Organic, Addlestones, Symonds Founders Reserve. ☗ 26 **Facilities** ◀ Children's portions Outside area ⋒ WiFi ▭ (notice required)

The Garricks Head

tel: 01225 318368 **7-8 St John's Place BA1 1ET**
email: info@garricksheadpub.com
dir: *Adjacent to Theatre Royal. Follow Theatre Royal brown tourist signs*

City centre pub with a dining room and outside terrace

Once the home of Beau Nash, the celebrated dandy who put the spa city on the map, The Garricks Head is named after 18th-century theatrical powerhouse David Garrick, and is adjacent to the Theatre Royal, for whose customers it provides pre-show dining facilities. The bar has a lot to commend it: a selection of natural wines from Europe, four real ales, Somerset ciders, and the largest selection of single malt whiskies in Bath. The food, locally sourced as far as possible, includes pub classics such as steak and chips, and a ploughman's, while the carte features pork rillettes and pickled vegetables; a rabbit dish of loin and cottage pie with creamed leek purée and purple sprouting broccoli; and sticky toffee pudding with double cream.

Open all day all wk Closed 25-26 Dec **Food** Lunch Mon-Sat 12-3, Sun 12-4 Dinner Mon-Sat 5.30-10, Sun 5.30-9 Av main course £11 Set menu available Restaurant menu available all wk ⊕ FREE HOUSE ◀ Otter Bitter, Palmers, Milk Street Funky Monkey ♂ Honey's Midford Cider, Broadoak Kingston Black. ☗ 20
Facilities Non-diners area ♨ (All areas) ◀ Children's menu Children's portions Garden Outside area ⋒ WiFi ▭ (notice required)

The Hare & Hounds ⊛

tel: 01225 482682 **Lansdown Rd BA1 5TJ**
email: info@hareandhoundsbath.com **web:** www.hareandhoundsbath.com
dir: *Phone for detailed directions*

Visit for the view, stay to eat and drink

Only a mile from Bath city centre, The Hare & Hounds sits high on Lansdown Hill with stunning views over the valley to Solsbury Hill. Happily the feast for the eyes extends to the pub's food and drink — so tarry awhile with an eponymous pint of ale or one of over 30 wines served by the glass. The welcome is warm, the staff and service friendly, and the food unpretentiously good. In summer the terrace is much sought after for alfresco dining as you'd expect; typical dishes are cod and crab fishcakes with pineapple salsa; chargrilled pork chop with bacon, potato fondant and cabbage; and rhubarb and Madeira doughnut with white chocolate.

Open all day all wk Open from 8.30am every day **Food** Contact pub for food times Restaurant menu available all wk ⊕ STAR PUBS ◀ St Austell Tribute, Caledonian Hare & Hounds (pub's own) ♂ Symonds. ☗ 31 **Facilities** Non-diners area ♨ (Bar Restaurant Garden) ◀ Children's menu Children's portions Play area Garden ⋒ Parking WiFi ▭ (notice required)

PICK OF THE PUBS

The Marlborough Tavern ⬡⬡

BATH — Map 4 ST76

tel: 01225 423731
35 Marlborough Buildings BA1 2LY
email: info@marlborough-tavern.com
web: www.marlborough-tavern.com
dir: *200mtrs from the western end of the Royal Crescent*

Agreeable hostelry well placed for Bath's best attractions

Just round the corner from the famous Royal Crescent, this 18th-century pub once refreshed foot-weary sedan-chair carriers. Today's clientele is more likely to need a break from the rigours of traipsing around Bath's shops, for which the Marlborough is handily placed. The interior is contemporary yet retro, with an abundance of mismatched chairs, sturdy solid wood tables and scrubbed floorboards. At the rear is a walled and trellised courtyard terrace, a secluded little spot ideal for whiling away a warm summer's evening. Butcombe and Box Steam Brewery's Piston Broke are the prime ales dispensed in the spotless bar, with Orchard Pig cider also very popular; the wine selection comprising 26 sold by the glass offers something for everyone. The lunch menu pleases too by not straying far from popular and traditional pub classics, such as Cornish haddock in Piston Broke batter with triple cooked chips, mushy peas and tartare. Other light bites range from sandwiches served with fries and salad; a venison

and beefburger with caramelised red onion and winter slaw; to Thai curried carrot soup with vegetable pakoras. This is one of the starters on the excellent value set lunch menu, which could be followed by Exmouth mussels in a cider, sage and smoked bacon sauce; conclude sweetly with a mocha brûlée served with chocolate biscotti and hazelnut cream. A typical three-course dinner may start with a trio of Brixham crab – crab bisque, chilli crab cake with salsa, and crab rillettes on toast with crab mayonnaise. Next may come a slow-cooked beef shin and ox kidney pudding, with pan-seared fillet, horseradish mash, squash purée, purple sprouting broccoli and confit shallots. Finish with a dark and white chocolate brownie with vanilla ice cream.

Open all day all wk 8am-11pm (Sat-Sun 9am-11pm) **Food** Lunch all wk 12-3 Dinner all wk 6-9.30 Set menu available Restaurant menu available all wk
⊕ FREE HOUSE ◖ Butcombe Bitter, Box Steam Piston Broke Ŏ The Orchard Pig.
🍷 26 **Facilities** Non-diners area
👫 Children's menu Children's portions Garden 🪑 WiFi 🚐 (notice required)

BATH *continued*

The Hop Pole
PICK OF THE PUBS

tel: 01225 446327 **7 Albion Buildings, Upper Bristol Rd BA1 3AR**
email: hoppole@bathales.co.uk
dir: *On A4 from city centre towards Bristol. Pub opposite Royal Victoria Park*

An oasis of calm plus top notch beer and food

Just off the River Avon towpath, opposite Royal Victoria Park, sits this delightful pub. Described as both a country pub in the heart of a city, and as a secret oasis, it has a stripped-down, stylish interior and a spacious beer garden with a grapevine canopy. Bath Ales supplies many beers from its stable — here you'll find Barnsey, Gem and Special Pale Ale. All food is home cooked, from the bar snacks to the main meals such as River Fowey mussels with cider and saffron sauce; honey and clove ham hock, piccalilli and cauliflower cheese; grilled cod with chorizo and haricot cassoulet; and grilled vegetable tart with rocket, parmesan shavings and potato salad. Children can be served smaller portions from the main menu.

Open all day all wk 12-11 (Fri-Sat 12-12) **Food** Lunch Mon-Sat 12-9.30, Sun 12-8 Dinner Mon-Sat 12-9.30, Sun 12-8 Set menu available ⊕ BATH ALES ◀ Gem, Special Pale Ale & Barnsey, Guest ales ♂ Bath Ciders Bounders & Traditional. ♥ 16 **Facilities** Non-diners area ♣ (Bar Garden Outside area) ♦ Children's menu Children's portions Garden Outside area ⊨ WiFi ▦ (notice required)

King William
PICK OF THE PUBS

tel: 01225 428096 **36 Thomas St BA1 5NN**
email: info@kingwilliampub.com
dir: *At junct of Thomas St & A4 (London Rd), on left from Bath towards London. 15 mins' walk from Bath Spa rail station*

Modern British cooking and well-kept local ales

A short stroll from the city centre on a busy main road, this unassuming Bath stone building offers a happy mix of destination dining inn and locals' pub. In the cosy snug and traditional bar, real ale buffs will generally find a regular Palmers ale, supplemented by guest beers from local microbreweries such as Stonehenge, Milk Street and Yeovil. The kitchen creates traditional dishes, with a contemporary twist, from locally produced seasonal ingredients. The bar menu offers lighter dishes such as a ploughman's or a good beef, pickle and horseradish sandwich, but serious diners will seek out the inspiring daily-changing menu served in the elegant upstairs dining room. A starter of white onion and cider soup, Bertinet bread might precede a main course of slow-cooked lamb belly, creamed potato, spiced carrot purée, roast turnip and thyme sauce. Upside down rhubarb cake is one highly comforting end to an evening, matched by a carefully chosen wine list.

Open all wk 12-3 5-close (Sat-Sun 12-close) Closed 25-26 Dec **Food** Lunch all wk 12-3 Dinner Mon-Sat 6-10, Sun 6-9 Av main course £11 Set menu available Restaurant menu available all wk ⊕ FREE HOUSE ◀ Stonehenge Danish Dynamite, Palmers Dorset Gold, Milk Street Funky Monkey, Yeovil Ales Star Gazer ♂ Pheasant Plucker, Westons Wyld Wood Organic, The Orchard Pig, Honey's Midford Cider. ♥ 14 **Facilities** Non-diners area ♣ (Bar) ♦ Children's portions WiFi ▦ (notice required)

The Marlborough Tavern ◉◉
PICK OF THE PUBS

See Pick of the Pubs on page 427

The Star Inn

tel: 01225 425072 **23 Vineyards BA1 5NA**
email: landlord@star-inn-bath.co.uk
dir: *On A4, 300mtrs from centre of Bath*

The city's oldest pub offering ales from its only brewery

Set amid glorious Georgian architecture and first licensed in 1760, the impressive Star Inn is one of Bath's oldest pubs and is of outstanding historical interest, with

a rare and totally unspoiled interior. Original features in the four drinking areas include 19th-century Gaskell and Chambers bar fittings, a barrel lift from the cellar, and even complimentary pinches of snuff found in tins in the smaller bar. Long famous for its pints of Bass served from the jug, these days Abbey Ales from Bath's only brewery are also popular. Fresh filled rolls are available and free snacks on Sundays. A beer festival focusing on Cornish beers is held twice a year.

Open all wk 12-2.30 5.30-12 (Fri-Sat noon-1am Sun 12-12) **Food** Contact pub for food times ⊕ PUNCH TAVERNS ◀ Abbey Bellringer, Bath Star, Twelfth Night & White Friar, Bass ♂ Abbey Ales Hells Bells. **Facilities** Non-diners area ♣ (Bar Restaurant) ♦ Beer festival WiFi ▦

■ BAWDRIP   Map 4 ST33

The Knowle Inn

tel: 01278 683330 **TA7 8PN**
email: toby@theknowleinn.co.uk
dir: *M5 junct 23 or A39 from Bridgwater towards Glastonbury*

A true community pub with amazing views

This 16th-century pub on the A39 sits beneath the Polden Hills and has far-reaching views across Sedgemoor to the Quantocks and Blackdown Hills. The live music, skittles and darts are popular with locals, while the seafood specials and Mediterranean-style garden attract visitors from further afield for summer alfresco meals. A full range of sandwiches and light meals is backed by pub favourites such as creamy garlic mushrooms; deep-fried plaice fillet; celery and cashew nut roast; smoked haddock with cheese and tomato topping; grilled steak with all the trimmings; and Malteser cheesecake.

Open all day all wk **Food** Lunch all wk 11-2.30 Dinner all wk 6-9 ⊕ ENTERPRISE INNS ◀ Otter, Guest ales ♂ Thatchers. **Facilities** Non-diners area ♣ (Bar Garden) ♦ Children's menu Children's portions Garden ⊨ Parking WiFi ▦ (notice required)

■ BECKINGTON   Map 4 ST85

Woolpack Inn ★★★★ INN

tel: 01373 831244 **BA11 6SP**
email: 6534@greeneking.co.uk **web:** www.oldenglish.co.uk
dir: *Just off A36 near junct with A361*

Former coaching inn with smart interior

This charming, stone-built coaching inn dates back to the 1500s. Standing in the middle of the village and a short drive from Bath, inside there's an attractive, flagstone floor in the bar and outside at the back, a delightful terraced garden. The menu offers sandwiches, jacket potatoes, burgers, steaks and dishes such as beef and ale pie; breaded scampi tails; and slow-cooked lamb shank. The evening menu is extensive. Twelve en suite bedrooms, including one four-poster room and one family room, are available.

Open all day all wk 11-11 (Sun 11-10) **Food** Lunch Mon-Fri 12-3, Sat-Sun 12-10 Dinner Mon-Fri 6-10, Sat-Sun 12-10 Set menu available ⊕ OLD ENGLISH INNS & HOTELS ◀ Greene King IPA, Butcombe, Guest ale ♂ Thatchers, Rekorderlig. ♥ 14 **Facilities** Non-diners area ♣ (Bar Garden) ♦ Children's menu Children's portions Garden Parking WiFi ▦ **Rooms** 12

■ BISHOP SUTTON   Map 4 ST55

The Red Lion

tel: 01275 333042 **Sutton Hill BS39 5UT**
email: redlionbishopsutton@aol.com
dir: *Between Pensford & Clutton on A37 take A368 to Bishop Sutton*

Innovative seasonal dishes in village pub

Duncan Ferguson has quickly built up a sound reputation at The Red Lion; many visitors are comment on its friendliness, the efficiency of its staff and how much they enjoy eating and drinking here. In the bar, Bath Ales Gem single-handedly raises the flag for Somerset. The menus offer choices such as chicken liver pâté with pear and date chutney on brioche; or Somerset Brie salad to start, followed by Jardaloo Boti (slowly braised lamb shank with apricots); gnocchi dumplings, salmon, broccoli florets and white wine cream sauce; or wild mushroom pie with roast potatoes, curly kale and garden peas. Game dishes, based on whatever's bagged on local shoots, crop up too.

Open all wk 12-2.30 4.30-11 (Fri-Sun 12-12 Mon 4.30-11) **Food** Contact pub for food times Set menu available ⊕ PUNCH TAVERNS ◀ Courage Best Bitter, Fuller's London Pride, Sharp's Doom Bar, Bath Ales Gem Ö Thatchers Dry & Gold. ♀ **Facilities** Non-diners area ☙ (All areas) ♦ Children's portions Play area Garden Outside area ⌕ Beer festival Parking WiFi ▭ (notice required)

■ **BISHOPSWOOD**   Map 4 ST21

Candlelight Inn

tel: 01460 234476 **TA20 3RS**
email: info@candlelight-inn.co.uk
dir: From A303 SW of Newtown, right a x-roads signed Bishopswood & Churchinford. Pub on right in village

Remote pub with excellent food

Debbie Lush and Tom Warren run this rustic rural local tucked away deep in the Blackdown Hills. A 17th-century flint-built inn with wooden floors, crackling log fires and a warm and friendly atmosphere, locals gather here for tip-top pints of Exmoor or Branscombe ale drawn straight from the cask. Food will not disappoint, with everything made on the premises, including vegetables grown in the pub's garden. Follow creamy cauliflower soup or devilled lamb's kidney on toast with venison haunch with mash and vegetables, plaice fillets with brown crab mousse, or smoked cheddar and leek cannelloni, leaving room for sticky toffee pudding with toffee sauce and double cream.

Open 12-3 6-11 (Sun all day) Closed 25-27 Dec, Mon **Food** Lunch Tue-Fri 12-2, Sat-Sun 12-2.30 Dinner Tue-Thu & Sun 7-9, Fri-Sat 7-9.30 Set menu available ⊕ FREE HOUSE ◀ Otter Bitter, Bass, Exmoor, Branscombe Ö Thatchers, Sheppy's, Tricky. ♀ 9 **Facilities** Non-diners area ☙ (Bar Garden) ♦ Children's portions Garden ⌕ Beer festival Parking WiFi ▭ (notice required)

■ **BLAGDON HILL**   Map 4 ST21

NEW The Blagdon Inn

tel: 01823 421296 **Honiton Rd TA3 7SG**
email: nigel@blagdoninn.co.uk **web:** www.blagdoninn.co.uk
dir: From Taunton, through Trull, over M5, to pub on right

On the edge of the Blackdown Hills

Standing well back from the road, this was The White Lion until 2014. Now, under its new name, landlord Nigel Capel raises some of the livestock and grows the fruit

and vegetables for chef Olivier Certain's tempting dishes. Provence-born Olivier serves the likes of South Coast pollock with chive and parmesan risotto cake, butternut squash and white wine cream sauce; venison stew with beetroot; crispy mussels with tartare sauce; pigeon breast with mash, greens, medlar jelly and candied walnuts; sea bream with salsa piccante and samphire; and beef shin and Otter Bitter pie with mash and kale. Somerset artist Camilla Clark's oils and watercolours are on display.

Open 12-3 5-11 (Sun 12-4) Closed Sun eve & Mon **Food** Lunch Tue-Sun 12-2.30 Dinner Tue-Sat 6-9 Restaurant menu available Tue-Sun ⊕ FREE HOUSE ◀ Butcome, Otter Bitter & Amber Ö Thatchers Gold, Katy, Rose, Red, Vintage, Old Rascal & Somerset Haze, Sheppy's. ♀ **Facilities** Non-diners area ☙ (Bar Restaurant Garden) ♦ Children's menu Children's portions Garden ⌕ Parking WiFi ▭ (notice required)

■ **CATCOTT**   Map 4 ST33

The Crown Inn

tel: 01278 722288 **1 The Nydon TA7 9HQ**
email: catcottcrownin@aol.com
dir: M5 junct 23, A39 towards Glastonbury. Turn left to Catcott

Venerable ale house with good home-cooked food

Originally a beer house serving local peat-cutters, this low-beamed, flagstoned pub in the Somerset levels is perhaps 400 years old. The winter log fire takes the chill off Bristol Channel winds; in summer the half-acre beer garden is great for families and sun worshippers. Food is plentiful, imaginative and home made; typical options include spicy battered chilli beef; lasagne; and cheesecake. Look out for specials such as fish pie au gratin; game casserole; or teriyaki belly pork. A good range of cask ales and ciders from regional suppliers completes the picture.

Open 12-2.30 6-late Closed Mon L **Food** Lunch Tue-Sun 12-2 (booking advisable Sun) Dinner all wk 6-9 ⊕ FREE HOUSE ◀ Sharp's Doom Bar, St Austell Proper Job, Molegrip Core Ö Pheasant Plucker, Thatchers Gold. ♀ 10 **Facilities** Non-diners area ☙ (Bar Garden) ♦ Children's menu Children's portions Play area Garden ⌕ Parking WiFi ▭

■ **CHEW MAGNA**   Map 4 ST56

The Bear and Swan   **PICK OF THE PUBS**

tel: 01275 331100 **South Pde BS40 8SL**
email: thebearandswan@ohhcompany.co.uk
dir: A37 from Bristol. Turn right signed Chew Magna onto B3130. Or from A38 turn left on B3130

Much loved by locals and visitors alike

On the main street in the bustling village of Chew Magna, a short hop from Bristol Airport, this early 18th-century pub boasts a warm and friendly atmosphere. Inside, the oak-beamed rooms with scrubbed wooden floors and diverse collection of reclaimed tables, chairs and assorted artefacts all contribute to its charm. Fuller's London Pride takes pride of place at the bar alongside the more local Butcombe Bitter, real Somerset ciders and a list of well selected wines. The restaurant has a good choice of fish, game, seafood, meats and vegetarian dishes. You might choose to start with pan-fried scallops, butternut squash, chorizo and pea shoots before moving on to roast duck breast with garlic roasted celeriac, beetroot, carrots, spinach and plum chutney, or wild mushroom risotto. Home-made desserts like passion fruit cheesecake with raspberry sorbet hit the sweet spot. Look out for the spring/summer beer and cider festivals.

Open all day all wk 9am-mdnt Closed 24-25 Dec **Food** Lunch 9am-10pm Dinner 9am-10pm Av main course £10.50 Set menu available Restaurant menu available all wk ⊕ FULLER'S ◀ London Pride, Butcombe Bitter, Guest ale Ö Westons Stowford Press, Cornish Orchards. ♀ 12 **Facilities** Non-diners area ☙ (Bar Garden) ♦ Children's menu Children's portions Garden ⌕ Beer festival Cider festival Parking WiFi ▭ (notice required)

CHEW MAGNA continued

The Pony and Trap ◎◎

PICK OF THE PUBS

tel: 01275 332627 **Knowle Hill, Newton BS40 8TQ**
email: info@theponyandtrap.co.uk
dir: *Take A37 S from Bristol. After Pensford turn right at rdbt onto A368 towards Weston-Super-Mare. In 1.5m right signed Chew Magna & Winford. Pub 1m on right*

Country cottage pub-restaurant with award-winning cuisine

This 200-year-old building benefits from a stunning location, enjoying fantastic views across the Chew Valley. The Pony and Trap still feels like a rural local despite the acclaim it has achieved with its food. Committed to sourcing all ingredients as locally as possible, everything on the menu is made on the premises, right down to the bread and the butter. The menu changes twice daily, but just to give an idea, you might see chargrilled pigeon with bresaola, carrot, apple and walnut; or braised squid and turnip risotto; followed by pollock, chargrilled ox tongue, broccoli and Worcestershire butter sauce; or wild sea bass, curried cauliflower, yogurt, raisin and almond. After all that, let's hope there's still room for one of the unusual desserts: celeriac burnt cream, walnut mousse and quince sorbet; or apple, white chocolate cheesecake and apple sorbet. The six-course tasting menu with wine pairings is a real treat. Fine wines, local real ales and a local cider sum up its appeal.

Open all wk 12-3 6.30-12 (Sun all day) **Food** Lunch Mon-Sat 12-2.30, Sun 12-3.30 Dinner Sun-Thu 7-9.30, Fri-Sat 6-9.30 ⊕ FREE HOUSE ◀ Butcombe Bitter, Guest ale ♂ Ashton Press. ▼ 26 **Facilities** Non-diners area ♥ (Bar Garden) ♦ Children's portions Garden ⊓ Parking WiFi

CHURCHILL	Map 4 ST45

The Crown Inn

tel: 01934 852995 **The Batch BS25 5PP**
dir: *From Bristol take A38 S. Right at Churchill lights, left in 200mtrs, up hill to pub*

Rural village pub with lovely gardens

This gem of a pub was once a stop on what was then the Bristol to Exeter coach road. A good selection of real ales is served straight from the cask in the two flagstone-floored bars, where open fires blaze on cold days. The freshly prepared bar lunches include sandwiches, soups, salads and ploughman's, all made from the best local ingredients. In fact the beef comes straight from the fields that can be seen from the pub's windows. You can enjoy a meal in the beautiful gardens in warmer weather, perhaps beef casserole; chilli; or cauliflower cheese.

Open all day all wk 11-11 (Fri 11am-mdnt) **Food** Lunch all wk 12-2.30 ⊕ FREE HOUSE ◀ Palmers IPA, Bass, RCH Hewish IPA, Bath Ales Gem, St Austell Tribute, Butcombe, Otter, Guest ale ♂ Thatchers, Ashton Press, Healey's Cornish Rattler, Bath Ciders Bounders. **Facilities** Non-diners area ♥ (Bar) ♦ Children's portions Garden Outside area ⊓ Parking WiFi ▭ Notes ⊕

CLAPTON-IN-GORDANO	Map 4 ST47

The Black Horse

PICK OF THE PUBS

tel: 01275 842105 **Clevedon Ln BS20 7RH**
email: theblackhorse@talktalkbusiness.net
dir: *M5 junct 19, A369 to Portishead. At rdbt left onto B3124. At 3rd rdbt left to Clapton-in-Gordano*

Real ales, short lunchtime menu, families welcome

The bars on one of the windows of this attractive, whitewashed inn near Bristol are a reminder that the Black Horse's Snug Bar was once the village lock-up. Built in the 14th century, the traditional bar of this pub features low beams, flagstone floors, wooden settles, and old guns above the big open fireplace. Real ales served straight from the barrel include local Butcombe Bitter and Bath Ales Gem, whilst cider fans will rejoice at the sight of Thatchers Heritage & Dry. The small kitchen in this listed building limits its output to traditional pub food served lunchtimes only (Monday to Saturday). The repertoire includes hot and cold filled baguettes and

rolls; home-made soup of the day; pies and seasonal specials. The large rear garden includes a children's play area, and there's a separate family room.

Open all day all wk **Food** Lunch Mon-Sat 12-2.30 ⊕ ENTERPRISE INNS ◀ Courage Best Bitter, Bath Ales Gem, Butcombe Bitter, Exmoor Gold, Otter Bitter ♂ Thatchers Heritage & Dry. ▼ 8 **Facilities** Non-diners area ♥ (Bar) ♦ Play area Family room Garden Parking WiFi

CLUTTON	Map 4 ST65

The Hunters Rest ★★★★ INN

PICK OF THE PUBS

See Pick of the Pubs on opposite page

COMBE HAY	Map 4 ST75

The Wheatsheaf Combe Hay ★★★★ INN ◎

PICK OF THE PUBS

tel: 01225 833504 **BA2 7EG**
email: info@wheatsheafcombehay.co.uk web: www.wheatsheafcombehay.co.uk
dir: *From Bath take A369 (Exeter road) to Odd Down, left at Park & Ride & immediately right towards Combe Hay. 2m to thatched cottage, turn left*

Grab a table in the tranquil garden

The Wheatsheaf was built in 1576 as a farmhouse, but not until the 18th century did it begin its life as an alehouse, and today its old persona rubs shoulders companionably with the country-chic interior. A long, whitewashed free house with a pantiled roof, the pub stands on a peaceful hillside. The building is decorated with flowers in summer, when the gorgeous south-facing garden makes an ideal spot for outdoor drinking and dining. In the stylishly decorated, rambling bar with its massive wooden tables, sporting prints and open fires, the resident real ale is Butcombe Bitter. The garden is home to free-range chickens and ducks, blissfully unaware of the importance of their various contributions to the daily menus prepared by head chef, Eddy Rains, who is wholly committed to the use of the freshest seasonal ingredients.

Open 10.30-3 6-11 (Sun 11-5.30) Closed 25-26 Dec & 1st wk Jan, Sun eve, Mon (ex BHs) **Food** Lunch Tue-Sat 12-2 Dinner Tue-Sat 6.30-9 Set menu available Restaurant menu available Tue-Sat ⊕ FREE HOUSE ◀ Butcombe Bitter, Otter, Guest ale ♂ Thatchers, Honey's Midford Cider Honey & Daughter, Ashton Press. ▼ 13 **Facilities** Non-diners area ♥ (Bar Restaurant Garden) ♦ Children's menu Children's portions Garden ⊓ Parking WiFi **Rooms** 3

COMPTON DANDO	Map 4 ST66

The Compton Inn

tel: 01761 490321 **Court Hill BS39 4JZ**
email: paul@huntersrest.co.uk
dir: *From A368 between Chelwood & Marksbury follow Hunstrete & Compton Dando signs*

Confident cooking in a picturesque location

A former farmhouse, the Grade II listed Compton Inn has only been a pub since World War II, but it has been sympathetically restored. Located in picturesque Compton Dando, with its imposing church and hump-backed bridge crossing the River Chew, it is only a few miles from the bustling city of Bristol. It's an ideal bolt-hole to enjoy local ale and cider, and well-cooked dishes like duck breast, Cognac prunes, dauphinoise potatoes, vegetables and red wine sauce; or chicken, ham and mushroom oggy with sauté potatoes. For pudding try apple and blackberry crumble and custard.

Open all day all wk 12-11 (Sun-Mon 12-9.30) **Food** Lunch Mon-Sat 12-2.15, Sun 12-5 Dinner Mon-Sat 6.15-9.15 Av main course £12 Restaurant menu available all wk ⊕ PUNCH TAVERNS ◀ Bath Ales Gem, Sharp's Doom Bar, Butcombe Bitter ♂ Thatchers Traditional & Dry. ▼ 10 **Facilities** Non-diners area ♥ (Bar Restaurant Garden) ♦ Children's menu Children's portions Garden ⊓ Parking WiFi ▭ (notice required)

PICK OF THE PUBS

The Hunters Rest ★★★★ INN

CLUTTON　　　　Map 4 ST65

tel: 01761 452303
King Ln, Clutton Hill BS39 5QL
email: info@huntersrest.co.uk
web: www.huntersrest.co.uk
dir: *On A37 follow signs for Wells through Pensford, at large rdbt left towards Bath, 100mtrs right into country lane, pub 1m up hill*

Traditional country inn with excellent views

Dating from 1750, The Earl of Warwick's former hunting lodge offers far-reaching views across the Cam Valley to the Mendip Hills and the Chew Valley towards Bristol. When the estate was sold in 1872, the building became a tavern serving the growing number of coal miners working in the area, but all the mines closed long ago and the place has been transformed into a popular and attractive inn. Paul Thomas has been running the place for more than 25 years, during which time he has established a great reputation for good home-made food, real ales – typically Butcombe, Bath Gem and Otter – and a well-stocked wine cellar. The menu includes warm chicken and bacon salad; coarse chicken liver pâté on warm granary toast; giant pastries called oggies, which might come with a variety of fillings, such as beef steak and Stilton, mixed smoked fish,

cauliflower cheese, and not for the faint hearted they say – the Welsh Dragon, casseroled beef with fiery chillies, peppers and tomatoes. Other dishes may include chilli burritos; and lamb's liver and bacon with onion gravy; and from the specials blackboard a selection of daily delivered, Brixham-landed sea bass and other fish; smoked duck and blood orange salad; beef steak kebab, garlic and chilli butter, lemon thyme rice and Greek salad; and game casserole with herb dumplings. Finish with a popular dessert such as blackcurrant cheesecake; Bakewell tart; or sticky toffee pudding. In summer you can sit out in the landscaped grounds, and if a longer visit is on the cards the inn has very stylish en suite bedrooms.

Open all day all wk **Food** all wk 12-9.45 🛢 FREE HOUSE 🍺 Bath Ales Gem, Otter Ale, Butcombe 🍎 Broadoak, Thatchers. 🍷 10 **Facilities** Non-diners area 🐾 (Bar Restaurant Garden) 👫 Children's menu Children's portions Play area Family room Garden Parking WiFi 🚌 (notice required) **Rooms** 5

CORTON DENHAM · Map 4 ST62

The Queens Arms ★★★★★ INN PICK OF THE PUBS

See Pick of the Pubs on opposite page

CRANMORE · Map 4 ST64

The Strode Arms

tel: 01749 880450 **BA4 4QJ**
email: info@thestrodearms.co.uk
dir: *S of A361, 3.5m E of Shepton Mallet, 7.5m W of Frome*

Country pub in pretty setting

The Strode Arms sits opposite the duck pond in the centre of the ancient village of Cranmore, close to the market towns of Frome and Shepton Mallet. This stone-built 18th-century inn is packed with character, with an open fire in winter and a sun-trap front terrace in the warmer months. Wherever you sit, it makes for a relaxed setting to enjoy local Wadworth ales and Thatchers Gold cider. Food is served lunch and dinner, with home-made pies and chilli con carne sitting alongside more creative dishes such as confit duck leg or chicken stuffed with blue cheese.

Open all wk 11.30-3 6-11 **Food** Lunch 11.30-2.30 Dinner Mon-Sat 6-9 Av main course £10 Set menu available Restaurant menu available all wk ⊕ WADWORTH ◾ Horizon, Henry's Original IPA, 6X, The Bishop's Tipple, Strong in the Arm & Swordfish Ô Thatchers Gold, Westons Old Rosie. **Facilities** Non-diners area ❤ (Bar Restaurant Garden) ⦁⧊ Children's menu Children's portions Play area Family room Garden ⌗ Parking WiFi ⛺ (notice required)

CREWKERNE · Map 4 ST40

The George Inn ★★★ INN

tel: 01460 73650 **Market Square TA18 7LP**
email: georgecrewkerne@btconnect.com **web:** www.thegeorgehotelcrewkerne.co.uk
dir: *Phone for detailed directions*

400 years of hospitality in busy market town

Situated in the heart of Crewkerne, The George has been welcoming travellers since 1541, though the present hamstone building dates from 1832, and the current landlord has held sway since 1994. Thatchers Gold cider sits alongside the real ales in the bar, while the kitchen produces an array of popular dishes for bar snacks and more substantial meals from the daily specials board. Vegetarian and vegan meals are always available. Comfortable en suite bedrooms are traditionally styled and include four-poster rooms.

Open all day all wk **Food** Lunch all wk 12-2 Dinner all wk 7-9 Restaurant menu available all wk ⊕ FREE HOUSE ◾ St Austell Trelawny, Exmoor Ales Ô Thatchers Gold. ⬤ 8 **Facilities** Non-diners area ⦁⧊ Children's menu Children's portions Outside area ⌗ WiFi ⛺ Rooms 13

The Manor Arms

tel: 01460 72901 **North Perrott TA18 7SG**
email: bookings@manorarms.net
dir: *From A30 (Yeovil to Honiton) take A3066 towards Bridport. North Perrott 1.5m*

A bastion of tradition in the country

On the Dorset/Somerset border, this 16th-century Grade II listed pub and its neighbouring hamstone cottages overlook the green in the conservation village of North Perrott. The inn has been lovingly restored and an inglenook fireplace, flagstone floors and oak beams are among the charming features inside. Dogs and children are welcome, there's a good beer garden for warmer days, and there are plenty of rambling opportunities on the doorstep. To accompany ales like Butcombe, and Ashton Press cider, expect wholesome traditional food such as steak and ale pie, pan-fried lamb's liver and beer-battered cod. There is also a specials board, and every month sees a different theme night.

Open 12-2 6-11 Closed Sun eve **Food** Lunch all wk 12-2 Dinner Mon-Sat 6.30-9 ⊕ FREE HOUSE ◾ Butcombe, St Austell Trelawny, Fuller's London Pride Ô Ashton Press. **Facilities** Non-diners area ❤ (Bar Garden) ⦁⧊ Children's menu Children's portions Garden ⌗ Parking WiFi

CROSCOMBE · Map 4 ST54

The George Inn

tel: 01749 342306 & 345189 **Long St BA5 3QH**
email: pg@thegeorgeinn.co.uk
dir: *On A371 midway between Shepton Mallet & Wells*

Traditional food and two beer festivals

This 17th-century village pub is a great place to enjoy local ales such as Moor Revival in the bar with its real hops, large inglenook fireplace and family grandfather clock. There are real ciders too, including Orchard Pig and Thatchers Gold, and diners can enjoy locally sourced quality food, with daily specials complementing old favourites such as smoked haddock fishcakes; steak and ale pie; and local rump steaks. The garden terrace incorporates an all-weather patio and children's area next to a function room, skittle alley and wood-fired pizza oven. There are beer festivals on the Spring Bank Holiday (late May) and in October, and a curry buffet the last Thursday of each month.

Open all wk 11-3 6-11 (Fri 11-3 5-12 Sat 11am-mdnt Sun 11.30-11) **Food** Lunch Mon-Fri 12-2.30, Sat 12-9, Sun 12-8 Dinner Mon-Fri 6-9, Sat 12-9, Sun 12-8 Av main course £11 ⊕ FREE HOUSE ◾ Butcombe Bitter, Moor Revival, Blindmans, Hop Back Summer Lightning, Cheddar Ales Potholer Ô Thatchers Cheddar Valley & Gold, The Orchard Pig, Bittersweet. ⬤ 9 **Facilities** Non-diners area ❤ (Bar Garden) ⦁⧊ Children's menu Children's portions Play area Family room Garden ⌗ Beer festival Parking WiFi

DINNINGTON · Map 4 ST41

Dinnington Docks

tel: 01460 52397 **TA17 8SX**
email: hilary@dinningtondocks.co.uk
dir: *S of A303 between South Petherton & Ilminster*

Traditional locals' pub in a small hamlet

This traditional village pub on the old Fosse Way has been licensed for over 250 years and has no loud music, pool tables or fruit machines to drown out the conversation. Inside you will find pictures, signs and memorabilia of its rail and maritime past. Good-quality cask ales and farmhouse cider are served, and freshly prepared food including the likes of crab cakes, faggots, snapper, steak, and lamb shank for two feature on the menu. There's a carvery every Sunday, and the pub is located in an ideal place for cycling and walking.

Open all wk 11.30-3 6-12 (Fri-Sun all day) **Food** Lunch all wk 12-2 Dinner all wk 7-9 ⊕ FREE HOUSE ◾ Butcombe Bitter, Guest ales Ô Burrow Hill, Westons, Thatchers Gold. **Facilities** Non-diners area ❤ (Bar Garden) ⦁⧊ Children's menu Children's portions Play area Family room Garden ⌗ Parking ⛺

PICK OF THE PUBS

The Queens Arms ★★★★★ INN ◉◉

CORTON DENHAM   Map 4 ST62

tel: 01963 220317 **DT9 4LR**
email: *relax@thequeensarms.com*
web: *www.thequeensarms.com*
dir: *A303 follow signs for Sutton Montis, South Cadbury & Corton Denham. Through South Cadbury, 0.25m, left, up hill signed Corton Denham. Left at hill top to village, approx 1m. Pub on right*

Award-winning country inn serving special food

Three miles from Sherborne, this late 18th-century, stone-built former cider house is set in stunning countryside on the Somerset/Dorset border. Beneath the beams in the bar and separate dining room are old scrubbed tables set with stylish china, grand open fireplaces, and leather chairs and sofas. Outside, the sheltered terrace and sunny garden are perfect for outdoor eating and drinking. The bar proffers an excellent range of real ales, such as Exmoor's Fox and Stag, or Gyle 59 Toujours, and local farm ciders include one from the village. These are augmented by truly remarkable ranges of bottled beer, gin, malt whiskey and world spirits. The exemplary wine list includes eight champagnes and a 'Vaulted Treasures' selection special occasions. Owners Gordon and Jeanette Reid also champion high-quality local produce, measuring the distances their food has travelled in metres rather than in miles. The back of the menu illustrates just

how close to the inn some suppliers are. Settle in with a Bloody Mary accompanied by a Portland oyster with shallot and Sea Buckthorne vinegar; or take your choice from tapas options such as buttermilk and fennel pollen chicken goujons. Pan-roasted Lyme Bay scallops with tempura fried soft shell crab, salsa rossa and Serrano ham combine in a mouthwatering fusion of textures and flavours. Continue perhaps with pot-roasted partridge breast and leg sausage, with garlic roasted potatoes, chestnut purée, roasted baby parsnips and smoked pancetta. Desserts are variations on accepted combinations: cappuccino crème brûlée with pistachio biscotti, for example; or mulled cider poached pear with nutmeg ice cream and hazelnut clusters.

Open all day all wk **Food** Lunch all wk 12-3 Dinner Mon-Sat 6-10, Sun 6-9 Restaurant menu available all wk ⊕ FREE HOUSE ◄ Exmoor Ales, Gyle 59, Otter Ale, Bath Ales Gem, Guest ales ♂ Thatchers Gold, Hecks, Wilkins Farmhouse, Burrow Hill, The Orchard Pig. ♀ 14 **Facilities** Non-diners area ✿ (Bar Garden) ♦♦ Children's menu & portions Garden ⋔ Beer festival Parking WiFi **Rooms** 8

DITCHEAT
Map 4 ST63

The Manor House Inn
PICK OF THE PUBS

tel: 01749 860276 **BA4 6RB**
email: landlord@manorhouseinn.co.uk
dir: *From Shepton Mallet take A371 towards Castle Cary, in 3m turn right to Ditcheat*

Local ales complement fine food in lovely Mendips setting

In the pretty village of Ditcheat, between Shepton Mallet and Castle Cary, this handsome red-brick, 17th-century free house belonged to the lord of the manor about 150 years ago when it was known as the White Hart. Convenient for the Royal Bath and West Showground and the East Somerset Steam Railway, it is also boasts views of the Mendips. Flagstone floors and warming log fires in winter add to the charm of the friendly bar, which serves local Butcombe Bitter and regular guest ales, Orchard Pig ciders and up to nine wines by the glass. The seasonal menu may offer starters such as home-baked ratatouille with rich provençale sauce; and scallops in shells with lemon and lime dressing; followed by main courses of braised brisket of beef with creamy horseradish mash and rich Guinness sauce; or guinea fowl breast with spinach, fondant potato and Marsala sauce.

Open all day all wk Mon-Sat 12-11 (Sun 12-9) **Food** Lunch all wk 12-9 Dinner all wk 12-9 ⊕ FREE HOUSE ◀ Butcombe Bitter, Guest ales ♂ Ashton Press, The Orchard Pig Reveller & Philosopher. ♀ 9 **Facilities** Non-diners area ♦ Children's portions Garden ⋒ Parking WiFi ➡ (notice required)

DULVERTON
Map 3 SS92

The Bridge Inn

tel: 01398 324130 **20 Bridge St TA22 9HJ**
email: info@thebridgeinndulverton.com
dir: *M5 junct 27, A361 towards Barnstaple. In Tiverton take A396 signed Dulverton. Left onto B3222 to Dulverton. Pub by river in village*

Walkers' choice on the southern edge of Exmoor

'Chris from the pet shop up the road' supplies this early-Victorian pub with gravy bones for 'all those visiting dogs'. Indeed, well-behaved dogs are welcome, as is everyone seeking award-winning cask ales, worldwide craft beers, sensibly priced wines and traditional pub food. Classics include fish pie, home-cooked ham, egg and chips, and venison sausages with parsnip mash. Grazing plates of meats, and River Exe mussels are designed as both main courses or for sharing. Check out the pies too. A beer festival is held over the Spring Bank Holiday (late May).

Open all wk 12-11 summer (Mon 12-3 Tue-Thu 12-3 6-11 Fri-Sun 12-11 winter) Closed 25 Dec **Food** Lunch all wk 12-2.30 Dinner all wk 6-9 ⊕ FREE HOUSE ◀ Exmoor Ale, St Austell Proper Job, Otter Ale ♂ Addlestones. ♀ 12 **Facilities** ♣ (Bar Restaurant Garden) ♦ Children's menu Children's portions Garden ⋒ Beer festival Parking WiFi ➡ (notice required)

Woods Bar and Restaurant ◉

tel: 01398 324007 **4 Bank Square TA22 9BU**
email: woodsdulverton@hotmail.com
dir: *From Tiverton take A396 N. At Machine Cross take B3222 to Dulverton. Establishment adjacent to church*

Serious food and a friendly atmosphere

In the rural town of Dulverton on the edge of Exmoor, this is a bar and restaurant where food and drink are taken seriously, but without detriment to its friendly atmosphere. It's run by owners with a passion for wine – every bottle on the comprehensive list (up to £25) can be opened for a single glass. The cosy bar crackles with conversation while dishes of modern British cooking with a French accent leave the kitchen. Typical of these one AA-Rosette dishes are roast chicken supreme with rösti potato, Savoy cabbage, pancetta and Jerusalem artichoke and wild mushroom fricassée.

Open all wk 11-3 6-11.30 (Sun 12-3 7-11) **Food** Lunch all wk 12-2 Dinner Mon-Sat 6-9.30, Sun 7-9.30 ⊕ FREE HOUSE ◀ St Austell Cornish Best & Proper Job, HSD ♂ Thatchers, Winkleigh Sam's Poundhouse. ♀ **Facilities** Non-diners area ♣ (Bar Restaurant Garden) ♦ Children's menu Children's portions Garden

DUNSTER
Map 3 SS94

The Luttrell Arms Hotel
PICK OF THE PUBS

See Pick of the Pubs on opposite page

The Stags Head Inn

tel: 01643 821229 **10 West St TA24 6SN**
email: info@stagsheadinnexmoor.co.uk
dir: *From A39 take A396 to Dunster. Pub on right*

Cosy, welcoming pub on edge of Exmoor

Dunster Castle dominates this historic village, the Gateway to Exmoor National Park. The inn itself is 16th century, as a fresco in a bedroom depicting Henry VIII as the devil confirms. The bar stocks Somerset real ciders and ales, including Wills Neck, named after the highest point in the Quantocks. Sandwiches and a ploughman's are served at lunchtime, while the main menu presents sweet potato, spinach and almond curry; coriander and garlic chicken; and pork, fennel and sage pie. This small inn has limited seating, so reservations for dinner and Sunday lunch are recommended.

Open all day all wk 12-11 **Food** Lunch all wk 12.30-9 Dinner all wk 12.30-9 Av main course £10.95 Restaurant menu available all wk ⊕ FREE HOUSE ◀ Exmoor Ale, Otter Ale, Quantock Wills Neck ♂ Addlestones, Thatchers Gold. **Facilities** Non-diners area ♣ (Bar Garden) ♦ Children's menu Children's portions Garden ⋒ Cider festival WiFi ➡ (notice required)

EAST BOWER
Map 4 ST33

The Bower Inn

tel: 01278 422926 **Bower Ln TA6 4TY**
email: enquiries@thebowerinn.co.uk
dir: *M5 junct 23, A39 signed Glastonbury & Wells. Right at lights signed Bridgwater. Over motorway, left into Bower Ln to pub on left*

Attractive 18th-century building in a picturesque cottage garden

The Bower Inn was converted from a private family home to a restaurant in the 1980s, then following two years of closure, it attracted the attention of Peter and Candida Leaver, who purchased and renovated it. Business is good, both in the bar (mind the tiger!), where Somerset's Butcombe and Devon's Otter real ales are served, and in the contemporary restaurant, renowned for home-made food such as grilled pork loin steak with black pepper and cider sauce; fresh battered cod with pea purée; and spinach and ricotta tortellini in white wine cream sauce.

Open 12-3 6-11 Closed Mon L **Food** Lunch Tue-Sun 12.30-2.30 Dinner Mon-Sat 6.30-9, Sun 6.30-8 ⊕ FREE HOUSE ◀ Otter, Butcombe. **Facilities** Non-diners area ♣ (Bar Garden) ♦ Children's menu Children's portions Garden ⋒ Parking WiFi ➡ (notice required)

PICK OF THE PUBS

The Luttrell Arms Hotel

DUNSTER Map 3 SS94

tel: 01643 821555 **High St TA24 6SG**
email: enquiry@luttrellarms.co.uk
web: www.luttrellarms.co.uk
dir: *From A39 (Bridgwater to Minehead), left onto A396 to Dunster (2m from Minehead)*

Ancient free house in memorable location

Dramatically sited on a wooded hill, Dunster Castle, the Luttrell family home for 600 years until 1976, looks down over the film-set village, where stands the imposing sandstone-built Luttrell Arms, and in the near distance, the Bristol Channel. In the street outside is the early 17th-century, timber-framed, octagonal Yarn Market. One of Britain's oldest post-houses, it retains its galleried courtyard, fine plasterwork ceiling, stone-mullioned windows, wood-panelled walls and open fireplaces; it was from here that Oliver Cromwell directed the siege of Dunster Castle during the English Civil War. Until the 1950s one would book a table by telephoning Dunster 2; the Luttrells had the pleasure of answering "Dunster 1". You can see the castle from the inn's hidden garden; here's as good a place as any to savour a pint of Exmoor Ale from nearby Wiveliscombe, or Thatcher's Cheddar Valley cider, while perusing the menu. The Old Kitchen Bar offers hot ciabattas and sandwiches; Salcombe

crab and coriander cake; chef's pie of the day; and Mediterranean tagliatelle. In Psalter's restaurant, the choice is narrower but more sophisticated, with starters that include duo of duck ballotine with candy beetroot tarte Tatin and crumbled goats' cheese; and mains such as free-range chicken supreme with wild mushroom mousse, fondant potato and chasseur sauce; pan-fried, sea-salt-cured cod loin with garlic-crushed potatoes, wilted baby spinach and tomato and caper dressing; and roasted courgette and forest mushroom gnocchi with toasted pine nuts and pecorino cheese. Finish with white chocolate and raspberry tart and vanilla ice cream; or rich sticky sponge pudding topped with butterscotch sauce and honeycomb ice cream.

Open all day all wk 8am-11pm **Food** all wk 11.30-9.30 Restaurant menu available all wk ⊕ FREE HOUSE ◾ Exmoor Ale, Sharp's Doom Bar, Guest ale Ŏ Thatchers Cheddar Valley. ♟ 12 **Facilities** Non-diners area ❖ (Bar Restaurant Garden) ⅰ Children's menu Children's portions Family room Garden ⟁ WiFi 🚐

PICK OF THE PUBS

The White Horse at Haselbury

HASELBURY PLUCKNETT Map 4 ST41

tel: 01460 78873 **North St TA18 7RJ**
email: whitehorsehaselbury
@hotmail.co.uk
web: www.thewhitehorsehaselbury.co.uk
dir: *Just off A30 between Crewkerne &
Yeovil on B3066*

Rural pub offering French and British classics

Until opening here a few years ago,
Rebecca and Richard Robinson were
part of the London restaurant scene but,
being a Dorset girl, Rebecca couldn't
resist the pull of the West Country. A
look at the surrounding countryside –
both Dorset and Somerset – is enough
to tell you why. The pub used to be a
rope works and flax store, then a cider
house, and now proves amenable to a
repertoire that, in addition to the French
and British classics, is prepared by
chef-proprietor Richard, and chef
Jonathan. Real ales are from Otter,
Palmers, Teignworthy and other
breweries, with ciders from Burrow Hill.
The excellent local produce, particularly
the abundant fine seafood from West
Bay and the Dorset coast, inspires
dishes that social media commentators
enthuse about. You'll get an idea of the
cooking style from dishes such as a
starter of Dorset snail bourguignon;
followed by roast partridge, Agen
prunes, Savoy cabbage and bacon. An
alternative pairing might be steamed

Cornish mussels with mulled cider
cream sauce, then rare breed pork belly,
honey and swede purée, pommes
dauphine and Madeira sauce. A third
course might be date and toffee
pudding with caramelised bananas, or a
selection of cheeses with home-made
chutney and biscuits, perhaps
accompanied by a glass of Churchill's
Finest Reserve port. Given Richard and
Rebecca's pledge that the "great British
pub experience is important to them",
they equally welcome those who just
want something simple, like a Dexter
beefburger and hand-cut chips, for
example, or a White Horse ploughman's.

Open 12-2.30 6.30-11 Closed Sun eve,
Mon **Food** Lunch Tue-Sun 12-2.30
Dinner Tue-Sat 6.30-9.30 Set menu

available Restaurant menu available
Tue-Sun ⊕ FREE HOUSE ◀ Palmers
Best Bitter, Otter Ale, Teignworthy,
Wadworth 6X, Sharp's Doom Bar,
Butcombe ♂ Thatchers, Burrow Hill.
♟ 10 **Facilities** Non-diners area
♣ (Garden) ♦ Children's menu
Children's portions Garden ⊼ Beer
festival Cider festival Parking WiFi
🚌 (notice required)

EAST HARPTREE
Map 4 ST55

NEW Castle of Comfort

tel: 01761 221321 **BS40 6DD**
email: castleofcomfort@yahoo.com
dir: On B3134

Traditional home cooking on the Mendips

During Judge Jeffreys' time in the 17th century, prisoners from nearby Wells jail were taken to the Castle of Comfort for their last meal and a pint before being hanged at Gibbets Brow. Thankfully, modern-day visitors to this charming country pub on top of The Mendips can enjoy their time without the worry of being taken away. Local Butcombe beer and Thatchers cider are amongst the regularly changing options at the bar, with local produce appearing in straightforward, enjoyable dishes like lamb chops with mushrooms and onions; ham, egg and chips; and chicken Kiev.

Open all wk 12-3 6-11 **Food** Lunch 12-2 Dinner 6.30-9 Av main course £10-£14 ⊕ FREE HOUSE ◄ Butcombe Bitter, Sharp's Doom Bar, Guest ale ⚬ Thatchers, Guest ciders. ℤ 9 **Facilities** Non-diners area ✿ (Bar Garden Outside area) ◀ Children's menu Children's portions Play area Garden Outside area ⊟ Parking ⌨ (notice required)

EXFORD
Map 3 SS83

The Crown Hotel ★★★ HL ◉
PICK OF THE PUBS

tel: 01643 831554 **TA24 7PP**
email: info@crownhotelexmoor.co.uk **web:** www.crownhotelexmoor.co.uk
dir: From M5 junct 25 follow Taunton signs. Take A358 then B3224 via Wheddon Cross to Exford

Dedicated to produce from the South West

A family-run, 17th-century coaching inn in the heart of Exmoor National Park, the Crown is a comfortable mix of elegance and tradition. With three acres of its own grounds and a tributary of the infant River Exe flowing through the woodland, it's popular with visiting outdoor pursuit enthusiasts. But the cosy bar is also very much the social hub of the village, where many of the patrons enjoy the range of Exmoor Ales from Wiveliscombe just down the road. The AA-Rosette cuisine promises much, especially with Exmoor's profuse organic produce on the doorstep and the kitchen's close attention to sustainable sources. A typical selection from the bar menu could include smoked salmon with dressed leaves, lime chantilly cream and Avruga caviar; wild mushroom risotto with truffle oil and parmesan crisp; and hot strawberry soufflé served with champagne sorbet and biscuit tuille.

Open all day all wk 12-11 **Food** Lunch all wk 12-2.30 Dinner all wk 5.30-9.30 Restaurant menu available all wk ⊕ FREE HOUSE ◄ Exmoor Ale & Gold, Guest ales ⚬ Thatchers Gold, St Austell Copper Press. ℤ 10 **Facilities** Non-diners area ✿ (Bar Garden Outside area) ◀ Children's portions Garden Outside area ⊟ Parking WiFi ⌨ (notice required) **Rooms** 16

FAULKLAND
Map 4 ST75

Tuckers Grave

tel: 01373 834230 **BA3 5XF**
dir: From Bath take A36 towards Warminster. Right onto A366, through Norton St Philip towards Faulkland. In Radstock, left at x-rds, pub on left

The smallest pub in Somerset in a lovely countryside setting

Tapped Butcombe ale and Cheddar Valley cider draw local aficionados to this unspoilt rural gem. Somerset's smallest pub has a tiny atmospheric bar with old settles but no counter, or music, TV or jukebox either. Lunchtime sandwiches are available, and a large lawn with flower borders makes an attractive outdoor seating area, with the countryside adjacent. The 'grave' in the pub's name is the unmarked one of Edward Tucker, who hung himself here in 1747.

Open 11.30-3 6-11 (Sun 12-3 7-10.30) Closed 25 Dec, Mon L **Food** Contact pub for food times ⊕ FREE HOUSE ◄ Fuller's London Pride, Butcombe Bitter ⚬ Thatchers Cheddar Valley. **Facilities** ◀ Family room Garden ⊟ Parking **Notes** ◉

HASELBURY PLUCKNETT
Map 4 ST41

The White Horse at Haselbury
PICK OF THE PUBS

See Pick of the Pubs on opposite page

HINTON BLEWETT
Map 4 ST55

Ring O'Bells

tel: 01761 452239 **BS39 5AN**
email: ringobellshinton@butcombe.com
dir: 11m S of Bristol on A37 towards Wells. Turn right from either Clutton or Temple Cloud to Hinton Blewett

A great walkers' pub with a welcoming atmosphere

On the edge of the Mendips, this 200-year-old inn describes itself as the 'archetypal village green pub' and offers good views of the Chew Valley. An all-year-round cosy atmosphere is boosted by a log fire in winter, and a wide choice of well-kept real ales. An extra dining area has been added. There's always something going on, whether it's a tour of the brewery, pig racing night or fishing competitions. Good-value pub classics include Ashton Press battered fish; Mexican beef chilli; lamb's liver, bacon and onions; and Somerset Blue chicken. Open sandwiches and a children's menu are also available.

Open all day all wk 12-3 5-11 (Fri-Sat 12-11 Sun 12-10.30) **Food** Lunch Tue-Sat 12-2.30, Sun 12-3 Dinner Tue-Sat 6-9 ⊕ BUTCOMBE ◄ Butcombe, Fuller's London Pride, Liberation Ale, Guest ales ⚬ Ashton Press & Still. ℤ 8 **Facilities** Non-diners area ✿ (Bar Outside area) ◀ Children's menu Children's portions Garden Outside area Parking WiFi ⌨

HINTON ST GEORGE
Map 4 ST41

The Lord Poulett Arms
PICK OF THE PUBS

See Pick of the Pubs on page 438

HOLCOMBE
Map 4 ST64

The Holcombe Inn ★★★★★ INN ◉

tel: 01761 232478 **Stratton Rd BA3 5EB**
email: bookings@holcombeinn.co.uk **web:** www.holcombeinn.co.uk
dir: On A367 to Stratton-on-the-Fosse, take concealed left turn opposite Downside Abbey signed Holcombe, take next right, pub 1.5m on left

Known for great food and glorious sunsets

A 17th-century, Grade II listed inn with views of nearby Downside Abbey, this is where to find some of the county's top locally-produced food, represented on the AA Rosette menus. Start with a pint of Bath Ales Gem in the log-fired, flagstone-floored bar, where local Orchard Pig cider is on tap and wines by the glass are plentiful. A typical meal might start with crispy breaded belly of Somerset pork, caramelised apple purée, fennel and caper salad, followed by pan-seared hake, Cornish fishcake, samphire and creamy pesto sauce. Linger in the evening as the the sunsets can be rather special here.

Open all wk 12-3 6-11 (Fri-Sun all day) **Food** Lunch Mon-Thu 12-2.30, Fri-Sun all day Dinner Mon-Thu 6.30-9.30, Fri-Sun all day ⊕ FREE HOUSE ◄ Otter Ale, Bath Ales Gem, Butcombe ⚬ Thatchers, The Orchard Pig, Hecks. ℤ 17 **Facilities** Non-diners area ✿ (Bar Garden) ◀ Children's menu Children's portions Garden ⊟ Parking WiFi ⌨ **Rooms** 10

PICK OF THE PUBS

The Lord Poulett Arms

HINTON ST GEORGE Map 4 ST41

tel: 01460 73149 **High St TA17 8SE**
email: reservations@lordpoulettarms.com
web: www.lordpoulettarms.com
dir: 2m N of Crewkerne, 1.5m S of A303

Award-winning pub between the A30 and A303

A pub since 1680, there's that certain something about this handsome stone village inn that we do so well in Britain: thatched roof, secluded garden; wisteria-draped pergola tucked in next to an old Fives court. Then inside, a magpie-mix of polished antique furniture distributed judiciously across timeworn boarded floors, shiny flagstones and a vast fireplace pumping out the heat into tastefully decorated rooms. The feel is so quintessentially, dare we say it, English. The inner bar is popular with locals, not least because it dispenses pints of Branscombe Vale and Otter ales, and West Country ciders straight from the cask. Such a traditional interior does not mean you'll necessarily get traditional food, although if you want fish, crushed peas and chips with tartare sauce, it could well be waiting for you to ask. Just as likely, though, are home-cured yuzu salmon, celery, orange and fennel salad, and citrus aïoli; cream of beetroot and fennel soup to start; confit pork belly, black pudding bubble-and-squeak,

heritage carrots and celeriac purée; or smoked lamb rump, aubergine caviar, red pepper and potato fondant as a main course; then twisted tart Tatin; broken rocky road; or a fine selection of West Country cheeses served with home-made oat cakes and chutney to round things off. The set two- and three-course Sunday lunches are good value, as is the Supper Club comfort food menu served from 5-7pm each evening. There's a decent wine list, too, and a summer beer festival. For outdoor dining there are picnic-sets in a wild flower meadow, and white metalwork tables and chairs in a lavender-fringed gravelled area reminiscent of somewhere in France.

Open all day all wk 12-11 Closed 25-26 Dec, 1 Jan **Food** Lunch all wk 12-2.30, bar menu 3-6.30 Dinner all wk 7-9.15 ⊕ FREE HOUSE ◖ Branscombe Vale, Otter, Dorset, Butcombe ☼ Thatchers Gold, Perry's. ☗ 14 **Facilities** Non-diners area ◦◦ Children's portions Garden ⅀ Beer festival Cider festival Parking WiFi

HOLTON
Map 4 ST62

The Old Inn

tel: 01963 32002 **BA9 8AR**
email: enquiries@theoldinnrestaurant.co.uk
dir: Exit A303 signed Wincanton. At rdbt left onto A371. At 2nd rdbt left, then right to Holton

Convivial village inn with enjoyable food

In the safe hands of locally renowned chef Sue Bloxham, this sympathetically restored coaching inn is at the heart of this small village near Wincanton. With Wessex produce to the fore, you'll be assured of tip-top beers from local microbrewers, Glastonbury Ales; an ideal accompaniment to a considered selection of tapas choices or a dish from the dependable modern European menu. Smoked chicken salad with honey and mustard dressing, or venison faggot, onion and red wine gravy, mash potato and baby carrots give a flavour of the range. Time a visit for the popular Fish Friday night.

Open all wk 12-3 6-11 (Sat 12-11 Sun 12-10.30) **Food** Lunch Tue-Sat 12-2.30, Sun 12-3 Dinner Tue-Sat 6.30-9 Set menu available Restaurant menu available Tue-Sat ⊕ FREE HOUSE ◀ Glastonbury Ales Lady of the Lake, Butcombe ◐ Thatchers, Harry's Cider. ♥ 10 **Facilities** Non-diners area ❤ (Bar) ◀ Children's menu Children's portions Outside area ⊓ Parking WiFi ▭ (notice required)

HUISH EPISCOPI
Map 4 ST42

Rose & Crown (Eli's)

tel: 01458 250494 **TA10 9QT**
dir: M5 junct 25, A358 towards Ilminster. Left onto A378. Huish Episcopi in 14m (1m from Langport). Pub near church in village

The pub with no bar but plenty of real ales

Locked in a glorious time-warp, this 17th-century thatched inn, affectionately known as Eli's, (named after the current licensees' grandfather) has been in the same family for over 150 years. Don't expect to find a bar counter, there's a flagstoned taproom where customers congregate. In the four parlour rooms you'll find an upright piano, dart board, time-honoured pub games, books and old family photographs. Home-made food includes popular steak and ale pie; pork, apple and cider cobbler, cauliflower cheese, home-made soups and ploughman's lunches. There's a pool table and jukebox in a large function room. Other attractions include a children's outdoor play area, skittle alley, regular live music nights and on Fridays, an organic food co-op.

Open all wk 11.30-3 5.15-11.30 (Fri-Sat 11.30-11.30 Sun 12-10.30) Closed 25 Dec eve **Food** Lunch all wk 12-2 Dinner Mon-Sat 5.30-7.30 ⊕ FREE HOUSE ◀ Teignworthy Reel Ale, Rotating Guest ales ◐ Burrow Hill, Thatchers Gold, Westons Stowford Press, Harry's Cider. **Facilities** Non-diners area ❤ (Bar Garden) ◀ Play area Family room Garden ⊓ Parking WiFi ▭ **Notes** ☺

ILCHESTER
Map 4 ST52

The Bull Inn

tel: 01935 840400 **The Square BA22 8LH**
dir: From A303 between Sparkford & Ilminster take A37 signed Ilchester. At rdbt left onto B3151. Pub in village on left

Unpretentious town centre watering hole for sports fans

Sitting in the heart of Ilchester's town square, the Bull is a traditional free house serving Yeovil Ales and Doom Bar, along with Thatchers and Brothers Pear ciders.

The menu is an unpretentious choice of favourite pub grub plates, but meats are supplied by local butchers and fresh fish is delivered daily from Brixham. It's properly child-friendly too, but note that the Bull opens at 2pm, serves food from 3pm, and stays open until way after bedtime. There are large TV screens for sporting events plus a pool table, bar football and a skittle alley.

Open all wk 2pm-mdnt Closed 25 Dec, 1 Jan **Food** Dinner Mon-Sat 3-9 ⊕ FREE HOUSE ◀ Sharp's Doom Bar, Yeovil Ales, Guest ales ◐ Thatchers Gold, Brothers Pear. ♥ **Facilities** Non-diners area ❤ (Bar Restaurant Garden) ◀ Children's menu Children's portions Garden ⊓ Beer festival Cider festival WiFi ▭

Ilchester Arms

tel: 01935 840220 **The Square BA22 8LN**
email: mail@ilchesterarms.com
dir: From A303 take A37 signed Ilchester & Yeovil, left at 2nd Ilchester sign. Pub 100yds on right

Smart hostelry close to A303

An elegant Georgian-fronted house with lots of character, this establishment was first licensed in 1686. Between 1962 and 1985 it was owned by the man who developed Ilchester cheese, and its association with good food continues: chef-proprietor Brendan McGee takes pride in producing modern British dishes such as pigeon with cauliflower purée; chicken liver pâté with red onion marmalade; Dexter beef steak cooked in Innis & Gunn ale with creamy mash; and medallions of venison, pumpkin purée, peppered sprouts, dauphinoise potatoes and red wine jus. There is a lovely walled garden.

Open all day all wk 7am-11pm Closed 26 Dec **Food** Lunch Mon-Sat 12-2.30 Dinner Mon-Sat 7-9 Restaurant menu available Mon-Sat ⊕ FREE HOUSE ◀ Yeovil Ales, Local ales ◐ Westons Mortimers Orchard. ♥ 14 **Facilities** Non-diners area ❤ (Bar Garden) ◀ Children's menu Children's portions Play area Family room Garden ⊓ Beer festival Cider festival Parking WiFi ▭

ILMINSTER
Map 4 ST31

New Inn ★★★★ INN

tel: 01460 52413 **Dowlish Wake TA19 0NZ**
email: newinn-ilminster@btconnect.com **web:** www.newinn-ilminster.co.uk
dir: From Ilminster follow Kingstone & Perry's Cider Museum signs, in Dowlish Wake follow pub signs

Recommended for its home-cooked food and local cider

Deep in rural Somerset, this 350-year-old stone-built pub is tucked away in the village of Dowlish Wake, close to Perry's thatched Cider Mill and Museum. Inside are two bars (serving Perry's Cider, of course) with wood-burning stoves and a restaurant, where menus of home-cooked food capitalise on the quality and freshness of local produce. You could opt for a signature dish such as fillet of salmon in a prawn and butter glaze; or perhaps stick to pub favourites like a giant Yorkshire pudding filled with pork sausages, served with new potatoes, vegetables and gravy. There are four guest rooms situated in an annexe overlooking the large secluded garden.

Open all wk 11.30-3 6-11 **Food** Lunch all wk 12-2.30 Dinner all wk 6-8.45 ⊕ FREE HOUSE ◀ Butcombe Bitter, Otter Ale ◐ Perry's, Thatchers Gold. ♥ 10 **Facilities** Non-diners area ❤ (All areas) ◀ Children's menu Children's portions Garden Outside area ⊓ Parking WiFi ▭ (notice required) **Rooms** 4

KILVE — Map 3 ST14

The Hood Arms

tel: 01278 741210 **TA5 1EA**
email: info@thehoodarms.com
dir: From M5 junct 23/24 follow A39 to Kilve. Village between Bridgwater & Minehead

Enjoyable food and beer betwixt the sea and the hills

Just an ammonite's throw from Kilve's fossil-rich beach, the Quantock Hills rise up behind this family-run 17th-century coaching inn. Real ales to enjoy in the beamed bar or in the garden include Exmoor Gold and Otter Head, plus local ciders, any of which will happily accompany a ciabatta roll, jacket potato or something from the main menu, such as pan-fried sea bass with saffron and shellfish broth; slow-roasted belly pork with black pudding, mashed potato, roasted pear and cider jus; or classic cod and chips. Specials are chalked up daily.

Open all day all wk 11-11 **Food** Lunch Mon-Sat 12-2, Sun 12-3 Dinner Mon-Sat 6-9, Sun 6-8 ⊕ FREE HOUSE ◀ Otter Head, Exmoor Gold, Fuller's London Pride, Guinness, Guest ales Ŏ Thatchers Gold, Rich's. ♟ 12 **Facilities** Non-diners area ♣ (Bar Garden) ♦ Children's menu Children's portions Play area Family room Garden ⊼ Parking WiFi

KINGSDON — Map 4 ST52

Kingsdon Inn

tel: 01935 840543 **TA11 7LG**
email: enquiries@kingsdoninn.co.uk
dir: A303 onto A372, right onto B3151, right into village, right at post office

Former cider house with very good food

Once a cider house, this pretty thatched pub is furnished with stripped pine tables and cushioned farmhouse chairs, and there are enough open fires to keep everywhere well warmed. The three charmingly decorated, saggy-beamed rooms have a relaxed and friendly feel. Hosts Adam Cain and Cinzia Iezzi have a wealth of experience in some of the UK's most respected hotels and restaurants, and they have made food a key part of the Kingsdon's appeal. Menus make excellent use of seasonal, local and often organic produce – maybe seared pigeon with pearl barley and cep risotto followed by pan-fried turbot with pea tortellini, baby vegetables and light shellfish bisque.

Open all wk 12-3 6-11 (Sun 12-3 7-10.30) **Food** Lunch all wk 12-2 Dinner all wk 6.30-9 Set menu available Restaurant menu available Mon-Sat ⊕ FREE HOUSE/ GAME BIRD INNS ◀ Sharp's Doom Bar, Butcombe, Otter Ŏ Thatchers, Ashton Press. ♟ 10 **Facilities** Non-diners area ♣ (Bar Garden) ♦ Children's menu Children's portions Garden ⊼ Parking WiFi ➡ (notice required)

LONG ASHTON — Map 4 ST57

NEW The Bird in Hand

tel: 01275 395222 **17 Weston Rd BS41 9LA**
email: info@birdinhand.co.uk
dir: Phone pub for detailed directions

Stylish recreation with a warm atmosphere and good food

Just to the west of Bristol, this newly redesigned pub's clean lines haven't smothered its former village-pub feel. To the left is the bar area, home of Bath Ales Gem, Tribute and guest ales; to the right the dining area. Here, with fish and shellfish delivered daily, meat sourced locally where possible, and much neighbourhood foraging, is a monthly-changing, modern British menu listing pressed pig's head, celeriac, apple and watercress; monkfish with Jerusalem

artichoke, broccoli and pickled mussels; and fried semolina, heritage beetroot, blue cheese and chicory. Home-made bar snacks include Scotch eggs, sausage rolls and crispy pigs' ears.

Open all day all wk **Food** Lunch all wk 12-3 Dinner all wk 6-9 Av main course £11 Restaurant menu available Mon-Sat ⊕ FREE HOUSE ◀ St Austell Tribute, Bath Ales Gem, 2 guest ales. ♟ 13 **Facilities** ♣ (Bar Outside area) ♦ Children's portions Outside area ⊼ WiFi ➡ (notice required)

LONG SUTTON — Map 4 ST42

The Devonshire Arms ★★★★ INN ⓦ — PICK OF THE PUBS

tel: 01458 241271 **TA10 9LP**
email: mail@thedevonshirearms.com **web:** www.thedevonshirearms.com
dir: Exit A303 at Podimore rdbt onto A372. 4m, left onto B3165

Excellent food and beers in a former hunting lodge

Wisteria, acers and lavender surround the walled courtyard at the rear of this lovely pub; croquet, boules and Jenga can be played by all the family on the garden's terraced lawns. Ales include regulars such as Cheddar Potholer, Otter Bitter and Adam Henson's Rare Breed from Butcombe. Burrow Hill and village-pressed Harry's are the draught ciders, and the wine list offers 10 by the glass. Locally sourced ingredients in modern British dishes have helped the Devonshire win an AA Rosette. Both lunch and dinner menus share a starter of fried, walnut-encrusted Somerset goats' cheese with beetroot and balsamic onions; and a main course of pan-fried hake, caper mash, greens, cockles with white wine and cream sauce. For the truly hungry, look to finish with the West Country cheeseboard accompanied by bread, oatcakes, water biscuits and quince jelly; otherwise take comfort in a sticky toffee pudding with Somerset cider brandy ice cream.

Open all wk 12-3 6-11 Closed 25-26 Dec, 1 Jan **Food** Lunch all wk 12-2.30 Dinner all wk 7-9.30 ⊕ FREE HOUSE ◀ Cheddar Potholer, Butcombe Adam Henson's Rare Breed, Otter Bitter Ŏ Burrow Hill, Harry's Cider. ♟ 10 **Facilities** Non-diners area ♣ (Bar Outside area) ♦ Children's menu Play area Garden Outside area ⊼ Parking WiFi **Rooms** 9

LOWER GODNEY — Map 4 ST44

The Sheppey

tel: 01458 831594 **BA5 1RZ**
email: hi@thesheppey.co.uk
dir: From Wells towards Wedmore on B3139. Through Bleadney. Left into Tilleys Drove to Godney. Or from Glastonbury & Street take B3151 to Meare, follow Godney signs

Enticing combination of ales, ciders, art and music

On the Somerset Levels and only a hippy's dance away from Glastonbury, the Sheppey sits beside its eponymous river like a cider barn crossed with a private members' club. The ales and craft beers are reassuringly real – around a dozen to tease the taste buds. Cider is taken seriously too – six barrels sit atop the bar, so there's no danger of running out as happened in 1976 resulting in a loss of trust by the locals towards the then landlords. Tasty dishes from the Spanish charcoal oven include lamb tagine with apricots; and braised ox cheek in red wine. Live music, cider and beer festivals in August, and decorative artworks on the walls complete the unique picture.

Open 12-2.30 5.30-12 (Sat-Sun all day) **Food** Lunch all wk 12-2.30 Dinner all wk 6.30-9.30 Set menu available Restaurant menu available all wk ⊕ FREE HOUSE ◀ Glastonbury Ales, Cheddar Ales, Arbor Ŏ Wilkins, Sheppeys own, Hecks, Harry's Cider, Tricky. **Facilities** Non-diners area ♣ (All areas) ♦ Children's menu Children's portions Family room Garden Outside area ⊼ Beer festival Cider festival Parking WiFi ➡ (notice required)

The Langford Inn ★★★★ INN

tel: 01934 863059 **BS40 5BL**
email: langfordinn@aol.com **web:** www.langfordinn.com
dir: *M5 junct 21, A370 towards Bristol. At Congresbury turn right onto B3133 to Lower Langford. Village on A38*

Traditional and international food

This acclaimed Mendip's pub and restaurant is owned by the Cardiff brewery, Brains, so expect a decent pint of SA in the bar. Brains beers are joined by local Butcombe ales in the bar, which is adorned with local memorabilia. The daily-changing menu proffers traditional dishes such as beef and ale pie; cod and chips; and a selection of grilled steaks; but rogan josh chicken curry; sizzling beef with oyster sauce; and vegetarian cottage pie offer something a little different. There's a good choice of 24 wines by the glass to accompany your meal. The inn also offers accommodation in converted 17th-century barns.

Open all day all wk **Food** Lunch all wk 12-9 Dinner all wk 12-9 Av main course £5.99 Set menu available ⊞ BRAINS ◀ SA, Butcombe, Guinness ⚬ Thatchers Gold & Katy. ▼ 24 **Facilities** Non-diners area ✿ (Bar Garden) ◀◗ Children's menu Children's portions Garden Parking WiFi 🚌 (notice required) **Rooms** 7

Vobster Inn ★★★★ INN ◉◉   PICK OF THE PUBS

tel: 01373 812920 **BA3 5RJ**
email: info@vobsterinn.co.uk **web:** www.vobsterinn.co.uk
dir: *4m W of Frome*

Historic village pub with Spanish twist

Set in four acres of glorious countryside in the pretty hamlet of Lower Vobster, it is believed the inn originated in the 16th century and was used by King James II and his army of Royalists prior to the battle of Sedgemoor in 1685. For lunch, choose a filled baguette, ploughman's, or a steak. On the main menu you may find veal escalope with Gentlemen's Relish; Cornish smoked haddock and poached egg risotto; and grilled garlic field mushrooms on ciabatta with French fries. The tapas menu offers roast Catalan tomato bread and Spanish meatballs. All desserts are home made, with choices like chocolate pannacotta and orange and mango sorbet. Special events like paella night and pudding night are popular. Individually furnished bedrooms are available.

Open 12-3 6.30-11 Closed Sun eve & Mon **Food** Lunch Tue-Sun 12-2 Dinner Tue-Thu & Sat 7-9, Fri 6.30-9 ⊞ FREE HOUSE ◀ Butcombe Bitter, Morland Old Golden Hen ⚬ The Orchard Pig, Thatchers Gold. ▼ 10 **Facilities** Non-diners area ✿ (Bar Garden) ◀◗ Children's menu Children's portions Family room Garden ⼹ Parking WiFi 🚌 (notice required) **Rooms** 4

The Nag's Head Inn

tel: 01935 823432 **East St TA12 6NF**
dir: *Phone for detailed directions*

Hamstone former cider house offering good grub, skittles and beer

This 16th-century former cider house is set in a lovely hamstone street in a picturesque south Somerset village. The large rear garden is partly walled and has pretty borders and trees. Ales, wines and home-cooked food are served in both the public and lounge/diner bars, where crib, dominoes, darts and pool are available. A sample menu includes Cajun chicken, burgers, quiche and sizzling garlic butter rump steak. The pub also has a separate skittle alley. There's a poker evening on Tuesday, and Sunday evening is quiz night.

Open all wk 12-3 6-11 (Fri-Sun 12-12) **Food** Lunch all wk 12-2 Dinner Mon-Tue 6-8, Wed-Sat 6-9 ⊞ FREE HOUSE ◀ Yeovil Ruby, Local guest ales ⚬ Thatchers Gold, Westons Stowford Press. **Facilities** Non-diners area ✿ (Bar Restaurant Garden) ◀◗ Children's menu Children's portions Family room Garden ⼹ Parking WiFi 🚌 (notice required)

The Talbot Inn

tel: 01373 812254 **Selwood St BA11 3PN**
email: info@talbotinn.com
dir: *A362 from Frome towards Radstock. Left signed Mells, Hapsford & Great Elm. Right at T-junct in Mells. Inn on right*

Traditional yet stylish coaching inn

In coaching days, this 15th-century inn was the stop before Wells. Perhaps some passengers mistakenly alighted here in Mells, a bonus for the innkeepers of the day. It has a main bar, snug and map rooms, all open for classic pub food and Talbot Ale. Across a cobbled courtyard is the Coach House Grill Room, where chef Pravin Nayar's fish and meats are grilled over a charcoal fire and, on Sundays, whole roast chickens and suckling pigs are carved at the table. His bar snacks – including deep-fried rabbit legs, and duck hearts on toast – are clearly not ordinary.

Open all day all wk 9am-11pm **Food** Lunch all wk 12-3 Dinner all wk 6-9.30 ⊞ FREE HOUSE ◀ Butcombe, Talbot Ale, Guest ales ⚬ Ashton Press, The Orchard Pig. ▼ 10 **Facilities** Non-diners area ✿ (Bar Restaurant Garden) ◀◗ Children's menu Children's portions Garden ⼹ Parking WiFi

The Globe ★★★ INN ◉   PICK OF THE PUBS

tel: 01823 400534 **Fore St TA4 1JX**
email: info@theglobemilverton.co.uk **web:** www.theglobemilverton.co.uk
dir: *On B3187*

Friendly, family-run inn close to Exmoor

Run by Mark and Adele Tarry for the past decade, this old coaching inn is a firm part of the community in Milverton. From the outside, the pub has all the character expected of a Grade II listed building, but the uncluttered interior is contemporary with paintings by local artists, a wood-burning stove and a tranquil sun terrace providing for all seasons. Local real ales are one of Mark's passions so expect tip-top local ales like Exmoor and Otter and heady cider from Sheppy's. The extensive menu makes good use of West Country produce and ranges from lunchtime sandwiches and ham, egg and chips, to evening specials such as Fowey mussels with cider, cream and parsley; or breast of local pheasant stuffed with sausage meat, streaky bacon, parsley and gravy. Stay over in one of the comfortable bedrooms and explore the Quantock Hills and Exmoor.

Open 12-3 6-11 (Fri-Sat 12-3 6-11.30) Closed Sun eve, Mon L **Food** Lunch Tue-Sun 12-2 Dinner Mon-Sat 6.30-9 Av main course £12.95 ⊞ FREE HOUSE ◀ Exmoor Ale, Butcombe Bitter, Otter Bitter, Guest ales ⚬ Sheppy's. ▼ 9 **Facilities** Non-diners area ◀◗ Children's menu Outside area ⼹ Parking WiFi **Rooms** 3

MONKTON COMBE | Map 4 ST76

Wheelwrights Arms

tel: 01225 722287 **BA2 7HB**
email: bookings@wheelwrightsarms.co.uk
dir: *SE of Bath*

Lovely valley and village setting for old pub

Sit in the lavender-scented garden with an Otter beer, or cosy up to the snug's log fire with a glass of Honey's cider in this attractive village inn set on the slopes of the Avon Valley just outside Bath. Handy for ramblers straying from the Kennet & Avon Canal towpath walk, the accomplished menu of home-prepared, locally sourced dishes means it's also a popular dining inn. Start with monkfish scampi with saffron mayonnaise and frisée; or consider a sharing plate of whole oven-baked camembert. Mains may stretch to root vegetable and hazelnut burger; or a minute steak, mustard mayo and red onion compôte sandwich, whilst desserts such as Bramley apple and vanilla tart make a memorable finale. The extensive wine list is equally satisfying.

Open all day all wk **Food** Lunch Mon-Fri 12-2, Sat-Sun 12-3 Dinner all wk 6-10 Set menu available Restaurant menu available all wk ⊕ FREE HOUSE ◀ Butcombe, Otter ♂ Honey's Midford Cider Honey & Daughter. ▾ 10 **Facilities** ♦ Children's portions Garden ⋒ Parking WiFi ▭ (notice required)

MONTACUTE | Map 4 ST41

The Kings Arms Inn

tel: 01935 822255 **49 Bishopston TA15 6UU**
email: info@thekingsarmsinn.co.uk
dir: *From A303 onto A3088 at rdbt signed Montacute. Inn in village centre*

17th-century village pub with cosy bar and good food

The hamstone-built Kings Arms has stood in this picturesque village, at the foot of Mons Acutus (thus, supposedly, Montacute) since 1632. Along with cask ales and fine wines, you can eat in several places as there are two restaurant areas, a bar/lounge, and a large beer garden which has games for both adults and children. Seasonal dishes based on locally sourced produce are offered on both the traditional bar menu and the à la carte. Perhaps try pan-roasted cod supreme with triple-cooked chips and confit tomatoes; pan-fried breast and confit of pheasant with rösti and braised red cabbage; and beef Stroganoff with basmati rice. There are plenty of events to watch out for.

Open all day all wk 7.30am-11pm **Food** Lunch all wk 12-3 Dinner all wk 6-9 Restaurant menu available all wk ⊕ GREENE KING ◀ Ruddles Best & IPA, Morland Old Speckled Hen, Timothy Taylor Landlord ♂ Thatchers. ▾ 11 **Facilities** Non-diners area ✿ (Bar Garden Outside area) ♦ Children's menu Children's portions Play area Garden Outside area ⋒ Parking WiFi ▭

The Phelips Arms

tel: 01935 822557 **The Borough TA15 6XB**
email: thephelipsarms@hotmail.com
dir: *From Cartgate rdbt on A303 follow signs for Montacute*

Pub classics in a classic setting

About 1598 Sir Edward Phelips, Master of the Rolls and the prosecutor during the Gunpowder Plot trial, built Montacute House, now owned by the National Trust. Next door, overlooking the village square, stands this 17th-century hamstone building, offering well-kept Palmers beers and Thatchers cider. The main menu features

chef's pie of the day; honey and mustard roasted ham and free-range eggs; and Somerset sausage and creamy mash. Sandwiches, baguettes and jacket potatoes are available too. The pub, with its beautiful walled garden, featured in the 1995 film *Sense and Sensibility* and the more recent BBC drama series, *Wolf Hall*.

Open all wk 12-2.30 6-11 (Sun 12-6) Closed 25 Dec **Food** Lunch Mon-Sat 12-2, 12-4 Dinner Mon-Sat 6.30-9 ⊕ PALMERS ◀ Best Bitter, 200, Copper Ale, Tally Ho! & Dorset Gold ♂ Thatchers Gold. ▾ 10 **Facilities** Non-diners area ✿ (Bar Restaurant Garden) ♦ Children's menu Children's portions Garden Parking WiFi ▭

NORTH CURRY | Map 4 ST32

The Bird in Hand

tel: 01823 490248 **1 Queen Square TA3 6LT**
dir: *M5 junct 25, A358 towards Ilminster, left onto A378 towards Langport. Left to North Curry*

Low beams, warming fires, friendly service

Cheerful staff provide a warm welcome to this friendly 300-year-old village inn, which boasts large inglenook fireplaces, flagstone floors, and exposed beams. The place is very atmospheric at night by candlelight, and the daily-changing blackboard menus feature local produce, including game casserole, curries and bubble-and-squeak with sausage, bacon, eggs and mushrooms. The à la carte menu always has two or three fresh fish dishes, steaks and home-made desserts. In season you can expect local game, as well as local lamb, chicken and pork. On Sunday, roast lunch is available.

Open all wk 12-3 6-11 (Fri 12-3 5.30-12 Sat 12-3 6-12) Closed 25 Dec eve & 26 Dec eve **Food** Lunch Mon-Sat 12-2, Sun 12-3 Dinner Sun-Thu 6.45-9, Fri-Sat 7-9.30 Restaurant menu available all wk ⊕ FREE HOUSE ◀ Otter Bitter & Ale, Exmoor Gold, Cotleigh Barn Owl, Butcombe Gold, North Curry Gold ♂ Parsons Choice, Ashton Press, Thatchers Gold. ▾ 9 **Facilities** Non-diners area ✿ (Bar Outside area) ♦ Children's portions Outside area ⋒ Parking WiFi

NORTON ST PHILIP | Map 4 ST75

George Inn | PICK OF THE PUBS

tel: 01373 834224 **High St BA2 7LH**
email: georgeinn@wadworth.co.uk
dir: *A36 from Bath to Warminster, 6m, right onto A366 to Radstock, village 1m*

Historic pub with a far-reaching reputation

Grade I listed, this truly remarkable building was built, so historians believe, in 1223 as temporary accommodation for Carthusian monks while they constructed Hinton Priory two miles away. In 1397, the Prior granted it a licence to sell ale, making it one of the country's oldest continuously licensed inns. When Wadworth, the Devizes brewery, carried out a major restoration, it uncovered medieval wall paintings, which are now preserved, as are other interesting features like the stone-tiled roof, massive doorway, turreted staircase, cobbled courtyard and open-air gallery. There are two menus, the carte and the more pocket-friendly and informal Monmouth's. For a lighter option, a selection of ciabattas is served until 6pm. Outside, you can eat in the ancient and atmospheric courtyard and from the beer garden watch cricket on the Mead.

Open all day all wk 9am-11pm (Sun 12-10.30) **Food** Lunch Mon-Sat 12-2.30, Sun 12-9 Dinner Mon-Sat 6-9, Sun 12-9 ⊕ WADWORTH ◀ 6X, Henry's Original IPA, The Bishop's Tipple, Guest ales ♂ Kingstone Press, Thatchers Gold. ▾ **Facilities** Non-diners area ✿ (Bar Garden) ♦ Children's menu Children's portions Play area Garden ⋒ Parking WiFi ▭

NUNNEY — Map 4 ST74

The George at Nunney

tel: 01373 836458 **Church St BA11 4LW**
email: info@thegeorgeatnunney.co.uk
dir: 0.5m N off A361, Frome/Shepton Mallet

The hub of the village's lively community

With views of 14th-century moated castle ruins, and a babbling brook and waterfall directly opposite, this rambling inn, run by the Hedges family, has the added attractions of landscaped gardens and a winter log fire. The stylish interior merges contemporary with traditional; the beamed bar has a choice of Wadworth ales, Thatchers cider and fine wines. Start with pan-seared king scallops or smooth duck liver parfait; continue to mains like wild mushroom and ricotta tortellini; a 28-day-aged steak; gourmet burger; or The George fish pie. Sandwiches are available at lunchtime and there are roasts on Sundays.

Open all day all wk **Food** Lunch all wk 12-2 Dinner all wk 7-9.30 Restaurant menu available all wk ⊕ WADWORTH ◀ 6X, Henrys IPA, Guest ale ♂ Thatchers Gold. ♀ 8
Facilities Non-diners area ❤ (Bar Restaurant Garden) ♦ Children's menu Children's portions Family room Garden ⊓ Parking WiFi ➡ (notice required)

OAKHILL — Map 4 ST64

The Oakhill Inn ★★★★ INN ⊛   PICK OF THE PUBS

tel: 01749 840442 **Fosse Rd BA3 5HU**
email: info@theoakhillinn.com **web:** www.theoakhillinn.com
dir: On A367 between Stratton-on-the-Fosse & Shepton Mallet

Mendips inn with a coveted AA Rosette

Spacious yet cosy, old but contemporary, this smart stone-built inn stands on a corner in the middle of the village. From the landscaped garden you can see the village church and the Mendip Hills; inside, the duck-egg blue interior features a display of over 20 clocks. Real ales from Butcombe and Palmers keep bar-top company with Pheasant Plucker and Lilley's Sunset ciders. Head chef Neil Creese's award-winning food conforms to free-range, organic and local-sourcing principles so, even though the menus are brief, the dishes are certainly not short on quality. Consider a three-course meal of honey-roast beetroot, goats' cheese truffles and toasted sesame seeds; pot-roast beef with Yorkshire pudding and horseradish cream; and hot chocolate pot with Midway Farm cream. The bar menu offers a good choice of steaks, as well as ploughman's, fish and chips, and sandwiches.

Open all wk 12-3 5-11 (Sat-Sun 12-12) **Food** Lunch all wk 12-3 Dinner all wk 6-9 Av main course £13 Restaurant menu available all wk ⊕ FREE HOUSE ◀ Butcombe Bitter, Palmers, Guest ale ♂ Pheasant Plucker, Lilley's Sunset, Thatchers Gold. ♀
Facilities Non-diners area ❤ (Bar Restaurant Garden) ♦ Children's menu Children's portions Garden ⊓ Parking WiFi ➡ (notice required) **Rooms** 5

OVER STRATTON — Map 4 ST41

The Royal Oak

tel: 01460 240906 **TA13 5LQ**
email: info@the-royal-oak.net
dir: Exit A303 at Hayes End rdbt (South Petherton). 1st left after Esso garage signed Over Stratton

Real ales and home-cooked food

With X-shaped tie-bar ends securing its aged hamstone walls, a thatched roof, blackened oak beams, flagstones, log fires, old church pews and settles, this 17th-century former farmhouse certainly looks like a textbook example of an English country pub. First licensed in the 1850s, the bar dispenses real ales from Hall & Woodhouse in Blandford, Dorset. With different prices for small or normal appetites, home-cooked dishes on the menu range from chicken tikka lahoori, via salmon en croûte, to beef and bacon pie. Added attractions are the good value two-course set lunch menu and large patio for enjoying in warmer weather.

Open Tue-Sun Closed Mon **Food** Lunch Tue-Sun 12-2 Dinner Tue-Sun 6-9 Set menu available ⊕ HALL & WOODHOUSE ◀ Badger Dorset Best, Tanglefoot, K&B Sussex.
Facilities Non-diners area ❤ (Bar Garden) ♦ Children's menu Children's portions Family room Garden Parking

PITNEY — Map 4 ST42

The Halfway House

tel: 01458 252513 **TA10 9AB**
dir: On B3153, 2m from Langport & Somerton

One for lovers of real ales and ciders

A delightfully old fashioned rural pub, The Halfway House has three homely rooms boasting open fires, books and traditional games, but no music or electronic games. This free house is largely dedicated to the promotion of quality brews, with an annual beer festival in March and cider festival in August. Eight to twelve top ales and ciders are served, including Teignworthy and Kingston Black cider. The home-cooked rustic fare is made using local ingredients. Sandwiches, pies, fish and chips, game casserole and soups are served at lunchtimes, while a great range of English pub food and specials are available for dinner. Sundays lunches stretch from 1 until 5.

Open all wk 11.30-3 4.30-11 (Fri 11.30-3 4.30-12 Sat-Sun all day) **Food** Lunch Mon-Sat 12-2.30, Sun 1-5 Dinner Mon-Sat 7-9.30 ⊕ FREE HOUSE ◀ Butcombe Bitter, Otter Ale, Hop Back Summer Lightning, Moor Northern Star, Teignworthy ♂ Kingston Black, Burrow Hill, Wilkins Farmhouse, Gold Rush. ♀ 8
Facilities Non-diners area ❤ (Bar Garden) ♦ Children's portions Play area Garden Beer festival Cider festival Parking WiFi

PORLOCK — Map 3 SS84

The Bottom Ship

tel: 01643 863288 **Porlock Weir TA24 8PB**
email: enquiries@shipinnporlockweir.co.uk
dir: Phone for detailed directions

Thatched inn at lovely Porlock Weir location

Enjoy superb views across the Bristol Channel to south Wales from the suntrap terrace at this thatched waterside pub, best enjoyed following a coastal path stroll. Exmoor ales are the mainstay in the beamed bar, with a couple of real ciders also on tap. Home-made food using fresh local produce includes most pub favourites, from deep-fried whitebait to steak and ale pie. Children have their own menu and dogs are welcome. Don't miss the music and ale festival in early July.

Open all day all wk 9am-10.45pm **Food** Lunch all wk 12-2.30 Dinner all wk 6-8.30 ⊕ FREE HOUSE ◀ Exmoor Ale & Stag, Otter Amber, Guest ales ♂ Thatchers.
Facilities Non-diners area ❤ (Bar Garden) ♦ Children's menu Children's portions Garden ⊓ Beer festival Cider festival Parking ➡

PORLOCK *continued*

The Ship Inn

tel: 01643 862507 **High St TA24 8QD**
email: enquiries@shipinnporlock.co.uk
dir: A358 to Williton, then A39 to Porlock. 6m from Minehead

Picture-postcard inn with sea-faring tales to tell

Reputedly one of the oldest inns on Exmoor, this 13th-century free house stands at the foot of Porlock's notorious hill, where Exmoor tumbles into the sea. In the past it's attracted the sinister attentions of Nelson's press gang, but now its thatched roof and traditional interior provide a more welcoming atmosphere. Regularly changing menus include an appealing selection of hot and cold baguettes, and hot dishes from home-made beef casserole with dumplings to risotto of the day. There's also a beer garden and children's play area.

Open all day all wk 9am-mdnt **Food** Lunch all wk 12-2.30 Dinner Sun-Thu 6.30-8.45, Fri-Sat 6-9 ⊕ FREE HOUSE ◀ St Austell Tribute & Proper Job, Exmoor Ale & Beast, Cotleigh Tawny Owl, Otter, Guest ales Ö Thatchers & Cheddar Valley. **Facilities** Non-diners area ❤ (Bar Garden) ◀❖ Children's menu Children's portions Play area Garden ⨯ Parking WiFi ▭

RODE	**Map 4 ST85**

The Mill at Rode

tel: 01373 831100 **BA11 6AG**
email: mill@butcombe.com
dir: 6m S of Bath

Impressive riverside building with alfresco eating terrace

A converted grist mill on the banks of the beautiful River Frome, this magnificent multi-storeyed Georgian building sits in its own landscaped grounds in the rural hinterland south of Bath. The dining-terrace overhangs the rushing waters, a great location in which to indulge in local beers or select from the West Country-based menu; maybe terrine of local game with apple chutney and warm toast, followed by fillets of Cornish plaice stuffed with mushrooms and spinach and topped with vintage cheddar sauce. A children's playroom offers grown-ups the chance of escape and have a peaceful chinwag.

Open all day all wk 11-11 (Sun 12-10.30) **Food** Lunch Mon-Sat 11-9, Sun 12-8 Dinner Mon-Sat 11-9, Sun 12-8 ⊕ BUTCOMBE ◀ Butcombe Bitter, Guest ales Ö Ashton Press, Thatchers Cheddar Valley. ♚ 35 **Facilities** Non-diners area ❤ (Bar Restaurant Garden) ◀❖ Children's menu Children's portions Play area Family room Garden Parking WiFi ▭

SHEPTON BEAUCHAMP	**Map 4 ST41**

Duke of York

tel: 01460 240314 **North St TA19 0LW**
email: sheptonduke@tiscali.co.uk
dir: N of A303 between Ilchester & Ilminster

Traditional village pub with plenty of reasons to visit

Husband and wife team Paul and Hayley Rowlands have established a good reputation over the years at this 17th-century free house. The bar stocks good West Country ales and local ciders, and the restaurant's traditional menu pleases locals and tourists alike with warm salad of wood pigeon; home-made steak and Stilton puff pastry pie, pot-roasted beef with Guinness and oyster mushroom sauce; Makhani chicken curry and lunchtime sandwiches. Gardens, a skittle alley, two steak nights a week, a Sunday carvery and the occasional beer festival round off the attractions of this homely pub.

Open all day Mon 5pm-11pm Tue-Wed 3.30pm-11pm Thu-Sun 12-12 Closed Mon L **Food** Lunch Thu-Sun 12-2 Dinner Tue-Sat 6.45-9 Av main course £9.95 ⊕ FREE HOUSE ◀ Teignworthy Reel Ale, Otter Ale & Bright Ö Thatchers Gold. ♚ 9 **Facilities** Non-diners area ❤ (Bar Garden) ◀❖ Children's menu Children's portions Family room Garden Beer festival Parking WiFi ▭ (notice required)

SHEPTON MALLET	**Map 4 ST64**

NEW The Natterjack Inn ★★★★ INN

tel: 01749 860253 **BA4 6NA**
email: natterjack@btconnect.com **web:** www.thenatterjackinn.co.uk
dir: Between Castle Cary & Shepton Mallet on A371

Family-owned hostelry with railway connection

Originally the Railway Hotel, which hosted passengers and goods yard workers on the Somerset and Dorset line for 100 years before closure in the 1960s. Its current name is based in a legend that a live toad was added to the cider barrel before the bung was inserted. Now in the capable hands of Adrian and Kate Brixey, the pub offers Butcombe and guest ales, along with Ashton Press cider and a dozen wines by the glass. The menu proffers staples like liver and bacon with black pudding and mash; round off with one of Kate's home-made desserts such as warm chocolate fudge cake with clotted cream ice cream.

Open all wk 11.30-3.30 6-11.30 **Food** Lunch 12-2.30 Dinner 6.30-9.30 ⊕ FREE HOUSE ◀ Bath Ales Gem, Butcombe, Guest ale Ö Ashton Press, The Orchard Pig Reveller. ♚ 12 **Facilities** Non-diners area ❤ (Bar Restaurant Garden) ◀❖ Children's menu Children's portions Garden ⨯ Parking WiFi ▭ (notice required) **Rooms** 5

The Three Horseshoes Inn   `PICK OF THE PUBS`

tel: 01749 850359 **Batcombe BA4 6HE**
email: info@thethreehorseshoesinn.com
dir: Take A359 from Frome to Bruton. Batcombe signed on right. Pub by church

Local produce drives the enjoyable menu here

Squirrelled away in the rural Batcombe Vale, this honey-coloured stone inn enjoys a peaceful position with a lovely rear garden overlooking the old parish church. The long and low-ceilinged main bar has exposed stripped beams, a huge stone inglenook with log fire, and is tastefully decorated, with pale blue walls hung with old paintings. From gleaming handpumps on the bar come pints of local brews including Plain Ales Innocence. Menus draw on the wealth of fresh seasonal produce available, including surplus vegetables from local allotments. Lunches take in broccoli and Dorset Blue Vinny soup; and beer battered fish and chips. Choice at dinner extends to steamed Cornish mussels in chilli, shallot, ginger and lemongrass cream; or a more traditional home-made beefburger. Desserts include chocolate fondant with salted caramel ice cream or a board of local cheeses.

Open all wk Mon-Fri 11-3 6-11 (Sat 11-11 Sun 12-10.30) ⊕ FREE HOUSE ◀ Butcombe Bitter, Plain Ales Innocence, Wild Beer Ö Rich's Farmhouse, Ashton Press. **Facilities** ❤ (Bar Garden) ◀❖ Children's menu Children's portions Garden Parking WiFi

PICK OF THE PUBS

The Carpenters Arms

STANTON WICK   Map 4 ST66

tel: 01761 490202 **BS39 4BX**
email: carpenters@buccaneer.co.uk
web: www.the-carpenters-arms.co.uk
dir: *From A37 at Chelwood rdbt take A368 signed Bishop Sutton. Right to Stanton Wick*

Good food and local ale in peaceful hamlet

The Carpenters Arms is well placed for visiting Bath, Bristol and the smaller cathedral city of Wells, but if you're already in one of these cities, then this quiet hamlet is equally well situated if you fancy pointing the car the other way and heading for somewhere rural. If you have your walking boots, nearby Chew Valley Lake is an established wildlife haven, where you can walk the Grebe and Bittern nature trails. A charming stone-built, pantile-roofed free house overlooking the Chew Valley, the pub was converted from a row of miners' cottages. Beyond the flower-hung exterior, in the rustic bar, you'll find low beams, old pews, squashy sofas, and precision-cut logs stacked neatly from floor to ceiling in the large fireplace. It all adds up to an appealing, music-free, chatty atmosphere. For a pint of local Butcombe Bitter, the bar is where you need to be, although you can always take it outside to the attractively landscaped patio. The menus are changed regularly to make the best of West Country, seasonal produce, incorporated into a menu that might feature duck liver and port pâté; spicy tomato and caramelised onion chutney; Doom Bar battered pollock fillet, chunky chips, peas and home-made tartare sauce; and six-hour brisket of beef, mash, green beans, roasted baby onion and thyme sauce. And then there are the delicious home-made desserts, especially the treacle tart with clotted cream, and the chocolate and raspberry brownie with honeycomb ice cream. The extensive wine list combines New and Old World favourites, with a lovely Chilean pudding wine available by the half bottle.

Open all day all wk 11-11 (Sun 12-10.30) Closed 25-26 Dec **Food** Lunch Mon-Sat 12-2.30, Sun 12-9 Dinner Mon-Thu 6-9.30, Fri-Sat 6-10, Sun 12-9 Restaurant menu available all wk ⊞ FREE HOUSE ◖ Butcombe Bitter, Sharp's Doom Bar. ♟ 10
Facilities Non-diners area ♠♦ Children's menu Children's portions Outside area ☴ Parking WiFi 🚐 (notice required)

SHEPTON MALLET *continued*

The Waggon and Horses | PICK OF THE PUBS

tel: 01749 880302 **Old Frome Rd, Doulting Beacon BA4 4LA**
email: waggon.horses09@googlemail.com
dir: *1.5m NE of Shepton Mallet. From Shepton Mallet take A37 N towards Bristol. At x-roads right into Old Frome Rd (follow brown pub sign)*

Family-run pub with a large enclosed garden

By a lonely crossroads with views towards Glastonbury Tor from its perch high in the Mendip Hills, this long, whitewashed building was a coaching inn in the 18th century. Its arched doorway once led into the blacksmith's forge. Beers include Butcombe and Box Steam brewery's Chuffin' Ale, with real ciders from Wilkins Farmhouse and Ashton Press. A bar menu lists lunchtime baguettes, jacket potatoes, ploughman's and cheesy chips, while among traditional, home-cooked mains are steak, ale and mushroom pie; home-made cod fishcakes; freshly made smoked salmon tagliatelle; and a range of beef and gammon steaks. Vegetarian lasagne is served with chips and garlic bread. Friday night is (motor) Bike Night, the second Wednesday of the month is Acoustic Night, and an Italian food evening is held on the last Thursday.

Open all wk Mon-Sat 12-2.30 6-11 (Sun 12-3 6-10) **Food** Lunch Mon-Sat 12-2.30, Sun 12-3 Dinner Mon-Sat 6-9, Sun 6-8 ⊕ FREE HOUSE ◼ Butcombe, Box Steam Brewery Chuffin' Ale ♻ Wilkins Farmhouse, Ashton Press. **Facilities** Non-diners area ✿ (Bar Garden) ♦ Children's menu Children's portions Garden ⊞ Parking WiFi ☞

SHEPTON MONTAGUE | Map 4 ST63

The Montague Inn | PICK OF THE PUBS

tel: 01749 813213 **BA9 8JW**
email: info@themontagueinn.co.uk
dir: *From Wincanton take A371 towards Castle Cary, right signed Shepton Montague. Or from A359, S of Bruton left signed Shepton Montague*

A treasure amongst the country lanes of Somerset

Located in rolling unspoilt Somerset countryside on the edge of sleepy Shepton Montague, this 18th-century stone-built village inn is hidden down winding country lanes. Tastefully decorated throughout, with the homely bar featuring old dark pine and an open log fire, and a cosy, yellow-painted dining room, the focus and draw of this rural dining pub is the careful sourcing of local foods from artisan producers and the kitchen's imaginative seasonal menus. Expect to find cask ales from Bath Ales; salads, fruit and vegetables from local farms, and free-range eggs from Blackacre Farm. This translates to lunchtime dishes like duck liver parfait and orange jelly; smoked haddock soufflé; and devilled chicken livers on toast. Evening specials might include rump of lamb with roasted garlic and parsley mash, ending with strawberry parfait and berry compôte. The attractive rear terrace with rural views is perfect for summer sipping. Families are most welcome.

Open 12-3 6-11.30 Closed Sun eve & BHs eve **Food** Lunch all wk 12-2.30 Dinner Mon-Sat 7-9 ⊕ FREE HOUSE ◼ Bath Ales Gem, Guest ales ♻ Thatchers Gold, Lilley's Apples & Pears, Local cider. ♛ **Facilities** Non-diners area ✿ (Bar Garden) ♦ Children's portions Family room Garden ⊞ Cider festival Parking WiFi

---

SOMERTON | Map 4 ST42

The White Hart

tel: 01458 272273 **Market Place TA11 7LX**
email: info@whitehartsomerton.com
dir: *In village centre*

500-year-old inn beside pretty market place

Chic modern lines blend easily with old beams, wooden flooring, matchboarding and other timeless features to produce a quality dining pub where beer drinkers aren't left on the back foot and children and dogs are welcome. Bath Ales and Cheddar beers, together with farmhouse ciders ensure the place is a thriving local; a great place to sup is the sheltered beer garden here. Diners can revel in a fine choice of dishes using West Country ingredients; Wiltshire rabbit with chorizo, or a platter of pickled, smoked, tartare and potted fish may tempt.

Open all day all wk 9am-11pm (Sun 9am-10.30pm) **Food** Lunch all wk 12-3 Dinner all wk 6-10 Restaurant menu available all wk ⊕ FREE HOUSE ◼ Cheddar Ales Potholer, Bath Ales Gem, Guest ales ♻ Thatchers Gold, The Orchard Pig, Harry's Cider. ♛ **Facilities** Non-diners area ✿ (Bar Garden) ♦ Children's menu Children's portions Garden ⊞ WiFi ☞ (notice required)

STANTON WICK | Map 4 ST66

The Carpenters Arms | PICK OF THE PUBS

See Pick of the Pubs on page 445

STOGUMBER | Map 3 ST03

The White Horse

tel: 01984 656277 **High St TA4 3TA**
email: info@whitehorsestogumber.co.uk
dir: *From Taunton take A358 to Minehead. In 8m left to Stogumber, 2m into village centre. Right at T-junct & right again. Pub opposite church*

Village local off the beaten track

This traditional free house on the edge of the Quantock Hills is ideally situated for walkers and visitors travelling on the West Somerset Steam Railway and who alight at Stogumber station. Formerly the village's Market Hall and Reading Room, the dining room is now the place to study a menu of home-cooked dishes such as Caribbean pork with apple, mango and ginger; steak and kidney pudding; or local gammon steak, egg and chips. Enjoy local ales such as Otter Bitter in the pretty courtyard garden.

Open all day all wk **Food** Lunch all wk 12-2 Dinner all wk 7-9 ⊕ FREE HOUSE ◼ St Austell Proper Job, Otter Bitter, Local & Guest ales ♻ Thatchers, Healey's Cornish Rattler, Lilley's Apples & Pears. **Facilities** Non-diners area ✿ (Bar Restaurant Garden) ♦ Children's menu Children's portions Garden ⊞ Parking WiFi ☞ (notice required)

STREET | Map 4 ST43

The Two Brewers ★★★★ INN

tel: 01458 442421 **38 Leigh Rd BA16 0HB**
email: thetwobrewers@yahoo.com **web:** www.thetwobrewers.co.uk
dir: *In town centre. From High St into Leigh Rd. 400mtrs to pub*

A country pub in a town

Located in a quiet area of Street, this country-style, creeper clad stone inn is an ideal touring base, with the fascinating Somerset Levels and the medieval glories of Glastonbury within easy reach. Over the years more than 500 guest beers have shared billing with the local favourite St Austell Tribute. Robust and traditional pub meals – some available as child portions – are the order of the day here; Mediterranean pasta; plaice, peas and jacket potato, or three-egg omelettes are home cooked, as are the changing daily specials. A final flourish could be a fantasy fudge sundae. The pub is proudly music and fruit-machine free; there's a grassy garden where dogs are welcome. En suite accommodation is available.

Open all wk 11-3 6-11 (Sun 11.30-3 6-10.30) Closed 25-26 Dec **Food** Lunch all wk 12-2 Dinner all wk 6-9 ⊕ FREE HOUSE ◼ St Austell Tribute, 3 guest ales ♻ Westons Stowford Press. **Facilities** Non-diners area ♦ Children's menu Children's portions Garden ⊞ Parking WiFi **Rooms** 3

PICK OF THE PUBS

The Rock Inn

WATERROW   Map 3 ST02

tel: 01984 623293 **TA4 2AX**
web: www.rockinnwaterrow.co.uk
dir: *From Taunton take B3227. Waterrow approx 14m W. Or from M5 junct 27, A361 towards Tiverton, then A396 N, right to Bampton, then B3227 to Waterrow*

Traditional food with a contemporary edge

A back-road between Taunton and South Molton brings you to this 400-year-old, half-timbered former smithy and coaching inn, built into the rock-face beside the River Tone. Successfully at the helm are husband and wife team Daren and Ruth Barclay, whose business philosophy is "to offer a more modern approach to dining... and to dispense with the set restaurant format". This doesn't mean there isn't a restaurant, because there is: it's up a few steps, with an open fire, scrubbed tables and a flexible menu. And, of course, there's a bar – dogs on leads welcome – where locals congregate on the well-worn floors in front of the log fire drinking real ales with appropriate West Country names like St Austell Tribute and Cotleigh Tawny Owl, or Thatchers Gold cider. Both eating areas share the same menu, which Daren changes according to whatever fine local produce he can source. Far from

untypical are lamb hotpot with roasted vegetables; Aberdeen Angus grilled sirloin steak with mushroom, tomato, hand-cut chips and truffle butter; pigs' cheeks braised in cider with greens and black pudding; and falafel with haloumi cheese, raita sauce, roasted butternut and pine kernels. Other dishes feature Brixham's best fish, delivered daily, such as deep-fried, beer-battered Cornish plaice. Local shoots provide the game, perhaps venison haunch steak with horseradish mash and braised red cabbage; and wild rabbit pie with woodland mushroom, truffle mash and roasted vegetables. A private dining room caters for up to 18 people.

Open 12-3 6-11 Closed Sun eve-Mon
Food Lunch Wed-Sun 12-2 Dinner Tue-Sat 6.30-9 ⊕ FREE HOUSE ◗ Cotleigh Tawny Owl, St Austell Proper Job & Tribute ♂ Thatchers Gold. ♟ 10
Facilities Non-diners area
🐾 (Bar Outside area) ♦♦ Children's menu Outside area ⌱ Parking WiFi
🚐 (notice required)

TAUNTON
Map 4 ST22

The Hatch Inn

tel: 01823 480245 **Village Rd, Hatch Beauchamp TA3 6SG**
dir: *M5 junct 25, S on A358 for 3m. Left to Hatch Beauchamp, pub in 1m*

A good reputation for quality pub food and ales

Surrounded by splendid Somerset countryside, the pub dates back to the mid-1700s and has its share of ghostly occupants. The inn prides itself on its friendly, community atmosphere and the quality of its wines and West Country beers. Wholesome home-made food is served, prepared from seasonally changing, local produce, with a good choice of snacks and meals such as breaded whitebait, vegetable chilli, chicken korma and gammon steak. There's a takeaway menu as well.

Open all day 12-3 6-11 (Sat 12-12 Sun 12-10.30) Closed Mon **Food** Lunch Tue-Sun 12-3 Dinner Tue-Sun 6-9 ⊕ FREE HOUSE ◀ Sharp's Doom Bar, Guest ales ○ Westons Stowford Press, Thatchers Gold. ♀ 9 **Facilities** Non-diners area ❖ (Bar Outside area) ◀ Children's menu Children's portions Outside area ⊓ Parking WiFi ▭ (notice required)

TINTINHULL
Map 4 ST41

The Crown and Victoria Inn ★★★★ INN ◉

PICK OF THE PUBS

tel: 01935 823341 **14 Farm St BA22 8PZ**
email: info@thecrownandvictoria.co.uk **web:** www.thecrownandvictoria.co.uk
dir: *1m S of A303. Adjacent to Tintinhull Garden (NT)*

Excellent food served in this family-friendly inn

Three hundred years old, and run by Isabel Thomas and Mark Hilyard, this lovely pub occupies an enviable position amidst the sweeping willow trees in its tranquil beer garden. The beer pumps belong exclusively to West Country real ales, such as Butcombe, Cheddar and Yeovil, while from the wine list, 10 are sold by the glass. Locally-sourced food, much of it organic and free-range, feature on the AA Rosette menus. Typical starters might include fried duck egg and foie gras with toasted brioche; and half a pint of prawns with garlic mayonnaise. Mains could include pan-fried chicken breast with wild mushroom sauce, potato hash brown and crispy proscuitto ham; chuck and brisket burger with smoked cheddar, bacon and chips; or mushroom Wellington with cranberry and port sauce. Finish with blueberry crumble tart with crème Anglaise or a board of West Country cheeses. Five spacious, well-equipped bedrooms complete the picture.

Open all wk 10-4 5.30-late **Food** Lunch all wk 12-2.30 Dinner Mon-Sat 6.30-9.30 ⊕ FREE HOUSE ◀ Sharp's Doom Bar, Butcombe, Cheddar, Cotleigh, Yeovil ○ Ashton Press. ♀ 10 **Facilities** Non-diners area ◀ Children's menu Children's portions Garden ⊓ Parking WiFi ▭ **Rooms** 5

TRISCOMBE
Map 4 ST13

The Blue Ball Inn
PICK OF THE PUBS

tel: 01984 618242 **TA4 3HE**
email: enq@blueballinn.info
dir: *From Taunton take A358 past Bishops Lydeard towards Minehead*

Inventive dishes with top quality, traceable ingredients

Although the 18th-century Blue Ball is still down the same narrow lane in the Quantock Hills, some years ago it moved into a pretty thatched barn across the road. The inn looks south to the Brendon Hills and serves regional ales such as Exmoor Stag, along with Thatchers and Mad Apple ciders. A change of hands has not detracted from the focus on reliably sourced, fully traceable produce, and cooking to order is still the order of the day. Share a board of nibbles at lunchtime, or choose your filling for a fresh sandwich made with home-baked bread. Look to

the restaurant carte for a proper three-course treat: Fowey River mussels with white wine, garlic and thyme; slow-cooked shank of lamb with Moroccan spices, couscous, apricots and pistachios; and a sticky toffee pudding with butterscotch and Somerset clotted cream.

Open 12-3 6-11 (Fri-Sat 12-11 Sun 12-6) Closed 25 Dec, 26 Dec eve, 1 Jan eve, Sun eve **Food** Lunch all wk 12-3 Dinner Mon-Sat 7-9 ⊕ FREE HOUSE ◀ Exmoor Stag, Courage Directors ○ Thatchers Gold, Mad Apple. ♀ 10 **Facilities** Non-diners area ❖ (Bar Garden) ◀ Children's menu Children's portions Garden ⊓ Parking WiFi ▭ (notice required)

WAMBROOK
Map 4 ST20

NEW The Cotley Inn

tel: 01460 62348 **TA20 3EN**
email: contact@cotleyinnwambrook.co.uk
dir: *Take A30 from Chard towards Yarcombe. At thatched roundhouse turn left to Wambrook. Pub on right*

Local fare served in Grade II listed building

Situated in classic Somerset countryside, The Cotley makes an ideal watering hole for lovers of peace and quiet. Walkers with dogs enjoy open fires in winter, and the raised terrace in summer with views over surrounding hills. Formerly the New Inn, it was bought and re-named the Cotley by Colonel Eames, after the Cotley Harriers. With a pint of Exmoor in hand, choose from pub fare such as home-made beef lasagne, or look to the specials list for dishes like plaice fillet stuffed with prawns and crabmeat. With spirit calmed and body replete, depart for a visit to the lovely gardens of Cricket St Thomas a short drive away.

Open 12-3 6-11 Closed Sun eve & Mon L **Food** Lunch 12-2, Sun 12-2.30 Dinner Mon-Sat 6.30-9 Av main course £12 ⊕ FREE HOUSE ◀ Otter Bitter & Amber, Exmoor Ales Fox ○ Hecks. **Facilities** ❖ (Bar Garden) ◀ Children's menu Children's portions Garden ⊓ Parking

WATERROW
Map 3 ST02

The Rock Inn
PICK OF THE PUBS

See Pick of the Pubs on page 447

WEDMORE
Map 4 ST44

The George Inn ★★★★ INN

tel: 01934 712124 **Church St BS28 4AB**
email: info@thegeorgewedmore.co.uk **web:** www.thegeorgewedmore.co.uk
dir: *M5 junct 22, follow Bristol/Cheddar signs (A38). From dual carriageway right, follow signs for Mark, then Wedmore. Pub in village centre*

Home-from-home philosophy at pretty village inn

At this former coaching inn all the original features, artwork, old and new furniture blend seamlessly, and there are four different dining areas, each with a warming open fire lit in the winter months. Food is sourced as locally and seasonally as possible – perhaps choose cream of mushroom and tarragon soup; pheasant, apple and Calvados pâté, onion confit; slow-braised shin of beef chilli con carne; rabbit and partridge pie; and roasted whole Cornish plaice, home-made chips, lemon and caper butter. As it's a free house, expect cask ales from Butcombe and Sharp's, and Wilkins Farmhouse real cider, together with an ever-changing choice of craft beers. Stylish accommodation is available.

Open all day all wk **Food** Lunch Mon-Fri 12-2, Sat-12-3, Sun 12-8 Dinner Mon-Sat 6-9, Sun 12-8 Av main course £12 Set menu available Restaurant menu available all wk ⊕ FREE HOUSE ◀ Butcombe, Sharp's Doom Bar ○ Thatchers, Symonds, Wilkins Farmhouse. **Facilities** Non-diners area ❖ (Bar Garden Outside area) ◀ Children's menu Children's portions Play area Garden Outside area ⊓ Beer festival Cider festival Parking WiFi ▭ (notice required) **Rooms** 4

The Swan

tel: 01934 710337 **Cheddar Rd BS28 4EQ**
email: info@theswanwedmore.com
dir: *In village centre*

Busy village pub with all-day food

Open fires, stripped wood floors and big mirrors now greet visitors to what in the early 1700s was a beer house, then by the mid 19th century had developed into a hotel. It's a free house, which allows boss Richard Hamblin to stock the bar with Cheddar Ales Potholer, Bath Ales Gem and Thatchers Gold cider. In the kitchen, head chef Tom Blake, ex-River Cottage Canteen, is now in charge of a team producing cider-steamed Dorset clams with watercress, soy and peanut dressing; merguez-spiced chickpea and butternut stew; and chargrilled Somerset rib-eye steak, roasted garlic, parsley butter and hand-cut chips.

Open all day all wk **Food** Contact pub for food times ⊕ FREE HOUSE ◖ Cheddar Ales Potholer, Bath Ales Gem ⌀ Thatchers Gold. ♟ 12 **Facilities** Non-diners area ❀ (Bar Garden) ♦♦ Children's menu Children's portions Garden ⋒ Parking WiFi

▮ WELLS   Map 4 ST54

The City Arms

tel: 01749 673916 **69 High St BA5 2AG**
email: cityofwellspubcoltd@hotmail.com
dir: *On corner of Queen St & Lower High St*

Cathedral city gem with a colourful past

Once the city jail, this pink-washed pub then became an abattoir. Owner Penny Lee says some people would argue that it was therefore only a matter of time before it became a hostelry. A true free house, it offers seven real ales, some rarely encountered outside Somerset, three draught ciders, and a good choice of wines and champagnes by the glass. Fresh local produce is paramount, with the menu offering black pudding and streaky bacon salad; Somerset faggots, bubble-and-squeak, garden peas and onion gravy; and creamy fish pie; lean-cut steak and ale pie; home-cooked honey- and mustard-glazed ham; and vegetarian options. The weekly-changing specials board incorporates fresh fish and speciality dishes, such as Somerset chicken casserole.

Open all day 9am-11pm (Fri-Sat 9am-mdnt Sun 10am-11pm) **Food** Lunch all wk 12-9.30 Dinner all wk 12-9.30 ⊕ FREE HOUSE ◖ Cheddar Potholer, Quantock Ale & Rorke's Drift, Glastonbury Hedge Monkey & Golden Chalice ⌀ Ashton Press, Addlestones, Soap Dodger. ♟ 10 **Facilities** Non-diners area ❀ (Bar Garden) ♦♦ Children's menu Children's portions Family room Garden WiFi ▤

The Crown at Wells ★★★★ INN

tel: 01749 673457 **Market Place BA5 2RP**
email: eat@crownatwells.co.uk **web:** www.crownatwells.co.uk
dir: *On entering Wells follow signs for Hotels & Deliveries. Left at lights into Sadler St, left into Market Place. For car park pass Bishop's Palace entrance, post office & town hall*

15th-century coaching inn with famous links

Overlooking the Market Place at Wells and a stone's throw from the magnificent cathedral, the exterior of this 15th-century inn, and indeed the entire Market Place itself, may be familiar to film fans, as they are featured in the 2007 British police comedy, *Hot Fuzz*. The inn's comfortable Penn Barr was named after William Penn, a Quaker who preached from The Crown and who later gave his name to

Pennsylvania. Anton's Bistrot menu choices include starters such as smooth chicken liver and wild mushroom pâté or goats' cheese with beetroot houmous; mains like pan-fried fillet of sea bass with prawn bisque, dressed crab; spinach gnocchi or a selection of burgers. There are also 15 en suite bedrooms.

Open all day all wk Closed 25 Dec **Food** Lunch all wk fr noon Dinner Mon-Sat 6-9.30, Sun 6-9 Restaurant menu available all wk ⊕ FREE HOUSE ◖ Sharp's Doom Bar, Glastonbury Holy Thorn, Butcombe, St Austell Tribute, Palmers Dorset Gold ⌀ Ashton Press, Thatchers Old Rascal. ♟ 11 **Facilities** Non-diners area ♦♦ Children's menu Children's portions Outside area ⋒ Parking WiFi ▤ (notice required) **Rooms** 15

The Fountain Inn   ▮ PICK OF THE PUBS ▮

tel: 01749 672317 **1 Saint Thomas St BA5 2UU**
email: eat@fountaininn.co.uk
dir: *In city centre, at A371 & B3139 junct. Follow signs for The Horringtons. Inn on junct of Tor St & Saint Thomas St*

A gastro-pub with a quirky interior

The tower of Wells Cathedral protrudes above the rooftops a short distance away from this attractive, three-storey, blue-shuttered pub with pretty window boxes. The interior is appealing, too, with a large open fire in the big, comfortable bar, interesting bric-à-brac, discreet music and board games. Owner Tessa Hennessey, who once had her own restaurant in South Africa, is one of the two chefs, the other being the Fountain's long-serving Julie Pearce. Together they maintain a winning repertoire of high quality, home-cooked food, among which are crispy squid with garlic mayo; chicken and butternut Madras curry with coconut rice; grilled salmon with seasonal stir-fry vegetables; and filo parcel with feta, sun-blushed tomatoes, olives and pine nuts. Some of these you'll also find at lunchtime, alongside savoury crêpes, and home-made lasagne. A meal could finish with pear tarte Tatin, or home-made cranberry and almond Bakewell tart. Off-street parking is available opposite the inn.

Open 12-3 6-11 (Sun 12-2.30 7-11) Closed 26 Dec, Mon L **Food** Lunch Tue-Sat 12-2, Sun 12-5 Dinner Mon-Sat 6-9 Restaurant menu available all wk ⊕ PUNCH TAVERNS ◖ Butcombe Bitter, Sharp's Doom Bar, Bath Ales Gem, Guest ales ⌀ Thatchers, Westons Stowford Press. **Facilities** Non-diners area ♦♦ Children's menu Children's portions Parking WiFi ▤ (notice required)

▮ WEST BAGBOROUGH   Map 4 ST13

The Rising Sun Inn

tel: 01823 432575 **TA4 3EF**
email: jon@risingsuninn.info
dir: *Phone for detailed directions*

Family-run pub serving West Country ales

This traditional, 16th-century village pub lies in the picturesque Quantock Hills and is run by the Brinkman family. After a fire the inn was rebuilt around the cob walls and magnificent door; the decor is both bold and smart. A good choice of ales and food, both sourced from local suppliers, is on offer. Main courses include 'Mr Pyne's very best 21-day matured rib steak' with black pepper and cream sauce; and butternut squash risotto, followed by caramelised oranges with honeycomb ice cream. A gallery restaurant above the bar is ideal for private functions.

Open all wk 10.30-3 6-11 **Food** Lunch all wk 12-2 Dinner all wk 6.30-9.30 ⊕ FREE HOUSE ◖ Exmoor Ale, St Austell Proper Job & Tribute. ♟ 8 **Facilities** Non-diners area ❀ (Bar) ♦♦ Children's portions Outside area ⋒ WiFi

---

WEST CAMEL
Map 4 ST52

The Walnut Tree
PICK OF THE PUBS

tel: 01935 851292 **Fore St BA22 7QW**
email: info@thewalnuttreehotel.com
dir: Exit A303 between Sparkford & Yeovilton Air Base at x-rds signed West Camel

Family-run village pub with good reputation for food

Just half a mile from the A303, this family-run country inn makes for an ideal pit stop for those weary travellers driving to and from the West Country. The eponymous tree provides the terrace with welcoming dappled shade on warm sunny days, while inside the black-beamed, part-oak, part-flagstone-floored bar sets the scene. As well as a carefully chosen wine list, West Country-brewed Otter and Sharp's real ales (and Thatchers Gold cider from Somerset) can accompany owner/chef Peter Ball's seasonal, locally sourced dishes in the comfortable, wood-panelled Rosewood restaurant. Typical starters of filo parcel filled with cheddar and red onion marmalade with tomato and basil sauce; or pigeon breast, bacon and mixed leaf salad might precede main courses of fillet of beef Rossini with rich Madeira sauce; or sea bass with prawns, mushrooms and lemon butter. Leave room for one of the 10 home-made desserts.

Open 11-3 5.30-11 Closed 25-26 Dec, 1 Jan, Sun eve, Mon L, Tue L **Food** Lunch Wed-Sun 12-2 Dinner Mon-Sat 6-9 Restaurant menu available Tue-Sat ⊕ FREE HOUSE ◗ Otter Ale & Bitter, Sharp's ♂ Thatchers Gold. **Facilities** Non-diners area ♦♦ Children's portions Garden ⌂ Parking WiFi

---

WEST HATCH
Map 4 ST22

The Farmers Arms

tel: 01823 480980 **TA3 5RS**
email: farmersarmswh@gmail.com
dir: M5 junct 25, A358 towards Ilminster. Approx 2m follow West Hatch & RSPCA Centre signs. Continue following RSPCA signs & brown pub sign (ignore West Hatch sign). Pub at brow of hill on left

Traditional pub that's a favourite retreat for walkers

A converted farmhouse dating from the 16th century in the countryside just a five-minute drive from Taunton. Walkers and riders are frequent visitors as the pub is on the 13.5 mile Neroche Staple Fitzpaine Herepath (meaning people's path). Either sit in the light and airy restaurant or in the beer garden to enjoy well kept Otter and Butcombe beers and food such as a starter of pork and wholegrain mustard terrine and apple purée, or tuna Thai fishcake. Then choose perhaps a main dish of bouillabaisse with grilled salmon, new potatoes, smoked paprika remoulade; or braised pork belly with bubble-and-squeak, honey roast beetroot, braised greens and cider sauce.

Open all day all wk 11am-11.30pm **Food** Lunch Mon-Sat 12-2, Sun 12-3, cream teas 3-5.30 Dinner Mon-Sat 6-9 ⊕ FREE HOUSE ◗ Otter, Exmoor Ales, Butcombe ♂ Westons Mortimers Orchard, Thatchers. **Facilities** Non-diners area ♥ (Bar Garden Outside area) ♦♦ Children's portions Garden Outside area ⌂ Parking WiFi ﹏ (notice required)

WEST HUNTSPILL
Map 4 ST34

Crossways Inn ★★★★ INN
PICK OF THE PUBS

See Pick of the Pubs on opposite page

WEST MONKTON
Map 4 ST22

The Monkton Inn
PICK OF THE PUBS

tel: 01823 412414 **Blundells Ln TA2 8NP**
dir: M5 junct 25 to Taunton, right at Creech Castle for 1m, left into West Monkton, right at Procters Farm, 0.5m on left

Pretty little pub offering hearty meals

A little bit tucked away on the edge of the village, this convivial pub is run by Peter and Val Mustoe who, for many years, lived in South Africa. Once inside you'll undoubtedly be struck by the polished floorboards, stone walls, log fire, leather sofas, smart dining furniture, in fact, by the whole set-up. At the bar you'll be able to order Exmoor and Sharp's real ales, as well as your food, but meals are served only in the restaurant or on the patio. Lunch could be springbok burger and hand-cut chips, or lamb's liver and mash, while the dinner menu offers tapas to share; grilled kingclip fillet with lemon butter; Thai-style chicken and prawn curry; chicken chasseur; or vegetarian choices of risotto, fresh tagliatelle and vegetable curry. Gluten free dishes are available too. On Sundays expect roasts, fish and chips, a curry and chargrills. Peter and Val say they are child, dog and horse friendly.

Open all wk 12-3 6-11 **Food** Lunch all wk 12-2 Dinner Mon-Sat 6-9, Sun 6-8 Restaurant menu available all wk ⊕ ENTERPRISE INNS ◗ Sharp's Doom Bar, Exmoor Ale, Otter Ale ♂ Thatchers Gold, Aspall. ♟ 10 **Facilities** Non-diners area ♥ (Bar Garden Outside area) ♦♦ Children's menu Children's portions Play area Garden Outside area ⌂ Parking WiFi ﹏ (notice required)

WHEDDON CROSS
Map 3 SS93

The Rest and Be Thankful Inn ★★★★ INN

tel: 01643 841222 **TA24 7DR**
email: stay@restandbethankful.co.uk **web:** www.restandbethankful.co.uk
dir: 5m S of Dunster

Traditional pub on Exmoor's heights

Almost 1,000 feet up in Exmoor National Park's highest village, this early 19th-century coaching inn blends old-world charm with friendly hospitality. Today's travellers are welcomed with log fires warming the bar in winter; traditional entertainments of skittle alley and pool table are at the disposal of the energetic. Menus of carefully prepared pub favourites may include deep-fried brie wedges; Exmoor sausages in red onion gravy; a 'taste of the West' cheeseboard; and Somerset farmhouse ice creams. The popular Sunday carvery is excellent value.

Open all wk 10-3 6-close **Food** Lunch all wk 12-2 Dinner all wk 6.30-9 ⊕ FREE HOUSE ◗ Exmoor Ale, St Austell Proper Job & Tribute, Sharp's Own, Guinness ♂ Thatchers & Gold, St Austell Copper Press. ♟ 9 **Facilities** Non-diners area ♦♦ Children's menu Children's portions Garden Beer festival Parking WiFi ﹏ (notice required) **Rooms** 8

PICK OF THE PUBS

Crossways Inn ★★★★ INN

WEST HUNTSPILL   Map 4 ST34

tel: 01278 783756
Withy Rd TA9 3RA
email: info@crosswaysinn.com
web: www.crosswaysinn.com
dir: *M5 juncts 22 or 23, on A38*

Good beer and cider choices plus classic pub food

A family-run 17th century, tile-hung coaching inn ideally positioned for visitors to the Somerset Levels or walkers looking for a cosy respite from the rigours of the Mendip Hills. Warmed by two open log fireplaces, the cosy, wavy-beamed interior has an array of fine old photos of the area. Draw close to the bar to inspect the ever-rotating selection of excellent beers, often from microbreweries in Somerset, such as Moor and RCH. The beer choice increases significantly during the pub's popular Summer Bank Holiday beer festival. Cider drinkers are spoiled for choice, too, with Thatchers on tap and Rich's Cider created at a local farm just a couple of miles away. The classic food here also tends to be very locally sourced, like Somerset rump and sirloin steaks, which come with home-made peppercorn, Stilton or white wine and mushroom sauce. Cottage pie, sausages and mash, curry of the day, and scampi and chips are all popular options, but you will need to check the specials

board for the daily pie. The pasta section of the menu offers lasagne, spaghetti bolognese and, for vegetarians, roasted vegetable and four-cheese bake. Lighter meals include sandwiches, baguettes, ploughman's and jacket potatoes. Interesting desserts are toffee and Dime Bar crunch pie, and Alabama chocolate fudge cake. Under-10s can have a menu of their own. In summer, the large enclosed beer garden and children's play area comes into its own, as does the heated gazebo.

Open all day all wk Closed 25 Dec
Food Lunch all wk 12-2.30 Dinner all wk 6-9 🛢 FREE HOUSE ◀ Exmoor Stag, Cotleigh Snowy, Sharp's Doom Bar,

Otter Ale, RCH Double Header, Moor, Butcombe, Cheddar Gorge Best ♂ Thatchers Gold, Dry & Heritage, Rich's. ♀ 16 **Facilities** Non-diners area ♣ (Bar Restaurant Garden) ♟ Children's menu Children's portions Play area Family room Garden ☴ Beer festival Parking WiFi 🚌 (notice required) **Rooms** 7

WINSFORD
Map 3 SS93

Royal Oak Inn ★★★★ INN

tel: 01643 851455 **TA24 7JE**
email: enquiries@royaloakexmoor.co.uk **web:** www.royaloakexmoor.co.uk
dir: *Follow Winsford signs from A396 (Minehead to Tiverton road)*

Local ales and seasonal produce in a delightful setting

Previously a farmhouse and dairy, the Royal Oak is a stunningly attractive thatched inn in one of Exmoor's prettiest villages, huddled beneath the rising moors beside the River Exe. Inside its all big fires, comfy chairs, restrained paraphernalia and restful decor. So, all the better to enjoy the twin treats of good honest Exmoor beers and rich local produce on the seasonal bar and restaurant menus, including slow-braised lamb shank with pan-fried gnocchi and red wine jus; butternut squash risotto cake; and deep-fried scampi in stout batter and chips.

Open all wk 11-3 6-11 **Food** Lunch all wk 12-2 Dinner all wk 6-9 ⊕ ENTERPRISE INNS ◂ Exmoor Ale, Stag & Gold ♂ Thatchers, Addlestones.
Facilities Non-diners area ◂ Children's menu Children's portions Garden ☰ Parking WiFi **Rooms** 14

WITHYPOOL
Map 3 SS83

The Royal Oak Inn

tel: 01643 831506 **TA24 7QP**
email: enquiries@royaloakwithypool.co.uk
dir: *Phone for detailed directions*

Local food and ales in village pub with literary links

Only four miles from the historic Tarr Steps, the Royal Oak Inn has been the hub of the pretty Exmoor village of Withypool for over 300 years. During that time, the pub has welcomed some notable guests including RD Blackmore, who stayed here whilst writing *Lorna Doone*. In the two bars with their real fires and wheelback chairs, join the locals over a pint of Exmoor Gold, or head to the restaurant for seasonal dishes such as roasted stuffed crown of pheasant with juniper jus; or steak and Exmoor Ale pie.

Open 12-3 6-11 (Summer all wk 12-11) Closed Mon in winter **Food** Lunch all wk 12-3 Dinner all wk 6.30-9 Av main course £12 ⊕ FREE HOUSE ◂ Exmoor Ale & Gold, Guest ale ♂ Sheppy's, Thatchers, Shepton Mallet Cider. ▾ 10
Facilities Non-diners area ♣ (Bar Outside area) ◂ Children's menu Children's portions Outside area ☰ Parking WiFi ▦ (notice required)

WOOKEY
Map 4 ST54

The Burcott Inn

tel: 01749 673874 **Wells Rd BA5 1NJ**
email: ian@burcottinn.co.uk
dir: *2m from Wells on B3139*

Homely stone-built inn offering a friendly welcome

On the edge of a charming village just two miles from the cathedral city of Wells, the age of this 300-year-old pub is confirmed by the low-beamed ceilings, flagstone floors and log fires. Another notable feature is its copper-topped bar with five real ales and Thatchers Gold on handpull. Here, you can have a snack or a daily special, while in the restaurant typical dishes include starters such as garlic mushrooms; pan-fried tiger prawns or warm mushroom and walnut salad; and main dishes like apricot chicken breast or poached salmon fillet. There are also specials board choices. The large enclosed garden enjoys views of the Mendip Hills.

Open 11.30-2.30 6-11 (Sun 12-3) Closed 25-26 Dec, 1 Jan, Sun eve **Food** Lunch all wk 12-2 Dinner Tue-Sat 6.30-9 Restaurant menu available Tue-Sun ⊕ FREE HOUSE ◂ Teignworthy Old Moggie, RCH Pitchfork, Hop Back Summer Lightning, Cheddar Potholer, Butts Barbus barbus ♂ Thatchers Gold. **Facilities** Non-diners area ◂ Children's menu Children's portions Family room Garden ☰ Parking ▦ (notice required)

WOOKEY HOLE
Map 4 ST54

Wookey Hole Inn

tel: 01749 676677 **High St BA5 1BP**
email: mail@wookeyholeinn.com
dir: *Opposite Wookey Hole caves*

A top selection of beers and noteworthy cuisine

Located opposite the famous caves, this family-run inn is outwardly traditional, although the interior looks and feels very laid-back. Somerset and continental draught and bottled beers include Glastonbury Ales Love Monkey and fruity Belgian Früli; local Wilkins Farmhouse tempts cider-heads. The menu offers something for everyone, from light bites like grilled goats' cheese and balsamic tomato bruschetta; to sandwiches (perhaps cheese and apple chutney or cold poached salmon and dill mayo); and hot grill dishes like wild boar burger with caramelised apple and smoked Applewood cheese; or herb marinated chicken breast, sweet potato chips and lemon mayo. Try to leave space for hot date and walnut pudding with toffee sauce, or caramelised poached pear with cinnamon ice cream.

Open all day Closed 25-26 Dec, Sun eve **Food** Lunch all wk 12-2.30 Dinner Mon-Sat 7-9.30 ⊕ FREE HOUSE ◂ Glastonbury Ales Love Monkey, Cheddar Ales, Yeovil, Cottage ♂ Wilkins Farmhouse. **Facilities** Non-diners area ♣ (Bar Garden) ◂ Children's menu Children's portions Garden ☰ Parking WiFi ▦ (notice required)

WRAXALL
Map 4 ST63

NEW The Battleaxes ★★★★ INN

tel: 01275 857473 **Bristol Rd BS48 1LQ**
email: thebattleaxes@flatcappers.co.uk **web:** www.flatcappers.co.uk
dir: *Take A370 from Bristol towards Weston-Super-Mare. Exit for B3130 signed Wraxall. Pub on left in village*

Fab building with great local ales

Built in 1882, The Battleaxes was originally staff quarters for the many servants working for the Gibbs family, who owned the now National Trust-run Tyntesfield Estate. A great example of Gothic Revival architecture, the pub was taken over by Flatcappers, a small local pub company, in 2011. Have a pint of Butcombe Bitter or

Flatcapper Ale while you peruse the menu. Breakfast is served between 8 and 12, but if it's lunch or dinner you're after, no problem. Black pudding Scotch egg might be a good place to start, followed by steak and chips; or roast Loch Duart salmon; desserts might include vanilla rice pudding with poached rhubarb, or a choice of West Country cheeses.

Open all day all wk **Food** Contact pub for food times Av main course £10 Set menu available ⊕ FREE HOUSE ◀ Butcombe Bitter, Three Castles Flatcapper Ale, Bath Ales Dark Side ♂ Bath Ciders Bounders, Westons Stowford Press.
Facilities Non-diners area ✿ (Bar Garden) ♦️ Children's menu Children's portions Garden ⌒ Parking WiFi ☷ (notice required) **Rooms** 6

YEOVIL   Map 4 ST51

The Half Moon Inn ★★★ INN

tel: 01935 850289 **Main St, Mudford BA21 5TF**
email: enquiries@thehalfmooninn.co.uk **web:** www.thehalfmooninn.co.uk
dir: A303 at Sparkford onto A359 to Yeovil, 3.5m on left

Long menu with something for everyone

The exposed beams and flagstone floors retain the character of this painstakingly restored 17th-century village pub just north of Yeovil. Local East Street Cream ale is one of the beers on tap and there are 10 wines by the glass to accompany the extensive menu of home-cooked food, which includes pub classics and main meals such as garlic cream cheese stuffed chicken breast with white wine sauce; oven-roasted barbecue pork ribs; or smoked haddock, cheese and chive mash, mornay sauce and poached egg. Sandwiches, hot paninis and jackets are also available. The large cobbled courtyard is ideal for alfresco dining and spacious, well-equipped bedrooms are also available.

Open all day all wk Closed 25-26 Dec **Food** Lunch Sun-Mon 12-9, Tue-Sat 12-9.30 Dinner Sun-Mon 12-9, Tue-Sat 12-9.30 ⊕ FREE HOUSE ◀ RCH Pitchfork, East Street Cream ♂ Thatchers, Westons Wyld Wood Organic. ♟ 10 **Facilities** Non-diners area ♦️ Children's menu Children's portions Outside area ⌒ Parking WiFi ☷ (notice required) **Rooms** 14

The Masons Arms ★★★★ INN   PICK OF THE PUBS

tel: 01935 862591 **41 Lower Odcombe BA22 8TX**
email: paula@masonsarmsodcombe.co.uk **web:** www.masonsarmsodcombe.co.uk
dir: A3088 to Yeovil, right to Montacute, through village, 3rd right after petrol station to Lower Odcombe

Strong green credentials and a microbrewery

Once a cider house and bolt-hole for local quarry workers, Paula and Drew's thatched, 16th-century pub serves an exclusive clutch of real ales – Odcombe No 1, Spring and Roly Poly – all brewed for it by Drew. The couple are big on green initiatives and grow many of their own vegetables and fruit, and offer organic, vegetarian, biodynamic and Fairtrade wines. Another string to Drew's bow is the modern British cooking that lies behind the dishes on his seasonal and daily-changing menus. Typically, these include honey and rosemary lamb rump with ratatouille and minted gnocchi; red wine-poached brill, herbed cream potatoes and braised cavolo nero with smoked bacon; and sweet potato, okra and spinach pasanda, Peshwari pilau rice and mushroom bhaji. Finish with sticky toffee pudding, butterscotch sauce and vanilla ice cream. The comfortable en suite letting rooms are set back from the road, overlooking the pretty garden.

Open all wk 12-3 6-12 **Food** Lunch all wk 12-2 Dinner all wk 6.30-9.30 ⊕ FREE HOUSE ◀ Odcombe No 1, Spring, Roly Poly, Winters Tail, Half Jack ♂ Thatchers Gold & Heritage. ♟ 8 **Facilities** Non-diners area ✿ (Bar Restaurant Garden) ♦️ Children's menu Children's portions Garden ⌒ Parking WiFi **Rooms** 6

STAFFORDSHIRE

ALSTONEFIELD   Map 16 SK15

The George   PICK OF THE PUBS

tel: 01335 310205 **DE6 2FX**
email: emily@thegeorgeatalstonefield.com
dir: 7m N of Ashbourne, signed Alstonefield to left off A515

An unspoilt, family-run pub in a Peak District village

Up above Dovedale, this attractive, stone-built pub offers a bar with a fire, historic artefacts, portraits of locals and a wide choice of real ales, including Banks's Sunbeam and Jennings Cumberland. There's an original simplicity about the dining room and snug, with their lime-plastered walls, farmhouse furniture, candlelight and fresh flowers. A warm welcome from Emily Brighton, whose family has run The George for three generations, may also contain a polite request to leave any muddy boots at the door – this is a popular walking area. The kitchen's passion for locally sourced food is evident from the organic garden, source of abundant vegetables, salad leaves and herbs. A winter lunch menu might offer potted native brown shrimps; and Derbyshire-reared flat-iron steak, while dinner might start with wood-pigeon breast with hazelnut and plum salad, followed by pan-fried market catch of the day with chorizo, white bean and winter greens cassoulet.

Open all wk Mon-Fri 11.30-3 6-11 (Sat 11.30-11 Sun 12-9.30) Closed 25 Dec **Food** Lunch all wk 12-2.30 Dinner Mon-Sat 7-9, Sun 6.30-9 ⊕ MARSTON'S ◀ Burton Bitter & Pedigree, Jennings Cumberland Ale, Brakspear Oxford Gold, Banks's Sunbeam, Guest ale ♂ Thatchers. ♟ 10 **Facilities** Non-diners area ✿ (Bar Garden) ♦️ Children's portions Garden ⌒ Parking

ALTON   Map 10 SK04

Bulls Head Inn

tel: 01538 702307 **High St ST10 4AQ**
email: janet@thebullsheadalton.co.uk
dir: M6 junct 14, A518 to Uttoxeter. Follow Alton Towers signs. Onto B5030 to Rocester, then B5032 to Alton. Pub in village centre

Family-run inn with a varied menu

This 18th-century coaching inn is handy for the Peak District, and Alton Towers theme park, which is less than a mile away. Oak beams and an inglenook fireplace set the scene for the old-world bar, where a rotating selection of real ales from three handpumps are on offer. In the country-style dining room with its pine furniture and slate floor, the evening menu might include smoked salmon and pesto tagliatelle; oven-roasted lemon and thyme chicken leg; vegetable fajitas; pan-fried sea bass with stir-fried noodles; and curry or pie of the day.

Open all wk 3pm-close (Fri-Sun 12-close) **Food** Lunch Fri-Sat 12-2, Sun 3-8 Dinner Mon-Sat 5-9, Sun 3-8 ⊕ FREE HOUSE ◀ Greene King Abbot Ale & Ruddles County, Sharp's Doom Bar, Guest ales. ♟ 8 **Facilities** Non-diners area ♦️ Children's menu Children's portions Garden ⌒ Parking WiFi

Looking for a beer or cider festival?
Check our listings at the end of this guide

BARTON-UNDER-NEEDWOOD
Map 10 SK11

The Waterfront

tel: 01283 711500 **Barton Marina DE13 8DZ**
email: info@waterfrontbarton.co.uk **web:** www.waterfrontbarton.co.uk
dir: *Exit A38 onto B5016 towards Barton-under-Needwood. 1st left signed Barton Turn. 1st right into Barton Marina*

Large modern pub overlooking a marina

This pub is part of a purpose-built marina complex, and is constructed with reclaimed materials to resemble a Victorian canalside warehouse. Overlooking busy moorings, it offers beers specially brewed for the pub and a fair few cocktails. Dine in the contemporary conservatory from an extensive menu of snacks, oven-fired pizzas, and old favourites like fish and chips, Waterfront beefburger and chargrilled spatchcock chicken. A walk along the Trent & Mersey towpath leads to the nearby National Memorial Arboretum, the UK's Centre of Remembrance.

Open all day all wk Sun-Thu 10am-11pm (Fri-Sat 10am-2am) **Food** Lunch 12-9.30 Dinner 12-9.30 ⊕ FREE HOUSE ◀ St Austell Tribute, Marston's Pedigree, Sharp's Doom Bar, Castle Rock Harvest Pale ♂ Thatchers. ⛀ 20 **Facilities** Non-diners area ♦ Children's menu Children's portions Garden ⋒ Parking WiFi ▭ (notice required)

See advert on opposite page

CAULDON
Map 16 SK04

Yew Tree Inn

tel: 01538 309876 **ST10 3EJ**
email: info@yewtreeinncauldon.co.uk
dir: *From either A52 or A523 follow Cauldon signs. Village approx 5m from Alton Towers*

Affectionately known as the 'junk shop with a bar'

An Aladdin's Cave of a pub, with its collection of antiques and curios, including Queen Victoria's stockings, a 3,000-year-old Grecian urn, penny-farthings, and a

Victorian polyphon. Sit on an old bench, settee or settle for a pint of Burton Bridge Bitter or guest ale, then turn to the modest menu to decide between a traditional Staffordshire pie or a made-to-order sandwich. Time a visit for the July beer festival. The family-owned Yew Tree is a popular meeting place for owners of vintage cars and motorcycles.

Open all wk 6-11 (Fri 6-mdnt Sat 12-12 Sun 12-11) **Food** Lunch Sat-Sun 12-9 Dinner Mon-Fri 6-9, Sat-Sun 12-9 Av main course £5 ⊕ FREE HOUSE ◀ Burton Bridge, Rudgate Ruby Mild, Guest ales ♂ Westons, Abrahalls. ⛀ 9 **Facilities** Non-diners area ♥ (Bar Garden Outside area) ♦ Children's portions Play area Family room Garden Outside area ⋒ Beer festival Cider festival Parking WiFi ▭

CHEADLE
Map 10 SK04

The Queens at Freehay

tel: 01538 722383 **Counslow Rd, Freehay ST10 1RF**
email: mail@queensatfreehay.co.uk
dir: *From Cheadle take A552 towards Uttoxeter. In Mobberley left, through Freehay to pub at next rdbt. Freehay also signed from B5032 (Cheadle to Denstone road)*

Family-run pub tucked away in a quiet village

Surrounded by mature trees and well-tended gardens, this 18th-century, family-run pub and restaurant has a refreshing, modern interior and it's just four miles from Alton Towers. Ringwood Fortyniner and the more local Alton Abbey are among the beers on handpump in the bar. With a good reputation for food, its main menu is supplemented by daily chef's specials on the fresh fish and meat boards. Expect crispy sweet chilli chicken; or moules marinière to start, followed by home-made beef and Merlot shortcrust pie; Barnsley lamb chops; a chargrilled steak; or red pepper and spicy bean enchiladas. At lunchtimes there are light bite options such as scampi and chips; and pork sausage, egg and chips.

Open all wk 12-3 6-11 (Sun 12-4 6.30-11) Closed 25-26, 31 Dec-1 Jan **Food** Lunch Mon-Sat 12-2, Sun 12-2.30 Dinner Mon-Sat 6-9.30, Sun 6.30-9.30 Restaurant menu available all wk ⊕ FREE HOUSE ◀ Peakstones Rock Alton Abbey, Marston's Pedigree & Oyster Stout, Ringwood Fortyniner. ⛀ **Facilities** Non-diners area ♦ Children's portions Garden ⋒ Parking WiFi

COLTON
Map 10 SK02

The Yorkshireman
PICK OF THE PUBS

tel: 01889 583977 **Colton Rd WS15 3HB**
email: theyorkshireman@wine-dine.co.uk
dir: *From A51 rdbt in Rugeley follow rail station signs, under rail bridge, to pub*

Try real ales from the local microbrewery

The pub's name comes from a scion of the White Rose county who was once landlord here although the heritage of this edge-of-town pub opposite Rugeley's Trent Valley railway station is lost in the mists of time. Many believe it may have been established as a tavern to serve the new railway in the 19th century and it's certainly seen a lot of life since those days, including a meeting place for farmers and soldiers. Walk through the doors today to find a panelled, wood-floored dining pub specialising in dishes using top Staffordshire produce and offering beers such as Blythe Brewery's Bagots Bitter. The eclectic furnishings are part of the charm, and the faux Stubbs paintings attract much comment. The seasonal menus are updated regularly, but a good range covering all the bases is assured.

Open all wk 12-2.30 5.30-10 (Sat 12-11 Sun 12-6) **Food** Lunch Mon-Sat 12-2.30, Sun 12-6 Dinner Mon-Sat 6-9 Set menu available ⊕ FREE HOUSE ◀ Blythe Bagots Bitter & Palmer's Poison ♂ Symonds. ⛀ 14 **Facilities** Non-diners area ♥ (Bar Garden) ♦ Children's portions Garden ⋒ Parking WiFi ▭ (notice required)

ELLASTONE

Map 10 SK14

NEW The Duncombe Arms

tel: 01335 324275 **Main Rd DE6 2GZ**
email: hello@duncombearms.co.uk web: www. duncombearms.co.uk
dir: *From Ashbourne take A515 towards Lichfield. 1m, take A52 towards Leek. Approx 1m left onto B5032 signed Ellastone. In village turn left, pub on left*

Beautifully refurbished village pub in the Dove Valley

George Eliot set her first novel *Adam Bede* in Ellastone. In this bucolic corner of Staffordshire, between the wooded Dove Valley and the shapely Weaver Hills, is where you'll find The Duncombe Arms, which re-opened in 2012 as a notable dining pub after a period of dereliction. Classic and contemporary architecture now blend seamlessly in the sturdy old inn. Over a glass of Duncombe Ale consider a comforting menu of pub stalwarts enhanced with modern dishes; start with Cropwell Bishop Blue Stilton twice baked soufflé before enjoying perhaps smoked haddock risotto with crispy Wootton egg; or lemon roasted chicken breast, pesto tagliatelle and sun-blushed tomatoes. The wine list is extensive.

The Duncombe Arms

Open all day all wk **Food** Lunch Mon-Sat 12-2.30, Sun 12-8 Dinner Mon-Thu 6-9, Fri-Sat 5.30-10, Sun 12-8 Av main course £15 Set menu available Restaurant menu available all wk ⊕ FREE HOUSE ◀ Marston's Pedigree, Duncombe Ale, Timothy Taylor Landlord ♻ Addlestones, Aspall Premier Cru. ♟ 21 **Facilities** Non-diners area ✿ (Bar Garden) ♦ Children's menu Children's portions Garden ⋔ Parking WiFi ▦ (notice required)

GREAT BRIDGEFORD
Map 10 SJ82

The Mill at Worston

tel: 01785 282710 **Worston Ln ST18 9QA**
email: info@themillatworston.co.uk **web:** www.themillatworston.co.uk
dir: *M6 junct 14, A5013 signed Eccleshall. 2m to Great Bridgeford. Turn right signed Worston Mill. Or from Eccleshall on A5013 towards Stafford. 3m to Great Bridgeford, turn left to Mill*

A restored corn mill serving good food

Documents can trace a mill on this site from 1279. The building that now occupies this rural spot beside the River Sow dates from 1814, when it was in daily use as a corn mill. Visitors can still see the original wheel and gearing that powered the mill stone. Drop in for meals that range from ciabatta or baguette sandwiches, jacket potatoes and grills to home-made steak and ale pie, wild mushroom carbonara and roasted field mushrooms with Welsh rarebit, all washed down with a pint of Greene King IPA perhaps? The pretty gardens, with duck pond, make a great place for alfresco eating in the warmer months.

Open all day all wk Closed 26 Dec **Food** Lunch all wk 12-6 Dinner Sun-Thu 6-9, Fri-Sat 6-10 Set menu available Restaurant menu available ⊕ FREE HOUSE ◀ Morland Old Speckled Hen, Greene King IPA, Rotating guest ales. ♀ 12
Facilities Non-diners area ◆▌ Children's menu Children's portions Play area Garden 🍴 Parking WiFi 🚌 (notice required)

See advert on opposite page

LEEK
Map 16 SJ95

Three Horseshoes Inn ★★★★ INN ◉◉

tel: 01538 300296 **Buxton Rd, Blackshaw Moor ST13 8TW**
email: enquiries@3shoesinn.co.uk **web:** www.3shoesinn.co.uk
dir: *On A53, 3m N of Leek*

Award-winning food at a well known inn

A family-run inn in the Peak District National Park, the Three Horseshoes offers breathtaking views of the moorlands, Tittesworth reservoir and rock formations from the attractive gardens. Inside this creeper-covered inn are ancient beams, gleaming brass, rustic furniture and wood fires in the winter, with a good selection of real ales. Using the best Staffordshire produce, visitors can choose from wide ranging lunch and dinner menus: locally-reared roast meat in the bar carvery and the bar and grill; the relaxed atmosphere of the brasserie offering modern British and Thai dishes, or Kirks Restaurant. Delicious afternoon teas are also available.

Open all day all wk **Food** Contact pub for food times Restaurant menu available ⊕ FREE HOUSE ◀ Morland Old Speckled Hen, Sharp's Doom Bar, Marston's Pedigree, Blue Moon, Guest ales. ♀ 12 **Facilities** Non-diners area ◆▌ Children's menu Children's portions Play area Garden 🍴 Parking WiFi 🚌 (notice required) **Rooms** 26

ONNELEY
Map 15 SJ74

The Wheatsheaf Inn

tel: 01782 751581 **Bar Hill Rd CW3 9QF**
email: pub@wheatsheafpub.co.uk
dir: *On A525 between Madeley & Woore*

Attractive inn offering good regional ales

Starting life as a coaching inn in the 18th century, this whitewashed pub with flower-filled window boxes lies in the hamlet of Onneley. Although it has been modernised, the old beams and fires are still in place, making for a cosy setting to enjoy real ales from Staffordshire breweries like Titanic and Peakstones. Meat from the local farm appears on the menu, which includes whole baby chicken glazed with honey and mustard, beefburger and lamb steak.

Open all day all wk **Food** Lunch Mon-Sat 12-9, Sun 12-8 Dinner Mon-Sat 12-9, Sun 12-8 ⊕ FREE HOUSE ◀ Wells Bombardier, Joule's, Titanic, Salopian, Peakstones, 2 guest ales Ò Westons. ♀ 8 **Facilities** Non-diners area ❀ (Bar Garden) ◆▌ Children's menu Children's portions Play area Family room Garden 🍴 Parking WiFi

STAFFORD
Map 10 SJ92

The Holly Bush Inn
PICK OF THE PUBS

See Pick of the Pubs on page 458

The Mill at Worston

Worston Lane, Great Bridgeford, Staffordshire ST18 9QA • **Tel:** 01785 282710
Website: www.themillatworston.co.uk • **Email:** info@themillatworston.co.uk

It is quite rare to stumble across a hidden gem as unique as *The Mill at Worston*. Nestled in some of our best Staffordshire countryside it sits beside the River Sow and has spectacular grounds, yet it is easily accessible, being just five minutes from junction 14 of the M6. The building itself is a 200 year old watermill and it has been tastefully converted retaining many features from its milling days. Thus, the lounge is dominated by the impressive original 10 foot pit wheel and full of character with enormous original beams spanning the ceiling and log burning stoves providing warmth on autumn and winter evenings. *The Mill at Worston* is cask marque accredited and has four cask ales on rotation, featuring beers from many local micro-breweries including Titanic, Lymestone and Peakstones.

The Mill at Worston is an avid supporter of local sourcing, and nearby farms and suppliers feature strongly on their menu. Starters include grilled black pudding topped with poached egg laced with a mustard dressing and oven baked field mushroom filled with welsh rarebit and served with rustic bread. For your main course their weekly specials currently feature such temptations as salmon au poivre with sauté potatoes, chargrilled vegetables and chervil hollandaise and mint glazed lamb cutlets with leek and potato cake, roast beetroot and spinach. If you've still got room desserts start from £4.25 and include the highly recommended sticky toffee pudding made to The Mill's own recipe, or for those wanting something more adventurous why not try the raspberry and basil cheesecake? Alternatively, the cheeseboard features traditional favourites, along with more local produce. Service is friendly and attentive without being too formal, making *The Mill at Worston* the perfect place to relax with family and friends.

The Mill at Worston serves food all day, seven days a week from 12pm. The venue's restaurant is open Wednesday to Saturday evenings from 6pm, and 12pm–4pm on Sundays when customers can enjoy a traditional Sunday carvery. Reservations are advisable, especially at peak times.

Directions to *The Mill at Worston* and further information can be downloaded
from www.themillatworston.co.uk.

PICK OF THE PUBS

The Holly Bush Inn

STAFFORD Map 10 SJ92

tel: 01889 508234 **Salt ST18 0BX**
email: geoff@hollybushinn.co.uk
web: www.hollybushinn.co.uk
dir: *From Stafford on A518 towards Weston. Left signed Salt. Pub on left in village*

Ancient pub with second oldest licence in England

This thatched inn is situated in the village of Salt, which has been a settlement since the Saxon period. It is thought to be only the second pub in the country to receive, back in Charles II's reign, a licence to sell alcohol, although the building itself may date from 1190; and when landlord Geoff Holland's son Joseph became a joint licensee at the age of 18 years and 6 days, he was the youngest person ever to be granted a licence. The pub's comfortably old fashioned interior contains all the essential ingredients: heavy carved beams, open fires, attractive prints and cosy alcoves. The kitchen has a strong commitment to limiting food miles by supporting local producers, and to ensuring that animals supplying meat have lived stress-free lives. The main menu features traditional dishes such as steak and ale pie; battered cod with mushy peas; and beefburger with beer battered onion rings; but also included are the still-traditional-but-less-well-known, such as grilled pork chop with

cheese, beer and mustard topping; and free range supreme of chicken with Guinness. Specials change every session, but usually include Staffordshire oatcakes stuffed with bacon and cheese; hand-made pork, leek and Stilton sausages with fried eggs and chips; roast topside of beef; or ham with sweet Madeira gravy. Evening specials may offer home-smoked fillet of Blythe Field trout with horseradish sauce; warm pan-fried duck and pear salad; Scottish mussels steamed with cider and cream; rabbit casserole with dumplings; or slow-cooked mutton with caper sauce. Seasonal puddings include traditional bread-and-butter pudding, and apple crumble. During the warmer months hand-made pizzas are cooked in a wood-fired brick oven.

Open all day all wk 12-11 (Sun 12-10.30) Closed 25-26 Dec
Food Mon-Sat 12-9.30, Sun 12-9
⊕ FREE HOUSE ◖ Marston's Pedigree, Adnams, Guest ales. ♟ 12
Facilities Non-diners area
♦♦ Children's menu Children's portions
Garden ⌒ Beer festival Cider festival
Parking WiFi

STOURTON — Map 10 SO88

The Fox Inn

tel: 01384 872614 & 872123 **Bridgnorth Rd DY7 5BH**
email: foxinnstourton@gmail.com
dir: *5m from Stourbridge town centre. On A458 (Stourbridge to Bridgnorth road)*

Forty-plus years behind the bar

Stefan Caron has been running this late 18th-century inn for more than 40 years. In unspoilt countryside on an estate once owned by Lady Jane Grey, it retains the style of an old country pub, with church pews in the bar, where Black Country brewers Bathams and Wye Valley put on a double act. Menus variously offer chicken balti; fresh tagliatelle; Tex Mex, a rib-eye steak with chilli and mozzarella; pie of the day with peas and chunky chips; and beer-battered cod with mushy peas. The large garden with weeping willow, gazebo and attractive patio area are the external attractions.

Open all wk 10.30-3 5-11 (Sat-Sun 10.30am-11pm) **Food** Lunch Mon-Sat 12-2.30, Sun 12.30-7 Dinner Tue-Sat 7-9.30, Sun 12.30-7 ⊕ FREE HOUSE ◀ Bathams, Wye Valley HPA, Guinness Ⓒ Robinsons, Thatchers. **Facilities** Non-diners area ❤ (Garden) ♦ Children's menu Children's portions Garden ⊓ Parking WiFi ➡ (notice required)

SUMMERHILL — Map 10 SK00

Oddfellows in the Boat

tel: 01543 361692 **The Boat, Walsall Rd WS14 0BU**
email: info@oddfellowsintheboat.com
dir: *A461 (Lichfield towards Walsall). At rdbt junct with A5 (Muckley Corner) continue on A461. 500mtrs, U-turn on dual carriageway back to pub*

An ale-lover's dream

Just four miles from Lichfield, this light and airy pub with country pine furnishings once served bargees on the now-disused 'Curly Wyrley' Canal to the rear. Real ale lovers can enjoy what amounts to a rolling beer festival all year thanks to an ever-changing choice from local microbreweries. Locally sourced dishes are prepared in an open kitchen and chalked up daily. Typical choices include spatchcock chicken, garlic butter and French fries; tandoori lamb culets, braised rice, mint yogurt and poppadoms; and peanut butter and caramel cheesecake. There is a large, attractive beer garden to enjoy on sunny days.

Open all wk 11-3 6-11 (Sun 12-11) Closed 25 Dec **Food** Lunch Mon-Sat 12-2.15, Sun 12-8.15 Dinner Mon-Sat 6-9.30, Sun 12-8.15 Restaurant menu available all wk ⊕ FREE HOUSE ◀ Backyard The Hoard, Blythe Staffie, 3 guest ales. ☗ 13 **Facilities** Non-diners area ♦ Garden ⊓ Beer festival Parking WiFi

TAMWORTH — Map 10 SK20

The Globe Inn ★★★ INN

tel: 01827 60455 **Lower Gungate B79 7AT**
email: info@theglobetamworth.com **web:** www.theglobetamworth.com
dir: *Phone for detailed directions*

Restored early 20th-century pub with a hearty menu of favourites

A popular meeting place in the 19th century, The Globe was rebuilt in 1901. The restored exterior shows off its original appearance, while interior decoration has followed design styles of the era – the elegant carved bar and fireplaces reinforce its period character; air conditioning in public areas and satellite TV are two concessions to 21st-century living. Beers from large breweries, menus of pub grub, a function room, and en suite accommodation complete the picture. Food-wise expect wraps, ciabattas, sandwiches, burgers, and jackets as well as vegetable lasagne, steak and kidney pie, pork steaks with honey and mustard sauce, and smoked haddock, bubble-and-squeak and a poached egg.

Open all day all wk 11-11 (Thu-Sat 11am-mdnt Sun 12-11) Closed 25 Dec, 1 Jan **Food** Lunch Mon-Sat 11-2, Sun 12-4 Dinner Mon-Sat 6-9 Set menu available Restaurant menu available Mon-Sat ⊕ FREE HOUSE ◀ Bass, Worthington's, Holden's Black Country Mild. **Facilities** Non-diners area ♦ Children's menu Children's portions Parking WiFi ➡ (notice required) **Rooms** 18

WALL — Map 10 SK10

The Trooper

tel: 01543 480413 **Watling St WS14 0AN**
email: info@thetrooperwall.co.uk
dir: *Phone for detailed directions*

Free house on a hillside overlooking Roman site

The Trooper is a Victorian pub in the Roman village of Wall, built on the original line of Watling Street, now superseded by the A5. Open fires welcome you to the bar, where you'll find local ales including Black Country brewer Holden's Golden Glow. There's a great terrace for fine days and the modern rustic restaurant serves mature steaks from local rump, rare breed and Kobe beef, as well as fresh pizza from the wood-fired oven. The large rear garden has a children's play area and views of Lichfield Cathedral's lofty spire.

Open all day all wk **Food** Lunch all wk 12-5 Dinner all wk 5-9.30 Av main course £9 Set menu available ⊕ FREE HOUSE ◀ Marston's Pedigree, Holden's Golden Glow, Black Sheep, Morland Old Speckled Hen Ⓒ Aspall, Westons Stowford Press. ☗ 13 **Facilities** Non-diners area ❤ (Bar Garden) ♦ Children's menu Children's portions Play area Garden ⊓ Beer festival Parking WiFi ➡

WETTON — Map 16 SK15

The Royal Oak

tel: 01335 310287 **DE6 2AF**
email: ian.lett@yahoo.co.uk
dir: *A515 from Ashbourne towards Buxton, left in 4m signed Alstonfield. In Alstonfield follow Wetton sign*

Old pub in astonishing Peak District countryside

Re-naming has lost the 'Olde' from the pub's name, but the long-established watering-hole in a pretty White Peak village continues to offer the most hospitable, time-honoured welcome. Flagged floors, beams and open fire within; tables outside that promise views to tree-studded limestone pastures. Tracks and byways wend down into the amazing gorge of the River Manifold, riddled by caves amidst memorable ash woods. No surprise then that the pub is popular with ramblers happy to sample beers from local producers like Whim. Filling pub stalwarts populate the menu here; Staffordshire chicken, and rustic beef and Guinness casserole are cases in point.

Open all day 12-close Closed Mon-Tue in winter **Food** Lunch Wed-Fri 12-2.30, Sat-Sun & BHs 12-8.30 Dinner Wed-Fri 6-8.30, Sat-Sun & BHs 12-8.30 Restaurant menu available all wk ⊕ FREE HOUSE ◀ Whim Ales Hartington Bitter & IPA, Local guest ales Ⓒ Thatchers Gold. **Facilities** Non-diners area ❤ (Bar Garden) ♦ Children's menu Family room Garden ⊓ Parking WiFi ➡ (notice required)

PICK OF THE PUBS

The Crown Inn

WRINEHILL   Map 15 SJ74

tel: 01270 820472 **Den Ln CW3 9BT**
email: info@thecrownatwrinehill.co.uk
web: www.thecrownatwrinehill.co.uk
dir: *On A531, 1m S of Betley. 6m S of Crewe; 6m N of Newcastle-under-Lyme*

Great ales and food at this family-run village pub

In the picturesque village of Wrinehill, The Crown is just six miles south of Crewe and the same distance from Newcastle-under-Lyme so it's well located for visitors crossing the borders of Staffordshire and Cheshire. The Davenhill family bought this 19th-century former coaching inn back in 1977 and it is now run by Anna and Mark Condliffe, the daughter and son-in-law of long-serving licensee Charles Davenhill. With an open-plan layout the pub retains its oak beams and famously large inglenook fireplace, always a welcome feature. The bar does a good line in well-kept real ales, with always a choice of seven, two each from Jennings and Marston's, one from Salopian Ales and every week two microbrewery guests including their own 'Legend' ale; 15 wines are offered by the glass. Food is a major reason for the success of The Crown, not just for its consistent quality but for the generosity of the portions. Regularly changing menus are jam-packed with choice: from modestly priced light meals, such as home-made veggie chilli and rice; or

marinated chicken tikka kebabs with onions, mushrooms and red and green peppers, to head chef Steve's trademark minced beef or vegetable lasagne al forno or his 'legendary' beef and ale pie with a hint of Stilton. Anna, a vegetarian herself, recognises that choice should extend beyond mushroom Stroganoff, so alternatives such as Cheddar cheese and onion pasty with balsamic roasted cherry tomatoes, caramelised onion chutney and potatoes will always make a showing on the menus. For pudding, try home-made raspberry Bakewell with cream; or a slice of Bramley apple pie with hot custard. On their own menu, children will find locally produced pork and leek sausage with mash, peas and gravy; or scampi, chips and peas.

Open 12-3 6-11 (Sun 12-4 6-10.30) Closed 25-26 Dec, Mon L **Food** Lunch Tue-Fri 12-2, Sat-Sun 12-3 Dinner Sun-Thu 6-9, Fri 6-9.30, Sat 6-10 ⊕ FREE HOUSE ◀ Marston's Pedigree & Burton Bitter, Jennings Sneck Lifter, Legend, Salopian, Guest ales ♂ Hogan's, Lyme Bay. ♟ 15 **Facilities** Non-diners area ♯ Children's menu Children's portions Outside area ⊼ Parking ▭ (notice required)

WRINEHILL
Map 15 SJ74

The Crown Inn
PICK OF THE PUBS

See Pick of the Pubs on opposite page

The Hand & Trumpet

tel: 01270 820048 **Main Rd CW3 9BJ**
email: hand.and.trumpet@brunningandprice.co.uk
dir: *M6 junct 16, A351, follow Keele signs, 7m, pub on right in village*

Smart pub with alfresco area overlooking the water

A deck to the rear of this relaxed country pub overlooks sizeable grounds, which include a large pond. The pub has a comfortable interior with original floors, old furniture, open fires and rugs. Six cask ales and over 70 malt whiskies are offered, along with a locally sourced menu. Typical dishes on the comprehensive menu are char sui belly pork and warm noodles salad; Cheshire Blue cheesecake with pear jelly; sharing platters; steak and ale pie; Moroccan roasted cod with spiced tabouleh; and dark chocolate and Bailey's torte. There is a cider festival and a hog roast in August.

Open all day all wk 11.30-11 (Sun 11.30-10.30) **Food** Lunch all wk 12-10 Dinner all wk 12-10 ⊕ BRUNNING & PRICE ◀ Original, Timothy Taylor Boltmaker, Salopian Oracle Ŏ Aspall. ♚ 12 **Facilities** Non-diners area ❄ (Bar Garden) ♦ Children's portions Garden ⊓ Cider festival Parking

SUFFOLK

ALDRINGHAM
Map 13 TM46

The Parrot and Punchbowl Inn & Restaurant

tel: 01728 830221 **Aldringham Ln IP16 4PY**
dir: *On B1122, 1m from Leiston, 3m from Aldeburgh, on x-roads to Thorpeness*

Former smugglers' haunt, now a welcoming pub and restaurant

If you thought bizarre pub names were a late 20th-century fad, think again. Originally called The Case is Altered, this 16th-century pink-washed smugglers' inn became The Parrot and Punchbowl in 1604 when Aldringham was a centre for smuggled contraband. East Anglian-brewed ales from Adnams and Woodforde's, and Suffolk's Aspall cider all feature in the bar line-up. The good-value menu offers chicken liver pâté with chutney and toast; steak and kidney pudding; lasagne; bangers and mash; and steaks. Daily specials and vegetarian meals also have very reasonable price tags. There are roasts on Sundays and quiz nights.

Open all wk 12-2.30 6-11 (Sun 12-4) **Food** Lunch all wk 12-2 Dinner Mon-Sat 6.30-9 Restaurant menu available Tue-Sun ⊕ ENTERPRISE INNS ◀ Woodforde's Wherry, Adnams, Guest ale Ŏ Aspall. ♚ 12 **Facilities** Non-diners area ❄ (Bar Garden) ♦ Children's menu Children's portions Play area Family room Garden ⊓ Parking WiFi 🚐

BRANDESTON
Map 13 TM26

The Queens Head
PICK OF THE PUBS

tel: 01728 685307 **The Street IP13 7AD**
dir: *From A14 take A1120 to Earl Soham, then S to Brandeston*

Family- and dog-friendly hostelry in a sleepy village

Created from four cottages and first opened in 1811, this smart pub stands slightly off the beaten track deep in peaceful Suffolk countryside. A detour is well worthwhile to sample one of the cracking Southwold ales, or a freshly prepared

meal. Outside is a well-furnished summer garden, while inside the warm and richly coloured decor complements the traditional homely features of wood panelling, quarry-tiled floors and open log fires. The modern British menu, described as 'pub food with a twist', is based on local produce where possible, and bristles with interest. How often do you come across fricassée of golden beetroot, pak choi, russet apples and parmesan cream? Or mushroom raviolo, braised oxtail, pickled mushrooms and shallot purée? Sunday lunches are always popular and family-based events are organised throughout the year, including barbecues in the garden and a beer festival in June to coincide with the village fête.

Open 12-3 5-12 (Sun 12-6) Closed Sun eve, Mon **Food** Lunch Tue-Sat 12-2, Sun 12-2.30 Dinner Tue-Sat 6-9 ⊕ FREE HOUSE ◀ Adnams Broadside & Southwold Bitter, Guest ales Ŏ Aspall. **Facilities** Non-diners area ❄ (Bar Garden) ♦ Children's menu Children's portions Garden ⊓ Beer festival Parking WiFi 🚐

BURY ST EDMUNDS
Map 13 TL86

The Nutshell

tel: 01284 764867 **17 The Traverse IP33 1BJ**
dir: *Phone for detailed directions*

Officially the smallest pub in Britain

Measuring just 15ft by 7ft, this unique pub has been confirmed as Britain's smallest by *Guinness World Records*; and somehow more than 100 people and a dog managed to fit inside in the 1980s. It has certainly become a tourist attraction and there's lots to talk about while you enjoy a drink – a mummified cat and the bar ceiling, which is covered with paper money. There have been regular sightings of ghosts around the building, including a nun and a monk who apparently weren't praying! No food is available, though the pub jokes about its dining area for parties of two or fewer.

Open all day all wk **Food** Contact pub for food times ⊕ GREENE KING ◀ IPA & Abbot Ale, Guest ales. **Facilities** Non-diners area WiFi 🚐 (notice required) **Notes** 🅰

The Old Cannon Brewery ★★★ INN
PICK OF THE PUBS

See Pick of the Pubs on page 462

CHILLESFORD
Map 13 TM35

The Froize Inn 🅰
PICK OF THE PUBS

tel: 01394 450282 **The Street IP12 3PU**
email: dine@froize.co.uk
dir: *On B1084 between Woodbridge (8m) & Orford (3m)*

Acclaimed Adnams free house near heritage coast

Nobody really knows what a froize is, or was. A savoury French pancake? Or Suffolk dialect for a friar? Anyhow, it's what this pantiled dining pub is called. Chef-patron David Grimwood worships at the same creative altar as his favourite chefs, Hugh Fearnley-Whittingstall, Jamie Oliver and Rick Stein, and his skills have earned him an AA Rosette. No printed menus here, simply changing blackboards listing 'very local' venison, ale and field mushroom pie; free-range Blythburgh pork; grilled Orford skate wing; and stuffed mushrooms, spinach and goats' cheese. A champion of 'Great British' puddings, David's sticky toffee with butterscotch sauce could prove irresistible.

Open Tue-Sun Closed Mon **Food** Contact pub for food times Restaurant menu available Tue-Sun ⊕ FREE HOUSE ◀ Adnams Ŏ Aspall. ♚ 12 **Facilities** ♦ Children's portions Garden ⊓ Parking WiFi 🚐 (notice required)

PICK OF THE PUBS

The Old Cannon Brewery ★★★ INN

BURY ST EDMUNDS   Map 13 TL86

tel: 01284 768769
86 Cannon St IP33 1JR
email: info@oldcannonbrewery.co.uk
web: www.oldcannonbrewery.co.uk
dir: *From A14 junct 43 follow signs to Bury St Edmunds town centre, 1st left at 1st rdbt into Northgate St, 1st right into Cadney Ln, left at end into Cannon St*

A free house with long brewing history

Brewing started at this Victorian pub over 160 years ago. Today it's brewing still, the only independent brewpub in Suffolk where you can see beer being brewed on a regular basis. Indeed, dominating the bar are two giant stainless steel brewing vessels, fount of Old Cannon Best Bitter, Gunner's Daughter and seasonal and special occasion beers, augmented by ever-rotating regular and other guest ales. In keeping with having a brewery inside the bar-cum-dining room, the decor and furnishings are easy on the eye, with rich, earth-coloured walls, wooden floors and scrubbed tables. Exploiting the obvious pun, the menu is headed 'Cannon Fodder', among which, all freshly prepared from local produce, are starters and light dishes of deep-fried whitebait and smoked ham hock, and main meals of home-made beef and smoked oyster pie; winter chicken and goats' cheese pasta; pan-fried sea bass

with chorizo and cherry tomatoes; and moules marinière. And the daily-changing specials board offers at least three more options. The possibility of a home-made pudding or a British cheeseboard is worth planning ahead for; otherwise, try a lighter locally produced ice cream. For the really keen, the pub offers a Brew Day experience giving two people the opportunity to work alongside the brewer, loading the malt, creating the wort and adding the hops, all during normal production hours. An August beer festival and tours of the brewery are added attractions. Overnight guests stay in the converted old brewery, just across the courtyard. Since the pub is tucked away in the back streets, follow the website directions carefully.

Open all day all wk 12-11 (Sun 12-10.30) Closed 26 Dec & 1 Jan **Food** Mon-Sat 12-9, Sun 12-3 Av main course £12.50 ⊕ FREE HOUSE ◧ The Old Cannon Best Bitter & Gunner's Daughter & Seasonal ales, Adnams Southwold Bitter, Guest ales Ö Aspall. ♟ 12 **Facilities** Non-diners area Garden ⋈ Beer festival Parking WiFi **Rooms** 7

CRATFIELD
Map 13 TM37

The Cratfield Poacher

tel: 01986 798206 **Bell Green IP19 OBL**
email: cratfieldpoacher@yahoo.co.uk
dir: *B1117 from Halesworth towards Eye. At Laxfield right, follow Cratfield signs. Or, A143 from Diss towards Bungay. Right at Harleston onto B1123 towards Halesworth. Through Metfield, 1m, right, follow Cratfield signs*

Family-run free house in rural location

A pub for the past 350 years, this handsome longhouse in deepest rural Suffolk is off the beaten track but well worth the detour. Boasting some impressive exterior plasterwork pargeting, it is just as charming inside, with low beams and tiled floors. There's always six draught beers available, often from the Adnams and Oakham breweries, plus local Aspall cider. Home-cooked food, such as smoked mackerel salad and shepherd's pie, with daily-changing specials complete the pleasing picture at this proper village local, which is the hub of the community.

Open 12-2.30 6-12 (Sat-Sun all day) Closed Mon, Tue L **Food** Lunch Fri 12-2.30 (Sat-Sun all day) Dinner Tue-Fri 6-9 (Sat-Sun all day) Av main course £8.95 Set menu available ⊕ FREE HOUSE ◀ Crouch Vale Brewers Gold, Oakham JHB, Earl Soham Victoria Bitter & Gannet Mild, Adnams Ö Aspall. **Facilities** Non-diners area ♣ (Bar Garden) ♦ Children's menu Children's portions Garden ⌷ Parking ▄ (notice required)

DENNINGTON
Map 13 TM26

Dennington Queen

tel: 01728 638241 **The Square IP13 8AB**
email: denningtonqueen@yahoo.co.uk
dir: *From Ipswich A14 to exit for Lowestoft (A12). Then B1116 to Framlingham, follow signs to Dennington*

Village centre pub worth seeking out

A 16th-century inn with bags of old-world charm including open fires, a coffin hatch, a bricked-up tunnel to the neighbouring church and a ghost. Locally brewed Aspall cider accompanies real ales from Adnams, plus Black Sheep, Timothy Taylor and Sharp's ales. Suggestions from the modern British menu include moules marinière; confit leek, blue cheese and sage bruschetta; seared calves' liver, bacon, parsley mash and onion gravy; and pan-seared sea bass fillet, coriander rösti and herb oil. A typical dessert might be chocolate fudge cake, pecan nut sauce and vanilla mascarpone.

Open all wk 12-3 6.30-10.30 **Food** Lunch all wk 12-2 Dinner all wk 6.30-9 Set menu available ⊕ FREE HOUSE ◀ Adnams, Timothy Taylor, Black Sheep, Sharp's Doom Bar, Wadworth Ö Aspall. **Facilities** Non-diners area ♣ (Bar Garden) ♦ Children's menu Children's portions Garden ⌷ Parking WiFi ▄ (notice required)

DUNWICH
Map 13 TM47

The Ship at Dunwich ★★ SHL ◉
PICK OF THE PUBS

See Pick of the Pubs on page 464

EARL SOHAM
Map 13 TM26

Victoria

tel: 01728 685758 **The Street IP13 7RL**
email: vic@earlsohamvictoria.co.uk
dir: *From A14 at Stowmarket take A1120 towards Yoxford, cross A40 at Stronham, through Pettaugh on A1120 to Earl Soham. Pub on right*

Microbrewery beers at their best

This friendly, down-to-earth free house is a showcase for Earl Soham beers, which for many years were produced from a microbrewery behind the pub. Some ten years ago the brewery moved to the Old Forge building a few yards away, where production still continues. Inside this traditional pub, simple furnishings, bare floorboards and an open fire set the scene for traditional home-cooked pub fare, including ploughman's, jacket potatoes and macaroni cheese. Heartier meals include a variety of curries and casseroles, local sausages and mash, and gammon and eggs, followed by home-made desserts. A specials board and vegetarian dishes add to the choices.

Open all wk 11.30-3 6-11 **Food** Lunch all wk 12-2 Dinner all wk 7-10 Av main course £9.50 ⊕ FREE HOUSE/EARL SOHAM BREWERY ◀ Earl Soham Victoria Bitter, Albert Ale, Brandeston Gold, Sir Roger's Porter Ö Aspall. ₮
Facilities Non-diners area ♣ (Bar Garden) ♦ Children's portions Garden ⌷ Parking WiFi ▄ (notice required)

ELVEDEN
Map 13 TL88

Elveden Inn ★★★★ INN
PICK OF THE PUBS

tel: 01842 890876 **Brandon Rd IP24 3TP**
email: enquiries@elvedeninn.com web: www.elvedeninn.com
dir: *From Mildenhall take A11 towards Thetford. Left onto B1106, pub on left*

Stylish inn showcasing produce from the estate

Located on the Elveden Estate, home to a direct descendent of the Guinness family, this village inn has a relaxed and contemporary bar, several dining areas, and four luxury bedrooms. Expect a family-friendly atmosphere, blazing log fires in winter, a range of guest ales on tap, and a modern pub menu that brims with produce sourced from the estate farm and surrounding area. Whether eating inside, or outside on the large patio area, a meal could kick off with smoked haddock brandade, lemon crème fraîche and crispy capers; or confit rabbit and pork bonbons with Guinness ketchup. Then estate venison haunch steak, parmesan polenta and sautéed chestnut mushrooms; or baked spinach, feta and red onion strudel. Children can choose from their own selection of 'fawn-size' portions.

Open all day all wk **Food** Lunch all wk 7.30am-9pm Dinner all wk 7.30am-9pm Av main course £10-£12 Restaurant menu available all wk ⊕ FREE HOUSE ◀ Adnams Southwold, Guest ales Ö Aspall. ₮ 14 **Facilities** Non-diners area ♣ (Bar Restaurant Garden) ♦ Children's menu Children's portions Play area Garden ⌷ Beer festival Cider festival Parking WiFi ▄ (notice required) **Rooms** 4

EYE
Map 13 TM17

The White Horse Inn ★★★★ INN

tel: 01379 678222 **Stoke Ash IP23 7ET**
email: mail@whitehorse-suffolk.co.uk web: www.whitehorse-suffolk.co.uk
dir: *On A140 between Ipswich & Norwich*

Family-run inn with good food

Midway between Norwich and Ipswich, this 17th-century coaching inn is set amid lovely Suffolk countryside. The heavily timbered interior accommodates an inglenook fireplace, two bars and a restaurant. An extensive menu is supplemented by lunchtime snacks, grills and daily specials from the blackboard. Try salmon pâté or smoked duck salad to start. Main courses include red pepper and goats' cheese lasagne; honey and mustard chicken; venison casserole; chicken Madras; and baked salmon with a sage and parmesan crust. There are 11 spacious motel bedrooms in the grounds, as well as a patio and secluded grassy area.

Open all day all wk 7am-11pm (Sat 8am-11pm Sun 8am-10.30pm) **Food** Contact pub for food times Av main course £8.95 ⊕ FREE HOUSE ◀ Greene King Abbot Ale, Adnams, Woodforde's Wherry Ö Aspall. **Facilities** Non-diners area ♦ Children's menu Children's portions Garden Parking WiFi ▄ **Rooms** 11

PICK OF THE PUBS

The Ship at Dunwich ★★ SHL ❀

DUNWICH	Map 13 TM47

tel: 01728 648219
Saint James St IP17 3DT
email: info@shipatdunwich.co.uk
web: www.shipatdunwich.co.uk
dir: *N on A12 from Ipswich through Yoxford, right signed Dunwich*

Coastal pub renowned for its fish and chips

Dunwich was at one time a medieval port of some size and importance, but then the original village was virtually destroyed by a terrible storm in 1326. Further storms and erosion followed and now the place is little more than a hamlet beside a shingle beach. Two minutes' stroll from the beach, The Ship at Dunwich is a well-loved old smugglers' inn overlooking the salt marshes and sea, and is popular with walkers and birdwatchers visiting the nearby RSPB Minsmere reserve. The Ship keeps Dunwich on the map with hearty meals and ales from Adnams, Woodforde's and St Peter's – to name just a few. Its delightful unspoilt public bar offers nautical bric-à-brac, a wood-burning stove in a huge fireplace, flagged floors and simple wooden furnishings. Sympathetically spruced up in recent years, with the addition of clean, comfortable and contemporary style bedrooms, it is locally renowned for its fish and chips, which include a

choice of cod, whiting, plaice or hake. Other dishes plough a traditional furrow. You could start with twice-baked Binham Blue soufflé with chicory, pear and hazelnuts, or salt cod fishcakes, crispy capers and home-made tartare sauce, followed perhaps by slow-braised Bramfield ox cheeks and bone marrow fritter with creamy mash, curly kale and cauliflower cheese; or grilled Suffolk lamb Barnsley chop with anchovy and rosemary dressing, pan-hagerty potatoes, braised red cabbage, carrot and swede purée. Desserts continue in a similar vein – maybe spiced apple crumble and custard, or a knickbocker glory. Look for the ancient fig tree in the garden, and take note of the inn's beer festivals.

Open all day all wk **Food** Lunch all wk 12-3 Dinner all wk 6-9 ⊕ FREE HOUSE 🍺 Adnams Southwold Bitter, Humpty Dumpty, Brandon Rusty Bucket, Earl Soham, Green Jack, Grain Norfolk Brewery, Woodforde's, St Peter's Ö Aspall. 🍷 9 **Facilities** Non-diners area 🐾 (Bar Restaurant Garden) 👪 Children's menu Children's portions Family room Garden 🎪 Beer festival Parking WiFi 🚌 (notice required) **Rooms** 15

FORWARD GREEN
Map 13 TM15

The Shepherd & Dog

tel: 01449 711685 **IP14 5HN**
email: info@theshepherdanddog.com
dir: *From Stowmarket (A14 junct 50) take A1120 signed Stowupland. Through Stowupland, approx 2m to pub*

A country bar, contemporary lounge and modern eatery

On the edge of the village, looking out over a field, this pub is very much part of the community. Bar meals include a half lobster with warm toast and roast garlic butter, and cauliflower risotto, but if you'd prefer the restaurant, its menu lists Suffolk lamb loin with salsify purée, slow-roast root vegetables and roast garlic polenta; pan-fried pork belly with pork croquette, roast pear and Brussels sprouts; and herb-crusted cod fillet with smoked eel gnocchi, whitebait, wilted greens and crispy kale. You don't have to be vegetarian to enjoy roasted Jerusalem artichoke with red cabbage.

Open all day Closed Mon-Tue **Food** Lunch Wed-Sun 12-9 Dinner Wed-Sun 12-9 Restaurant menu available Wed-Sun ⊕ FREE HOUSE ◀ Greene King IPA Ô Aspall. ♀ 12 **Facilities** Non-diners area ❖ (Bar Outside area) ♦♦ Children's menu Children's portions Outside area ⊨ Parking WiFi

FRAMLINGHAM
Map 13 TM26

NEW The Railway

tel: 01728 724760 **9 Station Rd IP13 9EA**
email: info@therailwayframlingham.co.uk
dir: *In village centre on B1116*

Good food and beer in a quirky pub

Dominated by the dramatic walls of its castle, which dates from the 12th century, the picturesque market town of Framlingham is the delightful location for this friendly, family-run pub. Stylish and quirky inside, there's a front patio and 'secret' garden for alfresco summer dining. They hold a beer festival at Easter, and in the bar you can find Adnams Southwold Bitter, as well as Fuller's London Pride and guest ales. A meal might begin with smoked salmon, or a pork and Suffolk cider terrine, followed by pan-fried sea bass or lamb's liver and smoked bacon.

Open all wk 12-3 5.30-11 **Food** Contact pub for food times Av main course £8 Set menu available ⊕ FREE HOUSE ◀ Adnams Southwold Bitter, Fuller's London Pride, Guest ales Ô Aspall. **Facilities** Non-diners area ❖ (Bar Restaurant Garden) ♦♦ Children's menu Children's portions Garden ⊨ Beer festival WiFi (notice required)

The Station Hotel

tel: 01728 723455 **Station Rd IP13 9EE**
email: framstation@btinternet.com
dir: *Bypass Ipswich towards Lowestoft on A12. Approx 6m, left onto B1116 to Framlingham*

Known for its bold and flavoursome dishes

Built as part of the local railway in the 19th century, The Station Hotel has been a pub since the 1950s, outliving the railway which closed in 1962. Inside, you will find scrubbed tables and an eclectic mix of furniture. During the last decade it has established a fine reputation for its gutsy and earthy food listed on the ever-changing blackboard menu. A typical lunch dish could be North African fish stew; dinner might include seared venison fillet with wild mushroom risotto; slow-roasted belly pork, mash, Savoy cabbage and apple sauce; pot-roasted rabbit and bean stew; pan-fried mullet with linguine clam chowder, or something cooked in wood-fired pizza oven. Several of the beers are supplied by Suffolk brewery, Earl Soham and there is a beer festival in mid July.

Open all wk 12-2.30 5-11 (Sun 12-3 7-10.30) **Food** Lunch all wk 12-2 Dinner Mon-Thu 6.30-9, Fri-Sat 6.30-9.30, Sun 7-9 ⊕ FREE HOUSE ◀ Earl Soham Victoria Bitter, Albert Ale & Gannet Mild, Veltins, Crouch Vale, Guinness Ô Aspall. **Facilities** ❖ (All areas) ♦♦ Children's portions Garden Outside area ⊨ Beer festival Parking WiFi

FRAMSDEN
Map 13 TM15

The Dobermann Inn

tel: 01473 890461 **The Street IP14 6HG**
dir: *S off A1120 (Stowmarket to Yoxford road). 10m from Ipswich on B1077 towards Debenham*

Thatched village inn with popular food

This pretty country pub was named by its current proprietor who is a prominent breeder and judge of Dobermanns. The thatched roofing, gnarled beams, open fire and assorted furniture reflect its 16th-century origins. With a selection of Adnams ales on offer and Mauldons Dickens bitter, food ranges from sandwiches, hearty ploughman's and salads to main courses featuring plenty of fish and vegetarian choices. Reliable favourites include chilli con carne, spicy nut loaf, and steak and mushroom pie.

Open 12-3 7-11 Closed 25-26 Dec, Sun eve, Mon **Food** Lunch Tue-Sun 12-2 Dinner Tue-Sat 7-9 ⊕ FREE HOUSE ◀ Adnams Southwold Bitter, Old Ale & Broadside, Mauldons Dickens Ô Aspall. **Facilities** Non-diners area Garden ⊨ Parking (notice required) **Notes** ☺

GREAT BRICETT
Map 13 TM05

The Veggie Red Lion
PICK OF THE PUBS

tel: 01473 657799 **Green Street Green IP7 7DD**
email: janwise@fsmail.net
dir: *4.5m from Needham Market on B1078*

Smart country inn with innovative approach to meals

Snuggled beside a thicket secluded in the rich wheat-fields outside Ipswich; Jan Wise's stylish country pub continues to attract discerning diners keen to experience the many-faceted menu of vegetarian and vegan dishes. The rustic heritage and real ales here reward lovers of traditional pubs, but it's the considered selection of dishes based on local produce that draws the accolades. The animal, fish and fowl-free fare benefits from Jan's long years of dedication to promoting alternatives to the catering mainstream. Starters might see lentil and coconut dhal, vegetable pakoras and mint raita setting a standard. Mains tempt with dishes such as cashew and apricot stuffed butternut squash, topped with goats' cheese accompanied by pumpkin seed and pomegranate slaw; or Mediterranean inspired haloumi and vegetable kebab with red peppers, courgettes and red onion with hazelnut and apple couscous. Rich, moreish puddings complete the repast. There's a garden here and a terrace for alfresco dining. Booking ahead is recommended.

Open 12-3 6-11 Closed Sun eve & Mon **Food** Lunch Tue-Sun 12-2 Dinner Tue-Sat 6-9 ⊕ HAWTHORN LEISURE ◀ Greene King IPA, Morland Old Speckled Hen, Rotating guest ales Ô Aspall. **Facilities** Non-diners area ❖ (Bar Garden) ♦♦ Children's menu Children's portions Play area Garden ⊨ Parking WiFi

HALESWORTH
Map 13 TM37

The Queen's Head
PICK OF THE PUBS

tel: 01986 784214 **The Street, Bramfield IP19 9HT**
email: info@queensheadbramfield.co.uk
dir: 2m from A12 on A144 towards Halesworth

Local produce gets pride of place on an ever-changing menu

In the centre of Bramfield on the edge of the Suffolk Heritage Coast near Southwold, the enclosed garden of this lovely Grade II listed pub is overlooked by the thatched village church with its unusual separate round bell tower. The pub's interior is welcoming, with scrubbed pine tables, a vaulted ceiling in the bar and enormous fireplaces. In the same hands for two decades, the pub's landlord enthusiastically supports local and organic producers, reflected by a constantly evolving menu which proudly names the farms and suppliers. Sample dishes include sweet-cured marinated herring fillets; twice-baked goats' cheese soufflé; home-made Thai fishcakes with sweet chilli sauce. In addition there's a big choice of sandwiches, filled baguettes and filled ciabatta, ploughman's and hamburgers. Take note of their popular live music events.

Open all wk 12-2.30 6.30-11 (Sun 12-4 7-10.30) **Food** Lunch Mon-Sat 12-2, Sun 12-4 Dinner Mon-Fri 6.30-9, Sat 6.30-9.30, Sun 7-9 Restaurant menu available all wk ⊕ ADNAMS ◀ Southwold Bitter, Broadside ♂ Aspall. ♥ 8
Facilities Non-diners area ♣ (Bar Restaurant Garden) ♦ Children's menu Children's portions Family room Garden ⋈ Parking WiFi ⬛ (notice required)

HAWKEDON
Map 13 TL75

The Queen's Head
PICK OF THE PUBS

tel: 01284 789218 **Rede Rd IP29 4NN**
dir: From A143 at Wickham St, between Bury St Edmunds & Haverhill, follow Stansfield sign. At junct left signed Hawkedon. 1m to village

Thriving village local with a butcher's shop

Off-the-beaten track by the green in a picture-book village deep in rural Suffolk, The Queen's Head is worth seeking out for its classic 15th-century character and charm – inglenook fireplace, stone floors, head-cracking timbers, scrubbed wooden tables – and top-notch hearty pub food prepared from the best local ingredients. The pub rears its own livestock (Suffolk sheep and Dexter cattle) and, like the pork, venison, poultry and wild boar sourced from local farms, they are hung and butchered at the butcher's shop in the pub grounds. This may translate to venison carpaccio; pork chops with Stilton, pear and sage; and pot-roasted beef with red wine and red onion marmalade; with butterscotch and almond pudding among the desserts. Sunday roast lunches, traditional bar snacks, and pizzas baked in the stone oven complete the culinary picture. A thriving community local, it also offers live music, a beer and cider festival in July, and game and wine tasting dinners.

Open 5-11 (Fri-Sun 12-11) Closed Mon-Thu L **Food** Lunch Fri-Sun 12-2.30 Dinner Wed-Thu 6-9, Fri-Sun 6.30-9 ⊕ FREE HOUSE ◀ Woodforde's Wherry, Adnams, Guest ales ♂ Westons Old Rosie & Country Perry, Guest cider. **Facilities** Non-diners area ♣ (Bar Garden) ♦ Children's portions Garden ⋈ Beer festival Cider festival Parking WiFi

Find out more about this county with *The AA Guide to Norfolk & Suffolk* – see shop.theAA.com

HITCHAM
Map 13 TL95

The White Horse Inn

tel: 01449 740981 **The Street IP7 7NQ**
email: lewis@thewhitehorse.wanadoo.co.uk
dir: 7m SW of Stowmarket on B1115; or from Hadleigh take A1141 towards Monks Eleigh, right onto B1115 to Hitcham

Friendly pub in the heart of the countryside

A blacksmith's forge was once attached to this 400-year-old inn, originally a staging post for London and Norwich coaches. In the late 17th century a notorious highwayman was arrested and tried in what nowadays is the public bar, found guilty and hanged from a nearby tree. Today, the bar is for more for hanging out, drinking Suffolk real ales, and playing traditional pub games. Freshly prepared meals include lamb and mint pudding; scampi, chips and peas; and lighter options of grilled paninis, sandwiches and ploughman's.

Open all wk 12-3 6-11 **Food** Lunch all wk 12-2.30 Dinner all wk 6-9 Restaurant menu available all wk ⊕ FREE HOUSE ◀ Adnams Southwold Bitter & Fisherman ♂ Aspall. ♥ **Facilities** Non-diners area ♣ (Bar Garden) ♦ Children's menu Children's portions Garden ⋈ Parking WiFi ⬛ (notice required)

HOLBROOK
Map 13 TM13

The Compasses

tel: 01473 328332 **Ipswich Rd IP9 2QR**
email: jayne.gooding@hotmail.co.uk
dir: From A137 S of Ipswich, take B1080 to Holbrook, pub on left. From Ipswich take B1456 to Shotley. At Freston Water Tower right onto B1080 to Holbrook. Pub 2m right

Proudly not a gastro-pub

On the spectacular Shotley peninsula bordered by the rivers Orwell and Stour, this traditional 17th-century country pub offers a simple, good-value menu. There's nothing self-consciously primped and styled about its interior or its food offerings; it prides itself on not being a gastro-pub but offering good value and plenty of choice. Typical starters include prawn cocktail and breaded mushrooms with garlic mayo. Follow this with minced beef and onion pie; crispy chicken mornay; or local sausages with egg and chips. There's a separate children's menu and some good vegetarian choices such as Cajun five bean chilli.

Open 11.30-2.30 6-11 (Sun 12-3 6-10.30) Closed 26 Dec, Tue eve **Food** Lunch all wk 12-2.15 Dinner Wed-Mon 6-9.15 ⊕ PUNCH TAVERNS ◀ Adnams Southwold Bitter, Sharp's Doom Bar ♂ Aspall. ♥ 12 **Facilities** Non-diners area ♦ Children's menu Children's portions Play area Garden ⋈ Parking WiFi ⬛ (notice required)

HONEY TYE
Map 13 TL93

The Lion

tel: 01206 263434 **CO6 4NX**
email: info@thelioncolchester.com
dir: On A134 midway between Colchester & Sudbury

Good food in dining pub with alfresco options

This traditional country dining pub occupies an enviable spot in an Area of Outstanding Natural Beauty. The spacious restaurant is decorated in a modern, comfortable style and the bar has low-beamed ceilings and wood-burner. The reasonably priced food here is sourced locally and the menu changes with the seasons. Start with twice-baked goats' cheese soufflé, perhaps, before a main course of oven-roasted rump of new season lamb with pearl barley risotto and salsa verde. The Lion has a walled beer garden for alfresco eating and drinking in the warmer summer months.

Open all day 11-11 Closed Mon **Food** Lunch Tue-Sun 12-9 Dinner Tue-Sun 12-9 Set menu available ⊕ FREE HOUSE ◀ Adnams ♂ Westons. ♥ 9 **Facilities** Non-diners area ♦ Children's menu Children's portions Garden ⋈ Parking WiFi ⬛ (notice required)

PICK OF THE PUBS

The Bull Inn ★★★★★ INN ✿

MILDENHALL   Map 12 TL77

tel: 01638 711001
The Street, Barton Mills IP28 6AA
email: reception@bullinn-bartonmills.com
web: www.bullinn-bartonmills.com
dir: *Exit A11 between Newmarket &
Mildenhall, signed Barton Mills*

An independent, quirky inn with something to suit everyone

With its fine roofline, dormer windows
and old coaching courtyard, this
rambling 16th-century building certainly
looks like a traditional roadside inn.
Stepping inside this historic building
you'll be wowed by an amazing interior
that blends original oak beams, wooden
floors and big fireplaces with funky
fabrics, designer wallpapers and bold
colours. This, along with their
dedication, is how family owners Cheryl,
Wayne and Sonia breathed new life into
an old inn, making the bar, with
scrubbed pine tables and cosy seats by
a winter fire, the hub of the building
(and indeed the village). Here you can
study the menus, perhaps with one of
the 11 wines by the glass, or an East
Anglian real ale from Adnams, Wolf or
Humpty Dumpty. Menus evolve with the
seasons, with every effort made to
reduce 'food miles' by sourcing locally.
In the AA Rosette dining rooms a meal
might begin with pulled Cajun turkey,
red onion and mayo tian; or brie fritters,
berry coulis, watercress and
caramelised walnuts, followed by pan-
fried halibut and king scallops, potato

and thyme rösti, tenderstem broccoli,
apple crisps, dried bacon, apple and
vanilla Madeira jus; or the signature
dish of fillet steak tower. Options
continue with roast Gressingham duck
breast, potato fondant, beetroot purée,
and port and sherry reduction; leek, pea,
red onion and Coastal mature cheese
risotto; and the Bull's 'famous' MOO pie
filled with slow-cooked fillet steak in
Brandon-brewed Rusty Bucket ale, with
creamy mash and roasted root
vegetables. The sticky toffee pudding,
rock salt caramel and toffee ice cream
is a must. Bar meals include classics
like Newmarket sausages with mash
and caramelised red onion gravy; and
chicken curry with basmati rice.

Open all day all wk 8am-11pm Closed
25 Dec **Food** Lunch Sun-Thu 12-9,

Fri-Sat 12-9.30 (bkfst 8-12) Dinner
Sun-Thu 12-9, Fri-Sat 12-9.30
Restaurant menu available all wk
🍺 FREE HOUSE 🍺 Adnams Broadside,
Greene King IPA, Brandon Rusty Bucket,
Humpty Dumpty, Wolf Ö Aspall. 🍷 11
Facilities Non-diners area 🚸 Children's
menu Children's portions Garden ⌁
Parking WiFi 🚐 (notice required)
Rooms 15

INGHAM
Map 13 TL87

The Cadogan ★★★★ INN ⊛

tel: 01284 728443 **The Street IP31 1NG**
email: info@thecadogan.co.uk **web:** www.thecadogan.co.uk
dir: *A14 junct 42, 1st exit onto B1106. At rdbt take 1st exit (A134). 3m to Ingham. Pub on left*

A welcoming place to stay or dine

A friendly and inviting pub with seven en suite bedrooms for those who want to stay longer, The Cadogan sits just four miles from the centre of Bury St Edmunds. The kitchen places an emphasis on seasonality and local produce; for something lighter there's grazing boards at both lunch and dinner (cheese; seafood; deli and puds). Dinner menu options could be winter spiced mackerel fillets and granary bread; or confit guinea fowl and wild mushroom terrine to start, followed by Norfolk turkey ballotine with potato fondant, roast carrots and bread sauce; or herb crust hake, roast butternut squash and pearl barley risotto. Open all day, the pub has a large garden, with a children's play area, perfect for alfresco dining.

Open all day all wk Closed 25-26 Dec & 31 Jan eve **Food** Lunch Mon-Sat 12-2.30, Sun 12-8.30 Dinner Mon-Sat 6-9.30, Sun 12-8.30 ⊕ GREENE KING ◼ Abbot Ale, Brewshed Pale Ale ♻ Aspall. ♟ 14 **Facilities** Non-diners area ♦ Children's menu Children's portions Play area Garden ⋒ Parking WiFi ➡ (notice required) **Rooms** 7

IPSWICH
Map 13 TM14

The Fat Cat

tel: 01473 726524 **288 Spring Rd IP4 5NL**
email: fatcatipswich@btconnect.com
dir: *From A12 take A1214 towards town centre, becomes A1071 (Woodbridge Road East). At mini rdbt 2nd left into Spring Rd*

One for the beer lover

Good beer and conversation are the two main ingredients in this no-frills free house. The Fat Cat is a mecca for beer aficionados, with a friendly atmosphere in the homely bar and a raft of real ales served in tip-top condition from the taproom behind the bar. The head-scratching choice – up to 20 every day – come from Adnams, Skinner's and Hop Back and a host of local microbreweries. Soak up the beer with simple bar snacks like home-made Scotch eggs, sausage rolls, pork pies and filled rolls.

Open all day all wk **Food** Contact pub for food times ⊕ FREE HOUSE ◼ Adnams Old Ale, Skinner's Betty Stogs, Green Jack Gone Fishing, Crouch Vale Yakima Gold, Oakham Inferno, Hop Back Summer lightning, Guest ales ♻ Aspall, Westons, Lilley's Cider Barn, Gwynt y Ddraig. ♟ 8 **Facilities** Non-diners area ♥ (Bar Garden) Garden WiFi ➡ (notice required) **Notes** ⊛

LAXFIELD
Map 13 TM27

The Kings Head (The Low House)   `PICK OF THE PUBS`

tel: 01986 798395 **Gorams Mill Ln IP13 8DW**
email: kingsheadlaxfield@yahoo.co.uk
dir: *On B1117*

Discover an authentic old pub with no bar

This unspoilt thatched 16th-century alehouse is a rare Suffolk gem that oozes charm and character. Locals know it as the Low House because it lies in a dip below the churchyard. Tip-top ales are served straight from the cask in the original taproom – this is one of the few pubs in Britain without a bar. Now in the capable hands of Sarah and Chris Cole, the traditional home-made approach to food continues. Typical dishes are button mushrooms in a creamy garlic sauce on toasted baguette; and rack of baby back ribs in the chef's Broadside barbecue sauce, served with herby sautéed potatoes and Low House coleslaw. Children are welcome and offered tempting specials and home-cooked favourites. Beer festivals in May and September are unforgettable occasions thanks to the beautiful situation of the pub overlooking the river; its grounds, with rose gardens and an arbour, were formerly the village bowling green.

Open all wk 11am-close (winter 12-3 6-close) **Food** Lunch Mon-Sat 12-2, Sun 12-3 Dinner Mon-Sat 6.30-9 ⊕ ADNAMS ◼ Southwold Bitter, Broadside & Ghost Ship ales, Guest ales ♻ Aspall. ♟ 11 **Facilities** Non-diners area ♥ (Bar Garden) ♦ Children's menu Children's portions Play area Family room Garden ⋒ Beer festival Parking WiFi ➡ (notice required)

MILDENHALL
Map 12 TL77

The Bull Inn ★★★★★ INN ⊛   `PICK OF THE PUBS`

See Pick of the Pubs on page 467

NAYLAND
Map 13 TL93

Anchor Inn   `PICK OF THE PUBS`

tel: 01206 262313 **26 Court St CO6 4JL**
email: info@anchornayland.co.uk
dir: *Follow A134 from Colchester towards Sudbury for 3.5m through Great Horkesley, at bottom of hill right into Horkesley Rd. Pub on right after bridge*

Eclectic modern dining in Constable Country

The inn, which enjoys a peaceful setting beside the alder-fringed meadows of the River Stour, is said to be the last remaining place from which press-gangs recruited their 'volunteers' in this area. Today's customers can rest easy, perhaps recovering from strolls around the idyllic village, which is close to the heart of 'Constable Country'. The Anchor is a light, airy destination where local and regional ales change monthly (there are also twice-yearly beer festivals), with the riverside decking and garden the ideal spot to tarry a while. The head chef presides over a progressive menu of pub favourites and modern European dishes, so anticipate smoked fish platter (the inn has its own smokehouse); trio of Kerridge sausages and mash; battered 'catch of the day' with hand-cut chips; a range of pizzas; and lemon posset with lime and lavender jelly.

Open all wk Tue-Sun all day (Mon 11-3 5-11) **Food** Lunch Mon-Fri 12-2, Sat 12-2.30, Sun 12-4 Dinner Mon-Fri 6.30-9, Sat 6.30-9.30 Set menu available Restaurant menu available all wk ⊕ FREE HOUSE/EXCLUSIVE INNS ◼ Greene King IPA, Adnams, Local & Guest ales ♻ Aspall, Carter's. ♟ 10 **Facilities** Non-diners area ♥ (Bar Garden) ♦ Children's menu Children's portions Garden ⋒ Beer festival Parking WiFi ➡ (notice required)

NEWMARKET
Map 12 TL66

The Packhorse Inn ★★★★★ INN ⊛⊛⊛ `PICK OF THE PUBS`

See Pick of the Pubs on opposite page

PICK OF THE PUBS

The Packhorse Inn ★★★★★ INN ❀❀❀

NEWMARKET　　　Map 12 TL66

tel: 01638 751818
Bridge St, Moulton CB8 8SP
email: info@thepackhorseinn.com
web: www.thepackhorseinn.com
dir: *A14 junct 39, B1506 signed*
Newmarket. Left onto B1085 to Moulton

Stylish country pub near Newmarket

Those who seek out dining establishments with three AA Rosettes should now head here, for in September 2014 the Packhorse acquired its third. That's not bad going, given that less than a year earlier village resident and former banker Philip Turner had reopened it following a six-month renovation. It acquired its new name too, having been the Kings Head, reflecting the nearby, pedestrian-only medieval bridge across the River Kennet. Just two miles from Newmarket Racecourse, this smart, family-friendly country pub and restaurant attracts all, from locals to out-of-town racegoers, to its large dining and bar area and individually designed, en suite bedrooms. Day-to-day running is in the hands of experienced husband-and-wife team Chris and Hayley Lee, who previously ran their own award-winning hotel and restaurant in Bildeston, Suffolk. The emphasis is on quality, locally sourced food and drink, including

game from shoots, lamb from Moulton, beers from Adnams and Woodforde's breweries, and Aspall cyder. The short but appealing, regularly changed menus might start with gravad lax, dill and pickled vegetables; venison carpaccio with quail's egg, parmesan and celeriac; or maybe half a dozen Dorset snails. Among the mains might be fillet of cod with confit cheek, fennel and Jerusalem artichoke; braised lamb shoulder 'hot-pot' with red cabbage; chargrilled Suffolk rib-eye steak and chips; and butternut squash and sage cannelloni with roasted chestnuts. Finish with pear and almond frangipane and Amaretto ice cream; or share a Packhorse 'retro' dessert plate.

Open all day all wk **Food** Lunch all wk 12-2.30 Dinner all wk 7-9.30 Av main course £15 ⊞ FREE HOUSE
◀ Woodforde's Wherry, Adnams Broadside, Fuller's London Pride, Guest ales ♻ Aspall Harry Sparrow. ♟ 19
Facilities Non-diners area ✿ (Bar Restaurant Garden) ♦ Children's portions Garden ⊼ Parking WiFi
🚌 (notice required) **Rooms** 4

REDE | Map 13 TL85

The Plough

tel: 01284 789208 **IP29 4BE**
dir: *On A143 between Bury St Edmunds & Haverhill*

Interesting menus in Suffolk's highest spot

Tucked away in the village on the green is this part-thatched, 16th-century pub easily identified by an old plough and a weeping willow at the front. On long-standing landlord Brian Desborough's ever-changing blackboard menu look for diced Highland beef with wholegrain mustard and whisky sauce; minted local venison with potato and cheese topping; and sea bass fillets with bacon, butterbean and sweetcorn sauce. The bar serves Fuller's, Adnams, Ringwood and Sharp's ales and 10 wines by the glass. At 128 metres above sea level, Rede is Suffolk's highest point – verified by *Guinness World Records*.

Open all wk 11-3 6-12 (Sun 12-3) **Food** Lunch all wk 12-2 Dinner Mon-Sat 6-9 ⊕ ADMIRAL TAVERNS ◀ Fuller's London Pride, Ringwood Best Bitter, Sharp's Cornish Coaster, Adnams Ȍ Aspall. ♚ 10 **Facilities** Non-diners area ◀♦ Children's portions Garden ⊨ Parking WiFi ▬ (notice required)

SIBTON | Map 13 TM36

Sibton White Horse Inn ★★★★ INN ☺ PICK OF THE PUBS

See Pick of the Pubs on opposite page

SNAPE | Map 13 TM35

The Crown Inn | PICK OF THE PUBS

tel: 01728 688324 **Bridge Rd IP17 1SL**
email: snapecrown@tiscali.co.uk
dir: *A12 from Ipswich towards Lowestoft, right onto A1094 towards Aldeburgh. In Snape right at x-rds by church, pub at bottom of hill*

Ancient village inn dedicated to using local produce

Getting on for 600 years old and once the haunt of smugglers using the nearby River Alde, this village stalwart shelters beneath a most extraordinary saltbox pantile roof. Inside, the public area threads beneath vast old beams and across mellow brick floors to cosy corners and an inglenook enclosed by the arms of a huge double settle. Folk musicians regularly take over this area for informal gigs; far more renowned is the nearby Snape Maltings complex where international performers are the order of the day. Pre- or post-concert meals are available for such concert goers. The Crown's owners Teresa and Garry Cook run their own livestock smallholding behind the pub, ensuring a very local supply chain. This is enhanced by locally sourced Limousin beef, seafood from Orford boats, game from nearby shoots, village vegetables and foraged specialities. Menus change frequently and a specials board adds spice to the mix – catch of the day with new potatoes and vegetables; pheasant wrapped in bacon with chestnuts and sage; or their own rare-breed pork sausages may feature.

Open all wk 12-3 6-11 **Food** Lunch all wk 12-2.30 Dinner all wk 6-9.30 ⊕ ADNAMS ◀ Southwold Bitter, Broadside, Seasonal ales Ȍ Aspall. ♚ 12 **Facilities** Non-diners area ◀ (Bar Garden) ◀♦ Children's portions Garden ⊨ Parking WiFi ▬ (notice required)

The Golden Key | PICK OF THE PUBS

tel: 01728 688510 **Priory Ln IP17 1SA**
email: info@goldenkeysnape.co.uk
dir: *Phone for detailed directions*

Dog-friendly, 16th-century cottage-style pub

This delightful village pub is a five-minute walk from Snape Maltings, home of the well-known Concert Hall, one of the focal points of the annual Aldeburgh Festival. The pub's low beamed ceilings and log fires not only attest to its age, but also help to generate its comfortable feel, especially in the quarry-tiled main bar, where you'll find villagers enjoying their pints of Southwold-brewed Adnams Broadside and Explorer. The food, both in the bar and in the pine-furnished dining room, owes much to the immediate locality, with fish delivered daily from Aldeburgh, lamb from a neighbouring farm and game supplied by the Benhall Shoot. Among the typical dishes are Richardson Smokehouse Suffolk ham with egg and chips; lamb curry with braised rice, tomato and coriander salad; and vegetable moussaka. Pre- and post-concert dining is available, but please remember to book.

Open all wk 12-3 5.30-11 (wknds all day) **Food** Lunch all wk 12-2.30 Dinner all wk 6-9 ⊕ ADNAMS ◀ Southwold Bitter, Broadside, Explorer, Old Ale, Ghost Ship Ȍ Aspall. ♚ 15 **Facilities** Non-diners area ◀ (All areas) ◀♦ Children's portions Garden Outside area ⊨ Parking WiFi ▬ (notice required)

Plough & Sail

tel: 01728 688413 **Snape Maltings IP17 1SR**
dir: *On B1069, S of Snape. Signed from A12*

Drawing in the crowds in Snape

Local twins, Alex (front of house) and Oliver (chef) Burnside own this pink, pantiled old inn at the heart of the renowned Snape Maltings complex; it's handy for cultural and shopping opportunities and close to splendid coastal walks. The interior is a comfy mix of dining and avant-garde destination pub; local ales and a good bin of wines accompany a solid menu, featuring a Mediterranean fish soup with rouille, gruyère and crostini, and home-made potted shrimps on toast to start; followed by seasonal fish pie; Gressingham duck (breast and confit leg), spiced pear, celeriac purée, sprouting broccoli and potato rösti; or Adnams beer battered fish and chips with crushed minted peas. A blackboard of specials adds to the choice.

Open all day all wk ⊕ FREE HOUSE ◀ Adnams Broadside, Southwold Bitter, Ghost Ship, Guest ale Ȍ Aspall. **Facilities** ◀ (Bar Garden) ◀♦ Children's menu Children's portions Garden Parking WiFi

SOMERLEYTON | Map 13 TM49

The Duke's Head

tel: 01502 733931 & 730281 **Slug's Ln NR32 5QR**
email: dukeshead@somerleyton.co.uk
dir: *From A143 onto B1074 signed Lowestoft & Somerleyton. Pub signed from B1074*

Rural estate-owned pub worth finding

Owned by and overlooking the Somerleyton Estate, this smart pub is tucked away down Slug's Lane on the edge of the village. Renowned locally for its imaginative seasonal menus, which champion game and meats reared on estate farms, it thrives as a dining-pub, and the rambling and very relaxed bar and dining areas fill early with those in the know. Savour the views over a pint of Wherry in the garden in the summer months.

Open all day all wk **Food** Lunch Mon-Sat 12-2.30, Sun 12-5 winter 12-8 summer (Jan-Mar Mon-Tue no food) Dinner Mon-Sat 6.30-9 (Jan-Mar Mon-Tue no food) ⊕ FREE HOUSE ◀ Adnams, Woodforde's Wherry, Guest ales Ȍ Aspall. ♚ 12 **Facilities** Non-diners area ◀ (Bar Restaurant Garden) ◀♦ Children's menu Children's portions Play area Garden ⊨ Beer festival Cider festival Parking WiFi ▬ (notice required)

PICK OF THE PUBS

Sibton White Horse Inn ★★★★ INN

SIBTON   Map 13 TM36

tel: 01728 660337
Halesworth Rd IP17 2JJ
email: info@sibtonwhitehorseinn.co.uk
web: www.sibtonwhitehorseinn.co.uk
dir: *A12 at Yoxford onto A1120, 3m to Peasenhall. Right opposite butchers, inn 600mtrs*

Delightful, award-winning inn

Off the beaten track in the heart of the Suffolk countryside, but just five minutes from the A12 at Yoxford and 10 miles from the coast, this rustic 16th-century inn retains much of its Tudor charm and incorporates stone floors, exposed brickwork and ships' timbers believed to have come from Woodbridge shipyard. A genuine free house, the bar with its raised gallery is the place to enjoy pints of Green Jack Trawlerboys or Woodforde's Once Bittern. There is a choice of dining areas to sample the award-winning food, while the secluded courtyard has a Mediterranean feel when the sun comes out. Owners Neil and Gill Mason are committed to producing high-quality food from fresh local ingredients — and, to prove it, they grow many of their own vegetables behind the pub. At lunch, you can order from the menu or from the selection of light bites and sandwiches. At dinner, a typical meal may offer old favourites like smoked mackerel pâté with sweet pickled cucumber and

Emmerdale 28-day-hung sirloin steak with thrice cooked, hand-cut chips. For something a little more special, there's lightly seared wood pigeon breast, thyme rösti potato, spinach and red wine jus; venison suet pudding, Parmentier potato, wilted greens and red onion gravy; or twice baked Binham Blue cheese soufflé, with Bramley apple, pear and red wine compôte. Finish, perhaps, with ginger sponge, toffee sauce and vanilla ice cream. Well behaved children are welcome; only those over six years old are permitted in the evening.

Open 12-2.30 6.30-11 (Sun 12-3.30 6.45-10.30) Closed 26-27 Dec, Mon L **Food** Lunch Tue-Sat 12-2, Sun 12-2.30 Dinner Mon-Sat 6.30-9, Sun 7-8.30

Set menu available Restaurant menu available Mon-Sat ⊕ FREE HOUSE ◀ Adnams Southwold Bitter, Woodforde's Once Bittern, Green Jack Trawlerboys Best Bitter ○ Aspall. ♀ 9 **Facilities** Non-diners area ♣ (Bar Garden) ♠♦ Children's menu/portions (lunchtime only) Please note: Only children over 6 years allowed in pub in evening Garden ⊟ Beer festival Parking WiFi **Rooms** 6

SOUTHWOLD
Map 13 TM57

The Crown Hotel
PICK OF THE PUBS

tel: 01502 722275 **The High St IP18 6DP**
email: crownhotelreception@adnams.co.uk
dir: A12 onto A1095 to Southwold. Hotel in town centre

The flagship hotel for the Adnams Brewery

Centrally located in the seaside town of Southwold, The Crown dates back to the 18th century, when it was a coaching inn. Buzzing with lively informality, it is owned by the Adnams Brewery (also based in Southwold), and offers a range of excellent ales on tap, as well as local Aspall cider. The location brings seafood options such as roulade of lemon sole, pan-fried sea bream fillet, and roasted scallops. Other choices from 'land' and 'garden' might include confit Gressingham duck leg, roast rack of lamb, goats' cheese risotto, and savoury pear tarte Tatin. Warm chocolate and peanut butter brownie is among the excellent puddings.

Open all wk 8am-11pm (Sun 8am-10.30pm) **Food** Lunch Mon-Fri 12-2, Sat-Sun 12-2.30 Dinner Sun-Fri 6-9, Sat 6-9.30 (5.30-9.30 summer) ⊕ ADNAMS ◀ Adnams Ŏ Aspall. ♟ 20 **Facilities** Non-diners area ♦️ Children's menu Children's portions Garden ♬ Parking WiFi

NEW The Harbour Inn

tel: 01502 722381 **Blackshore Quay IP18 6TA**
email: info@harbourinnsouthwold.co.uk
dir: From A12 (N of Blythburgh) take A1095 (Southwold). In Southwold right into York Rd to Southwold Harbour

Traditional old fishermen's pub with views of river and marshes

In contrast to pubs that don't tolerate wellies indoors, in winter this one actually recommends them because it stands right by the water, sometimes in it, as the sobering flood-level markers testify. Inside are two snug, photograph-plastered bars, the upper, nautically themed one with a wood-burner, while in the lower one staff must stoop to serve pints of Adnams through a hatch. Following one of the fish or seafood starters – 26 at the last count – continue with fish (lots of those, too); steak, Guinness and mushroom pudding; Thai-style vegetable curry; or a pizza, maybe to the accompaniment of live folk music.

Open all day all wk **Food** Lunch 12-9 Dinner 12-9 Av main course £12 ⊕ ADNAMS ◀ Southwold Bitter, Broadside, Ghost Ship & Spindrift Ŏ Aspall. ♟ 12 **Facilities** Non-diners area ♣ (Bar Garden) ♦️ Children's menu Children's portions Family room Garden ♬ Parking ▦ (notice required)

The Randolph
PICK OF THE PUBS

tel: 01502 723603 **41 Wangford Rd, Reydon IP18 6PZ**
email: reception@therandolph.co.uk
dir: A12 onto A1095 towards Southwold. Left into Wangford Rd

Family run with locally brewed beers

Easily walkable from Southwold, this majestic pub was built in 1899 by the town's well-known Adnams Brewery, whose directors were pally with Lord Randolph Churchill, Sir Winston's father. Showing no real sign today of its late-Victorian origins, the light and airy bar is furnished with contemporary high-backed chairs and comfortable sofas; the well-protected garden is lovely in the sun. In the bar and restaurant a concise modern British menu offers starters of spiced chickpea and vegetable stew topped with smoked cheese; and smoked chicken breast, carrot and caraway seed salad with tarragon crème fraîche. Mains include Hungarian beef goulash with mashed potato and soured cream; aromatic poached fillet of monkfish with pak choi, red pepper and noodle stir-fry; and honey-roasted parsnip and thyme risotto with mascarpone. Children can opt to select from their own menu.

Open all day all wk **Food** Lunch all wk 12-2 Dinner all wk 6.30-9 Restaurant menu available all wk ⊕ ADNAMS ◀ Southwold Bitter, Explorer, Old Ale & Ghost Ship Ŏ Aspall. **Facilities** Non-diners area ♦️ Children's menu Children's portions Garden ♬ Parking ▦ (notice required)

STOKE-BY-NAYLAND
Map 13 TL93

The Angel Inn ★★★★★ INN ◉
PICK OF THE PUBS

tel: 01206 263245 **CO6 4SA**
email: info@angelinnsuffolk.co.uk **web:** www.angelinnsuffolk.co.uk
dir: From Colchester take A134 towards Sudbury, 5m to Nayland. Or from A12 between juncts 30 & 31 take B1068, then B1087 to Nayland

Charming coaching inn in Constable Country

This substantial old inn has served the sublime village of gabled colour-washed houses and tall, slim chimneys since well before local lad John Constable put brush to canvas to capture the beauty of deepest rural Suffolk. Careful modernisation, like the air-conditioned conservatory, patio and sun terrace, harmonise happily with the ancient charm of The Angel's beamed bars, log fires and snug areas. The Well Room restaurant area, with its lofty, timbered ceiling and 52-ft deep well, is an astonishing centrepiece. Modern dishes and robust classics share billing on the seasonally-inspired menu which has gained head chef Mark Allen an AA Rosette. The good value prix fixe weekday lunch is a stalwart. From the à la carte, consider pan-seared sea bass with rice noodles, king prawns and lobster and ginger bisque; or trio of local venison with swede mash, honey-glazed carrots and game jus. Luxurious accommodation here offers scope for extended exploration of the scenic Stour Valley.

Open all day all wk 11-11 (Sun 11-10.30) **Food** Lunch Mon-Fri 12-3.30, Sat 12-9.30, Sun 12-9 Dinner Mon-Fri 6-9.30, Sat 12-9.30, Sun 12-9 Av main course £11 Set menu available Restaurant menu available all wk ⊕ FREE HOUSE/EXCLUSIVE INNS ◀ Adnams Southwold Bitter, Greene King, Nethergate, 2 guest ales Ŏ Aspall, Thatchers. ♟ 12 **Facilities** Non-diners area ♣ (Bar Garden) ♦️ Children's menu Children's portions Family room Garden Outside area ♬ Parking WiFi ▦ (notice required) **Rooms** 6

The Crown ★★★ SHL ◉◉
PICK OF THE PUBS

tel: 01206 262001 **CO6 4SE**
email: info@crowninn.net **web:** www.crowninn.net
dir: Exit A12 signed Stratford St Mary & Dedham. Through Stratford St Mary 0.5m, left, follow signs to Higham. At village green left, left again, 2m, pub on right

Delightful combination of village pub and boutique hotel

Slap bang in the heart of Constable Country and handy for the timeless villages of Lavenham, Kersey and Long Melford, this 16th-century free house sits above the Stour and Box Valleys on the Suffolk and Essex border. The stylish dining areas are informal, and there's a great choice of local ales in the contemporary bar. These are matched by an award-winning cellar of some 250 bins; over 30 of them can be bought by the glass. Tasty seasonal and local produce underpins a modern British menu. Typical starters are twice-baked wild mushroom and ricotta soufflé; and deep-fried whitebait with citrus mayonnaise and watercress. Children are welcome but dining is for adults only after 8pm. Dinner might feature West Devon lamb cutlets, pomegranate and herb tabbouleh, rocket and red onion salad and beetroot tzatziki. Finish with rhubarb crème brûlée. Eleven luxury en suite bedrooms complete the jewels in this crown.

Open all day all wk 7.30am-11pm (Sun 8am-10.30pm) Closed 25-26 Dec **Food** Lunch Mon-Sat 12-2.30, Sun 12-9 Dinner Mon-Thu 6-9.30, Fri-Sat 6-10, Sun 12-9 Set menu available Restaurant menu available all wk ⊕ FREE HOUSE ◀ Adnams Southwold Bitter, Crouch Vale Brewers Gold, Woodforde's Wherry, Guest ales Ŏ Aspall. ♟ 32 **Facilities** Non-diners area ♦️ Children's menu Children's portions Outside area ♬ Parking WiFi **Rooms** 11

STOWMARKET   Map 13 TM05

The Buxhall Crown

tel: 01449 736521 **Mill Rd, Buxhall IP14 3DW**
email: mail@thebuxhallcrown.co.uk
dir: *B1115 from Stowmarket, through Great Finborough to Buxhall*

Charming rural pub with exceptional menu

A fetching mix of cosy 17th-century cottage and Georgian artisan's house, this lavishly-beamed, wood-framed gastro-pub manages to retain the atmosphere of a traditional old village inn, complete with log fire and timeworn quarry tiles. There's a large, pergola-lined patio with restful views across the rich farmland, and Adnams beers are the order of the day. A typical menu includes starters like smoked salmon pie, or crayfish and prawn salad; following with wild and chestnut mushroom risotto, or free-range slow-roasted pork belly with bacon bubble-and-squeak; and finishes with winter berry posset or warm port poached Williams pear. Local provenance is assured; breads, chutneys and sweets are made at the pub.

Open 12-3 7-11 (Sat 12-3 6.30-11) Closed Sun eve & Mon **Food** Lunch Tue-Sun 12-2 Dinner Tue-Fri 7-9, Sat 6.30-9 ⊕ FREE HOUSE ◄ Adnams Southwold Bitter & Broadside Ö Aspall. ♈ 12 **Facilities** Non-diners area ♣ (Bar Restaurant Garden) ♦♦ Children's portions Garden Parking WiFi ⇔ (notice required)

STRADBROKE   Map 13 TM27

The Ivy House

tel: 01379 384634 **Wilby Rd IP21 5JN**
email: stensethhome@aol.com
dir: *Phone for detailed directions*

Interesting ales and wines in a pretty pub

Around the corner from Stradbroke's main street, this Grade II listed thatched pub with wooden beams dates from the Middle Ages. Real ales on handpump and wine from the Adnams wine cellar are the draw here. The weekly-changing menu makes good use of local and seasonal produce to offer both British and Asian-style dishes, and in warmer weather you can sit outside at the front or in the garden. Typical options include teriyaki-marinated chicken skewers with salsa to start; and pan-fried calves' liver with Suffolk dry-cured bacon, mash and onion gravy as a main course. Leave room for dark chocolate cake with praline ice cream. Curries and other dishes are available to take away.

Open all wk 12-3 6-11 **Food** Contact pub for food times ⊕ FREE HOUSE ◄ Adnams, Greene King, Fuller's London Pride Ö Aspall. **Facilities** Non-diners area ♣ (Bar Garden) Garden ⊨ Parking WiFi

SWILLAND   Map 13 TM15

Moon & Mushroom Inn

tel: 01473 785320 **High Rd IP6 9LR**
email: moonandmushroom@gmail.com
dir: *Take B1077 (Westerfield road) from Ipswich. Approx 6m, right to Swilland*

Tranquil escape in deepest Suffolk

The delightful sight of several firkins of East Anglian beer stillaged enticingly behind the bar welcomes drinkers to this 400-year-old free-house in the Suffolk countryside. Diners, too, relish the prospect of indulging in home-cooked specials such as Suffolk fish pie with salmon, cod, haddock and prawns; or slow-roasted

breast of lamb with lamb croquettes and redcurrant gravy. The pub was reputedly a staging post for the dispatch of convicts to Australia, and the records at Ipswich Assizes do indeed show that a previous landlord was deported for stealing two ducks and a pig. Today's guests are able to linger longer in the colourful, cottagey interior or the fragrant rose garden here.

Open Tue-Sat & Sun L Closed Sun eve & Mon **Food** Lunch Tue-Sat 12-2, Sun 12-2.30 Dinner Tue-Sat 6.30-9 Set menu available Restaurant menu available Tue-Sat ⊕ FREE HOUSE ◄ Nethergate Suffolk County, Woodforde's Wherry & Admiral's Reserve, Wolf Ale & Golden Jackal, Earl Soham Brandeston Gold & Victoria Bitter Ö Aspall. **Facilities** Non-diners area ♣ (Bar Garden) ♦♦ Children's portions Garden ⊨ Beer festival Parking ⇔ (notice required)

THORPENESS   Map 13 TM45

The Dolphin Inn

tel: 01728 454994 **Peace Place IP16 4NA**
email: dolphininn@hotmail.co.uk
dir: *A12 onto A1094 & follow Thorpeness signs*

At the community's heart and close to never-ending beaches

A stone's throw from the shingle of Suffolk's Heritage Coast and in a conservation area, this community-focused free house replaced a 1910 predecessor, destroyed by fire in 1995. At the bar are real ales from Adnams and Earl Soham, nearly 20 wines by the glass, and bourbons and single malts in abundance. Look forward to dressed crab salad; potted brown shrimps; seared Gressingham duck breast with sweet potato mash; grilled sea bass fillet; and lemon and elderflower cheesecake. After a bracing walk on the beach sit beside the fire and enjoy a pint of the local brew; in summer barbecues are held in the huge garden.

Open 11-3 6-11 (Sat all day Sun 11-5) Closed Sun eve & Mon in winter **Food** Lunch all wk 12-2.30 Dinner all wk 6.30-9.30 Set menu available ⊕ FREE HOUSE ◄ Adnams Southwold Bitter & Broadside, Brandon Rusty Bucket, Mauldons Midsummer Gold, Woodforde's Wherry Ö Aspall. ♈ 18 **Facilities** Non-diners area ♣ (Bar Garden) ♦♦ Children's menu Children's portions Garden ⊨ Parking WiFi ⇔

TUDDENHAM   Map 13 TM14

The Fountain

tel: 01473 785377 **The Street IP6 9BT**
email: fountainpub@btconnect.com
dir: *From Ipswich take B1077 (Westerfield Rd) signed Debenham. At Westerfield turn right for Tuddenham*

Informal bistro-style eating in a 16th-century country pub

In the lovely village of Tuddenham St Martin, only three miles north of Ipswich, this 16th-century country pub combines old fashioned pub hospitality with an informal bistro-style restaurant. The menu changes frequently and there is an emphasis on local produce in dishes such as twice baked Cromer crab soufflé; wild mushroom and tarragon risotto; and chocolate and pecan brownie with vanilla ice cream and caramel sauce. Wash it all down with pints of Adnams ale or Aspall cider.

Open all wk 12-3 6-11 (Sun 12-8) **Food** Lunch Mon-Sat 12-2, Sun 12-7 Dinner Mon-Fri 6-9, Sat 6-9.30, Sun 12-7 Set menu available Restaurant menu available all wk ⊕ FREE HOUSE ◄ Adnams Ö Aspall. ♈ 9 **Facilities** Non-diners area ♦♦ Children's menu Children's portions Garden ⊨ Parking WiFi

PICK OF THE PUBS

The Westleton Crown ★★★ HL 🌹🌹

WESTLETON   Map 13 TM46

tel: 01728 648777
The Street IP17 3AD
email: info@westletoncrown.co.uk
web: www.westletoncrown.co.uk
dir: *A12 N, turn right for Westleton just after Yoxford. Hotel opposite on entering Westleton*

Classic dishes with a twist and fine local ales

Standing opposite the parish church in a peaceful village close to the RSPB's Minsmere, this traditional coaching inn dates back to the 12th century and provides a comfortable base for exploring Suffolk's glorious Heritage Coast. The pub retains plenty of character and rustic charm, complemented by all the comforts of contemporary living. On winter days you'll find three crackling log fires, local real ales including Brandon Rusty Bucket and Adnams Southwold Bitter, as well as a good list of wines (with 11 available by the glass). There's also an extensive menu that includes innovative daily specials and classic dishes with a twist, freshly prepared from the best local produce. Eat in the cosy bar, in the elegant dining room, or in the garden room. Sandwiches are made with a choice of The Crown's own breads, and served with sea-salted crisps and a

dressed salad. More substantial appetites might choose from starters like Asian spiced beef salad, green papaya, peanuts, chilli and sesame dressing; or a smoked and cured fish plate with pickled vegetables. Follow up with main course choices such as braised Bunwell Wood venison bourguignon, truffle mash and red cabbage; or seafood casserole, saffron mash and fennel aïoli. Vegetarians have interesting options too – Binham Blue cheese soufflé, and wild mushroom and spinach tagliatelle, parmesan and truffle perhaps. Retire to one of the 34 comfortably and individually styled bedrooms. Outside, the large terraced gardens are floodlit in the evening.

Open all day all wk 7am-11pm (Sun 7.30am-10.30pm) **Food** Lunch all wk 12-2.30 Dinner all wk 6.30-9.30 🌐 FREE HOUSE 🍺 Adnams Southwold Bitter, Brandon Rusty Bucket 🍏 Aspall Harry Sparrow. 🍷 11 **Facilities** Non-diners area 🐾 (Bar Garden) 🚼 Children's menu Children's portions Garden 🎋 Parking WiFi 🚐 (notice required) **Rooms** 34

PICK OF THE PUBS

The White Horse

WHEPSTEAD Map 13 TL85

tel: 01284 735760 **Rede Rd IP29 4SS**
web: www.whitehorsewhepstead.co.uk
dir: *From Bury St Edmunds take A143 towards Haverhill. Left onto B1066 to Whepstead. In Whepstead right into Church Hill, leads into Rede Rd*

Delightful East Anglian pub with a loyal following

This village pub was built as a farmhouse in the early 17th century and extended during the Victorian era. As it is surrounded by rural public footpaths, many people take advantage of pub's short walk guides and then return here for lunch or dinner. The bright, spacious interior makes it a great space for the display and sale of artworks by local painters. The large, copper-topped bar, open fire and comfortable wooden chairs make you feel instantly at home, while nostalgic touches like the Tuck Shop – which sells ice cream, sweets and chocolate – appeal to adults and children alike. As well as reliable Suffolk ales and real cider behind the bar, the award-winning menus change on a daily basis. Owner Gary Kingshott oversees the kitchen, and his passion for great, uncomplicated food is evident in every dish. Quality seasonal ingredients are locally sourced where possible and always fresh; meat comes from the butcher in the next village. Starters could include cured salmon gravad lax with sweet chilli dressing; and pressed ham hock terrine with home-made piccalilli. Main course options might be rich venison ragout, juniper berries with a hint of dark chocolate; Madras-style fish curry, braised basmati and warm naan bread; or slow-roast pork belly with Bramley apple purée. For pudding the apricot bread and butter pudding will go down well. Front of house is run by Di Kingshott and her years of experience ensure quick and friendly service. Skye, the dog, can be found snoozing in a corner when he is not gently greeting customers.

Open 11.30-3 7-11 Closed 25-26 Dec, Sun eve **Food** Lunch all wk 12-2 Dinner Mon-Sat 7-9.30 FREE HOUSE Adnams Southwold Bitter & Broadside, Guest ale Aspall. 10 **Facilities** Non-diners area (Bar Garden) Children's portions Garden Parking

---

UFFORD
Map 13 TM25

The Ufford Crown

tel: 01394 461030 **High St IP13 6EL**
email: max@theuffordcrown.com
dir: *Just off A12 between Woodbridge & Wickham*

Friendly, family-run village pub and restaurant

Step though the doors of Max and Polly Durrant's handsome property and you'll find a spacious restaurant, cosy bar, stylish lounge area and, at the rear, a terrace and garden, where there's plenty to keep children amused. Adnams and Earl Soham badges adorn the real ale pumps, with Aspall cider alongside. A glass of sloe gin fizz would make a great intro for lunch or dinner here. Gifted chef Will Hardiman has a reputation for using all cuts of meat, including sweetbreads and ox cheeks, and Lowestoft-landed fish. Heavily reliant on seasonal produce from local suppliers, his menus feature harissa pork rillettes with fried quails's egg; grilled Ramsholt herring, caper buerre noisette and new potatoes; and BBQ short rib of beef, dauphinoise potatoes and greens.

Open 12-3 5-11 (Sat-Sun all day) Closed Tue **Food** Lunch Mon & Wed-Sat 12.30-2, Sun 12-3 Dinner Mon & Wed-Sat 6.30-9, Sun 6-8 ⊕ FREE HOUSE ◀ Adnams Southwold Bitter, Earl Soham Brandeston Gold & Victoria Bitter ⚬ Aspall. ♟ 15 **Facilities** Non-diners area ❤ (Bar Garden) ♦♦ Children's menu Children's portions Play area Garden Outside area ⋒ Parking WiFi ▭ (notice required)

WALBERSWICK
Map 13 TM47

The Bell Inn

tel: 01502 723109 **Ferry Rd IP18 6TN**
email: info@bellinnwalberswick.co.uk
dir: *From A12 take B1387 to Walberswick, after village green turn right into track*

Old inn where the menu captures top Suffolk produce

There's plenty of character here, with 600 years of history, oak-beamed ceilings, hidden alcoves, worn flagstone floors and open fires. Close to the Southwold ferry, the Suffolk Coastal Path and the marshes, the pub has a family-friendly garden overlooking a creek and the beach; here too is the Barn Café, offering everything for a picnic. Firm favourites on the menu are potted shrimps with granary toast; lamb shank tagine with couscous; and honey and mustard glazed ham with poached egg, chips and peas. Well-behaved dogs are welcome.

Open all day all wk **Food** Lunch all wk 12-2.30 Dinner all wk 6-9 Av main course £12 ⊕ ADNAMS ◀ Southwold Bitter, Broadside, Spindrift, Ghost Ship ⚬ Aspall. ♟ 15 **Facilities** Non-diners area ❤ (Bar Garden) ♦♦ Children's menu Children's portions Family room Garden ⋒ Parking ▭ (notice required)

WESTLETON
Map 13 TM46

The Westleton Crown ★★★ HL ◉◉ | **PICK OF THE PUBS**

See Pick of the Pubs on page 474

WHEPSTEAD
Map 13 TL85

The White Horse ◉ | **PICK OF THE PUBS**

See Pick of the Pubs on page 475

WOODBRIDGE
Map 13 TM24

Cherry Tree Inn ★★★★ INN

tel: 01394 384627 **73 Cumberland St IP12 4AG**
email: andy@thecherrytreepub.co.uk **web:** www.thecherrytreepub.co.uk
dir: *Phone for detailed directions*

Classically appealing hostelry with a caring approach

Winner of an AA Dinner Award and recognised for the sustainability of its operation, the Cherry Tree Inn features a large central counter, and several distinct seating areas amidst the twisting oak beams. The year sees around eight guest ales rotate, with Adnams and Aspall cider in permanent residence; a beer festival in early July confirms the pub's ale credentials. The focus on customer care manifests subtly in many ways: the availability of board games; play equipment for children in the large enclosed garden; wheelchair access; dog friendliness; free WiFi; and many gluten-free options among the locally-sourced and home-cooked menu dishes.

Open all day all wk 10.30am-11pm **Food** Lunch Mon-Sat 12-9, Sun 12-8 Dinner Mon-Sat 12-9, Sun 12-8 ⊕ ADNAMS ◀ Adnams ales, Guest ales ⚬ Aspall. ♟ 11 **Facilities** Non-diners area ❤ (Bar Outside area) ♦♦ Children's menu Children's portions Play area Garden Outside area ⋒ Beer festival Parking WiFi ▭ (notice required) **Rooms** 3

WOODDITTON
Map 12 TL65

The Three Blackbirds

tel: 01638 731100 **36 Ditton Green CB8 9SQ**
email: info@thethreeblackbirdswoodditton.co.uk
dir: *From Newmarket High Street (Cambridge end) take B1061 opposite Shell garage. In 300yds turn left, 2.5m to Woodditton. At x-roads turn right, pub 300yds on right*

Exciting food and local ales in beautiful thatched village inn

Mentioned in the Domesday Book, the beautiful village of Woodditton is just three miles from Newmarket, and the thatched Three Blackbirds, which has now changed hands, dates from 1642. The two cosy oak-beamed bars offer a range of real ales and diners can choose between the restaurant and private dining room to sample a daily-changing menu packed with local produce. Pheasant breast wrapped in Suffolk bacon; roasted sea trout; or local steaks from the grill are followed by treats like home-made profiteroles filled with Baileys Irish cream.

Open all wk 12-3 5-11 (Fri 12-3 5-mdnt Sat 12-3 5.30-12 Sun 12-7) **Food** Lunch Mon-Sat 12-2.30, Sun 12-4 Dinner Mon-Sat 6.30-9.30 Av main course £15 Set menu available ⊕ FREE HOUSE ◀ Adnams Best Bitter, Woodforde's Wherry, Sharp's Doom Bar ⚬ Aspall. ♟ 17 **Facilities** Non-diners area ❤ (Bar Garden Outside area) ♦♦ Children's menu Children's portions Garden Outside area ⋒ Beer festival Parking WiFi ▭ (notice required)

Read all about pubs and **their friendly ghosts in our feature on page 12**

SURREY

ABINGER
Map 6 TQ14

The Abinger Hatch

tel: 01306 730737 **Abinger Ln RH5 6HZ**
email: manager@theabingerhatch.com
dir: *A25 from Dorking towards Guildford. Left to Abinger Common*

Quintessentially English pub with something for everyone

Andy and Sarah run this lovely pub, aiming to please families with their special brand of hospitality. Plenty of variety is the key, from the children's choices to dishes based on fresh locally sourced produce. Traditionally English from its beams to its flagstone floors, the pub enjoys a light and airy atmosphere. There's lots of space outside too, with capacious car parking and a huge garden where a summer barbecue, wood-burning oven and outdoor bar make for a truly relaxing experience. Ringwood and guest ales head the refreshments list, with plenty of good wines to choose from.

Open all day all wk **Food** Lunch all wk 12-6 Dinner Mon-Sat 6-10, Sun 6-9 ⊕ FREE HOUSE ◀ Ringwood Best & Fortyniner, Cottage, Guest ales. ♟ 14 **Facilities** Non-diners area ❤ (Bar Restaurant Garden) ♦ Children's menu Children's portions Garden ♬ Parking WiFi ▄▄ (notice required)

ALBURY
Map 6 TQ04

The Drummond at Albury ★★★ INN

tel: 01483 202039 **The Street GU5 9AG**
email: drummondarms@aol.com web: www.thedrummondarms.co.uk
dir: *6m from Guildford on A248*

Riverside pub in the heart of the Surrey Hills

This eye-catching village inn, which has hanging flower baskets outside in summer, was reopened a few years ago by the Duke of Northumberland whose family have historic links to the pub. Its pleasant beer garden backs onto River Tillingbourne. Expect a comforting mix of great local (from Hogs Back) and national real ales. In the conservatory restaurant, the best of modern and traditional British cooking is on offer – herb-roasted chicken breast, trout from the Albury Estate lakes, and the popular home-made Drummond pies. Individually appointed letting rooms make the pub a good base from which to explore the North Downs.

Open all day all wk 11-11 (Fri-Sat 11am-mdnt Sun 12-10.30) **Food** Lunch Mon-Fri 12-3, Sat 12-6, Sun 12-8 Dinner Mon-Sat 6-9.30, Sun 12-8 ⊕ FREE HOUSE ◀ Courage Best Bitter, Fuller's London Pride, Hogs Back TEA, Adnams. ♟ 10 **Facilities** Non-diners area ❤ (Bar Garden) ♦ Children's portions Garden ♬ Parking WiFi **Rooms** 9

William IV

tel: 01483 202685 **Little London GU5 9DG**
dir: *Off A25 between Guildford & Dorking (for detailed directions contact pub)*

16th-century free house on a quiet country lane

Deep in the wooded Surrey Hills yet only a few miles from Guildford, this 16th-century free house provides 'proper pub food' made from mostly local produce. Look out for dishes of free-range pork (raised by landlord Giles) written on the blackboards, but also worth considering are the liver and bacon, beer-battered cod and chips, and pan-fried Cajun chicken, all served in the bar and dining room. Young's and two Surrey breweries supply the real ales. It is great walking and riding country, and the attractive garden is ideal for post-ramble relaxation.

Open all wk 11-3 5.30-11 (Sat 11-11 Sun 12-11) **Food** Lunch all wk 12-2 Dinner Mon-Sat 7-9 ⊕ FREE HOUSE ◀ Young's, Hogs Back, Surrey Hills Ŏ Westons Stowford Press, Addlestones. **Facilities** Non-diners area ❤ (Bar Garden) ♦ Children's portions Garden ♬ Parking WiFi ▄▄ (notice required)

BRAMLEY
Map 6 TQ04

Jolly Farmer Inn

tel: 01483 893355 **High St GU5 0HB**
email: enquiries@jollyfarmer.co.uk
dir: *From Guildford take A281 (Horsham road). Bramley 3.5m S of Guildford*

Welcoming and friendly pub

A 16th-century coaching inn steeped in character and history, this friendly family-run free house clearly has a passion for beer. Besides the impressive range of Belgian bottled beers, you'll always find up to eight constantly-changing cask real ales on the counter. The pub offers a high standard of food all freshly cooked, with daily specials board featuring dishes such as queen scallops, black pudding and pea purée; chorizo, ham and spinach omelette with salad; and rich lamb hot pot and seasonal vegetables.

Open all day all wk 11-11 **Food** Lunch all wk 12-2.30 Dinner all wk 6-9.30 Av main course £10 ⊕ FREE HOUSE ◀ 8 guest ales Ŏ Westons Stowford Press, Aspall. ♟ 16 **Facilities** Non-diners area ❤ (Bar Outside area) ♦ Children's menu Outside area ♬ Parking WiFi ▄▄ (notice required)

BROOK
Map 6 SU93

NEW The Dog & Pheasant

tel: 01428 682763 **Haslemere Rd GU8 5UJ**
email: info@dogandpheasant.com
dir: *From Godalming take A286 towards Haslemere. Pub approx 4.5m*

A truly English country pub

Four open fires warm this picturesque 15th-century pub, where over the inglenook on Wednesday nights the chef grills steaks and fish. Sixteen wines are served by the glass and real ales are sourced from Surrey to Cumbria. In addition to grills, the menu offers linguine with scallops, tiger prawns, crayfish tails and mussels in provençal sauce; thyme-roast pork tenderloin, braised cheek and ham-hock bonbon with apple mash, creamed cabbage, bacon and Calvados jus; and herbed pancake with wild mushrooms, goats' cheese, wilted spinach and walnut pesto. A 'cover drive' away from the lovely garden is the cricket pitch, the Surrey Hills beyond.

Open all day Closed Sun eve in winter **Food** Lunch Mon-Fri 12-2.30, Sat-Sun 12-4 Dinner Mon-Fri 6-9.30, Sat 5-9.30 Av main course £15 ⊕ PUNCH TAVERNS ◀ Ringwood Best Bitter, Sharp's Atlantic Ŏ Westons Old Rosie. ♟ 16 **Facilities** Non-diners area ❤ (Bar Garden) ♦ Children's menu Children's portions Play area Garden ♬ Parking WiFi ▄▄ (notice required)

BUCKLAND
Map 6 TQ25

The Jolly Farmers Eatery + Farm Shop

tel: 01737 221355 **Reigate Rd RH3 7BG**
email: info@thejollyfarmersreigate.co.uk
dir: *On A25 approx 2m from Reigate & 4m from Dorking*

Delightful deli, farm shop and pub combo

Beside the A25 between Reigate and Dorking, this unique free house may look like a traditional pub but step inside and you'll find a cracking deli and farm shop that showcases local foods and artisan producers smack next to the comfortable, wood-floored bar and restaurant. Choose from deli snacks such as a marinated sticky chicken wings, or Reigate Royal warm pork sausage roll, or plump for a full meal – maybe truffled wild mushrooms on toast followed by steam venison and juniper suet pudding. Wash it down with a pint of Dark Star Hophead or WJ King Horsham Best.

Open all day all wk **Food** Lunch all wk all day Dinner all wk all day Av main course £9.95 ⊕ FREE HOUSE ◀ Dark Star Hophead, WJ King Horsham Best, Dorking DB Number One, Pilgrim Surrey Bitter. ♟ 14 **Facilities** Non-diners area ❤ (Bar Garden Outside area) ♦ Children's menu Children's portions Play area Garden Outside area ♬ Parking WiFi ▄▄ (notice required)

CHIDDINGFOLD
Map 6 SU93

The Crown Inn ★★★★★ INN

tel: 01428 682255 **The Green GU8 4TX**
email: enquiries@thecrownchiddingfold.com **web:** www.thecrownchiddingfold.com
dir: On A283 between Milford & Petworth

Pretty as a picture timbered inn, more than 700 years old

Set by the village green and church, this beautifully appointed inn is one of the county's oldest buildings. It oozes charm and character, featuring ancient panelling, open fires, distinctive carvings, huge beams, and eight comfortable bedrooms. In addition to the house beer, Crown Bitter, ales come from Surrey, Hampshire and London breweries. Food ranges from enticing snacks like deep-fried haloumi skewers with tomato compôte; and honey and mustard glazed sausages, to dishes such as veal osso bucco with saffron rice; confit leg of duck and smoked bacon with potato rösti, buttered greens and clementine sauce, or a Crown favourite, pie or pudding of the week.

Open all day all wk **Food** Lunch Mon-Sat 12-2.30, Sun 12-3 Dinner Mon-Sat 6.30-10, Sun 6.30-9 Av main course £11.50 ⊕ FREE HOUSE/FGH INNS ◀ Crown Bitter, Fuller's London Pride, Triple fff Moondance, Hop Back Summer Lightning. ♟ 12 **Facilities** Non-diners area ♦♦ Children's menu Children's portions Outside area ⊼ Parking WiFi **Rooms** 8

The Swan Inn ★★★★ INN ◉◉
PICK OF THE PUBS

See Pick of the Pubs on opposite page

COLDHARBOUR
Map 6 TQ14

The Plough Inn
PICK OF THE PUBS

tel: 01306 711793 **Coldharbour Ln RH5 6HD**
email: theploughinn@btinternet.com
dir: M25 junct 9, A24 to Dorking. A25 towards Guildford. Coldharbour signed from one-way system

Well-established pub in pretty village

Set in the heart of the Surrey Hills Area of Outstanding Natural Beauty, this charming old coaching inn dates back to the 17th century, and has been home to the Abrehart family for more than 25 years. Nearby Leith Hill, at 965-ft the highest point in south-eastern England is popular with walkers and cyclists, many of whom pop into the Plough for some sustenance after their exertions. Earlier visitors were smugglers, en route from the south coast to London, which may be why the resident ghost is a sailor. Another high point is the Leith Hill Brewery – the landlord's own microbrewery, producing Tallywhacker porter, Crooked Furrow bitter and the lighter Beautiful South, as well as Biddenden cider. The Abreharts have created a family-friendly place with big fires and a pretty garden, serving great food. On the menus expect local butcher's Old English sausages, egg, chunky chips and salad; blackened Cajun spiced salmon fillet; and roasted vegetable and goats' cheese filo strudel, as well as their famous 6oz burgers. Home-made puddings include banoffee pie and a daily crumble.

Open all day all wk 11.30am-close Closed 25 Dec **Food** Lunch Mon-Fri 12-2.30, Sat-Sun 12-3 Dinner Mon-Sat 7-9.30 Av main course £11 ⊕ FREE HOUSE ◀ Leith Hill Crooked Furrow, Tallywhacker & The Beautiful South, Guest ale ⓑ Biddenden. **Facilities** Non-diners area ♦♦ Children's menu Children's portions Garden ⊼ Parking WiFi ➡ (notice required)

COMPTON
Map 6 SU94

The Withies Inn

tel: 01483 421158 **Withies Ln GU3 1JA**
dir: Phone for detailed directions

Eclectically furnished old village inn

This low-beamed inn has slumbered beside the wooded common for five centuries, maturing into a popular, cosy village local enhanced by an intimate restaurant area, where seasonal specials tumble from the menu. Start off with seafood crêpe mornay; mushrooms in garlic butter; or paw paw with fresh crab; then move on to mains like escalope of veal marsala; mushroom Stroganoff; grilled calves' liver with bacon and onions; or poached halibut with prawns and brandy sauce. After you've finished you could take a stroll in the lovely surrounding countryside, or relax in the garden with a pint of TEA from the local Hogs Back Brewery.

Open 11-3 6-11 (Fri 11-11) Closed Sun eve **Food** Lunch all wk 12-2.30 Dinner Mon-Sat 6-10 Restaurant menu available all wk ⊕ FREE HOUSE ◀ Hogs Back TEA, Greene King IPA, Adnams, Sharp's Doom Bar ⓑ Aspall. ♟ 12 **Facilities** Non-diners area ♦♦ Children's portions Garden ⊼ Parking WiFi ➡ (notice required)

CRANLEIGH
Map 6 TQ03

The Richard Onslow

tel: 01483 274922 **113-117 High St GU6 8AU**
email: hello@therichardonslow.co.uk
dir: From A281 between Guildford & Horsham take B2130 to Cranleigh, pub in village centre

A classy village gastro-pub

This grand old tile-hung pub stands at the heart of what claims to be England's largest village. While necessarily updating the interior, owners Peach Pubs worked hard to retain its period appeal, particularly the original brick inglenook in the bar, where you can enjoy Surrey-brewed Shere Drop (named after a nearby village) and Hogs Back TEA real ales. With the emphasis firmly on top-notch seasonal produce from breakfast to dinner, expect fillet of Loch Duart salmon; Cornish lamb rump; breast of chicken with crispy bread pudding; and pappardelle of sprouting broccoli, pine nuts, sun-dried tomato and Wensleydale Blue cheese.

Open all day all wk Closed 25 Dec **Food** Lunch Mon-Sat 12-10, Sun 12-9 Dinner Mon-Sat 12-10, Sun 12-9 Av main course £15.50 ⊕ FREE HOUSE ◀ Surrey Hills Shere Drop, Firebird Heritage XX, Hogs Back TEA ⓑ Hogs Back Hazy Hog, Aspall. ♟ **Facilities** Non-diners area �★ (Bar Outside area) ♦♦ Children's portions Outside area ⊼ Beer festival Parking WiFi ➡ (notice required)

PICK OF THE PUBS

The Swan Inn ★★★★ INN ❀❀

CHIDDINGFOLD   Map 6 SU93

tel: 01428 684688
Petworth Rd GU8 4TY
email: info@theswaninnchiddingfold.com
web: www.theswaninnchiddingfold.com
dir: *From A3 follow Milford/Petworth/ A283 signs. At rdbt 1st exit onto A283. Slight right onto Guildford & Godalming bypass. Right into Portsmouth Rd, left (continue on A283), to Chiddingfold*

Cosmopolitan food and drink in stylish village inn

The owners of The Swan Inn ran a pub in fashionable Knightsbridge for 20 years before taking over here and they have added luxurious boutique-style accommodation to this lovely old village inn. Nestling among the Surrey Hills in the village of Chiddingfold between Guildford and Petworth, The Swan is typical of the coaching inns that used to serve customers travelling to or from the south coast. Rebuilt in the 1880s and now appointed to a high standard, The Swan today offers weary travellers a friendly and relaxed welcome. In the bar, temptations include local ales such as Shere Drop brewed by the Surrey Hills Brewery, and from an international list, there are 16 wines served by the glass. The award-winning menu also has broad appeal, with top-notch produce such as Scottish salmon, Parma ham and foie gras. A typical meal might kick off with an appetiser of trompette

mushroom arancini, tarragon purée and red onion jam; a classic Caesar salad; or crispy pork belly and black pudding croquette. They might be followed by main course choices of lambs' kidneys turbigo, root vegetable gratin, Savoy cabbage and onion rings; fillet of hake, lemon tarragon crushed potatoes, mange tout and prawn bisque; or a classic burger with shoestring fries. Vegetarians might like to choose pumpkin, aubergine and chickpea tikka masala, aromatic rice, coriander naan, poppadoms and mango chutney. For dessert perhaps choose dark chocolate and orange torte, honeycomb and popcorn ice cream; or treacle cake, poppy seed pannacotta with plum compôte.

Open all day all wk 11-11 (Sun 12-10.30) **Food** Lunch all wk 12-3 Dinner Mon-Sat 6.30-10, Sun 6.30-9 ⊕ FREE HOUSE ◼ Adnams Southwold Bitter, Surrey Hills Shere Drop, Guest ale Ŏ Hogan's, Aspall. ♀ 16
Facilities Non-diners area ❖ (Bar Garden) ⷧ Children's menu Children's portions Garden ⍭ Beer festival Parking WiFi **Rooms** 10

DUNSFOLD
Map 6 TQ03

The Sun Inn

tel: 01483 200242 **The Common GU8 4LE**
email: suninn@dunsfold.net
dir: *A281 through Shalford & Bramley, take B2130 to Godalming. Dunsfold on left after 2m*

Traditional village pub charm

A 17th-century inn, with tables and benches on the green opposite, and well within earshot of "Howzat!" from the adjacent cricket pitch. High and low ceilings, beams, blazing fires and real ales from a tried and tested line-up of Adnams, Harvey's and Sharp's. The inn's own vegetable garden contributes generously to daily menus, typically featuring French onion soup; local venison liver pâté; various burgers; extra-mature British rib-eye steak; lemon chicken and tarragon risotto; beef vindaloo; and roast vegetable and coconut curry. Enjoy a Sunday evening quiz, Wednesday's pies and Friday's curries. Dogs will appreciate the free biscuits kept in the bar.

Open all day all wk **Food** Lunch all wk 12-2.30 Dinner Mon-Sat 7-9.15, Sun 7-8.30 ⊕ PUNCH TAVERNS ◀ Sharp's Doom Bar, Harvey's Sussex, Adnams, Thwaites Wainwright, Guest ales ♻ Westons Scrumpy & Old Rosie. ♟ 10
Facilities Non-diners area ♣ (Bar Garden) ♦♦ Children's menu Children's portions Garden ⋈ Parking WiFi ▭ (notice required)

EASHING
Map 6 SU94

The Stag on the River

tel: 01483 421568 **Lower Eashing GU7 2QG**
email: bookings@stagontherivereashing.co.uk
dir: *From A3 S'bound exit signed Eashing, 200yds over river bridge. Pub on right*

A good meeting place by the river

Located on the banks of the River Wye, this comfortable, well-appointed village inn takes full advantage, with a large garden and separate patio. Fixtures on handpump in the bar are Hogs Back TEA (Traditional English Ale) and Surrey Hills Shere Drop, others rotate. A seasonal menu might begin with home-made pork and black pudding Scotch egg, watercress salad and candied apple sauce; or a charcuterie sharing plate. Main courses include smoked haddock and salmon fishcakes; and a classic fish pie with chips and pea purée. For dessert try white chocolate and pistachio pannacotta with poached rhubarb.

Open all day all wk Closed 25 Dec **Food** Lunch Mon-Sat 12-3, Sun 12-8.30 Dinner Mon-Sat 6-9, Sun 12-8.30 Av main course £12 ⊕ FREE HOUSE ◀ Hogs Back TEA, Surrey Hills Shere Drop, Guest ales ♻ Hogs Back Hazy Hog. ♟ 12
Facilities Non-diners area ♣ (Bar Garden) ♦♦ Children's menu Children's portions Garden ⋈ Parking WiFi

EAST CLANDON
Map 6 TQ05

The Queens Head

tel: 01483 222332 **The Street GU4 7RY**
email: bookings@queensheadeastclandon.co.uk
dir: *4m E of Guildford on A246. Signed*

Village pub with a tree-shaded garden

With the North Downs Way that links Farnham to the White Cliffs of Dover passing nearby, you can expect fleece-clad rucksack wearers alongside the locals here. It's partly the Surrey, Kent and Oxfordshire real ales that appeal, and partly the locally sourced food, with starters including home-smoked duck salad; and caramelised red onion and sweet pepper tart. Surrounding farms and suppliers are also the main sources of British steak, real ale and mushroom pie; Scottish smoked haddock, crayfish and salmon fishcake; and home-dried cherry tomato and fennel risotto.

Open all wk 12-3 6-11 (Sat 12-11 Sun 12-9) **Food** Lunch Mon-Fri 12-2.30, Sat 12-9.30, Sun 12-8 Dinner Mon-Thu 6-9, Fri 6-9.30, Sat 12-9.30, Sun 12-8 Av main course £14.50 Set menu available ⊕ FREE HOUSE ◀ Surrey Hills Shere Drop, Hogs Back TEA, Brakspear Oxford Gold, Shepherd Neame Spitfire, Sharp's Doom Bar. ♟ 13
Facilities Non-diners area ♣ (All areas) ♦♦ Children's menu Children's portions Garden Outside area ⋈ Parking WiFi ▭

EFFINGHAM
Map 6 TQ15

The Plough

tel: 01372 458121 **Orestan Ln KT24 5SW**
email: info@theplougheffingham.co.uk
dir: *Between Guildford & Leatherhead on A246*

Off the beaten track, deep in the Surrey Hills

The cool neutral tones of the interior of this mid-1840s pub reflect the daylight; bookshelves, mirrors and prints line the walls. There are tables a-plenty inside, in the pretty garden and on the front terrace, where ramblers and cyclists are often to be found in the company of Naked Ladies and Redheads (both real ales, it should be explained). Monthly-changing menus offer freshly-prepared contemporary and traditional British favourites, such as pheasant cooked two ways; pan-fried sea bass; and pumpkin, spinach and ricotta cannelloni. The two Sunday roasts change weekly. Nearby is the National Trust's Polesden Lacey house and estate.

Open all wk 11-3 5.30-11 (Sun 12-5.30) Closed 25-26 Dec & 31 Dec eve **Food** Lunch Mon-Sat 12-2.30, Sun 12-4.30 Dinner Mon-Thu 6.30-9.30, Fri-Sat 6.30-10 ⊕ YOUNG'S ◀ Special, Twickenham Fine Ales, Redhead, Naked Ladies & Grandstand, Young's ♻ Aspall. ♟ 16 **Facilities** Non-diners area ♦♦ Children's menu Children's portions Garden Parking WiFi

ELSTEAD
Map 6 SU94

The Woolpack

tel: 01252 703106 **The Green, Milford Rd GU8 6HD**
email: info@woolpackelstead.co.uk
dir: *A3 S, take Milford exit, follow signs for Elstead on B3001*

Village local with an Italian flavour

Originally a wool exchange dating back to the 17th century, the attractive tile-hung Woolpack continues to display weaving shuttles and other artefacts relating to the wool industry. You'll also find open log fires, low beams, high-backed settles, comfortable window seats and cask-conditioned ales including local Hogs Back TEA and Ringwood Fortyniner. The menu features Italian dishes from the owners' home country, plus there's a sandwich menu and a wide selection of stone-baked pizzas. The surrounding common land attracts ramblers galore, especially at lunchtime.

Open all wk 12-3 5.30-late (Sun 12-late) ⊕ PUNCH TAVERNS ◀ Ringwood Fortyniner, Hogs Back TEA, Sharp's Doom Bar ♻ Westons Stowford Press.
Facilities ♣ (Bar Garden) ♦♦ Children's menu Children's portions Play area Garden Parking WiFi

ENGLEFIELD GREEN
Map 6 SU97

The Fox and Hounds

tel: 01784 433098 **Bishopsgate Rd TW20 0XU**
email: marketing@thefoxandhoundsrestaurant.com
dir: *M25 junct 13, A30 signed Basingstoke & Camberley. Right at lights onto A328 signed Englefield Green. With village green on left, left into Bishopsgate Rd*

Upmarket dining close to Windsor Great Park

Dating back to 1780, this pub is ideally situated next to the Bishopsgate entrance to Windsor Great Park in the village of Englefield Green. Enjoy a pint of Brakspear bitter in the stylish bar or enjoy a slap-up meal in the light and elegant conservatory restaurant. The locally sourced ingredients create a wide ranging choice of dishes, from the meze or charcuterie sharing boards to Chateaubriand for two. Leave room for one of the home-made desserts or the tasting plate of puddings that's for sharing.

Open all day all wk 8am-11pm **Food** Lunch all wk 12-9.30 Dinner all wk 12-9.30 Set menu available ⊕ FREE HOUSE/BRAKSPEAR ◄ Brakspear Bitter & Oxford Gold Ö Symonds. ♟ 14 **Facilities** Non-diners area ❀ (Bar Garden) ♦ Children's menu Children's portions Garden ⋒ Parking WiFi ☞ (notice required)

FARNHAM
Map 5 SU84

The Bat & Ball Freehouse
PICK OF THE PUBS

tel: 01252 792108 **15 Bat & Ball Ln, Boundstone GU10 4SA**
email: info@thebatandball.co.uk
dir: From A31 (Farnham bypass) onto A325 signed Birdworld. Left at Bengal Lounge. At T-junct right, immediately left into Sandrock Hill Rd. 0.25m left into Upper Bourne Ln. Follow signs

A mid-Victorian free house well worth seeking out

A little tricky to find – it's down a long cul-de-sac – but you'll be pleased you persevered. It's a real community pub, the interior featuring terracotta floors, oak beams, a warming fire and cricketing memorabilia, while in the garden you'll find a patio with picnic tables, a vine-topped pergola and a children's fort. Six frequently-changing real ales come from regional microbreweries, the ciders are Thatchers and Aspall, and plenty of wines are by the glass. Lizzy, daughter of owners Kevin and Sally Macready, masterminds a menu comprising both modern and traditional dishes. After a starter of ham hock terrine, maybe, main courses might include fisherman's pie; sticky slow-cooked pork ribs with pomegranate and chilli salsa and sweet potato fries; or triple mustard wood pigeon Stroganoff. A huge choice of ales and ciders is laid on during the beer, cider and music festival during the second weekend in June.

Open all day all wk 11-11 (Sun 12-10.30) **Food** Lunch Mon-Fri 12-2.15, Sat 12-9.30, Sun 12-8.30 Dinner Mon-Fri 7-9.30, Sat 12-9.30, Sun 12-8.30 ⊕ FREE HOUSE ◄ Hogs Back TEA, Triple fff, Bowman, Ballards, Andwell, Arundel, Weltons, Itchen Valley Ö Thatchers, Aspall. ♟ 8 **Facilities** Non-diners area ❀ (All areas) ♦ Children's menu Children's portions Play area Family room Garden Outside area ⋒ Beer festival Cider festival Parking WiFi

---

The Spotted Cow at Lower Bourne

tel: 01252 726541 **Bourne Grove, Lower Bourne GU10 3QT**
email: thespottedcow@btinternet.com **web:** www.thespottedcowpub.com
dir: From Farnham town centre, cross rail line, onto B3001. Right into Tilford Rd, up hill, at lights straight on, Bourne Grove 3rd right

Idyllic woodland and garden setting

Set in four acres of secluded, woodland-shaded grounds and two gardens, one of which is enclosed and especially suitable for young children, the Spotted Cow is a

perfect place to unwind. Indulge in some of the great TEA beer from nearby Hogs Back Brewery and consider the ever-changing menu of tried-and-tested favourites, all made fresh on the premises. Sandwiches and jackets are on the bar lunch menu, while regularly-changing specials could include oven-baked salmon with braised fennel; tomato, brie and spinach risotto; and the 'ultimate' veggie burger – roasted aubergine, beef tomato, onion marmalade and breaded goats' cheese in a brioche bun.

Open all wk 12-3 5.30-11 (Sat 12-11 Sun 12-10.30) **Food** Lunch Mon-Sat 12-2.30, Sun 12-7 Dinner Mon-Sat 6-9.15, Sun 12-7 ⊕ FREE HOUSE ◄ Timothy Taylor Landlord, Hogs Back TEA, Sharp's Doom Bar Ö Addlestones. ♟ **Facilities** Non-diners area ❀ (Bar Garden) ♦ Children's portions Play area Garden ⋒ Parking WiFi

---

FETCHAM
Map 6 TQ15

The Bell

tel: 01372 372624 **Bell Ln KT22 9ND**
email: bellfetcham@youngs.co.uk
dir: From A245 in Leatherhead take Waterway Rd (B2122). At rdbt 2nd exit into Guildford Rd (B2122). At mini rdbt right into Cobham Rd. Straight on at next 2 mini rdbts. Left into School Ln, left into Bell Ln

Something for everyone whether inside or outdoors

The striking 1930s building in the pretty Mole Valley is one of the Young's Brewery's 'flagship' dining pubs. Expect a smart terrace for alfresco drinking and dining, a light and airy wood-panelled restaurant, and a comfortable bar, replete with leather sofas and chairs. Using quality, seasonal produce, including vegetables from Secretts Farm and pork from Dingley Dell Farms, everything on the menus is cooked from scratch. The traditional British cuisine includes the likes roast Gressingham duck leg, and pan-fried sea bream on the main menu. Booking is essential for Sunday roasts.

Open all day all wk 11am-11.30pm (Fri-Sat 11am-mdnt Sun 12-11) **Food** Lunch Mon-Thu 12-3, Fri-Sat 12-9.30, Sun 12-8.30 Dinner Mon-Thu 6-9.30, Fri-Sat 12-9.30, Sun 12-8.30 ⊕ YOUNG'S ◄ Bitter & Special, Guest ales Ö Aspall. ♟ 22 **Facilities** Non-diners area ❀ (Bar Garden) ♦ Children's portions Garden ⋒ Beer festival Parking WiFi ☞ (notice required)

FOREST GREEN
Map 6 TQ14

The Parrot Inn
PICK OF THE PUBS

tel: 01306 621339 **RH5 5RZ**
email: drinks@theparrot.co.uk
dir: B2126 from A29 at Ockley, signed Forest Green

Inviting 17th-century country pub with its own farm

This tile-hung country pub overlooks a village green and cricket pitch up in the Surrey Hills. The traditional bar, with low-beamed ceilings, flagstone floor and huge brass fireplace is so typically English it could have been transported straight from a film set. From it, French doors lead to a sheltered, paved terrace. At owner Linda Gotto's farm in nearby Dorking, with her customers very much in mind, she raises rare-breed pigs, Shorthorn cattle and Dorset sheep. Now fast-forward to your plate, on which could appear a pork dish of home-dry-cured coppa with warm butterbean salad; pork, apple and Calvados pie with vegetables; or slow-cooked lamb shank with warm fennel and spelt salad. Some dishes need to be sourced from beyond Dorking, such as smoked haddock, mussel and prawn chowder; and skate wing with chorizo potatoes and cockle sauce. Butchers Hall, an on-site farm shop, opens daily.

Open all day all wk Closed 25 Dec **Food** Lunch Mon-Sat 12-3, Sun 12-5 Dinner Mon-Sat 6-10 ⊕ FREE HOUSE ◄ Ringwood Best Bitter & Old Thumper, Timothy Taylor Landlord, Dorking DB Number One, Fuller's London Pride Ö Aspall, Hogs Back Hazy Hog. ♟ 14 **Facilities** Non-diners area ❀ (Bar Garden) Children's portions Garden ⋒ Beer festival Parking WiFi

GUILDFORD   Map 6 SU94

The Weyside

tel: 01483 568024 **Millbrook GU1 3XJ**
email: weyside@youngs.co.uk
dir: *From Guildford take A281 towards Shalford. Pub on right*

When in Guildford, definitely one to head for

Overlooking the River Wey, this is one humdinger of a pub. The decor, the furnishings, the accessorising – all have been conceived and applied by people who understand good interior design. There are plenty of places to eat and drink, not least on the waterside decking (first grab some bread from the bowl on bar to feed the ducks). There's even a 'dog corner', with beds, treats and towels. Typical menu items are an 8oz hand-cut sirloin of Surrey Angus beef; coriander-dusted Dorset lamb rump; beer-battered North Sea cod and rustic chips; and purple sprouting broccoli and cauliflower bake.

Open all day all wk **Food** Lunch Sun-Fri 12-9, Sat 12-10 Dinner Sun-Fri 12-9, Sat 12-10 ⊕ YOUNG'S ◖ Bitter & Special ♂ Aspall. ♟ 15 **Facilities** Non-diners area ♣ (Bar Garden) ⬥ Children's menu Children's portions Garden ⌂ WiFi

HASLEMERE   Map 6 SU93

The Wheatsheaf Inn ★★★ INN

tel: 01428 644440 **Grayswood Rd, Grayswood GU27 2DE**
email: thewheatsheaf@aol.com **web:** www.thewheatsheafgrayswood.co.uk
dir: *Exit A3 at Milford, A286 to Haslemere. Grayswood approx 7.5m N*

Woodland-edge setting in the Surrey Hills

The Wheatsheaf Inn is a very distinctive, part hang-tiled Edwardian pub with enough vegetation to give Kew a run for its money. The hanging-basket festooned verandah, creeper-covered pergola and patio and colourful garden just invite a lingering visit with a pint of Langham Hip Hop bitter to hand, relaxing after a walk in the enfolding Surrey Hills beloved by Tennyson. There's opportunity to stay overnight here in one of the comfy rooms so creating an added excuse to engage with a wide-ranging menu of pub classics and thoughtful specials. Kick in with pan-fried field mushrooms with garlic and herb butter, moving along to lamb's liver and bacon, mash, vegetables and red wine gravy. There's also a selection of steaks, but be sure to leave room for some warmed treacle and walnut tart, or apple and rhubarb crumble.

Open all wk 11-3 6-11 (Sun 12-3 7-10.30) **Food** Lunch all wk 12-2 Dinner all wk 7-9.45 Av main course £11.95 ⊕ FREE HOUSE ◖ Fuller's London Pride, Sharp's Doom Bar, Greene King Abbot Ale, Langham Hip Hop ♂ Aspall. **Facilities** Non-diners area ♣ (Bar Garden) ⬥ Children's menu Children's portions Garden ⌂ Parking WiFi **Rooms** 7

LEIGH   Map 6 TQ24

The Plough

tel: 01306 611348 **Church Rd RH2 8NJ**
email: sarah@theploughleigh.wanadoo.co.uk
dir: *Phone for detailed directions*

Ramblers' retreat in the Surrey countryside

Some parts of this appealing, architecturally mixed building are known to date from the 15th century, whilst the popular locals' bar with its fire and traditional pub games is somewhat younger. Situated by a large green bordered by old houses and the medieval church, The Plough today is a cracking village pub. Beers from the Hall & Woodhouse list slake the thirst of walkers enjoying exploration of the Surrey

Weald, whilst the popular pub grub menu of bangers and mash or fish and chips is supplemented by chicken fillet, Black Forest ham or lamb steak dishes. The home-made pies also prove very popular.

Open all wk 11-11 (Sun 12-11) **Food** Lunch Mon-Sat 12-10, Sun 12-9 Dinner Mon-Sat 12-10, Sun 12-9 ⊕ HALL & WOODHOUSE ◖ Badger Dorset Best, Tanglefoot, K&B Sussex ♂ Westons Rosie's Pig. ♟ 11 **Facilities** Non-diners area ♣ (Bar Garden) ⬥ Children's menu Children's portions Garden ⌂ Parking WiFi 🚗

The Seven Stars   `PICK OF THE PUBS`

tel: 01306 611254 **Bunce Common Rd, Dawes Green RH2 8NP**
email: info@7starsleigh.co.uk
dir: *S of A25 (Dorking to Reigate road)*

Timeless tavern with high-quality food

This early 17th-century tile-hung tavern is tucked away in the rural southern reaches of the Mole Valley, its charm enhanced by the absence of games machines, TV screens and piped music. The older bar is centred on an inglenook fireplace at one end and a log-burning stove at the other. It's a tranquil spot to enjoy a pint of Harvey's Sussex ale or a glass of Mortimers Orchard cider. The restaurant has its own bar, which is always available to use when open. The food served is of high quality and is prepared by a team of chefs using local produce whenever possible. Typical dishes include pork and herb terrine, which might be followed by steak and ale pie or supreme of chicken. At the front is a garden for those with a drink, at the side a patio and garden for diners, and there's ample parking space.

Open all wk 12-11 (Sun 12-10) **Food** Lunch Mon-Sat 12-9.30, Sun 12-6 Dinner Mon-Sat 12-9.30 Restaurant menu available Mon-Sat ⊕ PUNCH TAVERNS ◖ Fuller's London Pride, Young's, Harvey's Sussex, Guest ales ♂ Westons Mortimers Orchard. ♟ 12 **Facilities** Non-diners area ♣ (Bar Garden) ⬥ Children's menu Children's portions Garden ⌂ Parking

LINGFIELD   Map 6 TQ34

Hare and Hounds   `PICK OF THE PUBS`

tel: 01342 832351 **Common Rd RH7 6BZ**
email: info@hareandhoundspublichouse.co.uk
dir: *From A22 follow Lingfield Racecourse signs into Common Rd*

Delightful country pub with excellent modern and classic food

Standing alone in open countryside, this 18th-century, pale-blue-washed country pub is a delight. Upholstered banquettes, leopard-spot-patterned fabrics, wooden tables and assorted chairs all come together pleasingly in the bar. In the dining room, a herring-bone parquet floor and a 'ceiling' of red ochre-coloured fabric swagging, reminiscent perhaps of a Bedouin tent. The pub's good name for modern and classic food stems from dishes such as stuffed rabbit Wellington with chorizo and chive mash; roast stone bass with artichoke and cherry tomato marmalade; and deep-fried olive dumpling; and pan-fried Sussex rib-eye steak with triple-cooked chips and red wine sauce. A brunch and light lunch selection offers creamed mushroom soup with croûtons; and cos lettuce salad with blue cheese mayonnaise, poached pear and toasted walnut. Barbecues and pizzas extend the choices. The decked patio is a good spot for a glass of wine, from a selection by a village-based merchant vintners' company.

Open all day Mon-Wed 10am-11.30pm Thu-Sat 10am-12.30am Sun 12-6 Closed 24 & 26 Dec, Sun eve **Food** Lunch Mon-Sat 12-2.30, Sun 12-3 Dinner Mon-Sat 7-9.30 Set menu available ⊕ PUNCH TAVERNS ◖ Harvey's Sussex, Sharp's Doom Bar, Guinness ♂ Westons Stowford Press. ♟ 12 **Facilities** Non-diners area ♣ (Bar Garden) ⬥ Children's portions Garden ⌂ Parking

LONG DITTON
Map 6 TQ16

The Ditton
PICK OF THE PUBS

tel: 020 8339 0785 **64 Ditton Hill Rd KT6 5JD**
email: goodfood@theditton.co.uk
dir: *Phone for detailed directions*

Suburban local not far from Hampton Court

With its large, south-facing beer garden, The Ditton is clearly a popular community local. Playing their part of course are beers from Sambrook's, Surrey Hills and Truman's and a good choice of wines by the glass. A typical menu offers ciabattas, wraps and jacket potatoes; potato skins topped with Stilton and bacon; toad-in-the-hole with bubble-and-squeak, fried onions and gravy; and vegetable lasagne with garlic bread and dressed salad. Fish dishes are there too, such as breaded wholetail scampi; as well as beef and Cajun chicken burgers; and home-made, hand-stretched pizzas. Children's main courses arrive with an ice lolly. Those irresistible old favourites, sticky date and toffee pudding, and chocolate and caramel tart, both with Yorvale vanilla ice cream, are characteristic desserts. Skittle alley league nights are every Monday, and quiz nights are Tuesday. Summer barbecues are held in the garden and live music backs a popular June beer and cider festival.

Open all day all wk 12-11 **Food** Lunch Mon-Sat 12-9, Sun 12-5 Dinner Mon-Sat 12-9 ⊕ ENTERPRISE INNS ◁ Sharp's Doom Bar, Sambrook's Wandle, Surrey Hills Shere Drop, Truman's Swift, Otter Bitter. ♀ 10 **Facilities** Non-diners area ☙ (Bar Garden) ◑ Children's menu Children's portions Play area Garden ⌰ Beer festival Cider festival Parking WiFi ▭ (notice required)

MICKLEHAM
Map 6 TQ15

The Running Horses

tel: 01372 372279 **Old London Rd RH5 6DU**
email: info@therunninghorses.co.uk
dir: *M25 junct 9, A24 towards Dorking. Left signed Mickleham & B2209*

Lovely country inn below Box Hill

Built in the 16th century, the inn had an important role as a coaching house, but it also sheltered highwaymen – a tiny ladder leading to the roof space was discovered during alterations. The inn acquired its name in 1825 after two horses, Colonel and Cadland, running in the Derby at Epsom, passed the post together. They appear on the inn sign, and the bars are named after them. Food includes home-smoked salmon; devilled kidneys; twice baked cheddar soufflé; Brixham bouillabaisse; grilled spatchcock chicken; and crisp roast pork belly with champ mash. Chunky sandwiches are available at lunchtime.

Open all day all wk 12-11 (Sun 12-10.30) Closed 25, 26 & 31 Dec eve, 1 Jan eve **Food** Lunch Mon-Fri 12-2.30, Sat-Sun 12-3 Dinner Mon-Sat 7-9.30, Sun 6.30-9 Restaurant menu available all wk ⊕ BRAKSPEAR ◁ Bitter & Special, Fuller's London Pride, Ringwood ♂ Symonds. ♀ 9 **Facilities** Non-diners area ☙ (Bar Garden) ◑ Children's menu Children's portions Garden ⌰ WiFi

NEWDIGATE
Map 6 TQ14

The Surrey Oaks

tel: 01306 631200 **Parkgate Rd RH5 5DZ**
email: visit-us@surreyoaks.co.uk
dir: *From A24 follow signs to Newdigate, at T-junct turn left, pub 1m on left*

Excellent beers in lovely country pub

This former wheelwright's shop is over 440 years old and still has wood fires burning in the inglenook fireplaces and original flagstones in the bar. Under new management since April 2014, The Surrey Oaks has won awards for its beers – the Surrey Hills Shere Drop is brewed six miles from the pub. Much of the food on the seasonal menu is cooked in the wood-fired oven, including the steak burger and fish pie. A separate list of 'Daily Doings' features specials from the butchers, fishmongers and gamekeepers. Time a visit for the Spring and August Bank Holiday beer festivals.

Open all wk 11.30-2.30 5.30-11 (Sat 11.30-11 Sun 12-9) **Food** Lunch Mon-Fri 12-2, Sat 12-9, Sun 12-6 Dinner Mon-Fri 6-9, Sat 12-9 ⊕ FREE HOUSE ◁ Surrey Hills Ranmore Ale & Shere Drop, Guest ales ♂ Snails Bank Tumbledown, Sandford Orchards Shaky Bridge, Guest perry. ♀ 22 **Facilities** Non-diners area ☙ (Bar Garden) ◑ Children's portions Play area Garden ⌰ Beer festival Parking WiFi ▭ (notice required)

OCKLEY
Map 6 TQ14

Bryce's The Old School House ⊛
PICK OF THE PUBS

tel: 01306 627430 **RH5 5TH**
email: fish@bryces.co.uk
dir: *8m S of Dorking on A29*

Smart country inn championing seafood

This Grade II listed former boarding school dates back to 1750, and owner Bill Bryce has been at the helm for over 20 years now. He is passionate about fresh fish and offers an appealing range, despite the land-locked location in rural Surrey. These days, it's more of a restaurant than a pub, although there is a bar with a choice of real ales including those from WJ King at Horsham, and 13 select wines sold by the glass. The dishes on the restaurant menu are nearly all fish, but the specials for non-piscivores such as calves' liver with bacon, black pudding and bubble-and-squeak; or parmesan breaded chicken breast with tomato and basil risotto are more than likely to please. If seafood is your thing, dive into Dorset crab cakes with mango and tomato salsa, followed by roast cod fillet with herb crust, creamed cabbage and chorizo. Puddings are all home made.

Open 12-3 6-11 Closed 25-26 Dec, 1 Jan, Sun pm & Mon Nov, Jan-Feb **Food** Lunch all wk 12-2.30 Dinner all wk 6-9.30 ⊕ FREE HOUSE ◁ Fuller's London Pride, WJ King Horsham Best ♂ Westons. ♀ 13 **Facilities** Non-diners area ☙ (Bar Outside area) ◑ Children's portions Outside area ⌰ Parking WiFi ▭ (notice required)

Silver Stars The AA Silver Star rating denotes a Hotel or B&B that we highly recommend. They have a superior level of quality within their star rating, high standards of hospitality, service and cleanliness.

RIPLEY
Map 6 TQ05

NEW The Anchor ◉◉

tel: 01483 211866 **High St GU23 6AE**
email: info@ripleyanchor.co.uk **web:** www.ripleyanchor.co.uk
dir: *M25 junct 10, A3 towards Guildford, then B2215 to Ripley*

Great food in a historic building

In the late 19th century, as cycling became increasingly popular, Ripley became a well-known stop on the London-Portsmouth road, and The Anchor was a favourite port of call. One of the town's most historic pubs, it was built as an almshouse in the early 16th century. Taken over by the owners of Drakes Restaurant a couple of years ago, the pub now has two AA Rosettes for its food. Local and regional produce features on the menus, appearing in dishes such as pheasant and ham terrine with pickled vegetables; roast cod with parsnip purée; or wild mushroom casserole. Finish with vanilla pannacotta, blackberries and Granny Smith apple sorbet.

Open all day Closed 25 Dec, Mon **Food** Contact pub for food times Set menu available ⊕ FREE HOUSE ◧ Timothy Taylor Landlord ⚬ Henney's Vintage. ♟ 10 **Facilities** Non-diners area ⬤ Children's menu Children's portions Outside area ⋈ Parking

Find out more about the AA's awards for food excellence on page 9

SHAMLEY GREEN
Map 6 TQ04

NEW The Red Lion

tel: 01483 892202 **The Green GU5 OUB**
email: debbieersser@gmail.com **web:** www.redlionshamleygreen.com
dir: *On B2128 between Guildford & Cranleigh*

Classic pub in the Surrey Hills

Film location scouts looking for a pub on a village green will find a prime candidate here. Although 17th century, it has been a pub only since the 1800s; before that it may have been tea rooms. Rich red ceilings and high-backed, red-upholstered settles help create that quintessential warm pubby feeling. A typical carte proposes pan-fried crispy duck salad with oranges, watercress and hoisin dressing; lamb shank cooked in red wine sauce, with shallots, wild mushrooms and redcurrant jelly; veal schnitzel with fried egg and fries; haddock in light beer batter; and Greek spinach and feta pie.

Open all day all wk **Food** Lunch Mon-Fri 12-2.30, Sat-Sun 12-3 Dinner Mon-Sat 6.30-9.30, Sun (Apr-Oct) 6.30-8.30 ⊕ PUNCH TAVERNS ◧ Young's IPA, Sharp's Doom Bar & Atlantic, Hogs Back TEA ⚬ Aspall, Westons Stowford Press. ♟ 9 **Facilities** Non-diners area ⬤ Children's menu Children's portions Garden ⋈ Parking WiFi

SOUTH GODSTONE
Map 6 TQ34

Fox & Hounds

tel: 01342 893474 **Tilburstow Hill Rd RH9 8LY**
email: info@foxandhounds.org.uk
dir: *M25 junct 6, A22 to South Godstone. Right into Harts Ln. At T-junct right into Tilburstow Hill Rd*

Haunted country pub serving home-cooked food

Dating in part to 1368, the Fox & Hounds has been a pub since 1601, and it is said that 17th-century pirate and smuggler John Trenchman haunts the building; he died here after being fatally wounded in an ambush nearby. A large inglenook in the restaurant and a real fire in the lower bar add to the old-world charm. Food-wise there's plenty to choose from, including a starter of crayfish and smoked salmon salad; baguettes; and mains ranging from applewood-smoked ham to whole sea bass. The ever-changing specials board might include beef Wellington and bouillabaisse, and a choice of roasts every Sunday. The large garden offers rural views and home-grown vegetables; marquees are erected in the summer for alfresco dining.

Open all day all wk **Food** Lunch all wk 12-9 Dinner all wk 12-9 ⊕ FREE HOUSE ◧ Greene King Abbot Ale & IPA, Guest ales. ♟ 12 **Facilities** Non-diners area ✿ (Bar Garden) ⬤ Children's menu Children's portions Garden ⋈ Parking WiFi ▦ (notice required)

PICK OF THE PUBS

The Inn West End ★★★★ INN

WEST END Map 6 SU96

tel: 01276 858652
42 Guildford Rd GU24 9PW
email: greatfood@the-inn.co.uk
web: www.the-inn.co.uk
dir: *On A322 towards Guildford. 3m from M3 junct 3, just beyond Gordon's School rdbt*

Destination restaurant and friendly local pub with bedrooms

It has been said that Gerry and Ann Price's renowned village pub out-manoeuvres many a competitor. In fact, it was this guide that said it last year, and we stick by our judgement. One particular attraction is its special wine events, linked to its own on-site wine shop (open on request) whose wide range includes Pinot Noir and Claret collections, magnums of reds, bin ends and own-label Labradouro Tinto, created by Gerry, who loves the Douro region of Portugal, and his Labrador dog. But don't let this passion deter you from just slipping in for a pint of West Berkshire's Good Old Boy, local Thurstons Horsell Gold, or Aspall cider, with a newspaper in the bar or out on the clematis-hung terrace overlooking the garden and boules pitch. The modern interior is open plan with wooden floors, crisp linen-clothed tables and an open fire. In the newly revamped kitchen, the brigade make great use of fish from the coast and game from Windsor Great Park, or

shot by Gerry himself. Seasonal menus reveal all with such dishes as Royal pigeon breasts with white pudding, baby beets and port reduction; wild mushroom, chestnut and spinach risotto, rocket and truffle oil; pan-fried selection of fresh British fish with crushed new potatoes, seasonal greens and lemon beurre blanc; and seared calves' liver with haggis mash, spinach, crispy bacon and port jus. At lunchtime, consider pairing Cornish mussels and hand-cut chips with a glass of white Rioja. There's a comprehensive bar menu, too. Weekly fish nights, monthly quizzes and 12 new boutique bedrooms further enhance the overall package. Children over five years old are welcome for meals.

Open all wk 7.30am-11pm (Sat 8.30am-11pm Sun 8.30am-10.30pm) **Food** Lunch Mon-Sat 12-2.30, Sun 12-3 Dinner Mon-Thu 6-9.30, Fri-Sat 6-10, Sun 6-9 ⊕ FREE HOUSE ◀ Fuller's London Pride, Dark Star Hophead, Thurstons Horsell Gold, West Berkshire Good Old Boy Ď Aspall. ♥ 15
Facilities Non-diners area ❖ (Bar Garden) Children's portions Garden ⊼ Beer festival Parking WiFi **Rooms** 12

STOKE D'ABERNON — Map 6 TQ15

The Old Plough

tel: 01932 866419 **2 Station Rd KT11 3BN**
email: info@oldploughcobham.co.uk
dir: From A245 into Station Rd. Pub on corner

Friendly, smart and independently owned community pub

Contemporary decor and traditional lines blend easily at this mature dining inn in the Mole Valley. In earlier times it was the village courthouse; it also features in the Sherlock Holmes story *The Adventure of The Speckled Band*. Local drinkers take summer shade in the peaceful garden and quaff beers from Surrey Hills brewery. Fulfilling meals are at the heart of the business, with a core menu available all day, supplemented by lighter bites available to 5.30pm in both bar and restaurant. A seafood thermidor gratin starter; then pan-roasted guinea fowl with butternut squash purée and haggis are tempting examples of the modern cuisine. Children are welcome in the restaurant area until 7.30pm.

Open all day all wk **Food** Lunch 12-9.30 Dinner 12-9.30 Av main course £14.50 ⊕ FULLER'S ◀ London Pride, Surrey Hills Shere Drop, George Gale & Co Seafarers Ö Aspall. ₹ 18 **Facilities** Non-diners area ⚘ (Bar Garden) ♦ Children's menu Children's portions Garden ⊓ Parking WiFi ▭

TILFORD — Map 5 SU84

The Duke of Cambridge

tel: 01252 792236 **Tilford Rd GU10 2DD**
email: amy.corstin@redmistleisure.co.uk
dir: From Guildford on A31 towards Farnham follow Tongham, Seale, Runfield signs. Right at end, follow Eashing signs. Left at end, 1st right (signed Tilford St). Over bridge, 1st left, 0.5m

Family-friendly pub offering wholesome local fodder

Set among pine trees with a lovely garden and terrace, this attractive pub in the Surrey countryside welcomes all, children and dogs included. Expect Surrey ales and hearty local food with much of the seasonal produce on the menu coming from the neighbouring farm. Typical of the menu are deli boards; pan-seared rump of venison; pesto and butternut squash tagliatelle; and bangers and mash. In May fundraising for a local charity is just one excuse for a beer and music festival. The Garden Bar & Grill is a summer feature (weather permitting), as well as garden parties and hog roasts.

Open all wk 11-3 5-11 (Sat 11-11 Sun 12-10.30) Closed 25 Dec & 31 Dec eve **Food** Lunch Mon-Fri 12-2.30, Sat 12-3.30, Sun 12-8.30 Dinner Mon-Fri 6-9, Sat 6-9.30 ⊕ FREE HOUSE/RED MIST LEISURE LTD ◀ Hogs Back, Guest ales Ö Hogs Back Hazy Hog, Somersby Cider. ₹ 15 **Facilities** ⚘ (Bar Restaurant Garden) ♦ Children's menu Children's portions Play area Garden ⊓ Beer festival Parking WiFi

WEST CLANDON — Map 6 TQ05

The Onslow Arms

tel: 01483 222447 **The Street GU4 7TE**
email: info@onslowarmsclandon.co.uk
dir: On A247, S of railway line

Eye-catching village pub with cosmopolitan appeal

Cyclists and ramblers; drinkers and diners all mix seamlessly at this vibrant and smart community local. The visually striking building retains much character, with a wealth of beams, huge open fire, squashy sofas and chairs set in a light, cool interior. Relax within or on the sheltered terrace with a glass of Tillingbourne Brewery bitter and choose from an all-day menu which offers a great mix of comfort meals and contemporary dishes. Stilton, spinach and avocado sandwiches with

chips or soup is a grand filler, or perhaps fillet of sea bream with potato cake, pak choi and king prawns.

Open all day all wk 11-11 (Wed & Fri-Sat 11am-11.30pm Sun 11-10.30) Closed 26 Dec **Food** Lunch Sun-Thu 12-9.30, Fri-Sat 12-10 Dinner Sun-Thu 12-9.30, Fri-Sat 12-10 ⊕ FREE HOUSE ◀ Surrey Hills Shere Drop, Sharp's Cornish Coaster, Tillingbourne Brewery Ales Ö Westons Stowford Press. ₹ 18 **Facilities** Non-diners area ⚘ (Bar Garden) ♦ Children's menu Children's portions Garden ⊓ Parking WiFi ▭

WEST END — Map 6 SU96

The Inn West End ★★★★ INN — PICK OF THE PUBS

See Pick of the Pubs on page 485

WEST HORSLEY — Map 6 TQ05

The King William IV — PICK OF THE PUBS

tel: 01483 282318 **83 The Street KT24 6BG**
dir: Off A246 (Leatherhead to Guildford road)

Relaxed and homely atmosphere in leafy Surrey

Named in honour of the monarch who relaxed England's brewing laws, this popular dining-pub is situated in a leafy Surrey village. The business was started by a miller, Edmund Collins, who knocked two cottages together to create an alehouse. Many of the original Georgian features have been preserved, but there is also an airy conservatory restaurant and a large garden and terrace to the rear, with colourful tubs and floral baskets. It's popular with walkers and is close to the Royal Horticultural Society's Wisley Gardens. Local beers include Surrey Hills Shere Drop and Courage Directors, plus a guest ale of the month, and a dozen wines are offered by the glass. The well-priced menu ranges from burgers and fish pie to platters, oven-baked salmon fillet and rump steak. Leave room for banoffee pie, chocolate fudge cake or crème brûlée.

Open all day all wk 11.30am-mdnt (Sun 12-10.30) **Food** Lunch Mon-Fri 12-3, Sat-Sun 12-4 Dinner Mon-Thu 6-9, Fri-Sat 6-9.30 ⊕ ENTERPRISE INNS ◀ Surrey Hills Shere Drop, Courage Best & Directors, Guest ales. ₹ 12 **Facilities** Non-diners area ⚘ (Bar Garden) ♦ Children's menu Children's portions Family room Garden ⊓ Parking WiFi ▭

WINDLESHAM — Map 6 SU96

The Half Moon

tel: 01276 473329 **Church Rd GU20 6BN**
email: c@sturt.tv
dir: M3 junct 3, A322 follow Windlesham signs into New Rd; right at T-junct into Church Rd, pub on right

Old-fashioned values and friendly service

Family-owned since 1909, Helga and Conrad Sturt's slate-floored, low-beamed, 17th-century free house offers the traditional country pub experience, including locally brewed Hogs Back real ale and Lilley's Bee Sting Pear cider from Somerset. There's plenty of choice at lunchtime, while dinner options include baked camembert with chilli jam; red Thai curry; calves' liver and smoked bacon with bubble-and-squeak; braised venison and ale ragout; and seared tuna niçoise. Go past the patio terrace into the well-kept beer garden with a children's play area. Check with the pub for beer festival dates.

Open all day all wk 9am-11pm **Food** Lunch all wk 9.30-9.30 Dinner all wk 9.30-9.30 Av main course £12 ⊕ FREE HOUSE ◀ Sharp's, Theakston, Fuller's, Timothy Taylor, Hogs Back, Palmers, Dark Star Ö Lilley's Bee Sting Pear, Westons Old Rosie. ₹ 10 **Facilities** ⚘ (Bar Garden Outside area) ♦ Children's menu Children's portions Play area Garden Outside area ⊓ Beer festival Parking WiFi ▭ (notice required)

EAST SUSSEX

ALCISTON
Map 6 TQ50

Rose Cottage Inn
PICK OF THE PUBS

tel: 01323 870377 **BN26 6UW**
email: ian@alciston.freeserve.co.uk
dir: Off A27 between Eastbourne & Lewes

Home-cooked food in a pretty cottage

Expect a warm welcome at this traditional village pub, housed in a 17th-century flint cottage complete with roses round the door and a lovely front garden. At the foot of the South Downs, ramblers will find it a good base for long walks in unspoilt countryside, especially along the old traffic-free coach road to the south. With its oak beams, and sloping walls and ceilings, the inn has been in the same family for over 40 years, and is well known for its good, home-cooked food, including organic vegetables and local meats, poultry and game. You might choose from the wide selection of fish – perhaps the 'jolly posh' fish pie, or opt for Keralan chicken curry; home-made steak and ale shortcrust pie; or wild Alciston rabbit casserole from the daily specials. Classic pub dishes, salads and light bites are also available. When in season, fresh mussels are delivered from Scotland every Friday, and are then cooked in French or Italian style. The inn sells a number of items from local suppliers for customers to buy, including honey and eggs.

Open 11.30-3 6.30-11 Closed 25-26 Dec, Sun eve **Food** Lunch all wk 12-2 Dinner Mon-Sat 7-9.30 Restaurant menu available Mon-Sat evening ⊕ FREE HOUSE ◀ Harvey's Sussex Best Bitter, Burning Sky Plateau ♂ Biddenden. ♀ 8 **Facilities** Non-diners area ✿ (Bar Garden Outside area) Children's portions Garden Outside area ⋈ Parking WiFi

ALFRISTON
Map 6 TQ50

George Inn

tel: 01323 870319 **High St BN26 5SY**
email: info@thegeorge-alfriston.com
dir: Phone for detailed directions

Period inn in a lovely location

First licensed to sell beer as far back as 1397, this splendid Grade II listed flint and half-timbered inn is set in a picturesque village with the South Downs Way passing its front door. The heavy oak beams and ancient inglenook fireplace add plenty of character to the bar, whilst the kitchen serves delights such as rustic boards to share; chicken liver parfait; Thai prawn and salmon fishcakes; sea bream fillets with hollandaise; belly pork and baked apple with cider reduction; quinoa, cherry tomato and spring onion stuffed red pepper; and sticky toffee pudding with butterscotch sauce and vanilla ice cream to finish. A network of smugglers' tunnels leads from the pub's cellars.

Open all day all wk Closed 25-26 Dec **Food** Lunch all wk 12-9 Dinner all wk 12-9 ⊕ GREENE KING ◀ Abbot Ale, Hardys & Hansons Olde Trip, Dark Star Hophead, Morland Old Speckled Hen ♂ Aspall. ♀ 14 **Facilities** Non-diners area ✿ (Bar Restaurant Garden) ⋔ Children's menu Children's portions Garden ⋈ WiFi ⋘ (notice required)

ASHBURNHAM PLACE
Map 6 TQ61

Ash Tree Inn

tel: 01424 892104 **Brownbread St TN33 9NX**
email: ashtreeinn@gmail.com
dir: From Eastbourne take A271 at Boreham Bridge towards Battle. Next left, follow pub signs

Country pub that welcomes walkers

Deep in the Sussex countryside on the delightfully named Brownbread Street, the 400-year-old Ash Tree is a hub of local activity, hosting everything from quiz nights to cricket club meetings. It boasts a warm and bright interior, replete with stripped wooden floors, four fireplaces (two of them inglenooks), exposed beams and a friendly local atmosphere. Expect to find Harvey's ale on tap and traditional home-cooked meals such as breaded tiger prawns with sweet chilli dip; or soup of the day followed by steak and kidney pudding; tagliatelle with bacon, mushroom and garlic cream sauce; or ham, free-range eggs and chips. Walkers and dogs are welcome.

Open 12-4 7-11 (Sat-Sun 11.30am-mdnt) Closed Mon pm (Sun pm winter) **Food** Lunch Mon-Sat 12-2.30, Sun 12-4 (summer Sun 12-5) Dinner Tue-Thu 7-9, Fri-Sat 6-9 (summer Fri-Sat 6-9.30) ⊕ FREE HOUSE ◀ Harvey's Sussex Best Bitter, Guest ales ♂ Westons Stowford Press. **Facilities** Non-diners area ✿ (Bar Restaurant Garden) ⋔ Children's portions Garden ⋈ Parking WiFi ⋘ (notice required)

BERWICK
Map 6 TQ50

The Cricketers Arms
PICK OF THE PUBS

tel: 01323 870469 **BN26 6SP**
email: info@cricketersberwick.co.uk
dir: At x-rds on A27 (between Polegate & Lewes) follow Berwick sign, pub on right

Popular with South Downs walkers

Previously two farmworkers' cottages dating from the 16th century, this flintstone building was an alehouse for 200 years, until around 50 years ago Harvey's of Lewes, Sussex's oldest brewery, bought it and turned it into a 'proper' pub. The Grade II listed building, in beautiful cottage gardens, is close to many popular walks – the South Downs Way runs along the crest of the chalk scarp between here and the sea. Three beamed, music-free rooms with stone floors and open fires are simply furnished with old pine furniture. A short menu of home-made food includes pork and pistachio terrine; and home-cured gravad lax as starters. Their home-made burger is an ever-popular main course, as are winter favourites such as a shortcrust pie with a variety of fillings (look to the blackboard for daily choices); and pork and herb sausages (served with a free-range egg and chunky chips) from the local butcher in Seaford. Nearby is Charleston Farmhouse, the country rendezvous of the Bloomsbury Group of writers, painters and intellectuals, and venue for an annual literary festival.

Open all wk Mon-Fri 11-3 6-11 Sat 11-11 Sun 12-9 (Etr-Sep Mon-Sat 11-11 Sun 12-10.30) Closed 25 Dec **Food** Lunch Oct-Apr Mon-Fri 12-2.15, Sat-Sun 12-9, Etr-Sep all wk 12-9 Dinner Oct-Apr Mon-Fri 6.15-9, Sat-Sun 12-9, Etr-Sep all wk 12-9 Av main course £10 ⊕ HARVEY'S OF LEWES ◀ Sussex Best Bitter, Armada Ale ♂ Thatchers, Westons Stowford Press. ♀ 12 **Facilities** ✿ (Bar Garden) ⋔ Children's portions Family room Garden ⋈ Parking ⋘ (notice required)

BLACKBOYS

Map 6 TQ52

The Blackboys Inn

tel: 01825 890283 **Lewes Rd TN22 5LG**
email: info@theblackboys.co.uk
dir: *From A22 at Uckfield take B2102 towards Cross in Hand. Or from A267 at Esso service station in Cross in Hand take B2102 towards Uckfield. Village 1.5m*

Hamlet pub known for its Sunday roasts

This inn was named after the local charcoal-burners, or the soot-caked 'blackboys', with whom the 14th-century pub was once a favourite. Today's well-scrubbed visitors enjoy beers from Harvey's of Lewes in one of two bars, and in the restaurant, vegetables from the garden, game from local shoots, and fish from Rye and Hastings. Typical dishes include trio of Framfield Farm sausages, caramelised onion gravy and creamed potatoes; blue cheese and leek crumble. Outside are rambling grounds with resident ducks and an orchard. There are quiz nights and live music every month, as well as an annual beer festival. A function room is available for larger parties to hire.

Open all day all wk 12-11 (Sun 12-10) **Food** Lunch Mon-Thu 12-2.30, Fri-Sat 12-9.30, Sun 12-8 Dinner Mon-Thu 6-9.30, Fri-Sat 12-9.30, Sun 12-8 Restaurant menu available all wk ⊕ HARVEY'S OF LEWES ◀ Sussex Best Bitter, Sussex Hadlow Bitter, Sussex Old Ale, Seasonal ales. ⍭ 12 **Facilities** Non-diners area ❅ (Bar Restaurant Garden) ⋔ Children's menu Children's portions Garden ⌂ Beer festival Cider festival Parking WiFi ⊷

BRIGHTON & HOVE

Map 6 TQ30

The Basketmakers Arms

tel: 01273 689006 **12 Gloucester Rd BN1 4AD**
email: bluedowd@hotmail.co.uk
dir: *From Brighton station main entrance 1st left (Gloucester Rd). Pub on right at bottom of hill*

Leave The Lanes to the tourists and find this cracker

Peter Dowd has run his Victorian back-street local, tucked away in the bohemian North Laine area, with passion and pride for nearly 30 years. Quirky customer messages left in vintage tins on the walls have made the pub a local legend. Expect to find a splendid selection of Fuller's and guest real ales, around 100 malt whiskies and rarely seen vodkas, gins and bourbons. Food is all prepared from locally sourced produce, such as the fish which comes in daily from Sussex fishermen. Hot mains include slow-cooked pulled pork in a bun; rib-eye and rump steaks; and authentic beef or vegetarian Mexican chilli.

Open all day all wk 11-11 (Fri-Sat 11am-mdnt Sun 12-11) **Food** Lunch all wk 12-9 Dinner all wk 12-9 ⊕ FULLER'S ◀ London Pride, ESB, Bengal Lancer, HSB & Seafarers, Castle Rock Harvest Pale, Butcombe, Guest ales. **Facilities** ❅ (Bar Restaurant) ⋔ Outside area ⌂ WiFi

Visit shop.theAA.com for the latest Hotel, B&B and Restaurant Guides

The Foragers ⊛

tel: 01273 733134 **3 Stirling Place BN3 3YU**
email: info@theforagerspub.co.uk
dir: *At lights on A259 (seafront road) onto A2023. Right into Stirling Place*

Smart Victorian corner pub

Since Paul Hutchinson's has been at the helm, The Foragers has become a much-loved Hove local once again. He likes to stock Harvey's Best straight from its brewery in Lewes, and Sharp's Doom Bar from Cornwall, as well as the 14 wines he offers by the glass. Behind the AA Rosette lies food sourced extensively from Sussex and Kent for dishes such as pea soup; chicken, walnut and blue cheese terrine with red onion marmalade; beef stew cobbler; pan-seared sea bass fillet, mussels, new potatoes and apples in a light prawn bisque; and rhubarb and custard sundae.

Open all day all wk **Food** Contact pub for food times Set menu available Restaurant menu available ⊕ PUNCH TAVERNS ◀ Harvey's Sussex Best Bitter, Sharp's Doom Bar ⍾ Westons Stowford Press. ⍭ 14 **Facilities** Non-diners area ❅ (Bar Garden) ⋔ Children's menu Children's portions Garden ⌂ WiFi

NEW The Ginger Pig

tel: 01273 736123 **3 Hove St, Hove BN3 2TR**
email: gingerpig@gingermanrestaurants.com
dir: *From A259 (seafront) into Hove St*

Excellent food and local ale

Very much a food pub, The Ginger Pig puts a lot of emphasis on seasonality and has a strong reputation for game and local sea food. The monthly-changing menu might offer starters including devilled chicken livers; or braised octopus; while for a main course you could have 35-day aged chargrilled rib-eye steak; tandoori crusted sea bass; or pan-fried venison. Follow that with blackberry tiramisù; individual treacle tart, or vanilla poached pear. There's a grand old bar at the front serving great cocktails and well-kept local ales, like Bedlam, Brighton Bier or Dark Star.

Open all day all wk Closed 25 Dec **Food** Lunch 12-2.30 Dinner 6.30-10 Av main course £12 Set menu available Restaurant menu available all wk ⊕ ENTERPRISE INNS ◀ Bedlam, Dark Star, Brighton Bier. ⍭ 12 **Facilities** Non-diners area ❅ (Bar Garden) ⋔ Children's menu Children's portions Garden ⌂ WiFi ⊷ (notice required)

The Urchin

tel: 01273 241881 **15-17 Belfast St BN3 3YS**
email: hello@urchinpub.co.uk
dir: *From A259 (coast road) into Hove St (A2023). Right into Blatchington Rd at lights. 4th right into Haddington St, right into Malvern St, left into Belfast St to pub (one-way system)*

Specialist craft beer and shellfish combo

An elegant and tasty addition to Brighton's already star-studded eating and drinking scene. In 2014 the pub, previously known as The Bell, underwent a complete refurbishment, along with a change of name more suited to its new destiny; the pub garden also received a makeover, re-opening in early 2015. Expect over 100 craft and speciality beers in addition to local real ales and wines to accompany your choice of shellfish. Mussels, scallops, prawns, crab and lobster are the core ingredients, prepared classically with flavourings of garlic, chilli, coconut, tomato, lemongrass and coriander as appropriate.

Open all day all wk **Food** Lunch Thu-Sun 12-3 Dinner Wed-Sat 6-10 Av main course £12 Restaurant menu available Wed-Sun ⊕ ENTERPRISE INNS ◀ Harvey's Sussex Best Bitter, Dark Star Hophead, Guest ale ⍾ Symonds. ⍭ 10
Facilities Non-diners area ❅ (Bar Garden) ⋔ Garden ⌂ WiFi ⊷ (notice required)

PICK OF THE PUBS

The Coach and Horses

DANEHILL   **Map 6 TQ42**

tel: 01825 740369 **RH17 7JF**
email: coachandhorses@danehill.biz
web: www.coachandhorses.danehill.biz
dir: *From East Grinstead, S through Forest Row on A22 to A275 junct (Lewes road), right on A275, 2m to Danehill, left into School Ln, 0.5m, pub on left*

Family-run country pub offering more than just beer

On the edge of Ashdown Forest, The Coach and Horses opened in 1847 when it was a simple alehouse with stabling. Today it ticks all the boxes for an attractive countryside inn. If you fancy a ramble to work up a thirst or an appetite, ask about the three routes that start at the pub door. Upon your return, you'll find a sunny child-free terrace at the rear dominated by an enormous maple tree; children can play in the peaceful front garden, where the undulating South Downs dominate the horizon. Understated and unspoilt, the pub's interior has retained the typical twin bar layout, with vaulted ceilings, wood-panelled walls and stone and oak flooring lending their quiet charm. The pub's dog lazing on a bar rug sets a friendly tone, along with locals supping weekly-changing guest ales from the likes of Isfield Brewery and Dark Star; local Danehill Black Pig cider is also popular, and English sparkling wines come from the Bluebell vineyard just up

the road. Relax with your drink or settle with a menu in the dedicated eating area. Dishes are traditionally English, but the cooking scores highly with the freshness of ingredients sourced as locally as possible. Lamb raised on the farm opposite makes one of the shortest trips from meadow to pot, in a lighter lunch of Danehill lamb stew served with crusty bread; other light options include baguettes and moules frites. For those of good appetite, a starter of smoked salmon and cream cheese roulade, and burnt lemon mayonnaise could be followed by braised beef cheek, tarragon mustard mash and roasted winter roots. English desserts may include roasted pear and almond tart, honeycomb and crème fraîche.

Open all wk 12-3 5.30-11 (Sat-Sun 12-11) Closed 26 Dec **Food** Lunch Mon-Fri 12-2, Sat 12-2.30, Sun 12-3 Dinner Mon-Thu 6.30-9, Fri-Sat 6.30-9.30 Set menu available ⊞ FREE HOUSE
◗ Harvey's, Hammerpot, Dark Star, Isfield Brewery, Turners Brewery, Long Man Best Bitter Ŏ Black Pig. ♟ 8
Facilities Non-diners area ✿ (Bar Garden) ♦♦ Children's menu & portions Play area Garden ⊨ Parking WiFi

CHELWOOD GATE
Map 6 TQ43

The Red Lion

tel: 01825 740836 & 740265 **Lewes Rd RH17 7DE**
email: redlion@outlook.com
dir: *On A275*

Popular Ashdown Forest destination

An attractive pub built in the early 1800s that includes among its famous visitors Prime Minister Harold Macmillan and President John F Kennedy. Although it is owned by Kent brewer Shepherd Neame, Harvey's of Lewes also gets a look in on the bar. A full menu is served in the conservatory dining room and on the patio, while a more limited selection applies at tables in the extensive gardens. Typical dishes are beer-battered cod and chips with mushy peas; steak burger with Emmental cheese, chunky chips and chef's burger relish; and risotto of butternut squash with fresh sage and goats' cheese.

Open all day all wk 11-11 (Fri-Sat 11am-mdnt Sun 11-10.30) **Food** Lunch Mon-Thu 12-9, Fri-Sat 12-9.30, Sun 12-8 Dinner Mon-Thu 12-9, Fri-Sat 12-9.30, Sun 12-8 ⊕ SHEPHERD NEAME ◀ Spitfire, Harvey's Sussex Best Bitter ♂ Thatchers Gold. **Facilities** Non-diners area ❄ (Bar Garden) ♦♦ Children's menu Children's portions Garden ⋒ Parking

CHIDDINGLY
Map 6 TQ51

The Six Bells

tel: 01825 872227 **BN8 6HE**
dir: *E of A22 between Hailsham & Uckfield. Turn opposite Golden Cross pub*

Popular pub with vintage car, music and jazz events

Inglenook fireplaces and plenty of bric-à-brac are to be found at this large free house, which is where various veteran car and motorbike enthusiasts meet on club nights. The jury in the famous 1852 Onion Pie Murder trial sat and deliberated in the bar before finding the defendant, Sarah Ann French, guilty. This is a popular pub with walkers who are out on the many great routes round here including the Vanguard Way. Enjoy live music on Tuesday, Friday and Saturday evenings plus jazz at lunchtime on Sundays.

Open all wk 10-3 6-11 (Fri-Sun all day) **Food** Lunch Mon-Thu 12-2.30, Fri-Sun all day Dinner Mon-Thu 6-10, Fri-Sun all day ⊕ FREE HOUSE ◀ Courage Directors, Harvey's Sussex Best Bitter, Guest ales. **Facilities** Non-diners area ❄ (Bar Garden) ♦♦ Children's portions Family room Garden Parking ▭

DANEHILL
Map 6 TQ42

The Coach and Horses
PICK OF THE PUBS

See Pick of the Pubs on page 489

DITCHLING
Map 6 TQ31

The Bull ★★★★ INN
PICK OF THE PUBS

See Pick of the Pubs on opposite page

EAST CHILTINGTON
Map 6 TQ31

The Jolly Sportsman ◉

tel: 01273 890400 **Chapel Ln BN7 3BA**
email: info@thejollysportsman.com
dir: *From Lewes take A275, left at Offham onto B2166 towards Plumpton, into Novington Ln, after approx 1m left into Chapel Ln*

Award-winning rustic food and local ales to match

Isolated but well worth finding, Bruce Wass's dining pub enjoys a lovely garden setting on a peaceful dead-end lane looking out to the South Downs. The bar retains some of the character of a Victorian alehouse, with Dark Star and Harvey's on tap, while the dining room strikes a cool, modern-rustic pose. Well-sourced food shines on daily-changing menus, served throughout the pub, from calves' liver in bacon and shallot sauce with colcannon, broccoli and potatoes, to Thai chickpea cakes with crispy aubergine and tofu kofta, garlic spinach, mint yogurt and pepper coulis. Good value fixed-price and children's menus are also available.

Open Tue-Sat 12-3 6-11 (Sat all day in summer Sun 12-5) Closed 25 Dec, Sun eve & Mon **Food** Lunch Tue-Sat 12-2.30, Sun 12-3.30 Dinner Tue-Sat 6.30-9.30 Set menu available ⊕ FREE HOUSE ◀ Dark Star Hophead, Harvey's Sussex Best Bitter ♂ Thatchers. ♟ 14 **Facilities** Non-diners area ❄ (Bar Garden) ♦♦ Children's menu Children's portions Play area Garden ⋒ Parking WiFi

EAST DEAN
Map 6 TV59

The Tiger Inn
PICK OF THE PUBS

tel: 01323 423209 **The Green BN20 0DA**
email: tiger@beachyhead.org.uk
dir: *From A259 between Eastbourne & Seaford. Pub 0.5m*

Village inn with splendid downland views

Set beside the large sloping green in one of the prettiest old villages on the South Downs, it's just a short stroll along downland paths from the inn to the magnificent coastal walk at the renowned Seven Sisters cliffs. The pub was once the base for smugglers landing contraband at the cove at nearby Birling Gap. The interior recalls such heady days, with log fires, beams, stone floors and ancient settles. With beers from the village's own Beachy Head microbrewery, the best local brews are guaranteed – 'Legless Rambler' celebrates walkers on the adjacent South Downs Way footpath. The menu too is laden with the promise of local ingredients cooked to hearty recipes. Fresh fish features in several choices; or look for pan-fried duck breast with new potatoes, vegetables and rhubarb and ginger sauce. Steamed puddings lead the sweet choice, while the daily specials board extends the appealing culinary fest.

Open all day all wk **Food** Lunch all wk 12-3 Dinner all wk 6-9 Av main course £10.95 ⊕ FREE HOUSE/BEACHY HEAD BREWERY ◀ Legless Rambler & Original Ale, Harvey's, Long Man Long Blonde & Crafty Blonde ♂ Kingstone Press. ♟ 10 **Facilities** Non-diners area ❄ (Bar Garden) ♦♦ Children's menu Children's portions Garden ⋒ Parking WiFi

PICK OF THE PUBS

The Bull ★★★★ INN

DITCHLING   Map 6 TQ31

tel: 01273 843147
2 High St BN6 8TA
email: info@thebullditchling.com
web: www.thebullditchling.com
dir: *From Brighton on A27 take A23,
follow Pyecombe/Hassocks signs, then
Ditchling signs, 3m*

Old inn with contemporary feel

Perfect for visitors to the South Downs National Park, within which The Bull stands, this cosy 450-year-old inn has been sympathetically restored with open fires, bare floorboards and candlelit scrubbed tables. With a choice of three bars and dining areas, locals and visitors have plenty of choice, whether it's to sample one of the 13 craft beers and local ales – including Bedlam from the pub's own brewery – or one of the 23 wines by the glass. If it's good food you're after, the friendly, knowledgeable staff will guide you to a table where you can order from new head chef Dion Scott's appealing menu, which showcases local produce from Sussex farms and estates, as well as vegetables, fruit and herbs from The Bull's own abundant kitchen garden. Starters could include salsify, pancetta and pullet egg salad, followed perhaps by roasted duck breast, potato rösti, cavolo nero and griottine sauce; or sea

bream, violet artichokes, clams and green olive tapenade. Vegetarian options are no less impressive with crisp polenta, spiced aubergine, fennel and pesto among the meat-free options. Leave room for seasonal desserts such as poached rhubarb, orange curd and coconut sorbet. You can walk it all off with a trek over the South Downs – walks provided at the bar will take you beyond the village up onto the hills of Ditchling Beacon and Brighton is just 15 minutes away by car. For those visitors who want to extend their visit, the newly renovated bedrooms upstairs have already won plaudits for their sumptuous 6ft beds, Egyptian cotton sheets, rain showers and other luxurious touches.

Open all day all wk 11-11 (Sat 8.30am-11pm Sun 8.30am-10.30pm) **Food** Lunch Mon-Fri 12-2.30, Sat 12-9.30, Sun 12-9 (Sat-Sun bkfst 8.30-10.30am) Dinner Mon-Fri 6-9.30, Sat 12-9.30, Sun 12-9 ⊞ FREE HOUSE ◼ Timothy Taylor Landlord, Dark Star, Bedlam Best Bitter ♂ Cornish Orchards, The Orchard Pig. ⚱ 23 **Facilities** Non-diners area ♟ Children's menu Children's portions Play area Garden ⏢ Parking WiFi **Rooms** 4

ERIDGE GREEN
Map 6 TQ53

The Nevill Crest and Gun

tel: 01892 864209 **Eridge Rd TN3 9JR**
email: nevill.crest.and.gun@brunningandprice.co.uk
dir: On A26 between Tunbridge Wells & Crowborough

Intriguingly named pub with a long history

This uniquely named, tile-hung pub was built on land owned by the Nevill family, the Earls of Abergavenny. So the 'Crest' is easily explained; a cannon that once stood outside accounts for the 'Gun'. The hamlet's balancing act on the Kent-Sussex border is reflected by the real ales dispensed in the low-beamed, wooden-floored bar: Larkins comes from the former, Harvey's and Black Cat from the latter. A springtime Sunday lunch menu advocates tempura of king prawns with a noodle and spring onion salad; braised shoulder of lamb with all the trimmings; and warm raspberry Bakewell tart with Chantilly cream.

Open all day all wk 11.30-11 (Sun 12-10.30) **Food** Lunch Mon-Thu 12-9.30, Fri-Sat 12-10, Sun 12-9 Dinner Mon-Thu 12-9.30, Fri-Sat 12-10, Sun 12-9 ⊕ FREE HOUSE ◀ Brunning & Price Original Bitter, Harvey's, Larkins, Black Cat ♥ Aspall, Biddenden. ☘ 16 **Facilities** Non-diners area ✿ (Bar Garden Outside area) ♦♦ Children's portions Play area Garden Outside area ⋈ Beer festival Cider festival Parking WiFi ▥ (notice required)

EWHURST GREEN
Map 7 TQ72

The White Dog

tel: 01580 830264 **Village St TN32 5TD**
email: info@thewhitedogewhurst.co.uk
dir: On A21 from Tonbridge towards Hastings, left after Hurst Green signed Bodiam. Straight on at x-rds, through Bodiam. Over rail crossing, left for Ewhurst Green

Family-run country inn overlooking Bodiam Castle

This tile-hung village pub is either the first in, or the last out of the village, depending on which way you are travelling. Its age is more apparent from the interior, particularly the huge fireplace, old oak beams and stone floors. Four hand-pumps dispense regularly-changing, mostly Sussex real ales and some 20 wines are available by the glass. The seasonal menus show how dependent the kitchen is on the local area: for example, roasted scallops with a ginger, chilli, garlic and soy butter; chargrilled chump of lamb, mustard mash with rosemary and garlic oil; linguine vongole with whole fresh clams; and Kentucky-fried rabbit with carrot purée and pesto potatoes.

Open all day all wk **Food** Lunch all wk 12-2.30 Dinner all wk 6.30-9.30 Restaurant menu available all wk ⊕ FREE HOUSE ◀ Harvey's, Growler Brewery Top Dog, Rother Valley Level Best, Pig and Porter Ashburnham Pale Ale ♥ Double Vision. ☘ 20 **Facilities** Non-diners area ✿ (Bar Garden Outside area) ♦♦ Children's menu Children's portions Play area Garden Outside area ⋈ Beer festival Cider festival Parking WiFi ▥ (notice required)

FLETCHING
Map 6 TQ42

The Griffin Inn
PICK OF THE PUBS

tel: 01825 722890 **TN22 3SS**
email: info@thegriffininn.co.uk
dir: M23 junct 10, A264 to East Grinstead, then A22, in Maresfield take A275. Village signed on left

Popular for its huge gardens and lovely country views

The unspoilt village of Fletching overlooks the Ouse Valley. This imposing Grade II listed inn has landscaped gardens with views over Ashdown Forest, the Sussex Downs and 'Capability' Brown-designed Sheffield Park Gardens. You might just hear a steam whistle, for the heritage Bluebell Railway is little more than a mile away. The 16th-century interior simply oozes charm from its beams, panelling, settles and log fires. The bar's handles dispense the best of local ales, while the

already generous wine list has grown since the introduction of the pub's highly popular wine club, which organises tastings, special dinners and excursions. Walkers and cyclists arriving to join destination diners will revel in the menu, created from the freshest of local produce. Look out for fresh crab linguine; penne with Mediterranean vegetables; whole plaice and new potatoes; and wild mushroom, baby spinach and taleggio tart. On fine summer days the barbecue is fired up and food can be served on the terrace.

Open all day all wk 12-11 (Sat 12-12) Closed 25 Dec **Food** Lunch Mon-Fri 12-2.30, Sat-Sun 12-3 Dinner all wk 7-9.30 Av main course £13-£14 Set menu available Restaurant menu available all wk (ex Sun eve) ⊕ FREE HOUSE ◀ Harvey's Sussex Best Bitter, WJ King, Hepworth & Co, Hogs Back ♥ Westons Stowford Press. ☘ 16 **Facilities** Non-diners area ✿ (Bar Garden) ♦♦ Children's menu Children's portions Play area Garden ⋈ Parking WiFi

GUN HILL
Map 6 TQ51

The Gun
PICK OF THE PUBS

tel: 01825 872361 **TN21 0JU**
email: enquiries@thegunhouse.co.uk
dir: From Heathfield on A267, after Horam turn right into Chiddingly Rd (signed Chiddingly). Follow to pub on left

First-class food in a charming setting

Where felons and miscreants were brought to face justice in the local courthouse centuries ago, it's discerning drinkers and diners who nowadays seek out this rambling, steeply-roofed old inn. Located high in the Sussex Downs, extensive views reward sitting in the tranquil, tree-shaded beer garden with a locally produced bitter or cider in hand. Inside, lots of beams, wooden floors and open log fireplaces picked out in old brick characterise an interior dressed with rustic furnishings. A beautifully panelled dining room is a particular draw, whilst numerous hideaway niches and corners offer dining privacy. Sharing platters are a fun way of sampling the wide ranging contemporary menu; the 'Winter Board' features duck leg ballotine and wild rabbit rillette, with ham hock terrine and spicy duck meatballs. Mains embrace wild boar burger with bacon and Weald smoked cheddar; good vegetarian choices may feature woodland mushroom and chestnut cobbler. Calorific sweets include orange bread and butter pudding.

Open all wk 11.30-3 5.30-11 (Sun 11.30-10.30) **Food** Lunch Mon-Sat 12-3, Sun 12-9.30 Dinner Mon-Sat 6-9.45, Sun 12-9.30 ⊕ FREE HOUSE ◀ Sharp's Doom Bar, Harvey's, Guinness ♥ Biddenden, Aspall. ☘ 14 **Facilities** Non-diners area ✿ (All areas) ♦♦ Children's menu Children's portions Play area Garden Outside area ⋈ Parking WiFi

HARTFIELD
Map 6 TQ43

Anchor Inn

tel: 01892 770424 **Church St TN7 4AG**
email: info@anchorhartfield.com
dir: On B2110

Friendly free house in the Ashdown Forest

This family-orientated pub is in the heart of 'Winnie the Pooh' country. It was built in 1465 and was at one time a workhouse before it became a pub in the late 19th century. Locals meet in the front bar with its stone floors and heavy wooden beams, plus the inglenook fireplace and library area give the back bar a more intimate feel. As well as hot and cold snacks, main courses such as Cumberland sausages and mash or battered haddock, chips and peas satisfy heartier appetites. Friday evening is steak night. The front verandah and large garden are a bonus on warm sunny days. Look out for the early May beer festival.

Open all day all wk **Food** Lunch Mon-Sat 12-3, Sun 12-6 Dinner Mon-Thu & Sat 6-9, Fri 6-9.30 ⊕ FREE HOUSE ◀ Harvey's Sussex Best Bitter, Larkins ♥ Westons Stowford Press. **Facilities** Non-diners area ✿ (Bar Garden) ♦♦ Children's menu Children's portions Play area Garden ⋈ Beer festival Parking WiFi ▥ (notice required)

PICK OF THE PUBS

The Hatch Inn

HARTFIELD
Map 6 TQ43

tel: 01342 822363
Coleman's Hatch TN7 4EJ
email: nickad@mac.com
web: www.hatchinn.co.uk
dir: *A22 at Forest Row rdbt, 3m to Coleman's Hatch, right by church*

Award-winning pub in the heart of Ashdown Forest

If AA Milne could populate Ashdown Forest with a bear called Winnie the Pooh, a tiger called Tigger and a kangaroo called Kanga, why shouldn't llamas and reindeer live here? Well, they do, on a farm in nearby Wych Cross, not far from this eye-catching old inn at the site of one of the medieval gates into what was then dense woodland with valuable iron and timber reserves. Built around 1430, the part-weatherboarded building may have been cottages for iron workers, although it has been a pub for nearly 300 years, it was no doubt much appreciated by the dry-throated charcoal burners who used to work in these parts, and even passing smugglers. Classic beams and open fires draw an appreciative crowd to sample beers from Fuller's, Larkins and Harvey's, and the food, a fusion of classic and modern, for which proprietor Nicholas Drillsma and partner Sandy Barton have built an enviable reputation. Their daily changing menus are complemented by an extensive wine

list, including 10 by the glass. With plenty of local suppliers to draw on, there is fresh seasonal produce features in just about everything. Lunchtime mains include roast breast of duck, served pink, with wild mushroom risotto; Thai green chicken curry, galangal, lime leaves and coconut milk with jasmine rice; and south coast tempura cod and chips, buttered peas and tartare sauce. A reservation is essential for evening dining where choices may include smoked haddock and chive fishcakes; or pan-fried black pudding, bacon and quail's egg followed by slow-roasted pork belly, mustard creamed potatoes, red cabbage and apple compôte; or taglietelle bolognaise. Finish with Belgian chocolate, sea salt and caramel torte perhaps.

Open all wk 11.30-3 5.30-11 (Sat-Sun all day) Closed 25 Dec drinks only **Food** Lunch all wk 12-2.15 Dinner Mon-Thu 7-9.15, Fri-Sat 7-9.30 Av main course £15 ⊕ FREE HOUSE ◼ Harvey's & Sussex Old Ale, Fuller's London Pride, Larkins, Black Cat Ŏ Westons Stowford Press. ♀ 10 **Facilities** Non-diners area ❤ (Bar Restaurant Garden) ♦♦ Children's portions Play area Garden ⌗ WiFi

HARTFIELD *continued*

The Hatch Inn

PICK OF THE PUBS

See Pick of the Pubs on page 493

See Pick of the Pubs on page 493

HEATHFIELD

Map 6 TQ52

Star Inn

tel: 01435 863570 **Church St, Old Heathfield TN21 9AH**
email: susiechappelle@aol.co.uk
dir: *From A265 between Cross in Hand & Broad Oak right onto B2096 signed Old Heathfield. Right signed Old Heathfield. At T-junct into School Hill. In Old Heathfield left into Church St*

Creeper-clad inn with great views and a welcoming interior

Built as an inn for the stonemasons who constructed the 14th-century church, this creeper-clad stone building has a stunning summer garden that affords impressive views across the High Weald. Equally appealing is the atmospheric, low-beamed main bar with its rustic furnishings and huge inglenook fireplace – all very cosy and welcoming in winter. Note the unusual barrel-vaulted ceiling in the upstairs dining room and the regularly-changing chalkboard menu that lists fresh fish and seafood from the day boats in Hastings; the pub uses only local seasonal ingredients.

Open all day all wk **Food** Lunch Mon-Sat 12-2.30, Sun 12-3 Dinner Mon-Sat 7-9.30, Sun 6-8.30 ⊕ FREE HOUSE ◀ Harveys, Young's, Whitstable Bay Pale Ale, John Smith's, Guest ale Ō Thatchers. ♚ 10 **Facilities** Non-diners area ♣ (All areas) ♦️ Children's menu Children's portions Garden Outside area ☎ Parking WiFi ▨ (notice required)

ICKLESHAM

Map 7 TQ81

The Queen's Head

tel: 01424 814552 **Parsonage Ln TN36 4BL**
dir: *Between Hastings & Rye on A259. Pub in village at x-rds near church*

A must for real ale lovers

This 17th-century tile-hung and oak-beamed pub enjoys magnificent views from its gardens of the Brede Valley and as far as the coast at Rye, and has been in the same hands for more than 30 years. The traditional atmosphere has been preserved, with vaulted ceilings, large inglenook fireplaces, split-level floors, church pews, antique farm implements, and a bar from the old Midland Bank in Eastbourne. Customers are kept happy with up to 10 real ales, an annual beer festival in October, and menus ranging from salads, sandwiches and ploughman's to a comprehensive main menu selection which includes chicken, chorizo, tomato and basil pasta; pan-fried soft herring roe with toast and garnish; and spinach and roasted vegetable lasagne.

Open all wk 11-11 (Sun 11-10.30) Closed 25 & 26 Dec (eve) **Food** Lunch Mon-Fri 12-2.30, Sat-Sun 12-9.30 Dinner Mon-Fri 6-9.30, Sat-Sun 12-9.30 ⊕ FREE HOUSE ◀ Rother Valley Level Best, Greene King Abbot Ale, Harvey's Sussex Best Bitter, Ringwood Fortyniner, Dark Star Ō Biddenden, Westons Rosie's Pig. ♚ 12 **Facilities** Non-diners area ♣ (Bar Restaurant Garden) ♦️ Children's menu Children's portions Play area Garden ☎ Beer festival Parking WiFi ▨ (notice required)

LANGNEY

Map 6 TQ60

The Farm @ Friday Street

tel: 01323 766049 **15 Friday St BN23 8AP**
email: enquiries@farmfridaystreet.com
dir: *From A22 onto B2247, left onto B2104. Approx 1m to pub on left*

Excellent find in Eastbourne's outer reaches

Although surrounded by the ever-expanding town, this Whiting & Hammond Group pub still looks like the elegant farmhouse it once was. Fishmongers call the kitchen daily to tell them what's looking good from the day's catch, while other possibilities are chicken, mushroom and ham shortcrust pastry pie; fillet of beef Stroganoff with pilau rice; braised oxtail suet pudding with black pudding mash; and gnocchi with quinoa, chestnut mushrooms, soft herbs and truffle cream. Desserts include sorbets; banoffee pie; and chocolate brownie. Sunday lunches, with live music, are hugely popular and a beer festival is held in August.

Open all day all wk 9am-11pm **Food** Lunch Mon-Sat 12-9.30, Sun 12-9 Dinner Mon-Sat 12-9.30, Sun 12-9 ⊕ ENTERPRISE INNS ◀ Sharp's Doom Bar, Timothy Taylor, Long Man, Guest ales Ō Aspall. ♚ **Facilities** Non-diners area ♣ (Bar Restaurant Garden) ♦️ Children's portions Garden ☎ Beer festival Parking WiFi

LEWES

Map 6 TQ41

The Snowdrop Inn

tel: 01273 471018 **119 South St BN7 2BU**
email: tony@thesnowdropinn.com
dir: *From A26 (Tesco) rdbt into South St. Pub on left*

Thriving ale house worth finding

In 1836 a large build-up of snow on the chalk cliff above South Street suddenly fell, burying buildings below and causing eight fatalities. It's this avalanche, not the pretty springtime white flower that's acknowledged in the name here. Today, a warm welcome awaits in a pub known for a big-hearted bar line-up that includes Lewes-brewed Harvey's, and Gwynt y Ddraig cider from Pontypridd. The menu offers over a dozen starters, such as Tangiers-style marinated sardine fillets, and a score of mains, including traditional Irish stew; bubble-and-squeak patty; sticky-glazed roasted salmon fillet; and vegetarian options. A beer festival takes place in October.

Open all day all wk **Food** Lunch all wk 12-9 Dinner all wk 12-9 ⊕ FREE HOUSE ◀ Harvey's Sussex Best Bitter, Burning Sky Plateau & Aurora Ō Gwynt y Ddraig Black Dragon, Westons Rosie's Pig. ♚ 15 **Facilities** ♣ (Bar Restaurant Garden) ♦️ Children's portions Garden ☎ Beer festival WiFi

MAYFIELD

Map 6 TQ52

The Middle House

PICK OF THE PUBS

See Pick of the Pubs on opposite page

See Pick of the Pubs on opposite page

PICK OF THE PUBS

The Middle House

MAYFIELD　　　　　　　　　Map 6 TQ52

tel: 01435 872146 **High St TN20 6AB**
email: info@themiddlehousemayfield.co.uk
web: www.themiddlehousemayfield.co.uk
dir: *E of A267, S of Tunbridge Wells*

Historic timber-framed hostelry

Once described as 'one of the finest examples of a timber-framed building in Sussex', this Grade I listed, 16th-century village inn dominates Mayfield's High Street. It has been here since 1575, when it was built for Sir Thomas Gresham, Elizabeth I's Keeper of the Privy Purse and founder of the London Stock Exchange. The entrance hall features a large ornately carved wooden fireplace by master carver Grinling Gibbons, wattle-and-daub infill, a splendid oak-panelled restaurant and secret priest holes. A private residence until the 1920s, it is now a family-run business. Real ale drinkers do well here, with a handsome choice, including Harvey's Sussex Best Bitter from Lewes and Adnams Southwold Bitter. As in all good kitchens, the meats, poultry, game and vegetables come from local farms and producers. The bar menu includes classic dishes of home-made steak, Harvey's and mushroom pie; deep-fried wholetail scampi with chunky chips; home-made sausages of the day; fresh salads, vegetarian options and children's healthy-eating options.

For something a little less traditional, try pan-seared pigeon with apricot purée and hazelnut salad; or guinea fowl supreme. The carte offers roasted mixed peppers and tomato gnocchi; seared swordfish loin steak vindaloo; and duo of Crainsden Farm pork — slow-cooked shredded pork spring roll and fanned tenderloin with Dijon mustard sauce. And of the desserts, special mention goes to glazed lemon tart, chocolate mousse and strawberry soup. It isn't just the building that has been described in superlative terms — the private chapel in the restaurant is regarded as 'one of the most magnificent in England'. Step outside onto the lovely terraced gardens to enjoy views of the rolling countryside.

Open all day all wk **Food** Lunch Mon-Fri 12-2.15, Sat 12-2.30, Sun all day Dinner Mon-Sat 6.30-9.30, Sun all day Restaurant menu available Tue-Sat ⊕ FREE HOUSE ◙ Harvey's Sussex Best Bitter, Greene King Abbot Ale, Black Sheep Best Bitter, Theakston Best Bitter, Adnams Southwold Bitter Ö Thatchers Gold. ♟ 9 **Facilities** Non-diners area ♦♦ Children's menu & portions Play area Garden ⊼ Parking WiFi

RINGMER
Map 6 TQ41

The Cock

tel: 01273 812040 **Uckfield Rd BN8 5RX**
email: matt@cockpub.co.uk web: www.cockpub.co.uk
dir: *Just off A26, approx 2m N of Lewes just outside Ringmer*

Step back in time at this historic pub

This 16th-century inn takes its name from the time when a 'cock horse' was a spare horse used by coachmen to pull heavy loads – immortalised in the nursery rhyme 'Ride a Cock Horse to Banbury Cross'. A mustering point during the Civil War, the interior of the main bar is pretty much unaltered since Cromwell's time, with oak beams, flagstone floors and a blazing fire in the inglenook. Harvey's, and two local guest ales accompany a truly extensive menu. Start with deep-fried whitebait or grilled sardines, followed by steak and ale pie, local venison burger, or three Sussex lamp chops. A good vegetarian choice is available.

Open all wk 11-3 6-11.30 (Sun 11-11) Closed 26 Dec **Food** Lunch Mon-Fri 12-2, Sat 12-2.30, Sun 12-9.30 Dinner Mon-Sat 6-9.30, Sun 12-9.30 ⊕ FREE HOUSE ◀ Harvey's Sussex Best Bitter, Hogs Back, Hammerpot, Local guest ales. ♟ 10 **Facilities** Non-diners area ♣ (Bar Garden) ◑ Children's menu Children's portions Play area Garden ⋒ Parking WiFi ⊞ (notice required)

See advert on opposite page

RYE
Map 7 TQ92

The George Tap

tel: 01797 222114 **98 High St TN31 7JT**
email: stay@thegeorgeinrye.com
dir: *M20 junct 10, A2070 to Brenzett, A259 to Rye*

16th-century inn in pretty Sussex town

This town centre inn can trace its origins back to 1575. Inside it offers a fascinating mix of old and new, with an exquisite original Georgian ballroom and plenty of antique and contemporary furnishings and locally produced art. In the bar, the draw is beers from Dark Star and Harvey's breweries and a tasty, light bar menu. Diners can enjoy fruits of the sea from local boats; perhaps sweetcorn chowder or salt and pepper squid, followed by classic fish and chips with mushy peas. Alternatively, try delicious grilled lamb from the wood charcoal oven or classic steak frites.

Open all day all wk **Food** Lunch all wk 12-6 Dinner all wk 6-10 Set menu available Restaurant menu available all wk ⊕ FREE HOUSE ◀ Dark Star American Pale Ale, Harvey's Sussex Best Bitter. ♟ 18 **Facilities** Non-diners area ◑ Children's menu Children's portions Garden ⋒ WiFi ⊞

Mermaid Inn ★★★ HL ◉◉ ⬛ PICK OF THE PUBS

tel: 01797 223065 **Mermaid St TN31 7EY**
email: info@mermaidinn.com web: www.mermaidinn.com
dir: *A259, follow signs to town centre, into Mermaid St*

Memorable seafood dishes in historic smugglers' inn

The aura of the smugglers' inn remains at the Mermaid, which is one of the most famous and photographed of England's ancient pubs. This venerable black and white timber-fronted building was a haunt of seafarers from the Cinque Port harbour. Its colourful history is reflected in ships' timbers for beams and huge open fireplaces carved from French stone ballast dredged from Rye harbour. A vast inglenook where the infamous Hawkshurst gang warmed themselves also has a hidden priest hole. British and French-style food is served in the bar, restaurant and under sunshades on the patio. Perhaps choose venison Scotch egg, remoulade and Kent salad; or potted mackerel and toast; followed by steak and kidney pudding, new potatoes, seasonal vegetables and red wine gravy; or sherry braised duck leg with celeriac and mushrooms. Superb wines, local Harvey's beer and comfortable bedrooms complete the package.

Open all day all wk 12-11 **Food** Lunch all wk 12-2.30 Dinner all wk 6-9 Restaurant menu available all wk ⊕ FREE HOUSE ◀ St Austell Tribute, Harvey's, Guest ale ○ Kingstone Press. ♟ 15 **Facilities** Non-diners area ♣ (Garden) ◑ Children's menu Children's portions Garden ⋒ Parking WiFi ⊞ (notice required) **Rooms** 31

The Cock

This is a 16th century family run dining pub where the landlords still find time to personally greet both new and returning customers. Walk into the pub and you are met by a huge blackboard that seems to list every pub dish that has ever existed! Should that not be enough choice then this is supplemented by a daily Specials Board and at lunchtimes (ex Sundays) sandwiches, rolls & Ploughman's – we try to offer something for all tastes, appetites and budgets and are also able to cater for Coeliacs and Vegans. The pub is well renowned for its wide choice of homemade dishes featuring locally produced ingredients, such as Steak & Ale Pie, Venison Sausages and Chicken Florentina. Vegetarians are well catered for with 6 regular Vegetarian dishes, 3 of which are prepared to Vegan standards. A variety of fish and steaks are always featured and a favourite is Val's Purse (named after the Landlady!) – Sirloin Steak stuffed with Stilton and with a Creamy Mushroom Sauce. There is always a choice of Sunday Roast with all the 'Trimmings' and if you still have room there are lovely homemade traditional puddings like Rhubarb Crumble, Sticky Toffee & Date Sponge with our own Butterscotch Sauce, Eton Mess or award winning Ice Creams from Downsview Farm (Toffee-Apple as featured on The Apprentice) available every day. And, if there is a dish that you particularly want, with a bit of notice, we will try to provide it.

The Specials Board is always well stocked with locally produced fare, representing the seasons – asparagus in Spring, Game in Autumn/Winter (Venison, Pheasant, Partridge, Guinea Fowl, etc), Winter warmers (Sausage casserole, Lamb's Hearts, Oxtail etc) and fresh salads and quiches in the Summer.

There is a well-stocked bar that always features Harvey's Best Bitter, together with two locally produced seasonal guests from The Hogsback Brewery, Hammerpot, WJ King, together with a number of locally emerging micro-breweries – details of which can be found on the pub's continually updated website at www.cockpub.co.uk. In addition, there is a choice of 12 wines by the glass, including Pinot Grigio, Sauvignon Blanc, Shiraz and Merlot, all at £4.20 per 175 ml glass plus Hot Mulled Wine in the winter and a wide selection of liqueurs, together with a selection of 12 Malt Whiskies.

There are three dining areas, which can accommodate up to 65 covers, plus the Bar area that can seat a further twelve people. The bar is a wonderful unspoilt area with original oak beams, a flagstone floor and an Inglenook fireplace, where a log fire can be found from October to April. Well-behaved children are welcomed in the restaurant and garden, keeping the bar for those who would like a quiet drink or bite to eat.

The garden has plenty of space to enjoy fine weather with patio areas and grass and views to the South Downs and if you are lucky spectacular sunsets on clear evenings. The pub welcomes dogs in the garden and bar area with dog chews and water bowls. The pub's own spaniels Tally & Bailey can often be seen returning through the bar after a walk on the nearby Wellingham Walk.

The Cock Inn takes its name from the bygone era when a spare horse (The Cock Horse) was kept ready at the foot of a steep hill to assist another horse with a heavy load up the hill. Old maps show that there was stabling in the car park area up until the later 1800's. The Cock Horse, of course, was immortalised in the favourite children's nursery rhyme that depicted Queen Elizabeth 1 riding into Banbury Cross aboard a large white stallion, after the Queen's carriage had broken a wheel on the steep climb up the hill.

Built in the mid-16th Century, The Cock has always been a thriving Coaching Inn. Although none of the original stables remain, it was once a mustering point during The Civil War, prior to the siege of Arundel.

The main bar and interior has changed little since Cromwell's time, with low oak beams and Inglenook fireplace. In its earliest days, four rooms within the building were licensed separately, each room identified by a small porcelain plate bearing a number. Two of these plates can still be seen in the main bar.

Uckfield Road, Ringmer, Lewes, East Sussex BN8 5RX • **Tel:** 01273 812040 • **Email:** matt@cockpub.co.uk
Website: www.cockpub.co.uk • **Twitter:** @CockInnRingmer • **Facebook:** TheCockInnRingmer

RYE *continued*

The Ypres Castle Inn

PICK OF THE PUBS

tel: 01797 223248 **Gun Garden TN31 7HH**
email: info@yprescastleinn.co.uk
dir: *Behind church & adjacent to Ypres Tower*

A well-kept secret in the ancient town of Rye

The pretty Ypres Castle Inn, known locally as 'The Wipers', sits beneath the castle's ramparts and has been providing hospitality since 1640. As you'd expect with such a long pedigree, the inn's atmosphere is relaxed and friendly, and the reading room is stocked with an eclectic literary mix and children's games. The bar, featuring the original timber frame of the building, serves Larkins and Harvey's, plus Biddenden cider, all to be savoured around the log fire. From the garden there are magnificent views of Romney Marsh and the River Rother; the Rye Bay fishing fleet moors close by. Light bites include baguettes, ciabattas and bruschettas; popular choices are a cold cured meat platter served with pitta bread, and English lamb hotpot, dumplings and mash. Booking is advisable for the traditional Sunday roasts. The pub hosts live music on Friday nights, Sundays and in the garden in summer.

Open all day Closed Mon in winter **Food** Lunch all wk 12-3 Dinner Mon-Sat 6-9 ⊕ FREE HOUSE ◀ Harvey's Sussex Best Bitter, Larkins Best Bitter, Adnams, Westerham Brewery, Long Man, Guest ales ♂ Biddenden Bushels. **Facilities** Non-diners area ❖ (Bar Garden) ♦ Children's menu Children's portions Garden ⌁ Beer festival WiFi

SALEHURST
Map 7 TQ72

Salehurst Halt

PICK OF THE PUBS

tel: 01580 880620 **Church Ln TN32 5PH**
dir: *0.5m from A21 (Tunbridge Wells to Hastings road). Exit at Robertsbridge rdbt to Salehurst*

Free house with hop growing connections

Built in the 1860s, when it was known as the Old Eight Bells. Legend puts the name change down to a church organist who commuted to the village from Bodiam, necessitating a new halt on the Robertsbridge to Tenterden line. Despite use by many a hop-picker thereafter, the steam railway eventually closed. Today the hop crop is sold to Harvey's in Lewes, and returned as one of the ales sold by the pub – its traditional cellar is much prized for maintaining ale in top condition. The hop-growing farm also supplies the pub's meats, including Buster's burgers; note that evening meals are only served from Wednesday to Saturday; the menus reflect the seasons. The landscaped garden has a wonderful terrace with beautiful views over the Rother Valley; here a wood-fired pizza oven (and outdoor griddle weather permitting) runs almost continually during the summer, with orders taken at the garden counter. Before leaving, have a stroll around this picturesque hamlet and the 12th-century church.

Open all day Closed Mon **Food** Contact pub for food times ⊕ FREE HOUSE ◀ Harvey's Sussex Best Bitter, Dark Star, Old Dairy, Guest ales ♂ Biddenden Bushels, East Stour. **Facilities** Non-diners area ❖ (Bar Restaurant Garden) ♦ Children's portions Garden ⌁

SHORTBRIDGE
Map 6 TQ42

The Peacock Inn

PICK OF THE PUBS

tel: 01825 762463 **TN22 3XA**
email: enquiries@peacock-inn.co.uk
dir: *Just off A272 (Haywards Heath to Uckfield road) & A26 (Uckfield to Lewes road)*

Pretty black and white pub with seasonally inspired menus

Mentioned in Samuel Pepys' diary, The Peacock Inn dates from 1567 but is these days more renowned for its food and its warm welcome. This traditional inn is full

of old-world charm, both inside and out. Long Man Best and a guest ale keep beer-lovers happy, and there are eight wines by the glass. For the hungry there are starters such as sweet chilli chicken and crispy bacon salad; chicken liver pâté; Sussex smokie, smoked haddock, cream and mustard sauce; followed by poached filled of hake, confit potatoes, clam chowder, buttered spinach and caramelised salsify; or pomegranate glazed duck breast, potato torte, baby leeks, spring greens and jus. Leave room for desserts such as blueberry cheesecake with honeycomb parfait, or toffee sponge pudding and apple ripple ice cream. The large rear patio garden is a delightful spot in summer.

Open all wk 11-3 6-11 (Sun all day) Closed 25-26 Dec **Food** Lunch Mon-Sat 12-3, Sun 12-8 Dinner Mon-Sat 6-9.30, Sun 12-8 ⊕ FREE HOUSE ◀ Harvey's Sussex Best Bitter, Long Man Best Bitter, Guest ale ♂ Westons Stowford Press. ♟ 8 **Facilities** Non-diners area ❖ (Bar Garden) ♦ Children's menu Children's portions Garden ⌁ Parking

THREE LEG CROSS
Map 6 TQ63

The Bull

tel: 01580 200586 **Dunster Mill Ln TN5 7HH**
email: enquiries@thebullinn.co.uk
dir: *From M25 exit at Sevenoaks toward Hastings, right at x-rds onto B2087, right onto B2099 through Ticehurst, right for Three Leg Cross*

Home-cooked food and large family-friendly garden

The Bull started life as a 14th-century Wealden Hall House, reputedly one of the oldest dwelling places in the country, and is set in a hamlet close to Bewl Water. The interior features oak beams, inglenook fireplaces, quarry-tiled floors, and a mass of small intimate areas in the bar. The extensive gardens are popular with families who enjoy the duck pond, petanque pitch, aviary and children's play area. Menus offer pub favourites ranging from freshly baked baguettes and bar snacks to hearty dishes full of comfort, such as bangers and mash and treacle tart.

Open all day all wk 12-12 **Food** Lunch all wk all day Dinner all wk all day Restaurant menu available all wk ⊕ FREE HOUSE ◀ Harvey's Sussex Best Bitter & Armada Ale, Timothy Taylor Landlord, Guest ales ♂ Westons Stowford Press, Symonds. ♟ 9 **Facilities** Non-diners area ❖ (Bar Garden) ♦ Children's menu Children's portions Play area Garden ⌁ Beer festival Parking WiFi ☎ (notice required)

TICEHURST
Map 6 TQ63

The Bell

PICK OF THE PUBS

tel: 01580 200234 **High St TN5 7AS**
email: info@thebellinticehurst.com
dir: *From A21 follow signs for Ticehurst. Pub in village centre*

A village inn to make you smile

This is certainly a quirky yet welcoming pub. The authentic 16th-century charm of the building has been preserved, with its rustic wooden floors, sagging beams, and a blazing log fire in the huge brick inglenook. Funky design touches abound, from the top hat lampshades and pillar of books in the bar, to the tubas for urinals in the Gents and the stuffed squirrel that appears to hold up a ceiling. A cosy snug is furnished with leather chesterfields and shelves of books, and the Stable with a Table is an inspired function room with long sunken table and benches, perfect for the pub's regular debate evenings and demonstration dinners. So, settle in with a pint of Old Dairy before ordering from the short but perfectly formed menu.

Open all day all wk **Food** Lunch all wk 12-6 Dinner all wk 6-9.30 Set menu available Restaurant menu available all wk ⊕ FREE HOUSE ◀ Harvey's, Old Dairy, Seasonal Guest ales ♂ Symonds. ♟ 12 **Facilities** Non-diners area ❖ (Bar Garden) ♦ Children's menu Garden ⌁ Parking WiFi ☎ (notice required)

WILMINGTON
Map 6 TQ50

The Giants Rest

tel: 01323 870207 **The Street BN26 5SQ**
email: giantsrest@hotmail.com
dir: *2m from Polegate on A27 towards Brighton*

An ideal spot for South Downs walkers

This traditional country pub is set back off the A27 in a pretty village close to the famous chalk figure of the Long Man of Wilmington. A family-owned Victorian free house, the pub is ideally situated for walkers exploring the South Downs Way. Furnished with pine tables and pews, the bar is decorated with Beryl Cook prints. Local ales from The Long Man brewery in nearby Litlington accompany a blackboard menu of traditional classics and daily specials. Typical choices include wild rabbit, bacon, apple and prune pie, and slow-roast belly of pork with spicy ginger and plum sauce.

Open all wk 12-3 6-11 (Sun all day) **Food** Lunch Mon-Sat 12-2, Sun all day Dinner Mon-Sat 6.30-9, Sun all day Av main course £12 ⊕ FREE HOUSE ◀ Long Man Best Bitter, Long Blonde, Old Man, American Pale Ale, Sussex Pride & Copper Hop ♂ Aspall, South Downs. ♥ 10 **Facilities** Non-diners area ❖ (Bar Restaurant Garden) ♦ Children's portions Garden ♠ Parking WiFi ➡

WITHYHAM
Map 6 TQ43

The Dorset Arms
PICK OF THE PUBS

tel: 01892 770278 **TN7 4BD**
email: enquiries@dorsetarms.co.uk
dir: *4m W of Tunbridge Wells on B2110 between Groombridge & Hartfield*

Good food in this buzzy village local

Licensed some 200 years ago when it took the name of the local landowning family, once Earls of Dorset, this centuries-old building is a jigsaw of styles. Slender chimney stacks, sharp gables, white weatherboarding and careworn tiles are reminders of its vintage, whilst the interior doesn't disappoint with its comfy, period mix of flagstone and oak-boarded floors, vast open fireplace and undulating beams. The Dorset Arms remains at heart a true village local, with darts, good Sussex ales from Harvey's and a vibrant community atmosphere. The produce of the kitchen is also a major draw, with a daily-changing specials board complementing the appealing carte menu. Starters include potted Cornish lobster and prawns; or Scotch egg with mustard mayonnaise. The main course options might be steak and kidney pudding or whole lemon sole with brown shrimps, samphire and frites. Tables on the green outside allow summertime alfresco dining.

Open all day all wk 12-11 (Sun 12-10.30) **Food** Lunch Mon-Sat 12-2.30, Sun 12-4 Dinner Mon-Sat 6-9 Av main course £12 ⊕ FREE HOUSE ◀ Harvey's Sussex Best Bitter, Larkins, Guest ales ♂ Aspall. **Facilities** Non-diners area ❖ (Bar Garden Outside area) ♦ Children's portions Garden Outside area ♠ Parking WiFi

WEST SUSSEX

ALBOURNE
Map 6 TQ21

NEW The Ginger Fox ◉

tel: 01273 857888 **Muddleswood Rd BN6 9EA**
email: gingerfox@gingermanrestaurants.com
dir: *On A281 at junct with B2117*

Pretty, thatched pub with no neighbours

The South Downs look glorious from the beer garden, where children can play safely, and mums and dads can admire the raised vegetable seed-bed if they have a mind to. Inside, walls and beams are painted in beige and oatmeal, a gentle contrast perhaps to the golden colour of a pint of Bedlam, the real ale brewed up nearby Shaves Wood Lane. Hogget (a young sheep) may be on the menu, specifically

saddle, shoulder and offal with goats' cheese, red peppers, aubergine and baby artichokes. Another possibility is sea bass with oyster beignet, braised leek, parsley root purée and red wine sauce. Cyclists may use the secure bike racks and top up their water bottles.

Open all day all wk Closed 25 Dec **Food** Lunch Mon-Fri 12-2, Sat 12-3, Sun 12-4 Dinner Mon-Fri 6-10, Sat 6.30-10, Sun 6-9 Set menu available Restaurant menu available all wk ⊕ FREE HOUSE ◀ Bedlam, Harvey's IPA, Dark Star Partridge Best Bitter ♂ Westons Wyld Wood Organic, Orchard Pig Reveller. ♥ 27 **Facilities** Non-diners area ❖ (Bar Garden) ♦ Children's menu Play area Garden ♠ Parking WiFi ➡ (notice required)

AMBERLEY
Map 6 TQ01

The Bridge Inn

tel: 01798 831619 **Houghton Bridge BN18 9LR**
email: bridgeamberley@btinternet.com **web:** www.bridgeinnamberley.com
dir: *5m N of Arundel on B2139. Adjacent to Amberley rail station*

Traditional downland free house in South Downs National Park

Over the road from this charming period pub is the fascinating Amberley Museum; adjacent is Houghton Bridge over the River Arun. The pub has a long association with the museum's industrial heritage theme as quarrymen and limekiln workers once bought their beer here. What attracts people to the pub today are its candlelit bar's log fires, real ales from Harvey's, Langham and Skinner's breweries, the sheltered garden with views of the South Downs countryside, and the extensive menu. This offers pub classics and daily specials, including fish, steaks, Mediterranean and vegetarian dishes, all prepared by Greek chef, George Koulouris.

Open all day all wk 11-11 (Sun 12-9) **Food** Lunch Mon-Fri 12-2.30, Sat-Sun 12-4 Dinner Mon-Sat 6-9, Sun 5.30-8 ⊕ FREE HOUSE ◀ Skinner's Betty Stogs, Harvey's Sussex Best Bitter, Langham Hip Hop, Guest ales ♂ Westons Stowford Press. **Facilities** Non-diners area ❖ (Bar Garden) ♦ Children's menu Children's portions Garden Outside area ♠ Parking WiFi ➡ (notice required)

ASHURST — Map 6 TQ11

The Fountain Inn — PICK OF THE PUBS

tel: 01403 710219 **BN44 3AP**
email: manager@fountainashurst.co.uk
dir: On B2135, N of Steyning

Traditional village pub with some famous customers

The South Downs and the village duck pond can be seen from the terrace of this lovely 16th-century listed building, which comes complete with wonky floorboards, inglenook fireplaces, beams and skittle alley. Acting legend Laurence Olivier was once a regular and Paul McCartney loved the place so much he filmed part of the video for *Wonderful Christmas Time* here. Local beers from Harvey's accompany the freshly cooked pub food that attracts walkers, cyclists, locals and those from further afield. At lunchtime there are light bites, or at lunch or dinner you could opt for the full three courses; maybe pan-seared scallops, shallot and wild garlic bhaji, mint dressing, curried aïoli followed by shepherd's pie or black olive and ricotta tortellini with baby tomato, wild garlic and asparagus. If you still have space, finish with sticky toffee pudding, butterscotch sauce and ice cream. Look out for live music events.

Open all day all wk 11-11 (Sun 11-10.30) **Food** Lunch Mon-Fri 12-2.30, Sat-Sun 12-9.30 Dinner Mon-Fri 6-9.30, Sat-Sun 12-9.30 Av main course £13 ⊕ ENTERPRISE INNS ◀ Harvey's Sussex, Sharp's Doom Bar, Fuller's, Seasonal & Guest ales Ő Symonds. ♀ **Facilities** Non-diners area ♣ (Bar Garden) ♦️ Children's menu Children's portions Play area Garden ⊨ Parking WiFi 🚌 (notice required)

BOSHAM — Map 5 SU80

The Anchor Bleu

tel: 01243 573956 **High St PO18 8LS**
dir: From A27 (SW of Chichester) take A259. Follow Fishbourne signs, then Bosham signs

Harbourside pub with plenty of real ales

If you park your car opposite The Anchor Bleu, check the tide times at this 17th-century inn, as that area floods during most high tides. Flagstone floors, low beams, an open log fire, an upstairs dining room with views and two terraces, one overlooking Chichester Harbour, add to the charm of this popular pub. A good choice of real ales is on offer, including Ringwood Fortyniner. Dishes are based on locally sourced, seasonal ingredients, such as Blackdown venison steak, salt and pepper squid, and brie and artichoke tartlet. Meals can be taken on the terraces during warmer weather. Reservations are recommended.

Open all wk all day (Mon-Thu 11.30-3 6-11 Nov-Mar) **Food** Lunch Mon-Sat 12-3, Sun all day Dinner all wk 6.30-9.30 ⊕ ENTERPRISE INNS ◀ Sharp's Cornish Coaster & Doom Bar, Ringwood Fortyniner, Otter Ale, Hop Back Summer Lightning, Anchor Springs Riptide Ő Westons Stowford Press. ♀ 10 **Facilities** Non-diners area ♦️ Children's menu Children's portions Garden ⊨ 🚌 (notice required)

BURGESS HILL — Map 6 TQ31

The Oak Barn

tel: 01444 258222 **Cuckfield Rd RH15 8RE**
email: enquiries@oakbarnrestaurant.co.uk **web:** www.oakbarnrestaurant.co.uk
dir: Phone for detailed directions

British produce in a restored barn

As its name suggests, this popular pub-restaurant occupies a 250-year-old barn that has been lovingly restored using salvaged timbers from wooden ships. Brimming with charm, the interior is rich in oak flooring, authentic wagon wheel chandeliers, and fine stained glass. Lofty raftered ceilings, a galleried restaurant, and leather chairs fronting a huge fireplace add to the atmosphere. Here, and in the bar and enclosed courtyard, you'll find sandwiches, pub classics and an à la carte menu at lunch and dinner. Sup a pint of Harvey's or Guinness and tuck into dishes created from seasonal British ingredients.

Open all day all wk 10am-11pm (Sun 11-11) **Food** Lunch all wk 12-2.30 Dinner all wk 6-9.30 Set menu available Restaurant menu available all wk ⊕ FREE HOUSE ◀ Dark Star, Harvey's, Fuller's London Pride, Guinness. ♀ 8 **Facilities** Non-diners area ♦️ Children's portions Garden Outside area ⊨ Parking WiFi

See advert on opposite page

BURPHAM
Map 6 TQ00

The George at Burpham
PICK OF THE PUBS

tel: 01903 883131 **Main St BN18 9RR**
email: info@georgeatburpham.co.uk
dir: Exit A27 1m E of Arundel signed Burpham, 2.5m, pub on left

Thriving village pub

Since being brought back from the brink of closure by three local businessmen, this village pub goes from strength to strength. Built in 1736, it stands opposite the 11th-century parish church, one of whose features is a lepers' window from which the afflicted could watch mass. Head for the bar with its wood-burning stove, safe in the knowledge that Sussex-sourced real ales, soft drinks and even champagne are waiting. Menus offer bar snacks of whitebait with chilli mayonnaise; starters of Spanish-style tortilla with mixed leaves and tangy tomato salsa; and mains that include whole baked local trout with new potatoes and sauce almondine; pork and leek sausages with mash, root vegetables and onion gravy; and gnocchi in gorgonzola cream sauce with spinach and pine nuts. Sunday roasts are supplemented by vegetarian dishes, including spiced vegetable tagine with couscous and yogurt.

Open all wk 10.30-3 6-11 (Sat 10.30am-11pm Sun 10.30-5.30) **Food** Lunch Mon-Fri 12-2.30, Sat 12-3, Sun 12-5.30 Dinner Mon-Fri 6-9, Sat 6-9.30 Av main course £17 Set menu available ⊕ FREE HOUSE ◀ Arundel, Guest ales ♻ Aspall. ▼ 25 **Facilities** Non-diners area ✿ (Bar) ♦ Children's menu Children's portions Outside area ᴙ Parking WiFi ▦ (notice required)

CHARLTON
Map 6 SU81

The Fox Goes Free ★★★★ INN
PICK OF THE PUBS

See Pick of the Pubs on page 502

CHICHESTER
Map 5 SU80

The Bull's Head ★★★★ INN

tel: 01243 839895 **99 Fishbourne Road West PO19 3JP**
email: enquiries@bullsheadfishbourne.net **web:** www.bullsheadfishbourne.net
dir: A27 onto A259, inn 0.5m on left

Good range of well-kept real ales

Only three minutes' walk from Chichester harbour, this traditional roadside pub with large open fire has been a hostelry since some time in the 17th century, and before that it was a farmhouse. Its position just outside Chichester is perfect for anyone visiting Fishbourne Roman Palace and Bosham Harbour. Traditional home-cooked food is based on locally sourced ingredients and baguettes and jacket potatoes are on offer as a lighter option; there's a chef's daily-changing special menu too. The pub serves five real ales all in tip-top condition. Live music and special events are hosted throughout the year. The comfortable accommodation is light and airy with modern decor and furnishings.

Open all wk 11-3 5.30-11 (Sat 11-11 Sun 12-11) **Food** Lunch Mon-Sat 12-2, Sun 12-3 Dinner Mon-Thu 6-9, Fri-Sat 6-9.30, Sun 6-8 ⊕ FULLER'S ◀ London Pride, ESB & George Gale & Co HSB, Guest ales ♻ Aspall. ▼ 10 **Facilities** Non-diners area ✿ (Bar Outside area) ♦ Children's menu Children's portions Outside area ᴙ Parking WiFi ▦ (notice required) **Rooms** 4

PICK OF THE PUBS

The Fox Goes Free ★★★★ INN

CHARLTON Map 6 SU81

tel: 01243 811461 **PO18 0HU**
email: enquiries@thefoxgoesfree.com
web: www.thefoxgoesfree.com
dir: *A286, 6m from Chichester towards Midhurst*

Friendly pub with William III, racing world and WI connections

Standing in unspoiled countryside at the foot of the South Downs, this lovely old brick and flint free house was a favoured hunting lodge of William III. With its three huge fireplaces, old pews and brick floors, the 15th-century building simply exudes charm and character. The pub, which hosted the first English Women's Institute meeting in 1915, lies close to the Weald and Downland Open Air Museum, where 50 historic buildings from around southern England have been reconstructed. Goodwood Estate is also close by, and The Fox attracts many customers during the racing season and the annual Festival of Speed. Away from the high life, you can watch the world go by from the solid timber benches and tables to the front, or relax under the apple trees in the lawned rear garden. Lest all this sounds rather extravagant, you'll find that The Fox is a friendly and welcoming drinkers' pub with a good selection of real ales that includes the eponymous Fox Goes Free bitter. Everything from the chips to the ice cream is home made

and, whether you're looking for a quick bar snack or something more substantial, the daily-changing menus offer something for every taste. Bar meals include Cumberland sausages with mash and red onion marmalade; and tomato and basil tagliatelle; as well as a selection of ciabattas. Further choices may be a mezze platter of the day, or whole baked camembert with confit of garlic and toast. Continue with a main course such as fish pie topped with cheesy mash and served with minted peas, roast chicken breast wrapped in parma ham with lyonnaise potatoes and wholegrain mustard jus; or pie of the day. Salads can be prepared for both small and large appetites, and there are some appealing vegetarian options, too.

Open all day all wk 11-11 (Sun 12-11) Closed 25 Dec eve **Food** Lunch Mon-Fri 12-2.30, Sat-Sun 12-10 Dinner Mon-Fri 6.30-10, Sat-Sun 12-10 Av main course £10.95 Restaurant menu available all wk ⊕ FREE HOUSE ◼ The Fox Goes Free, Shepherd Neame Spitfire, Local Guest ales ⏲ Addlestones, Aspall. ⬤ 15 **Facilities** Non-diners area ⁂ (Bar Garden) ⁙ Children's menu Children's portions Garden ⋔ Parking WiFi ⛟ (notice required) **Rooms** 5

CHICHESTER *continued*

The Earl of March ⓦ   PICK OF THE PUBS

tel: 01243 533993 **Lavant Rd, Lavant PO18 0BQ**
email: info@theearlofmarch.com
dir: *On A286, 1m N of Chichester*

Lots of style at former coaching inn

Named after the local landowning dynasty, the Earl sits at the foot of the South Downs National Park and is an inspirational place to visit. William Blake wrote the words to *Jerusalem* whilst sitting in the east-facing bay window here in 1803; today's visitors can enjoy much the same views that prompted his outpourings. The excellent choice of dishes is prepared from the bounty of local estates and the nearby Channel. An à la carte menu might have perhaps oak-smoked salmon with local cress, potato blini and dill crème fraîche; or steamed mussels in cider and parsley cream; followed by champagne risotto with mushrooms, slow-poached duck egg and truffle oil; or beer battered haddock and chips. Such dishes are crafted by Giles Thompson, former Executive Chef at London's Ritz Hotel and now proprietor of this delightful 18th-century coaching inn appointed in 'country plush' style.

Open all day all wk **Food** Lunch all wk 12-2.30 winter, 12-9 summer Dinner all wk 12-9 summer Av main course £19.50 Set menu available Restaurant menu available all wk ⊕ ENTERPRISE INNS ◀ Harvey's, Fuller's London Pride, Timothy Taylor Landlord, Guest ale Ŏ Westons Stowford Press, Aspall. ⓦ 24 **Facilities** Non-diners area ♣ (Bar Garden) ⓘ Children's menu Children's portions Garden ⋒ Parking WiFi

The George & Dragon Inn ★★★ INN

tel: 01243 785660 **51 North St PO19 1NQ**
email: info@thegeorgeanddragoninn.co.uk **web:** www.georgeanddragoninn.co.uk
dir: *Near Chichester Festival Theatre. Phone for detailed directions*

Stylish pub in the heart of Chichester

The George & Dragon stands next to the site of the original north walls' gatehouse in historic Chichester, and is well positioned near the Old Town Cross and cathedral. It dates from the early 18th century, and landlord Lee Howard has refurbished the place in the last few years – today you'll find open fires, comfortable sofas and a courtyard to enhance the family-friendly feel. In the light and airy conservatory dining room, the menus reveal traditional pub favourites such as breaded whitebait, rump of lamb or pork belly.

Open all day all wk Closed 25-26 Dec, 1 Jan **Food** Lunch Mon-Fri & Sun 12-3, Sat 12-5 Dinner Mon-Sat 5-9 Restaurant menu available all wk ⊕ PUNCH TAVERNS ◀ Sharp's Doom Bar, Timothy Taylor Landlord. ⓦ 18 **Facilities** Non-diners area ♣ (Bar Outside area) ⓘ Children's portions Outside area ⋒ WiFi ▬ (notice required) **Rooms** 10

Royal Oak Inn ★★★★★ INN ⓦⓦ   PICK OF THE PUBS

See Pick of the Pubs on page 504

COMPTON   Map 5 SU71

Coach & Horses

tel: 023 9263 1228 **The Square PO18 9HA**
dir: *On B2146, S of Petersfield. In village centre*

Appealing South Downs honeypot

David and Christiane Butler have run their 17th-century coaching inn in this pretty South Downs village since 1985. Popular with walkers, cyclists and, let's face it,

anyone looking for good food and drink, its unspoiled Victorian bar, with two open fires, is widely known for championing local microbreweries like Ballards and Langham. The oldest part of the pub, with many exposed beams, is the restaurant, where you'll find dishes such as chicken mushroom and tarragon pie; avocado and spinach bake; lamb rump with dauphinoise potatoes; steak and kidney pie; crackling pork belly, and local game choices in season.

Open Tue-Sun 11.30-3 6-11 Closed Mon **Food** Lunch Tue-Sun 12-2 Dinner 7-9 ⊕ FREE HOUSE ◀ Ballards Best Bitter, Bowmans, Guest ales Ŏ Thatchers. **Facilities** Non-diners area ♣ (Bar Outside area) ⓘ Children's portions Outside area ⋒ WiFi ▬ (notice required)

CUCKFIELD   Map 6 TQ32

The Talbot

tel: 01444 455898 **High St RH17 5JX**
email: info@thetalbotcuckfield.co.uk
dir: *B2036 into village centre*

Smart village pub showcasing the local larder

Once a staging post for travellers on the road between London and Brighton, The Talbot is still the hub in the historic village of Cuckfield. It's now a contemporary pub and restaurant that prides itself on making the most of the local larder, whether it's Dark Star ales or seasonal dishes such as pigs' cheeks, Puy lentils and home-made apple jelly; blackened salmon, chorizo, sugar snap and fennel velouté, saffron fondant with tomato and herb dressing; and blackcurrant crème brûlée with pistachio biscotti. There is a local producers' market in the courtyard on the second Saturday of the month.

Open all day all wk **Food** Lunch Mon-Sat 12-3, Sun 12-5 Dinner Mon-Sat 6-9.30 Restaurant menu available all wk ⊕ FREE HOUSE ◀ Harvey's Sussex Best Bitter, Dark Star, Guest ales Ŏ Symonds. ⓦ 14 **Facilities** Non-diners area ♣ (Bar Garden) ⓘ Children's menu Children's portions Garden ⋒ WiFi ▬ (notice required)

DIAL POST   Map 6 TQ11

The Crown Inn

tel: 01403 710902 **Worthing Rd RH13 8NH**
email: crowninndialpost@aol.com
dir: *8m S of Horsham. Village signed from A24*

Family heritage at real ale gastro-pub

The Crown Inn is owned by Penny and James Middleton-Burn; Penny's grandparents, were the previous owners of this tile-hung free house overlooking the village green. Penny's sister and husband rear the pigs and lambs that occasionally end up in the kitchen, strengthening the family involvement. Although it is food-led, if you just want a pint of Harvey's ale or a Thatchers cider, that's absolutely fine. Chef James and his team make nearly everything on the premises, including goats' cheese pannacotta, poached pear, honey toasted walnut and endive salad; potted crab and crayfish, fine bean salad and ciabatta crisp; luxury fisherman's pie; and individual chicken and mushroom puff pastry pie.

Open 12-3 6-11 (Sun 12-4) Closed contact pub for Xmas opening times, Sun eve **Food** Lunch Mon-Sat 12-2, Sun 12-3 Dinner Mon-Thu 6-9, Fri-Sat 6-9.30 Set menu available ⊕ FREE HOUSE ◀ Harvey's Sussex Best Bitter, Guest ales Ŏ Thatchers Gold. **Facilities** Non-diners area ♣ (Bar Restaurant Garden) ⓘ Children's portions Garden ⋒ Parking WiFi ▬ (notice required)

PICK OF THE PUBS

Royal Oak Inn ★★★★★ INN ❀❀

CHICHESTER　　　　　Map 5 SU80

tel: 01243 527434
Pook Ln, East Lavant PO18 0AX
email: info@royaloakeastlavant.co.uk
web: www.royaloakeastlavant.co.uk
dir: *2m N of Chichester. Exit A286 to East Lavant centre*

A smart dining pub with luxury accommodation

Starting life two centuries ago as a farmhouse, the Royal Oak is set within the South Downs National Park and is just up the hill from Goodwood racecourse; it is also perfectly situated for the nearby cathedral city of Chichester. The creeper-clad Georgian inn is at the heart of the beautiful, historic village of East Lavant and is known for offering great food to visitors and locals alike. The brick-lined restaurant and beamed bar achieve a crisp, rustic brand of chic: details include chunky wooden tables, leather chairs, open fires, fresh flowers, candles, and wine attractively displayed in alcoves set into the walls; local Sussex Gold and Horsham Best ales, whiskies and Gospel Green Champagne cider are among the thirst-quenchers on offer. The seasonal menu is an easy mix of modern European dishes and English classics with a twist, and much of the produce is grown by villagers in return for pints. The lovely patio is the perfect

place to enjoy pork and apricot ballotine, with spiced apricot compôte; or beetroot, orange and sorrel risotto perhaps accompanied by one of the 20 wines by the glass. Progress then to a main dish of guinea fowl breast, rösti potatoes, wilted greens with pancetta and wild mushroom jus; seared hake, white bean, chorizo and fennel cassoulet; or a 28-day aged rib-eye steak, thick hand cut chips, baked cherry tomatoes, roast field mushroom with a choice of sauces. Typical desserts are mascarpone and blueberry cheesecake with hedgerow compôte; and Madagascan vanilla seed crème brûlée. There are luxury guest rooms with large, comfortable beds and en suite bathrooms.

Open all day all wk 7am-11.30pm
Food Lunch all wk 11.30-3.30 Dinner all wk 5.30-9.30 Set menu available Restaurant menu available all wk ⊕ FREE HOUSE ◖ Skinner's Betty Stogs, Sharp's Doom Bar, Arundel Sussex Gold, WJ King Horsham Best ♂ Gospel Green Champagne & Cidermakers, Thatchers Gold. ♟ 20 **Facilities** Non-diners area ♦♦ Children's portions Garden ♉ Parking WiFi **Rooms** 8

DUNCTON
Map 6 SU91

The Cricketers

tel: 01798 342473 **GU28 0LB**
email: info@thecricketersduncton.co.uk
dir: On A285, 3m from Petworth, 8m from Chichester

Ideal rest stop when exploring the South Downs

Named to commemorate its one-time owner John Wisden, the first-class cricketer and creator of the famous sporting almanac, this attractive whitewashed pub sits in beautiful gardens behind Goodwood. Dating to the 16th century, with an inglenook fireplace, the inn has hardly changed over the years. Well-kept real ales include Arundel Sussex Gold, while the blackboard menu offers lunchtime sandwiches and traditional favourites, home-cooked from locally sourced ingredients. Look for the likes of a trio of Old English sausages, mash and onion gravy; sizzling pork, pear and parsnip skillet; and confit duck leg, bubble-and-squeak with spiced orange dressing. Children are welcome and there's a menu to suit younger tastes.

Open all day all wk **Food** Lunch Mon-Thu 12-2.30, Fri-Sun 12-9 Dinner Mon-Thu 6-9, Fri-Sun 12-9 Av main course £10.95 ⊕ FREE HOUSE ◀ Triple fff Moondance, Dark Star Partridge Best Bitter, Arundel Sussex Gold, Guest ale Ō Thatchers & Heritage. **Facilities** Non-diners area ✿ (Bar Restaurant Garden) ₦ Children's menu Children's portions Garden ⊨ Parking

EARTHAM
Map 6 SU90

NEW The George

tel: 01243 814340 **PO18 0LT**
email: bookings@thegeorgeeartham.com **web:** www.thegeorgeeartham.com
dir: From A283 (Petworth to Chichester Rd) follow Eartham signs. Inn on right. Or from A27 follow Great Ballard & Eartham signs

Privately owned free house with 'good, honest British food'

First appearing on an 1840 tithe map, this appealing pub is a tad off the beaten track in a quiet South Downs National Park village. Open fires act as magnets on cold days, on warm ones it's the pretty garden that attracts. Devoted to British produce, mostly local, one of its real ales is Langham's Hip Hop, from nine crow-flying miles away. The menu's an easy read, with pheasant breast in smoked bacon with crushed celeriac, roasted root vegetables, and cider and cream celery sauce; and red-wine-braised shin of beef with horseradish mash, roasted baby onions and baby carrots as typical dishes.

Open all day Closed Mon **Food** Lunch 12-3 Dinner 6-9 ⊕ FREE HOUSE ◀ Langham Hip Hop, Otter The George, Rotating Guest ales Ō Westons Old Rosie & Mortimers Orchard. ₹ 12 **Facilities** Non-diners area ✿ (Bar Garden) ₦ Children's portions Garden ⊨ Beer festival Parking WiFi ▭

EAST DEAN
Map 6 SU91

The Star & Garter
PICK OF THE PUBS

tel: 01243 811318 **PO18 0JG**
email: info@thestarandgarter.co.uk
dir: On A286 between Chichester & Midhurst. Exit A286 at Singleton. Village in 2m

Situated in charming downland village

Built as a pub from traditional Sussex flint in about 1740, The Star & Garter stands close to the village pond in the pretty downland village of East Dean. The interior is open and gives a light and airy atmosphere with original brickwork, antique panelling, scrubbed tables and a wood-burning stove. In the bar, two locally brewed real ales are served from the barrel alongside two ciders and a range of wines by the glass. Locally renowned for an excellent selection of fish and shellfish, the menu also includes fine meat and vegetarian dishes, plus sharing platters. Typical choices include roasted guinea fowl with creamy Shropshire Blue sauce; couscous-crusted goats' cheese with red onion salad; and dishes of Selsey crab and lobster. A sunny sheltered patio, an original well and attractive lawned gardens complete the picture. Goodwood's racecourse and motor racing venues are just a short hop by car from here.

Open all wk 11-3 6-11 (Fri 11-3 5-11 Sat-Sun all day) **Food** Lunch Mon-Fri 12-2.30, Sat-Sun 12-4 Dinner Mon-Fri 6.30-9.30, Sat-Sun 6-10 ⊕ FREE HOUSE ◀ Arundel Black Stallion, Castle & Sussex Gold, Guest ales Ō Westons 1st Quality & Stowford Press. ₹ 11 **Facilities** Non-diners area ✿ (Bar Garden) ₦ Children's menu Children's portions Garden ⊨ Parking WiFi ▭

EAST GRINSTEAD
Map 6 TQ33

The Old Dunnings Mill

tel: 01342 821080 **Dunnings Rd RH19 4AT**
email: enquiries@olddunningsmill.co.uk
dir: From High St into Ship St. At mini rdbt right into Dunnings Rd. Pub on right

Good food and local ale in converted water mill

A pub of two halves, parts of the ODM date from the original 16th-century flour mill that inspired its name, while the rest was added in the 1970s. As it's a Harvey's pub, you'll find their real ales in the bar, while on the menu look for a mix of pub classics and more contemporary dishes like chargrilled bacon chop, chorizo sausage cassoulet, winter greens and cider jus. The front garden is fenced, and a stream, which powers a working water-wheel, runs under the covered decking. The ODM holds beer festivals in June and September.

Open all day all wk **Food** Lunch Mon-Sat 12-3, Sun 12-4 Dinner all wk 6-9 Av main course £11 ⊕ HARVEY'S OF LEWES ◀ Sussex Best Bitter Ō Thatchers Gold Apple. **Facilities** Non-diners area ✿ (Bar Garden) ₦ Children's portions Garden ⊨ Beer festival Parking WiFi ▭

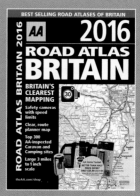

ELSTED — Map 5 SU81

The Three Horseshoes

tel: 01730 825746 **GU29 0JY**
dir: *A272 from Midhurst towards Petersfield, left in 2m signed Harting & Elsted, 3m to pub on left*

Game is a speciality here

With views across fields and woods, this 16th-century former drovers' alehouse is one of those quintessential English country pubs that Sussex specialises in. Tucked below the steep scarp slope of the South Downs National Park, expect unspoilt cottage-style bars, worn stone-flagged floors, low beams, latch doors, a vast inglenook, and a mix of antique furnishings. On fine days the extensive rear garden, with roaming bantams, is hugely popular. Tip-top real ales, including local Ballards, are drawn from the cask, and a daily-changing blackboard menu offers classic country cooking with game abundant in season and treacle tart being a typical dessert.

Open all wk 11-2.30 6-11 (Sun 12-3 7-10.30) **Food** Lunch all wk 12-2 Dinner Mon-Sat 6.30-9, Sun 7-8.30 summer only Av main course £12.95 ⊕ FREE HOUSE ◀ Ballards Best Bitter, Bowman Wallops Wood, Flower Pots, Young's, Langham Hip Hop ♂ Westons Stowford Press. **Facilities** Non-diners area ♣ (Bar Garden) ♦ Children's portions Garden ⋒ Parking

FERNHURST — Map 6 SU82

The Red Lion

tel: 01428 643112 **The Green GU27 3HY**
email: julianredlion@outlook.com
dir: *Just off A286 midway between Haslemere & Midhurst*

Tempting menu in South Downs village

In the dimpled shade of a huge maple, this attractive stone-and-whitewashed inn overlooks a corner of the green in this peaceful village set in the wooded hills of the South Downs National Park. Cricketers from the nearby ground amble here to enjoy Fuller's beers and guest ales, settling in the oak-beamed, fire-warmed heart of the 16th-century building to select from a menu finely balanced between good pub grub (fish and chips, grills) and enticing diversions such as jerk pulled pork; and BBQ piri piri half chicken, winter slaw and chunky chips. Finish with home-made bread and butter pudding perhaps.

Open all day all wk 11.30-11 (Sun 11.30-10.30) **Food** Lunch all wk 12-3 Dinner all wk 6-9.30 ⊕ FULLER'S ◀ ESB, Chiswick Bitter & London Pride, Guest ale ♂ Westons Stowford Press. ☂ 8 **Facilities** Non-diners area ♣ (Bar Garden) ♦ Children's menu Children's portions Garden ⋒ Parking WiFi ➡ (notice required)

HALNAKER — Map 6 SU90

The Anglesey Arms at Halnaker — PICK OF THE PUBS

tel: 01243 773474 **PO18 0NQ**
email: info@angleseyarms.co.uk
dir: *From centre of Chichester 4m E on A285 (Petworth road)*

Country pub with extensive gardens and fine dining

Standing on the Goodwood Estate, is this charming, red-brick Georgian country pub. The village name, in which the 'l' is silent, comes from the Old English for 'half an acre'. The Anglesey is set in its own two acres of landscaped grounds, which include a lovely tree-shaded beer garden. The kitchen team makes skilful use of meats from traceable and organically raised animals, including meat from the estate's farm, as well as locally caught sustainable fish and organic vegetables. The Anglesey has built a special reputation for its Sussex steaks, hung for at least 21 days. Hand-cut sandwiches and ploughman's are available at lunchtime along with a full menu including dressed Selsey crab salad and home-baked ham. For

dinner try a starter of duck and pork rillettes, follow with Thai-style red king prawn curry with basmati rice; or an organic beefburger served with blue cheese, onion rings and fries. At both lunch and dinner, blackboards list daily specials.

Open all wk 11-3 5.30-11 (Fri-Sat 11-11 Sun 12-11) **Food** Lunch Mon-Sat 12-2.30, Sun 12-3 Dinner Mon-Sat 6.30-9.30 ⊕ PUNCH TAVERNS ◀ Young's Bitter, Otter, Guest ales ♂ Westons Stowford Press. ☂ 12 **Facilities** Non-diners area ♣ (Bar Restaurant Garden) ♦ Children's portions Garden ⋒ Parking WiFi ➡

HENLEY — Map 6 SU82

Duke of Cumberland Arms — PICK OF THE PUBS

tel: 01428 652280 **GU27 3HQ**
email: info@thedukeofcumberland.com
dir: *From A286 between Fernhurst & Midhurst take single-track road signed Nicholsons & Aspinals. Pub on right*

'Pretty as a picture' inn with good beers and good food

In an absolutely delightful setting, this beautiful, 16th-century pub, perched on a wooded hillside in the South Downs National Park is a real gem. Inside are flagstones, brick floors, scrubbed tables, and ales served straight from the barrels Harvey's and Langham breweries deliver them in. There's a terrace, and the gardens are lovely, with fabulous views of the Weald, pools of trout, and plenty of places to sit, whether you're having a pint or stopping for something more substantial. The first-rate menus impress at lunchtime with Cornish moules marinière, or a slow-cooked pulled pork bap; while in the evening you might be choosing from hand-made Jerusalem artichoke and truffle ravioli, bacon and parmesan velouté, with wilted spinach and artichoke crisps; or pan-seared scallops with cauliflower purée and black pudding, followed by eight-hour braised lamb shank with roast garlic mash, green beans and mint jus; or spinach and mushroom stuffed wholemeal pancakes.

Open all day all wk **Food** Lunch all wk 12-2 Dinner Tue-Sat 7-9 ⊕ FREE HOUSE ◀ Harvey's Sussex, Langham Best Bitter & Hip Hop ♂ Westons Stowford Press. ☂ **Facilities** Non-diners area ♣ (Bar Garden) ♦ Children's portions Garden ⋒ Parking WiFi

HEYSHOTT — Map 6 SU81

Unicorn Inn — PICK OF THE PUBS

tel: 01730 813486 **GU29 0DL**
email: unicorninnheyshott@hotmail.co.uk
dir: *Phone for detailed directions*

A favourite with walkers and cyclists plus great views

Enjoying stunning views of the South Downs from its beautiful, south-facing rear garden, Jenni Halpin's 18th-century free house is the perfect spot to relax on sunny day with a pint of Adnams. This sleepy Sussex village is in the National Park, so it's a fair bet that you'll share the pub with walkers and cyclists (and, of course, some locals) seeking out the home-cooked food listed on seasonal menus that make sound use of locally sourced produce. The bar, with beams and a large log fire, is particularly atmospheric, while the subtly lit, cream-painted restaurant is where you can sample fresh fish from Selsey, or dishes like grilled pork belly with Stilton sauce; rib-eye steak; fish pie; or pheasant breast with apricot and date stuffing. Good sandwiches (perhaps roast beef and horseradish) and popular Sunday lunches complete the pleasing picture.

Open all day Tue-Sat all day (Sun 12-4) Closed 2wks Jan (contact pub for details), Sun eve & Mon (except BHs & Summer) **Food** Lunch Tue-Sat 11.30-2, Sun 12-2.30 Dinner Tue-Sat 6-9.30 Restaurant menu available Tue-Sun ⊕ FREE HOUSE ◀ Adnams, Sharp's Doom Bar, Arundel Sussex Gold ♂ Westons Stowford Press. **Facilities** Non-diners area ♣ (Bar Garden) ♦ Children's menu Children's portions Garden ⋒ Parking ➡ (notice required)

HORSHAM
Map 6 TQ13

The Black Jug

tel: 01403 253526 **31 North St RH12 1RJ**
email: black.jug@brunningandprice.co.uk
dir: Phone for detailed directions

Recommended for its eclectic menu

This handsome, tile-hung and gabled pub has served the discerning clientele of Horsham town centre for around 200 years. With a trim garden and copious flower displays outside; the interior is a delightful mix of panelling, classic time-worn pub furniture and a warm atmosphere free of music and gaming machines. Up to six beers and some cracking traditional ciders slake the thirst, whilst an indulgent, quality menu may feature ham hock and mozzarella arancini; chilli and prawn linguine; venison casserole; sweet potato curry; Malaysian fish stew; and steak and kidney pie. Lite bites, sandwiches, a children's menu, and a tempting range of puddings are available too. Please note that although dogs are welcome they are not allowed in the conservatory area.

Open all day all wk **Food** Contact pub for food times ⏣ BRUNNING & PRICE 🍺 Harvey's, Caledonian Deuchars IPA, Rotating Guest ales ⚗ Aspall, Westons Stowford Press, Rotating Guest ciders. ☙ 19 **Facilities** Non-diners area 🐾 (Bar Garden Outside area) ♦ Children's portions Garden Outside area ⊟ Beer festival Cider festival WiFi

HORSTED KEYNES
Map 6 TQ32

NEW The Crown Inn
PICK OF THE PUBS

tel: 01825 791609 **The Green RH17 7AW**
email: info@thecrown-horstedkeynes.co.uk
dir: From A272 at North Chailey (E of Haywards Heath) take A275 towards East Grinstead. In Daneshill left signed Horsted Keynes

Great food in a lovely old building

The Crown dates back to the 16th century, and has been serving locals and travellers for more than 250 years. Back in 2003 a lightning strike caused serious damage, and large parts of the building were destroyed. Fortunately the oldest parts were untouched and, after being closed for five years, it finally reopened. In 2013 Mark Raffan, former co-owner of Gravetye Manor, took over. His aim? To bring elegant yet relaxed fine dining to this cosy, traditional inn. There are comforting real fires in winter and a glorious patio garden overlooking the village cricket green for warmer days. Have a pint of Harvey's Sussex Best Bitter while you check out the menu; there are bar snacks and sandwiches, or you could have Portland Bay potted crab with smoked salmon to begin, followed by pan-fried calves' liver and bacon with bubble-and-squeak. Finish with blackcurrant cheesecake.

Open all wk 12-3 5-11 (Sat 12-11 Sun 12-9) Closed 25 Dec **Food** Lunch Mon-Fri 12-2, Sat 12-2.30, Sun 12-4 Dinner Mon-Thu 6-9, Fri-Sat 6-9.30 Av main course £16 Restaurant menu available all wk ⏣ FREE HOUSE 🍺 Harvey's Sussex Best Bitter, Sharp's Doom Bar. ☙ 10 **Facilities** Non-diners area 🐾 (Bar Outside area) ♦ Children's portions Outside area ⊟ Parking WiFi 🚐 (notice required)

HURSTPIERPOINT
Map 6 TQ21

The New Inn

tel: 01273 834608 **76 High St BN6 9RQ**
email: info@thenewinnhurst.com
dir: In village centre

Bustling village local with large beer garden

Despite its name, The New Inn actually dates back as far as 1450 and it has been a hub of the village ever since. Just off the A23 to the north of the South Downs National Park, this bustling village is also a short hop from Brighton. Whether it's one of the four areas in the pub or in the pretty beer garden, The New Inn is an ideal pitstop to enjoy local Harvey's ales or one of the 10 wines by the glass with dishes

such as tiger prawn and coconut curry or honey-glazed pheasant with Savoy cabbage and bacon.

Open all day all wk **Food** Lunch all wk 12-3 Dinner all wk 6-9 Restaurant menu available all wk ⏣ PUNCH TAVERNS 🍺 Harvey's ⚗ Symonds, Thatchers. ☙ 10 **Facilities** Non-diners area 🐾 (Bar Garden) ♦ Children's menu Children's portions Play area Garden ⊟ WiFi 🚐

KINGSFOLD
Map 6 TQ13

The Dog and Duck

tel: 01306 627295 **Dorking Rd RH12 3SA**
email: info@thedogandduck.fsnet.co.uk
dir: On A24, 3m N of Horsham

Children and dogs very welcome

The Dog and Duck is a 16th-century family-run and family-friendly country pub serving enjoyable food like cottage pie, home-made curry and chicken and bacon pie, washed down with Dorset Best. There's plenty of children's play equipment in the huge garden and three very large fields that encourage canines and energetic owners to stretch their legs. The rest of the year sees the diary chock-full of celebratory events, including the charity fundraising beer festival, summer camp, hallowe'en party and firework display.

Open all wk 12-3 6-11 (Fri 12-3 6-12 Sat 12-12 Sun 12-10) **Food** Lunch Mon-Sat 12-2, Sun 12-3 (bkfst all wk 9.30am-noon) Dinner Mon-Sat 6-9 Av main course £9.95 ⏣ HALL & WOODHOUSE 🍺 Badger K&B Sussex, Dorset Best, Seasonal ales ⚗ Westons Stowford Press. **Facilities** Non-diners area 🐾 (Bar Garden) ♦ Children's menu Children's portions Play area Garden ⊟ Beer festival Cider festival Parking 🚐 (notice required)

The Owl at Kingsfold

tel: 01306 628499 **Dorking Rd RH12 3SA**
email: info@theowl-kingsfold.co.uk **web:** www.theowl-kingsfold.co.uk
dir: On A24, 4m N of Horsham

In a hamlet just 20 minutes from the sea

A traditional country free house with wooden beams, flagstone floors and log burners. It occupies a prominent roadside site in the village, with plenty of parking and a garden with views to the Surrey Hills; composer Ralph Vaughan Williams reputedly arranged the hymn *Kingsfold* here. There are three real ales to choose from, while the frequently changing lunch menu might include West Sussex smokie or home-made liver pâté to start, followed by slow-roasted shoulder of lamb; home-made stout and Stilton pie, or roast, sticky lime, half chicken and chips; a specials board adds to the choices.

Open all day all wk 11-11 **Food** Lunch Mon-Sat 12-2.30, Sun 12-6 Dinner Mon-Sat 6-9 ⏣ FREE HOUSE 🍺 St Austell Tribute, Rotating guest ale ⚗ Westons. ☙ 12 **Facilities** Non-diners area ♦ Children's menu Children's portions Garden ⊟ Parking WiFi

LAMBS GREEN
Map 6 TQ23

The Lamb Inn

tel: 01293 871336 & 871933 **RH12 4RG**
email: lambinnrusper@yahoo.co.uk
dir: *6m from Horsham between Rusper & Faygate. 5m from Crawley*

Unspoilt village local with a long list of ciders and beers

Landlords Ben and Chris run a successful modern business within the ancient framework of their unspoilt, rustic country pub. They serve some great local beers and ciders in the beamed bar – too many to list, sadly, but there's Dark Star Hophead for one, while from Somerset comes Weston's Old Rosie. As much as possible, menus feature locally sourced produce, typical dishes being Sussex steak and ale pie; wild rabbit casserole; chargrilled sirloin steak; and pan-seared swordfish steak with chorizo, cherry tomatoes and sherry.

Open all wk Mon-Thu 11.30-3 5.30-11 (Fri-Sat 11.30-11 Sun 12-10.30) Closed 25-26 Dec **Food** Lunch Mon-Thu 12-2, Fri-Sat 12-9.30, Sun 12-9 Dinner Mon-Thu 6.30-9.30, Fri-Sat 12-9.30, Sun 12-9 Set menu available ⊕ FREE HOUSE ◀ WJ King Kings Old Ale, Weltons Old Cocky, Langham LSD, Dark Star Hophead & Partridge Best Bitter Ŏ Westons Stowford Press & Old Rosie, Biddenden, Rekorderlig. ♀ 12 **Facilities** Non-diners area ✿ (Bar Outside area) ♦♦ Children's menu Children's portions Outside area ☷ Beer festival Parking WiFi ➡ (notice required)

LODSWORTH
Map 6 SU92

The Halfway Bridge Inn ★★★★★ INN ◉ PICK OF THE PUBS

tel: 01798 861281 **Halfway Bridge GU28 9BP**
email: enquiries@halfwaybridge.co.uk **web:** www.halfwaybridge.co.uk
dir: *Between Petworth & Midhurst, adjacent to Cowdray Estate & Golf Club on A272*

Excellent food on South Downs National Park's doorstep

A pretty road, the A272 has many attractions, one being this renovated, 17th-century traditional pub and contemporary dining inn. It stands roughly equidistant from Midhurst, home of the Cowdray Estate and British polo, and Petworth, with its National Trust mansion. Travellers stopping at this inn will find tastefully furnished rooms with beamed ceilings, log fires and peaceful patio and garden. Those seeking a truly local pint will find real ales from Langham, brewed a mile away, and Sussex Gold from the Arundel Brewery. Lighter meals include grilled gammon steak, fried duck eggs and hand-cut chips; salmon and smoked salmon fishcakes with French-style peas; and open sandwiches, ciabattas and salads. From the mains selection there might be Moroccan braised lamb shank, apricots, prunes with toasted almond and minted pearl couscous; chicken green Thai curry and jasmine rice; and light beer battered haddock fillet with hand-cut chips and tartare sauce. Daily specials are listed on a blackboard. Leave room for one of the tempting desserts, perhaps honey, vanilla and cinnamon poached pear with cranberry sauce.

Open all day all wk 11-11 **Food** Lunch Mon-Fri 12-2.30, Sat-Sun 12-6 Dinner Mon-Thu 6-9.30, Fri-Sat 6-10, Sun 6-9 Av main course £15 Restaurant menu available all wk ⊕ FREE HOUSE ◀ Langham, Arundel Sussex Gold Ŏ Thatchers. ♀ 24 **Facilities** Non-diners area ✿ (Bar Garden) ♦♦ Children's menu Children's portions Garden ☷ Parking WiFi **Rooms** 7

LOWER BEEDING
Map 6 TQ22

The Crabtree

tel: 01403 892666 **Brighton Rd RH13 6PT**
email: info@crabtreesussex.com
dir: *On A281 between Cowfold & Horsham, opposite South Lodge Hotel*

Good, seasonal food in the lovely Sussex countryside

Visit the family-run Crabtree and you'll be following in the footsteps of author and poet Hilaire Belloc who was often to be found here. The inn, originally built in 1539, is located in beautiful countryside which is where the pub sources the vast majority of their produce. Trusty local companies supply meat from high welfare farms and the daily caught fish and shellfish come via the harbour at nearby Shoreham. Start perhaps with grilled South Coast mackerel and wasabi mayonnaise; followed by whole roast red legged partridge, creamed potato, smoked bacon, hispi cabbage and red wine sauce; or pan-fried sea bream, leek and mussel chowder, new potatoes and crispy leeks. The enticing dessert menu might include olive oil cake, chocolate mousse and white chocolate ice cream.

Open all day all wk **Food** Lunch all wk 12-9 Dinner all wk 12-9 Av main course £10 Set menu available Restaurant menu available all wk ⊕ HALL & WOODHOUSE ◀ Badger Tanglefoot, K&B Sussex Ŏ Westons Stowford Press, Wobblegate. ♀ 20 **Facilities** Non-diners area ✿ (Bar Garden) ♦♦ Children's portions Garden ☷ Parking WiFi

LURGASHALL
Map 6 SU92

The Noah's Ark

tel: 01428 707346 **The Green GU28 9ET**
email: amy@noahsarkinn.co.uk **web:** www.noahsarkinn.co.uk
dir: *B2131 from Haslemere follow signs to Petworth/Lurgashall. A3 from London towards Portsmouth. At Milford take A283 signed Petworth. Follow signs to Lurgashall*

16th-century inn at the height of country chic

In a picturesque village beneath Blackdown Hill, this attractive 16th-century inn overlooks the cricket green. The pretty, shabby-chic interior is full of warmth thanks to the charm of old beams, a large inglenook fireplace, muted colours, pale wooden furniture, fresh flowers and the enthusiasm of its owners. In addition to the Greene King ales is a regularly changing guest, and the traditional British food with a contemporary twist uses seasonal ingredients carefully sourced from the best local suppliers. The menu is concise but enticing: twice baked cheese soufflé may precede a main course of smoked haddock with potatoes, spinach, poached egg and hollandaise sauce.

Open all day all wk 11-11 (Sun 12-10 summer Sun 12-8 winter) **Food** Lunch Mon-Sat 12-2.30, Sun 12-3 Dinner Mon-Sat 7-9.30 ⊕ GREENE KING ◀ IPA & Abbot Ale,

Guest ale Ő Westons Stowford Press. **Facilities** Non-diners area ❤ (Bar Garden) ◉♦ Children's menu Children's portions Garden ⯗ Parking WiFi ⊞ (notice required)

See advert below

MAPLEHURST
Map 6 TQ12

The White Horse

tel: 01403 891208 **Park Ln RH13 6LL**
dir: *5m SE of Horsham, between A281 & A272*

Village-brewed cider and local ales prove a draw

This rural free house has been under the same family ownership for over 30 years and lies deep in the Sussex countryside. It offers a welcome haven free from music and fruit machines. Hearty home-cooked pub food, such as their popular chilli; and ham, free-range egg and chips plus an enticing selection of five real ales are served over what is reputed to be the widest bar counter in Sussex. Sip a pint of Harvey's Sussex Best Bitter or Weltons Pridenjoy whilst admiring the rolling countryside from the large, quiet, south-facing garden. Village-brewed cider is a speciality.

Open 12-2.30 6-11 (Sun 12-3 7-11) Closed Mon L **Food** Lunch Tue-Sun 12-2 Dinner Mon-Sat 6-9, Sun 7-9 Av main course £7 ⊕ FREE HOUSE ◄ Harvey's Sussex Best Bitter, Weltons Pridenjoy, Guest ales Ő JB, Local cider. ☍ 11 **Facilities** Non-diners area ❤ (Bar Garden) ◉♦ Children's menu Children's portions Play area Family room Garden ⯗ Parking WiFi ⊞ (notice required) **Notes** ☺

OVING
Map 6 SU90

The Gribble Inn

tel: 01243 786893 **PO20 2BP**
dir: *From A27 take A259. After 1m left at rdbt, 1st right to Oving, 1st left in village*

Pub and microbrewery with added extras

This charming 16th-century inn contains a village store, coffee shop and microbrewery, as well as a pub, within its walls. It is a peaceful spot to sup any of the own-brewed real ales plus a choice of five or six seasonal extras; takeaway polypins are also sold. The inn is named after school teacher, Rose Gribble, who up until her death, lived in the building. Today it has large open fireplaces, wood burners, low beams and no background music. From the daily-changing menu, enjoy traditional pub food such as beer-battered haddock or slow-roast pork belly. The inn hosts summer and winter beer festivals, and there is also a skittle alley, enjoyed by parties and works' social functions.

Open all day all wk 11-11 **Food** Lunch Mon-Sat 12-9, Sun 12-4 Dinner Mon-Sat 12-9 ⊕ HALL & WOODHOUSE ◄ Gribble Ale, Reg's Tipple, Pig's Ear, Fuzzy Duck, Plucking Pheasant & Sussex Quad Hopper, Gribble Wobbler & Pukka Mild Ő Westons Stowford Press & Rosie's Pig. ☍ 20 **Facilities** Non-diners area ❤ (Bar Garden) ◉♦ Children's menu Children's portions Family room Garden ⯗ Beer festival Parking ⊞

PETWORTH
Map 6 SU92

The Angel Inn ★★ HL

tel: 01798 344445 & 342153 **Angel St GU28 OBG**
email: enquiries@angelinnpetworth.co.uk **web:** www.angelinnpetworth.co.uk
dir: *From Petworth centre take A283 E towards Fittleworth, pub on left*

A real gem in a delightful town

Bowed walls, exposed beams, head-cracking doorways and sloping floors all testify
to the Angel's medieval origins, especially in the bedrooms. So too do the ships'
beams and three open fireplaces, one of which is used to spit-roast joints of meat.
Petworth's Langham Brewery supplies real ales. The modern British menu changes
four times a year; there are also fortnightly and daily specials. Expect dishes such
as crispy confit of duck with cherry liqueur sauce; Sussex wild venison casserole;
The Angel fish pie; and warm Thai beef salad. The walled patio garden can be a
real sun-trap.

Open all day all wk 10.30am-11pm (Sun 11.30-10.30) **Food** Lunch all wk 12-2.30
Dinner Mon-Sat 6.30-9.30, Sun 6-9 ⊕ FREE HOUSE ◀ Langham, Guest ales
Ö Aspall, Addlestones. ₹ 25 **Facilities** Non-diners area ✿ (Bar Garden) ♦ Children's
menu Children's portions Garden ⊣ Parking WiFi **Rooms** 6

POYNINGS
Map 6 TQ21

Royal Oak
PICK OF THE PUBS

tel: 01273 857389 **The Street BN45 7AQ**
email: mail@royaloakpoynings.pub
dir: *From A23 onto A281 signed Henfield & Poynings*

Dining pub in downland village

In a pretty South Downs National Park village and close to the remarkable Devil's
Dyke, this pub occupies a lovely spot that's handy for glorious downland walks. In
summer, the wonderful garden boasts excellent barbecue facilities, serene rural
views. Beyond the handsome exterior, the contemporary decor inside is an effortless
blend of solid oak floors, old beams hung with hop bines and sumptuous sofas. In
the bar, Harvey's Sussex Best Bitter sits alongside Westons cider and perry, and the
accessible wine list includes New and Old World wines with up to 14 by the glass.
The menu changes seasonally and is driven by local produce. Booking ahead for
meals is advised. Gregarious grazers will appreciate the shared charcuterie platter
of Serrano ham, Milano salami, pastrami, piccalilli, caper berries, and olives with
warm ciabatta; then mains could be beef, mushroom and ale pie; Royal Oak fish
pie; twice baked pork belly; or hand-made Sussex beefburger. Puddings are no less
tempting – perhaps the trio of bananas could round off an excellent meal.

Open all day all wk 11-11 (Sun 12-10.30) **Food** Lunch all wk 12-9.30 Dinner all wk
12-9.30 ⊕ FREE HOUSE ◀ Harvey's Sussex Best Bitter, Guest ale Ö Westons Family
Reserve & Country Perry. ₹ 14 **Facilities** Non-diners area ♦ Children's menu
Children's portions Play area Garden ⊣ Parking WiFi ▭ (notice required)

ROWHOOK
Map 6 TQ13

The Chequers Inn ◉
PICK OF THE PUBS

tel: 01403 790480 **RH12 3PY**
email: thechequersrowhook@googlemail.com
dir: *From Horsham A281 towards Guildford. At rdbt take A29 signed London. In 200mtrs
left, follow Rowhook signs*

Award-winning food in delightful country pub

A striking, 400-year-old higgledy-piggledy pub with a classic interior of flagstone
floor, low beams and blazing fire in the inglenook, The Chequers Inn is run by
Master Chef of Great Britain Tim Neal, also the holder of an AA Rosette. The bar
offers Harvey's Sussex and Long Man Best Bitter on tap and an impressive wine list
to partner the extensive bar menu (ploughman's, ciabattas, fish and chips, sausage
and mash), which may also be eaten in the inn's restaurant. Tim delights in using
only the best local produce, often sourcing seasonal wild mushrooms and even

truffles from the generous woodlands near the hamlet of Rowhook. From the
restaurant menu (also served in the bar), begin with Roquefort cheese pannacotta
with toasted walnuts and pear chutney, followed perhaps by crispy hake fillet with a
tomato, chorizo and butterbean ragu, buttered spinach and crisp potato; or local
sirloin steak with fondant potato, spinach, French beans, wild mushroom sauce and
foie gras.

Open 11.30-3.30 6-11.30 (Sun 12-3.30) Closed 25 Dec, Sun eve & BHs eve
Food Lunch all wk 12-2 Dinner Mon-Sat 7-9 Av main course £10.50 Restaurant
menu available all wk ⊕ FREE HOUSE ◀ Harvey's Sussex, Long Man Best Bitter,
Firebird Heritage XX Ö Thatchers Gold. ₹ 10 **Facilities** Non-diners area ✿ (Bar
Garden) Children's portions Garden ⊣ Parking

SHIPLEY
Map 6 TQ12

The Countryman Inn
PICK OF THE PUBS

See Pick of the Pubs on opposite page

SINGLETON
Map 5 SU81

The Partridge Inn

tel: 01243 811251 **PO18 0EY**
email: info@thepartridgeinn.co.uk
dir: *Phone for detailed directions*

Delightful country pub run by a former top London chef

Set within the picturesque Goodwood Estate in a South Downs' village, this pub
dates back to the 16th century when the huge hunting park was owned by the
FitzAlan family, Earls of Arundel. Today, the pub is popular with walkers enjoying
the rolling Sussex countryside and visitors to Goodwood's motor sports and
horseracing events. Run by Giles Thompson, former executive head chef of The Ritz
London, you can expect a friendly welcome, great ales from the likes of Hop Back,
and food firmly based in the English pub tradition. Perhaps try chicken liver parfait
with honey chutney; or deep-fried whitebait with home-made tartare sauce to start,
and follow with lamb's liver and smoked bacon, buttered mash, winter vegetables
and onion gravy; or pork belly slow roast, chilli and apple relish, fresh greens with
garlic and rosemary potatoes. Supper clubs, pie-and-a-pint and steak nights take
place every week.

Open all wk Mon-Fri 12-3 6-11 (Sat-Sun all day) **Food** Lunch Mon-Fri 12-2.30,
Sat-Sun 12-3 Dinner Mon-Thu & Sun 6-9, Fri-Sat 6-9.30 Av main course £13.50
⊕ ENTERPRISE INNS ◀ Fuller's London Pride, Harvey's Sussex, Hop Back Summer
Lightning Ö Westons Stowford Press. ₹ 19 **Facilities** Non-diners area ✿ (Bar
Garden) ♦ Children's menu Children's portions Garden ⊣ Parking WiFi

SLINDON
Map 6 SU90

The Spur

tel: 01243 814216 **BN18 0NE**
email: thespurslindon@btinternet.com
dir: *From A27 take A29 signed Slindon*

Pretty pub with lovely garden for alfresco drinking and eating

Set just outside the village of Slindon on top of the rolling South Downs, this
17th-century pub is a an ideal stopping-off point on a day out in the country. It has
been praised for its friendly atmosphere and for generous portions of food. Outside
are large pub gardens and a courtyard, inside is an open-plan bar and restaurant,
warmed by crackling log fires. Daily-changing bar meals are on the blackboard,
and may include lamb cutlets, steak and kidney pie, and fresh fish and shellfish.
A skittle alley and function room are also available.

Open all wk 11.30-3 6-11 (Sun 12-10) **Food** Lunch Mon-Sat 12-2, Sun 12-8 Dinner
Mon-Tue 7-9, Wed-Sat 7-9.30, Sun 12-8 ⊕ FREE HOUSE ◀ Sharp's Doom Bar,
Courage Directors Ö Thatchers Gold. ₹ 10 **Facilities** Non-diners area ✿ (Bar
Garden) ♦ Children's menu Children's portions Garden ⊣ Beer festival Parking ▭

PICK OF THE PUBS

The Countryman Inn

SHIPLEY   Map 6 TQ12

tel: 01403 741383
Countryman Ln RH13 8PZ
email: countrymaninn@btinternet.com
web: www.countrymanshipley.co.uk
dir: *A272 at Coolham into Smithers Hill Ln. 1m, left at T-junct*

A real old fashioned, traditional pub that ticks all the boxes

Alan Vaughan and his family, who have been successfully running this traditional rural free house for nearly 30 years, have certainly found the recipe for pleasing their customers. Surrounding the inn is the Knepp Castle Estate, 3,500 acres devoted to nature conservation through regeneration and restoration projects. In the pub's log fire-warmed bar, you'll find cask-conditioned beers from Sussex-brewed Harvey's, Langham and Long Man, Shepherd Neame from Kent. Making their way to the kitchen are fish landed at Shoreham and Newhaven, the two closest ports, free-range meats from local farms; game from the Knepp Estate, vegetables and salads grown in the pub's own half-acre garden, and through a 'swop shop' arrangement with villagers something unusual often appears on the menu, such as quince, kohlrabi or romanesco. Any surplus garden produce can be purchased in the bar. Country baguettes and flatbreads come filled with prawn and crayfish;

sausage and onion; and brie and redcurrant, while an alternative might be the all-day breakfast. Regular starters and grazing plates are hoi sin lamb wrap; salt 'n' pepper squid; and smörgåsbord of fish, which might be followed by one pot lamb stew with dumplings; vegetable Thai green curry; beef and mushroom shortcrust pie, mash and seasonal vegetables; or slow-roast pork belly, bubble-and-squeak, cabbage and bacon with caramelised onion and Calvados jus. Children are welcome in the restaurant, although the inn doesn't have a separate play area or family dining room. In the garden, weather permitting, an open-air kitchen serves grills, ploughman's and other snacks. In the pub's own farm shop you can buy free-range eggs and

home-made preserves, pickles and relishes.

Open all wk 10-4 6-11 **Food** Lunch all wk 11.30-3.30 Dinner all wk 6-9.30 Restaurant menu available all wk
🍺 FREE HOUSE 🍺 Harvey's, Langham, Shepherd Neame, Long Man, King Beer, Guest ales 🍏 Thatchers Gold. 🍷 18
Facilities Non-diners area 🚻 Children's portions Garden 🪑 Parking WiFi

SOUTH HARTING   Map 5 SU71

The White Hart

tel: 01730 825124 **The Street GU31 5QB**
email: info@the-whitehart.co.uk
dir: From Petersfield take B2146 to South Harting

A stylish interior at this cosy inn

An engaging mix of beams and timber framing, log-burners, rustic furnishings, deep leather chairs and an eye-catching stone fireplace set the scene at this 16th-century inn at the heart of a pretty village in the South Downs. Ramblers diverting from the nearby long-distance footpath sup beers from Upham Brewery's tasty range, kept well by the licensees who also tempt with a good menu. Home cooking and local producers ensure that both standard dishes and ever-changing specials have something for all tastes. Crispy duck salad, pomegranate, red onion and roast garlic mayo; or a meat and fish sharing board could kick things off, before moving on to pan-fried hake, wild mushrooms, watercress, new potatoes, clams and bacon marinière perhaps. Views from the garden encompass the rolling downland edges.

Open all day all wk **Food** Lunch all wk 12-2.30 Dinner all wk 6-9.30 ⊕ FREE HOUSE ◀ Upham Punter & Tipster Ò Somersby Cider. 🍷 9 **Facilities** Non-diners area 🐾 (Bar Garden Outside area) ♦♦ Children's menu Children's portions Garden Outside area ⋒ Parking WiFi

STEDHAM   Map 5 SU82

Hamilton Arms/Nava Thai Restaurant

tel: 01730 812555 **Hamilton Arms, School Ln GU29 0NZ**
email: hamiltonarms@hotmail.com **web:** www.thehamiltonarms.co.uk
dir: Follow Stedham sign from A272 between Midhurst & Petersfield. Pub on left in village

Well known for the excellent Thai food

Smiling Thai staff serve authentic Thai food and beers in this whitewashed free house opposite the village common – but if you prefer you can opt for English bar snacks and ales, including the Hamilton's own draught Armless. Thai food devotees will be spoilt for choice – the extensive menu ranges from soups, salads and curries through to the vegetarian menu. There's a £10 2-course lunch menu (Monday-Saturday) and takeaways are available too. The pub is home to the Mudita Trust, which helps abused and underprivileged children in Thailand.

Open all day Closed Mon (ex BHs) **Food** Lunch Tue-Sun 12-2.30 Dinner Tue-Sun 6-10 Av main course £8.50 Set menu available Restaurant menu available Tue-Sun ⊕ FREE HOUSE ◀ Fuller's London Pride, Triple fff Alton's Pride, Hamilton Armless, Dark Star Hophead, Skinner's Betty Stogs. 🍷 8 **Facilities** Non-diners area 🐾 (Bar Garden) ♦♦ Children's menu Children's portions Play area Garden ⋒ Parking WiFi 🚌

TILLINGTON   Map 6 SU92

The Horse Guards Inn ★★★★ INN ◉   PICK OF THE PUBS

tel: 01798 342332 **GU28 9AF**
email: info@thehorseguardsinn.co.uk **web:** www.thehorseguardsinn.co.uk
dir: From Petworth towards Midhurst on A272. 1m, right signed Tillington. Inn 300mtrs up hill opposite church

South Downs National Park village dining pub

Handy for the National Trust's Petworth House and its impressive art collection – Reynolds, Turner and Van Dyck – this 350-year-old inn's name recalls that the Household Cavalry would rest their horses in the parkland opposite. The tasteful interior features sagging beams, stripped floorboards, open fires (on one of which you can roast chestnuts), antique furnishings, fresh flowers and candles. The bar offers a fine range of real ales and ciders, while on the compact, seasonal, AA Rosette menu dishes often incorporate goodies from Sussex hedgerows and seashores. Begin with home-cured rose veal, celeriac and lovage remoulade; follow with South Downs pigeon breasts, gratin potatoes, baby carrots, curly kale, and beetroot and red wine gravy; or chickpea curry with red cabbage slaw, giant bean bhaji, and cucumber and pomegranate raita. Lastly, maybe, chocolate pistachio torte with hazelnut brittle. Deck-chairs, sheepskin-covered benches and even straw bales provide seating in the tree-shaded garden.

Open all day all wk **Food** Lunch Mon-Fri 12-2.30, Sat 12-3, Sun 12-3.30 Dinner all wk 6.30-9 Av main course £12-£15 ⊕ ENTERPRISE INNS ◀ Harvey's Sussex Best Bitter, Skinner's Betty Stogs, Staropramen, Otter Bitter, Guinness Ò Westons Stowford Press & Old Rosie. 🍷 16 **Facilities** Non-diners area 🐾 (Bar Restaurant Garden) ♦♦ Children's menu Children's portions Garden ⋒ WiFi 🚌 (notice required) **Rooms** 3

WALDERTON   Map 5 SU71

The Barley Mow

tel: 023 9263 1321 **PO18 9ED**
email: info@thebarleymowpub.co.uk
dir: From Chichester take B2178 (East Ashling). Through East Ashling (road becomes B2146). In Funtington right into Hares Ln signed Walderton. At T-junct right. 0.5m to Walderton. Turn right at Walderton village sign, pub 100yds on left

Popular Sunday carvery and pretty garden

Famous locally for its skittle alley, this 18th-century pub is a favourite with walkers, cyclists and horse-riders. Its secluded, stream-bordered garden is a real sun-trap; in the log-fire-warmed bar house beer Tichbourne Ale is accompanied by a rolling four-guest roster. Starters include home-made gravad lax with rye bread and marinated cucumber; and charcuterie sharing platter: among the mains are calves' liver, bacon and onion gravy; beer-battered cod fillet with chips and minted pea purée; and gnocchi caponata. Booking is strongly advised for the popular Sunday carvery. The nearby Kingley Vale Nature Reserve contains a grove of some of Britain's oldest trees.

Open all day all wk 11-11 **Food** Lunch all day Dinner all day Av main course £7-£15 Restaurant menu available all wk ⊕ FREE HOUSE ◀ Tichbourne, 4 rotating guest ales Ò Westons Stowford Press, Aspall. 🍷 13 **Facilities** Non-diners area 🐾 (Bar Garden) ♦♦ Children's menu Children's portions Garden ⋒ Parking WiFi 🚌 (notice required)

WARNINGLID
Map 6 TQ22

The Half Moon

tel: 01444 461227 **The Street RH17 5TR**
email: info@thehalfmoonwarninglid.co.uk
dir: 1m from Warninglid & Cuckfield junct on A23 & 6m from Haywards Heath

Family-owned country inn that's welcoming whatever the season

This picture-perfect Grade II listed building dates from the 18th century and has been sympathetically extended to preserve its traditional feel. Look out for the glass-topped well as you come in. Enjoy a pint of Harvey's or a real cider while perusing the menu, which offers specials and pub classics. Try chicken and rabbit liver parfait with red onion marmalade; pan-fried sea bass fillet, beetroot purée, orange braised chicory and sauté potatoes; wild mushroom, sun-blushed tomato and mozzarella potato gnocchi; or calves' liver, smoked bacon, bubble-and-squeak, kale and onion gravy. The pub garden is home to a 250-year-old cider press.

Open all wk 11.30-2.30 5.30-11 (Sat 11.30-11 Sun 11.30-10.30) **Food** Lunch Mon-Sat 12-2, Sun 12-3 Dinner Mon-Sat 6-9.30 ⊕ FREE HOUSE ◄ Harvey's Sussex & Old Ale, Dark Star ♂ The Orchard Pig. ♀ 12 **Facilities** Non-diners area ❤ (Bar Garden) ♦ Children's menu Children's portions Family room Garden ⊼ Parking WiFi (notice required)

WEST ASHLING
Map 5 SU80

The Richmond Arms ◉

tel: 01243 572046 **Mill Rd PO18 8EA**
email: richmondarms@gmail.com
dir: Phone for detailed directions

Raising the beer and pizza game

Thatched flint cottages and a quiet millpond characterise this old village. The Richmond Arms is young by comparison, but this welcoming pub is drawing custom from far afield with its attractive combination of happy interiors, Harvey's beers, sumptuous wine carte, and interesting menus. You might start with Keralan-style guinea fowl pie; followed by lamb cheeks, feta curd, peas, beans, and crispy mint. Outside there's the WoodFired family-friendly bar with a vintage Citroën van that houses a wood-fired pizza oven, stoked up on Friday and Saturday evenings.

Open 11-3 6-11 Closed 23 Dec-12 Jan, 23-30 Jul, Sun eve, Mon & Tue **Food** Lunch 12-2.30 Dinner 6-9.30 ⊕ FREE HOUSE ◄ Harvey's Sussex Hadlow Bitter, Star of Eastbourne, Armada Ale & Tom Paine Ale ♂ Aspall. ♀ 14 **Facilities** Non-diners area ❤ (Bar Outside area) ♦ Children's menu Children's portions Outside area ⊼ Parking WiFi

---

WEST DEAN
Map 5 SU81

The Dean Ale & Cider House ★★★★ INN

tel: 01243 811465 **Main Rd PO18 0QX**
email: thebar@thedeaninn.co.uk **web:** www.thedeaninn.co.uk
dir: Between Chichester & Midhurst on A286

Contemporary community pub on the downs

In a village of flint and thatch properties between the South Downs and Chichester Harbour, this 200-year-old contemporary country dining inn is a great place to relax and unwind. It maintains a community pub ethos, with drinkers revelling in the choice of real ales and a draught traditional cider. With a home-based smokery preserving meat, fish and cheese, the kitchen team produces an arresting range of pub stalwarts and modern dishes, using materials derived from the local catchment area. Smartly converted barns skirting the courtyard house the contemporary accommodation, handy for race-goers to nearby Goodwood.

Open all day Closed Mon (Sep-May) **Food** Lunch Sun-Fri 12-3, Sat 12-5 Dinner Mon-Sat 5-9.30 Restaurant menu available all wk ⊕ FREE HOUSE ◄ Sharp's Doom Bar, Dark Star Hophead ♂ Westons Old Rosie. ♀ 11 **Facilities** Non-diners area ❤ (Bar Garden) ♦ Children's menu Children's portions Garden ⊼ Beer festival Parking WiFi (notice required) **Rooms** 6

WEST HOATHLY
Map 6 TQ33

The Cat Inn
PICK OF THE PUBS

tel: 01342 810369 **North Ln RH19 4PP**
email: thecatinn@googlemail.com **web:** www.catinn.co.uk
dir: From East Grinstead centre take A22 towards Forest Row. Into left lane, into B2110 (Beeching Way) signed Turners Hill. Left into Vowels Ln signed Kingscote & West Hoathly. Left into Selsfield Rd, forward into Chapel Row, right into North Ln

Village hospitality at its best

This 16th-century tile-hung pub is in a great walking area, set high on the Sussex Weald, close to the edge of the Ashdown Forest. In the old bar you'll find two inglenook fireplaces, oak beams, fine wooden panelling and floors, and the sort of buzzy atmosphere village pubs are so good at generating. Local breweries in Groombridge (Black Cat), Litlington (Long Man), Lewes (Harvey's) and Chiddingstone (Larkins) deliver the excellent beers. The well-lit dining rooms are furnished with wooden dining chairs and tables on pale wood-strip flooring, and hops, china platters and brass and copper ornaments decorate the walls in homely style. Glass doors from the contemporary garden room open on to a terrace. The kitchen makes good use of South Downs lamb, Sussex coast fish and seafood, estate game and other locally-sourced produce, in addition to quality ingredients from further afield such as Shetland mussels, Hereford rib-eye steaks, and Loch Duart salmon. The Cat welcomes children over seven years of age.

Open all day 12-11.30 Closed Sun eve **Food** Lunch Mon-Thu 12-2, Fri-Sun 12-2.30 Dinner Mon-Thu 6-9, Fri-Sat 6-9.30 Av main course £15 ⊕ FREE HOUSE ◄ Harvey's Sussex Best Bitter, Black Cat, Larkins, Long Man ♂ Westons Stowford Press. ♀ 10 **Facilities** Non-diners area ❤ (Bar Garden) ♦ Children's portions Garden ⊼ Parking WiFi

TYNE & WEAR

NEWCASTLE UPON TYNE   Map 21 NZ26

NEW The Bridge Tavern

tel: 0191 232 1122 **7 Akenside Hill NE1 3UF**
email: contact@bridgetavern.com **web:** www.thebridgetavern.com
dir: *On A167 at Tyne Bridge*

Amazing location for bespoke beers beneath the Tyne Bridge

Built between the stanchions of the iconic Tyne Bridge, there has been an alehouse on this site for two hundred years – the original building being demolished to make way for the bridge and then rebuilt afterwards. There's a working microbrewery on site, where they brew bespoke, never repeated ales available exclusively in the pub. On the menu you'll find great bar snacks – pickled eggs with celery salt, and pork fried peanuts, for example, plus hearty dishes like ox cheek with bone marrow, toast and pickled walnuts; calves' liver and bacon; or beer battered haddock with triple cooked chips.

Open all day all wk Closed 25 Dec **Food** Lunch Mon-Thu 12-9, Fri-Sun 12-7 Dinner Mon-Thu 12-9, Fri-Sun 12-7 Av main course £10 ⊕ FREE HOUSE ◼ Wylam Tavernale. ♟ 10 **Facilities** Non-diners area ☻ (Bar Outside area) ♦ Children's menu Children's portions Outside area ⌂ Beer festival WiFi ▦ (notice required)

NEW Crown Posada

tel: 0191 232 1269 **31 Side NE1 3JE**
dir: *Phone pub for detailed directions*

Great local beer in a fantastic setting

This glorious Grade II listed building is one of the most famous pubs in Newcastle. The façade is Victorian, there's an elaborately panelled entrance and original stained glass windows, and the music comes courtesy of a 1940s gramophone. You can get a freshly made sandwich and a packet of crisps, but beer's the thing here.

Check out the well-kept real ales; Allendale Pennine Pale, Hadrian Border Tyneside Blonde or Blackgate Bitter, and three guest ales.

Open all day all wk **Food** Contact pub for food times ⊕ SIR JOHN FITZGERALD ◼ Allendale Pennine Pale, Hadrian Border Tyneside Blonde & Blackgate Bitter, Guest ales. **Facilities** Non-diners area Beer festival WiFi

WARWICKSHIRE

ALDERMINSTER   Map 10 SP24

The Bell ★★★★ INN   PICK OF THE PUBS
See Pick of the Pubs on opposite page

ALVESTON   Map 10 SP25

The Baraset Barn   PICK OF THE PUBS

tel: 01789 295510 **1 Pimlico Ln CV37 7RJ**
email: barasetbarn@lovelypubs.co.uk
dir: *Phone for detailed directions*

200-year-old history with contemporary refinements

Barn is what it's called, because barn is what it was. The original flagstones reflect its 200 years of history, but now it's a light and modern gastro-pub, the dramatic interior styled in granite, pewter and oak. Stone steps lead from the bar to the main dining area with brick walls and high oak beams, while the open mezzanine level offers a good view of the glass-fronted kitchen. The menu successfully blends classic British with Mediterranean ideas, such as sharing plates of meze; starters of confit duck, spring onion and potato hash, poached egg and black pepper hollandaise; and bourbon and cola braised pork ribs with Cajun sweetcorn and red cabbage slaw. Follow with roast loin of hake, butter bean, chorizo, king prawn and tomato cassoulet; or fennel roast belly pork. The patio garden is perfect for outdoor dining.

Open all day 11-11 (Fri-Sat 11am-mdnt Sun 12-6) Closed 1 Jan, Sun eve **Food** Lunch Mon-Sat 12-2.30, Sun 12-3.30 Dinner Mon-Sat 6.30-9.30 Set menu available Restaurant menu available all wk ⊕ FREE HOUSE ◼ Purity Gold. **Facilities** Non-diners area ☻ (Bar Garden) ♦ Children's portions Garden ⌂ Parking WiFi ▦

ARDENS GRAFTON   Map 10 SP15

The Golden Cross   PICK OF THE PUBS

tel: 01789 772420 **Wixford Rd B50 4LG**
email: info@thegoldencross.net
dir: *Phone for detailed directions*

Pretty pub with prized faggots

This traditional 18th-century country inn is the place to go to if you like faggots. The original recipe went missing but was then rediscovered; the tasty savouries are served with creamy mashed potato, mushed peas and onion gravy. Eat them in the pastel-toned dining room with attractive plasterwork on the ceiling, or in the rug-strewn, flagstone-floored and heavily beamed bar. The seasonally changing main menu of pub favourites is augmented by a daily changing specials board; ingredients for the freshly prepared dishes are sourced from best quality local suppliers. The single menu served throughout proffers a starter such as haddock and spring onion fishcake with dressed leaves and tartare sauce. Comforting mains include beef or chicken burgers served on a toasted bap with tomato and red pepper relish, double-dipped hand-cut chips and rocket salad. Sharing tapas platters brim with either fish or meats. Oven-baked camembert with red onion jam, olives and toasted farmhouse bread is a popular vegetarian option.

Open all wk Mon-Thu 12-3 5-11 (Fri-Sat 12-12 Sun 12-10.30) **Food** Lunch Mon-Fri 12-2.30, Sat 12-9, Sun 12-8 Dinner Mon-Fri 5-9, Sat 12-9, Sun 12-8 Set menu available ⊕ CHARLES WELLS ◼ Bombardier, Purity, Guest ales ♂ Thatchers Heritage. ♟ 10 **Facilities** Non-diners area ☻ (Bar Garden) ♦ Children's menu Children's portions Garden ⌂ Parking WiFi ▦ (notice required)

PICK OF THE PUBS

The Bell ★★★★ INN

ALDERMINSTER   Map 10 SP24

tel: 01789 450414
CV37 8NY
email: info@thebellald.co.uk
web: www.thebellald.co.uk
dir: *On A3400, 3.5m S of Stratford-upon-Avon*

Country pub chic with great food

Part of the Alscot Estate, this striking Georgian coaching inn is set in the heart of a picturesque village between Stratford-upon-Avon and Shipston on Stour. The interior is a refreshing mix of contemporary comforts and rustic charm, with the historic core of beamed ceilings, blazing log fires and flagged floors combining well with bold colours and stylish fabrics and the modern dining courtyard. The inn is located beside a grassy garden, and the riverside meadow that ripples down to the River Stour is perfect for enjoying summer picnics. The restaurant oozes charm and is cunningly designed into quirky zones, each with its own distinct atmosphere. Time to enjoy a pint of North Cotswold Windrush or the inn's locally-brewed Alscot Ale and nibble on a self-selected grazing platter, perhaps laden with hams, olives, mozzarella, pesto, balsamic shallots, vine tomatoes and garlic focaccia, before considering the indulgent daily-changing menu. Typically, begin with potted duck liver and orange pâté, carpaccio of smoked

duck and pink grapefruit salad, then follow with slow-roasted pork stuffed with pepperoni and sage, with crackling and pearl barley risotto. Round off with warm dark chocolate and fudge tart with strawberry ice cream, or a plate of local cheeses with home-made chutney. In the bar, sandwiches are served with hand-cut chips and salad, or you can try a Bell classic, perhaps the beef and thyme burger, or bangers and mash. Much of the produce is local, with vegetables and herbs harvested from Alscot's historic kitchen garden, and game and venison is reared on the estate.

Open all wk 9.30-3 6-11 (Fri-Sat 9.30am-11pm) **Food** Lunch Mon-Thu 12-2.30, Fri-Sun 12-3 Dinner Mon-Thu

6.30-9, Fri-Sat 6.30-9.30, Sun 6.30-8.30 Av main course £17 Set menu available Restaurant menu available all wk ⊕ FREE HOUSE ◀ Alscot Ale, North Cotswold Windrush ♂ Robinsons. ♟ 12
Facilities Non-diners area
⊶ Children's menu Children's portions Garden Outside area ⚞ Parking WiFi ➠ (notice required) **Rooms** 9

ARMSCOTE
Map 10 SP24

The Fuzzy Duck ★★★★ INN ☺
PICK OF THE PUBS

tel: 01608 682635 **Ilmington Rd CV37 8DD**
email: info@fuzzyduckarmscote.com **web:** www.fuzzyduckarmscote.com
dir: *From A429 (Fosse Way) N of Moreton-in-Marsh follow Armscote signs*

Innovative modern cooking in stylish village pub

In the picturesque hamlet of Armscote, a few miles south of historic Stratford-upon-Avon, this building once housed the local blacksmith before becoming a coaching inn in the 18th century. The pub is owned by the family behind the Baylis & Harding toiletries company; its range of luxury products take pride of place in the stylish bedrooms. In the buzzy bar, contemporary furnishings combine with exposed beams, flagstone floors and original fireplaces to create a relaxed setting to enjoy local ales such as Purity Mad Goose. The seasonal menu majors on local produce and robust, innovative dishes. Try the pork pie with date chutney; duck liver parfait; or leek and wild mushroom tart to start, followed by lamb shank with buttered mash, green beans and lamb gravy; or local venison pie. An attractive courtyard garden is a peaceful spot for alfresco dining but if the weather turns, you might be able to make use of the pub's quirky Hunter welly loan service.

Open 12-4 6-close Closed 1st wk Jan, Mon **Food** Lunch 12-2.30 Dinner 6.30-9 Av main course £14 Set menu available Restaurant menu available Tue-Fri Lunch ⊕ FREE HOUSE ◀ Purity Mad Goose, Guest ales ♂ Aspall, Westons Mortimers Orchard. ⬤ 11 **Facilities** Non-diners area ❀ (Bar Restaurant Garden) ♦♦ Children's menu Children's portions Family room Garden ⊨ Parking WiFi **Rooms** 4

ASTON CANTLOW
Map 10 SP16

The King's Head

tel: 01789 488242 **21 Bearley Rd B95 6HY**
email: info@thekh.co.uk **web:** www.thekh.co.uk
dir: *Exit A3400 between Stratford-upon-Avon & Henley-in-Arden. Follow Aston Cantlow signs*

Rustic Tudor pub steeped in history

Flanked by a huge spreading chestnut tree and oozing historic charm, this impressive black-and-white timbered Tudor building has been appointed in a modern style. Tastefully rustic inside, with lime-washed low beams, huge polished flagstones, painted brick walls, old scrubbed pine tables and crackling log fires, it draws diners for innovative pub food. Tuck into pub classics such as fish and chips and faggots, mash and peas or choose from the à la carte, dishes such duck breast, confit leg, seared foies gras and crispy egg, hand-cut chips and onion rings,

followed by a 'trio of chocolate'. If you don't want alcohol, try one of the specialist teas on offer. There's an area for alfresco dining.

The King's Head

Open all day all wk **Food** Lunch Mon-Sat 12-9.30, Sun 12-8 Dinner Mon-Sat 12-9.30, Sun 12-8 ⊕ ENTERPRISE INNS ◀ Purity Gold, Greene King Abbot Ale, M&B Brew XI ♂ Aspall. ⬤ 12 **Facilities** Non-diners area ❀ (Bar Garden) ♦♦ Children's menu Children's portions Garden ⊨ Parking WiFi ➡ (notice required)

See advert on opposite page

BARFORD
Map 10 SP26

The Granville @ Barford
PICK OF THE PUBS

tel: 01926 624236 **52 Wellesbourne Rd CV35 8DS**
email: info@granvillebarford.co.uk
dir: *M40 junct 15, A429 signed Stow, left to Barford*

Friendly and stylish village dining pub

Situated in the heart of Shakespeare country, this impressive brick building dates back to Georgian times. The comfortable dining pub benefits from stylish decor and warm, friendly service, which has made it a firm favourite with locals and visitors alike. Relax on the leather sofas in the lounge with a drink – Hook Norton Hooky Bitter perhaps, or choose from the accessible wine list. The Granville's ever-changing seasonal menus offer varied, interesting choices and good value. At lunch, there's doorstep sandwiches and wraps or starters like linguine in a lightly spiced crab broth with spring onion, lime and coriander. An evening meal might begin with salmon and haddock fishcakes, wilted spinach, lemon and butter sauce, followed by North African spiced lamb patties, winter fruit saffron couscous, mint and cucumber yogurt. Enjoy alfresco dining in the spacious patio garden.

Open all wk Mon-Fri 12-3 5-11 (Sat 12-11.30 Sun 12-11) **Food** Lunch Mon-Fri 12-2.30, Sat 12-3, Sun 12-4 Dinner Mon-Sat 6-9 ⊕ ENTERPRISE INNS ◀ Hook Norton Hooky Bitter, Fuller's London Pride, Purity ♂ Thatchers Gold, Guest ciders. ⬤ 17 **Facilities** Non-diners area ❀ (Bar Garden) ♦♦ Children's portions Play area Garden Parking WiFi ➡

BROOM
Map 10 SP05

The Broom Tavern

tel: 01789 778199 **32 High St B50 4HL**
email: enquiries@thebroomtavern.co.uk
dir: *From A46 onto B439 towards Bidford-on-Avon. Left into Victoria Rd to Broom. In Broom left into High St. Pub on right*

Historic food pub with links to Shakespeare

Reputed to be one of Shakespeare's drinking haunts, The Broom is a timber-framed, 16th-century pub in a pretty village. This venerable inn has great charm and character, with log fires in winter and three sunny beer gardens for alfresco drinking in the summer. Chef patron Fritz Ronnenburg showcases the best local produce and offers locally-brewed ales including Purity Mad Goose. Everything is made on the premises and a typical meal might include organic Scottish salmon 'three ways' with samphire, Jerusalem artichoke, potato, lemon and belly pork lardons, followed by breast of Gressingham duck, gastronome potatoes, confit duck straws, local Mudwalls Farm vegetables and winter berry sauce.

Open all wk 12-3 5-11 (Sat-Sun all day) **Food** Lunch Mon-Sat 12-2.30, Sun 12-6 Dinner Mon-Sat 6-9.30 ⊕ FREE HOUSE ◀ Sharp's Doom Bar, Wye Valley Butty Bach, Purity Mad Goose & Pure Gold ♂ Hogan's, Westons. ♚ 10 **Facilities** Non-diners area ✿ (Bar Garden) ◀ Children's menu Children's portions Garden ⊼ Beer festival Cider festival Parking WiFi ⊜ (notice required)

EARLSWOOD   **Map 10 SP17**

Bull's Head

tel: 01564 700368 **7 Limekiln Ln B94 6BU**
email: relax@bullsheadearlswood.co.uk **web:** www.bullsheadearlswood.co.uk
dir: *M42 junct 4, A34 signed Birmingham & Solihull. Left signed Chiswick Green. Through Chiswick Green, straight on at x-rds into Vicarage Rd. Left at T-junct signed Earlswood. On right bend turn left into Salter St. Pub on left*

Village food pub with large sun terrace

In the charming rural setting of Earlswood, near Solihull, the Bull's Head was built in the 18th century to house navvies building the Stratford-upon-Avon canal.

Rumoured to be haunted by the ghost of a lime kiln worker, it comprises a cluster of whitewashed cottages and became a pub in 1832. Popular with walkers, the pub is owned by the Daniel Thwaites Brewery and retains much of its original charm courtesy of log fires and a large sun terrace. Enjoy a glass of Lancaster Bomber as you choose from an extensive menu offering pizzas, deli boards, salads and chargrilled steaks.

Bull's Head

Open all day all wk **Food** Lunch all wk 12-10 (Bkfst 9am-11.45am) Dinner all wk 12-10 Restaurant menu available all wk ⊕ THWAITES INNS OF CHARACTER ◀ Lancaster Bomber, Wainwright, Nutty Black, Guest ales. ♚ 11 **Facilities** Non-diners area ✿ (Bar Garden) ◀ Children's menu Children's portions Garden ⊼ Parking WiFi ⊜ (notice required)

See advert on page 518

EDGEHILL

Map 11 SP34

Castle at Edgehill ★★★★ RR ◎◎

tel: 01295 670255 **OX15 6DJ**
email: enquiries@castleatedgehill.co.uk web: www.castleatedgehill.co.uk
dir: *M40 junct 11, A422 towards Stratford-upon-Avon. 6m to Upton House, next right, 1.5m to Edgehill*

A most unusual country pub

In 1742, a man called Sanderson Miller built this curious castellated property on top of Edgehill to mark the centenary of the English Civil War's first major skirmish. In 1822 it became an alehouse; fast-forward a hundred years and it was acquired by the Hook Norton Brewery, whose real ales you'll find to this day in the two bars. There are four dining areas including a glass-protected balcony with panoramic views. The modern menus are inviting and include dishes such as potted Cornish crab, mushroom loaf and samphire cream; and blade of beef, horseradish purée, shallots, broad beans, onion rings and garlic potato.

Open all day all wk **Food** Lunch Mon-Sat 12-2.30, Sun 12-4 Dinner Mon-Sat 6-9, Sun 6-8 Restaurant menu available all wk ⊕ HOOK NORTON ◀ Hooky Bitter, Old Hooky Ŏ Westons Old Rosie. **Facilities** Non-diners area ☺ (Bar Garden) ◑ Children's menu Children's portions Garden ⌷ Beer festival Cider festival Parking WiFi ▦ (notice required) **Rooms** 4

ETTINGTON

Map 10 SP24

The Chequers Inn
PICK OF THE PUBS

tel: 01789 740387 **91 Banbury Rd CV37 7SR**
email: hello@the-chequers-ettington.co.uk
dir: *Take A422 from Stratford-upon-Avon towards Banbury. Ettington in 5m, after junction with A429*

Tastefully decorated country inn serving classic fare

Thought to have once been a courthouse and probably named after the old chequer tree that used to stand in front of the building, this locals' pub is an elegant place to eat and drink. Go for a pint of Purity Mad Goose or Banks's Bitter in the bar, before moving on to the dining room, decorated in French style with ornate mirrors and chairs, rich tapestries and comfortable armchairs. A choice of interesting sandwiches might include chargrilled coriander and lime chicken flatbread with lemon mayo and spinach, and there are classics like beef chilli con carne; or

cheeseburger with gherkins. For something more substantial, kick off proceedings with goats' cheese and caramelised onion pithivier, potato, apple and walnut salad; followed by pan-fried sea bass fillets. Puddings along traditional lines may include dark chocolate and fudge brownie with ice cream.

Open 12-3 5-11 (Sat 12-11 Sun 12-6) Closed Sun eve, Mon **Food** Lunch Tue-Sat 12-2.30, Sun 12.30-3.30 Dinner Tue-Sat 6.30-9.30 ⊕ FREE HOUSE ◀ Purity Mad Goose, Banks's Bitter Ŏ Thatchers Gold. ▾ 8 **Facilities** Non-diners area ☺ (Bar Garden) ◑ Children's menu Children's portions Garden ⌷ Parking WiFi ▦ (notice required)

FARNBOROUGH

Map 11 SP44

The Inn at Farnborough
PICK OF THE PUBS

tel: 01295 690615 **OX17 1DZ**
email: enquiries@theinnfarnborough.co.uk
dir: *M40 junct 11 towards Banbury. Right at 3rd rdbt onto A423 signed Southam. 4m to A423. Left onto single track road signed Farnborough. Approx 1m, right into village, pub on right*

Stylish pub with tempting food

This Grade II listed, 16th-century property used to be the Butcher's Arms, having once belonged to the butcher on the now National Trust-owned Farnborough Park Estate. Built of locally quarried, honey-coloured stone, tasteful restoration has ensured the retention of a fine inglenook fireplace and other original features. The bar serves Hook Norton real ales, locally made Hogan's cider, and plenty of wines served by the glass. The concise menu lists British pub classic dishes, and others with a Mediterranean influence, but quality ingredients and high culinary skills ensure impressive results whatever your choice. Starters include slow-roasted pulled duck with green papaya salad; or spiced bubble-and-squeak; and among the mains are porcini mushroom, parsnip and Puy lentil casserole; and chargrilled Aberdeenshire rib steak medallions with garlic and parsley butter. Parents of small children will be glad to see the Little Gourmets menu. Enjoy good coffee in the terraced garden or on the covered decking area.

Open all wk 10-3 6-11 (Sat-Sun all day) **Food** Lunch all wk 12-3 Dinner all wk 6-10 Set menu available Restaurant menu available all wk ⊕ FREE HOUSE ◀ Hook Norton Hooky Bitter Ŏ Hogan's, Local ciders. ▾ 14 **Facilities** Non-diners area ☺ (Bar Garden) ◑ Children's menu Children's portions Play area Garden ⌷ Parking WiFi ▦ (notice required)

GAYDON
Map 11 SP35

The Malt Shovel

tel: 01926 641221 **Church Rd CV35 OET**
email: malt.shovel@btconnect.com
dir: M40 junct 12, B4451 to Gaydon

Village pub that gets it right

Richard and Debi Morisot's 16th-century village pub has a reputation for being friendly and reliable, qualities that have helped to make their venture a success. Another plus is the range of real ales, usually from Sharp's, Everards, Fuller's, Hook Norton, Timothy Taylor or Wadworth. Menu options include smoked haddock Welsh rarebit; slow braised beef with pancetta, mushroom and red wine sauce; three cheese vegetable lasagne; and chocolate, cherry and brandy fudge slice. If all you want is a lunchtime snack, there are chunky granary sandwiches, baguettes and hot paninis. Well-behaved children and dogs are welcome and can play with Molly, the Morisot's Jack Russell.

Open all wk 11-3 5-11 (Fri-Sat 11-11 Sun 12-10.30) **Food** Lunch all wk 12-2 Dinner all wk 6.30-9 ⊕ ENTERPRISE INNS ◀ Fuller's London Pride, Timothy Taylor Landlord, Everards Tiger, Wadworth 6X, Hook Norton, Sharp's Doom Bar ♂ South West Orchards, Thatchers Gold. ♟ 11 **Facilities** Non-diners area ❤ (Bar Outside area) ♦♦ Children's portions Outside area ⋒ Parking WiFi ➤ (notice required)

HENLEY-IN-ARDEN
Map 10 SP16

The Bluebell ◉◉

tel: 01564 793049 **93 High St B95 5AT**
email: info@bluebellhenley.co.uk
dir: Opposite police station on A3400 in town centre

Innovative food in pub with plenty of character

This rambling, half-timbered old coaching inn has fronted Henley's picturesque High Street for over 500 years. The interior retains much period character, with heavy beams, fireplaces and flagged floors contrasted with modern flourishes and an eclectic mix of furnishings. Behind is a secluded, lavender-scented beer-garden, where beers from Purity may hit the spot. The punchy, seasonal menu has gained the award of two AA Rosettes. Typically; a starter of lamb's kidneys on toast sets the scene for pan-fried fillet of Tamworth pork, shoulder rissole, roast apple, black pudding and Madeira sauce, with fig and almond tart to finish.

Open all day Closed Mon (ex BHs) **Food** Lunch Tue-Sat 12-2.30, Sun 12-3.30 Dinner Tue-Sat 6-9.30 ⊕ FREE HOUSE ◀ Purity Pure UBU & Mad Goose, Church End What The Fox's Hat, Hook Norton Hooky Bitter, Wye Valley HPA ♂ Hogan's. ♟ 12 **Facilities** Non-diners area ❤ (Bar Restaurant Garden) ♦♦ Children's portions Garden ⋒ Parking WiFi

HUNNINGHAM
Map 11 SP36

The Red Lion

tel: 01926 632715 **Main St CV33 9DY**
email: redllionhunningham@aol.com
dir: From Leamington Spa take B4453, through Cubbington to Weston under Wetherby. Follow Hunningham signs (turn sharp right as road bends left towards Princethorpe)

New owners at a popular village inn

Set in the heart of rural Warwickshire and beside a 14th-century bridge, this quirky country pub's beer garden leads down to the River Leam and offers views of sheep and cows grazing. New owners took over in February 2015 so there's bound to be a few changes. Examples on the concise winter-into-spring menus are starters of

baked Portland crab and leek gratin with toasted soldiers, then mains of steak and kidney pie, mash and cabbage; and wild mushroom, tarragon mac and cheese, winter leaf salad. A yummy dessert could be sticky toffee pudding, vanilla ice cream and warm butterscotch sauce.

Open all day all wk 11-11 (Fri-Sat 11am-mdnt) **Food** Lunch Mon-Sat 12-9, Sun 12-8 Dinner Mon-Sat 12-9, Sun 12-8 Av main course £9.50 ⊕ GREENE KING ◀ IPA, Abbot Ale, Guest ales ♂ Thatchers Gold. ♟ 28 **Facilities** Non-diners area ❤ (Bar Restaurant Garden) ♦♦ Children's menu Children's portions Garden ⋒ Beer festival Parking WiFi ➤ (notice required)

ILMINGTON
Map 10 SP24

The Howard Arms
PICK OF THE PUBS

tel: 01608 682226 **Lower Green CV36 4LT**
email: info@howardarms.com
dir: Exit A429 or A3400, 9m from Stratford-upon-Avon

A popular base for walkers

A stunning 400-year-old Cotswold-stone inn on Ilmington's picturesque village green. The pub is a popular start and finish to some fabulous circular walks; a detailed guide can be bought at the bar for a small donation to church funds. The flagstoned bar and open-plan dining room create a civilised yet informal atmosphere, all imbued with the warmth of a log fire that burns for most of the year. Award-winning ales come from famous local names such as Wye Valley and Hook Norton; wine drinkers can choose from a list of 30 sold by the glass; and cider lovers can indulge in a pint of Orchard Pig. Equally serious is the inn's kitchen, which moves with the seasons in a monthly-changing menu. Hungry hikers may look no further than an excellent sandwich of grilled steak, onion confit and mature cheddar; or a bap of home-made fish fingers with tartare sauce and lettuce.

Open all day all wk **Food** Lunch Mon-Sat 12-3, Sun 12-8 Dinner Mon-Sat 6-9.30, Sun 12-8 ⊕ FREE HOUSE ◀ Wye Valley Bitter, Hook Norton Old Hooky, Purity, Timothy Taylor ♂ The Orchard Pig. ♟ 30 **Facilities** Non-diners area ❤ (Bar Garden) ♦♦ Children's portions Garden ⋒ Parking WiFi ➤ (notice required)

KENILWORTH
Map 10 SP27

The Almanack

tel: 01926 353637 **Abbey End North CV8 1QJ**
email: hello@thealmanack-kenilworth.co.uk
dir: Exit A46 at Kenilworth & brown Castle sign, towards town centre. Left into Abbey Hill (B4104) signed Balsall Common. At rdbt into Abbey End. Opposite Holiday Inn

Modern British all-day eatery

Inspired by the 1960s Kinks hit Autumn Almanac, the stylish interior harks back to the 60s with its retro Danish teak and rosewood furniture and original album covers on the walls. The huge island bar separates the lounge from the eatery and open kitchen. The pub is open all day for breakfast, coffee and cake, lunch and dinner; menu choices include deli boards, a daily roast, a selection from the chargrill, and full meals such as Stilton rarebit, pear, watercress and hazelnut salad, followed by pan-fried sea bass with Bombay potatoes, Indian salad, and cucumber and mint yogurt; with pecan and pumpkin pie for dessert. The Almanack is part of the Peach Pubs 'family', not a chain, but 'a group of like-minded enthusiasts'.

Open all day all wk Closed 25 Dec **Food** Lunch all wk 12-6 Dinner all wk 6-10 ⊕ FREE HOUSE/PEACH PUBS ◀ Purity Pure UBU & Mad Goose, Sharp's Doom Bar ♂ Aspall. ♟ 16 **Facilities** Non-diners area ❤ (Bar Outside area) ♦♦ Children's portions Outside area ⋒ WiFi ➤ (notice required)

LAPWORTH
Map 10 SP17

The Boot Inn
PICK OF THE PUBS

tel: 01564 782464 **Old Warwick Rd B94 6JU**
email: thebootinn@lovelypubs.co.uk
dir: *Phone for detailed directions*

Stylish country pub by canal

Precision-cut logs and soft modern furnishings meet the eye in this convivial, 16th-century former coaching inn beside the Grand Union Canal. Beyond its smart interior is an attractive garden, on cooler days under a canopied patio with heaters. Free-house status means a good choice of real ales in the shape of Purity Pure UBU, Sharp's Doom Bar and Marston's EPA. But for many the draw is the brasserie-style food, and there's lots to choose from. For example, the first course could be Thai chicken patties with papaya salad, miso aïoli and black pepper crackers; mains include chargrilled 28-day-matured Hereford rib-eye steak with roast tomato, crispy onions, skin-on chips and béarnaise sauce; and South Indian spiced spit chicken with sweet potato and coconut curry with saffron and cashew pilaf. Children and well-behaved dogs are welcome.

Open all day all wk 11-11 (Thu-Sat 11am-mdnt Sun 12-10.30) **Food** Lunch Mon-Sat 12-2.30, Sun 12-3 Dinner Mon-Fri 7-9.30, Sat 6.30-9.30, Sun 7-9 ⊕ FREE HOUSE ◀ Purity Pure UBU, Marston's EPA, Sharp's Doom Bar ⎔ Thatchers Gold, Westons Stowford Press. ⬗ 9 **Facilities** Non-diners area ♥ (Bar Restaurant Garden) ♦️ Children's menu Children's portions Garden ⋒ Parking WiFi ⬛ (notice required)

NEW Navigation Inn

tel: 01564 783337 **Old Warwick Rd B94 6NA**
email: info@navigationlapworth.co.uk
dir: *On B4439 (Old Warwick Rd) between Lapworth & Rowington*

Family-run traditional pub with canalside beer garden

Right by Bridge 65 on the Grand Union Canal, the Navigation has a long history of refreshing narrowboat crews, walkers and cyclists. Keeping draught ales, lagers and ciders in optimum condition is second nature to landlord and former brewery engineer, Mark Ainley. Note to beer-hunters: unique to the pub is Coventry-brewed Lapworth Gold; also unique is Guinness on hand-pull, something Mark's expertise enabled him to devise. Fresh, home-made food served in the comfortable interior includes sandwiches and wraps with chips and dressed salad; lamb shank; grilled sea bass; apricot- and sage-stuffed chicken breast; and wild mushroom, pine nut and spinach tagliatelle.

Open all day all wk **Food** Lunch Mon-Fri 12-3, Sat 12-9.30, Sun 12-8 Dinner Mon-Fri 6-9.30, Sat 12-9.30, Sun 12-8 Av main course £9.95 Set menu available Restaurant menu available all wk ⊕ ENTERPRISE INNS ◀ Lapworth Gold, Timothy Taylor Landlord, Purity Mad Goose, Wadworth 6X, Guinness ⎔ Thatchers Gold, Aspall. ⬗ 9 **Facilities** Non-diners area ♥ (Bar Garden) ♦️ Children's menu Children's portions Garden ⋒ Parking WiFi ⬛

LEAMINGTON SPA (ROYAL)
Map 10 SP36

The Moorings at Myton

tel: 01926 425043 **Myton Rd CV31 3NY**
email: info@themoorings.co.uk
dir: *M40 junct 14 or 13, A452 towards Leamington Spa. At 4th rdbt after crossing canal, pub on left*

Anglo-French cuisine in waterside location

This food-led pub beside the Grand Union Canal is a popular stop for boaters on England's arterial waterway. Diners may look forward to dishes created by Raymond Blanc protégés Charles Harris and Nigel Brown, whose ever-evolving Anglo-French menu relies on local suppliers for the ingredients. A sharing charcuterie board is a substantial starter; mains include 28-day dry-aged Aberdeenshire steaks, or perhaps braised neck of Cornish lamb, parsnip purée, purple sprouting broccoli, button mushrooms and pearl barley jus. Fruit ciders, a decent wine list and beer from Warwickshire craft brewery slip down easily on the waterside terrace.

Open all day all wk **Food** Lunch all wk 12-2.30 Dinner all wk 6-9.30 Av main course £16 ⊕ CHARLES WELLS ◀ Bombardier, Young's London Gold, Courage Directors, Warwickshire Darling Buds. ⬗ 13 **Facilities** Non-diners area ♥ (Bar Garden) ♦️ Children's menu Children's portions Family room Garden ⋒ Parking WiFi ⬛ (notice required)

LONG COMPTON
Map 10 SP23

The Red Lion ★★★★ INN ◉
PICK OF THE PUBS

tel: 01608 684221 **Main St CV36 5JS**
email: info@redlion-longcompton.co.uk **web:** www.redlion-longcompton.co.uk
dir: *On A3400 between Shipston on Stour & Chipping Norton*

Cotswold character and award-winning cuisine

Wooded ridges ripple along the horizons enfolding this attractive north Cotswolds village. Ramblers challenge a web of recreational trails hereabouts, whilst folklorists home-in on the mysterious Rollright Stones monument just to the south. Explorers in-the-know then make a bee-line for the village's Red Lion pub. Its Georgian coaching inn origins bequeath an appealing mix of beams, stone-flags and honey-coloured stone, matchboarding, inglenook and log fires. The seasonal menu, complemented by daily specials, has the award of one AA Rosette for the considered mix of classic and contemporary dishes, and may offer starters such as smoked duck, watermelon and feta salad. Progress then with pancetta wrapped guinea fowl supreme with roasted vegetables, garlic and thyme jus; or duck leg cassoulet with Cotswold sausage and smoked bacon. In summer, the shrubby beer garden is just the place to enjoy beers from Hook Norton and Wickwar breweries. Dogs are well-liked here, whilst well-appointed accommodation is on hand for those on short breaks.

Open all wk Mon-Thu 10-2.30 6-11 (Fri-Sun all day) **Food** Lunch Mon-Thu 12-2.30, Fri-Sat 12-9.30, Sun 12-9 Dinner Mon-Thu 6-9, Fri-Sat 12-9.30, Sun 12-9 Set menu available ⊕ FREE HOUSE ◀ Hook Norton Hooky Bitter, Wickwar Cotswold Way. ⬗ 11 **Facilities** Non-diners area ♥ (Bar Restaurant Garden) ♦️ Children's menu Children's portions Play area Garden ⋒ Parking WiFi **Rooms** 5

■ MONKS KIRBY   Map 11 SP48

The Bell Inn

tel: 01788 832352 **Bell Ln CV23 0QY**
email: belindagb@aol.com
dir: From B4455 (Fosse Way) follow Monks Kirby signs

Timbered inn offering menus with strong Spanish influences

This quaint, timbered inn was once the gatehouse of a Benedictine priory and then a brewhouse cottage. The pine bar top came from a tree grown in Leire churchyard nearby. The Spanish owners describe their pub as "a corner of Spain in the heart of England". Mediterranean and traditional cuisine play an important role on the truly extensive menu. Enjoy a glass of Ruddles while taking time to make your choices — langostinos alioli; red snapper Gallega; fillet steak Rossini; chicken al Ajillo; and halibut Malageña all make a showing. Grills, pasta dishes and paella are readily available too.

Open 12-3 6.30-10.30 Closed 26 Dec, 1 Jan, Mon L **Food** Lunch Tue-Sat 12-2.30, Sun 12-3 Dinner Mon-Sat 6.30-10.30, Sun 6.30-8.30 Restaurant menu available all wk ⊕ FREE HOUSE ◀ Greene King IPA, Ruddles. **Facilities** Non-diners area ♣ (Garden) ♦ Children's portions Garden Outside area Parking WiFi ▭

■ OFFCHURCH   Map 11 SP36

The Stag at Offchurch

tel: 01926 425801 **Welsh Rd CV33 9AQ**
email: info@thestagatoffchurch.com
dir: From Leamington Spa take A425 towards Southam. At Radford Semele left into Offchurch Ln to Offchurch

Picturesque pub with progressive menu

The Stag is a charming thatched pub in a classic English village. Considerably modernised, it balances the feel of times long-gone with contemporary flourishes; diners, ramblers and locals all flock to the restaurant and bar. The imaginative menu offers plenty of choice — twice-baked Wookey Hole cheese soufflé; duck à l'orange, confit duck leg croquettes, wilted spinach and orange jus; and whisky marmalade bread and butter pudding with white chocolate ice cream. The head chef specialises in locally raised, 28-day, dry-aged Aberdeenshire beef steaks.

Open all day all wk **Food** Lunch all wk 12-2.30 Dinner all wk 6-9.30 Av main course £18 ⊕ FREE HOUSE ◀ Hook Norton, Warwickshire ♂ Somersby Cider. ☻ 13 **Facilities** Non-diners area ♣ (Bar Garden) ♦ Children's menu Children's portions Garden ▭ Parking WiFi

■ OXHILL   Map 10 SP34

The Peacock

tel: 01295 688060 **Main St CV35 0QU**
email: info@thepeacockoxhill.co.uk
dir: From Stratford-upon-Avon take A422 towards Banbury. Turn right to Oxhill

Destination pub in picturesque village

Yvonne Hamlett and Pam Farrell's objective is to run a classic English country pub. They can tick that one off, then. Their 16th-century, stone-built pub effortlessly combines its historic past with a relaxed modern atmosphere. Hand-pulled ales come from St Austell, Marston's and Wye Valley, and the popular food reflects the kitchen's focus on meats and vegetables from local farms, and fresh fish from Devon and Cornwall. Meal ideas include pan-fried chicken breast with brie, peppercorn, brandy and cream sauce; Moroccan spiced lamb chump with fruit couscous; or marinated salmon kebabs on stir-fry vegetables. There is also an extensive menu of 'free from' dishes, for diners with special dietary requirements.

Open all day all wk 12-11 **Food** Lunch Mon-Sat 12-2, Sun 12-8 Dinner Mon-Sat 6-9, Sun 12-8 Av main course £10 ⊕ FREE HOUSE ◀ Marston's Pedigree, St Austell Tribute, Sharp's Doom Bar, Wye Valley HPA, Salopian Darwin's Origin, Brakspear Bitter ♂ Thatchers Gold, Healey's Cornish Rattler. ☻ 12 **Facilities** Non-diners area ♣ (Bar Garden) ♦ Children's menu Children's portions Garden ▭ Parking WiFi ▭ (notice required)

■ PRESTON BAGOT   Map 10 SP16

The Crabmill

tel: 01926 843342 **B95 5EE**
email: thecrabmill@lovelypubs.co.uk
dir: M40 junct 16, A3400 towards Stratford-upon-Avon. Take A4189 at lights in Henley-in-Arden. Left, 1.5m pub on left

Richly varied menu in converted cider mill

Handy for a stroll in superb countryside alongside the Stratford-upon-Avon Canal, this carefully renovated former rural mill, where crab apples were perhaps mashed into cider, is a fine destination dining-pub presented in a modern rustic style. Colourwash, comfy seating and light beams offer an airy, informal interior. Contemporary dishes shine out from the extensive menu; commence with wasabi-cured salmon and pickled oriental salad, lime and ginger syrup, before tucking into a main of roasted cod with Puy lentils; slow-cooked lamb shoulder with dauphinoise potatoes; or spiced butternut squash, pumpkin and nut strudel with pomegranate.

Open all day 11-11 Closed Sun eve **Food** Lunch Mon-Thu 12-3, Fri-Sat 12-5, Sun 12-4 Dinner Mon-Sat 6-9.30 Set menu available ⊕ FREE HOUSE ◀ Purity Gold & Mad Goose, Sharp's Doom Bar, Guest ale ♂ Aspall. ☻ 14 **Facilities** Non-diners area ♣ (Bar Garden) ♦ Children's menu Children's portions Garden ▭ Parking WiFi

■ STRATFORD-UPON-AVON   Map 10 SP25

The One Elm   **PICK OF THE PUBS**

tel: 01789 404919 **1 Guild St CV37 6QZ**
email: theoneelm@peachpubs.com
dir: From rdbt on A46 take A3400 (Birmingham Rd) towards town centre. Pass Tesco, through lights, pub after mini rdbt on left

Quirky decor and a Mediterranean-style courtyard

Named after the elm tree that used to be a town boundary marker, The One Elm occupies a prime location, not far from the river and theatre. It mirrors the chic, contemporary look and style of menus to be found at other Peach Pubs, the innovative small pub group. Opening at 9.30am for coffee and breakfast, there's an informal, almost continental feel about the place, especially in the stylish front lounge, with its wood floor, bright painted walls, leather sofas and low tables displaying the day's newspapers. Beyond the central, open-to-view kitchen is the more formal dining area, while the upstairs seating area has an even grander feel. The menu is an eclectic list of modern pub food. Try air-dried British beef, cave-aged cheddar and watercress; pan-fried herb gnocchi, spring veg and seeded parmesan crisp; or barbecue pork belly rib steaks with wedges and crunchy vegetable slaw. The secluded terrace gives you a real feeling of being abroad.

Open all day all wk 9.30am-11pm (Thu 9.30am-mdnt Fri-Sat 9.30am-1am Sun 9.30am-10.30pm) Closed 25 Dec **Food** Lunch all wk 12-6 Dinner all wk 6-10 Av main course £12 Set menu available ⊕ FREE HOUSE/PEACH PUBS ◀ Purity Pure UBU & Gold, Sharp's Doom Bar, Church Farm Harry's Heifer, Guest ales ♂ Aspall. ☻ 14 **Facilities** Non-diners area ♣ (Bar Garden) ♦ Children's menu Children's portions Garden ▭ Parking WiFi ▭ (notice required)

TANWORTH IN ARDEN
Map 10 SP17

The Bell Inn

tel: 01564 742212 **The Green B94 5AL**
email: thebell@realcoolbars.com
dir: *M42 junct 8, A435 signed Evesham. Left signed Portway & Tanworth (Penn Ln). To T-junct, left signed Tanworth. 1st right signed Tanworth. Inn in village centre*

A popular village pub of both real and TV vintage

Older visitors might remember (or perhaps try to forget) a TV soap called *Crossroads*, many of whose outdoor scenes were shot in Tanworth, doubling as 'Kings Oak'. The pub overlooks the small village green and war memorial, and has stood here since the 17th century, so the cool grey tones of the thoroughly modern bar area might come as a surprise. Starters include liver, brandy and mushroom pâté and goats' cheese with parsley mousse on ciabatta; mains might be grilled sea bass on marinated peppers; tagliatelle with broccoli and pine nuts; or pub classics like Cumberland sausage and mash.

Open all day all wk **Food** Lunch Mon-Sat 12-2.30, Sun 12-8 Dinner Mon-Sat 6.30-9, Sun 12-8 ⊕ ENTERPRISE INNS ◄ Timothy Taylor Landlord Ö Sandford Orchards Devon Mist. ♟ **Facilities** Non-diners area ♣ (Bar Outside area) ♦ Children's menu Children's portions Outside area ⋒ Parking WiFi ⛟ (notice required)

TEMPLE GRAFTON
Map 10 SP15

The Blue Boar Inn ★★★ INN

tel: 01789 750010 **B49 6NR**
email: info@theblueboar.co.uk web: www.thebluboar.co.uk
dir: *From A46 (Stratford to Alcester) turn left to Temple Grafton. Pub at 1st x-rds*

Historic inn with Cotswolds views

The oldest part of this former ale house and now thriving village inn dates back to the early 1600s and includes a 35-foot deep well, now glassed over and illuminated, set into a flagstoned floor and home to goldfish. Warmth in the bar and restaurant comes from four open fires, while in the summer there is a patio garden with views of the Cotswold Hills. Extensive menus include steak from local Freeman's Farm, pork belly with cider jus, pub classics like chilli and coriander beefburger, and a steak and onion sandwich. Wash it down with a pint of Jennings or Wychwood Hobgoblin. There are 14 attractive bedrooms.

Open all day all wk 12-11.30 **Food** Lunch Mon-Fri 12-3, Sat 12-10, Sun 12-9 Dinner Mon-Fri 6-10, Sat 12-10, Sun 12-9 ⊕ MARSTON'S ◄ Pedigree, Wychwood Hobgoblin, Banks's Bitter, Jennings Ö Thatchers Gold. ♟ 10
Facilities Non-diners area ♣ (Bar Garden) ♦ Children's menu Children's portions Garden ⋒ Parking WiFi ⛟ (notice required) **Rooms** 14

WARWICK Map 10 SP26

The Rose & Crown PICK OF THE PUBS

tel: 01926 411117 **30 Market Place CV34 4SH**
email: roseandcrown@peachpubs.com
dir: *M40 junct 15 follow signs to Warwick. Pass castle car park entrance, up hill to West Gate, left into Bowling Green St, 1st right, follow one-way system to T-junct, right into Market Place, pub visible ahead*

Vibrant and stylish town-centre gastro-pub

In its major 2014 refit new seating, lighting and elegant stained glass were added to this popular meeting place. The makeover also saw a rear space converted into an eating and drinking area called The Yard. Overlooking Warwick's market place, its outside tables are in pole position for people-watching while sinking that pint of Harry's Heifer real ale or Harry Sparrow cider. In keeping with the pub's fresh image are new dishes on the modern British menu: mulled Cornish lamb casserole with creamy mash; and pan-fried sea bass with Bombay potatoes, onion bhaji and cardamom yogurt, for example. Deli boards offer selections of cheese, cold cuts, fish or vegetables; other possibilities include steaks from a Warwickshire butcher with a Royal Warrant; poached Loch Duart salmon; and French onion tart with Waldorf and blue cheese salad. On Finger Lickin' Fridays (last of the month) sliders and racks of ribs make an appearance.

Open all day all wk Mon-Wed 7am-11pm (Thu 7am-11.30pm Fri 7am-12.30am Sat 8am-12.30am Sun 8am-10pm) Closed 25 Dec **Food** Lunch all wk 12-6 Dinner Mon-Sat 6-10, Sun 6-9 Av main course £14.50 ⊕ FREE HOUSE ◀ Purity Pure UBU & Gold, Sharp's Doom Bar, Church Farm Harry's Heifer ◑ Aspall Draught & Harry Sparrow. ♟ **Facilities** Non-diners area ✿ (Bar) ♦♦ Children's portions Outside area ⋒ WiFi ⬛ (notice required)

WELFORD-ON-AVON Map 10 SP15

The Bell Inn PICK OF THE PUBS

tel: 01789 750353 **Binton Rd CV37 8EB**
email: info@thebellwelford.co.uk
dir: *Phone for detailed directions*

An enjoyably civilised pub

The interior of this appealing, early 16th-century pub is chock-full of signs of its age. Each distinct space displays its own character, with flagstones in one, and oak flooring in another; there's antique wood panelling in the bar, and three open fires, one an inglenook. Legend has it that William Shakespeare, having been drinking here with the dramatist Ben Jonson, contracted fatal pneumonia after returning to Stratford-upon-Avon in the pouring rain. It's a matter owners Colin and Teresa Ombler leave others to debate, while they focus on providing quality drink and food. For example, there are always four real ales and 16 wines served by the glass. Starters and light meals include smoked salmon with red onion and potato salad; and deep-fried brie with apricot and ginger compôte. Main courses include breaded garlic chicken breast stuffed with smoked cheddar with sweet potato mash and wilted spinach; shellfish paella topped with aïoli; or harissa and yogurt roasted salmon fillet on cucumber, watercress and baby spinach salad. Don't miss the hot-cross bun bread and butter pudding dessert.

Open all wk 11.30-3 6-11 (Sat 11.30-11 Sun 12-10.30) **Food** Lunch Mon-Fri 11.30-2.30, Sat-Sun all day Dinner Mon-Thu 6-9.30, Fri 6-10, Sat-Sun all day ⊕ ENTERPRISE INNS ◀ Hobsons Best Bitter, Purity Gold & Pure UBU, Morland Old Speckled Hen. ♟ 16 **Facilities** Non-diners area ♦♦ Children's menu Children's portions Garden ⋒ Parking WiFi ⬛ (notice required)

WITHYBROOK Map 11 SP48

The Pheasant Eating House

tel: 01455 220480 **Main St CV7 9LT**
email: thepheasant01@hotmail.com **web:** www.thepheasanteatinghouse.com
dir: *7m NE of Coventry, on B4112*

Crowd-pleasing pub grub in an idyllic location

A warm welcome awaits you at this 17th-century inn, idyllically situated beside the brook where withies were once cut for fencing, hence the village's name, Withybrook. The Pheasant is a popular free house, cosy and full of character with an inglenook fireplace, farm implements and horse-racing photographs on display. The chalkboard flags up specials, complementing a wealth of food choices from the extensive main menu. Take your pick from a range of steak and chicken grills (including fillet, rump and T-bone steaks; chicken Kiev, and Cajun chicken); a half roast duck with orange or plum sauce; and home-cooked lamb shank with root vegetables. Outside, the patio area is perfect for a leisurely lunch or a thirst-quenching pint of real ale after a walk in the beautiful countryside.

Open all wk 11-3 6-11.30 (Sun & BH 11-11) Closed 25-26 Dec **Food** Lunch Mon-Sat 12-2, Sun 12-9 Dinner Mon-Sat 6.30-10, Sun 12-9 Av main course £13 ⊕ FREE HOUSE ◀ Courage Directors, Theakston Smooth Dark, John Smith's Extra Smooth, Young's Bitter. ♟ 16 **Facilities** Non-diners area ✿ (Garden Outside area) ♦♦ Children's menu Children's portions Garden Outside area ⋒ Parking WiFi ⬛ (notice required)

See advert on opposite page

WEST MIDLANDS

BARSTON
Map 10 SP27

The Malt Shovel at Barston — PICK OF THE PUBS

See Pick of the Pubs on opposite page

BIRMINGHAM
Map 10 SP08

NEW The High Field

tel: 0121 227 7068 **22 Highfield Rd, Edgbaston B15 3DP**
email: highfield@peachpubs.com

Classy pub making its mark

The Peach Pubs group has renovated and extended this white-painted, early 20th-century Edgbaston villa to become a smart gastro-pub. With two patios to catch plenty of sun, a leafy garden and a light, contemporary orangery, it has rapidly grown very popular. Modern brasserie-style dishes, some available all day, include cheese, charcuterie, fish and veggie boards; 28-day aged steaks; free-range coq au vin; winter mulled lamb stew; and Loch Duart salmon fishcake. Warwickshire brewery Purity supplies UBU and Pure Gold, alongside Timothy Taylor Landlord and Aspall cider. Sundays offer far more than just roasts.

Open all day all wk Closed 25 Dec **Food** Lunch 12-6 Dinner 6-10 Av main course £10-£20 Restaurant menu available evenings ⊕ PEACH PUBS ◀ Timothy Taylor Landlord, Purity Pure Gold & UBU ○ Aspall. ♀ 16 **Facilities** Non-diners area ♣ (Bar Garden) ♦♦ Children's portions Garden ☞ Parking WiFi ➡ (notice required)

The Old Joint Stock

tel: 0121 200 1892 **4 Temple Row West B2 5NY**
email: oldjointstock@fullers.co.uk
dir: *Opposite main entrance to St Philip's Cathedral, just off Colmore Row*

Great for pies and pre-theatre drinks

A pub with its own theatre and art gallery, its high-Victorian Gothic interior incorporates an immense domed ceiling, stately-home fittings and towering mahogany island bar. Originally a library and later a bank, this impressively colonnaded building was designed by the same architect as part of St Philip's Cathedral opposite. Pies take up a chunk of the menu, which also features seared duck breast and pomegranate salad; pan-fried sea bass fillet with pearl barley and butterbean casserole, chorizo, salsa verde; and apple and blackberry crumble with custard. Beer festivals are held in both May and October.

Open all day (Sun 12-5) Closed Sun eve **Food** Lunch all wk 12-5 Dinner Mon-Sat 5-10 Av main course £10 ⊕ FULLER'S ◀ London Pride, ESB, Chiswick Bitter, Silhill Chatwin Golden Ale. ♀ 16 **Facilities** Non-diners area ♦♦ Family room Outside area ☞ Beer festival WiFi ➡ (notice required)

CHADWICK END
Map 10 SP27

The Orange Tree — PICK OF THE PUBS

tel: 01564 785364 **Warwick Rd B93 0BN**
email: theorangetree@lovelypubs.co.uk
dir: *3m from Knowle towards Warwick*

Informal modern revival with landscaped gardens

Part of the small, Warwickshire-centred Lovely Pubs chain, The Orange Tree adopts the house style of a light, modern interior, open kitchen, wooden floors, log fires and, here at least, old beams and antique mirrors. Wide-ranging menus group dishes according to type: 'grazing and sharing', 'hoof and fin', 'feather and fur' and 'pasta and flour'. Such generics embrace Mumbai meze of spiced aubergine dip, masala houmous, Bombay potato and spinach pakora; beef steak, stout, mushroom and black pudding pie; spit-roast chicken with winter slaw and fries; and king prawn and crab tagliatelle with chilli, spring onion and white wine cream. Puddings include sticky toffee pudding with butterscotch sauce and clotted cream; and Belgian waffle with banana, maple and walnut ice cream. Go for a 2-for-1 pizza deal (lunchtime and very early evening) on Monday to Fridays.

Open all day all wk 11-11 **Food** Lunch Mon-Sat 12-2.30, Sun 12-7 Dinner Mon-Sat 6-9.30, Sun 12-7 Set menu available ⊕ FREE HOUSE ◀ Sharp's Doom Bar, Greene King IPA. ♀ 10 **Facilities** Non-diners area ♣ (Bar Garden) ♦♦ Children's menu Children's portions Play area Garden ☞ Parking WiFi ➡ (notice required)

HAMPTON IN ARDEN
Map 10 SP28

The White Lion Inn — PICK OF THE PUBS

tel: 01675 442833 **10 High St B92 0AA**
email: info@thewhitelioninn.com
dir: *M42 junct 6, A45 towards Coventry. At rdbt take A452 towards Leamington Spa. At rdbt take B4102 towards Solihull. Approx 2m to Hampton in Arden*

Classic English, simple French and a bit of Jamaican

Once a farmhouse, this 17th-century, timber-framed pub first acquired a drinks licence in the early 1800s. Its bright, modern interior is today furnished with wicker chairs and decorated with fresh flowers. Landlord Chris Roach and his partner FanFan draw on their considerable experience of working in or visiting restaurants, bistros and gastro-pubs throughout England and France to present an ever-appealing combination of classic English pub grub and simple French bistro-style food. Black pudding St Malo would make a good starter, as would whitebait and Dijon mustard mayonnaise; a main of moules marinière à la crème and frites could continue the Gallic approach, or go Jamaican with curried goat and rice. There are also specials, jacket potatoes and toasted sandwiches. Real ales include Purity UBU, Banks's Sunbeam and Castle Rock Harvest Pale.

Open all day all wk noon-12.30am (Sun 12-10.30) **Food** Lunch Mon-Sat 12-2.30, Sun 12-4 Dinner all wk 6.30-9.30 ⊕ PUNCH TAVERNS ◀ M&B Brew XI, Purity UBU, Sharp's Doom Bar, Hobsons Best, Banks's Sunbeam, Castle Rock Harvest Pale ○ Westons Stowford Press, Aspall. ♀ 11 **Facilities** Non-diners area ♣ (Bar Restaurant Garden) ♦♦ Children's menu Children's portions Garden ☞ Parking WiFi ➡ (notice required)

SEDGLEY
Map 10 SO99

Beacon Hotel & Sarah Hughes Brewery — PICK OF THE PUBS

tel: 01902 883380 **129 Bilston St DY3 1JE**
dir: *Phone for detailed directions*

Enjoy a pint of ale brewed on the premises

Home of the Sarah Hughes Brewery, the Beacon Hotel is a restored Victorian tap house that has barely changed in 150 years. Proprietor John Hughes reopened the adjoining Sarah Hughes Brewery in 1987, 66 years after his grandmother became the licensee. The rare snob-screened island bar serves a simple taproom, with its old wall benches and a fine blackened range; a super cosy snug replete with a green-tiled marble fireplace, dark woodwork, velvet curtains and huge old tables; and a large smoke-room with an adjoining, plant-festooned conservatory. On a tour of the brewery you can see the original grist case and rare open-topped copper that add to the Victorian charm and give unique character to the brews. Flagship beers are Sarah Hughes Dark Ruby, Sedgley Surprise & Amber, with seasonal bitter and two guest beers from small microbreweries also available. Food in the pub is limited to filled cob rolls but there is a designated children's room and play area, as well as a large garden.

Open all wk 12-2.30 5.30-11 (Sat-Sun 12-3 6-11 Sun 12-3 7-10.30) **Food** Contact pub for food times ⊕ FREE HOUSE ◀ Sarah Hughes Dark Ruby, Sedgley Surprise & Amber, Guest ales. **Facilities** Non-diners area ♦♦ Play area Family room Garden Outside area ☞ Parking ➡ (notice required) **Notes** ⊛

PICK OF THE PUBS

The Malt Shovel at Barston

BARSTON Map 10 SP27

tel: 01675 443223
Barston Ln B92 0JP
email: themaltshovelatbarston
@gmail.com
web: www.themaltshovelatbarston.com
dir: *M42 junct 5, A4141 towards Knowle.
Left into Jacobean Ln, right at T-junct
(Hampton Ln). Left into Barston Ln,
0.5m to inn*

Smart, busy inn down the country lanes

The Malt Shovel is an airy, well designed free house with modern soft furnishings and interesting artefacts. An early 20th-century, stylishly converted mill building, it sits comfortably in the countryside outside Solihull. Natural wood and pastel colours characterise the interiors and flowers decorate the unclothed tables in the tiled dining area. The bar is cosy and relaxed with winter log fires, and there's an attractive garden for outdoor dining; at weekends the restaurant in the adjacent converted barn is opened. The extensive choice of modern British dishes makes the best of fresh seasonal ingredients, and, predictably, the daily fish specials board is popular with lovers of seafood. A look through the imaginative menu finds starters such as seared peppered tuna with celeriac, horseradish and enoki mushrooms; or harissa and honey

marinated chicken with winter slaw. Main course dishes are just as appetising: there could be pan-fried sea bass, new season Anya potatoes, chorizo, apple and pear salad; cocoa marinated venison, sour cherries, cabbage and bacon with fondant potatoes; and 12-hour braised beef, celeriac purée, bacon lardons and sherry jus. As for desserts, you could easily be tempted by wild berry risotto, honeycomb and vanilla ice cream; or apple and raisin bread and butter pudding with brandy custard, so tuck in. A board of English and European cheeses with grapes, celery, red onion chutney and artisan crackers will fill any remaining corners.

Open all day all wk **Food** Lunch Mon-Sat 12-2.30, Sun 12-4 Dinner Mon-Sat 6-9.30 Av main course £14.95
🍺 FREE HOUSE 🍺 St Austell Tribute, M&B Brew XI, Sharp's Doom Bar, Black Sheep. ♟ 15 **Facilities** Non-diners area
👬 Children's menu Children's portions Garden 🏠 Parking WiFi

WEST BROMWICH
Map 10 SP09

The Vine

tel: 0121 553 2866 **Roebuck St B70 6RD**
email: bharat@thevine.co.uk
dir: *M5 junct 1, follow West Bromwich/A41 signs. 1st left into Roebuck St. Pub at end on corner*

Spicy meals near West Brom's football ground

Certainly not the most attractive approach road to this pub, but keep going. Beers from reliable well-loved stalwarts such as Bathams and Holden's help this thriving, edge-of-town free house shine out. Equally adept at attracting customers to fill the surprisingly large open-plan interior and conservatory-style dining area is the remarkable menu created by Suki Patel, based around a pick 'n mix of firm Indian favourites. Channa massala, saag aloo, curried goat, kotmari lamb and mutter paneer all appear. The indoor barbecue is extremely popular, and there's also a range of traditional pub grub dishes like beef in ale pie, and fish and chips.

Open all wk 11.30-2.30 5-11 (Fri-Sat 12-11 Sun 12-10) **Food** Lunch Mon-Fri 11.30-2.30, Sat-Sun 12-10 Dinner Mon-Fri 5-10, Sat-Sun 12-10 Av main course £5.50 ⊕ FREE HOUSE ◀ Bathams, Holden's, Wye Valley, Burton Bridge. **Facilities** Non-diners area ◀▮ Garden ⌁ WiFi ▭ (notice required)

WILTSHIRE

ALDBOURNE
Map 5 SU27

The Blue Boar

tel: 01672 540237 **20 The Green SN8 2EN**
email: theblueboar@mail.com
dir: *From Salisbury take B4192 to Aldbourne. Or M4 junct 14 take A338 to Hungerford, B4192 to Aldbourne & follow brown signs*

The sort of pub to dream about when abroad

This Wadworth-owned, 16th-century pub stands on the village green, itself distanced from traffic, with views of pretty houses, the church and a Celtic cross. It couldn't wish for a better location, so outdoor drinking and eating are a particular pleasure, although there will be times when the two open fires inside beckon. Home-prepared food includes sandwiches and baguettes; chicken liver pâté; wild boar sausages, mash and onion gravy; and sweet potato chickpea and spinach peas. Landlords Michael and Joanne Hehir hold a beer festival over the first weekend in June, while local enthusiasts periodically relive wartime days when an American parachute regiment was billeted locally.

Open all wk 11.30-3 5.30-11 (Fri-Sun 11.30-11) **Food** Lunch Mon-Fri 12-2, Sat 12-2.30, Sun 12-4 Dinner Mon-Sat 6.30-9 ⊕ WADWORTH ◀ 6X & Henry's Original IPA, Guest ales ⚫ Westons Stowford Press. **Facilities** Non-diners area ❀ (Bar Garden) ◀▮ Children's menu Children's portions Garden ⌁ Beer festival Cider festival WiFi ▭ (notice required)

The Crown Inn

tel: 01672 540214 **The Square SN8 2DU**
email: bookings@thecrownaldbourne.co.uk
dir: *M4 junct 15, N on A419, signed Aldbourne*

Classic village-square inn in popular rambling area

This imposing coaching inn has served the village for over 400 years, and retains much period feel in the well-beamed old bar. In the Second World War, American NCOs made it their mess-room and enjoyed local beers and food; today's regulars

and visitors may indulge in White Horse or Bryden ales, whilst the home-prepared food majors on ingredients sourced from local suppliers. 'Pie of the Moment' and scampi and chips are favourites, as are the burgers and home-made stone-baked pizzas. There are beer festivals each May and September and a cider festival is held in July.

Open all day all wk 12-12 **Food** Lunch all wk, all day Dinner all wk, all day Av main course £10 Restaurant menu available all wk ⊕ ENTERPRISE INNS ◀ Timothy Taylor Landlord, Shepherd Neame Spitfire, Ramsbury Gold, Sharp's Doom Bar, Guest ales ⚫ Westons Stowford Press, Aspall. ♒ 16 **Facilities** Non-diners area ❀ (Bar Garden) ◀▮ Children's menu Children's portions Play area Garden ⌁ Beer festival Cider festival Parking WiFi ▭ (notice required)

BERWICK ST JAMES
Map 5 SU03

The Boot Inn

tel: 01722 790243 **High St SP3 4TN**
email: cathy@theboot.pub
dir: *From either A303 (Deptford to Winterbourne Stoke) or A36 (Deptford to Salisbury) take B3083 to Berwick St James. Pub in village centre*

Worth a detour if you're on the A303

Here in their picturesque 18th-century former coaching inn, formally trained chefs and landlords Giles and Cathy Dickinson aim to provide 'traditional British food', all home-made or locally sourced as far as possible. It's a Wadworth house which, as all the Devizes brewery's disciples know, means 6X and Henry's Original IPA. The Dickinson's say you won't find curry, chilli, lasagne or 'expensive gastro-pub concoctions'; instead, dishes like devilled ducks' hearts; peppered fig and Whitehaven cheese salad; whole grilled Cornish plaice with melted potted shrimps and purple sprouting broccoli; crayfish tail and orange salad; warm salad of slow-roast duck leg with caramelised orange and watercress and truffle oil; and apple and rhubarb crumble, or elderflower and butter milk pudding with fresh raspberries to finish.

Open 12-3 6-11 (Fri-Sat 12-3 6-12 Sun 12-4) Closed 1-13 Feb, Sun eve & Mon **Food** Lunch 12-2.15 Dinner 6.30-9.15 Av main course £12.50 ⊕ WADWORTH ◀ Henry's Original IPA & 6X. ♒ 9 **Facilities** Non-diners area ❀ (Bar Restaurant Garden) ◀▮ Children's menu Children's portions Garden ⌁ Parking

BERWICK ST JOHN
Map 4 ST92

The Talbot Inn

tel: 01747 828222 **The Cross SP7 0HA**
dir: *From Shaftesbury take A30 towards Salisbury. Right to Berwick St John. Pub 1.5m*

Traditional pub with lots of character

The Talbot Inn used to be three cottages, one of them the village shop, before becoming an alehouse in 1835. This typical old English country free house in the beautiful Chalke Valley dates from the 17th century and has the beams, low ceilings and huge inglenook fireplace so typical of its kind. Real ales plus good home-cooked food shown on the menus and specials board are on offer; try the crumbed butterfly prawns with sweet chilli dipping sauce or garlic mushrooms to start; followed by cooked ham, egg and chips; home-made lasagne or salmon and broccoli mornay.

Open 12-2.30 6.30-11 (Sun 12-4) Closed Sun eve & Mon **Food** Lunch Tue-Sun 12-2 Dinner Tue-Sat 6.30-9 ⊕ FREE HOUSE ◀ Ringwood Best Bitter, Wadworth 6X, Sixpenny Handley IPA ⚫ Westons Stowford Press. **Facilities** ❀ (Bar Garden) ◀▮ Children's portions Garden Parking

PICK OF THE PUBS

The Tollgate Inn ★★★★ INN

BRADFORD-ON-AVON   Map 4 ST86

tel: 01225 782326 **Holt BA14 6PX**
email: laura@tollgateinn.co.uk
web: www.tollgateinn.co.uk
dir: *M4 junct 18, A46 towards Bath, then A363 to Bradford-on-Avon, then B3107 towards Melksham, pub on right*

Sixteenth-century country inn with large grounds

Bradford-on-Avon was once at the heart of a thriving woollen textile industry, which is why one part of this stone-built village inn used to be a weaving shed, another the weavers' own chapel. Oak-floored and sofa-furnished, the main bar serves Ashton Press and Toodle Pip ciders, real ales from local breweries like Box Steam and Butcombe, and nigh on 20 wines by the glass. The two dining rooms, one upstairs in the old chapel, offer a seasonal menu based on the principle: 'If it isn't local, there will be a damn good reason why!' Expect therefore hand-reared, free-range meats from the farm opposite, day-boat fish from Lyme Bay and Brixham, and vegetables from nearby Bromham. A smoked haddock and anchovy fishcake comes with tartare dressing; and spinach, feta and herb roll with cucumber yoghurt and red onion salad. Main courses include Cumberland sausages with bubble-and-squeak, braised red cabbage and red onion gravy; slow-roast pork belly with apple

crisps, caramelised onion purée, mustard mash and honeyed carrots; and vegetarian risotto of the day. Listed among the daily specials are various dishes of the day, such as ham, pea and vegetable pie; pan-roasted pork loin steak; and fillet of roasted salmon. For dessert you could be fairly certain of chocolate and hazelnut brownie with ice cream and chocolate sauce; or date and walnut sticky toffee pudding. Sandwiches available at lunchtime include smoked salmon and crayfish, and tenderised striploin steak with caramelised onions; quiche of the day is another possibility. Wines are selected from all over the world. Pub quizzes are every other Tuesday and there's live music every Friday in July.

Open all day 9am-11.30pm (Sun 9-4.30) Closed 25 Dec, Sun eve **Food** Lunch Tue-Sat 12-2, Sun 12-2.30 Dinner Tue-Sat 6.30-9 Set menu available Restaurant menu available all wk ⊕ FREE HOUSE ◑ Butcombe Adam Henson's Rare Breed, Box Steam Tunnel Vision, Fuller's London Pride ♂ Ashton Press, Toodle Pip. ♟ 19 **Facilities** Non-diners area ♦ Children's menu & portions Garden ⋒ Parking WiFi 🚌 (notice required) **Rooms** 5

BISHOPSTONE
Map 5 SU28

The Royal Oak

tel: 01793 790481 **Cues Ln SN6 8PP**
email: royaloak@helenbrowningorganics.co.uk
dir: *M4 junct 15, A419 towards Swindon. At rdbt right into Pack Hill signed Wanborough. In Bishopstone left into Cues Ln. Pub on right*

Rustic, relaxed and friendly pub with its own farm

Organic farmer Helen Browning OBE rescued the delightful Royal Oak from closure. It stands tucked away in a glorious village below the Wiltshire Downs, and you can expect a cracking community atmosphere, Arkell's ales, Westons ciders, roaring log fires and daily-changing menus. Almost 60 per cent of produce comes from Helen's own farm, with the rest sourced from three other local organic farms and allotments. A three-course dinner could be pork rillettes, cornichons and dressed leaves; 40-day aged beef fillet with sauce béarnaise, hand-cut chips and salad; and caramelised apple and raspberry upside down cake with star anise custard. The child-friendly garden has a Wendy house and rope swing.

Open all wk 12-3 6-11 (Sat 12-12 Sun 12-10) **Food** Lunch all wk 12-3 Dinner all wk 6-9.30 ⊕ ARKELL'S ◀ Moonlight & 3B, Donnington SBA Ō Westons Old Rosie, Wyld Wood Organic & Perry. ♥ 12 **Facilities** Non-diners area ✿ (All areas) ♦♦ Children's menu Children's portions Play area Garden Outside area ☞ Parking WiFi ▭ (notice required)

BOX
Map 4 ST86

The Northey Arms ★★★★★ INN ⊚

tel: 01225 742333 **Bath Rd SN13 8AE**
email: thenorthey@ohhcompany.co.uk **web:** www.ohhcompany.co.uk
dir: *A4 from Bath towards Chippenham, 4m. Between M4 juncts 17 & 18*

Contemporary inn close to Bath

The former station hotel, built by Brunel for the workers who were building Box Tunnel, was transformed from a shabby roadside drinking pub to a stylish inn by Mark Warburton. The contemporary interior makes good use of wood and flagstone flooring, high-backed oak chairs, leather loungers and handcrafted tables around the bar, where inviting sandwiches (salmon, BLT or ham, tomato and mustard) and pub classics like poached eggs on toast hold sway. The main menu ranges from wood pigeon with rösti and carrots; and pan-fried calves' liver and bacon to the pub's speciality fish dishes and great steaks. Swish bedrooms complete the picture.

Open all day all wk Closed 25 Dec **Food** Lunch all wk 12-9.30 Dinner all wk 12-9.30 ⊕ FREE HOUSE ◀ Butcombe, Wadworth 6X, Guest ale Ō Ashton Press, Kingstone Press. ♥ 16 **Facilities** Non-diners area ✿ (Bar Garden) ♦♦ Children's menu Children's portions Garden ☞ Parking WiFi **Rooms** 5

The Quarrymans Arms

tel: 01225 743569 **Box Hill SN13 8HN**
email: pub@quarrymans-arms.co.uk
dir: *Phone for detailed directions*

Former miners' pub with excellent views

Superb views of the Box Valley can be enjoyed from this 300-year-old pub, from where you can also see Solsbury Hill. A display of Bath stone-mining memorabilia bears witness to the years Brunel's navvies spent driving the Great Western Railway through Box Tunnel (spot the bar's replica fireplace) deep beneath the pub. The resultant honeycomb of Bath stone workings attract potholers and cavers, who slake their thirsts on local ales and ciders, and replace lost calories with Thai chicken curry; Boxhill bangers with chips, beans, egg and salad; or something from

the comprehensive vegetarian selection. 'Mini ale weeks' are held throughout the year – check with the pub for details.

Open all day all wk 11am-11.30pm **Food** Lunch all wk 11-3 Dinner all wk from 6 ⊕ FREE HOUSE ◀ Butcombe Bitter, Wadworth 6X, Moles Best, Local guest ales Ō Black Rat, Ashton Press. ♥ 13 **Facilities** Non-diners area ✿ (All areas) ♦♦ Children's menu Children's portions Family room Garden Outside area ☞ Beer festival Cider festival Parking WiFi ▭ (notice required)

BRADFORD-ON-AVON
Map 4 ST86

The Dandy Lion

tel: 01225 863433 **35 Market St BA15 1LL**
email: Dandylion35@aol.com
dir: *Phone for detailed directions*

In bustling town near bridge over the River Avon

In the centre of the lovely market town of Bradford-on-Avon, this 18th-century inn was once a boot and shoe shop and a grocery. It is now a popular bar and restaurant offering well-kept Wadworth ales and continental lagers, together with a mix of traditional English and rustic European food. The bar menu offers hot filled flatbreads, light bites and salads, whilst the choice in the upstairs restaurant menu might include chicken Kiev, flash-fried hanger steak, seafood pot pie, nut and seed roast, or home-baked Wiltshire ham, free-range eggs and triple cooked chips.

Open all wk 11-3 6-11 (Fri-Sat 11-11 Sun 11.30-10.30) Closed 25 Dec **Food** Lunch Mon-Thu 12-2.15, Fri-Sat all day, Sun all day till 8.30 Dinner Mon Thu 6-9.30, Fri-Sat all day, Sun all day till 8.30 Restaurant menu available Fri-Sat eve ⊕ WADWORTH ◀ 6X, Henry's Original IPA, Seasonal ales Ō Westons Rosie's Pig. ♥ 21 **Facilities** Non-diners area ✿ (Bar) ♦♦ Children's portions

The Tollgate Inn ★★★★ INN
PICK OF THE PUBS

See Pick of the Pubs on page 527

BRINKWORTH
Map 4 SU08

The Three Crowns
PICK OF THE PUBS

tel: 01666 510366 **SN15 5AF**
email: info@threecrownsbrinkworth.co.uk
dir: *From Swindon take A3102 to Royal Wootton Bassett, take B4042, 5m to Brinkworth*

Traditional village inn serving not-so traditional food

The Three Crowns is a thriving community pub, welcoming locals and their dogs, and families set on celebrating a special occasion. Lots of greenery inside and out here, with the little village green at the front and the conservatory restaurant hosting some large pot-plants. The village sits in rich farming countryside on a low ridge above the River Avon and there are lovely views from the pub's secluded beer garden and tree-shaded patio, where heaters bring additional comfort as the evenings draw in. Amiable staff greet you in the cosy, beamed bar, where ales include Fuller's London Pride. The menu has long been recognised for its ambition and variety. Expect starters like pan-friend scallops with pea purée and fish cream; or chicken liver parfait. Follow with oven-roasted lamb rump, pavé of venison with horseradish mash; or salmon fillet with pesto mash and herb gnocchi.

Open all day all wk 10am-mdnt **Food** Lunch Mon-Sat 12-2.30, Sun 12-9 Dinner Mon-Sat 6-9.30, Sun 12-9 Set menu available ⊕ PRESTIGIOUS RESTAURANTS ◀ Sharp's Doom Bar, Fuller's London Pride, Greene King IPA Ō Westons Stowford Press. ♥ 27 **Facilities** Non-diners area ✿ (Bar Garden) ♦♦ Children's menu Children's portions Play area Garden ☞ Beer festival Cider festival Parking WiFi ▭ (notice required)

BROUGHTON GIFFORD
Map 4 ST86

The Fox

tel: 01225 782949 **The Street SN12 8PN**
email: alexgeneen@gmail.com
dir: *From Melksham take B3107 towards Holt. Turn right to Broughton Gifford. Pub in village centre*

Showing a commitment to home-grown and home-reared produce

The excellent ales at this village pub are augmented in the summer months when it hosts a beer and cider festival. Food standards are high too. The owners raise their own chickens, ducks and pigs, tend an extensive vegetable and herb garden, and barter with villagers for wildfowl and other produce. Bread is either baked in the kitchen or provided by the ethical Thoughtful Bread Company, and The Fox produces cured hams, charcuterie and sausages from its pigs. Typical dishes on the menus are smoked haddock Scotch egg with truffled cream leeks; and fillet of beef, boulangère potato, curly kale, garlic and shallot purée.

Open 12-3 5-9.30 Closed 26 Dec, 1 Jan, Mon **Food** Lunch Tue-Sun 12-2.30 Dinner Mon-Sat 6-9.30 Set menu available ⊕ FREE HOUSE ◀ Bath Gem, Butcombe Bitter. ♟ 18 **Facilities** Non-diners area ☕ (Bar Restaurant Garden) ♦♦ Children's menu Children's portions Garden ⌐ Beer festival Cider festival Parking WiFi ☎ (notice required)

BURTON
Map 4 ST87

The Old House at Home ★★★★★ INN

tel: 01454 218227 **SN14 7LT**
email: office@ohhcompany.co.uk **web:** www.ohhcompany.co.uk
dir: *On B4039 NW of Chippenham*

Family-run, traditional ivy-clad free house offering a warm welcome

This ivy-clad, stone built free house dates from the early 19th century and is run by the Warburton family. Dad David has been here for years and still happily pulls pints of Maiden Voyage, Wadworth 6X and Thatchers Gold in the low-beamed bar. The finest seasonal ingredients are used to create impressive menu favourites like venison casserole; peppered smoked haddock pilaf; lasagne verdi or home-cooked, honey-glazed ham. The beautifully landscaped gardens feature a waterfall. Six high quality bedrooms are available in a stylish annexe.

Open all day all wk **Food** Lunch all wk 12-9.30 Dinner all wk 12-9.30 ⊕ FREE HOUSE ◀ Ales of Scilly Maiden Voyage, Wadworth 6X, Guest ales ᵹ Thatchers Gold & Traditional. ♟ 12 **Facilities** Non-diners area ☕ (Bar Restaurant Garden) ♦♦ Children's menu Children's portions Garden ⌐ Parking WiFi ☎ (notice required) **Rooms** 6

CALNE
Map 4 ST97

The Lansdowne ★★★ INN

tel: 01249 812488 **The Strand SN11 OEH**
email: lansdowne@arkells.com **web:** www.lansdownestrand.co.uk
dir: *On A4 in town centre*

Traditional food and local ales close to the M4

Just 15 minutes from the M4 in the heart of Calne, this 16th-century former coaching inn was once home to the local brewery and the courtyard still retains the medieval brew house. Owned by Arkell's, the bar showcases that brewery's beers including Moonlight, alongside monthly guest ales. The straightforward and appealing food menu focuses on traditional pub meals and old favourites. Typical dishes include home-made lasagne; mac and cheese; homity pie with buttered

mash and buttered green beans; and sea bass fishcakes. At lunchtime, there is also a well-priced choice of sandwiches and jacket potatoes.

Open all day all wk **Food** Lunch all wk 9-2 Dinner Mon-Sat 6-9 Av main course £8.50 Restaurant menu available all wk (except Sun evening) ⊕ ARKELL'S ◀ 3B, Moonlight, Guest ale ᵹ Westons Stowford Press. **Facilities** Non-diners area ☕ (Bar Outside area) ♦♦ Children's menu Children's portions Outside area ⌐ Parking WiFi ☎ **Rooms** 25

The White Horse Inn ★★★★ INN ◉

tel: 01249 813118 **Compton Bassett SN11 8RG**
email: info@whitehorse-comptonbassett.co.uk
web: www.whitehorse-comptonbassett.co.uk
dir: *M4 junct 16 onto A3102, after Hilmarton turn left to Compton Bassett*

Civilised drinking and dining

A stone-built, whitewashed village pub, named after the equine figure cut out of the chalk on a nearby hillside in 1870. The bar's log-burner keeps customers warm in winter, while a year-round attraction is the ever-changing roster of local and national real ales. The kitchen relies on seasonal ingredients – their source, the closer to home the better – for braised oxtail, confit beef tongue, creamed mash, spinach and olive jus; braised shoulder of Wiltshire lamb with curly kale and ratatouille; and fillet of Cornish hake with risotto nero. Pecan tart with organic vanilla ice cream makes for a good finish.

Open all day all wk **Food** Lunch Mon-Sat 12-9, Sun 12-6 Dinner Mon-Sat 12-9 Restaurant menu available ⊕ FREE HOUSE ◀ Bath Ales Gem, Sharp's Doom Bar, Wadworth 6X, Adnams ᵹ Westons Old Rosie. ♟ 16 **Facilities** Non-diners area ☕ (Bar Garden) ♦♦ Children's menu Children's portions Garden ⌐ Parking WiFi ☎ (notice required) **Rooms** 8

COATE
Map 5 SU18

The Sun Inn ★★★★ INN

tel: 01793 523292 **Marlborough Rd SN3 6AA**
email: sun-inn@arkells.com **web:** www.suninn-swindon.co.uk
dir: *M4 junct 15, A419 towards Swindon. At 1st rdbt take A459 signed Swindon & hospital. Left lane at lights. Pub on left before next rdbt*

Ideal watering hole for families

The third Sun public house on this site since 1685, today's pre-war building is close to Arkell's Swindon brewery, which bought its predecessor in 1891. With a large garden and playground, and with Coate Water Country Park nearby, it is understandably popular with families, for whom the menus have clearly been designed. For example, there are takeaway fish and chips, sandwiches and hot drinks; chicken nuggets; giant fish fingers; cheeseburgers; and filled deli rolls. Main dishes include home-made three-cheese macaroni; Wiltshire pork sausages and mash; and scampi, chips and peas. An ever-changing specials board adds to the wide-ranging tally.

Open all day all wk **Food** Lunch all wk 12-9 Dinner all wk 12-9 ⊕ ARKELL'S ◀ 3B, Kingsdown & Wiltshire Gold ᵹ Westons Stowford Press & Old Rosie. ♟ 10 **Facilities** Non-diners area ☕ (Bar Restaurant Garden) ♦♦ Children's menu Play area Garden ⌐ Parking WiFi ☎ (notice required) **Rooms** 10

COLLINGBOURNE DUCIS
Map 5 SU25

The Shears Inn

tel: 01264 850304 **The Cadley Rd SN8 3ED**
email: info@theshears.co.uk
dir: Just off A338 between Marlborough & Salisbury

Delightful thatched pub with modern British menu

Dating from the 18th century, this traditional family-run country inn was once a shearing shed for market-bound sheep. The original part of the building is thatched, while inside you'll find wooden and slate floors, low-beamed ceilings and a large inglenook dominating the restaurant. Typical choices from the tasty modern British menu may include spiced potted beef with tangerine and chilli relish; slow-roast shoulder of lamb with cavolo nero and aubergine purée; fish pie with prawns and cheesy topping; and dark and white chocolate terrine with poached ginger pear; or blackberry and apple crumble with gingerbread ice cream for afters. The enclosed sunny garden is an ideal place for a quiet drink and for the annual cider festival held in late summer.

Open 11-3 6-11 (Sat 11-11 summer, Sun fr 12) Closed Sun eve **Food** Lunch Mon-Sat 12-2, Sun 12-3.30 Dinner Mon-Sat 6-9.30 Restaurant menu available Mon-Sat ⊕ BRAKSPEAR ◀ Brakspear, Ringwood, Local guest ales ♂ Addlestones, Aspall. ♀ 12 **Facilities** Non-diners area ✿ (Bar Restaurant Garden) ♦ Children's menu Children's portions Garden ⋈ Cider festival Parking WiFi ▭ (notice required)

CORTON
Map 4 ST94

The Dove Inn ★★★★ INN ◉
PICK OF THE PUBS

tel: 01985 850109 **BA12 0SZ**
email: info@thedove.co.uk **web:** www.thedove.co.uk
dir: 5m SE of Warminster. Exit A36 to Corton

Pub in the heart of the countryside

A warm welcome is guaranteed at this bustling 19th-century pub, tucked away in the delightful Wylye Valley. Plenty of original features are still in evidence such as the striking central fireplace and flagstone and oak floors. The appealing menu is based firmly on West Country produce, with many ingredients coming from just a few miles away. Popular lunchtime bar snacks give way to a full evening carte featuring well-made and hearty pub classics. Typical starters include whitebait with home-made lemon and tartare sauce; and mussels in creamy white wine and fresh crab sauce. These might be followed by slow-braised lamb shank with mustard mash, or the Dove Inn mixed grill. Fish and chips, and the famous Dove burger and chips are available to take away, traditionally wrapped in newspaper.

The garden is the perfect spot for barbecues or a drink on summer days while the bedrooms arranged around a courtyard make the Dove an ideal touring base.

Open all day all wk **Food** Lunch all wk 12-2.30 Dinner all wk 6-9 Restaurant menu available all wk ⊕ FREE HOUSE ◀ Otter, Atlantic, Guest ale ♂ Aspall. **Facilities** Non-diners area ✿ (Bar Garden) ♦ Children's portions Garden ⋈ Parking WiFi ▭ (notice required) **Rooms** 14

CRICKLADE
Map 5 SU09

The Red Lion Inn ★★★★ INN ◉

tel: 01793 750776 **74 High St SN6 6DD**
email: info@theredlioninncricklade.co.uk **web:** www.theredlioninncricklade.co.uk
dir: M4 junct 15, A419 towards Cirencester. Left onto B4040 into Cricklade. Right at T-junct (mini rdbt) into High St. Inn on right

On-site microbrewery and Saddleback pigs

Just off the Thames Path as it passes through historic Cricklade, this early 17th-century pub retains many historic features. Hop Kettle microbrewery in a barn behind the pub adds to the line-up of real ales and ciders, including Wadworth 6X and Mates Jackdaw. Home-prepared restaurant food is noteworthy for using locally foraged and wild ingredients, rare-breed meats and sustainable fish. Customers can even swap fruit and veg from their gardens for vouchers towards food and drink. Opt for hop-smoked Bibury rainbow trout with celeriac remoulade; Dorset spring lamb breast with lyonnaise potatoes, parsnip purée, caramelised baby carrots, spring cabbage and mint jelly; and a delicious warm citrus sponge with Grand Marnier syrup, candied orange, and elderflower sorbet to finish.

Open all day all wk **Food** Lunch Mon-Sat 12-2.30, Sun 12-3 Dinner Mon-Thu 6.30-9 Restaurant menu available Tue-Sat evenings ⊕ FREE HOUSE ◀ Hop Kettle North Wall & Tricerahops, Wadworth 6X ♂ Mates Ravens Roost & Jackdaw. ♀ 9 **Facilities** Non-diners area ✿ (Bar Garden) ♦ Children's menu Children's portions Garden ⋈ Beer festival WiFi **Rooms** 5

CRUDWELL
Map 4 ST99

The Potting Shed

tel: 01666 577833 **The Street SN16 9EW**
email: bookings@thepottingshedpub.com
dir: On A429 between Malmesbury & Cirencester

A warm welcome to all awaits at this dining pub

In addition to the grown-ups, children and dogs are very welcome at this Cotswold dining pub, which prides itself on offering good bitter, interesting wine and creative British food. Light pastel shades and beams scrubbed down to their natural hue characterise the appealing interior, where typical dishes include potted smoked mackerel, tarragon brown butter and sourdough toast; seared fallow deer, game sausage toad-in-the-hole, parsnips and red cabbage; and apple and cinnamon pie with clotted cream. Food and drink can be served outside; two acres of grounds allow plenty of space for lawns, fruit trees and vegetable plots which supply fresh produce for the kitchen.

Open all day all wk **Food** Lunch Mon-Sat 12-2.30, Sun 12-3 Dinner Mon-Sat 7-9.30, Sun 7-9 Av main course £14.50 ⊕ ENTERPRISE INNS ◀ Bath Ales Gem, Timothy Taylor Landlord, Flying Monk Elmers ♂ Thatchers, Bath Ciders Bounders. ♀ 25 **Facilities** Non-diners area ✿ (Bar Restaurant Garden) ♦ Children's portions Garden ⋈ Beer festival Parking WiFi ▭ (notice required)

PICK OF THE PUBS

The Fox and Hounds

EAST KNOYLE Map 4 ST83

tel: 01747 830573
The Green SP3 6BN
email: fox.hounds@virgin.net
web: www.foxandhounds-eastknoyle.co.uk
dir: *From A303 follow Blandford/East Knoyle signs onto A350, follow brown pub signs*

Traditional pub with lovely views

This partly thatched and half-timbered, rustic 15th-century inn makes the most of its stunning Blackmore Vale location. There are exceptional views from the patio beer garden and nearby East Knoyle village green across these Wiltshire and Dorset boundary-lands, where Sir Christopher Wren was born and the family of Jane Seymour (Henry VIII's third wife) were based. Hidden in a timeless village on a greensand ridge, the engaging exterior is well matched by the atmospheric interior, with lots of flagstone flooring, wood-burning fires and restful stripped wood furniture. Locals eager to partake of Thatchers Cheddar Valley cider or Hop Back Crop Circle rub shoulders with diners keen to make the acquaintance of the eclectic menu. Blackboard menus increase the choice, dependant entirely on the availability of the freshest local fare. Starters might include lightly dusted calamari with garlic mayonnaise; and deep-fried rosemary and garlic crusted

brie wedges with cranberry jelly. When it comes to main courses, good, wholesome pub grub like fish pie; chicken pie with chips and vegetables and home-made sausages, mash and gravy share the board with lamb shank braised in red wine; slow-roasted belly pork with an apple and cider sauce; duck breast with damson sauce and spring onion mash; or murgh makhani, basmati rice and chota naan. Stone-baked pizzas from a clay oven and a comprehensive children's menu add to the fray, whilst desserts include lemon posset and shortbread or rhubarb and apple crumble with vanilla ice cream. There is also a gluten-free chocolate fondant and ice cream.

Open all wk 11.30-3 5.30-11
Food Lunch all wk 12-2.30 Dinner all wk 6-9 Av main course £12 ⊕ FREE HOUSE
🍺 Hop Back Crop Circle & Summer Lightning, Palmers Dorset Gold & Copper Ale, Butcombe, Otter Amber ♉ Thatchers Cheddar Valley & Old Rascal. ☻ 12 **Facilities** Non-diners area ❀ (Bar Restaurant Garden)
♦♦ Children's menu Garden ⋒ Parking WiFi 🚌 (notice required)

DEVIZES   Map 4 SU06

The Raven Inn

tel: 01380 828271 **Poulshot Rd SN10 1RW**
email: theraveninnpoulshot@yahoo.co.uk
dir: *A361 from Devizes towards Trowbridge, left at Poulshot sign*

A warm welcome and ever-changing menus of home-cooked food

Worth noting if walking the Kennet & Avon Canal towpath (with or without your dog) or visiting the famous Caen Hill flight of locks, as this half-timbered 18th-century pub is just a short walk away. Divert for tip-top Wadworth ales and the weekly-changing menu, which offers a mixture of modern pub classics and more imaginative dishes. Expect to find ham, egg and chips; steak and kidney pie; and the Raven burger alongside Nasi Goreng and grilled sole with lemon and parsley butter. Leave room for warm sticky toffee pudding or pear and almond tart.

Open 11.30-2.30 6-11 (Sun 12-3 6-10) Closed Sun eve & Mon (Oct-Etr) **Food** Lunch all wk 12-2 Dinner all wk 6.30-9 ⊕ WADWORTH ◂ 6X, Henry's Original IPA, Horizon, Old Timer ♂ Thatchers Gold. ♈ 12 **Facilities** Non-diners area ✿ (Bar Garden) ♦♦ Children's menu Children's portions Garden ⌁ Beer festival Parking WiFi ⬛ (notice required)

DONHEAD ST ANDREW   Map 4 ST92

The Forester   PICK OF THE PUBS

tel: 01747 828038 **Lower St SP7 9EE**
email: possums1@btinternet.com
dir: *From Shaftesbury on A30 towards Salisbury. In approx 4.5m left, follow village signs*

Traditional pub specialising in West Country seafood

A dog-friendly watering hole, this lovely 15th-century pub is an ideal place to put your feet up after a long walk with your best friend. Close to Wardour Castle in a pretty village, The Forester has warm stone walls, a thatched roof, original beams and inglenook fireplace. Local Donhead Craft cider is a popular addition to the Butcombe and Otter ales served at the bar. An extension houses a restaurant plus a restaurant/meeting room, with double doors opening onto the lower patio area. The pub has a reputation for excellent cooking at reasonable prices, and for its use of fresh West Country ingredients, especially seafood. Dishes are constructed with a mix of traditional and cosmopolitan flavours, local rabbit, mushroom and cavolo nero linguine with crispy ham and parmesan is typical. Follow with a main course of pan-fried fillet of wild Cornish sea bass served with pressed potatoes, wild mushrooms and celeriac purée.

Open 12-2 6.30-11 Closed 25-26 Dec, Sun eve, Mon **Food** Lunch Tue-Sun 12-2 Dinner Tue-Sat 7-9 Av main course £13.50-£16.50 Set menu available ⊕ FREE HOUSE ◂ Butcombe, Otter ♂ Donhead Craft Cider, Westons Wyld Wood Organic. ♈ 15 **Facilities** Non-diners area ✿ (Bar Restaurant Garden) ♦♦ Children's menu Children's portions Garden ⌁ Parking WiFi ⬛ (notice required)

EAST CHISENBURY   Map 5 SU15

Red Lion Freehouse ★★★★★ INN ◉◉◉
PICK OF THE PUBS

tel: 01980 671124 **SN9 6AQ**
email: enquiries@redlionfreehouse.com **web:** www.redlionfreehouse.com
dir: *From A303 take A345 N. Exit at Enford. Left at T-junct towards East Chisenbury. Pub 1m on right*

Astonishing cuisine at a beautiful thatched village inn

Secluded in the upper Avon Valley in a fold of Salisbury Plain, this ancient inn shares a sleepy hollow with other eye-catching thatched properties. Elements of the Tudor pub remain, with plenty of character injected by bare brick, log-burner and other rustic flourishes. At the bar, beer-hounds will be delighted with a rolling

selection of local microbrewery beers like Keystone or Plain Ales – there's a May beer festival too. Equally content will be gastronomes seeking out the confident, contemporary menu which now has a three AA Rosette award. Licensees Guy and Brittany Manning have a distinguished pedigree in the restaurant world and bring particular flair to the range of dishes crafted from local, seasonal ingredients. Kick in with sika venison and pistachio terrine, then look for slow-cooked pigs' cheeks (from pub-raised pigs) with crisp polenta, roasted fennel, Burbage shiitakes and pork cracker. Tucked behind the Red Lion is a tranquil tree-shaded beer garden. Luxury riverside accommodation completes the dream here.

Open all day all wk **Food** Lunch all wk 12.30-2.30 Dinner Mon-Sat 6.30-9, Sun 6-8 Av main course £20 Set menu available ⊕ FREE HOUSE ◂ Stonehenge Ales, Ramsbury, Cottage, Guest ales ♂ Ty Gwyn, Black Rat, Perry's. ♈ 30 **Facilities** ✿ (All areas) ♦♦ Children's menu Children's portions Garden Outside area ⌁ Beer festival Parking WiFi **Rooms** 5

EAST KNOYLE   Map 4 ST83

The Fox and Hounds   PICK OF THE PUBS

See Pick of the Pubs on page 531

EBBESBOURNE WAKE   Map 4 ST92

The Horseshoe   PICK OF THE PUBS

tel: 01722 780474 **Handley St SP5 5JF**
dir: *Phone for detailed directions*

Well-kept beers and home-made food

Dating from the 17th century, the family-run Horseshoe is a genuine old English pub in the pretty village of Ebbesbourne Wake. The original building has not changed much, except for a conservatory extension to accommodate more diners, and there's a lovely flower-filled garden. Beyond the climbing roses are two rooms adorned with simple furniture, old farming implements and country bygones, linked to a central servery where well-kept cask-conditioned ales are dispensed straight from their barrels – Bowman Ales Swift One, Otter Bitter and Palmers Copper Ale – plus real ciders too. Good-value traditional bar food is offered from a varied menu. Freshly prepared from local produce, dishes include local faggots in onion gravy; ham, egg and chips; lamb hotpot; and lunchtime sandwiches. The home-made pies are a firm favourite – venison and mushroom; chicken, ham and mushroom; steak and kidney; and game. Ice creams are provided by the Buttercup & Daisy company in Wardour.

Open 12-3 6.30-11 (Sun 12-4) Closed 26 Dec, Sun eve & Mon L **Food** Lunch Tue-Sat 12-2 Dinner Tue-Sat 7-9 Restaurant menu available Tue-Sat evening ⊕ FREE HOUSE ◂ Otter Bitter, Bowman Ales Swift One, Palmers Copper Ale, Guest ales ♂ Thatchers Gold, Wessex Cider. **Facilities** Non-diners area ✿ (Bar Garden) ♦♦ Children's portions Garden ⌁ Parking

EDINGTON   Map 4 ST95

The Three Daggers ★★★★ INN

tel: 01380 830940 **Westbury Rd BA13 4PG**
email: hello@threedaggers.co.uk **web:** www.threedaggers.co.uk
dir: *A36 towards Warminster, A350 to Westbury, A303 to Edington*

Where locally sourced meals are kept simple

Opened as the Paulet Arms in 1750 by Harry Paulet, the Lord of Edington Manor, locals quickly christened it the Three Daggers, after the family's coat of arms. It has always been well known for its friendly atmosphere, and enjoyable meals. The interesting menus might include cured Cornish mackerel, cucumber jelly, Priory beetroot and roast walnut halves; day boat crab salad, English muffin melba toast; Downland Farm 'nose to tail' salad; and Penleigh Farm lamb and haloumi koftas with lemon and pepper couscous. Next door there is a farm shop selling locally sourced products, and also a microbrewery with a viewing gallery. There's was a change of hands here in late November 2014.

Open all day all wk 8am-11pm **Food** Lunch Mon-Sat 12-2.30, Sun 12-8.30 Dinner Mon-Thu 6-9, Fri-Sat 6-9.30, Sun 12-8.30 ⊕ FREE HOUSE ◀ Daggers Ale, Blonde & Edge ♂ Lilley's Apples & Pears, Pheasant Plucker, Westons Stowford Press. ♛ 14 **Facilities** Non-diners area ♣ (Bar Garden) ♦♦ Children's menu Children's portions Play area Garden ⚲ Beer festival Cider festival Parking WiFi ═ (notice required) **Rooms** 3

■ **FONTHILL GIFFORD**   Map 4 ST93

The Beckford Arms   PICK OF THE PUBS

See Pick of the Pubs on page 534

■ **FOXHAM**   Map 4 ST97

The Foxham Inn ★★★★ INN ◉

tel: 01249 740665 **SN15 4NQ**
email: info@thefoxhaminn.co.uk **web:** www.thefoxhaminn.co.uk
dir: M4 junct 17, B4122 (signed Sutton Benger). Onto B4069, through Sutton Benger. Right signed Foxham

Excellent Wiltshire countryside dining inn

This compact brick-built inn stands in a rural village close to the resurgent Wiltshire and Berkshire Canal. Real ales from the local Ramsbury brewery flow from the bar, but it's for the excellent cuisine created by Neil Cooper that customers beat a path to the door. The accomplished menu offers an extensive range of dishes from a starter of scallop and smoked haddock chowder to mains such as breast of duck with braised red cabbage, dauphinoise potatoes and red wine sauce; or roasted wood pigeon with salsify, beetroot, and Parma ham. There are equally fulfilling sweets to finish. Accommodation allows diners to rest easy after a classy repast.

Open 12-3 7-11 (Sun 12-3 7-10.30) Closed 1st 2wks Jan, Mon **Food** Lunch Tue-Sun 12-2 Dinner Tue-Sun 7-9.30 Av main course £12 Set menu available ⊕ FREE HOUSE ◀ Butcombe, Ramsbury ♂ Ashton Press. ♛ 10 **Facilities** Non-diners area ♣ (Bar Outside area) ♦♦ Children's menu Children's portions Outside area ⚲ Parking WiFi ═ (notice required) **Rooms** 2

■ **FROXFIELD**   Map 5 SU26

The Pelican Inn

tel: 01488 682479 **Bath Rd SN8 3JY**
email: enquiries@pelicaninn.co.uk **web:** www.pelicaninn.co.uk
dir: On A4 midway between Marlborough & Hungerford

Fresh food cooked well at this A4 inn

This 17th-century roadside inn has been serving the needs of locals and travellers alike for over three centuries. Being only 300 yards from the Kennet & Avon Canal, it

is also a popular refuelling stop for walkers, cyclists and the boating fraternity. Expect Ramsbury and local guest ales on tap, a raft of wines by the glass, and locally sourced food. The menu offers traditional pub favourites such as steak and ale pie; beer battered Cod and chips; local pork sausages and mash.

Open all day all wk 11-11 (Sun 12-10) **Food** Lunch Mon-Fri 12-3, Sat-Sun 12-9 Dinner Mon-Fri 6-9, Sat-Sun 12-9 ⊕ FREE HOUSE ◀ Ramsbury, Wickwar, Guest ales ♂ Westons Stowford Press. ♛ 9 **Facilities** Non-diners area ♣ (Bar Garden) ♦♦ Children's menu Garden ⚲ Parking WiFi ═ (notice required)

■ **HANNINGTON**   Map 5 SU19

The Jolly Tar

tel: 01793 762245 **Queens Rd SN6 7RP**
email: jolly.tar@sky.com
dir: M4 junct 15, A419 towards Cirencester. At Bunsdon/Highworth sign follow B4109. Towards Highworth, left at Freke Arms, follow Hannington & Jolly Tar pub signs

Local ales and a spacious garden

It may be far from the sea, but there's a nautical reason for this former farmhouse's name – a retired sea captain married into the Freke family, who once owned it. Old timbers and locally brewed Arkell's ales are served in its two bars, making this pretty inn an appealing destination. All food on the daily menu is freshly prepared; a meal could take in crispy chilli squid with garlic mayo followed by home-made steak and ale pie with chunky chips. The conservatory restaurant overlooks the sun terrace and spacious garden, replete with a children's play area.

Open 12-2 6-11 (Sun 12-3 7-11) Closed Mon L (ex BHs) **Food** Lunch Tue-Sun 12-2 Dinner Mon-Sat 6.30-9, Sun 7-9 (closed 1st Sun every month for village quiz) ⊕ ARKELL'S ◀ 3B, Wiltshire Gold, Bees Organic, Guest ales ♂ Westons Stowford Press. ♛ 9 **Facilities** Non-diners area ♣ (Bar Garden) ♦♦ Children's menu Play area Garden ⚲ Parking WiFi

---

■ **HEYTESBURY**   Map 4 ST94

The Angel   PICK OF THE PUBS

tel: 01985 840330 **High St BA12 OED**
email: admin@angelheytesbury.co.uk
dir: A303 onto A36 towards Bath, 8m, Heytesbury on left

Dining pub in an upmarket village

The wood-fringed slopes of Salisbury Plain rise steeply from the valley of the River Wylye, where this smart dining pub continues to make its mark with a punchy menu of modern British dishes. The Angel has stood at one end of Heytesbury's High Street for over 400 years; a comprehensive makeover a few years ago resulted in today's comfy mix of traditional and contemporary aspects of a village inn. Restrained bric-a-brac, exposed brick, wooden flooring, beams and on-trend furnishings are the building blocks that welcome drinkers to a range of Greene King beers. Diners may choose to eat in the bar or restaurant. A typical menu opener may be devilled lamb's kidneys on toast; or mussels with a cream, cider, shallot and chorizo sauce. Seasonal, locally sourced mains could include wild mushroom and chestnut cottage pie; or kedgeree Arancini (smoked haddock risotto balls, curry sauce and soft boiled egg). There's a strong hand of quality burgers here too, including one called 'mushoumi' for vegetarians. Booking is essential at weekends.

Open all day all wk 11.30-11 (Sun 11.30-8) **Food** Lunch Mon-Sat 12-2.30, Sun 12-3 Dinner Mon-Sat 6.30-9.30 ⊕ GREENE KING ◀ IPA, Morland Old Speckled Hen ♂ Thatchers Gold. ♛ 8 **Facilities** Non-diners area ♣ (Bar Outside area) ♦♦ Children's portions Outside area ⚲ Parking WiFi ═

PICK OF THE PUBS

The Beckford Arms

FONTHILL GIFFORD   Map 4 ST93

tel: 01747 870385 **SP3 6PX**
email: info@beckfordarms.com
web: www.beckfordarms.com
dir: *From A303 (E of Wincanton) follow Fonthill Bishop sign. At T-junct in village right, 1st left signed Fonthill Gifford & Tisbury. Through Fonthill Estate arch to pub*

Excellent food in elegant coaching inn with lovely garden

Just three minutes from the A303, this handsome 18th-century coaching inn is set on the edge of the beautiful rolling parkland of Lord Margadale's 10,000-acre Fonthill Estate. Once a stopping point for weary travellers on the way from London to the South West, this elegant dining pub is now a destination in its own right. You can eat wherever you want, either in the main bar with its huge fireplace and parquet floor or in the separate restaurant. In summer, head out into the rambling garden where hammocks hang between the trees, you can play pétanque and children can do what children do. In winter the huge open fire in the bar is used to spit-roast suckling pigs and warm mulled wine. Whatever the season, Keystone's Beckford Phoenix real ale is a permanent fixture in the bar, with other beers on tap including Dorset Piddle's Jimmy Riddle. Sheppy's is one of the real ciders on draught and

there are 12 wines available by the glass including the Fonthill Glebe, a local crisp white wine. Among the bar snacks is a very tempting sharing plate. Choosing from the daily-changing menu could prove pleasantly tricky: for example, do you start with pigeon with bacon, black pudding, roasted quince and hazelnut vinaigrette; or River Exe mussels with shallots, white wine and cream. Then there are the mains – red wine braised ox cheek, mash, root vegetables and bone marrow fritter; crispy shoulder of Boyton Farm mutton, smoked lamb sausage, white bean purée and fried wild garlic; or grilled 8oz rump steak and chips. Either way, leave room for white chocolate cheesecake with blackberries and honeycomb.

Open all day all wk **Food** Lunch all wk 12-2.30 Dinner all wk 6-9.30 ⊕ FREE HOUSE ◖ Keystone Beckford Phoenix, Dorset Piddle Jimmy Riddle, Butcombe, Erdinger Ŏ Ashton Press, Westons Wyld Wood Organic, Sheppy's. ♟ 12 **Facilities** Non-diners area ❖ (Bar Restaurant Garden) ♦ Children's menu Children's portions Play area Garden ☴ Parking WiFi

HORNINGSHAM
Map 4 ST84

The Bath Arms at Longleat ★★★★ INN ◉

PICK OF THE PUBS

tel: 01985 844308 **BA12 7LY**
email: enquiries@batharms.co.uk **web:** www.batharms.co.uk
dir: Off B3092 S of Frome

Quirky but stylish country inn on the Longleat Estate

Occupying a prime position at one of the entrances to Longleat Estate and the famous Safari Park, The Bath Arms dates back to the 17th century. An ivy-clad stone property, it features two beamed bars – one traditional with settles, old wooden tables and an open fire, and a bar for dining. In addition to sandwiches and sharing boards look out for main courses such as pan-fried sea bass with mussel, sweetcorn, potato and chive chowder; poached duck egg 'florentine' with buttered spinach on toasted muffin with hollandaise sauce; and pan-roast breast of Hayward Farm chicken wrapped in prosciutto stuffed with white apricot Stilton. Leave a space for elderflower and lime cheesecake and lemon sorbet or Eton Mess with Horningsham berry compôte and vanilla crème fraîche.

Open all day all wk 10am-11pm (Sun 10am-10.30pm) **Food** Lunch Sun-Thu 12-9, Fri-Sat 12-9.30 Dinner Sun-Thu 12-9, Fri-Sat 12-9.30 ⊕ WESSEX BREWERY ◀ Horningsham Pride & Golden Apostle, Sharp's Doom Bar ♂ Westons Stowford Press, Sharp's Orchard. ♀ 10 **Facilities** Non-diners area ♣ (Bar Garden) ♦♦ Children's menu Children's portions Garden ⋈ Beer festival Parking WiFi ☷ (notice required) **Rooms** 16

LOWER CHICKSGROVE
Map 4 ST92

Compasses Inn ★★★★ INN ◉
PICK OF THE PUBS

tel: 01722 714318 **SP3 6NB**
email: thecompasses@aol.com **web:** www.thecompassesinn.com
dir: On A30 (1.5m W of Fovant) 3rd right to Lower Chicksgrove. In 1.5m left into Lagpond Ln, pub 1m on left

Charming thatched inn amid beautiful rolling countryside

An old cobbled path leads to the low latched door of this 14th-century inn. Step inside and you walk into a delightful bar with worn flagstones, exposed stone walls and old beams. Snuggle up by the large inglenook fireplace or relax in the intimate booth seating, perfect on a winter's evening. You can be certain to find three or four local real ales on tap, perhaps from Wiltshire brewery Plain Ales, and the wine list is comprehensive. Be sure to try the food: the kitchen team has won an AA Rosette for their seasonal dishes; these are chalked up on a blackboard because they change so frequently. Examples of starters are chicken liver parfait with walnut bread and red onion marmalade; or baby aubergine stuffed with cream cheese. Main dishes could be Creedy Carver duck breast, courgettes, wild mushrooms and shallots with roasted new potatoes and blueberry jus; or fillet of sea trout, crab ravioli, gnocchi and summer vegetable broth. Five bedrooms are also available.

Open 12-3 6-11 (Sun 12-3 7-10.30) Closed 25-26 Dec, Mon L Jan-Mar **Food** Lunch all wk 12-2 Dinner all wk 6.30-9 Av main course £15.50 ⊕ FREE HOUSE ◀ Keystone Large One, Sixpenny Gold, Plain Ales Inntrigue, Butcombe ♂ Ashton Press & Still. **Facilities** Non-diners area ♣ (Bar Restaurant Garden) ♦♦ Children's menu Children's portions Garden ⋈ Parking WiFi ☷ **Rooms** 5

MALMESBURY
Map 4 ST98

Kings Arms ★★★ INN

tel: 01666 823383 **29 High St SN16 9AA**
email: thekingsarms.malmesbury@arkells.com **web:** www.thekahotel.co.uk
dir: M4 junct 17, A429 to Malmesbury. Follow town centre signs. Pub on left in town centre

16th-century coaching inn in a historic Cotswolds town

Close to Malmesbury Abbey, which was founded as a Benedictine monastery in the 7th century, the inn offers two very different bars, separated by a covered walkway: one is the residents' bar, within the Elmer Restaurant, while the other is the more contemporary Bar 29. The latter serves home-cooked meals throughout the day, including sausages and mash; pie of the day; fish and chips; omelettes; and the house speciality, double egg, Wiltshire ham and chips. There's live entertainment in the bar at weekends. The real ales – 3B and Wiltshire Gold – are from Arkell's, which owns the pub.

Open all day all wk **Food** Lunch Mon-Sat 12-9, Sun 12-4 Dinner Mon-Sat 12-9 Restaurant menu available all wk ⊕ ARKELL'S ◀ 3B, Wiltshire Gold & Moonlight, Angus Bitter (pub's own) ♂ Westons Stowford Press, Guest cider. **Facilities** Non-diners area ♦♦ Children's menu Children's portions Outside area ⋈ Beer festival Cider festival Parking WiFi **Rooms** 12

The Vine Tree
PICK OF THE PUBS

tel: 01666 837654 **Foxley Rd, Norton SN16 0JP**
email: tiggi@thevinetree.co.uk
dir: M4 junct 17, A429 towards Malmesbury. Turn left for village, after 1m follow brown signs

Former mill with great home cooking

This atmospheric pub was once a mill; workers reputedly passed beverages out through front windows to passing carriages. Today ramblers and cyclists exploring Wiltshire's charms are frequent visitors; the inn is situated on the official county cycle route. A large open fireplace burns wood all winter in the central bar, warming a wealth of old beams, flagstones and oak flooring. Here you'll find Flying Monk ales among others, and over three dozen wines served by the glass. The pub is also worth seeking out for its interesting modern British pub food and memorable outdoor summer dining. Nibble on free-range pork crackling with apple sauce while choosing from the carte. Start perhaps with lightly dusted salt and pepper squid with aïoli, griddled lemon and dressed leaves. Typical of the main courses is coq au vin, parsley creamed potatoes and garlic croûtons.

Open 12-3 6-12 (Sun 12-4) Closed Sun eve in Winter **Food** Lunch Mon-Sat 12-2.30, Sun 12-3.30 Dinner Mon-Thu 7-9.30, Fri-Sat 7-10 ⊕ FREE HOUSE ◀ Flying Monk Elmers, Sharp's Doom Bar ♂ Westons Stowford Press. ♀ 40 **Facilities** Non-diners area ♣ (Bar Restaurant Garden) ♦♦ Children's menu Children's portions Play area Garden ⋈ Parking WiFi ☷ (notice required)

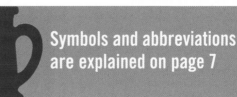

Symbols and abbreviations are explained on page 7

MARDEN
Map 5 SU05

The Millstream

tel: 01380 848490 **SN10 3RH**
email: themillstreammarden@gmail.com
dir: 6m E of Devizes, N of A342

Peaceful alfresco options here

Set in the heart of the Pewsey Vale, The Millstream is an attractive village pub near Devizes. The large garden is a wonderfully peaceful spot for an alfresco drink or meal. Inside, the three fireplaces make for a cosy and romantic atmosphere in which to sip a regional Thatchers cider and refuel with a bar snack or a light lunch of traditional ploughman's, or a cold roast beef and horseradish baguette. More substantial meal options include 8oz rib-eye steak, onion rings and peppercorn sauce; or wholetail Cornish scampi with salad and home-made tartare sauce.

Open 12-3 6.30-11 Closed Mon eve **Food** Lunch all wk 12-2.30 Dinner Tue-Sun 6.30-9.30 Set menu available Restaurant menu available Mon-Sat ⊕ WADWORTH ◀ 6X, IPA, Horizon Ö Thatchers Gold. **Facilities** Non-diners area ✿ (Bar Garden) ◀ Children's portions Play area Family room Garden ♬ Parking WiFi ▄ (notice required)

MARLBOROUGH
Map 5 SU16

The Lamb Inn ★★★ INN

tel: 01672 512668 **The Parade SN8 1NE**
email: thelambinnmarlboro@fsmail.net **web:** www.thelambinnmarlborough.com
dir: From High St (A4) into The Parade, pub 50yds on left

Flower-bedecked pub with home-cooked food

Just off Marlborough's impressively wide main street, this coaching inn dates from 1673. It's a dog-friendly and welcoming hostelry today, but the dining room, converted from the stable, is reputed to be haunted since a woman was killed when pushed down the stairs. Landlady and chef Jackie Scott uses prime local ingredients including Wiltshire beef, pork from farms close by, game in season, and herbs and berries from the hedgerows. Expect the likes of pigeon and wild mushroom pâté; and a home-made cassoulet of smoked ham, garlic sausage, lamb and duck.

Open all day all wk 12-12 **Food** Lunch all wk 12-2.30 Dinner Mon-Thu 6.30-9 ⊕ WADWORTH ◀ 6X, Guest ales. ☂ 10 **Facilities** ✿ (Bar Restaurant Garden) ◀ Children's portions Garden ♬ WiFi **Rooms** 6

MINETY
Map 5 SU09

Vale of the White Horse Inn
PICK OF THE PUBS

tel: 01666 860175 **SN16 9QY**
email: info@valeofthewhitehorseinn.co.uk
dir: On B4040 (3m W of Cricklade, 6m E of Malmesbury)

Popular with the local community

An eye-catching and beautifully restored inn overlooking a large pond. Built in the early 1800s, the building's true history is something of a mystery, but it was registered by its current name in the 1881 census. Today, sitting under a parasol on the large raised terrace, it's hard to think of a better spot. The village bar is popular with the local community, drawn by a good selection of real ales and events such as

skittles evenings, live music and quizzes. The ethos is to serve good home-cooked food at sensible prices. Upstairs, lunch and dinner are served in the stone-walled restaurant with its polished tables and bentwood chairs. The bar menu offers baguettes, ploughman's, nachos and daily specials. Most pub favourites will be found on the à la carte, ranging from chicken Caesar salad to home-made cottage pie and rib-eye steak. Mint chocolate chip cheesecake might tempt for dessert.

Open all wk 11.45-2.45 4.45-11 (Thu-Sat 11.45-11 Sun 11.45-10.30) **Food** Lunch all wk 12-2.30 Dinner all wk 6-9.15 ⊕ FREE HOUSE ◀ Cotswold Spring Stunner, Otter Bitter, Moles Best Ö Westons Stowford Press, Pheasant Plucker, Broadoak. ☂ 10 **Facilities** Non-diners area ✿ (Bar Garden) ◀ Children's menu Children's portions Family room Garden ♬ Parking WiFi ▄

MONKTON FARLEIGH
Map 4 ST86

NEW The Muddy Duck ★★★★ INN ◉

tel: 01225 858705 **BA15 2QH**
email: dishitup@themuddyduckbath.co.uk **web:** www.themuddyduckbath.co.uk
dir: Phone pub for detailed directions

Flying high following refurbishment

The doors of the former King's Arms, reputedly Wiltshire's most haunted pub, are again well and truly open for business following a rejuvenating makeover by its long-term landlord Simon Blagden, and catering supremo Nigel Harris. Inside is a fire-warmed, sunken snug, while picnic tables are set out in the wisteria-covered courtyard; the rear garden looks out over farmland. If Wiltshire can grow it or supply it, then that's where ingredients for the kitchen come from, destined to become, for example, slow-cooked pork belly with pan-seared scallops; chargrilled steak of the day; and tomato tart with ricotta and crispy courgettes.

Open all day all wk **Food** Lunch 12-2.30 Dinner 6-9.30 ⊕ PUNCH TAVERNS ◀ Butcombe, St Austell Proper Job, Guest ales. ☂ **Facilities** Non-diners area ✿ (Bar Garden) ◀ Children's menu Children's portions Garden ♬ Parking WiFi **Rooms** 5

NEWTON TONY
Map 5 SU24

The Malet Arms

tel: 01980 629279 **SP4 0HF**
email: info@maletarms.com
dir: 8m N of Salisbury on A338, 2m from A303

Pleasingly out of the way

In a quiet village on the River Bourne, this 17th-century inn was named after early Victorian lord of the manor, Sir Henry Malet. Fruit-machine- and piped-music-free, it has an enormous inglenook fireplace, and is bedecked with prints, trophies and myriad curiosities. Regional microbreweries are strongly supported, and most of the Mediterranean, Oriental and traditional English dishes on the ever-changing blackboard are locally sourced too. Game is plentiful in season, often shot by deer-stalker landlord, Noel. Other possibilities are scampi with home-made tartare sauce; and green chilli, ginger and cardamom chicken curry. In fine weather, you can sit in the garden.

Open 11-3 6-11 (Sun 12-3) Closed 25 Dec, 1 Jan, Sun eve **Food** Lunch all wk 12-2.30 Dinner Mon-Sat 6.30-9.30 Av main course £10-£12 ⊕ FREE HOUSE ◀ Butcombe, Ramsbury, Stonehenge, Triple fff, Palmers, Plain Ales, Butts, Fuller's, Guest ales Ö Westons Old Rosie & Stowford Press, Gwynt y Ddraig Orchard Gold. ☂ 9 **Facilities** Non-diners area ◀ Children's menu Garden Beer festival Parking

PICK OF THE PUBS

The Bell at Ramsbury ★★★★ INN

RAMSBURY Map 5 SU27

tel: 01672 520230 **The Square SN8 2PE**
email: thebell@thebellramsbury.com
web: www.thebellramsbury.com
dir: *M4 junct 14, A338 to Hungerford.*
B4192 towards Swindon. Left to
Ramsbury

Village-centre pub in the picturesque Kennet Valley

Newly refurbished, this 17th-century coaching inn looks straight down Ramsbury's old High Street. Just outside, a lovely old tree provides shade for a couple of benches; on the wall of a building opposite, one of the AA's pre-war enamel road signs informs motorists that Marlborough is seven miles away, London 68. The bar – shown a photo you'd think it was someone's comfortable living room – serves Ramsbury real ales, brewed in nearby Aldbourne, and Lilley's cider, from Bath. The bar menu offers Mediterranean-style nibbles, and meals such as fish and triple-cooked chips, and a daily pie. The restaurant is led by head chef Duncan Jones, formerly running the kitchen at one of Marco Pierre-White's flagship restaurants, and now guardian of the Bell's two AA Rosettes for its modern British fine-dining heritage. Among the dishes you may well find on Duncan's concise but inventive menus are haunch and braised shoulder of Ramsbury Estate venison with celeriac

and carrot rösti, parsnip purée and seasonal vegetables; free-range tenderloin of pork with apple and black pudding hash, Savoy cabbage and bacon; and roasted fillet of plaice with tenderstem broccoli, capers, lemon and beurre noisette. It might continue with, say, blackberry Eton mess; cherry chocolate torte with caramelised croûtons and cherry ice cream; or plum sponge with ginger crème Anglaise and caramelised plum. Children can have a half portion or even a dish without sauce if they want, although they do have their own small menu. High-chairs are available for toddlers. Breakfast, lunch, coffee and tea are served in the Bell's Shaker-influenced Café Bella. A mud room with welly washer declares the pub's popularity with ramblers.

Open all day all wk 12-11 (Sun 12-10) **Food** Lunch Mon-Sat 12-2.30 Dinner Mon-Sat 6-9, Sun 6-8 ⊞ FREE HOUSE 🍺 Ramsbury Bitter, Gold Ö Thatchers Gold, Lilley's Apples & Pears. 🍷 12 **Facilities** Non-diners area 🐾 (Bar Garden) 👶 Children's menu Children's portions Garden 🎍 Parking WiFi **Rooms** 9

OGBOURNE ST ANDREW | Map 5 SU17

Silks on the Downs

tel: 01672 841229 **Main Rd SN8 1RZ**
email: silks@silksonthedowns.com
dir: *M4 junct 15, A346 towards Marlborough. Approx 6m to Ogbourne St Andrew. Pub on A346*

Village pub with a horseracing theme

A mile north of the bustling market town of Marlborough can be found this pub, tucked away in rolling downland. The free house's name reflects the racing heritage of the Berkshire Downs (whose western boundary is on the border with Wiltshire). Framed silks of leading racehorse owners and jockeys adorn the walls and the pub offers local Ramsbury ales, fine wines and an informal dining experience. Sample dishes run along the lines of venison terrine, roasted pumpkin seed vinaigrette, rosemary butter and ciabatta; Wiltshire lamb rump, grain mustard mash and redcurrant sauce; and hot chocolate brownie, dark chocolate sauce and stem ginger ice cream. There was a change of hands in late 2014.

Open 12-3 6.30-11 Closed 25 & 26 Dec, Sun eve & BHs eve **Food** Lunch Mon-Tue 12-2, Wed-Sun 12-2.30 Dinner Mon-Tue 7-9, Wed-Sat 7-9.30 ⊕ FREE HOUSE ◀ Ramsbury Gold, Wadworth 6X, Smooth as Silk (pub's own) Ō Aspall. ☐ 11 **Facilities** Non-diners area ⦁ Children's menu Children's portions Garden ⋈ Parking WiFi

PEWSEY | Map 5 SU16

The Seven Stars Inn

tel: 01672 851325 **Bottlesford SN9 6LW**
email: info@thesevenstarsinn.co.uk
dir: *From A345 follow Woodborough sign. Through North Newnton. Right to Bottlesford. Pub on left*

Handsome thatched inn with seven acres of gardens

Close to two of Wiltshire's famous white horses, this 16th-century free house lies in the heart of the Vale of Pewsey between Salisbury Plain and the Marlborough Downs, and is a 15-minute drive from the stone circles of Avebury. The bar maintains its original character with low beams and oak panelling, and you can expect local Sharp's Doom Bar and guest ales on tap. The menu of home-made classics could list warm goats' cheese with beetroot, and walnut salad; followed by roast pork belly, ale-battered haddock, or grilled haloumi with summer vegetable salad. The chef's daily specials add to the choice.

Open 12-3 6-11 Closed Mon & Tue L **Food** Lunch Wed-Sun 12-3 Dinner Tue-Sat 6-9 Restaurant menu available Tue-Sun ⊕ FREE HOUSE ◀ Ramsbury Gold, Sharp's Doom Bar, Guest ales Ō Orchard Pig Reveller. ☐ 18 **Facilities** Non-diners area ⦁ (Bar Restaurant Garden) ⦁ Children's menu Children's portions Garden ⋈ Parking WiFi (notice required)

PITTON | Map 5 SU23

The Silver Plough | PICK OF THE PUBS

tel: 01722 712266 **White Hill SP5 1DU**
email: info@silverplough-pitton.co.uk
dir: *From Salisbury take A30 towards Andover, Pitton signed. Approx 3m*

Friendly village pub on the fringes of the Salisbury Downs

Close to the cathedral city of Salisbury and ideally situated for visitors to Stonehenge, there's a timeless atmosphere to this English country inn. At its heart is an elaborately moulded old dark-wood bar from which diverge rooms and a snug with rustic furniture, ancient beams, log fires and rustic country-style decor, whilst hop festoons are a reminder that this is the place to get a reliable pint of First Gold or K&B Sussex from Hall & Woodhouse's Dorset brewery. Local produce is to the fore in the menu of pub favourites given a modern twist, such as a half rack of ribs

slow-cooked with barbecue sauce, or garlic and tarragon king prawns with hot ciabatta. Mains may feature oven-baked salmon fillet with herbed new potatoes, sautéed baby spinach and lemon butter sauce. There's a traditional skittles alley here, too, and the gardens offer views over the villages' thatched roofs.

Open all wk 12-3 6-11 (Mon-Tue 12-3 6-10.30 Sun all day) **Food** Lunch Mon-Sat 12-2, Sun 12-8 Dinner Mon-Sat 6-9, Sun 12-8 ⊕ HALL & WOODHOUSE ◀ Badger Tanglefoot, First Gold & K&B Sussex, Guest ale Ō Westons Stowford Press. ☐ 15 **Facilities** Non-diners area ⦁ (Bar Garden) ⦁ Children's menu Children's portions Family room Garden ⋈ Parking WiFi (notice required)

RAMSBURY | Map 5 SU27

The Bell at Ramsbury ★★★★ INN ◉◉ PICK OF THE PUBS

See Pick of the Pubs on page 537

ROWDE | Map 4 ST96

The George & Dragon ★★★★ RR ◉◉ PICK OF THE PUBS

tel: 01380 723053 **High St SN10 2PN**
email: thegandd@tiscali.co.uk web: www.thegeorgeanddragonrowde.co.uk
dir: *1m from Devizes, take A342 towards Chippenham*

Fish and seafood a speciality

Narrowboaters from the nearby Kennet & Avon Canal enjoy coming here for a pint of Bath Ales Gem, especially after navigating through the 29 locks of the Caen Flight. In 1917 the writer Edward Hutton said that Rowde had a 'curious inn'; since this Wiltshire village possessed four at the time, it's not known whether he meant this 16th-century hostelry or another one. It is certainly interesting to note the Tudor Rose of Elizabeth I carved on the old beams in the cosy interior, where large open fireplaces, wooden floors, antique rugs and candlelit tables create a wonderful ambience. The award-winning restaurant specialises in fresh fish and seafood delivered daily from Cornwall: expect to find a starter like a simply grilled kipper with hot buttered toast, followed by the likes of whole grilled lemon sole with garlic and herb butter; or grilled skate wing with caper butter. Perhaps push the boat out and choose their famous seafood platter for two.

Open 12-3 6.30-10 (Sat 12-4 6.30-10 Sun 12-4) Closed Sun eve **Food** Lunch Mon-Fri 12-3, Sat-Sun 12-4 Dinner Mon-Sat 6.30-10 Av main course £8-£10 Set menu available Restaurant menu available all wk ⊕ FREE HOUSE ◀ Butcombe Bitter, Sharp's Doom Bar, Bath Ales Gem, Fuller's ESB & London Pride, Ringwood Fortyniner Ō Ashton Press. ☐ 10 **Facilities** Non-diners area ⦁ (Bar Garden) ⦁ Children's menu Children's portions Garden ⋈ Parking WiFi **Rooms** 3

ROYAL WOOTTON BASSETT | Map 5 SU08

The Angel ★★★★ INN

tel: 01793 851161 **47 High St SN4 7AQ**
email: theangel.wbassett@arkells.com web: www.theangelhotelwoottonbassett.co.uk
dir: *M4 junct 16, A3102 towards Royal Wootton Bassett. At 2nd rdbt left signed Royal Wootton Bassett. Pub on right after lights*

Historic coaching inn with good food and local ales

Slap bang on the high street in Royal Wootton Bassett, this former coaching inn is a contemporary establishment with traditional bar serving a range of Arkell's ales and an oak-panelled dining room showcasing local produce. Meat from named local farms and South Coast fish delivered daily are cooked on a charcoal grill that is the workhorse of the kitchen. Other options might be pan-fried duck breast, bubble-and-squeak with berry jus; slow-roast pork shank, root vegetable mash and apple crisps; or gnocchi and roast tomato sauce, with sandwiches served at lunchtime and throughout the afternoon. Sunday roasts are popular – booking is recommended.

Open all day all wk Closed 26 Dec, 1 Jan Food Lunch all wk 12-9.30 Dinner all wk 12-9.30 Av main course £11 ⊕ ARKELL'S ◄ 3B, Moonlight & Wiltshire Gold ♂ Westons Old Rosie. ♀ Facilities Non-diners area ❀ (Garden Outside area) ♦ Children's menu Children's portions Garden Outside area ⋒ Beer festival Cider festival WiFi ☞ Rooms 17

SALISBURY   Map 5 SU12

The Cloisters

tel: 01722 338102 83 Catherine St SP1 2DH
email: thecloisters83@gmail.com
dir: In city centre, near cathedral

A reputation for good honest food

Near the cathedral, the appropriately named Cloisters is a mid 18th-century pub. Its Victorian windows look into a beamed interior warmed by a pair of open fires. The choice of ales includes Hop Back Summer Lightning, Sharp's Doom Bar, and Butcombe Bitter. Thanks to a well-qualified chef, the menu will please everyone with its popular pub plates, from traditional fish and chips to ratatouille bake and the popular Cloisters beefburger, as well as meaty dishes like braised lamb shank, twice-cooked pork belly and rack of ribs. Booking is advised for the Sunday carvery. Doorstep sandwiches, baguettes and jacket potatoes are also available.

Open all day all wk 11-10 (Thu-Sat 11am-mdnt Sun 12-10) Food Lunch Mon-Fri 11-3, Sat 11-9, Sun 12-9 Dinner Mon-Fri 6-9, Sat 11-9, Sun 12-9 ⊕ ENTERPRISE INNS ◄ Butcombe Bitter, Sharp's Doom Bar, Hop Back Summer Lightning. ♀ Facilities Non-diners area ♦ Children's menu Children's portions WiFi ☞ (notice required)

The Wig and Quill

tel: 01722 335665 1 New St SP1 2PH
email: theofficialwigandquill2014@outlook.com
dir: On approach to Salisbury follow brown Old George Mall Car Park signs. Pub opposite car park

Charming old pub close to the cathedral

Following his mantra of 'traditional, stylish, relaxing and atmospheric', new landlord Robert Wood is building on the inherent qualities of this old city pub. The roomy, beamed bar with open fires, flagstones and wood flooring is as welcoming as ever. Ales include the ever-popular 6X alongside new arrivals from Wadworth such as Swordfish, and a beer festival is promised. Menus proffer happy pub grub, served all day every day. Light bites include fresh tiger-baguettes or jacket potatoes with a range of fillings; or choose plates such as hunter's chicken; braised lamb shank; or beer-battered fish and chips. A sheltered courtyard garden behind the pub is a restful spot in summer.

Open all day all wk 11am-close Food Lunch all day Dinner all day Set menu available Restaurant menu available all wk ⊕ WADWORTH ◄ 6X, The Bishop's Tipple, Henry's Original IPA, Horizon & Swordfish, Guest ales ♂ Westons Old Rosie, Thatchers, Aspall. ♀ 14 Facilities Non-diners area ❀ (All areas) ♦ Children's menu Children's portions Garden Outside area ⋒ Beer festival WiFi ☞

SEEND   Map 4 ST96

Bell Inn

tel: 01380 828338 Bell Hill SN12 6SA
email: thebellseend@live.com
dir: On A361 between Devizes & Semington

Historic village pub serving a wide range of food

This lovely red-brick pub in the pretty village of Seend has panoramic views of Salisbury Plain and the Westbury Valley. Oliver Cromwell and his troops reputedly

enjoyed breakfast at this inn in 1645 before attacking nearby Devizes Castle. Its other claim to fame is that John Wesley opened the chapel next door and preached against the 'evils' of drink outside the pub. Restaurant dishes could include sea bass fillet with Mediterranean salsa, rice and dressed leaves; crushed potato and trout salad; 10oz rib-eye steak, spring onion mash, green beans and peppercorn sauce; and Greek-style lamb casserole, rice and natural yogurt.

Open all wk 12-2.30 5.30-11.30 Food Lunch all wk 12-2 Dinner all wk 5.30-9 Restaurant menu available Tue-Sat ⊕ WADWORTH ◄ 6X, Henry's Original IPA ♂ Westons Stowford Press, Thatchers Gold. Facilities Non-diners area ❀ (Bar Garden) ♦ Children's menu Children's portions Play area Garden ⋒ Parking WiFi ☞

SEMINGTON   Map 4 ST86

The Lamb on the Strand

tel: 01380 870263 99 The Strand BA14 6LL
email: info@thelambonthestrand.co.uk
dir: 1.5m E on A361 from junct with A350

Craft brews and interesting tapas

This popular dining pub began life as a farmhouse in the 18th-century, later developing into a beer and cider house. Today, customers can choose a real ale from the Wiltshire craft brewery Box Steam, or a cider from Westons. Food is freshly prepared from locally sourced ingredients, with an appetising choice of hot dishes and open sandwiches at lunchtime. The Wiltshire tapas menu offers an interesting mix of British and global treats: pigs in blankets; deep-fried calamari with garlic aïoli; and cider-braised chorizo being just three.

Open all wk 12-3 6-11 ⊕ FREE HOUSE ◄ Box Steam ♂ Westons Stowford Press, Thatchers. Facilities ❀ (Bar Restaurant Garden) ♦ Children's menu Children's portions Play area Family room Garden Parking WiFi

---

SHERSTON   Map 4 ST88

The Rattlebone Inn

tel: 01666 840871 Church St SN16 0LR
email: eat@therattlebone.co.uk
dir: M4 junct 17, A429 to Malmesbury. 2m after passing petrol station at Stanton St Quentin, turn left signed Sherston

Lively village pub with robust country cooking

With fine beer from Flying Monk Brewery, alley-skittles and a strong menu of both old-style and contemporary dishes, who would ever want to leave this character, carefully refurbished Cotswold village retreat? Not John Rattlebone, that's for sure; this Saxon warrior's name lives on as does his restless spirit that occasionally manifests itself here. The interior is one of beams, flagged floors, log-burners and golden stone, and walled gardens enclose three boules pistes and sheltered patios, ideal for the July cider festival. Country bistro home cooking is the style here; kick-in with warm salad of seared pigeon breast, then chow down to Gloucester Old Spots pork belly and chorizo cassoulet.

Open all wk 12-3 5-11 (Fri-Sat 12-12 Sun 12-11) Food Lunch Mon-Sat 12-2.30, Sun 12-3 Dinner Mon-Sat 6-9.30 Av main course £11 Set menu available ⊕ YOUNG'S ◄ Bitter, St Austell Tribute, Flying Monk Elmers ♂ Westons Stowford Press & Wyld Wood Organic, Thatchers Gold, Pheasant Plucker. ♀ 14 Facilities Non-diners area ❀ (Bar Garden) ♦ Children's menu Children's portions Garden ⋒ Cider festival WiFi ☞ (notice required)

SOUTH WRAXALL   Map 4 ST86

The Longs Arms

tel: 01225 864450 **BA15 2SB**
email: info@thelongarms.com
dir: *From Bradford-on Avon take B3109 towards Corsham. Approx 3m, left to South Wraxall. Pub on left*

Character pub in lovely village location

This stunning-looking golden-stone pub commands the centre of a tiny village above the Avon Valley just outside Bath. A log-burner, slab flooring and country prints welcome you to the airy bar; the cosy dining room is pleasingly cottagey in character. The beers are from the Wadworth's stable; the cuisine equally local and proudly British, and each meal has a suggested beer to accompany. There's an on-site smokehouse, while the veg and herbs come from the grounds. Consider a starter of cold home-smoked salmon with horseradish, pickle and seaweed; leaving room for mains like Wiltshire lamb shoulder and cutlet, toasted almonds, Jersey Royals and spinach. The lavender-scented secluded garden is a summer delight.

Open 12-3.30 5.30-11.30 (Fri-Sun 12-11.30) Closed 3wks Jan, Mon **Food** Lunch Tue-Thu 12-2.30, Fri-Sat 12-9.30, Sun 12-5 Dinner Tue-Thu 5.30-9.30, Fri-Sat 12-9.30 ⊕ WADWORTH ◆ 6X, Henry's Original IPA, Guest ales Ö Thatchers. ♟ 10 **Facilities** ❦ (Bar Garden) ◖◗ Children's portions Garden ♜ Parking WiFi ⚍ (notice required)

STOURTON   Map 4 ST73

Spread Eagle Inn ★★★★ INN   PICK OF THE PUBS

tel: 01747 840587 **BA12 6QE**
email: enquiries@spreadeagleinn.com **web:** www.spreadeagleinn.com
dir: *N of A303 off B3092*

In the beautiful setting of the Stourhead Estate

This charming 19th-century inn is in an enviable position right at the heart of the 2,650-acre Stourhead Estate, one of the country's most loved National Trust properties. Before or after a walk through the magnificent gardens and landscapes, there is plenty on offer here, including real ales brewed in a nearby village and traditional countryside cooking using produce from local specialists in and around north Dorset, west Wiltshire and south Somerset. Even the simple ploughman's is prepared with local bread with a Dorset Blue cheese or Keene's mature cheddar served with home-made chutney. In the restaurant, expect oven-baked Cornish sea bass fillets with parmesan mash; free-range tarragon-stuffed chicken suprême with Parmentier potatoes; and chef's crème brûlée to finish. The interior is smartly traditional, and in the bedrooms, antiques sit side by side with modern comforts.

Open all day all wk 10am-11pm **Food** Lunch all wk 12-3 Dinner all wk 7-9 ⊕ FREE HOUSE ◆ Wessex Kilmington Best, Butcombe, Guest ales Ö Ashton Press. ♟ 8 **Facilities** ◖◗ Outside area ♜ Parking ⚍ **Rooms** 5

SWINDON   Map 5 SU18

The Runner

tel: 01793 523903 **Wootton Bassett Rd SN1 4NQ**
email: runninghorse@arkells.com
dir: *M4 junct 16, A3102 towards Swindon. At 2nd rdbt right signed town centre. Pub on right*

All-day food at this family pub

Arkell's Brewery owns this late 19th-century, family-friendly pub. Every Monday here is Steak Day, while lovers of chicken tikka masala, beef Madras and vegetable Thai curry should make a diary note for Tuesdays – Curry Day. A Lighter Bites menu offers filled baguettes, jacket potatoes and salads, while on Sundays two roasts are always available, as well as a selection of home-made desserts. There's a children's play area and plentiful parking, while on the River Rey, opposite the pub, Swindon's annual Duck Race is held at the end of May on the Bank Holiday.

Open all day all wk **Food** Lunch all wk 12-8.30 Dinner all wk 12-8.30 ⊕ ARKELL'S ◆ 3B & Kingsdown, Guest ale Ö Westons Stowford Press. ♟ **Facilities** Non-diners area ◖◗ Children's menu Children's portions Play area Family room Garden ♜ Parking WiFi ⚍ (notice required)

The Weighbridge Brewhouse

tel: 01793 881500 **Penzance Dr SN5 7JL**
email: info@weighbridgebrewhouse.co.uk
dir: *M4 junct 16, follow Swindon Centre signs, then Outlet Car Park West signs*

Striking pub and brewery in former railway building

Built in 1906, the former Great Western Railway Weighhouse was transformed by experienced operator Anthony Windle into a stunning pub-restaurant concept, complete with microbrewery. Many original features have been retained and the old railway building boasts brick walls and lofty ceilings, with a vast bar at one end, dispensing the six home-brewed ales and 25 wines by the glass, and an airy, smart and very comfortable dining room at the other. Extensive monthly menus may deliver beef and black pudding stack, or oriental-style belly pork. There are seasonal fresh fish dishes, a wide choice of house-aged steak; and interesting vegetarian options. Portions are very generous, so don't expect starters but, if you have room, there's home-made honeycomb cheesecake to finish.

Open all day all wk Closed 25-26 Dec **Food** Lunch Mon-Sat 12-2.30, Sun 12-8.30 Dinner Mon-Sat 6-9.30, Sun 12-8.30 Restaurant menu available all wk ⊕ FREE HOUSE ◆ Brinkworth Village, Weighbridge Best, Antsally's, Pooley's Golden, Seasonal ales. ♟ 25 **Facilities** Non-diners area ◖◗ Children's menu Children's portions Outside area ♜ Parking WiFi

TOLLARD ROYAL   Map 4 ST91

King John Inn ▣

tel: 01725 516207 **SP5 5PS**
email: info@kingjohninn.co.uk **web:** www.kingjohninn.co.uk
dir: *On B3081 (7m E of Shaftesbury)*

Stylish country pub with innovative modern menus

Named after the original hunting lodge built for King John, this brick-built Victorian inn luxuriates in its location on Cranborne Chase deep in stunning countryside outside Shaftesbury. Its airy, open-plan bar and dining areas have a crisp country feel, featuring rugs on quarry tile flooring, pine tables, snug alcoves and winter log fires. Lunchtime dining here offers a great choice of small-plate sharing options, whilst the contemporary dinner menu ranges from starters like Portland crab on toast to mains of venison haunch, beetroot, pearl barley and greens. Finish, perhaps, with chocolate and orange terrine.

Open all wk 12-3 6-11 **Food** Lunch Mon-Fri 12-2.30, Sat-Sun 12-3 Dinner all wk 7-9.30 ⊕ FREE HOUSE ◆ Ringwood Best Bitter, Sharp's Doom Bar, Guest ales Ö Ashton Press. ♟ 20 **Facilities** Non-diners area ❦ (Bar Restaurant Garden) ◖◗ Children's portions Garden ♜ Parking WiFi **Rooms** 8

UPTON LOVELL
Map 4 ST94

Prince Leopold Inn ★★★ INN

tel: 01985 850460 **BA12 0JP**
email: info@princeleopold.co.uk **web:** www.princeleopold.co.uk
dir: *From Warminster take A36 towards Salisbury 4.5m, left to Upton Lovell*

Beside the Wylye trout stream

Built here just west of Salisbury Plain in 1878, the Leo was named after Victoria and Albert's popular, but sickly, eighth child, who lived at nearby Boyton Manor. Local craftsman Matthew Burt's elm-topped bar counter is where to order Somerset-brewed Butcombe ale or Warminster-brewed Plain Ales Sheep Dip. There's a log fire, sofas and cameos of village life in the Victorian snug, while from the dining room beyond you can see the Wylye as you enjoy chicken wrapped in Parma ham; confit duck leg with pea and pancetta fricassée; fisherman's pie; or Portobello mushroom, feta and chilli burger.

Open all wk 12-3 6-11 Sat-Sun 12-11 summer (12-3 6-11 Sun 12-3 winter) **Food** Lunch all wk 12-2.30 Dinner Mon-Thu 6-8.30, Fri-Sat 6-9, Sun 6-8 ⊕ FREE HOUSE ◀ Butcombe, Plain Ales Sheep Dip ♂ Thatchers Dry, Ashton Press. ♟ 16
Facilities Non-diners area ♥ (Bar Garden) ♦♦ Children's menu Children's portions Garden ⌅ Parking WiFi (notice required) **Rooms** 6

Who are the AA's award-winning pubs? For details see pages 10 & 11

WANBOROUGH
Map 5 SU28

The Harrow Inn ★★★ INN

tel: 01793 791792 **SN4 0AE**
email: info@theharrowwanborough.co.uk **web:** www.theharrowwanborough.co.uk
dir: *M4 junct 15, A419 towards Cirencester. Exit at next junct signed Cirencester & Oxford. Follow Wanborough sign from rdbt*

Great local produce showcased on the menu here

This handsome thatched inn retains plenty of original character including exposed beams and inglenook fire, the grate of which is Grade II listed. Parts of The Harrow date back to 1747 and beer was brewed on site for the next century. Brewing ceased in 1863 but the pub still offers a range of ales such as Otter Bitter, which can be enjoyed with enticing dishes such as home-made parsnip and ginger soup; pheasant, chestnut and bacon terrine; puff-pastry steak and Otter pie; and braised ox cheeks with root vegetables and parsley and chive dumpling.

Open all day all wk **Food** Lunch all day Dinner all day ⊕ ENTERPRISE INNS ◀ Timothy Taylor Landlord, Otter Bitter ♂ Westons Stowford Press. ♟ 9
Facilities Non-diners area ♥ (Bar Garden) ♦♦ Children's menu Children's portions Garden ⌅ Parking WiFi (notice required) **Rooms** 3

WARMINSTER
Map 4 ST84

The Bath Arms

tel: 01985 212262 **Clay St, Crockerton BA12 8AJ**
email: batharms@aol.com
dir: *From Warminster on A36 take A350 towards Shaftesbury, left to Crockerton*

Family- and dog-friendly pub with a landscaped garden

This 17th-century pub was part of the Marquess of Bath's Longleat Estate, until death duties forced its sale in 1923. The bar, serving Hobdens Wessex Crockerton Classic and Potter's beers, has that genuine 'real local' feel; in winter the log burner can be an especially welcome sight. The Garden Suite, with views across the lawn, provides additional seating on busy weekends. An extensive menu offers light snacks and baguettes; signature dish 'Sticky Beef'; venison steak hâché with white asparagus and fried egg; shepherd's pie with crushed peas; grilled salmon, fennel and salad; and potato gnocchi with artichokes, peas and pecorino cheese.

Open all day all wk 11-3 6-11 (Sat-Sun 11-11) **Food** Lunch all wk 12-2 Dinner all wk 6.30-9 ⊕ FREE HOUSE ◀ Hobdens Wessex Crockerton Classic & Potter's Ale, Guest ales. **Facilities** Non-diners area ♥ (Bar Garden) ♦♦ Children's menu Children's portions Play area Garden ⌅ Beer festival Parking WiFi (notice required)

The George Inn

tel: 01985 840396 **Longbridge Deverell BA12 7DG**
email: info@the-georgeinn.co.uk
dir: *Phone for detailed directions*

Family-friendly pub near Longleat Safari Park

A member of the expanding Upham Pub group, this 17th-century coaching inn overlooks the grassy banks of the River Wylye. Upham started out as a brewery, so it's their beers that sit alongside guest ales and Orchard Pig Philosopher cider. Food is served in the oak-beamed Smithy Bar and in the two restaurants, where menus open with black pudding Scotch egg; and wild mushroom pâté with granary toast. They continue with tomato and fennel fish stew; chicken and leek shortcrust pastry pie with vegetables and potatoes; and Cumberland sausage with wholegrain mustard mash and onion gravy.

Open all day all wk 11-11 (Sun 12-10.30) Closed 25 Dec fr 3pm 26 Dec (1 Jan open 11-3) **Food** Lunch Mon-Thu 12-2.30, Fri-Sat 12-9.30, Sun 12-9 Dinner Mon-Thu 6-9.30, Fri-Sat 12-9.30, Sun 12-9 ⊕ UPHAM PUB CO ◀ Punter & Tipster, Guest ales ♂ Orchard Pig Philosopher. **Facilities** ♥ (Bar Garden) ♦♦ Children's menu Children's portions Play area Garden ⌅ Parking WiFi (notice required)

WEST OVERTON
Map 5 SU16

NEW The Bell at West Overton

tel: 01672 861099 **Bath Rd SN8 1QD**
email: hannah@thebellwestoverton.com
dir: 4m W of Marlborough on A4

Fast becoming well known for good food

Travellers on today's A4 near Marlborough have been passing or preferably stopping at The Bell since it was built as a coaching inn in 1812. Now renovated, some original features, including sarsen stone walls, remain. Hannah McNaughton and chef husband Andrew strongly support Wiltshire producers and suppliers in both the kitchen and the bar. Andrew has travelled the world and cooked in high profile restaurants; his seasonal menus list dishes such as roast Loch Duart salmon, soy and sesame noodles, shiitake mushrooms and pak choi; roast line-caught Cornish sea bream, chorizo and almonds; and spring onion, leek, pea and cheddar risotto. This is a great spot to just enjoy a drink in the garden or stay on for a three-course meal after exploring nearby Avebury Stone Circle.

Open 12-3 6-11 Closed Sun eve & Mon (ex BH) **Food** Lunch Tue-Sun 12-2.30 Dinner Tue-Sat 6-9 Restaurant menu available Tue-Sat ⊕ FREE HOUSE ◀ Moles Best, Ramsbury Flint Knapper, Twisted Gaucho. ♟ 15 **Facilities** Non-diners area ❀ (Bar Garden) ♦ Children's portions Garden ⋒ Parking WiFi 🚌 (notice required)

WOOTTON RIVERS
Map 5 SU16

Royal Oak
PICK OF THE PUBS

tel: 01672 810322 **SN8 4NQ**
email: royaloak35@hotmail.com
dir: 3m S from Marlborough

Pretty thatched pub, a favourite with walkers

This much expanded 16th-century thatched and timbered pub is perfectly situated for Stonehenge, Bath and Winchester and for exploring the ancient oaks of Savernake Forest. Only 100 yards from the Kennet & Avon Canal and the Mid-Wilts Way, it has an interior as charming as the setting, with low, oak-beamed ceilings, exposed brickwork and wide open fireplaces. In the bar you'll find Wadworth 6X and local ale, Ramsbury Bitter. The daily-changing menus cover all manner of pubby favourites and beyond. Look for starters like mixed salami with sweet and sour gherkins; fish cakes with chilli mayo; and crayfish and prawn salad, then continue with local game casserole; lamb cassoulet with creamy mash; whole grilled plaice; or pan-fried scallops with bacon and black pudding. To finish, maybe peach and Amaretto trifle.

Open all wk 12-2.30 6-11 (Sun 12-10) **Food** Lunch Mon-Sat 12-2.30, Sun 12-8 Dinner Mon-Sat 6-9, Sun 12-8 Set menu available ⊕ FREE HOUSE ◀ Ramsbury Bitter, Wadworth 6X, Local guest ales ♂ Westons Stowford Press.
Facilities Non-diners area ❀ (Bar Restaurant Outside area) ♦ Children's menu Children's portions Outside area ⋒ Parking WiFi 🚌 (notice required)

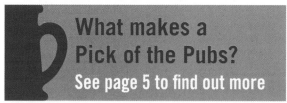

What makes a Pick of the Pubs?
See page 5 to find out more

ABBERLEY
Map 10 SO76

NEW The Manor Arms

tel: 01299 890300 **WR6 6BN**
email: info@themanorarms.co.uk **web:** www.themanorarms.co.uk
dir: From Ombersley take A443 towards Tenbury. After Great Witley right onto B4202. Right into Netherton Ln. Pub on left in village

Great beers and menus in sublime countryside

Tucked away opposite an ancient church in a peaceful village below the beautiful wooded Abberley Hills, this village pub dates back in parts over 400 years. Renovation in 2014 preserved the old world ambience, including an inglenook and timber framing, and a magpie collection of dark wood furniture and exposed brick add to the character. An enticing choice of local beers is a highlight here, while the wide-ranging menu covers traditional dishes and contemporary cuisine. On the one hand sausage and mash; on the other pan-fried salmon with crayfish and samphire linguine. Good-value, daily-changing set menus might tempt walkers in off the well-marked rambles that thread these secluded Worcestershire backwaters.

Open all day all wk **Food** Lunch Mon-Sat 12-2.30, Sun 12-5 Dinner Mon-Thu 6-9, Fri-Sat 6-9.30 Set menu available Restaurant menu available all wk ⊕ FREE HOUSE ◀ Ludlow Gold, Wye Valley HPA, Enville Ale, Hobsons, Wood's, Otter, St Austell Tribute ♂ Robinsons Flagon. ♟ 16 **Facilities** Non-diners area ❀ (Bar Restaurant Garden) ♦ Children's menu Children's portions Garden ⋒ Parking WiFi 🚌 (notice required)

PICK OF THE PUBS

The Mug House Inn & Angry Chef Restaurant ★★★★ INN ◉

BEWDLEY　　　　Map 10 S077

tel: 01299 402543
12 Severnside North DY12 2EE
email: drew@mughousebewdley.co.uk
web: www.mughousebewdley.co.uk
dir: *A456 from Kidderminster to Bewdley. Pub in town on river*

Unrivalled riverside location

Although unusual as a pub name today, a 'mug house' was a popular term for an alehouse in the 17th century. The Severnside address is a strong clue to its location – right on that river, with just a narrow cobbled road and some river's edge seating between it and the pub's flower-decked frontage. Bewdley Brewery's Worcestershire Way may be on duty at the bar alongside guest ales and regulars Timothy Taylor Landlord and Wye Valley HPA. Rosie's Pig cider offers a refreshing alternative, even during the Early May Bank Holiday beer festival held in the rear garden. The lunch time menu comprises a tummy-filling range of crusty bread sarnies such as the Mug House Sarnie (chicken, bacon, lettuce and tomato with garlic mayo), plus a range of Mug House platters that are served with salad, coleslaw, sweet pickled onion rings, Mug House pickle and a warm cut baguette: choose between the likes of house-cooked roast

beef; hot pork bangers; and smoked salmon with citrus and chive mayonnaise. For those who enjoy a proper lunch, look to the list of mains and desserts, which all follow classic pub lines. The AA Rosette-standard Angry Chef (provenance unknown) restaurant comes into its own in the evening, offering seasonally-based dishes such as pan-fried pigeon breast with boxty pancakes; beetroot and pumpkin risotto; or spiced lamb rump with minted couscous, roasted shallots and butternut squash. Desserts may include the likes of apple and blackberry parcels; or steamed chocolate and pear sponge.

Open all day all wk 12-11 **Food** Lunch Mon-Sat 12-2.30, Sun 12-5 Restaurant menu available Mon-Sat evening ⊕ FREE HOUSE ◀ Bewdley Worcestershire Way, Timothy Taylor Landlord, Wye Valley HPA, Purity Mad Goose, Guest ales ♻ Westons Rosie's Pig. ♟ 10 **Facilities** Non-diners area ☸ (Bar Garden) Garden ⊨ Beer festival WiFi **Rooms** 7

BECKFORD
Map 10 SO93

The Beckford

tel: 01386 881532 **Cheltenham Rd GL20 7AN**
email: enquiries@thebeckford.com
dir: *M5 junct 9, A46 towards Evesham, 5m to Beckford*

Cotswold country inn just off the A46

Midway between Tewkesbury and Evesham, this rambling Georgian country inn has the Cotswolds beckoning just to the east and shapely Bredon Hill rising immediately to the north. The Beckford is an enticing mix of contemporary comforts and traditional fixtures throughout. A typical meal might include rare roast beef and pickle salad; spicy Thai stir-fried prawns; platters to share; roast sea bass fillets, new potatoes and seasonal vegetable; and home-made bread and butter pudding with custard. Steaks and home-made burgers are also on the menu.

Open all day all wk **Food** Lunch all wk 12-6 Dinner all wk 6-9.30 Av main course £6.95-£10.95 ⊕ FREE HOUSE ◄ Fuller's London Pride, Courage Best Bitter, Wye Valley, Wickwar, Prescott, Goffs ♂ Westons Stowford Press. ♟ 14
Facilities Non-diners area ♣ (Bar Garden) ◀ Children's menu Children's portions Garden 戸 Beer festival Parking WiFi ➡ (notice required)

BEWDLEY
Map 10 SO77

Little Pack Horse

tel: 01299 403762 **31 High St DY12 2DH**
email: enquiries@littlepackhorse.co.uk
dir: *From Kidderminster follow ring road & Safari Park signs. Then follow Bewdley signs over bridge, turn left, then right at top of Lax Ln*

Homely old inn offering local beers and fabled pies

Close to an old ford through the River Severn, this timber framed inn tucked away in Bewdley's web of lanes has been catering for passing trade for over 480 years. It was a base for jaggers and their packhorses; the inside retains much character from those long-gone days, with cosy log fires and wizened beams. Today's time travellers can indulge in fine beers from the town's brewery and a range of ciders. Fulfilling fodder includes a wealth of pies – Desperate Dan Cow Pie with best Herefordshire beef for example – and savoury suet puddings: venison, port, cranberry and Shropshire Blue a real feast. Light bites cater for the less ravenous.

Open all wk 12-2.30 5.30-11 (Fri 12-2.30 5.30-12 Sat 12-12 Sun 12-10.30) **Food** Lunch Mon-Fri 12-2.15, Sat-Sun 12-4 Dinner Mon-Thu 5.30-9, Fri-Sat 5.30-9.30, Sun 5.30-8 Restaurant menu available all wk ⊕ PUNCH TAVERNS ◄ Bewdley Worcestershire Way, Hobsons Town Crier, Holden's Black Country Special, Guest ales ♂ Thatchers Katy, Westons Stowford Press & Mortimers Orchard. ♟ 16
Facilities Non-diners area ♣ (Bar Garden Outside area) ◀ Children's menu Children's portions Family room Garden Outside area 戸 Beer festival WiFi ➡ (notice required)

The Mug House Inn & Angry Chef
Restaurant ★★★★ INN ⊛
PICK OF THE PUBS

See Pick of the Pubs on page 543

Woodcolliers Arms ★★★ INN

tel: 01299 400589 **76 Welch Gate DY12 2AU**
email: roger@woodcolliers.co.uk **web:** www.woodcolliers.co.uk
dir: *3m from Kidderminster on A456*

17th-century free house with a Russian flavour

If you've never tried atbivnaya, you can at this 17th-century, family-run free house built into a hillside just across the river from the Severn Valley (steam) Railway.

Battered pork steak, it's one of the several dishes Russian chef Boris Rumba serves alongside largely locally sourced more traditional pub favourites, such as beef, chicken or mushroom Stroganoff ('made in the traditional Russian way'), sea bass fillet or steak. There's always a weekly-changing roll-call of local real ales on offer, and Herefordshire ciders. Comfortable accommodation includes the Secret Room, once blocked off and 'lost' for years.

Open all wk 5pm-12.30am (Sat 12.30-12.30 Sun 12.30-11) **Food** Lunch Sat-Sun 12.30-3 Dinner all wk 5-9 Av main course £10 Restaurant menu available all wk ⊕ FREE HOUSE/OLIVERS INNS LTD ◄ Ludlow Gold, Three Tuns 1642, Kinver Edge ♂ Thatchers Gold & Heritage, Westons Old Rosie & Country Perry. ♟ 20
Facilities Non-diners area ◀ Outside area 戸 Parking WiFi ➡ **Rooms** 5

BRANSFORD
Map 10 SO75

The Bear & Ragged Staff

tel: 01886 833399 **Station Rd WR6 5JH**
email: mail@bearatbransford.co.uk
dir: *3m from Worcester or Malvern, clearly signed from A4103 or A449*

Well-positioned free house with good reputation for food

Built in 1861 as an estate rent office and stables, this lovely old free house is easily reached from both Malvern and Worcester. The current owners have created a reputation for good food and beers, such as local Hobsons Twisted Spire (named after Cleobury Mortimer's parish church) and Cornish-brewed Sharp's Doom Bar. A typical meal might involve ham hock and root vegetable terrine, crispy quail egg and piccalilli; roast cod with salt cod fishcakes, braised green onions, sauté chestnut mushrooms, spinach and tarragon cream sauce. Sandwiches are available from Monday to Saturday at lunchtime only.

Open 11.30-2.30 6-10.30 (Fri-Sat 11.30-2.30 6-11 Sun 12-2.30) Closed 25 Dec eve, 1 Jan eve, Sun eve **Food** Lunch all wk 12-2 Dinner Mon-Sat 6.30-9 Av main course £12.50 Restaurant menu available all wk ⊕ FREE HOUSE ◄ Hobsons Twisted Spire, Sharp's Doom Bar ♂ Westons Stowford Press. ♟ 10 **Facilities** Non-diners area ♣ (Bar Garden) ◀ Children's menu Children's portions Garden 戸 Parking WiFi ➡ (notice required)

BRETFORTON
Map 10 SP04

The Fleece Inn
PICK OF THE PUBS

tel: 01386 831173 **The Cross WR11 7JE**
email: info@thefleeceinn.co.uk **web:** www.thefleeceinn.co.uk
dir: *From Evesham follow signs for B4035 towards Chipping Campden. Through Badsey into Bretforton. Right at village hall, past church, pub in open parking area*

Ancient village inn with seasonal menus

The first pub to be owned by the National Trust, the Fleece was built as a longhouse in Chaucer's time and was owned by the same family until the death in 1977 of Lola Taplin – a direct descendant of the farmer who built it. A quintessentially English pub, it is a beautiful timbered building. Real ale devotees will admire one of England's oldest pewter collections as they order a pint of Uley Pigs Ear or Wye Valley Bitter; and cider lovers can try the home-brewed Ark cider. Families enjoy summer sunshine in the apple orchard while children let off steam in the play area. Food is well priced yet notches above pub grub, when treats such as asparagus feature in seasonal menus; wintertime sees the likes of game pudding; pork and leek casserole; and pan-fried lamb's liver. Ale and cider festival in October.

Open all day all wk **Food** Lunch Mon-Sat 12-2.30, Sun 12-4 Dinner Mon-Sat 6.30-9, Sun 6.30-8.30 ⊕ FREE HOUSE ◀ Uley Pigs Ear, Wye Valley Bitter Ò Thatchers Heritage, The Ark. ♟ 20 **Facilities** Non-diners area ❄ (Bar Garden) ♦ Children's menu Children's portions Play area Garden ⚶ Beer festival Cider festival WiFi ⛟ (notice required)

Crown & Trumpet

tel: 01386 853202 **14 Church St WR12 7AE**
email: info@cotswoldholidays.co.uk
dir: *From High St follow Snowshill sign. Pub 600yds on left*

Ideally placed for exploring the Cotswolds

Just behind the green in this internationally-known picture-postcard village is the Crown & Trumpet, a traditional, 17th-century, mellow-stone inn. The classic beamed bar is just the place for a pint of Cotswold Spring Codrington Codger, or Stanway Broadway Artists Ale, or you can take it out into the peaceful patio garden; a winter alternative is a glass of mulled wine or a hot toddy by the fire. Classic, home-made pub food is available at lunch and dinner – try Evesham Vale pie; pan-fried chicken breast and chorizo; duck and apricot sausages with mash; or vegetable lasagne. There's musical entertainment every Saturday evening, and weekly jazz and blues evenings. Booking for meals is recommended.

Open all wk 11-3 5-11 (Fri-Sat 11am-mdnt Sun 12-11) **Food** Lunch Mon-Fri 12-2.30, Sat-Sun 12-5 Dinner Mon-Fri 6-9.30, Sat-Sun 5-9.30 Set menu available ⊕ ENTERPRISE INNS ◀ Stroud Tom Long, Cotswold Spring Codrington Codger, Stanway Cotteswold Gold & Broadway Artists Ale Ò Black Rat & Black Rat Perry. ♟ 9 **Facilities** Non-diners area ❄ (Bar Garden) ♦ Children's menu Children's portions Garden ⚶ Beer festival Parking WiFi ⛟ (notice required)

The Bell & Cross   PICK OF THE PUBS

tel: 01562 730319 **Holy Cross DY9 9QL**
dir: *Phone for detailed directions*

Good food near famous country park

Standing at the heart of a peaceful Worcestershire village, this character pub is the ideal culmination of a visit to the remarkable Clent Hills which rumble across the horizon just a mile from The Bell & Cross. Exploring the bald hills, wooded dingles and fabulous viewpoints can work up a healthy appetite; who better to help sate this than the former chef to the England football squad, host-patron Roger Narbett. Head for the bar for a rolling selection of hand-pulled beers and an inviting log fire in winter; the extensive garden, or the covered and heated patio for comfortable alfresco dining on cooler nights. The imaginative menu opens with a substantial range of starters and lite-bites such as pumpkin, carrot and ginger soup; or smoked chicken and pulled ham tian. Enticing mains include pot-roasted pork belly with Bramley apple, crumbled black pudding, crackling and cider; or aubergine and goats' cheese crumble with sweet potato and pumpkin. Booking is recommended.

Open all wk 12-3 6-11 (Sun 12-10.30) Closed 25 Dec, 26 Dec eve, 1 Jan eve **Food** Lunch all wk 12-2 Dinner Mon-Sat 6.30-9.15 Set menu available Restaurant menu available all wk ⊕ ENTERPRISE INNS ◀ Enville Ale, Marston's Pedigree & Burton Bitter, Timothy Taylor Landlord, Guest ales Ò Thatchers Gold. ♟ 15 **Facilities** Non-diners area ❄ (Bar Garden) ♦ Children's menu Children's portions Garden ⚶ Parking ⛟ (notice required)

Read all about pubs and their friendly ghosts in our feature on page 12

CLENT *continued*

The Vine Inn

tel: 01562 882491 **Vine Ln DY9 9PH**
email: info@vineinnclent.com **web:** www.vineinnclent.com
dir: *Phone for detailed directions*

Cracking pub secluded in marvellous hill country

Tucked into one of the sharp valleys which cleave the glorious Clent Hills, the Vine started life as a watermill at the dawn of the Industrial Revolution. Reborn as a pub in 1851, beers from Wye Valley, supplemented by cider and perry fresh from the Malvern Hills reward ramblers challenging the mini-mountain range that are the Clents. Recover in the tranquil wood-side gardens behind the flowerbasket-hung pub and consider a tempting menu offering the likes of Welsh rarebit stuffed mushrooms; Stilton and walnut stuffed chicken; game pie; or pan-fried, mead-marinated pork medallions with creamy apple, leek and brandy sauce. Leave space for chocolate and pear upside-down sponge pudding.

Open all day all wk **Food** Lunch Mon-Fri 12-3, Sat 12-9.30, Sun 12-8 Dinner Mon-Fri 6-9, Sat 12-9.30, Sun 12-8 Av main course £11 Set menu available ⊕ PUNCH TAVERNS ◼ Thwaites Wainwright, Wye Valley Butty Bach Ö Hogan's & Hogan's Perry, Thatchers Traditional. **Facilities** Non-diners area ♦ Children's portions Garden ⚲ Parking WiFi 🚍 (notice required)

See advert on page 545

See advert on page 545

| DROITWICH | Map 10 SO86 |

The Chequers
PICK OF THE PUBS

tel: 01299 851292 **Kidderminster Rd, Cutnall Green WR9 OPJ**
dir: *Phone for detailed directions*

Charming pub that's top of its league

Roger Narbett used to be the England football team chef; his soccer memorabilia can be found in the Players Lounge of this charming pub he now runs with wife Joanne. Its traditional look comes from the cranberry-coloured walls, open fire, church-panel bar and richly hued furnishings. Indeed, some might also make a case for including the range of real ales, such as Enville, Wye Valley HPA and Hook Norton in the bar, adjoining which is the country-style Garden Room with plush sofa and hanging tankards. The menus offer a wide choice, from sandwiches, deli platters and 'bucket food' to pub classics like pizza or cod and chips. Among the top performers are chicken breast marinated in honey and lemon thyme; carved ham with fried eggs; and Malaysian chicken curry. How sorry England's finest must have been to see Roger go.

Open all day all wk Closed 25 Dec, 26 Dec eve & 1 Jan eve **Food** Lunch Mon-Sat 12-2, Sun 12-2.30 (light bites 2-5.30) Dinner all wk 6.30-9.15 Set menu available Restaurant menu available all wk ⊕ FREE HOUSE ◼ Enville Ale, Greene King Ruddles, Wye Valley HPA, Timothy Taylor, Hook Norton, Otter Bitter, Marston's EPA Ö Thatchers Gold. ♟ 15 **Facilities** Non-diners area ❦ (Bar Garden) ♦ Children's menu Children's portions Family room Garden ⚲ Parking WiFi 🚍 (notice required)

The Honey Bee

tel: 01299 851620 **Doverdale Ln, Doverdale WR9 0QB**
email: honey@king-henrys-taverns.co.uk
dir: *From Droitwich take A442 towards Kidderminster. Left to Dovedale*

Spacious, modern and friendly pub

Set in four and half acres of grounds, you can go fishing for carp in this pub's two lakes – and even have your meal brought to you. The garden also has a great play area for children and there is a patio for outdoor drinking and dining. The contemporary interior has plenty of areas in which to enjoy freshly prepared dishes which will satisfy small and large appetites alike. Choose from a good selection of steaks and grills, fish and seafood options like swordfish steak, traditional favourites such as half a roast chicken, and international and vegetarian dishes, perhaps vegetable fajitas.

Open all day all wk 11.30-11 **Food** Lunch all wk 12-10 Dinner all wk 12-10 Set menu available Restaurant menu available all wk ⊕ FREE HOUSE/KING HENRY'S TAVERNS ◼ Greene King Abbot Ale, Fuller's London Pride, Sharp's Doom Bar, Guinness. ♟ 15 **Facilities** Non-diners area ♦ Children's menu Children's portions Play area Garden Parking 🚍

| ELDERSFIELD | Map 10 SO73 |

The Butchers Arms

tel: 01452 840381 **Lime St GL19 4NX**
dir: *A417 from Gloucester towards Ledbury. After BP garage take B4211. In 2m take 4th left into Lime St*

A real beer-lovers' pub with a concise menu

Dating from the 16th century this is a pub which values its beer-drinking customers. The low-ceilinged, wooden-floored bar offers a good choice of regional beers served from the cask and is the hub of local life (although, sorry, it's not for the under-10s). The seasonal menu may be small, but it sure offers diversity: for example, pan-fried squab pigeon breast with chorizo and creamed corn to start; then turbot roasted on the bone with mini oxtail pie and truffle mash; and rose water meringue with blood orange jelly, Amalfi lemon sorbet and lemon curd to finish. A spacious garden adds to its charm.

Open 12-2 7-11 Closed 1wk Jan, 1 wknd Aug, 24-26 Dec, Sun eve & Mon (incl BHs) **Food** Lunch Fri-Sun 12-1 Dinner Tue-Sat 7-9 ⊕ FREE HOUSE ◼ Wye Valley Dorothy Goodbody's Golden Ale, St Austell Tribute, Wickwar Sunny Daze Ö Westons Stowford Press. ♟ 11 **Facilities** Non-diners area Garden Parking

PICK OF THE PUBS

The Boot Inn ★★★★ INN

FLYFORD FLAVELL   Map 10 SO95

tel: 01386 462658
Radford Rd WR7 4BS
email: enquiries@thebootinn.com
web: www.thebootinn.com
dir: *A422 from Worcester towards Stratford. Turn right to village*

Friendly, family-run old coaching inn

Parts of this family-run, award-winning, traditional coaching inn can be traced back to the 13th century, and for evidence you need only to look at the heavy beams and slanting doorways. Keep an eye out too for the friendly ghost, age uncertain. The large bar area is comfortable, the pool table and TV having been banished to a separate room, while regulars like London Pride and Black Sheep, and an extensive wine list complement the varied and imaginative menus which change every six weeks. You can eat from the lunchtime sandwich and bar snack menu, from the extensive specials board, or from the full à la carte, but no matter which you choose, or indeed where – including the conservatory – only the best and freshest, mostly county-sourced, produce is used. A sample menu therefore may include starters of crispy pulled pork, black pudding, apple crisps and Colston

Bassett Stilton with honey-dressed leaves; followed by salmon supreme with apple, horseradish and hazelnut crust with creamy wild mushroom sauce; pork fillet stuffed with smoked Applewood, crushed walnuts and chilli flakes, wrapped in bacon, Stowford and Braeburn gravy; baked cod and king prawn mornay, mature cheddar, lemongrass and rosemary. Sundays are devoted to roasts – beef, pork and turkey are served, along with the specials menu. Gardens and a shaded patio area are especially suited to summer dining. The comfortable en suite bedrooms in the converted coach house are furnished in antique pine and equipped with practical goodies.

Open all day all wk **Food** Lunch all wk 12-2 Dinner all wk 6.30-10 Set menu available Restaurant menu available all wk ⊕ PUNCH TAVERNS ◀ Fuller's London Pride, Black Sheep, Sharp's Doom Bar ⚲ Westons Stowford Press. ♇ 8 **Facilities** Non-diners area ❖ (Bar Garden) ❙❙ Children's menu Children's portions Garden ⊼ Parking WiFi 🚌 (notice required) **Rooms** 5

FAR FOREST
Map 10 SO77

The Plough Inn

tel: 01299 266237 **Cleobury Rd DY14 9TE**
email: info@nostalgiainns.co.uk
dir: *From Kidderminster take A456 towards Leominster. Right onto A4117 towards Cleobury Mortimer. Approx 0.5m to pub on left*

Top notch carvery operation in lovely countryside setting

The location in beautiful rolling countryside, the excellent range of locally brewed real ales, and one of the best carvery dining operations for miles draw local foodies to this family-owned, 18th-century coaching inn. It's also popular with walkers and cyclists, so arrive early to get the pick of the four roasted joints, perhaps leg of lamb, Far Forest venison, local pork and Scottish beef, all served with a choice of 12 vegetables. The gorgeous summer garden comes with its own bar.

Open all wk 12-3 6-11 (Fri-Sat 12-11 Sun 12-9) **Food** Lunch Mon-Fri 12-2, Sat 12-9, Sun 12-6 Dinner Mon-Fri 6-9, Sat 12-9 ⊕ FREE HOUSE ◀ Greene King Abbot Ale, Hobsons Twisted Spire, Enville Ale, Guest ales Ö Healey's Cornish Rattler, Berry Rattler & Pear Rattler, Thatchers Gold. **Facilities** Non-diners area ♦ Children's menu Children's portions Garden ⊬ Parking WiFi ☞ (notice required)

FLADBURY
Map 10 SO94

Chequers Inn

tel: 01386 861854 **Chequers Ln WR10 2PZ**
email: tspchef85@gmail.com
dir: *Off A44 between Evesham & Pershore*

River Avon walkers can refuel here

With its beams and open fire, this lovely old inn has bags of rustic charm. Tucked away in a pretty village with views of the glorious Bredon Hills, local produce from the Vale of Evesham provides the basis for home-cooked dishes such as jumbo crayfish and prawn cocktail; boiled ham with two eggs and chunky chips; and a range of home-made desserts. There is also a traditional Sunday roast. The pretty walled garden enjoys outstanding views – a great setting for drinking or dining – and the nearby River Avon is ideal for walking and fishing.

Open 12-3 5-11 (Fri-Sat 12-11 Sun 12-late) Closed Mon L (Jan-May) **Food** Lunch Tue-Sat 12-2.30, Sun 12-3 Dinner Tue-Sat 6-9 Restaurant menu available Tue-Sat ⊕ ENTERPRISE INNS ◀ Sharp's Doom Bar, Wye Valley HPA Ö Thatchers Gold. ♈ **Facilities** Non-diners area ♦ (Bar Garden) ♦ Children's menu Children's portions Play area Family room Garden ⊬ Parking WiFi

FLYFORD FLAVELL
Map 10 SO95

The Boot Inn ★★★★ INN
PICK OF THE PUBS

See Pick of the Pubs on page 547

HARTLEBURY
Map 10 SO87

The Tap House @ The Old Ticket Office

tel: 01299 253275 **DY11 7YJ**
dir: *From A449 follow station signs*

Good pub grub in converted railway building

This is the flagship for the Worcestershire Brewing Company, whose Attwood Ales range of draught and bottled beers are brewed across from the pub. Until not long ago, it was Hartlebury's station building, a purpose recalled by the lounge bar's bench seating and railway-style signs. Meat, fish, Indian and dairy deli-boards and pub meals are served in the oak-panelled restaurant, where typical mains include roast breast of Gressingham duck with orange sauce; 28-day-matured Hereford steaks; fresh and smoked shellfish pie; and Portobello mushroom and spinach crumble. Tables on the outside terrace overlook the valley.

Open all day all wk **Food** Lunch all wk 12-3 Dinner Mon-Sat 6-9 Set menu available Restaurant menu available ⊕ WORCESTERSHIRE BREWING COMPANY ◀ Attwood Nectar Bitter, Pale Ale & Gold. **Facilities** Non-diners area ♦ (Bar Outside area) ♦ Children's menu Outside area ⊬ Beer festival Parking WiFi ☞ (notice required)

The White Hart

tel: 01299 250286 **The Village DY11 7TD**
email: skdiprose@fsmail.net
dir: *From Stourport-on-Severn take A4025 signed Worcester & Hartlebury. At rdbt take B4193. Pub in village centre*

At the community's centre and with really good food

Owner and top chef Simon Diprose runs this traditional country pub which has gone from strength to strength since his arrival. The concise menus might begin with garlic and mozzarella roasted field mushroom; smoked Scottish salmon with potato salad, pea shoots and prawns; or calamari rings with lime mayonnaise and salad leaves. Moving onto something more substantial there's wild mushroom leek and Stilton crumble; chicken with creamed potato, fresh vegetables and pea, bacon and marjoram sauce; slow-cooked shank of Welsh lamb with vegetables and creamy garlic and thyme sauce; or lemon roast salmon fillet, baby vegetables and light beetroot and horseradish sauce. At lunchtime you could opt for just filled baps, a ploughman's or a burger and chunky chips.

Open all day all wk **Food** Lunch all wk 12-3 Dinner all wk 6-9 Av main course £14 Set menu available Restaurant menu available all wk (ex Sun eve) ⊕ PUNCH TAVERNS ◀ Timothy Taylor Landlord, Wye Valley HPA, Purity Mad Goose. **Facilities** Non-diners area ♦ (Bar Garden) ♦ Children's menu Children's portions Garden ⊬ Parking WiFi

KEMPSEY
Map 10 SO84

Walter de Cantelupe Inn ★★★ INN
PICK OF THE PUBS

tel: 01905 820572 **Main Rd WR5 3NA**
email: info@walterdecantelupe.co.uk **web:** www.walterdecantelupe.co.uk
dir: *4m S of Worcester city centre on A38. Pub in village centre*

Village pub known for its personal touch

Just four miles from the centre of Worcester, this privately-owned free house commemorates a 13th-century bishop of that city, although he was strongly opposed to his parishioners brewing and selling ales to raise money for church funds. Whitewashed walls are bedecked with flowers in the summer, while the interior's wooden beams and stone floor testify to the inn's 17th-century origins. The daily menu on the blackboard testifies to the freshness of ingredients, with some produce being supplied by villagers. Worcestershire rare titbit (Welsh rarebit with a twist); and the plate-size gammon steak with fried free-range egg, pineapple and chips are two dishes to try. The walled and paved garden has been fragrantly planted with clematis, roses and honeysuckle, and its south-facing aspect can be a real suntrap. Cask ales include a particularly well-kept Timothy Taylor Landlord, and a beer festival is held in April.

Open Tue-Fri 5.30-11 Sat 12-2.30 5.30-11 Sun 12-9 Closed 25-26 Dec, 1 Jan, Mon (ex BHs) **Food** Lunch Sun 12-5 Dinner Tue-Sat 6-9.30 ⊕ FREE HOUSE ◀ Timothy Taylor Landlord Ö Westons Stowford Press. **Facilities** Non-diners area ♦ (Bar Outside area) ♦ Children's portions Outside area ⊬ Beer festival Parking WiFi **Rooms** 3

KNIGHTWICK

Map 10 SO75

The Talbot

PICK OF THE PUBS

tel: 01886 821235 **WR6 5PH**
email: info@the-talbot.co.uk **web:** www.the-talbot.co.uk
dir: *Take A44 from Worcester towards Bromyard. In 8m right on B4197 to Knightwick*

Family-run inn and brewery

Run by the Clift family for over 30 years, The Talbot is a traditional 14th-century coaching inn on the bank of the River Teme. Surrounded by hop yards and meadows, this peaceful inn is also home to the Teme Valley Brewery, which uses locally grown hops in a range of curiously named cask-conditioned ales called This, That, T'Other and Wot. Nearly everything on the menus is made in-house, including bread, preserves, black pudding and raised pies. Salads, herbs and vegetables are grown in the large organic kitchen garden, and everything else comes from a local source, with the exception of fish, which arrives from Cornwall and Wales. The bar menu offers ploughman's, filled rolls and hot dishes, whilst in the restaurant, starters might include pig's head brawn or French onion soup, followed by slow-roast pork belly served with griddled black pudding and apple fritters; or wild mushroom timbales with couscous. Leave space for the squidgy rhubarb or treacle hollygog (a 19th-century Cambridge University recipe). Three beer festivals a year.

Open all day all wk 7.30am-11.30pm **Food** Lunch all wk 12-9 Dinner all wk 12-9 Restaurant menu available all wk ⊕ FREE HOUSE ◀ Teme Valley This, That, T'Other & Wot, Hobsons Best Bitter ᕯ Kingstone Press, Robinsons. ☕ 12
Facilities Non-diners area ☣ (Bar Restaurant Garden) ♦♦ Children's portions Garden ♉ Beer festival Parking WiFi ☷

MALVERN

Map 10 SO74

The Inn at Welland

tel: 01684 592317 **Drake St, Welland WR13 6LN**
email: info@theinnatwelland.co.uk
dir: *M50 junct 1, A38 follow signs for Upton upon Severn. Left onto A4104, through Upton upon Severn, 2.5m. Pub on right*

Stylish inn with panoramic views

This 17th-century country inn close to the Three Counties Showground is appointed to a high standard with an eclectic mix of smart, contemporary furnishings and rustic chic. There are spectacular views of the Malvern Hills from the stylish terrace, where you can dine alfresco in the warmer months; and the pub has a wood-burner and open fire for the winter. Food centres around seasonal local produce accompanied by Wye Valley or Malvern Hills ales, plus guests. Typical dishes might be pressed terrine of duck and pigeon with clementine relish, mulled pear and brioche toast, followed by slow-cooked Herefordshire lamb shoulder, braised red cabbage, crushed minted new potatoes, glazed carrots and rich lamb cooking liquor. If there's still room, choose passion fruit parfait or sticky toffee pudding. There is a good children's menu.

Open 12-3.30 6-11 (Sun 12-3.30) Closed Sun eve & Mon **Food** Lunch Tue-Sun 12-2.30 Dinner Tue-Sat 6.30-9.30 ⊕ FREE HOUSE ◀ Otter Bitter, Wye Valley, Malvern Hills, Guest ales ᕯ Westons Stowford Press & Mortimers Orchard. ☕ 31
Facilities Non-diners area ♦♦ Children's menu Children's portions Garden ♉ Parking WiFi

The Nag's Head

tel: 01684 574373 **19-21 Bank St WR14 2JG**
email: enquiries@nagsheadmalvern.co.uk
dir: *Off A449*

An excellent choice of real ales

From this pub's garden, the looming presence of North Hill, northernmost top of the stunning Malvern Hills, takes the eye — if only momentarily — away from the panoply of delights at this enterprising free house. 'Real ale, real food, real people' is the motto at The Nag's Head. Fifteen real ales, many from local breweries, adorn the bar; eight are permanent fixtures and include three from the pub's own St George's microbrewery. The annual beer festival on St George's Day (23rd April) offers even more choice. The interior is dotted with snugs, log fires and a magpie's nest of artefacts to create a cosy atmosphere, and the marvellous menu features baked monkfish with roast fennel and courgette; and sweet potato, mushroom and salmon Wellington.

Open all day all wk **Food** Lunch all wk 12-2.30 Av main course £9-£13.50 Restaurant menu available Mon-Sat 6.30-8.30, Sun 7-8.30 ⊕ FREE HOUSE ◀ St George's Friar Tuck, Charger & Dragon's Blood, Bathams, Banks's, Wood's Shropshire Lad, Ringwood Fortyniner ᕯ Thatchers Gold, Westons Family Reserve, Robinsons. ☕ 10 **Facilities** Non-diners area ☣ (Bar Restaurant Garden) ♦♦ Children's portions Garden ♉ Beer festival Parking WiFi ☷ (notice required)

The Wyche Inn ★★★★ INN

tel: 01684 575396 **74 Wyche Rd WR14 4EQ**
email: thewycheinn@googlemail.com **web:** www.thewycheinn.co.uk
dir: *1.5m S of Malvern. On B4218 towards Malvern & Colwall. Off A449 (Worcester to Ledbury road)*

Spectacular views and home-cooked food

Start or end a walk in the Malvern Hills in this traditional, dog-friendly country inn, probably the highest in Worcestershire. Indeed, the views from various nearby high points are quite something; from Malvern Beacon, for instance, you can see seven counties. Beers come from Wye Valley among others, while home-cooked dishes include pie of the day, chicken curry and battered cod. Themed food nights feature sirloin steak (Tuesday/Saturday) and mixed grill (Wednesday), and roast lunches are served on Sundays. Well-behaved pets are welcome in the bar, garden and the bedrooms.

Open all day all wk **Food** Lunch Mon-Fri 12-2.30, Sat 12-8.30, Sun 12-3.30 Dinner Mon-Fri 6-8.30, Sat 5-8.30, Sun 6-7.30 ⊕ FREE HOUSE ◀ Wye Valley HPA, Guest ales ᕯ Robinsons. ☕ 9 **Facilities** Non-diners area ☣ (Bar Garden) ♦♦ Children's menu Children's portions Garden ♉ Parking WiFi **Rooms** 6

PERSHORE
Map 10 SO94

The Defford Arms

tel: 01386 750378 **Upton Rd, Defford WR8 9BD**
dir: *From Pershore take A4104 towards Upton upon Severn. Pub on left in village*

Popular village pub with much charm

Neil, Les and Sue Overton have certainly made a success of running The Defford Arms; they have said a firm 'no' to music, gambling machines and TV in favour of old fashioned hospitality values. It's in a great location too, so days out at Croome Park, the Three Counties Showground at Malvern, Cheltenham Racecourse or Pershore's plum festival could all include a welcome break here. Expect traditional home-made food such home-made shepherd's pie; oven braised lamb shank, mash with red wine and rosemary gravy; cheesy fish pie; and lemon meringue pie.

Open Mon 12-2 Tue 12-2.30 5.30-9 Wed 12-2.30 5.30-9.30 Thu 12-2.30 5.30-10 Fri 12-2.30 5.30-11 Sat 12-11 Sun 12-4 Closed Sun eve & Mon eve **Food** Lunch Mon 12-1.30, Tue-Sun 12-2 Dinner Tue-Sat 6-8 Restaurant menu available Tue-Sat ⊕ FREE HOUSE ◀ Guest ales ♂ Thatchers Gold & Heritage.
Facilities Non-diners area ✿ (Bar Garden) ♦♦ Children's menu Children's portions Garden ⏸ Parking ☻ (notice required)

POWICK
Map 10 SO85

The Halfway House Inn

tel: 01905 831098 **Bastonford WR2 4SL**
email: contact@halfwayhouseinnpowick.co.uk
dir: *M5 junct 7, A4440 then A449*

A warm welcome at this village pub

Standing halfway between Worcester and Malvern on the main road, this aptly named Georgian free house offers a range of bottled beers, winter log fires and a mature shady garden at the side. Steaks and seafood are a speciality, but the menu also features a good choice of fresh, locally sourced hot dishes such as escalope of chicken breast sweet peppers, basil and goats' cheese; Herefordshire rib-eye steak, chips, mushrooms, onion rings and tomatoes; and hand-carved home-cooked ham, new potatoes, parsley and Dijon mustard sauce. Round things off with steamed syrup sponge with custard; or summer fruit and cream meringue roulade.

Open 12-3 6-11 Closed Mon-Tue **Food** Lunch Sat-Sun 12-3 Dinner Wed-Sat 6-9 Av main course £13 Restaurant menu available Tue-Sun ⊕ FREE HOUSE ♂ Westons Stowford Press. **Facilities** Non-diners area ♦♦ Children's menu Children's portions Garden ⏸ Parking ☻ (notice required)

TENBURY WELLS
Map 10 SO56

Pembroke House

tel: 01584 810301 **Cross St WR15 8EQ**
dir: *Phone for detailed directions*

Modern menus and shoot dinners

Built as a farmhouse in the 16th century, by the year 1600 this was a cider house. When Andrew Mortimer bought this classic black and white timbered property he created the two intimate restaurants, where today lunch might be butternut squash roulade; slow-roasted belly pork; or smoked haddock and prawn pancake. For dinner, pan-fried king scallops with asparagus purée and crispy pancetta to start; then half a roast duckling with Grand Marnier and honey sauce; or baked salmon

steak with dill and cucumber pickle in puff pastry. Cider these days comes from Robinsons of Tenbury, the 'Town in the Orchard'; the real ales all come from hereabouts too.

Open 12-3 5-close (Mon 5-close Sat-Sun all day) Closed Mon L **Food** Lunch Tue-Sat 12-2, Sun 12-2.30 Dinner Tue-Sat 7-9.15 Restaurant menu available Tue-Sat evening ⊕ FREE HOUSE ◀ Hobsons, Wye Valley, Three Tuns, Wood's, Cannon Royall, Ludlow ♂ Robinsons, Thatchers Gold. ☻ 9 **Facilities** Non-diners area ✿ (Garden) ♦♦ Children's portions Garden ⏸ Parking WiFi ☻ (notice required)

Talbot Inn

tel: 01584 781941 **Newnham Bridge WR15 8JF**
email: info@talbotinnnewnhambridge.co.uk
dir: *3m E of Tenbury Wells*

Restored coaching inn in the beautiful Teme Valley

This 19th-century Teme Valley coaching inn was painstakingly restored by its current owners and its contemporary rustic style makes for a relaxed base to explore local market towns such as Ludlow and Leominster. Sup a pint of Wye Valley ale in the bar or bag a table and tuck into enjoyable dishes such as corned beef hash, fried duck egg and smokey beans; or pan-fried sea bass, white bean cassoulet, buttered greens and crushed potatoes. A light lunch menu includes wholetail scampi and chips; Welsh rarebit; and eggs Benedict.

Open all day all wk **Food** Lunch Mon-Sat 12-2.30, Sun 12-7.30 Dinner Mon-Sat 6-9.30, Sun 12-7.30 Av main course £13 Set menu available ⊕ FREE HOUSE ◀ Wye Valley Bitter & HPA, Hobsons Best Bitter ♂ Robinsons, Westons Stowford Press, Hobsons. ☻ 11 **Facilities** Non-diners area ✿ (All areas) ♦♦ Children's menu Children's portions Garden Outside area ⏸ Parking WiFi ☻ (notice required)

EAST RIDING OF YORKSHIRE

BARMBY ON THE MARSH
Map 17 SE62

The King's Head

tel: 01757 630705 **High St DN14 7HT**
email: rainderpubcoltd@tiscali.co.uk
dir: *M62 junct 37 follow A614/Bridlington/York/Howden signs. Left at A63. At rdbt 1st exit onto A614/Booth Ferry Rd towards Goole. At rdbt 4th exit on B1228/Booth Ferry Rd. Left, through Asselby to Barmby on the Marsh*

Look out for their Yorkshire tapas menu

In the 17th century this inn served a ferry that crossed the Rivers Ouse and Derwent. Nowadays this family-run village pub is a place that appeals to all tastes; from the beamed bar through a bright, modern lounge to the cosy, intimate restaurant. Several members of the family are trained chefs and make the most of Yorkshire's burgeoning larder; braised beef with clementines and ginger wine, herb cobbler and mash is just one of the tempting mains here. Their innovative Yorkshire tapas menu features haddock goujons, confit lamb croquettes, and baked mussels. There are great open sandwiches and a take-away deli menu (including ice creams), too.

Open Wed-Thu 12-2 5-11 (Mon-Tue 5-11 Fri 12-2 5-12 Sat 12-12 Sun 12-11) Closed Mon L, Tue L **Food** Lunch Wed-Fri 12-2, Sat-Sun all day Dinner Wed-Thu 5-8.30, Fri 5-9, Sat-Sun all day Set menu available Restaurant menu available Wed-Mon ⊕ FREE HOUSE ◀ Black Sheep Best Bitter, 3 guest ales.
Facilities Non-diners area ♦♦ Children's menu Children's portions Outside area ⏸ Parking WiFi ☻ (notice required)

BEVERLEY
Map 17 TA03

The Ferguson Fawsitt Arms & Country Lodge

tel: 01482 882665 **East End, Walkington HU17 8RX**

email: admin@fergusonfawsitt.com

dir: *M62 junct 38 onto B1230, left on A1034, right onto B1230, on left in centre of Walkington*

Well-positioned traditional inn where time stands still

Three miles from Beverley in the picturesque village of Walkington, there is a timeless quality to this Victorian pub named after two important local families. Parts of the pub used to form the village blacksmith's shop where carriage wheels were repaired. Open fires, dark-wood panelling, carved settles, beams and some decent tiling to the floor welcomes those set on sampling a pint of Black Sheep, or diners intent on a good Sunday roast, home-made steak pie from the carvery or a traditional pub meal from the bar food menu.

Open all day all wk 11-11 **Food** Lunch all wk 12-9 Dinner all wk 12-9 Restaurant menu available all wk ⊕ FREE HOUSE ◀ Courage Directors, Black Sheep, Guest ales. ☆ 10 **Facilities** Non-diners area ◉ Children's menu Children's portions Outside area 🍺 Beer festival Parking WiFi 🚗 (notice required)

FLAMBOROUGH
Map 17 TA27

The Seabirds Inn

tel: 01262 850242 **Tower St YO15 1PD**

email: philip.theseabirds@virgin.net **web:** www.theseabirds.com

dir: *On B1255 E of Bridlington*

Village pub that keeps it simple

Just east of this 200-year-old village pub is the famous chalk promontory of Flamborough Head and its equally famed lighthouse. With the North Sea so close you'd expect plenty of fish, and there is, namely, spicy Whitby creel king prawns; deep-fried dusted whitebait; salmon steak hollandaise; and battered haddock fillet. This is not a menu to overreach itself, instead keeping to staples like a good choice of steaks; chicken breast with bacon, barbecue sauce and cheese; gammon with

egg and pineapple; and steamed suet pudding with spinach, pine nuts, mozzarella cheese and cherry tomatoes. Guest ales are on tap in the bar.

Open 12-3 6-11 Closed Mon (winter) **Food** Lunch all wk 12-2 Dinner Sun-Fri 6-8.30, Sat 6-9.30 Set menu available ⊕ FREE HOUSE ◀ Wold Top, Greene King Abbot Ale & IPA, Morland Old Speckled Hen. ☆ 9 **Facilities** Non-diners area ☆ (Bar Garden) Children's menu Children's portions Garden 🍺 Parking WiFi 🚗

HUGGATE
Map 19 SE85

The Wolds Inn ★★★ INN

tel: 01377 288217 **YO42 1YH**

email: woldsinn@gmail.com **web:** www.woldsinn.co.uk

dir: *S off A166 between York & Driffield*

Yorkshire Wolds inn with hearty home-made food

Sixteenth century in origin, this family-run hostelry is, at 525 feet above sea level, the highest in the Yorkshire Wolds. Copper pans and gleaming brassware fill the wood-panelled interior, where the open fires still burn good old-fashioned coal. The restaurant is widely known for serving large portions of, among other things, locally sourced Barnsley chops; crispy fresh farm duckling; fillet of plaice; chicken breast stuffed with spinach; Wolds Topper, 'the mixed grill to remember' and their celebrated home-made steak pie. The overnight accommodation is particularly popular with those exploring the countryside and coast.

Open 12-2 5-11 (Sun 12-11) Closed Mon (ex BHs) **Food** Lunch Tue-Sat 12-2, Sun 12-8 Dinner Tue-Sat 6-9, Sun 12-8 Set menu available Restaurant menu available Tue-Sun ⊕ FREE HOUSE ◀ Timothy Taylor Landlord, Theakston Best Bitter, York Guzzler Ö Kingstone Press. ☆ **Facilities** Non-diners area ◉ Children's menu Children's portions Garden 🍺 Parking WiFi 🚗 (notice required) **Rooms** 3

LOW CATTON
Map 17 SE75

The Gold Cup Inn

tel: 01759 371354 **YO41 1EA**

dir: *1m S of A166 or 1m N of A1079, E of York*

Attractive, family-run country pub

A charming, family-run free house that is 300 years old but may not look it at first glance. Giveaways are the low beams and open fireplaces in the bar, now complemented by wooden floors, modern fabrics and wall-mounted coach-lamps. Bar meals are served every lunchtime (except Monday) and evening from the extensive menu. Equally extensive is the carte, whose options include half a crispy roast duck with plum and ginger sauce; home-baked Yorkshire ham with creamy Stilton sauce; wild mushroom Stroganoff with saffron rice; and seared salmon fillet with spinach and mushroom sauce. A paddock adjoining the large beer garden runs down to the River Derwent.

Open 12-2.30 6-11 (Sat-Sun 12-11) Closed Mon L **Food** Lunch Tue-Fri 12-2.30, Sat-Sun 12-6 Dinner all wk 6-9 Set menu available ⊕ FREE HOUSE ◀ Theakston Black Bull Bitter. ☆ 11 **Facilities** Non-diners area ☆ (Bar Garden) ◉ Children's menu Children's portions Play area Garden 🍺 Parking WiFi 🚗 (notice required)

LUND

Map 17 SE94

The Wellington Inn

tel: 01377 217294 **19 The Green YO25 9TE**
email: tellmemore@thewellingtoninn.co.uk
dir: *On B1248 NE of Beverley*

Exciting food in quintessential village inn

Occupying a wonderfully rural location, this country pub is popular with locals and visitors alike, whether for a pint of real ale, a glass of wine, or a plate of good food. Nicely situated opposite the picture-postcard village green, inside is a unique blend of old and new where you can choose from the traditional pub menu or from the carte in the more formal restaurant. Expect excellent dishes like smoked duck breast, bramble and apple salad with sloe dressing; pot roast pork belly, bacon and colcannon; and mixed fish, scampi and king prawn thermidor. Leave space for vanilla cheesecake, drunken cherries and chocolate.

Open 12-3 6.30-11 Closed Mon L **Food** Lunch Tue-Sun 12-2 Dinner Tue-Sat 6.30-9 Av main course £15.95 Restaurant menu available Tue-Sat evenings ⊕ FREE HOUSE ◀ Timothy Taylor Landlord, Theakston Best Bitter, Great Newsome Sleck Dust, Regular guest ale. ♀ 11 **Facilities** Non-diners area ◆♦ Children's menu Children's portions Outside area ⋒ Parking WiFi

SANCTON

Map 17 SE83

The Star

tel: 01430 827269 **King St YO43 4QP**
email: benandlindsey@thestaratsancton.co.uk
dir: *2m SE of Market Weighton on A1034*

Traditional local serving top-notch pub food

This stylishly modernised and extended old village pub stands at the heart of charming Sancton, past which the Wolds Way recreational footpath threads across the tranquil Yorkshire landscape. Beers from local microbreweries tempt ramblers to linger longer; more leisurely visits are rewarded by a reliable bar menu considerably enhanced by an evening restaurant choice. Smoked haddock risotto may start the repast; seared rib-eye steak from village-reared stock, or white onion tart with lovage pesto and Yorkshire cheddar are typical of the satisfying mains which chef-proprietor Ben Cox crafts from local produce. A forced rhubarb and parkin dessert seals the Yorkshire theme.

Open 12-3 6-11 (Sun all day) Closed 1st wk Jan, Mon **Food** Lunch Tue-Sat 12-2, Sun 12-3 Dinner Tue-Sat 6-9.30, Sun 6-8 Set menu available Restaurant menu available all wk ⊕ FREE HOUSE ◀ Black Sheep, Copper Dragon, Wold Top, Great Newsome Ö Moorlands Farm. ♀ 14 **Facilities** Non-diners area ◆♦ Children's menu Children's portions Garden Outside area ⋒ Parking

SOUTH DALTON

Map 17 SE94

The Pipe & Glass Inn ◉◉

PICK OF THE PUBS

tel: 01430 810246 **West End HU17 7PN**
email: email@pipeandglass.co.uk
dir: *Just off B1248 (Beverley to Malton road). 7m from Beverley*

Smart inn serving quality food and ales

Part 15th- and part 17th-century, the inn occupies the site of the original gatehouse to Dalton Hall, family seat of Lord Hotham. James and Kate Mackenzie's transformation of their inn has helped earn it two AA Rosettes, but it still retains the village pub feel, with Copper Dragon, Scarborough, Great Yorkshire and other local ales, and Moorlands Farm cider all served in the bar. The restaurant is more contemporary in style and the conservatory looks out over the garden. James

sources top-notch local and seasonal produce for a complete range of modern British menus, including one for vegetarians; here you'll find dishes such as baked Rothwell flat mushroom with cheddar rarebit and dandelion leaf salad. The specials board may proffer deep-fried monkfish cheeks with Jerusalem artichoke three ways. The unpretentiously-titled but equally alluring 'Afters' carte may list the Pipe & Glass chocolate plate – 'five reasons to love chocolate'.

Open all day 12-11 (Sun 12-10.30) Closed 2wks Jan, Mon (ex BHs) **Food** Lunch Tue-Sat 12-2, Sun 12-4 Dinner Tue-Sat 6-9.30 Av main course £20 ⊕ FREE HOUSE ◀ Wold Top, Copper Dragon, Black Sheep, York, Scarborough, Great Yorkshire Ö Moorlands Farm. ♀ 15 **Facilities** ◆♦ Children's menu Children's portions Garden ⋒ Parking WiFi

NORTH YORKSHIRE

AKEBAR

Map 19 SE19

The Friar's Head

tel: 01677 450201 & 450591 **Akebar Park DL8 5LY**
email: thefriarshead@hotmail.co.uk
dir: *From A1 at Leeming Bar onto A684, 7m towards Leyburn. Entrance at Akebar Park*

Stone-built Dales pub with a lovely conservatory

This 200-year-old pub lies in the heart of Wensleydale, known for its castles, abbeys and waterfalls. Located next to an 18-hole golf course and at the entrance to Akebar Holiday Park, The Friar's Head overlooks beautiful countryside and has grounds where you can play bowls or croquet. Inside you'll find exposed beams and stonework, and hand-pulled Yorkshire ales at the bar. The lush plants and vines of the Cloister conservatory dining room give it a tropical appearance; in the evening it looks magical in the candlelit. From the frequently changing menu, typical dishes include twice baked spinach and gruyère soufflé; slow-braised lamb shank; Yorkshire farmed venison steak served pink with caramelised onions and juniper sauce.

Open all wk 10-3 6-11.30 (Fri-Sun 10am-11.30pm Jul-Sep) Closed 25 Dec, 26 Dec eve **Food** Lunch all wk 12-2 Dinner all wk 5.30-9 ⊕ FREE HOUSE ◀ Theakston Best Bitter, Black Sheep Best Bitter, Timothy Taylor Landlord, Guinness Ö Somersby Cider. ♀ 12 **Facilities** Non-diners area ◆♦ Children's portions Garden ⋒ Parking WiFi

ALDWARK

Map 19 SE46

The Aldwark Arms ◉◉

tel: 01347 838324 **YO61 1UB**
email: peter@aldwarkarms.co.uk
dir: *From York ring road take A19 N. Left into Warehill Ln signed Tollerton & Helperby. Through Tollerton, follow Aldwark signs*

Warm welcomes abound at this family-run community pub

Successfully run by local boys the Hardisty brothers, this friendly free house has an inviting atmosphere. Keen to include locally sourced, season produce on his menus, the chef offers the likes of smooth duck liver and port pâté; Cumberland sausages and pepper mash; pan-seared Dutch calves' liver; and sea bass fillets with Moroccan chickpea, courgette and spinach ragu. On tap you'll find Black Sheep ales, as well as Yorkshire Cider and several wines by the glass. On warmer days food and drink can be enjoyed in the pub garden if you prefer.

Open all day all wk **Food** Lunch Mon-Sat 12-2, Sun 12-7 Dinner Mon-Sat 5.30-9, Sun 12-7 Set menu available Restaurant menu available Mon-Sat ⊕ FREE HOUSE ◀ Black Sheep, Guest ales Ö Yorkshire Cider. ♀ **Facilities** Non-diners area ◆♦ Children's menu Children's portions Play area Garden ⋒ Parking WiFi ▭ (notice required)

PICK OF THE PUBS

Charles Bathurst Inn ★★★★ INN ⊛

ARKENGARTHDALE | Map 18 NY90

tel: 01748 884567 **DL11 6EN**
email: info@cbinn.co.uk
web: www.cbinn.co.uk
dir: *A1 onto A6108 at Scotch Corner, through Richmond, left onto B6270 to Reeth. At Buck Hotel right signed Langthwaite, pass church on right, inn 0.5m on right*

Spectacular dale scenery at remote country inn

This 18th-century inn sits in possibly one of the North's finest dales, and takes its name from the son of Oliver Cromwell's physician who built it for his workers in what was once a busy lead mining area. In winter, it caters for serious ramblers tackling The Pennine Way and the Coast to Coast route, and it offers a welcome escape from the rigours of the moors and many a tale has been swapped over pints of Black Sheep or Theakston ale. The 'Terrace Room' features handcrafted tables and chairs from Robert Thompson's craftsmen in nearby Kilburn with their unique hand carved mouse on every item, watch out for them! English classics meet modern European dishes on a menu written up on the mirror hanging above the stone fireplace and the provenance is impeccable: Cogden Hill beef and Black Sheep Ale casserole, suet dumpling and leek mash; roasted globe artichoke and goats' cheese

risotto; and lemon posset with winter berries and shortbread biscuit. Choose the cheeseboard for the chance to taste local specialities such as mature and oak-smoked Wensleydale, and Shepherd Purse cheeses – Mrs Bell's Blue, Yorkshire Ryedale and Monk's Folly. The wine list is also excellent with well-written tasting notes. From April to September the local outdoor game of quoits can be played. The bedrooms have fabulous views overlooking the Stang and Arkengarthdale and are finished to a high standard with exposed beams, cast iron bed frames and warm colours.

Open all day all wk 11am-mdnt Closed 25 Dec **Food** Lunch Mon-Fri 12-2.30, Sat-Sun 12-6 Dinner all wk 6-9

Restaurant menu available all wk (evening) ⊕ FREE HOUSE ◖ Black Sheep Best Bitter, Black Sheep Golden Sheep, Black Sheep Riggwelter, Rudgate Jorvik Blonde, Theakston ♉ Symonds. ♟ 12 **Facilities** Non-diners area ☙ (Bar Garden) ♟ Children's menu Children's portions Play area Garden ☶ Parking WiFi ▭ (notice required) **Rooms** 19

APPLETREEWICK
Map 19 SE06

The Craven Arms

tel: 01756 720270 **BD23 6DA**
email: info@craven-cruckbarn.co.uk
dir: *2m E of Burnsall off B6160. 5m N of Bolton Abbey*

Interesting blackboard menus

Originally part of a farm, this 16th-century Dales pub has spectacular views of the Wharfedale and Simon's Seat. The building retains its original beams, flagstone floors, gas lighting and magnificent fireplace; the village stocks are still outside. Traditional real ales are served and there's a beer festival every October. The blackboard menu changes daily and offers plenty of choice. A heather-thatched cruck barn to the rear provides additional dining space and a function room for events, wedding receptions and concerts.

Open all day all wk **Food** Lunch Mon-Sat 12-9, Sun 12-8.30 Dinner Mon-Sat 12-9, Sun 12-8.30 ⊕ FREE HOUSE ◾ Dark Horse Craven Bitter & Hetton Pale Ale, Saltaire Raspberry Blonde, Moorhouse's Blond Witch & Black Witch Ö Aspall Harry Sparrow, Westons Old Rosie. **Facilities** Non-diners area ❖ (Bar Garden) ◗◗ Children's menu Children's portions Play area Garden ⋒ Beer festival Parking WiFi

ARKENGARTHDALE
Map 18 NY90

Charles Bathurst Inn ★★★★ INN ⊛ PICK OF THE PUBS

See Pick of the Pubs on page 553

ASKRIGG
Map 18 SD99

The King's Arms

tel: 01969 650113 **Main St DL8 3HQ**
email: info@kingsarmsaskrigg.co.uk
dir: *From A1 exit at Scotch Corner onto A6108, through Richmond, right onto B6270 to Leyburn. Follow Askrigg signs to Main St*

Stone-built Wensleydale inn on the Herriot Trail

This elegant, 18th-century coaching inn was used as the fictional Drover's Arms, vet James Herriot's favourite watering hole in the BBC drama *All Creatures Great and Small*. Owned by North Yorkshire hotelier Charles Cody, the inn has a big inglenook fireplace in the oak-panelled bar, where photographs show cast members relaxing between takes. The food, written up daily on an impressive mirror behind the bar, is based on top quality produce, such as game from the surrounding moors, and fish fresh from Hartlepool. Look also for loin of local lamb; pan-fried salmon; and wild mushroom risotto.

Open all day all wk **Food** Lunch all wk 12-2.30 Dinner Mon-Sat 5.30-9, Sun 5.30-8 ⊕ FREE HOUSE ◾ Black Sheep, Theakston, Yorkshire Dales Ö Thatchers Gold. ♚ 13 **Facilities** Non-diners area ❖ (Bar Outside area) ◗◗ Children's menu Children's portions Outside area WiFi ▄▄ (notice required)

Follow us on twitter
@TheAA_Lifestyle

AYSGARTH
Map 19 SE08

The George & Dragon Inn
PICK OF THE PUBS

tel: 01969 663358 **DL8 3AD**
email: info@georgeanddragonaysgarth.co.uk
dir: *On A684 midway between Leyburn & Hawes. Pub in village centre*

Perfect location for exploring Wensleydale

The George & Dragon Inn is a 17th-century Grade II listed building in a superb location in the Yorkshire Dales National Park, near the beautiful Aysgarth Falls. The area is perfect for walking, touring and visiting the many attractions, including Forbidden Corner, the Wensleydale Railway, and the cheese factory. The owners are proud to continue a centuries-long tradition of Yorkshire hospitality at the inn, with customers keeping cosy in winter by the fireside, and in summer enjoying their drinks and meals out on the furnished flower-filled patio. Well-kept real ales are served, and the inn has a great reputation for its traditional food, including steak pie and fish and chips. In the early evening a fixed-price menu meets the needs of ravenous walkers, while broader à la carte choices come into force after 7pm. Dishes could be home-made chicken liver pâté with apple chutney; Wensleydale pork sausages and mash; or braised pork belly, mash, choucroute and cider reduction.

Open all day all wk 12-close Closed Jan **Food** Lunch all wk 12-2 Dinner all wk 6-8.30, May-Sep 5.30-8.30 ⊕ FREE HOUSE ◾ Black Sheep Best Bitter, Theakston Best Bitter, Yorkshire Dales, Guest ales Ö Thatchers Gold. ♚ 16 **Facilities** Non-diners area ❖ (Bar Garden) ◗◗ Garden ⋒ Parking ▄▄

BEDALE
Map 19 SE28

The Castle Arms Inn

tel: 01677 470270 **Meadow Ln, Snape DL8 2TB**
email: castlearmsinn@gmail.com
dir: *From A1 (M) at Leeming Bar take A684 to Bedale. At x-rds in town centre take B6268 to Masham. Approx 2m, turn left to Thorp Perrow Arboretum. In 0.5m left for Snape*

Great base for walking or cycling

In the sleepy village of Snape, this family-run 18th-century pub is a good starting point for walking and cycling, and visiting local stately homes, castles and film locations. The homely interior has exposed beams, flagstoned floors and real fires in the bar, which is home to real ales from the Marston's Brewery. A meal in the restaurant selected from the ever-changing menu might feature a pub classic or something more cosmopolitan from the Italian chef. Afterwards, there is a range of home-made desserts and liqueur coffees to tempt you.

Open 12-3 5.30-12 (Sun 12-6) Closed Mon **Food** Lunch Mon-Sat 12-3, Sun 12-4 Dinner Mon-Sat 6-9 ⊕ MARSTON'S ◾ Pedigree New World, Ringwood Best, Brakspear Oxford Gold. **Facilities** Non-diners area ❖ (Bar Garden) ◗◗ Children's menu Children's portions Garden ⋒ Parking WiFi ▄▄ (notice required)

BOROUGHBRIDGE
Map 19 SE36

The Black Bull Inn
PICK OF THE PUBS

See Pick of the Pubs on opposite page

Crown Inn Roecliffe ★★★★ RR ⊛⊛ PICK OF THE PUBS

See Pick of the Pubs on page 556

PICK OF THE PUBS

The Black Bull Inn

BOROUGHBRIDGE   Map 19 SE36

tel: 01423 322413
6 St James Square YO51 9AR
web: www.blackbullboroughbridge.co.uk
dir: *A1(M) junct 48, B6265 E for 1m*

Traditional inn offering true Yorkshire hospitality

Using a false name, highwayman Dick Turpin stayed at this ancient inn which stands in a quiet corner of the market square and was one of the main stopping points for travellers on the long road between London and the North. Today you have to turn off the A1(M), but it's well worth it to discover an inn built in 1258 that retains its ancient beams, low ceilings and roaring open fires, not to mention one that also gives houseroom to the supposed ghosts of a monk, a blacksmith, a cavalier and a small boy. Tony Burgess is the landlord and the man responsible for high standards that exclude anything electronic which makes a noise, so settle back and enjoy a pint of Timothy Taylor Boltmaker, a guest ale from the Rudgate's brewery or a glass of wine from the list that shows all the signs of careful compilation. The hot and cold sandwich selection in the bar is wide (Cajun chicken; smoked frankfurter; and roast pork and apple being just three), while in the dining room expect a good choice of traditional pub food on menus such as home-made mince and onion pie; tenderloin of pork, new potatoes, seasonal vegetables with pink peppercorn and cream sauce; battered king prawns with sweet chilli dip; pork sausages, creamy mash and onion gravy; and gammon steak, fried egg, chips and salad. Frequently changing blackboard specials widen the choice to include halibut steak with smoked salmon and fresh prawns in white wine sauce; and wild button mushroom ragout with fresh salad. Possible followers are apple pie and custard, or chocolate fudge cake.

Open all day all wk 11-11 (Fri-Sat 11am-mdnt Sun 12-11) **Food** Lunch all wk 12-2 Dinner all wk 6-9 Restaurant menu available all wk ⊕ FREE HOUSE ◀ John Smith's, Timothy Taylor Boltmaker, Cottage, Rudgate Guest ale. ☙ 11 **Facilities** Non-diners area ☙ (Bar Restaurant) ♦ Children's menu Children's portions Parking WiFi ⛲

PICK OF THE PUBS

Crown Inn Roecliffe ★★★★★ RR ✿✿

BOROUGHBRIDGE   Map 19 SE36

tel: 01423 322300 **Roecliffe YO51 9LY**
email: info@crowninnroecliffe.co.uk
web: www.crowninnroecliffe.co.uk
dir: *A1(M) junct 48, follow
Boroughbridge signs. At rdbt to
Roecliffe*

Wonderful village just off the A1

Beside Roecliffe's neatly trimmed green, this handsome 16th-century former coaching inn has been put well and truly on the map by owners Karl and Amanda. The couple have worked wonders on the striking green-painted pub, which has been lovingly restored, with stone-flagged floors, oak beams and crackling log fires featuring prominently in the civilised bar and dining rooms. Children and dogs are welcome, and food and drink can be served in the garden during the summer months. The bar's beer handles tempt with some top Yorkshire brewers (Timothy Taylor, Theakston, Ilkley), but it's the wine list which may catch the eye – 20 pages long with a comprehensive choice of 30 wines sold by the glass. The two AA Rosettes are well deserved for the pub's enthusiastic use of fresh and local produce, from salad and vegetables to farm meats and game – all put to fine use on a clearly focused modern British menu. The bar lunch choice is a strong indicator of the pub's commitment to provenance and seasonality: sandwiches made with Boroughbridge seven seed granary cob are served with a little bowl of soup; fillings include roast pork, stuffing, crisp crackling and apple sauce. An extensive list of local suppliers appears at the top of the menu, which might start with home-made oxtail tortellini or fresh Whitby crab soup and follow on with steak and Timothy Taylor pie; rack of roasted Yorkshire Dales spring lamb; or fresh hake steamed with king prawns over a stock of tomato, chorizo and Shetland mussels. Delicious puddings may include a tangy lemon and lime tart; or chocolate and Grand Marnier 'Jaffa' cake. Alternatively, finish with a plate of excellent Yorkshire Dales cheeses.

Open all wk 12-3.30 5-12 (Sun 12-7)
Food Lunch Mon-Sat 12-2.30, Sun 12-7
Dinner Mon-Sat 6-9.30, Sun 12-7 Av
main course £14.95 Set menu available
⊕ FREE HOUSE ◀ Timothy Taylor
Landlord, Ilkley Gold & Mary Jane,
Theakston, Black Sheep. ♟ 30
Facilities Non-diners area ❀ (Bar
Garden) ♦ Children's menu Children's
portions Garden ⌁ Parking WiFi
🚍 (notice required) **Rooms** 4

BROUGHTON
Map 18 SD95

The Bull
PICK OF THE PUBS

tel: 01756 792065 **BD23 3AE**
email: enquiries@thebullatbroughton.com
dir: *3m from Skipton on A59, on right*

Destination dining and free house in an estate setting

The Bull is part of the historic Broughton Estate, 3,000 acres of prime Yorkshire parkland and countryside, owned by the Tempests for nine centuries. Their family seat, Broughton Hall, is close by. While essentially a dining pub, The Bull still loves to see beer drinkers, as its good selection of real ales proves – Dark Horse Hetton Pale Ale and Thwaites Original – and a real cider Westons Stowford Press. The chefs rely on carefully chosen local producers for modern English dishes such as seafood, game or ham sharing platters; Lancashire hotpot; Herdwick mutton with black pea suet pudding and bubble-and-squeak; North Sea fish pie; a range of chargrills; and Wensleydale cheese and onion pie. A comprehensive gluten-free menu includes battered line-caught haddock with marrowfat peas and dripping-fried chips.

Open all day all wk 12-11 (Sun 12-10) **Food** Lunch Mon-Fri 12-2, Sat-Sun & BHs 12-9 (afternoon bites Mon-Fri 2-5.30) Dinner Mon-Fri 5.30-9, Sat-Sun & BHs 12-9 Set menu available ⊕ FREE HOUSE ◀ Dark Horse Hetton Pale Ale, Thwaites Original, Copper Dragon Golden Pippin ♂ Westons Stowford Press. ⬤ 11 **Facilities** Non-diners area ❤ (Bar Outside area) ⬤ Children's menu Outside area ⌂ Parking

CALDWELL
Map 19 NZ11

Brownlow Arms

tel: 01325 718471 **DL11 7QH**
email: bookings@brownlowarms.co.uk
dir: *From A1 at Scotch Corner take A66 towards Bowes. Right onto B6274 to Caldwell. Or from A1 junct 56 take B6275 N. 1st left through Mesonby to junct with B6274. Right to Caldwell*

Family-friendly country inn

In the tiny village of Caldwell amidst the delightful rolling countryside between Barnard Castle and Darlington, this lovely stone inn is a great place to seek out. With 10 wines by the glass, plenty more bins and reliable Yorkshire real ales, time passes easily here. A blend of traditional and modern rooms is the setting for unpicking a phenomenally comprehensive, globally inspired menu. Start perhaps with avocado and chilli tiger prawns; then follow with home-made suet steak and kidney pudding; or smoked haddock and spinach cheese melt with roast tomatoes.

Open all wk 5.30-11 (Sat-Sun 12-11) **Food** Lunch Sat 12-11, Sun 12-8 Dinner Mon-Fri 5.30-9, Sat 12-11, Sun 12-8 Restaurant menu available all wk ⊕ FREE HOUSE ◀ Timothy Taylor Landlord, Black Sheep, Caffrey's Irish Ale, Sharp's Doom Bar, Guinness. ⬤ 10 **Facilities** Non-diners area ⬤ Children's menu Children's portions Garden Parking WiFi

CARTHORPE
Map 19 SE38

The Fox & Hounds
PICK OF THE PUBS

tel: 01845 567433 **DL8 2LG**
dir: *Off A1, signed on both N'bound & S'bound carriageways*

Vegetarians have their own extensive menu

In the sleepy village of Carthorpe, the cosy Fox & Hounds has been a country inn for over 200 years, and the old anvil and other tools from its time as a smithy are still evident. Landlady Helen Taylor's parents bought the pub over 30 years ago, and in her hands and that of her husband Vincent's, they have established an excellent reputation for their food which comes from named suppliers and the daily delivery of fresh fish. A typical dinner could begin with grilled black pudding with roasted apple, followed by half a roasted Gressingham duckling with orange sauce, and ending with bramble and almond tart. There is a separate vegetarian menu of dishes that can be chosen as a starter or a main, such as caramelised onion and goats' cheese tart. Beers include local Black Sheep, while the wine choice is global in scope. Home-made produce such as jams and chutneys are available to buy.

Open Tue-Sun 12-3 7-11 Closed 25 Dec & 1st 2wks Jan, Mon **Food** Lunch Tue-Sun 12-2 Dinner Tue-Sun 7-9.30 ⊕ FREE HOUSE ◀ Black Sheep Best Bitter, Worthington's, Guest ale ♂ Thatchers Gold. **Facilities** ⬤ Children's portions Parking

CHAPEL LE DALE
Map 18 SD77

The Old Hill Inn

tel: 015242 41256 **LA6 3AR**
email: sabena.martin@btopenworld.com
dir: *From Ingleton take B6255, 4m, pub on right*

An ancient Dales inn of great character

Beautiful views of the Dales await visitors to this former farmhouse, later a drovers' inn, parts dating from 1615, the rest from 1835. When Winston Churchill stayed here on huntin', shootin', fishin' holidays, he no doubt enjoyed the bar, which these days serves eminent Yorkshire real ales like Black Sheep and Dent Aviator. A family of three chefs run the inn (one of whom makes sculptures from sugar) producing lunchtime snacks of sandwiches and home-made sausages, and typical main dishes of beef and ale casserole; smoked haddock fishcakes; and specials of home-reared pork dishes and fish specials according to the daily catch.

Open Tue-Sun Closed 24-25 Dec, Mon (ex BHs) **Food** Lunch Tue-Sat 12-2.30, Sun 12-3 Dinner Tue-Fri & Sun 6.30-8.45, Sat 6-8.45 ⊕ FREE HOUSE ◀ Black Sheep Best Bitter, Dent Aviator & Golden Fleece, Guest beer ♂ Thatchers Gold, Aspall. **Facilities** Non-diners area ❤ (Bar Garden) ⬤ Children's menu Children's portions Garden Parking WiFi

COLTON
Map 16 SE54

Ye Old Sun Inn
PICK OF THE PUBS

See Pick of the Pubs on page 558

CRAYKE
Map 19 SE57

The Durham Ox
PICK OF THE PUBS

See Pick of the Pubs on page 559

CROPTON
Map 19 SE78

The New Inn

tel: 01751 417330 **YO18 8HH**
email: phil@thegreatyorkshirebrewery.co.uk
dir: *Phone for detailed directions*

Own brewery on site draws many real ale enthusiasts

On the edge of the North York Moors National Park, this family-run free house is fortunate to have the acclaimed The Great Yorkshire Brewery at the bottom of the garden. Popular with locals and visitors alike, the pub is a draw to ale lovers and there are beer festivals in May and November. Meals are served in the restored village bar and in the elegant Victorian restaurant: choices could include Yorkshire coast fishcakes or crisp belly pork with dauphinoise potatoes; an extensive range from the grill; plus lunchtime sandwiches and ciabatta rolls.

Open all day all wk 11-11 (Sun 11-10.30) **Food** Lunch Mon-Fri 12-2, Sat-Sun 12-3 Dinner Sun-Thu 5.30-8.30, Fri-Sat 5.30-9 ⊕ FREE HOUSE ◀ Cropton Yorkshire Classic, Yorkshire Golden, Yorkshire Pale, Yorkshire Warrior, Blackout & Monkmans Slaughter ♂ Yorkshire cider. **Facilities** Non-diners area ❤ (Bar Garden) ⬤ Children's menu Children's portions Play area Family room Garden ⌂ Beer festival Parking WiFi ▭ (notice required)

PICK OF THE PUBS

Ye Old Sun Inn

COLTON   Map 16 SE54

tel: 01904 744261 **Main St LS24 8EP**
email: yeoldsuninn@hotmail.co.uk
web: www.yeoldsuninn.co.uk
dir: *Approx 3.5m from York, off A64*

Country pub that goes from strength to strength

Ashley and Kelly McCarthy took over this 17th-century country pub around 10 years ago and have worked hard to transform it into a thriving inn. They added a bar area and extended the dining area, allowing them more space to increase the excellent themed events, cookery demonstrations and classes that have proved so popular. In the dining room they have a deli where freshly baked bread, home-made jams and chutneys, fresh fish and daily essentials can be bought. A marquee in the garden overlooks rolling countryside and is used for large functions, which includes a summer beer festival and regular farmers' markets. Ashley takes pride in sourcing food and ale from small local producers and suppliers, including salads from his own polytunnel, and his menus are innovative and exciting. Lunches include light bites such as sandwiches, salads and wraps, plus there's an excellent Sunday lunch menu featuring locally sourced roasted meats, chef's

specials and a dinner menu. Expect Yorkshire-style main courses such as braised beef cheeks with horseradish mash and casseroled vegetables; steak and Black Sheep Bitter pie with shortcrust pastry; or rack of Yorkshire lamb with bubble-and-squeak and red wine jus. Precede with roasted tomato and pesto soup and finish with upside-down plum sponge with home-made plum sorbet, or tuck into Ashley's tasting platter of desserts. All dishes come with a wine recommendation, or look to the handpumps – Rudgate Battle Axe and Timothy Taylor Landlord are among the choice of seven real ales.

Open all wk 12-2.30 6-11 (Sun 12-10.30) **Food** Lunch Mon-Sat 12-2, Sun 12-7 Dinner Mon-Sat 6-9.30 ⊕ FREE HOUSE ◧ Timothy Taylor Landlord & Golden Best, Rudgate Battle Axe, Black Sheep, Ossett, Moorhouse's, Guest ale Ŏ Aspall. ♟ 18
Facilities Non-diners area ♣ Children's menu Children's portions Garden ⋒ Beer festival Parking WiFi ▭

PICK OF THE PUBS

The Durham Ox

CRAYKE Map 19 SE57

tel: 01347 821506 **Westway YO61 4TE**
email: enquiries@thedurhamox.com
web: www.thedurhamox.com
dir: *From A19 through Easingwold to
Crayke. From market place left up hill,
pub on right*

Free house in the beautiful Howardian Hills

They don't do things by halves here. Not only is this 300-year-old, hilltop pub-restaurant named after a 189-stone ox that was exhibited all over the country, but it also features a steel and cast-iron, charcoal-fired oven nicknamed Big Bertha, weighing in at over a ton. The ox was born in 1796 and, as the pub sign shows, he was a hefty beast; his first owner was the Rt Hon Lord Somerville, a print of whom hangs in the bottom bar. Before entering the pub you somehow just know that inside you'll find flagstone floors, exposed beams, oak panelling and winter fires – and indeed you do. Also, this being Yorkshire, that the real ales will come from nowhere else, thus Timothy Taylor Boltmaker from Keighley, and Treboom from York. Sandwiches and pub classics like North Sea fish pie, and 'Ox' burger meet the need for something quick and easy, or if time is less of an issue you might want to work through the menu. Cured beef fillet carpaccio and celeriac remoulade is one starter option; another is home-

cured salmon, capers and horseradish cream. For a main course, there might be venison haunch steak, fondant potato, creamy Savoy cabbage and bitter chocolate sauce; pan-fried sea bass fillet, butter beans, chorizo and basil oil; or steak and ale suet pudding, hand-cut chips and garden peas. Desserts are no less appealing, typically plum and almond tart, mascarpone and Chantilly cream; and hot cherries, cherry ice cream, cherry mousse and a chocolate flake. There are noteworthy Yorkshire cheeses on the cheeseboard. Children have their own choices and there's a Magnificent Seven menu – '7 dishes, 7 pounds each, before 7pm'

Open all day all wk 12-11.30 (Sun 12-10.30) **Food** Lunch Mon-Sat

12-2.30, Sun 12-3 Dinner Mon-Sat 5.30-9.30, Sun 5.30-8.30 Av main course £13.95 Set menu available ⊕ FREE HOUSE ◀ Timothy Taylor Boltmaker, Black Sheep Best Bitter, Treboom Yorkshire Sparkle, York Guzzler ⚲ Symonds. ☙ 10 **Facilities** Non-diners area ❦ (Bar Garden) ♦ Children's menu Children's portions Garden ⚲ Parking WiFi ⚌ (notice required)

EASINGWOLD
Map 19 SE56

NEW The New Inn

tel: 01347 824007 **62-66 Long St YO61 3HT**
email: info@thenewinnateasingwold.co.uk
dir: *In town centre*

Taste of Yorkshire in small market town

New it isn't, of course, having been a coaching stop in the 19th century. On aptly named Long Street, it's owned by Yorkshire pub group, West Park Inns. The restaurant makes much of the fish and seafood available from the nearby coast, so home in on the day's catch, or the lightly battered haddock, triple-cooked chips and mushy peas. Also listed might be chicken, Yorkshire ham and leek pie, herb mash and seasonal vegetables; marinated duck breast, potato fondant, honey-roasted vegetables, curly kale and star anise jus; and beef tomatoes stuffed with winter root vegetables, chickpeas and herb couscous.

Open all day Closed Mon-Tue **Food** Lunch Wed-Sat 12-2.30, Sun 12-7 Dinner Wed-Sat 5-9, Sun 12-7 ⊕ FREE HOUSE ◄ Theakston Best Bitter, St Austell Tribute, Timothy Taylor Landlord. ♀ 13 **Facilities** Non-diners area ❤ (Bar) ♦♦ Children's menu Children's portions Outside area ♫ Parking WiFi ▄ (notice required)

EAST WITTON
Map 19 SE18

The Blue Lion
PICK OF THE PUBS

tel: 01969 624273 **DL8 4SN**
email: enquiries@thebluelion.co.uk
dir: *From Ripon take A6108 towards Leyburn*

Smart 18th-century hostelry with imaginative food

This well-maintained 18th-century coaching inn, tucked away in an unspoilt estate village close to Jervaulx Abbey, once catered to drovers and travellers journeying through Wensleydale. Ably run today by Paul and Helen Klein, it has built a reputation as one of North Yorkshire's finest inns. The interior is best described as rural chic, oozing stacks of atmosphere and charm. The classic bar with its open fire and flagstone floor is a beer drinker's haven, where the best of the county's breweries present a pleasant dilemma for the ale lover. A blackboard displays imaginative but unpretentious bar meals, while diners in the candlelit restaurant can expect culinary treats incorporating a variety of Yorkshire ingredients, notably seasonal game. A memorable meal may comprise Whitby crab and spinach raviolone with a shellfish bisque; whole roasted local partridge with sarladaise potatoes, bread sauce and game chips; and dark chocolate torte with passionfruit and coconut.

Open all day all wk 11-11 **Food** Lunch Mon-Sat 12-2.15, Sun all day Dinner Mon-Sat 7-9.30, Sun all day Set menu available ⊕ FREE HOUSE ◄ Black Sheep Best Bitter & Golden Sheep, Theakston Best Bitter ♂ Thatchers Gold. ♀ 12
Facilities Non-diners area ❤ (Bar Garden) ♦♦ Children's portions Garden ♫ Parking WiFi

The Cover Bridge Inn

tel: 01969 623250 **DL8 4SQ**
email: enquiries@thecoverbridgeinn.co.uk
dir: *On A6108 between Middleham & East Witton*

Welcoming Wensleydale pub with well-kept draught ales

The Harringtons have now owned this magnificent little pub at one end of a venerable arched bridge on the River Cover for nearly 20 years. The pub's oldest part was probably built around 1670, to cater for the increasing trade on the drovers' route from Coverdale. Watch out for the cunning door-latch, which befuddles many a first-time visitor. The ancient interior rewards with wrinkled

beams, a vast hearth and open log fires, settles and wholesome fodder, including home-made pies, daily specials, and their famous ham and eggs. Relax in the riverside garden with your choice from eight ales on tap, three of which are rotating guests.

Open all day all wk **Food** Lunch all wk 12-2 Dinner all wk 6-9 ⊕ FREE HOUSE ◄ Guest ales ♂ Westons Old Rosie, Gwynt y Ddraig Happy Daze & Two Trees Perry. **Facilities** Non-diners area ❤ (Bar Garden) ♦♦ Children's menu Children's portions Play area Garden ♫ Parking WiFi ▄ (notice required)

EGTON
Map 19 NZ80

The Wheatsheaf Inn
PICK OF THE PUBS

tel: 01947 895271 **YO21 1TZ**
email: info@wheatsheafegton.com
dir: *Off A169, NW of Grosmont*

Handsome pub at the centre of the community

This modest old pub is very popular with fishermen, as the River Esk runs along at the foot of the hill, and is a big draw for fly-fishers in particular. The pub sits back from the wide main road and it would be easy to drive past it, but that would be a mistake as the welcoming main bar is cosy and traditional, with low beams, dark green walls and comfy settles. The menu offers sandwiches, soup and hot focaccia rolls at lunchtime, as well as a range of light lunches, including wholetail Whitby scampi. In the evening, the supper menu might include a starter of lamb's kidneys with bacon, Madeira and redcurrant gravy and main courses such as chicken and smoked bacon puff pastry pie. There's a locals' bar too, but it only holds about a dozen people, so get there early.

Open 11.30-3 5.30-11.30 (Sat 11.30-11.30 Sun 11.30-11) Closed Mon **Food** Lunch Tue-Sun 12-2 Dinner Tue-Sat 6-8.30 ⊕ FREE HOUSE ◄ Black Sheep Best Bitter & Golden Sheep, John Smith's, Timothy Taylor Landlord, Guest ales ♂ Thatchers Gold. **Facilities** Non-diners area ♦♦ Garden ♫ Parking WiFi

EGTON BRIDGE
Map 19 NZ80

Horseshoe Hotel

tel: 01947 895245 **YO21 1XE**
email: horseshoehotel@yahoo.co.uk
dir: *From Whitby take A171 towards Middlesborough. Village signed in 5m*

Riverside hotel champions local ingredients and ales

The Horseshoe is an 18th-century country house set in beautiful grounds by the River Esk, handy for visiting Whitby, Robin Hood's Bay, the North Yorkshire Moors Railway and TV's *Heartbeat* country. Inside the welcoming bar are oak settles and tables, local artists' paintings, and plates around the picture rails. Along with some great beers, such as Durham Brewery ale, local ingredients are used to create the varied menu, try wholetail scampi and chips or medallion of pork fillet with woodchopper sauce.

Open all wk 11.30-3 6.30-11 (Sat 11.30-11 Sun 12-10.30) **Food** Lunch all wk 12-2 Dinner all wk 6-9 ⊕ FREE HOUSE ◄ John Smith's Cask, Durham, Black Sheep, Theakston, Guest ales. **Facilities** Non-diners area ♦♦ Children's menu Children's portions Family room Garden ♫ Parking WiFi ▄ (notice required)

The Postgate

tel: 01947 895241 **YO21 1UX**
dir: *Phone for detailed directions*

Walkers, families and dogs are very welcome

Set in the Esk Valley within a stone's throw of the river, The Postgate is a typical North York Moors country inn; it played the part of the Black Dog in TV's *Heartbeat*.

Being on the coast-to-coast trail, and becoming known as a food destination, the pub is popular with walkers who chat amiably with locals in the bar over their pints of Black Sheep. The menu offers an array of locally sourced fresh fish and seafood from Whitby fish market, excellent local meats, and game in season.

Open all wk 12-3 6-12 **Food** Lunch all wk 12-2.30 Dinner all wk 6-9 ⊕ PUNCH TAVERNS ◀ Timothy Taylor Landlord, Black Sheep Bitter ♂ Thatchers. **Facilities** Non-diners area ♣ (Bar Garden) ♦ Children's menu Children's portions Garden ⊼ Parking WiFi ▭ (notice required)

ELSLACK
Map 18 SD94

NEW The Tempest Arms

tel: 01282 842450 **BD23 3AY**
email: info@tempestarms.co.uk
dir: A59 from Skipton towards Gisburn. At rdbt left onto A56. Pub on left

Hand-pulled Yorkshire ales and a varied menu

A local landmark, the Tempest dates to the coaching days of the 17th century. The Yorkshire Dales and surrounding countryside bring walkers and cyclists, who enjoy the pub's warm welcome and convivial atmosphere. Wood fires, comfy cushions, alcoves and dining spaces set the interior's comfortable mood, completed by an array of Yorkshire ales at the bar and a vast menu of pub food. A Tempest staple is the seafood pancake with creamy sauce, salad and chipped potatoes. But there's no better place for a starter of Yorkshire puddings and onion gravy, with Bolton Abbey lamb and vegetable hotpot to follow.

Open all day all wk **Food** Lunch 12-2.30 Dinner 6-9 Av main course £9.95-£15 ⊕ FREE HOUSE ◀ Dark Horse Hetton Pale Ale, Theakston, Thwaites Wainwright ♂ Kingstone Press. ℗ 16 **Facilities** Non-diners area ♣ (Bar Outside area) ♦ Children's menu Children's portions Outside area ⊼ Parking WiFi ▭ (notice required)

FELIXKIRK
Map 19 SE48

The Carpenters Arms

tel: 01845 537369 **YO7 2DP**
email: enquiries@thecarpentersarmsfelixkirk.com **web:** www.carpentersarmsfelixkirk.com
dir: From Thirsk take A170 towards Helmsley. Left signed Felixkirk, 2.25m to village

Unpretentious village pub with lovely views

Felixkirk, in the Vale of Mowbray, has no shops, making this Provenance Inns owned pub the village's only retail establishment. To the east are the Hambleton Hills and the North Yorks Moors National Park, while west are the Yorkshire Dales. Bare stonework, slate flooring and rich red walls characterise the interior, and there are open fires in the dining areas and the bar. The restaurant and tiered terrace offer the best views. Menu descriptions are simple: pan-seared salmon fillet; braised pork cheeks; gourmet burgers; steak ciabattas; herb crusted haddock; devilled chicken livers; and fish and chips. Check out the Before Seven menu — seven main courses, each £7.

Open all day all wk **Food** Lunch Mon-Sat 12-2.30, Sun 12-3 Dinner Mon-Sat 5.30-9.30, Sun 6-8.30 ⊕ PROVENANCE INNS ◀ Black Sheep Best Bitter, Timothy Taylor Boltmaker ♂ Symonds. **Facilities** Non-diners area ♣ (Bar Garden) ♦ Children's menu Children's portions Garden ⊼ Parking WiFi ▭ (notice required)

GIGGLESWICK
Map 18 SD86

Black Horse Hotel

tel: 01729 822506 **32 Church St BD24 0BE**
email: theblackhorse-giggle@tiscali.co.uk
dir: Phone for detailed directions

Village centre inn with pub favourites on the menu

Set next to the church and behind the market cross in the 17th-century main street, this traditional free house is as charming as Giggleswick itself. Down in the warm and friendly bar you'll find a range of hand-pulled ales, with a local guest beer sometimes available. The menu of freshly prepared pub favourites ranges from home-made pizzas to main course dishes like home-made steak and ale pie; haddock and chips; and horseshoe of gammon with either eggs, pineapple, or both.

Open 12-2.30 5.30-11 (Sat-Sun 12-11) Closed Mon **Food** Lunch Tue-Sun 12-2 Dinner Tue-Thu 6.30-9, Fri-Sun 6-9 ⊕ FREE HOUSE ◀ Timothy Taylor Landlord & Golden Best, John Smith's, Tetley's, Settle Signal Main Line. **Facilities** Non-diners area ♦ Children's menu Children's portions Garden ⊼ Parking WiFi

---

GOATHLAND
Map 19 NZ80

Birch Hall Inn

tel: 01947 896245 **Beck Hole YO22 5LE**
email: glenys@birchhallinn.fsnet.co.uk
dir: 9m from Whitby on A169

One of the smallest bars in the country

Beck Hole is a tiny hamlet of nine cottages and a pub hidden in the steep Murk Esk Valley close to the North Yorkshire Moors (steam) Railway. This delightful little free house has just two tiny rooms separated by a sweet shop; no more than 30 people plus two small dogs have ever fitted inside with the door closed! The main bar offers well-kept local ales to sup beside an open fire in winter, including the pub's house ale, Beckwatter. The pub has been under the same ownership for over 30 years and the simple menu features the local butcher's pies, old-fashioned flatcakes filled with ham, cheese, corned beef or farmhouse pâté, and home-made scones and buttered beer cake. In warm weather, food and drink can be enjoyed in the large garden, which has countryside views. The local quoits team play on the village green on summer evenings.

Open 11-3 7.30-11 (11-11 summer) Closed Mon eve & Tue in winter **Food** All hours when open ⊕ FREE HOUSE ◀ Birch Hall Inn Beckwatter, Black Sheep Best Bitter, York Guzzler. **Facilities** ♣ (Bar Garden) ♦ Family room Garden ⊼ **Notes** ⊛

GRASSINGTON
Map 19 SE06

Grassington House ★★★★★ RR ◉◉

tel: 01756 752406 **5 The Square BD23 5AQ**
email: bookings@grassingtonhousehotel.co.uk **web:** www.grassingtonhousehotel.co.uk
dir: *A59 into Grassington, in town square opposite post office*

A destination pub with top-notch accommodation

Whoever commissioned this private house in 1760 chose the site well, for this elegant Georgian pub and restaurant stands imposingly in Grassington's cobbled square. Fresh local produce underpins the award-winning menu offering starters of taster slates of tapas-style nibbles; whipped goats' cheese, textures of beetroot and Thai basil. Mains might be beef fillet mignon, rag pudding, carrot purée and red wine onion jus; beer-battered Northumberland haddock, minted peas and hand-cut chips; and roasted aubergine, marinated tomatoes and herb couscous. For lighter options there's an interesting range of open and closed sandwiches, perhaps prawn, chilli and coriander with Marie Rose sauce will appeal. Thwaites Original and Wainwright, and Dark Horse Hetton Pale Ale are bar staples.

Open all day all wk **Food** Lunch Mon-Fri 12-2.30, Sat 12-4, Sun 12-8 Dinner Mon-Sat 6-9.30, Sun 12-8 Set menu available ⊕ FREE HOUSE ◀ Dark Horse Hetton Pale Ale, Thwaites Original & Wainwright, Black Sheep. ♀ 14 **Facilities** Non-diners area ♦❙ Children's menu Children's portions Garden ⊼ Parking WiFi ▭ (notice required) **Rooms** 9

GREAT HABTON
Map 19 SE77

The Grapes Inn

tel: 01653 669166 **YO17 6TU**
email: info@thegrapes-inn.co.uk
dir: *From Malton take B1257 towards Helmsley. In Amotherby right into Amotherby Ln. After Newsham Bridge right into Habton Ln & follow pub signs. 0.75m to pub*

Enjoyable food in a busy community pub

A welcoming village pub between the Howardian Hills and the North Yorkshire Moors near the bustling market town of Malton. Enjoy a pint of Marston's EPA with the locals in the lively taproom, separated from the dining room – once the village post office – by a double-sided log-burner. Chef-proprietor Adam Myers has gained an enviable reputation in Ryedale for his chargrilled steaks, but other hearty options are roast loin of pork, Yorkshire pudding and red wine gravy; and chicken breast with butternut squash and smoked cheddar risotto. Desserts are no less tempting – chocolate and Bailey's mousse; and apple crumble and custard.

Open Tue-Fri 6pm-close (Sat 12-2 6-close Sun open all day) Closed from 2 Jan for 2wks, Mon **Food** Lunch Sat-Sun 12-2 Dinner Tue-Sat 6-8.30, Sun 6.30-8.30 ⊕ MARSTON'S ◀ EPA, Wychwood Hobgoblin Ö Thatchers Gold. **Facilities** Non-diners area ♦❙ Children's menu Children's portions Outside area ⊼ Parking

GREEN HAMMERTON
Map 19 SE45

The Bay Horse Inn

tel: 01423 330338 **York Rd YO26 8BN**
email: enquiry@bayhorsegreenhammerton.co.uk
dir: *A1 junct 47 follow signs for A59 towards York. After 3m, turn left into village, inn on right opposite post office*

Hearty food in the Vale of York

This traditional inn is part of the original settlement of Green Hammerton, positioned on the old Roman road from York to Aldborough. The pub has served travellers and villagers for over 200 years; many features from those days remain in the beamed, fire-warmed interior. Reliable Yorkshire cask beers accompany home-made meals strong on local produce; excellent matured steaks, gammon and chicken grilled to order are always available. Daily-changing dishes include haunch

of venison steak with blackberry port sauce; and pork fillet with cider and apple sauce. Outside is a garden and patio area.

Open all wk 11.30-2.30 5.30-12 (Sat 11.30am-mdnt Sun 11.30-8) **Food** Lunch Mon-Fri 12-2.30, Sat 12-9, Sun 12-7.30 Dinner Mon-Fri 6-9, Sat 12-9, Sun 12-7.30 ⊕ GREENE KING ◀ Timothy Taylor, Black Sheep, Guest ale. **Facilities** Non-diners area ✿ (Bar Garden) ♦❙ Children's menu Children's portions Garden ⊼ Parking WiFi ▭ (notice required)

GRINTON
Map 19 SE09

The Bridge Inn
PICK OF THE PUBS

See Pick of the Pubs on opposite page

HARDRAW
Map 18 SD89

The Green Dragon Inn

tel: 01969 667392 **DL8 3LZ**
email: info@greendragonhardraw.com
dir: *From Hawes take A684 towards Sedbergh. Right to Hardraw, approx 1.5m*

If you're in the area, it's worth a visit

Entering the Bar Parlour is like stepping into a Tudor film-set, although parts of the inn are much older – 13th century in fact. Gravestones, forming part of the floor, were washed away from the neighbouring churchyard during floods. In a wooded site behind is Hardraw Force, England's highest single-drop waterfall, which JMW Turner painted while staying here in 1816. The choice of real ales and ciders is good, and pub food includes home-made steak and kidney pie; lamb shank, mash and veg; and a seasonal dish of pheasant bourguignon with horseradish mash and creamed cabbage. Beer festivals in June and July, a third with cider in October, and regular live folk music are all big draws.

Open all day all wk **Food** Lunch all wk 11.30-3 Dinner all wk 6-10 Av main course £9.95 ⊕ FREE HOUSE ◀ Timothy Taylor Landlord, Theakston Best Bitter & Old Peculier, Wensleydale, Yorkshire Dales Ö Olivers, Gwatkins, Dunkertons, Ralph's, Westons Stowford Press. **Facilities** Non-diners area ✿ (Bar Garden) ♦❙ Children's menu Children's portions Family room Garden ⊼ Beer festival Cider festival Parking ▭ (notice required)

HAROME
Map 19 SE68

The Star Inn ◉◉
PICK OF THE PUBS

tel: 01439 770397 **YO62 5JE**
email: reservations@thestarinnatharome.co.uk
dir: *From Helmsley take A170 towards Kirkbymoorside 0.5m. Turn right for Harome*

Renowned gastro-pub in prime walking country

On the fringe of the North Yorkshire Moors National Park, this 14th-century thatched gem sits in an idyllic village surrounded by wonderful walks. Although renowned as a foodie destination, the genuinely pubby bar is worth seeking out. Here both locals and visitors relax with well-kept pints of Hambleton or Cropton whilst awaiting the call to dine. Chef/patron Andrew Pern changes his dishes frequently according to seasonal availability. Treat yourself to a fixed-price market menu of corned beef terrine with brown ale jelly, duck egg, salad cream and home-made pickles; North Sea fish 'pye' with English mustard cream and flat-leaf parsley mash; and gooseberry charlotte with elderflower Anglaise. Alternatively choose from the carte which glows with the quality of dishes such as baked 'humble pie' of Gary Verity's 1,000-foot Coverdale lamb with cutlet, peppered neep purée, charred leeks, Lowna Dairy goats' curd and Wass Wood sorrel.

Open all wk 11.30-3 6.30-11 (Mon 6.30-11 Sun 12-11) Closed Mon L **Food** Lunch Tue-Sat 11.30-2, Sun 12-6 Dinner Mon-Sat 6.30-9.30 Set menu available ⊕ FREE HOUSE ◀ Theakston Best Bitter, Black Sheep, Copper Dragon, Hambleton, Cropton Ö Westons Stowford Press, Ampleforth Abbey. ♀ 24 **Facilities** Non-diners area ♦❙ Children's menu Children's portions Garden ⊼ Parking ▭ (notice required)

PICK OF THE PUBS

The Bridge Inn

GRINTON　　　　　Map 19 SE09

tel: 01748 884224 **DL11 6HH**
email: atkinbridge@btinternet.com
web: www.bridgeinn-grinton.co.uk
dir: *Exit A1 at Scotch Corner onto
A6108, through Richmond. Left onto
B6270 towards Grinton & Reeth*

Former coaching inn popular with ramblers and discerning diners

Close to one of Yorkshire's finest old churches, known as the Cathedral of the Dales, this 13th-century riverside pub is located in Grinton, which has stood here for almost 1,000 years. Two of the Yorkshire Dales' wildest and prettiest dales meet in Grinton; Arkengarthdale and Swaledale collide in a symphony of fells, moors, waterfalls and cataracts. Lanes and tracks slope down from the heights, bringing ramblers and riders to appreciate the good range of northern beers that landlord Andrew Atkin matches with his fine foods; Jennings Brewery's Cocker Hoop being a case in point. Locals enjoy the bustling games room and beamed old bar serving baguettes and toasted ciabattas, while a more tranquil restaurant area caters for those after a more intimate meal experience. The kitchen here is inspired by carefully chosen seasonal local game, meats, fish and other produce, including herbs plucked from the garden. Expect traditional and familiar

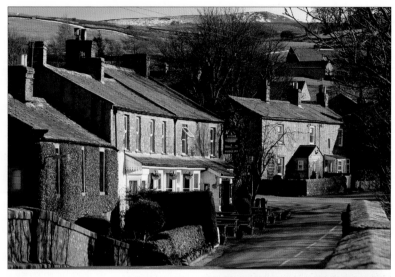

dishes with a modern twist, enhanced by daily-changing specials. Starters range from pork belly, chorizo, red onion and cinnamon marmalade with balsamic treacle, to a salad of cold-smoked salmon and crayfish with sun-blushed tomato and rocket. Mains reflect a similar scope, running from duck breast served with wholegrain mustard mash, spring greens and parsnip crisps, to pan-seared pork fillet medallions with bubble-and-squeak and black pudding. Finish with almond and apricot treacle tart; mascarpone and peppered strawberry mille feuille with coconut and ginger ice cream, or a selection of Swaledale cheeses with savoury biscuits and chutney.

Open all day all wk **Food** all wk 12-9 Av main course £12 Restaurant menu available all wk ⊕ JENNINGS ▐ Cumberland Ale & Cocker Hoop, Caledonian Deuchars IPA, York Yorkshire Terrier, Adnams.
Facilities Non-diners area ❖ (Bar Garden) ♦ Children's menu Children's portions Garden Beer festival Parking WiFi ▭

The Fat Badger

tel: 01823 505681 **The White Hart Hotel, Cold Bath Rd HG2 0NF**
email: dominicjackson@btconnect.com

Victorian-style grandeur in the heart of Harrogate

Just around the corner from Harrogate's Royal Pump Rooms in the heart of the spa town's Montpellier Quarter, The Fat Badger has the lofty ceilings and dark wood fixtures reminiscent of the grand gin palaces of more than a century ago. Animal-themed oil paintings, faux gas lamps and leather chesterfields give the place an elegant, clubby feel and makes for a relaxed setting to enjoy a pint of real ale or one of six world lagers. The food menu offers plenty of choice, with sharing dishes, pub classics, sandwiches and chef's specialities.

Open all day all wk **Food** Lunch all wk 12-9 Dinner all wk 12-9 Set menu available Restaurant menu available Mon-Sat ⊕ FREE HOUSE ◼ York Guzzler, Black Sheep, Timothy Taylor Landlord, Copper Dragon Golden Pippin. **Facilities** Non-diners area ◕◗ Children's menu Garden WiFi ⛟ (notice required)

The Moorcock Inn

tel: 01969 667488 **Garsdale Head LA10 5PU**
email: info@moorcockinn.com
dir: *On A684, 5m from Hawes, 10m from Sedbergh at junct with B6259 for Kirkby Stephen*

Old inn surrounded by open countryside

At the tip of Wensleydale, this 18th-century inn stands alone in open countryside, although it is only three-quarters of a mile from Garsdale Station. Inside is a traditional blend of original stonework, bright colours and comfortable sofas. Savour a glass of local real ale from the Tirril Brewery, draught lager or one of the 50 malt whiskies, and enjoy the spectacular views from the garden. Home-cooked lunches include jackets, sandwiches and pub classics. For dinner, start with giant Yorkshire pudding with onion gravy, then tuck into game and chestnut stew (a house speciality); or a vegetarian choice of cherry tomato, red onion and goats' cheese tart.

Open 12-12 Mar-Oct (Mon-Fri 12-3 6-12 Sat-Sun 12-12 Nov-Feb) Closed 25 Dec Mon & Wed in Nov & Jan **Food** Lunch all wk 12-3 Dinner all wk 6.30-8.30 Av main course £10 ⊕ FREE HOUSE ◼ Copper Dragon, Theakston, Tirril Ales, Nine Standards Brewery, Cumberland Corby Ale, Dent, Wensleydale, Guest ales ◔ Thatchers Gold. ♟ 12 **Facilities** Non-diners area ◕◗ (Bar Restaurant Garden) ◕◗ Children's menu Children's portions Family room Garden ⋈ Parking WiFi ⛟ (notice required)

The Inn at Hawnby ★★★★ INN ⊛   PICK OF THE PUBS

tel: 01439 798202 **YO62 5QS**
email: info@innathawnby.co.uk **web:** www.innathawnby.co.uk
dir: *From Helmsley take B1257 towards Stokesley. Follow Hawnby signs*

Stunning moor views and first-rate food

Perched on top of a hill and with panoramic country views of the North Yorkshire Moors, this charming 19th-century former drovers' inn is run by hands-on and welcoming proprietors Kathryn and David Young. The pub stocks some great Yorkshire-brewed ales, including Helmsley Howardian Gold and Timothy Taylor Landlord. In the kitchen local and seasonal produce steer the menu, with accomplished dishes served either in the Mexborough restaurant or in the cosy bar. Typical of dinner starters are ham hock terrine, pickled cauliflower, cider jelly and piccalilli dressing; or scrambled duck eggs on home-made brioche, Worcestershire cured ham and parmesan. These may be followed by roast rare breed pork chop,

potato and black pudding galette, buttered baby vegetables and cider sauce; or braised feather blade of beef bourguignon with horseradish mash, kale and kibbled onions. Finish with an old favourite like apple and blackberry crumble.

Open all wk 10-3 6-11 (Fri-Sun all day) Closed 25 Dec & Mon-Tue Feb-Mar **Food** Lunch all wk 12-2 Dinner all wk 7-9 Av main course £12.95 ⊕ FREE HOUSE ◼ Timothy Taylor Landlord, Black Sheep, Helmsley Howardian Gold ◔ Somersby Cider. ♟ 8 **Facilities** Non-diners area ◕◗ (Bar Garden) ◕◗ Children's menu Children's portions Garden ⋈ Parking WiFi ⛟ (notice required) **Rooms** 9

The Oak Tree Inn

tel: 01423 789189 **Raskelf Rd YO61 2PH**
email: enquiries@theoaktreehelperby.com **web:** www.theoaktreehelperby.com
dir: *A19 from York towards Thirsk. After Easingwold left signed Helperby.
Approx 5m to village*

No-nonsense pub food at the village inn

Depending on how you approach the village, the signs say either Helperby Brafferton or Brafferton Helperby, an apparent confusion which to locals probably makes perfect sense. At this village inn there is a spacious bar for informal dining, and a barn extension overlooking the rear courtyard for more formal meals. You'll find there's a similar menu to those at the sister Provenance Inns in Felixkirk and Marton, offering unfussy mains such as roasted chicken breast with artichoke and wild mushroom risotto; confit shoulder of lamb with braised red cabbage; butter roast Scottish salmon fillet; and a selection of pizzas.

Open all day all wk **Food** Lunch Mon-Sat 12-2.30, Sun 12-3 Dinner Mon-Sat 5.30-9.30, Sun 5.30-8.30 Set menu available ⊕ FREE HOUSE/PROVENANCE INNS ◼ Black Sheep Best Bitter, Timothy Taylor Landlord ◔ Symonds. ♟ **Facilities** Non-diners area ◕◗ (Bar Outside area) ◕◗ Children's menu Children's portions Outside area ⋈ Parking WiFi ⛟ (notice required)

The Malt Shovel

tel: 01653 628264 **Main St YO62 4LF**
email: info@themaltshovelhovingham.com
dir: *18m NE of York, 5m from Castle Howard*

Friendly roadside village pub

The stone-built 18th-century Malt Shovel offers a friendly atmosphere with well-kept ales and food prepared from quality local ingredients. There are two dining rooms where you can enjoy starters of whitebait with lime and chilli mayonnaise, chicken liver pâté with chutney, or black pudding and apple fritters, followed by swordfish with tomato and anchovy sauce, mustard chicken, or chickpea curry.

There is also a large beer garden at the rear of the pub where you can sit and enjoy a pint or two in lovely surroundings.

Open all wk winter 11.30-2 6-11 (summer 11.30-2.30 5.30-11) Sun all day **Food** Lunch Mon-Sat 11.30-2 (winter) 11.30-2.30 (summer), Sun 12-2.30 Dinner Mon-Sat 6-9 (winter) 5.30-9 (summer), Sun 5.30-7.45 Set menu available ⊕ PUNCH TAVERNS ◼ Copper Dragon Golden Pippin, Theakston Best Bitter, Black Sheep, Guest ale ♻ Thatchers. **Facilities** Non-diners area ♣ (Bar Restaurant Garden) ♦♦ Children's menu Children's portions Garden ♬ Parking WiFi ☞ (notice required)

The Worsley Arms Hotel — PICK OF THE PUBS

tel: 01653 628234 **Main St YO62 4LA**
email: enquiries@worsleyarms.co.uk
dir: On B1257 between Malton & Helmsley

Excellent base for exploring North Yorkshire

This village hotel and pub form part of the Worsley family's historic Hovingham Hall Estate, birthplace of the Duchess of Kent. Hambleton Stallion from nearby Thirsk, and Black Sheep from Masham are on tap in the Cricketers' Bar (the local team has played on the village green for over 150 years). You can eat here or in the restaurant; lunch and afternoon tea are also served in the large walled garden. Lunchtime choices could include a selection of sandwiches; while the à la carte lists estate venison with soy glazed beetroot and baby onion, honey parsnip purée and air-dried venison; halibut with potatoes, wild mushrooms and roast smoked salmon; and confit of braised lamb shank. The pub hosts regular wine evenings and a supper club.

Open all day all wk **Food** Lunch Mon-Sat 12-2, Sun 12-2.30 Dinner all wk 6.30-9 Av main course £14 ⊕ FREE HOUSE ◼ Hambleton Stallion, Black Sheep ♻ Ampleforth Abbey. ♀ 20 **Facilities** Non-diners area ♣ (Bar Garden) ♦♦ Children's portions Garden ♬ Parking WiFi ☞ (notice required)

◼ HUBBERHOLME — Map 18 SD97

The George Inn

tel: 01756 760223 **BD23 5JE**
email: visit@thegeorge-inn.co.uk
dir: From Skipton take B6265 to Threshfield. B6160 to Buckden. Follow signs for Hubberholme

Dales inn with bags of charm

Stunningly located beside the River Wharfe in the Yorkshire Dales National Park, this pub was built in the 1600s as a farmstead and still has flagstone floors, stone walls, mullioned windows and an open fire. To check if the bar is open, look for a lighted candle in the window. Beers are local, coming from the Black Sheep and Yorkshire Dales breweries. For lunch there's soup, sandwiches and baskets of chips; but the traditional choices for an evening meal are based on locally sourced produce; perhaps try an individual steak and kidney pie, and sticky toffee pudding and ice cream. Enjoy your drink on the terrace in the warmer summer months.

Open 12-3 6-10.30 (summer all day 12-11 check website) Closed last 3wks Jan, Tue **Food** Lunch Wed-Sun 12-2.30 Dinner Wed-Mon 6-8 ⊕ FREE HOUSE ◼ Black Sheep, Yorkshire Dales, Tetley's, Local guest ales ♻ Thatchers Gold. **Facilities** ♣ (Bar Outside area) ♦♦ Children's portions Outside area ♬ Parking

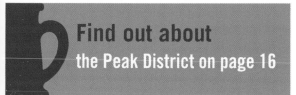

Find out about the Peak District on page 16

◼ KETTLEWELL — Map 18 SD97

NEW The Kings Head

tel: 01756 761600 **The Green BD23 5RD**
email: kingsheadkettlewell@outlook.com **web:** www.thekingsheadkettlewell.co.uk
dir: From A65 N of Skipton take B6265 signed Grassington. In Treshfield take B6160 to Kettlewell, right before river bridge. 1st left at maypole. Pub on left

Family-run pub in Wharfedale

The immense and venerable hearth and chimney breast are difficult to miss in the bar of this traditional family-run pub in the heart of the Yorkshire Dales; it's no wonder visitors and locals alike are drawn here to warm-up on cold wintery nights. Local beers include Dark Horse Hetton Pale Ale. Fresh, seasonal produce is used for dishes on the modern British menus. Seared breast of pigeon with black pudding, Scotch egg, celeriac and truffle, spinach and pancetta is an indicative starter. Follow with pork two ways with bubble-and-squeak croquette, apple and chorizo, and sherry sauce.

Open all day Closed 2wks beg Jan, 1wk end Nov, 25-26 Dec, Mon in winter **Food** Lunch 12-3 Dinner 5-9 Av main course £13 Set menu available ⊕ FREE HOUSE ◼ Dark Horse Hetton Pale Ale, Black Sheep, Tetley's ♻ Thatchers. ♀ 10 **Facilities** ♦♦ Children's menu Children's portions Outside area ♬ WiFi ☞ (notice required)

◼ KILBURN — Map 19 SE57

The Forresters Arms Inn

tel: 01347 868386 **The Square YO61 4AH**
email: admin@forrestersarms.com
dir: From Thirsk take A170, after 3m turn right signed Kilburn. At Kilburn Rd junct, turn right, inn on left in village square

Sturdy coaching inn with hearty food

Next door to the famous Robert Thompson craft carpentry workshop, The Forresters Arms has fine examples of his early work, with the distinctive trademark mouse evident in both bars. A sturdy stone-built former coaching inn still catering for travellers passing close by the famous White Horse of Kilburn on the North York Moors, it has log fires, cask ales and good food. Dishes include starters such as deep-fried brie with Kilburn chutney, and smoked chicken and roasted pepper salad; then mains like steak and ale pie, and game casserole with horseradish dumplings. There's also a specials board and a selection of lunchtime sandwiches and snacks.

Open all day all wk 9am-11pm **Food** Lunch Mon-Fri 12-3, off season 12-2.30, Sat-Sun all day Dinner all wk 6-9, off season 6-8 Av main course £10 ⊕ ENTERPRISE INNS ◼ John Smith's Cask, Wharfe Bank White Horse Blonde, Guest ales ♻ Addlestones, Westons Stowford Press. **Facilities** Non-diners area ♣ (Bar Outside area) ♦♦ Children's menu Children's portions Outside area ♬ Beer festival Parking WiFi ☞ (notice required)

KIRKBY FLEETHAM — Map 19 SE29

Black Horse Inn ★★★★★ INN ◉◉

tel: 01609 749010 **Lumley Ln DL7 0SH**
email: gm@blackhorsekirkbyfleetham.com **web:** www.blackhorsekirkbyfleetham.com
dir: *Signed from A1 between Catterick & Leeming Bar*

Charming and successful inn

Legend has it that Dick Turpin eloped with his lady from this village pub in the Swale Valley, just off the vast village green; the inn was named after the outlaw's steed in celebration. The pub garden adjoins fields, and the interior, including the seven character bedrooms, is appointed to create a pleasing mix of tradition and comfort. No surprise then that locals and visitors are encouraged to tarry a while, to sup a grand Yorkshire pint and enjoy accomplished food that covers all the bases. Look for signature starters such as chef's black pudding, crunchy hen's egg, with parsnip purée and caramelised apple, and main courses like braised Yorkshire pork belly, black pudding, grain mustard mash and cider jus, or a vegetarian choice of pea and mint risotto.

Open all day all wk **Food** Lunch Mon-Sat 12-2.30, Sun 12-7 Dinner Mon-Sat 5-9.30, Sun 12-7 Set menu available Restaurant menu available all wk ⊕ FREE HOUSE ◀ Black Sheep, Copper Dragon, Timothy Taylor Landlord. ⬥ 10 **Facilities** Non-diners area ❀ (Bar Garden) ◑ Children's menu Children's portions Garden ⋔ Parking WiFi ⛟ (notice required) **Rooms** 7

KIRKBYMOORSIDE — Map 19 SE68

George & Dragon Hotel — PICK OF THE PUBS

tel: 01751 433334 **17 Market Place YO62 6AA**
email: reception@georgeanddragon.net
dir: *Just off A170 between Scarborough & Thirsk. In town centre*

Charming, family-owned favourite

A whitewashed coaching inn that's welcoming and dog-friendly. Affectionately known as the G&D, it's full of charm – from the log fire in the bar, the collection of sporting paraphernalia, to the fountain in the sheltered courtyard – and there are five well-kept, hand-pulled real ales on offer, including an in-house brew. At lunchtime, enjoy a baguette or panini in the bar or, if you fancy contemporary decor and leather seats, Knight's Restaurant's short menu offers a haggis and Helmsley black pudding tower; a whole dressed crab; and confit of duck or slow-roasted belly pork. Home-made steak and Stilton pie, and Cajun chicken burgers are listed as pub classics. The traditional Sunday carvery is hugely popular.

Open all day all wk 10.30am-11pm **Food** Lunch all wk 12-2 Dinner all wk 6-9 Restaurant menu available all wk ⊕ FREE HOUSE ◀ Greene King Abbot Ale, Copper Dragon, Black Sheep, House Bitter, Guest ales. ⬥ 12 **Facilities** Non-diners area ❀ (Bar Garden) ◑ Children's menu Children's portions Garden ⋔ Parking WiFi ⛟

KIRKBY OVERBLOW — Map 19 SE34

NEW Shoulder of Mutton

tel: 01423 871205 **Main St HG3 1HD**
email: info@shoulderofmuttonharrogate.co.uk
web: www.shoulderofmuttonharrogate.co.uk
dir: *S from Harrogate on A61 towards Leeds, left for Kirkby Overblow*

Close to Harrogate, Harewood House and other attractions

For those who might be wondering, Overblow is a corruption of oreblow, a reference to the village's iron-smelting past. Built of local stone in the 1880s, this traditional country pub still offers open log fires and the attraction of an enclosed garden. Home-cooked, locally sourced food includes what the menu calls 'Shoulder of Mutton', but is in fact braised Masham lamb in mint and redcurrant gravy; grilled Wensleydale gammon and chips; chicken kohlpari biryani; and a generous selection of gluten-free dishes. On the specials board, look for pan-fried Nidderdale chicken fillet; and squid rings in spicy tomato sauce with tagliatelle.

Open 12-3 6-11 (Sun 12-10.30) Closed Mon **Food** Lunch Tue-Sat 12-2, Sun 12-7 Dinner Tue-Sat 6-9, Sun 12-7 Av main course £10.95 Set menu available Restaurant menu available Tue-Sun ⊕ PUNCH TAVERNS ◀ Black Sheep Best Bitter, Timothy Taylor Landlord ⓭ Thatchers Gold. ⬥ 12 **Facilities** Non-diners area ❀ (Bar Restaurant Garden) ◑ Children's menu Children's portions Garden ⋔ Parking WiFi

KNARESBOROUGH — Map 19 SE35

The General Tarleton Inn ★★★★★ RR ◉◉
PICK OF THE PUBS

See Pick of the Pubs on opposite page

PICK OF THE PUBS

The General Tarleton Inn ★★★★★ RR

KNARESBOROUGH   Map 19 SE35

tel: 01423 340284
Boroughbridge Rd, Ferrensby HG5 0PZ
email: gti@generaltarleton.co.uk
web: www.generaltarleton.co.uk
dir: *A1(M) junct 48 at Boroughbridge, take A6055 to Knaresborough. Inn 4m on right*

Local produce drives the award-winning menu here

Renamed in honour of General Banastre Tarleton who fought in the American War of Independence, this 18th-century coaching inn just north of Knaresborough is an ideal base for exploring the Yorkshire Dales. The renovated interior retains its old beams and original log fires, while the sofas encourage guests to settle down with a pint of Black Sheep Best Bitter and peruse the seasonal menus that have helped chef-proprietor John Topham and his team earn two AA Rosettes. Championing local produce, East Coast fish is delivered daily, local vegetables arrive the day they've been picked, and the game comes from nearby shoots when in season. The 'Food with Yorkshire Roots' menu is available in the Bar Brasserie, fine-dining restaurant, and terrace garden and courtyard. Typical starters include twice-baked Wendsleydale cheese soufflé; pork cheek with crispy ham hock, swede and mustard compôte; or roast pigeon breast, bourdin noir, girolles, cucumber and redcurrant jelly. These might precede mains of slow-braised beef cheek, creamed potatoes, textures of onion, vegetable crisps and port jus; pan-seared wild sea bass, truffle gnocchi, marinated artichoke and Jerusalem artichoke crisps; beetroot ravioli, rainbow chard, goats' cheese and beetroot crisps; or Norfolk quail — breast wrapped in ham and legs slow braised — with rösti potato, celeriac and game jus. Leave a space for mascarpone pannacotta, blackberry and apple sponge, compressed apple, apple sorbet and honeycomb; or dark chocolate fondant, cherry purée and cherry sorbet. Accompanying wines can be selected from a list of 150, with 11 served by the glass.

Open all wk 12-3 5.30-11
Food Lunch all wk 12-2 Dinner Mon-Sat 6-9.15, Sun 6-8.30 Av main course £18.50 Set menu available ⊕ FREE HOUSE ◖ Black Sheep Best Bitter, Timothy Taylor Landlord. ♟ 11
Facilities Non-diners area ♦ Children's menu Children's portions Garden ⊼ Parking WiFi **Rooms** 13

LANGTHWAITE
Map 19 NZ00

The Red Lion Inn

tel: 01748 884218 **DL11 6RE**
email: rlionlangthwaite@aol.com
dir: *From A6108 between Richmond & Leyburn follow Reeth signs. In Reeth follow Langthwaite sign*

Often used as a film and TV location

The Red Lion Inn is a traditional country community pub that has been owned by the same family for 50 years. It hosts two darts teams in winter, a quoits team in summer, and offers only bar snacks — although ice cream, chocolate and sweets are available too. There are some wonderful walks in this part of the Dales and relevant books and maps are on sale in the bar. In the tiny snug there are photographs relating to the various films and TV programmes filmed at this unusually photogenic — they include *All Creatures Great and Small*, *A Woman of Substance* and *Hold the Dream*.

Open all wk 11-3 7-11 **Food** Lunch all wk 11-3 ⊕ FREE HOUSE ◂ Black Sheep Best Bitter & Riggwelter, Guinness ♂ Thatchers Gold. **Facilities** Non-diners area Family room Outside area ⊟ Parking WiFi

LASTINGHAM
Map 19 SE79

Blacksmiths Arms

tel: 01751 417247 **YO62 6TN**
email: pete.hils@blacksmithslastingham.co.uk
dir: *7m from Pickering & 4m from Kirkbymoorside. A170 (Pickering to Kirkbymoorside road), follow Lastingham & Appleton-le-Moors signs*

Well-loved pub on the southern fringe of the North York Moors

With a cottage garden and decked outdoor seating area, this stone-built, 17th-century free house has a wonderful atmosphere. In the small front bar pewter mugs and beer pump clips hang from the low beams, and copper cooking pans decorate the open range. A snug and two delightful dining rooms make up the rest of the interior. Home-cooked dishes prepared from local supplies include Yorkshire hotpot; lamb and mint pie; and Whitby breaded scampi (also in takeaway form). Enjoy the food with Theakston Best Bitter or a guest ale. St Mary's Church, opposite the pub, is renowned for its Saxon crypt.

Open all day all wk **Food** Lunch all wk 12-5 Dinner all wk 6.30-8.45 ⊕ FREE HOUSE ◂ Theakston Best Bitter, 3 guest ales. **Facilities** Non-diners area ♦♦ Children's menu Children's portions Family room Garden ⊟ WiFi ⛟ (notice required)

LEVISHAM
Map 19 SE89

Horseshoe Inn ★★★★ INN

tel: 01751 460240 **Main St YO18 7NL**
email: info@horseshoelevisham.co.uk web: www.horseshoelevisham.co.uk
dir: *A169, 5m from Pickering. 4m, pass Fox & Rabbit Inn on right. In 0.5m left to Lockton. Follow steep winding road to village*

Family-run pub in tranquil village

On the edge of the North York Moors National Park, this village pub is an ideal overnight stop while touring the area, perhaps by steam train from Levisham station. Charles and Toby Wood have created an inviting atmosphere, especially apparent in the beamed and wooden-floored bar, where a gilt-edged mirror hangs above the open fire, and the real ales are from Black Sheep and Cropton. Local suppliers play a big part behind the scenes so that the kitchen can prepare hearty plates of Whitby scampi and chips, steak and ale pie, and sausage and mash with onion gravy.

Open all day all wk **Food** Lunch all wk 12-2 Dinner all wk 6-8.30 ⊕ FREE HOUSE ◂ Black Sheep Best Bitter, Cropton Yorkshire Moors, Two Pints, Yorkshire Warrior & Endeavour, Wold Top Headland Red, Brass Castle Cliffhanger ♂ Thatchers Gold. ♀ 12 **Facilities** Non-diners area ❀ (Bar Garden) ♦♦ Children's menu Children's portions Garden ⊟ Parking WiFi **Rooms** 9

LEYBURN
Map 19 SE19

The Queens Head ★★★★ INN

tel: 01677 450259 **Westmoor Ln, Finghall DL8 1QZ**
email: enquiries@queensfinghall.co.uk web: www.queensfinghall.co.uk
dir: *From Bedale follow A684 W towards Leyburn, just after pub & caravan park turn left signed Finghall*

Dales produce is high on the list

This pretty 18th-century country inn with beams and open fires is set on a hillside above Wensleydale and there are stunning views of the countryside from the terrace. The dining room overlooks Wild Wood — believed to be one of the inspirations for Kenneth Grahame's *Wind in the Willows*. Drinkers can quaff a pint of Theakston Black Bull Bitter by the fire and diners can create their own deli board while considering the menu, which demonstrates the kitchen team's passion for Dales produce. As well as sandwiches and pub favourites there are contemporary dishes like crab and ginger risotto with tempura king prawns; Hornby Park venison pudding; and Indian spiced salmon fillet. Spacious accommodation is located in the adjacent annexe.

Open all wk 12-3 6-close Closed 26 Dec, 1 Jan **Food** Lunch all wk 12-2 Dinner all wk 6-9 Set menu available ⊕ FREE HOUSE ◂ Theakston Black Bull Bitter, Pennine Brewing Co Hair of the Dog. ♀ 10 **Facilities** Non-diners area ♦♦ Children's menu Children's portions Garden Outside area ⊟ Parking WiFi ⛟ (notice required) **Rooms** 3

Sandpiper Inn
PICK OF THE PUBS

tel: 01969 622206 **Market Place DL8 5AT**
email: hsandpiper99@aol.com
dir: *A1 onto A684 to Leyburn*

Wensleydale market town inn

The ivy-clad Sandpiper may only have been a pub for 30 years or so, but it's Leyburn's oldest building, dating to the 17th century. Run by Jonathan and Janine Harrison, the bar and snug offer real ales from a small army of Yorkshire breweries, and some 100 single malts. The restaurant, distinguished by a huge stone lintel above an open fireplace, oak floors and candlelit tables, is where Jonathan has built on his excellent reputation for modern British food. Such reputations, of course, require using the finest ingredients, which he does for traditional and international dishes such as double baked cheese soufflé with roasted pear, butternut squash, red onion and rocket; roasted sea trout, courgette spaghetti and smoked salmon; pressed Dales lamb with dauphinoise potato, roast vegetables with cranberry and mint sauce. For dessert, why not one of the Sandpiper's own ice creams or sorbets, or warm chocolate and orange bread and butter pudding?

Open 10.30-3 6-11 (Sun 12-2.30 6-10) Closed 2wks from 1st Jan, Mon & occasionally Tue **Food** Lunch Tue-Sun 12-2.30 Dinner Tue-Fri 6-8.30, Sat 6-9, Sun 6-8 Av main course £18 Restaurant menu available ⊕ FREE HOUSE ◼ Black Sheep Best Bitter, Daleside, Copper Dragon, Archers, Yorkshire Dales, Rudgate Brewery, Wensleydale Ŏ Thatchers Gold. ♚ 10 **Facilities** Non-diners area ☺ (Restaurant Garden) ♦ Children's menu Family room Garden ⋒ WiFi

---

LITTON	**Map 18 SD97**

Queens Arms

tel: 01756 770096 **BD23 5QJ**
email: info@queensarmslitton.co.uk **web:** www.queensarmslitton.co.uk
dir: From Skipton N on B6265, through Threshfield & Kilnsey. Left signed Arncliffe & Litton

Whitewashed gem in a secret sylvan dale

Secluded Littondale is the Dales of yesteryear; the Queens radiates character and charm from its idyllic hamlet setting amidst wildflower meadows and limestone crags in one of the most secret of dales. Bag a table out-front and sip a Chinook Blonde whilst drinking in the views across the River Skirfare's valley. Inside is classical and compact, with open fire, slate floor and beams, all enhanced by contemporary fittings and fabrics. The dishes reflect the inn's setting and change daily; home-made beef, smoked bacon and Black Sheep ale pie a good example.

Queens Arms

Open 11-3 6-11 Closed Mon (winter) **Food** Lunch all wk 12-2 Dinner all wk 6-8 ⊕ FREE HOUSE ◼ Thwaites Original, Black Sheep, Goose Eye Chinook Blonde Ŏ Thatchers. **Facilities** Non-diners area ☺ (All areas) ♦ Children's portions Garden Outside area ⋒ WiFi ⛟ (notice required)

See advert below

LOWER DUNSFORTH	**Map 19 SE46**

NEW The Dunsforth

tel: 01423 320700 **Mary Ln YO26 9SA**
email: hello@thedunsforth.co.uk
dir: Phone pub for detailed directions

Village pub ticking all the right boxes

Paul Cunliffe, former head chef at Harvey Nichols in Leeds, runs this welcoming village pub with his wife Janine as their first joint venture. Inside are open coal fires, outside a terrace and gardens. It is hardly surprising that Paul, given his background, and Janine are passionate about food-sourcing; meats come from trusted local farms and estates, fish daily from Hartlepool. You may eat at the bar, or in the restaurant, where Shetland mussels might precede butter-roasted wild halibut with spinach, duck-fat potatoes, oyster beignet, brown shrimps and pancetta, and finish with Yorkshire rhubarb tart. The wine list nudges 100 bins.

Open 12-2.30 5.30-11 (Sat-Sun 12-11) Closed Mon **Food** Lunch Tue-Sat 12-2.30, Sun 12-6 Dinner Tue-Sat 5.30-9.30 Av main course £15 Set menu available Restaurant menu available all wk ⊕ FREE HOUSE ◼ Theakston Best Bitter & Black Bull Bitter, Adnams Ghost Ship. ♚ 14 **Facilities** Non-diners area ☺ (Bar Garden) ♦ Children's menu Children's portions Garden ⋒ Parking WiFi ⛟ (notice required)

LOW ROW   **Map 18 SD99**

The Punch Bowl Inn ★★★★ INN

tel: 01748 886233 **DL11 6PF**
email: info@pbinn.co.uk web: www.pbinn.co.uk
dir: A1 from Scotch Corner take A6108 to Richmond. Through Richmond then right onto B6270 to Low Row

Lots on offer at this Yorkshire Dales inn

With Wainwright's Coast to Coast Walk on the doorstep, this Grade II listed Swaledale pub dates back to the 17th century. As well as open fires and antique furniture, the bar and bar stools were hand-crafted by Robert 'The Mouseman' Thompson's company (see if you can spot the mice around the bar). Typical food choices include chicken liver and orange pâté; beef and ale casserole with herb dumplings and horseradish mash; and Yorkshire parkin with apple compôte. Local cask-conditioned ales also feature. If you would like to stay over for the Swaledale festivals, the 11 bedrooms all have spectacular views.

The Punch Bowl Inn

Open all day all wk 11am-mdnt Closed 25 Dec **Food** Lunch Mon-Sat 12-2.30, Sun 12-3 Dinner all wk 6-9 Restaurant menu available all wk ⊕ FREE HOUSE ◀ Theakston Best Bitter, Black Sheep Best Bitter & Riggwelter, Timothy Taylor Landlord Ò Thatchers Gold. ☕ 13 **Facilities** Non-diners area ❤ (Bar) ✚ Children's menu Children's portions Outside area ⋒ Parking WiFi ▬ (notice required) **Rooms** 11

MALHAM   **Map 18 SD96**

The Lister Arms ★★★★ INN   `PICK OF THE PUBS`

See Pick of the Pubs on opposite page and advert below

PICK OF THE PUBS

The Lister Arms ★★★★ INN

MALHAM   Map 18 SD96

tel: 01729 830330 **BD23 4DB**
email: relax@listerarms.co.uk
web: www.listerarms.co.uk
dir: *In village centre*

Close to majestic Malham Cove

For location alone, this handsome old coaching inn takes some beating, sitting as it does in some of Britain's most impressive, cavern-riddled limestone scenery. A dense covering of creepers masks its stone walls, and there's still the old mounting block from coaching days. Beyond the attractive tiled entrance are the little rooms with original beams, fireplaces, wooden floors and log-burning stoves that the exterior promises. One of Blackburn brewery Thwaites' Inns of Character, it's right on the village green, which presents much easier terrain for the fell-walkers, cavers and other outdoor types who drop in here for morning coffee or a pint of Wainwright bitter, named after fellow Blackburnian and fell-walking guide writer/illustrator, Alfred Wainwright. Traditional, home-cooked meals originating from trusted local suppliers might begin with venison parfait and parkin croûte; or smoked salmon with capers, shallots and horseradish cream. From there the choice broadens into sharing boards and salads, grills, classics and fish

dishes. Taking an example from each group, you could choose a Yorkshire Blue and roasted beetroot board; grilled pork chop with chimichurri sauce (a piquant South American concoction); Steve's shortcrust pie of the day (the Lister supports British Pie Week in March and other food-focused weeks throughout the year); or spiced hake and mussel stew. On Sundays giant Yorkshire puddings accompany the roasts. Puddings and cake are home made too, including apple and blackberry crumble, and vanilla crème brûlée. The children's Half Pints menu includes all their favourites, from fish and chips to creamy pea risotto. Feel free to arrive with a well-behaved dog and muddy boots – no-one will object.

Open all day all wk **Food** Contact pub for details ⊕ THWAITES INNS OF CHARACTER ◼ Wainwright, Original ♂ Westons Stowford Press. ♟ 8 **Facilities** Non-diners area ❤ (Bar Garden) ⫯ Children's menu Children's portions Garden ⊠ Parking WiFi **Rooms** 15

MALTON — Map 19 SE77

The New Malton

tel: 01653 693998 **2-4 Market Place YO17 7LX**
email: info@thenewmalton.co.uk
dir: *In town centre opposite church*

Family-friendly pub overlooking the market place

Overlooking the market place in Malton, this prominent 18th-century building has had an interesting history including a time as a tea room in the 1930s and as a tapas bar. Beer drinkers are spoilt for choice, with the range of local ales changing weekly. An extensive menu features a mix of pub classics and more ambitious dishes such as seared haloumi with roast cashew nuts, mild chilli, candied lemon and lime salad; steak burger with pancetta, Swiss cheese, dill pickle, coleslaw and chips; and pan-fried sea bass with saffron mash, mussel and dill butter sauce.

Open all day all wk Closed 25-26 Dec, 1 Jan **Food** Lunch Mon-Sat 12-9.30, Sun 12-9 Dinner Mon-Sat 12-9.30, Sun 12-9 Av main course £11.50 ⊕ FREE HOUSE ◖ Wold Top Bitter, Great Newsome Prickly Back Otchan, Rudgate Ruby Mild ♂ Westons Stowford Press & Wyld Wood Organic. ♟ 10 **Facilities** ❀ (Bar Restaurant Outside area) ♦ Children's portions Outside area ⋈ Parking WiFi

MARTON (NEAR BOROUGHBRIDGE) — Map 19 SE46

The Punch Bowl Inn

tel: 01423 322519 **YO51 9QY**
email: enquiries@thepunchbowlmartoncumgrafton.com
web: www.thepunchbowlmartoncumgrafton.com
dir: *In village centre*

Village pub with six eating areas

A Provenance Inns group member, the 16th-century Punch Bowl commands a central location in the village. Its beamed, wood-floored bar and tap-room's generous seating includes a settle, and there's a log fire in each of the six eating areas. The Yorkshire Plate starter features Harrogate Blue cheese, black pudding fritter, duck rillettes, beetroot salsa, Malham chorizo and griddled sourdough. Typical main dishes are a seafood platter; confit shoulder of lamb; and mushroom, spinach and ricotta Wellington, with roasts and baked Cajun salmon on Sundays. Summer barbecues are held in the courtyard.

Open all day all wk **Food** Lunch Mon-Sat 12-2.30, Sun 12-3 Dinner Mon-Sat 5.30-9.30, Sun 5.30-8.30 ⊕ PROVENANCE INNS ◖ Black Sheep Best Bitter, Timothy Taylor Landlord ♂ Symonds. **Facilities** Non-diners area ❀ (Bar Garden) ♦ Children's menu Children's portions Garden ⋈ Parking WiFi 🚌 (notice required)

MASHAM — Map 19 SE28

The Black Sheep Brewery

tel: 01765 680101 & 680100 **Wellgarth HG4 4EN**
email: sue.dempsey@blacksheep.co.uk
dir: *Off A6108, 9m from Ripon & 7m from Bedale*

Famous brewery site for over 20 years

Set up by Paul Theakston, a member of Masham's famous brewery family, in the former Wellgarth Maltings in 1992, the complex includes an excellent visitor centre and a popular bar-cum-bistro. Go on a fascinating tour of the brewery. Next take in the wonderful views over the River Ure and surrounding countryside as you sup tip-top pints of Riggwelter and Golden Sheep; then tuck into a good plate of food, perhaps duck confit, dauphinoise potatoes, braised Puy lentils and seasonal vegetables; locally made Hog and Hop sausages, sage mash, onion gravy and vegetables; or an oak-smoked salmon and prawn sandwich.

Open all wk 10-5 (Thu-Sat 10am-late) Closed 25-26 Dec **Food** Contact pub for food times Av main course £10.95 Restaurant menu available Mon-Sat ⊕ BLACK SHEEP BREWERY ◖ Best Bitter, Riggwelter Ale, Golden Sheep ♂ Aspall, Thatchers Gold. **Facilities** Non-diners area ❀ (Garden) ♦ Children's menu Children's portions Garden ⋈ Parking WiFi 🚌 (notice required)

The White Bear

tel: 01765 689319 **Wellgarth HG4 4EN**
email: sue@whitebearmasham.co.uk
dir: *Signed from A1 between Bedale & Ripon*

Theakston's flagship pub in bustling market town

Theakston Brewery's flagship inn stands just a short stroll from the legendary brewhouse and market square in this bustling market town and provides the perfect base for exploring the Yorkshire Dales. Handsome and stylish, there's a snug taproom for quaffing pints of Old Peculier by the glowing fire, oak-floored lounges with deep sofas and chairs for perusing the daily papers, and an elegant dining room. Menus take in pork fillet wrapped in bacon filled with black pudding served with parsnip and English mustard purée; butternut squash and spinach curry; sausage and mash with onion gravy; and mushroom and sweet pepper risotto with parmesan crisps. Expect live music and 30 cask ales at the late June beer festival.

Open all day all wk **Food** Lunch all wk 12-9 Dinner all wk 12-9 ⊕ FREE HOUSE/ THEAKSTON ◖ Best Bitter, Black Bull Bitter, Lightfoot & Old Peculier, Caledonian Deuchars IPA. **Facilities** Non-diners area ❀ (Bar Garden) ♦ Children's menu Children's portions Garden ⋈ Beer festival Parking WiFi 🚌 (notice required)

MAUNBY
Map 19 SE38

NEW The Buck Inn

tel: 01845 587777 **YO7 4HD**
email: info@thebuckinnmaunby.co.uk **web:** www.thebuckinnmaunby.co.uk
dir: *A1(M) junct 50, A61 towards Thirsk. Left onto A671 (Northallerton). In South Otterington left signed Maunby. Or A1(M) junct 53, A684 towards Northallerton. At rdbt right onto A167 to South Otterington, right signed Maunby*

Chef-led pub for quality eating and drinking

Chef Matthew Roath and partner Sammy Clark refurbished the Buck as soon as they arrived here. But the classic British country pub atmosphere has been preserved, with wing-backed chairs around two log fires and regularly changing ales from different Yorkshire breweries in the bar. Carefully sourced ingredients include organic vegetables from a neighbouring supplier. Indicative of the quality dishes on offer is the carte's starter of Gloucester Old Spots pork haslet with Yorkshire rhubarb, stout and date toast. Follow, perhaps, with East Coast halibut, slow-cooked oxtail and creamed celeriac. Look out for a famous trainer exercising his horses, or the locals playing quoits in the garden.

Open 12-2 5-11 (Fri-Sat 12-11, Sun 12-10.30) Closed 26 Dec & 1 Jan, Sun eve & Mon **Food** Lunch Tue-Sat 12-2, Sun 12-4 Dinner Tue-Fri 5-9.30, Sat 6-9.30 Av main course £11 Set menu available Restaurant menu available Tue-Sat ⊕ FREE HOUSE ◀ Theakston Best Bitter, Rudgate, Yorkshire Heart. ☐ 12 **Facilities** Non-diners area ❀ (Bar Garden) ◀◀ Children's menu Children's portions Garden ☐ Parking WiFi ☐ (notice required)

MIDDLEHAM
Map 19 SE18

The White Swan

tel: 01969 622093 **Market Place DL8 4PE**
email: enquiries@whiteswanhotel.co.uk
dir: *From A1, take A684 towards Leyburn then A6108 to Ripon, 1.5m to Middleham*

Popular and attractive inn

Paul Klein's Tudor coaching inn stands in the shadow of Middleham's ruined castle in the cobbled market square and, like the village, is steeped in the history of the turf, with several top horseracing stables located in the area. Oak beams, flagstones and roaring log fires all feature in the atmospheric bar, where you can quaff tip-top Black Sheep or Wensleydale ales and enjoy modern British and Italian food. Using quality Yorkshire produce the menu might feature pappardelle with wild boar ragu, saltimbocca (pork loin, sage and Parma ham with white wine and butter bean sauce), or braised rabbit with vegetable risotto. Finish with torta di mele — apple pie.

Open all day all wk 8am-11pm (mdnt at wknds) **Food** Contact pub for food times ⊕ FREE HOUSE ◀ Black Sheep Best Bitter, John Smith's, Theakston, Wensleydale ☐ Thatchers Gold. ☐ 9 **Facilities** Non-diners area ❀ (Bar Outside area) ◀◀ Children's menu Children's portions Family room Outside area ☐ Parking WiFi ☐ (notice required)

MIDDLESMOOR
Map 19 SE07

Crown Hotel

tel: 01423 755204 **HG3 5ST**
dir: *Phone for detailed directions*

Family run hotel at the top of the valley

This family-run traditional free house dates back to the 17th century and is in an ideal spot for anyone following the popular Nidderdale Way. There are great views towards Gouthwaite Reservoir from this breezy 900-ft high hilltop village with its cobbled streets. Visitors can enjoy a good pint of local beer and food by the cosy, roaring log fire, or in the sunny pub garden. A large selection of malt whiskies is also on offer.

Open Nov-Apr Tue-Thu 7-11 Fri-Sun all day (May-Oct Tue-Thu 12-2 7-11 Fri-Sun all day) Closed all day Mon, Tue-Thu L (winter) **Food** Lunch Tue-Sun 12-2 Dinner Tue-Sun 7-8.30 ⊕ FREE HOUSE ◀ Black Sheep Best Bitter, Wensleydale Bitter, Guinness ☐ Thatchers Gold. **Facilities** ❀ (Bar Restaurant Garden) ◀◀ Children's portions Garden ☐ Parking WiFi **Notes** ☐

NEWTON ON OUSE
Map 19 SE55

The Dawnay Arms

tel: 01347 848345 **YO30 2BR**
email: dine@thedawnay.co.uk
dir: *From A19 follow Newton on Ouse signs*

Great riverside location with a large garden

Right in the middle of a picture-perfect village, The Dawnay Arms dates back to Georgian times. It sits on the banks of the River Ouse, and its large rear garden runs down to moorings for those arriving by boat. The interior, all chunky beams and tables, hosts Black Sheep and guest ales, and the well-chosen wine list also deserves mention. Dishes are British in style and replete with quality ingredients. The hot fish platter, for example, comprises roast hand-dived scallop with cauliflower, smoked haddock chowder, warm potted shrimps on toast, and goujons of Scarborough Woof (wolf fish) with tartare sauce.

Open 12-3 6-11 (Sat all day Sun 12-8) Closed Mon ⊕ FREE HOUSE ◀ Black Sheep, Guest ales ☐ Westons Stowford Press. **Facilities** ❀ (Bar Garden) ◀◀ Children's portions Garden Parking WiFi

NUN MONKTON
Map 19 SE55

The Alice Hawthorn
PICK OF THE PUBS

tel: 01423 330303 **The Green YO26 8EW**
email: info@theforagerskitchen.com
dir: *From A59 between York & Harrogate follow Nun Monkton signs. Pub 2m on right*

Village pub going the extra mile for local sourcing

At the heart of village life in Nun Monkton for more than 200 years, The Alice Hawthorn has a team of chefs with an uncompromising passion for local sourcing. All the meat and vegetables used in the kitchen are from local farmers and all fish arrives from the east coast. The chefs have even joined forces with locals who knock on the kitchen door with apples from nearby orchards and just-caught trout — all of it destined for the 'foragers' specials board'. A smokehouse, chicken run and pub pigs complete the sustainable picture at the pub, where only local ales and ciders are served in the friendly bar. A lunchtime sandwich selection and set menu run alongside a carte that might include crispy belly pork Asian salad; steak and ale pie with honey-roasted root vegetables; finishing with ginger and treacle tartlet.

Open 12-3 5-11 (Sat all day Sun 12-6) Closed Jan, Sun eve, Mon & Tue L **Food** Lunch Wed-Sun 12-3 Dinner Tue-Sat 6-9 ⊕ FREE HOUSE ◀ Weekly changing local ales ☐ Rekorderlig, Local ciders. ☐ 12 **Facilities** Non-diners area ❀ (Bar Garden) ◀◀ Children's menu Children's portions Garden ☐ Parking WiFi ☐

OLDSTEAD
Map 19 SE57

The Black Swan at Oldstead ★★★★★ RR ⊛⊛⊛
PICK OF THE PUBS

See Pick of the Pubs on opposite page

OSMOTHERLEY
Map 19 SE49

The Golden Lion
PICK OF THE PUBS

tel: 01609 883526 **6 West End DL6 3AA**
email: goldenlionosmotherley@yahoo.co.uk
dir: *Phone for detailed directions*

Honest, well-cooked food

Standing in Osmotherley, the 'Gateway to the North Yorkshire Moors', The Golden Lion is a 250-year-old sandstone building. The atmosphere is warm and welcoming with open fires, a wooden bar, bench seating, whitewashed walls, mirrors and fresh flowers. As well as some 60 single malt whiskies, there are always three real ales on offer. The extensive menu ranges through basic pub grub to more refined dishes. Starters might include smoked salmon and prawn roulade; grilled aubergines filled with ratatouille; and fresh mussels in a white wine and cream sauce. Mains are along the lines of home-made chicken Kiev; sirloin steak, and fillets of plaice, supplemented by specials such as turkey roulade; duck, chestnut and thyme risotto; and sea bass with a samphire, crayfish and basil sauce. Popular desserts are raspberry ripple cheesecake, ginger sponge and crème brûlée.

Open 12-3 6-11 Closed 25 Dec, Mon L, Tue L **Food** Lunch Wed-Sun 12-2.30 Dinner all wk 6-9 ⊕ FREE HOUSE ◀ Timothy Taylor Landlord, York Guzzler, Salamander, Wall's Brewing Co ᵓ Herefordshire. **Facilities** ❀ (Bar Restaurant Outside area) ♦♠ Children's menu Children's portions Outside area WiFi

PICKERING
Map 19 SE78

Fox & Hounds Country Inn ★★★★ INN ⊛ **PICK OF THE PUBS**

tel: 01751 431577 **Sinnington YO62 6SQ**
email: fox.houndsinn@btconnect.com **web:** www.thefoxandhoundsinn.co.uk
dir: *3m W of town, off A170 between Pickering & Helmsley*

Great country pub atmosphere with award-winning food

This friendly, 18th-century coaching inn on the edge of the North York Moors is run by resident proprietors Andrew and Catherine Stephens. In the wood-panelled bar, under oak beams and, depending on the temperature, warmed by a double-sided log-burner called Big Bertha, a pint of Copper Dragon Best, or Black Sheep Special, could be waiting, or maybe a rarely encountered whisky. Making full use of locally farmed produce, light lunches (except Sundays) and early suppers (except Saturdays) include baked smoked haddock with herb crust; slow-braised shoulder of lamb; or a variety of omelettes. Differing only in part, the main menu also lists twice-baked cheddar soufflé with pear and walnut salad; prime rib steak with chips; and apricot glazed pear and almond tart with custard. Turn right along the village street past the village green to an ancient packhorse bridge over the gentle River Seven (yes, Seven).

Open all wk 12-2 5.30-11 (Sat 12-2 6-11 Sun 12-2.30 5.30-10.30) Closed 25-27 Dec **Food** Lunch all wk 12-2 Dinner Mon-Fri 5.30-9, Sat 6.30-9, Sun 5.30-8.30 Av main course £13.25 ⊕ FREE HOUSE ◀ Copper Dragon Best Bitter, Black Sheep ᵓ Thatchers Gold. ♟ 9 **Facilities** Non-diners area ❀ (Bar Garden) ♦♠ Children's menu Children's portions Garden ⊨ Parking WiFi ▬ **Rooms** 10

The Fox & Rabbit Inn

tel: 01751 460213 **Whitby Rd, Lockton YO18 7NQ**
email: info@foxandrabbit.co.uk
dir: *From Pickering take A169 towards Whitby. Lockton in 5m*

Reliable stop near Dalby Forest

On a wide ridge above wooded dales, the sound of steam trains may drift across pastures to this very traditional Yorkshire Inn near Pickering. The North York Moors Railway is just one of a string of attractions within easy reach of the limestone-built country pub. With beers sourced from nearby craft breweries and menu ingredients with a distinctly Yorkshire pedigree, the Wood brothers have an embarrassment of riches to offer their guests. Seasonally adjusted menus may offer slow-roasted Ginger Pig Farm belly pork or slow-braised lamb shank as filling mains, topped off with lemon and lime cheesecake.

Open all day all wk **Food** Lunch Mon-Thu 12-2.30, Fri-Sun 12.30-4 Dinner all wk 5-8.30 ⊕ FREE HOUSE ◀ Black Sheep Best Bitter, Marston's Oyster Stout, Cropton, Wold Top Ales, Tetley's Smooth Flow, Guest ales ᵓ Thatchers Gold. ♟ 13 **Facilities** Non-diners area ❀ (Bar Garden) ♦♠ Children's menu Children's portions Garden ⊨ Parking ▬ (notice required)

The White Swan Inn ★★★ HL ⊛⊛ **PICK OF THE PUBS**

tel: 01751 472288 **Market Place YO18 7AA**
email: welcome@white-swan.co.uk **web:** www.white-swan.co.uk
dir: *From N: A19 or A1 to Thirsk, A170 to Pickering, left at lights, 1st right onto Market Place. Pub on left. From S: A1 or A1(M) to A64 to Malton rdbt, A169 to Pickering*

Elegant market town inn with award-winning food

At the heart of pretty Pickering, The White Swan Inn fronts the steep main street dropping to the beck and steam railway station. With open fires, flagstone floors, panelling and eclectic furnishings, this sturdy coaching inn oozes character. Far from being a period piece, the owners have skilfully combined good contemporary design to produce a stylish destination dining inn. A creeper-clad courtyard snuggles behind, where browsers can enjoy Timothy Taylor Landlord bitter. It's for the exceptional menus, however, that guests travel to savour. The team led by Derren Clemmit scour the county for the best ingredients. Rare breed meats from the Ginger Pig Farm at Levisham; and lobster and fish from Whitby are crafted into a fine dining experience. A starter of ox tongue, pickled red onion and wild garlic purée is an appetiser for roast rack of spring lamb, Jersey Royal potato cake, minted new season carrots and caper sauce; or battered Whitby haddock with 'posh' peas and tartare sauce. A local cheeseboard is an ample conclusion, whilst the wine list has 65 bins.

Open all day all wk **Food** Lunch all wk 12-2 Dinner all wk 6.45-9 Av main course £19 ⊕ FREE HOUSE ◀ Black Sheep, Timothy Taylor Landlord ᵓ Westons Stowford Press. ♟ 19 **Facilities** Non-diners area ❀ (Bar Outside area) ♦♠ Children's menu Children's portions Outside area ⊨ Parking WiFi ▬ (notice required) **Rooms** 21

Find out more about the AA's awards for food excellence on page 9

PICK OF THE PUBS

The Black Swan at Oldstead ★★★★★ RR ✿✿✿

OLDSTEAD   Map 19 SE57

tel: 01347 868387 **Main St YO61 4BL**
email: enquiries@blackswanoldstead.
co.uk
web: www.blackswanoldstead.co.uk
dir: *A1 junct 49, A168, A19S, after 3m
left to Coxwold then Byland Abbey. In 2m
left for Oldstead, pub 1m on left*

Outstanding food in rural Yorkshire

Dating back to the 16th century and set
in a sleepy hamlet below the North York
Moors, The Black Swan is owned and
run by the Banks family, who have
farmed in the village for generations. In
the bar you'll find a stone-flagged floor,
an open log fire, original wooden window
seats, soft cushions, and fittings by
Robert 'Mousey' Thompson who, in the
1930s, was a prolific maker of
traditional handcrafted English oak
furniture. Expect tip-top real ales,
cracking wines by the glass, malt
whiskies and vintage port, while the
first-class food on offer changes with
the seasons, being sourced mainly from
local farms. The same award-winning
menus are offered in the bar and in the
comfortable restaurant where Persian
rugs line an oak floor, the furniture is
antique, and candles in old brass
holders create light soft enough to be
romantic, but bright enough to read the

innovative modern country menus by.
Start perhaps with langoustine soup,
crab and cheddar croûton; or butternut
squash cannelloni, langoustine, tomato
and basil; move on to ox cheek,
cauliflower cheese, macaroni, truffle
and salsify; or halibut, Jerusalem
artichoke, squid, pink fir potato and
samphire; and finish with dark
chocolate, vanilla and pear. The
bedrooms have solid oak floors and are
furnished with quality antiques, classy
soft fabrics, and paintings. Bathrooms
are fitted with an iron roll-top bath and
a walk-in wet room shower, which
sounds like just the place to head for
after one of the pleasant walks
radiating from the front of the building.

Open 12-3 6-11 Closed 1wk Jan, Mon
L-Fri L **Food** Lunch Sat-Sun 12-2
Dinner all wk 6-9 Set menu available
Restaurant menu available all wk
⊕ FREE HOUSE ◖ Black Sheep. ☙ 30
Facilities Non-diners area ♦♦ Children's
menu Children's portions Garden ⩎
Parking WiFi **Rooms** 4

PICKHILL

Map 19 SE38

Nags Head Country Inn

PICK OF THE PUBS

tel: 01845 567391 **YO7 4JG**
email: enquiries@nagsheadpickhill.co.uk
dir: *A1(M) junct 50, A61 towards Thirsk. Left onto B6267 signed Masham. Right signed Pickhill*

Renowned for excellent food, fine wines and real ales

For over 40 years the Boynton family have been welcoming visitors to their extended, former 17th-century coaching inn set in a peaceful village just off the A1 north of Thirsk. Synonymous with Yorkshire hospitality at its best, notably among weary travellers and the local racing fraternity, the inn comprises a beamed lounge and a traditional taproom bar with flagged and tiled floors, beams adorned with ties and a magpie selection of tables and chairs tucked around open fires. A terrific menu is the icing on the cake here; a small but perfectly formed taproom menu offers sandwiches and simple meals such as steak and chips with all the trimmings or Thai chicken, vegetable and noodle stir-fry. In the lounge or elegant restaurant, order mushroom and roasted garlic risotto to start, followed perhaps by corn-fed chicken with a small wing Kiev, buttered cabbage, potato dumplings and pearl barley broth. Tempting, calorific puddings seal the deal, perhaps forced Yorkshire rhubarb pithivier with frangipane and ewe's milk ice cream.

Open all wk 11-11 (Sun 11-10.30) Closed 25 Dec (drinks only available) **Food** Lunch Mon-Sat 12-2, Sun 12-3 Dinner Mon-Sat 6-9.30, Sun 5.30-8 ⊕ FREE HOUSE ◀ Black Sheep Best Bitter, Theakston Old Peculier & Best Bitter, Rudgate Viking ♻ Westons Stowford Press. ☕ 8 **Facilities** Non-diners area ♦♦ Children's menu Children's portions Garden ♯ Parking WiFi ☕ (notice required)

RIPON

Map 19 SE37

The George at Wath

tel: 01765 641324 **Main St, Wath HG4 5EN**
email: reception@thegeorgeatwath.co.uk
dir: *From A1 (dual carriageway) N'bound turn left signed Melmerby & Wath. From A1 S'bound exit at slip road signed A61. At T-junct right (signed Ripon). Approx 0.5m turn right signed Melmerby & Wath*

Welcoming free house with very good food

The George at Wath, a brick-built double-fronted free house dating from the 18th century, is just three miles from the cathedral city of Ripon. This traditional Yorkshire pub retains its flagstone floors, log-burning fires and cosy atmosphere, while the contemporary dining room proffers seasonal and locally sourced ingredients for its mix of classic and bistro-style dishes: salt cod fritters could be followed by glazed gammon with chips cooked in dripping; finish with a chocolate tart, or rhubarb and custard. The George is child and dog friendly.

Open 12-3 5-11 (Sat-Sun all day) Closed Mon L & Tue L **Food** Lunch Wed-Sun 12-2 Dinner Mon-Sat fr 5.30pm ⊕ FREE HOUSE ◀ Theakston, Guest ale ♻ Westons Stowford Press. ☕ 14 **Facilities** Non-diners area ♣ (Bar Garden) ♦♦ Children's menu Children's portions Garden ♯ Beer festival Parking WiFi ☕ (notice required)

The Royal Oak ★★★★ INN ◉

tel: 01765 602284 **36 Kirkgate HG4 1PB**
email: info@royaloakripon.co.uk **web:** www.royaloakripon.co.uk
dir: *In town centre*

Excellent ales and good food in this smart coaching inn

Built in the 18th century, this beautiful coaching inn in the centre of Ripon is an ideal base for exploring nearby Harrogate and York. Well-kept local cask ales from Timothy Taylor and Saltaire breweries can be enjoyed in the bar, as well as wines from a carefully chosen list. Sandwiches and 'pub classics' appear on the menu alongside local steaks and signature dishes such as pheasant en croûte with potato gratin; sticky Ripon beef; and crispy skinned sea trout with Whitby crab cake.

Open all day all wk **Food** Lunch Mon-Sat 12-9, Sun 12-8 Dinner Mon-Sat 12-9, Sun 12-8 Set menu available Restaurant menu available ◀ Timothy Taylor Landlord, Best Bitter & Golden Best, Saltaire Blonde, Guest ales ♻ Westons Stowford Press. ☕ 14 **Facilities** Non-diners area ♣ (Bar Garden) ♦♦ Children's menu Children's portions Garden ♯ Parking WiFi ☕ **Rooms** 8

ROBIN HOOD'S BAY

Map 19 NZ90

Laurel Inn

tel: 01947 880400 **New Rd YO22 4SE**
dir: *Phone for detailed directions*

On the winding street towards the sea

Given its location it's hardly surprising that this was once the haunt of smugglers who used a network of underground tunnels and secret passages to bring the booty ashore. Nowadays it's the haunt of holidaymakers and walkers, and the setting for this small, traditional pub which retains lots of character features, including beams and an open fire. The bar is decorated with old photographs, and an international collection of lager bottles. This popular free house serves Adnams and Theakston Old Peculier and Best Bitter.

Open all wk 4-12 (winter) 2-12 (summer) ⊕ FREE HOUSE ◀ Theakston Best Bitter & Old Peculier, Adnams. **Facilities** ♣ (Bar Outside area) ♦♦ Family room Outside area ♯ WiFi ☕ **Notes** ☺

SAWDON

Map 17 SE98

The Anvil Inn

PICK OF THE PUBS

tel: 01723 859896 **Main St YO13 9DY**
email: info@theanvilinnsawdon.co.uk
dir: *1.5m N of Brompton-by-Sawdon, on A170 (8m E of Pickering & 6m W of Scarborough)*

Attractive stone-built village pub

There's huge charm here in what until 1985 was still a working forge, with a history traceable back to the early 1700s. The bar, with its steeply pitched ceiling and stone walls, was the original blacksmith's workshop, and the furnace, anvil, bellows and tools are all still in place. Sit on an old pew and enjoy one of the weekly changing Yorkshire beers, such as Citra pale ale from the Scarborough brewery, or Anglers Reward from Wold Top in Driffield. Locally farmed beef and pork, game from Dalby Forest, and Whitby-landed fresh fish all appear on a menu that applies in both bar and dining room. Choices to weigh up include honey-roasted venison haunch with Merguez sausage, Puy lentil and sweet potato risotto; Moroccan-spiced lamb tagine with apricot, toasted almonds, parsley, preserved lemon, wheatberries and crème fraîche; and twice-baked soufflé of leek and Coquetdale cheese with red onion jam.

Open 12-2.30 6-11 Closed 25 & 26 Dec, 1 Jan & varying annual holiday, Mon-Tue **Food** Lunch Sat 12-2, Sun 12-2.30 Dinner Wed-Sat 6.30-9, Sun 6-8 ⊕ FREE HOUSE ◀ Daleside, Leeds, Scarborough Citra, Wold Top Anglers Reward, Guest ale ♻ Westons Stowford Press. ☕ 11 **Facilities** Non-diners area ♣ (Bar Garden) ♦♦ Children's portions Garden ♯ Parking

SCARBOROUGH

Map 17 TA08

Downe Arms Country Inn ★★★★ INN

tel: 01723 862471 **Main Rd, Wykeham YO13 9QB**
email: info@downearmshotel.co.uk **web:** www.downearmshotel.co.uk
dir: *On A170*

Hospitable stone-built hostelry with country-house interiors

A converted 17th-century farmhouse on the edge of the North Yorkshire Moors, within easy reach of the Scarborough coastline and Ryedale. Inside are lovely high ceilings, and large sash windows look down to the attractive stone village of Wykeham. Yorkshire ales populate the bar, and lunchtime plates represent excellent value. In the evening the charming restaurant is transformed into an intimate candle-lit dining room, where a Whitby smoked herring fishcake could precede the pork loin steak matador (served with Spanish-style patatas bravas). If a hazlenut and mochachino Pavlova cannot be resisted, one of the inn's 10 en suite and sumptuously furnished bedrooms may also prove tempting.

Open all day all wk **Food** Lunch all wk 12-2 Dinner all wk 6-9 Restaurant menu available Mon-Sat ⊕ FREE HOUSE ◀ Black Sheep, Theakston Best Bitter, Wold Top Bitter. **Facilities** Non-diners area ✿ (Bar Garden) ⬦ Children's menu Children's portions Garden ⌒ Parking WiFi ⬛ (notice required) **Rooms** 10

SCAWTON — Map 19 SE58

The Hare Inn ◉◉ — PICK OF THE PUBS

tel: 01845 597769 **YO7 2HG**
email: liz@thehare-inn.com
dir: *Exit A170 towards Rievaulx Abbey & Scawton. Pub 1m on right*

Historic inn near idyllic moorland dales

Local lore has it that in medieval times a witch lived here. Shape-shifting into a wandering hare, she was pursued home by the hunt, breathing her last in the cottage after changing back into a witch. Other legends and tales – including a resident ghost – abound at this pretty, pantiled pub, which may have been a brewhouse for local abbeys at Rievaulx and Byland. Things are more relaxed today at this secluded dining inn in the North York Moors National Park. You'll find low-beamed ceilings and flagstone floors, a wood-burning stove offering a warm welcome in the bar, with beers coming from Rudgate and other Yorkshire breweries. An old-fashioned kitchen range features in the dining area. A classy menu offers food that's been awarded two AA Rosettes from chef-patron Paul Jackson, relying on seasonal specialities; a scallop, celeriac, apple and smoked eel starter may precede rabbit with broccoli, eryngii (king oyster mushroom), salsify and black pudding.

Open Wed-Sat 12-2 6-9 (Sun 12-4) Closed 2wks end of Jan-beg of Feb, Sun eve, Mon-Tue **Food** Lunch Wed-Sun 12-3 Dinner Wed-Sat 6-9 Set menu available ⊕ FREE HOUSE ◀ Black Sheep, Rudgate Viking, Guest ales ⚘ Thatchers. ♟ 10 **Facilities** Non-diners area ✿ (Bar Garden) ⬦ Children's portions Garden ⌒ Parking WiFi ⬛ (notice required)

SETTLE — Map 18 SD86

The Lion at Settle ★★★★ INN

tel: 01729 822203 & 823459 **Duke St BD24 9DU**
email: relax@thelionsettle.co.uk **web:** www.thelionsettle.co.uk
dir: *Phone for detailed directions*

Stylish Dales coaching inn

Owned by Thwaites and set in the heart of Settle's 17th-century market place, this inn's interior oozes history and atmosphere, with original inglenook fireplaces, wooden floors and a grand staircase lined with pictures that trace back through the town's history. It's a comfortable base for exploring the Dales or the spectacular

Settle to Carlisle railway line. Expect decent cask ales and a classic pub menu offering freshly prepared pub favourites. Typical examples include devilled whitebait; venison cottage pie; the ever popular Settle pudding of beef steak and Wainwright Ale; and one of the deli boards – butcher's or fish maybe. Leave room for banoffee pecan sundae or warm chocolate and hazelnut brownie. There's a cider festival in August and one for the beer in September.

The Lion at Settle

Open all day all wk 8am-11pm **Food** Lunch all wk bkfst 8am-10am, Mon-Sat 12-9, Sun 12-8 Dinner Mon-Sat 12-9, Sun 12-8 Set menu available ⊕ THWAITES INNS OF CHARACTER ◀ Original, Lancaster Bomber & Wainwright, Guest ales ⚘ Kingstone Press. ♟ 9 **Facilities** Non-diners area ✿ (Bar Outside area) ⬦ Children's menu Children's portions Outside area ⌒ Beer festival Cider festival WiFi ⬛ (notice required) **Rooms** 14

See advert on page 578

SKIPTON — Map 18 SD95

Devonshire Arms at Cracoe

tel: 01756 730237 **Grassington Rd, Cracoe BD23 6LA**
email: devonshirearmscracoe@outlook.com
dir: *Phone for detailed directions*

Old beams and warming fires in traditional inn

Close to the famous village of Grassington at the gateway to the Dales, and famed for its association with the Rhylstone Ladies WI calendar. This convivial and lovingly renovated 17th-century inn is favoured by Three Peaks ramblers who enjoy a rotating selection of real ales; the drinks list also offers a generous choice of wines sold by the glass, and an eclectic collection of rare bottled refreshments. The inn's menu feature rare breed meats alongside pub classics. After a field mushroom fricassée, Mr Jackson's pork bangers with creamy mash and onion gravy go down well; or try succulent short-rib of beef and Burgundy stew with horseradish dumplings. The provenance of all ingredients is reassuringly identified on the menu; if you would like to pre-order something special, it can be sourced for you with just a few days' notice.

Open all day all wk 8.30am-11pm **Food** Lunch all wk 12-3 Dinner all wk 6-8.30 ⊕ MARSTON'S ◀ EPA, Pedigree, Mansfield Cask Ale, Guest ale. ♟ 12 **Facilities** Non-diners area ✿ (Bar Garden) ⬦ Children's portions Garden ⌒ Parking WiFi ⬛ (notice required)

STARBOTTON
Map 18 SD97

Fox & Hounds Inn

tel: 01756 760269 & 760367 **BD23 5HY**
email: starbottonfox@aol.com
dir: *Phone for detailed directions*

Traditional family-run pub in the glorious Yorkshire Dales

Built as a private house some 400 years ago, this pub has been serving this picturesque limestone Yorkshire Dales village since the 1840s. Make for the bar, with its large stone fireplace, oak beams and flagged floor to enjoy a pint of something from the local Yorkshire Dales brewery, or one of the wide selection of malts. Head to the dining room for dishes such as pork medallions cooked in brandy and mustard; garlic and herb cream cheese stuffed chicken fillet, wrapped in bacon; steak and ale pie; and balti chicken and rice. The area is renowned for its spectacular walks, and dogs are permitted in the inn's garden.

Open 12-3 6-11 (Sun 12-3.30 5.30-10.30) Closed 1-22 Jan, Mon **Food** Lunch Tue-Sun 12-2.30 Dinner Tue-Sat 6-9, Sun 5.30-8 Av main course £10 ⊕ FREE HOUSE ◀ Timothy Taylor Landlord, Moorhouse's, Yorkshire Dales, Guest ales ♂ Aspall. ♀ 10 **Facilities** Non-diners area ♣ (Garden Outside area) ♦ Children's menu Garden Outside area ⋒ Parking WiFi ➡ (notice required)

SUTTON-ON-THE-FOREST
Map 19 SE56

NEW The Rose and Crown ◉

tel: 01347 811333 **Main St YO61 1DP**
email: roseandcrownsutton@gmail.com
dir: *From A1237 take B1363 (Wigginton & Helmsley). In Sutton-on-the-Forest at T-junct right. Pub on right*

Quirky village pub for local seafood

The decor of this two-century-old village pub is inspirational, quirky bits and all. The carved wooden bar, for example, is a masterpiece to be admired as well as

leant on while ordering a locally brewed Naylor's or York Guzzler. In the oak-floored, candlelit dining room seasonal dishes, organically sourced where possible, include baked lemon sole with shallot and caper butter; braised ox cheek with seared goose liver, truffle and oxtail tortellini; and wild mushroom risotto with green kale and Madeira. Outside is an African-style gazebo and a large south-facing rose-filled garden with sofas and recliners.

Open 12-3 5-11 (Sat-Sun 12-11) Closed Mon **Food** Lunch Tue-Sat 12-3, Sun 12-3.30 Dinner Tue-Sat 5.30-9, Sun 5.30-8 Av main course £16 Set menu available ⊕ FREE HOUSE ◀ York Guzzler, Naylor's ♂ Westons Stowford Press. ♀ 12 **Facilities** Non-diners area ♣ (Bar Garden) ♦ Children's menu Children's portions Play area Garden ⋒ Beer festival Parking WiFi ➡ (notice required)

THIRSK
Map 19 SE48

NEW Little 3

tel: 01845 523782 **13 Finkle St YO7 1DA**
email: info@littlethree.co.uk

Bustling haven for real ale fans

Just off the market square in the centre of Thirsk, the quirkily named Little 3 was taken over in October 2014 by Sean Kirkley, who has turned the place into a haven for real ale drinkers but also diners. Yorkshire breweries such as Timothy Taylor and Theakston dominate the handpumps at the bar, and there is an extensive whisky selection. Away from the bustling bar, the upstairs brasserie serves seasonal dishes and themed specials boards such as 'Italian classics' and 'American smokehouse'. Start with lamb koftas, tzatziki and sweet chilli before moving onto spatchcock chicken or confit pork belly.

Open all day all wk **Food** Lunch Wed-Sat 12-2.30, Sun 12-4 Dinner Wed-Sat 5-9, Sun 4-7 Av main course £9.95 Set menu available ⊕ FREE HOUSE ◀ Timothy Taylor Landlord, Theakston, Rudgate, Bradfield. ♀ 10 **Facilities** Non-diners area ♣ (Bar Outside area) ♦ Children's menu Children's portions Outside area ⋒ Beer festival Parking WiFi ➡

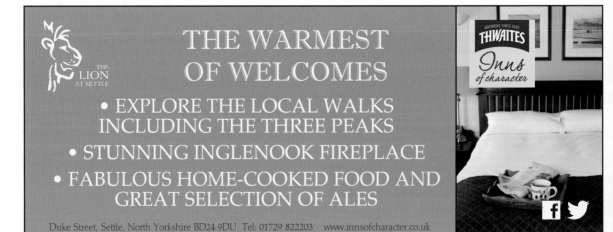

THORNTON-LE-DALE
Map 19 SE88

The New Inn

tel: 01751 474226 **Maltongate YO18 7LF**
email: enquire@the-new-inn.com
dir: *A64 N from York towards Scarborough. At Malton take A169 to Pickering. At Pickering rdbt right onto A170, 2m, pub on right*

Warm welcome at a Yorkshire favourite

Standing at the heart of a picturesque village complete with stocks and a market cross, this family-run Georgian coaching house dates back to 1720. The old-world charm of the location is echoed inside the bar and restaurant, with real log fires and exposed beams. Enjoy well-kept Theakston Best Bitter and guest ales, bitters, lagers and wines and tuck into beef and ale stew with herb scones; slow-braised lamb shoulder and minted gravy; and beer battered fish and fat-cut chips.

Open all day all wk **Food** Lunch Mon-Sat 12-2, Sun 12-3 Dinner Mon-Sat 6-8.30, Sun 5-8 ⊕ STAR PUBS & BARS ◖ Theakston Best Bitter, Guest ales.
Facilities Non-diners area ❤ (Bar Garden) ◗ Children's menu Children's portions Garden ⊓ Parking WiFi ⛟ (notice required)

THORNTON WATLASS
Map 19 SE28

The Buck Inn
`PICK OF THE PUBS`

tel: 01677 422461 **HG4 4AH**
dir: *From A1 at Leeming Bar take A684 to Bedale, B6268 towards Masham. Village in 2m*

Plenty of choice for real ale fans

Very much the heart of the local community, this refurbished traditional pub is welcoming and relaxed. New owners took over in May 2014, but you'll still see cricketing memorabilia in the Long Room, which overlooks the village green and cricket pitch (the pub is part of the boundary). You'll find up to five real ales in the bar with its open fire, including Theakston and a guest ale such as Wall's Gun Dog bitter. There are several separate dining areas and the menu ranges from sandwiches and light bites to traditional, freshly prepared pub fare. You might choose deep-fried whitebait or prawn cocktail to start, then mains of steak and ale pie; gammon steak with egg or pineapple, chips and peas; or Masham rarebit with home-made chutney. There's live jazz music most Sunday lunchtimes.

Open all wk 12-11 Closed 25 Dec eve **Food** Lunch Mon-Sat 12-2, Sun 12-3 Dinner Mon-Sat 6-9, Sun 6-8.30 Av main course £10 ⊕ FREE HOUSE ◖ Black Sheep Best Bitter, Theakston Best Bitter, 2 guest ales ♂ Westons Stowford Press.
Facilities Non-diners area ❤ (Bar Garden) ◗ Children's menu Children's portions Play area Garden ⊓ Parking ⛟ (notice required)

TOPCLIFFE
Map 19 SE47

NEW The Angel at Topcliffe

tel: 01845 578000 **YO7 3RW**
email: info@theangelattopcliffe.co.uk
dir: *A1(M) junct 49, A168 to Topcliffe. Over river, pub on right*

Bar and grill serving Yorkshire's best

The Angel is a country pub offering the best of Yorkshire's food and drink in relaxed surroundings. Spacious outdoor terraces are furnished with attractive parasol-shaded tables and chairs. The open-plan interior is equally appealing, with a mix of armchairs, alcove seats and stiff-backed chairs around dark wood tables. Hand-pulled Yorkshire ales include Copper Dragon, while menus embrace sandwiches, hot and cold snacks, and classics such as steak and kidney pie. Matured dry-edge Yorkshire beef steaks from the grill come with all the trimmings. Head for the Sports Room, separate from the bar, for the pool table or a big game on the flat-screen TV.

Open all day all wk **Food** Lunch Mon-Sat 12-2.30, Sun 12-7 Dinner Mon-Sat 5-9, Sun 12-7 Set menu available ⊕ FREE HOUSE ◖ Copper Dragon, Theakston, St Austell Tribute. ♚ 13 **Facilities** Non-diners area ❤ (Bar Garden) ◗ Children's menu Children's portions Garden ⊓ Parking WiFi ⛟ (notice required)

WASS
Map 19 SE57

Wombwell Arms
`PICK OF THE PUBS`

tel: 01347 868280 **YO61 4BE**
email: info@wombwellarms.co.uk
dir: *From A1 take A168 to A19 junct. Take York exit, then left after 2.5m, left at Coxwold to Ampleforth. Wass 2m*

Enjoyable home cooking in friendly family-run village inn

In the shadow of the Hambleton Hills, this white-painted village pub dates from the 17th century and was built using stones from the ruins of nearby Byland Abbey. One of the two oak-beamed, flagstone-floored bars has a huge inglenook fireplace, the other a wood-burning stove, and the atmosphere is relaxed and informal; popular with locals, walkers and cyclists, all can be found here enjoying a pint of Black Sheep Best Bitter. Modern British meals with a South African twist are prepared from high quality produce — sourced locally as far as possible. There's a great selection of sandwiches at lunchtime and for dinner choose one of the Wombwell classics — steak, mushroom and Guinness pie; or try the South African bobotie — mild and fruity curry with mango chutney. Leave room for one of the comforting home-made desserts, or a plate of local cheeses.

Open all wk 12-3 6-11 (Sat 12-11 Sun 12-10.30) **Food** Lunch Mon-Fri 12-2, Fri-Sat 12-2.30, Sun 12-3 Dinner Mon-Thu 6-8.30, Fri-Sat 6-9, Sun 6-8 Av main course £12 Set menu available ⊕ FREE HOUSE ◖ Black Sheep Best Bitter, Guest ales. ♚ 10 **Facilities** Non-diners area ❤ (Bar Outside area) ◗ Children's menu Children's portions Outside area ⊓ Parking WiFi ⛟ (notice required)

Silver Stars The AA Silver Star rating denotes a Hotel or B&B that we highly recommend. They have a superior level of quality within their star rating, high standards of hospitality, service and cleanliness.

WELBURN   Map 19 SE76

The Crown and Cushion

tel: 01653 618777 **YO60 7DZ**
email: enquiries@thecrownandcushionwelburn.com
web: www.thecrownandcushionwelburn.com
dir: A64 from York towards Malton. 13m left to Welburn

Traditional stone-built inn serving quality Yorkshire produce

Exposed stone walls and open log fires characterise the comfortable interior of this spacious yet homely village inn. It boasts a traditional tap room, a bar serving York Guzzler ale, and three separate dining areas. Menus are based on carefully sourced local produce, including Waterford Farm Limousin and Charolais beef hung for 40 days. So expect top quality steaks and the likes of oxtail cottage pie; four-hour rotisserie pork with apricot and raisin stuffing; and beer battered haddock and chips. At the rear, a tiered terrace offers superb views. An ideal stop before or after visiting Castle Howard a mile down the road.

Open all wk 12-3 5-11 (Fri-Sun all day from noon) **Food** Lunch Mon-Sat 12-2.30, Sun 12-4 Dinner Mon-Sat 5.30-9.30, Sun 4-8 ⊕ FREE HOUSE ◀ Black Sheep, York Guzzler ♂ Symonds. **Facilities** Non-diners area ♦ Children's menu Children's portions Garden ⊓ Parking WiFi ➡ (notice required)

WEST TANFIELD   Map 19 SE27

The Bruce Arms   `PICK OF THE PUBS`

tel: 01677 470325 **Main St HG4 5JJ**
email: halc123@yahoo.co.uk
dir: On A6108 between Ripon & Masham

Peaceful village inn with enticing home cooking

This homely pub sits at the heart of the pretty village of West Tanfield, which stands beside a languorous loop of the River Ure. The cathedral city of Ripon, Fountains Abbey and the famous spa at Harrogate are within easy reach and it's also handy for the glorious, undiscovered countryside of nearby Nidderdale Area of Outstanding Natural Beauty. The stone-built inn's interior is a comfy mix of traditional village pub, complete with beams, log fires and good Yorkshire-brewed ales such as Black Sheep. The contemporary bistro complements the stylish, modern European cooking of highly experienced chef-patron Hugh Carruthers. There's a regularly changing menu, formulated to make the most of locally available seasonal produce; home in on a starter of smoked haddock and prawn fishcake with cucumber, yogurt and

mint, leading to coq au vin with mash and spring greens; or ham hock, Savoy cabbage, white beans, boiled potatoes and parsley.

Open 12-2.30 6-9.30 (Sun 12-3.30) Closed 2wks Feb, Mon **Food** Lunch Tue-Sat 12-2.30 Dinner Tue-Sat 6-7.30 Set menu available Restaurant menu available Tue-Sun ⊕ FREE HOUSE ◀ Black Sheep Best Bitter, Guest ales ♂ Aspall. ♟ 10 **Facilities** Non-diners area ♣ (Bar Outside area) ♦ Children's portions Outside area ⊓ Parking

WEST WITTON   Map 19 SE08

The Wensleydale Heifer ★★★★★ RR ⊛ `PICK OF THE PUBS`

tel: 01969 622322 **Main St DL8 4LS**
web: www.wensleydaleheifer.co.uk
dir: A1 to Leeming Bar junct, A684 towards Bedale for approx 10m to Leyburn, then towards Hawes, 3.5m to West Witton

Stylish all-rounder

Built in 1631, this white-painted coaching inn is right in the heart of the Yorkshire Dales National Park. For a morning coffee, head for the Whisky Lounge, where you can indeed also enjoy a malt whisky, or a pint of Heifer Gold or Black Sheep real ale, if you prefer. Of the two dining areas the Fish Bar, with sea-grass flooring, wooden tables and rattan chairs, is the less formal, while the restaurant, which leads to the garden, is furnished with chocolate leather chairs and linen table cloths, and decorated with distinctive artworks by international artist, Doug Hyde. Whichever room you choose, the food is AA Rosette-quality; banana leaf baked Scottish salmon, Whitby crab, Thai peanut curry sauce and buttered rice; a whole menu of lobster dishes; and daily specials that might feature roast farm chicken with butter mash and Savoy cabbage.

Open all day all wk **Food** Lunch all wk 12.30-2.30 Dinner all wk 6-9.30 Set menu available Restaurant menu available all wk ⊕ FREE HOUSE ◀ Heifer Gold, Black Sheep ♂ Aspall. ♟ **Facilities** Non-diners area ♣ (Bar Garden) ♦ Children's menu Children's portions Garden ⊓ Parking WiFi ➡ **Rooms** 13

WHITBY   Map 19 NZ81

The Magpie Café

tel: 01947 602058 **14 Pier Rd YO21 3PU**
email: ian@magpiecafe.co.uk
dir: Phone for detailed directions

Fish-focussed in every way

The acclaimed Magpie Café has been the home of North Yorkshire's 'best-ever fish and chips' since the late 1930s. You could pop in for just a pint of Cropton, but the excellent views of the harbour from the dining room, together with the prospect of fresh, sustainably fished seafood, could prove too much of a temptation. An exhaustive list of fish and seafood dishes is offered daily; perhaps Whitby crab pâté with French bread and home-made chutney and then seafood paella, or your choice of fish simply battered and served with chips. Desserts include classics like sherry trifle or spotted dick.

Open all day all wk 11.30-9 summer (11.30-8 winter) Closed 6-31 Jan, 25 Dec **Food** Contact pub for food times ⊕ FREE HOUSE ◀ Bradfield Farmers Blonde, Brown Cow, Cropton Blackout & Scoresby Stout, The Captain Cook Slipway. ♟ 10 **Facilities** ♦ Children's menu Children's portions WiFi ➡

WOMBLETON

Map 19 SE68

NEW The Plough Inn

tel: 01751 431356 **Main St YO62 7RW**
email: ploughinnwombleton@mail.com **web:** www.theploughinnatwombleton.co.uk
dir: *From A170 between Helmsley & Kirkbymoorside follow signs to Wombleton*

A successful new venture

When he retired, the landlord bought this local, built a complete new kitchen and renovated the rest of it. Today the traditional warm and genuine Yorkshire hospitality continues, with the serving of fine ales and good food – a tradition started in the 15th century when monks brewed beer for weary travellers. Local produce features in the menus, which change seasonally. Starters may include salad of black pudding with poached egg and hollandaise sauce. The main courses range from roast rack of local lamb, shepherd's pie, pea purée and dauphinoise potatoes; to slow-braised belly pork with crackling, mustard mash and apple gravy.

The Plough Inn

Open 12-3 5.30-12 (Mon 5-12 Fri-Sun all day) Closed Mon L **Food** Lunch Tue-Sat 12-2, Sun 12-8 Dinner Mon-Sat 5.30-9, Sun 12-8 Av main course £10 Restaurant menu available all wk ⊕ FREE HOUSE ◼ Black Sheep Best Bitter, Theakston Best Bitter ☼ Symonds. **Facilities** Non-diners area ♣ (Bar Outside area) ♦ Children's menu Children's portions Outside area ⊼ Parking WiFi ▭ (notice required)

YORK

Map 16 SE65

Blue Bell

PICK OF THE PUBS

tel: 01904 654904 **53 Fossgate YO1 9TF**
email: robsonhardie@aol.com
dir: *In city centre*

Quaint city pub that's tucked away

Its slimline frontage is easy to miss, but don't walk past this charming pub – the smallest in York – which has been serving customers in the ancient heart of the city for 200 years. In 1903 it was given a typical Edwardian makeover, and since then almost nothing has changed – so the Grade II listed interior still includes varnished wall and ceiling panelling, cast-iron tiled fireplaces, and charming old settles. The layout is original too, with the taproom at the front and the snug down a long corridor at the rear, both with servery hatches. The only slight drawback is that the pub's size leaves no room for a kitchen, so don't expect anything more complicated than lunchtime sandwiches. However, there's a good selection of real ales: no fewer than seven are usually on tap, including rotating guests. The pub has won awards for its efforts in fund-raising.

Open all day all wk **Food** Lunch Mon-Sat 12-2.30 ⊕ PUNCH TAVERNS ◀ Timothy Taylor Landlord, Bradfield Farmers Blonde, Roosters Yankee ♂ Thatchers Heritage. ♀ 21 **Facilities** Non-diners area ♣ (Bar Restaurant) WiFi **Notes** ⊜

The Judge's Lodging ★★★★★ INN ◉

tel: 01904 638733 **9 Lendal YO1 8AQ**
web: www.judgeslodgingyork.co.uk
dir: *Phone for detailed directions*

Seasonal menu amidst period splendour

Iron-railed steps sweep up to the grand entrance to this former assize court, set off one of York's old town web of narrow lanes and byways. Owning brewery Thwaites carefully and tastefully upgraded this Grade I listed building, incorporating the vaulted cellar bar and secluded cask bar into a stunning period interior. The tree-shaded terrace to the front is a popular place to dine alfresco, selecting from a contemporary, seasonally adjusted menu. Fish pie; home-made lamb hotpot; or duck leg confit, chorizo and butter bean casserole may take the eye here; there's also a good range of small plate dishes and sharing boards.

The Judge's Lodging

Open all day all wk **Food** Lunch Mon-Sat 12-11, Sun 12-10 Dinner Mon-Sat 12-11, Sun 12-10 Set menu available ⊕ THWAITES INNS OF CHARACTER ◀ Wainwright & Lancaster Bomber ♂ Kingstone Press. ♀ 15 **Facilities** Non-diners area ♦ Children's menu Children's portions Garden ⌇ WiFi **Rooms** 23

See advert on page 581

Lamb & Lion Inn ★★★★ INN ◉◉

tel: 01904 612078 **2-4 High Petergate YO1 7EH**
email: gm@lambandlionyork.com **web:** www.lambandlionyork.com
dir: *From York Station, turn left. Stay in left lane, over Lendal Bridge. At lights left (Theatre Royal on right). At next lights pub on right under Bootham Bar (medieval gate)*

Right in the city's historical centre

This rambling Georgian inn has unrivalled views of nearby York Minster from its elevated beer garden. Conjoined to the medieval Bootham Bar gateway, it is furnished and styled in keeping with its grand heritage. A warren of snugs and corridors radiate from a bar which stocks a challenging array of beers; Great Heck Golden Mane is brewed especially for the inn. Equally enticing is the menu. Here you'll find comforting classics ranging from beer-battered fish to steak and ale pie; or more complex cooking in dishes such as duo of spring lamb, or basil and parmesan gnocchi.

Open all day all wk **Food** Lunch Mon-Sat 12-9, Sun 12-8 Dinner Mon-Sat 12-9, Sun 12-8 Av main course £11 Set menu available ⊕ FREE HOUSE ◀ Great Heck Golden Mane, Black Sheep Best Bitter, Copper Dragon Golden Pippin, Timothy Taylor Landlord. ♀ 10 **Facilities** Non-diners area ♣ (Bar Restaurant Garden) ♦ Children's menu Children's portions Garden ⌇ WiFi ⛬ **Rooms** 12

Lysander Arms

tel: 01904 640845 **Manor Ln, Shipton Rd YO30 5TZ**
email: christine@lysanderarms.co.uk
dir: *Phone for detailed directions*

British menu and a good range of beers

The pub stands on the former RAF Clifton airfield, where Westland Lysander aircraft were based until 1942. The long, fully air-conditioned bar incorporates a pool table, dartboard and large-screen TVs. Restaurant meals range from pan-seared pigeon breast with pickled brambles, spiced ginger waffle and pear purée; and blackened Cajun king prawns with coriander mayo and cherry tomato salad, to chargrilled gammon steak with fresh pineapple, beer-battered onion rings and hand-cut chips; and prime steak pie with button mushrooms, buttered carrots and redcurrant jus. A beer and cider festival takes place over the Early May Bank Holiday weekend.

Open all day all wk **Food** Lunch Tue-Sat 12-2, Sun 12-3 Dinner Tue-Sat 5.30-9 Restaurant menu available Tue-Sat ⊕ FREE HOUSE ◀ Sharp's Doom Bar, York Guzzler, Wychwood Hobgoblin, Copper Dragon, Black Sheep, Theakston, Roosters ♂ Rekorderlig. ♀ 8 **Facilities** Non-diners area ♣ (Bar Garden) ♦ Children's menu Children's portions Play area Garden ⌇ Beer festival Cider festival Parking WiFi

SOUTH YORKSHIRE

BRADFIELD
Map 16 SK29

The Strines Inn

tel: 0114 285 1247 **Bradfield Dale S6 6JE**
email: thestrinesinn@yahoo.co.uk
dir: *N off A57 between Sheffield & Manchester*

Popular free house overlooking Strines Reservoir

Although built as a manor house in 1275, most of the structure is 16th century; it has been an inn since 1771 – the public rooms contain artefacts from its bygone days. The name apparently means 'meeting of waters' in Old English. Locally brewed Bradfield Farmers Bitter shares bar space with ambassadors from the further-flung Marston's, Jennings and Wychwood. Traditional home-made food begins with sandwiches and salads, then by way of the Pie of the Day, and giant Yorkshire puddings arrives at the mammoth mixed grill; lasagne verdi; macaroni cheese; and home-made butter bean stew. Salads, jacket potatoes and burgers are also on the menu. A play area and an enclosure for peacocks, geese and chickens are outside.

Open all wk 10.30-3 5.30-11 (Sat-Sun 10.30am-11pm; all day Apr-Oct) Closed 25 Dec **Food** Lunch Mon-Fri 12-2.30, Sat-Sun 12-9 (summer all wk 12-9) Dinner Mon-Fri 5.30-9, Sat-Sun 12-9 (summer all wk 12-9) Av main course £9.25 ⊕ FREE HOUSE ◖ Marston's Pedigree, Jennings Cocker Hoop, Bradfield Farmers Bitter, Wychwood Hobgoblin. ☗ 10 **Facilities** Non-diners area ✿ (Bar Restaurant Garden) ◗ Children's menu Children's portions Play area Garden ♬ Parking ➡ (notice required)

CADEBY
Map 16 SE50

The Cadeby Pub & Restaurant

tel: 01709 864009 **Main St DN5 7SW**
email: info@cadebyinn.co.uk
dir: *A1(M) junct 37, A635 towards Rotherham. Follow Cadeby signs*

Mid 18th-century village destination pub

The Cadeby stands well back, buffered from the village's main street by a lovely long lawn with tables. Yorkshire-brewed real ales are usually Timothy Taylor Landlord and Black Sheep (plus weekly changing guest ales from the area), while Old Rosie is on cider duty. Snacks and light meals are available at lunchtime; and the evening à la carte menus showcase seasonal dishes prepared in house from the best locally sourced ingredients. Typical choices might be home-made oxtail ravioli; and assiette of local lamb – soused rump, rosemary marinated rack lamb and slow-braised shoulder.

Open all wk all wk **Food** Contact pub for food times Set menu available Restaurant menu available ⊕ FREE HOUSE ◖ Timothy Taylor Landlord, Black Sheep. Guest ales ♂ Westons Old Rosie & Stowford Press. ☗ 12 **Facilities** Non-diners area ✿ (Bar Garden) ◗ Children's portions Garden ♬ Beer festival Cider festival Parking WiFi ➡

PENISTONE
Map 16 SE20

Cubley Hall
PICK OF THE PUBS

tel: 01226 766086 **Mortimer Rd, Cubley S36 9DF**
email: info@cubleyhall.co.uk
dir: *M1 junct 37, A628 towards Manchester, or M1 junct 35a, A616. Hall just S of Penistone*

Impressive building with fascinating history

On the edge of the Peak District National Park, Cubley Hall was built as a farm in the 18th century and became a gentleman's residence in Queen Victoria's reign. It later became a children's home before being transformed into pub in 1982. Following that the massive, oak-beamed bar was converted into the restaurant and furnished with old pine tables, chairs and church pews, and the building was extended to incorporate the hotel, which was designed to harmonise with the original mosaic floors, ornate plaster ceilings, oak panelling and stained glass. Food-wise, take your pick from light bites, chalkboard specials and an extensive main menu listing pub classics and home-made pizzas. Typically, choose from a classic lasagne; meat and potato pie; traditional fish and chips; and Mexican chilli con carne. The hall is reputedly haunted by Florence Lockley, who married there in 1904 and is affectionately known as Flo.

Open all day all wk 7am-11.30pm **Food** Lunch all wk 12-9 Dinner all wk 12-9 Av main course £10 Restaurant menu available Sun ⊕ FREE HOUSE ◖ Tetley's Bitter, Black Sheep Best Bitter ♂ Somersby Cider. **Facilities** Non-diners area ✿ (Garden) ◗ Children's menu Children's portions Play area Family room Garden ♬ Parking WiFi ➡ (notice required)

SHEFFIELD
Map 16 SK38

NEW Broadfield Ale House

tel: 0114 255 0200 **452 Abbeydale Rd S7 1FR**
email: info@thebroadfield.co.uk
dir: *Phone pub for detailed directions*

An ale house worthy of the name

Silent movie-goers and steam railway passengers were among the first customers at the Broadfield, built just before Queen Victoria died. Millhouses and Ecclesall station no longer exists, but this distinctive pub on the Abbeydale Road is still very much in business. No fewer than nine handles proffer the discerning ale enthusiast a wonderful choice, from the likes of Stancill, Acorn, Black Iris and Blackjack breweries. Pride is taken in the food too, with home-made sausages and pies served with hand-cut chips and mushy peas always in demand; coeliacs, vegans, vegetarians and fish-lovers are also well catered for.

Open all day all wk Closed 25 Dec **Food** Lunch all wk 12-10 Dinner all wk 12-10 ⊕ FREE HOUSE ◖ Rotating guest ales ♂ Westons Old Rosie. **Facilities** Non-diners area ✿ (Bar Garden) ◗ Children's menu Children's portions Garden ♬ Beer festival WiFi ➡ (notice required)

The Fat Cat
PICK OF THE PUBS

tel: 0114 249 4801 **23 Alma St S3 8SA**
email: info@thefatcat.co.uk
dir: *Phone for detailed directions*

Own Kelham Island beers in Victorian pub

Built in 1832, it was known as The Alma Hotel for many years, then in 1981 it was the first Sheffield pub to introduce guest beers. The policy continues, with constantly changing, mainly microbrewery, guests from across the country, two handpumped ciders, unusual bottled beers, Belgian pure fruit juices and British country wines. The pub's own Kelham Island Brewery accounts for at least four of the 11 traditional draught real ales. The smart interior is very much that of a traditional, welcoming back-street pub, with real fires making it feel very cosy, while outside is an attractive walled garden with Victorian-style lanterns and bench seating. Except on Sunday evenings, typical home-cooked from a simple weekly menu is broccoli cheddar pasta; Mexican mince and nachos; and savoury bean casserole. Events include the Monday quiz and curry night and annual beer festival.

Open all wk 12-11 (Fri-Sat 12-12) Closed 25 Dec **Food** Lunch Mon-Fri & Sun 12-3, Sat 12-8 Dinner Mon-Fri 6-8, Sat 12-8 ⊕ FREE HOUSE ◖ Timothy Taylor Landlord, Kelham Island Best Bitter & Pale Rider, Guest ales ♂ Thatchers Gold. **Facilities** Non-diners area ✿ (Bar Garden) ◗ Children's portions Family room Garden Beer festival Parking WiFi ➡

SHEFFIELD *continued*

Kelham Island Tavern
PICK OF THE PUBS

tel: 0114 272 2482 **62 Russell St S3 8RW**
email: lewiskelham@gmail.com
dir: *Just off A61 (inner ring road). Follow brown tourist signs for Kelham Island*

City pub with good reputation for its real ales

This 1830s backstreet pub was built to quench the thirst of steelmakers who lived and worked nearby, and in the hands of Lewis Gonda and Trevor Wraith it's become a gem of a busy traditional local. The pub is in a conservation and popular walking area, where old buildings have been converted into stylish apartments, and The Kelham Island Museum round the corner tells the story of the city's industrial heritage. The real ale list is formidable: four residents including Barnsley Bitter and Bradfield Farmers Blonde are joined by 10 ever-changing guests, as well as Westons Old Rosie cider, and a midsummer beer festival is held every year at the end of June. Good quality pub grub is available six days a week and includes a good veggie choice. Great in the summer, the pub has won awards for its beer garden and floral displays. Folk nights on Sundays and a quiz night on Mondays pack in the punters.

Open all day all wk 12-12 **Food** Lunch Mon-Sat 12-3 Av main course £6 ⊕ FREE HOUSE ◀ Barnsley Bitter, Bradfield Farmers Blonde, Pictish Brewers Gold, 10 guest ales Ò Westons Old Rosie & Country Perry. **Facilities** Non-diners area ❤ (Bar Garden) ♦♦ Children's portions Family room Garden ╤ Beer festival Cider festival Parking ▭ (notice required)

The Sheffield Tap

tel: 0114 273 7558 **Platform 1B, Sheffield Station, Sheaf St S1 2BP**
email: info@sheffieldtap.com
dir: *Access from Sheaf St & from Platform 1B. (NB limited access from Platform 1B on Fri & Sat)*

Very much on track to serve the best beers

For more than 30 years disused and derelict, the former Edwardian refreshment room and dining rooms of Sheffield Midland Railway Station have become a much praised Grade II listed free house. Painstakingly restored to its former glory by the current custodians, with help from the Railway Heritage Trust, The Sheffield Tap is now a beer mecca with its own on-site microbrewery allowing customers to view the complete brewing process while supping a pint or two in comfort. There's 10 real ales, one real cider, 12 keg products and more than 200 bottled beers from around the world. Food is limited to bagged bar snacks, and children are welcome until 8pm every day.

Open all day all wk Closed 25-26 Dec, 1 Jan **Food** Contact pub for food times ⊕ FREE HOUSE ◀ Tapped Brew Company Ò Thistly Cross. **Facilities** Non-diners area ❤ (Bar Restaurant Outside area) ♦♦ Outside area WiFi ▭ (notice required)

▌ **TOTLEY** Map 16 SK37

The Cricket Inn
PICK OF THE PUBS

tel: 0114 236 5256 **Penny Ln S17 3AZ**
email: cricket@brewkitchen.co.uk
dir: *Follow A621 from Sheffield, 8m. Right into Hillfoot Rd, 1st left into Penny Ln*

Popular gastro-pub well known for seafood and game dishes

Down a country lane bordered by wooded hills and pastures, this former farmhouse became a pub for the navvies building the nearby Totley railway tunnel in the late 1880s. Walkers and cyclists flock here, while dogs and children are made to feel welcome too. Chef Richard Smith co-runs it with the Thornbridge Brewery in Bakewell, which naturally enough provides the real ales. Richard's kitchen team under Marco Caires produces smoked haddock omelette with gruyère, leeks, asparagus and parsley potatoes; spinach, pine nut and ricotta risotto; escalope of

veal rump with Parma ham, fontina cheese, roast Tuscan vegetables, polenta mash and roast tomato sauce; and espetada, Marco's Portuguese signature dish featuring herby pieces of chargrilled sirloin steak. They also smoke their own fish and meats. For a dessert alternative, try a whole baked Barncliffe Yorkshire Brie – it's enough for two. Summer barbecues are held in the field behind the pub and cricket is played next door.

Open all day all wk 11-11 **Food** Lunch all wk 12-9.30 Dinner all wk 12-9.30 Av main course £15 Set menu available ⊕ FREE HOUSE/BREWKITCHEN LTD ◀ Thornbridge Wild Swan, Lord Marples, Jaipur Ò Thatchers Gold, Aspall. ☻ 10 **Facilities** Non-diners area ❤ (Bar Restaurant Garden) ♦♦ Children's menu Children's portions Garden ╤ Beer festival Parking WiFi ▭ (notice required)

WEST YORKSHIRE

▌ **ADDINGHAM** Map 19 SE04

The Fleece
PICK OF THE PUBS

See Pick of the Pubs on opposite page

▌ **BRADFORD** Map 19 SE13

New Beehive Inn

tel: 01274 721784 **171 Westgate BD1 3AA**
email: newbeehiveinn+21@btinternet.com
dir: *Phone for detailed directions*

Step back in time at an inn with lots of character

Dating from 1901 and centrally situated with many tourist attractions nearby, this classic Edwardian inn retains its period Arts and Crafts atmosphere with five separate bars and gas lighting. It is on the national inventory list of historic pubs. Outside, with a complete change of mood, you can relax in the Mediterranean-style courtyard. The pub offers a good range of unusual real ales, such as Salamander Mudpuppy and Abbeydale Moonshine, and a selection of over 100 malt whiskies, served alongside some simple bar snacks. Music fans should attend the cellar bar, which is open at weekends and features regular live bands.

Open all day all wk ⊕ FREE HOUSE ◀ Kelham Island Best Bitter, Abbeydale Moonshine, Salamander Mudpuppy, Ilkley Mary Jane, Saltaire Cascade Pale Ale Ò Westons Old Rosie. **Facilities** Non-diners area ♦♦ Family room Garden ╤ Parking WiFi ▭

▌ **CALVERLEY** Map 19 SE23

Calverley Arms

tel: 0113 255 7771 **Calverley Ln LS28 5QQ**
email: calverleyarmspudsey@vintageinn.co.uk
dir: *Phone for detailed directions*

Victorian country house in landscaped grounds

Pleasantly located in the gently rolling countryside of the Aire Valley, with the popular Leeds & Liverpool Canal just across the fields. This very substantial village-edge inn makes the most of its situation, with restful views from the leafy beer garden. The rustic theme continues inside, with lots of wood, brick and fireplaces, where Leeds Pale or York Yorkshire Terrier are the beers of choice. Part of the Vintage Inns group, the fare reflects their quality menus. Aromatic braised pork belly or slow-cooked game and blackberry pie should take the chill off a bracing Yorkshire day.

Open all day all wk **Food** Lunch all wk 12-10 Dinner all wk 12-10 Set menu available Restaurant menu available all wk ⊕ MITCHELLS & BUTLERS ◀ Leeds Pale, York Yorkshire Terrier. ☻ **Facilities** Non-diners area ♦♦ Children's menu Children's portions Garden Outside area ╤ Parking WiFi ▭ (notice required)

PICK OF THE PUBS

The Fleece

ADDINGHAM   Map 19 SE04

tel: 01943 830491
154 Main St LS29 0LY
email: info@fleeceinnaddingham.co.uk
web: www.fleeceinnaddingham.co.uk
dir: *Between Ilkley & Skipton*

Real character, friendly service, tasty food

Close to where several well-tramped footpaths meet, this 17th-century coaching inn attracts many walkers. You'll see them supping their well-earned refreshments on the front terrace or throughout the interior of this welcoming hostelry, with children and dogs all adding to the friendly ambience. The stone-flagged bar has wooden settles, an enormous fireplace and real ales from Skipton's Saltaire Brewery and Black Sheep, among others. Modern British pub classics is the only phrase to describe the wholesome dishes on the menu, all prepared from local ingredients if possible. Expect starters such as crab millefeuille with tomato and red onion salsa and roasted red pepper purée; or chicken pistachio terrine with grilled peach. Abundant flavours continue in the main courses: examples are sea bass fillet with potato rösti and pea and mint fricassée; and confit pork belly with chargrilled celeriac and an apple and cider purée. Sunday lunch at The Fleece is hugely popular, with fixed price

menus promising great value. Start with The Fleece fishcake, market-fresh fish in buttery mash with samphire, soft herbs and tomato salsa; or a wild mushroom Scotch egg served with home-made piccalilli. Next comes the roast: choose between topside of beef, leg of lamb or glazed ham; they are all served with duck fat potatoes, Yorkshire pudding and proper gravy. Traditional desserts may include sticky toffee pudding sundae with Chantilly cream; or lemon posset with shortbread and fruit compôte. A covered courtyard makes a natural suntrap in summer, ideal for barbecues or a bottle of chilled white wine. The deli next door stocks many of the pub's raw ingredients, as well as Ilkley bottled beers such as the sought-after Mary Jane range.

Open all day all wk 12-11 (Sun 12-10.30) **Food** Lunch Mon-Sat 12-2.15, Sun 12-8 Dinner Mon-Sat 5-9, Sun 12-8 Av main course £14 Set menu available ⊕ PUNCH TAVERNS ◀ Timothy Taylor Landlord, Black Sheep, Ilkley, Saltaire ♂ Thatchers. � 30 **Facilities** Non-diners area ❀ (Bar Garden) ♟ Children's menu Children's portions Play area Garden ⊼ Parking WiFi 🚌 (notice required)

Shibden Mill Inn

Shibden Mill Fold, Shibden, Halifax, West Yorkshire HX3 7UL • **Tel:** 01422 365840 • Fax: 01422 362971
Website: www.shibdenmillinn.com • **Email:** enquiries@shibdenmillinn.com

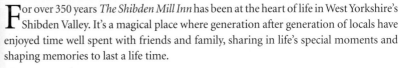

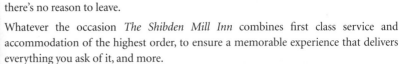

For over 350 years *The Shibden Mill Inn* has been at the heart of life in West Yorkshire's Shibden Valley. It's a magical place where generation after generation of locals have enjoyed time well spent with friends and family, sharing in life's special moments and shaping memories to last a life time.

The Inn's reputation for warm hospitality, premier gastro dining and first class accommodation draws people to the Shibden Valley from far and wide, and the Mill has naturally become a popular choice for those wishing to savour a sumptuous weekend break or mid-week stay.

Stunning countryside walks are in easy reach, as too the bright lights and city centre shopping on offer in Leeds. From its unique location, *The Shibden Mill Inn* offers easy access to the very best to be found in this delightful part of West Yorkshire. However there are those who during their stay simply wish to relax and unwind in the beautiful surrounds of this 17th Century property, where once you've arrived and unpacked, there's no reason to leave.

Whatever the occasion *The Shibden Mill Inn* combines first class service and accommodation of the highest order, to ensure a memorable experience that delivers everything you ask of it, and more.

Crowned Yorkshire's Favourite Pub • UK Food Pub of the Year

Inn of the Year • Sunday Lunch Pub of the Year

EMLEY

Map 16 SE21

The White Horse

tel: 01924 849823 **2 Chapel Ln HD8 9SP**
dir: *M1 junct 38, A637 towards Huddersfield. At rdbt left onto A636, then right to Emley*

The hub of the community

On the old coaching route to Huddersfield and Halifax on the edge of the village, this 18th-century pub has views towards Emley Moor Mast and the surrounding countryside. The pub, now in new hands, is popular with walkers, cyclists and locals — walking maps are available from the bar, which is warmed by a working Yorkshire range. Of the eight cask ales, four are permanent (including their own Ossett Brewery ales), and four are ever-rotating guests featuring microbreweries. A straightforward menu offers the likes of mushroom Stroganoff; chicken breast stuffed with Wensleydale; vegetable lasagne; and chorizo chicken with rice and salad. Look to the blackboards for daily specials and desserts.

Open all day all wk 12-11 **Food** Lunch all wk 12-9 Dinner all wk 12-9 ⊕ FREE HOUSE ◀ Ossett Excelsior & Silver King, Emley Cross, Yorkshire Blonde, Guest ales Ŏ Rotating guest ciders. ♀ 9 **Facilities** Non-diners area ♣ (Bar Garden) ♦ Children's portions Family room Garden ♬ Parking ☞ (notice required)

HALIFAX

Map 19 SE02

Shibden Mill Inn ★★★★★ INN ◉◉ **PICK OF THE PUBS**

See Pick of the Pubs on page 588 and advert on opposite page

HARTSHEAD

Map 16 SE12

The Gray Ox Inn

tel: 01274 872845 **15 Hartshead Ln WF15 8AL**
email: grayox@hotmail.co.uk
dir: *M62 junct 25, A644 signed Dewsbury. Take A62, branch left signed Hartshead & Moor Top/B6119. Left to Hartshead*

Pennine-fringe inn with great views and fine food

Originally a farmhouse that sold ale, this rural inn dating from 1709 occupies a commanding position overlooking the Calder Valley. Ales from Marston's, Jennings and a guest brewery are in the bar, where reminders of the pub's former life can be seen, in winter by the flickering light of the huge log fire. Fine locally-sourced dishes prepared by a five-strong kitchen team include Yorkshire Blue cheese and pear tartlet as a starter; Shipham House Farm trio of Yorkshire lamb cutlet, slow-braised shoulder and pan-seared liver; and roasted butternut squash gnocchi. Daily fish specials are also a fixture.

Open all wk 12-3.30 6-12 (Sun 12-10.30) **Food** Lunch Mon-Sat 12-2, Sun 12-7 Dinner Mon-Fri 6-9, Sat 6-9.30, Sun 12-7 Set menu available ⊕ MARSTON'S ◀ Jennings Cumberland Ale, Cocker Hoop & Sneck Lifter, Guest ale. ♀ 12 **Facilities** Non-diners area ♣ (Garden) ♦ Children's menu Children's portions Garden ♬ Parking WiFi ☞

HAWORTH

Map 19 SE03

NEW The Fleece Inn

tel: 01535 642172 **67 Main St BD22 8DA**
email: info@fleeceinnhaworth.co.uk
dir: *From B6142 in Haworth centre into Butt Ln. Left at T-junct into Main St*

Unchanging town stalwart in Brontë country

Solidly planted on the steep cobbled road in Haworth's old town, this gritstone inn dates from the days when the Brontë sisters were writing their novels in the village

vicarage. The enticing pub is owned by the Timothy Taylor Brewery; their award-winning Yorkshire beers as reliable as the steam trains on the famous heritage railway at the foot of the hill. Escape the hurly-burly and indulge in one of the pub's renowned home-made pies or maybe a fish butty: no-nonsense, filling fare (with some interesting starters) is the staple here. Each Monday evening the town's celebrated brass band practices upstairs.

Open all day all wk **Food** Lunch Mon-Fri 12-9, Sat 10-9, Sun 10am-noon (bkfst) 12-7 Dinner Mon-Fri 12-9, Sat 10-9, Sun 12-7 Av main course £9.95 Set menu available ⊕ TIMOTHY TAYLOR ◀ Landlord, Golden Best, Ram Tam & Boltmaker Ŏ Westons Stowford Press, Rekorderlig, Old Mout. ♀ 10 **Facilities** Non-diners area ♣ (Bar Restaurant Garden) ♦ Children's menu Children's portions Family room Garden ♬ WiFi ☞ (notice required)

The Old White Lion Hotel

tel: 01535 642313 **Main St BD22 8DU**
email: enquiries@oldwhitelionhotel.com
dir: *A629 onto B6142, 0.5m past Haworth Station*

Charming inn in the Brontë family's home town

This traditional family-run 300-year-old coaching inn looks down onto the cobbled Main Street of the famous Brontë town of Haworth. In the charming bar the ceiling beams are supported by timber posts, and locals appreciatively quaff their pints of guest ale. Food is taken seriously and 'dispensed with hospitality and good measure'. Bar snacks include baguettes, salads and jackets, while a meal in the Gimmerton Restaurant might include duck parcels with plum, spring onion and hoi sin chutney, followed by chicken and butternut squash roulade, or pan-fried duck breast, fondant potato and brandy, orange and cherry sauce. Vegetarians are well catered for.

Open all day all wk 11-11 (Sun 12-10.30) **Food** Lunch Mon-Fri 12-2.30, Sat-Sun all day Dinner Mon-Fri 6-9.30, Sat-Sun all day Set menu available Restaurant menu available all wk evenings only ⊕ FREE HOUSE ◀ Tetley's Bitter, John Smith's, Local guest ales. ♀ 9 **Facilities** Non-diners area ♦ Children's menu Children's portions Parking WiFi ☞

HOLMFIRTH

Map 16 SE10

Farmers Arms

tel: 01484 683713 **2-4 Liphill Bank Rd HD9 2LR**
email: farmersarms2@gmail.com
dir: *From Holmfirth take A635 (Greenfield Rd) on right signed Manchester. Left at Compo's Café. 2nd right into Liphill Bank Rd*

Great ales and home-cooked food

A small village pub run with pride by Sam Page and Danielle Montgomery, the Farmers Arms sits in typical *Last of the Summer Wine* country. There is a welcome emphasis on real ales, with an annual beer festival every autumn and regulars that include Timothy Taylor Landlord, Greene King IPA and Bradfield Farmers Blonde. The menu appeals too; settle by the log fire and enjoy fresh dishes prepared from scratch such as ham hock and guinea fowl terrine; stuffed chicken breast with Mexican cheese with patatas bravas; and apple crumble with custard.

Open Tue-Thu 12-3 5-12 (Fri-Sun 12-12 Mon 5-12) Closed Mon L **Food** Lunch Tue-Thu 12-2, Fri-Sat 12-3, Sun 12-8 Dinner Tue-Thu 6-9.30, Sat 5-9.30, Sun 12-8 ⊕ PUNCH TAVERNS ◀ Timothy Taylor Landlord, Bradfield Farmers Blonde, Greene King IPA, Guest ales Ŏ Thatchers Gold, Westons Wyld Wood Organic. ♀ 13 **Facilities** Non-diners area ♣ (Bar Garden) ♦ Children's portions Garden ♬ Beer festival Cider festival Parking WiFi ☞ (notice required)

PICK OF THE PUBS

Shibden Mill Inn ★★★★★ INN ✿✿

HALIFAX   Map 19 SE02

tel: 01422 365840
Shibden Mill Fold HX3 7UL
email: enquiries@shibdenmillinn.com
web: www.shibdenmillinn.com
dir: *From A58 into Kell Ln. 0.5m, left into Blake Hill*

Award-winning food in renovated corn mill

The Shibden Valley used to be an important wool production area, the waters of Red Beck powering this 17th-century, former spinning mill until the industry collapsed in the late 1800s. Now it's a charming inn, with open fires, oak beams, small windows and heavy tiles, happily enjoying a more civilised existence below overhanging trees in a wooded glen that makes Halifax just down the road seem a thousand miles away. The beer garden is extremely popular, not least with beer fans who come here to sample a real ale called Shibden Mill, brewed specially for the inn, Black Sheep or one of the three guest ales. With two AA Rosettes, the restaurant attracts those who enjoy food prepared from trusted local growers and suppliers, and a seasonal menu offering newly conceived dishes and old favourites. Two starters to consider might be partridge and chestnut pie, pickled red cabbage, cherry purée and grape chutney; or East Coast crab, beetroot, pickled carrot and courgette, burnt lime and crackers. Turn

over the page for possibilities such as mackerel and brown crab strudel, fennel, citrus butter and sweet potato purée; or Yorkshire Moor pheasant, black pudding, wild boar sausage, caramelised apple, creamed cabbage, cider sauce and game chips. Among the vegetarian choices you might find sweet potato and pumpkin seed risotto; and croquettes of Todmorden camembert and leeks. There's also a gourmet menu of Yorkshire artisan cheeses served with home-made chutney, oat biscuits, celery and Eccles cakes, ideally accompanied by a glass of vintage port. Gourmet diners are offered too. Stay overnight in one of the luxury bedrooms.

Open all day all wk Closed 25-26 Dec eve,1 Jan eve **Food** Bkfst Mon-Fri 7am-

10am Sat-Sun 8am-10am Lunch Mon-Thu 12-2, Fri-Sat 12-2.30, Sun 12-7.30 Dinner Mon-Thu 5.30-9, Fri 5.30-9.30, Sat 6-9.30, Sun 12-7.30 Av main course £16.50 Set menu, & restaurant menu available all wk ⊞ FREE HOUSE ◀ John Smith's, Black Sheep, Shibden Mill. ♀ 22 **Facilities** Non-diners area ♦♦ Children's & portions Garden ⊼ Parking WiFi **Rooms** 11

ILKLEY
Map 19 SE14

The Crescent Inn

tel: 01943 811250 **Brook St LS29 8DG**
email: manager@thecrescentinn.co.uk
dir: *On corner of A65 (Church St) & Brook St*

Vast range of local real ales here

Part of a hotel dating back to 1861, The Crescent is a landmark building in the centre of Ilkley and it shares the site with its sister restaurant next door. The pub blends original Victorian features such as an open fire with contemporary interiors including handcrafted furniture upholstered in local cloth. Choose from an ever-changing range of real ales from local breweries such as Saltaire or pick one of the 15 wines by the glass. Unpretentious and enjoyable dishes on the menu include pie of the day, home-made curry and steak-frites.

Open all day all wk **Food** Lunch Mon-Fri 12-3, Sat-Sun all day Dinner Mon-Fri 5.30-9, Sat-Sun all day ⊕ FREE HOUSE ◀ Saltaire Blonde, Crescent Gold, Copper Dragon Best Bitter, Leeds Pale, Guest ales. ☂ 15 **Facilities** Non-diners area ✿ (Bar Restaurant Outside area) ♦ Children's menu Children's portions Outside area ♠ WiFi ➤ (notice required)

Ilkley Moor Vaults

tel: 01943 607012 **Stockeld Rd LS29 9HD**
email: info@ilkleymoorvaults.co.uk
dir: *From Ilkley on A65 towards Skipton. Pub on right*

Proper pub, roaring fire, warm welcome

Known locally as The Taps, it sits at the start of the Dales Way above the old packhorse bridge across the River Wharfe. A popular and stylish establishment, it is equally good for a pint of real ale or a classic dish of pub food – expect the likes of beef and ale pie; a much prized rib of Lishman's beef for two; and home-made sticky toffee pudding with vanilla ice cream. An ever-changing specials board, full gluten-free menu, impressive children's menu and early bird deals complete the food offerings. A large function room caters for weddings and private parties.

Open 12-3 5-11 (Sat-Sun all day) Closed Mon (ex BHs) **Food** Lunch Tue-Sat 12-2.30, Sun 12-6 Dinner Tue-Sat 5.30-9 ⊕ STAR PUBS & BARS ◀ Timothy Taylor Landlord, Caledonian Deuchars IPA, Theakston Black Bull Bitter. ☂ 9 **Facilities** Non-diners area ✿ (Bar Restaurant Garden) ♦ Children's menu Children's portions Garden ♠ Parking WiFi ➤ (notice required)

KIRKBURTON
Map 16 SE11

The Woodman Inn ★★★★ INN

tel: 01484 605778 **Thunderbridge Ln HD8 0PX**
email: chris@woodman-inn.com **web:** www.woodman-inn.com
dir: *1.4m SW of Kirkburton. From Huddersfield take A629 towards Sheffield. Follow brown Woodman Inn signs*

Smart inn with proud Yorkshire provenance

Hidden in a charming hamlet of weavers' cottages in a secluded wooded valley, The Woodman Inn comes up trumps in any search for the perfect Yorkshire inn. Real ales are from county breweries, including the sublime Bradfield Farmers Blonde. Sup this in a long, cosy, log-fire warmed beamed room wrapped around the bar or in the restaurant, where rustic gastro-food makes the most of Yorkshire's produce. Featherblade and oxtail duo of beef, or the Yorkshire tapas sharing plate are just two dishes to try. Should you be loathe to leave, boutique-style bedrooms provide the perfect excuse for stopping over.

Open all day all wk **Food** Lunch Mon-Fri 12-2.30, Sat 12-4, Sun 12-7 Dinner Mon-Sat 5-9, Sun 12-7 ⊕ FREE HOUSE ◀ Small World, Bradfield Farmers Blonde. ☂ 14 **Facilities** Non-diners area ✿ (Bar Garden Outside area) ♦ Children's menu Children's portions Garden Outside area ♠ Parking WiFi ➤ (notice required) **Rooms** 13

LEEDS
Map 19 SE23

The Cross Keys
PICK OF THE PUBS

tel: 0113 243 3711 **107 Water Ln LS11 5WD**
email: info@the-crosskeys.com
dir: *0.5m from Leeds Station: right into Neville St, right into Water Ln. Pass Globe Rd, pub on left*

Robust food in a historic city centre pub

Hard to believe now but this historic landmark from the peak of Leeds' industrial history was closed in the 1980s and used as a tyre storage depot until it was restored in 2005. Built in 1802, The Cross Keys was a watering hole for local foundry workers and it's where steam engine inventor James Watt reputedly hired a room to spy on his competitor Matthew Murray. To learn Murray's trade secrets Watt bought drinks for foundry workers relaxing here after work. This city centre pub has a country pub atmosphere, with hand-pulled pints from local microbreweries complementing food recreated from long lost recipes for traditional British dishes. The best seasonal produce goes into dishes such as braised pig's cheek, mash, braised fennel and cider sauce, which might precede a main course of lamb belly with celeriac purée, celeriac fondant and roasted shallots.

Open all day all wk 12-11 (Fri-Sat 12-12 Sun 12-10.30) Closed 25-26 Dec, 1 Jan **Food** Lunch Mon-Sat 12-3, Sun 12-5 Dinner Mon-Sat 5.30-9.30 ⊕ FREE HOUSE ◀ Kirkstall, Rotating Guest ales Ŏ Aspall. ☂ 12 **Facilities** Non-diners area ✿ (Bar Restaurant Garden) ♦ Children's menu Children's portions Garden ♠ WiFi ➤

North Bar

tel: 0113 242 4540 **24 New Briggate LS1 6NU**
email: info@northbar.com
dir: *From rail station towards Corn Exchange, left into Briggate (main shopping area). At x-rds with The Headrow straight on into New Briggate. Bar 100mtrs on right*

Beers from around the world in upbeat atmosphere

This pioneering beer bar in the heart of Leeds is heaven for ale aficionados as it offers up to 130 bottled beers from around the globe at any one time, plus 16 draught beers. Yet, pride of place on the vast bar are hand-pumped beers from local microbreweries, notably Roosters ales. It's a trendy European-style bar, full of characters and great conversation, as well as a venue for music and local art exhibitions. Don't miss the regular beer festivals.

Open all day all wk 11am-2am (Sun 11am-mdnt Mon-Tue 11am-1am) Closed 25 Dec **Food** Lunch all wk 12-10 Dinner all wk 12-10 ⊕ FREE HOUSE ◀ Kirkstall, Roosters, Thornbridge, Buxton, Magic Rock Ŏ Pure North. **Facilities** Non-diners area ✿ (Bar) ♦ Beer festival Parking WiFi

---

LINTHWAITE
Map 16 SE11

The Sair Inn

tel: 01484 842370 **Lane Top HD7 5SG**
dir: *From Huddersfield take A62 (Oldham road) for 3.5m. Left just before lights at bus stop (in centre of road) into Hoyle Ing & follow sign*

Own-brewed ales and welcoming atmosphere

You won't be able to eat here, but this old hilltop alehouse has enough character in its four small rooms to make up for that; three are heated by hot Yorkshire ranges in winter. Landlord Ron Crabtree has brewed his own beers for over 33 years and they are much sought after by real ale aficionados. Imported German lagers are available, too. In summer the outside drinking area catches the afternoon sun and commands views across the Colne Valley.

Open all wk 5-11 (Sat 12-11 Sun 12-10.30) ⊕ FREE HOUSE ◀ Linfit Bitter, Special Bitter, Gold Medal, Autumn Gold, Old Eli Ŏ Pure North Original. **Facilities** Non-diners area ✿ (Bar Outside area) ♦ Outside area WiFi ➤ (notice required)

LINTON
Map 16 SE34

The Windmill Inn ★★★★ INN

tel: 01937 582209 **Main St LS22 4HT**
email: enquiries@thewindmillinnlinton.co.uk **web:** www.thewindmillinnlinton.co.uk
dir: *From A1 exit at Tadcaster/Otley junct, follow Otley signs. In Collingham follow Linton signs*

Historic pub with a diverse menu

Once the home of a long-forgotten miller, this pleasant village pub is made up of small beamed rooms that have been stripped back to bare stone, presumably the original 14th-century walls. A coaching inn since the 18th century, polished antique settles, log fires, oak beams and copper-topped cast-iron tables set the scene in which to enjoy good pub food in the bar or restaurant. A sample dinner menu features starters like chicken liver parfait with toast and plum and apple chutney; and warm pork and apple tart; then mains such as slow-roasted pork belly with black pudding mash and apple jus; or harissa chicken with salad, coleslaw and warm pitta bread. A beer festival is held in July. The Windmill also offers two spacious boutique bed and breakfast apartments.

Open all wk 11-3 5.30-11 (Fri-Sat 11-11 Sun 12-10.30) Closed 1 Jan **Food** Lunch Mon-Fri 12-2, Sat 12-9, Sun 12-5.45 Dinner Sat 12-9 ⊕ HEINEKEN ◀ Theakston Best Bitter, Caledonian, John Smith's. ♚ 12 **Facilities** Non-diners area ❖ (Bar Garden) ♦❙ Children's menu Children's portions Garden ⊼ Beer festival Parking WiFi ⛟ (notice required) **Rooms** 2

MARSDEN
Map 16 SE01

The Olive Branch

tel: 01484 844487 **Manchester Rd HD7 6LU**
email: eat@olivebranch.uk.com
dir: *On A62 between Marsden & Slaithwaite, 6m from Huddersfield*

Highly regarded brasserie-style food

Enter this traditional 19th-century inn on a former packhorse route above the River Colne and the Huddersfield Canal and you'll find yourself in a rambling series of rooms, fire-warmed in winter. The restaurant's brasserie-style food is exemplified by starters of parfait of chicken livers, and wood pigeon with garlic risotto and chocolate sauce, while typical main dishes include Gressingham duck breast, Chateaubriand to share, and pan-fried medallions of venison. The beef (proudly sourced from Yorkshire farms) is aged for up to 50 days. Enjoy a pint of Greenfield Dobcross Bitter from Saddleworth on the sun deck and admire the views of Marsden Moor Estate.

Open Tue-Sat 5.30pm-11pm (Sun 12-10.30) Closed Mon eve **Food** Lunch Sun 12-8 Dinner Tue-Sat 6.30-9, Sun 12-8 Restaurant menu available Tue-Sat ⊕ FREE HOUSE ◀ Greenfield Dobcross Bitter & Ale, Nook. ♚ 12 **Facilities** Non-diners area ♦❙ Children's menu Children's portions Garden ⊼ Parking WiFi

Find out more about the AA's accommodation rating schemes on page 8

RIPPONDEN
Map 16 SE01

Old Bridge Inn

tel: 01422 822595 **Priest Ln HX6 4DF**
email: tim@theoldbridgeinn.co.uk **web:** www.theoldbridgeinn.co.uk
dir: *In village centre by church*

Probably West Yorkshire's oldest hostelry

An inn has stood by Ripponden's old bridge, and even earlier ford, since at least 1307. The lower bar is of cruck-frame construction, and the top bar retains its wattle and daub walls, partly later encased in stone. In addition to Timothy Taylor real ales, including Ram Tam and two guests, 14 wines are offered by the glass. Expect main courses like smoked haddock and spinach pancakes; pan-fried chicken on a chorizo, red onion and sweet pepper cassoulet; and crisp belly pork roulade on colcannon mash, with parsnip and cider gravy. Seating outside overlooks the River Ryburn. Booking for meals is recommended.

Open all wk 12-3 5.30-11 (Fri-Sat 12-11.30 Sun 12-10.30) Closed 25 Dec **Food** Lunch Mon-Sat 12-2, Sun 12-4 Dinner Mon-Sat 6.30-9.30 ⊕ FREE HOUSE ◀ Timothy Taylor Landlord, Golden Best, Best Bitter, Ram Tam, Rotating Guest ales ♻ Aspall Harry Sparrow. ♚ 14 **Facilities** Non-diners area ♦❙ Children's portions Garden Outside area ⊼ Parking WiFi

SHELLEY
Map 16 SE21

The Three Acres Inn
PICK OF THE PUBS

tel: 01484 602606 **HD8 8LR**
email: info@3acres.com
dir: *From Huddersfield take A629 then B6116, turn left for village*

Welcoming old drovers' inn with a reputation for good food

Established in the late 1960s by the Ormes and Trueloves, this old drovers' inn is tucked away in the rolling green countryside of the Pennines. An ideal stopping off place for travellers heading north to the Yorkshire Dales, the pub has built a reputation for good quality food and a welcoming atmosphere. The spacious interior has a traditional feel with exposed beams and large fireplaces. On summer evenings, sit out on the deck with a pint of Black Sheep (to remind you of the drovers) or a glass of wine and soak up the fabulous views. The food served in both bar and restaurant successfully fuses traditional English with international influences. A typical three-course meal might be French onion soup; curried spatchcock of Wortley pheasant; and stem ginger and date pudding. A wide range of lighter meals, grills, rotisserie chickens and sandwiches makes a great lunchtime alternative.

Open all wk 12-3 6-11 (Fri-Sat 12-3 5-11) Closed 1 Jan eve, 25-26 Dec eve, 31 Dec L **Food** Lunch all wk 12-2 Dinner Sun-Thu 6.30-9.30, Fri-Sat 5.30-9.30 Av main course £15 Set menu available Restaurant menu available all wk ⊕ FREE HOUSE ◀ Timothy Taylor Landlord, Black Sheep, Copper Dragon, Bradfield Farmers Blonde, Small World. ♚ 19 **Facilities** ♦❙ Children's portions Garden ⊼ Parking WiFi

SOWERBY BRIDGE
Map 16 SE02

The Alma Inn

tel: 01422 823334 **Cotton Stones HX6 4NS**
email: info@almainn.co.uk
dir: *Exit A58 at Triangle between Sowerby Bridge & Ripponden. Follow signs for Cotton Stones*

Country inn with home-cooked Italian food

An old stone inn set in a dramatically beautiful location at Cotton Stones with stunning views of the Ryburn Valley. Outside seating can accommodate 200 customers, while the interior features stone-flagged floors and real fires. The cosy bar serves several ales including a guest, and a vast selection of Belgian bottled beers, each with its individual glass. The appeal of the restaurant area revolves around the wood-burning pizza oven which is on display, the only one in the Calderdale area.

Open all day all wk 12-10.30 **Food** Lunch Mon-Thu 12-10, Fri-Sat 12-10.30, Sun 12-9 Dinner Mon-Thu 12-10, Fri-Sat 12-10.30, Sun 12-9 ⊕ FREE HOUSE ◀ Timothy Taylor Landlord & Golden Best, Tetley's Bitter, Guest ales. ₹ 10
Facilities Non-diners area ✿ (Bar Garden) ◀ Children's portions Garden ⋒ Beer festival Parking WiFi ⛟ (notice required)

THORNTON
Map 19 SE03

Ring O'Bells Country Pub & Restaurant PICK OF THE PUBS

tel: 01274 832296 **212 Hilltop Rd BD13 3QL**
email: enquiries@theringobells.com
dir: *From M62 take A58 for 5m, right onto A644. 4.5m follow Denholme signs, into Well Head Rd into Hilltop Rd*

Dining pub in 'Wuthering Heights' country

The Brontë sisters and their brother were born, christened and lived for a while in Thornton, where their father was rector. With 40-mile views over the Pennines, this former Wesleyan chapel met the spiritual needs of its congregation of weavers. Today's rather more secular operation has been in Ann and Clive Preston's hands for more than 20 accolade-full years. Copper Dragon Golden Pippin is one of the popular ales pulled at the bar, where wood-panelled walls are decorated with prints of the village in the 1920s. Contemporary art is on display in the Brontë Restaurant, a full-length conservatory with glorious valley views. The traditional British menu is interspersed with modern continental dishes: salt and chilli calamari with rocket and red pepper jam salad and lime mayonnaise is a good example. The grill furnishes steaks and gammon served with hand-cut chips, roasted tomatoes, mushrooms and beer-battered onion rings; and chargrilled chicken breast, Caesar salad, crispy bacon, parmesan and croûtons.

Open all wk 11.30-4 5.30-11.30 (Sat-Sun 11.30-4 6.15-11.30) Closed 25 Dec
Food Lunch all wk 12-2 Dinner Mon-Fri 5.30-9.30, Sat-Sun 6.15-9 Set menu available ⊕ FREE HOUSE ◀ John Smith's, Black Sheep, Copper Dragon Golden Pippin, Timothy Taylor Landlord ♉ Kopparberg. ₹ 12 **Facilities** Non-diners area ◀ Children's menu Children's portions Parking WiFi ⛟ (notice required)

CHANNEL ISLANDS

GUERNSEY

CASTEL
Map 24

Fleur du Jardin PICK OF THE PUBS

tel: 01481 257996 **Kings Mills GY5 7JT**
email: info@fleurdujardin.com
dir: *2.5m from town centre*

Gastro-pub food with strong island provenance

This magnificent granite and golden stone property has slumbered in the peaceful Guernsey countryside for over 500 years, and curiously, its name comes from a long-gone Guernsey champion cow. The hotel's heritage is long, and the ambience of past centuries remains evident in the wooden beams, old fireplaces and stone features as well as a low-ceiling, character bar area. Such seasoned charm is matched by contemporary decor and design, producing a chic vibe for those seeking good Channel Islands' dining. Being so close to the coast, fresh seafood features strongly on the menu, with catch of the day perhaps included in the fish pie. Meat eaters are not short-changed either; the pork dishes may derive from pigs that are played soothing music during their local farm upbringing! Sun worshippers making the short walk from Vazon Bay can refresh themselves with beers from both island and mainland microbreweries or hand-crafted cider from a local farm producer.

Open all day all wk **Food** Lunch all wk 12-2 Dinner all wk 6-9 Av main course £14 Set menu available Restaurant menu available all wk ⊕ FREE HOUSE ◀ Arundel, Liberation Guernsey Sunbeam, Fuller's London Pride, Goose Eye Wonkey Donkey, Sharp's Doom Bar, Guest ales ♉ Rocquette. ₹ 12 **Facilities** Non-diners area ✿ (Bar Restaurant Garden) ◀ Children's menu Children's portions Garden ⋒ Parking WiFi ⛟ (notice required)

ST PETER PORT
Map 24

The Pickled Pig ★★★ HL

tel: 01481 721431 **Duke of Normandie Hotel, Lefebvre St GY1 2JP**
email: enquiries@dukeofnormandie.com **web:** www.dukeofnormandie.com
dir: *From harbour rdbt into St Julians Av, 3rd left into Anns Place, continue to right, up hill, left into Lefebvre St, archway entrance on right*

Maritime theme and good pub dishes

Part of the Duke of Normandie Hotel, this newly refurbished bar with a new name attracts a happy mix of Guernsey locals and hotel residents. You can be served your refreshments out in the suntrap beer garden in warmer weather. The lunch and dinner menus proffer traditional pub favourites, plus the likes of Guernsey sea bass with crab risotto; pork cutlet, chorizo mash and sautéed greens; or chicken jalfrezi with steamed rice. At least 80% of the Pickled Pig's produce is sourced locally, including beef from Meadow Court Farm, just a short drive away.

Open all day all wk 11am-11.30pm **Food** Lunch all wk 12-2 Dinner all wk 5.30-9.30 Av main course £12 ⊕ FREE HOUSE ◀ Liberation, Randall's of Guernsey Patois ♉ Rocquette. ₹ 14 **Facilities** Non-diners area ◀ Children's menu Children's portions Outside area ⋒ Parking WiFi ⛟ (notice required) **Rooms** 37

ST PETER PORT *continued*

The Ship & Crown, Crow's Nest Brasserie

tel: 01481 728994 **The Quay GY1 2NB**
email: ship_crown@hotmail.com
dir: *Opposite Crown Pier*

Waterfront pub with magnificent views

This busy Guernsey town pub and stylish brasserie occupies a historic building and benefits from stunning views across the Victoria Marina to the neighbouring islands. Run by the same family for well over 30 years, The Ship & Crown offers one of the widest ranges of beers and ciders on the island, but it is equally well known for its all-day bar meals. The friendly Crow's Nest Brasserie specialises in fish and seafood dishes, such as monkfish in tempura batter, but there are plenty of salad and meat options too.

Open all day all wk **Food** Lunch all wk 11-9 Dinner all wk 11-9 Set menu available Restaurant menu available all wk ⊕ FREE HOUSE ◀ Fuller's London Pride, Sharp's Doom Bar, Liberation, St Austell Tribute, Brains The Rev. James, Timothy Taylor Landlord ð Rocquette. ☻ 8 **Facilities** Non-diners area ↟ Children's portions Parking WiFi ⛟

JERSEY

| ▌ ST AUBIN | Map 24 |

Old Court House Inn

tel: 01534 746433 **St Aubin's Harbour JE3 8AB**
email: info@oldcourthousejersey.com
dir: *From Jersey Airport, right at exit, left at lights, 0.5m to St Aubin*

Harbour-side location on Jersey's stunning south coast

At low tide a path snakes across the foreshore to St Aubin's Fort, guarding the harbour overlooked by this old inn. Wizened beams and mellow stone walls testify to the building's medieval origins; its cellars were allegedly used to secrete contraband. A strong suite of seafood options feature on the menus available at the several bars and restaurant rooms here; local oysters grilled with cheese a prelude to asparagus and tiger prawn filled baked breast of chicken, or a locally caught plaice. Jersey-brewed Liberation Ale is a favoured tipple; there's a beer festival too.

Open all day all wk Closed 25 Dec, Mon (Jan-Mar) **Food** Lunch all wk 12.30-2.30, (all day May-Aug) Dinner Mon-Sat 7.30-10 Set menu available Restaurant menu available all wk ⊕ FREE HOUSE ◀ Courage Directors, Theakston, John Smith's, Liberation. ☻ 9 **Facilities** Non-diners area ↟ Children's menu Children's portions Outside area ㄇ Beer festival WiFi ⛟ (notice required)

Looking for a beer or cider festival?
Check our listings at the end of this guide

| ▌ ST BRELADE | Map 24 |

The Portelet Inn

tel: 01534 741899 **La Route de Noirmont JE3 8AJ**
email: portelet@randalls.je
dir: *Phone for detailed directions*

Family-friendly with carvery

Belonging to Jersey's Randalls group of privately owned public houses, the Portelet is a family-friendly pub a short walk from the coast. Since 1948, when it was transformed from a 17th-century farmhouse into the Portelet, much has changed – children can play in Pirate Pete's, while adults relax in the bar. Although young ones have their own menu, the Carvery restaurant is ideal for family dining, with a menu offering BBQ baby back ribs; braised lamb shank kleftiko; steak and Bombardier Ale filo pie; or a choice of burgers including a veggie spiced version. There's live entertainment on Fridays and some Saturday nights.

Open all day 11-11 Closed Tue (Jan-Mar) **Food** Lunch Mon-Sat 12-2.30, Sun 12-8 Dinner Mon-Thu 4.30-8.30, Fri-Sat 4.30-9, Sun 12-8 ⊕ RANDALLS ◀ Wells Bombardier, Guest ale. **Facilities** Non-diners area ↟ Children's menu Children's portions Play area Family room Garden ㄇ Parking WiFi ⛟ (notice required)

| ▌ ST MARTIN | Map 24 |

Royal Hotel

tel: 01534 856289 **La Grande Route de Faldouet JE3 6UG**
email: johnbarker2806@gmail.com
dir: *2m from Five Oaks rdbt towards St Martin. Pub on right next to St Martin's Church*

Log fires in winter, beer garden in summer

A friendly local in the heart of St Martin, this former coaching inn prides itself on offering quality food and drink. Landlord John Barker has been welcoming guests for many years. A roaring log fire in the spacious lounge warm winter visitors, and there's a sunny beer garden to enjoy during the summer months. On the menu are traditional home-made favourites such as steak and ale pie, chicken curry, beef burgers, pizzas and jacket potatoes, as well as local seafood available according to season and availability. Children's choices are on offer, too.

Open all day all wk **Food** Lunch all wk 12-2.15 Dinner Mon-Sat 6-8.30 Av main course £10 ⊕ RANDALLS ◀ Ringwood Best Bitter, Bass Cask, Guest ales ð Westons Stowford Press. ☻ 9 **Facilities** Non-diners area ↟ Children's menu Children's portions Play area Garden ㄇ Parking WiFi ⛟ (notice required)

| ▌ ST MARY | Map 24 |

St Mary's Country Inn

tel: 01534 482897 **La Rue des Buttes JE3 3DS**
email: stmarys@liberationpubco.com
dir: *Phone for detailed directions*

Smart inn with island-brewed ale and global menu

Jersey's Liberation Brewery owns this appealing country inn with smart, contemporary interior. The menu offers imaginative food at reasonable prices, including roasts and grills; espetadas (Portuguese chargrilled skewered meats and fish); and ale-battered cod with chunky chips. There are just three prices on the wine list, but choice extends to half-litre carafes and plenty by the glass. In the bar you'll find continental lagers, island-brewed Mary Ann Special and flagship cask-conditioned Liberation Ale. There's a delightful seating area outside.

Open all day all wk **Food** Lunch all wk 12-2.30 Dinner Mon-Sat 6-9, Sun 5-8 ⊕ LIBERATION GROUP ◀ Liberation Ale, Mary Ann Special, Guest ales. ☻ 19 **Facilities** Non-diners area ✿ (Bar Garden) ↟ Children's menu Children's portions Garden ㄇ Parking WiFi ⛟ (notice required)

ISLE OF MAN

PEEL   Map 24 SC28

The Creek Inn

tel: 01624 842216 **Station Place IM5 1AT**
email: thecreekinn@manx.net
dir: *On quayside opposite House of Manannan Museum*

A must for ale lovers

The family-run Creek Inn occupies a plum spot on the quayside overlooked by Peel Hill. A real ale drinkers' paradise, it has locally brewed Okells ales with up to four changing guests. Bands play every weekend, and nightly during the TT and Manx Grand Prix, when the pub becomes the town's focal point. There's a huge selection of dishes on the menu, from local fish, steaks and burgers, to vegetarian options and salads, alongside sandwiches, hot baguettes and toasties. A typical meal might be chilli and garlic crab claws followed by steak and Rory's ale pie with chips and peas.

Open all day all wk **Food** Lunch all wk 11-9.30 Dinner all wk 11-9.30 ⊕ FREE HOUSE ◀ Okells Bitter & Seasonal ales, Bushy's, 4 guest ales Ö Thatchers Green Goblin, St Helier, Manx Apple. ♟ 12 **Facilities** Non-diners area ❀ (Garden) ♦ Children's menu Children's portions Garden ⟗ Parking WiFi 🚌

PORT ERIN   Map 24 SC26

Falcon's Nest Hotel

tel: 01624 834077 **The Promenade, Station Rd IM9 6AF**
email: falconsnest@enterprise.net
dir: *Follow coast road S from airport or ferry. Hotel on seafront, immediately after steam railway station*

Family-run pub-hotel with an emphasis on local seafood

The Potts family has run the Falcon's Nest since 1984 and it has become very much a part of life in Port Erin. The magnificent building overlooks a beautiful sheltered harbour and sandy beach, and this waterside location means local seafood dishes dominate the menu in the Victorian-style dining room (once a ballroom). Local 'queenie' scallops turn up on the menu alongside a roast of the day; honey-roast Manx ham and many gluten-free options. Head for the saloon bar or the residents' lounge to sample local ales and over 70 whiskies. A beer festival is held in early May each year.

Open all day all wk 11am-mdnt (Fri-Sat 11am-12.45am) **Food** Lunch all wk 12-9 Dinner all wk 12-9 Set menu available Restaurant menu available all wk ⊕ FREE HOUSE ◀ John Smith's, Okells, Bushy's, Guinness, Guest ales.
Facilities Non-diners area ♦ Children's menu Children's portions Family room Beer festival Cider festival Parking WiFi 🚌 (notice required)

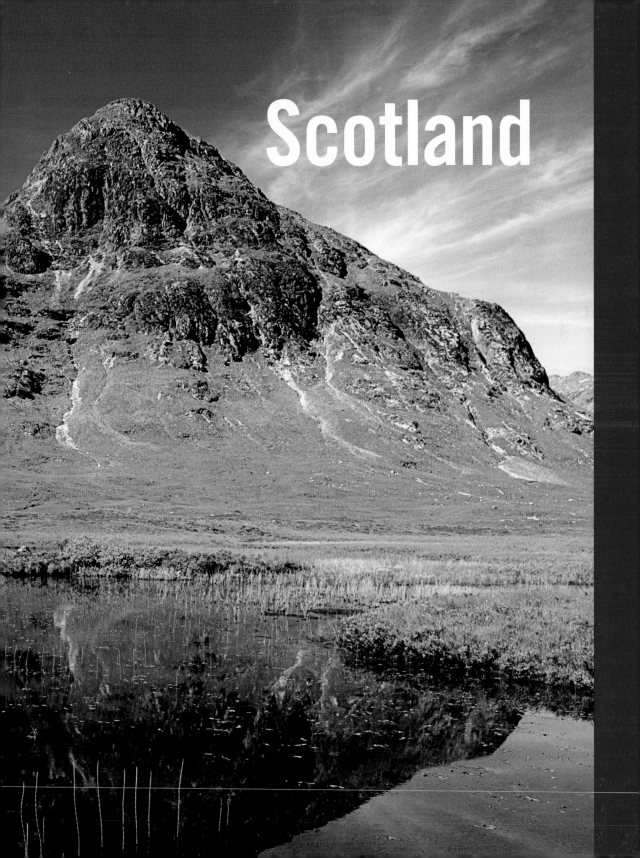

Scotland

CITY OF ABERDEEN

ABERDEEN
Map 23 NJ90

Old Blackfriars

tel: 01224 581922 **52 Castle St AB11 5BB**
email: oldblackfriars.aberdeen@belhavenpubs.net
dir: *From rail station right into Guild St left into Market St, at end right into Union St. Pub on right on corner of Marishal St*

Historic Castlegate-area pub with music nights

Situated in Aberdeen's historic Castlegate, this traditional split-level city centre pub stands on the site of property owned by Blackfriars Dominican monks, hence the name. Inside you'll find stunning stained glass, plus well-kept real ales (five handpumps) and a large selection of malt whiskies. The pub is also renowned for good food and an unobtrusive atmosphere. The wide-ranging menu has all the pub favourites and more – haggis bon bons; chicken satay skewers; black bean and jalapeño burger; and chilli burritos. There's a weekly quiz on Tuesdays and live music every Thursday.

Open all day all wk 11am-mdnt (Fri 11am-1am Sat 10am-1am Sun 10am-11pm) Closed 25 Dec **Food** Lunch all wk 11-9 Dinner all wk 11-9 ⊕ BELHAVEN ◀ Inveralmond Ossian, Old Blackfriars, Guest ales. ▼ 9 **Facilities** Non-diners area ◀♦ Children's menu Family room Outside area ☷ WiFi

ABERDEENSHIRE

ABOYNE
Map 23 NO59

NEW The Boat Inn

tel: 01339 886137 **Charleston Rd AB34 5EL**
email: enquiries@theboatinnaboyne.co.uk
dir: *A93 from Aberdeen to Aboyne. Left in Aboyne centre into Charleston Rd*

Full of Highland promise

A ferry once operated across the River Dee at this spot, where the inn has stood since 1720. Renovated in 2015, but you'd still know it was old – take those mounted stags' skulls, for example. Fresh produce comes from indisputably Scottish suppliers – Finzean Estate, Glen Tanar Estate, Turriff's of Montrose – and in the bar you're unlikely to find a real ale from south of the Border. Lunch and dinner menus both promise chorizo and black pudding Scotch egg with harissa and crispy leeks; 8oz Highland-reared sirloin steak with oven-roasted vine tomatoes, mushrooms and rustic fries; and Thai lentil curry.

Open all day all wk Closed 25 Dec, 1-2 Jan **Food** Lunch 12-1.50 Dinner 5.30-8.45 Av main course £11 ⊕ FREE HOUSE ◀ Inveralmond Ossian, Cairngorm Trade Winds, Brewmeister Supersonic IPA Ŏ Aspall. **Facilities** Non-diners area ✿ (Bar Outside area) ◀♦ Children's menu Children's portions Outside area ☷ Parking WiFi ⛟ (notice required)

BALMEDIE
Map 23 NJ91

The Cock & Bull Bar & Restaurant

tel: 01358 743249 **Ellon Rd, Blairton AB23 8XY**
email: info@thecockandbull.co.uk
dir: *11m N of city centre, on left of A90 between Balmedie junct & Foveran*

Country inn with great food of impeccable provenance

A cast-iron range warms the bar in this creeper-clad, stone-built coaching inn, standing quite alone in open farmland north of Aberdeen. Conversation is easily stimulated by local artist Irene Morrison's paintings, assorted hanging artefacts and good beer. Affordably priced food in the AA-Rosetted restaurant uses Marine Stewardship Council-approved white fish and Peterhead-landed shellfish; and beef and pork from the region's stock farms. A seasonal menu might list Scottish girolles in garlic butter with pea pancake, broad beans and parsley fritters; the Aberdeen Angus burger; or sweet-spiced breast of Gressingham duck with gooseberries and spätzle. Great wines and whiskies as well.

Open all day all wk 10am-11.30pm (Sun 12-7.30) Closed 2-3 Jan, 26-27 Dec **Food** Lunch Mon-Sat 10-8.45, Sun 12-7.30 Dinner Mon-Sat 10-8.45, Sun 12-7.30 ⊕ FREE HOUSE ◀ Burnside 3 Bullz Bitter Ale, Guinness. **Facilities** Non-diners area ✿ (Bar Garden) ♦ Children's menu Play area Garden ♠ Parking WiFi ➡ (notice required)

KILDRUMMY
Map 23 NJ41

NEW Kildrummy Inn ★★★★ INN ◉◉

tel: 01975 571227 **AB33 8QS**
email: enquiries@kildrummyinn.co.uk **web:** www.kildrummyinn.co.uk
dir: *Take A944 from Aberdeen, left onto A97 (Strathdon). Inn on right*

Former coaching inn with an all-round first-rate reputation

Brothers-in-law David Littlewood and Nigel Hake, together with their wives, have fulfilled their long-held ambition to own an inn. Thanks to David's expert cooking and Nigel's amiable hospitality, they have swiftly achieved a reputation for attentive service, highly praised modern Scottish food and excellent accommodation. A sample dinner menu lists Asian pork belly salad with apricot compôte; sirloin and featherblade of beef with dauphinoise potatoes and Grana Padano cheese; and beer-battered haddock with crispy fries, pea purée and tartare sauce. A fine selection from some of Scotland's smaller breweries and Thistly Cross ciders are sold in the tartan-carpeted bar.

Open 6pm-late (Sun 12-2.30 6-late) Closed Jan, Tue **Food** Lunch Sun 12-2.30 Dinner 6-8.45 Set menu available ⊕ FREE HOUSE ◀ Deeside Swift APA, Macbeth & Talorcan, Atlas Wayfarer Ŏ Thistly Cross. ♚ 12 **Facilities** Non-diners area ♦ Children's portions Garden Outside area ♠ Parking WiFi ➡ (notice required) **Rooms** 4

NETHERLEY
Map 23 NO89

The Lairhillock Inn
PICK OF THE PUBS

tel: 01569 730001 **AB39 3QS**
email: info@lairhillock.co.uk
dir: *From Aberdeen take A90. Right towards Durris on B9077 then left onto B979 to Netherley*

A bustling country inn serving seasonal food

Nooks and crannies pepper the rambling interior of this generously-beamed inn that has stood in rural Deeside for over 200 years. Rustic furnishings on quarry tile floors; wood smoke drifting off the highly unusual slab-mounted central fire grate, reliable real ales and a regularly updated food offering from the country kitchen ensure that it's a popular spot for Aberdonians escaping the nearby Granite City. The confident menu majors on Scottish produce, with robust starters such as hot smoked venison fillet or seared guinea fowl breast a meal in themselves. Unsurprisingly, grilled Aberdeen Angus steaks feature as mains, as does the Lairhillock's own pork, venison and beef lasagne dish; fish dishes include smoked haddock, pancetta and Applewood cheddar fishcakes with mild curry mayonnaise. There's a light, bright conservatory with garden views, or hunker down at candlelit tables beside gleaming brass and copper lamps, and bric-á-brac.

Open all day all wk Closed 25-26 Dec, 1-2 Jan **Food** Lunch all wk 12-2 Dinner all wk 6-9.30 ⊕ FREE HOUSE ◀ Timothy Taylor Landlord, Caledonian Deuchars IPA, Guest ales. **Facilities** Non-diners area ✿ (Bar Garden) ♦ Children's menu Children's portions Garden ♠ Parking ➡ (notice required)

OLDMELDRUM
Map 23 NJ82

The Redgarth

tel: 01651 872353 **Kirk Brae AB51 ODJ**
email: redgarth1@aol.com
dir: *From A947 (Oldmeldrum bypass) follow signs to Golf Club/Pleasure Park. Inn E of bypass*

Friendly, family-run inn with attractive garden

The Redgarth looks more like a house than a pub, because that's what it was built as in 1928. It became the Redgarth Cocktail Bar in the 1970s and has been further altered since, but not too much. A cask-conditioned ale, such as Highland Scapa Special or Kelburn Pivo Estivo, or a malt whisky from Glen Garioch, the village distillery, might precede haggis stuffed chicken with Glen Garioch sauce; lamb rump on braised red cabbage with rosemary jus; or catch of the day. Grills are well represented and vegetarians will very likely find a sun-dried tomato and black olive Mediterranean flan, or mozzarella and spinach stuffed cannelloni on the menu.

Open all wk 11-3 5-11 (Fri-Sat 11-3 5-11.45) Closed 25-26 Dec, 1-3 Jan **Food** Lunch all wk 12-2 Dinner Sun-Thu 5-9, Fri-Sat 5-9.30 ⊕ FREE HOUSE ◀ Inveralmond Thrappledouser, Timothy Taylor Landlord, Highland Scapa Special & Orkney Best, Kelburn Pivo Estivo Ŏ Aspall. **Facilities** Non-diners area ✿ (Garden) ♦ Children's menu Children's portions Garden ♠ Parking WiFi ➡

continued

STONEHAVEN
Map 23 NO88

The Ship Inn ★★★ INN

tel: 01569 762617 **5 Shorehead AB39 2JY**
email: enquiries@shipinnstonehaven.com **web:** www.shipinnstonehaven.com
dir: From A90 follow signs to Stonehaven, then signs to harbour

Fresh seafood a speciality

Overnight guests will surely testify that the Ship is in one of the best locations in town, for it overlooks the almost circular harbour, once an important centre of the herring trade. In the blue-carpeted bar you'll find real ales from Inveralmond, Orkney and elsewhere, as well as a hundred-plus malts. Seafood is served in the bar, the air-conditioned restaurant, and on the open-air terrace, all with harbour views. King prawn and chorizo salad; and goats' cheese with candy beets are typical starters, while main dishes include hake with mussels in herb cream sauce, baby potatoes and crispy kale; smoked haddock and leek fishcakes; mixed grill; and spicy veggie tortillas.

The Ship Inn

Open all day all wk **Food** Lunch Mon-Fri 12-2.15, Sat-Sun 12-9 Dinner Mon-Fri 5.30-9, Sat-Sun 12-9 ⊕ FREE HOUSE ◀ Inveralmond Thrappledouser, Orkney, Guest ales. **Facilities** ❀ (Bar Outside area) ⛟ Children's menu Children's portions Outside area ⊟ WiFi **Rooms** 11

See advert on page 596

ARGYLL & BUTE

ARDUAINE
Map 20 NM71

Chartroom II Bistro ★★★ CHH ◉◉ **PICK OF THE PUBS**

tel: 01852 200233 **Loch Melfort Hotel PA34 4XG**
email: reception@lochmelfort.co.uk **web:** www.lochmelfort.co.uk
dir: On A816, midway between Oban & Lochgilphead

West Coast seafood and far-reaching views out to sea

Seafood lovers flock to this modern bar and bistro, part of the Loch Melfort Hotel, next door to National Trust Scotland's Arduaine Garden. It's not just the langoustines, scallops and mussels they come for – the views over Asknish Bay towards Jura, Scarba and Shuna are a real treat, too. Enjoy Fyne Ales from Cairndow, soup of the day; an Ayrshire ham and Arran mustard sandwich; beer-battered Scottish haddock; Argyll beef stovies; spinach and ricotta tortellini; or one of the eight 12-inch pizzas. If sitting outside is out of the question, you can watch the waves crashing against the rocks from in front of the fire. Children's dishes include macaroni cheese, and fish, chips and beans. Sailors can moor free of charge from April to October; hang up their oilskins and freshen up with a shower. The hotel's Asknish Bay Restaurant has been awarded two AA Rosettes.

Open all wk 11-10 Closed Nov-Etr **Food** Lunch all wk 12-2.30 Dinner all wk 6-9 Av main course £10.95 ⊕ FREE HOUSE ◀ Belhaven, Fyne, Tennent's. ♟ 8 **Facilities** Non-diners area ⛟ Children's menu Children's portions Play area Garden ⊟ Parking WiFi 🚍 **Rooms** 25

ARROCHAR
Map 20 NN30

NEW Village Inn

tel: 01301 702279 **Shore Rd G83 7AX**
email: villageinn@maclay.co.uk
dir: From Arrochar take A814 towards Helensburgh. Inn in 1m

Traditional pub in the heart of the Loch Lomond National Park

On the east shore of Loch Long, just a few minutes from Loch Lomond, the Village Inn was originally built in 1872 as a church manse. There's a large beer garden and superb views of the 'Arrochar Alps'. Ideally located for the hills and trails of the National Park, the inn is popular with locals and visitors alike, all of whom appreciate the comfortable, friendly atmosphere and quality Scottish food. You'll find three Scottish cask ales in the cosy bar, and if you're hungry you can share an Italian meat platter, or enjoy something more substantial – start with whitebait or garlic mushrooms and move on to steak pie or cod and pancetta fishcakes. There are steaks and burgers as well, and there's even a choice of dishes 'under 500 calories'. Finish with the fig, plum and pistachio frangipane tart, or apple and blackberry crumble.

Open all day all wk **Food** Lunch all wk 12-3 (summer all day) Dinner all wk 5-8.30 (summer all day) Av main course £10 Set menu available ◀ Caledonian Deuchars IPA, Loch Lomond, St Andrews, Houston. ♟ 22 **Facilities** Non-diners area ⛟ Children's menu Children's portions Garden Outside area ⊟ Beer festival Parking WiFi 🚍 (notice required)

CAIRNDOW
Map 20 NN11

Cairndow Stagecoach Inn ★★★ INN

tel: 01499 600286 **PA26 8BN**
email: enq@cairndowinn.com **web:** www.cairndowinn.com
dir: N of Glasgow take A82, left on A83 at Arrochar. Through Rest and be Thankful to Cairndow. Follow signs for inn

An old coaching inn set in glorious scenery

On the upper reaches of Loch Fyne, this old coaching inn offers plenty of fine views of mountains, magnificent woodlands and rivers. Sample one of many malt whiskies in the friendly bar by the roaring fire, or idle away the time in the loch-side garden watching the oyster-catchers while sipping the local Fyne Ales. The menu in the candlelit Stables Restaurant offers steak and Fyne Ale pie; chicken breast stuffed with smoked Scottish cheddar and ham, wrapped in pancetta; roasted pepper, courgette and wild mushroom risotto; and pan-fried venison steak with shallot, mushroom and smoked bacon red wine sauce. Meals are also served all day in the bar and lounges. Accommodation is available if you would like to stay over and explore the area. On your way to the pub you should look out for Britain's tallest tree (Ardkinglas Grand Fir), which is taller than Nelson's Column.

Open all day all wk **Food** Lunch all wk 12-6 Dinner all wk 6-9 ⊕ FREE HOUSE ◄ Fyne Hurricane Jack, Avalanche, Piper's Gold, Maverick, Jarl. ☻ **Facilities** Non-diners area ☻ (Bar Garden) ◄ Children's menu Children's portions Family room Garden ⌐ Parking WiFi ☞ (notice required) **Rooms** 18

CONNEL
Map 20 NM93

The Oyster Inn
PICK OF THE PUBS

tel: 01631 710666 **PA37 1PJ**
email: stay@oysterinn.co.uk
dir: Phone for detailed directions

Excellent local seafood against a backdrop of views to Mull

This 18th-century inn once served ferry passengers, the cannier among them knowing they could be 'stuck' here between ferries and thus evade Oban's Sunday licensing laws. The stone-walled Ferryman's Bar next door is known as the Glue Pot, a reminder that the neighbouring blacksmith once boiled horses' hooves for glue. The pots still hang from the ceiling and tradition requires that on entering or leaving the pub, gentlemen touch the hanging glue pot, whilst ladies wink at the Ferryman. Overlooking the tidal whirlpools and white water of the Falls of Lora, the ferry is long gone, superseded by a modern road bridge, but seafood lovers will find plenty to enjoy on the menu here, with West Coast mussels, oysters and scallops in abundance. In addition, a starter of haggis, neeps and tatties with whisky cream sauce might be followed by chargrilled Scottish steaks.

Open all day all wk 11am-mdnt **Food** Lunch all wk 12-9.30 Dinner all wk 12-9.30 ⊕ FREE HOUSE ◄ Caledonian Deuchars IPA. ☻ 9 **Facilities** Non-diners area ☻ (Bar Garden) ◄ Children's menu Children's portions Family room Garden ⌐ Parking WiFi ☞ (notice required)

CRINAN
Map 20 NR79

Crinan Hotel
PICK OF THE PUBS

tel: 01546 830261 **PA31 8SR**
email: reservations@crinanhotel.com
dir: From M8, at end of bridge take A82, at Tarbert left onto A83. At Inveraray follow Campbeltown signs to Lochgilphead, follow signs for A816 to Oban. 2m, left to Crinan on B841

Stunning views and the freshest West Coast seafood

This romantic retreat enjoys a stunning location with fabulous views across the Sound of Jura. The hotel stands at the north end of the Crinan Canal, which connects Loch Fyne to the Atlantic Ocean. For over two hundred years this hostelry has been caring for the community needs of this tiny fishing village, and welcoming travellers. This sense of continuity has been lovingly provided by Nick and Frances Ryan for over 40 years. Relax with a drink in the Gallery Bar on a summer's evening, or settle in the Mainbrace, a wood-panelled seafood bar which extends to the patio overlooking the fishing boats. The Westward Restaurant's cuisine is firmly based on the freshest seafood – it's landed daily just 50 metres from the hotel. Look out for hot Arbroath smokie; risotto of crab with cream cheese and chives, and – if meat is preferred – pan-seared Scottish sirloin steak.

Open all day all wk 11-11 Closed 25 Dec **Food** Lunch all wk 12-2.30 Dinner all wk 6-8.30 Restaurant menu available all wk ⊕ FREE HOUSE ◄ Fyne, Tennent's, Caledonian, Guinness. ☻ 8 **Facilities** Non-diners area ☻ (Bar Garden Outside area) ◄ Children's menu Children's portions Garden Outside area ⌐ Parking WiFi ☞ (notice required)

DUNOON
Map 20 NS17

Coylet Inn

tel: 01369 840426 **Loch Eck PA23 8SG**
email: reservations@coylet-locheck.co.uk
dir: N of Dunoon on A815

Local produce in pub with loch views

Run by Craig Wilson, this charming, beautifully appointed 17th-century coaching inn has a timeless quality. Located on Loch Eck's shores you wouldn't want a television or games machines to disturb your drink or meal. Well, they won't, at least not in where you can relax with a glass of wine or a pint of Fyne Ales Highlander in peace by a real log fire. An appealing menu offers local favourites such as home-made Cullen skink soup and smoked salmon with rocket and caper salad, which might be followed by peat-smoked battered haddock and chips.

Open all day all wk **Food** Lunch all wk 12-2.30 Dinner all wk 6-8.30 ⊕ FREE HOUSE ◄ Fyne Ales Highlander & Jarl, Guest ales. **Facilities** Non-diners area ☻ (Bar Garden) ◄ Children's menu Children's portions Garden ⌐ Beer festival Cider festival Parking WiFi ☞ (notice required)

INVERARAY
Map 20 NN00

George Hotel

tel: 01499 302111 **Main Street East PA32 8TT**
email: info@thegeorgehotel.co.uk
dir: On A83

Family-owned gem offering many whiskies, and more

Built in 1776 and in the ownership of the Clark family since 1860, The George occupies a prime spot in the centre of a historic conservation town. Although there have been sensitive additions over the years, nothing detracts from the original flagstone floors and four roaring log fires. More than 100 whiskies and a range of Fyne Ales are complemented by an extensive bar menu that includes traditional haggis, neeps and tatties. The restaurant showcases local produce; try the fresh potted crab followed by slow-braised lamb shank in Loch Fyne ale. The George holds beer and music festivals on Bank Holidays in May and August.

Open all day all wk 11am-1am Closed 25 Dec **Food** Lunch all wk 12-6 Dinner all wk 6-9 Av main course £8-£23 ⊕ FREE HOUSE ◄ Fyne Ales, Harviestoun. ☻ 11 **Facilities** Non-diners area ☻ (Bar Restaurant Garden) ◄ Children's menu Children's portions Garden ⌐ Beer festival Parking WiFi ☞ (notice required)

LUSS
Map 20 NS39

The Inn on Loch Lomond ★★★★ INN

tel: 01436 860201 **G83 8PD**
email: inverbeg.reception@loch-lomond.co.uk **web:** www.innonlochlomond.co.uk
dir: 12m N of Balloch

Scottish hospitality and great views

Today a good road skirts Loch Lomond's western shore, but it wouldn't have been so good in 1814, when this wayside inn opened its doors. Today it incorporates Mr C's Fish & Whisky Bar where the menu might feature haggis, neeps and tatties; Cullen skink; pea and herb risotto; and roast salmon and haddock fishcakes; and for dessert, cranachan (a mixture of whipped cream, whisky, honey and fresh raspberries, with toasted oatmeal soaked overnight in a little bit of whisky) or deep-fried Mars Bars with ice cream. More than 200 whiskies are available, but if you prefer ale, there's Deuchars IPA, Fyne Highlander and Houston Killellan. Live folk music is played nightly throughout the summer.

Open all day all wk 11-11 (Fri-Sat 11am-mdnt) **Food** Lunch all wk 12-9 Dinner all wk 12-9 ⊕ FREE HOUSE ◄ Houston Killellan, Fyne Highlander, Caledonian Deuchars IPA. **Facilities** Non-diners area ☻ (Outside area) ◄ Children's menu Children's portions Outside area ⌐ Parking WiFi ☞ (notice required) **Rooms** 33

OBAN
Map 20 NM83

NEW Cuan Mor

tel: 01631 565078 **60 George St PA34 5SD**
email: info@cuanmor.co.uk
dir: *Phone pub for detailed directions*

Delightful views and good home-cooked food

Cuan Mor means 'big ocean', clearly a reference to the Atlantic, which stretches a finger called the Firth of Lorn towards Oban. Restaurant and bars make effective use of reclaimed Ballachulish slate and timbers from the old lighthouse pier. The on-site Oban Bay Brewery produces the real ales, there are 16 wines by the glass, and a hundred or so single malts and special blends – read the Brewery Bar's Whisky Bible for guidance. As you overlook Oban Bay enjoy West Coast crab pot, followed by braised Scottish beef with haggis Yorkshire pudding; or lightly smoked rainbow trout fillet with chargrilled pepper pesto dressing.

Open all day all wk **Food** Lunch all wk 12-4 Dinner all wk 4-9 (Etr-Sep 4-10) Av main course £10 ⊕ FREE HOUSE ◀ Oban Bay. ☝ 16 **Facilities** Non-diners area ◀◀ Children's menu Children's portions Outside area ⊨ WiFi ▬ (notice required)

The Lorne

tel: 01631 570020 **Stevenson St PA34 5NA**
email: lornebar@maclay.co.uk
dir: *Phone for detailed directions*

A place for refreshment before train or ferry

The Lorne is close to both Oban's train station and its terminal for the Mull ferry. It's a family-friendly haven with a sheltered and heated beer garden – an ideal spot to enjoy a pot of freshly brewed coffee or a pint Deuchars IPA before departing the town. From May to September the kitchen serves delicious plates of locally-caught seafood. At other times the menu of pub grub ranges from warm ciabattas or tortilla wraps, toasted paninis and baked potatoes, to pizzas, house burgers, and curries. If you can tarry awhile, The Lorne offers a busy programme of pub quizzes, DJ nights and live music, when the party continues into the early hours.

Open all day all wk **Food** Lunch all wk 12-3 Dinner all wk 5-9 ⊕ MACLAY ◀ Caledonian Deuchars IPA. ☝ 12 **Facilities** ◀◀ (All areas) ◀◀ Children's menu Children's portions Garden Outside area ⊨ WiFi ▬ (notice required)

PORT APPIN
Map 20 NM94

The Pierhouse Hotel & Seafood Restaurant ★★★ SHL ◉
PICK OF THE PUBS

tel: 01631 730302 **PA38 4DE**
email: reservations@pierhousehotel.co.uk web: www.pierhousehotel.co.uk
dir: *A828 from Ballachulish to Oban. In Appin right at Port Appin & Lismore ferry sign. After 2.5m left after post office, hotel at end of road by pier*

Delicious seafood on the shores of Loch Linnhe

Once home to the piermaster (hence the name), this distinctive whitewashed building boasts breathtaking views to the islands of Lismore and Mull. It would be hard to imagine a more spectacular setting for this family-run hotel and seafood restaurant; an AA Rosette being one its many awards, others recognising its green credentials. The popular bar is stocked with Belhaven beers and 50 malt whiskies; a pool room; and a dining area where the finest of Scottish seasonal seafood, meat, game and vegetables are served. Overlooking the pier, the Ferry Bar serves burgers and seafood dishes, plus ciabattas at lunchtime. An evening three-course meal in the restaurant could commence with the Cullen skink, followed by Highland game pie; roast fillet of Scottish salmon; or langoustine platter. For dessert, try the butterscotch pot or a board of local cheeses. Twelve individually designed bedrooms include some with superb loch views.

Open all wk 11-11 Closed 25-26 Dec **Food** Lunch all wk 12.30-2.30 Dinner all wk 6.30-9.30 Restaurant menu available all wk ⊕ FREE HOUSE ◀ Belhaven Best & Export, Guinness. **Facilities** Non-diners area ◀◀ (Bar Garden Outside area) ◀◀ Children's menu Children's portions Garden Outside area ⊨ Parking WiFi ▬ **Rooms** 12

STRACHUR
Map 20 NN00

Creggans Inn ★★★ HL ◉◉
PICK OF THE PUBS

tel: 01369 860279 **PA27 8BX**
email: info@creggans-inn.co.uk web: www.creggans-inn.co.uk
dir: *A82 from Glasgow, at Tarbet take A83 towards Cairndow, left onto A815 to Strachur*

Award-winning family-run inn on loch shores

Set between the woods and the water, guests at the centuries-old loch-side hotel can look forward to losing themselves in both the astounding view across Loch Fyne and the award-winning menus from Archie and Jill MacLellan's kitchen. The reputation of the area's provender is well-established; this is matched by beers from the Fyne microbrewery at the head of the loch. A pint of Highlander and a seat on the terrace is a restful way to pass time while considering the menu's seasonally adjusted, daily-changing dishes. Eat outside, dine in the bistro-style MacPhunn's bar or in the more formal Loch Fyne dining room; try Ramsay haggis, creamy mash, buttered neeps and whisky sauce; local venison sausages, leek and smoked bacon mash, and root vegetables with honey; or West Coast fillet of salmon, crushed potato, spinach with white wine and prawn sauce. Many of the bedrooms have views of the loch.

Open all day all wk 11am-mdnt **Food** Lunch all wk 12-2.30 Dinner all wk 6-8.30 Av main course £11 Restaurant menu available all wk ⊕ FREE HOUSE ◀ Fyne Highlander, Atlas Latitude, Caledonian Deuchars IPA, Harviestoun Bitter & Twisted. **Facilities** Non-diners area ◀◀ (Bar Garden) ◀◀ Children's menu Children's portions Garden ⊨ Parking WiFi **Rooms** 14

TAYVALLICH
Map 20 NR78

Tayvallich Inn

tel: 01546 870282 **PA31 8PL**
email: info@tayvallichinn.com
dir: *From Lochgilphead take A816 then B841, B8025*

Popular loch-side pub at the heart of a vibrant community

Established for over 30 years, the inn stands in a picturesque fishing village overlooking the natural harbour of Tayvallich Bay at the head of Loch Sween. There are unrivalled views, particularly from the outside area of decking, where food and a great selection of real ales can be enjoyed. Not surprisingly given the location, fresh seafood features strongly – the catch is landed from the boats right outside the front door! Lobster, crab and langoustine are available in the summer, while typical dishes in winter might be fragrant oven-baked salmon fillet with prawn and caper sauce or line-caught Tarbert haddock in batter with chips.

Open all wk all day in summer (closed 3-6 Tue-Fri in winter) Closed 25-26 Dec, Mon (Nov-Mar) **Food** Lunch all wk 12-2.30 Dinner all wk 6-9 ⊕ FREE HOUSE ◀ Caledonian Best, Loch Ness, Guinness. ☝ 8 **Facilities** Non-diners area ◀◀ (Bar Garden) ◀◀ Children's menu Children's portions Garden ⊨ Parking ▬ (notice required)

EAST AYRSHIRE

SORN
Map 20 NS52

The Sorn Inn
PICK OF THE PUBS

tel: 01290 551305 **35 Main St KA5 6HU**
email: craig@sorninn.com
dir: *A70 from S; or A76 from N onto B743 to Sorn*

A fusion of fine dining and brasserie-style food

The whitewashed Sorn Inn dates back to the 18th century when it was a coaching inn on the old Edinburgh to Kilmarnock route; today it's a smart gastro-pub that serves ales that include Corncrake from the Orkney Brewery. Menus offer the best of Scottish and seasonal ingredients. Choose medallion of beef confit, black pudding, smoked onion velouté and peas to start perhaps, then slow-cooked Shetland salmon fillet, crushed new potatoes, crab dumplings and dill mayonnaise; or chump of lamb, gratin potatoes, spiced green lentils, aubergine compôte and wild mushroom jus. Half a dozen classic dishes include smoked Ayrshire bacon carbonara; and 'Mum's' steak pie, mash, and buttered cabbage. Finish with spiced custard tart, dried fruit compôte and apricot ice cream; or Golden Delicious apple crumble baked Alaska.

Open 12-2.30 6-10 (Fri 12-2.30 6-12 Sat 12-12 Sun 12-10) Closed 2wks Jan, Mon **Food** Lunch Tue-Fri 12-2.30, Sat 12-9, Sun 12-8 Dinner Tue-Fri 6-9, Sat 12-9, Sun 12-8 Av main course £15 ⊕ FREE HOUSE ◀ John Smith's, Orkney Corncrake, Guinness. ♠ 12 **Facilities** Non-diners area ♣ (Bar) ♦ Children's menu Children's portions Outside area ⋒ Parking WiFi ▭ (notice required)

SOUTH AYRSHIRE

SYMINGTON — Map 20 NS33

Wheatsheaf Inn

tel: 01563 830307 **Main St KA1 5QB**
email: thewheatsheafinnsymington@gmail.com
dir: Off A77 between Ayr & Kilmarnock

Village free house with friendly service

Close to the Royal Troon Golf Course and one of Scotland's oldest churches, this charming 17th-century free house has been run by Martin and Marnie Thompson for over 25 years. Log fires burn in every room of the former coaching inn and the interior is decorated with the work of local artists. The varied menu offers plenty of choice, with dishes like haggis, neeps and tatties with a sweet whisky cream; fillet of haddock mornay; gammon steak with egg or pineapple; pan-fried lamb's liver with red wine and onions; or blackened Cajun salmon.

Open all day all wk 11-11 (Fri-Sat 11am-mdnt) Closed 1 Jan **Food** Lunch all wk 12-9 Dinner all wk 12-9 Av main course £10 Set menu available Restaurant menu available all wk ⊕ FREE HOUSE ◀ Belhaven Best, Morland Old Speckled Hen, Guinness. **Facilities** Non-diners area ♦ Children's menu Children's portions Garden ⋒ Parking WiFi ▭ (notice required)

DUMFRIES & GALLOWAY

BARGRENNAN — Map 20 NX37

House O'Hill Hotel

tel: 01671 840243 **DG8 6RN**
email: enquiries@houseohill.co.uk
dir: From Newton Stewart take A714 towards Girvan, 8m. Hotel signed

Secluded location in Galloway's forested hills

At the fringe of loch-speckled Galloway Forest and beautiful Glen Trool, this contemporary, homely little hotel makes the most of its setting in Europe's first 'Dark Sky' Park. The House O'Hill attracts cyclists and ramblers on the Southern Upland Way by offering an exceptional combination of local microbrewery beers such as Sulwath and a wide-ranging menu strong on Galloway produce. Chicken stuffed with locally smoked haggis with crushed new potatoes; or lamb shoulder shank hotpot are just two of the dishes on the hit list. There are themed world-food evenings and beer festivals occur in April and September.

Open all day all wk Closed 3-25 Jan **Food** Lunch all wk 12-2.45 Dinner all wk 5.30-8.30 Restaurant menu available all wk ⊕ FREE HOUSE ◀ Sulwath, Stewart's, Ayr, Fyne, Houston. **Facilities** Non-diners area ♣ (Bar Restaurant Garden) ♦ Children's menu Children's portions Family room Garden ⋒ Beer festival Parking WiFi ▭

BLADNOCH — Map 20 NX45

The Bladnoch Inn

tel: 01988 402200 **DG8 9AB**
email: thebladnochinn@hotmail.co.uk
dir: A714 S of Wigtown to Bladnoch. Inn at rdbt by river bridge

In a charming spot by the River Bladnoch

This traditional country inn is in the heart of the Machars peninsula, just down the road is Wigtown, home to some 20 bookshops. At lunchtime there are sandwiches and filled baked potatoes, while starters include haggis fritters; duck and orange pâté; and garlic mushrooms. Traditional pub favourites make up the mains' choices – home-made chicken curry; pork and leek sausages with mash and honey-roast vegetables; beer-battered fish, pea purée and fries; and macaroni cheese. A carvery is available on Sundays.

Open all day all wk **Food** Lunch all wk 12-3 Dinner all wk 6-9 Av main course £10 ⊕ FREE HOUSE ◀ Greene King & IPA, Timothy Taylor Landlord ☼ Kopparberg. ♠ 15 **Facilities** Non-diners area ♣ (Bar Outside area) ♦ Children's menu Children's portions Play area Outside area ⋒ Parking WiFi ▭ (notice required)

ISLE OF WHITHORN — Map 20 NX43

The Steam Packet Inn

tel: 01988 500334 **Harbour Row DG8 8LL**
email: steampacketinn@btconnect.com
dir: From Newton Stewart take A714, then A746 to Whithorn, then to Isle of Whithorn

Local seafood a specialty

Personally run by the Scoular family for over 30 years, this lively quayside pub stands in a picturesque village at the tip of the Machars peninsula. Sit in one of the comfortable bars and enjoy a real ale, a malt whisky or a glass of wine. Glance out of the picture windows and watch the fishermen at work, then look to the menu to sample the fruits of their labours. Extensive seafood choices – perhaps salmon and fishcake kebabs; or smoked haddock fillet wrapped with black pudding and bacon – are supported by the likes of wild mushroom risotto and corn-fed chicken breast with haggis and mash.

Open all day all wk 11-11 (Sun 12-11) Closed 25 Dec, winter Tue-Thu 2.30-6 **Food** Lunch Mon-Thu 12-2, Fri-Sun all day Dinner Mon-Thu 6.30-9, Fri-Sun all day Av main course £12 ⊕ FREE HOUSE ◀ Timothy Taylor Landlord, Belhaven IPA, Guest ales. ♠ 12 **Facilities** Non-diners area ♣ (Bar Garden Outside area) ♦ Children's menu Children's portions Garden Outside area ⋒ Parking WiFi ▭

KIRKCUDBRIGHT — Map 20 NX65

Selkirk Arms Hotel

tel: 01557 330402 **Old High St DG6 4JG**
email: reception@selkirkarmshotel.co.uk
dir: M74 & M6 to A75, halfway between Dumfries & Stranraer on A75

Choice of two bars and two restaurants

In 1794, when dining at what today is a tastefully refurbished town house, Robert Burns reputedly penned and delivered The Selkirk Grace. In the bar, Sulwath Brewery's eponymous ale celebrates the occasion. A good choice of dishes is offered in both the homely lounge and bistro, with comfy sofas and a living-flame fire, and the more intimate Artistas Restaurant. Locally sourced specialities include rump of lamb with ginger and liquorice; hay-baked chicken with spicy chorizo, barley risotto and roasted vegetables; and Galloway venison. Finish with lemon curd doughnuts and ginger yogurt.

Open all day all wk **Food** Lunch all wk 12-2 Dinner all wk 6-9 ⊕ FREE HOUSE ◀ Timothy Taylor Landlord, Sulwath Selkirk Grace, Dark Horse Hetton Pale Ale, Caledonian Deuchars IPA. **Facilities** Non-diners area ♦ Children's menu Children's portions Garden ⋒ Parking WiFi ▭

NEW GALLOWAY
Map 20 NX67

Cross Keys Hotel

tel: 01644 420494 **High St DG7 3RN**
email: enquiries@thecrosskeys-newgalloway.co.uk
dir: *At N end of Loch Ken, 10m from Castle Douglas on A712*

Great selection of real ales and malts

This 17th-century coaching inn sits in a stunning location at the top of Loch Ken on the edge of Galloway Forest Park, a superb area for walking, fishing, birdwatching, golf, watersports and photography. Part of the hotel was once the police station and in the beamed period bar the food is served in restored, stone-walled cells. Scottish ales are supplied by the Houston and Sulwath breweries, among others. The lunch menu includes sandwiches, pizzas, pastas and burgers, while the weekly-changing dinner specials feature the likes of soy, ginger and honey beef strips with steamed egg noodles. A grill menu and early supper menu are also available.

Open 6pm-11.30pm Closed Sun eve winter **Food** Dinner all wk 6.30-8.30 ⊕ FREE HOUSE ◀ Houston, Sulwath, Guest ales Ö Westons Stowford Press. ♟ 9
Facilities Non-diners area ✿ (Bar Garden) Children's menu Children's portions Garden WiFi ➡ (notice required)

SANDHEAD
Map 20 NX04

Tigh Na Mara Hotel

tel: 01776 830210 **Main St DG9 9JF**
email: mail@tighnamarahotel.co.uk
dir: *A75 from Dumfries towards Stranraer. Left onto B7084 to Sandhead. Hotel in village centre*

Bracing sea air and long sandy beaches

Tigh na Mara means 'house by the sea', which seems appropriate for this family-run village hotel is set in the tranquil seaside village of Sandhead and boasts breathtaking views of the Sands of Luce. A menu created from top-quality local ingredients might include crispy beer battered camembert with cranberry relish; breaded whitebait with garlic mayonnaise; slow-roasted sirloin of beef, Yorkshire pudding and gravy; and home-made steak and ale pie. Relax with a glass of Morland Old Speckled Hen in the garden, comfortable lounge or beside the fire in the public bar.

Open all day all wk **Food** Lunch all wk 12-2.30 Dinner all wk 6-9 Set menu available ⊕ BELHAVEN ◀ Best & IPA, Morland Old Speckled Hen, Seasonal Specials.
Facilities Non-diners area ✿ (Bar Garden) ♦ Children's menu Children's portions Family room Garden ⊭ Parking WiFi

CITY OF DUNDEE

BROUGHTY FERRY
Map 21 NO43

The Royal Arch Bar

tel: 01382 779741 **285 Brook St DD5 2DS**
dir: *On A930, 3m from Dundee at Broughty Ferry rail station*

Convivial local by the Tay Estuary

This long established street-corner inn is a pleasing mix of locals' saloon bar, complete with stained-glass windows and an eye-catching Victorian gantry, and a well-maintained art deco lounge long ago converted from the inn's stables. The Royal Arch itself was a monument built to commemorate Queen Victoria's Dundee visit in 1863; a fragment survives on display in the bar. Dispensed from this bar are quality Scottish beers such as from local micro MòR, as well as over 50 malt whiskies; satisfying pub meals can include chicken or beef lasagne; or macaroni cheese. There's a pavement terrace canopy for all-weather, alfresco eating and drinking. Beer, cider and sausage festivals are held.

Open all day all wk **Food** Lunch Mon-Fri 11.30-2.30, Sat 11.30-8, Sun 12.30-7 Dinner Mon-Fri 5-8, Sat 11.30-8, Sun 12.30-7 Av main course £8.50 Set menu available ⊕ FREE HOUSE ◀ McEwan's 80/-, Belhaven St Andrews, Caledonian Deuchars IPA, MòR Tea, Vicar?, Black Isle Blonde Ö Thistly Cross. ♟ 30
Facilities Non-diners area ♦ Children's portions Family room Garden Outside area ⊭ Beer festival Cider festival WiFi ➡

DUNDEE
Map 21 NO43

Speedwell Bar

tel: 01382 667783 **165-167 Perth Rd DD2 1AS**
dir: *From A92 (Tay Bridge), A991 signed Perth/A85/Coupar Angus/A923. At Riverside rdbt 3rd exit (A991). At lights left into Nethergate signed Parking/South Tay St. Becomes Perth Rd. Pass university. Bar on right*

Edwardian gem with unspoilt interior

This fine example of an unspoiled Edwardian art deco bar is worth visiting for its interior alone; all the fitments in the bar and sitting rooms are beautifully crafted mahogany – gantry, drink shelves, dado panelling and fireplace. Internal doors are all glazed with etched glass. The same family owned it for 90 years, until the present landlord's father bought it in the mid 90s. As well as the cask-conditioned ales, 157 whiskies and imported bottles are offered. A kitchen would be good, but since the pub is listed this is impossible. Visitors are encouraged to bring their own snacks from nearby bakeries. This community pub is home to several clubs and has live Scottish music from time to time on a Tuesday.

Open all day all wk 11am-mdnt ⊕ FREE HOUSE ◀ Caledonian Deuchars IPA, Harviestoun Bitter & Twisted, Williams Bros Seven Giraffes Ö Addlestones. ♟ 18
Facilities Non-diners area ✿ (Bar) ⊭ Beer festival WiFi ➡ Notes ⊛

CITY OF EDINBURGH

EDINBURGH   Map 21 NT27

The Bow Bar

tel: 0131 226 7667 **80 The West Bow EH1 2HH**
dir: *Phone for detailed directions*

A whisky and beer connoisseurs' delight

If there is one free house that reflects the history and traditions of Edinburgh's Old Town, it is The Bow Bar. With some 290 malt whiskies, eight real ales poured from traditional tall founts and 50 bottled beers, the focus may be on liquid refreshment but the range of snacks includes haggis, cheese and chilli pies and bridies (meat pastries). Tables from old train carriages and a church gantry add to the unique feel of a bar where the sound of conversation makes up for the lack of gaming machines and music. Twice a year in January and July, the pub holds ten-day long beer festivals.

Open all day all wk Closed 25-26 Dec **Food** Lunch Mon-Sat 12-3, Sun 12.30-3 ⊕ FREE HOUSE ◣ Alechemy, Stewart Edinburgh No 3, Fyne Avalanche & Jarl, Tempest, Thornbridge, Fallen Dragonfly, Black Isle Porter, Williams Bros Joker IPA, Cromarty Happy Chappy ♻ Westons Stowford Press. **Facilities** Non-diners area ❤ (Bar Restaurant) Beer festival WiFi

The Café Royal ◉   PICK OF THE PUBS

tel: 0131 556 1884 **19 West Register St EH2 2AA**
dir: *Off Princes St, in city centre*

Hearty Scottish fare in historic building

Designed by local architect Robert Paterson, The Café Royal is a glorious example of Victorian and Baroque, with an interior seemingly frozen in time. Elegant stained glass and fine late Victorian plasterwork dominate the building, as do irreplaceable Doulton ceramic murals in the bar and restaurant. The whole building and its interior were listed in 1970 so future generations can enjoy the unique building which still sticks to its early 19th-century roots by serving local ales such as Kelburn Ca'Canny and Goldihops, wine, coffee and fresh oysters in the bar and restaurant. Scottish produce dominates the menu, from starters of black pudding with king scallops to mains of Balmoral chicken wrapped in bacon and stuffed with haggis. Please note children are allowed in the restaurant but there are no changing facilities for babies.

Open all day all wk **Food** Lunch all wk 11-9.45 Dinner all wk 11-9.45 Restaurant menu available all wk ⊕ SPIRIT PUB COMPANY ◣ Edinburgh Pale Ale, Kelburn Ca'Canny & Goldihops, Williams Bros, Stewart, Broughton Ales ♻ Aspall. ♟ 9 **Facilities** Non-diners area WiFi ⛟ (notice required)

Doric Tavern   PICK OF THE PUBS

tel: 0131 225 1084 **15-16 Market St EH1 1DE**
email: info@the-doric.com
dir: *In city centre opposite Waverly Station & Edinburgh Dungeons*

Edinburgh's oldest gastro-pub

There's been a dining inn on this site close to the Royal Mile and the Scottish National Gallery since at least 1823. As such it's the oldest food-inn in Edinburgh, and it proudly continues to offer top-quality Scottish sourced produce. The building may be 400 years old and is apparently named from an old language once spoken in north-east Scotland, mainly Aberdeenshire. Award-winning Scottish beers are the mainstay here, including brews from Caledonian and micros like Cairngorm, while

real whisky-cask cider comes from Dunbar. Public rooms include a ground-floor bar, and a wine bar and bistro upstairs. In these pleasantly informal surroundings, a wide choice of fresh, locally sourced food is prepared by the chefs on site. Favourite starters include Cullen skink, or smoked salmon with capers. Mains from the chef's specials range could be haggis, neeps and tatties in light whisky juice, or home-made shepherd's pie topped with Isle of Mull cheddar cheese mash. Seafood is delivered fresh each morning; look for haddock fillet fried in pub-made beer batter.

Open all day all wk Sat-Thu 11.30am-1am (Fri 11am-1am) Closed 25-26 Dec **Food** Lunch all wk 12-10 Dinner all wk 12-10 Av main course £10 Set menu available Restaurant menu available all wk ⊕ FREE HOUSE ◣ Caledonian Deuchars IPA & Edinburgh Castle, Guest ales ♻ Thistly Cross, Westons Stowford Press. **Facilities** Non-diners area ❤ Children's menu Children's portions Family room WiFi ⛟

The Guildford Arms

tel: 0131 556 4312 **1-5 West Register St EH2 2AA**
email: guildfordarms@dmstewart.com
dir: *Opposite Balmoral Hotel at E end of Princes St*

Late-Victorian classic free house and galleried restaurant

Arrive at Edinburgh Waverley railway station and head straight here; miss a departing train, ditto — it's so close it would be almost criminal not to. Worthy of study are the bar's magnificent Jacobean-style ceiling, and 10 blue porcelain-handled real ale hand-pumps bearing the Stewart family crest. April and October beer festivals, and monthly brewery weekends underscore their commitment to the products of malted barley. The galleried restaurant offers Orkney Dark Island Ale and Aberdeen Angus steak pie; haggis, neeps and tatties; and Shetland mussels in creamy garlic and white wine sauce. However fascinated they might be, under-fives are not allowed in the bar.

Open all day all wk Closed 25-26 Dec, 1 Jan **Food** Lunch all wk 12-3, snacks 3-9 Dinner Sun-Thu 5.30-9.30, Fri-Sat 5.30-10 Av main course £13 Restaurant menu available all wk ⊕ FREE HOUSE ◣ Orkney Dark Island, Highland Island Hopping, Stewart Pentland IPA, Highland Brewing Co, Alechemy, Fyne Ales Jarl, Rotating Guest ales ♻ Westons 1st Quality, Farmer Jims. ♟ 12 **Facilities** Non-diners area ❤ (Bar) ❤ Children's portions Family room Beer festival WiFi

Halfway House

tel: 0131 225 7101 **24 Fleshmarket Close EH1 1BX**
email: stevewhiting@straitmail.co.uk
dir: *From Royal Mile (close to x-rds with North & South bridges) into Cockburn St. Into Fleshmarket Close, or take flight of steps off Cockburn St on right*

Edinburgh's smallest pub is an iconic institution

Hidden down one of the Old Town's 'closes' (a narrow alleyway, often with a flight of steps and enclosed by tall buildings), the cosy interior of this pub is adorned with railway memorabilia and throngs with locals, tourists, lawyers, students and beer aficionados supping interesting ales from Scottish microbreweries, perhaps Houston Peter's Well and Cairngorm Trade Winds. Mop up the ale with some traditional Scottish bar food made from fresh produce — Cullen skink; stovies and oatcakes; or haggis, tatties and neeps perhaps. Look out for the regular beer festivals, but if beer is not your thing, then perhaps sample a few of the 40 or so whiskies displayed behind the bar.

Open all day all wk **Food** Lunch all wk all day Dinner all wk all day ⊕ FREE HOUSE ◣ Stewart Pentland IPA, Harviestoun Bitter & Twisted, Cairngorm Trade Winds, Houston Peter's Well, Cromarty, Alechemy ♻ Addlestones. **Facilities** Non-diners area ❤ (Bar) ❤ Outside area ☂ Beer festival WiFi **Notes** ◉

EDINBURGH *continued*

NEW The Scran & Scallie ☻   PICK OF THE PUBS

tel: 0131 561 8686 **1 Comely Bank Rd EH4 1DT**
email: info@scranandscallie.com
dir: *On B900, in Stockbridge area, opposite Inverleith Park & Botanical Gardens*

Somewhere new and exciting with cutting-edge cooking

From the same team that brought you the award-winning Edinburgh restaurants The Kitchin and Castle Terrace, The Scran & Scallie (it means 'food and scallywag') opened in 2013 to instant acclaim. In keeping with the building's vintage, many of the original features have been blended with trendy Scandinavian influences, including distressed and reclaimed furnishings, Isle of Bute fabrics and touches of tartan and tweed. Top Scottish chefs Tom Kitchin and Dominic Jack, along with head chef James Chapman, have created a menu of contemporary seasonal dishes that reflect the pub's 'from nature to plate' philosophy, as well as breathing new life into forgotten regional classics. Open all week for lunch, bar 'scran' and dinner (with very late closing times so you can tarry awhile), as well as weekend brunches, typical dishes include ham hock and vegetable broth; fish pie; tripe and ox tongue; and Highland bavette steak and corned beef hash. Puddings include chocolate brownie and popcorn ice cream; or vanilla cheesecake with poached pear.

Open all day all wk 11.30am–1am Closed 25 Dec **Food** Lunch Mon-Fri 12-3, Sat-Sun 12-5 Dinner Mon-Fri 5-10, Sat-Sun 6-10 Av main course £14.50 Set menu available Restaurant menu available all wk ⊕ FREE HOUSE ◖ Isle of Skye Skye Red & Skye Black, Harviestoun Ale ♂ Thistly Cross. ⬤ 40 **Facilities** Non-diners area ❀ (Bar Restaurant) ⬤ Children's menu Children's portions Play area Family room WiFi ⬛ (notice required)

The Shore Bar & Restaurant

tel: 0131 553 5080 **3 Shore, Leith EH6 6QW**
email: theshorebar@fishersrestaurantgroup.co.uk
dir: *Phone for detailed directions*

Enjoyable food at Edinburgh's bustling port

This redoubtable old pub at the heart of Leith's bustling waterfront welcomes guests with a memorable wood-boarded interior. It's said that a lighthouse, guiding seafarers to the safety of Edinburgh's port, once shared this site, but now visitors are drawn here by the excellent Scottish seafood for which the place is famous. Haddock tempura might be a good place to start, coupled with mains like Scottish lobster and chips, or whole braised pigeon with pea, pancetta and baby onion fricassée. Scottish-brewed real ales feature, and from the outside seating you can look out on the promenade beside the Water of Leith.

Open all day all wk noon–1am (Sun 12.30pm-1am) Closed 25-26 Dec, 1 Jan **Food** Lunch Mon-Sat 12-10, Sun 12.30-10 Dinner Mon-Sat 12-10, Sun 12.30-10 Set menu available Restaurant menu available all wk ⊕ FREE HOUSE ◖ Harviestoun Bitter & Twisted, Orkney Dark Island, Guinness ♂ Kopparberg, Aspall. ⬤ 14 **Facilities** Non-diners area ❀ (Bar Outside area) ⬤ Children's portions Outside area ⛩ WiFi ⬛ (notice required)

Whiski Bar & Restaurant

tel: 0131 556 3095 **119 High St EH1 1SG**
email: info@whiskibar.co.uk **web:** www.whiskibar.co.uk
dir: *Phone for detailed directions*

Whisky, music and food galore on the Royal Mile

If you find yourself on Edinburgh's famous Royal Mile and in need of sustenance and a 'wee' dram, then seek out this highly acclaimed bar at number 119. Choose from over 300 malt whiskies (all available by the nip) and tuck into some traditional Scottish food. Served all day, the menu makes good use of Scottish Border beef and daily deliveries of seafood from local fishermen. Typically, try Cullen skink; Haggis tower with neeps and mash; or smoked salmon penne pasta; then cranachan (a blend of whisky, oatmeal, cream honey and raspberries) for pudding. Come for the traditional Scottish music in the evening – The Whiski is famous for its fiddle music.

Open all day all wk Closed 25 Dec **Food** Lunch Mon-Thu 10-10, Fri-Sun 10am-10.30pm Dinner Mon-Thu 10-10, Fri-Sun 10am-10.30pm ⊕ FREE HOUSE ◖ Caledonian Deuchars IPA, Innis & Gunn, Williams Bros Caesar Augustus ♂ Thistly Cross. ⬤ 9 **Facilities** Non-diners area ⬤ Children's menu Children's portions Outside area ⛩ WiFi ⬛ (notice required)

See advert on opposite page

RATHO   Map 21 NT17

The Bridge Inn ★★★★ INN ☻   PICK OF THE PUBS

tel: 0131 333 1320 **27 Baird Rd EH28 8RA**
email: info@bridgeinn.com **web:** www.bridgeinn.com
dir: *From Newbridge at B7030 junct, follow signs for Ratho & Edinburgh Canal Centre*

Canal-side inn offering restaurant cruises

The tree-lined Union Canal between Edinburgh and the Falkirk Wheel runs past this waterside inn, once used by the early 19th-century navvies who dug the cut. In both the bar and restaurant the menu offers dishes based on local produce, including from the pub's kitchen garden, and from its own chickens, ducks and Saddleback pigs, the latter providing a rich supply of pork loin, fillet, belly and sausages. Bar favourites are fresh haddock with hand-cut chips, and pie of the week, while the restaurant features Buccleuch sirloin and fillet steaks; caramelised shoulder of hogget; smoked coley risotto; and hand-dived scallops. Guest Scottish cask ales may include Trade Winds from Cairngorm Brewery, Dark Island from Orkney and beers from Arran. The pub's two renovated barges provide Sunday lunch, afternoon tea and dinner cruises. Children and dogs love the big grassy area outside.

Open all day all wk 11-11 (Fri-Sat 11am-mdnt) Closed 25 Dec **Food** Lunch Mon-Fri 12-3, Sat 12-9, Sun 12-8.30 Dinner Mon-Fri 5-9, Sat 12-9, Sun 12-8.30 ⊕ FREE HOUSE ◀ Belhaven, rotating Alechemy Ales, Guest ales Ö Aspall. ☂ 40 **Facilities** Non-diners area ❀ (Bar Garden) ◀❶ Children's menu Children's portions Play area Garden 🎪 Beer festival Parking WiFi ➾ (notice required) **Rooms** 4

FIFE

BURNTISLAND
Map 21 NT28

Burntisland Sands Hotel

tel: 01592 872230 **Lochies Rd KY3 9JX**
email: mail@burntislandsands.co.uk
dir: *Towards Kirkcaldy, Burntisland on A921. Hotel on right before Kinghorn*

Family-run hotel just a hop from the beach

Once a highly regarded girls' boarding school, this small, family-run hotel stands only 50 yards from an award-winning sandy beach. Visitors can expect reasonably priced meals throughout the day, including internationally themed evenings. Typical dishes served in the three dining areas include deep fried breaded mushrooms or king prawns to start; mains like seared tuna steak with lemon butter, or haggis, neeps and tatties; and bread and butter pudding or mint paradise for dessert. Relax and enjoy a Scottish ale in the bar and lounge area, perhaps on a live music night. There is also a patio garden and children can play with the rabbits in the activity area.

Open all day all wk **Food** Lunch Mon-Fri 12-2.30, Sat-Sun all day Dinner Mon-Fri 5-8.30, Sat-Sun all day Av main course £8 Set menu available Restaurant menu available all wk ⊕ FREE HOUSE ◀ Caledonian Deuchars IPA, Tennent's, Belhaven Best, Guinness, Guest ales. **Facilities** Non-diners area ❀ (Garden) ◀❶ Children's menu Children's portions Play area Garden 🎪 Parking WiFi ➾ (notice required)

ST ANDREWS
Map 21 NO51

Hams Hame Pub & Grill

tel: 01334 474371 **The Old Course Hotel, Golf Resort & Spa KY16 9SP**
email: reservations@oldcoursehotel.co.uk
dir: *M90 junct 8, A91 to St Andrews*

Finest Scottish produce at famous golf venue

Part of a famous complex, this pub, with low ceilings, beams and wooden floors, is over the road from the famous Old Course's 18th green. This being the 19th hole, your fellow diner or drinker might well be a golfing legend, sharing your enjoyment of some of Scotland's best breweries and menus showcasing its finest produce. Freshly landed North Sea fish and seafood is a given, typically shellfish and chorizo gumbo; other dishes include Dornoch rack of pork ribs; Cajun chicken burger; and grilled flat-cap mushroom with garlic potatoes.

Open all day all wk **Food** Lunch all wk 11.30-9.30 Dinner all wk 11.30-9.30 ⊕ FREE HOUSE ◀ Local ales. **Facilities** Non-diners area ◀❶ Children's menu Children's portions WiFi ➾ (notice required)

The Jigger Inn
PICK OF THE PUBS

tel: 01334 474371 **The Old Course Hotel, Golf Resort & Spa KY16 9SP**
email: reservations@oldcoursehotel.co.uk
dir: *M90 junct 8, A91 to St Andrews*

Possibly golf's best-known 19th hole

Golfing history is an all-embracing experience at this former stationmaster's lodge on the now long-disused railway line to Leuchars. It's now in the grounds of The Old Course Hotel, the course in question being the world-famous Royal & Ancient Golf Club of St Andrews. Belhaven brewery supplies the appropriately named St Andrews real ale, and Jigger, brewed exclusively for both the pub and its sister golfing resort in Wisconsin, USA. Available all day is seafood landed in nearby fishing villages, carefully selected pork, lamb, beef, game and poultry reared by award-winning Scottish producers, and seasonal fruit and vegetables from local farms. Main courses include rib-eye steak with grilled Portobello mushrooms and béarnaise sauce; and tabouleh and Mediterranean vegetable fusilli pasta.

Open all day all wk 11-11 (Sun 12-11) **Food** Lunch all wk 12-9.30 Dinner all wk 12-9.30 ⊕ FREE HOUSE ◀ The Jigger Inn Jigger Ale, St Andrews, Guinness. ☂ 8 **Facilities** Non-diners area ◀❶ Garden 🎪 Parking ➾

ST ANDREWS continued

The Inn at Lathones ★★★★ INN ◉◉ **PICK OF THE PUBS**

tel: 01334 840494 **Largoward KY9 1JE**
email: stay@innatlathones.com **web:** www.innatlathones.com
dir: 5m from St Andrews on A915

Old coaching inn that's big on music

The footprint of this late 17th-century coaching inn takes up most of the hamlet of Lathones in the East Neuk (meaning corner) of Fife. In 1718 a minister blessed a young couple's marriage here, and their wedding stone has served as the lintel over a fireplace ever since. The oldest part, the stone-walled Stables, is home to the Grey Lady, a friendly ghost with her equally spectral horse. More practically, it's also the bar and venue for frequent live music, with its own menu and real ales from Belhaven and Eden. For many years the restaurant has been awarded two AA Rosettes for its innovative cooking of well-sourced local ingredients. A three-course choice in the Stables could commence with Dunsyre Blue cheese brûlée with pear chutney; continue with roast breast of chicken with tian of haggis, crushed potatoes and peppercorn sauce; and round off nicely with rhubarb and vanilla cheesecake.

Open all day all wk 10-10 Closed 2wks Jan **Food** Lunch all wk 12-3 Dinner all wk 6-9 Restaurant menu available all wk ⊕ FREE HOUSE ◀ Belhaven Best, Eden Ales. **Facilities** Non-diners area ♦ Children's menu Children's portions Garden ⊼ Parking WiFi ▭ **Rooms** 21

CITY OF GLASGOW

| GLASGOW | Map 20 NS56 |

Bon Accord

tel: 0141 248 4427 **153 North St G3 7DA**
email: paul.bonaccord@ntlbusiness.com
dir: M8 junct 19 merge onto A804 (North Street) signed Charing Cross

An unmissable destination for malt whisky lovers

Visitors from all over the world come to the 'Bon', Paul McDonagh and son Thomas's acclaimed alehouse and malt whisky bar. The reason? To sample some of the annual tally of a 1,000-plus different beers, over 40 ciders (maybe at one of the four beer and cider festivals), or the 350-strong malts collection (a far cry from the original five on offer). Menus display all-day breakfasts, baguettes, giant Yorkshire puddings, chilli con carne, fish and chips, grilled steaks, chicken salads, macaroni cheese and vegetarian Glamorgan sausages (made with leek and Caerphilly).

Open all day all wk **Food** Lunch all wk 12-8 Dinner all wk 12-8 Av main course £6.95 Set menu available ⊕ FREE HOUSE ◀ Over 1,000 real ales per year ♂ Over 40 ciders per year. ♥ 11 **Facilities** Non-diners area ♦ Garden Outside area ⊼ Beer festival Cider festival WiFi ▭

Rab Ha's

tel: 0141 572 0400 **83 Hutchieson St G1 1SH**
email: management@rabhas.com
dir: Phone for detailed directions

A blend of Victorian character and contemporary Scottish decor

This hotel, restaurant and bar in the heart of Glasgow's revitalised Merchant City takes its name from Robert Hall, a local 19th-century character known as 'The Glasgow Glutton' who would earn a living by taking bets on the amount of food he could consume. The kitchen team prides itself on the extensive use of carefully sourced Scottish produce to create hearty Scottish dishes like breaded Scottish brie; smoked Loch Fyne trout and salmon rillette; Cullen skink; haggis, neeps and tatties; Angus sirloin steak and hand-cut chips; Rab's tomato and seafood broth; and Ailsa Craig cheese salad.

Open all day all wk 12-12 (Sun 12.30-12) ⊕ FREE HOUSE ◀ Tennent's, Blue Moon, West Brewery St Mungos, Belhaven Best, Guest ales ♂ Addlestones. **Facilities** ☀ (Bar Outside area) ♦ Children's portions Outside area WiFi

Stravaigin ◉◉ **PICK OF THE PUBS**

tel: 0141 334 2665 **26-30 Gibson St G12 8NX**
email: stravaigin@btinternet.com
dir: Phone for directions

Encouraging a policy of culinary curiosity

'Stravaig' is an old Scots' word meaning 'to wander aimlessly with intent' which fits the Stravaigin's 'think global, eat local' philosophy perfectly. Located in a busy street close to the university, this popular bar/restaurant has picked up two AA Rosettes for the food, and also an environmental award. The modern split-level basement restaurant draws the crowds with its contemporary decor, modern art and quirky antiques. The bar offers an extensive wine list and real ales like Fyne Chip 71. Expect innovative and exciting fusion food cooked from top-notch, seasonal Scottish ingredients – the same menu is served throughout. Embracing the flavours of the world are dishes of Masala chicken livers, chickpea and coriander polenta, neep relish and tamarind chutney; chilindron – a Spanish pheasant stew with chorizo and red peppers; steamed West Coast mussels in Keralan coconut, tamarind and curry leaf sauce; spiced caramel pineapple, coconut and lychee sorbet, pineapple purée and coriander salted peanuts.

Open all day all wk Closed 1 Jan, 25 Dec **Food** Lunch all wk 11-5 Dinner all wk 5-11 Restaurant menu available all wk ⊕ FREE HOUSE ◀ Caledonian Deuchars IPA, Belhaven Best, Fyne Chip 71 ♂ Westons Wyld Wood Organic Classic, Addlestones. ♥ 19 **Facilities** Non-diners area ☀ (Bar) ♦ Children's menu Children's portions ⊼ WiFi

Ubiquitous Chip ◉◉ **PICK OF THE PUBS**

tel: 0141 334 5007 **12 Ashton Ln G12 8SJ**
email: mail@ubiquitouschip.co.uk
dir: In West End of Glasgow, off Byres Rd. Beside Hillhead subway station

Iconic city pub with buzzing atmosphere and memorable menus

One of the city's most intriguing pubs stands hidden down a cobbled lane in Glasgow's Bohemian, trendy West End. Here; this mews property has morphed over four decades into a jigsaw of eating and drinking spaces to savour. The main dining area opens into a vine-covered courtyard, while upstairs is the brasserie-style, two AA-Rosette restaurant. There are three drinking areas: the traditional Big Pub, serving real ales such as Loch Fyne (there's a twice-yearly beer festival here too), nearly 30 wines by the glass and more than 150 malt whiskies; the Wee Bar, which lives up to its name by being possibly the 'wee-est' bar in Scotland; and the Corner Bar, which serves cocktails across a granite slab reclaimed from a mortuary. The menu is a Pandora's Box of delights and draws lavishly on Scotland's generous larder. Lead in with smoked haddock fishcake with Arbroath smokie mayonnaise; then turn attention to Ayrshire mallard breast, confit leg, roast celeriac, Savoy cabbage and bacon with mead gravy.

Open all day all wk 11am-1am Closed 1 Jan, 25 Dec **Food** Lunch all wk 11-11 Dinner all wk 11-11 Restaurant menu available all wk ⊕ FREE HOUSE ◀ Caledonian Deuchars IPA, Fyne Chip 71 ♂ Addlestones. ♥ 29 **Facilities** Non-diners area ☀ (Bar Outside area) ♦ Children's menu Children's portions Outside area ⊼ Beer festival WiFi ▭ (notice required)

WEST Brewery · PICK OF THE PUBS

tel: 0141 550 0135 **Templeton Building, Glasgow Green G40 1AW**
email: info@westbeer.com
dir: *Phone for detailed directions*

German-style brewpub in converted carpet factory

'Glaswegian heart, German head' is the strapline this buzzy brewpub/restaurant uses as the only UK brewery producing beers in accordance with Germany's Purity Law of 1516, which means no additives, colourings or preservatives. It occupies the old Winding House of a former carpet factory, modelled by its Victorian architect on the Doge's Palace in Venice. Look down into the brewhouse from the beer hall and watch the brewers making artisanal lagers and wheat beers, including St Mungo, Dunkel, Munich Red and Hefeweizen. Brewery tours are conducted on selected days of the week. The all-day menu has a German flavour too, offering Schinkenbrot, Currywurst and Käsebrot sandwiches; Brotaufstriche; Wiener Schnitzel; and Semmelknödel. If these choices don't appeal you can also choose from grills, burgers and other British pub grub. For dessert are Viennese apple strudel; baked Alaska; and, in a nod to the past, Black Forest gâteau. Brunch is available at weekends. October's Fridays are Oktoberfest beer festival days.

Open all day all wk Closed 25-26 Dec, 1-2 Jan **Food** Lunch all wk 12-5 Dinner all wk 5-9 Av main course £9.95 Set menu available Restaurant menu available all wk ⊕ FREE HOUSE ◀ WEST Munich Red & GPA. **Facilities** Non-diners area ♣ (Bar Restaurant Garden) ♦♦ Children's menu Children's portions Garden ♬ Beer festival WiFi ⇌ (notice required)

HIGHLAND

ACHILTIBUIE · Map 22 NC00

Summer Isles Hotel & Bar · PICK OF THE PUBS

tel: 01854 622282 **IV26 2YG**
email: summerisleshotel@gmail.com
dir: *Take A835 N from Ullapool for 10m, Achiltibuie signed on left, 15m to village. Hotel 1m on left*

Remote, but that's one of its attractions

With its wonderful views of Badentarbat Bay and the Summer Isles, this highly praised hotel is adored by seafood lovers. Why? Because within sight of the place, Andy the Diver hand-picks scallops from the Gulf Stream-warmed sea bed, Peter from nearby Polbain supplies crab and lobster, and Dan's the man for langoustines. Of course, the daily menus and specials blackboards offer plenty of alternatives to seafood, including rib-eye of Speyside beef; Highland venison burger; and traditional fish and chips. The informal all-day bar serves freshly ground coffee, snacks, lunch, afternoon tea and evening meals. Real ales come from the An Teallach brewery on a croft a few miles to the south at Dundonnell. As the weather can range from Aegean to Arctic inside a week, come prepared, not forgetting something for the midges that the Highlands host from late spring to late summer.

Open all wk 11-11 Closed 31 Oct-3 Apr **Food** Lunch all wk 12-3 (soup & snacks till 5) Dinner all wk 6-9.30 Restaurant menu available all wk ⊕ FREE HOUSE ◀ An Teallach Crofters' Pale Ale, Beinn Deorg. **Facilities** Non-diners area ♣ (Garden) ♦♦ Children's menu Children's portions Garden ♬ Parking WiFi ⇌ (notice required)

CAWDOR · Map 23 NH85

Cawdor Tavern · PICK OF THE PUBS

See Pick of the Pubs on page 608

FORTROSE · Map 23 NH75

The Anderson · PICK OF THE PUBS

tel: 01381 620236 **Union St IV10 8TD**
email: info@theanderson.co.uk
dir: *From Inverness take A9 N signed Wick. Right onto B9161 signed Munlochy, Cromarty & A832. At T-junct right onto A832 to Fortrose*

Coastal conservation village on the Black Isle

On the beautiful Black Isle to the north of Inverness, this striking black-and-white painted pub enjoys a tranquil seaside setting; a short walk from its door passes the gaunt, ruined cathedral before happening on the picturesque harbour at Fortrose, with sweeping views across the Moray Firth. Nearby Chanonry Point lighthouse is renowned as one of the best places from which to watch the dolphins in the Firth. But why leave an inn famed for its classic range of finest Scottish microbrewery beers, vast array of Belgian beers and 230 single malts selected by American proprietor Jim Anderson? The 'global cuisine' created with freshest Scottish produce is equally comprehensive. Aberdeen beef, West Coast seafood and Highland game are amongst ingredients on the daily-changing menu: seafood chowder or fried ravioli are typical starters, followed perhaps by Stornoway guinea fowl (stuffed with Munro's white pudding) and creamy leek and cider sauce. You could finish with apple rhubarb crumble tartlet with vanilla ice cream.

Open all wk 4pm-late Closed mid Nov-mid Dec & 25 Dec **Food** Dinner all wk 6-9.30 ⊕ FREE HOUSE ◀ Rotating ales ♂ Addlestones. ♛ 13 **Facilities** Non-diners area ♣ (Bar Garden) ♦♦ Children's menu Garden ♬ Beer festival Parking WiFi

FORT WILLIAM · Map 22 NN17

Moorings Hotel ★★★★ HL

tel: 01397 772797 **Banavie PH33 7LY**
email: reservations@moorings-fortwilliam.co.uk **web:** www.moorings-fortwilliam.co.uk
dir: *From A82 in Fort William follow signs for Mallaig, left onto A830 for 1m. Cross canal bridge, 1st right signed Banavie*

Canalside spot with panoramic views

The historic Caledonian Canal and Neptune's Staircase, the famous flight of eight locks, runs right beside this modern hotel and pub. On clear days it has panoramic views towards Ben Nevis, best savoured from the Upper Deck lounge bar and the bedrooms. Food, served in the lounge bar and the fine-dining Neptunes Restaurant, features local fish and seafood, with other choices such as steak and ale pie, and rib-eye of Highland beef. There is access to the canal towpath from the gardens.

Open all day all wk Closed 24-26 Dec **Food** Lunch all wk 12-9.30 Dinner all wk 12-9.30 Restaurant menu available ⊕ FREE HOUSE ◀ Tetley's Bitter, Caledonian Deuchars IPA, Guinness. ♛ 8 **Facilities** Non-diners area ♣ (Garden) ♦♦ Children's menu Children's portions Garden ♬ Parking WiFi ⇌ (notice required) **Rooms** 27

PICK OF THE PUBS

Cawdor Tavern

CAWDOR   Map 23 NH85

tel: 01667 404777 **The Lane IV12 5XP**
email: enquiries@cawdortavern.co.uk
web: www.cawdortavern.co.uk
dir: *Between Inverness and Nairn, take A96 onto B9006, follow Cawdor Castle signs. Tavern in village centre*

Scottish innkeeping at its best

The Tavern is tucked away in the heart of Cawdor's pretty conservation village; nearby is the castle where Macbeth held court. Pretty wooded countryside slides away from the pub, offering umpteen opportunities for rambles and challenging cycle routes. Exercise over, repair to this homely hostelry to enjoy the welcoming mix of fine Scottish food and island microbrewery ales that makes the pub a destination in its own right. There's an almost baronial feel to the bars, created from the Cawdor Estate's joinery workshop in the 1960s. The lounge bar's wonderful panelling came from Cawdor Castle's dining room as a gift from a former laird; log fires and stoves add winter warmth, as does the impressive choice of Orkney Brewery beers and Highland and Island malts. An accomplished menu balances meat, fish, game and vegetarian options, prepared in a modern Scottish style with first class Scottish produce. Settle in the delightful restaurant beneath wrought iron Jacobean chandeliers and contemplate starting with a trio of

Scottish puddings – black pudding, prize haggis and white pudding layered together and served with home-made chutney. Next maybe a venison burger from the grill, topped with smoked bacon, tomato relish and melting mozzarella. Classic sweets include sticky toffee pudding, and chocolate brownie with warm chocolate sauce. Alfresco drinking and dining is possible on the colourful patio area at the front of the Tavern during the warm summer months. Excellent value is a Sunday high tea starting at 4.30pm.

Open all wk 11-3 5-11 (Sat 11am-mdnt Sun 12.30-11) Mar-Dec all day Closed 25 Dec, 1 Jan **Food** Lunch Mon-Sat 12-2, Sun 12.30-3 (Mar-Dec all day) Dinner all wk 5.30-9 (Mar-Dec all day)

⊕ FREE HOUSE ◀ Orkney Red MacGregor, Raven Ale, Clootie Dumpling & Dark Island, Atlas Latitude Highland Pilsner, Three Sisters, Nimbus & Wayfarer ♂ Thatchers Gold. ♇ 9
Facilities Non-diners area ❀ (Bar) ♦♦ Children's menu Children's portions Outside area ⋻ Beer festival Parking WiFi ☞ (notice required)

GAIRLOCH Map 22 NG87

The Old Inn PICK OF THE PUBS

tel: 01445 712006 **IV21 2BD**
email: info@theoldinn.net
dir: *Just off A832, near harbour at south end of village*

Traditional coaching inn with its own brewery

Close to the small harbour in a sheltered bay at the northern fringe of the immense Torridon Mountains, fabulous walks percolate from this old coaching and drovers' inn to secluded bays and wooded crags with memorable views across to Skye and the outer islands. Owner Alastair Pearson operates the pub's own on-site microbrewery, so expect pints of The Erradale, Mike's Mild and Blind Piper alongside other Scottish micro's beers at the bar. It's not just the beer that's home-made: the pub has its own smokery producing smoked meats, fish and cheese, and bread is baked in-house. Highland game and West Coast seafood feature strongly in a comfortable menu of standards and modern dishes. Clams in a white wine cream sauce sets the tone; slow-cooked local venison casserole with herb dumplings, or pan-fried scallops with black pudding purée, beurre blanc and shoestring fries two of a regularly changing roll-call of mains.

Open all day all wk 11am-mdnt (Sun 12-12) Closed 21 Nov-Feb **Food** Lunch all wk 12-2.30, summer 12-4.30 Dinner all wk 5-9.30 Restaurant menu available all wk evening ⊕ FREE HOUSE ◀ The Old Inn The Erradale, The Flowerdale, The Slattadale, Mike's Mild & Blind Piper, An Teallach Beinn Dearg, Crofters' Pale Ale & Suilven, Cairngorm Nessie's Monster Mash, Trade Winds & Wildcat.
Facilities Non-diners area ☀ (Bar Garden) ♦♦ Children's menu Children's portions Garden 🎄 Parking WiFi 🚌 (notice required)

GLENCOE Map 22 NN15

Clachaig Inn

tel: 01855 811252 **PH49 4HX**
email: frontdesk@clachaig.com
dir: *Follow Glencoe signs from A82. Inn 3m S of village*

Real craic at this legendary Highland inn

In the heart of Glencoe, against a backdrop of spectacular mountains, this famous Highland inn has welcomed climbers, hill-walkers, skiers, kayakers and regular travellers for over 300 years. Real ales (sometimes as many as 15), nearly 300 malt whiskies, good food and fresh coffee are served in all three bars, each with its own distinctive and lively character. Local dishes on offer include Stornoway black pudding; oak-smoked West Coast salmon; Highland venison burger; and vegetarian haggis, neeps 'n' tatties. As well as beer and whisky tastings, the pub also holds a Hogmanay beer festival, and two others – FebFest and OctoberFest.

Open all day all wk Closed 24-26 Dec **Food** Lunch all wk 12-9 Dinner all wk 12-9 ⊕ FREE HOUSE ◀ Rotating Guest ales ♂ Westons, Thistly Cross.
Facilities Non-diners area ☀ (Bar Garden) ♦♦ Children's menu Children's portions Play area Family room Garden 🎄 Beer festival Parking WiFi 🚌

GLENUIG Map 22 NM67

Glenuig Inn

tel: 01687 470219 **PH38 4NG**
email: bookings@glenuig.com
dir: *From Fort William on A830 towards Mallaig through Glen Finnan. Left onto A861, 8m to Glenuig Bay*

A more spectacular setting you couldn't wish for

The newly renovated Glenuig Inn, on a no-through road and right beside a stunning beach on the Sound of Arisaig, is a popular base for sea-kayakers. The emphasis

here is 'as local as we can get it' and this philosophy applies to the bar, where only local real ale from Cairngorm is served, and the kitchen, where menus are prepared using organic seasonal ingredients wherever possible. A typical selection might include Glenuig hot smoked salmon, followed by Skye lamb tagine or home-made venison burger, and chocolate and chilli tart to finish. The inn's owners are committed to 'going green', and also welcome dogs throughout.

Open all day all wk **Food** Lunch all wk 12-9 Dinner all wk 12-9 ⊕ FREE HOUSE ◀ Cairngorm Trade Winds, Black Gold, Gold, Wild Cat, Nessie's Monster Mash & Stag ♂ Thistly Cross. ☗ 9 **Facilities** Non-diners area ☀ (Bar Restaurant Garden) ♦♦ Children's menu Children's portions Play area Family room Garden 🎄 Parking WiFi

INVERGARRY Map 22 NH30

The Invergarry Hotel

tel: 01809 501206 **PH35 4HJ**
email: info@invergarryhotel.co.uk
dir: *At junct of A82 & A87*

In a tranquil spot, ideal for walking

A real Highland atmosphere pervades this roadside inn set in glorious mountain scenery between Fort William and Fort Augustus. Welcoming bars make it a great base from which to explore Loch Ness, Glencoe and the West Coast. Relax by the crackling log fire with a wee dram or a pint of Garry Ale, then tuck into a good meal. Perhaps try Lochaber haggis, bashit neeps and tatties to start; followed by sea bream en papillote or a succulent 10oz rib-eye Scottish beefsteak and hand-cut chips. There are, of course, excellent walks from the front door. Please note that booking is required for dinner.

Open all day all wk **Food** Lunch all wk 8am-9.30pm Dinner all wk 8am-9.30pm Av main course £13 ⊕ FREE HOUSE ◀ The Invergarry Inn Garry Ale.
Facilities Non-diners area ♦♦ Children's menu Children's portions Family room Garden 🎄 Parking

KYLESKU Map 22 NC23

Kylesku Hotel PICK OF THE PUBS

tel: 01971 502231 **IV27 4HW**
email: info@kyleskuhotel.co.uk
dir: *A835, A837 & A894 to Kylesku. Hotel at end of road at Old Ferry Pier*

Wonderful local seafood by the loch

A major renovation and extension to the bar and restaurant has completely upgraded this 17th-century coaching inn at the centre of the North West Highlands Global Geopark. Surrounded by lochs, mountains and wild coast – and close to Britain's highest waterfall – it's a glorious location. Views from the bar and restaurant are truly memorable – you may catch sight of seals, dolphins, otters, eagles and terns. The fishing boats moor at the old ferry slipway to land the creel-caught seafood that forms the backbone of the daily-changing menu. So settle down with a pint of Isle of Skye, and ponder your choice of the morning's catch, perhaps starting with Loch Fyne oysters, Loch Glendhu langoustines or hand-dived local king scallops. Next, you could go for a paella of local seafood, chicken and barley; grilled Scottish rib-eye or fish pie. Gluten-free and vegetarian menus also available.

Open all day all wk Closed Dec-Jan **Food** Lunch all wk 12-6 Dinner all wk 6-9 Av main course £14 ⊕ FREE HOUSE ◀ An Teallach & Beinn Dearg Ale, Isle of Skye. ☗ 12 **Facilities** Non-diners area ☀ (Bar Restaurant Garden) ♦♦ Children's menu Children's portions Garden 🎄 WiFi

PICK OF THE PUBS

The Plockton Hotel

PLOCKTON   Map 22 NG83

tel: 01599 544274 **Harbour St IV52 8TN**
email: info@plocktonhotel.co.uk
web: www.plocktonhotel.co.uk
dir: *A87 towards Kyle of Lochalsh. At Balmacara follow Plockton signs, 7m*

Award-winning local seafood served here

Set with the mountains on one side and the deep blue waters of Loch Carron on the other, this lovely village is well known for its white-washed cottages and, of all things, palm trees. Dating from 1827, this original black fronted building is thought to have been a ships' chandlery before it was converted to serve as the village inn. Run by Alan Pearson and Mags Pearson, the couple have inherited a successful legacy from Alan's parents who were in charge for two decades. The hotel specialises in seafood — including freshly landed fish and locally caught langoustines (mid afternoon you can watch the catch being landed) — supplemented by Highland steaks and locally reared beef. Lunchtime features light bites and toasted paninis, as well as a good range of hot dishes. Evening dishes might include Talisker whisky pâté; sweet pickled herring and prawns; or grilled goats' cheese with beetroot chutney to

start, followed by Highland venison collops with Cumberland sauce; fillet of monkfish wrapped in bacon; chargrilled Aberdeen Angus steak with whisky sauce; or pan-fried medallions of pork with brandied apricots and cream sauce. Daily specials, written up on the blackboard, add to the tempting choices. There are four Scottish real ales on tap, and a fine range of malts is available to round off that perfect Highland day, perhaps accompanied by one of the 'basket' meals served every evening from 9pm-10pm — try the breaded scampi tails.

Open all day all wk 11am-mdnt (Sun 12-11) Closed 25 Dec, 1 Jan **Food** Lunch all wk 12-2.15 Dinner all wk 6-10 Av main course £12 ⊕ FREE HOUSE 🍺 Highland Scapa Special & Island Hopping, Cromarty Happy Chappy & Kowabunga. **Facilities** Non-diners area 🚼 Children's menu Children's portions Family room Garden ⴕ Beer festival WiFi

LEWISTON
Map 23 NH52

The Loch Ness Inn

tel: 01456 450991 **IV63 6UW**
email: info@staylochness.co.uk
dir: *Phone for detailed directions*

Comfy village inn in the famous Great Glen

A brisk stroll from here on the waymarked Great Glen Way heads towards the shoreline of the renowned loch. Try a few jars of the locally brewed Inndiginess bitter at the inn's bustling bar and who knows what you'll see in the shimmering waters? The place is a hive of activity and there's always an event of some kind going on. With haggis bobotie or curried crab and mango as a starter; then seafood linguine or Highland venison loin to follow, that appetite-building loch-side ramble to famous Urquhart Castle looks more and more desirable. Unusually, a range of Scottish distilled gins is available at the bar.

Open all day all wk **Food** Lunch all wk breakfast-9pm Dinner all wk breakfast-9pm Set menu available Restaurant menu available all wk ⊕ FREE HOUSE ◖ Loch Ness LightNess, LochNess & Inndiginess ♂ Thistly Cross. ⏹ 10 **Facilities** Non-diners area ♦ Children's menu Children's portions Garden ⋒ Parking WiFi ▭ (notice required)

NORTH BALLACHULISH
Map 22 NN06

Loch Leven Hotel

tel: 01855 821236 **Old Ferry Rd PH33 6SA**
email: reception@lochlevenhotel.co.uk
dir: *Off A82, N of Ballachulish Bridge*

Enjoy one of Scotland's most idyllic views

The slipway into Loch Leven at the foot of the garden recalls the origins of this 17th-century inn as one of the Road to The Isles staging points linked to the old ferry. Enjoy a pint of River Leven bitter onto the sundeck and drink-in one of the best views from a pub anywhere in Britain, or on chillier days sit beside the open fire. The extraordinary location, near the foot of Glencoe and with horizons peppered by Munro peaks rising above azure sea lochs, is gifted with superb seafood from the local depths. So you can enjoy scallop, sea bass, and mussel dishes and also classics such as an Aberdeen Angus burger with hand-cut chips. Adjoining the bar are family and games rooms.

Open all day all wk 11-11 (Thu-Sat 11am-mdnt Sun 12.30-11) **Food** Lunch all wk 12-3 Dinner all wk 6-9 Av main course £10 Restaurant menu available all wk ⊕ FREE HOUSE ◖ River Leven. ⏹ 16 **Facilities** Non-diners area ♣ (Bar Garden) ♦ Children's menu Children's portions Family room Garden ⋒ Parking WiFi ▭ (notice required)

PLOCKTON
Map 22 NG83

The Plockton Hotel
PICK OF THE PUBS

See Pick of the Pubs on opposite page

Plockton Inn & Seafood Restaurant
PICK OF THE PUBS

See Pick of the Pubs on page 612

SHIELDAIG
Map 22 NG85

Shieldaig Bar & Coastal Kitchen
PICK OF THE PUBS

See Pick of the Pubs on page 613

TORRIDON
Map 22 NG95

The Torridon Inn ★★★★ INN
PICK OF THE PUBS

tel: 01445 791242 **IV22 2EY**
email: info@thetorridon.com **web:** www.thetorridon.com/inn
dir: *From Inverness take A9 N, then follow signs to Ullapool. Take A835 then A832. In Kinlochewe take A896 to Annat. Pub 200yds on right after village*

Idyllic location and definitive Scottish menus

The island-fringed, azure waters of Loch Torridon and the striking mountains across the water are neighbours to this bustling inn. It makes it a convenient base to walk, mountaineer, kayak or rock climb, but its cosy comfortable atmosphere and good home-cooked food very much appeal to the less active too. Painstakingly converted from old farm buildings, a stable block and buttery, there's a good range of Highlands and Islands beer on tap, often from Cairngorm and An Teallach breweries, supplemented by an annual October beer festival. A cosy interior with wood fires and bright decor as well as an airy conservatory-diner is a restful place to consider a fine Scottish menu, much of it from the West Coast area. Isle of Ewe smoked salmon with caper and onion salad to start perhaps; then plump for steak and ale pie; broccoli risotto; or perhaps chargrilled local venison burger.

Open all day all wk Closed Jan **Food** Lunch all wk 12-2 Dinner all wk 6-9 ⊕ FREE HOUSE ◖ Isle of Skye Red Cuillin, Torridon Ale, Cairngorm Trade Winds, An Teallach & Crofters Pale Ale, Cromarty Happy Chappy. **Facilities** Non-diners area ♣ (Bar Garden) ♦ Children's menu Children's portions Play area Garden ⋒ Beer festival Parking WiFi ▭ (notice required) **Rooms** 12

NORTH LANARKSHIRE

CUMBERNAULD
Map 21 NS77

Castlecary House Hotel

tel: 01324 840233 **Castlecary Rd G68 0HD**
email: enquiries@castlecaryhotel.com
dir: *A80 onto B816 between Glasgow & Stirling. 7m from Falkirk, 9m from Stirling*

Friendly family-run hotel

Castlecary House Hotel is located close to the historic Antonine Wall and the Forth and Clyde Canal. Meals in the four lounge bars plough a traditional furrow with options such as deep-fried black pudding balls; bangers and mash; and baked gammon. Home-made puddings include sticky toffee pudding and profiteroles. More formal fare is available in Camerons Restaurant, where high tea is also served on Sundays. There is an excellent selection of real ales on offer, including Arran Blonde and Harviestoun Bitter. A beer festival is held once or twice a year – contact the hotel for details.

Open all day all wk Closed 1 Jan **Food** Lunch all wk 12-9 Dinner all wk 12-9 Av main course £8 Set menu available Restaurant menu available all wk ⊕ FREE HOUSE ◖ Arran Blonde, Harviestoun Bitter & Twisted, Inveralmond Ossian's Ale, Houston Peter's Well, Caledonian Deuchars IPA. ⏹ 8 **Facilities** Non-diners area ♦ Children's menu Children's portions Garden Outside area ⋒ Beer festival Parking WiFi ▭ (notice required)

PICK OF THE PUBS

Plockton Inn & Seafood Restaurant

PLOCKTON   Map 22 NG83

tel: 01599 544222 **Innes St IV52 8TW**
email: info@plocktoninn.co.uk
web: www.plocktoninn.co.uk
dir: *A87 towards Kyle of Lochalsh. At
Balmacara follow Plockton signs, 7m*

Friendly inn offering great seafood

Located in Plockton which is on Loch
Carron in the West Highlands, this inn is
owned and run by Mary Gollan, her
brother Kenny and his partner Susan
Trowbridge. The Gollans were born and
bred in the village and it was actually
their great-grandfather who built the
attractive stone free house as a manse.
The beautiful views can be enjoyed from
seats on the decking outside. The ladies
double up in the role of chef, while
Kenny manages the bar, where you'll
find winter fires, Plockton real ales from
the village brewery, and a selection of
over 50 malt whiskies. A meal in the
reasonably formal Dining Room or more
relaxed Lounge Bar is a must, with a
wealth of freshly caught local fish and
shellfish, West Highland beef, lamb,
game and home-made vegetarian
dishes on the menu, plus daily specials.
The Plockton prawns (called
langoustines here), which Martin the
barman catches in the sea loch, are
taken to Kenny's smokehouse to the rear
of the building to be cured along with
other seafood — the results can be

sampled in the seafood platter starter.
Other starters include cardamom spiced
mussel soup; oyster shooters; and baked
mini camembert with redcurrant jelly.
Among the main dishes are
langoustines, served hot with garlic
butter or cold with Marie Rose sauce;
skate wing and black butter, lemon and
capers with boiled baby potatoes or
chips; guinea fowl breast in red wine
sauce; and vegetarian haggis and
clapshot. Desserts include crannachan
ice cream, and Scottish cheeses served
with Orkney oatcakes. The public bar is
alive on Tuesdays and Thursdays with
music from local musicians, who are
often joined by talented youngsters from
the National Centre of Excellence in
Traditional Music in the village.

Open all day all wk **Food** Lunch all wk
12-2.15 Dinner all wk 6-9 ⊕ FREE
HOUSE ◼ Greene King Abbot Ale,
Fuller's London Pride, Young's Special,
Plockton Crags Ale & Bay.
Facilities Non-diners area 🐾 (Bar
Garden) 🚼 Children's menu Children's
portions Play area Garden 🪑 Parking
WiFi 🚐 (notice required)

PICK OF THE PUBS

Shieldaig Bar & Coastal Kitchen

SHIELDAIG Map 22 NG85

tel: 01520 755251 **IV54 8XN**
email: tighaneilean@keme.co.uk
web: www.tighaneilean.co.uk
dir: *Exit A896*

Remote and peaceful lochside pub, hotel and restaurants

Remote enough to make its Inverness postcode look totally inappropriate, the Shieldaig Bar & Coastal Kitchen is part of the famous Tigh an Eilean (House of the Island) Hotel. It's here that the majestic Torridon Mountains meet the western seas. Upper Loch Torridon is just round the corner. Wildlife is abundant, with otters, seals, white-tailed sea eagles, oyster catchers and pine martens. Then there are the deserted beaches and walking trails. From a croft at the magical-sounding Little Loch Broom, the An Teallach Brewery supplies real ales to the traditional bar, where live music and ceilidhs add a weekend buzz. The sea provides much of what appears on the menu, especially the shellfish landed daily by fishermen using environmentally responsible creel-fishing and hand-diving techniques. Ways of sampling this local bounty in the restaurant include gratin of crab with pink grapefruit; seared Hebridean scallops with Serrano ham; and escalope of West Coast sea bream with Provençal confit. The land also does a pretty good job with food, among other things rack of Scottish Blackface lamb with herb crust and lamb jus. An alternative eating place is the more casual Coastal Kitchen, not that the main restaurant is particularly formal. Here the local seafood is just as imaginatively prepared but with the emphasis on simplicity, such as the hearty seafood stew or one of the speciality pizzas from the wood-fired oven. To watch the often spectacular sunsets, choose a table in the courtyard or one of the first-floor decks. The hotel also owns the village's general store, where you can buy provisions, postcards and most-day-to-day necessities.

Open all day all wk 11-11
Food Lunch all wk 12-2.30 (all day summer) Dinner all wk 6-9 (all day summer) 🍺 FREE HOUSE 🛢 An Teallach. 🍷 8 **Facilities** Non-diners area 🚻 Children's menu Children's portions Garden 🪑 Parking WiFi 🚌 (notice required)

EAST LOTHIAN

GULLANE
Map 21 NT48

The Old Clubhouse

tel: 01620 842008 **East Links Rd EH31 2AF**
dir: *A198 into Gullane, 3rd right into East Links Rd, pass church, on left*

Pub favourites overlooking the Gullane Links

Established in 1890 as the home of Gullane Golf Club, this building had a chequered past after the golfers moved on to larger premises, including stints as a disco and as tea rooms. In the late 1980s the Campanile family took the reins and it hasn't looked back. Roaring winter fires and walls crammed with golfing memorabilia make a good first impression, and the menu delivers a lengthy list of pub classics including regional specialities such as venison haggis, Cullen skink and Stornoway black pudding. For dessert, maybe choose deconstructed lemon meringue pie.

Open all day all wk Closed 25 Dec, 1 Jan **Food** Lunch all wk 12-9.30 Dinner all wk 12-9.30 ⊕ FREE HOUSE ◀ Timothy Taylor Landlord, Caledonian Deuchars IPA ♂ Thistly Cross. ☗ 9 **Facilities** Non-diners area ♣ (Bar Garden) ♦ Children's menu Children's portions Garden Outside area ⌂ WiFi ☛ (notice required)

LONGNIDDRY
Map 21 NT47

The Longniddry Inn

tel: 01875 852401 **Main St EH32 0NF**
email: info@longniddryinn.com
dir: *On A198 (Main St), near rail station*

Comprehensive menu choices in historic buildings

This combination of a former blacksmith's forge and four cottages on Longniddry's Main Street continues to be a popular spot. Held in high esteem locally for friendly service and good food, it offers an extensive menu featuring the likes of roast chicken platter; pan-fried lamb's liver, crispy bacon, mash, vegetables and onion gravy; Mexican enchiladas; spaghetti carbonara; and haddock mornay. In warmer weather why not take your pint of Belhaven Best, glass of wine or freshly ground coffee outside.

Open all day all wk Closed 26 Dec, 1 Jan **Food** Lunch Mon-Sat 12-8.30, Sun 12.30-7.30 Dinner Mon-Sat 12-8.30, Sun 12.30-7.30 Av main course £9.95 ⊕ PUNCH TAVERNS ◀ Belhaven Best. **Facilities** Non-diners area ♦ Children's menu Children's portions Garden Parking WiFi ☛

WEST LOTHIAN

LINLITHGOW
Map 21 NS97

Champany Inn - The Chop and Ale House ⊛⊛
PICK OF THE PUBS

tel: 01506 834532 **Champany EH49 7LU**
email: reception@champany.com
dir: *2m NE of Linlithgow at junct of A904 & A803*

Renowned inn within striking distance of Edinburgh

Buildings here comprise a former mill-house, a farmer's bothy and some buildings dating from the 16th century. A talking point in the luxurious bar is a rock pond where oysters and lobsters fresh from the Western Isles consider their future, while you, your glass of Caledonia Best, or perhaps own-label South African pinotage in hand, consider your meal. In the Chop and Ale House starters include home-smoked chorizo sausage with tomato and smoked bacon chutney; pickled dill and tomato

herring fillets; or red onion and goats' cheese tart. The menu also makes it clear that they're big on Aberdeen Angus steaks and burgers here, but among alternatives to beef are lamb chops, South African farmer's sausages, or deep fried haddock in home-made batter. If there's still room have a sweet like hot waffles, fresh fruit Pavlova or chocolate and honeycomb brownie.

Open all wk 12-2 6.30-10 (Fri-Sun 12-10) Closed 25-26 Dec, 1 Jan **Food** Lunch all wk 12-2 Dinner all wk 6.30-10 Restaurant menu available Mon-Sat ⊕ FREE HOUSE ◀ Caledonia Best, St Mungos ♂ Thistly Cross. ☗ 8 **Facilities** Children's portions Garden ⌂ Parking

The Four Marys

tel: 01506 842171 **65/67 High St EH49 7ED**
email: fourmarys.linlithgow@belhavenpubs.net
dir: *M9 junct 3 or junct 4, A803 to Linlithgow. Pub in town centre*

Real ale paradise in historic town setting

This eye-catching building at the heart of Linlithgow has only been a pub since 1981, but its pedigree stretches back a further 500 years to when royalty lived at the nearby palace. The eponymous Marys were ladies-in-waiting to Linlithgow-born Mary, Queen of Scots. Low ceilings, striking dressed-stone walls, and period and antique furnishings give the pub, which changed hands in 2014, a real sense of atmosphere and history. You'll find a great selection of real ales in the bar, including Belhaven 80/- and Four Marys, and Caledonian Deuchars IPA; twice-yearly beer festivals are held, whilst robust pub grub includes steak and ale pie, burgers, hot dogs and jacket potatoes.

Open all day all wk **Food** Lunch all wk 12-5 Dinner all wk 5-9 Av main course £7.95 Set menu available ⊕ BELHAVEN/GREENE KING ◀ Belhaven 80/-, Four Marys & St Andrews, Morland Old Speckled Hen, Caledonian Deuchars IPA, Stewart Edinburgh Gold, St Andrews. ☗ 9 **Facilities** Non-diners area ♣ (Bar) ♦ Children's menu Children's portions Garden Outside area Beer festival WiFi ☛ (notice required)

MIDLOTHIAN

DALKEITH
Map 21 NT36

The Sun Inn ★★★★ INN ⊛
PICK OF THE PUBS

tel: 0131 663 2456 **Lothian Bridge EH22 4TR**
email: thesuninn@live.co.uk **web:** www.thesuninnedinburgh.co.uk
dir: *On A7 towards Galashiels, opposite Newbattle Viaduct*

A thoroughly modern dining-pub

Standing in wooded grounds close to the banks of the River Esk, this family-run former coaching inn is an expert blend of tradition and modernity. Here there's an original fireplace, oak beams, exposed stone walls with wooden floors given a contemporary twist. Scottish cask ales have pride of place behind the bar, which also offers an extensive wine list. Food in the more formal, AA-Rosetted restaurant is modern British with a strong Scottish accent, masterminded by owner and head chef Ian Minto and his son Craig. Locally sourced ingredients feature in lunch dishes such as pan-seared lamb's liver with creamy mash and onion gravy; while in the evening, try the house-cured salmon, beetroot and apple remoulade and horseradish fritter; and local pork fillet wrapped in Serrano ham, twice cooked belly, rolled shoulder, Hornig's black pudding and mash. High teas are served on weekday afternoons.

Open all day all wk Closed 1 Jan, 26 Dec **Food** Lunch Mon-Sat 12-2, Mon-Fri High Tea 2.30-5.30, Sun 12-7 Dinner Mon-Sat 6-9, Sun 12-7 Set menu available ⊕ FREE HOUSE ◀ Alechemy, Inveralmond, Eden Ales, Stewart ♂ Addlestones. ☗ 19 **Facilities** Non-diners area ♦ Children's menu Children's portions Garden ⌂ Parking WiFi ☛ (notice required) **Rooms** 5

PENICUIK
Map 21 NT25

The Howgate Restaurant

tel: 01968 670000 **Howgate EH26 8PY**
email: peter@howgate.com
dir: *10m N of Peebles. 3m E of Penicuik on A6094 between Leadburn junct & Howgate*

Fine food and ales in a former dairy

Formerly the home of Howgate cheeses, this beautifully converted farm building has a fire-warmed bar offering bistro-style meals, while the candlelit restaurant serves a full carte. The kitchen uses the finest Scottish produce, especially beef and lamb, which are cooked on the charcoal grill; other options might include brie filo pastry parcel with plum and vanilla sauce; Cullen skink; smoked haddock and wild mushroom risotto; Borders venison and pheasant game pie with Stilton; and chargrilled lamb's liver, chive mash, seasonal vegetables and onion sauce. There are fine beers to enjoy and an impressively produced wine list roams the globe.

Open all wk 12-2 6-9.30 Closed 25-26 Dec, 1 Jan **Food** Lunch all wk 12-2 Dinner all wk 6-9.30 ⊕ FREE HOUSE ◖ Belhaven Best, Broughton Ales Greenmantle Ale. ♟ 14 **Facilities** ♦ Children's menu Children's portions Garden ⤢ Parking ▭ (notice required)

ROSLIN
Map 21 NT26

The Original Rosslyn Inn ★★★★ INN

tel: 0131 440 2384 **2-4 Main St EH25 9LE**
email: enquiries@theoriginalhotel.co.uk **web:** www.theoriginalhotel.co.uk
dir: *Off city bypass at Straiton for A703*

A perfect city escape that's a stone's throw from Rosslyn Chapel

Just eight miles from central Edinburgh and a short walk from Rosslyn Chapel, this family-run village inn has been in the Harris family for 40 years. Robert Burns, the famous Scottish poet, stayed here in 1787 and wrote a two verse poem for the landlady about his visit. Today you have the chance to catch up with the locals in the village bar, or relax by the fire in the lounge whilst choosing from the menu. Soups, jackets and paninis are supplemented by main course options like haggis with tatties and neeps; breaded haddock and chips; and vegetarian harvester pie. Alternatively, the Grail Restaurant offers more comprehensive dining options. There are well-equipped bedrooms, four with four-posters.

Open all wk all wk **Food** Lunch all wk 12-9.15 Dinner all wk 12-9.15 Restaurant menu available Fri & Sat ⊕ FREE HOUSE ◖ Belhaven Best. ♟ 14 **Facilities** Non-diners area ♣ (Bar Garden) ♦ Children's menu Children's portions Garden ⤢ Parking WiFi ▭ **Rooms** 7

MORAY

FORRES
Map 23 NJ06

The Old Mill Inn

tel: 01309 641605 **Brodie IV36 2TD**
dir: *Between Nairn & Forres on A96*

Spacious, family-friendly pub and restaurant

Situated on the Scottish Riviera, officially recorded as one of the sunniest and driest places in the UK, this former watermill has acquired windows, panelling and a beautiful door from a demolished stately home across the Moray Firth. There's a wide choice of food, from 12-hour slow-roasted belly of pork to feta cheese and spinach tart; and pan-fried sea bream with pea and broad bean gnocchi to roast loin of venison with pommes Anna, red cabbage, black kale and 'gin and tonic' scented chocolate jus. There's an ever-changing selection of Scottish real ales at the bar; over 30, all through handpumps, can be tried during the June beer festival.

Open all day all wk Closed 25-26 Dec, 1 Jan **Food** Lunch all wk 11.30-5 Dinner all wk 5-9 Av main course £13.95 Restaurant menu available Tue-Sun ⊕ FREE HOUSE ◖ Rotating Guest ales. ♟ 9 **Facilities** ♦ Children's menu Children's portions Garden ⤢ Beer festival Parking WiFi ▭ (notice required)

PERTH & KINROSS

KILLIECRANKIE
Map 23 NN96

Killiecrankie House Hotel ★★★ SHL ◎◎ PICK OF THE PUBS

tel: 01796 473220 **PH16 5LG**
email: enquiries@killiecrankiehotel.co.uk **web:** www.killiecrankiehotel.co.uk
dir: *Take B8079 N from Pitlochry. Hotel in 3m*

Historic venue in stunning location

This white-painted Victorian hotel gleams amidst woodland at the Pass of Killiecrankie, the gateway to The Highlands. It is a magnificent gorge, famed for the battle in 1689 when the Jacobites routed the forces of King William III; today it is a stronghold for red squirrels and a renowned birdwatching area. There are walks bedside rivers and lochs, and countless hill walks, including on the majestic Ben Vrackie that rises behind the hotel. Standing in a four-acre estate, the hotel retains much of its old character and successfully blends it with modern comforts. The cosy, panelled bar is a popular haunt, while the snug sitting room opens on to a small patio. Arm yourself with a Scottish beer as you study a menu that makes the most of Scotland's diverse produce and which has gained the restaurant two AA Rosettes.

Open all day all wk Closed Jan & Feb **Food** Lunch all wk 12.30-2 Dinner all wk 6.30-8.30 ⊕ FREE HOUSE ◖ Orkney Red MacGregor, Caledonian Best, Belhaven Best ♥ Thistly Cross. ♟ 8 **Facilities** Non-diners area ♦ Children's menu Garden ⤢ Parking **Rooms** 10

MEIKLEOUR
Map 21 NO14

Meikleour Arms ★★★★ INN

tel: 01250 883206 **PH2 6EB**
email: contact@meikleourarms.co.uk **web:** www.meikleourarms.co.uk
dir: *From A93 N of Perth, approx 12m take A984 signed Caputh & Dunkeld to Meikleour*

A small country inn set in the heart of a conservation village

Although no longer called a hotel, overnight guests are still welcome at this former mail-coach stopover on the old Edinburgh to Inverness road. The flagstone-floored bar offers Perth-brewed Lure of Meikleour, and Dark Island from Orkney. Eat in the bar, the wood-panelled dining room, on the terrace or in the garden and enjoy vegetables, trout and game from the pub's own farm; seafood arrives daily from Aberdeen. Menus feature haggis, clapshot and whisky sauce; Scottish haddock deep fried in ale batter; and wild mushroom carbonara. A beer and cider festival is held in August.

Open all day all wk 11-11 **Food** Contact pub for food times ⊕ FREE HOUSE ◖ Inveralmond Lure of Meikleour, Orkney Dark Island ♥ Aspall. **Facilities** Non-diners area ♣ (Bar Restaurant Garden) ♦ Children's menu Garden ⤢ Beer festival Cider festival Parking WiFi ▭ **Rooms** 9

PITLOCHRY
Map 23 NN95

Moulin Hotel
PICK OF THE PUBS

tel: 01796 472196 **11-13 Kirkmichael Rd, Moulin PH16 5EH**
email: enquiries@moulinhotel.co.uk
dir: *From A9 at Pitlochry take A924. Moulin 0.75m*

Hearty local food in prime walking country

Dating from 1695, this welcoming inn located on an old drovers' road at the foot of Ben Vrackie is a popular base for walking and touring. Locals are drawn to the bar for the excellent home-brewed beers, with Moulin Ale of Atholl, Braveheart and Light, and Belhaven Best served on handpump. The interior boasts beautiful stone walls and lots of cosy niches, with blazing log fires in winter; while the courtyard garden is lovely in summer. Menus offer the opportunity to try something local such as mince and tatties; venison Braveheart (strips of local venison pan-fried with mushrooms and Braveheart beer); and Vrackie Grostel (sautéed potatoes with smoked bacon lightly herbed and topped with a fried egg). You might then round off your meal with Highland honey sponge and custard. A specials board broadens the choice further. 25 wines by the glass and more than 30 malt whiskies are available.

Open all day all wk 11-11 (Fri-Sat 11am-11.45pm Sun 12-11) **Food** Lunch all wk 12-9.30 Dinner all wk 12-9.30 ⊕ FREE HOUSE ◀ Moulin Braveheart, Old Remedial, Ale of Atholl & Light, Belhaven Best. ☗ 25 **Facilities** Non-diners area ♦ Children's menu Children's portions Garden ⼕ Parking WiFi ⛟ (notice required)

SCOTTISH BORDERS

ALLANTON
Map 21 NT85

Allanton Inn

tel: 01890 818260 **TD11 3JZ**
email: info@allantoninn.co.uk
dir: *From A1 at Berwick take A6105 for Chirnside (5m). At Chirnside Inn take Coldstream Rd for 1m to Allanton*

Informal dining in family-run Borders pub

Wooden floors, contemporary furnishings, artworks, subtle lighting and that all-important log fire characterise this 18th-century coaching inn. A huge silver spoon and fork dominate one wall of the modern bar, a subtle hint perhaps to study the menu, while enjoying that pint of Inveralmond Ossian. Beef may come from the family farm and the fish is fresh from Eyemouth, while receiving the garden smokehouse treatment are pork, salmon, chicken and even cheeses. Daily blackboard specials add to a regularly changing menu that typically features smoked duck breast and soft boiled duck egg; pan-seared scallops with red lentil, coconut and coriander dahl; and apple and caramel turnover with cinnamon ice cream and caramel sauce. A garden with fruit trees overlooks open countryside.

Open all day all wk 12-11 Closed 2wks Feb (dates vary) **Food** Lunch all wk 12-3 Dinner all wk 6-9 ⊕ FREE HOUSE ◀ Inveralmond Ossian, Scottish Borders Game Bird & Foxy Blonde, Harviestoun Bitter & Twisted, Fyne Piper's Gold ♂ Aspall. ☗ 10 **Facilities** Non-diners area ♦ Children's menu Children's portions Garden ⼕ WiFi

GALASHIELS
Map 21 NT43

Kingsknowes Hotel ★★★ HL

tel: 01896 758375 **1 Selkirk Rd TD1 3HY**
email: enquiries@kingsknowes.co.uk web: www.kingsknowes.co.uk
dir: *Exit A7 at Galashiels/Selkirk rdbt*

Traditional food on banks of the Tweed

An imposing Scots baronial mansion dating from 1869, the Kingsknowes is set in over three acres of grounds on the banks of the Tweed with lovely views of the Eildon Hills and Abbotsford House, Sir Walter Scott's ancestral home. Meals are served in two restaurants and the Courtyard Bar, where fresh local or regional produce is used as much as possible. Typical choices include haggis, potato rösti and quails' eggs; and pan-fried salmon with chive and king prawn risotto. The impressive glass conservatory is the ideal place to enjoy a glass of McEwan's 70/- or John Smith's.

Open all day all wk Mon-Wed & Sun 12-11 (Thu-Sat noon-1am) Closed 1-3 Jan **Food** Lunch Mon-Fri 12-2, Sat 12-9.30, Sun 12-8.30 Dinner Mon-Fri 5.45-9, Sat 12-9.30, Sun 12-8.30 ⊕ FREE HOUSE ◀ McEwan's 70/-, John Smith's. **Facilities** Non-diners area ♦ Children's menu Play area Garden Parking ⛟ (notice required) **Rooms** 12

INNERLEITHEN
Map 21 NT33

Traquair Arms Hotel

tel: 01896 830229 **Traquair Rd EH44 6PD**
email: info@traquairarmshotel.co.uk
dir: *From A72 (Peebles to Galashiels road) take B709 for St Mary's Loch & Traquair*

A taste of Italy in the Scottish Borders

Amidst heather-covered hills stands this imposing pub-hotel with a tranquil beer garden. Expect to share it with muddy mountain bikers – downhill and cross-country trails are right on the doorstep. It's one of only two places where you can drink Traquair Bear Ale, brewed a stone's throw away at Traquair House. The bar menu has dishes such as chicken and haggis with clapshot mash and whisky sauce; Aberdeen Angus sirloin; and fish pie. In the restaurant, an unusual combination of Scottish and Italian food is prepared by the resident Italian chef. Sample dishes include Italian sausage with borlotti beans, cherry tomatoes, toasted focaccia and salad; and roast haunch of Tweed Valley venison with garlic baby potatoes, root vegetables and redcurrant jus.

Open all day all wk Closed 25 Dec **Food** Lunch Mon-Fri 12-2.30, Sat-Sun all day Dinner Mon-Fri 5-9, Sat-Sun all day ⊕ FREE HOUSE ◀ Caledonian Deuchars IPA, Timothy Taylor Landlord, Traquair Bear Ale. **Facilities** Non-diners area ♣ (Bar Garden) ♦ Children's menu Children's portions Garden ⼕ Parking WiFi ⛟

JEDBURGH
Map 21 NT62

NEW The Ancrum Cross Keys ◎◎
PICK OF THE PUBS

tel: 01835 830242 **The Green, Ancrum TD8 6XH**
email: crosskeysdining@gmail.com
dir: *From Jedburgh take A68 towards St Boswells. Left onto B6400 to Ancrum*

Popular local, destination eatery, enchanting waterside garden

This friendly pub celebrated its 200th anniversary a couple of years ago. Its delightfully large garden bordering the idyllic Ale Water is a huge factor in its favour. Others are the Front Bar – proudly unrefurbished for over a century – which serves ales from the Scottish Borders Brewery; and chef David Malcolm's serious kitchen credentials, which have earned two AA Rosettes. David uses all manner of locally-sourced and foraged ingredients to create dishes not found anywhere else: quail, wigeon, venison and rabbit all make regular appearances on his carte. A starter of hand-dived scallop, braised ox cheeks, clementine marmalade and potato mousseline is memorable. Mains such as gurnard Véronique, which comprises cockles, mussels, razor clams, squid ink pasta and Treviso radicchio, surely cannot be resisted. Finish lightly with Earl Grey custard, lemon curd parfait, bergamot jelly and meringue; or a simple dish of home-made ice cream.

Open all day all wk **Food** Lunch 12-2.30 Dinner 6-9.30 Restaurant menu available Tue-Sun ⊕ SCOTTISH BORDERS ◀ Foxy Blonde & Dark Horse. ☗ 12 **Facilities** Non-diners area ♣ (Bar Garden) ♦ Children's menu Children's portions Garden ⼕ Parking WiFi

PICK OF THE PUBS

The Cobbles Freehouse & Dining ✸

KELSO Map 21 NT73

tel: 01573 223548
7 Bowmont St TD5 7JH
email: info@thecobbleskelso.co.uk
web: www.thecobbleskelso.co.uk
dir: *A6089 from Edinburgh to Kelso, right at rdbt into Bowmont St. Pub in 0.3m*

Accomplished food and well-kept beers

Tucked away in a corner of the town's rather fine square stands this modernised 19th-century coaching inn. For the last few years it has taken on the role as the brewery tap for proprietor Gavin Meiklejohn's Tempest Brewing Co. Gavin is married to Annika, Cobbles' landlady, and his real ales are always perfectly on song as they flow from the pumps in the log fire-warmed bar. The restaurant's AA Rosette was awarded for its mix of cuisines – British gastro-pub classics, Pacific Rim and modern European. Available in the bar are potted pâté, toasted ciabatta with grape and apple chutney as well as daily blackboard specials. Dishes on the frequently changing restaurant menu feature Scottish fish and shellfish, local lamb, beef and pork, and game in season, thus starters may be pheasant and rabbit terrine, pickled vegetables and spiced tomato ketchup mayo; and possible main courses could be Borders venison haunch, skirlie mash,

bourguignon sauce and Stornoway black pudding; and assiette of Gressingham duck, smoked Yukon Gold mash and roast salsify. Not far away in Galashiels is Overlangshaw Farmhouse, whence come the dessert ice creams, flavoured with butterscotch, pistachio and chocolate; alternatives include peanut butter chocolate fondant, rhubarb jam, peanut brittle and rhubarb ice cream; or sticky date pudding, steeped prunes, butterscotch sauce and Earl Grey ice cream. On Friday nights, starting at 10pm, the Kelso Folk & Live Music Club holds its weekly sessions in the restaurant. Acoustic guitarists are the mainstay, but pipes, accordion, bouzouki and many other instruments are also likely to appear. There is a private dining and function room.

Open all day all wk 11.30-11 Closed 25 Dec **Food** Lunch Mon-Sat 12-2.30, Sun 12-8 Dinner Mon-Sat 5.45-9, Sun 12-8 Av main course £10.95 Restaurant menu available Tue-Sat 🛢 FREE HOUSE ◄ Tempest Ŏ Thistly Cross. 💡 9 **Facilities** Non-diners area 🕯 Children's menu Children's portions Outside area 🛱 WiFi 🚐 (notice required)

KELSO
Map 21 NT73

The Cobbles Freehouse & Dining ◉ | PICK OF THE PUBS

See Pick of the Pubs on page 617

KIRK YETHOLM
Map 21 NT82

The Border Hotel

tel: 01573 420237 **The Green TD5 8PQ**
email: theborderhotel@yahoo.co.uk
dir: *From A698 in Kelso take B6352 for 7m to Kirk Yetholm*

A homely place to stop awhile

Standing at the end of the 268-mile-long Pennine Way walk, this 18th-century former coaching inn is a welcoming and most hospitable place to revive after any journey, be it on foot or by car. The menu features local game and farm meats, perhaps washed down with ales from Hadrian & Border Brewery. Try Cullen skink; steamed game pudding; breaded haggis fritters with spicy tomato salsa; or sausage and mash. Leave space for banoffee pie or apple crumble. The stone-flagged bar has a log fire, and the conservatory dining room looks over the patio and beer garden.

Open all day all wk Closed 25-26 Dec **Food** Lunch all wk 12-2 Dinner all wk 6-8.30 (winter), 6-9 (summer) Av main course £12 ⊕ FREE HOUSE ◀ Timothy Taylor Landlord, Greene King Abbot Ale, Hadrian & Border Pennine Pint. **Facilities** Non-diners area ❤ (Bar Garden) ♦ Children's menu Children's portions Garden ⊼ Parking WiFi ⛟ (notice required)

MELROSE
Map 21 NT53

Burts Hotel ★★★ HL ◉◉ | PICK OF THE PUBS

tel: 01896 822285 **Market Square TD6 9PL**
email: enquiries@burtshotel.co.uk **web:** www.burtshotel.co.uk
dir: *From A68 N of St Boswells take A6091 towards Melrose. approx 2m right signed Melrose & B6374, follow to Market Sq*

Family-owned, town-centre fixture

The Henderson family has owned this 18th-century hotel for around four decades. Overlooking the market square, it was built in 1722 by a local dignitary. Its age dictates listed-building status, which restoration, extension and upgrades have all respected in the Hendersons' quest for a modern hotel. After a day out, settle in with one of the 90 single malts, or a pint of Caledonian Deuchars IPA. The restaurant has held two AA Rosettes since 1995, thanks to starters such as herb-crusted hen's egg, confit tomato, spinach and Isle of Mull cheese sauce. This could be followed by harissa-marinated rump of Borders lamb, with lightly spiced couscous, yogurt, and courgette Charlotte. Light lunch specials may list breaded fishcakes with sweet chilli and lime sauce; or breaded chicken goujons with curried mayo dip, salad and fries. Puddings include a range of locally made ice creams, or savour the selection Scottish and Borders cheeses.

Open all wk 12-2.30 5-11 **Food** Lunch all wk 12-2 Dinner all wk 6-9.30 Restaurant menu available Lunch Sat-Sun, Dinner all wk ⊕ FREE HOUSE ◀ Caledonian Deuchars IPA & 80/-, Timothy Taylor Landlord, Fuller's London Pride, Scottish Borders Game Bird. ☻ 10 **Facilities** ❤ (Bar Garden) ♦ Children's menu Children's portions Garden ⊼ Parking WiFi **Rooms** 20

NEWCASTLETON
Map 21 NY48

Liddesdale ★★★★ INN

tel: 01387 375255 **17 Douglas Square TD9 0QD**
email: reception@theliddesdalehotel.co.uk **web:** www.theliddesdalehotel.co.uk
dir: *In village centre*

Set amidst beautiful countryside

This inn sits in Douglas Square at the heart of Newcastleton (sometimes referred to as Copshaw Holm), an 18th-century village planned by Henry Scott, the third Duke of Buccleuch. An ideal base for exploring the unspoiled countryside in this area, the inn has a bar stocked with over 20 malt whiskies and a different cask-conditioned ale every week in the summer. The menu is full of pub favourites – creamy garlic mushrooms; steak and ale pie; battered haddock and chips; and apple and cinnamon crumble.

Open all day all wk **Food** Lunch all wk 12-2 Dinner Mon-Thu 5-8, Fri-Sun 5-8.30 Set menu available Restaurant menu available Fri-Sun ⊕ FREE HOUSE ◀ Samuel Smith's ⌂ Samuel Smith's Organic. ☻ 9 **Facilities** Non-diners area ❤ (Bar Garden) ♦ Children's menu Children's portions Garden ⊼ Beer festival Parking WiFi ⛟ (notice required) **Rooms** 6

ST BOSWELLS
Map 21 NT53

Buccleuch Arms

tel: 01835 822243 **The Green TD6 0EW**
email: info@buccleucharms.com
dir: *On A68, 10m N of Jedburgh. Hotel on village green*

Friendly hotel serving local food

Originally an inn catering for the fox-hunting aristocracy, this smart and friendly country-house hotel dates from the 16th century. Set beside the village cricket pitch, it's an attractive brick and stone building with an immaculate garden. Inside, the large and comfortable lounge is warmed by a log fire in winter, while the spacious enclosed garden comes into its own during the warmer months. Extensive menus are served in the Blue Coo Bistrot, where the focus is on local meat dishes, and in particular steaks from local farms.

Open all day all wk 12-11 Closed 25 Dec **Food** Lunch all wk 12-2.30 Dinner Sun-Thu 5.30-9, Fri-Sat 5.30-9.30 Av main course £11 Restaurant menu available all wk ⊕ FREE HOUSE ◀ Scottish Borders Brewery Ales, Belhaven Best, Guinness. ☻ 20 **Facilities** Non-diners area ❤ (Bar Garden) ♦ Children's menu Children's portions Play area Garden ⊼ Parking WiFi ⛟ (notice required)

SWINTON
Map 21 NT84

The Wheatsheaf at Swinton | PICK OF THE PUBS

See Pick of the Pubs on opposite page

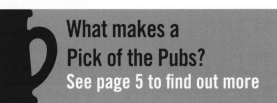

What makes a Pick of the Pubs?
See page 5 to find out more

PICK OF THE PUBS

The Wheatsheaf at Swinton

SWINTON Map 21 NT84

tel: 01890 860257 **Main St TD11 3JJ**
email:
reception@wheatsheaf-swinton.co.uk
web: www.wheatsheaf-swinton.co.uk
dir: *From Edinburgh A697 onto B6461.*
From East Lothian A1 onto B6461

Scottish hospitality and locally sourced food

Husband and wife team Chris and Jan Winson have built up an impressive reputation for their dining destination in this attractive village. Whether you choose to eat in the Sun Room or the Dining Room, the latter overlooking the village green, the menus feature home-made food using locally sourced produce, including daily delivered fresh seafood from Eyemouth 12 miles away, and beef from livestock raised on the surrounding Borders pastures. Also likely to appear, according to the season, are wild salmon, venison, partridge, pheasant, woodcock and duck. The bar and garden menu is likely to offer a club sandwich, steak and ale pie and beefburger. A restaurant meal might start with pan-seared woodland pigeon breast, Stornoway black pudding purée, crispy apple and light game jus; or home-made Thai crab cake with sweet chilli sauce. Head chef John Forrestier, from Nancy in France, specialises in fish, so a main course definitely worth considering is his baked

Dover sole with scallop mousse, clams, beurre blanc and pickled cockle salad. Alternatives might include roast Scottish venison with celeriac purée, seared poached pears, rösti potato and light beetroot and chocolate sauce; or pan-seared goats' cheese gnocchi and morel mushroom fricassée, buttered kale and truffle oil. Other regular meat dishes include oven-roast pork fillet, and slow-braised Borders beef blade. Finally, a couple of the desserts: glazed pomegranate tart and lemon sorbet; and baked Malteser cheesecake with passionfruit coulis. The bar stocks Belhaven IPA, draught Peroni, plus Stewart Brewery and Scottish Borders Brewery bottled beers. Here too is a whisky map and tasting notes to study before choosing your single malt.

Open 4-11 (Sat 12-12 Sun 12-11)
Closed 23-24 & 26 Dec, 2-3 Jan, Mon-Fri L **Food** Lunch Sat 12-3, Sun 12-4
Dinner Mon-Sat 6-9, Sun 6-8.30
🛢 FREE HOUSE 🍺 Belhaven IPA,
Scottish Borders Gamebird & Foxy Blonde, Stewart Brewing Hollyrood, Peroni. 🍷 12 **Facilities** Non-diners area
🚻 Garden 🎍 Parking 🚌

PICK OF THE PUBS

The Inn at Kippen

KIPPEN   **Map 20 NS69**

tel: 01786 870500 **Fore Rd FK8 3DT**
email: info@theinnatkippen.co.uk
web: www.theinnatkippen.co.uk
dir: *From Stirling take A811 to Loch
Lomond. 1st left at Kippen station rdbt,
1st right into Fore Rd. Inn on left*

Quality and caring approach to hospitality

A traditional white-painted village free
house at the foot of the Campsie Hills;
views across the Forth Valley to the
Highlands are stunning. In the capable
hands of owners Mark and Alice
Silverwood, this popular and caring inn
welcomes all comers, along with their
children and dogs. In the winter months
you'll be warmed by wood fires and
entertained by the locals in the stylish
bar. If you're a summer visitor, settle in
the pretty garden with a pint from the
Fallen Brewing Company or Loch
Lomond ales. Menus feature the best of
regional and seasonal produce. Beef,
pork and lamb all come from Cairnhill
farms; chicken from Gartmorn Farm just
outside Stirling; wild herbs and
mushrooms are foraged from the same
estate as the game; and seafood from
Scottish waters is fully traceable.
Special dietary needs can usually be
accommodated; the inn bakes its own
gluten- and dairy-free bread, and at
least one dessert is free of both gluten
and dairy too. Children have their own

menu, or can be served smaller portions
from the carte. The Kippen's sharing
boards showcase many of Scotland's
natural meat and smoked fish products:
venison salami, pastrami-cured
Shetland salmon, Dunlop cheddar,
chicken liver parfait, home-dried
tomatoes, pickles, house chutney,
Perthshire oatcakes and rapeseed
croûtes, and leaves dressed with Arran
mustard. Main course delights continue
with dishes of mussels; beer-battered
haddock; and feather blade of beef
braised in red wine, with smoked bacon,
potato pie and roasted roots. Perhaps a
hand-formed local venison burger will
suffice, served with tomato chutney,
hand-cut chips, and dressed salad with
cheese. On the specials and dessert
lists, look out for aged lamb three ways,

and ice creams from an award-winning
Scottish artisan producer.

Open all day all wk **Food** Lunch all wk
12-6 Dinner Sun-Tue 6-8, Wed-Sat 6-9
⊕ FREE HOUSE ◨ Fallen, Loch Lomond
♂ Addlestones. ♀ 9
Facilities Non-diners area
♣ (Bar Garden) ♦ Children's menu
Children's portions Garden ♠ Parking
WiFi ▭ (notice required)

TIBBIE SHIELS INN
Map 21 NT22

Tibbie Shiels Inn
PICK OF THE PUBS

tel: 01750 42231 **St Mary's Loch TD7 5LH**
email: tibbieshiels@hotmail.com
dir: From Moffat take A708. Inn 14m on right

Superbly located famous old inn

The first thing any first-time visitor to this lovely white-painted old inn between two lochs wants to know is: who was Tibbie Shiels? She was a young widow who, determined to support herself and her six bairns, took in lodgers and became the first licensee, catering in due course to Sir Walter Scott, Thomas Carlyle and Robert Louis Stevenson. Her spirit still keeps watch over the bar, which serves a real ale named after her, together with over 50 malt whiskies. The majority of the ingredients used in the kitchen are local, including venison, pheasant, partridge, hill-raised lamb and garden-grown herbs. Sandwiches, salads, ploughman's and paninis are all on offer, while the main menu lists Scottish smoked salmon on toasted crumpet; chicken, leek and smoked bacon pie; battered haddock and chips; and macaroni cheese.

Open all wk 6pm-mdnt (Sat-Sun 12-12) **Food** Lunch Sat-Sun 12-3 Dinner all wk 6-9 ⊕ FREE HOUSE ◀ Belhaven 80/-, Broughton Greenmantle Ale, Tibble Shiels Ale & The Reiver ♂ Westons Stowford Press. **Facilities** Non-diners area ☆ (Bar Garden) ♦ Children's menu Children's portions Play area Garden ⋒ Parking WiFi ⛺ (notice required)

STIRLING

CALLANDER
Map 20 NN60

The Lade Inn

tel: 01877 330152 **Kilmahog FK17 8HD**
email: info@theladeinn.com
dir: From Stirling take A84 to Callander. 1m N of Callander, left at Kilmahog Woollen Mills onto A821 towards Aberfoyle. Pub immediately on left

Warming fires in winter, a garden in summer

In the heart of the Trossachs National Park, the stone-built Lade Inn was built as a tearoom in 1935. The family-owned and run inn is known for its own real ales and for its 16-day beer festival from late August to mid September. There is also an on-site real ale shop selling bottled ales from microbreweries throughout Scotland. The home-cooked menu offers many smaller portions and allergen-free dishes. A typical menu offers crispy battered haggis balls with creamy whisky sauce; vegetable lasagne; Big Yin half-pound burger; and steak and ale pie. The beer garden with its three ponds and bird-feeding station is great for families.

Open all day all wk **Food** Lunch Mon-Sat 12-9, Sun 12.30-9 Dinner Mon-Sat 12-9, Sun 12.30-9 Set menu available ⊕ FREE HOUSE ◀ Waylade, LadeBack & LadeOut, Belhaven Best, Tennent's ♂ Thistly Cross. ☆ 9 **Facilities** Non-diners area ☆ (Bar Garden) ♦ Children's menu Children's portions Play area Family room Garden ⋒ Beer festival Parking WiFi ⛺ (notice required)

DRYMEN
Map 20 NS48

The Clachan Inn

tel: 01360 660824 **2 Main St G63 0BG**
email: info@clachaninndrymen.co.uk
dir: Phone for detailed directions

Scottish hospitality stretching back over the years

Established in 1734, The Clachan Inn is believed to be the oldest licensed pub in Scotland; this quaint white-painted cottage on the West Highland Way was once owned by Rob Roy's sister. Family-run for over 30 years the bar stocks frequently changing guest ales while a warming log fire keeps things cosy. More comfort comes with the food – choose from pub favourites such as deep-fried potato skins

with dips; jumbo sausage with baked beans and chips; and home-made toffee sponge pudding.

Open all day all wk 11am-mdnt (Fri-Sat 11am-1am Sun 12-12) Closed 1 Jan, 25 Dec **Food** Lunch Mon-Sat 12-3.45, Sun 12.30-3.45 Dinner Mon-Sat 6-9.45, Sun 5-9.45 ⊕ FREE HOUSE ◀ Harviestoun Bitter & Twisted, Cairngorm Trade Winds, Guinness. ☆ 9 **Facilities** Non-diners area ☆ (Bar) ♦ Children's menu Children's portions WiFi ⛺ (notice required)

KIPPEN
Map 20 NS69

Cross Keys Hotel

tel: 01786 870293 **Main St FK8 3DN**
email: info@kippencrosskeys.co.uk
dir: 10m W of Stirling, 20m from Loch Lomond off A811

Warming fires in winter, a garden in summer

The 300-year-old Cross Keys stands on Kippen's Main Street and offers seasonally changing menus and a good pint of cask ale. The pub's welcoming interior, warmed by three log fires, is perfect for resting your feet after a walk in nearby Burnside Wood, or you can sit in the garden when the weather permits. The menus take in soup and sandwiches; small plates such as Arbroath smokies fishcakes; and butternut squash and roasted chestnut risotto; and main courses of village bangers, herb mash and caramelised onions; and sage polenta cake, red pepper and aubergine casserole; Moroccan lamb tagine, flatbread, almond rice and crème fraîche; and cinnamon crème brûlée with mini stolen cake. Dogs are welcome in the top bar.

Open all wk 12-3 5-11 (Fri 12-3 5-1am Sat noon-1am Sun 12-12) Closed 1 Jan, 25 Dec **Food** Lunch Mon-Fri 12-3, Sat 12-9, Sun 12-8 Dinner Mon-Fri 5-9, Sat 12-9, Sun 12-8 ⊕ FREE HOUSE ◀ Belhaven Best & St Andrews, Harviestoun Bitter & Twisted, Fallen Brewing Co 1703 Archie's amber, Guinness, Guest ales ♂ Addlestones. ☆ 10 **Facilities** Non-diners area ☆ (Bar Garden) ♦ Children's menu Children's portions Play area Family room Garden ⋒ Parking WiFi ⛺ (notice required)

The Inn at Kippen
PICK OF THE PUBS

See Pick of the Pubs on opposite page

SCOTTISH ISLANDS

ISLE OF COLL

ARINAGOUR
Map 22 NM25

Coll Hotel
PICK OF THE PUBS

tel: 01879 230334 **PA78 6SZ**
email: info@collhotel.com
dir: Ferry from Oban. Hotel at head of Arinagour Bay, 1m from Pier (collections by arrangement)

Great for local seafood

The Coll Hotel has some stunning views over the sea to Jura and Mull, and being the Isle of Coll's only inn it is, naturally, the hub of the island community. Come here to mingle with the locals, soak in the atmosphere, and enjoy pints of Fyne Ale and malt whiskies. In the summer months the fabulous garden acts as an extension to the bar or the Gannet Restaurant; watch the yachts coming and going while enjoying a glass of Pimm's or something from the global wine selection. Fresh produce is landed and delivered from around the island every day and features on the specials board. Famed for its seafood, you'll find it in dishes such as crab cakes with wasabi mayonnaise; pan-fried grey sole fillets, lightly spiced Puy lentils, cherry tomatoes and spinach; or scallops with chorizo and cannellini bean ragout. Among the non-fish options, try the roast chicken pie or roasted butternut squash risotto.

Open all day all wk **Food** Lunch all wk 12-2 Dinner all wk 6-9 ⊕ FREE HOUSE ◀ Fyne Ales. **Facilities** Non-diners area ♦ Children's menu Children's portions Play area Garden ⋒ Parking WiFi ⛺ (notice required)

ISLE OF ISLAY

PORT CHARLOTTE Map 20 NR25

The Port Charlotte Hotel

tel: 01496 850360 **Main St PA48 7TU**
email: info@portcharlottehotel.co.uk
dir: *From Port Askaig take A846 towards Bowmore. Right onto A847, through Blackrock. Take unclassified road to Port Charlotte*

Beachside hotel displaying Scottish art

In an attractive conservation village, this sympathetically restored Victorian hotel is perfectly positioned on the west shore of Loch Indaal. A large conservatory opens out into the garden and directly onto the beach. Lovers of Scottish art will enjoy the work on display in the lounge and public bar. Islay ales and whiskies make a great way to warm up before enjoying menus focusing on local seafood – perhaps Lagavulin scallops, or vodka-cured sliced fresh Scottish salmon with radicchio and citrus salad, followed by supreme of guinea fowl with banana and corn gallette, or cannon of local lamb.

Open all day all wk Closed 24-26 Dec **Food** Lunch all wk 12-2 Dinner all wk 6-9 Restaurant menu available all wk ⊕ FREE HOUSE ◖ Islay ☌ Somersby Cider. ♟ 9 **Facilities** Non-diners area ✿ (Garden) ♦ Children's menu Children's portions Play area Family room Garden ♠ Parking WiFi ▭

ISLE OF MULL

DERVAIG Map 22 NM45

The Bellachroy Hotel

tel: 01688 400225 **PA75 6QW**
email: info@thebellachroy.co.uk
dir: *Take ferry from Oban to Craignure. A849 towards Tobermory. Left at T-junct onto B8073 to Dervaig*

Oldest inn on Mull specialising in local seafood

Near the foot of a hill road over from Mull's capital, Tobermory, and yards from the pretty sea loch Loch a' Chumhainn, the island's oldest hotel can trace its roots back to 1608. Today's visitors come to experience the wildlife including white-tailed sea eagles, which may well fly overhead as a pint of Fyne Avalanche is being enjoyed on the terrace in front of the inn. The chefs here take full advantage of the generous bounty from Mull's coastal waters and moors. Crab, mackerel and locally smoked haddock all feature on the menus when available, and seasonal dishes include venison and juniper casserole; and Ulva lamb shank, plus vegetarian options.

Open all day all wk **Food** Lunch all wk 12-2.30 Dinner all wk 6-8.30 ⊕ FREE HOUSE ◖ Fyne Avalanche, Highlander. **Facilities** Non-diners area ✿ (Bar Garden) ♦ Children's menu Children's portions Garden ♠ Parking WiFi ▭ (notice required)

ORKNEY

STROMNESS Map 24 HY20

Ferry Inn

tel: 01856 850280 **John St KW16 3AD**
email: info@ferryinn.com
dir: *Opposite ferry terminal*

Enjoy island ales overlooking the harbour

With its prominent harbour-front location, the Ferry Inn has long enjoyed a reputation for local ales. The pub has racking for a further 10 local ales on top of the five handpulls on the bar and although the beers change regularly look out for the island's own Dark Island and Skull Splitter. If beer isn't your thing, there are plenty of wines and malt whiskies to choose from, as well as an appealing menu that may include crunchy breaded Grimbister cheese with red onion and thyme marmalade to start, followed by burgers, steak, fish and chips, or roasted vegetable tart with cheese and salad.

Open all day all wk 9am-mdnt (Thu-Sat 9am-1am Sun 9.30am-mdnt) Closed 1-2 Jan, 25-26 Dec **Food** Lunch all wk 11.45-5 Dinner all wk 5-9.30 Av main course £10 Restaurant menu available all wk ⊕ FREE HOUSE ◖ Highland Scapa Special & Orkney IPA, Orkney Corncrake, Dark Island & Skull Splitter. **Facilities** Non-diners area ♦ Children's menu Children's portions Outside area ♠ Parking WiFi ▭

ISLE OF SKYE

ARDVASAR Map 22 NG60

Ardvasar Hotel ★★★ SHL

tel: 01471 844223 **IV45 8RS**
email: richard@ardvasar-hotel.demon.co.uk **web:** www.ardvasarhotel.com
dir: *From ferry terminal, 50yds & turn left*

Homely, welcoming and serving excellent Skye produce

Beside the road towards the southern tip of Skye, sit out front to drink in the extraordinary views to the rocky foreshore, Sound of Sleat and the mountains of the Knoydart Peninsula, a ferry ride away via Mallaig. Once you've sipped your Skye-brewed beer or local malt, retire to the comfy lounge bar or dining room to indulge in some of Skye's most renowned seafood meals; the local boats may land salmon, crab, lobster or scallops. Estate venison and Aberdeen Angus beef extend the choice. Residents in the individually designed rooms can look to a fine Scottish breakfast to set another day in paradise off to a good start.

Open all day all wk 11am-mdnt (Sun 12-11) **Food** Lunch all wk 12-2.30 Dinner all wk 5-9 ⊕ FREE HOUSE ◖ Isle of Skye Red Cuillin. **Facilities** Non-diners area ♦ Children's menu Children's portions Garden ♠ Parking **Rooms** 10

CARBOST Map 22 NG33

The Old Inn and Waterfront Bunkhouse PICK OF THE PUBS

tel: 01478 640205 **IV47 8SR**
email: enquiries@theoldinnskye.co.uk **web:** www.theoldinnskye.co.uk
dir: *From Skye Bridge follow A87 N. Take A863, then B8009 to inn*

Free house attracting locals, tourists and hill walkers

The Old Inn and Waterfront Bunkhouse, on the shores of Loch Harport near the Talisker distillery, is a charming, 200-year-old island cottage very popular among the walking and climbing fraternity. Arrive early for a table on the waterside patio and savour the breathtaking views of the Cuillin Hills with a pint of Hebridean ale in hand. Inside, open fires welcome winter visitors, and live Highland music is a regular feature most weekends. The menu includes daily home-cooked specials with numerous fresh fish dishes such as hot smoked salmon with lime and herb crème fraîche as a starter. Haggis, neeps and tatties strudel with whisky cream; a Highland burger (beef, venison or spicy bean); or an 8oz sirloin steak and chips could follow.

Open all day all wk Mon-Fri 11am-1am (Sat 11am-12.30am Sun 12.30-11.30) **Food** Lunch all wk 12-9 Dinner all wk 12-9 FREE HOUSE Isle of Skye Red Cuillin & Black Cuillin, Cuillin Skye Ale & Pinnacle Ale, Hebridean. **Facilities** Non-diners area (All areas) Children's menu Children's portions Family room Garden Outside area Parking WiFi

ISLEORNSAY Map 22 NG71

Hotel Eilean Iarmain ★★★ SHL PICK OF THE PUBS

tel: 01471 833332 **IV43 8QR**
email: hotel@eileaniarmain.co.uk **web:** www.eileaniarmain.co.uk
dir: *A851, A852 right to Isleornsay harbour*

Hebridean charm in spectacular setting

There's masses of Highland character at this well known hotel with its own pier overlooking Sleat Sound and the Knoydart Hills beyond. Step inside to find tartan carpets and stag antlers in the hallway, whilst elsewhere the decor is mainly cotton and linen chintzes with traditional furniture. More a small private hotel than a pub, the bar and restaurant ensure that the standards of food and drinks served here are exacting – the Gaelic Whiskies company is based here so sample a 'wee dram' or two. The head chef declares, 'We never accept second best, it shines through in the standard of food served in our restaurant'. Here you can try dishes like slow-braised venison shin with suet dumplings, glazed carrots and bone marrow mousse; or herb and truffle gnocchi with artichoke hearts, bell peppers, pine nuts and pesto dressing. Half portions from the main menu are served for children.

Open all day all wk 11am-11.30pm (Thu 11am-12.30am Fri 11am-1am Sat 11am-12.30am Sun 12-11.30) **Food** Lunch all wk 12-2.30 Dinner all wk 5.30-9 Av main course £12.95 Restaurant menu available all wk FREE HOUSE McEwan's 80/-, Isle of Skye, Guinness. **Facilities** Non-diners area Children's menu Children's portions Garden Parking WiFi (notice required) **Rooms** 16

STEIN Map 22 NG25

Stein Inn

tel: 01470 592362 **Macleod's Ter IV55 8GA**
email: angus.teresa@steininn.co.uk **web:** www.steininn.co.uk
dir: *A87 from Portree. In 5m take A850 for 15m. Right onto B886, 3m to T-junct. Turn left*

Skye's oldest inn set amid beautiful scenery

If your travels take you to Skye, then you just have to visit the Waternish peninsula and the island's oldest inn, for slap-bang in front of it, across a grassy foreshore, are the beautiful waters of Loch Bay. The wood-panelled bar, with peat fire a-smouldering, stocks 125 malts and Reeling Deck beer from the Isle of Skye Brewery. Daily-changing menus take full advantage of the abundant fresh fish and shellfish, sheep, wild deer and Highland cattle, with choices including breast of duck with garlic cider cream sauce; bean and nut patties with Angus' plum chutney; and Scottish salmon with vermouth and tarragon sauce. Home-made apple and blueberry crumble and custard makes a great finish to a meal.

Open all day all wk 11am-mdnt Closed 1 Jan, 25 Dec **Food** Lunch all wk 12-4 Dinner all wk 6-9.30 FREE HOUSE Isle of Skye Red Cuillin & Reeling Deck, Cairngorm Trade Winds, Caledonian Deuchars IPA, Orkney Dark Island. 9 **Facilities** Non-diners area (Bar Garden) Children's menu Children's portions Play area Family room Garden Parking WiFi

SOUTH UIST

LOCHBOISDALE Map 22 NF71

The Polochar Inn

tel: 01878 700215 **Polochar HS8 5TT**
email: polocharinn@aol.com
dir: *W from Lochboisdale, take B888. Hotel at end of road*

Cosy island pub overlooking the Sound

Standing virtually alone overlooking the Sound of Eriskay and a prehistoric standing stone, this white-painted inn is the former change-house, where travellers waited for the ferry to Barra. Owned by sisters Morag MacKinnon and Margaret Campbell, it serves Hebridean real ales and specialises in local seafood and meats, as well as pasta dishes, all made with fresh, seasonal ingredients and served in a dining room with outstanding views of the sea. The beer garden is the ideal spot for dolphin watching and for admiring the beautiful sunsets. On summer Saturday nights the sound of live music fills the bar.

Open all day all wk 11-11 (Fri-Sat 11am-1am Sun 12.30pm-1am) **Food** Lunch Mon-Sat 12.30-8.30, Sun 1-8.30 (winter all wk 12-2.30) Dinner Mon-Sat 12.30-8.30, Sun 1-8.30 (winter all wk 5-8.30) FREE HOUSE Hebridean, Guest ales. **Facilities** Non-diners area Children's menu Children's portions Family room Garden Parking WiFi (notice required)

Wales

ISLE OF ANGLESEY

| BEAUMARIS | Map 14 SH67 |

Ye Olde Bulls Head Inn ★★★★★ INN ⊛⊛⊛

PICK OF THE PUBS

tel: 01248 810329 **Castle St LL58 8AP**
email: info@bullsheadinn.co.uk **web:** www.bullsheadinn.co.uk
dir: *From Britannia Road Bridge follow A545. Inn in town centre*

Historic and award-winning inn on the island's coast

This 15th-century pub started life as a staging post and inn on the route to Ireland; it's just a stone's throw from the gates of Beaumaris' medieval castle. The bar transports drinkers back to Dickensian times (the man himself stayed here) with settles and antique furnishings; artefacts include the town's old ducking stool. The Bull's location in the midst of a rich larder of seafood and Welsh livestock farms has inspired the multi-talented kitchen team to produce exceptional menus, well deserving of three AA Rosettes. The light and airy Brasserie, created from the former stables, serves a good range of modern global dishes such as chargrilled bacon chop with Welsh cheddar macaroni, tenderstem broccoli, peas and oven-dried tomato. Push the boat out in the intimate Loft Restaurant by ordering grilled wild duck with smoked cabbage, crisp ham, glazed shallots and potato sauce, followed by poached fillet of sea trout with fennel risotto, kohlrabi, confit lemon and ginger velouté. Evening meals only served in the Brasserie and Loft Restaurant.

Open all day all wk Closed 25 Dec **Food** Lunch Mon-Sat 12-2, Sun 12-3 Av main course £15 Set menu available Restaurant menu available all wk ⊕ FREE HOUSE ◀ Bass, Hancock's, Guest ales. ☻ 20 **Facilities** Non-diners area ❤ (Bar) ◀◀ Children's menu Children's portions Parking WiFi **Rooms** 26

| LLANFAETHLU | Map 14 SH38 |

The Black Lion Inn ★★★★ INN ⊛

tel: 01407 730718 **LL65 4NL**
email: blacklion.admin@blacklionanglesey.co.uk **web:** www.blacklionanglesey.com
dir: *From A55 junct 3, A5 signed Valley. In Valley at lights right (A5025), 5m to pub on right*

An object lesson in pub restoration

A few years ago this derelict mid-terrace pub was bought by locals Leigh and Mari Faulkner who then restored it using slate and reclaimed oak, and filled it with auction-bought furniture. Even an old water trough found a new home. Today it has a snug, a patio, a bar with Welsh guest ales, an award-winning dining room with views of Snowdonia and AA-rated accommodation. Sourcing all food on Anglesey can be tricky, but luckily Mari's father and uncle raise livestock, mussels dwell in the Menai Strait, and fruit and vegetables do grow here. Mains (prif gwrs) include salmon and cod paupiette, crushed dill potatoes, Menai mussels and prawn broth; and roast topside of roast beef.

Open all day in holiday season Closed 10 days Jan, Mon & Tue Nov-Mar **Food** Lunch 12-2.30, Sat all day Dinner 6-8.30, Sat all day Av main course £13.95 ⊕ FREE HOUSE ◀ Marston's Pedigree & EPA, Local guest ales ☻ Thatchers Gold. **Facilities** Non-diners area ❤ (Bar Outside area) ◀◀ Children's menu Children's portions Outside area ⋒ Parking WiFi ▱ (notice required) **Rooms** 2

| RED WHARF BAY | Map 14 SH58 |

The Ship Inn

tel: 01248 852568 **LL75 8RJ**
dir: *Phone for detailed directions*

Walkers' and birdwatchers' favourite with lovely views

Wading birds flock here to feed on the extensive sands of Red Wharf Bay, making the Ship's waterside beer garden a birdwatcher's paradise. In the Kenneally family's hands for over 40 years, this traditional free house proffers carefully tended real ales, including the pub's own brewed by Conwy, and Facer's Flintshire. Local fish and seafood feature in dishes such as Menai mussels served in a classic marinière sauce. Otherwise plump for excellent Welsh beef in the form of a steak and ale pie; a steakwich with red onion and Dijon mustard sauce in toasted granary bread; or sirloin steak with home-made chips and pepper sauce.

Open all day all wk **Food** Lunch all wk 12-2.30 Dinner all wk 6-9 Av main course £12 Set menu available Restaurant menu available Sat ⊕ FREE HOUSE ◀ Conwy Kenneally's Bitter, Adnams, Facer's Flintshire, Guest ales ☻ Westons Wyld Wood Organic. **Facilities** Non-diners area ❤ (Bar Garden Outside area) ◀◀ Children's menu Children's portions Play area Family room Garden Outside area ⋒ Parking WiFi

BRIDGEND

| KENFIG | Map 9 SS88 |

Prince of Wales Inn

tel: 01656 740356 **CF33 4PR**
email: prince-of-wales@btconnect.com
dir: *M4 junct 37 into North Cornelly. Left at x-rds, follow signs for Kenfig & Porthcawl. Pub 600yds on right*

Inn with an intriguing history

Thought to be one of the most haunted pubs in Wales, this 16th-century stone-built free house was formerly the seat of local government for the lost city of Kenfig. Just as remarkably, it is also the only pub in Britain to have held a Sunday school continuously from 1857 to 2000. Welsh brunch; liver and onion casserole; poached cod in cream and tarragon sauce; and beef and Welsh ale pie are amongst the local dishes on the menu, and the daily blackboard specials are also worth attention. A list of suppliers is available for those wishing to check the provenance of the ingredients. In the summer of 2013, HRH The Prince of Wales visited his namesake pub, which is part of his The Pub is the Hub organisation, and enjoyed half a pint.

Open all day all wk **Food** Lunch Tue-Sat 12-2.30, Sun 12-3 Dinner Tue-Sat 6-8.30 Av main course £9-£14 ⊕ FREE HOUSE ◀ Bass, Sharp's Doom Bar, Worthington's, Local guest ales ☻ Gwynt y Ddraig Happy Daze, Tomos Watkin Taffy Apples. **Facilities** Non-diners area ❤ (Bar Garden) ◀◀ Children's menu Children's portions Garden ⋒ Beer festival Parking WiFi ▱ (notice required)

CARDIFF

| CREIGIAU | Map 9 ST08 |

Caesars Arms

PICK OF THE PUBS

tel: 029 2089 0486 **Cardiff Rd CF15 9NN**
email: info@caesarsarms.co.uk
dir: *M4 junct 34, A4119 towards Llantrisant/Rhondda. Approx 0.5m right at lights signed Groesfaen. Through Groesfaen, past Dynevor Arms pub. Next left, signed Creigiau. 1m, left at T-junct, pass Creigiau Golf Course. Pub 1m on left*

Country dining inn and farm shop handy for Cardiff

Well established for over 20 years, the Caesars Arms has a lot to offer. Vegetable gardens, polytunnels and a smallholding all form part of this enterprise, supplying a huge variety of greens, rare breed pork, honey, smoked meats and fish to the adjoining thriving farm shop (the former cricket pavilion) as well as the country pub and brasserie itself. The chefs here pride themselves in offering a progressive, modern menu combined with some old favourites, with seafood and exotic fish creating a good range of signature dishes which vary depending on the catch available. Sea bream, turbot or red mullet may feature, whilst a particular favourite is sea bass baked in rock salt then filleted at your table. Welsh game, beef and lamb satisfy the more traditional demands on the menu, whilst free-range chicken and duck come from Madgetts Farm in the Wye Valley. An extensive, quality wine list ensures that finding the perfect companion to your chosen main meal will be a breeze.

Open 12-2.30 6-10 (Sun 12-4) Closed 25-26 Dec, 1 Jan, Sun eve **Food** Lunch Mon-Sat 12-2.30 ⊕ FREE HOUSE ◄ Felinfoel Double Dragon, Brains Smooth, Guinness Ŏ Gwynt y Ddraig Orchard Gold. **Facilities** Non-diners area ◄ Children's menu Children's portions Garden ⊟ Parking ⚍ (notice required)

GWAELOD-Y-GARTH
Map 9 ST18

Gwaelod-y-Garth Inn

tel: 029 2081 0408 & 07855 313247 **Main Rd CF15 9HH**
email: gwaeloinn@outlook.com
dir: *From M4 junct 32, N on A470, left at next exit, at rdbt turn right 0.5m. Right into village*

Friendly pub with own ales in good walking country

This stone-built hillside cottage enjoys a wonderful position on the thickly wooded flank of Garth Hill, high above Taffs Well, with great walking and stunning views such as the fairytale Victorian sham castle of Castell Coch across the vale. At the bar guest ales from as far afield as Essex and Derbyshire rub shoulders with local brews, including some from their own microbrewery Violet Cottage, along with a farm cider from Pontypridd. A pleasing selection of home-cooked pub food produces dishes of grilled sea bass fillets on braised fennel, and Welsh Black steak and ale pie with puff pastry.

Open all day all wk 11am-mdnt (Sun 12-11) **Food** Lunch Mon-Thu 12-2, Fri-Sat 12-9.30, Sun 12-3.30 Dinner Mon-Thu 6.30-9, Fri-Sat 12-9.30 ⊕ FREE HOUSE ◄ Wye Valley Bitter, Swansea Three Cliffs Gold, Dark Star, Crouch Vale Brewers Gold, Thornbridge Jaipur, Gower Brewery Co, Tiny Rebel, Violet Cottage Shine On (pub's own), Total Eclipse & Zig Zag Ŏ Gwynt y Ddraig, Local cider. ₹ 10 **Facilities** Non-diners area ◄ (Bar Garden) ◄ Children's menu Children's portions Garden ⊟ Parking WiFi ⚍

PENTYRCH
Map 9 ST18

Kings Arms

tel: 029 2089 0202 **22 Church Rd CF15 9QF**
email: info@kingsarmspentyrch.co.uk
dir: *M4 junct 32, A470 (Merthyr Tydfil). Left onto B4262 signed Radyr then Pentyrch. Right at rdbt for Pentyrch. Or M4 junct 34, A4119 (dual carriageway) signed Llantrisant & Rhondda. Into right lane, right at lights signed Groes Farm. Left to Pentyrch*

Traditional Welsh longhouse pub

In a leafy village on the outskirts of Cardiff, this Grade II listed pub is full of traditional features, from the flagstoned snug to the exposed lime-washed walls and log fire of the lounge. The restaurant opens out onto the lovely landscaped gardens. Local brewery Brains supplies the real ales while there is also a choice of New and Old World wines. Promoting seasonal Welsh produce, the menus and daily blackboard specials could include Severn and Wye Valley smoked mackerel foccacia sandwich; confit leg of free-range duck; and loin of pork with sage and black pudding crust. The Sunday roasts are very popular.

Open all day all wk **Food** Lunch Mon-Fri 12-3, Sat all day, Sun 12-4 Dinner Mon-Fri 5.30-9.30, Sat all day Set menu available Restaurant menu available Tue-Sun ⊕ BRAINS ◄ Bitter, Guest ales Ŏ Symonds. **Facilities** Non-diners area ◄ (Bar Garden) ◄ Children's menu Children's portions Garden ⊟ Parking WiFi ⚍ (notice required)

ABERGORLECH
Map 8 SN53

The Black Lion

tel: 01558 685271 **SA32 7SN**
email: georgerashbrook@hotmail.com
dir: *A40 E from Carmarthen, then B4310 signed Brechfa & Abergorlech*

Cosy black-and-white pub in charming Welsh countryside

A drive through the pretty Cothi Valley brings you to this attractive, 16th-century village pub run by George and Louise Rashbrook. Louise does all the cooking and George wisely gives her generous credit for doing so. You can eat from an extensive menu in the flagstoned bar, while the evening menu in the more modern, candlelit dining room offers classic starters like prawn cocktail or fresh garlic mushrooms, followed by vegetable and Stilton crumble; lamb shank with red wine and rosemary gravy; chicken curry; or steak and Guinness pie. If there's room, go for banoffee pie, chocolate and Baileys cheesecake, or sherry trifle. The lovely beer garden overlooks a Roman bridge.

Open 12-3 7-11 (Sat-Sun & BH all day) Closed Mon (ex BHs) **Food** Lunch Tue-Sun 12-2.30 Dinner Tue-Sun 7-9 Av main course £8.95 Restaurant menu available Sun L ⊕ FREE HOUSE ◄ Rhymney Ŏ Westons Stowford Press, Gwynt y Ddraig. **Facilities** Non-diners area ◄ (Bar Garden Outside area) ◄ Children's menu Children's portions Garden Outside area ⊟ Parking WiFi ⚍ (notice required)

LLANDDAROG
Map 8 SN51

Butchers Arms

tel: 01267 275330 **SA32 8NS**
email: b5dmj@aol.com
dir: *From A48 between Carmarthen & Cross Hands follow Llanddarog/B4310 signs. Pub adjacent to church*

Country pub that's Welsh through and through

David and Mavis James's more than 30 years in this pretty village pub surely make them Old Favourites; as it happens, this is also the term David uses for some of his dishes – 'hearty' mixed grill; four pork sausages with eggs and home-made chips; beef and ale pie; and hot grilled chicken baguette with 'lashings of mayonnaise', for example. A further look at the menu reveals home-made tomato, onion and basil tart; pan-fried cockles with laver bread; chicken in home-made rustic Chasseur sauce; and 'sizzling' platter of king tiger prawns in garlic butter.

Open 12-3 6-11 Closed 24-26 Dec, Sun & Mon **Food** Lunch Tue-Sat 12-2.30 Dinner Tue-Sat 6-9.30 Restaurant menu available Tue-Sat ⊕ FREE HOUSE ◄ Felinfoel Cambrian Bitter, Double Dragon, Celtic Pride. ₹ 10 **Facilities** Non-diners area ◄ (Garden) ◄ Children's menu Garden ⊟ WiFi ⚍ (notice required)

Follow The AA on social media

twitter: @TheAA_Lifestyle
facebook: www.facebook.com/TheAAUK

LLANDEILO
Map 8 SN62

The Angel Hotel

tel: 01558 822765 **Rhosmaen St SA19 6EN**
email: capelbach@hotmail.com
dir: *In town centre adjacent to post office*

Reliable base in idyllic Welsh market town

This gabled inn commands a position near the crest of the long hill rising from Llandeilo's old bridge across the Towy, at the fringe of the Brecon Beacons National Park. Popular as both a locals' pub, with some reliable Welsh real ales and a good range of wines, and as an intimate place to dine in Y Capel Bach Bistro, an 18th-century gem tucked away at the rear of the hotel. Most diets are catered for on the ever-changing specials board and fixed price menu; perhaps chorizo, sauté potato and balsamic salad to start, followed by hake fillet with a mango, ginger and tomato sauce, or oven-roasted aubergine with a mixed bean chilli and melted blue cheese. There's pineapple upside-down pudding if you've left enough room.

Open 11.30-3 6-11 (Sun 11.30-4) Closed Sun eve **Food** Lunch Mon-Sat 11.30-2.30, Sun 12-3 Dinner Mon-Sat 6-9 Set menu available Restaurant menu available Mon-Sat evening ⊕ FREE HOUSE ◀ Evan Evans, Tomos Watkin, Wye Valley Ö Gwynt y Ddraig. ♀ 10 **Facilities** Non-diners area ✿ (Bar Garden) ♦♦ Children's menu Children's portions Garden ⊼ WiFi ▄ (notice required)

LLANDOVERY
Map 9 SN73

The Kings Head

tel: 01550 720393 **1 Market Square SA20 0AB**
email: info@kingsheadcoachinginn.co.uk
dir: *M4 junct 49, A483 through Ammanford, Llandeilo onto A40 to Llandovery. Pub in town centre opposite clock tower*

Former coaching inn with family-friendly food

Once the home of the Llandovery Bank, this 17th-century inn overlooks the town's cobbled market square. Step inside and the exposed beams and crooked floors are a reminder of the pub's heritage, with beers from the Gower Brewery representing the Principality. A good few menus are offered here, including lunchtime specials (all at £5, weekdays), light bites and children's. For your lunchtime fiver you could enjoy quality food from a menu that changes daily, perhaps a Welsh Black steak and onion sandwich. Choices from the à la carte menu include local Welsh lamb rack; or wild mushroom and parmesan linguine.

Open all day all wk 10am-mdnt **Food** Lunch all wk 12-2.30 Dinner all wk 6-9.30 Av main course £9 Restaurant menu available all wk ⊕ FREE HOUSE ◀ Sharp's Doom Bar, Tomos Watkin, Gower Gold Ö Kopparberg. **Facilities** Non-diners area ✿ (Bar Outside area) ♦♦ Children's menu Children's portions Outside area ⊼ Parking WiFi ▄

LLANLLWNI
Map 8 SN43

Belle @ Llanllwni

tel: 01570 480495 **SA40 9SQ**
email: food@thebelle.co.uk
dir: *Midway between Carmarthen & Lampeter on A485*

Well-cooked food at this cosy roadside inn

This cosy and welcoming roadside inn sits on the A485 between Carmarthen and Lampeter, surrounded by countryside and with stunning views. It's a great place to dine alfresco on a sunny day. There are two rotating ales here to enjoy along with Weston Stowford Press and local Welsh ciders. In the dining room, pan-seared

sewin fillet with chive mash and saffron lemon cream sauce; spinach and mozzarella tart, potato cake and pesto cream; or Welsh beef and mushroom pie with creamed spring onion mash could precede rich chocolate truffle tart; or fresh lemon cheesecake. Expect excellent ingredients including locally reared meats.

Open 12-3 5.30-11 Closed 25-26 Dec, Mon (ex BHs) **Food** Lunch Wed-Sat 12-3 Dinner Tue-Sun 6-9.30 Av main course £12.50 Set menu available Restaurant menu available Tue-Sun ⊕ FREE HOUSE ◀ Peroni, Guinness, Guest ales Ö Westons Stowford Press, Gwynt y Ddraig. ♀ 9 **Facilities** Non-diners area ♦♦ Children's menu Children's portions Outside area ⊼ Parking ▄ (notice required)

NANTGAREDIG
Map 8 SN42

Y Polyn ◉◉
PICK OF THE PUBS

tel: 01267 290000 **SA32 7LH**
email: ypolyn@hotmail.com
dir: *From A48 follow signs to National Botanic Garden of Wales. Then follow brown signs to Y Polyn*

Stylish but never stuffy, worth seeking out

Not far from the attractive county town of Carmarthen and just a couple of miles from the National Botanic Garden of Wales, Y Polyn is a former tollhouse, now well established as a destination pub for lovers of Welsh food. Recent development work has seen the conversion of the first floor to a couple of private dining rooms, ideal for family gatherings and parties. The bounty of West Wales is at the forefront of the uncomplicated, tempting dishes that come from the modest kitchen here, and 'Fat equals Flavour. Live with it' is the unapologetic ethos. Starters include ham hock bon-bons, poached egg, parsley sauce and Carmarthen ham, and roasted baby monkfish, vegetable and chickpea tagine with salsa verde; follow on with rump of salt marsh lamb, confit lamb breast, celeriac purée, and onion soubise. If you've room for pudding try one of the reinvented knickerbocker glories – tiramisù, for example. All this has gained the inn two AA Rosettes for its accomplished cooking. The excellent beers come from the local Handmade Brewery.

Open all wk 12-4 7-11 Closed Mon, Sun eve **Food** Contact pub for food times Set menu available Restaurant menu available Tue-Sun ⊕ FREE HOUSE ◀ Handmade Cwrw Sir Gâr & Pale Ale. ♀ 12 **Facilities** Non-diners area ♦♦ Children's portions Garden ⊼ Parking WiFi

PENDINE
Map 8 SN20

NEW Springwell Inn

tel: 01994 453274 **Marsh Rd SA33 4PA**
email: springwellinn@btinternet.com
dir: *A40 from Carmarthen to St Clears, onto A4066 to Pendine*

Local seafood a speciality

In the coastal village of Pendine, famous for hosting world land speed records, this 500-year-old pub offers far-reaching beach views and is only four miles from Laugharne, famous for its Dylan Thomas connections. Traditional with a cosy lounge warmed by a real fire in winter, the bar and restaurant offer a range of basket meals and pub classics, as well as main courses such as pan-fried sea bass with white wine sauce; and Gwendraeth Valley gammon steak with pineapple and egg. The Sunday lunch carvery is a popular option and children can choose from their own menu.

Open all day all wk **Food** Lunch all wk 12-3 Dinner all wk 6-9 Av main course £5.95-£9.95 ⊕ FREE HOUSE ◀ Sharp's Doom Bar, Brains The Rev. James Ö Gwynt y Ddraig Black Dragon. ♀ 12 **Facilities** Non-diners area ✿ (Bar Outside area) ♦♦ Children's menu Outside area ⊼ Parking WiFi ▄ (notice required)

PUMSAINT
Map 9 SN64

The Dolaucothi Arms

tel: 01558 650237 **SA19 8UW**
email: info@thedolaucothiarms.co.uk **web:** www.thedolaucothiarms.co.uk
dir: On A482 between Lampeter & Llandovery. From Llandeilo or Llandovery take A40

An authentic taste of Wales in an old village hostelry

Set in the rolling green Cothi Valley, the Dolaucothi Arms is a Grade II listed building owned by the National Trust. After closing for five years, it reopened with David Joy and Esther Hubert at the helm; both are passionate about Welsh food and drink. Choose an armchair in the cosy lounge bar, or sit at a large table in the main bar where Welsh real ales and ciders are on tap. Head for the separate dining room with wood-burning stove and eclectic mix of mismatched furniture to enjoy Dinewfr venison sausages; slow-cooked shin of beef; or partridge with cabbage and bacon. A beer and cider festival is held over the Summer Bank Holiday weekend.

Open all day Closed 25 Dec, Mon & Tue L winter **Food** Lunch 12.30-2.30 Dinner 6.30-8.30 Av main course £12 ⊕ FREE HOUSE ◀ Evan Evans Cwrw, Purple Moose Snowdonia Ale, Wye Valley Butty Bach, Jacobi Original Ŏ Gwynt y Ddraig Black Dragon. ⬗ 9 **Facilities** Non-diners area ❄ (Bar Garden) ⁅ Children's menu Children's portions Garden ♜ Beer festival Cider festival Parking WiFi ⛟ (notice required)

CEREDIGION

ABERAERON
Map 8 SN46

The Harbourmaster
PICK OF THE PUBS

tel: 01545 570755 **Pen Cei SA46 0BT**
email: info@harbour-master.com
dir: In Aberaeron follow Tourist Information Centre signs. Pub adjacent

Delightful quayside hotel overlooking Cardigan Bay

Close to the harbour-mouth, the grand sunsets of Cardigan Bay illuminate the pastel colours of this and other quayside buildings crowding in around the old port. It's an enchanting scene, the ideal culmination of a day's exploring the astonishing coastline and deep countryside here in west Wales. The owners make the most of the wealth of surf 'n turf produce available from this favoured locale. Weekly-changing bar menus might highlight Cardigan Bay crab, chilli and garlic linguine; or Welsh beef salad Asian style. The fare is an easy medley of traditional and contemporary dishes. The restaurant menu majors on seafood, but also carries loin of Brecon venison with parsnip purée red cabbage and Brecon gin sauce; or rib of Welsh beef on the bone. Beers are from first-rate microbreweries, whilst the real cider harks from the Ebbw Valley.

Open all day all wk 10am-11.30pm Closed 25 Dec **Food** Lunch all wk 12-2.30 Dinner all wk 6-9 Restaurant menu available all wk ⊕ FREE HOUSE ◀ Purple Moose Glaslyn Ale, HM Best Bitter Ŏ Hallets Real. ⬗ 15 **Facilities** Non-diners area ⁅ Children's menu Children's portions ♜ Parking WiFi

ABERYSTWYTH
Map 8 SN58

The Glengower Hotel

tel: 01970 626191 **3 Victoria Ter SY23 2DH**
email: info@glengower.co.uk
dir: Phone for detailed directions

Local ales and enjoyable food overlooking the bay

Literally a stone's throw from the beach, the sun terrace at 'The Glen' – as it's affectionately known by the locals – offers fabulous views across Cardigan Bay where you might possibly spot one of the friendly local dolphins. A traditional free house serving a wide range of home-made food all day, from sandwiches and paninis to local butchers' sausages and mash; smoked salmon and asparagus linguine; and home-made chilli con carne, The Glen has a good local reputation for its real ales, including beers from award-winning North Wales brewery Purple Moose. Look out for the pub's Bank Holiday beer festival in late May.

Open all day all wk **Food** Lunch Mon-Sat 12-8, Sun 12-6 Dinner Mon-Sat 12-8, Sun 12-6 ⊕ FREE HOUSE ◀ Wye Valley, Purple Moose Ŏ Gwynt y Ddraig. **Facilities** Non-diners area ❄ (Bar Outside area) ⁅ Children's menu Children's portions Outside area ♜ Beer festival WiFi

LLANFIHANGEL-Y-CREUDDYN
Map 9 SN67

y Ffarmers
PICK OF THE PUBS

tel: 01974 261275 **SY23 4LA**
email: bar@yffarmers.co.uk
dir: From Aberystwyth take B4340 towards Trawsgoed. After New Cross left signed Llanfihangel-y-Creuddyn

Excellent local food in the Welsh hills

Found down winding narrow lanes through stunning countryside, this traditional local is tucked away in Llanfihangel's gorgeous open square alongside listed whitewashed cottages and an imposing church. Since Rhodri Edwards and his wife Esther took over and spruced the place up with a contemporary feel, it has become an oasis for tip-top Welsh beer and quality food. Expect to find a buzzy community vibe and the place packed with local drinkers supping pints of Evan Evans or potent Gwynt y Ddraig cider, farmers from the hills and local foodies in the know. There's distinct Welsh flavour to the short monthly menus (written in Welsh and English, naturally), which champion produce from local farms and artisan producers. Typically, tuck into local honey and duck samosas with plum sauce; Ystwyth Valley lamb cutlets with dauphinoise potatoes, and warm gooseberry and almond cake with stem ginger ice cream. Don't miss the Sunday roasts.

Open 12-2 6-11 Closed 2-12 Jan, Mon (ex BH & school hols) **Food** Lunch Wed-Sun 12-2 Dinner Tue-Sat 6-9 Av main course £12.50 ⊕ FREE HOUSE ◀ Evan Evans, Felinfoel Ŏ Gwynt y Ddraig, Westons Stowford Press. **Facilities** Non-diners area ❄ (Bar Garden) ⁅ Children's menu Children's portions Garden ♜ WiFi ⛟ (notice required)

Read all about pubs and their friendly ghosts in our feature on page 12

LLWYNDAFYDD   Map 8 SN35

The Crown Inn & Restaurant

tel: 01545 560396 **SA44 6BU**
email: thecrowninnandrestaurant@hotmail.co.uk
dir: Follow Llwyndafydd signs from A487, NE of Cardigan

Amid exquisite countryside

A village pub since the 1800s, this traditional Welsh longhouse is only a short walk from Cwm Tydu beach and National Trust-owned cliffs. The award-winning garden is a delight, while inside are original beams, fireplaces and a pretty restaurant. Mains here include beef or three-cheese vegetarian lasagne; fillet of breaded or battered cod and chips; Thai-spiced fillet of salmon; and beetroot and butternut squash cupcake pie. There's a carvery every Sunday. Blackboard specials, a children's menu, light snacks and bar food are also available. Buckleys, Cottage, Evan Evans, Sharp's and guest breweries do the honours in the bar.

Open all day all wk Closed Mon (Winter) **Food** Lunch all wk 12-3 Dinner all wk 6-9 ⊕ FREE HOUSE ◀ Buckleys Best Bitter, Evan Evans, Cottage, Sharp's Doom Bar, Guest ales. ♟ 9 **Facilities** Non-diners area ♣ (Bar Garden Outside area) ♦ Children's menu Children's portions Play area Garden Outside area ⌂ Beer festival Parking WiFi ▥

PONTRHYDFENDIGAID   Map 9 SN76

NEW The Black Lion Hotel

tel: 01974 831624 **SY25 6BE**
email: alynjpugh@gmail.com
dir: On B4343 N of Tregaron

Where drovers, pilgrims and travellers have stayed for centuries

A mile away from this white-painted hotel lies the ruined abbey at Strata Florida, a most un-Welsh-sounding place-name that's actually a corruption of Ystrad Fflur, meaning 'valley of flowers'. Walkers, cyclists, fishermen and nature lovers attracted by the abbey and the other scenic delights of west Wales visit here and enjoy its Welsh-farmhouse-like interior, where Llandeilo brewery Evan Evans satisfies no doubt the many real-ale drinkers among them. Home-made food depends to a great extent on local produce, typical examples being Welsh beef lasagne; breaded wholetail scampi; and chickpea curry and rice. Board specials complement the printed menu.

Open 12-late (winter Mon-Wed 4-late Thu-Sun 12-late) Closed L Mon-Wed in winter **Food** Lunch 12-2 Dinner all wk 6-9 Av main course £10 ⊕ FREE HOUSE ◀ Evan Evans ♂ Westons Stowford Press. **Facilities** Non-diners area ♣ (Bar Garden) ♦ Children's menu Garden ⌂ Parking WiFi ▥ (notice required)

TREGARON   Map 9 SN65

Y Talbot ★★★★ INN

tel: 01974 298208 **The Square SY25 6JL**
email: info@ytalbot.com **web:** www.ytalbot.com
dir: On B4343 in village centre. (NB take caution in winter on mountain road from Beulah)

Timeless village inn with great Welsh beer and food

An arresting inn which dominates the compact square at the heart of Tregaron. Surrounded by a web of footpaths, bridleways and drovers' roads, the tiny town bustles with outdoor activity. This idyllic location also guarantees first class provender from local farms, lakes and the Afon Teifi which flows through the town at the fringe of the little-known Cambrian Mountains. Past customers here include the Victorian travel writer George Borrow and US President Jimmy Carter; perhaps they, too, enjoyed fare such as roast fillet of wild sea bass with wild mushrooms and celeriac purée; and braised chicken wings and red wine sauce from the contemporary Welsh menu. Beers are usually from local craft breweries, augmented by an October beer festival.

Open all day all wk **Food** Lunch all wk 12-2.30 Dinner all wk 6-9 Av main course £13 Restaurant menu available all wk ⊕ FREE HOUSE ◀ Purple Moose Glaslyn Ale, Wye Valley HPA, Buckley's Best, Cwrw Teifi ♂ Gwynt y Ddraig Happy Daze. **Facilities** Non-diners area ♣ (Bar Garden) ♦ Children's menu Children's portions Garden ⌂ Beer festival Parking WiFi ▥ (notice required) **Rooms** 13

CONWY
AA PUB OF THE YEAR FOR WALES
2015–2016

ABERGELE   Map 14 SH97

NEW The Kinmel Arms ★★★★★ RR ◎◎ PICK OF THE PUBS

tel: 01745 832207 **The Village, St George LL22 9BP**
email: info@thekinmelarms.co.uk **web:** www.thekinmelarms.co.uk
dir: From A55 junct 24a to St George. E on A55, junct 24. 1st left to Rhuddlan, 1st right into St George. 2nd right

Family-run pub that's a true winner

Situated between the mountains and the sea, this 17th-century pub occupies a lovely spot in the secluded hamlet of St George overlooking the north Wales coast. Tim and Lynn Cunnah-Watson took over here in 2002 with a vision to create a peaceful hideaway from which to eat, sleep and explore the area, and the hard work has paid off. The original sandstone frontage and mullion windows contrast well with the contemporary interior and the dining room is a relaxed space to enjoy enjoyable, locally-sourced food, perhaps accompanied by a glass of Facer's Flintshire ale or Gwynt y Ddraig cider. The pub's coastal location determines much of the menu, which majors on local seafood. An à la carte starter of king scallops, squash, miso glaze, black sesame and wild rice cracker might precede sea bass with salt-baked kohlrabi and celeriac purée. More traditional dishes include Menai mussels or home-made beefburger. Staying in the luxury accommodation rounds off a visit very nicely.

Open 12-3 5.45-11.30 Closed Sun & Mon **Food** Lunch Tue-Sat 12-2 Dinner Tue-Sat 6-9.30 Av main course £14 Set menu available Restaurant menu available Tue-Sat ⊕ FREE HOUSE ◀ Facer's Flintshire, Great Orme ♂ Gwynt y Ddraig. ♟ **Facilities** Non-diners area ♣ (Bar Garden Outside area) ♦ Children's menu Children's portions Garden Outside area ⌂ Parking WiFi ▥ (notice required) **Rooms** 4

BETWS-Y-COED   Map 14 SH75

Ty Gwyn Inn   PICK OF THE PUBS

tel: 01690 710383 & 710787 **LL24 0SG**
email: mratcl1050@aol.com
dir: At junct of A5 & A470, 100yds S of Waterloo Bridge

Local, seasonal food drive the menus

Located on the old London to Holyhead road, the Ty Gwyn was welcoming travellers long before Thomas Telford built his impressive cast iron Waterloo Bridge over the River Conwy in 1815. Much of the original 17th-century character is evident inside. The Ratcliffe family has owned and run this former coaching inn for the past 29 years, and today Martin (the chef for all that time) and his wife Nicola are in charge. Real ales come from as near as Conwy's Great Orme brewery, as well as from much further afield. Martin's cooking relies heavily on quality local produce including home-grown vegetables. Typical dishes include a starter of creamy scrambled free-range goose egg with smoked salmon and wild garlic, and main courses such as slow-roasted suckling pig with black pudding and hazelnut stuffing and thyme-scented roast root vegetables.

Open all wk 12-2 6.30-11 Closed 1wk Jan, 24-26 Dec **Food** Lunch all wk 12-2 Dinner all wk 6.30-9 Set menu available Restaurant menu available Sunday Lunch ⊕ FREE HOUSE ◀ Brains The Rev. James, Great Orme. **Facilities** ♦ Children's menu Children's portions Outside area ⌂ Parking WiFi ▥

CAPEL CURIG — Map 14 SH75

Bryn Tyrch Inn ★★★★ INN ◉

tel: 01690 720223 **LL24 0EL**
email: info@bryntyrchinn.co.uk web: www.bryntyrchinn.co.uk
dir: *On A5, 6m from Betws-y-Coed*

Smart inn with wonderful Snowdon views

Occupying an idyllic position in the heart of the Snowdonia National Park with breathtaking views of Snowdon and Moel Siabod, this remote inn is an ideal base for exploring the stunning mountains of the region. Welsh produce dominates the menu, which can be enjoyed in the informal bar or the terrace restaurant. Seared wood pigeon, chestnut and bacon tart, poached egg with port reduction; chargrilled rib-eye Welsh steak with hand-cut chips; and fish of the day are typical choices.

Open 4-11 (Fri-Sun all day) Closed 3-21 Jan, mid Dec-27 Dec, Mon-Thu L (excluding holidays) **Food** Lunch Fri-Sun & hols 12-9 Dinner Mon-Thu 5-9, Fri-Sun & hols 12-9 ⊕ FREE HOUSE ◀ Conwy Rampart, Welsh Pride & Clogwyn Gold ♻ Symonds. **Facilities** Non-diners area ◀◗ Children's menu Children's portions Garden ﬠ Parking WiFi **Rooms** 11

COLWYN BAY — Map 14 SH87

Pen-y-Bryn — PICK OF THE PUBS

tel: 01492 533360 **Pen-y-Bryn Rd LL29 6DD**
email: pen.y.bryn@brunningandprice.co.uk
dir: *1m from A55. Follow signs to Welsh Mountain Zoo. Establishment at top of hill*

Character interior and friendly atmosphere

A self-guided walk from the pub makes the most of the wooded hills and lanes here above Colwyn Bay. Alternatively, grab a seat in the garden and appreciate the views across to the gigantic headlands of The Little and Great Orme hills jutting out into silvery Liverpool Bay. Brunning & Price's designers have worked their usual magic on the interior of this plain-looking 1970s building, producing a character mix of Edwardian parlour and country inn. A new addition is a private dining room for small parties. Beer festivals are regularly held, complementing the already generous selection of real ales, many from North Wales breweries. The food side of the business is equally appealing, with daily-changing menus offering a liberal choice, from sandwiches upwards. Breeze in with a starter like chickpea falafel cakes with beetroot houmous. Mains cover all the bases; chicken, ham hock and leek pie, or beef feather braised with stout and honey roast onions are typical quality choices on the all-day menu.

Open all day all wk 12-11 (Sun 12-10.30) **Food** Lunch Mon-Sat 12-9.30, Sun 12-9 Dinner Mon-Sat 12-9.30, Sun 12-9 Av main course £11.95 ⊕ BRUNNING & PRICE ◀ Original, Purple Moose Snowdonia Ale, Guest ales ♻ Aspall. ♇ 14 **Facilities** Non-diners area ❖ (Bar Garden) ◀◗ Children's menu Children's portions Garden ﬠ Beer festival Parking WiFi

CONWY — Map 14 SH77

The Groes Inn ★★★★★ INN ◉ — PICK OF THE PUBS

tel: 01492 650545 **Ty'n-y-Groes LL32 8TN**
email: reception@groesinn.com web: www.groesinn.com
dir: *Exit A55 to Conwy, left at mini rdbt by Conwy Castle onto B5106, 2.5m inn on right*

Historic pub blessed with stunning views

Overlooking the sweeping Conwy estuary, the rambling, oak-beamed rooms of this 450-year-old, creeper-smothered inn — the first licensed house in Wales - are so full of careworn settles, log fires, military hats and historic cooking utensils that, mercifully perhaps, there's no room for jukebox or pool table. Study the nicely balanced menu in the well-groomed bar over a leisurely Groes Ale or Welsh Black beer from Llandudno's Great Orme brewery, or one of the 14 wines by the glass. Start with roasted beetroot and Pant-ysgawn goats' cheese salad; or grilled

sardines with marinated courgettes, tomato and garlic butter. Main dishes often have clear local provenance, such as prime Welsh beefburger with Bodnant cheese and onions; and pan-fried Anglesey sea bass with scallops and samphire. A former AA Pub of the Year for Wales, it offers luxurious accommodation.

Open all wk 12-3 6-11 **Food** Lunch all wk 12-2 Dinner all wk 6.30-9 Av main course £10 ⊕ FREE HOUSE ◀ Groes Ale, Great Orme Welsh Black, Orme, Tetley's ♻ Westons Stowford Press. ♇ 14 **Facilities** Non-diners area ❖ (Bar Garden) Children's menu Children's portions Family room Garden ﬠ Parking WiFi ☎ (notice required) **Rooms** 14

DOLWYDDELAN — Map 14 SH75

Elen's Castle Hotel

tel: 01690 750207 **LL25 0EJ**
email: stay@hotelinsnowdonia.co.uk
dir: *5m S of Betws-y-Coed, follow A470*

Relaxed and welcoming atmosphere at this village hostelry

Elen's Castle was once owned by the Earl of Ancaster, who sold it to his gamekeeper. The latter opened it as a coaching inn around 1880, specialising in hunting parties. Now a family-run free house, it boasts an old-world bar with a wood-burning stove and an intimate restaurant with breathtaking views of the mountains and Lledr River. Sample dishes include sweet potato and spinach curry; local Welsh chops with new potatoes and seasonal vegetables; and deep-filled Welsh Black shortcrust beef pie. The chocolate fudge cake or raspberry Pavlova should round things off nicely. Water from the on-site Roman well is said to have healing properties.

Open vary by season Closed 1st 2wks Jan, wk days in quiet winter periods **Food** Dinner 6.30-9 Av main course £8.95 ⊕ FREE HOUSE ◀ Shepherd Neame Spitfire, Wychwood Hobgoblin, Brains, Worthington's, Wadworth 6X ♻ Westons Stowford Press. **Facilities** Non-diners area ❖ (Bar) ◀◗ Children's menu Children's portions Play area Family room Garden ﬠ Parking WiFi ☎ (notice required)

LLANDUDNO — Map 14 SH78

The Cottage Loaf

tel: 01492 870762 **Market St LL30 2SR**
email: thecottageloaf@hotmail.co.uk
dir: *From A55 onto A470, then A456. Into Mostyn St, left into Market St*

Quirky seaside pub with good food and local ale

For years a bakery, this whitewashed building in the heart of Llandudno only became a pub in 1981 and much of its quirky interior is made up of salvaged materials from a ship-wrecked coal schooner. With a log fire for winter and a large garden and sun terrace for summer, this welcoming pub attracts visitors all year round. Local Conwy Welsh Pride is one of several ales on rotation, alongside a large range of whiskies and wines. Pan-fried Gressingham duck breast and crispy leg pastille; and treacle-roasted ham, eggs, triple-cooked chips, garden peas and bread and butter, are typical choices from the extensive food menu.

Open all day all wk **Food** Lunch all wk 12-9 Dinner all wk 12-9 Av main course £10.95 ⊕ FREE HOUSE ◀ Courage Directors, Conwy Welsh Pride, Guest ales ♻ Gwynt y Ddraig Black Dragon, Firey Fox, Dog Dancer & Happy Daze, Westons Old Rosie. **Facilities** Non-diners area ◀◗ Children's menu Children's portions Garden ﬠ WiFi ☎ (notice required)

LLANDUDNO JUNCTION — Map 14 SH77

The Queens Head ★★★★★ INN ◉ — PICK OF THE PUBS

See Pick of the Pubs on page 632

PICK OF THE PUBS

The Queens Head ★★★★★ INN ❀

tel: 01492 546570
Glanwydden LL31 9JP
email: enquiries@
queensheadglanwydden.co.uk
web: www.queensheadglanwydden.co.uk
dir: *A55 onto A470 towards Llandudno.*
At 3rd rdbt right towards Penrhyn Bay,
2nd right into Glanwydden, pub on left

A warm welcome, effortless charm and excellent service

This charming, 18th-century country pub, a former winner of AA Pub of the Year for Wales, was once the storehouse of the Llangwestennin Parish and is located in a pretty rural village just a five-minute drive from the Victorian seaside town of Llandudno. It is ideally placed for anyone enjoying country walks, cycling, or a day on the beach. The Queens Head continues to attract discerning customers with its warm welcome, effortless charm and excellent service. The stylish terrace is just the place to join friends on warmer summer evenings, whilst on colder nights the relaxed atmosphere in the bar is perfect for a pre-dinner drink by the log fire; or arrive early to bag a seat in the cosy snug. Real ales come from the Great Orme Brewery, located in the hills nearby, and you'll find that the lip-smacking wine list with helpful

description notes has plenty of choice. The dedicated kitchen makes excellent use of local produce in varied menus that might include a starter of smoked salmon and trout mousse; grilled Glanwydden goats' cheese tart; or crispy lamb and feta salad. Local fish and seafood is the cornerstone of the menu and typical examples are Conwy moules marinière; and monkfish and king prawn curry; and baked fillet of cod topped with Welsh rarebit. Meat-lovers are certainly not overlooked, with the likes of home-made lasagne; chicken korma; braised Welsh lamb shoulder with redcurrant and rosemary gravy; and sautéed calves' liver and crispy bacon.

Open all day all wk 12-10.30 Closed 25 Dec **Food** Contact pub for details ⊕ FREE HOUSE 🍺 Great Orme. ♟ 10 **Facilities** Non-diners area 🚻 Children's portions Garden ⊼ Parking WiFi 🚌 (notice required) **Rooms** 1

LLANELIAN-YN-RHÔS Map 14 SH87

The White Lion Inn

tel: 01492 515807 **LL29 8YA**
email: info@whitelioninn.co.uk
dir: *A55 junct 22, left signed Old Colwyn, A547. At rdbt 2nd exit onto B5383 signed Betwys-yn-Rhos. In 1m turn right into Llanelian Rd, follow to village. Pub on right*

One of the oldest country inns in north Wales

Incredibly, parts of this attractive family-run inn are reputed to date back over 1,200 years. It still retains its original slate floor and oak-beamed ceiling, and there is an old salt cellar by the inglenook fireplace. The Cole family have been running the inn for more than 25 years and have restored and preserved many aspects of traditional village life revolving around the pub, including reinstating the snug next to the bar (dogs are allowed in here). The food is traditional, home cooked, and wherever possible locally sourced. Look out for steak and kidney pie; roast beef with Yorkshire pudding; roast lamb shoulder, mash, vegetables and gravy; and scampi and chips.

Open Tue-Fri 11.30-3 6-11 (Sat 11.30-4 5-11.30 Sun 12-10.30) Closed Mon (ex BHs & school summer hols) **Food** Lunch Tue-Sat 12-2, Sun 12-9 Dinner Tue-Sat 6-9, Sun 12-9 Av main course £10.95 ⊕ FREE HOUSE ◀ Marston's Pedigree & Burton Bitter, Guest ale. ♀ 11 **Facilities** Non-diners area ♦♦ Children's menu Children's portions Garden ⋒ Parking WiFi ⬛ (notice required)

LLANNEFYDD Map 14 SH97

The Hawk & Buckle Inn

tel: 01745 540249 **LL16 5ED**
email: garethandsiwan@googlemail.com
dir: *Phone for detailed directions*

Old inn situated high in the hills of north Wales

From high in the north Wales hills, this lovingly restored 17th-century coaching inn enjoys spectacular views across the local countryside to Blackpool Tower and beyond. The real ale selection includes Heavy Industry and Purple Moose Glaslyn Ale, while a regularly changing menu uses the best of fresh local produce. Here's just a sample of what you might find: black pudding and goats' cheese stack with apple chutney; slow-roasted lamb chump with mint and cranberry gravy; the 8oz Hawk burger topped with Welsh cheese and smoked bacon; or red snapper fillet with citrus butter.

Open all wk Mon-Fri 6-11 (Sat 3.30-12 Sun 5-11) **Food** Dinner Mon-Fri 6-8.30, Sat 3.30-12, Sun 5-11 ⊕ FREE HOUSE ◀ Heavy Industry, Purple Moose Glaslyn Ale, Guest ales. **Facilities** Non-diners area ♦♦ Children's menu Children's portions Garden Outside area ⋒ Parking WiFi ⬛ (notice required)

TREFRIW Map 14 SH76

The Old Ship

tel: 01492 640013 **High St LL27 0JH**
email: rhian.barlow@btopenworld.com
dir: *From A470 between Tal-y-Bont & Betws-y-Coed follow Trefriw signs*

A great place to end a walk

A perfect refuelling stop following a tramp in the hills, this traditional inn is situated in a peaceful village in the wooded eastern edge of the Snowdonia National Park. Warm up by the log fire with a refreshing pint of Purple Moose Glaslyn Ale and peruse the daily chalkboard menu. Using locally sourced

ingredients, freshly prepared dishes take in pea and ham soup; coq au vin with dauphinoise potatoes and green beans; and pub classics such as fish and chips, or sausages with garlic mash and red wine gravy. For dessert, maybe dark and white chocolate cheesecake.

Open 12-3 6-11 (Sat-Sun 12-11) Closed Mon (ex BHs) **Food** Lunch Tue-Fri 12-2.30, Sat-Sun 12-9 Dinner Tue-Fri 6-9, Sat-Sun 12-9 ⊕ FREE HOUSE ◀ Banks's Bitter, Purple Moose Glaslyn Ale, 2 Guest Ales ♂ Thatchers Gold. ♀ **Facilities** Non-diners area ♦♦ Children's menu Children's portions Garden ⋒ Parking

DENBIGHSHIRE

RUTHIN Map 15 SJ15

NEW The White Horse

tel: 01824 790218 **Hendrerwydd LL16 4LL**
email: enquiries@whitehorserestaurant.co.uk
dir: *From Ruthin A494 (Mold Rd). Left at Llanbedr-Dyffryn-Clwyd onto B5429 (Llandyrnog). Right signed Gellifor. At x-rds in Hendrerwydd, pub on left. Or from Denbigh, A525 (Ruthin road). Left onto B5429 to Llandyrnog. Left to Hendrerwydd*

16th-century country pub deep in the Vale of Clwyd

Surrounded by the sublime scenery of the Clwydian hills, this pretty, whitewashed pub is the 'charming and friendly retreat from the world' that owners Lucy Hughes and Jason Stock set out to create. For the modern British food their unshakeable maxim is 'locally sourced', typically extra-mature Welsh steak, roast tomatoes, scrumpy-battered onions and grilled field mushrooms; baked haddock fillet on crushed new potatoes with white wine sauce; and spinach and ricotta tortellini in smoked cheese with wilted baby spinach and wild mushroom sauce. It follows then that real ales, such as Porthmadog's Purple Moose, should come only from local microbreweries.

Open 12-2 5-11 (Sat-Sun 12-11) Closed Mon & Tue **Food** Lunch Wed-Sat 12-2, Sun 12-8 Dinner Wed-Sat 5.30-9, Sun 12-8 Av main course £12.95 ⊕ FREE HOUSE ◀ Purple Moose Snowdonia Ale, Buzzard Vale Ale. **Facilities** Non-diners area ♣ (Bar Garden) ♦♦ Children's menu Children's portions Garden ⋒ Beer festival Parking WiFi ⬛ (notice required)

ST ASAPH Map 15 SJ07

The Plough Inn

tel: 01745 585080 **The Roe LL17 0LU**
email: ploughsa@gmail.com
dir: *Exit A55 at Rhyl & St Asaph signs, left at rdbt, pub 200yds on left*

A former coaching inn combining modern and traditional

The bar here is a quirky blend of modern and traditional, with open fires, blackboard menus, an unusual trompe l'oeil bar and real ales from north Wales; the restaurant, though very modern, retains a vaulted ceiling from its days as a ballroom. Dine here on chicken fillet with chicken mousse, mushrooms, spinach with leek and potato mash; grilled gammon steak with egg, pineapple, peas and chips; or braised lamb shank, dauphinoise potatoes, honey-glazed carrots and rosemary jus. There's live music on Friday and Saturday nights, as well as a cocktail bar and a wine shop.

Open all day all wk **Food** Lunch all wk 10-9 Dinner all wk 10-9 Av main course £8.95 Set menu available ⊕ FREE HOUSE ◀ Conwy, Great Orme, Facer's Brewery Flintshire, Heavy Industry Brewery, Weetwood Ales, Coach House Brewing Company. ♀ 10 **Facilities** Non-diners area ♣ (Garden Outside area) ♦♦ Children's menu Children's portions Garden Outside area ⋒ Parking WiFi ⬛

FLINTSHIRE

BABELL	Map 15 SJ17

Black Lion Inn

tel: 01352 720239 **CH8 8PZ**
email: reservations@theblacklioninn.uk.com
dir: A55 junct 31 to Caerwys. Left at x-rds signed Babell. In 3m turn right

Ancient coaching inn with ghostly residents

Surely no building can survive for 700 years without acquiring ghosts – and this former coaching inn has plenty, including that of a Canadian man forever asking to come in. From its rural location, it commands mind-blowing views across the Clwydian Range in an Area of Outstanding Natural Beauty. Comfy sofas and an open fire distinguish the bar, where locally-brewed cask ales complement an appealing modern British menu featuring local pork fritters with piccalilli; seafood risotto (served either as a starter or main course); Black Lion Welsh beef steak and ale pie; and home-made cheesecake of the day. Every Wednesday is pie night, Thursday night is grill night, and there's a September beer festival.

Open all day Closed Mon & Tue **Food** Lunch Wed-Sun 12-9 Dinner Wed-Sun 12-9 Av main course £7.95-£10 Restaurant menu available Wed-Sun ⊕ FREE HOUSE ◀ Purple Moose Myrica Gale, Black Lion Bitter, Great Orme Celtica. ₮ 8 **Facilities** Non-diners area ◆ Children's menu Children's portions Play area Garden ⨅ Beer festival Parking WiFi ▭ (notice required)

CILCAIN	Map 15 SJ16

White Horse Inn

tel: 01352 740142 **CH7 5NN**
email: christine.jeory@btopenworld.com
dir: From Mold take A541 towards Denbigh. After approx 6m turn left

Traditional inn, the hub of village life

This 400-year-old pub is the last survivor of five originally to be found in this lovely hillside village, probably because it was the centre of the local gold-mining industry in the 19th century. Today, the White Horse is popular with walkers, cyclists and horse-riders. Food here is home made by the landlord's wife using the best quality local ingredients, and is accompanied by a good range of real ales. A typical meal might start with crispy duck spring rolls or spicy lamb samosas, followed by home-made steak and kidney pie or, for a vegetarian option, sweet potato, spinach and chickpea curry.

Open all wk 12-3 6-11 (Sat 12-11 Sun 12-10.30) **Food** Lunch all wk 12-2.15 Dinner all wk 7-9 ⊕ FREE HOUSE ◀ Timothy Taylor Landlord, Banks's, Great Orme, Brimstage ♂ Thatchers Gold. ₮ 9 **Facilities** Non-diners area ◆ (Bar Garden) Garden ⨅ Parking WiFi

HAWARDEN	Map 15 SJ36

NEW The Glynne Arms

tel: 01244 569988 **3 Glynne Way CH5 3NS**
email: manager@theglynnearms.co.uk
dir: From North Wales Expressway junct 36a onto B5125 to Hawarden. Or from A494 onto A550 or B5125 to Hawarden. Pub in village centre

Excellent food and very dog-friendly too

Behind this fine-looking old coaching inn's 2012 revival are Charlie and Caroline Gladstone. Charlie's great-great grandfather was 19th-century prime minister Sir William Ewart Gladstone, who married into Hawarden Castle's Glynne dynasty. Meat, fruit and vegetables come from the couple's Estate Farm Shop down the road.

Real ales are local too. At the menu's simpler end are sandwiches, gourmet burgers and grills, while greater sophistication comes courtesy of baked monkfish, red mullet and baby fennel, Parmentier potatoes and samphire; pan-fried venison steak with roasted baby beets, sweet potatoes, spinach and redcurrant jus; and artichoke and quinoa rice salad with tempura courgettes. This is a dog-friendly establishment.

Open all day all wk **Food** Lunch all wk 12-9.30 Dinner all wk 12-9.30 Av main course £14 ⊕ FREE HOUSE ◀ Purple Moose, Spitting Feathers, Facer's Flintshire ♂ Rosie's. ₮ 16 **Facilities** Non-diners area ◆ (Bar Garden) ◆ Children's menu Children's portions Garden ⨅ Parking WiFi ▭ (notice required)

MOLD	Map 15 SJ26

Glasfryn | PICK OF THE PUBS |

tel: 01352 750500 **Raikes Ln, Sychdyn CH7 6LR**
email: glasfryn@brunningandprice.co.uk
dir: From Mold follow signs to Theatr Clwyd, 1m from town centre

Hill views, heavenly ales and great menus

With magical views from the gardens over the Alyn Valley towards the rippling hills of the Clwydian Range Area of Outstanding Natural Beauty, this imposing dining pub was converted from a judge's country residence some years ago by the Brunning & Price group. Their hallmark style of polished wood, country and quirky prints, quality antiquey furnishings and largely wood flooring complements the Arts and Crafts style of the original building. The pub's real ale pumps are the tip of the refreshment iceberg – the wine and malt whisky lists are comprehensive too. Fine pub grub is a given; there's a great range of starters and light bites, or investigate mains like slow-cooked shoulder of lamb with cinnamon, cumin and chickpeas, apricot and date couscous.

Open all day all wk **Food** Lunch Mon-Sat 12-9.30, Sun 12-9 Dinner Mon-Sat 12-9.30, Sun 12-9 ⊕ BRUNNING & PRICE ◀ Purple Moose Snowdonia Ale, Timothy Taylor ♂ Aspall. ₮ 16 **Facilities** Non-diners area ◆ (Bar Garden) ◆ Garden ⨅ Beer festival Parking WiFi

NORTHOP	Map 15 SJ26

NEW The Celtic Arms

tel: 01352 840423 **Northop Country Park CH7 6WA**
email: celticarms@woodwardandfalconer.com
dir: A55 junct 33a (W'bound), left into Northop Country Park. Or A55 junct 33 (E'bound) through Northop. At lights left (signed A5126) into Connah's Quay Rd, right signed Northop Country Park

Pub and restaurant in a beautiful country park

Converted from a golf clubhouse into this gastro-pub, Woodward & Falconer's sixth pub venture is impressive. The entrance leads into a long bar with areas each end for drinking and eating; walls are lined either with bookshelves or hung with prints and pictures. Among the portfolio of eight, mainly Welsh, cask beers are Piffle & Balderdash, brewed by the Conwy Brewery especially for this pub group. Chargrilled steaks; coq au vin; toad-in-the-hole; lobster thermidor gratin and chips; and vegetable enchilada are among dishes on the comprehensive menu. Modestly priced wines include 16 by the glass. Children eat well too and have an outdoor play area.

Open all day all wk 12-11 (Sun 12-10.30) Closed 1 Jan, 25 Dec **Food** Contact pub for food times ⊕ WOODWARD & FALCONER PUBS LTD ◀ Piffle & Balderdash, Conwy, Monty's. ₮ 16 **Facilities** Non-diners area ◆ Children's menu Children's portions Play area Garden ⨅ Parking WiFi ▭ (notice required)

Stables Bar Restaurant

tel: 01352 840577 **CH7 6AB**
email: info@soughtonhall.co.uk
dir: *From A55, take A119 through Northop*

Stable-block conversion makes an excellent eatery

This unusual free house dates from the 18th century and was created from Soughton Hall's stable block, and original features like the cobbled floors and roof timbers remain intact; the magnificent main house was built as a bishop's palace. The selection of real ales includes Stables Bitter, or diners can browse the wine shop for a bottle to accompany their meal. Examples from a winter carte menu include ham hock, baby leek and mustard terrine with pineapple piccalilli; and roast loin of cod, pan-fried scallops, creamed cauliflower, vine tomatoes and apple and cumin sauce. Enjoy the gardens in summer.

Open all day all wk Closed Mon-Tue in Winter **Food** Lunch all wk 12-9.30 Dinner all wk 12-9.30 ⊕ FREE HOUSE ◀ Coach House Honeypot Best Bitter & Dick Turpin Premium Bitter, Plassey Bitter, Stables Bitter. **Facilities** Non-diners area ♦ Children's menu Children's portions Family room Garden ♬ Parking WiFi ▭

GWYNEDD

ABERDYFI
Map 14 SN69

Penhelig Arms Hotel & Restaurant `PICK OF THE PUBS`

See Pick of the Pubs on page 636

BEDDGELERT
Map 14 SH54

Tanronnen Inn ★★★★ INN

tel: 01766 890347 **LL55 4YB**
email: guestservice@tanronnen.co.uk **web:** www.tanronnen.co.uk
dir: *In village centre opposite river bridge*

Great hospitality at the heart of Snowdonia

Originally part of the Beddgelert Estate, this stone building was the stables for the passing coach trade in 1809; after conversion to a cottage, it opened as a beer house in 1830. By the end of that century, it had two letting bedrooms and was serving meals for visitors; so setting the style of operation we see today. Today's inn has two attractive small bars serving Robinsons ales, a large lounge with open fire, a dining room open to non-residents in which to enjoy a wide range of home-cooked meals, and attractive accommodation.

Open all day all wk **Food** Lunch all wk 12.30-2 Dinner all wk 7-8.30 ⊕ ROBINSONS ◀ Unicorn & Double Hop ♂ Westons Stowford Press. **Facilities** Non-diners area ♦ Children's menu Children's portions Outside area ♬ Parking **Rooms** 7

BRITHDIR
Map 14 SH71

Cross Foxes

tel: 01341 421001 **LL40 2SG**
email: hello@crossfoxes.co.uk
dir: *At junct of A470 & A487, 4m from Dolgellau*

Strikingly modern inn, certainly worth finding

Grade II listed the Cross Foxes may be, but what an interior! It's true that traditional Welsh materials like slate and stone are used in the design, but the effect is light years from being Welsh Traditional. In the impressive bar you'll find regional real ales and ciders, and in the café a multiplicity of teas (including one from Wales), fresh coffees and finger sandwiches; here they also serve a traditional Welsh cream tea and a champagne afternoon tea. A meal in The Grill dining room might be

venison Scotch egg with mustard mayo; Welsh ale battered haddock and chunky chips; and banana fritter, toffee sauce and ice cream. Gaze at Cader Idris from the large decked area.

Open all day all wk **Food** Lunch all wk 12-9 Dinner all wk 12-9 Av main course £11.95 ⊕ FREE HOUSE ◀ Cader Ales, Evan Evans ♂ Kingstone Press. **Facilities** Non-diners area ♣ (Bar Garden) ♦ Children's menu Children's portions Garden ♬ Parking WiFi ▭ (notice required)

CAERNARFON
Map 14 SH46

Black Boy Inn ★★★★ INN

tel: 01286 673604 **Northgate St LL55 1RW**
email: reception@black-boy-inn.com **web:** www.black-boy-inn.com
dir: *A55 junct 9 onto A487, follow signs for Caernarfon. Within town walls between castle & Victoria Dock*

Old-fashioned values in the shadow of Caernarfon Castle

Character oozes from the very fabric of this ancient gabled inn, one of the oldest in Wales (built 1522). Relax with a pint of local Snowdonia Ale in the fire-warmed, low-ceilinged rooms strewn amidst beams and struts rescued from old ships. Meat and other products are generally local, and dishes from the long menu include field mushrooms and red onion compôte; vegetable cobbler; black pudding-stuffed chicken breast; and braised lamb shank. The well-proportioned bedrooms are ideal for those wishing to stay on and explore Mount Snowdon, the Lleyn Peninsula or catch the Welsh Highland Railway.

Open all day all wk **Food** Lunch all wk 12-9 Dinner all wk 12-9 Av main course £7 ⊕ FREE HOUSE ◀ Purple Moose Snowdonia Ale, Brains The Rev. James, Hancock's ♂ Aspall. **Facilities** Non-diners area ♦ Children's menu Children's portions Play area Garden ♬ Parking WiFi ▭ **Rooms** 26

PICK OF THE PUBS

Penhelig Arms Hotel & Restaurant

ABERDYFI Map 14 SN69

tel: 01654 767215 **Terrace Rd LL35 0LT**
email: info@penheligarms.com
web: www.penheligarms.com
dir: On A493, W of Machynlleth

Small hostelry with a big reputation

This popular waterside inn has been serving travellers and locals since 1870 and offers spectacular views over the mountain-backed tidal Dyfi Estuary, a nature reserve rich in birdlife. Aberdyfi is a charming little resort with a championship golf course, and sandy beach and harbour, making it a favourite with golfers and watersports enthusiasts; the Penhelig Arms is also perfectly situated for visitors to Cader Idris, the Snowdonia National Park and several historic castles in the area. Music and TV-free, the wood-panelled and log-fire-warmed Fisherman's Bar is a cosy and friendly bolt-hole to enjoy Brains real ales and bar meals such as smoked salmon salad, roast supreme of chicken, chargrilled rump steak burger and bloomer sandwiches. The waterfront restaurant offers a more brasserie-style experience with views over the estuary and menus showcasing the abundant Welsh seafood (a Penhelig speciality) and Welsh beef and lamb. The kitchen team emphasise the freshness of ingredients and fuse local and

cosmopolitan influences in a style of cooking that allows natural flavours to shine through. A typical menu might include seared scallops, chorizo and citrus dressing; roast rack of lamb, creamed potatoes, mange-tout, port and red wine sauce; or wild mushroom raviolini with truffle oil. Leave room for apple pie with clotted cream; orange and cardamom pannacotta; or a Welsh cheese slate with biscuits, fruit cake and honey. Daily specials are listed on the blackboard. On Sundays, expect a set menu featuring a traditional roast. The short wine list is attractively priced and complements the excellent food. In warmer weather, you can sit outside on the sea wall terrace.

Open all day all wk **Food** Lunch all wk 12-2.30 Dinner all wk 6-9 ⊕ BRAINS ▬ Bitter & The Rev. James, Guest ale ☼ Symonds. ♟ 25 **Facilities** Non-diners area ⚘ (Bar Outside area) ♦️ Children's menu Children's portions Outside area Parking WiFi

LLANBEDR
Map 14 SH52

Victoria Inn ★★★★ INN

tel: 01341 241213 **LL45 2LD**
email: vicinn@chessmail.co.uk **web:** www.vic-inn.co.uk
dir: On A496 between Barmouth & Harlech

Close to the beach and many mountain walks

Fascinating features for pub connoisseurs are the circular wooden settle, ancient stove, grandfather clock and flagged floors in the atmospheric bar of the Victoria. Home-made food is served in the lounge bar and restaurant, complemented by a range of Robinsons traditional ales. A children's play area has been incorporated into the well-kept garden, with a playhouse, slides and swings. Situated beside the River Artro, the Rhinog mountain range and the famous Roman Steps are right on the doorstep. If you would like to explore the area, there are five spacious and thoughtfully furnished bedrooms to stay in.

Open all day all wk 11-11 (Sun 12-10.30) **Food** Lunch Mon-Fri 12-3, Sat-Sun 12-9 (all wk 12-9 summer) Dinner Mon-Fri 5-9, Sat-Sun 12-9 (all wk 12-9 summer) ⊕ ROBINSONS ◀ Unicorn, Guest ales Ŏ Westons Stowford Press. ♚ 10
Facilities Non-diners area ⊕ Children's menu Children's portions Play area Garden ⛶ Parking ▭ (notice required) **Rooms** 5

PENNAL
Map 14 SH60

Glan yr Afon/Riverside

tel: 01654 791285 **Riverside Hotel SY20 9DW**
email: info@riverside-hotel-pennal.co.uk
dir: 3m from Machynlleth on A493 towards Aberdovey. Pub on left

Stylish 16th-century inn between sea and mountains

In the glorious Dyfi Valley close to Cader Idris and Cardigan Bay this family-run inn has slate floors, modern light oak furnishings and bold funky fabrics. There's a wood-burning stove pumping out heat in winter, Dark Side of the Moose ale on tap, and a good range of modern pub food. Relax and opt for a starter of warm duck and orange salad; garlic mushrooms on toast; or smoked salmon fishcake, then lamb steak with roasted root vegetables; pan-fried sea bass with king prawns; or Welsh sirloin steak with onion rings. There's a riverside garden, with views to the hills, for summer enjoyment.

Open 12-3 6-11 (Sat-Sun all day) Closed 2wks Jan, 25-26 Dec, Mon (Nov-Mar) **Food** Lunch all wk 12-2 Dinner all wk 6-9 Set menu available ⊕ FREE HOUSE ◀ Cwrw Cader, Tiny Rebel, Purple Moose Dark Side of the Moose & Snowdonia Ale, Salopian Golden Thread, Brewdog Ŏ Kingstone Press. ♚ 12
Facilities Non-diners area ⊕ (Bar Garden) ⊕ Children's menu Children's portions Garden ⛶ Parking WiFi ▭ (notice required)

TREMADOG
Map 14 SH53

The Union Inn

tel: 01766 512748 **7 Market Square LL49 9RB**
email: mail@union-inn.com
dir: From Porthmadog follow A487 & Caernarfon signs; then Tremadog signs. Inn on right before T-junct in village centre

Freehold, family-run pub in historic setting

Hefty local stones were used to build this early 19th-century pub, part of a row of cottages facing the main square of Wales' first planned town. Customers can thank these stones for the snugness of the interior, not least the bar, which offers a really good choice of Welsh real ales and ciders. Home-made food is fresh, locally sourced and seasonal, with Welsh lamb and beef dishes held in particularly high regard. You'll also find authentic curries, steak and ale pie, fresh fish, scampi and vegetarian dishes, such as mushroom Stroganoff, and daily specials.

Open all wk 12-2 5.30-11.30 **Food** Lunch all wk 12-2 Dinner all wk 5.30-9 ⊕ FREE HOUSE ◀ Purple Moose Snowdonia Ale & Madog's Ale, Great Orme, Big Bog Ŏ Gwynt y Ddraig Happy Daze, Dog Dancer & Farmhouse Scrumpy.
Facilities Non-diners area ⊕ (Bar Outside area) ⊕ Children's menu Children's portions Outside area ⛶ Parking WiFi ▭ (notice required)

TUDWEILIOG
Map 14 SH23

Lion Hotel

tel: 01758 770244 **LL53 8ND**
email: martlee.lion@gmail.com **web:** www.lionhoteltudweiliog.co.uk
dir: A487 from Caernarfon onto A499 towards Pwllheli. Right onto B4417 to Nefyn, through Edern to Tudweiliog

Family-run pub offering good-value dining

Standing at a tangent to the road, fronted by a garden with tables and chairs, the 300-year-old Lion has been run by the Lee family for the past 40 years. The bar features an extensive list of whiskies, alongside real ales from Big Bog, Cwrw Llyn and Purple Moose breweries, all Welsh of course. Typical pub meals include spare ribs in barbecue sauce; lamb or chicken balti; sweet chilli, prawn and cod fishcakes; and leek and mushroom crumble. Ample parking and a children's play area both help to make it popular with the many families holidaying in the beautiful Lleyn Peninsula.

Open all wk 11-3 6-11 (summer all day) **Food** Lunch all wk 12-2 Dinner all wk 6-9 ⊕ FREE HOUSE ◀ Cwrw Llyn Brenin Enlli, Big Bog, Purple Moose, Guinness.
Facilities Non-diners area ⊕ Children's menu Children's portions Play area Family room Garden ⛶ Parking WiFi ▭ (notice required)

WAUNFAWR
Map 14 SH55

Snowdonia Parc Brewpub & Campsite

tel: 01286 650409 & 650218 **LL55 4AQ**
email: info@snowdonia-park.co.uk
dir: Phone for detailed directions

Own microbrewery, wholesome food, beautiful location

In the heart of Snowdonia, a short drive from Mount Snowdon, this popular walkers' pub is located at Waunfawr Station on the Welsh Highland Railway. There are steam trains on site (the building was originally the stationmaster's house), plus a microbrewery and campsite. Home-cooked food ranges from chicken, leek and ham pie to vegetable curry or roast Welsh beef with all the trimmings. All real ales served are brewed on the premises. The Welsh Highland Railway Rail Ale Festival is held in mid-May.

Open all day all wk 11-11 (Fri-Sat 11am-11.30pm) **Food** Contact pub for food times ⊕ FREE HOUSE ◀ Snowdonia Welsh Highland Bitter, Summer Ale, Carmen Sutra, Cais, Gwyrfai, Theodore Stout, Dark & Delicious, Gold & Trithro.
Facilities Non-diners area ⊕ (Bar Garden) ⊕ Children's menu Children's portions Play area Family room Garden ⛶ Beer festival Parking WiFi ▭ (notice required)

MONMOUTHSHIRE

ABERGAVENNY
Map 9 SO21

Clytha Arms
PICK OF THE PUBS

tel: 01873 840206 **Clytha NP7 9BW**
email: theclythaarms@btinternet.com
dir: *From A449 & A40 junction (E of Abergavenny) follow Old Road Abergavenny & Clytha signs*

Excellent beers and stunning views

This converted dower house on the old Abergavenny to Raglan road stands on the edge of parkland dotted with small woods. From the large garden, there are captivating views across the lush and shapely Vale of Gwent. The main bar is full of character, with old pews, tables and rustic furnishings, as well as posters and a wood-burning stove. The pub is renowned for its range of real ales, with Rhymney Bitter and some great artisan ciders and perrys. Grazers can enjoy tapas or tuck into a full restaurant meal accompanied by a choice of over 100 wines. Starters like leek and laverbread rissoles with beetroot chutney might precede a main course of wild boar in Rioja with chorizo dumpling, then South Comfort pannacotta. Time a visit for the Welsh Cider Festival, or the Welsh Beer, Cheese and Music festival.

Open 12-3 6-12 (Fri-Sun 12-12) Closed 25 Dec, Mon L **Food** Lunch Tue-Sun 12.30-2.30 Dinner Mon-Sat 7-9.30 Av main course £14 Set menu available ⊕ FREE HOUSE ◀ Rhymney Bitter, Wye Valley Bitter, 4 guest ales (300+ per year) Ŏ Gwynt y Ddraig Black Dragon, Ragan Perry, Clytha Perry. ♀ 12 **Facilities** Non-diners area ♣ (Bar Garden) ♦♦ Children's menu Children's portions Play area Garden Beer festival Cider festival Parking WiFi ⊶

NEW Kings Arms ★★★★ INN

tel: 01873 855074 **29 Nevill St NP7 5AA**
email: enquiries@kingsarmsabergavenny.co.uk **web:** www.kingsarmsabergavenny.co.uk
dir: *M4 junct 25a, A4042 to Abergavenny. At rdbt 2nd exit (Abergavenny). At x-rds in town left into Lower Castle St. At T-junct right into Castle St, pub on right*

Rich history and a home-brewing tradition

This 300-year-old coaching inn has a plaster relief of Charles II's coat of arms on its frontage, and soldiers stationed here in the early 1800s scratched their names on one of the pub's beams. Records show the pub has brewed its own ales for at least 150 years; today they are named after neighbouring mountains. Menus of pub food start with lunchtime hot or cold sandwiches made from home-baked crusty bread; and finish with a dinner selection of smoked cod, Penclawdd cockle and mussel chowder, followed by loin and sausage of local pork with mustard greens and black pudding mash.

Open all day all wk **Food** Lunch Tue-Sat 12-3, Sun 12-4 Dinner Tue-Sat 6-9 Av main course £10-£12 Set menu available ⊕ FREE HOUSE ◀ Brains The Rev. James, Wye Valley HPA & Butty Bach. ♀ 13 **Facilities** Non-diners area ♣ (Bar Outside area) ♦♦ Children's menu Children's portions Outside area ⊓ WiFi **Rooms** 11

LLANGATTOCK LINGOED
Map 9 SO32

NEW The Hunters Moon Inn

tel: 01873 821499 **NP7 8RR**
email: thehuntersmooninn@btconnect.com
dir: *Phone pub for detailed directions*

Family-run village pub popular with walkers

In the peaceful village of Llangattock Lingoed on the Offa's Dyke Path, the Hunters Moon dates back to the 13th century and is now run by three generations of the Bateman family who have returned it to its former glory. Dog-friendly and with a large beer garden, this traditional inn focuses on doing the simple things well, from well-kept Wye Valley ale to unpretentious, good quality home cooking using local

produce. Try the sizzling flash-fried prawns in garlic, chillies and parsley before moving on to home-made steak and ale pie or pheasant casserole.

Open all day all wk **Food** Lunch 12-9 Dinner 12-9 Av main course £7 Restaurant menu available all wk ⊕ FREE HOUSE ◀ Wye Valley HPA, Sharp's Doom Bar Ŏ Addlestones, Westons Stowford Press. **Facilities** Non-diners area ♣ (Bar Garden Outside area) ♦♦ Children's menu Children's portions Play area Garden Outside area ⊓ Parking WiFi ⊶ (notice required)

LLANGYBI
Map 9 ST39

The White Hart Village Inn ⊛⊛
PICK OF THE PUBS

tel: 01633 450258 **NP15 1NP**
email: enquiries@thewhitehartvillageinn.com
dir: *M4 junct 25 onto B4596 (Caerleon road), through Caerleon High St, straight over rdbt into Usk Rd, continue to Llangybi*

Historic inn serving excellent food

The welcome is literally 'warm' at this picturesque historic inn in the beautiful Usk Valley, where no fewer than 11 fireplaces can be counted. Oliver Cromwell based himself here during local Civil War campaigns; so add a priest hole, exposed beams, precious Tudor plasterwork and a mention in T S Eliot's poem *Usk* and this is a destination to savour. Chef-patron Michael Bates offers reliable ales from the likes of Wye Valley Butty Bach, as well as unusual ciders such as Gwynt y Ddraig Farmhouse Scrumpy. Using fresh local produce, and combining exciting ingredients with complementary flavours, head chef Adam Whittle prepares dishes with the utmost attention to detail for his award-winning menus. Representative choices could include chicken liver parfait with apple and plum; pollock with confit potato, chestnuts, sprout leaves and mussels; and vanilla rice pudding with peanut brittle and blackberry. Extensive seating is available outside.

Open all day 12-11 (Sun 12-10) Closed Mon **Food** Lunch Tue-Sat 12-3, Sun 12-4 Dinner Tue-Sat 6-7 Av main course £8.95 Set menu available Restaurant menu available Tue-Sat ⊕ FREE HOUSE ◀ Wye Valley Butty Bach, Kite Brewery Cwrw Gorslas Ŏ Thatchers Gold, Ty Gwyn, Gwynt y Ddraig Farmhouse Scrumpy. ♀ 15 **Facilities** Non-diners area ♦♦ Children's menu Children's portions Garden ⊓ Parking WiFi ⊶ (notice required)

LLANTRISANT
Map 9 ST39

The Greyhound Inn
PICK OF THE PUBS

tel: 01291 672505 & 673447 **NP15 1LE**
email: enquiry@greyhound-inn.com
dir: *M4 junct 24, A449 towards Monmouth, exit at 1st junct signed Usk. 2nd left for Llantrisant. Or from Monmouth A40, A449 exit for Usk. In Usk left into Twyn Sq follow Llantrisant signs. 2.5m, under A449 bridge. Inn on right*

Charming country inn surrounded by farmland

In the 17th century a typical Welsh longhouse, then from 1845 an inn, the family-owned Greyhound stands just outside the town between the Rivers Usk and Wye. Free-house status ensures a range of real ales and ciders in the log-fire-warmed Stable Bar, where the tiled floor remains steadfastly impervious to muddy boots and soggy dogs. You can play darts, crib and dominoes here or just watch them being played. Owner Nick Davies heads the kitchen team, whose skills you can enjoy in the candlelit restaurant, or in one of three other dining areas. Among the starters are soup of the day; deep-fried breaded brie wedges; and duck spring rolls with hoisin sauce, while an idea of the main courses is conveyed by Welsh venison and ale pie; Usk salmon; coq au vin; chilli con carne; and vegetable chilli. Outside are two acres of lovingly-nurtured, award-winning gardens and a large paddock.

Open all day 11-11 Closed 25 & 31 Dec, 1 Jan, Sun eve **Food** Lunch all wk 12-2.15 Dinner Mon-Sat 6-10 Av main course £9.50 ⊕ FREE HOUSE ◀ Greene King Abbot Ale, Bass, Guest ale Ŏ Gwynt y Ddraig, Kingstone Press. ♀ 10 **Facilities** Non-diners area ♣ (Bar Garden) ♦♦ Children's menu Children's portions Family room Garden ⊓ Parking WiFi ⊶ (notice required)

PICK OF THE PUBS

The Inn at Penallt ★★★★ INN 🌹🌹

PENALLT   Map 4 SO51

tel: 01600 772765 **NP25 4SE**
email: enquiries@theinnatpenallt.co.uk
web: www.theinnatpenallt.co.uk
dir: *From Monmouth take B4293 to Trellech. Approx 2m, left at brown sign for inn. At next x-rds left. Right at war memorial*

An inn with a fast-growing collection of accolades

Originally a farmhouse in the 17th century, the inn stands between the village green and colourful wildflower meadows that head in the direction of the famous, thickly-wooded Wye Gorge. Owners Andrew and Jackie Murphy took only a few short years to make this inn a real success story and to become winners, along with other accolades, of AA Pub of the Year for Wales in 2013. For some, the reasons for its appeal start in the slate-floored bar, where monopolising the pumps are Welsh and border real ales Wye Valley Butty Bach, Kingstone Classic Bitter and Kite's Cwrw Gorslas. The ciders are Welsh too, with Ty Gwyn and Gwynt y Ddraig Black Dragon. You can look forward to nibbling olives and home-made bread with olive oil, before beginning perhaps with chorizo, pea and smoked Welsh bacon risotto; or Monmouthshire duck faggot, potato cake, Deeside black pudding, apple sauce and duck jus. For 'the middle bit' as the two AA Rosette menu

says, saddle of Bwlch venison, smoked Welsh bacon, château potatoes, girolles and port wine sauce; or seafood ragout of sea bass, mussels, prawns, crayfish tails and scallops with laverbread dumplings make excellent choices. Non-meat eaters often plump for the vegetarian cassoulet baked with smoked Applewood cheese. Desserts not meant to be overlooked include lemon scented treacle tart with ginger cream; and crème brûlée, red berries and short bread biscuit. There are regular gourmet evenings with tasting menus and wine matching. Children and dogs are welcome.

Open Tue 6-11 Wed-Sat 11-11 Sun 12-5 Closed 4-21 Jan, Mon (ex BHs)
Food Lunch Wed-Sat 12-2.30, Sun 12-3

Dinner Tue-Sat 6-9 Set menu available Restaurant menu available Tue-Sat ⊕ FREE HOUSE 🍺 Wye Valley Butty Bach, Kingstone Classic Bitter, Kite Brewery Cwrw Gorslas ♂ Ty Gwyn, Gwynt y Ddraig Black Dragon. 🍷 **Facilities** Non-diners area 🐾 (Bar Garden) 🚼 Children's menu Children's portions Play area Garden 🎋 Parking WiFi 🚌 **Rooms** 4

LLANVAIR DISCOED
Map 9 ST49

The Woodlands Tavern Country Pub & Dining
PICK OF THE PUBS

tel: 01633 400313 **NP16 6LX**
email: info@thewoodlandstavern.co.uk
dir: 5m from Caldicot & Magor

Modern British food and Welsh beers

Below Gray Hill, near the Roman fortress town of Caerwent, this friendly pub is popular with walkers, cyclists and fishermen. They like it, not just because it's close to the Wentwood Forest and plentiful rivers, but also because it has a good selection of Welsh real ales, such as Wye Valley, Felinfoel and regularly changing guests. In addition, there's its modern British food, with baguettes, all-day breakfasts, jacket potatoes and sausage and mash in the bar, and a main menu inviting you to try Parma and Serrano ham with feta and ricotta-stuffed bell peppers; extra-mature sirloin steak with tomato and mushrooms; steak and ale shortcrust pastry pie; or chicken curry with rice, mango chutney and a poppadom. Dressed Devon crab and prawn salad and other daily fish specials appear on a blackboard; vegetarian options are available too. Sunday roasts are always well received, especially out on the patio area.

Open 12-3 6-12 (Sat all day Sun 12-4) Closed 1 Jan, Sun eve, Mon **Food** Lunch Tue-Fri 12-2, Sat 12-2.30, Sun 12-4 Dinner Tue-Fri 6-9, Sat 6-9.30 Set menu available Restaurant menu available Tue-Sat ⊕ FREE HOUSE ◀ Felinfoel, Marston's & Pedigree, Wye Valley Butty Bach, Guest ales ♂ Westons Old Rosie, Thatchers Gold. ♟ 10 **Facilities** Non-diners area ♣ (Bar Outside area) ◀ Children's menu Children's portions Outside area ⋒ Parking WiFi ➡ (notice required)

PANTYGELLI
Map 9 SO31

The Crown

tel: 01873 853314 **Old Hereford Rd NP7 7HR**
email: crown@pantygelli.com
dir: Phone for detailed directions

Family-run free house with fine views

A charming family-run free house dating from the 16th century, The Crown has fine views of Skirrid (in Welsh, Ysgyrid Fawr) known also as Holy Mountain. Walkers and cyclists love it, but it's a genuine community pub too, serving Bass, Rhymney Bitter, Wye Valley HPA and guest real ales as well as Gwatkin cider, all ideal before or with garlic mushrooms on crostini or deep-fried squid with harissa mayo and rocket; venison sausages with mash, green beans and red onion gravy; or tenderloin pork with mange tout and Calvados sauce; and a dessert of sticky toffee pudding with butterscotch sauce; or poached pear with vanilla ice cream.

Open 12-2.30 6-11 (Sat 12-3 6-11 Sun 12-3 6-10.30) Closed Mon L **Food** Lunch Tue-Sun 12-2 Dinner Tue-Sat 7-9 ⊕ FREE HOUSE ◀ Rhymney, Wye Valley HPA, Bass, Guest ales ♂ Westons Stowford Press & Mortimers Orchard, Gwatkin Yarlington Mill. **Facilities** Non-diners area ♣ (Bar Garden) ◀ Children's portions Garden ⋒ Parking WiFi

PENALLT
Map 4 SO51

The Inn at Penallt ★★★★ INN ⊛⊛
PICK OF THE PUBS

See Pick of the Pubs on page 639

RAGLAN
Map 9 SO40

The Beaufort Arms Coaching Inn & Brasserie ⒰

tel: 01291 690412 **High St NP15 2DY**
email: enquiries@beaufortraglan.co.uk **web:** www.beaufortraglan.co.uk
dir: 0.5m from junct of A40 & A449 Abergavenny/Monmouth, midway between M50 & M4, signed Raglan

Ancient hostelry with a rich history

This grandly proportioned former coaching inn has always had strong links with nearby Raglan Castle; during the Civil War Roundhead soldiers frequented the bar during the siege of 1646. The inn has been beautifully appointed with many delightful design features, while holding strong to its traditional roots. A handsome display of fishing trophies dominates the country bar, where locals and visitors gather and chat over pints of Fuller's London Pride. Food is served in the lounge, with its carved bar, deep leather settees, and large stone fireplace ('lifted', some say, from the castle), as well as in the private dining room and brasserie. Enjoy well-presented modern dishes from a regularly changing menu.

Open all day all wk **Food** Lunch Mon-Thu 12-3, Fri-Sat 12-3 Dinner Mon-Thu 6-9, Fri-Sat 6-9.30, Sun 6-8.30 Set menu available ⊕ FREE HOUSE ◀ Fuller's London Pride, Wye Valley Butty Bach, Untapped Border, Untapped UPA ♂ Westons Stowford Press, Thatchers Gold. ♟ 16 **Facilities** Non-diners area ◀ Children's menu Children's portions Garden ⋒ Parking WiFi ➡ (notice required) **Rooms** 16

RHYD-Y-MEIRCH
Map 9 SO30

Goose and Cuckoo Inn

tel: 01873 880277 **Upper Llanover NP7 9ER**
email: llanovergoose@gmail.com
dir: From Abergavenny take A4042 towards Pontypool. Turn left after Llanover, follow signs for inn

Walkers' haven with food from the Aga

Popular with walkers, this friendly, whitewashed pub in the Brecon Beacons National Park has a garden with views of the Malvern Hills and a traditional interior with flagstoned bar area and a wood-burning stove. So, the perfect setting for a pint of well-kept Rhymney Bitter or one of the 85 single malt whiskies. All the food is home made on the Aga by landlady Carol Dollery; typical dishes include cauliflower soup; steak and ale pie; faggots; quiche; bread and butter pudding; and home-made ice cream. The pub hosts two beer festivals – in May and August.

Open Tue-Thu 11.30-3 7-11 (Fri-Sun all day) Closed Mon (ex BHs) **Food** Lunch Tue-Sun 11.30-3 Dinner Tue-Sun 7-9 ⊕ FREE HOUSE ◀ Rhymney Bitter, Celt Iron Age ♂ Kingstone Press. **Facilities** Non-diners area ♣ (Bar Garden) ◀ Children's portions Family room Garden ⋒ Beer festival Parking **Notes** ⊛

PICK OF THE PUBS

Newbridge on Usk

TREDUNNOCK   Map 9 ST39

tel: 01633 410262 **NP15 1LY**
email: bookings@celtic-manor.com
web: www.celtic-manor.com
dir: *M4 junct 24 follow Newport signs. Right at Toby Carvery, B4236 to Caerleon. Right over bridge, through Caerleon to mini rdbt. Straight ahead onto Llangibby/Usk road*

Two hundred-year-old inn, now a smart gastro-pub

The pub really is called this. It sounds like a town or village name, but apart from the pub, there's hardly even a hamlet. What there is, right in front, is a bridge over the River Usk that could only have been considered new several centuries ago. Roman Caerleon and the medieval town of Usk are nearby, as is the pub's parent, the famous Celtic Manor Resort. All of which means, this is exceedingly well located. The interior is a pleasing blend of traditional beamed ceilings, snug corners and open fires, with some modern touches. On a warm day, the riverside garden is the place for slipping into a pint of The Rev. James, or a glass of Tomos Watkin Taffy Apples cider. Catch the right time, and while you do so you could watch the golden light of the setting sun bathe the Monmouthshire hills. Enjoy starters such as the local fish market platter for two; and pigeon breast, caramelised leg, beetroot compôte and hazelnut dressing. Follow on with loin of Brecon venison, pumpkin chutney, red cabbage and potato terrine; pollock and mussel chowder; pie of the day with mash and vegetables; or rump of Welsh lamb, shepherd's pie, salsify and braised leeks. Two very hungry people can share fillet of Welsh beef with 24-hour braised cheek, Perl Las Blue cheese, shin and ale pie, corned beef croquette with greens, creamed mushrooms, red wine shallots and beef jus. A tempting dessert to follow all that would be dark chocolate fondant with coffee ice cream; or stem ginger cheesecake, poached rhubarb and mango gel. On Sundays a jazz band plays at lunchtimes.

Open all day all wk 12-12
Food Lunch all wk 12-2.30 Dinner all wk 5-10 Set menu available ⊕ FREE HOUSE ◖ Brains The Rev. James & Smooth, Guest ale ♂ Tomos Watkin Taffy Apples. ♟ 12 **Facilities** Non-diners area ♦ Children's menu Children's portions Garden ☰ Parking WiFi 🚍

SKENFRITH
Map 9 SO42

The Bell at Skenfrith ★★★★ RR ⊛ PICK OF THE PUBS

tel: 01600 750235 **NP7 8UH**
email: enquiries@skenfrith.co.uk **web:** www.skenfrith.co.uk
dir: *M4 junct 24 onto A449. Exit onto A40, through tunnel & lights. At rdbt take 1st exit, right at lights onto A466 towards Hereford road. Left onto B4521 towards Abergavenny, 3m on left*

An absolute must in the prettiest countryside

December 2014 saw Richard and Sarah Ireton's arrival as landlords of this 17th-century coaching inn — and it's easy to understand why they came. In lush countryside, it overlooks the River Monnow and Skenfrith Castle, with flagstone floors, oak beams and antique furniture all contributing to its delights. Real ales come from Kingstone, Wickwar and Wye Valley breweries and cider from the village's own Apple County. The award-winning restaurant uses organic vegetables, herbs, salad leaves and fruits from the kitchen garden for starters of tian of Lyme Bay crab, shaved fennel, spring onion and chilli slaw; and beetroot carpaccio with Pant-ys-gawn goats' cheese and candied walnuts, with mains of Trelleck Grange venison with roasted garlic pomme purée, Koffman cabbage and port jus; and classic fish pie with buttered leeks and gruyère-glazed mash. The acclaimed wine list ranges worldwide. There's free WiFi, but a patchy mobile signal.

Open all day all wk **Food** Lunch all wk 12-2.30 Dinner all wk 6.30-9.30 Restaurant menu available all wk ⊕ FREE HOUSE ◀ Wye Valley Bitter, Butty Bach & HPA, Kingstone Classic Bitter, Wickwar BOB ♂ Westons Stowford Press, Apple County Cider, Local cider. ♥ 13 **Facilities** Non-diners area ♣ (Bar Garden) ♦♦ Children's menu Garden ⨝ Parking WiFi ⛬ (notice required) **Rooms** 11

TINTERN PARVA
Map 4 SO50

Fountain Inn

tel: 01291 689303 **Trellech Grange NP16 6QW**
email: fountaininntrellech@btconnect.com
dir: *From M48 junct 2 follow Chepstow then A466 & Tintern signs. In Tintern turn by George Hotel for Raglan. Bear right, inn at top of hill, 2m from A466*

Good food and well-kept ales at this village pub

A fine old inn dating from 1611 in lovely countryside, with a garden overlooking the Wye Valley. The pub offers several curries, including chicken kashmiri, and fruit and vegetable jalfrezi; and Welsh Black beef, Welsh lamb and roasted ham, all with fresh vegetables, roast potatoes, Yorkshire pudding and beer gravy. There is also a fresh fish menu with whole griddled flounder; sizzling crevettes; and beer-battered cod and chips. The owners' passion for real ales and ciders is evident both in the great bar line-up, and at the September beer festival.

Open Tue-Sun all day Closed Mon **Food** Lunch Tue-Sun 12-2.30 Dinner all wk 6-8 Av main course £7.95 Set menu available ⊕ FREE HOUSE ◀ Wychwood Hobgoblin, Brains The Rev. James, Kingstone Classic Bitter, Whittingtons Cats Whiskers, Butcombe, Mayfields, Rhymney, Hook Norton, Hereford, Ring O'Bells, Bass, Guest ales ♂ Thatchers Gold & Traditional. ♥ 9 **Facilities** Non-diners area ♣ (Bar Garden) ♦♦ Children's menu Children's portions Family room Garden ⨝ Beer festival Parking WiFi ⛬ (notice required)

TREDUNNOCK
Map 9 ST39

Newbridge on Usk
PICK OF THE PUBS

See Pick of the Pubs on page 641

TRELLECH
Map 4 SO50

The Lion Inn
PICK OF THE PUBS

tel: 01600 860322 **NP25 4PA**
email: debs@globalnet.co.uk
dir: *From A40 S of Monmouth take B4293, follow Trellech signs. From M8 junct 2, straight across rdbt, 2nd left at 2nd rdbt, B4293 to Trellech*

A traditional inn with nautical links

Built in 1580 as a brewhouse and inn by a former sea captain, the Lion consists of two rooms, both with open fires; one is a traditional bar, the other a restaurant. Although best known for its food and drink, the pub also once showed true versatility by providing the best-dressed entry in the Monmouth raft race. Debbie Zsigo has run it for the past 20 years and knows instinctively what works. In the bar the answer is Wye Valley Butty Bach, and a number of local ciders including Raglan Cider Mill Snowy Owl. In the restaurant Debbie provides bar snacks, pizzas, light meals and a range of main dishes, typically home-made cottage pie; breaded whole tail scampi; home-cooked ham, egg and chips; and pasta carbonara. There's a stream and an aviary in the garden, and beautiful views from the suntrap courtyard. Time a visit for the beer festival in June or the cider festival in August.

Open all day 12-11 (Thu-Sat 12-12 Sun 12-4.30) Closed Sun eve **Food** Lunch Mon-Fri 12-2, Sat-Sun 12-2.30 Dinner Mon 7-9.30, Tue-Sat 6-9.30 Restaurant menu available all wk ⊕ FREE HOUSE ◀ Butcombe Bitter, Felinfoel Double Dragon, Wye Valley Butty Bach ♂ Springfield Red Dragon, Raglan Cider Mill Snowy Owl Sweet Perry. **Facilities** Non-diners area ♣ (Bar Garden) ♦♦ Children's portions Garden ⨝ Beer festival Cider festival Parking ⛬ (notice required)

USK
Map 9 SO30

The Nags Head Inn

tel: 01291 672820 **Twyn Square NP15 1BH**
email: keynags@tiscali.co.uk
dir: *On A472*

Bustling old town hostelry in the Vale of Gwent

Fronting the old town square mid-way between the castle and fine priory church, parts of the inn date from the 15th century. Saunter around the old town before sampling the largely Welsh real ales here, where the same family has held-sway for over 46 years, lovingly caring for the highly-traditional interior that's all beams and polished tables, rural artefacts and horse-brasses. The tempting menu draws on the wealth of produce the fertile Vale of Gwent can offer; seasonal game dishes are a speciality, whilst there's a good vegetarian selection; try the cheese and leek Glamorgan sausage perhaps.

Open all wk 10.30-2.30 5-11 Closed 25 Dec **Food** Lunch all wk 11.45-1.45 Dinner all wk 5.30-9.30 Restaurant menu available all wk ⊕ FREE HOUSE ◀ Brains Bitter, Buckley's Bitter, The Rev. James & Bread of Heaven, Sharp's Doom Bar ♂ Westons Stowford Press. ♥ 9 **Facilities** Non-diners area ♣ (Bar Restaurant Garden) ♦♦ Children's menu Children's portions Garden Outside area ⨝ Parking WiFi ⛬

The Raglan Arms | **PICK OF THE PUBS**

tel: 01291 690800 **Llandenny NP15 1DL**
email: info@raglanarms.co.uk
dir: *From Monmouth take A449 to Raglan, left in village. From M4 take A449 exit. Follow Llandenny signs on right*

Peaceful setting for good food in the Vale of Gwent

At the heart of a small village tucked between Tintern Forest and the rich agricultural lands of the Usk Valley, this neat, stone-built 19th-century pub continues to receive praise for its varied and frequently changing menu. The head chef and his small team use high quality ingredients for the imaginative menu. The pub is keen to reduce food miles and most suppliers are within a nine mile radius; from further afield, the fish is delivered from Cornwall each day. So try a starter of Cornish hand-dived scallops and Charley Barley black pudding, cauliflower purée and apple salad, then follow on with the chef's signature dish of duck, chips and gravy; or a vegetarian choice of crèpinette de Byaldi, garlic crisps, heritage tomatoes and goats' cheese dressing, and finish with Valronha dark, chocolate fondant, roast beetroot ice cream, caramel caviar and poppyseed tuile biscuit. Whether eating in, or just enjoying a pint brewed in Raglan just three miles away, visitors are sure of a warm welcome. A change of hands in early 2015.

Open Tue-Sat 12-3 6.30-11.30, (Sun 12-2.30) Closed 25-28 Dec, Sun eve & Mon **Food** Lunch Tue-Sat 12-3, Sun 12-2.30 Dinner Tue-Sat 6.30-9.30 ⊕ FREE HOUSE ◀ Untapped. ♟ 18 **Facilities** Non-diners area ❀ (Bar Garden) ♦ Children's portions Garden ⊼ Parking

NEWPORT

CAERLEON | Map 9 ST39

The Bell at Caerleon

tel: 01633 420613 **Bulmore Rd NP18 1QQ**
email: thebellinn@hotmail.co.uk
dir: *M4 junct 25, B4596 signed Caerleon. In Caerleon before river bridge right onto B4238 signed Christchurch. Left into Bulmore Rd (follow brown pub sign)*

Ancient riverbank inn with great range of local ciders

For more than 400 years this 17th-century coaching inn has stood in ancient Caerleon on the banks of the River Usk. Situated close to an ancient Roman burial ground (also believed by some to be the location of King Arthur's Camelot), the pub is particularly well known for its range of local ciders and perrys. It holds annual real ale and cider festivals with barbecues and free entertainment. Local produce drives the menu, which might include braised pork belly with rich Italian sausage and bean casserole; linguine prima vera; and potted rabbit with celery and carrots, crispy rabbit meatball and radish and beansprout slaw.

Open all day all wk **Food** Lunch Mon-Sat 12-2.30, Sun 12-4 Dinner all wk 6-9.30 Av main course £15 Set menu available ⊕ ENTERPRISE INNS ◀ Wye Valley HPA, Timothy Taylor Landlord, Tiny Rebel Cwtch ♂ Gwynt y Ddraig Black Dragon & Happy Daze, Hallets Real. ♟ 10 **Facilities** Non-diners area ❀ (Bar Garden) ♦ Children's portions Garden ⊼ Beer festival Cider festival Parking WiFi ▅▅ (notice required)

NEWPORT | Map 9 ST38

NEW The Ridgeway Bar & Kitchen

tel: 01633 266053 **2 Ridgeway Av NP20 5AJ**
email: theridgeway@storyinns.com **web:** www.storyinns.com
dir: *M4 junct 27, B4591 towards Newport. At rdbt 1st left into Fields Park Rd. 1st left into Ridgeway Ave*

Breezy New England looks and British dishes

Set in a quiet suburb of Newport, just a few miles from Cardiff, and handily situated just a couple of minutes from the M4, the Ridgeway was given a New England-style makeover a few years ago. There's a breezy coastal atmosphere, beautiful tiled floors and clever contemporary touches. Dogs and children are welcome in the garden and the south-facing patio is a popular spot for a drink. A variety of menus offer something for everyone; starters might be butternut squash and blue cheese en croûte with honeyed walnuts, maybe, or potted oak-smoked salmon with pickles and grilled brioche; followed by lemon and fennel marinated lamb rump, or chargrilled steak with triple-cooked chips. Finish with treacle tart.

Open all day all wk **Food** Lunch 12-2.30 Dinner 5.30-9.45 Av main course £11 Set menu available ⊕ ENTERPRISE INNS ◀ Sharp's Doom Bar, Tiny Rebel Fubar, Wye Valley HPA ♂ Thatchers Cheddar Valley, Westons Old Rosie. ♟ 12
Facilities Non-diners area ❀ (Bar Outside area) ♦ Children's menu Children's portions Outside area ⊼ Parking WiFi ▅▅ (notice required)

PEMBROKESHIRE

ABERCYCH
Map 8 SN24

Nags Head Inn

tel: 01239 841200 **SA37 0HJ**
email: samnags@hotmail.co.uk
dir: On B4332 (Carmarthen to Newcastle Emlyn road)

Classic Welsh riverside pub

Situated at the entrance to the enchanted valley in the famous Welsh folk tales of *Mabinogion*, this famous old inn is the first building you see over the county boundary when crossing into Pembrokeshire from the Teifi Falls at Cenarth. In one of the outbuildings the old forge still remains where the blacksmith crafted the first horse-drawn ploughs for export to America. Old Emrys ale is brewed on the premises ready for consuming in the beamed bars and riverside gardens. The fine fare includes home-made cawl with cheese and crusty bread; steak, Guinness and mushroom pie; and Cardigan Bay lobster.

Open Tue-Sun Closed Mon **Food** Lunch Tue-Sun 12-2 Dinner Tue-Sun 6-9 Set menu available ⊕ FREE HOUSE ◖ Cych Valley Old Emrys. **Facilities** Non-diners area ❖ (Bar Garden) ♦ Children's menu Children's portions Play area Garden Parking WiFi ▭

AMROTH
Map 8 SN10

The New Inn

tel: 01834 812368 **SA67 8NW**
email: paulluger@hotmail.com
dir: A48 to Carmarthen, A40 to St Clears, A477 to Llanteg then left, follow road to seafront, turn left. 0.25m on left

Old inn specialising in Welsh beef dishes

Originally a farmhouse, this 16th-century inn has been family run for 40 years. The pub has old-world charm with beamed ceilings, a Flemish chimney, a flagstone floor and an inglenook fireplace. It is close to the beach, with views towards Saundersfoot and Tenby from the dining room upstairs. Along with Welsh beef, home-made dishes include broccoli and cream cheese bake; pork and leek sausages; Greek salad; and minted lamb steak. There is even a toddlers' menu in addition to the children's menu. Enjoy food or drink outside on the large lawn complete with picnic benches.

Open all day all wk Mar-Oct 11-11 (Oct-Mar eve & wknds only) **Food** Contact pub for food times ⊕ FREE HOUSE ◖ Sharp's Doom Bar, Hancock's, Preseli Ales, Guinness, Guest ales. **Facilities** Non-diners area ❖ (Bar Garden) ♦ Children's menu Children's portions Family room Garden ⊼ Parking ▭

ANGLE
Map 8 SM80

The Old Point House

tel: 01646 641205 **East Angle Bay SA71 5AS**
email: croeso@theoldpointhouse.co.uk
dir: From Pembroke take B4320 signed Monkton & Hundleton. Right signed Angle. At T-junct left signed West Angle Bay. 1st right at pub sign on wall into narrow lane. Follow lane round bay to pub

Remote but well worth tracking down

It's all angles round here – Angle village, Angle Bay, Angle RNLI. Indeed, the 15th-century Old Point has been the lifeboatmen's local since 1868, when their boathouse was built nearby. At its uneven-floored heart is the snug, its walls covered in old photos and memorabilia, Felinfoel Best Bitter is on handpump, and real cider comes from Honey's in Somerset. Pub food includes sandwiches, jacket potatoes, pan-fried John Dory, curried chicken, Pembrokeshire rib-eye steak, pasta bolognese and daily specials. Picnic tables at the front look across Angle Bay. The track from the village skirts the foreshore and occasionally gets cut off by high spring tides.

Open all day May-Sep (12-3 6-10 autumn & winter) Closed 10-31 Jan, Mon & Tue 5 Nov-1 Mar **Food** Lunch all wk 12.30-2.30 (Mar-5 Oct) Dinner Mon-Sat 6.30-8.30 (Mar-5 Oct) ⊕ FREE HOUSE ◖ Felinfoel Best Bitter, Evan Evans ○ Honey's Midford Cider, Gwynt y Ddraig. **Facilities** Non-diners area ❖ (Bar Garden Outside area) ♦ Children's portions Garden Outside area ⊼ Parking WiFi ▭ (notice required)

CAREW
Map 8 SN00

Carew Inn

tel: 01646 651267 **SA70 8SL**
email: mandy@carewinn.co.uk
dir: From A477 take A4075. Inn 400yds opposite castle

One of Wales' best-kept secrets

Opposite the Carew Celtic cross and Norman castle, this traditional stone-built country inn is a great place to finish the one-mile circular walk around the castle and millpond. Mandy and Rob Scourfield have been here over 25 years, during which time they have built a strong reputation for quality ales and home-cooked food. A meal might include home-made smoked mackerel pâté with toast; pork tenderloin with chorizo sausage in a spicy sauce, served with crispy potatoes; and home-made lemon cheesecake. There's a children's play area in the garden, which also hosts regular barbecues in the summer.

Open all day all wk 11-11 (Sun 12-12) Closed 25 Dec **Food** Lunch all wk 12-2.30 Dinner all wk 6-9 ⊕ FREE HOUSE ◖ Worthington's, Brains The Rev. James, Sharp's Doom Bar ○ Westons Stowford Press. ♟ 9 **Facilities** Non-diners area ♦ Children's menu Children's portions Play area Garden ⊼ Parking WiFi ▭ (notice required)

DALE
Map 8 SM80

Griffin Inn

tel: 01646 636227 **SA62 3RB**
email: info@griffininndale.co.uk
dir: From end of M4 onto A48 to Carmarthen. A40 to Haverfordwest, B4327 to Dale. In Dale (with sea on left) pub on corner by slipway

By the sea in a hidden corner of west Wales

Standing opposite the sea wall in a pretty coastal village, the Griffin offers the pleasure of roaring log fires in the winter and, in the summer, the joy of eating out on the water's edge, looking across Dale Bay. On tap in the bar you'll find Buckleys Best Bitter, The Rev. James and Evan Evans Cwrw Haf (koo-roo - it's Welsh for beer). The kitchen's sourcing policy demands that produce is both local and sustainable: for example, the Griffin now has its own fishing boat to supply fresh fish and seafood from the bay. Arrive there when they land and you can perhaps choose from the catch.

Open all wk Apr-Sep all day (winter opening times vary) Closed Nov **Food** Lunch 12-2.30 Dinner all wk 5-8.30 summer, 6-8.30 winter ⊕ FREE HOUSE ◖ Brains The Rev. James, Evan Evans Cwrw Haf, Buckleys Best Bitter ○ Westons Stowford Press, Thatchers. **Facilities** Non-diners area ♦ Children's menu Children's portions Outside area ⊼ Parking WiFi ▭ (notice required)

LETTERSTON
Map 8 SM92

The Harp Inn

tel: 01348 840061 **31 Haverfordwest Rd SA62 5UA**
email: info@theharpatletterston.co.uk
dir: *On A40, 10m from Haverfordwest, 4m from Fishguard*

Modernised hostelry in the heart of Pembrokeshire

Formerly a working farm and home to a weekly market, this 15th-century free house remained largely unchanged for 500 years. Owned by the Sandall family for over 30 years, the building has a stylish conservatory restaurant where diners can enjoy local favourites like Welsh fillet steak; venison Roquefort; and whole sea bass. Alternatively, the bar lunch menu offers classic pub meals including crispy battered cod and chips. Enjoy lunch in all areas with your children.

Open all day all wk **Food** Lunch all wk 12-9 Dinner all wk 12-9 Set menu available ⊕ FREE HOUSE ◀ Tetley's, Greene King Abbot Ale ⚬ Thatchers Gold.
Facilities Non-diners area ◀ Children's menu Children's portions Play area Garden ⊓ Parking WiFi ⇌ (notice required)

LITTLE HAVEN
Map 8 SM81

St Brides Inn

tel: 01437 781266 **St Brides Rd SA62 3UN**
email: malcolmwhitewright@hotmail.co.uk
dir: *From Haverfordwest take B4341 signed Broad Haven. Through Broad Haven to Little Haven*

Great walkers' refuelling stop

An ideal stop for walkers on the nearby Pembrokeshire coastal path as it runs through the seaside village of Little Haven, the St Brides Inn has the added attraction of an indoor ancient well, as well as a pretty floral beer garden. Food-wise expect the likes of deep-fried breaded camembert with warm cranberry sauce; black pudding-stuffed pork loin with cider sauce; and home-made rhubarb and ginger crumble. Lunchtime light bites include a bacon and black pudding bap; and pork and apple sausage and mushroom bap with fried potatoes. Fresh fish is always available, together with locally caught lobster and crab, in season.

Open all day all wk **Food** Lunch all wk 12-2 Dinner all wk 6-9 Av main course £12.50 ⊕ FREE HOUSE ◀ Brains The Rev. James, Hancock's HB, Pembrokeshire Guest ales ⚬ Westons Stowford Press, Tomos Watkin Taffy Apples. ♥ 10
Facilities Non-diners area ◀ (Bar Garden Outside area) ◀ Children's menu Children's portions Garden Outside area ⊓ Beer festival WiFi ⇌ (notice required)

The Swan Inn

tel: 01437 781880 **Point Rd SA62 3UL**
email: enquiries@theswanlittlehaven.co.uk
dir: *B4341 from Haverfordwest. In Broad Haven follow seafront & Little Haven signs. 0.75m to inn*

Popular spot in an idyllic setting

Arrive early to bag a window table and savour one of the best views in Pembrokeshire from this 200-year-old pub perched above a rocky cove overlooking St Brides Bay. This free house buzzes with chatter and contented visitors enjoying well-kept real ales and a good choice of wines in the comfortably rustic bar, furnished with old settles, polished oak tables and leather armchairs. There's also an intimate dining room, with an elegant contemporary-style restaurant upstairs; cooking is modern British, with a commitment to seasonal and local produce.

Open all day all wk 11am-mdnt Closed early Jan-mid Feb **Food** Lunch all wk 12-2 Dinner all wk 6-9 ⊕ FREE HOUSE ◀ Brains The Rev. James, Bass.
Facilities Non-diners area ◀ (Bar) ◀ Children's menu Children's portions Garden ⊓ WiFi ⇌ (notice required)

NEWPORT
Map 8 SN03

Salutation Inn

tel: 01239 820564 **Felindre Farchog, Crymych SA41 3UY**
email: johndenley@aol.com **web:** www.salutationcountryhotel.co.uk
dir: *On A487 between Cardigan & Fishguard*

Top local produce served in former coaching inn

This tastefully modernised, 16th-century coaching inn stands on the River Nevern in the Pembrokeshire Coast National Park. Owners since 2000 are John Denley, a veteran of 20 years in restaurants in North Africa and the Middle East, and his wife Gwawr, born two miles away on the slopes of Carningli Mountain. There is an emphasis on fresh locally sourced produce for the menu, which lists pork liver pâté with home-made chutney; paprika chicken breast with tagliatelle; and grilled fillet of fresh salmon with lemon butter. Felinfoel, Brains and a local guest are on tap.

Open all day Closed Tue in winter, (reduced hours out of season) **Food** Lunch all wk 12.30-2.30 Dinner all wk 6.30-9 ⊕ FREE HOUSE ◀ Felinfoel, Brains, Local guest ales ⚬ Thatchers Gold. **Facilities** Non-diners area ✿ (Bar Garden) ◀ Children's menu Children's portions Garden ⊓ Parking WiFi ⇌ (notice required)

PORTHGAIN
Map 8 SM83

The Sloop Inn

tel: 01348 831449 **SA62 5BN**
email: matthew@sloop-inn.freeserve.co.uk
dir: *Take A487 NE from St Davids for 6m. Left at Croesgooch for 2m to Porthgain*

Cosy pub with a maritime history

Possibly the most famous pub on the north Pembrokeshire coast, The Sloop Inn is located in the beautiful quarrying village of Porthgain and is especially enticing on a cold winter's day. The walls and ceilings are packed with pictures and memorabilia from nearby shipwrecks. The harbour is less than 100 yards from the door and there is a village green to the front, a large south-facing patio and a children's football pitch. With ales like Felinfoel and The Rev. James on the pump, a varied menu includes breakfasts, snacks, pub favourites, steaks and home-caught fish. Just the place to call into when out for one of the amazing nearby walks.

Open all day all wk 9.30am-11pm (winter 11.30-10) Closed 25 Dec eve **Food** Lunch all wk 12-2.30 Dinner all wk 6-9.30 Restaurant menu available all wk ⊕ FREE HOUSE/B G BETTERSPOONS LTD ◀ Hancock's HB, Felinfoel, Brains The Rev. James, Sharp's Doom Bar ⚬ Gwynt y Ddraig. **Facilities** Non-diners area ✿ (Garden Outside area) ◀ Children's menu Children's portions Garden Outside area ⊓ Parking WiFi ⇌

PICK OF THE PUBS

The Stackpole Inn

STACKPOLE Map 8 SR99

tel: 01646 672324 **SA71 5DF**
email: info@stackpoleinn.co.uk
web: www.stackpoleinn.co.uk
dir: *From Pembroke take B4319, follow Stackpole signs, approx 4m*

A real find in beautiful Pembrokeshire

This traditional inn is a walker's delight, set in pristine gardens at the heart of the National Trust's Stackpole Estate and close to the spectacular Pembrokeshire coastal path. There's a rare George V postbox in the mellow stone wall outside, a survival from the time when one of the two original stone cottages was a post office. Nowadays the pub offers facilities for walkers, cyclists, fishermen and climbers, as well as those who simply prefer to relax and do nothing. Once inside, you'll find a slate bar, ceiling beams made from ash trees grown on the estate, and a wood-burning stove set within the stone fireplace. The pub's free house status means that there's always a guest beer from around the UK to accompany three Welsh ales, a couple of real ciders and a varied wine list. Chef Maciej 'Magic' Martyka oversees the creation of menus that use the best of local produce from the surrounding countryside and fish from the coast. Three-course appetites

might begin with pork and apricot terrine served with home-made piccalilli, Welsh Telifi cheese rarebit with chutney and tomato salad, or Stackpole fishcakes with lemon sauce. Main course options range from roasted butternut squash stuffed with root vegetables, Drewi Sant (a soft cheese washed with mead) and rosemary; to traditional cottage pie served with seasonal vegetables and gravy. Round things off with apple and sultana crème brûlée, steamed syrup sponge pudding with custard, or a rich chocolate brownie with chocolate sauce and vanilla ice cream. Walkers may enjoy the 'Walkers lunch', a selection of cheeses, ham, pickles, salad and bread.

Open all wk 12-3 6-11 (summer 12-11) Closed Sun eve (winter) **Food** Lunch Mon-Sat 12-2, Sun 12-2.30 (summer 12-11) Dinner all wk 6.30-9 (summer 12-11) ⊕ FREE HOUSE ◀ Brains The Rev. James, Felinfoel Double Dragon, Guest ale ☙ Gwynt y Ddraig, Westons Stowford Press. ♟ 12
Facilities Non-diners area ♗ Children's menu Children's portions Garden ⅋ Parking WiFi 🚌

ROSEBUSH
Map 8 SN02

Tafarn Sinc

tel: 01437 532214 **Preseli SA66 7QT**
email: briandavies2@btconnect.com
dir: *Phone for detailed directions*

Free house maintaining its nostalgic originality

Built to serve the railway that no longer exists, this large red corrugated-iron free house stands testament to its rapid construction in 1876. This idiosyncratic establishment refuses to be modernised and boasts wood-burning stoves, a sawdust floor, and a charming garden. Set high in the Preseli Hills amid stunning scenery, it is popular with walkers, who can refuel on traditional favourites like local lamb burgers; prime Welsh sirloin steak; home-cooked ham; and Glamorgan sausages with chutney.

Open all day 12-11 Closed Mon (ex BHs & summer) **Food** Lunch Tue-Sat 12-2 Dinner Tue-Sat 6-9 Av main course £10.50 ⊕ FREE HOUSE ◀ Worthington's, Tafarn Sinc, Guest ale. **Facilities** Non-diners area ♦ Children's menu Children's portions Garden ⏛ Parking ▭ (notice required)

ST DOGMAELS
Map 8 SN14

The Teifi Netpool Inn

tel: 01239 612680 **SA43 3ET**
email: jennyspangles@aol.com
dir: *From A487 follow St Dogmaels signs (B4546). Left signed St Dogmaels, Llandudoch & Poppit (B4546). Left into Maeshfryd St, to end, pub on left*

Family-friendly place for ale and non-stop food

Since Jenny Thomas took it over, this pub has concentrated on what it does best – stocking local guest ales and serving food for all the family from midday until the evening. It's on the banks of the River Teifi near the village green – a little off the beaten track but a good place to find for anything from a baked potato to Welsh rarebit; or a steaming plate of minted Welsh lamb casserole with mash and peas. Sunday lunches are popular, when the main event may proffer roasted Welsh beef topside with home-made Yorkshire pudding; or Celtic Pride pork leg with crispy crackling.

Open all day all wk **Food** Lunch all wk 12-9 Dinner all wk 12-9 Av main course £9 Set menu available ⊕ FREE HOUSE ◀ Greene King Abbot Ale, Local guest ales ⏾ Addlestones. **Facilities** Non-diners area ♣ (Bar Outside area) ♦ Children's menu Children's portions Play area Outside area ⏛ Parking WiFi ▭ (notice required)

Webley Waterfront Inn & Hotel

tel: 01239 612085 **Poppit Sands SA43 3LN**
email: webleyhotel@btconnect.com
dir: *A484 from Carmarthen to Cardigan, then to St Dogmaels, right in village centre to Poppit Sands on B4546*

Seafood in a magnificent setting

This long-established family business is spectacularly situated at the start of the Pembrokeshire Coast National Park, a haven for birdwatchers and watersports enthusiasts. The inn offers outstanding views across the River Teifi and Poppit Sands to Cardigan Bay, which supplies the daily catch for the menu. King scallops with crispy bacon and carrot purée, perhaps to start, followed by pan-seared salmon and sautéed new potatoes. The specials board might feature dressed lobster and crab. Other dishes include rump steak and five bean chilli. The bar serves Gwynt y Ddraig Welsh cider together with a selection of ales.

Open all day all wk **Food** Lunch all wk 12-2.30 Dinner all wk 6-8.30 Av main course £10-£15 ⊕ FREE HOUSE ◀ Brains Buckley's Bitter, Felinfoel, Guest ales ⏾ Gwynt y Ddraig. ☇ 8 **Facilities** Non-diners area ♣ (Bar Garden) ♦ Children's menu Children's portions Play area Family room Garden ⏛ Parking WiFi ▭

STACKPOLE
Map 8 SR99

The Stackpole Inn
PICK OF THE PUBS

See Pick of the Pubs on opposite page

TENBY
Map 8 SN10

Hope and Anchor

tel: 01834 842131 **Saint Julians St SA70 7AX**
dir: *A478 or A4139 into Tenby. Into High St, becomes Saint Julians St. Pub on left*

A popular pub with a good choice of fish dishes

Heading down towards the harbour and the beach at Tenby and you can't miss the blue Hope and Anchor pub. Traditionally a fishing pub it has remained popular with locals for years and years. They offer seven real ales that change throughout the week and the menus and special boards feature lots of fish. Tenby mackerel, pan fried in butter or with a Cajun seasoning; sea bass with rocket and couscous salad; or mussels cooked with bacon, onions, cider and cream; even locally caught lobster is featured. Meat eaters might choose minted lamb or rib eye steaks; steak and ale pie; or rosemary and garlic chicken.

Open all day all wk Closed 25 Dec L **Food** Lunch all wk 12-9.30 Dinner all wk 12-9.30 ⊕ FREE HOUSE ◀ Sharp's Atlantic, Felinfoel Double Dragon, Guest ales ⏾ Westons Scrumpy, Old Rosie, Orchard Pig The Hog Father. ☇ 13 **Facilities** Non-diners area ♦ Children's menu Children's portions Garden ⏛ WiFi ▭ (notice required)

POWYS

BEGUILDY
Map 9 SO17

NEW The Radnorshire Arms

tel: 01547 510634 **LD7 1YE**
email: radnorshirearmsbeguildy@gmail.com
dir: *8m from Knighton on B4355 towards Newtown*

Enjoyable food and local ales in a former drovers' inn

Tucked away in the Teme Valley, this centuries-old black and white timber framed pub started life as a drovers' inn and it retains an old world charm with mind-your-head beams, inglenook fireplace and wood-burner. Sup on pints of local Ludlow Best or Stonehouse Station Bitter and choose between the bar menu with its pub classics or the main menu. Typical dinner choices include leek and crab tartlet, which might precede venison haunch steak with braised red cabbage, herb mash and red wine sauce, or chicken and mango stir-fry with noodles and sweet chilli sauce.

Open 12-2.30 6-11 Closed Mon **Food** Lunch Tue-Sun 12-2 Dinner Tue-Sat 6.30-9, Sun 7-8 Av main course £10 Restaurant menu available Tue-Sun evenings ⊕ FREE HOUSE ◀ Stonehouse Station Bitter, Ludlow Best ⏾ Thatchers Gold. **Facilities** Non-diners area ♦ Children's menu Children's portions Garden ⏛ Parking WiFi ▭ (notice required)

BRECON
Map 9 SO02

The Usk Inn
PICK OF THE PUBS

tel: 01874 676251 **Talybont-on-Usk LD3 7JE**
email: stay@uskinn.co.uk
dir: *6m E of Brecon, just off A40 towards Abergavenny & Crickhowell*

An ideal stop for Brecon Beacon visitors

The Usk Inn enjoys an enviable position about 300 metres from the village centre at Talybont-on-Usk on the picturesque Abergavenny to Brecon road. Attracting locals and visitors to the Brecon Beacons National Park in equal number, the inn opened in the 1840s just as the Brecon to Merthyr railway line was being built alongside it. Another source of custom is the Brecon to Monmouthshire canal that passes through the village. Over the years the Usk has been transformed from an ordinary pub into a country inn with a restaurant. Expect a choice of guest ales at the bar, along with ciders and popular wines. Typical dinner dishes, based on carefully sourced ingredients, are confit of pheasant, pearl barley and fruit berry sauce; loin of lamb, dauphinoise potatoes and rosemary sauce; and steak and ale pie with mashed potatoes.

Open all day all wk 11am-11.30pm (Sun 11-10.30) Closed 25-26 Dec eve **Food** Lunch all wk 12-2.30 ⊕ FREE HOUSE ◀ Guinness, Guest ales ♂ Thatchers, Robinsons. ♟ 11 **Facilities** Non-diners area ♦️ Children's menu Children's portions Garden ⌖ Parking ▱ (notice required)

COEDWAY
Map 15 SJ31

The Old Hand and Diamond Inn

tel: 01743 884379 **SY5 9AR**
email: moz123@aol.com web: www.oldhandanddiamond.co.uk
dir: *From Shrewsbury take A458 towards Welshpool. Right onto B4393 signed Four Crosses. Coedway approx 5m*

One for all the family

On the Powys/Shropshire border, this 17th-century inn retains much of its original character, with exposed beams and an inglenook fireplace. Its reputation for good quality food owes much to local farmers who supply excellent meats, including lamb and mutton from rare-breed Jacob sheep. Enjoy local Shropshire Lad and guest real ales in the bar, while choosing from an extensive menu that lists grilled lamb chop and shepherd's pie; butternut squash stuffed with cannellini beans, mozarella, peppers and tomato; and Stonehouse ale and beef pie. Among the desserts are fresh fruit Pavlova and ginger and lime cheesecake. The beer garden has plenty of seating and a children's play area.

Open all day all wk 11am-1am **Food** Lunch Mon-Thu 12-2.30, Fri-Sun 12-9.30 Dinner Mon-Thu 6-9.30, Fri-Sun 12-9.30 Restaurant menu available all wk ⊕ FREE HOUSE ◀ Worthington's, Wood's Shropshire Lad, Guest ales. **Facilities** Non-diners area ♣ (Bar Garden) ♦️ Children's portions Play area Garden ⌖ Parking WiFi ▱

CRICKHOWELL
Map 9 SO21

The Bear ★★★★ INN ⦿
PICK OF THE PUBS

tel: 01873 810408 **Brecon Rd NP8 1BW**
email: bearhotel@aol.com web: www.bearhotel.co.uk
dir: *On A40 between Abergavenny & Brecon*

Quintessential market town coaching inn

This imposing white-painted inn has been run by the Hindmarsh family for over 35 years, although it dates back to the 15th century. The rug-strewn, antique-laden and award-winning bar offers sandwiches and baguettes on top of the main menu, and Welsh real ales take the lead at the pumps. Alternatively, dine in the original D Restaurant, intimately dressed with linen and fresh cut flowers, or at a table in the restored former kitchen. New head chef Adam Littlewort makes good use of Welsh produce, as in a starter of Black Mountain smoked salmon with horseradish cream; and home-made Welsh beefburger topped with smoked bacon and Gorwydd Caerphilly cheese. For vegetarians, perhaps cauliflower cheese and potato cake with red pepper and tomato sauce. Finish with local cheeses, or panettone bread and butter pudding made with rum and bananas.

Open all day all wk Closed 25 Dec **Food** Lunch all wk 12-2 Dinner Mon-Sat 6-10, Sun 7-9.30 Restaurant menu available Mon-Sat ⊕ FREE HOUSE ◀ Brains The Rev. James, Wye Valley Butty Bach, Hancock's HB, Guest ales ♂ Westons Stowford Press. ♟ 10 **Facilities** Non-diners area ♣ (Bar Garden) ♦️ Children's menu Children's portions Family room Garden ⌖ Parking WiFi ▱ (notice required) **Rooms** 34

DEFYNNOG
Map 9 SN92

The Tanners Arms

tel: 01874 638032 **LD3 8SF**
email: info@tannersarmspub.com
dir: *From Brecon take A40 towards Llandovery. Left onto A4067 to Defynnog*

Old inn not far from the glorious Brecon Beacons

In a tiny village and overlooking open countryside, this 17th-century inn derives its name from the tannery that was once in business up the road. In the foothills of the Brecon Beacons National Park it makes a good stopping point for those setting off to explore this mountain area. The pub has real ales and ciders changing very regularly and the menus offer whole prawns in tempura batter; home-made pâté and toast; French brie and tomato quiche; sweet and sour chicken; rack of roasted BBQ pork ribs; pan-fried sea bass fillet with buttered new potatoes. Lunchtime quick bites and sandwiches are offered too.

Open all wk 5-12 (Fri 4-12 Sat-Sun 12-12) **Food** Lunch Sat-Sun 12-2 Dinner all wk 6-9 Av main course £10.95 Restaurant menu available all wk ⊕ FREE HOUSE ◀ Constantly changing ales ♂ Constantly changing ciders. **Facilities** Non-diners area ♣ (Bar Garden) ♦️ Children's menu Children's portions Garden ⌖ Beer festival Parking WiFi ▱ (notice required)

GLANGRWYNEY
Map 9 SO21

The Bell

tel: 01873 811115 **NP8 1EH**
email: thebellinncrickhowell@gmail.com
dir: *On A40 halfway between Abergavenny & Crickhowell*

A warm retreat in a small rural village

Real ale lovers should visit this lovely Brecon Beacons National Park pub during the Easter or Summer Bank Holiday beer and cider festivals. In fact, at any time it's the perfect destination for anyone who wants somewhere comfortable for a decent pint and something to eat. In addition to a constantly-changing selection of local ales and ciders — Symonds, for example — the menu draws extensively on local produce for dishes such as the creamy cockles, bacon and laverbread on granary toast;

home-made steak and real Welsh ale pie; and oven-baked cod parcel with creamy white wine and cucumber sauce.

Open 12-3 6-11.30 (Sat 12-12 Sun 12-10.30) Closed Mon (ex holiday periods) **Food** Lunch Tue-Fri 12-2.30, Sat-Sun 12-4 Dinner Tue-Sat 6-9 ⊕ BRAINS ◀ Bitter & The Rev. James ♂ Gwynt y Ddraig Orchard Gold, Symonds. **Facilities** Non-diners area ✿ (Bar Garden) ◈ Children's menu Children's portions Garden ⚲ Beer festival Cider festival Parking WiFi ⛟ (notice required)

GLASBURY
Map 9 SO13

The Harp Inn

tel: 01497 847373 **HR3 5NR**
email: info@theharpinn.co.uk **web:** www.theharpinn.co.uk
dir: *In village centre on B4350, approx 3.5m from Hay-on-Wye*

Country pub with a long history

A pub since the 17th century, this comfortable inn overlooks the River Wye and is just a few miles from Hay-on-Wye itself. In the bar, grab a table and enjoy a pint of one of several local real ales, including Mayfields Glasbury Undaunted specially brewed for the pub. The tempting menu offers classics of spicy meatballs and spaghetti; steak and ale pie; and oven-baked vegetable lasagne. There's also a range of tasty pizzas and a specials board to watch out for. Regular music events include monthly folk and Irish sessions, and occasional jazz nights.

Open 12-3 6-12 (Sun 12-3 7-11 Mon 6-11) Closed Mon L **Food** Lunch Tue-Sun 12-2 Dinner Tue-Sat 6.30-8.30, Sun 7-8 Av main course £8.50 ⊕ FREE HOUSE ◀ Wye Valley Dorothy Goodbody's Golden Ale & Butty Bach, Mayfields Glasbury Undaunted ♂ Westons Stowford Press. **Facilities** Non-diners area ✿ (Bar Garden) ◈ Children's menu Children's portions Garden ⚲ Parking WiFi ⛟ (notice required)

HAY-ON-WYE
Map 9 SO24

The Old Black Lion ★★★★ INN ◉ | PICK OF THE PUBS

tel: 01497 820841 **HR3 5AD**
email: info@oldblacklion.co.uk **web:** www.oldblacklion.co.uk
dir: *From B4348 in Hay-on-Wye into Lion St. Inn on right*

Historic inn with very good food

Close to Lion Gate, one of the original entrances to the old walled town of Hay-on-Wye, parts of this charming whitewashed inn date from the 1300s, although structurally most of it is 17th century. The oak-timbered bar is furnished with scrubbed pine tables, comfy armchairs and a log-burner – perfect for savouring a pint of Wye Valley bitter. The inn has a long-standing reputation for its food, and the pretty dining room overlooking the garden terrace is where to enjoy grilled mackerel and rhubarb chutney followed by roast pork chop, bubble-and-squeak and Calvados gravy; or roast fillet of salmon, crushed potatoes, mushroom and white wine sauce. Hay, of course, has bookshops at every turn, and it is also home to a renowned annual literary festival. Please note that only children over eight are permitted in the pub.

Open all day all wk 8am-11pm Closed 24-26 Dec **Food** Lunch all wk 12-2.30 Dinner Sun-Thu 6.30-9, Fri-Sat 6.30-9.30 ⊕ FREE HOUSE ◀ Old Black Lion Ale, Wye Valley Bitter ♂ Westons Stowford Press. ☐ 8 **Facilities** Non-diners area ◈ Children's portions Garden ⚲ Parking WiFi **Rooms** 10

The Three Tuns

tel: 01497 821855 **4 Broad St HR3 5DB**
email: info@three-tuns.com
dir: *In town centre*

Stylish town pub with a warm welcome

This 16th-century, possibly older, pub has attracted an eclectic roll-call of famous, even infamous, visitors, from musician Jools Holland to the Great Train Robbers. In the bar is an old settle, reclaimed from a fire at the pub, and restored so that visitors can continue to sit and enjoy a welcome pint of Wye Valley Bitter or Butty Bach. The menus range from a home-made pizza, baked ciabatta or beer battered haddock and chips to choices such as Welsh rarebit, Caerphilly cheese, smoked bacon salad; mixed olive and fennel risotto, deep-fried poached egg, pecorino crackling; and lamb and apricot tagine, lemon couscous and mint yogurt.

Open 11-3 6-11 Closed 25 Dec, Mon & Tue (winter) **Food** Lunch all wk 11-2 Dinner all wk 6-9 ⊕ FREE HOUSE ◀ Wye Valley Bitter, Butty Bach ♂ Westons Old Rosie. **Facilities** Non-diners area ◈ Children's portions Garden ⚲ WiFi ⛟

LLANDRINDOD WELLS
Map 9 SO06

The Laughing Dog

tel: 01597 822406 **Howey LD1 5PT**
dir: *From A483 between Builth Wells & Llandrindod Wells follow Howey signs. Pub in village centre*

Village centre inn with adventurous cooking

All you'd expect from a thriving village local, from pub games in the fire-warmed bar to real ales from respected Welsh microbreweries such as Rhymney and The Celt Experience. Originating as a drovers' stopover some 300 years ago and reputedly haunted. The pub's varied menu combines the best of Welsh cooking with influences from Europe and further afield. Start with deep-fried garlic and herb filo prawns, or duck spring rolls with chilli dipping sauce; follow that with pot-roasted lamb shank with rosemary and garlic gravy; or traditional Welsh faggots in a blue cheese gravy. The pub is in superb walking country.

Open all wk Mon 7pm-10.30pm Tue-Thu 6-11 (Fri 5.30-11 Sat-Sun all day) **Food** Lunch Sun 12-2 Dinner Tue-Sat 6.30-9 Av main course £9.95 ⊕ FREE HOUSE ◀ Wye Valley Bitter & Butty Bach, The Celt Experience Celt-Bronze Ale, Felinfoel Double Dragon, Rhymney Bevan's Bitter & General Picton. **Facilities** Non-diners area ✿ (Bar Garden) ◈ Children's menu Children's portions Garden ⚲ ⛟ (notice required)

LLANFYLLIN
Map 15 SJ11

Cain Valley Hotel

tel: 01691 648366 **High St SY22 5AQ**
email: info@cainvalleyhotel.co.uk
dir: *From Shrewsbury & Oswestry follow signs for Lake Vyrnwy onto A490 to Llanfyllin. Hotel on right*

Traditional food in long-established hotel

A watering hole since the 17th century, this hotel offers the choice of an oak-panelled lounge bar and a heavily beamed restaurant. A full bar menu is available at lunchtime (sandwiches, salads, pub classics, vegetarian and children's choices) and the evening menu typically offers chef's chicken liver pâté, which might be followed by steak and ale pie, chips, peas or fresh vegetables; chicken or vegetable balti; grilled Welsh lamb double chop; or lasagne. Lovers of mild ale will find Ansell's in the bar, alongside The Rev. James and Westons Stowford Press cider.

Open all day all wk 11.30am-mdnt (Sun 12-11) Closed 25 Dec **Food** Lunch all wk 12-2 Dinner all wk 7-9 Av main course £10 Restaurant menu available all wk ⊕ FREE HOUSE ◀ Worthington's, Ansell's Mild, Brains The Rev. James, Guinness ♺ Westons Stowford Press. **Facilities** Non-diners area ♦ Children's menu Children's portions ⊟ Parking WiFi ➡ (notice required)

LLANGYNIDR
Map 9 SO11

The Coach & Horses

tel: 01874 730245 **Cwmcrawnon Rd NP8 1LS**
email: coachandhorses222@outlook.com
dir: *Take A40 from Abergavenny towards Brecon. At Crickhowell left onto B4558 to Llangynidr (NB narrow river bridge), or from Beaufort take B4560 through Brynmawr to Llangynidr*

Enjoy local ales close to the Brecon Beacons

Just two minutes' walk from the nearby canal moorings and surrounded by the Brecon Beacons, this early 18th-century free house is also a popular meeting place for car club members – the car park can accommodate over 70 vehicles. Changing real ales are sourced from a 40-mile radius, and the chefs prepare the likes of deep-fried brie followed by home-made venison faggots with horseradish mash and a red wine sauce, finishing with chilled banana terrine. The beer garden has lovely views over the countryside.

Open all day 12-12 Closed Mon in winter **Food** Lunch all wk 12-2 Dinner all wk 6-9 ⊕ FREE HOUSE ◀ Wye Valley Butty Bach, Sharp's Doom Bar, Bass. **Facilities** Non-diners area ♣ (Bar Garden) ♦ Children's menu Children's portions Garden ⊟ Parking WiFi ➡ (notice required)

MACHYNLLETH
Map 14 SH70

Wynnstay Hotel
PICK OF THE PUBS

tel: 01654 702941 **SY20 8AE**
email: info@wynnstay-hotel.com
dir: *At junct A487 & A489 in town centre. 5m from A470 (parking to rear)*

Strong commitment to Welsh food and drink

It was in 'Mach', as the locals helpfully call it, that in 1780 politician Sir Watcyn Williams-Wynne built his pied-à-terre, later to become the Wynnstay, Herbert Arms and Unicorn Hotel, a mouthful since abandoned. From its balcony in 1932 and 1937 Prime Minister David Lloyd George watched as the Eisteddfod processions passed by. Brothers Paul and Gareth Johns run this child- and dog-friendly hotel, whose bar

serves several Welsh real ales and 10 wines by the glass. Committed, as far as it can, to sourcing ingredients from within a 50-mile radius, Gareth ensures local origins are name-checked on the menus: for example, warm salad of Mathafarn mallard with smoked bacon; braised Braichithel lamb with caper sauce; Clywedog trout with cockles and bacon; and Llaeth-y-Llan yogurt pannacotta. Complete your gastronomic tour of mid-Wales with local cheeses and ice creams.

Open all wk 12-2.30 6-11 Closed 1wk over New Year **Food** Lunch all wk 12-2 Dinner all wk 6.30-9 Set menu available ⊕ FREE HOUSE ◀ Greene King IPA, The Celt Experience Celt-Golden Ale, Monty's Moonrise, Evan Evans Warrior, Guinness. ♀ 10 **Facilities** Non-diners area ♣ (Bar Outside area) ♦ Children's menu Children's portions Outside area ⊟ Parking WiFi ➡ (notice required)

OLD RADNOR
Map 9 SO25

The Harp
PICK OF THE PUBS

tel: 01544 350655 **LD8 2RH**
email: mail@harpinnradnor.co.uk
dir: *Old Radnor signed from A44 between Kington & New Radnor*

Enjoyable food in a Welsh longhouse with lovely views

With magnificent views across the Radnor Valley, this stone-built Welsh longhouse dates from the 15th century. Open the plain wooden door and you step into a cosy lounge and bars with original oak beams, crackling log fires, semi-circular wooden settles and slate floors; books, board games and hop bines complete the warm, traditional appeal. The food focus is on fresh and seasonal produce, and local sourcing is highlighted on the concise, refreshingly no-frills menu. Leek, mushroom and smoked cheddar tart with slow-roasted tomatoes makes for a tasty starter. Welsh lamb and beef will probably feature in the main course, alongside a pie or risotto, with grilled fillets of sea bream for fish lovers. Finish with a selection of Welsh cheeses; or warm ginger cake, caramel sauce, vanilla ice cream. Real ales from Shropshire and Herefordshire breweries are rotated, and an annual June beer festival is hugely popular.

Open Wed-Thu 6-11 (Fri-Sun 12-3 6-11) Closed Mon (ex BHs) Tue (ex summer hols) **Food** Lunch Fri-Sun 12-2.30 Dinner Wed-Sat 6-9 ⊕ FREE HOUSE ◀ Three Tuns, Wye Valley, Hobsons, Ludlow, Salopian ♺ Dunkertons. **Facilities** Non-diners area ♣ (Bar Garden) ♦ Children's portions Garden ⊟ Beer festival Parking WiFi

PAINSCASTLE
Map 9 SO14

The Roast Ox Inn

tel: 01497 851398 **LD2 3JL**
dir: *From Hay-on-Wye take B4351, through Clyro to Painscastle*

Classic pub food in restored rural local

In stunning countryside close to Hay-on-Wye and Brecon, the Roast Ox is traditional through and through – a country pub fully restored using venerable building materials and methods. Expect rustic brick floors, stone walls, old fireplaces and a classic pub atmosphere alongside comfortable furnishings and local Wye Valley Butty Bach ale tapped straight from the barrel. Head for the dining room, originally a blacksmith's workshop, for home-cooked and locally sourced fodder. Typical are twice-cooked pork spare ribs in barbecue sauce; Welsh faggots with creamy mash; and a board of Welsh cheeses to die for, served with apple chutney and oat biscuits.

Open pm Jan-Mar Closed Mon-Tue Jan-Mar **Food** Lunch all wk 12-2 Dinner all wk 6-9 Av main course £12.95 ⊕ FREE HOUSE ◀ Sharp's Doom Bar, Wye Valley Butty Bach, Guest ale ♺ Thatchers. ♀ 8 **Facilities** Non-diners area ♣ (Bar Outside area) ♦ Children's portions Outside area ⊟ Parking WiFi ➡ (notice required)

PICK OF THE PUBS

The Castle Coaching Inn

TRECASTLE   Map 9 SN82

tel: 01874 636354 **LD3 8UH**
email:
reservations@castle-coaching-inn.co.uk
web: www.castle-coaching-inn.co.uk
dir: *On A40, W of Brecon*

Ideal base for walking in the Brecon Beacons

Privately owned and run by the Porter family, this Georgian coaching inn sits on the old London to Carmarthen route in the northern part of the Brecon Beacons National Park. It makes an ideal base for the pursuit of outdoor activities or, for the less energetic, the simple appreciation of mountain views, lakes, waterfalls and wildlife. The inn has lovely old fireplaces and a remarkable bow-fronted window looking out from the bar, where an open log fire burns throughout the winter. The focus on customer satisfaction makes this a relaxing hostelry, even at weekends when it becomes especially lively. Two real ales on tap change weekly, ensuring a pint in tip-top condition; wines and a good selection of Scottish and Irish whiskies are also served. While settling back to enjoy your drink and the great atmosphere, take a look at the menu and specials board. Some guests prefer to stay in the bar to eat; the menu is the same both here and in the restaurant, although additional bar food includes fresh sandwiches, jackets, seafood, steak and ale pie, and lamb casserole. Starters range from home-made soup of the day with crusty bread, to duck and orange pâté; deep-fried camembert; and a salmon, cod and prawn fishcake served with home-made tartare sauce. Main courses typically include Welsh sirloin steak cooked to your liking with mushrooms, cherry tomatoes and onion rings; supreme of chicken stuffed with Stilton, wrapped in bacon, with white wine and cream sauce; and slow-roasted Welsh lamb. Desserts press all the right buttons with the likes of Belgian triple chocolate praline torte with vanilla ice cream; and lemon posset with shortbread. Outside, the peaceful terrace and garden beckon on sunny days.

Open all wk Sat-Sun 12-3 Mon-Sat 6-11 Sun 7-11 **Food** Lunch Sat-Sun 12-2 Dinner Mon-Sat 6.30-9, Sun 7-9 🌐 FREE HOUSE 🍺 Guest ale 🍏 Westons Stowford Press. **Facilities** Non-diners area 🐾 (Bar Garden) 🚻 Children's menu Children's portions Garden 🪑 Parking WiFi

TALYBONT-ON-USK · Map 9 SO12

Star Inn

tel: 01874 676635 **LD3 7YX**
email: anna@starinntalybont.co.uk
dir: *Take A40 from Brecon toward Crickhowell. 6m to pub in town centre*

An astonishing number of beers at Brecon Beacons' pub

In the National Park, with a garden right next to the Monmouthshire & Brecon Canal, and an ever-changing choice of real ales – over 500 guests a year – Ian and Anna Bell's village pub is extremely popular, and even that could be an understatement. Beer festivals pull in even more fans in mid-June and mid-October. But, of course, there's food too, in the shape of local venison faggots with creamed mash and winter greens; fresh beer battered fish and chips; and roast pumpkin and squash gnocchi. Under-12s have their own selection and the under-2s eat for free.

Open all wk 11.30-3 5-11 Fri-Sun 11.30-11 (summer Mon-Thu 11.30-11) **Food** Lunch Mon-Fri 12-2, Sat-Sun 12-2.30 Dinner all wk 6-9 (no food Sun eve Nov-Mar) ⊕ PUNCH TAVERNS ◀ Wye Valley, Brecon Brewing, Guest ales ♂ Gwynt y Ddraig, Guest ciders. **Facilities** Non-diners area ❖ (Bar Restaurant Garden) ♦♦ Children's menu Children's portions Garden ⛱ Beer festival WiFi

TRECASTLE · Map 9 SN82

The Castle Coaching Inn · PICK OF THE PUBS

See Pick of the Pubs on page 651

RHONDDA CYNON TAFF

PONTYPRIDD · Map 9 ST08

Bunch of Grapes · PICK OF THE PUBS

See Pick of the Pubs on opposite page

SWANSEA

LLANGENNITH · Map 8 SS49

Kings Head ★★★★ INN

tel: 01792 386212 **SA3 1HX**
email: info@kingsheadgower.co.uk **web:** www.kingsheadgower.co.uk
dir: *M4 junct 47, follow signs for Gower A483, 2nd exit at rdbt, right at lights onto B495 towards Old Walls, left at fork to Llangennith, pub on right*

A pub with it all, near glorious coastline

A lane to Rhossili Bay's magnificent beach starts just along from this 17th-century village inn, which still displays plenty of old beams, exposed stonework and a large open fire. The bar serves a weekly rotating schedule of real ales from the Gower Brewery, which pub landlord Chris Stevens co-founded. Expect much praised home-made food using local produce that includes Vietnamese, Goan and Thai curries; pizzas; gourmet burgers; salt marsh lamb; and Welsh beef and venison. Comfortable and stylish accommodation is available. A beer and cider festival is held during the last weekend of October.

Open all day all wk 9am-11pm (Sun 9am-10.30pm) **Food** Lunch all wk 9am-9.30pm Dinner all wk 9am-9.30pm ⊕ FREE HOUSE ◀ Gower Gold, Lighthouse & Power, Guinness ♂ Gwynt y Ddraig Black Dragon. **Facilities** Non-diners area ❖ (Bar Garden) ♦♦ Children's menu Children's portions Garden ⛱ Beer festival Cider festival Parking 🛏 **Rooms** 27

LLANMADOC · Map 8 SS49

NEW Britannia Inn

tel: 01792 386624 **SA3 1DB**
email: enquiries@britanniainngower.co.uk **web:** www.britanniainngower.co.uk

Welcoming pub adding to the attractions of the Gower

Landlords Martin and Lindsey Davies packed their early years with cooking and hospitality experience around the world. Ten years ago, after returning to home territory, they set about applying their skills at the Britannia. The pub's attractive whitewashed and flower-bedecked exterior features a terrace with lovely Gower views. Beer gardens front and back are home to a variety of pets. Inside, chunky wooden furniture and beamed ceilings make a welcoming ambience. Martin's fixed price lunch menu is indicative of the quality fare on offer: Penclawdd cockles and laverbread with samphire and quail egg could be followed perhaps by Weobly Castle salt marsh lamb burger, with salad, mint mayo and chips.

Open all day all wk **Food** Lunch all wk 12-3 Dinner all wk 6-9.30 Av main course £10 Set menu available Restaurant menu available all wk ⊕ ENTERPRISE INNS ◀ Gower Gold, Wadworth 6X, Marston's Pedigree. **Facilities** Non-diners area ❖ (Bar Garden) ♦♦ Children's menu Children's portions Play area Garden Parking WiFi 🛏 (notice required)

REYNOLDSTON · Map 8 SS48

King Arthur Hotel

tel: 01792 390775 **Higher Green SA3 1AD**
email: info@kingarthurhotel.co.uk
dir: *Just N of A4118, SW of Swansea*

A warm welcome and a delightful setting

Sheep graze on the village green opposite this charming inn set in a pretty village at the heart of the beautiful Gower Peninsula. Inside you'll find real log fires, bare wood floors and walls decorated with nautical memorabilia. Eat in the restaurant, main bar or family room, where choices range from pub favourites such as fillet of cod in a lager batter with home-made tartare sauce, or a Welsh Celtic Pride steak through to healthy salads (maybe Greek, ham or chicken Caesar). Enjoy the food with a choice of well-kept local ales, or one of 11 wines served by the glass.

Open all day all wk Closed 25 Dec **Food** Contact pub for food times ⊕ FREE HOUSE ◀ Felinfoel Double Dragon, Tomos Watkin OSB, Worthington's, Tiny Rebel, Mumbles. 🍷 11 **Facilities** Non-diners area ♦♦ Children's menu Children's portions Family room Garden Parking WiFi 🛏 (notice required)

PICK OF THE PUBS

Bunch of Grapes

PONTYPRIDD   Map 9 ST08

tel: 01443 402934
Ynysangharad Rd CF37 4DA
email: info@bunchofgrapes.org.uk
web: www.bunchofgrapes.org.uk
dir: *From A470 onto A4054 (Pentrebach Rd to Merthyr road) into Ynysangharad Rd*

Excellent beers and good food where the Rhondda meets the Taff

Eight hand pumps lining the bar are the first clue that this pub is an ale lover's paradise. It's owned by the local award-winning Otley Brewing Company, and is a previous winner of the AA Pub of the Year for Wales. The brewery's flagship 02 Croeso is one of four regular Otley ales on offer, alongside guests from other UK microbreweries and imported bottles and kegs from Europe and America. Beer festivals are hosted every two months, when the choice expands to more than 20; and two annual cider festivals showcase Welsh draught ciders among others. To complete the refreshments line-up, the wine list is no also-ran, with quality choices from around the world and seven served by the glass. Surrounded by the striking, wooded landscapes of South Wales, this 160-year-old market town pub includes many of the region's best ingredients in its dishes. The lunchtime bar menu keeps things simple with quality pub-grub offerings such as sandwiches, ploughman's, deep-fried cod fillet in Otley ale batter, and home-cooked ham with

free-range egg and hand-cut chips. Burgers, with melted Welsh cheddar as an option, and a full range of steak cuts feature Breconshire beef. In the evening the kitchen steps up the pace. Indicative starters are devilled lamb's kidneys with toasted focaccia; deep-fried lamb belly goujons, salsa verde and salad; pan-fried cockles, laverbread, leeks and home-cured pancetta on fried bread with charred lemon; and confit Wye Valley duck leg with chilli jam and watercress. Main courses too reflect the kitchen's serious credentials: typical are potted cider-braised rabbit, baked celeriac chips, Talgarth black pudding and caramelised Cox apple; and pan-fried fillet of gurnard, lemon, ginger and crab broth, charred red chilli, dehydrated curly kale and smoked new potatoes.

Open all day all wk **Food** Lunch Mon-Fri 12-2.30, Sat 12-3, Sun 12-3.30 Dinner Mon-Sat 6-9.30 Restaurant menu available all wk ⊞ FREE HOUSE ◧ Otley Ales, Guest ales ♻ Gwynt y Ddraig, Blaengawney. **Facilities** Non-diners area ❁ (Bar Garden) ❸ Children's menu Children's portions Garden ꠰ Beer festival Cider festival Parking WiFi

VALE OF GLAMORGAN

BARRY
Map 9 ST16

NEW Fox and Hounds ★★★★ INN

tel: 01446 781287 **Llancarfan CF62 3AD**
email: foxandhoundsllancarfan@gmail.com **web:** www.foxandhoundsllancarfan.co.uk
dir: Contact pub for detailed directions

Lovely surroundings and good beer

Beautiful countryside surrounds the little village of Llancarfan, and the church houses medieval paintings dating back to the 15th century. The pub was rescued from threat of closure by the villagers, and bought by the Millards. There's a light and airy restaurant and an ornate glass-roofed canopy means you can eat outside even if it happens to be raining. There's Butcombe Adam Henson's Rare Breed and Gold bitter on tap in the bar, while on the menu you'll find starters like avocado, crab and prawn cocktail or rillettes of duck with red onion marmalade, followed by cannon of Welsh lamb; or roasted butternut squash, spinach and pine nut risotto.

Open 12-2.30 6-11 (Sun 12-2.30 7-10.30 Mon 7-11) Closed Mon L **Food** Lunch Tue-Sat 12-2 Dinner Tue-Sat 6-9 Restaurant menu available Tue-Sat ⊕ FREE HOUSE ◀ Butcombe Adam Henson's Rare Breed & Gold ⚲ Ashton Press. ♟ 9
Facilities Non-diners area ♦♦ Children's portions Outside area ⋒ Parking WiFi **Rooms** 8

COWBRIDGE
Map 9 SS97

Cross Inn
PICK OF THE PUBS

See Pick of the Pubs on opposite page

Victoria Inn

tel: 01446 773943 **Sigingstone CF71 7LP**
email: oleary445@aol.com
dir: From Llantwit Major N on B4270. Right to Sigingstone

Bright and welcoming village inn with extensive menu

This inn stands near the top of an old village tucked away along country lanes in the Vale of Glamorgan, with the captivating coastline of the Bristol Channel just a short hop away. The eye-catching exterior beckons villagers and explorers into a cottagey, beamed interior with lots of prints, brass and antiques. At the bar there's a range of south Wales real ales including bitter from Evan Evans and beers from breweries in nearby Cardiff. The locally sourced menu, which is strong on seafood dishes, proffers modern twists on traditional mains.

Open all wk 9.30-3 6-11.30 **Food** Lunch all wk 11.45-2.30 Dinner all wk 6-9 Set menu available Restaurant menu available Mon-Sat ⊕ FREE HOUSE ◀ Hancock's HB, Worthington's Creamflow, Evan Evans. ♟ 10 **Facilities** Non-diners area ♨ (Bar Garden Outside area) ♦♦ Children's menu Garden Outside area ⋒ Parking WiFi ⇥ (notice required)

EAST ABERTHAW
Map 9 ST06

Blue Anchor Inn
PICK OF THE PUBS

tel: 01446 750329 **CF62 3DD**
email: blueanchor@gmail.com
dir: From Barry take A4226, then B4265 towards Llantwit Major. Follow signs, turn left for East Aberthaw. 3m W of Cardiff Airport

14th-century pub in the same family for generations

The grandfather of the present owners, Jeremy and Andrew Coleman, acquired this pretty, stone-built and heavily thatched inn in 1941, when he bought it from a large local estate. The inn has been trading almost continuously since 1380. The interior is warmly traditional: a warren of small rooms with low beamed ceilings and open fires, including a large inglenook. A selection of well-kept real ales is always on tap, and an enticing range of food is served in both the bar and the upstairs restaurant. Choose pub classics like grilled gammon steak with fried egg, pineapple and home-cut chips. Or look to the specials list, where a starter of confit pheasant leg with gem, black pudding and smoked bacon salad, could be followed by a main course of grilled whole plaice, tenderstem broccoli, tomato and tarragon beurre blanc, and new potatoes.

Open all day all wk 11-11 (25 Dec 12-2) **Food** Lunch Mon-Sat 12-2 Dinner Mon-Sat 6-9 Set menu available ⊕ FREE HOUSE ◀ Theakston Old Peculier, Wadworth 6X, Wye Valley HPA, Brains Bitter. ♟ 9 **Facilities** Non-diners area ♨ (Bar Restaurant Garden) ♦♦ Children's menu Garden ⋒ Parking WiFi ⇥ (notice required)

PENARTH
Map 9 ST17

The Pilot

tel: 029 2071 0615 **67 Queens Rd CF64 1DJ**
email: pilot@knifeandforkfood.co.uk
dir: Phone for detailed directions

Contemporary community pub with harbour views

Set on a hillside overlooking the watery wonder that is Cardiff Bay, The Pilot has seen immense changes since it originated as a dock-workers' pub. Transformed like the harbour and docklands at its feet, the pub is now a popular destination where drinkers and diners are equally welcome. With craft beers from the respected Otley Brewery in Pontypridd and ciders from Gwynt y Ddraig to slake a thirst, attention can turn to the ever-changing fare outlined on the chalkboard. Pub classics mix with modern British dishes on a pleasing choice that may feature pan-seared scallops, squash purée and truffle salad; and an 8oz Welsh rib-eye. A beer and cider festival is held twice a year.

Open all day all wk **Food** Lunch all day Dinner all day ⊕ BRAINS ◀ Otley, Tiny Rebel, The Celt Experience, Grey Trees ⚲ Gwynt y Ddraig, Guest ciders. ♟ 17 **Facilities** Non-diners area ♨ (Bar Outside area) ♦♦ Children's menu Children's portions Outside area ⋒ Beer festival Cider festival WiFi ⇥ (notice required)

Find out more
about the AA's awards for food excellence on page 9

PICK OF THE PUBS

Cross Inn

COWBRIDGE   Map 9 SS97

tel: 01446 772995
Church Rd, Llanblethian CF71 7JF
email: artherolry@aol.com
web: www.crossinncowbridge.co.uk
dir: *Take B4270 from Cowbridge towards Llantwit Major, pub 0.5m on right*

Ever popular country pub

Much loved by visitors, this 17th-century former coaching inn is set in a picturesque corner of the Vale of Glamorgan's countryside on the fringe of the ancient town of Cowbridge, just a few miles from the splendid Heritage Coast. A family-run pub, Cross Inn has a cosy restaurant and comfortable, character bar with welcoming log fires and a convivial atmosphere. The chefs take great pride in developing daily menus of essentially British food with European influences. Fresh produce is sourced from local farmers and other reliable suppliers, with fish, prime Welsh steaks, poultry and other ingredients delivered every day to supply the bar meals, children's meals and the frequently changing restaurant menu. Expect choices to include pub favourites such as home-made curried chicken, crispy beer battered fillet of cod, wholetail scampi, pies and steaks, local pork and leek sausages and mash.

Other choices could be ham hock terrine with red onion marmalade; and home-made lasagne al forno with hand-cut chips. The regularly changing specials board features a variety of fish, meat and game dishes, and the traditional Sunday lunch are always popular. There is a good wine list of regularly selected, quality wines. On arriving at Cross Inn particularly noticeable are the lovely hanging flower baskets which have won the pub several awards. Dogs are very welcome, and the pub, with a good sized car park, is an ideal starting and finishing point for walkers who enjoy exploring the many delightful country walks the area has to offer.

Open all day all wk 11-11 **Food** Lunch Tue-Fri 12-2.30, Sat 12-9, Sun 12-4 Dinner Tue-Fri 5.30-9, Sat 12-9 🛢 FREE HOUSE 🍺 Hancock's HB, Wye Valley Butty Bach, Evan Evans Crwr, Shepherd Neame Bishops Finger, Thornbridge Jaipur 🍏 Westons & Stowford Press, Thatchers Gold, Gwynt y Ddraig. **Facilities** Non-diners area 🐾 (Bar Garden) 👫 Children's menu & portions Garden 🪑 Beer festival Parking WiFi 🚐

WREXHAM

ERBISTOCK
Map 15 SJ34

The Boat Inn

tel: 01978 780666 **LL13 ODL**
email: info@boatondee.com
dir: *A483 Whitchurch/Llangollen exit, towards Whitchurch on A539. After 2m turn right at signs for Erbistock & The Boat Inn*

Local ales and modern food at riverside gem

A no-through lane past the Victorian church leads to the 13th-century Boat, in an unrivalled position on the banks of the River Dee; there was once a ferry crossing here. Expect to find a cosy flagstoned and oak beamed bar and several rambling rooms with open fires, stone walls and charming nooks and crannies. It's a fine spot for a pint of local Weetwood Cheshire Cat and some modern pub food, best enjoyed in the glorious riverside garden. From the extensive menu choose tempura prawns; deep-fried brie; salmon fishcakes or chef's soup of the day to start; follow with fresh sea bass; Boat fish and chips; Cajun chicken; beefburgers; pie of the day; or Welsh Black lamb.

Open all day all wk **Food** Contact pub for food times Av main course £15 ⊕ FREE HOUSE ◾ Weetwood Best & Cheshire Cat, Black Sheep ♂ Hereford Dry. ♟ 10 **Facilities** Non-diners area ✿ (Bar Garden Outside area) ♦️ Children's menu Children's portions Garden Outside area ⋔ Parking WiFi

GRESFORD
Map 15 SJ35

Pant-yr-Ochain
PICK OF THE PUBS

tel: 01978 853525 **Old Wrexham Rd LL12 8TY**
email: pant.yr.ochain@brunningandprice.co.uk
dir: *From Chester towards Wrexham on A483 take A5156 signed Nantwich (dual carriageway). 1st left into Old Wrexham Rd. Pub 500yds on right*

Good ale and good food in an elegant setting

Set in a country estate of gentle hills, woods and meres, this astonishing Tudor manor house stands at the end of a long, sweeping drive just outside Wrexham. Timber framed gables overlook award-winning gardens, whilst the interior retains many characteristics of its origins. Brick fireplaces, nooks and crannies, alcoves and quiet corners all help to create an overriding feel of an Edwardian country house. Countless prints and paintings, artefacts and bric-á-brac add considerable character and interest. The Brunning & Price partnership work their magic throughout. Splendid real ales from Marches breweries like Joule's and Weetwood head up a great selection of ales, with real ciders adding local colour. From the kitchen emerge contemporary British dishes. Starters chime in with seared chicken breast with beetroot risotto; the main event may be pan-roasted duck breast with duck hash cake; or lamb and mint suet pudding. Rich desserts and a tempting cheeseboard are a final flourish.

Open all day all wk 11.30-11 (Sun 11.30-10.30) **Food** Lunch all wk 12-5 Dinner Mon-Sat 5-9.30, Sun 5-9 Av main course £10.95 ⊕ FREE HOUSE/BRUNNING & PRICE ◾ Brunning & Price Original Bitter, Purple Moose, Weetwood Ales Eastgate Ale, Joule's Slumbering Monk ♂ Tomas Watkin Taffy Apples, Aspall. ♟ 22 **Facilities** Non-diners area ✿ (Bar Garden) ♦️ Children's menu Children's portions Play area Garden ⋔ Parking WiFi

LLANARMON DYFFRYN CEIRIOG
Map 15 SJ13

The Hand at Llanarmon ★★★★ INN ◉ PICK OF THE PUBS

See Pick of the Pubs on opposite page

NEW West Arms

tel: 01691 600665 **LL20 7LD**
email: info@thewestarms.co.uk
dir: *Exit A483 or A5 at Chirk, take B4500 to Ceiriog Valley*

Still extending warm hospitality after 500 years

Set against a stunning backdrop of Berwyn Mountain and originally built as a drovers' inn, the West Arms spent some time as a hotel and has been offering visitors a warm welcome for the past five centuries. Slate flagged floors, low beams and an original inglenook fireplace add to the charm of this lovely old free house, where ales from local Stonehouse brewery are on tap in the bar. In summer, the riverside gardens are an ideal spot for lunch, from a menu packed with local produce including braised Welsh lamb shanks, local pheasant or whole Ceiriog trout.

Open all day all wk **Food** Lunch Mon-Sat 12-2.30, Sun 12-6 Dinner all wk 6.30-9 Av main course £16 ⊕ FREE HOUSE ◾ Stonehouse, Black Sheep ♂ Somersby Cider. **Facilities** Non-diners area ✿ (Bar Garden) ♦️ Children's menu Children's portions Garden ⋔ Parking WiFi ⛟ (notice required)

ROSSETT
Map 15 SJ35

The Golden Lion

tel: 01244 571020 **Chester Rd LL12 OHN**
email: goldenlion@woodwardandfalconer.com
dir: *From Chester take A483 towards Wrexham, left onto B5102 signed Rossett, left onto B5445, pub on left in Rossett*

Attractive village inn with interesting heritage

Haunted by the mischievous ghost of a murderous ploughman, this village-centre pub in the northern Welsh Marches is an engaging mix of old and new. Lots of beams, trusses and wooden flooring offer great character within, melding seamlessly with tasteful decor, countlesss prints and framed ephemera amidst eclectic furnishings. Outside is an immense, tree-shaded beer garden where a pint of Piffle is amongst the choice brews to sample. The regularly changing fare has much for seafood fans, a good vegetarian choice and may feature meaty mains like venison bourguignon pie; an impressive wine list includes 16 by the glass.

Open all day all wk 12-11 (Sun 12-10.30) Closed 1 Jan & 25 Dec **Food** Contact pub for food times ⊕ WOODWARD & FALCONER PUBS LTD ◾ Piffle, Theakston Best Bitter, Guest ales. ♟ 16 **Facilities** Non-diners area ♦️ Children's menu Children's portions Play area Family room Garden ⋔ Parking WiFi ⛟

PICK OF THE PUBS

The Hand at Llanarmon ★★★★ INN ✿

LLANARMON DYFFRYN CEIRIOG Map 15 SJ13

tel: 01691 600666 **LL20 7LD**
email: reception@thehandhotel.co.uk
web: www.thehandhotel.co.uk
dir: *Exit A5 at Chirk follow B4500 for 11m. Through Ceiriog Valley to Llanarmon Dyffryn Ceiriog. Pub straight ahead*

Imaginative food and well-kept local ales

Jonathan and Jackie Greatorex spent years visiting this 16th-century free house and inn, once a rest stop for drovers and their flocks on the old road from Anglesey to London. Its warm atmosphere and delicious food really struck home, so when in 2014 the opportunity arose, they bought it. Up the remote Ceiriog Valley, known as The Valley of the Poets, in the shadow of the Berwyn Mountains, is where you'll find it and its original oak beams, plum-coloured walls, large fireplaces and mix-and-match furniture. The well-stocked bar offers Weetwood Cheshire Cat and Conwy Rampart real ales and plenty of malt whiskies, including a Welsh one. Head chef Grant Mulholland and his team have earned an AA Rosette for their impressive modern European dishes. Everything is prepared on the premises from fresh ingredients – everything, that is, except the steak and ale, and chicken and gammon pies that McArdle's of Chirk make specially for The Hand. Frequently changing menus include one for the bar, on which you're likely to find Welsh Celtic Pride beef lasagne; ale-battered cod fillet and home-made chips; tomato and Peri Las cheese crumble with onion bhajis; and traditional ploughman's with Llandymog mature cheddar and home-made bread. From the dinner menu, typical examples are Severn and Wye Valley oak-smoked salmon with lemon and capers; organic free-range chicken breast with pan-fried smoked gammon terrine and grain mustard sauce; and grilled Welsh lamb cutlets with tomato ratatouille, and red wine and redcurrant sauce. There's always at least one vegetarian option. To follow, baked Amaretto cheesecake; or bread and butter pudding with Chantilly cream. Few places can be quieter than the sunny terrace garden.

Open all day all wk **Food** Lunch Mon-Sat 12-2.20, Sun 12.30-2.45 Dinner all wk 6.30-8.45 Av main course £12.50 Set menu available ⬛ FREE HOUSE ⬛ Weetwood Cheshire Cat, Conwy Rampart. **Facilities** Non-diners area ☘ (Bar Garden) ♦ Children's portions Garden ⍭ Parking WiFi ▦ (notice required) **Rooms** 13

Beer festivals

Beer festivals, or their equivalent, are as old as the hills. The brewing of hops goes back to the beginning of human civilisation, and the combination of a common crop and a fermenting process that results in alcoholic liquid has long been a cause of celebration. Beer festivals officially began in Germany with the first Munich Oktoberfest in 1810. Wherever in the world beer is brewed, today and for the last few millennia, admirers, enthusiasts, aficionados – call them what you will – have gathered together to sample and praise its unique properties. It happens throughout Europe, in Australia, New Zealand, America and Canada, and annual events are held in pubs all over Britain.

Beer festivals are often occasions for the whole family, when entertainment is laid on for children as well as adults. Summer is naturally a popular season for festivals, when the action can take place outdoors, but many are held in October, traditionally harvest time. Beer festivals are sometimes large and well-advertised gatherings that attract a wide following and last several days; or they might be local but none the less enthusiastic neighbourhood get-togethers.

For up-to-date information, please check directly with the pub.

Abbreviations
Etr Easter; May BH (1st Monday in May); Spring BH (last Monday in May); Aug BH (last Monday in August); wk week; wknd weekend

Public Holidays 2015
New Year's Day January 1; Good Friday March 25; Easter Monday March 28; Early May Bank Holiday May 2; Spring Bank Holiday May 30; Summer Bank Holiday (August Bank Holiday) August 29 (August 1 Scotland only); St Andrew's Day November 30 (Scotland only); Christmas Day December 25; Boxing Day December 26

ENGLAND

BERKSHIRE

CURRIDGE
The Bunk Inn
01635 200400
Jun-Jul

HAMPSTEAD NORREYS
The White Hart
01635 202248
Last wknd Jun

HERMITAGE
The White Horse of Hermitage
01635 200325
Jun

KNOWL HILL
Bird In Hand Country Inn
01628 826622
Jun & Nov

MONEYROW GREEN
The White Hart
01628 621460
Summer

READING
The Flowing Spring
0118 969 9878
Midsummer & Autumn

WALTHAM ST LAWRENCE
The Bell
0118 934 1788
Annually (30 real ales, 10 ciders)

WOKINGHAM
The Broad Street Tavern
0118 977 3706
Twice a year

WOOLHAMPTON
The Rowbarge
0118 971 2213

BRISTOL

BRISTOL
The Alma Tavern & Theatre
0117 973 5171
Jul (summer fayre)

BUCKINGHAMSHIRE

AMERSHAM
Hit or Miss Inn
01494 713109
Mid Jul wknd

AYLESBURY
The King's Head
01296 718812

BEACONSFIELD
The Red Lion Knotty Green
01494 680888
Sep

The Royal Standard of England
01494 673382
Summer BH

CHESHAM
The Black Horse Inn
01494 784656

The Swan
01494 783075
Summer BH

CUBLINGTON
The Unicorn
01296 681261
May & Summer BHs

DENHAM
The Falcon Inn
01895 832125

DORNEY
The Palmer Arms
01628 666612

FARNHAM ROYAL
The Emperor
01753 643006

GERRARDS CROSS
The Three Oaks
01753 899016
Summer

GREAT HAMPDEN
The Hampden Arms
01494 488255
Summer

GREAT MISSENDEN
The Polecat Inn
01494 862253
Summer

HEDGERLEY
The White Horse
01753 643225
Etr, Spring BH & Summer BH

LACEY GREEN
The Whip Inn
01844 344060
May & Sep

LITTLE KINGSHILL
The Full Moon
01494 862397
Mid Jul

MOULSOE
The Carrington Arms
01908 218050
Jun

SEER GREEN
The Jolly Cricketers
01494 676308
Etr wknd & Summer BH

TURWESTON
The Stratton Arms
01280 704956

CAMBRIDGESHIRE

BALSHAM
The Black Bull Inn
01223 893844

BOURN
The Willow Tree
01954 719775
Summer

COTON
The Plough
01954 210489
Summer

DRY DRAYTON
The Black Horse
01954 782600
Apr (St George's Day wknd)

GLINTON
The Blue Bell
01733 252285

HEMINGFORD GREY
The Cock Pub and Restaurant
01480 463609
Wknd mid Aug

HISTON
Red Lion
01223 564437
Etr & 1st wk Sep

OFFORD D'ARCY
The Horseshoe Inn
01480 810293
Midsummer

PETERBOROUGH
Charters Bar & East Restaurant
01733 315700
Etr Thu-Etr Mon

SPALDWICK
The George
01480 890293

STRETHAM
The Lazy Otter
01353 649780
Jul

WHITTLESFORD
The Tickell Arms
01223 833025
May

CHESHIRE

ASTON
The Bhurtpore Inn
01270 780917
Jul (130 beers)

CHESTER
Old Harkers Arms
01244 344525
Mar (Pie & Champion Ale Wk)

GOOSTREY
The Crown
01477 532128
Summer

KETTLESHULME
Swan Inn
01663 732943
1st wknd Sep

KNUTSFORD
The Dog Inn
01625 861421

MOBBERLEY
The Bulls Head
01565 873395
Jun

SPURSTOW
The Yew Tree Inn
01829 260274
Etr wknd

STYAL
The Ship Inn
01625 444888
Summer

TARPORLEY
The Swan, Tarporley
01829 733838
Summer

CORNWALL & ISLES OF SCILLY

ALTARNUN
Rising Sun Inn
01566 86636
Mid-late Nov

BOLINGEY
Bolingey Inn
01872 571626
Apr & Oct

CADGWITH
Cadgwith Cove Inn
01326 290513
Oct

CHAPEL AMBLE
The Maltsters Arms
01208 812473
Spring BH

CONSTANTINE
Trengilly Wartha Inn
01326 340332

CUBERT
The Smugglers' Den Inn
01637 830209
Early May BH wknd

GUNNISLAKE
The Rising Sun Inn
01822 832201
Every 2-3 months

GWITHIAN
The Red River Inn
01736 753223
Etr wknd

HALSETOWN
The Halsetown Inn
01736 795583
Aug

MITCHELL
The Plume of Feathers
01872 510387
Oct

PENZANCE
The Coldstreamer Inn
01736 362072
Sep

The Turks Head Inn
01736 363093

PHILLEIGH
Roseland Inn
01872 580254
1st wknd Sep

ST AGNES
Driftwood Spars
01872 552428
Mid Mar (mini beer festival) &
Early May BH wknd

ST IVES
The Watermill
01736 757912
Jun & Nov

ST MAWGAN
The Falcon Inn
01637 860225
Jul (last full wknd)

ST MERRYN
The Cornish Arms
01841 532700
Mar (beer & mussel festival)

TRESCO (ISLES OF SCILLY)
The New Inn
01720 422849
Mid May & early Sep

TRURO
Old Ale House
01872 271122

CUMBRIA

BOOT
Brook House Inn
019467 23288
Early Jun

BROUGHTON-IN-FURNESS
Blacksmiths Arms
01229 716824
1st wknd Oct

CARTMEL
The Cavendish Arms
015395 36240

CONISTON
The Black Bull Inn & Hotel
015394 41335

ELTERWATER
The Britannia Inn
015394 37210
2wks mid Nov

HAWKSHEAD
Kings Arms
015394 36372
Jul & Dec

The Sun Inn
015394 36236
May

LOW LORTON
The Wheatsheaf Inn
01900 85199 & 85268
Late Mar

LOWESWATER
Kirkstile Inn
01900 85219

RAVENSTONEDALE
The Black Swan
015396 23204
Summer

SATTERTHWAITE
The Eagles Head
01229 860237

SEATHWAITE
Newfield Inn
01229 716208
Oct

ULVERSTON
Farmers Arms Hotel
01229 584469

WASDALE HEAD
Wasdale Head Inn
019467 26229

DERBYSHIRE

ASHOVER
The Old Poets Corner
01246 590888
Mar & Oct (Thu-Sun, 40 beers &
ciders, live music)

BAKEWELL
The Monsal Head Hotel
01629 640250
Sep

BAMFORD
The Yorkshire Bridge Inn
01433 651361
May

BIRCHOVER
The Druid Inn
01629 653836
May

Red Lion Inn
01629 650363
Mid Jul

BONSALL
The Barley Mow
01629 825685
BHs (3-4 times a year)

CASTLETON
The Peak Hotel
01433 620247
Etr

Ye Olde Nags Head
01433 620248
Summer

CHINLEY
Old Hall Inn
01663 750529
3rd wknd Feb, 3rd wknd Sep

The Paper Mill Inn
01663 750529
4th wknd Feb, 3rd wknd Sep

DALBURY
The Black Cow
01332 824297

EYAM
Miners Arms
01433 630853
3 times a year

FENNY BENTLEY
Bentley Brook Inn
01335 350278

HOPE
The Old Hall Hotel
01433 620160
BHs

LITTON
Red Lion Inn
01298 871458

MATLOCK
The Red Lion
01629 584888

ROWSLEY
The Grouse & Claret
01629 733233

SHARDLOW
The Old Crown Inn
01332 792392
Apr & Oct

DEVON

BLACKAWTON
The George Inn
01803 712342
Early May BH & Summer BH

BRANSCOMBE
The Fountain Head
01297 680359
Mid Jun

The Masons Arms
01297 680300
Jul (30 ales & ciders, live music,
BBQ)

BRIDFORD
The Bridford Inn
01647 252250
May & Aug

BROADHEMBURY
The Drewe Arms
01404 841267
Etr

CLAYHIDON
The Merry Harriers
01823 421270
Summer

CLEARBROOK
The Skylark Inn
01822 853258
Summer BH

CLOVELLY
Red Lion Hotel
01237 431237
Spring BH

CLYST HYDON
The Five Bells Inn
01884 277288
2nd wk Aug

COCKWOOD
The Anchor Inn
01626 890203
Etr & Halloween

EAST ALLINGTON
The Fortescue Arms
01548 521215

HONITON
The Holt
01404 47707

IDDESLEIGH
The Duke of York
01837 810253
Aug

KILMINGTON
The Old Inn
01297 32096
Spring BH Sat

KINGS NYMPTON
The Grove Inn
01769 580406
Jul

NEWTON ABBOT
The Wild Goose Inn
01626 872241
Early May BH wknd

PLYMTREE
The Blacksmiths Arms
01884 277474
Biannually

SANDFORD
The Lamb Inn
01363 773676

SLAPTON
The Tower Inn
01548 580216

TAVISTOCK
The Cornish Arms
01822 612145
Summer BH wknd

TOTNES
The Durant Arms
01803 732240
1st wknd Sep

Royal Seven Stars Hotel
01803 862125

Steam Packet Inn
01803 863880
Mid May (3 days)

Beer festivals *continued*

TUCKENHAY
The Maltsters Arms
01803 732350

WOODBURY SALTERTON
The Digger's Rest
01395 232375
May

DORSET

BUCKHORN WESTON
Stapleton Arms
01963 370396

CRANBORNE
The Inn at Cranborne
01725 551249
Jun

IWERNE COURTNEY OR SHROTON
The Cricketers
01258 860421
Early May BH

MILTON ABBAS
The Hambro Arms
01258 880233
Jul

NORTH WOOTTON
The Three Elms
01935 812881

STUDLAND
The Bankes Arms Hotel
01929 450225
Mid Aug

WEST STOUR
The Ship Inn
01747 838640
Aug

WORTH MATRAVERS
The Square and Compass
01929 439229
1st Sat Oct (beer & pumpkin festival)

DURHAM, COUNTY

BARNARD CASTLE
The Morritt Hotel
01833 627232

CASTLE EDEN
Castle Eden Inn
01429 835137
May/Jun

FROSTERLEY
The Black Bull Inn
01388 527784

LONGNEWTON
Vane Arms
01642 580401
Jul (mini beer festival), Oct (Blacksheep wknd)

STANLEY
The Stables Pub and Restaurant
01207 288750
3rd wknd Sep

THORPE THEWLES
The Vane Arms
01740 630458
Jun

ESSEX

BELCHAMP ST PAUL
The Half Moon
01787 277402
Summer BH

CASTLE HEDINGHAM
The Bell Inn
01787 460350
3rd wknd Jul

CHELMSFORD
Admiral J McHardy
01245 256783

CHRISHALL
The Red Cow
01763 838792
Spring BH

COPFORD GREEN
The Alma
01206 210607
Spring BH wknd

FEERING
The Sun Inn
01376 570442
End of Jun & Sep

FYFIELD
The Queen's Head
01277 899231
Summer BH

GOLDHANGER
The Chequers Inn
01621 788203
Mar & Sep

HASTINGWOOD
Rainbow & Dove
01279 415419
Sep

LITTLEBURY
The Queens Head Inn Littlebury
01799 520365
Etr

LITTLEY GREEN
The Compasses
01245 362308
2nd last wknd Aug

MARGARETTING TYE
The White Hart Inn
01277 840478
Jul & Nov

MOUNT BURES
The Thatchers Arms
01787 227460

NEWNEY GREEN
The Duck Pub & Dining
01245 421894
Summer BH

PURLEIGH
The Bell
01621 828348
Aug/Sep

STOCK
The Hoop
01277 841137
Spring BH

WENDENS AMBO
The Bell
01799 540382
Summer BH

WOODHAM MORTIMER
Hurdlemakers Arms
01245 225169
Last wknd Jun (25+ real ales & ciders)

GLOUCESTERSHIRE

ALDERTON
The Gardeners Arms
01242 620257
Spring BH & 26 Dec (both 5 days)

ALMONDSBURY
The Swan Hotel
01454 625671
Jul

BROCKHAMPTON
Craven Arms Inn
01242 820410
Sep

CHELTENHAM
The Gloucester Old Spot
01242 680321
Spring BH

The Royal Oak Inn
01242 522344
Spring BH

CLIFFORD'S MESNE
The Yew Tree
01531 820719
Oct

COATES
The Tunnel House Inn
01285 770280
1st wknd Aug

DURSLEY
The Old Spot Inn
01453 542870
May & Oct

EBRINGTON
The Ebrington Arms
01386 593223
Early Oct

EWEN
The Wild Duck
01285 770310
Summer

LECHLADE ON THAMES
The Trout Inn
01367 252313
Jun

LEIGHTERTON
The Royal Oak
01666 890250

MEYSEY HAMPTON
The Masons Arms
01285 850164

NORTH CERNEY
Bathurst Arms
01285 832150
Jan, Apr, Jul & Oct

SAPPERTON
The Bell at Sapperton
01285 760298

TETBURY
The Priory Inn
01666 502251
Early May BH (real ale & cider)

The Royal Oak Tetbury
01666 500021
Spring BH

GREATER MANCHESTER

MANCHESTER
Marble Arch
0161 832 5914
Aug

OLDHAM
The White Hart Inn
01457 872566

SALFORD
The King's Arms
0161 839 8726
Sep

STOCKPORT
The Nursery Inn
0161 432 2044
3 times a year (8 guests on handpump)

WALMERSLEY
The Lord Raglan
0161 764 6680
Summer & Autumn

HAMPSHIRE

ALTON
The George
01420 82331
Mid summer

BALL HILL
The Furze Bush Inn
01635 253228
24-26 Dec

BEAULIEU
The Drift Inn
023 8029 2342

BISHOP'S WALTHAM
The Hampshire Bowman
01489 892940
Last wknd Jul

BRAISHFIELD
The Wheatsheaf
01794 368652

BRANSGORE
The Three Tuns Country Inn
01425 672232
Last wk Sep

CHALTON
The Red Lion
023 9259 2246
1st wknd Aug

CHARTER ALLEY
The White Hart Inn
01256 850048

CHERITON
The Flower Pots Inn
01962 771318
Aug

CLANFIELD
The Rising Sun Inn
023 9259 6975
Sep

EAST BOLDRE
Turfcutters Arms
01590 612331
Aug

EAST STRATTON
Northbrook Arms
01962 774150
Early May BH

EVERSLEY
The Golden Pot
0118 973 2104

EVERSLEY CROSS
The Chequers
0118 402 7065

FORDINGBRIDGE
The Augustus John
01425 652098
Early May BH

FREEFOLK
The Watership Down Inn
01256 892254
Early May BH

HANNINGTON
The Vine at Hannington
01635 298525
Jul

HAWKLEY
The Hawkley Inn
01730 827205
1st wknd Jun

HURSLEY
The Kings Head
01962 775208
Summer BH

LITTLETON
The Running Horse
01962 880218

LYNDHURST
New Forest Inn
023 8028 4690
2nd wknd Jul

NORTH WALTHAM
The Fox
01256 397288
Late Apr

PETERSFIELD
The Old Drum
01730 300544
1st wknd in Aug

The White Horse Inn
01420 588387
Jun

SELBORNE
The Selborne Arms
01420 511247
1st wknd Oct

STOCKBRIDGE
The Three Cups Inn
01264 810527

SWANMORE
The Rising Sun
01489 896663
Summer BH (Sat)

TICHBORNE
The Tichborne Arms
01962 733760
Jun

UPHAM
The Brushmakers Arms
01489 860231
Aug

WINCHESTER
The Bell Inn
01962 865284
Summer

The Westgate Inn
01962 820222

HEREFORDSHIRE

BRINGSTY COMMON
Live and Let Live
01886 821462
Etr wknd

HOARWITHY
The New Harp Inn
01432 840900
BHs

KIMBOLTON
Stockton Cross Inn
01568 612509

MICHAELCHURCH ESCLEY
The Bridge Inn
01981 510646
Summer BH

ORLETON
The Boot Inn
01568 780228
Last wknd Jul

WELLINGTON
The Wellington
01432 830367
Jun

WOOLHOPE
The Crown Inn
01432 860468
Early May BH

HERTFORDSHIRE

ALDBURY
The Valiant Trooper
01442 851203
BHs

ARDELEY
Jolly Waggoner
01438 861350
Aug

HERONSGATE
The Land of Liberty, Peace
and Plenty
01923 282226
Mid Feb, Etr, Oct & Xmas

HERTFORD HEATH
The College Arms
01992 558856

HITCHIN
The Highlander
01462 454612
Late May

PERRY GREEN
The Hoops Inn
01279 843568
Aug

WATTON-AT-STONE
The Bull
01920 831032
May & Oct

WILLIAN
The Fox
01462 480233

ISLE OF WIGHT

NITON
Buddle Inn
01983 730243
Jun & Sep

NORTHWOOD
Travellers Joy
01983 298024
Jul & Sep

KENT

BADLESMERE
The Red Lion
01233 740320

CANTERBURY
Duke of Cumberland
01227 831396
Jul or Aug

CHILHAM
The White Horse
01227 730355
Jul

FAVERSHAM
Albion Taverna
01795 591411
Early Sep, annual hop festival

HALSTEAD
Rose & Crown
01959 533120
Spring, Summer & Autumn

HAWKHURST
The Great House
01580 753119

HOLLINGBOURNE
The Windmill
01622 889000

IDEN GREEN
The Peacock
01580 211233

LOWER HALSTOW
The Three Tuns
01795 842840
Summer BH

ROLVENDEN
The Bull
01580 241212

SISSINGHURST
The Milk House
01580 720200

STALISFIELD GREEN
The Plough Inn
01795 890256
Summer

TONBRIDGE
The Little Brown Jug
01892 870318
May & Sep

TUNBRIDGE WELLS (ROYAL)
Sankey's
01892 511422

WEST MALLING
The Farm House
01732 843257

WEST PECKHAM
The Swan on the Green
01622 812271
Oct

LANCASHIRE

BILSBORROW

Owd Nell's Tavern
01995 640010
1st wknd Jul (American
Beer Festival); 1st wk Sep
(Oyster Festival); last wk Oct
(Oktoberfest)

CHORLEY
The Yew Tree Inn
01257 480344
Etr

HEST BANK
Hest Bank Inn
01524 824339

LANCASTER
The Sun Hotel and Bar
01524 66006
Summer

The White Cross
01524 33999
Late Apr (beer & pie festival)

PARBOLD
The Eagle & Child
01257 462297
Early May BH

RAMSBOTTOM
Eagle + Child
01706 557181

TOCKHOLES
The Royal Arms
01254 705373
Sep

WADDINGTON
Waddington Arms
01200 423262
Oct

LEICESTERSHIRE

LONG WHATTON
The Royal Oak
01509 843694
Summer BH

MOUNTSORREL
The Swan Inn
0116 230 2340
May & Summer BHs

OADBY
The Cow & Plough
0116 272 0852
Quarterly

SHAWELL
The White Swan
01788 860357

SUTTON CHENEY
Hercules Revived
01455 699336

LINCOLNSHIRE

CLEETHORPES
The Nottingham House
01472 505150
Spring & Autumn

INGHAM
Inn on the Green
01522 730354
Summer

LINCOLN
The Victoria
01522 541000
Halloween & Winter

LITTLE BYTHAM
The Willoughby Arms
01780 410276
Summer BH

THEDDLETHORPE ALL SAINTS
Kings Head Inn
01507 339798
Jul

LONDON

E14
The Gun
020 7515 5222

EC1
Ye Olde Mitre
020 7405 4751
May, Aug & Dec

NW1
The Engineer
020 7483 1890

The Prince Albert
020 7485 0270
BHs

SE1
The George Inn
020 7407 2056

SE10
The Old Brewery
020 3327 1280
Twice a year

SE22
The Palmerston
020 8693 1629

SW6
The White Horse
020 7736 2115
4 times a year (American, Great
British, Old Ale & European)

SW10
The Hollywood Arms
020 7349 7840

W4
The City Barge
020 8994 2148

W5
The Grove
07896 231503
Feb & Oct

W8
The Windsor Castle
020 7243 8797

Beer festivals *continued*

W14
The Albion
020 7603 2826
Aug

LONDON, GREATER

CHELSFIELD
The Five Bells
01689 821044
Etr & Oct

PINNER
The Queens Head
020 8868 4607
Spring/Summer

NORFOLK

BRANCASTER STAITHE
The Jolly Sailors
01485 210314

BURSTON
The Crown
01379 741257
2 or 3 times a year

HEYDON
Earle Arms
01263 587376
23 Apr (St George's Day)

HUNSTANTON
The Ancient Mariner Inn
01485 536390
Jul

HUNWORTH
The Hunny Bell
01263 712300

KING'S LYNN
The Stuart House Hotel, Bar
& Restaurant
01553 772169
Jul

LARLING
Angel Inn
01953 717963
Early Aug

NORWICH
The Mad Moose Arms
01603 627687

The Reindeer Pub & Kitchen
01603 612995
Summer

THOMPSON
Chequers Inn
01953 483360

WINTERTON-ON-SEA
Fishermans Return
01493 393305
Summer BH

NORTHAMPTONSHIRE

FOTHERINGHAY
The Falcon Inn
01832 226254

NORTHAMPTON
Althorp Coaching Inn
01604 770651

OLD
The White Horse
01604 781297
Summer BH wknd

OUNDLE
The Chequered Skipper
01832 273494
Twice a year

THORNBY
The Red Lion
01604 740238
Last wknd Jul

TOWCESTER
The Saracens Head
01327 350414

UPPER BODDINGTON
Plough Inn
01327 260364
Summer BH

WADENHOE
The King's Head
01832 720024
Aug

NORTHUMBERLAND

BEADNELL
The Craster Arms
01665 720272
Last wknd Jul

CARTERWAY HEADS
The Manor House Inn
01207 255268
Last wknd Aug

HEDLEY ON THE HILL
The Feathers Inn
01661 843607
Etr wknd

HEXHAM
Battlesteads Hotel &
Restaurant
01434 230209
Summer

Miners Arms Inn
01434 603909

MILFIELD
The Red Lion Inn
01668 216224
Last wknd Jun

NOTTINGHAMSHIRE

BEESTON
The Victoria
0115 925 4049
Etr; last 2wks Jul (beer & music)
& Oct

KIMBERLEY
The Nelson & Railway Inn
0115 938 2177
BHs

NEWARK-ON-TRENT
The Prince Rupert
01636 918121
Mid May & late Jun

NOTTINGHAM
The Hand and Heart
0115 958 2456
Spring & Autumn

Ye Olde Trip to Jerusalem
0115 947 3171
2 or 3 times a year

SOUTHWELL
The Hearty Goodfellow
01636 919176
Jul

OXFORDSHIRE

ABINGDON-ON-THAMES
The Brewery Tap
01235 521655
Mar & Oct

BANBURY
Ye Olde Reindeer Inn
01295 270972
Etr, Summer BH

BLOXHAM
The Elephant & Castle
01295 720383
Early May (part of Bloxfest Music
Festival)

BRIGHTWELL-CUM-SOTWELL
The Red Lion
01491 837373
Summer, 2 days (local beer &
musicians)

BURFORD
The Angel at Burford
01993 822714
Summer

The Highway Inn
01993 823661
Early Jun

CUMNOR
The Vine Inn
01865 862567

DORCHESTER
The George
01865 340404

FERNHAM
The Woodman Inn
01367 820643

FRINGFORD
The Butchers Arms
01869 277363
Jun

GALLOWSTREE COMMON
The Reformation
0118 972 3126
May & Oct

GREAT TEW
The Falkland Arms
01608 683653

KINGHAM
The Wild Rabbit
01608 658389
Spring BH

MARSH BALDON
Seven Stars
01865 343337
Summer BH

MILTON
The Plum Pudding
01235 834443
Apr & Oct

NORTH HINKSEY VILLAGE
The Fishes
01865 249796

NORTHMOOR
The Red Lion
01865 300301

OXFORD
The Magdalen Arms
01865 243159

PISHILL
The Crown Inn
01491 638364
Late Sep

TETSWORTH
The Old Red Lion
01844 281274
Etr (mini festival)

THAME
The Thatch
01844 214340
Late Sep-early Oct (National
Cask Ale Week)

UFFINGTON
The Fox & Hounds
01367 820680

WEST HANNEY
Plough Inn
01235 868674
Etr, Spring BH, Summer BH

WYTHAM
White Hart
01865 244372

RUTLAND

OAKHAM
The Grainstore Brewery
01572 770065
Summer BH

SHROPSHIRE

BISHOP'S CASTLE
The Three Tuns Inn
01588 638797
2nd wknd Jul (town festival)

CLUN
The White Horse Inn
01588 640305
1st wknd Oct

CRAVEN ARMS
The Sun Inn
01584 861239
May BH

MUCH WENLOCK
The George & Dragon
01952 727312
23 April (St George's Day); late
Sep-early Oct (National Cask
Ale Week)

PAVE LANE
The Fox
01952 815940
Summer

SHREWSBURY
The Prince of Wales
01743 343301
Feb & Spring BH

STOTTESDON
Fighting Cocks
01746 718270
Early Nov

WENTNOR
The Crown Inn
01588 650613
Jul

SOMERSET

BATH
The Star Inn
01225 425072
Twice a year

BISHOP SUTTON
The Red Lion
01275 333042

BISHOPSWOOD
Candlelight Inn
01460 234476

CHEW MAGNA
The Bear and Swan
01275 331100
Spring/Summer

CORTON DENHAM
The Queens Arms
01963 220317

CROSCOMBE
The George Inn
01749 342306
Spring BH wknd, Oct

DULVERTON
The Bridge Inn
01398 324130
Spring BH

HASELBURY PLUCKNETT
The White Horse at
Haselbury
01460 78873

HINTON ST GEORGE
The Lord Poulett Arms
01460 73149

ILCHESTER
The Bull Inn
01935 840400

Ilchester Arms
01935 840220
BHs

LOWER GODNEY
The Sheppey
01458 831594
Aug

PITNEY
The Halfway House
01458 252513
Mar

PORLOCK
The Bottom Ship
01643 863288
1st wknd Jul

SHEPTON BEAUCHAMP
Duke of York
01460 240314
Sep (occasionally)

SHEPTON MALLET
The Three Horseshoes Inn
01749 850359
Etr, Summer BH

WEDMORE
The George Inn
01934 712124

WEST HUNTSPILL
Crossways Inn
01278 783756
Summer BH

WHEDDON CROSS
The Rest and Be
Thankful Inn
01643 841222

STAFFORDSHIRE

CAULDON
Yew Tree Inn
01538 309876
Jul

STAFFORD
The Holly Bush Inn
01889 508234
Jun & Sep

SUMMERHILL
Oddfellows in the Boat
01543 361692

WALL
The Trooper
01543 480413

SUFFOLK

BRANDESTON
The Queens Head
01728 685307
Jun

BURY ST EDMUNDS
The Old Cannon Brewery
01284 768769
Summer BH wknd

DUNWICH
The Ship at Dunwich
01728 648219
BH Sundays

ELVEDEN
Elveden Inn
01842 890876
Mid Jun

FRAMLINGHAM
The Railway
01728 724760
Etr

The Station Hotel
01728 723455
Mid Jul

HAWKEDON
The Queen's Head
01284 789218
3rd wknd Jul

LAXFIELD
The Kings Head
(The Low House)
01986 798395
May & Sep

NAYLAND
Anchor Inn
01206 262313
Father's Day (Jun), Sep,
Octoberfest

SIBTON
Sibton White Horse Inn
01728 660337
Jun & Aug

SOMERLEYTON
The Duke's Head
01502 733931

SWILLAND
Moon & Mushroom Inn
01473 785320
Summer

WOODBRIDGE
Cherry Tree Inn
01394 384627
Early Jul

WOODDITTON
The Three Blackbirds
01638 731100

SURREY

CARSHALTON
The Sun
020 8773 4549

CHIDDINGFOLD
The Swan Inn
01428 684688
Sep

CRANLEIGH
The Richard Onslow
01483 274922

FARNHAM
The Bat & Ball Freehouse
01252 792108
2nd wknd Jun

FETCHAM
The Bell
01372 372624
Late Sep-early Oct (National
Cask Ale Week)

FOREST GREEN
The Parrot Inn
01306 621339

LONG DITTON
The Ditton
020 8339 0785

NEWDIGATE
The Surrey Oaks
01306 631200
Spring BH & Summer BH

TILFORD
The Duke of Cambridge
01252 792236
May (CherryFest, charity beer &
music festival)

WEST END
The Inn West End
01276 858652

WINDLESHAM
The Half Moon
01276 473329

SUSSEX, EAST

BLACKBOYS
The Blackboys Inn
01825 890283

ERIDGE GREEN
The Nevill Crest and Gun
01892 864209

EWHURST GREEN
The White Dog
01580 830264

HARTFIELD
Anchor Inn
01892 770424
Early May

ICKLESHAM
The Queen's Head
01424 814552
Oct

LANGNEY
The Farm @ Friday Street
01323 766049
Jun & Aug

LEWES
The Snowdrop Inn
01273 471018
1st or 2nd wknd Oct

RYE
The Ypres Castle Inn
01797 223248
Aug

THREE LEG CROSS
The Bull
01580 200586

SUSSEX, WEST

EARTHAM
The George
01243 814340
Mid April

EAST GRINSTEAD
The Old Dunnings Mill
01342 821080
Jun & Sep

HORSHAM
The Black Jug
01403 253526
Sep

KINGSFOLD
The Dog and Duck
01306 627295
Annual charity event

LAMBS GREEN
The Lamb Inn
01293 871336
Aug

OVING
The Gribble Inn
01243 786893
Summer & Winter

SLINDON
The Spur
01243 814216

WEST DEAN
The Dean Ale & Cider House
01243 811465
Early May

TYNE & WEAR

NEWCASTLE UPON TYNE
The Bridge Tavern
0191 232 1122

Crown Posada
0191 232 1269
Feb

WARWICKSHIRE

BROOM
The Broom Tavern
01789 778199
Summer BH

EDGEHILL
Castle at Edgehill
01295 670255
Summer BH

HUNNINGHAM
The Red Lion
01926 632715
Jul

WEST MIDLANDS

BIRMINGHAM
The Old Joint Stock
0121 200 1892
May & Oct

WILTSHIRE

ALDBOURNE
The Blue Boar
01672 540237
1st wknd Jun

The Crown Inn
01672 540214
3rd wknd May & 3rd wknd Sep

BOX
The Quarrymans Arms
01225 743569
6 times a year

BRINKWORTH
The Three Crowns
01666 510366

BROUGHTON GIFFORD
The Fox
01225 782949
Spring BH

CRICKLADE
The Red Lion Inn
01793 750776
Last wknd Feb & Jun

CRUDWELL
The Potting Shed
01666 577833
Summer BH

DEVIZES
The Raven Inn
01380 828271
Early Aug (Wadworth Shire
Horses' holiday weeks)

EAST CHISENBURY
Red Lion Freehouse
01980 671124
May

EDINGTON
The Three Daggers
01380 830940

HORNINGSHAM
The Bath Arms at Longleat
01985 844308
Mid Jun

MALMESBURY
Kings Arms
01666 823383

NEWTON TONY
The Malet Arms
01980 629279
Jul

ROYAL WOOTTON BASSETT
The Angel
01793 851161
Sep

SALISBURY
The Wig and Quill
01722 335665

SEMINGTON
The Lamb on the Strand
01380 870263

WARMINSTER
The Bath Arms
01985 212262

WORCESTERSHIRE

BECKFORD
The Beckford
01386 881532
Oct

BEWDLEY
Little Pack Horse
01299 403762

The Mug House Inn & Angry
Chef Restaurant
01299 402543
Early May BH wknd

BRETFORTON
The Fleece Inn
01386 831173
Mid-late Oct

BROADWAY
Crown & Trumpet
01386 853202
Xmas & New Year

HARTLEBURY
The Tap House @ The Old
Ticket Office
01299 253275

KEMPSEY
Walter de Cantelupe Inn
01905 820572
Etr & Oct

KNIGHTWICK
The Talbot
01886 821235
Apr, Jun & Oct

MALVERN
The Nag's Head
01684 574373
23 Apr (St George's Day)

YORKSHIRE, EAST RIDING OF

BEVERLEY
The Ferguson Fawsitt Arms
& Country Lodge
01482 882665

YORKSHIRE, NORTH

APPLETREEWICK
The Craven Arms
01756 720270
Oct (over 25 beers)

COLTON
Ye Old Sun Inn
01904 744261
Summer

CROPTON
The New Inn
01751 417330
May & Nov

GRINTON
The Bridge Inn
01748 884224

HARDRAW
The Green Dragon Inn
01969 667392
Jun, Jul & Oct

KILBURN
The Forresters Arms Inn
01347 868386

MASHAM
The White Bear
01765 689319
Late Jun

RIPON
The George at Wath
01765 641324

SETTLE
The Lion at Settle
01729 822203
1st wknd Sep (folk festival)

SUTTON-ON-THE-FOREST
The Rose and Crown
01347 811333

THIRSK
Little 3
01845 523782

YORK
Lysander Arms
01904 640845
Early May BH wknd

YORKSHIRE, SOUTH

CADEBY
The Cadeby Pub &
Restaurant
01709 864009

SHEFFIELD
Broadfield Ale House
0114 255 0200

The Fat Cat
0114 249 4801
Aug

Kelham Island Tavern
0114 272 2482
Late Jun wknd

TOTLEY
The Cricket Inn
0114 236 5256

YORKSHIRE, WEST

HOLMFIRTH
Farmers Arms
01484 683713
Autumn

LEEDS
North Bar
0113 242 4540
Spring (Belgian/Dutch beers),
Summer (USA beers), Autumn/
Winter (German beers)

LINTON
The Windmill Inn
01937 582209
Jul

SOWERBY BRIDGE
The Alma Inn
01422 823334
Late Sep (Oktoberfest)

CHANNEL ISLANDS

JERSEY

ST AUBIN
Old Court House Inn
01534 746433
Nov

ISLE OF MAN

PORT ERIN
Falcon's Nest Hotel
01624 834077
Early May

SCOTLAND

ARGYLL & BUTE

ARROCHAR
Village Inn
01301 702279

DUNOON
Coylet Inn
01369 840426

INVERARAY
George Hotel
01499 302111
Early May BH & Summer BH

CITY OF DUNDEE

BROUGHTY FERRY
The Royal Arch Bar
01382 779741
1st wknd Oct (charity event)

DUNDEE
Speedwell Bar
01382 667783
1st wknd Oct (Rotary Charity
Oktoberfest)

CITY OF EDINBURGH

EDINBURGH
The Bow Bar
0131 226 7667
End Jan & end Jul (plus German
Beer Festival)

The Guildford Arms
0131 556 4312
Apr & Oct (plus monthly brewery
wknds)

Halfway House
0131 225 7101

RATHO
The Bridge Inn
0131 333 1320

CITY OF GLASGOW

GLASGOW
Bon Accord
0141 248 4427
4 times a year (90 beers &
ciders)

Ubiquitous Chip
0141 334 5007
Twice a year (dates vary)

WEST Brewery
0141 550 0135
Oct Fridays (OktoberFest)

DUMFRIES & GALLOWAY

BARGRENNAN
House O'Hill Hotel
01671 840243
Apr & Sep

HIGHLAND

CAWDOR
Cawdor Tavern
01667 404777

FORTROSE
The Anderson
01381 620236
Jan (Burns Weekend Real Ale
Festival), monthly mini-festivals

GLENCOE
Clachaig Inn
01855 811252
Hogmanay, FebFest &
OctoberFest

PLOCKTON
The Plockton Hotel
01599 544274
May

TORRIDON
The Torridon Inn
01445 791242
1st wknd Oct

LANARKSHIRE, NORTH

CUMBERNAULD
Castlecary House Hotel
01324 840233

LOTHIAN, WEST

LINLITHGOW
The Four Marys
01506 842171
last wknd May & Oct

MORAY

FORRES
The Old Mill Inn
01309 641605
Jun

PERTH & KINROSS

MEIKLEOUR
Meikleour Arms
01250 883206
Aug

SCOTTISH BORDERS

NEWCASTLETON
Liddesdale
01387 375255
1st wknd Jul

STIRLING

CALLANDER
The Lade Inn
01877 330152
Late Aug-mid Sep

WALES

BRIDGEND

KENFIG
Prince of Wales Inn
01656 740356

CARMARTHENSHIRE

PUMSAINT
The Dolaucothi Arms
01558 650237
Summer BH wknd

CEREDIGION

ABERYSTWYTH
The Glengower Hotel
01970 626191
Spring BH

LLWYNDAFYDD
The Crown Inn & Restaurant
01545 560396

TREGARON
Y Talbot
01974 298208
Early Oct

CONWY

COLWYN BAY
Pen-y-Bryn
01492 533360
Beer & bangers week; pie & ale week

DENBIGHSHIRE

RUTHIN
The White Horse
01824 790218
Jul

FLINTSHIRE

BABELL
Black Lion Inn
01352 720239
Apr & Sep (Annual Ale Trail)

MOLD
Glasfryn
01352 750500
Mar (Welsh Food & Drink week); Oct (Great British Pie & Champion Beers of Britain week)

GWYNEDD

WAUNFAWR
Snowdonia Parc Brewpub
01286 650409
Etr week & mid May (Welsh Highland Railway Raleigh Festival)

MONMOUTHSHIRE

ABERGAVENNY
Clytha Arms
01873 840206
Spring BH

RHYD-Y-MEIRCH
Goose and Cuckoo Inn
01873 880277
End May & end Aug

TINTERN PARVA
Fountain Inn
01291 689303
Etr & Sep

TRELLECH
The Lion Inn
01600 860322
Jun

NEWPORT

CAERLEON
The Bell at Caerleon
01633 420613

PEMBROKESHIRE

LITTLE HAVEN
St Brides Inn
01437 781266

POWYS

DEFYNNOG
The Tanners Arms
01874 638032
End May

GLANGRWYNEY
The Bell
01873 811115
Etr & Summer BH

OLD RADNOR
The Harp
01544 350655
Jun

TALYBONT-ON-USK
Star Inn
01874 676635
Mid Jun & mid Oct

RHONDDA CYNON TAFF

PONTYPRIDD
Bunch of Grapes
01443 402934
Every 2 months (20+ ales)

SWANSEA

LLANGENNITH
Kings Head
01792 386212
Last wknd Oct

VALE OF GLAMORGAN

COWBRIDGE
Cross Inn
01446 772995
Late Apr & Sep (mini beer & cider festival)

PENARTH
The Pilot
029 2071 0615
Twice a year

Cider festivals

ENGLAND

BEDFORDSHIRE

WOBURN
The Black Horse
01525 290210

BERKSHIRE

HERMITAGE
The White Horse of Hermitage
01635 200325

MONEYROW GREEN
The White Hart
01628 621460
Summer

READING
The Flowing Spring
0118 969 9878
Midsummer & Autumn

WOKINGHAM
The Broad Street Tavern
0118 977 3706
Summer

BRISTOL

BRISTOL
The Albion
0117 973 3522
Early May BH

The Alma Tavern & Theatre
0117 973 5171
Late Dec (Xmas fayre)

BUCKINGHAMSHIRE

AMERSHAM
Hit or Miss Inn
01494 713109
Mid Jul wknd

BEACONSFIELD
The Royal Standard of England
01494 673382
Summer BH

BRILL
The Pheasant Inn
01844 239370
Spring BH

DENHAM
The Falcon Inn
01895 832125

MOULSOE
The Carrington Arms
01908 218050
Jun

CAMBRIDGESHIRE

BOURN
The Willow Tree
01954 719775
Summer

HISTON
Red Lion
01223 564437
Etr & 1st wk Sep

PETERBOROUGH
Charters Bar & East Restaurant
01733 315700
Etr Thu-Etr Mon

SPALDWICK
The George
01480 890293

STRETHAM
The Lazy Otter
01353 649780
Jul

THORNEY
Dog In A Doublet
01733 202256
Early May BH

CHESHIRE

CHESTER
Old Harkers Arms
01244 344525
Mar (Pie & Champion Ale Wk)

CORNWALL & ISLES OF SCILLY

CADGWITH
Cadgwith Cove Inn
01326 290513
Oct

CHAPEL AMBLE
The Maltsters Arms
01208 812473
Spring BH

CONSTANTINE
Trengilly Wartha Inn
01326 340332

GUNNISLAKE
The Rising Sun Inn
01822 832201
Every 2-3 months

GWITHIAN
The Red River Inn
01736 753223
Etr wknd

PORTHLEVEN
The Ship Inn
01326 564204
Aug

ST MAWGAN
The Falcon Inn
01637 860225
Jul (last full wknd)

TRESCO (ISLES OF SCILLY)
The New Inn
01720 422849
Jun

TRURO
Old Ale House
01872 271122
Apr/May

CUMBRIA

ULVERSTON
Farmers Arms Hotel
01229 584469

Cider festivals *continued*

DERBYSHIRE

ASHOVER
The Old Poets Corner
01246 590888

BAMFORD
The Yorkshire Bridge Inn
01433 651361
May

BIRCHOVER
Red Lion Inn
01629 650363
Mid Jul

BONSALL
The Barley Mow
01629 825685
BHs (3-4 times a year)

CASTLETON
The Peak Hotel
01433 620247
Etr

CHINLEY
Old Hall Inn
01663 750529
3rd wknd Sep

The Paper Mill Inn
01663 750529
3rd wknd Sep

HOPE
The Old Hall Hotel
01433 620160
BHs

MATLOCK
The Red Lion
01629 584888

SHARDLOW
The Old Crown Inn
01332 792392
Oct

DEVON

BRANSCOMBE
The Masons Arms
01297 680300
Jul

BRIDFORD
The Bridford Inn
01647 252250
May & Aug

CLAYHIDON
The Merry Harriers
01823 421270
Summer

CLYST HYDON
The Five Bells Inn
01884 277288

DODDISCOMBSLEIGH
The NoBody Inn
01647 252394

EAST ALLINGTON
The Fortescue Arms
01548 521215

KINGS NYMPTON
The Grove Inn
01769 580406
Jul

TAVISTOCK
The Cornish Arms
01822 612145
Summer BH wknd

TOTNES
Royal Seven Stars Hotel
01803 862125

DORSET

BOURTON
The White Lion Inn
01747 840866
Jul

CHEDINGTON
Winyard's Gap Inn
01935 891244
Aug

STUDLAND
The Bankes Arms Hotel
01929 450225

WEST STOUR
The Ship Inn
01747 838640
Aug

WORTH MATRAVERS
The Square and Compass
01929 439229
1st Sat Nov

DURHAM, COUNTY

CASTLE EDEN
Castle Eden Inn
01429 835137
May/Jun

FROSTERLEY
The Black Bull Inn
01388 527784

STANLEY
The Stables Pub and
Restaurant
01207 288750
2nd wknd Dec

ESSEX

BELCHAMP ST PAUL
The Half Moon
01787 277402
Summer BH

FEERING
The Sun Inn
01376 570442
End of Jun & Sep

GLOUCESTERSHIRE

ALDERTON
The Gardeners Arms
01242 620257
Aug BH

ALMONDSBURY
The Swan Hotel
01454 625671
Jul

CHELTENHAM
The Gloucester Old Spot
01242 680321

The Royal Oak Inn
01242 522344
Summer BH

CLIFFORD'S MESNE
The Yew Tree
01531 820719
Oct

COATES
The Tunnel House Inn
01285 770280

DURSLEY
The Old Spot Inn
01453 542870
May

SHEEPSCOMBE
The Butchers Arms
01452 812113

TETBURY
The Priory Inn
01666 502251
Early May BH (cider & real ale)

The Royal Oak Tetbury
01666 500021
Spring BH

HAMPSHIRE

BEAULIEU
The Drift Inn
023 8029 2342

BISHOP'S WALTHAM
The Hampshire Bowman
01489 892940
Last wknd Jul

BRAISHFIELD
The Wheatsheaf
01794 368652

BRANSGORE
The Three Tuns Country Inn
01425 672232
Summer

EAST STRATTON
Northbrook Arms
01962 774150
Sep

EVERSLEY
The Golden Pot
0118 973 2104

LYNDHURST
New Forest Inn
023 8028 4690
Last wknd Mar

PETERSFIELD
The White Horse Inn
01420 588387
Sep

ROMSEY
The Three Tuns
01794 512639

STOCKBRIDGE
The Three Cups Inn
01264 810527

SWANMORE
The Rising Sun
01489 896663
Summer BH (Sat)

HEREFORDSHIRE

HOARWITHY
The New Harp Inn
01432 840900
Summer BH

MICHAELCHURCH ESCLEY
The Bridge Inn
01981 510646
Summer BH

ORLETON
The Boot Inn
01568 780228
Last wknd Jul

WOOLHOPE
The Crown Inn
01432 860468

HERTFORDSHIRE

PERRY GREEN
The Hoops Inn
01279 843568
Aug

WATTON-AT-STONE
The Bull
01920 831032
May & Oct

KENT

LOWER HALSTOW
The Three Tuns
01795 842840
Summer BH

SISSINGHURST
The Milk House
01580 720200

TONBRIDGE
The Little Brown Jug
01892 870318
May & Sep

LANCASHIRE

BILSBORROW
Owd Nell's Tavern
01995 640010
Last wk Jul

CHORLEY
The Yew Tree Inn
01257 480344
Etr

LEICESTERSHIRE

LONG WHATTON
The Royal Oak
01509 843694
Summer BH

LINCOLNSHIRE

CLEETHORPES
The Nottingham House
01472 505150
Spring & Autumn

LONDON

NW1
The Engineer
020 7483 1890

The Prince Albert
020 7485 0270
BHs

SW10
The Hollywood Arms
020 7349 7840

W4
The City Barge
020 8994 2148

W8
The Windsor Castle
020 7243 8797
Jul

NORFOLK

WINTERTON-ON-SEA
Fishermans Return
01493 393305

NORTHAMPTONSHIRE

OLD
The White Horse
01604 781297
Summer BH wknd

NORTHUMBERLAND

BEADNELL
The Craster Arms
01665 720272
Last wknd Jul

CARTERWAY HEADS
The Manor House Inn
01207 255268
Last wknd Aug

HEDLEY ON THE HILL
The Feathers Inn
01661 843607
Summer BH

NOTTINGHAMSHIRE

NEWARK-ON-TRENT
The Prince Rupert
01636 918121
Summer BH

NOTTINGHAM
The Hand and Heart
0115 958 2456

SOUTHWELL
The Hearty Goodfellow
01636 919176
Feb

OXFORDSHIRE

ABINGDON-ON-THAMES
The Brewery Tap
01235 521655
Mar & Oct

BANBURY
Ye Olde Reindeer Inn
01295 270972
Summer BH

BLOXHAM
The Elephant & Castle
01295 720383
Early May (part of Bloxfest Music Festival)

NORTH HINKSEY VILLAGE
The Fishes
01865 249796

WYTHAM
White Hart
01865 244372

RUTLAND

OAKHAM
The Grainstore Brewery
01572 770065
Spring BH

SHROPSHIRE

PAVE LANE
The Fox
01952 815940
Summer

SOMERSET

CHEW MAGNA
The Bear and Swan
01275 331100
Spring/Summer

DUNSTER
The Stags Head Inn
01643 821229
Dec

HASELBURY PLUCKNETT
The White Horse at Haselbury
01460 78873

HINTON ST GEORGE
The Lord Poulett Arms
01460 73149

ILCHESTER
The Bull Inn
01935 840400

Ilchester Arms
01935 840220

LOWER GODNEY
The Sheppey
01458 831594
Aug

PITNEY
The Halfway House
01458 252513
Aug

PORLOCK
The Bottom Ship
01643 863288
1st wknd Jul

SHEPTON MALLET
The Three Horseshoes Inn
01749 850359
Etr, Summer BH

SHEPTON MONTAGUE
The Montague Inn
01749 813213

WEDMORE
The George Inn
01934 712124

STAFFORDSHIRE

CAULDON
Yew Tree Inn
01538 309876
Jul

STAFFORD
The Holly Bush Inn
01889 508234
Jun & Sep

WRINEHILL
The Hand & Trumpet
01270 820048
Aug

SUFFOLK

ELVEDEN
Elveden Inn
01842 890876
Mid Aug

HAWKEDON
The Queen's Head
01284 789218
3rd wknd Jul

SOMERLEYTON
The Duke's Head
01502 733931

SURREY

FARNHAM
The Bat & Ball Freehouse
01252 792108

LONG DITTON
The Ditton
020 8339 0785

SUSSEX, EAST

BLACKBOYS
The Blackboys Inn
01825 890283

ERIDGE GREEN
The Nevill Crest and Gun
01892 864209

EWHURST GREEN
The White Dog
01580 830264
Late Sep (book & cider festival)

SUSSEX, WEST

HORSHAM
The Black Jug
01403 253526
Summer

KINGSFOLD
The Dog and Duck
01306 627295
Annual charity event

WARWICKSHIRE

BROOM
The Broom Tavern
01789 778199
Summer BH

EDGEHILL
Castle at Edgehill
01295 670255
Aug/Sep

WILTSHIRE

ALDBOURNE
The Blue Boar
01672 540237
1st wknd Jun

The Crown Inn
01672 540214
2nd week Jul

BOX
The Quarrymans Arms
01225 743569
Jul

BRINKWORTH
The Three Crowns
01666 510366

BROUGHTON GIFFORD
The Fox
01225 782949

COLLINGBOURNE DUCIS
The Shears Inn
01264 850304
Late summer

EDINGTON
The Three Daggers
01380 830940
Sep

MALMESBURY
Kings Arms
01666 823383

ROYAL WOOTTON BASSETT
The Angel
01793 851161
Sep

SHERSTON
The Rattlebone Inn
01666 840871
Jul

WORCESTERSHIRE

BRETFORTON
The Fleece Inn
01386 831173
Mid-late Oct

YORKSHIRE, NORTH

HARDRAW
The Green Dragon Inn
01969 667392
Oct

SETTLE
The Lion at Settle
01729 822203
Aug

YORK
Lysander Arms
01904 640845
Early May BH wknd

YORKSHIRE, SOUTH

CADEBY
The Cadeby Pub & Restaurant
01709 864009

SHEFFIELD
Kelham Island Tavern
0114 272 2482
Late Jun wknd

YORKSHIRE, WEST

HOLMFIRTH
Farmers Arms
01484 683713
Summer BH

ISLE OF MAN

PORT ERIN
Falcon's Nest Hotel
01624 834077
Early May

SCOTLAND

ARGYLL & BUTE

DUNOON
Coylet Inn
01369 840426

CITY OF DUNDEE

BROUGHTY FERRY
The Royal Arch Bar
01382 779741
Last wknd Apr

CITY OF GLASGOW

GLASGOW
Bon Accord
0141 248 4427

PERTH & KINROSS

MEIKLEOUR
Meikleour Arms
01250 883206
Aug

WALES

CARMARTHENSHIRE

PUMSAINT
The Dolaucothi Arms
01558 650237
Summer BH wknd

MONMOUTHSHIRE

ABERGAVENNY
Clytha Arms
01873 840206
Spring BH

TRELLECH
The Lion Inn
01600 860322
Aug

NEWPORT

CAERLEON
The Bell at Caerleon
01633 420613

POWYS

GLANGRWYNEY
The Bell
01873 811115

RHONDDA CYNON TAFF

PONTYPRIDD
Bunch of Grapes
01443 402934
Twice a year

SWANSEA

LLANGENNITH
Kings Head
01792 386212
Last wknd Oct

VALE OF GLAMORGAN

PENARTH
The Pilot
029 2071 0615
Twice a year

How to find a pub in the atlas section

Pubs are shown in the gazetteer under the name of their nearest town or village. If a pub is in a very small village, or in a remote rural area, it may appear under a larger town that is within five miles of its actual location.

The black dots in the atlas section match the location name in the gazetteer.

The county map shown opposite will help you identify the counties within each country. The county names are shown at the top of each page in the gazetteer.

The atlas section and the index that follow will help you find the towns featured in the guide.

Key to County Map

England

1 Bedfordshire
2 Berkshire
3 Bristol
4 Buckinghamshire
5 Cambridgeshire
6 Greater Manchester
7 Herefordshire
8 Hertfordshire
9 Leicestershire
10 Northamptonshire
11 Nottinghamshire
12 Rutland
13 Staffordshire
14 Warwickshire
15 West Midlands
16 Worcestershire

Scotland

17 City of Glasgow
18 Clackmannanshire
19 East Ayrshire
20 East Dunbartonshire
21 East Renfrewshire
22 Perth & Kinross
23 Renfrewshire
24 South Lanarkshire
25 West Dunbartonshire

Wales

26 Blaenau Gwent
27 Bridgent
28 Caerphilly
29 Denbighshire
30 Flintshire
31 Merthyr Tydfil
32 Monmouthshire
33 Neath Port Talbot
34 Newport
35 Rhondda Cynon Taff
36 Torfaen
37 Vale of Glamorgan
38 Wrexham

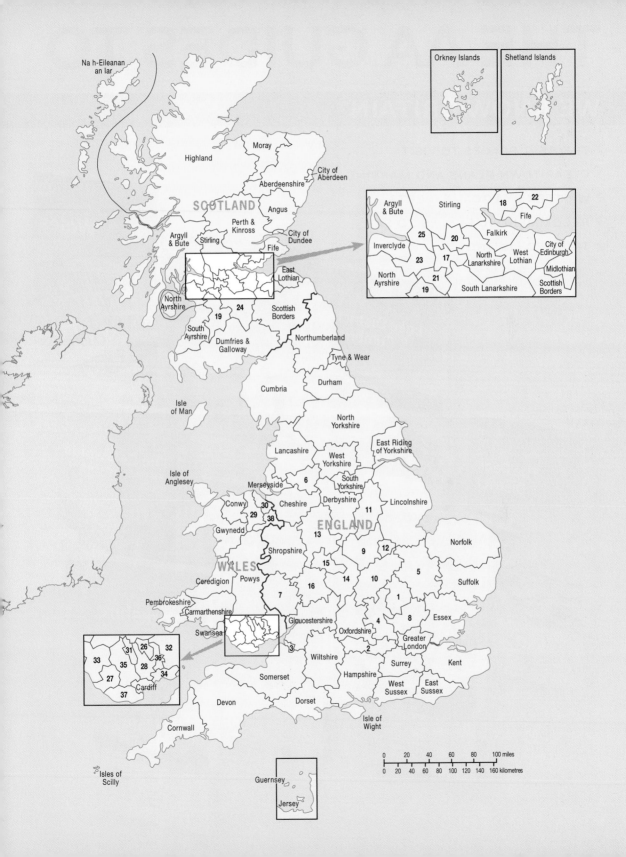

THE AA GUIDES TO

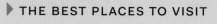

WE KNOW BRITAIN

▸ THE BEST PLACES TO VISIT

▸ CLEAR TOWN PLANS AND MAPPING

▸ WRITTEN BY LOCAL EXPERTS

▸ RECOMMENDED PLACES TO EAT

▸ TRUSTED LISTINGS

🐦 Follow @TheAA_Lifestyle

KEY TO ATLAS

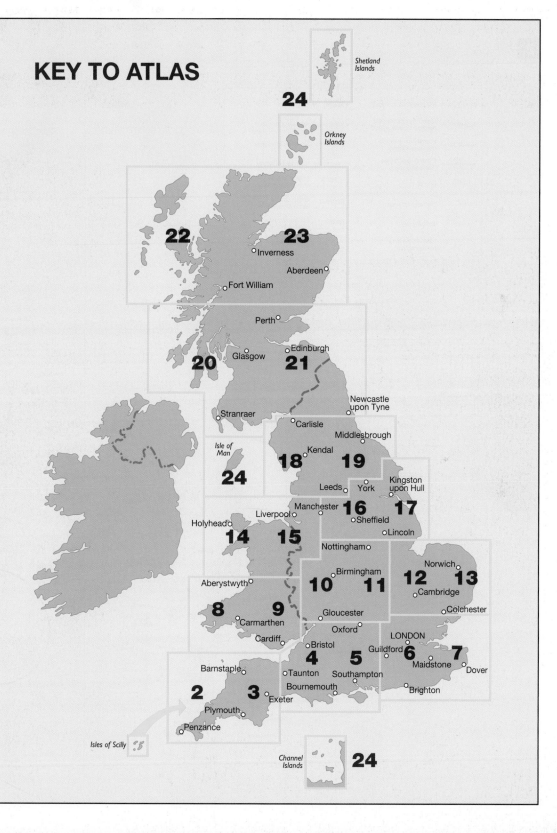

Shetland Islands — 24

Orkney Islands

22 23
Inverness
Aberdeen
Fort William
Perth
20 Glasgow Edinburgh 21
Stranraer Newcastle upon Tyne
Carlisle Middlesbrough
Isle of Man 18 Kendal 19
24 Leeds York Kingston upon Hull
Liverpool Manchester 16 17
Holyhead Sheffield Lincoln
14 15 Nottingham
Aberystwyth Birmingham Norwich
10 11 12 13
8 9 Cambridge
Carmarthen Gloucester Colchester
Cardiff Oxford LONDON
Bristol Guildford 6 7
Barnstaple 4 5 Maidstone Dover
Taunton Southampton Brighton
2 3 Bournemouth
Plymouth Exeter
Penzance
Isles of Scilly
Channel Islands 24

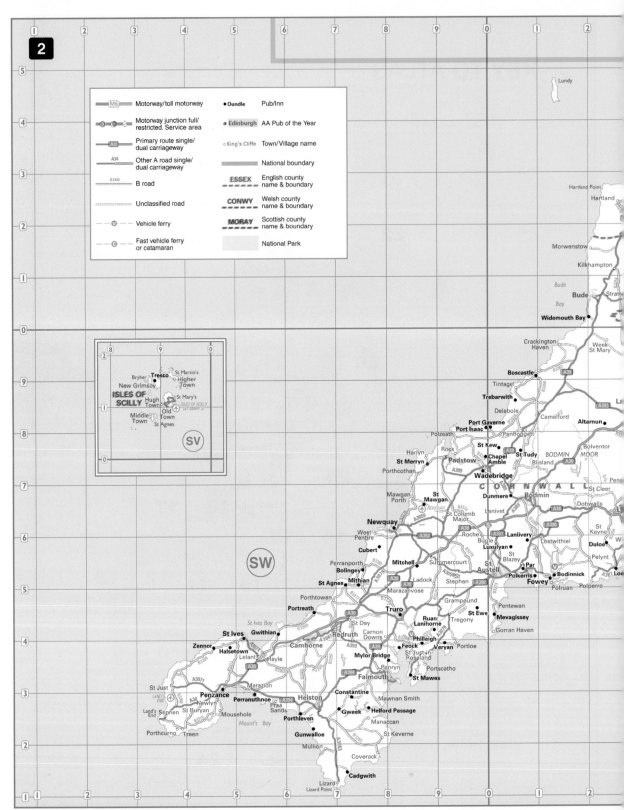

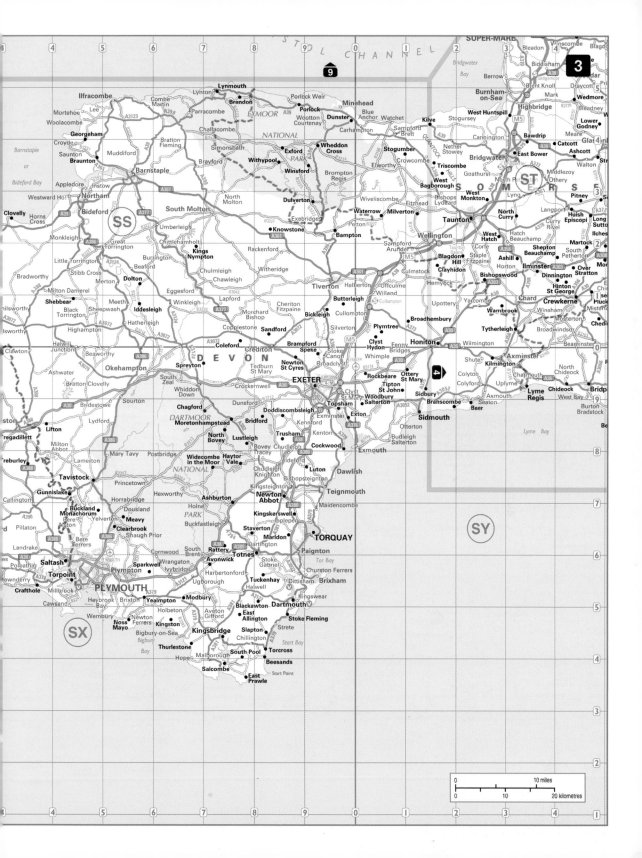

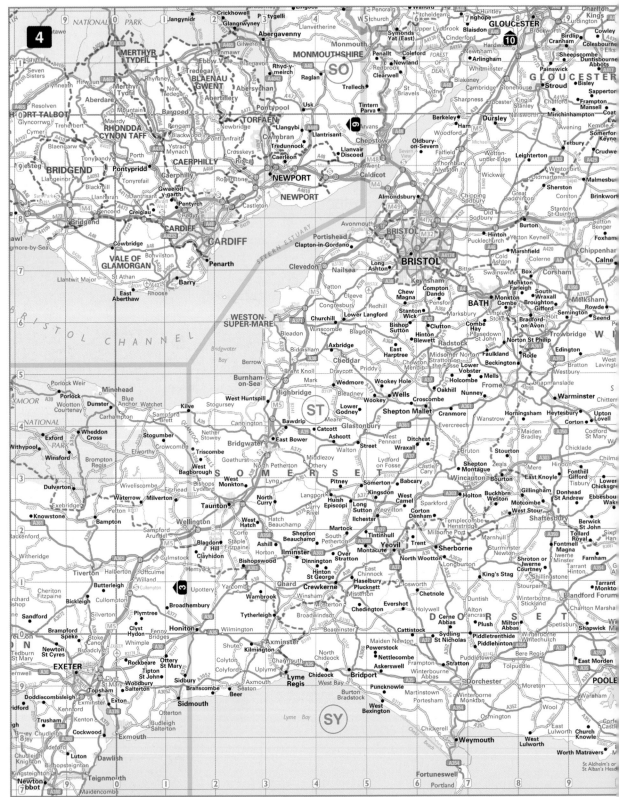

For continuation pages refer to numbered arrows

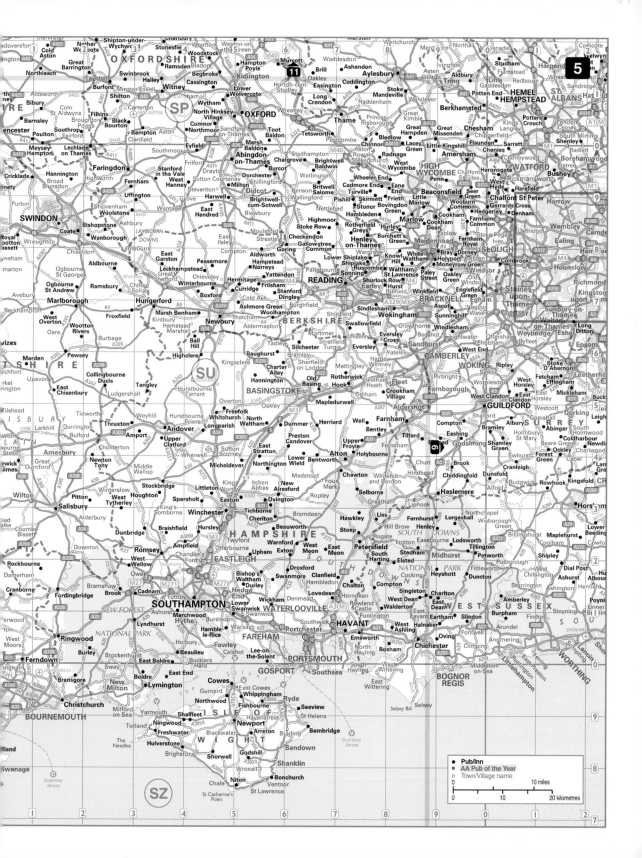

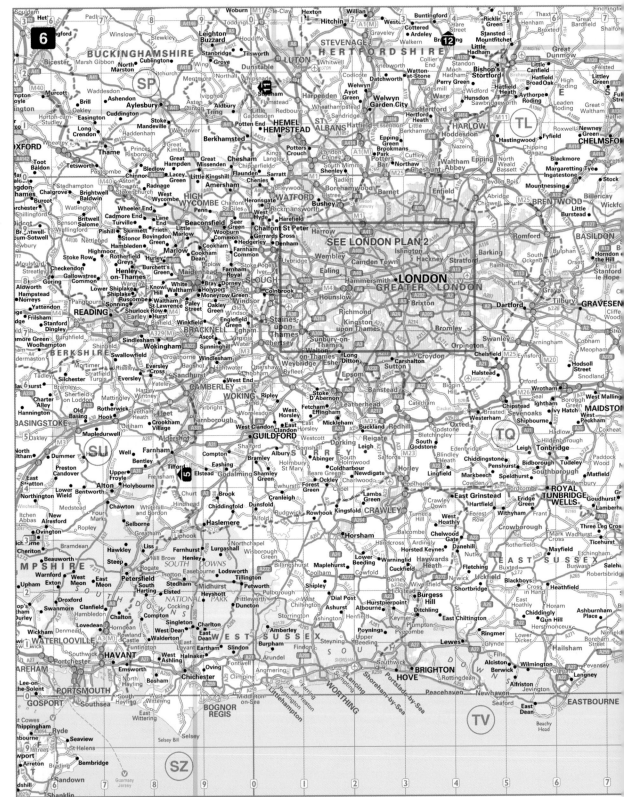

CARDIGAN BAY

Aberdyfi

Aberystwyth

Llandre
Llanfarian
Llanilar
Llanrhystud
Llansantffraid
Aberarth
Aberaeron
New Quay
Llwyndafydd
Llangranog
Aberporth
Tan-y-groes
Blaenporth
Talgarreg
Rhydowen
Llanybydder
Llandysul
CERE
Temple Bar
Lampeter
Llanllwni
Abergorlech
Talley
Brechfa

St Dogmaels
Cardigan
Llechryd
Abercych
Newcastle Emlyn
Llangeler
SN

SM

Strumble Head
Nevern
Newport
Goodwick
Fishguard
Eglwyswrw
PEMBROKESHIRE COAST NATIONAL PARK
MYNYDD PRESELI

Porthgain
Letterston
Wolf's Castle
Rosebush
Cynwyl Elfed
CARMARTHENSHIRE

St David's Head
St Davids
Solva
PEMBROKESHIRE
Newgale
Roch
Llandissilio
Carmarthen
Nantgaredig
Llande
Llanarthne
Llandybie

St Brides Bay
PEMBROKESHIRE COAST NATIONAL PARK
Broad Haven
Haverfordwest
Robeston Wathen
Whitland
St Clears
Llanddarog
Cross Hands

Little Haven
Johnston
Narberth
Red Roses
Laugharne
Llansteffan
Pontyberem
Pontyates

Marloes
Kilgetty
Amroth
Pendine
Kidwelly
Pont

Broad Sound
Dale
Milford Haven
Neyland
Saundersfoot
Carmarthen Bay
Pembrey
Burry Port
Llanelli
Gorseinon

Angle
Pembroke Dock
Carew
St Florence
Tenby
Pembrey
Pwll
M4

Pembroke
Castlemartin
PEMBROKESHIRE COAST NATIONAL PARK
Manorbier
Penally
Gowerton
Dunvant

Stackpole
Bosherston
Llanmadoc
Llanrhidian
SWANSEA
Bishopston

Llangennith
Reynoldston
Rhossili
Oxwich

Worms Head
Port Einon

SR
SS

Pub/Inn
AA Pub of the Year
Town/Village name
0 ___ 10 miles
0 ___ 10 ___ 20 kilometres

Lundy
Ilfracombe
Com
Lee
Mortehoe

For continuation pages refer to numbered arrows

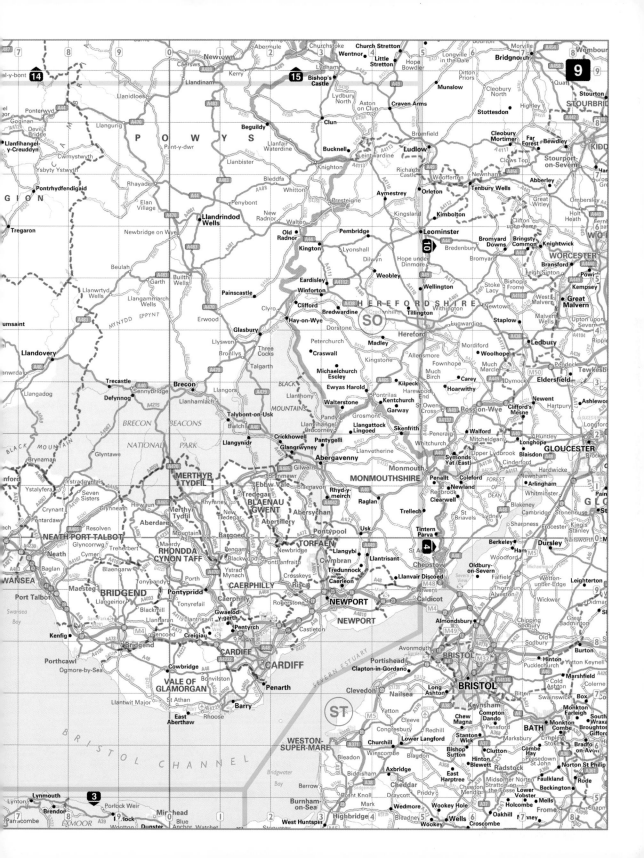

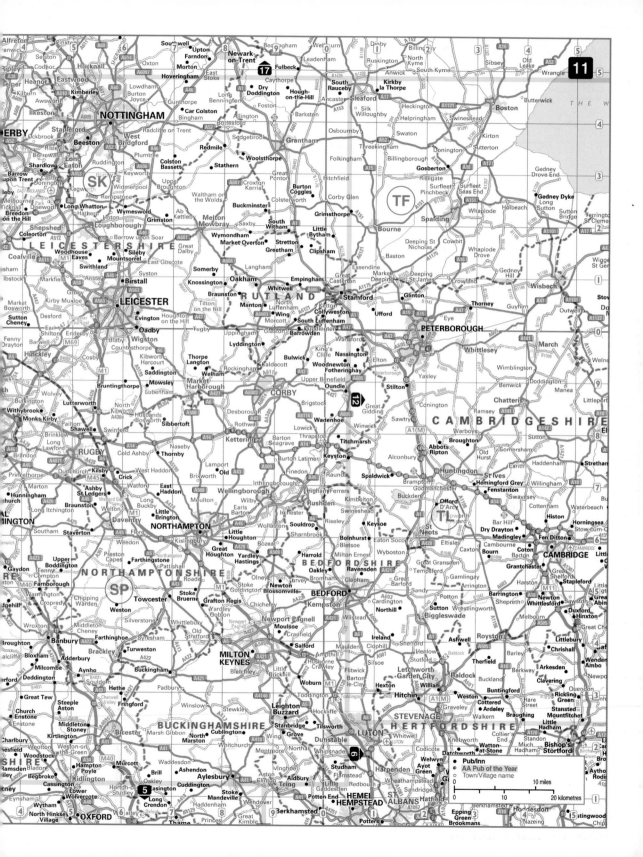

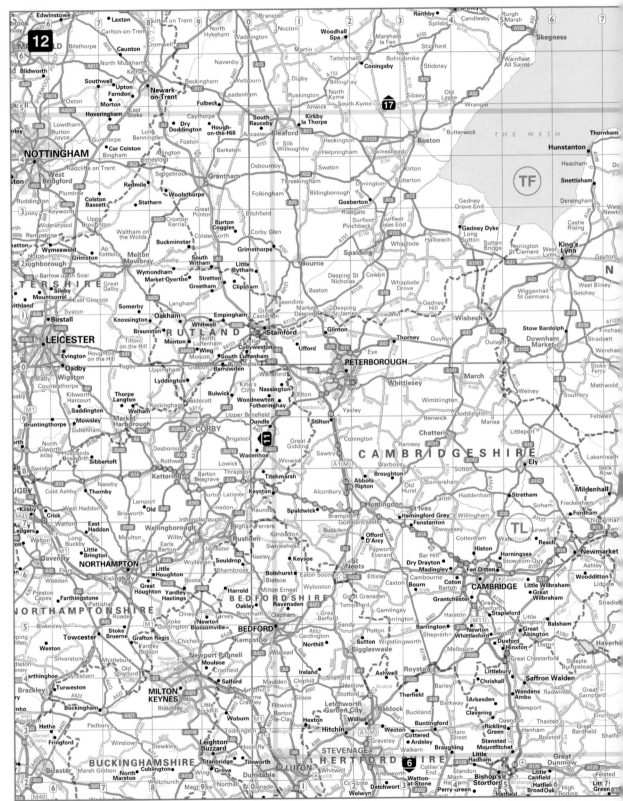

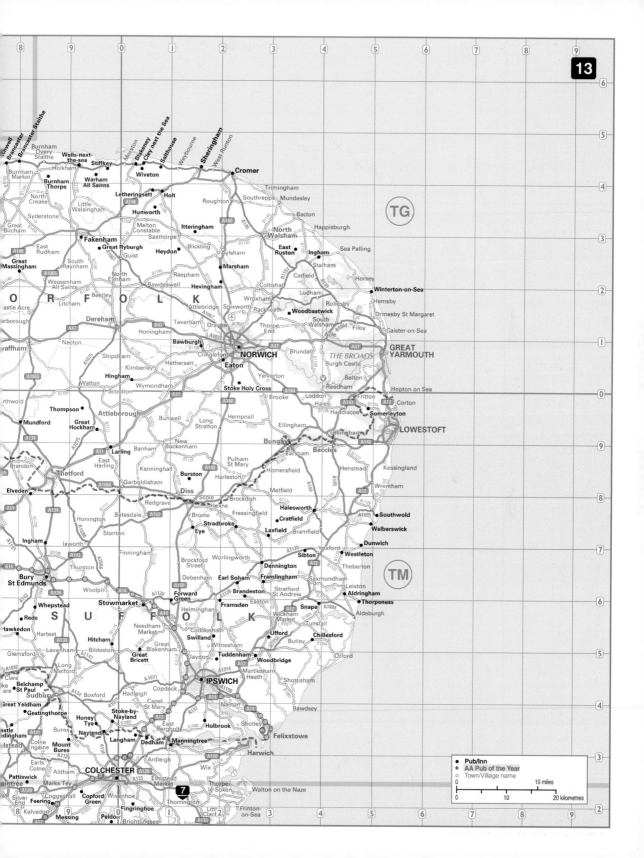

NORFOLK

Unwell
Brancaster
Brancaster Staithe
Burnham Overy Staithe
Burnham Market
Holkham
Wells-next-the-sea
Stiffkey
Morston
Blakeney
Cley next the Sea
Salthouse
Weybourne
Sheringham
West Runton
Cromer
North Creake
Burnham Thorpe
Warham All Saints
Wiveton
Trimingham
Southrepps
Mundesley
Great Bircham
Syderstone
Little Walsingham
Letheringsett
Holt
Roughton
Bacton
Happisburgh
Sea Palling
Fakenham
Hunworth
Melton Constable
Saxthorpe
Itteringham
Blickling
North Walsham
East Ruston
Ingham
Stalham
Catfield
Horsey
Great Raynham
South Raynham
Great Ryburgh
Heydon
Guist
Reepham
Aylsham
Coltishall
Ludham
Rollesby
Hemsby
Ormesby St Margaret
Winterton-on-Sea
astle Acre
arborough
Weasenham All Saints
Beetley
Litcham
Bawdeswell
Hevingham
Marsham
Wroxham
Spixworth
Rackheath
South Walsham
Filby
Caister-on-Sea
Dereham
Taverham
Drayton
Thorpe End
Acle
Woodbastwick
waffham
Necton
Honingham
NORWICH
Brundall
THE BROADS
GREAT YARMOUTH
Shipdham
Bawburgh
Cringleford
Eaton
Burgh Castle
Belton
Hingham
Hethersett
Yelverton
Reedham
Hopton on Sea
Watton
Kimberley
Wymondham
Stoke Holy Cross
Loddon
Fritton
Corton
rthwold
Thompson
Scoulton
Attleborough
Brooke
Hales
Haddiscoe
Somerleyton
Mundford
Great Hockham
Bunwell
Long Stratton
Hempnall
Ellingham
Gillingham
LOWESTOFT
A134
Larling
New Buckenham
Earsham
Beccles
Thetford
East Harling
Banham
Pulham St Mary
Homersfield
Henstead
Kessingland
Brandon
Kenninghall
Burston
Harleston
Metfield
Wrentham
Elveden
Garboldisham
Redgrave
Diss
Scole
Brockdish
Hexne
Fressingfield
Halesworth
Southwold
Honington
Botesdale
Stanton
Brome
Stradbroke
Eye
Laxfield
Bramfield
Cratfield
Walberswick
Ingham
Ixworth
Finningham
Brockford Street
Worlingworth
Sibton
Yoxford
Westleton
Dunwich
Bury St Edmunds
Thurston
Woolpit
Debenham
Dennington
Framlingham
Theberton
Whepstead
Stowmarket
Forward Green
Earl Soham
Brandeston
Stratford St Andrew
Saxmundham
Leiston
Aldringham
Thorpeness
Rede
Hitcham
Framsden
Easton
Snape
Aldeburgh
Hawkedon
Hartest
Needham Market
Coddenham
Wickham Market
Tunstall
Bildeston
Great Blakenham
Helmingham
Witnesham
Ufford
Butley
Chillesford
Orford
Glemsford
Lavenham
Great Bricett
Claydon
Swilland
Tuddenham
Woodbridge
Long Melford
Clare
Copdock
Martlesham Heath
Shottisham
Belchamp St Paul
Boxford
Hadleigh
Capel St Mary
IPSWICH
Nacton
Bawdsey
Sudbury
Great Yeldham
Gestingthorpe
Honey Tye
Stoke-by-Nayland
East Bergholt
Holbrook
Shotley
Castle dingham
Nayland
Langham
Dedham
Manningtree
Felixstowe
Mount Bures
Ardleigh
Harwich
stead
Bures
Wix
COLCHESTER
Elmstead Market
Thorpe-le-Soken
Walton on the Naze
Earls Colne
Aldham
Pattiswick
Copford Green
Wivenhoe
Frinton-on-Sea
aintree
Marks Tey
Coggeshall
Fingringhoe
Thorrington
Littl Clact
Silver End
Kelvedon
Feering
Peldon
Brightlingsea
Messing

TG

TM

NORFOLK

SUFFOLK

	Pub/Inn
	AA Pub of the Year
	Town/Village name

0   10 miles
0   10   20 kilometres

14

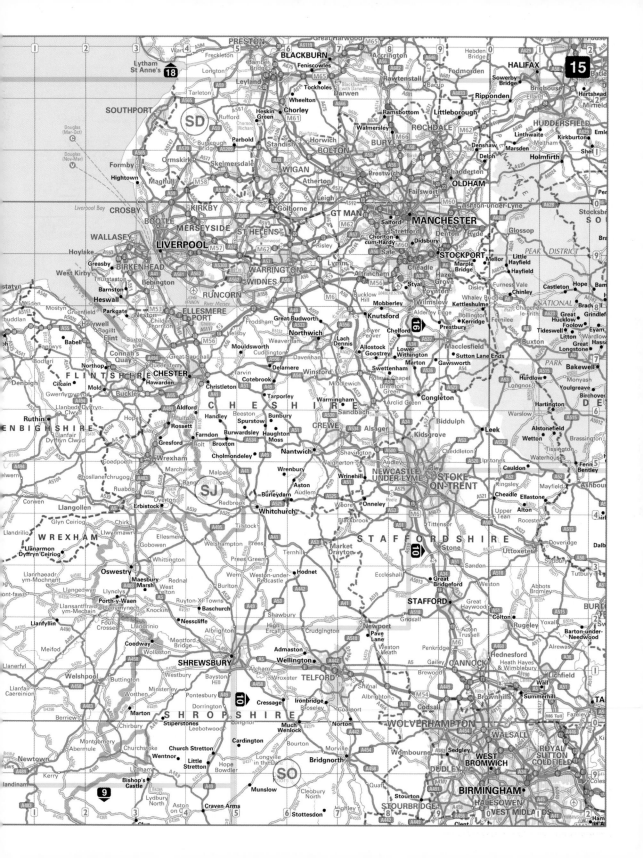

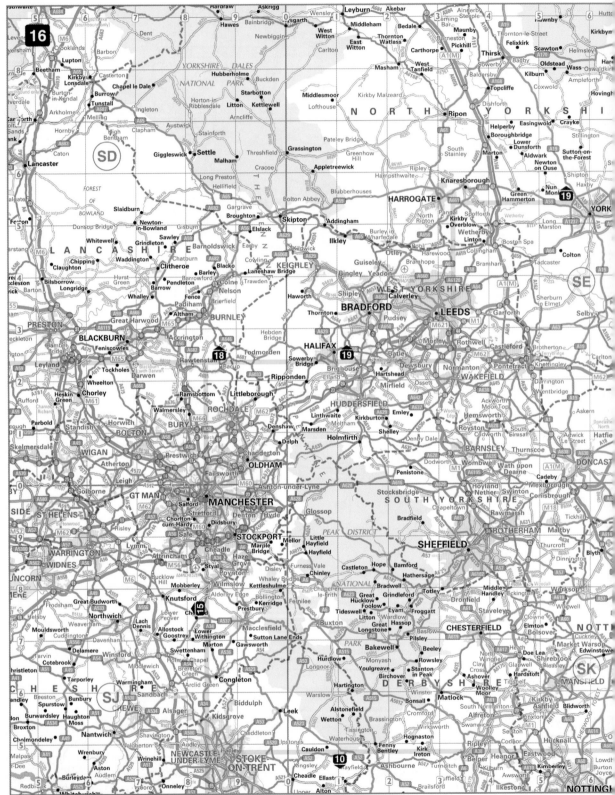

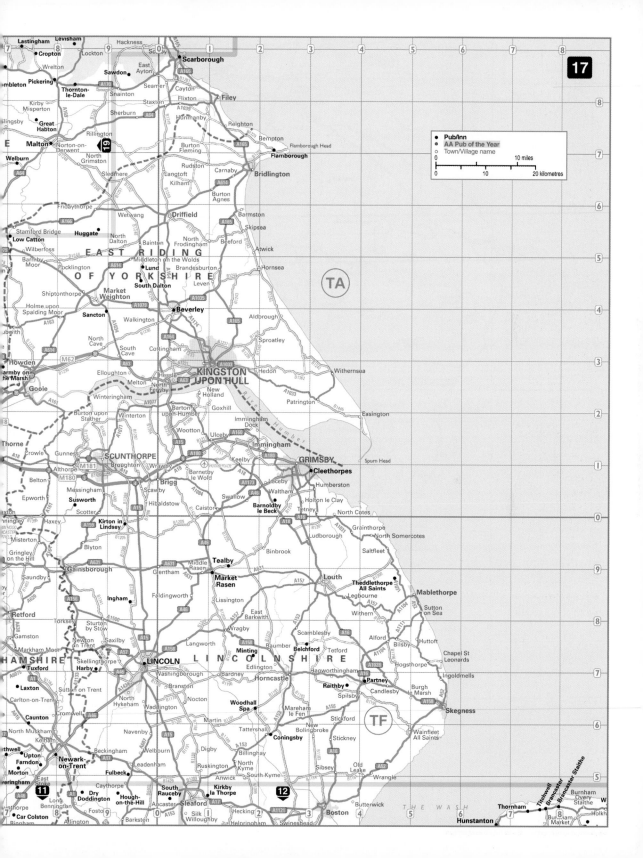

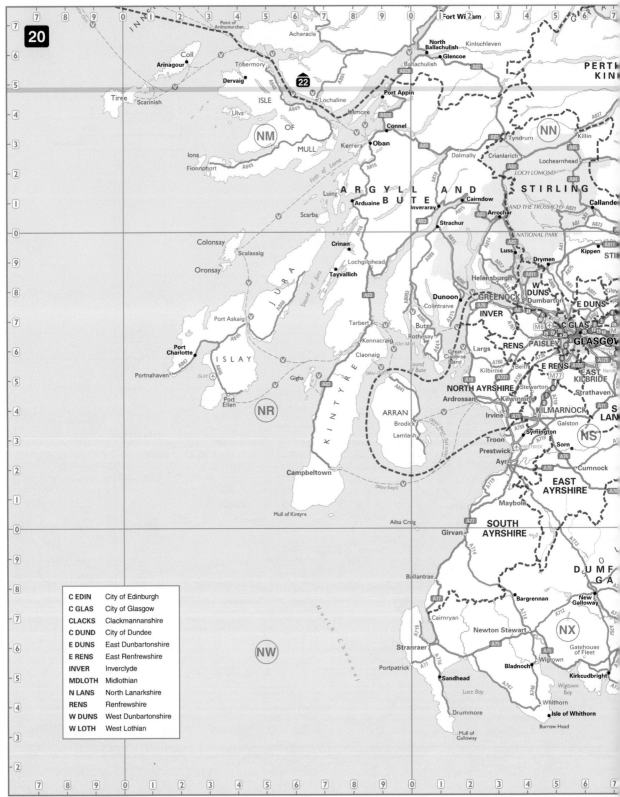

C EDIN   City of Edinburgh
C GLAS   City of Glasgow
CLACKS   Clackmannanshire
C DUND   City of Dundee
E DUNS   East Dunbartonshire
E RENS   East Renfrewshire
INVER   Inverclyde
MDLOTH   Midlothian
N LANS   North Lanarkshire
RENS   Renfrewshire
W DUNS   West Dunbartonshire
W LOTH   West Lothian

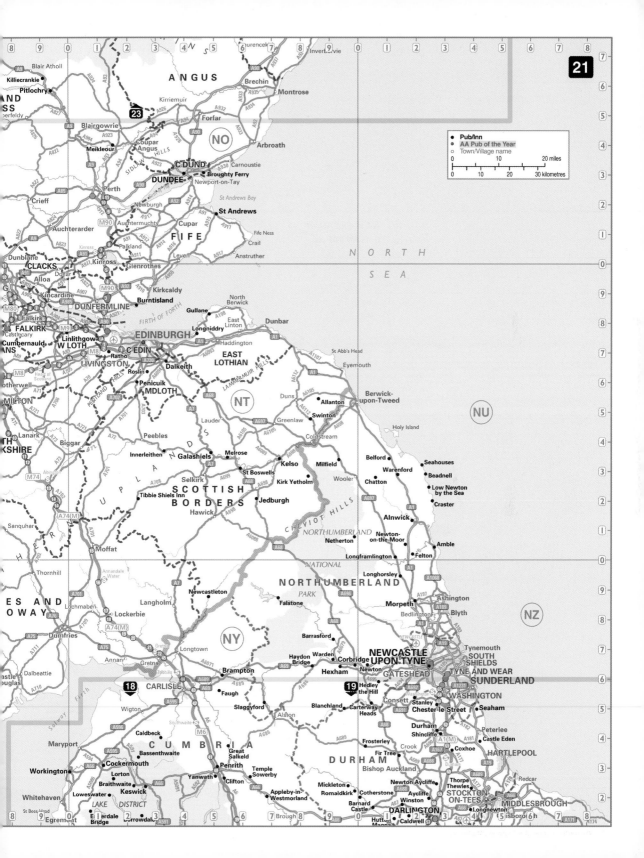

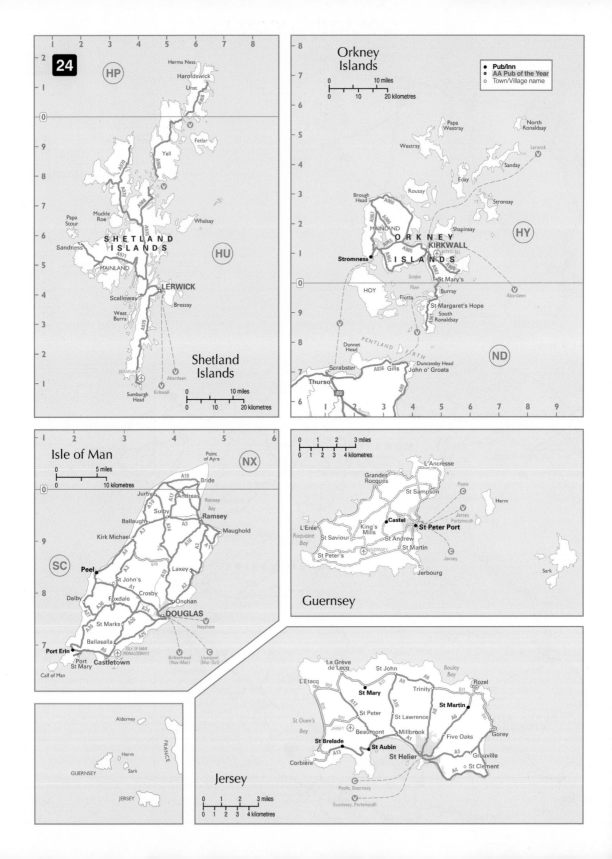

24

Shetland Islands

HP

Herma Ness
Haroldswick
Unst
Fetlar
Yell
Muckle Roe
Papa Stour
Whalsay
SHETLAND ISLANDS
Sandness
HU
MAINLAND
Scalloway
LERWICK
Bressay
West Burra
SUMBURGH
Sumburgh Head
Aberdeen
Kirkwall

Orkney Islands

Papa Westray
North Ronaldsay
Westray
Lerwick
Sanday
Eday
Stronsay
Rousay
Shapinsay
Brough Head
HY
MAINLAND
ORKNEY
KIRKWALL
Stromness
ISLANDS
St Mary's
Scapa Flow
HOY
Burray
Flotta
St Margaret's Hope
Aberdeen
South Ronaldsay
St Margaret's Hope
PENTLAND FIRTH
Dunnet Head
Duncansby Head
John o' Groats
ND
Scrabster
Gills
Thurso

Isle of Man

Point of Ayre
NX
Bride
Jurby
Andreas
Sulby
Ballaugh
Ramsey
Kirk Michael
Maughold
Ramsey Bay
SC
Peel
Laxey
St John's
Crosby
Dalby
Foxdale
○Onchan
St Marks
DOUGLAS
Ballasalla
Heysham
ISLE OF MAN (RONALDSWAY)
Port Erin
Birkenhead (Nov-Mar)
Liverpool (Mar-Oct)
Port St Mary
Castletown
Calf of Man

Guernsey

L'Ancresse
Grandes Rocques
St Sampson
Poole
Herm
L'Erée
Castel
King's Mills
St Peter Port
Jersey Portsmouth
Roquaine Bay
St Saviour
St Andrew
St Peter's
St Martin
GUERNSEY
Jersey
Jerbourg
Sark

Jersey

La Grève de Lecq
St John
Bouley Bay
L'Etacq
Rozel
St Mary
Trinity
St Peter
St Martin
St Lawrence
St Ouen's Bay
JERSEY
Beaumont
Five Oaks
St Brelade
Millbrook
Gorey
St Aubin
Corbière
St Helier
Grouville
Poole, Guernsey
St Clement
Guernsey, Portsmouth

Alderney
Herm
FRANCE
GUERNSEY
Sark
JERSEY

Legend:
- ● Pub/Inn
- ● AA Pub of the Year
- ○ Town/Village name

Scales:
- 10 miles / 20 kilometres (Orkney)
- 10 miles / 20 kilometres (Shetland)
- 5 miles / 10 kilometres (Isle of Man)
- 3 miles / 4 kilometres (Guernsey)
- 3 miles / 4 kilometres (Jersey)

Central London

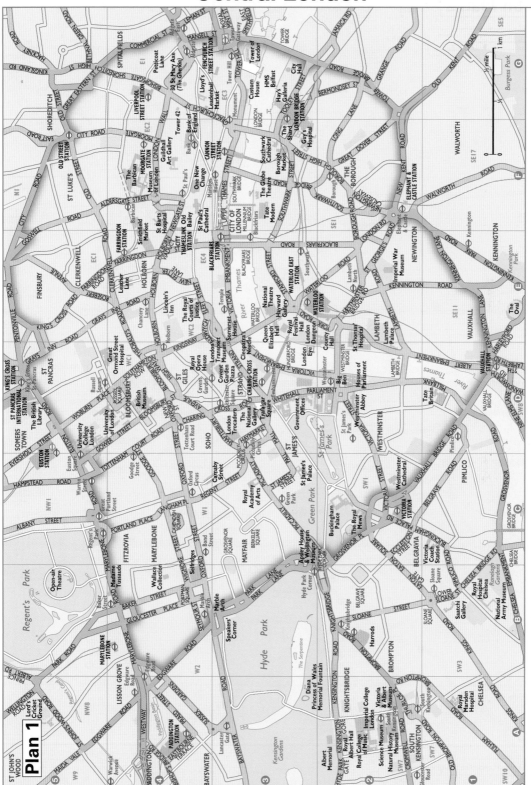

KEY TO PUB LOCATIONS

Each pub in London has a map reference, eg C2. The letter 'C' refers to the grid square located at the bottom of the map. The figure '2' refers to the grid square located at the left hand edge of the map. For example, where these two intersect, Buckingham Palace can be found. Due to the scale of the map, only a rough guide to the location of a pub can be given. A more detailed map will be necessary to be precise.

Congestion Charging Zone boundary

London Plan 2

0 —— 2 miles
0 —— 3 kilometres

The Queens Head

The Salusbury Pub and Dining Room

The Red Lemon

The Grove

Princess Victoria

Anglesea Arms

The Swan

The Dartmouth Castle

The Hampshire Hog

The Albion

The Stonemasons Arms

The Cumberland Arms

The City Barge

The Brown Dog

The Spencer

The White Swan

The Victoria

Prince of Wales

The Telegraph

Fox & Grapes

Central London Congestion Charging Zone

Index

Red entries are Pick of the Pubs

Acknowledgments

The Automobile Association would like to thank the following photographers, companies and picture libraries for their assistance in the preparation of this book.

Abbreviations for the picture credits are as follows – (t) top; (b) bottom; (c) centre; (l) left; (r) right; (AA) AA World Travel Library

Front & Back Cover: © Aleksandr Bryliaev / Alamy

England Opener AA/Tom Mackie;
Scotland Opener AA/Jim Henderson;
Wales Opener AA/Mark Bauer

003 Courtesy of The Fox and Hounds, Nottinghamshire; 004 Courtesy of Sibton White Horse Inn, Suffolk; 008 Courtesy of The Wellington Hotel, Cornwall; 009 Courtesy of The Treby Arms, Devon; 010-011 AA/Clive Sawyer; 010 Courtesy of The Porch House, Stow-on-the-Wold, Gloucestershire; 011l Courtesy of The Scran & Scallie, Edinburgh, Scotland; 011r Courtesy of The Kinmel Arms, Abergele, Wales; 012 Courtesy of Crown Inn, Henley; 012-013 Courtesy of The Crown, Pishill; 013 Courtesy of Adnams Brewery; 014 Alamy/Gary Doak; 015 Courtesy of The Crown Country Inn, Shropshire; 016-017 Alamy/Alan Novelli; 018-019 AA/Tom Mackie; 020-021 Alamy/Matt Gibson; 022-023 AA/Tom Mackie; 593 Alamy/Orange Elephant Photography; 594-5 AA/Jim Henderson; 624-5 AA/Mark Bauer.

Every effort has been made to trace the copyright holders, and we apologise in advance for any unintentional omissions or errors. We would be pleased to apply any corrections in a following edition of this publication

Readers' Report Form

Please send this form to:–
The Editor, The AA Pub Guide,
AA Lifestyle Guides,
13th Floor,
Fanum House,
Basingstoke RG21 4EA

e-mail: lifestyleguides@theAA.com

Please use this form to tell us about any pub or inn you have visited, whether it is in the guide or not currently listed. We are interested in the quality of food, the selection of beers and the overall ambience of the establishment.

Feedback from readers helps us to keep our guide accurate and up to date. However, if you have a complaint to make during a visit, we do recommend that you discuss the matter with the pub management there and then, so that they have a chance to put things right before your visit is spoilt.

Please note that the AA does not undertake to arbitrate between you and the pub management, or to obtain compensation or engage in protracted correspondence.

Date

Your name (BLOCK CAPITALS)

Your address (BLOCK CAPITALS)

Post code

E-mail address

Name of pub

Location

Comments

(please attach a separate sheet if necessary)

Please tick here ☐ if you DO NOT wish to receive details of AA offers or products   PTO

Readers' Report Form *continued*

Have you bought this guide before? ☐ YES ☐ NO

Do you regularly use any other pub, accommodation or food guides? ☐ YES ☐ NO
If YES, which ones?

....

....

What do you find most useful about The AA Pub Guide?

....

....

....

Do you read the editorial features in the guide? ☐ YES ☐ NO

Do you use the location atlas? ☐ YES ☐ NO

Is there any other information you would like to see added to this guide?

....

....

....

What are your main reasons for visiting pubs (tick all that apply)

Food ☐	Business ☐	Accommodation ☐
Beer ☐	Celebrations ☐	Entertainment ☐
Atmosphere ☐	Leisure ☐	
Other		

How often do you visit a pub for a meal?
more than once a week ☐
once a week ☐
once a fortnight ☐
once a month ☐
once in six months ☐

Readers' Report Form

Please send this form to:–
The Editor, The AA Pub Guide,
AA Lifestyle Guides,
13th Floor,
Fanum House,
Basingstoke RG21 4EA

e-mail: lifestyleguides@theAA.com

Please use this form to tell us about any pub or inn you have visited, whether it is in the guide or not currently listed. We are interested in the quality of food, the selection of beers and the overall ambience of the establishment.

Feedback from readers helps us to keep our guide accurate and up to date. However, if you have a complaint to make during a visit, we do recommend that you discuss the matter with the pub management there and then, so that they have a chance to put things right before your visit is spoilt.

Please note that the AA does not undertake to arbitrate between you and the pub management, or to obtain compensation or engage in protracted correspondence.

Date

Your name (BLOCK CAPITALS)

Your address (BLOCK CAPITALS)

Post code

E-mail address

Name of pub

Location

Comments

(please attach a separate sheet if necessary)

Please tick here ☐ if you DO NOT wish to receive details of AA offers or products

PTO

Readers' Report Form *continued*

Have you bought this guide before? ☐ YES ☐ NO

Do you regularly use any other pub, accommodation or food guides? ☐ YES ☐ NO
If YES, which ones?

....

....

What do you find most useful about The AA Pub Guide?

....

....

....

Do you read the editorial features in the guide? ☐ YES ☐ NO

Do you use the location atlas? ☐ YES ☐ NO

Is there any other information you would like to see added to this guide?

....

....

....

What are your main reasons for visiting pubs (tick all that apply)

Food ☐   Business ☐   Accommodation ☐
Beer ☐   Celebrations ☐   Entertainment ☐
Atmosphere ☐   Leisure ☐
Other

How often do you visit a pub for a meal?
more than once a week ☐
once a week ☐
once a fortnight ☐
once a month ☐
once in six months ☐